Oxford
STUDENT'S
Dictionary

Fourth edition

for intermediate to advanced
learners of English

OXFORD
UNIVERSITY PRESS

OXFORD
UNIVERSITY PRESS

Great Clarendon Street, Oxford, OX2 6DP, United Kingdom

Oxford University Press is a department of the University of Oxford. It furthers the University's objective of excellence in research, scholarship, and education by publishing worldwide. Oxford is a registered trade mark of Oxford University Press in the UK and in certain other countries

© Oxford University Press 2021

Database right Oxford University Press (maker)

First published 2001
Fourth edition 2021
2025 2024 2023
10 9 8 7 6 5

No unauthorized photocopying

ISBN: 978 0 19 440614 7

Typeset by Data Standards Limited

Printed in China

This book is printed on paper from certified and well-managed sources

ACKNOWLEDGEMENTS

Back cover photograph: Oxford University Press building/David Fisher

The publisher is grateful to those who have given permission to reproduce the following extracts and adaptations of copyright material: p WT14 Graph adapted from graph 'Huawei makes more phones than Apple' from www.bbc.co.uk and data from Canalys, reprinted by permission.

The publisher would like to thank the following for their kind permission to reproduce photographs and other copyright material: 123RF (bass drum/Wilawan Khasawong, bassoon/Sergei Furtcev, bricks/alekss, cable/saidin b jusoh, camper/deusexlupus, cymbals/Pavlo Baishev, French horn/nerthuz, hoe/belchonock, kettledrum/trodler, keyboard/scanrail, lorry/Thomas Lenne, megaphone/wabeno, metronome/bruno135, oboe/alenavlad, sword/genmike, tanker/nerthuz, turnstile/nerthuz, van/Vladimir Kramin, wood/Elenathewise); Advocate Art (aerosol/Fabian Slongo, arm in a sling/Fabian Slongo, atmosphere/Fabian Slongo, brain/Fabian Slongo, cells/Fabian Slongo, climate change/Fabian Slongo, leg in plaster/Fabian Slongo, lever (class 1)/Fabian Slongo, longshore drift/Fabian Slongo); Hardlines (accommodation, arm, carbon cycle, circulation, clouds, coastal erosion (causes)/Garret Nagle, diffraction, diffusion/Brian Arnold, distillation/Michael Lewis, ecosystems, energy/Brian Arnolds, floodplain/Garret Nagle, flower/George Bethell, food chain/W R Pickering, food web/Garret Nagle, generator/Brian Arnold, glacial features, glacial movement, heart, high-pitched, hydraulic jack/Brian Arnold, lenses, light bulb, limestone, long-sighted, low-pitched, magnetism, nitrogen cycle/George Bethell, ocean currents/Garret Nagle, periscope, pH, plug (with wires), prisms, reflection, refraction, resistor, rock cycle, seasons, seismic waves, shadow, short-sighted, solar system, sonar, speed, sound waves, switches, synovial joint/W R Pickering, vacuum flask, water cycle/Matthew Lewis, wave/Brian Arnold, wavelength); Hemera Technologies Inc. (dagger, hinge, minaret); Karen Hiscock (animal kingdom, cheetah, cub, ewe, goat, jellyfish, kid, lamb, leopard, lion, lioness, panther, sheep, squid, tiger); JB Illustrations (airliner, axis on a graph, body, dimensions, eye, face, pictograph); KJA-artists.com (barbed wire, block and tackle, cogwheel, dovetail, mitre, nut and bolt/Kevin Jones, plug (with socket), ratchet, sprocket wheel); Oxford University Press (acoustic guitar, adjustable spanner/Dennis Kitchen Studio, angles, bandage, bar chart, barcode, barrel, binoculars/Mike Stone, capitals, capsules, car, car transporter/Creativa Images, cello/C Squared Studios, cereals, chisel/amattel, circle, clarinet/OUP, coastal erosion (features), compass (for directions)/OUP, compass (for drawing)/macumazahn, concentric circles, conic sections, crane, cream, crocodile clip, doe/Ekaterina V. Borisova, dome/Iakov Kalinin, castle (drawbridge), drill/Kitch Bain, double bass/the palms, earth, electric guitar/ilker canikligil, flow chart, fork (for eating)/urfin, flute/Bombaert Patrick, fork (for gardening)/Roman Milert, geodesic dome, hammer/_LeS, harp/Dmitry Skutin, helix, hippopotamus, internal organs, joist, lines, line graph, lizard, lyre/James Steidl, magnifying glass, medicine, mug/DenisNata, musical notation, obelisk, orchestra/Roger Sutcliffe, overlapping tiles, oxbow, pagoda, parallelograms, photosynthesis, piano/James Steidl, piccolo/Alenavlad, pie chart, pills, plane/Dennis Kitchen Studio, plasters, pliers/Gareth Boden Photography, portico, pressure/Daniel Baty, pulley, recorder/Evgeny Tomeev, rhinoceros, rucksack/Gareth Boden Photography, saw/ekipaj, saxophone/Horiyan, scatter diagram, screwdriver/Dennis Kitchen Studio, skeleton, spade/Prapann, spanner/Art Konovalov, spiral, spiral staircase, sports equipment/Lola Barnard, stag/Eric Isselee, syringe, tambourine/Vereshchagin Dmitry, tractor/Bjorn Heller, trapezium, trapezoid, tree/Michael Woods, triangle/OUP, triangles, trombone/3drenderings, trumpet/Judith Collins, tuba/Photodisc, vault, Venn diagram/J Shaw, violin/Valery Evlakhov, volcano, washer/Dennis Kitchen Studio, wind turbine/zentilia, workbench, xylophone/C Squared Studios); Oxford University Press (OXED) (asymmetric bars, convection currents, digestive system, DNA, dry cell, ear, embryo, fertilization, filtration, fractional distillation, levers (class 2 and class 3), microscope, moon, parallel bars, petroleum formation, plate tectonics, pommel horse, respiratory system, safety symbols, skin, states of matter, teeth, tooth, water purification); Q2AMedia (corrugated roof, handles, hieroglyphics, Möbius strip, solids); P Schramm/P Harrison/Meiklejohn Illustration (laboratory equipment, springs); Shutterstock (ammonite/psamtik, arch/Geoff54, archway/ Andie_Alpion, axe/objectsforall, axis of symmetry/Lovely Bird, axis on a globe/Africa Studio, banjo/Vereshchagin Dmitry, cable car/superjoseph, canoe/Dja65, caravan/Nerthuz, cement/Shcherbakov Ilya, concrete/Sketchphoto, cushion (tassel)/nik7ch, circular flow of income/Pensiri, dodecahedron/vectortatu, door handle/Narudom Chaisuwon, fawn/sarayut_sy, file/Roblan, glass/noprati somchit, hatchet/Andrei Kuzmik, holdall/Serg64, hose/Take Photo, kayak/marekuliasz, loom/redknapper, lute/I Canikligil, mallet/Dan Kosmayer, oscilloscope/OhSurat, pickaxe/Stocksnapper, plough/Ton Bangkeaw, push-up/Jacek Chabraszewski, rake (for earth)/Africa Studio, rake (for leaves)/Ivan Asmalouski, sand/Photo Melon, secateurs/Love You Stock, shears/chungking, shovel/Vadym Zaitsev, sit-up/Branislav Nenin, spear/Phichai, salmon meal/Jacek Chabraszewski, spirit level/Audrius Merfeldas, stile/Garry Basnett, suitcase/anna-nt, telescope/Sandratsky Dmitriy, tiles/cherezoff, trowel/mihalec, vegan meal/Elena Veselova, viola/kongsky, watering can/Ficmajstr, wheelbarrow/Margo Harrison, windmill/Sanit Fuangnakhon)

Although every effort has been made to trace and contact copyright holders before publication, this has not been possible in some cases. We apologise for any apparent infringement of copyright and, if notified, the publisher will be pleased to rectify any errors or omissions at the earliest possible opportunity.

Contents

The Oxford 3000™ and Oxford 5000™

What is the Oxford 3000?

The **Oxford 3000** is a list of the 3 000 core words that every learner of English needs to know. The words have been carefully selected based on their frequency in the language and their relevance to learners. Every word has been assigned a level, from A1 to B2 on the CEFR, guiding students from beginner to upper-intermediate level on the most important words to learn.

The **frequency** of words was measured in the Oxford English Corpus (OEC). A corpus is an electronic database containing large numbers of written or spoken texts that can be searched, sorted and analysed. The OEC contains over 2 billion words from different subject areas and contexts, covering British, American and world English. Frequency is the most important criterion for deciding the importance of a word: the most frequent 2 000 words in English make up around 80 per cent of almost any English text.

For learners of English, another important criterion is **relevance**: which words are particularly important in the specific contexts in which students encounter and use English? To measure relevance, a second corpus was created, containing all the Secondary and Adult English courses published by Oxford University Press. This means that the Oxford 3000 list covers words that you will come across in class and in your study texts, even if they are less frequent in a general corpus. These include, for example, words for everyday things and places (e.g. *banana, cafe, T-shirt*), words for describing feelings (e.g. *amazed, annoyed, unhappy*) and words connected with studying (e.g. *dictionary, exam*).

What is the CEFR?

CEFR stands for the 'Common European Framework of Reference' for languages, which is a description of the language abilities of students at different levels of learning.

The CEFR grades language skills at six levels:

- A1 and A2 indicate elementary and pre-intermediate levels of ability
- B1 and B2 indicate lower- and upper-intermediate levels.
- C1 indicates advanced level.

- C2 indicates complete proficiency in the language.

The CEFR grades language skills — what students can do in the language, for example 'can understand the main ideas of complex text on both concrete and abstract topics' (at B2). It does not grade specific grammar points or vocabulary items. However, we have aligned the words in the Oxford 3000 to the levels of the CEFR from A1 to B2, in order to guide learners of English on the most important words to learn at each level. These levels are based on the same criteria of frequency and relevance: the corpus of Secondary and Adult English courses enabled us to track the frequency of vocabulary items at each level of a course.

What is the Oxford 5000?

The Oxford 3000 is the core word list for learners up to B2/upper-intermediate level. The **Oxford 5000** is an expanded core word list for advanced learners of English. It includes an additional 2 000 words at B2–C1 level on the CEFR, guiding advanced learners on the most useful high-level words to expand their vocabulary.

Keywords in the dictionary

The words of the Oxford 3000 are shown in the main section of the dictionary in larger print in blue and with a key symbol (🔑) immediately following. The CEFR level of the word is shown after the key. The words of the Oxford 5000 are also shown in blue and have a 'key plus' symbol (🔑+) and a CEFR level of B2 or C1.

In order to make the definitions in this dictionary easy to understand, we have written them using the keywords of the Oxford 3000. Numbers and proper names are also used in definitions, as are a few language study terms, such as *alphabet, noun* and *tense*. When it has been necessary to use a specialist term that is not in the Oxford 3000, the word is shown in SMALL CAPITALS. Where appropriate, a gloss (= a short explanation of the meaning) of the specialist term is included in brackets.

For more information on the Oxford 3000 and Oxford 5000, and to see the full lists, visit **www.oxford3000.com**.

The Oxford Phrasal Academic Lexicon™

What is OPAL?

The English used for studying different academic subjects in class, or for giving lectures at a university, is different from everyday conversation between friends, or the language used in popular fiction. If you are studying academic subjects in English, it is important to become familiar with the vocabulary that you will come across in class and in your study texts, and that you will need for writing essays and reports.

The **Oxford Phrasal Academic Lexicon**, or **OPAL** for short, is a collection of four word lists that together provide an essential guide to the most important words in written and spoken academic English. There are lists of written words, spoken words, written phrases and spoken phrases.

The words and phrases in OPAL are based on two main corpora. The written words and phrases are based on the 71-million-word Oxford Corpus of Academic English, a corpus composed of academic texts published by Oxford University Press across these four subject areas: physical sciences, life sciences, social sciences, and arts and humanities. The spoken words and phrases are based on the British Academic Spoken English (BASE) corpus[1]. This corpus was developed at the Universities of Warwick and Reading, and contains nearly 1.2 million words of spoken academic English, recorded and transcribed from lectures and seminars across the same four subject areas.

OPAL was developed using a method called 'keyword analysis'. By comparing the list of the most frequent words and phrases in each corpus with the list of the most frequent words and phrases in a contrasting reference corpus, we identified the words and phrases that are most important in an academic setting. For the written lists, we compared the OCAE with the fiction subcorpus of the Oxford English Corpus. For the spoken lists, we compared the BASE corpus with the spoken subcorpus of the British National Corpus, containing recordings of meetings and everyday conversation.

OPAL in the dictionary and online

Words that belong to the OPAL written and spoken word lists are indicated in the dictionary by symbols next to the headword: **W** indicates a word on the OPAL written word list; **S** indicates a word on the OPAL spoken word list; and **O** indicates are word on both the written and spoken word lists.

To see the full lists, visit **www.opalwordlist.com**. The written word list is divided into twelve sublists of 100 words each and the spoken word list is divided into six sublists of 100 words each. Sublist 1 of each list contains the most important academic words, with the next most important in Sublist 2, and so on.

It is often not the word itself that is 'academic', but the way it is used and combined with other words in an academic context. Therefore, besides the lists of single words, OPAL also includes a list of written phrases and a list of spoken phrases, which you can also find online. The phrase lists are grouped into academic functions, such as 'Explaining and defining' and 'Giving examples and presenting evidence'.

Whether you are using the print dictionary or accessing OPAL online, it is important to realize that learning a word involves more than just knowing its basic meaning. Some words may have specific meanings in particular contexts. For example, the word *culture* may have a different meaning, depending on whether the area of study is social studies, arts and media, or biology. The dictionary entry will guide you on the different meanings, with examples of use for each one.

---

[1]OPAL has been created with reference to the following corpora: the Oxford Corpus of Academic English (OCAE), the fiction subcorpus of the Oxford English Corpus (OEC), the spoken element of the British National Corpus (BNC) and a subset of the British Academic Spoken English (BASE) corpus, developed within the University of Warwick and for which relevant permissions have been obtained. BASE was developed at the Universities of Warwick and Reading under the directorship of Hilary Nesi and Paul Thompson. Corpus development of BASE was assisted by funding from BALEAP, EURALEX, the British Academic and the Arts and Humanities Research Council.

Guide to the dictionary

Headword ———————— **Pronunciation** is given at each headword.

Part of speech (= noun, adjective, etc.)

music ⚹ **A1** /'mjuːzɪk/ *noun* [U] **1** an arrangement of sounds in patterns to be sung or played on instruments: *What sort of music do you like?* ◇ *classical/pop/rock music* ◇ *to write/compose music* ◇ *a music lesson/teacher* **2** the written signs that represent the sounds of music: *Can you read music?*

The **definition** is the meaning of the word. This is shown in simple English.

Sense numbers separate different meanings.　　　　**Examples** show you how to use the word.

Words marked with a ⚹ symbol are part of the *Oxford 3000* list of important words (see page **iv**).

The **A2** tells you the CEFR level of the word.

Words from the *Oxford Phrasal Academic Lexicon* (OPAL) *written* and *spoken* word lists are marked with ⊙ (see page **v**).

ability ⚹ **A2** ⊙ /ə'bɪləti/ *noun* [C, U] (*pl.* -ies) ~ **(to do sth)** the mental or physical power or skill that makes it possible to do sth: *an ability to make decisions* ◇ *A person of his ability should have no difficulty at all in getting a job.* **OPP inability**

Words with a ⚹+ symbol are part of the *Oxford 5000* list of important words (see page **v**).

absent ⚹+ **C1** ⓦ /'æbsənt/ *adj.* **1** ~ **(from ...)** not present somewhere: *He was absent from work because of illness.* **OPP present¹** **2** showing that you are not really looking at or thinking about what is happening around you: *an absent expression/stare* ▸ absently *adv.*

Words from the *OPAL written* word list are marked with ⓦ (see page **v**).

Words from the *OPAL spoken* word list are marked with ⓢ (see page **v**).

actually ⚹ **A2** ⓢ /'æktʃuəli/ *adv.* **1** used to emphasize a fact or a comment, or that sth is really true: *It's not actually raining now.* ◇ *I can't believe that I'm actually going to America!* **2** used to show surprise about what is true: *The food was not actually that expensive.* **3** used to correct sb or say sth that sb might not like, in a polite way: *We're not American, actually.* ◇ *Actually, I'm busy at the moment.*

Stress marks show pronunciation in compounds.

Headwords are listed in alphabetical order whether they are written as one word or two, or with a hyphen.

'sound effect *noun* [C, usually pl.] (**ARTS AND MEDIA**) a sound that is made artificially, for example the sound of the wind, and used in a play, film or computer game to make it more realistic

soundly /'saʊndli/ *adv.* completely or deeply: *The children were sleeping soundly.*

soundproof /'saʊndpruːf/ *adj.* made so that no sound can get in or out: *a soundproof room*

soundtrack /'saʊndtræk/ *noun* [C] (**ARTS AND MEDIA, MUSIC**) the recorded sound and music from a film or computer game ⊃ look at **track¹** (5)

Subject labels show the words that relate to a particular subject.

Cross references direct you to related vocabulary.

drum¹ ɪ **B1** /drʌm/ *noun* [C] **1** (**MUSIC**) a musical instrument like an empty container with plastic or skin stretched across the ends. You play a drum by hitting it with your hands or with sticks: *She plays drums in a band.* ◇ *Tony Cox on drums* ⊃ picture at **instrument, orchestra 2** a round container: *an oil drum*

drum² /drʌm/ *verb* (-mm-) **1** [I] (**MUSIC**) to play a drum **2** [I, T] to make a noise like a drum by hitting sth many times: *to drum your fingers on the table* (= because you are annoyed, impatient, etc.)
PHR V **drum sth into sb** to make sb remember sth by repeating it many times **drum sth up** to try to get support or business: *to drum up more custom*

rhythm ɪ **B2** /'rɪðəm/ *noun* [C, U] (**MUSIC**) a regular repeated pattern of sound or movement: *I'm not keen on the tune but I love the rhythm.* ◇ *He's a terrible dancer because he has no sense of rhythm.* ◇ *He tapped his foot in rhythm with the music.* ▸ **rhythmic** /'rɪðmɪk/ (*also* **rhythmical** /-mɪkl/) *adj.*: *the rhythmic qualities of African music* ▸ **rhythmically** /-kli/ *adv.*

slip¹ ɪ **B2** /slɪp/ *verb* (-pp-)
• SLIDE/FALL **1** [I] ~ (**over**); ~ (**on sth**) to slide a short distance by accident and fall or nearly fall: *She slipped over on the wet floor.* ◇ *I slipped on the ice and twisted my ankle.*
• OUT OF POSITION **2** [I] (often used with an adverb or a preposition) to slide out of the correct position or out of your hand: *This hat's too big. It keeps slipping down over my eyes.* ◇ *The glass slipped out of my hand and smashed on the floor.*
• GO/PUT QUIETLY **3** [I] (used with an adverb or a preposition) to move or go somewhere quietly, quickly, and often without being noticed: *While everyone was dancing we slipped away and went home.* **4** [T] ~ **sth (to sb)**; ~ (**sb**) **sth** to put sth somewhere or give sth to sb quietly and often without being noticed: *She picked up the money and slipped it into her pocket.* ◇ *He slipped her a note under the table.*
• BECOME WORSE **5** [I] to fall a little in value, level, etc.
• CLOTHES **6** [I, T] ~ **into/out of sth**; ~ **sth on/off** to put on or take off a piece of clothing quickly and easily: *She slipped into her silk jacket.* ◇ *I slipped off my shoes.*
IDM **let sth slip** to give sb information that you should keep secret **slip your mind** if sth **slips your mind**, you forget it or forget to do it: *I'm sorry, the meeting completely slipped my mind.*
PHR V **slip out** when sth **slips out**, you say it without really intending to: *I didn't mean to tell them. It just slipped out.* **slip up** (*informal*) to make a mistake

American and other **different spellings** are shown in brackets.

flautist /ˈflɔːtɪst/ (*BrE*) (*AmE* **flutist**) *noun* [C] (**MUSIC**) a person who plays the FLUTE (= a musical instrument that you blow into)

Difficult words in definitions are explained.

high-ˈpitched *adj.* (used about sounds) very high: *a high-pitched voice/whistle* **OPP** **low-pitched**

Opposite (= a word with the opposite meaning)

hobby ⓘ **A1** /ˈhɒbi/ *noun* [C] (*pl.* **-ies**) something that you do regularly for pleasure in your free time: *Chloe's hobbies are gaming and mountain biking.* **SYN** **pastime**

Synonym (= a word with the same meaning)

Word family boxes show related words.

WORD FAMILY

produce *verb*
produce *noun*
producer *noun*
production *noun*
productive *adj.*
(≠ **unproductive**)

▼ COLLOCATIONS

the performing arts

A **composer** writes a **song/a musical/an opera**. A **playwright** or **dramatist** writes plays: *He's written a new musical.* A group **presents/performs/produces/puts on/ stages** a play, show, etc: *The drama group is putting on a show at the local school.* ◇ *We are proud to present Arthur Miller's 'The Crucible'.* A **director directs** a play, show, etc: *The theatre has got a new director.* ◇ *She is directing Mozart's 'Figaro' at La Scala.* A performer, an actor, etc. **acts/ appears/performs/sings/stars in** a play, show, etc: *She's appearing in 'The Seagull' at the New Theatre.* ◇ *He starred in the musical 'Guys and Dolls'.* A performer, an actor, etc. **rehearses (for)** a play, show, etc: *She had three weeks to rehearse for the concert.*

Note boxes help you to extend your vocabulary.

▼ SYNONYMS

ask

enquire/inquire ◆ demand ◆ query

All these words mean to say or write sth in the form of a question, in order to get information.

ask *Can I ask you a question?*

enquire/inquire (formal) *I emailed the company to enquire about work experience.*

demand *'Where have you been?' he demanded angrily.*

query (formal) *'Why ever not?' she queried.*

A a

A¹ /eɪ/ *noun* [C, U] (*pl.* A's) **1** (*also* a, *pl.* a's) the first letter of the English alphabet: *'Andy' begins with (an) 'A'.* **2** (MUSIC) the sixth note in the SCALE of C MAJOR **3** ~ (in/for sth) (EDUCATION) a grade given for an exam or a piece of work that shows that it is excellent: *I got an A for my essay.*
IDM from A to B from one place to another: *All I need is a car that gets me from A to B.*

A² *abbr.* (in writing) (*pl.* A) = AMP (1)

a [A1] /ə, *strong form* eɪ/ (*also* an) *indefinite article* ❶ The form an is used before a vowel sound: *an apple ◇ an hour ◇ an MP* **1** one: *A cup of coffee, please. ◇ We've got an apple, a banana and two oranges.* **2** used when you talk about one example of sth for the first time: *I saw a dog chasing a cat this morning. The cat climbed up a tree. ◇ Have you got a dictionary* (= any dictionary)? **3** used for saying what kind of person or thing sb/sth is: *He's a doctor. ◇ She's a Muslim. ◇ You are a clever boy. ◇ 'Is that an eagle?' 'No, it's a falcon.'* **4** (used with prices, rates and measurements) each: *I usually drink 2 litres of water a day. ◇ twice a week ◇ He was travelling at about 80 miles an hour.* **SYN per 5** used with some expressions of quantity: *a lot of money ◇ a few cars* **6** (used when you are talking about a typical example of sth) any; every: *An elephant can live for up to 80 years.* **HELP** You can also use the plural in this sense: *Elephants can live for up to 80 years.*

a- /eɪ/ *prefix* (in nouns, adjectives and adverbs) not; without: *atheist ◇ amoral*

A & E /ˌeɪ ənd ˈiː/ *abbr.* (*BrE*) (MEDICINE) **accident and emergency** (the part of a hospital where people who need immediate treatment are taken) ⊃ look at **ER** ⊃ note at **hospital**

aback /əˈbæk/ *adv.*
IDM be taken aback (by sb/sth) to be shocked or surprised by sb/sth

abacus /ˈæbəkəs/ *noun* [C] (MATHEMATICS) a frame with small balls that slide along wires. It is used as a tool or toy for counting.

abandon [B2] /əˈbændən/ *verb* [T] **1** to leave sb/sth that you are responsible for, usually permanently: *The bank robbers abandoned the car just outside the city.* **2** to stop doing sth without finishing it or without achieving what you wanted to do: *The search for the missing sailors was abandoned after two days.*
▸ **abandonment** *noun* [U]

abandoned /əˈbændənd/ *adj.* **1** left and no longer wanted, used or needed: *an abandoned car/house* **2** (used about people or their behaviour) wild; not following accepted standards

abashed /əˈbæʃt/ *adj.* feeling guilty and embarrassed because of sth that you have done: *'I'm sorry,' said Ali, looking abashed.*

abate /əˈbeɪt/ *verb* [I, T] (*formal*) to become less strong; to make sth less strong

abattoir /ˈæbətwɑː(r)/ = SLAUGHTERHOUSE

abbess /ˈæbes/ *noun* [C] (RELIGION) a woman who is the head of an ABBEY of NUNS (= religious women who often live apart from other people)

abbey /ˈæbi/ *noun* [C] (RELIGION) a large church together with a group of buildings where MONKS or NUNS (= members of a religious group of men or women) live or lived in the past

abbot /ˈæbət/ *noun* [C] (RELIGION) a man who is the head of an ABBEY of MONKS (= religious men who often live apart from other people)

abbreviate /əˈbriːvieɪt/ *verb* [T] to make sth shorter, especially a word or phrase: *'Kilometre' is usually abbreviated to 'km'.* ⊃ look at **abridge**

abbreviation /əˌbriːviˈeɪʃn/ *noun* [C] (LANGUAGE) a short form of a word or phrase: *In this dictionary 'sth' is the abbreviation for 'something'.*

ABC /ˌeɪ biː ˈsiː/ *noun* [sing.] **1** (LANGUAGE) all the letters of the alphabet **2** the simple facts about sth: *an ABC of Gardening*

abdicate /ˈæbdɪkeɪt/ *verb* [I] (HISTORY, POLITICS) to give up being king or queen: *The queen abdicated in favour of her son* (= her son became king). **2** to give sth up, especially power or a position: *to abdicate responsibility* (= to refuse to be responsible for sth) ▸ **abdication** /ˌæbdɪˈkeɪʃn/ *noun* [C, U]

abdomen /ˈæbdəmən/ *noun* [C] **1** (ANATOMY) a part of the body below the chest that contains the stomach, BOWELS, etc. **2** the end part of an insect's body ⊃ look at **thorax** (2) ⊃ picture at **animal** ▸ **abdominal** /æbˈdɒmɪnl/ *adj.*: *abdominal pains*

abdominals /æbˈdɒmɪnlz/ (*also informal* **abs**) *noun* [pl.] (ANATOMY) the muscles of the ABDOMEN

abduct /æbˈdʌkt/ *verb* [T] (LAW) to take hold of sb and take them away illegally ▸ **abduction** /-ˈdʌkʃn/ *noun* [C, U]

abductor /æbˈdʌktə(r)/ (*also* ab'ductor muscle) *noun* [C] (ANATOMY) a muscle that moves a body part away from the middle of the body or from another part ⊃ look at **adductor**

aberration /ˌæbəˈreɪʃn/ *noun* [C, U] (*formal*) a fact, an action or a way of behaving that is not usual, and that may be unacceptable

abet /əˈbet/ *verb* (-tt-)
IDM aid and abet → AID²

abhor /əbˈhɔː(r)/ *verb* [T] (not used in the progressive tenses) (-rr-) (*formal*) to hate sth very much

abhorrence /əbˈhɒrəns/ *noun* [U] (*formal*) a strong feeling of hate **SYN disgust¹**

abhorrent /əbˈhɒrənt/ *adj.* ~ (to sb) (*formal*) causing a strong feeling of hate: *The idea of slavery is abhorrent to us nowadays.*

abide /əˈbaɪd/ *verb* [T] (not used in the progressive tenses) used especially after *can/could* in negative sentences to emphasize that you do not like sth/sb **SYN stand¹**
PHRV abide by sth to obey a law, etc.; to do what sb has decided

ability [A2] ⊙ /əˈbɪləti/ *noun* [C, U] (*pl.* -ies) ~ (to do sth) the mental or physical power or skill that makes it possible to do sth: *an ability to make decisions ◇ A person of his ability should have no difficulty at all in getting a job.* **OPP inability**

abject /ˈæbdʒekt/ *adj.* (*formal*) **1** terrible and without hope: *abject poverty* **2** without any respect for yourself: *an abject apology*

ablation /əˈbleɪʃn/ *noun* [U] **1** (MEDICINE) the use of surgery to remove body TISSUE **2** (GEOLOGY) the loss of material from a large mass of ice, snow or rock as a result of the action of the sun, wind or rain ⊃ picture at **glacial**

ablaze /əˈbleɪz/ *adj.* [not before noun] burning strongly; completely on fire: *Soldiers used petrol to set the building ablaze. ◇* (*figurative*) *The lights were ablaze.*

able 🔊 **A2** /'eɪbl/ *adj.*
1 (used as a modal verb) ~ **to do sth** to have the ability, power, opportunity, time, etc. to do sth: *Will you be able to come to a meeting next week?* ◇ *I was able to solve the problem quickly.* ◇ *Many men don't feel able to express their emotions.* **OPP** **unable 2** (abler /-blə(r)/; ablest /-blɪst/) clever; doing your job well: *one of the ablest students in the class* ◇ *an able politician* ▸ **ably** /-bli/ *adv.*

WORD FAMILY

able *adj.* (≠**unable**)
ably *adv.*
ability *noun* (≠**inability**)
disabled *adj.*
disability *noun*

able-'bodied *adj.* (**HEALTH**) physically healthy and strong; having full use of your body

abnormal 🔟 /æb'nɔːml/ *adj.* different from what is normal or usual, in a way that worries you or that is unpleasant **OPP** **normal**¹ ▸ **abnormally** /-məli/ *adv.*: *abnormally high temperatures*

abnormality 🔟 /ˌæbnɔː'mæləti/ *noun* [C, U] (*pl.* -ies) (**HEALTH**) something that is not normal, especially in a person's body: *He was born with an abnormality of the heart.*

aboard /ə'bɔːd/ *adv., prep.* on or onto a train, ship, aircraft or bus: *We climbed aboard the train and found a seat.* ◇ *Welcome aboard this flight to Caracas.*

abode /ə'bəʊd/ *noun* [sing.] (*formal*) the place where you live
IDM **(of) no fixed abode/address** → FIXED

abolish 🔊+ **C1** /ə'bɒlɪʃ/ *verb* [T] (**LAW**) to end a law or system officially: *When was capital punishment abolished here?*

abolition /ˌæbə'lɪʃn/ *noun* [U] (**HISTORY, LAW**) the act of ending a law or system officially: *the abolition of slavery in the US*

A-bomb /'eɪ bɒm/ = ATOMIC BOMB

abominable /ə'bɒmɪnəbl/ *adj.* very bad; shocking ▸ **abominably** /-bli/ *adv.*

Aboriginal /ˌæbə'rɪdʒənl/ *noun* (*also* aboriginal) [C] (**SOCIAL STUDIES**) a member of a human group who were the original people living in a country, especially Australia ▸ **Aboriginal** (*also* aboriginal) *adj.*: *Aboriginal traditions*

aborigine /ˌæbə'rɪdʒəni/ *noun* [C] (**SOCIAL STUDIES**) **1** a member of a human group who were the original people living in a country **2** Aborigine a member of the human group who were the original people of Australia

abort /ə'bɔːt/ *verb* [T] **1** (**MEDICINE**) to end a PREGNANCY early in order to prevent a baby from developing and being born alive **2** to end sth before it is complete, especially because it is likely to fail: *The company aborted the project when they realized it was costing too much.*

abortion 🔊+ **C1** /ə'bɔːʃn/ *noun* [C, U] (**MEDICINE**) a medical operation that ends a PREGNANCY at an early stage so that a baby cannot develop: *to have an abortion* ◇ *Abortion is illegal in some countries.* ⊃ look at **miscarriage**

abortionist /ə'bɔːʃənɪst/ *noun* [C] a person who performs a medical operation, especially illegally, that ends a PREGNANCY at an early stage so that a baby cannot develop

abortive /ə'bɔːtɪv/ *adj.* (*formal*) (used about an action) not completed successfully; failed: *He made two abortive attempts to escape from prison.*
SYN **unsuccessful**

abound /ə'baʊnd/ *verb* [I] to exist in large numbers: *Animals abound in the forest.*
PHR V **abound with/in sth** to contain large numbers of sth: *The lake abounds with fish.*

about¹ 🔊 **A1** /ə'baʊt/ *adv.* **1** a little more or less than; approximately: *It's about 3 miles from the city centre.* ◇ *I got home at about half past seven.*
SYN **approximately** ⊃ note at **measure**² **2** (*informal*) almost; nearly: *Dinner's just about ready.* **3** (*especially BrE*) in many directions or places: *I could hear people moving about upstairs.* ◇ *Don't leave your clothes lying about all over the floor.* **4** (*especially BrE*) (used after certain verbs) without doing anything in particular: *The kids spend most evenings sitting about, bored.* **5** (*especially BrE*) present in a place; existing: *It was very late and there were few people about.* ◇ *There isn't much good music about these days.*

about² 🔊 **A1** /ə'baʊt/ *prep.* **1** on the subject of: *Let's talk about something else.* ◇ *What's your book about?* ◇ *He told me all about his family.* ◇ *I don't like it, but there's nothing I can do about it.* **2** busy with sth; doing sth: *Everywhere people were going about their daily business.* **3** (*especially BrE*) in many directions or places; in different parts of sth: *We wandered about the town for an hour or two.* ◇ *Lots of old newspapers were scattered about the room.* **4** in the character of sb/sth: *There's something about him that I don't quite trust.* ◇ *I like the food, the climate, and everything else about this country.*
IDM **how/what about ... ?** **1** (used when asking for information about sb/sth or for sb's opinion or wish): *How about Ruth? Have you heard from her lately?* ◇ *I'm going to have chicken. What about you?* **2** (used when making a suggestion): *What about going to see a film tonight?*

about³ /ə'baʊt/ *adj.*
IDM **be about to do sth** to be going to do sth very soon: *The film's about to start.* ◇ *I was just about to explain when she interrupted me.*

a,bout-'turn (*BrE*) (*AmE* a,bout-'face) *noun* [C] a complete change of opinion, plan or behaviour: *The government did an about-turn over tax.* ⊃ look at **U-turn** (2)

above¹ 🔊 **A1** /ə'bʌv/ *prep.*
• HIGHER PLACE **1** at or to a higher place than sb/sth: *the people in the flat above mine* ◇ *The coffee is in the cupboard above the sink.* **OPP** **below**
• MORE THAN **2** more than a number, an amount, a price, etc: *You must get above 50% to pass.* ◇ *Temperatures have been above average.* **OPP** **below** ⊃ look at **over**¹ (6)
• AT WORK **3** with a higher position in an organization, etc: *The person above me is the department manager.* **OPP** **below**
• PROUD **4** too proud to do sth: *He seems to think he's above helping with the cleaning.*
IDM **above all** (used to emphasize the main point) most important of all; especially: *Above all, stay calm!*

above² 🔊 **A1** 🔟 /ə'bʌv/ *adv.* **1** at or to a higher place: *The people in the flat above make a lot of noise.* **OPP** **below 2** more than a number, an amount, a price, etc: *children aged 11 and above* ◇ *A score of 70 and above will get you a grade B.* **OPP** **below** ⊃ look at **over**¹ (6) **3** earlier in something written or printed: *As was stated above, ...*

above³ 🔟 /ə'bʌv/ *adj.* [only before noun] mentioned or printed previously in a letter, book, etc: *Contact me at the above address.* ▸ **the above** 🔟 *noun* [sing. + sing./pl. verb]

a,bove 'board *adj., adv.* legal and honest; in a legal and honest way a,bove-'mentioned *adj.* [only before noun] mentioned or named earlier in the same letter, book, etc.

abrasion /əˈbreɪʒn/ *noun* **1** [C] (**HEALTH**) a damaged area of the skin where it has been rubbed against sth hard and rough **2** [U] (**GEOGRAPHY**) damage to a surface caused when sth is rubbed very hard against it ⊃ picture at **erosion**

abrasive /əˈbreɪsɪv/ *adj.* **1** rough and likely to damage a surface: *Do not use abrasive cleaners on the bath.* **2** (used about a person) rude and rather aggressive

abreast /əˈbrest/ *adv.* next to or level with sb/sth and going in the same direction: *The soldiers marched two abreast.*
IDM be/keep abreast of sth to have all the most recent information about sth

abridge /əˈbrɪdʒ/ *verb* [T] (**LITERATURE**) to make a book, play, etc. shorter by removing parts of it ⊃ look at **abbreviate**

abroad ȴ **A2** /əˈbrɔːd/ *adv.* (**TOURISM**) in or to another country or countries: *My mother has never been abroad.* ◇ *She often goes abroad on business.*

abrupt /əˈbrʌpt/ *adj.* **1** sudden and unexpected: *an abrupt change of plan* **2** ~ (with sb) seeming rude and unfriendly: *I'm sorry for being so abrupt with you.*
▸ abruptly *adv.* ▸ abruptness *noun* [U]

ABS /ˌeɪ biː ˈes/ *abbr.* **anti-lock braking system** (a system that stops the wheels of a vehicle from locking if you have to stop suddenly, and therefore make the vehicle easier to control)

abs /æbz/ (*informal*) = ABDOMINALS

abscess /ˈæbses/ *noun* [C] (**HEALTH**) a SWOLLEN (= larger than normal) and painful area on or in the body, containing PUS (= a thick yellow liquid)

abscond /əbˈskɒnd/ *verb* [I] ~ (from sth) (with sth) (*formal*) to run away from a place that you are not allowed to leave without permission: *to abscond from prison* ◇ *She absconded with all the company's money.*

abseil /ˈæbseɪl/ (*BrE*) (*AmE* **rappel**) *verb* [I] (**SPORT**) to go down a steep CLIFF or rock while you are fastened to a rope, pushing against the surface with your feet

absence ȴ+ **C1 W** /ˈæbsəns/ *noun* **1** [C, U] ~ (from …) a time when sb is away from somewhere; the fact of being away from somewhere: *Frequent absences due to illness meant he was behind with his work.* ◇ *absence from school* ◇ *I have to make all the decisions in his absence.* **2** [U] (in the) ~ (of sb/sth) the fact of sb/sth not being there; lack: *In the absence of a doctor, try to help the injured person yourself.* **OPP** presence

absent ȴ+ **C1 W** /ˈæbsənt/ *adj.* **1** ~ (from …) not present somewhere: *He was absent from work because of illness.* **OPP** present¹ **2** showing that you are not really looking at or thinking about what is happening around you: *an absent expression/stare* ▸ absently *adv.*

absentee /ˌæbsənˈtiː/ *noun* [C] a person who is not in the place where they should be

,absentee 'ballot (*AmE*) = POSTAL VOTE

absenteeism /ˌæbsənˈtiːɪzəm/ *noun* [U] the problem of workers or students often not going to work or school

,absent-'minded *adj.* often forgetting or not noticing things, perhaps because you are thinking about sth else **SYN** forgetful ▸ absent-mindedly *adv.*

absolute ȴ **B2** ⊙ /ˈæbsəluːt/ *adj.* **1** complete; total: *The trip was an absolute disaster.* **2** [only before noun] used, especially in spoken English, to give emphasis to what you are saying: *That's absolute nonsense!* **3** not measured in comparison with sth else: *House prices are falling in absolute terms.*

absolutely ȴ **B1** /ˈæbsəluːtli/ *adv.* **1** completely; totally: *It's absolutely freezing outside!* ◇ *I absolutely refuse to believe that.* ◇ *He made absolutely no effort* (= no effort at all) *to help me.* **2** /ˌæbsəˈluːtli/ (used when you are agreeing with sb) yes; certainly: *'It is a good idea, isn't it?' 'Oh, absolutely!'* **3** absolutely not used to show that you strongly disagree with sb, or to refuse permission to do sth: *'Do you think you'll apply for that job?' 'Absolutely not!'*

,absolute ma'jority *noun* [C] (**POLITICS**) more than half of the total number of votes or winning candidates in an election: *280 seats are needed for an absolute majority in the National Assembly.* **SYN** overall majority

,absolute 'zero *noun* [U] (**PHYSICS**) the lowest temperature that is thought to be possible

absolution /ˌæbsəˈluːʃn/ *noun* [U, C] (**RELIGION**) (especially in the Christian Church) a formal statement that a person is forgiven for what he or she has done wrong

absolutism /ˈæbsəluːtɪzəm/ *noun* [U] **1** (**POLITICS**) a political system in which a leader or government has total power at all times **2** (**POLITICS**, **RELIGION**) belief in a political, religious or moral idea that you think is true in all situations ▸ absolutist /-tɪst/ *adj.*, *noun* [C]

absolve /əbˈzɒlv/ *verb* [T] ~ sb (from/of sth) **1** to say formally that sb does not have to take responsibility for sth: *The court absolved the driver of all responsibility for the accident.* **2** (**RELIGION**) to give ABSOLUTION to sb: *I absolve you from all your sins.*

absorb ȴ+ **B2** /əbˈzɔːb/ *verb* [T]
• LIQUID/HEAT **1** ~ sth (into sth) to take in and hold a liquid, heat, etc: *a drug that is quickly absorbed into the bloodstream*
• INFORMATION **2** to take sth into the mind and understand it: *I found it impossible to absorb so much information so quickly.*
• INTO STH LARGER **3** [often passive] ~ sth (into sth) to take sth into sth larger, so that it becomes part of it: *Over the years many villages have been absorbed into the city.*
• INTEREST **4** to hold sb's attention completely or interest sb very much: *History is a subject that absorbs her.*
• A KNOCK/HIT **5** to reduce the effect of a sudden violent knock, hit, etc: *The front of the car is designed to absorb most of the impact of a crash.*

absorbed /əbˈzɔːbd/ *adj.* ~ (in sth) giving all your attention to sth: *He was absorbed in his work and didn't hear me come in.*

absorbent /əbˈzɔːbənt/ *adj.* able to take in and hold liquid: *an absorbent cloth* ▸ absorbency /-bənsi/ *noun* [U]

absorbing /əbˈzɔːbɪŋ/ *adj.* holding all your interest and attention: *an absorbing book*

absorption /əbˈzɔːpʃn/ *noun* [U] **1** the process of a liquid, gas or other substance being taken in: *Vitamin D is necessary to aid the absorption of calcium from food.* **2** ~ (of sb/sth) (into sth) (**SOCIAL STUDIES**) the process of a smaller group, country, etc., becoming part of a larger group or country: *the absorption of immigrants into the host country* **3** ~ (in sth) the fact of sb being very interested in sth so that it takes all their attention: *His work suffered because of his total absorption in sport.*

abstain /əbˈsteɪn/ *verb* [I] **1** ~ (from sth/doing sth) (*formal*) to stop yourself from doing sth that you enjoy: *The doctor said he should abstain from (eating) fatty foods until he was better.* ⊃ noun **abstinence** **2** (**POLITICS**) (in a vote) to say that you are not voting either for or against sth: *Two people voted in favour,* two voted against and one abstained. ➔ noun **abstention**

abstainer /əb'steɪnə(r)/ noun [C] **1** (POLITICS) a person who chooses not to vote either in favour of or against sth **2** a person who ABSTAINS from sth (= chooses not to do or have it), especially alcohol

abstention /əb'stenʃn/ noun [C, U] (POLITICS) an act of choosing not to vote either for or against sth

abstinence /'æbstɪnəns/ noun [U] ~ (from sth) (formal) the practice of stopping yourself from having or doing sth that you enjoy: The doctor advised total abstinence from dairy products. ➔ verb **abstain**

abstract¹ ʔ+ B2 /'æbstrækt/ adj. **1** existing only as an idea, not as a physical thing: It is hard to imagine an abstract idea like 'eternity'. OPP **concrete¹** **2** (used about art) not showing people and things as they really look, but showing the artist's feelings about them: an abstract painting

abstract² /'æbstrækt/ noun [C] **1** (ART) an example of ABSTRACT art **2** a short piece of writing that tells you the main contents of a book, speech, etc. SYN **summary¹** IDM **in the abstract** only as an idea, not in real life

abstract³ /æb'strækt/ verb [T] ~ sth (from sth) to remove sth from somewhere: She abstracted the main points from the argument.

abstract ex'pressionism noun [U] (ART) a style and movement in ABSTRACT art that developed in New York in the middle of the twentieth century and tries to express the feelings of the artist rather than showing a physical object ▸ abstract ex'pressionist noun [C], adj.: abstract expressionist art

abstraction /æb'strækʃn/ noun **1** [C, U] (formal) a general idea not based on any particular real person, thing or situation **2** [U] (formal) the state of thinking deeply about sth and not paying attention to what is around you **3** [U, C] the act of removing sth from sth else: water abstraction from rivers

abstract 'noun noun [C] (GRAMMAR) a noun, for example goodness or freedom, that refers to an idea or a general quality, not to a physical object

absurd ʔ+ C1 /əb'sɜːd/ adj. not at all logical or sensible: It would be absurd to spend all your money on one pair of shoes. ◇ Don't be absurd! I can't possibly do all that in one day. SYN **ridiculous** ▸ absurdity noun [C, U] (pl. -ies) ▸ absurdly adv.

abundance ʔ+ C1 /ə'bʌndəns/ noun [sing., U] a very large quantity of sth: There is an abundance of wildlife in the forest. SYN **profusion** IDM **in abundance** in large quantities: These flowers grow here in abundance.

abundant /ə'bʌndənt/ adj. existing in very large quantities; more than enough SYN **plentiful** ▸ abundantly adv.

abuse¹ ʔ+ C1 /ə'bjuːs/ noun **1** [U, sing.] using sth in a bad or dishonest way: the dangers of drug abuse ◇ an abuse of power **2** [U] (LAW) bad, usually violent treatment of sb: He subjected her to verbal and physical abuse. ◇ **child abuse** **3** [U] rude and offensive words, usually spoken when sb is angry: The other driver leaned out of the car and hurled abuse at me. ◇ racial abuse SYN **insult²**

abuse² ʔ+ C1 /ə'bjuːz/ verb [T] **1** to use sth in a bad or dishonest way: to abuse alcohol/drugs ◇ The politician was accused of abusing his position in order to become rich. **2** to say rude things to sb SYN **insult¹** **3** (LAW) to treat sb badly, often violently: The girl was being physically abused.

abusive /ə'bjuːsɪv/ adj. **1** (used about a person or what they say) rude and offensive: an abusive remark **2** involving violent behaviour: an abusive relationship

abysmal /ə'bɪzməl/ adj. very bad; of very poor quality ▸ abysmally /-məli/ adv.

abyss /ə'bɪs/ noun [C] (formal) a very deep hole that seems to have no bottom

abyssal /ə'bɪsl/ adj. (GEOGRAPHY) connected with the deepest parts of the ocean or the ocean floor

AC /ˌeɪ 'siː/ abbr. **1** = AIR CONDITIONING **2** = ALTERNATING CURRENT

a/c abbr. **1** /ˌeɪ 'siː/ = AIR CONDITIONING **2** (in writing) = ACCOUNT¹ (1)

acacia /ə'keɪʃə/ (also a'cacia tree) noun [C] a tree with yellow or white flowers. There are several types of acacia.

academia /ˌækə'diːmiə/ noun [U] (EDUCATION) the world of learning, research, etc. at universities, and the people involved in it

academic¹ ʔ B1 ⊙ /ˌækə'demɪk/ adj. **1** (EDUCATION) connected with education, especially in schools and universities: The academic year begins in September. **2** (EDUCATION) involving a lot of reading and studying rather than practical or technical skills: academic subjects such as history OPP **non-academic** **3** not connected with reality; not affecting the facts of a situation: It's academic which one I prefer because I can't have either of them. ▸ academically /-kli/ adv.

academic² ʔ B2 ⊙ /ˌækə'demɪk/ noun [C] (EDUCATION) a person who teaches and/or does research at a university or college

academician /əˌkædə'mɪʃn/ noun [C] (ARTS AND MEDIA) a member of an official group of people who are important in art, science or literature

academic 'year noun [C] (EDUCATION) the period of the year during which students go to school or university

academy ʔ+ C1 /ə'kædəmi/ noun [C] (pl. -ies) **1** (EDUCATION) a school for special training: a military academy **2** (usually Academy) (ARTS AND MEDIA) an official group of people who are important in art, science or literature: the Royal Academy of Arts **3** (EDUCATION) a school in England that is independent of local authority control

accede /ək'siːd/ verb [I] ~ (to sth) (formal) **1** to agree to a request, demand, etc: He acceded to demands for his resignation. **2** (HISTORY, POLITICS) to achieve a very high position, especially to become king or queen: Queen Victoria acceded to the throne in 1837. ➔ noun **accession**

accelerando /əkˌselə'rændəʊ/ adv., adj. (MUSIC) gradually increasing in speed ▸ accelerando noun [C] (pl. -os)

accelerate ʔ+ C1 /ək'seləreɪt/ verb [I, T] (PHYSICS) to go faster; to make sth go faster or happen more quickly: The driver slowed down for the bend then accelerated away. ◇ The government plans to accelerate the pace of reform. OPP **decelerate** ▸ acceleration /əkˌselə'reɪʃn/ noun [U, sing.]

accelerator /ək'seləreɪtə(r)/ noun [C] the control in a vehicle that you press with your foot in order to make it go faster

accent ʔ+ B2 /'æksent, -sənt/ noun **1** [C] (LANGUAGE, SOCIAL STUDIES) a particular way of pronouncing words that is connected with the country, area or social class that you come from: He speaks with a strong Scottish accent. **2** [C] (LANGUAGE) the greater force that you give to a particular word or part of a word when you speak: In the word 'because' the accent is on the second syllable. SYN **stress¹** **3** [C] (LANGUAGE) a mark, usually above a letter, that shows that it has to be pronounced in a certain way **4** [sing.] the particular importance that is given to sth: *In all our products the accent is on quality.* **SYN emphasis**

accentuate /əkˈsentʃueɪt/ *verb* [T] to make sth easier to notice: *Her short hair accentuates her eyes.*

accept ♫ **A2 ○** /əkˈsept/ *verb* **1** [T] to agree to take sth that sb offers you: *Please accept this small gift.* ◇ *Do I have to pay in cash or will you accept a credit card?* ◇ *Why won't you accept my advice?* **2** [I, T] to say 'yes' to sth or to agree to sth willingly: *Thank you for your invitation. I am happy to accept.* ◇ *He asked her to marry him and she accepted.* ◇ *She has accepted the job.* **OPP refuse**[1] **3** [T] to admit or recognize that sth difficult or unpleasant is true: *They refused to **accept responsibility** for the accident.* **4** [T] to make sb feel welcome or to allow sb to join a group or an organization: *The university has accepted me on the course.* **OPP reject**[1]

acceptable ♫ **B2 ○** /əkˈseptəbl/ *adj.* **1** agreed or approved of by most people in society: *That kind of behaviour is not **socially acceptable**.* **2** that sb agrees is good enough or allowed: *One or two mistakes are acceptable but no more than that.* **3** not very good but good enough: *The food was acceptable, but no more.* **SYN satisfactory OPP unacceptable** ▸ acceptability /əkˌseptəˈbɪləti/ *noun* [U] ▸ acceptably /əkˈseptəbli/ *adv.*

acceptance ♫+ **C1 ○** /əkˈseptəns/ *noun* [C, U] ~ **(of sth)** the act of accepting or being accepted: *His ready acceptance of the offer surprised me.* ◇ *He quickly **gained acceptance** in the group* (= the other people thought of him as equal to them).

access[1] ♫ **B1 ○** /ˈækses/ *noun* [U] ~ **(to sth) 1** a way of entering or reaching a place: *Access to the garden is through the kitchen.* **2** the chance or right to use or have sth: *internet access* ◇ *Do you have access to a computer?* **3** (LAW) legal or official permission to see sb: *They are divorced, but he has regular access to the children.*

access[2] ♫ **B1 ○** /ˈækses/ *verb* [T] **1** (COMPUTING) to open a computer file or use a computer system: *Click on the icon to access a file.* **2** to be able to have or use sth, especially sth that you have a right to: *Being informed is the first step toward **accessing** better health **services**.* **3** (often used with an adverb or a preposition) (*formal*) to reach, enter or use sth: *The cellar can be accessed from the kitchen.*

ˈaccess course *noun* [C] (*BrE*) (EDUCATION) a course of education that prepares students without the usual qualifications, so that they can study at university or college

accessible ♫+ **C1 ○** /əkˈsesəbl/ *adj.* **1** possible to be reached or entered: *The island is only accessible by boat.* **2** easy to get, use or understand: *This TV programme aims to make history more accessible to children.* **OPP inaccessible** ▸ accessibility /əkˌsesəˈbɪləti/ *noun* [U]: *Computers have given people greater accessibility to information.* ◇ *The building has limited wheelchair accessibility.*

accession /əkˈseʃn/ *noun* [U] (HISTORY, POLITICS) the act of achieving a very high position, especially as a king or a queen: *the accession of Queen Elizabeth to the throne in 1952* ➔ *verb* **accede**

accessory /əkˈsesəri/ *noun* [C] (*pl.* -ies) **1** an extra item that is added to sth and is useful or attractive but not of great importance: *a wide range of car accessories, such as alloy wheels and roof racks* **2** [usually pl.] a thing that you wear or carry that matches your clothes, for example a piece of jewellery, a bag, etc. **3** ~ **(to sth)** (LAW) a person who helps sb to do sth illegal: *He was charged with being an accessory to murder.*

accident ♫ **A2** /ˈæksɪdənt/ *noun* [C] an unpleasant event, especially in a vehicle, that happens unexpectedly and causes damage, injury or death: *a car accident* ◇ *I hope they haven't **had an accident**.* ◇ *a **serious/minor accident** ◇ a **fatal accident*** (= when sb is killed) ◇ *He broke his leg **in an accident**.* ◇ *I didn't mean to kick you; **it was an accident**.* ➔ note at **hospital**

IDM by accident by chance; without intending to: *I knocked the vase over by accident as I was cleaning.* **OPP deliberately**

accidental /ˌæksɪˈdentl/ *adj.* happening by chance; not planned: *Police do not know if the explosion was accidental or caused by a bomb.* ▸ accidentally ♫+ **B2** /-təli/ *adv.*: *She accidentally took the wrong coat.*

ˌaccident and eˈmergency *noun* [U] (*BrE*) = A & E

ˈaccident-prone *adj.* often having accidents

acclaim /əˈkleɪm/ *verb* [T, usually passive] **be acclaimed (as sth)** (used about a film, book, etc.) to be praised by many people: *a highly acclaimed new film* ◇ *The novel has been acclaimed as a modern classic.* ▸ acclaim *noun* [U]

acclamation /ˌækləˈmeɪʃn/ *noun* [U] (*formal*) loud and enthusiastic approval or welcome

acclimatize (*BrE also* -ise) /əˈklaɪmətaɪz/ *verb* [I, T] ~ **(yourself) (to sth)** to get used to a new climate, situation, etc. so that it is not a problem any more: *It took a while for me to acclimatize myself to the cold.* ▸ acclimatization (*BrE also* -isation) /əˌklaɪmətaɪˈzeɪʃn/ *noun* [U] ▸ acclimatized (*BrE also* -ised) *adj.*

accolade /ˈækəleɪd/ *noun* [C] a comment, prize, etc. that shows people's high opinion of sth that you have done

accommodate ♫+ **B2** /əˈkɒmədeɪt/ *verb* [T] **1** to have enough space for sb/sth, especially for a certain number of people: *Each apartment can accommodate up to six people.* **2** to provide sb with a place to stay, live or work: *During the conference you will be accommodated in a nearby hotel.* **3** (*formal*) to do or provide what sb wants or needs: *Should you have any special requirements, our staff will do their best to accommodate you.*

accommodating /əˈkɒmədeɪtɪŋ/ *adj.* (used about a person) agreeing to do or provide what sb wants

accommodation

viewing a close object

viewing a distant object

accommodation ♫ **B1** /əˌkɒməˈdeɪʃn/ *noun* **1** [U] (*BrE*) (TOURISM) a place for sb to live or stay: *We lived in rented accommodation before buying this house.* ◇ *The price of the holiday includes flights and accommodation.* **2** accommodations [pl.] (*AmE*) (TOURISM) somewhere to live or stay, often also providing food or other services **3** [U] the way in which the LENS (= a part of the eye) becomes flatter or thicker in order to create a clear image of the object that you want to look at

accompaniment /əˈkʌmpənimənt/ *noun* **1** [C, U] (MUSIC) music that is played to support singing or another instrument: *traditional songs with piano accompaniment* **2** [C] ~ **(to sth)** something that goes

...nore important thing: *Dill is an ...nent to fish dishes.*

...st /ə'kʌmpənɪst/ *noun* [C] (**MUSIC**) a person ...plays the piano, or another instrument, while sb else plays or sings the main part of the music

accompany ʔ **B2** /ə'kʌmpəni/ *verb* [T] (accompanying; accompanies; *pt, pp* accompanied) **1** to go together with sb/sth: *He went to America accompanied by his wife and three children.* ◇ *Massive publicity accompanied the film's release.* **2 ~ sb (on sth)** (**MUSIC**) to play music for a singer or another instrument: *She accompanied him on the guitar.*

accomplice /ə'kʌmplɪs/ *noun* [C] **~ (to/in sth)** (**LAW**) a person who helps sb to do sth bad, especially to commit a crime: *She was charged with being an accomplice to the murder.*

accomplish ʔ+ **B2** /ə'kʌmplɪʃ/ *verb* [T] to succeed in doing sth difficult that you planned to do: *I managed to accomplish my goal of starting my own business.*

accomplished /ə'kʌmplɪʃt/ *adj.* very good at a particular thing: *an accomplished actor*

accomplishment ʔ+ **C1** /ə'kʌmplɪʃmənt/ *noun* **1** [C] something that sb has succeeded in doing or learning: *It was a remarkable accomplishment to walk across America.* ◇ *What is your greatest accomplishment?* **SYN** **achievement** **2** [C, U] a skill or special ability **3** [U] **~ (of sth)** (*formal*) the act of completing sth successfully: *the accomplishment of a plan*

accord¹ /ə'kɔːd/ *noun* [C] (**POLITICS**) an agreement, especially between countries: *The two sides signed a peace accord.*
IDM **in accord (with sb/sth)** (*formal*) in agreement with sb/sth: *This action would not be in accord with our policy.* **of your own accord** without being forced or asked: *He wasn't sacked from his job — he left of his own accord.*

accord² /ə'kɔːd/ *verb* [T] **~ sth (to sb/sth)** (*formal*) to give sth to sb/sth: *Our society accords great importance to the family.*
PHRV **accord with sth** (*formal*) to agree with or match sth

accordance ʔ+ **C1** /ə'kɔːdns/ *noun*
IDM **in accordance with sth** (*formal*) in a way that follows or obeys sth: *to act in accordance with instructions*

accordingly ʔ+ **C1** **W** /ə'kɔːdɪŋli/ *adv.* **1** in a way that is suitable: *I realized that I was in danger and acted accordingly.* **2** (*formal*) therefore; for that reason

according to ʔ **A2** **O** /ə'kɔːdɪŋ tə, *before vowels* tu/ *prep.* **1** as stated by sb; as shown by sth: *According to Mick, it's a brilliant film.* ◇ *Standards of living are improving, according to the statistics.* **2** in a way that matches, follows or depends on sth: *Everything went according to plan* (= as we had planned it). ◇ *The salary will be fixed according to experience.*

accordion /ə'kɔːdiən/ *noun* [C] (**MUSIC**) a musical instrument that you hold in both hands and play by pulling the two sides apart and then pushing them together, while pressing the keys and/or buttons with your fingers

accost /ə'kɒst/ *verb* [T] to go up to a stranger and talk to them in a way that is rude or frightening

account¹ ʔ **B1** **O** /ə'kaʊnt/ *noun* [C] **1** (*abbr.* a/c) **~ (with/at …)** (**FINANCE**) the arrangement by which a bank looks after your money for you: *to open/close an account* ◇ *I have an account with Barclays.* **2** (**COMPUTING**) an arrangement that sb has with a

company that allows them to use the internet, buy things online, send and receive messages by email, **SOCIAL MEDIA**, etc: *an email account* ◇ *a Twitter account* ◇ *Please always use the same email address and password to log in to your account.* **3** [usually pl.] a record of all the money that a person or business has received or paid out: *If you are self-employed, you have to keep your own accounts.* **4** an arrangement with a shop, etc. that allows you to pay for goods or services at a later date: *Most customers settle/pay their account in full every month.* ◇ note at **bill¹** **5** somebody's report or description of sth that happened: *She gave the police a full account of the robbery.*
IDM **by all accounts** according to what everyone says: *By all accounts, she's a very good doctor.* **by your own account** according to what you say yourself: *By his own account, Peter was not very good at his job.* **on account of** because of: *Our flight was delayed on account of bad weather.* **on no account | not on any account** not for any reason: *On no account should you walk home by yourself.* **take account of sth | take sth into account** to consider sth, especially when deciding or judging sth: *We'll take account of your comments.*

account² ʔ **B2** **O** /ə'kaʊnt/ *verb*
PHRV **account for sth** **1** to explain or give a reason for sth: *How can we account for these changes?* **2** to form the amount that is mentioned: *Sales to Europe accounted for 80% of our total sales last year.*

accountable ʔ+ **C1** /ə'kaʊntəbl/ *adj.* **~ (for sth)** expected to give an explanation of your actions, etc.; responsible: *She is too young to be held accountable for what she did.* ▸ **accountability** ʔ+ **C1** **W** /ə,kaʊntə'bɪləti/ *noun* [U]

accountancy /ə'kaʊntənsi/ *noun* [U] (**FINANCE**) the work or profession of an ACCOUNTANT

accountant ʔ+ **B2** /ə'kaʊntənt/ *noun* [C] (**FINANCE**) a person whose job is to keep or examine the financial accounts of a business, etc.

accounting /ə'kaʊntɪŋ/ *noun* [U] (**FINANCE**) the process or work of keeping financial accounts: *a career in accounting* ◇ *accounting methods*

ac͵counts ˈpayable *noun* [pl.] (**FINANCE**) money that is owed by a company; the department of the company that deals with paying this money

accreditation /ə,kredɪ'teɪʃn/ *noun* [U] official approval given by an organization when sb/sth achieves a certain standard

accredited /ə'kredɪtɪd/ *adj.* officially recognized or approved: *a fully accredited course*

accrue /ə'kruː/ *verb* (*formal*) (**FINANCE**) **1** [I] to increase over a period of time: *Interest will accrue daily until payment is received in full.* **2** [T] to allow a sum of money or debts to grow over a period of time **SYN** **accumulate**

acculturation /ə,kʌltʃə'reɪʃn/ *noun* [U] **~ (of sb) (to sth)** (**SOCIAL STUDIES**) the process of learning to live successfully in a different culture, or of helping sb to do this: *the acculturation of immigrants to American society*

accumulate ʔ+ **C1** **W** /ə'kjuːmjəleɪt/ *verb* (*formal*) **1** [T] to collect a number or quantity of sth over a period of time: *Over the years, I've accumulated hundreds of books.* **SYN** **amass** ◇ note at **collect** **2** [I] to increase over a period of time ▸ **accumulation** ʔ+ **C1** **W** /ə,kjuːmjə'leɪʃn/ *noun* [C, U] ◇ picture at **glacial** ▸ **accumulative** /ə'kjuːmjələtɪv/ *adj.*

accurate ʔ **B2** **W** /'ækjərət/ *adj.* exact and correct; without mistakes: *He managed to give the police an accurate description of the robbers.* ◇ *That clock isn't*

very accurate. **OPP** **inaccurate** ⊃ note at **true**
▸ accuracy ɪ+ **B2** **W** /-rəsi/ *noun* [U] ⊃ look at
inaccuracy ▸ accurately ɪ+ **B2** **W** *adv.*

accusation ɪ+ **C1** /ˌækjuˈzeɪʃn/ *noun* [C, U] a statement
saying that sb has done sth wrong

accusative /əˈkjuːzətɪv/ *noun* [sing.] the form of a noun, a
pronoun, or an adjective in some languages when it is,
or is connected with, the direct object of a verb: *In the
sentence 'I bought them', 'them' is in the accusative.*
⊃ look at **dative**, **genitive**, **nominative**, **vocative**
▸ accusative *adj.*

accusatory /əˈkjuːzətəri, ˌækjuˈzeɪtəri/ *adj.* (*formal*)
suggesting that you think sb has done sth wrong

accuse ɪ **B2** /əˈkjuːz/ *verb*
[T] ~ sb (of sth/doing sth)
to say that sb has done sth
wrong or broken the law:
I accused her of cheating.
◇ *He was accused of
murder.* ▸ accuser
noun [C]

WORD FAMILY
accuse *verb*
accusation *noun*
accusing *adj.*
accusatory *adj.*

the accused ɪ+ **C1** /ði əˈkjuːzd/ *noun* [C] (*pl.* the accused)
(**LAW**) (used in a court of law) the person who is on trial
for committing a crime: *The jury found the accused
not guilty of murder.* ⊃ note at **court¹**, **crime**

accusing /əˈkjuːzɪŋ/ *adj.* showing that you think sb has
done sth wrong: *He gave me an accusing look.*
▸ accusingly *adv.*

accustom /əˈkʌstəm/ *verb*
PHR V accustom yourself/sb to sth to make
yourself/sb get used to sth: *It took him a while to
accustom himself to the idea.*

accustomed /əˈkʌstəmd/ *adj.* **1** ~ to sth/doing sth if
you are **accustomed** to sth, you are used to it and it is
not strange for you: *She's accustomed to travelling a
lot in her job.* ◇ *It took a while for my eyes to get
accustomed to the dark room.* **SYN** used **2** (*formal*)
usual; regular: *He took his accustomed seat by the fire.*

ace /eɪs/ *noun* [C] **1** a playing card that has a single
shape on it. An ace has the lowest or the highest
value in a game of cards: *the ace of spades* **2** (**SPORT**)
(in the sport of tennis) a **SERVICE** (= the first hit of the
ball) that the person playing against you cannot hit
back because it is so good: *to serve an ace*

acetate /ˈæsɪteɪt/ *noun* [U] (**CHEMISTRY**) a chemical
made from **ACETIC ACID**, used in making plastics, etc.
2 a chemical used to make **FIBRES** that are used to
make clothes, etc.

acetic acid /əˌsiːtɪk ˈæsɪd/ *noun* [U] (**CHEMISTRY**) a type of
ACID that is in **VINEGAR** (= a liquid with a bitter taste)

acetone /ˈæsɪtəʊn/ *noun* [U] (**CHEMISTRY**) a clear liquid
with a strong smell that is used for cleaning things,
making paint thinner and producing various
chemicals

acetylene /əˈsetəliːn/ (*also* ethyne) *noun* [U] (*symb.* C_2H_2)
(**CHEMISTRY**) a gas that burns with a very hot bright
flame, used for cutting or joining metal

ache¹ /eɪk/ *noun* [C] (**HEALTH**) a pain that lasts for a long
time: *aches and pains* ◇ *I felt a dull ache in my back.*
⊃ look at **backache**, **earache**, **headache**, **stomach
ache**, **toothache**

ache² /eɪk/ *verb* [I] (**HEALTH**) to feel a continuous pain:
His legs ached after playing football. ◇ *She was aching
all over.*

achieve ɪ **A2** **W** /əˈtʃiːv/ *verb* [T] **1** to complete sth
through hard work or skill: *They have achieved a lot
in a short time.* **2** to gain sth, usually by effort or skill:
You have achieved the success you deserve.
▸ achievable *adj.*: *Profits of $20m look achievable.*
◇ *achievable goals*

achievement ɪ **B1** **W** /əˈtʃiːvmənt/ *noun* **1** [C]
something that you have done successfully,
especially through hard work or skill: *She felt that
winning the gold medal was her greatest
achievement.* **2** [U] the act or process of achieving sth:
*He enjoys climbing mountains because it gives him a
sense of achievement.*

Achilles heel /əˌkɪliːz ˈhiːl/ *noun* [C, usually sing.] a weak
point or fault in sb/sth

Achilles tendon /əˌkɪliːz ˈtendən/ *noun* [C] (**ANATOMY**)
the strong thin material inside the leg that connects
the muscles at the **CALF** (= the back of the lower part of
the leg) to the heel

acid¹ ɪ+ **B2** /ˈæsɪd/ *noun* [U, C] (**CHEMISTRY**) a liquid
substance that contains **HYDROGEN** and has a **pH** value
of less than seven. Acids can burn or damage things
they touch: *sulphuric acid* ⊃ look at **alkali**, **base¹** (6)
⊃ picture at **pH** ▸ acidic /əˈsɪdɪk/ *adj.*

acid² ɪ+ **C1** /ˈæsɪd/ *adj.* **1** (used about a fruit, etc.) with a
bitter sharp taste **2** (**CHEMISTRY**) containing an **ACID**:
an acid solution ⊃ look at **alkaline**

acidify /əˈsɪdɪfaɪ/ *verb* [I, T] (acidifying; acidifies; *pt, pp*
acidified) (**CHEMISTRY**) to become or make sth become
an **ACID**

acidity /əˈsɪdəti/ *noun* [U] (**CHEMISTRY**) the quality of
being **ACID**: *to measure the acidity of soil*

ˌacid ˈrain *noun* [U] (**ENVIRONMENT**) rain that has
chemicals in it from factories, cars, etc. and that causes
damage to trees, buildings and rivers

ˌacid ˈtest *noun* [sing.] ~ (of sb/sth) a way of deciding
whether sb/sth is successful or true: *The acid test of a
good driver is whether he or she remains calm in an
emergency.*

acknowledge ɪ **B2** **W** /əkˈnɒlɪdʒ/ *verb* [T]
1 ~ (that …) to accept or admit that sth is true or
exists: *He acknowledged that he had made a mistake.*
◇ *They wouldn't acknowledge defeat.* ⊃ note at **admit**
2 to show that you have seen or noticed sb/sth, or
received sth: *The manager sent a card to all the staff to
acknowledge their hard work.*

acknowledgement (*also* acknowledgment)
/əkˈnɒlɪdʒmənt/ *noun* **1** [U] the act of showing that you
have seen or noticed sb/sth: *The president gave a
smile of acknowledgement to the photographers.* **2** [C]
an email, etc. that says that sth has been received or
noticed: *I haven't received (an) acknowledgement of
my job application yet.* **3** [C, usually pl.] (**LITERATURE**) a
few words, especially at the beginning of a book, in
which the writer thanks the people who have helped
them

acne /ˈækni/ *noun* [U] (**HEALTH**) a skin condition,
common among young people, that produces many
spots, especially on the face and neck

acorn /ˈeɪkɔːn/ *noun* [C] the small nut of the **OAK** (= a
large tree with hard wood), that grows in a base
shaped like a cup

acoustic /əˈkuːstɪk/ *adj.* **1** (**PHYSICS**) connected with
sound or the sense of hearing **2** (**MUSIC**) (used about a
musical instrument) not electric: *an acoustic guitar*
⊃ picture at **instrument**

acoustics /əˈkuːstɪks/ *noun* [pl.] (**PHYSICS**) the qualities of
a room, etc. that make it good or bad for you to hear
music, play, etc. in: *The theatre has excellent acoustics.*

acquaint /əˈkweɪnt/ *verb* [T] ~ sb/yourself with sth
(*formal*) to make sb or yourself become familiar with
sth: *I spent several hours acquainting myself with the
new computer system.*

acquaintance /əˈkweɪntəns/ noun **1** [C] a person that you know but who is not a close friend **2** [U, C] slight friendship **3** [U, C] ~ with sth (formal) knowledge of sth: I have little acquaintance with that subject.

acquainted /əˈkweɪntɪd/ adj. (formal) **1** ~ with sth knowing sth: I went for a walk to get acquainted with my new neighbourhood. **2** knowing sb, but usually not very closely

acquiesce /ˌækwiˈes/ verb [I] ~ (in/to sth) (formal) to accept sth without argument, although you may not agree with it: Senior officials acquiesced in the cover-up. ⊃ note at **agree** ▶ acquiescence /-ˈesns/ noun [U]

acquire ⚡ **B2** ⊙ /əˈkwaɪə(r)/ verb [T] (formal) to obtain or buy sth: She has acquired a good knowledge of English. ◇ The company has acquired shares in a rival business.

acquisition ⚡+ **C1** ⓦ /ˌækwɪˈzɪʃn/ noun (formal) **1** [U] the act of getting sth, especially knowledge, a skill, etc: a study of language acquisition in children **2** [C] something that sb buys to add to what they already own, usually sth valuable: This sculpture is the museum's latest acquisition. **3** [C, U] (BUSINESS) a company, piece of land, etc. bought by sb, especially another company; the act of buying it: They have made acquisitions in several EU countries. ◇ the acquisition of shares by employees

acquit /əˈkwɪt/ verb [T] (-tt-) **1** ~ sb (of sth) (LAW) to state formally that a person is not guilty of a crime: The jury acquitted her of murder. **OPP** convict¹ ⊃ note at **crime 2** ~ yourself well, badly, etc. (formal) to behave in the way that is mentioned: He acquitted himself well in his first match as a professional.

acquittal /əˈkwɪtl/ noun [C, U] (LAW) an official decision in court that a person is not guilty of a crime: The case resulted in an acquittal. ◇ The jury voted for acquittal. **OPP** conviction

acre ⚡+ **C1** /ˈeɪkə(r)/ noun [C] (AGRICULTURE) a measure of land; 4 840 square yards or about 4 050 square metres: a farm of 20 acres/a 20-acre farm

acrid /ˈækrɪd/ adj. having a strong and bitter smell or taste that is unpleasant: acrid smoke from the factory

acrimony /ˈækrɪməni/ noun [U] (formal) angry and bitter feelings or words: The dispute was settled without acrimony. ▶ acrimonious /ˌækrɪˈməʊniəs/ adj.: an acrimonious divorce

acrobat /ˈækrəbæt/ noun [C] (ARTS AND MEDIA) a person who performs difficult movements of the body, especially in a CIRCUS (= a show that travels to different towns)

acrobatic /ˌækrəˈbætɪk/ adj. performing or involving difficult movements of the body: an acrobatic dancer ◇ an acrobatic leap ▶ acrobatically /-kli/ adv.

acrobatics /ˌækrəˈbætɪks/ noun [pl.] (the art of performing) difficult movements of the body

acronym /ˈækrənɪm/ noun [C] ~ (for sth) (LANGUAGE) a short word that is made from the first letters of a group of words: TEFL is an acronym for 'Teaching English as a Foreign Language'.

acropolis /əˈkrɒpəlɪs/ noun [C] (ARCHITECTURE, HISTORY) (in an ancient Greek city) a castle or an area that is designed to resist attack, especially one on top of a hill

across ⚡ **A1** /əˈkrɒs/ adv., prep. **1** from one side of sth to the other: The stream was too wide to jump across. ◇ He walked across the field. ◇ A smile spread across his face. ◇ The river was about 20 metres across. ◇ The bank has 800 branches across (= in all parts of) the country. **2** on the other side of sth: There's a cafe just across the road. ◇ The house across the road from us is for sale.

IDM across the board involving or affecting all groups, members, cases, etc.

acrostic /əˈkrɒstɪk/ noun [C] (LITERATURE) a poem or other piece of writing in which particular letters in each line, usually the first letters, form a word or phrase

acrylic /əˈkrɪlɪk/ noun [C, U] (ART) **1** an artificial material that is used in making clothes, etc. **2** a type of paint used by artists ⊃ note at **art**

act¹ ⚡ **A2** ⓦ /ækt/ verb **1** [I] ~ (on sth) to do sth; to take action: The doctor knew he had to act quickly to save the child. ◇ I'm always giving my brother advice, but he never acts on it (= as a result of it). **2** [I] ~ as sth to perform a particular function: The man we met on the plane to Tokyo was kind enough to act as our guide. ◇ The elephant's trunk acts as a nose, a hand and an arm. **3** [I] ~ (like sth) to behave in the way that is mentioned: Stop acting like a child! ◇ Although she was trying to act cool, I could see she was really upset. ◇ He hasn't really hurt himself — he's just acting! ◇ Ali's acting strangely today — what's wrong with him? **4** [I, T] (ARTS AND MEDIA) to perform in a play or film: I acted in a play at school. ◇ He's always wanted to act the part of Hamlet. ⊃ note at **performing arts**
PHR V act for sb to be employed to deal with sb's affairs for them: His lawyers are continuing to act for him. **SYN** represent ⊃ note at **professional²**

act² ⚡ **B1** ⓦ /ækt/ noun
• STH YOU DO **1** [C] ~ (of sth) a thing that you do: In a typical act of generosity they refused to accept any money. ◇ to commit a violent act ⊃ note at **action¹**
• IN A PLAY **2** [C] (ARTS AND MEDIA) one of the main divisions of a play or an OPERA: How many scenes are there in Act 4?
• ENTERTAINMENT **3** [C] (ARTS AND MEDIA) a short piece of entertainment, especially as part of a show: Did you enjoy the clowns' act? **4** [C] (MUSIC) a musician or group of musicians: They are one of the most successful live acts ever to come out of the UK.
• LAW **5** Act [C] (LAW, POLITICS) a law made by a government: The parliament passed an act protecting the rights of tenants.
• BEHAVIOUR **6** [sing.] behaviour that hides your true feelings: She seems very happy but she's just putting on an act.
IDM be/get in on the act (informal) to become involved in an activity that is becoming popular get your act together (informal) to organize yourself so that you can do sth properly: If he doesn't get his act together, he's going to lose his job. a hard act to follow → HARD¹ in the act (of doing sth) while doing sth, especially sth wrong: He was looking through the papers on her desk and she caught him in the act.

acting¹ /ˈæktɪŋ/ adj. [only before noun] (BUSINESS) doing the job mentioned for a short time: James will be the acting director while Henry is away.

acting² /ˈæktɪŋ/ noun [U] (ARTS AND MEDIA) the art or profession of performing in plays or films

actinium /ækˈtɪniəm/ noun [U] (symb. Ac) (CHEMISTRY) a chemical element. Actinium is a RADIOACTIVE metal. ❶ For more information on the periodic table of elements, look at the **Reference Section** of this dictionary.

action¹ ⚡ **A1** ⊙ /ˈækʃn/ noun
• DOING STH **1** [U] doing things, often for a particular purpose: Now is the time for action! ◇ If we don't take action quickly, it'll be too late! **OPP** inaction **2** [C] something that you do: The doctor's quick action saved the child's life. ◇ They should be judged by their actions, not by what they say.

- IN A STORY/FILM/PLAY **3** [U] (**ARTS AND MEDIA**, **LITERATURE**) the most important events in a story, film or play: *The action takes place in London.*
- EXCITING EVENTS **4** [U] exciting things that happen: *There's not much action in this boring town.*
- IN A WAR **5** [U] fighting in a war: *Their son was killed in action.*
- EFFECT **6** [U] ~ of sth (on sth) (**CHEMISTRY**) the effect that one substance has on another: *They're studying the action of sunlight on the skin.*
- IN COURT **7** [C, U] (**LAW**) the process of settling an argument in court

IDM **in action** in operation; while working or doing sth: *We shall have a chance to see their new team in action next week.* **into action** if you put an idea or a plan **into action**, you start making it happen or work: *We'll put the plan into action immediately.* **out of action** not able to do the usual things; not working: *The coffee machine's out of action again.*

▼ SYNONYMS

action

act ◆ deed ◆ feat ◆ gesture ◆ move

These are all words for a thing that sb does.

action *Her quick action saved the child's life.*

act *a heroic act of bravery*

deed (*formal*) *heroic/evil deeds*

feat *The tunnel is a brilliant feat of engineering.*

gesture *They sent me some flowers as a gesture of sympathy.*

move *What's your next move?*

action² /ˈækʃn/ *verb* [T] to make sure that sth is done or dealt with: *Your request will be actioned.*

ˈaction-packed *adj.* full of exciting events and activity: *an action-packed weekend*

ˌaction ˈreplay (*BrE*) (*also* **instant replay** *BrE, AmE*) *noun* [C] (**SPORT**) part of sth, for example a recording of a sports game on TV, that is immediately repeated, often more slowly, so that you can see a goal or another exciting or important moment again

activate ⸿+ **C1** /ˈæktɪveɪt/ *verb* [T] to make sth start working: *A slight movement can activate the car alarm.* ▸ **activation** ⸿+ **C1** /ˌæktɪˈveɪʃn/ *noun* [U]

active ⸿ **A2** ⦿ /ˈæktɪv/ *adj.* **1** always doing things; lively: *My grandfather is very active for his age.* ◇ *I have a very active social life.* **OPP inactive 2** involved in sth: *She's very politically active.* ◇ *I was at the meeting, but I didn't take an active part in the discussion.* **3** having or causing a chemical effect **4** doing sth regularly: *an active volcano* (= likely to ERUPT) **5** (**GRAMMAR**) used about the form of a verb or sentence when the subject of the sentence performs the action of the verb: *In the sentence 'The dog bit him', the verb is active.* ⊃ look at **passive¹** (2) ▸ **actively** ⦿ *adv.*: *She was actively looking for a job.*

ˌactive ˈcitizen *noun* [C] (**SOCIAL STUDIES**) a person who is involved in trying to improve things in their local community

activist ⸿+ **C1** /ˈæktɪvɪst/ *noun* [C] (**POLITICS**) a person who takes action to cause political or social change, usually as a member of a group ▸ **activism** /-vɪzəm/ *noun* [U]

activity ⸿ **A1** ⦿ /ækˈtɪvəti/ *noun* (*pl.* -ies) **1** [C, usually pl.] something that you do for interest or pleasure: *The hotel offers a range of leisure activities.* **2** [C, usually pl.] a thing that sb does in order to achieve a particular aim: *criminal/illegal activities* ◇ *an activity that you can use in the classroom* **3** [U] a situation in which there is a lot of action or movement: *The house was*

full of activity on the morning of the wedding. **OPP inactivity**

actor ⸿ **A1** /ˈæktə(r)/ *noun* [C] (**ARTS AND MEDIA**) a person whose job is to act in a play or film, or on TV

actress ⸿ **A1** /ˈæktrəs/ *noun* [C] (**ARTS AND MEDIA**) a woman whose job is to act in a play or film, or on TV **❶** Many women now prefer to be called **actors**.

actual ⸿ **B2** ⦿ /ˈæktʃuəl/ *adj.* real; that happened: *The actual damage to the car was not as great as we had feared.* ◇ *They seemed to be good friends but in actual fact they hated each other.*

actually ⸿ **A2** ❸ /ˈæktʃuəli/ *adv.* **1** used to emphasize a fact or a comment, or that sth is really true: *It's not actually raining now.* ◇ *I can't believe that I'm actually going to America!* **2** used to show surprise about what is true: *The food was not actually that expensive.* **3** used to correct sb or say sth that sb might not like, in a polite way: *We're not American, actually.* ◇ *Actually, I'm busy at the moment.*

actuary /ˈæktʃuəri/ *noun* [C] (*pl.* -ies) (**FINANCE**) a person whose job involves calculating insurance risks and payments for insurance companies by studying how frequently accidents, fires, deaths, etc. happen

acumen /ˈækjəmən, əˈkjuːmən/ *noun* [U] the ability to understand and decide things quickly and well: *business/financial acumen*

acupressure /ˈækjupreʃə(r)/ *noun* [U] (**MEDICINE**) a form of medical treatment in which particular parts of the body are pressed with the hands

acupuncture /ˈækjupʌŋktʃə(r)/ *noun* [U] (**MEDICINE**) a way of treating an illness or stopping pain by putting thin needles into parts of the body ▸ **acupuncturist** /-tʃərɪst/ *noun* [C]

acute ⸿+ **C1** /əˈkjuːt/ *adj.* **1** very serious; very great: *an acute shortage of food* ◇ *acute pain* **2** (**HEALTH**) (used about an illness) becoming dangerous very quickly: *acute appendicitis* ⊃ look at **chronic** (1) **3** (used about feelings or the senses) very strong: *Dogs have an acute sense of smell.* **4** showing that you are able to understand things easily: *The report contains some acute observations on the situation.* ▸ **acutely** *adv.*

aˌcute ˈaccent *noun* [C] (**LANGUAGE**) the mark placed over a vowel to show how it should be pronounced, as over the *e* in *fiancé* ⊃ look at **circumflex**, **grave³**, **tilde**, **umlaut**

aˌcute ˈangle *noun* [C] (**GEOMETRY**) an angle of less than 90° ⊃ look at **obtuse angle**, **reflex angle**, **right angle** ⊃ picture at **angle¹**

AD /ˌeɪ ˈdiː/ *abbr.* (**HISTORY**, **RELIGION**) used in dates to show the number of years since the year when Jesus Christ was believed to have been born (from Latin 'Anno Domini'): *in (the year) AD 44* ⊃ look at **BC**

ad ⸿ **B1** /æd/ *noun* [C] (*informal*) = ADVERTISEMENT: *an expensive ad campaign* ◇ *an ad agency*

adage /ˈædɪdʒ/ *noun* [C] (**LANGUAGE**) a well-known phrase expressing sth that is always true about people or the world

adagio /əˈdɑːdʒiəʊ/ *noun* [C] (*pl.* -os) (**MUSIC**) a piece of music that you should play slowly ▸ **adagio** *adj., adv.* ⊃ look at **allegro**, **andante**

adamant /ˈædəmənt/ *adj.* (*formal*) very sure; refusing to change your mind ▸ **adamantly** *adv.*

Adam's apple /ˌædəmz ˈæpl/ *noun* [C] (**ANATOMY**) the part at the front of the throat that sticks out, particularly in men, and moves up and down when you SWALLOW

adapt 🔊 **B2** ⭕ /ə'dæpt/ *verb* **1** [I, T] ~ **(yourself) (to sth)** to change your behaviour because the situation you are in has changed: *They were quick to adapt (themselves) to the new system.* **2** [T] ~ **sth (for sth/sb)**; ~ **sth (to do sth)** to change sth so that you can use it in a different situation: *The bus was adapted for disabled people.* ◇ *The teacher adapted the coursebook to suit the needs of her students.*

adaptable /ə'dæptəbl/ *adj.* able to change to suit new situations ▸ **adaptability** /ə,dæptə'bɪləti/ *noun* [U]

adaptation 🔊+ **C1** 🔷 /,ædæp'teɪʃn/ *noun* **1** [C] (**ARTS AND MEDIA**) a play or film that is based on a novel, etc. **2** [U] the state or process of changing or changing sth to suit a new situation

adapter (*also* **adaptor**) /ə'dæptə(r)/ *noun* [C] **1** (**ENGINEERING**) a device for connecting pieces of electrical equipment that were not designed to be fitted together **2** (*BrE*) a device that allows you to connect more than one piece of electrical equipment to a SOCKET (= an electricity supply point)

adaptive /ə'dæptɪv/ *adj.* (**COMPUTING**) concerned with changing; able to change when necessary in order to deal with different situations

ADD /,eɪ di: 'di:/ (*also* **ADHD**) *noun* [U] (**PSYCHOLOGY**) a medical condition, especially in children, that makes it difficult for them to pay attention to what they are doing and to stay still for long (the abbreviation for 'attention deficit disorder' or 'attention deficit hyperactivity disorder')

add 🔊 **A1** 🔵 /æd/ *verb* **1** [I, T] ~ **(sth) (to sth)** to put sth together with sth else, so that you increase the size, number, value, etc: *I added a couple more items to the list.* ◇ *The juice contains no added sugar.* **2** [I, T] ~ **(A to B)**; ~ **(A and B together)** (**MATHEMATICS**) to put numbers or amounts together so that you get a total: *Add £8 to the total, to cover postage and packaging.* ◇ *If you add 3 and 3 together, you get 6.* ◇ *Messi cost more than all the other players added together.* **OPP** **subtract** **3** [T] to say sth more: '*By the way, please don't tell anyone I phoned you,*' *she added.*
IDM **add to this | added to this** in addition to sth; as well as: *Add to this his charm and charisma and you can see why he's become so successful.*
PHRV **add sth on (to sth)** to include sth: *10% will be added on to your bill as a service charge.* **add up** to seem to be a true explanation: *I'm sorry, but your story just doesn't add up.* **add (sth) up** to find the total of several numbers: *The waiter hadn't added up the bill correctly.* **add up to sth** to have as a total: *How much does all the shopping add up to?*

addendum /ə'dendəm/ *noun* [C] (*pl.* **addenda** /-də/) (*formal*) (**LITERATURE**) an item of extra information that is added to a book, contract, etc.

adder /'ædə(r)/ *noun* [C] a small poisonous snake

addict /'ædɪkt/ *noun* [C] (**PSYCHOLOGY, SOCIAL STUDIES**) a person who cannot stop taking or doing sth harmful: *a drug addict* ▸ **addicted** /ə'dɪktɪd/ *adj.* ~ **(to sth)**: *He is addicted to heroin.* **SYN** **hooked** ▸ **addiction** 🔊+ **B2** /ə'dɪkʃn/ *noun* [C, U]: *the problem of teenage drug addiction*

addictive /ə'dɪktɪv/ *adj.* (**SOCIAL STUDIES**) if a substance or an activity is **addictive**, people find it difficult to stop using it or doing it: *a highly addictive drug* ◇ *an addictive game*

addition 🔊 **B1** 🔷 /ə'dɪʃn/ *noun* **1** [U] (**MATHEMATICS**) adding sth, especially two or more numbers ◯ look at **subtraction** **2** [C] ~ **(to sth)** a person or thing that is added to sth: *They've got a new addition to the family* (= another child).

IDM **in addition (to sth)** as well as: *She speaks five foreign languages in addition to English.*

additional 🔊 **B2** 🔷 /ə'dɪʃənl/ *adj.* added: *a small additional charge for the use of the swimming pool* **SYN** **extra**[1] ▸ **additionally** 🔊+ **B2** 🔷 /-nəli/ *adv.*

additive /'ædətɪv/ *noun* [C] (**CHEMISTRY**) a substance that is added in small amounts to sth, especially food, in order to improve it, give it colour, etc: *food additives*

address[1] 🔊 **A1** /ə'dres/ *noun* [C] **1** the number of the building and the name of the street and place where sb lives or works: *my home/business address* ◇ *She no longer lives at this address.* ◇ *Please inform the office of any change of address.* **2** (**COMPUTING**) a series of words and/or numbers that tells you where you can find sb/sth using a computer or phone, for example on the internet: *What's your email address?* **3** a formal speech that is given to an audience

address[2] 🔊 **B2** 🔷 /ə'dres/ *verb* [T]
• DEAL WITH **1** (*formal*) to try to deal with a problem, etc: *The government is finally addressing the question of corruption.*
• WRITE ON A LETTER, ETC. **2** [often passive] ~ **sth (to sb/ sth)** to write the name and address of the person you are sending a letter, etc. to: *The package was addressed to my mother.*
• MAKE A SPEECH **3** to make an important speech to an audience
• USE A NAME **4** ~ **sb (as sth)** to talk or write to sb using a particular name or title: *She prefers to be addressed as 'Ms'.*
• COMMUNICATE **5** ~ **sth to sb** (*formal*) make a comment, etc. to sb: *Kindly address any complaints you have to the manager.*

ad'dress bar *noun* [C] (**COMPUTING**) a line near the top of a page on an internet BROWSER where you can type in the address of a website

ad'dress book *noun* [C] **1** a book in which you keep addresses, phone numbers, etc. **2** (**COMPUTING**) a computer file where you store email and internet addresses

adductor /ə'dʌktə(r)/ (*also* **ad'ductor muscle**) *noun* [C] (**ANATOMY**) a muscle that moves a body part towards the middle of the body or towards another part ⊃ look at **abductor**

adenine /'ædəni:n/ *noun* [U] (**BIOLOGY, CHEMISTRY**) one of the four COMPOUNDS that make up NUCLEIC ACIDS ⊃ picture at **DNA**

adenoids /'ædənɔɪdz/ *noun* [pl.] (**ANATOMY**) soft areas at the back of the nose and throat that can become larger than normal and cause breathing difficulties, especially in children

adept /ə'dept/ *adj.* ~ **(at sth/doing sth)** very good at doing sth that is quite difficult: *He's becoming very adept at French.* **SYN** **skilful** **OPP** **inept** ▸ **adeptly** *adv.*

adequate 🔊+ **B2** 🔷 /'ædɪkwət/ *adj.* **1** enough for what you need: *Make sure you take an adequate supply of water with you.* **2** just good enough; acceptable: *Your work is adequate, but I'm sure you could do better.* **OPP** **inadequate** ▸ **adequacy** /-kwəsi/ *noun* [U] ▸ **adequately** 🔊+ **B2** 🔷 *adv.*: *The mystery has never been adequately explained.*

ADHD /,eɪ di: eɪtʃ 'di:/ = ADD

adhere 🔊+ **C1** /əd'hɪə(r)/ *verb* [I] ~ **(to sth)** (*formal*) to stick FIRMLY to sth: *Make sure that the paper adheres firmly to the wall.*
PHRV **adhere to sth** to continue to support an idea, etc.; to follow a rule

adherent /əd'hɪərənt/ *noun* [C] (*formal*) somebody who supports a particular idea **SYN** **supporter** ▸ **adherence** /-rəns/ *noun* [U]

adhesion /ədˈhiːʒn/ *noun* **1** [U] the ability to stick or become attached to sth **2** [U, C] the sticking together of surfaces inside the body in a way that is not normal, caused by injury

adhesive¹ /ədˈhiːsɪv, -ˈhiːzɪv/ *noun* [C] a substance that makes things stick together

adhesive² /ədˈhiːsɪv, -ˈhiːzɪv/ *adj.* that can stick, or can cause two things to stick together: *He sealed the parcel with adhesive tape.* **SYN** sticky

ad hoc /ˌæd ˈhɒk/ *adj.* made or done suddenly for a particular purpose: *They set up an ad hoc committee to discuss the matter.* ◊ *Staff training takes place occasionally on an ad hoc basis.* ▸ ad hoc *adv.*

ad infinitum /ˌæd ɪnfɪˈnaɪtəm/ *adv.* forever; again and again: *We can't stay ad infinitum.* ◊ *The problem would be repeated ad infinitum.*

adipose /ˈædɪpəʊs, -pəʊz/ *adj.* (BIOLOGY) (used about body TISSUE) used for storing fat ⊃ picture at **skin¹**

adjacent 🔒+ **C1** /əˈdʒeɪsnt/ *adj.* ~ **(to sth)** (used about an area, a building, a room, etc.) next to sth: *She works in the office adjacent to mine.*

a,djacent ˈangle *noun* [C] (GEOMETRY) one of the two angles formed on the same side of a straight line when another line meets it ⊃ picture at **angle¹**

adjectival /ˌædʒekˈtaɪvl/ *adj.* (GRAMMAR) containing or connected with an adjective or adjectives: *The adjectival form of 'smell' is 'smelly'.*

adjective /ˈædʒɪktɪv/ *noun* [C] (GRAMMAR) a word that describes a person or a thing, for example *big* and *clever* in *a big house* and *a clever idea*: *The adjective 'reserved' is often applied to British people.* ◊ *What adjective would you use to describe my sister?*

adjoining /əˈdʒɔɪnɪŋ/ *adj.* next to or nearest to sth: *A scream came from the adjoining room.*

adjourn /əˈdʒɜːn/ *verb* [I, T, often passive] to stop a meeting, a trial, etc. for a short time and start it again later: *The meeting adjourned for lunch.* ◊ *The trial was adjourned until the following week.* ▸ adjournment *noun* [C, U]

adjudicate /əˈdʒuːdɪkeɪt/ *verb* [I, T] ~ **(on sth)** to act as an official judge in a competition; to decide who is right when two people or groups disagree about sth: *The review panel adjudicated on the matter.* ▸ adjudication /əˌdʒuːdɪˈkeɪʃn/ *noun* [U, C]

adjudicator /əˈdʒuːdɪkeɪtə(r)/ *noun* [C] a person who acts as a judge, for example in a competition or when two groups or organizations disagree

adjunct /ˈædʒʌŋkt/ *noun* [C] **1** (GRAMMAR) an adverb or a phrase that adds meaning to the verb in a sentence or part of a sentence: *In the sentence 'He ran away in a panic', 'in a panic' is an adjunct.* **2** (formal) a thing that is added or joined to sth larger or more important

adjust 🔒+ **B2** **W** /əˈdʒʌst/ *verb* **1** [T] to change sth slightly in order to achieve the appearance, result, etc. that you want: *The brakes on my bike need adjusting.* **2** [I] ~ **(to sth)** to get used to new conditions or a new situation: *She found it hard to adjust to working at night.* ▸ adjustment 🔒+ **C1** **W** *noun* [C, U]: *We'll just make a few minor adjustments and the room will look perfect.*

adjustable /əˈdʒʌstəbl/ *adj.* that can be moved to different positions or changed in shape or size: *an adjustable mirror*

ad justable ˈspanner (BrE) (also **monkey wrench** AmE, BrE) *noun* [C] a tool with a part that can be moved to hold and turn things of different WIDTHS ⊃ look at **spanner**, **wrench¹** ⊃ picture at **tool**

ad lib /ˌæd ˈlɪb/ *adj., adv.* done or spoken without preparation: *She had to speak ad lib because she couldn't find her notes.* ▸ ad lib *verb* [I, T] (-bb-): *He forgot his notes so he had to ad lib.*

administer 🔒+ **C1** **W** /ədˈmɪnɪstə(r)/ *verb* [T] (formal) **1** to control or manage sth **2** (MEDICINE) to give sb sth, especially medicine

administration 🔒 **B2** **W** /ədˌmɪnɪˈstreɪʃn/ *noun* **1** (also informal **admin** /ˈædmɪn/) [U] (BUSINESS) the process or act of managing sth, for example a system, an organization or a business: *The administration of a large project like this is very complicated.* ◊ *A lot of the teachers' time is taken up by admin.* **2** (often **Administration**) [C] (POLITICS) the government of a country, especially the US: *the Obama Administration* **3** [U] (BUSINESS) the group of people or part of a company that organizes or controls sth: *the hospital administration* **4** [U] (BrE) (BUSINESS, LAW) a situation in which the financial affairs of a business that cannot pay its debts are managed by an independent ADMINISTRATOR: *If it cannot find extra funds, the company will go into administration.*

administrative 🔒+ **C1** **W** /ədˈmɪnɪstrətɪv/ *adj.* connected with the organization of a country, business, etc., and the way in which it is managed

administrator 🔒+ **C1** /ədˈmɪnɪstreɪtə(r)/ *noun* [C] (BUSINESS) **1** a person whose job is to manage the business affairs of a company or an institution, or a person who works in an office dealing with phone calls, arranging meetings, etc. **2** (BUSINESS, LAW) a person legally APPOINTED (= chosen) to manage the financial affairs of a business that cannot pay its debts

admirable /ˈædmərəbl/ *adj.* (formal) having qualities that you admire; excellent ▸ admirably /-bli/ *adv.*: *She dealt with the problem admirably.*

admiral /ˈædmərəl/ *noun* [C] the most important officer in the NAVY

admiration /ˌædməˈreɪʃn/ *noun* [U] ~ **(for sb/sth)** a feeling of liking and respecting sb/sth very much: *I have great admiration for what he's done.*

admire 🔒 **B1** /ədˈmaɪə(r)/ *verb* [T] ~ **sb/sth (for sth/ doing sth)** to respect or like sb/sth very much; to look at sb/sth with pleasure: *We stopped at the top of the hill to admire the view.* ◊ *I've always admired her for being such a wonderful mother.*

admirer /ədˈmaɪərə(r)/ *noun* [C] a person who admires sb/sth: *I've always been a great admirer of her work.*

admiring /ədˈmaɪərɪŋ/ *adj.* showing respect for sb/sth for what they are or what they have done ▸ admiringly *adv.*

admissible /ədˈmɪsəbl/ *adj.* (LAW) that can be allowed or accepted, especially in court: *The judge ruled the tapes to be admissible in court.* ◊ *admissible evidence* **OPP** inadmissible

admission 🔒+ **C1** /ədˈmɪʃn/ *noun* **1** [C, U] ~ **(to sth)** the act of allowing sb to enter a school, club, public place, etc: *Admissions to British universities have increased by 15% this year.* ⊃ look at **entrance** (3) **2** [C] a statement that admits that sth is true **3** [C] ~ **(of sth)** (LAW) a statement in which sb admits that sth is true, especially sth wrong or bad that they have done: *an admission of guilt/failure/defeat* **4** [U] the amount of money that you have to pay to enter a place: *The museum charges half-price admission on Mondays.*

admit 🔒 **B1** /ədˈmɪt/ *verb* (-tt-) **1** [I, T] ~ **(to sth/doing sth)**; ~ **(that)** ... to agree that sth unpleasant is true or that you have done sth wrong: *He refused to admit to* the theft. ◇ You should admit your mistake. ◇ After trying four times to pass the exam, I finally **admitted defeat**. ◇ I have to admit (that) I was wrong. **OPP** deny ⊃ note at **crime 2** [T] ~ **sb/sth (into/to sth)** to allow sb/ sth to enter; to take sb into a place: He was admitted to hospital with suspected appendicitis.

▼ SYNONYMS

admit

acknowledge ♦ concede ♦ confess ♦ grant

These words all mean to agree, often unwillingly, that sth is true.

admit It was a stupid thing to do, I admit.

acknowledge (formal) to acknowledge the need for reform

concede (formal) He conceded that there might be difficulties.

confess She confessed that she'd scratched his car.

grant It's a fine painting, I grant you, but is it worth the money?

admittance /əd'mɪtns/ noun [U] ~ **(to sth)** (formal) being allowed to enter a place; the right to enter: The journalist tried to **gain admittance** to the minister's office.

admittedly /əd'mɪtɪdli/ adv. used, especially at the beginning of a sentence, when you are accepting that sth is true: The work is very interesting. Admittedly, I do get rather tired.

admonish /əd'mɒnɪʃ/ verb [T] (formal) **1** ~ **sb (for sth/ doing sth)** to tell sb FIRMLY that you do not approve of sth that they have done: He was admonished for arriving late at work. **2** ~ **sb (to do sth)** to strongly advise sb to do sth: She admonished the staff to call off the strike.

ad nauseam /ˌæd 'nɔːziəm/ adv. if a person says or does sth **ad nauseam**, they say or do it again and again so that it becomes boring and annoying

ado /ə'duː/ noun
IDM without further/more ado (old-fashioned) without delaying; immediately

adobe /ə'dəʊbi/ noun [U] (**ARCHITECTURE**) mud that is dried in the sun and used as a building material

adolescence /ˌædə'lesns/ noun [U] the period of a person's life between being a child and becoming an adult, between the ages of about 13 and 17 **SYN** puberty

adolescent ʔ+ **C1** /ˌædə'lesnt/ noun [C] a young person who is no longer a child and not yet an adult, between the ages of about 13 and 17: the problems of adolescents ◇ an adolescent daughter ⊃ look at **teenager**

adopt ʔ **B2** **W** /ə'dɒpt/ verb **1** [I, T] (**SOCIAL STUDIES**) to take a child into your family and treat them as your own child by law: They couldn't have children so they adopted. ◇ They're hoping to adopt a child. **2** [T] to take and use sth: What approach did you adopt when dealing with the problem? ▶ adopted adj.: an **adopted child** ◇ his **adopted country** (= where he lives, although he was not born there)

adoption ʔ+ **C1** /ə'dɒpʃn/ noun **1** [U, C] (**SOCIAL STUDIES**) the act of adopting a child; the fact of being adopted: She **put the baby up for adoption**. **2** [U] the decision to start using sth such as an idea, a plan or a name: the adoption of new technology

adoptive /ə'dɒptɪv/ adj. (**SOCIAL STUDIES**) (used about parents) having legally taken a child to live with them as part of their family: the baby's adoptive parents

adorable /ə'dɔːrəbl/ adj. very attractive and easy to feel love for: an adorable child **SYN** lovely ▶ adorably /-bli/ adv.

adore /ə'dɔː(r)/ verb [T] **1** to love and admire sb/sth very much: Kim adores her older sister. **2** to like sth very much: She adores Italy. ▶ adoration /ˌædə'reɪʃn/ noun [U] ▶ adoring adj.: his adoring fans

adorn /ə'dɔːn/ verb [T] ~ **sth (with sth)** (formal) to add sth in order to make a thing or person more attractive or beautiful: a building adorned with flags ▶ adornment noun [C, U]

adrenaline (also adrenalin) /ə'drenəlɪn/ noun [U] (**BIOLOGY**) a substance that the body produces when you are very angry, frightened or excited, and that makes the heart go faster: The excitement at the start of a race can really **get the adrenaline flowing**.

adrift /ə'drɪft/ adj. [not before noun] (used about a boat) not tied to anything or controlled by anyone

adroit /ə'drɔɪt/ adj. (formal) clever and showing skill, especially in dealing with people: an adroit negotiator

ADSL /ˌeɪ diː es 'el/ abbr. (**COMPUTING**) asymmetric digital subscriber line (a system for connecting a computer to the internet using a phone line)

adulation /ˌædju'leɪʃn/ noun [U] (formal) great praise, especially when it is greater than necessary: The band learned to deal with the adulation of their fans.

adult ʔ **A1** **S** /'ædʌlt, ə'dʌlt/ noun [C] a person or an animal that is fully grown: This film is suitable for both adults and children. **SYN** grown-up[2] ▶ adult ʔ **A2** **S** adj.

adult edu'cation (also continuing education) noun [U] (**EDUCATION**) education for adults that is available outside the formal education system, for example at evening classes

adulterate /ə'dʌltəreɪt/ verb [T] (often passive) ~ **sth (with sth)** to make food or drink less pure or of lower quality by adding sth to it: The butter had been adulterated with milk. **SYN** contaminate

adulterer /ə'dʌltərə(r)/ noun [C] (formal) a person who commits ADULTERY

adultery /ə'dʌltəri/ noun [U] (formal) sex between a married person and sb who is not their husband or wife: He was accused of **committing adultery**. ▶ adulterous /-rəs/ adj.: an adulterous relationship

adulthood /'ædʌlthʊd, ə'dʌlthʊd/ noun [U] the time in your life when you are an adult

advance¹ ʔ **B2** /əd'vɑːns/ verb **1** [I] to move forward: The army advanced towards the city. **OPP** retreat¹ **2** [I, T] to make progress or help sth make progress: Our research has not advanced much recently.

advance² ʔ **B2** /əd'vɑːns/ noun **1** [C, U] ~ **(in sth)** progress in sth: advances in computer technology **2** [C, usually sing.] ~ **(on sth)** forward movement: the army's advance on the capital **OPP** retreat² **3** [C] ~ **(on sth)** (**FINANCE**) an amount of money that is paid to sb before the time when it is usually paid: She asked for an advance on her salary.
IDM in advance (of sth) before a particular time or event: You should book tickets for the concert well in advance.

advance³ ʔ **B2** /əd'vɑːns/ adj. [only before noun] that happens before sth: There was no advance warning of the earthquake.

advanced ʔ **B1** /əd'vɑːnst/ adj. **1** of a high level: an advanced English class **2** highly developed: a country that is not very advanced industrially

ad'vanced level = A LEVEL

advancement /əd'vɑːnsmənt/ *noun* (*formal*) **1** [U, C] the process of helping sth to make progress or succeed; the progress that is made: *the advancement of knowledge/education/science* **2** [U] progress in a job, social class, etc: *There are good opportunities for advancement if you have the right skills.*

advantage 🔤 A2 ❂ /əd'vɑːntɪdʒ/ *noun* **1** [C] ~ (**over sb**) something that may help you to do better than other people: *Her experience gave her an advantage over the other applicants.* ◊ *Living abroad means he has the advantage of being fluent in two languages.* ◊ *Some runners try to gain an unfair advantage by taking drugs.* **2** [C, U] ~ (**of sth/doing sth**); ~ (**in/to sth/doing sth**) something that helps you or that will bring you a good result: *the advantages and disadvantages of a plan* ◊ *The traffic is so bad here that there is no advantage in having a car.* **OPP** **disadvantage**[1] ⊃ look at **pro**
IDM **take advantage of sb/sth** to make use of sb/sth in a way that is unfair or dishonest in order to get what you want **take advantage of sth** to make good or full use of sth: *We should take full advantage of these low prices while they last.* **turn sth to your advantage** to use or change a bad situation so that it helps you

advantageous /ˌædvən'teɪdʒəs/ *adj.* good or useful in a particular situation

advent /'ædvent/ *noun* **1** [sing.] **the ~ of sth/sb** the coming of an important event, person, new technology, etc: *This area was very isolated before the advent of the railway.* **2** Advent [U] (**RELIGION**) (in the Christian year) the period of approximately four weeks before Christmas

adventure 🔤 A2 /əd'ventʃə(r)/ *noun* [C, U] an experience or event that is very unusual, exciting or dangerous: *Our journey through the jungle was quite an adventure!* ◊ *She left home to travel, hoping for excitement and adventure.*

adventurer /əd'ventʃərə(r)/ *noun* [C] **1** (*old-fashioned*) a person who enjoys exciting new experiences, especially going to unusual places **2** a person who is capable of taking risks and perhaps acting dishonestly in order to gain money or power

adventurous /əd'ventʃərəs/ *adj.* **1** (used about a person) liking to try new things or have adventures **2** involving new and interesting things and ideas: *For a more adventurous holiday try mountain climbing.*

adverb /'ædvɜːb/ *noun* [C] (**GRAMMAR**) a word that adds more information about place, time, manner, cause or degree to a verb, an adjective, a phrase or another adverb: *In 'speak slowly', 'extremely funny', 'arrive late' and 'too quickly', 'slowly', 'extremely', 'late', 'too' and 'quickly' are adverbs.* ▶ **adverbial** /æd'vɜːbiəl/ *adj.*: *'Very quickly indeed' is an adverbial phrase.*

adversary /'ædvəsəri/ *noun* [C] (*pl.* **-ies**) (*formal*) an enemy, or an opponent in a competition

adverse 🔤+ C1 /'ædvɜːs, əd'vɜːs/ *adj.* (*formal*) negative and unpleasant: *Our flight was cancelled because of adverse weather conditions.* ⊃ look at **unfavourable** ▶ **adversely** *adv.*

adversity /əd'vɜːsəti/ *noun* [C, U] (*pl.* **-ies**) (*formal*) difficulties or problems

advertise 🔤 A2 /'ædvətaɪz/ *verb* (**ARTS AND MEDIA**) **1** [I, T] to tell the public about a product or a service in order to encourage people to buy or to use it: *It's very expensive to advertise on TV.* ◊ *a website that advertises cars* **2** [I] ~ (**for sb/sth**) to let people know that sth is going to happen, or that a job is available by giving details about it in a newspaper, on the internet, etc: *The shop is advertising for a sales assistant.* ◊ *The job was advertised on the company's website.*

advertisement 🔤 A2 /əd'vɜːtɪsmənt/ (*also informal* ad) (*also BrE, informal* advert /'ædvɜːt/) *noun* [C] ~ (**for sth**) (**ARTS AND MEDIA**) a piece of information on the internet, on TV, in a newspaper, etc. telling people about a product, job or service: *a TV/newspaper advertisement* ◊ *an online advertisement* ◊ *an advertisement for a new brand of shampoo*

▼ SYNONYMS

advertisement

ad ◆ advert ◆ commercial ◆ promotion ◆ trailer

These are all words for a notice, picture or film telling people about a product, job or service.

advertisement *an advertisement for a job*

ad *an ad for a new chocolate bar*

advert (*BrE, informal*) *I think there are too many adverts on TV.*

commercial *a commercial on TV for a new car*

promotion *a special promotion of our products*

trailer *The cinema usually shows three or four trailers before the main film.*

advertiser /'ædvətaɪzə(r)/ *noun* [C] (**ARTS AND MEDIA**) a person or company that pays to put an advertisement on the internet, on TV, etc.

advertising 🔤 A2 /'ædvətaɪzɪŋ/ *noun* [U] (**ARTS AND MEDIA**) the activity and industry of advertising things to people on TV, in newspapers, on the internet, etc: *an advertising campaign* ◊ *radio/TV advertising* ◊ *Val works for an advertising agency.*

advice 🔤 A1 /əd'vaɪs/ *noun* [U] an opinion that you give sb about what they should do: *She took her teacher's advice and worked hard for the exam.* ◊ *Let me give you some advice.* ⊃ note at **professional**[2]

ad'vice columnist (*AmE*) = AGONY AUNT

advisable /əd'vaɪzəbl/ *adj.* (*formal*) sensible and a good idea: *It is advisable to reserve a seat.* **OPP** **inadvisable**

advise 🔤 B1 /əd'vaɪz/ *verb* **1** [I, T] ~ (**sb**) (**against sth/doing sth**); ~ (**sb to do sth**) to tell sb what you think they should do: *The newspaper article advised against eating too much meat.* ◊ *He did what the doctor advised.* ◊ *I would strongly advise you to take the job.* ⊃ note at **recommend** **2** [I, T] ~ (**sb**) (**on/about sth**) to give sb help and information on a subject that you know a lot about: *She advises the government on economic affairs.* **3** [T] ~ **sb** (**of sth**); ~ **sb** (**that**) … (*formal*) to officially tell sb sth; to inform sb: *Please advise us of your arrival time.* ◊ *We would like to advise you that the goods are now ready for collection.*

adviser (*also* advisor) /əd'vaɪzə(r)/ *noun* [C] (**BUSINESS, POLITICS**) a person who gives advice to a company, government, etc: *an adviser on economic affairs*

advisory /əd'vaɪzəri/ *adj.* having the role of giving professional advice

advocacy /'ædvəkəsi/ *noun* [U] **1** ~ (**of sth**) (*formal*) the giving of public support to an idea, a course of action or a belief: *He is known for his advocacy of gender equality.* **2** (**LAW**) the work of lawyers who speak about cases in court

advocate[1] 🔤+ C1 /'ædvəkeɪt/ *verb* [T] (*formal*) to support sth publicly ⊃ note at **recommend**

advocate[2] 🔤+ C1 /'ædvəkət/ *noun* [C] **1** ~ (**of/for sth/sb**) a person who supports sth publicly: *an advocate of nuclear disarmament* **2** (**LAW**) a lawyer who defends sb in court

aeolian /i:'əuliən/ *adj.* (GEOLOGY) connected with or caused by the action of the wind

aeon (*BrE*) (*AmE* eon) /'i:ən, 'i:ɒn/ *noun* [C] (*formal*) an extremely long period of time; thousands of years

aerate /'eəreɪt/ *verb* [T] **1** (AGRICULTURE) to make it possible for air to become mixed with soil, water, etc. **2** (CHEMISTRY) to add a gas to a liquid under pressure: *aerated water*

aerial[1] /'eəriəl/ (*especially BrE*) (*also* antenna *especially in AmE*) *noun* [C] a piece of equipment made of wire or metal for receiving or sending radio and TV signals

aerial[2] /'eəriəl/ *adj.* from or in the air: *an aerial photo of the town*

aerobic /eə'rəubɪk/ *adj.* **1** (BIOLOGY) connected with or needing OXYGEN (= the gas that we need in order to live) **2** (SPORT) (used about physical exercise that we do to improve the way our bodies use OXYGEN ⊃ look at **anaerobic**(2)

aerobics /eə'rəubɪks/ *noun* [U] (SPORT) physical exercises intended to make the heart and lungs stronger, often done in classes, with music: *I do aerobics twice a week to keep fit.*

aerodrome /'eərədrəum/ (*BrE*) (*AmE* airdrome) *noun* [C] a small airport, used mainly by private planes

aerodynamics /ˌeərəudaɪ'næmɪks/ *noun* [U] (PHYSICS) the scientific study of the way that things move through the air ▸ aerodynamic *adj.*: *the aerodynamic design of a racing car* ▸ aerodynamically /-kli/ *adv.*

aeronautics /ˌeərə'nɔ:tɪks/ *noun* [U] (ENGINEERING, PHYSICS) the science or practice of building and flying aircraft ▸ aeronautical /-tɪkl/ *adj.*: *an aeronautical engineer*

aeroplane /'eərəpleɪn/ (*BrE*) = PLANE[1] (1)

aeroponics /ˌeərə'pɒnɪks/ *noun* [U] (AGRICULTURE) the process of growing plants in which the roots are hung in the air rather than buried in soil ⊃ look at **hydroponics**

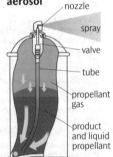

aerosol /'eərəsɒl/ *noun* [C] a liquid substance that is kept under pressure in a container. When you press a button, the liquid comes out in a fine SPRAY.

aerosol
nozzle
spray
valve
tube
propellant gas
product and liquid propellant

aerospace /'eərəuspeɪs/ *noun* [U] (often used as an adjective) the industry of building aircraft, vehicles and equipment to be sent into space

aesthete (*AmE also* esthete) /'es0i:t, 'i:s-/ *noun* [C] (*formal*) (ART) a person who has a love and an understanding of art and beautiful things

aesthetic[1] /i:s'0etɪk, es-/ *adj.* (*AmE also* esthetic) (ART) connected with beauty and art: *The columns are there for purely aesthetic reasons* (= only to look beautiful). ▸ aesthetically (*AmE also* esthetically) /-kli/ *adv.*: *The design is aesthetically pleasing as well as practical.*

aesthetic[2] (*AmE also* esthetic) /i:s'0etɪk, es-/ *noun* [U] (ART) **1** the qualities and ideas in a work of art or literature that relate to beauty and art **2** aesthetics (*AmE also* esthetics) the branch of philosophy that studies the principles of beauty, especially in art ▸ aestheticism (*AmE also* estheticism) /-tɪsɪzəm/ *noun* [U]

aetiology (*BrE*) (*AmE* etiology) /ˌi:ti'ɒlədʒi/ *noun* (*pl.* -ies) (MEDICINE) **1** [U, C] the cause of a disease or medical condition **2** [U] the scientific study of the causes of disease

afar /ə'fɑ:(r)/ *adv.* (*formal*)
IDM **from afar** from a long distance away

affable /'æfəbl/ *adj.* pleasant, friendly and easy to talk to SYN **genial** ▸ affability /ˌæfə'bɪləti/ *noun* [U] ▸ affably /'æfəbli/ *adv.*

affair ?B2 /ə'feə(r)/ *noun* **1** affairs [pl.] (POLITICS) events that are of public interest or political importance: *an expert on foreign affairs* (= political events in other countries) ◇ *affairs of state* ◇ *current affairs* (= the events and the social events that are happening at the present time) **2** [C, usually sing.] an event that people are talking about or describing in a particular way: *The newspapers exaggerated the whole affair wildly.* **3** [C] ~ (with sb) a sexual relationship between two people, usually when at least one of them is married to sb else: *She's having an affair with her boss.* **4** affairs [pl.] matters connected with a person's private business and financial situation: *I looked after my father's financial affairs.* **5** [sing.] a thing that sb is responsible for (and that other people should not be concerned with)
IDM **state of affairs** → STATE[1]

affect ?A2 ◐ /ə'fekt/ *verb* [T] **1** [often passive] make sb/sth change in a particular way; to influence sb/sth: *Her personal problems seem to be affecting her work.* ◇ *This disease affects the brain.* **2** to make sb feel very sad, angry, etc: *The whole community was affected by the tragedy.*

affected /ə'fektɪd/ *adj.* (used about a person or their behaviour) not natural or sincere OPP **unaffected** ▸ affectation /ˌæfek'teɪʃn/ *noun* [C, U]

affection ?+C1 /ə'fekʃn/ *noun* [U, sing.] ~ (for sb/sth) a feeling of loving or liking sb/sth: *She shows her daughter a lot of affection.* ◇ *I have a great affection for Paris.*

affectionate /ə'fekʃənət/ *adj.* showing that you love or like sb very much SYN **loving** ▸ affectionately *adv.*

affective /ə'fektɪv/ *adj.* (PSYCHOLOGY) connected with emotions and attitudes: *affective disorders*

affidavit /ˌæfə'deɪvɪt/ *noun* [C] (LAW) a written statement that you swear is true, and that can be used as evidence in court: *to make/swear/sign an affidavit*

affiliate[1] /ə'fɪlieɪt/ *verb* [T, usually passive] **be affiliated (with/to sb/sth)** (BUSINESS) (used about a group, an organization, etc.) to be connected to a larger group, organization, etc: *Our local club is affiliated to the national association.* ▸ affiliated *adj.* ▸ affiliation /əˌfɪli'eɪʃn/ *noun* [C, U]

affiliate[2] /ə'fɪliət/ *noun* [C] (BUSINESS) a group, an organization, etc. that is connected with or controlled by another larger one

affinity /ə'fɪnəti/ *noun* (*pl.* -ies) ~ (with sb/sth) **1** [sing.] a strong feeling that you like and understand sb/sth, usually because you feel similar to them or it in some way: *He had always had an affinity with nature.* **2** [C, U] a similar quality in two or more people or things: *His music has certain affinities with Brahms.*

affirm /ə'fɜ:m/ *verb* [T] (*formal*) to say formally or clearly that sth is true or that you support sth strongly

affirmation /ˌæfə'meɪʃn/ *noun* [U, C] **1** (*formal*) a statement that sth is true or that you support sth strongly: *She nodded in affirmation.* **2** (PSYCHOLOGY) emotional support: *Many children look to their parents for affirmation.* ◇ *Positive affirmations line the walls of her classroom.*

affirmative[1] /əˈfɜːmətɪv/ adj. (formal) an **affirmative** word or reply means 'yes' or expresses agreement **OPP** **negative**[1] ▸ affirmatively adv.: 90% voted affirmatively.

affirmative[2] /əˈfɜːmətɪv/ noun [C] (formal) (**GRAMMAR**) a word or statement that means 'yes'; an agreement or a CONFIRMATION: She answered **in the affirmative** (= said 'yes'). **OPP** **negative**[2]

af,firmative 'action (especially AmE) = POSITIVE DISCRIMINATION

affix[1] /əˈfɪks/ verb [T, often passive] ~ **sth (to sth)** (formal) to stick or join sth to sth else: The label should be firmly affixed to the package.

affix[2] /ˈæfɪks/ noun [C] (**GRAMMAR**) a letter or group of letters added to the beginning or end of a word to change its meaning. The prefix un- in unhappy and the suffix -less in careless are both affixes. ⊃ look at **prefix**, **suffix**

afflict /əˈflɪkt/ verb [T, usually passive] **be afflicted (with sth)** (formal) to be affected by sth in an unpleasant way: He had been afflicted with the illness since childhood. ▸ affliction /əˈflɪkʃn/ noun [C, U]

affluent /ˈæfluənt/ adj. having a lot of money **SYN** **wealthy** ▸ affluence /-əns/ noun [U]: Increased exports have brought new affluence.

afford ⟨**B1**⟩ /əˈfɔːd/ verb [T] (usually after can/could in negative sentences and questions) ~ **(to do sth)** **1** to have enough money or time to be able to do sth: We couldn't afford a car in those days. ◇ I can't afford to go on holiday this year. **2** to not be able to do sth or let sth happen because it would have a bad result for you: The other team was very good so we couldn't afford to make any mistakes. ▸ affordable ⟨**B2**⟩ adj.: affordable prices ◇ affordable housing

af,fordable 'housing noun [U] (**SOCIAL STUDIES**) houses or flats that people on low incomes can buy or rent at a low price

afforestation /ə,fɒrɪˈsteɪʃn/ noun [U] (**ENVIRONMENT**) planting trees on an area of land in order to form a forest ⊃ look at **deforestation**

affront /əˈfrʌnt/ noun [C, usually sing.] ~ **(to sb/sth)** something that you say or do that offends sb/sth: Losing his job was a real affront to Oscar's dignity.

afield /əˈfiːld/ adv.
IDM **far afield** → FAR[2]

afloat /əˈfləʊt/ adj. [not before noun] **1** on the surface of the water; not sinking: A life jacket helps you **stay afloat** if you fall in the water. **2** (**BUSINESS, FINANCE**) (used about a business, an economy, etc.) having enough money to survive

afoot /əˈfʊt/ adj. [not before noun] being planned or prepared

aforementioned /əˈfɔːmenʃənd, ə,fɔːˈmenʃənd/ (also **aforesaid** /əˈfɔːsed/, said) adj. [only before noun] (formal) (**LAW**) mentioned before, in an earlier sentence: The aforementioned person was seen acting suspiciously.

afraid ⟨**A1**⟩ /əˈfreɪd/ adj. [not before noun] **1** ~ **(of sb/ sth/doing sth); ~ (to do sth)** feeling fear; frightened: Are you afraid of dogs? ◇ Ben is afraid of going out after dark. ◇ I was too afraid to answer the door. **2** ~ **(that) … ; ~ (of doing sth)** worried about sth: We were afraid (that) you would be angry. ◇ to be afraid of offending somebody **3** ~ **for sb/sth** worried that sb/sth will be harmed, lost, etc: I'm not afraid for me, but for the baby.
IDM **I'm afraid** used for saying politely that you are sorry about sth: I'm afraid I can't come on Sunday. ◇ 'Is the factory going to close?' 'I'm afraid so.' ◇ 'Is this seat free?' 'I'm afraid not/it isn't.'

afresh /əˈfreʃ/ adv. (formal) again, in a new way: to start afresh

African[1] /ˈæfrɪkən/ adj. of or connected with Africa

African[2] /ˈæfrɪkən/ noun [C] a person from Africa, especially a black person

,African A'merican noun [C] an American citizen whose family was originally from Africa ▸ African American adj.

Afrikaans /,æfrɪˈkɑːns/ noun [U] (**LANGUAGE**) a language that has developed from Dutch, spoken in South Africa

Afro-Caribbean /,æfrəʊ kærɪˈbiːən, kəˈrɪbiən/ noun [C] a person whose family came originally from Africa, and who was born or whose parents were born in the Caribbean ▸ Afro-Caribbean adj.

aft /ɑːft/ adv., adj. (formal) at, near or towards the back of a ship or an aircraft ⊃ look at **fore**[2]

after[1] ⟨**A1**⟩ /ˈɑːftə(r)/ prep. **1** later than sth; following sth: Ian phoned just after six o'clock. ◇ the week after next ◇ I hope to arrive some time after lunch. ◇ After we had finished our dinner, we went into the garden. ◇ I went out yesterday morning, and **after that** I was at home all day. **2** repeated many times or continuing for a long time: **day after day** of hot weather ◇ I've told the children **time after time** not to do that. **3** following or behind sb/sth: Shut the door after you. ◇ C comes after B in the alphabet. **4** looking for or trying to catch or get sb/sth: The police were after him. ◇ Nicky is after a job in advertising. **5** as a result of sth: After the way he behaved I won't invite him here again. **6** used when sb/sth is given the name of another person or thing: We called our son William after his grandfather.
IDM **after all** **1** used when sth is different in reality to what sb expected or thought: So you decided to come after all! (= I thought you weren't going to come) **2** used for reminding sb of a certain fact: She can't understand. After all, she's only 2.

after[2] ⟨**A2**⟩ /ˈɑːftə(r)/ conj., adv. later than sth; afterwards: They arrived at the station after the train had left. ◇ That was in April. Soon after, I heard that he was ill.

afterbirth /ˈɑːftəbɜːθ/ noun [sing.] (**BIOLOGY**) the material that comes out of a woman or female animal's body after a baby has been born, and that was necessary to feed and protect the baby ⊃ look at **placenta**

'after-effect noun [C] an unpleasant result of sth that comes some time later ⊃ look at **effect**[1] (1), **side effect**

afterlife /ˈɑːftəlaɪf/ noun [sing.] (**RELIGION**) a life that some people believe exists after death

aftermath ⟨**C1**⟩ /ˈɑːftəmæθ, -mɑːθ/ noun [sing.] a situation that is the result of an important or unpleasant event ⊃ note at **disaster**

afternoon ⟨**A1**⟩ /,ɑːftəˈnuːn/ noun [C, U] the part of a day between twelve o'clock in the middle of the day and about six o'clock in the evening: I'll see you **tomorrow afternoon**. ◇ What are you doing **this afternoon**? ◇ I went shopping **yesterday afternoon**. ◇ I usually go for a walk **in the afternoon**. ◇ He goes swimming **every afternoon**. ◇ Tom works two afternoons a week. ◇ Are you busy **on Friday afternoon**? ❶ When you are talking about a particular afternoon you say **on Monday, Tuesday, Wednesday, etc. afternoon**, but when you are talking generally about doing sth at the time of day you say **in the afternoon**.
IDM **good afternoon** used when you see sb for the first time in the afternoon

aftershave /ˈɑːftəʃeɪv/ noun [C, U] a liquid with a pleasant smell that men put on their faces after they SHAVE

aftershock /ˈɑːftəʃɒk/ noun [C] (GEOLOGY) a smaller earthquake that happens after a bigger one

aftersun /ˈɑːftəsʌn/ noun [U] cream that you put on painful skin after you have spent too long in the sun

aftertaste /ˈɑːftəteɪst/ noun [sing.] a taste (usually an unpleasant one) that stays in your mouth after you have eaten or drunk sth

afterthought /ˈɑːftəθɔːt/ noun [C, usually sing.] something that you think of or add to sth else at a later time

afterwards ？ B2 /ˈɑːftəwədz/ (especially BrE) (AmE usually **afterward** /ˈɑːftəwəd/) adv. at a later time: He was taken to hospital and died shortly afterwards. ◇ Afterwards, I realized I'd made a terrible mistake.

again ？ A1 S /əˈɡen, əˈɡeɪn/ adv. 1 once more; another time: Could you say that again, please? ◇ Don't ever do that again! 2 in the place or condition that sb/sth was in before: It's great to be home again. ◇ I hope you'll soon be well again. 3 in addition to sth: 'Is that enough?' 'No, I'd like half as much again, please.'
IDM **again and again** many times: He said he was sorry again and again, but she wouldn't listen. **then/ there again** used to say that sth you have just said may not happen or be true: She might pass her test, but then again she might not. **yet again** → YET[1]

against ？ A2 /əˈɡenst, əˈɡeɪnst/ prep. 1 being an opponent to sb/sth in a game, competition, etc., or an enemy of sb/sth in a war or fight: We played football against a school from another district. 2 not agreeing with or supporting sb/sth: Are you for or against the plan? ◇ She felt that everybody was against her. **OPP** **for**[1] 3 what a law, rule, etc. says you must not do: It's against the law to steal. 4 in order to protect yourself from sb/sth: Take these pills as a precaution against malaria. 5 in the opposite direction to sth: We had to cycle against the wind. 6 touching sb/sth for support: I put the ladder against the wall.

agar /ˈeɪɡɑː(r)/ (also ˌagar-ˈagar) noun [U] (BIOLOGY) a substance like JELLY, used by scientists for growing CULTURES (= groups of cells or bacteria, grown for medical or scientific study)

agate /ˈæɡət/ noun [U, C] a hard stone with bands or areas of colour, used in jewellery

age[1] ？ A1 W /eɪdʒ/ noun [C, U] the length of time that sb has lived or that sth has existed: Children of all ages will enjoy this film. ◇ He needs some friends of his own age. ◇ Ali is 17 years of age. ◇ She left school at the age of 16. **HELP** When you want to ask about sb's age, you usually say: How old is she? and the answer can be: She's eighteen or: She's eighteen years old (but NOT: She's eighteen years). Here are some examples of other ways of talking about age: I'm nearly nineteen. ◇ a girl of eighteen ◇ an eighteen-year-old girl ◇ The robber is of medium height and aged about sixteen or seventeen. 2 [U, C] a particular period in sb's life: a problem that often develops in middle age ◇ Her sons will look after her in her old age. ◇ look at youth (1) 3 [U] the state of being old: a face lined with age ◇ The jacket was showing signs of age. ◇ look at youth (3) 4 [C] (HISTORY) a particular period of history: the computer age ◇ the history of art through the ages 5 ages [pl.] (informal) a very long time: We had to wait (for) ages at the hospital. ◇ It's ages since I've seen her.
IDM **at a tender age | at the tender age of …** → TENDER[1] **come of age** (LAW) to reach the age at which sb has an adult's rights and responsibilities in law **feel your age** → FEEL[1] **under age** (LAW) not old enough by law to do sth

age[2] ？ B1 /eɪdʒ/ verb [I, T] (ageing BrE, aging especially AmE; pt, pp aged) to become or look old; to cause sb to look old: My father seems to have aged a lot recently. ◇ an ageing aunt ◇ I could see her illness had aged her.

aged ？ B1 /eɪdʒd/ adj. [not before noun] 1 of the age mentioned: The woman, aged 26, was last seen in Victoria Station. 2 the aged /ði ˈeɪdʒɪd/ noun [pl.] very old people

ˈ**age group** noun [C] people of about the same age: This club is very popular with the 20–30 age group.

ageism (BrE) (AmE also **agism**) /ˈeɪdʒɪzəm/ noun [U] (SOCIAL STUDIES) unfair treatment of people because they are considered too old ▶ **ageist** /-dʒɪst/ adj.

ageless /ˈeɪdʒləs/ adj. (formal) 1 never seeming to grow old 2 existing for ever; impossible to give an age to: the ageless mystery of the universe

ˈ**age limit** noun [C] (LAW) the oldest or youngest age at which you are allowed to do sth: to be over/under the age limit

agency ？ B2 /ˈeɪdʒənsi/ noun [C] (pl. -ies) 1 (BUSINESS) a business or an organization that provides a particular service: an advertising agency 2 (AmE) (POLITICS) a government department

agenda ？ B2 W /əˈdʒendə/ noun [C] 1 a list of items to be discussed at a meeting: The first item on the agenda at the meeting was security. ◇ note at meeting 2 ~ (for sth) a plan of things to be done or problems to be addressed: The government have set an agenda for reform over the next ten years.

agent ？ B1 W /ˈeɪdʒənt/ noun [C] 1 (BUSINESS) a person whose job is to do business for a company or for another person: Our company's agent in Rio will meet you at the airport. ◇ a travel agent ◇ an estate agent 2 (BUSINESS) a person whose job is to arrange work for an actor, a musician, a sports player, etc: Most actors and musicians have their own agents. 3 = SECRET AGENT 4 (CHEMISTRY) a chemical or a substance that produces an effect or a change, or is used for a particular purpose: cleaning/oxidizing agents

ˌ**age of conˈsent** noun [sing.] (LAW) the age at which sb is legally old enough to agree to have a sexual relationship

ˌ**age-ˈold** adj. having existed for a very long time: an age-old custom/problem

agglomeration /əˌɡlɒməˈreɪʃn/ noun [C, U] (formal) a group of things put together in no particular order or arrangement

agglutinative /əˈɡluːtɪnətɪv/ adj. (LANGUAGE) an agglutinative language makes new words by joining words and parts of words together

aggravate /ˈæɡrəveɪt/ verb [T] 1 to make sth worse or more serious 2 (informal) to make sb angry or annoyed ▶ **aggravation** /ˌæɡrəˈveɪʃn/ noun [C, U]

aggregate[1] /ˈæɡrɪɡət/ noun 1 [C] a total number or amount made up of smaller amounts that are collected together 2 [U, C] sand or broken stone that is used to make CONCRETE or for building roads, etc. **IDM** **on aggregate** (BrE) (SPORT) when the scores of a number of games are added together: Our team won 3-1 on aggregate.

aggregate[2] /ˈæɡrɪɡət/ adj. [only before noun] made up of several amounts that are added together to form a total number: aggregate demand/investment/ turnover ◇ an aggregate win over their rivals

aggregate[3] /ˈæɡrɪɡeɪt/ verb [T] [usually passive] **be aggregated (with sth)** (formal) (used about different items, amounts, etc.) to be put together into a single group or total: *The scores were aggregated with the first round totals to decide the winner.*

aggression ⚡+ **C1** /əˈgreʃn/ *noun* [U] **1** angry feelings or behaviour that make you want to attack other people: *People often react to this kind of situation with fear or aggression.* **2** the act of starting a fight or war without reasonable cause

aggressive ⚡ **B2** /əˈgresɪv/ *adj.* **1** ready or likely to fight or argue: *an aggressive dog* ◇ *Some people get aggressive after drinking alcohol.* **2** using or showing force or pressure in order to succeed: *an aggressive salesman* ▶ **aggressively** *adv.*: *They responded aggressively when I asked them to make less noise.*

aggressor /əˈgresə(r)/ *noun* [C] a person or country that attacks sb/sth or starts fighting first

aggrieved /əˈgriːvd/ *adj.* (*formal*) upset or angry

aghast /əˈgɑːst/ *adj.* [not before noun] ~ **(at sth)** filled with horror and surprise when you see or hear sth: *He stood aghast at the sight of so much blood.*

agile /ˈædʒaɪl/ *adj.* **1** able to move quickly and easily **2** (**BUSINESS**) used to describe a way of working in which a project is divided into a series of short tasks, with regular reviews and changes to the plans: *We use an agile planning approach and organise all our tasks over two-week periods.* **3** (**BUSINESS**) used to describe a way of working in which the time and place of work, and the tasks that people do, can all be changed according to need: *A growing number of employers are now offering flexible and agile working.* ▶ **agility** /əˈdʒɪləti/ *noun* [U]: *This sport is a test of both physical and mental agility.*

agism /ˈeɪdʒɪzəm/ (*AmE*) = AGEISM

agitate /ˈædʒɪteɪt/ *verb* [I] ~ **(for/against sth)** to make other people feel very strongly about sth so that they want to help you achieve it: *to agitate for reform*

agitated /ˈædʒɪteɪtɪd/ *adj.* worried or nervous ▶ **agitation** /ˌædʒɪˈteɪʃn/ *noun* [U]

agitator /ˈædʒɪteɪtə(r)/ *noun* [C] (**POLITICS**) a person who tries to persuade people to take part in political protest

aglow /əˈgləʊ/ *adj.* [not before noun] ~ **(with sth)** shining with heat or happiness: *The children's faces were aglow with excitement.*

AGM /ˌeɪ dʒiː ˈem/ *noun* [C] (*BrE*) (**BUSINESS**) an important meeting that the members of an organization hold once a year in order to elect officers, discuss past and future activities, and examine the accounts (the abbreviation for 'annual general meeting')

agnostic /ægˈnɒstɪk/ *noun* [C] (**RELIGION**) a person who believes that it is not possible to know whether God exists or not

ago ⚡ **A1** /əˈgəʊ/ *adv.* in the past; back in time from now: *Patrick left ten minutes ago* (= if it is twelve o'clock now, he left at 11.50). ◇ *That was a long time ago.* ◇ *How long ago did this happen?*

agog /əˈgɒg/ *adj.* [not before noun] very excited while waiting to hear sth: *We were all agog when she said she had good news.*

agonize (*BrE also* -**ise**) /ˈægənaɪz/ *verb* [I] ~ **(over/about sth)** to worry or think about sth for a long time: *He agonized over the decision.*

agonized (*BrE also* -**ised**) /ˈægənaɪzd/ *adj.* showing extreme pain or worry: *an agonized cry*

agonizing (*BrE also* -**ising**) /ˈægənaɪzɪŋ/ *adj.* causing extreme worry or pain: *an agonizing choice* ◇ *an agonizing headache*

agony /ˈægəni/ *noun* [C, U] (*pl.* -**ies**) great pain or suffering: *to be/scream in agony*

agony aunt (*BrE*) (*AmE* **advice columnist**) *noun* [C] (**ARTS AND MEDIA**) a person who writes in a newspaper or magazine, or on a website, giving advice in reply to people's questions about their personal problems

agoraphobia /ˌægərəˈfəʊbiə/ *noun* [U] (**PSYCHOLOGY**) fear of being in public places where there are a lot of people ▶ **agoraphobic** /-bɪk/ *adj.*

agrarian /əˈgreəriən/ *adj.* (*formal*) (**AGRICULTURE**) connected with farming and the use of land for farming

agree ⚡ **A1** /əˈgriː/ *verb*
- SHARE AN OPINION **1** [I] ~ **(with sb/sth)**; ~ **(that)** ... to have the same opinion as sb/sth: *I agree with Paul.* ◇ *Do you agree (that) we should travel by train?* ◇ *I'm afraid I don't agree.* ◇ *'I think we should talk to the teacher about this.' 'Yes, I agree.'* **OPP disagree**
- SAY YES **2** [I] ~ **(to sth)**; ~ **(to do sth)** to say 'yes' to sth: *She agreed to my request.* ◇ *Alkis has agreed to lend me his car for the weekend.* **OPP refuse¹**
- ARRANGE **3** [I, T] ~ **(to do sth)**; ~ **(on) (sth)** to make an arrangement or decide sth with sb: *They agreed to meet again the following day.* ◇ *Can we agree (on) a price?* ⊃ note at **meeting**
- APPROVE OF **4** [I] ~ **with sth** to think that sth is right: *I don't agree with experiments on animals.* **OPP disagree**
- BE THE SAME **5** [I] to be the same as sth: *The two accounts of the accident do not agree.* **OPP disagree**
- IN GRAMMAR **6** [I] ~ **(with sth)** to match a word or phrase in NUMBER, GENDER or PERSON
IDM not agree with sb (used about food) to make sb feel ill

▼ **SYNONYMS**

agree

approve ◆ consent ◆ acquiesce

These words all mean to say that you will do what sb wants or that you will allow sth to happen.

agree *He agreed to let me go early.*

approve *The committee approved the plans.*

consent (*formal*) *He finally consented to answer our questions.*

acquiesce (*formal*) *Senior politicians must have acquiesced in the cover-up.*

agreeable /əˈgriːəbl/ *adj.* **1** pleasant; nice **OPP disagreeable 2** (*formal*) ready to agree: *If you are agreeable, we would like to visit your offices on 21 May.* ▶ **agreeably** /-bli/ *adv.*: *I was agreeably surprised by the film.*

agreement ⚡ **B1** **W** /əˈgriːmənt/ *noun* **1** [U] **(in)** ~ **(with sb) (on/about sth)** the state of agreeing with sb/sth: *She nodded her head in agreement.* ◇ *We are totally in agreement with you on that issue.* **OPP disagreement 2** [C] a contract or decision that two or more people have made together: *Please sign the agreement and return it to us.* ◇ *The leaders reached an agreement after five days of talks.* ◇ *We never break an agreement.* **3** [U] **(in)** ~ **(with sth)** (**GRAMMAR**) (used about words in a phrase) the state of having the same NUMBER, GENDER or PERSON: *In 'We love Italian food,' the plural form of the verb 'love' is in agreement with the plural subject 'they'.* **SYN concord**

agribusiness /ˈægrɪbɪznəs/ *noun* [U, C] (**AGRICULTURE**) the industry concerned with making and selling farm products, especially involving large companies

agriculture ⟨⁺ **B2** /ˈæɡrɪkʌltʃə(r)/ *noun* [U] keeping animals and growing crops for food; farming: *the Minister of Agriculture* ▸ **agricultural** ⟨⁺ **C1** **Ⓦ** /ˌæɡrɪˈkʌltʃərəl/ *adj.*

▼ **COLLOCATIONS**

agriculture

Fruit and vegetables **grow** or **are grown**: *Pineapples grow in tropical climates.* ◇ *We have been growing strawberries for many years.* When fruit is almost ready to pick and eat, it **ripens** or becomes **ripe**: *Peaches ripen in the sun.* ◇ *Those pears are not quite ripe yet.* A plant **produces** fruit or vegetables: *The tree produces very sweet plums.* The amount of fruit/vegetables collected is the **harvest/crop**: *Growers are expecting a plentiful harvest this year.* ◇ *Hereford enjoyed a bumper crop of apples.* Fruit that grows on trees grows in **orchards** or **groves**. Nuts grow in **groves**: *apple/cherry orchards* ◇ *almond/citrus/lemon/orange groves.* **Plantations** are large areas of land where fruit and other crops grow: *banana/coffee/rice/sugar/tea plantations*

agrochemical /ˌæɡrəʊˈkemɪkl/ *noun* [C] (**AGRICULTURE, ENVIRONMENT**) a chemical used in farming, especially for killing insects or for making plants grow better

agronomy /əˈɡrɒnəmi/ *noun* [U] (**AGRICULTURE, ENVIRONMENT**) the scientific study of the relationship between the plants that farmers grow and the environment ▸ **agronomist** /-mɪst/ *noun* [C]

aground /əˈɡraʊnd/ *adv.* if a ship **runs/goes aground**, it touches the ground in water that is not deep enough and it cannot move: *The oil tanker ran/went aground off the Spanish coast.* ▸ **aground** *adj.*

ah ⟨ **A2** /ɑː/ *exclamation* used for expressing surprise, pleasure, understanding, etc: *Ah, there you are.*

aha /ɑːˈhɑː/ *exclamation* used when you suddenly find or understand sth: *Aha! Now I understand.*

ahead ⟨ **B1** /əˈhed/ *adv.* **1** further forward in space or time; in front: *The path ahead looked narrow and steep.* ◇ *Look **straight ahead** and don't turn round!* ◇ *He's got a difficult time ahead of him.* **2** earlier: *We must **think ahead** and make a plan.* **3** (**SPORT**) winning in a game, competition, etc: *The goal put Argentina 2–1 **ahead** at half-time.* ⊃ look at **behind** (2) **IDM streets ahead** → STREET

a'head of *prep.* **1** further forward in space or time than sb/sth; in front of sb/sth: *I could see the other car about half a mile ahead of us.* **2** earlier than sb/sth: *We finished the task ahead of the deadline.* **3** in front of sb, for example in a race or competition: *She's well ahead of the rest of the class.*

ahistorical /ˌeɪhɪˈstɒrɪkl/ *adj.* (*formal*) (**HISTORY**) not showing any knowledge of history or of what has happened before

AI /ˌeɪ ˈaɪ/ *abbr.* **1** (**COMPUTING**) **artificial intelligence** (the study and development of computer systems that can copy the way humans think): *The company developed an AI system that could fly an aircraft.* **2** = ARTIFICIAL INSEMINATION

aid¹ ⟨ **B2** /eɪd/ *noun* **1** [U] money, food, etc. that is sent to a country or to people in order to help them: *We sent aid to the earthquake victims.* ◇ *economic aid* **2** [U] **(with/without the) ~(of sb/sth)** help: *to walk with the aid of a stick* ⊃ look at **first aid 3** [C] an object, a machine, etc. that you use to help you do sth: *a hearing aid* ◇ *dictionaries and other study aids* **IDM in aid of sb/sth** in order to collect money for sb/sth, especially for a charity: *a concert in aid of Children in Need*

aid² ⟨ **B2** /eɪd/ *verb* [T] (*formal*) **1 ~(sb/sth) (in sth/doing sth)** to help sb/sth to do sth, especially by making it easier: *A team of researchers aided him in his work.* **2** to help or encourage sth to happen: *Sleep aids recovery from illness.* **IDM aid and abet** to help sb to do sth that is not allowed by law

aide ⟨⁺ **C1** /eɪd/ *noun* [C] (**POLITICS**) a person who helps another person, especially a politician, in their job **SYN assistant¹**

AIDS ⟨⁺ **B2** /eɪdz/ (*BrE usually* **Aids**) *noun* [U] (**HEALTH**) an illness that destroys the body's ability to fight infection and that usually causes death (the abbreviation for 'Acquired Immune Deficiency Syndrome'): *the AIDS virus* ◇ *He was HIV positive for three years before developing **full-blown** AIDS.* ◇ *to contract Aids*

aileron /ˈeɪlərɒn/ *noun* [C] a part of the wing of a plane that moves up and down to control the plane's balance ⊃ picture at **airliner**

ailing /ˈeɪlɪŋ/ *adj.* not in good health; weak: *an ailing economy*

ailment /ˈeɪlmənt/ *noun* [C] (*formal*) (**HEALTH**) any illness that is not very serious ⊃ note at **disease**

aim¹ ⟨ **B1** **Ⓞ** /eɪm/ *noun* **1** [C] something that you intend to do; a purpose: *Our main aim is to increase sales in Europe.* ◇ *His only aim in life is to make money.* ⊃ note at **purpose 2** [U] to point or direct a weapon, camera, shot, etc. at sb/sth: *She picked up the gun, **took aim** and fired.* ◇ *Jo's aim was good and she hit the target.* ◇ *He aimed the camera and took a beautiful shot of the sunrise.*

aim² ⟨ **B1** **Ⓞ** /eɪm/ *verb* **1** [I] **~(to do sth); ~(at/for sth)** to intend to do or achieve sth: *We aim to leave after breakfast.* ◇ *The company is aiming at a 25% increase in profit.* **2** [T] **~ sth at sb/sth** to direct sth at a particular person or group: *The advertising campaign is aimed at young people.* **3** [I, T] **~(sth) (at sb/sth)** to point sth at sb/sth before trying to hit them or it with it: *She aimed (the gun) at the target and fired.* ⊃ note at **gun¹** **IDM be aimed at sth/doing sth** to be intended to achieve sth: *The new laws are aimed at reducing heavy traffic in cities.*

aimless /ˈeɪmləs/ *adj.* having no purpose: *an aimless discussion* ▸ **aimlessly** *adv.*

ain't /eɪnt/ *short form* (*informal*) **1** am not; is not; are not **2** has not; have not **HELP** Ain't is NOT considered to be correct English.

air¹ ⟨ **A1** /eə(r)/ *noun* **1** [U] the mixture of gases that surrounds the earth and that people, animals and plants breathe: *the pure mountain air* ◇ *Open a window—I need some **fresh air**.* ◇ *The air was polluted by smoke from the factory.* ⊃ picture at **convection, diffusion 2** [U] the space around and above things: *to throw a ball high into the air* **3** [U] travel or transport in an aircraft: *to travel by air* ◇ *an air ticket* **4** [sing.] **~(of sth)** the particular feeling or impression that is given by sb/sth: *She has an air of confidence.* **IDM a breath of fresh air** → BREATH **clear the air** → CLEAR³ **in the air** probably going to happen soon: *A feeling of change was in the air.* **in the open air** → OPEN¹ **off (the) air** no longer on the radio or TV: *The programme was taken off the air over the summer.* **on (the) air** sending out programmes on the radio or TV: *This radio station is on the air 24 hours a day.* **up in the air** not yet decided: *All of these questions are still up in the air.* **vanish, etc. into thin air** → THIN¹

air² /eə(r)/ *verb* **1** [T, I] to put clothes, etc. in a warm place or outside in the fresh air to make sure they are completely dry; to become dry in this way **2** [I, T] to make a room, etc. fresh by letting air into it; to become fresh in this way **3** [T] to tell people what you think about sth: *The discussion gave people a chance to air their views.*

air ambulance *noun* [C] (*especially BrE*) an aircraft, especially a helicopter, used for taking ill or injured people to a hospital quickly

airbag /ˈeəbæg/ *noun* [C] a safety device in a car that fills with air if there is an accident. It protects the people sitting in the front of the car.

airbase /ˈeəbeɪs/ *noun* [C] an airport for military aircraft where some staff live

airborne /ˈeəbɔːn/ *adj.* **1** (used about a plane or passengers) flying in the air: *Five minutes after getting on the plane we were airborne.* **2** [only before noun] carried through the air ⊃ look at **waterborne**

airbrush¹ /ˈeəbrʌʃ/ *noun* [C] (**ART**) an artist's tool for pushing tiny drops of paint onto a surface, that works by air pressure

airbrush² /ˈeəbrʌʃ/ *verb* [T, often passive] ~ **sth (out)** (**ART**) to paint sth with an AIRBRUSH; to change a detail in a photo using this tool: *Somebody had been airbrushed out of the picture.*

Airbus™ /ˈeəbʌs/ *noun* [C] (**TOURISM**) a large plane that carries passengers over short and medium distances

air conditioner *noun* [C] a machine that cools and dries air

air conditioning (*also* ˈair con) *noun* [U] (*abbr.* **AC**, a/c) the system that keeps the air in a building, car, etc. cool and dry ▶ ˈair-conditioned *adj.*: *air-conditioned offices*

aircraft ⚓ **B2** /ˈeəkrɑːft/ *noun* [C] (*pl.* aircraft) any vehicle that can fly in the air, for example a plane: *fighter/military aircraft* ◇ *The aircraft was flown by an experienced pilot.*

aircraft carrier *noun* [C] a ship that carries military aircraft and that has a long flat area where they can take off and land

aircrew /ˈeəkruː/ *noun* [C + sing./pl. verb] the pilot and other people who fly a plane, especially in the AIR FORCE

airdrome /ˈeədrəʊm/ (*AmE*) = AERODROME

airdrop /ˈeədrɒp/ *noun* [C] the act of dropping supplies, equipment, soldiers, etc. from an aircraft using a PARACHUTE (= a thing that helps them fall to the ground slowly)

airfare /ˈeəfeə(r)/ *noun* [C] (**TOURISM**) the money that you pay to travel by plane: *Take advantage of low-season airfares.* ⊃ look at **fare¹**

airfield /ˈeəfiːld/ *noun* [C] an area of land where aircraft can land or take off. An airfield is smaller than an airport.

air force *noun* [C + sing./pl. verb] the part of a country's military organization that fights in the air ⊃ look at **army** (1), **navy**

air gun (*also* ˈair rifle) *noun* [C] a gun that uses air pressure to fire PELLETS (= small metal balls)

airing cupboard *noun* [C] a warm cupboard that you put sheets, clothes, etc. in to make sure they are completely dry after being washed

airless /ˈeələs/ *adj.* not having enough fresh air: *The room was hot and airless.*

airlift /ˈeəlɪft/ *noun* [C] an operation to take people, soldiers, food, etc. to or from an area by aircraft, especially in an emergency or when roads are closed or dangerous ▶ airlift *verb* [T] ~ **sb/sth (to …)**: *Two casualties were airlifted to safety.*

airline ⚓ **A2** /ˈeəlaɪn/ *noun* [C] (**TOURISM**) a company that provides regular flights for people or goods in aircraft: *international airlines* ◇ *an airline pilot*

airliner /ˈeəlaɪnə(r)/ *noun* [C] (**TOURISM**) a large plane that carries passengers

airlock /ˈeəlɒk/ *noun* [C] (**ENGINEERING**) **1** a small room with a tightly closed door at each end, which you go through to reach another area at a different air pressure, for example on a SPACECRAFT or SUBMARINE (= a ship that can travel UNDERWATER) **2** a bubble of air that blocks the flow of liquid in a pipe or PUMP (= a machine used for forcing a gas or liquid in a particular direction)

airmail /ˈeəmeɪl/ *noun* [U] the system for sending letters, packages, etc. by plane: *I sent the parcel by airmail.*

airplane /ˈeəpleɪn/ (*especially AmE*) = PLANE¹ (1)

airplay /ˈeəpleɪ/ *noun* [U] (**MUSIC**) time that is spent playing a particular piece of music, music by a particular performer, etc. on the radio: *His songs are starting to get airplay on radio stations around the world.*

airliner

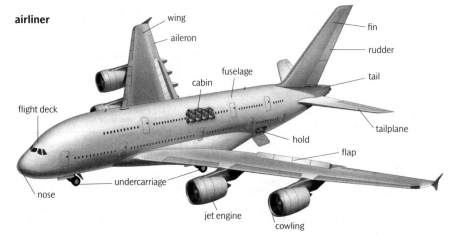

wing
aileron
fin
rudder
fuselage
cabin
tail
flight deck
hold
tailplane
flap
undercarriage
nose
jet engine
cowling

'air pocket *noun* [C] **1** a closed area that becomes filled with air: *Make sure there are no air pockets around the roots of the plant.* **2** an area of low air pressure that makes a plane suddenly drop while flying

airport 🔊 **A1** /'eəpɔːt/ *noun* [C] (**TOURISM**) a place where aircraft can land and take off and that has buildings for passengers to wait in: *He arrived at Bologna airport on Friday.* ◇ *the airport lounge/terminal*

'air raid *noun* [C] an attack by military aircraft

'air rifle = AIR GUN

airship /'eəʃɪp/ *noun* [C] a large aircraft without wings, filled with gas that is lighter than air, and driven by engines

airsick /'eəsɪk/ *adj.* feeling sick when you are travelling on a plane ◯ look at **carsick, seasick, travel-sick** ▸ **airsickness** *noun* [U]

airspace /'eəspeɪs/ *noun* [U] the part of the sky that is above a country and that belongs to that country by law

airstrip /'eəstrɪp/ (*also* landing strip) *noun* [C] a narrow piece of land where aircraft can take off and land

airtight /'eətaɪt/ *adj.* not allowing air to get in or out

airtime /'eətaɪm/ *noun* [U] **1** (**ARTS AND MEDIA**) the amount of time that is given to a subject on radio or TV **2** the amount of time that is paid for when you use a mobile phone: *This deal gives you 90 minutes free airtime a week.*

air-to-'air *adj.* from one aircraft to another while they are both flying: *an air-to-air missile*

air traffic con'troller *noun* [C] a person whose job is to organize routes for aircraft and to tell pilots by radio when they can land and take off

airwaves /'eəweɪvz/ *noun* [pl.] (**ARTS AND MEDIA**) radio waves that are used in sending out radio and TV programmes: *A well-known voice came over the airwaves.*

airway /'eəweɪ/ *noun* [C] (**ANATOMY**) the passage from your nose and throat down into your lungs, through which you breathe

airworthy /'eəwɜːði/ *adj.* (used about aircraft) safe to fly ▸ **airworthiness** *noun* [U]

airy /'eəri/ *adj.* (airier; airiest) having a lot of fresh air inside

aisle /aɪl/ *noun* [C] a passage between the rows of seats in a church, theatre, etc., or between rows of shelves in a large shop ◯ look at **gangway** (1)

ajar /ə'dʒɑː(r)/ *adj.* [not before noun] (used about a door) slightly open

aka /ˌeɪ keɪ 'eɪ/ *abbr.* also known as: *Antonio Fratelli, aka 'Big Tony'*

akin /ə'kɪn/ *adj.* ~ **to sth** (*formal*) similar to sth: *The new building was something akin to a spaceship.*

alabaster /'æləbɑːstə(r)/ *noun* [U] (**ART**) a type of white stone that is often used to make statues and other objects: *an alabaster tomb* ◇ (*figurative*) *her pale, alabaster* (= white and smooth) *skin*

à la carte /ˌɑː lɑː 'kɑːt/ *adj., adv.* (used about a meal in a restaurant) where each dish that is available has a separate price and there is not a fixed price for a complete meal

alarm¹ 🔊 **B1** /ə'lɑːm/ *noun* **1** [sing.] a warning of danger: *A small boy saw the smoke and **raised the alarm**.* **2** [C] a device that warns you of danger, or that a person is in danger: *The burglars **set off the alarm** when they broke the window.* ◇ *The **fire alarm** went off in the middle of the night.* ◇ *You should carry a*

personal alarm with you when you walk home at night. **3** [C] a ringing sound or a tune played by a clock or your phone after you have set it to play at a particular time to wake you up **4** [U] a sudden feeling of fear or worry: *She jumped up **in alarm**.* ◯ look at **false alarm**

alarm² 🔊 **B2** /ə'lɑːm/ *verb* [T] to make sb/sth feel suddenly frightened or worried

a'larm call *noun* [C] a phone call that is intended to wake you up: *Could I have an alarm call at 5.30 tomorrow morning, please?* **SYN** **wake-up call**

a'larm clock *noun* [C] a clock that you can set to make a noise at a particular time and wake you up: *She set the alarm clock for half past six.*

alarmed /ə'lɑːmd/ *adj.* ~ (**at/by sth**) frightened or worried: *She was alarmed at the thought of staying alone in the house.*

alarming /ə'lɑːmɪŋ/ *adj.* causing worry or fear: *The population of the world is increasing at an alarming rate.* ▸ **alarmingly** *adv.*

alarmist /ə'lɑːmɪst/ *adj.* causing unnecessary fear and worry: *The reports of a flu epidemic were alarmist.* ▸ **alarmist** *noun* [C]

alas /ə'læs/ *exclamation* (*old-fashioned*) used to show you are sad about sth

albatross /'ælbətrɒs/ *noun* [C] **1** a very large white bird with long wings that lives in the Pacific and Southern Oceans ◯ picture at **animal 2** [usually sing.] (*formal*) a thing that causes problems or that prevents you from doing sth: *The national debt is an albatross around the president's neck.*

albeit 🔊+ **C1** /ˌɔːl'biːɪt/ *conj.* (*formal*) although: *He finally agreed to come, albeit unwillingly.*

albino /æl'biːnəʊ/ *noun* [C] (*pl.* -os) (**BIOLOGY**) a person or an animal that is born with no PIGMENT (= colour) in the hair or skin, which are white, or in the eyes, which are pink

album 🔊 **B1** /'ælbəm/ *noun* [C] **1** (**MUSIC**) a collection of songs released as a single item, usually on a CD or on the internet: *The band are about to release their third album.* ◯ look at **single²** (4) **2** a book in which you can keep stamps, photos, etc. that you have collected

albumen /'ælbjʊmɪn/ *noun* [U] (**BIOLOGY**) the clear inside part of an egg that turns white when you cook it **SYN** **white²**

alchemist /'ælkəmɪst/ *noun* [C] a person who studied ALCHEMY

alchemy /'ælkəmi/ *noun* [U] **1** (**HISTORY**) a form of chemistry in the Middle Ages that involved trying to discover how to change ordinary metals into gold **2** magic power that can change things

alcohol 🔊 **B1** /'ælkəhɒl/ *noun* **1** [U] drinks such as beer, wine, etc. that can make people drunk: *He never drinks alcohol.* ◇ *alcohol abuse* **2** [U, C] (**CHEMISTRY**) the clear liquid that is found in drinks such as beer, wine, etc. and is used in medicines, cleaning products, etc: *Wine contains about 12% alcohol.* ◇ *alcohol-free beer*

alcoholic¹ 🔊 **B1** /ˌælkə'hɒlɪk/ *adj.* containing alcohol: *alcoholic drinks* **OPP** **non-alcoholic**

alcoholic² /ˌælkə'hɒlɪk/ *noun* [C] (**SOCIAL STUDIES**) a person who regularly drinks too much alcohol: *a programme to help alcoholics to overcome their addiction*

alcoholism /'ælkəhɒlɪzəm/ *noun* [U] (**SOCIAL STUDIES**) the medical condition caused by drinking too much alcohol regularly

alcove /'ælkəʊv/ *noun* [C] (**ARCHITECTURE**) a small area in a room where one part of the wall is further back than the rest of the wall

alderman /ˈɔːldəmən/ *noun* [C] (*pl.* **-men** /-mən/) (**HISTORY**, **POLITICS**) (in England and Wales in the past) an important member of the town or county council, chosen by other members of the council

ale /eɪl/ *noun* [U, C] a type of beer

aleatory /ˌæliˈeɪtəri, ˈeɪliətəri/ (*also* **aleatoric** /ˌæliəˈtɒrɪk, ˌeɪl-/) *adj.* (*formal*) (**MUSIC**) relating to music, etc. that includes elements of chance in the way it is created or performed

alert¹ ⟨+⟩ **C1** /əˈlɜːt/ *adj.* **~ (to sth) 1** able to think or notice things quickly: *Security guards must be alert at all times.* ◇ *to be alert to possible changes* **2 ~ (to sth)** aware of sth, especially a danger or a problem: *to be alert to possible changes*

alert² ⟨+⟩ **C1** /əˈlɜːt/ *noun* [C] a warning of danger or a problem: *a bomb alert*
IDM **on the alert (for sth)** ready or prepared for danger

alert³ ⟨+⟩ **C1** /əˈlɜːt/ *verb* [T, often passive] to warn sb of danger or a problem: *We quickly alerted the police.*

A level (*also* **advanced level**) *noun* [C, U] (**EDUCATION**) a British exam taken in a particular subject, usually in the final year of school at the age of 18: *How many A levels have you got?* ◇ *I'm doing my A levels this summer.* ◇ *You need two passes at A level to get onto this course.* ⊃ look at **GCSE**

Alexander technique /ˌælɪɡˈzɑːndə tekniːk, -ˈzæn-/ *noun* [sing., U] (**MEDICINE**) a method of improving sb's health by teaching them how to stand, sit and move correctly

alfalfa /ælˈfælfə/ *noun* [U] (**AGRICULTURE**) a plant with small divided leaves and purple flowers, grown as food for farm animals and as a salad vegetable

algae /ˈældʒiː, ˈælɡiː/ *noun* [U, pl.] (**BIOLOGY**) very simple plants that grow mainly in water ⊃ picture at **carbon cycle**, **erosion**

algebra /ˈældʒɪbrə/ *noun* [U] (**MATHEMATICS**) a type of mathematics in which letters and symbols are used to represent numbers ▶ **algebraic** /ˌældʒɪˈbreɪk/ *adj.: an algebraic equation*

algorithm /ˈælɡərɪðəm/ *noun* [C] (**COMPUTING**, **MATHEMATICS**) a set of rules that must be followed when solving a particular problem: *The company uses algorithms to determine who should see which adverts on its website.*

alias¹ /ˈeɪliəs/ *adv.* used when a person, especially a criminal or an actor, is known by two names: *Norma Jean Baker, alias Marilyn Monroe*

alias² /ˈeɪliəs/ *noun* [C] **1** a false or different name, especially one that is used by a criminal **2** (**COMPUTING**) a name that can be used instead of the actual name for a file, an internet address, etc: *On his website he uses the online alias 'Maddox'.*

alibi /ˈæləbaɪ/ *noun* [C] (*pl.* **alibis**) **~ (for sth)** (**LAW**) evidence that proves that you were in a different place at the time of a crime and so cannot be guilty of the crime: *He had a good alibi for the night of the robbery.*

alien¹ ⟨+⟩ **C1** /ˈeɪliən/ *adj.* **1 ~ (to sb)** strange and frightening; different from what you are used to: *The idea of eating meat was alien to her.* **2** from another country or society: *an alien land* **SYN** **foreign** **3** connected with creatures from another world

alien² ⟨+⟩ **B2** /ˈeɪliən/ *noun* [C] **1** (**LAW**) a person who is not a citizen of the country in which they live or work: *an illegal alien* **2** a creature that comes from another planet: *aliens from outer space*

alienate /ˈeɪliəneɪt/ *verb* [T] **1** to make people less friendly towards you: *The prime minister's new policies on defence have alienated many of his supporters.* **2 ~ sb (from sb/sth)** to make sb feel that they do not belong somewhere or are not part of sth: *Many young unemployed people feel completely alienated from the rest of society.* ▶ **alienation** /ˌeɪliəˈneɪʃn/ *noun* [U]

alight¹ /əˈlaɪt/ *adj.* [not before noun] on fire; burning: *A cigarette set the petrol alight.*

alight² /əˈlaɪt/ *verb* [I] (*formal*) **1 ~ (on/upon sth)** (used about a bird or an insect) to land on sth after flying to it: *The bee alighted on a flower.* **SYN** **land²** **2 ~ (from sth)** to get out of a bus, train or other vehicle: *Do not alight from a moving bus.* **SYN** **get off (sth)**

align ⟨+⟩ **C1** /əˈlaɪn/ *verb* [T, often passive] **~ sth (with sth)** to arrange things in the correct position in relation to sth else, especially in a straight line: *Make sure the shelf is aligned with the top of the wall.*
PHR V **align yourself with sb/sth** to say that you support the opinions of a particular group, country, etc.

alignment ⟨+⟩ **C1** /əˈlaɪnmənt/ *noun* **1** [U] arrangement in a straight line **2** [C, U] (**POLITICS**) an agreement between political parties, countries, etc. to support the same thing

alike¹ ⟨+⟩ **C1** /əˈlaɪk/ *adj.* [not before noun] very similar: *The two boys are very alike.*

alike² ⟨+⟩ **C1** /əˈlaɪk/ *adv.* in the same way; equally: *The book is popular with adults and children alike.*

alimentary canal /ˌælɪmentəri kəˈnæl/ *noun* [sing.] (**ANATOMY**) the long passage inside the body that food moves along, from the mouth to the opening where it leaves the body as waste

alimony /ˈælɪməni/ *noun* [U] (**FINANCE**, **LAW**) the money that a court orders sb to pay regularly to their former wife, husband or partner when the marriage or CIVIL PARTNERSHIP is ended

A-list *adj.* (**ARTS AND MEDIA**) used to describe a group of people who are considered to be the most famous, successful or important: *He only invited A-list celebrities to his party.*

alive ⟨+⟩ **A2** /əˈlaɪv/ *adj.* [not before noun] **1** not dead; living: *The young woman was still alive when the ambulance reached the hospital.* ◇ *The quick action of the doctors kept the child alive.* **2** continuing to exist: *Many old traditions are very much alive in this area of the country.* **3** full of life: *In the evening the town really comes alive.*

alkali /ˈælkəlaɪ/ *noun* [C, U] (**CHEMISTRY**) a chemical substance that reacts with ACIDS to form a SALT. An alkali has a pH value of more than seven when it is mixed with water. ⊃ look at **acid¹**, **base¹** (6) ▶ **alkaline** /-kəlaɪn/ *adj.* ⊃ picture at **pH**

alkaloid /ˈælkəlɔɪd/ *noun* [C] (**BIOLOGY**, **MEDICINE**) a poisonous substance that is found in some plants. Some alkaloids are used in drugs.

alkane /ˈælkeɪn/ *noun* [C] (**CHEMISTRY**) any of a series of COMPOUNDS that contain HYDROGEN and CARBON: *Methane and propane are alkanes.*

alkene /ˈælkiːn/ *noun* [C] (**CHEMISTRY**) any of a series of gases that contain HYDROGEN and CARBON, and that have a double BOND (= force of attraction) between two of the ATOMS of CARBON

all¹ ⟨+⟩ **A1** /ɔːl/ *det., pron.* **1** the whole of a thing or a period of time: *All (of) the food has gone.* ◇ *They've eaten all of it.* ◇ *They've eaten it all.* ◇ *This money is all yours.* ◇ *All of it is yours.* ◇ *all week/month/year* ◇ *He worked hard all his life.* **2** every one of a group: *All (of) my children can swim.* ◇ *My children can all swim.* ◇ *She's read all (of) these books.* ◇ *She's read them all.*

◇ *The people at the meeting all voted against the plan.* ◇ *All of them voted against the plan.* **3** everything that; the only thing that: *I wrote down all I could remember.* ◇ *All I've eaten today is one banana.*
IDM **above all** → ABOVE¹ **after all** → AFTER¹ **for all** **1** despite: *For all her wealth and beauty, she was never very happy.* **2** used to show that sth is not important or of no interest or value to you: ***For all I know**, he's probably remarried by now.* **in all** in total: *There were ten of us in all.* **not all that good, well, etc.** not very good, well, etc: *The film wasn't all that good.* **(not) at all** (not) in any way: *I didn't enjoy it at all.* **not at all** used as a polite reply when sb thanks you for sth

all² ℓ A2 /ɔːl/ *adv.* **1** completely; very: *He has lived all alone since his wife died.* ◇ *I didn't watch that programme — I forgot all about it.* ◇ *They got all excited about it.* **2** (**SPORT**) for each side: *The score was two all.*
IDM **all along** from the beginning: *I knew you were joking all along.* **all the better, harder, etc.** even better, harder, etc. than before: *It will be all the more difficult with two people missing.*

all- /ɔːl/ *prefix* (in adjectives and adverbs) **1** completely: *an all-American show* ◇ *an all-inclusive price* **2** in the highest degree: *all-important* ◇ *all-powerful*

Allah /ˈælə, əˈlɑː/ *noun* [sing.] (**RELIGION**) the name of God among Muslims

ˌall-aˈround (*AmE*) = ALL-ROUND

allay /əˈleɪ/ *verb* [T] (*formal*) to make sth, especially a feeling, less strong: *to allay concern/suspicion*

ˌall-ˈclear (*usually* **the all-clear**) *noun* [sing.] a signal or statement telling you that a situation is no longer dangerous

allege ℓ+ C1 /əˈledʒ/ *verb* [T, often passive] ~ **(that)...** (*formal*) (**LAW**) to say that sb has done sth wrong, but without having any proof that this is true: *The woman alleged (that) Williams had attacked her with a knife.* ◇ ***It is alleged (that)** he attempted to blackmail a former colleague.* ▸ **allegation** ℓ+ C1 /ˌæləˈɡeɪʃn/ *noun* [C] ~ **(of sth)**: *to **make allegations** of police corruption* ➲ note at **claim²** ▸ **alleged** *adj.* [only before noun] ▸ **allegedly** ℓ+ C1 /əˈledʒɪdli/ *adv.*: *The man was allegedly shot while trying to escape.* is said not

allegiance /əˈliːdʒəns/ *noun* [U, C] ~ **(to sb/sth)** (*formal*) (**POLITICS**) support for a leader, government, belief, etc: *Many people **switched allegiance** and voted against the government.* ◇ *He **pledged allegiance** to his country.* SYN **loyalty**

allegory /ˈæləɡəri/ *noun* [C, U] (*pl.* **-ies**) (**ART, LITERATURE**) a story, play, picture, etc. in which each character or event is a symbol representing an idea or a quality, such as truth, evil, death, etc.; the use of such symbols ▸ **allegorical** /ˌæləˈɡɒrɪkl/ *adj.*

allegro /əˈleɡrəʊ/ *noun* [C] (*pl.* **-os**) (**MUSIC**) a piece of music that you should play quickly and with energy ▸ **allegro** *adj., adv.* ➲ look at **adagio, andante**

allele /əˈliːl/ *noun* [C] (**BIOLOGY**) one of two or more possible forms of a GENE (= a unit inside a cell that controls a particular quality in a living thing) that are found at the same place on a CHROMOSOME

allergen /ˈælədʒən/ *noun* [C] (**HEALTH**) any substance that causes an ALLERGY in some people when they eat or touch it

allergic /əˈlɜːdʒɪk/ *adj.* (**HEALTH**) **1** ~ **(to sth)** having an ALLERGY: *I can't drink cow's milk. I'm allergic to it.* **2** [only before noun] caused by an ALLERGY: *an allergic reaction to house dust*

allergy /ˈælədʒi/ *noun* [C] (*pl.* **-ies**) ~ **(to sth)** (**HEALTH**) a medical condition that makes you ill when you eat or touch a particular substance: *an allergy to cats* ➲ look at **hay fever**

alleviate /əˈliːvieɪt/ *verb* [T] to make sth less strong or bad: *The doctor gave me an injection to alleviate the pain.* SYN **ease²** ▸ **alleviation** /əˌliːviˈeɪʃn/ *noun* [U]

alley /ˈæli/ (*also* **alleyway** /ˈæliweɪ/) *noun* [C] a narrow passage between buildings

alliance ℓ+ C1 /əˈlaɪəns/ *noun* [C] (**POLITICS**) an agreement between groups, countries, etc. to work together and support each other: *The two parties **formed an alliance**.* ➲ look at **ally¹** (1)

allied *adj.* **1** /ˈælaɪd/ (*also* **Allied**) [only before noun] (**POLITICS**) connected with countries that join together to fight a war, especially the countries that fought together against Germany in the First and Second World Wars: *Italy joined the war on the Allied side in 1915.* ◇ *allied forces/troops* **2** /ˈælaɪd, əˈlaɪd/ (*formal*) (used about two or more things) similar or existing together; connected with sth: *medicine, nursing, physiotherapy and other allied professions*

alligator /ˈælɪɡeɪtə(r)/ *noun* [C] a large REPTILE similar to a CROCODILE, with a long tail, hard skin and a big mouth with sharp teeth. Alligators live in the lakes and rivers of America and China.

ˈalligator clip (*especially AmE*) = CROCODILE CLIP

ˌall-ˈin *adj.* [only before noun] (*BrE*) including everything: *an all-in price*

ˌall-inˈclusive *adj.* (**TOURISM**) including everything or everyone: *Our trips are all-inclusive — there are no hidden costs.*

alliteration /əˌlɪtəˈreɪʃn/ *noun* [U] (**LITERATURE**) the use of the same letter or sound at the beginning of words that are close together, as in 'sing a song of sixpence'

allocate ℓ+ C1 /ˈæləkeɪt/ *verb* [T] ~ **sth (for sth)**; ~ **sth (to sb/sth)** to give sth to sb/sth as their share or to decide to use sth for a particular purpose: *The government has allocated half the budget for education.* ◇ *They have allocated 40 places to mature students.* ▸ **allocation** ℓ+ C1 /ˌæləˈkeɪʃn/ *noun* [C, U]

allot /əˈlɒt/ *verb* [T, often passive] (**-tt-**) ~ **sth (to sb/sth)**; ~ **sb/sth sth** to give a share of work, time, etc. to sb/sth: *Different tasks were allotted to each member of the class.* ◇ *We were allotted extra time to complete the task.*

allotment /əˈlɒtmənt/ *noun* [C] (*BrE*) (**AGRICULTURE**) a small area of land in a town that you can rent for growing vegetables on

allotrope /ˈælətrəʊp/ *noun* [C] (**CHEMISTRY**) one of the different physical forms in which certain substances can exist. For example, diamond and coal are allotropes of CARBON.

allotropy /əˈlɒtrəpi/ *noun* [U] (**CHEMISTRY**) the ability that certain substances have to exist in more than one physical form

ˌall ˈout *adj., adv.* using all your strength, etc: *an all-out effort* ◇ *We're going all out for victory.*

ˌall-ˈover *adj.* [only before noun] covering the whole of sth: *an all-over tan*

allow ℓ A2 W /əˈlaʊ/ *verb* [T, often passive] **1** ~ **sb/sth to do sth**; ~ **sth** to give permission for sb/sth to do sth or for sth to happen: *Children under 18 are not allowed to buy alcohol.* ◇ *I'm afraid we don't allow people to bring dogs into this restaurant.* ◇ *Photography is not allowed inside the cathedral.* **2** (often used with an adverb or a preposition) to give permission for sb/sth to be or go somewhere: *No dogs allowed.* ◇ *I'm only allowed out on Friday and Saturday nights.* **3** ~ **sb sth** to let sb have sth: *My contract allows me four weeks' holiday a year.*

4 ~ sb/sth to do sth to make it possible for sb/sth to do sth: *Working part-time would allow me to spend more time with my family.* **5 ~ sth (for sb/sth)** to provide money, time, etc. for sb/sth: *You should allow about 30 minutes for each question.*

PHRV allow for sb/sth to think about possible problems when you are planning sth and include extra time, money, etc. for them: *The journey should take about two hours, allowing for heavy traffic.*

allowable /əˈlaʊəbl/ *adj.* that is allowed, especially by law or by a set of rules

allowance ʔ+ **C1** /əˈlaʊəns/ *noun* [C] **1** an amount of sth that you are allowed: *Most flights have a 20kg* **baggage allowance.** **2** (*especially AmE*) = POCKET MONEY **3** an amount of money that you receive regularly to help you pay for sth that you need

IDM make allowance(s) for sth to consider sth, for example when you are making a decision or planning sth: *Good financial planning makes allowances for inflation.* make allowances (for sb) to judge a person or their actions in a kinder way than usual because they have a particular problem or disadvantage: *You really should make allowances for her. She's very inexperienced.*

alloy /ˈælɔɪ/ *noun* [C, U] (CHEMISTRY) a metal that is formed by mixing two types of metal together, or by mixing metal with another substance: *Brass is an alloy of copper and zinc .*

all ˈright¹ ʔ **A2** (*also informal* alright) *adj.* [not before noun], *adv.* **1** good enough; in a good enough manner: *'How was the film?' 'All right.'* ◇ *Is he getting on all right in his new school?* **SYN** OK¹ **2** safe and well: *I hope the children are all right.* ◇ *Do you feel all right?* ◇ *Do you feel all right?* **3** that can be allowed: *'Are you sure it's all right for me to leave early?'* **SYN** OK¹

all ˈright² ʔ **A2** (*also informal* alright) *exclamation* **1** used to check that sb agrees or understands: *We've got to leave on time, all right?* **SYN** OK¹ **2** used to show you agree to do what sb has asked: *'Can you get me some stamps?' 'Yes, all right.'* **SYN** OK¹ **3** used when sb thanks you for sth or when sb says sorry for sth: *'Thanks for the lift home.' 'That's all right.'* ◇ *'I'm so sorry I'm late.' 'That's all right. Don't worry.'*

all-ˈround (*BrE*) (*AmE* all-around) *adj.* [only before noun] able to do many different things well; good in many different ways: *a superb all-round athlete* ◇ *The school aims at the all-round development of the child.*

all-ˈrounder *noun* [C] (*BrE*) a person who can do many different things well

allspice /ˈɔːlspaɪs/ *noun* [U] the dried BERRIES of a West Indian tree, used in cooking as a SPICE

all-terrain ˈvehicle (*especially AmE*) = ATV

ˈall-time *adj.* [only before noun] (used when you are comparing things or saying how good or bad sb/sth is) of any time: *It's my all-time favourite song.* ◇ *He's one of the all-time great athletes.* ◇ *Unemployment is at an all-time high.*

allude /əˈluːd/ *verb*
PHRV allude to sb/sth (*formal*) to speak about sb/ sth in an indirect way: *He mentioned no names, but we all knew who he was alluding to.* ◇ note at **mention**

allure /əˈlʊə(r)/ *noun* [U, sing.] the quality of being attractive and exciting: *sexual allure* ◇ *the allure of the big city*

alluring /əˈlʊərɪŋ/ *adj.* attractive in an exciting way: *an alluring smile* ▶ alluringly *adv.*

allusion /əˈluːʒn/ *noun* [C, U] ~ (to sb/sth) (*formal*) (LITERATURE) something that is said or written that refers to or mentions another person or subject in an indirect way: *Her poetry is full of literary allusion.*

alluvial /əˈluːviəl/ *adj.* (GEOLOGY) made of sand and earth that is left by rivers or floods: *alluvial deposits/ soil/plains*

alluvium /əˈluːviəm/ *noun* [U] (GEOLOGY) sand and earth that is left by rivers or floods

all-ˈweather *adj.* (SPORT) suitable for all types of weather: *an all-weather football pitch*

ally¹ ʔ+ **C1** /ˈælaɪ/ *noun* [C] (*pl. -ies*) (POLITICS) **1** a country that has an agreement to support another country, especially in a war: *France and its European allies* ◇ look at **alliance 2** a person who helps and supports you, especially when other people are against you: *the prime minister's political allies*

WORD FAMILY
ally *verb, noun*
allied *adj.*
alliance *noun*

ally² /əˈlaɪ, ˈælaɪ/ *verb* [T] (allying; allies; *pt, pp* allied) ~ (yourself) with sb/sth to give your support to another group or country: *The prince allied himself with the Scots.*

almanac (*also* almanack) /ˈɔːlmənæk, ˈæl-/ *noun* [C] **1** a book or digital resource that is published every year, giving information for that year about a particular subject or activity **2** a book that gives information about the sun, moon, times of the TIDES (= the rise and fall of the sea level), etc. for each day of the year

almighty /ɔːlˈmaɪti/ *adj.* **1** (in prayers, etc.) having the power to do anything: *Almighty God* **2** [only before noun] (*informal*) very great: *Suddenly we heard the most almighty crash.*

almond /ˈɑːmənd/ *noun* [C] a flat pale nut

almost ʔ **A2** /ˈɔːlməʊst/ *adv.* very nearly; not quite: *By nine o'clock almost everybody had arrived.* ◇ *The film has almost finished.* ◇ *She almost always cycles to school.* ◇ *There's almost nothing left.* ◇ *Almost all the students passed the exam.* **SYN** nearly

aloft /əˈlɒft/ *adv.* (*formal*) high in the air

alone ʔ **A2** /əˈləʊn/ *adj.* [not before noun], *adv.* **1** without any other person: *The old man lives alone.* ◇ *Are you alone? Can I speak to you for a moment?* ◇ *I don't like walking home alone after dark.* **2** (after a noun or pronoun) used to emphasize one particular thing: *You alone can help us.* ◇ *The rent alone takes up most of my salary.*

IDM go it alone to start working on your own without the usual help leave sb/sth alone → LEAVE¹ let alone and certainly not: *We haven't decided where we're going yet, let alone booked the tickets.*

along ʔ **A2** /əˈlɒŋ/ *prep., adv.* **1** from one end to or towards the other end of sth: *I walked slowly along the road.* ◇ *David looked along the corridor to see if anyone was coming.* **2** on or in a line that follows the side of sth long: *Wild flowers grew along both sides of the river.* ◇ *Our house is about halfway along the street.* **3** forward: *We moved along slowly with the crowd.* **4** with sb: *We're going for a walk. Why don't you come along too?*

IDM all along → ALL² along with sb/sth together with sb/sth

alongside ʔ+ **B2** /əˌlɒŋˈsaɪd/ *prep.* **1** next to or at the side of sth: *The boat moored alongside the quay.* **2** together with sb/sth: *the opportunity to work alongside experienced musicians* ▶ alongside *adv.*

aloof /əˈluːf/ adj. not friendly or interested in other people: *Her shyness made her seem aloof.*
SYN distant
IDM keep/hold (yourself) aloof (from sb/sth) | remain/stand aloof (from sb/sth) to not become involved in sth: *He remained aloof from politics.*

alopecia /ˌæləˈpiːʃə/ noun [U] (**HEALTH**) loss of hair from the head and body, often caused by illness

aloud /əˈlaʊd/ adv. in a voice that other people can hear: *The teacher listened to the children reading aloud.*
OPP silently ⊃ look at **out loud** at **out**[1]

alpaca /ælˈpækə/ noun **1** [C] a South American animal whose long hair makes good quality wool **2** [U] the wool of the alpaca

alpha /ˈælfə/ noun [C] (**LANGUAGE**) the first letter of the Greek alphabet (A, α)

alphabet /ˈælfəbet/ noun [C] (**LANGUAGE**) a set of letters in a fixed order that you use when you are writing a language: *There are 26 letters in the English alphabet.*

alphabetical /ˌælfəˈbetɪkl/ adj. arranged in the same order as the letters of the alphabet: *The names are listed in alphabetical order.* ▶ alphabetically /-kli/ adv.

alphanumeric /ˌælfənjuːˈmerɪk/ (also **alphanumerical** /ˌælfənjuːˈmerɪkl/) adj. containing or using both numbers and letters: *alphanumeric data*

ˈalpha particle noun [C] (**PHYSICS**) a PARTICLE with a positive electric CHARGE that is EMITTED (= sent out) by some RADIOACTIVE substances

ˈalpha radiation noun [U] (**PHYSICS**) a type of RADIATION (= powerful and very dangerous energy) that comes from some substances when they start to break down ⊃ look at **gamma radiation**

alpine /ˈælpaɪn/ adj. (**GEOGRAPHY**) connected with or found in high mountains: *alpine flowers*

ˌAlpine ˈskiing noun [U] (**SPORT**) the sport of skiing down mountains ⊃ look at **Nordic skiing**

already ⚑ **A2** **S** /ɔːlˈredi/ adv. **1** used for talking about sth that has happened before now or before a particular time in the past: *'Would you like some lunch?' 'No, I've already eaten, thanks.' ◇ We got there at 6.30, but Marsha had already left. ◇ Sita was already awake when I went into her room.* **2** (used in negative sentences and questions for expressing surprise) so early; as soon as this: *Have you finished already? ◇ Surely you're not going already!*

alright /ɔːlˈraɪt/ (informal) = ALL RIGHT[1], ALL RIGHT[2]

Alsatian /ælˈseɪʃn/ (BrE) = GERMAN SHEPHERD

also ⚑ **A1** **S** /ˈɔːlsəʊ/ adv. (not in negative sentences) in addition; too: *He plays several instruments and also writes music. ◇ Bring summer clothing and also something warm to wear in the evenings. ◇ The food is wonderful, and also very cheap.*
IDM not only … but also → ONLY[1]

ˈalso-ran noun [C] (**POLITICS**, **SPORT**) a person who is not successful in a competition or an election

altar /ˈɔːltə(r)/ noun [C] (**RELIGION**) a high table that is the centre of a religious ceremony

altarpiece /ˈɔːltəpiːs/ noun [C] (**ART**, **RELIGION**) a painting or other piece of art, found near the ALTAR in a church

alter ⚑ **B2** ⚹ /ˈɔːltə(r)/ verb [I, T] to become different; to make sb/sth different: *We've altered our plan and will now arrive at 7.00 instead of 8.00. ◇ The village seems to have altered very little in the last 20 years.*

alteration ⚹ /ˌɔːltəˈreɪʃn/ noun [C, U] ~(to/in sth) a change to sth; the act of making a change to sth: *We want to make a few alterations to the house before we move in.*

altercation /ˌɔːltəˈkeɪʃn/ noun [C, U] (formal) a noisy argument or DISAGREEMENT

alternate[1] /ɔːlˈtɜːnət/ adj. **1** (used about two types of events, things, etc.) happening or following regularly one after the other: *alternate periods of sun and showers* **2** one of every two: *He works alternate weeks* (= he works the first week, he doesn't work the second week, he works again the third week, etc.). ▶ alternately adv.: *The bricks were painted alternately white and red.*

alternate[2] /ˈɔːltəneɪt/ verb **1** [T] ~A with/and B to cause two types of events or things to happen or follow regularly one after the other: *He alternated periods of work with periods of rest.* **2** [I] ~(with sth); ~(between A and B) (used about two types of events, things, etc.) to happen or follow regularly one after the other: *Busy periods in the hospital alternate with times when there is not much to do. ◇ She seemed to alternate between hating him and loving him.* ▶ alternation /ˌɔːltəˈneɪʃn/ noun [C, U]

alˌternate ˈangles noun [pl.] (**GEOMETRY**) two angles formed on opposite sides of a line that crosses two other lines. If the two lines that are crossed are PARALLEL (= always the same distance apart), the alternate angles are equal. ⊃ look at **corresponding angles** ⊃ picture at **angle**[1]

alternating current /ˌɔːltəneɪtɪŋ ˈkʌrənt/ noun [C, U] (abbr. AC) (**ENGINEERING**, **PHYSICS**) a flow of electricity that changes direction regularly many times a second ⊃ look at **direct current**

alternative[1] ⚑ **B1** ⚹ /ɔːlˈtɜːnətɪv/ adj. **1** [only before noun] that you can use, do, etc. instead of sth else: *The motorway was closed so we had to find an alternative route. ◇ alternative energy/fuel* **2** different to what is usual or traditional: *an alternative lifestyle*

alternative[2] ⚑ **A2** ⚹ /ɔːlˈtɜːnətɪv/ noun [C] ~(to sth) one of two or more things that you can choose between: *a healthy alternative to crisps ◇ Quinoa can be served as an alternative to rice. ◇ There are several alternatives open to us at the moment.*

alˌternative ˈenergy noun [U] (**ENVIRONMENT**) electricity or power that is produced from the sun, wind, water, etc. in ways that do not use up the earth's natural resources or harm the environment

alˌternative ˈfuel noun [C, U] (**ENVIRONMENT**) fuel that can be used instead of coal and oil, or instead of nuclear fuel ⊃ look at **fossil fuel**

alternatively ⚹ /ɔːlˈtɜːnətɪvli/ adv. used to introduce a suggestion that is a second choice or possibility: *The agency will make travel arrangements for you. Alternatively, you can organize your own transport.*

alˌternative ˈmedicine noun [C, U] (**MEDICINE**) any type of treatment that does not use the usual scientific methods of Western medicine, for example one using plants instead of artificial drugs

alternator /ˈɔːltəneɪtə(r)/ noun [C] (**ENGINEERING**) a device, used especially in a car, that produces an electrical current that moves in different directions

although ⚑ **A2** ⚹ /ɔːlˈðəʊ/ conj. **1** despite the fact that: *Although she was tired, she stayed up late watching TV.* **SYN** though **2** used to mean 'but' or 'however' when you are commenting on a statement: *I love dogs, although I wouldn't have one as a pet.*

altimeter /ˈæltɪmiːtə(r)/ noun [C] (**ENGINEERING**) an instrument for showing height above sea level, used especially in an aircraft

altitude /ˈæltɪtjuːd/ *noun* (**GEOGRAPHY**) **1** [C, usually sing.] the height of sth above sea level: *The plane climbed to an altitude of 10 000 metres.* **2** [C, usually pl., U] a place that is high above sea level: *You need to carry oxygen when you are climbing* **at high altitudes**.

alto /ˈæltəʊ/ *noun* [C] (*pl.* -os) (**MUSIC**) the lowest normal singing voice for a woman or the highest for a man; a woman or man with this voice

altogether Ⓑ+ **B2** /ˌɔːltəˈɡeðə(r)/ *adv.* **1** completely: *I don't altogether agree with you.* ◇ *At the age of 55 he stopped working altogether.* ◇ *This time the situation is altogether different.* **2** including everything; in total: *How much money will I need altogether?* ◇ *Altogether there were six of us.* **3** when you consider everything: *Altogether, this town is a pleasant place to live.* ⊃ look at **generally** (1)

altostratus /ˌæltəʊˈstrɑːtəs/ *noun* [U] (**GEOGRAPHY**) a layer of flat cloud that is formed at a height of between 2 and 7 kilometres ⊃ picture at **cloud**¹

altruism /ˈæltruɪzəm/ *noun* [U] (*formal*) the fact of caring about the needs and happiness of other people more than your own, even if it brings no advantage to yourself ▶ **altruistic** /ˌæltruˈɪstɪk/ *adj.*: *altruistic behaviour*

aluminium Ⓑ+ **C1** /ˌæljəˈmɪniəm, ˌælə-/ (*BrE*) (*AmE* **aluminum** /əˈluːmɪnəm/) *noun* [U] (*symb.* Al) (**CHEMISTRY**) a chemical element. Aluminium is a light silver-grey metal used for making cooking equipment, etc: *aluminium foil* ❶ For more information on the periodic table of elements, look at the **Reference Section** of this dictionary.

alumna /əˈlʌmnə/ *noun* [C] (*pl.* **alumnae** /-niː/) (*especially AmE*) (**EDUCATION**) a former female student of a school, college or university

alumnus /əˈlʌmnəs/ *noun* [C] (*pl.* **alumni** /-naɪ/) (*especially AmE*) (**EDUCATION**) a former male student of a school, college or university

alveolar /ˌælˈviːələ(r), ˌælviˈəʊlə(r)/ *noun* [C] (**LANGUAGE**) a speech sound made with the tongue touching the part of the mouth behind the upper front teeth, for example /t/ and /d/ in *tie* and *die* ▶ alveolar *adj.*

alveolus /ˌælˈviːələs, ˌælviˈəʊləs/ *noun* [C] (*pl.* **alveoli** /-laɪ, -liː/) (**ANATOMY**) one of the many small spaces in each lung where gases can pass into or out of the blood

always Ⓑ **A1** /ˈɔːlweɪz/ *adv.* **1** at all times; regularly: *I always get up at 6.30.* ◇ *Why is the train always late when I'm in a hurry?* **2** all through the past until now: *Tony has always been shy.* **3** for ever: *I shall always remember this moment.* **4** (only used in the progressive tenses) again and again, usually in an annoying way: *She's always complaining about something.* **5** used with *can* or *could* for suggesting sth that sb could do, especially if nothing else is possible: *If you haven't got enough money, I could always lend you some.*

Alzheimer's /ˈæltshaɪməz, ˈɔːlts-/ (*also* **Alzheimer's disease**) *noun* [U] (**HEALTH**) a disease that affects the brain and makes some people become more and more confused as they get older

AM /ˌeɪ ˈem/ *abbr.* (**PHYSICS**) one of the main methods of broadcasting sound by radio (the abbreviation for 'amplitude modulation')

am /əm, *strong form* æm/ → BE¹

a.m. /ˌeɪ ˈem/ *abbr.* between 12 o'clock at night and 12 o'clock in the day (from Latin 'ante meridiem'): *10 a.m.* ⊃ look at **p.m.**

amalgam /əˈmælɡəm/ *noun* **1** [C, usually sing.] (*formal*) a mixture or combination of things **2** [U] (**CHEMISTRY**, **MEDICINE**) a mixture of MERCURY (= a silver liquid metal) and another metal, used especially to fill holes in teeth

amalgamate /əˈmælɡəmeɪt/ *verb* [I, T] (**BUSINESS**) (used especially about organizations, groups, etc.) to join together to form a single organization, group, etc. ▶ **amalgamation** /əˌmælɡəˈmeɪʃn/ *noun* [C, U]

amass /əˈmæs/ *verb* [T] (*formal*) to collect or put together a large quantity of sth: *We've amassed a lot of information on the subject.* **SYN** **accumulate** ⊃ note at **collect**

amateur¹ Ⓑ+ **C1** /ˈæmətə(r), -tʃə(r)/ *noun* [C] **1** (**SPORT**) a person who takes part in a sport or an activity for pleasure, not for money as a job **OPP** **professional**² **2** (usually used when being critical) a person who does not have skill or experience when doing sth

amateur² Ⓑ+ **C1** /ˈæmətə(r), -tʃə(r)/ *adj.* **1** doing sth for pleasure, not as a job: *an amateur production of a play* ◇ *an amateur photographer* **OPP** **professional**¹ **2** (*also* **amateurish** /ˈæmətərɪʃ, -tʃə-/) done without skill or experience: *The performance sounded very amateur.*

amateur dramatics (*BrE*) (*AmE* **community theater**) *noun* [U] (**ARTS AND MEDIA**) the activity of producing and acting in plays for the theatre by people who do it as a hobby, not as a job

amaze /əˈmeɪz/ *verb* [T] to surprise sb very much; to be difficult for sb to believe: *Sometimes your behaviour amazes me!* ◇ *It amazes me that anyone could be so stupid!*

amazed Ⓑ **B1** /əˈmeɪzd/ *adj.* ~ (at/by sb/sth); ~ (to find, see, etc.); ~ (that) … very surprised: *I was amazed by the change in his attitude.* ◇ *She was amazed to discover the truth about her husband.* ◇ *I'm amazed (that) you couldn't guess what your present was.*

amazement /əˈmeɪzmənt/ *noun* [U] a feeling of great surprise: *He looked at me* **in amazement**.

amazing Ⓑ **A1** /əˈmeɪzɪŋ/ *adj.* **1** very surprising and difficult to believe: *She has shown amazing courage.* ◇ *I've got an amazing story to tell you.* **SYN** **incredible** **2** very impressive; excellent: *He makes the most amazing cakes.* **SYN** **fantastic** ▶ amazingly *adv.*

ambassador Ⓑ+ **C1** /æmˈbæsədə(r)/ *noun* [C] ~ (to …) (**POLITICS**) an important person who represents their country in a foreign country: *the Spanish Ambassador to Britain* ⊃ look at **consul** ❶ An ambassador lives and works in an **embassy**.

amber /ˈæmbə(r)/ *noun* [U] **1** a hard clear yellow-brown substance used for making jewellery or objects for decoration **2** a yellow-brown colour: *The three colours in traffic lights are red, amber and green.* ▶ amber *adj.*

ambi- /æmbi, æmbɪ, æmˈbɪ/ *prefix* (in nouns, adjectives and adverbs) referring to both of two: *ambivalent*

ambidextrous /ˌæmbiˈdekstrəs/ *adj.* able to use the left hand and the right hand equally well

ambience (*also* **ambiance**) /ˈæmbiəns/ *noun* [sing.] the character and atmosphere of a place

ambient /ˈæmbiənt/ *adj.* [only before noun] **1** relating to the surrounding area; on all sides: *ambient temperature/conditions* **2** (**MUSIC**) (used especially about music) creating a relaxed atmosphere: *ambient music/lighting*

ambiguity /ˌæmbɪˈɡjuːəti/ *noun* [C, U] (*pl.* -ies) the possibility of being understood in more than one way; sth that can be understood in more than one way

ambiguous /æmˈbɪɡjuəs/ *adj.* having more than one possible meaning ▶ **ambiguously** *adv.*

ambition ʔ **B1** /æmˈbɪʃn/ *noun* **1** [C] ~ **(to do sth)**; ~ **(of being/doing sth)** something that you want to do or achieve very much: *It has always been her ambition to travel the world.* ◇ *He finally **achieved** his **ambition** of becoming a doctor.* **2** [U] a strong desire to be successful, to have power, etc: *One problem of young people today is their lack of ambition.*

ambitious ʔ **B1** /æmˈbɪʃəs/ *adj.* **1** ~ **(to do sth)** having a strong desire to be successful, to have power, etc: *I'm not particularly ambitious — I'm content with my life the way it is.* ◇ *We are ambitious to succeed.* **2** difficult to achieve or do because it takes a lot of work or effort: *The company have announced ambitious plans for expansion.* ▸ **ambitiously** *adv.*

ambivalent /æmˈbɪvələnt/ *adj.* having or showing a mixture of feelings or opinions about sth or sb ▸ **ambivalence** /-ləns/ *noun* [C, U]

amble /ˈæmbl/ *verb* [I] to walk at a slow, relaxed speed: *We ambled down to the beach.* **SYN stroll**

ambulance ʔ+ **B2** /ˈæmbjələns/ *noun* [C] a special vehicle for taking ill or injured people to and from a hospital: *the ambulance service* ◇ *Call an ambulance!* ⊃ note at **hospital**

ambush /ˈæmbʊʃ/ *noun* [C, U] a surprise attack from a hidden position: *He was killed in an enemy ambush.* ◇ *The robbers were waiting **in ambush**.* ▸ **ambush** *verb* [T]

ameba /əˈmiːbə/ *noun* [C] (*pl.* amebas, amebae /-biː/) (*AmE*) = AMOEBA

ameliorate /əˈmiːliəreɪt/ *verb* [T] (*formal*) to make sth better: *Steps have been taken to ameliorate the situation.*

amen /ɑːˈmen, eɪˈm-/ *exclamation* (**RELIGION**) a word used at the end of prayers by Christians and Jews, meaning 'may it be so'

amenable /əˈmiːnəbl/ *adj.* ~ **(to sth)** happy to accept sth: *I'm amenable to any suggestions you may have.*

amend ʔ+ **C1** /əˈmend/ *verb* [T] (**LAW**) to change a law, document, statement, etc. slightly in order to make it better: *He asked to see the amended version.*

amendment ʔ+ **C1** /əˈmendmənt/ *noun* **1** [C, U] ~ **(to sth)** (**LAW**) a small change or improvement that is made to a law or document; the process of changing a law or document: *I've made a few small amendments to the document.* ◇ *The bill was passed **without amendment**.* **2** Amendment [C] (**POLITICS**) a statement of a change to the Constitution of the US: *The 19th Amendment gave women the right to vote.*

amends /əˈmendz/ *noun* [pl.]
IDM **make amends** to do sth for sb that shows that you are sorry for sth bad that you have done before

amenity /əˈmiːnəti/ *noun* [C, usually pl.] (*pl.* -ies) something that makes a place pleasant or easy to live in: *Among the town's amenities are two cinemas and a sports centre.*

Amerasian /æməˈreɪʒn, -ˈreɪʃn/ *noun* [C] a person with one parent from the US and one Asian parent ▸ **Amerasian** *adj.*

American[1] /əˈmerɪkən/ *adj.* of or connected with North or South America, especially the US: *Have you met Bob? He's American.* ◇ *an American accent*

American[2] /əˈmerɪkən/ *noun* [C] a person from America, especially the US

A̦merican ˈfootball (*BrE*) (*AmE* football) *noun* [U] (**SPORT**) a game that is played by two teams of eleven players, using an OVAL ball. Teams try to put the ball over the other team's line.

A̦merican ˈIndian = NATIVE AMERICAN

Americanism /əˈmerɪkənɪzəm/ *noun* [C] (**LANGUAGE**) a word, phrase or spelling that is typical of American English, used in another variety of English

Americanize (*BrE* also -ise) /əˈmerɪkənaɪz/ *verb* [T] to make sb/sth American in character

americium /æməˈrɪsiəm, -ˈrɪʃi-/ *noun* [U] (*symb.* Am) (**CHEMISTRY**) a chemical element. Americium is a RADIOACTIVE metal. ❶ For more information on the periodic table of elements, look at the **Reference Section** of this dictionary.

amethyst /ˈæməθɪst/ *noun* [C, U] a purple SEMI-PRECIOUS stone

amiable /ˈeɪmiəbl/ *adj.* friendly and pleasant ▸ **amiably** /-bli/ *adv.*

amicable /ˈæmɪkəbl/ *adj.* made or done in a friendly way, without argument ▸ **amicably** /-bli/ *adv.*

amid ʔ+ **C1** /əˈmɪd/ (*also* amidst /əˈmɪdst/) *prep.* (*formal*) in the middle of; among

amino acid /əˌmiːnəʊ ˈæsɪd/ *noun* [C] (**BIOLOGY**) any of the substances that are found in animals and plants and that combine to form a PROTEIN that is necessary for a healthy body and for growth

amir /eˈmɪə(r), ˈeɪmɪə(r)/ = EMIR

amiss /əˈmɪs/ *adj., adv.* wrong; not as it should be: *When I walked into the room, I could sense that something was amiss.*
IDM **not come/go amiss** (*BrE*) to be useful or pleasant: *Things are fine, although a bit more money wouldn't go amiss.* **take sth amiss** (*BrE*) to be upset by sth, perhaps because you have understood it in the wrong way: *Please don't take my remarks amiss.*

ammeter /ˈæmiːtə(r)/ *noun* [C] (**ENGINEERING**, **PHYSICS**) an instrument for measuring the strength of an electric current

ammonia /əˈməʊniə/ *noun* [U] (*symb.* NH_3) (**CHEMISTRY**) a gas with a strong smell; a clear liquid containing ammonia, used for cleaning

ammonite /ˈæmənaɪt/ *noun* [U] (**GEOLOGY**) a type of FOSSIL (= an animal that lived thousands of years ago that has turned into rock)

ammonium /əˈməʊniəm/ *noun* [U] (*symb.* NH_4^+) (**CHEMISTRY**) a chemical substance with a positive electrical charge that is found in liquids and salts that contain AMMONIA
⊃ picture at **nitrogen cycle**

ammonite

ammunition /ˌæmjəˈnɪʃn/ *noun* [U] **1** a supply of bullets, etc. to be fired from a weapon: *The troops surrendered because they had run out of ammunition.* **2** facts or information that can be used against sb/sth

amnesia /æmˈniːziə/ *noun* [U] (**HEALTH**) a medical condition in which sb partly or completely loses their memory

amnesty /ˈæmnəsti/ *noun* (*pl.* -ies) **1** [C, usually sing.] (**POLITICS**) a time when a government forgives political crimes **2** [C, usually sing.] (**LAW**) a time when people can give in illegal weapons without being arrested

amniocentesis /ˌæmniəʊsenˈtiːsɪs/ *noun* [U, sing.] (**MEDICINE**) a medical test in which some liquid is taken from a pregnant woman's WOMB (= the part where a baby grows before it is born) to find out if the baby has particular illnesses or health problems

amnion /'æmniən/ *noun* [C] (*pl.* amnions, amnia /'æmniə/) (**ANATOMY**) the MEMBRANE (= thin layer) that surrounds the EMBRYO of a human or an animal ⊃ picture at **fertilization**

amniotic fluid /ˌæmniɒtɪk 'fluːɪd/ *noun* [U] (**BIOLOGY**) the liquid that is around a baby when it is inside its mother's body ⊃ picture at **fertilization**

amoeba (*AmE also* ameba) /ə'miːbə/ *noun* [C] (*pl.* amoebas, amoebae /-biː/) (**BIOLOGY**) a very small living creature that consists of only one cell

amok /ə'mɒk/ *adv.*
IDM **run amok** to suddenly become very angry or excited and start behaving violently, especially in a public place: *Football fans ran amok in the centre of Brussels last night.* **SYN** **run riot**

among 🔒 **A2** **W** /ə'mʌŋ/ (*also* amongst /ə'mʌŋst/) *prep.*
1 surrounded by; in the middle of: *I often feel nervous when I'm among strangers.* ◊ *I found the missing letter amongst a heap of old newspapers.* **2** in or concerning a particular group of people or things: *Discuss it amongst yourselves and let me know your decision.* ◊ *There is a lot of anger among students about the new law.* ◊ *Among other things, the drug can cause headaches and sweating.* **3** used when you are dividing or choosing sth, and three or more people or things are involved: *On his death, his money will be divided among his children.*

amoral /ˌeɪ'mɒrəl/ *adj.* (used about people or their behaviour) not following any moral rules; not caring about right or wrong ⊃ look at **immoral**, **moral¹** (2)

amorous /'æmərəs/ *adj.* showing sexual desire and love towards sb: *She rejected his amorous advances.* ▸ amorously *adv.*

amorphous /ə'mɔːfəs/ *adj.* (*formal*) having no definite shape, form or structure: *an amorphous mass of cells with no identity at all*

amount¹ 🔒 **A2** **O** /ə'maʊnt/ *noun* [C] **1** a quantity of sth: *I spent an enormous amount of time preparing for the exam.* ◊ *I have a certain amount of sympathy with her.* ◊ *a large amount of money* **2** a total or sum of money: *You are requested to pay the full amount within seven days.*

amount² 🔒 **B2** **O** /ə'maʊnt/ *verb*
PHR V **amount to sth** **1** to add up to sth; to make sth as a total: *The cost of the repairs amounted to £5 000.* **2** to be equal to or the same as sth: *Whether I tell her today or tomorrow, it amounts to the same thing.*

amp /æmp/ *noun* [C] **1** (*also formal* ampere /'æmpeə(r)/) (*abbr.* A) (**ENGINEERING**, **PHYSICS**) a unit for measuring electric current: *a 13 amp fuse/plug* **2** (*informal*) = AMPLIFIER

ampersand /'æmpəsænd/ *noun* [C] (**LANGUAGE**) the symbol (&), used to mean 'and'

amphetamine /æm'fetəmiːn, -mɪn/ *noun* [C, U] (**MEDICINE**) a drug, sometimes taken illegally, that makes you feel excited and full of energy

amphibian /æm'fɪbiən/ *noun* [C] (**BIOLOGY**) an animal with cold blood that can live on land and in water: *Frogs, toads and newts are all amphibians.* ⊃ picture at **animal**

amphibious /æm'fɪbiəs/ *adj.* able to live or be used both on land and in water: *Frogs are amphibious.* ◊ *amphibious vehicles*

amphitheatre (*BrE*) (*AmE* amphitheater) /'æmfɪθɪətə(r)/ *noun* [C] (**ARCHITECTURE**, **HISTORY**) a round building without a roof and with rows of seats that rise in steps around an open space. Amphitheatres were used in ancient Greece and Rome for public entertainment.

amphora /'æmfərə/ *noun* [C] (*pl.* amphorae /-riː/, amphoras) (**HISTORY**) a tall ancient Greek or Roman container with two handles and a narrow neck

amphoteric /ˌæmfə'terɪk/ *adj.* (**CHEMISTRY**) (used about a chemical COMPOUND) able to act as an ACID or a BASE

ample /'æmpl/ *adj.* **1** enough or more than enough: *We've got ample time to make a decision.* ◊ *I'm not sure how much the trip will cost, but I should think £1 000 will be ample.* ◊ *There is ample parking.* **2** (used about a person's figure) large: *He's tall and has an ample waistline.* ▸ amply *adv.*

amplifier /'æmplɪfaɪə(r)/ (*also informal* amp) *noun* [C] (**ENGINEERING**, **MUSIC**) an electrical device or piece of equipment that makes sounds or radio signals louder

amplify /'æmplɪfaɪ/ *verb* (amplifying; amplifies; *pt, pp* amplified) **1** [T] (**PHYSICS**) to increase the strength of a sound using electrical equipment: *to amplify a guitar/ an electric current/a signal* **2** [I, T] (*formal*) to add details to a story, statement, etc. in order to explain it more fully ▸ amplification /ˌæmplɪfɪ'keɪʃn/ *noun* [U]

amplitude /'æmplɪtjuːd/ *noun* [U, C] (**PHYSICS**) the greatest distance that a wave, especially a sound or radio wave, moves up or down ⊃ picture at **sound wave**

amply /'æmpli/ → AMPLE

ampoule /'æmpjuːl, -puːl/ *noun* [C] (**MEDICINE**) a small container, usually made of glass, containing a drug, etc. that will be INJECTED into sb (= put into sb's body though a needle)

amputate /'æmpjuteɪt/ *verb* [I, T] (**MEDICINE**) to cut off sb's arm, leg, etc. for medical reasons ▸ amputation /ˌæmpju'teɪʃn/ *noun* [C, U]

amputee /ˌæmpju'tiː/ *noun* [C] (**HEALTH**) a person who has had an arm or a leg AMPUTATED (= cut off)

amulet /'æmjulət/ *noun* [C] a piece of jewellery that some people wear because they think it protects them from bad luck, illness, etc.

amuse /ə'mjuːz/ *verb* [T] **1** to make sb laugh or smile; to seem funny to sb: *Everybody laughed but I couldn't understand what had amused them.* **2** to make time pass pleasantly for sb; to stop sb from getting bored: *I did some crosswords to amuse myself on the journey.* ◊ *I've brought a few toys to amuse the children.*

amused /ə'mjuːzd/ *adj.* ~ (at/by sth); ~ (to do sth) thinking that sth is funny and wanting to laugh or smile: *We were amused by her stories.* ◊ *I was amused to hear his account of what happened.*
IDM **keep sb/yourself amused** to do sth in order to pass time pleasantly and stop sb/yourself getting bored

amusement /ə'mjuːzmənt/ *noun* **1** [U] the feeling caused by sth that makes you laugh or smile, or by sth that entertains you: *Much to the pupils' amusement, the teacher fell off his chair.* **2** [C, usually pl.] a game, an activity, etc. that provides entertainment and pleasure: *The holiday centre offers a wide range of amusements, including golf and tennis.*

a'musement arcade (*BrE*) (*also* arcade *AmE, BrE*) *noun* [C] an indoor place where you can play games on machines that you usually operate with coins

a'musement park *noun* [C] (**TOURISM**) a large park that has a lot of things that you can ride and play on and many different activities to enjoy

amusing 🔒+ **B2** /ə'mjuːzɪŋ/ *adj.* causing you to laugh or smile: *He's a very amusing person.* ◊ *The story was quite amusing.* ▸ amusingly *adv.*

amylase /ˈæmɪleɪz/ *noun* [U] (**BIOLOGY**) an ENZYME (= a substance that helps a chemical change take place) that allows the body to change some substances into simple SUGARS

an /ən, *strong form* æn/ → A

anabolic steroid /ˌænəbɒlɪk ˈsterɔɪd, ˈstɪər-/ *noun* [C] (**CHEMISTRY**) a chemical substance that increases the size of the muscles. It is sometimes taken illegally by people who play sports. ⊃ look at **steroid**

anachronism /əˈnækrənɪzəm/ *noun* [C] **1** a person, custom, etc. that seems old-fashioned and does not belong in the present **2** something that does not belong in the period of history in which it appears, for example in a book or a film: *The movie, which is set in Ancient Rome, is full of anachronisms and inaccuracies.* ▸ **anachronistic** /əˌnækrəˈnɪstɪk/ *adj.*

anaemia (*BrE*) (*AmE* **anemia**) /əˈniːmiə/ *noun* [U] (**HEALTH**) a medical condition in which there are not enough red cells in the blood ▸ **anaemic** (*BrE*) (*AmE* **anemic**) /-mɪk/ *adj.*

anaerobic /ˌænəˈrəʊbɪk/ *adj.* **1** (**BIOLOGY**) not needing OXYGEN: *anaerobic bacteria* **2** (**SPORT**) (used about physical exercise) not especially designed to improve the function of the heart and lungs **OPP** **aerobic**

anaesthesia (*BrE*) (*AmE* **anesthesia**) /ˌænəsˈθiːziə/ *noun* [U] (**MEDICINE**) the use of drugs that make you unable to feel pain during medical operations

anaesthetic (*BrE*) (*AmE* **anesthetic**) /ˌænəsˈθetɪk/ [C, U] (**MEDICINE**) a substance that stops you feeling pain, for example when a doctor is performing a medical operation on you: *The dentist gave me a local anaesthetic* (= one that only affects part of the body and does not make you unconscious). ◇ *Did you have a general anaesthetic* (= one that makes you unconscious) *for your operation?* ◇ *You'll need to be under anaesthetic for the operation.*

anaesthetist (*BrE*) (*AmE* **anesthetist**) /əˈniːsθətɪst/ *noun* [C] (**MEDICINE**) a person with the medical training necessary to give ANAESTHETICS to patients

anaesthetize (*also* **-ise**) (*both BrE*) (*AmE* **anesthetize**) /əˈniːsθətaɪz/ *verb* [T] (**MEDICINE**) to make a person or an animal unable to feel pain, etc., especially by giving them an ANAESTHETIC

anagram /ˈænəɡræm/ *noun* [C] (**LANGUAGE**) a word or phrase that is made by arranging the letters of another word or phrase in a different order: *'Worth' is an anagram of 'throw'.*

anal /ˈeɪnl/ *adj.* (**ANATOMY**) relating to or located near the ANUS (= the place where solid waste leaves the body)

analgesia /ˌænəlˈdʒiːziə/ *noun* [U] (**MEDICINE**) the loss of the ability to feel pain while still conscious

analgesic /ˌænəlˈdʒiːzɪk/ *noun* [C] (**MEDICINE**) a substance that reduces pain ▸ **analgesic** *adj.*

analogous /əˈnæləɡəs/ *adj.* ~ (**to/with sth**) (*formal*) similar in some way; that you can compare: *The present situation is not analogous to the situation we faced in the nineties.*

analogue *especially BrE* (*AmE usually* **analog**) /ˈænəlɒɡ/ *adj.* **1** (**COMPUTING**, **ENGINEERING**) (used about an electronic process) using a continuously changing range of physical quantities to measure or store data: *an analogue circuit/computer/signal* **2** (used about a clock or watch) showing the time using hands on a DIAL (= the round part) and not with a display of numbers ⊃ look at **digital** (3)

analogy ʔ+ **C1** /əˈnælədʒi/ *noun* [C] (*pl.* **-ies**) ~ (**between A and B**) (**LITERATURE**) a comparison between two things that shows a way in which they are similar: *You could make an analogy between the human body and a car engine.*
IDM **by analogy** by comparing sth to sth else and showing how they are similar

analyse ʔ **B1** ⊙ (*BrE*) (*AmE* **analyze**) /ˈænəlaɪz/ *verb* [T] to look at or think about the different parts or details of sth carefully in order to understand or explain it: *The water samples are now being analysed in a laboratory.* ◇ *to analyse statistics* ◇ *She analysed the situation and then decided what to do.*

analysis ʔ **B1** ⊙ /əˈnæləsɪs/ *noun* (*pl.* **analyses** /-ləsiːz/) **1** [C, U] the careful examination of the different parts or details of sth: *Some samples of the water were sent to a laboratory for analysis.* **2** [U] = PSYCHOANALYSIS **3** [C] the result of a careful examination of sth: *Your analysis of the situation is different from mine.*

analyst ʔ+ **B2** ⓦ /ˈænəlɪst/ *noun* [C] (**BUSINESS**) a person whose job is to examine sth carefully as an expert: *a food analyst* ◇ *a political analyst*

analytical ⓦ /ˌænəˈlɪtɪkl/ (*also* **analytic** /ˌænəˈlɪtɪk/) *adj.* **1** using a logical method of thinking about sth in order to understand it, especially by looking at all the parts separately: *She has a clear analytical mind.* **2** using scientific analysis in order to find out about sth: *analytical methods of research* ▸ **analytically** /-kli/ *adv.*

analyze /ˈænəlaɪz/ (*AmE*) = ANALYSE

anarchic /əˈnɑːkɪk/ *adj.* without rules or laws

anarchism /ˈænəkɪzəm/ *noun* [U] (**POLITICS**) the political belief that there should be no government or laws in a country ▸ **anarchist** /-kɪst/ *noun* [C]

anarchy /ˈænəki/ *noun* [U] (**POLITICS**) a situation in a country, an organization, etc. in which there is no government, order or control: *The overthrow of the military regime was followed by a period of anarchy.* ▸ **anarchic** (*also* **anarchical** /əˈnɑːkɪkl/) *adj.*

anathema /əˈnæθəmə/ *noun* [U, C, usually sing.] (*formal*) a thing or an idea that you hate because it is the opposite of what you believe: *Racial prejudice is (an) anathema to me.*

anatomist /əˈnætəmɪst/ *noun* [C] a scientist who studies ANATOMY

anatomy /əˈnætəmi/ *noun* (*pl.* **-ies**) (**BIOLOGY**) **1** [U] the scientific study of the structure of a human, an animal or a plant **2** [C] the structure of a living thing: *the anatomy of the frog* ▸ **anatomical** /ˌænəˈtɒmɪkl/ *adj.* ▸ **anatomically** /-kli/ *adv.*

ancestor ʔ+ **B2** /ˈænsestə(r)/ *noun* [C] (**HISTORY**) a person in your family who lived a long time before you: *My ancestors settled in this country 100 years ago.* **SYN** **forebear** ⊃ look at **descendant** ▸ **ancestral** /ænˈsestrəl/ *adj.*: *her ancestral home* (= that had belonged to her ancestors)

ancestry /ˈænsestri/ *noun* [C, U] (*pl.* **-ies**) all of a person's ANCESTORS: *He is of Irish ancestry.*

anchor[1] ʔ+ **C1** /ˈæŋkə(r)/ *noun* [C] **1** a heavy metal object at the end of a chain that you drop into the water from a boat in order to stop the boat moving **2** = ANCHORMAN **3** = ANCHORWOMAN

anchor[2] /ˈæŋkə(r)/ *verb* **1** [I, T] to drop an ANCHOR down from a boat or ship to prevent it from moving away: *They anchored off the coast of Spain.* **2** [T] to fix sth FIRMLY so that it cannot move

anchorage /ˈæŋkərɪdʒ/ *noun* [C, U] **1** a place where boats or ships can ANCHOR **2** the action of fastening sth securely in position; the fact of being securely fastened in position: *anchorage points for a baby's car seat*

anchorman /'æŋkəmæn/ (*pl.* -men /-men/) (*also* anchor) *noun* [C] (**ARTS AND MEDIA**) a man who presents a radio or TV programme and introduces reports by other people

anchorwoman /'æŋkəwʊmən/ (*pl.* -women /-wɪmɪn/) (*also* anchor) *noun* [C] (**ARTS AND MEDIA**) a woman who presents a radio or TV programme and introduces reports by other people

anchovy /'æntʃəvi/ *noun* [C, U] (*pl.* -ies) a small fish that is used for food, usually preserved in salt, giving it a strong SALTY taste

ancient ᵏ **A2** /'eɪnʃənt/ *adj.* **1** (**HISTORY**) belonging to a period of history that is thousands of years in the past: *ancient history ◇ the ancient world ◇ ancient Rome/Greece* **OPP** **modern 2** very old: *an ancient oak tree ◇ I can't believe he's only 30 — he looks ancient!*

ancillary /æn'sɪləri/ *adj.* **1** (**BUSINESS**) providing necessary support to the main work or activities of an organization: *Ancillary hospital staff such as cleaners are often badly paid.* **SYN** auxiliary¹ **2** in addition to sth else but not as important: *ancillary rights*

and ᵏ **A1** /ənd, ən, n, *strong form* ænd/ *conj.* **1** (used to connect words or parts of sentences) also; in addition to: *a boy and a girl ◇ Do it slowly and carefully. ◇ We were singing and dancing all evening. ◇ Come in and sit down.* **2** used between repeated words to show that sth is increasing or continuing: *The situation is getting worse and worse. ◇ I shouted and shouted but nobody answered.* **3** used instead of *to* after certain verbs, for example *go, come* and *try*: *Go and answer the door for me, will you? ◇ Why don't you come and stay with us one weekend? ◇ I'll try and find out what's going on.* **4** (used when you are saying numbers in sums) in addition to: *12 and 6 is 18 (12+6=18).* **SYN** plus¹ **HELP** When you are saying large numbers, **and** is used after the word **hundred**: You say 2 264 as *two thousand, two hundred and sixty-four*.

andante /æn'dænteɪ/ *noun* [C] (**MUSIC**) a piece of music that you should play fairly slowly ▸ andante *adj., adv.* ↻ look at **adagio, allegro**

androgynous /æn'drɒdʒənəs/ *adj.* looking neither very male nor very female

android /'ændrɔɪd/ *noun* [C] a type of robot that looks like a real person

anecdotal /ˌænɪk'dəʊtl/ *adj.* based on personal accounts and possibly not true or accurate: *The newspaper's 'monster shark' story was based on anecdotal evidence.*

anecdote /'ænɪkdəʊt/ *noun* [C, U] a short, interesting story about a real person or event

anemia, anemic (*AmE*) = ANAEMIA, ANAEMIC

anemometer /ˌænɪ'mɒmɪtə(r)/ *noun* [C] (**GEOGRAPHY, PHYSICS**) an instrument for measuring the speed of the wind or of a current of gas

anemone /ə'neməni/ *noun* [C] a small plant with white, red, blue or purple flowers that are shaped like cups ↻ look at **sea anemone**

anesthesia, anesthetic, anesthetist, anesthetize (*AmE*) = ANAESTHESIA, ANAESTHETIC, ANAESTHETIST, ANAESTHETIZE

anew /ə'njuː/ *adv.* again; in a new or different way

angel ᵏ⁺ **C1** /'eɪndʒl/ *noun* [C] **1** (**RELIGION**) a spirit who is believed to carry messages from God. In pictures angels are often dressed in white, with wings. **2** a person who is very kind **3** (*also* ˌangel in'vestor, business angel) (**BUSINESS**) a person who invests money in a business, especially a new small business

angelic /æn'dʒelɪk/ *adj.* good, kind or beautiful; like an ANGEL: *an angelic smile* ▸ angelically /-kli/ *adv.*

anger¹ ᵏ **B2** /'æŋgə(r)/ *noun* [U] ~ (**at/over/about sth**); ~ (**towards/against sb/sth**) the strong feeling that you have when sth has happened or sb has done sth that you do not like: *He could not hide his anger at the news. ◇ I felt no anger towards him. ◇ She was shaking with anger.*

angles

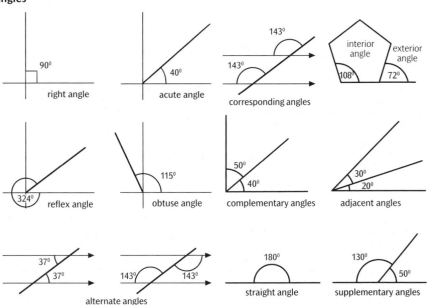

right angle

acute angle

corresponding angles

reflex angle

obtuse angle

complementary angles

adjacent angles

alternate angles

straight angle

supplementary angles

anger² /ˈæŋgə(r)/ *verb* [T, often passive] to make sb become angry: *It angers me that such things can be allowed to happen.* ◊ *She was angered by his lack of concern.*

angina /ænˈdʒaɪnə/ *noun* [U] (**HEALTH**) very bad pain in the chest caused by not enough blood going to the heart during exercise

angioplasty /ˈændʒiəʊplæsti/ *noun* [C, U] (*pl.* -ies) (**MEDICINE**) a medical operation to repair or open a blocked BLOOD VESSEL, especially either of the two ARTERIES that supply blood to the heart

angle¹ 🔒 **B2** /ˈæŋgl/ *noun* [C] **1** ~ (**of sth**) (**GEOMETRY**) the space between two lines or surfaces that meet, measured in degrees: *a right angle* (= an angle of 90°) ◊ *at an angle of 40°* ◊ *The three angles of a triangle add up to 180°.* ⊃ look at **acute angle, obtuse angle, reflex angle, right angle** ⊃ picture on **page 29 2** the direction from which you look at sth: *Viewed from this angle, the building looks bigger than it really is.* **3** the direction that sth is leaning or pointing in when it is not straight: *The tower leans at an angle.*

angle² /ˈæŋgl/ *verb* **1** [T] to put sth in a position that is not straight; to be in this position: *Angle the lamp towards the desk.* **2** [T, often passive] ~ **sth at/to/towards sb** to show sth from a particular point of view; to aim sth at a particular person or group: *The new magazine is angled at young professionals.*

PHRV angle for sth to try to make sb give you sth, without asking for it in a direct way: *She was angling for an invitation to our party.*

angler /ˈæŋglə(r)/ *noun* [C] a person who catches fish as a hobby ⊃ look at **fisherman**

Anglican /ˈæŋglɪkən/ *noun* [C] (**RELIGION**) a member of the Church of England or of a related church in another country ▶ **Anglican** *adj.*

Anglicism /ˈæŋglɪsɪzəm/ *noun* [C] (**LANGUAGE**) a word, phrase or spelling that is typical of British English, used in another variety of English or another language

anglicize (*BrE also* -ise) /ˈæŋglɪsaɪz/ *verb* [T] (**LANGUAGE**) to make sb/sth English in character: *Gutmann anglicized his name to Goodman.*

angling /ˈæŋglɪŋ/ *noun* [U] (**SPORT**) the art or sport of catching fish with a FISHING ROD: *He goes angling at weekends.* ⊃ look at **fishing**

Anglo- /ˈæŋgləʊ/ *prefix* (in nouns and adjectives) connected with England or Britain: *Anglo-American relations*

anglophone /ˈæŋgləʊfəʊn/ *noun* [C] (**LANGUAGE**) a person who speaks English, especially in countries where English is not the only language spoken ▶ **anglophone** *adj.*: *anglophone communities*

Anglo-Saxon /ˌæŋgləʊ ˈsæksn/ *noun* **1** [C] (**SOCIAL STUDIES**) a person whose ANCESTORS were English **2** [C] (**HISTORY**) an English person of the period before the Norman Conquest **3** (*also* Old English) [U] (**LANGUAGE**) the English language before about 1150 ▶ **Anglo-Saxon** *adj.*

angora /æŋˈgɔːrə/ *noun* [U] a type of soft wool or cloth

angry 🔒 **A1** /ˈæŋgri/ *adj.* (angrier; angriest) ~ (**with/at sb**) (**about sth**); ~ (**with/at sb**) (**for doing sth**) feeling or showing anger: *Calm down, there's no need to get angry.* ◊ *My parents will be angry with me if I get home late.* ◊ *He's always getting angry about something.* ◊ *I'm very angry with them for letting me down at the last moment.* ▶ **angrily** /-grəli/ *adv.*

angst /æŋst/ *noun* [U] a feeling of worry about a situation or about your life: *songs full of teenage angst*

angst-ridden *adj.* having feelings of worry about a situation or about your life: *a generation of angst-ridden adolescents*

anguish /ˈæŋgwɪʃ/ *noun* [U] (*formal*) great mental or physical pain or suffering ▶ **anguished** *adj.*

angular /ˈæŋgjələ(r)/ *adj.* with sharp points or corners

animal 🔒 **A1** 🌐 /ˈænɪml/ *noun* [C] (**BIOLOGY**) **1** a living creature that is not a bird, a fish, a REPTILE, an insect or a human: *the animals and birds of South America* ◊ *a small furry animal* ◊ *farm animals* **2** any living thing that is not a plant or a human: *the animal kingdom* ⊃ picture on **pages 32–33 3** any living creature, including humans: *Humans are the only animals to have developed speech.*

animate¹ /ˈænɪmeɪt/ *verb* [T] **1** to make sth have more life and energy: *Her enthusiasm animated the whole room.* **2** [usually passive] (**ARTS AND MEDIA**) to make models, toys, images, etc. seem to move in a film, either by rapidly showing slightly different pictures of them in a series, one after another, or by using computer techniques to create moving images

animate² /ˈænɪmət/ *adj.* (*formal*) living; having life: *animate beings* **OPP inanimate**

animated /ˈænɪmeɪtɪd/ *adj.* **1** interesting and full of energy: *an animated discussion* **2** (**ARTS AND MEDIA**) (used about films) using a process or method that makes pictures or models appear to move: *an animated cartoon*

animation 🔒+ **B2** /ˌænɪˈmeɪʃn/ *noun* **1** [U] (**ARTS AND MEDIA**) the method of making films, computer games, etc. with pictures or models that appear to move: *computer animation* **2** [C] (**ARTS AND MEDIA**) a film in which drawings of people and animals seem to move: *The electronic dictionary includes some animations.* **3** [U] the state of being full of energy and enthusiasm

animosity /ˌænɪˈmɒsəti/ *noun* [U, C] (*pl.* -ies) ~ (**between A and B**); ~ (**towards sb/sth**) a strong feeling of opposition, anger or hate: *There is still animosity between these two teams after last year's match.* **SYN hostility**

anion /ˈænaɪən/ *noun* [C] (**CHEMISTRY, PHYSICS**) an ION with a negative electrical CHARGE ⊃ look at **cation**

anise /ˈænɪs/ *noun* [U] a plant with seeds that smell sweet

aniseed /ˈænəsiːd/ *noun* [U] the dried seeds of the ANISE plant that are used to give a particular taste to sweets and alcoholic drinks

ankle 🔒 **A2** /ˈæŋkl/ *noun* [C] (**ANATOMY**) the part of the body where the foot joins the leg: *The water only came up to my ankles.* ◊ *to break/twist your ankle* ◊ *I tripped and sprained my ankle.* ⊃ picture at **body**

anklet /ˈæŋklət/ *noun* [C] a piece of jewellery worn around the ankle

annals /ˈænlz/ *noun* [pl.] (**HISTORY**) an official record of events or activities year by year; historical records: *The battle went down in the annals of British history.*

anneal /əˈniːl/ *verb* [T] to heat metal or glass and allow it to cool slowly, in order to make it harder

annex /ˈæneks, əˈneks/ *verb* [T] (**POLITICS**) to take control of another country or region by force: *Germany annexed Austria in 1938.* **SYN occupy** ▶ **annexation** /ˌænekˈseɪʃn/ *noun* [C, U]

annexe (*BrE*) (*also* annex *AmE, BrE*) /ˈæneks/ *noun* [C] (**ARCHITECTURE**) a building that is joined to, or is near, a larger one

annihilate /əˈnaɪəleɪt/ *verb* [I] to destroy or defeat sb/ sth completely ▶ **annihilation** /əˌnaɪəˈleɪʃn/ *noun* [U]

anniversary ʔ B2 /ˌænɪˈvɜːsəri/ *noun* [C] (*pl.* -ies) a day that is exactly a year or a number of years after a special or important event: *the hundredth anniversary of the country's independence* ◇ *a wedding anniversary*

annotate /ˈænəteɪt/ *verb* [T] (**LITERATURE**) to add notes to a book or text, giving explanations or comments ▶ **annotation** /ˌænəˈteɪʃn/ *noun* [C, U]

annotated /ˈænəteɪtɪd/ *adj.* (used about a book, etc.) with notes added to it that explain and give extra information about the contents

announce ʔ B1 /əˈnaʊns/ *verb* [T] **1** to tell people sth officially, especially about a decision, plans, etc: *The winners will be announced at the awards ceremony.* **2** to give information about sth in a public place, especially through a LOUDSPEAKER: *They announced that our train had been delayed.* **3** to say sth in a loud or serious way: *She stormed into my office and announced that she was leaving.* ⊃ note at **declare**

announcement ʔ B1 /əˈnaʊnsmənt/ *noun* **1** [C] a statement that tells people about sth: *Ladies and gentlemen, I'd like to **make an announcement**.* ⊃ note at **statement** **2** [U] an act of telling people about sth

announcer /əˈnaʊnsə(r)/ *noun* [C] (**ARTS AND MEDIA**) a person who introduces or gives information about programmes on the radio or TV

annoy ʔ B1 /əˈnɔɪ/ *verb* [T] to make sb angry or slightly angry: *Close the door if the noise is annoying you.* ◇ *It really annoys me when you act so selfishly.* **SYN irritate**

annoyance /əˈnɔɪəns/ *noun* **1** [U] the feeling of being annoyed **2** [C] something that annoys sb

annoyed ʔ B1 /əˈnɔɪd/ *adj.* ~ (with sb) (at/about sth); ~ with sb/yourself (for doing sth); ~ (that …); ~ (to find, see, etc.) feeling angry or slightly angry: *I'm really annoyed with him about this situation.* ◇ *She's annoyed with herself for making such a stupid mistake.* ◇ *He's annoyed that nobody believes him.* ◇ *I was annoyed to see that they had left the door open again.* ◇ *I shall be extremely annoyed if he turns up late again.* **SYN irritated**

annoying ʔ B1 /əˈnɔɪɪŋ/ *adj.* making you feel angry or slightly angry: *His most annoying habit is always arriving late.* ◇ *It's so annoying that I can't come with you!* ▶ **annoyingly** *adv.*

annual¹ ʔ B2 ⓦ /ˈænjuəl/ *adj.* **1** happening or done once a year: *the company's annual report* ◇ *an annual festival* **2** relating to a period of one year: *a person's annual salary* ◇ *the annual sales figures* ◇ *annual rainfall* ⊃ note at **income**

annual² /ˈænjuəl/ *noun* [C] **1** (**LITERATURE**) a book, especially one for children, that is published once each year, with the same title each time, but different contents: *a football annual* **2** (**BIOLOGY**) any plant that grows and dies within one year or season ⊃ look at **biennial²**, **perennial²**

annually ʔ+ B2 /ˈænjuəli/ *adv.* once a year: *The exhibition is held annually.*

annuity /əˈnjuːəti/ *noun* [C] (*pl.* -ies) (**FINANCE**) a fixed amount of money that is paid to sb each year, usually for the rest of their life

annul /əˈnʌl/ *verb* [T, usually passive] (-ll-) (**LAW**) to state officially that sth is not legally recognized: *Their marriage was annulled after just six months.* ▶ **annulment** *noun* [C, U]

anode /ˈænəʊd/ *noun* [C] (**CHEMISTRY, PHYSICS**) the ELECTRODE in an electrical device; the positive ELECTRODE in an ELECTROLYTIC CELL and the negative ELECTRODE in a battery ⊃ look at **cathode**

anoint /əˈnɔɪnt/ *verb* [T] (**RELIGION**) to put oil or water on sb's head as part of a religious ceremony

anomalous /əˈnɒmələs/ *adj.* (*formal*) different from what is normal

anomaly /əˈnɒməli/ *noun* [C, U] (*pl.* -ies) something that is different from what is normal or usual: *We discovered an anomaly in the sales figures for August.*

anonymity /ˌænəˈnɪməti/ *noun* [U] the state of being unknown to most other people: *The names of the participants in the study have been changed to preserve anonymity.* ◇ *the anonymity of the city* (= where people do not know each other)

anonymize (*BrE also* -ise) /əˈnɒnɪmaɪz/ *verb* [T] **1** if you **anonymize** a test result, you remove any information that shows who it belongs to **2** (**COMPUTING**) if you **anonymize** data that is sent or received over the internet, you remove any information that identifies which computer that data originally came from

anonymous ʔ+ C1 /əˈnɒnɪməs/ *adj.* **1** (used about a person) with a name that is not known or made public: *An anonymous caller told the police that a robbery was going to take place.* **2** (*abbr.* anon.) done, written, etc. by sb whose name is not known or made public: *He received an anonymous letter.* ▶ **anonymously** *adv.*

anonymous FTⁱP *noun* [U] (**COMPUTING**) a system that allows anybody to download files from the internet without having to give their name

anorak /ˈænəræk/ *noun* [C] (*BrE*) **1** a short coat with a covering for your head that protects you from rain, wind and cold **2** (*informal*) a person who enjoys learning boring facts

anorexia /ˌænəˈreksiə/ (*also* **anorexia nervosa** /ˌænəˌreksiə nɜːˈvəʊsə/) *noun* [U] (**PSYCHOLOGY**) an emotional DISORDER in which the person has an OBSESSIVE desire to lose weight and eats as little as possible ⊃ look at **bulimia** ▶ **anorexic** /ˌænəˈreksɪk/ *adj., noun* [C]

another ʔ A1 /əˈnʌðə(r)/ *det., pron.* **1** one more person or thing of the same kind: *Would you like another drink?* ◇ *They've got three children already and they're having another.* **2** a different thing or person: *I'm afraid I can't see you tomorrow. Could we arrange another day?* ◇ *If you've already seen that film, we can go and see another.* **IDM one after another/the other** → ONE¹ **yet another** → YET¹

answer¹ ʔ A1 ⓢ /ˈɑːnsə(r)/ *noun* [C] ~ (to sb/sth) **1** something that you say, write or do as a reply: *The answer to your question is that I don't know.* ◇ *They've made me an offer and I have to give them an answer by Friday.* ◇ *I wrote to them two weeks ago and I'm still waiting for an answer.* ◇ *I knocked on the door and waited but there was no answer.* **SYN reply** **2** a solution to a problem: *I think I know the answer to this problem.* **3** (**EDUCATION**) a reply to a question in a test or exam: *My answer to question 5 was wrong.* ◇ *How many answers did you get right?* **4** (**EDUCATION**) the correct reply to a question in a test or exam: *What was the answer to question 4?* **IDM in answer (to sth)** as a reply (to sth)

answer² ʔ A1 ⓢ /ˈɑːnsə(r)/ *verb* [I, T] ~ (that …) to say, write or do sth as a reaction to a question or situation: *I asked her what the matter was but she didn't answer.* ◇ *Answer all the questions on the form.* ◇ *When I asked him how much he earned, he answered that it was none of my business.* ◇ 'No!' he answered angrily. ◇ *He hasn't answered my email yet* (= written an email back to me). ◇ *I rang their doorbell but nobody*

The animal kingdom

birds

webbed foot
talons
beak/bill
wing
tail
claw
finch
crest
cockatoo
feather
egg
nest

birds of prey

carrion
eagle
vulture
owl

mammals

coat
mane
muzzle
dog
tail
snout
paw
claw
lion
badger
whisker
antlers
horn
goat
hooves
stag

cetacean

blowhole
whale
tusk
trunk
elephant

fish

tail
dorsal fin
ventral fin
scales
bat
trout
gill

poultry and game

pheasant
duck
turkey
chicken

seabirds

gull
albatross
puffin

primates

prehensile tail
chimpanzee
monkey

rodents

squirrel
beaver

marsupials

joey
pouch
koala
kangaroo

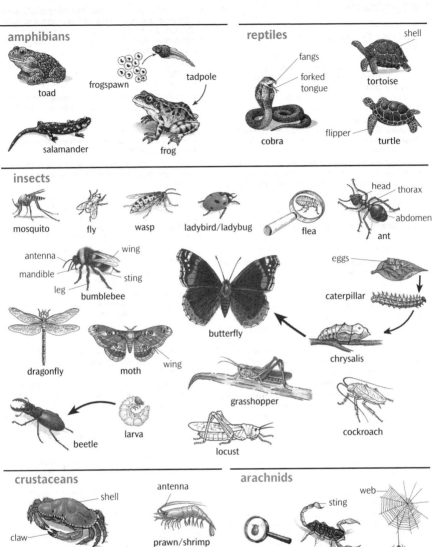

amphibians

toad

frogspawn

tadpole

frog

salamander

reptiles

fangs

forked tongue

cobra

shell

tortoise

flipper

turtle

insects

mosquito

fly

wasp

ladybird/ladybug

flea

head

thorax

abdomen

ant

antenna

mandible

wing

leg

sting

bumblebee

butterfly

eggs

caterpillar

dragonfly

moth

wing

chrysalis

grasshopper

beetle

larva

cockroach

locust

crustaceans

shell

antenna

claw

crab

prawn/shrimp

woodlouse

arachnids

web

sting

tick

scorpion

spider

taxonomy

Living things are grouped on the basis of their similarities and differences into smaller and smaller groups. This scientific process of classification is called **taxonomy**. The main groups, from the largest to the smallest, are:

- **kingdom** (*animal* or *plant*)
- **phylum** (e.g. *mollusc*, *arthropod*)
- **class** (e.g. *mammal*, *gastropod*)
- **order** (e.g. *primate*, *marsupial*)
- **family**
- **genus**
- **species**

gastropods

shell

snail

slug

cephalopod

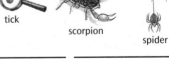

sucker

tentacle

octopus

answered. ◇ *She isn't **answering** her phone.* ◌ note at **phone**[1]

PHR V **answer back** to defend yourself against sth bad that has been written or said about you **answer (sb) back** to reply rudely to sb **answer for sb/sth 1** to accept responsibility for sth/sb: *Somebody will have to answer for all the damage that has been caused.* **2** to speak in support of sb/sth

answerable /ˈɑːnsərəbl/ *adj.* **~ (to sb) (for sth)** having to explain and give good reasons for your actions to sb; responsible for sth: *I'm no longer answerable to my parents for my actions.*

'answering machine (*BrE also* **answerphone** /ˈɑːnsəfəʊn/) *noun* [C] a machine that answers the phone and records messages from the people who call: *I rang him and left a message on his answering machine.* ◌ look at **voicemail**

ant /ænt/ *noun* [C] a very small insect that lives in highly organized groups ◌ picture at **animal**

antacid /æntˈæsɪd/ *noun* [C] (**MEDICINE**) a medicine that reduces the amount of ACID in the stomach

antagonism /ænˈtægənɪzəm/ *noun* [C, U] **~ (towards sb/ sth)** a feeling of hate and of being strongly against sb/ sth: *He still felt antagonism towards her.*
▸ antagonistic /ænˌtægəˈnɪstɪk/ *adj.*

antagonist /ænˈtægənɪst/ *noun* [C] (*formal*) a person who is strongly against sb/sth

antagonize (*BrE also* **-ise**) /ænˈtægənaɪz/ *verb* [T] to make sb angry or to annoy sb

the Antarctic /ði ænˈtɑːktɪk/ *noun* [sing.] (**GEOGRAPHY**) the area around the South Pole ◌ look at **Arctic**
▸ **Antarctic** *adj.* [only before noun]: *an Antarctic expedition* ◌ look at **Arctic** (1)

the Anˌtarctic 'Circle *noun* [sing.] (**GEOGRAPHY**) the line of LATITUDE 66° 33′ South ◌ look at **Arctic Circle** ◌ picture at **earth**[1]

ante- /ænti/ *prefix* (in nouns, adjectives and verbs) before; in front of: *anteroom* ◇ *antenatal* ◌ look at **post-, pre-**

anteater /ˈæntiːtə(r)/ *noun* [C] an animal with a long nose and tongue that eats ANTS (= small insects)

antecedent /ˌæntɪˈsiːdnt/ *noun* **1** [C] (*formal*) a thing or an event that exists or comes before another, and may have influenced it **2 antecedents** [pl.] (*formal*) the people in sb's family who lived a long time ago **SYN** **ancestor 3** [C] (**GRAMMAR**) a word or phrase to which the following word, especially a pronoun, refers: *In 'He grabbed the ball and threw it in the air', 'ball' is the antecedent of 'it'.*

antelope /ˈæntɪləʊp/ *noun* [C] (*pl.* antelope, antelopes) an African animal with HORNS and long, thin legs that can run very fast

antenatal /ˌæntiˈneɪtl/ *adj.* (*BrE*) (*also* prenatal *especially in AmE*) (**MEDICINE**) connected with the care of pregnant women: *an antenatal clinic* ◇ *antenatal care* ◌ look at **postnatal**

antenna /ænˈtenə/ *noun* [C] **1** (*pl.* antennae /-niː/) one of the two long thin parts on the heads of insects and some animals that live in shells. Antennae are used for feeling things with. **SYN** **feeler** ◌ picture at **animal 2** (*pl.* antennas) (*especially AmE*) = AERIAL[1]

anterior /ænˈtɪəriə(r)/ *adj.* [only before noun] (**ANATOMY**) (used about a part of the body) at or near the front

anthem /ˈænθəm/ *noun* [C] (**MUSIC**) a song that has a special importance for a country, an organization or a particular group of people, and is sung on special occasions: *The song became an anthem for teenagers.*

anther /ˈænθə(r)/ *noun* [C] (**BIOLOGY**) the part of a flower at the top of a STAMEN (= the male part in the middle of a flower) that produces POLLEN (= the powder that makes other flowers of the same type produce seeds) ◌ picture at **flower**[1]

anthology /ænˈθɒlədʒi/ *noun* [C] (*pl.* -ies) (**LITERATURE**) a book that contains pieces of writing or poems, often on the same subject, by different authors

anthracite /ˈænθrəsaɪt/ *noun* [U] a very hard type of coal that burns slowly without producing a lot of smoke or flames

anthrax /ˈænθræks/ *noun* [U] (**AGRICULTURE**, **HEALTH**) a serious disease that affects sheep and cows, and sometimes people, and can cause death

anthropo- /ænθrəpəʊ, ænθrəpə, ænθrəˈpɒ/ *prefix* (in nouns, adjectives and adverbs) connected with humans

anthropology /ˌænθrəˈpɒlədʒi/ *noun* [U] (**SOCIAL STUDIES**) the study of humans, especially of their origin, development, customs and beliefs
▸ anthropological /ˌænθrəpəˈlɒdʒɪkl/ *adj.*
▸ anthropologist /ˌænθrəˈpɒlədʒɪst/ *noun* [C]

anthropomorphism /ˌænθrəpəˈmɔːfɪzəm/ *noun* [U] (**LANGUAGE**, **LITERATURE**) the practice of treating gods, animals or objects as if they had human qualities
▸ anthropomorphic /-fɪk/ *adj.*

anti- /ænti, ænti, ænˈtɪ/ *prefix* (in nouns and adjectives) **1** against: *anti-tank weapons* ◌ look at **pro- 2** the opposite of: *anticlimax* **3** preventing: *antifreeze*

ˌanti-'aircraft *adj.* [only before noun] designed to destroy enemy aircraft: *anti-aircraft fire/guns/missiles*

antibacterial /ˌæntibækˈtɪəriəl/ *adj.* (**MEDICINE**) that kills bacteria that can cause disease: *antibacterial treatments*

antibiotic /ˌæntibaɪˈɒtɪk/ *noun* [C, usually pl.] (**MEDICINE**) a medicine that is used for destroying bacteria and curing infections

antibody /ˈæntibɒdi/ *noun* [C] (*pl.* -ies) (**BIOLOGY**, **HEALTH**) a substance that the body produces in the blood to fight disease, or as a reaction when certain substances are put in the body

anticipate 🔷+ **B2** /ænˈtɪsɪpeɪt/ *verb* [T] **1 ~ (that …)** to expect sth to happen: *to anticipate a problem* ◇ *I anticipate that the situation will get worse.* **2** to see what might happen in the future and prepare for it: *We try to anticipate what our customers need.*

anticipation /ænˌtɪsɪˈpeɪʃn/ *noun* [U] **1 (in) ~ (of sth)** the state of expecting sth to happen and perhaps preparing for it: *The government has reduced tax in anticipation of an early general election.* **2** excited feelings about sth that is going to happen: *They queued outside the stadium in excited anticipation.*

anticlimax /ˌæntiˈklaɪmæks/ *noun* [C, U] an event, etc. that is less exciting than you had expected or than what has already happened

anticline /ˈæntiklaɪn/ *noun* [C] (**GEOLOGY**) an area of ground where layers of rock in the earth's surface have been folded into a curve that is higher in the middle than at the ends ◌ look at **syncline**

anticlockwise /ˌæntiˈklɒkwaɪz/ (*BrE*) (*AmE* counterclockwise) *adv., adj.* in the opposite direction to the movement of the hands of a clock: *Turn the lid anticlockwise/in an anticlockwise direction.* **OPP** **clockwise** ◌ picture at **moon**

anticoagulant /ˌæntikəʊˈægjələnt/ *noun* [C] (**MEDICINE**) a substance that stops the blood from becoming thick and forming CLOTS (= solid pieces)

antics /ˈæntɪks/ *noun* [pl.] funny, strange or silly ways of behaving

anticyclone /ˌænti'saɪkləʊn/ *noun* [C] (**GEOGRAPHY**) an area of high air pressure that produces calm weather conditions with clear skies ↪ look at **depression** (4)

antidepressant /ˌæntidɪ'presnt/ *noun* [C] (**MEDICINE**) a drug that is used to treat DEPRESSION

antidote /'æntidəʊt/ *noun* [C] ~ (**to sth**) **1** a medical substance that is used to prevent a poison or disease from having an effect: *an antidote to snake bites* **2** anything that helps you to deal with sth unpleasant: *Many people find music to be an antidote to stress.*

antifreeze /'æntifriːz/ *noun* [U] a chemical that is added to the water in the cooling system of cars and other vehicles to stop it from freezing

antigen /'æntɪdʒən/ *noun* [C] (**BIOLOGY, MEDICINE**) a substance that enters the body and starts a process that can cause disease. The body then usually produces ANTIBODIES to fight the antigens.

anti-hero *noun* [C] (**ARTS AND MEDIA, LITERATURE**) the main character in a film, story or play who does not have the qualities that a hero normally has, such as courage. An anti-hero is more like an ordinary person or is very unpleasant. ↪ look at **hero** (2), **villain** (1)

antihistamine /ˌænti'hɪstəmiːn/ *noun* [C, U] (**MEDICINE**) a drug used to treat an ALLERGY (= a medical condition that makes you ill when you touch, eat or breathe sth): *antihistamine cream/injections* ↪ look at **histamine**

anti-inflammatory /ˌænti ɪn'flæmətri/ *adj.* (**MEDICINE**) (used about a drug) used to reduce INFLAMMATION

anti-lock *adj.* [only before noun] **anti-lock** BRAKES stop the wheels of a vehicle from locking if you have to stop suddenly, and therefore make the vehicle easier to control: *an anti-lock braking system*

antimatter /'æntimætə(r)/ *noun* [U] (**CHEMISTRY, PHYSICS**) MATTER that is made up of PARTICLES that have the same MASS as normal PARTICLES but the opposite electrical CHARGE ↪ look at **matter**[1] (4)

antimony /'æntɪməni/ *noun* [U] (*symb.* **Sb**) a chemical element. Antimony is a silver-white metal that breaks easily. ❶ For more information on the periodic table of elements, look at the **Reference Section** of this dictionary.

antioxidant /ˌænti'ɒksɪdənt/ *noun* [C] **1** (**BIOLOGY, MEDICINE**) a substance such as VITAMIN C that removes dangerous MOLECULES, etc. from the food **2** (**CHEMISTRY**) a substance that helps prevent OXYGEN combining with other substances and damaging them, especially one used to help prevent stored food products from going bad

antipathy /æn'tɪpəθi/ *noun* [C, U] ~ (**to/towards sb/sth**) a strong feeling of dislike: *I felt (a) deep antipathy towards her.* ⓢⓨⓝ **dislike**[2]

antiperspirant /ˌænti'pɜːspərənt/ *noun* [C, U] a substance that people use, especially under the arms, to prevent or reduce SWEAT

the Antipodes /ði æn'tɪpədiːz/ *noun* [pl.] (*BrE*) (**GEOGRAPHY**) a way of referring to Australia and New Zealand ▸ **Antipodean** /ˌæntɪpə'diːən/ *adj.*

antiquated /'æntɪkweɪtɪd/ *adj.* old-fashioned and not suitable for the modern world

antique /æn'tiːk/ *adj.* (used about furniture, jewellery, etc.) old and often valuable: *an antique vase/table* ◇ *antique furniture/jewellery* ▸ **antique** *noun* [C]: *That vase is an antique.* ◇ *an antique shop* (= one that sells antiques)

antiquity /æn'tɪkwəti/ *noun* (*pl.* -ies) **1** [U] (**HISTORY**) the ancient past, especially the times of the Ancient Greeks and Romans: *The statue was brought to Rome in antiquity.* **2** [U] the state of being very old or ancient **3** [C, usually pl.] (**HISTORY**) a building or object from ancient times: *Greek/Roman antiquities*

antiretroviral /ˌænti ˌretrəʊ'vaɪrəl/ *adj.* (**MEDICINE**) of or connected with a class of drugs designed to stop viruses such as HIV from damaging the body

anti-Semitism /ˌænti 'semətɪzəm/ *noun* [U] (**SOCIAL STUDIES**) hate that is felt towards Jewish people; unfair treatment of Jewish people ▸ **anti-Semite** /ˌænti 'siːmaɪt, 'sem-/ *noun* [C] ▸ **anti-Semitic** /ˌænti sə'mɪtɪk/ *adj.*

antiseptic /ˌænti'septɪk/ *noun* [C, U] (**MEDICINE**) a liquid or cream that helps to prevent infection in wounds: *Put an antiseptic/some antiseptic on that scratch.* ⓢⓨⓝ **disinfectant** ▸ **antiseptic** *adj.*: *antiseptic cream*

antisocial /ˌænti'səʊʃl/ *adj.* **1** harmful or annoying to other people: *antisocial behaviour* **2** not liking to be with other people

anti-tank *adj.* [only before noun] (used about weapons) designed to destroy enemy tanks: *anti-tank missiles/ mines/rockets*

antithesis /æn'tɪθəsɪs/ *noun* [C, U] (*pl.* antitheses /-θəsiːz/) (*formal*) **1** the opposite of sth: *Love is the antithesis of hate.* **2** a difference between two things

antiviral /ˌænti'vaɪrəl/ *noun* [C] (**MEDICINE**) a drug used to treat diseases caused by a virus ▸ **antiviral** *adj.*

antivirus /'æntivaɪrəs/ *adj.* (**COMPUTING**) designed to find and destroy computer viruses: *antivirus software*

antler /'æntlə(r)/ *noun* [C, usually pl.] one of the two HORNS that grow on the head of male DEER: *a pair of antlers* ↪ picture at **animal**

antonym /'æntənɪm/ *noun* [C] (**LANGUAGE**) a word that means the opposite of another word ⓢⓨⓝ **opposite** ↪ look at **synonym**

anus /'eɪnəs/ *noun* [C] (**ANATOMY**) the opening through which solid waste leaves the body ↪ picture at **body**, **digestive system**

anvil /'ænvɪl/ *noun* [C] **1** an iron block on which a BLACKSMITH (= a person who works with iron) puts hot pieces of metal before shaping them with a HAMMER **2** (**ANATOMY**) the second of three small bones in the MIDDLE EAR that carry sound to the INNER EAR ⓢⓨⓝ **incus** ↪ picture at **ear**

anxiety 🔤+ B2 W /æŋ'zaɪəti/ *noun* (*pl.* -ies) **1** [C, U] a feeling of worry or fear, especially about the future: *a feeling/state of anxiety* ◇ *There are anxieties over the effects of unemployment.* **2** [U] (**PSYCHOLOGY**) a mental health problem that causes sb to worry so much that it has a very negative effect on their life

anxious 🔤 B2 /'æŋkʃəs/ *adj.* **1** ~ (**about sth**) worried and afraid: *I began to get anxious when they still hadn't arrived at nine o'clock.* ◇ *an anxious look/ expression* ◇ *I'm anxious about my exam.* **2** causing worry and fear: *For a few anxious moments we thought we'd missed the train.* **3** ~ (**to do sth**) wanting sth very much: *Police are anxious to find the owner of the white car.* ▸ **anxiously** *adv.*

any[1] 🔤 A1 /'eni/ *det., pron.* **1** used instead of *some* in negative sentences and in questions: *We didn't have any lunch.* ◇ *I speak hardly any* (= almost no) *Spanish.* ◇ *Do you have any questions?* ◇ *I don't like any of his books.* **2** used for saying that it does not matter which thing or person you choose: *Take any book you want.* ◇ *Come round any time — I'm usually in.* ◇ *I'll take any that you don't want.* ⓘⓓⓜ **any moment/second/minute/day (now)** very soon: *She should be home any minute now.*

any[2] 🔤 A1 /'eni/ *adv.* (in negative sentences and questions) at all; to any degree: *I can't run any faster.* ◇ *Is your father any better?*

anybody ⚡ **A1** /'enibɒdi/ (*also* **anyone** /'eniwʌn/) *pron.* **1** (usually in negative sentences and questions) any person: *I didn't know anybody at the party.* ◊ *Is there anybody here who can speak Japanese?* ◊ *Would anybody else* (= any other person) *like to come with me?* **2** any person, it does not matter who: *Anybody* (= all people) *can learn to swim.* ◊ *Can anybody come, or are there special invitations?*

anyhow /'enihaʊ/ *adv.* **1** = ANYWAY **2** in a careless way; not arranged in any order: *Don't throw your clothes down just anyhow!*

any 'more ⚡ **A2** (*BrE*) (*also* **anymore** *BrE, AmE*) *adv.* often used at the end of negative sentences and at the end of questions, to mean 'any longer': *She doesn't live here any more.* ◊ *Why doesn't he speak to me any more?*

anything ⚡ **A1** /'eniθɪŋ/ *pron.* **1** (usually in negative sentences and questions) one thing (of any kind): *It was so dark that I couldn't see anything at all.* ◊ *Did you buy anything?* ◊ *'I'd like a kilo of apples please.' 'Anything else?'* (= any other thing?) **2** any thing at all, when it does not matter which: *I'm very hungry — I'll eat anything!* ◊ *I'll do anything you say.*
IDM **anything but** not at all: *Their explanation was anything but clear.* **anything like sb/sth** at all similar to sb/sth; nearly: *She isn't anything like her sister, is she?* ◊ *This car isn't anything like as fast as mine.* **as happy, quick, etc. as anything** (*informal*) very happy, quick, etc. **like anything** → LIKE[1] **not come to anything** → COME

anyway ⚡ **A2** /'eniweɪ/ (*also* **anyhow**) *adv.* **1** (used to add an extra point or reason) in any case: *It's too late now, anyway.* ◊ *I don't want to go out tonight, and anyway I haven't got any money.* **SYN** **besides 2** used for correcting sth you have just said and making it more accurate: *Everybody wants to be rich — well, most people anyway.* **3** despite sth; even so: *I'm afraid I can't come to your party, but thanks anyway.* **4** used when changing the subject or going back to a subject being discussed before: *Anyhow, as I was saying…* ◊ *Anyway, that's enough about my problems. How are you?* **5** used to correct or slightly change what you have said: *He works in a bank. He did when I last saw him, anyway.*

anywhere[1] ⚡ **A2** /'eniweə(r)/ (*AmE also* **anyplace** /'enipleɪs/) *adv.* **1** used in negative sentences and in questions instead of 'somewhere': *I can't find my keys anywhere.* ◊ *Is there a post office anywhere near here?* ◊ *You can't buy the book anywhere else* (= in another place). **2** any place; it does not matter where: *You can sit anywhere you like.*

anywhere[2] ⚡ **A2** /'eniweə(r)/ (*AmE also* **anyplace** /'enipleɪs/) *pron.* used in negative sentences and in questions instead of 'somewhere': *I don't have anywhere to stay.*

AOB /ˌeɪ əʊ 'biː/ *abbr.* (**BUSINESS**) **any other business** (the things that are discussed at the end of an official meeting that are not on the list of things to discuss) ⊃ note at **meeting**

aorta /eɪ'ɔːtə/ *noun* [C] (**ANATOMY**) the main ARTERY (= tube) that carries blood from the heart to the rest of the body ⊃ picture at **heart**

apart ⚡ **B1** /ə'pɑːt/ *adv.* **1** away from sb/sth or each other; not together: *The doors slowly slid apart.* ◊ *Stand with your feet apart.* ◊ *The houses are 10 metres apart.* ◊ *I'm afraid our ideas are too far apart.* ⊃ look at **tell** (7) **2** into pieces: *The material was so old that it just fell/came apart in my hands.*

IDM **take sth apart** to separate sth into pieces: *He took the whole bike apart.* **tell A and B apart** to see the difference between A and B: *It's very difficult to tell the twins apart.*

a'part from (*also* **aside from** *especially in AmE*) *prep.* **1** except for: *I've answered all the questions apart from the last one.* ◊ *There's nobody here apart from me.* **2** as well as; in addition to: *Apart from music, she also loves sport and reading.*

apartheid /ə'pɑːtaɪt, -teɪt/ *noun* [U] (**POLITICS**, **SOCIAL STUDIES**) the former political system in South Africa in which only white people had full political rights and other people, especially black people, were forced to live away from white people

aparthotel /ə'pɑːthəʊtel/ *noun* [C] (**TOURISM**) a type of hotel that has apartments where you can cook your own meals as well as ordinary hotel rooms

apartment ⚡ **A1** /ə'pɑːtmənt/ *noun* [C] **1** (*especially AmE*) = FLAT[1] (1): *an apartment building* **2** (**TOURISM**) a set of rooms rented for a holiday: *a self-catering apartment*

a'partment block (*BrE*) (*AmE* **a'partment building**) *noun* [C] a large building with flats on each floor

apathetic /ˌæpə'θetɪk/ *adj.* lacking interest or desire to act

apathy /'æpəθi/ *noun* [U] the feeling of not being interested in or enthusiastic about anything

ape[1] /eɪp/ *noun* [C] a type of animal like a large monkey, with no tail or only a very short tail: *Chimpanzees and gorillas are apes.*

ape[2] /eɪp/ *verb* [T] (*BrE*) to do sth in the same way as sb, especially when it is not done very well: *For years the British film industry merely aped Hollywood.*
SYN **imitate**

aperitif /ə,perə'tiːf/ *noun* [C] a drink, usually one containing alcohol, that people sometimes have just before a meal

aperture /'æpətʃə(r)/ *noun* [C] **1** (*formal*) a small opening in sth **2** a small opening that allows light to reach a lens inside a camera

apex /'eɪpeks/ *noun* [C, usually sing.] the top or highest part of sth: *the apex of a roof/triangle*

aphid /'eɪfɪd/ *noun* [C] a very small insect that is harmful to plants. There are several different types of aphid.

aphorism /'æfərɪzəm/ *noun* [C] (*formal*) (**LANGUAGE**) a short phrase that expresses in a clever way sth that is true

aphrodisiac /ˌæfrə'dɪziæk/ *noun* [C] a food or drug that is said to make people have a desire to have sex ▶ **aphrodisiac** *adj.*

apiece /ə'piːs/ *adv.* each

apocalypse /ə'pɒkəlɪps/ *noun* **1** [sing., U] the DESTRUCTION of the world **2 the Apocalypse** [sing.] (**RELIGION**) the end of the world, as described in the Bible **3** [sing.] a situation causing very serious damage and DESTRUCTION: *an environmental apocalypse* ▶ **apocalyptic** /ə,pɒkə'lɪptɪk/ *adj.*

apocryphal /ə'pɒkrɪfl/ *adj.* (used about a story) well known, but probably not true: *Most of the stories about him are apocryphal.*

apolitical /ˌeɪpə'lɪtɪkl/ *adj.* (**POLITICS**) **1** (used about a person) not interested in politics; not thinking politics are important **2** not connected with a political party: *an apolitical organization*

apologetic /ə,pɒlə'dʒetɪk/ *adj.* feeling or showing that you are sorry for sth you have done: *He was most apologetic about his son's bad behaviour.* ◊ *I wrote him an apologetic letter.* ▶ **apologetically** /-kli/ *adv.*

apologize ʔ **B1** (*BrE also* -ise) /əˈpɒlədʒaɪz/ *verb* [I] ~(to sb) (for sth/doing sth) to say that you are sorry for sth that you have done: *You'll have to apologize to your teacher for being late.*

apology ʔ+ **B2** /əˈpɒlədʒi/ *noun* [C, U] (*pl.* -ies) ~(for sth) a spoken or written statement that you are sorry for sth you have done, etc: *Please accept our apologies for the delay.* ◇ *a letter of apology*
IDM **make no apology/apologies for sth** to not feel that you have said or done anything wrong

apostle /əˈpɒsl/ *noun* [C] (**RELIGION**) (in the Bible) one of the twelve men chosen by Christ to tell people about him and his teaching

apostrophe /əˈpɒstrəfi/ *noun* [C] (**LANGUAGE**) **1** the mark (') used for showing that you have left a letter or letters out of a word as in *I'm*, *can't* or *we'll* **2** the mark (') used for showing who or what sth belongs to as in *John's chair*, *the boys' room* or *Russia's president*

app ʔ **A2** /æp/ *noun* [C] **1** (**COMPUTING**) a piece of software that you can download to a device such as a smartphone, for example to look up information: *I've got an English dictionary app on my phone.*
2 = APPLICATION (2)

appal (*BrE*) (*AmE* **appall**) /əˈpɔːl/ *verb* [T] (-ll-) to shock sb very much: *The idea of sharing a room appalled her.*

appalled /əˈpɔːld/ *adj.* feeling horror at sth unpleasant or wrong

appalling /əˈpɔːlɪŋ/ *adj.* extremely bad, especially from a moral point of view: *The prisoners were living in appalling conditions.* **SYN** **deplorable** ▶ **appallingly** *adv.*

apparatus ʔ+ **C1** /ˌæpəˈreɪtəs/ *noun* [U] (**SCIENCE**) the set of tools, instruments or equipment used for doing a job or an activity ◯ picture at **laboratory**

apparent ʔ **B2** **W** /əˈpærənt/ *adj.* **1** ~ (to sb) (that …) clear; easy to see: *It quickly became apparent to us that our teacher could not speak French.* ◇ *For no apparent reason she suddenly burst into tears.* **SYN** **obvious** ◯ note at **clear¹** ◯ *verb* **appear 2** [only before noun] that seems to be real or true but may not be: *His apparent interest in the proposal didn't last very long.*

apparently ʔ **B2** /əˈpærəntli/ *adv.* according to what people say or to how sth appears, but perhaps not true: *Apparently, he's already been married twice.* ◇ *He was apparently undisturbed by the news.*

apparition /ˌæpəˈrɪʃn/ *noun* [C] a ghost or a ghost-like image of a person who is dead

appeal¹ ʔ **B2** /əˈpiːl/ *noun* **1** [C] ~(to sb) (for sth) (**SOCIAL STUDIES**) a deeply felt request for money, help or information, especially one made by a charity or by the police: *to launch a TV appeal for donations to the charity* ◇ *The police have made an urgent appeal to the public for any information that may help them.* **2** [U] the attraction or interesting quality of sth/sb: *The Beatles have never really lost their appeal.* **3** [C, U] ~ (against sth) (**LAW**) a formal request to a court or to sb in authority for a judgement or a decision to be changed: *She has launched an appeal against her conviction.* ◇ *The judge turned down the defendant's appeal.* ◯ look at **court of appeal 4** [C] ~to sth a suggestion that tries to influence sb's feelings or thoughts so that they will do what you want: *an appeal to our sense of national pride*

appeal² ʔ **B2** /əˈpiːl/ *verb* [I] **1** ~(against/for sth) (**LAW**) to make a formal request to a court or to sb in authority for a judgement or a decision to be changed: *He decided to appeal against his conviction.* ◇ *The player fell down and appealed for a penalty.* **2** ~(to sb) to be attractive or interesting to sb: *The idea of living in the country doesn't appeal to me at all.*

3 ~(to sb) (for sth); ~(to sb to do sth) (**SOCIAL STUDIES**) to make a serious request for sth you need or want very much: *Relief workers in the disaster area are appealing for more supplies.* ◇ *She appealed to the kidnappers to let her son go.* **4** ~to sth to try to influence sb's feelings or thoughts so that they will do sth you want: *We aim to appeal to people's generosity.*

apˈpeal court 1 = COURT OF APPEAL (1) **2** **Appeal Court** = COURT OF APPEAL (2) **3** **appeals court** (*AmE*) = COURT OF APPEAL (3)

appealing ʔ+ **C1** /əˈpiːlɪŋ/ *adj.* **1** attractive or interesting: *The idea of lying on a beach sounds very appealing!* **2** showing that you need help, etc: *an appealing look* ▶ **appealingly** *adv.*

appear ʔ **A2** **O** /əˈpɪə(r)/ *verb* **1** [I] to suddenly be seen; to come into sight: *The bus appeared from round the corner.* **OPP** **disappear 2** linking verb ~(to be/do sth) to give the impression of being or doing sth: *She appears to be very happy in her job.* ◇ *It appears that you were given the wrong information.* ◇ *Everything appeared normal.* ◯ adjective **apparent 3** [I] to begin to exist: *When did mammals appear on the earth?* **4** [I] ~ (in sth) (**ARTS AND MEDIA**) to be published or printed: *The article appeared in this morning's paper.* **5** [I] (**ARTS AND MEDIA, LAW**) to perform or speak where you are seen by a lot of people: *to appear on TV/in a play* ◇ *I've been asked to appear in court.* ◯ note at **performing arts**

appearance ʔ **A2** /əˈpɪərəns/ *noun* **1** [C, U] the way that sb/sth looks or seems: *A different hairstyle can completely change your appearance.* ◇ *He gives the appearance of being extremely confident.* **2** [C, usually sing.] the coming of sb/sth: *the appearance of TV in the home in the 1950s* **3** [C] (**ARTS AND MEDIA**) an act of appearing in public, especially on stage, TV, etc. **IDM** **keep up appearances** to pretend that everything is going well, even though you are having problems: *Despite being short of money, she was determined to keep up appearances.*

appease /əˈpiːz/ *verb* [T] (*formal*) **1** to make sb calmer or less angry by agreeing to what they want **2** (**POLITICS**) to give a country what it wants in order to avoid war ▶ **appeasement** *noun* [U]: *a policy of appeasement*

append /əˈpend/ *verb* [T] ~ sth (to sth) (*formal*) to add sth to the end of a piece of writing: *Footnotes have been appended to the document.*

appendage /əˈpendɪdʒ/ *noun* [C] (*formal*) a smaller or less important part of sth larger

appendicitis /əˌpendəˈsaɪtɪs/ *noun* [U] (**HEALTH**) an illness in which the APPENDIX becomes extremely painful and usually has to be removed

appendix /əˈpendɪks/ *noun* [C] **1** (*pl.* **appendixes**) (**ANATOMY**) a small organ inside the body near the stomach. In humans, the appendix has no clear function. ◯ picture at **body 2** (*pl.* **appendices** /-dɪsiːz/) (**LITERATURE**) a section at the end of a book, etc. that gives extra information

appetite ʔ+ **C1** /ˈæpɪtaɪt/ *noun* [U, C, usually sing.] ~(for sth) a strong desire for sth, especially food: *Some fresh air and exercise should give you an appetite* (= make you hungry). ◇ *He has a great appetite for work/life.* ◇ *loss of appetite*
IDM **whet sb's appetite** → WHET

appetizer (*BrE also* -iser) /ˈæpɪtaɪzə(r)/ = STARTER

appetizing (*BrE also* -ising) /ˈæpɪtaɪzɪŋ/ *adj.* (used about food, etc.) that looks or smells attractive; making you feel hungry

applaud ⚡+ **C1** /ə'plɔːd/ *verb* **1** [I, T] to show that you like sb/sth by CLAPPING your hands (= hitting your open hands together several times): *The audience applauded loudly.* ◊ *The team was applauded as it left the field.* **2** [T, usually passive] to express approval of sth: *The decision was applauded by everybody.*

applause /ə'plɔːz/ *noun* [U] the noise made by a group of people CLAPPING their hands and sometimes shouting to show their approval: *The audience broke into rapturous applause.* ◊ *Let's all give a big round of applause to the cook!*

apple ⚡ **A1** /'æpl/ *noun* [C, U] a hard, round fruit with a smooth green, red or yellow skin: *apple juice* ◊ *an apple pie* ◊ *three apple trees*

applet /'æplət/ *noun* [C] (COMPUTING) a program that is run from within another program, for example from within an internet BROWSER

appliance /ə'plaɪəns/ *noun* [C] a piece of equipment for a particular purpose in the house: *washing machines and other domestic appliances*

applicable ⚡+ **C1** **W** /ə'plɪkəbl, 'æplɪkəbl/ *adj.* [not before noun] ~ (to sb/sth) that concerns sb/sth: *This part of the form is only applicable to married women.* **SYN** relevant

applicant ⚡+ **B2** /'æplɪkənt/ *noun* [C] a person who makes a formal request for sth, especially for a job or a place at a college, university, etc: *There were over 200 applicants for the job.*

application ⚡ **B1** **W** /ˌæplɪ'keɪʃn/ *noun* **1** [C, U] ~ (for sth); ~ (to do sth) a formal written request, especially for a job or a place in a school, club, etc: *To become a member, fill in the application form.* ◊ *a planning application* ◊ *an application for asylum* ◊ *The company has submitted an application to build a new car park.* **2** (*also* app) [C] (COMPUTING) a program designed to do a particular job; a piece of software: *a software application* **3** [C, U] ~ (of sth) the practical use (of sth): *the application of technology in the classroom* **4** [U] hard work; effort: *Success as a writer demands great application.*

applied /ə'plaɪd/ *adj.* (EDUCATION) (used about a subject) studied in a way that has a practical use: *You have to study applied mathematics as part of the engineering course.* ⊃ look at **pure** (4)

apˌplied linˈguistics *noun* [U] (LANGUAGE) the scientific study of language for practical uses, such as teaching and dealing with speech problems

apply ⚡ **A2** **O** /ə'plaɪ/ *verb* (applying; applies; *pt, pp* applied)
• FOR A JOB/COURSE **1** [I] ~ (for sth) to ask for sth in writing: *I've applied for that job.* ◊ *She's applying for a place at university.* ⊃ note at **job**
• BE RELEVANT **2** [I, T] (not used in the progressive tenses) ~ (to sb/sth) to affect or be relevant to sb/sth: *This information applies to all children born after 2017.*
• USE **3** [T] ~ sth (to sth) to make practical use of sth: *After the training, you should be able to apply what you have learned to your job.*
• PAINT/CREAM **4** [T] ~ sth (to sth) to put or spread sth onto sth: *Apply the cream to the infected area twice a day.*
• WORK HARD **5** [T] ~ yourself/sth (to sth/doing sth) to make yourself give all your attention to sth: *He applied himself to his studies.*

appoint ⚡+ **C1** /ə'pɔɪnt/ *verb* [T] **1** ~ sb (to sth); ~ sb (as) sth (BUSINESS) to choose sb for a job or position: *She has recently been appointed to the committee.* ◊ *The committee have appointed a new chairperson.* ◊ *He's been appointed (as) assistant to Dr Beale.* ⊃ note at **job, professional²** **2** [usually passive] be appointed (for

sth) (*formal*) if a date or a time for a meeting, etc. is appointed, it is arranged: *A date has been appointed for the next meeting.*

appointment ⚡ **B1** /ə'pɔɪntmənt/ *noun* **1** [C, U] ~ (with sb); ~ (to do sth) an arrangement to see sb at a particular time: *I have an appointment with Dr Sula at three o'clock.* ◊ *I'd like to make an appointment to see the manager.* ◊ *I realized I wouldn't be able to keep the appointment so I cancelled it.* ◊ *Visits are by appointment only* (= at a time that has been arranged in advance). **2** [C] (BUSINESS) a job or a position of responsibility: *a temporary/permanent appointment* **3** [C, U] ~ (of sb) (to sth) the act of choosing sb for a job: *Many people criticized the appointment of such a young woman to the post.*

apportion /ə'pɔːʃn/ *verb* [T] ~ sth (among/between/to sb) (*formal*) to divide sth among people; to give a share of sth to sb: *The land was apportioned between members of the family.* ◊ *The programme gives the facts but does not apportion blame.*

apposition /ˌæpə'zɪʃn/ *noun* [U] (in) ~ (to sth) (GRAMMAR) the use of a noun phrase immediately after another noun phrase that refers to the same person or thing: *In the phrase 'Paris, the capital of France', 'the capital of France' is in apposition to 'Paris'.*

appraisal /ə'preɪzl/ *noun* [C, U] (*formal*) **1** a judgement about the value or quality of sb/sth **2** (*BrE*) (BUSINESS) a meeting in which an employee discusses with their manager how well they have been doing their job; the system of holding such meetings

appraise /ə'preɪz/ *verb* [T] **1** (*formal*) to judge the value or quality of sb/sth **2** (BUSINESS) to make a formal judgement about the value of a person's work, usually after a discussion with them about it: *Managers must appraise all staff.*

appreciable /ə'priːʃəbl/ *adj.* large enough to be noticed or thought important: *an appreciable effect/increase/amount* **SYN** considerable ▸ appreciably /-bli/ *adv.*

appreciate ⚡ **B1** /ə'priːʃieɪt/ *verb* **1** [T] to enjoy sth or to understand the value of sb/sth: *My boss doesn't appreciate me.* ◊ *I don't appreciate good coffee — it all tastes the same to me.* **2** [T] to understand a problem, situation, etc: *I appreciate your problem but I'm afraid I can't help you.* **3** [T] to be grateful for sth: *Thanks very much. I really appreciate your help.* ◊ *Thanks for doing that. I appreciate it.* **4** [I] (FINANCE) to increase in value: *Their investments have appreciated over the years.*

appreciation ⚡+ **C1** /əˌpriːʃi'eɪʃn/ *noun* **1** [U] ~ (of sth) pleasure that you feel when you understand the value of sth: *I'm afraid I have little appreciation of modern architecture.* **2** [U] ~ (of/for sth) the feeling of being grateful for sth: *We bought him a present to show our appreciation for all the work he had done.* **3** [U, sing.] ~ of sth understanding of a situation, problem, etc. **4** [U, sing.] (FINANCE) an increase in value over a period of time

appreciative /ə'priːʃətɪv/ *adj.* **1** feeling or showing that you are grateful for sth: *an appreciative audience* **2** ~ (of sth) grateful for sth: *He was very appreciative of our efforts to help.* ▸ appreciatively *adv.*

apprehend /ˌæprɪ'hend/ *verb* [T] (*formal*) (LAW) (used about the police) to catch sb and arrest them

apprehensive /ˌæprɪ'hensɪv/ *adj.* ~ (about/of sth) worried or afraid that sth unpleasant may happen: *I'm feeling apprehensive about tomorrow's exam.* ▸ apprehension /-'henʃn/ *noun* [C, U]

apprentice /əˈprentɪs/ noun [C] a young person who works for a fixed period of time, in order to learn the skills needed in a particular job: *an apprentice electrician/chef/plumber*

apprenticeship /əˈprentɪʃɪp/ noun [C, U] the state or time of being an APPRENTICE

approach[1] ⚑ B2 Ⓦ /əˈprəʊtʃ/ verb **1** [I, T] to come near or nearer to sb/sth: *The day of the exam approached.* ◇ *When you approach the village, you will see a garage on your left.* **2** [T] to begin to deal with a problem, situation, etc: *What is the best way to approach this problem?* **3** [T] ~ **sb/sth (about sth)** to speak to sb, usually in order to ask for sth: *I'm going to approach my bank about a loan.*

approach[2] ⚑ B2 Ⓞ /əˈprəʊtʃ/ noun **1** [C] ~ **(to sth)** a way of dealing with sb/sth: *Parents don't always know what **approach** to **take** with teenage children.* ◇ *We're proposing a new approach to the problem.* **2** [sing.] ~ **(of sb/sth)** the act of coming nearer to sb/sth: *the approach of winter* **3** [C] ~ **(to sb) (for sth)** a request for sth: *The club has **made an approach** to a company for sponsorship.* **4** [C] ~ **to sth** a road or path leading to sth: *the approach to the village*

approachable /əˈprəʊtʃəbl/ adj. **1** friendly and easy to talk to OPP **unapproachable** **2** [not before noun] that can be reached SYN **accessible**

appropriate[1] ⚑ B2 Ⓦ /əˈprəʊpriət/ adj. ~ **(for sth)** suitable or right for a particular situation, person, use, etc: *The matter will be dealt with by the appropriate authorities.* ◇ *I don't think this film is appropriate for children.* OPP **inappropriate** ▸ **appropriately** ⚑+ B2 Ⓦ adv.

appropriate[2] /əˈprəʊprieɪt/ verb [T] ~ **sth (from sb/sth)** (*formal*) to take sth to use for yourself, usually without permission: *He appropriated the money from the company's pension fund.* ▸ **appropriation** /əˌprəʊpriˈeɪʃn/ noun [U, sing.]

approval ⚑ B2 /əˈpruːvl/ noun [U] **1** the feeling that sb/sth is good or acceptable: *She was always anxious to **win** her mother's **approval**.* ◇ *Her colleagues nodded **in approval**.* OPP **disapproval** **2** agreement to or permission for sth, especially a plan or request: *government approval* ◇ *Everybody gave their approval to the proposal.* ◇ *I'm afraid I can't sign these papers without my partner's approval.*

approve ⚑ B2 /əˈpruːv/ verb **1** [I] ~ **(of sb/sth)**; ~ **(of sb doing sth)** to be pleased about sth; to like sb/sth: *Her parents don't approve of her friends.* ◇ *His father didn't approve of him becoming a dancer.* OPP **disapprove** **2** [T] to agree formally to sth or to say that sth is correct: *We need to get an accountant to approve these figures.* ⊃ note at **agree, meeting**

approving /əˈpruːvɪŋ/ adj. showing that you believe that sb/sth is good or acceptable: *'Good,' he said with an approving smile.* OPP **disapproving** ▸ **approvingly** adv.

approximate[1] /əˈprɒksɪmət/ adj. (*abbr.* **approx.** /əˈprɒks/) almost correct but not completely accurate: *The approximate time of arrival is three o'clock.* ◇ *I can only give you an approximate idea of the cost.* OPP **exact**[1]

approximate[2] /əˈprɒksɪmeɪt/ verb (*formal*) **1** [T, I] ~ **(to) sth** to be similar or close to sth in nature, quality, amount, etc., but not exactly the same: *The animals were reared in conditions that approximated the wild as closely as possible.* ◇ *The total cost will approximate £15 billion.* ◇ *His story approximates to the facts that we already know.* **2** [T] to calculate or estimate sth fairly accurately: *a formula for approximating the weight of a horse*

approximately ⚑ B1 Ⓦ /əˈprɒksɪmətli/ adv. (*abbr.* **approx.** /əˈprɒks/) about; roughly: *It's approximately 50 miles from here.* SYN **roughly** ⊃ note at **measure**[2]

approximation Ⓦ /əˌprɒksɪˈmeɪʃn/ noun [C] an estimate of a number or an amount that is almost correct, but not exact: *That's just an approximation, you understand.*

APR /ˌeɪ piː ˈɑː(r)/ abbr. (**FINANCE**) **annual percentage rate** (the amount of interest a bank charges on money that it lends, calculated for a period of a year): *a rate of 26.4% APR*

apricot /ˈeɪprɪkɒt/ noun [C] a small round fruit with yellow or orange skin and a large STONE inside

April ⚑ A1 /ˈeɪprəl/ noun [U, C] (*abbr.* **Apr.**) the fourth month of the year, between March and May: *She was born in April.* ◇ *We went to Italy last April.*

April Fool's Day noun [sing.] 1 April

▼ CULTURE

On this day it is traditional for people to play tricks on each other, especially by inventing silly stories and trying to persuade other people that they are true. If sb believes such a story, they are called an **April Fool**.

---

a priori /ˌeɪ praɪˈɔːraɪ/ adj., adv. (*formal*) using facts or principles that we know are true in order to decide what the likely effects or results of sth will be, for example saying 'They haven't eaten anything all day so they must be hungry.': *an a priori assumption*

apron /ˈeɪprən/ noun [C] a piece of clothing that you wear over the front of your usual clothes in order to keep them clean, especially when cooking

apropos /ˌæprəˈpəʊ/ (*also* ˌaproˈpos of) prep. on the subject of sth/sb: *Apropos (of) what you were just saying…*

apse /æps/ noun [C] (**ARCHITECTURE**) a small area, often in the shape of a SEMICIRCLE, usually at the east end of a church

apt /æpt/ adj. **1** suitable in a particular situation: *I thought 'complex' was an apt description of the book.* **2** ~ **to do sth** often likely to do sth: *You'd better remind me. I'm rather apt to forget.* ◇ *She's apt to be forgetful.*

aptitude /ˈæptɪtjuːd/ noun [U, C] ~ **(for sth/doing sth)** natural ability or skill: *She has an aptitude for learning languages.* ◇ *an **aptitude test** (= one designed to show whether sb has the natural ability for a particular job or educational course)*

aptly /ˈæptli/ adv. in an appropriate way: *The winner of the race was aptly named Alan Speedy.* SYN **suitably**

aqualung /ˈækwəlʌŋ/ noun [C] (**SPORT**) a piece of breathing equipment that a DIVER wears on his or her back when swimming UNDERWATER

aquamarine /ˌækwəməˈriːn/ noun **1** [C, U] a pale blue-green SEMI-PRECIOUS stone **2** [U] a pale blue-green colour ▸ **aquamarine** adj.

aquarium /əˈkweəriəm/ noun [C] (*pl.* **aquariums, aquaria** /-riə/) **1** a glass container filled with water, in which fish and water animals are kept **2** a building where people can go to see fish and other water animals

Aquarius /əˈkweəriəs/ noun [U] the eleventh sign of THE ZODIAC (= twelve signs that represent the positions of the sun, moon and planets), the Water Bearer or Water Carrier; a person born under this sign

aquatic /əˈkwætɪk/ adj. (**BIOLOGY**) living or taking place in, on or near water: *aquatic plants* ◇ *windsurfing and other aquatic sports*

aqueduct /ˈækwɪdʌkt/ noun [C] (**ARCHITECTURE**) a structure for carrying water, usually one like a bridge across a valley or low ground

aqueous /ˈeɪkwiəs/ adj. (**CHEMISTRY**) containing water; like water

aquifer /ˈækwɪfə(r)/ noun [C] (**GEOLOGY**) a layer of rock or soil that can take in and hold water ⊃ picture at **water cycle**

AR /ˌeɪ ˈɑː(r)/ noun [U] (**COMPUTING**) a technology that combines images produced by a computer with the real object or scene that you are looking at (the abbreviation for 'augmented reality'): *an AR app/game/system*

Arab /ˈærəb/ noun [C] (**SOCIAL STUDIES**) a person from the Middle East or North Africa, whose ANCESTORS lived in the Arabian PENINSULA ▸ **Arab** adj.: *Arab countries*

Arabic /ˈærəbɪk/ noun [U] (**LANGUAGE**) the language of the Arabs

arable /ˈærəbl/ adj. (**AGRICULTURE**) connected with growing crops for sale, not keeping animals: *arable land/farmers*

arachnid /əˈræknɪd/ noun [C] (**BIOLOGY**) any of the CLASS of small creatures with eight legs that includes spiders ⊃ picture at **animal**

arbitrage /ˈɑːbɪtrɑːʒ, -trɪdʒ/ noun [U] (**FINANCE**) the practice of buying sth, for example foreign money, in one place and selling it in another place where the price is higher ▸ **arbitrageur** /ˌɑːbɪtraːˈʒɜː(r)/ (*also* **arbitrager** /ˈɑːbɪtrɪdʒə(r)/) noun [C]

arbitrary ⓘ+ **C1** /ˈɑːbɪtrəri, -tri/ adj. not seeming to be based on any reason or plan: *The choice of players for the team seemed completely arbitrary.* ▸ **arbitrarily** /ˌɑːbɪˈtrerəli, ˈɑːbɪtrəli/ adv. ▸ **arbitrariness** noun [U]

arbitrate /ˈɑːbɪtreɪt/ verb [I, T] ~ **(in/on) (sth)** to officially settle an argument between two people or groups by finding a solution that both can accept: *to arbitrate in a dispute* ▸ **arbitration** /ˌɑːbɪˈtreɪʃn/ noun [U]: *The union and the management decided to go to arbitration.*

arbitrator /ˈɑːbɪtreɪtə(r)/ noun [C] a person who is chosen to settle an argument between two people or two groups of people

arc /ɑːk/ noun [C] (**GEOMETRY**) a curved line that is part of a circle ⊃ picture at **circle**¹

arcade /ɑːˈkeɪd/ noun [C] **1** (**ARCHITECTURE**) a covered passage with ARCHES along the side of a row of buildings **2** = AMUSEMENT ARCADE: *arcade games* **3** a covered passage between streets, with shops on either side **4** (*also* **shopping arcade**) (*both BrE*) a large building with a number of shops in it ⊃ look at **shopping centre**

arcane /ɑːˈkeɪn/ adj. (*formal*) known to very few people and therefore difficult to understand: *the arcane rules of cricket*

arch¹ /ɑːtʃ/ noun [C] **1** (**ARCHITECTURE**) a curved structure that supports the weight of sth above it, such as a bridge or the upper part of a building ⊃ look at **archway 2** (**ARCHITECTURE**) a structure with a curved top that is supported by straight sides, sometimes forming an entrance or built as a MONUMENT: *Marble Arch is a famous London landmark.* **3** (**ANATOMY**) the curved bottom part of the foot

arch² /ɑːtʃ/ verb [I, T] if you **arch** part of your body, or if it **arches**, it moves and forms a curved shape: *The cat arched its back and hissed.*

arch- /ɑːtʃ/ prefix (in nouns) main, most important or most extreme: *archbishop* ◇ *arch-rival*

archaeology (*AmE also* **archeology**) /ˌɑːkiˈɒlədʒi/ noun [U] (**HISTORY**) the study of the past, based on objects or parts of buildings that are found in the ground ▸ **archaeological** (*AmE also* **archeological**) /ˌɑːkiəˈlɒdʒɪkl/ adj. ▸ **archaeologist** (*AmE also* **archeologist**) /ˌɑːkiˈɒlədʒɪst/ noun [C]

archaic /ɑːˈkeɪk/ adj. very old-fashioned; no longer used

archbishop /ˌɑːtʃˈbɪʃəp/ noun [C] (**RELIGION**) a BISHOP of the highest rank, who is responsible for all the churches in a large area of a country: *the Archbishop of Canterbury* (= the head of the Church of England) ⊃ look at **bishop** (1)

arched /ɑːtʃt/ adj. in the shape of an ARCH: *a chair with an arched back*

archeological, archeologist, archeology (*AmE*) = ARCHAEOLOGICAL, ARCHAEOLOGIST, ARCHAEOLOGY

archer /ˈɑːtʃə(r)/ noun [C] (**HISTORY**, **SPORT**) a person who shoots ARROWS (= pieces of wood or metal with a sharp point) through the air by pulling back a tight string on a BOW (= a curved piece of wood) and letting go.

archery /ˈɑːtʃəri/ noun [U] (**SPORT**) the sport of shooting ARROWS

archetypal /ˌɑːkiˈtaɪpl/ adj. (*formal*) having all the qualities that make sb/sth a typical example of a particular kind of person or thing: *He lived an archetypal rock star's lifestyle.*

archetype /ˈɑːkitaɪp/ noun [C] (*formal*) the most typical example of a particular kind of person or thing

archipelago /ˌɑːkɪˈpeləɡəʊ/ noun [C] (*pl.* **-os, -oes**) (**GEOGRAPHY**) a group of islands and the sea around them

architect ⓘ **A2** /ˈɑːkɪtekt/ noun [C] a person whose job is to design buildings

architectonic /ˌɑːkɪtekˈtɒnɪk/ adj. (**ARCHITECTURE**) relating to architecture or architects

architectural ⓘ+ **C1** /ˌɑːkɪˈtektʃərəl/ adj. connected with the design of buildings ▸ **architecturally** /-rəli/ adv.

architecture ⓘ **A2** /ˈɑːkɪtektʃə(r)/ noun [U] **1** the study of designing and making buildings **2** the style or design of a building or buildings: *modern architecture* **3** (**COMPUTING**) the design and structure of a computer system

architrave /ˈɑːkɪtreɪv/ noun [C] (**ARCHITECTURE**) the frame around a door or window

archive¹ ⓘ+ **C1** /ˈɑːkaɪv/ noun [C] (*also* **archives** [pl.]) (**HISTORY**) a collection of historical documents, etc. that show the history of a place or an organization; the place where they are kept: *archive material on the First World War*

archive² /ˈɑːkaɪv/ verb [T] **1** to put or store a document or other material in an ARCHIVE **2** (**COMPUTING**) to move information that is not often needed to a different disk, tape or other computer to store it

archway /ˈɑːtʃweɪ/ noun [C] (**ARCHITECTURE**) a passage or an entrance with an ARCH over it

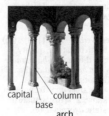

capital column
base
arch

archway

the Arctic *noun* [sing.] **(GEOGRAPHY)** the area around the North Pole ⊃ look at **Antarctic**

Arctic /ˈɑːktɪk/ *adj.* **1** **(GEOGRAPHY)** connected with the region around the North Pole (the most northern point of the world) ⊃ look at **Antarctic 2** arctic extremely cold

the Arctic Circle *noun* [sing.] **(GEOGRAPHY)** the line of LATITUDE 66° 33′ North ⊃ look at **Antarctic Circle** ⊃ picture at **earth**¹

ardent /ˈɑːdnt/ *adj.* showing strong feelings, especially a strong liking for sb/sth: *an ardent supporter of the local football team* ▸ **ardently** *adv.*

arduous /ˈɑːdʒuəs/ *adj.* full of difficulties; needing a lot of effort: *an arduous journey* ◇ *arduous work*

are /ə(r), *strong form* ɑː(r)/ → BE¹

area ?+ **A1** ❍ /ˈeəriə/ *noun* **1** [C] **(GEOGRAPHY)** a part of a town, a country or the world: *There are lots of restaurants in the area.* ◇ *The wettest areas are in the West of the country.* ◇ *built-up areas* (= where there are a lot of buildings) ◇ *Forests cover a large area of the country.* ◇ *Housing is very expensive in the Tokyo area.* **2** [C, U] **(GEOMETRY)** the size of a surface, which you can calculate by multiplying the length by the WIDTH: *The area of the office is 35 square metres.* ◇ *The office is 35 square metres in area.* ⊃ look at **volume** (1) ⊃ note at **measure**² ⊃ picture at **pressure**¹ **3** [C] a space used for a particular activity: *The hotel has a children's play area.* **4** [C] ~ **(of sth); ~ (for sth)** a particular part of a subject or activity: *Internet safety is an area of concern for many parents.* ◇ *We have identified several areas for improvement.*

arena ?+ **C1** /əˈriːnə/ *noun* [C] **1** **(SPORT)** an area with seats around it where people can watch sports and entertainment **2** (*formal*) an area of activity that concerns the public

aren't /ɑːnt/ *short form* are not

argon /ˈɑːɡɒn/ *noun* [U] (*symb.* Ar) **(CHEMISTRY)** a chemical element. Argon is a gas that does not react with anything and is used in electric lights. ❶ Argon is a **noble gas**. For more information on the periodic table of elements, look at the **Reference Section** of this dictionary.

argot /ˈɑːɡəʊ/ *noun* [U] **(LANGUAGE)** informal words and phrases that are used by a particular group of people and that other people do not easily understand

arguable /ˈɑːɡjuəbl/ *adj.* (*formal*) **1** that you can give reasons for: *It is arguable that all hospital treatment should be free.* **2** that you can give reasons against: *Whether the company should invest so much money is highly arguable.*

arguably ?+ **C1** ❍ /ˈɑːɡjuəbli/ *adv.* (often before a comparative or superlative adjective) used for giving an opinion, especially when you could give reasons to support this opinion: *He is arguably the best actor of his generation.*

argue ?+ **A2** ❍ /ˈɑːɡjuː/ *verb* **1** [I] ~ **(with sb) (about/over sth)** to say things, often angrily, that show that you do not agree with sb about sth: *The couple next door are always arguing.* ◇ *I never argue with my parents about money.* ⊃ look at **fight**¹ (4), **quarrel**² **2** [I, T] ~ **(that ...); ~ (for/against sth)** to give reasons that support your opinion about sth: *She argued that they needed more time to finish the project.* ◇ *He argued against buying a new computer.*

argument ?+ **A2** ❍ /ˈɑːɡjumənt/ *noun* **1** [C, U] ~ **(with sb) (about/over sth)** an angry discussion between two or more people who disagree with each other: *Sue had an argument with her father about politics.* ◇ *He accepted the decision without argument.* **2** [C] ~ **(for/against sth)** the reason(s) that you give to support your opinion about sth: *What are the arguments against lower taxes?*

argumentation /ˌɑːɡjumənˈteɪʃn/ *noun* [U] logical arguments used to support a theory, an action or an idea

argumentative /ˌɑːɡjuˈmentətɪv/ *adj.* often involved in or enjoying arguments

aria /ˈɑːriə/ *noun* [C] **(MUSIC)** a song for one voice, especially in an OPERA

arid /ˈærɪd/ *adj.* **(GEOGRAPHY)** (used about land or climate) very dry; with little or no rain

Aries /ˈeəriːz/ *noun* [U] the first sign of THE ZODIAC (= twelve signs that represent the positions of the sun, moon and planets), the Ram; a person born under this sign

arise ?+ **B2** ❍ /əˈraɪz/ *verb* [I] (*pt* arose /əˈrəʊz/; *pp* arisen /əˈrɪzn/) to begin to exist; to appear: *If any problems arise, let me know.*

aristocracy /ˌærɪˈstɒkrəsi/ *noun* [C + sing./pl. verb] (*pl.* -ies) **(SOCIAL STUDIES)** (in some countries) the people of the highest social class who often have special titles **SYN nobility** ▸ **aristocratic** /ˌærɪstəˈkrætɪk/ *adj.*

aristocrat /ˈærɪstəkræt/ *noun* [C] **(SOCIAL STUDIES)** (in some countries) a member of the highest social class, often with a special title

arithmetic /əˈrɪθmətɪk/ *noun* [U] **(MATHEMATICS)** the kind of mathematics that involves the adding, multiplying, etc. of numbers: *I'm not very good at mental arithmetic.*

arithmetical /ˌærɪθˈmetɪkl/ *adj.* **(MATHEMATICS)** relating to ARITHMETIC: *an arithmetical calculation*

arithmetic mean = MEAN³ (1)

arithmetic progression (*also* **arithmetic series**) *noun* [C] **(MATHEMATICS)** a series of numbers that decrease or increase by the same amount each time, for example 2, 4, 6, 8 ⊃ look at **geometric progression**

the ark /ðɪ ˈɑːk/ (*also* **Noah's ark**) *noun* [sing.] **(RELIGION)** (in the Bible) a large boat that Noah built to save his family and two of every type of animal from the flood

the arm

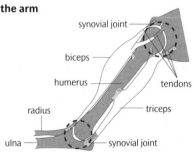

synovial joint
biceps
humerus — tendons
radius — triceps
ulna — synovial joint

arm¹ ?+ **A1** /ɑːm/ *noun* [C] **1** **(ANATOMY)** the long part at each side of the body connecting the shoulder to the hand: *He took her by the arm and led her away.* ◇ *He was carrying a magazine under his arm.* ◇ *They waved their arms in the air and shouted at us.* ◇ *I put my arm round her and tried to comfort her.* **2** the part of a piece of clothing that covers the arm **SYN sleeve 3** the part of a chair where you rest your arm

IDM arm in arm with your arm folded around sb else's arm: *The two friends walked arm in arm.* **cross/fold your arms** to cross your arms in front of your chest: *She folded her arms and waited.* ◇ *James was sitting with his arms crossed.* **twist sb's arm** → TWIST¹ **with open arms** → OPEN¹

arm² **℟+** **C1** /ɑːm/ *verb* [I, T] ~ **(yourself/sb) (with sth)** to prepare yourself/sb to fight by supplying or getting weapons: *They armed themselves with stones.* ⊃ look at **armed, arms** (1)

armadillo /ˌɑːməˈdɪləʊ/ *noun* [C] (*pl.* -os) an American animal with a hard shell, that eats insects and rolls into a ball if sth attacks it

armament /ˈɑːməmənt/ *noun* **1** [C, usually pl.] weapons, especially large guns, bombs, tanks, etc. **2** [U] (**POLITICS**) the process of increasing the amount of weapons an army or a country has, especially to prepare for war ⊃ look at **disarmament**

armature /ˈɑːmətʃə(r)/ *noun* [C] a frame that is covered to make a figure: *The figures are made from clay over a wire armature.*

armband /ˈɑːmbænd/ *noun* [C] **1** a piece of cloth that you wear around your arm: *The captain of the team wears an armband.* **2** a plastic ring filled with air that you can wear on each of your arms when you are learning to swim

armchair /ˈɑːmtʃeə(r)/ *noun* [C] a soft comfortable chair with sides that support your arms

armed **℟** **B2** /ɑːmd/ *adj.* carrying a gun or other weapon; involving weapons: *All the terrorists were armed.* ◇ *armed robbery* **OPP** **unarmed** ⊃ look at **arm², arms**

the ˌarmed ˈforces (*also* **the ˌarmed ˈservices**) *noun* [pl.] (**POLITICS**) a country's army, the **NAVY** and the **AIR FORCE**

armful /ˈɑːmfʊl/ *noun* [C] the amount that you can carry in your arms

armhole /ˈɑːmhəʊl/ *noun* [C] the opening in a piece of clothing where your arm goes through

armistice /ˈɑːmɪstɪs/ *noun* [C] (**POLITICS**) an agreement between two countries who are at war that they will stop fighting

armour (*BrE*) (*AmE* **armor**) /ˈɑːmə(r)/ *noun* [U] (**HISTORY**) clothing, often made of metal, that soldiers wore in earlier times to protect themselves: *a suit of armour*

armoured (*BrE*) (*AmE* **armored**) /ˈɑːməd/ *adj.* (used about a vehicle) covered with metal to protect it in an attack

armpit /ˈɑːmpɪt/ *noun* [C] (**ANATOMY**) the part of the body under the arm at the point where it joins the shoulder ⊃ picture at **body**

arms **℟** **B2** /ɑːmz/ *noun* [pl.] **1** weapons, especially those that are used in war ⊃ look at **arm², armed** **2** = **COAT OF ARMS**
IDM **up in arms** (*informal*) protesting angrily about sth: *The workers were up in arms over the news that the factory was going to close.*

army **℟** **A2** /ˈɑːmi/ *noun* [C + sing./pl. verb] (*pl.* -ies) **1** the military forces of a country that are trained to fight on land: *the British Army* ◇ *She joined the army at the age of 18.* ◇ *The army is/are advancing towards the border.* ◇ *an army officer* ⊃ look at **air force, navy 2** a large number of people, especially when involved in an activity together

ˈA-road *noun* [C] (in the UK) a main road, usually not as wide as a **MOTORWAY**

aroma /əˈrəʊmə/ *noun* [C] a smell, especially a pleasant one ▶ **aromatic** *adj.*

aromatherapy /əˌrəʊmədˈθerəpi/ *noun* [U] (**MEDICINE**) the use of natural oils with a pleasant smell to improve physical, emotional or mental health
▶ **aromatherapist** /-pɪst/ *noun* [C]

aromatic /ˌærəˈmætɪk/ *adj.* having a pleasant smell that is easy to notice: *aromatic oils/herbs* **SYN** **fragrant**

arose /əˈrəʊz/ past tense of **arise**

around **℟** **A1** /əˈraʊnd/ *adv.*, *prep.* **1** (*especially AmE*) (*BrE usually* **round**) surrounding sb/sth; on all sides of sth: *The park has a wall all around.* ◇ *He put his arms around her.* ◇ *We sat down around the table.* **2** (*especially AmE*) (*BrE usually* **round**) (moving) in a circle: *They walked around the lake.* **3** (*especially AmE*) (*BrE usually* **round**) on, to or from the other side of sb/sth: *We walked around to the back of the house.* ◇ *She turned around to face me.* **4** (*especially AmE*) (*BrE usually* **round**) in or to many places: *This is our office — David will show you around* (= show you the different parts of it). ◇ *They wandered around the town, looking at the shops.* **5** present in a place; available: *Is there a bank around here?* ◇ *I went to the house, but there was nobody around.* **6** approximately: *I'll see you around seven* (= at about seven o'clock). ⊃ note at **measure²** **7** used for activities with no real purpose: *'What are you doing?' 'Nothing, just lazing around.'*

arouse /əˈraʊz/ *verb* [T] **1** to cause a particular reaction in people: *to arouse somebody's curiosity/interest* **2** to make sb feel sexually excited ▶ **arousal** /əˈraʊzl/ *noun* [U]

arpeggio /ɑːˈpedʒiəʊ/ *noun* [C] (*pl.* -os) (**MUSIC**) the notes of a **CHORD** played quickly one after the other

arr. *abbr.* (in writing) arrives; arrival: *arr. York 07.15*

arraign /əˈreɪn/ *verb* [T, usually passive] to bring a person to court in order to formally accuse them of a crime ▶ **arraignment** *noun* [C, U]

arrange **℟** **A2** /əˈreɪndʒ/ *verb* **1** [T] to put sth in order or in a particular pattern: *The books were arranged in alphabetical order.* ◇ *Arrange the chairs in a circle.* ◇ *She arranged the flowers in a vase.* **2** [I, T] ~ **(for sb/sth) (to do sth)** to make plans and preparations so that sth can happen in the future: *We're arranging a surprise party for Aisha.* ◇ *He arranged for his mother to look after the baby.* ⊃ note at **meeting**

arˌranged ˈmarriage *noun* [C, U] (**SOCIAL STUDIES**) a marriage in which the parents choose the husband or wife for their child

arrangement **℟** **A2** **ⓦ** /əˈreɪndʒmənt/ *noun* **1** [C, usually pl.] ~ **(for sth)** a plan or preparation for sth that will happen in the future: *Come round this evening and we'll make arrangements for the party.* **2** [C, U] ~ **(between A and B); ~ (with sb) (to do sth)** an agreement with sb to do sth: *an arrangement between the bank and the customer* ◇ *They worked out an arrangement with another company to handle things.* ◇ *We both need to use the computer so we'll have to come to an arrangement.* ◇ *Use of the swimming pool will be by arrangement only.* **3** [C, U] ~ **(of sth)** a group of things that have been placed in a particular pattern: *an arrangement of stones in a circle* ◇ *the art of flower arrangement*

arranger /əˈreɪndʒə(r)/ *noun* [C] (**MUSIC**) a person who arranges music that has been written by sb different

array **℟+** **C1** /əˈreɪ/ *noun* [C, usually sing.] **1** a large collection of things, especially one that is impressive and is seen by other people **2** (**COMPUTING**) a way of organizing and storing related data in a computer memory **3** (**MATHEMATICS**) a set of numbers, signs or values arranged in rows and columns

arrears /əˈrɪəz/ *noun* [pl.] (**FINANCE**) money that sb owes that they should have paid earlier
IDM **be in arrears | fall/get into arrears** to be late in paying money that you owe **in arrears** if money or a person is paid **in arrears** for work, the money is paid after the work has been done

arrest¹ **℟** **B1** /əˈrest/ *verb* [T, often passive] ~ **sb (for sth/ doing sth)** (**LAW**) when the police **arrest** sb, they take them to a police station in order to question them about a crime: *The man was arrested for carrying a weapon.* ➔ note at **crime**

arrest² **ʔ** **B1** /əˈrest/ *noun* [C, U] (**LAW**) the act of arresting sb: *The police made ten arrests after the riot.* ◇ *The wanted man is now under arrest on suspicion of murder.*

arrival **ʔ** **B1** /əˈraɪvl/ *noun* **1** [C, U] (*abbr.* arr.) reaching the place to which you were travelling: *We were told on arrival that our rooms had not been reserved.* **OPP departure** (1) **2** arrivals [U] the part of an airport that you go through when you arrive on a plane: *I made my way through arrivals.* ➔ look at **departure** (4) **3** [C] people or things that have arrived: *We brought in extra chairs for the late arrivals.*

arrive **ʔ** **A1** /əˈraɪv/ *verb* [I] **1** (*abbr.* arr.) ~ (at/in ...) to reach the place to which you were travelling: *We arrived home at about midnight.* ◇ *What time does the train arrive in Newcastle?* ◇ *They arrived at the station ten minutes late.* **2** to come or happen: *The day of the wedding had finally arrived.*
PHR V arrive at sth to decide on or find sth, especially after discussion or thought: *We finally arrived at a decision.*

arrogant /ˈærəɡənt/ *adj.* thinking that you are better and more important than other people **SYN self-important** ▸ arrogance /-ɡəns/ *noun* [U] ▸ arrogantly *adv.*

arrow **ʔ+** **B2** /ˈærəʊ/ *noun* [C] **1** a thin piece of wood or metal, with a sharp point at one end, that is shot by pulling back the string on a BOW (= a curved piece of wood) and letting go: *a bow and arrow* ◇ *to fire/shoot an arrow* ➔ look at **archer** ➔ picture at **speed¹** **2** a mark or sign like an arrow (→) that is used to show direction or position: *Follow the arrows.* ◇ *Use the arrow keys to move the cursor.*

arsenal /ˈɑːsənl/ *noun* [C] **1** a collection of weapons such as guns and EXPLOSIVES **2** a building where military weapons and EXPLOSIVES are made or stored

arsenic /ˈɑːsnɪk/ *noun* [U] (*symb.* As) (**CHEMISTRY**) a chemical element. Arsenic is a grey METALLOID (= has properties of both metals and other solid substances) and is very poisonous. ❶ For more information on the periodic table of elements, look at the **Reference Section** of this dictionary.

arson /ˈɑːsn/ *noun* [U] (**LAW**) the crime of setting fire to a building deliberately

arsonist /ˈɑːsənɪst/ *noun* [C] (**LAW**) a person who deliberately sets fire to a building

art **ʔ** **A1** /ɑːt/ *noun* **1** [U] the activity or skill of producing things such as paintings, designs, etc.; the objects that are produced: *an art class* ◇ *modern art* ◇ *I've never been good at art.* ◇ *She studied history of art at university.* ◇ *an art gallery* ➔ look at **work of art 2** [C] ~ (to doing sth) a skill or sth that needs skill: *There's an art to writing a good letter.* **3** the arts [pl.] (**ARTS AND MEDIA**) art, literature, music, theatre, etc. when you think of them as a group: *The government has agreed to spend twice as much on the arts next year.* **4** [C, usually pl.] (**EDUCATION**) the subjects that you study at school or university that are not scientific, such as history or languages: *an arts degree* ➔ look at **science** (2)

art deco /ˌɑːt ˈdekəʊ/ (*also* Art Deco) *noun* [U] (**ART**) a popular style of art in the 1920s and 1930s that has GEOMETRIC (= regular) shapes with clear outlines and bright strong colours

artefact (*also* artifact *especially in AmE*) /ˈɑːtɪfækt/ *noun* [C] (**HISTORY**) an object that is made by a person, especially sth of historical or cultural interest

arteriosclerosis /ɑːˌtɪəriəʊskləˈrəʊsɪs/ *noun* [U] (**HEALTH**) a condition in which the walls of the ARTERIES (= the tubes that carry blood from the heart to the other parts of the body) become thick and hard, making it difficult for blood to flow

artery /ˈɑːtəri/ *noun* [C] (*pl.* -ies) (**ANATOMY**) one of the tubes that take blood from the heart to other parts of the body ➔ look at **carotid artery, vein** (1) ➔ picture at **circulation** ▸ arterial /ɑːˈtɪəriəl/ *adj.*: *arterial blood/disease*

artful /ˈɑːtfl/ *adj.* clever at getting what you want, sometimes by not telling the truth **SYN crafty**

art gallery (*also* gallery) *noun* [C] (**ART**) a building where paintings and other works of art are shown to the public ➔ note at **art**

art history *noun* [U] (**ART, HISTORY**) the study of the history of painting, sculpture, etc.

arthritis /ɑːˈθraɪtɪs/ *noun* [U] (**HEALTH**) a disease that causes the JOINTS (= places where the bones are connected) to become SWOLLEN (= larger than normal) and painful ▸ arthritic /-ˈθrɪtɪk/ *adj.*

arthropod /ˈɑːθrəpɒd/ *noun* [C] (**BIOLOGY**) any of the PHYLUM (= group) of animals that have a hard body without a BACKBONE in it. Arthropods have legs that are made of more than one part and that can bend where the parts join together: *Spiders, insects and crustaceans are arthropods.*

artichoke /ˈɑːtɪtʃəʊk/ *noun* [C] a green vegetable with a lot of thick pointed leaves. You can eat the bottom part of the leaves and its centre.

article **ʔ** **A1** **⊙** /ˈɑːtɪkl/ *noun* **1** [C] ~ (by sb) (on/about sth) (**ARTS AND MEDIA**) a piece of writing in a newspaper or magazine, on a website, etc: *I read an article by a well-known physicist on the subject of radiation.* **2** [C] (**LAW**) a separate item in an agreement or a contract: *Article 10 of the European Convention guarantees free speech.* **3** [C] (*formal*) an object, especially one of a set: *articles of clothing* **SYN item 4** [C] (**GRAMMAR**) the words *a, an* (= the indefinite article) or *the* (= the definite article)

articulate¹ /ɑːˈtɪkjələt/ *adj.* good at expressing your ideas clearly **OPP inarticulate**

articulate² **ʔ+** **C1** /ɑːˈtɪkjuleɪt/ *verb* [I, T] to say sth clearly or to express your ideas or feelings ▸ articulation /ɑːˌtɪkjuˈleɪʃn/ *noun* [U]

▼ COLLOCATIONS

art

An **artist** works in a **studio**. A **painter** paints **pictures**, for example **portraits** (= pictures of people), **landscapes** (= pictures of the countryside) or **abstract paintings**: *Constable was a famous landscape painter.* ◇ *Velazquez painted many portraits of King Philip IV of Spain.* A picture might be a **watercolour**, an **acrylic** or an **oil painting**. A **sculptor** makes **sculptures** of figures or objects in materials such as **marble** (= a type of stone) or **bronze** (= a type of metal). Some people collect **works of art**: *She collects nineteenth-century watercolours.* An **exhibition** is a **collection** of **works of art** which is **on display/show** for a short time in an **art gallery**: *Cezanne's landscapes will be on display at the Musée d'Orsay from 8 May.* ◇ *Kandinsky's abstract paintings were on show at MOMA last year.* Many **public galleries** have **permanent collections**. A great work of art is called a **masterpiece**: *The National Gallery has a fine collection of Impressionist masterpieces.*

articulated /ɑːˈtɪkjuleɪtɪd/ adj. (used about a large vehicle such as a lorry) with two or more sections joined together in a way that makes it easier to turn corners

artifact /ˈɑːtɪfækt/ (especially AmE) = ARTEFACT

artifice /ˈɑːtɪfɪs/ noun [U, C] (formal) the use of clever methods to trick sb

artificial ? B2 /ˌɑːtɪˈfɪʃl/ adj. **1** made or produced to copy sth natural; not real: an artificial limb ◊ artificial sweetener/fertilizer **2** created by people; not happening naturally: A job interview is a very artificial situation. ▸ **artificially** /-ʃəli/ adv.

▼ SYNONYMS

artificial

synthetic ◆ false ◆ man-made ◆ fake ◆ imitation

These words all describe things that are not real, or not naturally produced or grown.

artificial artificial flowers

synthetic synthetic drugs

false false teeth

man-made man-made fibres such as nylon

fake a fake-fur jacket

imitation imitation pearls

artificial insemination /ˌɑːtɪfɪʃl ɪnˌsemɪˈneɪʃn/ noun [U] (abbr. AI) (BIOLOGY) the scientific process of making a woman or a female animal pregnant by putting male SPERM inside her so that babies or young can be produced without sexual activity

artificial inˈtelligence = AI (1)

artificial ˈlanguage noun [C] (LANGUAGE) a language invented for international communication or for use with computers

artificial respiˈration noun [U] (MEDICINE) the process of helping a person who has stopped breathing begin to breathe again, usually by blowing into their mouth or nose

artillery /ɑːˈtɪləri/ noun **1** [U] large, heavy guns that are moved on wheels **2** the artillery [sing.] the part of the army that uses artillery

artisan /ˌɑːtɪˈzæn/ noun [C] a person who does work that needs a special skill, especially with their hands **SYN** craftsman

artist ? A1 /ˈɑːtɪst/ noun [C] **1** (ART) somebody who produces art, especially paintings or drawings ⊃ note at **art 2** (also artiste /ɑːˈtiːst/) (ARTS AND MEDIA, MUSIC) a person who is a professional singer, dancer, actor, etc: After the band broke up, Joe relaunched his career as a solo artist.

artistic ? B2 /ɑːˈtɪstɪk/ adj. (ART) **1** connected with art or artists: a work of great artistic merit **2** showing a skill in art: Elizabeth is very artistic — her drawings are excellent. ▸ **artistically** /-kli/ adv.

artistry /ˈɑːtɪstri/ noun [U] the skill of an artist

art nouveau /ˌɑːt nuːˈvəʊ, ˌɑː/ (also Art Nouveau) noun [U] (ARCHITECTURE, ART) a style of art and architecture popular in Europe and the US at the end of the nineteenth century and beginning of the twentieth century that uses complicated designs and curved patterns based on natural shapes like leaves and flowers

arts and ˈcrafts noun [pl.] (ART) activities that need both artistic and practical skills, such as making cloth, jewellery and furniture

the ˌArts and ˈCrafts Movement noun [sing.] (ART, HISTORY) a group of people in England at the end of the nineteenth century who wanted to show the importance and value of ARTS AND CRAFTS at a time when machines were being used more and more

artwork ? B2 /ˈɑːtwɜːk/ noun **1** [U] (ARTS AND MEDIA) photos, drawings, etc. that have been prepared for a book or magazine: a piece of artwork **2** [C, U] (ART) a work of art, especially one in a museum or an exhibition; a collection of works of art

arty /ˈɑːti/ adj. (artier; artiest) (informal) seeming or wanting to be very artistic or interested in the arts

arugula /əˈruːɡjələ/ (AmE) = ROCKET¹ (4)

as¹ ? A1 /əz, strong form æz/ prep. **1** used to describe sb/sth appearing to be sb/sth else: The robbers were disguised as security guards. **2** used for talking about sb/sth's job, role or function: He works as a train driver. ◊ Think of me as your friend, not as your boss. ◊ You could use this white sheet as a tablecloth.

as² ? A2 /əz, strong form æz/ conj., adv. **1** while sth else is happening: As she walked along the road, she thought about her father. **2 as … as …** used for comparing people or things: Todor's almost as tall as me. ◊ Todor's almost as tall as I am. ◊ It's not as cold as it was yesterday. ◊ I'd like an appointment **as soon as possible**. ◊ She earns twice **as much as** her husband. ◊ I haven't got as many books as you have. **3** in a particular way, state, etc.; like: Please do as I tell you. ◊ Leave the room **as it is**. Don't move anything. **4** because: I didn't buy the dress as I decided it was too expensive. **5** used at the beginning of a comment about what you are saying: **As you know**, I've decided to leave at the end of the month. **IDM as for** used when you are starting to talk about a different person or thing: Gianni's upstairs. As for Andreas, I've no idea where he is. **as from** | **as of** starting from a particular time: As from next week, Tim Shaw will be managing this department. **as if** | **as though** used for saying how sb/sth appears: She looks as if/though she's just got out of bed. **as it were** used for saying that sth is only true in a certain way: She felt, as it were, a stranger in her own house. **as to** about a particular thing; concerning: I was given no instructions as to how to begin. **as yet** → YET¹

ASA /ˌeɪ es ˈeɪ/ abbr. **Advertising Standards Authority** (an organization in the UK that controls the standard of advertising)

asap /ˌeɪ es eɪ ˈpiː, ˈeɪsæp/ abbr. as soon as possible

asbestos /æsˈbestɒs/ noun [U] a soft grey material that does not burn and was used in the past to protect against heat

ascend /əˈsend/ verb [I, T] (formal) to go up: The road ascends steeply from the harbour. ◊ (figurative) to ascend the throne (= become king or queen) **OPP descend** ▸ ascending adj.: The questions are arranged **in ascending order** of difficulty (= the most difficult ones are at the end). ▸ **ascension** /əˈsenʃn/ noun [C]

Asˈcension Day noun [U, C] (RELIGION) (in the Christian religion) the 40th day after Easter when Christians remember Christ leaving the earth and going to heaven

ascent /əˈsent/ noun [C, usually sing.] **1** the act of climbing or going up: the ascent of Mont Blanc **2** a path or hill leading upwards: There was a steep ascent before the path became flat again. **OPP descent**

ascertain /ˌæsəˈteɪn/ verb [T] ~ (that …) (formal) to find sth out: Experts ascertained that the portrait was by Leonardo Da Vinci.

find out certain information

ascetic /ə'setɪk/ adj. (**RELIGION**) not allowing yourself physical pleasures, especially for religious reasons
▶ ascetic noun [C]

ASCII /'æski/ abbr. (**COMPUTING**) **American Standard Code for Information Interchange** (a system that allows data to be moved between computers that use different programs)

ascorbic acid /ə,skɔːbɪk 'æsɪd/ = VITAMIN C

ascribe /ə'skraɪb/ verb
PHR V ascribe sth to sb to say that sth was written by or belonged to sb: Many people ascribe this play to Shakespeare. ascribe sth to sb/sth to say what caused sth: He ascribed his forgetfulness to old age.

ASD /,eɪ es 'diː/ noun [U] (**PSYCHOLOGY**) a mental DISORDER in which a person finds it very difficult to communicate or form relationships with others and often shows limited or repeated patterns of thought and behaviour (the abbreviation for 'autism/autistic spectrum disorder') **SYN** autism

ASEAN /'æsiæn/ abbr. **Association of Southeast Asian Nations** (an economic and political association of certain countries in south-east Asia)

aseptic /,eɪ'septɪk/ adj. (**HEALTH**) not having any harmful bacteria

asexual /,eɪ'sekʃuəl/ adj. **1** (**BIOLOGY**) not involving sex; not having sex organs: asexual reproduction **2** not having sexual qualities; not interested in sex
▶ asexually /-ʃəli/ adv.: to reproduce asexually

ash ﾟ+ **C1** /æʃ/ noun **1** [U] the grey or black powder that is left after sth has burned: cigarette ash ◇ the ashes of a fire ⇒ picture at **volcano 2** ashes [pl.] what is left after a dead person has been CREMATED (= burned after death) **3** (also 'ash tree) [C] a type of forest tree that grows in cool countries

ashamed ﾟ **B2** /ə'ʃeɪmd/ adj. [not before noun] ~ (of sth/sb/yourself) (for doing sth); ~ (that …) feeling guilty or embarrassed about sb/sth or because of sth you have done: She was ashamed of her old clothes. ◇ He was ashamed of himself for having lied. ◇ She felt ashamed that she hadn't helped him.
OPP unashamed

ashen /'æʃn/ adj. (used about sb's face) very pale; without colour because of illness or fear

ashore /ə'ʃɔː(r)/ adv. onto the land from the sea, a river, etc: The passengers went ashore for an hour while the ship was in port. ⇒ look at **shore**[1]

ashram /'æʃrəm/ noun [C] (**RELIGION**) a place where Hindus who want to live away from society live together as a group; a place where other Hindus go for a short time to say prayers

Asian[1] /'eɪʒn, 'eɪʃn/ adj. of or connected with Asia

Asian[2] /'eɪʒn, 'eɪʃn/ noun [C] a person from Asia, or whose family came from Asia

Asian A'merican noun [C] a person from America whose family was originally from Asia, especially East Asia ▶ Asian-A'merican adj.

aside[1] ﾟ+ **B2** /ə'saɪd/ adv. **1** on or to one side; out of the way: We stood aside to let the man go past. **2** to be kept separately, for a special purpose: I try to set aside a little money each month. **3** used after nouns to say that except for one thing, sth is true: Money worries aside, things are going well.

aside[2] /ə'saɪd/ noun [C] (**ARTS AND MEDIA**) (in the theatre) something that a character in a play says to the audience, but that the other characters on stage are not intended to hear

a'side from (especially AmE) = APART FROM

ask ﾟ **A1** /ɑːsk/ verb
• A QUESTION **1** [I, T] ~ (sb) (sth); ~ (sb) (about sth/sb) to put a question to sb in order to find out some

information: He asked me the time. ◇ I asked him about the festival. ◇ Ask him how old he is. ◇ She asked if I wanted tea or coffee. ◇ 'What's the time?' he asked. ◇ He asked what the time was.
• REQUEST **2** [I, T] ~ (sb) (for sth); ~ (sth) (of sb); ~ (sb) (to do sth) to request that sb gives you sth or does sth for you: She sat down and asked for a cup of coffee. ◇ Don't ask Joe for money — he hasn't got any. ◇ You are asking too much of him — he can't possibly do all that! ◇ I asked him to drive me home. ◇ I asked him if he would drive me home. ⇒ note at **demand**[2]
• PERMISSION **3** [I] ~ (to do sth) to request permission to do sth: I'm sure she'll let you go if you ask. ◇ I asked to speak to a supervisor. ◇ We asked the teacher if we could go home early.
• INVITE **4** [T] ~ sb (to sth) to invite sb: They've asked us to dinner. ◇ We must ask the neighbours round (= to our house).
• SAY A PRICE **5** [T] ~ sth (for sth) to say the price that you want for sth: How much are they asking for their car?
IDM be asking for trouble | be asking for it to behave in a way that will almost certainly cause you problems: Driving when you're tired is just asking for trouble. if you ask me if you want my opinion
PHR V ask after sb to ask about sb's health or to ask for news of sb: Tina asked after you today. ask sb out to invite sb to go out with you, especially as a way of starting a romantic relationship: Harry's too shy to ask her out.

▼ SYNONYMS

ask

enquire/inquire • demand • query

All these words mean to say or write sth in the form of a question, in order to get information.

ask Can I ask you a question?

enquire/inquire (formal) I emailed the company to enquire about work experience.

demand 'Where have you been?' he demanded angrily.

query (formal) 'Why ever not?' she queried.

askew /ə'skjuː/ adv., adj. [not before noun] not in a straight or level position

'asking price noun [C] (**FINANCE**) the price that sb wants to sell sth for ⇒ look at **cost price**, **selling price**

asleep ﾟ **A2** /ə'sliːp/ adj. [not before noun] sleeping: The baby is fast/sound asleep. ◇ It didn't take me long to fall asleep last night. **OPP** awake[1]

asp /æsp/ noun [C] a small poisonous snake found especially in North Africa

asparagus /ə'spærəgəs/ noun [U] a plant with green or white STEMS (= the long thin parts) that are cooked and eaten as a vegetable

aspect ﾟ **B2** ⦿ /'æspekt/ noun **1** [C] one of the qualities or parts of a situation, an idea, a problem, etc: the most important aspect of the debate **2** [U, sing.] (formal) the appearance of a place, situation or person: Events began to take on a more sinister aspect.

'Asperger's syndrome (also Asperger's /'æspɜːgəz/) noun [U] (**PSYCHOLOGY**) a mental DISORDER related to AUTISM in which a person finds it difficult to communicate or form relationships with others

asphalt /'æsfælt/ noun [U] a thick black substance that is used for making the surface of roads

asphyxia /əs'fɪksiə/ noun [U] (**HEALTH**) the state of being unable to breathe, causing death or loss of CONSCIOUSNESS

asphyxiate /əsˈfɪksieɪt/ *verb* [T] to make sb become unconscious or die by preventing them from breathing: *He was asphyxiated by the smoke.* ▶ **asphyxiation** /əsˌfɪksiˈeɪʃn/ *noun* [U]

aspic /ˈæspɪk/ *noun* [U] clear JELLY (= a soft, solid substance), that food is sometimes put into when it is being served cold

aspirate /ˈæspərət/ *noun* [C] (**LANGUAGE**) a consonant pronounced with a clear breath sound that can be heard, for example /h/ in *house* ▶ **aspirate** /-reɪt/ *verb* [T]

aspire 🔒+ **C1** /əˈspaɪə(r)/ *verb* [I] ~ **(to do sth)** (*formal*) to have a strong desire to have or do sth: *an aspiring actor* ◇ *She aspired to become managing director.* ▶ **aspiration** 🔒+ **C1** /ˌæspəˈreɪʃn/ *noun* [C, U]

aspirin /ˈæsprɪn, ˈæspərɪn/ *noun* [C, U] (**MEDICINE**) a drug used to reduce pain and a high temperature

assailant /əˈseɪlənt/ *noun* [C] (*formal*) (**LAW**) a person who attacks sb

assassin /əˈsæsɪn/ *noun* [C] a person who kills a famous or important person, especially for money or for political reasons

assassinate /əˈsæsɪneɪt/ *verb* [T, often passive] to kill a famous or important person, especially for money or for political reasons: *The politician was assassinated by an extremist.* ⊃ note at **kill**[1] ▶ **assassination** 🔒+ **C1** /əˌsæsɪˈneɪʃn/ *noun* [C, U]

assault 🔒+ **C1** /əˈsɔːlt/ *noun* [C, U] ~ **(on sb/sth)** a sudden attack on sb/sth: *Assaults on elderly people are becoming more common.* ▶ **assault** 🔒+ **C1** *verb* [T]: *He was charged with assaulting a police officer.*

asˈsault course (*BrE*) (*AmE* **obstacle course**) *noun* [C] (**SPORT**) an area of land with many objects that are difficult to climb, jump over or go through, that is used, especially by soldiers, for improving physical skills and strength

assemble 🔒+ **C1** /əˈsembl/ *verb* **1** [I, T] to come together or bring sb/sth together in a group: *The management team assembled in the main meeting room.* ◇ *I've assembled all the information I need for my essay.* **2** [T] to fit the parts of sth together: *We spent hours trying to assemble our new bookshelves.* ⊃ note at **build**[1]

assembly 🔒+ **C1** /əˈsembli/ *noun* (*pl.* -ies) **1** (*also* **Assembly**) [C] (**POLITICS**) a group of people who have been elected to meet together regularly and make decisions or laws for a particular region or country: *state/legislative/federal/local assemblies* ◇ *the UN General Assembly* **2** [U, C] (**EDUCATION**) the meeting together of a group of people for a particular purpose; a group of people who meet together for a particular purpose: *freedom of assembly* (= the right to have public meetings) ◇ *school assembly* (= a regular meeting for all the students and teachers of a school) ◇ *an assembly point* (= a place where people have been asked to meet) **3** [U] the process of putting together the parts of sth such as a vehicle or piece of furniture

asˈsembly line *noun* [C] (**BUSINESS**) a line of people and machines in a factory that fit the parts of sth together in a fixed order

assemblyman /əˈsemblimən/, **assemblywoman** /əˈsembliwʊmən/ *noun* [C] (*pl.* -men /-mən/, -women /-wɪmɪn/) (**POLITICS**) a person who is an elected representative in a state ASSEMBLY in the US

assent /əˈsent/ *noun* [U] ~ **(to sth)** (*formal*) official agreement to sth: *The committee gave their assent to the proposed changes.* ▶ **assent** *verb* [I] ~ **(to sth)**: *Nobody would assent to the terms he proposed.*

assert 🔒+ **C1** **W** /əˈsɜːt/ *verb* [T] **1** ~ **(that …)** to say sth clearly and FIRMLY: *He asserted that the allegations were untrue.* **2** ~ **yourself/sth** to behave in a determined and confident way in order to make people listen to you or to get what you want: *You ought to assert yourself more.* ◇ *to assert your authority*

assertion 🔒+ **C1** **W** /əˈsɜːʃn/ *noun* (*formal*) **1** [C] ~ **(that …)** a statement that says you strongly believe that sth is true: *his confident assertion that he would win* ⊃ note at **claim**[2] **2** [U, C] ~ **of sth** the act of showing, using or stating sth strongly: *the assertion of power*

assertive /əˈsɜːtɪv/ *adj.* expressing your opinion clearly and FIRMLY so that people listen to you or do what you want ▶ **assertively** *adv.* ▶ **assertiveness** *noun* [U]

assess 🔒 **B2** **W** /əˈses/ *verb* [T] **1** to judge or form an opinion about sth: *It's too early to assess the effects of the price rises.* **2** ~ **sth (at …)** to guess or decide the amount or value of sth: *The damage was assessed at £10 000.* ▶ **assessable** *adj.*

assessment 🔒 **B2** **W** /əˈsesmənt/ *noun* **1** [C] an opinion or a judgement about sb/sth that has been thought about very carefully: *I made a careful assessment of the risks involved.* **2** [U] the act of judging or forming an opinion about sb/sth **3** [U] (**EDUCATION**) the process of testing students: *written exams and other forms of assessment* ⊃ look at **continuous assessment**

assessor /əˈsesə(r)/ *noun* [C] **1** (**LAW**) an expert in a particular subject who is asked by a court or another official group to give advice **2** (**FINANCE**) a person who calculates the value or cost of sth or the amount of money to be paid: *an insurance/a tax assessor* **3** a person who judges how well sb has done in an exam, a competition, etc: *Marks are awarded by an external assessor.*

asset 🔒+ **B2** /ˈæset/ *noun* [C] **1** ~ **(to sb/sth)** a person or thing that is useful to sb/sth: *She's a great asset to the organization.* **2** [usually pl.] (**FINANCE**) something of value that a person, company, etc. owns

assiduous /əˈsɪdʒuəs/ *adj.* (*formal*) working very hard and taking great care that everything is done as well as it can be **SYN** **diligent** ▶ **assiduously** *adv.*

assign 🔒+ **B2** **W** /əˈsaɪn/ *verb* [T] **1** ~ **sth to sb/sth**; ~ **sb sth** to give sth to sb for a particular purpose: *We have assigned 20% of our budget to the project.* ◇ *They have been assigned a classroom.* **2** ~ **sb to sth** to give sb a particular job to do: *A detective was assigned to the case.*

assignment 🔒 **B1** /əˈsaɪnmənt/ *noun* [C, U] a job or type of work that you are given to do: *The reporter disappeared while on (an) assignment in the war zone.*

assimilate /əˈsɪməleɪt/ *verb* **1** [I, T] ~ **(to/into sth)** (**SOCIAL STUDIES**) to become, or allow sb/sth to become, part of a country, a social group, etc. rather than remaining in a separate group: *Many immigrants find it difficult to assimilate into society.* ◇ *to assimilate people of other cultures* **2** [T] to learn and understand sth: *to assimilate new facts/information/ideas* ▶ **assimilation** /əˌsɪməˈleɪʃn/ *noun* [U]

assist 🔒 **B1** /əˈsɪst/ *verb* [I, T] ~ **(sb) (in sth/doing sth)**; ~ **(sb) (with sth)** (*formal*) to help: *Volunteers assisted the police in the search for the boy.* ◇ *Ben pays a student to assist him with his research.*

assistance 🔒+ **B2** /əˈsɪstəns/ *noun* [U] **(with the)** ~ **(of sb/ sth)** (*formal*) help or support: *financial assistance for poorer families* ◇ *Can I be of any assistance?* ◇ *She shouted for help but nobody came to her assistance.*

◇ *The suspects were tracked down with the assistance of a police dog.*

assistant¹ ? 🅐🅐 /əˈsɪstənt/ *noun* [C] **1** (*abbr.* Asst) **~(to sb)** a person who helps or supports sb, usually in their job: *The director is away today. Would you like to speak to her assistant?* ◇ *He's assistant to the Sales Manager.* ⊃ look at **personal assistant 2** (*BrE*) = SHOP ASSISTANT

assistant² ? 🅐🅐 /əˈsɪstənt/ *adj.* [only before noun] (often in titles) (*abbr.* Asst) having a rank below that of a senior person and helping them in their work: *the assistant manager* ◇ *Assistant Attorney General William Weld*

Assoc. *abbr.* (in writing) = ASSOCIATION (1)

associate¹ ? 🅑🅲 🅦 /əˈsəʊsieɪt, əˈsəʊʃi-/ *verb* **1** [T] **~sth/sb (with sth/sb)** to make a connection between people or things in your mind: *I always associate the smell of the sea with my childhood.* **2** [I] **~with sb** to spend time with sb: *I prefer not to associate with colleagues outside work.* **3** [T] **~yourself with sth** (*formal*) to say that you support sth or agree with sth **OPP disassociate**

associate² /əˈsəʊsiət, əˈsəʊʃi-/ *adj.* (BUSINESS) **1** a person that you work with, do business with or spend a lot of time with: *business associates* **2** of a lower rank or having fewer rights in a particular profession or organization: *associate membership of the European Union* ◇ *an associate member/director*

associate³ /əˈsəʊsiət, əˈsəʊʃi-/ *noun* [C] (BUSINESS) a person that you meet and get to know through your work: *a business associate*

associated ? 🅑🅲 🅢 /əˈsəʊsieɪtɪd, əˈsəʊʃi-/ *adj.* **1 ~(with sth/doing sth)** if one thing is **associated** with another, the two things are connected: *the risks associated with taking drugs* ◇ *illnesses associated with obesity* **2 ~with sth** if a person is associated with an organization, etc. they support it: *He no longer wished to be associated with the firm.*

association ? 🅑🅲 🅦 /əˌsəʊsiˈeɪʃn, əˌsəʊʃi-/ *noun* **1** [C] (*abbr.* Assoc.) a group of people or organizations who work together for a particular purpose: *the National Association of Language Teachers* **2** [C, U] **~(with sb/sth)** a connection or relationship between people or organizations: *his alleged association with terrorist groups* ◇ *We work in association with our New York office.* **3** [C, usually pl.] **~(with sb/sth); ~(between A and B)** an idea or a memory that sb/sth makes you think about; the act of connecting one person or thing with another in your mind: *Many people have positive associations with music.* ◇ *The cat soon made the association between human beings and food.*

assonance /ˈæsənəns/ *noun* [U] (LANGUAGE) the effect created when two syllables in words that are close together have the same vowel sound, but different consonants, or the same consonants but different vowels, for example, *seen* and *beat* or *cold* and *killed*

assorted /əˈsɔːtɪd/ *adj.* of different types; mixed

assortment /əˈsɔːtmənt/ *noun* [C, usually sing.] a group of different things or of different types of the same thing **SYN mixture**

Asst *abbr.* (in writing) = ASSISTANT²

assuage /əˈsweɪdʒ/ *verb* [T] (*formal*) to make an unpleasant feeling less strong: *He hoped that by confessing he could assuage his guilt.*

assume ? 🅑🅲 🅞 /əˈsjuːm/ *verb* **1 ~(that) … ; ~(sb/ sth to be, have, etc. sth)** to accept or believe that sth is true even though you have no proof; to expect sth to be true: *I assume (that) you have the necessary documents.* ◇ *Everyone assumed Ralph to be guilty.* **2** (*formal*) to pretend to have or be sb/sth: *to assume a*

false name **3** (*formal*) to begin to use power or to have a powerful position: *to assume control of something*

assuming /əˈsjuːmɪŋ/ *conj.* **~(that) …** used to suppose that sth is true so that you can talk about what the results might be: *Assuming (that) he's still alive, how old would he be now?*

assumption ? ＋ 🅑🅲 🅞 /əˈsʌmpʃn/ *noun* **1** [C] **~(that …);** **~(about sb/sth)** something that you accept is true even though you have no proof: *We'll work on the assumption that the guests will be hungry when they arrive.* ◇ *a reasonable/false assumption* ◇ *It's unfair to make assumptions about somebody's character before you know them.* **2** [U] **~of sth** (*formal*) the act of taking power or of starting an important job: *the assumption of power by the army*

assurance ? ＋ 🅲🅵 /əˈʃʊərəns, əˈʃɔːr-/ *noun* **1** [C] **~(that …)** a promise that sth will certainly happen or be true: *They gave me an assurance that the work would be finished by Friday.* **SYN guarantee¹** **2** (also self-assurance) [U] the belief that you can do or succeed at sth **SYN confidence**

assure ? ＋ 🅑🅲 /əˈʃʊə(r), əˈʃɔː(r)/ *verb* [T] **1 ~sb (that) … ;** **~sb (of sth)** to promise sb that sth will certainly happen or be true, especially if they are worried: *I assure you (that) it is perfectly safe.* ◇ *Let me assure you of my full support.* **2** to make sth sure or certain: *The success of the new product assured the survival of the company.*

assured /əˈʃʊəd, əˈʃɔːd/ (also self-assured) *adj.* believing that you can do sth or succeed at sth **SYN confident**

astatine /ˈæstətiːn/ *noun* [U] (*symb.* At) (CHEMISTRY) a chemical element. Astatine is a RADIOACTIVE substance found in small amounts in nature and produced artificially for use in medicine. ❶ For more information on the periodic table of elements, look at the **Reference Section** of this dictionary.

asterisk /ˈæstərɪsk/ *noun* [C] (LANGUAGE) the symbol (*) that you use to make people notice sth in a piece of writing

asteroid /ˈæstərɔɪd/ *noun* [C] (ASTRONOMY) a very large piece of rock that goes around the sun ⊃ picture at **solar system**

asthma /ˈæsmə/ *noun* [U] (HEALTH) a medical condition of the chest that makes breathing difficult

asthmatic /æsˈmætɪk/ *noun* [C] (HEALTH) a person who has ASTHMA ▸ **asthmatic** *adj.*

astigmatism /əˈstɪɡmətɪzəm/ *noun* [C] (HEALTH) a fault in the shape of a person's eye that prevents them from seeing clearly

astonish /əˈstɒnɪʃ/ *verb* [T] to surprise sb very much: *She astonished everybody by announcing her engagement.* **SYN amaze** ▸ **astonished** *adj.*: *I was astonished by the decision.*

astonishing ? ＋ 🅑🅲 /əˈstɒnɪʃɪŋ/ *adj.* very surprising **SYN amazing** ▸ **astonishingly** *adv.*

astonishment /əˈstɒnɪʃmənt/ *noun* [U] very great surprise: *He dropped his book in astonishment.* **SYN amazement**

astound /əˈstaʊnd/ *verb* [T, usually passive] to surprise sb very much: *We were astounded by how well he performed.* **SYN amaze**

astounded /əˈstaʊndɪd/ *adj.* feeling or showing great surprise

astounding /əˈstaʊndɪŋ/ *adj.* causing sb to feel extremely surprised ▸ **astoundingly** *adv.*

astray /əˈstreɪ/ adv.
IDM **go astray** to become lost or be stolen **lead sb astray** → LEAD¹

astride /əˈstraɪd/ prep., adv. with one leg on each side of sth: *to sit astride a horse*

astringent /əˈstrɪndʒənt/ adj. **1** (MEDICINE) (used about a liquid or cream) able to stop the loss of blood from a cut, or to make the skin tighter so that it feels less OILY: *an astringent cream* **2** (formal) critical in a severe or clever way: *astringent comments* **3** (formal) slightly bitter but fresh in taste or smell ▶ **astringent** noun [C]

astrobiology /ˌæstrəʊbaɪˈɒlədʒi/ noun [U] (ASTRONOMY, BIOLOGY) the scientific study of life on other planets ▶ **astrobiologist** /-dʒɪst/ noun [C]

astrolabe /ˈæstrəleɪb/ noun [C] (ASTRONOMY) a device used in the past for measuring the distances of stars, planets etc. from the earth, and for calculating the position of a ship

astrologer /əˈstrɒlədʒə(r)/ noun [C] a person who uses the positions of the stars and the movements of the planets to tell people about their character, what might happen to them in the future, etc.

astrology /əˈstrɒlədʒi/ noun [U] the study of the positions and movements of the stars and planets and the way that some people believe they affect people and events ⊃ look at **horoscope**, **zodiac**

astronaut /ˈæstrənɔːt/ noun [C] a person who works and travels in a SPACECRAFT

astronomer /əˈstrɒnəmə(r)/ noun [C] (ASTRONOMY) a scientist who studies the sun, moon, stars, etc.

astronomical /ˌæstrəˈnɒmɪkl/ adj. **1** (ASTRONOMY) connected with ASTRONOMY **2** (also astronomic /ˌæstrəˈnɒmɪk/) (informal) (used about an amount, a price, etc.) extremely large: *astronomical house prices* ▶ **astronomically** /-kli/ adv.

astronomy /əˈstrɒnəmi/ noun [U] the scientific study of the sun, moon, stars, etc.

astrophysics /ˌæstrəʊˈfɪzɪks/ noun [U] (ASTRONOMY, PHYSICS) the scientific study of the physical and chemical structure of the stars, planets, etc. ▶ **astrophysicist** /-zɪsɪst/ noun [C]

astute /əˈstjuːt/ adj. very clever; good at judging people or situations

asylum ⭐+ **C1** /əˈsaɪləm/ noun **1** (also formal political asylum) [U] (POLITICS, SOCIAL STUDIES) protection that a government gives to people who have left their own country, usually because they were in danger for political reasons: *to seek/apply for/be granted asylum* **2** [C] (old-fashioned) (MEDICINE) a hospital where people who were mentally ill could be cared for, often for a long time

aˈsylum seeker noun [C] (POLITICS, SOCIAL STUDIES) a person who has been forced to leave their own country because they are in danger and who arrives in another country asking to be allowed to stay there

asymmetric /ˌeɪsɪˈmetrɪk/ (also asymmetrical /ˌeɪsɪˈmetrɪkl/) adj. (GEOMETRY) having two sides or parts that are not the same in size or shape **OPP** **symmetrical** ▶ **asymmetrically** /-kli/ adv. ▶ **asymmetry** /ˌeɪˈsɪmətri/ noun [U]

ˌasymmetric ˈbars (BrE) (also uneven bars BrE, AmE) noun [pl.] (SPORT) two bars on posts of different heights that are used by women for doing GYMNASTIC exercises ⊃ look at **parallel bars**

asymptomatic /ˌeɪsɪmptəˈmætɪk/ adj. (HEALTH) (used about a person or an illness) having no symptoms

at ⭐ **A1** /ət, strong form æt/ prep. **1** used to show where sb/sth is or where sth happens: *at the bottom/top of the page* ◇ *He was standing at the door.* ◇ *Change trains at Chester.* ◇ *We were at home all weekend.* ◇ *Are the children at school?* ◇ *'Where's Peter?' 'He's at Sue's.'* (= at Sue's house) **2** used to show when sth happens: *I start work at nine o'clock.* ◇ *at the weekend* ◇ *at night* ◇ *at Easter* ◇ *She got married at 18* (= when she was 18). **3** in the direction of sb/sth: *What are you looking at?* ◇ *He pointed a gun at the policeman.* ◇ *Don't shout at me!* **4** because of sth: *I was surprised at her behaviour.* ◇ *We laughed at his jokes.* **5** used to show what sb is doing or what is happening: *They were hard at work.* ◇ *The two countries were at war.* **6** used to show the price, rate, speed, etc. of sth: *We were travelling at about 50 miles per hour.* **7** used with adjectives that show how well sb/sth does sth: *She's not very good at French.* **8** /æt/ (COMPUTING) the symbol (@) used in email addresses

ate /et, eɪt/ past tense of **eat**

atheism /ˈeɪθiɪzəm/ noun [U] (RELIGION) the belief that there is no God ▶ **atheist** /-θiɪst/ noun [C] ▶ **atheistic** /ˌeɪθiˈɪstɪk/ adj.

athlete ⭐ **A2** /ˈæθliːt/ noun [C] (SPORT) **1** a person who takes part in sports competitions **2** (BrE) a person who takes part in sports competitions that involve running, jumping and throwing **3** a person who is good at sports and physical exercise

athletic /æθˈletɪk/ adj. (SPORT) **1** connected with athletes or ATHLETICS: *athletic ability* **2** (used about a person) having a fit, strong, and healthy body ▶ **athletically** /-kli/ adv. ▶ **athleticism** /-tɪsɪzəm/ noun [U]: *She moved with great athleticism about the court.*

athletics /æθˈletɪks/ (BrE) (AmE track and field) noun [U] (SPORT) sports such as running, jumping and throwing

atlas /ˈætləs/ noun [C] (pl. atlases) (GEOGRAPHY) a book of maps: *a road atlas of Europe*

ATM /ˌeɪ tiː ˈem/ noun [C] a machine in or outside a bank, shop, etc., from which you can get money from your bank account using a special plastic card (the abbreviation for 'automated/automatic teller machine') **SYN** **cash machine**

ˈATM card (AmE) = CASH CARD

atmosphere ⭐ **B1** /ˈætməsfɪə(r)/ noun **1** (usually the atmosphere) [C, usually sing.] (ASTRONOMY) the mixture of gases that surrounds the earth or another planet, star, etc: *the earth's atmosphere* ◇ *Saturn's atmosphere* ⊃ note at **water**¹ **2** [C] the air in a place: *a smoky atmosphere* **3** [sing.] the mood or feeling of a place or situation: *The atmosphere of the meeting was relaxed.*

atmospheric /ˌætməsˈferɪk/ adj. **1** [only before noun] (ASTRONOMY) connected with the earth's atmosphere: *atmospheric pollution/conditions/pressure* **2** creating a particular feeling or emotion: *atmospheric music*

atoll /ˈætɒl/ noun [C] (GEOGRAPHY, GEOLOGY) an island made of CORAL (= a hard red, pink or white substance that forms in the sea from the bones of very small sea animals) and shaped like a ring with a lake of salt water in the middle

asymmetric bars/uneven bars   parallel bars

atom /ˈætəm/ *noun* [C] (**CHEMISTRY, PHYSICS**) the smallest part into which a chemical element can be divided: *the splitting of the atom* ◇ *Two atoms of hydrogen combine with one atom of oxygen to form a molecule of water.* ◇ (*figurative*) *There isn't an atom of* (= there is no) *truth in these rumours.* ⊃ look at **molecule**

atomic /əˈtɒmɪk/ *adj.* (**CHEMISTRY, PHYSICS**) **1** connected with ATOMS or an ATOM: *atomic structure* ⊃ look at **nuclear** (2) **2** related to the energy that is produced when ATOMS are split; related to weapons that use this energy: *atomic energy/power* ⊃ look at **nuclear** (1)

a‚tomic 'bomb (*also* **A-bomb**, '**atom bomb**) *noun* [C] a bomb that explodes using the energy that is produced when an ATOM or ATOMS are split

a‚tomic 'clock *noun* [C] an extremely accurate clock that uses the movement of ATOMS or MOLECULES to measure time

a‚tomic 'energy = NUCLEAR ENERGY

a‚tomic 'mass *noun* [C] (**CHEMISTRY**) the average MASS of all the ATOMS of a chemical element: *Oxygen has an atomic mass of 16.*

a‚tomic 'number *noun* [C] (**CHEMISTRY, PHYSICS**) the number of PROTONS in the NUCLEUS (= central part) of an ATOM of a particular chemical element ❶ Elements are arranged in the **periodic table** according to their **atomic number**. For more information on the periodic table of elements, look at the **Reference Section** of this dictionary.

atonal /eɪˈtəʊnl/ *adj.* (**MUSIC**) (used about a piece of music) not written in any particular KEY (= a set of musical notes based on one note)

atone /əˈtəʊn/ *verb* [I] ~ (**for sth**) (*formal*) to act in a way that shows you are sorry for doing sth wrong: *to atone for your crimes* ▸ **atonement** *noun* [U]

atrium /ˈeɪtriəm/ *noun* [C] (*pl.* atria /-triə/) **1** (**ARCHITECTURE**) a large high open space in the centre of a modern building **2** (**HISTORY**) an open space in the centre of an ancient Roman VILLA (= a large house) **3** (**ANATOMY**) either of the two upper spaces in the heart ⊃ look at **ventricle** (1) ⊃ picture at **heart**

layers of the earth's atmosphere

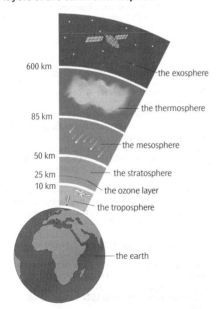

- 600 km — the exosphere
- 85 km — the thermosphere
- — the mesosphere
- 50 km
- 25 km — the stratosphere
- 10 km — the ozone layer
- — the troposphere
- — the earth

atrocious /əˈtrəʊʃəs/ *adj.* extremely bad: *atrocious weather* **SYN terrible** ▸ **atrociously** *adv.*

atrocity 𝄞+ **C1** /əˈtrɒsəti/ *noun* [C, U] (*pl.* **-ies**) a cruel and violent act: *Both sides were accused of committing atrocities during the war.*

atrophy /ˈætrəfi/ *noun* [U] (**HEALTH**) the medical condition of losing fat, muscle, strength, etc. in a part of the body because it does not have enough blood

attach 𝄞 **B1** /əˈtætʃ/ *verb* [T] **1** ~ **sth (to sth)** to fasten or join sth to sth: *I attach a copy of the spreadsheet* (= send it with an email). ◇ *I attached a label to each bag.* **OPP detach 2** (**COMPUTING**) to send an electronic document with an email: *I attach a copy of the spreadsheet.* **3** ~ **importance, significance, value, weight to sth** to think that sth is important or worth thinking about: *Don't attach too much importance to what they say.*
IDM (**with**) **no strings attached** → STRING[1]

attaché /əˈtæʃeɪ/ *noun* [C] (**POLITICS**) a person who works in an EMBASSY and who usually has special responsibility for a particular area of activity: *a cultural/military attaché*

attached /əˈtætʃt/ *adj.* **1** ~ **(to sth)** joined to sth: *Please complete the attached application form.* ◇ *The board was attached to the wall.* **2** [not before noun] ~ **(to sb/ sth)** liking sb/sth very much **3** ~ **to sth** working for or forming part of an organization: *The research unit is attached to the university.*

attachment 𝄞+ **B2** /əˈtætʃmənt/ *noun* **1** [C] (**COMPUTING**) a document that you send to sb using email **2** [C] something that you can fit on sth else to make it do a different job: *an electric drill with a range of attachments* **3** [C, U] ~ **(to sb/sth)** the feeling of liking sb/sth very much: *emotional attachment* ◇ *I feel a strong attachment to this house.*

attack¹ 𝄞 **A2 ⑤** /əˈtæk/ *noun* **1** [C, U] ~ **(on/against sb/ sth)**; ~ **(from sb/sth)** an act of trying to hurt or defeat sb/sth by using force: *The rebel forces **launched an attack** on the capital.* ◇ *The town was **under attack** from all sides.* **2** [C, U] ~ **(on sb/sth)** an act of saying strongly that you do not like or agree with sb/sth: *an outspoken attack on government policy* **3** [C] ~ **(of sth)** (**HEALTH**) a sudden, short period of illness, usually severe: *an attack of fever* ◇ *to **suffer an** asthma **attack**.* ⊃ look at **heart attack 4** [C] (**SPORT**) the act of trying to score a point in a game of sport

attack² 𝄞 **A2 ⑤** /əˈtæk/ *verb* **1** [I, T] to try to hurt or defeat sb/sth by using force: *The child was attacked by a dog.* ◇ *The enemy attacked at night.* **2** [T] to say strongly that you do not like or agree with sb/sth **3** [T] to have a harmful effect on sth: *a virus that attacks the nervous system* **4** [I] (**SPORT**) to try to score a point in a game of sport: *This team attacks better than it defends.*

attacker /əˈtækə(r)/ *noun* [C] a person who tries to hurt sb using force: *The victim of the assault didn't recognize his attackers.*

attain 𝄞+ **C1** /əˈteɪn/ *verb* [T] **1** to succeed in getting sth, usually after a lot of effort: *Most of our students attained five 'A' grades in their exams.* **2** (*formal*) to reach a particular age, level or condition

attainable /əˈteɪnəbl/ *adj.* that can be achieved: *realistically attainable targets*

attainment /əˈteɪnmənt/ *noun* **1** [U] success in achieving sth: *the attainment of the government's objectives* **2** [C, usually pl.] (*formal*) a skill or sth you have achieved

attempt[1] ʔ **B2** **S** /ə'tempt/ *verb* [T] ~ **(to do sth)** to try to do sth that is difficult: *Don't attempt to make him change his mind.* ◇ *The army attempted a rescue operation to free the hostages.*

attempt[2] ʔ **B2** **S** /ə'tempt/ *noun* [C] **1 (in an)~ (to do sth)** an act of trying to do sth: *The thief made no attempt to run away.* ◇ *The students are carrying out the challenge in an attempt to raise money for charity.* ◇ *I failed the exam once but passed at the second attempt.* **2 ~ on sb/sb's life** an act of trying to kill sb: *They made an attempt on the prime minister's life.* **3 ~ (on sth)** an effort to achieve the best result that has ever been reached, especially in sport: *She hopes to make an attempt on the world record in tomorrow's race.*

attempted /ə'temptɪd/ *adj.* [only before noun] (**LAW**) (used about a crime, etc.) that sb has tried to do but without success: *attempted rape/murder/robbery*

attend ʔ **A2** /ə'tend/ *verb* [I, T] to go to or be present at a place: *The children attend the local school.* ⊃ note at **subject**[1]

PHR V **attend to sb/sth** to give your care, thought or attention to sb/sth or look after sb/sth: *Please attend to this matter immediately.*

attendance ʔ+ **C1** /ə'tendəns/ *noun* **1** [U, C] being present somewhere: *Attendance at lectures is compulsory.* **2** [C, U] the number of people who go to or are present at a place: *There was a poor attendance at the meeting.*

attendant[1] /ə'tendənt/ *noun* [C] a person whose job is to serve or help people in a public place: *a car park attendant*

attendant[2] /ə'tendənt/ *adj.* [only before noun] (*formal*) closely connected with sth that has just been mentioned: *unemployment and all its attendant social problems*

attendee /əˌten'diː/ *noun* [C] a person who attends a meeting, etc.

attention[1] ʔ **A2** **S** /ə'tenʃn/ *noun* [U] **1 ~ (to sth/sb)** watching, listening to or thinking about sb/sth carefully: *I shouted in order to attract her attention.* ◇ *The report lacks attention to detail.* ◇ *Shy people hate to be the centre of attention* (= the person that everybody is watching). **2** special care or action: *The hole in the roof needs urgent attention.* ◇ *to require medical attention* **3** a position in which a soldier stands up straight and still: *to stand/come to attention* **IDM** **catch sb's attention/eye** → CATCH[1] **draw (sb's) attention to sth** → DRAW[1] **pay attention** → PAY[1]

attention[2] ʔ **A2** /ə'tenʃn/ *exclamation* used for asking people to listen to sb carefully

attention deficit disorder (*also* **attention deficit hyperactivity disorder**) = ADD

attentive /ə'tentɪv/ *adj.* ~ **(to sb/sth)** watching, listening to or thinking about sb/sth carefully: *The hotel staff were very attentive to our needs.* **OPP** **inattentive** ▸ **attentively** *adv.*: *to listen attentively to something*

attest /ə'test/ *verb* [I, T] (*formal*) **1 ~ (to sth)** to show or prove that sth is true: *Her long fight against cancer attested to her courage.* **2 ~ (that…)** (**LAW**) to state that you believe that sth is true or what sb claims it is, for example in court: *I attest that I understand the options that are available to me.*

attic /'ætɪk/ *noun* [C] the space or room under the roof of a house ⊃ look at **loft**

attire /ə'taɪə(r)/ *noun* [U] (*formal*) clothes, especially fine or formal ones

attitude ʔ **B1** **O** /'ætɪtjuːd/ *noun* [C] ~ **(to/towards sb/ sth)** the way that you think, feel or behave: *She has a very positive attitude to her work.* ◇ *People's attitude to marriage is changing.*

attn *abbr.* (in writing) (**BUSINESS**) for the attention of: *Sales Dept, attn M Holland*

attorney ʔ+ **C1** /ə'tɜːni/ *noun* [C] (**LAW**) **1** (*especially AmE*) a lawyer, especially one who can act for sb in court ⊃ look at **district attorney** ⊃ note at **lawyer** **2** a person who is given the power to act for another person in business or legal matters: *She was made her father's attorney when he became ill.* ⊃ look at **power of attorney**

Attorney General *noun* [C] (*pl.* **Attorneys General**, **Attorney Generals**) (**LAW, POLITICS**) **1** the most senior legal officer in some countries or states, for example the UK or Canada, who advises the government or head of state on legal matters **2** the Attorney General the head of the US Department of Justice and a member of the president's CABINET (= a group of senior politicians who advise the president)

attract ʔ **B1** /ə'trækt/ *verb* [T] **1** [usually passive] if you **are attracted** by sth, it interests you and makes you want it: *I was attracted by the challenge of learning something new.* **2** [usually passive] **be attracted (to sb)** to have a sexual or romantic interest in sb: *She's attracted to older men.* **3** to make sb/sth come somewhere: *It is hoped that the new marina will attract more tourists to the area.* **4** to make people have a particular reaction: *I waved to attract the waiter's attention.* ◇ *The new film has attracted a lot of publicity.* **5** (**PHYSICS**) if a MAGNET or GRAVITY attracts sth, it makes it move towards it. **OPP** **repel**

attraction ʔ **B1** /ə'trækʃn/ *noun* **1** [U, sing.] a feeling of liking sb/sth: *sexual attraction* **2** [C] a thing that is interesting or that you enjoy: *The city offers all kinds of tourist attractions.* **3** [U] (**PHYSICS**) a force that pulls things towards each other: *gravitational/magnetic attraction* ⊃ look at **repulsion** (2) ⊃ picture at **magnetism**

attractive ʔ **A2** /ə'træktɪv/ *adj.* **1** (used about a thing) pleasant: *an attractive part of the country* ◇ *an attractive idea* **2** (used about a person) beautiful or nice to look at ▸ **attractively** *adv.* ▸ **attractiveness** *noun* [U]

attributable /ə'trɪbjətəbl/ *adj.* [not before noun] ~ **to sb/ sth** probably caused by the thing mentioned: *Their illnesses are attributable to poor diet.*

attribute[1] ʔ+ **C1** **W** /ə'trɪbjuːt/ *verb* [T] ~ **sth to sth/sb** to say or believe that sth was caused by sth or created by sb: *Mustafa attributes his success to hard work.* ◇ *a poem attributed to Shakespeare*

attribute[2] ʔ+ **C1** **W** /'ætrɪbjuːt/ *noun* [C] a quality or feature of sb/sth: *physical attributes* **SYN** **feature**[1]

attributive /ə'trɪbjətɪv/ *adj.* (**GRAMMAR**) (used about adjectives or nouns) used before a noun to describe it: *In 'the blue sky' and 'a family business', 'blue' and 'family' are attributive.* ⊃ note at **predicative** ▸ **attributively** *adv.*

attrition /ə'trɪʃn/ *noun* [U] (*formal*) a process of making sb/sth, especially your enemy, weaker by attacking them or causing problems for them over a period of time: *It was a war of attrition.*

ATV /ˌeɪ tiː 'viː/ *noun* [C] (*especially AmE*) a small open motor vehicle, usually with one seat and four wheels with very thick tyres, designed especially for use on rough ground without roads (the abbreviation for 'all-terrain vehicle') ⊃ look at **quad bike**

atypical /ˌeɪ'tɪpɪkl/ *adj.* (*formal*) not typical of a particular type, group, etc. **OPP** **typical** ⊃ look at **untypical**

aubergine /ˈəʊbəʒiːn/ (*BrE*) (*AmE* **eggplant**) *noun* [C, U] a long vegetable with dark purple skin

auburn /ˈɔːbən/ *adj.* (used about hair) red-brown in colour ▸ **auburn** *noun* [U]

auction¹ ⌂+ **B2** /ˈɔːkʃn, ˈɒk-/ *noun* [C, U] a public sale at which items are sold to the person who offers to pay the most money: *The house was sold at auction.* ◇ *an internet auction site*

auction² /ˈɔːkʃn, ˈɒk-/ *verb* [T, usually passive] to sell sth at an AUCTION

auctioneer /ˌɔːkʃəˈnɪə(r), ˌɒk-/ *noun* [C] a person who organizes the selling of goods at an AUCTION

audacious /ɔːˈdeɪʃəs/ *adj.* (*formal*) willing to take risks or to do sth that shocks people: *an audacious decision* **SYN** **daring** ▸ **audaciously** *adv.*

audacity /ɔːˈdæsəti/ *noun* [U] behaviour that shows courage but that is also likely to shock or offend people: *He had the audacity to tell me I was fat!* **SYN** **nerve**

audible /ˈɔːdəbl/ *adj.* that can be heard: *Her speech was barely audible.* **OPP** **inaudible** ▸ **audibly** /-bli/ *adv.*

audience ⌂ **A2** /ˈɔːdiəns/ *noun* [C] **1** [+ sing./pl. verb] (**ARTS AND MEDIA**) all the people who are watching or listening to a play, a concert, a speech, the TV, etc: *The audience was/were wild with excitement.* ◇ *There were only about 200 people in the audience.* **2** a number of people who watch, read or listen to the same thing: *TV/television/cinema/movie audiences* ◇ *His book reached an even wider audience when it was made into a movie.* ◇ *The target audience for this advertisement was mainly teenagers.* **3** ~ **with sb** a formal meeting with a very important person: *He was granted an audience with the president.*

audio ⌂+ **B2** /ˈɔːdiəʊ/ *adj.* connected with the recording of sound: *audio equipment*

audio- /ɔːdiəʊ, ɔːdiˈɒ/ *prefix* (in nouns, adjectives and adverbs) connected with hearing or sound: *audiovisual*

audiobook /ˈɔːdiəʊbʊk/ *noun* [C] (**LITERATURE**) a recording of a book being read ALOUD (= in a voice that other people can hear), made available to download or on a CD

audiovisual /ˌɔːdiəʊˈvɪʒuəl/ *adj.* using both sound and pictures

audit ⌂+ **C1** /ˈɔːdɪt/ *noun* [C] (**FINANCE**) an official examination of the present state of sth, especially of a company's financial records: *to carry out an audit* ▸ **audit** *verb* [T]: *We have just had our accounts audited.*

audition¹ /ɔːˈdɪʃn/ *noun* [C] (**ARTS AND MEDIA**) a short performance by a singer, an actor, etc., so that sb can decide if they are suitable to be in a play, show, etc.

audition² /ɔːˈdɪʃn/ *verb* [I, T] ~ **(sb) (for sth)** (**ARTS AND MEDIA**) to do or to watch sb do an AUDITION: *I auditioned for a part in the play.* ◇ *They're auditioning singers for the band.*

auditor /ˈɔːdɪtə(r)/ *noun* [C] (**FINANCE**) a person whose job is to examine a company's financial records

auditorium /ˌɔːdɪˈtɔːriəm/ *noun* [C] (*pl.* **-toriums, -toria** /-riə/) (**ARTS AND MEDIA**) the part of a theatre, concert hall, etc. where the audience sits

auditory /ˈɔːdətri/ *adj.* connected with hearing ◌ picture at **ear**

au fait /ˌəʊ ˈfeɪ/ *adj.* [not before noun] ~ **(with sth)** completely familiar with sth: *Are you au fait with this type of computer system?*

Aug. *abbr.* (in writing) = AUGUST

augment /ɔːɡˈment/ *verb* [T] (*formal*) to increase the amount, value, size, etc. of sth ▸ **augmentation** /ˌɔːɡmenˈteɪʃn/ *noun* [U, C]

augmented reality /ɔːɡˌmentɪd riˈæləti/ = AR

augur /ˈɔːɡə(r)/ *verb*
IDM **augur well/ill for sb/sth** (*formal*) to be a good/bad sign of what will happen in the future

August ⌂ **A1** /ˈɔːɡəst/ *noun* [U, C] (*abbr.* **Aug.**) the eighth month of the year, between July and September

aunt ⌂ **A1** /ɑːnt/ *noun* [C] your father's or mother's sister; your uncle's wife: *Aunt Ellen*

au pair /ˌəʊ ˈpeə(r)/ *noun* [C] (*BrE*) a young person, usually a woman from another country, who comes to live with a family in order to learn the language. An au pair helps to clean the house and look after the children, and receives a small wage.

aura /ˈɔːrə/ *noun* [C] (*formal*) the particular quality that sb/sth seems to have: *These hills have a magical aura.*

aural /ˈɔːrəl/ *adj.* connected with hearing and listening: *an aural comprehension test* ◌ look at **oral¹** (1) ▸ **aurally** /-rəli/ *adv.*

auricle /ˈɔːrɪkl/ *noun* [C] (**ANATOMY**) **1** either of the two upper spaces in the heart used to send blood around the body **SYN** **atrium** ◌ look at **ventricle** (1) **2** the outer part of the ear

aurora australis /əˌrɔːrə ɒˈstreɪlɪs/ *noun* [sing.] = SOUTHERN LIGHTS

aurora borealis /əˌrɔːrə ˌbɔːriˈeɪlɪs/ *noun* [sing.] = NORTHERN LIGHTS

auspices /ˈɔːspɪsɪz/ *noun* [pl.]
IDM **under the auspices of sb/sth** with the help and support of sb/sth

auspicious /ɔːˈspɪʃəs/ *adj.* showing signs that sth is likely to be successful in the future **OPP** **inauspicious**

Aussie /ˈɒzi/ *noun* [C] (*informal*) a person from Australia

austere /ɒˈstɪə(r), ɔːˈs-/ *adj.* **1** very simple; without decoration **2** (used about a person) very strict and serious **3** not having anything that makes your life more comfortable: *The nuns lead simple and austere lives.*

austerity /ɒˈsterəti, ɔːˈs-/ *noun* [U] **1** (**ECONOMICS**) difficult economic conditions created when a government cuts public spending by a large amount: *War was followed by many years of austerity.* **2** the quality of being AUSTERE: *the austerity of the monks' life*

Australasia /ˌɒstrəˈleɪʒə, -ˈleɪʃə/ *noun* [sing.] (**GEOGRAPHY**) the region consisting of Australia, New Zealand, New Guinea, and the islands of the south-west Pacific

Australasian /ˌɒstrəˈleɪʒn, -ˈleɪʃn/ *noun* [C] a person from Australasia ▸ **Australasian** *adj.*

Australian Rules /ɒˌstreɪliən ˈruːlz/ (*also* Au ˌstralian Rules ˈfootball) *noun* [U] (**SPORT**) an Australian game played by two teams of 18 players with an OVAL ball that can be kicked, carried or hit with the hand

aut- /ɔːt/ → AUTO-

authentic ⌂+ **C1** /ɔːˈθentɪk/ *adj.* **1** that you know is real or what sb claims it is: *an authentic Van Gogh painting* **2** true or accurate: *an authentic model of the building* ▸ **authentically** /-kli/ *adv.* ▸ **authenticity** /ˌɔːθenˈtɪsəti/ *noun* [U]

authenticate /ɔːˈθentɪkeɪt/ *verb* [T, often passive] ~ **sth (as sth)** to prove that sth is real, true or what sb claims it is: *The picture has been authenticated as a genuine Picasso.* ▸ **authentication** /ɔːˌθentɪˈkeɪʃn/ *noun* [U]

author¹ 🔊 ❷ ⦿ /ˈɔːθə(r)/ *noun* [C] (LITERATURE) a person who writes a book, play, etc: *a well-known author of detective novels* ◊ *Who's your favourite author?* ▶ **authorship** *noun* [U]

author² /ˈɔːθə(r)/ *verb* [T] (*formal*) to be the author of a book, report, etc.

authoritarian /ɔːˌθɒrɪˈteəriən/ *adj.* believing that people should obey authority and rules, even when these are unfair: *authoritarian parents* ◊ *The **authoritarian government** crushed all signs of opposition.* ▶ **authoritarianism** *noun* [U]

authoritative /ɔːˈθɒrətətɪv/ *adj.* **1** having authority; demanding or expecting that people obey you: *an authoritative tone of voice* **2** that you can trust and respect as true and correct: *the most authoritative book on the subject*

authority 🔊 B1 ⓦ /ɔːˈθɒrəti/ *noun* (*pl.* -ies)
• POWER **1** [U] (LAW) the power and right to give orders and make others obey: *Children often begin to question their parents' authority at a very early age.* ◊ *You must get this signed by a person **in authority**.*
• PERMISSION **2** [U] ~ (**to do sth**) the right or permission to do sth: *The police **have the authority** to question anyone they wish.* ◊ *He was sacked for using a company vehicle **without authority**.*
• OFFICIAL GROUP **3** [C, usually pl.] (LAW) a person, group or government department that has the power to give orders, make official decisions, etc: *I have to report this to the authorities.*
• KNOWLEDGE **4** [U] the power to influence people because they respect your knowledge or official position: *He spoke **with authority** and everybody listened.*
• EXPERT **5** [C] ~ (**on sth**) a person with special knowledge: *He's an authority on criminal law.*

authorize 🔊+ C1 (*BrE also* -ise) /ˈɔːθəraɪz/ *verb* [T] ~ (**sb to do sth**) to give official permission for sth or for sb to do sth: *She authorized her PA to respond to emails in her absence.* ▶ **authorization** (*BrE also* -isation) /ˌɔːθəraɪˈzeɪʃn/ *noun* [U, C]

autism /ˈɔːtɪzəm/ *noun* [U] (PSYCHOLOGY) a mental DISORDER in which a person finds it very difficult to communicate or form relationships with others and often shows limited or repeated patterns of thought and behaviour SYN ASD ▶ **autistic** /ɔːˈtɪstɪk/ *adj.*

auto 🔊+ C1 /ˈɔːtəʊ/ *noun* [C] (*pl.* -os) (*especially AmE*) a car: *the auto industry*

auto- /ɔːtəʊ, ɔːtə, ɔːˈtɒ/ (*also* aut-) *prefix* (in nouns, adjectives and adverbs) **1** about or by yourself: *an autobiography* **2** by itself without a person to operate it: *automatic*

autobiography /ˌɔːtəbaɪˈɒɡrəfi/ *noun* [C, U] (*pl.* -ies) (LITERATURE) the story of a person's life, written by that person; this type of writing ⊃ look at **biography** ▶ **autobiographical** /ˌɔːtəˌbaɪəˈɡræfɪkl/ *adj.*

autoclave /ˈɔːtəʊkleɪv/ *noun* [C] (SCIENCE) a strong closed container, used for processes that involve high temperatures or pressure

autocorrect /ˌɔːtəʊkəˈrekt/ *verb* [T, I] (COMPUTING) (used about a software feature) to correct mistakes in spelling or grammar that the user has made: *The phone will autocorrect as you type for improved accuracy.* ▶ **autocorrect** /ˈɔːtəʊkərekt/ *noun* [U]: *From this screen you can disable autocorrect.*

autocracy /ɔːˈtɒkrəsi/ *noun* (*pl.* -ies) (POLITICS) **1** [U] a system of government of a country in which one person has complete power **2** [C] a country that is ruled by one person who has complete power

autocrat /ˈɔːtəkræt/ *noun* [C] **1** (POLITICS) a leader who has complete power ⊃ look at **despot 2** a person who expects to be obeyed by other people and does not care about their opinions or feelings ▶ **autocratic** /ˌɔːtəˈkrætɪk/ *adj.*

Autocue™ /ˈɔːtəʊkjuː/ (*BrE*) (*also* **teleprompter** *especially in AmE*) *noun* [C] (ARTS AND MEDIA) a device used by people who are speaking in public, especially on TV, that shows them the words they have to say

autograph /ˈɔːtəɡrɑːf/ *noun* [C] a famous person's SIGNATURE (= their name, written by them) especially when written for sb else to keep: *The players stopped outside the stadium to **sign autographs**.* ▶ **autograph** *verb* [T]: *The whole team have autographed the football.*

autoimmune /ˌɔːtəʊɪˈmjuːn/ *adj.* [only before noun] (HEALTH) an **autoimmune** disease or medical condition is caused by ANTIBODIES (= substances produced in the blood to fight disease) attacking substances that are naturally present in the body: *an autoimmune response*

automate /ˈɔːtəmeɪt/ *verb* [T, usually passive] to make sth operate by machine, without needing people: *The system in the factory has been **fully automated**.*

automatic¹ 🔊+ B2 /ˌɔːtəˈmætɪk/ *adj.* **1** (used about a machine) having controls that work without needing a person to operate them: *automatic doors* ◊ *an automatic washing machine* **2** done without thinking: *Rapid breathing is an automatic reaction to stress.* **3** always happening as a result of a particular action or situation: *All the staff have an automatic right to a space in the car park.* ▶ **automatically** 🔊+ B2 /-kli/ *adv.*: *The lights will come on automatically when it gets dark.*

automatic² /ˌɔːtəˈmætɪk/ *noun* [C] **1** a gun that can fire bullets continuously **2** (*BrE*) a vehicle with a system of GEARS that works without direct action from the driver

automatic ˈpilot = AUTOPILOT

automation /ˌɔːtəˈmeɪʃn/ *noun* [U] the use of machines and computers instead of people to do work

automobile /ˈɔːtəməbiːl/ (*AmE*) = CAR (1)

automotive /ˌɔːtəˈməʊtɪv/ *adj.* (*formal*) connected with cars and other motor vehicles: *the automotive industry*

autonomy 🔊+ C1 /ɔːˈtɒnəmi/ *noun* [U] **1** (POLITICS) the freedom for a country, a region or an organization to govern itself independently **2** the ability to act and make decisions without being controlled by anyone else: *giving learners greater autonomy in the classroom* ▶ **autonomous** /-məs/ *adj.*

autopilot /ˈɔːtəʊpaɪlət/ (*also* **automatic pilot**) *noun* [C, U] a device in an aircraft or a ship that keeps it on a fixed course without the need for a person to control it **IDM do sth/be on autopilot** (*also* **do sth/be on automatic pilot**) (*informal*) to do sth without thinking because you have done the same thing many times before: *I tidied up and made the dinner on autopilot.*

autopsy /ˈɔːtɒpsi/ *noun* [C] (*pl.* -ies) (MEDICINE) an examination of a dead body by a specially trained doctor to find out the cause of death SYN post-mortem

autosuggestion /ˌɔːtəʊsəˈdʒestʃən/ *noun* [U] (PSYCHOLOGY) a process that makes you believe sth or do sth according to ideas that come from within yourself without you realizing it

autotroph /ˈɔːtətrəʊf/ *noun* [C] (BIOLOGY) a living thing that is able to feed itself using simple chemical substances such as CARBON DIOXIDE ▶ **autotrophic** /ˌɔːtəˈtrɒfɪk/ *adj.*

autumn ʔ **A1** /ˈɔːtəm/ (*especially BrE*) (*AmE usually* **fall**) *noun* [C, U] the season of the year between summer and winter, when leaves change colour and the weather becomes colder: *It was a very cold autumn that year.* ◇ *In autumn the leaves on the trees begin to fall.* ◇ *We met in the autumn of 2017.* ➲ picture at **season**¹ ▶ **autumnal** /ɔːˈtʌmnəl/ *adj.*

auxiliary¹ /ɔːgˈzɪliəri/ *adj.* [only before noun] **1** (used about workers) giving help or support to the main group of workers: *auxiliary nurses/troops/staff* **SYN** **ancillary** **2** (used about a piece of equipment) used if there is a problem with the main piece of equipment: *an auxiliary pump*

auxiliary² /ɔːgˈzɪliəri/ *noun* [C] (*pl.* **-ies**) **1** (*also* auˈxiliary **verb**) (**GRAMMAR**) a verb such as *be*, *do* and *have* that is used with a main verb to show tense, etc. or to form questions and negatives **2** a worker who gives help or support to the main group of workers: *nursing auxiliaries*

auxin /ˈɔːksɪn/ *noun* [U] (**BIOLOGY**) a chemical substance in plants that helps control their growth

avail /əˈveɪl/ *noun* (*formal*)
IDM **of little/no avail** not helpful; having little or no effect **to little/no avail** without success: *They searched everywhere, but to no avail.*

availability ʔ+ **C1** **W** /əˌveɪləˈbɪləti/ *noun* [U] the fact that sth is possible to get, buy or find: *You will receive the colour you order,* **subject to availability** (= if it is available).

available ʔ **A2** **W** /əˈveɪləbl/ *adj.* **1** ~ (to sb); ~ (for sth) (used about things) that you can get, buy, use, etc: *Is this information is going to be* **made available** *to the public?* ◇ *Refreshments are available at the snack bar.* ◇ *The following files are available for download.* **2** ~ (to do sth); ~ (for sth) (used about people) free to be seen, talked to, etc: *Our team of consultants is available to answer any questions you may have.* ◇ *The minister was not available for comment.*

avalanche /ˈævəlɑːnʃ/ *noun* [C] (**GEOGRAPHY**) a very large amount of snow that slides quickly down the side of a mountain

the avant-garde /ˌði ˌævɒ̃ ˈɡɑːd/ *noun* [sing.] (**ARTS AND MEDIA**) extremely modern works of art, music or literature, or the artists who create these ▶ **avant-garde** *adj.*

avarice /ˈævərɪs/ *noun* [U] (*formal*) extreme desire for money **SYN** **greed** ▶ **avaricious** /ˌævəˈrɪʃəs/ *adj.*

avatar /ˈævətɑː(r)/ *noun* [C] **1** (**RELIGION**) (in Hinduism and Buddhism) a god appearing in a physical form **2** a picture of a person or an animal that represents a particular person on a computer screen, especially on SOCIAL MEDIA

avenge /əˈvendʒ/ *verb* [T] to punish sb for hurting you, your family, etc. in some way: *He wanted to avenge his father's murder.*

avenue /ˈævənjuː/ *noun* [C] **1** (*abbr.* **Ave.**) a wide street, especially one with trees or tall buildings on each side: *I live on Tennyson Avenue.* **2** a way of doing or getting sth: *We must explore every avenue open to us* (= try every possibility).

average¹ ʔ **A2** **O** /ˈævərɪdʒ/ *noun* [C, U]
1 (**MATHEMATICS**) the number you get when you add two or more amounts together and then divide the total by the number of figures you added: *The average of 14, 3 and 1 is 6* (= 18 divided by 3 is 6). ◇ *He has scored 93 goals at* **an average of** *1.55 per game.* **2** the normal standard, amount or quality: *I sleep for about seven hours a night* **on average**. ◇ *Temperatures are* **below average** *for this time of year.*

average² ʔ **A2** **O** /ˈævərɪdʒ/ *adj.* **1** [only before noun] (**MATHEMATICS**) calculated by adding two or more amounts together and then dividing the total by the number of figures you added: *What's the average age of your students?* **2** normal or typical: *children of* **above/below average** *intelligence*

average³ ʔ **B1** **W** /ˈævərɪdʒ/ *verb* [T] **1** to do, get, etc. a certain amount as an average: *If we average 50 miles an hour, we should arrive at about four o'clock.* **2** [usually passive] to calculate the average of sth: *Earnings are averaged over the whole period.*
PHR V **average out (at sth)** to result in an average (of sth): *Her training runs average out at about 10 kilometres a day.*

averse /əˈvɜːs/ *adj.* [not before noun] **not ~ to sth/doing sth** (*formal*) not opposed to doing sth: *He is not averse to trying out new ideas.*

aversion /əˈvɜːʃn/ *noun* [C, U] **~ (to sb/sth)** a strong feeling of not liking sb/sth: *Some people* **have an aversion** *to spiders.*

aˈversion therapy *noun* [U] (**PSYCHOLOGY**) a way of helping sb to lose a bad habit, by connecting the habit with an unpleasant effect

avert /əˈvɜːt/ *verb* [T] to prevent sth unpleasant: *The accident could have been averted.*

avian /ˈeɪviən/ *adj.* (**BIOLOGY**) relating to or connected with birds

ˌavian ˈflu = **BIRD FLU**

aviary /ˈeɪviəri/ *noun* [C] (*pl.* **-ies**) a large CAGE or area in which birds are kept

aviation /ˌeɪviˈeɪʃn/ *noun* [U] the designing, building and flying of aircraft

avid /ˈævɪd/ *adj.* **1** very enthusiastic about sth (usually a hobby): *an avid collector of antiques* **SYN** **keen** **2** ~ for sth wanting to get sth very much: *Journalists crowded round the entrance, avid for news.* ▶ **avidly** *adv.*: *He read avidly as a child.*

avocado /ˌævəˈkɑːdəʊ/ (*pl.* **-os**) (*BrE also* ˌavocado ˈpear) *noun* [C] a tropical fruit that is wider at one end than the other, with a hard green skin and a large seed inside

avoid ʔ **A2** **O** /əˈvɔɪd/ *verb* [T] **1** ~ (doing sth) to prevent sth bad from happening: *He always tried to avoid an argument if possible.* ◇ *I just managed to avoid crashing into the tree.* **2** ~ (doing sth) to keep away from sb/sth; to try not to do sth: *I leave home early to avoid the rush hour.* ◇ *She has to avoid eating fatty food.* ▶ **avoidance** *noun* [U]

avoidable /əˈvɔɪdəbl/ *adj.* that can be prevented; unnecessary **OPP** **unavoidable**

avow /əˈvaʊ/ *verb* [I, T] (*formal*) to say FIRMLY and often publicly what your opinion is, what you think is true, etc. ▶ **avowal** /-əl/ *noun* [C]

await ʔ+ **C1** /əˈweɪt/ *verb* [T] (*formal*) to wait for sb/sth: *We sat down to await the arrival of the guests.*

awake¹ /əˈweɪk/ *adj.* [not before noun] not sleeping: *I was sleepy this morning but I'm* **wide awake** *now.* ◇ *They were so tired that they found it difficult to* **stay awake**. ◇ *I hope our singing didn't* **keep** *you* **awake** *last night.* **OPP** **asleep**

awake² /əˈweɪk/ *verb* [I, T] (*pt* **awoke** /əˈwəʊk/; *pp* **awoken** /əˈwəʊkən/) (*formal*) to wake up; to make sb/sth wake up: *I awoke to find that it was already nine o'clock.* ◇ *A sudden loud noise awoke us.*

awaken /əˈweɪkən/ *verb* (*formal*) **1** [I, T, often passive] to wake up; to make sb/sth wake up: *We were awakened by a loud knock at the door.* **2** [T] to produce a

particular feeling, attitude, etc. in sb: *The film awakened memories of her childhood.*
PHR V **awaken sb to sth** to make sb notice or realize sth for the first time

awakening /əˈweɪkənɪŋ/ *noun* **1** [C, U] the act of starting to feel or understand sth: *the awakening of an interest in the opposite sex* **2** [C, usually sing.] a moment when sb notices or realizes sth for the first time: *It was a rude awakening* (= unpleasant) *when I suddenly found myself unemployed.*

award¹ **A2** /əˈwɔːd/ *noun* [C] **1** (often in names of particular awards) a prize, etc. that sb gets for doing sth well: *This year the awards for best actor and actress went to two Americans.* ◇ *an awards ceremony* **2** (LAW) an amount of money given to sb as the result of a court decision: *She received an award of £5 000 for damages.*

award² **B1** /əˈwɔːd/ *verb* [T] ~ **sth (to sb)** to give sth to sb as a prize, payment, etc: *She was awarded first prize in the gymnastics competition.* ◇ *The court awarded £10 000 each to the workers injured in the accident.*

a'ward-winning *adj.* [only before noun] having won a prize: *an award-winning TV drama*

aware **B1** **W** /əˈweə(r)/ *adj.* **1** [not before noun] ~ **(of sb/sth)**; ~ **(that …)** knowing about or realizing sth; conscious of sb/sth: *I am well aware of the problems you face.* ◇ *I suddenly became aware that somebody was watching me.* ◇ *There is no other entrance, as far as I am aware.* **OPP** **unaware** **2** interested in and knowing about sth: *Many young people are very politically aware.*

awareness **B2** **W** /əˈweənəs/ *noun* [U, sing.] ~ **(of sth)** knowing sth; knowing that sth exists and is important; being interested in sth: *People's awareness of healthy eating has increased in recent years.* ◇ *There was an almost complete lack of awareness of the issues involved.* **SYN** **consciousness**

awash /əˈwɒʃ/ *adj.* [not before noun] ~ **(with sth)** covered with water: *The downstairs area of the building was awash after the floods.* ◇ (*figurative*) *The city was awash with rumours.*

away¹ **A1** /əˈweɪ/ *adv.* **1** to a different place or in a different direction: *Go away! I'm busy!* ◇ *I asked him a question, but he just looked away.* **2** ~ **(from sb/sth)** to or at a distance from sb/sth in space or time: *The village is 2 miles away from the sea.* ◇ *My parents live five minutes away.* **3** ~ **(from sth)** (used about people) not present: *My neighbours are away on holiday at the moment.* ◇ *Aki was away from school for two weeks with measles.* **SYN** **absent 4** in the future: *Our summer holiday is only three weeks away.* **5** into a place where sth is usually kept: *Put your books away now.* ◇ *They cleared the dishes away* (= off the table). ⊃ look at **throw sth away** at **throw 6** continuously, without stopping: *They chatted away for hours.* **7** (SPORT) (used about a football, etc. match) on the other team's ground: *Our team's playing away on Saturday.* **OPP** **at home 8** until sth disappears: *The crash of thunder slowly died away.*
IDM **right/straight away** immediately; without any delay: *I'll phone the doctor right away.*
PHR V **do away with sb/sth** (*informal*) to kill sb/ yourself **do away with sth** (*informal*) to stop doing or having sth; to make sth end: *He thinks it's time we did away with the monarchy.* **SYN** **abolish**

away² /əˈweɪ/ *adj.* (SPORT) (used about a football, etc. match) played or scored on the other team's ground: *an away match/game* **OPP** **home²**

a'way day *noun* [C] (*BrE*) (**BUSINESS**) a day that a group of workers spend together away from their usual place of work in order to discuss ideas or plans

awe /ɔː/ *noun* [U] feelings of respect and slight fear; feelings of being very impressed by sb/sth: *We watched in awe as the rocket took off.* ◇ *His students regarded him with awe.*
IDM **be in awe of sb/sth** to admire sb/sth and be slightly frightened of them or it

'awe-inspiring *adj.* extremely impressive; making you admire it very much

awesome /ˈɔːsəm/ *adj.* **1** impressive and sometimes frightening: *an awesome task* **2** (*especially AmE, informal*) very good; excellent

awful **A2** /ˈɔːfl/ *adj.* **1** very bad or unpleasant: *We had an awful holiday. It rained every day.* ◇ *I feel awful — I think I'll go to bed.* ◇ *What an awful thing to say!* **2** that shocks people very much: *I'm afraid there's been some awful news.* **SYN** **terrible 3** [only before noun] (*informal*) used to say that there is a large amount or too much of sth: *We've got an awful lot of work to do.*

awfully /ˈɔːfli/ *adv.* (*informal*) very; extremely: *I'm awfully sorry.* **SYN** **terribly**

awkward **B2** /ˈɔːkwəd/ *adj.* **1** difficult to deal with: *That's an awkward question.* ◇ *You've put me in an awkward position.* ◇ *an awkward customer* ◇ *The box isn't heavy but it's awkward to carry.* **SYN** **difficult 2** not convenient: *My mother always phones at an awkward time.* ◇ *This tin-opener is very awkward to clean.* **SYN** **inconvenient 3** embarrassed or embarrassing: *I often feel awkward in a group of people.* ◇ *There was an awkward silence.* **4** not using the body in the best way; not comfortable: *I was sitting with my legs in an awkward position.*
▸ **awkwardly** *adv.* ▸ **awkwardness** *noun* [U]

awning /ˈɔːnɪŋ/ *noun* [C] a sheet of cloth that stretches out from above a door or window to keep off the sun or rain

awoke /əˈwəʊk/ past tense of **awake²**

awoken /əˈwəʊkən/ past participle of **awake²**

AWOL /ˈeɪwɒl/ *abbr.* **absent without leave** (used especially when sb in the army, etc. has left their group without permission): *He's gone AWOL from his base.*

awry /əˈraɪ/ *adv., adj.* [not before noun] wrong, not in the way that was planned; untidy

axe¹ (*AmE usually* **ax**) /æks/ *noun* [C] a tool with a wooden handle and a heavy metal head with a sharp edge, used for cutting wood, etc.

axe² (*AmE usually* **ax**) /æks/ *verb* [T, often passive] **1** to remove sb/sth: *Hundreds of jobs have been axed.* **2** to reduce sth by a great amount: *Budgets are to be axed.*

axes

pickaxe   axe   hatchet

axiom /ˈæksiəm/ *noun* [C] (*formal*) a rule or principle that most people believe to be true

axiomatic /ˌæksiəˈmætɪk/ *adj.* (*formal*) true in such an obvious way that you do not need evidence to show that it is true

axis /ˈæksɪs/ *noun* [C] (*pl.* **axes** /ˈæksiːz/) **1** an imaginary line through the middle of an object, around which the object turns: *The earth rotates on its axis.* **2** (MATHEMATICS) a fixed line used for marking measurements on a GRAPH: *the horizontal/vertical axis* **3** a line that divides a shape into two equal parts:

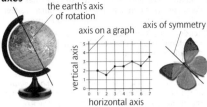

the earth's axis of rotation

axis on a graph   axis of symmetry

vertical axis

horizontal axis

an *axis of symmetry* ◊ *The axis of a circle is its diameter.*

axle /ˈæksl/ *noun* [C] a bar that connects a pair of wheels on a vehicle

ayatollah /ˌaɪəˈtɒlə/ *noun* [C] (**RELIGION**) a religious leader of Shiite Muslims, especially in Iran

Ayurvedic medicine /ˌaɪəˌveɪdɪk ˈmedsn, ˈmedɪsn/ (*also* Ayurveda, ayurveda /ˌaɪəˈveɪdə/) *noun* [U] (**MEDICINE**) a type of traditional medicine from India that treats illnesses using a combination of foods, HERBS (= a type of plant) and breathing exercises

azalea /əˈzeɪliə/ *noun* [C] a plant or bush with large flowers that may be pink, purple, white or yellow

azure /ˈæʒə(r), ˈæzjʊə(r)/ *adj.* (*formal*) bright blue in colour like the sky ▶ **azure** *noun* [U]

B b

B /biː/ *noun* [C, U] (*pl.* B's) **1** (*also* b, *pl.* b's) the second letter of the English alphabet: *'Bicycle' begins with (a) 'B'.* **2** (**MUSIC**) the seventh note in the SCALE of C MAJOR **3** ~ (**in/for sth**) (**EDUCATION**) a grade given for an exam or a piece of work that shows that it is good but not excellent: *She got a B in history.*

b. *abbr.* (in writing) = BORN[1] (1): *J S Bach, b. 1685*

B2B /ˌbiː tə ˈbiː/ *abbr.* (**BUSINESS**) **business-to-business** (used to describe the buying, selling and exchanging over the internet of products, services or information between companies): *B2B transactions*

B2C /ˌbiː tə ˈsiː/ *abbr.* (**BUSINESS**) **business-to-consumer** (used to describe the selling of products, services or information to consumers over the internet): *B2C e-commerce*

BA (*BrE*) (*AmE usually* **B.A.**) /ˌbiː ˈeɪ/ *noun* [C] (**EDUCATION**) a second university degree in an arts subject (the abbreviation for 'Bachelor of Arts') ⊃ look at **BSc, MA**

baa /bɑː/ *noun* [C] the sound that a sheep makes ⊃ note at **sheep**

babble[1] /ˈbæbl/ *noun* [sing.] **1** the sound of many voices talking at the same time **2** talking that is confused or silly and is difficult to understand **3** the sound of water running over stones

babble[2] /ˈbæbl/ *verb* [I] **1** to talk quickly or in a way that is difficult to understand **2** to make the sound of water running over stones

babe /beɪb/ *noun* [C] **1** (*also* baby *especially in AmE*) (*slang*) a word used to address a young woman or your wife, husband, etc., usually expressing love but sometimes considered offensive if used by a man to a woman he does not know: *It's OK, babe.* **2** (*informal*) an attractive young woman **3** (*old-fashioned*) a baby

baboon /bəˈbuːn/ *noun* [C] a large African or Asian monkey with a long face like a dog's

baby 🔊 **A1** /ˈbeɪbi/ *noun* [C] (*pl.* -ies) **1** a very young child: *I'm going to have a baby.* ◊ *She's expecting a baby early next year.* ◊ *When's the baby due?* (= when will it be born?) ◊ *a baby boy/girl* **2** a very young animal or bird **3** (*especially AmE, slang*) = BABE (1)

baby boom *noun* [C, usually sing.] (**SOCIAL STUDIES**) a time when more babies are born than usual

baby boomer (*also informal* boomer *especially in AmE*) *noun* [C] (**SOCIAL STUDIES**) a person born during a BABY BOOM (= a period when more babies were born than usual), especially after the Second World War

baby carriage (*AmE*) = PRAM

babyhood /ˈbeɪbihʊd/ *noun* [U] the time of your life when you are a baby

babyish /ˈbeɪbiɪʃ/ *adj.* suitable for or behaving like a baby

baby shower *noun* [C] a party given for a woman who is going to have a baby, at which her friends give her presents for the baby

babysit /ˈbeɪbisɪt/ *verb* [I, T] (babysitting; *pt, pp* babysat /-sæt/) ~ (**for sb**) to look after a child for a short time while the parents are out: *I sometimes babysit for our neighbours at weekends.* ◊ *She has to babysit her little brother on Saturday.* ▶ **babysitter** *noun* [C]

baccalaureate /ˌbækəˈlɔːriət/ *noun* [C] (**EDUCATION**) the last SECONDARY SCHOOL exam in France and other countries, and in some international schools: *to sit/take/pass/fail your baccalaureate* ⊃ look at **International Baccalaureate™**

bachelor /ˈbætʃələ(r)/ *noun* [C] **1** (**SOCIAL STUDIES**) a man who has not yet married ⊃ look at **spinster** **2** Bachelor (**EDUCATION**) a person who has a Bachelor's degree (= a first university degree): *a Bachelor of Arts/Science*

bachelor pad *noun* [C] (*informal*) a house or flat where a man who is not married lives

bacillus /bəˈsɪləs/ *noun* [C] (*pl.* bacilli /-laɪ/) (**BIOLOGY**) a type of bacteria. There are several types of bacillus, some of which cause diseases.

back[1] 🔊 **A1** /bæk/ *noun* **1** [C] (**ANATOMY**) the part of the human body that is on the opposite side to the chest, between the neck and the bottom: *Do you sleep on your back or on your side?* ◊ *She had her back to me so I couldn't see her face.* ◊ *He stood with his hands behind his back.* ◊ *A camel has a hump on its back.* **2** [C, usually sing.] the part or side of sth that is furthest from the front: *I sat at the back of the class.* ◊ *The answers are in the back of the book.* ◊ *Leave your bike around the back of the house.* **3** [C] the part of a chair that supports your upper body when you sit down **IDM** **at/in the back of your mind** if sth is at the back of your mind, it is in your thoughts but is not the main thing that you are thinking about **back to front** with the back where the front should be: *Wait a minute — you've got your jumper on back to front.* ⊃ look at **way**[1] (4) **behind sb's back** without sb's knowledge or agreement: *They criticized her behind her back.* **OPP** **to sb's face** **get off sb's back** (*informal*) to stop annoying sb, for example when you keep asking them to do sth: *I've told her I'll do the job by Monday, so I wish she'd get off my back!* **know sth like the back of your hand →** KNOW[1] **a pat on the back →** PAT[2] **turn your back on sb/sth** to refuse to be involved with sb/sth

back[2] 🔊 **A2** /bæk/ *adj.* [only before noun] **1** furthest from the front: *Have you locked the back door?* ◊ *the back row of the theatre* ◊ *back teeth* **2** owed from a time in the past: *back pay/rent*

IDM on the back burner (*informal*) (used about an idea, a plan, etc.) left for the present time, to be done or considered later take a back seat to allow sb to play a more important or active role than you in a particular situation

back³ **A1** /bæk/ *adv.* **1** in or to a place or state that sb/sth was in before: *I'm going out now — I'll be back at about six o'clock.* ◇ *It started to rain so I came back home.* ◇ *Go back to sleep.* ◇ *Could I have my pen back, please?* ◇ *I've got to take these books back to the library.* **2** away from the direction you are facing or moving in: *She walked away without looking back.* ◇ *Could everyone move back a bit, please?* **OPP** forward¹ **3** away from sth; under control: *The police were unable to keep the crowds back.* ◇ *She tried to hold back her tears.* **4** in return or in reply: *He said he'd phone me back in half an hour.* **5** in or into the past; ago: *I met her a few years back, in Madrid.* ◇ *Think back to your first day at school.*
IDM back and forth from one place to another and back again, all the time: *Travelling back and forth to work takes up quite a bit of time.*

back⁴ **B2** /bæk/ *verb* **1** [I, T] to move backwards or to make sth move backwards: *I'll have to back into that parking space.* ◇ *He backed the car into the garage.* **2** [T] to give help or support to sb/sth: *We can go ahead with the scheme if the bank will agree to back us.* **3** [T] (SPORT) to bet money that a particular horse, team, etc. will win in a race or game: *Which horse are you backing in the two o'clock race?*
PHRV back away (from sb/sth) to move backwards because you are afraid, shocked, etc. back down to stop saying that you are right: *I think you are right to demand an apology. Don't back down now.* back onto sth (used about a building) to have sth directly behind it: *Many of the colleges back onto the river.* back out (of sth) to decide not to do sth that you had promised to do: *You promised you would come with me. You can't back out of it now!* back (sth) up to move backwards, especially in a vehicle: *Back up a little so that the other cars can get past.* back sb/sth up to support sb; to say or show that sth is true: *I'm going to say exactly what I think at the meeting. Will you back me up?* ◇ *All the evidence backed up what the woman had said.* back sth up (COMPUTING) to make a copy of a computer file, etc. that can be used if the original one is lost or damaged

backache /'bækeɪk/ *noun* [U] (HEALTH) a pain in the back

back bench *noun* [C, usually pl.] (POLITICS) (in the British and certain other parliaments) any of the seats for Members of Parliament who do not have senior positions in the government or the other parties: *He resigned as Home Secretary and returned to the back benches.*

backbencher /ˌbæk'bentʃə(r)/ *noun* [C] (POLITICS) (in the British and certain other parliaments) a member who sits in the rows of seats at the back, and who does not have an important position in the government or the Opposition

backbone /'bækbəʊn/ *noun* **1** [C] (ANATOMY) the row of small bones that are connected together down the middle of the back **SYN** spine ◇ picture at body **2** [sing.] the most important part of sth: *Agriculture is the backbone of the country's economy.*

back-breaking *adj.* (used about physical work) very hard and making you tired

back catalogue (AmE also back catalog) *noun* [C] (MUSIC) all the recorded music that a musician has produced in the past: *The entire Beatles' back catalogue has been put online.*

backdate /ˌbæk'deɪt/ *verb* [T] ~ sth (to …) to make a document, payment, etc. take effect from an earlier date: *The pay rise will be backdated to 1 April.*

backdrop **C1** /'bækdrɒp/ (BrE also backcloth /'bækklɒθ/) *noun* [C] **1** everything that can be seen around an event or a scene: *The mountains provided a dramatic backdrop for our picnic.* **2** (against a) ~ (of sth) the general conditions in which an event takes place: *The agreement was signed against a backdrop of conflict.* **3** (ARTS AND MEDIA) a painted piece of cloth that is hung at the back of the stage in a theatre

backer /'bækə(r)/ *noun* [C] (FINANCE) a person, an organization or a company that gives support to sb, especially financial support

backfire /ˌbæk'faɪə(r)/ *verb* [I] to have a result that is unexpected and unpleasant and, often the opposite of what was intended

backgammon /'bækgæmən/ *noun* [U] a game for two people, played by moving pieces around a board marked with long thin TRIANGLES

background **A2** /'bækgraʊnd/ *noun* **1** [C] the type of family and social class you come from and the education and experience you have: *We get on very well together in spite of our different backgrounds.* **2** [C, usually sing., U] (against a) ~ (of sth) the facts or events that are connected with a situation: *The talks are taking place against a background of increasing tension.* ◇ *I need some background information.* **3** [C, usually sing.] the part of a view, scene, picture, etc. that is furthest away from the person looking at it: *You can see the mountains in the background of the photo.* **OPP** foreground **4** [sing.] a position where sb/sth can be seen, heard, etc. but is not the centre of attention: *All the time I was speaking to her, I could hear a child crying in the background.* ◇ (*figurative*) *The film star's husband prefers to stay in the background.* ◇ *I like to have background music when I'm studying.* ⊃ look at foreground (2)

backhand /'bækhænd/ *noun* [C, usually sing.] (SPORT) a way of hitting the ball in sports such as tennis that is made with the back of your hand facing forward **OPP** forehand

back-heel *verb* [T] (SPORT) to kick a ball using your heel: *He back-heeled the ball to Hughes.* ▶ back-heel *noun* [C]

backing **C1** /'bækɪŋ/ *noun* **1** [U] help or support to do sth, especially financial support: *The police gave the proposals their full backing.* ◇ *financial backing* **2** [U, C, usually sing.] (MUSIC) (in pop songs) music that accompanies the main singer or tune: *a backing group/singer/track*

backlash /'bæklæʃ/ *noun* [sing.] a strong negative reaction by a large number of people against a political or social event or development

backlog /'bæklɒg/ *noun* [C, usually sing.] an amount of work, etc. that has not yet been done and should have been done already

backpack¹ /'bækpæk/ *noun* [C] = RUCKSACK

backpack² /'bækpæk/ *verb* [I] ~ (round/around …) (TOURISM) to go walking or travelling with your clothes, etc. in a BACKPACK: *We went backpacking round Europe last summer.* ▶ backpacker *noun* [C]

back-pedal *verb* [I] (-ll-, AmE -l-) **1** ~ (on sth) to change an earlier statement or opinion; to not do sth that you promised to do: *The protests have forced the government to back-pedal on plans to introduce a new tax.* **2** to move your feet backwards when you are riding a bicycle

backside /'bæksaɪd/ *noun* [C] (*informal*) the part of the body that you sit on **SYN** bottom¹

backslash /'bækslæʃ/ *noun* [C] (**COMPUTING, LANGUAGE**) a symbol (\) used in computer commands ⊃ look at **forward slash, slash**² (3)

backstage /ˌbæk'steɪdʒ/ *adv.* (**ARTS AND MEDIA**) in the part of a theatre where the actors get dressed, wait to perform, etc.

backstroke /'bækstrəʊk/ *noun* [U] (**SPORT**) a style of swimming that you do on your back: *Can you* **do** *backstroke?*

back-to-'back *adj.* [only before noun] (used about events) following one after another in a continuous series: *The women's hockey team is playing back-to-back games this weekend.*

backtrack /'bæktræk/ *verb* [I] **1** to go back the same way you came **2 ~ (on sth)** to change your mind about a plan, promise, etc. that you have made: *Unions forced the company to backtrack on its plans to close the factory.*

backup 🔒+ **C1** /'bækʌp/ *noun* **1** [U] extra help or support that you can get if necessary **2** [C] (**COMPUTING**) a copy of a file, etc. that you can use if the original one is lost or damaged: *Always* **make a backup** *of your files.*

backward /'bækwəd/ *adj.* **1** [only before noun] directed towards the back: *a backward step/glance* **OPP forward**² **2** slow to develop or learn: *Our teaching methods are backward compared to some countries.*

backwards 🔒 **B1** /'bækwədz/ (*also* **backward** *especially in AmE*) *adv.* **1** towards a place or a position that is behind: *Could everybody take a step backwards?* **2** in the opposite direction to usual: *Can you say the alphabet backwards?* **OPP forwards**
IDM backward(s) and forward(s) first in one direction and then in the other, many times: *The dog ran backwards and forwards, barking loudly.*

backwash /'bækwɒʃ/ *noun* [U] (**GEOGRAPHY**) waves caused by a boat moving through water; the movement of water back into the sea after a wave has hit the beach ⊃ look at **swash** ⊃ picture at **longshore drift**

backwater /'bækwɔːtə(r)/ *noun* [C] a place that is away from the places where most things happen and so is not affected by new ideas or outside events

backyard /ˌbæk'jɑːd/ *noun* [C] **1** (*especially BrE*) an area behind a house, with a hard surface and a wall or fence around it **2** (*AmE*) a piece of land behind a house, usually with an area of grass

bacon /'beɪkən/ *noun* [U] meat from the back or sides of a pig, that has been CURED (= treated with salt or smoke to keep it fresh), usually served in thin slices ⊃ note at **meat**

bacteria 🔒 **B2** /bæk'tɪəriə/ *noun* [pl.] (*sing.* **bacterium** /-riəm/) (**BIOLOGY**) very small living things that can only be seen with a MICROSCOPE (= a piece of equipment that makes small objects look bigger). Bacteria exist in large numbers in air, water, soil, plants and the bodies of people and animals. Some bacteria cause disease: *More than 15 per cent of the water samples contained* **harmful bacteria**. ◇ *Food poisoning can be caused by eating food contaminated* **with bacteria**. ⊃ look at **germ** (1), **virus** ⊃ picture at **food chain, nitrogen cycle** ▸ **bacterial** /-riəl/ *adj.*: *bacterial infections*

bad 🔒 **A1** /bæd/ *adj.* (**worse** /wɜːs/; **worst** /wɜːst/)
• UNPLEASANT **1** not good; unpleasant: *Our family's had a bad time recently.* ◇ *bad weather* ◇ *I'm afraid I've got some bad news for you.*
• POOR QUALITY **2** of poor quality; of a low standard: *Many accidents are caused by bad driving.* ◇ *Some of the company's problems are the result of bad management.*
• NOT SKILFUL **3 ~ (at sth/doing sth)** not able to do sth well or easily: *a bad teacher/driver/cook* ◇ *I've always been bad at sport.* **SYN poor**
• SERIOUS **4** serious; severe: *The traffic was very bad on the way to work.* ◇ *She went home with a bad headache.* ◇ *That was a bad mistake!*
• FOOD **5** not fresh or suitable to eat: *These eggs will go bad if we don't eat them soon.*
• PART OF THE BODY **6** (**HEALTH**) (used about parts of the body) not healthy; painful: *He's always had a bad heart.* ◇ *Keith's off work with a bad back.*
• PERSON/BEHAVIOUR **7** (used about a person or behaviour) not good; morally wrong: *He was not a bad man, just rather lazy.*
• HARMFUL **8** [not before noun] **~ for sb/sth** likely to damage or hurt sb/sth: *Sugar is bad for your teeth.*
• NOT SUITABLE **9 ~ (to do sth)** difficult or not suitable: *This is a bad time to phone — I'm in the middle of making dinner.*
IDM not bad (*informal*) quite good: *'What was the film like?' 'Not bad.'* **too bad** (*informal*) used to show that nothing can be done to change a situation: *'I'd much rather stay at home.' 'Well that's just too bad. We've said we'll go.'* ❶ For other idioms containing **bad**, look at the entries for the nouns, adjectives, etc. For example, **go through a bad patch** is at **patch**.

baddy (*also* **baddie**) /'bædi/ *noun* [C] (*pl.* **-ies**) (*informal*) (**ARTS AND MEDIA**) a bad person in a film, book, etc. **OPP goody**

badge 🔒+ **B2** /bædʒ/ *noun* [C] a small piece of metal, cloth or plastic with a design or words on it that you wear on your clothing or carry: *The players all have jackets with the club badge on.*

badger /'bædʒə(r)/ *noun* [C] an animal with black and white lines on its head, that lives in a hole in the ground and comes out at night ⊃ picture at **animal**

bad 'language *noun* [U] (**LANGUAGE**) words that are used for swearing

badly 🔒 **A2** /'bædli/ *adv.* (**worse** /wɜːs/; **worst** /wɜːst/) **1** in a way that is not good enough; not well: *She did badly in the exams.* **OPP well**¹ **2** seriously; severely: *He was badly hurt in the accident.* **3** very much: *He badly needed a holiday.*

badly 'off *adj.* not having much money: *They don't seem too badly off — they have smart clothes and a nice house.* **OPP well off**

badminton /'bædmɪntən/ *noun* [U] (**SPORT**) a game for two or four people in which players hit a SHUTTLECOCK (= a type of light ball, originally with feathers around it) over a high net, using a RACKET (= a piece of equipment that is held in the hand) ⊃ picture at **sport**

bad-'tempered *adj.* often angry or impatient: *a bad-tempered old man*

baffle /'bæfl/ *verb* [T] to be impossible to understand; to confuse sb very much: *His illness baffled the doctors.* ▸ **baffled** *adj.*: *The instructions were so complicated that I was completely baffled.* ▸ **baffling** *adj.*

bag¹ 🔒 **A1** /bæg/ *noun* **1** [C] (often in compounds) a container made of cloth, leather, plastic or paper, used to carry things in, especially when shopping or travelling: *She brought some sandwiches in a* **plastic bag**. ◇ *a* **shopping bag** ◇ *She took her purse out of her bag* (= HANDBAG). ◇ *Don't forget your* **school bag**. **2** [C] (**TOURISM**) a bag or case that you take when you are travelling: *Have you* **packed your bags** *yet?* ◇ *We checked in two bags at the airport.* **3** [C] the amount contained in a bag: *She's eaten a whole bag of sweets!*

◇ *a bag of crisps/sugar/flour* **4** bags [pl.] (**HEALTH**) dark circles or folds of skin under the eyes, often caused by lack of sleep **5** bags [pl.] ~ **(of sth)** (*BrE, informal*) a large amount or number of sth: *There's no hurry, we've got bags of time.*

bag² /bæg/ *verb* [T] (-gg-) **1** to put sth into bags: *The fruit is bagged at the farm.* **2** (*informal*) to try to get sth for yourself so that other people cannot have it: *Somebody's bagged the seats by the pool!*

bagel /ˈbeɪgl/ *noun* [C] a type of bread roll in the shape of a ring

baggage/luggage

holdall/duffel bag   suitcase   rucksack/backpack

baggage /ˈbægɪdʒ/ *noun* [U] (**TOURISM**) bags, cases, etc. used for carrying sb's clothes and things on a journey: *excess baggage* (= baggage weighing more than the airline's permitted limit) ◇ *baggage handlers* (= people employed to load and UNLOAD baggage at airports) **SYN** luggage

baggage carousel *noun* [C] (**TOURISM**) a moving belt from which you collect your bags at an airport

baggage reclaim (*BrE*) (*AmE* **baggage claim**) *noun* [U] (**TOURISM**) the place at an airport where you get your bags, cases, etc. again after you have flown

baggy /ˈbægi/ *adj.* (**baggier**; **baggiest**) (used about a piece of clothing) fitting loosely **OPP** tight¹

bagpipes /ˈbægpaɪps/ *noun* [pl.] (**MUSIC**) a musical instrument, popular in Scotland, that is played by blowing air through a pipe into a bag and then pressing the bag so that the air comes out of other pipes, producing a noise

baguette /bæˈget/ (*also* **French stick**) *noun* [C] a type of bread in the shape of a long thick stick

bail¹ ¹ ⁺ **C1** /beɪl/ *noun* [U] (**LAW**) money that sb agrees to pay if a person accused of a crime does not appear in court on the day they are called. When bail has been arranged, the accused person can go free until the trial: *She was released on bail of £2 000.* ◇ *The judge set bail at £10 000.* ◇ *The judge felt that he was a dangerous man and refused him bail.* ◇ *She was granted bail.*

bail² /beɪl/ *verb* [T] (**LAW**) to free sb on BAIL
PHR V **bail sb out 1** (**LAW**) to pay sb's BAIL for them: *Her parents went to the police station and bailed her out.* **2** to rescue sb from a difficult situation (especially by providing money)

bailey /ˈbeɪli/ *noun* [C] (**HISTORY**) the open area of a castle, inside the outer wall ⊃ look at **motte-and-bailey castle**

bailiff /ˈbeɪlɪf/ *noun* [C] **1** (*BrE*) (**LAW**) a law officer whose job is to take the possessions and property of people who cannot pay their debts **2** (*BrE*) (**AGRICULTURE**) a person employed to manage land or a large farm for sb else **3** (*AmE*) (**LAW**) an official who keeps order in court, takes people to their seats, watches prisoners, etc.

bailout /ˈbeɪlaʊt/ *noun* [C] (**FINANCE**) an act of giving money to a company, a foreign country, etc. that has very serious financial problems

bait /beɪt/ *noun* [U] **1** food, or sth that looks like food, that is put onto a HOOK (= a curved piece of metal) to catch fish, or in nets, TRAPS, etc. to catch other animals **2** something that is used for persuading or attracting sb: *Free offers are often used as bait to attract customers.*

baize /beɪz/ *noun* [U] a type of thick cloth made of wool that is usually green, used especially for covering card tables and BILLIARD, SNOOKER or POOL tables

bake ⁷ **B1** /beɪk/ *verb* [I, T] **1** to cook food in an oven without extra fat or liquid; to be cooked in this way: *I could smell bread baking in the oven.* ◇ *On his birthday she baked him a cake.* ⊃ note at **cook¹ 2** to become hard when heated; to make sth hard by heating it: *The hot sun baked the earth.*

baked 'beans *noun* [pl.] (*especially BrE*) small white beans cooked in a tomato sauce and sold in cans

baked po'tato (*BrE also* **jacket potato**) *noun* [C] a potato that has been cooked in the oven in its skin

baker /ˈbeɪkə(r)/ *noun* [C] **1** a person who bakes bread, cakes, etc. to sell in a shop **2** **baker's** (*pl.* **bakers**) a shop that sells bread, cakes, etc: *Get a loaf at the baker's.*

bakery /ˈbeɪkəri/ *noun* [C] (*pl.* -**ies**) a place where bread, cakes, etc. are baked to be sold

baking /ˈbeɪkɪŋ/ (*also* **baking 'hot**) *adj.* (*informal*) very hot: *The workers complained of the baking heat in the office in the summer.*

baking powder *noun* [U] a mixture of powders used to make cakes rise and become light as they are baked

baking soda = SODIUM BICARBONATE

balance¹ ⁷ **B1** ❶ /ˈbæləns/ *noun* **1** [C, U, usually sing.] ~ **(between A and B)** a situation in which different or opposite things are of equal importance, size, etc: *The course provides a good balance between academic and practical work.* ◇ *Tourism has upset the delicate balance of nature on the island.* **2** [U] the ability to keep steady with an equal amount of weight on each side of the body: *to lose your balance* ◇ *It's very difficult to keep your balance when you start learning to ski.* ◇ *You need a good sense of balance to ride a motorbike.* **3** [sing.] (**FINANCE**) the amount that still has to be paid; the amount that is left after sth has been used, taken, etc: *You can pay a 10% deposit now, with the balance due in one month.* ◇ *to check your bank balance* (= to find out how much money you have in your account) **4** [C] an instrument for weighing things, with a bar that is supported in the middle and has dishes hanging from each end
IDM **(be/hang) in the balance** uncertain: *Following poor results, the company's future hangs in the balance.* **(catch/throw sb) off balance** (to find or put sb) in a position that is not safe and from which it is easy to fall: *A strong gust of wind caught me off balance and I nearly fell over.* **on balance** having considered all sides, facts, etc: *On balance, I've had a pretty good year.* **strike a balance (between A and B)** → STRIKE²

balance² ⁷ **B1** ⓦ /ˈbæləns/ *verb* **1** [I, T] ~ **(sth) (on sth)** to put your body or sth else into a position where it is steady and does not fall: *I had to balance on the top step of the ladder to paint the ceiling.* ◇ *Carefully, she balanced a glass on top of the pile of plates.* **2** [I, T] (**FINANCE**) to have equal totals of money spent and money received: *I must have made a mistake — the accounts don't balance.* ◇ *She is always very careful to balance her weekly budget.* **3** [I, T] ~ **(sth) (out); ~ (A with B)** to have or give sth equal value, importance, etc. in relation to other parts: *The loss in the first half of the year was balanced out by the profit in the second half.* ◇ *It's difficult to balance the demands of a career with caring for an elderly relative.* **4** [T] ~ **sth against sth** to consider and compare one matter in relation to another: *In planning the new road, we have to balance the benefit to motorists against the damage to the environment.*

'balance beam (*AmE*) = BEAM¹ (4)

balanced ⓘ+ B2 /'bælənst/ *adj.* keeping or showing a balance so that different things, or different parts of things exist in equal or correct amounts: *I like this newspaper because it gives a balanced view.* ◊ *A balanced diet plays an important part in good health.* OPP **unbalanced**

,balance of 'payments *noun* [sing.] (ECONOMICS) the difference between the amount of money a country receives from other countries for things it sells and the amount it pays other countries for things it buys, in a particular period of time

,balance of 'power *noun* [sing.] (POLITICS) **1** a situation in which political power or military strength is divided between two countries or groups of countries: *There was a dramatic shift in the balance of power.* **2** the power that a smaller political party has when the larger parties need its support because they do not have enough votes on their own: *The Democratic Party now holds the balance of power in this region.*

,balance of 'trade (*also* trade balance) *noun* [sing.] (ECONOMICS) the difference in value between the amount that a country buys from other countries and the amount that it sells to them

'balance sheet *noun* [C] (FINANCE) a written statement showing the amount of money and property that a company has, and how much has been received and paid out

balcony /'bælkəni/ *noun* [C] (*pl.* -ies) **1** a platform built on an upstairs outside wall of a building, with a wall or RAIL around it **2** = CIRCLE¹ (4)

bald /bɔːld/ *adj.* **1** (used about people) having little or no hair on the head: *I hope I don't go bald like my father did.* ◊ *He has a bald patch on the top of his head.* **2** (used about sth that is said) simple; without extra words: *the bald truth*

balding /'bɔːldɪŋ/ *adj.* starting to lose the hair on your head: *a balding man in his fifties*

baldly /'bɔːldli/ *adv.* in a few words with nothing extra or unnecessary: *He told us baldly that he was leaving.*

bale /beɪl/ *noun* [C] a large quantity of sth pressed tightly together and tied up: *a bale of hay/cloth/paper*

the 'Balkans *noun* [pl.] (GEOGRAPHY) a region of south-east Europe ▸ Balkan /'bɔːlkən, 'bɒl-/ *adj.*

ball ⓘ A1 /bɔːl/ *noun* [C]
- ROUND OBJECT **1** (SPORT) a round object that you hit, kick, throw, etc. in games and sports: *a tennis/golf/rugby ball* ◊ *a football* ⊃ picture at **sport 2** a round object or a thing that has been formed into a round shape: *a ball of wool* ◊ *The children threw snowballs at each other.* ◊ *We had meatballs and pasta for dinner.*
- THROW/KICK **3** (SPORT) one throw, kick, etc. of the ball in some sports: *That was a great ball from the defender.*
- PART OF THE BODY **4** ~ of the foot/hand (ANATOMY) the part below the big toe or the THUMB
- PARTY **5** a large formal party at which people dance IDM **be on the ball** (*informal*) to always know what is happening and be able to react to or deal with it quickly **play ball** (*informal*) to be willing to work with other people in a helpful way **set/start the ball rolling** to start an activity, conversation, etc. that involves or is done by a group

ballad /'bæləd/ *noun* [C] (LITERATURE, MUSIC) a long song or poem that tells a story, often about love

,ball-and-'socket joint *noun* [C] (ANATOMY) a JOINT (= place where two bones meet) in which a piece of bone in the shape of a ball that moves inside a curved hollow part, for example at the top of the leg

ballast /'bæləst/ *noun* [U] heavy material placed in a ship or HOT-AIR BALLOON to make it heavier and keep it steady

,ball 'bearing *noun* [C] (ENGINEERING) a ring of small metal balls used in a machine to enable the parts to turn smoothly; one of these small metal balls

ballboy /'bɔːlbɔɪ/ *noun* [C] (SPORT) a boy who picks up the balls for the players in a tennis match

ballerina /,bælə'riːnə/ *noun* [C] (ARTS AND MEDIA) a woman who dances in BALLETS

ballet ⓘ+ B2 /'bæleɪ/ *noun* (ARTS AND MEDIA) **1** [U] a style of dancing that tells a story with music but without words: *He wants to be a ballet dancer.* **2** [C] a performance or work that consists of this type of dancing

'ball game *noun* [C] (SPORT) **1** any game played with a ball **2** (*AmE*) a baseball match IDM **a (whole) new/different ball game** (*informal*) something completely new or different

ballgirl /'bɔːlgɜːl/ *noun* [C] (SPORT) a girl who picks up the balls for the players in a tennis match

ballistic /bə'lɪstɪk/ *adj.* connected with BALLISTICS IDM **go ballistic** (*informal*) to become very angry: *He went ballistic when I told him.*

bal,listic 'missile *noun* [C] a MISSILE (= a powerful exploding weapon that can be sent long distances) that is fired into the air at a particular speed and angle in order to fall in the right place

ballistics /bə'lɪstɪks/ *noun* [U] (PHYSICS) the scientific study of things that are shot or fired through the air, for example bullets

balloon ⓘ+ B2 /bə'luːn/ *noun* [C] **1** a small coloured object made of very thin rubber that you blow air into and use as a toy or for decoration: *to blow up/burst/pop a balloon* **2** (*also* hot-air balloon) a large balloon made of strong material that is filled with gas or hot air so that it can fly through the sky, usually carrying people in a BASKET (= a container) under it: *They crossed the Atlantic in a balloon.*

ballot ⓘ+ C1 /'bælət/ *noun* (POLITICS) **1** [U, C] ~ (on sth) a secret written vote: *The union will hold a ballot on the new pay offer.* ◊ *The committee are elected by ballot every year.* **2** (*BrE also* ballot paper) [C] the piece of paper on which sb marks who they are voting for: *What percentage of eligible voters cast their ballots?* ▸ ballot *verb* [T] ~ sb (on sth): *The union is balloting its members on strike action.*

'ballot box *noun* (POLITICS) **1** [C] the box into which people put the piece of paper with their vote on **2** the ballot box [sing.] the system of voting in an election: *People will express their opinion through the ballot box.*

ballpark /'bɔːlpɑːk/ *noun* [C] (SPORT) a place where baseball is played IDM **a ballpark estimate/figure** a number, amount, etc. that is likely to be correct **in the ballpark** (*informal*) (used about figures or amounts) within a range that is likely to be correct: *All the bids for the contract were in the same ballpark.*

ballpoint /'bɔːlpɔɪnt/ (*also* ,ballpoint 'pen) *noun* [C] a pen with a very small metal ball at the end that rolls INK (= coloured liquid for writing) onto paper ⊃ look at **Biro™**

ballroom /ˈbɔːlruːm, -rʊm/ noun [C] a large room used for dancing on formal occasions

ˌballroom ˈdancing noun [U] a formal type of dance in which couples dance together using particular steps and movements

balm /bɑːm/ noun [U, C] (**MEDICINE**) a liquid, cream, etc. with a pleasant smell, used to make wounds less painful or skin softer

balsa /ˈbɔːlsə/ (also ˈbalsa wood) noun [U] the light wood of the tropical American balsa tree, used especially for making models

balustrade /ˌbæləˈstreɪd/ noun [C] (**ARCHITECTURE**) a row of posts, joined together at the top, built along the edge of a structure such as a bridge, etc. to stop you from falling, or as a decoration

bamboo /ˌbæmˈbuː/ noun [C, U] (pl. -oos) a tall plant that is a member of the grass family. The plant has hard hollow STEMS that are used for making furniture, etc: a bamboo chair

BAME /beɪm, ˌbiː eɪ em ˈiː/ abbr. (BrE) (**SOCIAL STUDIES**) black, Asian and minority ethnic (used in the UK to refer to people who are not white): Around 20% of the teachers are from BAME backgrounds.

ban ʔ B1 /bæn/ verb [T] (-nn-) (**LAW**) **1** ~ sth (from sth) to officially say that sth is not allowed, often by law: The city has banned private cars from the historic centre. **SYN** prohibit **2** [usually passive] be banned (from sth/doing sth) to be officially ordered not to do sth, go somewhere, etc: He was fined £2 000 and banned from driving for a year. ▸ ban ʔ B1 noun [C] ~ (on sth): There is a ban on smoking in this office. ◇ to impose/lift a ban

banal /bəˈnɑːl/ adj. not original or interesting: a banal comment

banana ʔ A1 /bəˈnɑːnə/ noun [C, U] a curved fruit with yellow skin that grows in hot countries: a bunch of bananas ◇ a banana milkshake
IDM go bananas (informal) to become angry, crazy or silly: When he walked on stage, the crowd went bananas.

band ʔ A1 /bænd/ noun [C]
• **MUSICIANS 1** [+ sing./pl. verb] (**MUSIC**) a small group of musicians who play popular music together, often with a singer or singers: a rock/jazz band ◇ He plays the drums in a band. ◇ The band has/have released a new album.
• **GROUP OF PEOPLE 2** [+ sing./pl. verb] a group of people who do sth together or have the same ideas: A small band of rebels is/are hiding in the hills.
• **THIN PIECE OF MATERIAL/COLOUR 3** ~ (round/around sth) a thin flat piece or circle of any material that is put around things, for example to hold them together: She rolled up the papers and put an elastic band round them. ◇ All babies in the hospital have name bands round their wrists. **4** a line of colour or material on sth that is different from what is around it: She wore a red pullover with a green band across the middle.
• **RADIO WAVES 5** (also waveband) a set of radio waves of similar length
• **RANGE 6** a range of numbers, ages, prices, etc. within which people or things are counted or measured: the 25–35 age band ◇ tax bands

bandage /ˈbændɪdʒ/ noun [C] (**MEDICINE**) a long, narrow piece of soft cloth that you tie round a part of the body that has been hurt ◇ picture at **health** ▸ bandage verb [T] ~ sth (up): The nurse bandaged my hand up.

ˈBand-Aid™ noun [C] (AmE) = PLASTER¹ (2)

bandana (also **bandanna**) /bænˈdænə/ noun [C] a piece of brightly coloured cloth worn around the neck or head

B and B (also **B & B**) /ˌbiː ən ˈbiː/ abbr. (especially BrE, informal) = BED AND BREAKFAST

bandit /ˈbændɪt/ noun [C] a member of an armed group of thieves who attack travellers

bandwagon /ˈbændwæɡən/ noun (informal)
IDM climb/jump on the bandwagon to copy what other people are doing because it is fashionable or successful

bandwidth /ˈbændwɪdθ, -wɪtθ/ noun [C, U]
1 (**ENGINEERING**) a BAND of FREQUENCIES used for sending electronic signals **2** (**COMPUTING**) a measurement of the amount of information that a particular computer network or internet connection can send in a particular time. It is often measured in BITS per second.

bandy¹ /ˈbændi/ adj. (used about a person's legs) curving towards the outside so that the knees are wide apart

bandy² /ˈbændi/ verb (bandying; bandies; pt, pp bandied)
PHR V bandy sth about/around [usually passive] if a name, word, story, etc. is bandied about/around, it is mentioned frequently by many people

bang¹ /bæŋ/ verb [I, T] (often used with an adverb or a preposition) **1** to make a loud noise by hitting sth hard; to close sth or to be closed with a loud noise: Somewhere in the house, I heard a door bang. ◇ He banged his fist on the table and started shouting. **SYN** slam **2** to knock against sth by accident; to hit a part of the body against sth by accident: Be careful not to bang your head on the ceiling. It's quite low. ◇ As I was crossing the room in the dark I banged into a table.

bang² /bæŋ/ noun [C] **1** a sudden, short, very loud noise: There was an enormous bang when the bomb exploded. **2** a short, strong knock or hit, especially one that causes pain and injury: a nasty bang on the head **3** bangs (AmE) = FRINGE¹ (1)
IDM with a bang (informal) in a successful or exciting way: Our team's season started with a bang when we won our first five matches.

bang³ /bæŋ/ adv. (especially BrE, informal) exactly; directly; right: Our computers are bang up to date. ◇ The shot was bang on target.
IDM bang goes sth (informal) used for expressing the idea that sth is now impossible: 'It's raining!' 'Ah well, bang goes our picnic!'

bang⁴ /bæŋ/ exclamation used to sound like the noise of a gun, etc.

banger /ˈbæŋə(r)/ noun [C] (BrE, informal) **1** a SAUSAGE **2** an old car that is in very bad condition **3** a small, noisy FIREWORK (= a device that burns or explodes, used for entertainment)

bangle /ˈbæŋɡl/ noun [C] a circle of metal that is worn round the arm or WRIST for decoration

banish /ˈbænɪʃ/ verb [T] (formal) **1** [usually passive] (**LAW**) to send sb away, especially out of the country, usually as a punishment **SYN** exile **2** to make sb/sth go away; to get rid of sb/sth: She banished all hope of winning from her mind.

banister (also **bannister**) /ˈbænɪstə(r)/ noun [C] (BrE also banisters [pl.]) the posts and RAIL that you can hold for support when going up or down stairs: The children loved sliding down the banister at the old house.

banjo /ˈbændʒəʊ/ noun [C] (pl. -os) (**MUSIC**) a musical instrument like a guitar, with a long thin NECK, a round BODY and four or more STRINGS ◇ picture at **instrument**

bank[1] 🔊 **A1** /bæŋk/ *noun* [C]
- FOR MONEY **1** (**FINANCE**) an organization that keeps money safely for its customers; the office or building of such an organization. You can take money out, save, borrow or exchange money at a bank: *I need to go to the bank to get some money out.* ◇ *a bank account/loan* ⊃ look at **bank account** ⊃ note at **mortgage**[1]
- STORE **2** a store of things that you keep to use later: *a blood bank in a hospital*
- BESIDE A RIVER **3** (**GEOGRAPHY**) the ground along the side of a river or CANAL: *People were fishing on the banks of the river.* ⊃ note at **river**
- HIGHER GROUND **4** (**GEOGRAPHY**) a higher area of ground that goes down or up at an angle, often at the edge of sth or dividing sth: *There were grassy banks on either side of the road.*
- OF CLOUD/SNOW **5** a mass of cloud, snow, etc: *The sun disappeared behind a bank of clouds.*

bank[2] /bæŋk/ *verb* **1** [T] (**FINANCE**) to put money into a bank account: *She is believed to have banked (= been paid) £10 million in two years.* **2** [I] ~ (**with/at ...**) (**FINANCE**) to have an account with a particular bank: *I've banked with Lloyds for years.* **3** [I] to travel with one side higher than the other when turning: *The plane banked steeply to the left.*
PHR V **bank on sb/sth** to expect and trust sb to do sth, or sth to happen: *Our boss might let you have the morning off, but I wouldn't bank on it.*

bank account *noun* [C] (**FINANCE**) an arrangement that you have with a bank that allows you to keep your money there, to pay in or take out money, etc: *to open/close a bank account*

banker /ˈbæŋkə(r)/ *noun* [C] (**FINANCE**) a person who owns a bank or has an important job in a bank

bank holiday *noun* [C] (*BrE*) a public holiday, for example Christmas Day or New Year's Day

banking /ˈbæŋkɪŋ/ *noun* [U] (**BUSINESS**, **FINANCE**) the type of business done by banks: *a career in banking*

banknote /ˈbæŋknəʊt/ (*especially BrE*) = NOTE[1] (4)

bankrupt[1] /ˈbæŋkrʌpt/ *adj.* (**FINANCE**) not having enough money to pay what you owe: *The company must cut its costs or it will go bankrupt.* ► **bankrupt** *verb* [T]: *The failure of the new product almost bankrupted the firm.*

bankrupt[2] /ˈbæŋkrʌpt/ *noun* [C] (**LAW**) a person who has been judged by a court to be unable to pay his or her debts

bankruptcy /ˈbæŋkrʌptsi/ *noun* [C, U] (*pl.* -ies) (**FINANCE**) the state of being BANKRUPT: *The company filed for bankruptcy (= asked to be officially declared BANKRUPT) in 2020.*

bank statement *noun* [C] (**FINANCE**) a printed list of all the money going into or out of your bank account during a certain period

banner 🔊+ **C1** /ˈbænə(r)/ *noun* [C] a long piece of cloth with words or signs on it, that can be hung up or carried on two POLES: *The demonstrators carried banners saying 'Stop the War'.*

banner ad *noun* [C] (**BUSINESS**, **COMPUTING**) an advertisement across the top or bottom or down the side of a page on the internet

bannister /ˈbænɪstə(r)/ (*BrE also* **bannisters** [pl.]) = BANISTER

banquet /ˈbæŋkwɪt/ *noun* [C] a formal meal for a large number of people, usually at a special event at which speeches are made

banter /ˈbæntə(r)/ *noun* [U] friendly comments and jokes ► **banter** *verb* [I]

baobab /ˈbeɪəʊbæb/ *noun* [C] an African tree with a very thick TRUNK (= central part)

baptism /ˈbæptɪzəm/ *noun* [C, U] (**RELIGION**) a ceremony in which a person becomes a member of the Christian Church by being covered with water for a short time or having drops of water put onto their head. Often they are also formally given a name. ⊃ look at **christening** ► **baptize** (*BrE also* -ise) /bæpˈtaɪz/ *verb* [T, usually passive]: *She was baptized a Catholic.* ⊃ look at **christen** (1)

Baptist /ˈbæptɪst/ *noun* [C] (**RELIGION**) a member of a Christian Protestant Church that believes that people should only be BAPTIZED when they are old enough to understand what it means ► **Baptist** *adj.*

bar[1] 🔊 **A2** /bɑː(r)/ *noun*
- FOR DRINKS/FOOD **1** [C] a place where you can buy and drink alcoholic and other drinks: *They had a drink in the bar before the meal.* **2** [C] (in compounds) a place where a particular type of food or drink is the main thing that is served: *a wine/coffee/sandwich bar* **3** [C] a long, narrow, high surface where drinks are served: *She went to the bar and ordered a drink.* ◇ *We sat on stools at the bar.* ◇ *He works behind the bar in the local pub.*
- OF SOAP/CHOCOLATE **4** [C] a small block of solid material, longer than it is wide: *a bar of soap/chocolate*
- ON A WINDOW **5** [C] a long, thin, straight piece of metal, often placed across a window or door, etc. to stop sb from getting through it
- THAT STOPS YOU **6** [C, usually sing.] ~ (**to sth**) something that stops you from doing sth: *Lack of education is not always a bar to success in business.*
- IN COMPUTING **7** [C] a long narrow area, usually at the top or side of a computer screen, that contains links or menus, or displays information about the website or program that you are using
- IN MUSIC **8** (*BrE*) (*AmE* **measure**) [C] one of the short sections of equal length that a piece of music is divided into, and the notes that are in it: *If you sing a few bars of the song, I might recognize it.* ⊃ picture at **music**
- IN LAW **9** **the Bar** [sing.] (*BrE*) the profession of a BARRISTER (= a lawyer in a higher court): *to be called to the Bar (= allowed to work as a qualified BARRISTER)* **10** **the Bar** [sing.] (*AmE*) the profession of any kind of lawyer
- MEASUREMENT **11** [C] (**PHYSICS**) a unit for measuring the pressure of the atmosphere, equal to 100 thousand NEWTONS per square metre ⊃ look at **millibar**
- LINE OF SAND/MUD **12** [C] (**GEOGRAPHY**) a long thin line of sand or mud that sticks out into the sea
IDM **behind bars** (*informal*) in prison: *The criminals are now safely behind bars.* **raise the bar** → RAISE[1] **set the bar** to set a standard of quality or performance: *The movie really sets the bar for special effects.*

bar[2] 🔊 **B2** /bɑː(r)/ *verb* [T] (-rr-) **1** [usually passive] to close sth with a bar or bars: *All the windows were barred.* **2** to block a road, path, etc. so that nobody can pass: *A line of police officers barred the entrance to the embassy.* **3** ~ **sb (from sth/doing sth)** to say officially that sb is not allowed to do, use or enter sth: *He was barred from the club for fighting.*

bar[3] /bɑː(r)/ *prep.* (*especially BrE*) except: *All the seats were taken, bar one.*

barb /bɑːb/ *noun* [C] **1** the point of an ARROW (= a thin stick with a sharp point at one end) or a HOOK that is curved backwards to make it difficult to pull out **2** something that sb says that is intended to hurt another person's feelings

barbarian /bɑːˈbeəriən/ *noun* [C] a wild person with no culture, who behaves very badly

barbaric /bɑːˈbærɪk/ *adj.* very cruel and violent: *barbaric treatment of prisoners* ▶ **barbarism** /ˈbɑːbərɪzəm/ *noun* [U]: *acts of barbarism committed in war*

barbarity /bɑːˈbærəti/ *noun* [U, C] (*pl.* -ies) extremely cruel and violent behaviour

barbecue /ˈbɑːbɪkjuː/ *noun* [C] (*abbr.* **BBQ**) **1** a metal frame on which food is cooked outdoors over flames **2** an outdoor party at which food is cooked in this way: *Let's have a barbecue on the beach.* ⊃ look at **roast**¹(2) ▶ **barbecue** *verb* [T]: *barbecued steak* ⊃ note at **cook**¹

barbed wire /ˌbɑːbd ˈwaɪə(r)/ *noun* [U] strong wire with sharp points on it: *a barbed wire fence*

barbed wire

barber /ˈbɑːbə(r)/ *noun* [C] **1** a person whose job is to cut men's hair and sometimes to SHAVE them ⊃ look at **hairdresser**(1) **2** **barber's** (*pl.* **barbers**) (*BrE*) a shop where men go to have their hair cut

barbiturate /bɑːˈbɪtʃərət/ *noun* [C] (**MEDICINE**) any of several types of powerful drug that make you feel calm and relaxed or put you to sleep

'bar chart (*also* **bar graph**) *noun* [C] (**MATHEMATICS**) a diagram that uses narrow bands of different heights to show different amounts so that they can be compared ⊃ picture at **chart**¹

barcode /ˈbɑːkəʊd/ *noun* [C] (**COMPUTING**) a pattern of thick and thin lines that is printed on things you buy. It contains information that a computer can read.

barcode

bard /bɑːd/ *noun* [C] (**LITERATURE**) a person who writes poems

bare 🔒 **C1** /beə(r)/ *adj.* **1** not covered by any clothes: *bare arms/feet/shoulders* ⊃ look at **naked**(1), **nude**¹ **2** without anything covering it or in it: *They had taken the pictures down, so the walls were bare.* ◇ *I looked for some food but the cupboards were bare.* **3** [only before noun] just enough; the most basic or simple: *I don't take much luggage when I travel, just the bare essentials.* ◇ *You won't pass your exams if you just do the bare minimum.*
IDM **with your bare hands** without weapons or tools: *She killed the snake with her bare hands.*

bareback /ˈbeəbæk/ *adj., adv.* riding a horse without a SADDLE (= seat): *bareback riders in the circus*

barefoot /ˈbeəfʊt/ *adj., adv.* not wearing anything on your feet: *We walked barefoot along the beach.*

bareheaded /ˌbeəˈhedɪd/ *adj., adv.* not wearing anything to cover your head

barely 🔒 **B2** /ˈbeəli/ *adv.* **1** used especially after *can* and *could* to emphasize that sth is possible, but only with difficulty: *I was so tired I could barely stand up.* **2** just; almost not: *I earn barely enough money to pay my rent.* ◇ *There was barely any smell.* ⊃ look at **hardly**

bargain¹ 🔒 **B2** /ˈbɑːgən/ *noun* [C] **1** something that is cheaper or at a lower price than usual: *At that price, it's an absolute bargain!* ◇ *I found a lot of bargains in the sale.* **2** an agreement between people or groups about what each of them will do for the other or others: *Let's make a bargain — I'll lend you the money*

if you'll help me with my work. ◇ *I lent him the money but he didn't keep his side of the bargain.*
IDM **into the bargain** (used for emphasizing sth) as well; in addition; also: *They gave me free tickets and a free meal into the bargain.* **strike a bargain (with sb)** → **STRIKE**²

bargain² /ˈbɑːgən/ *verb* [I] ~ **(with sb) (about/over/for sth)** (**BUSINESS**) to discuss prices, conditions, etc. with sb in order to reach an agreement that suits each person: *They bargained over the price.*
PHR V **bargain for/on sth/doing sth** (usually in negative sentences) to expect sth to happen and be ready for it: *I didn't bargain on all these meetings.* ◇ *He didn't bargain on having to help set up the event.*

barge¹ /bɑːdʒ/ *noun* [C] a long narrow boat with a flat bottom, that is used for carrying goods or people on a CANAL or river

barge² /bɑːdʒ/ *verb* [I, T] (used with an adverb or a preposition) to push people out of the way in order to get past them: *He barged (his way) angrily through the crowd.*

'bar graph = **BAR CHART**

barista /bəˈriːstə, -ˈrɪs-/ *noun* [C] a person who works in a COFFEE BAR

baritone /ˈbærɪtəʊn/ *noun* [C] (**MUSIC**) a man's singing voice with a range between a TENOR and a BASS; a man with this voice

barium /ˈbeəriəm/ *noun* [U] (*symb.* Ba) (**CHEMISTRY**) a chemical element. Barium is a soft silver-white metal. ❶ For more information on the periodic table of elements, look at the **Reference Section** of this dictionary.

bark¹ /bɑːk/ *noun* **1** [U] the hard outer covering of a tree ⊃ picture at **tree 2** [C] the short, loud noise that a dog makes

bark² /bɑːk/ *verb* **1** [I] ~ **(at sb/sth)** (used about dogs) to make a loud, short noise or noises **2** [T] ~ **sth (out) (at sb)** to give orders, ask questions, etc. in a loud, unfriendly way: *The boss came in, barked out some orders and left again.*

barley /ˈbɑːli/ *noun* [U] (**AGRICULTURE**) **1** a plant that produces grain that is used for food or for making beer and other drinks ⊃ picture at **cereal 2** the grain produced by this plant

barmaid /ˈbɑːmeɪd/ (*BrE*) (*AmE* **bartender**) *noun* [C] a woman who serves drinks from behind a bar in a pub, etc.

barman /ˈbɑːmən/ (*pl.* -men /-mən/) (*especially BrE*) (*AmE usually* **bartender**) *noun* [C] a man who works in a bar, serving drinks

bar mitzvah /ˌbɑː ˈmɪtsvə/ *noun* [C] (**RELIGION**) a ceremony in the Jewish religion for a boy who has reached the age of 13. At the ceremony he accepts the religious responsibilities of an adult. ⊃ look at **bat mitzvah**

barn /bɑːn/ *noun* [C] (**AGRICULTURE**) a large building on a farm in which crops or animals are kept

barometer /bəˈrɒmɪtə(r)/ *noun* [C] **1** (**GEOGRAPHY**) an instrument that measures air pressure and indicates changes in weather **2** something that indicates the state of a situation, a feeling, etc: *Results of local elections are often a barometer of the government's popularity.*

baron /ˈbærən/ *noun* [C] **1** a NOBLEMAN of the lowest rank. In the UK, barons use the title 'Lord'; in other countries they use the title 'Baron'. **2** (**BUSINESS**) a person who controls a large part of a particular industry or type of business: *drug/oil barons*

baroness /ˈbærənəs/ *noun* **1** [C, usually sing.] a woman who has the same rank as a BARON. In the UK, baronesses use the title 'Lady' or 'Baroness'. **2** [sing.] the wife of a BARON

baroque /bəˈrɒk/ (*also* **Baroque**) *adj.* (**ARTS AND MEDIA**) used to describe a highly decorated style of European architecture, art and music of the seventeenth and early eighteenth centuries

barracks /ˈbærəks/ *noun* [C + sing./pl. verb] (*pl.* **barracks**) a building or group of buildings in which soldiers live: *Guards were on duty at the gate of the barracks.*

barrage /ˈbærɑːʒ/ *noun* [C] **1** the continuous firing of a large number of guns in a particular direction, especially to protect soldiers while they are attacking or moving towards the enemy **2 ~ of sth** a large number of questions, comments, etc., directed at a person very quickly: *The minister faced a barrage of questions from reporters.* **3** a wall or barrier built across a river to store water, prevent a flood, etc.

barrel + C1 /ˈbærəl/ *noun* [C] **1** a large round wooden, plastic or metal container for liquids, that has a flat top and bottom and is wider in the middle: *a beer/wine barrel* **2** a unit of measurement in the oil industry equal to between 120 and 159 LITRES: *The price of oil is usually given per barrel.* **3** the long metal part of a gun that is like a tube, through which the bullets are fired

barrel

ˈ**barrel vault** *noun* [C] (**ARCHITECTURE**) an ARCHED roof in a church, etc. that has the shape of half of a tube

barren /ˈbærən/ *adj.* (**AGRICULTURE**) **1** (used about land or soil) not good enough for plants to grow on **2** (used about trees or plants) not producing fruit or seeds

barricade[1] /ˈbærɪkeɪd, ˌbærɪˈkeɪd/ *noun* [C] a line of objects that is placed across a road, an entrance, etc. to stop people getting through: *The demonstrators **put up barricades** to keep the police away.*

barricade[2] /ˈbærɪkeɪd, ˌbærɪˈkeɪd/ *verb* [T] to defend or block sth by building a BARRICADE
PHR V **barricade yourself in** to defend yourself by building a BARRICADE: *Demonstrators took over the building and barricaded themselves in.*

barrier B2 (O) /ˈbæriə(r)/ *noun* [C] **1 ~ (between A and B)** an object that keeps people or things separate or prevents them moving from one place to another: *The mountains form a natural barrier between the two countries.* ◇ *The crowd were kept **behind barriers**.* ➲ look at **crash barrier** **2 ~ (to sth)** something that causes problems or makes it impossible for sth to happen: *Narrow-mindedness is a barrier to progress.* ◇ *When you live in a foreign country, the **language barrier** can be a difficult problem to overcome.*

barring /ˈbɑːrɪŋ/ *prep.* except for; unless there is/are: *Barring any unforeseen problems, we'll be moving house in a month.*

barrister /ˈbærɪstə(r)/ *noun* [C] (**LAW**) a lawyer in the UK who is trained to argue cases in the higher courts ➲ note at **lawyer**

barrow /ˈbærəʊ/ *noun* [C] **1** (*BrE*) a small vehicle on two wheels on which fruit, vegetables, etc. are moved or sold in the street, especially in markets **2** = WHEELBARROW

bartender /ˈbɑːtendə(r)/ (*AmE*) = BARMAID, BARMAN

barter /ˈbɑːtə(r)/ *verb* [I, T] **~ sth (for sth); ~ (with sb) (for sth)** (**BUSINESS**) to exchange goods, services, property, etc. for other goods, etc., without using money: *The farmer bartered his surplus grain for machinery.* ◇ *The prisoners bartered with the guards for writing paper and books.* ▶ **barter** *noun* [U]

basalt /ˈbæsɔːlt/ *noun* [U] (**GEOLOGY**) a type of dark rock that comes from VOLCANOES

base[1] B1 (W) /beɪs/ *noun* **1** [C] the lowest part of sth, especially the part on which it stands or at which it is fixed or connected to sth: *I felt a terrible pain **at the base** of my spine.* ◇ *the base of a column/glass/box* ➲ picture at **arch**[1], **microscope** **2** [C] an idea, fact, etc. from which sth develops or is made: *With these ingredients **as a base**, you can create all sorts of interesting dishes.* ◇ *The country needs a strong economic base.* ➲ note at **basis** **3** [C] **~ (for sth/doing sth)** a place used as a centre from which activities are done or controlled: *This hotel is an ideal base for touring the region.* **4** [U, C] a military centre from which an army, a NAVY, etc. operates: *an army base* **5** [C] (**SPORT**) (in baseball) one of the four points that a runner must reach in order to score points **6** [C, usually sing.] (**CHEMISTRY**) a chemical substance, for example an ALKALI, that can combine with an ACID to form a SALT ➲ look at **acid**[1], **alkali** ➲ picture at **pH** **7** [C, usually sing.] (**MATHEMATICS**) a number on which a system of counting and expressing numbers is built up, for example 10 in the DECIMAL system and 2 in the BINARY system

base[2] B1 (W) /beɪs/ *verb* [T, usually passive] **~ (yourself/sth in …)** to make one place the centre from which sb/sth can work or move around: *They decided to base the company in Milan.*
PHR V **base sth on sth** [usually passive] to form or develop sth from a particular starting point or source: *This film is based on a true story.*

baseball A2 /ˈbeɪsbɔːl/ *noun* [U] (**SPORT**) a team game that is popular in the US, in which players hit the ball with a BAT (= a piece of wood or metal) and run around the four BASES (= points) before the other team can return the ball

baseboard /ˈbeɪsbɔːd/ (*AmE*) = SKIRTING BOARD

based A2 (O) /beɪst/ *adj.* [not before noun] **1 ~ (on sth)** if one thing is **based** on another, it uses it or is developed from it: *The book is based on a real-life story.* **2 ~ (in …)** if a person or business is **based** in a place, that is where they live or work: *She's based in New York.* ◇ *a Bristol-based company* **3 -based** (in compounds) containing sth as an important part: *a plant-based diet*

baseline /ˈbeɪslaɪn/ *noun* [C, usually sing.] **1** (**SPORT**) a line that marks each end of the court in games such as tennis, or the edge of the area where a player can run in baseball **2 ~ (for sth)** a line or measurement that is used as a starting point when comparing facts: *The figures for 2017 were used **as a baseline** for the study.*

basement + B2 /ˈbeɪsmənt/ *noun* [C] a room or rooms in a building that are partly or completely below ground level: *a basement flat* ➲ look at **cellar**

ˌ**base** ˈ**metal** *noun* [C] (**CHEMISTRY**) a metal that is not a PRECIOUS METAL such as gold

ˈ**base rate** *noun* [C] (**ECONOMICS, FINANCE**) a rate of interest, set by a central bank, that all banks in the UK use when calculating the amount of interest that they charge on the money they lend

bases **1** /ˈbeɪsiːz/ plural of **basis** **2** /ˈbeɪsɪz/ plural of **base**[1]

bash[1] /bæʃ/ *verb* (*informal*) **1** [I, T] (used with an adverb or a preposition) to hit sb/sth very hard: *I didn't stop in time and bashed into the car in front.* ◇ *The old lady* bashed the thief on the head with her bag. **2** [T] to criticize sb/sth strongly: *The candidate continued to bash her opponent's policies.*

bash² /bæʃ/ *noun* [C] (*informal*) **1** ~ (on/over sth) a hard hit: *He gave Alex a bash on the nose.* **2** a large party or celebration (*informal*)
IDM **have a bash (at sth/doing sth)** (*BrE, informal*) to try: *I'll get a screwdriver and have a bash at mending the light.*

bashful /'bæʃfl/ *adj.* shy and embarrassed

BASIC /'beɪsɪk/ *noun* [U] (**COMPUTING**) a simple language, using familiar English words, for writing computer programs (the abbreviation for 'Beginners' All-purpose Symbolic Instruction Code')

basic ⚹ **B1** ● /'beɪsɪk/ *adj.* **1** forming the part of sth that is most necessary and from which other things develop: *The basic question is, can we afford it?* ◇ *basic information/facts/ideas* **2** of the simplest kind or level; including only what is necessary without anything extra: *This course teaches basic computer skills.* ◇ *The basic pay is £200 a week — with extra for overtime.*

basically ⚹ **B2** ⓢ /'beɪsɪkli/ *adv.* used to say what the most important or most basic aspect of sb/sth is: *The two designs are basically the same.* ◇ *She's a little strange but basically a very nice person.*
SYN **essentially**

basics /'beɪsɪks/ *noun* [pl.] ~ (of sth) the simplest or most important facts or aspects of sth; things that you need the most: *So far, I've only learnt the basics of computing.*

basil /'bæzl/ *noun* [C] a plant with shiny green leaves that smell sweet and are used in cooking as a HERB

basilica /bə'zɪlɪkə/ *noun* [C] (**ARCHITECTURE**) a large church or hall with a curved end and two rows of columns inside

basin /'beɪsn/ *noun* [C] **1** (*especially BrE*) = WASHBASIN **2** a round open bowl often used for mixing or cooking food **3** (**GEOGRAPHY**) an area of land from which water flows into a river: *the Amazon Basin*

basis ⚹ **B1** ● /'beɪsɪs/ *noun* (*pl.* bases /'beɪsiːz/) **1** [sing.] the principle or reason that lies behind sth: *We made our decision on the basis of the reports which you sent us.* **2** [sing.] the way sth is done or organized: *They meet on a regular basis.* ◇ *to employ somebody on a temporary/voluntary/part-time basis* **3** [C] ~ (for sth) a starting point, from which sth can develop: *She used her diaries as a basis for her book.*

▼ SYNONYMS

basis

foundation • base

These are all words for ideas or facts that sth is based on.
basis *the basis for a discussion*
foundation *He laid the foundation of Japan's modern economy.*
base *a sound economic base*

---

bask /bɑːsk/ *verb* [I] ~ (in sth) to sit or lie in a place where you can enjoy the heat: *The snake basked in the sunshine on the rock.*
PHR V **bask in sth** to enjoy the good feelings you have when other people admire you, give you a lot of attention, etc: *The team was still basking in the glory of winning the cup.*

basket ⚹+ **B2** /'bɑːskɪt/ *noun* [C] **1** a container for carrying or holding things, made of thin pieces of material that bends easily, for example wood, plastic or wire: *a waste-paper basket* ◇ *a shopping basket* ◇ *a clothes/laundry basket* (= in which you put dirty clothes before they are washed) **2** (*also* cart *especially in AmE*) a facility on a website that records the items that you select to buy **3** (**SPORT**) a net and the metal ring it hangs from, high up at each end of a basketball court ⊃ picture at **sport** **4** (**SPORT**) a score of one, two or three points in basketball, made by throwing the ball through one of the nets
IDM **put all your eggs in one basket** → EGG¹

basketball ⚹ **A2** /'bɑːskɪtbɔːl/ *noun* [U] (**SPORT**) a game for two teams of five players, in which players score points by throwing a large ball into a high net hanging from a ring

basketwork /'bɑːskɪtwɜːk/ (*BrE*) (*also* basketry /'bɑːskɪtri/ *especially in AmE*) *noun* [U] the skill of making BASKETS

bas mitzvah /ˌbæs 'mɪtsvə/ = BAT MITZVAH

bas-relief /ˌbæs rɪ'liːf/ *noun* [U, C] (**ART**) a form of sculpture in which the shapes are cut so that they are slightly raised from the background; a sculpture made in this way

bass¹ ⚹+ **C1** /beɪs/ *noun* **1** [U] (**MUSIC**) the lowest tone or part in music, for instruments or voices; a singer with this voice ⊃ look at **baritone, tenor¹, treble²** **2** [C] = DOUBLE BASS **3** [C] (*also* ˌbass gui'tar) (**MUSIC**) an electric guitar that plays very low notes ▶ bass *adj.* [only before noun]: *a bass drum* ◇ *Can you sing the bass part in this song?*

bass drum /ˌbeɪs 'drʌm/ *noun* [C] (**MUSIC**) a large drum that makes a very low sound, used in ORCHESTRAS ⊃ picture at **instrument**

bassist /'beɪsɪst/ *noun* [C] (**MUSIC**) a person who plays the BASS or the DOUBLE BASS

bassoon /bə'suːn/ *noun* [C] (**MUSIC**) a musical instrument of the WOODWIND group. When you blow into the instrument, it produces notes with a very low sound. ⊃ picture at **instrument, orchestra**

bastard /'bɑːstəd, 'bæs-/ *noun* [C] (*old-fashioned*) a person whose parents were not married to each other when that person was born

baste /beɪst/ *verb* [T] to pour liquid fat or juices over meat, etc. while it is cooking

bat¹ ⚹+ **B2** /bæt/ *noun* [C] **1** (**SPORT**) a piece of wood with a handle for hitting the ball in sports such as TABLE TENNIS, CRICKET or baseball: *a cricket bat* ⊃ look at **club¹** (4), **racket** (3), **stick²** (3) ⊃ picture at **sport 2** a small animal like a mouse with wings, that flies and hunts at night ⊃ picture at **animal**
IDM **off your own bat** (*BrE, informal*) without anyone asking you or helping you

bat² ⚹+ **C1** /bæt/ *verb* [I] (-tt-) (**SPORT**) (used about one player or a whole team) to have a turn hitting the ball in sports such as CRICKET or baseball ⊃ look at **field²** (1)
IDM **not bat an eyelid** (*AmE*) | **not bat an eye** to show no surprise or concern when sth unusual happens

batch¹ /bætʃ/ *noun* [C] **1** a number of things or people that belong together as a group: *The bus returned to the airport for the next batch of tourists.* **2** (**COMPUTING**) a set of jobs that are done together on a computer: *to process a batch job* ◇ *a batch file/program*

batch² /bætʃ/ *verb* [T] to put things into groups in order to deal with them: *The service will be improved by batching and sorting enquiries.*

bated /ˈbeɪtɪd/ adj.
IDM **with bated breath** (formal) excited or afraid, because you are waiting for sth to happen

bath[1] 🔊 **A1** /bɑːθ/ noun (pl. baths /bɑːðz/) **1** [C] (BrE) (also **bathtub** AmE, BrE) a large long container for water in which you sit to wash your body: Can you answer the phone? I'm **in the bath**! **2** [C] an act of washing the whole of your body when you sit or lie in a bath filled with water: to **have a bath 3** baths [pl.] (BrE, old-fashioned) a public building where you can go to swim **4** baths [pl.] (HISTORY) a public place where people went in past times to wash or have a bath: Roman baths

bath[2] /bɑːθ/ verb **1** [T] to give sb a bath: to bath the baby **2** [I] (old-fashioned) to have a bath

bathe /beɪð/ verb **1** [T] to wash or put part of the body in water, often for medical reasons: She bathed the wound with antiseptic. **2** [I] (old-fashioned) to swim in the sea or in a lake or river ➔ look at **sunbathe**

bathed /beɪðd/ adj. [not before noun] **~ in sth** (formal) covered with sth: The room was bathed in moonlight.

bathos /ˈbeɪθɒs/ noun [U] (formal) (LITERATURE) a sudden change, that is not usually deliberate, from a serious subject or feeling to sth silly or not important

bathrobe /ˈbɑːθrəʊb/ noun [C] **1** a loose piece of clothing worn before and after taking a bath **2** (AmE) = DRESSING GOWN

bathroom 🔊 **A1** /ˈbɑːruːm, -rʊm/ noun [C] **1** a room where there is a bath and/or a shower, a WASHBASIN (= a place to wash your hands) and often a toilet: Go and wash your hands in the bathroom. ◇ Our bedroom has an **en-suite bathroom**. **2** (AmE) a room in which there is a toilet, a sink and sometimes a bath or shower

bathtub /ˈbɑːθtʌb/ = BATH[1] (1)

batik /bəˈtiːk/ noun [U, C] (ART) a method of printing patterns on cloth by putting WAX (= a solid substance made from fat or oil) on the parts of the cloth that will not have any colour; a piece of cloth that is printed in this way

bat mitzvah /ˌbæt ˈmɪtsvə/ (also **bas mitzvah**) noun [C] (RELIGION) a ceremony in the Jewish religion for a girl who is about 13 years old ➔ look at **bar mitzvah**

baton /ˈbætɒn, ˈbætɒ̃/ noun [C] **1** = TRUNCHEON **2** (MUSIC) a short thin stick used by the person who is in control of an ORCHESTRA (= a large group of musicians who play together) **3** (SPORT) a stick that a runner in a RELAY (= a race in which each member of the team runs one part of the race) passes to the next person to run

batsman /ˈbætsmən/ noun [C] (pl. -men /-mən/) (SPORT) (in CRICKET) the player who is hitting the ball

battalion /bəˈtæliən/ noun [C] a large group of soldiers that form part of a BRIGADE (= a unit of an army)

batter[1] /ˈbætə(r)/ verb [I, T] (often used with an adverb or a preposition) to hit sb/sth hard many times: The wind battered against the window. ◇ He battered the door down.

batter[2] /ˈbætə(r)/ noun [U, C] a mixture of flour, eggs and milk used to cover food such as fish, vegetables, etc. before frying them, or to make PANCAKES

battered /ˈbætəd/ adj. no longer looking new; damaged or out of shape: a battered old hat

battery 🔊 **B1** /ˈbætri, -təri/ noun (pl. -ies) **1** [C] (ENGINEERING, PHYSICS) a device that provides electricity for a toy, radio, car, etc: to recharge a **flat battery** (= no longer producing electricity) ➔ note at **electricity 2** [C] (BrE) (often used as an adjective) (AGRICULTURE) a large number of very small CAGES in which chickens, etc. are kept on a farm: a battery hen/ farm ➔ look at **free-range 3** [U] (LAW) the crime of

attacking sb physically: He was charged with **assault and battery**.

battle[1] 🔊 **B1** /ˈbætl/ noun **1** [C, U] (HISTORY, POLITICS) a fight, especially between armies in a war: the battle of Trafalgar ◇ to die/be killed **in battle 2** [C] **~ (with sb) (for sth)** a competition, argument or fight between people or groups of people trying to win power or control: a legal battle for custody of the children **3** [C, usually sing.] **~ (against sth)**; **~ (for sth)** a determined effort to solve a difficult problem or to succeed in a difficult situation: After three years she lost her battle against cancer. ◇ They now face a battle for survival. ➔ note at **campaign**[1]
IDM **a losing battle** → LOSE

battle[2] 🔊 **B2** /ˈbætl/ verb [I] **~ (with sb/sth) (for sth)**; **~ (against sb/sth)**; **~ (on)** to try very hard to achieve sth difficult or to deal with sth unpleasant or dangerous: He was battling with his brother for control of the family business. ◇ The little boat battled against the wind. ◇ Life is hard at the moment but we're battling on.

battlefield 🔊+ **C1** /ˈbætlfiːld/ (also **battleground** /ˈbætlɡraʊnd/) noun [C] (HISTORY) the place where a battle is being fought or has been fought

battlements /ˈbætlmənts/ noun [pl.] (HISTORY) a low wall around the top of a castle, with spaces in it that people inside could shoot through ➔ picture at **drawbridge**

battleship /ˈbætlʃɪp/ noun [C] a very large ship with big guns, used in war

bauble /ˈbɔːbl/ noun [C] **1** a piece of cheap jewellery **2** (BrE) a decoration in the shape of a ball that is hung on a Christmas tree

Bauhaus /ˈbaʊhaʊs/ noun [U] (ARCHITECTURE, ART) a style and movement in German architecture and design in the early twentieth century that was influenced by the methods and materials used in industry and placed emphasis on how things would be used

baulk (also **balk** especially in AmE) /bɔːk/ verb [I] **~ (at sth/ doing sth)** to not want to do or agree to sth because it seems too difficult, dangerous or unpleasant: They baulked at paying $100 for a ticket.

bauxite /ˈbɔːksaɪt/ noun [U] (GEOLOGY) a soft rock from which we get ALUMINIUM (= a light metal)

bawdy /ˈbɔːdi/ adj. (bawdier; bawdiest) (old-fashioned) (LITERATURE) (used about songs, plays, etc.) loud and dealing with sex in a way that makes people laugh

bawl /bɔːl/ verb [I, T] to shout or cry loudly

bay 🔊+ **C1** /beɪ/ noun **1** [C] (GEOGRAPHY) a part of the coast where the land goes in to form a curve: the Bay of Bengal ◇ The harbour was in a sheltered bay. **2** [C] a part of a building, an aircraft or an area that has a particular purpose: a parking/loading bay **3** [U] the leaves of the bay tree, used in cooking as a HERB
IDM **hold/keep sb/sth at bay** to stop sb/sth dangerous from getting near you; to prevent a situation or problem from getting worse

bayonet /ˈbeɪənət/ noun [C] a knife that can be fixed to the end of a gun

bay window noun [C] (ARCHITECTURE) a window in a part of a room that sticks out from the wall of a house

bazaar /bəˈzɑː(r)/ noun [C] **1** (in some Eastern countries) a street or an area of a town where there are many small shops **2** (BrE) a sale where the money that is made goes to charity: The school held a bazaar to raise money for the hospital.

bazooka /bəˈzuːkə/ *noun* [C] a long gun, shaped like a tube, that is held on the shoulder and used to fire ROCKETS (= weapons that travel through the air)

BBC /ˌbiː biː ˈsiː/ *abbr.* (**ARTS AND MEDIA**) **British Broadcasting Corporation** (a national organization that broadcasts TV and radio programmes): *a BBC documentary* ◊ *to watch a programme on BBC1*

BBQ *abbr.* (in writing) = BARBECUE

BC /ˌbiː ˈsiː/ *abbr.* (**HISTORY**, **RELIGION**) **before Christ** (used in dates to show the number of years before the time when Christians believe Jesus Christ was born): *300 BC* ◌ look at **AD**

be¹ 🔊 **A1** /bi, *strong form* biː/ *verb* ❶ For the forms of 'be', look at the irregular verbs section of this dictionary. **1** *linking verb* **there is/are** to exist; to be present: *I tried phoning them but there was no answer.* ◊ *There are some people outside.* ◊ *There are a lot of trees in our garden.* **2** [I] (used with an adverb or a preposition) used to give the position of sb/sth or the place where sb/sth is: *Katrina's in her office.* ◊ *Where are the scissors?* ◊ *The bus stop is five minutes' walk from here.* ◊ *St Tropez is on the south coast.* **3** *linking verb* **it is/was** used to give the date or age of sb/sth or to talk about time: *My birthday is on April 24th.* ◊ *It's six o'clock.* ◊ *It was Tuesday yesterday.* ◊ *Stacey will be 21 in June.* ◊ *He's older than Miranda.* ◊ *It's ages since I last saw him.* **4** used when you are giving the name of people or things, describing them or giving more information about them: *This is my father, John.* ◊ *I'm Alison.* ◊ *He's Italian. He's from Milan.* ◊ *He's a doctor.* ◊ *What's that? A lion is a mammal.* ◊ *'What colour is your car?' 'It's green.'* ◊ *How much was your ticket?* ◊ *The film was excellent.* ◊ *She's very friendly.* ◊ *'How is your wife?' 'She's fine, thanks.'* **5** [I] (only used in the perfect tenses; used with an adverb or a preposition) to go to a place (and return): *Have you ever been to Japan?* ◌ look at **been**
IDM **be yourself** to act naturally: *Don't be nervous; just be yourself and the interview will be fine.* **-to-be** (in compounds) future: *his bride-to-be* ◊ *mothers-to-be* (= pregnant women)

be² 🔊 **A1** /bi, *strong form* biː/ *auxiliary verb* **1** used with a past participle to form the passive; used with a present participle to form the progressive tenses: *He was killed in the war.* ◊ *Where were they made?* ◊ *The house was still being built.* ◊ *You will be told what to do.* ◊ *I am studying Italian.* ◊ *What have you been doing?* **2 ~ to do sth** used to show that sth must happen or that sth has been arranged: *You are to leave here at ten o'clock at the latest.* **3 if sb/sth were to do sth** used to show that sth is possible but not very likely: *If they were to offer me the job, I'd probably take it.*

be- /bɪ/ *prefix* **1** (in verbs) to make or treat sb/sth as: *They befriended him.* **2** (in adjectives) wearing or covered with: *bejewelled*

beach 🔊 **A1** /biːtʃ/ *noun* [C] (**GEOGRAPHY**) an area of sand or small stones next to the sea: *to sit on the beach* ◊ *We were at the beach when that photo was taken.* ◊ *a sandy beach*

beachfront /ˈbiːtʃfrʌnt/ *noun* [sing.] (*especially AmE*) the part of a town facing the beach: *The hotel is on the beachfront.*

beacon /ˈbiːkən/ *noun* [C] a fire or light on a hill or tower, that is used as a signal

bead /biːd/ *noun* **1** [C] a small round piece of wood, glass or plastic with a hole in the middle for putting a string through to make jewellery, etc. **2 beads** [pl.] a NECKLACE (= a piece of jewellery that you wear around your neck) made of beads **3** [C] **~ (of sth)** a drop of liquid: *There were beads of sweat on his forehead.*

beady /ˈbiːdi/ *adj.* (used about eyes) small, round and bright; watching everything closely

beak /biːk/ *noun* [C] the hard pointed part of a bird's mouth ◌ picture at **animal**

beaker /ˈbiːkə(r)/ *noun* [C] **1** a plastic or paper drinking cup, usually without a handle **2** (**SCIENCE**) a glass container, used in scientific experiments, etc. for pouring liquids ◌ picture at **laboratory**, **refraction**

beam¹ 🔊⁺ **C1** /biːm/ *noun* [C] **1** (**PHYSICS**) a line of light: *the beam of a torch* ◊ *The car's headlights were on full beam* (= giving the most light possible and not directed downwards). ◊ *a laser beam* **2** (**ARCHITECTURE**) a long piece of wood, metal, etc. that is used to support weight, for example in the floor or ceiling of a building **3** a happy smile **4** (*especially BrE*) (*AmE usually* **balance beam**) (**SPORT**) a wooden bar that is used in the sport of GYMNASTICS for people to move and balance on: *The gymnast performed a somersault on the beam.*

beam² /biːm/ *verb* **1** [I] **~ (at sb)** to smile happily: *I looked at Sam and he beamed back at me.* **2** [T] (used with an adverb or a preposition) to send out radio or TV signals: *The programme was beamed live by satellite to many different countries.* **3** [I] (used with an adverb or a preposition) to send out light and heat: *The sun beamed down on them.*

bean 🔊 **A2** /biːn/ *noun* [C] **1** a seed or POD (= a long thin case filled with seeds) from a climbing plant, that is eaten as a vegetable: *soya beans* ◊ *a tin of baked beans* (= beans in a tomato sauce) ◊ *green beans* **2** a seed from a coffee plant, or some other plants: *coffee beans*
IDM **full of beans/life** → FULL¹ **spill the beans** → SPILL

ˈbean sprouts *noun* [pl.] bean seeds that are just beginning to grow, often eaten without being cooked

bear¹ 🔊 **B2** /beə(r)/ *verb* (*pt* **bore** /bɔː(r)/; *pp* **borne** /bɔːn/)

• ACCEPT **1** [T] (usually after *can/could* in negative sentences and questions) **~ (doing sth)**; **~ (to do sth)** to be able to accept and deal with sth unpleasant: *The pain was almost more than he could bear.* ◊ *I can't bear getting up early.* ◊ *How can you bear to listen to that music?* **SYN** **endure**, **stand¹**

• NOT BE SUITABLE **2** [T] to not be suitable for sth; to not allow sth: *These figures won't bear close examination* (= when you look closely, you will find mistakes). ◊ *What I would do if I lost my job doesn't bear thinking about* (= is too unpleasant to think about).

• BE RESPONSIBLE **3** [T] (*formal*) to take responsibility for sth: *Customers will bear the full cost of the improvements.*

• FEEL **4** [T] **~ sth (towards/against sb)** to have a feeling, especially a negative feeling: *Despite what they did, she bears no resentment towards them.* ◊ *He's not the type to bear a grudge against anyone.*

• SUPPORT **5** [T] to support the weight of sth: *Twelve pillars bear the weight of the roof.*

• SHOW/CARRY **6** [T] (*formal*) to show sth; to carry sth so that it can be seen: *The waiters came in bearing trays of food.* ◊ *He still bears the scars of his accident.* ◊ *She bore a strong resemblance to her mother* (= she looked like her).

• HAVE A CHILD **7** [T] (*formal*) to give birth to children: *She bore four children, all sons.*

• TURN **8** [I] **~ left, north, etc.** to turn or go in the direction that is mentioned: *Where the road forks, bear left.*
IDM **bear the brunt of sth** to suffer the main force of sth: *Her sons usually bore the brunt of her anger.* **bear fruit** to be successful; to produce results **bear in**

mind (that) | bear/keep sb/sth in mind → MIND[1] bear witness (to sth) to show evidence of sth: *The burning buildings and empty streets bore witness to a recent attack.*

PHR V bear down (on sb/sth) **1** to move closer to sb/sth in a frightening way: *We could see the hurricane bearing down on the town.* **2** to push down hard on sb/sth bear sth out to show that sb is correct or that sth is true bear up to be strong enough to continue at a difficult time: *How is he bearing up after his accident?* bear with sb/sth to be patient with sb: *Bear with me — I won't be much longer.*

bear[2] Ỻ **A2** /beə(r)/ *noun* [C] **1** a large, heavy wild animal with thick fur and sharp teeth: *a polar/grizzly/brown bear* ⊃ look at **teddy bear 2** (FINANCE) a person who sells shares in a company, hoping to buy them back later at a lower price ⊃ look at **bull** (3)

bearable /'beərəbl/ *adj.* that you can accept or deal with, although it is unpleasant: *It was extremely hot, but the breeze made it more bearable.*
OPP **unbearable**

beard /bɪəd/ *noun* [C, U] the hair that grows on a man's CHIN and the side of his face: *I'm going to grow a beard.* ◇ *a week's growth of beard* ⊃ look at **goatee, moustache**

bearded /'bɪədɪd/ *adj.* with a BEARD

bearer /'beərə(r)/ *noun* [C] a person who carries or brings sth: *I'm sorry to be the bearer of bad news.*

bearing /'beərɪŋ/ *noun* **1** [sing.] ~ (on sth) a relation or connection to the subject being discussed: *Her comments had no bearing on our decision.* **2** [U, sing.] the way in which sb stands or moves: *a man of dignified bearing* **3** [C] (GEOGRAPHY) a direction measured from a fixed point using a COMPASS (= an instrument that shows direction) **4** bearings [pl.] knowledge of where you are in relation to everything that around you: *to get/find your bearings* ◇ *I lost my bearings in the forest.* **5** [C] (ENGINEERING) a part of a machine that supports a moving part, especially one that is turning ⊃ look at **ball bearing**

beast Ỻ+ **C1** /biːst/ *noun* [C] (*formal*) an animal, especially a large one: *a wild beast*

beat[1] Ỻ **A2** /biːt/ *verb* (*pt* beat; *pp* beaten /'biːtn/) **1** [T] ~ sb (at sth); ~ sth to defeat sb; to be better than sth: *He always beats me at tennis.* ◇ *We're hoping to beat the world record.* ◇ *If you want to keep fit, you can't beat swimming.* **2** [I, T] (often used with an adverb or a preposition) to hit sb/sth hard several times: *The rain was beating on the roof of the car.* ◇ *I could hear somebody beating a drum.* ◇ *The man had been severely beaten.* **3** [I, T] to make a regular sound or movement: *Her heart beat faster as she ran to pick up her child.* ◇ *We could hear the drums beating in the distance.* ◇ *The bird beat its wings* (= moved them up and down quickly). **4** [T] to mix sth quickly with a fork, etc: *Beat the eggs and sugar together.*

IDM beat about the bush (*informal*) to talk about sth for a long time without mentioning the main point (it) beats me (*informal*) I do not know: *It beats me where he's gone.* ◇ *'Why is she angry?' 'Beats me!'* beat time (to sth) (MUSIC) to mark or follow the rhythm of music, by waving a stick, moving your foot, etc: *She beat time with her fingers.* off the beaten track in a place where people do not often go **PHR V** beat sb/sth off to fight until sb/sth goes away: *The thieves tried to take his wallet but he beat them off.* beat sb to sth to get somewhere or do sth before sb else: *She beat me back to the house.* ◇ *I wanted to get there first but Aisha beat me to it.* beat sb up to attack sb by hitting or kicking them many times

beat[2] Ỻ **B2** /biːt/ *noun* **1** [C] ~ (on sth) a single hit on sth such as a drum or the movement of sth, such as your heart; the sound that this makes: *several loud beats on the drum* ◇ (*figurative*) *Her heart skipped a beat when she saw him.* **2** [sing.] ~ (of sth) a series of regular hits on sth such as a drum, or of movements of sth; the sound that this makes: *the beat of the drums* ⊃ look at **heartbeat 3** [C] (MUSIC) the strong rhythm that a piece of music has **4** [C, usually sing.] the area that a police officer walks around regularly: *Having more policemen on the beat helps reduce crime.*

beatbox[1] /'biːtbɒks/ *noun* (MUSIC) **1** [C] (*informal*) an electronic machine that produces drum sounds **2** [U] music that is created using sounds made with the human voice

beatbox[2] /'biːtbɒks/ *verb* [I] (MUSIC) to copy the sound of a drum with the voice: *He taught us how to beatbox.*

beaten /'biːtn/ past participle of **beat[1]**

beating /'biːtɪŋ/ *noun* [C] **1** a punishment that you give to sb by hitting them **2** (SPORT) a defeat **IDM** take a lot of/some beating to be so good that it would be difficult to find sth better: *Mary's cooking takes some beating.*

the Beaufort scale /ðə 'bəʊfət skeɪl/ *noun* [sing.] (GEOGRAPHY) a range of numbers used for measuring how strongly the wind is blowing. The lowest number (0) means that there is no wind and the highest number (12) means that there is a violent storm with very strong winds.

beautician /bjuː'tɪʃn/ *noun* [C] a person whose job is to give beauty treatments

beautiful Ỻ **A1** /'bjuːtɪfl/ *adj.* very pretty or attractive; giving pleasure to the senses: *The view from the top of the hill was really beautiful.* ◇ *What a beautiful day — the weather's perfect!* ◇ *He has a beautiful voice.* ◇ *A beautiful perfume filled the air.* ◇ *a beautiful woman*

beautifully /'bjuːtɪfli/ *adv.* **1** in a beautiful way: *a beautifully decorated house* ◇ *He plays the piano beautifully.* ◇ *She was beautifully dressed.* **2** very well; in a pleasing way: *It's all working out beautifully.*

beautify /'bjuːtɪfaɪ/ *verb* [T] (beautifying; beautifies; *pt, pp* beautified) to make sb/sth beautiful or more beautiful

beauty Ỻ **B1** /'bjuːti/ *noun* (*pl.* -ies) **1** [U] ~ (of sth) the quality that gives pleasure to the senses; the state of being beautiful: *I was amazed by the beauty of the mountains.* ◇ *music of great beauty* ◇ *beauty products/treatments* (= intended to make a person more beautiful) **2** [C] a beautiful woman: *She grew up to be a beauty.* **3** [C] a particularly good example of sth: *Look at this tomato — it's a beauty!*

'**beauty contest** *noun* [C] (*BrE*) a competition to choose the most beautiful from a group of women ⊃ look at **pageant** (2)

'**beauty queen** *noun* [C] a woman who is judged to be the most beautiful in a BEAUTY CONTEST

'**beauty salon** (*also* beauty parlour /'bjuːti pɑːlə(r)/, *AmE also* '**beauty shop**) *noun* [C] a place where you can pay for treatment to your face, hair, nails, etc. that is intended to make you more beautiful

'**beauty spot** *noun* [C] (*BrE*) a place in the countryside that is famous because it is beautiful

beaver /'biːvə(r)/ *noun* [C] an animal with brown fur, a wide, flat tail and sharp teeth. It lives in water and on land and uses branches to build DAMS (= walls across rivers to hold back the water). ⊃ picture at **animal**

became /bɪ'keɪm/ past tense of **become**

because ?[A1]⑤ /bɪˈkəz, -ˈkɒz/ *conj.* for the reason that: *They didn't go for a walk because it was raining.*

beˈcause of *prep.* as a result of; on account of: *They didn't go for a walk because of the rain.*

beck /bek/ *noun*
IDM **at sb's beck and call** always ready to obey sb's orders

beckon /ˈbekən/ *verb* [I, T] (often used with an adverb or a preposition) to show sb with a movement of your finger or hand that you want them to come closer: *She beckoned me over to speak to her.*

become ?[A1]⑤ /bɪˈkʌm/ *linking verb* (*pt* became /-ˈkeɪm/; *pp* become) to begin to be sth: *Mr Saito became Chairman in 2015.* ◇ *She wants to become a pilot.* ◇ *They became friends.* ◇ *She became nervous as the exam date came closer.* ◇ *He is becoming more like you every day.*
PHR V **become of sb/sth** to happen to sb/sth: *What became of Alima? I haven't seen her for years!*

BEd (*also* B.Ed. *especially in AmE*) /ˌbiː ˈed/ *noun* [C] (**EDUCATION**) a first university degree in education for people who want to be teachers (the abbreviation for 'Bachelor of Education')

bed¹ ?[A1] /bed/ *noun* **1** [C, U] a piece of furniture that you lie on when you sleep: *to make the bed* (= to arrange the sheets, etc. so that the bed is tidy and ready for sb to sleep in) ◇ *What time do you usually go to bed?* ◇ *She was lying on the bed* (= on top of the covers). ◇ *When he rang I was already in bed* (= under the covers). ◇ *It's late. It's time for bed.* ◇ *to get into/ out of bed* **2** -bedded having the type or number of beds mentioned: *a twin-bedded room* **3** [C] (**GEOGRAPHY**) the bottom of a river, the sea, etc: *the ocean bed* **4** [C] = FLOWER BED **5** [C] (**GEOLOGY**) a layer of rock in the earth's surface
IDM **go to bed with sb** (*informal*) to have sex with sb

bed² /bed/ *verb* [T] (-dd-) to fix sth FIRMLY in sth
PHR V **bed down** to sleep in a place where you do not usually sleep: *We couldn't find a hotel so we bedded down for the night in the van.*

ˌbed and ˈbreakfast *noun* [U, C] (*abbr.* B and B, B & B /ˌbiː ən ˈbiː/) (*all especially BrE*) (**TOURISM**) a service that provides a place to stay and a meal the next morning in a private house or small hotel; a place that provides this service ⊃ note at **hotel**

bedclothes /ˈbedkləʊðz/ (*BrE also* bedcovers /ˈbedkʌvəz/) *noun* [pl.] the sheets, covers, etc. that you put on a bed

bedding /ˈbedɪŋ/ *noun* [U] everything that you put on a bed and need for sleeping

bedpan /ˈbedpæn/ *noun* [C] (**MEDICINE**) a container used as a toilet by sb in hospital who is too ill to get out of bed

bedraggled /bɪˈdrægld/ *adj.* very wet and untidy or dirty: *bedraggled hair*

ˈbed rest *noun* [U] (**MEDICINE**) time spent resting in bed as a way to recover from an illness or injury: *She was put on bed rest after a car accident.*

bedridden /ˈbedrɪdn/ *adj.* (**HEALTH**) being too old or ill to get out of bed

bedrock /ˈbedrɒk/ *noun* **1** [sing.] ~ of sth a strong base for sth, especially the facts or principles on which it is based: *The poor suburbs traditionally formed the bedrock of the party's support.* **2** [U] (**GEOLOGY**) the solid rock in the ground below the soil and sand ⊃ picture at **floodplain**

bedroom ?[A1] /ˈbedruːm, -rʊm/ *noun* [C] a room that is used for sleeping in: *the spare/guest bedroom.* ◇ *a double/single bedroom* ◇ *the bedroom window/door*

bedside /ˈbedsaɪd/ *noun* [sing.] the area that is next to a bed: *She sat at his bedside all night long.* ◇ *A book lay open on the bedside table.*

bedsit /ˈbedsɪt/ *noun* [C] (*BrE*) a room that a person rents and uses for both living and sleeping in

bedsore /ˈbedsɔː(r)/ *noun* [C] (**HEALTH**) a painful place on a person's skin that is caused by lying in bed for a long time

bedspread /ˈbedspred/ *noun* [C] an attractive cover for a bed that you put on top of the sheets and other covers

bedtime /ˈbedtaɪm/ *noun* [U] the time that you normally go to bed

bee ?[B1] /biː/ *noun* [C] a black and yellow insect that lives in large groups and that makes HONEY (= a sweet substance that is spread on bread, etc.)

beech /biːtʃ/ *noun* **1** (*also* ˈbeech tree) [C] a large tree with smooth grey BARK and small nuts **2** [U] the wood of the beech tree

beef ?[A2] /biːf/ *noun* [U] the meat from a cow: *a slice of roast beef* ◇ *a joint of beef* ⊃ note at **meat**

beefburger /ˈbiːfbɜːɡə(r)/ *noun* [C] beef that has been cut up very small and pressed into a flat round shape that is then fried ⊃ look at **burger** (1)

beefeater /ˈbiːfiːtə(r)/ *noun* [C] a guard who dresses in a traditional red uniform at the Tower of London

beefy /ˈbiːfi/ *adj.* (beefier; beefiest) (*informal*) having a strong body with big muscles

beehive /ˈbiːhaɪv/ (*also* hive) *noun* [C] a type of box made for bees to live in

beekeeper /ˈbiːkiːpə(r)/ *noun* [C] a person who owns and takes care of bees ▸ beekeeping *noun* [U]

been /biːn, bɪn/ past participle of **be¹, go¹**

beep¹ /biːp/ *noun* [C] a short high noise such as that made by the HORN of a car

beep² /biːp/ *verb* **1** [I] (used about an electronic machine) to make a short high noise: *The microwave beeps when the food is cooked.* **2** [I, T] when a car HORN **beeps**, or when you **beep** it, it makes a short noise: *I beeped my horn at the dog, but it wouldn't get off the road.*

beer ?[A1] /bɪə(r)/ *noun* **1** [U, C] a type of alcoholic drink that is made from MALT (= a type of grain) and HOPS: *a pint/can/bottle of beer* ◇ *a beer glass/bottle/can* ◇ *This pub serves a wide range of beers.* ⊃ look at **wine** **2** [C] a glass, bottle or can of beer: *We went out for a couple of beers.*

beeswax /ˈbiːzwæks/ *noun* [U] a yellow sticky substance that is produced by bees. It is used to make CANDLES and POLISH for wood.

beet /biːt/ (*BrE*) **1** = SUGAR BEET **2** (*AmE*) = BEETROOT

beetle /ˈbiːtl/ *noun* [C] an insect, often large, shiny and black, with a hard case on its back covering its wings. There are many different types of beetle. ⊃ picture at **animal**

beetroot /ˈbiːtruːt/ (*BrE*) (*AmE* beet) *noun* [C, U] a dark red root that is cooked and eaten as a vegetable

befall /bɪˈfɔːl/ *verb* [T] (*pt* befell /-ˈfel/; *pp* befallen /-ˈfɔːlən/) (*formal*) (used about sth bad) to happen to sb

before¹ ?[A1] /bɪˈfɔː(r)/ *prep.* **1** earlier than sb/sth: *You can call me any time before ten o'clock.* ◇ *the week before last* ◇ *They should be here before long* (= soon). **2** ahead of sb/sth in an order or in the future: *'H' comes before 'N' in the alphabet.* ◇ *A very difficult task lies before us.* ◇ *a company that puts profit before* safety (= thinks profit is more important than safety) **3** (*formal*) in a position in front of sb/sth: *They knelt before the altar.* ◊ *You will appear before the judge tomorrow.*

before² 🔊 **A2** /bɪˈfɔː(r)/ *conj.* **1** earlier than the time when: *Turn the lights off before you leave.* **2** until: *It was some time before I realized the truth.* **3** rather than: *I'd die before I apologized to him!*

before³ 🔊 **A2** /bɪˈfɔː(r)/ *adv.* at an earlier time; already: *I think we've met somewhere before.* ◊ *It was fine yesterday, but it rained the day before.*

beforehand /bɪˈfɔːhænd/ *adv.* at an earlier time than sth: *If you visit us, phone beforehand to make sure we're in.*

befriend /bɪˈfrend/ *verb* [T] to become sb's friend; to be kind to sb

beg 🔊 **B2** /beg/ *verb* [I, T] (-gg-) **1** ~ (**sb**) **for sth; ~ sth** (**of/from sb**); ~ (**sb**) **to do sth** to ask sb for sth strongly, or with great emotion: *He begged for forgiveness.* ◊ *Can I beg a favour of you?* ◊ *We begged him to lend us the money.* **SYN** entreat, implore ⊃ look at **plead** (1) **2** ~ (**for sth**) (**from sb**) to ask people for food, money, etc. because you are very poor: *People were begging for food in the streets.*
IDM **I beg your pardon** (*formal*) **1** I am sorry: *I beg your pardon. I picked up your bag by mistake.* **2** used for asking sb to repeat sth because you did not hear it

beggar¹ /ˈbegə(r)/ *noun* [C] a person who lives by asking people for money or food on the streets

beggar² /ˈbegə(r)/ *verb*
IDM **beggar belief** to be too extreme, shocking, etc. to believe: *It beggars belief how things could have got this bad.*

begin 🔊 **A1** 🅂 /bɪˈɡɪn/ *verb* (**beginning**; *pt* **began** /-ˈgæn/; *pp* **begun** /-ˈgʌn/) **1** [I, T] ~ (**doing sth**); ~ (**to do sth**) to start doing sth; to do the first part of sth: *Shall I begin or will you?* ◊ *I began* (= started reading) *this novel last month and I still haven't finished it.* ◊ *I began teaching in 1998.* ◊ *The carpet is beginning to look dirty.* **2** [I] to start to happen or exist, especially from a particular time: *What time does the concert begin?* **3** [I] ~ (**with sth**) to start in a particular way, with a particular event, or in a particular place: *My name begins with 'W' not 'V'.* ◊ *The fighting began with an argument about money.* ◊ *This is where the footpath begins.* ▸ **beginner** *noun* [C]
IDM **to begin with 1** at first: *To begin with, they were very happy.* **2** used for giving your first reason for sth or to introduce your first point: *We can't possibly go. To begin with, it's too far and we can't afford it either.*

beginning 🔊 **A1** 🅂 /bɪˈɡɪnɪŋ/ *noun* [C, usually sing.] the first part of sth; the time when or the place where sth starts: *We're going away at the beginning of the school holidays.* ◊ *I'm going to start again from the beginning.*

begrudge /bɪˈɡrʌdʒ/ *verb* [T] ~ (**sb**) **sth 1** to feel angry or upset because sb has sth that you think that they should not have: *He's worked hard. I don't begrudge him his success.* **2** to be unhappy that you have to do sth: *I begrudge paying so much money in tax each month.*

behalf 🔊+ **C1** /bɪˈhɑːf/ *noun*
IDM **on behalf of sb | on sb's behalf 1** for sb; instead of sb: *Emma couldn't be present so her husband accepted the prize on her behalf.* ◊ *I would like to thank you all on behalf of my colleagues and myself.* **2** in order to help sb: *They campaigned on behalf of asylum seekers.*

behave 🔊 **A2** ⦾ /bɪˈheɪv/ *verb* **1** [I] ~ (**well, badly, etc.**) (**towards sb**) to act in a particular way: *Don't you think that Ellen has been behaving very strangely recently?* ◊ *I think you behaved very badly towards your father.* ◊ *He behaves as if/though he was the boss.* **2** [I, T] ~ (**yourself**) to act in the correct or appropriate way: *I want you to behave yourselves while we're away.*
OPP misbehave **3** -behaved /bɪheɪvd/ (in adjectives) behaving in the way mentioned: *a well-behaved child* ◊ *a badly behaved class*

behaviour 🔊 **A2** ⦾ (*AmE* **behavior**) /bɪˈheɪvjə(r)/ *noun* **1** [U] the way that you act or behave: *He was sent out of the class for bad behaviour.* **2** [U, C] (**BIOLOGY**) the way a person, an animal, a plant, a chemical, etc. behaves or functions in a particular situation: *studying human and animal behaviour* ◊ *the behaviour of chromosomes* ◊ *to study learned behaviours*
▸ **behavioural** (*AmE* **behavioral**) /-jərəl/ *adj.*: *children with behavioural difficulties*

behead /bɪˈhed/ *verb* [T] to cut off sb's head, especially as a punishment **SYN** decapitate

behind 🔊 **A1** /bɪˈhaɪnd/ *prep., adv.* **1** in, at or to the back of sb/sth: *There's a small garden behind the house.* ◊ *The sun went behind a cloud.* ◊ *You go on ahead. I'll follow on behind.* ◊ *Look behind you before you drive off.* ◊ *He ran off but the police were close behind.* **2** ~ (**in/with**) (**sth**) later or less good than sb/sth; making less progress than sb/sth: *The train is 20 minutes behind schedule.* ◊ *Jane is behind in maths.* ◊ *We are a month behind with the rent.* ⊃ look at **ahead 3** supporting or agreeing with sb/sth: *Whatever she decides, her family will be behind her.* **4** responsible for causing or starting sth: *What is the reason behind his sudden change of opinion?* **5** used to say that sth is in sb's past: *It's time you put your problems behind you* (= forgot about them). **6** in the place where sb/sth is or was: *Oh no! I've left the tickets behind* (= at home).

beige /beɪʒ/ *adj.* light yellow-brown in colour ▸ **beige** *noun* [U]

being 🔊 **B2** /ˈbiːɪŋ/ *noun* **1** [U] the state of existing: *When did the organization come into being?* **SYN** existence **2** [C] a living creature: *a human being*

belated /bɪˈleɪtɪd/ *adj.* coming late: *a belated apology* ▸ **belatedly** *adv.*: *They have realized, rather belatedly, that they have made a mistake.*

belch /beltʃ/ *verb* **1** [I] to let gas out from your stomach through your mouth with a sudden noise **SYN** burp **2** [I, T] to send out a lot of smoke, etc: *The volcano belched smoke and ashes.* ▸ **belch** *noun* [C]

belie /bɪˈlaɪ/ *verb* [T] (**belying**; **belies**; *pt, pp* **belied**) (*formal*) to give an idea of sth that is false: *His smiling face belied his true feelings.*

belief 🔊 **B1** 🅦 /bɪˈliːf/ *noun* **1** [U] ~ (**in sb/sth**) (**RELIGION**) a feeling that sb/sth is true, morally good or right, or that sb/sth really exists: *She has lost her belief in God.* ⊃ look at **disbelief 2** [sing., U] ~ (**that …**) (*formal*) something you accept as true; what you believe: *It's my belief that people are basically good.* ◊ *There is a general belief that things will soon get better.* ◊ *Contrary to popular belief* (= despite what many people think), *the north of the country is not poorer than the south.* **3** [C, usually pl.] (**POLITICS, RELIGION**) an idea about religion, politics, etc: *Divorce is against their religious beliefs.* ⊃ note at **religion**
IDM **beyond belief** (in a way that is) too great, difficult, etc. to be believed

believable /bɪˈliːvəbl/ *adj.* that can be believed
OPP unbelievable

believe ⟨A1⟩ /bɪˈliːv/ *verb* (not used in the progressive tenses) **1** [T] to feel sure that sth is true or that sb is telling the truth: *He said he hadn't taken any money, but I didn't believe him.* ◇ *Nobody believes a word she says.* **OPP** **disbelieve** ⊃ note at **think**¹ **2** [T] ~ **(that)** … ; **be believed to be, have, etc. sth** to think that sth is true or possible, although you are not certain: *I believe they have moved to Italy.* ◇ *'Does Pat still work there?' 'I believe so.'* ◇ *The escaped prisoner is believed to be in this area.* ◇ *Four people are still missing, believed drowned.* **3** [T] ~ **(that)** … used to show anger or surprise at sth: *I can't believe (that) you're telling me to do it again!* **4** [I] **(RELIGION)** to have religious beliefs **IDM** **believe it or not** (*informal*) used to introduce information that may be surprising but is true: *Believe it or not, he asked me to marry him!* **give sb to believe/understand (that)** [often passive] (*formal*) to give sb the impression or idea that sth is true: *I was given to believe that I had got the job.*
PHR V **believe in sb** to feel that you can trust sb and/or that they will be successful: *They need a leader they can believe in.* ⊃ note at **trust**² **believe in sb/sth** **(RELIGION)** to be sure that sb/sth exists: *Do you believe in God?* **believe in sth/doing sth** to think that sth is good, right or acceptable: *He doesn't believe in killing animals for their fur.*

believer /bɪˈliːvə(r)/ *noun* [C] **(RELIGION)** a person who has religious beliefs
IDM **be a (great/firm) believer in sth** to think that sth is good or right: *He is a great believer in getting things done on time.*

belittle /bɪˈlɪtl/ *verb* [T] to make sb or the things they do seem unimportant or not very good

bell ⟨B1⟩ /bel/ *noun* [C] **1** a metal object, often shaped like a cup, that makes a ringing sound when it is hit by a small piece of metal inside it: *the sound of church bells* ◇ *Her voice came back clear as a bell.* ⊃ picture at **goat** **2** an electrical device that makes a ringing sound when the button on it is pushed; the sound that it makes
IDM **ring a bell** → **RING**²

bellboy /ˈbelbɔɪ/ (*AmE also* **bellhop** /ˈbelhɒp/) *noun* [C] **(TOURISM)** a person whose job is to carry people's cases to their rooms in a hotel

belligerent /bəˈlɪdʒərənt/ *adj.* **1** unfriendly and aggressive **SYN** **hostile** **2** [only before noun] (*formal*) **(POLITICS)** (used about a country) fighting a war

bellow /ˈbeləʊ/ *verb* **1** [I, T] to shout in a loud deep voice, especially because you are angry **2** [I] when a large animal such as a bull (= a male cow) **bellows**, it makes a deep low sound ▸ **bellow** *noun* [C]

bell pepper (*AmE*) = **PEPPER**¹ (2)

belly /ˈbeli/ *noun* [C] (*pl.* **-ies**) (*informal*) the part of the body below the chest **SYN** **stomach**¹

belly button (*informal*) = **NAVEL**

belong ⟨A2⟩ /bɪˈlɒŋ/ *verb* [I] (often used with an adverb or a preposition) to have a right or usual place: *The plates belong in the cupboard over there.* ◇ *It took quite a long time before we felt we belonged in the village* (= until we felt comfortable).
PHR V **belong to sb** to be owned by sb **belong to sth** to be a member of a group, an organization, etc.

belongings /bɪˈlɒŋɪŋz/ *noun* [pl.] the things that you own that can be moved, for example not land and buildings

beloved ⟨+⟩ ⟨C1⟩ /bɪˈlʌvd/ *adj.* (*formal*) much loved: *He was beloved by all who knew her.* ❶ When **beloved** comes before a noun, the pronunciation is /bɪˈlʌvɪd/.

below ⟨A1⟩ ⟨W⟩ /bɪˈləʊ/ *prep., adv.* at or to a lower position or level than sb/sth: *Do not write below this line.* ◇ *The temperature fell below freezing during the night.* ◇ *Her marks in the exam were below average.* ◇ *I don't live on the top floor. I live on the floor below.* ◇ *temperatures of 30° and below* **OPP** **above**²

belt¹ ⟨A2⟩ /belt/ *noun* [C] **1** a thin piece of cloth, leather, etc. that you wear around the middle part of your body: *I need a belt to keep these trousers up.* ⊃ look at **seat belt** **2** a continuous band of material that moves round and is used to carry things along or to make parts of a machine move: *The suitcases were carried round on a conveyor belt.* ◇ *the fan belt of a car* (= that operates the MACHINERY that cools a car engine) **3** **(GEOGRAPHY)** an area of land that has a particular quality or where a particular group of people live: *the green belt around London* (= an area of countryside where you are not allowed to build houses, factories, etc.) ◇ *a country's corn/industrial belt* ◇ *the commuter belt*
IDM **below the belt** (*informal*) unfair or cruel: *That remark was rather below the belt.* **have sth under your belt** (*informal*) to have already done or achieved sth: *She's already got four tournament wins under her belt.* **tighten your belt** → **TIGHTEN**

belt² /belt/ *verb* (*informal*) **1** [T] to hit sb/sth hard **2** [I] (*BrE*) to run or go somewhere very fast: *I was belting along on my bike.*
PHR V **belt sth out** (*informal*) to sing, shout or play sth loudly **belt up** (*informal*) used to tell sb rudely to be quiet: *Belt up! I can't think with all this noise.*

beltway /ˈbeltweɪ/ *noun* [C] (*AmE*) a road that goes around a town or city, especially the road around Washington DC

belying /bɪˈlaɪɪŋ/ present participle of **belie**

bemused /bɪˈmjuːzd/ *adj.* confused and unable to think clearly

bench ⟨+⟩ ⟨C1⟩ /bentʃ/ *noun* **1** [C] a long wooden or metal seat for two or more people, often outdoors: *a park bench* **2** **the bench** [sing.] **(LAW)** a way of referring to a judge in court or the seat where he/she sits; the position of being a judge or MAGISTRATE: *His lawyer turned to address the bench.* **3** [C, usually pl.] **(POLITICS)** (in the British Parliament) a seat where a particular group of politicians sit: *the government front bench* ◇ *There was cheering from the Opposition benches.* ⊃ look at **back bench** **4** **the bench** [sing.] **(SPORT)** the seats where players sit when they are not playing in the game **5** [C] a long narrow table that people work at, for example in a factory: *a carpenter's bench* ⊃ look at **workbench**

benchmark ⟨+⟩ ⟨C1⟩ /ˈbentʃmɑːk/ *noun* [C] a standard that other things can be compared to: *These new safety features set a benchmark for other manufacturers to follow.*

bend¹ ⟨B1⟩ /bend/ *verb* (*pt, pp* **bent** /bent/) **1** [I] (used with an adverb or a preposition) to move your body or head forwards and downwards: *He bent down to tie up his shoelaces.* ◇ *She had to bend forward to hear what the child was saying.* **2** [T] ~ **sth (into sth)** to move sth so that it is no longer straight: *to bend a piece of wire into an S shape* ◇ *It hurts when I bend my knee.* **3** [I] ~ **(to the right/left)** to change direction to form a curve or an angle: *The road bends to the left here.*
IDM **bend the rules** to do sth that is not normally allowed by the rules

bend² ⟨B1⟩ /bend/ *noun* [C] ~ **(in sth)** a curve or turn, for example in a road: *a sharp bend in the road.*
IDM **round the bend** (*informal*) crazy: *His behaviour is driving me round the bend* (= annoying me very much). **SYN** **mad**

beneath ĩ+ **C1** /bɪˈniːθ/ *prep.* (*formal*) **1** in, at or to a lower position than sb/sth; under: *The ship disappeared beneath the waves.* ◇ *He seemed a nice person but there was a lot of anger beneath the surface.* **SYN** **under 2** not good enough for sb: *She felt that cleaning for other people was beneath her.* ▶ **beneath** *adv.* (*formal*): *His calm exterior hid the anger beneath.*

benefactor /ˈbenɪfæktə(r)/ *noun* [C] (*formal*) a person who helps or gives money to a person or an organization

beneficial ĩ+ **B2** **W** /ˌbenɪˈfɪʃl/ *adj.* ~ (to sb/sth) improving a situation; having a helpful or useful effect: *a good diet is beneficial to health* **SYN** **advantageous** **OPP** **detrimental**

beneficiary ĩ+ **C1** **O** /ˌbenɪˈfɪʃəri/ *noun* [C] (*pl.* -ies /ˌbenəˈfɪʃəriz/) ~ (of sth) (**LAW**) **1** a person who gains as a result of sth: *Who will be the main beneficiary of the cuts in income tax?* **2** a person who receives money or property when sb dies

benefit[1] ĩ **A2** **O** /ˈbenɪfɪt/ *noun* **1** [U, C] ~ (of sth/doing sth) an advantage or useful effect that sth has: *I can't see the benefit of doing things this way.* ◇ *the benefits of modern technology* ◇ *The proposed changes would be to their benefit.* **2** [C, usually pl., U] (*BrE*) (**POLITICS**, **SOCIAL STUDIES**) money that the government gives to people who are ill, poor, unemployed, etc: *child/sickness/disability benefit* ◇ *I'm not entitled to unemployment benefit.* ◇ *to claim benefits* **3** [C, usually pl.] (**BUSINESS**) advantages that you get from your company in addition to the money you earn: *a company car and other benefits*
IDM **for sb's benefit** especially to help, please, etc. sb: *For the benefit of the newcomers, I will start again.* **give sb the benefit of the doubt** to believe what sb says although there is no proof that it is true

benefit[2] ĩ **B1** **O** /ˈbenɪfɪt/ *verb* (-t-, -tt-) **1** [T] to produce a good or useful effect for sb: *The new tax laws will benefit people on low wages.* **2** [I] ~ (from sth) to receive an advantage from sth: *Small businesses have benefited from the changes in the law.*

benevolent /bəˈnevələnt/ *adj.* (*formal*) kind, friendly and helpful to others ▶ **benevolence** /-ləns/ *noun* [U]

benign /bɪˈnaɪn/ *adj.* **1** (*formal*) (used about people) kind or gentle **2** (**HEALTH**) (used about a disease, etc.) not dangerous or likely to cause death: *a benign tumour* **SYN** **non-malignant** **OPP** **malignant**

bent[1] /bent/ past tense, past participle of **bend**[1]

bent[2] ĩ **B2** /bent/ *adj.* **1** not straight: *Do this exercise with your knees bent.* ◇ *This knife is bent.* ◇ *It was so funny we were bent double with laughter.* **2** (*BrE, informal*) (used about a person in authority) dishonest: *a bent policeman* **SYN** **corrupt**[1]
IDM **bent on sth/doing sth** determined to do sth, especially sth bad

bent[3] /bent/ *noun* [sing.] ~ for sth/doing sth a natural skill at sth or interest in sth: *She has a bent for music.*

benzene /ˈbenziːn/ *noun* [U] (**CHEMISTRY**) a clear liquid obtained from PETROLEUM and used in making plastics and many chemical products

benzene ring *noun* [C] (**CHEMISTRY**) a ring of six CARBON ATOMS that is flat, found in BENZENE and many other COMPOUNDS

bequeath /bɪˈkwiːð/ *verb* [T] ~ sth (to sb) (*formal*) (**LAW**) to say in a WILL (= a legal document) that you want sb to have your property, money, etc. after you die: *He bequeathed £1 000 to his favourite charity.* **SYN** **leave**[1]

bequest /bɪˈkwest/ *noun* [C] ~ (to sb) (*formal*) (**LAW**) money or property that you ask to be given to a particular person when you die: *He left a bequest to each of his grandchildren.*

bereaved /bɪˈriːvd/ *adj.* (*formal*) **1** having lost a relative or close friend who has recently died **2** the bereaved *noun* [C] (*pl.* the bereaved) the people whose relative or close friend has died recently

bereavement /bɪˈriːvmənt/ *noun* (*formal*) **1** [U] the state of having lost a relative or close friend who has recently died **2** [C] the death of a relative or close friend: *There has been a bereavement in the family.*

bereft /bɪˈreft/ *adj.* [not before noun] **1** ~ of sth (*formal*) completely lacking sth; having lost sth: *bereft of ideas/hope* **2** (used about a person) sad and lonely because you have lost sb/sth: *He was utterly bereft when his wife died.*

beret /ˈbereɪ/ *noun* [C] a soft flat round hat

bergschrund /ˈbɜːɡʃrʊnd/ *noun* [C] (**GEOLOGY**) a deep narrow space formed where a GLACIER (= a large moving mass of ice) meets the side of a mountain

berkelium /bɜːˈkiːliəm, ˈbɜːkliəm/ *noun* [U] (*symb.* Bk) (**CHEMISTRY**) a chemical element. Berkelium is a RADIOACTIVE metal produced artificially from AMERICIUM and HELIUM. ❶ For more information on the periodic table of elements, look at the **Reference Section** of this dictionary.

berry /ˈberi/ *noun* [C] (*pl.* -ies) a small soft fruit with seeds. There are several types of berry: *Those berries are poisonous.* ◇ *a raspberry/strawberry/blueberry*

berserk /bəˈzɜːk, -ˈsɜːk/ *adj.* [not before noun] very angry, often in a violent way or without control: *If the teacher finds out what you've done he'll go berserk.*

berth /bɜːθ/ *noun* [C] **1** a place to sleep on a ship or train, or in a CARAVAN: *a cabin with four berths* **SYN** **bunk 2** a place where a ship or boat can stop and stay

beryllium /bəˈrɪliəm/ *noun* [U] (*symb.* Be) (**CHEMISTRY**) a chemical element. Beryllium is a hard grey metal. ❶ For more information on the periodic table of elements, look at the **Reference Section** of this dictionary.

beseech /bɪˈsiːtʃ/ *verb* [T] (*pt, pp* besought /-ˈsɔːt/, beseeched) (*formal*) to ask sb for sth in a worried way because you want or need it very much **SYN** **beg, implore**

beset /bɪˈset/ *verb* [T, usually passive] (besetting; *pt, pp* beset) (*formal*) to affect sb/sth in a bad way: *The team has been beset by injuries all season.*

beside ĩ+ **B2** /bɪˈsaɪd/ *prep.* at the side of or next to sb/sth: *Come and sit beside me.* ◇ *He kept his bag close beside him at all times.*
IDM **be beside the point** not connected with the subject you are discussing **beside yourself (with sth)** not able to control yourself because of a very strong emotion: *Emily was almost beside herself with grief.*

besides ĩ+ **B2** /bɪˈsaɪdz/ *prep., adv.* **1** in addition to sb/sth: *There will be six people coming, besides you and David.* **2** used for making an extra comment that adds to what you have just said: *I don't want to go out tonight. Besides, I haven't got any money.* ⊃ look at **anyway**(1)

besiege /bɪˈsiːdʒ/ *verb* [T] **1** (**HISTORY**) to surround a place with an army **2** [usually passive] (used about sth unpleasant or annoying) to surround sb/sth in large numbers: *The actor was besieged by fans and reporters.*

besotted /bɪˈsɒtɪd/ *adj.* [not before noun] ~ (with/by sb/sth) so much in love with sb/sth that you cannot think or behave normally

besought /bɪˈsɔːt/ past tense, past participle of
beseech

bespectacled /bɪˈspektəkld/ adj. (formal) wearing
glasses

bespoke /bɪˈspəʊk/ adj. (especially BrE, formal) (AmE usually
custom-made) (used about a product) made according
to the needs of an individual customer: bespoke
software ◇ a bespoke suit **SYN** **tailor-made**

best¹ 🔒 **A1** /best/ adj. (superlative of good) of the
highest quality or level; most suitable: His latest book
is by far his best. ◇ I'm going to wear my best shirt to
the interview. ◇ Who in the class is best at maths? ◇ It's
best to arrive early if you want a good seat. ◇ What's
the best way to get to York from here? ◇ Who's your
best friend?
IDM your best bet (informal) the most sensible or
appropriate thing for you to do in a particular
situation: There's nowhere to park in the city centre.
Your best bet is to go in by bus. the best/better part
of sth → PART¹

best² 🔒 **A2** /best/ adv. 1 (superlative of well) to the
greatest extent; most: Which of these dresses do you
like best? ◇ one of Britain's best-loved TV stars 2 in the
most excellent way; to the highest standard: He
works best in the morning.
IDM as best you can as well as you can, even if it is
not perfectly

best³ 🔒 **A2** /best/ (usually the best) noun [sing.] the
person or thing that is of the highest quality or level
or better than all others: When you pay that much for a
meal you expect the best. ◇ Even the best of us make
mistakes sometimes. ◇ I think James is the best!
◇ They are the best of friends. ◇ The best we can hope
for is that the situation doesn't get any worse. ⊃ look at
second best¹, **second best²**
IDM all the best (informal) used when you are saying
goodbye to sb or ending a letter or an email, to give
sb your best wishes: All the best! Keep in touch,
won't you? at best if everything goes as well as
possible; taking the most positive view: We won't be
able to deliver the goods before March, or, at best, the
last week in February. at its/your best in its/your
best state or condition: This is an example of
Beckett's work at its best. ◇ No one is at their best
first thing in the morning. be (all) for the best used to
say that although sth appears bad now, it will be
good in the end: I didn't get the job, but I'm sure it's
all for the best. bring out the best/worst in sb to show
sb's best/worst qualities: The crisis really brought out
the best in Tony. do/try your best to do all or the
most that you can look your best to look as beautiful
or attractive as possible make the best of sth/a bad
job to accept a difficult situation and try to be as
happy as possible to the best of your knowledge/
belief as far as you know: He never made a will, to
the best of my knowledge.

best man noun [sing.] a man who helps and supports the
BRIDEGROOM (= the man who is getting married) at a
wedding

bestow /bɪˈstəʊ/ verb [T] ~ sth (on/upon sb) (formal) to
give sth to sb, especially to show how much they are
respected: The title was bestowed on him by the king.

bestseller /ˌbestˈselə(r)/ noun [C] (**ARTS AND MEDIA**,
LITERATURE) a book or other product that is bought by
large numbers of people ▸ **bestselling** adj. [only before
noun]: a bestselling novel

bet¹ 🔒 **B2** /bet/ verb (betting; pt, pp bet) 1 [I, T] ~ (sth) (on
sth) to risk money on a race or an event by trying to
predict the result. If you are right, you win money: I

wouldn't bet on them winning the next election. ◇ I bet
him £50 he couldn't beat me at tennis. **SYN** **gamble¹**,
put money on sth 2 [I] ~ (that) … (informal) used to say
that you are almost certain that sth is true or that sth
will happen: I bet he arrives late — he always does. ◇ I
bet you're worried about your exam, aren't you?
IDM I/I'll bet (informal) used to show that you can
understand what sb is feeling or describing: 'I'm
going to tell her what I think of her.' 'Yeah, I bet!' you
bet (informal) a way of saying 'Yes, of course!': 'Are
you coming too?' 'You bet (I am)!'

bet² 🔒 **B2** /bet/ noun [C] 1 ~ (on sth) an act of betting: to
win/lose a bet ◇ She had never placed a bet on a horse
before. 2 an opinion: My bet is that he's missed the
train.
IDM your best bet → BEST¹ hedge your bets
→ HEDGE²

beta /ˈbiːtə/ noun [C] (**LANGUAGE**) 1 the second letter of
the Greek alphabet (B, β) 2 = BETA VERSION

beta decay noun [sing.] (**PHYSICS**) the breaking up of an
ATOM in which an ELECTRON is EMITTED (= sent out)

beta particle noun [C] (**PHYSICS**) a fast-moving ELECTRON
that is EMITTED (= sent out) when some RADIOACTIVE
substances break down

beta version (also **beta**) noun [C] (**COMPUTING**) a product,
especially computer software, that is almost ready
for the public to buy or use, and that is tested by
customers to check that it works properly

betide /bɪˈtaɪd/ verb
IDM woe betide sb → WOE

betray 🔒 **C1** /bɪˈtreɪ/ verb [T] 1 to give information
about sb/sth to an enemy; to make a secret known: She
betrayed all the members of the group to the secret
police. ◇ He refused to betray their plans. ◇ to betray
your country 2 to hurt sb who trusts you, especially by
lying to or about them: If you take the money, you'll
betray her trust. ◇ When parents get divorced the
children often feel betrayed. 3 to show a feeling or
quality that you would like to keep hidden: Her steady
voice did not betray the emotion she was feeling.
▸ **betrayal** /-əl/ noun [C, U]

betrothal /bɪˈtrəʊðl/ noun [C] ~ (to sb) (formal, old-
fashioned) an agreement to marry sb
SYN **engagement**

betrothed /bɪˈtrəʊðd/ adj. ~ (to sb) (formal, old-fashioned)
having promised to marry sb **SYN** **engaged**

better¹ 🔒 **A1** /ˈbetə(r)/ adj. 1 (comparative of good) of
a higher quality or level or more suitable than sb/sth: I
think her second novel was much better than her first.
◇ It's a long way to drive. It would be better to take the
train. 2 ~ (at sth) more able: He's far better at English
than me. 3 (**HEALTH**) less ill; fully recovered after an
illness: You can't go swimming until you're better. ◇ I
hope you get better soon.
IDM the bigger, smaller, faster, slower, etc. the
better used to say that sth should be as big, small,
etc. as possible

better² 🔒 **A2** /ˈbetə(r)/ adv. (comparative of well) in a
better way; to a greater or higher degree: I think you
could have done this better. ◇ Sylvie speaks English
better than I do.
IDM (be) better off (comparative of well off) with
more money: We're much better off now I go out to
work too. (be) better off (doing sth) to be in a more
pleasant or suitable situation: You look terrible. You'd
be better off at home in bed. you, etc. had better (do
sth) used to tell sb what you think they should or
should do; you ought to: I think we'd better go before it
gets dark. ❶ For other idioms containing better, look at
the entries for the nouns, adjectives, etc. For example,
think better of sth/doing sth is at **think**.

better³ 🔊 **B1** /'betə(r)/ *noun* [sing., U] something that is of higher quality: *The hotel wasn't very good. I must say we'd expected better.*
IDM **get the better of sb/sth** to defeat or be stronger than sb/sth: *When we have an argument, she always gets the better of me.*

better⁴ /'betə(r)/ *verb* [T] **1** [often passive] to be better or do sth better than sb/sth else **2** ~ **yourself** to improve your social position through education, a better job, etc.

'**betting shop** *noun* [C] (*BrE*) a shop where you can go to put money on a race or an event

between¹ 🔊 **A1** 🔘 /bɪ'twiːn/ *prep.* **1** in the space in the middle of two things, people, places etc: *I was sitting between Sam and Charlie.* ◊ *a village between Girona and Palamos* **2** (used about two amounts, distances, ages, times, etc.) at a point that is greater or later than the first and smaller or earlier than the second; somewhere in the middle: *They said they would arrive between four and five o'clock.* **3** from one place to another: *There aren't any direct trains between here and Manchester.* **4** involving or connecting two people, groups or things: *There's some sort of disagreement between them.* ◊ *There may be a connection between the two crimes.* **5** choosing one and not the other (of two things): *to choose between two jobs* ◊ *What's the difference between 'some' and 'any'?* **6** by putting together the actions, efforts, etc. of two or more people: *Between us we saved up enough money to buy a car.* **7** giving each person a share: *The money was divided equally between the two children.* ◊ *We ate all the chocolates between us.*

between² **A2** /bɪ'twiːn/ *adv.* (*usually* in between /ˌɪn bɪ'twiːn/) in the space in the middle of two things, places etc: *The house was near a park but there was a road in between.*

bevel /'bevl/ *noun* [C] **1** an edge or a surface that is cut at an angle, for example at the side of a picture frame or sheet of glass **2** a tool for cutting edges or surfaces at an angle on wood or stone

beverage /'bevərɪdʒ/ *noun* [C] (*formal*) any type of drink except water

beware /bɪ'weə(r)/ *verb* [I] (in infinitives and orders) ~ **(of sb/sth)** (used for giving a warning) to be careful: *Beware of the dog!* (= written on a sign) ◊ *We were told to beware of strong currents in the sea.*

bewilder /bɪ'wɪldə(r)/ *verb* [T, usually passive] to confuse and surprise sb: *I was completely bewildered by his sudden change of mood.* ▸ **bewildered** *adj.*: *a bewildered expression* ▸ **bewildering** *adj.*: *a bewildering experience* ▸ **bewilderment** *noun* [U]: *to stare at somebody in bewilderment*

bewitch /bɪ'wɪtʃ/ *verb* [T, often passive] to attract and interest sb very much so that they cannot think in a sensible way

beyond¹ 🔊 **B2** 🔘 /bɪ'jɒnd/ *prep.* **1** on or to the other side of sth: *beyond the distant mountains* **2** more than sth: *The house was far beyond what I could afford.* ◊ *I haven't heard anything beyond a few rumours.* **3** further than; later than: *Does the motorway continue beyond Birmingham?* ◊ *Most people don't go on working beyond the age of 65.* **4** used to say that sth is not possible: *The car was completely beyond repair* (= too badly damaged to repair). ◊ *The situation is beyond my control.* **5** too far or too advanced for sb/sth: *The activity was beyond the students' abilities.*
IDM **be beyond sb** (*informal*) to be impossible for sb to understand or imagine: *Why she wants to go and live there is quite beyond me.*

beyond² 🔊 **B2** 🔵 /bɪ'jɒnd/ *adv.* on the other side: *We could see the mountains and the sea beyond.*

bhangra /'bɑːŋɡrə/ *noun* [U] (**MUSIC**) a type of popular music that combines traditional Punjabi music from India and Pakistan with Western pop music

bi /baɪ/ (*informal*) = BISEXUAL

bi- /baɪ/ *prefix* (in nouns and adjectives) two; twice; double: *bicentenary* ◊ *bilingual*

bias¹ 🔊+ **B2** 🌐 /'baɪəs/ *noun* (*pl.* biases) **1** [U, C, usually sing.] ~ **(towards/against sb/sth)** a strong feeling in favour of or against one group of people, or on one side in an argument, often not based on fair judgement or facts: *a bias against women drivers* ◊ *The BBC has been accused of political bias.* **2** [C, usually sing.] an interest in one thing more than others: *a course with a strong scientific bias*

bias² /'baɪəs/ *verb* [T, often passive] (-s-, -ss-) ~ **sth** **(towards/against sb/sth)** to influence sb/sth, especially unfairly; to give an advantage to one group, etc: *Good newspapers should not be biased towards a particular political party.* ▸ **biased** *adj.*: *a biased report*

biathlon /baɪ'æθlən/ *noun* [C] (**SPORT**) a sports event that combines CROSS-COUNTRY SKIING and RIFLE shooting ⊃ look at **decathlon, pentathlon, triathlon**

bib /bɪb/ *noun* [C] a piece of cloth or plastic that you fasten around the neck of a baby or small child to protect its clothes while it is eating

the Bible /ðə 'baɪbl/ *noun* [sing.] (**RELIGION**) **1** the holy book of the Christian religion, consisting of the Old Testament and the New Testament **2** the holy book of the Jewish religion, consisting of the Torah (or Law), the Prophets, and the Writings ▸ **biblical** /'bɪblɪkl/ *adj.*

bibliography /ˌbɪbli'ɒɡrəfi/ *noun* [C] (*pl.* -ies) (**EDUCATION, LITERATURE**) **1** a list of books or articles on a particular subject or by a particular author **2** a list of the books and articles that a writer used when they were writing an article, etc.

bicameral /ˌbaɪ'kæmərəl/ *adj.* (**POLITICS**) (used about a parliament) having two main parts, such as the Senate and the House of Representatives in the US, and the House of Commons and the House of Lords in the UK: *a bicameral assembly/legislature/congress*

bicarbonate /ˌbaɪ'kɑːbənət/ *noun* [U] (**CHEMISTRY**) a SALT that contains CARBON, HYDROGEN and OXYGEN together with another element

bi,**carbonate of** 'soda = SODIUM BICARBONATE

bicentenary /ˌbaɪsen'tiːnəri/ (*pl.* -ies) (*BrE*) (*AmE* **bicentennial** /ˌbaɪsen'teniəl/) *noun* [C] the day or the year 200 years after an important event happened or began: *the bicentenary of the French Revolution*

biceps /'baɪseps/ *noun* [C] (*pl.* biceps) (**ANATOMY**) the large muscle at the front of the top part of the arm ⊃ look at **triceps** ⊃ picture at **arm¹**

bicker /'bɪkə(r)/ *verb* [I] ~ **(about/over sth)** to argue about things that are not important: *My parents are always bickering about something or other.*

bicycle 🔊 **A1** /'baɪsɪkl/ (*also informal* **bike**) *noun* [C] a vehicle with two wheels, that you sit on and ride by pushing PEDALS with your feet: *Did you come by bicycle?* ◊ *He got on his bicycle and rode off.* ◊ *We went for a bicycle ride on Sunday.*

'**bicycle lane** (*AmE*) = CYCLE LANE

bid¹ 🔊+ **B2** /bɪd/ *verb* (bidding; *pt, pp* bid) (**FINANCE**) **1** [I, T] ~ **(sth) (for sth)**; ~ **(against sb)** to offer to pay a particular price for sth, especially at an AUCTION (= a public sale where things are sold to the person who offers the most money): *Somebody bid £5 000 for the painting.* ◊ *I wanted to buy the vase but another man* *was bidding against me.* **2** [I] ~ **(for/on sth)** to offer to do work or provide a service for a particular price, in competition with other companies, etc: *A French firm will be bidding for the contract.*

bid² 🔊+ **B2** /bɪd/ *noun* [C] **1** ~ **(for sth)** **(BUSINESS, FINANCE)** an offer by a person or a business company to pay a certain amount of money for sth: *Granada mounted a hostile takeover bid* (= when one company tries to buy another company) *for Forte.* ◇ *At the auction we made a bid of £100 for the chair.* **2** ~ **(for sth)** **(BUSINESS)** an offer to do work or provide a service for a particular price, in competition with other companies, etc: *The company submitted a bit for the contract.* **SYN** **tender²** **3** ~ **for sth;** ~ **to do sth** an effort to do or obtain sth: *His bid for freedom had failed.* ◇ *Tonight the Ethiopian athlete will make a bid to break the world record.* **SYN** **attempt²** ▸ **bidder** *noun* [C]: *The house was sold to the highest bidder* (= the person who offered the most money).

bide /baɪd/ *verb* **IDM** **bide your time** to wait for a good opportunity: *I'll bide my time until the situation improves.*

bidet /ˈbiːdeɪ/ *noun* [C] a low bowl in the bathroom, usually with TAPS, that you fill with water and sit on to wash your bottom

biennial¹ /baɪˈeniəl/ *adj.* happening once every two years ⊃ look at **annual¹**

biennial² /baɪˈeniəl/ *noun* [C] **(BIOLOGY)** any plant that lives for two years, producing flowers in the second year ⊃ look at **annual² (2), perennial²**

bifocals /ˌbaɪˈfəʊklz/ *noun* [pl.] a pair of glasses with each LENS made in two parts. The upper part is for looking at things at a distance, and the lower part is for looking at things that are close to you. ▸ **bifocal** *adj.*

big 🔊 **A1** /bɪg/ *adj.* (**bigger; biggest**) **1** large; not small: *a big house/town/salary* ◇ *This dress is too big for me.* **OPP** **small** **2** great or important: *They had a big argument yesterday.* ◇ *That was the biggest decision I've ever had to make.* ◇ *some of the big names in Hollywood* **3** [only before noun] (*informal*) older: *a big brother/sister* **OPP** **little¹** **IDM** **a big deal/no big deal** (*informal*) something that is (not) very important or exciting: *Birthday celebrations are a big deal in our family.* ◇ *We may lose, I suppose, but it's no big deal.* **big deal!** (*informal*) used to say that you think sth is not important or interesting: *'Look at my new bike!' 'Big deal! It's not as nice as mine.'* **give sb a big hand** → HAND¹

bigamy /ˈbɪgəmi/ *noun* [U] **(LAW)** the crime of marrying sb when you are still married to sb else ⊃ look at **monogamy, polygamy** ▸ **bigamist** /-mɪst/ *noun* [C]

Big Bang (*usually the Big Bang*) *noun* [sing.] **(ASTRONOMY, PHYSICS)** the single large explosion that some scientists believe created the universe

big data *noun* [U, pl.] **(COMPUTING)** very large and complex sets of information: *The company uses big data to improve its services.*

big game *noun* [U] large wild animals that people hunt for sport, for example elephants and lions

big-head (*informal*) *noun* [C] a person who thinks they are very important or clever because of sth they have done ▸ **big-headed** *adj.*

big mouth (*informal*) *noun* [C] a person who talks too much and cannot keep a secret

bigot /ˈbɪgət/ *noun* [C] **(SOCIAL STUDIES)** a person who has very strong and unreasonable opinions, and refuses to change them or listen to other people: *a religious bigot* ▸ **bigoted** *adj.* ▸ **bigotry** /-gətri/ *noun* [U]

the big screen *noun* [sing.] **(ARTS AND MEDIA)** the cinema (when contrasted with television): *The movie hits the big screen in July.*

the big time *noun* [sing.] (*informal*) **(ARTS AND MEDIA)** great success in a profession, especially the entertainment business: *This is the role that could help her make it to the big time in Hollywood.*

big time *adv.* (*especially AmE, informal*) very much: *You screwed up big time, Wayne!*

big toe *noun* [C] **(ANATOMY)** the largest toe on a person's foot ⊃ picture at **body**

big wheel (*usually the Big Wheel*) *noun* [C] (*BrE*) **(TOURISM)** a large wheel that stands on its side at an AMUSEMENT PARK, with seats on the edge for people to ride in

bike 🔊 **A1** /baɪk/ (*informal*) (*also* bicycle) *noun* [C] a vehicle with two wheels, that you sit on and ride by pushing PEDALS with your feet: *Hasan's just learnt to ride a bike.* ◇ *We went by bike.* ◇ *He came on his bike.*

bike lane (*AmE, informal*) = CYCLE LANE

bikini /bɪˈkiːni/ *noun* [C] a piece of clothing, in two pieces, that women wear for swimming and lying in the sun

bilabial /ˌbaɪˈleɪbiəl/ *noun* [C] **(LANGUAGE)** a speech sound made by using both lips, for example /b/, /p/ and /m/ in *buy, pie* and *my* ▸ **bilabial** *adj.*

bilateral /ˌbaɪˈlætərəl/ *adj.* **1** **(POLITICS)** involving two groups of people or two countries: *bilateral relations/agreements/trade/talks* **2** **(ANATOMY)** involving both sides of the body or brain ▸ **bilaterally** /-rəli/ *adv.*

bile /baɪl/ *noun* [U] **(BIOLOGY)** **1** a green-brown liquid with a bitter unpleasant taste that is produced by the LIVER (= one of the body's main organs) to help the body break down the fats we eat **2** (*formal*) a strong feeling of anger or hating sb/sth

bile duct *noun* [C] **(ANATOMY)** the tube that carries BILE from the LIVER and the GALL BLADDER to the upper part of the small INTESTINE ⊃ picture at **body**

bilge /bɪldʒ/ *noun* **1** [C] (*also* bilges [pl.]) the almost flat part of the bottom of a boat or a ship, inside or outside **2** (*also* bilge water) [U] dirty water that collects in a ship's bilge

bilingual /ˌbaɪˈlɪŋgwəl/ *adj.* **(LANGUAGE)** **1** having or using two languages: *a bilingual dictionary* ⊃ look at **monolingual** **2** ~ **(in sth)** able to speak two languages equally well: *Our children are bilingual in English and Spanish.* ⊃ look at **monolingual, multilingual**

bill¹ 🔊 **A1** /bɪl/ *noun* [C] **1** **(BUSINESS, FINANCE)** a piece of paper that shows how much money you owe sb for goods or services: *to pay a bill* ◇ *an electricity bill* **2** (*especially BrE*) (*AmE* check) a piece of paper that shows how much you have to pay for the food and drinks that you have had in a restaurant: *Can I have the bill, please?* **3** (*AmE*) = NOTE¹ (4): *a ten-dollar bill* **4** **(POLITICS)** a plan for a possible new law: *The bill was passed/defeated.* **5** **(ARTS AND MEDIA)** a programme of entertainment offered in a show, concert, etc: *Topping the bill* (= the most important performer) *is Ariana Grande.* **6** a bird's BEAK (= the hard pointed part of a bird's mouth) ⊃ picture at **animal 7** (*AmE*) = PEAK¹ (2) **IDM** **foot the bill** → FOOT²

bill² 🔊 **B2** /bɪl/ *verb* [T] **1** ~ **sb (for sth)** to send sb a bill for sth: *Please bill me for the books.* ◇ *We are changing the way that we bill our customers.* ◇ *He only billed me £130.* **2** [usually passive] **be billed as sth** to describe sb/sth to the public in an advertisement, etc: *This young player is being billed as 'the new Messi'.*

billboard /ˈbɪlbɔːd/ (*especially AmE*) (*BrE also* **hoarding**) *noun* [C] a large board near a road where advertisements are put

billet /ˈbɪlɪt/ *noun* [C] a place, often in a private house, where soldiers live temporarily ▸ **billet** *verb* [T, usually passive] (used with an adverb or a preposition): *The troops were billeted in the town with local families.*

billfold /ˈbɪlfəʊld/ (*AmE*) = WALLET

billiards /ˈbɪliədz/ *noun* [U] (**SPORT**) a game played on a big table covered with cloth. You use a CUE (= a long thin stick) to hit three balls against each other and into pockets at the edge of the table: *to have a game of billiards ◇ to play billiards* ⊃ look at **pool**¹ (4), **snooker** ▸ **billiard** *adj.*

billing /ˈbɪlɪŋ/ *noun* [U] **1** an important position that sb is described as having in a show, etc: *to have top/star billing* **2** (**BUSINESS**) the act of preparing and sending bills to customers

billion ⚡ 🅰🔢 /ˈbɪljən/ *number* one thousand million **HELP** Note that when you are counting you use **billion** without 's'. You use **billions** when you mean 'a lot': *three billion yen ◇ billions of dollars* Formerly, **billion** was used with the meaning 'one million million'. Now you should say **trillion** for this. ❶ For more information about numbers, look at the **Reference Section** of this dictionary.

billionaire /ˌbɪljəˈneə(r)/ *noun* [C] a person who has at least a thousand million pounds, dollars, etc. in money or property

bill of exˈchange *noun* [C] (*pl.* **bills of exchange**) (**FINANCE**) a written order to pay a sum of money to a particular person on a particular date

bill of lading /ˌbɪl əv ˈleɪdɪŋ/ *noun* [C] (*pl.* **bills of lading**) (**FINANCE**) a list giving details of the goods that a ship, etc. is carrying

bill of ˈsale *noun* [C] (*pl.* **bills of sale**) (**FINANCE**) an official document showing that sth has been bought

billow /ˈbɪləʊ/ *verb* [I] (often used with an adverb or a preposition) **1** to fill with air and move in the wind: *curtains billowing in the breeze* **2** to move in large clouds through the air: *Smoke billowed from the chimneys.*

billy goat /ˈbɪli gəʊt/ *noun* [C] a male GOAT (= an animal like a sheep that lives wild in mountain areas or is kept on farms)

bimetallic strip /ˌbaɪmetælɪk ˈstrɪp/ *noun* [C] (**ENGINEERING**) a STRIP made of two different types of metal that bends when it is heated, used in THERMOSTATS (= a device that controls the temperature in a house or machine by switching the heat on and off as necessary)

bin ⚡🅰 /bɪn/ *noun* [C] **1** a container that you put rubbish in: *to throw something in the bin ◇ a litter bin ◇ The dustmen come to empty the bins on Wednesdays.* **2** a container, usually with a LID (= cover), for storing bread, flour, etc: *a bread bin*

binary /ˈbaɪnəri/ *adj.* **1** (**COMPUTING, MATHEMATICS**) using only 0 and 1 as a system of numbers: *the binary system ◇ binary arithmetic* **2** based on only two

numbers; consisting of two parts: *binary code/ numbers* ▸ **binary** *noun* [U]: *The computer performs calculations in binary and converts the results to decimal.*

bin bag *noun* [C] (*BrE, informal*) a large plastic bag for putting rubbish in

bind¹ ⚡+ 🔵 /baɪnd/ *verb* [T] (*pt, pp* **bound** /baʊnd/) **1** ~ sb/sth (to sb/sth) to tie or fasten with string or rope: *They bound him to a chair.* **2** ~ (A and B) (together) to join people, organizations, etc. together so that they live or work together more happily or with better effect: *The two countries are bound together by a common language.* **3** [usually passive] **be bound (to sth)** to be forced to promise to do sth or to make it your duty to do it: *to be bound by a law/an agreement ◇ The contract binds you to completion of the work within two years.* **4** [usually passive] **be bound (in sth)** (used about the pages of a book) to be fastened together into a cover to form a book: *The book was bound in leather.*

bind² /baɪnd/ *noun* [sing.] (*BrE, informal*) a situation or task that you find boring or annoying **SYN** nuisance

binder /ˈbaɪndə(r)/ *noun* [C] a hard cover for holding sheets of paper, magazines, etc. together: *a ring binder*

binding¹ /ˈbaɪndɪŋ/ *adj.* (**LAW**) making it necessary for sb to do sth they have promised or to obey a law, etc: *This contract is legally binding.*

binding² /ˈbaɪndɪŋ/ *noun* **1** [C] a cover that holds the pages of a book together **2** [C, U] material that you fasten to the edge of sth to protect or decorate it **3** **bindings** [pl.] (**SPORT**) a device that fastens your boot to your ski

binge¹ /bɪndʒ/ *noun* [C] a period of time when sb does too much of a particular activity, especially eating or drinking alcohol: *to go on a binge*

binge² /bɪndʒ/ *verb* [I] (**bingeing, binging**) ~ (on sth) to eat or drink too much, especially without being able to control yourself

bingo /ˈbɪŋgəʊ/ *noun* [U] a game in which each player has a different card with numbers on it. The person in charge of the game calls numbers out and the winner is the first player to have all the numbers on their card called out.

bin liner *noun* [C] (*BrE*) a bag that you put inside a container for holding rubbish ⊃ look at **bin bag**

binoculars /bɪˈnɒkjələz/ *noun* [pl.] an instrument with two LENSES that you look through in order to see objects that are in the distance more clearly: *a pair of binoculars* ⊃ look at **telescope**

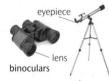

eyepiece

lens

binoculars

telescope

binomial /baɪˈnəʊmiəl/ *noun* [C] (**MATHEMATICS**) an expression in mathematics that has two groups of numbers or letters, joined by the symbol (+) or (−) ▸ **binomial** *adj.*

bio- /baɪəʊ, baɪə, baɪˈɒ/ *prefix* (in nouns, adjectives and adverbs) connected with living things or human life: *biology ◇ biodegradable ◇ biography*

biochemist /ˌbaɪəʊˈkemɪst/ *noun* [C] (**BIOLOGY, CHEMISTRY**) a scientist who studies the chemistry of living things

biochemistry /ˌbaɪəʊˈkemɪstri/ *noun* (*pl.* -ies) (**BIOLOGY, CHEMISTRY**) **1** [U] the scientific study of the chemistry of living things **2** [C, U] the chemical structure of a living thing ▸ **biochemical** /-mɪkl/ *adj.*

biodegradable /ˌbaɪəʊdɪˈgreɪdəbl/ adj. (BIOLOGY, ENVIRONMENT) a substance or chemical that is **biodegradable** can be changed to a natural state and so not harm the environment **OPP** **non-biodegradable**

biodegrade /ˌbaɪəʊdɪˈgreɪd/ verb [I] (ENVIRONMENT) (used about a substance or chemical) to change back, by the action of bacteria, to a natural state that will not harm the environment

biodiesel /ˈbaɪəʊdiːzl/ noun [U] (ENVIRONMENT) a type of fuel made from plant or animal matter and used in engines

biodiversity /ˌbaɪəʊdaɪˈvɜːsəti/ noun [U] (BIOLOGY, ENVIRONMENT) the existence of a large number of different kinds of animals and plants that together make a balanced environment ▶ **biodiverse** /-ˈvɜːs/ adj.: It is one of the world's most biodiverse areas.

biofuel /ˈbaɪəʊfjuːəl/ noun [C, U] (ENVIRONMENT) fuel made from plant or animal sources and used in engines: Ministers are promoting the use of biofuels for transport to reduce greenhouse gas emissions.

biogas /ˈbaɪəʊgæs/ noun [U] (ENVIRONMENT) gas such as METHANE that is produced by dead plants, etc. and that can be burned to produce heat

biographer /baɪˈɒgrəfə(r)/ noun [C] (LITERATURE) a person who writes the story of sb else's life

biography ⓘ+ ⓒ1 /baɪˈɒgrəfi/ noun [C, U] (pl. -ies) (LITERATURE) the story of a person's life written by sb else; this type of writing: a biography of Napoleon ◇ I enjoy reading science fiction and biography. ⊃ look at **autobiography** ▶ **biographical** /ˌbaɪəˈgræfɪkl/ adj.

biohazard /ˈbaɪəʊhæzəd/ noun [C] (ENVIRONMENT) a risk to human health or to the environment from a disease, bacteria, etc.

biological ⓘ+ ⓑ2 /ˌbaɪəˈlɒdʒɪkl/ adj. (BIOLOGY) **1** connected with the scientific study of animals, plants and other living things: biological research ◇ the biological sciences **2** connected with the processes that take place within living things: the biological effects of radiation **3** (used about a member of a person's family) related by blood: a child's **biological father**

ˌbiological ˈwarfare (also germ warfare) noun [U] the use of weapons of war that spread disease

ˌbioˌlogical ˈweapon noun [C] a weapon of war that spreads disease ⊃ look at **chemical weapon**

biology ⓘ ⓐ2 /baɪˈɒlədʒi/ noun [U] (EDUCATION, SCIENCE) **1** the scientific study of living things ⊃ look at **botany, zoology 2** the way in which the body and cells of a living thing behave: How far is human nature determined by biology? ▶ **biologist** /-dʒɪst/ noun [C]

biomass /ˈbaɪəʊmæs/ noun [U, sing.] **1** (BIOLOGY) the total quantity or weight of plants and animals in a particular area or volume **2** (ENVIRONMENT) natural materials from plants, trees and animals, used especially to produce electricity

biome /ˈbaɪəʊm/ noun [C] (ENVIRONMENT) the characteristic plants and animals that exist in a particular type of environment, for example in a forest or desert

biomedical /ˌbaɪəʊˈmedɪkl/ adj. (BIOLOGY, MEDICINE) connected with how biology affects medicine

biometric /ˌbaɪəʊˈmetrɪk/ adj. (BIOLOGY) using measurements of human features, such as fingers or eyes, in order to identify people: Biometric systems have several advantages over conventional identification methods.

biomolecule /ˌbaɪəʊˈmɒlɪkjuːl/ noun [C] (BIOLOGY, CHEMISTRY) a chemical COMPOUND that is found in animals and plants and that is necessary for a healthy body and growth

bionic /baɪˈɒnɪk/ adj. (BIOLOGY, ENGINEERING) having parts of the body that are electronic, and therefore able to do things that are not possible for normal humans

biophysics /ˌbaɪəʊˈfɪzɪks/ noun [U] (BIOLOGY, PHYSICS) the science that uses the laws and methods of physics to study biology ▶ **biophysical** /-zɪkl/ adj. ▶ **biophysicist** /-zɪsɪst/ noun [C]

biopic /ˈbaɪəʊpɪk/ noun [C] (ARTS AND MEDIA) a film about the life of a particular person

biopolymer /ˌbaɪəʊˈpɒlɪmə(r)/ noun [C] (CHEMISTRY) a natural substance consisting of large MOLECULES that are made from repeating combinations of small MONOMERS. Biopolymers occur in living things. ⊃ look at **polymer**

biopsy /ˈbaɪɒpsi/ noun [C] (pl. -ies) (MEDICINE) the process of removing and examining some cells from sb's body in order to find out about a disease that they may have

biorhythm /ˈbaɪəʊrɪðəm/ noun [C, usually pl.] a regular series of changes in the life of a living creature, for example sleeping and waking

BIOS /ˈbaɪɒs/ abbr. (COMPUTING) **Basic Input-Output System** (a set of basic instructions in a computer that controls how it starts up when you first switch it on)

bioscience /ˈbaɪəʊsaɪəns/ noun [C, U] (BIOLOGY) any of the LIFE SCIENCES (= the scientific study of humans, animals or plants)

biosphere /ˈbaɪəʊsfɪə(r)/ noun [sing.] (ASTRONOMY, BIOLOGY) the part of the earth's surface and atmosphere in which plants and animals can live

biotechnology /ˌbaɪəʊtekˈnɒlədʒi/ (also informal **biotech** /ˈbaɪəʊtek/) noun [U] (BIOLOGY, ENGINEERING) the use of living cells and bacteria in industrial and scientific processes ▶ **biotechnological** /ˌbaɪəʊteknəˈlɒdʒɪkl/ adj.: biotechnological research

biotype /ˈbaɪəʊtaɪp/ noun [C] (BIOLOGY) a group of living things with exactly the same combination of GENES (= the units inside a cell that control particular qualities)

bipartisan /ˌbaɪˈpɑːtɪzæn, ˌbaɪpɑːtɪˈzæn/ adj. (POLITICS) involving two political parties: a bipartisan policy

biped /ˈbaɪped/ noun [C] (BIOLOGY) any creature with two feet ⊃ look at **quadruped**

bipolar /ˌbaɪˈpəʊlə(r)/ adj. (PSYCHOLOGY) suffering from or connected with BIPOLAR DISORDER

biˈpolar disorder noun [U, C] (PSYCHOLOGY) a mental illness causing sb to change suddenly from being extremely depressed to being extremely happy

biracial /ˌbaɪˈreɪʃl/ adj. (especially AmE) = MIXED-RACE: a biracial child (= with parents of different races)

birch /bɜːtʃ/ noun **1** (also ˈbirch tree) [C] a type of tree with smooth thin branches **2** [U] the wood from the birch tree

bird ⓘ ⓐ1 /bɜːd/ noun [C] a creature that is covered with feathers and has two wings and two legs. Most birds can fly: I could hear the birds singing outside. ◇ There was a bird's nest in the hedge with four eggs in it. ⊃ picture at **animal, food web** **IDM** kill two birds with one stone → KILL[1]

ˈbird flu (also formal avian flu) noun [U] (HEALTH) a serious illness that affects birds, especially chickens, and that can be spread from birds to humans, sometimes causing death: Ten new cases of bird flu were reported yesterday.

birdsong /ˈbɜːdsɒŋ/ _noun_ [U] the musical sounds made by birds

birdwatcher /ˈbɜːdwɒtʃə(r)/ _noun_ [C] a person who studies birds in their natural environment and identifies different species as a hobby **SYN** **ornithologist** ▶ **birdwatching** _noun_ [U]

Biro™ /ˈbaɪrəʊ/ _noun_ [C] (_pl._ -os) (_BrE_) a type of pen in which INK (= coloured liquid for writing) comes out of a small metal ball at the end ⊃ look at **ballpoint**

birth ⚐ A2 /bɜːθ/ _noun_ **1** [C, U] being born; coming out of a mother's body: _It was a difficult birth._ ◇ _The baby weighed 3 kilos **at birth** (= when it was born)._ ◇ _What's your **date of birth** (= the date on which you were born)?_ **2** [U] a person's origin or the social position of their family: _She's always lived in England but she's German by birth._ **3** [sing.] the beginning of sth: _the birth of an idea_
IDM **give birth (to sb)** to produce a baby: _She gave birth to her second child at home._

ˈbirth certificate _noun_ [C] an official document that shows when and where a person was born

ˈbirth control _noun_ [U] ways of limiting the number of children you have ⊃ look at **contraception**, **family planning**

birthday ⚐ A1 /ˈbɜːθdeɪ/ _noun_ [C] the day in each year that is the same date as the one when you were born: _My birthday's on 15 November._ ◇ _my 18th birthday_ ◇ _a birthday present/card/cake_

birthmark /ˈbɜːθmɑːk/ _noun_ [C] a red or brown mark on a person's skin that has been there since they were born

birthplace /ˈbɜːθpleɪs/ _noun_ **1** [C] the house or town where a person was born **2** [sing.] the place where sth began: _Greece is the birthplace of the Olympic Games._

ˈbirth rate _noun_ [C] (SOCIAL STUDIES) the number of births every year for every 1 000 people in the population of a place

biscuit ⚐ A2 /ˈbɪskɪt/ _noun_ [C] **1** (_BrE_) (_AmE_ **cookie**) a type of small cake that is thin, hard and usually sweet: _a chocolate biscuit_ ◇ _a packet of biscuits_ **2** (_AmE_) a soft bread roll that is not sweet

bisect /baɪˈsekt/ _verb_ [T] (MATHEMATICS) to divide sth into two equal parts

bisexual /ˌbaɪˈsekʃuəl/ (_also informal_ **bi**) _adj._ sexually attracted to people of more than one GENDER ⊃ look at **heterosexual**, **homosexual** ▶ **bisexual** _noun_ [C]

bishop ⚐+ C1 /ˈbɪʃəp/ _noun_ [C] **1** (RELIGION) a priest with a high position in some branches of the Christian Church, who is responsible for all the churches in a city or a district ⊃ look at **archbishop** **2** a piece used in the game of CHESS that is shaped like a bishop's mitre

bismuth /ˈbɪzməθ/ _noun_ [U] (_symb._ Bi) (CHEMISTRY) a chemical element. Bismuth is a silver-grey metal that breaks easily. ➊ For more information on the periodic table of elements, look at the **Reference Section** of this dictionary.

bison /ˈbaɪsn/ _noun_ [C] a large wild animal that looks like a cow and is covered with hair

bistro /ˈbiːstrəʊ/ _noun_ [C] (_pl._ -os) a small informal restaurant

bit¹ ⚐ A2 /bɪt/ _noun_
• SMALL AMOUNT **1** a bit [sing.] (_especially BrE_) slightly; a little: _I was a bit annoyed with him._ ◇ _I'm afraid I'll be a little bit late tonight._ ◇ _Could you be a bit quieter, please?_ **2** a bit [sing.] (_especially BrE_) a short time or distance: _I'm just going out for a bit._ ◇ _Could you move forward a bit?_ **3** [C] ~ **(of sth)** (_especially BrE_) a small piece, amount or part of sth: _There were bits of broken glass all over the floor._ ◇ _Could you give me a bit of advice?_ ◇ _Which bit of the film did you like best?_
• LARGE AMOUNT **4** a bit [sing.] (_especially BrE, informal_) a lot: _It must have rained **quite a bit** during the night._
• IN COMPUTING **5** [C] the smallest unit of information that is stored in a computer's memory
• FOR A HORSE **6** [C] a metal bar that you put in a horse's mouth when you ride it in order to control it
IDM **bit by bit** slowly or a little at a time: _Bit by bit we managed to get the information we needed._ **a bit much** (_informal_) annoying or unpleasant: _It's a bit much expecting me to work on Sundays._ **a bit of a …** (_especially BrE, informal_) used when talking about unpleasant or negative things or ideas, to mean 'rather a … ': _I've got a bit of a problem._ **bits and pieces** (_BrE, informal_) small things of different kinds: _I've finished packing except for a few bits and pieces._ **do your bit** (_informal_) to do your share of sth; to help with sth: _It won't take long to finish if we all do our bit._ **not a bit** not at all: _The holiday was not a bit what we had expected._ **to bits 1** into small pieces: _She angrily tore the letter to bits._ **2** (_informal_) very; very much: _I was **thrilled to bits** when I won the competition._

bit² /bɪt/ past tense of **bite**¹

bitch¹ /bɪtʃ/ _verb_ [I] ~ **(about sb/sth)** (_informal_) to say unkind and critical things about sb, especially when they are not there

bitch² /bɪtʃ/ _noun_ [C] a female dog

bitchy /ˈbɪtʃi/ _adj._ (**bitchier**; **bitchiest**) (_informal_) talking about other people in an unkind way: _a bitchy remark_

bitcoin /ˈbɪtkɔɪn/ _noun_ [U, C] (_abbr._ BTC) (ECONOMICS) a system of electronic money used for buying and selling online; a unit of the bitcoin system of money

bite¹ ⚐ B1 /baɪt/ _verb_ (_pt_ bit /bɪt/; _pp_ bitten /ˈbɪtn/) **1** [I, T] ~ **(into sth)** to cut or attack sb/sth with your teeth: _Don't worry about the dog — she never bites._ ◇ _The cat bit me._ ◇ _He picked up the bread and bit into it hungrily._ **2** [I, T] (used about some insects and animals) to push a sharp point into your skin and cause pain: _He was bitten by a snake/mosquito/spider._ ➊ Wasps, bees and jellyfish do not bite you. They **sting** you. **3** [I] to begin to have an unpleasant effect: _In the South the job losses are starting to bite._
IDM **bite sb's head off** to answer sb in a very angry way **bite your tongue** to stop yourself from saying sth that might upset sb or cause an argument, although you want to speak

bite² ⚐ B1 /baɪt/ _noun_ **1** [C] an act of biting: _He ate the cupcake in two bites._ **2** [C] a piece of food that you can put into your mouth: _She took a big bite of the apple._ **3** [C] (HEALTH) a painful place on the skin made by an insect, snake, dog, etc: _I'm covered in mosquito bites._ **4** [sing.] (_informal_) a small meal; a small amount of food: _Would you like **a bite to eat** before you go?_ **SYN** **snack**

bitten /ˈbɪtn/ past participle of **bite**¹

bitter¹ ⚐ B2 /ˈbɪtə(r)/ _adj._ **1** caused by anger or hate: _a bitter quarrel_ **2** (used about a person) very unhappy or angry about sth that has happened because you feel you have been treated unfairly: _She was very bitter about not getting the job._ **3** causing unhappiness or anger for a long time; difficult to accept: _Failing the exam was **a bitter disappointment** to him._ ◇ _I've learnt **from bitter experience** not to trust him._ **4** having a sharp, unpleasant taste; not sweet: _bitter coffee_ ⊃ look at **sour** (1) **5** (used about the weather) very cold: _a bitter wind_ ▶ **bitterness** _noun_ [U]: _The pay cut caused bitterness among the staff._

bitter² /ˈbɪtə(r)/ *noun* [U] (*BrE*) a type of dark beer with a bitter taste that is popular in Britain: *A pint of bitter, please.*

bitterly /ˈbɪtəli/ *adv.* **1** (used for describing strong negative feelings or cold weather) extremely: *bitterly disappointed/resentful* ◇ *a bitterly cold winter/wind* **2** in an angry and disappointed way: *'I've lost everything,'* he said bitterly .

bitty /ˈbɪti/ *adj.* (bittier; bittiest) (*informal*) made up of a lot of parts that do not seem to fit well together: *Your essay is rather bitty.*

bitumen /ˈbɪtʃumən/ *noun* [U] (**CHEMISTRY**) a black substance made from petrol, used for covering roads or roofs ⊃ picture at **fractional distillation**

bivalve /ˈbaɪvælv/ *noun* [C] (**BIOLOGY**) any SHELLFISH (= a creature with a shell that lives in water) with a shell in two parts: *Mussels and clams are bivalves.*

bizarre 🔒 **C1** /bɪˈzɑː(r)/ *adj.* very strange: *The story had a most bizarre ending.* **SYN** **weird**

black¹ 🔒 **A1** /blæk/ *adj.* **1** having the darkest colour, like the sky at night or coal **2** (*also* Black) (**SOCIAL STUDIES**) belonging to any human group that has dark skin: *the black population of Britain* ◇ *black culture* **3** (used about coffee or tea) without milk or cream: *black coffee with sugar* **4** very angry: *to give somebody a black look* **5** (used about a situation) without hope: *The economic outlook for the coming year is rather black.* **SYN** **depressing** **6** dealing with unpleasant or terrible things in a funny way: *The film was a black comedy.*
IDM **black and blue** covered with BRUISES (= purple marks on the body) because you have been hit by sb/sth **black and white** (used about TV, photos, etc.) showing no colours except black, white and grey

black² 🔒 **A1** /blæk/ *noun* **1** [U] the darkest colour, like the sky at night or coal: *People often wear black* (= black clothes) *at funerals* . **2** (*also* Black) [C] a member of a human group that has dark skin ❶ Many people find this word offensive. Use the adjective instead: *black people.* ▸ **blackness** *noun* [U]
IDM **be in the black** (**FINANCE**) to have some money, for example in the bank **OPP** **be in the red** **in black and white** in writing or in print: *I won't believe I've passed the exam till I see it in black and white.*

black³ /blæk/ *verb*
PHRV **black out** to become unconscious for a short time **SYN** **faint¹**

black belt *noun* [C] (**SPORT**) **1** a belt that you can earn in some fighting sports such as JUDO or KARATE that shows that you have reached a very high standard **2** a person who has gained a black belt

blackberry /ˈblækbəri/ *noun* [C] (*pl.* -ies) a small black fruit that grows on bushes and can be eaten

blackbird /ˈblækbɜːd/ *noun* [C] a common European bird. The male is black with a yellow BEAK (= the hard pointed part of a bird's mouth) and the female is brown.

blackboard /ˈblækbɔːd/ (*also* chalkboard *especially in AmE*) *noun* [C] a large board with a smooth black or dark green surface that teachers write on with a piece of CHALK (= a small white or coloured stick) ⊃ look at **whiteboard**

blackcurrant /ˌblækˈkʌrənt/ *noun* [C] a small round black fruit that grows on bushes and can be eaten

blacken /ˈblækən/ *verb* **1** [T, I] to make sth black; to become black: *Smoke had blackened the walls.* **2** [T] to make sb seem bad by saying unpleasant things about them: *to blacken somebody's name*

black eye *noun* [C] (**HEALTH**) an area of dark-coloured skin around sb's eye where they have been hit: *He got a black eye in the fight.*

blackhead /ˈblækhed/ *noun* [C] a small spot on the skin with a black centre

black hole *noun* [C] (**ASTRONOMY**) an area in space that nothing, not even light, can escape from, because GRAVITY (= the force that pulls objects in space towards each other) is so strong there

black ice *noun* [U] ice in a thin layer on the surface of a road

blackleg /ˈblækleg/ *noun* [C] (*BrE*) a person who continues to work when the people they work with are on strike; a person who is employed to work instead of those who are on strike

blacklist /ˈblæklɪst/ *noun* [C] a list of people, companies, etc. that are considered bad or dangerous and that should be avoided: *to be on somebody's blacklist*
▸ **blacklist** *verb* [T]: *She was blacklisted by all the major Hollywood studios.*

blackly /ˈblækli/ *adv.* ~ **comic/funny/humorous** (**ARTS AND MEDIA**, **LITERATURE**) dealing with unpleasant things in a funny way: *The movie takes a blackly humorous look at death.*

black magic *noun* [U] a type of magic that is used for evil purposes

blackmail /ˈblækmeɪl/ *noun* [U] (**LAW**) the crime of forcing a person to give you money or do sth for you, usually by threatening to make known sth that they want to keep secret ▸ **blackmail** *verb* [T]: ~**sb (into sth/doing sth)**: *He was blackmailed into betraying state secrets.* ▸ **blackmailer** *noun* [C]

black mark *noun* [C] a note, either in writing on an official record, or in sb's mind, of sth you have done or said that makes people think badly of you: *She earned a black mark for turning up late to the meeting.*

black market *noun* [C, usually sing.] (**ECONOMICS**) the buying and selling of goods or foreign money in a way that is not legal: *to buy/sell something on the black market*

blackout /ˈblækaʊt/ *noun* [C] **1** a period when there is no light as a result of an electrical power failure **2** (**HEALTH**) a period when you are unconscious for a short time: *to have a blackout*

blacksmith /ˈblæksmɪθ/ *noun* [C] a person whose job is to make and repair things made of iron

bladder /ˈblædə(r)/ *noun* [C] (**ANATOMY**) the part of the body where URINE (= waste liquid) collects before leaving the body ⊃ picture at **body**

blade 🔒 **C1** /bleɪd/ *noun* [C] **1** the flat, sharp part of a knife, etc. ⊃ picture at **gardening**, **tool** **2** (**ENGINEERING**) one of the flat parts that turn around in a device such as a PROPELLER: *the blades of a propeller* ⊃ picture at **windmill** **3** the flat, wide part of an OAR (= one of the long straight pieces of wood that are used to move a boat through water) ⊃ picture at **canoe** **4** a long, thin leaf of grass: *a blade of grass* ⊃ look at **shoulder blade**

blag /blæg/ *verb* [T] (-gg-) (*BrE*, *informal*) to persuade sb to give you sth, or to let you do sth, by talking to them in a clever or funny way: *I blagged some tickets for the game.*

blame¹ 🔒 **B2** /bleɪm/ *verb* [T] ~ **sb (for sth)**; ~ **sth on sb/sth** to think or say that a certain person or thing is responsible for sth bad that has happened: *The teacher blamed me for the accident.* ◇ *Police are blaming the accident on dangerous driving.*
IDM **be to blame (for sth)** to be responsible for sth bad: *The police say that careless driving was to*

blame for the accident. I don't blame you/her, etc. (for doing sth) used to say that you think that sb is not wrong to do sth

blame² ͜ **B2** /bleɪm/ noun [U] ~ **(for sth)** responsibility for sth bad: *The government must **take the blame** for the economic crisis.* ◊ *The report **put the blame on** rising prices.* ◊ *Why do I always **get the blame**?* **IDM** shift the blame/responsibility (for sth) (onto sb) → SHIFT¹

blameless /'bleɪmləs/ adj. not guilty; that should not be blamed: *He insisted that his wife was blameless and hadn't known about his crimes.* **SYN innocent**

blanch /blɑːntʃ/ verb 1 [I] ~ **(at sth)** (formal) to become pale because you are shocked or frightened 2 [T] to prepare food, especially vegetables, by putting it into boiling water for a short time

bland /blænd/ adj. 1 ordinary or not very interesting: *a rather bland style of writing* 2 (used about food) mild or lacking in taste 3 not showing any emotion ▶ blandly adv.

blank¹ ͜ **A2** /blæŋk/ adj. 1 empty, with nothing written, printed or recorded on it: *a blank screen/ piece of paper/page* 2 without feelings, understanding or interest: *a blank expression on his face* ◊ *My mind **went blank** when I saw the exam questions* (= I couldn't think properly or remember anything). ▶ blankly adv.: *She stared at me blankly, obviously not recognizing me.*

blank² ͜ **A2** /blæŋk/ noun [C] an empty space: ***Fill in the blanks** in the following exercise.* ◊ (figurative) *I couldn't remember his name — my mind was a complete blank.* **IDM** draw a blank → DRAW¹

blanket¹ ͜+ **B2** /'blæŋkɪt/ noun [C] 1 a cover made of wool, etc. that is put on beds to keep people warm 2 a thick layer or covering of sth: *a blanket of snow* ▶ blanket verb [T, often passive] **be blanketed (in/with sth)**: *The countryside was blanketed in snow.* **IDM** a wet blanket → WET¹

blanket² /'blæŋkɪt/ adj. [only before noun] affecting everyone or everything: *There is a **blanket ban** on journalists reporting the case.*

‚blank 'verse noun [U] (LITERATURE) poetry that has a regular rhythm but whose lines do not end with the same sound ◯ look at **free verse**

blare /bleə(r)/ verb [I, T] ~ **(sth) (out)** to make a loud unpleasant noise: *Car horns were blaring in the street outside.* ◊ *The loudspeaker blared out pop music.* ▶ blare noun [U, sing.]: *the blare of a siren*

blasphemy /'blæsfəmi/ noun [U] (RELIGION) writing or speaking about God or religion in a way that shows a lack of respect ▶ blasphemous /-məs/ adj.

blast¹ ͜+ **C1** /blɑːst/ noun [C] 1 an explosion, especially one caused by a bomb 2 a sudden strong current of air: *a blast of cold air* 3 a loud sound made by a musical instrument, etc: *The driver gave a few blasts on his horn.*

blast² ͜+ **C1** /blɑːst/ verb [T] 1 to make a hole, a tunnel, etc. in sth with an explosion: *They blasted a tunnel through the mountainside.* 2 (informal) to criticize sb/ sth very strongly **PHR V** blast off (used about a SPACECRAFT) to leave the ground **SYN lift off, take off**

‚blast furnace noun [C] a large structure like an oven in which iron ORE (= rock containing iron) is heated at high temperatures in order to take out the metal

‚blast-off noun [U] the time when a SPACECRAFT leaves the ground

blatant /'bleɪtnt/ adj. (used about actions that are considered bad) done in an obvious and open way without caring if people are shocked: *a blatant lie* ▶ blatantly adv.

blaze¹ /bleɪz/ noun 1 [C] a large and often dangerous fire: *It took firefighters four hours to put out the blaze.* 2 [sing.] ~ **of sth** a very bright show of light or colour: *The garden was a **blaze of colour**.* ◊ (figurative) *The new theatre was opened in a **blaze of publicity*** (= the media gave it a lot of attention).

blaze² /bleɪz/ verb [I] 1 to burn with bright strong flames 2 ~ **(with sth)** to be extremely bright; to shine brightly: *I woke up to find that the room was blazing with sunshine.* ◊ (figurative) *'Get out!' she shouted, her eyes blazing with anger.*

blazer /'bleɪzə(r)/ noun [C] a jacket, especially one that has the colours or BADGE (= symbol) of a school, club or team on it: *a school blazer*

bleach¹ /bliːtʃ/ verb [T] to make sth white or lighter in colour by using a chemical or by leaving it in the sun

bleach² /bliːtʃ/ noun [C, U] a strong chemical substance used for making clothes, etc. whiter or for cleaning things

bleachers /'bliːtʃəz/ noun [pl.] (AmE) (SPORT) rows of seats at a sports ground that are cheaper and not covered by a roof

bleak /bliːk/ adj. 1 (used about a situation) not giving any reason to have hope: *a bleak future for the next generation* 2 (used about a place) cold, empty and with no pleasant features: *the bleak Arctic landscape* 3 (used about the weather) cold and unpleasant: *a bleak winter's day* ▶ bleakly adv. ▶ bleakness noun [U]

bleary /'blɪəri/ adj. (blearier; bleariest) (used about the eyes) red, tired and unable to see clearly: *We were all rather bleary-eyed after the overnight journey.* ▶ blearily /-rəli/ adv.

bleat /bliːt/ verb 1 [I] to make the sound of a sheep ◯ note at **sheep** 2 [I, T] to speak in a weak or complaining voice ▶ bleat noun [C]

bleed ͜+ **C1** /bliːd/ verb [I] (pt, pp bled /bled/) to lose blood from the body ▶ bleeding noun [U]: *He wrapped a scarf around his arm to stop the bleeding.*

‚bleeding 'edge noun [sing.] **the ~ (of sth)** (COMPUTING) technology that is so new and advanced that there may be problems when you use it: *They were working at the bleeding edge of chip design.*

bleep¹ /bliːp/ noun [C] a short high sound made by a piece of electronic equipment

bleep² /bliːp/ verb [I] (used about machines) to make a short high sound

blemish /'blemɪʃ/ noun [C] a mark that makes sth look less beautiful or perfect ▶ blemish verb [T]: (figurative) *The defeat has blemished the team's perfect record.*

blend¹ ͜+ **C1** /blend/ verb 1 [T] ~ **A with B; ~ A and B (together)** to mix two or more substances together: *First blend the flour and the melted butter together.* 2 [I] ~ **(in) with sth** to combine with sth in an attractive or suitable way: *The new room is decorated to blend in with the rest of the house.* **PHR V** blend (into sth) to look so similar to the background that it is difficult for you to see it

blend² ͜+ **C1** /blend/ noun [C] a mixture: *He had the right blend of enthusiasm and experience.*

‚blended 'learning noun [U] (EDUCATION) a way of studying a subject that combines being taught in class with the use of different technologies, including learning over the internet ◯ look at **flipped classroom**

blender /'blendə(r)/ (*BrE also* **liquidizer**) *noun* [C] an electric machine that is used for making solid food into liquid

bless ᵢ+ **C1** /bles/ *verb* [T] (**RELIGION**) to ask God to protect sb/sth
IDM **be blessed with sth/sb** to be lucky enough to have sth/sb: *The West of Ireland is an area blessed with many fine sandy beaches.* **Bless you!** what you say to a person who has just SNEEZED (= made air come out of their nose suddenly and with a noise)

blessed /'blesɪd/ *adj.* **1** (**RELIGION**) holy: *the Blessed Virgin Mary* **2** (**RELIGION**) (in religious language) lucky: *Blessed are the pure in heart.* **SYN** **fortunate** **3** (*formal*) giving great pleasure: *The cool breeze brought blessed relief from the heat.*

blessing ᵢ+ **C1** /'blesɪŋ/ *noun* [C] **1** a thing that you are grateful for or that brings happiness: *It's a great blessing that we have two healthy children.* ◇ *Not getting that job was a blessing in disguise* (= something which seems to be a problem at first, but that has good results in the end). **2** [usually sing.] approval or support: *They got married without their parents' blessing.* **3** [usually sing.] (**RELIGION**) (a prayer asking for) God's help and protection: *The priest said a blessing.*

blew /bluː/ past tense of **blow**[1]

blight[1] /blaɪt/ *verb* [T] to have a bad effect on sth, especially by causing a lot of problems: *an area blighted by unemployment*

blight[2] /blaɪt/ *noun* **1** [U, C] (**AGRICULTURE**) any disease that kills plants, especially crops: *potato blight* **2** [sing., U] ~ (**on sb/sth**) something that has a bad effect on a situation, a person's life or the environment

blimp /blɪmp/ *noun* [C] (*especially AmE*) a small AIRSHIP (= an aircraft without wings that is filled with gas)

blind[1] ᵢ **B2** /blaɪnd/ *adj.* **1** unable to see: *a blind person* ◇ *to be completely/partially blind* **2** **the blind** *noun* [pl.] people who are unable to see **3** ~ (**to sth**) not wanting to notice or understand sth: *He was completely blind to her faults.* **4** without reason or thought: *He drove down the motorway in a blind panic.* **5** impossible to see round: *You should never overtake on a blind corner.* ▸ **blindly** *adv.* ▸ **blindness** *noun* [U]
IDM **turn a blind eye (to sth)** to pretend not to notice sth bad is happening so that you do not have to do anything about it

blind[2] /blaɪnd/ *verb* [T] **1** to make sb unable to see: *Her grandfather had been blinded in an accident* (= permanently). ◇ *Just for a second I was blinded by the sun* (= for a short time). **2** ~ **sb (to sth)** to make sb unable to think clearly or behave in a sensible way

blind[3] /blaɪnd/ *noun* [C] a piece of cloth or other material that you pull down to cover a window

blind date *noun* [C] an arranged meeting between two people who have never met before. The meeting is sometimes organized by their friends because they want them to begin a romantic relationship.

blinders /'blaɪndəz/ (*AmE*) = BLINKER (2)

blindfold /'blaɪndfəʊld/ *noun* [C] a piece of cloth, etc. that is used for covering sb's eyes ▸ **blindfold** *verb* [T]

blind spot *noun* [C] **1** the part of the road just behind you that you cannot see when driving a car **2** [usually sing.] if you have a blind spot about sth, you cannot understand or accept it **3** (**ANATOMY**) the part of the RETINA in the eye that is not sensitive to light

bling /blɪŋ/ (*also* **bling-'bling**) *noun* [U] (*informal*) expensive shiny jewellery and fashionable clothes ▸ **bling** (*also* **bling-bling**) *adj.*

blink /blɪŋk/ *verb* **1** [I, T] to shut your eyes and open them again very quickly: *Oh dear! You blinked just as I took the photo!* ◇ *He blinked his eyes to clear his vision.* ◒ look at **wink** 2 [I] (used about a light) to come on and go off again quickly ▸ **blink** *noun* [C]

blinker /'blɪŋkə(r)/ *noun* **1** [C] (*informal*) = INDICATOR (2) **2 blinkers** (*AmE also* **blinders**) [pl.] pieces of leather that are placed at the side of a horse's eyes to stop it from looking to the side

blinkered /'blɪŋkəd/ *adj.* not considering every aspect of a situation; not willing to accept different ideas about sth: *a blinkered policy/attitude/approach* **SYN** **narrow-minded**

blip /blɪp/ *noun* [C] **1** a light flashing on the screen of a piece of equipment, sometimes with a short high sound **2** a small problem that does not last for long

bliss /blɪs/ *noun* [U] perfect happiness ▸ **blissful** /'blɪsfl/ *adj.* ▸ **blissfully** /-fəli/ *adv.*

blister[1] /'blɪstə(r)/ *noun* [C] (**HEALTH**) a small painful area of skin that looks like a bubble and contains clear liquid. Blisters are usually caused by rubbing or burning.

blister[2] /'blɪstə(r)/ *verb* [I, T] **1** (**HEALTH**) to get or cause BLISTERS **2** when a surface **blisters**, it becomes covered with round areas that are filled with liquid or air and break open: *The paint is starting to blister.*

blistering /'blɪstərɪŋ/ *adj.* very strong or extreme: *the blistering midday heat* ◇ *The runners set off at a blistering pace.*

blitz /blɪts/ *noun* **1** [C, usually sing.] ~ (**on sth**) (*informal*) a sudden effort or attack on sb/sth **2 the Blitz** [sing.] (**HISTORY**) the German air attacks on the UK in 1940–1941

blizzard /'blɪzəd/ *noun* [C] a very bad storm with strong winds and a lot of snow ◒ note at **storm**[1]

bloated /'bləʊtɪd/ *adj.* unusually large and uncomfortable because of liquid, food or gas inside: *I felt a bit bloated after all that food.*

blob /blɒb/ *noun* [C] a small piece of a thick liquid: *a blob of paint/cream/ink*

bloc /blɒk/ *noun* [C + sing./pl. verb] (**POLITICS**) a group of countries that work closely together because they have the same political interests

block[1] ᵢ **B1** /blɒk/ *noun* [C]
• PIECE OF STH **1** a large, heavy piece of sth, usually with flat sides: *a block of wood* ◇ *huge concrete blocks*
• BUILDING **2** a large building that is divided into separate flats or offices: *a block of flats* ◒ look at **apartment block**, **office block** ◒ note at **building**
• GROUP OF BUILDINGS **3** a group of buildings in a town that has streets on all four sides: *The restaurant is three blocks away.*
• QUANTITY/AMOUNT **4** a quantity of sth or an amount of time that is considered as a single unit: *The class is divided into two blocks of 50 minutes.*
• THAT STOPS YOU **5** [usually sing.] ~ (**to sth**) a thing that makes movement or progress difficult or impossible: *a block to further progress in the talks* ◇ *I had a complete mental block. I just couldn't remember his name.* ◒ look at **roadblock**

block[2] ᵢ **B1** /blɒk/ *verb* [T] **1** to stop sth from moving or flowing through a pipe, a passage, a road, etc. by being in the way: *An overturned lorry is blocking the road.* ◇ *a blocked sink* **2** to prevent sth from being done: *The management tried to block the deal.* **3** to prevent sth from being seen by sb: *Get out of the way, you're blocking the view!*
PHR V **block sth off** to separate one area from another with sth solid: *This section of the motorway*

has been blocked off by the police. **block sth out to** stop yourself thinking about sth unpleasant: *She tried to block out the memory of the crash.*

blockade /blɒˈkeɪd/ *noun* [C] a situation in which a place is surrounded by soldiers or ships in order to prevent sb/sth from reaching it or coming out ▸ **blockade** *verb* [T]

blockage /ˈblɒkɪdʒ/ *noun* [C] a thing that is preventing sth from passing; the state of being blocked: *a blockage in the drainpipe* ◇ *There are blockages on some major roads.*

block and ˈtackle *noun* [sing.] a piece of equipment for lifting heavy objects that works by a system of ropes and PULLEYS (= small wheels around which the ropes are stretched)

pulley

blockbuster /ˈblɒkbʌstə(r)/ *noun* [C] (**ARTS AND MEDIA**, **LITERATURE**) a book or film with an exciting story that is very successful and popular

block and tackle

block ˈcapitals *noun* [C] separate big letters such as 'A' (not 'a'): *Please write your name in block capitals.*

blog¹ 🔊 **A1** /blɒg/ *noun* [C] (**COMPUTING**) a website where an individual person, or sb representing an organization, writes regularly about events or topics that interest them

blog² /blɒg/ *verb* [I] (-gg-) (**COMPUTING**) to write a blog ▸ **blogger** *noun* [C]

blogosphere /ˈblɒgəsfɪə(r)/ *noun* [sing.] (*informal*) (**COMPUTING**) all the personal websites that exist on the internet, seen as a network of people communicating with each other: *The story moved from the blogosphere to the mainstream press.*

blog post *noun* [C] (**ARTS AND MEDIA**) a piece of writing that forms part of a blog: *She posted a link to one of her blog posts about her recent trip.*

bloke /bləʊk/ *noun* [C] (*BrE, informal*) a man: *He's a really nice bloke.*

blonde 🔊 **A1** (*also* blond) /blɒnd/ *adj.* with fair or yellow hair: *Both my sisters have blonde hair.* ◇ *a small, blond boy* ▸ **blonde** *noun* [C] ⊃ look at **brunette**

blood 🔊 **A2** /blʌd/ *noun* [U] (**HEALTH**) the red liquid that flows through the bodies of humans and animals: *The heart pumps blood around the body.* ◇ *Blood was pouring from a cut on his knee.* ⊃ look at **bleed** **IDM** **be in your blood** to be a strong part of your character: *A love of the countryside was in his blood.* **your (own) flesh and blood** → **FLESH** **in cold blood** → **COLD¹** **shed blood** → **SHED²**

bloodbath /ˈblʌdbɑːθ/ *noun* [sing.] a situation in which many people are killed violently

blood count *noun* [C] (**HEALTH**) the number of red and white cells in the blood; a medical test to count these: *to have a high/low/normal blood count*

blood-curdling *adj.* very frightening: *a blood-curdling scream*

blood donor *noun* [C] (**MEDICINE**) a person who gives some of their blood for use in medical treatment

blood group (*also* blood type) *noun* [C] (**HEALTH**) any of several different types of human blood: *'What blood group are you?' 'Blood group/type O.'*

bloodless /ˈblʌdləs/ *adj.* **1** without killing or violence: *a bloodless coup* **2** (used about a part of the body) very pale

blood poisoning *noun* [U] (**HEALTH**) an illness in which harmful bacteria get into the blood, especially because of an injury to the skin **SYN** **septicaemia**

blood pressure *noun* [U] (**BIOLOGY**, **HEALTH**) the force with which the blood travels round the body: *to have high/low blood pressure*

bloodshed /ˈblʌdʃed/ *noun* [U] the killing or harming of people, usually after fighting or a war: *Both sides in the war want to avoid further bloodshed.*

bloodshot /ˈblʌdʃɒt/ *adj.* (used about the white part of the eyes) full of red lines, for example when sb is tired

blood sport *noun* [C] (**SPORT**) a sport in which animals or birds are killed

bloodstain /ˈblʌdsteɪn/ *noun* [C] a mark or spot of blood on sth ▸ **bloodstained** *adj.*

bloodstream /ˈblʌdstriːm/ *noun* [sing.] (**BIOLOGY**) the blood as it flows through the body: *drugs injected straight into the bloodstream*

blood test *noun* [C] (**MEDICINE**) an examination of a small amount of your blood by doctors in order to make judgements about your medical condition

bloodthirsty /ˈblʌdθɜːsti/ *adj.* wanting to use violence or to watch scenes of violence

blood transfusion *noun* [C] (**MEDICINE**) the process of putting new blood into a person's body

blood type = BLOOD GROUP

blood vessel *noun* [C] (**ANATOMY**) any of the tubes in the body that blood flows through ⊃ look at **artery**, **capillary**, **vein** (1) ⊃ picture at **tooth**

bloody /ˈblʌdi/ *adj.* (bloodier; bloodiest) **1** involving a lot of violence and killing: *a bloody war* **2** covered with blood: *a bloody knife*

bloody-ˈminded *adj.* (*BrE, informal*) (used about a person) deliberately difficult; not helpful ▸ **bloody-mindedness** *noun* [U]

bloom¹ /bluːm/ *noun* [C] (*formal*) a flower (usually one on a plant that people admire for its flowers) **IDM** **in bloom** with its flowers open: *All the wild plants are in bloom.*

bloom² /bluːm/ *verb* [I] to produce flowers: *This shrub blooms in May.* **SYN** **flower²**

blossom¹ /ˈblɒsəm/ *noun* [C, U] a flower or a mass of flowers, especially on a fruit tree in the spring: *The apple tree is in blossom.* ⊃ picture at **tree**

blossom² /ˈblɒsəm/ *verb* [I] **1** (used especially about trees) to produce flowers **2** ~ (into sth) to become more healthy, confident or successful: *This young runner has blossomed into a top-class athlete.*

blot¹ /blɒt/ *noun* [C] **1** a spot of sth, especially one made by INK (= coloured liquid in a pen), etc.; a dirty mark **SYN** **stain** **2** ~ (on sth) a thing that damages other people's opinion of you, or your happiness

blot² /blɒt/ *verb* [T] (-tt-) **1** to make a spot or a mark on sth, especially of INK on paper **2** to remove liquid from a surface by pressing soft paper or cloth on it **PHR V** **blot sth out** to cover or hide sth: *Fog blotted out the view completely.* ◇ *She tried to blot out the memory of what happened.*

blotch /blɒtʃ/ *noun* [C] a mark, usually not regular in shape, on skin, plants, material, etc: *The blotches on* *his face showed that he had been crying.* ▶ **blotchy** (**blotchier**; **blotchiest**) (*also* **blotched**) *adj.*

blouse /blaʊz/ *noun* [C] a piece of clothing like a shirt, worn by women

blow¹ ⏚ **A2** /bləʊ/ *verb* (*pt* **blew** /bluː/; *pp* **blown** /bləʊn/)

• OUT OF THE MOUTH **1** [I, T] (used with an adverb or a preposition) to send air out of the mouth: *The policeman asked me to blow into the breathalyser.* ◇ *She blew the candles out on her birthday cake.*
• OF WIND/AIR **2** [I, T] (used about wind, air, etc.) to be moving or to cause sth to move: *A gentle breeze was blowing.* ◇ *It was blowing a gale.* **3** [I] (used with an adverb or a preposition) to move because of the wind or a current of air: *The balloons blew away.* ◇ *My papers blew all over the garden.*
• MAKE/SHAPE **4** [T] to make or shape sth by blowing air out of your mouth: *to blow bubbles/smoke rings* ◇ *to blow (somebody) a kiss* (= to kiss your hand and pretend to blow the kiss towards sb)
• INSTRUMENT **5** [I, T] to produce sound from a musical instrument, etc. by blowing air into it: *The referee's whistle blew for the end of the match.* ◇ *He blew a few notes on the trumpet.*
• OPPORTUNITY **6** [T] (*informal*) to waste an opportunity: *I think I've blown my chances of promotion.* ◇ *You had your chance and you blew it.*
• MONEY **7** [T] ~ **sth (on sth)** (*informal*) to spend or waste a lot of money on sth: *She blew all her savings on a trip to China.*
• STOP FLOWING **8** [I, T] (**ENGINEERING**) when a FUSE (= a thin piece of wire in an electrical system) **blows**, the electricity has stopped flowing suddenly because the electric current was too strong: *A fuse has blown.* ◇ *I think the kettle's blown a fuse.*
IDM **blow your nose** to clear your nose by blowing strongly through it into a TISSUE (= a piece of paper) or a HANDKERCHIEF (= a piece of cloth)
PHRV **blow over** to disappear without having a serious effect: *The scandal will soon blow over.* **blow up 1** to explode or be destroyed in an explosion: *The car blew up when the door was opened.* **2** to start suddenly and strongly: *A storm blew up in the night.* ◇ *A huge row blew up about money.* **blow sth up 1** to make sth explode or to destroy sth in an explosion: *The terrorists tried to blow up the plane.* **2** to fill sth with air or gas: *to blow up a balloon* **3** to make a photo bigger **blow sth apart** to completely destroy sth in an explosion **blow up (at sb)** (*informal*) to become very angry with sb: *The teacher blew up at me when I said I'd forgotten my homework.*

blow² ⏚+ **B2** /bləʊ/ *noun* [C] **1** a hard hit from sb's hand, a weapon, etc: *She aimed a blow at me.* **2** ~ **(to sb/sth)** a sudden event that causes people to be sad or disappointed: *It was a blow to his pride when he didn't get the job.* **3** an act of blowing: *Give your nose a blow!*
IDM **a blow-by-blow account, description, etc.** (**of sth**) an account, etc. of an event that gives all the exact details of it **come to blows (with sb) (over sth)** to start fighting (about sth) **deal sb/sth a blow** | **deal a blow to sb/sth** → DEAL¹

blow-dry *verb* [T] (**blow-dries**; *pt, pp* **blow-dried**) to dry and shape sb's hair using a HAIRDRYER (= a machine that produces hot air) and a brush

blowhole /ˈbləʊhəʊl/ *noun* [C] **1** (**BIOLOGY**) a hole in the top of the head of a WHALE (= a large sea creature) through which it breathes ⊃ picture at **animal** **2** (**GEOGRAPHY**) a hole in a large area of ice through which sea animals, for example SEALS, breathe

blown /bləʊn/ past participle of **blow¹**

blowout /ˈbləʊaʊt/ *noun* [C] (*informal*) **1** an occasion when a tyre suddenly BURSTS (= explodes) on a vehicle while it is moving: *We had a blowout on the motorway.* **SYN** **puncture** **2** a very large meal at which people eat too much; a large party or social event

blowtorch /ˈbləʊtɔːtʃ/ (*BrE*) (*AmE also* **torch**) *noun* [C] a tool with a very hot flame that you can point at a surface, for example to remove paint

blubber /ˈblʌbə(r)/ *noun* [U] the fat of WHALES and other sea animals

bludgeon /ˈblʌdʒən/ *verb* [T] **1** to hit sb several times with a heavy object **2** ~ **sb (into sth/doing sth)** to force sb to do sth, especially by arguing with them: *They tried to bludgeon me into joining their protest.*

blue¹ ⏚ **A1** /bluː/ *adj.* **1** having the colour of a clear sky when the sun shines: *His eyes were bright blue.* ◇ *light/dark blue* **2** (*informal*) (often used in songs) sad
IDM **black and blue** → BLACK¹ **once in a blue moon** → ONCE¹

blue² ⏚ **A1** /bluː/ *noun* [C, U] the colour of a clear sky when the sun shines: *a deep blue* ◇ *dressed in blue* (= blue clothes)
IDM **out of the blue** suddenly; unexpectedly: *I didn't hear from him for years and then this email came out of the blue.*

blueberry /ˈbluːbəri/ *noun* [C] (*pl.* -ies) a small, sweet, dark blue BERRY that grows on bushes and can be eaten

blue-ˈchip *adj.* (**BUSINESS**, **FINANCE**) a **blue-chip** investment is thought to be safe and likely to make a profit: *blue-chip companies*

blue-ˈcollar *adj.* (**BUSINESS**) doing or involving physical work with the hands rather than office work ⊃ look at **white-collar**

blueprint /ˈbluːprɪnt/ *noun* [C] **1** (**ARCHITECTURE**, **ENGINEERING**) a PHOTOGRAPHIC print of a plan for a building or a machine, with white lines on a blue background: *blueprints of a new aircraft* **2** ~ **(for sth)** a plan that shows what can be achieved and how it can be achieved: *a blueprint for the privatization of health care* **3** (**BIOLOGY**) the pattern in every living cell that decides how the plant, animal or person will develop and what it will look like: *DNA carries the blueprint which tells any organism how to build itself.*

blues /bluːz/ *noun* **1** (*often* the blues) [U] (**MUSIC**) a type of slow sad music with strong rhythms, developed by African American musicians in the southern US: *a blues band/singer* **2** [C] (*pl.* blues) (**MUSIC**) a blues song **3** the blues [pl.] sad feelings: *the Monday morning blues*

Bluetooth™ /ˈbluːtuːθ/ *noun* [U] (**COMPUTING**) a radio technology that makes it possible for mobile phones, computers and other electronic devices to be linked over short distances, without needing to be connected by wires: *Bluetooth-enabled devices*

bluff¹ /blʌf/ *verb* [I, T] to try to make people believe that you will do sth that you do not intend to do, or that you know sth when you do not
IDM **bluff your way through (sth)** to succeed in dealing with a difficult situation by making other people believe sth that is not true

bluff² /blʌf/ *noun* **1** [U, C] an attempt to make sb believe that you will do sth when you really have no intention of doing it, or that you know sth when, in fact, you do not know it: *John keeps threatening to leave home but I'm sure it's only bluff!* **2** [C] (**GEOGRAPHY**) a steep CLIFF, especially by the sea or a river ⊃ picture at **floodplain**
IDM **call sb's bluff** → CALL¹

bluish /ˈbluːɪʃ/ *adj.* slightly blue: *bluish green*

blunder¹ /ˈblʌndə(r)/ *noun* [C] a stupid mistake: *I'm afraid I've made a terrible blunder.*

blunder² /ˈblʌndə(r)/ *verb* [I] to make a stupid mistake

PHR V **blunder about, around, etc.** to move in an uncertain or careless way, as if you cannot see where you are going: *We blundered about in the dark, trying to find the light switch.*

blunt /blʌnt/ *adj.* **1** (used about a knife, pencil, tool, etc.) without a sharp edge or point **OPP** **sharp**[1] **2** (used about a person, comment, etc.) very direct; saying what you think without trying to be polite: *I'm sorry to be so blunt, but I'm afraid you're just not good enough.* ▸ **blunt** *verb* [T] ▸ **bluntly** *adv.* ▸ **bluntness** *noun* [U]

blur[1] /blɜː(r)/ *noun* [C, usually sing.] something that you cannot see clearly or remember well: *Without my glasses, their faces were just a blur.*

blur[2] /blɜː(r)/ *verb* [I, T] (-rr-) if the shape or outline of sth blurs, or if sth **blurs** it, it becomes less clear: *The words on the page blurred as tears filled her eyes.* ◇ *His thoughts were blurred and confused.* ▸ **blurred** *adj.* ⊃ picture at **short-sighted**

Blu-ray /'bluː reɪ/ *noun* [U] technology that uses a blue LASER (= a very strong line of light) to record and play large amounts of high-quality data on a type of DVD: *These high-definition movies are all out on Blu-ray.* ◇ *a Blu-ray disc*

blurt /blɜːt/ *verb*
PHR V **blurt sth out** to say sth suddenly or without thinking: *We didn't want to tell Mum but Ann blurted the whole thing out.*

blush /blʌʃ/ *verb* [I] to become red in the face, especially because you are embarrassed or feel guilty: *She blushed with shame.* ▸ **blush** *noun* [C]

blusher /'blʌʃə(r)/ *noun* [U, C] a coloured cream or powder that some people put on their CHEEKS (= the sides of their faces below their eyes) to give them more colour

blustery /'blʌstəri/ *adj.* (used to describe the weather) with strong winds: *The day was cold and blustery.*

BMI /ˌbiː em 'aɪ/ *abbr.* (HEALTH) **body mass index** (a measure of whether you are too heavy or too light, based on the relationship between your height and your weight)

BMX /ˌbiː em 'eks/ *noun* **1** [C] a strong bicycle that can be used for riding on rough ground **2** (*also* **BMXing**) [U] (SPORT) the sport of racing BMX bicycles on rough ground

BO /ˌbiː 'əʊ/ *noun* [U] the unpleasant smell from a person's body, especially of SWEAT (the abbreviation for 'body odour')

boa constrictor /ˌbəʊə kən'strɪktə(r)/ *noun* [C] a large South American snake that kills animals for food by wrapping its body tightly around them

boar /bɔː(r)/ *noun* [C] (*pl.* boar, boars) **1** a male pig ⊃ note at **pig**[1] **2** a wild pig

board[1] ⟨ **A2** /bɔːd/ *noun* **1** [C] a long thin flat piece of wood used for making floors, walls, etc: *She noticed a loose board in the fence.* ⊃ look at **floorboard 2** [C] (especially in compounds) a thin flat piece of wood, etc. used for a particular purpose: *Can you please write it on the board?* ◇ *a diving board* ⊃ look at **blackboard, bulletin board, chopping board, noticeboard, whiteboard 3** [C + sing./pl. verb] (BUSINESS) a group of people who control an organization, a company, etc: *the board of directors* ◇ *a board meeting* ◇ *She is on the board of a British port authority.* **4** [U] (TOURISM) the meals that are provided when you stay in a hotel, etc: *The prices are for a double room and full board* (= all the meals). **IDM** **across the board** → ACROSS **bring/get sb on board** to persuade sb to support an idea or a project or to join a team: *We need to get more sponsors on board.* **on board** on a ship or an aircraft: *All the passengers were safely on board.*

board[2] ⟨ **B1** /bɔːd/ *verb* (TOURISM) **1** [T, I] to get on a plane, ship, bus, etc: *We said goodbye and boarded the train.* ◇ *Passengers are now boarding.* **2** [I] when a plane or ship **is boarding**, it is ready for passengers to get on: *Lufthansa flight LH120 to Hamburg is now boarding at Gate 27.*
PHR V **board sth up** to cover sth with boards: *Nobody lives there now — it's all boarded up.*

boarder /'bɔːdə(r)/ *noun* [C] (*BrE*) **1** (EDUCATION) a child who lives at school and goes home for the holidays **2** a person who pays to live at sb's house ⊃ look at **lodger**

boarding card (*BrE*) (*also* **boarding pass** *BrE, AmE*) *noun* [C] a card that you must show in order to get on a plane or ship

boarding house *noun* [C] a private house where you can pay to stay and have meals for a period of time

boarding school *noun* [C] (EDUCATION) a school that children live at while they are studying, going home only in the holidays

boardroom /'bɔːdruːm, -rʊm/ *noun* [C] (BUSINESS) a room in which the meetings of the board of a company are held

boast ⟨+ **C1** /bəʊst/ *verb* **1** [I] ~ (about sth); ~ (that ...) to talk in a way that shows you are too proud of sth that you have or can do: *I wish she wouldn't boast about her family so much.* ◇ *He's always boasting that he's the fastest runner in the school.* **2** [T] (used about a place) to have sth that it can be proud of: *The town boasts over a dozen restaurants.* ▸ **boast** *noun* [C]

boastful /'bəʊstfl/ *adj.* talking about yourself in a way that is too proud

boat ⟨ **A1** /bəʊt/ *noun* [C] **1** a small vehicle that is used for travelling across water: *The cave can only be reached by boat/in a boat.* ◇ *a rowing/fishing boat* **2** any ship: *When does the next boat to France sail?* **IDM** **rock the boat** → ROCK[2]

boathouse /'bəʊthaʊs/ *noun* [C] a building next to a river or lake for keeping a boat in

bob /bɒb/ *verb* [I, T] (-bb-) to move quickly up and down; to make sth do this: *The boats in the harbour were bobbing up and down in the water.* ◇ *She bobbed her head down below the top of the wall.*
PHR V **bob up** to appear suddenly from behind or under sth: *He disappeared and then bobbed up again on the other side of the pool.*

bobsleigh /'bɒbsleɪ/ (*BrE*) (*AmE* **bobsled** /'bɒbsled/) *noun* [C] (SPORT) a racing vehicle for two or more people that slides over snow along a track ⊃ look at **sledge, sleigh, toboggan**

bode /bəʊd/ *verb*
IDM **bode well/ill (for sb/sth)** to be a sign that sb/sth will have a good/bad future

bodice /'bɒdɪs/ *noun* [C] the top part of a woman's dress, covering the upper part of the body

bodily[1] /'bɒdɪli/ *adj.* [only before noun] of the human body; physical: *First we must attend to their bodily needs* (= make sure that they have a home, enough to eat, etc.).

bodily[2] /'bɒdɪli/ *adv.* by taking hold of the body: *She picked up the child and carried him bodily from the room.*

body ⟨ **A1** **⑤** /'bɒdi/ *noun* (*pl.* -ies)
• PERSON/ANIMAL **1** [C] (ANATOMY) the whole physical form of a person or an animal: *the human body* ⊃ picture on **page 84 2** [C] (ANATOMY) the part of a person that is not their legs, arms or head: *She had injuries to her head and body.* **3** [C] a dead person: *The police have found a body in the canal.*

The body

the face

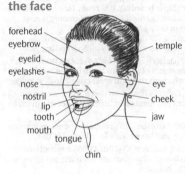

forehead
eyebrow
eyelid
eyelashes
nose
nostril
lip
tooth
mouth
tongue
chin
temple
eye
cheek
jaw

the body

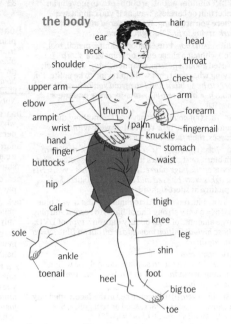

hair
head
ear
neck
throat
shoulder
chest
upper arm
arm
elbow
forearm
armpit
thumb
fingernail
wrist
palm
knuckle
hand
stomach
finger
waist
buttocks
hip
thigh
calf
knee
leg
sole
shin
ankle
toenail
heel
foot
big toe
toe

the skeleton

skull/cranium
jawbone/mandible
cheekbone
breastbone/sternum
collarbone/clavicle
shoulder blade/
scapula
ribcage
humerus
rib
backbone/
spine
vertebra
radius
pelvis
ulna
hip bone
tailbone/
coccyx
carpals
metacarpals
thigh bone/femur
kneecap/patella
shin bone/tibia
fibula
tarsals
metatarsals

the internal organs

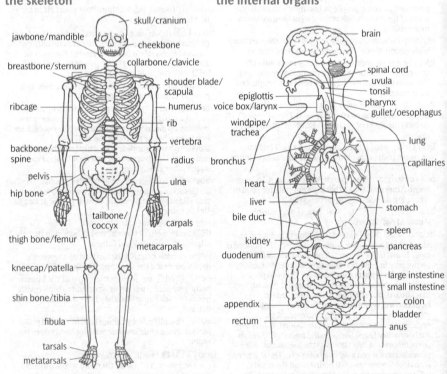

brain
spinal cord
uvula
tonsil
epiglottis
pharynx
voice box/larynx
gullet/oesophagus
windpipe/
trachea
lung
bronchus
capillaries
heart
liver
stomach
bile duct
spleen
kidney
pancreas
duodenum
large instestine
small instestine
appendix
colon
rectum
bladder
anus

• GROUP OF PEOPLE **4** [C + sing./pl. verb] a group of people who work or act together, especially in an official way: *The **governing body** of the college meets/meet once a month.*
• MAIN PART **5** [sing.] the main part of sth: *We agree with the body of the report, although not with certain details.*
• OBJECT **6** [C] (*formal*) an object: ***heavenly bodies*** (= stars, planets, etc.) ◇ *The doctor removed a **foreign body*** (= something that would not usually be there) *from the child's ear.*

bodyboard /ˈbɒdibɔːd/ *noun* [C] (**SPORT**) a short light type of SURFBOARD that you ride lying on your front ▶ **bodyboarding** *noun* [U]

bodybuilding /ˈbɒdibɪldɪŋ/ *noun* [U] (**SPORT**) making the muscles of the body stronger and larger by exercise ▶ **bodybuilder** /-bɪldə(r)/ *noun* [C]

bodyguard /ˈbɒdigɑːd/ *noun* [C + sing./pl. verb] a person or group of people whose job is to protect sb

ˈ**body language** *noun* [U] (**SOCIAL STUDIES**) showing how you feel by the way you move, stand, sit, etc., rather than by what you say: *I could tell by his body language that he was scared.*

ˈ**body mass index** *noun* [U] = BMI

ˈ**body odour** = BO

ˈ**body scanner** *noun* [C] an electronic machine that produces a picture of a person's body through their clothes on a screen. It is used to search for illegal drugs or weapons, for example at an airport.

ˈ**body search** *noun* [C] (**LAW**) a search of a person's body and clothes by the police or another official, to check for drugs, weapons, etc.

bodysuit /ˈbɒdisuːt/ *noun* [C] a piece of clothing that fits tightly over a woman's upper body and bottom, usually fastening between the legs

bodywork /ˈbɒdiwɜːk/ *noun* [U] the main outside structure of a vehicle, usually made of painted metal

bog¹ /bɒg/ *noun* [C, U] (**GEOGRAPHY**) an area of ground that is very soft and wet: *a peat bog*

bog² /bɒg/ *verb* (-gg-)
PHR V **bog sb/sth down (in sth)** [usually passive] **1** (used about a vehicle) to make sth sink into mud or wet ground **2** (used about a person) to prevent sb from making any progress

bogey /ˈbəʊgi/ *noun* [C] **1** something that causes fear, often without reason **2** (*informal*) a piece of MUCUS (= a sticky substance) from inside the nose

boggle /ˈbɒgl/ *verb* [I] ~ **(at sth)** to be unable to imagine sth; to be impossible to imagine or believe: *'What will happen if his plan doesn't work?' '**The mind boggles**!'* ➲ look at **mind-boggling**

boggy /ˈbɒgi/ *adj.* (**boggier**; **boggiest**) (used about land) soft and wet, so that your feet sink into it

BOGOF /ˈbɒgɒf/ *abbr.* (*BrE, informal*) **buy one, get one free** (a type of special offer in shops): *He can't resist those BOGOF offers.*

ˌ**bog-ˈstandard** *adj.* (*BrE, informal*) ordinary; with no special features: *It's just a bog-standard camera.*

bogus /ˈbəʊgəs/ *adj.* pretending to be real or true: *a bogus policeman* SYN **false**

bohrium /ˈbɔːriəm/ *noun* [U] (*symb.* **Bh**) (**CHEMISTRY**) a RADIOACTIVE chemical element ❶ For more information on the periodic table of elements, look at the **Reference Section** of this dictionary.

boil¹ 🔑 A2 /bɔɪl/ *verb* **1** [I] (used about a liquid) to reach a high temperature where bubbles rise to the surface and the liquid changes to a gas: *Water boils at 100°C.* ◇ (*BrE*) *The kettle's boiling* (= the water inside it is boiling). ➲ note at **water¹** ➲ picture at **state¹** **2** [T] to heat a liquid until it boils and let it keep boiling: *Boil all drinking water for five minutes.* **3** [I, T] to cook (sth) in boiling water: *Put the potatoes on to boil, please.* ◇ *to boil an egg* ➲ note at **cook¹** **4** [I] (used about a person) to feel very angry: *She was boiling with rage.*
PHR V **boil down to sth** to have sth as the most important point: *What it all boils down to is that you don't want to spend too much money.* **boil over** **1** (used about a liquid) to boil and flow over the sides of a pan: *You let the soup boil over.* **2** (used about an argument or sb's feelings) to become more serious or angry

boil² /bɔɪl/ *noun* **1** [sing.] a period of boiling; the point at which a liquid boils: ***Bring** the soup **to the boil*** (= heat it until it boils), *then allow to simmer for five minutes.* **2** [C] (**HEALTH**) a small painful SWELLING (= an area that is larger and rounder than normal) under the skin that is full of PUS (= a thick yellow liquid)

boiler /ˈbɔɪlə(r)/ *noun* [C] a container in which water is heated to provide hot water or heating in a building or to produce STEAM in an engine ➲ picture at **generator**

ˈ**boiler suit** *noun* [C] a piece of clothing that you wear over your normal clothes to protect them when you are doing dirty work ➲ look at **overall²** (2)

boiling /ˈbɔɪlɪŋ/ (*also* ˌ**boiling ˈhot**) *adj.* (*informal*) very hot: *Open a window — it's boiling hot in here.* ◇ *Can I open a window? I'm boiling.* ➲ note at **cold¹**

ˈ**boiling point** *noun* [C] (**CHEMISTRY**) the temperature at which a liquid starts to boil ➲ picture at **fractional distillation**

boisterous /ˈbɔɪstərəs/ *adj.* (used about a person or their behaviour) noisy and full of energy: *Their children are very nice but they can get a bit too boisterous.*

bold 🔑+ B2 /bəʊld/ *adj.* **1** (used about a person or their behaviour) confident and not afraid: *Not many people are bold enough to say exactly what they think.* **2** that you can see clearly: *bold, bright colours* **3** (used about printed letters) in thick dark type: *Make the important text **bold**.* ▶ **bold** *noun* [U]: *The important words are highlighted **in bold**.* ▶ **boldly** *adv.* ▶ **boldness** *noun* [U]

bole /bəʊl/ *noun* [C] (**BIOLOGY**) the main part of a tree that grows up from the ground SYN **trunk**

bollard /ˈbɒlɑːd/ *noun* [C] a short thick post that is used to stop motor vehicles from going into an area that they are not allowed to enter

Bollywood /ˈbɒliwʊd/ *noun* [U] (**ARTS AND MEDIA**) used to refer to the Hindi film industry, which is mainly based in the Indian city of Mumbai (formerly called Bombay) ➲ look at **Hollywood**

bolshie (*also* **bolshy**) /ˈbɒlʃi/ *adj.* (*BrE, informal*) (used about a person) creating difficulties or arguments deliberately and refusing to be helpful

bolster /ˈbəʊlstə(r)/ *verb* [T] ~ **sb/sth (up)** to support or encourage sb/sth; to make sth stronger: *His remarks did nothing to bolster my confidence.*

bolt¹ /bəʊlt/ *noun* [C] **1** (**ENGINEERING**) a small piece of metal that is used with a NUT (= a small circle of metal) for fastening things together ➲ picture on **page 86** **2** a bar of metal that you can slide across the inside of a door in order to fasten it

bolt² /bəʊlt/ *verb* **1** [T] to fasten a door, etc. with a BOLT: *Make sure that the door is locked and bolted.* **2** [T] ~ **(A to B)** (**ENGINEERING**) to fasten one thing to another using a BOLT: *All the tables have been bolted to the floor so that nobody can steal them.* **3** [I] (used

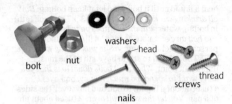

washers | head

bolt | nut

thread
screws

nails

especially about a horse) to run away very suddenly, usually in fear **4** [T] ~ **sth (down)** to eat sth very quickly

bolt³ /bəʊlt/ *adv.*

IDM **bolt upright** sitting or standing very straight

bomb¹ ʔ+ **B1** /bɒm/ *noun* **1** [C] a container that is filled with material that will explode when it is thrown or dropped, or when a device inside it makes it explode: *Fortunately, the car bomb failed to go off.* **2** the bomb [sing.] nuclear weapons: *How many countries have the bomb now?* **3** a bomb [sing.] (*BrE, informal*) a lot of money: *That car must have cost you a bomb!*

bomb² ʔ+ **B1** /bɒm/ *verb* **1** [T] to attack a city, etc. with bombs: *Enemy forces have bombed the bridge.* **2** [I] (*BrE, informal*) (used with an adverb or a preposition) to move along very fast in the direction mentioned, especially in a vehicle: *He was bombing along at 100 miles an hour when the police stopped him.*

bombard /bɒmˈbɑːd/ *verb* [T] to attack a place with bombs or guns: *They bombarded the city until the enemy surrendered.* ◇ (*figurative*) *The reporters bombarded the minister with questions.* ▸ **bombardment** *noun* [C, U]: *The main radio station has come under enemy bombardment.*

bomb disposal *noun* [U] the removing or exploding of bombs in order to make an area safe: *a bomb disposal expert*

bomber /ˈbɒmə(r)/ *noun* [C] **1** a type of plane that drops bombs **2** a person who puts a bomb somewhere illegally

bombing ʔ+ **B2** /ˈbɒmɪŋ/ *noun* [C, U] an occasion when a bomb is dropped or left somewhere; the act of doing this: *recent bombings in major cities* ◇ *enemy bombing*

bombshell /ˈbɒmʃel/ *noun* [C, usually sing.] (*informal*) an unexpected piece of news, usually about sth unpleasant: *The head teacher dropped a bombshell when he said he was resigning.*

bona fide /ˌbəʊnə ˈfaɪdi/ *adj.* real or true: *This car park is for the use of bona fide customers only.*

bond¹ ʔ+ **B2** /bɒnd/ *noun* [C] **1** ~ (between A and B) something that joins two or more people or groups of people together, such as a feeling of friendship: *the bond between mother and child* **2** (**FINANCE**) an agreement by a government or a company to pay you interest on the money you have lent; a document containing this agreement: *government bonds* **3** (*especially AmE*) (**LAW**) a sum of money that is paid as BAIL: *He was released on a $5 000 bond.* **4** (**CHEMISTRY**) the way in which ATOMS are held together in a chemical COMPOUND

bond² /bɒnd/ *verb* [I, A] **1** ~ (A and B) (together); ~ (A) to B to join two things FIRMLY together; to join FIRMLY to sth else: *The atoms bond together to form a molecule.* ◇ *Will this glue bond wood to metal?* **2** ~ (with sb) to develop or create a relationship of trust with sb: *Mothers who are depressed sometimes fail to bond with their children.*

bone¹ ʔ **A2** /bəʊn/ *noun* **1** [C] (**ANATOMY**) one of the hard parts that form the SKELETON of the body of a human or an animal: *He's broken a bone in his hand.* ◇ *This fish has got a lot of bones in it.* ◑ picture at **synovial** **2** [U] the substance that bones are made of **IDM** **have a bone to pick with sb** (*informal*) to have sth that you want to complain to sb about **make no bones about sth/doing sth** (*informal*) to do sth in an open honest way without feeling nervous or worried about it: *She made no bones about telling him exactly what she thought about him.*

bone² /bəʊn/ *verb* [T] to take the bones out of fish or meat: *to bone a fish*

bone dry *adj.* completely dry

bone marrow (*also* **marrow**) *noun* [U] (**ANATOMY**) the soft substance that is inside the bones of a person or an animal

bonemeal /ˈbəʊnmiːl/ *noun* [U] (**AGRICULTURE**) a substance made from animal bones that is used to make soil better for growing plants

bonfire /ˈbɒnfaɪə(r)/ *noun* [C] a large fire that you build outside to burn rubbish or as part of a festival, etc.

Bonfire Night *noun* [C] in the UK, the night of 5 November

▼ CULTURE

On this day people in the UK light fireworks and sometimes burn a model of a man (called a **guy**) on top of a **bonfire**, to celebrate the failure of Guy Fawkes to blow up the Houses of Parliament in the seventeenth century.

---

bonkers /ˈbɒŋkəz/ *adj.* (*informal*) crazy and silly: *I'd go bonkers if I worked here full-time.* **SYN** **mad**

bonnet /ˈbɒnɪt/ *noun* [C] **1** (*BrE*) (*AmE* **hood**) the front part of a car that covers the engine **2** a type of hat that covers the sides of the face and is fastened with strings under the CHIN

bonus ʔ+ **C1** /ˈbəʊnəs/ *noun* [C] **1** (**FINANCE**) a payment that is added to what is usual, especially to sb's wages or salary as a reward: *All our employees receive an annual bonus.* **2** something good that you get in addition to what you expect: *I enjoy my job, and having my own office is an added bonus.*

bony /ˈbəʊni/ *adj.* (**bonier**; **boniest**) so thin that you can see the shape of the bones: *long bony fingers*

boo /buː/ *exclamation, noun* [C] (*pl.* **boos**) **1** a sound you make to show that you do not like sb/sth: *The minister's speech was met with boos from the audience.* **2** a sound you make to frighten or surprise sb: *He jumped out from behind the door and said 'boo'.* ▸ **boo** *verb* [I, T] (**booing**; **boos**; *pt, pp* **booed**)

boob /buːb/ *noun* [C] (*BrE, informal*) **1** a silly mistake **2** (*slang*) a woman's breast

booby prize /ˈbuːbi praɪz/ *noun* [C] a prize that is given as a joke to the person or team that comes last in a competition

booby trap /ˈbuːbi træp/ *noun* [C] a device that will kill, injure or surprise sb when they touch the object that it is connected to ▸ **booby-trap** *verb* [T] (-pp-)

boogie¹ /ˈbuːgi/ (*also* **boogie-woogie** /ˌbuːgi ˈwuːgi/) *noun* [U] (**MUSIC**) a type of BLUES music played on the piano, with a fast strong rhythm

boogie² /ˈbuːgi/ *verb* [I] (*informal*) to dance to fast pop music

book¹ ʔ **A1** /bʊk/ *noun* **1** [C] ~ (on/about sth) (by sb) (**LITERATURE**) a written work that is published on printed pages fastened together inside a cover, or in electronic form: *I'm reading a book on astrology.* ◇ *She's writing a book about her life abroad.* ◇ *Do you have any books by William Golding?* ◇ *hardback/*

paperback books ➔ look at **audiobook, e-book 2** [C] a number of pieces of paper, fastened together inside a cover, for people to write or draw on: *Please write down all the new vocabulary in your exercise books.* ◇ *a notebook* ◇ *a sketch book* **3** [C] a number of things fastened together in the form of a book: *a book of stamps* **4** books [pl.] (**FINANCE**) the records that a company, etc., keeps of the amount of money it spends and receives: *We employ an accountant to keep the books.*

IDM be in sb's good/bad books (*informal*) to have sb pleased/angry with you: *He's been in his girlfriend's bad books since he forgot her birthday.* by the book exactly according to the rules: *A policeman must always do things by the book.* (be) on sb's books (to be) on the list of an organization

book² 🔊 **A2** /bʊk/ *verb* **1** [I, T] to arrange to have or do sth at a particular time: *Have you booked a table, sir?* ◇ *to book a seat on a plane/train/bus* ◇ *I've booked a hotel room for you/I've booked you a hotel room.* ◇ *I'm sorry, but this evening's performance is fully booked (= there are no seats left).* **2** [T] ~ **sb (for sth)** to officially write down the name of a person who has done sth wrong: *The police booked her for (= charged her with) dangerous driving .* ◇ *The player was booked for a foul and then sent off for arguing.*

PHR V book in to say that you have arrived at a hotel, etc., and sign your name on a list book sb in to arrange a room for sb at a hotel, etc. in advance: *I've booked you in at the George Hotel.*

bookcase /'bʊkkeɪs/ *noun* [C] a piece of furniture with shelves to keep books on

bookie /'bʊki/ (*informal*) = BOOKMAKER

booking 🔊 **B2** /'bʊkɪŋ/ *noun* [C, U] (**TOURISM**) the arrangement you make in advance to have a hotel room, a seat on a plane, etc: *Did you manage to make a booking?* ◇ *No advance booking is necessary.*

booking office *noun* [C] an office where you buy tickets

bookkeeper /'bʊkkiːpə(r)/ *noun* [C] (**BUSINESS, FINANCE**) a person whose job is to keep an accurate record of the accounts of a business

bookkeeping /'bʊkkiːpɪŋ/ *noun* [U] the job of keeping a record of the money that a company, etc. spends or receives

booklet /'bʊklət/ *noun* [C] a small thin book, usually with a soft cover, that gives information about sth

bookmaker /'bʊkmeɪkə(r)/ (*also informal* bookie) *noun* [C] a person whose job is to take bets on the result of horse races, etc. and pay out money to people who win

bookmark¹ /'bʊkmɑːk/ *noun* [C] **1** (**COMPUTING**) a record of the address of a file, a page on the internet, etc. that you keep on your computer so that you can find it quickly **SYN** favourite² **2** a narrow piece of card, etc. that you put between the pages of a book so that you can find the same place again easily

bookmark² /'bʊkmɑːk/ *verb* [T] (**COMPUTING**) to record the address of a file, a page on the internet, etc. so that you can find it quickly: *Do you want to bookmark this site?*

bookseller /'bʊkselə(r)/ *noun* [C] a person whose job is selling books

bookshelf /'bʊkʃelf/ *noun* [C] (*pl.* bookshelves /-ʃelvz/) a shelf that you keep books on

bookshop /'bʊkʃɒp/ (*BrE*) (*AmE* bookstore /'bʊkstɔː(r)/) *noun* [C] a shop that sells books ➔ look at **library** (1)

bookstall /'bʊkstɔːl/ (*especially BrE*) (*AmE usually* newsstand /'njuːzstænd/) *noun* [C] a type of small shop that is open at the front, selling newspapers, magazines and books, for example at a station

bookworm /'bʊkwɜːm/ *noun* [C] a person who likes reading books very much

Boolean /'buːliən/ *adj.* (**COMPUTING, MATHEMATICS**) connected with a system, used especially in COMPUTING and ELECTRONICS, that uses only the numbers 1 (to show sth is true) and 0 (to show sth is false)

Boolean operator *noun* [C] (**COMPUTING**) a symbol or word such as *or* or *and*, used in computer programs and searches to show what is or is not included

boom¹ 🔊 **C1** /buːm/ *noun* [C] **1** ~ **(in sth)** (**ECONOMICS**) a period in which sth increases or develops very quickly; a period of wealth and success: *a boom in car sales* ◇ *a boom year for exports* ➔ look at **slump²** (2) **2** [usually sing.] a loud deep sound: *the boom of distant guns* **3** a long POLE to which the sail of a boat is fixed. You move the boom to change the position of the sail.

IDM boom and bust (**ECONOMICS**) a situation in which a period of fast economic growth is followed by one of sudden decline

boom² /buːm/ *verb* **1** [I, T] ~ **(sth) (out)** to make a loud deep sound: *The loudspeaker boomed out instructions to the crowd.* **2** [I] (**ECONOMICS**) to grow very quickly in size or value: *Business is booming in the computer industry.*

boomer /'buːmə(r)/ *noun* (*especially AmE, informal*) = BABY BOOMER

boomerang /'buːməræŋ/ *noun* [C] a curved piece of wood that returns to you when you throw it in a particular way

boon /buːn/ *noun* [C] a thing that is very helpful and that you are grateful for

boorish /'bʊərɪʃ, 'bɔːr-/ *adj.* (used about people and their behaviour) very unpleasant and rude

boost¹ 🔊 **B2** /buːst/ *verb* [T] to increase sth in number, value or strength: *If we lower the price, that should boost sales.* ◇ *The good exam result boosted her confidence.*

boost² 🔊 **B2** /buːst/ *noun* [C, usually sing.] ~ **(in sth)**; ~ **(to sth)** something that encourages people; an increase: *The fall in the value of the pound has led to a boost in exports.* ◇ *The president's visit gave a boost to the soldiers' morale.*

booster /'buːstə(r)/ *noun* [C] **1** a device that gives extra power to a piece of electrical equipment **2** (**MEDICINE**) a small amount of a VACCINE that is given to increase the effect of one given earlier: *a tetanus booster*

boot¹ 🔊 **A1** /buːt/ *noun* [C] **1** a type of shoe that covers the foot and ankle and often part of the leg: *ski boots* ◇ *walking/climbing boots* ◇ *football boots* **2** (*BrE*) (*AmE* trunk) the space at the back of a car where you put bags, cases, etc.

boot² /buːt/ *verb* **1** [T] (*informal*) to kick sth/sb hard: *He booted the ball over the fence.* **2** [I, T] ~ **(sth) (up)** (**COMPUTING**) to prepare a computer for use when it is first switched on; to be prepared in this way

PHR V boot sb out (*informal*) to force sb to leave a place

booth /buːð/ *noun* [C] a small place with thin walls that divide it from the rest of the room or area, where you can do sth that is private, for example make a phone call or vote: *a voting booth*

booty /'buːti/ *noun* [U] things that are taken by thieves or captured by soldiers in a war

booze¹ /buːz/ *noun* [U] (*informal*) alcoholic drinks

booze² /buːz/ *verb* [I] (*informal*) to drink a lot of alcohol

'booze-up noun [C] (*BrE, informal*) an occasion when people drink a lot of alcohol

border¹ ⓕ **B1** /'bɔːdə(r)/ *noun* [C] **1 ~ (between A and B); ~ (with sth)** (**GEOGRAPHY**) a line that divides two countries, etc.; the land close to this line: *The refugees escaped across/over the border.* ◇ *the Moroccan border* ◇ *the border between France and Italy* ◇ *Italy's border with France* **2** a band or narrow line around the edge of sth, often for decoration: *a white tablecloth with a blue border*

border² ⓕ **B2** /'bɔːdə(r)/ *verb* [T] **1** to share a border with another country or area: *Which countries border Hungary?* **2** to form a line around the edge of sth: *The hedge borders the garden.*
PHR V **border on sth 1** to be almost the same as sth: *The dictator's ideas bordered on madness.* **2** to be next to sth: *Our garden borders on the railway line.*

borderline¹ /'bɔːdəlaɪn/ *noun* [sing.] **~ (between A and B)** the line that marks a division between two different cases, conditions, etc: *The novel is on the borderline between fiction and non-fiction.*

borderline² /'bɔːdəlaɪn/ *adj.* not clearly belonging to a particular condition or group; not clearly acceptable: *In borderline cases teachers will take the final decision, based on the student's previous work.* ◇ *a borderline pass/fail in an exam*

bore¹ /bɔː(r)/ *verb* **1** [T] to make sb feel bored, especially by talking too much: *I hope I'm not boring you.* **2** [I, T] to make a long deep hole with a tool or by digging: *This drill can bore (a hole) through solid rock.*

bore² /bɔː(r)/ *noun* **1** [C] a person who talks a lot in a way that is not interesting **2** [sing.] (*informal*) something that you have to do that you do not find interesting: *It's such a bore having to learn these lists of irregular verbs.* **3** (*also* **borehole**) [C] (**GEOGRAPHY**) a deep hole made in the ground, especially to find water or oil

bore³ /bɔː(r)/ past tense of **bear¹**

boreal /'bɔːriəl/ *adj.* (**GEOGRAPHY**) relating to or typical of the climate near the Arctic: *northern boreal forest*

bored ⓕ **A1** /bɔːd/ *adj.* **~ (with/of sth)** feeling tired and perhaps slightly annoyed because sth is not interesting or because you do not have anything to do: *I'm bored with eating the same thing every day.* ◇ *The children get bored on long journeys.* ◇ *He gave a bored yawn.* ◇ *The play was awful — we were bored stiff* (= extremely bored).

boredom /'bɔːdəm/ *noun* [U] the state of being bored; the fact of being very boring: *I sometimes eat out of boredom.* ◇ *the boredom of life in a small town*

borehole /'bɔːhəʊl/ = BORE² (3)

boring ⓕ **A1** /'bɔːrɪŋ/ *adj.* not at all interesting: *a boring film/job/speech/man* **SYN** dull¹

born¹ ⓕ **A1** /bɔːn/ *verb* **1 be born** (*abbr.* b.) to come into the world by birth; to start to exist: *Where were you born?* ◇ *I was born in London, but I grew up in Leeds.* ◇ *I'm going to give up work after the baby is born.* ◇ *His unhappiness was born out of a feeling of frustration.* ◇ *The idea of free education for all was born in the nineteenth century.* **2 -born** (in adjectives) born in the place or state mentioned: *This Kenyan-born athlete now represents Denmark.*

born² /bɔːn/ *adj.* [only before noun] having a natural ability to do sth: *She's a born leader.*

born-a'gain *adj.* [only before noun] (**RELIGION**) having found new, strong religious belief: *a born-again Christian*

borne /bɔːn/ past participle of **bear¹**

-borne /bɔːn/ *adj.* (in adjectives) carried by the thing mentioned: *water-borne diseases*

boron /'bɔːrɒn/ *noun* [U] (*symb.* B) (**CHEMISTRY**) a chemical element. Boron is a solid substance used in making steel ALLOYS. ❶ For more information about the periodic table of elements, look at the **Reference Section** of this dictionary.

borough /'bʌrə/ *noun* [C] a town, or an area inside a large town, that has some form of local government

borrow ⓕ **A2** /'bɒrəʊ/ *verb* [I, T] **~ (sth) (from sb/sth)** **1** (**FINANCE**) to take or receive sth from sb/sth that you intend to give back, usually after a short time: *I had to borrow from the bank to pay for my car.* ◇ *We'll have to borrow a lot of money to buy a car.* ◇ *Could I borrow your pen for a minute?* ◇ *I borrowed a book from the library.* ⊃ look at **lend** (1) **2** to take sth and use it as your own; to copy sth: *That idea is borrowed from another book.*

borrower /'bɒrəʊə(r)/ *noun* [C] (**FINANCE**) a person who borrows money, especially from a bank

borrowing /'bɒrəʊɪŋ/ *noun* [C, U] (**FINANCE**) the money that a company, an organization or a person borrows; the act of borrowing money: *an attempt to reduce bank borrowings* ◇ *High interest rates help to keep borrowing down.*

bosom /'bʊzəm/ *noun* [C] (**ANATOMY**) a woman's chest or breasts: *She clutched the child to her bosom.*
IDM **in the bosom of sth** close to; with the protection of: *He was glad to be back in the bosom of his family.*

boss¹ ⓕ **A2** /bɒs/ *noun* [C] (*informal*) **1** a person who is in charge of other people at work and tells them what to do: *I'm going to ask the boss for a day off work.* ◇ *OK. You're the boss* (= you make the decisions). **2** a person who is in charge of a large organization: *the new boss at IBM* ◇ *Hospital bosses protested at the government's decision.*

boss² /bɒs/ *verb* [T] **~ sb (about/around)** to give orders to sb, especially in an annoying way: *I wish you'd stop bossing me around.*

bossy /'bɒsi/ *adj.* (**bossier; bossiest**) liking to give orders to other people, often in an annoying way: *Don't be so bossy!* ▸ **bossily** /-səli/ *adv.* ▸ **bossiness** *noun* [U]

bot /bɒt/ *noun* [C] (**COMPUTING**) a computer program that runs AUTOMATED tasks (= without needing people) over the internet

botany /'bɒtəni/ *noun* [U] (**BIOLOGY**) the scientific study of plants ⊃ look at **biology, zoology** ▸ **botanical** /bə'tænɪkl/ *adj.*: *botanical gardens* (= a type of park where plants are grown for scientific study) ▸ **botanist** /'bɒtənɪst/ *noun* [C]

botch /bɒtʃ/ *verb* [T] **~ sth (up)** (*informal*) to do sth badly: *The waiter completely botched up my order.* ◇ *a botched* (= failed) *robbery attempt* **SYN** mess sth up

both ⓕ **A1** /bəʊθ/ *det., pron.* **1** the two; the one as well as the other: *Both women were French.* ◇ *Both the women were French.* ◇ *Both of the women were French.* ◇ *I liked them both.* ◇ *We were both very tired.* ◇ *Both of us were tired.* ◇ *I've got two sisters. They both live in London/Both of them live in London.* **2 ~ both … and …** not only … but also …: *Both he and his wife are vegetarian.*

bother¹ ⓕ **B1** /'bɒðə(r)/ *verb* **1** [T] to interrupt, annoy or worry sb: *I'm sorry to bother you, but could I speak to you for a moment?* ◇ *Don't bother Geeta with that now — she's busy.* **SYN** trouble² **2** [I] **~ (to do sth/doing sth); ~ (about/with sth)** (often in negative sentences and questions) to make the effort to do sth: *'Shall I make you something to eat?' 'No, don't bother — I'm not hungry.'* ◇ *He didn't even bother to say thank you.* ◇ *Don't bother waiting for me — I'll catch you up* later. ◇ *Don't bother about the washing-up. I'll do it later.*

89

bout B

IDM **be bothered (about sth)** (*especially BrE, informal*) to think that sb/sth is important: *'What would you like to do this evening?' 'I'm not bothered really.'* ◇ *Sam doesn't seem too bothered about losing his job.* **can't be bothered (to do sth)** used to say that you do not want to spend time or energy doing sth: *I can't be bothered to do my homework now. I'll do it tomorrow.*

bother² /'bɒðə(r)/ *noun* [U] trouble or difficulty: *Thanks for all your help. It's saved me a lot of bother.*

Botox™ /'bəʊtɒks/ *noun* [U] a substance that makes muscles relax. It is sometimes INJECTED into the skin (= put into the skin through a needle) on sb's face in order to remove lines and make the skin look younger. ▸ **Botox** *verb* [T, usually passive]: *Do you think she's been Botoxed?*

bottle¹ ʔ**A1** /'bɒtl/ *noun* [C] **1** a glass or plastic container with a narrow neck for keeping liquids in: *a beer bottle* ◇ *an empty bottle* **2** the amount of liquid that a bottle can hold: *a bottle of beer*

bottle² /'bɒtl/ *verb* [T] to put sth into bottles: *After three or four months the wine is bottled.* ◇ *bottled water* (= that you can buy in bottles) **PHR V** **bottle sth up** to not allow yourself to express strong emotions: *You'll make yourself ill if you keep your feelings bottled up.*

'**bottle bank** *noun* [C] (**ENVIRONMENT**) a large container in a public place where people can leave their empty bottles so that the glass can be recycled

bottleneck /'bɒtlnek/ *noun* [C] **1** a narrow piece of road that causes traffic to slow down or stop **2** (**BUSINESS**) something that makes progress slower, especially in business or industry

bottom¹ ʔ**A2** /'bɒtəm/ *noun* **1** [C, usually sing.] the lowest part of sth: *The house is **at the bottom** of a hill.* ◇ *I think I've got a pen in the bottom of my bag.* ◇ *The sea is so clear that you can see the bottom.* **OPP** top¹ **2** [C] the flat surface on the outside of an object, on which it stands: *There's a label on the bottom of the box.* **OPP** top¹ **3** [sing.] the far end of sth: *The bus stop is **at the bottom** of the road.* **OPP** top¹ **4** [sing.] the lowest position in relation to other people, teams, etc: *She started **at the bottom** and now she's the Managing Director.* ◇ *Which team is at the bottom of the league?* **OPP** top¹ **5** [C] (**ANATOMY**) the part of the body that you sit on: *He fell over and landed on his bottom.* **6** bottoms [pl.] the lower part of a piece of clothing that is in two parts: *pyjama bottoms* ◇ *tracksuit bottoms* **IDM** **be/lie at the bottom of sth** to be the cause of sth **from the (bottom of your) heart** → HEART **get to the bottom of sth** to find out the real cause of sth

bottom² ʔ**A2** /'bɒtəm/ *adj.* [only before noun] in the lowest position: *the bottom shelf* ◇ *I live on the bottom floor.*

bottomless /'bɒtəmləs/ *adj.* very deep; without limit

,**bottom 'line** *noun* **1 the bottom line** [sing.] the most important thing to consider when you are discussing or deciding sth, etc: *A musical instrument should look and feel good, but the bottom line is how it sounds.* **2** [C] (**BUSINESS, FINANCE**) the final profit or loss that a company has made in a particular period of time: *The bottom line for 2017 was a pre-tax profit of £85 million.*

botulism /'bɒtʃəlɪzəm/ *noun* [U] (**HEALTH**) a serious illness caused by diseases in food that is old and has gone bad

bough /baʊ/ *noun* [C] (*formal*) one of the main branches of a tree

bought /bɔːt/ past tense, past participle of **buy¹**

boulder /'bəʊldə(r)/ *noun* [C] (**GEOLOGY**) a very large rock

boulevard /'buːləvɑːd/ *noun* [C] a wide street in a city, often with trees on each side

bounce ʔ+ **C1** /baʊns/ *verb* **1** [I, T] (used about a ball, etc.) to move away quickly after it has hit a hard surface; to make a ball do this: *The stone bounced off the wall and hit her on the head.* ◇ *A small boy came down the street, bouncing a ball.* **2** [I] to jump up and down continuously: *The children were bouncing on their beds.* **3** [I, T] ~ (sth) (back) (**COMPUTING**) if an email **bounces** or the system **bounces** it, it returns to the person who sent it because the system cannot deliver it **4** [I, T] (**FINANCE**) (used about a CHEQUE) to be returned by a bank without payment because there is not enough money in the account ▸ **bounce** *noun* [C, U] **PHR V** **bounce back** to become healthy, successful or happy again after being ill or having difficulties

bouncer /'baʊnsə(r)/ *noun* [C] a person who is employed to stand at the entrance to a club, pub, etc. to stop people who are not wanted from going in, and to throw out people who are causing trouble inside

bouncy /'baʊnsi/ *adj.* (**bouncier; bounciest**) **1** that BOUNCES well or that can make things BOUNCE: *a bouncy ball/surface* **2** (used about a person) full of energy: *She's a very bouncy person.* **SYN** lively

bound¹ ʔ+ **B2** /baʊnd/ *adj.* [not before noun] **1** ~ to do sth certain to do sth: *You've done so much work that you're bound to pass the exam.* ⊃ note at **certain** **2** ~ (by sth) (to do sth) having a legal or moral duty to do sth: *They are legally bound to appear in court* ◇ *She felt bound to refuse the offer.* **3** ~ (for ...) travelling to a particular place: *a ship bound for Australia* **IDM** **bound up with sth** very closely connected with sth

bound² /baʊnd/ *verb* [I] to run quickly with long steps: *She bounded out of the house to meet us.* ▸ **bound** *noun* [C]: *With a couple of bounds he had crossed the room.*

bound³ /baʊnd/ past tense, past participle of **bind¹**

boundary ʔ+ **C1** /'baʊndri/ *noun* [C] (*pl.* -ies) ~ (between A and B) a real or imagined line that marks the limits of sth and divides it from other places or things: *national boundaries* ◇ *The main road is the boundary between the two districts.* ◇ *Scientists continue to push back the boundaries of human knowledge.* ⊃ picture at **plate tectonics**

boundless /'baʊndləs/ *adj.* having no limit: *boundless energy*

bounds /baʊndz/ *noun* [pl.] limits that cannot or should not be passed: *Price rises must be kept within reasonable bounds.* **IDM** **out of bounds (to sb)** (*BrE*) (used about a place) where people are not allowed to go: *This area is out of bounds to all staff.* ⊃ look at **off-limits**

bouquet /bu'keɪ/ *noun* [C] a bunch of flowers that is arranged in an attractive way

bourbon /'bɜːbən/ *noun* [C, U] a type of WHISKY (= strong alcoholic drink) that is made mainly in the US

bourgeois /'bʊəʒwɑː, ˌbʊə'ʒwɑː/ *adj.* **1** belonging to the middle class **2** interested mainly in having more money and a higher social position: *bourgeois attitudes/ideas/values*

the bourgeoisie /ˌðə ˌbʊəʒwɑː'ziː/ *noun* [sing. + sing./pl. verb] (**SOCIAL STUDIES**) the group of people in society whose members are neither very rich nor very poor and that includes professional and business people **SYN** middle class

bout /baʊt/ *noun* [C] **1** a short period of great activity: *a bout of hard work* **2** (**HEALTH**) a period of illness: *I'm just recovering from a bout of flu.*

boutique¹ /buːˈtiːk/ *noun* [C] a small shop that sells fashionable clothes or expensive presents

boutique² /buːˈtiːk/ *adj.* [only before noun] (used about a business) small and offering products or services of a high quality to a small number of customers: *a boutique hotel*

bovine /ˈbəʊvaɪn/ *adj.* (**AGRICULTURE**) connected with cows: *bovine diseases*

bow¹ ʔ+ **C1** /baʊ/ *verb* [I, T] ~ (sth) (to sb) to bend your head or the upper part of your body forward and down, as a sign of respect: *The speaker bowed to the guests and left the stage.* ◇ *He bowed his head respectfully.*
PHR V **bow out (of sth/as sth)** to leave an important position or stop taking part in sth: *After a long and successful career, she has decided to bow out of politics.* ◇ *He finally bowed out as chairman after ten years.* **bow to sb/sth** to agree to do sth because other people want you to: *They finally bowed to pressure from the public.*

bow² ʔ+ **C1** /baʊ/ *noun* [C] **1** an act of BOWING: *The director of the play came on stage to take a bow.* **2** (*also* **bows** [pl.]) the front part of a ship ◌ look at **stern²**

bow³ /bəʊ/ *noun* [C] **1** a KNOT with two loose round parts and two loose ends that is used for decoration on clothes, in hair, etc. or for tying shoes, etc: *He tied his laces in a bow.* **2** a weapon used for shooting ARROWS (= thin sticks with a sharp point at one end). A bow is a long curved piece of wood or metal with a tight string joining its ends: *He was armed with a bow and arrow.* **3** (**MUSIC**) a long thin piece of wood with thin string stretched across it that you use for playing some musical instruments: *a violin bow* ◌ picture at **instrument**

bowel /ˈbaʊəl/ *noun* [C, usually pl.] (**ANATOMY**) the tube that carries waste food away from the stomach to the place where it leaves the body

bowel movement *noun* [C] (**MEDICINE**) an act of emptying waste material from the BOWELS; the waste material that is emptied

bowl¹ ʔ **A2** /bəʊl/ *noun* **1** [C] a deep round dish that is used for holding food or liquid: *a soup bowl* ◌ look at **plate¹**(1) **2** [C] the amount of sth that is in a bowl: *I usually have a bowl of cereal for breakfast.* **3** [C] a large plastic container that is used for washing dishes, washing clothes, etc. **4** bowls [U] (**SPORT**) a game in which you try to roll large wooden balls as near as possible to a smaller ball: *to play bowls*

bowl² /bəʊl/ *verb* [I, T] (**SPORT**) (in games such as CRICKET) to throw the ball in the direction of the person with the BAT (= a piece of wood or metal)
PHR V **bowl sb over 1** to knock sb down when you are moving quickly **2** to surprise sb very much in a pleasant way

bow legs /ˌbəʊ ˈlegz/ *noun* [pl.] legs that curve out at the knees ▸ **bow-legged** /-ˈlegɪd/ *adj.*

bowler /ˈbəʊlə(r)/ *noun* [C] **1** (**SPORT**) (in CRICKET) the player who throws the ball in the direction of the person with the BAT (= a piece of wood or metal) **2** (*also* **bowler ˈhat**) (*both especially BrE*) (*AmE usually* **derby**) a round hard black hat, usually worn by men

bowling /ˈbəʊlɪŋ/ *noun* [U] (**SPORT**) a game in which you roll a heavy ball down a LANE (= a special track) towards a group of PINS (= wooden objects shaped like bottles) and try to knock them all down: *to go bowling*

bowling alley *noun* [C] a building or part of a building where people can go BOWLING

bowser /ˈbaʊzə(r)/ *noun* [C] (*especially BrE*) a container on wheels that is used for holding water or fuel, often because the normal supply is not available: *400 bowsers have been set up in the area to provide clean water.*

bow tie /ˌbəʊ ˈtaɪ/ *noun* [C] a tie in the shape of a BOW that is worn by men, especially on formal occasions

box¹ ʔ **A1** /bɒks/ *noun* **1** [C] a container made of wood, thick card, metal, etc. with a flat stiff base and sides and often a LID (= cover): *a cardboard box* ◇ *a shoebox* **2** [C] a box and the things inside it: *a box of chocolates/matches/tissues* **3** [C] a square or RECTANGLE on a page or computer screen in which you have to write sth: *Write your name in the box below.* **4** [C] a small area with walls on all sides that is used for a particular purpose: *the jury/witness box* (= in a court of law)

box² /bɒks/ *verb* **1** [I, T] (**SPORT**) to fight in the sport of BOXING **2** [T] to put sth into a box: *He boxed the old photos and put them away.*
PHR V **box sb/sth in** to prevent sb/sth from getting out of a small space: *Somebody parked behind us and boxed us in.*

boxer /ˈbɒksə(r)/ *noun* [C] (**SPORT**) a person who fights in the sport of BOXING

boxer shorts (*also* **boxers** /ˈbɒksəz/) (*AmE also* **shorts**) *noun* [pl.] a piece of men's underwear, similar to the SHORTS worn by BOXERS

boxing /ˈbɒksɪŋ/ *noun* [U] (**SPORT**) a sport in which two people fight by hitting each other with their hands inside large gloves: *the world middleweight boxing champion* ◇ *boxing gloves* ◌ picture at **sport**

Boxing Day *noun* [C] (*BrE*) the first day after Christmas Day. Boxing Day is an official holiday in the UK and some other countries.

box number *noun* [C] a number used as an address, especially in newspaper advertisements

box office *noun* [C] the place in a cinema, theatre, etc. where the tickets are sold

boy ʔ **A1** /bɔɪ/ *noun* [C] a male child or a young male person: *They've got three children — two boys and a girl.* ◇ *I used to play here when I was a boy.*

boycott /ˈbɔɪkɒt/ *verb* [T] to refuse to buy things from a particular company, take part in an event, etc. as a way of protesting: *Several countries boycotted the Olympic Games in protest.* ▸ **boycott** *noun* [C]: *a boycott of the local elections*

boyfriend ʔ **A1** /ˈbɔɪfrend/ *noun* [C] a man or boy that sb has a romantic or sexual relationship with: *That's Melissa's boyfriend.*

boyhood /ˈbɔɪhʊd/ *noun* [U] the time when sb is a boy: *My father told me some of his boyhood memories.*

boyish /ˈbɔɪɪʃ/ *adj.* like a boy: *a boyish smile*

Boy ˈScout = SCOUT (2)

bps /ˌbiː piː ˈes/ *abbr.* (**COMPUTING**) **bits per second** (a measure of the speed at which data is sent or received)

bra /brɑː/ *noun* [C] a piece of women's underwear worn to support their breasts

brace¹ /breɪs/ *noun* (*BrE*) **1** [C] (*AmE* **braces** [pl.]) a device that people, especially children, wear inside the mouth in order to make their teeth straight ◌ note at **tooth 2** braces (*AmE* **suspenders** /səˈspendəz/) [pl.] a pair of long, narrow pieces of cloth, leather, etc. that go over your shoulders to hold your trousers up **3** [C, usually pl.] = CALLIPER (2)

brace² /breɪs/ *verb* [T] ~ sth/yourself (for sth) to prepare yourself for sth unpleasant: *You'd better brace yourself for some bad news.*

bracelet /'breɪslət/ *noun* [C] a piece of jewellery, for example a metal chain or band, that you wear around your WRIST or arm

bracing /'breɪsɪŋ/ *adj.* (used especially about weather) making you feel healthy and full of energy: *bracing sea air*

bracken /'brækən/ *noun* [U] a wild plant with large leaves that grows on hills and in woods and turns brown in the autumn ⊃ look at **fern**

bracket¹ /'brækɪt/ *noun* [C] **1** [usually pl.] (*BrE*) (*also* **parenthesis** *AmE or formal*) (**LANGUAGE**) one of two marks, () or [ ], that you put round extra information in a piece of writing: *A translation of each word is given in brackets.* **2** a category of people or things that are between two limits: *to be in a high income bracket* ◇ *The magazine is aimed at people in the 30–40 age bracket* (= people aged between 30 and 40). **3** a piece of metal or wood that is fixed to a wall and used as a support for a shelf, lamp, etc.

bracket² /'brækɪt/ *verb* [T] **1** to put a word, number, etc. between BRACKETS **2** ~**A and B (together)**; ~**A with B** to think of two or more people or things as similar in some way: *It is unfair to bracket together those who cannot work and those who will not.*

brackish /'brækɪʃ/ *adj.* (used about water) containing salt and tasting of it in an unpleasant way: *brackish lakes/lagoons/marshes*

brag /bræɡ/ *verb* [I] (-gg-) ~**(to sb) (about/of sth)** to talk in a very proud way about sth: *She's always bragging to her friends about how clever she is.*

braid¹ /breɪd/ *noun* **1** [U] thin coloured rope that is used to decorate military uniforms, etc. **2** [C] (*especially AmE*) = PLAIT

braid² /breɪd/ *verb* [T] = PLAIT

Braille /breɪl/ *noun* [U] a system of printing for blind people, using little round marks that are higher than the level of the paper they are on and that can be read by touch: *The signs were written in Braille.*

the brain

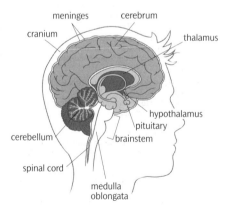

meninges
cerebrum
cranium
thalamus
hypothalamus
pituitary
brainstem
cerebellum
spinal cord
medulla oblongata

brain ⚡ **A2** /breɪn/ *noun* **1** [C] (**ANATOMY**) the part of the body inside the head that controls thoughts, feelings and movements: *He suffered serious brain damage in a road accident.* ◇ *a brain surgeon* **2** [C, usually pl., U] the ability to think clearly; intelligence: *He hasn't got the brains to be a doctor.* ◇ *It doesn't take much brain to work that out.* **3** [C, usually pl.] (*informal*) a very clever person: *He's one of the best brains in the country.* **4 the brains** [sing.] the person who plans or organizes sth: *She's the real brains in the organization.*

IDM **have sth on the brain** (*informal*) to think about sth all the time **rack your brains** → RACK²

brainchild /'breɪntʃaɪld/ *noun* [sing.] the idea or invention of a particular person

brain-dead *adj.* **1** (**HEALTH**) having serious brain damage and needing a machine to stay alive **2** (*informal*) unable to think clearly; stupid

brain drain *noun* [sing.] (*informal*) (**SOCIAL STUDIES**) the movement of highly SKILLED and educated people to a country where they can work in better conditions and earn more money

brainless /'breɪnləs/ *adj.* (*informal*) very silly; stupid

brainstem /'breɪnstem/ *noun* [C] (**ANATOMY**) the part of the brain that joins the SPINAL CORD to the CEREBELLUM and the CEREBRUM ⊃ picture at **brain**

brainstorm¹ /'breɪnstɔːm/ *noun* [sing.] **1** a sudden failure to think clearly: *I had a brainstorm in the exam and couldn't answer any questions.* **2** (*AmE*) = BRAINWAVE

brainstorm² /'breɪnstɔːm/ *verb* [I, T] to solve a problem or make a decision by thinking of as many ideas as possible in a short time: *We'll spend five minutes brainstorming ideas on how we can raise money.*

brainteaser /'breɪntiːzə(r)/ *noun* [C] a problem that is difficult but fun to solve

brainwash /'breɪnwɒʃ/ *verb* [T] ~**sb (into doing sth)** to force sb to believe sth by using strong mental pressure: *TV advertisements try to brainwash people into buying things that they don't need.* ▶ **brainwashing** *noun* [U]

brainwave /'breɪnweɪv/ (*AmE also* **brainstorm**) *noun* [C] (*informal*) a sudden clever idea: *If I have a brainwave, I'll let you know.*

brainy /'breɪni/ *adj.* (**brainier**; **brainiest**) (*informal*) intelligent

braise /breɪz/ *verb* [T] to cook meat or vegetables slowly in a little liquid in a covered dish

brake¹ /breɪk/ *noun* [C] **1** the part of a vehicle that makes it go slower or stop: *She put her foot on the brake and just managed to stop in time.* **2** something that makes sth else slow down or stop: *The government must try to put a brake on inflation.*

brake² /breɪk/ *verb* [I] to make a vehicle go slower or stop by using the BRAKES: *If the driver hadn't braked in time, the car would have hit me.*

brake light *noun* [C] a red light on the back of a vehicle that comes on when the BRAKES are used

bramble /'bræmbl/ *noun* [C] (*especially BrE*) a wild bush on which BLACKBERRIES grow

bran /bræn/ *noun* [U] the brown outer covering of grains that is left when the grain is made into flour

branch¹ ⚡ **B1** /brɑːntʃ/ *noun* [C] **1** (**BIOLOGY**) a part of a tree that grows out from the TRUNK (= the thick central part) ⊃ picture at **tree 2** (**BUSINESS**) a local office or shop belonging to a large company or organization: *The company I work for has branches in Paris, Milan and New York.* **3** a part of a government or other large organization that deals with one particular aspect of its work: *the anti-terrorist branch* **SYN** **department 4** a division of an area of knowledge or a group of languages: *Psychiatry is a branch of medicine.* **5** a smaller or less important part of a river, road, railway, etc. that leads away from the main part: *a branch of the Rhine*

branch² /brɑːntʃ/ *verb*

PHR V **branch off** (used about a road) to leave a larger road and go off in another direction: *A bit* *further on, the road branches off to the left.* **branch out (into sth)** to start doing sth new and different from the things you usually do

brand¹ ⟨B1⟩ /brænd/ *noun* [C] **1** (**BUSINESS**) the name of a product that is made by a particular company: *a well-known brand of coffee ◇ a fashion/beauty/clothing brand ◇* **brand loyalty** (= when customers continue buying the same brand) **2** a particular type of sth: *a strange brand of humour*

brand² ⟨B1⟩ /brænd/ *verb* [T, often passive] **1** ~ **sth (with sth); ~ sth (as sth)** (**BUSINESS**) to give a BRAND NAME, image or identity to sth: *Stadiums are branded with corporate logos. ◇ Their products are branded as organic.* **2** ~ **sb/sth (as sth)** to say that sb has a bad character so that people have a bad opinion of them: *She was branded as a troublemaker after she complained about her long working hours.* **3** (**AGRICULTURE**) to mark an animal with a hot iron to show who owns it

branded /'brændɪd/ *adj.* [only before noun] (used about a product) made by a company that many people know and having that company's name on it: **branded drugs/ goods/products**

branding /'brændɪŋ/ *noun* [U] (**BUSINESS**) the activity of giving a particular name and image to goods and services so that people will be attracted to them and want to buy them

brandish /'brændɪʃ/ *verb* [T] to wave sth in the air in an aggressive or excited way: *The robber was brandishing a knife.*

brand name (*also* **trade name**) *noun* [C] (**BUSINESS**) the name given to a product by the company that produces it

brand 'new *adj.* completely new

brandy /'brændi/ *noun* [C, U] (*pl.* **-ies**) a strong alcoholic drink that is made from wine

brash /bræʃ/ *adj.* too confident and direct: *Her brash manner makes her unpopular with strangers.* ▶ **brashness** *noun* [U]

brass /brɑːs/ *noun* **1** [U] a hard yellow metal that is a mixture of COPPER and ZINC: *brass buttons on a uniform* **2** [U + sing./pl. verb] (**MUSIC**) the group of musical instruments that are made of metal ⊃ note at **instrument** ⊃ picture at **instrument, orchestra**

brat /bræt/ *noun* [C] (*informal*) a child who behaves badly and annoys you

bravado /brəˈvɑːdəʊ/ *noun* [U] a confident way of behaving that is intended to impress people, sometimes as a way of hiding a lack of confidence

brave¹ ⟨B1⟩ /breɪv/ *adj.* **1** ready to do things that are dangerous or difficult without showing fear: *the brave soldiers who fought in the war ◇ 'This may hurt a little, so try and be brave,' said the dentist.* **2** needing or showing courage: *a brave decision* ▶ **bravely** *adv.*: *The men bravely defended the town for three days.* **IDM** **put on a brave face | put a brave face on sth** to pretend that you feel confident and happy when you do not

brave² /breɪv/ *verb* [T] to face sb/sth unpleasant, dangerous or difficult without showing fear

bravery /'breɪvəri/ *noun* [U] actions that are brave or the quality of being brave: *After the war he received a medal for bravery.* **SYN** **courage**

bravo /ˌbrɑːˈvəʊ/ *exclamation* a word that people shout to show that they have enjoyed sth that sb has done, especially a performance

brawl /brɔːl/ *noun* [C] a noisy fight among a group of people, usually in a public place ▶ **brawl** *verb* [I]: *We saw some football fans brawling in the street.*

brawn /brɔːn/ *noun* [U] physical strength: *To do this kind of job you need more brawn than brain* (= you need to be strong rather than clever). ▶ **brawny** *adj.* (**brawnier; brawniest**)

braze /breɪz/ *verb* [T] to join pieces of metal using a mixture of metals that is heated and melted

brazen /'breɪzn/ *adj.* without shame, especially in a way that shocks people: *Don't believe a word she says — she's a brazen liar!* **SYN** **shameless** ▶ **brazenly** *adv.*

brazil /brəˈzɪl/ (*also* **braˈzil nut**) *noun* [C] a curved nut with a very hard shell with three sides.

breach¹ ⟨C1⟩ /briːtʃ/ *noun* **1** [C, U] ~ (**of sth**) (**LAW**) an act that breaks an agreement, a law, etc: *Giving private information about clients is a breach of confidence. ◇ The company was found to be in breach of contract.* **2** [C] ~ **between A and B** a break in friendly relations between people, groups, etc: *The incident caused a breach between the two countries.* **3** [C] an opening in a wall, etc. that defends or protects sb/sth: *The waves made a breach in the sea wall.*

breach² ⟨C1⟩ /briːtʃ/ *verb* [T] **1** (**LAW**) to break an agreement, a law, etc: *He accused the government of breaching international law.* **2** to make an opening in a wall, etc. that defends or protects sb/sth

bread ⟨A1⟩ /bred/ *noun* [U] a type of food made from flour, water and usually YEAST (= a substance that makes the bread rise), mixed together and baked in an oven: *a piece/slice of bread ◇ a loaf of bread ◇ white/ brown/wholemeal bread*

breadcrumbs /'bredkrʌmz/ *noun* [pl.] very small pieces of bread that are used in cooking

breadline /'bredlaɪn/ *noun* [sing.] (**SOCIAL STUDIES**) the lowest level of income on which it is possible to live: *They are living on the breadline* (= are very poor).

breadth /bredθ/ *noun* **1** [C, U] the distance between the two sides of sth: *We measured the length and breadth of the garden.* **SYN** **width 2** [U] the wide variety of things, subjects, etc. that sth includes: *I was amazed by the breadth of her knowledge.* ⊃ adjective **broad** **IDM** **the length and breadth of sth → LENGTH**

breadwinner /'bredwɪnə(r)/ *noun* [C, usually sing.] the person who earns most of the money that their family needs: *When his dad died, Steve became the breadwinner.*

break¹ ⟨A1⟩ /breɪk/ *verb* (*pt* **broke** /brəʊk/; *pp* **broken** /'brəʊkən/)

• INTO PIECES **1** [I, T] to be damaged and separated into two or more parts; to damage sth in this way: *She dropped the vase onto the floor and it broke. ◇ He broke his leg in a car accident.*

• STOP WORKING **2** [I, T] (used about a machine, etc.) to stop working; to stop a machine, etc. working: *The photocopier has broken. ◇ Be careful with my camera — I don't want you to break it.*

• LAW/PROMISE **3** [T] to do sth that is against the law, or against what has been agreed or promised: *to break the law/rules/speed limit ◇ Don't worry — I never break my promises.*

• STOP **4** [I, T] to stop doing sth for a short time: *Let's break for coffee now. ◇ We decided to break the journey and stop for lunch.*

• END **5** [T] to make sth end: *Once you start smoking it's very difficult to break the habit. ◇ Suddenly, the silence was broken by the sound of a bird singing.*

• OF DAY/DAWN/A STORM **6** [I] when the day or DAWN (= the time of day when light first appears) or a storm **breaks**, it begins: *The day was breaking as I left the house. ◇ We ran indoors when the storm broke.*

• OF NEWS **7** [I] if a piece of news **breaks**, it becomes known: *When the story broke in the newspapers, nobody could believe it.* ⊃ look at **break the news (to sb)** at **news**

• OF A WAVE **8** [I] (used about a wave) to reach its highest point and begin to fall: *I watched the waves breaking on the rocks.*

• OF THE VOICE **9** [I] if sb's voice **breaks**, it changes its tone because of emotion: *His voice was breaking with emotion as he told us the awful news.* **10** [I] when a boy's voice **breaks**, it becomes permanently deeper at the age of about 13 or 14

• RECORD **11** [T] **~a record** to do sth better, faster, etc. than anyone has ever done it before: *She had broken the world 100 metres record.*

IDM ❶ For idioms containing **break**, look at the entries for the nouns, adjectives, etc. For example, **break even** is at **even**.

PHR V **break away (from sb/sth) 1** to escape suddenly from sb who is holding you **2** (POLITICS) to leave a political party, state, etc. in order to form a new one **break down 1** (used about a vehicle or machine) to stop working: *Akram's car broke down on the way to work this morning.* **2** (used about a system, discussion, etc.) to fail: *Talks between the two countries have completely broken down.* **3** to lose control of your feelings and start crying: *He broke down in tears when he heard the news.* **4** to divide into parts to be analysed: *Costs for the project break down as follows: wages $20m, plant $4m, raw materials $5m.* ⊃ noun **breakdown** **break sth down 1** to destroy sth by using force: *The police had to break down the door to get into the house.* **2** (BIOLOGY, CHEMISTRY) to make a substance separate into parts or change into a different form in a chemical process: *Food is broken down in our bodies by the digestive system.* **3** to divide sth into parts in order to analyse it or make it easier to do: *Each lesson is broken down into several units.* ⊃ noun **breakdown** **break in** to enter a building by force, usually in order to steal sth **break in (on sth)** to interrupt when sb else is speaking: *She longed to break in on their conversation but didn't want to appear rude.* **break into sth 1** to enter a place that is closed: *Thieves broke into his car and stole the radio.* ◊ (*figurative*) *The company is trying to break into the Japanese market.* ⊃ note at **criminal**[1] **2** to start doing sth suddenly: *to break into song/a run* **break off** to suddenly stop doing or saying sth: *He started speaking and then broke off in the middle of a sentence.* **break (sth) off** to remove a part of sth by force; to be removed in this way: *Could you break off another bit of chocolate for me?* **break sth off** to end a relationship suddenly: *After a bad argument, they decided to break off their engagement.* **break out** (used about fighting, wars, fires, etc.) to start suddenly **break out in sth** (HEALTH) to suddenly have a skin problem: *to break out in spots/a rash* **break out (of sth)** to escape from a prison, etc. **break through (sth)** to manage to get past sth that is stopping you **break up 1** to separate into smaller pieces: *The ship broke up on the rocks.* **2** (used about events that involve a group of people) to end or finish: *The meeting broke up just before lunch.* **3** (*BrE*) (EDUCATION) to start school holidays: *When do you break up for the summer holidays?* **4** when a person who is talking on a mobile phone **breaks up**, you can no longer hear them clearly because the signal has been interrupted: *Sorry, I can't hear you — you're breaking up.* **break sth up 1** to make sth separate into smaller pieces **2** to make people leave sth or stop doing sth, especially by using force: *The police arrived and broke up the fight.* **break up (with sb)** to end a relationship with sb **break with sth** to end a relationship or connection with sb/sth: *to break with tradition/the past*

break² ⫶ A1 /breɪk/ *noun*

• BROKEN PART **1** [C] **~ (in sth)** a place where sth has been broken: *a break in a pipe*

• OPENING **2** [C] **~ (in sth)** an opening or a space in sth: *Wait for a break in the traffic before you cross the road.*

• SHORT REST **3** [C] a short period of rest: *We worked all day without a break.* ◊ *to take a break*

• HOLIDAY **4** [C] (TOURISM) a short holiday: *We had a weekend break in New York.* ◊ *a well-earned break*

• CHANGE **5** [sing.] **~ (in sth)**; **~ (with sb/sth)** a change from what usually happens or an end to sth: *The incident led to a break in diplomatic relations.* ◊ *She wanted to make a complete break with the past.*

• GOOD LUCK **6** [C] (*informal*) a piece of good luck: *to give somebody a break* (= to help sb by giving them a chance to be successful)

IDM **break of day** the time when light first appears in the morning **SYN** **dawn**[1] **give me a break! 1** used to tell sb to stop saying things that are annoying or not true: *Give me a break and stop nagging, OK!* **2** (*especially AmE*) to be fair to sb

breakage /'breɪkɪdʒ/ *noun* [C, usually pl.] something that has been broken: *Customers must pay for any breakages.*

breakaway /'breɪkəweɪ/ *adj.* [only before noun] (POLITICS) (used about a political group, an organization, or a part of a country) that has separated from a larger group or country: *a breakaway group on the left of the party* ▶ **breakaway** *noun* [sing.]

breakdown ⫶+ C1 /'breɪkdaʊn/ *noun* [C] **1** a time when a vehicle, machine, etc. stops working: *I hope we don't have a breakdown on the motorway.* **2** the failure or end of sth: *The breakdown of the talks means that a strike is likely.* **3** = NERVOUS BREAKDOWN **4** a list of all the details of sth: *I would like a full breakdown of how the money was spent.*

breakdown lane (*AmE*) = HARD SHOULDER

breakdown truck (*BrE*) (*AmE* **tow truck**) *noun* [C] a lorry that is used to take away cars that need to be repaired

breaker /'breɪkə(r)/ *noun* [C] a large wave covered with white bubbles that is moving towards the beach

break-even *noun* [U] (FINANCE) the point at which a business activity earns just enough money to pay for its costs: *The company expects to reach break-even next year.*

breakfast ⫶ A1 /'brekfəst/ *noun* [C, U] the meal that you have when you get up in the morning: *to have breakfast* ◊ *What do you usually have for breakfast?* ◊ *to eat a big breakfast*

▼ CULTURE

In a hotel an **English breakfast** means cereal, fried eggs, bacon, sausages, tomatoes, toast, etc. A **continental breakfast** means bread and jam with coffee.

---

break-in *noun* [C] the act of entering a building by force, especially in order to steal sth

breakneck /'breɪknek/ *adj.* [only before noun] very fast and dangerous: *He drove her to the hospital at breakneck speed.*

breakout[1] /'breɪkaʊt/ *noun* [C] an escape from prison, usually by a group of prisoners

breakout[2] /'breɪkaʊt/ *adj.* [only before noun] suddenly very successful and making sb/sth very popular: *her breakout movie*

breakthrough ?+ **C1** /'breɪkθruː/ *noun* [C] ~ (**in sth**) an important discovery or development: *Scientists are hoping to **make a breakthrough** in cancer research.*

'**break-up** *noun* [C] **1** the ending of a relationship between two people: *the break-up of a marriage* **2** the division of a country or an organization into smaller parts

breakwater /'breɪkwɔːtə(r)/ *noun* [C] a wall built out into the sea to protect the land from the force of the waves

breast ? **B2** /brest/ *noun* **1** [C] (**ANATOMY**) either of the two round soft parts at the front of a woman's body that produce milk when she has had a baby **2** [C] a word used especially in literature for the top part of the front of the body, below the neck **SYN** **chest** **3** [C] the front part of the body of a bird **4** [C, U] meat from the front part of the body of a bird or an animal

breastbone /'brestbəʊn/ *noun* [C] (**ANATOMY**) the long flat bone in the middle of the chest that the seven top pairs of RIBS (= curved bones that surround the chest) are connected to **SYN** **sternum** ⊃ picture at **body**

breastfeed /'brestfiːd/ *verb* [I, T] (*pt, pp* **breastfed** /-fed/) to feed a baby with milk from the breast

breaststroke /'breststrəʊk/ *noun* [U] (**SPORT**) a style of swimming on your front in which you start with your hands together, push both arms forward and then move them out and back through the water: *to do (the) breaststroke* ⊃ look at **backstroke**, **butterfly** (2), **crawl²** (2)

breath ? **B1** /breθ/ *noun* **1** [U] the air that you take into and blow out of your lungs: *to **have bad breath** (= breath that smells unpleasant)* **2** [C] an act of taking air into the lungs: *Take a few deep breaths before you start running.*
IDM **a breath of fresh air** the clean air that you breathe outside, especially when compared to the air inside a room or building: *Let's go for a walk. I need a breath of fresh air.* ◇ (*figurative*) *The child's happy face was like a breath of fresh air on that miserable day.* **catch your breath** → CATCH¹ **get your breath (again/back)** to rest after physical exercise so that your breathing returns to normal **hold your breath** to stop breathing for a short time: *How long can you hold your breath for?* **(be/get) out of/short of breath** (to be/start) breathing very quickly, for example after physical exercise **say sth, speak, etc. under your breath** to say sth very quietly, usually because you do not want people to hear you **take sb's breath away** to be very surprising or beautiful ⊃ adjective **breathtaking** **take a deep breath** → DEEP¹ **with bated breath** → BATED

breathalyse (*BrE*) (*AmE* **breathalyze**) /'breθəlaɪz/ *verb* [T, usually passive] (**LAW**) to check how much alcohol a driver has drunk by making him or her breathe into a BREATHALYSER: *Both drivers were breathalysed at the scene of the accident.*

breathalyser (*BrE*) (*AmE* **Breathalyzer™**) /'breθəlaɪzə(r)/ *noun* [C] (**LAW**) a device used by the police to measure how much alcohol is in a driver's breath

breathe ? **B1** /briːð/ *verb* [I, T] to take air, etc. into your lungs and blow it out again: *She was unconscious but still breathing.* ◇ *If you start to feel anxious, **breathe deeply** and slowly.*
IDM **breathe (new) life into sth** to improve sth by introducing new ideas and making people more interested in it: *Her illustrations breathe new life into these familiar stories.* **not breathe a word (of/about sth) (to sb)** to not tell sb about sth that is secret

PHRV **breathe in** to take air into your lungs through your nose or mouth: *Breathe in and hold your breath for as long as possible.* **breath sth in** to take air, smoke, etc. into your lungs through your nose or mouth: *None of us want to breathe in exhaust fumes from heavy traffic.* **breathe out** to send air out of your lungs through your nose or mouth: *Breathe out as you lift the weight.*

breather /'briːðə(r)/ *noun* [C] (*informal*) a short rest: *to have/take a breather*

breathing ? **B1** /'briːðɪŋ/ *noun* [U] the action of taking air into the lungs and sending it out again: *irregular breathing* ◇ *These deep breathing exercises will help you relax.* ◇ *Heavy (= loud) breathing was all I could hear.*

breathless /'breθləs/ *adj.* **1** (**HEALTH**) having difficulty breathing: *I was hot and breathless when I got to the top of the hill.* **2** ~ (**with sth**) not able to breathe because you are so excited, frightened, etc: *to be breathless with excitement* ▶ **breathlessly** *adv.* ▶ **breathlessness** *noun* [U]

breathtaking /'breθteɪkɪŋ/ *adj.* extremely surprising, beautiful, etc: *breathtaking scenery*

'**breath test** *noun* [C] a test by the police on the breath of a driver to measure how much alcohol they have drunk ⊃ look at **breathalyse**

breed¹ ?+ **C1** /briːd/ *verb* (*pt, pp* **bred** /bred/) **1** [I] (**BIOLOGY**) (used about animals) to have sex and produce young animals: *Many animals won't breed in zoos.* **SYN** **mate¹** **2** [T] (**AGRICULTURE**) to keep animals in order to produce young ones for a particular purpose: *These cattle are bred to produce high yields of milk.* **3** [T] to cause sth: *This kind of thinking breeds intolerance.* ▶ **breeding** *noun* [U]: *the breeding of horses*

breed² ?+ **C1** /briːd/ *noun* [C] a particular variety of an animal: *a breed of cattle/dog*

breeder /'briːdə(r)/ *noun* [C] a person who BREEDS animals: *a dog breeder*

'**breeding ground** *noun* [C] **1** a place where wild animals go to produce their young **2** a place where sth can develop: *a breeding ground for crime*

breeze¹ /briːz/ *noun* [C] a light wind: *A warm breeze was blowing.* ⊃ picture at **convection**

breeze² /briːz/ *verb* [I] (*informal*) (used with an adverb or a preposition) to move in a confident and relaxed way: *He just breezed in 20 minutes late without a word of apology.*

breezy /'briːzi/ *adj.* (**breezier**; **breeziest**) **1** with the wind blowing quite strongly **2** (*informal*) happy and relaxed: *You're bright and breezy this morning!*

breve /briːv/ *noun* [C] (**MUSIC**) a note that lasts as long as eight CROTCHETS and that is rarely used in modern music

brevity /'brevəti/ *noun* [U] (*formal*) the state of being short or quick: *The report is a masterpiece of brevity.* ⊃ adjective **brief**

brew /bruː/ *verb* **1** [T] to make beer **2** [T] to make a drink of tea or coffee by adding hot water: *to brew a pot of tea* **3** [I] (used about tea) to be mixed with hot water before it is ready to drink: *Leave it to brew for a few minutes.*
IDM **be brewing** (used about sth bad) to be developing or growing: *There's **trouble brewing**.*

brewery /'bruːəri/ *noun* [C] (*pl.* **-ies**) a place where beer is made

Brexit /'breksɪt, 'bregzɪt/ *noun* [U] (**POLITICS**) used to refer to the departure of the United Kingdom from the European Union

bribe /braɪb/ *noun* [C] money, etc. that is given to sb such as an official to persuade them to help you, especially by doing sth dishonest: *to accept/take bribes* ▸ **bribe** *verb* [T] ~ **sb (with sth):** *They got their visas by bribing an official.* ▸ **bribery** /ˈbraɪbəri/ *noun* [U]

bric-a-brac /ˈbrɪk ə bræk/ *noun* [U] small items of little value, for decoration in a house

brick ʔ+ B2 /brɪk/ *noun* [C, U] (**ARCHITECTURE**) CLAY that is used for building houses, etc.; an individual block of this: *a lorry carrying bricks* ◇ *a house built of red brick* ⊃ picture at **building**

bricklayer /ˈbrɪkleɪə(r)/ *noun* [C] a person whose job is to build walls with BRICKS

brickwork /ˈbrɪkwɜːk/ *noun* [U] (**ARCHITECTURE**) the part of a building that is made of BRICKS

bricolage /ˌbrɪkəˈlɑːʒ/ *noun* [U, C] (**ART**) the process of creating art using a variety of different objects; a piece of art that has been made in this way

bridal /ˈbraɪdl/ *adj.* [only before noun] connected with a bride or a wedding

bride ʔ B1 /braɪd/ *noun* [C] a woman on or just before her wedding day: *a bride-to-be* (= a woman whose wedding is soon)

bridegroom /ˈbraɪdɡruːm/ = GROOM¹ (1)

bridesmaid /ˈbraɪdzmeɪd/ *noun* [C] a woman or girl who helps a bride before and during the marriage ceremony

bridge¹ ʔ A2 /brɪdʒ/ *noun* **1** [C] a structure that carries a road or railway across a river, valley, road or railway: *a bridge over the River Danube* **2** [sing.] the high part of a ship where the captain and the people who control the ship stand **3** [U] a card game for four people **4** [sing.] **the~ of sb's nose** (**ANATOMY**) the hard part at the top of the nose, between the eyes

bridge² /brɪdʒ/ *verb* [T] to build a bridge over sth **IDM** **bridge the gap (between A and B)** to reduce or get rid of the differences that exist between two things or groups of people

bridle /ˈbraɪdl/ *noun* [C] the narrow pieces of leather that you put around a horse's head so that you can control it when you are riding it

brief¹ ʔ B2 /briːf/ *adj.* short or quick: *a brief description* ◇ *Please be brief. We don't have much time.* ⊃ *noun* **brevity** **IDM** **in brief** using only a few words: *In brief, the meeting was a disaster.*

brief² /briːf/ *noun* [C] **1** (*BrE*) the instructions that a person is given explaining what their job is and what their duties are: *He was given the brief of improving the image of the organization.* **2** (*BrE*) (**LAW**) a legal case that is given to a lawyer to argue in court; a piece of work for a BARRISTER **3** (*AmE*) (**LAW**) a written summary of the facts that support one side of a legal case that will be presented to a court **4** (*BrE, informal*) (**LAW**) a SOLICITOR or a defence lawyer: *I want to see my brief.*

brief³ /briːf/ *verb* [T] ~ **sb (on/about sth)** to give sb information about sth so that they are prepared to deal with it: *The minister has been fully briefed on what questions to expect.* ⊃ look at **debrief**

briefcase /ˈbriːfkeɪs/ *noun* [C] a flat case that you use for carrying papers, etc., especially when you go to work

briefing /ˈbriːfɪŋ/ *noun* [C] a meeting in which people are given instructions or information: *a press/news briefing* (= where information is given to journalists) ⊃ look at **debriefing**

briefly ʔ+ B2 ⑤ /ˈbriːfli/ *adv.* **1** for a short time; quickly: *She glanced briefly at the letter.* **2** using only a few words: *I'd like to comment very briefly on that last statement.*

briefs /briːfs/ *noun* [pl.] a piece of men's or women's underwear that covers the body from the middle part to the tops of the legs

brigade /brɪˈɡeɪd/ *noun* [C] **1** a large group of soldiers that forms a unit in the army **2** used, always with a word or phrase in front of it, to describe a group of people who share the same opinions or are similar in some other way: *the anti-smoking brigade*

brigadier /ˌbrɪɡəˈdɪə(r)/ *noun* [C] an important officer in the British army

bright ʔ A2 /braɪt/ *adj.*
• FULL OF LIGHT **1** having a lot of light: *a bright, sunny day* ◇ *eyes bright with happiness*
• OF A COLOUR **2** (used about a colour) strong and easy to see: *a bright yellow jumper*
• INTELLIGENT **3** intelligent; able to learn things quickly; showing these qualities: *a bright child* ◇ *a bright idea*
• POSITIVE **4** likely to be pleasant or successful: *The future looks bright.* **5** happy; cheerful: *a bright smile* ▸ **brightly** *adv.*: *brightly coloured clothes* ▸ **brightness** *noun* [U]
IDM **look on the bright side** → LOOK¹

brighten /ˈbraɪtn/ *verb* [I, T] ~ **(sth) (up)** to become brighter or happier; to make sth brighter: *His face brightened when he saw her.* ◇ *to brighten up somebody's day* (= make it happier)

brilliant ʔ A2 /ˈbrɪliənt/ *adj.* **1** having a lot of light; very bright: *brilliant sunshine* **2** very clever, successful or showing a lot of skill: *a brilliant young scientist* ◇ *That's a brilliant idea!* **3** (*informal*) very good: *That was a brilliant film!* ▸ **brilliance** /-əns/ *noun* [U] ▸ **brilliantly** *adv.*

brim¹ /brɪm/ *noun* [C] **1** the top edge of a cup, glass, etc: *The cup was full to the brim.* **2** the bottom part of a hat that is wider than the rest

brim² /brɪm/ *verb* [I] (-mm-) ~ **(with sth)** to be full of sth: *His eyes were brimming with tears.* **PHR V** **brim over (with sth)** (used about a cup, glass, etc.) to have more liquid than it can hold: *The bowl was brimming over with water.* ◇ (*figurative*) *to be brimming over with health/happiness*

brine /braɪn/ *noun* [U] water that contains a lot of salt, used especially for keeping food fresh

bring ʔ A1 /brɪŋ/ *verb* [T] (*pt, pp* **brought** /brɔːt/)
• CARRY/TAKE **1** ~ **sb/sth (to sth)**; ~ **sb/sth (with you)**; ~ **sb/sth (back)** to carry or take sb/sth to a place with you: *Is it all right if I bring a friend to the party?* ◇ *Bring some sandwiches with you.* ◇ *Could you bring us some water, please?* ◇ *My sister went to Spain and brought me back a present.*
• GIVE/PROVIDE **2** ~ **(sb/sth) sth**; ~ **sth (to sb/sth)** to give or provide sb/sth with sth: *They brought us some good news.* ◇ *He will bring valuable skills and experience to the team.*
• CAUSE **3** ~ **sth (to sth)** to cause or result in sth: *The sight of her brought a smile to his face.* ◇ *Money doesn't always bring happiness.* **4** ~ **sb/sth (to sth)** to cause sb/sth to be in a certain place or condition: *Their screams brought people running from all directions.* ◇ *Add water to the mixture and bring it to the boil.* ◇ *An injury can easily bring an athlete's career to an end.*
• MOVE **5** (used with an adverb or a preposition) to move sth somewhere: *She brought the book down off the shelf.*

• FORCE YOURSELF **6 ~ yourself to do sth** to force yourself to do sth: *The film was so horrible that I couldn't bring myself to watch it.*

IDM ❶ For idioms containing **bring**, look at the entries for the nouns, adjectives, etc. For example, **bring up the rear** is at **rear**.

PHR V **bring sth about** to cause sth to happen: *to bring about changes in people's lives* **bring sb around** (*AmE*) = BRING SB ROUND **bring sb around (to sth)** (*AmE*) = BRING SB ROUND (TO STH) **bring sth around to sth** (*AmE*) = BRING STH ROUND TO STH **bring sth back 1** to cause sth that existed before to be introduced again: *Nobody wants to bring back the days of child labour.* **2** to cause sb to remember sth: *The photos brought back memories of his childhood.* **bring sb/sth down** to defeat sb/sth; to make sb/sth lose a position of power: *to bring down the government* **bring sth down** to make sth lower in level: *to bring down the price of something* ⊃ note at **price**¹ **bring sth forward 1** to move sth to an earlier time: *The date of the meeting has been brought forward by two weeks.* **OPP** **put sth back 2** to suggest sth for discussion **bring sb in** to ask or employ sb to do a particular job: *A specialist was brought in to set up the new computer system.* **bring sth in** to introduce sth: *The government have brought in a new law on dangerous dogs.* **bring sth off** to manage to do sth difficult: *The team brought off an amazing victory.* **bring sth on** to cause sth: *Her headaches are brought on by stress.* **bring sth out** to produce sth or cause sth to appear: *When is the company bringing out its next new model?* **bring sb round** (*BrE*) (*AmE* **bring sb around**) to make sb become conscious again: *I splashed cold water on his face to try to bring him round.* **bring sb round (to sth)** (*BrE*) (*AmE* **bring sb around (to sth)**) to persuade sb to agree with your opinion: *After a lot of discussion we finally brought them round to our point of view.* **bring sth round to sth** (*AmE* **bring sth around to sth**) to direct a conversation to a particular subject: *I finally brought the conversation round to the subject of money.* **bring sb up** [often passive] to look after a child until they are an adult and to teach them how to behave: *After her parents were killed the child was brought up by her uncle.* ◊ *a well-brought-up child* **SYN raise**¹ **bring sth up 1** to bring food from the stomach back out through the mouth **SYN vomit 2** to introduce sth into a discussion or conversation: *I intend to bring the matter up at the next meeting.*

brink /brɪŋk/ *noun* [sing.] **the ~ (of sth/doing sth)** if you are on the **brink** of sth, you are almost in a very new, exciting or dangerous situation: *Just when the band were on the brink of becoming famous, they split up.*

brinkmanship /'brɪŋkmənʃɪp/ *noun* [U] (**POLITICS**) the activity of getting into a situation that could be very dangerous in order to frighten people and make them do what you want

brisk /brɪsk/ *adj.* **1** quick or using a lot of energy; busy: *They set off at a brisk pace.* ◊ *Trading has been brisk this morning.* **2** confident and practical; wanting to get things done quickly: *a brisk manner* ▶ **briskly** *adv.* ▶ **briskness** *noun* [U]

bristle¹ /'brɪsl/ *noun* [C] **1** a short thick hair: *The bristles on my chin hurt the baby's face.* **2** one of the short thick hairs of a brush

bristle² /'brɪsl/ *verb* [I] **1** (used about hair or an animal's fur) to stand up straight because of fear, anger, cold, etc. **2** ~ **(with sth)** to show that you are angry: *Her comment made him bristle with rage.*
PHR V **bristle with sth** to be full of sth

Brit /brɪt/ *noun* [C] (*informal*) a British person

Britain /'brɪtn/ *noun* [sing.] (**GEOGRAPHY**) the island containing England, Scotland and Wales ⊃ look at **Great Britain**, **United Kingdom**

British /'brɪtɪʃ/ *adj.* **1** of the United Kingdom (= Great Britain and Northern Ireland): *British industry* ◊ *to hold a British passport* **2 the British** *noun* [pl.] the people of the United Kingdom

the British Isles *noun* [pl.] (**GEOGRAPHY**) Great Britain and Ireland with all the islands that are near their coasts ⊃ note at **United Kingdom ❶** The British Isles are only a geographical unit, not a political unit.

Briton /'brɪtn/ *noun* [C] (*formal*) a person who comes from Britain

brittle /'brɪtl/ *adj.* hard but easily broken: *The bones become brittle in old age.*

broach /brəʊtʃ/ *verb* [T] to start talking about a particular subject, especially one that is difficult or embarrassing: *How will you broach the subject of the money he owes us?*

'B-road *noun* [C] (in Britain) a road that is not as important as an A-ROAD (= a main road) and usually joins small towns and villages

broad ⅞ B2 ❶ /brɔːd/ *adj.* **1** wide: *a broad street/river* ◊ *broad shoulders* ◊ *a broad smile* **OPP narrow**¹ ⊃ noun **breadth 2** including many different people or things: *We sell a broad range of products.* **3** without a lot of detail; general: *I'll explain the new system in broad terms.* **4** if sb has a **broad** ACCENT (= a particular way of pronouncing words), you can hear very easily which area they come from
IDM (**in**) **broad daylight** during the day, when it is easy to see

broadband ⅞⁺ C1 /'brɔːdbænd/ *noun* [U] **1** (**COMPUTING**) a way of connecting to the internet that allows you to receive information, including pictures, etc., very quickly: *We have broadband at home now.* **2** signals that use a wide range of FREQUENCIES

,broad 'bean *noun* [C] a type of round, pale green bean

broadcast ⅞ B2 /'brɔːdkɑːst/ *verb* [I, T] (*pt, pp* **broadcast**) (**ARTS AND MEDIA**) to send out radio or TV programmes: *The Olympics are broadcast live around the world.* ◊ *The BBC World Service broadcasts to most countries in the world.* ▶ **broadcast** ⅞ B2 *noun* [C]: *We watched a live broadcast of the ceremony* (= one shown at the same time as the ceremony) ▶ **broadcasting** *noun* [U]: *She works in broadcasting.*

broadcaster ⅞⁺ B2 /'brɔːdkɑːstə(r)/ *noun* [C] (**ARTS AND MEDIA**) **1** a person who speaks on the radio or on TV **2** a company that sends out radio or TV programmes

broaden /'brɔːdn/ *verb* [I, T] ~ **(sth) (out)** to become wider; to make sth wider: *The river broadens out beyond the bridge.* ◊ (*figurative*) *Travel broadens the mind* (= it makes you understand other people better).

broadly ⅞⁺ B2 ❻ /'brɔːdli/ *adv.* **1** (used to describe a way of smiling) with a big, wide smile: *He smiled broadly as he shook everyone's hand.* **2** generally: *Broadly speaking, the scheme will work as follows …*

,broad-'minded *adj.* happy to accept beliefs and ways of life that are different from your own **OPP narrow-minded**

broadsheet /'brɔːdʃiːt/ *noun* [C] (**ARTS AND MEDIA**) a newspaper printed on a large size of paper, generally considered more serious than smaller newspapers ⊃ look at **tabloid**

broccoli /'brɒkəli/ *noun* [U] a vegetable with a thick STEM (= the main long part of a plant) and green or purple flower heads

brochure /'brəʊʃə(r)/ noun [C] a small magazine or book containing pictures and information about sth or advertising sth: *a travel brochure*

broil /brɔɪl/ (*AmE*) = GRILL² (1)

broke¹ /brəʊk/ past tense of **break¹**

broke² /brəʊk/ adj. [not before noun] (*informal*) having no money: *I can't come out tonight — I'm absolutely broke.*

broken¹ /'brəʊkən/ past participle of **break¹**

broken² 🔺A2 /'brəʊkən/ adj. **1** damaged or in pieces; not working: *Watch out! There's broken glass on the floor.* ◊ *a broken leg* ◊ *How did the window get broken?* ◊ *The washing machine's broken.* ⊃ note at **hospital 2** (used about a promise or an agreement) not kept **3** not continuous; interrupted: *a broken line* ◊ *a broken night's sleep* **4** (used about a foreign language) spoken slowly with a lot of mistakes: *to speak in broken English* ⊃ note at **language**

broken-'down adj. **1** in a very bad condition: *a broken-down old building* **2** (used about a vehicle) not working: *A broken-down bus was blocking the road.*

broken-'hearted = HEARTBROKEN

broken 'home noun [C] a family in which the parents do not live together because they are divorced or separated: *Many of the children came from broken homes.*

broken 'marriage noun [C] a marriage that has ended

broker¹ /'brəʊkə(r)/ noun [C] (**FINANCE**) a person who buys and sells things, for example shares in a company, for other people: *an insurance broker* ⊃ look at **stockbroker**

broker² /'brəʊkə(r)/ verb [T] to arrange the details of an agreement, especially between different countries: *a peace plan brokered by the UN*

bromide /'brəʊmaɪd/ noun [U] (**MEDICINE**) a chemical that contains BROMINE, used in medicine, especially in the past, to make people feel calm

bromine /'brəʊmiːn/ noun [U] (*symb.* Br) (**CHEMISTRY**) a chemical element. Bromine is a dark red, poisonous liquid with a strong smell. ❶ For more information on the periodic table of elements, look at the **Reference Section** of this dictionary.

bronchial /'brɒŋkiəl/ adj. (**ANATOMY**) connected with or affecting the BRONCHI: *bronchial tube*

bronchiole /'brɒŋkiəʊl/ noun [C] (**ANATOMY**) one of many very small tubes connected to the BRONCHI ⊃ picture at **respiratory**

bronchitis /brɒŋ'kaɪtɪs/ noun [U] (**HEALTH**) an illness that affects the BRONCHI and causes a very bad COUGH

bronchus /'brɒŋkəs/ noun [C] (*pl.* bronchi /-kaɪ/) (**ANATOMY**) any of the main tubes that carry air in and out of the lungs ⊃ picture at **body, respiratory**

bronze¹ /brɒnz/ noun **1** [U] (**CHEMISTRY**) a dark red-brown metal that is made by mixing tin with COPPER (= another red-brown metal) **2** [U] a dark red-brown colour, like bronze **3** [C] (**ART**) a work of art made of bronze, for example a statue ⊃ note at **art 4** [U, C] = BRONZE MEDAL

bronze² /brɒnz/ adj. dark red-brown in colour

the 'Bronze Age noun [sing.] (**HISTORY**) the period in human history between the Stone Age and the Iron Age when people used tools and weapons made of BRONZE

bronzed /brɒnzd/ adj. having skin that has been turned brown, in an attractive way, by the sun **SYN** **suntanned** ⊃ look at **tan¹** (1)

bronze 'medal noun [C] (*also* bronze [U, C]) a MEDAL that you get as a prize for coming third in a race or competition ⊃ look at **gold medal, silver medal** ▸ **bronze 'medallist** noun [C]

brooch /brəʊtʃ/ noun [C] a piece of jewellery with a pin at the back that can be fastened to your clothes

brood¹ /bruːd/ verb **1** [I] ~ (**on/over/about sth**) to worry, or to think a lot about sth that makes you worried or sad: *to brood on a failure* **2** [I, T] if a bird **broods** or **broods** its eggs, it sits on them

brood² /bruːd/ noun [C] all the young birds that a mother produces at one time

broody /'bruːdi/ adj. (**broodier; broodiest**) **1** (used about a woman) wanting to have a baby **2** (used about a female bird) ready to have or sit on eggs: *a broody hen*

brook /brʊk/ noun [C] a small river **SYN** **stream¹**

broom /bruːm/ noun [C] a brush with a long handle that you use for removing dirt from the floor

broomstick /'bruːmstɪk/ noun [C] a BROOM with a long handle and small thin sticks at the end. In stories, WITCHES (= women with evil magic powers) ride through the air on broomsticks.

Bros /brɒs/ abbr. (**BUSINESS**) **Brothers** (used in the name of a company): *Wentworth Bros Ltd*

broth /brɒθ/ noun [U] thick soup: *chicken broth*

brothel /'brɒθl/ noun [C] a place where people pay to have sex with PROSTITUTES (= people who earn money in this way)

brother 🔺A1 /'brʌðə(r)/ noun [C] **1** a man or boy who has the same parents as another person: *Michael and Jim are brothers.* ◊ *Michael is Jim's brother.* ◊ *a younger/an older brother* ⊃ look at **half-brother, stepbrother 2** (**RELIGION**) a man who is a member of a Christian religious COMMUNITY **3** (*informal*) a man who you feel close to because he is a member of the same society, group, etc. as you

brotherhood /'brʌðəhʊd/ noun **1** [U] a feeling of great friendship and understanding between people: *the brotherhood of man* (= a feeling of friendship between all the people in the world) **2** [C + sing./pl. verb] an organization that is formed for a particular, often religious, purpose

'brother-in-law noun [C] (*pl.* brothers-in-law) your husband's or wife's brother; your sister's or brother's husband

brotherly /'brʌðəli/ adj. being kind and showing the feelings of love that you would expect a brother to show: *brotherly love/advice*

brought /brɔːt/ past tense, past participle of **bring**

brow /braʊ/ noun [C] **1** = EYEBROW **2** = FOREHEAD **3** [usually sing.] (**GEOGRAPHY**) the top part of a hill: *Suddenly a car came over the brow of the hill.*

browbeat /'braʊbiːt/ verb [T] (*pt* browbeat; *pp* browbeaten /-biːtn/) ~ **sb (into doing sth)** to frighten or threaten sb in order to make them do sth: *They were browbeaten into accepting the offer.*

brown¹ 🔺A1 /braʊn/ adj. **1** having the colour of earth or coffee: *brown eyes/hair* ◊ *brown bread* ◊ *a package wrapped in brown paper* **2** having skin that is naturally brown or has been made brown by the sun: *Although I often sunbathe, I never seem to go brown.*

brown² 🔺A1 /braʊn/ noun [U, C] the colour of earth or coffee: *Brown doesn't* (= brown clothes do not) *suit you.* ◊ *the yellows and browns of the trees in autumn*

brown³ /braʊn/ verb [I, T] to become brown; to make sth brown: *First, brown the meat in a frying pan.*

brownfield /'braʊnfiːld/ adj. [only before noun] (GEOGRAPHY) used to describe an area of land in a city that was used by industry in the past and where new buildings can now be built: *Developers are encouraged to build on brownfield sites.* ⊃ look at **greenfield**

Brownian motion /ˌbraʊniən 'məʊʃn/ noun [U] (PHYSICS) the movement without any regular pattern made by very small pieces of matter in a liquid or gas

brownie /'braʊni/ noun **1** [C] a type of heavy chocolate cake that is served in small squares **2 the Brownies** [pl.] an organization for girls between the ages of 7 and 10 that trains them in practical skills and does a lot of activities with them **3 Brownie** (BrE also 'Brownie Guide) [C] a member of the Brownies

brownish /'braʊnɪʃ/ adj. fairly brown: *She has brownish eyes.*

browse /braʊz/ verb **1** [I] to look at a lot of things in a shop rather than looking for one particular thing: *I spent hours browsing in the local bookshop.* **2** [I, T] ~ (through sth) (COMPUTING) to look through a book, newspaper, website, etc. without reading everything: *I enjoyed browsing through the catalogue but I didn't order anything.* ◇ *I've just been browsing the internet for information on Iceland.* ▶ browse noun [sing.]

browser ℝ+ 🅒🅘 /'braʊzə(r)/ noun [C] (COMPUTING) a computer program that lets you look at or read documents on the internet: *an internet browser*

bruise /bruːz/ noun [C] (HEALTH) a blue, brown or purple mark that appears on the skin after sb has fallen, been hit, etc. ❶ A bruise around your eye is a **black eye**. ▶ bruise verb [I, T]: *I've got the sort of skin that bruises easily.* ◇ *I fell over and bruised my arm.* ⊃ note at **injure**

brunch /brʌntʃ/ noun [C, U] (informal) a meal that you eat in the late morning as a combination of breakfast and lunch

brunette /bruːˈnet/ noun [C] a white woman with dark brown hair ⊃ look at **blonde**

brunt /brʌnt/ noun
IDM bear the brunt of sth → BEAR¹

brush¹ ℝ 🅐🅑 /brʌʃ/ noun **1** [C] an object made of BRISTLES (= short thick hairs) set in a block of wood or plastic. Brushes are used for cleaning things, painting, tidying your hair, etc: *Apply the paint with a fine brush.* ◇ *a toothbrush* ◇ *a paintbrush* ◇ *a hairbrush* ⊃ look at **broom 2** [sing.] an act of cleaning, tidying the hair, etc. with a brush: *Your hair needs a brush.* **IDM** (have) a brush with sb/sth (to have or almost have) an unpleasant meeting with sb/sth: *My only brush with the law was when I was stopped for speeding.*

brush² ℝ 🅐🅑 /brʌʃ/ verb **1** [T] to clean, tidy, etc. sth with a brush: *Make sure you brush your teeth twice a day.* ◇ *Brush your hair before you go out.* ⊃ note at **clean¹, tooth 2** [I, T] to touch sb/sth lightly when passing: *Her hand brushed his cheek.* ◇ *Leaves brushed against the car as we drove along the narrow road.*
PHR V brush sb/sth aside **1** to refuse to pay attention to sb/sth: *She brushed aside the protests and continued with the meeting.* **2** to push past sb/sth: *He hurried through the crowd, brushing aside the reporters who tried to stop him.* brush sth off/away to remove sth with a brush or with the hand, as if using a brush: *I brushed the dust off my jacket.* brush sth up/brush up on sth to study or practise sth in order to get back knowledge or skill that you had before and have lost: *She took a course to brush up her Spanish.*

brush-off noun [sing.] (informal) rude or unfriendly behaviour: *I'd ask her to go out with me but I'm scared she'll give me the brush-off.*

brushwork /'brʌʃwɜːk/ noun [U] (ART) the particular way in which an artist uses a brush to paint

brusque /bruːsk, brʊsk/ adj. using very few words and sounding rude: *He gave a brusque 'No comment!' and walked off.* ▶ brusquely adv.

Brussels sprout /ˌbrʌslz 'spraʊt/ (also sprout) noun [C, usually pl.] a round green vegetable that looks like a very small CABBAGE (= a large round vegetable with thick green leaves)

brutal ℝ+ 🅒🅘 /'bruːtl/ adj. very cruel and/or violent: *a brutal murder* ◇ *a brutal dictatorship* ▶ brutally /-təli/ adv.: *He was brutally honest and told her that he didn't love her any more.*

brutalism /'bruːtəlɪzəm/ noun [U] (ARCHITECTURE) a style of architecture that uses large CONCRETE blocks, steel, etc., and is sometimes considered ugly ▶ brutalist /-lɪst/ adj.

brutality /bruːˈtæləti/ noun [C, U] (pl. -ies) very cruel and violent behaviour

brute¹ /bruːt/ noun [C] **1** a cruel, violent man **2** a large strong animal

brute² /bruːt/ adj. [only before noun] using strength to do sth rather than thinking about it: *I think you'll have to use brute force to get this window open.*

brutish /'bruːtɪʃ/ adj. cruel and unpleasant

BSc /ˌbiː es 'siː/ (BrE) (AmE B.S. /ˌbiː 'es/) noun [C] (EDUCATION) a first university degree in science (the abbreviation for 'Bachelor of Science') ⊃ look at **BA, MSc**

BSE /ˌbiː es 'iː/ noun [U] (AGRICULTURE, HEALTH) a disease of cows that affects their brains and usually kills them (the abbreviation for 'bovine spongiform encephalopathy') ⊃ look at **CJD**

BST /ˌbiː es 'tiː/ abbr. **British Summer Time** (the time used in the UK in the summer that is one hour ahead of UTC)

BTC abbr. (in writing) = BITCOIN

BTEC /'biːtek/ noun [C] (EDUCATION) an exam for young people who have left secondary school and are training in commercial or technical subjects (the abbreviation for 'Business and Technology Education Council'): *She's doing a BTEC in design.*

BTW abbr. (in writing) = BY THE WAY

bubble¹ ℝ 🅑🅘 /'bʌbl/ noun [C] a ball of air or gas, in liquid or floating in the air: *We knew there where fish because of the bubbles on the surface.*

bubble² /'bʌbl/ verb [I] **1** to produce bubbles or to rise with bubbles: *Cook the pizza until the cheese starts to bubble.* ◇ *The clear water bubbled up out of the ground.* **2** ~ (over) (with sth) to be full of happy feelings

bubble bath noun [U] a liquid that you can add to the water in a bath to produce a mass of white bubbles

bubblegum /'bʌblgʌm/ noun [U] a type of CHEWING GUM (= a sweet that you bite many times but do not eat) that can be blown into bubbles ⊃ look at **chewing gum**

bubbly /'bʌbli/ adj. **1** full of bubbles **2** (used about a person) happy and full of energy

buck¹ ℝ+ 🅒🅘 /bʌk/ noun **1** [C] (AmE, informal) a US dollar: *Could you lend me a few bucks?* **2** [C] a male DEER, HARE or RABBIT ⊃ note at **deer 3 the buck** [sing.] used in some expressions to refer to the responsibility or blame for sth: *The government should accept responsibility instead of passing the buck.*

buck² /bʌk/ *verb* [I] (used about a horse) to jump into the air or to kick the back legs in the air
PHR V **buck your ideas up** (*informal*) to start behaving in a more acceptable way: *Unless you buck your ideas up, you'll never pass the exam.*

bucket /'bʌkɪt/ *noun* [C] **1** an open container with a handle, used for carrying or holding liquids, sand, etc. **2** (*also* **bucketful** /'bʌkɪtfʊl/) the amount that a bucket contains: *How many buckets of water do you think we'll need?*
IDM **a drop in the bucket** → DROP²

buckle¹ /'bʌkl/ *noun* [C] a piece of metal or plastic used for fastening a belt, shoe, etc.

buckle² /'bʌkl/ *verb* [I, T] **1** to fasten or be fastened with a BUCKLE **2** to become damaged or bent because of heat, force, weakness, etc.; to damage or bend sth in this way: *Some railway lines buckled in the heat.*

buckwheat /'bʌkwiːt/ *noun* [U] a type of grain that is small and dark and that is grown as food for animals and for making flour

bud /bʌd/ *noun* [C] (**BIOLOGY**) a small closed part on a tree or plant that opens and develops into a flower or leaf: *rosebuds* ⊃ picture at **flower¹**, **tree**
IDM **nip sth in the bud** → NIP

Buddhism /'bʊdɪzəm/ *noun* [U] (**RELIGION**) an Asian religion based on the teaching of Siddhartha Gautama (or Buddha) ⊃ note at **religion** ▶ **Buddhist** /-dɪst/ *noun* [C], *adj.*: *a Buddhist temple* ⊃ note at **religion**

budding /'bʌdɪŋ/ *adj.* [only before noun] wanting or starting to develop and be successful: *Have you got any tips for budding young photographers?*

buddy 𝄞+ **C1** /'bʌdi/ *noun* [C] (*pl.* **-ies**) (*informal*) a friend

budge /bʌdʒ/ *verb* [I, T] **1** to move or make sth move a little: *I tried as hard as I could to loosen the screw but it simply wouldn't budge.* ◇ *We just couldn't budge the car when it got stuck in the mud.* **2** to change or make sb change a strong opinion: *Neither side in the dispute is prepared to budge.*

budgerigar /'bʌdʒərɪgɑː(r)/ (*also informal* **budgie**) *noun* [C] a small bird of the PARROT family, often kept in a CAGE as a pet

budget¹ 𝄞 **B2** /'bʌdʒɪt/ *noun* **1** [C, U] (**FINANCE**) a plan of how to spend an amount of money over a particular period of time; the amount of money that is mentioned: *What's your monthly budget for food?* ◇ *a country's defence budget* ◇ *The work was finished on time and* **within budget**. ◇ *The builders are already 20 per cent* **over budget**. **2** (*BrE also* **Budget**) [C, usually sing.] (**FINANCE**, **POLITICS**) an official statement by the government of a country's income from taxes, etc. and how it will be spent: *Do you think taxes will go up in this year's budget?*

budget² /'bʌdʒɪt/ *verb* [I, T] **~ (sth) (for sth)** (**FINANCE**) to plan carefully how much money to spend on sth: *The government has budgeted an extra £3 billion for education.*

budget³ /'bʌdʒɪt/ *adj.* [only before noun] low in price; not charging high prices: *a budget hotel* ◇ *budget airlines*

budgetary /'bʌdʒɪtəri/ *adj.* (**FINANCE**) connected with plans for how to spend money during a particular period of time ⊃ note at **economic**

budgie /'bʌdʒi/ (*informal*) = BUDGERIGAR

buff¹ /bʌf/ *noun* [C] (*informal*) a person who knows a lot about a particular subject and is very interested in it: *a film/computer buff*

buff² /bʌf/ *adj.* (*informal*) physically fit and attractive with big muscles

buffalo /'bʌfələʊ/ *noun* [C] (*pl.* **buffalo**, **buffaloes**) **1** a large wild animal that looks like a cow with wide, curved HORNS: *a herd of buffalo* **2** (*AmE*) = BISON

buffer 𝄞+ **C1** /'bʌfə(r)/ *noun* [C] **1 ~ (against sth)**; **~ (between A and B)** a thing or person that reduces a shock or protects sb/sth against difficulties: *Meditation is a buffer against stress.* ◇ *UN forces are acting as a buffer between the two sides in the war.* ◇ *a* **buffer state** (= a small country between two powerful states that helps keep peace between them) **2** (*BrE*) one of two round metal devices on the front or end of a train, or at the end of a railway track, that reduce the shock if the train hits sth **3** (**COMPUTING**) an area in a computer's memory where data can be stored for a short time

buffet¹ /'bʌfeɪ, 'bʊf-/ *noun* [C] **1** a meal (usually at a party or a special occasion) at which food is placed on a long table and people serve themselves: *Lunch was a cold buffet.* ◇ *a buffet lunch* **2** part of a train or a place at a station where you can buy food and drinks

buffet² /'bʌfɪt/ *verb* [T, often passive] to knock or push sth in a rough way from side to side: *The boat was buffeted by the rough sea.*

bug¹ 𝄞+ **B2** /bʌg/ *noun* **1** [C] (*especially AmE*) any small insect **2** [C] (*informal*) (**HEALTH**) an illness that is not very serious and that people get from each other: *I don't feel very well — I think I've got the bug that's going round.* ⊃ note at **disease** **3** [C] (**COMPUTING**) something wrong in a system or machine, especially a computer: *There's a bug in the software.* **4** (*usually* **the … bug**) [sing.] (*informal*) a sudden interest in sth: *They've been bitten by the golf bug.* **5** [C] a small hidden device secretly listening to and recording people's conversations

bug² /bʌg/ *verb* [T] (**-gg-**) **1** to hide a MICROPHONE somewhere so that people's conversations can be recorded secretly: *Be careful what you say. This room is bugged.* **2** (*informal*) to annoy or worry sb

buggy /'bʌgi/ *noun* [C] (*pl.* **-ies**) = PUSHCHAIR

▼ SYNONYMS

build

construct ♦ assemble ♦ erect ♦ put up ♦ put together

These words all mean to make sth, especially by putting different parts together.

build *to build a house*

construct *When was the bridge constructed?*

assemble *The cupboard is easy to assemble.*

erect (*formal*) *Police erected barriers to keep the crowds back.*

put up *They're putting up new hotels to boost tourism in the area.*

put together *to put together a model plane*

---

build¹ 𝄞 **A1** /bɪld/ *verb* (*pt, pp* **built** /bɪlt/) **1** [T] to make sth by putting pieces, materials, etc. together: *The house is built of stone.* ◇ *How long ago was your house built?* **2** [I] to use land for building on: *There's plenty of land to build on around here.* **3** [T] to develop or increase sth: *The government is trying to build a more modern society.* ◇ *This book claims to help people to build their self-confidence.*
PHR V **build sth in/on | build sth into/onto sth** to make sth a part of sth else: *They've made sure that a large number of checks are built into the system.* ◇ *We're planning to build two more rooms onto the back of the house.* **build on sth** to use sth as a base

from which you can make further progress: *Now that we're beginning to make a profit, we must build on this success.* **build sth on sth** to base sth on sth: *a society built on the principle of freedom and democracy* **build up (to sth)** to become greater in amount or number; to increase: *The traffic starts to build up at this time of day.* **build sth up** **1** to make sth seem more important or greater than it really is: *I don't think it's a very serious matter, it's just been built up in the newspapers.* **2** to increase or develop sth over a period: *You'll need to build up your strength again slowly after the operation.*

build² /bɪld/ *noun* [C, U] the shape and size of sb's body: *She **has a** very athletic **build**.*

builder /ˈbɪldə(r)/ *noun* [C] a person whose job is to build houses and other buildings

building materials

tiles
bricks
wood
sand
cement
glass
concrete

building 🔑 A1 /ˈbɪldɪŋ/ *noun* **1** [C] a structure, such as a house, shop or school, that has a roof and walls: *There are a lot of very old buildings in this town.* **2** [U] the process or business of making buildings: *building materials* ◇ *the building industry* ◇ *the building of the school*

▼ **SYNONYMS**

building

property • **premises** • **complex** • **structure** • **block** • **edifice**

These are all words for a structure such as a house, an office block or a factory that has a roof and walls.

building *an industrial building*
property *Several buyers viewed the property.*
premises *The company needs larger premises.*
complex *a leisure complex*
structure *a wooden structure*
block *a block of flats*
edifice (*formal*) *an imposing edifice*

ˈ**building site** *noun* [C] an area of land on which a building is being built

ˈ**building society** *noun* [C] (*BrE*) (**FINANCE**) an organization like a bank that lends money to people who want to buy a house. People can also save money with a building society. ➲ note at **mortgage¹**

ˈ**build-up** *noun* **1** [sing., U] an increase of sth over a period: *The build-up of tension in the area has made war seem more likely.* **2** [C, usually sing.] **~ (to sth)** a period of preparation or excitement before an event: *The players started to get nervous in the build-up to the big game.*

built¹ /bɪlt/ *suffix* [only before noun] (after an adverb; in adjectives) made in the particular way that is mentioned: *a newly built station* ◇ *American-built cars*

built² /bɪlt/ past tense, past participle of **build¹**

ˌ**built-ˈin** *adj.* that is a part of sth and cannot be removed: *built-in cupboards*

ˌ**built-ˈup** *adj.* (used about an area of land) covered with buildings, roads, etc: *a built-up area*

bulb /bʌlb/ *noun* [C] **1** = LIGHT BULB **2** (**BIOLOGY**) the round underground part of some plants that grows into a new plant every year: *a tulip bulb* ➲ picture at **flower¹**

bulbous /ˈbʌlbəs/ *adj.* fat, round and ugly: *a bulbous red nose*

bulge¹ /bʌldʒ/ *noun* [C] a round shape that sticks out from sth

bulge² /bʌldʒ/ *verb* [I] **1 ~ (with sth)** to be full of sth: *His bags were bulging with presents for the children.* **2** to stick out from sth in a round shape: *My stomach is starting to bulge. I must get more exercise.*

bulging /ˈbʌldʒɪŋ/ *adj.* that sticks out from sth in a round shape: *He had a thin face and rather bulging eyes.*

bulimia /buˈlɪmiə, -ˈliːm-/ (*also* **bulimia nervosa** /buˌlɪmiə nɜːˈvəʊsə, -ˌliːm-/) *noun* [U] (**PSYCHOLOGY**) an emotional DISORDER in which the person has an OBSESSIVE desire to lose weight and repeatedly eats too much and then forces themself to VOMIT (= bring up food from the stomach) ➲ look at **anorexia** ▶ **bulimic** /buˈlɪmɪk, -ˈliːm-/ *adj.*, *noun* [C]

bulk 🔑+ C1 /bʌlk/ *noun* **1** [sing.] **the ~ (of sth)** the main part of sth; most of sth: *The bulk of the work has been done, so we should finish this week.* **2** [U] the size, quantity or weight of sth large: *He slowly lifted his vast bulk out of the chair.* ◇ *The cupboard isn't especially heavy — what makes it hard to move is its bulk.*
IDM **in bulk** in large quantities: *If you buy in bulk, it's 10% cheaper.*

bulky /ˈbʌlki/ *adj.* (**bulkier**; **bulkiest**) large and heavy and therefore difficult to move or carry

bull /bʊl/ *noun* [C] **1** an adult male of any animal in the cow family ➲ note at **cow** **2** the male of the elephant, WHALE (= a very large sea animal) and some other large animals **3** (**FINANCE**) a person who buys shares in a company, hoping to sell them soon afterwards at a higher price: *a **bull market*** (= in which prices are rising) ➲ look at **bear²** (2)

bulldog /ˈbʊldɒɡ/ *noun* [C] a strong dog with short legs, a large head and a short, thick neck

ˈ**Bulldog clip™** *noun* [C] (*BrE*) a metal device for holding papers together

bulldoze /ˈbʊldəʊz/ *verb* [T] to make ground flat or knock down a building with a BULLDOZER: *The old buildings were bulldozed and new ones were built.*

bulldozer /ˈbʊldəʊzə(r)/ *noun* [C] a large, powerful vehicle with a broad piece of metal at the front, used for moving earth or knocking down buildings

bullet 🔑 B2 /ˈbʊlɪt/ *noun* [C] a small metal object that is fired from a gun: *The bullet hit her in the arm.* ◇ *a bullet wound*

bulletin /ˈbʊlətɪn/ *noun* [C] **1** a short news report on TV or radio; an official statement about a situation: *The next **news bulletin** is at nine o'clock.* **2** a report that a club or an organization produces

ˈ**bulletin board** *noun* [C] **1** (*AmE*) = NOTICEBOARD **2** a place in a computer system where you can write or read messages

bullet point *noun* [C] (**LANGUAGE**) an item in a list in a document, that is printed with a square, diamond or circle in front of it in order to show that it is important. The square, etc. is also called a **bullet point**.

bulletproof /ˈbʊlɪtpruːf/ *adj.* made of a strong material that stops bullets from passing through it

bullfight /ˈbʊlfaɪt/ *noun* [C] a traditional public entertainment, especially in Spain, Portugal and Latin America, in which a BULL (= an adult male cow) is fought and usually killed ▶ **bullfighter** *noun* [C] ▶ **bullfighting** *noun* [U]

bullion /ˈbʊliən/ *noun* [U] bars of gold or silver

bullock /ˈbʊlək/ *noun* [C] a young BULL (= an adult male cow) that has been CASTRATED (= had part of its sexual organs removed)

bullring /ˈbʊlrɪŋ/ *noun* [C] the large round area, like an outdoor theatre, where BULLFIGHTS take place

bullseye /ˈbʊlzaɪ/ *noun* [C] (**SPORT**) the centre of the target that you shoot or throw at in sports such as ARCHERY; a shot or throw that hits this

bully[1] /ˈbʊli/ *noun* [C] (*pl.* -ies) a person who uses their strength or power to hurt or frighten people who are weaker: *the school bully*

bully[2] /ˈbʊli/ *verb* [T] (**bullying; bullies;** *pt, pp* **bullied**) ~ **sb (into sth/doing sth)** to use your strength or power to hurt or frighten sb who is weaker or to make them do sth: *Don't try to bully me into making a decision.* ▶ **bullying** *noun* [U]: *Bullying is a serious problem in many schools.*

bum /bʌm/ *noun* [C] (*informal*) **1** (*BrE*) the part of the body that you sit on SYN **backside, bottom**[1] **2** (*especially AmE*) a person who has no home or job and who asks other people for money or food **3** a lazy person who does nothing for society: *a beach bum* (= somebody who spends all their time on the beach)

bumbag /ˈbʌmbæɡ/ (*BrE*) (*AmE* **fanny pack**) *noun* [C] (*informal*) a small bag worn around the the middle part of the body to keep money, etc. in

bumblebee /ˈbʌmblbiː/ *noun* [C] a large bee covered with small hairs that makes a loud noise as it flies ⊃ picture at **animal**

bump[1] /bʌmp/ *verb* **1** [I] ~ **against/into sb/sth** to hit sb/ sth by accident when you are moving: *She bumped into a lamp post because she wasn't looking where she was going.* **2** [T] ~ **sth (against/on sth)** to hit sth against or on sth by accident: *I bumped my knee on the edge of the table.* **3** [I] to move along over a rough surface: *The car bumped along the track to the farm.* PHR V **bump into sb** (*informal*) to meet sb by chance: *I bumped into an old friend on the bus today.* **bump sb off** (*informal*) to murder sb **bump sth up** (*informal*) to increase or make sth go up: *All this publicity will bump up sales of our new product.*

bump[2] /bʌmp/ *noun* [C] **1** the action or sound of sth hitting a hard surface: *She fell and hit the ground with a bump.* **2** an area on the body that is larger and rounder than normal, often caused when you have been hit **3** a part of a surface that is higher than the rest of it: *There are a lot of bumps in the road, so drive carefully.*

bumper[1] /ˈbʌmpə(r)/ *noun* [C] the bar fixed to the front and back of a motor vehicle to protect it if it hits sth

bumper[2] /ˈbʌmpə(r)/ *adj.* larger than usual: *The unusually fine weather has produced a bumper harvest this year.*

bumpy /ˈbʌmpi/ *adj.* (**bumpier; bumpiest**) not flat or smooth: *a bumpy road* ◊ *Because of the stormy weather, it was a very bumpy flight.* OPP **smooth**[1]

bun /bʌn/ *noun* [C] **1** a small round sweet cake: *a currant bun* **2** a small soft bread roll: *a hamburger bun* **3** hair fastened tightly into a round shape at the back of the head: *She wears her hair in a bun.*

bunch[1] [B2] /bʌntʃ/ *noun* **1** [C] a number of things, usually of the same type, fastened or growing together: *He bought her a bunch of flowers for her birthday.* ◊ *a bunch of bananas/grapes* ◊ *a bunch of keys* **2 bunches** [pl.] (*BrE*) long hair that is divided into two and tied on each side of the head **3** [sing.] (*informal*) a group of people: *My colleagues are the best bunch of people I've ever worked with.*

bunch[2] /bʌntʃ/ *verb* [I, T] ~ **(sth) (up)** to become tight or to form tight folds; to make sth do this: *These jeans tend to bunch (up) around the ankles.* PHR V **bunch (sb/sth) up/together** to move closer and form into a group; to make people or things do this: *The runners bunched up as they came round the final bend.*

bundle[1] /ˈbʌndl/ *noun* [C] **1** a number of things tied or folded together: *a bundle of letters with an elastic band round them* **2** a number of things that belong, or are sold together

bundle[2] /ˈbʌndl/ *verb* [T] **1** (used with an adverb or a preposition) to put or push sb/sth quickly and in a rough way in a particular direction: *He was arrested and bundled into a police car.* **2** ~ **sth (with sth)** (**COMPUTING**) to supply extra equipment, especially software when selling a new computer, at no extra cost: *A further nine applications are bundled with the system.* PHR V **bundle sb up (in sth)** to put warm clothes or a cover on sb: *I bundled her up in a blanket and gave her a hot drink.* **bundle sth up/together** to make or tie sth a number of things together: *I bundled up the old newspapers and threw them away.*

bung[1] /bʌŋ/ *verb* [T] (*BrE, informal*) to put or throw sth somewhere, carelessly and quickly PHR V **bung sth up (with sth)** [usually passive] to block sth: *My nose is all bunged up.*

bung[2] /bʌŋ/ *noun* [C] **1** a round piece of wood, rubber, etc. used for closing the hole in a container such as a BARREL or JAR **2** (*BrE, informal*) an amount of money that is given to sb to persuade them to do sth illegal

bungalow /ˈbʌŋɡələʊ/ *noun* [C] (*BrE*) a house that is all on one level, without stairs

bunged up *adj.* (*informal*) blocked, so that nothing can get through

bungee jumping /ˈbʌndʒi dʒʌmpɪŋ/ *noun* [U] (**SPORT**) a sport in which you jump from a high place, for example a bridge, with a thick ELASTIC rope tied round your feet

bungle /ˈbʌŋɡl/ *verb* [I, T] to do sth badly or fail to do sth: *a bungled robbery*

bunk /bʌŋk/ *noun* [C] **1** a bed that is fixed to a wall, especially on a ship or train **2** (*also* **bunk bed**) one of a pair of single beds built as a unit with one above the other IDM **do a bunk** (*BrE, informal*) to run away or escape; to leave without telling anyone

bunker /ˈbʌŋkə(r)/ *noun* [C] **1** a strong underground building that gives protection, for example in a war **2** a small area filled with sand on a GOLF COURSE

bunny /ˈbʌni/ *noun* [C] (*pl.* -ies) a child's word for a RABBIT

Bunsen burner /ˌbʌnsn ˈbɜːnə(r)/ *noun* [C] (**SCIENCE**) an instrument used in scientific work that produces a hot gas flame ⊃ picture at **laboratory**

buoy¹ /bɔɪ/ *noun* [C] an object that floats on the sea or a river to mark the places where it is dangerous for boats to go

buoy² /bɔɪ/ *verb* [T] ~ **sb/sth (up) 1** to keep sb happy and confident: *His encouragement buoyed her up during that difficult period.* **2** to keep sb/sth floating on water **3** to keep sth at a high level: *Share prices were buoyed by news of a takeover.*

buoyant /ˈbɔɪənt/ *adj.* **1** (**ECONOMICS**) (used about prices, business activity, etc.) staying at a high level or increasing, so that people make more money: *a buoyant economy/market* **2** happy and confident: *The team were in buoyant mood after their win.* **3** floating, able to float or able to keep things floating ▸ **buoyancy** /-ənsi/ *noun* [U]: *the buoyancy of the market*

bur /bɜː(r)/ **1** = BURR (2) **2** = BURR (3)

burden¹ ⟨ᵗ⟩ **C1** **Ⓦ** /ˈbɜːdn/ *noun* [C] **1** a responsibility or difficult task that causes a lot of work or worry **2** (*formal*) something that is heavy and difficult to carry

burden² /ˈbɜːdn/ *verb* [T] ~ **sb/yourself (with sth)** to give sb/yourself a responsibility or task that causes a lot of work or worry

the ˌburden of ˈproof *noun* [sing.] (**LAW**) the task or responsibility of proving that sth is true

bureau /ˈbjʊərəʊ/ *noun* [C] (*pl.* **bureaux** /-rəʊz/, **bureaus**) **1** (*BrE*) a writing desk with DRAWERS and a top that opens to form a flat surface to write on **2** an office or organization that provides information on a particular subject: *an employment bureau* **3** (**POLITICS**) (in the US) a government department or part of a government department: *the Federal Bureau of Investigation*

bureaucracy ⟨ᵗ⟩ **C1** /bjʊəˈrɒkrəsi/ *noun* (*pl.* **-ies**) **1** [U] (often used in a critical way) the system of official rules that an organization has for doing sth, that people often think is too complicated: *Getting a visa involves a lot of unnecessary bureaucracy.* **2** [C, U] (**POLITICS**) a system of government by a large number of officials who are not elected; a country with this system

bureaucrat /ˈbjʊərəkræt/ *noun* [C] (**POLITICS**) an official working in an organization or a government department, especially one who follows the rules of the department too strictly

bureaucratic /ˌbjʊərəˈkrætɪk/ *adj.* connected with a BUREAUCRACY or BUREAUCRATS and involving complicated official rules that may seem unnecessary: *You have to go through a complex bureaucratic procedure if you want to get your money back.*

bureau de change /ˌbjʊərəʊ də ˈʃɑːnʒ/ *noun* [C] (*pl.* **bureaux de change** /ˌbjʊərəʊ də ˈʃɑːnʒ/) (*BrE*) (**TOURISM**) an office at an airport, in a hotel, etc. where you can change the money of one country to the money of another country

burette (*AmE also* **buret**) /bjʊəˈret/ *noun* [C] (**CHEMISTRY**) a glass tube with measurements marked on it and a TAP at one end ⇨ picture at **laboratory**

burger /ˈbɜːɡə(r)/ *noun* [C] **1** (*also* **hamburger**) meat that has been cut up small and pressed into a flat round shape. Burgers are often eaten in a bread roll. ⇨ look at **beefburger 2** (in compounds) fish, vegetables, etc. cut into small pieces and made into a flat round shape like a HAMBURGER

burglar /ˈbɜːɡlə(r)/ *noun* [C] a person who enters a building illegally in order to steal ⇨ note at **criminal¹** ▸ **burgle** /-ɡl/ *verb* [T] (*BrE*) (*AmE* **burglarize** /-ɡləraɪz/): *Our flat was burgled while we were out.*

burglar alarm *noun* [C] a piece of equipment, usually fixed on a wall, that makes a loud noise if sb enters a building

burglary /ˈbɜːɡləri/ *noun* [C, U] (*pl.* **-ies**) (**LAW**) the crime of entering a building illegally in order to steal: *There was a burglary next door last week.* ◇ *He is in prison for burglary.* ⇨ note at **criminal¹**

burgundy /ˈbɜːɡəndi/ *adj.* dark red in colour ▸ **burgundy** *noun* [U]

burial ⟨ᵗ⟩ **C1** /ˈberiəl/ *noun* [C, U] the act or ceremony of burying a dead body

burka (*also* **burkha**) /ˈbʊəkə, ˈbɜːkə/ *noun* [C] (**RELIGION**) a long, loose piece of clothing that covers the whole body and that is worn by some Muslim women

burlap /ˈbɜːlæp/ (*AmE*) = HESSIAN

burly /ˈbɜːli/ *adj.* (**burlier**; **burliest**) (used about a person or their body) strong and heavy

burn¹ ⟨ᵗ⟩ **A2** /bɜːn/ *verb* (*pt, pp* **burnt** /bɜːnt/, **burned**) **1** [T] to destroy, damage or injure sb/sth with fire or heat: *We took all the rubbish outside and burned it.* ◇ *It was a terrible fire and the whole building was burnt to the ground* (= completely destroyed). ◇ *If you get too close to the fire you'll burn yourself.* ◇ *Two people were burnt to death in the hotel fire.* **2** [I] to be destroyed, damaged or injured by fire or heat: *If you leave the cake in the oven for much longer, it will burn.* ◇ *I can't spend too much time in the sun because I burn easily.* ◇ *They were trapped by the flames and they burned to death.* **3** [T] to produce a hole or mark in or on sth by burning: *He dropped his cigarette and it burned a hole in the carpet.* **4** [I] to be on fire: *Firemen raced to the burning building.* **5** [T] to use sth as fuel: *an oil-burning lamp* **6** [I] to produce light: *I don't think he went to bed at all — I could see his light burning all night.* **7** [I] to feel very hot and painful: *You have a temperature — your forehead's burning.* **8** [I] ~ **(with sth)** to be filled with a very strong feeling: *She was burning with indignation.* **9** [T] to put information onto a CD, etc. **IDM** **sb's ears are burning** → EAR **PHR V** **burn down** (used about a building) to be completely destroyed by fire **burn sth down** to completely destroy a building by fire **burn (sth) off** to remove sth or to be removed by burning **burn sth out** [usually passive] to completely destroy sth by burning: *the burnt-out wreck of a car* **burn yourself out** to work, etc., until you have no more energy or strength **burn (sth) up** to destroy or to be destroyed by fire or strong heat: *The space capsule burnt up on its re-entry into the earth's atmosphere.*

burn² ⟨ᵗ⟩ **B2** /bɜːn/ *noun* [C] damage or an injury caused by fire or heat: *severe burns* ◇ *There's a cigarette burn on the carpet.* ◇ *He has been treated for **third-degree burns*** (= the most serious kind of burns) *to his face and hands.* ◇ *He was taken to hospital with **minor burns**.*

burner /ˈbɜːnə(r)/ *noun* [C] the part of a cooker, etc. that produces a flame **IDM** **on the back burner** → BACK²

burning /ˈbɜːnɪŋ/ *adj.* [only before noun] **1** (used about a feeling) extremely strong: *a burning ambition/desire* **2** very important or needing immediate attention: *a burning issue/question* **3** feeling very hot: *the burning sun*

burnt /bɜːnt/ past tense, past participle of **burn¹**

burp /bɜːp/ *verb* [I] to make a noise with the mouth when air rises from the stomach and is forced out: *He sat back when he had finished his meal and burped loudly.* **SYN** belch ▸ **burp** *noun* [C]

burr /bɜː(r)/ *noun* [C] **1** [usually sing.] (**LANGUAGE**) a strong pronunciation of the 'r' sound, typical of some ACCENTS (= a particular way of pronouncing words that shows where a person comes from) in English; an ACCENT with this type of pronunciation **2** (*also* bur) a small tool for cutting that can be used with a DRILL (= a tool or machine that is used for making holes in wood, etc.) **3** (*also* bur) (**BIOLOGY**) the seed container of some plants that sticks to clothes or fur

burrow[1] /'bʌrəʊ/ *noun* [C] a hole in the ground made by certain animals, for example RABBITS, in which they live

burrow[2] /'bʌrəʊ/ *verb* [I] to dig a hole in the ground, to make a tunnel or to look for sth: *These animals burrow for food.* ◊ (*figurative*) *She burrowed in her handbag for her keys.*

bursar /'bɜːsə(r)/ *noun* [C] (**EDUCATION**) the person who manages the financial matters of a school, college or university

bursary /'bɜːsəri/ *noun* [C] (*pl.* -ies) (**EDUCATION**) a sum of money given to a specially chosen student to pay for his/her studies at a college or university ⊃ look at **scholarship**

burst[1] ⓘ+ **C1** /bɜːst/ *verb* (*pt, pp* burst) **1** [I, T] to break open suddenly and violently, usually because there is too much pressure inside; to cause this to happen: *The ball burst when I kicked it.* ◊ *You'll burst that tyre if you blow it up any more.* ◊ (*figurative*) *If I eat any more I'll burst!* ◊ *If it rains much more, the river will burst its banks.* **2** [I] ~**into/out of/through sth** to move suddenly in a particular direction, often using force: *She burst into the manager's office and demanded to speak to him.*
IDM **be bursting (with sth)** to be very full of sth: *I packed so many clothes that my suitcase was bursting.* ◊ *She was bursting with pride when she won the race.* **be bursting to do sth** (*informal*) to want to do sth very much **burst (sth) open** to open or make sth open suddenly or violently
PHR V **burst in on sb/sth** to interrupt sb/sth by arriving suddenly: *The police burst in on the gang as they were counting the money.* **burst into sth** to start doing sth suddenly: *On hearing the news she burst into tears* (= started crying). ◊ *The lorry hit a wall and burst into flames* (= started burning). **burst out 1** to start doing sth suddenly: *He looked so ridiculous that I burst out laughing.* **2** to say sth suddenly and with strong feeling: *Finally he burst out, 'I can't stand it any more!'*

burst[2] /bɜːst/ *noun* [C] **1** a short period of a particular activity, that often starts suddenly: *a burst of energy/enthusiasm/speed* ◊ *a burst of applause/gunfire* ◊ *He prefers to work in short bursts.* **2** an occasion when sth BURSTS or explodes; a hole caused by this: *a burst in a water pipe*

bury ⓘ **B1** /'beri/ *verb* [T] (**burying**; **buries**; *pt, pp* **buried**) **1** to put a dead body in the ground: *She wants to be buried in the village graveyard.* **2** to put sth in a hole in the ground and cover it: *Our dog always buries its bones in the garden.* **3** [usually passive] to cover or hide sth/sb: *At last I found the photo, buried at the bottom of a drawer.*

bus ⓘ **A1** /bʌs/ *noun* [C] a large public vehicle, especially one that takes passengers along a fixed route and stops regularly to let people get on and off: *Where do you usually get on/off the bus?* ◊ *We'll have to hurry up if we want to catch the nine o'clock bus.* ◊ *We'd better run or we'll miss the bus.* ◊ *a school bus* ◊ *a bus company/driver*

bush ⓘ **B2** /bʊʃ/ *noun* **1** [C] (**BIOLOGY**) a plant like a small, thick tree with many low branches: *a rose bush* ◊ *The house was surrounded by thick bushes.* **2** (*often* the bush) [U] (**GEOGRAPHY**) wild land that has not been cleared, especially in Africa and Australia
IDM **beat about the bush** → BEAT[1]

bushy /'bʊʃi/ *adj.* (**bushier**; **bushiest**) growing thickly: *bushy hair/eyebrows*

busily /'bɪzɪli/ → BUSY[1]

business ⓘ **A1** /'bɪznəs/ *noun*
• TRADE **1** [U] buying and selling as a way of earning money: *She's planning to set up in business as a hairdresser.* ◊ *I'm going to go into business with my brother.* ◊ *They are very easy to do business with.*
SYN **commerce, trade**[1]
• WORK **2** [U] the work that you do as your job: *The manager will be away on business next week.* ◊ *a business trip*
• CUSTOMERS **3** [U] the number of customers that a person or company has had: *Business has been good for the time of year.*
• COMPANY **4** [C] a firm, a shop, a factory, etc. that produces or sells goods or provides a service: *She aims to start a business of her own.* ◊ *Small businesses are finding it hard to survive at the moment.* ⊃ picture at **income**
• RESPONSIBILITY **5** [U] something that concerns a particular person: *The friends I choose are my business, not yours.* ◊ *Our business is to collect the information, not to comment on it.* ◊ *'How much did it cost?' 'It's none of your business!'* (= I don't want to tell you. It's private.)
• IMPORTANT MATTERS **6** [U] important matters that need to be dealt with or discussed: *First we have some unfinished business from the last meeting to deal with.* ⊃ note at **meeting**
• EVENT **7** [sing.] a situation or an event, especially one that is strange or unpleasant: *The divorce was an awful business.* ◊ *I found the whole business very depressing.*
IDM **get down to business** to start the work that has to be done **go out of business** to have to close because there is no more money available: *The shop went out of business because it couldn't compete with the new supermarket.* **have no business to do sth/doing sth** to have no right to do sth: *You have no business to read/reading my letters without asking me.* **mind your own business** → MIND[2] **monkey business** → MONKEY

'business angel = ANGEL (3)

'business card (*also* card) *noun* [C] (**BUSINESS**) a small card printed with sb's name and details of their job and company: *We exchanged business cards.*

businesslike /'bɪznəslaɪk/ *adj.* dealing with matters in a direct and practical way, without trying to be friendly: *She has a very businesslike manner.*

businessman ⓘ **A2** /'bɪznəsmæn, -mən/ *noun* [C] (*pl.* -men /-men, -mən/) **1** (**BUSINESS**) a man who works in business, especially in a top position **2** a man who is good at dealing with business and financial matters

'business model *noun* [C] (**BUSINESS**) a plan for running a business, showing where the money will come from, who the customers are, etc.

'business person *noun* [C] (**BUSINESS**) a person who works in business, especially in a top position ⊃ look at **businessman** **HELP** Business people is usually used to talk about a group of men and women to avoid having to say **businessmen and businesswomen. Business person/people** is also used in more formal language.

'business plan *noun* [C] (**BUSINESS**) a document that describes a business's aims for the future and how the business will achieve those aims

'business school *noun* [C] (**EDUCATION**) a part of a college or university that teaches business, often to graduates

business studies noun [U] (**EDUCATION**) the study of subjects connected with managing a business: *a course in business studies*

businesswoman /ˈbɪznəswʊmən/ noun [C] (*pl.* -women /-wɪmɪn/) **1** (**BUSINESS**) a woman who works in business, especially in a top position **2** a woman who is good at dealing with business and financial matters

busk /bʌsk/ verb [I] to sing or play music in the street so that people will give you money

busker /ˈbʌskə(r)/ noun [C] a street musician who asks for money

bus lane noun [C] a part of a road that only buses are allowed to use

bust¹ /bʌst/ verb [T] (*pt, pp* bust, busted) (*informal*) **1** to break or damage sth so that it cannot be used **2** to arrest sb: *He was busted for possession of heroin.*

bust² /bʌst/ adj. **1** (*informal*) broken or not working: *The zip on these trousers is bust.* **2** (used about a business) closed because it has lost so much money: *During the recession thousands of businesses went bust.*
SYN **bankrupt¹**

bust³ /bʌst/ noun [C] **1** (**ART**) a model in stone, etc. of a person's head, shoulders and chest **2** a woman's breasts; the measurement round a woman's chest: *This blouse is a bit too tight around the bust.* **3** (*informal*) an unexpected visit by the police in order to arrest people for doing sth illegal: *a drugs bust*
IDM boom and bust → **BOOM¹**

bustle¹ /ˈbʌsl/ verb **1** [I, T] to move in a busy, noisy or excited way; to make sb move somewhere quickly: *He bustled about the kitchen making tea.* ◇ *They bustled her out of the room before she could see the body.* **2** [I] ~(with sth) to be full of people, noise or activity: *The streets were bustling with shoppers.*

bustle² /ˈbʌsl/ noun [U] excited and noisy activity: *She loved the bustle of city life.*

bust-up noun [C] (*informal*) an argument: *He had a bust-up with his boss over working hours.*

busy¹ ⁊ **A1** /ˈbɪzi/ adj. (busier; busiest) **1** ~(at/with sth); ~(doing sth) having a lot of work or tasks to do; not free; working on sth: *Mr Khan is busy until four o'clock but he could see you after that.* ◇ *Don't disturb him. He's busy.* ◇ *She's busy with her preparations for the party.* ◇ *We're busy decorating the spare room before our visitors arrive.* **2** (used about a period of time) full of activity and things to do: *I've had rather a busy week.* **3** (used about a place) full of people, movement and activity: *The town centre was so busy that you could hardly move.* **4** (*especially AmE*) = **ENGAGED** (3): *The line's busy at the moment. I'll try again later.* ▶ **busily** adv.: *When I came in she was busily typing something on her laptop.*
IDM get busy (*informal*) to start working: *We'll have to get busy if we're going to be ready in time.*

busy² /ˈbɪzi/ verb [T] (busying; busies; *pt, pp* busied) ~yourself (with sth); ~yourself (with) (doing sth) to keep yourself busy; to find sth to do: *She busied herself with the preparations for the party.*

busybody /ˈbɪzibɒdi/ noun [C] (*pl.* -ies) a person who is too interested in other people's private lives

but¹ ⁊ **A1** /bət, *strong form* bʌt/ conj. **1** used for introducing an idea that contrasts with or is different from what has just been said: *The weather will be sunny but cold.* ◇ *Theirs is not the first but the second house on the left.* ◇ *James hasn't got a car but his sister has.* **2** however; and yet: *She's been learning Italian for five years but she doesn't speak it very well.* ◇ *I'd love to come but I can't make it till eight o'clock.*

3 used when you are saying sorry for sth: *Excuse me, but is your name Cynthia Waters?* ◇ *I'm sorry, but I can't stay any longer.* **4** used for introducing a statement that shows that you are surprised or annoyed or that you disagree: '*But that's not possible!*' ◇ '*Here's the book you lent me.*' '*But it's all dirty and torn!*'
IDM but for sb/sth (*formal*) except for or without sb/sth: *We wouldn't have managed but for your help.* but then however; on the other hand: *We could go swimming. But then perhaps it's too cold.* ◇ *He's brilliant at the piano. But then so was his father.* (= so it's not surprising)

but² ⁊ **B2** /bət, *strong form* bʌt/ prep. except: *I've told no one but you about this.* ◇ *We've had nothing but trouble with this washing machine!*

butane /ˈbjuːteɪn/ noun [U] a gas produced from **PETROLEUM**, used in liquid form as a fuel for cooking etc.

butcher¹ /ˈbʊtʃə(r)/ noun [C] **1** a person who sells meat: *The butcher cut me four lamb chops.* **2** butcher's (*pl.* butchers) a shop that sells meat: *She went to the butcher's for some sausages.* ◇ note at **meat** **3** a person who kills a lot of people in a cruel way

butcher² /ˈbʊtʃə(r)/ verb [T] to kill a lot of people in a cruel way

butchery /ˈbʊtʃəri/ noun [U] **1** cruel killing **2** the work of preparing meat to be sold

butler /ˈbʌtlə(r)/ noun [C] the main male servant in a large house

butt¹ /bʌt/ verb [T] to hit sb/sth with your head
PHR V butt in (on sb/sth) to interrupt sb/sth or to join in sth without being asked: *I'm sorry to butt in but could I speak to you urgently for a minute?*

butt² /bʌt/ noun [C] **1** the thicker, heavier end of a weapon or tool: *the butt of a rifle* **2** the short piece of a cigarette that is left when it has been smoked **3** (*especially AmE, informal*) the part of the body that you sit on: *Get up off your butt and do some work!*
SYN **bottom¹** **4** the act of hitting sb/sth with your head
IDM be the butt of sth the person who is often laughed at or talked about in an unkind way

butter¹ ⁊ **A1** /ˈbʌtə(r)/ noun [U] a soft yellow fat that is made from cream and used for spreading on bread, etc. or in cooking: *First, melt a little butter in the pan.* ◇ look at **margarine**

butter² /ˈbʌtə(r)/ verb [T] to spread butter on bread, etc: *I'll cut the bread and you butter it.* ◇ *hot buttered toast*

buttercup /ˈbʌtəkʌp/ noun [C] a wild plant with small shiny yellow flowers that look like cups

butterfly /ˈbʌtəflaɪ/ noun (*pl.* -ies) **1** [C] an insect with a long, thin body and four brightly coloured wings: *Caterpillars develop into butterflies.* ◇ picture at **animal** **2** [U] (**SPORT**) a style of swimming in which both arms are brought over the head at the same time, and the legs move up and down together
IDM have butterflies (in your stomach) (*informal*) to feel very nervous before doing sth

buttermilk /ˈbʌtəmɪlk/ noun [U] the liquid that is left when butter is made from cream

buttock /ˈbʌtək/ noun [C, usually pl.] (**ANATOMY**) either of the two round soft parts at the top of a person's legs ◇ picture at **body**

button ⁊ **A2** /ˈbʌtn/ noun [C] **1** a small, often round, piece of plastic, wood or metal that you use for fastening your clothes: *One of the buttons on my jacket has come off.* ◇ *This blouse is too tight — I can't fasten the buttons.* **2** a small part of a machine, etc. that you press in order to operate sth: *Press the button* to ring the bell. ◇ *Which button turns the volume down?* ◇ *Double-click the right mouse button.* **3** (**COMPUTING**) a small area on a screen that you click on or touch in order to do sth: *To print a file, simply click on the 'print' button.*

buttonhole /ˈbʌtnhəʊl/ *noun* [C] **1** a hole in a piece of clothing that you push a button through in order to fasten it **2** (*BrE*) a flower worn in the buttonhole of a coat or jacket

buttress¹ /ˈbʌtrəs/ *noun* [C] (**ARCHITECTURE**) a stone or BRICK structure that is built against a wall to support it

buttress² /ˈbʌtrəs/ *verb* [T] (*formal*) to support or give strength to sb/sth

buy¹ 🔊 **A1** /baɪ/ *verb* [T] (*pt, pp* **bought** /bɔːt/) ~ **sth (for sb); ~ sb sth** to get sth by paying money for it: *I'm going to buy a new dress for the party.* ◇ *We bought this book for you in London.* ◇ *Can I buy you a coffee?* ◇ *He bought the car from a friend.* ◇ *Did you buy your car new or second-hand?* ◇ *He bought the necklace as a present for his wife.* **OPP** **sell**
IDM **buy time** to do sth in order to delay an event, a decision, etc.
PHR V **buy sb off** (*informal*) to pay sb money, especially dishonestly, to stop them from doing sth you do not want them to do **buy sb out** to pay sb for their share in a house, business, etc. in order to get full control of it yourself

buy² /baɪ/ *noun* [C] an act of buying sth or a thing that you can buy: *I think your house was **a good buy** (= worth the money you paid).*

buyer /ˈbaɪə(r)/ *noun* [C] **1** a person who buys sth, especially sth expensive: *I think we've found a buyer for our house!* **SYN** **purchaser** **OPP** **seller, vendor 2** a person whose job is to choose and buy goods to be sold in a large shop

buyout /ˈbaɪaʊt/ *noun* [C] (**BUSINESS, FINANCE**) the act of buying enough or all of the shares in a company in order to get control of it

buzz¹ /bʌz/ *verb* **1** [I] (used about a bee) to make a low continuous sound **2** [I] to make a sound like a bee buzzing: *The doorbell buzzed loudly.* **3** [I] ~ **(with sth)** to be full of excitement, activity, thoughts, etc: *Her head was buzzing with questions that she wanted to ask.* ◇ *The room was buzzing with activity.* **4** [I, T] to call sb by using an electric bell, etc: *The doctor will buzz for you when he's ready.*

buzz² /bʌz/ *noun* **1** [C] the sound that a bee, etc. makes when flying: *the buzz of insects* **2** [sing.] the low sound made by many people talking at the same time: *I could hear the buzz of conversation in the next room.* **3** [sing.] (*informal*) a strong feeling of excitement or pleasure: *a buzz of expectation* ◇ *Flying first class gave her a real buzz.* ◇ *She **gets a buzz out of** shopping for expensive clothes.*

buzzer /ˈbʌzə(r)/ *noun* [C] a piece of equipment that makes a BUZZING sound: *Press your buzzer if you know the answer to a question.*

buzzword /ˈbʌzwɜːd/ *noun* [C] (**LANGUAGE**) a word or phrase, especially one connected with a particular subject, that has become fashionable and popular

by¹ 🔊 **A1** /baɪ/ *prep.* **1** through doing or using sth; by means of sth: *Turn it on by pressing this button.* ◇ *Will you be paying by cash or card?* ◇ *The house is heated by electricity.* ◇ *'How do you go to work?' 'By train, usually.'* ◇ *by bus/car/plane/bike* ◇ *We went in by the back door.* **2** next to; very near: *Come and sit by me.* ◇ *We stayed in a cottage by the sea.* **3** not later than; before: *I'll be home by seven o'clock.* ◇ *He should have phoned by now/by this time.* **4** (usually used without *the*) during a period of time; in a particular situation: *By day we covered about 30 miles and by night we*

rested. ◇ *The electricity went off so we had to work by candlelight.* **5** used after a passive verb for showing who or what did or caused sth: *She was knocked down by a car.* ◇ *The event was organized by local people.* ◇ *I was deeply shocked by the news.* ◇ *Who was the book written by?/Who is the book by?* **6** used to say that sth happens as a result of sth: *I got on the wrong bus by mistake/accident.* ◇ *I met an old friend by chance.* **7** according to sth: *It's eight o'clock by my watch.* ◇ *By law you have to attend school from the age of 5.* ◇ *She's French by birth.* ◇ *She's a doctor by profession.* **8** (**MATHEMATICS**) used for multiplying or dividing: *4 multiplied by 5 is 20.* ◇ *6 divided by 2 is 3.* **9** used for showing the measurements of an area: *The table is 6 feet by 3 feet* (= 6 feet long and 3 feet wide). **10** (used with *the*) in the quantity or period mentioned: *You can rent a car by the day, the week or the month.* ◇ *Copies of the book have sold by the million.* ◇ *They came in one by one.* ◇ *Day by day she was getting better.* **11** to the amount mentioned: *Prices have gone up by 10 per cent.* ◇ *I missed the bus by a few minutes.* **12** (used with a part of the body or an article of clothing) holding: *He grabbed me by the arm.*
IDM **by the way** → WAY¹

by² 🔊 **B1** /baɪ/ *adv.* past: *He walked straight by without speaking.* ◇ *We stopped to let the ambulance get by.*
IDM **by and large** → LARGE

by- (*also* **bye-**) /baɪ/ *prefix* (in nouns and verbs) **1** less important: *a by-product* **2** near: *a bystander*

bycatch /ˈbaɪkætʃ/ *noun* [U] fish that are caught by ships by accident when other types of fish are being caught: *Thousands of small fish are thrown back into the sea as bycatch.*

bye 🔊 **A1** /baɪ/ (*also* **bye-'bye**) *exclamation* (*informal*) goodbye: *Bye! See you tomorrow.*

bye-law = BY-LAW

by-election *noun* [C] (*BrE*) (**POLITICS**) an election to choose a new Member of Parliament to replace sb who has died or left parliament ⊃ look at **general election**

bygone /ˈbaɪɡɒn/ *adj.* [only before noun] that happened a long time ago: *a bygone era*

bygones /ˈbaɪɡɒnz/ *noun* [pl.]
IDM **let bygones be bygones** to decide to forget arguments that happened in the past

by-law (*also* **bye-law**) *noun* [C] (*BrE*) (**LAW**) a law that is made by a local authority and that has to be obeyed only in that area

bypass¹ /ˈbaɪpɑːs/ *noun* [C] **1** (*especially BrE*) a road that traffic can use to go round a town, instead of through it ⊃ look at **ring road 2** (**MEDICINE**) a medical operation to send blood along a different route so that it does not go through a part that is damaged or blocked, especially to improve blood flow to the heart: *a triple bypass operation* ◇ *heart bypass surgery*

bypass² /ˈbaɪpɑːs/ *verb* [T] to go around or to avoid sth using a BYPASS: *Let's try to bypass the city centre.* ◇ (*figurative*) *It's no good trying to bypass the problem.*

by-product *noun* [C] **1** something that is formed during the making of sth else **2** something that happens as the result of sth else

bystander /ˈbaɪstændə(r)/ *noun* [C] a person who is standing near and sees sth that happens, without being involved in it: *Several **innocent bystanders** were hurt when the two gangs attacked each other.*

byte /baɪt/ *noun* [C] (**COMPUTING**) a unit of information stored in a computer, equal to 8 BITS. Computer memory is measured in bytes.

byword /ˈbaɪwɜːd/ *noun* [C, usually sing.] **1** ~ **for sth** a person or a thing that is a typical or well-known example of a particular quality: *A limousine is a byword for luxury.* **2** (*especially AmE*) a word or phrase that is often used

Byzantine /baɪˈzæntaɪn, bɪ-/ *adj.* **1** (HISTORY) connected with Byzantium or the Eastern Roman Empire **2** (ARCHITECTURE) used to describe architecture of the fifth to the fifteenth centuries in the Byzantine Empire: *a Byzantine church*

C c

C¹ /siː/ *noun* [C, U] (*pl.* C's) **1** (*also* c, *pl.* c's) the third letter of the English alphabet: *'Car' begins with (a) 'C'.* **2** (MUSIC) the first note in the SCALE of C MAJOR **3** ~ (in/ for sth) (EDUCATION) a grade given for an exam or a piece of work that shows that it is acceptable but not good or excellent: *She got a C in physics.*

C² *abbr.* (in writing) **1** = CELSIUS: *Water freezes at 0°C.* **2** (*also* c) = CENTURY (1) **3** (*pl.* C) = COULOMB

c *abbr.* (in writing) **1** (*pl.* c) = CENT **2** = CIRCA: *c 1770*

cab /kæb/ *noun* [C] **1** = TAXI¹: *Let's take a cab/go by cab.* **2** the part of a lorry, train, bus, etc. where the driver sits

cabaret /ˈkæbəreɪ/ *noun* [C, U] (ARTS AND MEDIA) entertainment with singing, dancing, etc. in a restaurant or club

cabbage /ˈkæbɪdʒ/ *noun* [C, U] a large round vegetable with thick green, dark red or white leaves: *Cabbages are easy to grow.* ◇ *Do you like cabbage?*

cabin 🔑 B2 /ˈkæbɪn/ *noun* [C] **1** a small room on a ship in which you live or sleep **2** one of the areas for passengers to sit in a plane ◯ picture at **airliner** **3** a small house or shelter, usually made of wood: *a log cabin*

cabin crew *noun* [C + sing./pl. verb] (TOURISM) the people whose job is to take care of passengers on a plane: *A member of the cabin crew demonstrated the safety procedures.*

cabin cruiser = CRUISER (2)

cabinet 🔑+ C1 /ˈkæbɪnət/ *noun* [C] **1** (*usually* the Cabinet) [+ sing./pl. verb] (POLITICS) a group of senior members of a government that is responsible for advising and deciding on government policy: *a cabinet meeting* ◇ (*BrE*) **the shadow Cabinet** (= the most important members of the opposition party) ◇ (*BrE*) *a cabinet minister* **2** a cupboard with shelves or DRAWERS, used for storing things: *a medicine cabinet* ◇ *a filing cabinet*

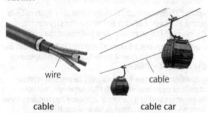

wire

cable

cable

cable car

cable 🔑 B2 /ˈkeɪbl/ *noun* **1** [C, U] a set of wires covered with plastic, etc., for carrying electricity or signals: *underground/overhead cables* ◇ *a phone cable*

◇ *2 metres of cable* **2** [C] a thick strong metal rope **3** [U] = CABLE TV

cable car *noun* [C] a vehicle like a box that hangs on a moving metal cable and carries passengers up and down a mountain ◯ picture at **cable**

cable TV (*also* cable, ˌcable ˈtelevision) *noun* [U] (ARTS AND MEDIA) a system of sending out TV programmes along wires instead of by radio waves

cache¹ /kæʃ/ *noun* [C] **1** a hidden store of things such as weapons **2** (COMPUTING) a part of a computer's memory that stores copies of data that is often needed while a program is running. This data can be found very quickly.

cache² /kæʃ/ *verb* [T] **1** to store things in a secret place, especially weapons **2** (COMPUTING) to store data in a CACHE

cackle /ˈkækl/ *verb* [I] to laugh in a loud, unpleasant way ▶ **cackle** *noun* [C]

cactus /ˈkæktəs/ *noun* [C] (*pl.* cactuses, cacti /-taɪ/) a type of plant that grows in hot, dry areas, especially deserts. A cactus has a thick STEM (= the central part) and sharp, pointed parts but no leaves.

CAD /kæd, ˌsiː eɪ ˈdiː/ *noun* [U] (COMPUTING) the use of computers to design machines, buildings, vehicles, etc. (the abbreviation for 'computer-aided design')

cadaver /kəˈdævə(r)/ *noun* [C] (*formal*) the body of a dead person

cadence /ˈkeɪdns/ *noun* [C] **1** (*formal*) the rise and fall of the voice in speaking **2** (MUSIC) the end of a musical phrase

cadenza /kəˈdenzə/ *noun* [C] (MUSIC) a short passage that is put into a piece of music to be played by one musician alone, and that shows the skill of that musician

cadet /kəˈdet/ *noun* [C] a young person who is training to be in the police or the armed forces

cadge /kædʒ/ *verb* [I, T] ~ (sth) (from/off sb) (*BrE*, *informal*) to try to persuade sb to give or lend you sth: *He's always trying to cadge money off me.*

cadmium /ˈkædmiəm/ *noun* [U] (*symb.* Cd) (CHEMISTRY) a chemical element. Cadmium is a soft poisonous blue-white metal used in batteries. ❶ For more information on the periodic table of elements, look at the **Reference Section** of this dictionary.

caesarean (*also* caesarian) (*both BrE*) (*AmE* cesarean) /sɪˈzeəriən/ = CAESAREAN SECTION

cae,sarean ˈsection (*also* caesarian section) (*both BrE*) (*AmE* cesarean section) (*also* C-section *especially in AmE*) *noun* [C, U] (MEDICINE) a medical operation in which an opening is cut in a mother's body in order to take out the baby when a normal birth would be impossible or dangerous

caesium (*BrE*) (*AmE* cesium) /ˈsiːziəm/ *noun* [U] (*symb.* Cs) (CHEMISTRY) a chemical element. Caesium is a soft silver-white metal that reacts strongly in water. ❶ For more information on the periodic table of elements, look at the **Reference Section** of this dictionary.

cafe 🔑 A1 (*also* café) /ˈkæfeɪ/ *noun* [C] a small restaurant that serves drinks and light meals

cafeteria /ˌkæfəˈtɪəriə/ *noun* [C] a restaurant, especially one for workers, where people collect their meals themselves and carry them to their tables ◯ look at **canteen**

cafetière /ˌkæfəˈtjeə(r)/ (*BrE*) (*AmE* French press™) *noun* [C] a special glass container for making coffee with a FILTER (= a metal part that you push down) ◯ look at **percolator**

caffeine /'kæfi:n/ *noun* [U] the substance found in coffee and tea that makes you feel more active ⊃ look at **decaffeinated**

cage /keɪdʒ/ *noun* [C] a box made of bars or wire, or a space surrounded by wire or metal bars, in which a bird or animal is kept so that it cannot escape: *a birdcage* ▸ **cage** *verb* [T] ▸ **caged** *adj.*: *He felt like a caged animal in the tiny office.*

cagey /'keɪdʒi/ *adj.* (cagier; cagiest) ~ **(about sth)** (*informal*) not wanting to give information or to talk about sth

cagoule /kə'ɡu:l/ *noun* [C] a long, light jacket with a HOOD (= a part that covers your head) that protects you from the rain or wind

cajole /kə'dʒəʊl/ *verb* [T, I] ~ **(sb) (into sth/doing sth)**; ~ **sth out of sb** to make sb do sth by talking to them and being very nice to them: *He cajoled me into agreeing to do the work.* ◊ *I managed to cajole their address out of him.* **SYN** coax

cake¹ 🔊 **A1** /keɪk/ *noun* **1** [C, U] a sweet food made by mixing flour, eggs, butter, sugar, etc. together and baking the mixture in the oven: *to make/bake a cake* ◊ *a wedding cake* ◊ *a piece/slice of birthday cake* ◊ *Would you like some more cake?* **2** [C] a mixture of other food, cooked in a round, flat shape: *fish/potato cakes*
IDM **have your cake and eat it** (*BrE*) to enjoy the advantages of sth without its disadvantages; to have both things that are available **a piece of cake** → PIECE¹

cake² /keɪk/ *verb* [T, usually passive] **be caked (in/with sth)** to be covered with a thick layer of sth soft that becomes hard when it dries: *boots caked in mud*

calamity /kə'læməti/ *noun* [C, U] (*pl.* -ies) a terrible event that causes a lot of damage or harm **SYN** disaster

calcify /'kælsɪfaɪ/ *verb* [I, T] (calcifying; calcifies; *pt, pp* calcified) (CHEMISTRY, GEOLOGY) to become hard when CALCIUM salts are added; to make sth hard by adding CALCIUM salts ▸ **calcification** /ˌkælsɪfɪ'keɪʃn/ *noun* [U]

calcium /'kælsiəm/ *noun* [U] (*symb.* Ca) (CHEMISTRY) a chemical element. Calcium is a soft silver-white metal found in bones, teeth and CHALK. ❶ For more information on the periodic table of elements, look at the **Reference Section** of this dictionary.

calcium carbonate *noun* [U] (*symb.* CaCO₃) (CHEMISTRY) a white solid that exists naturally as CHALK, LIMESTONE and MARBLE

calculate 🔊 **B2** /'kælkjuleɪt/ *verb* [T] **1** (MATHEMATICS) to find sth out by using mathematics; to work sth out: *It's difficult to calculate how long the project will take.* **2** ~ **(that)** to consider or expect sth: *We calculated that the advantages would be greater than the disadvantages.*
IDM **be calculated to do sth** to be intended or designed to do sth: *His remark was clearly calculated to annoy me.*

calculating /'kælkjuleɪtɪŋ/ *adj.* planning things in a very careful way in order to achieve what you want, without considering other people: *Her cold, calculating approach made her many enemies.*

calculation 🔊+ **C1** /ˌkælkju'leɪʃn/ *noun* **1** [C, U] (MATHEMATICS) (the act of) finding an answer by using mathematics: *I'll have to do a few calculations before telling you how much I can afford.* ◊ *Calculation of the exact cost is impossible.* **2** [U] (*formal*) careful planning in order to achieve what you want, without considering other people: *His actions were clearly the result of deliberate calculation.*

calculator /'kælkjuleɪtə(r)/ *noun* [C] a small electronic device or piece of software used for calculating with numbers: *a pocket calculator*

calculus /'kælkjələs/ *noun* [U] (MATHEMATICS) a type of mathematics that deals with rates of change, for example the speed of a falling object

caldron /'kɔːldrən/ (*especially AmE*) = CAULDRON

calendar /'kælɪndə(r)/ *noun* [C] **1** a list that shows the days, weeks and months of a particular year **2** a system for dividing time into fixed periods and for marking the beginning and end of a year: *the Islamic calendar* **3** [usually sing.] a list of dates and events in a year that are important in a particular area of activity: *Wimbledon is a major event in the sporting calendar.*

calendar month = MONTH

calendar year = YEAR (1)

calf /kɑːf/ *noun* [C] (*pl.* calves /kɑːvz/) **1** a young cow ⊃ note at COW **2** a young animal of some other type such as a young elephant or WHALE (= a very large sea animal) **3** (ANATOMY) the back of the leg, between the ankle and the knee: *I've strained a calf muscle.* ⊃ picture at **body**

calibrate /'kælɪbreɪt/ *verb* [T] to mark units of measurement on an instrument such as a THERMOMETER so that it can be used for measuring sth accurately

calibration /ˌkælɪ'breɪʃn/ *noun* **1** [U] the act of CALIBRATING: *a calibration error* **2** [C] the units of measurement marked on a THERMOMETER or other instrument

calibre (*AmE* caliber) /'kælɪbə(r)/ *noun* **1** [U] the quality of sth, especially a person's ability: *He was impressed by the high calibre of applicants for the job.* **2** [C] the measurement from one side of the inside of a tube or gun to the other; the measurement from one side of a bullet to the other

calico /'kælɪkəʊ/ *noun* [U] **1** (*especially BrE*) a type of heavy cotton cloth that is usually plain white **2** (*especially AmE*) a type of rough cotton cloth that has a pattern printed on it

californium /ˌkælɪ'fɔːniəm/ *noun* [U] (*symb.* Cf) (CHEMISTRY) a chemical element. Californium is a RADIOACTIVE metal produced artificially from CURIUM or AMERICIUM. ❶ For more information on the periodic table of elements, look at the **Reference Section** of this dictionary.

caliper /'kælɪpə(r)/ = CALLIPER

CALL /kɔːl/ *abbr.* (EDUCATION) **computer-assisted language learning** (the use of computers to help people learn languages)

call¹ 🔊 **A1** ❺ /kɔːl/ *verb*
• SHOUT **1** [I, T] ~ **(out) to sb**; ~ **(sth) (out)** to say sth loudly or to shout in order to attract attention: *'Hello, is anybody there?' she called.* ◊ *He called out the names and the winners stepped forward.* ◊ *I could hear a man calling his dog.*
• PHONE **2** [I, T] to phone sb: *Who's calling, please?* ◊ *I'll call you tomorrow.* **SYN** phone², phone²
• NAME **3** [T] ~ **sb sth** to give sb/sth a particular name or describe them/it in a certain way: *They called the baby Evie.* ◊ *It was very rude to call her fat.* ◊ *Are you calling me a liar?*
• ORDER SB TO COME **4** [T] to order or ask sb to come to a certain place: *Can you call everybody in for lunch?* ◊ *I think we had better call the doctor.*
• ARRANGE **5** [T] to arrange for sth to take place at a certain time: *to call a meeting/an election/a strike* ⊃ note at **meeting**
• VISIT **6** [I] ~ **(in/round) (on sb/at …)** to make a short visit to a person or place: *I called in on Mike on my way*

home. ◇ *We called at his house but there was nobody in.*

IDM bring/call sb/sth to mind → MIND[1] call sb's bluff to tell sb to actually do what they are threatening to do (believing that they will not risk doing it) call it a day (*informal*) to decide to stop doing sth: *Let's call it a day. I'm exhausted.* call sb names to use offensive words about sb call the shots/tune (*informal*) to be in a position to control a situation and make decisions about what should be done

PHR V call at … (*BrE*) (used about a train, etc.) to stop at a place for a short time: *This train calls at Didcot and Reading.* call back | call sb back to phone sb again or to phone sb who phoned you early: *She said she'd call back.* ◇ *We're just in the middle of dinner. Can I call you back later?* call by (*informal*) to make a short visit to a place or person as you pass: *I'll call by to pick up the book on my way to work.* call for sb (*BrE*) to collect sb in order to go somewhere together: *I'll call for you when it's time to go.* call for sth to demand or need sth: *The crisis calls for immediate action.* ◇ *This calls for a celebration!* call sth off to cancel sth: *The football match was called off because of the bad weather.* ⊃ note at **meeting** call sb out to ask sb to come, especially to an emergency: *We had to call out the doctor in the middle of the night.* call sb up **1** (*especially AmE*) to phone sb: *He called me up to tell me the good news.* **2** to make sb join the army, etc. call sth up to look at sth that is stored in a computer: *The bank clerk called up my account details on screen.*

call² ʔ **A1** /kɔːl/ *noun*

• ACT OF PHONING **1** (*also* phone call) [C] an act of phoning or a conversation on a phone: *Were there any calls for me while I was out?* ◇ *I'll give you a call at the weekend.* ◇ *to make a local call* ◇ *a long-distance call*

• SHOUT **2** [C] ~ (for sth) a loud sound that is made to attract attention; a shout: *a call for help* ◇ *That bird's call is easy to recognize.*

• VISIT **3** [C] a short visit, especially to sb's house: *We could pay a call on Dave on our way home.*

• REQUEST/DEMAND **4** [C] ~ for sth a request or demand for sth: *There have been calls for the president to resign.* **5** [C, U] no ~ (for sth) no demand for sth; no reason for sb's behaviour: *The doctor said there was no call for concern.*

IDM at sb's beck and call → BECK (be) on call (to be) ready to work if necessary: *Dr Young will be on call this weekend.*

'call centre (*BrE*) (*AmE* call center) *noun* [C] (BUSINESS) an office in which many people work using telephones, for example taking customers' orders or answering questions

called /kɔːld/ *adj.* [not before noun] to have a particular name: *His wife is called Vanessa.* ◇ *I don't know anyone called Alex.*

caller /ˈkɔːlə(r)/ *noun* [C] a person who phones or visits sb

calligraphy /kəˈlɪɡrəfi/ *noun* [U] (ART) beautiful HANDWRITING that you do with a special pen or brush; the art of producing this

calliper (*BrE*) (*also* caliper *BrE, AmE*) /ˈkælɪpə(r)/ *noun* **1** callipers [pl.] (GEOMETRY) an instrument with two long thin parts joined at one end, used for measuring the DIAMETER of tubes and round objects (= the distance across them) **2** (*AmE* brace) [C, usually pl.] (MEDICINE) a metal support for weak or injured legs

callous /ˈkæləs/ *adj.* not caring about the suffering of other people **SYN** cruel

callus /ˈkæləs/ *noun* [C] an area of thick hard skin on a hand or foot, usually caused by rubbing

calm¹ ʔ **B1** /kɑːm/ *adj.* **1** not excited, worried or angry; quiet: *Try to keep calm — there's no need to panic.* ◇ *She spoke in a calm voice.* ◇ *The city is calm again after last night's riots.* **2** (used about the sea) without big waves: *a calm sea* **OPP** rough¹ **3** (used about the weather) without much wind: *a calm, cloudless day* ▸ calmly *adv.*: *'I'll call the doctor,' he said calmly.* ▸ calmness *noun* [U]

calm² ʔ **B1** /kɑːm/ *verb* [I, T] ~ (sb/sth) (down) to become or to make sb quiet or calm: *Calm down! Shouting at everybody won't help.* ◇ *I did some breathing exercises to calm my nerves.*

calm³ ʔ **B1** /kɑːm/ *noun* [C, U] a period of time or a state when everything is peaceful: *After living in the city, I enjoyed the calm of country life.*

Calor gas™ /ˈkælə ɡæs/ (*BrE*) (*AmE* cooking gas) *noun* [U] a type of gas that is kept in special containers and used for heating and cooking in places where there is no gas supply

calorie /ˈkæləri/ *noun* [C] **1** a unit for measuring how much energy food will produce: *A fried egg contains about 100 calories.* ◇ *a low-calorie drink/yogurt/diet* **2** (PHYSICS) a unit for measuring a quantity of heat; the amount of heat needed to increase the temperature of a GRAM of water by one degree Celsius

calorific /ˌkæləˈrɪfɪk/ *adj.* **1** (PHYSICS) connected with or producing heat: *the calorific value of food* (= the amount of heat or energy produced by a particular amount of food) **2** (used about food and drink) containing a lot of CALORIES (= units for measuring energy) and likely to make you fat: *calorific chocolate cake*

calque /kælk/ (*also* loan translation) *noun* [C] (LANGUAGE) a word or expression in a language that translates exactly a word or expression in another language: *'Traffic calming' is a calque of the German 'Verkehrsberuhigung'.*

calve /kɑːv/ *verb* **1** [I] (used about a cow) to give birth to a CALF (= a young cow) **2** [I, T] (GEOGRAPHY) (used about a large piece of ice) to break away from an ICEBERG or a GLACIER (= a mass of ice that moves slowly down a valley); to lose a piece of ice in this way ⊃ picture at **glacial**

calves /kɑːvz/ *plural of* **calf**

calypso /kəˈlɪpsəʊ/ *noun* [C, U] (pl. -os) (MUSIC) a Caribbean song about a subject of current interest; this type of music

calyx /ˈkeɪlɪks/ *noun* [C] (pl. calyxes, calyces /-lɪsiːz/) (BIOLOGY) the ring of SEPALS (= small green leaves) that protect a flower before it opens

CAM /kæm/ *abbr.* (COMPUTING) computer-aided manufacturing (the use of computers to make products in factories)

camber /ˈkæmbə(r)/ *noun* [C] a slight curve that goes downwards from the middle of a road to each side

cambium /ˈkæmbiəm/ *noun* [U] (BIOLOGY) a layer of cells inside the STEM of a plant. Cambium cells grow into material that is needed to feed the plant.

came /keɪm/ *past tense of* **come**

camel /ˈkæml/ *noun* [C] an animal that lives in the desert and has a long neck and either one or two HUMPS (= large masses of fat) on its back. Camels are used for carrying people and goods.

cameo /ˈkæmiəʊ/ *noun* [C] (pl. -os) **1** (ARTS AND MEDIA) a small part in a film or play that is usually played by a famous actor: *Ryan Reynolds plays a cameo role as the dying king.* **2** a piece of jewellery that has a raised design in one colour and a background in a different colour

camera 🔊 **A1** /'kæmrə/ *noun* [C] a piece of equipment that you use for taking photos or moving pictures: *I took the photo with the camera on my phone.* ◇ *a digital/video/TV camera*

cameraman /'kæmrəmæn/ *noun* [C] (*pl.* -men /-men/) (**ARTS AND MEDIA**) a man whose job is to operate a camera for a film or a TV company ◑ look at **photographer**

camerawoman /'kæmrəwʊmən/ *noun* [C] (*pl.* -women /-wɪmɪn/) (**ARTS AND MEDIA**) a woman whose job is to operate a camera for a film or a TV company ◑ look at **photographer**

camerawork /'kæmrəwɜːk/ *noun* [U] (**ARTS AND MEDIA**) the style in which sb takes photos or uses a film camera

camouflage /'kæməflɑːʒ/ *noun* [U] **1** materials or colours that soldiers use to make themselves and their equipment difficult to see **2** the way in which an animal's colour or shape matches what is around it and makes it difficult to see: *The polar bear's white fur provides effective camouflage against the snow.*
▶ **camouflage** *verb* [T]

camp¹ 🔊 **A2** /kæmp/ *noun* **1** [C, U] a place where people live in tents or simple buildings away from their usual home: *The climbers set up camp at the foot of the mountain.* **2** [C] (in compounds) a place where people are kept in temporary buildings or tents, especially by a government and often for long periods: *a refugee camp* ◇ *camp guards* ◑ look at **concentration camp**

camp² 🔊 **A2** /kæmp/ *verb* [I] ~ **(out)** to sleep without a bed, especially outside in a tent: *We camped next to a river.* ◇ *Shoppers camped out on the pavement waiting for the store to open.* ◇ *They're going camping next week.*

campaign¹ 🔊 **B1** /kæm'peɪn/ *noun* [C] **1** (**BUSINESS, POLITICS**) a plan to do a number of things in order to achieve a special aim: *to launch an advertising/election campaign* **2** a planned series of attacks in a war: *a bombing campaign*

▼ SYNONYMS

campaign

battle ♦ **struggle** ♦ **drive** ♦ **war** ♦ **fight**

These are all words for an effort made to achieve or prevent sth.

campaign *the campaign for reform*

battle *to win a legal battle*

struggle *the struggle for independence*

drive *a drive to reduce carbon emissions*

war *the war against drugs*

fight *a fight for justice*

campaign² 🔊 **B1** /kæm'peɪn/ *verb* [I] ~ **(for/against sb/sth)** (**POLITICS**) to take part in a planned series of activities in order to make sth happen or to prevent sth: *Local people are campaigning for lower speed limits in the town.* ▶ **campaigner** *noun* [C]: *an animal rights campaigner*

'**camp bed** (*BrE*) (*AmE* cot) *noun* [C] a light narrow bed that you can fold up and carry easily

camper /'kæmpə(r)/ *noun* [C] **1** (**TOURISM**) a person who stays in a tent on holiday **2** (*also* 'camper van) (*both BrE*) (*AmE* **RV, recreational vehicle**) (**TOURISM**) a large vehicle in which you can sleep, cook, etc. when you are on holiday **3** (*AmE*) = CARAVAN (1)

camping 🔊 **A2** /'kæmpɪŋ/ *noun* [U] (**TOURISM**) living in a tent, etc. on holiday: *Camping is cheaper than staying in hotels.* ◇ *to go on a camping holiday*

campsite /'kæmpsaɪt/ *noun* [C] (**TOURISM**) a place where people on holiday can put up their tents, park their CARAVAN, etc., often with toilets, water, etc.

campus 🔊 **B1** /'kæmpəs/ *noun* [C, U] (**EDUCATION**) the area of land where the main buildings of a college or university are: *She lives on campus* (= within the main university area) ◇ *the college campus* ◇ *strategies for safety on and off campus*

can¹ 🔊 **A1** ❺ /kən, *strong form* kæn/ *modal verb* (*negative* cannot /'kænɒt/; *short form* can't /kɑːnt/; *pt, pp* could /kəd, *strong form* kʊd/; *negative* could not /'kʊd nɒt/; *short form* couldn't /'kʊdnt/)

• ABILITY **1** used to say that it is possible for sb/sth to do sth or that sb/sth has the ability to do sth: *Can you ride a bike?* ◇ *He can't speak French.*
• PERMISSION **2** used to ask for or give permission: *Can I have a drink, please?* ◇ *He asked if he could have a drink.*
• REQUEST **3** used to ask sb to do sth: *Can you help me carry these books?*
• OFFER **4** used for offering to do sth: *Can I help at all?*
• POSSIBILITY **5** used to talk about sb's typical behaviour or about a typical effect: *You can be very annoying.* ◇ *Wasp stings can be very painful.*
• PROBABILITY **6** used in the negative for saying that you are sure sth is not true: *That can't be Maria — she's in London.* ◇ *Surely you can't be hungry. You've only just had lunch.*
• SENSES **7** used with the verbs *feel, hear, see, smell, taste*: *I can smell something burning.*

can² 🔊 **A2** /kæn/ *noun* [C] **1** a metal container in which food or drink is kept without air so that it stays fresh; the contents of one of these containers: *a can of sardines* ◇ *a can of coke* **2** a metal or plastic container that is used for holding or carrying liquid: *an oil can* ◇ *a watering can*

can³ /kæn/ *verb* [T] (-nn-) to put food, drink, etc. into a can in order to keep it fresh for a long time: *canned fruit*

canal 🔊+ **B2** /kə'næl/ *noun* [C] **1** (**GEOGRAPHY**) a deep cut that is made through land and filled with water for boats or ships to travel along; a smaller cut used for carrying water to fields, crops, etc. **2** (**ANATOMY**) a tube inside the body through which liquid, food or air can pass ◑ look at **alimentary canal, ear canal**

ca'**nal boat** *noun* [C] a long narrow boat used on CANALS

cancel 🔊 **B2** /'kænsl/ *verb* [T] (-ll-, *AmE* -l-) **1** to decide that sth that has been planned or arranged will not happen: *All flights have been cancelled because of the bad weather.* ◑ look at **postpone** ◑ note at **meeting** **2** to stop sth that you asked for or agreed to: *to cancel a reservation* ◇ *I wish to cancel my order for these books.* ◇ *There is no charge if you cancel within two weeks.*

camper/RV   caravan/camper

PHR V cancel (sth) out to be equal or have an equal effect: *What I owe you is the same as what you owe me, so our debts cancel each other out.*

cancellation /ˌkænsəˈleɪʃn/ *noun* [C, U] the act of cancelling sth: *We had to make a last-minute cancellation.* ◇ *Call the doctor and see it there are any cancellations. You might get an appointment today.*

Cancer /ˈkænsə(r)/ *noun* [C, U] the fourth sign of THE ZODIAC (= twelve signs that represent the positions of the sun, moon and planets), the Crab; a person born under this sign

cancer 🔒 **B2** /ˈkænsə(r)/ *noun* [U, C] (**HEALTH**) a very serious disease in which cells that kill normal body cells grow in the body: *She has lung cancer.* ◇ *He died of cancer.* ◇ *Most skin cancers can be cured.*

cancerous /ˈkænsərəs/ *adj.* (**HEALTH**) (used especially about a part of the body or sth growing in the body) having cancer: *a cancerous growth* ◇ *cancerous cells*

candid /ˈkændɪd/ *adj.* saying exactly what you think **SYN** frank ⊃ noun **candour** ▶ candidly *adv.*

candidacy /ˈkændɪdəsi/ *noun* [C, U] (*pl.* -ies) (**POLITICS**) the fact of being a candidate in an election

candidate 🔒 **B1** /ˈkændɪdət, -deɪt/ *noun* [C] 1 ~ (for sth) a person who is trying to be elected or is applying for a job: *We have some very good candidates for the post.* ⊃ note at **election** 2 (**EDUCATION**) a person who is taking an exam

candle 🔒+ **B2** /ˈkændl/ *noun* [C] a round stick of WAX (= solid oil or fat) with a WICK (= a piece of string) through the middle that you can burn to give light: *to light/blow out a candle*

candlelight /ˈkændllaɪt/ *noun* [U] light that comes from a CANDLE: *They had dinner by candlelight.*

candlestick /ˈkændlstɪk/ *noun* [C] an object for holding a CANDLE or CANDLES

candour (*BrE*) (*AmE* candor) /ˈkændə(r)/ *noun* [U] the quality of being honest; saying exactly what you think ⊃ adjective **candid**

candy /ˈkændi/ *noun* [U, C] (*pl.* -ies) (*AmE*) = SWEET² (1): *You eat too much candy.*

cane /keɪn/ *noun* 1 [C, U] the long, hard central part of certain plants, for example BAMBOO (= a tall tropical plant), that is like a tube and is used as a material for making furniture, etc: *sugar cane* ◇ *a cane chair* 2 [C] a stick that is used to help sb walk

canine¹ /ˈkeɪnaɪn/ *adj.* (**BIOLOGY**) connected with dogs

canine² /ˈkeɪnaɪn/ (*also* ˈcanine tooth) *noun* [C] (**ANATOMY**) one of the four pointed teeth in the front of a person's or an animal's mouth ⊃ look at **incisor, molar, premolar** ⊃ picture at **tooth**

canister /ˈkænɪstə(r)/ *noun* [C] a small round metal container: *a gas canister*

cannabis /ˈkænəbɪs/ *noun* [U] a drug made from HEMP (= a type of plant) that some people smoke in order to feel relaxed, but that is illegal in many countries

cannibal /ˈkænɪbl/ *noun* [C] a person who eats other people ▶ cannibalism /-bəlɪzəm/ *noun* [U]

cannon /ˈkænən/ *noun* [C] (*pl.* cannon, cannons) 1 a gun that fires many shots from an aircraft, etc. 2 a large, heavy gun that was used in the past for firing large stone or metal balls

cannot 🔒 **A1** /ˈkænɒt/ → CAN¹

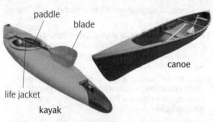

paddle blade canoe life jacket kayak

canoe /kəˈnuː/ *noun* [C] a light narrow boat for one or two people that you can move through the water using a PADDLE (= a flat piece of wood) ▶ canoe *verb* [I] (canoeing; canoes; *pt, pp* canoed): *They canoed down the river.*

canoeing /kəˈnuːɪŋ/ *noun* [U] (**SPORT**) the sport of travelling in or racing a CANOE: *We're going canoeing on the river tomorrow.*

canola /kəˈnəʊlə/ *noun* [U] a kind of RAPESEED seed that is grown widely in North America

canon /ˈkænən/ *noun* [C] 1 (**RELIGION**) a Christian priest with special duties in a CATHEDRAL (= the largest church in a district) 2 (*formal*) a generally accepted rule, standard or principle by which sth is judged: *the canons of good taste* 3 (**LITERATURE**) a list of books or other works that are generally accepted as the real work of a particular writer or as being important: *the Shakespeare canon* 4 (**MUSIC**) a piece of music in which singers or instruments take it in turns to repeat the tune

ˈcan opener (*especially AmE*) = TIN OPENER

canopy /ˈkænəpi/ *noun* [C] (*pl.* -ies) 1 a cover that hangs or spreads above sth: *The canopy will be installed to provide shade over the playground.* 2 (**ENVIRONMENT**) a thick layer of branches and leaves that spreads over a forest like a roof: *The highest branches in the rainforest form a dense canopy.*

can't /kɑːnt/ *short form* can not

canteen /kænˈtiːn/ *noun* [C] the place in a school, factory, office, etc. where the people who work there can get meals: *the staff canteen* ⊃ look at **cafeteria**

canter /ˈkæntə(r)/ *verb* [I] (used about a horse and its rider) to run fairly fast but not very: *We cantered along the beach.* ⊃ look at **gallop, trot¹** (1) ▶ canter *noun* [sing.]

cantilever /ˈkæntɪliːvə(r)/ *noun* [C] (**ARCHITECTURE**) a long piece of metal, concrete or wood that sticks out from a wall to support a bridge, roof, or other structure: *a cantilever bridge*

Cantonese /ˌkæntəˈniːz/ *noun* [U] (**LANGUAGE**) a form of Chinese spoken mainly in southern China, including Hong Kong

canvas 🔒+ **C1** /ˈkænvəs/ *noun* 1 [U] a type of strong cloth that is used for making sails, bags, tents, etc. 2 [C] (**ART**) a piece of strong material used by artists for painting a picture on

canvass /ˈkænvəs/ *verb* 1 [I, T] ~ (sb) (for sth) (**POLITICS**) to try to persuade people to vote for a particular person or party in an election or to support sb/sth: *to canvass for votes* ◇ *He's canvassing for the Conservative Party.* ◇ *Party activists are canvassing voters in the run-up to the election.* ◇ *The prime minister is trying to canvass support for the plan.* 2 [T] ~ (sb/sth) (for sth) to find out what people's opinions are about sth: *The council canvassed residents for their views on the new bridge.*

canyon /ˈkænjən/ *noun* [C] (**GEOGRAPHY**) a deep valley with very steep sides of rock

canyoning /ˈkænjənɪŋ/ (*AmE also* **canyoneering** /ˌkænjəˈnɪərɪŋ/) *noun* [U] (**SPORT**) a sport in which you jump into a mountain stream and allow yourself to be carried down at high speed

cap¹ ⟨A1⟩ /kæp/ *noun* [C] **1** a type of soft hat with a PEAK (= a hard part sticking out in front): *a baseball cap* **2** a soft hat that is worn for a particular purpose: *a shower cap* **3** (*BrE*) (**SPORT**) a hat that is given to a player who is chosen to play for their country: *She won her first cap against France.* **4** a covering for the end or top of sth: *Please put the cap back on the bottle.*

cap² /kæp/ *verb* [T] (**-pp-**) **1** [usually passive] to cover the top of sth: *mountains capped with snow* **2** to limit the amount of money that can be spent on sth: *a capped mortgage* **3** to follow sth with sth bigger or better **4** [usually passive] (**MEDICINE**) to put an artificial covering on a tooth to make it look more attractive or to protect it: *He's had his front teeth capped.* **5** [usually passive] (*BrE*) (**SPORT**) to choose sb to play in their country's national team for a particular sport **IDM to cap it all** (*informal*) as a final piece of bad luck: *I had a row with my boss, my bike was stolen, and now to cap it all I've lost my keys!*

capability ⟨C1⟩ **W** /ˌkeɪpəˈbɪləti/ *noun* [C, U] (*pl.* **-ies**) **~ (to do sth/of doing sth)** the quality of being able to do sth: *I tried to fix the computer, but it was **beyond** my capabilities.* ◇ *Animals in the zoo have lost the capability to catch/of catching food for themselves.*

capable ⟨B2⟩ **W** /ˈkeɪpəbl/ *adj.* **1 ~ of (doing) sth** having the ability or qualities necessary to do sth: *He's capable of passing the exam if he tries harder.* ◇ *That car is capable of 180 miles per hour.* ◇ *I do not believe that she's capable of stealing.* **2** having a lot of skill; good at doing sth: *She's a very capable teacher.* **SYN competent OPP incapable** ▶ **capably** /-bli/ *adv.*

capacitor /kəˈpæsɪtə(r)/ *noun* [C] (**ENGINEERING**, **PHYSICS**) a device used to store an electric charge

capacity ⟨B2⟩ **W** /kəˈpæsəti/ *noun* (*pl.* **-ies**) **1** [C, usually sing., U] the amount that a container or space can hold: *The tank has a capacity of 1 000 litres.* ◇ *The stadium was **filled** to capacity.* **2** [sing.] **~ (for sth/doing sth); ~ (to do sth)** the ability to understand or do sth: *That book is beyond the capacity of young children.* ◇ *a capacity for hard work/for learning languages* **3** [C, usually sing.] the official position that sb has: *In his capacity as chairman of the council …* **SYN role 4** [sing., U] the amount that a factory or machine can produce: *The power station is working **at full capacity**.*

cape /keɪp/ *noun* [C] **1** a piece of clothing with no SLEEVES (= parts covering the arms) that hangs from the shoulders ○ look at **cloak** (1) **2** (**GEOGRAPHY**) a piece of high land that sticks out into the sea: *the Cape of Good Hope*

caper /ˈkeɪpə(r)/ *noun* [C] the small green BUD (= the part that will develop into a flower) of a Mediterranean bush, used in cooking

capillary /kəˈpɪləri/ *noun* [C] (*pl.* **-ies**) (**ANATOMY**) any of the smallest tubes in the body that carry blood ○ picture at **body**, **skin¹**

capital¹ ⟨A1⟩ /ˈkæpɪtl/ *noun* **1** (*also* ˌcapital ˈcity) [C] (**GEOGRAPHY**, **POLITICS**) the town or city where the government of a country or region is: *Madrid is the capital of Spain.* **2** [U] (**FINANCE**) an amount of money that can be invested or used to start a business: *When she had enough capital, she bought a shop.* **3** (*also* capital letter) [C] the large form of a letter of the alphabet: *Write your name in capitals.* **4** [C] a place that is well known for a particular thing: *Niagara Falls is the honeymoon capital of the world.* **5** [C] (**ARCHITECTURE**) the top part of a column

capital² ⟨A1⟩ /ˈkæpɪtl/ *adj.* **1** (**LAW**) connected with punishment by death: *a **capital offence** (= a crime for which sb can be sentenced to death)* **2** (used about letters of the alphabet) written in the large form: *'David' begins with a capital 'D'.*

ˌcapital ˈgain *noun* [C, usually pl., U] (**FINANCE**) a profit that is made from the sale of property or an investment: *unearned income such as capital gains*

ˌcapital ˈgains tax *noun* [C, U] (*abbr.* **CGT**) (**FINANCE**) a tax that a person must pay when they have made a profit above a particular level by selling sth of value such as a building, vehicle, shares in a company, etc.

ˌcapital inˈvestment *noun* [U] (**FINANCE**) money that a business spends on buildings, vehicles, etc.

capitalism ⟨C1⟩ /ˈkæpɪtəlɪzəm/ *noun* [U] (**ECONOMICS**, **POLITICS**) the economic system in which businesses are owned and run for profit by private owners and not by the state ○ look at **communism**, **Marxism**, **socialism** ▶ **capitalist** ⟨C1⟩ /-lɪst/ *noun* [C], *adj.*

capitalize (*BrE also* **-ise**) /ˈkæpɪtəlaɪz/ *verb* [T] **1** to write or print a letter of the alphabet as a capital; to begin a word with a capital letter **2** to sell possessions in order to change them into money **3** [usually passive] (**FINANCE**) to provide a company etc. with the money it needs to function ▶ **capitalization** (*BrE also* **-isation**) /ˌkæpɪtəlaɪˈzeɪʃn/ *noun* [U] **PHR V capitalize on sth** to use sth to your advantage: *We can capitalize on the mistakes that our rivals have made.*

ˌcapital ˈletter = CAPITAL¹ (3)

ˌcapital ˈpunishment *noun* [U] (**LAW**) punishment by death ○ look at **corporal punishment**, **death penalty**

capitulate /kəˈpɪtʃuleɪt/ *verb* [I] (*formal*) to stop fighting and accept that you have lost; to give in to sb **SYN surrender** ▶ **capitulation** /kəˌpɪtʃuˈleɪʃn/ *noun* [C, U]

cappuccino /ˌkæpəˈtʃiːnəʊ/ (*pl.* **-os**) *noun* [C, U] a type of coffee made with hot milk

capricious /kəˈprɪʃəs/ *adj.* (*formal*) changing behaviour suddenly in a way that is difficult to predict **SYN unpredictable**

Capricorn /ˈkæprɪkɔːn/ *noun* [U] the tenth sign of THE ZODIAC (= twelve signs that represent the positions of the sun, moon and planets), the Goat; a person born under this sign

capsicum /ˈkæpsɪkəm/ *noun* [C] a type of plant that has hollow fruits. Some types of these are eaten as vegetables, either raw or cooked, for example RED PEPPERS or CHILLIES.

capsid /ˈkæpsɪd/ *noun* [C] (**BIOLOGY**) the outer layer that surrounds the NUCLEIC ACID in a virus PARTICLE ○ picture at **virus**

capsize /kæpˈsaɪz/ *verb* [I, T] (used about boats) to turn over in the water; to make sth turn over in the water: *The canoe capsized.* ◇ *A big wave capsized the yacht.*

capsule /ˈkæpsjuːl/ *noun* [C] **1** (**MEDICINE**) a very small closed tube of medicine that you SWALLOW ○ picture at **health 2** a small plastic container with a substance or liquid inside **3** the part of a SPACECRAFT in which people travel and that often separates from the main

capitals

Doric

Corinthian

Ionic

ROCKET **4** (BIOLOGY) a shell or container for seeds or eggs in some plants and animals

captain¹ ⚡ **B1** /ˈkæptɪn/ *noun* [C] (*abbr.* Capt.) **1** the person who is in command of a ship or an aircraft **2** an officer at a middle level in the army, NAVY and the US AIR FORCE **3** (SPORT) a person who is the leader of a group or team: *Who's (the) captain of the French team?*

captain² /ˈkæptɪn/ *verb* [T] to be the captain of a group, team or ship

caption /ˈkæpʃn/ *noun* [C] the words that are written above or below a picture, photo, etc. to explain what it is about

captivate /ˈkæptɪveɪt/ *verb* [T, often passive] to attract and hold sb's attention ▸ **captivating** *adj.*

captive¹ /ˈkæptɪv/ *adj.* **1** kept as a prisoner or in a space that you cannot get out of; unable to escape: *captive animals* **2** not free to leave a particular place or to choose what you want to do: *A salesman loves a captive audience* (= listening because they have no choice).
IDM **hold/take sb captive/prisoner** to keep sb as a prisoner and not allow them to escape **take sb captive** to catch sb and hold them as your prisoner

captive² /ˈkæptɪv/ *noun* [C] a person who is kept as a prisoner, especially in a war

captivity /kæpˈtɪvəti/ *noun* [U] the state of being kept in a place that you cannot escape from: *Wild animals are often unhappy when kept in captivity.*

captor /ˈkæptə(r)/ *noun* [C] (*formal*) a person who takes or keeps a person as a prisoner

capture¹ ⚡ **B2** /ˈkæptʃə(r)/ *verb* [T] **1** to catch a person or an animal and keep them as a prisoner or shut them in a space that they cannot escape from: *The lion was captured and taken back to the zoo.* **SYN** **catch¹ 2** to take control of sth: *The town has been captured by the rebels.* ◇ *The company has captured 90% of the market.* **3** to make sb interested in sth: *The story captured the children's imagination/interest/attention.* **4** to succeed in representing or recording sth in words, pictures, etc: *This poem captures the atmosphere of the carnival.* ◇ *The robbery was captured on video.* **5** (COMPUTING) to put sth into a computer in a form that it can use

capture² ⚡ **B2** /ˈkæptʃə(r)/ *noun* [U] the act of capturing sth or being captured: *data capture*

car ⚡ **A1** /kɑː(r)/ *noun* [C] **1** (*AmE, formal* automobile) a road vehicle with four wheels that can carry a small number of people: *a new/second-hand car* ◇ *Where can I park the car?* ◇ *They had a car crash.* ◇ *to get into/out of a car* ◇ *Shall we go in the car/by car?* **2** (*AmE*) = CARRIAGE (1) **3** (*AmE*) = TRUCK (4) **4** a section of a train that is used for a particular purpose: *a dining/sleeping car*

carafe /kəˈræf/ *noun* [C] a glass container like a bottle with a wide neck, in which wine or water is served

caramel /ˈkærəmel/ *noun* **1** [U] burnt sugar that is used to add taste and colour to food **2** [C, U] a type of sticky sweet that is made from boiled sugar, butter and milk

carapace /ˈkærəpeɪs/ *noun* [C] (BIOLOGY) the hard shell on the back of some animals, for example CRABS, that protects them

carat (*especially BrE*) (*AmE* karat) /ˈkærət/ *noun* [C] a unit for measuring how pure gold is or how heavy JEWELS (= valuable stones) are: *a 20-carat gold ring*

caravan /ˈkærəvæn/ *noun* [C] (*BrE*) **1** (*BrE*) (*AmE* camper) (TOURISM) a road vehicle without an engine that is pulled by a car, designed for people to live and sleep in, especially when they are on holiday: *a caravan site/park* ⊃ picture at **camper 2** a group of people and animals that travel together, for example across a desert

caravanning /ˈkærəvænɪŋ/ *noun* [U] (*BrE*) (TOURISM) the activity of spending a holiday in a CARAVAN

caraway /ˈkærəweɪ/ *noun* [U] the dried seeds of a plant from the PARSLEY family, used in cooking: *caraway seeds*

carbohydrate /ˌkɑːbəʊˈhaɪdreɪt/ *noun* [C, U] (BIOLOGY) one of the substances in food, for example sugar, that gives the body energy: *Athletes need a diet that is high in carbohydrate.*

carbon ⚡+ **B2** /ˈkɑːbən/ *noun* [U] **1** (*symb.* C) (CHEMISTRY) a chemical element. Carbon is a substance found in all living things, and also in diamonds, coal, petrol, etc. ❶ For more information on the periodic table of elements, look at the **Reference Section** of this dictionary. **2** (ENVIRONMENT) used to refer to the gas CARBON DIOXIDE when talking about the harmful effect it has on the environment: *carbon emissions/levels*

carbonate /ˈkɑːbənət/ *noun* [C] (CHEMISTRY) a SALT that contains CARBON and OXYGEN together with another chemical

carbonated /ˈkɑːbəneɪtɪd/ *adj.* (used about a drink) containing small bubbles of CARBON DIOXIDE **SYN** **fizzy**

carbon ˈcopy *noun* [C] **1** (BUSINESS) a copy of a document, letter, etc. made with CARBON PAPER ⊃ look at **cc¹ 2** a person or thing that is very similar to sb/sth else

carbon credit *noun* [C] (ENVIRONMENT) a way of expressing how much CARBON DIOXIDE and other gases a country or organization is allowed to produce. Carbon credits can be bought and sold between countries or organizations.

carbon cycle *noun* [usually sing.] (BIOLOGY, CHEMISTRY) the processes by which CARBON is changed from one form to another within the environment

carbon ˈdating (*also* radiocarbon dating) *noun* [U] (SCIENCE) a method of calculating the age of very old objects by measuring the amounts of different forms of CARBON in them

carbon ˈdebt *noun* [C] (ENVIRONMENT) the difference between the CARBON FOOTPRINT of a country, business, etc. and anything that has been done to reduce the effects of this

carbon diˈoxide *noun* [U] (*symb.* CO_2) (CHEMISTRY) a gas breathed out by people and animals from the lungs or produced by burning CARBON ⊃ picture at **photosynthesis**

carbon ˈfootprint *noun* [C] (ENVIRONMENT) a measure of the amount of CARBON DIOXIDE that is produced by the daily activities of a person or company: *Companies are looking at ways to reduce their carbon footprints.* ⊃ look at **carbon-neutral** (2), **carbon offset**, **ecological footprint**

carbonic acid /kɑːˌbɒnɪk ˈæsɪd/ *noun* [U] (CHEMISTRY) a very weak ACID that is formed when CARBON DIOXIDE DISSOLVES (= becomes liquid) in water ⊃ picture at **erosion**

carboniferous /ˌkɑːbəˈnɪfərəs/ *adj.* (GEOLOGY) **1** producing or containing coal **2** Carboniferous belonging to the period in the earth's history when layers of coal were formed underground

carbon monoxide /ˌkɑːbən məˈnɒksaɪd/ *noun* [U] (*symb.* CO) (**CHEMISTRY**) a poisonous gas formed when CARBON burns partly but not completely. It is produced when petrol is burnt in car engines.

carbon-ˈneutral *adj.* (**ENVIRONMENT**) **1** producing no CARBON DIOXIDE or an amount that is balanced by actions that protect the environment **SYN** **zero-carbon** **2** balancing the damage to the environment that we do when travelling by car or plane, using electricity, etc. by such actions as planting trees ⊃ look at **carbon footprint**, **carbon offset**

carbon ˈoffset *noun* [C, U] (**ENVIRONMENT**) a way for a company or person to reduce the level of CARBON DIOXIDE for which they are responsible. They pay money to a company that works to reduce the total amount produced in the world, for example by planting trees: *carbon offset initiatives for air travellers*

carbon paper *noun* [U] thin paper with a dark substance on one side that you put between two sheets of paper to make a copy of what you are writing

carbon trading *noun* [U] (**ENVIRONMENT**) a system that gives countries and organizations the right to produce a particular amount of CARBON DIOXIDE, and allows them to sell this right

car ˈboot sale *noun* [C] an outdoor sale where people sell things they do not want using tables or the back of their cars to put the goods on

carburettor (*BrE*) (*AmE* **carburetor**) /ˌkɑːbəˈretə(r)/ *noun* [C] the piece of equipment in a car's engine that mixes petrol and air

carcass /ˈkɑːkəs/ *noun* [C] the dead body of an animal ⊃ look at **corpse**

carcinogen /kɑːˈsɪnədʒən/ *noun* [C] (**HEALTH**) a substance that can cause cancer

carcinogenic /ˌkɑːsɪnəˈdʒenɪk/ *adj.* (**HEALTH**) likely to cause cancer

carcinoma /ˌkɑːsɪˈnəʊmə/ *noun* [C] (**HEALTH**) a cancer that affects the top layer of the skin or the LINING of the body's internal organs

card 🔑 **A1** /kɑːd/ *noun* **1** [U] (*BrE*) thick stiff paper: *a piece of card* **2** [C] = POSTCARD **3** [C] a piece of card or plastic that has information on it, especially information about sb's identity: *a membership/identity/loyalty card* **4** [C] = BUSINESS CARD **5** [C] a small piece of plastic, especially one given by a bank or shop, used for buying things or obtaining money: *a debit/credit card* ◇ *The customer paid by card.* ◇ *Do taxis there accept card payment?* **6** [C] a piece of card

with a picture on it that you use for sending a special message to sb: *a Christmas/birthday card* ◇ *a get-well card* (= one that you send to sb who is ill) **7** (*also* playing card) [C] one of a set of 52 small pieces of card with shapes or pictures on them that are used for playing games: *a pack of cards* **8** cards [pl.] games that are played with cards: *Let's play cards.* ◇ *Let's have a game of cards.* ◇ *I never win at cards!*
IDM **on the cards** (*BrE*) (*AmE* **in the cards**) (*informal*) likely to happen: *Their marriage break-up has been on the cards for some time now.*

cardamom /ˈkɑːdəməm/ *noun* [U] the dried seeds of a south-east Asian plant, used in cooking as a SPICE

cardboard /ˈkɑːdbɔːd/ *noun* [U] very thick paper that is used for making boxes, etc: *The goods were packed in cardboard boxes.*

card catalog (*AmE*) = CARD INDEX

cardholder /ˈkɑːdhəʊldə(r)/ *noun* [C] a person who uses a card from a bank, etc. to pay for things

cardiac /ˈkɑːdiæk/ *adj.* (**HEALTH**) connected with the heart: *cardiac surgery* ◇ *a cardiac arrest* (= when the heart stops temporarily or permanently)

cardigan /ˈkɑːdɪɡən/ *noun* [C] a warm piece of clothing, often made of wool, that you wear on the top half of your body. Cardigans fasten at the front, usually with buttons.

cardinal /ˈkɑːdɪnl/ *noun* [C] **1** (**RELIGION**) a priest at a high level in the Roman Catholic church **2** (*also* ˌcardinal ˈnumber) (**LANGUAGE**, **MATHEMATICS**) a whole number, such as 1, 2 and 3, that shows quantity rather than order ⊃ look at **ordinal**

ˌcardinal ˈpoints *noun* [pl.] (**GEOGRAPHY**) the four main points (North, South, East and West) on a COMPASS (= an instrument that shows direction)

card index (*also* **index**) (*both BrE*) (*AmE* **card catalog**) *noun* [C] a box of cards with information on them, arranged in the order of the alphabet

cardio- /ˈkɑːdiəʊ, kɑːdiə, kɑːdiˈɒ/ *prefix* (in nouns, adjectives and adverbs) (**ANATOMY**) relating to the heart: *a cardiogram*

cardiologist /ˌkɑːdiˈɒlədʒɪst/ *noun* [C] (**MEDICINE**) a doctor who studies and treats heart diseases ▶ **cardiology** /-dʒi/ *noun* [U]

cardiovascular /ˌkɑːdiəʊˈvæskjələ(r)/ *adj.* (**ANATOMY**) connected with the heart and the BLOOD VESSELS (= the tubes that carry blood around the body)

the carbon cycle

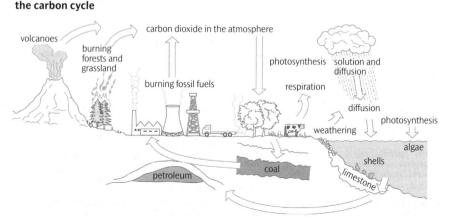

care¹ 🔊 A2 ⊙ /keə(r)/ *noun* **1** [U] ~ **(for sb)** the process of looking after sb/sth and providing what they need for their health or protection: *All the children in their care were healthy and happy.* ◇ *This hospital provides free medical care.* ◇ *She's in intensive care* (= the part of the hospital for people who are very seriously ill). ◇ *care for the elderly* ◇ *a care assistant* ◇ *health and social care* ◇ *skin/hair care products* **2** [U] ~ **(over sth/ in doing sth)** thinking about what you are doing so that you do it well or do not make a mistake: *You should take more care over your homework.* ◇ *This box contains glasses — please handle it with care.* **3** [C, U] something that makes you feel worried or unhappy: *Since Charlie retired he doesn't have a care in the world.* ◇ *It was a happy life, free from care.* **IDM** **in care** (used about children) living in an institution run by the local authority or with another family, and not with their parents: *They were taken into care after their parents died.* **take care (that … / to do sth)** to be careful: *Goodbye and take care!* ◇ *Take care that you don't spill your tea.* ◇ *He took care not to arrive too early.* **take care of sb/sth** to deal with sb/sth; to organize or arrange sth: *I'll take care of the food for the party.* **take care of yourself/sb/sth** to keep yourself/sb/sth safe from injury, illness, damage, etc.; to look after sb/sth: *My mother took care of me when I was ill.* ◇ *She always takes great care of her books.*

▼ SYNONYMS

care

caution • prudence • discretion • wariness

These are all words for attention or thought that you give to sth in order to avoid mistakes or accidents.

care *She chose her words with care.*

caution *Proceed with the utmost caution.*

prudence (*formal*) *We need to exercise financial prudence.*

discretion *Can I rely on your complete discretion?*

wariness *Her wariness soon turned to mistrust.*

care² 🔊 A2 /keə(r)/ *verb* [I, T] ~ **(about sb/sth)** to be worried about or interested in sb/sth: *Money is the thing that she cares about most.* ◇ *He really cares about his staff.* ◇ *I don't care what you do.* **IDM** **I, etc. couldn't care less** (*informal*) it does not matter to me, etc. at all: *I couldn't care less what Barry thinks.* **who cares?** (*informal*) nobody is interested; it is not important to anyone: 'I wonder who'll win the match.' 'Who cares?' **would you care for … /to do sth** (*formal*) a polite way to ask if sb would like to do sth **PHR V** **care for sb** to look after sb: *Who cared for her while she was ill?* **care for sb/sth** to like or love sb/ sth: *She still cares for Liam although he married somebody else.* ◇ *I don't care for that colour very much.*

career¹ 🔊 A1 /kə'rɪə(r)/ *noun* [C] **1** the series of jobs that sb has in a particular area of work ~ **in sth**: *Sarah is considering a career in engineering.* ◇ *a successful career in politics* **2** the period of your life that you spend working: *She spent most of her career working in India.*

career² /kə'rɪə(r)/ *verb* [I] to move quickly and in a dangerous way: *The car careered off the road and crashed into a wall.*

carefree /'keəfriː/ *adj.* with no problems or worries

careful 🔊 A2 /'keəfl/ *adj.* **1** ~ **(of/with sth)**; ~ **(to do sth)** thinking about what you are doing so that you do not have an accident or make mistakes: *Be careful! There's a car coming.* ◇ *Please be very careful of the traffic.* ◇ *Be careful with that knife — it's very sharp.* ◇ *That ladder doesn't look very safe. Be careful you don't fall.* ◇ *I was careful not to say anything about the money.* ◇ *a careful driver* **OPP** **careless 2** giving a lot of attention to details to be sure sth is right: *I'll need to give this matter some careful thought.* ◇ *a careful worker* **OPP** **careless** ▶ **carefully** 🔊 A2 /-fəli/ *adv.*: *Please listen carefully. It's important that you remember all this.*

care home *noun* [C] (*BrE*) a place that provides care for people who cannot live at home or look after themselves: *a care home for the elderly*

careless 🔊 B1 /'keələs/ *adj.* **1** ~ **(about/with sth)** not thinking enough about what you are doing so that you make mistakes: *Jo's very careless.* ◇ *The accident was caused by careless driving.* ◇ *They've always been careless with money.* **OPP** **careful 2** resulting from a lack of thought or attention to detail: *a careless mistake* ▶ **carelessly** *adv.*: *She threw her coat carelessly on the chair.* ▶ **carelessness** *noun* [U]

carer /'keərə(r)/ (*BrE*) (*AmE* **caregiver** /'keəgɪvə(r)/) *noun* [C] (HEALTH) a person who takes care of a sick or an old person at home

caress /kə'res/ *verb* [T] to touch sb/sth in a gentle and loving way ▶ **caress** *noun* [C]

caretaker /'keəteɪkə(r)/ (*BrE*) (*AmE* **janitor**) *noun* [C] a person whose job is to look after a large building, for example a school or a block of flats

cargo 🔊+ C1 /'kɑːgəʊ/ *noun* [C, U] (*pl.* -oes, *AmE also* -os) the goods that are carried in a ship or an aircraft: *Luggage is carried in the cargo hold of the plane.* ◇ *a cargo ship*

cargo pants (*also* **cargoes** /'kɑːgəʊz/, *BrE also* **combats**, **combat trousers**) *noun* [pl.] loose trousers that have pockets in various places, for example on the side of the leg above the knee

the Caribbean /ðə ˌkærɪ'biːən, ðə kə'rɪbiən/ *noun* [sing.] (GEOGRAPHY) the region consisting of the Caribbean Sea and its islands, including the West Indies, and the coasts that surround it ▶ **Caribbean** /ˌkærɪ'biːən, kə'rɪbiən/ *adj.*

caricature /'kærɪkətʃʊə(r)/ *noun* [C] a picture or description of sb that makes their appearance or behaviour funnier and more extreme than it really is: *Many of the people in the book are caricatures of the author's friends.*

caring /'keərɪŋ/ *adj.* showing that you care about other people: *We must work towards a more caring society.*

carjacking /'kɑːdʒækɪŋ/ *noun* [U, C] the crime of forcing the driver of a car to take you somewhere or give you their car, using threats and violence ⊃ look at **hijacking** ▶ **carjack** /-dʒæk/ *verb* [T] ▶ **carjacker** *noun* [C]

carnage /'kɑːnɪdʒ/ *noun* [U] the violent killing of a large number of people **SYN** **slaughter**

carnation /kɑː'neɪʃn/ *noun* [C] a white, pink, red or yellow flower with a pleasant smell

carnival /'kɑːnɪvl/ *noun* [C] a public festival that takes place in the streets with music and dancing: *the carnival in Rio*

carnivore /'kɑːnɪvɔː(r)/ *noun* [C] (BIOLOGY) any animal that eats meat ⊃ look at **herbivore**, **insectivore**, **omnivore** ▶ **carnivorous** /kɑː'nɪvərəs/ *adj.*: *Lions are carnivorous animals.*

carol /'kærəl/ *noun* [C] (MUSIC) a Christian religious song that people sing at Christmas

carotid artery /kəˌrɒtɪd ˈɑːtəri/ *noun* [C] (**ANATOMY**) either of the ARTERIES (= two large tubes in the neck) that carry blood to the head

carousel /ˌkærəˈsel/ *noun* [C] **1** (*AmE*) = MERRY-GO-ROUND **2** (**TOURISM**) a moving belt at an airport from which you collect your bags

carp /kɑːp/ *noun* [C, U] (*pl.* carp) a large fish that is often kept in PONDS (= small artificial areas of water)

carpal /ˈkɑːpl/ *noun* [C] (**ANATOMY**) any of the eight small bones in the WRIST ⊃ picture at **body**

ˈcar park (*BrE*) (*AmE* **parking lot**) *noun* [C] an area or a building where you can leave your car: *a multi-storey car park*

carpel /ˈkɑːpl/ *noun* [C] (**BIOLOGY**) the female REPRODUCTIVE organ of a flower ⊃ picture at **flower**[1]

carpenter /ˈkɑːpəntə(r)/ *noun* [C] a person whose job is to make things from wood or to repair them ⊃ look at **joiner**

carpentry /ˈkɑːpəntri/ *noun* [U] the skill or work of a CARPENTER

carpet 🔑 **A2** /ˈkɑːpɪt/ *noun* **1** [C, U] (a piece of) thick material that is used for covering floors and stairs: *a fitted carpet* (= one that is cut to the exact shape of a room) ◇ *a square metre of carpet* ⊃ look at **rug** (1) **2** [C] a thick layer of sth that covers the ground: *The fields were under a carpet of snow.* ▶ **carpeted** *adj.*: *All the rooms are carpeted.*

carpool /ˈkɑːpuːl/ *verb* [I] (**ENVIRONMENT**) if a group of people **carpool**, they travel to work together in one car and divide the cost between them

carriage 🔑+ **C1** /ˈkærɪdʒ/ *noun* [C] **1** (*also* **coach**) (*BrE*) (*AmE* **car**) one of the separate parts of a train where people sit: *a first-class carriage* **2** a vehicle with wheels that is pulled by horses ⊃ look at **coach**[1] (4)

carriageway /ˈkærɪdʒweɪ/ *noun* [C] (*BrE*) one of the two sides of a MOTORWAY (= a wide road for fast traffic) or other large road, used by vehicles travelling in the same direction: *the southbound carriageway of the motorway* ⊃ look at **dual carriageway**

carrier /ˈkæriə(r)/ *noun* [C] **1** (**BUSINESS**) a company that transports people or goods: *the Dutch carrier, KLM* **2** a military vehicle or ship that is used for transporting soldiers, planes, weapons, etc: *an aircraft carrier* **3** (**HEALTH**) a person or an animal that can pass a disease to others but does not show the signs of the disease: *Some insects are carriers of tropical diseases.* **4** (*BrE*) = CARRIER BAG **5** (**BUSINESS**) a company that provides a phone or internet service: *a telecoms carrier*

ˈcarrier bag (*also* **carrier**) *noun* [C] (*BrE*) a plastic or paper bag for carrying shopping

carrion /ˈkæriən/ *noun* [U] the bodies of animals that have been dead for some time ⊃ picture at **animal**

carrot 🔑 **A1** /ˈkærət/ *noun* **1** [C, U] a long thin orange vegetable that grows under the ground: *A pound of carrots, please.* ◇ *grated carrot* **2** [C] something attractive that is offered to sb in order to persuade them to do sth

carry 🔑 **A1** /ˈkæri/ *verb* (carrying; carries; *pt, pp* carried) **1** [T] to hold sb/sth in your hand, arms or on your back while you are moving from one place to another: *Could you carry this bag for me? It's terribly heavy.* ◇ *She was carrying a rucksack on her back.* **2** [T] to have sth with you as you go somewhere: *I never carry much cash with me.* ◇ *Do the police carry guns in your country?* **3** [T] to transport sb/sth from one place to another: *A train carrying hundreds of passengers crashed yesterday.* ◇ *Strong winds carried the boat off course.* **4** [T] (**HEALTH**) to have a disease that can be given to others, usually without showing any signs of

the disease yourself **5** [T, usually passive] (**POLITICS**) to officially approve of sth in a meeting, etc., because the largest number of people vote for it: *The motion was carried by twelve votes to nine.* **6** [I] (used about a sound) to reach a long distance: *You'll have to speak louder if you want your voice to carry to the back of the room.*

IDM **be/get carried away** to be so excited that you forget what you are doing **carry weight** to have influence on the opinion of sb else: *Nick's views carry a lot of weight with the boss.*

PHR V **carry it/sth off** to succeed in doing sth difficult: *He felt nervous before he started his speech but he carried it off very well.* **carry on (with sth/ doing sth)** to continue: *They ignored me and carried on with their conversation.* ◇ *She intends to carry on studying after the course has finished.* **carry on sth** to do an activity: *to carry on a conversation/a business* **carry out sth 1** to do sth that you have been asked to do: *The soldiers carried out their orders without question.* **2** to do and complete a task: *to carry out tests/an investigation*

carrycot /ˈkærikɒt/ *noun* [C] a small bed, like a box with handles, that you can carry a baby in

ˈcarry-on *noun* [C] (**TOURISM**) a small bag or case that you carry onto a plane with you: *Only one carry-on is allowed.* ◇ *carry-on baggage*

ˈcarry-on baggage (*especially AmE*) = HAND LUGGAGE

ˈcarry-out (*AmE*) = TAKEAWAY

carsick /ˈkɑːsɪk/ *adj.* feeling sick or VOMITING as a result of travelling in a car: *to get/feel/be carsick* ⊃ look at **airsick, seasick, travel-sick**

cart[1] /kɑːt/ *noun* [C] **1** a vehicle with wheels that is used for transporting things: *a horse and cart* **2** (*AmE*) = TROLLEY (1): *a baggage cart* **3** (*especially AmE*) = BASKET (2)

cart[2] /kɑːt/ *verb* [T] (*informal*) to take or carry sth/sb somewhere, often with difficulty: *We left our luggage at the station because we didn't want to cart it around all day.*

cartel /kɑːˈtel/ *noun* [C + sing./pl. verb] (**BUSINESS**) a group of separate companies that agree to increase profits by fixing prices and not competing with each other

cartilage /ˈkɑːtɪlɪdʒ/ *noun* [C, U] (**ANATOMY**) a strong substance in the places where the bones join ⊃ picture at **respiratory, synovial**

cartographer /kɑːˈtɒɡrəfə(r)/ *noun* [C] (**GEOGRAPHY**) a person who draws or makes maps

cartography /kɑːˈtɒɡrəfi/ *noun* [U] (**GEOGRAPHY**) the art or process of drawing or making maps ▶ **cartographic** /ˌkɑːtəˈɡræfɪk/ *adj.*

carton /ˈkɑːtn/ *noun* [C] a small container made of CARDBOARD (= very thick paper that is used for making boxes) or plastic: *a carton of milk/orange juice*

cartoon 🔑 **A2** /kɑːˈtuːn/ *noun* [C] **1** (**ART**) a funny drawing, especially in a newspaper or magazine **2** (**ARTS AND MEDIA**) a film or TV show made by photographing a series of gradually changing drawings or models, so that they look as if they are moving **3** (**ART**) a drawing made by an artist as a preparation for a painting

cartoonist /kɑːˈtuːnɪst/ *noun* [C] a person who draws cartoons

cartridge /ˈkɑːtrɪdʒ/ *noun* [C] **1** a small tube that contains powder that can explode and a bullet. You put a cartridge into a gun when you want to fire it. **2** a closed container that holds sth that is used in a machine, for example film for a camera, INK for printing, etc. Cartridges can be removed and replaced when they are finished or empty.

cartwheel /'kɑːtwiːl/ *noun* [C] a fast movement in which you turn in a circle to the side by putting your hands on the ground and bringing your legs, one at a time, over your head: *to **do/turn cartwheels*** ▶ **cartwheel** *verb* [I]

carve ᴵ+ **C1** /kɑːv/ *verb* [T, I] **1** ~ (sth) (out of sth) (ART) to cut wood or stone in order to make an object or to put a pattern or writing on it: *The statue is carved out of marble.* ◊ *He carved his name on the desk.* **2** to cut a piece of cooked meat into slices: *to carve a chicken* ⊃ note at **meat**

carving /'kɑːvɪŋ/ *noun* [C, U] (ART) an object or a design that has been CARVED; the art of making objects in this way: *There are ancient carvings on the walls of the cave.*

cascade¹ /kæ'skeɪd/ *noun* [C] **1** (GEOGRAPHY) a small WATERFALL (= water that falls down the side of a mountain, etc.), especially one of several falling down a steep slope with rocks **2** (*formal*) a large quantity of sth that falls or hangs down: *a cascade of blond hair*

cascade² /kæ'skeɪd/ *verb* [I] to fall or hang down, especially in large amounts or in stages: *Water cascaded from the roof.*

case ᴵ **A2** ⊙ /keɪs/ *noun*
• SITUATION **1** [C] a particular situation or example of sth: *In some cases, people have had to wait two weeks for a doctor's appointment.* ◊ *Most of us travel to work by tube — or, in Jim's case, by train and tube.* ◊ *Cases of the disease are very unusual in this country.* ⊃ note at **example 2** the case [sing.] the true situation: *The man said he worked in Cardiff, but we discovered later that this was not the case.*
• LEGAL MATTER **3** [C] (LAW) a crime or legal matter: *The police deal with hundreds of murder cases a year.* ◊ *The case will come to court in a few months.* ⊃ note at **court¹**
• REASONS **4** [C, usually sing.] ~ **for** the facts and reasons that support one side in a discussion or legal matter: *She tried to **make a case for** shorter working hours, but the others disagreed.*
• CONTAINER **5** [C] (especially in compounds) a container or cover for sth: *a pencil case* ◊ *a pillowcase* ◊ *a bookcase* ◊ *She put her glasses back in the case.* **6** [C] = SUITCASE: *Would you like me to carry your case?*
• GRAMMAR **7** [C, U] (in some languages) the form of a noun, an adjective or a pronoun that shows its relationship to another word: *The object of the verb is in the accusative case.* ⊃ look at **accusative, dative, genitive, nominative, vocative**
IDM (be) a case of sth/doing sth (be) a situation in which sth is needed: *There's no secret to success in this business. It's just a case of hard work.* in any case whatever happens or may have happened: *I don't know how many tickets for the match cost, but I'm going in any case.* **SYN** anyway (just) in case (…) because sth might happen: *I think I'll take an umbrella in case it rains.* ◊ *I wasn't intending to buy anything but I took my credit card **just in case**.* in case of sth (*formal*) if sth happens: *In case of fire, break this glass.* in that case if that is the situation: *'I'm busy on Tuesday.' 'Oh well, in that case we'll have to meet another day.'*

case history *noun* [C] (MEDICINE) a record of a person's background, past illnesses, etc.

case law *noun* [U] (LAW) law based on decisions made by judges in earlier cases ⊃ look at **common law, statute law**

case study *noun* [C] (SOCIAL STUDIES) a detailed study of a person, group, situation, etc. over a period of time

cash¹ ᴵ **A2** /kæʃ/ *noun* [U] **1** money in the form of coins or notes and not plastic cards, CHEQUES, etc: *Would you prefer me to pay **in cash**?* ◊ *How much cash have you got with/on you?* **2** (*informal*) money in any form: *I'm a bit short of cash this month so I can't afford to go out much.*

cash² /kæʃ/ *verb* [T] to exchange a CHEQUE for the amount of money that it is worth: *to cash a cheque* **PHR V** cash in (on sth) to gain an advantage for yourself in a situation, especially in a way that other people think is wrong

cashback /'kæʃbæk/ *noun* [U] **1** if you ask for **cashback** when you are paying for goods in a shop with a DEBIT CARD (= a plastic card that takes money directly from your bank account), you get a sum of money in cash, that is added to your bill **2** an offer of money as a present that is made by some banks and companies in order to persuade customers to do business with them

cash card (*BrE*) (*AmE* **ATM card**) *noun* [C] a plastic card given by a bank to its customers so that they can get money from a CASH MACHINE (= a special machine in or outside a bank) ⊃ look at **credit card, debit card**

cash cow *noun* [C] (BUSINESS) the part of a business that always makes a profit and that provides money for the rest of the business

cash crop *noun* [C] (AGRICULTURE) plants that people grow to sell, and not to eat or use themselves ⊃ look at **subsistence**

cash desk *noun* [C] the place in a large shop where you pay for things

cash dispenser (*BrE*) = CASH MACHINE

cashew /'kæʃuː, kæ'ʃuː/ (*also* **cashew nut**) *noun* [C] a small curved nut that can be eaten

cash flow *noun* [C, U] (FINANCE) the movement of money into and out of a business as goods are bought and sold: *The company had cash-flow problems and could not pay its bills.*

cashier /kæ'ʃɪə(r)/ *noun* [C] the person in a bank, shop, etc. that customers pay money to or get money from

cash machine (*BrE also* **cash dispenser, Cashpoint™**) *noun* [C] a machine inside or outside a bank that you can get money from at any time of day by putting in a CASH CARD **SYN** ATM

cashmere /'kæʃmɪə(r), ˌkæʃ'mɪə(r)/ *noun* [U] a type of wool that made from the long hair of a type of GOAT and is very fine and soft

Cashpoint™ /'kæʃpɔɪnt/ (*BrE*) = CASH MACHINE

cash register = TILL²

casing /'keɪsɪŋ/ *noun* [C, U] a layer of material that protects sth: *The keyboard has a black plastic casing.* ⊃ picture at **dry cell, vacuum flask**

casino ᴵ+ **C1** /kə'siːnəʊ/ *noun* [C] (*pl.* -os) a place where people play card games, etc. in which you can win or lose money

cask /kɑːsk/ *noun* [C] a small BARREL (= a round wooden container with flat ends) in which alcoholic drinks, etc. are stored

casket /'kɑːskɪt/ *noun* [C] **1** a small decorated box for holding JEWELS or other valuable things, especially in the past **2** (*AmE*) = COFFIN

cassava /kə'sɑːvə/ (*also* **manioc**) *noun* [U] **1** a tropical plant with many branches and long roots that you can eat **2** the roots of this plant, which can be cooked or made into flour

casserole /ˈkæsərəʊl/ *noun* **1** [C, U] a hot dish made by cooking meat, vegetables, etc. in liquid for a long time in the oven: *chicken casserole* **2** [C] a large dish with a LID (= cover) for cooking casseroles in

cassette /kəˈset/ *noun* [C] a small flat plastic case containing tape for playing or recording music or sound: *to put on/play/listen to a cassette* ◇ *a video cassette* SYN **tape¹** ⊃ look at **video** (5)

cast¹ ᵻ B2 /kɑːst/ *verb* (*pt, pp* cast) **1** [T, often passive] (ARTS AND MEDIA) to choose an actor for a particular role in a play, film, etc: *She always seems to be cast in the same sort of role.* **2** [I, T] to throw a fishing line or net into the water **3** [T] to make an object by pouring hot liquid metal into a MOULD (= a shaped container): *a statue cast in bronze*
IDM **cast doubt on sth** to make people less sure about sth: *New evidence casts doubt on the truth of the prime minister's statement.* **cast an eye/your eye(s) over sb/sth** to look at sb/sth quickly **cast light on sth** to help to explain sth: *Can you cast any light on the problem?* **cast your mind back** to make yourself remember sth: *She cast her mind back to the day she met her husband.* **cast a shadow (across/over sth)** to cause an area of shade to appear somewhere: *(figurative) The accident cast a shadow over the rest of the holiday* (= stopped people enjoying it fully). **cast a/your vote** (POLITICS) to vote: *The MPs will cast their votes in the leadership election tomorrow.*
PHRV **cast about/around for sth** to try to find sth: *Jack cast around desperately for a solution to the problem.*

cast² ᵻ B2 /kɑːst/ *noun* [C] **1** [+ sing./pl. verb] (ARTS AND MEDIA) all the actors in a play, film, etc: *The entire cast was/were excellent.* **2** (ART) a container that you use to make an object in a particular shape by pouring hot liquid metal, etc. into it; an object that is made in this way SYN **mould¹**

castanets /ˌkæstəˈnets/ *noun* [pl.] (MUSIC) a musical instrument that consists of two small round pieces of wood that you hold in the hand and hit together with the fingers to make a noise. Castanets are used especially by Spanish dancers.

castaway /ˈkɑːstəweɪ/ *noun* [C] a person who is left alone somewhere after their ship has sunk: *a castaway on a desert island*

caste /kɑːst/ *noun* [C, U] (SOCIAL STUDIES) a social class or group based on your position in society, how much money you have, family origin, etc.; the system of dividing people in this way: *Hindu society is based on a caste system.*

caster sugar (*also* castor sugar) /ˈkɑːstə ʃʊɡə(r)/ *noun* [U] (*BrE*) white sugar in the form of very small grains, used in cooking

cast iron *noun* [U] a hard type of iron that is shaped by pouring the hot liquid metal into a MOULD (= a shaped container) ⊃ look at **wrought iron**

cast-iron *adj.* **1** made of CAST IRON **2** (*BrE*) very strong or certain; that cannot be broken or fail: *a cast-iron alibi/excuse*

castle ᵻ A2 /ˈkɑːsl/ *noun* [C] **1** (HISTORY) a large building with high walls and towers that was built in the past to defend people against attack: *a medieval castle* ◇ *Edinburgh Castle* **2** (in the game of CHESS) any of the four pieces placed in the corner squares of the board at the start of the game, usually made to look like a castle

cast-off *noun* [C, usually pl.] (*especially BrE*) a piece of clothing that you no longer want and that you give to sb else or throw away: *When I was little I had to wear my sister's cast-offs.*

castor sugar /ˈkɑːstə ʃʊɡə(r)/ = CASTER SUGAR

castrate /kæˈstreɪt/ *verb* [T] to remove part of the sexual organs of a male animal so that it cannot produce young ⊃ look at **neuter²** ▶ **castration** /-ˈstreɪʃn/ *noun* [U, C]

casual ᵻ B2 /ˈkæʒuəl/ *adj.* **1** relaxed and not worried; not showing great effort or interest: *I'm not happy about your casual attitude to your work.* ◇ *It was only a casual remark so I don't know why he got so angry.* **2** (used about clothes) not formal: *I always change into casual clothes as soon as I get home from work.* **3** (used about work) done only for a short period; not regular or permanent: *a casual job* ◇ *Most of the building work was done by casual labour.* ▶ **casually** /-əli/ *adv.*: *She walked in casually and said, 'I'm not late, am I?'* ◇ *Dress casually, it won't be a formal party.*

casualty ᵻ+ C1 /ˈkæʒuəlti/ *noun* (*pl.* -ies) **1** [C] (MEDICINE) a person who is killed or injured in a war or an accident: *After the accident the casualties were taken to hospital.* **2** [U] (*BrE*) = A & E **3** [C] a person or thing that suffers as a result of sth else: *Many small companies became casualties of the economic crisis.* SYN **victim**

cat ᵻ A1 /kæt/ *noun* [C] **1** a small animal with soft fur that people often keep as a pet **2** a wild animal of the cat family: *the big cats* (= lions, TIGERS, etc.)

catabolism /kəˈtæbəlɪzəm/ *noun* [U] (BIOLOGY) the process by which chemical structures are broken down and energy is released

catacombs /ˈkætəkuːmz/ *noun* [pl.] (HISTORY) a series of underground tunnels used for burying dead people, especially in ancient times

catalogue ᵻ+ C1 (*AmE also* catalog) /ˈkætəlɒɡ/ *noun* [C] **1** a list of all the things that you can buy, see, etc. somewhere **2** a series, especially of bad things: *a catalogue of disasters/errors/injuries* ▶ **catalogue** *verb* [T]: *She started to catalogue all the new library books.*

catalyse (*BrE*) (*AmE* catalyze) /ˈkætəlaɪz/ *verb* [T] (CHEMISTRY) to make a chemical reaction happen faster ▶ **catalysis** *noun* [U]

catalysis /kəˈtæləsɪs/ *noun* [U] (CHEMISTRY) an increase in the rate of a chemical reaction that is caused by a CATALYST

catalyst /ˈkætəlɪst/ *noun* [C] **1** ~ (for sth) a person or a thing that causes change: *The scandal was the catalyst for the president's election defeat.* **2** (CHEMISTRY) a substance that makes a chemical reaction happen faster without being changed itself ▶ **catalytic** *adj.*

catalytic /ˌkætəˈlɪtɪk/ *adj.* [only before noun] (CHEMISTRY) causing a chemical reaction to happen faster

catalytic converter /ˌkætəˌlɪtɪk kənˈvɜːtə(r)/ *noun* [C] (ENVIRONMENT) a device used in motor vehicles to reduce the damage caused to the environment by poisonous gases

catamaran /ˌkætəməˈræn/ *noun* [C] a fast sailing boat with two HULLS (= with two main parts to its structure, like two boats joined together)

catapult¹ /ˈkætəpʌlt/ *noun* [C] **1** (*BrE*) (*AmE* slingshot) a stick that has the shape of a Y with a rubber band attached to it, used by children for shooting stones **2** (HISTORY) a weapon used in the past to throw heavy stones

catapult² /ˈkætəpʌlt/ *verb* [T, I] (used with an adverb or a preposition) to throw sb/sth suddenly and with great force: *When the car crashed the driver was catapulted through the windscreen.* ◇ *(figurative) The success of his first film catapulted him to fame.*

cataract /'kætərækt/ *noun* [C] **1** (**HEALTH**) a medical condition that affects the LENS (= the clear part of the front of the eye) so that you gradually lose your sight **2** (*formal*) a large WATERFALL (= a place where a river falls from a high place)

catarrh /kə'tɑː(r)/ *noun* [U] (**HEALTH**) a thick liquid that forms in the nose and throat when you have a cold

catastrophe /kə'tæstrəfi/ *noun* [C] **1** a sudden disaster that causes great suffering or damage: *major catastrophes such as floods and earthquakes* **2** an event that causes people to suffer, or makes difficulties: *It'll be a catastrophe if I fail the exam again.* ▸ **catastrophic** /ˌkætə'strɒfɪk/ *adj.*: *The war had a catastrophic effect on the whole country.*

catastrophism /kə'tæstrəfɪzəm/ *noun* [U] (**GEOLOGY**) the theory that changes to the earth's CRUST (= surface) in the history of the planet were caused by sudden violent and unusual events

catatonic /ˌkætə'tɒnɪk/ *adj.* (**HEALTH**) not able to move or show any reaction to things because of illness, shock, etc: *a catatonic state*

catch¹ ⸂ A2 /kætʃ/ *verb* (*pt, pp* caught /kɔːt/)
• TAKE HOLD OF **1** [T] to take hold of sth that is moving, usually with your hand or hands: *The dog caught the ball in its mouth.*
• CAPTURE **2** [T] to capture sb/sth that you have been following or looking for: *Two policemen ran after the thief and caught him at the end of the street.* ◇ *to catch a fish*
• NOTICE **3** [T] to notice or see sb doing sth bad: *I caught her taking money from my purse.* **4** [T] to notice sth only for a moment: *I caught sight of him as he was leaving.* ◇ *He caught a glimpse of himself in the mirror.*
• BUS, TRAIN, ETC. **5** [T] to get on a bus, train, etc: *I caught the bus into town.* **OPP** miss¹
• BE IN TIME **6** [T] to be in time for sth; not to miss sb/sth: *We arrived just in time to catch the beginning of the film.* ◇ *I'll phone her now. I might just catch her before she leaves the office.* **OPP** miss¹
• GET STUCK **7** [I, T] to become stuck in or on sth; to make sth become stuck: *His jacket caught on a nail and ripped.* ◇ *If we leave early we won't get caught in the traffic.*
• HIT **8** [T] to hit sb/sth: *The branch caught him on the head.*
• ILLNESS **9** [T] (**HEALTH**) to get an illness: *to catch a cold/flu/measles*
• HEAR/UNDERSTAND **10** [T] to hear or understand sth that sb says: *I'm sorry, I didn't quite catch what you said. Could you repeat it?*
IDM **catch sb's attention/eye** to make sb notice sth: *I tried to catch the waiter's eye so that I could get the bill.* **catch your breath 1** (*BrE*) to rest after physical exercise so that your breathing returns to normal **2** to breathe in suddenly because you are surprised **catch your death (of cold)** to get very cold **catch fire** to start burning, often in a way that is not planned: *Nobody knows how the building caught fire.* **catch sb red-handed** to find sb just as they are doing sth wrong: *The police caught the burglars red-handed with the stolen jewellery.* **catch the sun 1** to shine brightly in the SUNLIGHT: *The panes of glass flashed as they caught the sun.* **2** (used about people) to become red or brown because of spending time in the sun: *Your face looks red. You've really caught the sun, haven't you?*
PHR V **catch on** (*informal*) **1** to become popular or fashionable: *The idea has never really caught on in this country.* **2** to understand or realize sth: *She's sometimes a bit slow to catch on.* **catch sb out** to cause sb to make a mistake by asking a clever

question: *Ask me anything you like — you won't catch me out.* **catch up (with sb)** | **catch sb up** to reach sb who is in front of you: *Sharon's missed so much school she'll have to work hard to catch up with the rest of the class.* ◇ *Go on ahead. I'll catch you up in a minute.* **catch up on sth** to spend time doing sth that you have not been able to do for some time: *I'll have to go into the office at the weekend to catch up on my work.* **be/get caught up in sth** to be or get involved in sth, usually without intending to: *I seem to have got caught up in a rather complicated situation.*

catch² ⸂ B2 /kætʃ/ *noun* [C] **1** (**SPORT**) an act of catching sth, for example a ball **2** the amount of fish that sb has caught: *The fishermen brought their catch to the harbour.* **3** a device for fastening sth and keeping it closed: *I can't close my suitcase — the catch is broken.* ◇ *a window catch* **4** (*informal*) a hidden disadvantage or difficulty in sth that seems attractive: *It looks like a good offer but I'm sure there must be a catch in it.*
IDM **(a) catch-22** | **a catch-22 situation** (*informal*) a difficult situation that you cannot escape from because you need to do one thing before doing a second, and you cannot do the second thing before doing the first

catching /'kætʃɪŋ/ *adj.* [not before noun] (**HEALTH**) (used about a disease or an emotion) passing easily or quickly from one person to another **SYN** **infectious**

catchment area *noun* [C] **1** the area from which a school gets its students, a hospital gets its patients, etc. **2** (*also* catchment /'kætʃmənt/) (**GEOGRAPHY**) the area from which rain flows into a particular river or lake

catchphrase /'kætʃfreɪz/ *noun* [C] a phrase that becomes famous because it is used by a famous person

catchy /'kætʃi/ *adj.* (catchier; catchiest) (used about a tune or song) easy to remember

catechism /'kætəkɪzəm/ *noun* [sing.] (**RELIGION**) a set of questions and answers that are used for teaching people about the beliefs of the Christian Church

categorical /ˌkætə'ɡɒrɪkl/ *adj.* very definite: *The answer was a categorical 'no'.* ▸ **categorically** /-kli/ *adv.*: *The Minister categorically denied the rumour.*

categorize ⓦ (*BrE also* -ise) /'kætəɡəraɪz/ *verb* [T] to divide people or things into groups; to say that sb/sth belongs to a particular group

category ⸂ B1 ⓞ /'kætəɡəri/ *noun* [C] (*pl.* -ies) a group of people or things that are similar to each other: *This painting won first prize in the junior category.* ◇ *These books are divided into categories according to subject.*

cater ⸂+ C1 /'keɪtə(r)/ *verb* [I] **1** ~ **for sb/sth**; ~ **to sth** to provide what sb/sth needs or wants: *The class caters for all ability ranges.* ◇ *The menu caters to all tastes.* **2** ~ (**for sb/sth**) to provide and serve food and drink at an event or in a place that a lot of people go to: *Can we cater for 20?*

caterer /'keɪtərə(r)/ *noun* [C] a person or business that provides food and drink at events or in places that a lot of people go to

catering /'keɪtərɪŋ/ *noun* [U] the activity or business of providing food and drink at events or in places that a lot of people go to: *the hotel and catering industry* ◇ *Who's going to do the catering at the wedding?*

caterpillar /'kætəpɪlə(r)/ *noun* [C] a small animal with a long body and a lot of legs, that eats the leaves of plants. A caterpillar later develops into a BUTTERFLY or MOTH (= flying insects with large, sometimes brightly coloured, wings) ⸦ picture at **animal**

catharsis /kəˈθɑːsɪs/ *noun* [U, C] (*pl.* **catharses** /-ˈθɑːsiːz/) (**LITERATURE**) the process of expressing strong feeling, for example through plays or other artistic activities, as a way of getting rid of anger, reducing suffering, etc. ▶ **cathartic** /-ˈθɑːtɪk/ *adj.*: *It was a cathartic experience.*

cathedral /kəˈθiːdrəl/ *noun* [C] a large church that is the most important one in a district

catheter /ˈkæθətə(r)/ *noun* [C] (**MEDICINE**) a thin tube that is put into the body in order to remove liquid such as URINE

cathode /ˈkæθəʊd/ *noun* [C] (**CHEMISTRY, PHYSICS**) an ELECTRODE in an electrical device; the negative ELECTRODE in an ELECTROLYTIC CELL and the positive ELECTRODE in a battery ⊃ look at **anode**

cathode ray tube *noun* [C] (**PHYSICS**) a VACUUM tube in the past inside a TV or computer screen, etc. from which a stream of ELECTRONS produces images on the screen

Catholic /ˈkæθlɪk/ = ROMAN CATHOLIC

Catholicism /kəˈθɒlɪsɪzəm/ = ROMAN CATHOLICISM

cation /ˈkætaɪən/ *noun* [C] (**CHEMISTRY, PHYSICS**) an ION with a positive electrical charge ⊃ look at **anion**

catkin /ˈkætkɪn/ *noun* [C] a long thin hanging bunch, or short standing group, of soft flowers on the branches of trees such as the WILLOW

CAT scan /ˈkæt skæn/ = CT SCAN

cattle ʔ+ **C1** /ˈkætl/ *noun* [pl.] cows that are kept as farm animals for their milk or meat: *a herd of cattle* (= a group of them) ⊃ note at **cow**

catwalk /ˈkætwɔːk/ (*also* **runway** *especially in AmE*) *noun* [C] (**ARTS AND MEDIA**) the long stage that models walk on during a fashion show

Caucasian /kɔːˈkeɪʒn/ *noun* [C] (**SOCIAL STUDIES**) a member of a human group that has pale skin ▶ **Caucasian** *adj.*

caucus /ˈkɔːkəs/ *noun* [C] (*especially AmE*) **1** (**POLITICS**) a meeting of the members or leaders of a political party to choose candidates or to decide policy; the members or leaders of a political party as a group **2** a group of people with similar interests, often within a larger organization or political party

caught /kɔːt/ *past tense, past participle of* **catch**[1]

cauldron (*AmE also* **caldron**) /ˈkɔːldrən/ *noun* [C] a large deep metal pot that is used for cooking things over a fire

cauliflower /ˈkɒliflaʊə(r)/ *noun* [C, U] a large vegetable with green leaves and a round white centre

causal ◑ /ˈkɔːzl/ *adj.* **1** (*formal*) connected with the relationship between two things, where one causes the other to happen: *the causal relationship between poverty and disease* **2** a word like *because* that introduces a statement about the cause of sth

causation ◑ /kɔːˈzeɪʃn/ *noun* [U] (*formal*) the process of one event causing another event

cause[1] ʔ **A2** ◑ /kɔːz/ *noun* **1** [C] ~ (**of sth**) a thing or person that makes sth happen: *The police do not know the cause of the accident.* ◊ *Smoking is one of the causes of heart disease.* **2** [U] ~ (**for sth**) reason for feeling sth or behaving in a particular way: *The doctor assured us that there was no cause for concern.* ◊ *I don't think you have any real cause for complaint.* ⊃ note at **reason**[1] **3** [C] an idea or organization that a group of people believe in and support: *We are all committed to the cause of racial equality.*
IDM **be for/in a good cause** to be worth doing because it will help other people **a lost cause** → LOST[2]

cause[2] ʔ **A2** ◑ /kɔːz/ *verb* [T] ~ **sth (for sb)**; ~ **sth (to sb/ sth)**; ~ **sb/sth to do sth** to make sth happen: *The fire was caused by an electrical fault.* ◊ *Is your leg causing you any pain?* ◊ *I don't want to cause trouble for her.* ◊ *The earthquake caused widespread damage to property.* ◊ *High winds caused many trees to fall during the night.*

'cause /kəz, kɒz/ (*BrE, informal*) = COS

causeway /ˈkɔːzweɪ/ *noun* [C] a raised road or path across water or wet ground: *The island is connected to the mainland by a causeway.*

caustic /ˈkɔːstɪk/ *adj.* **1** (**CHEMISTRY**) (used about a chemical substance) able to destroy or DISSOLVE other substances **SYN** **corrosive** **2** critical in a cruel way: *a caustic remark*

caustic soda *noun* [U] (**CHEMISTRY**) a chemical used in making paper and soap

caution[1] ʔ+ **C1** /ˈkɔːʃn/ *noun* **1** [U] great care, because of possible danger: *Any advertisement that asks you to send money should be treated with caution.* ⊃ note at **care**[1] **2** [C] (*BrE*) (**LAW**) a warning given by a police officer to sb who has committed a small crime: *As a first offender, she got off with a caution.*

caution[2] /ˈkɔːʃn/ *verb* [I, T] **1** ~ (**sb**) **against sth** to warn sb not to do sth: *The president's advisers have cautioned against calling an election too early.* **2** to give sb an official warning: *Dixon was cautioned by the referee for wasting time.*

cautionary /ˈkɔːʃənəri/ *adj.* giving a warning: *The teacher told us a cautionary tale about a girl who cheated in her exams.*

cautious ʔ+ **C1** /ˈkɔːʃəs/ *adj.* taking great care to avoid possible danger or problems: *I'm very cautious about expressing my opinions in public.* ▶ **cautiously** *adv.*

cavalry /ˈkævlri/ *noun* [sing. + sing./pl. verb] the part of the army that fought on horses in the past; the part of the modern army that uses heavily protected vehicles

cave[1] ʔ+ **B2** /keɪv/ *noun* [C] (**GEOGRAPHY**) a large hole in the side of a hill or CLIFF, or under the ground

cave[2] /keɪv/ *verb*
PHR V **cave in 1** to fall in: *The roof of the tunnel had caved in and we could go no further.* **2** to suddenly stop arguing or being against sth: *He finally caved in and agreed to the plan.*

caveman /ˈkeɪvmæn/ *noun* [C] (*pl.* **-men** /-men/) **1** a person who lived many thousands of years ago in CAVES **2** (*informal*) a man who behaves in an aggressive way

cavern /ˈkævən/ *noun* [C] (**GEOGRAPHY**) a large, deep hole in the side of a hill or under the ground; a big CAVE ⊃ picture at **limestone**

caviar (*also* **caviare**) /ˈkæviɑː(r)/ *noun* [U] the eggs of some types of fish, that are preserved using salt and eaten as a very special and expensive type of food

cavity /ˈkævəti/ *noun* [C] (*pl.* **-ies**) **1** an empty space inside sth solid: *the abdominal cavity* ◊ *a wall cavity* **2** (**HEALTH**) a hole in a tooth

cayenne /keɪˈen/ (*also* **cayenne pepper**) *noun* [U] a type of red pepper used in cooking to give a hot taste to food

CBI /ˌsiː biː ˈaɪ/ *abbr.* (**BUSINESS**) **Confederation of British Industry** (an important organization to which businesses and industries belong)

CBT /ˌsiː biː ˈtiː/ *noun* [U] (**PSYCHOLOGY**) a type of therapy in which you try to change negative ways of thinking in order to change your behaviour or to treat conditions such as stress (the abbreviation for 'cognitive behavioural therapy')

cc[1] /ˌsiː ˈsiː/ *abbr.* (**BUSINESS**, **COMPUTING**) **carbon copy (to)** (used on business letters and emails to show that a copy is being sent to another person): *to Monika Davies, cc Penny Burgess*

cc[2] /ˌsiː ˈsiː/ *verb* [T] (cc'ing; cc's; *pt, pp* cc'd) to send sb a copy of a letter or email message that you are sending to sb else: *He cc'd me on the email he sent to his manager.*

CCTV /ˌsiː siː tiː ˈviː/ *abbr.* **closed-circuit television** (a TV system used in a limited area, for example a shopping centre, to protect it from crime): *He was caught on CCTV leaving the store.* ◇ *CCTV cameras/footage*

CD ⁊ **A1** /ˌsiː ˈdiː/ *noun* [C] a small disc on which sound or information is recorded (the abbreviation for 'compact disc') ⊃ look at **CD player**

CD burner (*also* **CD writer**) *noun* [C] a piece of equipment used for copying sound or information from a computer onto a CD

CD player *noun* [C] a piece of equipment that you use for playing CDs

CD-ROM /ˌsiː diː ˈrɒm/ *noun* [C, U] a type of CD used with a computer on which information, sound and pictures can only be read and not written by the computer (the abbreviation for 'compact disc read-only memory')

cease ⁊+ **C1** /siːs/ *verb* [I, T] (*formal*) to stop or end: *Fighting in the area has now ceased.* ◇ *That organization has ceased to exist.*

ceasefire /ˈsiːsfaɪə(r)/ *noun* [C] an agreement between two groups to stop fighting each other **SYN** truce

ceaseless /ˈsiːsləs/ *adj.* (*formal*) continuing for a long time without stopping ▸ **ceaselessly** *adv.*

cedar /ˈsiːdə(r)/ *noun* **1** [C] a tall EVERGREEN tree (= one that has green leaves all through the year) that has wide spreading branches **2** (*also* **cedarwood** /ˈsiːdəwʊd/) [U] the hard red wood of the cedar

cede /siːd/ *verb* [T] (*formal*) to give land or control of sth to another country or person

cedilla /sɪˈdɪlə/ *noun* [C] (**LANGUAGE**) the mark placed under the letter *c* in French, Portuguese, etc. to show that it is pronounced like an *s* rather than a *k*; a similar mark under *s* in Turkish and some other languages

ceiling ⁊ **B1** /ˈsiːlɪŋ/ *noun* [C] **1** the top surface of the inside of a room: *a room with a high/low ceiling* **2** a top limit: *The government has put a 3 per cent ceiling on wage increases.*

celeb /səˈleb/ (*informal*) = CELEBRITY

celebrate ⁊ **A2** /ˈselɪbreɪt/ *verb* [I, T] to do sth to show that you are happy about sth that has happened or because it is a special day: *When I got the job we celebrated by going out for a meal.* ◇ *Nora celebrated her 90th birthday yesterday.* ▸ **celebratory** /ˌselɪˈbreɪtəri/ *adj.*: *We went out for a celebratory meal after the match.*

celebrated /ˈselɪbreɪtɪd/ *adj.* (*formal*) famous: *a celebrated poet*

celebration ⁊ **B1** /ˌselɪˈbreɪʃn/ *noun* [C, U] the act or occasion of doing sth that you enjoy because sth good has happened or because it is a special day: *Christmas celebrations* ◇ *I think this is an occasion for celebration!*

celebrity ⁊ **A2** /səˈlebrəti/ *noun* [C] (*pl.* -ies) (**ARTS AND MEDIA**) a famous person: *a TV celebrity* **SYN** personality

celery /ˈseləri/ *noun* [U] a vegetable with long green STEMS that can be eaten without being cooked: *a stick of celery*

celestial /səˈlestiəl/ *adj.* (*formal*) of the sky or of heaven: *celestial bodies* (= the sun, moon, stars, etc.) ⊃ look at **terrestrial** (2)

celiac /ˈsiːliæk/ (*AmE*) = COELIAC

celibate /ˈselɪbət/ *adj.* (*formal*) (**RELIGION**) never having sexual relations, often because of religious beliefs ▸ **celibacy** /-bəsi/ *noun* [U]

typical plant cell   typical animal cell

chloroplast
vacuole membrane
cell membrane
large vacuole
cell wall
cell membrane
nucleus
nuclear membrane
mitochondrion
cytoplasm
small vacuole
centriole

cell ⁊ **B2** /sel/ *noun* [C] **1** a small room in a prison or police station in which a prisoner is locked **2** a small room without much furniture in which a MONK or NUN (= a member of a religious group of men or women) lives **3** (**BIOLOGY**) the smallest living part of an animal or a plant: *The human body consists of millions of cells.* ◇ *red blood cells* **4** (**PHYSICS**) a device for producing an electric current, for example by the action of chemicals or light: *solar cells* ◇ *a photoelectric cell* ⊃ picture at **dry cell**, **resistor**, **switch**[1] **5** (**POLITICS**) a small group of people who work as part of a larger political organization, especially secretly: *a terrorist cell* **6** (**COMPUTING**) one of the small squares in a SPREADSHEET computer program in which you enter a single piece of data **7** (*especially AmE, informal*) = CELL PHONE

cellar /ˈselə(r)/ *noun* [C] an underground room that is used for storing things ⊃ look at **basement**

cellist /ˈtʃelɪst/ *noun* [C] (**MUSIC**) a person who plays the CELLO

cello /ˈtʃeləʊ/ *noun* [C] (*pl.* -os) (**MUSIC**) a large musical instrument with strings. You sit down to play it and hold it between your knees. ⊃ picture at **instrument**, **orchestra**

Cellophane™ /ˈseləfeɪn/ *noun* [U] a thin, clear plastic material used for wrapping things

cell phone (*especially AmE*) = MOBILE PHONE

cellular /ˈseljələ(r)/ *adj.* **1** (**BIOLOGY**) connected with or consisting of the cells of plants or animals: *cellular tissue* **2** (**COMPUTING**) connected with a phone system that works by radio instead of wires: *a cellular network*

cellulose /ˈseljuləʊs/ *noun* [U] (**BIOLOGY**) a natural substance that forms the cell walls of all plants and trees and is used in making plastics, paper, etc.

Celsius /ˈselsiəs/ (*also* **centigrade**) *adj.* (*abbr.* C) (**SCIENCE**) the name of a scale for measuring temperatures, in which water freezes at 0° and boils at 100°: *The temperature tonight will fall to 7°C.* ⊃ look at **Fahrenheit**, **kelvin**

Celtic /ˈkeltɪk/ *adj.* (**HISTORY**) connected with the Celts (= the people who lived in Wales, Scotland, Ireland and Brittany in ancient times) or with their language

cement[1] /sɪˈment/ *noun* [U] **1** a grey powder that becomes hard after it is mixed with water and left to dry. It is used in building for sticking BRICKS or stones together or for making very hard surfaces. ⊃ picture at **building** **2** the hard substance that is formed when cement becomes dry and hard: *a floor of cement* ◇ *a* *cement floor* ⊃ look at **concrete²**, **mortar** (1) **3** a soft substance that becomes hard when dry and is used for sticking things together or filling in holes: *dental cement* (= for filling holes in teeth) **4** (**ANATOMY**) a thin layer of material similar to bone that covers the root of a tooth and holds it in place ⊃ picture at **tooth**

cement² /sɪˈment/ *verb* [T] **1** to join two things together using CEMENT, or a strong sticky substance **2** to make a relationship, an agreement, etc. very strong: *This agreement has cemented the relationship between our two countries.*

cementation /ˌsiːmenˈteɪʃn/ *noun* [U] (**GEOLOGY**) the process in which grains of sand, etc. stick together to form SEDIMENTARY rocks

ceˈment mixer (*also* concrete mixer) *noun* [C] a machine with a DRUM (= a large metal container) that holds sand, water and CEMENT, and turns to mix them all together

cemetery ʔ+ **C1** /ˈsemətri/ *noun* [C] (*pl.* -ies) a place where dead people are buried, especially a place that does not belong to a church ⊃ look at **churchyard**, **graveyard**

cenotaph /ˈsenətɑːf/ *noun* [C] (**ARCHITECTURE**) a MONUMENT built in memory of soldiers killed in a war who are buried somewhere else

censor¹ /ˈsensə(r)/ *verb* [T, often passive] to remove the parts of a book, film, etc. that might offend people or that are considered to be offensive or a political threat ▶ **censorship** *noun* [U]: *state censorship of radio and TV programmes*

censor² /ˈsensə(r)/ *noun* [C] an official who CENSORS books, films, etc.

censure /ˈsenʃə(r)/ *verb* [T] (*formal*) to tell sb, in a strong and formal way, that they have done sth wrong: *The attorney was censured for not revealing the information earlier.* ▶ **censure** *noun* [U]

census /ˈsensəs/ *noun* [C] (**SOCIAL STUDIES**) an official count of the people who live in a country, including information about their ages, jobs, etc.

cent ʔ **A1** /sent/ *noun* [C] (*abbr.* c, ct) a unit of money that is worth 1% part of the main unit of money in many countries, for example of the US dollar or of the euro ⊃ look at **per cent¹**

centenarian /ˌsentɪˈneəriən/ *noun* [C] a person who is 100 years old or more

centenary /senˈtiːnəri/ (*pl.* -ies) (*especially BrE*) (*AmE usually* centennial /senˈteniəl/) *noun* [C] the year that comes exactly 100 years after an important event or the beginning of sth: *The school will celebrate its centenary next year.*

center /ˈsentə(r)/ (*AmE*) = CENTRE¹, CENTRE²

centi- /senti/ *prefix* (in nouns) **1** one hundred: *centipede* **2** (often in units of measurement) one HUNDREDTH: *centilitre*

centigrade /ˈsentɪgreɪd/ *adj.* = CELSIUS: *a temperature of 40 degrees centigrade*

centilitre (*BrE*) (*AmE* centiliter) /ˈsentiliːtə(r)/ *noun* [C] (*abbr.* cl) a unit for measuring liquids. There are 100 centilitres in a LITRE.

centimetre (*BrE*) (*AmE* centimeter) /ˈsentimiːtə(r)/ *noun* [C] (*abbr.* cm) a measure of length. There are 100 centimetres in a metre.

centipede /ˈsentɪpiːd/ *noun* [C] a small creature like an insect, with a long thin body and many legs

central ʔ **B1** ⊙ /ˈsentrəl/ *adj.* **1** in the centre of sth: *a map of central Europe ◇ Our flat is very central* (= near the centre of the city and therefore very convenient). **2** most important; main: *The film's central character is a 15-year-old girl.* ⊃ note at **main¹ 3** [only before noun] having control over all other parts: *central government* (= the government of a whole country, not local government) ◇ *the central nervous system* ⊃ note at **government**

ˌcentral ˈbank *noun* [C] (**FINANCE**) a national bank that does business with the government and other banks, controls the amount of money in the country's economy and issues the country's coins and paper money

ˌcentral ˈheating *noun* [U] a system for heating a building from one main point. Air or water is heated and carried by pipes to all parts of the building. ⊃ picture at **fractional distillation**

centralize ⓦ (*BrE also* -ise) /ˈsentrəlaɪz/ *verb* [T, usually passive] (**BUSINESS**, **POLITICS**) to give control of a country or an organization to a group of people in one place: *Our education system is becoming increasingly centralized.* **OPP** **decentralize** ▶ **centralization** (*BrE also* -isation) /ˌsentrəlaɪˈzeɪʃn/ *noun* [U]

centrally /ˈsentrəli/ *adv.* in a place that is easily reached from many areas: *The hotel is centrally located for all major attractions.*

ˌcentral ˈnervous system *noun* [C] (**ANATOMY**) the part of the system of nerves in the body that consists of the brain and the SPINAL CORD ⊃ look at **nervous system**

ˌcentral ˈprocessing unit = CPU

ˌcentral reserˈvation (*BrE*) (*AmE* median) *noun* [C] a narrow piece of land with a barrier that separates the two sides of a main road such as a MOTORWAY

centre¹ ʔ **A1** ⊙ (*BrE*) (*AmE* center) /ˈsentə(r)/ *noun* **1** [C, usually sing.] the middle point or part of sth: *I work in the centre of Bangkok. ◇ Which way is the town centre, please?* ⊃ picture at **circle¹ 2** [C] a building or place where a particular activity or service is based: *a sports/health/shopping centre ◇ This university is a centre of excellence for medical research.* **3** [C] a place where sb/sth is collected together; the point towards which sth is directed: *major urban/industrial centres ◇ She always likes to be the centre of attention. ◇ You should bend your legs to keep a low centre of gravity.* **4** [sing.] (**POLITICS**) a political position that is not extreme: *a party of the centre ◇ Her views are left of centre.*

centre² ʔ **B1** ⓦ (*BrE*) (*AmE* center) /ˈsentə(r)/ *verb* [I, T] **~(around/round/on sb/sth); be centred (around/round/on sb/sth)** to be the person or thing around which most activity takes place; to make sb/sth the central person or thing: *Life in the village centres around the church and the school. ◇ His interests were centred on Irish history.*

-centric /sentrɪk/ *suffix* (in adjectives) based on a particular way of thinking: *Eurocentric policies* (= concerned with Europe)

centrifugal /ˌsentrɪˈfjuːgl, senˈtrɪfjəgl/ *adj.* (**PHYSICS**) moving or tending to move away from a centre: *centrifugal force*

centrifuge /ˈsentrɪfjuːdʒ/ *noun* [C] a machine with a part that turns round very quickly to separate substances, for example liquids from solids, by forcing the heavier substance to the outer edge

centriole /ˈsentriəʊl/ *noun* [C] (**BIOLOGY**) a structure in a cell that helps the cell to divide into two parts ⊃ picture at **cell**

centripetal /ˌsentrɪˈpiːtl, senˈtrɪpɪtl/ *adj.* (**PHYSICS**) moving or tending to move towards a centre: *centripetal force*

centrist /ˈsentrɪst/ *noun* [C] (**POLITICS**) a person with political views that are not extreme ▶ **centrist** *adj.*: *His more moderate policies will appeal to centrist voters.*

century ⓘ **A1** Ⓦ /ˈsentʃəri/ *noun* [C] (*pl.* -ies) **1** a particular period of 100 years that is used for giving dates: *We live in the 21st century* (= the period between the years 2000 and 2099 after the birth of Christ). **2** any period of 100 years: *People have been making wine in this area for centuries.*

CEO /ˌsiː iː ˈəʊ/ *noun* [C] (*pl.* CEOs) (**BUSINESS**) the person with the most powerful position in a company or business (the abbreviation for 'chief executive officer')

cephalopod /ˈsefələpɒd, ˈke-/ *noun* [C] (**BIOLOGY**) any of the class of sea animals that have a large soft head, large eyes and eight or ten TENTACLES (= long thin legs): *Octopus and squid are cephalopods.* ⊃ picture at **animal**

ceramic /səˈræmɪk/ *noun* (**ART**) **1** [C, usually pl.] a pot or other object made of CLAY that has been made permanently hard by heat: *an exhibition of ceramics by Picasso* **2** ceramics [U] the art of making and decorating pots, etc ⊃ look at **pottery** (2) ▸ ceramic *adj.*: *ceramic tiles*

cereals

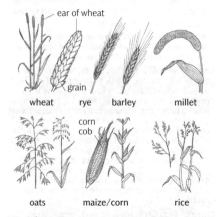

ear of wheat

grain

wheat   rye   barley   millet

corn
cob

oats   maize/corn   rice

cereal /ˈsɪəriəl/ *noun* [C, U] **1** (**AGRICULTURE**) any type of grain that can be eaten or made into flour, or the grass that the grain comes from: *Wheat, barley and rye are cereals.* **2** a food that is made from grain, often eaten for breakfast with milk: *a bowl of cereal*

cerebellum /ˌserəˈbeləm/ *noun* [C] (*pl.* cerebellums, cerebella /-lə/) (**ANATOMY**) the part of the brain at the back of the head that controls the movement of the muscles ⊃ picture at **brain**

cerebral /səˈriːbrəl, ˈserəbrəl/ *adj.* (**ANATOMY**) relating to the brain

cerebral palsy /ˌserəbrəl ˈpɔːlzi/ *noun* [U] (**HEALTH**) a medical condition, usually caused by brain damage before or at birth, that causes the loss of control of the arms and legs

cerebrum /səˈriːbrəm, ˈserəbrəm/ *noun* [C] (*pl.* cerebra /-brə/) (**ANATOMY**) the front part of the brain, responsible for thoughts, emotions and personality ⊃ picture at **brain**

ceremonial /ˌserɪˈməʊniəl/ *adj.* connected with a ceremony: *a ceremonial occasion* ▸ ceremonially /-niəli/ *adv.*

ceremony ⓘ **B1** /ˈserəməni/ *noun* (*pl.* -ies) **1** [C] a formal public or religious event: *the opening ceremony of the Olympic Games* ◇ *a wedding*

ceremony **2** [U] formal behaviour, speech, actions, etc. that are expected on special occasions: *The new hospital was opened with great ceremony.*

cerium /ˈsɪəriəm/ *noun* [U] (*symb.* Ce) (**CHEMISTRY**) a chemical element. Cerium is a silver-white metal used in the production of glass and CERAMICS. ❶ For more information on the periodic table of elements, look at the **Reference Section** of this dictionary.

certain ⓘ **A2** Ⓞ /ˈsɜːtn/ *adj.* **1** [not before noun] **~ (that …); ~ (of sth)** completely sure; without any doubts: *She's absolutely certain that there was somebody outside her window.* ◇ *We're not quite certain what time the train leaves.* ◇ *I'm certain of one thing — he didn't take the money.* **OPP** **uncertain** ⊃ note at **sure¹** **2 ~ (that …); ~ (to do sth)** sure to happen or to do sth; definite: *It is almost certain that unemployment will increase this year.* ◇ *The Director is certain to agree.* ◇ *We must rescue them today, or they will face certain death.* **3** [only before noun] used for talking about a particular thing or person without naming it or them: *You can only contact me at certain times of the day.* ◇ *There are certain reasons why I'd prefer not to meet him again.* **4** [only before noun] some, but not very much: *I suppose I have a certain amount of respect for Mr Nolan.* **5** easy to notice but difficult to describe: *There was a certain feeling of autumn in the air.* **6** (*formal*) used before a person's name to show that you do not know them: *I received a letter from a certain Ms Groves.*

IDM **for certain** without doubt: *I don't know for certain what time we'll arrive.* **make certain (that …)** **1** to do sth in order to be sure that sth else happens: *They're doing everything they can to make certain that they win.* **2** to do sth in order to be sure that sth is true: *We'd better phone Akram before we go to make certain he's expecting us.*

certainly ⓘ **A2** /ˈsɜːtnli/ *adv.* **1** without doubt; definitely: *The number of students will certainly increase after next year.* **2** (used in answer to questions) of course: '*Do you think I could borrow your notes?*' '*Certainly.*'

certainty ⓘ+ **B2** Ⓦ /ˈsɜːtnti/ *noun* (*pl.* -ies) **1** [U] the state of being completely sure about sth: *We can't say with certainty that there is life on other planets.* **OPP** **uncertainty** **2** [C] something that is sure to happen: *It's now almost a certainty our team will win the league.*

certificate ⓘ+ **B2** /səˈtɪfɪkət/ *noun* [C] **1** (**LAW**) an official document that may be used to prove that the facts it states are true: *a birth/death/medical certificate* **2** (**EDUCATION**) an official document proving that you have completed a course of study or passed an exam; a qualification obtained after a course of study or an exam: *a Postgraduate Certificate in Education* (= a British qualification for teachers)

certify /ˈsɜːtɪfaɪ/ *verb* [T] (certifying; certifies; *pt, pp* certified) **1 ~ (that)** (**LAW**) to state officially, especially in writing, that sth is true: *We need somebody to certify that this is her signature.* **2** [usually passive] (**EDUCATION**) to give sb a CERTIFICATE to show that they have successfully completed a course of training for a particular profession: *a certified accountant* **3** [usually passive] (*BrE*) (**LAW, MEDICINE**) to officially state that sb is mentally ill, so that they can be given medical treatment

certiorari /ˌsɜːʃiəˈreəraɪ/ *noun* [U] (**LAW**) a COURT ORDER by which a case TRIED in a lower court is reviewed in a higher court: *an application for an order of certiorari*

certitude /ˈsɜːtɪtjuːd/ *noun* (*formal*) **1** [U] a feeling of being certain about sth **2** [C] a thing about which you are certain

cervix /ˈsɜːvɪks/ *noun* [C] (*pl.* **cervices** /-vɪsiːz/) (**ANATOMY**) the narrow passage at the opening of the UTERUS (= the place where a baby grows inside a woman's body) ▶ **cervical** /ˈsɜːvɪkl, səˈvaɪkl/ *adj.*

ceˌsarean ˈsection (*also* **cesarean** /sɪˈzeəriən/) (*AmE*) = CAESAREAN SECTION

cesium /ˈsiːziəm/ (*AmE*) = CAESIUM

cessation /seˈseɪʃn/ *noun* [U, C] (*formal*) the stopping of sth; a break in sth: *The UN have demanded an immediate cessation of hostilities.*

cesspit /ˈsespɪt/ (*also* **cesspool** /ˈsespuːl/) *noun* [C] a covered hole or container in the ground for collecting waste from a building, especially from the toilets

cetacean /sɪˈteɪʃn/ *noun* [C] (**BIOLOGY**) a WHALE, DOLPHIN or other sea creature that belongs to the same group ⊃ picture at **animal**

cf. *abbr.* (in writing) = COMPARE (1)

CFC /ˌsiː ef ˈsiː/ *noun* [C, U] (**ENVIRONMENT**) a type of gas, previously found for example in AEROSOLS (= cans that release liquid in very small drops), that is harmful to the environment (the abbreviation for 'chlorofluorocarbon') ⊃ look at **ozone layer**

CGI /ˌsiː dʒiː ˈaɪ/ *abbr.* **computer-generated imagery** (unusual or exciting pieces of action in films or TV programmes, that are created by computers to show things that do not normally exist or happen): *The movie is full of stunts and has some amazing CGI special effects.*

CGT /ˌsiː dʒiː ˈtiː/ *abbr.* = CAPITAL GAINS TAX

ch *abbr.* (in writing) = CHAPTER (1)

chador /ˈtʃɑːdɔː(r)/ *noun* [C] a large piece of cloth that covers a woman's head and upper body so that only the face can be seen, worn by some Muslim women

chain[1] 🔒 **B1** ⊙ /tʃeɪn/ *noun* **1** [C, U] a line of metal rings that are joined together: *a bicycle chain* ◇ *She was wearing a silver chain round her neck.* ◇ *a length of chain* **2** [C] a series of connected things or people: *a chain of mountains/a mountain chain* ◇ *The book examines the complex chain of events that led to the Russian Revolution.* ◇ *The Managing Director is at the top of the chain of command.* **3** [C] a group of shops, hotels, etc. that are owned by the same company: *a chain of supermarkets* ◇ *a fast-food chain*

chain[2] 🔒 **B2** /tʃeɪn/ *verb* [T, often passive] ~ **sb/sth (to sth); ~ sb/sth (up)** to fasten sb/sth to sth else with a chain: *The demonstrators chained themselves to the railings.* ◇ *The dog is kept chained up outside.*

ˈchain mail *noun* [U] (**HISTORY**) ARMOUR (= covering to protect the body when fighting) made of small metal rings linked together

ˌchain reˈaction *noun* [C] **1** (**CHEMISTRY**) a chemical change that forms products which themselves cause more changes and new products **2** a series of events, each of which causes the next

chainsaw /ˈtʃeɪnsɔː/ *noun* [C] a tool made of a chain with sharp teeth set in it that is driven by a motor and used for cutting wood

ˈchain-smoke *verb* [I] to smoke continuously, lighting one cigarette after another ▶ **chain-smoker** *noun* [C]

ˈchain store *noun* [C] one of a number of similar shops that are owned by the same company

chair[1] 🔒 **A1** /tʃeə(r)/ *noun* **1** [C] a piece of furniture for one person to sit on, with a seat, a back and four legs: *a kitchen chair* ◇ *Sit on your chair!* ◇ *an old man asleep in a chair* (= an ARMCHAIR) **2** [C, usually singular] = CHAIRMAN (1) **3** [C] (**EDUCATION**) the position of being in charge of a department in a university; a special position as a university professor

chair[2] 🔒 **B2** /tʃeə(r)/ *verb* [T] to be the person who is in charge of a meeting: *Who's chairing the meeting this evening?*

chairman 🔒 **B2** /ˈtʃeəmən/ *noun* [C] (*pl.* **-men** /-mən/) **1** the person in charge of a meeting, who tells people when they can speak, etc. **2** (**BUSINESS**) the person in charge of a committee, a company, etc: *The chairman of the company presented the annual report.* ▶ **chairmanship** *noun* [C, U]

chairperson /ˈtʃeəpɜːsn/ *noun* [C] (*pl.* **-persons**) a chairman or CHAIRWOMAN ⊃ note at **meeting**

chairwoman /ˈtʃeəwʊmən/ *noun* [C] (*pl.* **-women** /-wɪmɪn/) **1** the woman in charge of a meeting, who tells people when they can speak, etc. **2** (**BUSINESS**) the woman in charge of a committee, a company, etc.

chalet /ˈʃæleɪ/ *noun* [C] (**TOURISM**) a wooden house, especially one built in a mountain area or used by people on holiday

chalk[1] /tʃɔːk/ *noun* **1** [U] (**GEOLOGY**) a type of soft white stone: *chalk cliffs* **2** [U, C] a substance similar to chalk that is made into white or coloured sticks for writing or drawing

chalk[2] /tʃɔːk/ *verb* [T] to write or draw sth with CHALK: *Somebody had chalked a message on the wall.* **PHR V** **chalk sth up** (*informal*) to succeed in getting sth: *The team have chalked up five wins this summer.*

chalkboard /ˈtʃɔːkbɔːd/ (*especially AmE*) = BLACKBOARD

challenge[1] 🔒 **B1** ⓦ /ˈtʃælɪndʒ/ *noun* [C] **1** ~ **(of sth)** something new and difficult that forces you to make a lot of effort: *Rob found his new job an exciting challenge.* ◇ *The company will have to face many challenges in the coming months.* ◇ *How will this government meet the challenge of rising unemployment?* **2** ~ **(to sth)** an invitation from sb to fight, play, argue, etc. against them: *She accepted his challenge to a debate.*

challenge[2] 🔒 **B2** ⓦ /ˈtʃælɪndʒ/ *verb* [T] **1** ~ **sb (to sth/ to do sth)** to invite sb to fight, play, argue, etc. against you: *They've challenged us to a football match this Saturday.* **2** to question if sth is true, right, etc., or not: *She hates anyone challenging her authority.*

challenger /ˈtʃælɪndʒə(r)/ *noun* [C] a person who invites you to take part in a competition or election, because they want to win a title or position that you hold

challenging 🔒+ **B2** /ˈtʃælɪndʒɪŋ/ *adj.* forcing you to make a lot of effort: *a challenging job* ⊃ note at **difficult**

chamber 🔒+ **C1** /ˈtʃeɪmbə(r)/ *noun* [C] **1** a hall in a public building that is used for formal meetings: *The members left the council chamber.* ◇ *the Senate/ House chamber* ⊃ look at **Chamber of Commerce** **2** (**POLITICS**) one of the parts of a parliament: *the Lower/Upper Chamber* (= in Britain, the House of Commons/House of Lords) ◇ *Under Senate rules, the chamber must vote on the bill by this Friday.* **3** a room used for the particular purpose that is mentioned: *a* burial chamber ⊃ look at **gas chamber 4** a space in the body, in a plant or in a machine, that is separated from the rest: *the four chambers of the heart* **5** (*old-fashioned*) a bedroom or private room

chambermaid /ˈtʃeɪmbəmeɪd/ *noun* [C] (**TOURISM**) a woman whose job is to clean and tidy hotel bedrooms

chamber music *noun* [U] (**MUSIC**) a type of classical music that is written for a small group of instruments

Chamber of Commerce *noun* [C] a group of local business people who work together to help business and trade in a particular town

chameleon /kəˈmiːliən/ *noun* [C] a small LIZARD (= an animal with four legs, dry skin and a long tail) that can change colour according to what is around or near it

chamfer /ˈtʃæmfə(r)/ *noun* [C] a cut made along an edge or on a corner so that it slopes rather than being at 90°

champagne /ʃæmˈpeɪn/ *noun* [U, C] a French white wine that has a lot of bubbles in it and is often very expensive

champion¹ B1 /ˈtʃæmpiən/ *noun* [C] **1** (**SPORT**) a person, team, etc. that has won a competition: *a world champion* ◇ *a champion swimmer* **2** (**POLITICS**) a person who speaks and fights for a particular group, idea, etc: *a champion of free speech*

champion² /ˈtʃæmpiən/ *verb* [T] (**POLITICS**) to support or fight for a particular group or idea: *to champion the cause of human rights*

championship B2 /ˈtʃæmpiənʃɪp/ *noun* [C] (*also* championships [pl.]) (**SPORT**) a competition or series of competitions to find the best player or team in a sport or game: *the World Hockey Championships*

chance¹ A2 /tʃɑːns/ *noun* **1** [C, U] ~ **of (doing) sth**; ~ **(that …)** a possibility: *to have a slim/an outside chance of success* ◇ *Is there any chance of getting tickets for tonight's concert?* ◇ *I think we **stand a** good chance of winning the competition.* ◇ *I think there's a good chance that she'll be the next prime minister.* **2** [C] ~ **(of doing sth/to do sth)** an opportunity: *If somebody invited me to America, I'd **jump at the chance** (= accept enthusiastically).* ◇ *Be quiet and **give her a chance** to explain.* ◇ *I think you should tell him now. You may not **get** another **chance**.* ◇ *If you have the chance to speak to Jo, give her my best wishes.* **3** [C] a risk: *We may lose some money but we'll just have to take that chance.* ◇ *Fasten your seat belt — you shouldn't take (any) chances.* ◇ *I didn't want to **take a chance on** anyone seeing me, so I closed the curtains.* **4** [U] luck; the way that some things happen without any cause that you can see or understand: *We have to plan every detail — I don't want to **leave** anything **to chance**.* ◇ *We met **by chance** (= we had not planned to meet) as I was walking down the street.* **IDM by any chance** (used for asking sth politely) perhaps or possibly: *Are you, by any chance, going into town this afternoon?* **the chances are (that) …** (*informal*) it is likely that … : *The chances are that it will rain tomorrow.* **no chance** (*informal*) there is no possibility of that happening: *'Perhaps your mother will give you the money.' 'No chance!'* **on the off chance** in the hope that sth might happen, although it is not very likely: *I didn't think you'd be at home, but I just called in on the off chance.*

chance² /tʃɑːns/ *verb* **1** [T] ~ **sth/doing sth** (*informal*) to risk sth: *'Take an umbrella.' 'No, I'll **chance it** (= take the risk that it may rain).'* **2** [I] ~ **to do sth** (*formal*) to happen or to do sth by chance: *They chanced to be staying at the same hotel.*

IDM chance your arm (*BrE, informal*) to take a risk although you will probably fail

chance³ /tʃɑːns/ *adj.* [only before noun] not planned: *a chance meeting*

chancel /ˈtʃɑːnsl/ *noun* [C] (**ARCHITECTURE**) the part of a church near the ALTAR, where the priests and the CHOIR (= singers) sit during services

chancellor /ˈtʃɑːnsələ(r)/ (*also* Chancellor) *noun* [C] (often in a title) **1** (**POLITICS**) the head of government in Germany or Austria: *the German chancellor* **2** (*BrE*) = CHANCELLOR OF THE EXCHEQUER: *MPs waited for the chancellor's announcement.* **3** (**EDUCATION**) (in Britain) the official head of a university ⊃ look at **vice chancellor 4** (**EDUCATION**) the head of some American universities **5** (in Britain) a senior state official: *the Lord Chancellor* (= a senior law official)

Chancellor of the Exchequer (*also* Chancellor) *noun* [C] (**FINANCE, POLITICS**) (in the UK) the government minister who is responsible for financial affairs

chandelier /ˌʃændəˈlɪə(r)/ *noun* [C] a large round frame with many branches for lights or CANDLES hanging from the ceiling and sometimes decorated with small pieces of glass

change¹ A1 ⊙ /tʃeɪndʒ/ *verb*

- BECOME/MAKE DIFFERENT **1** [I, T] to become different or to make sb/sth different: *This town has changed a lot since I was young.* ◇ *Our plans have changed — we leave in the morning.* ◇ *His lottery win has not changed him at all.* **SYN** alter **2** [I, T] ~ **(sb/sth) to/into sth**; ~ **(from A) (to/into B)** to become a different thing; to make sb/sth take a different form: *They changed the spare bedroom into a study.* ◇ *The new job changed him into a more confident person.* ◇ *The traffic lights changed from green to red.*
- REPLACE **3** [T] ~ **sth (for sth)** to take, have or use sth instead of sth else: *Could I change this blouse for a larger size?* ◇ *to change jobs* ◇ *to change a wheel on a car* ◇ *to change direction* ◇ *Can I change my appointment from Wednesday to Thursday?*
- EXCHANGE **4** [T] ~ **sth (with sb)** (used with a plural object) to exchange sth with sb, so that you have what they had, and they have what you had: *The teams change ends at half-time.* ◇ *If you want to sit by the window I'll change seats with you.* **SYN** swap
- CLOTHES **5** [I, T] ~ **(out of sth) (into sth)** to take off your clothes and put different ones on: *He's changed his shirt.* ◇ *I had a shower and changed before going out.* ◇ *She changed out of her work clothes and into a clean dress.* ◇ *You can **get changed** in the bedroom.*
- BABY/BED **6** [T] to put clean things onto sb/sth: *The baby's nappy needs changing.* ◇ *to **change the bed** (= to put clean sheets on)*
- MONEY **7** [T] ~ **sth (for/into sth)** to give sb money and receive the same amount back in money of a different type: *Can you change a ten pound note for two fives?* ◇ *I'd like to change 50 euros into US dollars.*
- BUS, TRAIN, ETC. **8** [I, T] to get out of one bus, train, etc. and get into another: *Can we get to Mumbai direct or do we have to change (trains)?*

IDM change hands to pass from one owner to another **change your mind** to change your decision or opinion: *I'll have the green one. No, I've changed my mind — I want the red one.* **change/swap places (with sb)** → PLACE¹ **change the subject** to start talking about sth different **change your tune** (*informal*) to change your opinion or feelings about sth **change your ways** to start to live or behave in a different and better way from before **chop and change** → CHOP¹ **PHR V change over (from sth) (to sth)** to stop doing or using one thing and start doing or using sth else: *The theatre has changed over to a new booking system.*

change² ℇ A1 ⊙ /tʃeɪndʒ/ *noun* **1** [C, U] ~ (in/to sth) the process of becoming or making sth different: *There was little change in the patient's condition overnight.* ◊ *After two hot summers, people were talking about a change in the climate.* ◊ *There will be a slight change to tonight's programme.* **2** [C] ~ (of sth) something that you take, have or use instead of sth else: *We must notify the bank of our change of address.* ◊ *I packed my toothbrush and a change of clothes.* **3** [U] the money that you get back if you pay more than the amount sth costs **4** [U] coins rather than paper money: *He needs some change for the parking meter.* ◊ *Have you got change for a 100 dollar bill?* (= coins or notes of lower value that together make 100 dollars) **IDM** a change for the better/worse a person, thing or situation that is better/worse than the one before **a change of heart** a change in your opinion or the way that you feel **for a change** in order to do sth different from usual: *I usually cycle to work, but today I decided to walk for a change.* **make a change** used to say that an activity is interesting or fun because it is different from what you usually do

changeable /'tʃeɪndʒəbl/ *adj.* likely to change; often changing

changeover /'tʃeɪndʒəʊvə(r)/ *noun* [C] a change from one system or situation to another

'**changing room** *noun* [C] (*especially BrE*) a room for changing clothes in, for example before or after playing sport ⊃ look at **fitting room**

channel¹ ℇ B1 ⓦ /'tʃænl/ *noun* [C] **1** (**ARTS AND MEDIA**) a TV station: *Which channel is the film on?* ⊃ look at **station¹** (4) **2** (**ARTS AND MEDIA**) a band of radio waves used for sending out radio or TV programmes **3** a way or route along which news, information, etc. is sent: *a channel of communication* ◊ *You have to order new equipment through the official channels.* **4** a passage that water can flow along, especially in the ground, on the bottom of a river, etc: *drainage channels in the rice fields* **5** a deep passage of water in a river or near the coast that can be used as a route for ships **6** (**GEOGRAPHY**) a passage of water that connects two areas of water, especially two seas **7** (*usually* **the Channel**) (*also* **the English Channel**) (**GEOGRAPHY**) the area of sea between England and France: *a cross-Channel ferry*

channel² /'tʃænl/ *verb* [T] (-ll-, *AmE* -l-) to make sth move along a particular path or route: *Water is channelled from the river to the fields.* ◊ (*figurative*) *You should channel your energies into something constructive.*

the ˌChannel ˈTunnel *noun* [sing.] the tunnel under the sea that connects England and France

chant¹ /tʃɑːnt/ *noun* **1** [C] a word or phrase that is sung or shouted many times: *A chant of 'we are the champions' went round the stadium.* **2** [C, U] (**RELIGION**) a religious song or prayer or a way of singing, using only a few notes that are repeated many times: *a Buddhist chant* ⊃ look at **Gregorian chant**

chant² /tʃɑːnt/ *verb* [I, T] **1** to sing or shout a word or phrase many times: *The protesters marched by, chanting slogans.* **2** (**RELIGION**) to sing or say a religious song or prayer using only a few notes that are repeated many times

chanterelle /ˌʃɑːntəˈrel/ *noun* [C] a yellow MUSHROOM that grows in woods

chantey /'ʃænti/ (*AmE*) = SHANTY

chaos ℇ+ C1 /'keɪɒs/ *noun* [U] a complete lack of order: *The country was in chaos after the war.* ◊ *The heavy snow has caused chaos on the roads.*

chaotic /keɪˈɒtɪk/ *adj.* without any order; in a completely confused state: *With no one in charge of the situation became chaotic.*

chap /tʃæp/ *noun* [C] (*especially BrE, old-fashioned, informal*) a man or boy

chap. *abbr.* (in writing) = CHAPTER (1)

chapatti (*also* **chapati**) /tʃəˈpɑːti/ *noun* [C] a type of flat round Indian bread

chapel /'tʃæpl/ *noun* [C, U] (**RELIGION**) a small building or room that is used by some Christians as a church or for prayer: *a Methodist chapel*

chaperone /'ʃæpərəʊn/ *noun* [C] (**SOCIAL STUDIES**) in the past, an older person, usually a woman, who went to public places with a young woman who was not married, to look after her and to make sure that she behaved correctly ▸ **chaperone** *verb* [T]

chaplain /'tʃæplɪn/ *noun* [C] (**RELIGION**) a priest who is responsible for the religious needs of people in prison, hospital, the army, etc: *an army chaplain* ⊃ look at **priest**

chapped /tʃæpt/ *adj.* (**HEALTH**) (used about the lips or skin) rough, dry and painful, especially because of wind or cold weather

chapter ℇ B1 /'tʃæptə(r)/ *noun* [C] **1** (*abbr.* **ch, chap.**) (**LITERATURE**) a separate section of a book, usually with a number or title: *Please read Chapter 2 for homework.* **2** a period of time in a person's life or in history: *The last few years have been a difficult chapter in the country's history.*

character ℇ A2 ⓦ /'kærəktə(r)/ *noun*
• QUALITIES **1** [C, usually sing., U] the qualities that make sb/sth different from other people or things; the nature of sb/sth: *Although they are twins, their characters are quite different.* ◊ *These two songs are very different in character.* **2** [U] strong personal qualities: *The match developed into a test of character rather than just physical strength.* **3** [U] qualities that make sb/sth interesting: *Modern houses often seem to lack character.*
• GOOD OPINION **4** [U] the good opinion that people have of you: *The article was a vicious attack on the president's character.*
• PERSON **5** [C] (*informal*) an interesting, funny, strange or unpleasant person: *Neil's quite a character — he's always making us laugh.* ◊ *I saw a suspicious-looking character outside the bank, so I called the police.* **6** [C] (**ARTS AND MEDIA, LITERATURE**) a person in a book, story, etc: *The main character in the film is a boy who meets an alien.*
• SYMBOL/LETTER **7** [C] (**LANGUAGE**) a letter or sign that you use when you are writing or printing: *Chinese characters* **IDM** in/out of character typical/not typical of sb/sth: *Emma's rude reply was completely out of character.*

'**character actor** *noun* [C] (**ARTS AND MEDIA**) an actor who always takes the parts of interesting or unusual people, rather than one of the main parts

characteristic¹ ℇ B2 ⊙ /ˌkærəktəˈrɪstɪk/ *noun* [C] ~ (of sb/sth) a quality that is typical of sb/sth and that makes them or it different from other people or things: *The chief characteristic of fish is that they live in water.*

characteristic² ℇ B2 ⊙ /ˌkærəktəˈrɪstɪk/ *adj.* ~ (of sb/sth) very typical of sb/sth: *The flat landscape is characteristic of this part of the country.* **OPP** uncharacteristic ▸ characteristically /-kli/ *adv.*: *'No' he said, in his characteristically direct manner.*

characterization Ⓦ (BrE also -isation) /ˌkærəktəraɪˈzeɪʃn/ noun [U, C] **1** (LITERATURE) the way that a writer makes the characters in a book or play seem real **2** (formal) the way in which sb/sth is described

characterize ᴦ+ **C1** Ⓦ (BrE also -ise) /ˈkærəktəraɪz/ verb [T] (formal) **1** [often passive] to be typical of sb/sth: the tastes that characterize Thai cooking ◇ His poems are characterized by their simple language and strange imagery. **2** ~ sb/sth (as sth) to describe what sb/sth is like: The president characterized the meeting as friendly and positive.

charade /ʃəˈrɑːd/ noun **1** [C] a situation in which people pretend that sth is true when it clearly is not: They pretend to be friends but it's all a charade. Everyone knows they hate each other. **2** charades [U] a party game in which people try to guess the title of a book, film, etc. that one person must represent using actions but not words

charcoal /ˈtʃɑːkəʊl/ noun [U] a black substance that is produced from burned wood. It can be used for drawing with or as a fuel.

charge¹ ᴦ **B1** /tʃɑːdʒ/ noun
• MONEY **1** [C, U] ~ (for sth) (FINANCE) the amount of money that you must pay for sth: The hotel makes a small charge for changing currency. ◇ We deliver free of charge. ⊃ note at **price¹**
• RESPONSIBILITY **2** [U] a position of control over sb/sth; responsibility for sb/sth: Who is in charge of the office while Alan's away? ◇ The assistant manager had to take charge of the team when the manager resigned. ◇ My mother had charge of the family finances.
• OF A CRIME **3** [C, U] (on a) ~ (of sth) a statement that says that sb has done sth illegal or bad: He was arrested on a charge of murder. ◇ The writer dismissed the charge that his books were childish. ⊃ note at **crime**
• ATTACK **4** [C] a sudden attack where sb/sth runs straight at sb/sth else
• ELECTRICITY **5** [C, U] (PHYSICS) the amount of electricity that is put into a battery or carried by a substance: a positive/negative charge
IDM bring/press charges (against sb) (LAW) to formally accuse sb of a crime so that there can be a trial in a court

charge² ᴦ **B1** /tʃɑːdʒ/ verb **1** [I, T] ~ (sb/sth) for sth (FINANCE) to ask sb to pay a particular amount of money: We charge £35 per night for a single room. ◇ They forgot to charge us for the drinks. ⊃ look at **overcharge 2** [T] ~ sb (with sth) (LAW) to accuse sb officially of doing sth that is against the law: Six men have been charged with attempted robbery. ⊃ note at **crime 3** [I, T] (often used with an adverb or a preposition) to run straight at sb/sth, or in a particular direction, in an aggressive or noisy way: The bull put its head down ready to charge (us). ◇ The children charged into the room. **4** [T] to put electricity into sth: to charge a battery ◇ I need to find somewhere to charge my phone. ⊃ look at **recharge**

charged /tʃɑːdʒd/ adj. ~ (with sth) full of or causing strong feelings or opinions: a highly charged atmosphere ◇ The dialogue is charged with menace.

charger /ˈtʃɑːdʒə(r)/ noun [C] a piece of equipment for loading a battery with electricity: a mobile phone charger

chariot /ˈtʃæriət/ noun [C] (HISTORY) an open vehicle with two wheels that was pulled by a horse or horses in ancient times

charisma /kəˈrɪzmə/ noun [U] a powerful personal quality that some people have to attract and influence other people: The president is not very clever, but he has great charisma. ▶ charismatic /ˌkærɪzˈmætɪk/ adj.

charitable /ˈtʃærətəbl/ adj. **1** kind; generous: Some people accused him of lying, but a more charitable explanation was that he had made a mistake. **2** connected with a charity: charitable donations

charity ᴦ **A2** /ˈtʃærəti/ noun (pl. -ies) **1** [C, U] (SOCIAL STUDIES) an organization that collects money to help people who are poor, sick, etc. or to do work that is useful to society: We went on a sponsored walk to raise money for charity. **2** [U] (formal) kind behaviour towards other people: to act out of charity

charity shop (BrE) (also thrift shop, thrift store both AmE) noun [C] a shop that sells clothes, books, etc. given by people to make money for charity

charlatan /ˈʃɑːlətən/ noun [C] a person who pretends to have knowledge or skills that they do not really have

charm¹ ᴦ+ **C1** /tʃɑːm/ noun **1** [C, U] a quality that pleases and attracts people: The charm of the island lies in its unspoilt beauty. ◇ Frank found it hard to resist Olivia's charms. **2** [C] something that you wear because you believe it will bring you good luck: a charm bracelet ◇ a lucky charm

charm² /tʃɑːm/ verb [T] **1** to please and attract sb: Her drawings have charmed children all over the world. **2** to protect sb/sth as if by magic: He has led a charmed life, surviving serious illness and a plane crash.

charming ᴦ+ **B2** /ˈtʃɑːmɪŋ/ adj. very pleasing or attractive ▶ charmingly adv.

charred /tʃɑːd/ adj. burnt black by fire

chart¹ ᴦ **A1** /tʃɑːt/ noun **1** [C] a drawing that shows information in the form of a diagram, etc: a temperature chart ◇ This chart shows the company's sales for this year. **2** [C] (GEOGRAPHY) a map of the sea or the sky: navigation charts **3** the charts [pl.] (MUSIC) a list, produced each week, of the songs or albums that have sold the most copies or been downloaded or listened to via STREAMING the most frequently

chart² ᴦ+ **B2** /tʃɑːt/ verb [T] **1** to follow or record sth carefully and in detail: This TV series charts the history of the country since independence.
2 (GEOGRAPHY) to make a map of one area of the sea or sky: an uncharted coastline

charter¹ ᴦ+ **C1** /ˈtʃɑːtə(r)/ noun **1** [C] (POLITICS) a written statement describing the rights that a particular group of people should have: the European Union's Social Charter of workers' rights **2** [C] (POLITICS) a written statement of the principles and aims of an organization: the United Nations Charter
SYN constitution **3** [C] (POLITICS) an official document stating that a leader or government allows a new organization, town or university to be established and gives it particular rights: Certain towns were allowed to hold weekly markets, by royal charter. **4** [U] the hiring of a plane, boat, etc: a charter airline ◇ a yacht available for charter

charter² /ˈtʃɑːtə(r)/ verb [T] to rent a ship, plane, etc. for a particular purpose or for a particular group of people: As there was no regular service to the island we had to charter a boat.

chartered /ˈtʃɑːtəd/ adj. [only before noun] (BrE) (used about people in certain professions) fully trained; qualified according to the rules of a professional organization that has a royal CHARTER: a chartered accountant/surveyor/engineer, etc.

charter flight noun [C] (TOURISM) a flight in an aircraft in which all seats are paid for by a travel company and then sold to their customers

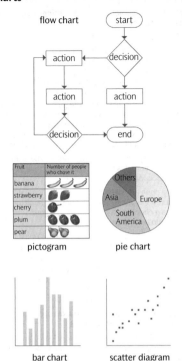

flow chart

pictogram   pie chart

bar chart   scatter diagram

chase¹ ʔ+ B2 /tʃeɪs/ verb 1 [I, T] ~ (after) (sb/sth) to run after sb/sth in order to catch them or it: *The dog chased the cat up a tree.* ◇ *The police car chased after the stolen van.* 2 [I] to run somewhere fast: *The kids were chasing around the park.*

chase² ʔ+ B2 /tʃeɪs/ noun [C] the act of following sb/sth in order to catch them or it: *an exciting car chase* **IDM** give chase to run after sb/sth in order to try to catch them or it: *The robber ran off and the policeman gave chase.*

chasm /ˈkæzəm/ noun [C] (formal) 1 a deep opening or break in the ground 2 a wide difference of feelings, interests, etc. between two people or groups

chassis /ˈʃæsi/ noun [C] (pl. chassis /-siz/) the metal frame of a vehicle onto which the other parts fit

chaste /tʃeɪst/ adj. 1 (old-fashioned) not having sex with anyone; only having sex with the person that you are married to: *to remain chaste* 2 (formal) not expressing sexual feelings: *She gave him a chaste kiss on the cheek.* ▶ chastity /ˈtʃæstəti/ noun [U]

chastise /tʃæˈstaɪz/ verb [T] 1 ~ sb (for sth/doing sth) (formal) to criticize sb for doing sth wrong 2 (old-fashioned) to punish sb physically ▶ chastisement /tʃæˈstaɪzmənt, ˈtʃæstɪzmənt/ noun [U]

chat¹ ʔ A2 /tʃæt/ verb [I] (-tt-) ~ (with/to sb) (about sth) 1 to talk to sb in a friendly, informal way: *The two grandmothers sat chatting about the old days.* ◇ *Helen chats away for hours on the phone to her friends.* 2 (COMPUTING) to exchange messages with sb on the internet, when you can see and reply to messages immediately and have a written conversation: *He's been on the computer all morning, chatting with his friends.*

PHRV chat sb up (BrE, informal) to talk to sb in a friendly way because you are sexually attracted to them

chat² ʔ A2 /tʃæt/ noun [C, U] 1 a friendly informal conversation; talking: *I'll have a chat with Jim about the arrangements.* 2 (COMPUTING) communication between people on the internet in which they see and reply to messages immediately and have a written conversation: *Fans are invited to an online chat.*

chatbot /ˈtʃætbɒt/ noun [C] (COMPUTING) a computer program that can hold a conversation with a person, usually over the internet

'chat room noun [C] (COMPUTING) an area on the internet where people can communicate with each other, usually about one particular topic

'chat show noun [C] (BrE) (ARTS AND MEDIA) a TV or radio programme on which famous people are invited to talk about themselves

chatter /ˈtʃætə(r)/ verb [I] 1 to talk quickly or for a long time about sth unimportant 2 (used about the teeth) to knock together because you are cold or frightened ▶ chatter noun [U]

chatty /ˈtʃæti/ adj. (chattier; chattiest) (informal) 1 talking a lot in a friendly way 2 in an informal style: *a chatty letter*

chauffeur /ˈʃəʊfə(r)/ noun [C] a person whose job is to drive a car for sb else: *a chauffeur-driven limousine* ▶ chauffeur verb [T]

chauvinism /ˈʃəʊvɪnɪzəm/ noun [U] 1 (POLITICS) an aggressive and unreasonable belief that your own country is better than all others 2 (also male chauvinism) (SOCIAL STUDIES) the belief held by some men that men are more important, intelligent, etc. than women ▶ chauvinist /-nɪst/ noun [C], adj.

chav /tʃæv/ noun [C] (BrE, slang) (SOCIAL STUDIES) a young person of a low social class and without a high level of education, who wears fashionable clothes and behaves in a rude, loud way

cheap¹ ʔ A1 /tʃiːp/ adj. 1 costing little money or less money than you expected: *Oranges are cheap at the moment.* ◇ *Computers are getting cheaper all the time.* **SYN** inexpensive **OPP** expensive 2 charging low prices: *a cheap hotel/restaurant* **OPP** expensive 3 low in price and quality and therefore not attractive: *The clothes in that shop look cheap.*

cheap² ʔ B1 /tʃiːp/ adv. (informal) for a low price: *I got this coat cheap in the sale.* **IDM** be going cheap (informal) to be on sale at a lower price than usual

cheapen /ˈtʃiːpən/ verb [T] 1 to make sb lose respect for himself or herself: *She felt cheapened by his treatment of her.* **SYN** degrade 2 to make sth lower in price 3 to make sth appear to have less value: *The film was accused of cheapening human life.*

cheaply /ˈtʃiːpli/ adv. without spending or costing much money: *I'm sure I could buy this more cheaply elsewhere.*

cheapskate /ˈtʃiːpskeɪt/ noun [C] (informal) a person who likes to spend as little money as possible on sth

cheat¹ ʔ B1 /tʃiːt/ verb 1 [T] to trick sb or make them believe sth that is not true: *The wine company cheated customers by replacing the labels on the bottles.* 2 [I] ~ (at sth) to act in a dishonest way in order to gain an advantage, especially in a game, a competition, an exam, etc: *Paul was caught cheating in the exam.* ◇ *to cheat at cards* 3 [I] ~ (on sb) (used about sb who is married or has a regular partner) to have a secret sexual relationship with sb else: *He found out that his wife had been cheating on him.*

PHR V **cheat sb (out) of sth** to take sth from sb in a dishonest or unfair way: *They cheated him out of his share of the profits.*

cheat² 🅱1 /tʃiːt/ *noun* [C] a person who cheats: *The man's a liar and a cheat!*

check¹ 🅰1 /tʃek/ *verb* **1** [I, T] ~ **(sth) (for sth)** to examine or test sth in order to make sure that it is safe or correct, in good condition, etc: *Check your work for mistakes before you hand it in.* ◇ *The doctor X-rayed me to check for broken bones.* **2** [I, T] ~ **(sth) (with sb)** to find out if sth/sb is there, correct or true, or if sth is how you think it is: *You'd better check with Tim that it's OK to borrow his bike.* ◇ *I'll phone and check what time the bus leaves.* ◇ *I need to check my email.* **3** [T] to control sth; to stop sth from increasing or getting worse: *She almost told her boss what she thought of him, but checked herself in time.* ◇ *Phil checked his pace as he didn't want to tire too early.* **4** [T] (*especially AmE*) = TICK¹ (2)

PHR V **check in (at …) | check into …** (**TOURISM**) to go to a desk in a hotel or an airport and tell an official that you have arrived: *Can we check in online for this flight?* ◇ note at **hotel** **check sth off** to mark names or items on a list **check (up) on sb/sth** to find out how sb/sth is: *We call my grandmother every evening to check up on her.* **check out (of …)** (**TOURISM**) to pay your bill and leave a hotel, etc. ◇ note at **hotel** **check sb/sth out 1** to find out more information about sb/ sth, especially to find out if sth is true or not: *We need to check out these rumours of possible pay cuts.* **2** (*informal*) to look at or examine a person or thing that seems interesting or attractive: *Check out the prices at our new store!* **check up on sb/sth** to make sure that sb/sth is working correctly, behaving well, etc., especially if you think they are not

check² 🅰2 /tʃek/ *noun*
- CLOSE LOOK **1** [C] ~ **(on sth)** a close look at sth to make sure that it is safe, correct, in good condition, etc: *We carry out/do regular checks on our products to make sure that they are of high quality.* ◇ *I don't go to games, but I like to keep a check on my team's results.*
- MARK **2** [C] (*especially AmE*) = TICK² (1)
- MONEY **3** [C] (*AmE*) = BILL¹ (2) **4** [C] (*AmE*) = CHEQUE
- PATTERN **5** [C, U] a pattern of squares, often of different colours: *a check jacket* ◇ *a pattern of blue and red checks*
- IN A GAME **6** [U] the position in CHESS (= a game for two players played on a black and white board) in which a player's king (= the most important piece) can be directly attacked by the other player's pieces ◇ look at **checkmate**

IDM **hold/keep sth in check** to keep sth under control so that it does not get worse

checkbook /'tʃekbʊk/ (*AmE*) = CHEQUEBOOK

checkbox /'tʃekbɒks/ *noun* [C] (**COMPUTING**) a small square on a computer screen that you click on with the mouse in order to choose whether a particular function is switched on or off

checked /tʃekt/ *adj.* with a pattern of squares: *a red-and-white checked tablecloth*

checkers /'tʃekəz/ (*AmE*) = DRAUGHT¹

check-in *noun* (**TOURISM**) **1** [C, U] the place where you go first when you arrive at an airport, to show your ticket, etc. **2** [U] the act of confirming your intention to take a particular flight and your personal details either at an airport or using a computer: *Online check-in is now open for your flight.* **3** [C, U] the time when you arrive at a hotel at the start of your stay

checking account (*AmE*) = CURRENT ACCOUNT

checklist /'tʃeklɪst/ *noun* [C] a list of things that you must remember to do

check mark (*AmE*) = TICK² (1)

checkmate /ˌtʃek'meɪt, 'tʃekmeɪt/ *noun* [U] the position in CHESS (= a game for two players played on a black and white board) in which one player cannot prevent their king (= the most important piece) from being captured and so loses the game ◇ look at **check²** (6)

checkout /'tʃekaʊt/ *noun* **1** [C] the place where you pay for the things that you are buying in a supermarket **2** [U] (**TOURISM**) the time when you leave a hotel at the end of your stay **3** [U] part of the process of online shopping in which the customer pays for an item

checkpoint /'tʃekpɔɪnt/ *noun* [C] a place where all people and vehicles must stop and be checked: *an army checkpoint*

check-up *noun* [C] (**MEDICINE**) a general medical examination to make sure that you are healthy: *to go for/have a check-up* ◇ *You should visit your dentist for a check-up twice a year.*

Cheddar /'tʃedə(r)/ (*also* Cheddar 'cheese) *noun* [U] a type of hard yellow cheese

cheek 🅱+ 🅱2 /tʃiːk/ *noun* **1** [C] (**ANATOMY**) either side of the face below the eyes ◇ picture at **body 2** (*sing., U*) (*BrE*) rude behaviour; lack of respect: *He's got a cheek, asking to borrow money again!*

IDM **(with) tongue in cheek** → TONGUE

cheekbone /'tʃiːkbəʊn/ *noun* [C] (**ANATOMY**) the bone below the eye ◇ picture at **body**

cheeky /'tʃiːki/ *adj.* (*BrE, informal*) (**cheekier; cheekiest**) not showing respect; rude: *Don't be so cheeky! Of course I'm not fat!* ▸ cheekily /-kɪli/ *adv.*

cheer¹ 🅱+ 🅱2 /tʃɪə(r)/ *noun* [C] a loud shout to show that you like sth or to encourage sb who is taking part in a competition, sport, etc: *A great cheer went up from the crowd.* ◇ look at **hip, hip, hooray/hurrah** at **hip²**

cheer² 🅱+ 🅱2 /tʃɪə(r)/ *verb* **1** [I, T] to shout to show that you like sth or to encourage sb who is taking part in competition, sport, etc: *Everyone cheered the winner as he crossed the finishing line.* **2** [T, usually passive] to give hope or comfort to sb; to encourage sb: *They were all cheered by the good news.*

PHR V **cheer sb on** to shout in order to encourage sb in a race, competition, etc: *As the runners started the last lap the crowd cheered them on.* **cheer (sb/sth) up** to become or to make sb happier; to make sth look more attractive: *Cheer up! Things aren't that bad.* ◇ *A few pictures would cheer this room up a bit.*

cheerful 🅱1 /'tʃɪəfl/ *adj.* **1** happy, and showing it by the way that you behave: *Caroline is always very cheerful.* ◇ *a cheerful smile* **2** giving you a feeling of happiness: *walls painted in cheerful colours* ▸ cheerfully /-fəli/ *adv.* ▸ cheerfulness *noun* [U]

cheerily /'tʃɪərəli/ → CHEERY

cheerio /ˌtʃɪəri'əʊ/ *exclamation* (*BrE, informal, old-fashioned*) goodbye

cheerleader /'tʃɪəliːdə(r)/ *noun* [C] (especially in the US) one of the members of a group of young people (usually women) wearing special uniforms, who encourage the crowd to CHEER for their team (= shout to encourage them) at a sports event

cheers /tʃɪəz/ *exclamation* (*informal*) **1** a word that people say to each other as they lift up their glasses to drink: *'Cheers,' she said, raising her wine glass.* **2** (*BrE*) goodbye **3** (*BrE*) thank you

cheery /'tʃɪəri/ *adj.* (**cheerier; cheeriest**) happy and cheerful: *a cheery remark/wave/smile* ▸ cheerily *adv.*

cheese 🔊 **A1** /tʃiːz/ *noun* **1** [U] a type of food made from milk. Cheese is usually white or yellow in colour and can be soft or hard: *a chunk/piece/slice of cheese* ◇ *a cheese sandwich* **2** [C] a type of cheese: *a wide selection of cheeses*

cheesecake /'tʃiːzkeɪk/ *noun* [C, U] a type of cake that is made from soft cheese and sugar on a PASTRY or biscuit base, sometimes with fruit on top

cheesy /'tʃiːzi/ *adj.* (**cheesier; cheesiest**) (*informal*) not very good or original and without style, in a way that is embarrassing but sometimes funny: *an incredibly cheesy love song*

cheetah /'tʃiːtə/ *noun* [C] a large wild cat with black spots that can run very fast ➔ picture at **lion**

chef 🔊 **A2** /ʃef/ *noun* [C] a professional cook, especially the head cook in a hotel, restaurant, etc.

chemical¹ 🔊 **B1** /'kemɪkl/ *adj.* (**CHEMISTRY**)
1 connected with chemistry: *a chemical element*
2 produced by or using processes that involve changes to ATOMS or MOLECULES: *chemical reactions/ processes* **3** using or connected with chemicals: *the chemical industry* ◇ *chemical weapons/warfare*
▶ **chemically** /-kli/ *adv.*: *The raw sewage is chemically treated.*

chemical² 🔊 **B1** /'kemɪkl/ *noun* [C] (**CHEMISTRY**) a substance that is used or produced in a chemical process: *Sulphuric acid is a dangerous chemical.* ◇ *Farmers are being urged to reduce their use of chemicals and work with nature to combat pests.* ➔ picture at **fractional distillation**

,chemical 'warfare *noun* [U] the use of poisonous gases and chemicals as weapons in a war

,chemical 'weapon *noun* [C] a weapon that uses poisonous gases and chemicals to kill and injure people ➔ look at **biological weapon**

chemist /'kemɪst/ *noun* [C] **1** (*BrE*) (*also* **pharmacist** *AmE, BrE*) a person who prepares and sells medicines **2** **chemist's** (*pl.* **chemists**) (*BrE*) (*AmE* **drugstore**) a shop that sells medicines, soap, MAKE-UP, etc: *Take this prescription to the chemist's.* ➔ note at **doctor¹** **3** a scientist who studies chemistry

chemistry 🔊 **A2** /'kemɪstri/ *noun* [U] **1** (**EDUCATION, SCIENCE**) the scientific study of the structure of substances and what happens to them in different conditions or when mixed with each other **2** (**SCIENCE**) the structure of a particular substance **3** the relationship between two people, usually a strong sexual attraction

chemosynthesis /ˌkiːməʊˈsɪnθəsɪs/ *noun* [U] (**BIOLOGY**) the process by which some ORGANISMS (= living things) that live in dark places at the bottom of the sea feed themselves using energy from SULPHIDES mixed with OXYGEN ➔ look at **photosynthesis**
▶ **chemosynthetic** /ˌkiːməʊsɪnˈθetɪk/ *adj.*: *chemosynthetic microbes*

chemotherapy /ˌkiːməʊˈθerəpi/ (*also informal* **chemo** /'kiːməʊ/) *noun* [U] (**MEDICINE**) the treatment of disease, especially cancer, using chemical substances: *She was suffering from leukaemia and undergoing chemotherapy.* ➔ look at **radiation** (3), **radiotherapy**

cheque (*BrE*) (*AmE* **check**) /tʃek/ *noun* [C, U] (**FINANCE**) a piece of paper printed by a bank that you sign and use to pay for things: *She wrote out a cheque for £1000.* ◇ *I went to the bank to cash a cheque.* ◇ *Can I pay by cheque?*

chequebook (*BrE*) (*AmE* **checkbook**) /'tʃekbʊk/ *noun* [C] (**FINANCE**) a book of CHEQUES (= pieces of paper printed by a bank that you sign and use to pay for things)

cherish /'tʃerɪʃ/ *verb* [T] (*formal*) **1** to love sb/sth and look after them or it carefully **2** to keep a thought, feeling, etc. in your mind and think about it often: *a cherished memory*

cherry /'tʃeri/ *noun* [C] (*pl.* **-ies**) **1** a small soft round fruit with shiny red or black skin and a large hard seed inside **2** (*also* 'cherry tree) the tree that produces cherries

cherub /'tʃerəb/ *noun* [C] (**RELIGION**) a type of ANGEL (= a spirit who is believed to be a servant of God), shown as a small fat, usually male, child with wings

chervil /'tʃɜːvɪl/ *noun* [U] a plant with leaves that are used in cooking as a HERB

chess /tʃes/ *noun* [U] a game for two people played on a board marked with black and white squares on which each playing piece (representing a king, queen, castle, etc.) is moved according to special rules: *Can you play chess?*

chest 🔊 **B1** /tʃest/ *noun* [C] **1** (**ANATOMY**) the top part of the front of the body between the neck and the stomach ➔ picture at **body** **2** a large strong box that is used for storing or carrying things
IDM **get sth off your chest** (*informal*) to talk about sth that you have been thinking or worrying about

chestnut /'tʃesnʌt/ *noun* [C] **1** (*also* 'chestnut tree) a tree with large leaves that produces smooth brown nuts in shells with sharp points on the outside ➔ look at **horse chestnut** (1) **2** a smooth brown nut from the chestnut tree. You can eat some types of chestnut: *roast chestnuts* ➔ look at **conker**, **horse chestnut** (2)

,chest of 'drawers *noun* [C] (*pl.* **chests of drawers**) a piece of furniture with DRAWERS (= containers like boxes that you can pull out) in it that is used for storing clothes, etc.

chevron /'ʃevrən, -rɒn/ *noun* [C] a line or pattern in the shape of a V

chew /tʃuː/ *verb* [I, T] **1** to break up food in your mouth with your teeth before you SWALLOW it **2** ~ (on) sth to bite sth continuously: *The dog was chewing on a bone.*

'chewing gum (*also* **gum**) *noun* [U] a sweet sticky substance that you CHEW in your mouth but do not eat ➔ look at **bubblegum**

chewy /'tʃuːi/ *adj.* (**chewier; chewiest**) (used about food) difficult to break up with your teeth before it can be eaten: *chewy meat/toffee*

chi *noun* **1** /kaɪ/ [C] the 22nd letter of the Greek alphabet (Χ, χ) **2** /tʃiː/ [U] (in Chinese philosophy and medicine) the life force that is part of everything

chiaroscuro /kiˌɑːrəˈskʊərəʊ/ *noun* [U] (**ART**) the way light and shade are shown; the contrast between light and shade

chiasmus /kaɪˈæzməs/ *noun* [U, C] (*pl.* **chiasmi** /-maɪ/) (**LANGUAGE, LITERATURE**) a technique used in writing or in speeches, in which words, ideas, etc. are repeated in the opposite order, for example in the phrase 'What's mine is yours, and what's yours is mine'

chic /ʃiːk/ *adj.* fashionable and attractive **SYN** **stylish**
▶ **chic** *noun* [U]

chick /tʃɪk/ *noun* [C] **1** a baby bird, especially a young chicken **2** (*old-fashioned, slang*) a way of referring to a young woman

chicken¹ 🔊 **A1** /'tʃɪkɪn/ *noun* **1** [C] a bird that people often keep for its eggs and its meat ➔ note on **page 130** ➔ picture at **animal** **2** [U] the meat of a chicken: *roast chicken* ◇ *chicken soup*
IDM **Don't count your chickens (before they're hatched)** → COUNT¹

Note that **chicken** is the general word for the bird and its meat. A male chicken is called a **cock** or **rooster**, a female is called a **hen**, and a young bird is called a **chick**.

chicken² /'tʃɪkɪn/ *verb*
PHR V **chicken out (of sth)** (*informal*) to decide not to do sth because you are afraid

chickenpox /'tʃɪkɪnpɒks/ *noun* [U] (**HEALTH**) a disease, especially of children. When you have **chickenpox** you have a high temperature and get many red spots on your skin.

chickpea /'tʃɪkpiː/ (*especially BrE*) (*AmE usually* **garbanzo**, **gar'banzo bean**) *noun* [C] a hard round seed, like a light brown PEA, that can be cooked and eaten as a vegetable

chicory /'tʃɪkəri/ (*BrE*) (*AmE* **endive**) *noun* [U] a small pale green plant with bitter leaves that can be eaten cooked or not cooked

chief¹ 🔒 **B2** /tʃiːf/ *adj.* [only before noun] **1** most important; main: *One of the chief reasons for his decision was money.* ⊃ note at **main¹** **2** (*often* Chief) of the highest level or position: *the chief executive of a company* ◇ *Detective Chief Inspector Garcia*

chief² 🔒 **B2** /tʃiːf/ *noun* [C] **1** the person who has command or control over an organization: *the chief of police* **2** (*often as a title*) the leader of a community or a TRIBE

chief e'xecutive *noun* [C] **1** (**BUSINESS**) the person with the highest rank in a company or an organization: *The chief executive addressed the board.* **2** Chief Executive (**POLITICS**) the president of the US

chief e,xecutive 'officer = CEO

chiefly /'tʃiːfli/ *adv.* mostly: *His success was due chiefly to hard work.* **SYN** **mainly**

chieftain /'tʃiːftən/ *noun* [C] (**SOCIAL STUDIES**) the leader of a TRIBE

chiffon /'ʃɪfɒn/ *noun* [U] a very thin type of cloth that you can see through, used for making clothes, etc.

chilblain /'tʃɪlbleɪn/ *noun* [C] (**HEALTH**) a painful red area on the foot, hand, etc. that is caused by cold weather

child 🔒 **A1** /tʃaɪld/ *noun* [C] (*pl.* children) **1** a young boy or girl who is not yet an adult: *A group of children were playing in the park.* ◇ *a 6-year-old child* ◇ *the children's room* **2** a son or daughter of any age: *She has two children but both are married and have moved away.*

child 'benefit *noun* [U] (in the UK) money that the government regularly pays to parents of children up to a particular age

childbirth /'tʃaɪldbɜːθ/ *noun* [U] the act of giving birth to a baby: *His wife died in childbirth.*

childcare /'tʃaɪldkeə(r)/ *noun* [U] the job of looking after children, especially while the parents are at work: *Some employers provide childcare facilities.*

childhood 🔒 **B1** /'tʃaɪldhʊd/ *noun* [C, U] the time when you are a child: *Harriet had a very unhappy childhood.* ◇ *childhood memories*

childish /'tʃaɪldɪʃ/ *adj.* **1** connected with or typical of a child: *childish handwriting* **2** (used about an adult) behaving in a stupid or silly way **SYN** **immature** **OPP** **mature¹** ▸ childishly *adv.*

childless /'tʃaɪldləs/ *adj.* having no children

childlike /'tʃaɪldlaɪk/ *adj.* having the qualities that children usually have, especially INNOCENCE: *childlike enthusiasm/delight* ⊃ look at **childish**

childminder /'tʃaɪldmaɪndə(r)/ *noun* [C] (*BrE*) a person whose job is to care for children while their parents are at work, usually in his or her own home ⊃ look at **babysitter**

childproof /'tʃaɪldpruːf/ *adj.* designed so that young children cannot open, use or damage it: *childproof containers for medicine*

children /'tʃɪldrən/ plural of **child**

'children's home *noun* [C] an institution where children live whose parents cannot look after them

chili /'tʃɪli/ *noun* [C] (*pl.* chilies) (*AmE*) = CHILLI

chill¹ /tʃɪl/ *noun* **1** [sing.] an unpleasant cold feeling: *There's a chill in the air.* ◇ (*figurative*) *A chill of fear went down my spine.* **2** [C] (*informal*) (**HEALTH**) an illness caused by being cold and wet, causing a high temperature and SHIVERING (= shaking of the body): *to catch a chill*

chill² /tʃɪl/ *verb* **1** [I, T] to become or to make sb/sth colder: *Let the pudding chill for an hour in the fridge.* **2** [I] (*informal*) = CHILL OUT
PHR V **chill out** (*also* chill) (*informal*) to spend time relaxing; to stop feeling angry or nervous about sth: *I work hard all week so on Sundays I just chill out.* ◇ *Sit down and chill out!*

chillax /tʃɪ'læks/ *verb* [I] (*slang*) to relax and stop feeling angry or nervous about sth: *Chillax, dude — I'm in your team.*

chilli (*BrE*) (*AmE* **chili**) /'tʃɪli/ *noun* [C, U] (*pl.* chillies) a small green or red vegetable that has a very strong hot taste: *chilli powder*

chilling /'tʃɪlɪŋ/ *adj.* frightening: *a chilling ghost story*

chilly /'tʃɪli/ *adj.* (chillier; chilliest) **1** (used about the weather but also about people) too cold to be comfortable: *It's a chilly morning. You need a coat on.* **2** unfriendly: *We got a very chilly reception.*

chime /tʃaɪm/ *verb* [I, T] (used about a bell or clock) to ring ▸ chime *noun* [C]
PHR V **chime in (with sth)** (*informal*) to interrupt a conversation and add your own comments

chimney /'tʃɪmni/ *noun* [C] a structure through which smoke or STEAM is carried up and out through the roof of a building

'chimney pot *noun* [C] a short wide pipe that is placed on top of a CHIMNEY

'chimney sweep *noun* [C] a person whose job is to clean the inside of CHIMNEYS with long brushes

chimpanzee /ˌtʃɪmpæn'ziː/ (*also informal* **chimp** /tʃɪmp/) *noun* [C] a small intelligent African APE (= an animal like a large monkey without a tail) ⊃ look at **monkey** ⊃ picture at **animal**

chin /tʃɪn/ *noun* [C] (**ANATOMY**) the part of the face below the mouth ⊃ picture at **body**
IDM **(keep your) chin up** (*informal*) used to tell sb to try to stay cheerful even though they are in a difficult or unpleasant situation

china /'tʃaɪnə/ *noun* [U] **1** white CLAY of good quality that is used for making cups, plates, etc: *a china vase* **2** cups, plates, etc. that are made from china

,china 'clay = KAOLIN

chink /tʃɪŋk/ *noun* [C] a small narrow opening: *Daylight came in through a chink between the curtains.*

chintz /tʃɪnts/ *noun* [U] a shiny cotton cloth with a printed design, usually of flowers, used for making curtains, covering furniture, etc.

chip¹ 🔒 **A2** /tʃɪp/ *noun* [C] **1** (*BrE*) (*also* **French fry**, **fry** *BrE*, *AmE*) [usually pl.] a thin piece of potato that is fried in hot fat or oil **2** (*AmE*) = CRISP¹ **3** = MICROCHIP: *chip technology* **4** the place where a small piece of stone, glass, wood, etc. has broken off sth: *This dish has a* *chip in it.* **5** a small piece of stone, glass, wood, etc. that has broken off sth **6** a flat round piece of plastic that you use to represent a particular amount of money in some types of GAMBLING

IDM have a chip on your shoulder (about sth) (*informal*) to feel angry about sth that happened a long time ago because you think it is unfair

chip² /tʃɪp/ *verb* [I, T] (-pp-) **1** to break a small piece off the edge or surface of sth; to become damaged in this way: *They chipped the paint trying to get the table through the door.* **2** (SPORT) to hit or kick the ball so that it goes high in the air and then lands within a short distance

PHRV chip in (*informal*) **1** to interrupt when sb else is talking **2** to give some money as part of the cost of sth: *We all chipped in and bought him a present when he left.*

chipmunk /'tʃɪpmʌŋk/ *noun* [C] a small North American animal with a long, thick tail and bands of dark and light colour on its back

chip shop (*also* **chippy** /'tʃɪpi/ *informal*) *noun* [C] (in the UK) a shop that cooks and sells fish and chips and other fried food to take away and eat

chiropody /kɪ'rɒpədi/ (*especially BrE*) (*AmE usually* **podiatry**) *noun* [U] (MEDICINE) the care and treatment of people's feet ▸ **chiropodist** /-dɪst/ (*AmE usually* **podiatrist**) *noun* [C]

chiropractor /'kaɪərəʊpræktə(r)/ *noun* [C] (MEDICINE) a person whose job involves treating some diseases and physical problems by pressing and moving the bones in a person's SPINE or JOINTS ⊃ look at **osteopath**

chirp /tʃɜːp/ *verb* [I] (used about small birds and some insects) to make short high sounds

chisel /'tʃɪzl/ *noun* [C] a tool with a sharp end that is used for shaping wood or stone ⊃ picture at **tool**

chivalry /'ʃɪvəlri/ *noun* [U] polite and kind behaviour by men that shows respect towards women ▸ **chivalrous** /-rəs/ *adj.*

chives /tʃaɪvz/ *noun* [pl.] the long thin leaves of a plant that taste like onions and are used in cooking

chlamydia /klə'mɪdiə/ *noun* [U] (HEALTH) a disease caused by bacteria that is caught by having sex with a person who already has the disease

chloride /'klɔːraɪd/ *noun* [U, C] (CHEMISTRY) a COMPOUND of CHLORINE and another chemical element

chlorinate /'klɔːrɪneɪt/ *verb* [T] to put CHLORINE in sth, especially water, or to treat sth with CHLORINE: *a chlorinated swimming pool ◇ chlorinated chicken* ▸ **chlorination** /ˌklɔːrɪ'neɪʃn/ *noun* [U] ⊃ picture at **purification**

chlorine /'klɔːriːn/ *noun* [U] (*symb.* Cl) (CHEMISTRY) a chemical element. Chlorine is a green gas with a strong smell, used for making water safe to drink or swim in. ❶ For more information on the periodic table of elements, look at the **Reference Section** of this dictionary.

chlorofluorocarbon /ˌklɔːrəʊˈfluərəʊkɑːbən/ *noun* [C] a CFC; a COMPOUND of CARBON, FLUORINE and CHLORINE that is harmful to the environment ⊃ look at **fluorocarbon**

chloroform /'klɒrəfɔːm/ *noun* [U] (*symb.* CHCl₃) (CHEMISTRY) a clear liquid with a strong smell used by doctors in the past to make people unconscious, for example before an operation

chlorophyll /'klɒrəfɪl/ *noun* [U] (BIOLOGY) the green substance in plants that takes in light from the sun to help them grow ⊃ look at **photosynthesis** ⊃ picture at **photosynthesis**

chloroplast /'klɒrəplɑːst/ *noun* [C] (BIOLOGY) the part of a green plant cell that contains CHLOROPHYLL and in which PHOTOSYNTHESIS (= the changing of light from the sun into energy) takes place ⊃ picture at **cell**

chock-a-block /ˌtʃɒk ə 'blɒk/ *adj.* [not before noun] completely full: *The High Street was chock-a-block with shoppers.*

chocoholic /ˌtʃɒkə'hɒlɪk/ *noun* [C] (*informal*) a person who loves chocolate and eats a lot of it

chocolate ⚠ A1 /'tʃɒklət/ *noun* **1** [U] a sweet brown substance made from COCOA beans that you can eat as a sweet or use to add taste to food and drinks: *a bar of milk/plain chocolate ◇ a chocolate milkshake* **2** [C] a small sweet that is made from or covered with chocolate: *a box of chocolates* **3** [C, U] a drink made by mixing chocolate powder with hot milk or water: *a mug of hot chocolate* **4** [U] a dark brown colour

choice¹ ⚠ A2 ⊙ /tʃɔɪs/ *noun* **1** [C] ~ (between A and B) an act of choosing between two or more people or things: *David was forced to make a choice between moving house and losing his job.* **2** [U] the right or chance to choose: *There is a rail strike so we have no choice but to cancel our trip. ◇ to have freedom of choice* **SYN** option **3** [C, U] two or more things from which you can or must choose: *This cinema offers a choice of six different films every night.* **4** [C] a person or thing that is chosen: *Harry would be my choice as team captain.* ⊃ verb **choose**

IDM by choice because you have chosen: *I wouldn't go there by choice.*

choice² /tʃɔɪs/ *adj.* of very good quality: *choice beef*

choir ⚠+ B2 /'kwaɪə(r)/ *noun* [C + sing./pl. verb] (MUSIC) an organized group of people who sing together in churches, schools, etc.

choke¹ /tʃəʊk/ *verb* **1** [I, T] ~ (on sth) to be or to make sb unable to breathe because sth is stopping air getting into the lungs: *She was choking on a fish bone. ◇ He almost choked to death. ◇ He put the scarf around her neck and tried to choke her.* ⊃ look at **strangle** (1) **2** [T, usually passive] be choked (up) (with sth) if a passage, space, etc. **is choked** up or **is choked** with sth, nothing can pass through: *The roads to the coast were choked with traffic.* **3** [I] (*informal*) (SPORT) to fail to win a sports contest, especially because you lose your confidence: *He should have won, but he seemed to choke in the final set.*

PHRV choke sth back to hide or control a strong emotion: *to choke back tears/anger*

choke² /tʃəʊk/ *noun* [C] **1** the device in a car, etc. that controls the amount of air going into the engine **2** an act or the sound of sb CHOKING

cholera /'kɒlərə/ *noun* [U] (HEALTH) a serious disease that causes DIARRHOEA and VOMITING and can cause death. Cholera is most common in hot countries and is carried by water.

cholesterol /kə'lestərɒl/ *noun* [U] (BIOLOGY, HEALTH) a FATTY substance that is found in the blood, etc. of people and animals. Too much cholesterol in the blood is thought to be a cause of heart disease.

choose ⚠ A1 ⓢ /tʃuːz/ *verb* [I, T] (*pt* chose /tʃəʊz/; *pp* chosen /'tʃəʊzn/) **1** ~ (between A and/or B); ~ (A) (from B); ~ sb/sth (as sth) to decide which thing or person you want out of the ones that are available: *Choose carefully before you make a final decision. ◇ Amy had to choose between getting a job or going to college. ◇ You can choose three questions from the five on the exam paper. ◇ The viewers chose this programme as their favourite.* **2** ~ (to do sth) to decide or prefer to do sth: *You are free to leave whenever you*

choose. ◊ *They chose to resign rather than work for the new manager.* ᴐ noun **choice**
IDM pick and choose → PICK¹

choosy /'tʃuːzi/ *adj.* (choosier; choosiest) (*informal*) (used about a person) difficult to please

chop¹ ɛ̃+ **B2** /tʃɒp/ *verb* [T] (-pp-) ~ **sth (up) (into sth)** to cut sth into pieces with a knife, etc.: *finely chopped herbs* ◊ *Chop the onions up into small pieces.*
IDM chop and change (*BrE, informal*) to change your plans or opinions several times
PHR V chop sth down to cut a tree, etc. at the bottom so that it falls down chop sth off (sth) to remove sth from sth by cutting it with a knife or a sharp tool

chop² /tʃɒp/ *noun* [C] **1** a thick slice of meat with a piece of bone in it ᴐ look at **steak** **2** an act of hitting sth with a quick, short DOWNWARD movement: *a karate chop*

chopper /'tʃɒpə(r)/ (*informal*) = HELICOPTER

chopping board (*BrE*) (*AmE* **chopping block**) *noun* [C] a piece of wood or plastic used for cutting meat or vegetables on

choppy /'tʃɒpi/ *adj.* (choppier; choppiest) (used about the sea) with a lot of small waves; not calm

chopstick /'tʃɒpstɪk/ *noun* [C, usually pl.] one of the two thin pieces of wood or plastic that are used for eating with, especially in Asian countries

choral /'kɔːrəl/ *adj.* (MUSIC) connected with, written for or sung by a CHOIR (= a group of singers)

chorale /kɒ'rɑːl/ *noun* [C] (MUSIC) **1** a piece of church music sung by a group of singers **2** (*especially AmE*) a group of singers ᴐ look at **choir**

chord /kɔːd/ *noun* [C] **1** (MUSIC) two or more musical notes that are played at the same time ᴐ look at **arpeggio** **2** (MATHEMATICS) a straight line that joins two points on a curve ᴐ picture at **circle¹**

chore /tʃɔː(r)/ *noun* [C] a job that is not interesting but that you must do: *household chores*

choreograph /'kɒriəgrɑːf/ *verb* [T] (ARTS AND MEDIA) to design and arrange the movements of a dance ▸ **choreographer** /ˌkɒri'ɒgrəfə(r)/ *noun* [C]

choreography /ˌkɒri'ɒgrəfi/ *noun* [U] (ARTS AND MEDIA) the arrangement of movements for a dance performance

chorister /'kɒrɪstə(r)/ *noun* [C] (MUSIC) a person, especially a boy, who sings in the CHOIR of a church

chorus¹ /'kɔːrəs/ *noun* **1** [C] (MUSIC) the part of a song that is repeated at the end of each VERSE: *The audience joined in with the choruses.* **SYN** **refrain²** ᴐ look at **verse** (2) **2** [C] (MUSIC) a piece of music, usually part of a larger work, that is written for a CHOIR (= a group of singers) **3** [C + sing./pl. verb] (MUSIC) a large group of people who sing together **SYN** **choir** **4** [C + sing./pl. verb] (ARTS AND MEDIA) a group of people who sing and dance in a musical show: *the chorus line* (= a line of singers and dancers performing together) **5** [sing.] ~ **of sth** something that a lot of people say together: *a chorus of cheers/criticism/disapproval*

chorus² /'kɔːrəs/ *verb* [T] (used about a group of people) to sing or say sth together: *'That's not fair!' the children chorused.*

chose /tʃəʊz/ past tense of **choose**

chosen /'tʃəʊzn/ past participle of **choose**

Christ /kraɪst/ (*also* Jesus, Jesus 'Christ) *noun* (RELIGION) the man that Christians believe is the son of God and on whose teachings the Christian religion is based

christen /'krɪsn/ *verb* [T] **1** (RELIGION) to give a person, usually a baby, a name during a Christian ceremony in which he or she is made a member of the Church:

The baby was christened James Harry. ᴐ look at **baptize 2** to give sb/sth a name: *People drive so dangerously on this stretch of road that they've christened it 'The Mad Mile'.*

christening /'krɪsnɪŋ/ *noun* [C] (RELIGION) the church ceremony in the Christian religion in which a baby is given a name ᴐ look at **baptism**

Christian /'krɪstʃən/ *noun* [C] (RELIGION) a person whose religion is Christianity ᴐ note at **religion** ▸ **Christian** *adj.*

Christianity /ˌkrɪsti'ænəti/ *noun* [U] (RELIGION) the religion that is based on the ideas taught by Jesus Christ ᴐ note at **religion**

Christian name (*also* given name *especially in AmE*) *noun* [C] the name given to a child when he or she is born; first name

Christmas /'krɪsməs/ *noun* **1** [C, U] the period of time before and after 25 December: *Where are you spending Christmas this year?* ◊ *What did you get for Christmas?* ◊ *Christmas presents* **2** Christmas 'Day [C] a public holiday on 25 December. It is the day on which Christians celebrate the birth of Christ each year.

Christmas card *noun* [C] a card with a picture on the front and a message inside that people send to their friends and relatives at Christmas

Christmas 'carol = CAROL

Christmas 'cracker = CRACKER

Christmas 'dinner *noun* [C] the traditional meal eaten on Christmas Day: *We had a traditional Christmas dinner that year, with roast turkey, Christmas pudding and all the trimmings.*

Christmas 'Eve *noun* [C] 24 December, the day before Christmas Day, or the evening of this day

Christmas 'pudding *noun* [C, U] a hot sweet dish made from dried fruit and traditionally eaten in the UK at Christmas

Christmas tree *noun* [C] a real or an artificial tree that people bring into their homes and cover with coloured lights and decorations at Christmas

chromatic /krə'mætɪk/ *adj.* (MUSIC) used to describe a series of musical notes that rise and fall in SEMITONES (= notes that are next to each other on a piano): *the chromatic scale*

chromatography /ˌkrəʊmə'tɒgrəfi/ *noun* [U] (CHEMISTRY) the process of separating a liquid mixture by passing it through a material through which some parts of the mixture travel further than others

chrome /krəʊm/ *noun* [U] (CHEMISTRY) a hard shiny metal that is used for covering other metals; CHROMIUM or an ALLOY of CHROMIUM and other metals

chromium /'krəʊmiəm/ *noun* [U] (*symb.* Cr) (CHEMISTRY) a chemical element. Chromium is a hard grey metal that shines brightly when POLISHED (= made smooth and shiny by being rubbed). ❶ For more information on the periodic table of elements, look at the **Reference Section** of this dictionary.

chromosomal /ˌkrəʊmə'səʊml/ *adj.* (BIOLOGY) relating to one or more CHROMOSOMES: *chromosomal abnormalities*

chromosome /'krəʊməsəʊm/ *noun* [C] (BIOLOGY) a part of a cell in living things that decides the sex, character, shape, etc. that a person, an animal or a plant will have. Chromosomes carry the GENES. ᴐ look at **X chromosome, Y chromosome**

chronic ɛ̃+ **C1** /'krɒnɪk/ *adj.* (HEALTH) **1** (used especially about a disease) lasting for a long time; difficult to cure or get rid of: *chronic bronchitis/arthritis/asthma* ◊ *the country's chronic unemployment problem* ᴐ look

2 having had a disease for a long time: *a chronic alcoholic/depressive* ▶ chronically /-kli/ *adv.*

chronicle /ˈkrɒnɪkl/ *noun* [C] (**HISTORY**) a written record of historical events describing them in the order in which they happened: *the Anglo-Saxon Chronicle* ▶ chronicle *verb* [T] (*formal*): *Her achievements are chronicled in a new biography out this week.*

chronological /ˌkrɒnəˈlɒdʒɪkl/ *adj.* (**HISTORY**) arranged in the order in which the events happened: *This book describes the main events in his life **in chronological order**.* ▶ chronologically /-kli/ *adv.*

chronology /krəˈnɒlədʒi/ *noun* [U, C] (*pl.* -ies) (**HISTORY**) the order in which a series of events happened; a list of these events in order: *The exact chronology of these events is a subject for debate.* ◊ *a chronology of Kennedy's life*

chrysalis /ˈkrɪsəlɪs/ *noun* [C] (*pl.* chrysalises) (**BIOLOGY**) the form of an insect, especially a BUTTERFLY (= an insect with large brightly coloured wings) or a MOTH (= an insect similar to a BUTTERFLY), while it is changing into an adult inside a hard case, which is also called a chrysalis ⊃ look at **pupa** ⊃ picture at **animal**

chrysanthemum /krɪˈzænθəməm/ *noun* [C] a large garden flower that is brightly coloured and shaped like a ball

chubby /ˈtʃʌbi/ *adj.* (chubbier; chubbiest) slightly fat in an attractive way: *a baby with chubby cheeks*

chuck /tʃʌk/ *verb* [T] (*informal*) to throw sth in a careless way: *You can chuck those old shoes in the bin.* **PHR V** chuck sth in (*informal*) to give sth up: *He's chucked his job in because he was fed up.* chuck sb out (of sth) (*informal*) to force sb to leave a place: *They were chucked out of the cinema for making too much noise.*

chuckle /ˈtʃʌkl/ *verb* [I] to laugh quietly: *Bruce chuckled to himself as he read the message.* ▶ chuckle *noun* [C]

chug /tʃʌg/ *verb* [I] (-gg-) **1** (used about a machine or an engine) to make short repeated sounds while it is working or moving slowly **2** ~ along, down, up, etc. to move making the sound of an engine running slowly: *The train chugged out of the station.*

chunk ？+ **C1** /tʃʌŋk/ *noun* [C] a large or thick piece of sth: *chunks of bread and cheese*

chunky /ˈtʃʌŋki/ *adj.* (chunkier; chunkiest) **1** thick and heavy: *chunky jewellery* **2** (used about a person) short and strong **3** (used about food) containing thick pieces: *chunky banana milkshake*

church ？ **A2** /tʃɜːtʃ/ *noun* (**RELIGION**) **1** [C, U] a building where Christians go to pray, etc: *Do you go to church regularly?* **2** Church [C] a particular group of Christians: *the Anglican/Catholic/Methodist Church* **3** (the) Church [sing.] the ministers or the institution of the Christian religion: *the conflict between Church and State*

churchgoer /ˈtʃɜːtʃɡəʊə(r)/ *noun* [C] (**RELIGION**) a person who goes to church regularly

the Church of England /ðə ˌtʃɜːtʃ əv ˈɪŋɡlənd/ *noun* [sing.] (*abbr.* C. of E.) (**RELIGION**) the Protestant Church that is the official church in England, whose leader is the Queen or King ⊃ look at **Anglican**

churchyard /ˈtʃɜːtʃjɑːd/ *noun* [C] (**RELIGION**) the area of land around a church, often used for burying people in ⊃ look at **cemetery, graveyard**

churn /tʃɜːn/ *verb* **1** [I, T] ~ (sth) (up) to move around violently; to make water, mud, etc. move like this: *The dark water churned beneath the huge ship.* ◊ *Quad bikes had churned the path up.* **2** [I] if your stomach **churns** or sth makes it **churn**, you feel a strong feeling of worry or fear: *Reading about the murder made my*

stomach churn. **3** [T] to make butter from milk or cream
PHR V churn sth out (*informal*) to produce large numbers of sth very quickly: *Modern factories can churn out cars at an amazing speed.*

chute /ʃuːt/ *noun* [C] a tube or passage down which people or things can slide: *a laundry/rubbish chute* (= from the upper floors of a high building) ◊ *a water chute* (= at a swimming pool)

chutney /ˈtʃʌtni/ *noun* [U] a thick sauce that is made from fruit or vegetables, sugar, SPICES and VINEGAR (= a liquid with a bitter taste). You eat chutney cold with cheese or meat.

CIA /ˌsiː aɪ ˈeɪ/ *abbr.* (**POLITICS**) **Central Intelligence Agency** (a department of the US government that collects information about other countries, often secretly)

ciabatta /tʃəˈbætə, -ˈbɑːtə/ *noun* [U, C] a type of Italian bread made in a long flat shape; a sandwich made with this type of bread

cicada /sɪˈkɑːdə/ *noun* [C] a large insect that lives in hot countries. The male makes a continuous high sound after dark by making two MEMBRANES (= pieces of thin skin) on its body move very fast

-cide /saɪd/ *suffix* (in nouns) **1** the act of killing: *suicide* ◊ *genocide* **2** a person or thing that kills: *insecticide*

cider /ˈsaɪdə(r)/ *noun* [U, C] **1** (*BrE*) an alcoholic drink made from apples: *dry/sweet cider* **2** (*AmE*) a drink made from apples that does not contain alcohol

cigar /sɪˈɡɑː(r)/ *noun* [C] a roll of dried TOBACCO leaves that people smoke. Cigars are larger than cigarettes.

cigarette ？ **A2** /ˌsɪɡəˈret/ *noun* [C] a thin tube of paper filled with TOBACCO (= a type of dried leaf) that people smoke: *a packet/pack of cigarettes*

ciga'rette lighter (*also* lighter) *noun* [C] an object that produces a small flame for lighting cigarettes, etc.

ciliary muscle /ˈsɪliəri mʌsl/ *noun* [C] (**ANATOMY**) a muscle in the eye that controls how much the LENS (= the clear part of the front of the eye) curves ⊃ picture at **eye¹**

C.-in-C. /ˌsiː ɪn ˈsiː/ = COMMANDER-IN-CHIEF

cinder /ˈsɪndə(r)/ *noun* [usually pl.] a small piece of ASH or partly burnt coal, wood, etc. that is no longer burning but may still be hot

cinema ？ **A1** /ˈsɪnəmə, -mɑː/ *noun* (**ARTS AND MEDIA**) **1** [C] (*BrE*) a place where you go to see a film: *What's on at the cinema this week?* ◊ *Let's go to the cinema this evening* (= go and see a film). ❶ In American English, you use **movie theater** to talk about the building where films are shown but the **movies** when you are talking about going to see a film there: *There are five movie theaters in this town.* ◊ *Let's go to the movies this evening.* **2** [U] films in general; the film industry: *one of the great successes of British cinema*

cinematography /ˌsɪnəməˈtɒɡrəfi/ *noun* [U] (**ARTS AND MEDIA**) the art or process of making films, especially the CAMERAWORK

cinnamon /ˈsɪnəmən/ *noun* [U] the BARK of a south-east Asian tree, used in cooking as a SPICE, especially in sweet food

circa /ˈsɜːkə/ *prep.* (*abbr.* c) (*formal*) (used with dates) about; approximately: *The vase was made circa 600 AD.*

circle¹ ？ **A2** /ˈsɜːkl/ *noun* **1** [C] a line that forms the edge of a round shape like a ring: *The children were drawing circles and squares on a piece of paper.* ◊ *We all stood **in a circle** and held hands.* **2** [C] a completely

circles

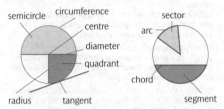

semicircle circumference sector

centre arc

diameter

quadrant

chord

radius tangent segment

round flat shape: *She cut out a circle of paper.* **3** [C] a group of people who are friends, or who have the same interest or profession: *He has a large circle of friends.* ◇ *Her name was well known in artistic circles.* **4** (*also* balcony) [sing.] (**ARTS AND MEDIA**) an area of seats that is upstairs in a cinema, theatre, etc.
IDM **come full circle** to return to the original situation, after a series of events or experiences **go round in circles** to work hard at sth or discuss sth without making any progress **a vicious circle** → VICIOUS

circle² 🔊 **A2** /'sɜːkl/ *verb* **1** [I, T] to move, or to move round sth, in a circle: *The plane circled the town several times before it landed.* **2** [T] to draw a circle round sth: *There are three possible answers to each question. Please circle the correct one.*

circuit 🔊+ **B2** /'sɜːkɪt/ *noun* **1** [C] a line, route, or journey around a place: *The cars have to complete ten circuits of the track.* ◇ *The earth takes a year to make a circuit of* (= go round) *the sun.* **2** [C] (**PHYSICS**) the complete path of wires and equipment along which an electric current flows: *an electrical circuit* ⊃ picture at **resistor, switch¹** **3** [sing.] (**SPORT**) a series of sports competitions, meetings or other organized events that are regularly visited by the same people: *She's one of the best players on the tennis circuit.*

'**circuit board** *noun* [C] (**ENGINEERING**) a board inside a piece of electrical equipment that holds CIRCUITS around which electric currents can flow

'**circuit breaker** *noun* [C] (**ENGINEERING**) a safety device that will stop the flow of electricity if there is danger

'**circuit training** *noun* [U] (**SPORT**) a type of training in sport in which different exercises are each done for a short time

circular¹ /'sɜːkjələ(r)/ *adj.* **1** shaped like a circle; round: *a circular table* **2** moving around in a circle: *a circular tour of Oxford* ⊃ picture at **income**

circular² /'sɜːkjələ(r)/ *noun* [C] a letter, notice or advertisement that is sent to a large number of people

circulate 🔊+ **C1** /'sɜːkjəleɪt/ *verb* [I, T] **1** (**SCIENCE**) when a liquid, gas, or air **circulates** or **is circulated**, it moves continuously around a place or system: *Blood circulates round the body.* ◇ *Hot water is circulated through pipes to the buildings.* **2** to go or to pass sth from one person to another: *Rumours were circulating about the Minister's private life.* ◇ *We've circulated a copy of the report to each department.* ⊃ note at **meeting**

circulation 🔊+ **C1** /ˌsɜːkjə'leɪʃn/ *noun* **1** [U] (**BIOLOGY**) the movement of blood around the body **2** [U] the passing or spreading of sth from one person or place to another: *the circulation of news/information/rumours* ◇ *Those coins are no longer in circulation* (= being used by people). **3** [C, usually sing.] (**ARTS AND MEDIA**) the usual number of copies of a newspaper or magazine that are sold each day, week, etc.

circulatory /ˌsɜːkjə'leɪtəri/ *adj.* (**BIOLOGY**) connected with the movement of blood around the body

circum- /'sɜːkəm/ *prefix* (in verb, nouns and adjectives) around: *to circumnavigate* (= sail around) *the world*

circumcise /'sɜːkəmsaɪz/ *verb* [T] **1** to remove the skin at the end of the PENIS (= the male sexual organ) of a boy or man for religious or medical reasons **2** to cut off part of the sex organs of a girl or woman
▶ **circumcision** /ˌsɜːkəm'sɪʒn/ *noun* [C, U]

circumference /sə'kʌmfərəns/ *noun* [C, U] (**GEOMETRY**) a line that goes around a circle or sth in the shape of a circle: *The Earth is about 40 000 kilometres in circumference.* ⊃ look at **diameter, radius** (1) ⊃ picture at **circle¹**

circumflex /'sɜːkəmfleks/ (*also* circumflex 'accent) *noun* [C] (**LANGUAGE**) the mark placed over a vowel in some languages to show how it should be pronounced, as over the *o* in *rôle* ⊃ look at **acute accent, grave³, tilde, umlaut**

circumlocution /ˌsɜːkəmlə'kjuːʃn/ *noun* [U, C] (*formal*) using more words than are necessary, instead of speaking or writing in a clear, direct way
▶ **circumlocutory** /ˌsɜːkəm'lɒkjʊtəri, -kəmlə'kjuːt-/ *adj.*

circumnavigate /ˌsɜːkəm'nævɪgeɪt/ *verb* [T] (*formal*) to sail all the way around sth, especially all the way around the world ▶ **circumnavigation** /ˌsɜːkəmˌnævɪ'geɪʃn/ *noun* [U]

circumspect /'sɜːkəmspekt/ *adj.* (*formal*) thinking very carefully about sth before doing it, because there may be risks involved **SYN** **cautious**

circumstance 🔊 **B2** 🔴 /'sɜːkəmstəns, -stɑːns, -stæns/ *noun* **1** [C, usually pl.] the facts and events that affect what happens in a particular situation: *Police said there were no suspicious circumstances surrounding the boy's death.* ◇ **In normal circumstances** *I would not have accepted the job, but at that time I had very little money.* ⊃ note at **situation** **2** circumstances [pl.] (*formal*) the conditions of your life, especially the amount of money that you have: *The company has promised to repay the money when its financial circumstances improve.*
IDM **in/under no circumstances** never; not for any reason: *Under no circumstances should you lend Paul any money.* **in/under the circumstances** as the result of a particular situation: *It's not an ideal solution, but it's the best we can do in the circumstances.* ◇ *My father was ill at that time, so under the circumstances I decided not to go on holiday.*

circulation

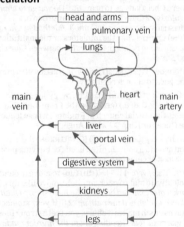

head and arms

pulmonary vein

lungs

main vein

heart

main artery

liver

portal vein

digestive system

kidneys

legs

circumstantial /ˌsɜːkəmˈstænʃl/ *adj.* (**LAW**) containing information and details that strongly suggest that sth is true but do not prove it: *They only had circumstantial evidence. ◊ The case against him was largely circumstantial.*

circumvent /ˌsɜːkəmˈvent/ *verb* [T] (*formal*) **1** to find a clever way of avoiding a difficulty or rule **2** to go round sth that is in your way

circus /ˈsɜːkəs/ *noun* [C] a group of people, sometimes with trained animals, who perform acts with skill in a show that travels around to different places; the show that they perform, usually in a large tent

cirque /sɜːk/ *noun* [C] (**GEOGRAPHY**) a round area shaped like a bowl in the side of a mountain ⊃ look at **corrie**, **cwm** ⊃ picture at **glacial**

cirrhosis /səˈrəʊsɪs/ *noun* [U] (**HEALTH**) a serious disease of the LIVER (= the organ in the body that cleans the blood), caused especially by drinking too much alcohol

cirrostratus /ˌsɪrəʊˈstrɑːtəs/ *noun* [U] (**GEOGRAPHY**) a type of cloud that forms a thin layer at a very high level in the sky ⊃ picture at **cloud**[1]

cirrus /ˈsɪrəs/ *noun* [U] (**GEOGRAPHY**) a type of light cloud that forms high in the sky ⊃ picture at **cloud**[1]

cistern /ˈsɪstən/ *noun* [C] a container for storing water, especially one that is connected to a toilet

citadel /ˈsɪtədəl, -del/ *noun* [C] (**HISTORY**) (in past times) a castle with high ground in or near a city where people could go when the city was being attacked: (*figurative*) *citadels of private economic power*

cite ʔ **B2** ⓦ /saɪt/ *verb* [T] (*formal*) **1** ~ **sth (as sth)** to mention sth as a reason or an example, or in order to support what you are saying: *He cited his heavy workload as the reason for his breakdown.* ⊃ note at **mention 2** to speak or write the exact words from a book, an author, etc: *She cited a passage from the president's speech.* **SYN** **quote**[1] **3** (**LAW**) to order sb to appear in court; to name sb officially in a legal case: *She was cited in the divorce proceedings.* ▸ **citation** /saɪˈteɪʃn/ *noun* [C, U]

citizen ʔ **B2** /ˈsɪtɪzn/ *noun* [C] **1** (**SOCIAL STUDIES**) a person who has the legal right to belong to a particular country: *She was born in Japan, but became an American citizen in 1991.* **2** a person who lives in a town or city: *the citizens of Rome* ⊃ look at **senior citizen**

citizenship ʔ+ **C1** /ˈsɪtɪzənʃɪp/ *noun* [U] (**SOCIAL STUDIES**) **1** the legal right to belong to a particular country: *You can apply for citizenship after five years' residency.* **2** the state of being a citizen of a particular country **3** the state of being a citizen and accepting the responsibilities of it: *an education that prepares young people for citizenship*

citric acid /ˌsɪtrɪk ˈæsɪd/ *noun* [U] (**CHEMISTRY**) a weak ACID that is found in the juice of oranges, lemons and other similar fruits

citrus /ˈsɪtrəs/ *adj.* used to describe fruit such as oranges and lemons

city ʔ **A1** /ˈsɪti/ *noun* (*pl.* -ies) **1** [C] a large and important town: *Venice is one of the most beautiful cities in the world. ◊ the city centre ◊ the country's capital city* ⊃ look at **inner city 2 the City** [sing.] (*BrE*) (**BUSINESS**, **FINANCE**) the UK's financial and business centre, in the oldest part of London: *a City stockbroker*

cityscape /ˈsɪtiskeɪp/ *noun* [C] (**ART**) a picture or view of a city ⊃ look at **landscape**[1] (2), **townscape**

civic ʔ+ **C1** /ˈsɪvɪk/ *adj.* **1** officially connected with a city or town: *civic buildings/leaders* **2** connected with the people who live in a town or city: *civic pride* (= feeling

proud because you belong to a particular town or city) ◊ *civic duties/responsibilities*

civics /ˈsɪvɪks/ *noun* [U] (*especially AmE*) (**EDUCATION**) a school subject in which you study the way government works and the rights and duties that you have as a citizen

civil ʔ **B2** /ˈsɪvl/ *adj.* **1** [only before noun] (**POLITICS**) connected with the people who live in a country: *civil disorder* (= involving groups of people within the same country) ⊃ look at **civil war 2** [only before noun] connected with the state, not with the army or the Church: *They were married in a civil ceremony* (= one that was not religious) **3** (**LAW**) [only before noun] connected with the personal legal matters of ordinary people, and not criminal law: *civil courts* **4** polite, but not very friendly: *The less time I have to spend being civil to him the better!* ▸ **civility** /səˈvɪləti/ *noun* [U]: *Staff members are trained to treat customers with civility at all times.* ▸ **civilly** /ˈsɪvəli/ *adv.*

civil disobedience *noun* [U] (**LAW**, **POLITICS**) the act by a large group of people of refusing to obey particular laws or pay taxes, usually as a form of political protest

civil engineering *noun* [U] the design, building and repair of roads, bridges, etc.; the study of this as a subject

civilian ʔ+ **C1** /səˈvɪliən/ *noun* [C] a person who is not in the armed forces or the police: *Two soldiers and one civilian were killed when the bomb exploded.* ▸ **civilian** ʔ+ **C1** *adj.*: *He left the army and returned to civilian life.*

civilization ʔ+ **B2** (*BrE also* -isation) /ˌsɪvəlaɪˈzeɪʃn/ *noun* (**SOCIAL STUDIES**) **1** [C, U] a society that has its own highly developed culture and way of life: *the civilizations of ancient Greece and Rome ◊ Western civilization* **2** [U] an advanced state of social and cultural development, or the process of reaching this state: *the civilization of the human race* **3** [U] all the people in the world and the societies they live in considered as a whole: *Global warming poses a threat to the whole of civilization.*

civilize (*BrE also* -ise) /ˈsɪvəlaɪz/ *verb* [T] (**SOCIAL STUDIES**) to educate and improve a person or a society; to make sb's manners or behaviour better

civilized (*BrE also* -ised) /ˈsɪvəlaɪzd/ *adj.* **1** (**SOCIAL STUDIES**) (used about a society) well organized; having a high level of social and cultural development **2** polite and reasonable: *a civilized conversation*

civil law *noun* [U] (**LAW**) law that deals with the rights of private citizens rather than with crime ⊃ look at **criminal law**

civil liberty *noun* [C, usually pl., U] (**SOCIAL STUDIES**) the right of people to be free to say or do what they want while respecting others and staying within the law

civil partnership (*BrE*) (*AmE* **civil union**) *noun* [C] (in some countries) a legal relationship between two people, usually of the same sex, that is similar to a marriage

civil rights *noun* [pl.] (**SOCIAL STUDIES**) the rights that every person in society has, for example to be treated equally: *the civil rights leader Martin Luther King*

civil servant *noun* [C] (*especially BrE*) a person who works in THE CIVIL SERVICE

the civil service *noun* [sing.] (**POLITICS**) all the government departments (except for the armed forces, judges and elected politicians) and all the people who work in them

,civil 'war *noun* [C, U] (**POLITICS**) a war between groups of people who live in the same country

CJD /ˌsiː dʒeɪ 'diː/ *noun* [U] (**HEALTH**) a disease of the brain, believed to be caused by very small units of PROTEIN (the abbreviation for 'Creutzfeldt-Jakob disease') ⊃ look at **BSE**

cl *abbr.* (in writing) (*pl.* **cl**) = CENTILITRE

clad /klæd/ *adj.* [not before noun] (*formal*) dressed (in); wearing a particular type of clothing: *The children were warmly clad in coats, hats and scarves.*

claim[1] ʔ B1 ○ /kleɪm/ *verb* 1 [T] ~ (**that**); ~ (**to be sth**) to say that sth is true, without having any proof: *Mark claims the book belongs to him.* ◊ *The woman claims to be the oldest person in Britain.* 2 [T] ~ (**for sth**) to demand or ask for sth because you believe it is your legal right to own or to have it: *He claimed political asylum.* ◊ *A lot of lost property is never claimed.* ◊ (*figurative*) *No one has* **claimed responsibility** *for the bomb attack.* 3 [I, T] ~ **sth from sb**; ~ **for sth** to ask for money from the government or a company because you have a right to it: *He's not entitled to claim housing benefit.* ◊ *Motorists have claimed for damage caused by potholes.* 4 [T] (used about a disaster, an accident, etc.) to cause sb's death: *The earthquake claimed thousands of lives.*

claim[2] ʔ B1 ○ /kleɪm/ *noun* [C] 1 ~ (**that**) a statement that sth is true although it has not been proved and other people may not agree with or believe it: *a report examining claims that politicians acted dishonestly* 2 ~ (**to sth**) (**LAW**) a right that sb believes they have to sth, especially property, land, etc: *You will have to prove your claim to the property in court.* 3 ~ (**for sth**) a demand for money that you think you have a right to, especially from the government, a company, etc: *to* **make an insurance claim** ◊ *After the accident he decided* **to put in a claim** *for compensation.*
IDM **stake (out) a/your claim (to/for/on sth)** → STAKE[2]

▼ SYNONYMS

claim

allegation • assertion • contention

These are all words for a statement that sth is true, although it has not been proved.

claim *A claim of corruption was made.*

allegation (*formal*) *Officials denied the allegations.*

assertion (*formal*) *He was correct in his assertion that she was lying.*

contention (*formal*) *The result was a matter of some contention.*

claimant /ˈkleɪmənt/ *noun* [C] 1 (**LAW**) a person who believes they have the right to have sth: *The insurance company refused to pay the claimant any money.* 2 (*BrE*) a person who is receiving money from the state because they are unemployed, etc.

clairvoyant /kleəˈvɔɪənt/ *noun* [C] a person who some people believe have special mental powers and can see what will happen in the future

clam[1] /klæm/ *noun* [C] a SHELLFISH (= a creature with a shell that lives in water) that can be eaten. Its shell is in two parts that can open and close.

clam[2] /klæm/ *verb* (-mm-)
PHR V **clam up (on sb)** (*informal*) to stop talking and refuse to speak especially when sb asks you about sth

clamber /ˈklæmbə(r)/ *verb* [I] ~ **up, down, out** etc. to move or climb with difficulty, usually using both your hands and feet

clammy /ˈklæmi/ *adj.* (**clammier; clammiest**) cold, slightly wet and sticky in an unpleasant way: *clammy hands*

clamour (*BrE*) (*AmE* **clamor**) /ˈklæmə(r)/ *verb* [I] ~ **for sth** (*formal*) to demand sth in a loud or angry way: *The public are clamouring for answers to all these questions.* ▶ **clamour** (*AmE* **clamor**) *noun* [sing.]: *the clamour of angry voices*

clamp[1] /klæmp/ *noun* [C] 1 a tool that you use for holding two things together very tightly ⊃ picture at **laboratory, workbench** 2 (*also* **wheel clamp**) (*BrE*) a metal object that is fixed to the wheel of a car that has been parked illegally, so that it cannot drive away

clamp[2] /klæmp/ *verb* [T] 1 ~ **A and B (together)**; ~ **A to B** to fasten two things together with a CLAMP: *The metal rods were clamped together.* ◊ *Clamp the wood to the table so that it doesn't move.* 2 to hold sth very FIRMLY in a particular position: *Her lips were clamped tightly together.* 3 [usually passive] (*BrE*) to fix a metal object to the wheel of a vehicle that has been parked illegally, so that it cannot move: *Oh no! My car's been clamped.*
PHR V **clamp down on sb/sth** (*informal*) to take strong action in order to stop or control sth ⊃ look at **clampdown**

clampdown /ˈklæmpdaʊn/ *noun* [usually sing.] ~ **on sth** strong action to stop or control sth: *a clampdown on corruption*

clan /klæn/ *noun* [C + sing./pl. verb] (**SOCIAL STUDIES**) a group of families who are related to each other, especially in Scotland

clandestine /klænˈdestɪn, ˈklændəstaɪn/ *adj.* (*formal*) secret and often not legal: *a clandestine meeting*

clang /klæŋ/ *verb* [I, T] to make a loud ringing sound like that of metal being hit; to cause sth to make this sound: *The iron gates clanged shut.* ▶ **clang** *noun* [C]

clank /klæŋk/ *verb* [I, T] to make a loud sound like pieces of metal hitting each other; to cause sth to make this sound: *The lift clanked its way up to the seventh floor.* ▶ **clank** *noun* [C]

clap[1] /klæp/ *verb* (-pp-) 1 [I, T] to hit your hands together many times, usually to show that you like sth: *The audience clapped as soon as the singer walked onto the stage.* 2 [T] to put sth onto sth quickly and FIRMLY: *'Oh no, I shouldn't have said that,' she said, clapping a hand over her mouth.*

clap[2] /klæp/ *noun* 1 [C] a sudden loud noise: *a clap of thunder* 2 [sing.] an act of hitting your hands together

claret /ˈklærət/ *adj.* dark red in colour ▶ **claret** *noun* [U]

clarification /ˌklærəfɪˈkeɪʃn/ *noun* [U, C] an act of making sth clear and easier to understand: *We'd like some clarification of exactly what your company intends to do.* ⊃ look at **clarity**

clarify ʔ+ B2 /ˈklærəfaɪ/ *verb* [T] (**clarifying; clarifies;** *pt, pp* **clarified**) to make sth become clear and easier to understand: *I hope that what I say will clarify the situation.* ⊃ adjective **clear**

clarinet /ˌklærəˈnet/ *noun* [C] (**MUSIC**) a musical instrument that is made of wood. You play a clarinet by blowing through it. ⊃ look at **woodwind** ⊃ picture at **instrument, orchestra**

clarity ʔ+ C1 /ˈklærəti/ *noun* [U] the quality of being clear and easy to understand: *clarity of expression* ⊃ look at **clarification**

clash[1] /klæʃ/ *verb* 1 [I] ~ (**with sb**) (**over sth**) to fight or disagree seriously about sth: *A group of demonstrators clashed with police outside the Town Hall.* ◊ *Conservative and Labour politicians have* clashed again over defence cuts. **2** [I] **~ (with sth)** (used about two events) to happen at the same time: *Her party clashes with the concert.* **3** [I] **~ (with sth)** (used about colours, etc.) to not match or look nice together: *I don't think you should wear that tie — it clashes with your shirt.* **4** [I, T] (used about two metal objects) to hit together with a loud noise; to cause two metal objects to do this: *Their swords clashed.*

clash² ᵻ+ **C1** /klæʃ/ *noun* [C] **1** a fight or serious argument: *a clash between police and demonstrators* **2** a big difference: *a clash of opinions* ◇ *There was a* **personality clash** *between the two men* (= they did not get well on together or like each other). **3** a loud noise, made by two metal objects hitting each other

clasp¹ /klɑːsp/ *noun* [C] an object, usually of metal, that fastens or holds sth together: *the clasp on a necklace/ brooch/handbag*

clasp² /klɑːsp/ *verb* [T] to hold sb/sth tightly: *Kevin clasped the child in his arms.*

class¹ ᵻ **A1** ⊙ /klɑːs/ *noun*
• IN SCHOOL **1** [C + sing./pl. verb] (**EDUCATION**) a group of students who are taught together: *Jane and I are in the same class at school.* ◇ *The whole class is/are going to the theatre tonight.* **2** [C, U] (**EDUCATION**) a lesson: *Classes begin at nine o'clock in the morning.* ◇ *We watched an interesting video* **in class** (= during the lesson) *yesterday.*
• SOCIAL GROUP **3** [U, C, + sing./pl. verb] (**SOCIAL STUDIES**) the way people are divided into social groups; one of these groups: *the* **working/middle/upper class** ◇ *class differences*
• GROUP OF ANIMALS, ETC. **4** [C] (**BIOLOGY**) a group of animals, plants, etc. of a similar type: *There are several different classes of insects.* ⊃ picture at **animal**
• QUALITY **5** [U] (*informal*) high quality or style: *Pele was a football player of great class.*
• OF TRANSPORT **6** [C, U] (especially in compounds) each of several different levels of comfort that are available to travellers on a plane, train, etc: *a first-class carriage on a train* ◇ *He always travels business class.*
• OF A UNIVERSITY DEGREE **7** [C] (especially in compounds) (**EDUCATION**) (in the UK) a level that you are given when you pass your final university exam: *a first-/ second-/third-class degree*

class² /klɑːs/ *verb* [T] **~ sb/sth (as sth)** to put sb/sth in a particular group or type: *Certain animals and plants are now classed as 'endangered species'.*

ˌclass ˈaction *noun* [U] (*AmE*) (**LAW**) a type of LAWSUIT (= a legal argument in court) that is started by a group of people who have the same problem

classic¹ ᵻ **B2** ⊙ /ˈklæsɪk/ *adj.* **1** very typical; with all the features you would expect to find: *It was a classic case of bad management.* **2** attractive but traditional in style or design: *a classic grey suit* **3** (used about a book, play, etc.) important and having a value that will last: *the classic film 'Casablanca'*

classic² ᵻ **B2** ⑤ /ˈklæsɪk/ *noun* **1** (**ARTS AND MEDIA**, **LITERATURE**) a famous book, play, etc. that has a value that will last: *All of Charles Dickens' novels are classics.* **2** Classics [U] (**EDUCATION**) the study of ancient Greek and Roman culture, especially their languages and literature

classical ᵻ **A2** ⊙ /ˈklæsɪkl/ *adj.* **1** widely accepted and used for a long time; traditional, not modern: *the classical theory of unemployment* ◇ *classical and modern ballet* **2** (**ART**) connected with or influenced by the culture of ancient Greece and Rome: *classical studies* ◇ *classical architecture* **3** (**MUSIC**) relating to music written in a Western musical tradition, usually using an established form: *I prefer* **classical music** *to*

pop. ◇ *a* **classical composer/violinist** ⊃ look at **jazz¹**, **pop²** (1), **rock¹** (5) ▶ **classically** /-kli/ *adv.*

classicism /ˈklæsɪsɪzəm/ *noun* [U] (**ART**, **LITERATURE**) a style of art and literature that is simple and beautiful and is based on the styles of ancient Greece and Rome. Classicism was popular in Europe in the eighteenth century.

classified /ˈklæsɪfaɪd/ *adj.* officially secret: *classified information*

ˌclassified adˈvertisement (*BrE, informal* ˌclassified ˈad, small ad) *noun* [usually pl.] a small advertisement that you put in a newspaper or on a website if you want to buy or sell sth, employ sb, find a flat, etc.

classify ᵻ+ **B2** ⓦ /ˈklæsɪfaɪ/ *verb* [T] (classifying; classifies; *pt, pp* classified) **~ sb/sth (as sth)** to put sb/sth into a group with other people or things of a similar type: *Would you classify it as an action film or a thriller?* ▶ **classification** ᵻ+ **C1** ⓦ /ˌklæsɪfɪˈkeɪʃn/ *noun* [C, U]: *the classification of the different species of butterfly*

classless /ˈklɑːsləs/ *adj.* (**SOCIAL STUDIES**) **1** with no division into social classes: *It is hard to imagine a truly classless society.* **2** not clearly belonging to any particular social class: *a classless accent*

classmate /ˈklɑːsmeɪt/ *noun* [C] a person who is in the same class as you at school or college

classroom ᵻ **A1** /ˈklɑːsruːm, -rʊm/ *noun* [C] a room in a school, college, etc. where lessons are taught: *classroom activities* ◇ *technology in the classroom*

classy /ˈklɑːsi/ *adj.* (classier; classiest) (*informal*) of high quality; expensive and fashionable: *a classy restaurant*

clatter /ˈklætə(r)/ *verb* [I, T] to make a series of short loud repeated sounds; to cause sth hard to make these sounds: *The horses clattered down the street.* ▶ **clatter** *noun* [sing.]

clause ᵻ **B1** /klɔːz/ *noun* [C] **1** (**GRAMMAR**) a group of words that includes a subject and a verb, and forms a sentence or part of a sentence: *The sentence 'After we had finished eating, we watched a film.' contains two clauses.* ⊃ look at **subordinate clause 2** (**LAW**) an item in a legal document that says that a particular thing must or must not be done: *There is a clause in the contract forbidding tenants to sublet.*

claustrophobia /ˌklɒstrəˈfəʊbiə, ˌklɔːs-/ *noun* [U] (**PSYCHOLOGY**) an extreme fear of being in a small space

claustrophobic /ˌklɒstrəˈfəʊbɪk, ˌklɔːs-/ *adj.* **1** (**PSYCHOLOGY**) extremely afraid of being in a small space: *I always feel claustrophobic in lifts.* **2** used about sth that makes you feel afraid in this way: *a claustrophobic little room*

clavicle /ˈklævɪkl/ *noun* [C] (**ANATOMY**) one of the two bones that connect the chest bones to the shoulder ⊃ picture at **body**

claw¹ /klɔː/ *noun* [C] **1** one of the long curved nails on the end of an animal's or a bird's foot ⊃ picture at **animal**, **lion 2** a long sharp curved part of the body that some types of SHELLFISH (= creatures with shells that live in water) have. They use them for holding or picking things up: *the claws of a crab* ⊃ picture at **animal**

claw² /klɔː/ *verb* [I, T] **~ (at) sb/sth** to SCRATCH or tear sb/ sth with CLAWS or with your nails: *The cat was clawing at the furniture.*

clay /kleɪ/ *noun* [U] heavy earth that is soft and sticky when it is wet and becomes hard when it is baked or dried: *clay pots*

clean¹ 🔊 **A1** /kliːn/ *adj.* **1** not dirty: *The whole house was beautifully clean.* ◇ *Cats are very clean animals.* **OPP** dirty¹ ⊃ noun **cleanliness 2** free from harmful or unpleasant substances **3** not offensive or referring to sex; not doing anything that is considered bad or wrong: *a clean joke* **OPP** dirty¹ **4** having no record of offences or crimes: *a clean driving licence* **IDM** **a clean sweep** a complete victory in a sports competition, an election, etc. that you get by winning all the different parts of it

clean² 🔊 **A1** /kliːn/ *verb* [T, I] to remove dirt or dust from sth: *to clean the windows* ◇ *Don't forget to clean your teeth!* ◇ *Mr Burrows comes in to clean after office hours.* ◇ *I do the cleaning once a week.* ⊃ look at **dry-clean, spring-clean** ⊃ note at **tooth** **PHR V** **clean sth off/from sth | clean sth off** to remove sth by brushing, rubbing, etc: *I cleaned the mud off my shoes.* **clean sth out** to clean the inside of sth: *I'm going to clean out all the cupboards next week.* **clean (sth) up** to remove dirt from somewhere: *I'm going to clean up the kitchen before Mum and Dad get back.* ◇ *Oh no, you've spilt coffee on the new carpet! Can you clean it up?* ⊃ look at **dry-clean, spring-clean**

clean³ /kliːn/ *adv.* (*informal*) used to emphasize that an action takes place completely: *I clean forgot it was your birthday.* **IDM** **come clean (with sb) (about sth)** (*informal*) to tell the truth about sth that you have been keeping secret **go clean out of your mind** to be completely forgotten

clean-ˈcut *adj.* (used especially about a young man) having a clean, tidy appearance that is attractive and socially acceptable: *The girls all go for James' clean-cut good looks.*

cleaner /ˈkliːnə(r)/ *noun* [C] **1** a person whose job is to clean the rooms and furniture inside a house or other building: *an office cleaner* **2** a substance or a special machine that you use for cleaning sth: *liquid floor cleaners* ◇ *a carpet cleaner* ⊃ look at **vacuum cleaner 3** cleaner's (*pl.* cleaners) = DRY-CLEANER'S: *Could you take my coat to the cleaner's?*

cleanliness /ˈklenlinəs/ *noun* [U] being clean or keeping things clean: *High standards of cleanliness are important in a hotel kitchen.*

cleanly /ˈkliːnli/ *adv.* easily or smoothly in one movement: *The knife cut cleanly through the rope.*

cleanse /klenz/ *verb* [T] to clean your skin or a wound ⊃ look at **ethnic cleansing**

cleanser /ˈklenzə(r)/ *noun* [C] a substance that you use for cleaning your skin, especially your face

clean-ˈshaven *adj.* a man who is **clean-shaven** does not have a BEARD or other hair growing on his face

clean-up *noun* [C, usually sing.] the process of removing dirt or other bad things from a place: *the clean-up operation after the oil spill*

clear¹ 🔊 **A2 O** /klɪə(r)/ *adj.*
• EASY TO HEAR, ETC. **1** easy to understand and not confusing: *His voice wasn't very clear on the phone.* ◇ *She gave me clear directions on how to get there.*

WORD FAMILY
clear *adj.*
clarity *noun*
clarify *verb*

• SURE **2** ~ **(about/on sth)** sure or definite; without any doubts; not confused: *I'm not quite clear about the arrangements for tomorrow.* ⊃ verb **clarify**

• WITHOUT DOUBT **3** ~ **(to sb)** obvious: *It was clear to me that he was not telling the truth.* ◇ *His height gives him a clear advantage.*
• EASY TO SEE THROUGH **4** that you can see through: *The water was so clear that we could see the bottom of the lake.*
• NOT BLOCKED **5** ~ **(of sth)** free from things that are blocking the way: *The police say that most roads are now clear of snow.*
• NOT MARKED **6** free from marks: *a clear sky* (= without clouds) ◇ *clear skin* (= without spots)
• NOT GUILTY **7** if you have a **clear** CONSCIENCE or your CONSCIENCE is **clear**, you do not feel guilty
IDM **make yourself clear | make sth clear/plain (to sb)** to speak so that there can be no doubt about what you mean: *'I do not want you to go to that concert,' said my mother. 'Do I make myself clear?'* ◇ *He made it quite clear that he was not happy with the decision.*

▼ SYNONYMS

clear

obvious • apparent • evident • plain

These words all describe sth that is easy to see or understand and leaves no doubts or confusion.

clear *It was clear that she wasn't welcome.*

obvious *It's obvious to me that something is wrong.*

apparent *It was apparent from her face that she was upset.*

evident (*formal*) *The choir sang with evident enjoyment.*

plain *He made it plain that he wanted us to leave.*

clear² /klɪə(r)/ *adv.* ~ **(of sth)** away from sth; not touching sth: *stand clear of the doors* (= on a train) **IDM** **keep/stay/steer clear (of sb/sth)** to avoid sb/sth because they or it may cause problems **loud and clear** in a way that is very easy to understand: *We can hear you loud and clear from here.*

clear³ 🔊 **B1** /klɪə(r)/ *verb*
• REMOVE **1** [T] to remove sth that is not wanted or needed: *to clear the roads of snow/to clear snow from the roads* ◇ *It's your turn to clear the table* (= to take away the dirty plates, etc. after a meal). **2** [T] to make people leave a place: *After the bomb warning, police cleared the streets.*
• OF SMOKE, WEATHER, ETC. **3** [I] (used about smoke, etc.) to disappear: *The fog slowly cleared and the sun came out.* **4** [I] when the sky or the weather **clears**, it becomes brighter and free of cloud or rain: *After a cloudy start, the weather will clear during the afternoon.*
• FIND SB NOT GUILTY **5** [T] ~ **sb (of sth)** (LAW) to provide proof that sb is innocent of sth: *The man has finally been cleared of murder.*
• GET OVER/PAST **6** [T] to jump over or get past sth without touching it
• GIVE/GET PERMISSION **7** [T] to give official permission for a plane, ship, etc. to enter or leave a place: *At last the plane was cleared for take-off.* **8** [T] ~ **sth (with sb)** to get official approval for sth to be done: *I'll have to clear it with the manager before I can refund your money.*
• OF MONEY **9** [I, T] if a payment that is made into your bank account **clears**, or a bank **clears** it, the money is available for you to use
IDM **clear the air** to improve a difficult or uncomfortable situation by talking honestly about worries, doubts, etc: *I'm sure if you discuss your feelings with her it will help to clear the air between you.* **clear your throat** to COUGH (= to send air out of your throat with a sudden noise) slightly in order to make it easier to speak
PHR V **clear off** (*informal*) used to tell sb to go away **clear sth out** to tidy sth and throw away things that

you do not want clear up (used about the weather or an illness) to get better clear (sth) up to make sth tidy: *Make sure you clear up properly before you leave.* clear sth up to solve or explain sth: *There's been a slight misunderstanding but we've cleared it up now.*

clearance /ˈklɪərəns/ *noun* [U, C] **1** the removing of sth that is old or not wanted: *The shop is having a clearance sale* (= selling things cheaply in order to get rid of them). **2** the distance between an object and sth that is passing under or next to it, for example a ship or vehicle: *There was not enough clearance for the bus to pass under the bridge safely.* **3** official permission for sb/sth to do sth: *All employees at the submarine base require security clearance.*

clear-ˈcut *adj.* definite and easy to see or understand

clear-ˈheaded *adj.* able to think clearly, especially if there is a problem

clearing /ˈklɪərɪŋ/ *noun* **1** [C] (**GEOGRAPHY**) a small area without trees in the middle of a wood or forest **2** [U] (**EDUCATION**) (in the UK) the system used by universities to find students for the places on their courses that have not been filled before the beginning of the academic year: *She got into university through clearing.*

clearly ɪ A2 O /ˈklɪəli/ *adv.* **1** in a way that is easy to see, hear or understand: *It was so foggy that we couldn't see the road clearly.* ◇ *Please speak clearly.* ◇ *He explained it all very clearly.* **2** in a way that is not confused: *I'm so tired that I can't think clearly.* **3** used to emphasize that what you are saying is obvious and true: *She clearly doesn't want to speak to you any more.* **SYN** obviously

clear-ˈsighted *adj.* understanding or thinking clearly; able to make good decisions and judgements

cleavage /ˈkliːvɪdʒ/ *noun* [C, U] (**ANATOMY**) the space between a woman's breasts

clef /klef/ *noun* [C] (**MUSIC**) a sign (𝄞, 𝄢) at the beginning of a line of written music that shows the area of sound that the notes are in: *the bass/treble clef* ◌ picture at **music**

cleft /kleft/ *noun* [C] a natural opening or line, especially in rock or in a person's CHIN (= the part of the face below the mouth)

clemency /ˈklemənsi/ *noun* [U] (*formal*) (**LAW**) kind treatment of sb when they are being punished

clementine /ˈkleməntiːn/ *noun* [C] a fruit like a small orange

clench /klentʃ/ *verb* [T, I] when you clench your hands, teeth, etc., or when they clench, you press them together tightly, usually showing that you are angry, determined or upset: *She clenched her fists and looked as if she was going to hit him.*

clergy /ˈklɜːdʒi/ *noun* [pl.] (**RELIGION**) the people who perform religious ceremonies in the Christian church: *a member of the clergy*

clergyman /ˈklɜːdʒimən/ *noun* [C] (*pl.* -men /-mən/) (**RELIGION**) a male priest or minister in the Christian church

clergywoman /ˈklɜːdʒiwʊmən/ *noun* [C] (*pl.* -women /-wɪmɪn/) (**RELIGION**) a female priest or minister in the Christian church

cleric /ˈklerɪk/ *noun* [C] (**RELIGION**) **1** a religious leader in any religion: *Muslim clerics* **2** (*old-fashioned or formal*) a priest in the Christian church **SYN** clergyman

clerical /ˈklerɪkl/ *adj.* **1** connected with office work: *clerical work* **2** (**RELIGION**) connected with the CLERGY

clerk ɪ+ B2 /klɑːk/ *noun* [C] **1** a person whose job is to keep the records or accounts and do other routine duties in an office, a shop, etc. **2** an official in charge of

the records of a council, court, etc. **3** (*AmE*) = SHOP ASSISTANT **4** (*AmE*) (*also* desk clerk) (**TOURISM**) a person whose job is dealing with people arriving at or leaving a hotel **SYN** receptionist

clever ɪ A2 /ˈklevə(r)/ *adj.* **1** (*especially BrE*) able to learn, understand or do sth quickly and easily; intelligent: *a clever student* ◇ *How clever of you to mend my watch!* **2** (used about things, ideas, etc.) showing skill or intelligence: *a clever device* ◇ *a clever plan* ▸ cleverly *adv.* ▸ cleverness *noun* [U]

cliché (*also* cliche) /ˈkliːʃeɪ/ *noun* [C] (**LANGUAGE**) a phrase or idea that has been used so many times that it no longer has any real meaning or interest

click¹ ɪ B1 /klɪk/ *verb* **1** [I, T] (**COMPUTING**) to choose a particular function or item on a computer screen, etc., by pressing one of the buttons on a mouse or TOUCHPAD: *To open a file, click on the menu.* ◇ *Just click the link below.* ◌ look at double-click **2** [I, T] to make a short sharp sound; to cause sth to do this: *The door clicked shut.* ◇ *He clicked his fingers at the waiter.* **3** [I] (*BrE, informal*) (used about two people) to become friendly immediately: *We met at a party and just clicked.* **4** [I] (*informal*) (used about a problem, etc.) to become suddenly clear or understood: *Once I'd found the missing letter, everything clicked into place.* **PHR V** click through (to sth) (**COMPUTING**) to visit a web page by clicking on an electronic link or advertisement on another web page: *We had to click through to the fifth page of results to find the entry.*

click² ɪ B1 /klɪk/ *noun* [C] **1** (**COMPUTING**) the act of pressing the button on a computer mouse or TOUCHPAD **2** a short sharp sound: *the click of a switch*

clickable /ˈklɪkəbl/ *adj.* (**COMPUTING**) (used about text or an image) that you can click on with the mouse or TOUCHPAD in order to make sth happen

clickbait /ˈklɪkbeɪt/ *noun* [U] (*informal*) (**ARTS AND MEDIA**) material put on the internet in order to attract attention and encourage visitors to click on a link to another web page: *The article was pure clickbait and fake news.* ◇ *clickbait headlines*

client ɪ B1 /ˈklaɪənt/ *noun* [C] **1** somebody who receives a service from a professional person, for example a lawyer: *to act on behalf of a client* **2** (**COMPUTING**) a computer that is linked to a SERVER

▼ **VOCABULARY BUILDING**

Be careful. **Client** cannot be used for people in shops or restaurants. Those people are **customers**. **Clientele** is a general, formal word that includes both clients and customers.

---

clientele /ˌkliːənˈtel/ *noun* [sing. + sing./pl. verb] all the customers, guests or clients who regularly go to a particular shop, hotel, organization, etc.

cliff ɪ+ B2 /klɪf/ *noun* [C] (**GEOGRAPHY**) a high, very steep area of rock, especially one next to the sea ◌ picture at **erosion**

cliffhanger /ˈklɪfhæŋə(r)/ *noun* [C] (**ARTS AND MEDIA**) an exciting situation in a story, film, etc. when you cannot guess what is going to happen next and you have to wait until the next part in order to find out

climactic /klaɪˈmæktɪk/ *adj.* (*formal*) (used about an event or a point in time) very exciting, most important

climate ɪ A2 W /ˈklaɪmət/ *noun* [C] **1** (**GEOGRAPHY**) the normal weather conditions of a particular region: *a dry/humid/tropical climate* **2** an area with particular weather conditions: *They wanted to move to a warmer* *climate.* **3** a general attitude or feeling; an atmosphere or a situation that exists in a particular place: *What is the current* **climate of opinion** *regarding the death penalty?* ◇ *the political climate* ◇ *in today's economic climate*

'climate change *noun* [U] (**ENVIRONMENT**) changes in the earth's weather, including changes in temperature, wind patterns and RAINFALL (= the total amount of rain that falls in a particular place during a month, year, etc.), especially the increase in the temperature of the earth's atmosphere that is caused by the increase of particular gases, especially CARBON DIOXIDE: *the threat of global climate change* ⊃ look at **global warming**

'climate crisis (*also* **'climate emergency**) *noun* [C] (**ENVIRONMENT**) a situation in which immediate action is needed to reduce or stop CLIMATE CHANGE

'climate strike *noun* [C] (**ENVIRONMENT**) the act of not going to school or work in order to join a public protest to demand action against CLIMATE CHANGE: *Millions of people around the world joined the climate strike on Friday.*

climatic /klaɪˈmætɪk/ *adj.* (**GEOGRAPHY**) connected with the climate of a particular area: *climatic changes/conditions* ▶ **climatically** /-kli/ *adv.*

climatology /ˌklaɪməˈtɒlədʒi/ *noun* [U] (**GEOGRAPHY, SCIENCE**) the scientific study of climate ▶ **climatological** /ˌklaɪmətəˈlɒdʒɪkl/ *adj.* ▶ **climatologist** /ˌklaɪməˈtɒlədʒɪst/ *noun* [C]

climax /ˈklaɪmæks/ *noun* [C] **1** the most exciting or important event or point in time: *to come to a climax* ◇ *the climax of his political career* **2** (**ARTS AND MEDIA**) the most important and exciting part of a book, a play, a piece of music, an event, etc: *The novel reaches a dramatic climax in the final chapter.* **OPP** **anticlimax** ▶ **climax** *verb* [I]

climb¹ 🔊 **A1** /klaɪm/ *verb* **1** [I, T] ~ **(up) (sth)** to move up towards the top of sth: *to climb a tree/mountain/rope* ◇ *She climbed the stairs to bed.* ◇ *to climb up a ladder* **2** go climbing [I] (**SPORT**) to go up mountains or climb rocks as a hobby or sport: *He likes to go climbing most weekends.* **3** [I] to move, with difficulty or effort, in the direction mentioned, using hands as well as feet: *I managed to climb out of the window.* **4** [I] to rise to a higher position: *The plane climbed steadily.* ◇ *The road climbed steeply up the side of the mountain.* ◇ (*figurative*) *The value of the dollar climbed against the pound.* ⊃ note at **rise²**, **trend¹** **IDM** **climb/jump on the bandwagon** → BANDWAGON **PHRV** **climb down (over sth)** to admit that you have made a mistake; to change your opinion about sth in an argument ⊃ look at **climbdown**

climb² 🔊 **B1** /klaɪm/ *noun* [C] an act of climbing or a journey made by climbing: *The monastery could only be reached by a three-hour climb.*

climbdown /ˈklaɪmdaʊn/ *noun* [C] an act of admitting you have been wrong; a change of opinion in an argument

climber /ˈklaɪmə(r)/ *noun* [C] **1** (**SPORT**) a person who climbs mountains as a sport **2** a climbing plant

climbing /ˈklaɪmɪŋ/ *noun* [U] (**SPORT**) the sport or activity of climbing rocks or mountains: *a climbing accident*

clinch /klɪntʃ/ *verb* [T] (*informal*) to manage to get what you want in an argument or business agreement: *to clinch a deal*

climate change

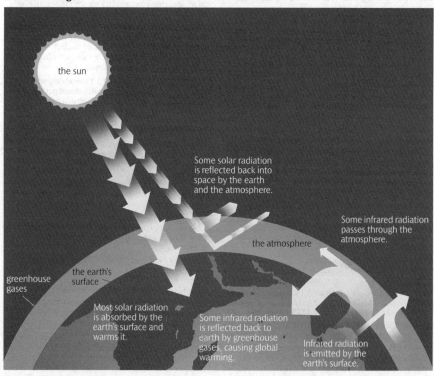

the sun

Some solar radiation is reflected back into space by the earth and the atmosphere.

Some infrared radiation passes through the atmosphere.

the atmosphere

greenhouse gases

the earth's surface

Most solar radiation is absorbed by the earth's surface and warms it.

Some infrared radiation is reflected back to earth by greenhouse gases, causing global warming.

Infrared radiation is emitted by the earth's surface.

cline /klaɪn/ *noun* [C] a continuous series of things, in which each one is only slightly different from the things next to it, but the last is very different from the first

cling 🔊 **C1** /klɪŋ/ *verb* [I] (*pt, pp* **clung** /klʌŋ/) **1 ~ (on) to sb/sth; ~ together** to hold on tightly to sb/sth: *She clung to the rope with all her strength.* ◇ *They clung together for warmth.* **2 ~ (on) to sth** to continue to believe sth, often when it is not reasonable to do so: *They were still clinging to the hope that the child would be found alive.* **3 ~ to sb/sth** to stick to sb/sth: *Her wet clothes clung to her.*

'cling film *noun* [U] a thin clear plastic material that sticks to a surface and to itself, used for covering food to keep it fresh

clingy /'klɪŋi/ *adj.* (**clingier; clingiest**) **1** (used about clothes or material) sticking to the body and showing its shape: *a clingy sweater* **2** needing another person too much: *a clingy child*

clinic 🔊+ **B2** /'klɪnɪk/ *noun* [C] (**MEDICINE**) **1** a small hospital or a part of a hospital where you go to receive special medical treatment: *He's being treated at a private clinic.* **2** (*especially BrE*) a time when a doctor sees patients and gives special treatment or advice: *The antenatal clinic is held on Thursdays.*

clinical 🔊+ **C1** /'klɪnɪkl/ *adj.* **1** (**MEDICINE**) connected with the examination and treatment of patients at a CLINIC or hospital: *Clinical trials of the new drug have proved successful.* **2** (used about a person) cold and not emotional

clinically /'klɪnɪkli/ *adv.* **1** (**MEDICINE**) according to medical examination: *to be clinically dead* (= judged to be dead from the condition of the body) ◇ *clinically depressed* **2** in a cold way; without showing any emotion

clink /klɪŋk/ *noun* [sing.] the short sharp ringing sound that objects made of glass, metal, etc. make when they touch each other: *the clink of glasses* ▶ **clink** *verb* [I, T]

clip¹ 🔊+ **B2** /klɪp/ *noun* **1** [C] a small object, usually made of metal or plastic, used for holding things together: *a paper clip* ◇ *a hair clip* **2** [C] (**ARTS AND MEDIA**) a small section of a film that is shown so that people can see what the rest of the film is like ⊃ look at **trailer** (4) **3** [C] (*informal*) a quick hit with the hand: *She gave the boy a clip round the ear.* **4** [sing.] the act of cutting sth to make it shorter

clip² /klɪp/ *verb* (**-pp-**) **1** [I, T] to be fastened with a CLIP; to fasten sth to sth else with a CLIP: *Clip the photo to the letter, please.* ◇ *I'll clip the pages together.* **2** [T] to cut sth, especially by cutting small parts off: *The hedge needs clipping.* **3** [T] to hit sb/sth quickly: *My wheel clipped the pavement and I fell off my bike.*

clipboard /'klɪpbɔːd/ *noun* **1** [C] a small board with a CLIP at the top for holding papers, used by sb who wants to write while standing or moving around **2** (**COMPUTING**) a place where information from a computer file is stored for a time until it is added to another file

clippers /'klɪpəz/ *noun* [pl.] a tool used for cutting small pieces off things: *a pair of nail clippers*

clipping /'klɪpɪŋ/ (*especially AmE*) = CUTTING¹

clique /kliːk/ *noun* [C + sing./pl. verb] a small group of people with the same interests who do not want others to join their group

clitoris /'klɪtərɪs/ *noun* [C] (**ANATOMY**) the small sensitive part of the female sex organs just above the entrance to the VAGINA

cloak /kləʊk/ *noun* **1** [C] a type of loose coat without SLEEVES (= parts that cover your arms) that was more common in former times ⊃ look at **cape 2** [sing.] (*formal*) a thing that hides sth else: *a cloak of mist*

cloakroom /'kləʊkruːm, -rʊm/ *noun* [C] (*especially BrE*) a room near the entrance to a building where you can leave your coat, bags, etc.

clobber /'klɒbə(r)/ *verb* [T] (*informal*) to hit sb hard

clock¹ 🔊 **A1** /klɒk/ *noun* [C] **1** an instrument that shows you what time it is: *an alarm clock* ◇ *a church clock* ⊃ look at **watch²** (1) **2** (*informal*) = MILOMETER: *My car has only 10 000 miles on the clock.* **IDM against the clock** if you do sth against the clock, you do it fast in order to finish before a certain time: *It was a race against the clock to get the building work finished on time.* **around/round the clock** all day and all night: *They are working round the clock to repair the bridge.* **put the clock/clocks forward/back** to change the time, usually by one hour, at the beginning/end of summer

clock² /klɒk/ *verb* **PHR V clock in/on | clock off** to record the time that you arrive at or leave work, especially by putting a card into a type of clock **clock sth up** to achieve a certain number or total: *Our car clocked up over 2 000 miles while we were on holiday.*

'clock tower *noun* [C] a tall tower, usually part of another building, with a clock at the top

clockwise /'klɒkwaɪz/ *adv., adj.* in the same direction as the hands of a clock: *Turn the handle clockwise.* ◇ *to move in a clockwise direction* **OPP anticlockwise, counterclockwise**

clockwork /'klɒkwɜːk/ *noun* [U] parts of a machine found in certain toys, etc. that you operate by turning a key: *a clockwork toy* ◇ *The plan went like clockwork* (= smoothly and without any problems).

clog¹ /klɒg/ *noun* [C] a type of shoe made completely of wood or with a thick wooden base

clog² /klɒg/ *verb* [I, T, often passive] (**-gg-**) **~ (sth) (up) (with sth)** to block or become blocked: *The drain is always clogging up.* ◇ *The roads were clogged with traffic.*

cloister /'klɔɪstə(r)/ *noun* [C, usually pl.] (**ARCHITECTURE**) a covered passage with ARCHES around a square garden, usually forming part of a religious building

clone¹ /kləʊn/ *noun* [C] **1** (**BIOLOGY**) an exact copy of a plant or an animal that is produced from one of its cells by scientific methods **2** (**COMPUTING**) a computer that is designed to work in exactly the same way as another one

clone² /kləʊn/ *verb* [T] **1** to produce an exact copy of a plant or an animal from one of its cells **2** to illegally copy information from sb's credit card or mobile phone so that you can use it but the owner of the card or phone receives the bill

close¹ 🔊 **A1** /kləʊz/ *verb* [I, T] **1** to shut: *The door closed quietly.* ◇ *to close a door/window* ◇ *Close your eyes — I've got a surprise.* **2** to be not open to the public; to make sth not open to the public: *What time do the shops close?* ◇ *The police have closed the road to traffic.* **3** to end or to bring sth to an end: *The meeting closed at 10pm.* ◇ *Detectives have closed the case on the missing girl.* **OPP open²** ⊃ note at **meeting PHR V close (sth) down** (**BUSINESS**) to stop all business or work permanently at a shop or factory: *The factory has had to close down.* ◇ *Health inspectors have closed the restaurant down.* **close in (on sb/sth)** to come nearer and gradually surround sb/sth, especially in order to attack **close sth off** to prevent people from entering a place or an area: *The police closed off the city centre because of a bomb alert.*

close² ɪ **B2** /kləʊz/ *noun* [sing.] the end, especially of a period of time or an activity: *the close of trading on the stock market*
IDM **bring sth/come/draw to a close** to end: *The chairman brought the meeting to a close.* ◇ *The guests began to leave as the evening drew to a close.*

close³ ɪ **A2** /kləʊs/ *adj.* **1** [not before noun] **~ (to sb/ sth)**; **~ (together)** near: *Is our hotel close to the beach?* ◇ *The tables are quite close together.* **2** (used about a friend, etc.) known very well and liked: *They invited only close friends to the wedding.* **3** near in a family relationship: *a close relative* **OPP** **distant 4** (used about a competition, etc.) only won by a small amount: *a close match* **5** careful and complete: *On close examination, you could see that the banknote was a forgery.* **6** (used about the weather, etc.) heavy and with little movement of air: *It's so close today that there might be a storm.* ▸ **closely** ɪ **B2** **S** *adv.*: *to watch somebody closely* ◇ *The insect closely resembles a stick.* ▸ **closeness** *noun* [U]
IDM **at close quarters** at or from a position that is very near **a close shave/thing** (*informal*) a situation in which a bad thing that almost happened: *I wasn't injured, but it was a close shave.* **close/near/dear to sb's heart → HEART**

close⁴ ɪ **B1** /kləʊs/ *adv.* near: *to follow close behind somebody* ◇ *I held her close* (= tightly).
IDM **close by (sb/sth)** at a short distance from sb/ sth: *She lives close by.* **close on nearly; almost:** *He's close on 100.* **close up (to sb/sth)** at or from a very short distance to sb/sth **come close (to sth/to doing sth)** to almost do sth: *We didn't win but we came close.*

close⁵ ɪ **B2** /kləʊs/ *noun* [C] a street that is closed at one end: *5 Devon Close*

closed ɪ **A2** /kləʊzd/ *adj.* not open; shut: *Keep your mouth closed.* ◇ *The supermarket is closed.* ◇ *The road was closed to traffic while the gas leak was mended.* **OPP** **open¹**

closed-circuit television *noun* [U] = CCTV

closet /ˈklɒzɪt/ *noun* [C] (*especially AmE*) a large cupboard that is built into a room

close-up /ˈkləʊs ʌp/ *noun* [C] a photo or film of sb/sth that you take from a very short distance away

closing¹ /ˈkləʊzɪŋ/ *adj.* [only before noun] coming at the end of a speech, a period of time or an activity: *his closing remarks* ◇ *The football season is now in its closing stages.* **OPP** **opening**

closing² /ˈkləʊzɪŋ/ *noun* [U] the act of permanently shutting sth such as a factory, hospital, school, etc: *the closing of the local school* **OPP** **opening**

closing time *noun* [C] the time when a shop, pub, etc. closes

closure ɪ+ **C1** /ˈkləʊʒə(r)/ *noun* [C, U] **1** the situation when a factory, school, etc. shuts permanently **2** the temporary closing of a road or bridge: *There will be road closures in the areas from 8 p.m.*

clot¹ /klɒt/ *noun* [C] (**BIOLOGY**) a thick mass that is formed when blood dries or becomes thicker: *They removed a blood clot from his brain.*

clot² /klɒt/ *verb* [I, T] (-tt-) when blood or another liquid **clots** or when sth **clots** it, it forms thick masses: *a drug that stops blood from clotting during operations*

cloth ɪ **B1** /klɒθ/ *noun* (*pl.* **cloths**) **1** [U] a material made of cotton, wool, etc. that you use for making clothes, curtains, etc: *a metre of cloth* **SYN** **fabric 2** [C] a piece of material that you use for a particular purpose: *Wipe the table with a damp cloth.* ◑ look at **tablecloth**

clothe /kləʊð/ *verb* [T] (*formal*) to provide clothes for sb: *to feed and clothe a child*

clothed /kləʊðd/ *adj.* **~ (in sth)** dressed; wearing sth: *He was clothed in black from head to foot.*

clothes ɪ **A1** /kləʊðz, kləʊz/ *noun* [pl.] the things that you wear, for example trousers, shirts, dresses, coats, etc: *Take off those wet clothes.* ◇ *She was wearing new clothes.* ◇ *I need to put on some clean clothes before dinner.* ◑ look at **garment**

clothes hanger = HANGER

clothes line *noun* [C] a thin rope attached to posts that you hang clothes on so that they can dry

clothespin /ˈkləʊðzpɪn, ˈkləʊz-/ = PEG¹ (3)

clothing ɪ **A2** /ˈkləʊðɪŋ/ *noun* [U] the clothes that you wear, especially for a particular activity: *waterproof/ outdoor/winter clothing* ◇ *a piece/an article of clothing*

clotted cream *noun* [U] (*BrE*) a type of thick rich cream

cloud¹ ɪ **A2** /klaʊd/ *noun* **1** [C, U] (**GEOGRAPHY**) a mass of very small drops of water that floats in the sky and is usually white or grey: *The sun disappeared behind a cloud.* ◇ *A band of thick cloud is spreading from the west.* ◑ note at **water¹** **2** [C] a mass of smoke, dust, sand, etc: *Clouds of smoke were pouring from the burning building.* **3 the cloud** [sing.] (**COMPUTING**) a network of SERVERS (= computers that control or supply information to other computers) on which data and software can be stored or managed and to which users have access over the internet: *Key company documents are now stored in the cloud.*
IDM **every cloud has a silver lining** every sad or difficult situation has a positive side **under a cloud** with the people around you thinking that you have done sth wrong: *She left her job under a cloud because she'd been accused of stealing.*

cloud² /klaʊd/ *verb* **1** [I, T] to become difficult to see through; to make sth difficult to see through: *His eyes clouded with tears.* **2** [T] to make sth less clear or easy to understand: *Her personal involvement in the case*

clouds

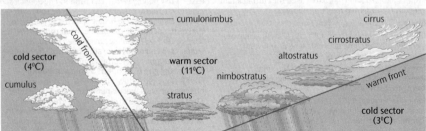

was beginning to **cloud her judgement**. **3** [T] to make sth less pleasant: *Illness has clouded the last few years of his life.*

PHR V cloud over (used about the sky) to become full of clouds

cloudburst /'klaʊdbɜːst/ *noun* [C] a sudden heavy fall of rain

'cloud computing *noun* [U] (**COMPUTING**) a system of storing data and programs on a central computer. People can find the data and programs on the internet and use them on their own computers

cloudless /'klaʊdləs/ *adj.* (used about the sky, etc.) clear; without any clouds

cloudy /'klaʊdi/ *adj.* (cloudier; cloudiest) **1** (used about the sky, etc.) full of clouds **2** (used about liquids, etc.) not clear: *cloudy water*

clout /klaʊt/ *noun* **1** [C] (*especially BrE, informal*) a hard hit, usually with the hand: *to give somebody a clout* **2** [U] influence and power: *He's an important man — he has a lot of clout in the company.*

clove /kləʊv/ *noun* [C] **1** the small dried flower of a tropical tree, used as a SPICE in cooking **2** one of the small separate sections into which GARLIC (= a vegetable of the onion family with a strong taste and smell) is divided

cloven hoof /ˌkləʊvn 'huːf/ *noun* [C] the foot of an animal such as a cow or a sheep, that is divided into two parts

clover /'kləʊvə(r)/ *noun* [U, C] a small plant with pink or white flowers and leaves with three parts to them

clown¹ /klaʊn/ *noun* [C] a person who wears funny clothes and a big red nose and does silly things to make people laugh: (*figurative*) *At school, Bob was always the class clown.*

clown² /klaʊn/ *verb* [I] ~ (**about/around**) to behave in a silly way, especially in order to make other people laugh: *Stop clowning around and get some work done!*

cloying /'klɔɪɪŋ/ *adj.* (*formal*) **1** (used about food, a smell, etc.) so sweet that it is unpleasant **2** using emotion in a very obvious way, so that the result is unpleasant: *Her novels are full of cloying sentimentality.*

cloze test /'kləʊz test/ *noun* [C] a type of test in which you have to put suitable words in spaces in a text where words have been left out

club¹ 🔓 **A1** /klʌb/ *noun* **1** [C + sing./pl. verb] a group of people who meet regularly to share an interest, do sport, etc.; the place where they meet: *to join a club* ◇ *to be a member of a club* ◇ *a tennis/football/golf club* **2** [C] a place where people, especially young people, go and listen to music, dance, etc: *the club scene in Ibiza* **3** [C] a heavy stick, usually with one end that is thicker than the other, used as a weapon **4** [C] = GOLF CLUB **5** clubs [pl.] one of the four SUITS (= sets) in a PACK of cards. The clubs have black shapes like three leaves on them: *the two/ace/queen of clubs* **6** [C] one of the cards from this SUIT: *I played a club.*

club² /klʌb/ *verb* (-bb-) **1** [T] to hit sb/sth hard with a heavy object **2** go clubbing [I] to go dancing and drinking in a club: *She goes clubbing every Saturday.*

PHR V club together (to do sth) to share the cost of sth, for example a present: *We clubbed together to buy him a leaving present.*

cluck /klʌk/ *noun* [C] the noise made by a chicken ▶ cluck *verb* [I]

clue 🔓 **B1** /kluː/ *noun* [C] ~ (**to sth**) a piece of information that helps you solve a problem or a crime, answer a question, etc: *The police were looking for clues to his disappearance.* ◇ *a crossword clue*

IDM not have a clue (*informal*) to know nothing about sth

clued-up /ˌkluːd 'ʌp/ (*BrE*) (*AmE* ˌclued-'in) *adj.* ~ (**on sth**) (*informal*) knowing a lot about sth: *I'm not really clued-up on the technical details.*

clueless /'kluːləs/ *adj.* (*informal*) not able to understand; stupid: *I'm absolutely clueless about computers.*

clump¹ /klʌmp/ *noun* [C] a small group of things or people very close together, especially trees or plants; a bunch of sth such as grass or hair

clump² /klʌmp/ *verb* [I, T] ~ (**together**); ~ A and B (**together**) to come together or be brought together to form a tight group: *Galaxies tend to clump together in clusters.*

clumsy /'klʌmzi/ *adj.* (clumsier; clumsiest) **1** (used about a person) careless and likely to knock into, drop or break things: *His clumsy fingers couldn't untie the knot.* **2** (used about a comment, etc.) likely to upset or offend people: *He made a clumsy apology.* **3** large, difficult to use, and not attractive in design: *a clumsy piece of furniture* ▶ clumsily /-zɪli/ *adv.* ▶ clumsiness *noun* [U]

clung /klʌŋ/ past tense, past participle of **cling**

clunk /klʌŋk/ *noun* [C] a short low sound made when two hard objects hit each other: *The car door shut with a clunk.*

cluster¹ 🔓+ **C1** /'klʌstə(r)/ *noun* [C] a group of people, plants or things that stand or grow close together

cluster² /'klʌstə(r)/ *verb* [I] ~ (**around/round sb/sth**) to come together in a small group or groups: *The tourists clustered around their guide.*

'cluster bomb *noun* [C] a type of bomb that throws out smaller bombs when it explodes

clutch¹ /klʌtʃ/ *verb* [T] to hold sth tightly, especially because you are in pain, afraid or excited: *He clutched his mother's hand in fear.*

PHR V clutch at sth to try to take hold of sth: *She clutched at the money but the wind blew it away.*

clutch² /klʌtʃ/ *noun* **1** [C] the part of a vehicle that you press with your foot when you are driving in order to change the GEAR; the part of the engine that it is connected to: *to press/release the clutch* **2** clutches [pl.] (*informal*) power or control over sb: *He fell into the enemy's clutches.*

clutter¹ /'klʌtə(r)/ *noun* [U] things that are where they are not wanted or needed and make a place untidy: *Who left all this clutter on the floor?* ▶ cluttered *adj.*: *a cluttered desk*

clutter² /'klʌtə(r)/ *verb* [T] ~ sth (**up**) to fill a place or an area with too many things, so that it is untidy ➷ look at **declutter**

cm *abbr.* (in writing) (*pl.* cm, cms) = CENTIMETRE

Co. *abbr.* **1** /kəʊ/ = COMPANY (1): *W Smith & Co.* **2** (in writing) = COUNTY: *Co. Down*

co- /kəʊ/ *prefix* (in verbs, nouns, adjectives and adverbs) together with: *co-pilot* ◇ *coexist*

c/o *abbr.* (in writing) **care of** (used for addressing a letter to sb who is staying at another person's house): *Sandra Garcia, c/o Mrs Nolan*

coach¹ 🔓 **A2** /kəʊtʃ/ *noun* [C] **1** (**SPORT**) a person who trains people to compete in certain sports: *a tennis coach* **2** (*BrE*) (**TOURISM**) a comfortable bus used for long journeys: *It's cheaper to travel by coach than by train.* **3** = CARRIAGE (1) **4** a large vehicle with four wheels pulled by horses, used in the past for carrying passengers ➷ look at **carriage** (2)

coach[2] 🔊 **B1** /kəʊtʃ/ *verb* [I, T] ~ **sb (in/for sth)** (**SPORT**) to train or teach sb, especially to compete in a sport or to pass an exam: *She is being coached for the Olympics by a former champion.*

coaching /ˈkəʊtʃɪŋ/ *noun* [U] **1** the process of training sb to play a sport, to do a job better or to improve a skill **2** (*especially BrE*) the process of giving a student extra teaching in a particular subject

coagulate /kəʊˈæɡjuleɪt/ *verb* [I] (used about a liquid) to become thick and partly solid: *The blood was starting to coagulate inside the cut.* ▶ **coagulation** /kəʊˌæɡjuˈleɪʃn/ *noun* [U]

coal 🔊 **B1** /kəʊl/ *noun* **1** [U] (**GEOLOGY**) a hard black mineral that is MINED (= dug) from the ground and burned to give heat: *a lump of coal* ◇ *a coal fire* ⊃ picture at **carbon cycle**, **energy**, **generator** **2** [C] a piece of coal: *A hot coal fell out of the fire and burnt the carpet.*

coalesce /ˌkəʊəˈles/ *verb* [I] ~ **(into sth)**; ~ **(with sth)** (*formal*) to come together to form one larger group, substance, etc. ▶ **coalescence** /-ˈlesns/ *noun* [U]

coalface /ˈkəʊlfeɪs/ *noun* [C] the place deep inside a mine where the coal is cut out of the rock

coalition 🔊+ **C1** /ˌkəʊəˈlɪʃn/ *noun* [C + sing./pl. verb] (**POLITICS**) a government formed by two or more political parties working together: *a coalition between the Socialists and the Green Party* ⊃ note at **government**

'coal mine (*also* **pit**) *noun* [C] a place, usually underground, where coal is dug from the ground ⊃ look at **colliery**

'coal miner (*also* **miner**) *noun* [C] a person whose job is to dig coal from the ground

coarse /kɔːs/ *adj.* **1** consisting of large pieces; rough, not smooth: *coarse salt* ◇ *coarse cloth* **OPP** **fine**[1], **smooth**[1] **2** (used about a person or their behaviour) rude, likely to offend people; having bad manners ▶ **coarsely** *adv.*: *Chop the onion coarsely* (= into pieces which are not too small). ◇ *He laughed coarsely.*

coarsen /ˈkɔːsn/ *verb* [I, T] to become or to make sth COARSE

coast[1] 🔊 **A2** /kəʊst/ *noun* [C] (**GEOGRAPHY**) the area of land that is next to or close to the sea: *Scarborough is on the east coast.* ◇ *an island off the coast of Italy* ◇ *We spent the day at the coast.*

coast[2] /kəʊst/ *verb* [I] **1** to travel in a car, on a bicycle, etc. (especially down a hill) without using power **2** to achieve sth without much effort: *They coasted to victory.*

coastal 🔊+ **C1** /ˈkəʊstl/ *adj.* (**GEOGRAPHY**) on or near a coast: *coastal areas* ⊃ picture at **erosion**

coaster /ˈkəʊstə(r)/ *noun* [C] a small flat object that you put under a glass to protect the top of a table

coastguard /ˈkəʊstɡɑːd/ *noun* [C] a person or group of people whose job is to watch the sea near the coast in order to help people or ships that are in danger or to stop illegal activities

coastline /ˈkəʊstlaɪn/ *noun* [C] (**GEOGRAPHY**) the edge or shape of a coast: *a rocky coastline*

coat[1] 🔊 **A1** /kəʊt/ *noun* [C] **1** a piece of clothing that you wear over your other clothes to keep warm when you are outside: *Put your coat on — it's cold outside.* ⊃ look at **overcoat**, **raincoat** **2** the fur or hair covering an animal's body: *a dog with a smooth coat* ⊃ picture at **animal** **3** a layer of sth covering a surface: *The walls will probably need two coats of paint.*

coat[2] /kəʊt/ *verb* [T, often passive] ~ **sth (with/in sth)** to cover sth with a layer of sth else: *biscuits coated with milk chocolate*

'coat hanger = HANGER

coating /ˈkəʊtɪŋ/ *noun* [C] a thin layer of sth that covers sth else: *wire with a plastic coating*

coat of 'arms *noun* [C] (*pl.* **coats of arms**) (*also* **arms** [pl.]) a design that is used as the symbol of a family, a town, a university, etc.

co-'author (**LITERATURE**) *noun* [C] a person who writes a book or an article with sb else ▶ **co-author** *verb* [T]

coax /kəʊks/ *verb* [T] ~ **sb (into/out of sth/doing sth)**; ~ **sth out of/from sb** to persuade sb gently: *The child wasn't hungry, but his mother coaxed him into eating a little.* ◇ *At last he coaxed a smile out of her.*

coaxial /kəʊˈæksiəl/ *adj.* **1** (**GEOMETRY**) sharing a common AXIS (= an imaginary line through the middle of an object) **2** (*informal* **coax** /ˈkəʊæks/) (**ENGINEERING**) (used about a cable) sending signals using two wires inside one cable, one of which is wrapped around the other. Coaxial cable is used by TV, phone and internet companies.

cob /kɒb/ *noun* [C] **1** the long hard part of the MAIZE (CORN) plant that the rows of yellow grains grow on ⊃ look at **corn on the cob 2** a strong horse with short legs

cobalt[1] /ˈkəʊbɔːlt/ *noun* [U] **1** (*symb.* Co) (**CHEMISTRY**) a chemical element. Cobalt is a hard silver-white metal that is often mixed with other metals and used to give a deep blue-green colour to glass. ❶ For more information on the periodic table of elements, look at the **Reference Section** of this dictionary. **2** (*also* **cobalt 'blue**) a deep blue-green colour

cobalt[2] /ˈkəʊbɔːlt/ (*also* **cobalt 'blue**) *adj.* deep blue-green in colour

cobble /ˈkɒbl/ *verb*
PHR V **cobble sth together** to make sth or put sth together quickly and without much care

cobbler /ˈkɒblə(r)/ *noun* [C] (*old-fashioned*) a person who repairs shoes

cobbles /ˈkɒblz/ (*also* **cobblestones** /ˈkɒblstəʊnz/) *noun* [pl.] small ROUNDED stones used to make the surfaces of roads, especially in the past ▶ **cobbled** /-bld/ *adj.*: *cobbled streets*

cobra /ˈkəʊbrə/ *noun* [C] a poisonous snake that can spread out the skin at the back of its neck. Cobras live in India and Africa. ⊃ picture at **animal**

cobweb /ˈkɒbweb/ *noun* [C] a net of THREADS made by a spider in order to catch insects ⊃ look at **web** (2)

cocaine /kəʊˈkeɪn/ (*also informal* **coke**) *noun* [U] a dangerous drug that some people take for pleasure but that is ADDICTIVE (= difficult to stop using)

coccus /ˈkɒkəs/ *noun* [C] (*pl.* **cocci** /-kaɪ/) (**BIOLOGY**) a type of bacteria. There are several types of coccus, some of which cause serious infections and illnesses. ⊃ look at **streptococcus**

coccyx /ˈkɒksɪks/ *noun* [C] (**ANATOMY**) the small bone at the bottom of the SPINE **SYN** **tailbone** ⊃ picture at **body**

cochineal /ˌkɒtʃɪˈniːl/ *noun* [U] a bright red substance used to give colour to food

cochlea /ˈkɒkliə/ *noun* [C] (**ANATOMY**) the part of the INNER EAR (= the inside of the ear) that is shaped like a shell and is very important for hearing ⊃ picture at **ear**

cock[1] /kɒk/ *noun* [C] **1** (*BrE*) (*also* **rooster** *AmE, BrE*) an adult male chicken ⊃ note at **chicken**[1] **2** an adult male bird of any type

cock² /kɒk/ *verb* [T] to hold up a part of the body: *The horse cocked its ears on hearing the noise.*
PHR V **cock sth up** (*BrE, slang*) to do sth very badly, often by making a stupid mistake ⊃ **cock-up**

cock-a-doodle-doo /ˌkɒk ə ˌduːdl ˈduː/ *noun* [sing.] the word for the sound that an adult male chicken makes

cockatoo /ˌkɒkəˈtuː/ *noun* [C] (*pl.* -oos) a large bird of the PARROT family, with a row of feathers standing up on its head ⊃ picture at **animal**

cockerel /ˈkɒkərəl/ *noun* [C] a young male chicken

cockle /ˈkɒkl/ *noun* [C] a small SHELLFISH (= a creature with a shell that lives in water) that can be eaten

cockney /ˈkɒkni/ *noun* **1** [C] a person who was born and grew up in the East End of London **2** [U] (**LANGUAGE**) the way of speaking English that is typical of people living in this area: *a cockney accent*

cockpit /ˈkɒkpɪt/ *noun* [C] the area in a plane, boat or racing car where the pilot or driver sits

cockroach /ˈkɒkrəʊtʃ/ (*AmE* roach) *noun* [C] a large insect with wings, that lives in houses, especially where there is dirt ⊃ picture at **animal**

cocktail 𝄞+ **C1** /ˈkɒkteɪl/ *noun* [C] **1** a drink made from a mixture of alcoholic drinks and fruit juices: *a cocktail bar/party* **2** a mixture of small pieces of food that is served cold: *a prawn cocktail* **3** a mixture of different substances, usually ones that do not mix together well: *a lethal cocktail of drugs*

cock-up *noun* [C] (*BrE, informal*) something that was badly done; a mistake that causes sth to be a failure ⊃ look at **cock¹**

cocoa /ˈkəʊkəʊ/ *noun* **1** [U] a dark brown powder made from the seeds of a tropical tree and used in making chocolate **2** [U, C] a hot drink made from this powder mixed with milk or water; a cup of this drink: *a cup of cocoa*

coconut /ˈkəʊkənʌt/ *noun* [C, U] the large nut of a tropical tree called a 'coconut palm'. It grows inside a hard shell and contains a soft white substance that can be eaten and juice that can be drunk

cocoon¹ /kəˈkuːn/ *noun* [C] (**BIOLOGY**) **1** a cover or case of silk THREADS that some insects make to protect themselves before they become adults ⊃ look at **chrysalis 2** a layer of sth soft that wraps all around sb/sth and keeps them safe (*figurative*): *the cocoon of a caring family*

cocoon² /kəˈkuːn/ *verb* [T] ~ **sb/sth (in sth)** to surround sb/sth completely with sth for protection

cod /kɒd/ *noun* [C, U] (*pl.* cod) a large sea fish that is white inside and used for food

coda /ˈkəʊdə/ *noun* [C] (**MUSIC**) the final passage of a piece of music

code¹ 𝄞 **A2** ⊙ /kəʊd/ *noun* **1** [C, U] a system of words, letters, numbers, etc. that are used instead of the real letters or words to make a message or information secret: *They managed to* **break/crack** *the enemy* **code** (= find out what it means). ◇ *They wrote letters to each other in* **code**. **2** [C] a group of numbers, letters, etc. that is used for identifying sth: *What's the code* (= the phone number) *for Stockholm?* ⊃ look at **barcode** ⊃ note at **phone¹ 3** a set of rules for behaviour: *a* **code of practice** (= a set of standards agreed and accepted by a particular profession) ◇ *the* **Highway Code** (= the rules for driving on the roads) **4** [U] (**COMPUTING**) a system of computer programming instructions: *lines of code*

code² 𝐖 /kəʊd/ *verb* [T] **1** to put or write sth in code: *coded messages* **OPP** **decode 2** to use a particular system for identifying things: *The files are colour-coded: blue for Europe, green for Africa.* **3** (**COMPUTING**)

to write a computer program by putting one system of numbers, words and symbols into another system

codec /ˈkəʊdek/ *noun* [C] (**COMPUTING**) a device or program that reduces the size of a file, etc. so that it can be sent more quickly, and returns it to its original form so that it can be used

codeine /ˈkəʊdiːn/ *noun* [U] (**MEDICINE**) a drug that is used to reduce pain

codify /ˈkəʊdɪfaɪ/ *verb* [T] (codifying; codifies; *pt, pp* codified) to arrange laws, rules, etc. into a system ▶ **codification** /ˌkəʊdɪfɪˈkeɪʃn/ *noun* [U]

co-edu'cational *adj.* (**EDUCATION**) (used about a school) where girls and boys are taught together **SYN** **mixed** ▶ **co-edu'cation** *noun* [U]

coefficient /ˌkəʊɪˈfɪʃnt/ *noun* [C] **1** (**MATHEMATICS**) a number that is placed before another quantity and that multiplies it, for example 3 in the quantity 3x **2** (**PHYSICS**) a number that measures a particular PROPERTY (= characteristic) of a substance: *the coefficient of friction/expansion*

coeliac (*BrE*) (*AmE* celiac) /ˈsiːliæk/ *adj.* (**HEALTH**) having or connected with coeliac disease, a condition in which food containing GLUTEN (= a substance found in some grains) causes sb to become ill ▶ **coeliac** (*BrE*) (*AmE* celiac) *noun* [C]

coerce /kəʊˈɜːs/ *verb* [T] ~ **sb (into sth/doing sth)** (*formal*) to force sb to do sth, for example by threatening them ▶ **coercion** /-ˈɜːʃn/ *noun* [U]

coexist /ˌkəʊɪɡˈzɪst/ *verb* [I] to live or be together at the same time or in the same place as sb/sth ▶ **coexistence** *noun* [U]

C. of E. /ˌsiː əv ˈiː/ *abbr.* = CHURCH OF ENGLAND

coffee 𝄞 **A1** /ˈkɒfi/ *noun* **1** [U] the cooked seeds (called coffee beans) of a tropical bush; a powder made from them: *Coffee is the country's biggest export.* ◇ *decaffeinated/instant coffee* **2** [U] a drink made by adding hot water to this powder: *Would you prefer tea or coffee?* ◇ *a cup of coffee* **3** [C] a cup of this drink: *Two coffees please.*

'coffee pot *noun* [C] a container in which coffee is made and served

'coffee shop (*also* **'coffee bar**) *noun* [C] (*BrE*) a place, sometimes inside a hotel, a large shop, etc., where simple food, coffee, tea and other drinks without alcohol are served

'coffee table *noun* [C] a small low table for putting magazines, cups, etc., on

coffin /ˈkɒfɪn/ (*especially BrE*) (*AmE usually* casket) *noun* [C] a box in which a dead body is buried or CREMATED (= burned)

cog /kɒɡ/ *noun* [C] (**ENGINEERING**) **1** one of a series of teeth on the edge of a wheel that fit between the teeth on the next wheel and cause it to move ⊃ picture at **cogwheel 2** = COGWHEEL

cogent /ˈkəʊdʒənt/ *adj.* (*formal*) strongly and clearly expressed in a way that influences what people believe: *a cogent argument/reason*

cognac /ˈkɒnjæk/ *noun* **1** [U] a type of BRANDY (= a strong alcoholic drink) that is made in France **2** [C] a glass of this drink

cognition /kɒɡˈnɪʃn/ *noun* [U] (**PSYCHOLOGY**) the process by which knowledge and understanding is developed in the mind

cognitive 𝄞+ **C1** /ˈkɒɡnətɪv/ *adj.* (**PSYCHOLOGY**) connected with mental processes of understanding: *cognitive abilities* ◇ *the* **cognitive process** *of absorbing new information*

,cognitive be,havioural 'therapy (*BrE*) (*AmE* cognitive behavioral therapy) = CBT

cognitive dissonance /ˌkɒgnətɪv 'dɪsənəns/ *noun* [U] (**PSYCHOLOGY**) the state of having beliefs and attitudes that are not consistent with your experiences and behaviour: *Most of us suffer from cognitive dissonance: we want to do something about global warming, but think we can continue our energy-guzzling lives.*

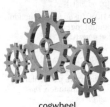

cogwheel

sprocket wheel

cogwheel /'kɒgwiːl/ (*also* cog) *noun* [C] a wheel with a series of teeth on its edge that fit into the teeth in the next wheel and cause it to move

cohabit /kəʊ'hæbɪt/ *verb* [I] (*formal*) (used about a couple) to live together as if they are married

coherent /kəʊ'hɪərənt/ *adj.* **1** (used about ideas, thoughts, arguments, etc.) logical and well organized; easy to understand and clear: *a coherent narrative/ explanation* **OPP** incoherent **2** (used about a person) able to talk and express yourself clearly: *He only became coherent again two hours after the attack.* **OPP** incoherent ▸ coherence /-rəns/ *noun* [U] ▸ coherently *adv.*

cohesion /kəʊ'hiːʒn/ *noun* [U] **1** the act or state of keeping together: *What the team lacks is cohesion — all the players play as individuals.* ◇ *social/political/ economic cohesion* **SYN** unity **2** (**CHEMISTRY**, **PHYSICS**) the force causing MOLECULES of the same substance to stick together

cohesive /kəʊ'hiːsɪv/ *adj.* (*formal*) forming a united whole: *We're a very cohesive group and we have been playing together for a few years.*

cohort /'kəʊhɔːt/ *noun* [C + sing./pl. verb] a group of people who share a common feature or type of behaviour: *the 1999 birth cohort* (= all those born in 1999)

coil¹ /kɔɪl/ *verb* [I, T] to wind into a series of circles; to make sth do this: *a snake coiled under a rock*

coil² /kɔɪl/ *noun* [C] a series of circles formed by winding up a length of rope, wire, etc: *a coil of rope*

coin¹ ? **B1** /kɔɪn/ *noun* [C] a piece of money made of metal: *a pound coin*

coin² /kɔɪn/ *verb* [T] (**LANGUAGE**) to invent a new word or phrase: *Who was it who coined the phrase 'a week is a long time in politics'?*

coinage /'kɔɪnɪdʒ/ *noun* [U] the system of coins used in a country: *Game developers introduced their own virtual coinage.*

coincide ? + **C1** /ˌkəʊɪn'saɪd/ *verb* [I] ~ (with sth) **1** (used about events) to happen at the same time as sth else: *The Queen's visit is timed to coincide with the country's centenary celebrations.* **2** to be exactly the same or very similar: *Our views coincide completely.*

coincidence ? + **C1** /kəʊ'ɪnsɪdəns/ *noun* [C, U] two or more similar things happening at the same time by chance, in a surprising way: *What a coincidence!* ◇ *We hadn't planned to meet. It was just coincidence.*

coincident /kəʊ'ɪnsɪdənt/ *adj.* ~ (with sth) (*formal*) happening in the same place or at the same time

coincidental /kəʊˌɪnsɪ'dentl/ *adj.* resulting from two similar or related events happening at the same time by chance ▸ coincidentally /-təli/ *adv.*

coitus /'kɔɪtəs, 'kəʊɪ-/ (*formal*) = SEXUAL INTERCOURSE

coke /kəʊk/ *noun* [U] **1** a solid black substance produced from coal and used as a fuel **2** (*informal*) = COCAINE

Col. *abbr.* (in writing) = COLONEL: *Col. Stewart*

col /kɒl/ *noun* [C] (**GEOGRAPHY**) a low point between two higher points in a line or group of mountains

cola /'kəʊlə/ *noun* [C, U] a sweet brown drink that does not contain alcohol; a glass or can of this

colander /'kʌləndə(r)/ *noun* [C] a metal or plastic bowl with a lot of small holes in it that is used for removing the water in which food has been boiled or washed

cold¹ ? **A1** /kəʊld/ *adj.* **1** having a low temperature; not hot or warm: *I'm not going into the sea, the water's too cold.* ◇ *Shall I put the heating on? I'm cold.* **2** (used about food or drink) not heated or cooked; having become cold after being heated or cooked: *a cold drink* ◇ *Have your soup before it gets cold.* **3** (used about a person or sb's behaviour) very unfriendly; not being kind, understanding, etc: *She gave him a cold, hard look.*

IDM cold turkey (**HEALTH**) suddenly and completely, without getting used to sth gradually: *I gave up smoking and went cold turkey.* get/have cold feet (*informal*) to become/be afraid to do sth: *She started to get cold feet as her wedding day approached.* in cold blood in a cruel way and without PITY: *to kill somebody in cold blood*

▼ VOCABULARY BUILDING

Hot describes a high temperature: *I can't drink this yet. It's too hot.* **Warm** means 'fairly hot' in a pleasant way: *Come and sit by the fire, you'll soon get warm again.* **Boiling** is an informal word for 'very hot': *Could you turn the heating down? It's boiling in here.* **Cool** means 'fairly cold, especially in a pleasant way': *It's hot outside, but it's nice and cool in here.* **Freezing** means 'extremely cold': *It's absolutely freezing outside.* It can mean that the temperature is below 0° Celsius.

---

cold² ? **A1** /kəʊld/ *noun* **1** [sing., U] lack of heat; low temperature; cold weather: *We walked home in the snow, shivering with cold.* ◇ *Come on, let's get out of the cold and go indoors.* **2** [C, U] (**HEALTH**) a common illness of the nose and throat. When you have a **cold** your throat hurts and you often cannot breathe through your nose: *I think I'm getting a cold.* ◇ *Wear some warm clothes when you go out or you'll catch cold.*

,cold-'blooded *adj.* **1** (**BIOLOGY**) having a blood temperature that changes with the temperature of the surrounding air or water: *Reptiles are cold-blooded.* **OPP** warm-blooded **2** cruel; having or showing no PITY: *cold-blooded killers*

,cold-'calling *noun* [U] (**BUSINESS**) the practice of phoning or visiting sb you do not know in order to sell them sth: *One million people have said no to junk mail and cold-calling.* ▸ 'cold call *noun* [C] ▸ ,cold-'call *verb* [I, T]: *I cold-called 500 companies.* ▸ ,cold-'caller *noun* [C]

,cold 'cash (*AmE*) = HARD CASH

'cold cuts *noun* [pl.] (*especially AmE*) slices of cooked meat that are served cold

,cold-'hearted *adj.* unkind; not showing love or understanding for other people

coldly /'kəʊldli/ *adv.* in an unfriendly way; in a way that is not kind or understanding

coldness /'kəʊldnəs/ *noun* [U] the lack of warm feelings; unfriendly behaviour

'cold snap *noun* [C] a sudden short period of very cold weather

'cold sore *noun* [C] (**HEALTH**) a small painful area on the lips or inside the mouth that is caused by a virus

,cold 'storage *noun* [U] a place where food, etc. can be kept fresh or frozen until it is needed; the keeping of sth in a place like this: *to keep meat **in cold storage***

,cold 'war (*often* Cold War) *noun* [sing., U] (**HISTORY**, **POLITICS**) a very unfriendly relationship between two countries who are not actually fighting each other, usually used about the situation between the US and the Soviet Union after the Second World War

colic /'kɒlɪk/ *noun* [U] (**HEALTH**) severe pain in the stomach area, suffered especially by babies

collaborate ʔ+ **C1** /kə'læbəreɪt/ *verb* [I] **1** ~ (**with sb**) (**on sth**) to work together (with sb), especially to create or produce sth: *She collaborated with another author on the book.* **2** ~ (**with sb**) to help the enemy forces who have taken control of your country
▸ collaboration ʔ+ **C1** /kə,læbə'reɪʃn/ *noun* [U, C]
▸ collaborator *noun* [C]

collaborative /kə'læbərətɪv/ *adj.* (*formal*) involving, or done by, several people or groups of people working together: *collaborative projects/studies/research*
▸ collaboratively *adv.*

collage /'kɒlɑːʒ/ *noun* [C, U] (**ART**) a picture made by fixing pieces of paper, cloth, photos, etc. onto a surface; the art of making a picture like this

collagen /'kɒlədʒən/ *noun* [U] (**BIOLOGY**) a PROTEIN found in skin and bone, sometimes INJECTED into the body (= put into the body through a needle), especially the face, to improve its appearance

collapse¹ ʔ **B2** /kə'læps/ *verb* **1** [I] to fall down or break into pieces suddenly: *A lot of buildings collapsed in the earthquake.* **2** [I] to fall down and often become unconscious, usually because you are very ill: *The winner collapsed at the end of the race.* **3** [I] (used about a business, plan, etc.) to fail suddenly or completely: *The company collapsed, leaving hundreds of people out of work.* **4** [I, T] to fold sth or be folded into a shape that uses less space

collapse² ʔ **B2** /kə'læps/ *noun* **1** [C, U] the sudden or complete failure of sth, such as a business, plan, etc: *The peace talks were on the brink/verge of collapse.* **2** [sing., U] (used about a building) a sudden fall: *the collapse of the motorway bridge* **3** [sing., U] (**HEALTH**) a medical condition when a person becomes very ill and suddenly falls down

collapsible /kə'læpsəbl/ *adj.* that can be folded into a shape that makes it easy to store: *a collapsible bed*

collar¹ /'kɒlə(r)/ *noun* [C] **1** the part of a shirt, coat, dress, etc. that fits round the neck and is often folded over: *a coat with a fur collar* ⊃ look at blue-collar, white-collar **2** a band of leather that is put round an animal's neck (especially a dog or cat)

collar² /'kɒlə(r)/ *verb* [T] (*informal*) to catch hold of sb who does not want to be caught

collarbone /'kɒləbəʊn/ *noun* [C] (**ANATOMY**) one of the two bones that connect the chest bones to the shoulder **SYN** clavicle ⊃ picture at body

collate /kə'leɪt/ *verb* [T] **1** to collect information from different places in order to put it together, examine and compare it: *to collate data/information/figures* **2** to collect pieces of paper or pages from a book and

arrange them in the correct order ▸ collation /-'leɪʃn/ *noun* [U]: *the collation of data*

collateral¹ /kə'lætərəl/ *noun* [U] (**FINANCE**) property or sth valuable that you promise to give to sb if you cannot pay back money that you borrow

collateral² /kə'lætərəl/ *adj.* (*formal*) connected with sth else, but in addition to it and less important: *collateral benefits* ◇ *The government denied that there had been any **collateral damage** (= injury to ordinary people or buildings) during the bombing raid.*

colleague ʔ **A2** /'kɒliːg/ *noun* [C] a person that you work with, especially in a profession or a business

collect ʔ **A2** /kə'lekt/ *verb* **1** [T] to bring a number of things together: *All the exam papers will be collected at the end.* **2** [T] to get and keep together a number of objects of a particular type over a period of time as a hobby: *He used to collect stamps.* **3** [I, T] to ask for money from a number of people: *to collect for charity* ◇ *The landlord collects the rent at the end of each month.* **4** [I] to come together: *A crowd collected to see what was going on.* **SYN** gather **5** [T] (*especially BrE*) to go and get sb/sth from a particular place; to pick sb/ sth up: *to collect the children from school* **6** [T] ~ (**yourself**) to get control of yourself, your feelings, thoughts, etc: *She collected herself and went back into the room as if nothing had happened.* ◇ *I tried to **collect my thoughts** before the exam.*

▼ SYNONYMS

collect

gather • accumulate • amass

These words all mean to get more of sth over a period of time, or to increase in quantity over a period of time.

collect *He collected data from various sources.*

gather *Detectives were gathering evidence.*

accumulate (*formal*) *Debts began to accumulate.*

amass (*formal*) *He amassed a large fortune.*

collected /kə'lektɪd/ *adj.* calm and in control of yourself, your feelings, thoughts, etc: *She felt cool, calm and collected before the interview.*

collection ʔ **B1** /kə'lekʃn/ *noun* **1** [C] a group of objects of a particular type that sb has collected as a hobby: *a stamp collection* ⊃ note at art **2** [C, U] the act of getting sth from a place or from people: *rubbish collections* **3** [C] a group of people or things: *a large collection of papers on the desk* **4** [C] (**LITERATURE**) a number of poems, stories, letters, etc. published together in one book: *a collection of modern poetry* **5** [C] the act of asking for money from a number of people (for charity, in church, etc.): *a collection for the poor* **6** [C] a variety of new clothes or items for the home that are specially designed and sold at a particular time: *Armani's stunning new autumn collection*

collective¹ ʔ+ **C1** /kə'lektɪv/ *adj.* shared by a group of people together; not individual: *collective responsibility* ▸ collectively *adv.*: *We took the decision collectively at a meeting.*

collective² /kə'lektɪv/ *noun* [C + sing./pl. verb] (**AGRICULTURE**, **BUSINESS**) a group of people who own a business or a farm and run it together; the business that they run

col,lective 'bargaining *noun* [U] (**POLITICS**) discussions between a TRADE UNION (= an organization that protects the rights of workers) and an employer about the pay and working conditions of the union members

col,lective 'farm noun [C] (**AGRICULTURE**) a large farm, or a group of farms, especially one owned by the state, that is run by a group of people

col,lective 'noun noun [C] (**GRAMMAR**) a singular noun, such as *committee* or *team*, that refers to a group of people, animals or things and, in British English, can be used with either a singular or a plural verb

collectivism /kə'lektɪvɪzəm/ noun [U] (**POLITICS**) the political system in which all farms, businesses and industries are owned by the government or by all the people ▶ **collectivist** /-vɪst/ adj.

collectivize (*BrE also* -ise) /kə'lektɪvaɪz/ verb [T, often passive] (**POLITICS**) to join several private farms, industries, etc. together so that they are controlled by the community or by the government
▶ **collectivization** (*BrE also* -isation) /kə,lektɪvaɪ'zeɪʃn/ noun [U]

collector 🔊+ **B2** /kə'lektə(r)/ noun [C] (often in compounds) a person who collects things as a hobby or as part of their job: *a stamp collector* ◇ *a ticket/rent/ tax collector*

college 🔊 **A1** /'kɒlɪdʒ/ noun (**EDUCATION**) **1** [C, U] (in the UK) an institution where you can study after you leave school (at the age of 16): *an art college* ◇ *a sixth-form college* (= an institution where pupils aged 16 to 18 can prepare for A Levels) ◇ *She's studying Spanish at the college of further education* (= a college that is not a university where people who have left school can study). **2** [C] (in Britain) one of the separate institutions into which certain universities are divided: *King's College, London* **3** [C] (in the US) a university, or part of one, where students can study for a degree

collide /kə'laɪd/ verb [I] ~ **(with sb/sth)** to crash; to hit sb/ sth very hard while moving: *He ran along the corridor and collided with his music teacher.*

colliery /'kɒliəri/ noun [C] (*pl.* -ies) (*especially BrE*) a coal mine and its buildings

collision 🔊+ **C1** /kə'lɪʒn/ noun [C, U] an accident in which two vehicles or people crash into each other: *It was a head-on collision and the driver was killed instantly.* ◇ *a collision between a bicycle and a van* ◇ *He was injured in a collision with the goalkeeper.*
IDM **be on a collision course (with sb/sth) 1** to be in a situation that is certain to end in an argument **2** to be moving in a direction which is certain to cause a crash: *The ship was on a collision course with an iceberg.*

collocate /'kɒləkeɪt/ verb [I] ~ **(with sth)** (**LANGUAGE**) (used about a word) to be often used with another word: *'Bitter' collocates with 'enemies' but 'sour' does not.* ▶ **collocate** /-kət/ noun [C]: *'Bitter' and 'enemies' are collocates.*

collocation /,kɒlə'keɪʃn/ noun [C, U] (**LANGUAGE**) a combination of words in a language, that happens very often and more frequently than would happen by chance: *A 'resounding success' and a 'crying shame' are English collocations.*

colloquial /kə'ləʊkwiəl/ adj. (**LANGUAGE**) (used about words, phrases, etc.) used in spoken conversation, not in formal situations ▶ **colloquially** /-kwiəli/ adv.

colloquialism /kə'ləʊkwiəlɪzəm/ noun [C] (**LANGUAGE**) a word or phrase that is used in conversation but not in formal speech or writing

collusion /kə'luːʒn/ noun [U] (*formal*) secret agreement, especially in order to do sth dishonest: *The drugs were brought into the country with the collusion of customs officials.*

colon /'kəʊlən, -lɒn/ noun [C] **1** (**LANGUAGE**) the mark (:) used before a list, an explanation, an example, etc., before reporting what sb has said **2** (**ANATOMY**) the lower part of the large INTESTINE that carries food away from the stomach to the ANUS (= the place where it leaves the body) ⊃ picture at **body**, **digestive system**

colonel /'kɜːnl/ noun [C] (*abbr.* **Col.**) an officer of a high level in the army or the US AIR FORCE

colonial 🔊+ **C1** /kə'ləʊniəl/ adj. (**POLITICS**) connected with or belonging to a country that controls another country: *Spain used to be a major colonial power.*

colonialism /kə'ləʊniəlɪzəm/ noun [U] (**POLITICS**) the practice by which a powerful country controls another country or countries

colonist /'kɒlənɪst/ noun [C] a person who goes to live in a country that has become a COLONY

colonize (*BrE also* -ise) /'kɒlənaɪz/ verb [T] (**POLITICS**) to take control of another country or place and make it a COLONY ▶ **colonization** (*BrE also* -isation) /,kɒlənaɪ'zeɪʃn/ noun [U]

colonnade /,kɒlə'neɪd/ noun [C] (**ARCHITECTURE**) a row of stone columns with equal spaces between them, usually supporting a roof

colony 🔊+ **B2** /'kɒləni/ noun (*pl.* -ies) **1** [C] (**POLITICS**) a country or an area that is ruled by another, more powerful country **2** [sing. + sing./pl. verb] (**SOCIAL STUDIES**) a group of people who go to live permanently in a colony **3** [C + sing./pl. verb] (**BIOLOGY**) a group of the same type of animals, insects or plants living or growing in the same place: *a colony of ants*

color /'kʌlə(r)/ (*AmE*) = COLOUR¹, COLOUR²

coloratura /,kɒlərə'tʊərə/ noun [U] (**MUSIC**) complicated passages for a singer, for example in OPERA

'color-blind (*AmE*) = COLOUR-BLIND

colored, colorful, coloring, colorless (*AmE*) = COLOURED, COLOURFUL, COLOURING, COLOURLESS

'color scheme (*AmE*) = COLOUR SCHEME

colossal /kə'lɒsl/ adj. extremely large: *a colossal building* ◇ *a colossal amount of money*

colour¹ 🔊 **A1** (*BrE*) (*AmE* color) /'kʌlə(r)/ noun **1** [C, U] the fact that sth is red, green, yellow, blue, etc: *'What colour is your car?' 'Red.'* ◇ *What colours do the Swedish team play in?* ◇ *a dark/deep colour* ◇ *a bright colour* ◇ *a light/pale colour* ◇ *Those flowers certainly give the room a bit of colour.* ⊃ picture at **prism 2** [U] the use of all the colours, not just black and white: *All the pictures in the book are in colour.* **3** [U] a red or pink colour in your face, particularly when it shows how healthy you are or that you are embarrassed: *You look much better now, you've got a bit more colour.* ◇ *Colour flooded her face when she thought of what had happened.* **4** [U] interesting or exciting details: *It's a busy area, full of activity and colour.*
IDM **off colour** ill with flying colours → FLYING¹

colour² (*BrE*) (*AmE* color) /'kʌlə(r)/ verb [T] **1** to put colour on sth, for example by painting it: *Colour the picture with your crayons.* ◇ *The area coloured yellow on the map is desert.* **2** to influence thoughts, opinions, etc: *You shouldn't let one bad experience colour your attitude to everything.*
PHRV **colour sth in** to fill a shape, a picture, etc. with colour using pencils, paint, etc: *The children were colouring in pictures of animals.*

'colour-blind (*BrE*) (*AmE* color-blind) adj. (**BIOLOGY**) unable to see the difference between certain colours, especially red and green

coloured 🔊 **B1** (*BrE*) (*AmE* **colored**) /'kʌləd/ *adj.*
1 having colour or a particular colour: *a coffee-coloured dress* ◇ *brightly-coloured lights* **2** (*old-fashioned*) (used about a person) belonging to a human group that does not have white skin ❶ This word is now considered offensive.

colourful 🔊+ **B2** (*BrE*) (*AmE* **colorful**) /'kʌləfl/ *adj.* **1** with bright colours; full of colour: *a colourful shirt* **2** full of interest or excitement: *a colourful story* ◇ *He has a rather colourful past.*

colouring (*BrE*) (*AmE* **coloring**) /'kʌlərɪŋ/ *noun* **1** [U] the colour of a person's hair, skin, etc: *to have fair/dark colouring* **2** [C, U] a substance that is used to give a particular colour to sth, especially food

colourless (*BrE*) (*AmE* **colorless**) /'kʌlələs/ *adj.* **1** without any colour: *a colourless liquid, like water* **2** not interesting or exciting: *a colourless description* **SYN** dull¹

'**colour scheme** (*BrE*) (*AmE* **color scheme**) *noun* [C] the way in which colours are arranged, especially in a room

colt /kəʊlt/ *noun* [C] a young male horse ⊃ look at **filly**

column 🔊 **A2** ❶ /'kɒləm/ *noun* [C]
• PIECE OF STONE **1** (**ARCHITECTURE**) a tall solid POST made of stone, supporting or decorating a building or standing alone: *Nelson's Column is a monument in London.* ⊃ picture at **arch¹**
• SHAPE **2** something that has the shape of a column: *a column of smoke* (= smoke rising straight up)
• ON A PAGE **3** one of the straight sections from top to bottom into which text on a page or screen is divided
• IN A NEWSPAPER **4** a piece of writing in a newspaper or magazine that is part of a regular series or always written by the same writer: *the travel/gossip column*
• OF NUMBERS **5** a series of numbers written one under the other: *to add up a column of figures*
• OF PEOPLE/VEHICLES **6** a long line of people, vehicles, etc., one following behind another: *a column of troops*

columnist 🔊+ **C1** /'kɒləmnɪst/ *noun* [C] (**ARTS AND MEDIA**) a journalist who writes regular articles in a newspaper or magazine: *a gossip columnist*

coma /'kəʊmə/ *noun* [C] (**HEALTH**) a deep unconscious state, often lasting for a long time and caused by serious illness or injury: *to go into/be in a coma*

comatose /'kəʊmətəʊs/ *adj.* **1** (*informal*) deeply asleep: *He had drunk a bottle of vodka and was comatose.* **2** (**HEALTH**) deeply unconscious; in a COMA

comb¹ /kəʊm/ *noun* **1** [C] a flat piece of metal or plastic with teeth that you use for making your hair tidy **2** [C, usually sing.] an act of COMBING of the hair: *Give your hair a comb before you go out.*

comb² /kəʊm/ *verb* [T] **1** to make your hair tidy using a COMB **2** ~ **sth** (**for sb/sth**) to search an area carefully: *Police are combing the woodland for the murder weapon.*

combat¹ 🔊+ **C1** /'kɒmbæt/ *noun* [U, C] a fight, especially in war: *unarmed combat* (= without weapons)

combat² 🔊+ **C1** /'kɒmbæt/ *verb* [T] to fight against sth; to try to stop or defeat sth: *to combat terrorism* ◇ *new medicines to combat heart disease*

combatant /'kɒmbətənt/ *noun* [C] a person who takes part in fighting, especially in war

combats /'kɒmbæts/ (*also* '**combat trousers**) (*BrE*) = CARGO PANTS

combination 🔊 **B2** ❶ /ˌkɒmbɪ'neɪʃn/ *noun* [C, U] a number of people or things mixed or joined together; a mixture: *The team manager still hasn't found the right combination of players.* ◇ *On this course, you may study French in combination with Spanish or Italian.*

combine¹ 🔊 **B1** ❶ /kəm'baɪn/ *verb* **1** [I, ~] ~ **(sth) (with sb/sth)** to join or mix two or more things together; to come together to form a single thing or group: *The two organizations combined to form one company.* ◇ *Bad planning, combined with bad luck, led to the company's collapse.* **2** [T] ~ **A and/with B** to do or have two or more things at the same time: *This car combines speed and reliability.*

combine² /'kɒmbaɪn/ (*BrE also* ˌcombine 'harvester) *noun* [C] (**AGRICULTURE**) a large farm machine that both cuts CORN and separates the grain from the rest of the plant ⊃ look at **harvest**

combined /kəm'baɪnd/ *adj.* done by a number of people joining together, resulting from the joining of two or more things: *The combined efforts of the emergency services prevented a major disaster.*

combustible /kəm'bʌstəbl/ *adj.* (**CHEMISTRY**) able to begin burning easily **SYN** inflammable

combustion /kəm'bʌstʃən/ *noun* [U] (**CHEMISTRY**) the process of burning

come 🔊 **A1** /kʌm/ *verb* [I] (*pt* came /keɪm/; *pp* come) **1** to move to or towards the person who is speaking or the place that sb is talking about: *Come here, please.* ◇ *Come and see what I've found.* ◇ *I hope you can come to my party.* ◇ *They're coming to stay for a week.* ◇ *The children came running into the room.* **2** ~ **(to …)** to arrive somewhere or reach a particular place or time: *What time are you coming home?* ◇ *Has the post come yet?* ◇ *After a few hours in the jungle, we came to a river.* ◇ *Her hair comes down to her waist.* ◇ *The water in the pool came up to our knees.* ◇ *The time has come to say goodbye.* **3** to be in a particular position in a series: *March comes after February.* ◇ *Charlie came second in the exam.* ◇ *I can't wait to find out what comes next in the story.* **4** ~ **in sth** to be available: *This blouse comes in a choice of four colours.* ◇ *Do these trousers come in a larger size?* **5** to be produced by or from sth: *Wool comes from sheep.* **6** to become open or loose: *Your blouse has come undone.* ◇ *Her hair has come untied.* **7** ~ **to do sth** used for talking about how, why or when sth happened: *How did you come to lose your passport?* **8** ~ **to/into sth** to reach a particular state: *We were all sorry when the holiday came to an end.* ◇ *The military government came to power in a coup d'état.*
IDM **come and go** to be present for a short time and then go away: *The pain in my ear comes and goes.* **come easily/naturally to sb** to be easy for sb to do: *Apologizing does not come easily to her.* **come to nothing | not come to anything** to fail; to not be successful: *Unfortunately, all his efforts came to nothing.* **how come … ?** (*informal*) why or how: *How come you're back so early?* **to come** (after a noun) in the future: *You'll regret it in years to come.* **when it comes to sth/doing sth** when it is a question of sth: *When it comes to value for money, these prices are hard to beat.* ❶ For other idioms containing **come**, look at the entries for the nouns, adjectives, etc. For example, **come to a head** is at **head**.
PHR V **come about** to happen: *How did this situation come about?*
come across sb/sth to meet or find sb/sth by chance: *I came across this book in a second-hand shop.* **come across/over (as sth)** to make an impression of a particular type: *Elizabeth comes across as being rather shy.*
come along 1 to arrive or appear: *When the right job comes along, I'll apply for it.* **2** = COME ON (2) **3** = COME ON (3)
come apart to break into pieces

come around (*also* **come round** *especially in BrE*) **1** (used about an event that happens regularly) to happen: *The end of the holidays always comes round very quickly.* **2** (*also* **come to**) (HEALTH) to become conscious again OPP **pass out** **come around (to …)** (*also* **come round (to …)** *especially in BrE*) to visit a person or place not far away **come around (to sth)** (*also* **come round (to sth)** *especially in BrE*) to change your opinion so that you agree with sb/sth: *They finally came round to our way of thinking.*

come away (from sth) to become separated from sth: *The wallpaper is coming away from the wall in the corner.* **come away with sth** to leave a place with a particular opinion or feeling: *We came away with a very favourable impression of Cambridge.*

come back 1 to return: *I don't know what time I'll be coming back.* **2** to become popular or fashionable again: *Flared trousers are coming back again.* **come back (to sb)** to be remembered: *When I went to Italy again, my Italian started to come back to me.*

come before sb/sth to be more important than sb/sth else: *Mark feels his family comes before his career.*

come between sb and sb to damage the relationship between two people: *Arguments over money came between the two brothers.*

come by sth to manage to get sth: *Fresh vegetables are hard to come by in the winter.*

come down 1 to fall down: *The power lines came down in the storm.* **2** (used about an aircraft or SPACECRAFT) to land: *The helicopter came down in a field.* **3** (used about prices) to become lower: *The price of land has come down in the past year.* **come down to sth/doing sth** to be able to be explained by a single important point: *It all comes down to having the right qualifications.* **come down with sth** (HEALTH) to become ill with sth: *I think I'm coming down with flu.*

come forward to offer help: *The police are asking witnesses to come forward.*

come from … to live in or have been born in a place: *Where do you come from originally?* **come from sth/ doing sth** to be the result of sth: *'I'm tired.' 'That comes from all the late nights you've had.'*

come in 1 to enter a place: *Come in and sit down.* **2** (used about the TIDES of the sea) to move towards the land and cover the beach ⊃ look at **tide¹** (1) **3** to become popular or fashionable: *Punk fashions came in during the seventies.* **4** (used about news or information) to be received: *Reports are coming in of fighting in the capital.* **come in for sth** to receive sth, especially sth unpleasant: *The government came in for a lot of criticism.*

come of sth/doing sth to be the result of sth: *We've written to several companies asking for help but nothing has come of it yet.*

come off 1 to be able to be removed: *Does the hood come off?* **2** (*informal*) to happen or to be successful: *The deal seems unlikely to come off.* **come off (sth) 1** to fall off sth: *Kim came off her bike and broke her leg.* **2** to become removed from sth: *One of the legs has come off this table.* **come off badly, well, etc.** (*informal*) to be in a good, bad, etc. situation as a result of sth: *Unfortunately, Dennis came off worst in the fight.* **come off it** (*informal*) used to say that you do not believe sb/sth or that you strongly disagree with sb: *'I thought it was quite a good performance.' 'Oh, come off it — it was awful!'*

come on 1 to start to act, play in a game of sport, etc: *The audience jeered every time the villain came on.* ◇ *The substitute came on in the second half.* **2** (*also* **come along**) to make progress or to improve: *Your* English is coming on nicely. **3** Come on! (*also* Come along!) used to tell sb to hurry up, try harder, etc: *Come on or we'll be late!* **4** to begin: *I think I've got a cold coming on.*

come out 1 to appear; to be published: *The rain stopped and the sun came out.* ◇ *The report came out in 2018.* **2** if a person **comes out**, they no longer hide the fact that they are GAY (= sexually attracted to people of the same sex) **3** to become known: *It was only after his death that the truth came out.* **4** to say publicly whether you agree or disagree with sth: *He came out against the plan.* ◇ *The minister came out in favour of the new airport.* **5** (used about a photo, etc.) to be produced successfully **come out (of sth)** to be removed from sth: *Red wine stains don't come out easily.* **come out in sth** (HEALTH) to become covered in spots, etc: *Heat makes him come out in a rash.* **come out with sth** to say sth unexpectedly: *The children came out with all kinds of stories.*

come over = COME ACROSS/OVER (AS STH) **come over (to …) (from …)** to visit people or a place a long way away: *Why don't you come over to England for a holiday?* **come over sb** (used about a feeling) to affect sb: *A feeling of despair came over me.*

come round (*especially BrE*) = COME AROUND **come round (to …)** (*especially BrE*) = COME AROUND (TO …) **come round (to sth)** (*especially BrE*) = COME AROUND (TO STH)

come through (used about news, information, etc.) to arrive: *Reports are coming through of a major fire.* **come through (sth)** to escape injury or death in a dangerous situation, illness, etc: *to come through an enemy attack*

come to = COME ROUND **come to sth 1** to equal or total a particular amount: *The bill for the meal came to £35.* **2** to result in a bad situation: *We will sell the house to pay our debts if we have to but we hope it won't come to that.*

come under to be included in a particular group: *Which category does this word come under?*

come up 1 to happen or be going to happen in the future: *Something's come up at work so I won't be home until late tonight.* **2** to be discussed or mentioned: *The subject of religion came up.* **3** (used about the sun and moon) to rise **4** (used about a plant) to appear above the soil **come up against sb/ sth** to find a problem or difficulty that you have to deal with **come up to sth** to be as good as usual or as necessary: *This piece of work does not come up to your usual standard.* **come up with sth** to find an answer or solution to sth: *Engineers have come up with new ways of saving energy.*

come under sth to be included in a particular group

comeback /'kʌmbæk/ *noun* [C] a return to a position of strength or importance that you had before: *The former world champion is hoping to make a comeback.*

comedian /kə'miːdiən/ (*also* **comic**) *noun* [C] (ARTS AND MEDIA) a person whose job is to entertain people and make them laugh, for example by telling jokes

comedown /'kʌmdaʊn/ *noun* [C, usually sing.] (*informal*) loss of importance or social position: *It's a bit of a comedown for her having to move to a smaller house.*

comedy ⭧ A2 /'kɒmədi/ *noun* (*pl.* -ies) **1** [C] (ARTS AND MEDIA) a play, film, etc. that makes you laugh and that has a happy ending ⊃ look at **tragedy** (2) **2** [U] professional entertainment with jokes, etc. that is intended to be funny **3** [U] the quality of being funny or making people laugh SYN **humour¹**

comet /'kɒmɪt/ *noun* [C] (ASTRONOMY) an object in space that looks like a bright star with a tail and that moves around the sun

comfort¹ 🔊 **B2** /ˈkʌmfət/ *noun* **1** [U] the state of having everything your body needs, or of having a pleasant life: *Most people expect to live **in comfort** in their old age.* ◇ *to travel in comfort* **2** [U] the feeling of being physically relaxed and in no pain: *This car has been specially designed for extra comfort.* **OPP** **discomfort** **3** [U] help and support to sb who is suffering: *I tried to offer a few words of comfort.* **4** [sing.] **a ~ (to sb)** a person or thing that helps you when you are very sad or worried: *You've been a real comfort to me.* **5** [C] something that makes your life easier or more pleasant: *the comforts of home*

comfort² 🔊 **B2** /ˈkʌmfət/ *verb* [T] to try to make sb feel less worried or unhappy: *to comfort a crying child*

comfortable 🔊 **A2** /ˈkʌmftəbl, ˈkʌmfət-/ *adj.* **1** (*also informal* **comfy** /ˈkʌmfi/) that makes you feel physically relaxed and in no pain; that provides you with everything your body needs: *a comfortable temperature* (= not too hot or too cold) ◇ *Sit down and make yourselves comfortable.* ◇ *a comfortable pair of shoes* **OPP** **uncomfortable** **2** not having or causing worry, difficulty, etc: *He didn't feel comfortable making speeches in public.* ◇ *Consumers are becoming more comfortable with technology.* ◇ *I didn't feel comfortable about accepting the money.* **3** having or providing enough money for all your needs: *My parents are not wealthy but they're quite comfortable.*

comfortably /ˈkʌmftəbli, ˈkʌmfət-/ *adv.* **1** in a comfortable way: *All the rooms were comfortably furnished.* ◇ *If you're all sitting comfortably, then I'll begin.* **2** with no problem: *He can comfortably afford the extra expense.* **SYN** **easily** **IDM** **comfortably off** having enough money to buy what you want without worrying too much about the cost

comic¹ 🔊 **B2** /ˈkɒmɪk/ *adj.* making you laugh; connected with comedy: *a comic scene in a play*

comic² 🔊 **B2** /ˈkɒmɪk/ *noun* [C] **1** = COMEDIAN **2** (*AmE also* **comic book**) a magazine that tells stories through pictures

comical /ˈkɒmɪkl/ *adj.* that makes you laugh; funny ▸ **comically** /-kli/ *adv.*

comic strip *noun* [C] (**ARTS AND MEDIA**) a short series of pictures that tell a funny story, for example in a newspaper

coming /ˈkʌmɪŋ/ *noun* [C] the moment when sth new arrives or begins: *The coming of the computer meant the loss of many jobs.* ▸ **coming** *adj.*: *We've got a lot of plans for the coming year.*

comma /ˈkɒmə/ *noun* [C] (**LANGUAGE**) the mark (,) used for separating parts of a sentence or items in a list

command¹ 🔊 **B2** /kəˈmɑːnd/ *noun* **1** [C] an order: *The captain's commands must be obeyed without question.* **2** [C] (**COMPUTING**) an instruction given to a computer **3** [U] control over sb/sth: *Who is **in command** of the expedition?* ◇ *to **take command** of a situation* **4** [sing.] the state of being able to do or use sth well: *She has a good command of French.* ◇ note at **language**

IDM **at/by sb's command** (*formal*) because you were ordered by sb: *At the command of their officer the troops opened fire.* **be at sb's command** to be ready to obey sb: *I'm completely at your command.*

command² 🔊 **B2** /kəˈmɑːnd/ *verb* **1** [I, T] **~ (sb to do sth)** (*formal*) to tell or order sb to do sth: *I command you to leave now!* **2** [T] to control or be in charge of sth: *to command a ship/a regiment/an army* **3** [T] to deserve and get sth: *The old man commanded great respect.*

---

commandant /ˈkɒməndænt/ *noun* [C] the officer in charge of a particular military group or institution

command economy = PLANNED ECONOMY

commandeer /ˌkɒmənˈdɪə(r)/ *verb* [T] to take control or possession of sth for military or police use

commander 🔊+ **B2** /kəˈmɑːndə(r)/ *noun* [C] **1** a person who controls or is in charge of a military organization or group **2** (*BrE*) an officer at a fairly high level in the NAVY

commander-in-chief *noun* [C] (*pl.* **commanders-in-chief**) (*abbr.* **C.-in-C.**) the officer who commands all the armed forces of a country or all its forces in a particular area

commanding /kəˈmɑːndɪŋ/ *adj.* **1** in charge or having control of sb/sth: *Who is your commanding officer?* **2** strong or powerful: *to speak in a commanding tone of voice*

commandment /kəˈmɑːndmənt/ (*also* **Commandment**) *noun* [C] (*formal*) (**RELIGION**) a law given by God, especially any of the Ten Commandments given to the Jews in the Bible

commando /kəˈmɑːndəʊ/ *noun* [C] (*pl.* **-os**) one of a group of soldiers who is trained to make sudden attacks in enemy areas

commemorate /kəˈmeməreɪt/ *verb* [T] to exist or take place in order to make people remember a special event: *a statue commemorating all the soldiers who died in the last war* ▸ **commemoration** /kəˌmeməˈreɪʃn/ *noun* [C, U]: *The concerts were held **in commemoration** of the 200th anniversary of Mozart's death.*

commence 🔊+ **C1** /kəˈmens/ *verb* [I, T] **~ (sth/doing sth)** (*formal*) to start or begin ▸ **commencement** *noun* [C, U]

commend /kəˈmend/ *verb* [T] (*formal*) to say officially that sb/sth is very good: *Dean was commended for his excellent work.*

commendable /kəˈmendəbl/ *adj.* (*formal*) that people think is good and deserves praise: *She acted with commendable honesty and fairness.* ▸ **commendably** /-bli/ *adv.*

comment¹ 🔊 **A2** /ˈkɒment/ *noun* [C, U] **~ (about/on sth)** something that you say or write that gives your opinion or feeling about sth: *I heard somebody **make a rude comment** about my clothes.* ◇ *I **posted a comment** on their website.* ◇ *The chancellor was not available for comment.* ◇ look at **observation** (3), **remark²** ◇ note at **statement**

IDM **no comment** used in reply to a question when you do not want to say anything at all: *'Mr President, how do you feel about these latest developments?' 'No comment.'*

comment² 🔊 **B1** /ˈkɒment/ *verb* [I] **~ (on sth)** to say what you think or feel about sth: *Several people commented on how ill David looked.*

▼ **SYNONYMS**

comment

note ◆ remark ◆ observe

These words all mean to say or write a fact or an opinion.

comment *He refused to comment.*

note (*formal*) *He noted in passing that the company's record on safety issues was not good.*

remark *Critics remarked that the play was not original.*

observe (*formal*) *She observed that it was getting late.*

commentary ⮕+ **C1** /'kɒməntri/ *noun* (*pl.* -ies) **1** [C, U] (ARTS AND MEDIA) a spoken description of sth as it is happening, especially on the radio or TV: *a sports commentary* **2** [C] (LITERATURE) a written explanation or discussion of sth such as a book or play **3** [C] something that shows what sth is like: *These petty quarrels are a sad commentary on the state of the government.*

commentate /'kɒmənteɪt/ *verb* [I] ~ **(on sth)** (ARTS AND MEDIA) to give a spoken description of sth as it is happening, especially on the radio or TV

commentator ⮕+ **C1** /'kɒmənteɪtə(r)/ *noun* [C] **1** a person who gives a spoken description of sth as it is happening, especially on the radio or TV: *a sports commentator* **2** (ARTS AND MEDIA) a person who gives their opinion about sth on the radio, on TV, in a newspaper or on SOCIAL MEDIA: *a political commentator*

commerce ⮕+ **C1** /'kɒmɜːs/ *noun* [U] the business of buying and selling things

commercial¹ ⮕ **B1** **W** /kə'mɜːʃl/ *adj.* (BUSINESS) **1** connected with buying and selling goods and services: *commercial law* ⊃ note at **economic** **2** [only before noun] making or trying to make money: *Although it won a lot of awards, the film was not a commercial success.* ⊃ note at **successful** **3** more interested in profit and being popular than in quality: *Is Mother's Day becoming too commercial?*
▶ **commercially** /-ʃəli/ *adv.*: *The factory was closed down because it was no longer commercially viable.*

commercial² ⮕ **B1** /kə'mɜːʃl/ *noun* [C] (ARTS AND MEDIA) an advertisement on TV, on the radio or on a website ⊃ note at **advertisement**

com,mercial 'farming *noun* [U] (AGRICULTURE) a method of farming that produces crops or animals for sale, usually on a large scale and using modern methods and equipment

commercialism /kə'mɜːʃəlɪzəm/ *noun* [U] the attitude that making money is more important than anything else

commercialize (*BrE also* -ise) /kə'mɜːʃəlaɪz/ *verb* [T, often passive] to try to make money out of sth, especially in a way that other people do not approve of: *Christmas has become very commercialized.*
▶ **commercialization** (*BrE also* -isation) /kə,mɜːʃəlaɪ'zeɪʃn/ *noun* [U]

commis /'kɒmi/ (*pl.* commis) (*also* 'commis chef) *noun* [C] a junior cook who works in a kitchen ⊃ look at **chef**, **sous-chef**

commiserate /kə'mɪzəreɪt/ *verb* [I] ~ **(with sb) (on/over/ for sth)** (*formal*) to feel sorry for and show understanding towards sb who is unhappy or in difficulty: *I commiserated with Debbie over losing her job.*

commission¹ ⮕ **B2** /kə'mɪʃn/ *noun* **1** (*often* Commission) [C + sing./pl. verb] an official group of people who have been given responsibility to control sth, or to find out about sth, usually for the government: *A Commission was appointed to investigate the causes of the accident.* **2** [C, U] (FINANCE) money that you get for selling sth: *Agents get 10% commission on everything they sell.* **3** [C, U] (FINANCE) money that a bank, etc. charges for providing a particular service **4** [C] (ARTS AND MEDIA) a formal request to an artist, writer, etc. to produce a piece of work: *He received a commission to write a play for the festival.*

commission² ⮕ **B2** /kə'mɪʃn/ *verb* [T] ~ **sb (to do sth)**; ~ **sth (from sb)** to ask an artist, a writer, etc. to do a piece of work: *to commission an architect to design a building* ◇ *The BBC commissioned short works from ten composers.*

commissionaire /kə,mɪʃə'neə(r)/ *noun* [C] (*BrE, old-fashioned*) a person in uniform whose job is to stand at the entrance to a hotel, theatre, cinema, etc. and open the door for visitors **SYN** **doorman**

commissioner ⮕+ **C1** /kə'mɪʃənə(r)/ *noun* [C] the head of the police or of a government department in some countries ⊃ look at **High Commissioner**

commit ⮕ **B1** **W** /kə'mɪt/ *verb* (-tt-) **1** to do sth wrong or illegal: *to commit a crime* ◇ *to commit suicide* ⊃ note at **criminal¹** **2** ~ **sb/yourself (to sth/ doing sth)** to make a definite agreement or promise to do sth: *I can't commit myself to helping you tomorrow.* **3** ~ **yourself (on sth)** to make a decision or give an opinion publicly so that it is then difficult to change it: *I'm not going to commit myself on who will win the election.* ⊃ look at **non-committal** **4** (*formal*) to decide to use money or time in a certain way: *The government has committed £2 billion to education.* **5** ~ **sb to sth** (*formal*) to send sb to a prison, mental hospital, etc.

commitment ⮕ **B2** **W** /kə'mɪtmənt/ *noun* **1** [U] ~ **(to sth)** being prepared to give a lot of your time and attention to sth because you believe it is right or important: *I admire Gary's commitment to protecting the environment.* **2** [C, U] a promise or an agreement to do sth; a responsibility: *When I make a commitment I always stick to it.* ◇ *Many people work fewer hours because of family commitments.*

committed /kə'mɪtɪd/ *adj.* ~ **(to sth)** prepared to give a lot of your time and attention to sth because you believe it is right or important: *The company is committed to providing quality products.*

committee ⮕ **B2** /kə'mɪti/ *noun* [C + sing./pl. verb] a group of people who have been chosen to discuss sth or decide sth: *to be/sit on a committee* ◇ *The planning committee meets/meet twice a week.*

commodity ⮕+ **C1** /kə'mɒdəti/ *noun* [C] (*pl.* -ies) (BUSINESS) a product or material that can be bought and sold: *Salt was once a very valuable commodity.* ⊃ note at **product**

commodore /'kɒmədɔː(r)/ *noun* [C] an officer at a high level in the NAVY

common¹ ⮕ **A1** **O** /'kɒmən/ *adj.* **1** happening or found often or in many places; usual: *Pilot error is the commonest/most common cause of plane crashes.* ◇ *The daisy is a common wild flower.* **OPP** **uncommon** **2** ~ **(to sb/sth)** shared by or belonging to two or more people or groups; shared by most or all people: *This type of behaviour is common to most children of that age.* ◇ *We have a common interest in gardening.* **3** [only before noun] not special; ordinary: *The officers had much better living conditions than the common soldiers.* **4** (*BrE, informal*) having or showing a lack of education: *Don't speak like that. It's common!*
IDM **be common/public knowledge** → KNOWLEDGE

common² /'kɒmən/ *noun* [C] an area of open land that anyone can use
IDM **have sth in common (with sb/sth)** to share sth with sb/sth else: *to have a lot in common with somebody* **in common with sb/sth** (*formal*) in the same way as sb/sth else; like sb/sth: *This company, in common with many others, is losing a lot of money.*

common de'nominator *noun* [C] (MATHEMATICS) a number that can be divided exactly by all the numbers below the line in a set of FRACTIONS ⊃ look at **denominator**

,common 'ground *noun* [U] beliefs, interests, etc. that two or more people or groups share

,common 'law *noun* [U] (**LAW**) laws in England that are based on customs and on decisions that judges have made, not laws that were made by Parliament ➔ look at **case law**, **statute law**

,common-law 'husband, ,common-law 'wife *noun* [C] a person that a woman or man has lived with for a long time and who is recognized in some countries as a husband or wife, without a formal marriage ceremony

commonly ⓘ **B2** ⓦ /'kɒmənli/ *adv.* usually; very often; by most people: *This is one of the most commonly used methods.*

,common 'market *noun* [C, usually sing.] (**ECONOMICS**) a group of countries that have free trade between countries in the group, and higher taxes on goods imported from countries outside the group

,common 'noun *noun* [C] (**GRAMMAR**) a word, such as *book* or *town*, that refers to an object or a thing but is not the name of a particular person, place or thing

commonplace /'kɒmənpleɪs/ *adj.* not exciting or unusual; ordinary

'common room *noun* [C] (*especially BrE*) a room in a school, university, etc. where students or teachers can go to relax when they are not in class

the Commons /ðə 'kɒmənz/ *noun* [pl.] = HOUSE OF COMMONS

,common 'sense *noun* [U] the ability to make good, sensible decisions or to behave in a sensible way

the Commonwealth /ðə 'kɒmənwelθ/ *noun* [sing.] (**POLITICS**) an organization consisting of the United Kingdom and other countries, including most of the countries that used to be part of the British Empire

commotion /kə'məʊʃn/ *noun* [sing., U] great noise or excitement

communal /kə'mju:nl, 'kɒmjənl/ *adj.* shared by a group of people: *a communal kitchen*

commune /'kɒmju:n/ *noun* [C + sing./pl. verb] (**SOCIAL STUDIES**) a group of people, not from the same family, who live together and share their property and responsibilities

communicable /kə'mju:nɪkəbl/ *adj.* (*formal*) that sb can pass on to other people or communicate to sb else: *communicable diseases*

communicate ⓘ **A2** ⓦ /kə'mju:nɪkeɪt/ *verb* **1** [I, T] ~ (**with sb**); ~ (**sth to sb**) to share and exchange information, ideas or feelings with sb: *Parents often have difficulty communicating with their teenage children .* ◊ *Our boss is good at communicating her ideas to the team.* **2** [T, usually passive] (*formal*) (**HEALTH**) to pass a disease from one person or animal to another: *The disease is communicated though dirty drinking water.* **3** [I] to lead from one place to another: *two rooms with a communicating door*

communication ⓘ **B1** ⓞ /kə,mju:nɪ'keɪʃn/ *noun* **1** [U] the act of sharing or exchanging information, ideas or feelings: *Radio is the only means of communication in remote areas.* ◊ *We are in regular* **communication with** *our head office in New York.* **2** communications [pl.] methods of sending information, especially phones, radio, computers, etc. or roads and railways: *The phone lines are down so communications are very difficult.* **3** [C] (*formal*) a message: *a communication from head office*

communicative /kə'mju:nɪkətɪv/ *adj.* willing and able to talk and share ideas, etc: *Emma seems shy and not very communicative.*

communion /kə'mju:niən/ *noun* [U] **1** (*formal*) the sharing of thoughts or feelings **2** Communion (*also* ,Holy Com'munion) (**RELIGION**) a Christian church ceremony in which people share bread and wine

communiqué /kə'mju:nɪkeɪ/ *noun* [C] (**POLITICS**) an official statement, especially from a government, a political group, etc.

communism /'kɒmjənɪzəm/ (*also* Communism) *noun* [U] (**POLITICS**) the political system in which the state owns and controls all factories, farms, services, etc. and aims to treat everyone equally ➔ look at **capitalism**, **Marxism**, **socialism**

communist /'kɒmjənɪst/ (*also* Communist) *noun* [C] (**POLITICS**) a person who believes in or supports COMMUNISM; a member of the Communist Party ▶ communist ⓘ+ **C1** (*also* Communist) *adj.*: *communist sympathies* ➔ note at **government**

community ⓘ **A2** ⓞ /kə'mju:nəti/ *noun* (*pl.* -ies) **1** [C, sing] (**SOCIAL STUDIES**) all the people who live in a particular place, area, etc. when considered as a group: *Recent increases in crime have disturbed the whole community.* ◊ *She was given an award for her work with young people* **in the community**. **2** [C + sing./ pl. verb] (**SOCIAL STUDIES**) a group of people who have sth in common: *the Asian community in Britain* ◊ *the business community* **3** [U] the feeling of belonging to a group in the place where you live: *There is a strong sense of community in the neighbourhood.*

com'munity centre *noun* [C] (*BrE*) a building that local people can use for meetings, classes, sports, etc.

com'munity college *noun* [C] (**EDUCATION**) **1** (in Britain) a secondary school where adults from the local community can attend classes in the evening **2** (in the US) a college that is mainly for students from the local community and that offers programmes that are two years long, including programmes in practical skills

com,munity 'service *noun* [U] (**LAW**) work helping people in the local community that sb does without being paid, often because they have been ordered to do it by a court as a punishment

com,munity 'theater (*AmE*) = AMATEUR DRAMATICS

commutative /kə'mju:tətɪv/ *adj.* (**MATHEMATICS**) (used about a CALCULATION) giving the same result whatever the order in which the quantities are shown

commutator /'kɒmjuteɪtə(r)/ *noun* [C] **1** (**ENGINEERING**) a device that connects a motor to the electricity supply **2** (**PHYSICS**) a device for changing the direction in which electricity flows

commute /kə'mju:t/ *verb* [I] to travel regularly by bus, train, car, etc. from home to work and back: *A lot of people commute to London from nearby towns.* ▶ commuter *noun* [C]

compact /kəm'pækt, 'kɒmpækt/ *adj.* smaller than is usual for things of the same kind: *a compact car*

,compact 'disc = CD

companion ⓘ+ **C1** /kəm'pænjən/ *noun* [C] a person or an animal who you spend a lot of time or go somewhere with: *a travelling companion*

companionship /kəm'pænjənʃɪp/ *noun* [U] the pleasant feeling of having a friendly relationship with sb and not being alone

company ⓘ **A1** /'kʌmpəni/ *noun* (*pl.* -ies) **1** [C + sing./pl. verb] (**BUSINESS**) a business organization selling goods or services: *The company is/are planning to build a new factory.* ➔ note at **organization** ⓞ In names **company** is written with a capital letter. The abbreviation is

Co.: *the Walt Disney Company* ◊ *Milton & Co.* **2** [C + sing./ pl. verb] (**ARTS AND MEDIA**) a group of actors, singers, dancers, etc.: *a ballet company* ◊ *the Royal Shakespeare Company* **3** [U] being with a person: *I always enjoy Rachel's company.* ◊ *Jeff is very good company* (= pleasant to be with). **4** [U] (*formal*) a visitor or visitors: *Sorry, I wouldn't have called if I'd known you had company.*
IDM **keep sb company** to go or be with sb so that they are not alone: *She was nervous so I went with her to keep her company.* **part company** → PART²

comparable ?+ **C1** **W** /'kɒmpərəbl/ *adj.* **~ (to/with sb/ sth)** of a similar standard or size; that can be compared with sth: *The population of Britain is comparable to that of France.* ◊ *A comparable flat in my country would be a lot cheaper.*

comparably /'kɒmpərəbli/ *adv.* in a similar way or to a similar extent: *a comparably priced phone*

comparative¹ ?+ **A2** **W** /kəm'pærətɪv/ *adj.* **1** that compares things of the same kind: *a comparative study of systems of government* **2** compared with sth else or with what is usual or normal: *He had problems with the written exam but passed the practical exam with comparative ease.* **3** (**GRAMMAR**) (used about the form of an adjective or adverb) expressing a greater amount, quality, size, etc: *'Hotter' and 'more quickly' are the comparative forms of 'hot' and 'quickly'.*

comparative² /kəm'pærətɪv/ *noun* [C] (**GRAMMAR**) the form of an adjective or adverb that expresses a greater amount, quality, size, etc: *'Bigger' is the comparative of 'big'.*

comparatively /kəm'pærətɪvli/ *adv.* when compared with sth else or with what is usual: *The disease is comparatively rare nowadays.* **SYN** **relatively**

compare ? **A1** **O** /kəm'peə(r)/ *verb* **1** [T] (*abbr.* cf.) **~ A and B; ~ A with/to B** to consider people or things in order to see how they are similar or how they are different: *If you compare the old and the new models, you'll see the changes we've made.* ◊ *I'm quite a patient person, compared with him.* ◊ *Compared to the place where I grew up, this town is exciting.* **2** [T] **~ A to B** to say that sb/sth is similar to sb/sth else: *When it was built, people compared the stadium to a spaceship.* **3** [I] **~ (with/to sb/sth)** to be as good as sb/ sth: *Her last film was brilliant but this one simply doesn't compare.* ◊ *There is nothing to compare with the taste of bread fresh from the oven.*
IDM **compare notes (with sb)** to discuss your opinions, ideas, experiences, etc. with sb else

comparison ? **B1** **W** /kəm'pærɪsn/ *noun* [C, U] **~ (between A and B); ~ of A with/and/to B** an act of comparing; a statement in which people or things are compared: *It's hard to make comparisons between two athletes from different sports.* ◊ *a comparison of men's salaries with those of women* ◊ *Put the new one and the old one side by side, for comparison.*
IDM **by/in comparison (with sb/sth)** when compared: *In comparison with many other people, they're quite well off.*

compartment /kəm'pɑːtmənt/ *noun* [C] **1** one of the separate sections which railway CARRIAGES (= the parts of a train) are divided into: *a first-class compartment* **2** one of the separate sections into which certain containers are divided: *The drugs were discovered in a secret compartment in his suitcase.*

compass /'kʌmpəs/ *noun* [C] **1** (**GEOGRAPHY**) an instrument for finding direction, with a needle that always points north: *They had to find their way back to the camp using a map and a compass.* **2** (*also* **compasses**

[pl.]) (**GEOMETRY**) a V-shaped instrument that is used for drawing circles: *Use a pair of compasses.*

compassion ?+ **C1** /kəm'pæʃn/ *noun* [U] **~ (for sb)** understanding or PITY for sb who is suffering: *to have/ feel/show compassion for others* ▶ **compassionate** /-ʃənət/ *adj.*

compatible /kəm'pætəbl/ *adj.* **~ (with sb/sth)** suitable to be used together, or to live or exist together: *These two computer systems are not compatible.* ◊ *Lee's diet is not compatible with his active lifestyle.*
OPP **incompatible** ▶ **compatibility** /kəm,pætə'bɪləti/ *noun* [U]

compatriot /kəm'pætriət/ *noun* [C] a person who comes from the same country as you

compel ?+ **C1** /kəm'pel/ *verb* (-ll-) **~ sb to do sth** (*formal*) to force sb to do sth: *I felt compelled to tell her what I really thought of her.* Ͻ *noun* **compulsion**

compelling ?+ **C1** /kəm'pelɪŋ/ *adj.* that forces or persuades you to do or to believe sth: *compelling evidence*

compensate ?+ **C1** /'kɒmpenseɪt/ *verb* **1** [I] **~ (for sth)** to remove or reduce the bad effect of sth: *His willingness to work hard compensates for his lack of skill.* **2** [T] **~ sb (for sth)** (**LAW**) to pay sb money because you have injured them or lost or damaged their property: *The airline offered to compensate me for losing my luggage.* ▶ **compensatory** /,kɒmpen'seɪtəri/ *adj.*: *He received a compensatory payment of $20 000.*

compensation ?+ **C1** /,kɒmpen'seɪʃn/ *noun* **1** [U] **~ (for sth)** (**LAW**) money that you pay to sb because you have injured them or lost or damaged their property: *I got £5 000 (in) compensation for my injuries.* **2** [C, U] a fact or an action that removes or reduces the bad effect of sth: *City life can be very tiring but there are compensations* (= good things about it).

compère /'kɒmpeə(r)/ *noun* [C] (*BrE*) (**ARTS AND MEDIA**) a person who entertains the audience and introduces the different people who perform in a show ▶ **compère** *verb* [T]: *Who compèred the show?*

compete ? **A2** **W** /kəm'piːt/ *verb* [I] **~ (in sth) (against/ with sb) (for sth)** to try to win or achieve sth, or to try to be better than sb else: *The world's best athletes*

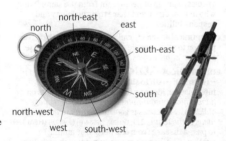

compasses

---

compass

A person or a place can **look** or **face** north, south, etc: *The garden faces south-east.* ◊ *Looking north, she could see the mountains.* Somebody or something can **live in/come from/be to** the north/south, etc. of a place: *I live in the south (of Poland).* ◊ *The wind is coming from the east.* ◊ *Oxford is to the north-west of London.* You can **drive, fly, go, run, travel, walk, continue** or **proceed** north, south, etc: *From Durham drive north for a couple of miles.* ◊ *The road continues west for 3 kilometres.* ◊ *Birds fly south in the winter.*

compete in the Olympic Games. ◇ We'll be competing against seven other teams for the trophy.
◇ Supermarkets have such low prices that small shops just can't compete.

competence ῑ+ **C1** /ˈkɒmpɪtəns/ noun [U] the fact of having the ability or skill that is needed for sth: She quickly proved her competence in her new position. **OPP** incompetence

competent ῑ+ **C1** /ˈkɒmpɪtənt/ adj. **1** having the ability or skill needed for sth ~ **(at sth)**: a highly competent player ◇ She is competent at her job. **OPP** incompetent **2** good enough, but not excellent: The singer gave a competent, but not particularly exciting, performance. ▶ competently adv.

competition ῑ **A2** **W** /ˌkɒmpəˈtɪʃn/ noun **1** [C] (**SPORT**) an organized event in which people try to win sth: They hold a competition every year to find the best young artist. ◇ to take part in/go in for/enter a competition ◇ She came second in an international piano competition. **2** [U] (**BUSINESS**) a situation where two or more people or organizations are trying to achieve, obtain, etc. the same thing or to be better than sb else: He is in competition with three other people for promotion. ◇ Competition from the supermarkets means that many small shops have had to close. **3** the competition [sing. + sing./pl. verb] (**BUSINESS**) the other people, companies, etc. who are trying to achieve the same as you: If we are going to succeed, we must offer a better product than the competition.

competitive ῑ **B1** /kəmˈpetətɪv/ adj. **1** (**SPORT**) involving people or organizations competing against each other: The travel industry is a highly competitive business. ◇ competitive sports **2** able to be as successful as or more successful than others: They are trying to make the company more competitive in the international market. ◇ Our prices are highly competitive (= as low as or lower than those of the others). **3** (**SPORT**) (used about people) wanting very much to win or to be more successful than others: She's a very competitive player. ▶ competitively adv.: Their products are competitively priced.
▶ competitiveness noun [U]

competitor ῑ **B1** /kəmˈpetɪtə(r)/ noun [C] (**BUSINESS**, **SPORT**) a person or organization that is competing against others: There are ten competitors in the first race. ◇ Two local companies are our main competitors.

compilation /ˌkɒmpɪˈleɪʃn/ noun **1** [C] a collection of pieces of music, writing, film, etc. that are taken from different places and put together: a compilation of the band's greatest hits **2** [U] the act of COMPILING sth

compile ῑ+ **C1** /kəmˈpaɪl/ verb **1** [I] to collect information and arrange it in a list, book, etc: to compile a dictionary/a report/a list **2** [I, T] (**COMPUTING**) to translate instructions from one computer language into another for a computer to understand

compiler /kəmˈpaɪlə(r)/ noun [C] **1** a person who COMPILES sth **2** (**COMPUTING**) a program that translates instructions from one computer language into another for a computer to understand

complacent /kəmˈpleɪsnt/ adj. feeling too satisfied with yourself or with a situation, so that you think that there is no need to worry: Our company is market leader at the moment, but we mustn't get complacent. ▶ complacency /-snsi/ noun [U] ▶ complacently adv.

complain ῑ **A2** /kəmˈpleɪn/ verb [I] ~ **(to sb) (about sth/that …)**) to say that you are not satisfied with or happy about sth: People are always complaining about the weather. ◇ We complained to the hotel manager that the room was too noisy.

PHR V complain of sth (formal) to say that you have a pain or illness: He went to the doctor, complaining of chest pains.

complainant /kəmˈpleɪnənt/ = PLAINTIFF

complaint ῑ **B1** /kəmˈpleɪnt/ noun **1** [C] ~ **(about sth)**; ~ **(that …)** a statement that you are not satisfied with sth: You should make a complaint to the council about the noise. ◇ We are looking into complaints that the goods were faulty. **2** [U] the act of complaining: I wrote a letter of complaint to the manager about the terrible service I had received. ◇ Jim's behaviour never gave the teachers cause for complaint. **3** [C] (**HEALTH**) an illness or a disease: a heart complaint

complement¹ /ˈkɒmplɪmənt/ noun [C] **1** ~ **(to)** (formal) a thing that goes together well with sth else: Ice cream is the perfect complement to this dessert. **2** the total number that makes a group complete: Without a full complement of players, the team will not be able to take part in the match. **3** (**GRAMMAR**) a word or words, especially a noun or adjective, used after a verb such as be or become and describing the subject of that verb: In 'I'm angry' and 'He became a teacher', 'angry' and 'teacher' are complements.

complement² ῑ+ **C1** /ˈkɒmplɪment/ verb [T] to go together well with: The colours of the furniture and the carpet complement each other.

complementary /ˌkɒmplɪˈmentri/ adj. going together well with sb/sth; adding sth that the other person or thing does not have: They work well together because their skills are complementary: he's practical and she's creative.

complementary ˈangle noun [C] (**GEOMETRY**) either of two angles that together make 90° ⊃ look at **supplementary angle** ⊃ picture at **angle¹**

complementary ˈcolour (BrE) (AmE **complementary color**) noun [C] a colour that, when mixed with another colour, gives black or white

complementary ˈmedicine noun [U] (**MEDICINE**) medical treatment that is not part of the usual scientific treatment used in Western countries, for example ACUPUNCTURE

complete¹ ῑ **A1** /kəmˈpliːt/ adj. **1** having or including all parts; with nothing missing: I gave a complete list of the stolen items to the police. ◇ The book explains the complete history of the place. **OPP** incomplete **2** [not before noun] finished or ended: The repair work should be complete by Wednesday. **OPP** incomplete **3** ~ **(with sth)** including sth extra, in addition to what is expected: The house come complete with a games room, cinema and sauna. **4** [only before noun] as great as possible; total; in every way: It was a complete waste of time. ◇ The room is a complete mess. ▶ completeness noun [U]

complete² ῑ **A1** /kəmˈpliːt/ verb [T] **1** to make sth whole: We need two more players to complete the team. **2** to finish sth; to bring sth to an end: When the building has been completed, it will look impressive. ◇ He completed his teacher training course in June 2016. ⊃ note at **job 3** to write all the necessary information on sth (for example a form): Please complete the following in capital letters.

completely ῑ **A2** **S** /kəmˈpliːtli/ adv. in every way; fully; totally: The building was completely destroyed by fire.

completion ῑ+ **B2** /kəmˈpliːʃn/ noun [U] (formal) the act of finishing sth or the state of being finished: You will be paid on completion of the work. ◇ The new motorway is due for completion within two years.

complex¹ ℹ️ **B1** ⊙ /ˈkɒmpleks/ adj. made up of several connected parts and often difficult to understand: a complex problem/subject **SYN** complicated

complex² ℹ️ **B2** ⓦ /ˈkɒmpleks/ noun [C] **1** a group of connected things, especially buildings: a shopping/sports complex ⊃ note at **building 2 ~ (about sth)** (**PSYCHOLOGY**) a mental problem that makes sb worry a lot about sth: He's got a complex about his height. ◇ an inferiority complex

complexion /kəmˈplekʃn/ noun [C] **1** the natural colour and condition of the skin on your face: a dark/fair complexion ◇ a healthy complexion **2** [usually sing.] the general nature or character of sth: These recent announcements **put a different complexion on** our situation.

complexity ℹ️+ **C1** ⓦ /kəmˈpleksəti/ noun (pl. -ies) **1** [U] the state of being complex and difficult to understand: an issue of great complexity **2** [C] one of the many details that make sth complicated: I haven't time to explain the complexities of the situation now.

compliant /kəmˈplaɪənt/ adj. **~ (with sth)** (formal) working or done in agreement with particular rules, orders, etc: All new products must be compliant with EU specifications. ▶ **compliance** ℹ️+ **C1** /-əns/ noun [U]: A hard hat must be worn at all times **in compliance with** safety regulations. ⊃ look at **comply**

complicate /ˈkɒmplɪkeɪt/ verb [T] to make sth difficult to understand or deal with: Let's not complicate things by adding too many details.

complicated ℹ️ **B2** /ˈkɒmplɪkeɪtɪd/ adj. made of many different things or parts that are connected; difficult to understand: a novel with a very complicated plot ◇ The instructions look very complicated. ◇ It's all very complicated, but I'll try and explain. **SYN** complex¹

complication ℹ️+ **C1** /ˌkɒmplɪˈkeɪʃn/ noun [C] **1** something that makes a situation hard to understand or to deal with: Unless there are any unexpected complications, I'll be arriving next month. **2** [usually pl.] (**HEALTH**) a new illness that you get when you are already ill: Unless he develops complications, he'll be out of hospital in a week.

complicit /kəmˈplɪsɪt/ adj. **~ (in sb)** involved with other people in sth wrong or illegal: Several officers were complicit in the cover-up.

complicity /kəmˈplɪsəti/ noun [U] (formal) (**LAW**) the fact of being involved with sb else in a crime

compliment¹ /ˈkɒmplɪmənt/ noun **1** [C] **~ (on sth)** a statement or action that shows praise for sb: People often **pay** her **compliments** on her piano playing. **2** compliments [pl.] (formal) polite words or good wishes, especially when used to express praise and approval: Tea and coffee are provided **with the compliments of** the hotel management (= without charge). ◇ My compliments to the chef!

compliment² /ˈkɒmplɪment/ verb [T] **~ sb (on sth)** to say that you think sb/sth is very good: She complimented them on their smart appearance.

complimentary /ˌkɒmplɪˈmentri/ adj. **1** showing that you think sb/sth is very good: He made several complimentary remarks about her work. **2** given free of charge: a complimentary theatre ticket

comply ℹ️+ **C1** /kəmˈplaɪ/ verb [I] (complying; complies; pt, pp complied) **~ (with sth)** (formal) to obey an order or request: All school buildings must comply with the fire and safety regulations. ⊃ look at **compliance**

component ℹ️ **B2** ⊙ /kəmˈpəʊnənt/ noun [C] one of several parts of which sth is made: the components of a machine/system ▶ component adj.: the component parts of an engine

compose ℹ️+ **B2** /kəmˈpəʊz/ verb **1** [T] to be the parts that together form sth: the parties that compose the coalition government **2** [I, T] (**MUSIC**) to write music: Mozart composed 41 symphonies. **3** [T] to produce a piece of writing, usually using careful thought: I sat down and composed an email to the manager. **4** [T] to make yourself, your feelings, etc. become calm and under control: The news came as such a shock that it took me a while to **compose myself**.

composed /kəmˈpəʊzd/ adj. **1 ~ of sth** (formal) made or formed from several different parts, people, etc: The committee is composed of politicians from all parties. **2** calm, in control of your feelings: Although he felt very nervous, he managed to appear composed.

composer ℹ️+ **B2** /kəmˈpəʊzə(r)/ noun [C] (**MUSIC**) a person who writes music, especially classical music ⊃ note at **performing arts**

composite /ˈkɒmpəzɪt/ adj. consisting of different parts or materials ▶ composite noun [C]

composition ℹ️+ **C1** ⓦ /ˌkɒmpəˈzɪʃn/ noun **1** [U] the parts that form sth; the way in which the parts of sth are arranged: the chemical composition of a substance ◇ the composition of the population ⊃ note at **structure** **2** [C] (**ARTS AND MEDIA**) a piece of music or art, or a poem: Chopin's best-known compositions **3** [U] the act or skill of writing a piece of music or text: She studied both musical theory and composition. **4** [C] (**EDUCATION**) a short piece of writing done at school, in an exam, etc: Write a composition of about 300 words on one of the following subjects.

compost /ˈkɒmpɒst/ noun [U] (**AGRICULTURE, BIOLOGY**) a mixture of dead plants, old food, etc. that is added to soil to help plants grow

composure /kəmˈpəʊʒə(r)/ noun [U] the state of being calm and having your feelings under control

compound¹ ℹ️+ **B2** /ˈkɒmpaʊnd/ noun [C] **1** a thing consisting of two or more separate things combined together: compounds derived from plants **2** (**CHEMISTRY**) a substance formed by a chemical reaction of two or more elements in fixed amounts relative to each other: Common salt is a compound of sodium and chlorine. ⊃ look at **element** (5), **mixture** (3) ⊃ picture at **nitrogen cycle 3** (**GRAMMAR**) a noun, an adjective or a verb made of two or more words or parts of words, written as one or more words, or joined by a HYPHEN: 'Car park', 'bad-tempered' and 'bathroom' are all compounds. **4** an area surrounded by a fence or wall in which a factory or other group of buildings stands: a prison compound

compound² /ˈkɒmpaʊnd/ adj. [only before noun] (**GRAMMAR**) formed of two or more parts: a compound adjective, such as 'fair-skinned' ◇ A compound sentence contains two or more clauses.

compound³ /kəmˈpaʊnd/ verb [T] to make sth bad become even worse by causing further damage or problems: The problems were compounded by severe food shortages.

compound 'eye noun [C] (**BIOLOGY**) an eye like that of most insects, made up of several parts that work separately: the compound eye of a wasp

compound 'interest noun [U] (**FINANCE**) interest that is paid both on the original amount of money saved and on the interest that has been added to it ⊃ look at **simple interest**

comprehend /ˌkɒmprɪˈhend/ verb [T] (formal) to understand sth completely: She's too young to comprehend what has happened.

comprehensible /ˌkɒmprɪˈhensəbl/ *adj.* (*formal*) easy to understand: *The book is written in clear, comprehensible language.* **OPP incomprehensible**

comprehension /ˌkɒmprɪˈhenʃn/ *noun* **1** [U] (*formal*) the ability to understand: *The horror of war is beyond comprehension.* **OPP incomprehension 2** [C, U] (**EDUCATION**) an exercise that tests how well you understand spoken or written language: *The first part of the exam is reading comprehension.*

comprehensive¹ 🔒+ B2 W /ˌkɒmprɪˈhensɪv/ *adj.* **1** including everything or nearly everything that is connected with a particular subject: *a guidebook giving comprehensive information on the area* **2** (*BrE*) (**EDUCATION**) educating children of all levels of ability in the same school: *a comprehensive education system*

comprehensive² /ˌkɒmprɪˈhensɪv/ (*also* ˌcompreˈhensive school) *noun* [C] (**EDUCATION**) (in the UK) a secondary school in which children of all levels of ability are educated: *I went to the local comprehensive.*

comprehensively /ˌkɒmprɪˈhensɪvli/ *adv.* completely **SYN thoroughly**

compress /kəmˈpres/ *verb* [T] **1** ~ **sth (into sth)** to make sth fill less space than usual: *Divers breathe compressed air from tanks.* ◇ *He found it hard to compress his ideas into a single page.* **2** (**COMPUTING**) to make computer files, etc. smaller so that they use less space on a disk, etc. **OPP decompress**
▶ **compression** /-ˈpreʃn/ *noun* [U]: *Nurses used bandages to achieve compression at the ankle.* ◇ *data compression* ◯ picture at **erosion**

compressor /kəmˈpresə(r)/ *noun* [C] a machine that COMPRESSES air or other gases

comprise 🔒+ B2 W /kəmˈpraɪz/ *verb* [T] (*formal*) **1** (*also* be comprised of) to consist of; to have as parts or members: *a house comprising three bedrooms, a kitchen, a bathroom and a living room* ◇ *The committee is comprised of parents, staff and students.* **2** to form or be part of sth: *Women comprise 62% of the staff.*

compromise¹ 🔒+ C1 /ˈkɒmprəmaɪz/ *noun* [C, U] ~ **(on sth)** an agreement that is reached when each person gets part, but not all, of what they wanted: *to reach a compromise* ◇ *Both sides will have to be prepared to make compromises on some issues.*

compromise² 🔒+ C1 /ˈkɒmprəmaɪz/ *verb* **1** [I] ~ **(with sb) (on sth)** to accept less than you want or are aiming for, especially in order to reach an agreement: *Unless both sides are prepared to compromise, there will be no peace agreement.* ◇ *The company never compromises on the quality of its products.* **2** [T] ~ **(yourself)** to put sb/sth/yourself in a bad or dangerous position, especially by doing sth that is not very sensible: *He compromised himself by accepting money from them.*

compulsion /kəmˈpʌlʃn/ *noun* **1** [U] (*formal*) the act of forcing sb to do sth or being forced to do sth: *There is no compulsion to take part. You can decide yourself.* ◯ verb **compel 2** [C] a strong desire that you cannot control, often to do sth that you should not do **SYN urge²**

compulsive /kəmˈpʌlsɪv/ *adj.* **1** (used about a bad or harmful habit) caused by a strong desire that cannot be controlled: *compulsive eating* **2** (used about a person) having a bad habit that they cannot control: *a compulsive gambler/shoplifter* **3** so interesting or exciting that you cannot take your attention away from it: *This book makes compulsive reading.*
▶ **compulsively** *adv.*

compulsory 🔒+ B2 /kəmˈpʌlsəri/ *adj.* that must be done by law, according to rules, etc: *Maths and English are compulsory subjects at this level.* ◇ *It is compulsory for all motorcyclists to wear helmets.* **SYN obligatory OPP optional, voluntary**

computation /ˌkɒmpjuˈteɪʃn/ *noun* [C, U] (*formal*) (**MATHEMATICS**) an act or the process of calculating sth: *All the statistical computations were performed by the new software system.* ◇ *an error in the computation*

computational /ˌkɒmpjuˈteɪʃənl/ *adj.* (**COMPUTING**) using or connected with computers: *computational methods*

compute 🔒+ C1 /kəmˈpjuːt/ *verb* [T] (*formal*) to calculate sth

computer 🔒 A1 /kəmˈpjuːtə(r)/ *noun* [C] an electronic machine that can store, find and arrange information, calculate amounts and control other machines: *The bills are all done by computer.* ◇ *a computer program* ◇ *a personal computer* ◇ *computer software/games* ◇ *First of all, the details are fed into a computer.*

comˌputer-ˈgenerated *adj.* (**COMPUTING**) produced by a computer after data or instructions are put into it: *a computer-generated image of a bridge* ◯ look at **CGI**

computerize (*BrE also* -ise) /kəmˈpjuːtəraɪz/ *verb* [T] (**COMPUTING**) to use computers to do a job or to store information: *The firm has computerized its records.*
▶ **computerization** (*BrE also* -isation) /kəmˌpjuːtəraɪˈzeɪʃn/ *noun* [U]

comˌputer-ˈliterate *adj.* (**COMPUTING**) able to use a computer

comˌputer ˈscience *noun* [U] (**COMPUTING**) the study of computers and how they can be used: *She has a degree in computer science.* ▶ **comˌputer ˈscientist** *noun* [C]

computing /kəmˈpjuːtɪŋ/ *noun* [U] the study or use of computers: *They were given training in basic computing.*

comrade /ˈkɒmreɪd/ *noun* [C] **1** a person who is a member of the same political party as the person speaking: *Comrades, we will fight against injustice!* **2** (*old-fashioned*) a friend or other person that you work with, especially as soldiers during a war
▶ **comradeship** *noun* [U]: *He enjoys the comradeship of the army.*

con¹ /kɒn/ *verb* [T] (-nn-) ~ **sb (into doing sth); ~ sb (out of sth)** (*informal*) to cheat sb, especially in order to get money: *He conned them into investing in a company that didn't really exist.* ◇ *The old lady was conned out of her life savings.*

con² /kɒn/ *noun* [C] (*informal*) a trick, especially in order to cheat sb out of some money
IDM the pros and cons → PRO

con- /kən, kɒn/ *prefix* (in verbs, nouns, adjectives and adverbs) with; together: *concurrent* ◇ *conurbation* ◇ *convene*

concave /kɒnˈkeɪv/ *adj.* having a surface that curves towards the inside of sth, like the inside of a bowl ◯ look at **convex** ◯ picture at **lens, short-sighted**

conceal 🔒+ C1 /kənˈsiːl/ *verb* [T] ~ **sth/sb (from sb/sth)** (*formal*) to hide sth/sb; to prevent sth/sb from being seen or discovered: *She tried to conceal her anger from her friend.* ▶ **concealment** *noun* [U]: *the concealment of the facts of the case*

concede 🔒+ C1 /kənˈsiːd/ *verb* (*formal*) **1** [T] ~ **(that)** to admit that sth is true although you do not want to: *She conceded that the problem was mostly her fault.* ◯ note at **admit 2** [T] ~ **sth (to sb)** to allow sb to take sth although you do not want to: *Despite conceding two late goals, they still won.* **3** [T, I] ~ **(defeat)** to admit that you have lost a game, an election, etc: *When it was clear that he would lose the election, he conceded defeat.* ⊃ noun **concession**

conceit /kənˈsiːt/ *noun* [U] the fact of being too proud of yourself and your abilities and importance
▸ **conceited** *adj.*: *He's so conceited — he thinks he's the best at everything!*

conceivable /kənˈsiːvəbl/ *adj.* possible to imagine or believe: *I made every conceivable effort to succeed in my new career.* **SYN** possible **OPP** inconceivable
▸ **conceivably** /-bli/ *adv.*: *She might just conceivably be telling the truth.*

conceive 🔑+ **C1** 🔟
/kənˈsiːv/ *verb* [T]
(*formal*) to think of a new idea or plan: *He conceived the idea for the novel during his journey through India.* **2** [I, T] ~ **of sb/sth (as sth)**; ~ **(that)**
(*formal*) to think about sb/sth in a particular way; to imagine: *He started to conceive of the world as a dangerous place.* ◊ *I cannot conceive that she would lie to me.* **3** [I, T] (**BIOLOGY**) to become pregnant: *Tests showed that she was unable to conceive.* ◊ *Their first child was conceived soon after they got married.*
⊃ noun **conception**

WORD FAMILY
conceive *verb*
concept *noun*
conceivable *adj.*
(≠inconceivable)
conceptual *adj.*

concentrate 🔑 **B1** ⓢ /ˈkɒnsntreɪt/ *verb* [I, T] **1** ~ **(sth) (on/doing sth)** to give all your attention or effort to sth: *I need to concentrate on passing this exam.* ◊ *I tried to concentrate my thoughts on the problem.* **2** to bring people or things together in one place: *Most factories are concentrated in one small area of the town.*

concentrated /ˈkɒnsntreɪtɪd/ *adj.* **1** showing that you are determined to do sth: *With one concentrated effort we can finish the work by tonight.* **2** made stronger by removing some liquid: *This is concentrated orange juice. You have to add water before you drink it.*

concentration 🔑 **B2** /ˌkɒnsnˈtreɪʃn/ *noun* **1** [U] ~ **(on sth)** the ability to give all your attention or effort to sth: *This type of work requires total concentration on the task.* ◊ *Don't lose your concentration or you might make a mistake.* **2** [C] ~ **(of sth)** a large amount of people or things in one place: *There is a high concentration of chemicals in the drinking water here.*

concenˈtration camp *noun* [C] (**HISTORY, POLITICS**) a type of prison, often consisting of a number of buildings inside a fence, where political prisoners, etc. are kept in extremely bad conditions: *a Nazi concentration camp*

concentric /kənˈsentrɪk/ *adj.* (**GEOMETRY**) (used about circles of different sizes) having the same centre point

concept 🔑 **B2** ⓞ /ˈkɒnsept/ *noun* [C] ~ **(of sth)**; ~ **(that …)** an idea; a basic principle: *It is difficult to grasp the concept of eternity.* ◊ *the concept that bigger is better*

concentric circles

conception 🔑+ **C1** 🔟 /kənˈsepʃn/ *noun* **1** [C, U] ~ **(of sth)** an understanding of how or what sth is: *Young children have no conception of history.* **2** [U] the process of forming an idea or a plan **3** [U, C] (**BIOLOGY**) the moment when a woman or female animal becomes pregnant ⊃ verb **conceive**

conceptual 🔟 /kənˈseptʃuəl/ *adj.* (*formal*) related to or based on ideas

conˌceptual ˈart *noun* [U] (**ART**) art in which the idea that the work of art represents is considered to be the most important thing about it

conceptualize 🔟 (*BrE also* -ise) /kənˈseptʃuəlaɪz/ *verb* [T, I] ~ **(sth as sth)** (*formal*) to form an idea of sth in your mind: *Try to conceptualize your thought processes as a series of connected circles.*

concern¹ 🔑 **B2** ⓞ /kənˈsɜːn/ *verb* [T] **1** to affect or involve sb/sth: *This does not concern you. Please go away.* ◊ *It is important that no risks are taken where safety is concerned.* **2** (*also* be concerned with sth) to be about sth: *The main problem concerns the huge cost of the project.* ◊ *Tonight's programme is concerned with the effects of the law on ordinary people.* **3** to worry sb: *What concerns me is that we have no long-term plan.* **4** ~ **yourself with sth** to give your attention to sth: *You needn't concern yourself with the details. There isn't time.*

concern² 🔑 **B2** 🔟 /kənˈsɜːn/ *noun* **1** [C, U] ~ **(for/ about/over sb/sth)**; ~ **(that …)** a feeling of worry; sth that causes worry: *She hasn't been seen for four days and there is concern for her safety.* ◊ *The safety officer assured us that there was no cause for concern.* ◊ *Our concern that the bridge wasn't safe proved unfounded.* **2** [C] something that is important to you or that involves you: *Financial matters are not my concern.* **3** [C] (**BUSINESS**) a company or business: *a large industrial concern*
IDM a going concern → GOING²

concerned 🔑 **B2** /kənˈsɜːnd/ *adj.* **1** worried and feeling concern about sth ~ **(about/for sth)**; ~ **(that …)**: *If you are concerned about your baby's health you should consult a doctor immediately.* ◊ *I'm concerned that we won't be able to find their house.* **OPP** unconcerned **2** affected by sth; involved in sth: *The closure of the factory came as a shock to all concerned.* ◊ *As far as I'm concerned, you can do what you like.* ◊ *Tonight's programme is concerned with the effects of the law on ordinary people.* **3** interested in sth; involved in sth

concerning /kənˈsɜːnɪŋ/ *prep.* about; on the subject of: *She refused to answer questions concerning her private life.*

concert 🔑 **A1** /ˈkɒnsət/ *noun* [C] (**MUSIC**) a public performance of music: *The band is on tour doing concerts all over the country.* ⊃ look at **recital**
IDM in concert (with sb/sth) (*formal*) working together with sb/sth

concerted /kənˈsɜːtɪd/ *adj.* [only before noun] done by a group of people working together: *We must all make a concerted effort to finish the work on time.*

concertina /ˌkɒnsəˈtiːnə/ *noun* [C] (**MUSIC**) a musical instrument that you hold in your hands and play by pressing the ends together and pulling them apart ⊃ look at **accordion**

concerto /kənˈtʃeətəʊ/ *noun* [C] (*pl.* -os) (**MUSIC**) a piece of music for one or more SOLO instruments playing with an ORCHESTRA (= a large group of musicians who play different musical instruments together): *a piano concerto*

concession 🔑+ **C1** /kənˈseʃn/ *noun* **1** [C, U] ~ **(to sb/sth)** something that you agree to do in order to end an argument: *Employers have been forced to make concessions to the union.* ⊃ verb **concede 2** [C] (*BrE*) a lower price for certain groups of people: *Concessions are available for students.*

concessionary /kənˈseʃənəri/ *adj.* (*BrE*) having a lower price for certain groups of people: *a concessionary fare*

conciliation /kənˌsɪliˈeɪʃn/ noun [U] (formal) the process of ending an argument: All attempts at conciliation have failed and civil war seems inevitable.

conciliatory /kənˈsɪliətəri/ adj. (formal) that tries to end an argument: a conciliatory speech/gesture

concise /kənˈsaɪs/ adj. giving a lot of information in a few words; brief: He gave a clear and concise summary of what had happened. ▸ **concisely** adv. ▸ **conciseness** noun [U]

conclude ʔ **B1** ● /kənˈkluːd/ verb **1** [T] ~ (that); ~ sth **from sth** to form an opinion as the result of thought or study: From the man's strange behaviour I concluded that he was drunk. ◊ What do we conclude from her reaction? **2** [I, T] (formal) to end or to bring sth to an end: May I conclude by thanking our guest speaker. ◊ The prince concluded his tour by attending a charity concert. **3** [T] ~ sth (with sb) to formally arrange or agree to sth: conclude a business deal/treaty

conclusion ʔ **B1** ● /kənˈkluːʒn/ noun **1** [C] ~ (that …) an opinion that you reach after thinking about sth carefully: After trying to phone Bob for days, I **came to the conclusion** that he was on holiday. ◊ Have you **reached** any **conclusions** from your studies? **2** [C, usually sing.] (formal) an end to sth: Let us hope the peace talks **reach a** successful **conclusion**. **3** [U] an act of arranging or agreeing to sth formally: The summit ended with the conclusion of an arms-reduction treaty. **IDM** a foregone conclusion → FOREGONE in conclusion finally: In conclusion, I would like to wish you continued success in the future. jump to conclusions → JUMP[1]

conclusive /kənˈkluːsɪv/ adj. that shows sth is definitely true or real: The blood tests gave conclusive proof of Roy's guilt. **OPP** inconclusive ▸ conclusively adv.

concoct /kənˈkɒkt/ verb [T] **1** to make sth unusual by mixing different things together **2** to make up or invent sth (an excuse, a story, etc.) ▸ concoction /-ˈkɒkʃn/ noun [C]

concord /ˈkɒŋkɔːd/ noun [U] **1** ~ (with sth) (formal) peace and agreement: The two countries now live in concord. **SYN** harmony **2** ~ (with sth) (GRAMMAR) (used about words in a phrase) the fact of having the same NUMBER, GENDER or PERSON **SYN** agreement

concordance /kənˈkɔːdəns/ noun **1** [C] an alphabetical list of the words used in a book, etc. showing where and how often they are used **2** [C] (COMPUTING) a list produced by a computer that shows all the examples of an individual word in a book, etc. **3** [U] the state of being similar to or agreeing with sth: There is reasonable concordance between the results.

concourse /ˈkɒŋkɔːs/ noun [C] (ARCHITECTURE) a large hall or space inside a building such as a station or an airport

concrete[1] ʔ+ **B2** /ˈkɒŋkriːt/ adj. **1** based on facts, not on ideas or guesses: Can you give me a concrete example of what you mean? **OPP** abstract[1] **2** made of CONCRETE ▸ concretely adv.

concrete[2] ʔ+ **B2** /ˈkɒŋkriːt/ noun [U] a hard substance made from CEMENT (= a grey powder) mixed with sand, water and small stones, that is used in building: a modern office building of glass and concrete �‌➲ picture at building

concrete[3] /ˈkɒŋkriːt/ verb [T] ~ sth (over) to cover sth with CONCRETE

ˈconcrete mixer = CEMENT MIXER

concur /kənˈkɜː(r)/ verb [I] (-rr-) (formal) to agree

concurrence /kənˈkʌrəns/ noun (formal) **1** [U, sing.] agreement: The doctor must seek the concurrence of a relative before carrying out the procedure. **2** [sing.] an example of two or more things happening at the same time: an unfortunate concurrence of events

concurrent /kənˈkʌrənt/ adj. existing or happening at the same time as sth else ▸ **concurrently** adv.: The semi-finals are played concurrently, so it is impossible to go to both.

concuss /kənˈkʌs/ verb [T, usually passive] (HEALTH) to hit sb on the head, making them become unconscious or confused for a short time: I was slightly concussed when I fell off my bike.

concussion /kənˈkʌʃn/ noun [U, C] (HEALTH) a temporary injury to the brain that was caused by a blow to the head; the effects of a severe blow to the head such as not being able to think clearly and temporary loss of physical and mental abilities: He was taken to the hospital with a concussion. ◊ He was rushed to hospital, but only suffered mild concussion.

condemn ʔ+ **C1** /kənˈdem/ verb [T] **1** ~ sb/sth (for/as sth) to say strongly that you think sb/sth is very bad or wrong: A government spokesman condemned the bombing as a cowardly act of terrorism. **2** ~ sb (to sth/ to do sth) (LAW) to say what sb's punishment will be; to sentence sb: The murderer was condemned to death. ◊ (figurative) Their poor education condemns them to a series of low-paid jobs. **3** ~ sth (as sth) to say officially that sth is not safe enough to use: The building was condemned as unsafe and was demolished.

condemnation /ˌkɒndemˈneɪʃn/ noun [C, U] an expression of very strong DISAPPROVAL: The bombing brought condemnation from all around the world.

condensation /ˌkɒndenˈseɪʃn/ noun [U] **1** small drops of liquid that are formed when warm air touches a cold surface **2** (CHEMISTRY) the process of a gas changing to a liquid ➲ picture at water cycle

condense /kənˈdens/ verb **1** [I, T] (CHEMISTRY) to change or make sth change from gas to liquid: Steam condenses into water when it touches a cold surface. ➲ look at evaporate (1) ➲ note at water[1] ➲ picture at state[1] **2** [T] ~ sth (into sth) to make sth smaller or shorter so that it fills less space: We'll have to condense these three chapters into one.

condenser /kənˈdensə(r)/ noun [C] **1** (CHEMISTRY) a piece of equipment that cools gas in order to turn it into liquid ➲ picture at distillation, generator **2** (ENGINEERING) a device that stores electricity, especially in a car engine

condescend /ˌkɒndɪˈsend/ verb [I] **1** ~ to sb to behave towards sb in a way that shows that you think you are better or more important than them: The teacher must explain things at the right level for the children without condescending to them. **SYN** patronize **2** ~ to do sth to do sth that you believe is below your level of importance: Celia only condescends to speak to me when she wants me to do something for her. ▸ condescending adj.: a condescending smile ▸ condescension /-ˈsenʃn/ noun [U]

condiment /ˈkɒndɪmənt/ noun [C, usually pl.] a substance such as salt or pepper or a sauce that is used to give extra taste to food

condition[1] ʔ **A2** ● /kənˈdɪʃn/ noun **1** [U, sing.] the state that sb/sth is in: to be **in poor/good/excellent condition** ◊ He looks really ill. He is certainly not in a condition to drive home. **2** [C] something that must happen so that sth else can happen or be possible: One of the conditions of the job is that you agree to work on Sundays. ◊ He said I could borrow his bike **on one condition** — that I didn't let anyone else ride it. **3** conditions [pl.] the situation or environment in which people live, work or do things or in which things happen: The prisoners were kept **in terrible conditions**. ◊ poor **living/housing/working conditions** ◊ The plants *grow best in cool, damp conditions.* ➲ note at **situation** **4** [C] (**HEALTH**) a medical problem that you have for a long time: *to have a heart/lung condition* ➲ note at **disease**

IDM **on condition (that …)** only if: *I agreed to help on condition that I got half the profit.* **on no condition** (*formal*) not for any reason: *On no condition must the press find out about this.* **out of condition** not physically fit

condition² /kən'dɪʃn/ *verb* [T] to affect or control the way that sb/sth behaves: *Pavlov conditioned dogs to respond to the sound of a bell.*

conditional ⓦ /kən'dɪʃənl/ *adj.* **1** ~ **(on/upon sth)** that only happens if sth else is done or happens first: *My university place is conditional on my getting good grades in the exams.* **OPP** **unconditional 2** (**GRAMMAR**) describing a situation that must exist before sth else can happen. A **conditional** sentence often contains the word *if*: *'If you don't study, you won't pass the exam' is a conditional sentence.* ▶ **conditionally** /-nəli/ *adv.*: *The offer was made conditionally.*

conditioner /kən'dɪʃənə(r)/ *noun* [C, U] a substance that keeps sth in a good condition or makes it softer: *Do you use conditioner on your hair?*

condolence /kən'dəʊləns/ *noun* [pl., U] an expression of how sorry you feel for sb whose relative or close friend has just died: *to offer your condolences* ◊ *a message of condolence*

condom /'kɒndɒm/ *noun* [C] a thin rubber covering that a man wears over his PENIS (= sexual organ) during sex to prevent a woman from becoming pregnant or to protect against disease

condominium /ˌkɒndə'mɪniəm/ (*also informal* **condo** /'kɒndəʊ/) *noun* [C] (*AmE*) a flat or block of flats owned by the people who live in them

condone /kən'dəʊn/ *verb* [T] to accept or agree with sth that most people think is wrong: *I can never condone violence — no matter what the circumstances are.*

conducive /kən'djuːsɪv/ *adj.* ~ **(to sth)** (*formal*) helping or making sth happen: *This hot weather is not conducive to hard work.*

conduct¹ 🔊 **B2** ⓦ /kən'dʌkt/ *verb* [T] **1** (*formal*) to organize and do sth, especially research: *to conduct tests/a survey/an inquiry* **2** (**MUSIC**) to direct a group of people who are singing or playing music: *a concert by the Philharmonic Orchestra, conducted by Sir Colin Davis* **3** ~ **yourself well, badly, etc.** (*formal*) to behave in a particular way: *He conducted himself far better than expected.* **4** (**CHEMISTRY**, **PHYSICS**) to allow heat or electricity to pass along or through sth: *Rubber does not conduct electricity.*

conduct² 🔊 **B2** ⓦ /'kɒndʌkt/ *noun* [U] **1** a person's behaviour: *His conduct has always been of the highest standard.* ◊ *a code of conduct* (= a set of rules for behaviour) ➲ look at **misconduct 2** ~ **of sth** (*formal*) the act of controlling or organizing sth: *She was criticized for her conduct of the bank's affairs.*

conduction /kən'dʌkʃn/ *noun* [U] (**PHYSICS**) the process by which heat or electricity passes through a material

conductive /kən'dʌktɪv/ *adj.* (**PHYSICS**) able to conduct electricity, heat, etc. ▶ **conductivity** /ˌkɒndʌk'tɪvəti/ *noun* [U]

conductor /kən'dʌktə(r)/ *noun* [C] **1** (**MUSIC**) a person who stands in front of an ORCHESTRA (= a large group of musicians who play together), a group of singers, etc. and directs their performance ➲ picture at **orchestra 2** a person whose job is to collect money

from passengers on a bus or train or to check their tickets **3** (**PHYSICS**) a substance that allows heat or electricity to pass through or along it: *Wood is a poor conductor.* ➲ look at **semiconductor**

cone /kəʊn/ *noun* [C] **1** (**GEOMETRY**) a shape or object that has a round base and a point at the top: *traffic cones* ◊ *an ice cream cone* ➲ picture at **solid²** ➲ adjective **conical 2** the hard fruit of a PINE tree or a FIR tree (= trees with thin sharp leaves that stay green all through the year) ➲ look at **conifer** ➲ picture at **tree**

confectionery /kən'fekʃənəri/ *noun* [U] sweets, cakes, chocolates, etc.

confederacy /kən'fedərəsi/ *noun* [sing.] (**POLITICS**) a union of states, groups of people or political parties with the same aim

confederate¹ /kən'fedərət/ *noun* [C] a person who helps sb, especially to do sth illegal or secret **SYN** **accomplice**

confederate² /kən'fedərət/ *adj.* (**POLITICS**) belonging to a CONFEDERACY

confederation /kənˌfedə'reɪʃn/ *noun* [C, U] an organization of smaller groups that have joined together: *a confederation of independent republics*

confer 🔊+ **C1** /kən'fɜː(r)/ *verb* (**-rr-**) **1** [I] ~ **(with sb) (on/ about sth)** to discuss sth with sb before making a decision: *The president is conferring with his advisers.* **2** [T] ~ **sth (on sb)** (*formal*) to give sb a special right or advantage, or an award: *The Queen conferred the title of Duke of Sussex on him.*

conference 🔊 **A2** /'kɒnfərəns/ *noun* [C] ~ **on sth** a large official meeting, often lasting several days, at which members of an organization, profession, etc. meet to discuss important matters: *an international conference on global warming*

'conference call *noun* [C] a phone call in which three or more people take part

confess 🔊+ **B2** /kən'fes/ *verb* [I, T] ~ **(to sth/doing sth)**; ~ **(sth) (to sb)** to admit that you have done sth bad or wrong: *The young woman confessed to the robbery.* ◊ *He confessed his guilt to us.* **SYN** **own up (to sth)** ➲ note at **admit, crime**

confession 🔊+ **C1** /kən'feʃn/ *noun* [C, U] an act of admitting that you have done sth bad or wrong: *The police persuaded the man to make a full confession.*

confetti /kən'feti/ *noun* [U] small pieces of coloured paper that people throw over people who have just got married, or (in the US) at other special events

confide /kən'faɪd/ *verb* [T] ~ **sth (to sb)** to tell sb sth that is secret: *She did not confide her love to anyone — not even to her best friend.*

PHR V **confide in sb** to talk to sb that you trust about sth secret or private

confidence 🔊 **B2** /'kɒnfɪdəns/ *noun* [U] **1** ~ **(in sb/sth)** trust or strong belief in sb/sth: *The public is losing confidence in the present government.* ◊ *I have every confidence in Emily's ability to do the job.* **2** the feeling that you are sure about your own abilities, opinion, etc: *I didn't have the confidence to tell her I thought she was wrong.* ◊ *to be full of confidence* ◊ *'Of course we will win,' the team captain said with confidence.* ➲ look at **self-confidence 3** a feeling of trust in sb to keep sth a secret: *The information was given to me in strict confidence.* ◊ *It took a while to win/gain her confidence.*

'confidence trick *noun* [C] (*especially BrE*) a way of getting money by cheating sb

confident 🔊 **B1** /'kɒnfɪdənt/ *adj.* ~ **(of sth/that …)**; ~ **(about sth)** **1** feeling or showing that you are sure about your own abilities, opinions, etc: *Kate feels*

confident of passing/that she can pass the exam. ◊ to be confident of success ◊ You should feel confident about your own abilities. ◊ Dillon has a very confident manner. ➔ look at **self-confident** ➔ note at **sure**[1]
2 feeling certain that sth will happen in the way that you want or expect: I'm confident that she will get the job. ▸ **confidently** adv.: She stepped confidently onto the stage and began to sing.

confidential /ˌkɒnfɪˈdenʃl/ adj. **1** meant to be kept secret and not told to or shared with other people: **confidential information/documents** ◊ Your medical records are strictly confidential. **2** secret; not to be shown or told to other people ▸ **confidentiality** /ˌkɒnfɪˌdenʃiˈæləti/ noun [U] ▸ **confidentially** /ˌkɒnfɪˈdenʃəli/ adv.: She told me confidentially that she is going to retire early.

configuration ⓘ+ **C1** /kənˌfɪɡəˈreɪʃn/ noun [C] **1** (formal) the way in which the parts of sth, or a group of things, are arranged **2** (COMPUTING) the equipment and programs that form a computer system and the particular way that these are arranged

configure /kənˈfɪɡə(r)/ verb [T] to arrange sth in a particular way, especially computer equipment

confine ⓘ+ **C1** /kənˈfaɪn/ verb [T] **1** ~ sb/sth (in/to sth) to keep a person or an animal in a particular, usually small, place: The prisoners are confined to their cells for long periods at a time. **2** ~ sb/sth/yourself to sth to stay within the limits of sth: Please confine your questions to the topic we are discussing. **SYN** **restrict**

confined /kənˈfaɪnd/ adj. (used about a space or an area) small and surrounded by walls or sides: It is cruel to keep animals in confined spaces.

confinement /kənˈfaɪnmənt/ noun [U] being kept in a small space: to be kept **in solitary confinement** (= in a prison)

confines /ˈkɒnfaɪnz/ noun [pl.] (formal) the limits of sth: Patients are not allowed beyond the confines of the hospital grounds.

confirm ⓘ **B1** **ⓦ** /kənˈfɜːm/ verb [T] **1** ~ (that) to say or show that sth is true; to make sth definite: Seeing the two of them together **confirmed our suspicions**. ◊ Can you confirm (that) you will be able to attend? ◊ Our booking was confirmed within minutes. **2** to make sb feel or believe sth even more strongly: The climb up the tower confirmed my fear of heights. **3** [often passive] (RELIGION) to perform the Christian ceremony of CONFIRMATION: He was confirmed at the age of 13.

confirmation ⓘ+ **C1** /ˌkɒnfəˈmeɪʃn/ noun [U, C] **1** a statement, letter, etc. that shows that sth is true or definite: We are waiting for confirmation of the report. **2** (RELIGION) a ceremony at which a person becomes a full member of the Christian Church

confirmed /kənˈfɜːmd/ adj. [only before noun] fixed in a particular habit or way of life: a confirmed bachelor (= a man who is not likely to get married)

confiscate /ˈkɒnfɪskeɪt/ verb [T] to take sth away from sb as a punishment: Any cigarettes found in school will be confiscated. ▸ **confiscation** /ˌkɒnfɪˈskeɪʃn/ noun [C, U]

conflict¹ ⓘ **B2** **ⓞ** /ˈkɒnflɪkt/ noun [C, U] **1** ~ with sb/sth (over sth) a fight or an argument: an armed conflict ◊ The new laws have brought the government **into conflict** with the unions over pay increases. **2** a difference between two or more ideas, wishes, etc: Many women have to cope with the conflict between their career and their family. ◊ a **conflict of interests** (= a situation in which there are two jobs, aims, roles, etc. and it is not possible for both of them to be treated equally and fairly at the same time)

conflict² ⓘ **B2** **ⓞ** /kənˈflɪkt/ verb [I] ~ with sth if two ideas, beliefs, stories, etc. **conflict**, it is not possible for them to exist together or both be true: The statements of the two witnesses conflict. ◊ John's statement conflicts with yours. ◊ conflicting results

confluence /ˈkɒnfluəns/ noun [C, usually sing.] (GEOGRAPHY) the place where two rivers flow together and become one

conform /kənˈfɔːm/ verb [I] ~ (to/with sth) **1** to obey a rule or law: This building does not conform to fire regulations. **2** to behave in the way that other people and society expect you to behave: Children are under a lot of pressure to conform when they first start school.

conformation /ˌkɒnfɔːˈmeɪʃn/ noun [U, C] (formal) the way in which sth is formed; the structure of sth, especially an animal

conformist /kənˈfɔːmɪst/ noun [C] (SOCIAL STUDIES) a person who behaves in the way that people are expected to behave by society **OPP** **nonconformist** ▸ **conformist** adj.

conformity /kənˈfɔːməti/ noun [U] (formal) (SOCIAL STUDIES) behaviour or actions that follow the accepted rules of society

confront ⓘ+ **C1** /kənˈfrʌnt/ verb [T] **1** ~ sb with sth to think about, or to make sb think about, sth that is difficult or unpleasant: to confront a problem/a difficulty/an issue ◊ When the police confronted him with the evidence, he confessed. **2** to stand in front of sb, for example because you want to fight them: The unarmed demonstrators were confronted by a row of soldiers.

confrontation ⓘ+ **C1** /ˌkɒnfrʌnˈteɪʃn/ noun [C, U] a fight or an argument

confuse ⓘ **B1** /kənˈfjuːz/ verb [T] **1** to make sb unable to think clearly or to know what to do: He confused everybody with his pages of facts and figures. **2** ~ A and/with B to mistake sb/sth for sb/sth else: I often confuse Lee with his brother. They look very much alike. **3** to make sth complicated: The situation is confused by the fact that so many organizations are involved.

confused ⓘ **B1** /kənˈfjuːzd/ adj. **1** not able to think clearly: When he regained consciousness he was dazed and confused. **2** difficult to understand: The article is very confused — I don't know what the main point is. ▸ **confusedly** /-ˈfjuːzədli/ adv.

confusing ⓘ **B2** /kənˈfjuːzɪŋ/ adj. difficult to understand: Her instructions were contradictory and confusing. ▸ **confusingly** adv.

confusion ⓘ+ **B2** /kənˈfjuːʒn/ noun [U] **1** the state of not being able to think clearly or not understanding sth: He stared **in confusion** at the exam paper. ◊ There is still a great deal of confusion as to the true facts. **2** a confused situation in which people do not know what action to take: Their unexpected visit threw all our plans into confusion. **3** the act of mistaking sb/sth for sb/sth else: To avoid confusion, all luggage should be labelled with your name and destination.

congeal /kənˈdʒiːl/ verb [I, T] (used about a liquid) to become solid; to make a liquid solid: congealed blood

congenial /kənˈdʒiːniəl/ adj. (formal) pleasant: We spent an evening in congenial company.

congenital /kənˈdʒenɪtl/ adj. (HEALTH) (used about a disease) beginning at and continuing since birth

congested /kənˈdʒestɪd/ adj. **1** crowded; full of traffic: The streets are congested with traffic. **2** (HEALTH) (used about a part of the body) blocked with blood or MUCUS (= a thick liquid that is produced in parts of the body such as the nose)

congestion /kənˈdʒestʃən/ *noun* [U] the state of being blocked or very full of sth: *severe traffic congestion* ◇ *medicine to relieve nasal congestion*

conˈgestion charge *noun* [C] (*BrE*) an amount of money that people have to pay for driving their cars into the centre of some cities as a way of stopping the city centre from becoming too full of traffic ▶ **congestion charging** *noun* [U]

conglomerate /kənˈglɒmərət/ *noun* **1** [C] (**BUSINESS**) a large company formed by joining together different firms **2** [U] (**GEOLOGY**) a type of rock made of small stones held together by dried CLAY

conglomeration /kənˌglɒməˈreɪʃn/ *noun* [C] (*formal*) a mixture of different things that are found all together

congratulate ᵻ+ **C1** /kənˈɡrætʃəleɪt/ *verb* [T] ~ **sb (on sth)** to tell sb that you are pleased about sth they have done: *Colin congratulated Sue on passing her driving test.*

congratulations /kənˌgrætʃəˈleɪʃnz/ *noun* [pl.] used for telling sb that you are pleased about sth they have done: ***Congratulations on** the birth of your baby boy!* ◇ *to offer/send your congratulations*

congregate /ˈkɒŋgrɪgeɪt/ *verb* [I] to come together in a crowd or group

congregation ᵻ+ **C1** /ˌkɒŋgrɪˈgeɪʃn/ *noun* [C + sing./pl. verb] (**RELIGION**) the group of people who are gathered in a particular church or who regularly attend a particular church

congress /ˈkɒŋgres/ *noun* [C + sing./pl. verb] **1** a large formal meeting or series of meetings: *a medical congress* **2 Congress** (**LAW**, **POLITICS**) the name in some countries (for example the US) for the group of people who are elected to make the laws **❶** The US Congress consists of the **Senate** and the **House of Representatives.** ▶ **congressional** ᵻ+ **C1** /kənˈgreʃənl/ *adj.*: *a **congressional committee/bill*** ◇ *the midterm Congressional elections*

congressman /ˈkɒŋgrəsmən/ (*often* Congressman) *noun* [C] (*pl.* -men /-mən/) (**POLITICS**) a man who is a member of Congress in the US, especially the House of Representatives

congresswoman /ˈkɒŋgrəswʊmən/ (*often* Congresswoman) *noun* [C] (*pl.* -women /-wɪmɪn/) (**POLITICS**) a woman who is a member of Congress in the US, especially the House of Representatives

congruent /ˈkɒŋgruənt/ *adj.* **1** (**GEOMETRY**) having exactly the same size and shape: *congruent triangles* **2** ~ **(with sth)** (*formal*) similar to sth or agreeing with it ▶ **congruence** /-əns/ *noun* [U]

conic /ˈkɒnɪk/ *adj.* (**GEOMETRY**) relating to CONES

conical /ˈkɒnɪkl/ *adj.* (**GEOMETRY**) having a round base and getting narrower towards a point at the top ⊃ *noun* **cone**

ˌconic ˈsection *noun* [C] (**GEOMETRY**) a shape formed when a flat surface meets a CONE with a round base

conifer /ˈkɒnɪfə(r)/ *noun* [C] (**BIOLOGY**) any tree that produces hard dry fruit called CONES. Most conifers are EVERGREEN (= have leaves that stay on the tree all year) ▶ **coniferous** /kəˈnɪfərəs/ *adj.*: *coniferous trees/forests* ⊃ picture at **ecosystem**

conjecture /kənˈdʒektʃə(r)/ *verb* [I, T] (*formal*) to guess about sth without any real proof or evidence ▶ **conjecture** *noun* [C, U]

conjoin /kənˈdʒɔɪn/ *verb* [I, T] (*formal*) to join together; to join two or more things together

conjugal /ˈkɒndʒəgl/ *adj.* (*formal*) connected with marriage and the relationship between a married couple

conjugate /ˈkɒndʒəgeɪt/ *verb* [T] (**GRAMMAR**) to give the different forms of a verb ▶ **conjugation** /ˌkɒndʒuˈgeɪʃn/ *noun* [C, U]

conjunction /kənˈdʒʌŋkʃn/ *noun* [C] (**GRAMMAR**) a word that is used for joining other words, phrases or sentences: *'And', 'but' and 'or' are conjunctions.* **IDM** **in conjunction with sb/sth** (*formal*) together with sb/sth

conjunctivitis /kənˌdʒʌŋktɪˈvaɪtɪs/ *noun* [U] (**HEALTH**) an eye disease that causes part of the eye to become red and painful, and that can be passed from one person to another

conjure /ˈkʌndʒə(r)/ *verb* [I] to do tricks by clever, quick hand movements, that appear to be magic ▶ **conjuring** *noun* [U]: *a **conjuring trick*** **PHR V** **conjure sth up 1** to cause an image to appear in your mind: *Hawaiian music conjures up images of sunshine, flowers and sandy beaches.* **2** to make sth appear quickly or suddenly: *Mum can conjure up a meal out of almost anything.*

conjuror (*also* **conjurer**) /ˈkʌndʒərə(r)/ *noun* [C] a person who does clever tricks that appear to be magic ⊃ look at **magician** (1)

conker /ˈkɒŋkə(r)/ (*BrE*, *informal*) *noun* [C] the smooth shiny brown nut of the HORSE CHESTNUT tree **SYN** **horse chestnut**

connect ᵻ **A2** **W** /kəˈnekt/ *verb* **1** [I, T] ~ **(sth) (up) (to/ with sth)** to be joined to sth; to join sth to sth else: *The tunnels connect (up) 10 metres further on.* ◇ *Connect the printer to the computer.* ◇ *This motorway connects Oxford with Birmingham.* ⊃ look at **disconnect 2** [T, I] ~ **(sth) (to sth)** (**COMPUTING**) to join a computer or a mobile device to the internet or to a computer network: *You can also connect wirelessly over Wi-Fi .* **3** [T] ~ **sb/sth (with sb/sth)** to have an association with sb/sth else; to realize or show that sb/sth is involved with sb/sth else: *There was no evidence to connect her with the crime.* **4** [I] ~ **(with sth)** (used about a bus, train, plane, etc.) to arrive at a particular time so that passengers can change to another bus, train, plane, etc: *This train connects with the ferry to Le Havre.* ◇ *a connecting flight* ▶ **connected** ᵻ **A2** *adj.* ~ **(with/to sb/ sth)**: *Police believe that the incidents are connected.* ◇ *All records connected with the case have been destroyed.*

connection ᵻ **B1** **W** /kəˈnekʃn/ *noun* **1** [C] ~ **(between A and B)**; ~ **with/to sth** an association or relationship between two or more people or things: *Is there any connection between the two organizations?* ◇ *What's your connection with Brazil? Have you worked there?*

conic sections

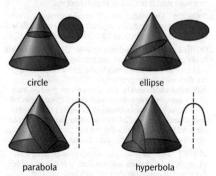

circle

ellipse

parabola

hyperbola

2 [U, C] (**COMPUTING**) the act of connecting or the state of being connected: *A computer with a high-speed internet connection has become an essential study tool.* ◊ *a broadband/network/wireless connection* **3** [C] a place where two wires, pipes, etc. join together: *The TV doesn't work. There must be a loose connection somewhere.* **4** [C] a bus, train, plane, etc. that leaves soon after another arrives: *Our bus was late so we missed our connection.* **IDM** **in connection with sb/sth** (*formal*) about or concerning: *I am writing to you in connection with your application.* **in this/that connection** (*formal*) about or concerning this/that

connective tissue /kəˌnektɪv ˈtɪʃuː/ *noun* [U] (**ANATOMY**) any fat, CARTILAGE or other material that supports, connects or separates organs or other parts of the body

connectivity /kəˌnekˈtɪvəti/ *noun* [U] ~ (**to sth**) **1** (**COMPUTING**) the ability of computer systems, applications, etc. to be connected to each other: *wireless/broadband/Bluetooth connectivity* ◊ *high-speed connectivity to the internet* **2** the state of being connected; the degree to which two things are connected: *There is a need to improve road, rail and air connectivity to the rest of the country.*

connive /kəˈnaɪv/ *verb* [I] ~ **at/in sth**; ~ (**with sb**) (**to do sth**) (*formal*) to work secretly with sb to do sth that is wrong; to do nothing to stop sb doing sth wrong: *They had connived in the kidnapping.* ◊ *The two parties connived to get rid of the president.*

connoisseur /ˌkɒnəˈsɜː(r)/ *noun* [C] a person who knows a lot about art, good food, music, etc.

connotation /ˌkɒnəˈteɪʃn/ *noun* [C] (**LANGUAGE**) an idea expressed by a word in addition to its main meaning: *'Spinster' means a single woman but it has negative connotations.*

conquer ʔ+ **C1** /ˈkɒŋkə(r)/ *verb* [T] **1** to take control of a country or city and its people by force, especially in a war: *Napoleon's ambition was to conquer Europe.* ◊ (*figurative*) *The young singer conquered the hearts of audiences all over the world.* **2** to succeed in controlling or dealing with a strong feeling, problem, etc: *He's trying to conquer his fear of flying.*

conqueror /ˈkɒŋkərə(r)/ *noun* [C] a person who has CONQUERED sth: *William the Conqueror* (= King William I of England)

conquest /ˈkɒŋkwest/ *noun* **1** [C, U] an act of CONQUERING sth: *the Norman conquest* (= of England in 1066) ◊ *the conquest of Mount Kilimanjaro* **2** [C] an area of land that has been taken in a war: *the Spanish conquests in South America*

conscience ʔ+ **C1** /ˈkɒnʃəns/ *noun* [C, U] the part of your mind that tells you if what you are doing is right or wrong: *a clear/a guilty conscience* **IDM** **have sth on your conscience** to feel guilty because you have done sth wrong

conscientious /ˌkɒnʃiˈenʃəs/ *adj.* **1** (used about people) careful to do sth correctly and well: *He's a conscientious worker.* **2** (used about actions) done with great care and attention: *conscientious work* ▸ **conscientiously** *adv.*

conscientious ob'jector *noun* [C] a person who refuses to join the army, etc. because they believe it is morally wrong to kill other people

conscious ʔ **B2** /ˈkɒnʃəs/ *adj.* **1** able to see, hear, feel, etc. things: *The injured driver was still conscious when the ambulance arrived.* **OPP** **unconscious** **2** [not before noun] ~ **of sth/that ...** noticing or realizing that sth exists; aware of sth: *She didn't seem conscious of the danger.* ◊ *Bill suddenly became conscious that somebody was following him.* **3** that you do on purpose or for a particular reason: *We made a conscious effort*

to treat both children equally. **SYN** **deliberate**[1] ▸ **consciously** *adv.*

consciousness ʔ+ **C1** /ˈkɒnʃəsnəs/ *noun* **1** [U] the state of being able to see, hear, feel, etc: *As he fell, he hit his head and lost consciousness.* ◊ *She regained consciousness after two weeks in a coma.* **2** [U, sing.] ~ (**of sth**) the state of realizing or noticing that sth exists: *There is (a) growing consciousness of the need to save energy.*

conscript[1] /kənˈskrɪpt/ *verb* [T, usually passive] (*especially BrE*) to order sb to join the armed forces ▸ **conscription** *noun* [U]

conscript[2] /ˈkɒnskrɪpt/ *noun* [C] (*especially BrE*) a person who has been CONSCRIPTED into the armed forces: *conscript soldiers/armies* ⊃ look at **volunteer**[1] (2)

conscription /kənˈskrɪpʃn/ *noun* [U] (*especially BrE*) (*AmE usually* **the draft** /ðə ˈdrɑːft/ [sing.]) the process of ordering people by law to join the armed forces

consecrate /ˈkɒnsɪkreɪt/ *verb* [T] (**RELIGION**) to state formally in a special ceremony that a place or an object can be used for religious purposes ▸ **consecration** /ˌkɒnsɪˈkreɪʃn/ *noun* [C, U]

consecutive ʔ+ **C1** /kənˈsekjətɪv/ *adj.* coming or happening one after the other: *This is the team's fourth consecutive win.* ▸ **consecutively** *adv.*

consensus ʔ+ **C1** **W** /kənˈsensəs/ *noun* [sing., U] (**a**) ~ (**among/between sb**) (**on/about sth**) an opinion that all members of a group agree with: *to reach a consensus* ◊ *There is no consensus among experts about the causes of the disease.*

consent[1] ʔ+ **C1** /kənˈsent/ *verb* [I] ~ (**to sth**) to agree to sth; to allow sth to happen ⊃ note at **agree**

consent[2] ʔ+ **C1** **W** /kənˈsent/ *noun* [U] agreement; permission: *The child's parents had to give their consent to the operation.* ⊃ look at **age of consent**

consequence ʔ **B1** **O** /ˈkɒnsɪkwəns/ *noun* **1** [C] something that happens or follows as a result of sth else: *Many people may lose their jobs as a consequence of recent poor sales.* ◊ *The error had tragic consequences.* ⊃ note at **effect**[1] **2** [U] (*formal*) importance: *It is of no consequence.*

consequent /ˈkɒnsɪkwənt/ *adj.* [only before noun] (*formal*) following as the result of sth else: *The lack of rain and consequent poor harvests have led to food shortages.* ▸ **consequently** ʔ+ **B2** **W** *adv.*: *She didn't work hard enough, and consequently failed the exam.*

conservation ʔ+ **B2** **W** /ˌkɒnsəˈveɪʃn/ *noun* [U] **1** (**ENVIRONMENT**) the protection of the natural world: *Conservation groups are protesting against the plan to build a road through the forest.* ◊ *wildlife conservation* **2** not allowing sth to be wasted, damaged or destroyed: *the conservation of energy* ⊃ verb **conserve**

conservationist /ˌkɒnsəˈveɪʃənɪst/ *noun* [C] (**ENVIRONMENT**) a person who takes an active part in protecting the natural world

conservatism /kənˈsɜːvətɪzəm/ *noun* [U] **1** the wish to resist new ideas and change **2 Conservatism** (**POLITICS**) the beliefs of the Conservative Party

conservative[1] ʔ **B2** **W** /kənˈsɜːvətɪv/ *adj.* **1** not liking change; traditional ⊃ note at **government** **2 Conservative** (**POLITICS**) connected with the British Conservative Party: *Conservative voters* **3** (used when you are guessing how much sth costs) lower than what is probably the real figure or amount: *Even a conservative estimate would put the damage at about £4 000 to repair.* ▸ **conservatively** *adv.*

conservative² 🔑 **B2** /kənˈsɜːvətɪv/ *noun* [C] **1** a person who does not like change **2** Conservative (POLITICS) a member or supporter of the British Conservative Party

the Conˈservative Party *noun* [C] (POLITICS) one of the main political parties in Britain. The Conservative Party supports a free market and is against the state controlling industry. ⊃ look at **Labour Party**, **Liberal Democrats** ⊃ note at **party**

conservatory /kənˈsɜːvətri/ *noun* [C] (*pl.* -ies) a room with glass walls and a glass roof that is built onto the outside of a house

conserve 🔑+ **C1** 🔑 /kənˈsɜːv/ *verb* [T] to protect sth and prevent it from being changed, destroyed or wasted: *to conserve water* ⊃ noun **conservation**

consider 🔑 **A2** ⊙ /kənˈsɪdə(r)/ *verb* [T] **1** ~ sb/sth (for/as sth); ~ doing sth to think about sb/sth carefully, often before making a decision: *She had never considered nursing as a career.* ◇ *They are considering him for the part of Romeo.* ◇ *He is still considering what material to include in the book.* **2** ~ sb/sth (as/to be) sth; ~ that ... to think about sb/sth in a particular way: *He considered the risk (to be) too great.* ◇ *Jane considers herself an expert on the subject.* ◇ *They considered that it would be better to wait.* ⊃ note at **regard¹ 3** to remember or pay attention to sth, especially sb's feelings: *I can't just move abroad. I have to consider my family.*

considerable 🔑+ **B2** 🔑 /kənˈsɪdərəbl/ *adj.* great in amount or size: *A considerable number of people preferred the old building to the new one.*

considerably 🔑+ **B2** 🔑 /kənˈsɪdərəbli/ *adv.* much; a lot: *This flat is considerably larger than our last one.* ◇ *The need for sleep varies considerably from person to person.*

considerate /kənˈsɪdərət/ *adj.* ~ (towards sb); ~ (of sb) (to do sth) careful not to upset people; thinking of others: *She is always considerate towards her employees.* ◇ *It was very considerate of you to offer to drive me home.* **SYN** **thoughtful** **OPP** **inconsiderate**

consideration 🔑 **B2** 🔑 /kənˌsɪdəˈreɪʃn/ *noun* **1** [U] (*formal*) an act of thinking about sth carefully or for a long time: *I have given some consideration to the idea but I don't think it would work.* **2** [C] something that you think about when you are making a decision: *If he changes his job, the salary will be an important consideration.* **3** [U] ~ (for sb/sth) the quality of thinking about what other people need or feel: *Most drivers show little consideration for cyclists.* **IDM** take sth into consideration to think about sth when you are forming an opinion or making a decision

considering /kənˈsɪdərɪŋ/ *prep.*, *conj.* (used for introducing a surprising fact) when you think about or remember sth: *Considering you've only been studying for a year, you speak English very well.*

consign /kənˈsaɪn/ *verb* [T] ~ sb/sth to sth (*formal*) to put or send sb/sth somewhere, especially in order to get rid of them/it: *I think I can consign this junk mail straight to the recycling bin.*

consignment /kənˈsaɪnmənt/ *noun* [C] a quantity of goods that are being sent to sb/sth: *a new consignment of books*

consist 🔑 **B1** 🔑 /kənˈsɪst/ *verb* (not used in the progressive tenses) **PHR V** consist in sth (*formal*) to have sth as the main or only part or feature: *The beauty of the city consists in its magnificent buildings.* consist of sth to be formed from the things or people mentioned: *The band consists of a singer, two guitarists and a drummer.* ◇ *It's a full-time course consisting of six different modules.*

consistency 🔑+ **C1** 🔑 /kənˈsɪstənsi/ *noun* (*pl.* -ies) **1** [U] the quality of always having the same standard, opinions, behaviour, etc: *Your work lacks consistency. Sometimes it's excellent but at other times it's full of mistakes.* **OPP** inconsistency **2** [C, U] how thick or smooth a liquid substance is: *The mixture should have a thick, sticky consistency.*

consistent 🔑 **B2** 🔑 /kənˈsɪstənt/ *adj.* **1** always having the same opinions, standard, behaviour, etc.; not changing **2** ~ (with sth) agreeing with or similar to sth: *I'm afraid your statement is not consistent with what the other witnesses said.* **OPP** inconsistent ▸ consistently 🔑+ **B2** 🔑 *adv.*: *We must try to maintain a consistently high standard.*

consolation /ˌkɒnsəˈleɪʃn/ *noun* [C, U] a thing or person that makes you feel better when you are sad: *It was some consolation to me to know that I wasn't the only one who had failed the exam.* **SYN** comfort¹

console¹ /kənˈsəʊl/ *verb* [T] to make sb happier when they are very sad or disappointed **SYN** comfort²

console² /ˈkɒnsəʊl/ *noun* [C] (ENGINEERING) a flat surface that contains all the controls and switches for a machine, a piece of electronic equipment, etc.

consolidate 🔑+ **C1** /kənˈsɒlɪdeɪt/ *verb* [T, I] to make sth stronger; to become stronger so that it is more likely to continue: *We're going to consolidate what we've learnt so far by doing some revision exercises today.* ▸ consolidation /kənˌsɒlɪˈdeɪʃn/ *noun* [U]

consonant /ˈkɒnsənənt/ *noun* [C] (LANGUAGE) any of the letters of the English alphabet except a, e, i, o, and u ⊃ look at **vowel**

consortium /kənˈsɔːtiəm/ *noun* [C] (*pl.* consortiums, consortia /kənˈsɔːtiə, -ˈsɔːʃə/) a group of people, countries, companies, etc. who are working together on a particular project: *Our company forms part of a consortium of local businesses working for environmental change.*

conspicuous /kənˈspɪkjuəs/ *adj.* easily seen or noticed **OPP** inconspicuous ▸ conspicuously *adv.*

conspiracy 🔑+ **B2** /kənˈspɪrəsi/ *noun* [C, U] (*pl.* -ies) a secret plan by a group of people to do sth bad or illegal

conspirator /kənˈspɪrətə(r)/ *noun* [C] a member of a group of people who are planning to do sth bad or illegal

conspire /kənˈspaɪə(r)/ *verb* [I] **1** ~ (with sb) (to do sth) to plan to do sth bad or illegal with another person or a group of people: *A group of terrorists were conspiring to blow up the plane.* **2** ~ (against sb/sth) (used about events) to seem to work together to make sth bad happen: *When we both lost our jobs in the same week, we felt that everything was conspiring against us.*

constable /ˈkʌnstəbl/ (*BrE*) = POLICE CONSTABLE

constabulary /kənˈstæbjələri/ *noun* [C + sing./pl. verb] (*pl.* -ies) the police force of a particular area in the UK: *the West Yorkshire Constabulary*

constancy /ˈkɒnstənsi/ *noun* [U] (*formal*) **1** the quality of staying the same and not changing **2** the quality of being FAITHFUL **SYN** fidelity

constant¹ 🔑 **B2** 🔑 /ˈkɒnstənt/ *adj.* **1** happening or existing all the time or again and again: *The constant noise gave me a headache.* **2** that does not change: *You use less petrol if you drive at a constant speed.*

constant² /ˈkɒnstənt/ *noun* [C] (MATHEMATICS) a number or quantity that does not vary **OPP** variable²

constantly 🔑 **B2** /ˈkɒnstəntli/ *adv.* always; again and again: *The situation is constantly changing.*

constellation /ˌkɒnstəˈleɪʃn/ *noun* [C] (**ASTRONOMY**) a group of stars that forms a pattern and has a name

consternation /ˌkɒnstəˈneɪʃn/ *noun* [U] a feeling of shock or worry: *We stared at each other in consternation.*

constipated /ˈkɒnstɪpeɪtɪd/ *adj.* (**HEALTH**) not able to empty waste from the body ▸ **constipation** /ˌkɒnstɪˈpeɪʃn/ *noun* [U]: *to suffer from/have constipation*

constituency 🔒+ **C1** /kənˈstɪtʃuənsi/ *noun* [C] (*pl.* -ies) (*especially BrE*) (**POLITICS**) a district and the people who live in it that a politician represents ⊃ note at **parliament**

constituent[1] /kənˈstɪtʃuənt/ *noun* [C] **1** one of the parts that form sth: *Hydrogen and oxygen are the constituents of water.* **2** (**POLITICS**) a person who lives and can vote in the district that a politician represents

constituent[2] /kənˈstɪtʃuənt/ *adj.* [only before noun] (*formal*) forming or helping to make a whole: *to break something up into its constituent parts/elements*

conˌstituent asˈsembly *noun* [C + sing./pl. verb] (**POLITICS**) a group of elected representatives with the power to make or change a country's **CONSTITUTION**

constitute 🔒+ **C1** 🔊 /ˈkɒnstɪtjuːt/ *linking verb* (*formal*) (not used in the progressive tenses) **1** to be one of the parts that form sth: *Women constitute a high proportion of part-time workers.* **2** to be considered as sth; to be equal to sth: *The presence of the troops constitutes a threat to peace.* ◇ *Management has to fix a maximum number of hours as constituting a day's work.*

constitution 🔒+ **C1** /ˌkɒnstɪˈtjuːʃn/ *noun* **1** [C] (**POLITICS**) the basic laws or rules of a country or an organization: *the United States Constitution* **2** [C] (**HEALTH**) the condition of a person's body and how healthy it is **3** [U, C] (*formal*) the way the parts of sth are put together; the structure of sth: *the constitution of DNA* **SYN** **structure**[1]

constitutional 🔒+ **C1** /ˌkɒnstɪˈtjuːʃənl/ *adj.* (**POLITICS**) connected with or allowed by the CONSTITUTION of a country, etc: *They argued that the ban was not constitutional.*

constrain 🔊 /kənˈstreɪn/ *verb* [T] ~ **sb/sth (to do sth)** (*formal*) **1** to force sb/sth to do sth: *We felt constrained to follow the regulations.* **2** to limit sb/sth: *The company's growth has been constrained by high taxes.*

constrained /kənˈstreɪnd/ *adj.* (*formal*) not natural; forced or too controlled: *constrained emotions*

constraint 🔒+ **C1** 🔊 /kənˈstreɪnt/ *noun* [C, U] ~ **(on sth)** something that limits you: *There are always some financial constraints on a project like this.* **SYN** **restriction** ⊃ note at **limit**[1]

constrict /kənˈstrɪkt/ *verb* **1** [I, T] to become tighter, narrower or less; to make sth tighter, narrower or less: *She felt her throat constrict with fear.* ◇ *The valve constricts the flow of air.* **2** [T] to limit what sb is able to do ▸ **constriction** /-ˈstrɪkʃn/ *noun* [C, U]

construct[1] 🔒 **B2** 🎯 /kənˈstrʌkt/ *verb* [T] **1** [often passive] to build or make sth: *Early houses were constructed out of mud and sticks.* ⊃ note at **build**[1] **2** to form sth by putting different things together

construct[2] 🔊 /ˈkɒnstrʌkt/ *noun* [C] **1** (*formal*) an idea or a belief that is based on various pieces of evidence that are not always true: *a contrast between lived reality and the construct held in the mind* **2** a group of words that form a phrase **3** a thing that is built or made

construction 🔒 **B2** 🔊 /kənˈstrʌkʃn/ *noun* **1** [U] (**ARCHITECTURE**) the process or method of building or making sth, especially roads, buildings, bridges, etc:

A new bridge is now under construction. ◇ *He works in the construction industry.* ⊃ note at **structure**[1] **2** [C] (*formal*) a thing that has been built or made: *The summer house was a simple wooden construction.* **3** [C] (**GRAMMAR**) the way that words are used together in a phrase or sentence: *a grammatical construction*

constructive 🔊 /kənˈstrʌktɪv/ *adj.* useful or helpful: *constructive suggestions/criticism/advice* ▸ **constructively** *adv.*

construe /kənˈstruː/ *verb* [T, usually passive] ~ **sth (as sth)** (*formal*) to understand the meaning of sth in a particular way: *Her confident manner is sometimes construed as arrogance.* ⊃ look at **misconstrue**

consul /ˈkɒnsl/ *noun* [C] (**POLITICS**) a government official who is the representative of his or her country in a foreign city: *the British consul in Miami* ⊃ look at **ambassador** ▸ **consular** /-sjələ(r)/ *adj.*

consulate /ˈkɒnsjələt/ *noun* [C] (**POLITICS**) the building where a CONSUL works ⊃ look at **embassy**

consult 🔒+ **B2** /kənˈsʌlt/ *verb* **1** [T] ~ **sb/sth (about sth)** to ask sb for some information or advice, or to look for it in a book, etc: *If the symptoms continue, consult your doctor.* ⊃ note at **medical**[1], **professional**[2] **2** [I] ~ **(with sb)** to discuss sth with sb to get their permission for sth, or to help you make a decision: *Sarah consulted with her sisters before selling the family business.*

consultancy /kənˈsʌltənsi/ *noun* (*pl.* -ies) **1** [C] (**BUSINESS**) a company that gives expert advice on a particular subject **2** [U] expert advice that sb is paid to provide on a particular subject

consultant 🔒+ **B2** /kənˈsʌltənt/ *noun* [C] **1** a person who gives advice to people on business, law, etc: *a firm of management consultants* **2** (*BrE*) (**MEDICINE**) a hospital doctor at a very high level who is a specialist in a particular area of medicine: *a consultant psychiatrist*

consultation 🔒+ **C1** /ˌkɒnslˈteɪʃn/ *noun* **1** [U, C] a discussion between people before a decision is taken: *Diplomats met for consultations on the hostage crisis.* ◇ *The measures were introduced without consultation.* **2** [C] a meeting with an expert, especially a doctor, to get advice or treatment **3** [U] the act of looking for information in a book, etc.

consultative /kənˈsʌltətɪv/ *adj.* giving advice or making suggestions: *a consultative committee/body/ document* **SYN** **advisory**

conˈsulting room *noun* [C] (**MEDICINE**) a room where a doctor talks to and examines patients

consumable /kənˈsjuːməbl/ *adj.* (**BUSINESS**) intended to be bought, used and then replaced

consumables /kənˈsjuːməblz/ *noun* [pl.] (**BUSINESS**) goods that are intended to be used fairly quickly and then replaced

consume 🔒 **B1** 🔊 /kənˈsjuːm/ *verb* [T] **1** to use sth such as fuel, energy or time **2** (*formal*) to eat or drink sth: *Wrestlers can consume up to 10 000 calories in a day.* ⊃ noun **consumption** **3** (*formal*) (used about fire) to destroy sth **4** [often passive] (*formal*) (used about an emotion) to affect sb very strongly: *She was consumed by grief when her son died.*

consumer 🔒 **B1** /kənˈsjuːmə(r)/ *noun* [C] **1** (**BUSINESS**) a person who buys things or uses services: *The regulations aim to protect consumers from misleading advertising.* **2** a person or an animal that eats or uses sth ⊃ picture at **food chain**

conˌsumer eˈconomy *noun* [C] (**ECONOMICS**) an economic system that depends on people buying and selling goods and services rather than producing goods

consumerism /kənˈsjuːmərɪzəm/ noun [U] (**ECONOMICS**) the buying and using of goods and services; the belief that it is good for a society or an individual person to buy and use a large quantity of goods and services ▸ **consumerist** /-rɪst/ adj.: consumerist values

conˌsumer ˈspending noun [U] (**ECONOMICS**) the amount of money that consumers spend on goods and services, expressed as a percentage of the total economy: Consumer spending accounts for about 70% of US economic activity.

consuming /kənˈsjuːmɪŋ/ adj. [only before noun] that takes up a lot of your time and attention: Sport is her consuming passion.

consummate¹ /kənˈsʌmət, ˈkɒnsəmət/ adj. [only before noun] (formal) extremely SKILLED; perfect: a consummate performer/professional

consummate² /ˈkɒnsəmeɪt/ verb [T] (formal) to make a marriage or relationship complete by having sex ▸ **consummation** /ˌkɒnsəˈmeɪʃn/ noun [C, U]

consumption 🔒+ B2 W /kənˈsʌmpʃn/ noun [U] **1** (**ENVIRONMENT**) the amount of fuel, etc. that sth uses: a car with low fuel consumption **2** the act of using, eating, etc. sth: The meat was declared unfit for human consumption (= for people to eat). ➲ verb **consume 3** (old-fashioned) (**HEALTH**) a serious disease of the lungs **SYN tuberculosis**

cont. abbr. (in writing) continued: cont. on p 91

contact¹ 🔒 B1 W /ˈkɒntækt/ noun **1** [U] ~ (with sb/sth) meeting, talking to or writing to sb else: They are trying to **make contact** with the kidnappers. ◇ We keep **in contact** with our office in New York. ◇ It's a pity to **lose contact** with old school friends. **2** [U] ~ (with sb/sth) the state of touching sb/sth: This product should not **come into contact** with food. ➲ look at **contact sport 3** [C] a person that you know, especially sb who may be able to help you: business contacts ◇ I added the number to my contacts (= in my phone). **4** [C] (**PHYSICS**) an electrical connection: The switches close the contacts and complete the circuit. ➲ picture at **light bulb** ▸ **contact** adj.: contact dermatitis (= caused by touching an INFECTED person)

contact² 🔒 B1 /ˈkɒntækt/ verb [T] to phone, email or write to sb: You can contact me on this number.

ˈcontact lens noun [C] a small piece of plastic that fits onto your eye to help you to see better

contactless /ˈkɒntæktləs/ adj. connected with the technology that allows a DEBIT CARD, mobile phone, etc. to contact an electronic device in order to make a payment: contactless cards ◇ a contactless payment

ˈcontact sport noun [C] (**SPORT**) a sport in which players have physical contact with each other **OPP non-contact sport**

ˈcontact tracing noun [U] the process of trying to identify anyone who has recently been near sb with a disease and may have caught the infection

contagious /kənˈteɪdʒəs/ adj. (**HEALTH**) (used about a disease) that spreads through close contact between people: a highly contagious virus ➲ look at **infectious** ▸ **contagion** /-dʒən/ noun [U]

contain 🔒 A2 ⊙ /kənˈteɪn/ verb [T] (not used in the progressive tenses) **1** to have sth inside or as part of itself: Each box contains 24 tins. ◇ This product may contain nuts. ◇ a jar containing olives **2** to keep sth within limits; to control sth: efforts to contain inflation ◇ She found it hard to contain her anger.

container 🔒 B1 /kənˈteɪnə(r)/ noun [C] **1** a box, bottle, PACKET, etc. in which sth is kept: a plastic container **2** a large metal box that is used for transporting goods on a ship, lorry or train: a container lorry/ship

containment /kənˈteɪnmənt/ noun [U] (formal) **1** the act of keeping sth under control so that it cannot spread in a harmful way: the containment of the epidemic **2** (**POLITICS**) the act of keeping another country's power within limits so that it does not become too powerful: a policy of containment

contaminant /kənˈtæmɪnənt/ noun [C] any substance that makes sth dirty or not pure

contaminate /kənˈtæmɪneɪt/ verb [T] ~ sth (with sth) to add a substance that will make sth dirty or harmful: The town's drinking water was contaminated with poisonous chemicals. ▸ **contamination** /kənˌtæmɪˈneɪʃn/ noun [U]

contemplate 🔒+ C1 /ˈkɒntəmpleɪt/ verb [T] **1** to think carefully about sth or the possibility of doing sth: Before her illness she had never contemplated retiring. **SYN consider 2** to look at sb/sth, often quietly or for a long time ▸ **contemplation** /ˌkɒntəmˈpleɪʃn/ noun [U]

contemporary¹ 🔒 B1 ⊙ /kənˈtemprəri/ adj. **1** (**HISTORY**) belonging to the same time as sb/sth else: The programme includes contemporary film footage of the First World War. **2** of the present time; modern: contemporary music/art/society

contemporary² ⊙ /kənˈtemprəri/ noun [C] (pl. -ies) a person who lives or does sth at the same time as sb else: The Beatles and their contemporaries changed popular music in the 60s.

contempt 🔒+ C1 /kənˈtempt/ noun [U] **1** ~ (for sb/sth) the feeling that sb/sth does not deserve any respect or is without value: Some players show contempt for the rules. ◇ The teacher treated my question with contempt. **2** = CONTEMPT OF COURT: She was held in contempt for refusing to testify. ▸ **contemptuous** /-ˈtemptʃuəs/ adj.: The boy just gave a contemptuous laugh when I asked him to be quiet.

contemptible /kənˈtemptəbl/ adj. (formal) not deserving any respect at all: contemptible behaviour **SYN despicable**

conˌtempt of ˈcourt (also contempt) noun [U] (**LAW**) the crime of refusing to obey an order made by a court; not showing respect for a court or judge: Any person who disregards this order will be in contempt of court.

contend 🔒+ C1 /kənˈtend/ verb **1** [I] ~ with sb/sth to have to deal with a problem or a difficult situation: She's had a lot of problems to contend with. **2** [T] (formal) to say or argue that sth is true: The young man contended that he was innocent. **SYN maintain 3** [I] ~ (for sth) to compete against sb to win or gain sth: Two athletes are contending for first place.

contender 🔒+ C1 /kənˈtendə(r)/ noun [C] a person who may win a competition: There are only two serious contenders for the leadership.

content¹ 🔒 B1 ⊙ /ˈkɒntent/ noun **1** contents [pl.] the thing or things that are inside sth: Add the contents of this packet to a pint of cold milk and mix well. **2** contents [pl.] the different sections that are contained in a book: a table of contents (= the list at the front of a book) **3** [U] (**ARTS AND MEDIA**) the main subject, ideas, etc. of a book, an article, a TV programme, etc: The content of the essay is good, but there are too many grammatical mistakes. **4** [sing.] the amount of a particular substance that sth contains: Many processed foods have a high sugar content. **5** [U] the information or other material contained on a website or other digital media: online content ◇ We plan to spend more on creating content for the website.

content[2] ᵏ⁺ **C1** /kənˈtent/ adj. [not before noun] **~ (with sth)**; **~ to do sth** happy or satisfied with what you have or do: *I don't need a new car — I'm perfectly content with the one I've got.* ◇ *He was content to let her do all the talking.*

content[3] /kənˈtent/ noun
IDM to your heart's content → HEART

content[4] /kənˈtent/ verb [T] **~ yourself with sth** to accept sth even though it was not exactly what you wanted: *The restaurant was closed, so we had to content ourselves with a sandwich.*

contented /kənˈtentɪd/ adj. happy or satisfied: *The baby gave a contented chuckle.* ▸ **contentedly** adv.

contention ᵏ⁺ **C1** /kənˈtenʃn/ noun (formal) **1** [U] anger between people who disagree **2** [C] your opinion; sth that you say is true: *The government's contention is that unemployment will start to fall next year.* ⊃ note at **claim**[2]
IDM in contention (for sth) having a chance of winning a competition: *Four teams are still in contention for the cup.*

contentious /kənˈtenʃəs/ adj. (formal) likely to cause argument: *a contentious issue*

contentment /kənˈtentmənt/ noun [U] a feeling of happiness and SATISFACTION

contest[1] ᵏ **B2** /ˈkɒntest/ noun [C] **1** a competition to find out who is the best, strongest, most beautiful, etc: *I've decided to **enter** that writing **contest**.* **2** a struggle to gain control or power

contest[2] ᵏ **B2** /kənˈtest/ verb [T] **1** to take part in a competition or try to win sth: *24 teams will contest next year's World Cup.* **2** to say that sth is wrong or that it was not done correctly: *They contested the decision, saying that the judges had not been fair.*

contestant /kənˈtestənt/ noun [C] a person who takes part in a contest or competition: *Four contestants appear on the quiz show each week.*

context ᵏ **A2** **O** /ˈkɒntekst/ noun [C, U] **1** the situation in which sth happens or that caused sth to happen: *To **put** our company **in context**, we are now the third largest in the country.* **2** (**LANGUAGE**) the words that come before or after a word, phrase or sentence that help you to understand its meaning: *You can often guess the meaning of a word from its context.* ◇ *Taken **out of context**, his comment made no sense.*

contextual /kənˈtekstʃuəl/ adj. (formal) connected with a particular context: *contextual information* ◇ *contextual clues to the meaning*

contextualize (BrE also -ise) /kənˈtekstʃuəlaɪz/ verb [T] (formal) to consider sth in relation to the situation in which it happens or exists

continent ᵏ **A2** /ˈkɒntɪnənt/ noun (**GEOGRAPHY**) **1** [C] one of the main areas of land on the earth: *Asia, Africa and Antarctica are continents.* **2 the Continent** [sing.] (BrE) the main part of Europe, not including the British Isles

continental /ˌkɒntɪˈnentl/ adj. (**GEOGRAPHY**) **1** relating to or typical of a continent: *Moscow has a continental climate: hot summers and cold winters.* ⊃ picture at **plate tectonics 2** (BrE) relating to the main part of Europe not including Britain or Ireland: *Britain's continental neighbours*

continental ˈbreakfast noun [C] a light breakfast, usually consisting of bread and jam with coffee ⊃ look at **English breakfast**

continental ˈdrift noun [U] (**GEOLOGY**) the slow movement of the continents towards and away from each other during the history of the earth ⊃ look at **plate tectonics**

continental ˈshelf noun [sing.] (**GEOLOGY**) the area of land under the sea on the edge of a continent

continental ˈslope noun [sing.] (**GEOLOGY**) the steep surface that goes down from the outer edge of the CONTINENTAL SHELF to the ocean floor

contingency /kənˈtɪndʒənsi/ noun [C] (pl. -ies) a possible future situation or event: *We'd better make **contingency plans** just in case something goes wrong.* ◇ *We've tried to prepare for every possible contingency.*

contingent /kənˈtɪndʒənt/ noun [C + sing./pl. verb] **1** a group of people from the same country, organization, etc. who are attending an event: *the Irish contingent at the conference* **2** a group of armed forces forming part of a larger force

continual /kənˈtɪnjuəl/ adj. happening again and again: *His continual phone calls started to annoy her.* ⊃ look at **incessant** ▸ **continually** ᵏ⁺ **C1** /-əli/ adv.

continuation /kənˌtɪnjuˈeɪʃn/ noun [sing., U] something that continues or follows sth else; the act of continuing or making sth continue: *Continuation of the current system will be impossible.* ◇ *Her second novel is a continuation of her first.*

continue ᵏ **A2** /kənˈtɪnjuː/ verb **1** [I] to keep happening or existing without stopping: *If the pain continues, see your doctor.* **2** [I, T] **~ (doing/to do sth)**; **~ (with sth)** to keep doing sth without stopping: *He continued working/to work late into the night.* ◇ *Will you continue with the lessons after the exam?* ◇ *They ignored me and continued their conversation.* **3** [I, T] to begin to do or say sth again after you had stopped: *The meeting will continue after lunch.* **4** [I, T] to go further in the same direction: *We continued along the path until we came to the river.*

continued /kənˈtɪnjuːd/ adj. [only before noun] going on without stopping: *We are grateful for your continued support.*

conˌtinuing eduˈcation = ADULT EDUCATION

continuity **O** /ˌkɒntɪˈnjuːəti/ noun [U] the fact of continuing without stopping or of staying the same: *The pupils will have the same teacher for two years to ensure continuity.*

continuo /kənˈtɪnjuəʊ/ noun [U] (**MUSIC**) music that is played as a background to the main voice or instrument

continuous ᵏ **B1** **O** /kənˈtɪnjuəs/ adj. **1** happening or existing without stopping: *There was a continuous line of cars stretching for miles.* **2** (informal) repeated many times **3** = PROGRESSIVE (3) ◇ **continuously** adv.: *It has rained continuously here for three days.*

conˌtinuous asˈsessment noun [U] (BrE) (**EDUCATION**) a system of giving a student a final mark based on work done during a course of study rather than on one exam

continuum /kənˈtɪnjuəm/ noun [C] (pl. continua /-njuə/) a continuous series of things, in which each one is only slightly different from the things next to it, but the last is very different from the first

contort /kənˈtɔːt/ verb [I, T] to move into a strange or unusual shape; to make sth move into a strange or unusual shape: *His face contorted/was contorted with pain.* ▸ **contortion** /-ˈtɔːʃn/ noun [C]

contortionist /kənˈtɔːʃənɪst/ noun [C] a performer who moves their body into strange or unusual shapes to entertain people

contour /ˈkɒntʊə(r)/ *noun* [C] **1** the shape of the outer surface of sth: *I could just make out the contours of the house in the dark.* **2** (*also* ˈcontour line) (**GEOGRAPHY**) a line on a map joining places of equal height

contra- /ˈkɒntrə/ *prefix* (in verbs, nouns and adjectives) against; opposite: *contradict ◇ contraflow*

contraband /ˈkɒntrəbænd/ *noun* [U] goods that are taken into or out of a country illegally: *contraband cigarettes*

contraception /ˌkɒntrəˈsepʃn/ *noun* [U] (**MEDICINE**) the ways of preventing a woman from becoming pregnant: *a reliable form of contraception ◇* look at **birth control, family planning**

contraceptive /ˌkɒntrəˈseptɪv/ *noun* [C] (**MEDICINE**) a drug or a device that prevents a woman from becoming pregnant ▸ **contraceptive** *adj.*

contract¹ 🔊 **B2** /ˈkɒntrækt/ *noun* [C] (**BUSINESS, LAW**) a written legal agreement: *They signed a three-year contract with a major record company. ◇ a temporary contract ◇ The company is hoping to win a contract to supply machinery to the government.*

contract² 🔊 **B2** /kənˈtrækt/ *verb* **1** [I, T] to become smaller or shorter; to make sth smaller or shorter: *Metals contract as they cool.* **OPP** **expand 2** [T] (**HEALTH**) to get an illness or disease, especially a serious one: *to contract pneumonia* **3** [I, T] (**LAW**) to make a written legal agreement with sb to do sth: *His firm has been contracted to supply all the furniture for the new building.*
PHR V **contract sth out (to sb)** to arrange for work to be done by sb outside your own company

contraction /kənˈtrækʃn/ *noun* **1** [U] the process of becoming or of making sth become smaller or shorter: *the expansion and contraction of a muscle* **2** [C] (**BIOLOGY**) a strong movement of the muscles that happens to a woman as her baby is born **3** [C] a shorter form of a word or words: *'Mustn't' is a contraction of 'must not'.*

contractor 🔊+ **C1** /kənˈtræktə(r), ˈkɒntræktə(r)/ *noun* [C] a person or company that has a contract to do work or provide goods or services for another company

contractual /kənˈtræktʃuəl/ *adj.* (**LAW**) connected with the conditions of a legal written agreement; agreed in a contract

contradict /ˌkɒntrəˈdɪkt/ *verb* [T] to say that sth is wrong or not true; to say the opposite of sth: *These instructions seem to contradict previous ones.*

contradiction 🔊+ **C1** /ˌkɒntrəˈdɪkʃn/ *noun* [C, U] ~ (**between A and B**); ~ (**to sth**) a statement, a fact or an action that is opposite to or different from another one: *There is a contradiction between his public and private personalities. ◇ There were a number of contradictions in what he told the police. ◇ This letter is in complete contradiction to their previous one.*

contradictory /ˌkɒntrəˈdɪktəri/ *adj.* being opposite to or not matching sth else: *Contradictory reports appeared in the newspapers.*

contraflow /ˈkɒntrəfləʊ/ *noun* [C] the system that is used when one half of a wide road is closed for repairs, and traffic going in both directions has to use the other side

contralto /kənˈtræltəʊ/ *noun* [C, U] (*pl.* -os) (**MUSIC**) the lowest female singing voice; a woman with this voice

contraption /kənˈtræpʃn/ *noun* [C] a strange or complicated piece of equipment: *The first aeroplanes were dangerous contraptions.*

contrapuntal /ˌkɒntrəˈpʌntl/ *adj.* (**MUSIC**) having two or more tunes played together to form a whole ◇ *noun* **counterpoint**

contrary¹ 🔊+ **C1** /ˈkɒntrəri/ *adj.* **1** [only before noun] completely different; opposite: *I thought it was possible, but she took the contrary view.* **2** ˈcontrary to completely different from; opposite to; against: *Contrary to popular belief* (= to what many people think), *many cats dislike milk.*

contrary² 🔊+ **C1** /ˈkɒntrəri/ *noun*
IDM **on the contrary** the opposite is true; certainly not: *'You don't look as though you're enjoying yourself.' 'On the contrary, I'm having a great time.'* **to the contrary** (*formal*) saying the opposite: *Unless I hear anything to the contrary, I shall assume that the arrangements haven't changed.*

contrast¹ 🔊 **B1** 🔊 /ˈkɒntrɑːst/ *noun* **1** [U] comparison between two people or things that shows the differences between them: *In contrast to previous years, we've had a very successful summer.* **2** [C, U] ~ (**to/with sb/sth**); ~ (**between A and B**) a clear difference between two things or people that is seen when they are compared: *The area is quiet, a real contrast to the hectic capital city. ◇ There is a tremendous contrast between the climate in the valley and the climate in the hills.* **3** [C] something that is clearly different from sth else when the two things are compared: *This house is quite a contrast to your old one!*

contrast² 🔊 **B1** 🔊 /kənˈtrɑːst/ *verb* **1** [T] ~ (**A and/with B**) to compare people or things in order to show the differences between them: *The film contrasts his poor childhood with his later life as a millionaire. ◇ Compare and contrast the two poems* (= discuss how they are similar and how they are different). **2** [I] ~ **with sb/sth** to be clearly different when compared: *This comment contrasts sharply with his previous remarks.*

contrasting /kənˈtrɑːstɪŋ/ *adj.* very different in style, colour or attitude: *bright, contrasting colours ◇ The book explores contrasting views of the poet's early work.*

contravene /ˌkɒntrəˈviːn/ *verb* [T] (*formal*) (**LAW**) to break a law or a rule ▸ **contravention** /-ˈvenʃn/ *noun* [C, U]

contribute 🔊 **B2** 🔊 /kənˈtrɪbjuːt, ˈkɒntrɪbjuːt/ *verb* **1** [I, T] ~ (**sth**) (**to/towards sth**) to give a part of the total, together with others: *The research has contributed a great deal to our knowledge of cancer. ◇ We each contributed some money towards a retirement present for her.* **2** [I] ~ **to sth** to be one of the causes of sth: *It is not known whether the bad weather contributed to the accident.* **3** [I, T] ~ (**sth**) (**to sth**) (**ARTS AND MEDIA**) to write articles for a magazine, website or newspaper

contribution 🔊 **B2** 🔊 /ˌkɒntrɪˈbjuːʃn/ *noun* [C] ~ (**to/ toward sth**) something that you give, especially money or help, or do together with other people: *We all made a small contribution to Ray's present.*

contributor 🔊+ **C1** /kənˈtrɪbjətə(r)/ *noun* [C] a person who contributes to sth

contributory /kənˈtrɪbjətəri/ *adj.* helping to cause or produce sth: *Tiredness is a contributory factor in many road accidents.*

contrive /kənˈtraɪv/ *verb* [T] (*formal*) **1** to manage to do sth, although there are difficulties: *Somehow they contrived to live on her tiny income.* **2** to plan or invent sth in a clever and/or dishonest way: *He contrived a scheme to cheat insurance companies.*

contrived /kən'traɪvd/ *adj.* hard to believe; not natural or realistic: *The ending of the film seemed rather contrived.*

control¹ ⓘ A2 ⊙ /kən'trəʊl/ *noun* **1** [U] ~ **(of/over sb/ sth)** power and ability to make sb/sth do what you want: *Rebels managed to* **take control** *of the radio station.* ◇ *Some teachers find it difficult to* **keep control** *of their class.* ◇ *He* **lost control** *of the car and crashed.* ◇ *I was late because of circumstances* **beyond** *my* **control.** **2** [C, U] ~ **(on/over sth)** a limit on sth; a way of keeping sb/sth within certain limits: *The province wants greater control over immigration.* ◇ *price controls* ◇ *The faults forced the company to review its* **quality control** *procedures.* ⊃ note at **limit¹** **3** [C] one of the parts of a machine that is used for operating it: *the controls of a plane/a TV* ◇ *a control panel* **4** [sing.] the place from which sth is operated or where sth is checked: *We went through* **passport control** *and then got onto the plane.* **5** [U] (*also* con'trol key [sing.]) (**COMPUTING**) a computer key that you press at the same time as another key when you want to perform a particular operation: *Hold down the control key and click.* **IDM** **be in control (of sth)** to direct or manage a situation: *Who is in control of the project?* **be/get out of control** to be/become impossible to deal with: *The demonstration got out of control and fighting broke out.* **under control** being dealt with successfully: *It took several hours to bring the fire under control.*

control² ⓘ A2 ⊙ /kən'trəʊl/ *verb* [T] (-ll-) **1** to have power and ability to make sb/sth do what you want: *One family controls the company.* ◇ *Police struggled to control the crowd.* ◇ *I couldn't control myself any longer and burst out laughing.* ◇ *This button controls the volume.* **2** to keep sth within certain limits: *measures to control price rises* ▶ **controller** *noun* [C]: *air traffic controllers*

con'trol freak *noun* [C] (*informal*) (used in a critical way) a person who always wants to be in control of their own and other people's lives, and to organize how things are done

controlled /kən'trəʊld/ *adj.* **1** done or arranged in a very careful way: *a controlled explosion* **2** limited, or managed by law or by rules **3** -controlled /kən'trəʊld/ (in compounds) managed by a particular group or in a particular way: *a British-controlled company* **4** remaining calm and not getting angry or upset: *She remained quiet and controlled.* ⊃ look at **uncontrolled** (1)

con'trol tower *noun* [C] a building at an airport from which the movements of aircraft are controlled

controversial ⓘ+ B2 /ˌkɒntrə'vɜːʃl/ *adj.* causing public discussion and argument: *a controversial issue/decision/plan*

controversy ⓘ+ B2 /'kɒntrəvɜːsi, kən'trɒvəsi/ *noun* [C, U] (*pl.* -ies) ~ **(over/about) sth** public discussion and argument about sth that people strongly disagree about: *the controversy over the site of the new airport* ◇ *The plans for the city centre caused a great deal of controversy.*

conundrum /kə'nʌndrəm/ *noun* [C] a confusing problem or question that is very difficult to solve

conurbation /ˌkɒnə'beɪʃn/ *noun* [C] (**GEOGRAPHY**) a very large area of houses and other buildings where towns have grown and joined together

convalesce /ˌkɒnvə'les/ *verb* [I] (*formal*) (**HEALTH**) to rest and get better over a period of time after an illness ▶ **convalescence** /-'lesns/ *noun* [sing., U] ▶ **convalescent** /-snt/ *adj.*

169

convection currents

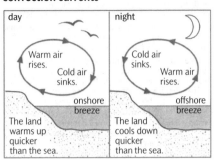

convection /kən'vekʃn/ *noun* [U] (**PHYSICS**) the process in which heat moves through a gas or a liquid as the hotter part rises and the cooler, heavier part sinks: *convection currents*

convene /kən'viːn/ *verb* [I, T] (*formal*) to come together or to bring people together for a formal meeting, etc. ⊃ note at **meeting**

convenience ⓘ+ B2 /kən'viːniəns/ *noun* **1** [U] the quality of being easy, useful or suitable for sb: *a building designed* **for the convenience of** *disabled people* ◇ **For convenience,** *you can pay for everything at once.* **2** [C] something that makes things easier, quicker or more comfortable: *houses with all the modern conveniences* (= central heating, hot water, etc.) ⊃ look at **public convenience**

con'venience food *noun* [C, U] food that you buy frozen or in a box or can, that you can prepare very quickly and easily

convenient ⓘ B1 /kən'viːniənt/ *adj.* **1** ~ **(for sb/sth)** suitable or practical for a particular purpose; not causing difficulty: *I'm willing to meet you on any day that's convenient for you.* ◇ *It isn't convenient to talk at the moment. I'm in a meeting.* **OPP** **inconvenient** **2** close to sth; in a useful position: *Our house is convenient for the shops.* ▶ **conveniently** *adv.*

convent /'kɒnvənt/ *noun* [C] (**RELIGION**) a place where a Christian community of NUNS (= members of a religious group of women) live together ⊃ look at **monastery**

convention ⓘ+ B2 Ⓦ /kən'venʃn/ *noun* **1** [C, U] a traditional way of behaving or of doing sth: *A speech by the bride's father is one of the conventions of a wedding.* ◇ *The film shows no respect for convention.* **2** [C] a large meeting of the members of a profession, political party, etc: *the Democratic Party Convention* **SYN** **conference** **3** [C] (**LAW**) a formal agreement, especially between different countries: *the Geneva Convention* ◇ *the United Nations Convention on the Rights of the Child*

conventional ⓘ+ B2 Ⓦ /kən'venʃənl/ *adj.* **1** always behaving in a traditional or normal way: *conventional attitudes* ◇ *I quite like him but he's so conventional* (= boring, because of this). **OPP** **unconventional** **2** following what is traditional or the way sth has been done for a long time ▶ **conventionally** /-ʃənəli/ *adv.*

converge /kən'vɜːdʒ/ *verb* **1** [I] ~ **(on …)** to move towards a place from different directions and meet: *Thousands of supporters converged on London for the rally.* **2** [I, T] to move towards each other and meet at a point; to make things move towards each other and meet at a point: *There was a signpost where the two*

paths converged. **OPP diverge** ⊃ picture at **short-sighted** ▶ convergence /-'vɜːdʒəns/ *noun* [U]
▶ convergent /-dʒənt/ *adj.* ⊃ picture at **plate tectonics**

conversant /kən'vɜːsnt/ *adj.* ~ **with sth** (*formal*) knowing about sth; familiar with sth: *All employees should be conversant with basic accounting.*

conversation ⓘ **A1** /ˌkɒnvə'seɪʃn/ *noun* [C, U] a talk between two or more people: *I had a long conversation with her about her plans for the future.* ◇ *His job is his only topic of conversation.*
IDM deep in thought/conversation → **DEEP**[1]

conversational /ˌkɒnvə'seɪʃənl/ *adj.* **1** not formal; as used in conversation: *I learned conversational Spanish at evening classes.* **SYN colloquial 2** [only before noun] connected with conversation: *He has a direct conversational style.* ▶ conversationally /-nəli/ *adv.*

converse /kən'vɜːs/ *verb* [I] ~ **(with sb)** (*formal*) to talk to sb; to have a conversation: *He conversed with Sophie in French.*

conversely /'kɒnvɜːsli/ *adv.* (*formal*) in a way that is opposite to sth: *People who earn a lot of money have little time to spend it. Conversely, many people with limitless time do not have enough money to do what they want.*

conversion ⓘ+ **C1** Ⓦ /kən'vɜːʃn/ *noun* [C, U] **1** ~ **(from sth) (into/to sth)** the act or process of changing, or of changing sth, from one form, system or use to another: *How do you do the conversion from miles to kilometres?* **2** ~ **(from sth) (to sth)** (**RELIGION**) becoming a member of a different religion

convert[1] ⓘ **B2** Ⓦ /kən'vɜːt/ *verb* [I, T] **1** ~ **(sth) (from sth) (into/to sth)** to change, or to change sth, from one form, system or use to another: *a sofa that converts into a double bed* ◇ *How do you convert pounds into kilos?* **2** ~ **(sb) (from sth) (to sth)** (**RELIGION**) to change or to persuade sb to change to a different religion: *As a young man he converted to Islam.* ◇ *to convert people to Christianity* ⊃ note at **religion**

convert[2] /'kɒnvɜːt/ *noun* [C] ~ **(to sth)** (**RELIGION**) a person who has changed their religion

convertible[1] /kən'vɜːtəbl/ *adj.* able to be changed into another form: *convertible currencies* (= those that can be exchanged for other currencies)

convertible[2] /kən'vɜːtəbl/ *noun* [C] a car with a roof that can be folded down or taken off

convex /'kɒnveks/ *adj.* having a surface that curves towards the outside of sth, like an eye: *a convex lens* ⊃ look at **concave** ⊃ picture at **lens, short-sighted**

convey ⓘ+ **B2** /kən'veɪ/ *verb* [T] **1** ~ **sth (to sb)** to make ideas, thoughts, feelings, etc. known to sb: *The film conveys a lot of information but in an entertaining way.* ◇ *Please convey my sympathy to her at this sad time.* **2** (*formal*) to take sb/sth from one place to another, especially in a vehicle

conveyor belt /kən'veɪə belt/ *noun* [C] a moving belt that carries objects from one place to another, for example in a factory

convict[1] ⓘ+ **C1** /kən'vɪkt/ *verb* [T, often passive] ~ **sb (of sth)** (**LAW**) to say officially in court that sb is guilty of a crime: *He was convicted of armed robbery and sent to prison.* **OPP acquit** ⊃ note at **crime**

convict[2] /'kɒnvɪkt/ *noun* [C] (**LAW**) a person who has been found guilty of a crime and put in prison

conviction ⓘ+ **C1** /kən'vɪkʃn/ *noun* **1** [C, U] ~ **(for sth)** (**LAW**) the act of finding sb guilty of a crime in court: *He has several previous convictions for burglary.* **2** [C, U] a very strong opinion or belief: *religious*

convictions **3** [U] the feeling of being certain about what you are doing or saying: *He played without conviction and lost easily.*

convince ⓘ **B1** /kən'vɪns/ *verb* [T] **1** ~ **sb (of sth/ that …)** to succeed in making sb believe sth: *She convinced him of the need to go back.* ◇ *I couldn't convince her that I was right.* **2** ~ **sb (to do sth)** to persuade sb to do sth: *The salesman convinced them to buy a new cooker.*

convinced ⓘ **B2** /kən'vɪnst/ *adj.* [not before noun] completely sure about sth: *He's convinced of his ability to win.* ⊃ note at **sure**[1]

convincing ⓘ+ **B2** /kən'vɪnsɪŋ/ *adj.* **1** able to make sb believe sth: *Her explanation for her absence wasn't very convincing.* **2** (used about a victory) complete; clear: *a convincing win* ▶ convincingly *adv.*

convivial /kən'vɪviəl/ *adj.* (*formal*) happy and friendly in atmosphere or character **SYN sociable**
▶ conviviality /kənˌvɪvi'æləti/ *noun* [U]

convoluted /'kɒnvəluːtɪd/ *adj.* extremely complicated and difficult to follow: *a convoluted argument/ explanation*

convoy /'kɒnvɔɪ/ *noun* [C, U] a group of vehicles or ships travelling together: *a convoy of lorries* ◇ *warships travelling in convoy*

convulse /kən'vʌls/ *verb* [I, T] to make sudden violent movements that you cannot control; to cause sb to move in this way: *He was convulsed with pain.*

convulsion /kən'vʌlʃn/ *noun* [C, usually pl.] (**HEALTH**) a sudden violent movement that you cannot control: *Children sometimes have convulsions when they are ill.*

convulsive /kən'vʌlsɪv/ *adj.* (used about movements or actions) sudden and impossible to control

coo /kuː/ *verb* [I] (cooing; coos; *pt, pp* cooed) **1** to make a soft, low sound like a DOVE (= a type of bird) **2** to speak in a soft, gentle voice: *He went to the cot and cooed over the baby.*

cook[1] ⓘ **A1** /kʊk/ *verb* **1** [I, T] to prepare food for eating by heating it: *My mother taught me how to cook.* ◇ *The sauce should be cooked on a low heat for 20 minutes.* ◇ *He cooked us a meal.* **2** [I] (used about food) to be prepared for eating by being heated: *I could smell something cooking in the kitchen.*
PHR V cook sth up (*informal*) to invent sth that is not true: *She cooked up an excuse for not arriving on time.*

▼ VOCABULARY BUILDING

Food can be cooked in various ways. You can **boil** or **steam** vegetables with water in a **saucepan** and you can **fry** meat, fish and vegetables in oil in a **frying pan**. You **roast** meat or **bake** bread and cakes in the **oven**. You can **grill** meat or fish under the **grill**, but **toast** is usually made in a **toaster**. If you want an easy meal you can **microwave** a **ready meal** (= a complete meal bought from a supermarket) in a special oven called a **microwave**. In the summer you can **barbecue** burgers, etc. on an outside grill, also called a **barbecue**.

---

cook[2] ⓘ **A2** /kʊk/ *noun* [C] a person who cooks, or whose job is cooking: *My sister is an excellent cook.*

cookbook /'kʊkbʊk/ (*BrE also* 'cookery book) *noun* [C] a book that gives instructions on cooking and how to cook individual dishes

cooker ⓘ **A2** /'kʊkə(r)/ (*BrE*) (*AmE range*) (*also* stove *AmE, BrE*) *noun* [C] a large piece of kitchen equipment for cooking using gas or electricity. It consists of an oven, a flat top on which pans can be placed and often a GRILL (= a device that heats the food from above).

cookery /'kʊkəri/ *noun* [U] the skill or activity of preparing and cooking food: *Chinese/French/Italian cookery*

cookie /'kʊki/ *noun* [C] **1** (*AmE*) = BISCUIT (1) **2** (**COMPUTING**) a computer file with information in it that is sent to the central SERVER each time a particular person uses a network or the internet

cooking ξ **A1** /'kʊkɪŋ/ *noun* [U] **1** the preparation of food for eating: *Cooking is one of her hobbies.* **2** food produced by cooking: *He missed his mother's cooking when he left home.*

'cooking gas (*AmE*) = CALOR GAS™

cool¹ ξ **A1** /kuːl/ *adj.* **1** fairly cold; not hot or warm: *It was a cool evening so I put on a pullover.* ◇ *What I'd like is a long cool drink.* ⊃ note at **cold¹** **2** calm; not excited or angry: *She always manages to remain cool under pressure.* **3** unfriendly; not showing interest: *When we first met, she was rather cool towards me, but later she became friendlier.* **4** (*informal*) very good or fashionable: *Those are cool shoes you're wearing!* **5** (*informal*) used to show that you approve of sth or agree to sth: '*Can you come at 10.30 tomorrow?*' '*That's cool.*' ◇ *I was surprised that she got the job, but I'm cool with it* (= it's not a problem for me).

cool² ξ **B1** /kuːl/ *verb* **1** [I, T] ~ (**sth/sb**) (**down/off**) to lower the temperature of sth; to become cool: *Let the soup cool (down).* ◇ *After the game we needed to cool off.* ◇ *A nice cold drink will soon cool you down.* **2** [I] (used about feelings) to become less strong **PHR V cool (sb) down/off** to become calmer; to make sb become calmer

the cool /ðə 'kuːl/ *noun* [sing.] a cool temperature or place; the quality of being cool: *We sat in the cool of a cafe, out of the sun.* **IDM keep/lose your cool** (*informal*) to stay calm/to stop being calm and become angry, nervous, etc.

coolant /'kuːlənt/ *noun* [C, U] a liquid that is used for cooling an engine, a nuclear REACTOR, etc.

'cooling-'off period *noun* [C] (**BUSINESS**) **1** a period of time during which two sides that disagree try to reach an agreement before taking further action **2** a period of time after sb has agreed to buy sth, during which they can change their mind: *He cancelled his order within the 14-day cooling-off period.*

coolly /'kuːlli/ *adv.* in a calm way; without showing much interest or excitement

coolness /'kuːlnəs/ *noun* [U] the quality or state of being cool: *the coolness of the water* ◇ *his coolness under stress* ◇ *their coolness towards strangers* ◇ *The brand's coolness appealed to millennials.*

coop¹ /kuːp/ *noun* [C] a CAGE for chickens, etc.

coop² /kuːp/ *verb* **PHR V coop sb/sth up (in sth)** [usually passive] to keep sb/sth inside a small space: *The children were cooped up indoors all day because the weather was so bad.*

cooperate ξ **C1** (*BrE also* co-operate) /kəʊ'ɒpəreɪt/ *verb* [I] **1** ~ (**with sb/sth**) (**on sth**) to work with sb else to achieve sth: *Our company is cooperating with a Danish firm on this project.* **2** ~ (**with sb/sth**) to be helpful by doing what sb asks you to do: *The bank is cooperating with the police nvestigation.*

cooperation **W** (*BrE also* co-operation) /kəʊˌɒpə'reɪʃn/ *noun* [U] **1** ~ (**with sb**) working together with sb else to achieve sth: *Schools are working in close cooperation with parents to improve standards.* **2** help that you give by doing what sb asks you to do: *The police asked the public for their cooperation in the investigation.*

cooperative¹ ξ+ **C1** **W** (*BrE also* co-operative) /kəʊ'ɒpərətɪv/ *adj.* **1** involving working together with others towards a shared aim: *The project was a cooperative effort involving the government and a team of researchers.* **2** helpful; doing what sb asks you to do: *My firm were very cooperative and allowed me to have time off.* **3** (**BUSINESS**) (used about a business, etc.) owned and run by the people involved: *a cooperative business venture* ◇ *a cooperative farm* ▸ **cooperatively** (*BrE also* co-operatively) *adv.*

cooperative² (*BrE also* co-operative) /kəʊ'ɒpərətɪv/ *noun* [C] (**BUSINESS**) a business or organization that is owned and run by all of the people who work for it: *The factory is now a workers' cooperative.*

coordinate¹ ξ+ **C1** **W** (*BrE also* co-ordinate) /kəʊ'ɔːdɪneɪt/ *verb* [T] to organize different things or people so that they work together: *It is her job to coordinate the various departments.* ◇ *the part of the brain that coordinates body movements*

coordinate² **W** (*BrE also* co-ordinate) /kəʊ'ɔːdɪnət/ *noun* [C] (**GEOGRAPHY**, **MATHEMATICS**) one of the two sets of numbers and/or letters that are used for finding the position of a point on a map or GRAPH

coordination ξ+ **C1** **W** (*BrE also* co-ordination) /kəʊˌɔːdɪ'neɪʃn/ *noun* [U] **1** the organization of different things or people so that they work together well **2** the ability to control the movements of your body well

coordinator ξ+ **C1** (*BrE also* co-ordinator) /kəʊ'ɔːdɪneɪtə(r)/ *noun* [C] a person who is responsible for organizing different things or people so that they work together well

cop¹ ξ+ **C1** /kɒp/ *noun* [C] (*informal*) a police officer

cop² /kɒp/ *verb* (-pp-) **PHR V cop out (of sth)** (*informal*) to avoid sth that you should do, because you are afraid or lazy: *She was going to help me with the cooking but she copped out at the last minute.*

co-'parent *verb* [T, I] (**SOCIAL STUDIES**) to share the duties of bringing up a child, especially when a couple are separated or not married: *The former couple continue to co-parent their 2-year-old daughter.* ◇ *They are learning to co-parent after their decision to divorce.* ▸ **co-parent** *noun* [C]: *They divorced in 2016 but have remained friendly co-parents to their children.*

cope ξ+ **B2** /kəʊp/ *verb* [I] ~ (**with sb/sth**) to deal successfully with a difficult matter or situation: *She finds it difficult to cope with the pressure of exams.* **SYN manage**

copier /'kɒpiə(r)/ (*especially AmE*) = PHOTOCOPIER

copious /'kəʊpiəs/ *adj.* in large amounts: *She made copious notes at the lecture.* **SYN abundant** ▸ **copiously** *adv.*

'cop-out *noun* [C] (*informal*) a way of avoiding sth that you should do

copper ξ+ **C1** /'kɒpə(r)/ *noun* **1** [U] (*symb.* Cu) (**CHEMISTRY**) a chemical element. Copper is a soft red-brown metal used for making electric wires, pipes and coins: *water pipes made of copper* ❶ For more information on the periodic table of elements, look at the **Reference Section** of this dictionary. **2** [C] (*BrE*) a coin of low value made of brown metal: *I only had a few coppers left.* **3** [C] (*BrE, informal*) a police officer

copra /'kɒprə/ *noun* [U] the dried white part of a COCONUT

copse /kɒps/ *noun* [C] a small area of trees or bushes

copulate /'kɒpjuleɪt/ *verb* [I] (**BIOLOGY**) to have sex ▸ **copulation** /ˌkɒpju'leɪʃn/ *noun* [U]

copy¹ 🔊 **A2** /'kɒpi/ *noun* [C] (*pl.* -ies) **1** something that is made to look exactly like sth else: *I kept a copy of the letter I wrote.* ◇ *the **master copy** (= the original piece of paper from which copies are made) ◇ *to **make a copy** of a computer file* ⊃ look at **hard copy, photocopy** **2** one book, newspaper, etc. of which many have been printed or produced: *I managed to buy the last copy of the book left in the shop.*

copy² 🔊 **A2** /'kɒpi/ *verb* (copying; copies; *pt, pp* copied) **1** [T] to make sth exactly the same as sth else: *The children copied pictures from a book.* ◇ *Is it illegal to copy computer programs?* ◇ *Copy the text and paste it into the new document.* **2** [T] = PHOTOCOPY **3** [T] ~ **sth (down/out)** to write down sth exactly as it is written somewhere else: *I copied down the address on the brochure.* ◇ *I copied out the essay more neatly.* **4** [T] to do or try to do the same as sb else: *She copies everything her friends do.* **SYN imitate 5** [I] ~ **(from sb)** to cheat in an exam or test by writing what sb else has written: *He was caught copying from another student in the exam.*

copyright¹ 🔊 **C1** /'kɒpiraɪt/ *noun* [C, U] (**LAW**) if a person or an organization holds the **copyright** on a piece of writing, music, etc., they are the only people who have the legal right to publish, broadcast, perform it, etc., and other people must ask their permission to use it or any part of it ▶ copyright *verb* [T]

copyright² /'kɒpiraɪt/ *adj.* protected by COPYRIGHT; not allowed to be copied without permission: *copyright material*

copywriter /'kɒpiraɪtə(r)/ *noun* [C] a person whose job is to write the words for advertising material

coral /'kɒrəl/ *noun* [U] (**BIOLOGY**, **GEOGRAPHY**) a hard red, pink or white substance that forms in the sea from the bones of very small sea animals: *a coral reef* (= a line of rock in the sea formed by coral)

corbel /'kɔːbl/ *noun* [C] (**ARCHITECTURE**) a piece of stone or wood that sticks out from a wall to support sth, for example an ARCH

cord /kɔːd/ *noun* **1** [C, U] (a piece of) strong, thick string **2** [C, U] (*especially AmE*) = FLEX¹ **3** [C, U] (*especially AmE*) (a piece of) wire covered with plastic **4** cords [pl.] trousers made of CORDUROY (= a thick soft cotton cloth with raised lines on it) ⊃ look at **vocal cords**

cordial /'kɔːdiəl/ *adj.* pleasant and friendly: *a cordial greeting/smile* ▶ cordially /-əli/ *adv.*

cordless /'kɔːdləs/ *adj.* (used about a phone or an electrical tool) not connected to its power supply by wires: *a cordless phone/kettle/iron*

cordon¹ /'kɔːdn/ *noun* [C] a line or ring of police or soldiers that prevents people from entering an area

cordon² /'kɔːdn/ *verb*
PHR V cordon sth off to stop people entering an area by surrounding it with a ring of police or soldiers: *The street where the bomb was discovered was quickly cordoned off.*

corduroy /'kɔːdərɔɪ/ *noun* [U] a thick soft cotton cloth with lines on it, used for making clothes: *a corduroy jacket*

core¹ 🔊 **B2** 🌐 /kɔː(r)/ *noun* **1** [C] the hard central part of a fruit such as an apple, that contains the seeds **2** [C] the central part of an object: *the earth's core* ◇ *the core of a nuclear reactor* ⊃ picture at **seismic 3** [sing.] the central or most important part of sth: *Concern for the environment is at the core of our policies.*
IDM to the core completely; in every way: *The news shook him to the core* (= shocked him very much).

core² **B2** /kɔː(r)/ *adj.* **1** most important; main or essential: *core subjects* (= subjects that all the students have to study) *such as English and maths* ◇ *We need to concentrate on our core business.* **2** used to describe the most important or central beliefs, etc. of a person or group: *The party is losing touch with its core values.*

coriander /ˌkɒri'ændə(r)/ *noun* [U] a plant whose leaves and seeds are used in cooking to give taste to food

Corinthian /kə'rɪnθiən/ *adj.* (**ARCHITECTURE**) used to describe a style of architecture in ancient Greece that has thin columns with decorations of leaves at the top: *Corinthian columns/capitals* ⊃ look at **Doric, ionic (3)** ⊃ picture at **capital¹**

cork /kɔːk/ *noun* **1** [U] a light soft material that comes from the outside of a type of tree: *cork floor tiles* **2** [C] a round piece of cork that you push into the end of a bottle to close it, especially a bottle of wine

corkscrew /'kɔːkskruː/ *noun* [C] a tool that you use for pulling CORKS out of bottles

corn /kɔːn/ *noun* **1** [U] (*especially BrE*) (**AGRICULTURE**) any plant that is grown for its grain, such as WHEAT: *a field of corn* ◇ *a cornfield* **2** [U] (*AmE*) = MAIZE **3** [U] (*AmE*) = SWEETCORN **4** [C] (**HEALTH**) a small, painful area of hard skin on the foot, especially the toe

cornea /'kɔːniə/ *noun* [C] (**ANATOMY**) the clear layer that covers and protects the outer part of the eye ⊃ picture at **eye¹** ▶ corneal /-əl/ *adj.*

corner¹ 🔊 **A2** /'kɔːnə(r)/ *noun* [C] **1** a place where two lines, edges, surfaces or roads meet: *Put the lamp in the corner of the room.* ◇ *Write your address in the top right-hand corner.* ◇ *The shop is on the corner of Wall Street and Long Road.* ◇ *He went round the corner at top speed.* **2** a quiet or secret place or area: *a remote corner of Scotland* **3** a difficult situation from which you cannot escape: *to get yourself into a corner* **4** (**SPORT**) (used in football and hockey) a free kick or hit from the corner of the field
IDM cut corners to do sth quickly and not as well as you should (just) **round the corner** very near: *There's a cafe just round the corner.*

corner² /'kɔːnə(r)/ *verb* [T] **1** to get a person or an animal into a position from which they/it cannot escape: *He cornered me at the party and started telling me all his problems.* **2** (**BUSINESS**) to get control in a particular area of business so that nobody else can have any success in it: *That company's really cornered the market in health foods.*

cornerstone /'kɔːnəstəʊn/ *noun* [C] **1** (**ARCHITECTURE**) a stone at the corner of the base of a building, often put there in a special ceremony **2** the most important part of sth that the rest depends on

cornet /'kɔːnɪt/ *noun* [C] (**MUSIC**) a metal musical instrument like a small TRUMPET that you play by blowing into it

cornflakes /'kɔːnfleɪks/ *noun* [pl.] food made of small pieces of dried MAIZE and eaten with milk for breakfast

cornflour /'kɔːnflaʊə(r)/ (*BrE*) (*AmE* cornstarch /'kɔːnstɑːtʃ/) *noun* [U] very fine flour made from MAIZE, often used to make sauces, etc. thicker

cornice /'kɔːnɪs/ *noun* [C] (**ARCHITECTURE**) a border around the top of the walls in a room or on the outside walls of a building

corn on the 'cob *noun* [U] SWEETCORN (= a type of vegetable) that is cooked with all the yellow grains still on the inner part and eaten

cornucopia /ˌkɔːnju'kəʊpiə/ *noun* [C] **1** (**ART**) an object shaped like an animal's HORN, shown in art as full of fruit and flowers **2** (*formal*) something that is or contains a large supply of good things: *The book is a cornucopia of good ideas.*

corny /ˈkɔːni/ *adj.* (**cornier; corniest**) (*informal*) too ordinary or familiar to be interesting or to make people laugh: *a corny joke*

corollary /kəˈrɒləri/ *noun* [C] (*pl.* **-ies**) (*formal*) a situation, a statement or a fact that is the natural and direct result of another one

corona /kəˈrəʊnə/ *noun* [C] (**ASTRONOMY**) a ring of light seen around the sun or moon, especially during an ECLIPSE

coronary[1] /ˈkɒrənri/ *adj.* (**HEALTH**) relating to the heart

coronary[2] /ˈkɒrənri/ *noun* [C] (*pl.* **-ies**) (**HEALTH**) a type of heart attack

coronary artery *noun* [C] (**ANATOMY**) either of the two ARTERIES that supply blood to the heart

coronation /ˌkɒrəˈneɪʃn/ *noun* [C] an official ceremony at which sb is made a king or queen

coronavirus /kəˈrəʊnəvaɪrəs/ *noun* [C, U] (**HEALTH**) a type of virus that can cause PNEUMONIA and other diseases ⊃ look at **COVID-19**

coroner /ˈkɒrənə(r)/ *noun* [C] (**LAW**) a person whose job is to find out the causes of death of people who have died in violent or unusual ways

Corp. *abbr.* (in writing) = CORPORATION: *West Coast Motor Corp.*

corporal /ˈkɔːpərəl/ *noun* [C] a person at a low level in the army, the MARINES or the British AIR FORCE

corporal punishment *noun* [U] the punishment of people by hitting them, especially the punishment of children by parents or teachers ⊃ look at **capital punishment**

corporate ⟨+ B2⟩ /ˈkɔːpərət/ *adj.* (**BUSINESS**) connected with a large business company: *corporate finance/profits/tax* ◇ **corporate identity** (= the image of a company, which all its members share)

corporate responsibility *noun* [U] (**BUSINESS**) the idea that a large company has a duty to treat people fairly and to play a positive part in society: *The company is committed to promoting corporate responsibility in all aspects of its business.*

corporation ⟨+ B2⟩ /ˌkɔːpəˈreɪʃn/ *noun* [C + sing./pl. verb] **1** (*abbr.* **Corp.**) (**BUSINESS**) a large business company: *multinational corporations* ◇ *the British Broadcasting Corporation* **2** (*BrE*) (**POLITICS**) a group of people elected to govern a particular town or city

corps /kɔː(r)/ *noun* [C + sing./pl. verb] (*pl.* **corps** /kɔːz/) **1** a part of an army with special duties: *the medical corps* **2** a group of people involved in a special activity: *the volunteer corps*

corpse /kɔːps/ *noun* [C] a dead body, especially of a person ⊃ look at **carcass**

corpus /ˈkɔːpəs/ *noun* [C] (*pl.* **corpora** /-pərə/, **corpuses**) (**LANGUAGE**) a collection of written or spoken texts

corpuscle /ˈkɔːpʌsl/ *noun* [C] (**ANATOMY**) any of the red or white cells found in blood: *red/white corpuscles*

correct[1] ⟨ A1 W⟩ /kəˈrekt/ *adj.* **1** with no mistakes; right or true: *Well done! All your answers were correct.* ◇ *Have you got the correct time, please?* ⊃ note at **true 2** (used about behaviour, manners, dress, etc.) suitable, proper or right OPP **incorrect** ▸ **correctly** ⟨ A2 W⟩ *adv.* ▸ **correctness** *noun* [U]

correct[2] ⟨ A1⟩ /kəˈrekt/ *verb* [T] **1** to make a mistake, fault, etc. right or better: *to correct a spelling mistake* ◇ *to correct a test* (= mark the mistakes in it) **2** to tell sb what mistakes they are making or what faults they have: *He's always correcting me when I'm talking to people.*

correction ⟨+ C1 W⟩ /kəˈrekʃn/ *noun* **1** [C] **~ (to sth)** a change that makes a mistake, fault, etc. right or better: *I've made a few small corrections to your report.* **2** [U] the act or process of correcting sth: *Some parts of the report needed correction.*

correction fluid *noun* [U] a white liquid that you use to cover mistakes that you make when you are writing or typing, and that you can write on top of ⊃ look at **Tipp-Ex™**

corrective /kəˈrektɪv/ *adj.* (*formal*) intended to make sth right that is wrong: *to take corrective action*

correlate ⟨+ C1 W⟩ /ˈkɒrəleɪt/ *verb* [I, T] (*formal*) to have or to show a relationship or connection between two or more things: *The increase in price correlates with a fall in demand.* ▸ **correlation** ⟨+ C1 W⟩ /ˌkɒrəˈleɪʃn/ *noun* [C, U]: *There is a correlation between a person's diet and height.*

correspond ⟨+ C1 O⟩ /ˌkɒrəˈspɒnd/ *verb* [I] **1 ~ (to/with sth)** to be the same as or equal to sth; to match: *American high schools correspond to British comprehensives.* **2 ~ (with sb)** (*formal*) to write letters or emails to and receive them from sb: *He corresponded with Paola for a year before they met.*

correspondence ⟨+ C1⟩ /ˌkɒrəˈspɒndəns/ *noun* **1** [U, C] (*formal*) the act of writing letters and emails; the letters and emails themselves: *There hasn't been any correspondence between them for years.* **2** [C, U] a close connection or relationship between two or more things: *There is no correspondence between the two sets of figures.*

correspondence course *noun* [C] (**EDUCATION**) a course of study that you do at home, using books and exercises sent to you by post or by email

correspondent ⟨+ C1⟩ /ˌkɒrəˈspɒndənt/ *noun* [C] **1** (**ARTS AND MEDIA**) a person who provides news or writes articles for a newspaper, etc., especially from a foreign country: *our Middle East correspondent, Anna Jenkins* **2** a person who writes letters or emails to sb

corresponding ⟨+ C1 W⟩ /ˌkɒrəˈspɒndɪŋ/ *adj.* [only before noun] related or similar to sth: *Sales are up 10% compared with the corresponding period last year.* SYN **equivalent** ▸ **correspondingly** *adv.*

corresponding angles *noun* [pl.] (**GEOMETRY**) equal angles formed on the same side of a line that crosses two PARALLEL lines ⊃ look at **alternate angles** ⊃ picture at **angle**[1]

corridor ⟨+ B2⟩ /ˈkɒrɪdɔː(r)/ (*AmE also* **hallway**) *noun* [C] a long narrow passage in a building or some trains, with doors that open into rooms, etc.

corrie /ˈkɒri/ *noun* [C] a round area shaped like a bowl in the side of a mountain, especially in Scotland ⊃ look at **cirque, cwm**

corroborate /kəˈrɒbəreɪt/ *verb* [T] (*formal*) (**LAW**) to support a statement, an idea, etc. by providing new evidence: *The witness corroborated Mr Patton's statement about the night of the murder.* ▸ **corroboration** /kəˌrɒbəˈreɪʃn/ *noun* [U]

corrode /kəˈrəʊd/ *verb* [I, T] (**CHEMISTRY**) (used about metals) to become weak or to be destroyed by chemical action; to cause a metal to do this: *Parts of the car were corroded by rust.* ▸ **corrosion** /-ˈrəʊʒn/ *noun* [U]

corrosive /kəˈrəʊsɪv/ *adj.* (**CHEMISTRY**) tending to destroy sth slowly by chemical action: *corrosive acid* ⊃ picture at **safety** ▸ **corrosive** *noun* [C]

corrugated /ˈkɒrəgeɪtɪd/ *adj.* (used about metal or CARDBOARD) shaped into folds

corrugated iron

corrupt¹ ⚡+ **C1** /kəˈrʌpt/ *adj.* **1** doing or involving illegal or dishonest things in exchange for money, etc: *corrupt officials who accept bribes* ◊ *corrupt business practices* **2** (COMPUTING) containing changes or faults and no longer in the original state: *corrupt software* ◊ *The file seems to be corrupt.*

corrupt² /kəˈrʌpt/ *verb* **1** [T] to cause sb/sth to start behaving in a dishonest or IMMORAL way: *Too many people are corrupted by power.* **2** [T, I] (COMPUTING) to cause mistakes to appear in a computer file, etc. with the result that the information in it is no longer correct: *The program has somehow corrupted the system files.* ◊ *corrupted data* ◊ *The disk will corrupt if it is overloaded.*

corruption ⚡+ **C1** /kəˈrʌpʃn/ *noun* [U] **1** dishonest or IMMORAL behaviour or activities: *There were accusations of corruption among senior police officers.* **2** the process of making sb/sth CORRUPT

corset /ˈkɔːsɪt/ *noun* [C] a piece of women's clothing worn especially in the past to make the middle part of the body look smaller

cortex /ˈkɔːteks/ *noun* [C] (*pl.* cortices /-tɪsiːz/) (ANATOMY) the outer layer of an organ in the body, especially the brain: *the cerebral cortex* (= around the brain)

cortisol /ˈkɔːtɪzɒl/ = HYDROCORTISONE

cortisone /ˈkɔːtɪzəʊn/ *noun* [U] (MEDICINE) a HORMONE (= a natural substance produced by the body) that is used to reduce SWELLING caused by certain diseases and injuries

cos (*also* ˈcause) /kəz, kɒz/ *conj.* (BrE, informal) because: *I can't come to the party cos I've got too much homework.*

cosine /ˈkəʊsaɪn/ *noun* [C] (MATHEMATICS) (*abbr.* cos) the RATIO of the length of the side next to an ACUTE ANGLE (= one that is less than 90°) to the length of the HYPOTENUSE (= the longest side) in a RIGHT-ANGLED TRIANGLE ⊃ look at sine, tangent

cosmetic¹ /kɒzˈmetɪk/ *noun* [C, usually pl.] a substance that you put on your face or hair to make yourself look more attractive ⊃ look at make-up (1)

cosmetic² /kɒzˈmetɪk/ *adj.* **1** used or done in order to make your face or body more attractive: *cosmetic products* ◊ *cosmetic surgery* **2** done in order to improve only the appearance of sth, without changing it in any other way: *changes in government policy which are purely cosmetic*

cosmic /ˈkɒzmɪk/ *adj.* (ASTRONOMY) connected with space or the universe

cosmic ˈrays *noun* [pl.] (ASTRONOMY) RAYS (= lines of energy) that reach the earth from outer space

cosmology /kɒzˈmɒlədʒi/ *noun* [U] (ASTRONOMY) the scientific study of the universe and its origin and development ▶ **cosmological** /ˌkɒzməˈlɒdʒɪkl/ *adj.* ▶ **cosmologist** /kɒzˈmɒlədʒɪst/ *noun* [C]

cosmonaut /ˈkɒzmənɔːt/ *noun* [C] (ASTRONOMY) an ASTRONAUT (= a person who travels in space) from the former Soviet Union

cosmopolitan /ˌkɒzməˈpɒlɪtən/ *adj.* **1** containing people from all over the world: *a cosmopolitan city* **2** influenced by the culture of other countries: *a cosmopolitan and sophisticated young woman*

the cosmos /ðə ˈkɒzmɒs/ *noun* [sing.] (ASTRONOMY) the universe: *Computers can help scientists unlock the mysteries of the cosmos.*

cost¹ ⚡ **A1** /kɒst/ *noun* **1** [C, U] the money that you have to pay for sth: *The cost of petrol has gone up again.* ◊ *The hospital was built at a cost of £10 million.* ◊ *The damage will have to be repaired regardless of cost.* ◊ *The company had to raise prices because of rising costs.* ⊃ note at price¹ **2** [sing., U] what you have to give or lose in order to obtain sth else: *He achieved great success but only at the cost of a happy family life.* **3** costs [pl.] (LAW) the amount of money that sb is ordered to pay for lawyers, etc. in a legal case **IDM at all costs/at any cost** using whatever means are necessary to achieve sth: *We must win at all costs.* **cover the cost (of sth)** → COVER¹ **to your cost** in a way that is unpleasant or bad for you: *Life can be lonely at university, as I found out to my cost.*

cost² ⚡ **A1** /kɒst/ *verb* [T] (*pt, pp* cost) **HELP** In sense 3 **costed** is used for the past tense and past participle. **1** to have the price of: *How much does a return ticket to London cost?* ◊ *It costs £10.* ◊ *We'll take the bus — it won't cost much.* ◊ (*informal*) *How much did your car cost you?* **2** to make you lose sth: *That one mistake cost him his job.* **3** to estimate how much money will be needed for sth or the price that should be charged for sth: *The project needs to be costed in detail.* **IDM cost the earth/a fortune** to be very expensive

co-star *verb* (-rr-) (ARTS AND MEDIA) **1** [I] (used about actors) to be one of two or more stars in a film, play, etc: *Emma Stone co-stars with Ryan Gosling in the film.* **2** [T] (used about a film, play, etc.) to have two or more famous actors as its stars: *a film co-starring Ryan Gosling and Emma Stone* ▶ **co-star** *noun* [C]: *His co-star was Lily James.*

cost-efˈfective *adj.* giving the best possible profit or results in comparison with the money that is spent: *This alarm system is the most cost-effective way of protecting your property.*

costly ⚡+ **C1** /ˈkɒstli/ *adj.* (costlier; costliest) **1** costing a lot of money **SYN expensive**: *a costly repair bill* **2** involving great loss of time, effort, etc: *a costly mistake* **SYN expensive**

the ˌcost of ˈliving *noun* [sing.] (ECONOMICS) the amount of money that people need to pay for food, clothing and somewhere to live: *Despite the high cost of living, New York is a great place to live.*

cost ˈprice *noun* [U] (BUSINESS, FINANCE) the cost of producing sth or the price at which it is sold without profit ⊃ look at asking price, selling price

costume ⚡ **B1** /ˈkɒstjuːm/ *noun* **1** [C, U] a set or style of clothes worn by people in a particular country or in a particular historical period: *seventeenth-century costume* ◊ *Welsh national costume* **2** [C, U] the clothes that actors wear in a play or film, or that sb wears to make them look like sb/sth else: *One of the children was dressed in a pirate's costume.* ◊ *The last rehearsal of the play will be done in costume.* **3** [C] (BrE) = SWIMSUIT

cosy (BrE) (AmE cozy) /ˈkəʊzi/ *adj.* (cosier; cosiest) warm and comfortable: *The room looked cosy and inviting in the firelight.*

cot /kɒt/ *noun* [C] **1** (AmE crib) a bed with high sides for a baby **2** (AmE) = CAMP BED

cottage ⚡ **B1** /ˈkɒtɪdʒ/ *noun* [C] a small and usually old house, especially in the country: *a country cottage with roses round the door*

cottage ˈcheese *noun* [U] a type of soft white cheese that has small thick pieces in it

cotton 🔊 **B1** /ˈkɒtn/ *noun* [U] **1** a natural cloth or THREAD made from the thin white hairs of the cotton plant: *a cotton shirt* **2** (*AmE*) = COTTON WOOL

ˌcotton ˈwool (*BrE*) (*AmE* cotton) *noun* [U] a soft mass of cotton, used for cleaning the skin, cuts, etc.

cotyledon /ˌkɒtɪˈliːdn/ *noun* [C] (**BIOLOGY**) a part inside a seed that looks like a small leaf, which the developing plant uses as a store of food. Cotyledons are the first parts of the seed to appear above the ground when it begins to grow.

couch¹ /kaʊtʃ/ *noun* [C] a long seat, often with a back and arms, for sitting or lying on: *They were sitting on the couch in the living room.* **SYN** sofa

couch² /kaʊtʃ/ *verb* [T, usually passive] (*formal*) to express a thought, idea, etc. in the way mentioned: *His reply was couched in very polite terms.*

ˈcouch potato *noun* [C] (*informal*) a person who spends a lot of time sitting and watching TV

cougar /ˈkuːgə(r)/ (*AmE*) = PUMA

cough¹ /kɒf/ *verb* **1** [I] to send air out of your throat and mouth with a sudden loud noise, especially when you have a cold, have sth in your throat, etc. ⊃ note at ill¹ **2** [T] ~ (up) sth to send sth out of your throat and mouth with a sudden loud noise: *When I started coughing (up) blood I went to the doctor's.*
PHR V cough (sth) up (*informal*) to give money when you do not want to: *Come on, cough up what you owe me!*

cough² /kɒf/ *noun* [C] **1** an act or the sound of COUGHING: *He gave a nervous cough before he started to speak.* **2** (**HEALTH**) an illness or infection that makes you COUGH a lot: *Kevin's got a bad cough.*

could 🔊 **A1** /kəd, *strong form* kʊd/ *modal verb* (*negative* could not; *short form* couldn't /ˈkʊdnt/)
• PAST OF CAN **1** used as the past tense of *can*: *I could run 3 miles without stopping when I was younger.*
• POSSIBILITY **2** used for saying that sth may be or may have been possible: *I could do it now if you like.* ◇ *She could be famous one day.* ◇ *He could have gone to university but he didn't want to.* ◇ *You could have said you were going to be late* (= I'm annoyed that you didn't)!
• REQUEST **3** used for asking permission politely: *Could I possibly borrow your car?* **4** used for asking sb politely to do sth for you: *Could you open the door? My hands are full.*
• SUGGESTION **5** used for making a suggestion: *'What do you want to do tonight?' 'We could go to the cinema or we could just stay in.'*
• SENSES **6** used with the verbs *feel, hear, see, smell* and *taste*: *We could hear children playing outside.*

coulomb /ˈkuːlɒm/ *noun* [C] (*abbr.* C) (**PHYSICS**) a unit of electric charge, equal to the quantity of electricity carried in one second by one AMPERE (= one unit of current)

council 🔊 **B2** /ˈkaʊnsl/ (*also* Council) *noun* [C + sing./pl. verb] **1** (**POLITICS**) a group of people who are elected to govern an area such as a town or county: *a town council* ◇ *a council house* (= one that a council owns and rents to people who do not have much money) ◇ *My dad's on the local council.* ◇ *The county council has/have decided to build a new road.* **2** a group of people chosen to give advice, manage affairs, etc. for a particular organization or activity: *the Arts Council* ◇ *a student council*

councillor 🔊 **C1** /ˈkaʊnsələ(r)/ *noun* [C] (**POLITICS**) a member of a council: *to elect new councillors*

counsel¹ /ˈkaʊnsl/ *verb* [T] (-ll-, *AmE* -l-) **1** to give professional advice and help to sb with a problem **2** (*formal*) to tell sb what you think they should do; to advise: *Mr Dean's lawyers counselled him against making public statements.*

counsel² /ˈkaʊnsl/ *noun* [U, C] **1** (*formal*) advice, especially given by older people or experts; a piece of advice **2** (**LAW**) a lawyer or group of lawyers representing sb in court: *the counsel for the defence/prosecution* ⊃ note at **lawyer**

counselling 🔊 **C1** (*BrE*) (*AmE* counseling) /ˈkaʊnsəlɪŋ/ *noun* [U] professional advice and help given to people with problems: *Many students come to us for counselling.*

counsellor 🔊 **C1** (*BrE*) (*AmE* counselor) /ˈkaʊnsələ(r)/ *noun* [C] a person whose job is to give advice to people with problems: *a marriage counsellor*

count¹ 🔊 **A2** /kaʊnt/ *verb* **1** [I] to say numbers one after another in order: *Close your eyes and count (up) to 20.* **2** [T] to calculate the total number or amount of sth: *The teacher counted the children as they got on the bus.* **3** [T] to include sb/sth when you are calculating an amount or a number: *There were 30 people on the bus, not counting the driver.* **4** [I] ~ (for sth) to be important or valuable: *I sometimes think my opinion counts for nothing at work.* **5** [I] ~ (as sth) to be officially accepted: *The referee had already blown his whistle so the goal didn't count.* ◇ *Will my driving licence count as identification?* **6** [I, T] to consider sb/sth in a particular way; to be considered in a particular way: *You should count yourself lucky to have a good job.* ◇ *On this airline, children over 12 count/are counted as adults.*
IDM Don't count your chickens (before they're hatched) used to say that you should not be too confident that sth will be successful because sth might still go wrong
PHR V count against sb to be considered as a disadvantage: *Do you think my age will count against me?* count on sb/sth to expect sth with confidence; to depend on sb/sth: *Can I count on you to help me?* ⊃ note at **trust²** count sb/sth out **1** to count things slowly, one by one: *She carefully counted out the money into my hand.* **2** (*informal*) to not include sb/sth: *If you're going swimming, you can count me out!*

count² 🔊 **B1** /kaʊnt/ *noun* [C] **1** [usually sing.] an act of counting or a number that you get after counting: *On the count of three, all lift together.* ◇ *At the last count, there were nearly 2 million unemployed.* **2** [usually pl.] a point that is made in a discussion, argument, etc: *I proved her wrong on all counts.*
IDM keep/lose count (of sth) to know/not know how many there are of sth: *I've lost count of the number of times he's told that joke!*

countable /ˈkaʊntəbl/ *adj.* (**GRAMMAR**) a countable noun can be made plural or used with *a* or *an*, for example *table, cat* and *idea* **OPP** uncountable

countdown /ˈkaʊntdaʊn/ *noun* [C] the act of saying numbers backwards to zero just before sth important happens: *the countdown to the lift-off of a rocket* ◇ (*figurative*) *The countdown to this summer's Olympic Games has started.*

countenance¹ /ˈkaʊntənəns/ *noun* [C] (*formal*) a person's face or their expression

countenance² /ˈkaʊntənəns/ *verb* [T] (*formal*) to support sth or agree to sth happening

counter- /ˈkaʊntə(r)/ *prefix* (in verbs, nouns, adjectives and adverbs) **1** against; opposite: *counterterrorism* ◇ *counter-argument* **2** related or similar to sth: *counterpart/countersign*

counter¹ 🔊 **B2** /ˈkaʊntə(r)/ *noun* [C] **1** a long, flat surface in a shop, bank, etc., where customers are served: *The man behind the counter in the bank was* *very helpful.* **2** (*AmE*) = WORKTOP **3** a small object (usually round and made of plastic) that is used in some games to show where a player is on the board **4** an electronic device for counting sth: *The rev counter is next to the speedometer.* ⊃ look at **Geiger counter**

IDM **over the counter** (**MEDICINE**) (used about medicines) able to be bought without a PRESCRIPTION (= a paper on which a doctor has written the name of the medicine you need): *These tablets are available over the counter.*

counter² 🔒+ **C1** /ˈkaʊntə(r)/ *verb* **1** [I, T] to reply or react to criticism: *He countered our objections with a powerful defence of his plan.* **2** [T] to try to reduce or prevent the bad effects of sth: *The shop has installed security cameras to counter theft.*

counter³ /ˈkaʊntə(r)/ *adv.* ~ **to sth** in the opposite direction to sth: *The results of these experiments* **run counter to** *previous findings.*

counteract /ˌkaʊntərˈækt/ *verb* [T] to reduce the effect of sth by acting against it: *measures to counteract traffic congestion*

counter-attack *noun* [C] an attack made in reaction to an enemy or opponent's attack ▸ **counter-attack** *verb* [I, T]

counterclockwise /ˌkaʊntəˈklɒkwaɪz/ (*AmE*) = ANTICLOCKWISE

counterfeit /ˈkaʊntəfɪt/ *adj.* (*formal*) copied so that it looks like the real thing: *counterfeit money*

counterfoil /ˈkaʊntəfɔɪl/ *noun* [C] the part of a ticket, CHEQUE, etc. that you keep when you give the other part to sb else

counterpart 🔒+ **C1** /ˈkaʊntəpɑːt/ *noun* [C] a person or thing that has a similar position or function in a different country or organization: *the French president and his Italian counterpart* (= the Italian president)

counterpoint /ˈkaʊntəpɔɪnt/ *noun* (**MUSIC**) **1** [U] the combination of two or more tunes to form a whole: *The two melodies are played in counterpoint.* ⊃ adjective **contrapuntal** **2** [C] ~ (**to sth**) a tune played in combination with another one

counterproductive /ˌkaʊntəprəˈdʌktɪv/ *adj.* having the opposite effect to the one you want ⊃ look at **productive** (2)

countersign /ˈkaʊntəsaɪn/ *verb* [T] (**LAW**) to sign a document that has already been signed by another person, especially in order to show that it is officially acceptable

countertenor /ˈkaʊntətenə(r)/ *noun* [C] (**MUSIC**) a man who is trained to sing with a very high voice

counterterrorism /ˌkaʊntəˈterərɪzəm/ *noun* [U] action taken to prevent the activities of political groups who use violence to try to achieve their aims ▸ **counterterrorist** /-ˈterərɪst/ *adj.*

countless 🔒+ **C1** /ˈkaʊntləs/ *adj.* [only before noun] very many: *I've tried to phone him countless times but he's not there.*

country 🔒 **A1** 🔘 /ˈkʌntri/ *noun* (*pl.* -ies) **1** [C] (**GEOGRAPHY, POLITICS**) an area of land that has or used to have its own government and laws: *France, Spain and other European countries* ◇ *There was snow over much of the country during the night.* **2** [U] (**GEOGRAPHY**) an area of land, especially with particular physical features, suitable for a particular purpose or connected with a particular person or people: *We looked down over miles of open country.* ◇ *hilly country* ◇ *Navajo country* **SYN terrain** **3** the

country [*sing.*] the people who live in a country: *a survey to find out what the country really thinks* **4** the country [*sing.*] any area outside towns and cities, with fields, woods, farms, etc: *Do you live in a town or in the country?* ⊃ look at **countryside** **5** [U] (**MUSIC**) = COUNTRY AND WESTERN

▼ **VOCABULARY BUILDING**

Nation is another word for country, or the people who live in a country: *The entire nation, it seemed, was watching TV.* **State** is used for talking about a country as an organized political community controlled by one government. It can also mean the government itself: *a politically independent state* ◇ *the member states of the EU* ◇ *You get a pension from the state when you retire.* ◇ *state education.* **Land** is more formal or literary: *Explorers who set out to discover new lands.*

---

country and western (*also* country) *noun* [U] (**MUSIC**) a type of music based on traditional music from the southern and western US

country house *noun* [C] (*BrE*) a large house in the country, usually owned by an important family and often with a lot of land

countryman /ˈkʌntrimən/ *noun* [C] (*pl.* -men /-mən/) a person from your own country: *The Italian Castorri beat his fellow countryman Rossi in the final.*

countryside 🔒 **B1** /ˈkʌntrisaɪd/ *noun* [U] (**GEOGRAPHY**) land that is away from towns and cities, where there are fields, woods, etc: *From the hill there is a magnificent view of the surrounding countryside.* ⊃ look at **country** (4)

countrywoman /ˈkʌntriwʊmən/ *noun* [C] (*pl.* -women /-wɪmɪn/) a woman from your own country

county 🔒 **B2** /ˈkaʊnti/ *noun* [C] (*pl.* -ies) (*abbr.* Co.) an area in Britain, Ireland or the US that has its own local government: *the county of Nottinghamshire* ◇ *Orange County, California* ⊃ look at **province** (1), **state¹** (5)

coup 🔒+ **C1** /kuː/ *noun* [C] **1** (*also* coup d'état /ˌkuː deɪˈtɑː/) (**POLITICS**) a sudden, illegal and often violent change of government: *a coup to overthrow the president* ◇ *an attempted coup* (= one that did not succeed) **2** a clever and successful thing to do: *Getting that promotion was a real coup.*

couple¹ 🔒 **A2** /ˈkʌpl/ *noun* [C + sing./pl. verb] **1** two people who are together because they are married or in a relationship: *a married couple* ◇ *Is/Are that couple over there part of our group?* ⊃ look at **pair¹** **2** two people or things: *I need a couple of glasses.* **3** a few: *I last saw her a couple of months ago.*

couple² /ˈkʌpl/ *verb* [T, usually passive] to join or connect sb/sth to sb/sth else: *The fog, coupled with the amount of traffic on the roads, made driving very difficult.*

couplet /ˈkʌplət/ *noun* [C] (**LITERATURE**) two lines of poetry of equal length one after the other: *a poem written in rhyming couplets*

coupon /ˈkuːpɒn/ *noun* [C] **1** a small piece of paper that you can use to buy goods at a lower price, or that you can collect and then exchange for goods: *a coupon worth 10% off your next purchase* **2** a printed form in a newspaper or magazine that you use to order goods, enter a competition, etc.

courage 🔒 **B2** /ˈkʌrɪdʒ/ *noun* [U] the ability to control fear in a situation that may be dangerous or unpleasant: *It took real courage to go back into the burning building.* ◇ *She showed great courage all through her long illness.* **SYN bravery** ▸ **courageous** /kəˈreɪdʒəs/ *adj.*

IDM **pluck up courage** → PLUCK¹

courgette /kʊəˈʒet, kɔːˈʒ-/ (*BrE*) (*AmE* **zucchini**) *noun* [C] a long vegetable with dark green skin that is white inside

courier /ˈkʊriə(r)/ *noun* [C] **1** a person or company whose job is to carry letters or important papers and packages: *The package was delivered by motorcycle courier.* **2** (*BrE*) (**TOURISM**) a person who is employed by a travel company to give advice and help to a group of tourists on holiday ▶ **courier** *verb* [T]: *Courier that letter — it needs to get there today* (= send it by courier).

course A1 S /kɔːs/ *noun* **1** [C] ~ **(in/on sth)** (**EDUCATION**) a complete series of lessons or studies: *a degree course* ◇ *I've decided to* ***enrol on a*** *computer* ***course***. ◇ *I'm going to* ***take/do a course*** *in self-defence.* ➲ note at **subject**[1] **2** [C, U] the route or direction that sth, especially an aircraft, a ship or a river, takes: *The hijackers forced the captain to* ***change course*** *and head for Cuba.* ◇ *to be* ***on/off course*** (= going in the right/wrong direction) ◇ (*figurative*) *I'm* ***on course*** (= making the right amount of progress) *to finish this work by the end of the week.* ◇ *The road follows the course of the river.* **3** (*also* **ˌcourse of ˈaction**) [C] a way of dealing with a particular situation: *In that situation resignation was the only course open to him.* **4** [sing.] the development of sth over a period of time: *events that changed* ***the course of history*** ◇ ***In the normal course of events*** (= the way things normally happen) *such problems do not arise.* **5** [C] any of the separate parts of a meal: *a three-course lunch* ◇ *I had chicken for the* ***main course***. **6** [C] (**SPORT**) an area where the game of golf is played or where certain types of race take place: *a golf course* ◇ *a racecourse* **7** [C] ~ **(of sth)** (**MEDICINE**) a series of medical treatments: *The doctor put her on* ***a course of antibiotics***.
IDM **be on a collision course (with sb/sth)** → COLLISION **in the course of sth** during sth: *He mentioned it in the course of conversation.* **in the course of time** when enough time has passed **SYN** **eventually** **in due course** → DUE[1] **a matter of course** → MATTER[1] **of course** naturally; certainly: *Of course, having children has changed their lives a lot.* ◇ *'Can I use your phone?' 'Of course (you can).'* ◇ *'You're not annoyed with me, are you?' 'Of course (I'm) not.'*

coursebook /ˈkɔːsbʊk/ *noun* [C] (*BrE*) (**EDUCATION**) a book for studying from that is used regularly in class

coursework /ˈkɔːswɜːk/ *noun* [U] (**EDUCATION**) work that students do during a course of study, not in exams, that is included in their final mark: *Coursework accounts for 50% of the final marks.*

court[1] B1 /kɔːt/ *noun* **1** [C, U] (*also* **court of law**) (*BrE also* **law court** [C]) (**LAW**) a place where legal trials take place and crimes, etc. are judged: *A man has been charged and will* ***appear in court*** *tomorrow.* ◇ *Bill's company are refusing to pay him so he's decided to* ***take them to court***. ➲ look at **court of appeal** ➲ note at **crime** **2** **the court** [sing.] (**LAW**) the people in a court, especially those taking part in the trial: *Please tell the court exactly what you saw.* **3** [C, U] (**SPORT**) an area where certain ball games are played: *a tennis/squash/badminton court* ➲ look at **pitch**[1] (1)

court[2] /kɔːt/ *verb* [T] **1** to try to gain sb's support by paying special attention to them: *Politicians from all parties will be courting voters this week.* **2** to do sth that might have a very bad effect: *Britain is* ***courting*** *ecological* ***disaster*** *if it continues to dump waste in the North Sea.*

courteous /ˈkɜːtiəs/ *adj.* polite and pleasant, showing respect for other people **OPP** **discourteous** ▶ **courteously** *adv.*

courtesy[1] ♀+ C1 /ˈkɜːtəsi/ *noun* (*pl.* **-ies**) **1** [U] polite and pleasant behaviour that shows respect for other people: *She didn't even* ***have the courtesy*** *to say that she was sorry.* **2** [C, usually pl.] (*formal*) a polite thing that you say or do when you meet people in formal situations: *The two presidents exchanged courtesies before their meeting.*
IDM **(by) courtesy of sb** (*formal*) with the permission of sb and as a favour: *These pictures are being shown by courtesy of BBC TV.*

courtesy[2] /ˈkɜːtəsi/ *adj.* [only before noun] provided free, at no cost to the person using it: *A* ***courtesy bus*** *operates between the hotel and the town centre.* ◇ *The dealer will provide you with a* ***courtesy car*** *while your vehicle is being repaired.*

ˌcourt ˈmartial *noun* [C] (*pl.* **courts martial**) (**LAW**) a military court that deals with matters of military law; a trial that takes place in such a court: *His case will be heard by a court martial.* ▶ **court-martial** *verb* [T] (**-ll-**, *AmE* **-l-**)

ˌcourt of apˈpeal *noun* (**LAW**) **1** (*pl.* **courts of appeal**) (*also* **appeal court**) [C] a court that people can go to in order to try and change decisions that have been made by a lower court **2** **Court of Appeal** (*also* **Appeal Court**) [sing.] (*BrE*) the highest court in England and Wales (apart from the Supreme Court), which can change decisions made by a lower court **3** **court of appeals** (*also* **appeals court**) [C] (*AmE*) one of the courts in the US that can change decisions made by a lower court

ˌcourt of ˈlaw *noun* [C] (*pl.* **courts of law**) = COURT[1] (1)

ˈcourt order *noun* [C] a decision that is made in court about what must happen in a particular situation: *He failed to meet four court orders to pay debts of £4 000.*

courtroom /ˈkɔːtruːm, -rʊm/ *noun* [C] (**LAW**) the place or room in which trials or other legal cases are held

courtship /ˈkɔːtʃɪp/ *noun* [C, U] (*old-fashioned*) the relationship between two people before they get married

courtyard /ˈkɔːtjɑːd/ *noun* [C] an area of ground, without a roof, that has walls or buildings around it, for example in a castle or between houses or flats

couscous /ˈkʊskʊs, ˈkuːskuːs/ *noun* [U] a type of North African food made from WHEAT in very small round pieces

cousin ♀ A1 /ˈkʌzn/ (*also* **first cousin**) *noun* [C] the child of your aunt or uncle: *That's my cousin Julia.* ◇ *Paul and I are cousins.* ➲ look at **second cousin**

▼ **COLLOCATIONS**

court

The **accused** (= a person charged with a crime) has the right to a **trial** which is held in a **court**. All trials have a **judge** (= the official in charge of the court) and some have a **jury** (= a group of members of the public), who **try** the **case**. One group of lawyers (the **prosecution**) tries to prove the guilt of the accused (= to show that they did it), while another group (the **defence**) tries to defend the person. The jury listens to the **evidence** to see if there is **proof** that the accused committed the crime. **Witnesses** (= people who saw the crime being committed) **give evidence** to the court. At the end of the trial the judge or the jury will **return** (= give) a **verdict** and decide if the accused is **guilty** or **not guilty**. If the person is found guilty, the judge **passes sentence** (= decides how sb is to be punished). They may be **fined** (= forced to pay money) or sent to **jail/prison**.

covalent /ˌkəʊˈveɪlənt/ *adj.* (**CHEMISTRY, PHYSICS**) (used about a chemical BOND) sharing a pair of ELECTRONS

cove /kəʊv/ *noun* [C] (**GEOGRAPHY**) a small BAY (= an area of the sea that is partly surrounded by land): *a sandy cove*

covenant /ˈkʌvənənt/ *noun* [C] a promise to sb, or a legal agreement, especially one to pay a regular amount of money to sb/sth ▸ **covenant** *verb* [T]: *All profits are covenanted to local charities.*

cover¹ 🔒 **A2** /ˈkʌvə(r)/ *verb*
- HIDE/PROTECT **1** [T] ~ **sb/sth (up/over) (with sth)** to put sth on or in front of sth to hide or protect it: *Could you cover the food and put it in the fridge?* ◇ *She couldn't look any more and covered her eyes.* ◇ *I covered the floor with newspaper before I started painting.* ◇ (*figurative*) *Paula laughed to cover* (= hide) *her embarrassment.* **OPP** uncover
- SPREAD OVER **2** [T] ~ **sth in/with sth** to lie or spread over the surface of sth: *A car went through the puddle and covered me with mud.* ◇ *Graffiti covered the walls.* ◇ *The eruption of the volcano covered the town in a layer of ash.* **3** [T] to fill or spread over a certain area: *The floods cover an area of about 15 000 square kilometres.*
- INCLUDE **4** [T] to include or to deal with sth: *All the papers covered the election in depth.* ◇ *The course covered both British and European history.*
- TRAVEL **5** [T] to travel a certain distance: *We covered about 500 kilometres that day.*
- BE ENOUGH MONEY **6** [T] to be enough money for sth: *We'll give you some money to cover your expenses.*
- IN INSURANCE **7** [T] ~ **sb/sth against/for sth** to protect sb/sth by insurance: *The insurance policy covers us for any damage to our property.*
- DO SB'S JOB **8** [I] ~ **(for sb)** to do sb's job while they are away from work: *Matt's phoned in sick so we'll have to find somebody to cover (for him).*
IDM **cover the cost (of sth)** to have or make enough money to pay for sth
PHR V **cover sth up** to prevent people hearing about a mistake or sth bad: *The police have been accused of trying to cover up the facts of the case.* **cover up for sb** to hide a person's mistakes or crimes in order to protect them

cover² 🔒 **B1** /ˈkʌvə(r)/ *noun*
- PROTECTION **1** [C] something that is put on or over sth, especially in order to protect it: *disposable cups with plastic covers* ◇ *a duvet cover* **2** [U] protection from the weather, damage, etc: *When the storm started we had to take cover in a shop doorway.* ◇ *When the gunfire started everyone ran for cover.* **SYN** shelter¹
- OF A BOOK, ETC. **3** [C] the outside part of a book or magazine: *I read the magazine from cover to cover* (= from beginning to end).
- INSURANCE **4** (*BrE*) (*AmE* coverage) [U] ~ **(against sth)** insurance against sth, so that if sth bad happens you get money or help in return: *The policy provides cover against theft.*
- ON A BED **5** the covers [pl.] the sheets, etc. on a bed
- HIDING STH **6** [C, usually sing., U] ~ **(for sth)** something that hides what sb is really doing: *The whole company was just a cover for all kinds of criminal activities.* ◇ *police officers working under cover*
- FOR A JOB **7** [U] doing sb's job for them while they are away from work: *Joanne's off next week so we'll have to arrange cover.*
IDM **under (the) cover of sth** hidden by sth: *They attacked under cover of darkness.*

coverage 🔒+ **B2** 🌐 /ˈkʌvərɪdʒ/ *noun* [U] **1** (**ARTS AND MEDIA**) the act or amount of reporting on an event in the media: *TV coverage of the Olympic Games was excellent.* **2** the amount or quality of information included in a book, magazine, etc: *The grammar section provides coverage of all the most problematic areas.* **3** (*AmE*) = COVER² (4)

coveralls /ˈkʌvərɔːlz/ (*AmE*) = OVERALL² (2)

covered 🔒 **B1** /ˈkʌvəd/ *adj.* **1** ~ **in/with sth** having a layer or a large amount of sth on sb/sth: *covered in mud/sweat/dust* ◇ *nuts covered with chocolate* **2** having a cover, especially a roof: *a covered shopping centre*

covering /ˈkʌvərɪŋ/ *noun* [C] something that covers the surface of sth: *There was a thick covering of dust over everything.*

covering letter (*BrE*) (*AmE* ˈcover letter) *noun* [C] a letter that you send with sth explaining the contents of the document, etc. that you are sending

covert /ˈkʌvət, ˈkəʊvɜːt/ *adj.* (*formal*) done secretly: *a covert police operation* **OPP** overt ▸ **covertly** *adv.*

cover-up *noun* [C] an act of preventing sth bad or dishonest from becoming known: *Several newspapers claimed that there had been a government cover-up.*

covet /ˈkʌvət/ *verb* [T] (*formal*) to want to have sth very much (especially sth that belongs to sb else)

Covid-19 (*also* **COVID-19**) /ˌkəʊvɪd naɪnˈtiːn/ *noun* [U] (**HEALTH**) a disease caused by a CORONAVIRUS that was first reported in 2019 and became a PANDEMIC

cow 🔒 **A1** /kaʊ/ *noun* [C] **1** a large female animal that is kept on farms to produce milk or beef: *to milk a cow* ◇ *a herd of cows* **2** (*slang*) an offensive word for a woman **3** the adult female of certain large animals, for example elephants

---

▼ VOCABULARY BUILDING

A male cow is called a **bull** and a young cow is a **calf**. However, **cows** is often used to talk about both male and female animals. A group of cows is a **herd**. An **ox** is a male cow that cannot produce young and which is used for pulling heavy loads. Cows and bulls that are kept as farm animals can be called **cattle**. When cows make a noise, they **moo**.

---

coward /ˈkaʊəd/ *noun* [C] a person who has no courage and is afraid in dangerous or unpleasant situations ▸ **cowardly** *adj.*

cowardice /ˈkaʊədɪs/ *noun* [U] a lack of courage; behaviour that shows that you are afraid

cowboy /ˈkaʊbɔɪ/ *noun* [C] **1** a man whose job is to look after cows (usually on a horse) in certain parts of the US **2** (*BrE, informal*) a person in business who is not honest or who does work of bad quality

cower /ˈkaʊə(r)/ *verb* [I] to move back or into a low position because of fear: *The dog cowered under the table when the storm started.*

cowl /kaʊl/ *noun* [C] (**RELIGION**) a covering for the head that is worn especially by a MONK (= a member of a religious group of men)

cowling /ˈkaʊlɪŋ/ *noun* [C] a metal cover for an engine, especially on an aircraft ⊃ picture at **airliner**

co-worker *noun* [C] a person that sb works with, doing the same kind of job **SYN** colleague

coy /kɔɪ/ *adj.* **1** pretending to be shy or innocent: *She lifted her head a little and gave him a coy smile.* **2** not wanting to give information about sth or to answer questions that tell people too much about you: *Don't be coy. Tell me how much you earn.* ▸ **coyly** *adv.*

CPR /ˌsiː piː ˈɑː(r)/ *noun* [U] (**MEDICINE**) breathing air into the mouth of an unconscious person and pressing on their chest to keep them alive by sending air around their body (the abbreviation for 'cardiopulmonary resuscitation')

CPU /ˌsiː piː ˈjuː/ *abbr.* (**COMPUTING**) **central processing unit** (the part of a computer that controls all the other parts of the system)

crab /kræb/ *noun* **1** [C] a sea animal with a flat shell and ten legs that moves SIDEWAYS (= towards the side). The front two legs have PINCERS (= long curved points) on them. ⊃ picture at **animal 2** [U] the meat from a crab

crack¹ ʕ+ B2 /kræk/ *verb*
• BREAK **1** [I, T] to break or to make sth break so that a line appears on the surface, but without breaking into pieces: *Don't put boiling water into that glass — it'll crack.* ◇ *The stone cracked the window but didn't break it.* **2** [T] to break sth open: *Crack two eggs into a bowl.*
• MAKE A SOUND **3** [I, T] to make a sudden loud, sharp sound; to cause sth to make this sound: *to crack a whip/your knuckles* ◇ *He heard the twigs crack under his feet.*
• HIT **4** [T] to hit a part of your body against sth; to hit sb with sth: *She stood up and cracked her head on the cupboard door.* ◇ *She cracked the thief over the head with her umbrella.*
• UNDER PRESSURE **5** [I] to no longer be able to deal with pressure and so lose control: *He cracked under the strain of all his problems.*
• OF THE VOICE **6** [I] (used about sb's voice) to suddenly change in a way that is not controlled: *Her voice cracked as she spoke about her parents' death.*
• FIND A SOLUTION **7** [T] (*informal*) to solve a problem: *to crack a code* ◇ *The police have cracked an international drug-smuggling ring.*
• JOKE **8** [T] to tell or make a joke: *Stop **cracking jokes** and do some work!*
IDM **get cracking** (*BrE, informal*) to start doing sth immediately: *I have to finish this job today so I'd better get cracking.*
PHR V **crack down (on sb/sth)** (used about people in authority) to start dealing strictly with bad or illegal behaviour: *The police have started to crack down on street crime.* **crack up** (*informal*) **1** (**HEALTH**) to be unable to deal with pressure and so lose control and become mentally ill: *He cracked up when his wife left him.* **2** to suddenly start laughing, especially when you should be serious

crack² ʕ+ B2 /kræk/ *noun*
• BREAK **1** [C] a line on the surface of sth where it has broken, but not into separate pieces: *a pane of glass with a crack in it* ◇ (*figurative*) *They had always seemed happy together, but then cracks began to appear in their relationship.* ⊃ picture at **plate tectonics**
• OPENING **2** [C] a narrow opening: *a crack in the curtains*
• SOUND **3** [C] a sudden loud, sharp sound
• HIT **4** [C] a hard hit on a part of the body: *He got a nasty crack on the head from a golf ball.*
• JOKE **5** [C] (*informal*) a funny, often critical, comment; a joke: *She **made a crack** about his bald head and he got angry.*
• DRUG **6** (*also* ˌcrack coˈcaine*) [U] a dangerous and illegal drug that some people take for pleasure and cannot then stop taking: *a crack addict*
IDM **the crack of dawn** (*informal*) very early in the morning **have a crack (at sth/doing sth)** (*informal*) to try to do sth: *I'm not sure how to play but I'll have a crack at it.*

crack³ /kræk/ *adj.* (used about soldiers or sports players) very well trained and having a lot of skill: ***crack troops*** ◇ *He's **a crack shot** (= very accurate at shooting) with a rifle.*

crackdown /ˈkrækdaʊn/ *noun* [C] **~ (on sth)** action to stop bad or illegal behaviour: *50 people have been arrested in a police crackdown on street crime.*

cracked /krækt/ *adj.* damaged with lines in its surface but not completely broken

cracker /ˈkrækə(r)/ *noun* [C] **1** a thin dry biscuit that is often eaten with cheese **2** (*also* **Christmas cracker**) a CARDBOARD (= very thick paper) tube covered in coloured paper and containing a small present. Crackers are pulled apart by two people, each holding one end, at Christmas parties. They make a loud noise as they break. **3** (*BrE, informal*) a very good example of sth: *That story he told was a real cracker.*

crackle /ˈkrækl/ *verb* [I] to make a series of short sharp sounds: *The radio started to crackle and then it stopped working.* ▸ **crackle** *noun* [sing.]: *the crackle of dry wood burning*

cradle¹ /ˈkreɪdl/ *noun* [C] a small bed for a baby that can be pushed gently from side to side

cradle² /ˈkreɪdl/ *verb* [T] to hold sb/sth carefully and gently in your arms

craft¹ ʕ+ B2 /krɑːft/ *noun* **1** [C, U] a job or an activity for which you need skill with your hands: *an arts and crafts exhibition* ◇ *I studied **craft and design** at school.* ⊃ look at **handicraft 2** [C] any job or activity for which you need skill: *He regards acting as a craft.* **3** [C] (*pl.* craft) (*formal*) a boat, an aircraft or a SPACECRAFT

craft² ʕ+ C1 /krɑːft/ *verb* [T, usually passive] to make sth using special skills, especially with your hands: *All the furniture is crafted from natural materials.*

craftsman /ˈkrɑːftsmən/ (*pl.* -men /-mən/) (*also* **craftsperson** /ˈkrɑːftspɜːsn/, *pl.* -people /-piːpl/) *noun* [C] a person who makes things with a lot of skill, especially with their hands SYN **artisan**

craftsmanship /ˈkrɑːftsmənʃɪp/ *noun* [U] the skill used by sb to make sth of high quality with their hands

crafty /ˈkrɑːfti/ *adj.* (craftier; craftiest) clever at getting or achieving things, especially by using unfair or dishonest methods ▸ **craftily** /-tɪli/ *adv.*

crag /kræg/ *noun* [C] (**GEOGRAPHY**) a steep rough rock on a hill or mountain

craggy /ˈkrægi/ *adj.* (craggier; craggiest) **1** (**GEOGRAPHY**) having a lot of steep rough rock **2** (used about a man's face) strong and with deep lines, especially in an attractive way

cram /kræm/ *verb* (-mm-) **1** [T, I] **~ (sth) into/onto sth; ~ (sth) in** to push people or things into a small space; to move into a small space with the result that it is full: *I managed to cram all my clothes into the bag but I couldn't close it.* ◇ (*figurative*) *We only spent two days in Rome but we managed to cram a lot of sightseeing in.* ◇ *He only had a small car but they all managed to cram in.* **2** [I] **~ (for sth)** (*old-fashioned*) (**EDUCATION**) to study very hard and learn a lot in a short time before an exam SYN **swot¹**

crammed /kræmd/ *adj.* very or too full: *That book is crammed with useful information.*

cramp /kræmp/ *noun* [U, C] (**HEALTH**) a sudden pain that you get in a muscle, that makes it difficult to move

cramped /kræmpt/ *adj.* not having enough space: *The flat was terribly cramped with so many of us living there.*

cranberry /'krænbəri/ noun [C] (pl. -ies) a small round red fruit with a bitter sharp taste that is used in cooking

crane¹ /kreɪn/ noun [C] a large machine with a long metal arm that is used for moving or lifting heavy objects

crane² /kreɪn/ verb [I, T] to stretch your neck forward in order to see or hear sth: We all craned forward to get a better view.

crane

crane fly noun [C] a flying insect with very long legs

cranium /'kreɪniəm/ noun [C] (pl. craniums, crania /-niə/) (**ANATOMY**) the bone that forms the head and surrounds the brain **SYN** skull ⊃ picture at **body** ▶ cranial /-əl/ adj.

crank /kræŋk/ noun [C] **1** a person with strange ideas or who behaves in a strange way **2** (**ENGINEERING**) a bar and handle in the shape of an L that you pull or turn to produce movement in a machine, etc.

crankshaft /'kræŋkʃɑːft/ noun [C] a long straight piece of metal in a vehicle that connects the engine to the wheels and helps turn the engine's power into movement

cranny /'kræni/ noun [C] (pl. -ies) a small opening in a wall, rock, etc.
IDM every nook and cranny → NOOK

crash¹ ⓘ **B2** /kræʃ/ verb **1** [I, T] to have an accident in a vehicle; to drive a vehicle into sth: He braked too late and crashed into the car in front. ◊ She crashed her motorbike. **2** [I] to hit sth hard, making a loud noise: The tree crashed to the ground. **3** [I] to make a loud noise: I could hear thunder crashing outside. **4** [I] (**BUSINESS**, **FINANCE**) (used about money or business) to suddenly lose value or fail ⊃ note at **trend¹** **5** [I] (**COMPUTING**) (used about a computer) to suddenly stop working; to stop sth working: We lost the data when the computer crashed. ◊ The demand for tickets crashed the website.

crash² ⓘ **B2** /kræʃ/ noun [C] **1** a sudden loud noise made by sth breaking, hitting sth, etc: I heard a crash and ran outside. **2** an accident when a car or other vehicle hits sth and is damaged: She was injured in a serious car crash. ◊ a plane crash with no survivors **3** (used about money or business) a sudden fall in the value or price of sth: the stock market crash of 2020 **4** a sudden failure of a machine, especially a computer

crash³ /kræʃ/ adj. done in a very short period of time and involving a lot of work and effort: She did a **crash course** in Spanish before going to work in Madrid.

crash barrier noun [C] (BrE) a strong low fence or wall at the side of a road or between two halves of a major road

crash helmet noun [C] a hard hat worn by motorcycle riders, racing drivers, etc.

crash-land verb [I] if a plane **crash-lands** or a pilot **crash-lands** it, the pilot lands it roughly in an emergency, usually because it is damaged and cannot land normally ▶ crash-'landing noun [C]: to make a crash-landing

crass /kræs/ adj. stupid, showing that you have no sympathy and do not understand sth: It was a crass comment to make when he knew how upset she was.

crate /kreɪt/ noun [C] a large box in which goods are carried or stored

crater /'kreɪtə(r)/ noun [C] **1** (**GEOGRAPHY**, **GEOLOGY**) the hole in the top of a VOLCANO, through which hot gases and liquid rock are forced ⊃ picture at **volcano 2** a large hole in the ground caused by the explosion of a bomb or by sth large hitting it: The bomb left a large crater. ◊ a meteorite crater ◊ craters on the moon

cravat /krə'væt/ noun [C] a wide piece of cloth that some men tie around their neck and wear inside the COLLAR of their shirt

crave /kreɪv/ verb [I, T] ~ (for) sth to want and need to have sth very much

craving /'kreɪvɪŋ/ noun [C] ~ (for sth) a strong desire for sth

crawl¹ ⓘ+ **C1** /krɔːl/ verb [I] **1** to move slowly with your body on or close to the ground, or on your hands and knees: Their baby has just started to crawl. ◊ An insect crawled across the floor. **2** (used about vehicles) to move very slowly: The traffic crawls through the centre of town in the rush hour. **3** ~ (to sb) (informal) to be very polite or pleasant to sb in order to be liked or to gain sth: He only got promoted because he crawled to the manager.
IDM be crawling with sth to be completely full of or covered with unpleasant animals: The kitchen was crawling with insects. ◊ (figurative) The village is always crawling with tourists at this time of year.

crawl² /krɔːl/ noun **1** [sing.] a very slow speed: The traffic slowed to a crawl. **2** (often the crawl) [sing., U] (**SPORT**) a style of swimming that you do on your front. When you do **the crawl**, you move first one arm and then the other over your head, turn your face to one side so that you can breathe and kick up and down with your legs.

crayfish /'kreɪfɪʃ/ (especially BrE) (also crawfish /'krɔːfɪʃ/ especially in AmE) noun [C, U] (pl. crayfish, crawfish) a SHELLFISH that lives in rivers, lakes or the sea and that can be eaten. Crayfish are similar to LOBSTERS but smaller.

crayon /'kreɪən, 'kreɪɒn/ noun [C, U] (**ART**) a soft, thick, coloured pencil that is used for drawing or writing, especially by children ▶ crayon verb [I, T]

craze /kreɪz/ noun [C] ~ (for sth) **1** a strong interest in sth, that usually only lasts for a short time: There was a craze for that kind of music last year. **2** something that a lot of people are very interested in

crazy ⓘ **A2** /'kreɪzi/ adj. (crazier; craziest) (informal) **1** not sensible; stupid: You must be crazy to turn down such a wonderful offer. **2** very angry: She goes crazy when people criticize her. ◊ That noise is driving me crazy. **3** very enthusiastic or excited about sth: The fans went crazy when their team scored the first goal. ◊ He's football-crazy. **4** ~ about sb/sth liking sb/sth very much; in love with sb: I've been crazy about him since the first time I saw him. **5** mentally ill ▶ crazily /-zɪli/ adv. ▶ craziness noun [U]

creak /kriːk/ verb [I] to make the noise of wood bending or of sth not moving smoothly: The floorboards creaked when I walked across the room. ▶ creak noun [C] ▶ creaky adj. (creakier; creakiest): creaky stairs

cream¹ ⓘ **A1** /kriːm/ noun **1** [U] the thick white or pale yellow liquid that rises to the top of milk: coffee with cream ◊ whipped cream (= cream that has been beaten) **2** [C, U] a substance that you rub into your skin to keep it soft or as a medical treatment: (an) antiseptic cream ⊃ picture at **health 3** [U] a pale colour between yellow and white **4** the cream [sing.] the best part of sth or the best people in a group

cream² ⓘ **B1** /kriːm/ adj. between yellow and white in colour

cream[3] /kriːm/ *verb*
PHR V **cream sb/sth off** to take away the best people or part from sth for a particular purpose: *The big clubs cream off the country's best young players.*

creamy /ˈkriːmi/ *adj.* (creamier; creamiest) **1** containing cream; thick and smooth like cream: *a creamy sauce* **2** between yellow and white in colour: *creamy skin*

crease[1] /kriːs/ *noun* [C] **1** an untidy line on paper, material, a piece of clothing, etc. that should not be there: *Your shirt needs ironing. It's full of creases.* ◇ *When I unrolled the poster, there was a crease in it.* **2** a tidy straight line that you make in sth, for example when you fold it: *He had a sharp crease in his trousers.*

crease[2] /kriːs/ *verb* [I, T] to get CREASES; to make sth get CREASES: *I creased my skirt by sitting on the floor.* ◇ *Crease the paper carefully down the middle.*

create ⟨A1⟩ **⊙** /kriˈeɪt/ *verb* [T] **1** to cause sth new to happen or exist: *a plan to create new jobs in the area* ◇ *The chef has created a new dish.* ➷ note at **make**[1], **organization 2** to produce a particular feeling

creation ⟨B2⟩ **Ⓦ** /kriˈeɪʃn/ *noun* **1** [U] the act of causing sth new to happen or exist: *the creation of new independent states* **2** (*usually* the Creation) [sing.] (**RELIGION**) the act of making the whole universe, as described in the Bible **3** [C] something new that sb has made or produced

creative ⟨A2⟩ **Ⓦ** /kriˈeɪtɪv/ *adj.* **1** using skill or imagination to make or do new things: *She's a fantastic designer — she's so creative.* **2** connected with producing new things: *His creative life went on until he was well over 80.* ▸ **creatively** *adv.*

creativity ⟨+ B2⟩ /ˌkriːeɪˈtɪvəti/ *noun* [U] the ability to make or produce new things using skill or imagination: *We want teaching that encourages children's creativity.*

creator ⟨+ C1⟩ /kriˈeɪtə(r)/ *noun* [C] a person who makes or produces sth new

creature ⟨B2⟩ /ˈkriːtʃə(r)/ *noun* [C] a living thing such as an animal, a bird, a fish or an insect, but not a plant: *sea creatures*

crèche /kreʃ/ *noun* [C] a place where small children are looked after while their parents are working, shopping, etc.

credentials /krəˈdenʃlz/ *noun* [pl.] **1** the qualities, experience, etc. that make sb suitable for sth: *He has the perfect credentials for the job.* **2** documents that prove that you have the training, education, etc. necessary to do sth, or that you are who you say you are

credibility ⟨+ C1⟩ /ˌkredəˈbɪləti/ *noun* [U] the quality that sb has that makes people believe or trust them: *The prime minister had lost all credibility and had to resign.*

credible ⟨+ C1⟩ /ˈkredəbl/ *adj.* **1** that you can believe: *It's hardly credible that such a thing could happen without him knowing it.* **OPP** **incredible 2** that seems possible: *We need to think of a credible alternative to nuclear energy.* **SYN** **viable**

credit[1] ⟨A2⟩ /ˈkredɪt/ *noun*
- PAYING LATER **1** [U] (**FINANCE**) a way of buying goods or services and not paying for them until later: *I bought the TV on credit.*
- MONEY BORROWED **2** [C, U] (**FINANCE**) a sum of money that a bank, etc. lends to sb: *The company was not able to get any further credit and went bankrupt.*
- MONEY IN A BANK **3** [U] (**FINANCE**) having money in an account at a bank: *No bank charges are made if your account remains in credit.* **4** [C] (**FINANCE**) a payment made into an account at a bank: *There have been several credits to her account over the last month.* **OPP** **debit**[1]
- MONEY PAID IN ADVANCE **5** [U] the right to use a service up to a certain limit, paid for in advance: *My phone's run out of credit.*
- PRAISE **6** [U] an act of saying that sb has done sth well: *He got all the credit for the success of the project.* ◇ *I can't take any credit; the others did all the work.* ◇ *She didn't do very well but at least give her credit for trying.*
- PERSON **7** [sing.] **a ~ to sb/sth** a person or thing that you should be proud of: *She is a credit to her school.*
- AT UNIVERSITY **8** [C] (*AmE*) (**EDUCATION**) a part of a course at a college or university; a part of a course that a student has completed successfully: *The credits she's earning count towards her high school diploma.*
- IN A FILM/PROGRAMME **9** the credits [pl.] (**ARTS AND MEDIA**) the list of the names of the people who made a film or TV programme, shown at the beginning or end of the film/programme
IDM **do sb credit** (used about sb's qualities or achievements) to be so good that people should be proud of them: *Her courage and optimism do her credit.* **have sth to your credit** to have finished sth that is successful: *He has three bestselling novels to his credit.* **(be) to sb's credit** making sb deserve praise or respect: *The company, to its credit, apologized and refunded my money.*

credit[2] ⟨B2⟩ /ˈkredɪt/ *verb* [T] **1** (**FINANCE**) to add money to an account: *Has the payment been credited to my bank account yet?* **2 ~ sb/sth with sth; ~ sth to sb/sth** to believe or say that sb/sth has a particular quality or has done sth well: *Of course I wouldn't do such a stupid thing — credit me with a bit more sense than that!* ◇ *He credited his success to a lot of hard work.* **3** (especially in negative sentences and questions) to believe sth: *I simply cannot credit that he has made the same mistake again!*

creditable /ˈkredɪtəbl/ *adj.* of a quite good standard that cannot be criticized, though not excellent

ˈcredit agency (*BrE*) (*AmE* ˈcredit bureau) *noun* [C] (**FINANCE**) a company that collects information that helps credit card companies, banks, etc. decide how much money people can afford to borrow

ˈcredit card *noun* [C] (**FINANCE**) a small plastic card that you can use to buy goods or services and pay for them later: *Can I pay by credit card?* ◇ *He put it on his credit card* (= paid for it using his credit card). ➷ look at **cash card**, **debit card**

ˈcredit crunch *noun* [sing.] (**ECONOMICS, FINANCE**) a time when a country's economic situation is bad and it becomes difficult and expensive to borrow money

ˈcredit note *noun* [C] (*BrE*) a letter that a shop gives you when you have returned sth and that allows you to have goods of the same value in exchange

creditor /ˈkredɪtə(r)/ *noun* [C] (**FINANCE**) a person or company from whom you have borrowed money

ˈcredit rating *noun* [C] (**FINANCE**) a judgement made by a bank, etc. about how likely sb is to pay back money that they borrow, and how safe it is to lend money to them

creed /kriːd/ *noun* [C] (**RELIGION**) a set of beliefs or principles (especially religious ones)

creek /kriːk/ *noun* [C] (**GEOGRAPHY**) **1** (*BrE*) a narrow piece of water where the sea flows into the land **2** (*AmE*) a small river or stream

creep¹ ⟨+ **C1** /kriːp/ *verb* [I] (used with an adverb or a preposition) (*pt, pp* crept /krept/) **1** to move very quietly and carefully so that nobody will notice you: *The cat crept silently towards the bird.* **2** to move forward slowly: *The traffic was only creeping along.* **IDM** make your flesh creep → FLESH
PHR V creep in | creep into sth to begin to appear: *All sorts of changes are beginning to creep into the education system.*

creep² /kriːp/ *noun* [C] (*informal*) **1** a person that you find very unpleasant **2** a person who tries too hard to be liked by people, especially people in authority
IDM give sb the creeps (*informal*) to make sb feel frightened or nervous

creeper /ˈkriːpə(r)/ *noun* [C] a plant that grows up trees or walls or along the ground

creepy /ˈkriːpi/ *adj.* (creepier; creepiest) (*informal*) that makes you feel nervous or frightened **SYN** spooky

cremate /krəˈmeɪt/ *verb* [T, often passive] to burn the body of a dead person as part of a FUNERAL service ▶ cremation /-ˈmeɪʃn/ *noun* [C, U]

crematorium /ˌkreməˈtɔːriəm/ *noun* [C] (*pl.* -toria /-riə/, -toriums) a building in which the bodies of dead people are burned

Creole /ˈkriːəʊl/ (*also* creole) *noun* **1** [C] (**SOCIAL STUDIES**) a person who belongs to both a European and an African human group, especially one who lives in the West Indies **2** [C] (**SOCIAL STUDIES**) a person whose ANCESTORS (= relatives who lived a long time ago) were among the first Europeans to live in the Caribbean and South America, or among the first French or Spanish people to live in the southern states of the US: *the Creole cooking of New Orleans* **3** [C, U] (**LANGUAGE**) a language that was originally a mixture of a European language and a local, especially African, language

creosote /ˈkriːəsəʊt/ *noun* [U] a thick brown liquid that is painted onto wood to protect it from rain, etc. ▶ creosote *verb* [T]

crêpe (*also* crepe) /kreɪp/ *noun* **1** [U] a type of light thin cloth, made especially from cotton or silk, with a surface that is covered in lines and folds: *a crêpe bandage* **2** [C] a thin PANCAKE (= a flat cake made of flour, eggs and milk and fried in a pan) **3** [U] a type of strong rubber with a rough surface, used for making the bottoms of shoes: *crêpe-soled shoes*

crept /krept/ past tense, past participle of **creep¹**

crescendo /krəˈʃendəʊ/ *noun* [C, U] (*pl.* -os) (**MUSIC**) a noise or piece of music that gets louder and louder **OPP** diminuendo

crescent /ˈkresnt, ˈkreznt/ *noun* [C] **1** a curved shape that is pointed at both ends, like the moon in its first and last stages **2** (often in street names) a curved street with a row of houses on it

cress /kres/ *noun* [U] a small plant with very small green leaves that does not need to be cooked and is eaten in salads and sandwiches

crest /krest/ *noun* [C] **1** a group of feathers on the top of a bird's head ⊃ picture at **animal 2** (**HISTORY**) a design used as the symbol of a particular family, organization, etc., especially one that has a long history: *the family/school crest* **3** [usually sing.] (**GEOGRAPHY**) the top part of a hill or wave: *surfers riding the crest of the wave* ⊃ picture at **wave¹**

crestfallen /ˈkrestfɔːlən/ *adj.* disappointed or sad because you have failed and did not expect to

Cretaceous /krɪˈteɪʃəs/ *adj.* (**GEOLOGY**) connected with the period between around 146 to 65 million years ago, when DINOSAURS lived

crevasse /krəˈvæs/ *noun* [C] (**GEOGRAPHY**) a deep CRACK in a very thick layer of ice

crevice /ˈkrevɪs/ *noun* [C] a narrow CRACK in a rock, wall, etc.

crew ⟨ **B2** /kruː/ *noun* [C + sing./pl. verb] **1** all the people who work on a ship, an aircraft, etc: *The captain and crew were rescued after the ship ran aground.* ◊ *a plane carrying 271 passengers and crew* **2** a group of people who work together: *a camera crew* (= people who film things for television, etc.) ◊ *Police, fire and ambulance crews are at the scene.*

crew cut *noun* [C] a HAIRSTYLE for men in which the hair is cut very short

crib¹ /krɪb/ *noun* [C] (*especially AmE*) = COT (1)

crib² /krɪb/ *verb* [I, T] (-bb-) ~ (sth) (from/off sb) to copy sb else's work and pretend it is your own

crick /krɪk/ *noun* [sing.] a sudden painful stiff feeling in the muscles of your neck or back ▶ crick *verb* [T]: *I've cricked my neck.*

cricket /ˈkrɪkɪt/ *noun* **1** [U] (**SPORT**) a game played on grass by two teams of eleven players. Players score points (called RUNS) by hitting the ball with a wooden BAT (= a piece of wood) and running between two sets of VERTICAL wooden sticks, called STUMPS: *a cricket match/team/club/ball* ⊃ picture at **sport 2** [C] an insect that makes a loud noise by rubbing its wings together

cricketer /ˈkrɪkɪtə(r)/ *noun* [C] (**SPORT**) a person who plays CRICKET

crime ⟨ **A2** /kraɪm/ *noun* **1** [C] (**LAW**) something that is illegal and that people are punished for, for example by being sent to prison: *to commit a crime* ⊃ look at **cybercrime** ⊃ note at **criminal¹ 2** [U] (**LAW**) illegal behaviour or activities: *There has been an increase in car crime recently.* ◊ *to fight crime* **3** (usually a crime) [sing.] (*informal*) something that is morally wrong: *It is a crime to waste food when people are starving.*

▼ COLLOCATIONS

crime

A crime is an act that is **illegal** or **against the law**. It is the job of the police to **investigate** a crime and try to **solve** it: *The public helped the police to solve the murder case.* When the police have enough **evidence** they can **arrest a suspect** and **charge him/her with** a crime: *A suspect was arrested this morning and charged with assault and robbery.* A **suspect** can **admit**, **confess to** or **deny the charge**: *All three men have denied assault.* ◊ *She admitted 3 charges of theft.* ◊ *He confessed to the murder.* **The accused** or the **defendant** (= the person the police have charged) must **stand trial** in **court** where he/she **pleads guilty** or **not guilty**: *The accused is charged with gross indecency and will stand trial on 3 April.* ◊ *Do you plead guilty or not guilty?* The defendant may be **acquitted** (= allowed to go free) or **found guilty** or **not guilty**: *The driver was acquitted of manslaughter.* ◊ *She was found guilty of arson.* A defendant who is **found guilty** is **convicted** and then **sentenced to** a **term of imprisonment** or some other form of punishment: *He was convicted of fraud.* ◊ *She was sentenced to life imprisonment.*

crime wave *noun* [sing.] a sudden increase in the number of crimes that are committed

criminal¹ ⟨ **A2** /ˈkrɪmɪnl/ *noun* [C] a person who has done sth illegal

criminal

A person who **commits a crime** is a **criminal**. Different types of criminal have different names. A **murderer** commits **murder** (= kills sb). A **thief steals from** a person or a place and commits **theft**: *A thief broke into our car and stole the radio.* A **robber robs** a person or place, often with violence or threats, and commits **robbery**: *A man was robbed of his wallet yesterday in Woodstock Road.* A **burglar breaks into** a property, committing **burglary**: *There was a burglary at the bookshop on Monday and the burglar escaped through a small window in a storeroom.* ◇ *We were broken into while we were away on holiday.* A **shoplifter** goes into a shop when it is open and takes things without paying. A **mugger mugs** sb in the street and steals from them using violence or threats: *She had been mugged in the street in broad daylight.* A **terrorist** commits **acts of terrorism**: *Terrorists attempted to blow up the plane.* A **vandal** commits **acts of vandalism** (= damage to property for no reason). A **kidnapper kidnaps** sb and **holds him/her to ransom**: *Three tourists were kidnapped and held to ransom for $30 000.*

criminal[2] 🔒 **B1** /ˈkrɪmɪnl/ *adj.* **1** [only before noun] connected with crime: *Deliberate damage to public property is a criminal offence.* ◇ **criminal law** **2** morally wrong: *a criminal waste of taxpayers' money*

criminality /ˌkrɪmɪˈnæləti/ *noun* [U] (**LAW**) the fact of people being involved in crime; criminal acts: *There is little evidence that juvenile criminality is increasing at a very much greater rate than crime in general.*

criminal 'law *noun* [U] (**LAW**) law that deals with the punishment of people who commit crimes: *This is an offence **under criminal law** and is punishable by three years in prison.* ⊃ look at **civil law**

criminally /ˈkrɪmɪnəli/ *adv.* (**LAW**) according to the laws that deal with crime: *criminally insane*

criminology /ˌkrɪmɪˈnɒlədʒi/ *noun* [U] the scientific study of crime and criminals ▸ **criminological** /ˌkrɪmɪnəˈlɒdʒɪkl/ *adj.* ▸ **criminologist** /ˌkrɪmɪˈnɒlədʒɪst/ *noun* [C]

crimson /ˈkrɪmzn/ *adj.* dark red in colour ▸ **crimson** *noun* [U]

cringe /krɪndʒ/ *verb* [I] **1** to feel embarrassed: *awful family photos that make you cringe* **2** to move away from sb/sth because you are frightened: *The dog cringed in terror when the man raised his arm.*

crinkle /ˈkrɪŋkl/ *verb* [I, T] ~ **(sth) (up)** to have, or to make sth have, thin folds or lines in it: *He crinkled the silver paper up into a ball.* ▸ **crinkly** /ˈkrɪŋkli/ *adj.*: *crinkly material*

cripple /ˈkrɪpl/ *verb* [T, usually passive] **1** (**HEALTH**) to damage sb's body so that they are no longer able to walk or move normally: *to be **crippled with** arthritis* **2** to seriously damage or harm sb/sth: *The recession has crippled the motor industry.*

crippling /ˈkrɪplɪŋ/ *adj.* that causes serious damage or has a very bad effect: *They had crippling debts and had to sell their house.*

crisis 🔒 **B2** /ˈkraɪsɪs/ *noun* [C, U] (*pl.* **crises** /ˈkraɪsiːz/) a time of great danger or difficulty; the moment when things change and either improve or get worse: *the international crisis caused by the invasion* ◇ *a friend you can rely on in times of crisis* ◇ *The economy is in crisis, with 50% of young people unemployed.*

crisp[1] /krɪsp/ *adj.* **1** (*also* **crispy**) pleasantly hard and dry: *Store the biscuits in a tin to keep them crisp.* **2** firm and fresh or new: *a crisp salad/apple* ◇ *a crisp cotton dress* **3** (used about the air or weather) cold and dry: *a crisp winter morning* **4** (used about the way sb speaks)

quick, clear but not very friendly: *a crisp reply* ▸ **crisply** *adv.*: *'I disagree,' she said crisply.*

crisp[2] /krɪsp/ (*BrE*) (*AmE* **chip, po'tato chip**) *noun* [C] a very thin, round piece of potato that is fried in oil, then dried and eaten cold. Crisps are sold in bags and have salt on them or are made to taste of many different foods: *a packet of crisps*

criss-cross /ˈkrɪs krɒs/ *adj.* with many straight lines that cross over each other: *a criss-cross pattern* ▸ **criss-cross** *verb* [I, T]: *Many footpaths criss-cross the countryside.*

criterion 🔒 **B2** 🅦 /kraɪˈtɪəriən/ *noun* [C] (*pl.* **criteria** /-riə/) the standard that you use when you make a decision or form an opinion about sb/sth: *The main criterion is value for money.* ◇ *What are the criteria for deciding who gets a place on the course?*

critic 🔒 **B2** /ˈkrɪtɪk/ *noun* [C] **1** ~ **of sth** a person who says what is bad or wrong with sb/sth: *He is a long-standing critic of the council's transport policy.* **2** (**ARTS AND MEDIA**) a person whose job is to give their opinion about a play, film, book, work of art, etc: *a film/restaurant/art critic*

critical 🔒 **B2** 🅞 /ˈkrɪtɪkl/ *adj.* **1** ~ **(of sb/sth)** saying what is wrong with sb/sth: *The report was very critical of safety standards on the railways.* **2** [only before noun] (**ARTS AND MEDIA**) describing the good and bad points of a play, film, book, work of art, etc: *a critical guide to this month's new films* **3** dangerous or serious: *The patient is **in a critical condition**.* **4** very important; at a time when things can suddenly become better or worse: *The talks between the two leaders have **reached a critical stage**.* ⊃ note at **essential** ▸ **critically** 🔒+ **B2** 🅦 /-kli/ *adv.*: *a critically ill patient* ◇ *a critically important decision*

criticism 🔒 **B2** /ˈkrɪtɪsɪzəm/ *noun* **1** [C, U] ~ **(of sth)** (an expression of) what you think is bad about sb/sth: *My main criticism of the plan is that it is too expensive.* ◇ *The council has **come in for** severe criticism over the plans.* **2** [U] (**ARTS AND MEDIA**) the act of describing the good and bad points of a play, film, book, work of art, etc: *literary criticism*

criticize 🔒 **B2** 🅦 (*BrE also* -**ise**) /ˈkrɪtɪsaɪz/ *verb* [I, T] ~ **(sb/sth) (for sth/doing sth)** to say what is bad or wrong with sb/sth: *The doctor was criticized for not sending the patient to hospital.* ◇ *Stop criticizing!* **OPP** **praise**[1]

critique 🔒+ **C1** /krɪˈtiːk/ *noun* [C] a piece of writing that describes the good and bad points of sb/sth

croak /krəʊk/ *verb* [I] to make a rough low sound like a frog; to speak in a rough low voice ▸ **croak** *noun* [C]

crochet /ˈkrəʊʃeɪ/ *noun* [U] a way of making clothes, etc. by using wool or cotton and a special thick needle with a HOOK at one end ▸ **crochet** *verb* [I, T] ⊃ look at **knit**

crockery /ˈkrɒkəri/ *noun* [U] cups, plates and dishes ⊃ look at **cutlery**

crocodile /ˈkrɒkədaɪl/ *noun* [C] a large REPTILE with a long tail and a big mouth with sharp teeth. Crocodiles live in rivers and lakes in hot countries. ⊃ look at **alligator**

'crocodile clip (*especially BrE*) (*also* **alligator clip** *especially in AmE*) *noun* [C] an object with sharp teeth used for

crocodile clip/ alligator clip

holding things together. It is held closed by a spring that you SQUEEZE to open: *Use the crocodile clips to attach the cables to the battery.*

crocus /ˈkrəʊkəs/ *noun* [C] a small yellow, purple or white flower that appears in early spring

crofting /ˈkrɒftɪŋ/ *noun* [U] (**AGRICULTURE**) a system of farming on a small scale in Scotland: *In the Scottish Highlands people struggled to make a living from crofting.*

croissant /ˈkwæsɒ̃/ *noun* [C] a type of bread roll, shaped in a curve, that is often eaten with butter for breakfast

crony /ˈkrəʊni/ *noun* [C] (*pl.* -ies) (*informal*) (often used in a critical way) a friend

crook /krʊk/ *noun* [C] **1** (*informal*) a dishonest person; a criminal **2** a bend or curve in sth: *the crook of your arm* (= the inside of your ELBOW)

crooked /ˈkrʊkɪd/ *adj.* **1** not straight or even: *That picture is crooked.* ◊ *crooked teeth* **2** (*informal*) not honest: *a crooked accountant*

crop¹ 🔊 B2 /krɒp/ *noun* **1** [C] (**AGRICULTURE**) all the grain, fruit, vegetables, etc. of one type that are grown on a farm at one time: *a crop of apples* ○ note at **agriculture 2** [C] (**AGRICULTURE**) plants that are grown on farms for food: *Rice and soya beans are the main crops here.* **3** [sing.] a number of people or things that have appeared at the same time: *the recent crop of movies about aliens*

crop² /krɒp/ *verb* (-pp-) **1** [T] to cut sth very short: *cropped hair* **2** [T] to cut off part of a photo or picture **3** [I] (**AGRICULTURE**) to produce a crop
PHRV **crop up** to appear suddenly, when you are not expecting it: *We should have finished this work yesterday but some problems cropped up.*

crop dusting *noun* [U] (**AGRICULTURE**) the practice of SPRAYING crops with chemicals such as PESTICIDES (= substances used for killing insects, etc. that eat food crops), especially from a plane

cropper /ˈkrɒpə(r)/ *noun*
IDM **come a cropper** (*informal*) **1** to fall over or have an accident **2** to fail

croquet /ˈkrəʊkeɪ/ *noun* [U] a game that you play on grass. When you play **croquet**, you use MALLETS (= sticks with a block of wood at one end) to hit balls through HOOPS (= curved pieces of metal).

cross¹ 🔊 A2 /krɒs/ *noun* **1** [C] a mark that you make by drawing one line across another (X or +). The sign is used for showing the position of sth, for showing that sth is not correct, etc: *I drew a cross on the map to show where our house is.* ◊ *Incorrect answers were marked with a cross.* ○ look at **noughts and crosses 2 the Cross** [sing.] (**RELIGION**) the two pieces of wood in the shape of a cross on which people were killed as a punishment in the past, or sth in this shape that is used as a symbol of the Christian religion **3** [C] (**RELIGION**) something in the shape of a cross that is used as a symbol of the Christian religion: *She wore a gold cross round her neck.* ○ look at **crucifix 4** [C, usually sing.] **~(between A and B)** something (especially a plant or an animal) that is a mixture of two different types of thing: *a fruit that is a cross between a peach and an apricot* **5** [C] (**SPORT**) (in sports such as football) a kick or hit of the ball that goes across the field rather than up or down it

cross² 🔊 A2 /krɒs/ *verb*
• GO/PUT ACROSS **1** [I, T] **~(over) (sth) (from sth/to sth)** to go from one side of sth to the other: *to cross the road*

◊ *Where did you cross the border?* ◊ *Which of the runners crossed the finishing line first?* ◊ *She crossed over to the other side of the street.* **2** [I] (used about lines, roads, etc.) to pass across each other: *The two roads cross just north of the village.* **3** [T] to put sth across or over sth else: *to cross your arms*
• OPPOSE **4** [T] to make sb angry by refusing to do what they want you to do: *He's an important man. It could be dangerous to cross him.*
• MIX **5** [T] **~ sth with sth** (**BIOLOGY**) to produce a new type of plant or animal by mixing two different types: *If you cross a horse with a donkey, you get a mule.*
• IN SPORT **6** [I, T] (in sports such as football and hockey) to pass the ball to the side across the field
IDM **cross your fingers** | **keep your fingers crossed** → FINGER¹ **cross my heart (and hope to die)** (*informal*) used for emphasizing that what you are saying is true **cross your mind** (used about a thought, an idea, etc.) to come into your mind: *It never once crossed my mind that she was lying.*
PHRV **cross sth off (sth)** to remove sth from a list, etc. by drawing a line through it: *Cross Dave's name off the guest list — he can't come.* **cross sth out** to draw a line through sth that you have written because you have made a mistake, etc.

cross³ /krɒs/ *adj.* **~(with sb) (about sth)** (*especially BrE, informal*) angry or annoyed: *I was really cross with her for leaving me with all the work.* ▶ **crossly** *adv.*: *'Be quiet,' Dad said crossly.*

cross- /krɒs/ *prefix* (in verbs, nouns, adjectives and adverbs) involving movement or action from one thing to another or between two things: *cross-fertilize* ◊ *crossfire* ◊ *cross-Channel ferries*

crossbar /ˈkrɒsbɑː(r)/ *noun* [C] **1** (**SPORT**) the piece of wood over the top of a goal in football, etc. **2** the metal bar that joins the front and back of a bicycle

cross-border *adj.* [only before noun] (**POLITICS**) involving activity across a border between two countries: *The peace process relies on cross-border co-operation.*

cross-breed¹ *verb* [I, T] (*pt, pp* **cross-bred** /ˈkrɒs bred/) (**BIOLOGY**) to make an animal or a plant BREED (= produce young animals/new plants) with a different type of animal or plant; to BREED with an animal or plant of a different type: *cross-bred sheep* ▶ **cross-breeding** *noun* [U]

cross-breed² *noun* [C] (**BIOLOGY**) an animal or a plant that has been produced from two different types of animal or plant

cross-check *verb* [T] **~ sth (against sth)** to make sure that information, figures, etc. are correct by using a different method or system to check them: *Cross-check your measurements against those suggested in the manual.*

cross-country *adj., adv.* (**SPORT**) across fields and natural land; not using roads or tracks: *We walked about 10 miles cross-country before we saw a village.*

cross-country skiing *noun* [U] (**SPORT**) the sport of skiing across the countryside, rather than down mountains

cross-examine *verb* [T] (**LAW**) (especially in court) to ask sb questions in great detail about answers they have already given in order to find out the truth about sth ▶ **cross-examination** *noun* [C, U]

cross-eyed *adj.* having one or both eyes looking towards the nose

cross-fertilize (*BrE also* -ise) *verb* [T] (**BIOLOGY**) to make a plant develop and grow fruit or seeds using POLLEN from a different plant of the same species ▶ **cross-fertilization** (*BrE also* -isation) *noun* [U, sing.]

crossfire /ˈkrɒsfaɪə(r)/ noun [U] a situation in which guns are being fired from two or more different directions: *The journalist was killed in crossfire.* ◇ (*figurative*) *When my parents argued, I sometimes got caught in the crossfire.*

cross-ˈfunctional adj. (**BUSINESS**) relating to a way of working in which people from different teams across an organization work together: *The projects require cross-functional teams to come together and work as a unit.*

crossing /ˈkrɒsɪŋ/ noun [C] **1** a place where you can cross a road, river, etc., or from one country to another: *You should cross the road at the pedestrian crossing.* ◇ *a border crossing* ➔ look at **level crossing 2** a journey from one side of a sea or river to the other: *We had a rough crossing.*

cross-legged /ˌkrɒs ˈlegd, ˈlegɪd/ adj., adv. sitting with your legs pulled up in front of you and with one leg or foot over the other: *to sit cross-legged*

ˈcross link noun [C] (**CHEMISTRY**) a chemical BOND between different chains of ATOMS in a POLYMER

crossover /ˈkrɒsəʊvə(r)/ noun [C] the process or result of changing from one area of activity or style of doing sth to another: *The album was an exciting jazz-pop crossover.*

ˌcross-ˈplatform adj. (**COMPUTING**) (used about a computer program or an electronic device) that can be used with different types of computers or programs

ˌcross-ˈpollinate verb [T] (**BIOLOGY**) to move POLLEN from a flower or plant onto another flower or plant so that it produces seeds ▸ **ˌcross-polliˈnation** noun [U]

ˌcross ˈpurposes noun
IDM **at cross purposes** if two people are **at cross purposes**, they do not understand each other because they are talking about different things, without realizing it

ˌcross ˈreference noun [C] a note in a text that tells you to look in another place in the text for more information

crossroads /ˈkrɒsrəʊdz/ noun [C] (*pl.* **crossroads**) a place where two or more roads cross each other: *When you come to the next crossroads, turn right.* ◇ (*figurative*) *I knew I was at the crossroads of my career.*

ˈcross section noun [C] **1** a picture of what the inside of sth would look like if you cut through it: *a cross section of the human brain* ➔ picture at **flower**[1] **2** a group of people or things that are typical of a larger group: *The families we studied were chosen to represent a cross section of society.* ▸ **cross-sectional** /ˌkrɒs ˈsekʃənl/ adj.

crosswalk /ˈkrɒswɔːk/ (*AmE*) = PEDESTRIAN CROSSING

crosswind /ˈkrɒswɪnd/ noun [C] a wind that is blowing across the direction that you are moving in

crossword /ˈkrɒswɜːd/ (*also* **ˈcrossword puzzle**) noun [C] a game in which you have to fit words across and downwards into spaces with numbers in a square diagram. You find the words by solving clues: *Every morning I try to do the crossword in the newspaper.*

crotch /krɒtʃ/ (*also* **crutch**) noun [C] (**ANATOMY**) the place where the legs, or a pair of trousers, join at the top

crotchet /ˈkrɒtʃɪt/ (*BrE*) (*AmE* **quarter note**) noun [C] (**MUSIC**) a note that lasts half as long as a MINIM ➔ picture at **music**

▼ **VOCABULARY BUILDING**

A **semibreve** is a musical note that lasts as long as four **crotchets**. A **minim** lasts twice as long as a **crotchet**. A **quaver** lasts half as long as a **crotchet** and a **semiquaver** lasts half as long as a **quaver**.

---

crouch /kraʊtʃ/ verb [I] ~ **(down)** to bend your legs and body so that you are close to the ground: *He crouched down behind the sofa.*

crow[1] /krəʊ/ noun [C] a large black bird that makes a loud unpleasant noise
IDM **as the crow flies** (used for describing distances) in a straight line: *It's a kilometre as the crow flies but 3 kilometres by road.*

crow[2] /krəʊ/ verb [I] **1** to make a loud noise like a COCK (= an adult male chicken) **2** (*informal*) to talk too proudly about sth you have achieved, especially when sb else has been unsuccessful **SYN** **boast**

crowbar /ˈkrəʊbɑː(r)/ noun [C] a long iron bar that is used for forcing sth open ➔ picture at **lever**

crowd[1] ⓘ **A2** /kraʊd/ noun **1** [C + sing./pl. verb] a large number of people in one place: *The crowd was/were extremely noisy.* ◇ *He pushed his way through the crowd.* ◇ *I go shopping early in the morning to avoid the crowds.* **2 the crowd** [sing.] ordinary people: *He wears weird clothes because he wants to stand out from the crowd.* **3** [C + sing./pl. verb] (*informal*) a group of people who know each other: *Bob, Liz and Chris will be there — all the usual crowd.*

crowd[2] /kraʊd/ verb **1** [I] ~ **around/round (sb)** (used about a lot of people) to stand in a large group around sb/sth: *Fans crowded round the singer hoping to get his autograph.* **2** [T] (used about a lot of people) to fill an area: *Groups of tourists crowded the main streets.* ◇ (*figurative*) *Memories crowded her mind.*
PHR V **crowd into sth** | **crowd in** to go into a small place and make it very full: *Somehow we all crowded into their small living room.* **crowd sb/sth into sth** | **crowd sb/sth in** to put a lot of people into a small place: *Ten prisoners were crowded into one small cell.* **crowd sth out** | **crowd sb out (of sth)** to completely fill a place so that nobody else can enter: *Grasses can crowd out the wild flowers.* ◇ *Smaller companies are being crowded out of the market.*

crowded ⓘ **A2** /ˈkraʊdɪd/ adj. full of people; having too many people: *a crowded bus* ◇ *people living in poor and crowded conditions*

crowdfunding /ˈkraʊdfʌndɪŋ/ noun [U] the practice of paying for a project or an activity by raising many small amounts of money from a large number of people, usually using the internet: *They raised the money for the film through crowdfunding.* ▸ **crowdfund** /-fʌnd/ verb [T]: *She's planning to crowdfund her next research project.*

crowdsourcing /ˈkraʊdsɔːsɪŋ/ noun [U] the use of a large group of people, especially members of the public, to help deal with a particular problem or task, often by using the internet

crown[1] ⓘ+ **C1** /kraʊn/ noun **1** [C] an object in the shape of a circle, usually made of gold and PRECIOUS STONES, that a king or queen wears on his or her head on official occasions **2 the Crown** [sing.] (**POLITICS**) the government of a country, thought of as being represented by a king or queen: *an area of land belonging to the Crown* **3** [sing.] (**MEDICINE**) the top of the head or of a hat **4** [sing.] the highest part of sth: *the crown of a hill* **5** [C] (**ANATOMY, MEDICINE**) the part of a tooth that is above the GUM ➔ picture at **tooth** **6** [C] (**MEDICINE**) an artificial cover for a damaged tooth

crown[2] /kraʊn/ verb [T, often passive] **1** (**POLITICS**) to put a CROWN on the head of a new king or queen in a ceremony at which they officially become king or queen: *Queen Elizabeth was crowned in 1953.* ◇ (*figurative*) *the newly crowned champion* **2** [often passive] ~ **sth (with sth)** to have or put sth on the top of sth: *The mountain was crowned with snow.* ◇ (*figurative*) *Her years of hard work were finally crowned with success.*

crowning /ˈkraʊnɪŋ/ *adj.* [only before noun] the best or most important: *Winning the World Championship was the crowning moment of her career.*

crown prince, crown princess *noun* [C] (**POLITICS**) (in some countries), a prince or princess who will become king or queen when the present king or queen dies

crucial 🔲 **B2** ⊙ /ˈkruːʃl/ *adj.* ~ (to/for sth) extremely important: *Early diagnosis of the illness is crucial for successful treatment.* **SYN** vital ⊃ note at **essential** ▸ **crucially** /-ʃəli/ *adv.*

crucible /ˈkruːsɪbl/ *noun* [C] **1** (**SCIENCE**) a pot in which substances are heated to high temperatures, metals are melted, etc. ⊃ picture at **laboratory** **2** (*formal*) a place or situation in which people or ideas are tested, often creating sth new or exciting in the process

crucifix /ˈkruːsəfɪks/ *noun* [C] (**RELIGION**) a small model of a cross with a figure of Jesus on it as a symbol of the Christian religion

crucifixion /ˌkruːsəˈfɪkʃn/ (*also* Crucifixion) *noun* **1** [C, U] (**RELIGION**) the act of killing sb by fastening them to a cross: *the Crucifixion* (= of Jesus) **2** [C] (**ART**) a painting or other work of art representing the crucifixion of Jesus Christ

cruciform /ˈkruːsɪfɔːm/ *adj.* (**ARCHITECTURE**) in the shape of a cross

crucify /ˈkruːsɪfaɪ/ *verb* [T] (crucifying; crucifies; *pt, pp* crucified) to kill sb by fastening them to a cross

crude 🔲 **C1** /kruːd/ *adj.* **1** simple and basic, without much detail, skill, etc: *The method was crude but very effective.* ◇ *She explained how the system worked **in crude terms**.* **2** referring to sex or the body in a way that would offend many people: *He's always telling crude jokes.* **3** (used about oil and other natural substances) in a natural state, before it has been treated with chemicals: *crude oil/metal* ⊃ picture at **fractional distillation** ▸ **crudely** *adv.*: *a crudely drawn face*

cruel 🔲 **B1** /ˈkruːəl/ *adj.* (crueller; cruellest) causing physical or mental pain or suffering to sb/sth: *I think it's cruel to keep animals in cages.* ◇ *a cruel punishment* **OPP** kind² ▸ **cruelly** /-əli/ *adv.*

cruelty /ˈkruːəlti/ *noun* (*pl.* -ies) **1** [U] ~ (to sb/sth) behaviour that causes physical or mental pain or suffering to sb/sth: *cruelty to children* **OPP** kindness **2** [C, usually pl.] a cruel act: *the cruelties of war*

cruise¹ 🔲+ **B2** /kruːz/ *verb* [I] **1** (**TOURISM**) to travel by ship, visiting a number of places, as a holiday: *to cruise around the Caribbean* **2** to stay at the same speed in a car, plane, etc: *cruising at 80 kilometres an hour*

cruise² 🔲+ **B2** /kruːz/ *noun* [C] (**TOURISM**) a holiday in which you travel on a ship and visit a number of different places: *They're planning to **go on a cruise**.*

cruise control *noun* [U] a device in a vehicle that allows it to stay at the speed that the driver has chosen

cruiser /ˈkruːzə(r)/ *noun* [C] **1** a large fast ship used in a war **2** (*also* cabin cruiser) a motor boat that has room for people to sleep in it

crumb /krʌm/ *noun* [C] a very small piece of bread, cake or biscuit

crumble /ˈkrʌmbl/ *verb* [I, T] ~ (sth) (up) to break into very small pieces; to make sth break into very small pieces: *The walls of the church are beginning to*

crumble. ◇ *We crumbled up the bread and threw it to the birds.* ◇ (*figurative*) *Support for the government is beginning to crumble.* ▸ **crumbly** /-bli/ *adj.* (crumblier; crumbliest): *This cheese has a crumbly texture.*

crumpet /ˈkrʌmpɪt/ *noun* [C] (*BrE*) a flat round type of bread roll with holes in the top that you eat hot with butter

crumple /ˈkrʌmpl/ *verb* [I, T] ~ (sth) (into sth); ~ (sth) (up) to be pressed or to press sth into an untidy shape: *The front of the car crumpled when it hit the wall.* ◇ *She crumpled the letter into a ball and threw it away.*

crunch¹ /krʌntʃ/ *verb* **1** [T] ~ sth (up) to make a loud noise when you are eating sth hard: *to crunch an apple* **2** [I] to make a loud noise like the sound of sth being CRUSHED: *We crunched through the snow.* ▸ **crunchy** *adj.* (crunchier; crunchiest): *a crunchy apple*

crunch² /krʌntʃ/ *noun* [sing.] an act or the noise of CRUNCHING: *There was a loud crunch as the car ran into the back of the lorry.* **IDM** if/when it comes to the crunch (*informal*) if/ when you are in a difficult situation and must make a difficult decision: *If it comes to the crunch, I'll stay and fight.*

crusade /kruːˈseɪd/ *noun* [C] **1** a fight for sth that you believe to be good or against sth that you believe to be bad: *Mr Khan is leading a crusade against crime in his neighbourhood.* **SYN** campaign¹ **2** (*also* Crusade) (**HISTORY, RELIGION**) one of the wars fought in Palestine by European Christians against Muslims in the Middle Ages ▸ **crusader** (*also* Crusader) *noun* [C]

crush¹ 🔲+ **C1** /krʌʃ/ *verb* [T] **1** to press sb/sth so hard that they are damaged or injured: *All the eggs got crushed when she sat on them.* ◇ *He was crushed to death in the accident.* **2** ~ sth (up) to break sth into very small flat pieces or a powder by pressing hard: *Crush the garlic and fry in oil.* **3** to defeat sb/sth completely: *The army was sent in to crush the rebellion.*

crush² /krʌʃ/ *noun* **1** [sing.] a large group of people in a small space: *There was such a crush that I couldn't get near the bar.* **2** [C] ~ (on sb) (*informal*) a strong feeling of love for sb that only usually lasts for a short time: *Maria **had a huge crush** on him.*

crushing /ˈkrʌʃɪŋ/ *adj.* [only before noun] that defeats sb/ sth completely; very bad: *a crushing defeat*

crust /krʌst/ *noun* [C, U] **1** the hard part on the outside of a piece of bread, a PIE, etc. **2** a hard layer or surface, especially above or around sth soft or liquid: *the earth's crust*

crustacean /krʌˈsteɪʃn/ *noun* [C] (**BIOLOGY**) any creature with a soft body in several sections and a hard outer shell. Most crustaceans live in water. CRABS, LOBSTERS and SHRIMPS are crustaceans. ⊃ picture at **animal**

crusty /ˈkrʌsti/ *adj.* (crustier; crustiest) **1** (used about food) having a hard layer on the outside: *crusty bread* **2** (*informal*) impatient and easily made angry: *a crusty old man*

crutch /krʌtʃ/ *noun* [C] **1** a type of stick that you put under your arm to help you walk when you have hurt your leg or foot: *She was **on crutches** for two months after she broke her ankle.* ⊃ look at **walking stick** **2** = CROTCH

crux /krʌks/ *noun* [sing.] the most important or difficult part of a problem: *The **crux of the matter** is how to stop this from happening again.*

cry¹ 🔲 **A2** /kraɪ/ *verb* (crying; cries; *pt, pp* cried) **1** [I] ~ (for sb/sth) to make a noise and produce tears in your eyes, for example because you are unhappy or have hurt yourself: *The baby never stops crying.* ◇ *The child was crying for* (= because she wanted) *her mother.* **2** [I, T] ~ (out) to shout or make a loud noise: *We could* hear somebody **crying for help.** ◊ '*Look!*' he cried, '*There they are.*' ◊ *to cry out in pain*

187

IDM **cry your eyes out** (*informal*) to cry a lot for a long time it's/there's **no use crying over spilt milk** used to tell sb not to waste time worrying about sth that has happened that they cannot do anything about **a shoulder to cry on** → SHOULDER[1]

PHR V **cry out for sth** to need sth very much: *The company is crying out for fresh new talent.*

cry² 💬 **B2** /kraɪ/ *noun* (*pl.* **cries**) **1** [C] a shout or loud high noise: *the cries of the children in the playground* ◊ *We heard Adam give a **cry** of pain as the dog bit him.* ◊ (*figurative*) *Her suicide attempt was really **a cry for help.*** **2** [sing.] an action or a period of crying: *After a good cry I felt much better.*

IDM **a far cry from sth/doing sth** → FAR[1]

crying /ˈkraɪɪŋ/ *adj.* [only before noun] (*informal*) (used to talk about a bad situation) very great: *There's a crying need for more doctors.* ◊ *It's **a crying shame** that so many young people can't find jobs.*

cryogenics /ˌkraɪəˈdʒenɪks/ *noun* [U] (PHYSICS) the scientific study of the production and effects of very low temperatures

crypt /krɪpt/ *noun* [C] (ARCHITECTURE) a room that is under a church, where people were sometimes buried in the past

cryptic /ˈkrɪptɪk/ *adj.* having a hidden meaning that is not easy to understand **SYN** **mysterious** ▸ **cryptically** /-kli/ *adv.*

crypto- /ˈkrɪptəʊ, krɪptə, krɪpˈtɒ/ *prefix* (in nouns) hidden; secret

cryptocurrency /ˈkrɪptəʊkʌrənsi/ *noun* [U, C] (*pl.* -ies) (ECONOMICS) any system of electronic money used for buying and selling online without a central bank

crystal 💬+ **C1** /ˈkrɪstl/ *noun* **1** [C] (CHEMISTRY) a regular shape that some mineral substances form when they become solid: *salt crystals* **2** [U, C] (GEOLOGY) a clear mineral that can be used in making jewellery **3** [U] glass of very high quality: *a crystal vase*

crystal 'ball *noun* [C] a clear glass ball used by people who claim they can predict what will happen in the future by looking into it

crystal 'clear *adj.* **1** (used about water, glass, etc.) completely clear and bright **2** very easy to understand: *The meaning is crystal clear.*

crystalline /ˈkrɪstəlaɪn/ *adj.* (GEOLOGY) made of or similar to CRYSTALS (= small pieces of a substance with many even sides)

crystallize (*BrE also* -ise) /ˈkrɪstəlaɪz/ *verb* [I, T] **1** (used about thoughts, beliefs, plans, etc.) to become clear and fixed; to make thoughts, etc. become clear and fixed: *Our ideas gradually began to crystallize into a definite shape.* **2** (CHEMISTRY) to form or to make sth form into CRYSTALS: *The salt crystallizes as the water evaporates.* ◊ picture at **rock**[1] ▸ **crystallization** (*BrE also* -isation) /ˌkrɪstəlaɪˈzeɪʃn/ *noun* [U] ◊ picture at **erosion**

crystallized (*also* **crystallised**) /ˈkrɪstəlaɪzd/ *adj.* (used about fruit) covered with sugar CRYSTALS

'C-section (*especially AmE*) = CAESAREAN SECTION

ct *abbr.* (in writing) (*pl.* **ct, cts**) = CENT

CT scan /ˌsiː ˈtiː skæn/ (*also* CAT scan) *noun* [C] (MEDICINE) a medical examination that uses a computer to produce an image of the inside of sb's body from X-RAY or ULTRASOUND pictures

cu. *abbr.* (in writing) = CUBIC: *a volume of 2 cu. m* (= 2 cubic metres)

cub /kʌb/ *noun* **1** [C] a young bear, lion, etc. ◊ picture at **lion** **2 the Cubs** [pl.] an organization for boys and girls between the ages of 8 and 10 or 11, that trains them in

practical skills and does a lot of activities with them **3** **Cub** (*also* Cub Scout) [C] a member of the Cubs

cube¹ /kjuːb/ *noun* [C] **1** (GEOMETRY) a solid shape that has six equal square sides **2** (MATHEMATICS) the number that you get if you multiply a number by itself twice: *the cube of 5 (5^3) is 125 ($5 \times 5 \times 5 = 125$).* ◊ look at **square²** (3) ◊ picture at **solid²**

cube² /kjuːb/ *verb* [T, usually passive] (MATHEMATICS) to multiply a number by itself twice: *4 cubed (4^3) is 64 ($4 \times 4 \times 4 = 64$).* ◊ look at **cube root**

ˌcube 'root *noun* [C] (MATHEMATICS) a number that, when multiplied by itself twice, produces a particular number: *The cube root of 64 ($\sqrt[3]{64}$) is 4.* ◊ look at **square root**

cubic /ˈkjuːbɪk/ *adj.* (*abbr.* cu.) used to show that a measurement is the volume of sth: *If a box is 4 cm long, 4 cm wide and 4 cm high, its volume is 64 cubic centimetres.* ◊ *The lake holds more than a million cubic metres of water.*

cubicle /ˈkjuːbɪkl/ *noun* [C] a small room or area that is made by separating off part of a larger room: *There are cubicles at the swimming pool for changing your clothes.*

cubism /ˈkjuːbɪzəm/ (*also* Cubism) *noun* [U] (ART) a style and movement in early twentieth-century art in which objects and people are represented as GEOMETRIC shapes, often shown from many different angles at the same time ▸ **cubist** /-bɪst/ (*also* Cubist) *noun* [C], *adj.*: *The exhibition includes works by the Cubists.* ◊ *cubist paintings*

cuboid /ˈkjuːbɔɪd/ *noun* [C] (GEOMETRY) a solid object that has six RECTANGULAR sides at RIGHT ANGLES to each other ▸ **cuboid** *adj.*

'Cub Scout = CUB (3)

cuckoo /ˈkʊkuː/ *noun* [C] (*pl.* -oos) a bird that makes a sound like its name. Cuckoos put their eggs into the NESTS of other birds.

cucumber /ˈkjuːkʌmbə(r)/ *noun* [C, U] a long thin vegetable with dark green skin that does not need to be cooked

cud /kʌd/ *noun* [U] the food that cows and similar animals bring back from the stomach into the mouth to eat again: *cows chewing the cud*

cuddle /ˈkʌdl/ *verb* [I, T] to hold sb/sth closely in your arms: *The little girl was cuddling her favourite doll.* ◊ *A couple of teenagers were kissing and cuddling on the doorstep.* ▸ **cuddle** *noun* [C]: *He gave the child **a cuddle** and kissed her goodnight.*

PHR V **cuddle up (to/against sb/sth)** | **cuddle up (together)** to move close to sb and sit or lie in a comfortable position: *They cuddled up together for warmth.*

cuddly /ˈkʌdli/ *adj.* (**cuddlier; cuddliest**) soft and pleasant to hold close to you: *a cuddly toy*

cue 💬+ **B2** /kjuː/ *noun* [C] **1** a word or movement that is the signal for sb else to say or do sth, especially in a play: *When Julia puts the tray on the table, that's your cue to come on stage.* **2** an example of how to behave: *I'm not sure how to behave at a Japanese wedding, so I'll take my **cue** from the hosts.* **3** (SPORT) a long thin wooden stick used to hit the ball in SNOOKER and BILLIARDS (= games that are played on a special table) ◊ picture at **sport**

IDM **(right) on cue** at exactly the moment expected: *Just as I was starting to worry about Stan, he phoned right on cue.*

cuff /kʌf/ noun [C] **1** the end part of a SLEEVE, which often fastens at the WRIST **2** cuffs = HANDCUFFS **3** a light hit with the open hand
IDM off the cuff (used about sth you say) without thought or preparation before you say it: *I haven't got the figures here, but, off the cuff, I'd say the rise is about 10%.*

cufflink /'kʌflɪŋk/ noun [C, usually pl.] one of a pair of small objects used instead of a button to fasten the CUFF of a shirt together at the WRIST

cuisine /kwɪ'ziːn/ noun [U] (formal) the style of cooking of a particular country, restaurant, etc: *Italian cuisine*

cul-de-sac /'kʌl də sæk/ noun [C] (pl. cul-de-sacs) a street that is closed at one end

culinary /'kʌlɪnəri/ adj. (formal) connected with cooking

cull¹ /kʌl/ verb [T] **1** to kill a number of animals in a group, especially in order to prevent the group from becoming too large **2** to collect information, ideas, etc., from different places: *I managed to cull some useful addresses from the internet.*

cull² /kʌl/ noun [C] the act of killing some animals in order to stop a group becoming too large

culminate /'kʌlmɪneɪt/ verb [I] ~ in sth (formal) to reach a final result: *The team's efforts culminated in victory in the championships.* ▶ culmination /ˌkʌlmɪ'neɪʃn/ noun [sing.]: *The joint space mission was the culmination of years of research.*

culottes /kjuː'lɒts/ noun [pl.] women's wide short trousers that are made to look like a skirt: *a pair of culottes*

culpable /'kʌlpəbl/ adj. (formal) responsible for sth bad that has happened

culprit /'kʌlprɪt/ noun [C] a person who has done sth wrong

cult ʔ+ **C1** /kʌlt/ noun [C] **1** (RELIGION) a small group of people who have extreme religious beliefs and who are not part of any established religion **2** a way of life, an attitude, an idea, etc. that has become very popular ▶ cult ʔ+ **C1** adj. [only before noun]: *cult movies/books* ◊ *The singer has become a cult figure in the US.*

cultivar /'kʌltɪvɑː(r)/ noun [C] (AGRICULTURE) a type of plant that has been deliberately developed to have particular features

cultivate ʔ+ **C1** /'kʌltɪveɪt/ verb [T] **1** (AGRICULTURE) to prepare and use land for growing plants for food or to sell: *to cultivate the soil* **2** (AGRICULTURE) to grow plants for food or to sell: *Olives have been cultivated for centuries in Mediterranean countries.* **3** to try to develop a friendship with sb: *He cultivated links with colleagues abroad.* ▶ cultivation /ˌkʌltɪ'veɪʃn/ noun [U] ⊃ look at **shifting cultivation**

cultivated /'kʌltɪveɪtɪd/ adj. **1** (used about people) well educated, with good manners **SYN** cultured **2** (AGRICULTURE) (used about land) used for growing plants for food or to sell **3** (AGRICULTURE) (used about plants) grown on a farm, not wild

cultural ʔ **B1** ⊙ /'kʌltʃərəl/ adj. **1** (SOCIAL STUDIES) connected with the customs, ideas, beliefs, etc. of a society or country: *The country's cultural diversity is a result of taking in immigrants from all over the world.* ⊃ look at **multicultural** **2** (ARTS AND MEDIA) connected with art, music, literature, etc: *The city has a rich cultural life, with many theatres, concert halls and art galleries.* ▶ culturally ⊙ /-rəli/ adv.

culture ʔ **A1** ⊙ /'kʌltʃə(r)/ noun **1** [C, U] (SOCIAL STUDIES) the customs, ideas, beliefs, etc. of a particular society, country, etc: *the language and culture of the Aztecs* ◊ *people from many different cultures* **2** [U] (ARTS AND MEDIA) art, literature, music, etc: *London has always been a centre of culture.* **3** [C] (BIOLOGY) a group of cells or bacteria, especially taken from a person or an animal and grown for medical or scientific study: *Yogurt is made from active cultures.*

cultured /'kʌltʃəd/ adj. well educated, showing a good knowledge of art, music, literature, etc. **SYN** cultivated

'culture shock noun [U, C] (SOCIAL STUDIES) a feeling of CONFUSION, etc. that you may have when you go to live in or visit a country that is very different from your own

culvert /'kʌlvət/ noun [C] a pipe for water that goes under a road, etc.

cum /kʌm/ prep. (used for joining two nouns together) also used as; as well as: *a bedroom-cum-study*

cumbersome /'kʌmbəsəm/ adj. **1** heavy and difficult to carry, use, wear, etc. **2** (used about a system, etc.) slow and complicated: *cumbersome legal procedures*

cumin /'kjuːmɪn, 'kʌm-/ noun [U] the dried seeds of the cumin plant, used in cooking as a SPICE

cumulative ⊙ /'kjuːmjələtɪv/ adj. increasing steadily in amount, degree, etc: *a cumulative effect*

cumulonimbus /ˌkjuːmələʊ'nɪmbəs/ noun [U] (GEOGRAPHY) a type of cloud that forms a large, very high mass, with a flat base at a fairly low level, and often a flat top. It is seen, for example, during THUNDERSTORMS. ⊃ picture at **cloud¹**

cumulus /'kjuːmjələs/ noun [U] (GEOGRAPHY) a type of thick white cloud ⊃ picture at **cloud¹**

cunning /'kʌnɪŋ/ adj. clever in a dishonest or bad way: *He was as cunning as a fox.* ◊ *a cunning trick* **SYN** sly, wily ▶ cunning noun [U] ▶ cunningly adv.

cup¹ ʔ **A1** /kʌp/ noun [C] **1** a small container usually with a handle, used for drinking liquids: *a cup of coffee* **2** (SPORT) a large metal cup given as a prize; the competition for such a cup: *Our team won the cup in the basketball tournament.* ◊ *the World Cup* **3** an object shaped like a cup: *an egg cup*
IDM not sb's cup of tea (informal) not what sb likes or is interested in: *Horror films aren't my cup of tea.*

cup² /kʌp/ verb [T] (-pp-) **1** ~ your hand(s) (around/over something) to make your hands into the shape of a bowl: *I cupped my hands to take a drink from the stream.* **2** ~ sth in your hands to make your hands into the shape of a bowl: *He cupped her face in his hands and kissed her.*

cupboard ʔ **A2** /'kʌbəd/ noun [C] a piece of furniture, usually with shelves inside and a door or doors at the front, used for storing food, clothes, etc: *a kitchen cupboard* ◊ *built-in cupboards*

'cup final noun [C] (BrE) (SPORT) (especially in football) the last match in a series of matches in a competition that gives a cup as a prize to the winner

cupful /'kʌpfʊl/ noun [C] the amount that a cup will hold: *two cupfuls of water*

Cupid /'kjuːpɪd/ noun [C] (ART) **1** the Roman god of love who is shown as a beautiful baby boy with wings, carrying a BOW and ARROW (= a thin piece of wood with a sharp point at one end) **2** cupid a picture or statue of a baby boy who looks like Cupid: *little cupids painted in the clouds on the ceiling*

cupola /'kjuːpələ/ noun [C] (ARCHITECTURE) a round part on top of a building (like a small DOME) ⊃ picture at **dome**

'cup tie noun [C] (*BrE*) (**SPORT**) (especially in football) a match between two teams in a competition that gives a cup as a prize to the winner

curable /'kjʊərəbl/ adj. (**MEDICINE**) (used about a disease) that can be made better **OPP incurable**

curate¹ /'kjʊərət/ noun [C] (**RELIGION**) (in the Church of England) an assistant to a VICAR (= a priest who is in charge of the church or churches in a particular area)

curate² /kjʊə'reɪt/ verb [T] (**ARTS AND MEDIA**) to choose, organize and look after things that are kept or shown in a museum, etc: *The exhibition is curated by Robin Muir.*

curator /kjʊə'reɪtə(r)/ noun [C] a person whose job is to look after the things that are kept in a museum

curb¹ /kɜːb/ verb [T] to limit or control sth, especially sth bad: *He needs to learn to curb his anger.*

curb² /kɜːb/ noun [C] ~ (**on sth**) a control or limit on sth: *a curb on local government spending* **2** (*AmE*) = KERB

curd /kɜːd/ noun [U] (*also* **curds** [pl.]) a thick soft substance that forms when milk turns SOUR (= not fresh)

curdle /'kɜːdl/ verb [I, T] (used about liquids, especially milk) to separate into solid and liquid parts; to make sth do this: *She heated the sauce for too long and it curdled.* ⊃ look at **blood-curdling**

cure¹ ʔ**B2** /kjʊə(r)/ verb [T] **1** ~ **sb** (**of sth**) (**MEDICINE**) to make sb healthy again after an illness: *The treatment cured him of cancer.* **2** (**MEDICINE**) to make an illness, injury, etc. end or disappear: *It is still not possible to cure the common cold.* ◇ (*figurative*) *The plumber cured the problem with the central heating.* **3** to make certain types of food last longer by drying them, or treating them with smoke or salt: *cured ham*

cure² ʔ**B2** /kjʊə(r)/ noun [C] ~ (**for sth**) (**MEDICINE**) **1** a medicine or treatment that can cure an illness, etc: *There is no cure for this illness.* **2** a return to good health; the process of being cured: *The new drug brought about a miraculous cure.*

curfew /'kɜːfjuː/ noun [C, U] **1** a time after which people are not allowed to go outside their homes, for example during a war: *The government imposed a dusk-to-dawn curfew.* **2** (*AmE*) a time by which children must arrive home in the evening: *She has a ten o'clock curfew.*

curiosity ʔ+**C1** /ˌkjʊəri'ɒsəti/ noun (pl. **-ies**) **1** [U] a desire to know or learn: *I was full of curiosity about their plans.* ◇ *Out of curiosity, he checked her email.* **2** [C] an unusual and interesting person or thing: *The museum was full of historical curiosities.*

curious ʔ+**B2** /'kjʊəriəs/ adj. **1** ~ (**about sth**); ~ (**to do sth**) wanting to know or learn sth: *They were very curious about the people who lived upstairs.* ◇ *He was curious to know how the machine worked.* **2** unusual or strange: *It was curious that she didn't tell anyone about the incident.* ▶ **curiously** adv.

curium /'kjʊəriəm/ noun [U] (symb. Cm) (**CHEMISTRY**) a chemical element. Curium is a RADIOACTIVE metal produced artificially from PLUTONIUM. ❶ For more information on the periodic table of elements, look at the **Reference Section** of this dictionary.

curl¹ /kɜːl/ verb **1** [I, T] to form into a curved or round shape; to make sth form this shape **2** [I] to move round in a curve: *The snake curled around his arm.* ◇ *Smoke curled up into the sky.*
PHR V curl up | **be curled up** to pull your arms, legs and head close to your body: *The cat curled up in front of the fire.* ◇ *He was curled up on the sofa.*

curl² /kɜːl/ noun [C] **1** a piece of hair that curves round: *Her hair fell in curls round her face.* **2** a thing that has a curved round shape: *a curl of blue smoke*

curler /'kɜːlə(r)/ noun [C] a small plastic or metal tube that you roll your hair around in order to make it curly

curly ʔ**A2** /'kɜːli/ adj. (**curlier; curliest**) full of CURLS; shaped like a CURL (= a piece of hair that curves round): *curly hair* **OPP straight¹**

currant /'kʌrənt/ noun [C] **1** a very small dried GRAPE used in cakes, etc. **2** (in compounds) a small black, red or white fruit that grows in bunches on bushes: *blackcurrants*

currency ʔ**B1** /'kʌrənsi/ noun (pl. **-ies**) **1** [C, U] (**ECONOMICS, FINANCE**) the system or type of money that a particular country uses: *a single European currency* ◇ *foreign currency* ◇ *a weak/strong/stable currency* **2** [U] the state of being believed, accepted or used by many people: *The new ideas soon gained currency.*

▼ COLLOCATIONS

currency

In financial markets currencies can be **high/rising/strong** or **falling/low/weak**: *Business should benefit from a strong euro.* ◇ *The yen gained ten points against a weak dollar.* Currencies can **strengthen** and **weaken**: *The peso strengthened on the foreign exchanges.* ◇ *The rand weakened by 5% to the euro.* One currency can **come under pressure against** another: *The pound came under pressure against the euro yesterday.* A currency may be **floated**, **devalued** or **revalued**: *The government allowed the peso to float freely.* ◇ *The Fiji dollar may have to be devalued.* ◇ *The yen is to be revalued.* The **exchange rate** is the relation in value of one currency against another: *The current exchange rate is 80 rupees to the euro.* ◇ *a high/low/stable/strong/weak exchange rate*

current¹ ʔ**B1** **W** /'kʌrənt/ adj. **1** [only before noun] of the present time; happening now: *current fashions/events* **2** generally accepted; in common use: *Is this word still current?*

current² ʔ**B2** **W** /'kʌrənt/ noun **1** [C] (**GEOGRAPHY**) a continuous flowing movement of water, air, etc: *to swim against/with the current* ◇ (*figurative*) *a current of anti-government feeling* ⊃ picture on **page 190** **2** [C, U] (**PHYSICS**) the flow of electricity through a wire, etc. ⊃ picture at **resistor**

'current account (*BrE*) (*AmE* **checking account**) noun [C] (**FINANCE**) a bank account that you can take money out of at any time, and that provides you with a DEBIT CARD (= a special card that can be used to take money directly from your bank account)

'current affairs noun [pl.] (**POLITICS, SOCIAL STUDIES**) important political or social events that are happening at the present time

currently ʔ**B1** **W** /'kʌrəntli/ adv. at present; at the moment: *He is currently working in Spain.*

curriculum ʔ**B2** /kə'rɪkjələm/ noun [C] (pl. **curriculums**, **curricula** /-lə/) (**EDUCATION**) all the subjects that are taught in a school, college or university; the contents of a particular course of study: *Latin is not on the curriculum at our school.* ⊃ look at **syllabus**

curriculum vitae /kəˌrɪkjələm 'viːtaɪ/ = CV

curry /'kʌri/ noun [C, U] (pl. **-ies**) a South Asian dish of meat, vegetables, etc. containing a lot of SPICES and usually served with rice: *a hot/mild curry* ▶ **curried** adj.: *curried chicken*

'curry powder noun [U] a fine mixture of SPICES that is used to make CURRY taste hot

curse¹ /kɜːs/ noun [C] **1** (LANGUAGE) a word used for expressing anger **SYN** swear word **2** a word or words expressing a wish that sth terrible will happen to sb: *The family seemed to be* **under a curse** (= lots of bad things happened to them). **3** something that causes great harm: *the curse of poverty*

curse² /kɜːs/ verb **1** [I, T] ~ **(sb/sth) (for sth)** to swear at sb/sth; to use rude language to express your anger: *He dropped the box, cursing himself for his clumsiness.* **2** [T] to use a magic word or phrase against sb because you want sth bad to happen to them: *She cursed his family.*

cursor /'kɜːsə(r)/ noun [C] (COMPUTING) a small sign on a computer screen that shows the position you are at

cursory /'kɜːsəri/ adj. quick and short; done in a hurry: *a cursory glance*

curt /kɜːt/ adj. short and not polite: *She gave him a curt reply and slammed the phone down.* ▶ **curtly** adv. ▶ **curtness** noun [U]

curtail /kɜːˈteɪl/ verb [T] (formal) to make sth shorter or smaller; to reduce: *I had to curtail my answer as I was running out of time.* ▶ **curtailment** noun [C, U]

curtain ⌀ **B1** /'kɜːtn/ noun [C] **1** (AmE also **drape**) a piece of material that you can move to cover a window, etc: *Could you* **draw the curtains**, *please?* (= Could you open/close the curtains?) ◊ **The curtain goes up** *at 7pm* (= in a theatre, the play begins). **2** a thing that covers or hides sth: *a curtain of mist*

curtsy (also **curtsey**) /'kɜːtsi/ noun [C] (pl. **-ies**, **-eys**) a movement made by a woman as a sign of respect, done by bending the knees, with one foot behind the other ▶ **curtsy** (also **curtsey**) verb [I] (curtsying, curtseying; curtsies, curtseys; pt, pp curtsied, curtseyed)

curve¹ ⌀ **B2** /kɜːv/ noun [C] a line that bends round: *a curve on a graph* ◊ *a pattern of straight lines and curves*

curve² ⌀ **B2** /kɜːv/ verb [I, T] to bend or to make sth bend in a curve: *The bay curved round to the south.* ▶ **curved** ⌀ **B2** adj.: *a curved line* ○ picture at **line¹**

cushion¹ /'kʊʃn/ noun [C] **1** a bag filled with soft material, for example feathers, that you put on a chair, etc. to make it more comfortable **2** something that acts or is shaped like a cushion: *A hovercraft rides on a cushion of air.*

cushion² /'kʊʃn/ verb [T] **1** to make a fall, hit, etc. less painful: *The snow cushioned his fall.* **2** to reduce the unpleasant effect of sth: *She spent her childhood on a farm, cushioned from the effects of the war.*

cushy /'kʊʃi/ adj. (cushier; cushiest) (informal) too easy, needing little effort (in a way that seems unfair to others): *a cushy job*

custard /'kʌstəd/ noun [U] a sweet yellow sauce made from milk, eggs and sugar. In the UK it is eaten hot or cold with sweet dishes.

custodial /kʌˈstəʊdiəl/ adj. (LAW) **1** involving sending sb to prison: *The judge gave him a* **custodial sentence** (= sent him to prison). **2** connected with the right or duty of taking care of sb; having CUSTODY: *The mother is usually the custodial parent after a divorce.*

custodian /kʌˈstəʊdiən/ noun [C] **1** (formal) a person who looks after or protects sth, such as a museum, library, etc: (figurative) *Farmers, besides being food producers, are custodians of the countryside.* **2** (AmE) = CARETAKER

custody ⌀+ **C1** /'kʌstədi/ noun [U] (LAW) **1** the legal right or duty to take care of sb/sth: *After the divorce, the mother* **had custody of** *the children.* **2** the state of being guarded, or kept in prison temporarily, especially by the police: *The man was* **kept in custody** *until his trial.*

custom¹ ⌀ **B1** /'kʌstəm/ noun **1** [C, U] (SOCIAL STUDIES) a way of behaving that a particular group or society has had for a long time: *the custom of giving presents at Christmas* ◊ *according to* **local custom** **2** [sing.] (formal) something that a person does regularly: *It's* **my custom** *to drink tea in the afternoon.* **3** [U] (BrE) (BUSINESS) commercial activity; the practice of people buying things regularly from a particular shop, etc: *The local shop lost a lot of custom when the new supermarket opened.* ○ look at **customs**

custom² /'kʌstəm/ adj. (especially AmE) **1** = CUSTOM-MADE **2** = CUSTOM-BUILT

ocean currents in the North Atlantic Ocean

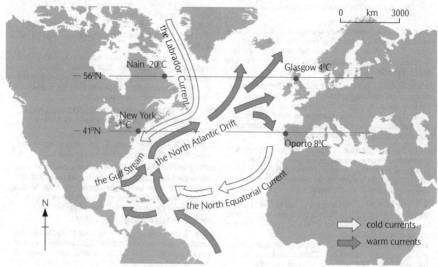

the Labrador Current · Nain -20°C · 56°N · Glasgow 4°C · the North Atlantic Drift · New York 1°C · 41°N · Oporto 8°C · the Gulf Stream · the North Equatorial Current · 0 km 3000 · N · ▷ cold currents · ▷ warm currents

customary /ˈkʌstəməri/ *adj.* according to custom; usual: *Is it customary to send cards at Christmas in your country?* ▸ **customarily** /-rəli/ *adv.*

custom-'built (*also* **custom** *especially in AmE*) *adj.* designed and built for a particular person

customer 🔒 **A1** /ˈkʌstəmə(r)/ *noun* [C] (**BUSINESS**) a person who buys goods or services in a shop, restaurant, online, etc: *The shop assistant was serving a customer.* ◇ *We send vouchers to all our clients as a way of strengthening customer loyalty.* ➔ note at **client**

customer en'gagement *noun* [U] (**BUSINESS**) the process of encouraging people to be interested in a company and its products or services: *Loyalty programs have become one of the most popular ways to improve customer engagement.*

customer satis'faction *noun* [U] (**BUSINESS**) a measure of how happy people are with the goods or services they pay for: *We are working hard to improve customer satisfaction, and to resolve all the issues.*

customer 'service (*also* **customer 'care**) *noun* [U] (**BUSINESS**) **1** the way in which a company treats its customers and answers their questions, complaints, etc: *The company provides excellent customer service.* **2** **customer services** [+ sing./pl. verb] the department in a company that deals with customers' complaints, questions, etc.

customize (*BrE also* **-ise**) /ˈkʌstəmaɪz/ *verb* [T] to make or change sth so that it is exactly what the owner or user needs: *You can customize the software in several ways.*

custom-'made (*also* **custom** *especially in AmE*) *adj.* designed and made for a particular person ➔ look at **bespoke**

customs /ˈkʌstəmz/ (*also* **Customs**) *noun* [pl.] **1** the government department that collects taxes on goods from other countries: *a customs officer* ➔ look at **excise** **2** (**TOURISM**) the place at a port or an airport where your bags are checked to make sure you are not bringing goods into the country illegally

cut¹ 🔒 **A1** /kʌt/ *verb* (**cutting**; *pt, pp* **cut**)

• MAKE AN OPENING, ETC. **1** [I, T] to make an opening, a wound or a mark in sth using a sharp tool, for example a pair of SCISSORS or a knife: *Be careful not to cut yourself on that broken glass!* ◇ *This knife doesn't cut very well.* ◇ *She fell and cut her head open.* ➔ note at **hospital**

• REMOVE **2** [T] ~ **sth (from sth)** to remove sth or a part of sth, using a knife, etc: *She cut two slices of bread (from the loaf).*

• DIVIDE **3** [T] ~ **sth (in/into sth)** to divide sth into pieces with a knife, etc: *She cut the cake into eight (pieces).* ◇ *He cut the rope in two.*

• MAKE SHORTER **4** [T] to make sth shorter by cutting: *I cut my own hair.* ◇ *to have your hair cut* (= at the HAIRDRESSER'S). ◇ *to cut the grass*

• SHAPE/FORM **5** [T] to make or form sth by removing material with a sharp tool: *She cut a hole in the card and pushed the string through.* ◇ *They cut a path through the jungle.*

• REDUCE/REMOVE **6** [T] (**ECONOMICS**) to reduce sth or make it shorter: *to cut taxes/costs/spending* ◇ *Train services have been cut because of the strike.* **7** [T] to remove sth from sth: *Several violent scenes in the film were cut.*

• IN COMPUTING **8** [T] to remove a piece of text from the screen: *Use the cut and paste buttons to change the order of the paragraphs.*

• GO ACROSS **9** [I] (used with an adverb or a preposition) to go in the direction mentioned, in order to make your route shorter: *It's much quicker if we cut across the field.*

• STOP **10** [T] (*informal*) to stop sth: *Cut the chat and get on with your work!*

• UPSET **11** [T] to deeply offend sb or hurt their feelings: *His cruel remarks cut her deeply.*

IDM ⓘ For idioms containing **cut**, look at the entries for the nouns, adjectives, etc. For example, **cut corners** is at **corner**.

PHR V **cut across sth** to affect or be true for different groups that usually remain separate: *The question of aid for the earthquake victims cuts across national boundaries.* **cut back** | **cut back (on sth)** to reduce sth: *to cut back on public spending* ➔ look at **cutback** **cut sth down** **1** to make sth fall down by cutting it: *to cut down a tree* **2** to make sth shorter: *I have to cut my essay down to 2 000 words.* **cut down** | **cut down (on sth)** to reduce the quantity or amount of sth; to do sth less often: *You should cut down on fatty foods.* **cut in (on sb/sth)** to interrupt sb/sth: *She kept cutting in on our conversation.* **cut sb off** [often passive] to stop or interrupt sb's phone conversation: *We were cut off before I could give her my message.* **cut sth off** [often passive] to stop the supply of sth to sb: *The electricity/gas/water has been cut off.* **cut sth off** to block a road, etc. so that nothing can pass: *We must cut off all possible escape routes.* **cut sth off (sth)** to remove sth from sth larger by cutting: *Be careful you don't cut your fingers off with that electric saw.* **cut sb/sth off (from sb/sth)** [often passive] to prevent sb/sth from moving from a place or contacting people outside: *The farm was cut off from the village by heavy snow.* **cut sth out** **1** to remove sth or to form sth into a particular shape by cutting: *to cut out a dress from a piece of cloth* **2** to not include sth: *Cut out the boring details!* **3** (*informal*) to stop saying or doing sth that annoys sb: *Cut that out and leave me alone!* **4** (*informal*) to stop doing or using sth: *You'll only lose weight if you cut out sweet things from your diet.* **be cut out for sth** | **be cut out to be sth** to have the qualities needed to do sth; to be suitable for sth/sb: *You're not cut out to be a teacher.* **cut sth up** to cut sth into small pieces with a knife, etc.

cut² 🔒 **B1** /kʌt/ *noun* [C]

• INJURY **1** an injury or opening in the skin made with a knife, etc: *He had a deep cut on his forehead.*

• OF HAIR **2** an act of cutting: *to have a cut and blow-dry* (= at a HAIRDRESSER'S)

• REDUCTION **3** ~ **(in sth)** (**ECONOMICS**) a reduction in size, amount, etc: *a cut in government spending* ◇ *a power cut* (= when the electric current is stopped temporarily)

• MEAT **4** a piece of meat from a particular part of an animal: *cheap cuts of lamb*

• MONEY **5** (*informal*) (**FINANCE**) a share of the profits from sth, especially sth dishonest ➔ look at **shortcut**

cutback /ˈkʌtbæk/ *noun* [C] a reduction in amount or number: *The management were forced to make cutbacks in staff.*

cut-'down *adj.* [only before noun] reduced in length or size: *a cut-down version of the program*

cute 🔒+ **B2** /kjuːt/ *adj.* attractive; pretty: *Your little girl is so cute!* ◇ *a cute smile*

cuticle /ˈkjuːtɪkl/ *noun* [C] **1** (**ANATOMY**) an area of hard skin at the base of the nails on the fingers and toes **2** (**BIOLOGY**) a hard outer layer that covers and protects parts of a plant

cutlery /ˈkʌtləri/ *noun* [U] (*especially BrE*) the knives, forks and spoons that you use for eating food ➔ look at **crockery**

cutlet /ˈkʌtlət/ *noun* [C] a small, thick piece of meat, often with bone in it, that is cooked

'cut-off *noun* [C] the level or time at which sth stops: *The cut-off date is 12 May. After that we'll end the offer.*

,cut-'price (*especially BrE*) (*AmE usually* ,cut-'rate) *adj.* (**FINANCE**) sold at a reduced price; selling goods at low prices: *cut-price offers ◇ a cut-price store*

cutters /'kʌtəz/ *noun* [pl.] a tool that you use for cutting through sth, for example metal: *a pair of wire cutters*

'cut-throat *adj.* caring only about success and not worried about hurting anyone: *cut-throat business practices*

cutting¹ ?+ 🔤 /'kʌtɪŋ/ *noun* [C] **1** (*BrE*) (*also* **clipping** *especially in AmE*) a piece cut out from a newspaper, etc: *press cuttings* **2** (**AGRICULTURE**) a piece cut off from a plant that you use for growing a new plant

cutting² /'kʌtɪŋ/ *adj.* (used about sth you say) unkind; meant to hurt sb's feelings: *a cutting remark*

,cutting 'edge *noun* [sing.] **1** the ~ (of sth) the newest, most advanced stage in the development of sth: *working at the cutting edge of computer technology* **2** an aspect of sth that gives it an advantage: *We're relying on him to give the team a cutting edge.*

CV /,si: 'vi:/ (*BrE*) (*AmE* **résumé**) *noun* [C] a formal list of your education and the jobs you have done, often used when you are trying to get a new job (the abbreviation for 'curriculum vitae')

cwm /kʊm/ *noun* [C] a round area shaped like a bowl in the side of a mountain, especially in Wales ⊃ look at **cirque**

cwt *abbr.* (in writing) (*pl.* **cwt**) = HUNDREDWEIGHT

cyanide /'saɪənaɪd/ *noun* [U] (**CHEMISTRY**) a poisonous chemical

cyber- /saɪbə(r)/ *prefix* (in nouns and adjectives) (**COMPUTING**) connected with electronic communication networks, especially the internet: *cybernetics ◇ cybercrime*

cyberbully /'saɪbəbʊli/ *noun* [C] (*pl.* **-ies**) a person who uses the internet to threaten and frighten sb else with unpleasant messages ⊃ look at **bully¹**

cyberbullying /'saɪbəbʊliɪŋ/ *noun* [U] (**COMPUTING**, **SOCIAL STUDIES**) sending unkind messages to sb using SOCIAL MEDIA in order to hurt or frighten them

cybercrime /'saɪbəkraɪm/ *noun* [C, U] (**COMPUTING**, **LAW**) crime that is committed using the internet, for example by stealing sb's bank details or sending a virus to sb's computer

cybernetics /,saɪbə'netɪks/ *noun* [U] (**BIOLOGY**, **COMPUTING**) the scientific study of communication and control systems, in which, for example, human and animal brains are compared with machines and electronic devices

cyberspace /'saɪbəspeɪs/ *noun* [U] the internet considered as an imaginary space without a physical location in which communication over computer networks takes place

cycle¹ ? 🔤 ⊙ /'saɪkl/ *noun* [C] **1** a bicycle or motorcycle: *a cycle shop* **SYN** **bike** **2** a series of events, etc. that happen again and again in the same order: *the carbon/nitrogen cycle* ⊃ picture at **carbon cycle, nitrogen cycle, rock¹**

cycle² ? 🔤 /'saɪkl/ *verb* [I] to ride a bicycle: *He usually cycles to school.*

'cycle lane (*BrE*) (*AmE* **bicycle lane, bike lane**) *noun* [C] a part of a road that only bicycles are allowed to use

cyclic /'saɪklɪk, 'sɪ-/ (*also* **cyclical** /'saɪklɪkl, 'sɪ-/) *adj.* repeated many times and always happening in the same order: *the cyclic processes of nature ◇ Economic*

activity often follows a cyclical pattern. ▶ **cyclically** /'saɪklɪkli, 'sɪ-/ *adv.*: *events that occur cyclically*

cycling /'saɪklɪŋ/ *noun* [U] (**SPORT**) the sport or activity of riding a bicycle: *We go cycling most weekends.* ◇ *Cycling is Europe's second most popular sport.*

cyclist /'saɪklɪst/ *noun* [C] (**SPORT**) a person who rides a bicycle

cyclone /'saɪkləʊn/ *noun* [C] (**GEOGRAPHY**) a violent tropical storm in which strong winds move in a circle ⊃ note at **storm¹** ▶ **cyclonic** /saɪ'klɒnɪk/ *adj.*

cygnet /'sɪgnət/ *noun* [C] a young SWAN (= a large white bird with a long neck that lives on or near water)

cylinder /'sɪlɪndə(r)/ *noun* [C] **1** (**GEOMETRY**) a solid or hollow figure with round ends and long straight sides ⊃ picture at **solid²** **2** an object shaped like a cylinder, especially one used as a container: *a gas/an oxygen cylinder ◇ a measuring cylinder* (= a container used in a laboratory) **3** a part of an engine that is shaped like a tube, for example in a car: *a six-cylinder engine* ▶ **cylindrical** /sə'lɪndrɪkl/ *adj.*

cymbal /'sɪmbl/ *noun* [C, usually pl.] (**MUSIC**) one of a pair of round metal plates used as a musical instrument. Cymbals make a loud ringing sound when you hit them together or with a stick. ⊃ picture at **instrument, orchestra**

cynic /'sɪnɪk/ *noun* [C] a person who believes that people only do things for themselves, rather than to help others: *Don't be such a cynic. He did it to help us, not for the money.* ▶ **cynical** ?+ 🔤 /-nɪkl/ *adj.*: *a cynical remark* ▶ **cynically** /-kli/ *adv.* ▶ **cynicism** /-nɪsɪzəm/ *noun* [U]

cypress /'saɪprəs/ *noun* [C] a tall, straight EVERGREEN tree (= a tree of the kind that does not lose its leaves in winter)

Cyrillic /sə'rɪlɪk/ *noun* [U] (**LANGUAGE**) the alphabet that is used in languages such as Russian

cyst /sɪst/ *noun* [C] (**HEALTH**) a SWELLING (= an area that is larger and rounder than normal) filled with liquid in the body or under the skin

cystic fibrosis /,sɪstɪk faɪ'brəʊsɪs/ *noun* [U] (**HEALTH**) a serious medical condition that some people are born with, in which some organs do not work correctly. It can cause death.

cystitis /sɪ'staɪtɪs/ *noun* [U] (**HEALTH**) an infection, especially in women, of the BLADDER (= the organ in which liquid waste collects before leaving the body) that makes it painful to go to the toilet

cytology /saɪ'tɒlədʒi/ *noun* [U] (**BIOLOGY**) the scientific study of the structure and function of cells from living things

cytoplasm /'saɪtəʊplæzəm/ *noun* [U] (**BIOLOGY**) all the living material in a cell, except for the NUCLEUS (= central part) ⊃ picture at **cell, fertilization**

cytosine /'saɪtəsi:n/ *noun* [U] (**BIOLOGY**, **CHEMISTRY**) one of the four COMPOUNDS that make up DNA and RNA ⊃ picture at **DNA**

czar, czarina = TSAR, TSARINA

D d

D /di:/ *noun* [C, U] (*pl.* **D's**) **1** (*also* **d**, *pl.* **d's**) the fourth letter of the English alphabet: *'David' begins with (a) 'D'.* **2** (**MUSIC**) the second note in the SCALE of C MAJOR **3** ~(in/for sth) (**EDUCATION**) a grade given for an exam or a piece of work that shows that it is not very good: *He got a D in geography.*

d. *abbr.* (in writing) died: *W A Mozart, d. 1791*

DA (*AmE* **D.A.**) /ˌdiː ˈeɪ/ = DISTRICT ATTORNEY

dab¹ /dæb/ *verb* [I, T] (**-bb-**) to touch sth lightly, usually several times: *He dabbed the cut with some cotton wool.*
PHR V **dab sth on/off (sth)** to put sth on or to remove sth lightly: *to dab some antiseptic on a wound*

dab² /dæb/ *noun* [C] **1** a light touch: *She gave her eyes a dab with a handkerchief.* **2** a small quantity of sth that is put on a surface: *a dab of paint/perfume*

dabble /ˈdæbl/ *verb* **1** [I] to become involved in sth in a way that is not very serious: *to dabble in politics* **2** [T] to put your hands, feet, etc. in water and move them around: *We sat on the bank and dabbled our toes in the river.*

dad ᵃ **A1** /dæd/ *noun* [C] (*informal*) used often as a name to mean 'father': *Is that your dad?* ◇ *Come on, Dad!*

Dada /ˈdɑːdɑː/ (*also* **Dadaism**) *noun* [U] (**ARTS AND MEDIA**) an early twentieth-century movement in art, literature, music and film that made fun of social and artistic behaviour and traditions ▶ **Dadaism** *noun* [U] ▶ **Dadaist** *noun* [C]

daddy /ˈdædi/ *noun* [C] (*pl.* **-ies**) (*informal*) used especially by and to young children, and often as a name, to mean 'father': *I want my daddy!*

daffodil /ˈdæfədɪl/ *noun* [C] a tall yellow flower that grows in the spring

daft /dɑːft/ *adj.* (*informal*) silly, often in a way that makes people laugh: *Don't be daft.* ◇ *a daft idea*

dagger /ˈdægə(r)/ *noun* [C] a type of knife used as a weapon, especially in past times ↪ picture at **weapon**

daily¹ ᵃ **A2** /ˈdeɪli/ *adj.* [only before noun] done, made or happening every day: *a daily routine/delivery/newspaper*

daily² ᵃ **B1** /ˈdeɪli/ *adv.* every day: *Our airline flies to Japan daily.*

daily³ /ˈdeɪli/ *noun* [C] (*pl.* **-ies**) (*informal*) a newspaper that is published every day except Sunday

dainty /ˈdeɪnti/ *adj.* (**daintier**; **daintiest**) **1** small and pretty: *a dainty lace handkerchief* **2** (used about a person's movements) very careful in a way that tries to show good manners: *Veronica took a dainty bite of her cucumber sandwich.* ▶ **daintily** /-tɪli/ *adv.*

dairy¹ ᵃ⁺ **B2** /ˈdeəri/ *noun* [C] (*pl.* **-ies**) **1** a company that sells milk, butter, eggs, etc. **2** [U] food made from milk: *The doctor told me to eat less dairy.* **3** [C] a place on a farm where milk is kept and butter, cheese, etc. are made

dairy² ᵃ⁺ **B2** /ˈdeəri/ *adj.* [only before noun] **1** made from milk: *dairy products/produce* (= milk, butter, cheese, etc.) **2** connected with the production of milk: *dairy cattle* ◇ *a dairy farm*

daisy /ˈdeɪzi/ *noun* [C] (*pl.* **-ies**) a small white flower with a yellow centre, that usually grows wild in grass

dam ᵃ⁺ **C1** /dæm/ *noun* [C] a wall built across a river to hold back the water and form a RESERVOIR (= a lake) behind it ↪ picture at **energy** ▶ **dam** *verb* [T] (**-mm-**)

damage¹ ᵃ **B1** /ˈdæmɪdʒ/ *noun* **1** [U] ~ (**to sth**) harm or injury caused to sth which makes it less attractive, useful or valuable: *Earthquakes can **cause** terrible **damage** in urban areas.* ◇ *Scandals such as this do considerable **damage** to the government's reputation.* ◇ *It will take weeks to **repair the damage** done by the vandals.* **2 damages** [pl.] (**LAW**) an amount of money that a court decides should be paid to sb by the person, company, etc. that has caused them harm or injury: *Mrs Rees, who lost a leg in the crash, was awarded damages of £100 000.*

damage² ᵃ **B1** /ˈdæmɪdʒ/ *verb* [T] to harm sth, for example by breaking it: *The roof was damaged by the storm.* ▶ **damaging** ᵃ⁺ **C1** *adj.*: *These rumours could be damaging to her reputation.*

dame /deɪm/ *noun* [C] **1 Dame** (in the UK) a title given to a woman as an honour because of sth special that she has done: *Dame Agatha Christie* **2** (*AmE*, *old-fashioned*, *informal*) a woman

damn¹ /dæm/ *exclamation*, *verb* [I, T] (*informal*) a swear word that people use to show that they are angry: *Damn (it)! I've left my phone behind.* ◇ *Damn that stupid printer!*

damn² /dæm/ (*also* **damned**) *adj.*, *adv.* (*informal*) **1** (a swear word that people use for emphasizing what they are saying) very: *Read it! It's a damn good book.* **2** a swear word that people use to show that they are angry: *Some damn fool has parked too close to me.*

damn³ /dæm/ *noun*
IDM **not give a damn (about sb/sth)** (*informal*) not care at all: *I don't give a damn what he thinks about me.*

damning /ˈdæmɪŋ/ *adj.* that criticizes sth very much: *There was a damning article about the book online.*

damp¹ /dæmp/ *adj.* a little wet, often in an unpleasant way: *The house had been empty and felt rather damp.* ▶ **damp** *noun* [U]: *She hated the damp and the cold of the English climate.*

damp² /dæmp/ *verb* [T] ~ **sth (down) 1** to make a fire burn less strongly or stop burning: *He tried to damp (down) the flames.* **2** to make sth less strong: *He tried to damp down their expectations in case they failed.*

dampen /ˈdæmpən/ *verb* [T] <u>1 to make sth less strong:</u> *Even the awful weather did not dampen their enthusiasm for the trip.* **2** to make sth a little wet: *He dampened his hair to try to stop it sticking up.*

damson /ˈdæmzn/ *noun* [C] a type of PLUM (= a small dark purple fruit)

dance¹ ᵃ **A1** /dɑːns/ *noun* **1** [C] a series of steps and movements which you do to music **2** [U] dancing as a form of art or entertainment: *She's very interested in modern dance.* **3** [C] (*old-fashioned*) a social meeting at which people dance with each other: *My parents met at a dance.*

dance² ᵃ **A1** /dɑːns/ *verb* **1** [I, T] to move around to the rhythm of music by making a series of steps: *I can't dance very well.* ◇ *to dance the samba* **2** [I] to jump and move around with energy: *She was dancing up and down with excitement.*

ˈ**dance music** *noun* [U] (**MUSIC**) music for dancing to, especially electronic music

dancer ᵃ **A1** /ˈdɑːnsə(r)/ *noun* [C] a person who dances, often as a job: *a ballet dancer* ◇ *She's a good dancer.*

dancing ᵃ **A1** /ˈdɑːnsɪŋ/ *noun* [U] moving your body to music

dandelion /ˈdændɪlaɪən/ *noun* [C] a small wild plant with a bright yellow flower that becomes a soft white ball of seeds called a 'dandelion clock'

dandruff /ˈdændrʌf/ *noun* [U] small pieces of dead skin in the hair that look like white powder

D & T /ˌdiː ən ˈtiː/ *noun* [U] (*BrE*) (**EDUCATION**) a school subject in which you learn about technology and also design and make things for yourself (the abbreviation for 'design and technology')

danger ᵃ **A2** /ˈdeɪndʒə(r)/ *noun* **1** [U, C] the chance that sb/sth may be hurt, killed or damaged or that sth bad may happen: *When he saw the men had knives, he* realized his life was **in danger**. ◇ *They kept on running until they thought they were **out of danger**.* ◇ *If things carry on as they are, **there's a danger that** the factory may have to close.* ⊃ picture at **safety 2** [C] **~ (to sb/ sth)** a person or thing that can cause injury, pain or damage to sb: *Drunk drivers are a danger to everyone on the road.*

dangerous ʔ **A1** /ˈdeɪndʒərəs/ *adj.* likely to cause injury or damage: *a dangerous animal/road/illness* ◇ *Police warn that the man is highly dangerous.* ◇ *It is dangerous to assume that people of the same age are alike.* ▸ **dangerously** *adv.*: *He was standing dangerously close to the cliff edge.*

dangle /ˈdæŋɡl/ *verb* [I, T] to hang freely; to hold sth so that it hangs down in this way: *She sat on the fence with her legs dangling.* ◇ *The police dangled a rope from the bridge and the man grabbed it.*

dank /dæŋk/ *adj.* wet, cold and unpleasant

dare¹ ʔ+ **B2** /deə(r)/ *verb* [I] (usually in negative sentences) **~ (to) do sth** to have enough courage to do sth: *Nobody dared (to) speak.* ◇ *I daren't ask her to lend me any more money.* ◇ *We were so frightened that we didn't dare (to) go into the room.* **2** [T] **~ sb (to do sth)** to ask or tell sb to do sth in order to see if they have the courage to do it: *Can you jump off that wall? Go on, I dare you!* ◇ *He dared his friend to put a mouse in the teacher's bag.*
IDM **don't you dare** (*informal*) used for telling sb very strongly not to do sth: *Don't you dare tell my parents about this!* **how dare you** used when you are angry about sth that sb has done: *How dare you speak to me like that!* **I dare say** used when you are saying sth is likely: *'I think you should accept the offer.' 'I dare say you're right.'*

dare² /deə(r)/ *noun* [C, usually sing.] something dangerous that sb asks you to do, to see if you have the courage to do it: *'Why did you try to swim across the river?' 'For a dare.'*

daredevil /ˈdeədevl/ *noun* [C] a person who likes to do dangerous things

daring /ˈdeərɪŋ/ *adj.* involving or taking risks; brave: *a daring attack* ▸ **daring** *noun* [U]: *The climb required skill and daring.*

dark ʔ **A1** /dɑːk/ *adj.* **1** with no light or very little light: *It was a dark night, with no moon.* ◇ *What time does it get dark in winter?* **2** (used about a colour) not light; nearer black than white: *dark blue* **OPP** **light²**, **pale 3** (*especially BrE*) (used about a person's hair, skin or eyes) brown or black; not fair: *She was small and dark with brown eyes.* ◇ *a handsome, dark-skinned man* ⊃ look at **skin¹** (2) **4** [only before noun] hidden and frightening; mysterious: *He seemed friendly, but there was a dark side to his character.* **5** [only before noun] sad; without hope: *the dark days of the recession*

the dark ʔ **A2** *noun* [sing.] the state of having no light: *He's afraid of the dark.* ◇ *Why are you sitting alone in the dark?*
IDM **before/after dark** before/after the sun goes down in the evening **(be/keep sb) in the dark (about sth)** (be/keep sb) in a position of not knowing about sth: *Don't keep me in the dark. Tell me!*

the dark ages *noun* [pl.] **1 the Dark Ages** (**HISTORY**) the period in western Europe between the end of the Roman Empire (about 500 AD) and the end of the tenth century AD **2** a period of history or a time when sth was not developed or modern: *Back in the dark ages of computing, in about 1980, they started a software company.*

darken /ˈdɑːkən/ *verb* [I, T] to become or to make sth darker: *The sky suddenly darkened and it started to rain.*

dark glasses = SUNGLASSES

darkly /ˈdɑːkli/ *adv.* **1** in a frightening or unpleasant way: *He hinted darkly that somebody would soon be going to hospital.* **2** showing a dark colour

dark matter *noun* [U] (**ASTRONOMY**) according to some scientists, material that exists in space but does not reflect any light ⊃ look at **matter¹** (4)

darkness ʔ+ **B2** /ˈdɑːknəs/ *noun* [U] the state of being dark: *A cat ran past her then disappeared into the darkness.* ◇ *We sat in total darkness, waiting for the lights to come back on.*

darkroom /ˈdɑːkruːm, -rʊm/ *noun* [C] a room that can be made completely dark so that film can be taken out of a camera and photos can be produced there

the Dark Web *noun* [sing.] (**COMPUTING**) the part of the internet that you cannot find with ordinary search engines, allowing users to remain secret. The Dark Web is often used for criminal activities.

darling /ˈdɑːlɪŋ/ *noun* [C] a way of addressing sb you love: *Hello darling! Have you had a nice day?*

darmstadtium /ˈdɑːmʃtætiəm/ *noun* [U] (*symb.* **Ds**) (**CHEMISTRY**) a chemical element. Darmstadtium is a RADIOACTIVE element that is produced artificially.
ⓘ For more information on the periodic table of elements, look at the **Reference Section** of this dictionary.

darn /dɑːn/ *verb* [I, T] to repair a hole in clothes by SEWING across it in one direction and then in the other: *I hate darning socks.*

dart¹ /dɑːt/ *noun* **1** [C] an object like a small ARROW (= a thin piece of metal with a sharp point at one end). It is thrown in a game or shot as a weapon: *The keeper fired a tranquillizer dart into the tiger to send it to sleep.* **2 darts** [U] a game in which you throw darts at a DARTBOARD

dart² /dɑːt/ *verb* [I, T] to move or make sth move suddenly and quickly in a certain direction: *A rabbit darted across the field.* ◇ *She darted an angry glance at me.*

dartboard /ˈdɑːtbɔːd/ *noun* [C] a round board used in the game of DARTS

dash¹ /dæʃ/ *noun* **1** [sing.] **~ for sth** an act of going somewhere suddenly and quickly: *Here comes our bus! Let's make a dash for it!* **2** [C, usually sing.] a small amount of sth that you add to sth else: *a dash of lemon juice* **3** [C] (**LANGUAGE**) the mark (—) used to separate parts of a sentence ⊃ look at **hyphen**

dash² /dæʃ/ *verb* **1** [I] to go somewhere suddenly and quickly: *I must dash — I'm late.* ◇ *I must dash — I'm late.* **2** [I, T] to hit sth with great force; to throw sth so that it hits sth else very hard: *The waves dashed against the harbour wall.*
IDM **dash sb's hopes (of sth/doing sth)** to completely destroy sb's hopes of doing sth
PHR V **dash sth off** to write or draw sth very quickly: *I dashed off a note to my boss and left.*

dashboard /ˈdæʃbɔːd/ *noun* [C] the part in a car in front of the driver where most of the switches, etc. are

data ʔ **A2** ⊘ /ˈdeɪtə, ˈdɑːtə/ *noun* [U, pl.] (used as a plural noun in technical English, when the singular is *datum*) (**COMPUTING**) facts or information: *to gather/ collect data* ◇ *data capture/retrieval* (= ways of storing and looking at information on a computer) ◇ *data processing* ◇ *The privacy notice sets out how the company uses your personal data.* ◇ *Businesses must comply with the data protection laws.* ◇ *Millions of customers had their personal information stolen in a data breach.*

database ʔ+ **B2** /'deɪtəbeɪs, 'dɑːt-/ *noun* [C] (**COMPUTING**) a large amount of data that is stored in a computer and can easily be used, added to, etc: *You can search the database by keyword or date.*

data processing *noun* [U] (**COMPUTING**) a series of actions that a computer performs on data to produce results

dataset (*also* **data set**) /'deɪtəset, 'dɑːt-/ *noun* [C] (**COMPUTING**) a collection of data that is treated as a single unit by a computer

date¹ ʔ **A1** /deɪt/ *noun* **1** [C] a particular day of the month or year: *What's the date today?/What date is it today?/What's today's date?* ◇ *What's your* **date of birth***?* ◇ *We'd better* **fix a date** *for the next meeting.* ◇ *What was the date of the Wall Street Crash?* **2** [sing.] a particular time: *We can discuss this* **at a later date.** ◯ look at **sell-by date 3** [C] an arrangement to meet sb, especially a boyfriend or girlfriend: *Shall we* **make a date** *to have lunch together?* ◇ *I've got a date with her on Friday night.* ◯ look at **blind date 4** [C] a small, sweet, dark brown fruit that comes from a tree that grows in hot countries
IDM **out of date 1** not fashionable; no longer useful: *out-of-date methods/machinery* **2** no longer able to be used: *I must renew my passport. It's out of date.* **to date** (*formal*) until now: *We've had very few complaints to date.* **up to date 1** completely modern: *The new kitchen will be right up to date, with all the latest gadgets.* **2** with all the most recent information; having done everything that you should: *Are you up to date with your homework?*

date² ʔ **B2** /deɪt/ *verb* **1** [T, often passive] to discover or guess how old sth is: *The skeleton has been dated at about 3 000 BC.* **2** [T] to write or print the day's date on sth: *The letter is dated 24 March, 2020.* **3** [I, T] to seem, or to make sb/sth seem, old-fashioned: *We chose a simple style so that it wouldn't date as quickly.*
PHR V **date back to …** | **date from …** to have existed since … : *The house dates back to the seventeenth century.* ◇ *photos dating from before the war*

dated /'deɪtɪd/ *adj.* old-fashioned; belonging to a time in the past: *This sort of jacket looks rather dated now.*

Date Line = INTERNATIONAL DATE LINE

dative /'deɪtɪv/ *noun* [sing.] (**GRAMMAR**) the form of a noun, a pronoun or an adjective in some languages when it is, or is connected with, the INDIRECT OBJECT of a verb: *In the sentence 'Give me the book', 'me' is in the dative.* ◯ look at **accusative, genitive, nominative, vocative**

datum /'deɪtəm/ → DATA

daub /dɔːb/ *verb* [T] **~ A on B; ~ B with A** to spread a substance such as paint, mud, etc. thickly and/or carelessly onto sth: *Protesters daubed red paint on the statue.* ◇ *The walls had been daubed with graffiti.*

daughter ʔ **A1** /'dɔːtə(r)/ *noun* [C] a female child: *I have two sons and one daughter.* ◇ *Janet's daughter is a doctor.*

daughter-in-law *noun* [C] (*pl.* **daughters-in-law**) your son's or daughter's wife

daunt /dɔːnt/ *verb* [T, usually passive] to frighten or to worry sb by being too big or difficult: *Don't be daunted by all the controls — in fact it's a simple machine to use.* **SYN** **intimidate** ▸ **daunting** *adj.*: *a daunting task*

dawdle /'dɔːdl/ *verb* [I] to go somewhere very slowly: *Stop dawdling! We've got to be at school by eight.*

dawn¹ ʔ+ **C1** /dɔːn/ *noun* [U, C] the time in the early morning, when light first appears in the sky: *before/at dawn* ◇ *Dawn was breaking* (= it was starting to get

light) *as I set off to work.* **SYN** **daybreak 2** [sing.] the beginning: *the dawn of civilization*
IDM **the crack of dawn** → CRACK²

dawn² /dɔːn/ *verb* [I] **1** (*formal*) to begin to grow light, after the night: *The day dawned bright and cold.* ◇ (*figurative*) *A new era of peace is dawning.* **2 ~ (on sb)** to become clear (to sb): *Suddenly it dawned on her. 'Of course!' she said. 'You're Mike's brother!'*

day ʔ **A1** /deɪ/ *noun* **1** [C] a period of 24 hours. Seven days make up a week: *'What day is it today?' 'Tuesday.'* ◇ *We went to Italy for ten days.* ◇ *We're meeting again* **the day after tomorrow/in two days' time.** ◇ *The next/following day I saw Mark again.* ◇ *I'd already spoken to him* **the day before/the previous day.** ◇ *I have to take these pills twice a day.* ◇ *I work six days a week. Sunday's* **my day off** (= when I do not work). **2** [C, U] the time when the sky is light; not night: *The days were warm but the nights were freezing.* ◇ *It's been raining all day (long).* ◇ *Owls sleep* **by day** (= during the day) *and hunt at night.* **3** [C] the hours of the day when you work: *She's expected to work a seven-hour day.* **4** [C] (*also* days [pl.]) a particular period of time in the past: *in Shakespeare's day* ◇ *There weren't so many cars in those days.*
IDM **at the end of the day** → END¹ **break of day** → BREAK² **call it a day** → CALL¹ **day by day** every day; as time passes: *Day by day, she was getting a little bit stronger.* **day in, day out** every day, without any change: *He sits at his desk working, day in, day out.* **from day to day** | **from one day to the next** within a short period of time: *Things change so quickly that we never know what will happen from one day to the next.* **have a field day** → FIELD DAY **it's early days (yet)** → EARLY¹ **make sb's day** (*informal*) to make sb very happy **one day** | **some day** at some time in the future: *Some day we'll go back and see all our old friends.* **the other day** a few days ago; recently: *I bumped into him in town the other day.* **these days** in the present age **SYN** **nowadays**

daybreak /'deɪbreɪk/ *noun* [U] the time in the early morning when light first appears **SYN** **dawn¹**

daydream /'deɪdriːm/ *noun* [C] thoughts that are not connected with what you are doing; often pleasant scenes in your imagination: *The child stared out of the window, lost in a daydream.* ▸ **daydream** *verb* [I]: *Don't just sit there daydreaming — do some work!*

daylight /'deɪlaɪt/ *noun* [U] the light that there is during the day: *The colours look quite different* **in daylight.** ◇ *daylight hours*
IDM **broad daylight** → BROAD

daylight saving time (*also* **daylight time**) *noun* [U] (*abbr.* DST) (*all AmE*) (**GEOGRAPHY**) the period during which in some countries the clocks are put forward one hour, so that it is light for an extra hour in the evening ◯ look at **summer time**

day return *noun* [C] (*BrE*) a train or bus ticket for going somewhere and coming back on the same day. It is cheaper than a normal return ticket.

daytime /'deɪtaɪm/ *noun* [U] the time when it is light; not night: *These flowers open* **in the daytime** *and close again at night.* ◇ *daytime TV*

day-to-day *adj.* **1** planning for only one day at a time: *I have organized the cleaning* **on a day-to-day basis,** *until our usual cleaner returns.* **2** involving the usual events or tasks of each day: *She has been looking after the* **day-to-day running** *of the school.*

'day trading *noun* [U] (**FINANCE**) buying and selling shares in companies very quickly on the same day using the internet in order to make a profit from small price changes ▸ **'day trader** *noun* [C]

daze /deɪz/ *noun*
IDM **in a daze** unable to think or react normally; confused

dazed /deɪzd/ *adj.* unable to think or react normally, for example because you have been hit on the head; confused: *He had a dazed expression on his face.*

dazzle /'dæzl/ *verb* [T, often passive] **1** (used about a bright light) to make sb unable to see for a short time: *She was dazzled by the other car's headlights.* **2** to impress sb very much: *He had been dazzled by her beauty.* ▸ **dazzling** *adj.*: *a dazzling light*

DC /ˌdiː 'siː/ *abbr.* = DIRECT CURRENT

de- /diː/ *prefix* (in verbs, nouns, adjectives and adverbs) **1** the opposite of: *decompress* **2** taking sth away: *decaffeinated coffee*

deacon /'diːkən/ *noun* [C] (**RELIGION**) (in some Christian churches) a religious leader just below the rank of a priest

dead¹ ⒧+ A2 /ded/ *adj.* **1** no longer alive: *My father's dead. He died two years ago.* ◇ *Police found a dead body under the bridge.* ◇ *The man was shot dead by a masked gunman.* ◇ *dead leaves* ⊃ *noun* **death**, *verb* **die 2** no longer used; finished: *Latin is a dead language.* **OPP** **living¹ 3** [not before noun] (used about a part of the body) no longer able to feel anything: *Oh no, my foot's gone dead. I was sitting on it for too long.* **SYN** **numb 4** [not before noun] (used about a piece of equipment) no longer working: *I picked up the phone but the line was dead.* ◇ *This battery's dead.* **5** (informal) without movement, activity or interest: *This town is completely dead after 11 o'clock at night.* **6** [only before noun] complete or exact: *a dead silence/calm* ◇ *The arrow hit the dead centre of the target.*
IDM **drop dead** → DROP¹

dead² /ded/ *adv.* completely, exactly or very: *The car made a strange noise and then stopped dead.* ◇ (informal) *He's dead keen to start work.*

the 'dead *noun* [pl.] people who have died: *A church service was held in memory of the dead.*
IDM **in the dead of night** in the middle of the night, when it is very dark and quiet

deaden /'dedn/ *verb* [T] to make sth less strong, painful, etc: *The thick walls deaden the noise of the traffic.*

dead 'end *noun* [C] **1** a road, passage, etc. that is closed at one end: *We came to a dead end and had to turn back.* a point, situation, etc. from which you can make no further progress: *The police had reached a dead end in their investigations.* ◇ *He felt he was in a* **dead-end job** (= one with low wages and no hope of PROMOTION), *so he left.*

dead 'heat *noun* [C] (**SPORT**) the result of a race when two people, etc. finish at exactly the same time

deadline ⒧+ B2 /'dedlaɪn/ *noun* [C] a time or date before which sth must be done or finished: *I usually set myself a* **deadline** *when I have a project to do.* ◇ *A journalist is used to having to* **meet deadlines.**

deadlock /'dedlɒk/ *noun* [sing., U] a situation in which two sides cannot reach an agreement: *Talks have reached a* **deadlock**. ◇ *to try to break the deadlock*

dead 'loss *noun* [C, usually sing.] (informal) a person or thing that is not helpful or useful

deadly¹ ⒧+ B2 /'dedli/ *adj.* (**deadlier**; **deadliest**) **1** causing or likely to cause death: *a deadly poison/weapon/disease* **2** very great; complete: *They're*

deadly enemies. **3** extremely accurate, so that no defence is possible: *That player is deadly when he gets in front of the goal.*

deadly² /'dedli/ *adv.* (informal) extremely: *I'm not joking. In fact I'm deadly serious.*

deadpan /'dedpæn/ *adj.* without any expression on your face or in your voice: *He told the joke with a completely deadpan face.*

dead 'weight *noun* [C, usually sing.] **1** a thing that is very heavy and difficult to lift or move **2** a person or thing that makes it difficult to make progress or succeed

dead 'wood *noun* [U] people or things that are no longer useful or necessary in an organization

deaf /def/ *adj.* **1** (**HEALTH**) unable to hear anything or unable to hear very well: *You'll have to speak louder. My father's a bit deaf.* ◇ *to* **go deaf 2** *the* **deaf** *noun* [pl.] people who cannot hear **3 ~to sth** not wanting to listen to sth: *I've told her what I think but she's deaf to my advice.* ▸ **deafness** *noun* [U]

deafen /'defn/ *verb* [T] to make sb unable to hear by making a very loud noise: *We were deafened by the loud music.* ▸ **deafening** *adj.*: *deafening music*

deal¹ ⒧ A2 ◉ /diːl/ *verb* (*pt, pp* **dealt** /delt/) **1** [I, T] **~(sth) (out)**; **~(sth) (to sb)** to give cards to players in a game of cards: *Whose turn is it to deal?* ◇ *Start by dealing seven cards to each player.* **2** [I] **~(in sth)**; **~(with sb)** (**BUSINESS**) to do business, especially buying and selling goods: *He deals in second-hand cars.* ◇ *Our firm deals with customers all over the world.* **3** [I, T] (informal) to buy and sell illegal drugs
IDM **deal sb/sth a blow | deal a blow to sb/sth 1** to hit sb/sth: *He was dealt a nasty blow to the head in the accident.* **2** to give sb a shock, etc: *This news dealt a terrible blow to my father.*
PHRV **deal sth out** to give sth to a number of people: *The profits are being dealt out among us.* **deal with sb** to treat sb in a particular way; to handle sb: *He's a difficult man. Nobody quite knows how to deal with him.* **deal in sth** to buy and sell a particular product **deal with sb/sth 1** to do business with a person or an organization **2** to take suitable action in a particular situation in order to solve a problem, etc: *My PA will deal with my correspondence while I'm away.* **SYN** **handle¹ 3** to have sth as its subject: *This chapter deals with essay writing.*

deal² ⒧ B1 /diːl/ *noun* [C] **1** (**BUSINESS**) an agreement or arrangement, especially in business: *We're hoping to* **do a deal** *with an Italian company.* ◇ *Let's* **make a deal** *not to criticize each other's work.* ◇ *'I'll help you with your essay if you'll fix my bike.' 'OK, it's a deal!'* **2** [usually sing.] the way that sb is treated: *With high fares and unreliable services, rail users are getting a* **raw deal** (= unfair treatment). ◇ *The new law aims to give older people a* **fair deal.** **3** the action of giving cards to players in a card game
IDM **a big deal/no big deal** → BIG **a good/great deal (of sth)** a lot (of sth): *I've spent a great deal of time on this report.*

dealer ⒧+ B2 /'diːlə(r)/ *noun* [C] **1** a person whose business is buying and selling things: *a dealer in gold and silver* ◇ *an art dealer* **2** a person who sells illegal drugs **3** the person who gives the cards to the players in a game of cards

dealing /'diːlɪŋ/ *noun* (**BUSINESS**) **1 dealings** [pl.] relations, especially in business: *We had some dealings with that firm several years ago.* **2** [U] buying and selling: *share dealing*

dealt /delt/ past tense, past participle of **deal¹**

dean /diːn/ *noun* [C] **1** (**RELIGION**) a priest who is responsible for a large church or a number of small churches **2** (**EDUCATION**) a person in a university who is in charge of a department of studies **3** (**EDUCATION**) (in a college or university, especially at Oxford or Cambridge) a person who is responsible for the discipline of students

dear¹ 🔊 **A1** /dɪə(r)/ adj. **1** used at the beginning of a letter or an email before the name or title of the person you are writing to: *Dear Sarah,* … ◇ *Dear Sir or Madam,* … **2 ~ (to sb)** loved by or important to sb: *It was a subject that was very dear to him.* ◇ *She's one of my dearest friends.* **3** (*BrE*) expensive
IDM close/dear/near to sb's heart → HEART

dear² 🔊 **A2** /dɪə(r)/ exclamation used in expressions to show that you are surprised, disappointed, sad, etc: *Oh dear! I've left my wallet at home.* ◇ *Dear me! Aren't you ready?*

dear³ /dɪə(r)/ noun (*old-fashioned*) used when speaking to sb you know well: *Would you like a cup of tea, dear?*

dearly /ˈdɪəli/ adv. **1** very much: *I'd dearly like to go there again.* **2** (*formal*) in a way that causes damage or suffering, or costs a lot of money: *I've already paid dearly for that mistake.*

dearth /dɜːθ/ noun [sing.] **~ (of sb/sth)** (*formal*) a lack of sth; not enough of sth: *There's a dearth of reliable information on this topic.*

death 🔊 **A2** /deθ/ noun **1** [C, U] the end of sb/sth's life; dying: *There were two deaths and many other people were injured in the accident.* ◇ *The police do not know the cause of death.* ◇ *There was no food and people were starving to death.* ⊃ adjective **dead**, verb **die** **2** [U] the end (of sth): *the death of fascism*
IDM catch your death → CATCH¹ a matter of life and/or death → MATTER¹ put sb to death [usually passive] (*formal*) to kill sb as a punishment sick to death of sb/sth → SICK¹ sudden death → SUDDEN

deathbed /ˈdeθbed/ noun [C] the bed in which sb is dying or dies

death certificate noun [C] (**LAW**) an official document signed by a doctor that states the time and cause of sb's death

deathly /ˈdeθli/ adj., adv. like death: *There was a deathly silence.* ◇ *Jessica went deathly pale.*

the ˈdeath penalty noun [sing.] (**LAW**) the punishment of being killed that is used in some countries ⊃ look at **capital punishment**

death rate noun [C] **1** (**SOCIAL STUDIES**) the number of deaths every year for every 1 000 people in the population of a place: *a high/low death rate* **2** (**HEALTH**) the number of deaths every year from a particular disease or in a particular group: *Death rates from heart disease have risen considerably in recent years.*

death ˈrow noun [U] (especially in the US) the cells in a prison for prisoners who are waiting to be killed as punishment for a serious crime: *prisoners on death row*

death toll noun [C] the number of people killed in a disaster, a war, an accident, etc.

death trap (*also* deathtrap) noun [C] a building, road, vehicle, etc. that is dangerous and could cause sb's death

debacle /dɪˈbɑːkl, deɪ-/ noun [C] an event or a situation that fails completely in a way that makes people feel embarrassed

debase /dɪˈbeɪs/ verb [T] (*formal*) to reduce the quality or value of sth

debatable /dɪˈbeɪtəbl/ adj. not certain; that you could argue about: *It's debatable whether people have a better lifestyle these days.*

debate¹ 🔊 **B2** 🔊 /dɪˈbeɪt/ noun **1** [C] a formal argument or discussion of a question at a public meeting or in a parliament **2** [U] general discussion about sth expressing different opinions: *There's been a lot of debate about the causes of violent crime.*

debate² 🔊 **B2** /dɪˈbeɪt/ verb **1** [I, T] to discuss sth in a formal way or at a public meeting **2** [T] to think about or discuss sth before deciding what to do: *They debated whether to go or not.*

debauched /dɪˈbɔːtʃt/ adj. a **debauched** person is not moral in their sexual behaviour, drinks a lot of alcohol, takes drugs, etc: *debauched sexual practices* **SYN** depraved

debenture /dɪˈbentʃə(r)/ noun [C] (*BrE*) (**ECONOMICS**) an official document that is given by a company, showing it has borrowed money from a person and stating the interest payments that it will make to them: *Payment of interest is made to the debenture holder at a specified rate and at clearly defined intervals.*

debilitate /dɪˈbɪlɪteɪt/ verb [T] (*formal*) **1** to make sb's body or mind weaker: *a debilitating disease* **2** to make a country, an organization, etc. weaker

debit¹ /ˈdebɪt/ noun [C] (**FINANCE**) an amount of money paid out of a bank account, etc. **OPP** credit¹ ⊃ look at **direct debit**

debit² /ˈdebɪt/ verb [T] (**FINANCE**) to take an amount of money out of a bank account, etc. usually as a payment; to record this

ˈdebit card noun [C] (**FINANCE**) a plastic card that can be used to take money directly from your bank account when you pay for sth ⊃ look at **credit card**

debrief /ˌdiːˈbriːf/ verb [T] **~ sb (on sth)** to ask sb questions officially, in order to get information about the task that they have just completed: *He was taken to a US airbase to be debriefed on the mission.* ⊃ look at **brief³** ▸ **debriefing** noun [C, U]: *a debriefing session* ⊃ look at **briefing**

debris 🔊 **C1** /ˈdebriː, ˈdeɪb-/ noun [U] pieces from sth that has been destroyed, especially in an accident

debt 🔊 **B2** /det/ noun **1** [C] (**FINANCE**) an amount of money that you owe to sb: *She borrowed a lot of money and she's still paying off the debt.* **2** [U] (**FINANCE**) the state of owing money: *She was heavily in debt.* ◇ *After he lost his job, he got into debt.* **3** [C, usually sing.] (*formal*) the fact that you should feel grateful to sb, for example because they have helped or been kind to you: *In his speech he acknowledged his debt to his family and friends for their support.*
IDM be in sb's debt (*formal*) to feel grateful to sb for sth that they have done for you

debtor /ˈdetə(r)/ noun [C] a person, a country or an organization who owes money

debug /ˌdiːˈbʌg/ verb [T] (-gg-) (**COMPUTING**) to look for and remove the faults in a computer program

debut¹ 🔊 **C1** /ˈdeɪbjuː, ˈdeb-/ noun [C] (**ARTS AND MEDIA**) a first appearance in public of an actor, etc: *She made her debut in London in 1959.*

debut² /ˈdeɪbjuː, ˈdeb-/ verb [I] (**ARTS AND MEDIA**) (used about a performer or show) to make a first appearance in public: *The ballet will debut next month in New York.*

Dec. abbr. (in writing) = DECEMBER

deca- /ˈdekə, dɪˈkæ/ prefix (in nouns) ten; having ten: *decathlon* (= a competition in which people do ten different sports)

decade 🔊 **B1** 🔊 /ˈdekeɪd, dɪˈkeɪd/ noun [C] a period of ten years, especially a continuous period such as 1910-1919: *the last decade of the twentieth century*

decadence /'dekədəns/ *noun* [U] behaviour, attitudes, etc. that show low moral standards ▸ **decadent** /-dənt/ *adj.*: *a decadent society*

decaffeinated /diː'kæfɪneɪtɪd/ (*also* **decaf** /'diːkæf/) *adj.* (used about coffee or tea) with most or all of the CAFFEINE (= the substance that makes you feel more active) removed

decagon /'dekəgən/ *noun* [C] (**GEOMETRY**) a flat shape with ten straight sides and ten angles ⊃ look at **decahedron**

decahedron /ˌdekə'hiːdrən/ *noun* [C] (**GEOMETRY**) a solid shape with ten flat sides ⊃ look at **decagon**

decant /dɪ'kænt/ *verb* [T] ~ **sth (into sth)** to gradually pour a liquid from one container into another, for example to separate solid material from the liquid

decapitate /dɪ'kæpɪteɪt/ *verb* [T] (*formal*) to cut off sb's head **SYN** **behead**

decathlon /dɪ'kæθlən/ *noun* [C] (**SPORT**) a sports event in which people compete in ten different sports ⊃ look at **biathlon, pentathlon, triathlon**

decay¹ /dɪ'keɪ/ *verb* [I] **1** to be slowly destroyed by natural causes or not being cared for: *the decaying carcass of a dead sheep* **SYN** **rot** **2** to become weaker or less powerful: *His business empire began to decay.* ▸ **decayed** *adj.*: *a decayed tooth*

decay² /dɪ'keɪ/ *noun* [U] the process or state of being slowly destroyed by natural causes or not being cared for: *tooth decay* ◇ *The old farm was in a terrible state of decay.* ⊃ note at **tooth** ⊃ picture at **nitrogen cycle**

deceased /dɪ'siːst/ *adj.* (*formal*) **1** dead **2** **the deceased** *noun* [C] (*pl.* **the deceased**) a person who has died, especially one who has died recently: *Many friends of the deceased were present at the funeral.*

deceit /dɪ'siːt/ *noun* [U] dishonest behaviour; trying to make sb believe sth that is not true: *Their marriage eventually broke up because she was tired of his lies and deceit.*

deceitful /dɪ'siːtfl/ *adj.* dishonest; trying to make sb believe sth that is not true ▸ **deceitfully** /-fəli/ *adv.* ▸ **deceitfulness** *noun* [U]

deceive /dɪ'siːv/ *verb* [T] ~ **sb/yourself (into doing sth)** to try to make sb/ yourself believe sth that is not true: *He deceived his mother into believing that he had earned the money, not stolen it.*

WORD FAMILY

deceive *verb*
deceit *noun*
deceitful *adj.*
deception *noun*
deceptive *adj.*

◇ *You're deceiving yourself if you think there's an easy solution to the problem.* ⊃ noun **deception** or **deceit**

decelerate /ˌdiː'seləreɪt/ *verb* [I, T] (**PHYSICS**) to go more slowly; to make sth go more slowly or happen more slowly: *The engine can be turned off when decelerating, to save fuel.* ◇ *The pilot rapidly decelerates the aircraft as it lands.* **OPP** **accelerate** ▸ **deceleration** /ˌdiːselə'reɪʃn/ *noun* [U]

December 🔊 **A1** /dɪ'sembə(r)/ *noun* [U, C] (*abbr.* **Dec.**) the twelfth month of the year, between November and January

decency /'diːsnsi/ *noun* [U] moral or correct behaviour: *She had the decency to admit that it was her fault.*

decent 🔊 **B2** /'diːsnt/ *adj.* **1** of a good enough standard: *All she wants is a decent job with decent wages.* **2** (used about people or behaviour) honest and fair; treating people with respect **3** not likely to offend or shock sb: *I can't come to the door, I'm not decent* (= I'm not dressed). **OPP** **indecent** ▸ **decently** *adv.*

decentralize (*BrE also* -ise) /ˌdiː'sentrəlaɪz/ *verb* [T, I] (**BUSINESS, POLITICS**) to give some of the power of a central government, organization, etc. to smaller parts or organizations around the country: *decentralized authority/administration* **OPP** **centralize** ▸ **decentralization** (*BrE also* -isation) /ˌdiːˌsentrəlaɪ'zeɪʃn/ *noun* [U, sing.]

deception /dɪ'sepʃn/ *noun* [C, U] making sb believe or being made to believe sth that is not true; a trick to make sb believe sth that is not true: *He had obtained the secret papers by deception.* ◇ *She was fired when the deception was uncovered.* **SYN** **deceit** ⊃ verb **deceive**

deceptive /dɪ'septɪv/ *adj.* likely to make you believe sth that is not true: *The water is deceptive. It's much deeper than it looks.* ▸ **deceptively** *adv.*: *She made the task sound deceptively easy.*

deci- /desɪ/ *prefix* (in nouns) one tenth: *a decilitre*

decibel /'desɪbel/ *noun* [C] (**PHYSICS**) a measurement of how loud a sound is

decide 🔊 **A1** /dɪ'saɪd/ *verb* **1** [I, T] ~ **(to do sth)**; ~ **against (doing) sth**; ~ **about/on sth**; ~ **that ...** to think about two or more possibilities and choose one of them: *There are so many to choose from — I can't decide!* ◇ *We've decided not to invite Isabel.* ◇ *She decided against borrowing the money.* ◇ *They decided on a name for the baby.* ◇ *He decided that it was too late to go.* ◇ *The date hasn't been decided yet.* **2** [T] to influence sth so that it produces a particular result: *Your votes will decide the winner.* **3** [T] to cause sb to make a decision: *What finally decided you to leave?* ⊃ noun **decision**, adjective **decisive**

WORD FAMILY

decide *verb*
decision *noun*
(≠**indecision**)
decisive *adj.*
(≠**indecisive**)
undecided *adj.*

decided /dɪ'saɪdɪd/ *adj.* [only before noun] clear; definite: *There has been a decided improvement in his work.* ⊃ look at **undecided** (2) ▸ **decidedly** *adv.*

deciduous /dɪ'sɪdʒuəs/ *adj.* (**BIOLOGY**) (used about a tree) of a type that loses its leaves every autumn ⊃ look at **evergreen** ⊃ picture at **ecosystem**

decimal¹ /'desɪml/ (*also* ˌdecimal 'fraction) *noun* [C] (**MATHEMATICS**) a FRACTION (= a number less than one) that is shown as a DECIMAL POINT followed by the number of TENTHS, HUNDREDTHS, etc: *Three quarters expressed as a decimal is 0.75.* ⊃ look at **vulgar fraction**

decimal² /'desɪml/ *adj.* (**MATHEMATICS**) based on or counted in units of ten or TENTHS: *the decimal system*

ˌdecimal 'place *noun* [C] (**MATHEMATICS**) the position of a number after a DECIMAL POINT: *The figure is accurate to two decimal places.*

ˌdecimal 'point *noun* [C] (**MATHEMATICS**) a small round mark used to separate the whole number from the TENTHS, HUNDREDTHS, etc. of a DECIMAL, for example in 0.61

decimate /'desɪmeɪt/ *verb* [T] **1** [usually passive] to kill large numbers of animals, plants or people in a particular area: *The rabbit population was decimated by the disease.* **2** to badly damage sth or make sth weaker

decimetre (*BrE*) (*AmE* **decimeter**) /'desɪmiːtə(r)/ *noun* [C] a unit for measuring length. There are ten decimetres in a metre.

decipher /dɪ'saɪfə(r)/ *verb* [T] to succeed in reading or understanding sth that is not clear: *It's impossible to decipher his handwriting.*

decision 🔒 A2 ⊙ /dɪˈsɪʒn/ noun **1** [C, U] ~ **(to do sth); ~ on/about sth; ~ that …** a choice or judgement that you make after thinking about various possibilities: *Have you **made a decision** yet?* ◇ *There were good reasons for his decision to leave.* ◇ *We need your decision on this matter as soon as possible.* ◇ *They **took the decision** that schools should close.* ◇ *The moment of decision has arrived.* **2** [U] being able to decide clearly and quickly: *We are looking for somebody with decision for this job.* ➔ verb **decide**

deˈcision-making 🔒+ C1 noun [U] the process of deciding about sth important, especially in a group of people or in an organization

decisive 🔒+ C1 /dɪˈsaɪsɪv/ adj. **1** very important for the final result of a particular situation: *the decisive battle of the war* ➔ note at **essential 2** having the ability to make clear decisions quickly: *It's no good hesitating. Be decisive.* OPP **indecisive** ➔ verb **decide** ▸ **decisively** adv. ▸ **decisiveness** noun [U]

deck[1] 🔒+ B2 /dek/ noun [C] **1** one of the floors of a ship or bus ➔ look at **flight deck 2** (AmE) = PACK[2] (6): *a deck of cards* **3** part of a machine that records and/or plays sounds
IDM **on deck** on the part of a ship that you can walk on outside: *I'm going out on deck for some fresh air.*

deck[2] /dek/ verb [T, often passive] **be decked (out) in sth** to decorate sb/sth with sth: *The room was decked out in flowers and balloons.*

deckchair /ˈdektʃeə(r)/ noun [C] a chair that you use outside, especially on the beach. You can fold it up and carry it.

declaration 🔒+ C1 /ˌdekləˈreɪʃn/ noun (formal) **1** [C, U] an official statement about sth: *a declaration of war* ◇ *In his speech he made a strong declaration of support for free education.* ➔ note at **statement 2** [C] (FINANCE) a written statement giving information on goods or money you have earned, on which you have to pay tax: *a customs declaration*

declare 🔒 B2 /dɪˈkleə(r)/ verb [T] **1** ~ **(that)** to state sth publicly and officially or to make sth known in a firm, clear way: *to **declare war** on another country* ◇ *I declare that the winner of the award is Jenni Taylor.* **2** (FINANCE) to give information about goods or money you have earned, on which you have to pay tax: *You must declare all your income on this form.*

▼ **SYNONYMS**

declare

state ♦ indicate ♦ announce
These words all mean to say sth, usually firmly and clearly and often in public.
declare (formal) *The picture was declared to be a forgery.*
state (formal) *He stated his intention to run for election.*
indicate (formal) *He indicated his interest in the project.*
announce *The winner will be announced next month.*

declension /dɪˈklenʃn/ noun (GRAMMAR) **1** [U] (in some languages) the way in which some sets of nouns, adjectives and pronouns change their form or endings to show the case, number or GENDER of the word **2** [C] (in some languages) a set of nouns, adjectives or pronouns that change in the same way to show case, number and GENDER: *Latin nouns of the second declension*

decline[1] 🔒 B2 ⊙ /dɪˈklaɪn/ verb **1** [I] to become weaker, smaller or less good: *declining profits* ◇ *The standard of education has declined in this country.* ➔ note at **fall**[1], **trend**[1] **2** [I, T] (formal) to refuse, usually politely: *Thank you for the invitation but I'm afraid I have to decline.* **3** [I, T] (GRAMMAR) if a noun, an adjective or a pronoun **declines**, it has different forms according to whether it is the subject or the object of a verb, whether it is in the singular or plural, etc. When you decline a noun, etc., you list these forms.

decline[2] 🔒 B2 ⊙ /dɪˈklaɪn/ noun [C, usually sing., U] ~ **(in sth)** a process or period of becoming weaker, smaller or less good: *a decline in sales* ◇ *As an industrial power, the country is **in decline**.*

declutter (also **de-clutter**) /ˌdiːˈklʌtə(r)/ verb [I, T] to remove things that you do not use so that you have more space and can easily find things: *Moving house is a good opportunity to declutter.*

decode /ˌdiːˈkəʊd/ verb [T] **1** to find the meaning of sth, especially sth that has been written in code OPP **encode 2** to receive an electronic signal and change it into pictures that can be shown on a TV screen: *decoding equipment*

decoder /ˌdiːˈkəʊdə(r)/ noun [C] a device that changes an electronic signal into a form that people can understand, such as sound and pictures: *a satellite/ video decoder*

decolonization (BrE also **-isation**) /ˌdiːˌkɒlənaɪˈzeɪʃn/ noun [U] (POLITICS) the process of a COLONY (= a country or an area that is ruled by another, more powerful country) or COLONIES becoming independent

decompose /ˌdiːkəmˈpəʊz/ verb [I, T] to slowly be destroyed by natural chemical processes: *The body was so badly decomposed that it couldn't be identified.* SYN **decay**[1], **rot** ▸ **decomposition** /ˌdiː.kɒmpəˈzɪʃn/ noun [U]: *the decomposition of organic waste* ➔ picture at **food chain**

decompress /ˌdiːkəmˈpres/ verb **1** [I, T] to have the air pressure in sth reduced to a normal level or to reduce it to its normal level **2** [T] (COMPUTING) to give files their original size again after they have been made smaller to fit into less space on a disk, etc. SYN **unzip** OPP **compress**

decompression /ˌdiːkəmˈpreʃn/ noun [U] **1** a reduction in air pressure: *decompression sickness* (= the problems that people experience when they come up to the surface after swimming very deep in the sea) **2** the act of reducing the pressure of the air **3** the process of allowing sth that has been made smaller to fill the space that it originally needed

decor /ˈdeɪkɔː(r)/ noun [U, sing.] the style in which the inside of a building is decorated

decorate 🔒 B1 /ˈdekəreɪt/ verb **1** [T] ~ **sth (with sth)** to add sth in order to make a thing more attractive to look at: *Decorate the cake with cherries and nuts.* **2** [I, T] (especially BrE) to put paint and/or WALLPAPER onto walls, ceilings and doors in a room or building

decoration 🔒 B2 /ˌdekəˈreɪʃn/ noun **1** [C, U] something that is added to sth in order to make it look more attractive: *Christmas decorations* ◇ *the elaborate decoration on the carved wooden door* **2** [U] the process of decorating a room or building; the style in which sth is decorated: *The house is in need of decoration.*

decorative /ˈdekərətɪv/ adj. attractive or pretty to look at: *The cloth had a decorative lace edge.*

ˌdecorative ˈarts noun [pl.] (ART) artistic activities that produce objects that are useful and beautiful at the same time

decorator /ˈdekəreɪtə(r)/ noun [C] a person whose job is to paint and decorate houses and buildings

decoy /ˈdiːkɔɪ/ *noun* [C] a person or object that is used in order to trick sb/sth into doing what you want, going where you want, etc. ▶ **decoy** /dɪˈkɔɪ/ *verb* [T]

decrease¹ 🔊 **B2** Ⓦ /dɪˈkriːs/ *verb* [I, T] to become smaller or less; to make sth smaller or less: *Profits have decreased by 15%.* ◇ *Decrease speed when you are approaching a road junction.* **OPP increase¹** ⊃ note at **fall¹**

decrease² 🔊 **B2** Ⓦ /ˈdiːkriːs/ *noun* [C, U] ~ **(in sth)** the process of becoming or making sth smaller or less; the amount that sth is reduced by: *a decrease in the number of students* **OPP increase²**

decree /dɪˈkriː/ *noun* [C] **1** (**LAW, POLITICS**) an official order from a ruler or a government that becomes the law **2** (**LAW**) a decision that is made in court ▶ **decree** *verb* [T]: *The government decreed a state of emergency.*

de,cree ˈabsolute *noun* [sing.] (*BrE*) (**LAW**) an order from a court that finally ends a marriage, making the two people divorced: *The period between the decree nisi and the decree absolute was six weeks.*

decree nisi /dɪˌkriː ˈnaɪsaɪ/ *noun* [sing.] (*BrE*) (**LAW**) an order from a court that a marriage will end after a fixed amount of time unless there is a good reason why it should not

decrepit /dɪˈkrepɪt/ *adj.* (used about a thing or person) old and in very bad condition or poor health

dedicate /ˈdedɪkeɪt/ *verb* [T] **1** ~ **sth to sth** to give all your energy, time, efforts, etc. to sth: *He dedicated his life to helping the poor.* **2** ~ **sth to sb** to say that sth is specially for sb: *He dedicated the book he had written to his brother.*

dedicated 🔊+ **C1** /ˈdedɪkeɪtɪd/ *adj.* giving a lot of your energy, time, efforts, etc. to sth that you believe to be important: *dedicated nurses and doctors*

dedication 🔊+ **C1** /ˌdedɪˈkeɪʃn/ *noun* **1** [U] ~ **(to sth)** wanting to give your time and energy to sth because you feel it is important: *I admire her dedication to her career.* **2** [C] a message at the beginning of a book, piece of music, etc. saying that it is for a particular person

deduce /dɪˈdjuːs/ *verb* [T] (*formal*) to form an opinion using the facts that you already know: *From his name I deduced that he was Polish.* ⊃ noun **deduction**

deduct /dɪˈdʌkt/ *verb* [T] ~ **sth (from sth)** to take sth such as money or points away from a total amount: *Marks will be deducted for untidy work.* ⊃ noun **deduction**

deduction /dɪˈdʌkʃn/ *noun* [C, U] **1** something that you work out from facts that you already know; the ability to think in this way: *It was a brilliant piece of deduction by the detective.* ⊃ look at **induction** (3) ⊃ verb **deduce 2** ~ **(from sth)** taking away an amount or number from a total; the amount or number taken away from the total: *What is your total income after deductions?* (= when tax, insurance, etc. are taken away) ⊃ verb **deduct**

deductive /dɪˈdʌktɪv/ *adj.* using knowledge about things that are generally true in order to think about and understand particular situations or problems ⊃ look at **inductive** (1)

deed 🔊+ **C1** /diːd/ *noun* [C] **1** (*formal*) something that you do; an action: *a brave/good/evil deed* ⊃ note at **action¹** **2** (often plural in British English) (**LAW**) a legal document that shows that you own a house or building

deem 🔊+ **C1** /diːm/ *verb* [T] (*formal*) to have a particular opinion about sb/sth: *He did not even deem it necessary to apologize.* **SYN consider**

deep¹ 🔊 **A2** /diːp/ *adj.*
- TOP TO BOTTOM **1** going a long way down from the surface: *to dig a deep hole* ◇ *That's a deep cut.* ◇ *a coat with deep pockets* ⊃ note at **measure²** ⊃ noun **depth**
- FRONT TO BACK **2** going a long way from front to back: *deep shelves*
- MEASUREMENT **3** measuring a particular amount from top to bottom or from front to back: *The water is only a metre deep at this end of the pool.* ◇ *shelves 40 centimetres deep*
- SOUND **4** (used about sounds) low: *a deep voice*
- COLOUR **5** (used about colours) dark; strong: *a deep red* **OPP light¹**
- EMOTION **6** (used about an emotion) strongly felt: *He felt a very deep love for the child.* **SYN sincere**
- SLEEP **7** (used about sleep) not easy to wake from: *I was in a deep sleep and didn't hear the phone ringing.* **OPP light¹**
- THOROUGH **8** showing great knowledge or understanding: *His books show a deep understanding of human nature.* **SYN profound**
▶ **the deep** *noun* [U]: *in the deep of the night* (= in the middle of the night) ◇ *the deep* (= a LITERARY way of referring to the sea)
IDM deep in thought/conversation thinking very hard or giving sb/sth your full attention **take a deep breath** to breathe in a lot of air, especially in preparation for doing sth difficult: *He took a deep breath then walked on stage.*

deep² 🔊 **B1** /diːp/ *adv.* a long way down or inside sth: *He gazed deep into her eyes.* ◇ *He dug his hands deep into his pockets.*
IDM deep down if you know sth **deep down**, you know your true feelings about it: *I tried to appear optimistic but deep down I knew there was no hope.* **dig deep** → **DIG¹**

deepen /ˈdiːpən/ *verb* [I, T] to become or to make sth deep or deeper: *The river deepens here.*

,deep ˈfreeze = **FREEZER**

,deep-ˈfried *adj.* cooked in oil that covers the food completely

deeply 🔊 **B2** /ˈdiːpli/ *adv.* **1** very; very much: *a deeply unhappy person* ◇ *Opinion is deeply divided on this issue.* **2** used with some verbs to show that sth is done in a very complete way: *to breathe/sigh/exhale deeply* (= using all of the air in your lungs) ◇ *to sleep deeply* (= in a way that makes it difficult for you to wake up) **3** to a depth that is quite a long way from the surface of sth: *to drill deeply into the wood*

,deep-ˈrooted (*also* ,deep-ˈseated) *adj.* strongly felt or believed and therefore difficult to change: *deep-rooted fears*

ˈdeep-sea *adj.* of or in the deeper parts of the sea: *deep-sea fishing/diving*

the ,Deep ˈSouth *noun* [sing.] the southern states of the US

,deep vein thromˈbosis *noun* [U, C] (*abbr.* DVT) (**HEALTH**) a serious condition caused by a blood CLOT (= a thick mass of blood) forming in a VEIN (= one of the tubes that carry blood from all parts of the body towards the heart): *Passengers on long-haul flights are being warned about the risks of deep vein thrombosis.*

deer /dɪə(r)/ *noun* [C] (*pl.* deer) an animal with long legs that eats grass, leaves, etc. and can run fast. Most male deer have ANTLERS (= parts on their heads that are shaped like branches).

▼ VOCABULARY BUILDING

A male **deer** is called a **buck** or, especially if it has fully grown antlers, a **stag**. The female is a **doe** and a young deer a **fawn**. **Venison** is the meat from deer.

deface /dɪˈfeɪs/ *verb* [T] to damage the appearance of sth by writing on or marking its surface

de facto /ˌdeɪ ˈfæktəʊ/ *adj.* (*formal*) (**LAW**) a Latin expression used to say that sth exists as a fact although it may not be legally accepted as existing: *The general took de facto control of the country.* ▸ **de facto** *adv.*: *He continued to rule the country de facto.*

defaecate /ˈdefəkeɪt, ˈdiːf-/ (*BrE*) = DEFECATE

defamatory /dɪˈfæmətri/ *adj.* (*formal*) (used about speech or writing) intended to harm sb by saying or writing bad or false things about them

defame /dɪˈfeɪm/ *verb* [T] (*formal*) to harm sb by saying or writing bad or false things about them ▸ **defamation** /ˌdefəˈmeɪʃn/ [U, C]: *The company sued the paper for defamation.*

default¹ ⓘ+ **C1** /dɪˈfɔːlt, ˈdiːfɔːlt/ *noun* [U, sing.] (**COMPUTING**) what happens or appears if you do not make any other choice or change, especially in a computer program

IDM **by default 1** a game or competition can be won **by default** if there are no other people, teams, etc. taking part: *They won by default, because the other team didn't turn up.* **2** if something happens **by default**, it happens because you have not made any other decision or choices that would make things happen in a different way: *I became a teacher almost by default.*

default² /dɪˈfɔːlt/ *verb* [I] **1 ~ (on sth)** (**LAW**) to not do sth that you should do by law: *If you default on the credit payments (= you don't pay them), the car will be taken back.* **2 ~ (to sth)** (**COMPUTING**) to happen when you do not make any other choice or change: *The progam defaults to the standard style each time you open it.*

defeat¹ ⓘ **B2** /dɪˈfiːt/ *verb* [T] **1** to win a game, a fight, a vote, etc. against sb: *The army defeated the rebels after three days of fighting.* ◇ *In the last match France defeated Wales.* **SYN** **beat¹ 2** to be too difficult for sb to do or understand: *I've tried to work out what's wrong with the car but it defeats me.* **3** to prevent sth from succeeding: *The local residents are determined to defeat the council's building plans.*

defeat² ⓘ **B2** /dɪˈfiːt/ *noun* **1** [C] an occasion when sb fails to win or be successful against sb else: *This season they have had two victories and three defeats.* **2** [U] the act of losing or not being successful: *She refused to admit defeat and kept on trying.*

defeatist /dɪˈfiːtɪst/ *adj.* expecting not to succeed: *a defeatist attitude/view* ▸ **defeatism** /-ˈfiːtɪzəm/ *noun* [U] ▸ **defeatist** *noun* [C]: *Don't be such a defeatist. We haven't lost yet!*

defecate (*BrE also* **defaecate**) /ˈdefəkeɪt, ˈdiːf-/ *verb* [I] (*formal*) (**BIOLOGY**) to get rid of solid waste from the body; to go to the toilet

defect¹ ⓘ **C1** /ˈdiːfekt/ *noun* [C] something that is wrong with or missing from sb/sth: *a speech defect* ◇ *defects in the education system* ▸ **defective** /dɪˈfektɪv/ *adj.*

deer

stag
doe
fawn

defect² /dɪˈfekt/ *verb* [I] (**POLITICS**) to leave your country, a political party, etc. and join one that is considered to be the enemy ▸ **defection** /-ˈfekʃn/ *noun* [C, U] ▸ **defector** *noun* [C]

defence ⓘ **B2** (*BrE*) (*AmE* **defense**) /dɪˈfens/ *noun*
• PROTECTION **1** [U] something that you do or say to protect sb/sth from attack, bad treatment, criticism, etc: *Would you fight in defence of your country?* ◇ *When her brother was criticized she leapt to his defence.* ◇ *I must say in her defence that I have always found her very reliable.* ᴐ look at **self-defence 2** [C, U] **~ (against sth)** something that protects sb/sth from sth, or that is used to fight against attack: *the body's defences against disease* **3** [U] (**POLITICS**) the military equipment, forces, etc. for protecting a country: *Spending on defence needs to be reduced.*
• SUPPORT **4** [C] something that is said or written in order to support sth: *a defence of Marxism*
• IN LAW **5** [C, usually sing.] an argument in support of the accused person in court: *His defence was that he was only carrying out orders.* **6** the defence [sing. + sing./pl. verb] the lawyer or lawyers who are acting for the accused person in court: *The defence claims/claim that many of the witnesses were lying.* ᴐ look at **prosecution** (2) ᴐ note at **court¹**
• IN SPORT **7** [sing., U] action to prevent the other team scoring; the players who try to do this: *She plays in defence.*

defenceless (*BrE*) (*AmE* **defenseless**) /dɪˈfensləs/ *adj.* unable to defend yourself against attack

defend ⓘ **B2** /dɪˈfend/ *verb*
• PROTECT **1** [T] **~ sb/sth/yourself (against/from sb/sth)** to protect sb/sth from harm or danger: *Would you be able to defend yourself against an attacker?* ◇ *The organization works to defend human rights.*
• SUPPORT **2** [T] **~ sb/sth/yourself (against/from sb/sth)** to say or write sth to support sb/sth that has been criticized: *The minister went on TV to defend the government's policy.*
• IN LAW **3** [T] to speak for sb who is accused of a crime in court ᴐ note at **professional²**
• IN SPORT **4** [I, T] to try to stop the other team or player scoring: *They defended well and managed to hold onto their lead.*
• IN A COMPETITION **5** [T] to take part in a competition that you won before and try to win it again: *She successfully defended her title.* ◇ *He is the defending champion.*

defendant /dɪˈfendənt/ *noun* [C] (**LAW**) a person who is accused of a crime in a court of law or who is being SUED by another person ᴐ look at **accused**, **plaintiff** ᴐ note at **crime**

defender ⓘ+ /dɪˈfendə(r)/ *noun* [C] a person who defends sb/sth, especially in sport

defense, defenseless (*AmE*) = DEFENCE, DEFENSELESS

defensible /dɪˈfensəbl/ *adj.* **1** that can be supported by reasons or arguments that show that it is right or should be allowed: *morally defensible* **2** (used about a place) that can be defended against an attack

defensive¹ ⓘ+ **C1** /dɪˈfensɪv/ *adj.* **1** that protects sb/sth from attack: *The troops took up a defensive position.* **OPP** **offensive¹ 2** showing that you feel that sb is criticizing you: *When I asked him about his new job, he became very defensive and tried to change the subject.*

defensive² /dɪˈfensɪv/ *noun*
IDM **on the defensive** acting in a way that shows that you expect sb to attack or criticize you: *My questions about her past immediately put her on the defensive.*

defer /dɪˈfɜː(r)/ *verb* [T] (-rr-) (*formal*) to leave sth until a later time: *She deferred her place at university for a year.*

deference /ˈdefərəns/ *noun* [U] polite behaviour that you show towards sb/sth, usually because you respect them
IDM **in deference to sb/sth** because you respect and do not wish to upset sb: *In deference to her father's wishes, she didn't mention the subject again.*

defiance /dɪˈfaɪəns/ *noun* [U] open REFUSAL to obey sb/sth: *an act of defiance*

defiant /dɪˈfaɪənt/ *adj.* showing open REFUSAL to obey sb/sth ⊃ verb **defy** ▸ **defiantly** *adv.*

defibrillator /diːˈfɪbrɪleɪtə(r)/ *noun* [C] (MEDICINE) a piece of equipment used to control the movements of the heart muscles by giving the heart a controlled electric shock

deficiency ℓ+ C1 /dɪˈfɪʃnsi/ *noun* (*pl.* -ies) ~ (in/of sth) 1 [C, U] the state of not having enough of sth; a lack: *a deficiency of vitamin C* 2 [C] a fault or a weakness in sb/sth: *The problems were caused by deficiencies in the design.*

deficient /dɪˈfɪʃnt/ *adj.* 1 ~ (in sth) not having enough of sth: *food that is deficient in minerals* 2 not good enough or not complete

deficit ℓ+ C1 /ˈdefɪsɪt/ *noun* [C] (FINANCE) the amount by which the money you receive is less than the money you have spent: *a budget deficit*

define ℓ B1 ○ /dɪˈfaɪn/ *verb* [T] 1 to say exactly what a word or an idea means: *How would you define 'happiness'?* 2 to explain the exact nature of sth clearly: *We need to define the problem before we can attempt to solve it.*

defining /dɪˈfaɪnɪŋ/ *adj.* 1 that describes or shows the essential meaning of sth: *Advertising is one of the defining features of our age.* 2 (used about clauses) explaining which particular person or thing you are talking about rather than giving extra information about them 3 a set of carefully chosen words used to write the explanations in some dictionaries

definite ℓ B1 /ˈdefɪnət/ *adj.* 1 fixed and unlikely to change; certain: *I'll give you a definite decision in a couple of days.* **OPP** **indefinite** ⊃ note at **certain** 2 easy to see or notice: *There has been a definite change in her attitude recently.* **SYN** **clear¹**

definite article *noun* [C] (GRAMMAR) the word *the* in English, or a similar word in another language ⊃ look at **indefinite article**

definitely ℓ A2 /ˈdefɪnətli/ *adv.* certainly; without doubt: *I'll definitely consider your advice.*

definition ℓ B1 ○ /ˌdefɪˈnɪʃn/ *noun* [C, U] a description of the exact meaning of a word or idea: *This dictionary has clear, simple definitions.* ◇ *Neighbours, by definition, live close by.*

definitive /dɪˈfɪnətɪv/ *adj.* in a form that cannot be changed or that cannot be improved: *This is the definitive version.* ◇ *the definitive performance of Hamlet* ▸ **definitively** *adv.*

deflate /dɪˈfleɪt, diːˈfleɪt/ *verb* [T, I] 1 to make sth smaller by letting the air or gas out of it; to become smaller because the air or gas is let out of it: *Someone had deflated the tyres of his bike.* ◇ *The balloon slowly deflated.* **OPP** **inflate** 2 [T, often passive] to make sb feel less confident, proud or excited: *I felt really deflated when I got my exam results.* 3 [T] (ECONOMICS) to reduce the amount of money in a country so that prices fall or stay steady ⊃ look at **inflate** (2), **reflate** ▸ **deflationary** /diːˈfleɪʃənri/ *adj.*

deflation /diːˈfleɪʃn/ *noun* [U] 1 (ECONOMICS) a reduction in the amount of money in a country's economy so that prices fall or remain the same 2 the action of air being removed from sth **OPP** **inflation**

deflect /dɪˈflekt/ *verb* 1 [I, T] to change direction after hitting sb/sth; to make sth change direction in this way: *The ball deflected off a defender and into the goal.* 2 [T] to turn sb's attention away from sth: *Nothing could deflect her from her aim.*

deflection /dɪˈflekʃn/ *noun* [C, U] a change of direction after hitting sb/sth

defoliate /diːˈfəʊlieɪt/ *verb* [T] to destroy the leaves of trees or plants, especially with chemicals ▸ **defoliation** /diːˌfəʊliˈeɪʃn/ *noun* [U]

deforestation /diːˌfɒrɪˈsteɪʃn/ *noun* [U] (ENVIRONMENT) cutting down or burning trees over a large area ⊃ look at **afforestation**

deform /dɪˈfɔːm/ *verb* [T] to change or damage the natural shape of sth

deformed /dɪˈfɔːmd/ *adj.* having a shape that is not normal because it has grown wrongly

deformity /dɪˈfɔːməti/ *noun* [C, U] (*pl.* -ies) the condition in which a part of the body is an unusual shape because of disease, injury, etc.

defrag /diːˈfræg/ (*also formal* **defragment** /ˌdiːfrægˈment/) *verb* [T] (COMPUTING) to organize the files on a computer so that information connected with each file is stored in the same area and the computer therefore works faster

defraud /dɪˈfrɔːd/ *verb* [T] ~ sb (of sth) to get sth from sb in a dishonest way: *He defrauded the company of millions.*

defriend /ˌdiːˈfrend/ = UNFRIEND

defrost /diːˈfrɒst/ *verb* 1 [T] to remove the ice from sth: *to defrost a fridge* ⊃ look at **de-ice** 2 [I, T] (used about frozen food) to return to a normal temperature; to make food do this: *Defrost the chicken thoroughly before cooking.*

deft /deft/ *adj.* (used especially about movements) quick and showing skill ▸ **deftly** *adv.*

defunct /dɪˈfʌŋkt/ *adj.* (*formal*) no longer existing or in use

defuse /ˌdiːˈfjuːz/ *verb* [T] 1 to remove part of a bomb so that it cannot explode: *Army experts defused the bomb safely.* 2 to make a situation calmer or less dangerous: *She defused the tension by changing the subject.*

defy ℓ+ C1 /dɪˈfaɪ/ *verb* [T] (defying; defies; *pt, pp* defied) 1 to refuse to obey sb/sth: *She defied her parents and continued seeing him.* ⊃ adjective **defiant**, noun **defiance** 2 ~ sb to do sth to ask sb to do sth that you believe to be impossible: *I defy you to prove me wrong.* 3 to make sth impossible or very difficult: *It's such a beautiful place that it defies description.*

WORD FAMILY
defy *verb*
defiance *noun*
defiant *adj.*

degenerate¹ /dɪˈdʒenəreɪt/ *verb* [I] to become worse, lower in quality, etc: *The calm discussion degenerated into a nasty argument.* **SYN** **deteriorate** ▸ **degeneration** /dɪˌdʒenəˈreɪʃn/ *noun* [U]

degenerate² /dɪˈdʒenərət/ *adj.* having moral standards that have fallen to a very low level

degenerative /dɪˈdʒenərətɪv/ *adj.* (HEALTH) (used about an illness) getting or likely to get worse as time passes: *degenerative diseases such as arthritis*

degradation /ˌdegrəˈdeɪʃn/ *noun* [U] 1 a situation in which sb has lost all SELF-RESPECT and the respect of other people: *the degradation of being in prison*

2 the process of causing the condition of sth to become worse: *environmental degradation*

degrade /dɪˈɡreɪd/ *verb* [T] to make people respect sb less: *It's the sort of film that really degrades women.* ▶ **degrading** *adj.*

degree 🔊 **A2 ⊙** /dɪˈɡriː/ *noun* **1** [C] (**SCIENCE**) a measurement of temperature: *Water boils at 100 degrees Celsius (100°C).* ◇ *three degrees below zero/minus 3 degrees (-3°)* **2** [C] (**GEOMETRY**) a measurement of angles: *a 45 degree (45°) angle* ◇ *An angle of 90 degrees (90°) is called a right angle.* **3** [C, U] ~ (**of sth**) a certain amount or level: *There is always a degree of risk involved in mountaineering.* ◇ *I sympathize with her to some degree.* **4** [C] ~ (**in sth**) (**EDUCATION**) a qualification that students gain by successfully completing a course at university or college: *She's got a degree in Philosophy.* ◇ *to do a Chemistry degree* ⊃ note at **subject**[1]

dehumanize (*BrE also* -ise) /ˌdiːˈhjuːmənaɪz/ *verb* [T] to make sb lose their human qualities such as KINDNESS, PITY, etc. ▶ **dehumanization** (*BrE also* -isation) /ˌdiːˌhjuːmənaɪˈzeɪʃn/ *noun* [U]

dehydrate /ˌdiːhaɪˈdreɪt/ *verb* **1** [T, usually passive] to remove all the water from sth: *Dehydrated vegetables can be stored for months.* **2** [I, T] (**HEALTH**) to lose or to make sb lose too much water from the body: *If you run for a long time in the heat, you start to dehydrate.* ▶ **dehydration** /-ˈdreɪʃn/ *noun* [U]: *Several of the runners were suffering from severe dehydration.*

de-ice /ˌdiːˈaɪs/ *verb* [T] to remove the ice from sth: *The car windows need de-icing.* ⊃ look at **defrost** (2)

deign /deɪn/ *verb* [T] ~ **to do sth** to do sth although you think you are too important to do it: *He didn't even deign to look up when I entered the room.* **SYN condescend**

deity /ˈdeɪəti, ˈdiːəti/ *noun* [C] (*pl.* -ies) (*formal*) (**RELIGION**) a god

dejected /dɪˈdʒektɪd/ *adj.* very unhappy, especially because you are disappointed: *The fans went home dejected after watching their team lose.* ▶ **dejectedly** *adv.* ▶ **dejection** /-ˈdʒekʃn/ *noun* [U]

delay[1] 🔊 **B2** /dɪˈleɪ/ *verb* **1** [T] to make sb/sth slow or late: *The plane was delayed for several hours because of bad weather.* **2** [I, T] ~ (**sth/doing sth**) to decide not to do sth until a later time: *Don't delay — call us today!* ◇ *I was forced to delay the trip until the following week.*

delay[2] 🔊 **B2** /dɪˈleɪ/ *noun* [C, U] a situation or period of time where you have to wait: *Delays are likely on the roads because of heavy traffic.* ◇ *If you smell gas, report it **without delay** (= immediately).*

delegate[1] 🔊+ **C1** /ˈdelɪɡət/ *noun* [C] a person who has been chosen to speak or take decisions for a group of people, especially at a meeting

delegate[2] /ˈdelɪɡeɪt/ *verb* [I, T] to give part of your work, power or authority to sb in a lower position than you: *You can't do everything yourself. You must learn how to delegate.*

delegation 🔊+ **C1** /ˌdelɪˈɡeɪʃn/ *noun* **1** [C + sing./pl. verb] a group of people who have been chosen to speak or take decisions for a larger group of people, especially at a meeting: *The British delegation walked out of the meeting in protest.* **2** [U] the process of giving sb work or responsibilities that would usually be yours

delete 🔊+ **B2** /dɪˈliːt/ *verb* [T] to remove sth that has been written or printed, or that has been stored on a computer: *Your name has been deleted from the list.* ◇ *This command deletes files from the directory.* ▶ **deletion** /-ˈliːʃn/ *noun* [C, U]

deli /ˈdeli/ (*also* delicatessen) *noun* [C] a shop, or part of a shop, that sells special, unusual or foreign foods, especially cold cooked meat, cheeses, etc.

deliberate[1] 🔊 **B2** /dɪˈlɪbərət/ *adj.* **1** done on purpose; planned: *Was it an accident or was it deliberate?* **SYN intentional 2** done slowly and carefully, without hurrying: *She spoke in a calm, deliberate voice.*

deliberate[2] /dɪˈlɪbəreɪt/ *verb* [I, T] (*formal*) to think about or discuss sth fully before making a decision: *The judges deliberated for an hour before announcing the winner.*

deliberately 🔊 **B2** /dɪˈlɪbərətli/ *adv.* **1** done in a way that was planned, not by chance: *I didn't break it deliberately. It was an accident.* **SYN intentionally**, **on purpose OPP by accident 2** slowly and carefully, without hurrying

deliberation /dɪˌlɪbəˈreɪʃn/ *noun* (*formal*) **1** [C, U] discussion or thinking about sth in detail: *After much deliberation I decided to reject the offer.* **2** [U] the quality of being very slow and careful in what you say and do: *He spoke with great deliberation.*

delicacy /ˈdelɪkəsi/ *noun* (*pl.* -ies) **1** [U] the quality of being easy to damage or break **2** [U] the fact that a situation is difficult and sb may be easily offended: *Be tactful! It's a matter of some delicacy.* **3** [U] great care; a gentle touch **4** [C] a type of food that is considered very special in a particular place: *Try this dish, it's a local delicacy.*

delicate 🔊+ **C1** /ˈdelɪkət/ *adj.* **1** easy to damage or break: *delicate skin* ◇ *delicate china teacups* **2** frequently ill or hurt: *He was a delicate child and often in hospital.* **3** (used about colours, tastes, etc.) light and pleasant; not strong: *a delicate shade of pale blue* **4** needing careful treatment: *Repairing this is going to be a very delicate operation.* ▶ **delicately** *adv.*: *She stepped delicately over the broken glass.*

delicatessen /ˌdelɪkəˈtesn/ *noun* [C] = DELI

delicious 🔊 **A1** /dɪˈlɪʃəs/ *adj.* having a very pleasant taste or smell: *This soup is absolutely delicious.*

delight[1] 🔊 **B2** /dɪˈlaɪt/ *noun* **1** [U] great pleasure; joy: *She laughed with delight as she opened the present.* **2** [C] something that gives sb great pleasure: *The story is a delight to read.* ▶ **delightful** /-fl/ *adj.*: *a delightful view* ▶ **delightfully** /-fəli/ *adv.*

delight[2] 🔊 **B2** /dɪˈlaɪt/ *verb* [T] to give sb great pleasure: *She delighted the audience by singing all her old songs.* **PHR V delight in sth/doing sth** to get great pleasure from sth: *He delights in playing tricks on people.*

delighted 🔊 **B2** /dɪˈlaɪtɪd/ *adj.* ~ (**at/with/about sth**); ~ **to do sth/that** ... extremely pleased: *She was delighted at getting the job/she got the job.* ◇ *They're absolutely delighted with their baby.* ◇ *I'm delighted to be here to speak to you today.*

delinquency /dɪˈlɪŋkwənsi/ *noun* [U] (*formal*) bad or criminal behaviour, especially among young people

delinquent /dɪˈlɪŋkwənt/ *adj.* (*formal*) (usually used about a young person) behaving badly and often breaking the law ▶ **delinquent** *noun* [C]: *a juvenile delinquent*

delirious /dɪˈlɪriəs, -ˈlɪər-/ *adj.* **1** (**HEALTH**) not able to think or speak clearly, usually because of a high temperature: *She started to become delirious and incoherent.* ◇ *He was delirious with a high fever.* **2** extremely happy ▶ **deliriously** *adv.* ▶ **delirium** /-əm/ *noun* [U]: *Many patients fell into delirium.*

deliver 𝄆 **B1** /dɪˈlɪvə(r)/ *verb* **1** [T, I] to take sth (goods, letters, etc.) to the place requested or to the address on it: *Your order will be delivered within five days.* ◇ *We deliver free within the local area.* ◇ *Online training sessions are delivered directly to your desktop.* **2** [T] to help a mother to give birth to her baby: *to deliver a baby* **3** [T] (*formal*) to say sth formally: *to deliver a speech/lecture/warning* **4** [I, T] ~ **(on sth)** (*informal*) to do or give sth that you have promised: *The new leader has made a lot of promises, but can he deliver on them?* ◇ *If you can't deliver improved sales figures, you're fired.*
IDM come up with/deliver the goods → GOODS

deliverable /dɪˈlɪvərəbl/ *noun* [usually pl.] (**BUSINESS**) a product that a company promises to have ready for a customer: *computer software deliverables*

delivery 𝄆 **B2** /dɪˈlɪvəri/ *noun* (*pl.* -ies) **1** [U] the act of taking sth (goods, letters, etc.) to the place or person who has ordered it or whose address is on it: *Please allow 28 days for delivery.* ◇ *a delivery van* ◇ *plans to improve the delivery of public services.* ◇ *Place your order before 3 p.m. and choose Next Day Delivery.* **2** [C] an occasion when sth is delivered: *Are there mail deliveries on Saturdays?* **3** [C] something (goods, letters, etc.) that is delivered: *The shop is waiting for a new delivery of apples.* **4** [C] (**HEALTH**) the process of giving birth to a baby: *an easy delivery*

delta /ˈdeltə/ *noun* [C] (**GEOGRAPHY**) an area of flat land shaped like a TRIANGLE where a river divides into smaller rivers as it goes into the sea

deltoids /ˈdeltɔɪdz/ *noun* [pl.] (**ANATOMY**) the thick muscles in the shape of TRIANGLES that cover the shoulder JOINTS (= the places where the shoulders are connected to the body)

delude /dɪˈluːd/ *verb* [T] to make sb believe sth that is not true: *If he thinks he's going to get rich quickly, he's deluding himself.* **SYN** deceive ◇ noun **delusion**

deluge¹ /ˈdeljuːdʒ/ *noun* [C, usually sing.] **1** a sudden very heavy fall of rain **2** ~ **(of sth)** a very large number of things that happen or arrive at the same time: *The programme was followed by a deluge of complaints from the public.* **SYN** flood¹

deluge² /ˈdeljuːdʒ/ *verb* [T, usually passive] to send or give sb/sth a very large quantity of sth, all at the same time: *They were deluged with applications for the job.* **SYN** flood¹

delusion /dɪˈluːʒn/ *noun* [C, U] a false belief or opinion about yourself or your situation: *He seems to be under the delusion that he's popular.* ◇ *He was suffering from paranoid delusions and hallucinations.* ◇ verb **delude**

deluxe /dɪˈlʌks, -ˈlʊks/ *adj.* of extremely high quality and more expensive than usual: *a deluxe hotel* **SYN** luxury²

delve /delv/ *verb* [I] (used with an adverb or a preposition) to search inside sth: *She delved into the bag and brought out a tiny box.* ◇ (*figurative*) *We must delve into the past to find the origins of the custom.*

Dem. *noun* [C] (in writing) = DEMOCRAT (2)

demand¹ 𝄆 **B2** ◉ /dɪˈmɑːnd/ *noun* **1** [C] ~ **(for sth/ that …)** a strong request or order that must be obeyed: *a demand for changes in the law* ◇ *I was amazed by their demand that I should leave immediately.* ◇ note at **ask 2** demands [pl.] something that sb/sth makes you do, especially sth that is difficult or makes you tired: *Running a marathon makes huge demands on the body.* **3** [U, sing.] ~ **(for sth/ sb)** (**BUSINESS**) the desire or need for sth among a group of people: *We no longer sell that product because there is no demand for it.*

IDM in demand wanted by a lot of people: *I'm in demand this weekend — I've had three invitations!* on demand whenever you ask for it: *This treatment is available from your doctor on demand.* ◇ *The service allows you to watch video on demand.*

demand² 𝄆 **B2** /dɪˈmɑːnd/ *verb* [T] **1** ~ **to do sth/ that …** ; ~ **sth** to ask for sth in an extremely firm or aggressive way: *I walked into the office and demanded to see the manager.* ◇ *She demanded that I pay her immediately.* ◇ *Your behaviour was disgraceful and I demand an apology.* **2** to need sth: *a sport that demands skill as well as strength*

demanding /dɪˈmɑːndɪŋ/ *adj.* **1** (used about a job, task, etc.) needing a lot of effort, care, skill, etc: *It will be a demanding schedule — I have to go to six cities in six days.* ◇ note at **difficult 2** (used about a person) always wanting attention or expecting very high standards of people: *Young children are very demanding.* ◇ *a demanding boss*

demarcation /ˌdiːmɑːˈkeɪʃn/ *noun* [U, C] a border or line that separates two things, such as types of work, groups of people or areas of land

dementia /dɪˈmenʃə/ *noun* [U] (**PSYCHOLOGY**) a serious mental DISORDER caused by brain disease or injury, that affects the ability to think, remember and behave normally: *patients with dementia* ◇ *dementia care*

demi- /demi/ *prefix* (in nouns) half; partly

demise /dɪˈmaɪz/ *noun* [C, usually sing.] **1** the end or failure of sth: *Poor business decisions led to the company's demise.* **2** (*formal*) the death of a person

demo¹ /ˈdeməʊ/ *noun* [C] (*informal*) (*pl.* -os) **1** = DEMONSTRATION (2) **2** = DEMONSTRATION (3): *They all went on the demo.* **3** (**COMPUTING**) a version of an app or computer program that you can try before you buy the full program: *You can download the free demo from the game's page.* **4** (**MUSIC**) a recording of an example of sb's music: *The band has recorded one demo and a full-length album.*

demo² /ˈdeməʊ/ *verb* [T] (*informal*) (**BUSINESS**, **COMPUTING**) to use something, especially a piece of software, to show sb or to see for yourself how it works: *They will demo the phone at this year's technology fair.* ◇ *We got to demo a bit of the game in the summer.*

demo- /demə, dɪˈmɒ/ *prefix* (in verbs, nouns and adjectives) connected with people or population: *democracy*

democracy 𝄆+ **B2** /dɪˈmɒkrəsi/ *noun* (*pl.* -ies) (**POLITICS**) **1** [U] a system in which the government of a country is elected by the people **2** [C] a country that has this system **3** [U] the right of everyone in an organization, etc. to be treated equally and to vote on matters that affect them: *There is a need for more democracy in the company.*

democrat /ˈdeməkræt/ *noun* [C] (**POLITICS**) **1** a person who believes in and supports DEMOCRACY **2** Democrat (*abbr.* **Dem.**) a member of, or sb who supports, the Democratic Party of the US ◇ look at **republican** (2)

democratic ᵇ⁺ B2 /ˌdeməˈkrætɪk/ *adj.* (**POLITICS**) **1** based on the system of DEMOCRACY: *democratic elections* ◇ *a democratic government* ⊃ note at **government** **2** having or supporting equal rights for all people: *a democratic decision* (= made by all the people involved) ◇ *a democratic society* **OPP** **undemocratic** ▶ **democratically** /-kli/ *adv.*: *a democratically elected government*

the ˌDemoˈcratic Party *noun* [sing.] (**POLITICS**) one of the two main political parties of the US ⊃ note at **party** ❶ The other main party is **the Republican Party.**

demographic /ˌdeməˈɡræfɪk/ *noun* **1 demographics** [pl.] (**SOCIAL STUDIES**) information about the members of a group of people, such as how old, rich, etc. they are, how many males and females there are, etc: *the demographics of radio listeners* **2** [C] (**BUSINESS**) a group of people who are of a similar age, the same sex, etc: *The publication is popular within the 15 to 24-year-old male demographic.* ▶ **demographic** *adj.*: *demographic changes/trends/factors*

demography /dɪˈmɒɡrəfi/ *noun* [U] (**SOCIAL STUDIES**) the changing number of births, deaths, diseases, etc. in a community over a period of time; the scientific study of these changes: *the social demography of Africa*

demolish /dɪˈmɒlɪʃ/ *verb* [T] to destroy sth, for example a building: *The old shops were demolished and a supermarket was built in their place.* ◇ (*figurative*) *She demolished his argument in one sentence.* ▶ **demolition** /ˌdeməˈlɪʃn/ *noun* [U,C]

demon ᵇ⁺ C1 /ˈdiːmən/ *noun* [C] an evil spirit

demonic /dɪˈmɒnɪk/ *adj.* connected with, or like, a DEMON

demonstrable /dɪˈmɒnstrəbl, ˈdemənstrəbl/ *adj.* (*formal*) that can be shown or proved: *There is no demonstrable link between the two events.*

demonstrate ᵇ⁺ B2 🔴 /ˈdemənstreɪt/ *verb* **1** [T] ~ **sth (to sb)**; ~ **that** to show sth clearly by giving proof: *Using this chart, I'd like to demonstrate to you what has happened to our sales.* ◇ *Tests demonstrated that the product was safe to use.* **2** [T] ~ **sth (to sb)** to show and explain to sb how to do sth or how sth works: *The crew demonstrated the use of life jackets just before take-off.* **3** [I] ~ **(against/for sb/sth)** (**POLITICS, SOCIAL STUDIES**) to take part in a public protest for or against sb/sth: *Enormous crowds have been demonstrating against the government.* **SYN** **protest**¹

demonstration ᵇ⁺ B2 /ˌdemənˈstreɪʃn/ *noun* **1** [C, U] something that shows clearly that sth exists or is true: *This accident is a clear demonstration of the system's faults.* **2** (*also informal* **demo**) [C, U] an act of showing or explaining to sb how to do sth or how sth works: *The salesman gave me a demonstration of what the phone could do.* **3** (*also informal* **demo**) [C] ~ **(against/for sb/sth)** (**POLITICS, SOCIAL STUDIES**) a public protest for or against sb/sth: *demonstrations against a new law*

demonstrative /dɪˈmɒnstrətɪv/ *adj.* **1** (used about a person) showing feelings, especially loving feelings, in front of other people **2** (**GRAMMAR**) used to identify the person or thing that is being referred to: *'This' and 'that' are demonstrative pronouns.*

demonstrator /ˈdemənstreɪtə(r)/ *noun* [C] (**POLITICS, SOCIAL STUDIES**) a person who takes part in a public protest **SYN** **protester**

demoralize (*BrE also* -ise) /dɪˈmɒrəlaɪz/ *verb* [T] to make sb lose confidence or the courage to continue doing sth: *Repeated defeats demoralized the team.* ▶ **demoralization** (*BrE also* -isation) /dɪˌmɒrəlaɪˈzeɪʃn/ *noun* [U] ▶ **demoralizing** (*BrE also* -ising) *adj.*: *Constant criticism can be extremely demoralizing.*

demote /diːˈməʊt/ *verb* [T, often passive] ~ **sb (from sth) (to sth)** to move sb to a lower position or less important job, often as a punishment **OPP** **promote** ▶ **demotion** /-ˈməʊʃn/ *noun* [C, U]

demure /dɪˈmjʊə(r)/ *adj.* (used especially about a girl or young woman) shy, quiet and polite

den /den/ *noun* [C] **1** the place where certain wild animals live, for example lions **2** a secret place, especially for illegal activities: *a gambling den*

deniable /dɪˈnaɪəbl/ *adj.* able to be denied: *The party's links to the rebels were no longer deniable.*

denial ᵇ⁺ C1 /dɪˈnaɪəl/ *noun* **1** [C] a statement that sth is not true: *The minister issued a denial that he was involved in the scandal.* **2** [C, U] **(a)** ~ **(of sth)** an act of refusing to allow sb to have or do sth: *a denial of personal freedom* **3** [U] a REFUSAL to accept that sth unpleasant or painful has happened: *He's been in denial ever since the accident.* ⊃ verb **deny**

denim /ˈdenɪm/ *noun* [U] thick cotton cloth (often blue) that is used for making clothes, especially jeans: *a denim jacket*

denitrify /ˌdiːˈnaɪtrɪfaɪ/ *verb* [T] (**denitrifying; denitrifies;** *pt, pp* **denitrified**) (**CHEMISTRY**) to remove NITRATES or NITRITES from sth, especially from soil, air or water ⊃ picture at **nitrogen cycle** ▶ **denitrification** /diːˌnaɪtrɪfɪˈkeɪʃn/ *noun* [U]

denizen /ˈdenɪzn/ *noun* [C] (*formal*) (**SOCIAL STUDIES**) a person, an animal or a plant that lives, grows or is often found in a particular place: *Tigers and black bears are among the denizens of the forest.* ◇ *I'm not a denizen of Twitter, but I know a lot of people who are.* ⊃ look at **inhabitant**

denomination /dɪˌnɒmɪˈneɪʃn/ *noun* [C] (**RELIGION**) a branch of the Christian church

denominator /dɪˈnɒmɪneɪtə(r)/ *noun* [C] (**MATHEMATICS**) the number below the line in a FRACTION showing how many parts the whole is divided into, for example the 4 in ¾ ⊃ look at **common denominator, numerator**

denote 🔴 /dɪˈnəʊt/ *verb* [T] to mean or be a sign of sth: *The red triangle denotes danger.*

denouement (*also* **dénouement**) /deɪˈnuːmɒ̃/ *noun* [C] (**LITERATURE**) the end of a play, book, etc., where everything is explained or settled; the end result of a situation: *an exciting/unexpected denouement*

denounce ᵇ⁺ C1 /dɪˈnaʊns/ *verb* [T] **1** to say publicly that sth is wrong; to be very critical of a person in public: *The actor has been denounced as a bad influence on young people.* ⊃ noun **denunciation** **2** ~ **sb (as sth)** to tell the police, people in power, etc. about sb's illegal political activities: *They were denounced as spies.*

dense ᵇ⁺ C1 /dens/ *adj.* **1** containing a lot of things or people close together: *dense forests* ◇ *areas of dense population* **2** difficult to see through: *dense fog* **3** (*informal*) not intelligent; stupid ▶ **densely** *adv.*: *densely populated areas*

density ᵇ⁺ C1 /ˈdensəti/ *noun* (*pl.* -**ies**) **1** [U] the number of things or people in a place in relation to its area: *There is a high density of wildlife in this area.* **2** [C, U] (**PHYSICS**) how thick a solid, liquid or gas is, measured by its mass per unit of volume: *Lead has a high density.*

dent¹ /dent/ *noun* [C] a place where a flat surface, especially metal, has been hit and damaged but not broken

dent² /dent/ *verb* [T] to damage a flat surface by hitting it but not breaking it: *I hit a wall and dented the front of the car.*

dental /'dentl/ *adj.* relating to teeth and their care: *dental care/treatment*

dental floss *noun* [U] a type of THREAD that is used for cleaning between the teeth ⊃ note at **tooth**

dentine /'denti:n/ *noun* [U] (**ANATOMY**) the hard substance that forms the main part of a tooth under the ENAMEL (= the hard white outer covering of a tooth) ⊃ picture at **tooth**

dentist 🔊 **A2** /'dentɪst/ *noun* (**MEDICINE**) **1** [C] a person whose job is to look after people's teeth ⊃ note at **tooth 2 the dentist's** [sing.] the place where a dentist works: *I have to go to the dentist's today.*

dentistry /'dentɪstri/ *noun* [U] (**MEDICINE**) **1** the medical study of the teeth and mouth **2** the work of a dentist **3** the care and treatment of people's teeth

dentition /den'tɪʃn/ *noun* [U] (**BIOLOGY**) the arrangement or condition of a person's or an animal's teeth

dentures /'dentʃəz/ = FALSE TEETH

denunciation /dɪ,nʌnsi'eɪʃn/ *noun* [C, U] (*formal*) an act of criticizing sb/sth strongly in public ⊃ verb **denounce**

deny 🔊 **B2** /dɪ'naɪ/ *verb* [T] (denying; denies; *pt, pp* denied) **1** ~ **sth/doing sth; ~ that …** to state that sth is not true; to refuse to admit or accept sth: *In court he denied all the charges.* ◇ *She denied telling lies/that she had told lies.* ◇ *They denied all knowledge of the payment* (= said they knew nothing about it). **OPP** admit ⊃ note at **crime 2** ~ **sb sth; ~ sth (to sb)** (*formal*) to refuse to allow sb to have sth: *She was denied permission to remain in the country.* ⊃ noun **denial**

> **WORD FAMILY**
> **deny** *verb*
> **denial** *noun*
> **undeniable** *adj.*

deodorant /di:'əʊdərənt/ *noun* [C, U] a chemical substance that you put onto your body to prevent bad smells

deoxyribonucleic acid /di:,ɒksi,raɪbəʊnju:,kleɪk 'æsɪd/ = DNA

dep. *abbr.* (in writing) DEPARTS; departure: *dep. London 15.32*

depart 🔊 **B2** /dɪ'pɑ:t/ *verb* [I] (*abbr.* dep.) (*formal*) to leave a place, usually at the beginning of a journey: *Ferries depart for Spain twice a day.* ◇ *The next train to the airport departs from platform 2.* ⊃ noun **departure**

department 🔊 **A2** **S** /dɪ'pɑ:tmənt/ *noun* [C] (*abbr.* Dept) **1** (**BUSINESS**) one of the sections into which an organization, for example a school or a business, is divided: *the Modern Languages department* ◇ *She works in the accounts department.* ⊃ note at **subject¹ 2** (**POLITICS**) a division of the government responsible for a particular subject: *the Department of Health* ⊃ look at **ministry**

departmental /,di:pɑ:'mentl/ *adj.* connected with a department: *There is a departmental meeting once a month.*

de'partment store *noun* [C] a large shop that is divided into sections selling different types of goods

departure 🔊 **B1** /dɪ'pɑ:tʃə(r)/ *noun* **1** [C, U] (*abbr.* dep.) (**TOURISM**) the act of leaving a place; an example of this: *Helen's sudden departure meant I had to do her job as well as mine.* ◇ *Passengers should check in at least one hour before departure.* **OPP** arrival ⊃ verb **depart 2** [C] (**TOURISM**) a plane, train, etc. leaving a place at a particular time: *All departures are from London.* ◇ *the departure lounge/time/gate* **OPP** arrival

3 [C] ~ **(from sth)** an action that is different from what is usual or expected: *a departure from normal practice* **4 departures** [U] (**TOURISM**) the part of an airport where you go before catching a plane: *There were long delays in departures.* ⊃ look at **arrival** (2)

depend 🔊 **A2** **O** /dɪ'pend/ *verb*
IDM **depending on** according to: *Starting salary varies from £25 000 to £30 000, depending on experience.* **that depends** | **it (all) depends** used to say that you are not certain of sth until other things have been considered: *'Can you lend me some money?' 'That depends. How much do you want?'* ◇ *I don't know whether I'll see him. It depends what time he gets here.*
PHR V **depend on sb/sth** to be able to trust sb/sth to do sth; to rely on sb/sth: *If you ever need any help, you know you can depend on me.* ◇ *You can't depend on the trains. They're always late.* ◇ *I was depending on getting the money today.* **SYN** rely on/upon sb/sth (to do sth) ⊃ note at **trust² depend on sb/sth (for sth)** to need sb/sth to provide sth: *Our organization depends on donations from the public.* **depend on sth** to be decided or influenced by sb/sth: *His whole future depends on these exams.*

dependable /dɪ'pendəbl/ *adj.* that can be trusted: *The bus service is very dependable.* **SYN** reliable ▸ **dependably** /-bli/ *adv.*

dependant (*BrE*) (*also* **dependent** *especially in AmE*) /dɪ'pendənt/ *noun* [C] a person who depends on sb else for money, a home, food, etc: *insurance cover for you and all your dependants*

dependence 🔊+ **C1** **W** /dɪ'pendəns/ *noun* [U] ~ **(on sb/ sth)** the state of needing sb/sth: *The country wants to reduce its dependence on imported oil.* **OPP** independence

dependency /dɪ'pendənsi/ *noun* [U] the state of needing sb/sth; the state of being unable to live without sth, especially a drug

dependent 🔊+ **B2** **W** /dɪ'pendənt/ *adj.* **1** ~ **(on sb/sth)** needing sb/sth to support you: *The industry is heavily dependent on government funding.* ◇ *Do you have any dependent children?* **2** ~ **on sb/sth** influenced or decided by sth: *The price you pay is dependent on the number in your group.* **OPP** independent¹

depict 🔊+ **C1** /dɪ'pɪkt/ *verb* [T] **1** to show sb/sth in a painting or drawing: *a painting depicting a country scene* **2** to describe sb/sth in words: *The novel depicts rural life a century ago.*

deplete /dɪ'pli:t/ *verb* [T] to reduce the amount of sth so that there is not much left: *We are depleting the world's natural resources.* ▸ **depletion** /-'pli:ʃn/ *noun* [U]

depleted /dɪ'pli:tɪd/ *adj.* reduced in amount so that there is not much left: *depleted fish stocks*

deplorable /dɪ'plɔ:rəbl/ *adj.* (*formal*) very bad and unacceptable: *They are living in deplorable conditions.* **SYN** appalling ▸ **deplorably** /-bli/ *adv.*

deplore /dɪ'plɔ:(r)/ *verb* [T] (*formal*) to feel or say that sth is morally bad: *I deplore such dishonest behaviour.*

deploy 🔊+ **C1** /dɪ'plɔɪ/ *verb* [T] **1** to put soldiers or weapons in a position where they are ready to fight **2** to use sth in a useful and successful way ▸ **deployment** 🔊+ **C1** *noun* [U]: *the deployment of troops*

depopulate /,di:'pɒpjuleɪt/ *verb* [T, usually passive] (*formal*) (**SOCIAL STUDIES**) to reduce the number of people living in a place ▸ **depopulation** /,di:,pɒpju'leɪʃn/ *noun* [U]

deport /dɪˈpɔːt/ *verb* [T] (**LAW, POLITICS, SOCIAL STUDIES**) to force sb to leave a country because they have no legal right to be there ▸ **deportation** /ˌdiːpɔːˈteɪʃn/ *noun* [C, U]: *The illegal immigrants face deportation.*

depose /dɪˈpəʊz/ *verb* [T] (**POLITICS**) to remove a ruler or leader from power: *There was a revolution and the dictator was deposed.*

deposit¹ ⯑+ **C1** /dɪˈpɒzɪt/ *verb* [T] **1** to put sth down somewhere: *He deposited his bags on the floor and sat down.* **2** (**GEOGRAPHY**) (used about liquid or a river) to leave sth lying on a surface, as the result of a natural or chemical process: *mud deposited by a flood* **3** (**FINANCE**) to put money into an account at a bank: *Millions were deposited in Swiss bank accounts.* **4** ~ **sth (in sth)**; ~ **sth (with sb/sth)** to put sth valuable in an official place where it is safe until needed again: *Valuables can be deposited in the hotel safe.*

deposit² ⯑+ **B2** /dɪˈpɒzɪt/ *noun* [C] **1** ~ **(on sth)** (**FINANCE**) a sum of money that is the first payment for sth, with the rest of the money to be paid later: *Once you have paid a deposit, the booking will be confirmed.* ◇ *We've put down a 5% deposit on the house.* **2** [usually sing.] ~ **(on sth)** (**FINANCE**) a sum of money that you pay when you rent sth and get back when you return it without damage: *Boats can be hired for £5 an hour, plus £20 deposit.* **3** (**FINANCE**) a sum of money paid into a bank account **4** (**GEOLOGY**) a substance that has been left on a surface or in the ground as the result of a natural or chemical process: *mineral deposits* ➔ picture at **glacial**

deˈposit account *noun* [C] (*BrE*) (**FINANCE**) a type of bank account where your money earns interest. You cannot take money out of a deposit account without arranging it first with the bank. ➔ look at **current account**

deposition /ˌdepəˈzɪʃn/ *noun* **1** [U, C] (**GEOLOGY**) the natural process of leaving a layer of a substance on rocks or soil; a substance left in this way: *marine/river deposition* ➔ picture at **oxbow lake** **2** [U, C] (**POLITICS**) the act of removing sb, especially a ruler, from power: *the deposition of the king* **3** [C] (**LAW**) a formal statement, taken from sb and used in court

depot /ˈdepəʊ/ *noun* [C] **1** (*BrE*) a place where large numbers of vehicles (buses, lorries, etc.) are kept when not in use **2** a place where large amounts of food, goods or equipment are stored **3** (*AmE*) a small bus or railway station

depraved /dɪˈpreɪvd/ *adj.* (*formal*) morally bad **SYN** evil¹, wicked

depravity /dɪˈprævəti/ *noun* [U] (*formal*) the state of being morally bad: *a life of depravity*

depreciate /dɪˈpriːʃieɪt/ *verb* [I] to become less valuable over a period of time: *New cars start to depreciate the moment they are on the road.* ▸ **depreciation** /dɪˌpriːʃiˈeɪʃn/ *noun* [C, U]

depress /dɪˈpres/ *verb* [T] **1** to make sb unhappy and without hope or enthusiasm: *All this wet weather really depresses me.* **2** (**BUSINESS**) to make trade, business, etc. less active: *The reduction in the number of tourists has depressed local trade.* **3** (*formal*) to press sth down on a machine, etc.: *To switch off the machine, depress the lever.*

depressed ⯑ **B2** /dɪˈprest/ *adj.* **1** very unhappy, often for a long period of time: *He's been very depressed since he lost his job.* **2** (**ECONOMICS**) (used about a place or an industry) without enough economic activity or jobs for people

depressing ⯑ **B2** /dɪˈpresɪŋ/ *adj.* making you feel very sad and without enthusiasm: *a depressing sight/thought/experience* ◇ *Looking for a job these days can be very depressing.* ▸ **depressingly** *adv.*: *a depressingly familiar experience*

depression ⯑+ **B2** /dɪˈpreʃn/ *noun* **1** [U] a feeling of unhappiness that lasts for a long time. Depression can be a medical condition and may have physical signs, for example being unable to sleep, etc: *clinical/post-natal depression* **2** [C, U] (**ECONOMICS**) a period when the economic situation is bad, with little business activity and many people without a job: *The country was in the grip of (an) economic depression.* **3** [C] a part of a surface that is lower than the parts around it: *Rainwater collects in shallow depressions in the ground.* **4** [C] (**GEOGRAPHY**) a weather condition in which the pressure of the air becomes lower, often causing rain ➔ look at **anticyclone**

deprivation /ˌdeprɪˈveɪʃn/ *noun* [U] (**SOCIAL STUDIES**) the fact of not having sth that you need, like enough food or money, or a home: *sleep deprivation* ◇ *children suffering from social deprivation*

deprive ⯑+ **C1** /dɪˈpraɪv/ *verb* **PHR V** deprive **sb/sth of sth** to prevent sb/sth from having sth; to take away sth from sb: *The prisoners were deprived of food.*

deprived /dɪˈpraɪvd/ *adj.* not having enough of the basic things in life, such as food, money, etc: *He came from a deprived background.*

Dept *abbr.* (in writing) = DEPARTMENT: *the Sales Dept*

depth ⯑ **B2** /depθ/ *noun* **1** [C, U] the distance down from the top to the bottom of sth: *The hole should be 3cm in depth.* **2** [C, U] the distance from the front to the back of sth: *the depth of a shelf* ➔ picture at **dimension** **3** [U] the amount of emotion, knowledge, etc. that a person has: *He tried to convince her of the depth of his feelings for her.* **4** [C, usually pl.] the deepest, most extreme or serious part of sth: *in the depths of winter* (= when it is coldest) ➔ adjective **deep** **IDM** in depth looking at all the details; in a careful and complete way: *to discuss a problem in depth* out of your depth **1** (*BrE*) in water that is too deep for you to stand up in **2** in a situation that is too difficult for you

deputation /ˌdepjuˈteɪʃn/ *noun* [C + sing./pl. verb] a group of people sent to sb to act or speak for others

deputize (*BrE also* -ise) /ˈdepjutaɪz/ *verb* [I] ~ **(for sb)** to act for sb in a higher position, who is away or unable to do sth

deputy ⯑+ **C1** /ˈdepjuti/ *noun* [C] (*pl.* -ies) the second most important person in a particular organization, who does the work of their manager if the manager is away: *the deputy head of a school*

derail /diːˈreɪl/ *verb* [I, T] (used about a train) to come off a railway track; to cause a train to come off a railway track

derailment /diːˈreɪlmənt/ *noun* [C, U] an occasion when a train comes off a railway track

deranged /dɪˈreɪndʒd/ *adj.* thinking and behaving in a way that is not normal, especially because of mental illness

derby /ˈdɑːbi/ *noun* [C] (*pl.* -ies) **1** (*BrE*) a race or sports competition: *a motorcycle derby* **2** (*AmE*) = BOWLER (2)

deregulate /ˌdiːˈregjuleɪt/ *verb* [T, often passive] (**ECONOMICS**) to free a commercial or business activity from rules and controls: *deregulated financial markets* ▸ **deregulation** /ˌdiːˌregjuˈleɪʃn/ *noun* [U] ▸ **deregulatory** /ˌdiːˈregjələtəri/ *adj.*

derelict /ˈderəlɪkt/ *adj.* no longer used and in bad condition: *a derelict house*

deride /dɪˈraɪd/ verb [T, often passive] (formal) to say that sb/sth is silly; to laugh at sb/sth in a cruel way ▶ **derision** /-ˈrɪʒn/ noun [U]: Her comments were met with derision. ▶ **derisive** /-ˈraɪsɪv/ adj.: 'What rubbish!' he said with a derisive laugh.

de rigueur /də rɪˈɡɜː(r)/ adj. considered to be necessary, especially if you wish to be accepted socially: Evening dress is de rigueur at the casino.

derisory /dɪˈraɪsəri/ adj. too small or of too little value to be considered seriously: Union leaders rejected the derisory pay offer.

derivation /ˌderɪˈveɪʃn/ noun [C, U] (LANGUAGE) the origin from which a word or phrase has developed

derivative¹ /dɪˈrɪvətɪv/ noun [C] **1** (GRAMMAR) a form of sth (especially a word) that has developed from the original form: 'Sadness' is a derivative of 'sad'. **2** (MATHEMATICS) an expression representing the rate of change of a function with respect to an independent VARIABLE (= a quantity that varies in value)

derivative² /dɪˈrɪvətɪv/ adj. copied from sth else; not having new or original ideas: a derivative design/style

derive ʔ+ B2 ⦿ /dɪˈraɪv/ verb
PHR V **derive from sth** | **be derived from sth** (LANGUAGE) (used about a word or name) to come from sth; to have sth as its origin: 'Mutton' derives from the French word 'mouton'. ◇ The town's name is derived from the river on which it was built. **derive sth from sth** (formal) to get sth (especially a feeling or an advantage) from sth: I derive great satisfaction from my work.

dermatitis /ˌdɜːməˈtaɪtɪs/ noun [U] (HEALTH) a skin condition in which the skin becomes red, SWOLLEN (= larger or rounder than normal) and painful

dermatologist /ˌdɜːməˈtɒlədʒɪst/ noun [C] (MEDICINE) a doctor who studies and treats skin diseases

dermatology /ˌdɜːməˈtɒlədʒi/ noun [U] (MEDICINE) the scientific study of skin diseases ▶ **dermatological** /ˌdɜːmətəˈlɒdʒɪkl/ adj.

dermis /ˈdɜːmɪs/ noun [sing., U] (ANATOMY) the thick layer of skin just under the EPIDERMIS ⊃ picture at **skin¹**

derogatory /dɪˈrɒɡətri/ adj. expressing a lack of respect for, or a low opinion of sth: derogatory comments about the standard of my work

derrick /ˈderɪk/ noun [C] **1** a tall machine used for moving or lifting heavy weights, especially on a ship; a type of CRANE **2** a tall structure over an OIL WELL for holding the DRILL (= the machine that makes the hole in the ground for getting the oil out)

desalination /ˌdiːˌsælɪˈneɪʃn/ noun [U] (GEOGRAPHY) the process of removing salt from sea water

descant /ˈdeskænt/ noun [C] (MUSIC) a tune that is sung or played at the same time as, and usually higher than, the main tune

descend ʔ+ C1 /dɪˈsend/ verb [I, T] (formal) to go down to a lower place; to go down sth: The plane started to descend and a few minutes later we landed. ◇ She descended the stairs slowly. **OPP** ascend
IDM **be descended from sb** to have sb as a relative in past times: He says he's descended from a Russian prince.

descendant /dɪˈsendənt/ noun [C] (HISTORY) a person who belongs to the same family as sb who lived a long time ago: Her family are descendants of one of the first Englishmen to arrive in America. ⊃ look at **ancestor**

descent ʔ+ C1 /dɪˈsent/ noun **1** [C] a movement down to a lower place: The pilot informed us that we were about to begin our descent. **OPP** ascent **2** [U] a person's family origins: He is of Italian descent. **SYN** ancestry

describe ʔ A1 ⦿ /dɪˈskraɪb/ verb [T] ~ sb/sth (to/for sb); ~ sb/sth (as sth) to say what sb/sth is like or what happened: Can you describe the bag you lost? ◇ It's impossible to describe to you how I felt. ◇ The thief was described as tall, thin, and aged about 20.

description ʔ A1 ⦿ /dɪˈskrɪpʃn/ noun **1** [C, U] a picture in words of sb/sth or of sth that happened: The man gave the police a detailed description of the burglar. **2** [C] a type or kind of sth: It must be a tool of some description, but I don't know what it's for.

descriptive ⦿ /dɪˈskrɪptɪv/ adj. that describes sb/sth, especially in an interesting way: a piece of descriptive writing ◇ She gave a highly descriptive account of the journey.

desecrate /ˈdesɪkreɪt/ verb [T] (RELIGION) to damage a thing or place of religious importance or treat it without respect: desecrated graves ▶ **desecration** /ˌdesɪˈkreɪʃn/ noun [U]: the desecration of a cemetery

desert¹ ʔ A2 /ˈdezət/ noun [C, U] (GEOGRAPHY) a large area of land, usually covered with sand, that is hot and has very little water and very few plants ⊃ picture at **ecosystem**

desert² ʔ B2 /dɪˈzɜːt/ verb **1** [T] to leave sb/sth, usually for ever: Many people have deserted the countryside and moved to the towns. **2** [I, T] (used especially about sb in the armed forces) to leave without permission: He deserted because he didn't want to fight. ▶ **desertion** /-ˈzɜːʃn/ noun [C, U]

deserted /dɪˈzɜːtɪd/ adj. empty, because all the people have left: a deserted house **SYN** abandoned

deserter /dɪˈzɜːtə(r)/ noun [C] a person who leaves the armed forces without permission

desertification /dɪˌzɜːtɪfɪˈkeɪʃn/ noun [U] (ENVIRONMENT) the process of becoming a desert or of making an area of land into a desert

desert island noun [C] an island, especially a tropical one, where nobody lives

deserve ʔ B2 /dɪˈzɜːv/ verb [T] (not used in the progressive tenses) to earn sth, either good or bad, because of sth that you have done: We've done a lot of work and we deserve a break. ◇ He deserves to be punished severely for such a crime.

deservedly /dɪˈzɜːvɪdli/ adv. in a way that is right because of what sb has done: He deservedly won the Best Actor award.

deserving /dɪˈzɜːvɪŋ/ adj. ~ (of sth) (formal) that you should give help, money, etc. to: This charity is a most deserving cause.

desiccated /ˈdesɪkeɪtɪd/ adj. **1** (used about food) dried in order to keep it for a long time: desiccated coconut **2** (ENVIRONMENT) completely dry: desiccated soil

desiccation /ˌdesɪˈkeɪʃn/ noun [U] (ENVIRONMENT) the process of becoming completely dry: the dramatic desiccation of North Africa

design¹ ʔ A1 ⦿ /dɪˈzaɪn/ noun **1** [U, C] the way in which sth is planned and made or arranged: Design faults have been discovered in the car. ◇ The website will have a new design from next month. **2** [U] the process and skill of making drawings or computer models that show how sth should be made, how it will work, etc: to study industrial design ◇ graphic design **3** [C] ~ (for sth) a drawing or plan that shows how sth should be made, built, etc: The architect showed us her design for the new theatre. **4** [C] a pattern of lines, shapes, etc. that decorate sth: *a T-shirt with a geometric design on it* **SYN** **pattern**

design² 🔉 **A1** ⊙ /dɪˈzaɪn/ *verb* [T] **1** to plan and make a drawing or computer model of how sth will be made: *to design cars/dresses/houses* **2** [often passive] to invent, plan and develop sth for a particular purpose: *The bridge wasn't designed for such heavy traffic.*

designate 🔉+ **C1** /ˈdezɪɡneɪt/ *verb* [T] **1** [often passive] ~ **sth (as) sth** (*formal*) to give sth a name to show that it has a particular purpose: *This has been designated (as) a conservation area.* **2** ~ **sb (as) sth** to choose sb to do a particular job or task: *Who has she designated (as) her deputy?* **3** [often passive] to show or mark sth: *The emergency exits are designated by arrows.*

,designated 'driver *noun* [C] the person who agrees to drive and not drink alcohol when people go to a party, a bar, etc.

designer¹ 🔉 **A2** /dɪˈzaɪnə(r)/ *noun* [C] a person whose job is to make drawings or plans showing how sth will look or be made: *a fashion/jewellery designer*

designer² /dɪˈzaɪnə(r)/ *adj.* [only before noun] made by a famous designer; expensive and fashionable and having a famous brand name: *designer jeans*

desirable 🔉+ **C1** 🆆 /dɪˈzaɪərəbl/ *adj.* **1** wanted, often by many people; worth having: *Experience is desirable but not essential for this job.* **OPP** **undesirable** **2** sexually attractive **OPP** **undesirable**

desire¹ 🔉 **B2** 🆆 /dɪˈzaɪə(r)/ *noun* [C, U] ~ **(for sth/to do sth)** **1** the feeling of wanting sth very much; a strong wish: *the desire for a peaceful solution to the crisis* ◇ *I have no desire to visit that place again.* **2** the wish for a sexual relationship with sb

desire² 🔉 **B2** 🆆 /dɪˈzaɪə(r)/ *verb* [T] **1** (*formal*) (not used in the progressive tenses) to want; to wish for: *They have everything they could possibly desire.* ◇ *The service in the restaurant left a lot to be desired* (= was very bad). **2** to find sb/sth sexually attractive

desk 🔉 **A1** /desk/ *noun* [C] **1** a type of table, often with DRAWERS (= containers like boxes, that you can pull out to put things in), that you sit at to write or work: *The students put their books on their desks.* ◇ *He used to be a pilot but now he has a desk job* (= he works in an office). **2** a table or place in a building where a particular service is provided: *an information desk*

'desk clerk (*AmE*) = CLERK (4)

desktop 🔉+ **C1** /ˈdesktɒp/ *noun* [C] **1** (**COMPUTING**) a computer screen on which you can see ICONS (= symbols) showing the programs, etc. that are available to be used **2** the top of a desk **3** (*also* ,desktop com'puter) (**COMPUTING**) a computer with a keyboard, screen and main processing unit that can fit on a desk ⊃ look at **laptop**, **tablet** (1)

desolate /ˈdesələt/ *adj.* **1** (used about a place) empty in a way that seems very sad: *desolate wasteland* **2** (used about a person) lonely, very unhappy and without hope ▸ desolation /ˌdesəˈleɪʃn/ *noun* [U]: *a scene of desolation* ◇ *He felt utter desolation when his wife died.*

despair¹ /dɪˈspeə(r)/ *noun* [U] the state of having lost all hope: *I felt like giving up in despair.* ▸ despairing *adj.*: *a despairing cry* ⊃ look at **desperate**

despair² /dɪˈspeə(r)/ *verb* [I] ~ **(of sb/sth)**; ~ **(of doing sth)** to lose all hope that a situation will change or improve: *We began to despair of ever finding somewhere to live.* ▸ despairing *adj.*: *a despairing cry* ⊃ look at **desperate**

despatch /dɪˈspætʃ/ (*BrE*) = DISPATCH¹, DISPATCH²

desperate 🔉 **B2** /ˈdespərət/ *adj.* **1** out of control and ready to do anything to change the situation you are in because it is so bad: *She became desperate when her*

money ran out. **2** done with little hope of success, as a last thing to try when everything else has failed: *I made a desperate attempt to persuade her to change her mind.* **3** ~ **(for sth/to do sth)** wanting or needing sth very much: *Let's go into a cafe. I'm desperate for a drink.* **4** terrible, very serious: *There is a desperate shortage of skilled workers.* ▸ desperately 🔉+ **B2** *adv.*: *She was desperately* (= extremely) *unlucky not to win.* ▸ desperation /ˌdespəˈreɪʃn/ *noun* [U]

despicable /dɪˈspɪkəbl, ˈdespɪkəbl/ *adj.* (*formal*) very unpleasant or evil: *a despicable act of terrorism*

despise /dɪˈspaɪz/ *verb* [T] (not used in the progressive tenses) to hate sb/sth very much: *I despise him for lying to me.*

despite 🔉 **B1** /dɪˈspaɪt/ *prep.* without being affected by the thing mentioned: *Despite having very little money, they enjoy life.* ◇ *The scheme went ahead despite public opposition.* **SYN** **in spite of**

despondent /dɪˈspɒndənt/ *adj.* ~ **(about/over sth)** without hope; expecting no improvement: *She was becoming increasingly despondent about finding a job.* ▸ despondency /-dənsi/ *noun* [U]

despot /ˈdespɒt/ *noun* [C] (**POLITICS**) a ruler with great power, especially one who uses it in a cruel way ⊃ look at **autocrat** (1) ▸ despotic /dɪˈspɒtɪk/ *adj.*: *despotic power/rule*

dessert /dɪˈzɜːt/ *noun* [C, U] something sweet that is eaten after the main part of a meal: *What would you like for dessert — ice cream or fresh fruit?* ⊃ look at **pudding** (1), **sweet²** (2)

dessertspoon /dɪˈzɜːtspuːn/ *noun* [C] a spoon of medium size used for eating sweet food after the main part of a meal

destabilize (*BrE also* -ise) /ˌdiːˈsteɪbəlaɪz/ *verb* [T] (**POLITICS**) to make a system, government, country, etc. become less safe and successful: *Terrorist attacks were threatening to destabilize the government.* ⊃ look at **stabilize**

destination 🔉 **B1** /ˌdestɪˈneɪʃn/ *noun* [C] (**TOURISM**) the place where sb/sth is going: *I finally reached my destination two hours late.* ◇ *popular holiday destinations like the Bahamas*

,desti'nation wedding *noun* [C] (**TOURISM**) a wedding held in an exciting or unusual place in a foreign country where all the people who travel to the wedding can also have a holiday

destined /ˈdestɪnd/ *adj.* **1** ~ **for sth/to do sth** having a future that has been decided or planned at an earlier time: *I think she is destined for success.* ◇ *He was destined to become one of the country's leading politicians.* **2** ~ **for ...** travelling towards a particular place: *I boarded a bus destined for New York.*

destiny /ˈdestəni/ *noun* (*pl.* -ies) **1** [C] the things that happen to you in your life, especially things that you cannot control: *She felt that it was her destiny to be a great singer.* **2** [U] a power that people believe controls their lives **SYN** **fate**

destitute /ˈdestɪtjuːt/ *adj.* without any money, food or a home ▸ destitution /ˌdestɪˈtjuːʃn/ *noun* [U]

destroy 🔉 **A2** 🅢 /dɪˈstrɔɪ/ *verb* [T] **1** to damage sth so badly that it can no longer be used or no longer exists: *The building was destroyed by fire.* ◇ *The defeat destroyed his confidence.*

2 to kill an animal, especially because it is injured or

WORD FAMILY
destroy *verb*
destroyer *noun*
destruction *noun*
destructive *adj.*
indestructible *adj.*

dangerous: *The horse broke its leg and had to be destroyed.*

destroyer /dɪˈstrɔɪə(r)/ *noun* [C] **1** a small ship that is used in war **2** a person or thing that destroys sth

destruction ⓘ+ **B2** /dɪˈstrʌkʃn/ *noun* [U] the act of destroying sth: *The war brought **death and destruction** to the city.* ◇ *the destruction of the rainforests* ◇ *weapons of mass destruction*

destructive ⓘ+ **C1** /dɪˈstrʌktɪv/ *adj.* causing a lot of harm or damage

detach /dɪˈtætʃ/ *verb* [T, I] ~ **(sth) (from sth)** to separate sth from sth it is connected to; to become separated from sth: *Detach the form at the bottom of the page and send it to this address …* ◇ *The hood detaches from the coat.* **OPP** **attach**

detachable /dɪˈtætʃəbl/ *adj.* that can be separated from sth it is connected to: *a coat with a detachable hood*

detached /dɪˈtætʃt/ *adj.* **1** (used about a house) not joined to any other house ⊃ look at **semi-detached** **2** not being or not feeling personally involved in sth; without emotion

detachment /dɪˈtætʃmənt/ *noun* **1** [U] the fact or feeling of not being personally involved in sth **2** [C] a group of soldiers who have been given a particular task away from the main group

detail¹ ⓘ **A1** ⓞ /ˈdiːteɪl/ *noun* **1** [C] one fact or piece of information: *Just give me the basic facts. Don't worry about the details.* ◇ *On the application form you should give details of your education and experience.* **2** [U] the small facts or features of sth: *The work involves close attention to detail.*
IDM **go into detail(s)** to talk or write about the details of sth; to explain sth fully: *I can't go into detail now because it would take too long.* **in detail** including the details: *We haven't discussed the matter in detail yet.* **SYN** **thoroughly**

detail² ⓘ **B2** /ˈdiːteɪl/ *verb* [T] to give a full list of sth; to describe sth completely: *He detailed all the equipment he needed for the job.*

detailed ⓘ **B2** ⓦ /ˈdiːteɪld/ *adj.* giving many details and a lot of information; paying great attention to details: *a **detailed description/analysis/study*** ◇ *He gave me **detailed instructions** on how to get there.*

detain ⓘ+ **C1** /dɪˈteɪn/ *verb* [T] to stop sb from leaving a place; to delay sb: *A man has been detained by the police for questioning* (= kept at the police station). ◇ *Don't let me detain you if you're busy.* ⊃ look at **detention** ⊃ note at **demand²** ⊃ noun **detention**

detainee /ˌdiːteɪˈniː/ *noun* [C] (**LAW, POLITICS**) a person who is kept in prison, usually because of his or her political opinions

detect ⓘ **B2** /dɪˈtekt/ *verb* [T] to notice or discover sth that is difficult to see, feel, etc.: *I detected a slight change in his attitude.* ◇ *Traces of blood were detected on his clothes.* ▶ **detectable** *adj.* ▶ **detection** ⓘ+ **C1** /-ˈtekʃn/ *noun* [U]: *The crime escaped detection* (= was not discovered) *for many years.*

detective ⓘ **A2** /dɪˈtektɪv/ *noun* [C] a person, especially a police officer, who tries to solve crimes

deˈtective story *noun* [C] (**LITERATURE**) a story about a crime, often a murder, in which sb tries to find out who the guilty person is

detector /dɪˈtektə(r)/ *noun* [C] a machine that is used for finding or noticing sth: *a **smoke/metal/lie detector***

detente (*also* **détente**) /ˌdeɪˈtɑːnt/ *noun* [U] (*formal*) (**POLITICS**) an improvement in the relationship between two or more countries that have been unfriendly towards each other in the past

detention ⓘ+ **C1** /dɪˈtenʃn/ *noun* **1** [U] (**LAW**) the act of stopping a person leaving a place, especially by keeping them in prison: *They were kept **in detention** for ten days.* **2** [C, U] the punishment of being kept at school for a time after other students have gone home ⊃ verb **detain**

deˈtention centre (*BrE*) (*AmE* **detention center**) *noun* [C] (**LAW, SOCIAL STUDIES**) **1** a place like a prison where people, especially people who have entered a country without the necessary documents, are kept for a time **2** a prison for people who have been accused of a crime and are waiting for their trial

deter /dɪˈtɜː(r)/ *verb* [T] (-rr-) ~ **sb (from doing sth)** to make sb decide not to do sth, especially by telling them that it would have bad results: *The council is trying to deter visitors from bringing their cars into the city centre.* ⊃ noun **deterrent**

detergent /dɪˈtɜːdʒənt/ *noun* [C, U] a chemical liquid or powder that is used for cleaning things

deteriorate ⓘ+ **C1** /dɪˈtɪəriəreɪt/ *verb* [I] ~ **(into sth)** to become worse: *The political tension is deteriorating into civil war.* ▶ **deterioration** /dɪˌtɪəriəˈreɪʃn/ *noun* [U, C]

determinant ⓦ /dɪˈtɜːmɪnənt/ *noun* [C] (*formal*) a factor that decides whether or how sth happens: *Income levels are an important determinant of demand for luxury goods.*

determination ⓘ+ **B2** ⓦ /dɪˌtɜːmɪˈneɪʃn/ *noun* [U] **1** ~ **(to do sth)** the quality of having FIRMLY decided to do sth and continuing to do it, even if it is very difficult: *her determination to win* ◇ *You need great determination to succeed in business.* **2** (*formal*) the process of deciding sth officially: *the determination of future government policy*

determine ⓘ **B1** ⓞ /dɪˈtɜːmɪn/ *verb* [T] (*formal*) **1** to discover the facts about sth: *We need to determine what happened immediately before the accident.* **2** to make sth happen in a particular way or be of a particular type: *The results of the tests will determine what treatment you need.* ◇ *Age and experience will be **determining factors** in our choice of candidate.* **3** to decide sth officially: *A date for the meeting has yet to be determined.*

determined ⓘ **B1** /dɪˈtɜːmɪnd/ *adj.* ~ **(to do sth)** having FIRMLY decided to do sth or to succeed, even if it is difficult: *He is determined to leave school, even though his parents want him to stay.* ◇ *She's a very determined athlete.*

determiner /dɪˈtɜːmɪnə(r)/ *noun* [C] (**GRAMMAR**) a word that comes before a noun to show how the noun is being used: *'Her', 'most' and 'those' are all determiners.*

deterrent /dɪˈterənt/ *noun* [C] something that makes sb less likely to do sth: *Their punishment will be a deterrent to others.* ⊃ verb **deter** ▶ **deterrence** /-rəns/ *noun* [U] (*formal*) ▶ **deterrent** *adj.*

detest /dɪˈtest/ *verb* [T] (not used in the progressive tenses) to hate or not like sb/sth at all: *They absolutely detest each other.* **SYN** **loathe**

detonate /ˈdetəneɪt/ *verb* [I, T] to explode or to make a bomb, etc. explode

detonator /ˈdetəneɪtə(r)/ *noun* [C] a device for making sth, especially a bomb, explode

detour /ˈdiːtʊə(r), -tɔː(r)/ *noun* [C] **1** a longer route from one place to another that you take in order to avoid sth/sb or in order to see or do sth: *Because of the*

accident we had to make a five-kilometre detour.
2 (AmE) = DIVERSION (2)

detox /ˈdiːtɒks/ noun [U, C] (informal) **1** the process of removing harmful substances from your body by only eating and drinking particular things **2** (also **detoxification** /ˌdiːˌtɒksɪfɪˈkeɪʃn/) treatment given to people to help them stop drinking alcohol or taking drugs: He's gone into detox.

detract /dɪˈtrækt/ verb
PHR V detract from sth to make sth seem less good or important: These criticisms in no way detract from the team's achievements.

detriment /ˈdetrɪmənt/ noun [U, C, usually sing.] (formal) the act of causing harm or damage; sth that causes harm or damage
IDM to the detriment of sb/sth resulting in harm or damage to sb/sth: Doctors claim that the changes will be to the detriment of patients.

detrimental /ˌdetrɪˈmentl/ adj. ~ (to sb/sth) (formal) harmful: Too much alcohol is detrimental to your health.

detritus /dɪˈtraɪtəs/ noun [U] (ENVIRONMENT) natural waste material that is left after sth has been used or broken up

deuce /djuːs/ noun [U] (SPORT) a score of 40 points to each player in a game of tennis

deus ex machina /ˌdeɪʊs eks ˈmækɪnə/ noun [sing.] (LITERATURE) an unexpected power or event that saves a situation that seems without hope, especially in a play or novel

deuterium /djuːˈtɪəriəm/ noun [U] (symb. D) (CHEMISTRY) a type of HYDROGEN that is twice as heavy as the usual type

devalue /ˌdiːˈvæljuː/ verb [T] **1** (ECONOMICS) to reduce the value of the money of one country in relation to the value of the money of other countries: The pound has been devalued against the dollar. ⊃ note at **currency 2** to reduce the value or importance of sth: The refusal of the top players to take part devalues this competition. ▸ **devaluation** /ˌdiːˌvæljuˈeɪʃn/ noun [U, C]

devastate ᴿ+ C1 /ˈdevəsteɪt/ verb [T] **1** to destroy sth or damage it badly: a land devastated by war **2** to make sb extremely upset and shocked: This tragedy has devastated the community. ▸ **devastation** /ˌdevəˈsteɪʃn/ noun [U]: a scene of total devastation ⊃ note at **disaster**

devastated /ˈdevəsteɪtɪd/ adj. extremely shocked and upset: He was devastated when his brother died.

devastating /ˈdevəsteɪtɪŋ/ adj. **1** that destroys sth completely: a devastating explosion **2** that shocks or upsets sb very much: The closure of the factory was a devastating blow to the workers.

develop ᴿ A2 O /dɪˈveləp/ verb
• GROW **1** [I, T] to grow slowly, increase, or change into sth else; to make sb/sth do this: to develop from a child into an adult ◇ a scheme to help pupils develop their natural talents ◇ Over the years, she's developed her own unique singing style.
• NEW IDEA/PRODUCT **2** [T] to think of or produce a new idea or product: Scientists have developed a drug against this disease. ⊃ note at **make**¹
• PROBLEM/DISEASE **3** [I, T] to begin to have a problem or disease; to start to affect sb/sth: to develop cancer/ Aids ◇ Trouble is developing along the border.
• IDEA/STORY **4** [T] to make an idea, a story, etc. clearer or more detailed by writing or talking about it more: She went on to develop this theme later in the lecture.
• BUILD HOUSES, ETC. **5** [T] to build houses, shops, factories, etc. on a piece of land: This site is being developed for offices.

developed S /dɪˈveləpt/ adj. **1** (ECONOMICS) (used about a country, a society, etc.) having many industries and a complicated economic system: financial aid to less developed countries ⊃ look at **developing**, **underdeveloped** ⊃ note at **HDI 2** in an advanced state: children with highly developed problem-solving skills

developer /dɪˈveləpə(r)/ (also **property developer**) noun [C] **1** a person or company that builds houses, shops, etc. on a piece of land **2** a person or company that designs and creates new products: a software developer

developing /dɪˈveləpɪŋ/ adj. [only before noun] (ECONOMICS) (used about a poor country) that is trying to develop or improve its industry and economy: a developing country ◇ the developing world ⊃ look at **developed** (1), **underdeveloped** ⊃ note at **HDI**

development ᴿ B1 O /dɪˈveləpmənt/ noun **1** [U] the process of becoming bigger, stronger, better, etc., or of making sb/sth do this: a child's intellectual development ◇ the development of tourism in Cuba **2** [U] (ECONOMICS) the growth of the economy of a country or region: Increased tourism will promote economic development. **3** [U, C] the process of creating sth more advanced; a more advanced product: the latest developments in space technology **4** [C, usually pl.] a new event that changes a situation: This week has seen a number of new developments in the crisis. **5** [C, U] a piece of land with new buildings on it; the process of building on a piece of land: a new housing development ◇ The land has been bought for development.

developmental /dɪˌveləpˈmentl/ adj. **1** in a state of developing or being developed: The product is still at a developmental stage. **2** connected with the development of sb/sth: developmental psychology

deviant /ˈdiːviənt/ adj. different from what most people consider to be normal and acceptable: deviant behaviour ▸ **deviance** /-əns/ (also **deviancy** /-ənsi/) noun [U]: a study of social deviance and crime ▸ **deviant** noun [C]: sexual deviants

deviate /ˈdiːvieɪt/ verb [I] ~ (from sth) to change or become different from what is normal or expected: He never once deviated from his original plan.

deviation W /ˌdiːviˈeɪʃn/ noun [C, U] a difference from what is normal or expected, or from what is approved of by society: a deviation from our usual way of doing things ◇ sexual deviation

device ᴿ A2 W /dɪˈvaɪs/ noun [C] **1** a tool or piece of equipment made for a particular purpose: a security device which detects any movement ◇ labour-saving devices such as washing machines and vacuum cleaners ⊃ note at **tool 2** (COMPUTING) a piece of computer equipment, especially a small one such as a smartphone: The waiter takes orders on a hand-held device. ⊃ look at **mobile device 3** a bomb or weapon that will explode: A powerful device exploded outside the station. **4** a clever method for getting the result you want: Critics dismissed the speech as a political device for winning support.

devil ᴿ+ C1 /ˈdevl/ noun [C] **1** the Devil (RELIGION) the most powerful evil being, according to the Christian, Jewish and Muslim religions ⊃ look at **Satan 2** (RELIGION) an evil being; a spirit
IDM be a devil (BrE) used to encourage sb to do sth that they are not sure about doing: Go on, be a devil — buy both of them. speak/talk of the devil used when the person who is being talked about appears unexpectedly

devious /'diːviəs/ *adj.* clever but not honest or direct: *I wouldn't trust him — he can be very devious.* ◇ *a devious trick/plan* ▸ **deviously** *adv.*

devise 🔒+ **C1** /dɪ'vaɪz/ *verb* [T] to invent a new way of doing sth: *They've devised a plan for keeping traffic out of the city centre.*

devoid /dɪ'vɔɪd/ *adj.* **~ of sth** (*formal*) not having a particular quality; without sth: *devoid of hope/ ambition/imagination*

devolution /ˌdiːvə'luːʃn/ *noun* [U] (**POLITICS**) the act of giving political power from central to local government ➔ verb **devolve**

devolve /dɪ'vɒlv/ *verb*
PHR V **devolve on/upon sb** **1** (**LAW**) if property, money, etc. **devolves on/upon** you, you receive it after sb dies **2** (*formal*) if a duty, responsibility, etc. **devolves on/upon** you, it is given to you by sb at a higher level of authority **devolve sth to/on/upon sb/sth** to give a duty, responsibility, power, etc. to sb/sth who has less authority: *The central government devolved most tax-raising powers to the regional authorities.* ➔ noun **devolution**

devote 🔒+ **B2** /dɪ'vəʊt/ *verb*
PHR V **devote sth to sth** to give a lot of time, energy, etc. to sth: *Schools should devote more time to science subjects.* **devote yourself to sb/sth** to give most of your time, energy, etc. to sb/sth: *She gave up work to devote herself full-time to her music.*

devoted /dɪ'vəʊtɪd/ *adj.* **~ (to sb/sth)** loving sb/sth very much and supporting them/it in everything: *Neil's absolutely devoted to his wife.*

devotee /ˌdevə'tiː/ *noun* [C] **~ (of sb/sth)** a person who likes sb/sth very much: *Devotees of science fiction will enjoy this new film.*

devotion /dɪ'vəʊʃn/ *noun* [U] **~ (to sb/sth)** **1** great love for sb/sth: *a mother's devotion to her children* **SYN** **dedication** **2** the act of giving a lot of your time, energy, etc. to sb/sth: *devotion to duty* **SYN** **dedication** **3** (**RELIGION**) very strong religious feeling

devour /dɪ'vaʊə(r)/ *verb* [T] **1** to eat sth quickly because you are very hungry **2** to read or look at sth with great interest and enthusiasm: *Lisa devours two or three novels a week.*

devout /dɪ'vaʊt/ *adj.* (**RELIGION**) very religious: *a devout Muslim family* ▸ **devoutly** *adv.*

dew /djuː/ *noun* [U, sing.] small drops of water that form on plants, leaves, etc. during the night

dew point *noun* [sing.] (**GEOGRAPHY**) the temperature at which air can hold no more water. Below this temperature the water comes out of the air in the form of drops.

dexterity /dek'sterəti/ *noun* [U] skill at doing things, especially with your hands

dexterous (*also* **dextrous**) /'dekstrəs/ *adj.* (*formal*) showing or having skill, especially with your hands ▸ **dexterously** (*also* **dextrously**) *adv.*

dextrose /'dekstrəʊz, -strəʊs/ *noun* [U] (**BIOLOGY**) a form of **GLUCOSE** (= a natural type of sugar) ➔ look at **fructose, glucose, lactose, sucrose**

di- /daɪ/ *prefix* (in nouns) (**CHEMISTRY**) used to refer to substances that contain two **ATOMS** of the type mentioned: *dioxide*

diabetes /ˌdaɪə'biːtiːz/ *noun* [U] (**HEALTH**) a serious disease in which a person's body cannot control the level of sugar in the blood

diabetic¹ /ˌdaɪə'betɪk/ *noun* [C] (**HEALTH**) a person who suffers from **DIABETES**

diabetic² /ˌdaɪə'betɪk/ *adj.* (**HEALTH**) connected with **DIABETES** or **DIABETICS**: *diabetic chocolate* (= safe for **DIABETICS**)

diacritic /ˌdaɪə'krɪtɪk/ *noun* [C] (**LANGUAGE**) a mark such as an **ACCENT**, placed over, under or through a letter in some languages, to show that the letter should be pronounced in a different way from the same letter without a mark ▸ **diacritical** /-tɪkl/ *adj.*: *diacritical marks*

diagnose 🔒+ **C1** /'daɪəgnəʊz, ˌdaɪəg'nəʊz/ *verb* [T] **~ sth (as sth); ~ sb as/with sth** (**MEDICINE**) to find out and say exactly what illness a person has or what the cause of a problem is: *His illness was diagnosed as bronchitis.* ◇ *I've been diagnosed as (a) diabetic/with diabetes.*

diagnosis 🔒+ **C1** /ˌdaɪəg'nəʊsɪs/ *noun* [C, U] (*pl.* **diagnoses** /-'nəʊsiːz/) (**MEDICINE**) the act of saying exactly what illness a person has or what the cause of a problem is: *to make a diagnosis*

diagnostic /ˌdaɪəg'nɒstɪk/ *adj.* (**MEDICINE**) connected with identifying sth, especially an illness: *to carry out diagnostic tests*

diagonal /daɪ'ægənl/ *adj.* (**GEOMETRY**) (used about a straight line) at an angle; joining two opposite sides of sth at an angle: *Draw a diagonal line from one corner of the square to the opposite corner.* ➔ picture at **line¹** ▸ **diagonal** *noun* [C] ▸ **diagonally** /-nəli/ *adv.*

diagram 🔒 **B1** 🅢 /'daɪəgræm/ *noun* [C] a simple picture that is used to explain how sth works or what sth looks like: *a diagram of the body's digestive system* ▸ **diagrammatic** /ˌdaɪəgrə'mætɪk/ *adj.*

dial¹ /'daɪəl/ *noun* [C] **1** the round part of a clock, watch, control on a machine, etc. that shows a measurement of time, amount, temperature, etc: *a dial for showing air pressure* **2** the round control on a radio, cooker, etc. that you turn to change sth

dial² /'daɪəl/ *verb* [I, T] (-ll-, *AmE* -l-) to push the buttons on a phone in order to call a phone number: *Dial 0033 for France.* ◇ *to dial the wrong number* ➔ note at **phone¹**

dialect /'daɪəlekt/ *noun* [C, U] (**LANGUAGE**) a form of a language that is spoken in one part of a country: *a local dialect* ➔ look at **idiolect**

dialling code *noun* [C] (*BrE*) the numbers that are used for a particular town, area or country, in front of an individual phone number: *international dialling codes*

dialling tone *noun* [C, U] the sound that you hear when you pick up a phone to make a call

dialog box (*BrE also* **dialogue box**) *noun* [C] (**COMPUTING**) a box that appears on a computer screen asking you to choose what you want to do next

dialogue 🔒 **A1** (*AmE also* **dialog**) /'daɪəlɒg/ *noun* [C, U] **1** (a) conversation between people in a book, play, etc: *This movie is all action, with very little dialogue.* ◇ *On the tape you will hear a short dialogue between a shop assistant and a customer.* **2** (a) discussion between people who have different opinions: *(a) dialogue between the major political parties*

dialysis /daɪ'æləsɪs/ *noun* [U] (**MEDICINE**) a process for separating substances from a liquid, especially for taking waste substances out of the blood of people with damaged **KIDNEYS**

diameter /daɪ'æmɪtə(r)/ *noun* [C] (**GEOMETRY**) a straight line that goes from one side to the other of a circle, passing through the centre ➔ look at **circumference**, **radius**(1) ➔ picture at **circle¹**

diamond 🔒 **B1** /'daɪəmənd/ *noun* **1** [C, U] a hard, bright **PRECIOUS** (= rare and valuable) stone that is used for making jewellery and in industry. A diamond usually has no colour: *a diamond ring* **2** [C] (**GEOMETRY**) a flat

shape that has four sides of equal length and points at two ends: *a sweater with a diamond pattern*
3 diamonds [pl.] one of the four SUITS (= sets) in a PACK of cards. The diamonds are marked with red diamond shapes: *the seven of diamonds* **4** [C] one of the cards from this SUIT: *I haven't got any diamonds.*

ˌdiamond ˈwedding *noun* [C] the 60th anniversary of a wedding ⊃ look at **golden wedding, ruby wedding, silver wedding**

diaper /ˈdaɪpə(r)/ (AmE) = NAPPY

diaphragm /ˈdaɪəfræm/ *noun* [C] **1** (ANATOMY) the muscle between the lungs and the stomach that helps you to breathe ⊃ picture at **respiratory 2** a rubber or plastic device that a woman puts inside her body before having sex to prevent her from becoming pregnant

diarrhoea (BrE) (AmE diarrhea) /ˌdaɪəˈrɪə/ *noun* [U] (HEALTH) an illness that causes you to get rid of waste matter from your body very often and in a more liquid form than usual: *Symptoms include diarrhoea and vomiting.*

diary ⚲ A2 /ˈdaɪəri/ *noun* [C] (pl. -ies) **1** (BrE) a book or an app in which you record things that you have to do, remember, etc: *I'll just check in my diary to see if I'm free that weekend.* **2** a book in which you write down what happens to you each day: *Do you keep a diary?*

diastole /daɪˈæstəli/ *noun* [C] (HEALTH) the stage of the heart's rhythm when its muscles relax and the heart fills with blood ⊃ look at **systole** ▸ diastolic /ˌdaɪə ˈstɒlɪk/ *adj*: *diastolic blood pressure* ⊃ look at **systolic**

diatomic /ˌdaɪəˈtɒmɪk/ *adj*. (CHEMISTRY) consisting of two ATOMS

dice /daɪs/ (*also* die *especially in AmE*) *noun* [C] (pl. dice) a small solid square object with six sides and a different number of spots (from one to six) on each side, used in certain games: *Throw the dice to see who goes first.*

dichotomy /daɪˈkɒtəmi/ *noun* [C, usually sing.] (pl. -ies) ~ (between A and B) (*formal*) a division or contrast that exists between two groups or things that are completely opposite to and different from each other

dictate ⚲+ C1 /dɪkˈteɪt/ *verb* **1** [I, T] ~ (sth) (to sb) to tell sb what to do in a way that seems unfair: *Parents can't dictate to their children how they should run their lives.* **2** [T] to control or influence sth: *The kind of house people live in is usually dictated by how much they earn.* **3** [T, I] ~ (sth) (to sb) to say sth in a normal speaking voice so that sb else can write or type it: *She dictated the letter to her assistant.*

dictation /dɪkˈteɪʃn/ *noun* [U, C] (EDUCATION) spoken words that sb else must write or type: *We had a dictation in English today* (= a test in which we had to write down what the teacher said).

dictator ⚲+ C1 /dɪkˈteɪtə(r)/ *noun* [C] (POLITICS) a ruler who has total power in a country, especially one who rules the country by force ▸ dictatorship /ˌdɪkˈteɪtəʃɪp/ *noun* [C, U]: *a military dictatorship*

dictatorial /ˌdɪktəˈtɔːriəl/ *adj*. **1** (POLITICS) connected with or controlled by a ruler who has total power, especially a DICTATOR: *a dictatorial regime* **2** using power in an unreasonable way by telling people what to do and not listening to their views or wishes

dictionary ⚲ A1 /ˈdɪkʃənri/ *noun* [C] (pl. -ies) **1** a book or electronic resource that contains a list of the words in a language in the order of the alphabet and that tells you what they mean, in the same or another language: *to look up a word in a dictionary* ◇ *a bilingual/ monolingual dictionary* **2** a book or electronic resource that lists the words connected with a particular subject and tells you what they mean: *a dictionary of idioms* ◇ *a medical dictionary*

did /dɪd/ *past tense of* **do**¹

didactic /daɪˈdæktɪk/ *adj*. (*formal*) **1** (EDUCATION) designed to teach people sth, especially a moral lesson: *didactic art/poetry* **2** telling people things rather than letting them find out for themselves: *Her way of teaching literature is too didactic.* ▸ didactically /-kli/ *adv*.

didn't /ˈdɪdnt/ *short form* did not

die¹ ⚲ A1 /daɪ/ *verb* (dying; dies; *pt, pp* died) **1** [I, T] ~ (from/of sth) to stop living: *My father died when I was three.* ◇ *Thousands of people have died from this disease.* ◇ *to die of hunger* ◇ *to die for what you believe in* ◇ *to die a natural/violent death* ⊃ adjective **dead**, noun **death 2** [I] to stop existing; to disappear: *The old customs are dying.* ◇ *Our love will never die.* **3** [I] (used about a machine) to stop working: *My phone died and I had no way to contact you.*
IDM be dying for sth/to do sth (*informal*) to want sth/ to do sth very much: *I'm dying for a cup of coffee.* die **hard** to change or disappear only slowly or with difficulty: *Old attitudes towards women die hard.* die **laughing** to find sth very funny: *I thought I'd die laughing when he told that joke.* to die for (*informal*) if you think that sth is to die for, you really want it and would do anything to get it: *They have a house in town that's to die for.*
PHR V die away to slowly become weaker before stopping or disappearing: *The sound of the engine died away as the car drove into the distance.* die **down** to slowly become less strong: *Let's wait until the storm dies down before we go out.* die **off** to die one by one until there are none left die **out** to stop happening or disappear: *The use of horses on farms has almost died out in this country.*

die² /daɪ/ *noun* [C] **1** (ART) a block of metal with a special shape, or with a pattern cut into it, that is used for shaping other pieces of metal such as coins, or for making patterns on paper or leather **2** (*especially AmE*) = DICE

diesel /ˈdiːzl/ *noun* **1** [U] a type of heavy oil used in some engines instead of petrol: *a diesel engine* ◇ *a taxi that runs on diesel* ⊃ picture at **fractional distillation 2** [C] a vehicle that uses diesel: *My new car's a diesel.* ⊃ look at **petrol**

diet¹ ⚲ A1 /ˈdaɪət/ *noun* **1** [C, U] (BIOLOGY) the food that a person or animal usually eats: *They live on a diet of rice and vegetables.* ◇ *I always try to have a healthy, balanced diet* (= including all the different types of food that our body needs). ◇ *Poor diet is a cause of ill health.* **2** [C] (HEALTH) certain foods that a person who is ill or who wants to lose weight eats; a time when you only eat these foods: *He's following a low-fat diet.* ◇ *a sugar-free diet* ◇ *I won't have a cake, thank you. I'm on a diet.* ◇ *He decided to go on a diet* (= to lose weight) *before his holiday.* ▸ dietary /-əteri/ *adj*.: *dietary habits/ requirements*

diet² /ˈdaɪət/ *verb* [I] to try to lose weight by eating less food or only certain kinds of food

dietetics /ˌdaɪəˈtetɪks/ *noun* [U] (BIOLOGY) the scientific study of the food we eat and its effect on our health

dietician (*also* dietitian) /ˌdaɪəˈtɪʃn/ *noun* [C] a person whose job is to advise people on what kind of food they should eat to keep healthy

differ ⚲+ B2 ⊙ /ˈdɪfə(r)/ *verb* [I] **1** ~ (from sb/sth) to be different: *How does this car differ from the more expensive model?* **2** ~ (with sb) (about/on sth) to have a different opinion: *I'm afraid I differ with you on that question.*

difference ʔ A1 ⦿ /'dɪfrəns/ *noun* **1** [C, U] ~ **(between A and B); ~ (in sth)** the way that people or things are not the same or the way that sb/sth has changed: *What's the difference between this computer and that cheaper one?* ◊ *From a distance it's hard to **tell the difference** between the twins.* ◊ *There's no difference in the results.* **OPP** **similarity** **2** [sing., U] ~ **(between A and B); ~ (in sth)** the amount by which people or things are not the same or by which sb/sth has changed: *There's **an age difference** of three years between the two children.* ◊ *There's very little difference in price since last year.* ◊ *We gave a 30% deposit and must **pay the difference** when the work is finished* (= the rest of the money). **3** [C] a DISAGREEMENT that is not very serious: *All couples **have their differences** from time to time.* ◊ *There was **a difference** of opinion over how much we owed.*
IDM **make no difference (to sb/sth)** | **not make any difference** to not be important (to sb/sth); to have no effect **make a, some, etc. difference (to sb/sth)** to have an effect (on sb/sth): *Marriage made a big difference to her life.* **split the difference** → SPLIT[1]

different ʔ A1 ⦿ /'dɪfrənt/ *adj.* **1** ~ **(from/to sth)** not the same: *The play was different from anything I had seen before.* ◊ *The two houses are very different in style.* ◊ *You'd look completely different with short hair.* **OPP** **similar ❶** In American English **different than** is also used. **2** [only before noun] separate; individual: *This coat is available in three different colours.*
▶ **differently** ʔ A2 Ⓦ *adv.*: *I think you'll feel differently about it tomorrow.*

differential[1] /ˌdɪfə'renʃl/ *noun* [C] **1** ~ **(between A and B)** a difference in the amount, value or size of sth, especially the difference in rates of pay for people doing different work in the same industry or profession **2** (*also* differential 'gear) a GEAR that makes it possible for a vehicle's back wheels to turn around at different speeds when going around corners

differential[2] /ˌdɪfə'renʃl/ *adj.* [only before noun] (*formal*) showing or depending on a difference; not equal

differentiate ʔ+ C1 Ⓦ /ˌdɪfə'renʃieɪt/ *verb* **1** [I, T] ~ **between A and B; ~ A (from B)** to see or show how things are different: *It is hard to differentiate between these two types of seed.* ◊ *I can't differentiate one variety from another.* **2** [T] ~ **sth (from sth)** to make one thing different from another: *The coloured feathers differentiate the male bird from the plain brown female.* **SYN** **distinguish 3** [I] ~ **(between A and B)** to treat one person or group differently from another: *We don't differentiate between the two groups — we treat everybody alike.* **SYN** **discriminate**
▶ **differentiation** Ⓦ /ˌdɪfəˌrenʃi'eɪʃn/ *noun* [U]

difficult ʔ A1 ⦿ /'dɪfɪkəlt/ *adj.* **1** ~ **(for sb) (to do sth)** not easy to do or understand: *a difficult test/problem* ◊ *I **find it difficult** to get up early in the morning.* ◊ *It was difficult for us to hear the speaker.* **2** full of problems: *I'm in a difficult situation. Whatever I do, somebody will be upset.* **3** (used about a person) not friendly, reasonable or helpful: *a difficult customer* **SYN** **awkward**

difficulty ʔ B1 Ⓦ /'dɪfɪkəlti/ *noun* (*pl.* -ies) **1** [U, C] ~ **(in sth/doing sth)** a problem; a situation that is hard to deal with: *I'm sure you won't **have any difficulty** getting a visa for America.* ◊ *We **had no difficulty** selling our car.* ◊ *We found a hotel **without difficulty**.* ◊ ***With difficulty**, I managed to persuade Alice to lend us the money.* ◊ *I could see somebody **in difficulty** in the water so I went to help them.* ◊ *If you borrow too much money you may **get into** financial **difficulties**.*

difficult

hard ♦ challenging ♦ demanding ♦ taxing

These words all describe sth that is not easy and requires a lot of effort or skill to do.

difficult *a difficult exam*

hard *hard work*

challenging *a challenging task*

demanding *a demanding job*

taxing *a physically taxing role*

2 [U] how hard sth is to do or to deal with: *The questions start easy and then increase in difficulty.*

diffident /'dɪfɪdənt/ *adj.* not having confidence in their own strengths or abilities: *He has a very diffident manner.* ▶ **diffidence** /-dəns/ *noun* [U]

diffraction

➡ wavelength
◀— path of waves

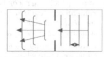

narrow opening, similar in size to wavelength = greater diffraction

wide opening, much larger than wavelength = less diffraction

diffract /dɪ'frækt/ *verb* [T] (**PHYSICS**) to break up a stream of light or another system of waves by passing it through a narrow opening or across an edge ▶ **diffraction** /-'frækʃn/ *noun* [U]

diffuse[1] /dɪ'fjuːz/ *verb* **1** [I, T] (*formal*) to spread sth or become spread widely in all directions **2** [I, T] (**PHYSICS**) if a gas or liquid **diffuses** or **is diffused** in a substance, it becomes slowly mixed with that substance **3** [T] (*formal*) to make light shine less brightly by spreading it in many directions ▶ **diffusion** /-'fjuːʒn/ *noun* [U]

diffusion

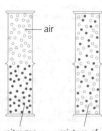

air

nitrogen dioxide

mixture of nitrogen dioxide and air

diffuse[2] /dɪ'fjuːs/ *adj.* spread over a wide area ⊃ picture at **reflection**

dig[1] ʔ B2 /dɪg/ *verb* [I, T] (digging; *pt, pp* dug /dʌg/) to move earth and make a hole in the ground: *The children are busy digging in the sand.* ◊ *to dig a hole*
IDM **dig deep** to try harder, give more, go further, etc. than is usually necessary: *Charities for the homeless are asking people to dig deep into their pockets in this cold weather.* **dig your heels in** to refuse to do sth or to change your mind about sth
PHRV **dig (sth) in** | **dig sth into sth** to push or press (sth) into sb/sth: *My neck is all red where my collar is digging in.* ◊ *He dug his hands deep into his pockets.* **dig sb/sth out (of sth) 1** to get sb/sth out of sth by moving the earth, etc. that covers them or it: *Rescue workers dug the survivors out of the rubble.* **2** to get or find sb/sth by searching: *I dug out some old photos from the attic.* **dig sth up 1** to remove sth from the earth by digging: *to dig up potatoes* **2** to make a hole or take away soil by digging: *Workmen are digging*

up the road in front of our house. **3** to find information by searching or studying: *Newspapers have dug up some embarrassing facts about his private life.*

dig² /dɪg/ *noun* [C] **1** a hard push: *to give somebody **a dig in the ribs** (= with your* ELBOW) **2** something that you say to upset sb: *The others kept **making digs** at him because of the way he spoke.* **3** an occasion or place where a group of people try to find things of historical or scientific interest in the ground in order to study them: *an archaeological dig*

digest /daɪˈdʒest, dɪ-/ *verb* [T] **1** (BIOLOGY) when you **digest** food, it is changed into substances that you body can use **2** to think about new information so that you understand it fully: *The lecture was interesting, but too much to digest all at once.*

digester /daɪˈdʒestə(r), dɪ-/ *noun* [C] (CHEMISTRY) a container in which substances are treated with heat or chemicals in order to break them down or release other substances: *We built two anaerobic digesters to process food waste.* ◊ *The kitchen is powered by a biogas digester .*

digestible /daɪˈdʒestəbl, dɪ-/ *adj.* (used about food) easy for the body to DIGEST

digestion /daɪˈdʒestʃən, dɪ-/ *noun* [U] (BIOLOGY) the process of DIGESTING food ▶ **digestive** *adj.*: *digestive problems*

digestive /daɪˈdʒestɪv, dɪ-/ *adj.* (BIOLOGY) connected with the DIGESTION of food; helping the process of DIGESTION

di'gestive system *noun* [C] (ANATOMY) the series of organs inside the body that DIGEST food

digger /ˈdɪgə(r)/ *noun* [C] **1** a large machine that is used for digging up the ground **2** a person or an animal that digs

digit /ˈdɪdʒɪt/ *noun* [C] **1** (MATHEMATICS) any of the numbers from 0 to 9: *a six-digit phone number* **2** (ANATOMY) a finger, THUMB or toe

digital 🔊 **A2** **ⓦ** /ˈdɪdʒɪtl/ *adj.* **1** (COMPUTING) using an electronic system that uses the numbers 1 and 0 to record sound or store information, showing that an electronic signal is there or not there: *a digital camera* ◊ *digital media/content/platforms* **2** connected with the use of computer technology, especially the internet: *communication in **the digital age*** ◊ *Digital technology continues to evolve rapidly.* **3** showing information by using numbers: *a digital watch* ⊃ look at **analogue** (2) ▶ **digital** *noun* [U]: *The world of digital* (= digital technology) *is constantly changing.* ▶ **digitally** /-təli/ *adv.*: *The photo has been digitally enhanced.*

the digestive system

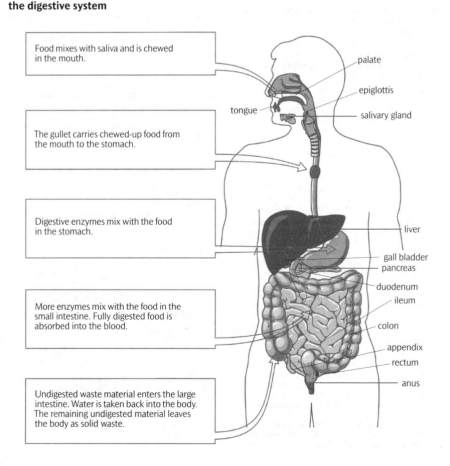

Food mixes with saliva and is chewed in the mouth.

The gullet carries chewed-up food from the mouth to the stomach.

Digestive enzymes mix with the food in the stomach.

More enzymes mix with the food in the small intestine. Fully digested food is absorbed into the blood.

Undigested waste material enters the large intestine. Water is taken back into the body. The remaining undigested material leaves the body as solid waste.

palate
epiglottis
tongue
salivary gland
liver
gall bladder
pancreas
duodenum
ileum
colon
appendix
rectum
anus

digital 'art noun [U] (**ART**) art that is created using computers or other digital media: *There are plenty of great apps you can use to create digital art.* ◇ *a digital art installation*

digital 'signature noun [C] (**COMPUTING**) a way of secretly adding sb's name to an electronic message or document to prove the identity of the person who is sending it and show that the data has not been changed at all

digitize (*BrE also* -ise) /'dɪdʒɪtaɪz/ (*also* digitalize) (*BrE also* -ise /'dɪdʒɪtəlaɪz/) verb [T] (**COMPUTING**) to change data into a digital form that can be easily read and processed by a computer: *a digitized map*

dignified /'dɪgnɪfaɪd/ adj. behaving in a calm, serious way that makes other people respect you: *dignified behaviour* **OPP** **undignified**

dignity ⌑+ **C1** /'dɪgnəti/ noun [U] **1** calm, serious behaviour that makes other people respect you: *to behave* **with dignity** **2** the quality of being serious and formal: *the quiet dignity of the funeral service*

digress /daɪ'gres/ verb [I] (*formal*) to stop talking or writing about the main subject under discussion and start talking or writing about another less important one ▸ **digression** /-'greʃn/ noun [C, U]

dike /daɪk/ = DYKE

dilapidated /dɪ'læpɪdeɪtɪd/ adj. (used about buildings, furniture, etc.) old and broken ▸ **dilapidation** /dɪˌlæpɪ'deɪʃn/ noun [U]

dilate /daɪ'leɪt/ verb [I, T] to become larger, wider or more open; to make sth larger, wide or more open: *Her eyes dilated with fear.* ◇ *dilated pupils/nostrils* **OPP** **contract²** ▸ **dilation** /-'leɪʃn/ noun [U]

dilemma ⌑+ **C1** /dɪ'lemə, daɪ-/ noun [C] a situation in which you have to make a difficult choice between two or more things: *Doctors* **face a** moral **dilemma** *of when to keep patients alive artificially and when to let them die.* ◇ *to be* **in a dilemma**

diligent /'dɪlɪdʒənt/ adj. (*formal*) showing care and effort in your work or duties: *a diligent student/worker* ▸ **diligently** adv.

dilute /daɪ'luːt/ verb [T] **~ sth (with sth)** to make a liquid weaker by adding water or another liquid ▸ **dilute** (*also* diluted) adj. (**CHEMISTRY**): *dilute acid/solution* ▸ **dilution** /-'luːʃn/ noun [U]: *the dilution of sewage*

dim¹ /dɪm/ adj. (dimmer; dimmest) **1** not bright or easy to see; not clear: *The light was too dim to read by.* ◇ *a dim shape in the distance* **2** (*informal*) not very clever; stupid: *He's a bit dim.* **3** (*informal*) (used about a situation) not giving any reason to have hope; not good: *The prospects of the two sides reaching an agreement look dim.* ▸ **dimly** adv.

dim² /dɪm/ verb [I, T] (-mm-) to become less bright or clear; to make sth less bright or clear: *The lights dimmed.* ◇ *to dim the lights*

dime /daɪm/ noun [C] a coin used in the US and Canada that is worth 10 cents

dimension ⌑+ **C1** **◉** /daɪ'menʃn, dɪ-/ noun **1** [C] (**GEOMETRY**) a measurement in space, for example how high, wide or long sth is: *to measure the dimensions of a room* ◇ (*figurative*) *The full dimensions of this problem are only now being recognized.* **2** [C] something that affects the way you think about a problem or situation: *to add a new dimension to a problem/situation* **3** -dimensional /daɪmenʃənl, dɪmenʃnl/ (in adjectives) having the number of dimensions mentioned: *a three-dimensional object*

diminish ⌑+ **C1** /dɪ'mɪnɪʃ/ verb [I, T] (*formal*) to become smaller or less important; to make sth smaller or less important: *The world's rainforests are diminishing fast.* ◇ *The bad news did nothing to diminish her enthusiasm for the plan.* **SYN** **decrease¹** ⊃ note at **fall¹**

diminuendo /dɪˌmɪnju'endəʊ/ noun [C, U] (*pl.* -os) (**MUSIC**) a slow steady decrease in how loudly a piece of music is played or sung **OPP** **crescendo**

diminution /ˌdɪmɪ'njuːʃn/ noun **~ (of/in sth)** (*formal*) **1** [U] the act of reducing sth or of being reduced: *the diminution of political power* **2** [C, usually sing.] a reduction in sth: *a diminution in population growth*

diminutive /dɪ'mɪnjətɪv/ adj. (*formal*) much smaller than usual

dimple /'dɪmpl/ noun [C] a round area in the skin on the CHEEK (= the side of the face), etc. that often only appears when you smile

din /dɪn/ noun [sing.] a lot of unpleasant noise that continues for some time

dine /daɪn/ verb [I] (*formal*) to eat a meal, especially in the evening: *We dined at an exclusive French restaurant.*
PHR V **dine out** to eat in a restaurant

diner /'daɪnə(r)/ noun [C] **1** a person who is eating at a restaurant **2** (*AmE*) a restaurant that serves simple, cheap food

dinghy /'dɪŋi, 'dɪŋgi/ noun [C] (*pl.* -ies) **1** a small open boat that you sail or ROW ⊃ look at **yacht** **2** a small open boat made of plastic of rubber that is filled with air: *an inflatable dinghy*

dingy /'dɪndʒi/ adj. (dingier; dingiest) dirty and dark: *a dingy room/hotel*

'dining room noun [C] a room where you eat meals

dinner ⌑ **A1** /'dɪnə(r)/ noun **1** [U, C] the main meal of the day, eaten either in the middle of the day or in the evening: *Would you like to* **go out for/to dinner** *one evening?* ◇ *What's for dinner, Mum?* ◇ *I never eat a big dinner.* **2** [C] a formal occasion in the evening during which a meal is served: *The club is holding its annual dinner next week.*

'dinner jacket (*AmE also* tuxedo) noun [C] a black or white jacket that a man wears on formal occasions. A dinner jacket is usually worn with a BOW TIE.

dinosaur /'daɪnəsɔː(r)/ noun [C] one of a number of very large animals that became EXTINCT (= disappeared from the earth) millions of years ago

diocese /'daɪəsɪs/ noun [C] (**RELIGION**) an area containing a number of churches, for which a BISHOP is responsible

dimensions

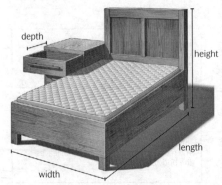

depth | height | length | width

diode /ˈdaɪəʊd/ *noun* [C] (ENGINEERING) an electronic device in which the electric current flows in one direction only

dioptre (*BrE*) (*AmE* **diopter**) /daɪˈɒptə(r)/ *noun* [C] (PHYSICS) a unit for measuring the power of a LENS to REFRACT light (= make it change direction)

dioxide /daɪˈɒksaɪd/ *noun* [C, U] (CHEMISTRY) a COMPOUND formed by combining two ATOMS of OXYGEN and one ATOM of another chemical element: *carbon dioxide*

dip¹ ẖ+ **C1** /dɪp/ *verb* (-pp-) **1** ~ sth (into sth); ~ sth (in) to put sth into liquid and immediately take it out again: *Julie dipped her toe into the pool to see how cold it was.* **2** [I, T] to go down or make sth go down to a lower level: *The road suddenly dipped down to the river.* ◊ *The company's sales have dipped slightly this year.*
PHR V **dip into sth** **1** to use part of an amount of sth that you have: *Tim had to dip into his savings to pay for his new suit.* **2** to read parts, but not all, of sth: *I've only dipped into the book. I haven't read it all the way through.*

dip² /dɪp/ *noun* **1** [C] ~ (in sth) a fall to a lower level, especially for a short time: *a dip in sales/temperature* **2** [C] an area of lower ground: *The cottage was in a dip in the hills.* **3** [C] (*informal*) a short swim: *We went for a dip before breakfast.* **4** [C, U] a thick sauce into which you DIP biscuits, vegetables, etc. before eating them: *a cheese/chilli dip*

diphtheria /dɪfˈθɪəriə, dɪpˈθ-/ *noun* [U] (HEALTH) a serious disease of the throat that makes it difficult to breathe

diphthong /ˈdɪfθɒŋ, ˈdɪpθ-/ *noun* [C] (LANGUAGE) two vowel sounds that are pronounced together to make one sound, for example the /aɪ/ sound in *fine*

diploid /ˈdɪplɔɪd/ *adj.* (BIOLOGY) (used about a cell) containing two complete sets of CHROMOSOMES, one from each parent ⊃ look at **haploid**

diploma /dɪˈpləʊmə/ *noun* [C] ~ (in sth) (EDUCATION) a course of study, often at a college; a CERTIFICATE that you receive when you complete the course of study: *I'm studying for a diploma in hotel management.* ⊃ note at **subject¹**

diplomacy /dɪˈpləʊməsi/ *noun* [U] **1** (POLITICS) the activity of managing relations between different countries: *If diplomacy fails, there is a danger of war.* **2** skill in dealing with people without upsetting or offending them: *He handled the tricky situation with tact and diplomacy.*

diplomat ẖ+ **C1** /ˈdɪpləmæt/ *noun* [C] (POLITICS) an official who represents his or her country in a foreign country: *a diplomat at the embassy in Rome*

diplomatic ẖ+ **C1** /ˌdɪpləˈmætɪk/ *adj.* **1** (POLITICS) connected with managing relations between different countries: *to break off diplomatic relations* **2** showing skill in dealing with people: *He searched for a diplomatic reply so as not to offend her.* **SYN** **tactful** ▶ **diplomatically** /-kli/ *adv.*

diplomatic corps (*usually* **the diplomatic corps**) *noun* [C + sing./pl. verb] (*pl.* **diplomatic corps**) (POLITICS) all the DIPLOMATS who work in a particular country or city

diptych /ˈdɪptɪk/ *noun* [C] (ART) a painting, especially a religious one, with two wooden panels that can be closed like a book

dire /ˈdaɪə(r)/ *adj.* (*formal*) very bad or serious: *dire consequences/poverty* **SYN** **terrible**

direct¹ ẖ **A2** ◑ /dəˈrekt, daɪˈr-/ *adj.* **1** going from one place to another without turning or stopping: *a direct flight to Hong Kong* **OPP** **indirect** **2** with nobody/ nothing in between; not involving anyone/anything else: *The British prime minister is in direct contact*

with the US president. ◊ *a direct attack on the capital* ◊ *As a direct result of the new road, traffic jams in the centre have been reduced.* ◊ *You should protect your skin from direct sunlight.* **OPP** **indirect** **3** saying exactly what you mean: *Politicians never give a direct answer to a direct question.* ◊ *She sometimes offends people with her direct way of speaking.* **OPP** **indirect** **4** [only before noun] complete; exact: *What she did was in direct opposition to my orders.*

direct² ẖ **B1** /dəˈrekt, daɪˈr-/ *adv.* **1** without turning or stopping: *This bus goes direct to London.* **2** with nobody/nothing in between; not involving anyone/ anything else: *I prefer to deal with him direct.* ◊ *Customers can buy produce direct from the farmer.*

direct³ ẖ **B1** ◑ /dəˈrekt, daɪˈr-/ *verb* **1** ~ sth to/ towards sb/sth; ~ sth at sb/sth to point or send sth towards sb/sth or in a particular direction: *In recent weeks the media's attention has been directed towards events abroad.* ◊ *The advert is directed at young people.* **2** to manage or control sb/sth: *A policeman was in the middle of the road, directing the traffic.* ◊ *to direct a play/film* ⊃ note at **performing arts** **3** ~ sb (to ...) to tell or show sb how to get somewhere: *I was directed to an office at the end of the corridor.* **4** (*formal*) to tell or order sb to do sth: *Take the tablets as directed by your doctor.*

direct action *noun* [U, C] (POLITICS) the use of strikes, protests, etc. instead of discussion in order to get what you want

direct cost *noun* [C, usually pl.] (BUSINESS) the cost of the materials and workers involved in making a product or providing a service **OPP** **indirect cost**

direct current *noun* [C, U] (*abbr.* DC) (ENGINEERING, PHYSICS) a flow of electricity that goes in one direction only ⊃ look at **alternating current**

direct debit *noun* [C, U] (FINANCE) an order to your bank that allows sb else to take a particular amount of money out of your account on certain dates

direction ẖ **A2** ◑ /dəˈrekʃn, daɪˈr-/ *noun* **1** [C, U] the path, line or way along which a person or thing is moving, looking, pointing, developing, etc: *A woman was seen running in the direction of the station.* ◊ *We met him coming in the opposite direction.* ◊ *I think the new speed limit is still too high, but at least it's a step in the right direction.* ◊ *I think the wind has changed direction.* ◊ *I've got such a hopeless sense of direction — I'm always getting lost.* **2** [U] a purpose; an aim: *I want a career that gives me a sense of direction in life.* **3** [C, usually pl.] information or instructions about how to do sth or how to get to a place: *I'll give you directions to my house.* **4** [U] the act of managing or controlling sth: *This department is under the direction of Mrs Walters.*

▼ COLLOCATIONS

direction

You can ask sb **the way**: *Can you tell me the way to the town centre?* ◊ *Which way is the station?* A place can be **near**, **not far** or **a long way from** another place: *The station is near the centre of town.* ◊ *The bus stop isn't far from the theatre.* ◊ *Our hotel was a long way from the sea.* A place can be **nearby** or **a long way away**. You can **turn right/left** or **go straight on**: *Turn right at the crossroads.* ◊ *Go straight on along the high street.* You can **take the first/second**, etc. **road/ turning/exit**, etc: *Take the second exit at the roundabout.* ◊ *Take the next left.* ◊ *Take the third turning on the right.* A place can be **on the right/left**: *You'll see the cinema on the left.*

directive /də'rektɪv, daɪ'r-/ *noun* [C] an official order to do sth: *an EU directive on safety at work*

directly¹ ⚡**B1** 〇 /də'rektli, daɪ'r-/ *adv.* **1** in a direct line or way: *The bank is directly opposite the supermarket.* ◇ *He refused to answer my question directly.* ◇ *Lung cancer is directly related to smoking.* **OPP indirectly 2** (*BrE, old-fashioned*) immediately; very soon: *Wait where you are. I'll be back directly.*

directly² /də'rektli, daɪ'r-/ *conj.* (*BrE*) as soon as: *I phoned him directly I heard the news.*

di,rect 'mail *noun* [U] (**BUSINESS**) advertisements that are sent to people through the post

di,rect 'marketing *noun* [U] (**BUSINESS**) the business of selling products or services directly to customers who order by mail, phone or email, or over the internet, instead of going to a shop

di,rect 'object *noun* [C] (**GRAMMAR**) a noun or phrase that refers to a person or thing that is affected by the action of a verb: *In the sentence 'Anna bought a jacket', 'a jacket' is the direct object.* ⊃ look at **indirect object**

director ⚡**A2** /də'rektə(r), daɪ'r-/ *noun* [C] **1** (**BUSINESS**) a person who manages or controls a company or organization: *the **managing director** of Rolls-Royce* ◇ *She's on the **board of directors** (= group of directors) of a large computer company.* **2** a person who is responsible for a particular activity or department in a company, a college, etc: *the director of studies of a language school* **3** (**ARTS AND MEDIA**) a person who tells the actors, etc. what to do in a film, play, etc: *a film/ theatre director* ⊃ note at **performing arts**

directory ⚡+ **C1** /də'rektəri, daɪ'r-/ *noun* [C] (*pl.* -ies) **1** a list of names, addresses and phone numbers in the order of the alphabet: *an online directory of local businesses* **2** (**COMPUTING**) a file containing a group of other files or programs in a computer

di,rect 'speech *noun* [U] (**GRAMMAR**) the actual words that a person said ⊃ look at **indirect speech** ⊃ look at **reported speech**

dirt ⚡**B1** /dɜːt/ *noun* [U] **1** a substance that is not clean, such as dust or mud: *His face and hands were covered in dirt.* **2** earth or soil: *a dirt track* **3** damaging information about sb: *The press are always trying to **dig up dirt** on the president's love life.*

dirty¹ ⚡**A1** /'dɜːti/ *adj.* (dirtier; dirtiest) **1** not clean: *Your hands are dirty. Go and wash them!* ◇ *Gardening is dirty work* (= it makes you dirty). **OPP clean¹** **2** referring to sex in a way that may upset or offend people: *to tell a dirty joke* **3** unpleasant or dishonest: *He's a dirty player.* ◇ *I'm not going to tell her you don't want to go. You **do** your own **dirty work**.* **IDM a dirty word** an idea or thing that you do not like or agree with: *Work is a dirty word to Frank.*

dirty² /'dɜːti/ *verb* [T] (dirtying; dirties; *pt, pp* dirtied) to make sth dirty **OPP clean²**

dirty³ /'dɜːti/ *adv.* **IDM dirty great/big** (*BrE, informal*) used to emphasize how large sth is: *When I turned around he was pointing a dirty great gun at me.* **play dirty** (*informal*) to behave or play a game in an unfair way

dis- /dɪs/ *prefix* (in verbs, nouns, adjectives and adverbs) not; the opposite of: *discontinue* ◇ *disarmament*

disability ⚡+ **B2** /ˌdɪsə'bɪləti/ *noun* [C, U] (*pl.* -ies) (**HEALTH**) a physical or mental condition that makes you unable to use a part of your body completely or easily, or that means you cannot learn easily: *Because of his disability, he needs constant care.* ◇ *people with severe disabilities* ◇ *physical/mental disability*

disable /dɪs'eɪbl/ *verb* [T, often passive] to make sb unable to use part of their body completely or easily, usually because of injury or disease: *Many soldiers were disabled in the war.*

disabled ⚡+ /dɪs'eɪbld/ *adj.* (**HEALTH**) **1** unable to use a part of your body completely or easily; unable to learn easily: *A car accident left her permanently disabled.* ◇ *mentally disabled* **2** the disabled *noun* [pl.] people who are disabled: *The hotel has improved facilities for the disabled.*

disadvantage¹ ⚡**B1** 〇 /ˌdɪsəd'vɑːntɪdʒ/ *noun* [C] something that causes problems; sth that may stop sb/sth from being successful or effective: *The main disadvantage of the job is the long hours.* ◇ *What are the advantages and disadvantages of nuclear power?* ◇ *Your qualifications are good. Your main disadvantage is your lack of experience.* **OPP advantage** **IDM put sb/be at a disadvantage** to put sb/be in a situation where they or you may be less successful than other people: *The fact that you don't speak the language will put you at a disadvantage in France.* **to sb's disadvantage** (*formal*) not good or helpful for sb: *The agreement will be to your disadvantage — don't accept it.*

disadvantage² 〇 /ˌdɪsəd'vɑːntɪdʒ/ *verb* [T] to cause problems and stop sb/sth from being successful or making progress: *Many people will be disadvantaged by the new tax system.*

disadvantaged /ˌdɪsəd'vɑːntɪdʒd/ *adj.* (**SOCIAL STUDIES**) in a bad social or economic situation; poor: *extra help for the most disadvantaged members of society* **SYN deprived**

disadvantageous /ˌdɪsædvən'teɪdʒəs/ *adj.* (*formal*) causing sb to be in a worse situation compared to other people

disagree ⚡**A2** /ˌdɪsə'griː/ *verb* [I] **1** ~ (**with sb/sth**) (**about sth**) to have a different opinion from sb/ sth; to not agree: *Stephen often disagrees with his father about politics.* ◇ *They strongly disagreed with my idea.* ◇ *'We have to tell him.' 'No, I disagree. I don't think we should tell him at all.'* **2** to be different; to give different information: *These two sets of statistics disagree.* **OPP agree** **PHRV disagree with sb** (used about sth you have eaten or drunk) to make you feel ill; to have a bad effect on you **disagree with sth** to believe that sth is bad: *I disagree with violent protests.*

disagreeable /ˌdɪsə'griːəbl/ *adj.* (*formal*) unpleasant **OPP agreeable** ▸ **disagreeably** /-bli/ *adv.*

disagreement ⚡+ **B2** /ˌdɪsə'griːmənt/ *noun* [C, U] ~ (**with sb**) (**about/on/over sth**) a situation in which people have a different opinion about sth and often also argue: *It's normal for couples to **have disagreements**.* ◇ *Mandy resigned after a disagreement with her boss.* ◇ *The conference ended in disagreement.* **OPP agreement**

disallow /ˌdɪsə'laʊ/ *verb* [T, often passive] to not allow or accept sth: *The goal was disallowed because the player was offside.*

disappear ⚡**A2** /ˌdɪsə'pɪə(r)/ *verb* [I] **1** to become impossible to see or to find: *He walked away and disappeared into a crowd of people.* ◇ *My purse was here a moment ago and now it's disappeared.* **SYN vanish OPP appear 2** to stop existing: *Plant and animal species are disappearing at an alarming rate.* **SYN vanish OPP appear** ▸ **disappearance** *noun* [C, U]: *The mystery of her disappearance was never solved.*

disappoint ⚡+ **B2** /ˌdɪsə'pɔɪnt/ *verb* [T] to make sb feel sad because what they had hoped for has not happened or is less good, interesting, etc. than they had hoped: *I'm sorry to disappoint you but I'm afraid you haven't won the prize.*

disappointed 🔊 **B1** /ˌdɪsəˈpɔɪntɪd/ *adj.* ~ **(about/at sth); ~ (in/with sb/sth); ~ that … ; ~ to see, hear, etc.** sad because you/sb/sth did not succeed or because sth was not as good, interesting, etc. as you had hoped: *Lucy was deeply disappointed at not being chosen for the team.* ◇ *We were disappointed with our hotel.* ◇ *I'm disappointed in you. I thought you could do better.* ◇ *They are very disappointed that they can't stay longer.* ◇ *I was disappointed to hear that you can't come to the party.*

disappointing 🔊 **B1** /ˌdɪsəˈpɔɪntɪŋ/ *adj.* making you feel sad because sth was not as good, interesting, etc. as you had hoped: *It has been a disappointing year for the company.* ▶ **disappointingly** *adv.*

disappointment 🔊+ **B2** /ˌdɪsəˈpɔɪntmənt/ *noun* **1** [U] the feeling of being sad because sth has not happened or been as good, successful, etc. as you expected or hoped: *To his great disappointment he failed to get the job.* **2** [C] ~ **(to sb)** a person or thing that is disappointing: *I always felt I was a disappointment to my father.* ◇ *She has suffered many disappointments in her career.*

disapproval /ˌdɪsəˈpruːvl/ *noun* [U] a feeling that sth is bad or that sb is behaving badly: *She shook her head in disapproval.*

disapprove /ˌdɪsəˈpruːv/ *verb* [I] ~ **(of sb/sth)** to think that sb/sth is not good or suitable; to not approve of sb/ sth: *His parents strongly disapproved of him leaving college before he had finished his course.* **OPP** approve

disapproving /ˌdɪsəˈpruːvɪŋ/ *adj.* **1** showing that you do not approve of sb/sth: *a disapproving glance/tone/look* ◇ *She sounded disapproving as we discussed my plans.* **2** showing that you think sth is bad, silly, etc. ▶ **disapprovingly** *adv.*: *He looked disapprovingly at the row of empty wine bottles.*

disarm /dɪsˈɑːm/ *verb* **1** [T] to take weapons away from sb: *The police caught and disarmed the terrorists.* **2** [I] (used about a country) to reduce the number of weapons it has **3** [T] to make sb feel less angry: *Jenny could always disarm the teachers with a smile.*

disarmament /dɪsˈɑːməmənt/ *noun* [U] reducing the number of weapons that an army or a country has: *nuclear disarmament*

disassociate /ˌdɪsəˈsəʊsieɪt, -ˈsəʊʃi-/ = DISSOCIATE

disaster 🔊 **A2** /dɪˈzɑːstə(r)/ *noun* **1** [C] an event that causes a lot of harm or damage: *earthquakes, floods and other natural disasters* **2** [C, U] a bad situation that causes problems: *Losing your job is unfortunate, but it's not a disaster.* ◇ *This year's lack of rain could spell disaster for the region.* **3** [C, U] (*informal*) a complete failure: *The school play was an absolute disaster. Everything went wrong.*

disastrous 🔊+ **C1** /dɪˈzɑːstrəs/ *adj.* terrible, harmful or failing completely: *Our mistake had disastrous results.* ▶ **disastrously** *adv.*: *The plan went disastrously wrong.*

disband /dɪsˈbænd/ *verb* [I, T] to stop existing as a group; to stop sb/sth from operating as a group

disbelief /ˌdɪsbɪˈliːf/ *noun* [U] the feeling of not believing sb/sth: *'It can't be true!' he shouted in disbelief.*

disbelieve /ˌdɪsbɪˈliːv/ *verb* [T] (not used in the progressive tenses) (*formal*) to think that sth is not true or that sb is not telling the truth: *I have no reason to disbelieve her.* **OPP** believe

disc 🔊 **B2** (*also* disk *especially in AmE*) /dɪsk/ *noun* [C] **1** a round flat object **2** = DISK (1) **3** (**ANATOMY**) one of the pieces of CARTILAGE (= thin strong material) between the bones in the back

discard 🔊+ **C1** /dɪˈskɑːd/ *verb* [T] (*formal*) to throw sth away because it is not useful

discern /dɪˈsɜːn/ *verb* [T] (*formal*) to see or notice sth with difficulty: *I discerned a note of anger in his voice.* **SYN** detect ▶ **discernible** /-ˈsɜːnəbl/ *adj.*: *The shape of a house was just discernible through the mist.*

discerning /dɪˈsɜːnɪŋ/ *adj.* able to recognize the quality of sb/sth: *The discerning music lover will appreciate the excellence of this recording.*

discharge¹ 🔊+ **C1** /dɪsˈtʃɑːdʒ/ *verb* **1** [T, often passive] to allow sb officially to leave; to send sb away: *to be discharged from hospital/the army* **2** [T, often passive] (**LAW**) to allow sb to leave prison or court: *He was conditionally discharged after admitting the theft.* **3** [I, T] when a gas or a liquid **discharges** or **is discharged**, or sb **discharges** it, it flows somewhere: *The factory was fined for discharging chemicals into the river.* **4** [T] (*formal*) to do everything that is necessary to perform and complete a particular duty: *to discharge a duty/task*

discharge² /ˈdɪstʃɑːdʒ/ *noun* [C, U] **1** the act of sending sb away or officially allowing them to leave: *The wounded soldier was given a medical discharge.* **2** the action of a gas or liquid flowing from somewhere: *The discharge of oil from the leaking tanker could not be prevented.* **3** a substance that has come out of somewhere: *yellowish discharge from a wound*

disciple /dɪˈsaɪpl/ *noun* [C] (**RELIGION**) a person who follows a teacher, especially a religious one **SYN** follower

disciplinary /ˌdɪsəˈplɪnəri, ˈdɪsəplɪnəri/ *adj.* connected with punishment for breaking rules

discipline¹ 🔊 **B2** **W** /ˈdɪsəplɪn/ *noun* **1** [U] the practice of training people to obey rules and behave well and punishing them if they do not: *A good teacher must be able to maintain discipline in the classroom.* **2** [U] the practice of training your mind and body so that you control your actions and obey rules; a way of doing this: *It takes a lot of self-discipline to study for three hours a day.* ◇ *Having to get up early every day is good discipline for a child.* **3** [C] (**EDUCATION**) a subject of study; a type of sporting event: *Barry's a good all-round athlete, but the long jump is his strongest discipline.* ◇ *academic disciplines*

▼ **COLLOCATIONS**

disaster

Disaster **strikes** in a number of forms, including **earthquakes, hurricanes, lightning** and **tsunamis/tidal waves:** *A massive earthquake struck on Monday.* ◇ *As a result, a tsunami struck much of Indonesia.* ◇ *The building was struck by lightning.* **Forest fires rage** and **volcanoes erupt** causing **devastation:** *Forest fires raged out of control for weeks devastating parts of the country.* ◇ *The volcano began erupting late last night.* After a tsunami or other disaster, areas may be **flooded** or **inundated** (= badly affected by floods): *Severe floods inundated dozens of villages.* **Relief efforts** (= money, food and other help from many organizations) begin in **the immediate aftermath of** (= the time straight after) a disaster: *A massive relief effort is under way to help victims of a tropical cyclone.* ◇ *The president visited the village in the immediate aftermath of the hurricane.*

discipline² /ˈdɪsəplɪn/ *verb* [T] **1** to train sb to obey and to behave in a controlled way: *You should discipline yourself to practise the piano every morning.* **2** to punish sb

'**disc jockey** = DJ

disclaim /dɪsˈkleɪm/ *verb* [T] (*formal*) to say that you do not have sth: *to disclaim responsibility/knowledge* **SYN deny**

disclaimer /dɪsˈkleɪmə(r)/ *noun* [C] **1** (*formal*) a statement in which sb says that they are not responsible for sth, or that they do not know anything about it **2** (LAW) an official statement in which sb says officially that they do not claim the right to do sth

disclose ⁀+ 🄲🄸 /dɪsˈkləʊz/ *verb* [T] (*formal*) to tell sth to sb or to make sth known publicly: *The newspapers did not disclose the victim's name.* **SYN reveal**

disclosure ⁀+ 🄲🄸 /dɪsˈkləʊʒə(r)/ *noun* [C, U] (*formal*) making sth known; the facts that are made known: *the disclosure of secret information* ◇ *He resigned following disclosures about his private life.* **SYN revelation**

disco /ˈdɪskəʊ/ *noun* [C] (*pl.* -os) a party or place where people dance to pop music: *Are you going to the school disco?* ⊃ look at **club¹** (2)

discolour (*BrE*) (*AmE* **discolor**) /dɪsˈkʌlə(r)/ *verb* [I, T] to change or to make sth change colour (often by the effect of light, age or dirt)

discomfort /dɪsˈkʌmfət/ *noun* [U, C] **1** a slight feeling of pain: *There may be some discomfort after the operation.* **OPP comfort¹** **2** a feeling of being embarrassed: *I could sense John's discomfort when I asked him about his job.*

disconcert /ˌdɪskənˈsɜːt/ *verb* [T, usually passive] to make sb feel confused or worried: *She was disconcerted when everyone stopped talking and looked at her.* ▸ **disconcerting** *adj.* ▸ **disconcertingly** *adv.*

disconnect /ˌdɪskəˈnekt/ *verb* [T] **1** to stop a supply of water, gas or electricity going to a piece of equipment or a building **2** to separate sth from sth: *The brake doesn't work because the cable has become disconnected from the lever.*

discontent /ˌdɪskənˈtent/ (*also* **discontentment**) *noun* [U] the state of being unhappy with sth: *The management could sense growing discontent among the staff.* ▸ **discontented** *adj.*: *to be/feel discontented*

discontinue /ˌdɪskənˈtɪnjuː/ *verb* [T] (*formal*) to stop sth or stop producing sth

discord /ˈdɪskɔːd/ *noun* [U] (*formal*) a situation in which people disagree and argue

discordant /dɪsˈkɔːdənt/ *adj.* (*formal*) not in agreement: *Her criticism was the only discordant note in the discussion.*

discount¹ ⁀ 🄱🄸 /ˈdɪskaʊnt/ *noun* [C, U] ~ (**on/off sth**) a lower price than usual: *to offer a discount* ◇ *They were selling everything at a discount* (= at reduced prices). ◇ *Staff get 20 per cent discount on all goods.* **SYN reduction**

discount² 🄱🄸 /dɪsˈkaʊnt/ *verb* [T] **1** [usually passive] to sell sth at a lower price than usual: *Students can get discounted tickets.* **2** to consider sth not true or not important: *I think we can discount that idea. It's just not practical.*

discourage ⁀+ 🄱🄸 /dɪsˈkʌrɪdʒ/ *verb* [T] ~ **sb (from doing sth) 1** to stop sb doing sth, especially by making them realize that it would not be successful or a good idea: *I tried to discourage Jake from giving up his job.* **OPP encourage 2** to make sb feel less confident or excited about doing sth: *Don't let these little problems discourage you.* **OPP encourage** ▸ **discouraged** *adj.*: *After failing the exam again Paul felt very discouraged.* ▸ **discouraging** *adj.*: *Constant criticism can be very discouraging.*

discouragement /dɪsˈkʌrɪdʒmənt/ *noun* [C, U] a thing that makes you not want to do sth; the act of trying to stop sb from doing sth

discourse ⁀+ 🄲🄸 /ˈdɪskɔːs/ *noun* [C, U] (*formal*) **1** a long and serious discussion of a subject in speech or writing **2** (LANGUAGE) the use of language in speech and writing in order to produce meaning; language that is studied, usually in order to see how the different parts of a text are connected: *discourse analysis*

discourteous /dɪsˈkɜːtiəs/ *adj.* (*formal*) not polite or showing respect for people **SYN impolite** **OPP courteous**

discover ⁀ 🄰🄶 🄢 /dɪsˈkʌvə(r)/ *verb* [T] **1** to find or learn sth that nobody had found or known before: *Who discovered the lost city of Machu Picchu?* ◇ *Scientists are hoping to discover the cause of the epidemic.* **2** to find sb/sth that was hidden and that you did not expect to find **3** to find out about sth; to find some information about sth ▸ **discoverer** /-vərə(r)/ *noun* [C]: *Parkinson's disease was named after its discoverer.*

discovery ⁀ 🄰🄶 /dɪsˈkʌvəri/ *noun* (*pl.* -ies) (SCIENCE) **1** [U] the act of finding sb/sth, or learning about sth that was not known before: *The discovery of fingerprints in the car helped the police to find the thief.* ◇ *The discovery of X-rays changed the history of medicine.* **2** [C] something that has been found and learnt about for the first time: *scientific discoveries*

discredit /dɪsˈkredɪt/ *verb* [T] to make people stop respecting or believing sb/sth: *He has been trying to discredit the company by spreading false information.* ▸ **discredit** *noun* [U]: *The government, to its discredit, tried to keep the mistake secret.*

discreet /dɪsˈkriːt/ *adj.* careful in what you say and do so as to avoid causing difficulty for sb or making them feel embarrassed: *I don't want anyone to find out about this, so please be discreet.* **OPP indiscreet** ▸ **discreetly** *adv.*

WORD FAMILY
discreet *adj.* (≠ **indiscreet**)
discretion *noun* (≠ **indiscretion**)

discrepancy /dɪsˈkrepənsi/ *noun* [C, U] (*pl.* -ies) ~ (**in sth**) ~ (**between A and B**) a difference between two things that should be the same: *discrepancies in the witnesses' stories* ◇ *Something is wrong here. There is a discrepancy between these two sets of figures.*

discrete /dɪsˈkriːt/ *adj.* (*formal*) independent of other things of the same type: *The organisms can be divided into discrete categories.* **SYN separate¹**

discretion ⁀+ 🄲🄸 /dɪsˈkreʃn/ *noun* [U] **1** the freedom and power to make decisions by yourself: *You must decide what is best. Use your discretion.* **2** care in what you say and do so as not to cause difficulty for sb or make them feel embarrassed: *This is confidential but I know I can rely on your discretion.* ⊃ note at **care¹** ⊃ adjective **discreet** **IDM at sb's discretion** depending on what sb thinks or decides: *Pay increases are awarded at the discretion of the director.*

discretionary /dɪsˈkreʃənəri/ *adj.* (*formal*) decided according to the judgement of a person in authority about what is necessary in each particular situation; not decided by rules: *You may be eligible for a discretionary grant for your university course.*

discriminate /dɪˈskrɪmɪneɪt/ verb **1** [I] ~ **(against sb)** (**SOCIAL STUDIES**) to treat one person or group worse than others: *It is illegal to discriminate against any ethnic or religious group.* **2** [I, T] ~ **(between A and B)** to see or make a difference between two people or things: *the need to discriminate between fact and fiction*

discriminating /dɪˈskrɪmɪneɪtɪŋ/ adj. able to judge that the quality of sth is good: *a discriminating audience/ customer* **SYN** **discerning**

discrimination ⓘ+ **C1** **Ⓦ** /dɪˌskrɪmɪˈneɪʃn/ noun [U] **1** ~ **(against sb)** (**SOCIAL STUDIES**) treating one person or group worse than others: *sexual/racial/religious discrimination* ◇ *Discrimination against disabled people is illegal.* **2** (*formal*) the ability to see a difference between two people or things: *discrimination between right and wrong*

discriminatory /dɪˈskrɪmɪnətəri/ adj. (**SOCIAL STUDIES**) unfair; treating one person or a group of people worse than others: *discriminatory practices*

discursive /dɪˈskɜːsɪv/ adj. (**LANGUAGE**) (used about a style of writing or speaking) moving from one point to another without any strict structure

discus /ˈdɪskəs/ noun (**SPORT**) **1** [C] a heavy round flat object that is thrown as a sport **2** the discus [sing.] the sport or event of throwing a discus as far as possible

discuss ⓘ **A1** **Ⓞ** /dɪˈskʌs/ verb [T] ~ **sth (with sb)** to talk or write about sth seriously or formally: *I must discuss the matter with my parents before I make a decision.*

discussion ⓘ **A2** **Ⓞ** /dɪˈskʌʃn/ noun [C, U] ~ **(with sb) (about/on sth)** the process of discussing sth/sb; a conversation about sth/sb: *I had a long discussion with Anna about art.* ◇ *The two leaders met for informal discussions.* ◇ *After much discussion we all agreed to share the cost.*
IDM **under discussion** being talked about: *Plans to reform the Health Service are under discussion in Parliament.*

disdain /dɪsˈdeɪn/ noun [U] the feeling that sb/sth is not good enough to be respected: *Monica felt that her boss always treated her ideas with disdain.* ▸ disdainful /-fl/ adj. ▸ disdainfully /-fəli/ adv.

disease ⓘ **A2** /dɪˈziːz/ noun [C, U] (**HEALTH**) an illness of the body in humans, animals or plants: *an infectious/ contagious disease* ◇ *These children suffer from a rare disease.* ◇ *Rats and flies spread disease.* ◇ *Smoking causes heart disease.* ▸ diseased adj.: *His diseased kidney had to be removed.*

▼ SYNONYMS

disease

illness ◆ disorder ◆ infection ◆ condition ◆ ailment ◆ bug

These are all words for a medical problem.

disease *heart/liver/kidney disease*

illness *a long/severe illness* ◇ *mental illness*

disorder (*formal*) *a personality disorder*

infection *a throat infection*

condition *a heart condition*

ailment (*formal*) *childhood ailments*

bug (*informal*) *a nasty stomach bug*

▼ VOCABULARY BUILDING

A **disease** is a medical problem which has a name and may be caused by bacteria, viruses, etc. Diseases can often be caught and passed on to other people. An **illness** can be either a medical problem or a period of ill health.

---

disembark /ˌdɪsɪmˈbɑːk/ verb [I] (*formal*) to get off a ship or an aircraft **OPP** **embark** ▸ disembarkation /ˌdɪsˌembɑːˈkeɪʃn/ noun [U]

disembodied /ˌdɪsɪmˈbɒdid/ adj. coming from a person or place that cannot be seen or identified: *a disembodied voice*

disenchanted /ˌdɪsɪnˈtʃɑːntɪd/ adj. ~ **(with sb/sth)** having lost your good opinion of sb/sth: *Fans are already becoming disenchanted with the new team manager.* ▸ disenchantment /-ˈtʃɑːntmənt/ noun [U]

disenfranchise /ˌdɪsɪnˈfræntʃaɪz/ verb [T, often passive] (**POLITICS**) to take away sb's rights, especially their right to vote **OPP** **enfranchise**

disentangle /ˌdɪsɪnˈtæŋgl/ verb [T] ~ **(A from B)** to free sb/sth that had become connected to sb/sth else in a confused and complicated way: *My scarf got caught up in some bushes and I couldn't disentangle it.* ◇ (*figurative*) *Listening to the woman's story, I found it hard to disentangle the truth from the lies.*

disfigure /dɪsˈfɪɡə(r)/ verb [T] to damage the appearance of sb/sth: *His face was permanently disfigured by the fire.*

disgrace¹ /dɪsˈɡreɪs/ noun **1** [U] the state of not being respected by other people, usually because you have behaved badly: *She left the company in disgrace after admitting stealing from colleagues.* **2** [sing.] **a ~ (to sb/ sth)** a person or thing that gives a very bad impression and makes you feel sorry and embarrassed: *The streets are covered in litter. It's a disgrace!* ◇ *Politicians who tell lies are a disgrace to their profession.*

disgrace² /dɪsˈɡreɪs/ verb [T] ~ **yourself** to behave badly in a way that makes you or other people feel sorry and embarrassed: *My brother disgraced himself by starting a fight at the wedding.*

disgraceful /dɪsˈɡreɪsfl/ adj. very bad, making other people feel sorry and embarrassed: *The behaviour of the team's fans was absolutely disgraceful.* ▸ disgracefully /-fəli/ adv.

disgruntled /dɪsˈɡrʌntld/ adj. disappointed and annoyed

disguise¹ /dɪsˈɡaɪz/ verb [T] ~ **sb/sth (as sb/sth)** to change the appearance, sound, etc. of sb/sth so that people cannot recognize them or it: *They disguised themselves as fishermen and escaped in a boat.* ◇ (*figurative*) *His smile disguised his anger.*

disguise² /dɪsˈɡaɪz/ noun [C, U] something that you wear or use to change your appearance so that nobody recognizes you: *The robbers were wearing heavy disguises so that they could not be identified.* ◇ *She is so famous that she has to go shopping in disguise.*

disgust¹ /dɪsˈɡʌst/ noun [U] ~ **(at sth)** a strong feeling of not liking or approving of sth/sb that you feel is unacceptable, or sth/sb that has smells, etc. unpleasant: *She felt disgust at the state of the filthy room.* ◇ *The film was so bad that we walked out in disgust.* ◇ *Much to my disgust, I found a hair in my soup.*

disgust² /dɪsˈɡʌst/ verb [T] to make sb feel shocked and almost sick: *Cruelty towards animals absolutely disgusts me.* ◇ *The way he eats with his mouth open completely disgusts me.*

disgusted /dɪsˈɡʌstɪd/ adj. ~ **(at/with sb/sth)** not liking or approving of sb/sth at all: *We were disgusted at the standard of service we received.*

disgusting /dɪsˈɡʌstɪŋ/ adj. very unpleasant; making you feel shocked, upset or angry: *What a disgusting smell!* **SYN** **revolting**

disgustingly /dɪsˈɡʌstɪŋli/ *adv.* **1** (often used to show you are JEALOUS of sb/sth) extremely: *Our neighbours are disgustingly rich.* **2** in a way that you do not like or approve of or that makes you feel sick: *The kitchen was disgustingly dirty.*

dish¹ ⟨ A1 ⟩ /dɪʃ/ *noun* **1** [C] a round container for food that is deeper than a plate **2** [C] a type of food prepared in a particular way: *The main dish was chicken curry. It was served with a selection of side dishes.* ◇ *a vegetarian/fish/meat/pasta dish* **3** the dishes [pl.] all the plates, cups, etc. that you use during a meal: *I'll cook and you can wash the dishes.* **4** [C] = SATELLITE DISH

dish² /dɪʃ/ *verb*
PHR V **dish sth out** (*informal*) to give away a lot of sth: *to dish out advice* **dish (sth) up** (*informal*) to serve food

dishcloth /ˈdɪʃklɒθ/ *noun* [C] a cloth for washing dishes

dishearten /dɪsˈhɑːtn/ *verb* [T] to make sb lose hope or confidence **SYN** **discourage** **OPP** **hearten**

disheartened /dɪsˈhɑːtnd/ *adj.* sad or disappointed; having lost confidence or hope

disheartening /dɪsˈhɑːtnɪŋ/ *adj.* making you lose hope and confidence **OPP** **heartening**

dishevelled (*especially BrE*) (*AmE usually* **disheveled**) /dɪˈʃevld/ *adj.* (used about a person's appearance) very untidy **SYN** **unkempt**

dishonest ⟨ B2 ⟩ /dɪsˈɒnɪst/ *adj.* that you cannot trust; likely to lie, steal or cheat: *Beware of dishonest traders in tourist areas.* **OPP** **honest** ▸ **dishonestly** *adv.* ▸ **dishonesty** *noun* [U]

dishonour¹ (*BrE*) (*AmE* **dishonor**) /dɪsˈɒnə(r)/ *noun* [U] (*formal*) the state of no longer being respected, especially because you have done sth bad: *Her cheating in exams has brought dishonour on the school.* **OPP** **honour¹** ▸ **dishonourable** (*BrE*) (*AmE* **dishonorable**) *adj.*

dishonour² (*BrE*) (*AmE* **dishonor**) /dɪsˈɒnə(r)/ *verb* [T] (*formal*) to make sb/sth lose the respect of other people

dishwasher /ˈdɪʃwɒʃə(r)/ *noun* [C] a machine that washes plates, cups, knives, forks, etc.

disillusion /ˌdɪsɪˈluːʒn/ *verb* [T] to destroy sb's belief in or good opinion of sb/sth ▸ **disillusion** (*also* **disillusionment**) *noun* [U]: *I feel increasing disillusion with the government.*

disillusioned /ˌdɪsɪˈluːʒnd/ *adj.* disappointed because sb/sth is not as good as you first thought: *She's disillusioned with nursing.*

disinfect /ˌdɪsɪnˈfekt/ *verb* [T] to clean sth with a substance that destroys bacteria: *to disinfect a wound* ▸ **disinfection** /-ˈfekʃn/ *noun* [U]

disinfectant /ˌdɪsɪnˈfektənt/ *noun* [C, U] a substance that destroys bacteria and is used for cleaning

disinherit /ˌdɪsɪnˈherɪt/ *verb* [T] (*LAW*) to prevent sb, especially your son or daughter, from receiving your money or property after your death ◇ look at **inherit** (1)

disintegrate /dɪsˈɪntɪɡreɪt/ *verb* [I] to break into many small pieces or parts: *The plane disintegrated as it fell into the sea.* ▸ **disintegration** /dɪsˌɪntɪˈɡreɪʃn/ *noun* [U]: *the disintegration of the empire*

disinterest /dɪsˈɪntrəst, -trest/ *noun* [U] **1** lack of interest **2** the fact of not being involved in sth and therefore able to be fair

disinterested /dɪsˈɪntrəstɪd, -tres-/ *adj.* fair, not influenced by personal feelings: *disinterested advice* ◇ look at **uninterested**

disjointed /dɪsˈdʒɔɪntɪd/ *adj.* (used especially about ideas, writing or speech) not clearly connected and therefore difficult to follow ▸ **disjointedly** *adv.*

disk ⟨ B2 ⟩ /dɪsk/ *noun* [C] **1** (*AmE*) = DISC (2) **2** (COMPUTING) a device for storing information on a computer, in the shape of a round flat plate that SPINS (= turns) ◇ look at **floppy disk**, **hard disk**

disk drive *noun* [C] (COMPUTING) a piece of electrical equipment that passes information to or from a computer disk

dislike¹ ⟨ B1 ⟩ /dɪsˈlaɪk/ *verb* [T] ~ (doing) sth to not like sb/sth: *I really dislike flying.* ◇ *What is it that you dislike about living here?* **OPP** **like²**

dislike² ⟨ B1 ⟩ /dɪsˈlaɪk/ *noun* [C, U, sing.] ~ (of/for sb/sth) the feeling of not liking sb/sth; a thing that you do not like: *She couldn't hide her dislike for him.* ◇ *He seems to have a strong dislike of hard work.* ◇ *I've told you all your likes and dislikes.*
IDM **take a dislike to sb/sth** to start disliking sb/sth: *He took an instant dislike to his boss.*

dislocate /ˈdɪsləkeɪt/ *verb* [T] (HEALTH) to put sth (usually a bone) out of its correct position: *He dislocated his shoulder during the game.* ▸ **dislocation** /ˌdɪsləˈkeɪʃn/ *noun* [C, U]

dislodge /dɪsˈlɒdʒ/ *verb* [T] ~ sth (from sth) to make sb/sth move from its correct fixed position: *The strong wind dislodged several tiles from the roof.*

disloyal /dɪsˈlɔɪəl/ *adj.* ~ (to sb/sth) not supporting your friends, family, country etc.; doing sth that will harm them: *It was disloyal to your friends to repeat their conversation to Peter.* **OPP** **loyal** ▸ **disloyalty** /-ti/ *noun* [U]

dismal /ˈdɪzməl/ *adj.* **1** causing sb to be sad; showing that you are sad: *dismal surroundings* **SYN** **gloomy**, **miserable** **2** (*informal*) of low quality; poor: *a dismal standard of work*

dismantle /dɪsˈmæntl/ *verb* [T] to take sth to pieces; to separate sth into the parts it is made from: *The photographer dismantled his equipment and packed it away.*

dismay /dɪsˈmeɪ/ *noun* [U] a worried, sad feeling after you have received an unpleasant surprise: *I realized to my dismay that I was going to miss the plane.* ▸ **dismay** *verb* [T, usually passive]: *I was dismayed to hear that my old school had been knocked down.*

dismember /dɪsˈmembə(r)/ *verb* [T] to cut a dead body into pieces

dismiss ⟨ B2 ⟩ /dɪsˈmɪs/ *verb* [T] **1** ~ sb/sth (as sth) to decide that sb/sth is not important and not worth thinking or talking about: *He dismissed the idea as nonsense.* **2** ~ sb (from sth) to officially remove sb from their job: *He was dismissed for refusing to obey orders.* **SYN** **fire²**, **sack²** **3** to send sb away: *The lesson ended and the teacher dismissed the class.* **4** (LAW) to say that a trial or court case should not continue, usually because there is not enough evidence: *The case was dismissed.*

dismissal ⟨+ C1 ⟩ /dɪsˈmɪsl/ *noun* **1** [U, C] the act of dismissing sb from their job; an example of this: *He still hopes to win his claim against unfair dismissal.* **2** [U] the failure to consider sth as important: *She was hurt at their dismissal of her offer of help.* **3** [C] (LAW) the act of not allowing a trial or legal case to continue, usually because there is not enough evidence: *the dismissal of the appeal*

dismissive /dɪsˈmɪsɪv/ *adj.* ~ (of sb/sth) saying or showing that you think that sb/sth is not worth considering seriously: *The boss was dismissive of all the efforts I had made.* ▸ **dismissively** *adv.*

dismount /dɪsˈmaʊnt/ *verb* [I] to get off sth that you ride (a horse, a bicycle, etc.) **OPP** **mount**[1]

disobedient /ˌdɪsəˈbiːdiənt/ *adj.* refusing or failing to obey **OPP** **obedient** ▸ **disobedience** /-əns/ *noun* [U]

disobey /ˌdɪsəˈbeɪ/ *verb* [I, T] to refuse to do what you are told to do: *He was punished for disobeying orders.* **OPP** **obey**

disorder ᴦ+ 🄱🄲 /dɪsˈɔːdə(r)/ *noun* **1** [U] (*formal*) an untidy, confused or badly organized state: *His financial affairs are in complete disorder.* **OPP** **order**[1] **2** [U] (*formal*) violent behaviour by a large number of people: *Disorder broke out on the streets of the capital.* **3** [C, U] (**PSYCHOLOGY**) an illness in which the mind or part of the body is not working correctly: *Parties can be particularly stressful for people with anxiety disorders.* ◇ *a kind of **mental disorder*** ⊃ note at **disease**

disordered /dɪsˈɔːdəd/ *adj.* untidy, confused or badly organized

disorderly /dɪsˈɔːdəli/ *adj.* **1** (used about people or behaviour) out of control and violent; causing trouble in public: *They were arrested for being **drunk and disorderly**.* **OPP** **orderly**[1] **2** untidy **OPP** **orderly**[1]

disorganization (*BrE also* -isation) /dɪsˌɔːɡənaɪˈzeɪʃn/ *noun* [U] a lack of careful planning and order **OPP** **organization**

disorganized (*BrE also* -ised) /dɪsˈɔːɡənaɪzd/ *adj.* badly planned; not able to plan well **OPP** **organized**

disorientate /dɪsˈɔːriənteɪt/ (*BrE*) (*also* **disorient** /dɪsˈɔːrient/ *especially in AmE*) *verb* [T] to make sb become confused about where they are: *The road signs were very confusing and I soon became disorientated.* ▸ **disorientation** /dɪsˌɔːriənˈteɪʃn/ *noun* [U]

disown /dɪsˈəʊn/ *verb* [T] to say that you no longer want to be connected with or responsible for sb/sth: *When he was arrested, his family disowned him.*

disparage /dɪˈspærɪdʒ/ *verb* [T] (*formal*) to talk about sb/sth in a critical way; to say that sb/sth is of little value or importance **SYN** **belittle** ▸ **disparaging** *adj.*: *disparaging remarks*

disparate /ˈdɪspərət/ *adj.* (*formal*) **1** made up of parts or people that are very different from each other: *a disparate group of individuals* **2** (used about two or more things) so different from each other that they cannot be compared or cannot work together

disparity /dɪˈspærəti/ *noun* [U, C] (*pl.* -ies) (*formal*) a difference, especially one connected with unfair treatment

dispatch[1] (*BrE also* **despatch**) /dɪˈspætʃ/ *verb* [T] (*formal*) to send sb/sth somewhere: *Troops have been dispatched to the area.* ◇ *Your order will be dispatched within seven days.*

dispatch[2] (*BrE also* **despatch**) /dɪˈspætʃ/ *noun* **1** [U] (*formal*) the act of sending sb/sth somewhere **2** [C] (**POLITICS**) a message or report sent quickly from one military officer to another or between government officials **3** [C] (**ARTS AND MEDIA**) a report sent to a newspaper by a journalist who is working in a foreign country: *dispatches from the war zone*

dispel /dɪˈspel/ *verb* [T] (-ll-) to make sth, especially a feeling or a belief, disappear: *His reassuring words dispelled all her fears.*

dispensable /dɪˈspensəbl/ *adj.* not necessary: *I suppose I'm dispensable. Anybody could do my job.* **OPP** **indispensable**

dispensary /dɪˈspensəri/ *noun* [C] (*pl.* -ies) (**MEDICINE**) a place in a hospital, shop, etc. where medicines are prepared for patients

dispense /dɪˈspens/ *verb* [T] (*formal*) to give or provide people with sth: *a machine that dispenses hot and cold drinks*
PHR V **dispense with sb/sth** to get rid of sb/sth that is not necessary: *They decided to dispense with luxuries and live a simple life.*

dispenser /dɪˈspensə(r)/ *noun* [C] a machine or container from which you can get sth: *a cash dispenser at a bank* ◇ *a soap dispenser*

dispersal /dɪˈspɜːsl/ *noun* [U, C] (*formal*) the process of sending sb/sth in different directions; the process of spreading sth over a wide area: *police trained in crowd dispersal* ◇ *the dispersal of seeds*

disperse /dɪˈspɜːs/ *verb* [I, T] to separate and go in different directions; to make sb/sth do this: *When the meeting was over, the group dispersed.* ◇ *The police arrived and quickly dispersed the crowd.*

dispersion /dɪˈspɜːʃn/ *noun* [U] (**BIOLOGY**, **PHYSICS**) the process by which people or things are spread over a wide area: *population dispersion* ◇ *the dispersion of light*

dispirited /dɪˈspɪrɪtɪd/ *adj.* having lost confidence or hope

displace ᴦ+ 🄲🄳 /dɪsˈpleɪs/ *verb* [T, often passive] (*formal*) **1** to remove and take the place of sb/sth: *Gradually factory workers have been displaced by machines.* **2** to force sb/sth to move from the usual or correct place: *refugees displaced by the war*

disˌplaced ˈperson *noun* [C] (*pl.* displaced persons) (**POLITICS**) a person who has been forced to leave his/her country for political or religious reasons, or because there is a war, not enough food, etc. ⊃ look at **refugee**

displacement /dɪsˈpleɪsmənt/ *noun* **1** [U] (*formal*) the act of DISPLACING sb/sth; the process of being DISPLACED: *the largest displacement of civilian population since World War Two* **2** [C] (**PHYSICS**) the amount of a liquid moved out of place by sth floating or put in it, especially a ship floating in water: *a ship with a displacement of 10 000 tonnes*

display[1] ᴦ 🄱🄲 /dɪˈspleɪ/ *verb* [T] **1** to put sth in a place where people will see it or where it will attract attention: *Posters for the concert were displayed throughout the city.* **2** to show signs of sth (for example a feeling or a quality): *She displayed no interest in the discussion.* **3** (used about a computer, etc.) to show information: *Giant screens displayed images of cheering crowds.*

display[2] ᴦ 🄱🄲 /dɪˈspleɪ/ *noun* **1** [C] an arrangement of things in a public place for people to see: *a window display in a shop* **2** [C] a public event in which sth is shown in action: *a firework display* **3** [C] behaviour that shows a particular feeling or quality: *a sudden display of aggression* **4** [C, U] (**COMPUTING**) words, pictures, etc. that can be seen on a computer screen **IDM** **on display** in a place where people will see it and where it will attract attention: *Treasures from the sunken ship were put on display at the museum.* ⊃ note at **art**

displease /dɪsˈpliːz/ *verb* [T] (*formal*) to annoy sb or to make sb angry or upset **OPP** **please**[2] ▸ **displeased** *adj.*

displeasure /dɪsˈpleʒə(r)/ *noun* [U] ~ (at/with sb/sth) (*formal*) the feeling of being annoyed or not satisfied: *I wrote to express my displeasure at not having been informed sooner.*

disposable /dɪˈspəʊzəbl/ *adj.* **1** made to be thrown away after being used once or for a short time: *a disposable razor* **2** (**FINANCE**) available for use: *disposable assets/*

capital/resources ◇ a person's **disposable income**
(= money they are free to spend after paying taxes,
etc.)

disposal ଢ+ **C1** /dɪˈspəʊzl/ *noun* [U] the act of getting rid
of sth or throwing sth away: *the disposal of dangerous
chemical waste* ◇ *a kitchen* **waste disposal** *unit*
◇ *bomb disposal*
IDM **at sb's disposal** available for sb to use at any
time

dispose ଢ+ **C1** /dɪˈspəʊz/ *verb*
PHRV **dispose of sb/sth** to throw away or sell sth; to
get rid of sth

disposed /dɪˈspəʊzd/ *adj.* [not before noun] **1** ~ **(to do
sth)** (*formal*) willing or prepared to do sth: *I'm not
disposed to argue.* **2** (after an adverb) ~ **to/towards sb/
sth** having a good/bad opinion of sb/sth: *The company
is* **well disposed to** (= has a positive attitude towards)
the idea of partnership.

disposition /ˌdɪspəˈzɪʃn/ *noun* (*formal*) **1** [C, usually sing.]
the natural qualities of a person's character: *to have a
cheerful disposition* ◇ *people of a nervous disposition*
SYN **temperament 2** [C, usually sing.] ~ **to/towards sth;
~ to do sth** a usual way of behaving: *to have/show a
disposition towards acts of violence* **3** [C, U] (LAW) a
formal act of giving property or money to sb

disproportion /ˌdɪsprəˈpɔːʃn/ *noun* [U] ~ **(between A and
B)** (*formal*) the state of two things not being at an
equally high or low level; an example of this: *the
disproportion between the extra responsibilities and
the small salary increase*

disproportionate /ˌdɪsprəˈpɔːʃənət/ *adj.* ~ **(to sth)** too
large or too small when compared to sth else
▶ **disproportionately** *adv.*

disprove /ˌdɪsˈpruːv/ *verb* [T] to show that sth is not true
OPP **prove**

dispute¹ ଢ+ **C1** /ˈdɪspjuːt, dɪˈspjuːt/ *noun* [C, U]
~ **(between A and B) (over/about sth)** a situation in
which two people, groups or countries disagree and
argue: *a pay dispute* ◇ *There was some dispute
between John and his boss about whose fault it was.*
IDM **in dispute** in a situation of arguing or being
argued about: *He is in dispute with the tax office
about how much he should pay.*

dispute² ଢ+ **C1** /dɪˈspjuːt/ *verb* [T] to argue about sth and
to question if it is true or right: *The player disputed the
referee's decision.*

disqualify /dɪsˈkwɒlɪfaɪ/ *verb* [T] (disqualifying;
disqualifies; *pt, pp* disqualified) ~ **sb (from sth/doing
sth); ~ sb (for sth)** to officially prevent sb from doing
sth or taking part in sth, usually because they have
broken a rule or law: *He was disqualified from driving
for two years.* ◇ *The team were disqualified for
cheating.* ▶ **disqualification** /dɪsˌkwɒlɪfɪˈkeɪʃn/ *noun*
[C, U]

disregard /ˌdɪsrɪˈɡɑːd/ *verb* [T] (*formal*) to take no notice
of sb/sth; to treat sth as unimportant: *These are the
latest instructions. Please disregard any you received
before.* ▶ **disregard** *noun* [U, sing.] ~ **(for sb/sth):** *He
rushed into the burning building with complete
disregard for his own safety.*

disrepair /ˌdɪsrɪˈpeə(r)/ *noun* [U] the state of being in
bad condition where repairs have not been made:
Over the years the building **fell into disrepair.**

disreputable /dɪsˈrepjətəbl/ *adj.* not to be trusted; well
known for being bad or dishonest: *disreputable
business methods* **OPP** **reputable, respectable**

disrepute /ˌdɪsrɪˈpjuːt/ *noun* [U] (*formal*) the situation
when people no longer respect sb/sth: *The players'
bad behaviour* **brings the game into disrepute.**

disrespect /ˌdɪsrɪˈspekt/ *noun* [U] ~ **(for/to sb/sth)** a lack
of respect for sb/sth that is shown in what you do or
say: *their disrespect for the law* ◇ *I meant no
disrespect to you.* **OPP** **respect¹** ▶ **disrespectful** /-fl/
adj. **OPP** **respectful** ▶ **disrespectfully** /-fəli/ *adv.*

disrupt ଢ+ **C1** /dɪsˈrʌpt/ *verb* [T] to stop sth happening as
or when it should: *The strike severely disrupted flights
to Spain.* ▶ **disruption** ଢ+ **C1** /-ˈrʌpʃn/ *noun* [C, U]

disruptive /dɪsˈrʌptɪv/ *adj.* **1** causing problems, noise,
etc. so that sth cannot continue normally: *She had a
disruptive influence on the rest of the class.* **2** new and
original, in a way that causes major changes to how
sth is done: *disruptive technologies*

dissatisfaction /ˌdɪsˌsætɪsˈfækʃn/ *noun* [U] ~ **(with/at sb/
sth)** the feeling of not being satisfied or pleased: *There
is some dissatisfaction among teachers with the plans
for the new exam.* **OPP** **satisfaction**

dissatisfied /dɪsˈsætɪsfaɪd, dɪˈs-/ *adj.* ~ **(with sb/sth)** not
satisfied or pleased: *complaints from customers
dissatisfied with the service* **OPP** **satisfied**

dissect /dɪˈsekt, daɪ-/ *verb* [T] (BIOLOGY) to cut up a dead
body, a plant, etc. in order to study it ▶ **dissection**
/-ˈsekʃn/ *noun* [C, U]

disseminate /dɪˈsemɪneɪt/ *verb* [T] (*formal*) to spread
information, knowledge, etc. so that it reaches many
people: *Their findings have been* **widely disseminated.**
▶ **dissemination** /dɪˌsemɪˈneɪʃn/ *noun* [U]

dissent¹ /dɪˈsent/ *noun* [U] (*formal*) the fact of having or
expressing opinions that are different from those
that are officially accepted: *There is some dissent
within the Labour Party on these policies.*

dissent² /dɪˈsent/ *verb* [I] ~ **(from sth)** (*formal*) to have
opinions that are different to those that are officially
held ▶ **dissenting** *adj.*

dissertation /ˌdɪsəˈteɪʃn/ *noun* [C] (EDUCATION) a long
piece of writing on sth that you have studied,
especially as part of a university degree ⊃ look at
thesis (1)

disservice /dɪsˈsɜːvɪs, dɪˈs-/ *noun*
IDM **do sb/sth a disservice | do a disservice to sb/
sth** to do sth that harms sb and the opinion other
people have of them

dissident /ˈdɪsɪdənt/ *noun* [C] (POLITICS) a person who
strongly disagrees with and criticizes their
government, especially in a country where it is
dangerous to do this ▶ **dissidence** /-dəns/ *noun* [U]

dissimilar /dɪˈsɪmɪlə(r)/ *adj.* ~ **(from/to sb/sth)** not the
same; different: *Your situation is* **not dissimilar** (= is
similar) *to mine.* **OPP** **similar**

dissociate /dɪˈsəʊsieɪt, -ˈsəʊʃi-/ (*also* disassociate) *verb* [T]
~ **sb/sth/yourself (from sth)** to show that you are not
connected with or do not support sb/sth; to show that
two things are not connected with each other: *He was
determined to dissociate his firm from any
involvement with the disgraced politician.*
OPP **associate¹**

dissolution /ˌdɪsəˈluːʃn/ *noun* [U] (*formal*) (LAW) the act of
officially ending a marriage, a business agreement or
a parliament

dissolve ଢ+ **C1** /dɪˈzɒlv/ *verb* **1** [I, T] (SCIENCE) (used
about a solid) to become liquid; to make a solid
become liquid: *Sugar dissolves in water.* ◇ *Dissolve
two tablets in cold water.* ⊃ picture at **erosion 2** [T]
(LAW) to officially end a marriage, business
agreement or parliament: *Their marriage was
dissolved in 2016.* ⊃ note at **organization**

dissuade /dɪˈsweɪd/ *verb* [T] ~ **sb (from doing sth)** to
persuade sb not to do sth: *I tried to dissuade her from
spending the money, but she insisted.* **OPP** **persuade**

distal /ˈdɪstl/ *adj.* (**ANATOMY**) located away from the centre of the body or at the far end of sth: *the distal end of the tibia* ⊃ look at **proximal**

distance¹ 🔊 **A2** 🔵 /ˈdɪstəns/ *noun* **1** [C, U] the amount of space between two places or things: *It's only a short distance from my home to work.* ◇ *The map tells you the distances between the major cities.* ◇ *We can walk home from here — it's no distance* (= it isn't far). ◇ *The house is within walking distance of the shops.* ⊃ picture at **speed¹** **2** [sing.] a point that is a long way from sb/sth: *At this distance I can't read the number on the bus.* ◇ *From a distance the village looks quite attractive.* **IDM** **in the distance** far away: *I could just see Paul in the distance.* **keep your distance** to stay away from sb/sth **within striking distance** → **STRIKE²**

distance² /ˈdɪstəns/ *verb* [T] **~ yourself from sb/sth** to become less involved or connected with sb/sth: *She was keen to distance herself from the views of her colleagues.*

distance ˈlearning (*also* ˌdistance eduˈcation) *noun* [U] (**EDUCATION**) a system of education in which people study at home and send or email work to their teachers

distant 🔊 **B2** /ˈdɪstənt/ *adj.* **1** a long way away in space or time: *travel to distant parts of the world* ◇ *in the not-too-distant future* (= quite soon) **2** (used about a relative) not closely related: *a distant cousin* **3** not very friendly: *He has a rather distant manner and it's hard to get to know him well.* **4** seeming to be thinking about sth else: *She had a distant look in her eyes and clearly wasn't listening to me.*

distaste /dɪsˈteɪst/ *noun* [U, sing.] not liking sth; the feeling that sb/sth is unpleasant or offends you: *She looked around the dirty kitchen with distaste.*

distasteful /dɪsˈteɪstfl/ *adj.* (*formal*) unpleasant or causing offence: *a distasteful remark*

distemper /dɪˈstempə(r)/ *noun* [U] (**HEALTH**) a disease of animals, especially dogs, that causes a high temperature and COUGHING (= sending air out of the throat and mouth with a loud noise)

distend /dɪˈstend/ *verb* [I, T] (*formal*) to SWELL (= become larger or rounder than before) or make sth SWELL because of pressure from inside: *starving children with distended bellies* ▶ **distension** /-ˈstenʃn/ *noun* [U]

distillation

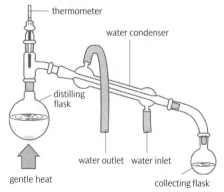

- thermometer
- water condenser
- distilling flask
- water outlet
- water inlet
- gentle heat
- collecting flask

distil (*BrE*) (*AmE* **distill**) /dɪˈstɪl/ *verb* [T] (-ll-) (**CHEMISTRY**) to make a liquid pure by heating it until it becomes a gas and then collecting the liquid that forms when the gas cools ▶ **distillation** /ˌdɪstɪˈleɪʃn/ *noun* [C, U]

distillery /dɪˈstɪləri/ *noun* [C] (*pl.* -**ies**) a factory where strong alcoholic drink is made by the process of DISTILLING

distinct 🔊 **B2** 🔵 /dɪˈstɪŋkt/ *adj.* **1** clear; easily seen, heard or understood: *There has been a distinct improvement in your work recently.* ◇ *I had the distinct impression that she was lying.* **OPP** **indistinct** **2 ~ (from sth)** clearly different: *Her books fall into two distinct groups: the novels and the travel stories.* ◇ *This region, as distinct from other parts of the country, relies heavily on tourism.*

distinction 🔊 **C1** 🔵 /dɪˈstɪŋkʃn/ *noun* [C, U] **1 ~ (between A and B)** a clear or important difference between things or people: *We must draw a distinction between classical and popular music here.* ◇ *The new law makes no distinction between married and unmarried couples.* **2** [C, U] the quality of being excellent or important: *a violinist of distinction* **3** [C, U] (**EDUCATION**) the highest mark that is given to students in some exams for excellent work: *James got a distinction in maths.*

distinctive 🔊 **C1** 🔊 /dɪˈstɪŋktɪv/ *adj.* clearly different from others and therefore easy to recognize: *The soldiers were wearing their distinctive red berets.* ▶ **distinctively** *adv.*

distinctly /dɪˈstɪŋktli/ *adv.* **1** clearly: *I distinctly heard her say that she would be here on time.* **2** very; particularly: *His behaviour has been distinctly odd recently.*

distinguish 🔊 **B2** 🔵 /dɪˈstɪŋgwɪʃ/ *verb* **1** [I, T] **~ (between A and B); ~ (A from B)** to recognize the difference between two things or people: *He doesn't seem able to distinguish between what's important and what isn't.* ◇ *People who are colour-blind often can't distinguish red from green.* **SYN** **differentiate** **2** [T] **~ A (from B)** to make sb/sth different from others: *The power of speech distinguishes humans from animals.* ◇ *distinguishing features* (= things by which sb/sth can be recognized) **3** [T] to see, hear or recognize with effort: *I listened carefully but they were too far away for me to distinguish what they were saying.* **4** [T] **~ yourself** to do sth that causes you to be noticed and admired: *She distinguished herself in the exams.*

distinguishable /dɪˈstɪŋgwɪʃəbl/ *adj.* **1** possible to recognize as different from sb/sth else: *The male bird is distinguishable from the female by the colour of its beak.* **OPP** **indistinguishable** **2** possible to see, hear or recognize with effort: *The letter is so old that the signature is barely distinguishable.*

distinguished /dɪˈstɪŋgwɪʃt/ *adj.* important, successful and respected by other people

distort 🔊 **C1** /dɪˈstɔːt/ *verb* [T] **1** to change the shape or sound of sth so that it seems strange or is not clear: *Her face was distorted with grief.* **2** to change facts, ideas, etc. so that they are no longer correct or true: *Foreigners are often given a distorted view of this country.* ▶ **distortion** /-ˈstɔːʃn/ *noun* [C, U]

distract 🔊 **B2** /dɪˈstrækt/ *verb* [T] **~ sb/sth (from sth)** to take sb's attention away from sth: *Could you stop talking please? You're distracting me from my work.* ◇ *It was an attempt to distract attention from the truth.*

distracted /dɪˈstræktɪd/ *adj.* unable to give your full attention to sth because you are worried or thinking about sth else

distraction /dɪˈstrækʃn/ *noun* [C, U] something that takes your attention away from what you were doing or thinking about

IDM **to distraction** with the result that you become upset, excited, or angry and unable to think clearly: *The noise of the traffic outside at night is **driving me to distraction**.*

distraught /dɪˈstrɔːt/ *adj.* extremely upset and anxious so that you cannot think clearly

distress¹ ʕ+ **C1** /dɪˈstres/ *noun* [U] **1** the state of being very upset or of suffering great pain or difficulty: *Their distress on hearing the bad news was obvious.* ◊ *She was **in** such **distress** that I didn't want to leave her on her own.* **2** the state of being in great danger and needing immediate help: *The ship's captain radioed that it was **in distress**.*

distress² ʕ+ **C1** /dɪˈstres/ *verb* [T] to make sb very upset or unhappy: *Try not to say anything to distress the patient further.* ▶ distressed *adj.*: *She was too distressed to talk.* ▶ distressing *adj.*: *a distressing experience/illness*

distribute ʕ **B2** **W** /dɪˈstrɪbjuːt, ˈdɪstrɪbjuːt/ *verb* [T] **1** ~ sth (to/among sb/sth) to give things to a number of people: *Tickets will be distributed to all club members.* ◊ *They distributed emergency food supplies to the areas that were most in need.* **2** (BUSINESS) to transport and supply goods to shops, companies, etc: *Which company distributes this product in your country?* **3** to spread sth equally over an area: *Make sure that the weight is **evenly distributed**.*

distribution ʕ **B2** **W** /ˌdɪstrɪˈbjuːʃn/ *noun* **1** [U, C] the way sth is shared out; the pattern in which sth is found: *a map to show the distribution of rainfall in Africa* **2** [U, C] the act of giving sth to a number of people: *the distribution of food parcels to the refugees* **3** [U] the system of transporting and delivering goods: *worldwide distribution systems*

distributor /dɪˈstrɪbjətə(r)/ *noun* [C] (BUSINESS) a person or company that transports and supplies goods to a number of shops and companies

district ʕ **B2** /ˈdɪstrɪkt/ *noun* [C] **1** (GEOGRAPHY) a part of a town or country that is special for a particular reason or is of a particular type: *rural districts* ◊ *the financial district of the city* **2** an official division of a town or country: *the district council* ◊ *postal districts*

district at'torney *noun* [C] (*abbr.* DA) (LAW) (in the US) a lawyer who is responsible for bringing criminal charges against sb in a particular area or state

distrust /dɪsˈtrʌst/ *noun* [U, sing.] ~ (of sb/sth) the feeling that you cannot believe sb/sth; a lack of trust ▶ distrust *verb* [T]: *She distrusts him because he lied to her once before.* ⊃ look at **mistrust** ▶ distrustful /-fl/ *adj.*

disturb ʕ+ **B2** /dɪˈstɜːb/ *verb* [T] **1** to interrupt sb while they are doing sth or sleeping: *I'm sorry to disturb you but there's a phone call for you.* ◊ *Their sleep was disturbed by a loud crash.* **2** to cause sb to worry: *It disturbed her to think that he might be unhappy.* **3** to move sth or change its position: *I noticed a number of things had been disturbed and realized that there had been a burglary.*

disturbance /dɪˈstɜːbəns/ *noun* [C, U] something that makes you stop what you are doing, or that upsets the normal condition of sth: *They were arrested for causing a disturbance (= fighting) in the town centre.* ◊ *emotional disturbance*

disturbed /dɪˈstɜːbd/ *adj.* (HEALTH) **1** having mental or emotional problems: *a school for emotionally disturbed young people* **2** very anxious and unhappy about sth: *I was deeply disturbed by the news of his accident.*

disturbing ʕ+ **C1** /dɪˈstɜːbɪŋ/ *adj.* making you worried or upset

disuse /dɪsˈjuːs/ *noun* [U] the state of not being used any more: *The farm buildings had been allowed to **fall into disuse**.*

disused /ˌdɪsˈjuːzd/ *adj.* not used any more: *a disused railway line*

ditch¹ /dɪtʃ/ *noun* [C] a long narrow hole that has been dug into the ground, especially along the side of a road or field for water to flow along

ditch² /dɪtʃ/ *verb* [T] (*informal*) to get rid of or leave sb/ sth: *She ditched her old friends when she became famous.*

dither /ˈdɪðə(r)/ *verb* [I] to be unable to decide sth: *Stop dithering and make up your mind!* **SYN** hesitate

ditto /ˈdɪtəʊ/ *noun* [C] (*pl.* -os) used, especially in a list, below a particular word or phrase, to show that it is repeated and to avoid having to write it again ▶ ditto *adv.*: *'I'm starving.' 'Ditto (= me too).'*

diurnal /daɪˈɜːnl/ *adj.* **1** (BIOLOGY) (used about animals) active during the day **OPP** nocturnal **2** (ASTRONOMY) taking one day: *the diurnal rotation of the earth*

diva /ˈdiːvə/ *noun* [C] **1** a famous female singer, especially an OPERA singer **2** a person who is difficult to please and demands a lot of attention

dive¹ ʕ+ **B2** /daɪv/ *verb* [I] (*pt* dived, *AmE also* dove /dəʊv/; *pp* dived) **1** ~ (off/from sth) (into sth); ~ in to jump into water with your arms and head first: *In Acapulco, men dive off the cliffs into the sea.* ◊ *A passer-by dived in and saved the drowning man.* **2** to swim under the surface of the sea, a lake, etc., usually wearing breathing equipment: *people diving for pearls* **3** to move quickly and suddenly downwards: *He dived under the table and hid there.* ◊ *The goalkeeper dived to save the penalty.* **PHR V** dive into sth (*informal*) to put your hand quickly into a pocket or bag in order to find or get sth

dive² ʕ+ **B2** /daɪv/ *noun* [C] **1** the act of DIVING into water **2** a quick and sudden downwards movement

diver /ˈdaɪvə(r)/ *noun* [C] **1** a person who swims under the surface of water using special equipment **2** a person who jumps into water with their arms and head first

diverge /daɪˈvɜːdʒ/ *verb* ~ (from sth) **1** [I, T] (used about roads, lines, etc.) to separate and go in different directions; to make sth separate and go in different directions: *The paths suddenly diverged and I didn't know which one to take.* **OPP** converge ⊃ picture at **short-sighted** **2** [I] to be or become different: *When I reached my teens, my interests began to diverge from those of my friends.* ▶ divergent /-ˈvɜːdʒənt/ *adj.* ⊃ picture at **plate tectonics**

diverse ʕ+ **B2** **W** /daɪˈvɜːs/ *adj.* very different from each other: *people from diverse social backgrounds* ◊ *My interests are very diverse.* ⊃ noun **diversity**

diversify /daɪˈvɜːsɪfaɪ/ *verb* [I, T] (diversifying; diversifies; *pt, pp* diversified) ~ (sth) (into sth) to increase or develop the number or types of sth: *To remain successful in the future, the company will have to diversify.* ◊ *Latin diversified into several different languages.* ▶ diversification /daɪˌvɜːsɪfɪˈkeɪʃn/ *noun* [C, U]

diversion /daɪˈvɜːʃn/ *noun* **1** [C, U] the act of changing the direction or purpose of sth, especially in order to solve or avoid a problem: *the diversion of a river to prevent flooding* ◊ *the diversion of government funds to areas of greatest need* **2** [C] (*BrE*) (*AmE* detour) a different route that traffic can take when a road is closed: *For London, follow the diversion.* **3** [C] something that takes your attention away from sth:

Some prisoners created a diversion while others escaped.

diversity ⓘ+ B2 Ⓦ /daɪˈvɜːsəti/ *noun* [U, C] (**SOCIAL STUDIES**) the wide variety of sth: *cultural and ethnic diversity* ◇ *There is a great diversity of opinion on this question.* ◇ *to promote* **diversity and inclusion** *in the workplace* (= offering equal opportunities to people from minority groups) ⊃ adjective **diverse**

divert ⓘ+ C1 /daɪˈvɜːt/ *verb* [T, often passive] ~ **sb/sth (from sth) (to sth)**; ~ **sth (away from sth)** to change the direction or purpose of sb/sth, especially to avoid a problem: *During the road repairs, all traffic is being diverted.* ◇ *Government money was diverted from defence to education.* ◇ *Politicians often criticize each other to divert attention away from their own mistakes.*

divide¹ ⓘ B1 Ⓞ /dɪˈvaɪd/ *verb*

	WORD FAMILY
	divide verb, noun
	division noun
	divisive adj.

• SEPARATE INTO PARTS **1** [I, T] ~ **(sth) (up) (into sth)** to separate or make sth separate into different parts: *The egg divides into two cells.* ◇ *The house was divided up into flats.* **2** [T] ~ **sth (out/up) (between/among sb)** to separate sth into parts and give a part to each of a number of people: *The robbers divided the money out between themselves.* ◇ *When he died, his property was divided up among his children.* **3** [T] ~ **sth (between A and B)** to use different parts or amounts of sth for different purposes: *They divide their time between their two homes.* **4** [T] to separate two places or things: *The river divides the old part of the city from the new.*

• CAUSE DISAGREEMENT **5** [T] to cause people to disagree: *The question of immigration has divided the country.* **SYN split¹**

• IN MATHEMATICS **6** [T] ~ **sth (by sth)** to calculate how many times a number will go into another number: *10 divided by 5 is 2 (10÷5=2).* **OPP multiply**

divide² ⓘ B2 /dɪˈvaɪd/ *noun* [C] ~ **(between A and B)** a difference between two groups of people that separates them from each other: *a divide between the rich and poor*

di‚vided 'highway (*AmE*) = DUAL CARRIAGEWAY

dividend /ˈdɪvɪdend/ *noun* [C] (**ECONOMICS, FINANCE**) a part of a company's profits that is paid to the people who own shares in the company ⊃ picture at **income**

divine ⓘ+ C1 /dɪˈvaɪn/ *adj.* (**RELIGION**) connected with God or a god

diving /ˈdaɪvɪŋ/ *noun* [U] (**SPORT**) the activity or sport of jumping into water or swimming under the surface of the sea, a lake, etc: *to go diving* ◇ *the diving world championships*

'diving board *noun* [C] a board at the side of a swimming pool from which people can jump or DIVE into the water

divisible /dɪˈvɪzəbl/ *adj.* (**MATHEMATICS**) that can be divided: *12 is divisible by 3.*

division ⓘ B2 Ⓦ /dɪˈvɪʒn/ *noun*

• INTO SEPARATE PARTS **1** [U, sing.] ~ **(of sth) (into sth)**; ~ **(of sth) (between A and B)** the process or result of separating into different parts; the sharing of sth between different people, groups, places, etc: *The organism begins as a single cell and grows by cell division.* ◇ *an unfair division of the profits* ◇ *We need a greater division of responsibility between central and local government.*

• IN MATHEMATICS **2** [U] dividing one number by another: *the teaching of multiplication and division*

• DISAGREEMENT **3** [C] ~ **(in/within sth)**; ~ **(between A and B)** a situation in which there is a difference of opinion

between sb/sth: *deep divisions within the Labour Party*

• PART OF AN ORGANIZATION **4** [C] a part or section of an organization: *the company's sales division*

• BORDER **5** [C] ~ **(between A and B)** a line that separates sth; a border: *The river marks the division between Europe and Asia.*

divisive /dɪˈvaɪsɪv/ *adj.* (*formal*) likely to cause people to be split into groups that disagree with or oppose each other: *a divisive policy*

divisor /dɪˈvaɪzə(r)/ *noun* [C] (**MATHEMATICS**) a number by which another number is divided

divorce¹ ⓘ+ B2 /dɪˈvɔːs/ *noun* [C, U] (**LAW**) the legal end of a marriage: *Their marriage ended in divorce.* ◇ *to get a divorce*

divorce² ⓘ+ B2 /dɪˈvɔːs/ *verb* **1** [T, I] (**LAW**) to legally end your marriage: *My parents got divorced when I was three.* ◇ *She divorced him a year after their marriage.* **2** [T, often passive] ~ **sb/sth from sth** to separate sb/sth from sth: *Sometimes these modern novels seem completely divorced from everyday life.*

divorced ⓘ A2 /dɪˈvɔːst/ *adj.* **1** no longer married because your marriage has been legally ended: *Many divorced men remarry and have second families.* ◇ *My parents are divorced.* ◇ *Are they going to get divorced?* **2** ~ **from sth** (*formal*) appearing not to be affected by sth; separate from sth: *He seems completely divorced from reality.*

divorcee /dɪˌvɔːˈsiː/ *noun* [C] a person who is divorced, especially a woman

divulge /daɪˈvʌldʒ/ *verb* [T] (*formal*) to tell sth that is secret: *The phone companies refused to divulge details of their costs.*

Diwali /dɪˈwɑːli/ *noun* [sing.] (**RELIGION**) a Hindu festival that takes place in October or November, in which people decorate their homes with lights

DIY /ˌdiː aɪ ˈwaɪ/ *noun* [U] the activity of making, repairing or decorating things in the home yourself, instead of paying sb to do it (the abbreviation for 'do-it-yourself'): *a DIY expert*

dizzy /ˈdɪzi/ *adj.* (**dizzier; dizziest**) **1** feeling as if everything is turning round and that you might fall: *I feel/get dizzy in high places.* **2** very great; making you feel that a situation is changing very fast: *the dizzy pace of life in London* ◇ *The following year, the band's popularity reached* **dizzy heights**. ▶ **dizziness** *noun* [U]

DJ /ˈdiː dʒeɪ/ (*also* **disc jockey**) *noun* [C] (**MUSIC**) a person who plays and talks about recorded music on radio or TV or at a club or party (the abbreviation for 'disc jockey')

DM /ˌdiː ˈem/ *noun* [C] (*pl.* **DMs**) (*informal*) a private message that you send on SOCIAL MEDIA that will only be seen by the person you send it to (the abbreviation for 'direct message') ▶ **DM** *verb* [T] (**DMing; DMs;** *pt, pp* **DM'd**)

DNA /ˌdiː en ˈeɪ/ *noun* [U] (**BIOLOGY**) the chemical in the cells of an animal or a plant that controls the characteristics that animal or plant will have (the abbreviation for 'deoxyribonucleic acid'): *a DNA test* ◇ *Police produced a DNA profile of the wanted man.* ⊃ picture on **page 228**

DNA 'fingerprinting (*also* **genetic fingerprinting**) *noun* [U] the method of finding the particular pattern of GENES (= the units inside a cell that control particular qualities) in an individual person, particularly to identify sb or find out if sb has committed a crime

do¹ ⓘ A1 /də, du, *strong form* duː/ *auxiliary verb* (*negative* **do not**; *short form* **don't** /dəʊnt/; **does** /dʌz/; *negative*

structure of part of a DNA double helix

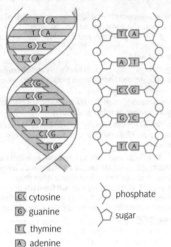

C cytosine

G guanine

T thymine

A adenine

phosphate

sugar

does not; *short form* **doesn't** /'dʌznt/; *pt* **did** /dɪd/; *negative* **did not**; *short form* **didn't** /'dɪdnt/; *pp* **done** /dʌn/) **1** used with other verbs to form questions and negative sentences, also in short answers and QUESTION TAGS (= short questions at the end of a sentence): *I don't like fish.* ◇ *Does she speak Italian?* ◇ *You don't like milk in your coffee, do you?* ◇ *She lives in New York, doesn't she?* **2** used for emphasizing the main verb: *I can't remember exactly when but I'm sure I did tell him about it.* **3** used to avoid repeating the main verb: *He earns a lot more than I do.* ◇ *She's feeling much better than she did last week.*

do² ⚡ **A1** /duː/ *verb* (*negative* **do not**; *short form* **don't** /dəʊnt/; **does** /dʌz/; *negative* **does not**; *short form* **doesn't** /'dʌznt/; *pt* **did** /dɪd/; *negative* **did not**; *short form* **didn't** /'dɪdnt/; *pp* **done** /dʌn/) **1** [T] to perform an action, activity or job: *What are you doing?* ◇ *What is the government doing about pollution* (= what action are they taking)? ◇ *What do you do* (= what is your job)? ◇ *Have you done your homework?* ◇ *I do 20 minutes exercise every morning.* ◇ *to do the cooking/cleaning/ironing* ◇ *to do judo/aerobics/windsurfing* ◇ *What did you do with the keys* (= where did you put them)? **2** [I, T] to make progress or develop; to improve sth: *'How's your daughter doing at school?' 'She's doing well.'* ◇ *Last year's win has done wonders for the team's confidence.* ◇ *This latest scandal will do nothing for* (= will harm) *this government's reputation.* **3** [T] to make or produce sth: *The photocopier does 60 copies a minute.* ◇ *to do a painting/drawing* **4** [T] to provide a service: *Do you do eye tests here?* **5** [T] to study sth: *to do French/a course/a degree* **6** [T] to find the answer to sth: *I can't do question 3.* **7** [T] to travel a certain distance or at a certain speed: *I normally do about 5 miles when I go running.* ◇ *This car does 120 miles an hour.* **8** [T] to have a particular effect: *A holiday will do you good.* ◇ *The storm did a lot of damage.* **9** [I, T] to be enough or suitable: *If you haven't got a pen, a pencil will do.*
IDM **be/have (got) to do with sb/sth** to be connected with sb/sth: *I'm not sure what Paola's job is, but I think it's something to do with animals.* ◇ *'How much do you earn?' 'It's nothing to do with you!'* **could do with sth** to want or need sth: *I could do*

with a holiday. **how do you do?** → HOW **make do with sth** → MAKE¹ **that does it** (*informal*) used to show that you will not accept sth any longer: *That does it! I'm leaving!* **that's done it** (*informal*) used to say that an accident, a mistake, etc. has had a very bad effect on: *That's done it. You've broken it now.* ❶ For other idioms containing **do**, look at the entries for the nouns, adjectives, etc. For example, **do sb credit** is at **credit**.
PHR V **do away with sth** (*informal*) to get rid of sth: *Most European countries have done away with their royal families.* **do sb out of sth** to prevent sb having sth in an unfair way; to cheat sb: *They've done me out of my share of the money!* **do sth up 1** to fasten a piece of clothing: *Hurry up. Do up your jacket and we can go!* **OPP undo 2** to repair a building and make it more modern **do without (sth)** to manage without having sth: *If there isn't any coffee left, we'll just have to do without.*

do³ /duː/ *noun* [C] (*pl.* **-os**) (*BrE*, *informal*) a party or other social event
IDM **dos and don'ts** things that you should and should not do: *the dos and don'ts of mountain climbing*

docile /'dəʊsaɪl/ *adj.* (used about a person or animal) quiet and easy to control

dock¹ /dɒk/ *noun* **1** [C, U] an area of a port where ships stop to be loaded, repaired, etc. **2** [C] (*AmE*) = JETTY **3 docks** [pl.] a group of docks with all the buildings, offices, etc. that are around them: *He works down at the docks.* **4** [C, usually sing.] the place in a court of law where the person who is accused sits or stands

dock² /dɒk/ *verb* **1** [I, T] if a ship **docks** or you **dock** a ship, it sails into a port and stops at the dock: *The ship had docked/was docked at Lisbon.* **2** [T] to take away part of the money sb earns, especially as a punishment: *They've docked £20 off my wages because I was late.*

docker /'dɒkə(r)/ *noun* [C] (*BrE*) a person whose job is moving goods on and off ships

docking station *noun* [C] (**COMPUTING**) a device to which a laptop computer can be connected so that it can be used like a DESKTOP computer; a device with speakers that you can connect to some types of small equipment for listening to music

doctor¹ ⚡ **A1** /'dɒktə(r)/ *noun* **1** [C] (*abbr.* **Dr**) a person who has been trained in medicine and who treats people who are ill: *Our family doctor is Dr Young.* ◇ *I've got a doctor's appointment at 10 o'clock.* ➔ note at **hospital**, **ill¹**, **medical¹** **2 the doctor's** [sing.] the place where a doctor sees her patients; a doctor's surgery: *I'm going to the doctor's today.* **3** [C] (**EDUCATION**) a person who has got a DOCTORATE (= the highest degree from a university): *a Doctor of Philosophy*

▼ **VOCABULARY BUILDING**

In Britain a **doctor** who looks after general health problems is called a **GP**. He/she works in a **surgery**. When you **go to the doctor's**, you describe your **symptoms**: *My head hurts.* ◇ *I've got stomach ache.* The doctor may **prescribe** a particular **medicine**. This is written on an official piece of paper called a **prescription**, which you take to a **chemist's** and show when you buy the medicine. If you are feeling very **ill** or if you are in a lot of **pain**, the doctor may send you to **hospital** for more **treatment**.

---

doctor² /'dɒktə(r)/ *verb* [T] **1** to change sth that should not be changed in order to gain an advantage: *The results of the survey had been doctored.* **2** to add sth harmful to food or drink

doctorate /'dɒktərət/ *noun* [C] (**EDUCATION**) the highest university degree

doctrine ʔ+ 🄲1 /'dɒktrɪn/ *noun* [C, U] (**POLITICS**, **RELIGION**) a set of beliefs that is taught by a Church, political party, etc.

docudrama /'dɒkjudrɑːmə/ *noun* [C] (**ARTS AND MEDIA**) a film, usually made for TV, in which real events are shown in the form of a story

document¹ ʔ 🄰2 🅦 /'dɒkjumənt/ *noun* [C] **1** an official piece of writing that gives information, proof or evidence: *Her solicitor asked her to read and sign a number of documents.* **2** (**COMPUTING**) a computer file that contains text that has a name that identifies it: *Save the document before closing.*

document² 🄱2 🅦 /'dɒkjument/ *verb* [T] **1** to record the details of sth: *Causes of the disease have been well documented.* **2** to prove or support sth with documents: *documented evidence*

documentary ʔ 🄱1 /ˌdɒkju'mentri/ *noun* [C] (**ARTS AND MEDIA**) (*pl.* -ies) a film, TV or radio programme that gives facts or information about a particular subject

documentation ʔ+ 🄲1 /ˌdɒkjumen'teɪʃn/ *noun* [U] the documents that are required for sth, or that give evidence or proof of sth: *I couldn't enter the country because I didn't have all the necessary documentation.*

doddle /'dɒdl/ *noun* [sing.] (*BrE, informal*) something that is very easy to do: *The exam was an absolute doddle!*

dodecagon /dəʊ'dekəgən/ *noun* [C] (**GEOMETRY**) a flat shape with twelve straight sides and twelve angles

dodecahedron /ˌdəʊdekə'hiːdrən/ *noun* [C] (**GEOMETRY**) a solid shape with twelve flat sides

dodge¹ /dɒdʒ/ *verb* **1** [I, T] to move quickly in order to avoid sb/sth: *I had to dodge between the cars to cross the road.* **2** [T] to avoid doing sth that you should do: *Don't try to dodge your responsibilities!*

dodecahedron

dodge² /dɒdʒ/ *noun* [C] (*informal*) a clever way of avoiding sth: *The man had been involved in a massive tax dodge.*

dodgy /'dɒdʒi/ *adj.* (dodgier; dodgiest) (*BrE, informal*) involving risk; not honest or not to be trusted: *a dodgy business deal*

doe /dəʊ/ *noun* [C] a female DEER (= a large wild animal that eats grass), RABBIT (= a small animal with long ears) or HARE (= an animal like a large RABBIT with strong back legs) or ↄ note at **deer** ↄ picture at **deer**

does /dʌz/ → DO¹

doesn't /'dʌznt/ *short form* does not

dog¹ ʔ 🄰1 /dɒg/ *noun* [C] **1** an animal that many people keep as a pet, or for working on farms, hunting, etc: *I'm just going to walk the dog.* ◊ *dog food* ↄ picture at **animal** **2** a male dog or FOX

dog² /dɒg/ *verb* [T] (-gg-) to follow sb closely: *A shadowy figure was dogging their every move.* ◊ (*figurative*) *Bad luck and illness have dogged her career from the start.*

dog-eared *adj.* (used about a book or piece of paper) in bad condition with untidy corners and edges because it has been used a lot

dogged /'dɒgɪd/ *adj.* refusing to give up even when sth is difficult: *I was impressed by his dogged determination to succeed.* ▶ **doggedly** *adv.*: *She doggedly refused all offers of help.*

dogma /'dɒgmə/ *noun* [C, U] (**RELIGION**) a belief or set of beliefs that people are expected to accept as true without questioning

dogmatic /dɒg'mætɪk/ *adj.* being certain that your beliefs are right and that others should accept them, without considering any other opinions or evidence ▶ **dogmatically** /-kli/ *adv.*

do-it-your'self (*especially BrE*) = DIY

doldrums /'dɒldrəmz/ (*usually the doldrums*) *noun* [pl.] **1** the state of feeling sad or depressed: *He's been in the doldrums ever since she left him.* **2** not active or busy: *Business has been in the doldrums recently.*

dole¹ /dəʊl/ *verb*
PHR V **dole sth out** (*informal*) to give sth, especially food, money, etc. in small amounts to a number of people

dole² /dəʊl/ (*usually the dole*) *noun* [sing.] (*BrE, informal*) money that the state gives every week to people who are unemployed: *I lost my job and had to go on the dole.*

doleful /'dəʊlfl/ *adj.* sad or unhappy: *She looked at him with doleful eyes.* ▶ **dolefully** /-fəli/ *adv.*

doll /dɒl/ *noun* [C] a child's toy that looks like a small person or a baby

dollar ʔ 🄰1 /'dɒlə(r)/ *noun* (**ECONOMICS**) **1** [C] (*symb.* $) the unit of money in some countries, for example the US, Canada and Australia: *Can I pay in US dollars?* **2** [C] a note or coin that is worth one dollar **3** the dollar [sing.] the value of the US dollar on international money markets

dollop /'dɒləp/ *noun* [C] (*informal*) an amount of sth soft, especially food: *a dollop of ice cream*

dolphin /'dɒlfɪn/ *noun* [C] a sea animal that lives in the sea and looks like a large fish with a pointed mouth. Dolphins are very intelligent and often friendly towards humans.

domain ʔ+ 🄲1 🅦 /də'meɪn, dəʊ'm-/ *noun* [C] **1** an area of knowledge or activity: *I don't know — that's outside my domain.* ◊ *This issue is now in the public domain* (= the public knows about it). **2** (**COMPUTING**) a set of websites on the internet that end with the same group of letters, for example *.com* or *.org* **3** (**MATHEMATICS**) the range of possible values of a particular VARIABLE (= a quantity that can vary)

do'main name *noun* [C] (**COMPUTING**) a name that identifies a website or group of websites on the internet

dome /dəʊm/ *noun* [C] (**ARCHITECTURE**) a round roof on a building: *the dome of St Paul's in London* ▶ **domed** *adj.*: *a domed roof*

dome on a church

cupola

dome

domestic ʔ 🄱2 /də'mestɪk/ *adj.* **1** not international; only within one country: *domestic flights* ◊ *domestic affairs/politics* **2** [only before noun] connected with the home or family: *domestic chores/tasks* ◊ *the growing problem of domestic violence* (= violence between members of the same family) ◊ *domestic water/gas/electricity supplies* **3** (used about animals) kept as pets or on farms; not wild: *domestic animals such as* *cats, dogs and horses* **4** (used about a person) enjoying doing things in the home, such as cooking and cleaning

domesticate /dəˈmestɪkeɪt/ *verb* [T, often passive] **1** to make a wild animal used to living with or working for humans **SYN** **tame²** **2** (AGRICULTURE) to grow plants or crops for human use **SYN** **cultivate**

domesticated /dəˈmestɪkeɪtɪd/ *adj.* **1** (used about animals) happy being near people and being controlled by them: *domesticated animals* **2** (used about people) to be good at cleaning the house, cooking, etc.

dominance ⫯+ **C1** **W** /ˈdɒmɪnəns/ *noun* [U] the fact of being more important, powerful or easy to notice than sb/sth else: *Japan's dominance of the car industry*

dominant ⫯+ **B2** **W** /ˈdɒmɪnənt/ *adj.* **1** more powerful, important or easy to notice than others: *His mother was the dominant influence in his life.* **2** (BIOLOGY) a **dominant** physical characteristic, for example brown eyes, appears in a child even if they has only one GENE (= a unit inside a cell that controls a particular quality) for this characteristic ⊃ look at **recessive**

dominate ⫯ **B2** **W** /ˈdɒmɪneɪt/ *verb* **1** [I, T] to be more powerful, important or NOTICEABLE than others: *The Italian team dominated throughout the second half of the game.* ◊ *She always tends to dominate the conversation.* **2** [T] (used about a building or place) to be much higher than everything else: *The cathedral dominates the area for miles around.* ▶ **domination** /ˌdɒmɪˈneɪʃn/ *noun* [U]

domineering /ˌdɒmɪˈnɪərɪŋ/ *adj.* having a very strong character and wanting to control other people **SYN** **overbearing**

dominion /dəˈmɪnjən/ *noun* (formal) **1** [U] the power to rule and control: *to have dominion over an area* **2** [C] (POLITICS) an area controlled by one government or ruler: *the dominions of the Roman empire*

domino /ˈdɒmɪnəʊ/ *noun* [C] (pl. -oes) one of a set of small flat pieces of wood or plastic, marked on one side with two groups of spots representing numbers, that are used for playing a game called **dominoes**

donate ⫯ **B1** /dəʊˈneɪt/ *verb* [T] ~ **sth (to sb/sth)** **1** to give money or goods to an organization, especially one for people or animals who need help: *She donated a large sum of money to Cancer Research.* **2** (MEDICINE) to allow doctors to remove blood or a body organ in order to help sb who needs it: *I've been donating blood regularly for a few years now.*

donation ⫯+ **B2** /dəʊˈneɪʃn/ *noun* **1** [C, U] money, etc. that is given to a person or an organization such as a charity, in order to help people or animals in need: *Would you like to make a small donation to the Red Cross?* **2** [U] (MEDICINE) the act of allowing doctors to remove blood or a body organ in order to help sb who needs it: *organ donation*

done¹ /dʌn/ past participle of **do¹**

done² /dʌn/ *adj.* [not before noun] **1** finished: *I've got to go out as soon as this job is done.* **2** (used about food) cooked enough: *The meat's ready but the vegetables still aren't done.*
IDM **over and done with** completely finished; in the past

done³ /dʌn/ *exclamation* used for saying that you accept an offer: *'I'll give you 20 pounds for it.' 'Done!'*

dongle /ˈdɒŋgl/ *noun* [C] (COMPUTING) a device that you connect to a computer so that you can use a particular program, the internet, etc.

donkey /ˈdɒŋki/ *noun* [C] an animal like a small horse, with long ears
IDM **donkey's years** (BrE, old-fashioned, informal) a very long time

donor ⫯+ **C1** **W** /ˈdəʊnə(r)/ *noun* [C] **1** (MEDICINE) a person who gives blood or a part of their own body for medical use: *a blood/kidney donor* **2** a person who gives money or goods to a charity

don't /dəʊnt/ *short form* do not

donut /ˈdəʊnʌt/ (AmE) = DOUGHNUT

doodle /ˈduːdl/ *verb* [I] to draw lines, patterns, etc. without thinking, especially when you are bored ▶ **doodle** *noun* [C]

doom /duːm/ *noun* [U] death or a terrible event in the future that you cannot avoid: *a sense of impending doom* (= that sth bad is going to happen) ◊ *Don't listen to her. She's always full of* **doom and gloom** (= expecting bad things to happen). ▶ **doomed** *adj.*: *The plan was* **doomed to failure.** ◊ *The project was doomed from the start.*

door ⫯ **A1** /dɔː(r)/ *noun* [C] **1** a piece of wood, glass, etc. that you open and close to get in or out of a room, building, car, etc: *to open/shut/close the door* ◊ *to bolt/ lock the door* ◊ *I could hear somebody knocking on the door.* ◊ *There's someone* **at the door** (= just outside the door, knocking or ringing the bell) ◊ *to* **answer the door** (= to open the door when sb knocks or rings the bell) ◊ *Please don't* **slam the door.** ◊ *the front/back door* ◊ *the fridge door* **2** the entrance to a building, room, car, etc: *I looked through the door and saw her sitting there.*
IDM **(from) door to door** (from) house to house: *The journey takes about five hours, door to door.* **next door (to sb/sth)** in the next house, room, etc: *Do you know the people who live next door?* **out of doors** outside: *Shall we eat out of doors today?* **SYN** **outdoors** **OPP** **indoors**

doorbell /ˈdɔːbel/ *noun* [C] a bell with a button outside a house that you push to let the people inside know that you are there

doorman /ˈdɔːmən/ *noun* [C] (pl. -men /-mən/) a man, often in uniform, whose job is to stand at the entrance to a large building such as a hotel or a theatre, and open the door for visitors, find them taxis, etc.

doormat /ˈdɔːmæt/ *noun* [C] **1** a piece of material on the floor in front of a door that you can clean your shoes on before going inside **2** (informal) a person who allows other people to treat them badly without complaining

doorstep /ˈdɔːstep/ *noun* [C] a step in front of a door outside a building
IDM **on your/the doorstep** very near to you: *The sea was right on our doorstep.*

doorway /ˈdɔːweɪ/ *noun* [C] an opening filled by a door leading into a building, room, etc: *She was standing in the doorway.*

dopamine /ˈdəʊpəmiːn/ *noun* [U] (BIOLOGY, CHEMISTRY) a chemical produced by nerve cells that has an effect on other cells

dope¹ /dəʊp/ *noun* (informal) **1** [U] an illegal drug, especially CANNABIS or MARIJUANA **2** [U] (SPORT) a drug that is taken by a person or given to an animal to affect their performance in a race or sport: *The athlete failed a* **dope test** (= a medical test showed that he had taken such drugs). **3** [C] (informal) a stupid person: *What a dope!*

dope² /dəʊp/ *verb* [T] to give a drug to a person or an animal, especially in order to affect their performance in a race or sport

dopey /ˈdəʊpi/ *adj.* (dopier; dopiest) **1** tired and not able to think clearly, especially because of drugs, alcohol or lack of sleep **2** (informal) stupid; not intelligent

doping /'dəʊpɪŋ/ *noun* [U] (**SPORT**) the practice of using drugs to affect performance in a race or other sport

Doric /'dɒrɪk/ *adj.* (**ARCHITECTURE**) used to describe the oldest style of architecture in ancient Greece that has thick plain columns and no decoration at the top: *a Doric column/temple* ➔ picture at **capital**[1]

dormant /'dɔːmənt/ *adj.* not active for some time: *a dormant volcano*

dormer window (*also* dormer /'dɔːmə(r)/) *noun* [C] (**ARCHITECTURE**) a VERTICAL window in a room that is built into a sloping roof

dormitory /'dɔːmətri/ (*pl.* -ies) *noun* [C] **1** (*also informal* dorm /dɔːm/) a large bedroom with a number of beds in it, especially in a school, etc. **2** (*AmE*) = HALL OF RESIDENCE

dormouse /'dɔːmaʊs/ *noun* [C] (*pl.* dormice /-maɪs/) a small animal like a mouse, with a tail covered in fur

dorsal /'dɔːsl/ *adj.* [only before noun] (**BIOLOGY**) on or connected with the back of a fish or an animal: *a shark's dorsal fin* ➔ look at **pectoral**, **ventral** ➔ picture at **animal**

dosage /'dəʊsɪdʒ/ *noun* [C, usually sing.] (**MEDICINE**) the amount of a medicine you should take over a period of time: *The recommended dosage is one tablet every four hours.*

dose[1] ⸿ **C1** /dəʊs/ *noun* [C] **1** (**MEDICINE**) an amount of medicine that you take at one time ➔ look at **overdose** **2** an amount of sth, especially sth unpleasant: *a dose of the flu* ◇ *I can only stand him in small doses.*

dose[2] /dəʊs/ *verb* [T] (**MEDICINE**) to give sb/yourself some medicine or a drug: *She dosed herself with aspirin and went to work.*

doss /dɒs/ *verb*
PHR V doss about/around (*BrE, informal*) to waste time not doing very much doss down (*BrE, informal*) to lie down to sleep, without a proper bed: *Do you mind if I doss down on your floor tonight?*

dossier /'dɒsieɪ/ *noun* [C] ~ (on sb/sth) (*formal*) a collection of documents that contain information about a person, an event or a subject: *to assemble/compile a dossier on somebody* ➔ look at **file**[1] (3)

dot[1] ⸿ **B2** /dɒt/ *noun* [C] **1** (**LANGUAGE**) a small, round mark, like a full stop: *a white dress with black dots* ◇ *The letters i and j have dots above them.* **2** something that looks like a dot: *He watched until the plane was just a dot in the sky.*
IDM on the dot (*informal*) at exactly the right time or at exactly the time mentioned

dot[2] /dɒt/ *verb* [T] (-tt-) **1** [usually passive] to mark sth with a DOT **2** [usually passive] to spread things or people over an area; to be spread over an area
IDM be dotted about/around to be spread over an area: *There are restaurants dotted about all over the centre of town.* be dotted with to have several things or people in or on it: *a hillside dotted with sheep*

dot-com /ˌdɒt 'kɒm/ *noun* [C] (**BUSINESS**) a company that sells goods and services on the internet, especially one whose address ends .com: *The weaker dot-coms have collapsed.* ◇ *a dot-com millionaire* ➔ look at **start-up** (1)

dote /dəʊt/ *verb*
PHR V dote on sb to have or show a lot of love for sb and think they are perfect: *He's always doted on his eldest son.*

doting /'dəʊtɪŋ/ *adj.* [only before noun] showing a lot of love for sb, often ignoring their faults: *doting parents*

dotted line *noun* [C] a line of DOTS (= small round marks) that show where sth is to be written on a form, etc: *Sign on the dotted line.* ➔ picture at **line**[1]

double[1] ⸿ **A2** /'dʌbl/ *adj., det.* **1** twice as much or as many (as usual): *a double helping of ice cream* ◇ *His income is double hers.* ◇ *We'll need double the amount of wine.* **2** having two equal or similar parts: *double doors* ◇ *Does 'necessary' have (a) double 's'?* ◇ *My phone number is two eight four double three four* (= 284334). **3** made for or used by two people or things: *a double garage* ➔ note at **hotel**

double[2] ⸿ **A2** /'dʌbl/ *pron.* twice the (usual) number or amount: *When you work overtime, you get paid double.*

double[3] ⸿ **A2** /'dʌbl/ *verb* **1** [I, T] to become twice as much or as many; to make sth twice as much or as many; to multiply by two: *The price of houses has almost doubled.* ◇ *Think of a number and double it.* **2** [I] ~ (up) as sth to have a second use or function: *The small room doubles (up) as a study.*
PHR V double (sb) up/over (to cause sb) to bend the body: *to be doubled up with pain/laughter*

double[4] ⸿ **B1** /'dʌbl/ *adv.* in twos or two parts: *When I saw her with her twin sister I thought I was seeing double.*

double[5] /'dʌbl/ *noun* **1** [C] a glass of strong alcoholic drink containing twice the usual amount **2** [C] a person who looks very much like another: *I thought it was you I saw in the supermarket. You must have a double.* **3** [C] an actor who replaces another actor in a film to do dangerous or other special things **4** [C] a bedroom for two people in a hotel, etc. ➔ look at **single**[1] (4) **5** doubles [pl.] (in some sports, for example tennis) with two pairs playing: *the Men's Doubles final* ➔ look at **single**[2] (5)

double-barrelled (*BrE*) (*AmE* double-barreled) *adj.* **1** (used about a gun) having two BARRELS (= long metal tubes through which bullets are fired) **2** (used about a family name) having two parts, sometimes joined by a HYPHEN, for example *Mr Day-Lewis*

double bass (*also* bass) *noun* [C] (**MUSIC**) the largest musical instrument in the VIOLIN family, which you can play either standing up or sitting down ➔ picture at **instrument, orchestra**

double-blind *adj.* [only before noun] (**SCIENCE**) (used about a test) organized so that neither the people responsible for the test nor the people being tested know any information that might affect the results

double-breasted *adj.* (used about a coat or jacket) having two rows of buttons down the front ➔ look at **single-breasted**

double-check *verb* [I, T] to check sth again, or with great care

double chin *noun* [C] fat under a person's CHIN (= the part of the face below the mouth), which looks like another CHIN

double-click *verb* [I, T] ~ (on sth) (**COMPUTING**) to choose a particular function or item on a computer screen by pressing one of the buttons on a mouse twice quickly: *To run an application, just double-click on the icon.*

double-cross *verb* [T] to cheat sb who believes that they can trust you, usually after you have agreed to do sth dishonest together

double-decker *noun* [C] a bus with two floors

double-dip recession *noun* [C] (**ECONOMICS**) a period when a country's economy becomes weaker, then improves for a short time before becoming weaker again

double figures (*especially BrE*) (*AmE usually* double digits) *noun* [U] a number that is between 10 and 99: *Inflation is in double figures.*

double ˈglazing noun [U] two layers of glass in a window to keep a building warm or quiet ▶ **double-ˈglazed** adj.

double ˈhelix noun [C] (**BIOLOGY**) the structure of DNA, consisting of two connected long thin pieces that form a SPIRAL shape ⊃ picture at **DNA**

doubly /ˈdʌbli/ adv. **1** in two ways: He was doubly blessed with both good looks and talent. **2** more than usually: I made doubly sure that the door was locked.

doubt¹ ? **B1** /daʊt/ noun [C, U] ~ (**about sth**); ~ (**as to sth**); ~ (**that**) ... a feeling of being uncertain about sth: If you have any doubts about the job, feel free to ring me and discuss them. ◇ There was some doubt as to whether she was the right person for the job. ◇ There is no doubt that we did the right thing.
IDM **cast doubt on sth** → **CAST¹** **give sb the benefit of the doubt** → **BENEFIT¹** **in doubt** not sure or definite **no doubt 1** (used when you expect sth to happen but you are not sure that it will) probably: No doubt she'll write when she has time. **2** used when you are saying that sth is certainly true **without (a) doubt** definitely: It was, without doubt, the coldest winter for many years.

doubt² ? **B1** /daʊt/ verb [T] ~ (**that** ...); ~ (**if/whether** ...) to think sth is unlikely or to feel uncertain about sth: 'Do you think he'll win?' '**I doubt it.'** ◇ She never doubted that he was telling the truth. ◇ I doubt if I'll have time to go to the shops today. ◇ He had never doubted her support.

doubtful /ˈdaʊtfl/ adj. **1** unlikely or uncertain: It's doubtful whether/if we'll finish in time. ◇ It was doubtful that he was still alive. **2** ~ (**about sth/doing sth**) (used about a person) not sure: He still felt doubtful about his decision. ▶ **doubtfully** /-fəli/ adv.: 'I suppose it'll be all right,' she said doubtfully.

doubtless /ˈdaʊtləs/ adv. almost certainly: Doubtless she'll have a good excuse for being late!

dough /dəʊ/ noun [U] a mixture of flour, water, etc. used for baking into bread, etc.

doughnut (also **donut** especially in AmE) /ˈdəʊnʌt/ noun [C] a small cake in the shape of a ball or a ring, made from a sweet DOUGH cooked in very hot oil

dour /dʊə(r), ˈdaʊə(r)/ adj. (used about a person's manner or expression) cold and unfriendly

douse /daʊs/ verb [T] **1** ~ **sth (with sth)** to stop a fire from burning by pouring liquid over it: The firefighters managed to douse the flames. **2** ~ **sb/sth (in/with sth)** to cover sb/sth with liquid: to douse yourself in perfume (= wear too much of it)

dove¹ /dʌv/ noun [C] a bird of the PIGEON family, often used as a sign of peace

dove² /dəʊv/ (AmE) past tense of **dive¹**

dovetail¹ /ˈdʌvteɪl/ verb [I, T] ~ (**sth**) (**with/into sth**) (formal) if two things **dovetail** or if one thing **dovetails** with/into another, they fit together well

dovetail   mitre

dovetail² /ˈdʌvteɪl/ (also **dovetail ˈjoint**) noun [C] a JOINT for fixing two pieces of wood together

dowdy /ˈdaʊdi/ adj. (**dowdier**; **dowdiest**) (used about a person or the clothes they wear) not attractive or fashionable

the Dow Jones Index /ðə ˌdaʊ dʒəʊnz ˈɪndeks/ (also **Dow Jones ˈaverage, the ˈDow**) noun [sing.] (**BUSINESS**) a list of the share prices of 30 US industrial companies that can be used to compare the prices to previous levels

down¹ ? **A1** /daʊn/ adv., prep. **1** to or at a lower level or place; from the top towards the bottom of sth: Can you get that book down from the top shelf? ◇ 'Where's Mary?' 'She's down in the basement.' ◇ Her hair hung down her back. ◇ The rain was running down the window. **2** along: We sailed down the river towards the sea. ◇ 'Where's the nearest garage?' 'Go down this road and take the first turning on the right.' **3** from a standing or VERTICAL position to a sitting or lying one: to sit/lie down **4** to or in the south: We went down to Devon for our holiday. **5** used for showing that the level, amount, strength, etc. of sth is less or lower: Do you mind if I turn the heating down a bit? **6** on paper; on a list: Did you get that down? **7** (informal) to or at a local place such as a shop, pub, etc: I'm just going down to the shops. **8** ~ **to sb/sth** even including: We had everything planned down to the last detail.
IDM **be down to sb** to be sb's responsibility: When my father died it was down to me to look after the family's affairs. **be down to sth** to have only the amount mentioned left: I need to do some washing — I'm down to my last shirt. **down and out** having no money, job or home **down under** (informal) (in) Australia

down² /daʊn/ verb [T] (informal) to finish a drink quickly: She **downed** her drink **in one** (= she drank the whole glass without stopping).

down³ /daʊn/ adj. **1** (informal) sad: You're looking a bit down today. **2** lower than before: Unemployment figures are down again this month. ⊃ note at **trend¹** **3** (**COMPUTING**) (used about computers) not working: I can't access the file as our computers have been down all morning.

down⁴ /daʊn/ noun [U] very soft feathers: a duvet filled with duck down
IDM **ups and downs** → **UP²**

ˈdown-and-out noun [C] a person who has got no money, job or home

downcast /ˈdaʊnkɑːst/ adj. **1** (used about a person) sad and without hope **2** (used about eyes) looking down

downfall /ˈdaʊnfɔːl/ noun [sing.] a loss of a person's money, power, social position, etc.; the thing that causes this: The government's downfall seemed inevitable. ◇ Greed was her downfall.

downgrade /ˌdaʊnˈɡreɪd/ verb [T] ~ **sb/sth (from sth) (to sth)** to reduce sb/sth to a lower level or position of importance: Tom's been downgraded from manager to assistant manager. ⊃ look at **upgrade** (2)

downhearted /ˌdaʊnˈhɑːtɪd/ adj. sad

downhill /ˌdaʊnˈhɪl/ adj., adv. (going) in a direction that goes downwards; towards the bottom of a hill: downhill skiing ◇ It's an easy walk. The road runs downhill most of the way. **OPP** **uphill**
IDM **go downhill** to get worse: Their relationship has been going downhill for some time now.

download¹ ? **A2** /ˌdaʊnˈləʊd/ verb [T] ~ **sth (from/to sth)** (**COMPUTING**) to get data from another computer, usually using the internet: to download files/music/software ◇ If you download pictures from the internet, check the terms of use. **OPP** **upload¹** ▶ **downloadable** adj.

download² ? **A2** /ˈdaʊnləʊd/ noun (**COMPUTING**) **1** [C] data that is copied from another computer system, usually using the internet: It's one of the most popular free software downloads. ⊃ look at **upload²** **2** [C, U] the act or process of copying data from another computer system: *app/file downloads* ◇ *More songs will soon be available for download.*

downmarket /ˌdaʊnˈmɑːkɪt/ *adj.* (*BrE*) cheap and of low quality ▶ **downmarket** *adv.*

ˌ**down ˈpayment** *noun* [C] (**FINANCE**) a sum of money that is given as the first part of a larger payment: *We are saving for a down payment on a house.*

downpour /ˈdaʊnpɔː(r)/ *noun* [C, usually sing.] a sudden, heavy fall of rain

downright /ˈdaʊnraɪt/ *adj.* [only before noun] (used about sth bad or unpleasant) complete: *The holiday was a downright disaster.* ▶ **downright** *adv.*: *The way he spoke to me was downright rude!*

downside /ˈdaʊnsaɪd/ *noun* [C, usually sing.] the disadvantages or negative aspects of sth: *All good ideas have a downside.*

downsize /ˈdaʊnsaɪz/ *verb* [I, T] (**BUSINESS**) to reduce the number of people who work in a company, business, etc. in order to reduce costs ▶ **downsizing** *noun* [U]

Down's syndrome /ˈdaʊnz sɪndrəʊm/ (*especially BrE*) (*AmE usually* **Down syndrome**) *noun* [U] (**HEALTH**) a medical condition in which a person is born with a flat, wide face and mental ability that is below average

downstairs¹ ʔ⚐**A1** /ˌdaʊnˈsteəz/ *adv.* towards or on a lower floor of a house or building: *He fell downstairs and broke his arm.* ◇ *Wait for me downstairs, in the kitchen.* **OPP** **upstairs**

downstairs² ʔ⚐**A2** /ˌdaʊnˈsteəz/ *adj.* on a lower floor of a house or building: *a downstairs toilet* **OPP** **upstairs**

downstream /ˌdaʊnˈstriːm/ *adv., adj.* (**GEOGRAPHY**) in the direction in which a river flows: *We were rowing downstream.* **OPP** **upstream**

ˈ**Down syndrome** (*AmE*) = **DOWN'S SYNDROME**

ˌ**down to ˈearth** *adj.* (used about a person) sensible, realistic and practical

downtown ʔ+⚐**B2** /ˌdaʊnˈtaʊn/ *adv., adj.* (*especially AmE*) in or towards the centre of a city, especially its main business area: *to go/work downtown* ▶ **downtown** ʔ+⚐**B2** *noun* [U]: *a hotel in the heart of downtown*

downtrend /ˈdaʊntrend/ *noun* [C, usually sing.] (**ECONOMICS**) a situation in which business activity or performance decreases or becomes worse over a period of time: *We have seen a significant downtrend in the price of oil.*

downtrodden /ˈdaʊntrɒdn/ *adj.* (used about a person) treated so badly by people with authority and power that you no longer have the ability to fight back

downturn /ˈdaʊntɜːn/ *noun* [C, usually sing.] ~ **(in sth)** (**ECONOMICS**) a drop in the amount of business that is done; a time when the economy becomes weaker: *a downturn in sales/trade/business* **OPP** **upturn**

downward /ˈdaʊnwəd/ *adj.* [only before noun] towards the ground or a lower level: *a downward movement*

downwards ʔ⚐**B2** /ˈdaʊnwədz/ (*also* **downward** *especially in AmE*) *adv.* towards the ground or towards a lower level: *She was lying face downwards on the grass.* ◇ *The garden sloped gently downwards to the river.* **OPP** **upwards**

dowry /ˈdaʊri/ *noun* [C] (*pl.* **-ies**) money and/or property that, in some countries, a wife or her family gives to the man she is marrying

doze /dəʊz/ *verb* [I] to sleep lightly and/or for a short time: *He was dozing in front of the TV.* ▶ **doze** *noun* [sing.]
PHRV **doze off** to go to sleep, especially during the day: *I'm sorry — I must have dozed off for a minute.*

dozen ʔ⚐**B2** /ˈdʌzn/ *noun det.* **1** [C] (*pl.* **dozen**) (*abbr.* doz.) a group of twelve of the same thing: *A dozen eggs, please.* ◇ *half a dozen* (= six) ◇ *two dozen sheep* **2** **dozens** [pl.] ~ **(of sth)** (*informal*) a lot of people or things: *I've tried phoning her dozens of times.*

dozy /ˈdəʊzi/ *adj.* **1** wanting to sleep; not feeling AWAKE **2** (*BrE, informal*) stupid; not intelligent: *You dozy thing — look what you've done!*

DPhil /ˌdiː ˈfɪl/ (*BrE*) = PHD

Dr *abbr.* (in writing) = DOCTOR¹ (1): *Dr John Waters*

drab /dræb/ *adj.* not interesting or attractive: *a drab grey office building*

draft¹ ʔ⚐**B2** /drɑːft/ *noun* **1** [C] a piece of writing, etc. that will probably be changed and improved; not the final version: *the first draft of a speech/essay* **2** **the draft** [sing.] (*especially AmE*) = CONSCRIPTION **3** [C] (**FINANCE**) a written order to a bank to pay money to sb: *Payment must be made by bank draft.* **4** [C] (*AmE*) = DRAUGHT¹

draft² ʔ⚐**B2** /drɑːft/ *verb* [T] **1** to make a first or early copy of a piece of writing: *I'll draft an email and show it to you before I send it.* **2** to choose people and send them somewhere for a special task **3** [usually passive] (*AmE*) to force sb to join the armed forces: *He was drafted into the army.*

draftsman /ˈdrɑːftsmən/ *noun* [C] (*pl.* **-men** /-mən/) (*AmE*) = DRAUGHTSMAN

draftswoman /ˈdrɑːftswʊmən/ *noun* [C] (*pl.* **-women** /-wɪmɪn/) (*AmE*) = DRAUGHTSWOMAN

drafty /ˈdrɑːfti/ *adj.* (**draftier; draftiest**) (*AmE*) = DRAUGHTY

drag¹ ʔ⚐**B2** /dræg/ *verb* (**-gg-**) **1** [T] to pull sb/sth along with difficulty: *The box was so heavy we had to drag it along the floor.* **2** [T] to make sb come or go somewhere: *She's always trying to drag me along to museums, but I'm not interested.* **3** [I] (used about time or an event) to pass very slowly: *The afternoon really dragged.* **4** [T] (**COMPUTING**) to move sth across the screen of a computer or phone using the mouse or your finger: *Click on the file and drag it into the new folder.*
PHRV **drag on** to go on for too long: *The speeches dragged on for hours.* **drag sth out** to make sth last longer than necessary: *Let's not drag this decision out — shall we go or not?* **drag sth out (of sb)** to force or persuade sb to give you information

drag² /dræg/ *noun* **1** [sing.] (*informal*) a person or situation that is boring or annoying: *'The car's broken down.' 'Oh no! What a drag!'* **2** [U] women's clothes worn by a man, especially as part of a show, etc: *men in drag* **3** [C] an act of breathing in cigarette smoke: *He took a long drag on his cigarette.* **4** [U] (**ENGINEERING**, **PHYSICS**) the force of the air that acts against the movement of an aircraft or other vehicle ⊃ look at **lift²** (4)

ˌ**drag-and-ˈdrop** *adj.* (**COMPUTING**) relating to the moving of ICONS (= small pictures or symbols that represents programs), etc. on a screen using the mouse or your finger

dragon /ˈdrægən/ *noun* [C] (in stories) a large animal with wings, that can breathe fire

dragonfly /ˈdrægənflaɪ/ *noun* [C] (*pl.* **-ies**) an insect with a long thin body, often brightly coloured, and two pairs of large wings. Dragonflies often live near water. ⊃ picture at **animal**

drain¹ /dreɪn/ *noun* [C] a pipe or hole in the ground that dirty water, etc. goes down to be carried away

IDM **(go) down the drain** (*informal*) (to be) wasted: *All that hard work has gone down the drain.* **a drain on sb/sth** something that uses up time, money, strength, etc: *The cost of travelling is a great drain on our budget.*

drain² ʔ+ **C1** /dreɪn/ *verb* **1** [T, I] to make sth empty or dry by removing the liquid from it; to become empty or dry in this way: *The whole area will have to be drained before it can be used for farming.* ◇ *Drain the pasta and add the sauce.* **2** [T, I] **~ (sth) (from/out of sth); ~ (sth) (away/off)** to make a liquid flow away; to flow away: *The plumber had to drain the water from the heating system.* ◇ *The sink's blocked—the water won't drain away at all.* ◇ (*figurative*) *He felt all his anger begin to drain away.* **3** [T] to drink all the liquid in a glass, cup, etc: *He drained his glass in one gulp.* **4** [T] **~ sb/sth (of sth)** to make sb/sth weaker, poorer, etc. by slowly using all the strength, money, etc. available: *My mother's hospital expenses were slowly draining my funds.* ◇ *The experience left her **emotionally drained.***

drainage /ˈdreɪnɪdʒ/ *noun* [U] the system used for making water, etc. flow away from a place

draining board *noun* [C] the place in the kitchen where you put plates, cups, knives, etc. to dry after washing them

drainpipe /ˈdreɪnpaɪp/ *noun* [C] a pipe that goes down the side of a building and carries water from the roof into the DRAIN (= a hole in the ground)

drake /dreɪk/ *noun* [C] a male DUCK (= a bird that lives on or near water)

drama ʔ **A2** /ˈdrɑːmə/ *noun* **1** [C] a play for the theatre, radio or TV: *a powerful **TV drama** about city life* ◇ *a **drama series*** **2** [U] (**EDUCATION, LITERATURE**) plays as a form of writing; the performance of plays: *He wrote some drama, as well as poetry.* **3** [C, U] an exciting event; exciting things that happen: *a real-life courtroom drama* ◇ *Her life was full of drama.*

dramatic ʔ **B2** /drəˈmætɪk/ *adj.* **1** sudden, very great and often surprising: *a dramatic change/increase/fall/improvement* **2** exciting or impressive: *the film's dramatic opening scene* **3** (**ARTS AND MEDIA**) connected with plays or the theatre: *Shakespeare's dramatic works* **4** (used about a person, a person's behaviour, etc.) showing feelings, etc. in a very obvious way because you want other people to notice you: *Calm down. There's no need to be so dramatic about everything!* ▸ **dramatically** ʔ+ **B2** /-kli/ *adv.*

dramatist /ˈdræmətɪst/ *noun* [C] (**ARTS AND MEDIA**) a person who writes plays for the theatre, radio or TV **SYN** **playwright** ⊃ note at **performing arts**

dramatize (*BrE also* **-ise**) /ˈdræmətaɪz/ *verb* **1** [T] (**ARTS AND MEDIA**) to make a book, an event, etc. into a play: *The novel has been dramatized for TV.* **2** [T, I] to make sth seem more exciting or important than it really is: *The newspaper was accused of dramatizing the situation.* ▸ **dramatization** (*BrE also* **-isation**) /ˌdræmətaɪˈzeɪʃn/ *noun* [C, U]

drank /dræŋk/ past tense of **drink¹**

drape¹ /dreɪp/ *verb* [T] **1 ~ sth round/over sth** to put a piece of material, clothing, etc. loosely on sth: *He draped his coat over the back of his chair.* **2** [usually passive] **~ sb/sth (in/with sth)** to cover sb/sth (with cloth, etc.): *The furniture was draped in dust sheets.*

drape² /dreɪp/ *noun* [C] (*especially AmE*) a long thick curtain

drastic /ˈdræstɪk/ *adj.* extreme, and having a sudden very strong effect: *There has been a drastic rise in crime in the area.* ▸ **drastically** /-kli/ *adv.*

draught¹ /drɑːft/ *noun* (*BrE*) **1** (*AmE* **draft**) [C] a flow of cold air that comes into a room: *Can you shut the door? There's a draught in here.* **2** **draughts** (*AmE* **checkers**) [U] a game for two players that you play on a black and white board using round black and white pieces

draught² (*BrE*) (*AmE* **draft**) /drɑːft/ *adj.* (used about beer, etc.) served from a BARREL (= a large container) rather than in a bottle: *draught beer*

draughtsman (*BrE*) (*AmE* **draftsman**) /ˈdrɑːftsmən/ *noun* [C] (*pl.* **-men** /-mən/) a person whose job is to make detailed technical plans or drawings

draughtswoman (*BrE*) (*AmE* **draftswoman**) /ˈdrɑːftswʊmən/ *noun* [C] (*pl.* **-women** /-wɪmɪn/) a woman whose job is to make detailed technical plans or drawings

draughty (*BrE*) (*AmE* **drafty**) /ˈdrɑːfti/ *adj.* (**draughtier**; **draughtiest**) (used about a room, etc.) uncomfortable because cold air is blowing through

draw¹ ʔ **A1** **S** /drɔː/ *verb* (*pt* **drew** /druː/; *pp* **drawn** /drɔːn/)
• PICTURE **1** [I, T] to do a picture or diagram of sth with a pencil, pen, etc. but not paint: *Shall I draw you a map of how to get there?* ◇ *I'm good at painting but I can't draw.*
• MOVE **2** [I] to move in the direction mentioned: *The train drew into the station.* ◇ (*figurative*) *I became more anxious as my exams drew nearer.*
• PULL **3** [T] to pull sth/sb into a new position or in the direction mentioned: *She drew the letter out of her pocket and handed it to me.* ◇ *to draw* (= open or close) *the curtains* ◇ *He drew me by the hand into the room.*
• LEARN **4** [T] **~ sth (from sth)** to learn or decide sth as a result of study, research or experience: *Can we **draw any conclusions** from this survey?* ◇ *There are important **lessons to be drawn** from this tragedy.* ◇ *It's important to **draw a distinction** between the methods used now and those used previously.*
• GET/TAKE **5** [T] **~ sth (from sb/sth)** to get or take sth from sb/sth: *He draws the inspiration for his stories from his family.*
• ATTRACT **6** [T] **~ sth (from sb); ~ sb (to sb/sth)** to make sb react to or be interested in sb/sth: *The advertisement has drawn criticism from people all over the country.* ◇ *The musicians drew quite a large crowd.* ◇ *The noise drew people to the scene.*
• IN A GAME, ETC. **7** [I, T] to finish a game, competition, etc. with equal scores so that neither person or team wins: *The two teams drew.* ◇ *The match was drawn.* **IDM** **bring sth/come/draw to an end → END¹** **draw (sb's) attention to sth** to make sb notice sth: *The article draws attention to the problem of homelessness.* **draw a blank** to get no result or find no answer: *Detectives investigating the case have drawn a blank so far.* **draw the line at sth** to say 'no' to sth even though you are happy to help in other ways: *I do most of the cooking but I draw the line at washing up as well!* **draw lots** to decide sth by chance: *They drew lots to see who should stay behind.* **PHR V** **draw in** to become dark earlier in the evening as winter gets nearer: *The **days/nights** are drawing in.* **draw out** to become lighter in the evening as summer gets nearer: *The **days/evenings** are drawing out.* **draw sth out** to take money out of a bank account: *A police car drew up outside the building.* **draw up** (used about a car, etc.) to drive up and stop in front of or near sth: *A police car drew up outside the building.* **draw sth up** to prepare and write a document, list, etc: *Our solicitor is going to draw up the contract.* ⊃ note at **meeting**

draw² /drɔː/ *noun* [C] **1** a result of a game or competition in which both players or teams get the same score so that neither of them wins: *The match ended in a draw.* **2** an act of deciding sth by chance by pulling out names or numbers from a bag, etc: *She won her bike in a prize draw.*

drawback /'drɔːbæk/ *noun* [C] a disadvantage or problem: *His lack of experience is a major drawback.* **SYN** disadvantage[1]

drawbridge /'drɔːbrɪdʒ/ *noun* [C] a bridge that can be pulled up, for example to stop people from entering a castle or to allow ships to pass under it: *to raise/lower a drawbridge*

drawbridge outside a castle

battlements

drawbridge   moat

drawer /drɔː(r)/ *noun* [C] a container that forms part of a piece of furniture such as a desk, that you can pull out to put things in: *There's some paper in the top drawer of my desk.*

drawing ⟨A2⟩ /'drɔːɪŋ/ *noun* (ART) **1** [C] a picture made with a pencil, pen, etc. but not paint ᴐ note at **painting 2** [U] the art of drawing pictures: *She's good at drawing and painting.*

'**drawing pin** (*BrE*) (*AmE* thumbtack) *noun* [C] a short pin with a flat top, used for fastening paper, etc. to a board or wall

'**drawing room** *noun* [C] (*old-fashioned*) a living room, especially in a large house

drawl /drɔːl/ *verb* [I, T] to speak slowly, making the vowel sounds very long ▸ **drawl** *noun* [sing.]: *to speak with a drawl*

drawn[1] /drɔːn/ past participle of **draw**[1]

drawn[2] /drɔːn/ *adj.* (used about a person or their face) looking tired, worried or ill

,**drawn-'out** *adj.* lasting longer than necessary: *long drawn-out negotiations*

drawstring /'drɔːstrɪŋ/ *noun* [C] a piece of string that is SEWN inside the material at the top of a bag, pair of trousers, etc. that can be pulled tighter in order to make the opening smaller: *The trousers fasten with a drawstring.*

dread[1] /dred/ *verb* [T] ~ (**doing sth**) to be very afraid of or worried about sth: *I'm dreading the exams.* ◇ *She dreaded having to tell him what had happened.* ◇ *I dread to think what my father will say.* ▸ **dreaded** *adj.*

dread[2] /dred/ *noun* [U, sing.] great fear: *He lived in dread of the same thing happening to him one day.*

dreadful /'dredfl/ *adj.* (*especially BrE*) very bad or unpleasant: *We had a dreadful journey — traffic jams all the way!* ◇ *I'm afraid there's been a dreadful* (= very serious) *mistake.* **SYN** terrible

dreadfully /'dredfəli/ *adv.* (*especially BrE*) **1** very; extremely: *I'm dreadfully sorry — I didn't mean to upset you.* **2** very badly: *The party went dreadfully and everyone left early.*

dreadlocks /'dredlɒks/ *noun* [pl.] hair worn in long thick pieces, especially by some black people

dream[1] ⟨A2⟩ /driːm/ *noun* **1** [C] ~ (**about sb/sth**) a series of events or pictures that happen in your mind while you are asleep: *I had a strange dream last night.* ◇ *That horror film has given me bad dreams.* ◇ *a vivid dream about my old school* ᴐ look at **nightmare 2** [C] something that you want very much to happen, although it is not likely: *His dream was to give up his job and live in the country.* ◇ *My dream house would have a huge garden and a swimming pool.* ◇ *Becoming a professional dancer was a dream come true for Nicola.* **3** [sing.] a state of mind in which you are not

thinking about what you are doing: *You've been in a dream all morning!*

dream[2] ⟨A2⟩ /driːm/ *verb* [I, T] (*pt, pp* dreamt /dremt/, dreamed) **1** ~ (**about sb/sth**); ~ (**that ...**) to see or experience pictures and events in your mind while you are asleep: *I dreamt about the house that I lived in as a child.* ◇ *I dreamed that I was running but I couldn't get away.* ᴐ look at **daydream 2** ~ (**about/of sth/doing sth**); ~ (**that ...**) to imagine sth that you would like to happen: *I've always dreamt about winning lots of money.* **3** ~ (**of doing sth/that ...**) to imagine that sth might happen: *I wouldn't dream of telling Stuart that I don't like his music.* ◇ *When I watched the Olympics on TV, I never dreamt that one day I'd be here competing!*

PHRV dream sth up (*informal*) to think of a plan, an idea, etc., especially sth strange

dreamer /'driːmə(r)/ *noun* [C] a person who thinks a lot about ideas, plans, etc. that may never happen instead of thinking about real life

dreamlike /'driːmlaɪk/ *adj.* as if existing or happening in a dream

dreamy /'driːmi/ *adj.* (dreamier; dreamiest) looking as though you are not paying attention to what you are doing because you are thinking about sth else: *a dreamy look/expression* ▸ **dreamily** /-mɪli/ *adv.*

dreary /'drɪəri/ *adj.* (drearier; dreariest) not at all interesting or attractive; boring **SYN** dull[1]

dredge /dredʒ/ *verb* [T] to clear the mud, etc. from the bottom of a river, CANAL, etc. using a special machine **PHRV** dredge sth up to mention sth unpleasant from the past that sb would like to forget: *The newspaper had dredged up all sorts of embarrassing details about her private life.*

dredger /'dredʒə(r)/ *noun* [C] a boat or machine that is used to clear mud, etc. from the bottom of a river, or to make the river wider

dregs /dregz/ *noun* [pl.] **1** the last drops in a container of liquid, containing small pieces of solid waste **2** the worst parts of sth that have no use or value: *These people were regarded as the dregs of society.*

drench /drentʃ/ *verb* [T, often passive] to make sb/sth completely wet: *Don't go out while it's raining so hard or you'll get drenched.*

dress[1] ⟨A1⟩ /dres/ *noun* **1** [C] a piece of women's clothing that covers the body from the shoulders to the knees or below: *a wedding dress* **2** [U] clothes for either men or women: *formal/casual dress* ◇ *He was wearing Bulgarian national dress.*

dress[2] ⟨A1⟩ /dres/ *verb* **1** [I, T] to put clothes on sb or yourself: *He dressed quickly and left the house.* ◇ *My husband dressed the children while I got breakfast ready.* **OPP** undress **2** [I, T] to put on or have clothes on, in the way or style mentioned: *to dress well/badly/casually* **3** [T] to put a clean covering on the place on sb's body where they have been hurt: *to dress a wound*

PHRV dress up to put on formal clothes, usually for a special occasion: *You don't need to dress up for the party.* dress up (as sb/sth) to put on special clothes, especially in order to look like sb/sth else: *The children decided to dress up as pirates.*

'**dress circle** (*especially BrE*) (*AmE* first balcony) *noun* [C] (ARTS AND MEDIA) the first level of seats above the ground floor in a theatre

dressed ⟨B1⟩ /drest/ *adj.* [not before noun] **1** wearing clothes: *Get up and get dressed!* ◇ *Hurry up, Simon! Aren't you dressed yet?* **2** ~ (**in sth**) wearing clothes of a particular type: *to be well dressed/badly dressed/*

casually dressed ◇ The people at the funeral were all dressed in black.

dresser /'dresə(r)/ noun [C] (BrE) a piece of furniture with cupboards at the bottom and shelves above. It is used for holding dishes, cups, etc.

dressing /'dresɪŋ/ noun **1** [C] a covering that you put on a part of sb's body that has been hurt to protect it and keep it clean **2** [C, U] a sauce for food, especially for salads

dressing gown (BrE) (AmE **bathrobe, robe**) noun [C] a piece of clothing like a loose coat with a belt, that you wear before or after a bath, before you get dressed in the morning, etc.

dressing room noun [C] a room for changing your clothes in, especially one for actors or, in British English, for sports players

dressing table noun [C] a piece of furniture in a bedroom with DRAWERS (= parts like boxes that you can pull out) and a mirror

drew /dru:/ past tense of **draw¹**

dribble /'drɪbl/ verb **1** [I, T] (used about a liquid) to move downwards in a thin flow; to make a liquid move in this way: The paint dribbled down the side of the pot. **2** [I] to allow SALIVA (= liquid that is produced in the mouth) to run out of the mouth: Small children often dribble. **3** [I, T] (used in ball games) to make a ball move forward by using many short kicks or hits: He dribbled round the goalkeeper and scored. ◇ She dribble the ball down the pitch.

dried² /draɪd/ adj. (used about food) with all the liquid removed from it: dried milk ◇ dried fruit

drier /'draɪə(r)/ = DRYER

drift¹ ᵉ➕ **C1** /drɪft/ verb [I] **1** to be carried or moved along by wind or water: The boat drifted out to sea. **2** to move slowly or without any particular purpose: He drifted from room to room. ◇ She drifted into acting almost by accident. **3** (used about snow or sand) to be moved into piles by wind or water: The snow drifted up to 2 metres deep in some places.
PHR V **drift apart** to slowly become less close or friendly with sb

drift² /drɪft/ noun **1** [sing.] a slow movement towards sth: the country's drift into economic decline **2** [sing.] the general meaning of sth: I don't understand all the details of the plan but I get the drift. **3** [C] a pile of snow or sand that was made by wind or water

drill¹ /drɪl/ noun **1** [C] a tool or machine that is used for making holes in things: a dentist's drill ⊃ picture at **tool 2** [C] (**EDUCATION**) something that you repeat many times in order to learn sth **3** [C, U] practice for what you should do in an emergency: a fire drill **4** [U] exercise in MARCHING, etc. that soldiers do

drill² /drɪl/ verb **1** [I, T] to make a hole in sth with a DRILL: to drill a hole in something **2** [I] ~ (for sth) to try to get oil or water by drilling in the ground or sea bed: to drill for oil **3** [T] (**EDUCATION**) to teach sb by making them repeat sth many times

drily (especially BrE) (also **dryly** AmE, BrE) /'draɪli/ adv. (used about the way sb says sth) in a way that makes people laugh although it sounds serious: 'I can hardly contain my excitement,' Peter said drily (= he was not excited at all).

drink¹ ᵉ **A1** /drɪŋk/ verb (pt **drank** /dræŋk/; pp **drunk** /drʌŋk/) **1** [T, I] to take liquid into your body through your mouth: Would you like anything to drink? ◇ We sat drinking coffee and chatting for hours. **2** [I, T] to drink alcohol: I never **drink and drive** so I'll have an orange juice. ◇ What do you drink — beer or wine?

◇ Her father used to **drink heavily** but he's teetotal now. ◇ She doesn't drink.
PHR V **drink to sb/sth** to wish sb/sth good luck by holding your glass up in the air before you drink: We all drank to the future of the bride and groom. ⊃ look at **toast** (2) **drink (sth) up** to finish drinking sth: Drink up your tea — it's getting cold.

drink² ᵉ **A1** /drɪŋk/ noun [C, U] **1** liquid for drinking; an amount that you drink: Can I **have a drink** please? ◇ a drink of milk ◇ soft drinks (= cold drinks without alcohol) ◇ food and drink **2** alcoholic drink: He's got a drink problem. ◇ Shall we **go for a drink**?

drink-'driver (BrE) (also **drunk driver** AmE, BrE) noun [C] a person who drives after drinking too much alcohol

drink-'driving (BrE) (also **drunk driving, drunken 'driving** especially in AmE) noun [U] the crime of driving a vehicle after drinking too much alcohol: He was convicted of drink-driving and was banned for two years.

drinker /'drɪŋkə(r)/ noun [C] a person who drinks a lot of sth, especially alcohol: a heavy drinker ◇ I'm not a big coffee drinker.

drinking /'drɪŋkɪŋ/ noun [U] drinking alcohol: Her drinking became a problem.

drinking water noun [U] water that is safe to drink

drip¹ /drɪp/ verb (-pp-) **1** [I] (used about a liquid) to fall in small drops: Water was dripping down through the roof. **2** [I, T] to produce drops of liquid: The tap is dripping. ◇ Her finger was dripping blood.

drip² /drɪp/ noun **1** [sing.] the act or sound of water falling continuously in small drops **2** [C] a drop of water that falls down from sb/sth: We put a bucket under the hole in the roof to catch the drips. **3** (also IV especially in AmE) [C] (**MEDICINE**) a piece of medical equipment, like a tube, that is used for putting liquid food or medicine straight into a person's blood: She's **on a drip**.

drive¹ ᵉ **A1** /draɪv/ verb (pt **drove** /drəʊv/; pp **driven** /'drɪvn/)
• VEHICLE **1** [I, T] to control or operate a car, train, bus, etc: Can you drive? ◇ to drive a car/train/bus/lorry **2** [I, T] to go or take sb somewhere in a car, etc: I usually drive to work. ◇ We drove Aisha to the airport. **3** [I] (used about a vehicle) to travel under the control of a driver: A stream of cars drove by.
• MAKE SB/STH MOVE **4** [T] to force people or animals to move in a particular direction: The dogs drove the sheep into the field.
• HIT **5** [T] to force sth into a particular position by hitting it: to drive a post into the ground
• MAKE SB DO STH **6** [T] to cause sb to be in a particular state or to do sth: His constant stupid questions **drive me mad**. ◇ to drive somebody to despair **7** [T] to make sb/sth work very hard: You shouldn't drive yourself so hard.
• MACHINE **8** [T] to make a machine work, by giving it power: What drives the wheels in this engine?
IDM **drive sth home (to sb)** to make sth clear so that people understand it **what sb is driving at** (informal) what sb means; what sb wants to say: I'm afraid I don't understand what you're driving at.
PHR V **drive off** (used about a car, driver, etc.) to leave the car **drive sb/sth off** to make sb/sth go away

drive² ᵉ **A2** /draɪv/ noun
• IN A VEHICLE **1** [C] a journey in a car or other road vehicle: The supermarket is only a five-minute drive away. ◇ Let's **go for a drive**. **2** [U] the equipment in a vehicle that takes power from the engine to the wheels: a car with four-wheel drive
• OUTSIDE A HOUSE **3** [C] a wide path or short road that leads to the door of a house: We keep our car on the drive.

- ROAD **4** [C] a street, usually where people live: *They live at 23 Woodlands Drive.*
- EFFORT **5** [C] a big effort by a group of people in order to achieve sth: *The company is launching a big sales drive.* ⊃ note at **campaign**[1]
- ENERGY **6** [U] a strong desire to do things and achieve sth; great energy: *You need lots of drive to run your own company.*
- DESIRE **7** [C, U] a strong natural need or desire: *a strong sex drive*
- IN SPORT **8** [C] a long hard hit or kick: *This player has the longest drive in golf.*
- IN COMPUTING **9** [C] the part of a computer that reads and stores information: *a 300 GB hard drive* ⊃ look at **disk drive**

'drive-by *adj.* [only before noun] (used about a shooting) done from a moving car: *drive-by killings*

'drive-in *noun* [C] (*AmE*) a place where you can eat, watch a film, etc. in your car

driven[1] /'drɪvn/ past participle of **drive**[1]

driven[2] /'drɪvn/ *adj.* **1** determined to succeed, and working very hard to do so **2** -driven /drɪvn/ (in adjectives) influenced or caused by a particular thing: *a market-driven economy*

driver 🔊 **A1** /'draɪvə(r)/ *noun* [C] a person who drives a vehicle: *a bus/train driver* ◇ *a good/careful driver*

driverless /'draɪvələs/ (*also* self-driving) *adj.* (used about a vehicle) that has the technology to drive itself without a person in control

'driver's license (*AmE*) = DRIVING LICENCE

'drive-through *noun* [C] (*AmE*) a restaurant, bank, etc. where you can be served without getting out of your car

driving[1] 🔊 **A2** /'draɪvɪŋ/ *noun* [U] the action or skill of controlling a car, etc: *She was arrested for dangerous driving.* ◇ *Joe's having **driving lessons**.* ◇ *She works as a **driving instructor**.* ◇ *a **driving school**
IDM be in the driving seat → SEAT[1]

driving[2] 🔊+ **C1** /'draɪvɪŋ/ *adj.* very strong: *driving rain* ◇ *driving ambition* ◇ *Who's the **driving force** behind this plan?*

'driving licence (*BrE*) (*AmE* **'driver's license**) *noun* [C] an official document that shows that you are qualified to drive

'driving test *noun* [C] a test that you must pass before you are qualified to drive a car, etc: *Did you pass your driving test first time?*

drizzle /'drɪzl/ *noun* [U] light rain with very small drops ▶ **drizzle** *verb* [I] ⊃ note at **weather**[1]

drone[1] /drəʊn/ *verb* [I] to make a continuous low sound: *the sound of the tractors droning away in the fields*
PHR V **drone on** to talk in a flat or boring voice: *We had to listen to the chairman drone on about sales for hours.*

drone[2] /drəʊn/ *noun* [C] **1** [usually sing.] a continuous low noise: *the distant drone of traffic* **2** [usually sing.] (MUSIC) a continuous low sound made by some musical instruments, for example the BAGPIPES, over which other notes are played or sung; the part of the instrument that makes this noise **3** an aircraft without a pilot, controlled from the ground, used for taking photos, delivering goods, etc: *aerial/surveillance drones*

drool /druːl/ *verb* [I] **1** to let SALIVA (= liquid) come out from the mouth, usually at the sight or smell of sth good to eat **2** ~ **(over sb/sth)** to show in a silly or EXAGGERATED way that you want sth or admire sb/sth very much: *teenagers drooling over photos of their favourite pop stars*

237

dropper D

droop /druːp/ *verb* [I] to bend or hang downwards, especially because of weakness or because you are tired: *The flowers were drooping without water.*
▶ **drooping** *adj.*: *a drooping moustache*

drop[1] 🔊 **A2** /drɒp/ *verb* (-pp-) **1** [T] to let sth fall: *That vase was very expensive. Whatever you do, don't drop it!* **2** [I] to fall: *The parachutist dropped safely to the ground.* ◇ *At the end of the race she dropped to her knees exhausted.* **3** [I, T] to become lower; to make sth lower: *The temperature will drop to minus 3 overnight.* ◇ *They ought to drop their prices.* ◇ *to drop your voice* (= speak more quietly) ⊃ note at **fall**[1], **trend**[1] **4** [T] ~ **sb/ sth (off)** to stop your car, etc. so that sb can get out; to deliver or leave sth in a particular place, especially on the way to somewhere else: *Drop me off at the traffic lights, please.* ◇ *I'll drop the parcel at your house.* **5** [T] ~ **sb/sth (from sth)** to no longer include sb/sth in sth: *Joe has been dropped from the team.* **6** [T] to stop doing sth: *I'm going to drop geography next term* (= stop studying it).
IDM **drop dead** (*informal*) to die suddenly **drop sb a line** (*informal*) to write an email or a letter to sb
PHR V **drop back | drop behind (sb)** to move into a position behind sb else, because you are moving more slowly: *Towards the end of the race she dropped behind the other runners.* **drop by | drop in (on sb)** to go to sb's house on an informal visit or without having told them you were coming **drop off** (*informal*) to fall into a light sleep: *I dropped off in front of the TV.* **drop out (of sth)** to leave or stop doing sth before you have finished: *His injury forced him to drop out of the competition.*

drop[2] 🔊 **B1** /drɒp/ *noun* **1** [C] a very small amount of liquid that forms a round shape: *a drop of blood/rain* **2** [C, usually sing.] a small amount of liquid: *I just have a drop of milk in my coffee.* **3** [sing.] ~ **(in sth)** a fall to a smaller amount or level: *The job is much more interesting but it will mean a drop in salary.* ◇ *a drop in prices/temperature* **4** [C, usually sing.] a distance down from a high point to a lower point: *a sheer drop of 40 metres to the sea* **5** drops [pl.] (MEDICINE) liquid medicine that you put into your eyes, ears or nose: *The doctor prescribed me drops to take twice a day.*
IDM **at the drop of a hat** immediately; without having to stop and think about it **a drop in the ocean** (*AmE*) | **a drop in the bucket** an amount of sth that is too small or unimportant to make any real difference to a situation

,drop-'dead *adv.* (*informal*) used before an adjective to emphasize how attractive sb/sth is: *She's drop-dead gorgeous.*

,drop-down 'menu *noun* [C] (COMPUTING) a list of choices that appears on a computer screen and stays there until you choose one of the functions on it

droplet /'drɒplət/ *noun* [C] a small amount of a liquid that forms a round shape

'drop-off *noun* [C] **1** ~ **(in sth)** a reduction or fall: *There has been a 50% drop-off in bookings.* **2** a place where vehicles can stop to deliver sth or for sb to get out; the action of doing this: *She got out of the taxi at one of the airport **drop-off points***

dropout /'drɒpaʊt/ *noun* [C] **1** (EDUCATION) a person who leaves school, university, etc. before finishing their studies **2** (SOCIAL STUDIES) a person who does not accept the ideas and ways of behaving of the rest of society

dropper /'drɒpə(r)/ *noun* [C] (SCIENCE) a short glass tube that has a rubber end with air in it. A dropper is used for measuring drops of liquids, especially medicines. ⊃ picture at **laboratory**

droppings /'drɒpɪŋz/ *noun* [pl.] waste material from the bodies of small animals or birds

drought ₤+ **B2** /draʊt/ *noun* [C, U] a long period without rain

drove /drəʊv/ past tense of **drive¹**

drown ₤+ **C1** /draʊn/ *verb* **1** [I, T] to die in water because it is not breathing; to make sb die in this way: *The girl fell into the river and drowned.* ◊ *20 people were drowned in the floods.* **2** [T] to make sth very wet; to completely cover sth in water or another liquid **3** [T] ~**sb/sth (out)** (used about a sound) to be so loud that you cannot hear sb/sth else: *His answer was drowned out by the music.*

drowse /draʊz/ *verb* [I] to be in a light sleep or to be almost asleep

drowsy /'draʊzi/ *adj.* (**drowsier**; **drowsiest**) tired and almost asleep **SYN** **sleepy** ▶ **drowsily** /-zɪli/ *adv.* ▶ **drowsiness** *noun* [U]

drudgery /'drʌdʒəri/ *noun* [U] hard and boring work

drug¹ ₤ **A2** /drʌg/ *noun* [C] **1** a chemical that people use to give them pleasant or exciting feelings. It is illegal in many countries to use drugs: *He doesn't drink or take drugs.* ◊ *She suspected her son was on drugs.* ◊ *hard drugs* such as heroin and cocaine ◊ *soft drugs* ◊ *a drug dealer* **2** (**MEDICINE**) a chemical that is used as a medicine: *drug companies* ◊ *Some drugs can only be obtained with a prescription from a doctor.*

drug² /drʌg/ *verb* [T] (**-gg-**) **1** to give a person or an animal a chemical to make them or it go to sleep or become unconscious: *The lion was drugged before the start of the journey.* **2** to put a drug into food or drink: *I think his drink was drugged.*

drugstore /'drʌgstɔ:(r)/ *noun* [C] (*AmE*) = CHEMIST

drum¹ ₤ **B1** /drʌm/ *noun* [C] **1** (**MUSIC**) a musical instrument like an empty container with plastic or skin stretched across the ends. You play a drum by hitting it with your hands or with sticks: *She plays drums in a band.* ◊ *Tony Cox on drums* ⊃ picture at **instrument, orchestra** **2** a round container: *an oil drum*

drum² /drʌm/ *verb* (**-mm-**) **1** [I] (**MUSIC**) to play a drum **2** [I, T] to make a noise like a drum by hitting sth many times: *to drum your fingers on the table* (= because you are annoyed, impatient, etc.) **PHRV** **drum sth into sb** to make sb remember sth by repeating it many times **drum sth up** to try to get support or business: *to drum up more custom*

drum and 'bass (*also* **drum 'n' bass**) *noun* [U] (**MUSIC**) a type of electronic dance music with a fast drum beat and a strong slower BASS beat

drumlin /'drʌmlɪn/ *noun* [C] (**GEOGRAPHY**) a very small hill formed by the movement of a GLACIER (= a large moving mass of ice)

drummer /'drʌmə(r)/ *noun* [C] (**MUSIC**) a person who plays a drum or drums

drumstick /'drʌmstɪk/ *noun* [C] **1** (**MUSIC**) a stick used for playing the drums **2** the lower leg of a chicken or similar bird that we cook and eat

drunk¹ ₤ **B1** /drʌŋk/ *adj.* [not before noun] having drunk too much alcohol: *to get drunk* **OPP** **sober¹** ▶ **drunk** (*also old-fashioned* **drunkard** /'drʌŋkəd/) *noun* [C]: *There were two drunks asleep under the bridge.*

drunk² /drʌŋk/ past participle of **drink¹**

drunk 'driver = DRINK-DRIVER

drunk 'driving (*also* **drunken 'driving**) (*both especially AmE*) = DRINK-DRIVING

drunken /'drʌŋkən/ *adj.* [only before noun] **1** having drunk too much alcohol **2** showing the effects of too much alcohol: *drunken singing* ▶ **drunkenly** *adv.* ▶ **drunkenness** *noun* [U]

dry¹ ₤ **A2** /draɪ/ *adj.* (**drier**; **driest**)
• NOT WET **1** without liquid in it or on it; not wet: *The washing isn't dry yet.* ◊ *The paint is dry now.* ◊ *Rub your hair dry with a towel.* **OPP** **wet¹**
• WITHOUT RAIN **2** having little or no rain: *a hot, dry summer* ◊ *a dry climate* **OPP** **wet¹**
• HAIR/SKIN **3** (used about hair or skin) not having enough natural oil
• ALCOHOL **4** (used about wine) not sweet **5** without alcohol; where no alcohol is allowed: *a dry country/state*
• HUMOUR **6** (used about what sb says, or sb's way of speaking) funny, although it sounds serious: *a dry sense of humour*
• BORING **7** not interesting: *dry legal documents* ▶ **dryness** *noun* [U]
IDM **be left high and dry** → HIGH¹

dry² ₤ **A2** /draɪ/ *verb* [I, T] (**drying**; **dries**; *pt, pp* **dried**) to become dry; to make sth dry: *I hung my shirt in the sun to dry.* ◊ *to dry your hands on a towel* **PHRV** **dry (sth) out** to become or make sth become completely dry: *Don't allow the soil to dry out.* **dry up 1** (used about a river, etc.) to have no more water in it **2** to stop being available: *Because of the recession a lot of building work has dried up.* **3** to forget what you were going to say, for example because you are very nervous **dry (sth) up** to dry plates, knives, forks, etc. with a small piece of cloth after they have been washed

dry cell

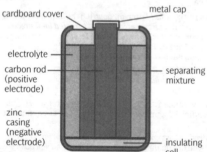

cardboard cover

metal cap

electrolyte

carbon rod (positive electrode)

separating mixture

zinc casing (negative electrode)

insulating cell

,dry 'cell *noun* [C] (**PHYSICS**) an electric cell in which the ELECTROLYTE (= a liquid that an electric current can pass through) is ABSORBED in a thick or solid substance inside its container

,dry-'clean *verb* [T] to clean clothes using special chemicals, without using water

,dry-'cleaner's (*also* **cleaner's** /'kli:nəz/) *noun* [C] a shop where you take your clothes to be cleaned

dryer (*also* **drier**) /'draɪə(r)/ *noun* [C] (often in compounds) a machine that you use for drying sth: *a hairdryer*

,dry 'land *noun* [U] land, not the sea: *I was glad to be back on dry land again.*

dryland farming /'draɪlənd fɑ:mɪŋ/ (*also* **dry farming**) *noun* [U] (**AGRICULTURE**) a method of farming in areas where there is very little rain, that involves growing crops that do not need much water

dryly /'draɪli/ = DRILY

DST /,di: es 'ti:/ *abbr.* = DAYLIGHT SAVING TIME

dual ₤+ **C1** /'dju:əl/ *adj.* [only before noun] having two parts; double: *to have dual nationality*

dual 'carriageway (*BrE*) (*AmE* **divided highway**) *noun* [C] a wide road that has an area of grass or a fence in the middle to separate the traffic going in one direction from the traffic going in the other direction

duality /dju:ˈæləti/ *noun* [U, C] (*pl.* -ies) (*formal*) the state of having two parts or aspects

dub ʒ+ **C1** /dʌb/ *verb* [T] (-bb-) **1** to give sb/sth a new or funny name: *Margaret Thatcher was dubbed 'the Iron Lady'.* **2** ~ **sth (into sth)** to change the sound in a film so that what the actors said originally is spoken by actors using a different language: *I don't like foreign films when they're dubbed into English. I prefer subtitles.* ⊃ look at **subtitle** 3 (**MUSIC**) to make a piece of music by mixing different pieces of recorded music together

dubious /ˈdju:biəs/ *adj.* **1** ~ **(about sth/doing sth)** not sure or certain: *I'm very dubious about whether we're doing the right thing.* **SYN** **doubtful** **2** that may not be honest or safe: *dubious financial dealings* **SYN** **suspicious** ▸ **dubiously** *adv.*

duchess /ˈdʌtʃəs/ (*also* **Duchess**) *noun* [C] a woman who has the same position as a DUKE, or who is the wife of a DUKE

duck[1] /dʌk/ *noun* (*pl.* **ducks**, **duck**) **1** [C, U] a common bird that lives on or near water; the meat of this bird. Ducks have short legs, WEBBED feet (= with pieces of skin between the toes) for swimming and a wide BEAK (= the hard pointed part of a bird's mouth). ⊃ picture at **animal** **2** [C] a female duck ❶ A male duck is called a **drake**. However, duck is often used for both males and females. A young duck is called a **duckling**. The sound a duck makes is a **quack**.

duck[2] /dʌk/ *verb* **1** [I, T] to move your head down quickly so that you are not seen or hit by sb/sth: *The boys ducked out of sight behind a hedge.* ◇ *I had to duck my head down to avoid the low doorway.* **2** [I, T] ~ **(out of) sth** (*informal*) to try to avoid sth difficult or unpleasant: *She tried to duck out of apologizing.* ◇ *The president is trying to duck responsibility for the crisis.* **3** [T] to push sb's head under water for a short time, especially when playing: *The kids were ducking each other in the pool.*

duckling /ˈdʌklɪŋ/ *noun* [C, U] a young DUCK (= a bird that lives on or near water); the meat of a young DUCK

duct /dʌkt/ *noun* [C] (**ANATOMY**) a tube that carries liquid, gas, etc: *They got into the building through the air duct.* ◇ *tear ducts* (= in the eye) ◇ *sweat ducts* ⊃ picture at **skin**[1]

ductile /ˈdʌktaɪl/ *adj.* (**PHYSICS**) (used about a metal) that can be made into a thin wire

dud /dʌd/ *noun* [C] (*informal*) a thing that cannot be used because it is not real or does not work correctly

dude /du:d/ *noun* [C] (*especially AmE, informal*) a man

due[1] **B1** **ⓦ** /dju:/ *adj.*
- EXPECTED **1** [not before noun] ~ **(to do sth)**; ~ **(for sth)** expected or planned to happen or arrive: *The conference is due to start in four weeks' time.* ◇ *What time is the next train due (in)?* ◇ *The baby is due in May.* ◇ *The album is due for release next month.*
- OWED **2** [not before noun] having to be paid: *Payment is due on 15 October.* **3** ~ **(to sb)** that is owed to you because it is your right to have it: *Make sure you claim all the benefits that are due to you.* **4** ~ **for sth** expecting sth or having the right to sth: *I think that I'm due for a pay rise.*
- CAUSED BY **5** ~ **to sb/sth** caused by or because of sb/sth: *His illness is probably due to stress.*
IDM **in due course** at some time in the future, quite soon: *All applicants will be informed of our decision in due course.*

due[2] /dju:/ *adv.* (used before *north, south, east* and *west*) exactly: *The plane was flying due east.*

due[3] /dju:/ *noun*
IDM **give sb his/her due** to be fair to a person: *She doesn't work very quickly, but to give Sarah her due, she is very accurate.*

due diligence /ˌdju: ˈdɪlɪdʒəns/ *noun* [U] **1** (**LAW**) actions taken by a person or an organization to avoid breaking the law: *These companies failed to exercise due diligence by not checking the applicants' right to work.* **2** (**BUSINESS**) a careful investigation of a business by a person or an organization that is thinking of buying it or employing it: *He conducted due diligence on the company before buying it.*

duel /ˈdju:əl/ *noun* [C] (**HISTORY**) a formal type of fight with guns or other weapons that was used in the past to decide an argument between two men

duet /dju'et/ (*also* **duo**) *noun* [C] (**MUSIC**) a piece of music for two people to sing or play ⊃ look at **solo**[2]

duffel bag /ˈdʌfl bæg/ (*AmE*) = HOLDALL

dug /dʌg/ past tense, past participle of **dig**[1]

dugout /ˈdʌgaʊt/ *noun* [C] **1** a rough shelter made by digging a hole in the ground and covering it, used by soldiers **2** (**SPORT**) a shelter by the side of a football or baseball field where a team's manager, etc. can sit and watch the game

duke /dju:k/ (*also* **Duke**) *noun* [C] a NOBLEMAN of the highest rank ⊃ look at **duchess**

dull[1] ʒ+ **B2** /dʌl/ *adj.* **1** not interesting or exciting; boring: *Miss Potter's lessons are always so dull.* **2** not bright: *a dull and cloudy day* **3** not loud, sharp or strong: *Her head hit the floor with a dull thud.* ◇ *a dull pain* **OPP** **sharp**[1] ▸ **dullness** *noun* [U] ▸ **dully** /ˈdʌlli/ *adv.*

dull[2] /dʌl/ *verb* [I, T] (used about pain or an emotion) to become less strong; to make a pain or an emotion less strong: *The tablets they gave him dulled the pain for a while.*

duly /ˈdju:li/ *adv.* (*formal*) in the correct or expected way: *We all duly assembled at 7.30 as agreed.*

dumb ʒ+ **C1** /dʌm/ *adj.* **1** (*especially AmE, informal*) stupid: *What a dumb thing to do!* **2** not able to speak: *to be deaf and dumb* ◇ (*figurative*) *They were struck dumb with amazement.* ❶ Some people find this word offensive. ▸ **dumbly** *adv.*: *Ken did all the talking, and I just nodded dumbly.*

dumbfounded /dʌmˈfaʊndɪd/ *adj.* very surprised

dummy /ˈdʌmi/ *noun* [C] (*pl.* -ies) **1** a model of the human body used for putting clothes on in a shop window or while you are making clothes: *a tailor's dummy* **2** (*especially AmE, informal*) a stupid person **3** (*BrE*) (*AmE* **pacifier**) a rubber or plastic object that you put in a baby's mouth to keep them quiet and happy **4** something that is made to look like sth else but that is not the real thing: *The guns the robbers used in the raid were all dummies.*

dump[1] ʒ+ **B2** /dʌmp/ *verb* [T] **1** to get rid of sth that you do not want, especially in a place that is not suitable: *Nuclear waste should not be dumped in the sea.* ◇ (*figurative*) *I wish you wouldn't keep dumping the extra work on me.* **2** (*informal*) to put sth down quickly or in a careless way: *The children dumped their bags in the hall and ran off to play.* **3** (*informal*) to end a relationship with sb, especially a boyfriend or girlfriend: *Did you hear that Laura dumped Chris last night?*

dump[2] /dʌmp/ *noun* [C] **1** a place where rubbish or waste material from factories, etc. is left: *a rubbish dump* **SYN** **tip**[1] **2** (*informal*) a place that is very dirty, untidy or unpleasant: *The flat is cheap but it's a real dump.* **SYN** **tip¹**

IDM **down in the dumps** (*informal*) unhappy or sad

'dumper truck (*BrE*) (*AmE* **'dump truck**) *noun* [C] a lorry that carries material such as stones or earth in a special container that can be lifted up so that the load can fall out

dumpling /'dʌmplɪŋ/ *noun* [C] a small ball of DOUGH (= a mixture of flour, fat and water) that is cooked and served with meat dishes or in soup

dune /djuːn/ (*also* **sand dune**) *noun* [C] (**GEOGRAPHY**) a low hill of sand by the sea or in the desert

dung /dʌŋ/ *noun* [U] waste material from the bodies of large animals: *cow dung*

dungarees /ˌdʌŋɡəˈriːz/ (*BrE*) (*AmE* **overalls** /ˈəʊvərɔːlz/) *noun* [pl.] a piece of clothing, similar to trousers, but covering the chest as well as the legs and with narrow pieces of cloth that go over the shoulders: *a pair of dungarees*

dungeon /'dʌndʒən/ *noun* [C] an old underground room used as a prison, especially in a castle

duo /'djuːəʊ/ *noun* [C] (*pl.* -os) (**MUSIC**) **1** two people who perform together **2** = **DUET**

duodenum /ˌdjuːəˈdiːnəm/ *noun* [C] (**ANATOMY**) the first part of the small INTESTINE (= the tube that carries food from the stomach), next to the stomach ⊃ picture at **body**, **digestive system**

dupe /djuːp/ *verb* [T] ~ **sb (into doing sth)** to lie to sb in order to make them believe sth or do sth: *The woman was duped into carrying the drugs.*

duplex /'djuːpleks/ *noun* [C] (**ARCHITECTURE**) **1** (*AmE*) a building divided into two separate homes **2** (*BrE*) a flat with rooms on two floors

duplicate¹ /'djuːplɪkeɪt/ *verb* [T] **1** to make an exact copy of sth **2** to do sth that has already been done: *We don't want to duplicate the work of other departments.* ▶ **duplication** /ˌdjuːplɪˈkeɪʃn/ *noun* [U, C]

duplicate² /'djuːplɪkət/ *noun* [C] something that is exactly the same as sth else ▶ **duplicate** *adj.* [only before noun]: *a duplicate key*

IDM **in duplicate** with two copies (for example of an official piece of paper) that are exactly the same: *The contract must be in duplicate.* ⊃ look at **in triplicate** at **triplicate**

durable /'djʊərəbl/ *adj.* likely to last for a long time without breaking or getting weaker: *a durable fabric* ▶ **durability** /ˌdjʊərəˈbɪləti/ *noun* [U]

duration /dju'reɪʃn/ *noun* [U] (*formal*) the time that sth lasts: *Please remain seated for the duration of the flight.*

duress /dju'res/ *noun* [U] (*formal*) threats or force that are used to make sb do sth: *He signed the confession under duress.*

during /'djʊərɪŋ/ *prep.* all through or within the period of time mentioned: *During the summer holidays we went swimming every day.* ◇ *Grandpa was taken very ill during the night.*

dusk /dʌsk/ *noun* [U] the time in the evening when the sun has already gone down and it is nearly dark ⊃ look at **dawn¹** (1), **twilight**

dust¹ /dʌst/ *noun* [U] **1** very small pieces of dry dirt, sand, etc. in the form of a powder: *chalk/coal dust* ◇ *The tractor came up the track in a cloud of dust.* **2** very small pieces of dirt in the form of a powder in buildings, on furniture, floors, etc: *There was a thick layer of dust on the table.* ◇ *There wasn't a speck of*

dust (= any dust) *anywhere in the room.* ▶ **dusty** *adj.* (**dustier**; **dustiest**): *This shelf has got very dusty.*

dust² /dʌst/ *verb* [I, T] to clean a room, furniture, etc. by removing dust with a cloth: *Let me dust those shelves before you put the books on them.* ⊃ note at **clean¹**

dustbin /'dʌstbɪn/ (*BrE*) (*AmE* **garbage can**) *noun* [C] a large container for rubbish that you keep outside your house

'dust bowl *noun* [C] (**GEOGRAPHY**) an area of land that has become desert because there has been too little rain or too much farming

duster /'dʌstə(r)/ *noun* [C] a soft dry cloth that you use for removing dust from furniture

dustman /'dʌstmən/ *noun* [C] (*pl.* -**men** /-mən/) (*BrE*) a person whose job is to take away the rubbish that people put outside their houses

dustpan /'dʌstpæn/ *noun* [C] a flat container with a handle into which you brush dirt from the floor: *Where do you keep your dustpan and brush?*

Dutch /dʌtʃ/ *adj.* from the Netherlands

dutiful /'djuːtɪfl/ *adj.* willing to respect and obey sb: *a dutiful son* ▶ **dutifully** /-fəli/ *adv.*

duty /'djuːti/ *noun* [C, U] (*pl.* -**ies**) **1** ~ **(to do sth)** something that you have to do because people expect you to do it or because you think it is right: *A soldier must do his duty.* ◇ *It's your duty to look after your parents when they get older.* ◇ *a sense of moral duty* **2** the tasks that you do when you are at work: *the duties of a policeman* ◇ *Which nurses are on night duty this week?* **3** ~ **(on sth)** (**ECONOMICS**) a tax that you pay, especially on goods that you bring into a country

IDM **on/off duty** (used about doctors, nurses, police officers, etc.) to be working/not working: *The porter's on duty from eight till four.* ◇ *What time does she go off duty?*

duty-'free *adj., adv.* (**TOURISM**) (used about goods) that you can bring into a country without paying tax: *an airport duty-free shop* ◇ *How much wine can you bring into Britain duty-free?* ⊃ look at **tax-free**

duty of 'care *noun* [sing.] ~ **(to sb) (to do sth)** (*especially BrE*) (**LAW**) a legal obligation to protect other people from physical or mental danger: *Employers have a duty of care to workers to keep the workplace safe.*

'duty officer *noun* [C] the officer, for example in the police, army, etc., who is on duty at a particular time in a particular place

duvet /'duːveɪ/ *noun* [C] a thick cover filled with feathers or another soft material that you sleep under to keep warm in bed ⊃ look at **quilt**

DVD /ˌdiː viː 'diː/ *noun* [C] (**COMPUTING**) a disk on which large amounts of information, especially films, photos and video, can be stored, for use in a computer or DVD PLAYER (the abbreviation for 'digital videodisc' or 'digital versatile disc'): *a DVD-ROM drive*

DV'D player *noun* [C] a piece of equipment that you use for playing DVDs

DVT /ˌdiː viː 'tiː/ = **DEEP VEIN THROMBOSIS**

dwarf¹ /dwɔːf/ *noun* [C] (*pl.* **dwarfs, dwarves** /dwɔːvz/) **1** (in stories) a very small person with magic powers **2** an extremely small person who will never grow to a normal size because of a physical problem ❶ Some people find this word offensive.

dwarf² /dwɔːf/ *adj.* [only before noun] (used about a plant or an animal) much smaller than the normal size: *dwarf conifers*

dwarf³ /dwɔːf/ *verb* [T] (used about a large object) to make sth seem very small in comparison: *The skyscraper dwarfs all the other buildings around.*

dwarf ˈplanet *noun* [C] (**ASTRONOMY**) a round object in space that moves around the sun but is not as large as a planet ⊃ note at **Pluto**

dwell /dwel/ *verb* [I] (*pt, pp* **dwelt** /dwelt/, **dwelled**) (*old-fashioned, formal*) to live or stay in a place
PHR V **dwell on/upon sth** to think or talk a lot about sth that it would be better to forget: *I don't want to dwell on the past. Let's think about the future.*

dweller /ˈdwelə(r)/ *noun* [C] (especially in compounds) a person or an animal that lives in the place mentioned: *city-dwellers*

dwelling /ˈdwelɪŋ/ *noun* [C] (*formal*) a house, flat, etc. where a person lives

dwindle /ˈdwɪndl/ *verb* [I] ~ (**away**) to become smaller or weaker: *Their savings dwindled away to nothing.*

dye¹ /daɪ/ *verb* [T] (**dyeing**; **dyes**; *pt, pp* **dyed**) to make sth a different colour, especially by using a special liquid or substance: *Does she dye her hair?* ◇ *I'm going to dye this blouse black.*

dye² /daɪ/ *noun* [C, U] a substance that is used to change the colour of sth

dying /ˈdaɪɪŋ/ *adj.* [only before noun] connected with or happening at the time of sb's death: *her dying wishes/words* ⊃ look at **die¹**

dyke (*also* **dike**) /daɪk/ *noun* [C] **1** a long thick wall that is built to prevent the sea or a river from flooding low land **2** (*especially BrE*) a long narrow space dug in the ground and used for taking water away from land

dynamic¹ ⫫+ **B2** ⓦ /daɪˈnæmɪk/ *adj.* **1** (used about a person) full of energy and ideas; active **2** (**PHYSICS**) (used about a force or power) that causes movement **OPP** **static¹**

dynamic² ⫫+ **C1** ⓦ /daɪˈnæmɪk/ *noun* **1** dynamics [pl.] the way in which people or things behave and react to each other in a particular situation **2** dynamics [U] (**PHYSICS**) the scientific study of the forces involved in movement: *fluid dynamics* **3** [sing.] (*formal*) a force that produces change, action or effects **4** dynamics [pl.] (**MUSIC**) changes in volume in music

dynamism /ˈdaɪnəmɪzəm/ *noun* [U] energy and enthusiasm to make new things happen or to make things succeed: *The freshness and dynamism of her approach was welcomed by all her students.*

dynamite /ˈdaɪnəmaɪt/ *noun* [U] **1** a powerful substance that can explode **2** a thing or person that causes great excitement, shock, etc: *His news was dynamite.*

dynamo /ˈdaɪnəməʊ/ *noun* [C] (*pl.* **-os**) (**ENGINEERING**, **PHYSICS**) a device that changes energy from the movement of sth such as wind or water into electricity

dynasty /ˈdɪnəsti/ *noun* [C] (*pl.* **-ies**) a series of RULERS who are from the same family: *the Ming dynasty in China*

dysentery /ˈdɪsəntri/ *noun* [U] (**HEALTH**) a serious disease that causes you to have severe DIARRHOEA with loss of blood

dysfunctional /dɪsˈfʌŋkʃənl/ *adj.* (*formal*) not working normally or correctly: *children from dysfunctional families*

dyslexia /dɪsˈleksiə/ *noun* [U] (**PSYCHOLOGY**) a brain condition that causes difficulty with reading and spelling ▸ **dyslexic** /-sɪk/ *noun* [C], *adj.*

dysmorphia /dɪsˈmɔːfiə/ *noun* [U] (**HEALTH**) a medical condition in which part of sb's body is the wrong size or shape

dyspraxia /dɪsˈpræksiə/ *noun* [U] (**HEALTH**) a brain condition that develops in childhood, causing difficulties with physical movement and activities such as writing

---

dysprosium /dɪsˈprəʊziəm/ *noun* [U] (*symb.* Dy) (**CHEMISTRY**) a chemical element. Dysprosium is a soft silver-white metal used in nuclear research. ❶ For more information on the periodic table of elements, look at the **Reference Section** of this dictionary.

E e

E¹ /iː/ *noun* [C, U] (*pl.* **E's**) **1** (*also* **e**, *pl.* **e's**) the fifth letter of the English alphabet: *'Egg' begins with (an) 'E'.* **2** (**MUSIC**) the third note in the SCALE of C MAJOR **3** ~ (**in/for sth**) (**EDUCATION**) a grade given for an exam or a piece of work that shows that it is very bad: *He got an E in French.*

E² *abbr.* (in writing) = EAST¹ (1), EASTERN (1): *E Asia*

e- /iː/ *prefix* (**COMPUTING**) (in verbs and nouns) connected with the use of electronic communication, especially the internet, for sending information, doing business, etc: *e-business/e-commerce* ⊃ look at **email**

each ⫫ **A1** /iːtʃ/ *det., pron., adv.* used to refer to every individual person or thing: *Each lesson lasts an hour.* ◇ *Each of the lessons lasts an hour.* ◇ *The lessons each last an hour.* ◇ *These T-shirts are £5 each.*

each ˈother *pron.* used for saying that A does the same thing to B as B does to A: *Emma and Dave love each other very much* (= Emma loves Dave and Dave loves Emma). ◇ *We looked at each other.*

eager ⫫+ **C1** /ˈiːgə(r)/ *adj.* ~ (**to do sth**); ~ (**for sth**) full of desire or interest: *We're all eager to start work on the new project.* ◇ *eager for success* **SYN** **keen** ▸ **eagerly** *adv.* ▸ **eagerness** *noun* [U]

eagle /ˈiːgl/ *noun* [C] a very large bird that can see very well. Eagles eat small birds and animals. ⊃ picture at **animal** ❶ An eagle is a type of **bird of prey**.

EAL /ˌiː eɪ ˈel/ *abbr.* (**EDUCATION**) **English as an Additional Language** (used in the UK and Ireland to refer to the teaching of English in schools to children whose first language is not English)

EAP /ˌiː eɪ ˈpiː/ *abbr.* (**EDUCATION**) **English for Academic Purposes** (teaching English to people who are using English for study, but whose first language is not English)

the ear

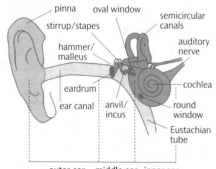

pinna, oval window, semicircular canals, stirrup/stapes, auditory nerve, hammer/malleus, eardrum, cochlea, ear canal, anvil/incus, round window, Eustachian tube

outer ear, middle ear, inner ear

ear ⫫ **A1** /ɪə(r)/ *noun* **1** [C] (**ANATOMY**) one of the two parts of the body of a person or animal that are used for hearing: *Elephants have large ears.* ◇ *He pulled his* hat down over his ears. **2** [sing.] **an ~ (for sth)** an ability to recognize and repeat sounds, especially in music or language: *Yuka has a good ear for languages.* **3** [C] (**AGRICULTURE**) the top part of a plant that produces grain: *an ear of corn* ⊃ picture at **cereal**

IDM **sb's ears are burning** used when a person thinks that other people are talking about them, especially in an unkind way **go in one ear and out the other** (*informal*) (used about information, etc.) to be forgotten quickly: *Everything I tell him seems to go in one ear and out the other.* **play (sth) by ear** (**MUSIC**) to play a piece of music that you have heard without using written notes **play it by ear** (*informal*) to decide what to do as things happen, instead of planning in advance: *We don't know what Alan's reaction will be, so we'll just have to play it by ear.* **prick up your ears** → **PRICK¹**

earache /ˈɪəreɪk/ *noun* [U, C] a pain in the ear: *I've got earache.*

ear canal *noun* [C] (**ANATOMY**) the passage inside the body that carries sound from the outside of the ear to the **MIDDLE EAR** ⊃ picture at **ear**

eardrum /ˈɪədrʌm/ *noun* [C] (**ANATOMY**) a thin piece of skin inside the ear that is tightly stretched and that allows you to hear sound ⊃ picture at **ear**

earl /ɜːl/ *noun* [C] a British **NOBLEMAN** of a high rank

earlobe /ˈɪələʊb/ (*also* **lobe**) *noun* [C] (**ANATOMY**) the round soft part at the bottom of the ear

early¹ 🔒 **A1** ⊙ /ˈɜːli/ *adj.* (**earlier; earliest**) **1** near the beginning of a period of time, a piece of work, a series, etc: *I think John's in his early twenties.* ◇ *The project is still in its early stages.* **2** arriving, or done before the usual or expected time

IDM **it's early days (yet)** used to say that it is too soon to know how a situation will develop **the early/ small hours** very early in the morning in the hours after midnight **an early/a late night** → **NIGHT** **an early riser** a person who usually gets up early in the morning

early² 🔒 **A1** /ˈɜːli/ *adv.* (**earlier; earliest**) **1** near the beginning of a period of time, a piece of work, a series, etc: *I have to get up early on weekday mornings.* **2** before the usual, expected or planned time: *She arrived five minutes early for her interview.*

IDM **at the earliest** not before the date or time mentioned: *I can repair it by Friday at the earliest.* **early on** soon after the beginning: *He achieved fame early on in his career.*

earmark /ˈɪəmɑːk/ *verb* [T] **~ sb/sth (for sth/sb); be earmarked as sth** to decide that sth will happen to sb/ sth; to choose sb/sth for a particular purpose: *The shop has been earmarked for closure.* ◇ *Everybody says Elena has been earmarked as the next manager.*

earn 🔒 **A2** /ɜːn/ *verb* **1** [T, I] to get money by working: *How much does a dentist earn?* ◇ *I earn £20 000 a year.* ◇ *It's hard to* **earn a living** *as an artist.* ⊃ note at **pay²** **2** [T] to get money as profit or interest on money you lend, have in a bank, etc. **3** [T] to win the right to sth, for example by working hard: *The team's victory today has earned them a place in the final.*

earnest /ˈɜːnɪst/ *adj.* serious or determined: *He's such an earnest young man — he never makes a joke.* ◇ *They were having a very earnest discussion.* ▸ **earnestly** *adv.*

IDM **in earnest** **1** serious and sincere about what you are going to do: *He was in earnest about wanting to leave university.* **2** happening more seriously or with more force than before: *After two weeks work began in earnest on the project.*

earnings 🔒+ **C1** /ˈɜːnɪŋz/ *noun* [pl.] **1** the money that a person earns by working: *Average earnings have increased by 5%.* ⊃ note at **pay²** **2** the profit that a company makes: *the company's export earnings*

earphones /ˈɪəfəʊnz/ *noun* [pl.] a piece of equipment that fits over or in the ears and is used for listening to music, the radio, etc. ⊃ look at **headphones**

earring /ˈɪərɪŋ/ *noun* [C] a piece of jewellery that is worn in or on the lower part of the ear: *Do these earrings clip on or are they for pierced ears?*

earshot /ˈɪəʃɒt/ *noun*

IDM **(be) out of/within earshot** where a person cannot/can hear: *Wait until he's out of earshot before you say anything about him.*

the earth

the northern hemisphere

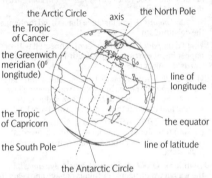

the Arctic Circle · axis · the North Pole
the Tropic of Cancer
the Greenwich meridian (0⁰ longitude)
line of longitude
the Tropic of Capricorn
the equator
the South Pole · line of latitude
the Antarctic Circle

the southern hemisphere

earth¹ 🔒 **A2** /ɜːθ/ *noun* **1** (*also* **Earth, the Earth**) [U, sing.] (**ASTRONOMY**) the world; the planet on which we live: *life on Earth* ◇ *The earth goes round the sun.* ⊃ look at **solar system** **2** [U, sing.] the surface of the world; land: *The spaceship fell towards earth.* ◇ *I could feel the earth shake when the earthquake started.* **3** [U] the substance that plants grow in: *The earth around here is very fertile.* **SYN** **soil¹** **4** [C, usually sing.] (*BrE*) (*AmE* **ground**) (**ENGINEERING**, **PHYSICS**) a wire that makes a piece of electrical equipment safer by connecting it to the ground ⊃ picture at **plug¹**

IDM **charge/pay the earth** (*informal*) to charge/pay a very large amount of money **cost the earth/a fortune** → **COST²** **how/why/where/who etc. on earth** (*informal*) used for emphasizing sth or expressing surprise: *Where on earth have you been?*

earth² /ɜːθ/ (*BrE*) (*AmE* **ground**) *verb* [T] (**ENGINEERING**, **PHYSICS**) to make a piece of electrical equipment safer by connecting it to the ground with a wire

earthenware /ˈɜːθənweə(r)/ *adj.* made of very hard baked **CLAY**: *an earthenware bowl* ▸ **earthenware** *noun* [U]

earthquake 🔒 **B1** /ˈɜːθkweɪk/ (*also informal* **quake**) *noun* [C] (**GEOLOGY**) a sudden, violent movement of the earth's surface: *Much of the town was destroyed in the earthquake.* ⊃ note at **disaster** ⊃ picture at **plate tectonics**

earth science *noun* [C, U] (**SCIENCE**) a science that involves studying the earth or part of it. Geography and **GEOLOGY** are earth sciences. ⊃ look at **life science, natural science**

earthworm /ˈɜːθwɜːm/ *noun* [C] a small, long, thin animal with no legs or eyes that lives in the soil

earwig /ˈɪəwɪɡ/ *noun* [C] a small brown insect with a long body and two PINCERS (= curved pointed parts that stick out) at the back end of its body

ease¹ ɬ+ **C1** /iːz/ *noun* [U] a lack of difficulty: *She answered the questions* ***with ease***. **OPP** **unease**
⊃ adjective **easy**
IDM **(be/feel) at (your) ease** to be/feel comfortable, relaxed, etc: *They were all so kind and friendly that I felt completely at ease.*

ease² ɬ+ **C1** /iːz/ *verb* **1** [I, T] to become less painful or serious; to make sth less painful or serious: *The pain should ease by this evening.* ◇ *This money will ease their financial problems a little.* ⊃ adjective **easy** **2** [T] to move sth slowly and gently: *He eased the key into the lock.*
IDM **ease sb's mind** to make sb feel less worried
PHR V **ease off/up** to become less strong or unpleasant: *Let's wait until the rain eases off.*

easel /ˈiːzl/ *noun* [C] (**ART**) a wooden frame that holds a picture while it is being painted

easily ɬ **A2** **S** /ˈiːzəli/ *adv.* **1** without difficulty: *I can easily ring up and check the time.* **2** ~ **the best, worst, nicest, etc.** without doubt: *It's easily his best novel.*

east¹ ɬ **A1** /iːst/ *noun* [U, sing.] (*abbr.* E) (**GEOGRAPHY**)
1 (*usually* the east) ~ **(of …)** the direction you look towards in order to see the sun rise; one of the points of the COMPASS (= the four main directions that we give names to): *Which way is east?* ◇ *a cold wind from the east* ◇ *Which county is* ***to the east*** *of Oxfordshire?* ⊃ look at **north¹** (1), **south¹** (1), **west¹** (1) ⊃ note at **compass** ⊃ picture at **compass 2** the east, the East the eastern part of a country, region or city: *Norwich is in the east of England.* **3** the East the countries of Asia, for example China, Japan and India ⊃ look at **Far East, Middle East**

east² ɬ **A1** /iːst/ *adj., adv.* (**GEOGRAPHY**) **1** in or towards the east: *They headed east.* ◇ *the East Coast of America* **2** ~ **(of …)** nearer to the east than sth: *We live east of the city.* **3** (used about a wind) coming from the east

eastbound /ˈiːstbaʊnd/ *adj.* travelling or leading towards the east: *The eastbound carriageway of the motorway is blocked.*

Easter /ˈiːstə(r)/ *noun* [U] (**RELIGION**) a festival on a Sunday in March or April when Christians celebrate Christ's return to life; the time before and after Easter Sunday: *the Easter holidays* ◇ *Are you going away* ***at Easter***?

Easter egg *noun* [C] an egg, usually made of chocolate, that you give as a present at Easter

easterly /ˈiːstəli/ *adj.* (**GEOGRAPHY**) **1** towards or in the east: *They travelled in an easterly direction.* **2** (used about winds) coming from the east: *cold easterly winds*

eastern ɬ **B1** /ˈiːstən/ (*also* Eastern) *adj.* **1** (*abbr.* E) (**GEOGRAPHY**) of, in or from the east of a place: *Eastern Scotland* ◇ *the eastern shore of the lake* **2** from or connected with the countries of the East: *Eastern cookery*

east-north-east *noun* [U] (*abbr.* ENE) (**GEOGRAPHY**) the direction that lies at an equal distance between east and north-east ▸ **east-north-east** *adv.*

east-south-east *noun* [U] (**GEOGRAPHY**) (*abbr.* ESE) the direction that lies at an equal distance between east and south-east ▸ **east-south-east** *adv.*

eastwards /ˈiːstwədz/ (*also* eastward /ˈiːstwəd/) *adv.* towards the east: *The Amazon flows eastwards.*
▸ **eastward** *adj.: to travel in an eastward direction*

east-west (*also* East-West) *adj.* (**GEOGRAPHY**) extending between or relating to the east and the west of a place: *The opening of London's new east-west railway has been delayed.* ◇ *East-west relations deteriorated in the years following the war.*

easy¹ ɬ **A1** /ˈiːzi/ *adj.* (easier; easiest) **1** ~ **(for sb) (to do sth)** not difficult: *an easy question* ◇ *It isn't easy to explain the system.* ◇ *The system isn't easy to explain.* ◇ *It's easy for you — you don't have to work with him.* **OPP** **hard¹ 2** comfortable, relaxed and not worried: *an easy life* ◇ *My mind's easier now.* ⊃ look at **uneasy** (1) ⊃ noun, verb **ease**
IDM **free and easy** → FREE¹ I'm easy (*informal*) used to say that you do not have a strong opinion when sb offers you a choice: *'Would you like to go first or second?' 'I'm easy.'*

easy² /ˈiːzi/ *adv.* (easier; easiest)
IDM **easier said than done** (*informal*) more difficult to do than to talk about: *'You should get her to help you.' 'That's easier said than done.'* **go easy on sb/ on/with sth** (*informal*) **1** to be gentle or less strict with sb: *Go easy on him; he's just a child.* **2** to avoid using too much of sth: *Go easy on the salt; it's bad for your heart.* **take it/things easy** (*informal*) to relax and not work too hard or worry too much

easy chair *noun* [C] a large comfortable chair with arms

easy-going *adj.* (used about a person) calm, relaxed and not easily worried or upset by what other people do **SYN** **laid-back**

eat ɬ **A1** /iːt/ *verb* (*pt* ate /et, eɪt/; *pp* eaten /ˈiːtn/) **1** [I, T] to put food into your mouth, then CHEW and SWALLOW it: *Who ate all the biscuits?* ◇ *I don't eat meat.* ◇ *Eat your dinner up, Joe* (= finish it all). ◇ *She doesn't eat properly. No wonder she's so thin.* **2** [I] to have a meal: *What time shall we eat?*
IDM **have sb eating out of your hand** to have control and power over sb **have your cake and eat it** → CAKE¹
PHR V **eat sth away/eat away at sth** to damage or destroy sth slowly over a period of time: *The sea had eaten away at the cliff.* **eat out** to have a meal in a restaurant

eater /ˈiːtə(r)/ *noun* [C] a person who eats in a particular way: *My uncle's a big eater* (= he eats a lot). ◇ *We're not great meat eaters in our family.*

eating disorder *noun* [C] (*abbr.* ED) (**PSYCHOLOGY**) an emotional DISORDER that causes eating habits that are not normal

eaves /iːvz/ *noun* [pl.] the edges of a roof that stick out over the walls

eavesdrop /ˈiːvzdrɒp/ *verb* [I] (-pp-) ~ **(on sb/sth)** to listen secretly to other people talking: *They caught her eavesdropping on their conversation.*

eBay™ /ˈiːbeɪ/ *noun* [U] a website on the internet where people can sell goods to other users of the website
▸ **eBay** *verb* [T]

ebb /eb/ *verb* [I] **1** (used about sea water) to flow away from the land, which happens twice a day **SYN** **go out 2** ~ **(away)** (used about a feeling, etc.) to become weaker: *The crowd's enthusiasm began to ebb away.*

the ebb *noun* [sing.] the time when sea water flows away from the land ⊃ look at **high tide ❶** The movement of sea water twice a day is called the **tide**.
IDM **the ebb and flow (of sth)** (used about a situation, noise, feeling, etc.) a regular increase and decrease in the progress or strength of sth

Ebola /iːˈbəʊlə/ *noun* [U] (**HEALTH**) a very serious disease, caused by a virus, that causes internal parts of the body to lose blood and usually ends in death

ebony /ˈebəni/ *noun* [U] a hard black wood from tropical trees

e-book *noun* [C] (**COMPUTING**, **LITERATURE**) a book that you can read on a computer screen or on an electronic device that you hold in your hand ⊃ look at **e-reader**

e-business = E-COMMERCE

eccentric /ɪkˈsentrɪk/ *adj.* (used about people or their behaviour) strange or unusual: *People said he was mad but I think he was just slightly eccentric.* ▸ **eccentric** *noun* [C]: *She's just an old eccentric.* ▸ **eccentricity** /ˌeksenˈtrɪsəti/ *noun* [C, U] (*pl.* -ies)

ecclesiastical /ɪˌkliːziˈæstɪkl/ *adj.* (**RELIGION**) connected with or belonging to the Christian Church: *ecclesiastical law*

ECG /ˌiː siː ˈdʒiː/ *noun* [C] (**MEDICINE**) a medical test that measures and records electrical activity of the heart (the abbreviation for 'electrocardiogram')

echo¹ ₹+ 🅲🅰 /ˈekəʊ/ *noun* [C] (*pl.* -oes) a sound that is repeated as it is sent back off a surface such as the wall of a tunnel: *I could hear the echo of footsteps somewhere in the distance.*

echo² ₹+ 🅲🅰 /ˈekəʊ/ *verb* **1** [I] (used about a sound) to be repeated; to come back as an ECHO: *Their footsteps echoed in the empty church.* **2** [I, T] ~ (**with/to sth**); ~ **sth** (**back**) to repeat or send back a sound; to be full of a particular sound: *The hall echoed with their laughter.* ◇ *The tunnel echoed back their calls.* **3** [T] to repeat what sb has said, done or thought: *The child echoed everything his mother said.* ◇ *The newspaper article echoed my views completely.*

echo sounder *noun* [C] (**PHYSICS**) a device for finding how deep the sea is or where objects are in the water by measuring how quickly sound waves are reflected ▸ **echo-sounding** *noun* [C, U] ⊃ picture at **sonar**

e-cigarette (*also* **electronic cigarette**) *noun* [C] an electronic device, like a cigarette in shape, that contains NICOTINE that you can take into your body through your mouth

eclair /ɪˈkleə(r)/ *noun* [C] a type of long thin cake, usually filled with cream and covered with chocolate

eclectic /ɪˈklektɪk/ *adj.* (*formal*) not following one style or set of ideas, but choosing from or using a wide variety: *She has very eclectic tastes in literature.*

eclipse¹ /ɪˈklɪps/ *noun* [C] an occasion when the moon passes between the earth and the sun so that you cannot see all or part of the sun for a time; an occasion when the earth passes between the moon and the sun so that you cannot see all or part of the moon for a time: *a total/partial eclipse* of the sun ⊃ picture at **shadow¹**

eclipse² /ɪˈklɪps/ *verb* [T] (**ASTRONOMY**) (used about the moon or the earth) to cause an ECLIPSE of the sun or the moon

eco- /iːkəʊ, iːkə, iːˈkɒ/ *prefix* (in nouns, adjectives and adverbs) (**ENVIRONMENT**) connected with the environment: *eco-friendly* ◇ *eco-warriors* (= people who protest about damage to the environment) ◇ *eco-terrorism* (= the use of force or violent action in order to protest about damage to the environment)

eco-friendly /ˌiːkəʊ ˈfrendli/ *adj.* (**ENVIRONMENT**) not harmful to the environment: *eco-friendly products/ fuel*

ecological footprint (*also* ˌeco ˈfootprint, footprint) *noun* [C] (**ENVIRONMENT**) a measure of the amount of

the earth's resources used by a particular person or a population ⊃ look at **carbon footprint**

ecology /iˈkɒlədʒi/ *noun* [U] (**BIOLOGY**, **ENVIRONMENT**) the relationship between living things and their environment; the study of this subject ▸ **ecological** ₹+ 🅲🅰 🆆 /ˌiːkəˈlɒdʒɪkl/ *adj.*: *an ecological disaster* ▸ **ecologically** /-kli/ *adv.* ▸ **ecologist** /iˈkɒlədʒɪst/ *noun* [C]

e-commerce (**e-business**) *noun* [U] (**BUSINESS**, **FINANCE**) the business of buying and selling things using the internet: *to be involved in/move into e-commerce* ◇ *an e-commerce business/company*

economic 🎧 🅱🅰 🅾 /ˌiːkəˈnɒmɪk, ek-/ *adj.* **1** [only before noun] (**ECONOMICS**) connected with the supply of money, business, industry, etc: *The country faces growing economic problems.* **2** producing a profit: *The mine was closed because it was not economic.* **OPP** **uneconomic** ⊃ look at **economical** ⊃ note at **successful**

▼ SYNONYMS

economic

financial ✦ **commercial** ✦ **monetary** ✦ **budgetary**

These words all describe activities or situations that are connected with the use of money, especially by a business or country.

economic *the current economic situation*

financial *in financial difficulties*

commercial *the commercial heart of the city*

monetary (*formal*) *closer European monetary union*

budgetary *budgetary control/reform*

---

economical /ˌiːkəˈnɒmɪkl, ek-/ *adj.* providing good service or value in relation to the amount of time or money spent: *an economical car to run* **OPP** **uneconomical** ⊃ look at **economic**

economically 🆆 /ˌiːkəˈnɒmɪkli, ek-/ *adv.* **1** in a way that is connected with the supply of money, business, industry, etc: *The country was economically very underdeveloped.* **2** in a way that provides good service or value in relation to the amount of time or money spent: *The train service could be run more economically.*

economic migrant *noun* [C] (**SOCIAL STUDIES**) a person who moves from their own country to a new country in order to find work or have a better standard of living: *The government claimed they were economic migrants and not political refugees.* ⊃ look at **refugee**

economics ₹+ 🅱🅲 /ˌiːkəˈnɒmɪks, ek-/ *noun* [U] (**EDUCATION**) the study or principles of the way money, business and industry are organized: *a degree in economics* ◇ *the economics of a company*

economist ₹+ 🅱🅲 /ɪˈkɒnəmɪst/ *noun* [C] (**ECONOMICS**) a person who studies or is an expert in ECONOMICS (= the study of how money, trade and industry is organized)

economize (*BrE also* -**ise**) /ɪˈkɒnəmaɪz/ *verb* [I] ~ (**on sth**) to save money, time, fuel, etc.; to use less of sth: *Older people often try to economize on heating.*

economy 🎧 🅱🅰 /ɪˈkɒnəmi/ *noun* (*pl.* -ies) **1** (*often the economy*) [C] (**ECONOMICS**) the operation of a country's money supply, commercial activities and industry: *There are signs of improvement in the economy.* ◇ *the economies of America and Japan* **2** [C, U] careful spending of money, time, fuel, etc.; trying to save, not waste sth: *Our department is making economies in the amount of paper it uses.* ◇ *economy class* (= the cheapest class of air travel)

ecosystem /ˈiːkəʊsɪstəm/ *noun* [C] (**BIOLOGY, ENVIRONMENT**) all the plants and living creatures in a particular area considered in relation to their physical environment

ecoterrorism /ˈiːkəʊterərɪzəm/ *noun* [U] (**ENVIRONMENT**) violent activities that are carried out in order let people know about companies, governments, etc. that are damaging the environment ▸ **ecoterrorist** /-terərɪst/ *noun* [C]

ecotourism /ˈiːkəʊtʊərɪzəm, -tɔːr-/ *noun* [U] (**ENVIRONMENT, TOURISM**) organized holidays that are designed so that the tourists damage the environment as little as possible, especially when some of the money they pay is used to protect the local environment and animals: *Ecotourism is financing rainforest preservation.* ▸ **ecotourist** /-rɪst/ *noun* [C]

eco-warrior /ˈiːkəʊ wɒriə(r)/ *noun* [C] (**ENVIRONMENT**) a person who actively tries to prevent damage to the environment: *Eco-warriors plan to stop flights at the airport with drones.*

ecstasy /ˈekstəsi/ *noun* [U, C] (*pl.* -ies) a feeling or state of great happiness: *to be in ecstasy ◇ She went into ecstasies about the ring he had bought her.*

ecstatic /ɪkˈstætɪk/ *adj.* extremely happy

ecumenical /ˌekjuˈmenɪkl, ˌiːk-/ *adj.* (**RELIGION**) connected with the idea of UNITING all the different parts of the Christian Church

eczema /ˈeksmə/ *noun* [U] (**HEALTH**) a disease that makes the skin red and dry so that you want to SCRATCH it

ED /ˌiː ˈdiː/ *abbr.* = EATING DISORDER

ed. *abbr.* (in writing) edited by; edition

eddy /ˈedi/ *noun* [C] (*pl.* -ies) a movement of air, dust or water in a circle

edema /ɪˈdiːmə/ (*AmE*) = OEDEMA

edge¹ ⓘ **B1** /edʒ/ *noun* **1** [C] the place where sth, especially a surface, ends: *the edge of a table ◇ The leaves were brown and curling at the edges. ◇ I stood at the water's edge.* **2** [C] the sharp cutting part of a knife, etc. **3** (*usually the edge*) [sing.] **~(on/over sb/sth)** a small advantage over sb/sth: *She knew she had the edge over the other candidates.*
IDM (**be**) **on edge** to be nervous, worried or quick to become upset or angry: *I'm a bit on edge because I get my exam results today.*

edge² /edʒ/ *verb* **1** [T, usually passive] **~ sth (with sth)** to put sth along the edge of sth else: *The cloth was edged with lace.* **2** [I, T] **~ (your way/sth) across, along, away, back, etc.** to move yourself/sth somewhere slowly and carefully: *She edged closer to get a better view. ◇ She edged her chair up to the window.*

edgeways /ˈedʒweɪz/ (*BrE*) (*AmE* **edgewise** /ˈedʒwaɪz/) *adv.*
IDM **not get a word in edgeways/edgewise** → WORD¹

edgy /ˈedʒi/ *adj.* (**edgier; edgiest**) (*informal*) **1** nervous, worried or quick to become upset or angry **2** (used about a film, piece of music, etc.) having a sharp exciting quality: *a clever, edgy film*

edible /ˈedəbl/ *adj.* good or safe to eat: *Are these mushrooms edible?* **OPP** **inedible**

edifice /ˈedɪfɪs/ *noun* [C] (*formal*) a large impressive building ⊃ note at **building**

edit ⓘ **B2** /ˈedɪt/ *verb* [T] **1** (**LITERATURE**) to prepare a piece of writing to be published, making sure that it is correct, the right length, etc: *This draft text will need to be edited.* **2** (**COMPUTING**) to make changes to text or

ecosystems

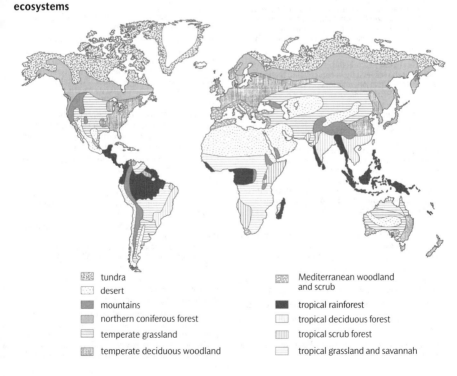

tundra		Mediterranean woodland and scrub
desert		tropical rainforest
mountains		tropical deciduous forest
northern coniferous forest		tropical scrub forest
temperate grassland		tropical grassland and savannah
temperate deciduous woodland		

data on screen on a computer: *You can download the file and edit it on your computer.* **3** (ARTS AND MEDIA) to prepare a film, TV or radio programme by cutting and arranging recorded material in a particular order **4** (ARTS AND MEDIA) to be in charge of a newspaper, magazine, etc.

edition ? B2 /ɪˈdɪʃn/ *noun* [C] **1** (*abbr.* ed.) the form in which a book, newspaper, etc. is published; all the books, newspapers, etc. published in the same form at the same time: *a paperback/hardback edition* ◇ *the morning edition of a newspaper* **2** one of a series of newspapers, magazines, TV or radio programmes: *And now for this week's edition of 'Panorama'* …

editor ? B1 /ˈedɪtə(r)/ *noun* [C] **1** (ARTS AND MEDIA) the person who is in charge of all or part of a newspaper, magazine, etc. and who decides what should be included: *the financial editor* ◇ *Who is the editor of 'The Times'?* ⊃ note at **newspaper 2** (LITERATURE) a person whose job is to prepare a book or other material to be published by checking for mistakes and correcting the text **3** (ARTS AND MEDIA) a person whose job is to prepare a film, TV or radio programme by cutting and arranging recorded material in a particular order

editorial¹ ?+ B2 /ˌedɪˈtɔːriəl/ *adj.* (ARTS AND MEDIA) connected with the task of preparing sth such as a newspaper, a book or a TV or radio programme, to be published or broadcast: *the magazine's editorial staff*

editorial² /ˌedɪˈtɔːriəl/ *noun* [C] (ARTS AND MEDIA) an important article in a newspaper that expresses the EDITOR's opinion about an item of news or an issue; in the US also a comment on radio or TV that expresses the opinion of the station or network

educate ? B1 /ˈedʒukeɪt/ *verb* [T, often passive] to teach or train sb, especially in school: *Young people should be educated to care for their environment.* ◇ *All their children were educated at private schools.*
▶ **educator** ?+ C1 *noun* [C]: *adult educators* (= who teach adults)

educated ? B1 /ˈedʒukeɪtɪd/ *adj.* **1** (*also* -educated /edʒukeɪtɪd/) (especially in compounds) having had the kind of education mentioned: *privately educated children* ◇ *a British-educated lawyer* **2** having studied and learnt a lot of things to a high standard: *a highly educated woman*

education ? A2 W /ˌedʒuˈkeɪʃn/ *noun* **1** [U, C] the teaching or training of people, especially in schools, colleges or universities: *primary/secondary/higher/adult education* ◇ *She received an excellent education.* ◇ *a public health education campaign* (= to educate the public about health issues) ⊃ note at **HDI 2** (*also* Education) [U] the subject of study that deals with how to teach; the institutions or people involved in this ▶ **educational** ? B1 W /-ʃənl/ *adj.*: *an educational toy/visit/experience*

Edwardian /edˈwɔːdiən/ *adj.* (HISTORY) from the time of the British king Edward VII (1901–1910): *an Edwardian terraced house* ▶ **Edwardian** *noun* [C]

EEG /ˌiː iː ˈdʒiː/ *noun* [C] (MEDICINE) a medical test that measures and records electrical activity in the brain (the abbreviation for 'electroencephalogram')

eel /iːl/ *noun* [C, U] a long thin fish that looks like a snake

eerie /ˈɪəri/ *adj.* strange and frightening: *an eerie noise* ▶ **eerily** /-rəli/ *adv.* ▶ **eeriness** /-rinəs/ *noun* [U]

efface /ɪˈfeɪs/ *verb* [T] (*formal*) to make sth disappear; to remove sth

effect¹ ? A2 O /ɪˈfekt/ *noun* **1** [C, U] **~(on sb/sth)** a change that is caused by sth; a result: *the effects of acid rain on the lakes and forests* ◇ *Her shouting had little or no effect on him.* ◇ *Despite her terrible experience, she seems to have suffered no ill effects.* ⊃ look at **after-effect, greenhouse effect, side effect 2** [C, U] a particular look, sound or impression that an artist, a writer, etc. wants to create: *How does the artist create the effect of moonlight?* ◇ *He likes to say things just for effect* (= to impress people). ⊃ look at **sound effect, special effects 3 effects** [pl.] (*formal*) your personal possessions
IDM **bring/put sth into effect** to cause sth to come into use **come into effect** (used especially about laws or rules) to begin to be used **in effect 1** in fact: *Though they haven't made an official announcement, she is, in effect, the new director.* **2** (used about a rule, a law, etc.) in operation; in use: *The new rules will be in effect from next month.* **take effect 1** (used about a drug, etc.) to begin to work; to produce the result you want: *The anaesthetic took effect immediately.* **2** (used about a law, etc.) to come into operation: *The ceasefire takes effect from midnight.* **to this/that effect** with this/that meaning: *I told him to leave her alone, or words to that effect.*

▼ SYNONYMS

effect

result ♦ consequence ♦ outcome ♦ repercussion

These are all words for a thing that is caused because of sth else.

effect *His criticism had the effect of discouraging her.*

result *She died as a result of her injuries.*

consequence *This decision could have serious consequences for everyone.*

outcome *We're waiting to hear the final outcome.*

repercussion *His dismissal will have serious repercussions.*

---

effect² /ɪˈfekt/ *verb* [T] (*formal*) to make sth happen: *to effect a cure/change/recovery*

effective ? B1 O /ɪˈfektɪv/ *adj.* **1** successfully producing the result that you want: *a medicine that is effective against the common cold* ◇ *That picture would look more effective on a dark background.* **2** real or actual, although perhaps not official: *The soldiers gained effective control of the town.* ▶ **effectiveness** ?+ C1 W *noun* [U]
OPP **ineffective**

effectively ? B1 O /ɪˈfektɪvli/ *adv.* **1** in a way that successfully produces the result you wanted: *She dealt with the situation effectively.* **2** in fact; in reality: *It meant that, effectively, they had lost.*

effector /ɪˈfektə(r)/ *noun* [C] (BIOLOGY) an organ or a cell in the body that is made to react by sth outside the body

effeminate /ɪˈfemɪnət/ *adj.* (used about a man or his behaviour) looking, behaving or sounding like a woman

effervescent /ˌefəˈvesnt/ *adj.* **1** (used about people and their behaviour) excited, enthusiastic and full of energy **SYN** **bubbly 2** (used about a liquid) having or producing small bubbles of gas **SYN** **fizzy** ▶ **effervescence** /-sns/ *noun* [U]

efficacy W /ˈefɪkəsi/ *noun* [U] (*formal*) the ability of sth to produce the results that are wanted: *to test the efficacy and safety of the medication*

efficient ? B2 W /ɪˈfɪʃnt/ *adj.* able to work well without making mistakes or wasting time and energy: *Our administrative assistant is very efficient.* ◇ *You must find a more efficient way of organizing your time.* ◇ *energy-efficient lighting* (= that does not use much energy **OPP** inefficient ▸ efficiency ʔ+ **C1** **W** /-ʃnsi/ noun [U, pl.] (pl. -ies) ▸ efficiently ʔ+ **B2** **W** adv.

effigy /ˈefɪdʒi/ noun [C] (pl. -ies) **1** (RELIGION) a statue of a famous or religious person or a god, often shown lying down **2** a model of a person that makes them look ugly

effluent /ˈefluənt/ noun [U] (ENVIRONMENT) liquid waste, especially chemicals produced by factories

effort ʔ **B1** **W** /ˈefət/ noun **1** [U] the physical or mental strength or energy that you need to do sth; sth that takes a lot of energy: *They have put a lot of effort into their studies this year.* ◇ *He made no effort to contact his parents.* **2** [C] **an ~ (to do sth)** an attempt to do sth, especially when it is difficult to do: *It was a real effort to stay awake in the lecture.* **3** [U] (PHYSICS) a FORCE applied by a machine or in a process ⊃ picture at **lever, pulley**

effortless /ˈefətləs/ adj. needing little or no effort so that sth seems easy ▸ effortlessly adv.

EFL /ˌiː ef ˈel/ abbr. (EDUCATION) **English as a Foreign Language** (refers to the teaching of English to people who do not speak it as a first language) ⊃ look at **ESL**

e.g. abbr. (in writing) = FOR EXAMPLE

egalitarian /iˌɡælɪˈteəriən/ adj. (POLITICS, SOCIAL STUDIES) (used about a person, system, society, etc.) following the principle that everyone should have equal rights

egg¹ ʔ **A1** /eɡ/ noun **1** [C] an almost round object with a hard shell that contains a young bird; a similar object (without a hard shell) that contains a young fish, insect, etc. ⊃ picture at **animal 2** [C, U] a bird's egg, especially one from a chicken, etc. that is used for food **3** [C] (in women and female animals) the small cell that can join with a SPERM (= a male seed) to make a baby ⊃ picture at **fertilization**
IDM **put all your eggs in one basket** to risk everything by depending completely on one thing, plan, etc. instead of giving yourself several possibilities

egg² /eɡ/ verb
PHR V **egg sb on (to do sth)** to encourage sb to do sth that they should not do

ˈegg cup noun [C] a small cup for holding a boiled egg

eggplant /ˈeɡplɑːnt/ (AmE) = AUBERGINE

eggshell /ˈeɡʃel/ noun [C, U] the hard outside part of an egg

ego ʔ+ **C1** /ˈiːɡəʊ, ˈeɡ-/ noun [C] (pl. -os) the (good) opinion that you have of yourself: *It was a blow to her ego when she lost her job.*

egocentric /ˌiːɡəʊˈsentrɪk, ˌeɡ-/ adj. (PSYCHOLOGY) thinking only about yourself and not what other people need or want **SYN** selfish

egoism /ˈiːɡəʊɪzəm, ˈeɡ-/ (also egotism /ˈiːɡətɪzəm, ˈeɡ-/) noun [U] thinking about yourself too much; thinking that you are better or more important than anyone else ▸ egoist /-ɡəʊɪst/ (also egotist /-ɡətɪst/) noun [C]: *I hate people who are egoists.* ▸ egoistic /ˌiːɡəʊˈɪstɪk, ˌeɡ-/ (also egotistical /ˌiːɡəˈtɪstɪkl, ˌeɡ-/) adj.

eh /eɪ/ exclamation (BrE, informal) **1** used for asking sb to agree with you: *'Good party, eh?'* **2** used for asking sb to repeat sth: *'Did you like the film?' 'Eh?' 'I asked if you liked the film!'*

Eid (also Id) /iːd/ noun [C] (RELIGION) one of the two main Muslim festivals, especially one that celebrates the end of Ramadan (= a month when people do not eat during the day)

eight ʔ **A1** /eɪt/ number 8

eighteen ʔ **A1** /ˌeɪˈtiːn/ number 18 ▸ eighteenth /-ˈtiːnθ/ ordinal number, noun [C]

eighth¹ /eɪtθ/ ordinal number 8th

eighth² /eɪtθ/ noun [C] one of eight equal parts of sth

ˈeighth note (AmE) = QUAVER²

eighty ʔ **A1** /ˈeɪti/ **1** number 80 **2** the eighties noun [pl.] numbers, years or temperatures from 80 to 89 ▸ eightieth /-əθ/ ordinal number, noun [C]
IDM **in your eighties** between the ages of 80 and 89

einsteinium /aɪnˈstaɪniəm/ noun [U] (symb. Es) (CHEMISTRY) a chemical element. Einsteinium is a RADIOACTIVE element produced artificially from PLUTONIUM and other elements. ❶ For more information on the periodic table of elements, look at the **Reference Section** of this dictionary.

either¹ ʔ **A2** /ˈaɪðə(r), ˈiːð-/ det., pron. **1** one or the other of two; it does not matter which: *You can choose either soup or salad, but not both.* ◇ *You can ask either of us for advice.* ◇ *Either of us is willing to help.* **2** both: *It is a pleasant road, with trees on either side.*

either² ʔ **A2** /ˈaɪðə(r), ˈiːð-/ adv. **1** (used after two negative statements) also: *I don't like Pat and I don't like Nick much either.* ◇ *'I can't remember his name.' 'I can't either.'* **2** used for emphasizing a negative statement: *The restaurant is quite good. And it's not expensive either.*

either³ /ˈaɪðə(r), ˈiːð-/ conj. **either ... or ...** used when you are giving a choice, usually of two things: *Either you leave or I do.* ◇ *You can either email or phone.*

ejaculate /iˈdʒækjuleɪt/ verb **1** [I] (BIOLOGY) to send out SEMEN (= liquid) from the PENIS (= the male sexual organ) **2** [I, T] (old-fashioned) to say sth suddenly ▸ ejaculation /iˌdʒækjuˈleɪʃn/ noun [C, U]

eject /iˈdʒekt/ verb **1** [T, often passive] **~ sb (from sth)** (formal) to push or send sb/sth out of a place (usually with force): *The protesters were ejected from the building.* **2** [I, T] to remove a disk from a machine, usually by pressing a button: *To eject the CD, press this button.* ◇ *After recording for three hours, the DVD will eject automatically.* **3** [I] to escape from an aircraft that is going to crash

eke /iːk/ verb
PHR V **eke sth out** to make a small amount of sth last a long time

elaborate¹ ʔ+ **C1** /iˈlæbərət/ adj. very complicated; done or made very carefully: *an elaborate pattern* ◇ *elaborate plans*

elaborate² /iˈlæbəreɪt/ verb [I] **~ (on sth)** (formal) to give more details about sth: *Could you elaborate on that idea?*

elapse /iˈlæps/ verb [I] (formal) (used about time) to pass

elastic¹ /iˈlæstɪk/ noun [U] material with rubber in it that can stretch and then return to its original size

elastic² /iˈlæstɪk/ adj. **1** (used about material, etc.) that returns to its original size and shape after being stretched **2** that can be changed; not fixed: *Our rules are quite elastic.*

eˌlastic ˈband (BrE) = RUBBER BAND

elasticity /ˌiːlæˈstɪsəti, iˌlæ-/ noun [U] the quality that sth has of being able to stretch and return to its original size and shape

elated /iˈleɪtɪd/ adj. very happy and excited ▸ elation /iˈleɪʃn/ noun [U]

elbow¹ ʔ+ **B2** /ˈelbəʊ/ noun [C] **1** (ANATOMY) the place where the bones of the arm join and the arm bends **2** the part of the SLEEVE of a coat, jacket, etc. that covers the ELBOW

elbow² /ˈelbəʊ/ verb [T] to push sb with your ELBOW: *She elbowed me out of the way.* ⊃ look at **nudge**

'elbow room noun [U] (*informal*) enough space to move freely

elder¹ /'eldə(r)/ adj. **1** [only before noun] older (of two members of a family): *My elder daughter is at university now but the other one is still at school.* ◇ *an elder brother/sister* **2** the elder [not before noun] the older of two people: *Who is the elder of the two?*

elder² /'eldə(r)/ noun **1** my, etc. elder [sing.] a person who is older than me, etc: *He is her elder by several years.* **2** elders [pl.] older people: *Do children still respect the opinions of their elders?*

elderly ⓘ B2 /'eldəli/ adj. **1** (used about a person) old **2** the elderly noun [pl.] old people in general: *The elderly need special care in winter.* ⊃ look at **old** (3)

eldest /'eldɪst/ adj. [C] (the) oldest (of three or more members of a family): *Their eldest child is a boy.* ◇ *John's got four boys. The eldest has just gone to university.*

elect ⓘ B2 /ɪ'lekt/ verb [T] **1** ~ sb (to sth); ~ sb (as sth) (**POLITICS**) to choose sb to have a particular job or position by voting for them: *He was elected to Parliament in 2015.* ◇ *The committee elected her as their representative.* **2** ~ to do sth (*formal*) to decide to do sth

-elect /ɪ'lekt/ adj. used after nouns to show that sb has been chosen for a job, but is not yet doing that job: *the president-elect*

election ⓘ B1 /ɪ'lekʃn/ noun (**POLITICS**) **1** [C, U] (the time of) choosing a Member of Parliament, president, etc. by voting: *In America, presidential elections are held every four years.* ◇ *to call* (= announce) *an election* ◇ *to vote in an election* ◇ *If you're interested in politics why not stand for election yourself?* **2** [U] ~as/ to sth the fact of having been chosen by election: *We welcome her as president.* ◇ *his election to the Senate*

electioneering /ɪ,lekʃə'nɪərɪŋ/ noun [U] (**POLITICS**) the activity of trying to persuade people to vote for a particular politician or political party in an election

elective /ɪ'lektɪv/ adj. **1** (*formal*) (**POLITICS**) using or chosen by election: *an elective democracy* ◇ *an elective member* **2** having the power to elect: *an elective body* **3** (used about medical treatment) that you choose to have; that does not have to be done immediately: *elective surgery* **4** (**EDUCATION**) (used about a course or subject) that a student can choose

elector /ɪ'lektə(r)/ noun [C] (**POLITICS**) a person who has the right to vote in an election ▸ **electoral** ⓘ+ C1 /-tərəl/ adj.: *the electoral register/roll* (= the list of electors in an area)

electorate /ɪ'lektərət/ noun [C + sing./pl. verb] (**POLITICS**) all the people who can vote in a region, country, etc.

electric ⓘ A2 /ɪ'lektrɪk/ adj. **1** producing or using electricity: *an electric current* ◇ *an electric kettle/car* **2** very exciting: *The atmosphere in the room was electric.*

electrical ⓘ A2 /ɪ'lektrɪkl/ adj. producing, using or relating to electricity: *an electrical appliance* (= a machine that uses electricity) ◇ *an electrical engineer* (= a person who designs and builds electrical systems and equipment)

e,lectric 'chair (*usually* the electric chair) noun [sing.] a chair used in some states of the US for killing criminals with a very strong electric current

electrician /ɪ,lek'trɪʃn/ noun [C] a person whose job is to connect and repair electrical systems and equipment

electricity ⓘ A2 /ɪ,lek'trɪsəti/ noun [U] (**PHYSICS**) a type of energy that we use to make heat, light and power to work machines, etc: *Turn that light off. We don't want to waste electricity.* ⊃ picture at **energy**

e,lectric 'razor = SHAVER

e,lectric 'shock (*also* shock) noun [C] (**HEALTH**) a sudden flow of electricity through a part of the body, causing pain and sometimes death ⊃ picture at **safety**

electrify /ɪ'lektrɪfaɪ/ verb [T] (electrifying; electrifies; pt, pp electrified) **1** [usually passive] (**PHYSICS**) to supply sth with electricity: *The railways are being electrified.* **2** to make sb very excited: *Mbappé electrified the crowd with his pace and skill.*

electro- /ɪlektrəʊ, ɪlektrə, ɪlek'trɒ/ prefix (in verbs, nouns, adjectives and adverbs) (**PHYSICS**) relating to electricity: *electromagnetism*

electrocute /ɪ'lektrəkjuːt/ verb [T, usually passive] to kill sb with electricity that goes through the body ▸ **electrocution** /ɪ,lektrə'kjuːʃn/ noun [U]

electrode /ɪ'lektrəʊd/ noun [C] (**PHYSICS**) one of two TERMINALS (= points where an electric current enters or leaves a battery, etc.) ⊃ look at **anode**, **cathode** ⊃ picture at **dry cell**

electrolysis /ɪ,lek'trɒləsɪs/ noun [U] (**PHYSICS**) a way of separating a liquid into its different chemical parts by passing an electric current through it

electrolyte /ɪ'lektrəlaɪt/ noun [C] (**PHYSICS**) a liquid that an electric current can pass through, especially in an electric cell or battery ⊃ picture at **dry cell**

electrolytic cell /ɪ,lektrə,lɪtɪk 'sel/ noun [C] (**CHEMISTRY**, **PHYSICS**) a device that produces an electric current caused by the chemical reaction between an ELECTROLYTE and two ELECTRODES

electromagnet /ɪ'lektrəʊmægnət/ noun [C] (**PHYSICS**) a piece of metal that becomes MAGNETIC (= having the ability to attract metal objects) when electricity is passed through it

electromagnetic /ɪ,lektrəʊmæg'netɪk/ adj. (**PHYSICS**) having both electrical characteristics and the ability to attract metal objects: *an electromagnetic wave/field* ▸ **electromagnetism** noun [U]

electromagnetism /ɪ,lektrəʊ'mægnətɪzəm/ noun [U] (**PHYSICS**) a MAGNETIC FIELD that is produced by electricity, or the science connected with this ⊃ look at **gravity** (1), **strong force**, **weak force**

electron /ɪ'lektrɒn/ noun [C] (**PHYSICS**) one of the three types of PARTICLES that form the NUCLEUS (= central part) of an ATOM. Electrons have a negative electric CHARGE. ⊃ look at **neutron**, **proton** ⊃ picture at **switch¹**

electronic ⓘ A2 /ɪ,lek'trɒnɪk/ adj. **1** (**COMPUTING**, **PHYSICS**) (used about a device) having many small parts, such as MICROCHIPS, that control and direct a small electric current: *Please turn off all electronic devices.* ◇ *electronic voting machines* **2** (**COMPUTING**) done or produced using a computer or other electronic device: *electronic banking/payments* ◇ *electronic dance music* ▸ **electronically** /-kli/ adv.

e,lectronic ciga'rette = E-CIGARETTE

electronics ⓘ+ B2 /ɪˌlekˈtrɒnɪks/ *noun* (**ENGINEERING, PHYSICS**) **1** [U] the technology used to produce computers, radios, etc.; the study of this technology: *the electronics industry* **2** electronics [pl.] the electronic CIRCUITS and other parts used in electronic equipment

eˌlectronic ˈtagging *noun* [U] (**LAW**) the system in which an electronic device is attached to a person, an animal or an object so that the police, etc. always know where that person, animal or object is

electrostatic /ɪˌlektrəʊˈstætɪk/ *adj.* (**PHYSICS**) used to talk about electric charges that are not moving, rather than electric currents

elegant ⓘ+ B2 /ˈelɪɡənt/ *adj.* having a good or attractive style: *She looked very elegant in her new dress.* ◇ *an elegant coat* SYN **stylish** ▶ elegance /-ɡəns/ *noun* [U] ▶ elegantly *adv.*

elegy /ˈelədʒi/ *noun* [C] (*pl.* -ies) (**LITERATURE, MUSIC**) a poem or song that expresses sad feelings, especially for sb who has died

element ⓘ B1 ⓞ /ˈelɪmənt/ *noun*
• PART/AMOUNT **1** [C] one important part of sth: *Cost is an important element when we're thinking about holidays.* **2** elements [pl.] the basic principles of a subject that you have to learn first SYN **basics** **3** [C, usually sing.] ~ **of sth** a small amount of sth: *There was an element of truth in what he said.*
• GROUP OF PEOPLE **4** [C] people of a certain type: *The criminal element at football matches causes a lot of trouble.*
• IN CHEMISTRY **5** [C] a simple chemical substance that consists of ATOMS of only one type and that cannot be split by chemical means into a simpler substance. Gold, OXYGEN and CARBON are all elements. ⊃ look at **compound¹ (2)**
• ELECTRICAL PART **6** [C] the metal part of a piece of electrical equipment that produces heat
• WEATHER **7** the elements [pl.] (bad) weather: *to be exposed to the elements*
IDM **in/out of your element** in a situation where you feel comfortable/uncomfortable: *Bill's in his element speaking to a large group of people, but I hate it.*

elementary ⓘ+ B2 /ˌelɪˈmentri/ *adj.* **1** (**EDUCATION**) connected with the first stages of learning sth: *an elementary course in English* ◇ *a book for elementary students* **2** basic; not difficult: *elementary physics*

ˌelementary ˈparticle *noun* [C] (**PHYSICS**) a very small piece of MATTER (= a substance), such as a QUARK, that does not contain within it any even smaller pieces of MATTER

eleˈmentary school (*also informal* **grade school**) *noun* [C] (**EDUCATION**) (in the US) a school for children between the ages of about 6 and 12

elephant ⓘ A1 /ˈelɪfənt/ *noun* [C] a very large grey animal with big ears, two TUSKS (= long curved teeth) and a TRUNK (= a very long nose) ⊃ picture at **animal**

elevate ⓘ+ C1 ⓦ /ˈelɪveɪt/ *verb* [T] (*formal*) **1** to move sb/ sth to a higher place or more important position: *an elevated platform* ◇ *He was elevated to the Board of Directors.* **2** to make the level of sth increase: *Smoking often elevates blood pressure.*

elevation /ˌelɪˈveɪʃn/ *noun* **1** [C, U] (*formal*) the process of moving sb/sth or being moved to a higher place or more important position: *his elevation to the presidency* **2** [C] (**GEOGRAPHY**) the height of a place, especially its height above sea level: *The city is at an elevation of 2 000 metres.* **3** [C] (*formal*) a piece of ground that is higher than the area around **4** [C] (**ARCHITECTURE**) one side of a building, or a drawing of this by an architect: *the front/rear/side elevation of a*

house 5 [U, sing.] (*formal*) an increase in the level or amount of sth: *elevation of blood sugar levels*

elevator /ˈelɪveɪtə(r)/ *noun* [C] **1** (*AmE*) = LIFT² (1) **2** a part in the tail of an aircraft that is moved to make it go up or down

eleven ⓘ A1 /ɪˈlevn/ *number* 11 ▶ eleventh /-vnθ/ *ordinal number, noun* [C]

elf /elf/ *noun* [C] (*pl.* elves /elvz/) (in stories) a small creature with pointed ears who has magic powers

elicit /ɪˈlɪsɪt/ *verb* [T] ~ **sth (from sb)** (*formal*) to manage to get information, facts, a reaction, etc. from sb

elide /ɪˈlaɪd/ *verb* [T] (**LANGUAGE**) to leave out the sound of part of a word when you are pronouncing it ▶ elision /ɪˈlɪʒn/ *noun* [U, C]

eligible ⓘ+ C1 /ˈelɪdʒəbl/ *adj.* ~ **(for sth/to do sth)** having the right to do or have sth: *In Britain, you are eligible to vote when you are 18.* OPP **ineligible** ▶ eligibility /ˌelɪdʒəˈbɪləti/ *noun* [U]: *Marriage to a national gave automatic eligibility for citizenship.*

eliminate ⓘ+ B2 ⓦ /ɪˈlɪmɪneɪt/ *verb* [T] **1** ~ **sb/sth (from sth)** to remove sb/sth that is not wanted or needed: *We must try and eliminate the problem.* ◇ *The police have eliminated two suspects from their investigation.* **2** [usually passive] to stop sb going further in a competition, etc: *The school team was eliminated in the first round of the competition.* ▶ elimination /ɪˌlɪmɪˈneɪʃn/ *noun* [U, C]

elite ⓘ+ C1 /eɪˈliːt, ɪ-/ *noun* [C + sing./pl. verb] a social group that is thought to be the best or most important because of its power, money, intelligence, etc: *an intellectual elite* ◇ *the ruling elite* ▶ elite *adj.* [only before noun]: *an elite group of artists*

elitism /eɪˈliːtɪzəm, ɪˈl-/ *noun* [U] (**SOCIAL STUDIES**) the belief that some people should be treated in a special way ▶ elitist /-tɪst/ *noun* [C], *adj.*

Elizabethan /ɪˌlɪzəˈbiːθən/ *adj.* (**HISTORY**) connected with the time when Queen Elizabeth I was queen of England (1558–1603): *Elizabethan drama/music* ◇ *The Elizabethan age was a time of exploration and discovery.* ▶ Elizabethan *noun* [C]: *Shakespeare was an Elizabethan.*

elk /elk/ (*BrE*) (*AmE* **moose**) *noun* [C] a very large DEER (= a large wild animal that eats grass) with large flat ANTLERS (= parts on its head that are shaped like branches)

ellipse /ɪˈlɪps/ *noun* [C] (**GEOMETRY**) a regular OVAL, like a circle that has been pressed in from two sides

ellipsis /ɪˈlɪpsɪs/ *noun* [C, U] (*pl.* ellipses /ɪˈlɪpsiːz/) **1** (**GRAMMAR**) the act of leaving out a word or words from a sentence deliberately, when the meaning can be understood without them **2** (**LANGUAGE**) three DOTS (...) used to show that a word or words have been left out

elliptical /ɪˈlɪptɪkl/ *adj.* **1** having a word or words left out of a sentence deliberately: *an elliptical remark* (= one that suggests more than is actually said) **2** (*also* elliptic /ɪˈlɪptɪk/) (**GEOMETRY**) connected with or in the form of an ELLIPSE ▶ elliptically /-kli/ *adj.*: *to speak/write elliptically*

elm /elm/ (*also* **ˈelm tree**) *noun* [C] a tall tree with broad leaves

El Niño /ˌel ˈniːnjəʊ/ *noun* [C, usually sing.] (**GEOGRAPHY**) a series of changes in the weather system near the coast of northern Peru and Ecuador that happens every few years and affects the weather in many parts of the world

elocution /ˌeləˈkjuːʃn/ *noun* [U] the ability to speak clearly, correctly and without a strong ACCENT (= a particular way of pronouncing words that is connected with the country, area or social class that you come from)

elongate /ˈiːlɒŋɡeɪt/ *verb* [I, T] to become longer; to make sth longer: *The seal pup's body elongates as it gets older.* **SYN** **lengthen** ▸ **elongation** /ˌiːlɒŋˈɡeɪʃn/ *noun* [U]: *the elongation of vowel sounds*

elongated /ˈiːlɒŋɡeɪtɪd/ *adj.* long and thin

elope /ɪˈləʊp/ *verb* [I] ~ **(with sb)** to run away secretly to get married

eloquent /ˈeləkwənt/ *adj.* (*formal*) able to use language and express your opinions well, especially when you speak in public ▸ **eloquence** /-kwəns/ *noun* [U] ▸ **eloquently** *adv.*

else ʔ **A1** /els/ *adv.* (in questions or after *nobody, something, anything,* etc.) another, different person, thing or place: *This isn't mine. It must be somebody else's.* ◇ *Was it you who phoned me, or somebody else?* ◇ *Everybody else is allowed to stay up late.* ◇ *You'll have to pay. Nobody else will.* ◇ *What else would you like?* ◇ *I'm tired of that cafe — shall we go somewhere else for a change?*
IDM **or else** otherwise; if not: *You'd better go to bed now or else you'll be tired in the morning.* ◇ *He's either forgotten or else he's decided not to come.*

elsewhere ʔ **B2** ⓦ /ˌelsˈweə(r)/ *adv.* in or to another place: *He's travelled a lot — in Europe and elsewhere.*

ELT /ˌiː el ˈtiː/ *abbr.* (**EDUCATION**) **English Language Teaching** (teaching English to people whose first language is not English)

elude /ɪˈluːd/ *verb* [T] (*formal*) **1** to manage to avoid being caught: *The escaped prisoner eluded the police for three days.* **2** to be difficult or impossible to remember: *I remember his face but his name eludes me.*

elusive /ɪˈluːsɪv/ *adj.* not easy to catch, find or remember

elves /elvz/ plural of **elf**

'em /əm/ (*informal*) = THEM

em- /ɪm/ → EN-

emaciated /ɪˈmeɪsieɪtɪd, ɪˈmeɪʃi-/ *adj.* (**HEALTH**) extremely thin and weak because of illness, lack of food, etc. ▸ **emaciation** /ɪˌmeɪsiˈeɪʃn/ *noun* [U]

email ʔ **A1** /ˈiːmeɪl/ *noun* **1** [U] (**COMPUTING**) a way of sending electronic messages or data from one computer to another: *to send a message by email* ◇ *What's your email address?* **2** (*also* mail) [C, U] a message or messages sent by email: *I'll send you an email tomorrow.* ◇ *to receive/get/open an email* ◇ *I have to check my email.* ▸ **email** ʔ **A1** *verb* [T] ~ **sth (to sb)**; ~ **sb sth**: *I'll email the information to you.* ◇ *I'll email you the information.*

emanate /ˈe||||||əneɪt/ *verb* [T] (*formal*) to produce or show sth: *He emanates power and confidence.*
PHR V **emanate from sth** to come from sth or somewhere: *The sound of loud music emanated from the building.*

emancipate /ɪˈmænsɪpeɪt/ *verb* [T, often passive] (*formal*) (**SOCIAL STUDIES**) to give sb the same legal, social and political rights as other people ▸ **emancipation** /ɪˌmænsɪˈpeɪʃn/ *noun* [U]

embalm /ɪmˈbɑːm/ *verb* [T] to treat a dead body with special substances in order to keep it in good condition

embankment /ɪmˈbæŋkmənt/ *noun* [C] a wall of stone or earth that is built to stop a river from flooding or to carry a road or railway

embargo /ɪmˈbɑːɡəʊ/ *noun* [C] (*pl.* -oes) ~ **(on sth)** (**BUSINESS, POLITICS**) an official order to stop doing business with another country: *to impose an embargo on arms sales* ◇ *to lift* (= remove) *an embargo*

embark ʔ+ **C1** /ɪmˈbɑːk/ *verb* [I] (*formal*) to get on a ship or plane: *Passengers with cars must embark first.* **SYN** **board** **OPP** **disembark** ▸ **embarkation** /ˌembɑːˈkeɪʃn/ *noun* [U, C]
PHR V **embark on sth** to start sth (new): *I'm embarking on a completely new career.*

embarrass /ɪmˈbærəs/ *verb* [T] **1** to make sb feel uncomfortable or shy: *Don't ever embarrass me in front of my friends again!* **2** to cause problems or difficulties for sb: *The minister's mistake embarrassed the government.*

embarrassed ʔ **B1** /ɪmˈbærəst/ *adj.* ~ **(about/at sth)**; ~ **(to do sth)** feeling uncomfortable or shy because of sth silly you have done, because people are looking at you, etc: *He's embarrassed about his height.* ◇ *Some women are too embarrassed to consult their doctor about the problem.*

embarrassing ʔ **B1** /ɪmˈbærəsɪŋ/ *adj.* making you feel uncomfortable or shy: *an embarrassing question/mistake/situation* ▸ **embarrassingly** *adv.*

embarrassment ʔ+ **C1** /ɪmˈbærəsmənt/ *noun* **1** [U] shy, uncomfortable or guilty feelings: *I nearly died of embarrassment when he said that.* **2** [C] ~ **(to sb)** a situation that causes problems for sb: *Here resignation will be a severe embarrassment to the party.*

embassy ʔ+ **C1** /ˈembəsi/ *noun* [C] (*pl.* -ies) (**POLITICS**) a group of DIPLOMATS (= officials who represent their country) and the AMBASSADOR (= the official with the highest position), who represent their government in a foreign country; the official building where they work ⊃ look at **consulate**

embed ʔ+ **C1** /ɪmˈbed/ *verb* [T, usually passive] (-dd-) to fix sth FIRMLY and deeply (in sth else): *The axe was embedded in the piece of wood.*

embellish /ɪmˈbelɪʃ/ *verb* [T] (*formal*) **1** to make sth more beautiful by adding decoration to it **SYN** **decorate** **2** to make a story more interesting by adding details that are not always true ▸ **embellishment** *noun* [U, C]: *Good meat needs very little embellishment.*

ember /ˈembə(r)/ *noun* [C, usually pl.] a piece of wood or coal that is not burning, but is still red and hot after a fire has died

embezzle /ɪmˈbezl/ *verb* [T] (**LAW**) to steal money that you are responsible for or that belongs to your employer ▸ **embezzlement** *noun* [U]

embitter /ɪmˈbɪtə(r)/ *verb* [T] to make sb feel angry or disappointed about sth over a long period of time ▸ **embittered** *adj.*: *a sick and embittered old man*

emblem /ˈembləm/ *noun* [C] an object or a symbol that represents sth: *The dove is the emblem of peace.*

embody ʔ+ **C1** /ɪmˈbɒdi/ *verb* [T] (embodying; embodies; *pt, pp* embodied) (*formal*) **1** to be a very good example of sth: *To me she embodies all the best qualities of a teacher.* **2** to include or contain sth: *This latest model embodies many new features.* ▸ **embodiment** /-mənt/ *noun* [C]: *She is the embodiment of a caring mother.*

emboss /ɪmˈbɒs/ *verb* [T, usually passive] ~ **A with B**; ~ **B on A** (**ART**) to put a raised design or piece of writing on paper, leather, etc: *stationery embossed with the hotel's name* ◇ *The hotel's name was embossed on the stationery.* ▸ **embossed** *adj.*: *embossed stationery*

embrace ⚡+ **B2** /ɪmˈbreɪs/ *verb* **1** [I, T] to put your arms around sb as a sign of love, happiness, etc. **2** [T] (*formal*) to include: *His report embraced all the main points.* **3** [T] (*formal*) to accept sth with enthusiasm: *She embraced Christianity in her later years.* ⊃ note at **religion** ▶ **embrace** *noun* [C]: *He held her in a warm embrace.*

embroider /ɪmˈbrɔɪdə(r)/ *verb* **1** [T, I] to decorate cloth by SEWING a pattern or picture on it **2** [T] to add details that are not true to a story to make it more interesting ▶ **embroidery** /-dəri/ *noun* [U]

embryo /ˈembriəʊ/ *noun* [C] (*pl.* -os) (BIOLOGY) a baby, an animal or a plant in the early stages of development before birth ⊃ look at **fetus** ⊃ picture at **fertilization** ▶ **embryonic** /ˌembriˈɒnɪk/ *adj.*

emcee /emˈsiː/ *noun* [C] **1** (*AmE, informal*) a person who introduces guests or ENTERTAINERS at a formal occasion **SYN** master of ceremonies **2** an MC at a club or party

emerald /ˈemərəld/ *noun* **1** [C, U] a bright green PRECIOUS STONE **2** (*also* emerald ˈgreen*) [U] a bright green colour ▶ **emerald** (*also* emerald green) *adj.*: *an emerald green dress*

emerge ⚡ **B2** ⊙ /ɪˈmɜːdʒ/ *verb* **1** [I] ~ (from sth) to appear or come out from somewhere: *A man emerged from the shadows.* ◇ (*figurative*) *The country emerged from the war in ruins.* **2** [I, T] ~ (that ...) to become known: *During investigations it emerged that she was lying about her age.* ▶ **emergence** ⚡+ **C1** **W** /ɪˈmɜːdʒəns/ *noun* [U]: *the emergence of new technologies*

emergency ⚡ **B1** /ɪˈmɜːdʒənsi/ *noun* [C, U] (*pl.* -ies) a serious event that needs immediate action: *In an emergency phone 112 for help.* ◇ *an emergency exit* ◇ *The pilot made an emergency landing in a field.* ◇ *The government has declared a state of emergency* (= a time when special plans or actions can be put into effect) *following the earthquake.*

eˈmergency brake (*AmE*) = HANDBRAKE

eˈmergency room *noun* [C] (*AmE*) = ER

eˈmergency services *noun* [pl.] (*BrE*) the public organizations that deal with EMERGENCIES (= serious events that need immediate action), the police, fire, AMBULANCE and COASTGUARD services

emergent /ɪˈmɜːdʒənt/ (*also* emerging /ɪˈmɜːdʒɪŋ/) *adj.* new and still developing: *emergent nations/states*

emigrant /ˈemɪɡrənt/ *noun* [C] (SOCIAL STUDIES) a person who has gone to live permanently in another country ⊃ look at **immigrant**

emigrate /ˈemɪɡreɪt/ *verb* [I] ~ (from ...) (to ...) (SOCIAL STUDIES) to leave your own country to go and live permanently in another: *They emigrated from Ireland to Australia 20 years ago.* ⊃ look at **immigrate**, **migrate** (2) ▶ **emigration** /ˌemɪˈɡreɪʃn/ *noun* [U, C] ⊃ look at **immigration**

eminent /ˈemɪnənt/ *adj.* (*formal*) (used about a person) famous and important: *an eminent scientist*

eminently /ˈemɪnəntli/ *adv.* (*formal*) very; extremely: *She is eminently suitable for the job.*

emir (*also* amir) /eˈmɪə(r), ˈemɪə(r)/ *noun* [C] (POLITICS) the title given to some Muslim RULERS: *the Emir of Kuwait*

emirate /ˈemɪrət, ˈemɪr-/ *noun* [C] **1** (POLITICS) the position held by an EMIR; the period of time that he is in power **2** an area of land that is ruled over by an EMIR: *the United Arab Emirates*

emissary /ˈemɪsəri/ *noun* [C] (*pl.* -ies) (*formal*) (POLITICS) a person who is sent somewhere, especially to another country, in order to give sb an official message or to perform a special task

emission ⚡+ **B2** /ɪˈmɪʃn/ *noun* (ENVIRONMENT, PHYSICS) **1** [U] (*formal*) the production or sending out of light, heat, gas, etc: *the emission of carbon dioxide into the atmosphere* **2** [C] gas, etc. that is sent out into the air: *The government has pledged to clean up industrial emissions.*

emit /iˈmɪt/ *verb* [T] (-tt-) (*formal*) to send out sth, for example a smell, a sound, smoke, heat or light: *The volcano emitted a huge plume of ash.*

emo /ˈiːməʊ/ *noun* (*pl.* -os) **1** [U] (MUSIC) a type of rock music that is like PUNK but deals more with personal feelings **2** [C] a person who likes emo music and often wears black clothes

emoji /ɪˈməʊdʒi/ *noun* [C] (*pl.* emoji, emojis) (COMPUTING) a small digital image used to express an idea or emotion in emails, on SOCIAL MEDIA, etc: *He responded with a red heart emoji.*

emoticon /ɪˈməʊtɪkɒn/ *noun* [C] (COMPUTING) a symbol that shows your feelings when you send an email or text message. For example :-) represents a smiling face. ⊃ look at **smiley** (2)

emotion ⚡ **B1** /ɪˈməʊʃn/ *noun* [C, U] a strong feeling such as love, anger, fear, etc: *to control/express your emotions* ◇ *His voice was filled with emotion.* ◇ *He showed no emotion as the police took him away.*

emotional ⚡ **B2** **W** /ɪˈməʊʃənl/ *adj.* **1** connected with people's feelings: *emotional problems* **2** causing strong feelings: *an emotional issue* **SYN** emotive **3** having strong emotions and showing them in front of people: *She always gets very emotional when I leave.* ▶ **emotionally** ⚡+ **B2** /-nəli/ *adv.*: *She felt physically and emotionally drained after giving birth.*

eˌmotional inˈtelligence *noun* [U] (PSYCHOLOGY) the ability to understand your emotions and those of other people: *Children need to develop emotional intelligence.*

emotive /ɪˈməʊtɪv/ *adj.* causing strong feelings: *emotive language* ◇ *an emotive issue* **SYN** emotional

empathy /ˈempəθi/ *noun* [U] ~ (with/for sb/sth); ~ (between A and B) the ability to understand another person's feelings, experience, etc: *Some adults have (a) great empathy with children.* ◇ *the empathy between a dog and its owner* ▶ **empathize** (*BrE also* -ise) /-θaɪz/ *verb* [I] ~ (with sb/sth): *He's a popular teacher because he empathizes with his students.*

emperor /ˈempərə(r)/ *noun* [C] (HISTORY, POLITICS) the ruler of an EMPIRE

emphasis ⚡ **B2** ⊙ /ˈemfəsɪs/ *noun* [U, C] (*pl.* emphases /-fəsiːz/) ~ (on sth) **1** (giving) special importance or attention (to sth): *There's a lot of emphasis on science at our school.* ◇ *You should put a greater emphasis on quality rather than quantity when you write.* **2** the force that you give to a word or phrase when you are speaking; a way of writing a word to show that it is important: *In the word 'photographer' the emphasis is on the second syllable.* ◇ *I underlined the key phrases of my letter for emphasis.* **SYN** stress[1]

emphasize ⚡ **B2** ⊙ (*BrE also* -ise) /ˈemfəsaɪz/ *verb* [T] ~ (that ...) to give special importance to sth: *They emphasized that healthy eating is important.* ◇ *They emphasized the importance of healthy eating.* **SYN** stress[2]

emphatic /ɪmˈfætɪk/ *adj.* said or expressed in a strong way: *an emphatic refusal/denial* ▶ **emphatically** /-kli/ *adv.*

emphysema /ˌemfɪˈsiːmə/ *noun* [U] (HEALTH) a condition that affects the lungs, making it difficult to breathe

empire ⚡+ B2 /ˈempaɪə(r)/ *noun* [C] **1** (HISTORY, POLITICS) a group of countries that is governed by one country: *the Roman Empire* ⊃ look at **emperor, empress** **2** (BUSINESS) a very large company or group of companies

empirical ⚡+ C1 ⊙ /ɪmˈpɪrɪkl/ *adj.* (*formal*) based on experiments and practical experience, not on ideas: *empirical evidence* ▸ **empirically** ⊙ /-kli/ *adv.*

empiricism /ɪmˈpɪrɪsɪzəm/ *noun* [U] (*formal*) the use of experiments or experience as the basis for your ideas; the belief in these methods ▸ **empiricist** /-sɪst/ *noun* [C]: *the English empiricist, John Locke*

employ ⚡ A2 ⊙ /ɪmˈplɔɪ/ *verb* [T] **1 ~ sb (as sth); ~ sb (in/on sth)** (ECONOMICS, SOCIAL STUDIES) to pay sb to work for you: *He is employed as a lorry driver.* ◇ *They employ 600 workers.* ◇ *18 per cent of the workforce is employed in agriculture.* ◇ *Three people are employed on the task of designing a new computer system.* ⊃ look at **unemployed 2 ~ sth (as sth)** (*formal*) to use: *to employ a technique/strategy/tactic* ◇ *In an emergency, an umbrella can be employed as a weapon.*

employee ⚡ A2 /ɪmˈplɔɪiː/ *noun* [C] (ECONOMICS, SOCIAL STUDIES) a person who is paid to work for sb: *The factory has 500 employees.*

employer ⚡ A2 /ɪmˈplɔɪə(r)/ *noun* [C] (ECONOMICS, SOCIAL STUDIES) a person or company that employs other people: *The car factory is the largest employer in this town.*

employment ⚡ B1 /ɪmˈplɔɪmənt/ *noun* [U] **1** (ECONOMICS, SOCIAL STUDIES) the state of having a paid job: *to be in/out of employment* ◇ *This bank can give employment to ten extra staff.* ◇ *It is difficult to find employment in the north of the country.* ⊃ look at **unemployment** ⊃ note at **work²** **2** the act of employing sb: *The law prevented the employment of children under ten.* **3** (*formal*) the use of sth: *the employment of force*

em'ployment agency *noun* [C] a company that helps people to find work and other companies to find workers

em'ployment tribunal (*also* industrial tribunal) *noun* [C] (*BrE*) (LAW) a type of court that can decide what happens when employees and employers disagree about sth

empower ⚡+ C1 ⊙ /ɪmˈpaʊə(r)/ *verb* [T, often passive] (*formal*) to give sb power or authority (to do sth) ▸ **empowerment** *noun* [U]

empress /ˈemprəs/ *noun* [C] (HISTORY, POLITICS) **1** a woman who rules an EMPIRE **2** the wife of an EMPEROR (= a man who rules an EMPIRE)

empty¹ ⚡ A2 /ˈempti/ *adj.* (emptier; emptiest) **1** with no things or people inside: *an empty box* ◇ *The bus was half empty.* ◇ *I couldn't see any empty seats* (= with nobody sitting in them). **2** without meaning or value: *It was an empty threat* (= it was not meant seriously). ◇ *My life feels empty now the children have left home.* **SYN hollow¹** ▸ **emptiness** *noun* [U]

empty² ⚡ B1 /ˈempti/ *verb* (emptying; empties; *pt, pp* emptied) **1** [T] **~ sth (out/out of sth)** to remove everything that is inside a container, etc: *I've emptied a wardrobe for you to use.* ◇ *Luke emptied everything out of the box.* **2** [I] to become empty: *The cinema emptied very quickly once the film was finished.*

empty-'handed *adj.* without getting what you wanted; without taking sth to sb: *The robbers fled empty-handed.*

EMU /ˌiː em ˈjuː/ *abbr.* (ECONOMICS) **E**conomic and **M**onetary **U**nion (the economic policies shared by the countries of the European Union) ⊃ look at **euro** (1)

emulate /ˈemjuleɪt/ *verb* [T] (*formal*) to try to do sth as well as sb else because you admire them

emulsifier /ɪˈmʌlsɪfaɪə(r)/ *noun* [C] a substance that is added to mixtures of food to make the different liquids or substances in them combine to form a smooth mixture

emulsify /ɪˈmʌlsɪfaɪ/ *verb* [I, T] (emulsifying; emulsifies; *pt, pp* emulsified) (CHEMISTRY) if two liquids, one of which is thicker than the other, **emulsify** or **are emulsified**, they combine to form a smooth mixture

emulsion /ɪˈmʌlʃn/ *noun* [C, U] **1** (CHEMISTRY) any mixture of liquids that do not normally mix together, such as oil and water **2** (*also* eˈmulsion paint) a type of paint used on walls and ceilings that dries without leaving a shiny surface (*BrE*)

en- /ɪn/ (*also* em-) *prefix* **1** to put into the thing or condition mentioned: *encase* ◇ *endanger* ◇ *empower* **2** to cause to be: *enlarge* ◇ *embolden*

enable ⚡ B2 ⊙ /ɪˈneɪbl/ *verb* [T] **~ sb/sth to do sth 1** to make sth possible: *The software enables you to manage the lighting remotely.* ◇ *The new train line enables easier access to the stadium.* **SYN allow 2** (COMPUTING) to make a system, device or feature ready to use: *To enable this feature, go to Account Settings and click 'Security'.* ◇ *Bluetooth-enabled devices*

enact ⚡+ C1 /ɪˈnækt/ *verb* [T] **1** (LAW) to pass a law: *legislation enacted by parliament* **2** (*formal*) to perform a play or act a part in a play: *scenes from history enacted by local residents* **3 be enacted** (*formal*) to take place: *They were unaware of the drama being enacted a few feet away from them.*

enamel /ɪˈnæml/ *noun* [U] **1** (ART) a hard, shiny substance used for protecting or decorating metal, etc: *an enamel bowl* **2** the hard white outer covering of a tooth ⊃ picture at **tooth**

enc. (in writing) = ENCLOSED (2)

encephalitis /enˌsefəˈlaɪtɪs, -ˌke-/ *noun* [U] (HEALTH) a condition in which the brain becomes SWOLLEN (= larger than normal), caused by an infection or ALLERGIC reaction

encephalopathy /enˌsefəˈlɒpəθi, -ˌke-/ *noun* [U] (HEALTH) a disease in which the functioning of the brain is affected by infection, BLOOD POISONING, etc. ⊃ look at **BSE**

enchanted /ɪnˈtʃɑːntɪd/ *adj.* **1** (in stories) affected by magic powers **2** (*formal*) pleased or very interested: *The audience was enchanted by her singing.*

enchanting /ɪnˈtʃɑːntɪŋ/ *adj.* very nice or pleasant; attractive **SYN delightful**

encircle /ɪnˈsɜːkl/ *verb* [T] (*formal*) to make a circle round sth: *London is encircled by the M25 motorway.* **SYN surround**

enclose /ɪnˈkləʊz/ *verb* [T] **1** [usually passive] **~ sth (in sth)** to surround sth with a wall, fence, etc.; to put one thing inside another: *The garden is enclosed by a high hedge.* ◇ *The jewels were enclosed in a strong box.* **2 ~ sth (with sth)** to put sth in an ENVELOPE, package, etc. with sth else: *Can I enclose a letter with this parcel?*

enclosed /ɪnˈkləʊzd/ *adj.* **1** with walls, etc. all around **2** (*abbr.* encl., enc.) sent with a letter, etc.

enclosure /ɪnˈkləʊʒə(r)/ *noun* [C] **1** a piece of land inside a wall, fence, etc. that is used for a particular purpose: *a wildlife enclosure* **2** something that is placed inside an ENVELOPE together with the letter

encode ⓦ /ɪnˈkəʊd/ *verb* [T] **1** to change ordinary language into letters, symbols, etc. in order to send secret messages **2** (**COMPUTING**) to change information into a form that a computer can deal with ▸ **encoder** *noun* [C]

encompass ⓘ+ ⓒ⓵ /ɪnˈkʌmpəs/ *verb* [T] (*formal*) **1** to include a large number or range of things: *The job encompasses a wide range of responsibilities.* **2** to surround or cover sth completely: *The fog soon encompassed the whole valley.*

encore¹ /ˈɒŋkɔː(r)/ *exclamation* called out by an audience that wants the performers in a concert, etc. to sing or play sth extra

encore² /ˈɒŋkɔː(r)/ *noun* [C] an extra, short performance at the end of a concert, etc.

encounter¹ ⓘ ⓑ⓶ ⓦ /ɪnˈkaʊntə(r)/ *verb* [T] **1** to experience sth (a danger, difficulty, etc.): *I've never encountered any discrimination at work.* **SYN** **meet with sth 2** (*formal*) to meet sb unexpectedly; to experience or find sth unusual or new **SYN** **come across sb/sth**

encounter² ⓘ ⓑ⓶ ⓦ /ɪnˈkaʊntə(r)/ *noun* [C] ~ (**with sb/sth**); ~ (**between A and B**) an unexpected (often unpleasant) meeting or event: *I've had a number of close encounters* (= situations that could have been dangerous) *with bad drivers.* ◇ *the semifinal encounter* (= match) *between Brazil and Japan*

encourage ⓘ ⓑ⓵ ⓦ /ɪnˈkʌrɪdʒ/ *verb* [T] **1** ~ **sb/sth (in sth/to do sth)** to give hope, support or confidence to sb: *She encouraged many young writers and artists.* ◇ *His friends encouraged him in his attempt to stop smoking.* **OPP** **discourage 2** ~ **sb/sth to do sth** to persuade sb to do sth by making them believe it is a good thing to do: *The teacher encouraged her students to ask questions.* **OPP** **discourage 3** to make sth happen more easily: *to encourage development/ investment/growth* ◇ *The government should encourage the use of renewable energy resources.* **OPP** **discourage** ▸ **encouraging** ⓘ+ ⓒ⓵ *adj.*

encouragement ⓘ+ ⓒ⓵ /ɪnˈkʌrɪdʒmənt/ *noun* [U, C, usually sing.] ~ (**to sb**) (**to do sth**) the act of encouraging sb to do sth; sth that encourages sb: *a few words of encouragement* ◇ *Her words were an encouragement to me to continue.*

encroach /ɪnˈkrəʊtʃ/ *verb* [I] ~ (**on/upon sth**) (*formal*) to use more of sth than you should: *I do hope that I am not encroaching too much upon your free time.*

encrypt /ɪnˈkrɪpt/ *verb* [T] (**COMPUTING**) to put information into a special code, especially in order to stop people being able to look at or understand it ▸ **encryption** /-ˈkrɪpʃn/ *noun* [U]

encyclopedia (*BrE also* **encyclopaedia**) /ɪnˌsaɪkləˈpiːdiə/ *noun* [C] a book or set of books that gives information about very many subjects, arranged in the order of the alphabet; a similar collection of information in digital form

end¹ ⓘ ⓐ⓵ ⓢ /end/ *noun* [C] **1** the furthest or last part of sth; the place or time where sth stops: *My house is at the end of the street.* ◇ *There are some seats at the far end of the room.* ◇ *I'm going on holiday at the end of October.* ◇ *He promised to give me an answer by the end of the week.* ◇ *She couldn't wait to hear the end of the story.* **HELP** The noun **finish** is used to mean **end** only in connection with races and competitions. **2** a situation in which sth does not exist any more: *It was the end of all his dreams.* ◇ *The war was finally at an end.* ◇ *The meeting came to an end* (= finished). ◇ look at **dead end** (2) **3** (*formal*) an aim or purpose: *They were prepared to do anything to achieve their ends.* ◇ note at **target¹ 4** one of the two halves of a sports field: *The teams changed ends at half-time.* **5** (*BrE*) a little piece

of sth that is left after the rest has been used: *a cigarette end*

IDM at the end of the day (*informal*) used to say the most important fact in a situation: *At the end of the day, you have to make the decision yourself.* **at the end of your tether** feeling that you cannot deal with a difficult situation any more, because you are too tired, worried, etc. **at a loose end** → **LOOSE¹ at your wits' end** → **WIT bring sth/come/draw to an end** (to cause sth) to finish: *His stay in England was coming to an end.* **end to end** in a line with the ends touching: *They put the tables end to end.* **in the end** finally; after a long period of time or series of events: *He wanted to get home early but in the end it was midnight before he left.* **make ends meet** to have enough money for your needs: *It's hard for us to make ends meet.* **make sb's hair stand on end** → **HAIR a means to an end** → **MEANS no end of sth** (*informal*) too many or much; a lot of sth: *She has given us no end of trouble.* **odds and ends** → **ODDS on end** (used about time) continuously: *He sits and reads for hours on end.* **put an end to sth** to stop sth from happening any more

end² ⓘ ⓐ⓵ ⓢ /end/ *verb* [I, T] ~ (**in/with sth**) to finish; to reach a point and go no further; to make sth finish: *The road ends here.* ◇ *How does this story end?* ◇ *The match ended in a draw.* ◇ *I think we'd better end this conversation now.*

PHRV end up (as sth) | **end up (doing sth)** to find yourself in a place/situation that you did not plan or expect: *We got lost and ended up in the centre of town.* ◇ *She had always wanted to be a writer but ended up as a teacher.* ◇ *There was nothing to eat at home so we ended up getting a takeaway.*

endanger /ɪnˈdeɪndʒə(r)/ *verb* [T] to cause danger to sb/ sth: *Smoking endangers your health.*

endangered /ɪnˈdeɪndʒəd/ *adj.* (used about animals, plants, etc.) in danger of becoming **EXTINCT** (= no longer alive in the world): *The giant panda is an endangered species.*

endear /ɪnˈdɪə(r)/ *verb* [T] ~ **sb/yourself to sb** (*formal*) to make sb/yourself liked by sb: *She managed to endear herself to everybody by her kindness.* ▸ **endearing** *adj.* ▸ **endearingly** *adv.*

endeavour (*AmE* **endeavor**) /ɪnˈdevə(r)/ *verb* [T] ~ **to do sth** (*formal*) to try hard: *She endeavoured to finish her work on time.* ▸ **endeavour** ⓘ+ ⓒ⓵ (*AmE* **endeavor**) *noun* [C, U]

endemic /enˈdemɪk/ *adj.* (**HEALTH**) (often used about a disease or problem) regularly found in a particular place or among a particular group of people and difficult to get rid of: *Malaria is endemic in many hot countries.* ◇ look at **epidemic, pandemic**

ending ⓘ ⓐ⓶ /ˈendɪŋ/ *noun* [C] **1** (**ARTS AND MEDIA**) the end (of a story, play, film, etc.): *That film made me cry but I was pleased that it had a happy ending.* **2** (**GRAMMAR**) the last part of a word, that can change: *When nouns end in '-ch' or '-sh' or '-x', the plural ending is '-es', not '-s'.*

endive /ˈendaɪv, -dɪv/ (*AmE*) = **CHICORY**

endless ⓘ+ ⓒ⓵ /ˈendləs/ *adj.* **1** very large in size or amount and seeming to have no end: *The possibilities are endless.* **2** lasting for a long time and seeming to have no end: *Our plane was delayed for hours and the wait seemed endless.* **SYN** **interminable** ▸ **endlessly** *adv.*

endorse ⓘ+ ⓒ⓵ /ɪnˈdɔːs/ *verb* [T] **1** to say publicly that you give official support or agreement to a plan, statement, decision, etc: *Members of all parties endorsed a ban on firearms.* **2** (**ARTS AND MEDIA**) to say in an advertisement that you use and like a particular product so that other people will want to buy it: *I wonder how many celebrities actually use the products they endorse.* **3** [usually passive] (*BrE*) (**LAW**) to add a note to a DRIVING LICENCE (= the document that allows you to drive a vehicle) to say that the driver has broken the law ▸ **endorsement** ⓘ+ **C1** *noun* [C, U]

endoscope /ˈendəskəʊp/ *noun* [C] (**MEDICINE**) an instrument used in medical operations that consists of a very small camera on a long thin tube that can be put into a person's body so that the parts inside can be seen

endoscopy /enˈdɒskəpi/ *noun* [C, U] (*pl.* -ies) (**MEDICINE**) a medical operation in which an ENDOSCOPE (= a very small camera) is put into a person's body so that the parts inside can be seen

endoskeleton /ˈendəʊskelɪtn/ *noun* [C] the bones inside the body of animals that give it shape and support ⊃ look at **exoskeleton**

endosperm /ˈendəʊspɜːm/ *noun* [U] (**BIOLOGY**) the part of a seed that stores food for the development of a plant

endothermic /ˌendəʊˈθɜːmɪk/ *adj.* (**CHEMISTRY**) (used about a chemical reaction or process) needing heat in order to take place ⊃ look at **exothermic** ⊃ picture at **water cycle**

endow /ɪnˈdaʊ/ *verb* [T] to give a large sum of money to a school, a college or another institution **PHR V** **be endowed with sth** to naturally have a particular characteristic, quality, etc: *She was endowed with courage and common sense.*

endowment /ɪnˈdaʊmənt/ *noun* [C, U] money that sb gives to a school, a college or another institution; the act of giving this money

ˈend point *noun* [C] the final stage of a period or process

ˈend product *noun* [C] something that is produced by a particular process or activity

endurance /ɪnˈdjʊərəns/ *noun* [U] the ability to continue doing sth painful or difficult for a long period of time without complaining

endure ⓘ+ **C1** /ɪnˈdjʊə(r)/ *verb* (*formal*) **1** [T] to suffer sth painful or uncomfortable, usually without complaining: *She endured ten years of loneliness.* **SYN** **bear¹** **2** [I] to continue **SYN** **last⁴** ▸ **enduring** *adj.*

ˈend user *noun* [C] (**COMPUTING**) a person who uses a product, especially one connected with computers, rather than one who makes or sells it: *Programs are tailored to meet the needs of end users.*

ENE *abbr.* (in writing) = EAST-NORTH-EAST

enemy ⓘ **B1** /ˈenəmi/ *noun* (*pl.* -ies) **1** [C] a person who hates and tries to harm you: *They used to be friends but became bitter enemies.* ◇ *He has made several enemies during his career.* ⊃ noun **enmity** **2** the enemy [sing. + sing./pl. verb] the army or country that your country is fighting against: *The enemy is/are approaching.* ◇ *enemy forces*

energetic /ˌenəˈdʒetɪk/ *adj.* full of or needing energy and enthusiasm: *Jogging is a very energetic form of exercise.* ▸ **energetically** /-kli/ *adv.*

energy ⓘ **A2** ⓦ /ˈenədʒi/ *noun* **1** [U] the ability to be very active or do a lot of work without getting tired: *Children are usually full of energy.* **2** energies [pl.] the effort and attention that you give to doing sth: *She*

energy resources

Radiant heat energy from the sun creates convection currents (kinetic energy) in the atmosphere. This energy can be used to turn wind turbines and so generate electricity.

When it rains, some of the water's potential energy is kept by storing the water behind dams.

When the water is released, it loses potential energy, which can be used to turn turbines and generate electricity.

Water from seas, rivers, etc. evaporates and rises, gaining potential energy.

Over millions of years the energy stored in plants and trees may be converted into fossil fuels such as coal, oil or gas.

Light energy is changed into chemical energy by a process called photosynthesis. This energy is stored by plants and trees.

Solar cells can be used to change sunlight directly into electricity.

Animals eat plants, trees or other animals in order to gain the energy they need to survive.

Solar panels contain water, which is heated by the sun. This warm water can then be used in the home for heating.

devoted all her energies to helping the blind. **3** [U] (**PHYSICS**) the power that comes from coal, electricity, gas, etc. that is used for producing heat, driving machines, etc: *solar/wind/renewable energy* ◊ *Employees are encouraged to* **save energy***.* ◊ *the country's total energy consumption* **4** [U] (**PHYSICS**) the ability of a substance or system to produce movement: *kinetic/potential energy*

enforce ⁰⁺ **C1** /ɪnˈfɔːs/ *verb* [T] to make people obey a law or rule or do sth that they do not want to: *How will they enforce the new law?* ▶ **enforced** *adj.*: *enforced redundancies* ▶ **enforcement** ⁰⁺ **C1** *noun* [U]

enfranchise /ɪnˈfræntʃaɪz/ *verb* [T, usually passive] (*formal*) (**POLITICS**) to give sb the right to vote in an election **OPP** **disenfranchise** ▶ **enfranchisement** /-tʃɪzmənt/ *noun* [U]

engage ⁰ **B2** ⓦ /ɪnˈɡeɪdʒ/ *verb* (*formal*) **1** [T] to interest or attract sb: *You need to engage the students' attention right from the start.* **2** [T] ~ **sb (as sth)** to give work to sb: *They engaged him as a cook.* ⊃ note at **job, professional²** **3** [I, T] ~ **(sth) (with sth)** when a part of a machine **engages**, or when you **engage** it, it fits together with another part of the machine and the machine begins to work: *Engage the clutch before selecting a gear.*
PHR V **engage in sth** (*formal*) to take part in sth: *I don't engage in that kind of gossip!*

engaged ⁰ **B1** /ɪnˈɡeɪdʒd/ *adj.* **1** ~ **(in/on sth)** (*formal*) (used about a person) busy doing sth: *They are engaged in talks with the Irish government.* **2** ~ **(to sb)** having agreed to get married: *We've just got engaged.* ◊ *Susan is engaged to Jim.* **3** (*BrE*) (*also* busy *especially in AmE*) (used about a phone line) being used: *I can't get through — the line is engaged.* ⊃ note at **phone¹** **4** (used about a public toilet) in use **OPP** **vacant**

engagement ⁰⁺ **C1** /ɪnˈɡeɪdʒmənt/ *noun* **1** [C] an agreement to get married; the time when you are engaged: *He broke off their engagement.* **2** [C] (*formal*) an arrangement to go somewhere or do sth at a fixed time; an appointment: *I can't come on Tuesday as I have a prior engagement.* **SYN** **appointment 3** [U] ~ **(with sb/sth)**; ~ **(in sth)** (*formal*) being involved with sb/sth in an attempt to understand them/it: *She has great connection and engagement with her young audience.* ◊ *their lack of engagement in politics*

en'gagement ring *noun* [C] a ring, usually with **PRECIOUS STONES** in it, that a man traditionally gives to a woman when they agree to get married

engaging ⁰⁺ **C1** /ɪnˈɡeɪdʒɪŋ/ *adj.* interesting or pleasant in a way that attracts your attention: *an engaging smile*

engine ⁰ **A2** /ˈendʒɪn/ *noun* [C] **1** (**PHYSICS**) the part of a vehicle that produces power to make the vehicle move: *This engine runs on diesel.* ◊ *a carjet engine* **2** (*also* locomotive) a vehicle that pulls a railway train

engineer¹ ⁰ **A2** /ˌendʒɪˈnɪə(r)/ *noun* [C] **1** a person whose job is to design, build or repair engines, machines, etc: *a civil/chemical/electrical/mechanical engineer* **2** a person who is trained to repair machines and electrical equipment: *They're sending an engineer to fix the problem with the heating.*

engineer² /ˌendʒɪˈnɪə(r)/ *verb* [T] **1** (*formal*) to arrange for sth to happen by careful secret planning: *Her promotion was engineered by her father.* **2** (**BIOLOGY**) to change the **GENETIC** structure of sth: *genetically engineered crops* **SYN** **genetically modified**

engineering ⁰ **B1** /ˌendʒɪˈnɪərɪŋ/ *noun* [U] (**EDUCATION, SCIENCE**) (the study of) the work that is done by an engineer: *mechanical/civil/chemical engineering* ◊ *an engineering company*

English¹ /ˈɪŋɡlɪʃ/ *noun* **1** [U] (**LANGUAGE**) the language, originally of England, now spoken in many other countries and used as a language of international communication: *Do you speak English?* ◊ *I've been learning English for five years.* **2** [U] English language or literature as a subject of study: *a degree in English* **3** the English [pl.] the people of England

English² /ˈɪŋɡlɪʃ/ *adj.* belonging to England, the English people, the English language, etc: *She's English.* ◊ *English history* ◊ *the English countryside*

English 'breakfast *noun* [C] a large breakfast of hot cooked food such as **BACON** and eggs ⊃ look at **continental breakfast**

the English 'Channel = **CHANNEL¹** (7)

English 'muffin (*AmE*) = **MUFFIN**

engrave /ɪnˈɡreɪv/ *verb* [T, often passive] ~ **B on A**; ~ **A with B** (**ART**) to cut words or designs on metal, stone, etc: *His name is engraved on the cup.* ◊ *The cup is engraved with his name.*

engraving /ɪnˈɡreɪvɪŋ/ *noun* (**ART**) **1** [C] a design that is cut into a piece of metal or stone; a picture made from this **2** [U] the art or process of cutting designs into wood, metal, etc.

engrossed /ɪnˈɡrəʊst/ *adj.* ~ **(in/with sth)** so interested in sth that you give it all your attention: *She was completely engrossed in her book.*

engulf /ɪnˈɡʌlf/ *verb* [T] (*formal*) **1** to surround or to cover sb/sth completely: *He was engulfed by a crowd of reporters.* **2** to affect sb/sth very strongly

enhance ⁰ **B2** ⓦ /ɪnˈhɑːns/ *verb* [T] to make the quality of sth even better or to make sb/sth more attractive: *This is an opportunity to enhance the reputation of the company.* ◊ *the skilled use of make-up to enhance your best features* ▶ **enhanced** *adj.*: *enhanced efficiency*

enigma /ɪˈnɪɡmə/ *noun* [C] (*pl.* enigmas) a person, thing or situation that is difficult to understand **SYN** **mystery** ▶ **enigmatic** /ˌenɪɡˈmætɪk/ *adj.*

enjoy ⁰ **A1** /ɪnˈdʒɔɪ/ *verb* [T] **1** ~ **sth/doing sth** to get pleasure from sth: *I really enjoyed that meal.* ◊ *He enjoys listening to music while he's driving.* **2** ~ **yourself** to be happy; to have a good time: *I enjoyed myself at the party last night.*

enjoyable ⁰⁺ **B2** /ɪnˈdʒɔɪəbl/ *adj.* giving pleasure: *an enjoyable experience/weekend*

enjoyment /ɪnˈdʒɔɪmənt/ *noun* [U, C] pleasure or a thing that gives pleasure: *She gets a lot of enjoyment from teaching.* ◊ *One of her main enjoyments is foreign travel.*

enlarge /ɪnˈlɑːdʒ/ *verb* [T, I] to make sth bigger or to become bigger: *I'm going to have this photo enlarged.*

enlargement /ɪnˈlɑːdʒmənt/ *noun* [C, U] making sth bigger or sth that has been made bigger: *an enlargement of a photo* **OPP** **reduction**

enlighten /ɪnˈlaɪtn/ *verb* [T] (*formal*) to give sb information so that they understand sth better

enlightened /ɪnˈlaɪtnd/ *adj.* having an understanding of people's needs, a situation, etc. that shows a modern attitude to life

the Enlightenment /ðiː ɪnˈlaɪtnmənt/ *noun* [sing.] (**HISTORY**) the period in the eighteenth century when many writers and scientists began to argue that science and reason were more important than religion and tradition

enlist /ɪnˈlɪst/ verb 1 [T] to get help, support, etc: *We need to enlist your support.* 2 [I, T] to join the armed forces; to make sb join the armed forces: *They enlisted as soon as war was declared.*

enmity /ˈenməti/ noun [U] feelings of hate towards an enemy

enormity /ɪˈnɔːməti/ noun [sing.] (formal) the very great size, effect, etc. of sth; the fact that sth is very serious: *the enormity of a task/decision/problem*

enormous 🕮 A2 /ɪˈnɔːməs/ adj. very big or very great: *an enormous building ◇ enormous pleasure* SYN **huge** ▸ **enormously** adv.

enough¹ 🕮 A1 /ɪˈnʌf/ det., pron. 1 as much or as many of sth as necessary: *I didn't have enough money to stay in a hotel. ◇ Not everybody can have a book — there aren't enough. ◇ If enough of you are interested, we'll arrange a trip to the theatre.* 2 as much or as many as you want: *I've had enough of living in a city (= I don't want to live in a city any more). ◇ Don't give me any more work. I've got quite enough already.*

enough² 🕮 A1 /ɪˈnʌf/ adv. (after a verb, an adjective or an adverb) 1 to the necessary amount or degree: *You don't practise enough. ◇ He's not old enough to travel alone. ◇ Does she speak Italian well enough to get the job?* SYN **sufficiently** 2 quite, but not very: *She plays well enough, for a beginner.*
IDM **fair enough** → FAIR¹ **funnily, strangely, etc. enough it is funny, etc. that …** : *Funnily enough, I thought exactly the same myself.* **sure enough** → SURE²

enquire 🕮+ C1 (especially BrE) (also **inquire** AmE, BrE) /ɪnˈkwaɪə(r)/ verb [I, T] ~(**about sb/sth**) (formal) to ask for information about sth: *Could you enquire when the trains to Cork leave? ◇ We need to enquire about hotels in Vienna.* ⸰ note at **ask**
PHR V **enquire after sb** to ask about sb's health **enquire into sth** to study sth in order to find out all the facts: *The journalist enquired into the politician's financial affairs.*

enquirer (especially BrE) (also **inquirer** AmE, BrE) /ɪnˈkwaɪərə(r)/ noun [C] (formal) a person who asks for information

enquiring (especially BrE) (also **inquiring** AmE, BrE) /ɪnˈkwaɪərɪŋ/ adj. 1 interested in learning new things: *We should encourage children to have enquiring minds.* 2 asking for information: *He gave me an enquiring look.*

enquiry 🕮 B2 (especially BrE) (also **inquiry** AmE, BrE) /ɪnˈkwaɪəri/ noun (pl. -ies) 1 [C] ~(**about/concerning/ into sb/sth**) (formal) a request for information about sth; a question that you ask about sth: *I'll make some enquiries into English language courses in Oxford.* 2 [U] the act of asking about sth: *After weeks of enquiry he finally found what he was looking for.* 3 [C] ~(**into sth**) an official process to find out the cause of sth: *After the accident there was an enquiry into safety procedures.*

enrage /ɪnˈreɪdʒ/ verb [T] (formal) to make sb very angry SYN **infuriate**

enrich 🕮+ C1 /ɪnˈrɪtʃ/ verb [T] 1 to improve the quality, taste, etc. of sth by adding sth: *These cornflakes are enriched with vitamins/are vitamin-enriched.* 2 to make sb/sth rich or richer OPP **impoverish** ▸ **enrichment** noun [U]

enrol 🕮+ C1 (BrE) (AmE **enroll**) /ɪnˈrəʊl/ verb [I, T] (-ll-) ~(**on/in sth**) (EDUCATION) to become a member of a club, school, etc.; to make sb a member of a club, school, etc: (BrE) *I've enrolled on an Italian course.*

◇ (AmE) *to enroll in a program of study ◇ They enrolled 100 new students last year.* ▸ **enrolment** (AmE **enrollment**) noun [C, U]: *Enrolment for the course will take place next week.*

en route /ˌɒn ˈruːt, ˌɒ̃ ˈruːt/ adv. ~(**from …**) (**to …**); ~(**for …**) on the way; while travelling from/to a place: *They were en route from Boston to New York. ◇ The car broke down when we were en route for Dover.*

ensemble /ɒnˈsɒmbl/ noun [C] 1 [+ sing./pl. verb] (MUSIC) a small group of musicians, dancers or actors who perform together: *a brass/wind/string ensemble* ◇ *The ensemble is/are based in Leeds.* 2 [usually sing.] (formal) a number of things considered as a group 3 [usually sing.] a set of clothes that are worn together

ensue 🕮+ C1 /ɪnˈsjuː/ verb [I] (formal) to happen after (and often as a result of) sth else SYN **follow**

en suite /ˌɒn ˈswiːt, ˌɒ̃ ˈswiːt/ adj., adv. (used about a bedroom and bathroom) forming one unit: *The bedroom has a bathroom en suite.*

ensure 🕮 B2 🆆 (also **insure** especially in AmE) /ɪnˈʃʊə(r), -ˈʃɔː(r)/ verb [T] ~(**that …**) to make sure that sth happens or is definite: *Please ensure that the door is locked before you leave.*

entail /ɪnˈteɪl/ verb [T] (formal) to make sth necessary: *The job sounds interesting but I'm not sure what it entails.* SYN **involve**

entangled /ɪnˈtæŋgld/ adj. caught in sth else: *The bird was entangled in the net.* ◇ (figurative) *I've got myself entangled in some financial problems.*

entente /ɒnˈtɒnt/ noun [U, sing.] (POLITICS) a friendly relationship between two countries: *the Franco-Russian entente*

enter 🕮 A2 🆂 /ˈentə(r)/ verb
• COME/GO IN 1 [I, T] (formal) to come or go into a place: *Don't enter without knocking. ◇ They all stood up when he entered the room.* ⸰ nouns **entrance** and **entry**
• BECOME A MEMBER 2 [T] to become a member of sth, especially a profession or an institution: *She entered the legal profession in 2015. ◇ to enter school/college/ university* ⸰ noun **entrant**
• BEGIN AN ACTIVITY 3 [T] to begin or become involved in an activity, a situation, etc: *When she entered the relationship, she had no idea he was already married. ◇ We have just entered a new phase in international relations.*
• EXAM/COMPETITION 4 [T, I] ~**sb/sth (in/for sth)**; ~(**for**) **sth** to put your name or sb's name on the list for an exam, race, competition, etc: *Irish trainers have entered several horses in the race. ◇ I entered a competition in the Sunday paper and I won £100! ◇ Only four British players have entered for the championship.*
• WRITE INFORMATION 5 [T] ~**sb/sth (in/into/on/onto sth)** to put names, numbers, details, etc. in a list, book, computer, etc: *I've entered all the data into the spreadsheet. ◇ Enter your password and press return.*
PHR V **enter into sth** (formal) 1 to start to think or talk about sth: *I don't want to enter into details now.* 2 to be part of sth; to be involved in sth: *This is a business matter. Friendship doesn't enter into it.* **enter into sth (with sb)** (formal) to begin sth: *The government has entered into negotiations with the unions.*

enterprise 🕮+ C1 /ˈentəpraɪz/ noun (BUSINESS) 1 [C] a company or business: *state-owned/public enterprises* ◇ *The organization has a lot of experience working with large enterprises.* ⸰ look at **social enterprise** 2 [C] a large project, especially one that is difficult: *It's a very exciting new enterprise. ◇ a joint enterprise* SYN **venture**¹ 3 [U] the development of businesses by the people of a country rather than by the government: *They provide grants to encourage enterprise in the region.* ➔ look at **free enterprise, private enterprise** **4** [U] the ability to think of new projects or create new businesses and make them successful: *We need men and women of enterprise and energy.*

enterprising /'entəpraɪzɪŋ/ *adj.* having or showing the ability to think of new projects or new ways of doing things and make them successful: *One enterprising farmer opened up his field as a car park and charged people to park there.*

entertain ⚡ **B1** /ˌentə'teɪn/ *verb* **1** [T] ~ **(sb) (with sth)** to interest sb or make sb laugh in order to please them: *He entertained us with jokes all evening.* ◇ *I find it very hard to keep my class entertained on a Friday afternoon.* **2** [I, T] to welcome sb as a guest, especially to your home; to give sb food and drink: *They entertain a lot./They do a lot of entertaining.* ◇ *Barbecues are a favourite way of entertaining friends.*

entertainer /ˌentə'teɪnə(r)/ *noun* [C] (**ARTS AND MEDIA**) a person whose job is to sing, dance or perform for people so that they enjoy themselves: *a street entertainer*

entertaining ⚡+ **B2** /ˌentə'teɪnɪŋ/ *adj.* interesting and funny: *an entertaining speech* ◇ *She was always so funny and entertaining.*

entertainment ⚡ **B1** /ˌentə'teɪnmənt/ *noun* [U, C] (**ARTS AND MEDIA**) film, music, etc. used to interest people or make them laugh: *There isn't much entertainment for young people in this town.* ◇ *There's a full programme of entertainments every evening.*

enthral (*BrE*) (*AmE* **enthrall**) /ɪn'θrɔːl/ *verb* [T, often passive] (-ll-) to hold sb's interest and attention completely: *He was enthralled by her story.* ▸ **enthralling** *adj.*

enthusiasm ⚡ **B2** /ɪn'θjuːziæzəm/ *noun* [U] ~ **(for/ about sth/doing sth)** a strong feeling of excitement or interest in sth and a desire to become involved in it: *Jan showed great enthusiasm for the new project.*

enthusiast ⚡+ **C1** /ɪn'θjuːziæst/ *noun* [C] a person who is very interested in an activity or subject

enthusiastic ⚡ **B2** /ɪnˌθjuːzi'æstɪk/ *adj.* ~ **(about sth/ doing sth)** full of excitement and interest in sth: *The kids are very enthusiastic about sport.* ▸ **enthusiastically** /-kli/ *adv.*

entice /ɪn'taɪs/ *verb* [T] ~ **sb (into sth/doing sth)** to persuade sb to do sth or to go somewhere by offering them sth nice: *Advertisements try to entice people into buying more things than they need.* ▸ **enticement** *noun* [C, U]

enticing /ɪn'taɪsɪŋ/ *adj.* attractive and interesting

entire ⚡ **B2** /ɪn'taɪə(r)/ *adj.* [only before noun] (used when you are emphasizing that the whole of sth is involved) including everything, everyone or every part: *He managed to read the entire book in two days.* ◇ *We invited the entire village to the party.* **SYN** **whole**[1] ▸ **entirety** /-ərəti/ *noun* [sing.] (*formal*): *We must consider the problem in its entirety* (= as a whole).

entirely ⚡ **B2** ⑤ /ɪn'taɪəli/ *adv.* in every way possible; completely: *I entirely agree with you.* ◇ *That's an entirely different matter.* ◇ *The audience was almost entirely female.*

entitle ⚡+ **C1** /ɪn'taɪtl/ *verb* [T, often passive] ~ **sb (to sth)** to give sb the right to have or do sth: *I think I'm entitled to a day's holiday — I've worked hard enough.*

entitled /ɪn'taɪtld/ *adj.* (used about books, plays, etc.) with the title: *Duncan's first book was entitled 'Aquarium'.*

entitlement /ɪn'taɪtlmənt/ *noun* (*formal*) **1** [U] ~ **(to sth)** the official right to have or do sth: *This may affect your entitlement to compensation.* **2** [C] something that you have the official right to; the amount that you have the right to receive: *The contributions will affect your pension entitlements.*

entity ⚡+ **C1** **W** /'entəti/ *noun* [C] (*pl.* -**ies**) (*formal*) something that exists separately from sth else and has its own identity: *The kindergarten and the school are in the same building but they're really separate entities.*

entomology /ˌentə'mɒlədʒi/ *noun* [U] (**BIOLOGY**) the scientific study of insects

entourage /'ɒntʊrɑːʒ/ *noun* [C + sing./pl. verb] a group of people who travel with an important person

entrails /'entreɪlz/ *noun* [pl.] (**ANATOMY**) the organs inside the body of a person or an animal, especially the INTESTINES (= the tubes that carry food away from the stomach)

entrance ⚡ **B1** /'entrəns/ *noun* **1** [C] ~ **(to/of sth)** the door, gate or opening where you go into a place: *I'll meet you at the entrance to the theatre.* **OPP** **exit**[1] **2** [C] ~ **(into/onto sth)** the act of coming or going into a place, especially in a way that attracts attention: *He made a dramatic entrance onto the stage.* **OPP** **exit**[1] **3** [U] ~ **(to sth)** the right to enter a place: *They refused entrance to the club because they were wearing shorts.* ◇ *an entrance fee* **SYN** **entry** ➔ look at **admission** (1), **admittance** **4** [U] ~ **(into/to sth)** permission to join a club, society, university, etc: *students hoping to gain entrance to college* ◇ *You don't need to take an entrance exam to get into university.* ➔ look at **admission** (1)

entrant /'entrənt/ *noun* [C] a person who enters a profession, competition, exam, university, etc.

entreat /ɪn'triːt/ *verb* [T] (*formal*) to ask sb to do sth, often in an emotional way **SYN** **beg**

entrepreneur ⚡+ **B2** /ˌɒntrəprə'nɜː(r)/ *noun* [C] (**BUSINESS**) a person who makes money by starting or running businesses, especially when this involves taking financial risks ▸ **entrepreneurial** /-'nɜːriəl/ *adj.* ▸ **entrepreneurship** *noun* [U] ➔ picture at **income**

entropy /'entrəpi/ *noun* [U] (*symb.* S) (**PHYSICS**) a measurement of the energy that is present in a system or process but is not available to do work

entrust /ɪn'trʌst/ *verb* [T] ~ **A with B/~ B to A** (*formal*) to make sb responsible for sth: *I entrusted Rachel with the arrangements for the party./I entrusted the arrangements for the party to Rachel.*

entry ⚡ **B1** ⊘ /'entri/ *noun* (*pl.* -**ies**)
• INTO A PLACE **1** [C, U] ~ **(into/to sth)** the act of coming or going into a place: *She made her entry to the sound of applause.* ◇ *How did the thieves gain entry into the building?* **SYN** **entrance** **2** [U] ~ **(into/to sth)** the right to enter a place: *The immigrants were refused entry at the airport.* ◇ *Entry to the museum is free.* ◇ *The sign says 'No Entry'.* ◇ *an entry visa* ➔ look at **admission** (1), **admittance**
• JOINING A GROUP **3** [U] ~ **(to/into sth)** the right to take part in sth or become a member of a group: *Entry to the competition is open to anyone over 18.* ◇ *countries seeking entry into the European Union*
• IN A COMPETITION **4** [C] a person or thing that is entered for a competition, etc: *There were 50 entries for the Eurovision song contest.* ◇ *The winning entry is number 45!*
• WRITTEN INFORMATION **5** [C] one item that is written down in a list, account book, dictionary, etc: *an entry in a diary* ◇ *You'll find 'ice-skate' after the entry for 'ice'.*

6 [U] an act of recording information in a computer, book, etc: *More keyboarding staff are required for data entry.*

• DOOR **7** [C] (*AmE*) a door, gate, passage, etc. where you enter a building, etc. **SYN** **entrance**

'**entry-level** *adj.* **1** (used about a product) basic and suitable for new users who may later move on to a more advanced product: *an entry-level computer* **2** (BUSINESS) (used about a job) at the lowest level in a company

'**E-number** *noun* [C] (*BrE*) a number beginning with the letter E that is printed on PACKETS and containers to show what artificial tastes and colours have been added to food and drink; an artificial taste, colour, etc. added to food and drink

envelop /ɪnˈveləp/ *verb* [T] (*formal*) to cover or surround sb/sth completely (in sth): *The hills were enveloped in mist.*

envelope 🔒+ **B2** /ˈenvələʊp, ˈɒn-/ *noun* [C] the paper cover for a letter ⊃ look at **stamped addressed envelope**

enviable /ˈenviəbl/ *adj.* (used about sth that sb else has and that you would like) attractive ⊃ verb and noun **envy**

envious /ˈenviəs/ *adj.* ~(of sb/sth) wanting sth that sb else has: *She was envious of her sister's success.* **SYN** **jealous** ⊃ verb and noun **envy** ▶ **enviously** *adv.*

environment 🔒 **A2** ⊙ /ɪnˈvaɪrənmənt/ *noun* **1** [C, U] the conditions in which you live, work, etc: *a pleasant working environment* **2** the environment [sing.] the natural world, for example the land, air and water, in which people, animals and plants live: *We need stronger laws to protect the environment.* ⊃ look at **surroundings**

environmental 🔒 **B1** ⊙ /ɪnˌvaɪrənˈmentl/ *adj.* **1** (ENVIRONMENT) connected with the natural conditions in which people, animals and plants live; connected with the environment: *the environmental impact of pollution* ◇ *environmental issues/problems* ◇ *an environmental group/movement* (= that aims to improve or protect the natural environment) **2** connected with the conditions that affect the behaviour and development of sb/sth: *environmental influences* ◇ *an environmental health officer* ▶ **environmentally** /-təli/ *adv.*: *an environmentally sensitive area* (= one that is easily damaged or that contains rare animals, plants, etc.)

en,vironmental 'art *noun* [U] (ART) art that is meant to enhance the environment or draw attention to environmental issues

environmentalist /ɪnˌvaɪrənˈmentəlɪst/ *noun* [C] (ENVIRONMENT) a person who wants to protect the environment ▶ **environmentalism** /-lɪzəm/ *noun* [U]

en,vironmentally 'friendly (*also* en,vironment-'friendly) *adj.* (ENVIRONMENT) (used about products) not harming the environment

envisage /ɪnˈvɪzɪdʒ/ *verb* (*especially BrE*) (*also* envision /ɪnˈvɪʒn/ *especially in AmE*) [T] (*formal*) to think of sth as being possible in the future; to imagine: *I don't envisage any problems with this.*

envoy /ˈenvɔɪ/ *noun* [C] (POLITICS) a person who is sent by a government or an organization to talk to other governments, etc.

envy[1] /ˈenvi/ *noun* [U] ~(of sb); ~(at/of sth) the feeling that you have when sb else has sth that you want: *It was difficult for her to hide her envy of her friend/of her friend's success.* ⊃ look at **enviable, envious**

IDM **be the envy of sb** to be the thing that causes sb to feel envy: *The city's transport system is the envy of many of its European neighbours.*

envy[2] /ˈenvi/ *verb* [T] (envying; envies; *pt, pp* envied) ~(sb) (sth) to want sth that sb else has; to feel ENVY: *I've always envied your good luck.* ◇ *I don't envy you that job* (= I'm glad that I don't have it).

enzyme /ˈenzaɪm/ *noun* [C] (BIOLOGY) a substance, produced by all living things, that helps a chemical change to happen more quickly, without being changed itself ⊃ picture at **digestive system, virus**

eon /ˈiːən, ˈiːɒn/ (*AmE*) = AEON

ephemeral /ɪˈfemərəl/ *adj.* (*formal*) lasting or used for only a short period of time: *ephemeral pleasures* **SYN** **short-lived**

epic[1] /ˈepɪk/ *noun* **1** [C, U] (LITERATURE) a long poem about the actions of great men and women or about a nation's history; this style of poetry: *one of the great Hindu epics* ⊃ look at **lyric**[1] (1) **2** [C] (ARTS AND MEDIA) a long film/movie or book that contains a lot of action, usually about a historical subject **3** [C] a long and difficult job or activity that you think people should admire: *Their four-hour match on Centre Court was an epic.*

epic[2] /ˈepɪk/ *adj.* very long and exciting: *an epic struggle/journey*

epicentre (*BrE*) (*AmE* epicenter) /ˈepɪsentə(r)/ *noun* [C] (GEOLOGY) the point on the earth's surface where the effects of an earthquake are felt most strongly ⊃ picture at **seismic**

epicurean /ˌepɪkjʊəˈriːən/ *adj.* (*formal*) taking great pleasure in things, especially food and drink, and enjoying yourself

epidemic 🔒+ **C1** /ˌepɪˈdemɪk/ *noun* [C] (HEALTH) a large number of cases of people or animals suffering from the same disease at the same time ⊃ look at **endemic, pandemic**

epidemiology /ˌepɪˌdiːmiˈɒlədʒi/ *noun* [U] (MEDICINE) the scientific study of the spread and control of diseases ▶ **epidemiological** /ˌepɪˌdiːmiəˈlɒdʒɪkl/ *adj.* ▶ **epidemiologist** /ˌepɪˌdiːmiˈɒlədʒɪst/ *noun* [C]

epidermis /ˌepɪˈdɜːmɪs/ *noun* [sing., U] **1** (ANATOMY) the outer layer of the skin ⊃ picture at **skin**[1] **2** the outer layer of TISSUE in a plant ⊃ picture at **flower**[1] ▶ **epidermal** /-məl/ *adj.*

epidural /ˌepɪˈdjʊərəl/ *noun* [C] (MEDICINE) an ANAESTHETIC (= a drug that stops you feeling pain) that is put into the lower part of the back so that no pain is felt in the lower half of the body: *Some mothers choose to have an epidural when giving birth.*

epiglottis /ˌepɪˈɡlɒtɪs/ *noun* [C] (ANATOMY) a small part behind the tongue that moves to prevent food or drink from entering the lungs ⊃ picture at **body, digestive system**

epigram /ˈepɪɡræm/ *noun* [C] (LITERATURE) a short poem or phrase that expresses an idea in a clever or funny way ▶ **epigrammatic** /ˌepɪɡrəˈmætɪk/ *adj.*

epilepsy /ˈepɪlepsi/ *noun* [U] (HEALTH) a DISORDER of the NERVOUS SYSTEM that can cause a person to become unconscious, sometimes with violent movements that they cannot control

epileptic /ˌepɪˈleptɪk/ *noun* [C] (HEALTH) a person who suffers from EPILEPSY ▶ **epileptic** *adj.*: *an epileptic fit*

epilogue /ˈepɪlɒɡ/ *noun* [C] (LITERATURE) a short piece that is added at the end of a book, play, etc. and that comments on what has gone before ⊃ look at **prologue**

6 January, when Christians celebrate the time when three wise men came to see the baby Jesus in Bethlehem

episode 🔵 B1 /ˈepɪsəʊd/ noun [C] **1** one separate event in sb's life, a novel, etc: *That's an episode in my life I'd rather forget.* **2** (**ARTS AND MEDIA**) one part of a TV or radio story that is shown or told in several parts

epistolary /ɪˈpɪstələri/ adj. (*formal*) (**LITERATURE**) written or expressed in the form of letters: *an epistolary novel*

epitaph /ˈepɪtɑːf/ noun [C] (**LITERATURE**) words that are written or said about a dead person, especially words written on a stone where they are buried

epithet /ˈepɪθet/ noun [C] (**LANGUAGE**) **1** an adjective or a phrase that is used to describe sb/sth's character or most important quality, especially in order to say sth good or bad about sb/sth: *The novel is neither old enough nor good enough to deserve the epithet 'classic'.* **2** (*especially AmE*) an offensive word or phrase that is used about a person or group of people: *Racial epithets were written all over the wall.*

epitome /ɪˈpɪtəmi/ noun [sing.] **the ~ (of sth)** (*formal*) a perfect example of sth: *Her clothes are the epitome of good taste.*

epitomize (*BrE also* -**ise**) /ɪˈpɪtəmaɪz/ verb [T] to be a perfect example of sth: *This building epitomizes modern trends in architecture.*

epoch /ˈiːpɒk/ noun [C] (*formal*) (**HISTORY**) a period of time in history, especially one during which important events or changes happen

eponymous /ɪˈpɒnɪməs/ adj. [only before noun] the **eponymous** character of a book, play, film, etc. is the one mentioned in the title: *Don Quixote is the eponymous hero of the great novel by Cervantes.*

equal¹ 🔵 B1 ⊙ /ˈiːkwəl/ adj. **1 ~ (to sb/sth)** the same in size, amount, value, number, level, etc: *This animal is equal in weight to a small car.* ◇ *They are equal in weight.* ◇ *They are of equal weight.* ◇ *Divide it into two equal parts.* **OPP** **unequal 2** having the same rights or being treated the same as other people; giving all people the same rights and opportunities: *Everyone is born equal.* ◇ *This company has an **equal opportunities** policy* (= gives the same chance of employment to everyone). **3 ~ to sth** (*formal*) having the strength, ability etc. to do sth: *I'm afraid Bob just isn't equal to the job.*
IDM **be on equal terms (with sb)** to have the same advantages and disadvantages as sb else

equal² 🔵 B1 ⊙ /ˈiːkwəl/ verb (-**ll-**, *AmE* -**l-**) **1** *linking verb* (**MATHEMATICS**) (used about numbers, etc.) to be the same as sth: *44 plus 17 equals 61* (44 + 17 = 61). **2** [T] to be as good as sb/sth: *He ran an excellent race, equalling the world record.*

equal³ 🔵 B2 🟢 /ˈiːkwəl/ noun [C] a person who has the same ability, rights, etc. as you do: *to treat somebody as an equal*

equality 🔵 C1 /iˈkwɒləti/ noun [U] the situation in which everyone has the same rights and advantages: *racial equality* (= between people of different races) ◇ *We need to ensure equality of opportunity.* **OPP** **inequality**

equalize (*BrE also* -**ise**) /ˈiːkwəlaɪz/ verb [I] (*BrE*) (**SPORT**) to score a goal that makes the score of both teams equal

equalizer (*BrE also* -**iser**) /ˈiːkwəlaɪzə(r)/ noun [C, usually sing.] (**SPORT**) a goal that makes the score of both teams equal: *Kane scored the equalizer.*

equally 🔵 B1 🟠 /ˈiːkwəli/ adv. **1** to the same degree or amount: *They both worked equally hard.* **2** in equal parts: *His money was divided equally between his children.* **3** (*formal*) (used when you are comparing two

ideas or commenting on what you have just said) at the same time; but/and also: *I do not think what he did was right. Equally, I can understand why he did it.*

equals sign (also **equal sign**) noun [C] (**MATHEMATICS**) the symbol (=), used in mathematics

equate /iˈkweɪt/ verb [T] **~ sth (with sth)** to consider one thing as being the same as sth else: *You can't always equate money with happiness.*

equation 🔵 C1 /iˈkweɪʒn/ noun [C] (**MATHEMATICS**) a statement that two quantities are equal: *2x + 5 = 11 is an equation.*

equator /iˈkweɪtə(r)/ noun (*usually* **the equator**) noun [sing.] (**GEOGRAPHY**) the imaginary line around the earth at an equal distance from the North and South Poles: *north/south of the equator* ◇ *The island is on the equator.* ⊃ picture at **earth**¹, **season**¹

equatorial /ˌekwəˈtɔːriəl/ adj. (**GEOGRAPHY**) near the EQUATOR: *equatorial rainforests*

equestrian /iˈkwestriən/ adj. (*formal*) (**SPORT**) connected with horse riding

equidistant /ˌiːkwɪˈdɪstənt, ˌek-/ adj. [not before noun] **~ (from sth)** (*formal*) equally far from two or more places

equilateral triangle /ˌiːkwɪˌlætərəl ˈtraɪæŋgl/ noun [C] (**GEOMETRY**) a TRIANGLE whose three sides are all the same length ⊃ picture at **triangle**

equilibrium /ˌiːkwɪˈlɪbriəm, ˌek-/ noun [U, sing.] **1** (**CHEMISTRY**, **PHYSICS**) a state of balance, especially between forces or influences that are working in opposite ways: *The point at which the solid and the liquid are **in equilibrium** is called the freezing point.* **2** a calm state of mind and a balance of emotions

equine /ˈekwaɪn, ˈiːk-/ adj. (*formal*) connected with horses; like a horse

equinox /ˈekwɪnɒks, ˈiːk-/ noun [C] (**ASTRONOMY**) one of the two times in the year (around 20 March and 22 September) when the sun is above the EQUATOR (= the imagined line around the middle of the earth) and day and night are of equal length: *the spring/autumn equinox* ⊃ look at **solstice** ⊃ picture at **season**¹

equip 🔵 B2 /iˈkwɪp/ verb [T] (-**pp-**) **~ sb/sth (with sth)** **1** to supply sb/sth with what is needed for a particular purpose: *We shall equip all schools with new computers over the next year.* ◇ *The flat has a **fully equipped** kitchen.* **2** to prepare sb for a particular task: *The course equips students with all the skills necessary to become a chef.*

equipment 🔵 A2 /iˈkwɪpmənt/ noun [U] the things that are needed to do a particular activity: *office/sports/computer equipment* ◇ *a useful **piece of equipment** for the kitchen* ⊃ picture at **gardening**

equitable /ˈekwɪtəbl/ adj. (*formal*) fair and reasonable; treating everyone in an equal way: *an equitable distribution of resources*

equity /ˈekwəti/ noun **1** [U] (**BUSINESS**) the value of a company's shares; the value of a property after all charges and debts have been paid ⊃ look at **negative equity 2 equities** [pl.] (**BUSINESS**) shares in a company that do not pay a fixed amount of interest

equivalent 🔵 B2 🟠 /iˈkwɪvələnt/ adj. **~ (to sth)** equal in value, amount, meaning, importance, etc: *The British House of Commons is roughly equivalent to the American House of Representatives.*
▶ **equivalence** 🟠 /-ləns/ noun [U] (*formal*)
▶ **equivalent** 🔵 B2 🟠 noun [C]: *There is no English equivalent to the French 'bon appétit'.*

ER /ˌiː ˈɑː(r)/ *abbr.* (*AmE*) **emergency room** (the part of a hospital where people who need immediate treatment are taken) ⊃ look at **A & E**

er /ɜː(r)/ *exclamation* used in writing to show the sound that sb makes when they cannot decide what to say next

era 🔊+ **B2** /ˈɪərə/ *noun* [C] (**HISTORY**) a period of time in history (that is special for some reason): *We are living in the era of the smartphone.*

eradicate /ɪˈrædɪkeɪt/ *verb* [T] (*formal*) to destroy or get rid of sth completely: *Some diseases, such as smallpox, have been completely eradicated.* ▶ **eradication** /ɪˌrædɪˈkeɪʃn/ *noun* [U]

erase /ɪˈreɪz/ *verb* [T] (*formal*) to remove sth completely (a pencil mark, a recording, a computer file, etc.): *Parts of the recording have been erased.* ◇ (*figurative*) *He tried to erase the memory of those terrible years from his mind.*

eraser /ɪˈreɪzə(r)/ *noun* [C] = RUBBER (2)

erbium /ˈɜːbiəm/ *noun* [U] (*symb.* Er) (**CHEMISTRY**) a chemical element. Erbium is a soft silver-white metal. ❶ For more information on the periodic table of elements, look at the **Reference Section** of this dictionary.

e-reader *noun* [C] (**COMPUTING, LITERATURE**) a device on which you can read electronic books, newspapers, etc.

erect¹ /ɪˈrekt/ *adj.* **1** (*formal*) standing straight up: *He stood with his head erect.* **SYN** **upright** **2** (used about the male sexual organ) hard and standing up because of sexual excitement

erect² 🔊+ **C1** /ɪˈrekt/ *verb* [T] (*formal*) to build sth or to stand sth straight up: *to erect a statue* ◇ *Huge TV screens were erected above the stage.* ⊃ note at **build¹**

erection /ɪˈrekʃn/ *noun* **1** [C] if a man has an **erection**, his PENIS (= his sexual organ) becomes hard and stands up because he is sexually excited: *to get/have an erection* **2** [U] (*formal*) the act of building sth or standing sth straight up

ergonomic /ˌɜːɡəˈnɒmɪk/ *adj.* designed to make people's working environment more comfortable and to help them work more efficiently: *ergonomic design* ▶ **ergonomically** /-kli/ *adv.*: *The layout is hard to fault ergonomically.*

ergonomics /ˌɜːɡəˈnɒmɪks/ *noun* [U] the study of working environments, especially the design of equipment and furniture, in order to help people work more efficiently

features of coastal erosion

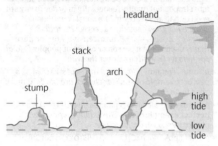

erode /ɪˈrəʊd/ *verb* [T, usually passive, I] (**GEOLOGY**) (used about the sea, the weather, etc.) to destroy sth slowly; to be destroyed in this way: *The cliff has been eroded by the sea.* ◇ *The rocks have eroded away over time.* ▶ **erosion** /ɪˈrəʊʒn/ *noun* [U]: *the erosion of rocks by the sea*

erotic /ɪˈrɒtɪk/ *adj.* causing sexual excitement: *an erotic film/poem/dream*

causes of coastal erosion

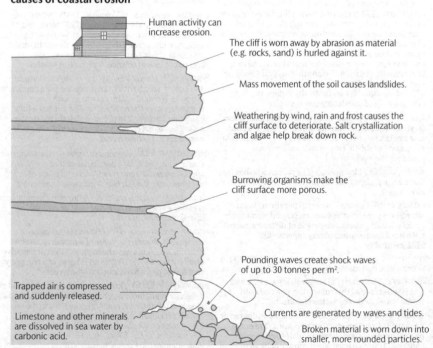

Human activity can increase erosion.

The cliff is worn away by abrasion as material (e.g. rocks, sand) is hurled against it.

Mass movement of the soil causes landslides.

Weathering by wind, rain and frost causes the cliff surface to deteriorate. Salt crystallization and algae help break down rock.

Burrowing organisms make the cliff surface more porous.

Trapped air is compressed and suddenly released.

Limestone and other minerals are dissolved in sea water by carbonic acid.

Pounding waves create shock waves of up to 30 tonnes per m².

Currents are generated by waves and tides.

Broken material is worn down into smaller, more rounded particles.

err /ɜː(r)/ *verb* [I] (*formal*) to be or do wrong; to make mistakes

IDM **err on the side of sth** to do more of sth than is necessary in order to avoid the opposite happening: *It is better to err on the side of caution* (= it is better to be too careful rather than not careful enough).

errand /'erənd/ *noun* [C] a short journey to take or get sth for sb, for example to buy sth from a shop

erratic¹ /ɪ'rætɪk/ *adj.* (used about a person's behaviour, or about the quality of sth) changing without reason; that you can never be sure of: *Jones is a talented player but he's very erratic* (= sometimes he plays well, sometimes badly). ▶ **erratically** /-kli/ *adv.*

erratic² /ɪ'rætɪk/ *noun* [C] (**GEOLOGY**) a large rock that is different from the rock around it and was left behind when a GLACIER (= a large moving mass of ice) melted

erroneous /ɪ'rəuniəs/ *adj.* (*formal*) not correct; based on wrong information: *erroneous conclusions/ assumptions* ▶ **erroneously** *adv.*

error ʔ **A2** **◐** /'erə(r)/ *noun* **1** [C] (*formal*) a mistake: *The phone bill was far too high due to a computer error.* ◊ *factual/grammatical errors* ◊ *an error of judgement* ◊ *to make an error* **2** [U] the state of being wrong: *The letter was sent to you in error.* ◊ *The accident was the result of human error.*

IDM **trial and error** → TRIAL

▼ **COLLOCATIONS**

Error is more formal than **mistake**. There are some expressions such as *error of judgement* and *human error* where only **error** can be used.

'**error message** *noun* [C] a message that appears on a computer screen that tells you that you have done sth wrong or that the program cannot do what you want it to do

erupt ʔ+ **B2** /ɪ'rʌpt/ *verb* [I] **1** (**GEOLOGY**) (used about a VOLCANO) to explode and throw out fire, LAVA (= hot liquid rock), smoke, etc. ⊃ note at **disaster** **2** (used about violence, shouting, etc.) to start suddenly: *The demonstration erupted into violence.* **3** (used about a person) to suddenly express your feelings very strongly, especially by shouting ▶ **eruption** /ɪ'rʌpʃn/ *noun* [C, U]: *a volcanic eruption*

erythrocyte /ɪ'rɪθrəsaɪt/ *noun* [C] (**BIOLOGY**) a red blood cell

escalate ʔ+ **C1** /'eskəleɪt/ *verb* [I, T] (*formal*) **1** ~ (**sth**) (**into sth**) (to cause sth) to become stronger or more serious: *The demonstrations are escalating into violent protest in all the major cities.* ◊ *The terrorist attacks escalated tension in the capital.* **2** (to cause sth) to become greater or higher; to increase: *The cost of housing has escalated in recent years.* ⊃ note at **rise²** ▶ **escalation** /ˌeskə'leɪʃn/ *noun* [C, U]

escalator /'eskəleɪtə(r)/ *noun* [C] moving stairs that carry people between different floors of a shop, etc.

escapade /'eskəpeɪd/ *noun* [C] an exciting experience that may be dangerous

escape¹ ʔ **B1** /ɪ'skeɪp/ *verb* [I, T] **1** ~ (**from sb/sth**) to manage to get away from a place where you do not want to be; to get free: *Two prisoners have escaped.* ◊ *They managed to escape from the burning building.* ◊ *She managed to escape her captors.* **2** [I, T] to manage to avoid sth dangerous or unpleasant: *The two men in the other car escaped unhurt in the accident.* ◊ *Ben Hales escaped injury when his car skidded off the road.* ◊ *to escape criticism/punishment* **3** [T] to be forgotten or not noticed by sb: *His name escapes me.* ◊ *to escape somebody's notice* **4** [I] (used about gases or liquids) to come or get out of a

container, etc: *There's gas escaping somewhere.* ▶ **escaped** *adj.* [only before noun]: *an escaped prisoner*

escape² ʔ **B1** /ɪ'skeɪp/ *noun* **1** [C, U] ~ (**from sth**) the act or a method of escaping from a place or from an unpleasant or dangerous situation: *There have been twelve escapes from the prison this year.* ◊ *She had a narrow/lucky escape when a lorry crashed into her car.* ◊ *When the guard fell asleep they were able to make their escape.* ⊃ look at **fire escape** **2** [U, sing.] ~ (**from sth**) something that helps you forget your normal life: *For him, listening to music is a means of escape.* ◊ *an escape from reality* **3** [U] (*also* e'**scape key** [C]) (**COMPUTING**) a computer key that you press to stop a particular operation or to leave a program: *Press escape to get back to the menu.*

escapism /ɪ'skeɪpɪzəm/ *noun* [U] an activity, a form of entertainment, etc. that helps you to avoid or forget unpleasant or boring things: *For John, reading is a form of escapism.* ▶ **escapist** /-pɪst/ *adj.*

escarpment /ɪ'skɑːpmənt/ *noun* [C] (**GEOGRAPHY**, **GEOLOGY**) a very steep piece of ground that separates an area of high ground from an area of lower ground

escort¹ /'eskɔːt/ *noun* [C] **1** [+ sing./pl. verb] one or more people or vehicles that go with and protect sb/sth, or that go with sb/sth as an honour: *an armed escort* ◊ *He arrived under police escort.* **2** (*formal*) a person who takes sb to a social event **3** a person, especially a woman, who is paid to go out socially with sb: *an escort agency*

escort² /ɪ'skɔːt/ *verb* [T] to go with sb to protect or guard them or to show them the way: *The president's car was escorted by several police cars.* ◊ *Philip escorted her to the door.*

ESE *abbr.* (in writing) = EAST-SOUTH-EAST

esker /'eskə(r)/ *noun* [C] (**GEOLOGY**) a long line of small stones and earth that has been left by a large mass of ice that has melted

Eskimo /'eskɪməu/ *noun* [C] (*pl.* Eskimo, Eskimos) a member of a human group from northern Canada, and parts of Alaska, Greenland and Siberia. ⊃ look at **Inuit ◐** Some people find this word offensive.

ESL /ˌiː es 'el/ *abbr.* (**EDUCATION**) English as a Second Language: (refers to the teaching of English as a foreign language to people who are living in a country in which English is either the first or the second language) ⊃ look at **EFL**

ESOL /'iːsɒl/ *abbr.* **English for speakers of other languages**; (used especially in the UK and Ireland to refer to the teaching of English as a foreign language to people who are living in the UK or Ireland)

esophagus /iː'sɒfəgəs/ *noun* [C] (*pl.* esophaguses, esophagi /-gaɪ/) (*AmE*) = OESOPHAGUS

ESP /ˌiː es 'piː/ *abbr.* **English for Specific/Special Purposes** (refers to the teaching of English to people who need it for a special reason, such as scientific study, a technical job, etc.)

especial /ɪ'speʃl/ *adj.* [only before noun] (*formal*) not usual; special: *This will be of especial interest to you.*

especially ʔ **A2** **◐** /ɪ'speʃəli/ *adv.* **1** (*abbr.* esp.) more than other things, people, situations, etc: *She loves animals, especially dogs.* ◊ *Teenage boys especially can be very competitive.* ◊ *He was very disappointed with his mark in the exam, especially as he had worked so hard for it.* **SYN** **particularly 2** for a particular purpose or person: *I made this especially for you.* **3** very (much): *It's not an especially difficult exam.* ◊ *'Do you like jazz?' 'Not especially.'* **SYN** **particularly**

espionage /ˈespiənaːʒ/ *noun* [U] the activity of finding out secret information about another country or organization ➲ verb **spy**

esplanade /ˌespləˈneɪd/ *noun* [C] a level area of ground in a town for people to walk along, often by the sea or a river

espresso /eˈspresəʊ/ *noun* [C, U] (*pl.* -os) a strong black coffee made by forcing STEAM or boiling water through ground coffee

essay ⚡**A2** /ˈeseɪ/ *noun* [C] ~ **(on/about sth)** (**EDUCATION**) a short piece of writing on one subject: *We have to write a 1 000-word essay on tourism for homework.*

essence ⚡+ **C1** **W** /ˈesns/ *noun* **1** [U] the basic or most important quality of sth: *The essence of the problem is that there is not enough money available.* ◊ *Although both parties agree in essence, some minor differences remain.* **2** [U, C] a substance (usually a liquid) that is taken from a plant or food and that has a strong smell or taste of that plant or food: *coffee/vanilla essence* ➲ look at **extract**²

essential ⚡**B1** **O** /ɪˈsenʃl/ *adj.* ~ **(for sth)**; ~ **(that …)** completely necessary; that you must have or do: *essential medical supplies* ◊ *Maths is essential for a career in computers.* ◊ *It is essential that all school-leavers should have a qualification.* ▶ **essential** *noun* [C, usually pl.]: *food, and other essentials such as clothing and heating*

▼ SYNONYMS

essential

vital ◆ crucial ◆ critical ◆ decisive ◆ indispensable

These words all describe sb/sth that is extremely important and completely necessary because a particular situation or activity depends on them.

essential *Experience is essential for this job.*

vital *The police play a vital role in society.*

crucial *It is crucial that we get this right.*

critical *Your decision is critical to our future.*

decisive *She played a decisive role in the investigations.*

indispensable *Cars have become an indispensable part of our lives.*

---

essentially ⚡+ **B2** **O** /ɪˈsenʃəli/ *adv.* when you consider the basic or most important part of sth: *The problem is essentially one of money.* **SYN** **basically**

establish ⚡**B2** **O** /ɪˈstæblɪʃ/ *verb* [T] **1** to start or create an organization, a system, etc: *The school was established in 1875.* ◊ *Before we start on the project we should establish some rules.* ➲ note at **organization** **2** to make sth exist (especially a formal relationship with sb/sth): *The government is trying to establish closer links between the two countries.* **3** ~ **sb/sth (as sth)** to cause sb/sth to be accepted: *The festival has become established as one of the most popular events in the town.* **4** ~ **(that …)** to discover or find proof of the facts of a situation: *The police have not been able to establish the cause of the crash.* ◊ *They have established that his injuries were caused by a fall.*

established /ɪˈstæblɪʃt/ *adj.* respected or given official status because it has existed or been used for a long time: *They are an established company with a good reputation.*

establishment ⚡+ **C1** **W** /ɪˈstæblɪʃmənt/ *noun* **1** [C] (*formal*) an organization, a large institution or a hotel: *an educational establishment* **2 the Establishment** [sing. + sing./pl. verb] the people in positions of power

in a country, who usually do not support change **3** [U] the act of creating or starting a new organization, system, etc: *the establishment of new laws on taxes*

estate ⚡**B2** /ɪˈsteɪt/ *noun* [C] **1** (*BrE*) an area of land that has a lot of houses or factories of the same type on it: *an industrial estate* (= where there are a lot of factories) ➲ look at **housing estate** **2** a large area of land in the countryside that is owned by one person or family: *He owns a large estate in Scotland.* ◊ *She receives rent from all the people whose cottages are on estate land.* **3** all the money and property that a person owns, especially everything that is left when they die: *Her estate was left to her daughter.*

esˈtate agent (*BrE*) (*AmE* Realtor™, real estate agent) *noun* [C] a person whose job is to buy and sell houses and land for other people

esˈtate car (*BrE*) (*AmE* station wagon) *noun* [C] a car with a door at the back and a long area for LUGGAGE behind the back seat

esteem /ɪˈstiːm/ *noun* [U] (*formal*) great respect; a good opinion of sb

ester /ˈestə(r)/ *noun* [C] (**CHEMISTRY**) a type of natural substance that is formed by combining an ACID and an alcohol

esthete (*AmE*) = AESTHETE

esthetic (*AmE*) = AESTHETIC¹, AESTHETIC²

esthetically, estheticism (*AmE*) = AESTHETICALLY, AESTHETICISM

estimate¹ ⚡**B2** **W** /ˈestɪmət/ *noun* [C] **1** ~ **(of sth)** a guess or judgement about the size, cost, etc. of sth, without having all the facts and figures: *Can you give me a rough estimate of how many people will be at the meeting?* ◊ *At a conservative estimate* (= the real figure will probably be higher), *the job will take six months to complete.* **2** ~ **(for sth/doing sth)** a written statement from a person who is going to do a job for you, for example a BUILDER, telling you how much it will probably cost: *They gave me an estimate for repairing the roof.* ➲ look at **quotation** (2)
IDM **a ballpark figure/estimate** → BALLPARK

estimate² ⚡**B2** **W** /ˈestɪmeɪt/ *verb* [T] ~ **sth (at sth)**; ~ **that …** to calculate the size, cost, etc. of sth approximately, without having all the facts and figures: *The police estimated the crowd at 10 000.* ◊ *She estimated that the work would take three months.*

estimation **W** /ˌestɪˈmeɪʃn/ *noun* [U] (*formal*) opinion or judgement: *Who is to blame, in your estimation?*

estranged /ɪˈstreɪndʒd/ *adj.* **1** no longer living with your husband, wife or partner: *her estranged husband* **2** ~ **(from sb)** no longer friendly or in contact with sb who was close to you: *He became estranged from his family following an argument.*

estrogen /ˈiːstrədʒən/ (*AmE*) = OESTROGEN

estuary /ˈestʃuəri/ *noun* [C] (*pl.* -ies) (**GEOGRAPHY**) the wide part of a river where it flows into the sea

ETA /ˌiː tiː ˈeɪ/ *abbr.* **estimated time of arrival** (the time at which an aircraft, a ship, etc. is expected to arrive)

et al. /ˌet ˈæl/ *abbr.* used especially after names to mean 'and other people or things' (from Latin 'et alii/alia'): *research by West et al., 1996*

etc. /ˌet ˈsetərə, ˌɪt/ *abbr.* used after a list to show that there are other things that you could have mentioned (from Latin 'et cetera'): *sandwiches, biscuits, cakes, etc.*

etch /etʃ/ *verb* [T] (**ART**) to cut lines into a piece of glass, metal, etc. in order to make words or a picture: *a beer glass with his initials etched on it*

etching /'etʃɪŋ/ *noun* [C, U] (**ART**) a picture that is printed from an ETCHED piece of metal; the art of making these pictures

eternal ⟨+ **C1** /ɪ'tɜːnl/ *adj.* **1** without beginning or end; existing or continuing for ever: *Some people believe in eternal life* (= after death). **2** [only before noun] happening too often; seeming to last for ever: *I'm tired of these eternal arguments!* ▸ **eternally** /-nəli/ *adv.*: *I'll be eternally grateful if you could help me.*

eternity /ɪ'tɜːnəti/ *noun* **1** [U] time that has no end; the state or time after death **2** an eternity /æn ɪ'tɜːnəti/ [sing.] (*informal*) a period of time that never seems to end: *It seemed like an eternity before the ambulance arrived.*

ethane /'iːθeɪn/ *noun* [U] (*symb.* C_2H_6) (**CHEMISTRY**) a gas that has no colour or smell and that can burn. Ethane is found in natural gas and in PETROLEUM (= oil that can be made into fuel).

ethanol /'eθənɒl/ (*also* **ethyl alcohol**) *noun* [U] (**CHEMISTRY**) the type of alcohol in alcoholic drinks, also used as a fuel or as a SOLVENT (= for making other substances liquid)

ether /'iːθə(r)/ *noun* [U] **1** a clear liquid made from alcohol, used in industry as a SOLVENT (= a liquid that can make another substance liquid) and, in the past, in medicine to make people unconscious before an operation **2** the ether the air, when it is thought of as the place in which radio or electronic communication takes place

ethereal /ɪ'θɪəriəl/ *adj.* (*formal*) extremely DELICATE and light; seeming to belong to another, more spiritual, world: *her ethereal beauty*

Ethernet /'iːθənet/ *noun* [sing.] (**COMPUTING**) a system for connecting a number of computer systems to form a network

ethic ⟨+ **B2** **W** /'eθɪk/ *noun* **1** ethics [pl.] moral principles that control or influence a person's behaviour: *business/professional/medical ethics* ◇ *to draw up a code of ethics* **2** [sing.] a system of moral principles or rules of behaviour: *a strongly defined work ethic* **3** ethics [U] the branch of philosophy that deals with moral principles

ethical ⟨ **B2** **W** /'eθɪkl/ *adj.* **1** connected with beliefs of what is right or wrong: *That is an ethical problem.* **2** morally correct: *Although she didn't break the law, her behaviour was certainly not ethical.* ▸ **ethically** /-kli/ *adv.*

ethnic¹ ⟨+ **B2** **W** /'eθnɪk/ *adj.* (**SOCIAL STUDIES**) **1** connected with or belonging to a particular nation or people that share a cultural tradition: *ethnic groups/communities* **2** typical of a country or culture that is very different from modern Western culture and therefore interesting for people in Western countries: *ethnic food/music/clothes*

ethnic 'cleansing *noun* [U] (**SOCIAL STUDIES**) the policy of forcing people who belong to a certain human group or have a certain religion to leave an area or a country

ethnicity **W** /eθ'nɪsəti/ *noun* [U, C] (*pl.* -ies) (**SOCIAL STUDIES**) the fact of belonging to a particular nation or people that shares a cultural tradition: *There should not be any discrimination on the basis of race, gender or ethnicity.* ◇ *I have made many friends of different ethnicities.*

ethnic mi'nority *noun* [C] (**SOCIAL STUDIES**) a group of people who have a particular culture or belong to a particular human group living in a country where the main group has a different culture or belongs to a different human group

ethnography /eθ'nɒgrəfi/ *noun* [U] (**SOCIAL STUDIES**) the scientific description of different peoples and cultures ▸ **ethnographic** /ˌeθnə'græfɪk/ *adj.*: *ethnographic research/studies*

ethnology /eθ'nɒlədʒi/ *noun* [U] (**SOCIAL STUDIES**) the scientific study and comparison of different peoples ▸ **ethnological** /ˌeθnə'lɒdʒɪkl/ *adj.* ▸ **ethnologist** /eθ'nɒlədʒɪst/ *noun* [C]

ethos /'iːθɒs/ *noun* [sing.] (*formal*) the moral ideas and attitudes that belong to a particular group, society or person

ethyl alcohol /ˌeθɪl 'ælkəhɒl, ˌiːθaɪl/ = ETHANOL

ethyne /'iːθaɪn/ = ACETYLENE

e-ticket *noun* [C] (**TOURISM**) a ticket, for example for a plane or train journey, that you buy on the internet and receive by email or on your phone

etiology /ˌiːti'ɒlədʒi/ (*AmE*) = AETIOLOGY

etiquette /'etɪkət, -ket/ *noun* [U] the rules of polite and correct behaviour: *social/professional etiquette* ⟳ look at **netiquette**

etymology /ˌetɪ'mɒlədʒi/ *noun* (*pl.* -ies) **1** [U] (**LANGUAGE**) the study of the origins and history of words and their meanings **2** [C] an explanation of the origin and history of a particular word

EU /ˌiː 'juː/ *abbr.* = EUROPEAN UNION: *the member states of the EU* ◇ *EU laws/regulations*

eucalyptus /ˌjuːkə'lɪptəs/ *noun* [C, U] (*pl.* eucalyptuses, eucalypti /-taɪ/) a tall straight tree that grows especially in Australia. Its leaves produce an oil with a strong smell, that is used in medicine.

eukaryote (*also* **eucaryote**) /juː'kæriəʊt/ *noun* [C] (**BIOLOGY**) an ORGANISM (= living thing) consisting of one or more cells in which DNA is contained inside a clear NUCLEUS (= central part). Eukaryotes include most living things except bacteria. ⟳ look at **prokaryote** ▸ **eukaryotic** /juːˌkæri'ɒtɪk/ *adj.*

eulogy /'juːlədʒi/ *noun* (*pl.* -ies) **1** [C, U] ~ (of/to sb/sth) (**LITERATURE**) a speech or piece of writing that says good things about sb/sth: *a eulogy to marriage* **2** [C] ~ (for/to sb) a speech given at a FUNERAL saying good things about the person who has died

euphemism /'juːfəmɪzəm/ *noun* [C] (**LANGUAGE**) an indirect word or expression that you use instead of a more direct one when you are talking about sth that is unpleasant or embarrassing: *'Pass away' is a euphemism for 'die'.* ▸ **euphemistic** /ˌjuːfə'mɪstɪk/ *adj.*: *euphemistic language* ▸ **euphemistically** /-kli/ *adv.*

euphoria /juː'fɔːriə/ *noun* [U] (*formal*) an extremely strong feeling of happiness ▸ **euphoric** /-'fɒrɪk/ *adj.*: *My euphoric mood could not last.*

Eurasian /juː'reɪʒn, -'reɪʃn/ *adj.* (**SOCIAL STUDIES**) **1** of or connected with both Europe and Asia **2** having one Asian parent and one parent who is white or from Europe ▸ **Eurasian** *noun* [C]: *Singapore Eurasians*

euro ⟨ **A1** /'jʊərəʊ/ *noun* (*pl.* euros, euro) (**ECONOMICS**) **1** [C] (*symb.* €) the unit of money of some countries of the European Union: *The price is given in dollars or euros.* ⟳ look at **EMU** **2** the euro [sing.] the value of the euro on international money markets: *The euro fell against the dollar.*

Euro- /jʊərəʊ/ *prefix* (in nouns and adjectives) connected with Europe or the European Union: *a Euro-MP* ◇ *Euro-elections*

European¹ /ˌjʊərə'piːən/ *adj.* **1** of or connected with Europe: *European languages* **2** (**POLITICS**) of or connected with the European Union: *European law*

European² /ˌjʊərə'piːən/ *noun* [C] a person from Europe

the ¦European ¦Parliament *noun* [sing.] (**POLITICS**) the group of people who are elected in the countries of the European Union to make and change its laws

the ¦European ¦Union *noun* [sing.] (*abbr.* **EU**) (**POLITICS**) an economic and political association of certain European countries

europium /juə'rəupiəm/ *noun* [U] (*symb.* **Eu**) (**CHEMISTRY**) a chemical element. Europium is a silver-white metal used in TV screens. ❶ For more information on the periodic table of elements, look at the **Reference Section** of this dictionary.

the eurozone /ðə 'juərəuzəun/ *noun* [sing.] (**ECONOMICS**) the countries in the European Union that use the euro as a unit of money

Eustachian tube /juː'steɪʃn tjuːb/ *noun* [C] (**ANATOMY**) a narrow tube that joins the throat to the middle ear ⊃ picture at **ear**

euthanasia / juːθə'neɪziə/ *noun* [U] (**SOCIAL STUDIES**) the practice of killing without pain a person or an animal who is suffering from a disease that cannot be cured. Euthanasia of people is illegal in most countries.

eutrophication / juːtrəfɪ'keɪʃn/ *noun* [U] (**BIOLOGY**, **ENVIRONMENT**) the process of too many plants growing on the surface of a river, lake, etc., often because chemicals that are used to help crops grow have been carried there by rain

evacuate ⍰+ **C1** /ɪ'vækjueɪt/ *verb* [T, I] to move people from a dangerous place to somewhere safer; to leave a place because it is dangerous: *Thousands of people were evacuated from the war zone.* ◇ *The village had to be evacuated when the river burst its banks.* ◇ *Locals were told to evacuate.* ▶ evacuation /ɪˌvækju'eɪʃn/ *noun* [C, U]

evacuee /ɪˌvækju'iː/ *noun* [C] (**POLITICS**) a person who is sent away from a place because it is dangerous, especially during a war

evade /ɪ'veɪd/ *verb* [T] **1** to manage to escape from or to avoid meeting sb/sth: *They managed to evade capture and escaped to France.* **2** to avoid dealing with or doing sth: *to evade responsibility* ◇ *I asked her directly, but she evaded the question.* ⊃ noun **evasion**

evaluate ⍰ **B2** ⓦ /ɪ'væljueɪt/ *verb* [T] (*formal*) to form an opinion of the amount, value or quality of sth after thinking about it carefully: *We evaluated the situation very carefully before we made our decision.* ▶ evaluation ⍰+ **B2** ⓦ /ɪˌvælju'eɪʃn/ *noun* [C, U]

evangelical / iːvæn'dʒelɪkl/ *adj.* (**RELIGION**) belonging to a Christian group that emphasizes the authority of the Bible

evangelist /ɪ'vændʒəlɪst/ *noun* [C] a person who tries to persuade people to become Christians, especially by travelling around the country holding religious meetings, etc. ▶ evangelism /-lɪzəm/ *noun* [U]

evaporate /ɪ'væpəreɪt/ *verb* **1** [I, T] (**CHEMISTRY**) (used about a liquid) to change into STEAM or gas; to change a liquid into STEAM or gas: *The water evaporated in the sunshine.* ⊃ look at **condense** (1) ⊃ picture at **energy 2** [I] to disappear completely: *All her confidence evaporated when she saw the exam paper.* ▶ evaporation /ɪˌvæpə'reɪʃn/ *noun* [U] ⊃ note at **water¹** ⊃ picture at **water cycle**

evasion /ɪ'veɪʒn/ *noun* [C, U] **1** the act of avoiding sth that you should do: *You can be imprisoned for not paying fare evasion fines.* ◇ *an evasion of responsibility* **2** a statement that avoids dealing with a question or subject in a direct way: *The president's reply was full of evasions.* ⊃ verb **evade**

evasive /ɪ'veɪsɪv/ *adj.* trying to avoid sth; not direct: *Ann gave an evasive answer.*

eve /iːv/ *noun* [C] the day or evening before a religious festival, important event, etc: *Christmas Eve* ◇ *He injured himself on the eve of the final.*

even¹ ⍰ **A1** /'iːvn/ *adv.* **1** used for emphasizing sth that is surprising: *It isn't very warm here even in summer.* ◇ *He didn't even open the letter.* **2 ~ more, less, bigger, nicer, etc.** used when you are comparing things, to make the comparison stronger: *You know even less about it than I do.* ◇ *It is even more difficult than I expected.* ◇ *We are even busier than yesterday.* **IDM** even if despite the possibility that; no matter whether: *I wouldn't ride a horse, even if you paid me.* even so (used for introducing a new idea, fact, etc. that is surprising) despite that: *There are a lot of spelling mistakes; even so it's quite a good essay.* **SYN** nevertheless even though/if although: *I like her very much even though she can be very annoying.* ⊃ note at **although**

even² ⍰ **B2** /'iːvn/ *adj.* **1** (**MATHEMATICS**) (used about numbers) that can be divided by two: *2, 4, 6, 8, 10, etc. are even numbers.* **OPP** odd **2** (used about a competition, etc.) equal, with one side being as good as the other: *The contest was very even until the last few minutes of the game.* **OPP** uneven **3** not changing; regular: *He's very even-tempered — in fact I've never seen him angry.* ◇ *This wine must be stored at an even temperature.* **OPP** uneven **4** flat, level or smooth: *The game must be played on an even surface.* **OPP** uneven **IDM** be/get even (with sb) (*informal*) to hurt or harm sb who has hurt or harmed you break even to make neither a loss nor a profit

evening ⍰ **A1** /'iːvnɪŋ/ *noun* [C, U] the part of the day between the afternoon and the time that you go to bed: *What are you doing this evening?* ◇ *We were out yesterday evening.* ◇ *I went to the cinema on Saturday evening.* ◇ *Tom usually goes swimming on Wednesday evenings.* ◇ *They often watch TV in the evening.* ◇ *an evening class* (= a course of lessons for adults that takes place in the evening) **IDM** good evening used when you see sb for the first time in the evening

¦evening dress *noun* **1** [U] smart clothes worn for formal occasions in the evening: *Everyone was in evening dress.* **2** [C] a woman's long formal dress

evenly /'iːvnli/ *adv.* in a smooth, regular or equal way: *The match was very evenly balanced.* ◇ *Spread the cake mixture evenly in the tin.*

event ⍰ **A1** ⊙ /ɪ'vent/ *noun* [C] **1** something that happens, especially sth important or unusual: *a historic event* ◇ *The events of the past few days have made things very difficult for the government.* **2** a planned public or social occasion: *a fund-raising event* **3** one of the races, competitions, etc. in a sports programme: *The next event is the 800 metres.* **IDM** at all events | in any event whatever happens: *I hope to see you soon, but in any event I'll phone you on Sunday.* in the event of sth (*formal*) if sth happens: *In the event of fire, leave the building as quickly as possible.*

eventful /ɪ'ventfl/ *adj.* full of important, dangerous or exciting things happening

eventual /ɪ'ventʃuəl/ *adj.* [only before noun] happening at the end of a period of time or a process: *It is impossible to say what the eventual cost will be.*

eventuality /ɪˌventʃu'æləti/ *noun* [C] (*pl.* **-ies**) (*formal*) something that may possibly happen, especially sth unpleasant: *We were prepared for every eventuality.*

eventually 🔊 **B1** /ɪˈventʃuəli/ *adv.* in the end; after a long time: *He eventually managed to persuade his parents to let him buy a motorbike.* **SYN** **finally**

ever 🔊 **A1** /ˈevə(r)/ *adv.* **1** (used in questions and negative sentences, and in sentences with *if*) at any time: *Do you ever wish you were famous?* ◇ *Nobody ever comes to see me.* ◇ *Have you ever been to Spain?* ◇ *She hardly ever* (= almost never) *goes out.* ◇ *Today is hotter than ever.* ◇ *This is the best meal I have ever had.* ◇ *If you ever visit England, you must come and stay with us.* **2** used after *when, why,* etc., to show that you are surprised or shocked: *Why ever did you agree?* ⊃ look at **forever, however, whatever¹, whenever¹**

IDM **(as) bad, good, etc. as ever** (as) bad, good, etc. as usual or as always: *In spite of his problems, Andrew is as cheerful as ever.* **ever after** (used especially at the end of stories) from that moment on for always: *The prince married the princess and they lived happily ever after.* **ever since …** all the time from … until now: *She has had a car ever since she was at university.* **ever so/ever such (a)** (*BrE, informal*) very: *He's ever so kind.* ◇ *He's ever such a kind man.*

ever- /ˈevə(r)/ *prefix* (in adjectives) always; continuously: *the ever-growing problem of pollution*

evergreen /ˈevəɡriːn/ *noun* [C] (**BIOLOGY**) a tree or bush with green leaves all through the year ⊃ look at **deciduous** ▸ **evergreen** *adj.*

everlasting /ˌevəˈlɑːstɪŋ/ *adj.* (*formal*) continuing for ever; never changing: *everlasting life/love*

every 🔊 **A1** /ˈevri/ *det.* **1** used with singular nouns to refer to all of the people or things in a group of three or more: *She knows every student in the school.* ◇ *There are 200 students in the school, and she knows every one of them.* ◇ *I've read every book in this house.* ◇ *I get that wrong every single time.* **2** all that is possible: *You have every chance of success.* **3** used for saying how often sth happens: *We see each other every day.* ◇ *Take the medicine every four hours* (= at eight, twelve, four o'clock, etc.). ◇ *One in every three marriages ends in divorce.*

IDM **every other** each ALTERNATE one (= the first, third, fifth, etc. one, but not the second, fourth, sixth, etc.): *I work every other day* (= on Monday, Wednesday, Friday, etc.).

everybody 🔊 **A1** /ˈevribɒdi/ (*also* **everyone**) *pron.* (used with a singular verb) every person; all people: *Is everybody here?* ◇ *The police questioned everyone who was at the party.* ◇ *I'm sure everybody else* (= all the other people) *will agree with me.*

everyday 🔊 **A2** /ˈevrideɪ/ *adj.* [only before noun] normal or usual: *Change is a part of everyday life in business.*

everyone 🔊 **A1** /ˈevriwʌn/ = **EVERYBODY**

everything 🔊 **A1** /ˈevriθɪŋ/ *pron.* (used with a singular verb) **1** each thing; all things: *Sam lost everything in the fire.* ◇ *Everything is very expensive in this shop.* ◇ *We can leave everything else* (= all the other things) *until tomorrow.* **2** the most important thing: *Money isn't everything.*

everywhere 🔊 **A2** /ˈevriweə(r)/ *adv., pron., conj.* in or to every place: *I've looked everywhere, but I still can't find it.* ◇ *We'll have to eat here — everywhere else is full.* ◇ *Everywhere we went was full of tourists.*

evict /ɪˈvɪkt/ *verb* [T] to force sb (officially) to leave the house or land that they are renting: *They were evicted for not paying the rent.* ▸ **eviction** /ɪˈvɪkʃn/ *noun* [U, C]

evidence 🔊 **A2** **⊙** /ˈevɪdəns/ *noun* [U] **1** ~ (of/for sth); ~ that … (**SCIENCE**) the facts, signs, etc. that make you believe that sth is true: *Researchers found clear scientific evidence of the link between smoking and lung cancer.* ◇ *You have absolutely no evidence for what you're saying!* ◇ *There is not a shred of evidence that the meeting actually took place.* ⊃ look at **proof**(1) **2** the information that is used in court to try to prove sth: *There was not enough evidence to prove him guilty.* ◇ *Her statement to the police was used in evidence against him.* ◇ *The witnesses to the accident will be asked to give evidence in court .* ⊃ note at **court¹, crime**

IDM **(to be) in evidence** that you can see; present in a place: *When we arrived there was no ambulance in evidence.*

evident 🔊+ **B2** **⊙** /ˈevɪdənt/ *adj.* (*formal*) clear (to the eye or mind): *It was evident that the damage was very serious.* **SYN** **obvious** ⊃ note at **clear¹**

evidently /ˈevɪdəntli/ *adv.* **1** clearly; that can be easily seen or understood: *She was evidently extremely shocked at the news.* **SYN** **obviously 2** according to what people say: *Evidently he has decided to leave.* **SYN** **apparently**

evil¹ 🔊 **B2** /ˈiːvl, -vɪl/ *adj.* morally bad; causing trouble or harming people: *In the play Richard is portrayed as an evil king.* **OPP** **good¹**

evil² 🔊 **B2** /ˈiːvl, -vɪl/ *noun* [U, C, usually sing.] a force that causes bad or harmful things to happen; a bad or harmful thing: *The play is about the good and evil in all of us.* ◇ *Drugs and alcohol are two of the evils of modern society.* **OPP** **good²**

IDM **the lesser of two evils** → **LESSER**

evocative /ɪˈvɒkətɪv/ *adj.* ~ **(of sth)** making you think of or remember a strong image or feeling, in a pleasant way: *evocative smells/sounds/music* ◇ *Her book is wonderfully evocative of village life.*

evoke 🔊+ **C1** /ɪˈvəʊk/ *verb* [T] (*formal*) to produce a memory, feeling, etc. in sb: *For me, that music always evokes hot summer evenings.* ◇ *Her novel evoked a lot of interest.*

evolution 🔊+ **B2** **⊙** /ˌiːvəˈluːʃn, ˌev-/ *noun* [U] **1** (**BIOLOGY**) the development of plants, animals, etc. during the history of the earth, as they adapt to changes in their environment: *Darwin's theory of evolution* **2** the slow steady process of change and development of sth: *Political evolution is a slow process.* ▸ **evolutionary** 🔊+ **C1** **⊙** /-ʃənri/ *adj.*: *evolutionary theory*

evolve 🔊+ **B2** **⊙** /ɪˈvɒlv/ *verb* **1** [I, T] (*formal*) to develop or to make sth develop gradually, from a simple to a more advanced form: *His style of painting has evolved gradually over the past 20 years.* **2** [I] ~ **(from sth)** (**BIOLOGY**) (used about plants, animals, etc.) to develop over a long period of time into forms that are better adapted to survive changes in their environment

ewe /juː/ *noun* [C] a female sheep ⊃ note at **sheep** ⊃ picture at **sheep**

ex- /eks/ *prefix* (in nouns) former: *ex-wife* ◇ *ex-president*

exacerbate /ɪɡˈzæsəbeɪt/ *verb* [T] (*formal*) (**HEALTH**) to make sth worse, especially a disease or problem **SYN** **aggravate** ▸ **exacerbation** /ɪɡˌzæsəˈbeɪʃn/ *noun* [U, C]

exact¹ 🔊 **A2** /ɪɡˈzækt/ *adj.* **1** (completely) correct; accurate: *He's in his mid-fifties. Well, 56 to be exact.* ◇ *I can't tell you the exact number of people who are coming.* ◇ *She's the exact opposite of her sister.* **SYN** **precise** ⊃ note at **true 2** able to work in a way that is completely accurate: *You need to be very exact*

when you calculate the costs. **SYN** **precise**
▸ **exactness** *noun* [U]

exact² /ɪɡˈzækt/ *verb* [T] ~ **sth (from sb)** (*formal*) to demand and get sth from sb

exacting /ɪɡˈzæktɪŋ/ *adj.* needing a lot of care and attention: *exacting work* **SYN** **demanding**

exactly 🔑 A2 **S** /ɪɡˈzæktli/ *adv.* **1** (used to emphasize that sth is correct in every way) just: *You've arrived at exactly the right moment.* ◇ *I found exactly what I wanted.* **SYN** **precisely** **2** (*informal*) used to ask for more information about sth: *Where exactly did you stay in France?* **3** (*informal*) (used for agreeing with a statement) yes; you are right: *'I don't think she's old enough to travel on her own.' 'Exactly.'* **SYN** **precisely** **IDM** **not exactly** (*informal*) **1** (used when you are saying the opposite of what you really mean) not really; not at all: *He's not exactly the most careful driver I know.* **2** (used as an answer to say that sth is almost true): *'So you think I'm wrong?' 'No, not exactly, but …'*

exaggerate 🔑+ C1 /ɪɡˈzædʒəreɪt/ *verb* [I, T] to make sth seem larger, better, worse, etc. than it really is: *Don't exaggerate. I was only two minutes late, not 20.* ◇ *The problems have been greatly exaggerated.*
▸ **exaggeration** /ɪɡˌzædʒəˈreɪʃn/ *noun* [C, usually sing., U]: *It's rather an exaggeration to say that all the students are lazy.*

exam 🔑 A1 **S** /ɪɡˈzæm/ (*also formal* **examination**) *noun* [C] ~ **(in sth)** (**EDUCATION**) a written, spoken or practical test of what you know or can do: *an English exam* ◇ *the exam results* ◇ *to* ***do/take/sit an exam*** ◇ *to* ***pass/fail an exam*** ◇ *Every term we would have exams in maths, English, French, etc.* ◑ note at **study²**

examination 🔑 B2 **W** /ɪɡˌzæmɪˈneɪʃn/ *noun* **1** [C] (*formal*) = **EXAM** **2** [U, C] the act of looking at sth carefully, especially to see if there is anything wrong or to find the cause of a problem: *On close examination, it was found that the passport was false.* ◇ *a medical examination*

examine 🔑 B1 **W** /ɪɡˈzæmɪn/ *verb* [T] **1** to consider or study an idea, a subject, etc. very carefully: *These theories will be examined in more detail later on in the lecture.* **2** ~ **sb/sth (for sth)** to look at sb/sth carefully in order to find out sth: *The detective examined the room for clues.* **3** ~ **sb (in/on sth)** (*formal*) (**EDUCATION**) to test what sb knows or can do: *You will be examined on everything that has been studied in the course.*

▼ SYNONYMS

examine

review • study • take stock • survey

These words all mean to think about, study or describe sb/ sth carefully, especially in order to understand them, form an opinion of them or make a decision about them.

examine *He examined the letter in detail.*

review *Let us review the situation.*

study *Study the report carefully.*

take stock *It was time to stand back and take stock of his career.*

survey *This chapter surveys the current state of Finnish politics.*

examinee /ɪɡˌzæmɪˈniː/ *noun* [C] (**EDUCATION**) a person who is taking an exam

examiner /ɪɡˈzæmɪnə(r)/ *noun* [C] (**EDUCATION**) a person who tests sb in an exam

example 🔑 A1 **O** /ɪɡˈzɑːmpl/ *noun* [C] **1** ~ **(of sth)** something such as an object, a fact or a situation that shows, explains or supports what you say: *I don't quite understand you. Can you give me* ***an example of*** *what you mean?* ◇ *This is* ***a typical example of*** *a Victorian house.* **2** ~ **(to/for sb)** a person or thing or a type of behaviour that is good and should be copied: *Joe's bravery should be an example to us all.* ◇ *She* ***sets an example*** *for the other students.*
IDM **follow sb's example/lead** → FOLLOW **for example** (*abbr.* e.g. /ˌiː ˈdʒiː/) used for giving a fact, situation, etc., that explains or supports what you are talking about: *In many countries, Italy for example, family life is much more important than here.* **set a good/bad example (to/for sb)** to behave in a way that should/should not be copied: *Parents should always take care when crossing roads in order to set a good example to their children.*

▼ SYNONYMS

example

case • instance • specimen • illustration

These are all words for a thing or situation that is typical of a particular group or set, and is sometimes used to support an argument.

example *Give an example of what you mean.*

case *In some cases people have had to wait several weeks for an appointment.*

instance (*formal*) *It was an instance of terrible injustice.*

specimen *The aquarium has some interesting specimens of unusual fish.*

illustration *The statistics are a clear illustration of the point I am trying to make.*

exasperate /ɪɡˈzæspəreɪt, -ˈzɑːs-/ *verb* [T] to make sb angry; to annoy sb very much: *She was exasperated by the lack of progress.* **SYN** **infuriate** ▸ **exasperating** *adj.*: *an exasperating problem* ▸ **exasperation** /ɪɡˌzæspəˈreɪʃn, -ˌzɑːs-/ *noun* [U]: *She finally threw the book across the room* ***in exasperation***.

excavate /ˈekskəveɪt/ *verb* [T] (**HISTORY**) to dig in the ground to look for old objects or buildings that have been buried for a long time; to find sth by digging in this way: *A Roman villa has been excavated in a valley near the village.* ▸ **excavation** /ˌekskəˈveɪʃn/ *noun* [C, U]: *Excavations on the site have revealed Saxon objects.*

excavator /ˈekskəveɪtə(r)/ *noun* [C] **1** a large machine that is used for digging and moving earth **2** (**HISTORY**) a person who digs in the ground to look for old buildings and objects

exceed 🔑+ B2 **W** /ɪkˈsiːd/ *verb* [T] (*formal*) **1** to be more than a particular number or amount: *The weight should not exceed 20 kilos.* **2** to do more than the law, a rule, an order, etc. allows you to do: *He was stopped by the police for exceeding the speed limit* (= driving faster than is allowed). ◑ noun and adjective **excess**, adjective **excessive**

exceedingly /ɪkˈsiːdɪŋli/ *adv.* (*formal*) very: *an exceedingly difficult problem*

excel /ɪkˈsel/ *verb* (-ll-) (*formal*) **1** [I] ~ **(in/at sth/doing sth)** to be very good at doing sth: *Anne excels at sports.* **2** [T] ~ **yourself** (*BrE*) to do sth even better than you usually do: *Rick's cooking is always good but this time he really excelled himself.*

excellence 🔑+ C1 /ˈeksələns/ *noun* [U] the quality of being very good: *The head teacher said that she wanted the school to be a centre of academic excellence.*

Excellency /ˈeksələnsi/ (*pl.* -ies) **His/Her/Your Excellency** *noun* [C] a title used when talking to or about an AMBASSADOR (= somebody who has a very important official position as the representative of his or her own country in another country)

excellent ɪ A2 /'eksələnt/ adj. ~ (at/for sth) extremely good: *He speaks excellent French.* ◇ *She was great at sport and excellent at art.* ◇ *The experience was excellent for students' self-confidence.* ▸ **excellently** adv.

except¹ ɪ A2 /ɪk'sept/ prep. ~ (for) sb/sth not including sb/sth: *The museum is open every day except Mondays.* ◇ *I can answer all of the questions except for the last one.*

except² ɪ B1 /ɪk'sept/ conj. ~ (that) … apart from the fact that: *It was a good hotel except that it was rather noisy.*

except³ /ɪk'sept/ verb [T, often passive] ~ sb/sth (from sth) (*formal*) to leave sb/sth out; to not include sb/sth: *Nobody is excepted from helping with the housework.* ▸ **excepting** prep.: *Excepting a year spent travelling as a student, Green has always lived in the UK.*

exception ɪ+ B2 ⓦ /ɪk'sepʃn/ noun [C] a person or thing that is not included in a general statement: *Most of his songs are awful but this one is an exception.* ◇ *Everybody was poor as a student and I was no exception.*
ɪᴅᴍ **make an exception (of sb/sth)** to treat sb/sth differently: *We don't usually allow children under 14 but we'll make an exception in your case.* **with the exception of** except for; apart from: *He has won every major tennis championship with the exception of Wimbledon.* **without exception** in every case; including everyone/everything: *Everybody without exception must take the test.*

exceptional ɪ+ C1 /ɪk'sepʃənl/ adj. very unusual; unusually good: *You will only be allowed to leave early in exceptional circumstances.* ꜱʏɴ **outstanding** ◝ look at **unexceptional** ▸ **exceptionally** /-nəli/ adv.: *The past year has been exceptionally difficult for us.*

excerpt /'eksɜːpt/ noun [C] (**LITERATURE**) a short piece taken from a book, film, piece of music, etc.

excess¹ ɪ+ C1 ⓦ /ɪk'ses/ noun **1** [sing.] **an ~ (of sth)** more of sth than is necessary or usual; too much of sth: *An excess of fat in your diet can lead to heart disease.* **2** [C, usually sing., U] an amount by which sth is larger than sth else: *We cover costs up to £600 and then you pay the excess.*
ɪᴅᴍ **in excess of** more than: *Her debts are in excess of £1 000.* ◝ verb **exceed**

excess² ɪ+ C1 /'ekses/ adj. [only before noun] more than is usual or allowed; extra: *Cut any excess fat off the meat.* ◝ verb **exceed**

ˌexcess ˈbaggage noun [U] (**TOURISM**) bags, cases, etc. taken from a plane that weigh more than the amount each passenger is allowed to carry without paying extra: *The baggage allowance is 20kg, after which excess baggage charges apply.*

excessive ɪ+ B2 ⓦ /ɪk'sesɪv/ adj. too much; too great or extreme: *He was driving at excessive speed when he crashed.* ▸ **excessively** adv.

exchange¹ ɪ B1 ⓞ /ɪks'tʃeɪndʒ/ noun **1** [C, U] giving or receiving sth in return for sth else: *a useful exchange of information* ◇ *We can offer free accommodation in exchange for some help in the house.* **2** [U] (**FINANCE**) the process of changing an amount of one currency for an equal value of another: *What's the exchange rate/rate of exchange for dollars?* ◝ look at **foreign exchange** ◝ note at **currency** **3** [C] (**EDUCATION**) an arrangement when two people or groups from different countries visit each other's homes or do each other's jobs for a short time: *She went on a school exchange to Germany when she was 16.* **4** [C] an angry conversation or argument: *She*

had a **heated exchange** with her neighbours about the noise the night before.

exchange² ɪ B1 /ɪks'tʃeɪndʒ/ verb [T] ~ A for B; ~ sth (with sb) to give or receive sth in return for sth else: *I would like to exchange this skirt for a bigger size.* ◇ *They exchanged glances* (= they looked at each other). ◇ *Claire and Molly exchanged phone numbers with the boys.*

exchequer /ɪks'tʃekə(r)/ (*often the Exchequer*) noun [sing.] (**POLITICS**) (in the UK in the past) the government department that controlled public money. This department is now called THE TREASURY. ◝ look at **Chancellor of the Exchequer**

excise /'eksaɪz/ noun [U] (**ECONOMICS**) a government tax on certain goods that are produced or sold inside a country, for example TOBACCO, alcohol, etc. ◝ look at **customs** (1)

excitable /ɪk'saɪtəbl/ adj. likely to get excited easily

excite /ɪk'saɪt/ verb [T] **1** to make sb feel happy and enthusiastic or nervous: *Don't excite the baby too much or we'll never get him off to sleep.* **2** to make sb feel a particular emotion or react in a particular way: *The programme excited great interest.*

excited ɪ A1 /ɪk'saɪtɪd/ adj. ~ (about/at/by sth) feeling or showing happiness and enthusiasm; not calm: *Are you getting excited about your holiday?* ◇ *We're all very excited at the thought of moving house.* ▸ **excitedly** adv.

excitement ɪ B1 /ɪk'saɪtmənt/ noun [U] the state of being excited, especially because sth interesting is happening or will happen: *There was great excitement as the winner's name was announced.* ◇ *The match was full of excitement until the very last minute.*

exciting ɪ A1 /ɪk'saɪtɪŋ/ adj. causing strong feelings of pleasure and interest: *That's very exciting news.* ◇ *Berlin is one of the most exciting cities in Europe.*

exclaim /ɪk'skleɪm/ verb [I, T] to say sth suddenly and loudly because you are surprised, angry, etc: 'I just don't believe it!' he exclaimed.

exclamation /ˌekskləˈmeɪʃn/ noun [C] a short sound, word or phrase that you say suddenly because of a strong emotion, pain, etc: 'Ouch!' is an exclamation. ꜱʏɴ **interjection**

excla̱ˈmation mark (*especially BrE*) (*AmE usually* ˌexclaˈmation point*) noun [C] (**LANGUAGE**) a mark (!) that is written after an EXCLAMATION

exclude ɪ+ B2 ⓦ /ɪk'skluːd/ verb [T] **1** to leave out; not include: *The price excludes all extras such as drinks or excursions.* ᴏᴘᴘ **include** **2** [often passive] ~ sb/sth (from sth) to prevent sb/sth from entering a place or taking part in sth: *Women are excluded from the temple.* ◇ *children who are excluded from school* (= not allowed to attend because of bad behaviour) **3** to decide that sth is not possible: *The police had excluded the possibility that the child had run away.*

excluding /ɪk'skluːdɪŋ/ prep. leaving out; without: *Lunch costs £20 per person excluding drinks.* ᴏᴘᴘ **including**

exclusion ɪ+ ⓦ /ɪk'skluːʒn/ noun [U] keeping or leaving sb/sth out

exclusive¹ ɪ+ C1 ⓦ /ɪk'skluːsɪv/ adj. **1** [only before noun] only to be used by or given to one person, group, etc.; not to be shared: *This car is for the Director's exclusive use.* ◇ *Tonight we are showing an exclusive interview with the new leader of the Labour Party* (= on only one television station). **2** expensive and not welcoming people who are thought to be of a lower social class:

an exclusive restaurant ◇ *a flat in an exclusive part of the city* **3** not including anything else: *He had an exclusive focus on making money.* ◇ *This list is not exclusive.* **4** ~ **of sb/sth** not including sb/sth; without: *Lunch costs £20 per person exclusive of drinks.* **OPP** **inclusive 5** not able to exist or be a true statement at the same time as sth else: *The two statements are not mutually exclusive* (= they can both be true).

exclusive² /ɪkˈskluːsɪv/ *noun* [C] (**ARTS AND MEDIA**) a news story that is given to and published by only one newspaper or TV station

exclusively ⚡+ **C1** ⓦ /ɪkˈskluːsɪvli/ *adv.* only; not involving anyone/anything else: *The swimming pool is reserved exclusively for members of the club.*

excrement /ˈekskrɪmənt/ *noun* [U] (*formal*) (**BIOLOGY**) the solid waste matter that you get rid of from the body when you go to the toilet **SYN** **faeces**

excrete /ɪkˈskriːt/ *verb* [T] (*formal*) (**BIOLOGY**) to get rid of solid or liquid waste material from the body
▶ **excretion** /-ˈskriːʃn/ *noun* [U, C] ⊃ picture at **nitrogen cycle**

excruciating /ɪkˈskruːʃieɪtɪŋ/ *adj.* extremely painful

excursion /ɪkˈskɜːʃn/ *noun* [C] (**TOURISM**) a short journey or trip that a group of people make for pleasure: *to go on an excursion to the seaside* ⊃ note at **travel²**

excusable /ɪkˈskjuːzəbl/ *adj.* that you can forgive: *The mistake was excusable.* **OPP** **inexcusable**

excuse¹ ⚡ **B2** /ɪkˈskjuːs/ *noun* [C] ~ **(for sth/doing sth)** a reason (that may or may not be true) that you give in order to explain your behaviour: *There's no excuse for rudeness.* ◇ *He always finds an excuse for not helping with the housework.* ◇ *You don't have to make excuses for her* (= try to think of reasons for her behaviour). ⊃ note at **reason¹**

excuse² ⚡ **B2** /ɪkˈskjuːz/ *verb* [T] **1** ~ **sb/sth (for sth/ doing sth)** to forgive sb for sth they have done wrong that is not very serious: *Please excuse the interruption but I need to talk to you.* ◇ *I hope you'll excuse me for being so late.* **HELP** The expression **excuse me** is used when you interrupt sb or when you want to start talking to sb that you don't know: *Excuse me, can you tell me the way to the station?* In American English, and occasionally in British English, **excuse me** is used when you apologize for sth: *Did I tread on your toe? Excuse me.* **2** to explain sb's bad behaviour and make it seem less bad: *Nothing can excuse such behaviour.* **SYN** **justify 3** ~ **sb (from sth)** to free sb from a duty, responsibility, etc: *She excused herself* (= asked if she could leave) *and left the meeting early.* ◇ *He was excused from military service because of poor health.*

execute ⚡+ **C1** /ˈeksɪkjuːt/ *verb* [T] **1** [usually passive] ~ **sb (for sth)** (**LAW**) to kill sb as an official punishment: *He was executed for murder.* **2** (*formal*) to perform a task, etc. or to put a plan into action

execution ⚡+ **C1** /ˌeksɪˈkjuːʃn/ *noun* **1** [U, C] (**LAW**) the act of killing sb, especially as a legal punishment **2** [U] (*formal*) the act of doing a piece of work, performing a duty or putting a plan into action: *He had failed in the execution of his duty.*

executioner /ˌeksɪˈkjuːʃənə(r)/ *noun* [C] a person whose job is to **EXECUTE** criminals

executive¹ ⚡ **B2** /ɪgˈzekjətɪv/ *adj.* **1** (used in connection with people in business, government, etc.) concerned with managing, making plans, decisions, etc: *an executive director of the company* ◇ *executive decisions/jobs/duties* **2** (used about goods, buildings,

etc.) designed to be used by important people: *an executive briefcase/car/home*

executive² ⚡ **B2** /ɪgˈzekjətɪv/ *noun* **1** [C] (**BUSINESS**) a person who has an important position as a manager of a business or organization: *She's a senior executive in a computer company.* **2** **the executive** [sing. + sing./pl. verb] the part of a government responsible for putting new laws into effect ⊃ look at **judiciary**, **legislature 3** [sing.] the group of people who are in charge of an organization or a company

exemplary /ɪgˈzempləri/ *adj.* very good; that can be an example to other people: *exemplary behaviour*

exemplify ⓦ /ɪgˈzemplɪfaɪ/ *verb* [T] (**exemplifying**; **exemplifies**; *pt, pp* **exemplified**) to be a typical example of sth

exempt¹ /ɪgˈzempt/ *adj.* [not before noun] ~ **(from sth)** free from having to do sth or pay for sth: *Children under 16 are exempt from dental charges.*
▶ **exemption** /-ˈzempʃn/ *noun* [C, U]

exempt² /ɪgˈzempt/ *verb* [T] ~ **sb/sth (from sth)** (*formal*) to say officially that sb does not have to do sth or pay for sth

exercise¹ ⚡ **A1** ⓦ /ˈeksəsaɪz/ *noun*
• ACTIVITY **1** [U] (**SPORT**) physical activity that keeps you healthy and strong: *The doctor advised him to take regular exercise.* ◇ *Swimming is a good form of exercise.* **2** [C] (**SPORT**) a movement or activity that you do in order to stay healthy or to become SKILLED at sth: *I do keep-fit exercises every morning.* ◇ *breathing/ stretching/relaxation exercises*
• STUDY **3** [C] (**EDUCATION**) a piece of work that is intended to help you learn or practise sth: *an exercise on phrasal verbs*
• FOR A PARTICULAR AIM **4** [C] ~ **in sth** an activity or a series of actions that has a particular aim: *The project is an exercise in getting the best results at a low cost.*
• USE OF POWER, ETC. **5** [U] ~ **of sth** (*formal*) the use of sth, for example a power, right, etc: *the exercise of patience/judgement/discretion*
• FOR SOLDIERS **6** [C, usually pl.] a set of activities for training soldiers: *military exercises*

exercise² ⚡ **A1** ⓦ /ˈeksəsaɪz/ *verb* **1** [I, T] (**SPORT**) to do some form of physical activity in order to stay fit and healthy: *It is important to exercise regularly.* **2** [T] (*formal*) to make use of sth, for example a power, right, etc: *You should exercise your right to vote.*

ˈexercise bike *noun* [C] a bicycle that does not move forward but is used for getting exercise indoors

ˈexercise book (*BrE*) (*AmE* **notebook**) *noun* [C] a small book for students to write their work in

exert ⚡+ **C1** /ɪgˈzɜːt/ *verb* [T] **1** to make use of sth, for example influence, strength, etc., to affect sb/sth: *Parents exert a powerful influence on their children's opinions.* **2** ~ **yourself** to make a big effort: *You won't make any progress if you don't exert yourself a bit more.*

exertion /ɪgˈzɜːʃn/ *noun* [U] (*also* **exertions** [pl.]) using your body in a way that takes a lot of effort; sth that you do that makes you tired: *At his age physical exertion was dangerous.* ◇ *I'm tired after the exertions of the past few days.*

ex gratia /ˌeks ˈɡreɪʃə/ *adj.* (**LAW**) given or done as a gift or favour, not because there is a legal duty to do it: *ex gratia payments* ▶ **ex gratia** *adv.*: *The sum was paid ex gratia.*

exhale /eksˈheɪl/ *verb* [I, T] (*formal*) (**BIOLOGY**) to breathe out the air, smoke, etc. in the lungs **OPP** **inhale**
▶ **exhalation** /ˌekshəˈleɪʃn/ *noun* [U, C]

exhaust¹ /ɪgˈzɔːst/ *noun* **1** [U] the waste gas that comes out of a vehicle, an engine or a machine: *car exhaust fumes/emissions* **2** (*also* **exhaust pipe, tailpipe** *especially*

through which waste gas escapes from an engine or machine

exhaust² ⁀+ /ɪɡ'zɔːst/ *verb* [T] **1** to make sb very tired: *The long journey to work every morning exhausted him.* **2** to use sth up completely; to finish sth: *All the supplies of food have been exhausted.* **3** to say everything you can about a subject, etc: *Well, I think we've exhausted that topic.*

exhausted /ɪɡ'zɔːstɪd/ *adj.* very tired

exhausting /ɪɡ'zɔːstɪŋ/ *adj.* making sb very tired: *Teaching young children is exhausting work.*

exhaustion /ɪɡ'zɔːstʃən/ *noun* [U] the state of being extremely tired

exhaustive /ɪɡ'zɔːstɪv/ *adj.* including everything possible: *This list is certainly not exhaustive.*

ex'haust pipe = EXHAUST¹ (2)

exhibit¹ ⁀+ B2 /ɪɡ'zɪbɪt/ *noun* [C] (**ART**) an object that is shown in a museum, etc. or as a piece of evidence in court

exhibit² ⁀+ B2 /ɪɡ'zɪbɪt/ *verb* [T] **1** (**ART**) to show sth in a public place for people to enjoy or to give them information: *His paintings have been exhibited in the local art gallery.* **2** (*formal*) to show clearly that you have a particular quality, feeling, etc: *The refugees are exhibiting signs of exhaustion and stress.*

exhibition ⁀ B1 /ˌeksɪ'bɪʃn/ *noun* **1** [C, U] (**ART**) a collection of objects, for example works of art, that are shown to the public: *an exhibition of photos* ◇ *Her paintings will be on exhibition in London for the whole of April.* ⊃ note at **art 2** [C] an occasion when a particular skill is shown to the public: *We saw an exhibition of Scottish dancing last night.* **3** [sing.] (*formal*) the act of showing a quality, feeling, etc: *It was just an exhibition of stupidity and bad manners.*

exhibitor /ɪɡ'zɪbɪtə(r)/ *noun* [C] (**ART**) a person or a company that shows their work or products to the public

exhilarate /ɪɡ'zɪləreɪt/ *verb* [T, usually passive] to make sb feel very excited and happy: *We felt exhilarated by our walk along the beach.* ▶ **exhilarating** *adj.* ▶ **exhilaration** /ɪɡ,zɪlə'reɪʃn/ *noun* [U]

exhume /eks'hjuːm, ɪɡ'zjuːm/ *verb* [T, usually passive] (*formal*) to remove a dead body from the ground especially in order to examine how the person died ▶ **exhumation** /ˌekshjuː'meɪʃn/ *noun* [U]

exile ⁀+ C1 /'eksaɪl, 'eɡzaɪl/ *noun* (**POLITICS**) **1** [U] the state of being forced to live outside your own country (especially for political reasons): *He went into exile after the revolution of 1968.* ◇ *They lived in exile in London for many years.* **2** [C] a person who is forced to live outside their own country (especially for political reasons) ⊃ look at **refugee** ▶ **exile** *verb* [T, usually passive]: *After the revolution the king was exiled.*

exist ⁀ A2 ◐ /ɪɡ'zɪst/ *verb* [I] **1** (not used in the progressive tenses) to be real; to be found in the real world; to live: *Dreams only exist in our imagination.* ◇ *Fish cannot exist out of water.* **2 ~ (on sth)** to manage to live: *I don't know how she exists on the wage she earns.*

existence ⁀ B2 ◐ /ɪɡ'zɪstəns/ *noun* **1** [U] the state of being real or living or of being present: *This is the oldest human skeleton in existence.* ◇ *How did the universe come into existence?* **2** [C] a way of living, especially when it is difficult: *They lead a miserable existence in a tiny flat in London.*

existing /ɪɡ'zɪstɪŋ/ *adj.* [only before noun] that is already there or being used; present: *Under the existing law you are not allowed to work in this country.*

exit¹ ⁀+ B2 /'eksɪt, 'eɡzɪt/ *noun* [C] **1** a door or way out of a public building or vehicle: *The emergency exit is at the back of the bus.* **OPP entrance 2** the act of leaving sth: *If I see her coming I'll make a quick exit.* ◇ *an exit visa* (= one that allows you to leave a country) **OPP entrance 3** a place where traffic can leave a road to join another road: *At the roundabout take the third exit.* ⊃ note at **direction**

exit² ⁀+ C1 /'eksɪt, 'eɡzɪt/ *verb* [I, T] (*formal*) **1** to leave a place: *He exited through the back door.* **2** (**COMPUTING**) to finish using a computer program: *I exited the database and switched off the computer.*

'exit exam (*also formal* 'exit ex,amination) *noun* [C] (*especially AmE*) (**EDUCATION**) an exam that you take at the end of the last year in school or at the end of a period of training: *a high school exit exam*

exodus /'eksədəs/ *noun* [sing.] (*formal*) a situation in which many people leave a place at the same time

exonerate /ɪɡ'zɒnəreɪt/ *verb* [T, often passive] (*formal*) to say officially that sb was not responsible for sth bad that happened

exoplanet /'eksəʊplænɪt/ *noun* [C] (**ASTRONOMY**) a planet outside the solar system

exorbitant /ɪɡ'zɔːbɪtənt/ *adj.* (*formal*) (used about the cost of sth) much more expensive than it should be

exoskeleton /'eksəʊskelɪtn/ *noun* [C] (**BIOLOGY**) a hard outer covering that protects the bodies of certain animals, such as insects ⊃ look at **endoskeleton**

the exosphere /ðɪ 'eksəʊsfɪə(r)/ *noun* [sing.] (**ASTRONOMY**) the region near the edge of a planet's atmosphere ⊃ picture at **atmosphere**

exothermic /ˌeksəʊ'θɜːmɪk/ *adj.* (**CHEMISTRY**) (used about a chemical reaction or process) producing heat ⊃ look at **endothermic** ⊃ picture at **water cycle**

exotic ⁀+ B2 /ɪɡ'zɒtɪk/ *adj.* unusual or interesting because it comes from a different country or culture: *exotic plants/animals/fruits*

expand ⁀ B1 ◐ /ɪk'spænd/ *verb* [I, T] (**BUSINESS**) to become bigger or to make sth bigger: *Metals expand when they are heated.* ◇ *We hope to expand our business this year.* **OPP contract²** **PHRV expand on sth** to give more details of a story, plan, idea, etc.

expanse /ɪk'spæns/ *noun* [C] a large open area (of land, sea, sky, etc.)

expansion ⁀+ B2 ◐ /ɪk'spænʃn/ *noun* [U, C] the act of becoming bigger or of making sth become bigger: *The rapid expansion of the university has caused a lot of problems.*

expansionism /ɪk'spænʃənɪzəm/ *noun* [U] (**POLITICS**) the belief in and process of increasing the size and importance of sth, especially in a country or a business: *military/territorial expansionism* ▶ **expansionist** /-ʃənɪst/ *noun* [C], *adj.*: *He was a ruthless expansionist.* ◇ *expansionist policies*

expansive /ɪk'spænsɪv/ *adj.* (*formal*) (used about a person) talking a lot in an interesting way; friendly

expatriate /ˌeks'pætriət/ (*also informal* **expat** /'ekspæt/) *noun* [C] (**POLITICS**) a person who lives outside their own country: *American expatriates in London*

expect ⁀ A2 ◐ /ɪk'spekt/ *verb* [T] **1 ~ (that); ~ (to do sth)** to think or believe that sb/sth will come or that sth will happen: *She was expecting a letter from the bank this morning but it didn't come.* ◇ *I expect (that) it will rain this afternoon.* ◇ *I know the food's not so good, but what did you expect from such a cheap restaurant?* (= it's not surprising) ◇ *I expected to hear from her last* *week, but there's been no news.* ◇ *She's expecting a baby in the spring* (= she's pregnant). ◯ note at **demand**[2] **2 ~ sth (from sb); ~ sb to do sth** to feel confident that you will get sth from sb or that they will do what you want: *He expects a high standard of work from everyone.* ◇ *Factory workers are often expected to work at night.* **3** I expect (*BrE*) (not used in the progressive tenses) to think that sth is true or correct; to suppose: *'Whose is this suitcase?' 'Oh it's Maureen's, I expect.'* ◇ *'Will you be able to help me later on?' 'I expect so.'*

expectancy /ɪkˈspektənsi/ *noun* [U] the state of expecting sth, especially sth good, to happen; hope: *a look/feeling of expectancy* ◯ look at **life expectancy**

expectant /ɪkˈspektənt/ *adj.* **1** hoping for sth good and exciting: *an expectant audience* ◇ *expectant faces* **2** (HEALTH) having a baby soon: *Expectant mothers need a lot of rest.* ▸ **expectantly** *adv.*

expectation 🔊 B2 🆆 /ˌekspekˈteɪʃn/ *noun* (*formal*) **1** [U, C] **~ (of sth)** the belief that sth will happen or come: *The dog was sitting under the table in expectation of food.* **2** [C, usually pl.] hope for the future: *They had great expectations for their daughter, but she didn't really live up to them.*
IDM against/contrary to (all) expectation(s) very different to what was expected **not come up to (sb's) expectations | not meet (sb's) expectations** to not be as good as expected

expected 🔊 B1 /ɪkˈspektɪd/ *adj.* that you think will happen **OPP** unexpected

expedient /ɪkˈspiːdiənt/ *adj.* (*formal*) (used about an action) convenient or helpful for a purpose, but possibly not completely honest or moral: *The government decided that it was expedient not to increase taxes until after the election.* ▸ **expediency** /-ənsi/ *noun* [U]

expedition 🔊 B1 /ˌekspəˈdɪʃn/ *noun* [C] **1** a long journey for a special purpose: *a scientific expedition to Antarctica* **2** (TOURISM) a short journey that you make for pleasure: *a fishing expedition*

expel /ɪkˈspel/ *verb* [T] (**-ll-**) **1** to force sb to leave a country, school, club, etc: *The government has expelled all foreign journalists.* ◇ *The boy was expelled from school for fighting.* **2** to send sth out by force: *to expel air from the lungs* ◯ *noun* **expulsion**

expend /ɪkˈspend/ *verb* [T] **~ sth (on sth)** (*formal*) to spend or use money, time, care, etc. in doing sth

expendable /ɪkˈspendəbl/ *adj.* (*formal*) not considered important enough to be saved: *In a war human life is expendable.*

expenditure 🔊+ C1 /ɪkˈspendɪtʃə(r)/ *noun* [U, sing.] (*formal*) (FINANCE) the act of spending money; the amount of money that is spent: *Government expenditure on education has been cut.*

expense 🔊 B2 /ɪkˈspens/ *noun* **1** [C, U] (FINANCE) the cost of sth in time or money: *Running a car is a great expense.* ◇ *The movie was filmed in Tahiti at great expense.* ◇ *They spared no expense in sending their daughter to the best school.* **2** expenses [pl.] (FINANCE) money that is spent in doing a particular job, or for a particular purpose: *You can claim back your travelling expenses.*
IDM at sb's expense **1** (FINANCE) with sb paying; at sb's cost: *My trip is at the company's expense.* **2** against sb, so that they look silly: *They were always making jokes at Paul's expense.* **at the expense of sth** harming or damaging sth: *He was a successful businessman, but it was at the expense of his family life.*

expensive 🔊 A1 /ɪkˈspensɪv/ *adj.* costing a lot of money **OPP** cheap[1], inexpensive ▸ expensively *adv.*

experience[1] 🔊 A2 🆆 /ɪkˈspɪəriəns/ *noun* **1** [U] **~ (of sth); ~ (as sth); ~ (in doing sth)** the things that you have done in your life; the knowledge or skill that you get from seeing or doing sth: *She has five years' teaching experience.* ◇ *Do you have experience of working with teenagers?* ◇ *She has 36 years of experience as a diplomat.* ◇ *doctors with experience in treating these diseases* ◇ *We all learn by experience.* ◇ *I know from experience what will happen.* **2** [C] something that has happened to you (often sth unusual or exciting): *She wrote a book about her experiences in Africa.*

experience[2] 🔊 B1 🆆 /ɪkˈspɪəriəns/ *verb* [T] to have sth happen to you; to feel: *It was the first time I'd ever experienced failure.* ◇ *to experience pleasure/pain/difficulty*

experienced 🔊 B1 /ɪkˈspɪəriənst/ *adj.* having the knowledge or skill that is necessary for sth: *He's an experienced diver.* **OPP** inexperienced

experiment[1] 🔊 A2 🆆 /ɪkˈsperɪmənt/ *noun* [C, U] (SCIENCE) a scientific test that is done in order to get proof of sth or new knowledge: *to carry out/perform/conduct/do an experiment* ◇ *We need to prove this theory by experiment.* ▸ **experimentally** /ɪkˌsperɪˈmentəli/ *adv.*

experiment[2] 🔊 B1 /ɪkˈsperɪment/ *verb* [I] **~ (on/with sth)** to do tests to see if sth works or to try to improve it: *Is it really necessary to experiment on animals?* ◇ *We're experimenting with a new timetable this month.*

experimental 🔊+ C1 /ɪkˌsperɪˈmentl/ *adj.* (SCIENCE) connected with experiments or with trying new ideas: *We're still at the experimental stage with the new product.* ◇ *experimental schools*

experimentation /ɪkˌsperɪmenˈteɪʃn/ *noun* [U] (*formal*) (SCIENCE) the activity or process of doing scientific experiments or testing new ideas, methods, etc. to find out what effect they have: *experimentation with new teaching methods* ◇ *Many people object to experimentation on embryos.*

expert 🔊 A2 🆆 /ˈekspɜːt/ *noun* [C] **~ (at/in/on sth)** a person who has a lot of special knowledge or skill: *She's a leading expert in the field of genetics.* ◇ *a computer expert* ◇ *Let me try — I'm an expert at parking cars in small spaces.* ▸ **expert** 🔊 A2 🆆 *adj.*: *He's an expert cook.* ◇ *I think we should get expert advice on the problem.* ▸ **expertly** *adv.*

expertise 🔊+ B2 🆆 /ˌekspɜːˈtiːz/ *noun* [U] a high level of special knowledge or skill

expert system *noun* [C] (COMPUTING) a computer system that can provide information and expert advice on a particular subject. The program asks the people who use it a series of questions about their problem and gives them advice based on its store of knowledge: *expert systems to aid medical diagnosis*

expire 🔊+ C1 /ɪkˈspaɪə(r)/ *verb* [I] (*formal*) (used about an official document, agreement, etc.) to come to the end of the time when you can use it or in which it has effect: *My passport's expired. I'll have to renew it.* **SYN** run out (of sth)

expiry /ɪkˈspaɪəri/ *noun* [U] the end of a period when you can use sth: *They had stayed on in the country after the expiry of their visas.*

ex'piry date (*BrE*) (*AmE* **expiration date** /ˌekspəˈreɪʃn deɪt/) *noun* [C] the date after which an official document, agreement, etc. is no longer legally acceptable, or after which sth should not be used

explain 🔊 A1 ⊙ /ɪkˈspleɪn/ verb [T, I]
~ (that ...); ~ (sth) (to sb)
1 to make sth clear or easy to understand: *He explained that someone would meet me at the airport.* ◇ *She explained how I should fill in the form.* ◇ *I don't understand this. Can you explain it to me?* **2** to give a reason for sth: *'This work isn't very good.' 'I wasn't feeling very well.' 'Oh, that explains it then.'* ◇ *The manager explained to the customers why the goods were late.*
IDM **explain yourself 1** to give reasons for your behaviour, especially when it has upset sb **2** to say what you mean in a clear way
PHR V **explain sth away** to give reasons why sth is not your fault or is not important

WORD FAMILY
explain *verb*
explanation *noun*
explanatory *adj.*
explicable *adj.*
(≠ **inexplicable**)

explanation 🔊 A2 ⊙ /ˌekspləˈneɪʃn/ noun **1** [C, U]
~ (for sth) a statement, fact or situation that gives a reason for sth: *He could not give an explanation for his behaviour.* ◇ *That idea needs some explanation.* **2** [C] a statement or a piece of writing that makes sth easier to understand: *For a full explanation of how the machine works, turn to page 5.*

explanatory 🔊 /ɪkˈsplænətri/ adj. giving an explanation: *There are some explanatory notes at the back of the book.* ◇ *Those instructions are self-explanatory* (= they don't need explaining).

expletive /ɪkˈspliːtɪv/ noun [C] (formal) a word, especially a rude word, that you use when you are angry or in pain **SYN** **swear word**

explicable /ɪkˈsplɪkəbl, ˈeksplɪkəbl/ adj. (formal) that can be explained: *Barry's strange behaviour is only explicable in terms of the stress he is under.*
OPP **inexplicable**

explicit 🔊 C1 🔊 /ɪkˈsplɪsɪt/ adj. **1** clear, making sth easy to understand: *I gave you explicit instructions not to touch anything.* ◇ *She was quite explicit about her feelings on the subject.* ⊃ look at **implicit** (1) **2** not hiding anything, especially details of sexual activity: *Some of the sex scenes in that TV play were very explicit.* ▶ **explicitly** 🔊 C1 🔊 adv.: *He was explicitly forbidden to stay out later than midnight.*

explode 🔊 B1 /ɪkˈspləʊd/ verb [I, T] to BURST (= break apart) or make sth BURST with a loud noise: *The bomb exploded without warning.* ◇ *The army exploded the bomb at a safe distance from the houses.* ◇ (figurative) *My father exploded* (= became very angry) *when I told him how much the car would cost to repair.* **SYN** **blow up** ⊃ noun **explosion**

WORD FAMILY
explode *verb*
explosion *noun*
explosive *adj., noun*
unexploded *adj.*

exploit¹ 🔊 B2 🔊 /ɪkˈsplɔɪt/ verb [T] **1** to use sth or to treat sb unfairly for your own advantage: *Some employers exploit foreign workers, making them work long hours for low pay.* **2** to develop sth or make the best use of sth: *This region has been exploited for oil for 50 years.* ◇ *Solar energy is a source of power that needs to be exploited more fully.* ▶ **exploitation** 🔊 C1 🔊 /ˌeksplɔɪˈteɪʃn/ noun [U]: *They're making you work 80 hours a week? That's exploitation!*

exploit² /ˈeksplɔɪt/ noun [usually pl.] something exciting or interesting that sb has done

exploration 🔊 B2 🔊 /ˌekspləˈreɪʃn/ noun [C, U] the act of travelling around a place in order to learn about it: *space exploration*

exploratory /ɪkˈsplɒrətri/ adj. done in order to find sth out: *The doctors are doing some exploratory tests to try and find out what's wrong.*

explore 🔊 B1 ⊙ /ɪkˈsplɔː(r)/ verb [T, I] to travel around a place, etc. in order to learn about it: *They went on an expedition to explore the River Amazon.* ◇ *I've never been to Paris before — I'm going out to explore.* ◇ (figurative) *We need to explore* (= look carefully at) *all the possibilities before we decide.*

explorer /ɪkˈsplɔːrə(r)/ noun [C] a person who travels around a place in order to learn about it

explosion 🔊 B1 /ɪkˈspləʊʒn/ noun [C] **1** the sudden violent BURSTING (= breaking apart) and loud noise of sth such as a bomb exploding: *Two people were killed in the explosion.* **2** a sudden dramatic increase in sth: *the population explosion* ⊃ verb **explode**

explosive¹ 🔊 C1 /ɪkˈspləʊsɪv, -ˈspləʊzɪv/ adj. **1** (CHEMISTRY) capable of exploding and therefore dangerous: *Hydrogen is highly explosive.* **2** causing strong feelings or having dangerous effects

explosive² 🔊 C1 /ɪkˈspləʊsɪv, -ˈspləʊzɪv/ noun [C] a substance that is used for causing explosions

exponent /ɪkˈspəʊnənt/ noun [C] **1** a person who supports an idea, a theory, etc. and persuades others that it is good: *She was a leading exponent of free trade during her political career.* **2** a person who is able to perform a particular activity with skill: *the most famous exponent of the art of mime* **3** (MATHEMATICS) a small number or symbol that shows how many times a quantity must be multiplied by itself, for example the figure 4 in a^4

exponential /ˌekspəˈnenʃl/ adj. **1** (MATHEMATICS) of or shown by an EXPONENT: *an exponential curve/function* ◇ 22^4 *is an exponential expression.* **2** (formal) (used about a rate of increase) becoming faster and faster: *exponential growth/increase* ▶ **exponentially** /-ʃəli/ adv.: *to increase exponentially*

export¹ 🔊 B1 /ɪkˈspɔːt/ verb [T, I] (ECONOMICS) to send goods, etc. to another country, usually for sale: *India exports tea and cotton.* **OPP** **import²** **2** [T] (COMPUTING) to move information from one program to another

export² 🔊 B1 /ˈekspɔːt/ noun (ECONOMICS) **1** [U] sending goods to another country for sale: *Most of our goods are produced for export.* ◇ *the export trade* **2** [C, usually pl.] something that is sent to another country for sale: *What are Brazil's main exports?* **OPP** **import¹** ▶ **exporter** /ekˈspɔːtə(r)/ noun [C]: *Japan is the largest exporter of electronic goods.* **OPP** **importer**

expose 🔊 B2 🔊 /ɪkˈspəʊz/ verb [T] **1** ~ sth (to sb); ~ sb/sth (as sth) to show sth that is usually hidden; to tell sth that has been kept secret: *This is an injustice which needs to be exposed.* ◇ *The politician was exposed as a liar on TV.* **SYN** **reveal 2** ~ sb/sth to sth to put sb/sth or yourself in a situation that could be difficult or dangerous: *to be exposed to radiation/danger* **3** ~ sb to sth to give sb the chance to experience sth: *I like jazz because I was exposed to it as a child.* **4** (ARTS AND MEDIA) (in photography) to allow light onto the film inside a camera when taking a photo

exposed /ɪkˈspəʊzd/ adj. (used about a place) not protected from the wind and bad weather

exposition /ˌekspəˈzɪʃn/ noun [C] (formal) a full explanation of a theory, plan, etc.

exposure 🔊 B2 /ɪkˈspəʊʒə(r)/ noun **1** [U, C] the act of making sth public; the thing that is made public: *The new movie has been given a lot of exposure in the media.* ◇ *The politician resigned because of the exposures about his private life.* **2** [U] being allowed or forced to experience sth: *Exposure to radiation is* almost always harmful. ◊ *TV can give children exposure to other cultures from an early age.* **3** [U] (**HEALTH**) a harmful condition when a person becomes very cold because they have been outside in very bad weather: *The climbers all died of exposure.*

express¹ 🔒 **A2** **W** /ɪk'spres/ *verb* [T] **1** to show sth such as a feeling or an opinion by words or actions: *I found it very hard to express what I felt about her.* ◊ *to express fears/concern about something* **2** ~ **yourself** to say or write your feelings, opinions, etc: *I don't think she expresses herself very well in that article.*

express² /ɪk'spres/ *adj.* [only before noun], *adv.* **1** going or sent quickly: *an express coach* ◊ *We'd better send the parcel express if we want it to get there on time.* **2** (used about a wish, command, etc.) clearly and definitely stated: *It was her express wish that he should have the picture after her death.*

express³ /ɪk'spres/ (*also* **express train**) *noun* [C] a fast train that does not stop at all stations

expression 🔒 **A2** **O** /ɪk'spreʃn/ *noun* **1** [U, C] something that you say that shows your opinions or feelings: *Freedom of expression is a basic human right.* ◊ *an expression of gratitude/sympathy/anger* **2** [C] the look on a person's face that shows what they are thinking or feeling: *He had a puzzled expression on his face.* **3** [C] (**LANGUAGE**) a word or phrase with a particular meaning: *'I'm starving' is an expression meaning 'I'm very hungry'.* ◊ *a slang/an idiomatic expression*

expressionism /ɪk'spreʃənɪzəm/ (*also* **Expressionism**) *noun* [U] (**ARTS AND MEDIA**) a style and movement in early twentieth-century art, theatre, cinema and music that tries to express people's feelings and emotions rather than showing events or objects in a realistic way ▸ **expressionist** /-nɪst/ (*also* **Expressionist**) *noun* [C], *adj.*

expressive /ɪk'spresɪv/ *adj.* showing feelings or thoughts: *That is a very expressive piece of music.* ◊ *Dave has a very expressive face.* ▸ **expressively** *adv.*

expressly /ɪk'spresli/ *adv.* (*formal*) **1** clearly; definitely: *I expressly told you not to do that.* **2** for a special purpose; specially: *These scissors are expressly designed for left-handed people.*

ex'press train = EXPRESS³

expressway /ɪk'spreswei/ (*AmE*) = MOTORWAY

expulsion /ɪk'spʌlʃn/ *noun* [U, C] the act of making sb leave a place or an institution: *There have been three expulsions from school this year.* ⊃ verb **expel**

exquisite /ɪk'skwɪzɪt, 'ekskwɪzɪt/ *adj.* extremely beautiful and pleasing: *She has an exquisite face.* ◊ *I think that ring is exquisite.* ▸ **exquisitely** *adv.*

extend 🔒 **B2** **W** /ɪk'stend/ *verb* **1** [T] to make sth longer or larger (in space or time): *Could you extend your visit for a few days?* ◊ *We're planning to extend the back of the house to give us more space.* ◊ *The company is planning to extend its operations into Asia.* ◊ *Since my injury I can't extend this leg fully* (= make it completely straight). **2** [I] (used with an adverb or a preposition) to cover the area or period of time mentioned: *The desert extends over a huge area of the country.* **3** [T] ~ **sth to sb** (*formal*) to offer sth to sb: *to extend hospitality/a warm welcome/an invitation to somebody*

ex,tended 'family *noun* [C + sing./pl. verb] (**SOCIAL STUDIES**) a family group with a close relationship among the members that includes not only parents and children but also uncles, aunts, grandparents, etc. ⊃ look at **nuclear family**

extension 🔒+ **B2** **W** /ɪk'stenʃn/ *noun* **1** [U, C] the act of increasing the area of activity, group of people, etc. that is affected by sth: *The extension of new technology into developing countries.* ◊ *gradual extension of the powers of central government* **2** [C] an extra period of time that you are allowed for sth: *I've applied for an extension to my work permit.* **3** [C] (**ARCHITECTURE**) a part that is added to a building: *They're building an extension to the hospital.* **4** (*abbr.* **ext.**) [C] a phone that is connected to a central phone in a house or to a SWITCHBOARD (= a central point where all telephone calls are answered) in a large office building: *What's your extension number?* ◊ *Can I have extension 4342, please?* **5** [C, usually pl.] pieces of artificial hair that are added to sb's own hair to make it longer: *I'm thinking of getting hair extensions.*

extensive 🔒+ **B2** **W** /ɪk'stensɪv/ *adj.* **1** large in area or amount: *The house has extensive grounds.* ◊ *Most of the buildings suffered extensive damage.* **2** (**AGRICULTURE**) (used about methods of farming) producing a small amount of food from a large area of land with a small amount of money and effort: *extensive agriculture* ⊃ look at **intensive** (2) ▸ **extensively** 🔒+ **B2** *adv.*

extensor /ɪk'stensə(r)/ (*also* **ex'tensor muscle**) *noun* [C] (**ANATOMY**) a muscle that allows you to make part of your body straight or stretched out ⊃ look at **flexor**

extent 🔒 **B2** **O** /ɪk'stent/ *noun* [U] **the ~ of sth** the length, area, size or importance of sth: *I was amazed at the extent of his knowledge.* ◊ *The full extent of the damage is not yet known.*
IDM **to a certain/to some extent** used to show that sth is only partly true: *I agree with you to a certain extent but there are still a lot of points I disagree with.* **to what extent** how far; how much: *I'm not sure to what extent I believe her.*

exterior¹ /ɪk'stɪəriə(r)/ *adj.* on the outside: *the exterior walls of a house* **OPP** **interior**

exterior² /ɪk'stɪəriə(r)/ *noun* [C] the outside of sth; the appearance of sb/sth: *The exterior of the house is fine but inside it isn't in very good condition.* ◊ *Despite his calm exterior, Steve suffers badly from stress.*

ex,terior 'angle *noun* [C] (**GEOMETRY**) an angle formed between the side of a shape and the line next to it, when this side is made longer ⊃ look at **interior angle** ⊃ picture at **angle¹**

exterminate /ɪk'stɜːmɪneɪt/ *verb* [T] to kill all the members of a group of people or animals **SYN** **wipe sth out** ▸ **extermination** /ɪkˌstɜːmɪ'neɪʃn/ *noun* [U]

external 🔒 **B2** **O** /ɪk'stɜːnl/ *adj.* **1** connected with the outside of sth: *The cream is for external use only* (= to be used on the skin). **OPP** **internal 2** coming from another place: *You will be tested by an external examiner.* **OPP** **internal** ▸ **externally** /-nəli/ *adv.* **OPP** **internally**

externalize (*BrE also* **-ise**) /ɪk'stɜːnəlaɪz/ *verb* [T] (*formal*) (**PSYCHOLOGY**) to show what you are thinking and feeling by what you say or do ⊃ look at **internalize**

extinct /ɪk'stɪŋkt/ *adj.* **1** (used about a type of animal, plant, etc.) no longer existing: *Rhinoceros are nearly extinct in the wild.* **2** (**GEOLOGY**) (used about a VOLCANO) no longer active ▸ **extinction** /-'stɪŋkʃn/ *noun* [U]: *The giant panda is in danger of extinction.*

extinguish /ɪk'stɪŋgwɪʃ/ *verb* [T] (*formal*) to cause sth to stop burning: *The fire was extinguished very quickly.* **SYN** **put sth out** ▸ **extinguisher** (*also* **fire extinguisher**) *noun* [C]

extort /ɪkˈstɔːt/ *verb* [T] ~ **sth (from sb)** (*formal*) to get sth by using threats or violence: *The gang were found guilty of extorting money from small businesses.*
▸ **extortion** /-ˈstɔːʃn/ *noun* [U]

extortionate /ɪkˈstɔːʃənət/ *adj.* (used especially about prices) much too high **SYN excessive**

extra¹ 🔒 **A1** /ˈekstrə/ *adj.* more than is usual, expected, or than exists already: *I'll need some extra money for the holidays.* ⊃ look at **additional**

extra² 🔒 **B1** /ˈekstrə/ *adv.* **1** in addition; more than is usual, expected, or than exists already: *Is wine included in the price of the meal or is it extra?* **2** (with an adjective or adverb) more than usually: *'What size is this sweater?' 'Extra large.'* ◇ *I tried to be extra nice to him yesterday because it was his birthday.*

extra³ 🔒 **B1** /ˈekstrə/ *noun* [C] **1** something that costs more, or that is not normally included: *Metallic paint is an optional extra.* **2** (ARTS AND MEDIA) a person in a film, etc. who has a small unimportant part, for example as a member of a crowd

extra- /ekstrə, ɪkˈstræ/ *prefix* **1** outside; beyond: *extramarital sex* ◇ *extraterrestrial beings* **2** very; more than usual: *extra-thin* ◇ *extra-special*

extract¹ 🔒 **C1** /ɪkˈstrækt/ *verb* [T] (*formal*) to take sth out, especially with difficulty: *I think this tooth will have to be extracted.* ◇ *a machine that extracts excess moisture from the air* ◇ *I wasn't able to extract an apology from her.* ⊃ note at **tooth**

extract² 🔒+ **B2** /ˈekstrækt/ *noun* (ARTS AND MEDIA) **1** [C] a part of a book, piece of music, etc., that has often been specially chosen to show sth: *The newspaper published extracts from the controversial novel.* **2** [U, C] a substance that has been taken from sth else using a particular process: *vanilla extract* ⊃ look at **essence**

extraction /ɪkˈstrækʃn/ *noun* (*formal*) **1** [U, C] the act of taking sth out: *extraction of salt from the sea* ◇ *Dentists report that children are requiring fewer extractions.* **2** [U] family origin: *He's an American but he's of Italian extraction.*

extracurricular /ˌekstrəkəˈrɪkjələ(r)/ *adj.* (EDUCATION) not part of the usual course of work or studies at a school or college: *The school offers many extra-curricular activities such as yoga and chess.*

extradite /ˈekstrədaɪt/ *verb* [T] ~ **sb (to …) (from …)** (LAW, POLITICS) to send a person who may be guilty of a crime from the country in which they are living to the country that wants to put them on trial for the crime: *The suspected terrorists were captured in Spain and extradited to France.* ▸ **extradition** /ˌekstrəˈdɪʃn/ *noun* [U, C]

extraordinary 🔒 **B2** /ɪkˈstrɔːdnri/ *adj.* **1** very unusual; greater or better than usual: *She has an extraordinary ability to whistle and sing at the same time.* ◇ *an extraordinary achievement* **SYN incredible 2** not what you would expect in a particular situation; very strange or unusual: *That was extraordinary behaviour for a teacher!* **SYN incredible** ⊃ look at **ordinary** ▸ **extraordinarily** /-dnrəli/ *adv.: He was an extraordinarily talented musician.*

extrapolate /ɪkˈstræpəleɪt/ *verb* [I, T] ~ **(sth) (from/to sth)** (*formal*) to form an opinion or make a judgement about a situation by using facts that you know from a different situation: *The figures were obtained by extrapolating from past trends.* ▸ **extrapolation** /ɪkˌstræpəˈleɪʃn/ *noun* [U, C]: *Their age can be determined by extrapolation from their growth rate.*

extraterrestrial /ˌekstrətəˈrestriəl/ *noun* [C] (in stories) a creature that comes from another planet; a creature that may exist on another planet ▸ **extraterrestrial** *adj.*

extravagant /ɪkˈstrævəgənt/ *adj.* **1** spending or costing too much money: *He's terribly extravagant — he travels everywhere by taxi.* ◇ *an extravagant present* **2** more than is usual, true or necessary: *The advertisements made extravagant claims for the new medicine.* ▸ **extravagance** /-gəns/ *noun* [U, C] ▸ **extravagantly** *adv.*

extra 'virgin *adj.* used to describe the good quality oil obtained the first time that OLIVES (= small green or black fruit with a bitter taste) are pressed

extreme 🔒 **A2 ⦿** /ɪkˈstriːm/ *adj.* **1** [only before noun] very great or strong: *You must take extreme care when driving at night.* ◇ *extreme heat/difficulty/poverty* **2** much stronger than is considered usual, acceptable, etc: *Her extreme views on immigration are shocking to most people.* ◇ *Extreme weather events are becoming more frequent.* **3** [only before noun] as far away as possible from the centre in the direction mentioned: *There could be snow in the extreme north of the country.* ◇ *politicians on the extreme left of the party* ⊃ look at **moderate**¹ (2), **radical**¹ (2) ▸ **extreme** 🔒 **B2 ⦿** *noun* [C]: *extremes of temperature* ◇ *Alex used to be very shy but now she's gone to the opposite extreme.*

extremely 🔒 **A2 ⦿** /ɪkˈstriːmli/ *adv.* very: *Listen carefully because this is extremely important.*

ex,treme 'sport *noun* [C, U] (SPORT) a very dangerous sport or activity that some people do for fun: *He enjoys extreme sports, such as bungee jumping and hang-gliding.*

extremist 🔒+ **C1** /ɪkˈstriːmɪst/ *noun* [C] (POLITICS) a person who has extreme political opinions and who may do sth violent or illegal ⊃ look at **moderate**³, **radical**² ▸ **extremism** /-mɪzəm/ *noun* [U]

extremity /ɪkˈstreməti/ *noun* [C] (*pl.* -ies) the part of sth that is furthest from the centre

extricate /ˈekstrɪkeɪt/ *verb* [T] to manage to free sb/sth from a difficult situation or position

extrovert /ˈekstrəvɜːt/ *noun* [C] a person who is confident and full of life and who prefers being with other people to being alone **OPP introvert**

extrusive /ɪkˈstruːsɪv/ *adj.* (GEOLOGY) (used about rock) that has been pushed out of the earth by a VOLCANO

exuberant /ɪɡˈzjuːbərənt/ *adj.* (used about a person or their behaviour) full of energy and excitement ▸ **exuberance** /-rəns/ *noun* [U]

eye¹ 🔒 **A1** /aɪ/ *noun* [C] **1** (ANATOMY) one of the two organs of the body that you use to see with: *She opened/closed her eyes.* ◇ *He's got blue eyes.* ⊃ look at **black eye** ⊃ picture on **page 274 2** the ability to see sth: *He has sharp eyes* (= he can see very well). ◇ *She has an eye for detail* (= she notices small details). **3** the hole at one end of a needle that the THREAD goes through

IDM as far as the eye can see → FAR² **be up to your eyes in sth** (*informal*) to have more of sth than you can easily do or manage **before sb's very eyes** in front of sb so that they can clearly see what is happening **cast an eye/your eye(s) over sb/sth** → CAST¹ **catch sb's attention/eye** → CATCH¹ **cry your eyes out** → CRY¹ **an eye for an eye** used to say that you should punish sb by doing to them what they have done to you or to sb else **have (got) your eye on sb** to watch sb carefully to make sure that they do nothing wrong **have (got) your eye on sth** to be thinking about buying sth **in the eyes of sb/in sb's eyes** in the opinion of sb: *She was still a child in her mother's eyes.* **in the public eye** → PUBLIC¹ **keep an eye on sb/sth** to make sure that sb/sth is safe; to look after sb/sth: *Please could you keep an eye on the*

the eye

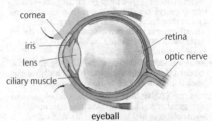

cornea
iris
lens
ciliary muscle
retina
optic nerve
eyeball

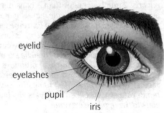

eyelid
eyelashes
pupil
iris

house while we're away? **keep an eye open/out (for sb/sth)** to watch or look out for sb/sth **keep your eyes peeled/skinned (for sb/sth)** (*informal*) to watch carefully for sb/sth **look sb in the eye** → LOOK¹ **the naked eye** → NAKED **not bat an eye** → BAT² **see eye to eye (with sb)** → SEE **set eyes on sb/sth** to see sb/sth: *He loved the house the moment he set eyes on it.* **turn a blind eye** → BLIND¹ **with your eyes open** knowing what you are doing: *You went into the new job with your eyes open, so you can't complain now.*

eye² /aɪ/ *verb* [T] (eyeing, eying; *pt, pp* eyed) to look at sb/sth closely: *She eyed him with suspicion.*

eyeball /'aɪbɔːl/ *noun* [C] (**ANATOMY**) the whole of the eye (including the part that is hidden inside the head)

eyebrow /'aɪbraʊ/ (*also* brow) *noun* [C] (**ANATOMY**) the line of hair that is above the eye ⊃ picture at **body**
IDM **raise your eyebrows** → RAISE¹

'**eye-catching** *adj.* (used about a thing) attracting your attention immediately because it is interesting, bright or pretty

eyeglasses /'aɪglɑːsɪz/ (*AmE*) = GLASS (3)

eyelash /'aɪlæʃ/ (*also* lash) *noun* [C] (**ANATOMY**) one of the hairs that grow on the edges of the EYELIDS ⊃ picture at **body, eye¹**

'**eye level** *noun* [U] at the same height as sb's eyes when they are standing up: *Computer screens should be at eye level.* ◊ *an eye-level grill*

eyelid /'aɪlɪd/ (*also* lid) *noun* [C] (**ANATOMY**) the piece of skin that can move to cover the eye ⊃ picture at **body, eye¹**
IDM **not bat an eyelid** → BAT²

eyeliner /'aɪlaɪnə(r)/ *noun* [U] a substance that you use to draw a dark line around your eyes to make them look more attractive

'**eye-opener** *noun* [C] something that makes you realize the truth about sth

eyepiece /'aɪpiːs/ *noun* [C] (**SCIENCE**) the LENS at the end of a TELESCOPE or MICROSCOPE that you look through ⊃ picture at **binoculars, laboratory, microscope**

eyeshadow /'aɪʃædəʊ/ *noun* [U] colour that is put on the skin above the eyes to make them look more attractive

eyesight /'aɪsaɪt/ *noun* [U] the ability to see: *good/poor eyesight*

eyesore /'aɪsɔː(r)/ *noun* [C] something that is ugly and unpleasant to look at: *All this litter in the streets is a real eyesore.*

eyewitness /'aɪwɪtnəs/ = WITNESS¹ (1)

eying /'aɪɪŋ/ present participle of **eye²**

e-zine /'iː ziːn/ *noun* [C] a magazine that you can pay to read in electronic form on the internet

F f

F¹ /ef/ *noun* [C, U] (*pl.* F's) **1** (*also* f, *pl.* f's) the sixth letter of the English alphabet: *'Father' begins with (an) 'F'.* **2** (**MUSIC**) the fourth note in the SCALE of C MAJOR **3** ~ (**in/for sth**) (**EDUCATION**) a grade given for an exam or a piece of work that shows that it is very bad: *She got an F in chemistry.*

F² *abbr.* (in writing) = FAHRENHEIT: *Water freezes at 32°F*

f *abbr.* (in writing) **1** = FEMALE¹ (2) **2** = FEMININE

FA /ˌef 'eɪ/ *abbr.* (*BrE*) **Football Association** (the organization that controls the sport of football in England and Wales): *the FA Cup*

fable /'feɪbl/ *noun* [C] (**LITERATURE**) a short story that teaches a moral lesson and that often has animals as the main characters: *Aesop's fables*

fabric ?+ B2 /'fæbrɪk/ *noun* **1** [C, U] (a type of) cloth or soft material that is used for making clothes, curtains, etc: *cotton fabrics* **2** [sing.] the basic structure of a building or system: *The Industrial Revolution changed the fabric of society.* ⊃ note at **structure¹**

fabulous ?+ B2 /'fæbjələs/ *adj.* **1** (*informal*) very good; excellent: *It was a fabulous concert.* **2** (*formal*) very great: *fabulous wealth/riches/beauty*

facade (*also* façade) /fə'sɑːd/ *noun* [C] **1** (**ARCHITECTURE**) the front wall of a large building that you see from the outside **2** [usually sing.] the way sb/sth appears to be, which is different from the way sb/sth really is: *His good humour was just a facade.*

face¹ ?⊞ A1 /feɪs/ *noun* [C] **1** (**ANATOMY**) the front part of the head; the expression that is shown on it: *Go and wash your face.* ◊ *She has a very pretty face.* ◊ *He came in with a smile on his face.* ◊ *Her face lit up* (= showed happiness) *when John came into the room.* ◊ *I tried to put on a happy face.* **2** the front or one side of sth: *the north face of the mountain* ◊ *He put the cards face up/down on the table.* ◊ *a clock face* **3** -faced (in adjectives) having the type of face or expression mentioned: *red-/round-/sour-faced*
IDM **face to face (with sb/sth)** close to and looking at sb/sth **keep a straight face** → STRAIGHT¹ **lose face** → LOSE **make/pull faces** to make rude expressions with your face: *The children made faces behind the teacher's back.* **make/pull faces/a face (at sb/sth)** to make an expression that shows that you do not like sb/sth **put on a brave face** | **put a brave face on sth** → BRAVE¹ **save face** → SAVE¹ **to sb's face** if you say sth to sb's face, you do it when that person is with you **OPP** **behind sb's back**

face² ?⊞ B1 /feɪs/ *verb* **1** [T, I] (used with an adverb or a preposition) to have your face or front pointing towards sb/sth or in a particular direction: *The garden faces south.* ◊ *Can you all face the front, please?* ⊃ note at **compass 2** [T] to have to deal with sth unpleasant; to deal with sb in a difficult situation: *We're facing a*

financial crisis. ◇ *He couldn't face going to work yesterday — he felt too ill.* ◇ *They faced a lot of problems when they moved house.* ◇ *I didn't know how to face my mother after I'd crashed her car.* **3** [T] to need attention or action from sb: *There are several problems facing the government.* ◇ *We are faced with a difficult decision.*
IDM **let's face it** (*informal*) we must accept it as true: *Let's face it, we can't afford a holiday this year.* **PHR V** **face up to sth** to accept a difficult or unpleasant situation and do sth about it

Facebook™ /ˈfeɪsbʊk/ *noun* [U] a very popular SOCIAL MEDIA website: *Are you on Facebook?* ◇ *I posted an update on Facebook.*

facecloth /ˈfeɪsklɒθ/ (*also* **flannel**) *noun* [C] (*BrE*) a small square piece of cloth that is used for washing yourself

faceless /ˈfeɪsləs/ *adj.* without individual character or identity: *faceless civil servants*

facelift /ˈfeɪslɪft/ *noun* [C] (MEDICINE) a medical operation in which the skin on a person's face is made tighter in order to make them look younger ⊃ look at **plastic surgery**

face-off *noun* [C] **1** (*especially AmE, informal*) an argument or a fight: *a face-off between the presidential candidates* **2** (SPORT) the way of starting play in a game of ICE HOCKEY

face-saving *adj.* [only before noun] said or done in order to avoid looking silly or losing other people's respect: *In his interview, the captain made face-saving excuses for his team's defeat.*

facet /ˈfæsɪt/ *noun* [C] **1** one part or particular aspect of sth **2** one side of a PRECIOUS STONE

face time *noun* [U] (*AmE, informal*) (BUSINESS) time that you spend talking in person to people you work with, rather than speaking on the phone or sending emails

facetious /fəˈsiːʃəs/ *adj.* trying to be funny about a subject at a time that is not appropriate so that other people become annoyed: *He kept making facetious remarks during the lecture.* ▶ **facetiously** *adv.*

face-to-face *adj.* involving people who are close together and looking at each other: *a face-to-face conversation*

face value *noun* [U, sing.] the cost or value that is shown on the front of tickets, stamps, coins, etc.
IDM **take sb/sth at (its, his, etc.) face value** to accept sb/sth as it, he, etc. appears to be: *Don't take his story at face value. There's something he hasn't told us yet.*

facial /ˈfeɪʃl/ *adj.* connected with a person's face: *a facial expression* ◇ *facial hair*

facile /ˈfæsaɪl/ *adj.* (used about a comment, an argument, etc.) not carefully thought out

facilitate ⟨↑⟩ C1 ⓦ /fəˈsɪlɪteɪt/ *verb* [T] (*formal*) to make an action or a process possible or easier: *The new trade agreement should facilitate more rapid economic growth.*

facilitator /fəˈsɪlɪteɪtə(r)/ *noun* [C] **1** a person who helps sb do sth more easily by discussing problems, giving advice, etc. rather than telling them what to do: *The teacher acts as a facilitator of learning.* **2** (*formal*) a thing that helps a process take place

facility ⟨↑⟩ B2 ⓦ /fəˈsɪləti/ *noun* (*pl.* -ies) **1 facilities** [pl.] (TOURISM) services, buildings, equipment, etc. that make it possible to do sth: *Our town has excellent sports facilities* (= a stadium, swimming pool, etc.). ◇ *healthcare facilities* **2** [C] a special feature of a machine, service, etc. that makes it possible to do sth extra: *a facility that allows you to check in for your flight online*

facsimile /fækˈsɪməli/ *noun* [C, U] an exact copy of a picture, piece of writing, etc. ⊃ look at **fax¹**

fact ⟨↑⟩ A1 ⓞ /fækt/ *noun* **1** [C] something that you know has happened or is true: *It is a scientific fact that light travels faster than sound.* ◇ *We need to know all the facts before we can decide.* ◇ *I know **for a fact** that Peter wasn't ill yesterday.* ◇ **The fact that** *I am older than you makes no difference at all.* ◇ *You must **face facts** and accept that he has gone.* **2** [U] true things; reality: *The film is based on fact.* **OPP** **fiction**
IDM **as a matter of fact** → MATTER¹ **the fact (of the matter) is (that)** … the truth is that … : *I would love a car, but the fact is that I just can't afford one.* **a fact of life** something unpleasant that you must accept because you cannot change it **facts and figures** detailed information: *Before we make a decision, we need some more facts and figures.* **the facts of life** the details of sexual behaviour and how babies are born **hard facts** → HARD¹ **in (actual) fact 1** (used for emphasizing that sth is true) really; actually: *I thought the lecture would be boring but in actual fact it was rather interesting.* **2** used for introducing more detailed information: *It was cold. In fact it was freezing.*

faction ⟨↑⟩ C1 /ˈfækʃn/ *noun* [C] (POLITICS) a small group of people within a larger one whose members have some different aims and beliefs to those of the larger group: *rival factions within the organization* ▶ **factional** /-ʃənl/ *adj.*: *factional rivalries/disputes*

factor¹ ⟨↑⟩ A2 ⓞ /ˈfæktə(r)/ *noun* [C] **1** one of the things that influences a decision, situation, etc: *His unhappiness at home was a major factor in his decision to go abroad.* **2** (MATHEMATICS) a whole number (except 1) by which a larger number can be divided: *2, 3, 4 and 6 are factors of 12.*

factor² /ˈfæktə(r)/ *verb*
PHR V **factor sth in** | **factor sth into sth** to include a particular fact or situation when you are thinking about or planning sth: *Remember to factor in staffing costs when you are planning the project.*

factorize (*BrE also* **-ise**) /ˈfæktəraɪz/ *verb* [T] (MATHEMATICS) to express a number in terms of its FACTORS

factory ⟨↑⟩ A2 /ˈfæktri, -təri/ *noun* [C] (*pl.* -ies) a building or group of buildings where goods are made in large quantities by machine: *a car factory* ◇ *factory workers*

▼ SYNONYMS

factory

plant ◆ **mill** ◆ **works** ◆ **yard** ◆ **workshop** ◆ **foundry**

These are all words for buildings or places where things are made or where industrial processes take place.

factory *a chocolate/clothing factory*

plant *a nuclear processing plant*

mill *a cotton/paper/textile mill*

works *a brickworks* ◇ *a steelworks*

yard *a shipyard*

workshop *a car repair workshop*

foundry *an iron foundry*

---

factory farm *noun* [C] (*BrE*) (AGRICULTURE) a type of farm in which animals are kept inside in small spaces and a large amount of meat, milk, etc. is produced as quickly and cheaply as possible ▶ **factory farming** *noun*

fact sheet *noun* [C] a piece of paper or an electronic document giving information about a subject: *Our fact sheet on hurricanes is available online.*

factual /ˈfæktʃuəl/ *adj.* based on or containing things that are true or real: *a factual account of the events* ⊃ look at **fictional** ▸ **factually** /-əli/ *adv.*: *factually correct*

faculty ʔ+ **C1** /ˈfæklti/ *noun* [C] (*pl.* -ies) **1** one of the natural abilities of a person's body or mind: *the faculty of hearing/sight/speech* **2** (*often* Faculty) (**EDUCATION**) one department in a university, college, etc: *the Faculty of Law/Arts* **3** [+ sing./pl. verb] all the teachers in a faculty of a university, college, etc.

fad /fæd/ *noun* [C] (*informal*) a fashion, interest, etc. that will probably not last long **SYN** **craze**

fade ʔ+ **C1** /feɪd/ *verb* **1** [I, T] to become or make sth become lighter in colour or less strong or fresh: *Jeans fade when you wash them.* ◇ *Look how the sunlight has faded these curtains.* **2** [I] ~ (**away**) to disappear slowly (from sight, hearing, memory, etc.): *The cheering of the crowd faded away.* ◇ *The smile faded from his face.*

faeces (*BrE*) (*AmE* feces) /ˈfiːsiːz/ *noun* [pl.] (*formal*) (**BIOLOGY**) the solid waste matter that you get rid of from the body when you go to the toilet **SYN** **excrement**

fag /fæg/ *noun* (*BrE*) **1** [C] (*informal*) a cigarette **2** [sing.] (*informal*) a piece of work that you do not want to do

Fahrenheit /ˈfærənhaɪt/ *noun* [U] (*abbr.* F) the name of a scale that measures temperatures: *Water freezes at 32° Fahrenheit (32°F).* ⊃ look at **Celsius**

fail¹ ʔ **A2** ⊙ /feɪl/ *verb* **1** [I, T] (**BUSINESS**) to not be successful in sth: *I feel that I've failed — I'm 25 and I still haven't got a steady job.* ◇ *She failed her driving test.* ⊃ look at **pass¹** (1), **succeed** (1) ⊃ note at **study²** **2** [T] (**EDUCATION**) to decide that sb is not successful in a test, exam, etc: *The examiners failed half of the candidates.* **OPP** **pass¹ 3** [I] ~ **to do sth** to not do sth: *She never fails to do her homework.* **4** [I, T] to not be enough or not do what people are expecting or wanting: *If the crops fail, people will starve.* ◇ *I think the government has failed us.* **5** [I] (**HEALTH**) (used about health, EYESIGHT, etc.) to become weak: *His health is failing.* **6** [I] to stop working: *My brakes failed on the hill but I managed to stop the car.* ▸ **failed** ʔ+ **B2** *adj.* [only before noun]: *a failed writer* ◇ *a failed attempt at beating the record*

fail² /feɪl/ *noun* [C] (**EDUCATION**) the result of an exam in which sb is not successful **OPP** **pass²** **IDM** **without fail** always, even if there are difficulties: *The postman always arrives at eight o'clock without fail.*

failing¹ /ˈfeɪlɪŋ/ *noun* [C] a weakness or fault: *She's not very patient — that's her only failing.*

failing² /ˈfeɪlɪŋ/ *prep.* if sth is not possible: *Ask Jackie to go with you, or failing that, try Anne.*

failure ʔ **B2** ⊙ /ˈfeɪljə(r)/ *noun* **1** [U] lack of success: *All my efforts ended in failure.* **OPP** **success 2** [C] a person or thing that is not successful: *His first attempt at skating was a miserable failure.* **OPP** **success 3** [U, C] ~ **to do sth** not doing sth that people expect you to do: *I was very disappointed at his failure to come to the meeting.* **4** [U, C] an example of sth not working correctly: *She died of heart failure.* ◇ *There's been a failure in the power supply.*

faint¹ /feɪnt/ *adj.* **1** (used about things that you can see, hear, feel, etc.) not strong or clear: *a faint light/sound* ◇ *There is still a faint hope that they will find more people alive.* **2** [not before noun] (used about people) likely to become unconscious; very weak: *I feel faint — I'd better sit down.* **3** (used about actions, etc.) done without much effort: *He made a faint protest.* ▸ **faintly** *adv.*

IDM **not have the faintest/foggiest (idea)** (*informal*) to not know at all: *I haven't the faintest idea where they've gone.*

faint² /feɪnt/ *verb* [I] to become unconscious when not enough blood is going to your brain, usually because of the heat, a shock, etc: *Suddenly the woman in front of me fainted.* **SYN** **pass out** **OPP** **come around**

fair¹ ʔ **A2** /feə(r)/ *adj., adv.* **1** appropriate and acceptable in a particular situation: *That's a fair price for that house.* ◇ *I think it's fair to say that the number of homeless people is increasing.* **OPP** **unfair 2** ~ (**to/on sb**) treating each person or side equally, according to the law, the rules, etc: *That's not fair — he got the same number of mistakes as I did and he's got a better mark.* ◇ *It wasn't fair on her to ask her to stay so late.* ◇ *a fair trial* ◇ **To be fair**, *she did ask me first.* **OPP** **unfair 3** quite good, large, etc: *They have a fair chance of success.* **4** (used about the skin or hair) light in colour: *Chloe has fair hair and blue eyes.* ⊃ look at **skin¹** (2) **5** (used about the weather) good, without rain ⊃ look at **skin¹** (2) **IDM** **fair enough** (*BrE, informal*) used to show that you agree with what sb has suggested **fair play** (**SPORT**) equal treatment of both/all sides according to the rules: *The referee is there to ensure fair play during the match.* **(more than) your fair share of sth** (more than) the usual or expected amount of sth

fair² /feə(r)/ *adv.* according to the rules; in a way that is considered to be acceptable and appropriate: *You must play fair in all team games.*

fair³ /feə(r)/ *noun* [C] **1** (*BrE* funfair) a type of entertainment in a field or park. At a fair you can ride on machines or try and win prizes at games. Fairs usually travel from town to town. **2** (**BUSINESS**) a large event where people, businesses, etc. show and sell their goods: *a trade fair* ◇ *the Frankfurt book fair*

fair ˈdealing (*BrE*) = **FAIR USE**

fairground /ˈfeəɡraʊnd/ *noun* [C] a large outdoor area where FAIRS are held

fair-ˈhaired *adj.* with light or blonde hair **SYN** **blonde**

fairly ʔ **B1** ⊙ /ˈfeəli/ *adv.* **1** in an acceptable way; in a way that treats people equally or according to the law, rules, etc: *I felt that the teacher didn't treat us fairly.* **OPP** **unfairly 2** quite, not very: *He is fairly tall.* ⊃ note at **rather**

fairness ʔ+ **C1** /ˈfeənəs/ *noun* [U] treating people equally or according to the law, rules, etc.

fair-ˈtrade *adj.* (**BUSINESS**, **ECONOMICS**) involving trade that supports producers in developing countries by paying fair prices and making sure that workers have good working conditions and fair pay

fair ˈuse (*AmE*) (*BrE* fair dealing) *noun* [C] (**LAW**) a legal statement that allows people to copy sb else's material without permission for news reporting, teaching, research, etc: *The defendants said their use of the photos should qualify as fair use.*

fairway /ˈfeəweɪ/ *noun* [C] (**SPORT**) the long STRIP of short grass that you hit the ball along in golf before you get to the GREEN and the HOLE

fairy /ˈfeəri/ *noun* [C] (*pl.* -ies) (in stories) a creature like a small person with wings and magic powers

ˈfairy tale (*also* **ˈfairy story**) *noun* [C] (**LITERATURE**) a story that is about FAIRIES, magic, etc.

faith ʔ **B2** /feɪθ/ *noun* **1** [U] ~ (**in sb/sth**) strong belief (in sb/sth); trust: *I've got great/little faith in his ability to do the job.* ◇ *I have lost faith in him.* **2** [U] (**RELIGION**) strong religious belief: *I've lost my faith.* **3** [C] (**RELIGION**) a particular religion: *the Jewish faith* ⊃ note at **religion**

IDM in good faith with honest reasons for doing sth: *I bought the car in good faith. I didn't know it was stolen.*

faithful /ˈfeɪθfl/ *adj.* **1** ~ **(to sb/sth)** always staying with and supporting a person, an organization or a belief: *Peter has been a faithful friend.* **SYN** loyal **2** ~ **(to sb)** not having a sexual relationship with anyone else: *He was always faithful to his wife.* **OPP** unfaithful **3** ~ **(to sth)** true to the facts; accurate: *a faithful description* ▶ faithfulness *noun* [U] ⊃ look at **fidelity**

faithfully /ˈfeɪθfəli/ *adv.* **1** accurately; carefully: *to follow instructions faithfully* ◇ *The events were faithfully recorded in her diary.* **2** in a way that shows commitment; in a way that you can rely on: *He had supported the local team faithfully for 30 years.* ◇ *She promised faithfully not to tell anyone my secret.* ❶ Yours faithfully is used to end formal letters.

'faith school *noun* [C] (*BrE*) (**EDUCATION**) a school especially for children of a particular religion

fake¹ /feɪk/ *noun* [C] **1** a work of art, etc. that seems to be sth that it is not **2** a person who is not really what they appear to be ▶ fake ⓘ+ **B2** *adj.*: *a fake passport* ⊃ note at **artificial**

fake² /feɪk/ *verb* [T] **1** to copy sth and try to make people believe it is the real thing: *He faked his father's signature.* **2** to make people believe that you are feeling sth that you are not: *I faked surprise when he told me the news.*

fake 'news *noun* [U] (**ARTS AND MEDIA**) false reports of events, usually spread on the internet: *The president dismissed the report as fake news.*

falcon /ˈfɔːlkən/ *noun* [C] a BIRD OF PREY (= a bird that kills other creatures for food) with long pointed wings

fall¹ ⓘ **A1** /fɔːl/ *verb* [I] (*pt* fell /fel/; *pp* fallen /ˈfɔːlən/)
• DROP DOWN **1** to drop down towards the ground: *He fell off the ladder onto the grass.* ◇ *The rain was falling steadily.* **2** ~ **(down/over)** to suddenly stop standing and drop to the ground: *She slipped on the ice and fell.* ◇ *I fell down the steps.* ◇ *The little boy fell over and hurt his knee.*
• OF HAIR/CLOTH **3** (used with an adverb or a preposition) to hang down: *Her hair fell down over her shoulders.*
• DECREASE **4** to become lower or less: *The temperature is falling.* ◇ *The price of coffee has fallen again.* **OPP** price¹, rise², trend¹
• BE DEFEATED **5** to be defeated or captured: *The government fell because of the scandal.*
• DIE IN WAR **6** (*formal*) to be killed in battle: *Millions of soldiers fell in the war.*
• BECOME **7** to change into a different state; to become: *He fell asleep on the sofa.* ◇ *They fell in love with each other in Spain.* ◇ *I must get some new shoes — these ones are falling to pieces.*
• HAPPEN **8** (*formal*) to come or happen: *My birthday falls on a Sunday this year.*
• BELONG TO A GROUP **9** (used with an adverb or a preposition) to belong to a particular group, type, etc: *Animals fall into two groups, those with backbones and those without.*
IDM ❶ For idioms containing fall, look at the entries for the nouns, adjectives, etc. For example, fall flat is at flat. **PHR V** fall apart to break (into pieces): *My old book was falling apart.* fall back on sb/sth to use sb/sth when you are in difficulty: *When the electricity was cut off we fell back on candles.* fall for sb (*informal*) to be strongly attracted to sb; to fall in love with sb fall for sth (*informal*) to be tricked into believing sth that is not true: *He makes excuses and she falls for them every time.* fall out (with sb) to argue and stop being friendly (with sb) fall through to fail or not happen: *Our trip to Japan has fallen through.*

▼ SYNONYMS

fall

decline ✦ drop ✦ diminish ✦ slump ✦ decrease

These are all words that can be used when the amount, level or number of sth goes down.

fall *Profits have fallen by 30 per cent.*

decline *The market for these products has slowly declined.*

drop *The Dutch team dropped to fifth place.*

diminish *The world's resources are rapidly diminishing.*

slump *Oil prices have slumped badly in recent months.*

decrease *The number of students decreased significantly last year.*

fall² ⓘ **A2** /fɔːl/ *noun*
• DOWN/OFF STH **1** [C] an act of falling down or off sth: *She had a nasty fall from her horse.*
• AMOUNT/DISTANCE **2** [C] ~ **(of sth)** the amount of sth that has fallen or the distance that sth has fallen: *We have had a heavy fall of snow.* ◇ *a fall of 4 metres*
• DECREASE **3** [C] ~ **(in sth)** a decrease (in value, quantity, etc.): *There has been a sharp fall in the price of oil.* **SYN** drop² **OPP** rise¹
• DEFEAT **4** [sing.] the ~ of sth a (political) defeat; a failure: *the fall of the Roman Empire*
• WATER **5** falls [pl.] a large amount of water that falls from a height down the side of a mountain, etc: *Niagara Falls* **SYN** waterfall
• SEASON **6** [C, U] (*AmE*) = AUTUMN

fallacy /ˈfæləsi/ *noun* [C, U] (*pl.* -ies) (*formal*) a false belief or a wrong idea: *It's a fallacy that money brings happiness* (= it's not true).

fallible /ˈfæləbl/ *adj.* able or likely to make mistakes: *Even our new computerized system is fallible.* **OPP** infallible

fallopian tube /fəˈləʊpiən tjuːb/ *noun* [C] (**ANATOMY**) one of the two tubes in the body of a woman or a female animal along which eggs travel from the OVARIES (= the place where they are produced) to the UTERUS (= the place where a baby is formed) ⊃ picture at **fertilization**

fallout /ˈfɔːlaʊt/ *noun* [U] (**PHYSICS**) dangerous RADIOACTIVE waste that is carried in the air after a nuclear explosion

fallow /ˈfæləʊ/ *adj.* (**AGRICULTURE**) (used about land) not used for growing plants for a time, especially so that the quality of the land will improve: *The farmer let the field lie fallow for two years.*

false ⓘ **A1** /fɔːls/ *adj.* **1** not true; not correct: *I think the information you have given is false.* ◇ *I got a completely false impression of him from our first meeting.* **OPP** true **2** not real; artificial: *false hair/eyelashes/teeth* **OPP** natural¹, real¹ ⊃ note at **artificial** **3** made to look real in order to trick people: *This suitcase has a false bottom.* ◇ *a false name/passport* **4** (used about sb's behaviour or expression) not sincere or honest: *a false smile* ◇ *false modesty* ⊃ look at **false alarm** ⊃ look at **false friend** ▶ falsely *adv.*: *She was falsely accused of stealing a wallet.* **IDM** under false pretences pretending to be or to have sth in order to trick people: *She got into the club under false pretences — she isn't a member at all!*

false a'larm *noun* [C] a warning about a danger that does not happen

false 'friend *noun* [C] (**LANGUAGE**) a word in another language that looks similar to a word in your own but has a different meaning

false 'teeth (*also* **dentures**) *noun* [pl.] artificial teeth that are worn by sb who has lost their natural teeth ➲ note at **tooth**

falsify /'fɔːlsɪfaɪ/ *verb* [T] (**falsifying; falsifies;** *pt, pp* **falsified**) (*formal*) to change a document, information, etc. so that it is no longer true in order to trick sb

falter /'fɔːltə(r)/ *verb* [I] **1** to become weak or move in a way that is not steady: *The engine faltered and stopped.* **2** to lose confidence: *Zverev faltered and missed the ball.*

fame Ⓘ+ **B2** /feɪm/ *noun* [U] being known or talked about by many people because of what you have achieved: *Pop stars achieve fame at a young age.* ◇ *The town's only claim to fame is that there was a riot there.*

famed /feɪmd/ *adj.* ~ **(for sth)** well known (for sth): *Welsh people are famed for their singing.* **SYN** **famous**

familiar Ⓘ **B1** Ⓢ /fə'mɪliə(r)/ *adj.* **1** ~ **(to sb)** well known to you; often seen or heard and therefore easy to recognize: *Does that sound familiar to you?* ◇ *It was a relief to see a familiar face in the crowd.* **OPP** **unfamiliar 2** ~ **with sth** having a good knowledge of sth: *People in Europe aren't very familiar with Chinese music.* **OPP** **unfamiliar 3** ~ **(with sb)** (used about a person's behaviour) too friendly and informal: *I was annoyed by the waiter's familiar behaviour.*

familiarity /fə,mɪli'ærəti/ *noun* [U] **1** ~ **(with sth)** having a good knowledge of sth: *His familiarity with the area was an advantage.* **2** a friendly and informal manner

familiarize (*BrE also* **-ise**) /fə'mɪliəraɪz/ *verb* [T] ~ **sb/ yourself (with sth)** to teach sb about sth or learn about sth until you know it well: *I want to familiarize myself with the plans before the meeting.* ▶ **familiarization** (*BrE also* **-isation**) /fə,mɪliəraɪ'zeɪʃn/ *noun* [U]

family¹ Ⓘ **A1** /'fæməli/ *noun* (*pl.* **-ies**) **1** [C + sing./pl. verb] a group of people who are related to each other: *I have quite a large family.* ◇ *a family of four* ◇ *the Dawson family* **2** [C, U] children: *We are planning to start a family next year* (= to have our first baby). ◇ *to bring up/raise a family* ◇ *Do you have any family?* **3** [C] a group of animals, plants, etc. that are of a similar type; a group of related things, especially languages: *Lions belong to the cat family.* ➲ picture at **animal** **IDM** **run in the family** to be found very often in a family: *Red hair runs in the family.*

family² Ⓘ **A1** /'fæməli/ *adj.* [only before noun] **1** connected with the family or a particular family: *family life* **2** owned by a family: *a family business* **3** suitable for both adults and children: *a family show*

family 'court *noun* [C] (**LAW**) a court that deals with cases that affect families, for example when people get divorced

family name *noun* [C] the name that is shared by members of a family **SYN** **surname**

family 'planning *noun* [U] (**HEALTH**) controlling the number of children you have by using birth control ➲ look at **contraception**

family room *noun* [C] **1** (*AmE*) a room in a house where the family can relax, watch TV, etc. **2** (**TOURISM**) a room in a hotel for three or four people to sleep in, especially parents and children

family 'tree *noun* [C] (**SOCIAL STUDIES**) a diagram that shows the relationship between different members of a family over a long period of time

famine /'fæmɪn/ *noun* [C, U] (**SOCIAL STUDIES**) a lack of food over a long period of time in a large area that can cause the death of many people: *There is a severe famine in the area.* ◇ *The long drought* (= a lack or rain or water) *was followed by famine.*

famished /'fæmɪʃt/ *adj.* [not before noun] (*informal*) very hungry

famous Ⓘ **A1** Ⓢ /'feɪməs/ *adj.* ~ **(for sth)** known about by many people: *a famous singer* ◇ *Glasgow is famous for its museums and art galleries.*

famously /'feɪməsli/ *adv.* in a way that is famous: *the words Nelson famously uttered just before he died* **IDM** **get on/along famously** (*old-fashioned, informal*) to have a very good relationship with sb

fan¹ Ⓘ **A2** /fæn/ *noun* [C] **1** somebody who admires and is very enthusiastic about a sport, a film star, a singer, etc: *football fans* ◇ *She's an Ed Sheeran fan.* ◇ *fan mail* (= letters from fans to the person they admire) **2** a machine with parts that turn around very quickly to create a current of cool or warm air: *an electric fan* ◇ *a fan heater* **3** an object in the shape of a SEMICIRCLE made of paper, feathers, etc. that you wave in your hand to create a current of cool air

fan² /fæn/ *verb* [T] (**-nn-**) **1** to make air blow on sb/sth by waving a FAN , your hand, etc. in the air: *She used a newspaper to fan her face.* **2** to make a fire burn more strongly by blowing on it: *The strong wind really fanned the flames.* **PHRV** **fan out** to spread out: *The police fanned out across the field.*

fanatic /fə'nætɪk/ *noun* [C] (**POLITICS**, **RELIGION**) a person who is very enthusiastic about sth and may have extreme or dangerous opinions (especially about religion or politics): *a religious fanatic* ◇ *She's a health food fanatic.* ▶ **fanatical** /-tɪkl/ *adj.*: *He's fanatical about keeping things tidy.* ▶ **fanatically** /-kli/ *adv.* ▶ **fanaticism** /-tɪsɪzəm/ *noun* [U]

fan base *noun* [U, sing.] the group of people who very much admire a particular musican, band, team, writer, etc.

fan belt *noun* [C] the belt that operates the machines that cool a car engine

fancy¹ Ⓘ **B1** /'fænsi/ *verb* [T] (**fancying; fancies;** *pt, pp* **fancied**) **1** (*BrE, informal*) to like the idea of having or doing sth; to want sth or to want to do sth: *What do you fancy to eat?* ◇ *I don't fancy going out in this rain.* **2** (*BrE, informal*) to be sexually attracted to sb: *Jack keeps looking at you. I think he fancies you.* **3** ~ **yourself (as) sth** (*informal*) to think that you would be good at sth; to think that you are sth (although this may not be true): *He fancied himself (as) a poet.*

fancy² Ⓘ **B1** /'fænsi/ *adj.* (**fancier; fanciest**) not simple or ordinary: *My father doesn't like fancy food.* ◇ *I just want a pair of black shoes — nothing fancy.* **OPP** **plain¹**

fancy³ /'fænsi/ *noun* **IDM** **take sb's fancy** to attract or please sb: *If you see something that takes your fancy I'll buy it for you.* **take a fancy to sb/sth** to start liking sb/sth: *I think that Laura's really taken a fancy to you.*

fancy 'dress *noun* [U] (*BrE*) special clothes that you wear to a party at which people dress up to look like a different person (for example from history or a story): *It was a Hallowe'en party and everyone went in fancy dress.*

fanfare /'fænfeə(r)/ *noun* [C] (**MUSIC**) a short loud piece of music that is used for introducing sb important, for example a king or queen

fang /fæŋ/ *noun* [C] a long sharp tooth of a dog, snake, etc. ➲ picture at **animal**

fanlight /'fænlaɪt/ *noun* [C] (**ARCHITECTURE**) a small window above a door or another window

fanny pack /'fæni pæk/ (*AmE*) = BUMBAG

fantasize (*BrE also* -ise) /'fæntəsaɪz/ *verb* [I, T] to imagine sth that you would like to happen: *He liked to fantasize that he had won a gold medal at the Olympics.*

fantastic 🔤 **A1** /fæn'tæstɪk/ *adj.* **1** (*informal*) very good; excellent: *She's a fantastic swimmer.* ◊ *You passed your test. Fantastic!* **SYN** **wonderful 2** strange and difficult to believe: *a story full of fantastic creatures from other worlds* **3** (*informal*) very large or great: *A Rolls-Royce costs a fantastic amount of money.* ▶ **fantastically** /-kli/ *adv.*

fantasy 🔤+ **B2** /'fæntəsi/ *noun* [C, U] (*pl.* -ies) **1** a situation that you imagine but that is not true: *I have a fantasy about going to live in the Bahamas.* ◊ *They live in a world of fantasy.* **2** (**LITERATURE**) a type of story that is set in an imaginary world and that involves magic, strange creatures, etc: *a sci-fi fantasy about three kids who build their own spaceship* ◊ *It's a series of epic fantasy novels for young adults.*

fanzine /'fænziːn/ *noun* [C] (**ARTS AND MEDIA**) a magazine that is written by and for people who like a particular sports team, singer, etc.

FAQ /ˌef eɪ 'kjuː, fæk/ *abbr.* (**COMPUTING**) **frequently asked questions** (a list of questions and answers about a particular subject, especially one giving basic information for users of a website)

far¹ 🔤 **B1** /fɑː(r)/ *adj.* [only before noun] (**farther** /'fɑːðə(r)/, **further** /'fɜːðə(r)/; **farthest** /'fɑːðɪst/, **furthest** /'fɜːðɪst/) **1** at a greater distance away from you: *the far side of the river* ◊ *My friend lives at the far end of the street.* **2** at the furthest point in a particular direction: *In the far north, days are short in winter.* ◊ *politicians from the far left of the party*

IDM **a far cry from sth/doing sth** an experience that is very different from sth/doing sth

far² 🔤 **A1** /fɑː(r)/ *adv.* (**farther** /'fɑːðə(r)/, **further** /'fɜːðə(r)/; **farthest** /'fɑːðɪst/, **furthest** /'fɜːðɪst/) **1** a long distance away: *London's not far from here.* ◊ *How far did we walk yesterday?* ◊ *If we sit too far away from the screen I won't be able to see the film.* ◊ *I can't swim as far as you.* ◊ *How much further is it?* ➔ note at **direction 2** very much: *She's far more intelligent than I thought.* ◊ *There's far too much salt in this soup.* **3** (to) a certain degree: *How far have you got with your homework?* ◊ *The company employs local people as far as possible.* **4** a long time: *We danced far into the night.*

IDM **as far as** to the place mentioned but not further: *We walked as far as the river and then turned back.* **as/so far as** used for giving your opinion or judgement of a situation: *As far as I know, she's not coming, but I may be wrong.* ◊ *So far as school work is concerned, he's hopeless.* ◊ *As far as I'm concerned, this is the most important point.* ◊ *As far as I can see, the accident was John's fault, not Ann's.* **as far as the eye can see** to the furthest place you can see **by far** (used for emphasizing comparative or superlative words) by a large amount: *Carmen is by far the best student in the class.* **far afield** far away, especially from where you live or from where you are staying: *You can hire a car if you want to explore further afield.* **far from doing sth** instead of doing sth: *Far from enjoying the film, he fell asleep in the middle.* **far from sth** almost the opposite of sth; not at all: *He's far from happy* (= he's very sad or angry). **far from it** (*informal*) certainly not; just the opposite: *'Did you enjoy your holiday?' 'No, far from it. It was awful.'* **few and far between** → FEW **go far 1** to be enough: *This food won't go very far between three of us.* **2** to be successful in life: *Dan is very talented and should go far.* **go too far** to behave in a way that causes trouble or upsets other people: *He's always being naughty*

but this time he's gone too far. **so far** until now: *So far the weather has been good but it might change.* **so far so good** everything has gone well until now

faraway /'fɑːrəweɪ/ *adj.* [only before noun] **1** a great distance away: *He told us stories of faraway countries.* **SYN** **distant 2** (used about a look in a person's eyes) as if you are thinking of sth else: *She stared out of the window with a faraway look in her eyes.*

farce /fɑːs/ *noun* [C] **1** something important or serious that is not organized well or treated with respect: *The meeting was a farce — everyone was shouting at the same time.* **2** (**ARTS AND MEDIA**) a funny play for the theatre full of silly situations and events ▶ **farcical** /'fɑːsɪkl/ *adj.*

fare¹ 🔤+ **B2** /feə(r)/ *noun* [C, U] the amount of money you pay to travel by bus, train, taxi, plane, etc: *What's the fare to Birmingham?* ◊ *Adults pay full fare, children pay half fare.* ➔ look at **airfare**

fare² /feə(r)/ *verb* [I] (*formal*) to be successful or not successful in a particular situation: *How did you fare in your examination* (= did you do well or badly)? **SYN** **get on/along**

the Far East *noun* [sing.] (**GEOGRAPHY**) China, Japan and other countries in East and South East Asia ➔ look at **Middle East**

farewell /ˌfeə'wel/ *noun* [C, U] the act of saying goodbye to sb: *He said his farewells and left.* ◊ *a farewell party/drink* ▶ **farewell** *exclamation* (*old-fashioned*)

far-fetched *adj.* not easy to believe: *It's a good book but the story's too far-fetched.*

farm¹ 🔤 **A1** /fɑːm/ *noun* [C] (**AGRICULTURE**) an area of land with fields and buildings that is used for growing crops and/or keeping animals: *to work on a farm* ◊ *farm buildings/workers/animals*

farm² 🔤 **A2** /fɑːm/ *verb* [I, T] (**AGRICULTURE**) to use land for growing crops and/or keeping animals: *The family have farmed in this area for centuries.* ◊ *She farms 200 acres.*

farmer 🔤 **A1** /'fɑːmə(r)/ *noun* [C] (**AGRICULTURE**) a person who owns or manages a farm: *a dairy farmer*

farmhand /'fɑːmhænd/ (*AmE also* **field hand**) *noun* [C] (**AGRICULTURE**) a person who works for a farmer

farmhouse /'fɑːmhaʊs/ *noun* [C] (**AGRICULTURE**) the house on a farm where the farmer lives

farming 🔤 **A2** /'fɑːmɪŋ/ *noun* [U] (**AGRICULTURE**) managing a farm or working on it: *farming methods/areas* ◊ *organic/sheep/dairy farming*

farmland /'fɑːmlænd/ *noun* [U, pl.] (**AGRICULTURE**) land that is used for farming: *250 acres of farmland*

farmyard /'fɑːmjɑːd/ *noun* [C] (**AGRICULTURE**) an outside area near a FARMHOUSE surrounded by buildings or walls

far-reaching *adj.* having a great influence on a lot of other things: *far-reaching changes*

far-sighted *adj.* **1** being able to see what will be necessary in the future and making plans for it **2** (*AmE*) = LONG-SIGHTED

fart /fɑːt/ *verb* [I] (*slang*) to suddenly let gas from the stomach escape from the bottom **HELP** Some people find this word offensive. A more polite way of saying this is 'to break wind'. ▶ **fart** *noun* [C]

farther /'fɑːðə(r)/ = FURTHER² (1)

farthest /'fɑːðɪst/ (*also* **furthest**) *adv.* at or to the greatest distance

fascinate /'fæsɪneɪt/ verb [T] to attract or interest sb very much: *Chinese culture has always fascinated me.* ▶ **fascinating** ⚡**B1** adj. ▶ **fascination** /ˌfæsɪ'neɪʃn/ noun [C, U]

fascism /'fæʃɪzəm/ (also **Fascism**) noun [U] (**POLITICS**) an extreme RIGHT-WING political system that is in favour of strong central government and does not allow anyone to speak against it ▶ **fascist** /-ɪst/ (also **Fascist**) noun [C], adj.

fashion ⚡**A2** /'fæʃn/ noun 1 [U, C] the style of dressing or behaving that is the most popular at a particular time: *What is **the latest fashion** in hairstyles?* ◇ *a fashion show/model/magazine* ◇ *Jeans are always **in fashion**.* ◇ *I think hats will **come back into fashion**.* ◇ *That colour is **out of fashion** this year.* 2 [U] the business of making or selling clothes in new and different styles: *a fashion magazine* ◇ *the fashion industry* 3 [sing.] the way you do sth: *Watch him. He's been behaving **in a very strange fashion**.*

fashionable ⚡**B1** /'fæʃnəbl/ adj. 1 popular or in a popular style at a particular time: *a fashionable area/dress/opinion* **OPP** **unfashionable** ⊃ look at **old-fashioned** (1) 2 used or visited by people following a current fashion, especially by rich people: *That restaurant has become fashionable recently.* ◇ *fashionable society* **OPP** **unfashionable** ▶ **fashionably** /-bli/ adv.

fashion designer noun [C] a person who designs fashionable clothes

fashionista /ˌfæʃn'iːstə/ noun [C] a person who dresses in a fashionable way or designs fashionable clothes

fast¹ ⚡**A1** /fɑːst/ adj. 1 moving or able to move or act at great speed: *a fast car/worker/runner/reader* 2 [not before noun] (used about a clock or watch) showing a time that is later than the real time: *The clock is five minutes fast.* **OPP** **slow¹** 3 [not before noun] FIRMLY fixed: *He made the boat fast* (= he tied it to sth) *before he got out.* ◇ *Do you think the colour in this T-shirt is fast* (= will not come out when washed)? **IDM** **fast and furious** very fast and exciting **hard and fast** → HARD¹

fast² ⚡**A1** /fɑːst/ adv. 1 quickly: *She ran very fast.* 2 FIRMLY or deeply: *Sam was fast asleep by ten o'clock.* ◇ *Our car was stuck fast in the mud.* **IDM** **hold fast to sth** (formal) to continue to believe in an idea

fast³ /fɑːst/ verb [I] to eat no food for a certain time, especially for religious or medical reasons: *Muslims fast during Ramadan.* ▶ **fast** noun [C]

fasten ⚡**B1** /'fɑːsn/ verb 1 [T, I] ~ **(sth) (up)** to close or join the two parts of sth; to become closed or joined: *Please fasten your seat belts.* ◇ *Fasten your coat up — it's cold outside.* ◇ *My dress fastens at the back.* **OPP** **unfasten** 2 [T] ~ **sth (on/to sth); ~ A and B (together)** to fix or tie sth to sth, or two things together: *Fasten this badge on your jacket.* ◇ *How can I fasten these pieces of wood together?* 3 [T] to close or lock sth FIRMLY so that it will not open: *Close the window and fasten it securely.* **OPP** **unfasten**

fastener /'fɑːsnə(r)/ (also **fastening**) noun [C] something that fastens things together

fast food noun [U] food that can be served very quickly in special restaurants and is often taken away to be eaten in the street: *a fast-food restaurant*

fast-forward verb [T] to move a recording forwards to a later point without playing it ▶ **fast forward** noun [U]: *the fast-forward button*

fastidious /fæ'stɪdiəs/ adj. difficult to please; wanting everything to be perfect

fat¹ ⚡**A1** /fæt/ adj. (fatter; fattest) 1 (used about people's or animals' bodies) weighing too much; covered with too much FLESH: *You'll **get fat** if you eat too much.* **OPP** **thin¹** 2 (used about a thing) thick or full: *a fat wallet/book*

fat² ⚡**A2** /fæt/ noun 1 [U] (**BIOLOGY**) the soft white substance under the skins of animals and people: *I don't like meat with fat on it.* ⊃ adjective **fatty** 2 [C, U] the substance containing oil that we obtain from animals, plants or seeds and use for cooking: *Cook the onions in a little fat.*

fatal ⚡**C1** /'feɪtl/ adj. 1 causing or ending in death: *a fatal accident/disease/crash* ⊃ look at **mortal¹** (2) 2 causing trouble or a bad result: *She made the fatal mistake of trusting him.* ▶ **fatally** /-təli/ adv.: *fatally injured*

fatality /fə'tæləti/ noun [C] (pl. -ies) a person's death caused by an accident, in war, etc: *There were no fatalities in the fire.*

fat cat noun [C] (informal) a person who earns, or who has, a lot of money (especially when compared to people who do not earn so much)

fate ⚡**C1** /feɪt/ noun 1 [U] the power that some people believe controls everything that happens: *It was fate that brought them together again after 20 years.* ⊃ look at **providence** 2 [C] your future; sth that happens to you: *Both men suffered the same fate — they both lost their jobs.*

fateful /'feɪtfl/ adj. having an important effect on the future: *a fateful decision*

father¹ ⚡**A1** /'fɑːðə(r)/ noun [C] 1 a person's male parent: *John looks exactly like his father.* ◇ *Tim's a wonderful father.* 2 **Father** (**RELIGION**) the title of certain priests: *Father O'Reilly*

father² /'fɑːðə(r)/ verb [T] to become the father of a child by making a woman pregnant: *to father a child*

Father Christmas (BrE) (also **Santa Claus**) noun [C] an imaginary old man with a red coat and a long white BEARD (= hair on the sides and bottom part of his face) who, children believe, brings presents at Christmas

fatherhood /'fɑːðəhʊd/ noun [U] the state of being a father

father-in-law noun [C] (pl. fathers-in-law) your husband's or wife's father

fatherly /'fɑːðəli/ adj. like or typical of a good father: *Would you like a piece of fatherly advice?*

Father's Day /'fɑːðəz deɪ/ noun [C] a day when fathers receive cards and gifts from their children, usually the third Sunday in June

fathom¹ /'fæðəm/ verb [T] (usually in negative sentences) to understand sth: *I can't fathom what he means.*

fathom² /'fæðəm/ noun [C] a measure of the depth of water; 6 feet (1.8 metres)

fatigue /fə'tiːg/ noun [U] 1 the feeling of being extremely tired: *He was suffering from mental and physical fatigue.* **SYN** **exhaustion** 2 (**CHEMISTRY, PHYSICS**) weakness in metals caused by a lot of use: *The plane crash was caused by metal fatigue in a wing.*

fatten /'fætn/ verb [T] ~ **sb/sth (up)** to make sb/sth fatter: *He's fattening the pigs up for market.*

fattening /'fætnɪŋ/ adj. (used about food) that makes people fat: *Chocolate is very fattening.*

fatty /'fæti/ adj. (fattier; fattiest) (used about food) having a lot of fat in or on it ⊃ note at **meat**

fatty acid noun [C] (**BIOLOGY, CHEMISTRY**) an ACID that is found in fats and oils

fatwa /ˈfætwɑː/ *noun* [C] an official decision or order made by a Muslim leader

faucet /ˈfɔːsɪt/ (*AmE*) = TAP² (1)

fault¹ ʔ B2 /fɔːlt/ *noun* **1** [C] something wrong or not perfect in a person's character or in a thing: *One of my faults is that I'm always late.* ◊ *a fault in the electricity supply* ◊ *a technical fault* **2** [U] responsibility for a mistake: *It will be your own fault if you don't pass your exams.* **3** ('fault line) [C] (GEOLOGY) a place where there is a break in the layers of rock in the earth's surface. Earthquakes are more likely to happen in these places: *the San Andreas fault* ⊃ picture at **limestone, plate tectonics** IDM **be at fault** to be wrong or responsible for a mistake: *The other driver was at fault — he didn't stop at the traffic lights.* **find fault (with sb/sth)** → FIND¹

fault² /fɔːlt/ *verb* [T] (usually after *can/could* in negative sentences) to find sth wrong with sb/sth: *I couldn't fault his dedication to the job.*

faultless /ˈfɔːltləs/ *adj.* without any mistakes: *The pianist gave a faultless performance.* SYN **perfect¹**

faulty /ˈfɔːlti/ *adj.* (used especially about electricity or machines) not working correctly: *a faulty switch*

fauna /ˈfɔːnə/ *noun* [U] (BIOLOGY) all the animals of an area or a period of time: *the flora and fauna of South America* ⊃ look at **flora**

Fauvism /ˈfəʊvɪzəm/ *noun* [U] (ART) a style of painting that uses bright colours and in which objects and people are represented in a non-realistic way. It was popular in Paris for a short period from 1905.

faux pas /ˌfəʊ ˈpɑː/ *noun* [C] (*pl.* faux pas /-ˈpɑːz/) something you say or do that is embarrassing or offends people: *to make a faux pas*

favor (*AmE*) = FAVOUR¹, FAVOUR²

favorable, favorably (*AmE*) = FAVOURABLE, FAVOURABLY

favorite (*AmE*) = FAVOURITE¹, FAVOURITE²

favoritism (*AmE*) = FAVOURITISM

favour¹ ʔ B1 (*BrE*) (*AmE* favor) /ˈfeɪvə(r)/ *noun* **1** [C] something that helps sb: *Would you do me a favour and pick Amy up from school today?* ◊ *Could I ask you a favour?* ◊ *Are they paying you for the work, or are you doing it as a favour?* **2** [U] ~ (with sb) liking or approval: *I'm afraid I'm out of favour with my neighbour since our last argument.* ◊ *The new boss's methods didn't find favour with the staff.* ◊ *He seems to be be back in favour with the voters.* IDM **in favour (of sb/sth)** supporting and in agreement with sb/sth: *Are you in favour of private education?* **in sb's favour** to the advantage of sb: *The committee decided in their favour.*

favour² ʔ B2 W (*BrE*) (*AmE* favor) /ˈfeɪvə(r)/ *verb* [T] **1** to support sb/sth; to prefer: *Which suggestion do you favour?* **2** to treat one person very well and so be unfair to others: *Parents must try not to favour one of their children.*

favourable ʔ+ C1 W (*BrE*) (*AmE* favorable) /ˈfeɪvərəbl/ *adj.* **1** showing liking or approval; making people have a good opinion of sb/sth: *Did you get a favourable report on your work?* ◊ *He made a favourable impression on the interviewers.* **2** (often used about the weather) suitable or helpful: *Conditions are favourable for skiing today.* OPP **adverse, unfavourable** ▸ **favourably** (*AmE* favorably) /-bli/ *adv.*

favourite¹ ʔ A1 (*BrE*) (*AmE* favorite) /ˈfeɪvərɪt/ *adj.* liked more than any other: *What is your favourite colour?* ◊ *Who is your favourite singer?*

favourite² ʔ A1 (*BrE*) (*AmE* favorite) /ˈfeɪvərɪt/ *noun* [C] **1** a person or thing that you like more than any others: *The other kids were jealous of Rose because she was*

the teacher's favourite. **2** = BOOKMARK¹ (1) **3** ~ (for sth/ to do sth) the horse, team, person, etc. that is expected to win: *Mimms is the hot favourite for the leadership of the party.* OPP **outsider**

favouritism (*BrE*) (*AmE* favoritism) /ˈfeɪvərɪtɪzəm/ *noun* [U] giving unfair advantages to the person or people that you like best: *The referee was accused of showing favouritism to the home side.*

fawn¹ /fɔːn/ *adj.* light yellow-brown in colour

fawn² /fɔːn/ *noun* **1** [C] a young DEER ⊃ note at **deer** ⊃ picture at **deer 2** [U] a light yellow-brown colour

fax¹ /fæks/ *noun* **1** [C, U] a copy of a letter, etc. that you can send by phone lines using a special machine **2** (*also* 'fax machine) [C] the machine that you use for sending faxes

fax² /fæks/ *verb* [T] ~ sth (to sb); ~ sb (sth) to send sb a FAX: *We will fax our order to you tomorrow.* ◊ *I've faxed her a copy of the letter.*

faze /feɪz/ *verb* [T] (*informal*) to make sb worried or nervous

FBI /ˌef biː ˈaɪ/ *abbr.* **Federal Bureau of Investigation** (the police department in the US that is controlled by the government and that is responsible for dealing with crimes that affect more than one state)

FC /ˌef ˈsiː/ *abbr.* (*BrE*) football club: *Everton FC*

FCDO /ˌef siː diː ˈəʊ/ *abbr.* = FOREIGN, COMMONWEALTH AND DEVELOPMENT OFFICE

FE /ˌef ˈiː/ *abbr.* (*BrE*) = FURTHER EDUCATION

fear¹ ʔ A2 /fɪə(r)/ *noun* [U, C] the feeling that you have when sth dangerous, painful or frightening might happen: *He was shaking with fear after the accident.* ◊ *People in this area live in constant fear of crime.* ◊ *This book helped me overcome my fear of dogs.* ◊ *She showed no fear.* ◊ *My fears for his safety were unnecessary.* IDM **no fear** (*BrE, informal*) (used when answering a suggestion) certainly not

fear² ʔ B1 /fɪə(r)/ *verb* **1** [T] to be afraid of sb/sth or of doing sth: *We all fear illness and death.* **2** [T, I] to feel that sth bad might happen or might have happened: *The government fears that it will lose the next election.* ◊ *Thousands of people are feared dead in the earthquake.* ◊ *It is not as bad as we had feared.* PHR V **fear for sb/sth** to be worried about sb/sth: *Parents often fear for the safety of their children.*

fearful /ˈfɪəfl/ *adj.* (*formal*) **1** ~ (of sth/doing sth); ~ that … afraid or worried about sth: *You should never be fearful of starting something new.* ◊ *They were fearful that they would miss the plane.* **2** [only before noun] (*formal*) terrible: *the fearful consequences of war* ▸ **fearfully** /-fəli/ *adv.* ▸ **fearfulness** *noun* [U]

fearless /ˈfɪələs/ *adj.* never afraid ▸ **fearlessly** *adv.* ▸ **fearlessness** *noun* [U]

feasible /ˈfiːzəbl/ *adj.* possible to do: *a feasible plan* ▸ **feasibility** /ˌfiːzəˈbɪləti/ *noun* [U]

feast /fiːst/ *noun* [C] a large, special meal, especially to celebrate sth ▸ **feast** *verb* [I] ~ (on sth): *They feasted on exotic dishes.*

feat ʔ+ C1 /fiːt/ *noun* [C] something you do that shows great strength, skill or courage: *That new bridge is a remarkable feat of engineering.* ◊ *Persuading Helen to give you a pay rise was no mean feat* (= difficult to do). ⊃ note at **action¹**

feather ʔ B2 /ˈfeðə(r)/ *noun* [C] one of the light soft things that grow in a bird's skin and cover its body: *tail/flight/wing feathers* ⊃ picture at **animal**

feature¹ 🔉 **A2** 🔵 /'fiːtʃə(r)/ noun [C] **1** an important or interesting part of sth: *Mountains and lakes are the main features of the landscape of Wales.* ◇ *Noise is a feature of city life.* **2** a part of the face: *Her eyes are her best feature.* **3** ~ (**on sth**) (**ARTS AND MEDIA**) an article or TV programme about sth: *There's a feature on kangaroos in this magazine.*

feature² 🔉 **B1** 🔵 /'fiːtʃə(r)/ verb **1** [T] ~ **sb/sth (as/sb/ sth)** to include sb/sth as an important part: *The musical features Hugh Jackman as Barnum.* **2** [I] ~ **in sth** to have a part in sth: *Does marriage feature in your future plans?* **SYN** figure²

'**feature film** noun [C] (**ARTS AND MEDIA**) a main film with a story, rather than a documentary, etc.

'**feature-length** adj. (**ARTS AND MEDIA**) of the same length as a typical film: *a feature-length documentary*

featureless /'fiːtʃələs/ adj. without any qualities or characteristics that are easy to notice: *a dull, featureless landscape*

February 🔉 **A1** /'februəri/ noun [U, C] (*abbr.* **Feb.**) the second month of the year, between January and March

feces /'fiːsiːz/ (*AmE*) = FAECES

fed /fed/ past tense, past participle of **feed¹**

federal 🔉 **B2** 🔵 /'fedərəl/ adj. (**POLITICS**) **1** organized as a FEDERATION: *a federal system of rule* ⊃ note at **government 2** connected with the central government of a FEDERATION: *That is a federal not a state law.*

federalist /'fedərəlɪst/ noun [C] (**POLITICS**) a supporter of a system of government in which the individual states of a country have control of their own affairs, but are controlled by a central government for national decisions ▶ **federalism** /-lɪzəm/ noun [U]: *European federalism* ▶ **federalist** adj.: *a federalist future for Europe*

federate /'fedəreɪt/ verb [I] (**POLITICS**) (used about states, organizations, etc.) to UNITE under a central government or organization while keeping some local control

federation /ˌfedəˈreɪʃn/ noun [C] a group of states, etc. that have joined together to form a single group

,**fed 'up** adj. [not before noun] ~ (**with sb/sth/doing sth**) (*informal*) bored or unhappy; tired of sth: *What's the matter? You look really fed up.* ◇ *I'm fed up with waiting for the phone to ring.* **HELP** In informal English, people sometimes also say **fed up of** sb/sth/doing sth: *When I get fed up of studying, I play my guitar.*

fee 🔉 **B2** /fiː/ noun [C] **1** [usually pl.] the money you pay for professional advice or service from private doctors, lawyers, schools, universities, etc: *We can't afford private school fees.* ◇ *Most ticket agencies will charge a small fee.* ⊃ note at **pay² 2** the cost of an exam, the cost of becoming a member of a club, the amount you pay to go into certain buildings, etc: *How much is the entrance fee?*

feeble /'fiːbl/ adj. (**feebler** /-blə(r)/; **feeblest** /-blɪst/) **1** with no energy or power; weak: *a feeble old man* ◇ *a feeble cry* **2** not effective: *a feeble argument/excuse* ▶ **feebly** /-bli/ adv.: *He shook his head feebly.*

feed¹ 🔉 **A2** /fiːd/ verb (*pt, pp* **fed** /fed/) **1** [T] ~ **sb/sth (on) (sth)** to give food to a person or an animal: *Don't forget to feed the dog.* ◇ *I can't come yet. I haven't fed the baby.* ◇ *Some of the snakes in the zoo are fed (on) rats.* **2** [I] ~ (**on sth**) (used about animals or babies) to eat: *What do horses feed on in the winter?* ◇ *Bats feed at night.* **3** [T] ~ **A (with B)**; ~ **B into/to/through A** to supply sb/sth with sth; to put sth into sth else: *This channel feeds us with news and information 24 hours a day.* ◇ *The electricity line is fed with power through an underground cable.* ◇ *Metal sheets are fed through the machine one at a time.*

feed² 🔉 **B2** /fiːd/ noun **1** [C] a meal for an animal or a baby: *When's the baby's next feed due?* **2** [U] (**AGRICULTURE**) food for animals: *cattle feed* **3** a special feature on a blog, news website, SOCIAL MEDIA site, etc. that allows you to see new information that has been added without having to visit the website: *the film's official Twitter feed* ⊃ look at **newsfeed**

feedback 🔉 **B2** /'fiːdbæk/ noun [U] ~ **on sth** information or comments about sth that sb has done that tells them how good or bad it is: *The teacher spent five minutes with each of us to give us feedback on our homework.*

feeder /'fiːdə(r)/ noun [C] **1** an animal or a plant that eats a particular thing or eats in a particular way: *plankton feeders* **2** a container filled with food for birds or animals: *a bird feeder*

feel¹ 🔉 **A1** /fiːl/ verb (*pt, pp* **felt** /felt/) **1** linking verb (usually before an adjective) to be in the state that is mentioned: *to feel cold/sick/tired/happy* ◇ *How are you feeling today?* ◇ *You'll feel better in the morning.* **2** linking verb used to say how sth seems to you when you touch, see, smell, experience, etc. it: *My new coat feels like leather but it's not.* ◇ *He felt as if he had been there before.* **3** [T] to notice or experience sth physical or emotional: *I damaged the nerves and now I can't feel anything in this hand.* ◇ *I felt something crawling up my back.* ◇ *I don't feel any sympathy for Matt at all.* ◇ *You could feel the tension in the courtroom.* **4** [T] to touch sth in order to find out what it is like: *Feel this material. Is it cotton or silk?* ◇ *I felt her forehead to see if she had a temperature.* **5** [I] ~ (**about**) (**for sb/sth**) to try to find sth with your hands instead of your eyes: *She felt about in the dark for the light switch.* **6** [T, I] to think or believe that something is the case; to have a particular opinion or attitude: *I felt (that) it was a mistake not to ask her advice.* ⊃ note at **think¹ 7** [T] to be affected by sth: *Do you feel the cold in winter?* ◇ *She felt it badly when her mother died.*
IDM **feel your age** to realize that you are getting old, especially compared to other younger people around you **feel free (to do sth)** (*informal*) used to tell sb they are allowed to do sth: *Feel free to use the phone.* **feel like sth/doing sth** to want sth or to want to do sth: *Do you feel like going out?* **not feel yourself** to not feel healthy or well
PHR V **feel for sb** to understand sb's feelings and situation and feel sorry for them: *I really felt for him when his wife died.* **feel up to sth/doing sth** to have the strength and the energy to do or deal with sth: *I really don't feel up to eating a huge meal.*

feel² 🔉 **B2** /fiːl/ noun [sing.] **1** the impression sth gives you when you touch it; the impression that a place or situation gives you: *You can tell it's wool by the feel.* ◇ *The town has a friendly feel.* **2** an act of touching sth in order to learn about it: *Let me have a feel of that material.*

feeler /'fiːlə(r)/ noun [C, usually pl.] either of the two long thin parts on the heads of some insects and of some animals that live in shells that they use to feel and touch things with **SYN** antenna
IDM **put out feelers** (*informal*) to try to find out what people think about sth before you do it

feeling 🔉 **A1** /'fiːlɪŋ/ noun **1** [C] ~ (**of sth**) something that you feel in your mind or body: *a feeling of hunger/ happiness/fear/helplessness* ◇ *I've got a funny feeling in my leg.* **2** [sing.] a belief or idea that sth is true or is likely to happen: *I get the feeling that Ian doesn't like me much.* ◇ *I have a nasty feeling that Jan didn't get*

our message. **3** [C, U] ~ **(about/on sth)** an attitude or opinion about sth: *What are your feelings on this matter?* ◊ *My own feeling is that we should postpone the meeting.* ◊ *Public feeling seems to be against the new road.* **4** [C, usually pl., U] a person's emotions; strong emotion: *I have to tell Jeff his work's not good enough but I don't want to* **hurt** *his feelings.* ◊ *Let's practise that song again, this time* **with feeling. 5** [C, U] ~ **(for sb/sth)** love or understanding for sb/sth: *She doesn't have much (of a) feeling for music.* ◊ *He still has feelings for his ex-wife.* **6** [U] the ability to feel in your body: *After the accident he lost all feeling in his legs.*
IDM **bad/ill feeling** unhappy relations between people: *The decision caused a lot of bad feeling at the factory.* **no hard feelings** → HARD¹

feet /fiːt/ plural of **foot**¹

feisty /ˈfaɪsti/ *adj.* (**feistier; feistiest**) (*informal*) (used about people) strong, determined and not afraid to argue

feldspar /ˈfeldspɑː(r)/ *noun* [U, C] (**GEOLOGY**) a type of white or red rock

feline /ˈfiːlaɪn/ *adj.* (**BIOLOGY**) relating to an animal of the cat family; like a cat

fell¹ /fel/ past tense of **fall**¹

fell² /fel/ *verb* [T] to cut down a tree

fella (*also* **feller**) /ˈfelə(r)/ *noun* [C] (*informal*) a man or boyfriend

fellow¹ /ˈfeləʊ/ *noun* [C] **1** (**EDUCATION**) a member of an academic or professional organization, or a senior member of some universities: *a fellow of the Royal College of Surgeons* **2** (**EDUCATION**) a person who is paid to study a particular thing at a university: *Jill is a research fellow in the biology department.* **3** (*old-fashioned*) a man

fellow² ⟨ **B2** /ˈfeləʊ/ *adj.* [only before noun] used to describe another or others like yourself in the same situation: *Her fellow students were all older than her.* ◊ *fellow workers/passengers/citizens*

fellowship /ˈfeləʊʃɪp/ *noun* **1** [U] a feeling of friendship between people who share an interest **2** [C] a group or society of people who share the same interest or belief **3** [C] (**EDUCATION**) the state of being a member of an academic or professional organization

felon /ˈfelən/ *noun* [C] (*especially AmE*) (**LAW**) a person who commits a serious crime such as murder

felony /ˈfeləni/ *noun* [C, U] (*pl.* -**ies**) (*especially AmE*) (**LAW**) the act of committing a serious crime such as murder; a crime of this type ◌ look at **misdemeanour** (2)

felt¹ /felt/ past tense, past participle of **feel**¹

felt² /felt/ *noun* [U] a type of soft cloth made from wool or hair that has been pressed tightly together: *a felt hat*

felt-tip ˈpen (*also* ˌfelt ˈtip) *noun* [C] a type of pen with a point made of felt

female¹ ⟨ **A2** ◉ /ˈfiːmeɪl/ *adj.* (**BIOLOGY**) **1** being a woman or a girl: *a female artist/employer/student* ◌ look at **feminine** (1) **2** (*abbr.* f) being of the sex that can produce eggs or give birth to babies: *a female cat* ◌ picture at **fertilization 3** (used about plants and flowers) that can produce fruit

female² ⟨ **A2** ◉ /ˈfiːmeɪl/ *noun* [C] (**BIOLOGY**) **1** an animal that can produce eggs or give birth to babies; a plant that can produce fruit **2** a woman or a girl

feminine /ˈfemənɪn/ *adj.* **1** typical of or looking like a woman; connected with women: *My daughter always dresses like a boy. She hates looking feminine.* **2** (*abbr.* f) (**GRAMMAR**) (in English) of the forms of words used to describe females: '*Lioness*' *is the feminine form of*

'*lion*'. **3** (*abbr.* f) (**GRAMMAR**) (in the grammar of some languages) belonging to a certain class of nouns, adjectives or pronouns: *The German word for a flower is feminine.* ◌ look at **masculine** (3), **neuter**¹
▶ **femininity** /ˌfeməˈnɪnəti/ *noun* [U]

feminism /ˈfemənɪzəm/ *noun* [U] (**SOCIAL STUDIES**) the belief that women should have the same rights and opportunities as men; the struggle to achieve this aim
▶ **feminist** ⟨+ **C1** /-nɪst/ *noun* [C], *adj.*

femur /ˈfiːmə(r)/ *noun* [C] (**ANATOMY**) the large thick bone in the top part of the leg above the knee
SYN **thigh bone** ◌ picture at **body**

fence¹ ⟨ **B1** /fens/ *noun* [C] a line of wooden or metal posts joined by wood, wire, metal, etc. to divide land or to keep animals in or to keep people/animals out
IDM **sit on the fence** → SIT

fence² /fens/ *verb* **1** [T] (**ARCHITECTURE**) to surround land with a fence **2** [I] to fight with a FOIL (= a long thin pointed weapon) as a sport
PHR V **fence sb/sth in 1** to surround sb/sth with a fence: *They fenced in their garden to make it more private.* **2** to limit sb's freedom: *She felt fenced in by so many responsibilities.* **fence sth off** to separate one area from another with a fence

fencing /ˈfensɪŋ/ *noun* [U] (**SPORT**) the sport of fighting with FOILS (= long thin pointed weapons)

fend /fend/ *verb*
PHR V **fend for yourself** to look after yourself without help from anyone else: *It's time Ben left home and learned to fend for himself.* **fend sb/sth off** to defend yourself from sb/sth that is attacking you: *Politicians usually manage to fend off awkward questions.*

fender /ˈfendə(r)/ *noun* [C] **1** (*AmE*) = WING (4) **2** a low metal frame in front of an open fire that stops coal or wood falling out

feng shui /ˌfeŋ ˈʃuːi, ˌfʊŋ ˈʃweɪ/ *noun* [U] a Chinese system for deciding the right position for a building and for placing objects inside a building in order to make people feel comfortable and happy

fennel /ˈfenl/ *noun* [U] a plant that has a thick round part at the base of the leaves with a strong taste. The base is used as a vegetable and the seeds and leaves are also used in cooking.

feral /ˈferəl/ *adj.* (used about animals) living wild, especially after escaping from life as a pet or on a farm

ferment¹ /fəˈment/ *verb* [I, T] (**BIOLOGY**, **CHEMISTRY**) to experience a chemical change because of the action of YEAST or bacteria, often changing sugar to alcohol; to make sth change in this way: *The wine is starting to ferment.* ▶ **fermentation** /ˌfɜːmenˈteɪʃn/ *noun* [U]

ferment² /ˈfɜːment/ *noun* [U] (*formal*) a state of political or social excitement and change: *The country is in ferment and nobody's sure what will happen next.*

fermium /ˈfɜːmiəm/ *noun* [U] (*symb.* Fm) (**CHEMISTRY**) a chemical element. Fermium is a very rare RADIOACTIVE metal. ❶ For more information on the periodic table of elements, look at the **Reference Section** of this dictionary.

fern /fɜːn/ *noun* [C] (**BIOLOGY**) a green plant with no flowers and a lot of long thin leaves

ferocious /fəˈrəʊʃəs/ *adj.* very aggressive and violent: *a ferocious beast/attack/storm/war* ▶ **ferociously** *adv.*

ferocity /fəˈrɒsəti/ *noun* [U] violence; cruel and aggressive behaviour ◌ adjective **fierce**

ferret¹ /ˈferɪt/ *noun* [C] a small aggressive animal with a long thin body, used for hunting RATS and RABBITS

ferret² /ˈferɪt/ *verb* [I] ~ **(about/around) (for sth)** (*informal*) to search for sth that is lost or hidden among a lot of things
PHR V **ferret sb/sth out** (*informal*) to discover information or to find sb/sth by searching THOROUGHLY, asking a lot of questions, etc.

ferrite /ˈferaɪt/ *noun* [U] **1** (**ENGINEERING**) a chemical containing iron, used in electrical devices such as radio and TV AERIALS **2** (**CHEMISTRY**) a form of pure iron that is found in steel that contains low amounts of CARBON

ferrous /ˈferəs/ *adj.* (**CHEMISTRY**) containing iron

ferry¹ /ˈferi/ *noun* [C] (*pl.* -ies) (**TOURISM**) a boat that carries people, vehicles or goods across a river or across a narrow part of the sea: *a car ferry*

ferry² /ˈferi/ *verb* [T] (**ferrying; ferries;** *pt, pp* **ferried**) (used with an adverb or a preposition) to carry people or goods in a boat or other vehicle from one place to another, usually for a short distance: *Could you ferry us across to the island?* ◇ *We share the job of ferrying the children to school.*

fertile /ˈfɜːtaɪl/ *adj.* **1** (**AGRICULTURE**) (used about land or soil) that plants grow well in **OPP** **infertile 2** (**BIOLOGY**) (used about people, animals or plants) that can produce babies, fruit or new plants
⊃ **OPP** **infertile** (1) **3** (used about a person's mind) full of ideas: *a fertile imagination*

fertility /fəˈtɪləti/ *noun* [U] **1** (**AGRICULTURE**) the quality in land or soil of making plants grow well **OPP** **infertility 2** (**BIOLOGY**) the ability to produce babies, young animals, fruit or new plants **OPP** **infertility**

fertilize (*BrE also* -ise) /ˈfɜːtəlaɪz/ *verb* [T] **1** (**BIOLOGY**) to put a male seed into an egg, a plant or a female animal so that a baby, fruit or a young animal starts to develop **2** (**AGRICULTURE**) to put natural or artificial substances on soil in order to make plants grow better ▶ **fertilization** (*BrE also* -isation) /ˌfɜːtəlaɪˈzeɪʃn/ *noun* [U]

fertilization

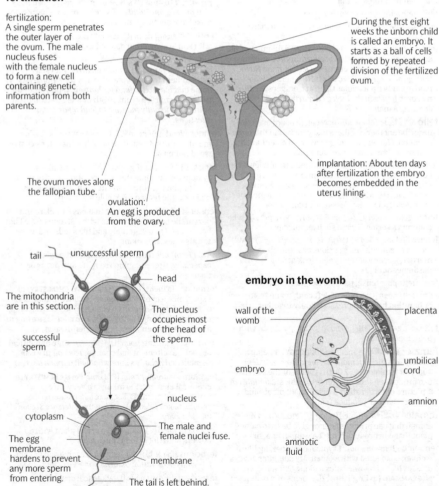

fertilization:
A single sperm penetrates the outer layer of the ovum. The male nucleus fuses with the female nucleus to form a new cell containing genetic information from both parents.

During the first eight weeks the unborn child is called an embryo. It starts as a ball of cells formed by repeated division of the fertilized ovum.

The ovum moves along the fallopian tube.

ovulation:
An egg is produced from the ovary.

implantation: About ten days after fertilization the embryo becomes embedded in the uterus lining.

tail

unsuccessful sperm

head

The mitochondria are in this section.

The nucleus occupies most of the head of the sperm.

successful sperm

embryo in the womb

wall of the womb

placenta

embryo

umbilical cord

amnion

nucleus

cytoplasm

The male and female nuclei fuse.

The egg membrane hardens to prevent any more sperm from entering.

membrane

amniotic fluid

The tail is left behind.

fictional F

fertilizer (*BrE also* **-iser**) /'fɜːtəlaɪzə(r)/ *noun* [C, U] (**AGRICULTURE**) a natural or chemical substance that is put on land or soil to make plants grow better ⊃ look at **manure**

fervent /'fɜːvənt/ *adj.* having or showing very strong feelings about sth: *She's a fervent believer in women's rights.* ◇ *a fervent belief/hope/desire* **SYN** **ardent** ▶ **fervently** *adv.*

fervour (*BrE*) (*AmE* **fervor**) /'fɜːvə(r)/ *noun* [U] very strong feelings about sth **SYN** **enthusiasm**

fess /fes/ *verb*
PHR V **fess up (to sth)** (*informal*) to tell sb that you have done sth wrong: *She called last night to fess up.* **SYN** **own up (to sth)**

fester /'festə(r)/ *verb* [I] **1** (used about a cut or an injury) to become **INFECTED** (= full of bacteria): *a festering sore/wound* **2** (used about an unpleasant situation, feeling or thought) to become more unpleasant because you do not deal with it successfully

festival /'festɪvl/ *noun* [C] **1** (**ARTS AND MEDIA**) a series of plays, films, musical performances, etc. often held regularly in one place: *the Cannes Film Festival* ◇ *a jazz festival* **2** a day or time when people celebrate sth (especially a religious event): *Christmas is an important Christian festival.*

festive /'festɪv/ *adj.* happy, because people are enjoying themselves celebrating sth: *the festive season* (= Christmas)

festivity /fe'stɪvəti/ *noun* **1** festivities [pl.] happy events when people celebrate sth: *The festivities went on until dawn.* **2** [U] being happy and celebrating sth: *The wedding was followed by three days of festivity.*

fetal (*BrE also* **foetal**) /'fiːtl/ *adj.* (**BIOLOGY**) relating to or typical of a baby that is still developing in its mother's body

fetal 'alcohol syndrome *noun* [U] (**HEALTH**) a condition in which a child's development is damaged because the mother drank too much alcohol while she was pregnant

fetch /fetʃ/ *verb* [T] **1** (*especially BrE*) to go to a place and bring back sb/sth: *Shall I fetch you your coat?/Shall I fetch your coat for you?* ◇ *It's my turn to fetch the children from school.* **2** (used about goods) to be sold for the price mentioned: *'How much will your car fetch?' 'It should fetch about £2000.'*

fete (*also* **fête**) /feɪt/ *noun* [C] (*BrE*) an outdoor event with competitions, entertainment and things to buy, often organized to make money for a particular purpose: *the school/village/church fete*

fetus (*BrE also* **foetus**) /'fiːtəs/ *noun* [C] (**BIOLOGY**) a young human or animal that is still developing in its mother's body ❶ An **embryo** is at an earlier stage of development.

feud /fjuːd/ *noun* [C] **~ (between A and B); ~ (with sb) (over sb/sth)** an angry and serious argument between two people or groups that continues over a long period of time: *a family feud* (= within a family or between two families) ▶ **feud** *verb* [I]

feudal /'fjuːdl/ *adj.* (**HISTORY, POLITICS**) connected with the system of **FEUDALISM**: *the feudal system*

feudalism /'fjuːdəlɪzəm/ *noun* [U] (**HISTORY, POLITICS**) the social system that existed in the Middle Ages in Europe, in which people worked and fought for a person who owned land and received land and protection from them in return

fever /'fiːvə(r)/ *noun* **1** [C, U] (**HEALTH**) a condition of the body when it is too hot because of illness: *A high fever can be dangerous, especially in small children.* ⊃ look at **temperature 2** [sing.] **a ~ (of sth)** a state of nervous excitement

feverish /'fiːvərɪʃ/ *adj.* **1** (**HEALTH**) suffering from or caused by a **FEVER**: *a feverish cold/dream* **2** showing great excitement ▶ **feverishly** *adv.*

few /fjuː/ *det., adj., pron.* **1** a few used with plural nouns and a plural verb to mean 'a small number', 'some': *a few people* ◇ *a few hours/days/years* ◇ *I'll meet you later. I've got a few things to do first.* ◇ *I knew a few of the people there.* **2** used with plural nouns and a plural verb to mean 'not many': *Few people live to be 100.* ◇ *Few of the players played really well.* **3** fewer not so many; not as many as: *There are fewer cars here today than yesterday.* ◇ *Fewer than 20 students passed all the exams.*
IDM **few and far between** not happening very often; not common **quite a few** (*BrE also* **a good few**) a fairly large amount or number (of): *It's been a good few years since I saw him last.*

ff. *abbr.* (in writing) used after the number of a page or line to mean 'and the following pages or lines': *British Politics, pp. 10 ff.*

fiancé /fi'ɒnseɪ/ *noun* [C] a man who has promised to marry sb

fiancée /fi'ɒnseɪ/ *noun* [C] a woman who has promised to marry sb

fiasco /fi'æskəʊ/ *noun* [C] (*pl.* -os, *AmE also* -oes) an event that does not succeed, often in a way that makes people feel embarrassed: *Our last party was a complete fiasco.* **SYN** **disaster**

fib /fɪb/ *noun* [C] (*informal*) something you say that is not true: *Please don't tell fibs.* **SYN** **lie** ▶ **fib** *verb* [I] (-bb-)

fibre (*BrE*) (*AmE* **fiber**) /'faɪbə(r)/ *noun* **1** [U] (**BIOLOGY**) parts of plants that you eat that are good for you because they help to move food quickly through the body: *Wholemeal bread is high in fibre.* **2** [C, U] a material or a substance that is made from natural or artificial **THREADS**: *natural fibres* (= for example, cotton and wool) ◇ *man-made/synthetic fibres* (= for example, NYLON, POLYESTER, etc.) **3** [C] one of the thin **THREADS** that form a natural or an artificial substance: *cotton/wood/nerve/muscle fibres*

fibreglass (*BrE*) (*AmE* **fiberglass**) /'faɪbəɡlɑːs/ (*also* **glass fibre**) *noun* [U] a material made from small **THREADS** of plastic or glass, used for making small boats, parts of cars, etc.

fibre 'optics (*BrE*) (*AmE* **fiber optics**) *noun* [U] (**PHYSICS**) the use of thin **FIBRES** of glass, etc. for sending information in the form of light signals ▶ **fibre-'optic** (*BrE*) (*AmE* **fiber-optic**) *adj.*: *fibre-optic cables*

fibrin /'faɪbrɪn/ *noun* [U] a substance that forms in the blood to help stop the blood from flowing, for example when there is a cut

fibrinogen /faɪ'brɪnədʒən/ *noun* [U] (**BIOLOGY**) a substance in the blood from which **FIBRIN** is made

fibula /'fɪbjələ/ *noun* [C] (**ANATOMY**) the outer bone of the two bones in the lower part of the leg, between the knee and the foot ⊃ look at **tibia** ⊃ picture at **body**

fickle /'fɪkl/ *adj.* always changing your mind or your feelings so you cannot be trusted: *a fickle friend*

fiction /'fɪkʃn/ *noun* [U] (**LITERATURE**) stories, novels, etc. that describe events and people that are not real: *I don't read much fiction.* **OPP** **non-fiction** ⊃ look at **fact** (2)

fictional /'fɪkʃnl/ *adj.* (**LITERATURE**) not real or true; only existing in stories, novels, etc: *The book gave a fictional account of a doctor's life.* ⊃ look at **factual**

fictionalize (*BrE also* -ise) /ˈfɪkʃənəlaɪz/ *verb* [T] (**ARTS AND MEDIA**) to write a book or make a film about a true story, but changing some of the details, characters, etc: *a fictionalized account of the 2007 financial crisis*

fictitious /fɪkˈtɪʃəs/ *adj.* invented; not real: *The novel is set in a fictitious village called Paradise.*

fiddle¹ /ˈfɪdl/ *noun* [C] (*informal*) **1** = VIOLIN **2** (*BrE*) a dishonest action, especially one connected with money: *a tax fiddle*

fiddle² /ˈfɪdl/ *verb* **1** [I] ~ (**about/around**) (**with sth**) to play with sth carelessly, because you are nervous or not thinking: *He sat nervously, fiddling with a pencil.* **2** [T] (*informal*) to change the details or facts of sth (business accounts, etc.) in order to get money dishonestly: *She fiddled her expenses form.*

fiddler /ˈfɪdlə(r)/ *noun* [C] (**MUSIC**) a person who plays the VIOLIN (= a musical instrument with STRINGS), especially to play FOLK music

fiddly /ˈfɪdli/ *adj.* (**fiddlier; fiddliest**) (*informal*) difficult to do or manage with your hands (because small or complicated parts are involved)

fidelity /fɪˈdeləti/ *noun* [U] (*formal*) **1** ~ (**to sb/sth**) the quality of being FAITHFUL to your husband, wife or partner by not having a sexual relationship with anyone else **OPP** **infidelity** **HELP** A less formal word is **faithfulness**. **2** (used about translations, the REPRODUCTION of music, etc.) the quality of being accurate or close to the original ⸫ look at **hi-fi**

fidget /ˈfɪdʒɪt/ *verb* [I] ~ (**with sth**) to keep moving your body, hands or feet because you are nervous, bored, excited, etc: *She fidgeted nervously with her keys.* ▸ **fidgety** *adj.*

fiefdom /ˈfiːfdəm/ *noun* [C] (**LAW**) (in the past) an area of land, especially a rented area for which the payment is work, not money

field¹ ⚡ **A2** ⓦ /fiːld/ *noun* [C] **1** (**AGRICULTURE**) an area of land on a farm, usually surrounded by fences or walls, used for growing crops or keeping animals in: *People were working in the fields.* ◇ *a field of cows* **2** (**EDUCATION**) an area of study or knowledge: *He's an expert in the field of economics.* ◇ *That question is outside my field* (= not one of the subjects that I know about). **3** an area of land used for sports, games or some other activity: *a football field* ◇ *an airfield* (= where planes land and take off) ◇ *a battlefield* ⸫ look at **pitch¹** (1) **4** an area affected by or included in sth: *a magnetic field* ◇ *It's outside my field of vision* (= I can't see it). **5** (**GEOLOGY**) an area of land where oil, coal or other minerals are found: *a coalfield* ◇ *a North Sea oilfield*

field² /fiːld/ *verb* (**SPORT**) **1** [I, T] (in CRICKET, baseball, etc.) to (be ready to) catch and throw back the ball after sb has hit it ❶ When one team is **fielding**, the other is **batting**. **2** [T] to choose a team for a game of football, CRICKET, etc: *New Zealand is fielding an excellent team for the next match.*

field day *noun*

IDM **have a field day** to get the opportunity to do sth you enjoy, especially sth other people do not approve of: *The newspapers always have a field day when there's a political scandal.*

fielder /ˈfiːldə(r)/ *noun* [C] (**SPORT**) (in sports such as CRICKET and baseball) a player who is trying to catch the ball rather than hit it

field event *noun* [C] (**SPORT**) a sport, such as jumping and throwing, that is not a race and does not involve running ⸫ look at **track event**

field hand (*AmE*) = FARMHAND

field hockey (*AmE*) = HOCKEY (1)

field sports *noun* [pl.] (*BrE*) outdoor sports such as hunting, fishing and shooting

field trip *noun* [C] (**EDUCATION**) a journey made to study sth in its natural environment: *We went on a geography field trip.*

fieldwork /ˈfiːldwɜːk/ *noun* [U] (**EDUCATION**) practical research work done outside school, college, etc.

fiend /fiːnd/ *noun* [C] **1** a very cruel person **2** (*informal*) a person who is very interested in one particular thing: *a health fiend* **SYN** **fanatic**

fiendish /ˈfiːndɪʃ/ *adj.* **1** very unpleasant or cruel **2** (*informal*) clever and complicated: *a fiendish plan* ▸ **fiendishly** *adv.*

fierce ⚡+ **C1** /fɪəs/ *adj.* **1** angry, aggressive and frightening: *The house was guarded by fierce dogs.* **2** very strong; violent: *fierce competition for jobs* ◇ *a fierce attack* ⸫ *noun* **ferocity** ▸ **fiercely** *adv.*

fiery /ˈfaɪəri/ *adj.* (**fierier; fieriest**) **1** looking like fire: *She has fiery red hair.* **2** quick to become angry: *a fiery temper* **SYN** **passionate**

FIFA /ˈfiːfə/ *abbr.* (**SPORT**) the organization that is in charge of international football (from French 'Fédération Internationale de Football Association')

fifteen ⚡ **A1** /ˌfɪfˈtiːn/ *number* 15 ▸ **fifteenth** /-ˈtiːnθ/ *ordinal number, noun* [C]

fifth¹ ⚡ **A1** /fɪfθ/ *ordinal number* 5th

fifth² /fɪfθ/ *noun* [C] one of five equal parts of sth

fifty ⚡ **A1** /ˈfɪfti/ **1** *number* 50 **2** the **fifties** *noun* [pl.] numbers, years or temperatures from 50 to 59: *She was born in the fifties.* ▸ **fiftieth** /-əθ/ *ordinal number, noun* [C]

IDM **in your fifties** between the ages of 50 and 59

fifty-fifty *adj., adv.* equal or equally (between two people, groups, etc.): *You've got a fifty-fifty chance of winning.* ◇ *We'll divide the money fifty-fifty .*

fig /fɪg/ *noun* [C] (a type of tree with) a soft sweet fruit full of small seeds that grows in warm countries and is sometimes eaten dried: *a fig tree*

fig. *abbr.* (in writing) **1** = FIGURE¹ (7): *See diagram at fig.* **2.** **2** = FIGURATIVE (1)

fight¹ ⚡ **A2** /faɪt/ *verb* (*pt, pp* **fought** /fɔːt/) **1** [I, T] ~ (**against sb**); ~ (**over sth**); ~ (**for sth**) to use physical strength, guns, weapons, etc. against sb/sth: *Government troops were fighting against rebel groups.* ◇ *My younger brothers were always fighting.* ◇ *The dogs often fight over food.* ◇ *They were fighting for freedom.* ◇ *They gathered soldiers to fight the invading army.* **2** [I, T] ~ (**against sth**) to try very hard to stop or prevent sth: *to fight against crime/disease* ◇ *to fight a fire/a decision/prejudice* **3** [I] ~ (**for sth/to do sth**) to try very hard to get or keep sth: *to fight for your rights* ◇ *The doctors fought to save his life.* **4** [I] ~ (**with sb**) (**about/over sth**) to argue: *It's not worth fighting about money.* ⸫ look at **argue** (1), **quarrel²**

PHR V **fight back** to attack sb who has attacked you: *If he hits you again, fight back!*

fight² ⚡ **A2** /faɪt/ *noun* **1** [C] ~ (**with sb/sth**); ~ (**between A and B**) the act of using physical force against sb/sth: *Don't get into a fight with the boys at school, will you?* ◇ *Fights broke out between rival groups of fans.* **2** [sing.] ~ (**against/for sth**) (**to do sth**) the work done trying to destroy, prevent or achieve sth: *Workers won their fight to stop the factory from closing down.* ◇ *his fight against cancer* ⸫ note at **campaign¹** **3** [C] ~ (**with sb/sth**) (**about/over sth**) (*especially AmE*) an argument about sth: *I had a fight with my mum over what time I had to be home.* **4** [U] the desire to continue trying or fighting: *I've had some bad luck but I've still got plenty of fight in me.*

IDM **pick a fight** → PICK¹

fighter /'faɪtə(r)/ *noun* [C] **1** (*also* 'fighter plane) a small fast military aircraft used for attacking enemy aircraft: *a fighter pilot* ◇ *a jet fighter* **2** a BOXER (= a person who fights as a sport) or a person who fights in a war

fighting ⟨B1⟩ /'faɪtɪŋ/ *noun* [U] an occasion when people fight: *There has been street fighting in many parts of the city today .* ◇ *At least 50 were killed in fierce fighting with terrorist groups.* ◇ *The fighting between the rebels and our troops continues.*

figurative /'fɪɡərətɪv/ *adj.* **1** (*abbr.* fig. /fɪɡ/) (**LANGUAGE**) (used about a word or an expression) not used with its exact meaning but used for giving an IMAGINATIVE description or a special effect: *'He exploded with rage' is a figurative use of the verb 'to explode'.* ⊃ look at **literal** (1), **metaphor** **2** (**ART**) showing people, animals and objects as they really look: *a figurative artist* ⊃ look at **abstract**[1] ▸ **figuratively** *adv.*

figure[1] ⟨A2⟩ /'fɪɡə(r)/ *noun*
• NUMBER **1** [C, usually pl.] an amount (in numbers) or a price: *The unemployment figures are lower this month.* ◇ *What sort of figure are you thinking of for your house?* **2** [C] (**MATHEMATICS**) a written sign for a number (0 to 9): *Write the numbers in figures, not words.* ◇ *He has a six-figure income/an income in six figures* (= £100 000 or more). ◇ *Interest rates are now down to single figures* (= less than 10 per cent). ◇ *double figures* (= 10 to 99) **3** figures [pl.] (*informal*) (**MATHEMATICS**) mathematics: *I don't* **have a head for figures** (= I'm not very good with numbers).
• PERSON **4** [C] a well-known or important person: *an important political figure* **5** [C] a person that you cannot see very clearly or do not know: *Two figures were coming towards us in the dark.* ◇ *There were two figures on the right of the photo that I didn't recognize.*
• BODY **6** [C] the shape of the human body, especially a woman's body that is attractive: *She's got a beautiful slim figure.*
• PICTURE **7** [C] (*abbr.* fig.) a diagram or picture used in a book to explain sth: *Figure 3 shows the major cities of Italy.*
IDM a ballpark figure/estimate → BALLPARK facts and figures → FACT in round figures/numbers → ROUND[1]

figure[2] ⟨B2⟩ /'fɪɡə(r)/ *verb* **1** [I] ~ (as sth) (in/among sth) to be included in sth; to be an important part of sth: *Women figure only as minor characters in his novels.* **SYN** feature[1] [T] ~ (that) (*informal*) to think or decide that sth is true: *I figured he was here because I saw his car outside.*
IDM it/that figures (*informal*) that is what I expected; that makes sense
PHR V figure on sth/doing sth (*especially AmE*) to include sth in your plans: *I figure on arriving in New York on Wednesday.* figure sb/sth out to find an answer to sth or to understand sb: *I can't figure out why she married him in the first place.*

figure of eight (*pl.* figures of eight) (*BrE*) (*AmE* figure eight) *noun* [C] something in the shape of the number 8

figure of speech *noun* [C] (*pl.* figures of speech) (**LANGUAGE**) a word or an expression used not with its original meaning but in an IMAGINATIVE way to make a special effect

figure skating *noun* [U] (**SPORT**) a type of SKATING on ice in which you cut patterns in the ice and do jumps and turns ⊃ look at **speed skating**

filament /'fɪləmənt/ *noun* [C] **1** (**ENGINEERING**) a thin wire in a LIGHT BULB (= the glass part of an electric lamp) that produces light when electricity is passed through it ⊃ picture at **light bulb** **2** a long thin piece of

sth that looks like a THREAD: *glass/metal filaments* **3** (**BIOLOGY**) a long thin part of the STAMEN (= the male part of a flower) that supports the part where POLLEN is produced ⊃ picture at **flower**[1]

file[1] ⟨B1⟩ /faɪl/ *noun* [C] **1** a box or a cover that is used for keeping papers together **2** (**COMPUTING**) a collection of information or material on one subject that is stored together in a computer or on a disk, with a particular name: *to open/close a file* ◇ *to create/delete/save/copy a file* **3** ~ (on sb/sth) a collection of papers or information about sb/sth kept inside a file: *The police are now keeping a file on all known football hooligans.* **4** a metal tool with a rough surface used for shaping hard substances or for making surfaces smooth: *a nail file* ⊃ picture at **tool**
IDM in single file in a line, one behind the other on file kept in a file: *We have all the information you need on file.* the rank and file → RANK[1]

file[2] ⟨B2⟩ /faɪl/ *verb* **1** [T] ~ sth (away) to put and keep documents, etc. in a particular place so that you can find them easily; to put sth into a file: *I filed the letters away in a drawer.* **2** [I, T] ~ (for sth) (**LAW**) to present sth so that it can be officially recorded and dealt with: *to file for divorce* ◇ *to file a claim/complaint/lawsuit* **3** [I] ~ in, out, past, etc. to walk or march in a line: *The children filed out of the classroom.* **4** [T] ~ sth (away, down, etc.) to shape sth hard or make sth smooth with a FILE: *to file your nails*

'file cabinet (*AmE*) = FILING CABINET

filename /'faɪlneɪm/ *noun* [C] (**COMPUTING**) a name you give to a computer file to identify it

'file sharing *noun* [U] (**COMPUTING**) the practice of sharing computer files with other people over the internet or a computer network

filet /'fɪlɪt/ (*AmE*) = FILLET

filibuster /'fɪlɪbʌstə(r)/ *noun* [C] (*especially AmE*) (**POLITICS**) a long speech made in a parliament in order to delay a vote ▸ **filibuster** *verb* [I]

filing /'faɪlɪŋ/ *noun* **1** [U] the act of putting documents, letters, etc. into a file **2** [C] (*especially AmE*) something that is placed into an official record: *a bankruptcy filing* **3** filings [pl.] very small pieces of metal, made when a larger piece of metal is filed: *iron filings*

'filing cabinet (*BrE*) (*AmE* file cabinet) *noun* [C] a piece of office furniture with deep DRAWERS (= parts like boxes that you can pull out) for storing files

fill ⟨A1⟩ /fɪl/ *verb* **1** [T, I] ~ (sth/sb) (with sth) to make sth full or to become full: *Can you fill the kettle for me?* ◇ *The news filled him with excitement.* ◇ *The room filled with smoke within minutes.* **2** [T] ~ sth (with sth) to block a hole with a substance: *They used putty to fill the holes.* ◇ *The crack in the wall had been filled with plaster.* **3** [T] to use up your time doing sth **4** [T] to do a job, have a role or position, etc: *I'm afraid that teaching post has just been filled* (= somebody has got the job).
PHR V fill sth in (*BrE*) (*also* fill sth out *especially in AmE*) to complete a form, etc. by writing information on it: *Could you fill in the application form, please?* **2** to fill a hole or space completely to make a surface flat: *You had better fill in the cracks in the wall before you paint it.* fill (sth) up to become or to make sth completely full: *There weren't many people at first but then the room filled up.*

fillet (*also* **filet** *especially in AmE*) /'fɪlɪt/ *noun* [C, U] a piece of meat or fish with no bones in it

filling¹ /ˈfɪlɪŋ/ *noun* **1** [C] the material that a dentist uses to fill a hole in a tooth: *a gold filling* ⊃ note at **tooth** **2** [C, U] the food inside a sandwich, PIE, cake, etc.

filling² /ˈfɪlɪŋ/ *adj.* (used about food) that makes you feel full: *Pasta is very filling.*

filly /ˈfɪli/ *noun* [C] (*pl.* -ies) a young female horse ⊃ look at **colt**

film¹ ʔ **A1** /fɪlm/ *noun*
- MOVING PICTURES **1** (*especially BrE*) (*AmE usually* **movie**) [C] (**ARTS AND MEDIA**) a story, play, etc. shown in moving pictures at the cinema or on TV or another device: *Let's go to the cinema — there's a good film on this week.* ◊ *to* **watch a film** *on TV* ◊ *to* **see a film** *at the cinema* ◊ *a horror/documentary/feature film* ◊ *a film director/producer/critic* **2** (*especially BrE*) (*AmE usually* the movies /ðə ˈmuːviz/ [pl.]) [U] (**ARTS AND MEDIA**) the art or business of making films: *She's studying film and theatre.* ◊ *the* **film industry** **3** [U] (**ARTS AND MEDIA**) moving pictures of real events
- IN A CAMERA **4** [U, C] thin plastic used especially in the past to take photos and make films; a roll of this plastic
- THIN LAYER **5** [C, usually sing.] a thin layer of a substance or material

film² ʔ **A2** /fɪlm/ *verb* [I, T] (**ARTS AND MEDIA**) to record moving pictures of an event, story, etc. with a camera: *A lot of westerns are filmed in Spain.*

ˈfilm-maker ʔ+ **C1** *noun* [C] (**ARTS AND MEDIA**) a person who makes films

film noir /ˌfɪlm ˈnwɑː(r)/ *noun* [U, C] (*pl.* films noirs /ˌfɪlm ˈnwɑː(r)/) (**ARTS AND MEDIA**) a style of making films in which there are strong feelings of fear or danger; a film made in this style ⊃ look at **noir**

ˈfilm star *noun* [C] (**ARTS AND MEDIA**) a male or female actor who is famous for being in films

filter¹ ʔ+ **C1** /ˈfɪltə(r)/ *noun* [C] **1** (**SCIENCE**) a device for holding back solid substances from a liquid or gas that passes through it: *a coffee filter* ◊ *an oil filter* ⊃ picture at **purification** **2** (**ARTS AND MEDIA**) a piece of coloured glass used with a camera to hold back some types of light **3** (**COMPUTING**) a program that stops certain types of electronic information, email, etc. being sent to a computer

filter² ʔ+ **C1** /ˈfɪltə(r)/ *verb* **1** [T] to pass a liquid through a FILTER, especially to remove sth that is not wanted: *Do you filter your water?* **2** [T] (**COMPUTING**) to use a special program to check the content of emails or websites before they are sent to your computer **3** [I] ~ **in, out, through, etc.** to move slowly and/or in small amounts: *Sunlight filtered into the room through the curtains.* ◊ (*figurative*) *News of her illness filtered through to her friends.*
PHR V **filter sth out (of sth)** to remove sth that you do not want from a liquid, light, etc. using a special device or substance: *This chemical filters impurities out of the water.* ◊ (*figurative*) *This test is designed to filter out weaker candidates before the interview stage.*

ˈfilter paper *noun* [U] (**CHEMISTRY**) a type of paper used for separating solids from liquids ⊃ picture at **filtration, laboratory**

filth /fɪlθ/ *noun* [U] **1** unpleasant dirt: *The room was covered in filth.* **2** words or pictures that cause offence

filthy /ˈfɪlθi/ *adj.* (filthier; filthiest) **1** very dirty **2** (used about language, books, films, etc.) connected with sex in a way that causes offence

filtrate /ˈfɪltreɪt/ *noun* [C] (**CHEMISTRY**) a liquid that has passed through a FILTER (= a device containing paper, sand, chemicals, etc. to remove material that is not wanted from the liquid that is passed through it)

filtration

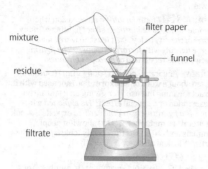

mixture · filter paper · funnel · residue · filtrate

filtration /fɪlˈtreɪʃn/ *noun* [U] (**CHEMISTRY**) the process of passing a liquid or gas through a FILTER (= a device containing paper, sand, chemicals, etc. that remove material that is not wanted from the liquid or gas that is passed through it)

fin /fɪn/ *noun* [C] **1** (**BIOLOGY**) one of the parts of a fish that it uses for swimming ⊃ picture at **animal 2** a thin flat part that sticks out of an aircraft or other vehicle to improve its balance and movement through the air or water ⊃ picture at **airliner**

final¹ ʔ **A1** ⑤ /ˈfaɪnl/ *adj.* **1** [only before noun] last (in a series): *This will be the final lesson of our course.* ◊ *The series is currently in its fourth and final season.* **2** not to be changed: *The judge's decision is always final.* ◊ *I'm not lending you the money, and that's final!*
IDM **the last/final straw** → STRAW

final² ʔ **A2** /ˈfaɪnl/ *noun* **1** [C] (**SPORT**) the last game or match in a series of competitions or sporting events: *The first two runners in this race go through to the final.* ⊃ look at **semi-final 2** finals [pl.] (*BrE*) (**EDUCATION**) the exams you take in your last year at university

finale /fɪˈnɑːli/ *noun* [C] (**ARTS AND MEDIA, MUSIC**) the last part of a piece of music, an OPERA, a show, etc.

finalist /ˈfaɪnəlɪst/ *noun* [C] (**SPORT**) a person who is in the last of a series of competitions ⊃ look at **semi-finalist** at **semi-final**

finality /faɪˈnæləti/ *noun* [U] the fact of being final and impossible to change: *the finality of death*

finalize (*BrE also* -ise) /ˈfaɪnəlaɪz/ *verb* [T] to make firm decisions about plans, dates, etc: *Have you finalized your holiday arrangements yet?*

finally ʔ **A2** ⑤ /ˈfaɪnəli/ *adv.* **1** after a long time or delay: *It was getting dark when the plane finally took off.* **SYN** **eventually 2** used to introduce the last in a list of things: *Finally, I would like to say how much we have all enjoyed this evening.* **SYN** **lastly 3** in a definite way so that sth will not be changed: *We haven't decided finally who will get the job yet.*

finance¹ ʔ **B2** /ˈfaɪnæns, faɪˈnæns, fəˈn-/ *noun* **1** [U] the money you need to start or support a business, etc: *How will you raise the finance to start the project?* **2** [U] the activity of managing money: *Who is the new Minister of Finance?* ◊ *an expert in finance* **3** finances [pl.] the money a person, company, country, etc. has to spend: *What are our finances like at the moment* (= how much money have we got)?

finance² ʔ **B2** /ˈfaɪnæns, faɪˈnæns, fəˈn-/ *verb* [T] to provide the money to pay for sth: *Your trip will be financed by the company.* ⊃ look at **fund²**

financial ⓘⒷ1 Ⓦ /faɪˈnænʃl, fə'n-/ *adj.* (**FINANCE**) connected with money and finance: *I have three years' experience in the **financial services** industry.* ◇ *The economy was quick to recover after the global financial crisis.* ⊃ note at **economic** ▸ **financially** /-ʃəli/ *adv.*

the Financial Times 'index = FTSE INDEX™

financial 'year (*BrE*) (*AmE* **fiscal year**) *noun* [C, usually sing.] (**BUSINESS**, **FINANCE**) a period of twelve months over which the accounts and taxes of a company or a person are calculated

financier /faɪˈnænsiə(r), fə'n-/ *noun* [C] (**FINANCE**) a person who lends large amounts of money to businesses

finch /fɪntʃ/ *noun* [C] a small bird with a short strong BEAK (= the hard pointed part of a bird's mouth). There are several types of finch. ⊃ picture at **animal**

find¹ ⓘⒶ1 Ⓢ /faɪnd/ *verb* [T] (*pt, pp* **found** /faʊnd/)
• BY SEARCHING **1** to discover sth or sb that you want or that you have lost after searching for it: *Did you find the pen you lost?* ◇ *After six months she finally found a job.* ◇ *Scientists haven't yet found a cure for colds.* ◇ *It's hard to find a babysitter.* ⊃ note at **job**
• BY CHANCE **2** to discover sth by chance: *I've found a piece of glass in this milk.* ◇ *We went into the house and found her lying on the floor.* ◇ *This particular species can be found* (= exists) *all over the world.*
• FROM EXPERIENCE **3** to have an opinion about sth because of your own experience: *I find that book very difficult to understand.* ◇ *We didn't find the film at all funny.* ◇ *How are you finding life as a student?* ◇ *I find it difficult to believe that her parents don't know what's happening.*
• REALIZE **4** to suddenly realize or see sth: *I got home to find that I'd left the tap on all day.* ◇ *When Shirin walked on stage she found that she'd forgotten all her lines.*
• REACH **5** to arrive at sth naturally; to reach sth: *Water always finds its own level.* ◇ *These birds find their way to Africa every winter.*
ⒾⒹⓂ **find fault (with sb/sth)** to look for things that are wrong with sb/sth and complain about them **find your feet** to become confident and independent in a new situation
ⓅⒽⓇⓋ **find (sth) out** to get some information; to discover a fact: *Have you found out how much the tickets cost?* ◇ *I later found out that Will had been lying to me.* ◇ *If I cannot answer your question, I can find out.* **find sb out** to discover that sb has done sth wrong: *He had used a false name for years before they found him out.*

find² /faɪnd/ *noun* [C] a thing or a person that has been found, especially one that is valuable or useful: *Archaeologists made some interesting finds when they dug up the field.* ◇ *This new young player is quite a find!*

finder /'faɪndə(r)/ *noun* [C] a person that finds sth

finding ⓘⒷ2 Ⓦ /'faɪndɪŋ/ *noun* [C, usually pl.] information that is discovered as a result of research into sth: *the findings of a survey/report/committee*

fine¹ ⓘⒶ1 /faɪn/ *adj.*
• IN GOOD HEALTH **1** in good health, or happy and comfortable: *'How are you?' 'Fine, thanks.'* ◇ *'Do you want to change places?' 'No, I'm fine here, thanks.'*
• ACCEPTABLE **2** all right; acceptable: *'Do you want some more milk in your coffee?' 'No, that's fine, thanks.'* ◇ *Don't cook anything special — a sandwich will be fine.* ◇ *The hotel rooms were fine but the food was awful.*
• WEATHER **3** (used about weather) bright with SUNLIGHT; not raining: *Let's hope it stays fine for the match tomorrow.*
• GOOD QUALITY **4** of very good quality, with great beauty or detail: *a fine piece of work* ◇ *fine detail/carving/china*
• VERY THIN **5** very thin or narrow: *That hairstyle's no good for me — my hair's too fine.* ◇ *You must use a fine pencil for the diagrams.* ⓄⓅⓅ **thick¹**
• WITH SMALL GRAINS **6** made of very small pieces, grains, etc: *Salt is finer than sugar.* ⓄⓅⓅ **coarse**
• DETAIL **7** difficult to notice or understand: *I couldn't understand the finer points of his argument.* ◇ *There's a fine line between being reserved and being unfriendly.*

fine² ⓘ Ⓒ1 /faɪn/ *noun* [C] (**LAW**) a sum of money that you have to pay for breaking a law or rule: *a parking fine* ◇ *You'll get a fine if you park your car there.*
▸ **fine** ⓘ Ⓒ1 *verb* [T] ~ **sb (for sth/doing sth)**: *He was fined £50 for driving without lights.* ⊃ note at **court¹**

fine³ /faɪn/ *adv.* (*informal*) in a way that is acceptable or good enough: *Keep going like that — you're doing fine.* ◇ *Things were going fine until you showed up.*

fine 'art *noun* [U] (*also* **fine arts** [pl.]) (**ART**) forms of art, especially painting, drawing and sculpture, that are created to be beautiful rather than useful

finely /'faɪnli/ *adv.* **1** into small pieces: *The onions must be finely chopped for this recipe.* **2** very accurately: *a finely tuned instrument*

the fine 'print (*AmE*) = SMALL PRINT

finger¹ ⓘ Ⓐ2 /'fɪŋɡə(r)/ *noun* [C] (**ANATOMY**) one of the four parts at the end of each hand (or five if the THUMB is included): *little finger, ring finger, middle finger, forefinger (or index finger), thumb* ⊃ picture at **body**
ⒾⒹⓂ **cross your fingers** | **keep your fingers crossed** to hope that sb/sth will be successful or lucky: *I'll keep my fingers crossed for you in your exams.* ◇ *There's nothing more we can do now — just cross our fingers and hope for the best.* **have green fingers** → GREEN¹ **snap your fingers** → SNAP¹

finger² /'fɪŋɡə(r)/ *verb* [T] to touch or feel sth with your fingers

fingering /'fɪŋɡərɪŋ/ *noun* [U, C] (**MUSIC**) the positions in which you put your fingers when playing a musical instrument

fingermark /'fɪŋɡəmɑːk/ *noun* [C] a mark on sth made by a dirty finger

fingernail /'fɪŋɡəneɪl/ (*also* **nail**) *noun* [C] (**ANATOMY**) the thin hard layer that covers the outer end of each finger ⊃ picture at **body**

fingerprint /'fɪŋɡəprɪnt/ *noun* [C] (**LAW**) the mark that is made by the pattern of lines on the tip of sb's finger, used for identifying people: *The burglar left his fingerprints all over the house.*

fingertip /'fɪŋɡətɪp/ *noun* [C] (**ANATOMY**) the end of a finger
ⒾⒹⓂ **have sth at your fingertips** to have sth ready for quick and easy use: *They asked some difficult questions but luckily I had all the facts at my fingertips.*

finish¹ ⓘ Ⓐ1 /'fɪnɪʃ/ *verb* **1** [I, T] ~ **(sth/doing sth)** to complete sth or reach the end of sth: *Haven't you finished yet? You've taken ages!* ◇ *The Ethiopian runner won and the Kenyans finished second and third.* ◇ *Finish your work quickly!* ◇ *Have you finished writing that report?* **2** [I] *noun*: *What time does the film finish?* **3** [T] ~ **sth (off/up)** to eat, drink or use the last part of sth: *Finish up your milk, Tony!* ◇ *Who finished off all the bread?* **4** [T] ~ **sth (off)** to complete the last details of sth or make sth perfect: *He stayed up all*

night to finish off the article he was writing. ◇ He's just **putting the finishing touches to** his painting.
PHR V **finish sb/sth off** (*informal*) to kill sb/sth; to be the thing that makes sb unable to continue: *The cat played with the mouse before finishing it off.* ◇ *I was very tired towards the end of the race, and that last hill finished me off.* **finish with sb** (*BrE, informal*) to end a relationship with sb: *Sally's not going out with David any more — she finished with him last week.* **finish with sth** to stop needing or using sth: *I'll borrow that book when you've finished with it.*

finish² A2 /ˈfɪnɪʃ/ *noun* [C, usually sing.] **1** the last part or end of sth: *There was a dramatic finish to the race when two runners fell.* ◇ *I enjoyed the film* ***from start to finish***. **2** the last covering of paint, POLISH, etc. that is put on a surface to make it look good

finished /ˈfɪnɪʃt/ *adj.* **1** [not before noun] **~ (with sb/sth)** having stopped doing sth, using sth or dealing with sb/sth: *'Are you using the computer?' 'Yes, I won't be finished with it for another hour or so.'* **2** [not before noun] not able to continue: *The business is finished — there's no more money.* **3** made; completed: *the finished product/article*

finite /ˈfaɪnaɪt/ *adj.* having a definite limit or a fixed size: *The world's resources are finite.* OPP **infinite**

fiord /fjɔːd/ = FJORD

fir /fɜː(r)/ (*also* **fir tree**) *noun* [C] a tree with NEEDLES (= thin leaves) that are EVERGREEN (= do not fall off in winter)

ˈ**fir cone** *noun* [C] the fruit of the FIR tree

fire¹ A1 /ˈfaɪə(r)/ *noun* **1** [C, U] the flames, light and heat, and often smoke that are produced when sth burns, especially flames that are out of control and destroy buildings, trees, etc: *Firemen struggled for three hours to* ***put out the fire***. ◇ *It had been a dry summer so there were many forest fires.* ◇ *In very hot weather, dry grass can* ***catch fire*** (= start burning). ◇ *Did somebody* ***set fire to*** *that pile of wood?* ◇ *Help! The frying pan's* ***on fire***! ➲ note at **disaster** **2** [C] a pile of burning wood or coal used for warming people or cooking food: *They tried to* ***light a fire*** *to keep warm.* ◇ *It's cold — don't let the fire go out!* **3** [C] a machine for heating a room: *a gas/an electric fire* **4** [U] shooting from guns: *The soldiers came* ***under fire*** *from all sides.*
IDM **come/be under fire** be strongly criticized: *The government has come under fire from all sides for its foreign policy.* **get on/along like a house on fire** → HOUSE¹ **open fire** → OPEN²

fire² B1 /ˈfaɪə(r)/ *verb* **1** [I, T] **~ (sth) (on/into sb/sth); ~ (sth) (at sb/sth)** to shoot bullets, etc. from a gun or other weapon: *Can you hear the guns firing?* ◇ *The soldiers fired on the crowd, killing 20 people.* ◇ *She fired an arrow at the target.* ◇ (*figurative*) *If you stop firing questions at me I might be able to answer!* ➲ note at **gun¹** **2** [T] (*informal*) to remove an employee from a job: *He was fired for always being late.* SYN **sack²** ➲ note at **job** **3** [T] **~ sb with sth** to produce a strong feeling in sb: *Her speech fired me with determination.* **4** [T] (**ART**) to heat a CLAY object to make it hard and strong: *to fire pottery* ◇ *to fire bricks in a kiln*

ˈ**fire alarm** *noun* [C] a bell or other signal to warn people that there is a fire

firearm + C1 /ˈfaɪərɑːm/ *noun* [C] a gun that you can carry

ˈ**fire brigade** (*also* **fire service**) (*both BrE*) (*AmE* ˈ**fire department**) *noun* [C + sing./pl. verb] an organization of people trained to deal with fires

-fired /ˈfaɪəd/ *suffix* (in adjectives) using the fuel mentioned: *gas-fired central heating*

ˈ**fire engine** *noun* [C] a special vehicle that carries equipment for dealing with large fires

ˈ**fire escape** *noun* [C] metal stairs on the outside of a building that people can go down if there is a fire

ˈ**fire extinguisher** (*also* **extinguisher** /ɪkˈstɪŋgwɪʃə(r)/) *noun* [C] a metal container with water or chemicals inside that you use for stopping small fires

firefighter + B2 /ˈfaɪəfaɪtə(r)/ *noun* [C] a person whose job is to stop fires

firefly /ˈfaɪəflaɪ/ *noun* [C] (*pl.* **-ies**) a flying insect with a tail that shines in the dark

firelight /ˈfaɪəlaɪt/ *noun* [U] the light that comes from a fire

fireman /ˈfaɪəmən/ *noun* [C] (*pl.* **-men** /-mən/) a person, usually a man, whose job is to stop fires

fireplace /ˈfaɪəpleɪs/ *noun* [C] the open place in a room where you light a fire

fireproof /ˈfaɪəpruːf/ *adj.* able to take great heat without burning or being badly damaged: *a fireproof door*

ˈ**fire service** = FIRE BRIGADE

fireside /ˈfaɪəsaɪd/ *noun* [sing.] the part of a room next to the fire: *Come and sit by the fireside.*

ˈ**fire station** *noun* [C] a building where FIREFIGHTERS wait to be called, and where the vehicles that they use are kept

firewall /ˈfaɪəwɔːl/ *noun* [C] (**COMPUTING**) a part of a computer system that is designed to prevent people from getting information without authority but still allows them to receive information that is sent to them

firewood /ˈfaɪəwʊd/ *noun* [U] wood used for burning on fires

firework + B2 /ˈfaɪəwɜːk/ *noun* [C] a small object that burns or explodes with coloured lights and loud sounds, used for entertainment

ˈ**firing line** *noun*
IDM **be in the firing line** **1** to be in a position where you can be shot at **2** to be in a position where people can criticize you or say that sth is your fault

ˈ**firing squad** *noun* [C] a group of soldiers who have been ordered to shoot and kill a prisoner

firm¹ B2 /fɜːm/ *noun* [C + sing./pl. verb] (**BUSINESS**) a business or company: *Which firm do you work for?* ◇ *a firm of solicitors* ◇ *an international law firm* ➲ note at **organization**

firm² + B2 /fɜːm/ *adj.* **1** able to stay the same shape when pressed; quite hard: *a firm mattress* ◇ *firm muscles* **2** strong and steady or not likely to change: *She kept a firm grip on her mother's hand.* ◇ *a firm commitment/decision/offer* **3 ~ (with sb)** strong and in control: *He's very firm with his children.* ◇ *You have to show the examiner that you have a firm grasp* (= good knowledge) *of grammar.* ▶ **firmness** *noun* [U]
IDM **a firm hand** strong control or discipline

firm³ /fɜːm/ *verb* **1** [T] to make sth become stronger or harder: *Firm the soil around the plant.* ◇ *This product claims to firm your body in six weeks.* **2** [I] **~ (to/at …)** (**BUSINESS, FINANCE**) to become steady or rise steadily: *Rank's shares firmed 3p to 696p.*
PHR V **firm sth up** **1** to make arrangements more final and fixed: *The company has not yet firmed up its plans for expansion.* ◇ *The precise details still have to be firmed up.* **2** to make sth harder or more solid: *A few weeks of aerobics will firm up that flabby stomach.* ◇ *Put the mixture in the fridge to firm it up a bit.*

firmly ʔ+ B2 /'fɜːmli/ adv. in a strong or definite way: '*I can manage,*' *she said firmly.* ◊ *It is now firmly established as one of the leading brands in the country.* ◊ *Keep your eyes firmly fixed on the road ahead.*

first¹ ʔ A1 /fɜːst/ det., *ordinal number* happening or coming before all other similar things or people; 1st: *She's expecting her first baby.* ◊ *the first half of the game* ◊ *You've won first prize!* ◊ *What were your first impressions of this country when you arrived?* ◊ *King Charles I (= King Charles the First)* **IDM at first glance/sight** when first seen or examined: *The task seemed impossible at first glance, but it turned out to be quite easy.* **first/last thing** → THING

first² ʔ A1 /fɜːst/ adv. **1** before any others: *Sue arrived first at the party.* ◊ *Mike's very competitive — he always wants to come first when he plays a game.* ◊ *Do you want to go first or second?* **2** before doing anything else: *I'll come out later. I've got to finish my homework first.* **3** the time before all the other times; for the first time: *Where did you first meet your husband?* **4** at the beginning: *When I first started my job I hated it.* **5** used for introducing the first thing in a list: *There are several people I would like to thank: First, my mother.* **SYN firstly** **IDM at first** at the beginning: *At first I thought he was joking, but then I realized he was serious.* **come first** to be more important to sb than anything else **first and foremost** more than anything else **first come, first served** (*informal*) people will be dealt with, served, seen, etc. strictly in the order in which they arrive: *Tickets can be bought here on a first come, first served basis.* **first of all** as the first thing (to be done or said): *In a moment I'll introduce our guest speaker, but first of all, let me thank you all for coming.* **first off** (*informal*) before anything else: *First off, let's decide who does what.* **head first** → HEAD¹

first³ ʔ A2 /fɜːst/ noun **1** the first [C] (*pl.* the first) the first person or thing, people or things: *Are we the first to arrive?* ◊ *I'd be the first to admit* (= I will most willingly admit) *I might be wrong.* **2** a first [C, usually sing.] an important event that is happening for the first time: *This operation is a first in medical history.* **3** [C] (*BrE*) (**EDUCATION**) the highest mark given for a university degree: *He got a first in History.* **IDM from the (very) first** from the beginning

first aid noun [U] (**MEDICINE**) simple medical help that you give as soon as possible to sb who is hurt or ill: *a first aid kit/course* ◊ *to give somebody first aid* ⊃ picture at **safety**

the First Amendment noun [sing.] (**LAW**) the statement in the US Constitution that protects freedom of speech and religion, and the right to meet in peaceful groups

first balcony (*AmE*) = DRESS CIRCLE

firstborn /'fɜːstbɔːn/ noun [C] (*old-fashioned*) a person's first child ▶ **firstborn** adj. [only before noun]

first-class adj. **1** of the best quality; of the highest standard: *a first-class player* **SYN excellent 2** [only before noun] used about the best and most expensive seats on a train, ship or plane: *a first-class cabin/seat/ticket* **3** [only before noun] (*BrE*) used about the way of sending letters, etc. that is faster but more expensive than SECOND-CLASS: *first-class mail/letters/stamps* **4** [only before noun] used to describe a university degree of the highest class from a British university: *She was awarded a first-class degree in French.*

first class noun [U] **1** the best and most expensive seats or accommodation on a train, ship, etc. **2** (in the UK) the way of sending letters, etc. that is faster but more expensive than SECOND CLASS: *First class costs more.* **3** (**EDUCATION**) the highest degree of degree given

by a British university ▶ **first class** adv.: *to travel first class* ◊ *I sent the letter first class on Tuesday.*

first cousin = COUSIN

first degree noun [C] (*especially BrE*) (**EDUCATION**) an academic qualification given by a university or college, for example a BA or BSc, that is given to sb who does not already have a degree in that subject: *What was your first degree in?* ◊ *to study geography at first-degree level*

first-degree adj. [only before noun] **1** (*especially AmE*) (**LAW**) (used about murder or other serious crimes) of the most serious kind **2** (**HEALTH**) (used about burns) of the least serious of three kinds, affecting only the surface of the skin ⊃ look at **second-degree** (2), **third-degree** (1)

first floor (*usually* the first floor) noun [sing.] **1** (*BrE*) the floor of a building above the GROUND FLOOR (= the floor at street level): *I live in a flat on the first floor.* ◊ *a first-floor flat* **2** (*AmE*) = GROUND FLOOR

first gear noun [C] the lowest GEAR (= the equipment that turns power into movement) on a car, bicycle, etc: *To move off, put the car into first gear and slowly release the clutch.*

first generation noun [sing.] (**SOCIAL STUDIES**) people who have left their country to go and live in a new country, or the children of these people ▶ **first-generation** adj.: *first-generation Caribbeans in the UK*

first-hand adj., adv. (used about information, experience, a story, etc.) heard, seen or learnt by yourself, not from other people: *He gave me a first-hand account of the accident* (= he had seen it). ◊ *I've experienced the problem first-hand, so I know how you feel.*

the First Lady noun [C, usually sing.] (**POLITICS**) (in the US) the wife of the president or the leader of a state

first language noun [C] (**LANGUAGE**) the language that you learn to speak first as a child; the language that you speak best ⊃ look at **second language**

firstly ʔ A2 /'fɜːstli/ adv. used to introduce the first point in a list: *They were angry, firstly because they had to pay extra, and secondly because no one had told them about it.* **SYN first²**

first name noun [C] the first of your names that come before your family name: *'What's Mr Munn's first name?' 'Robert, I think.'*

the first person noun [sing.] **1** (**GRAMMAR**) the set of pronouns and verb forms used by a speaker to refer to himself or herself, or to a group including himself or herself: *'I am' is the first person singular of the verb 'to be'.* ◊ *'I', 'me', 'we' and 'us' are first-person pronouns.* **2** (**LITERATURE**) the style of writing a novel, telling a story, etc. as if it happened to you: *The author writes in the first person.* ⊃ look at **second person**, **third person**

first-rate adj. of the best quality **SYN excellent**

first responder noun [C] (*especially AmE*) (**MEDICINE**) a person such as a member of the police or fire department who arrives first at an emergency and can give basic medical treatment ⊃ look at **paramedic**

First World noun [sing.] the rich industrial countries of the world ⊃ look at **Third World**

fir tree = FIR

fiscal /'fɪskl/ adj. (**ECONOMICS**, **FINANCE**) connected with government or public money, especially taxes

fiscal year (*AmE*) = FINANCIAL YEAR

fish¹ 🔊 **A1** /fɪʃ/ *noun* (*pl.* **fish**, **fishes**) **1** [C] a creature that lives in water and swims. It breathes through GILLS: *How many fish have you caught?* ◇ *The list of endangered species includes nearly 600 fishes.* ⊃ picture at **animal 2** [U] fish as food: *We're having fish for dinner.* ◇ *a fish and chip shop*

fish² 🔊 **A1** /fɪʃ/ *verb* [I] **1** ~ **(for sth)** to try to catch fish: *He's fishing for trout.* ◇ *They often go fishing at weekends.* **2** ~ **(around) (in sth) (for sth)** to search for sth in water or in a deep or hidden place: *She fished (around) for her keys in the bottom of her bag.*
PHR V **fish for sth** to try to get sth you want in an indirect way: *to fish for an invitation* **fish sth out (of sth)** to take or pull sth out (of sth) especially after searching for it: *After the accident they fished the car out of the canal.*

fishcake /'fɪʃkeɪk/ *noun* [C] (*especially BrE*) pieces of fish mixed with potato that are made into a flat round shape, covered with BREADCRUMBS (= very small pieces of bread) and fried

fisherman /'fɪʃəmən/ *noun* [C] (*pl.* -**men** /-mən/) a person who catches fish either as a job or as a sport ⊃ look at **angler**

ˌfish ˈfinger (*BrE*) (*AmE* **fish stick**) *noun* [C] a narrow piece of fish covered with BREADCRUMBS (= very small pieces of bread) or BATTER (= a mixture of flour, eggs and milk), usually frozen and sold in packs

fishing 🔊 **A2** /'fɪʃɪŋ/ *noun* [U] (**SPORT**) catching fish as a job, sport or hobby: *Fishing is a major industry in Iceland.* ◇ *a fishing boat* ⊃ look at **angling**

ˈfishing line *noun* [C, U] a long THREAD with a sharp HOOK attached, used for catching fish

ˈfishing rod *noun* [C] a long thin stick with a long THREAD and a HOOK on it, used for catching fish ⊃ picture at **lever**

fishmeal /'fɪʃmiːl/ *noun* [U] (**AGRICULTURE**) dried fish made into powder and used as animal food or used by farmers to make plants grow well

fishmonger /'fɪʃmʌŋɡə(r)/ *noun* [C] (*especially BrE*) **1** a person whose job is to sell fish **2** **fishmonger's** (*pl.* **fishmongers**) a shop that sells fish

ˈfish stick (*AmE*) = FISH FINGER

fishy /'fɪʃi/ *adj.* (**fishier; fishiest**) **1** tasting or smelling like a fish: *a fishy smell* **2** (*informal*) seeming wrong, dishonest or illegal: *The police thought the man's story sounded extremely fishy.* **SYN** **suspicious**

fissile /'fɪsaɪl/ *adj.* (**PHYSICS**) capable of nuclear FISSION

fission /'fɪʃn/ *noun* [U] **1** (*also* **nuclear fission**) (**PHYSICS**) the action or process of dividing the NUCLEUS (= central part) of an ATOM, when a large amount of energy is created ⊃ look at **fusion** (2) **2** (**BIOLOGY**) the division of cells as a method of creating more cells

fissure /'fɪʃə(r)/ *noun* [C] (**GEOLOGY**) a long deep CRACK in sth, especially in rock or in the earth

fist /fɪst/ *noun* [C] a hand with the fingers closed together tightly: *She clenched her fists in anger.*

fit¹ 🔊 **A2** /fɪt/ *verb* (**fitting**; *pt, pp* **fitted**, *AmE usually* **fit**) **1** [I, T] to be the right size or shape for sb/sth: *These jeans fit very well.* ◇ *This dress doesn't fit me any more.* ◇ *This key doesn't fit in the lock.* **2** [T, I] ~ **(sb/sth) in/ into/on/onto sth** to find or have enough space for sb/ sth: *Can you fit one more person in the car?* ◇ *I can't fit all these books onto the shelf.* ◇ *I can't fit into these trousers any more.* **3** [T] to put or fix sth in the right place: *The builders are fitting new windows today.* ◇ *I can't fit these pieces of the model together.* **4** [T] to be or make sb/sth right or suitable: *I don't think Ruth's*

fitted for such a demanding job. ◇ *That description fits Jim perfectly.*
PHR V **fit sb/sth in** | **fit sb/sth in/into sth** to find time to see sb or to do sth: *The doctor managed to fit me in this morning.* **fit in (with sb/sth)** to be able to live, work, etc. in an easy and natural way (with sb/ sth): *The new girl found it difficult to fit in (with the other children) at school.*

fit² 🔊 **A2** /fɪt/ *adj.* (**fitter; fittest**) **1** ~ **(for sth/to do sth)** (**HEALTH**) strong and in good physical health (especially because of exercise): *Swimming is a good way to keep fit.* ◇ *My dad's almost recovered from his illness, but he's still not fit enough for work.* ◇ *She goes to keep-fit classes.* **OPP** **unfit 2** ~ **for sb/sth; ~ to do sth** good enough; suitable: *This food isn't fit for human consumption.* ◇ *These houses are not fit (for people) to live in.* **3** (*BrE, informal*) sexually attractive

fit³ 🔊+ **B2** /fɪt/ *noun* **1** [C] (**HEALTH**) a sudden attack of an illness, in which sb becomes unconscious and their body may make violent movements: *to have fits* **2** [C] a sudden short period of COUGHING (= sending air out of your throat with a loud sound), laughing, etc. that you cannot control: *a fit of laughter/anger* **3** [C, U] (usually after an adjective) the way in which sth (for example a piece of clothing) fits: *a good/bad/tight/loose fit* ◇ *It was a tight fit with six of us in the boat.*

fitness 🔊 **B1** /'fɪtnəs/ *noun* [U] **1** (**HEALTH**) the condition of being strong and healthy: *Fitness is important in most sports.* **2** ~ **for sth/to do sth** the quality of being suitable: *The directors were not sure about his fitness for the job.*

ˈfitness centre (*BrE*) (*AmE* **fitness center**) *noun* [C] (**SPORT**) a place where people go to do physical exercise in order to stay or become healthy and fit ⊃ look at **gym** (1)

fitted /'fɪtɪd/ *adj.* made or cut to fit a particular space and fixed there: *a fitted carpet* ◇ *a fitted kitchen* (= one with fitted cupboards)

fitting¹ /'fɪtɪŋ/ *adj.* **1** (*formal*) right; suitable: *It would be fitting for the Olympics to be held in Greece, as that is where they originated.* **2** -**fitting** /fɪtɪŋ/ used in compounds to describe how clothes, etc. fit: *a tight-fitting dress* ◇ *loose-fitting trousers*

fitting² /'fɪtɪŋ/ *noun* [C, usually pl.] (*BrE*) (**ARCHITECTURE**) the things that are fixed in a building or on a piece of furniture but that can be changed or moved if necessary ⊃ look at **fixture** (2)

ˈfitting room *noun* [C] a room in a shop where you can put on clothes to see how they look ⊃ look at **changing room**

five 🔊 **A1** /faɪv/ *number* 5

fiver /'faɪvə(r)/ *noun* [C] (*BrE, informal*) a five-pound note; £5

ˈfive-star *adj.* (**TOURISM**) having five stars in a system that measures quality. Five stars usually represents the highest quality: *a five-star hotel* ◇ *Our restaurant has a five-star rating on this website.*

fix¹ 🔊 **A2** /fɪks/ *verb* [T]
- FASTEN **1** (used with an adverb or a preposition) to put sth FIRMLY in place so that it will not move: *Can you fix this new handle to the door?* ◇ (*figurative*) *I found it difficult to keep my mind fixed on my work.*
- REPAIR **2** to repair sth: *The electrician's coming to fix the cooker.* **SYN** **repair¹**
- ARRANGE **3** ~ **sth (up)** to decide or arrange sth: *We need to fix the price.* ◇ *Have you fixed (up) a date for the party?*
- PREPARE **4** ~ **sth (up)** to get sth ready: *They're fixing up their spare room for the new baby.* **5** ~ **sb sth; sth (for sb)** (*especially AmE*) to prepare sth, especially food or drink: *Can I fix you a drink* ◇ *Can I fix a drink for you?*

• RESULT **6** [often passive] (*informal*) (**SPORT**) to arrange the result of sth in a way that is not honest or fair: *Fans of the losing team suspected that the match had been fixed.*

PHR V **fix sb up (with sth)** (*informal*) to arrange for sb to have sth: *I can fix you up with a place to stay.* **fix sth (up)** to get sth ready

fix² ⓘ **B2** /fɪks/ *noun* **1** [C] a solution to a problem, especially one that is easy or temporary: *There's no quick fix to this problem.* **2** [sing.] (*informal*) a difficult situation: *I was in a real fix — I'd locked the car keys inside the car.* **3** [sing.] (*informal*) a result that is dishonestly arranged

fixation /fɪkˈseɪʃn/ *noun* [C] ~ (**with sth**) an interest in sth that is too strong and not normal

fixative /ˈfɪksətɪv/ *noun* [C, U] **1** (**ART**) a substance that is used to prevent colours or smells from changing or becoming weaker, for example in photography, art or the making of PERFUME **2** a substance that is used to stick things together or keep things in position

fixed ⓘ **B1** /fɪkst/ *adj.* **1** already decided and not able to be changed: *a fixed date/price/rent* **OPP** **movable** ⊃ picture at **resistor** **2** not easily changed: *He has such fixed ideas that you can't discuss anything with him.* ◊ *She looked at him with a fixed smile.*
IDM **how are you, etc. fixed (for sth)?** (*informal*) used to ask how much of sth a person has, or to ask about arrangements: *How are you fixed for cash?* ◊ *How are we fixed for Saturday?* **(of) no fixed abode/address** (*formal*) (with) no permanent place to live: *Stephens, of no fixed abode, was found guilty of robbery.*

fixed 'assets *noun* [pl.] (**BUSINESS**) land, buildings and equipment that are owned and used by a company

fixed 'costs *noun* [pl.] (**FINANCE**) the costs that a business must pay that do not change even if the amount of work produced changes

fixed 'mindset *noun* [C, usually sing.] (**EDUCATION**, **PSYCHOLOGY**) the belief that your natural abilities are fixed and cannot be developed just by working hard, listening to advice from others, etc. ⊃ look at **growth mindset**

fixture ⓘ **C1** /ˈfɪkstʃə(r)/ *noun* [C] **1** (**SPORT**) a sporting event arranged for a particular day: *to arrange/ cancel/play a fixture* **2** [usually pl.] (**ARCHITECTURE**) a piece of furniture or equipment such as a bath or toilet that is fixed in a house or building and sold with it: *Does the price of the house include fixtures and fittings?* ⊃ look at **fitting¹**

fizz /fɪz/ *noun* [U, sing.] the bubbles in a liquid and the sound they make: *This lemonade's lost its fizz.* ▸ **fizz** *verb* [I]

fizzle /ˈfɪzl/ *verb*
PHR V **fizzle out** to end in a weak or disappointing way: *The game started well but it fizzled out in the second half.*

fizzy /ˈfɪzi/ *adj.* (**fizzier**; **fizziest**) (used about a drink) containing many small bubbles of gas ⊃ look at **still¹**

fizzy 'drink (*BrE*) (*AmE* **soda**) *noun* [C] a sweet drink without alcohol that contains many small bubbles

fjord (*also* **fiord**) /fjɔːd/ *noun* [C] (**GEOGRAPHY**) a long narrow piece of sea between CLIFFS, especially in Norway

flabbergasted /ˈflæbəɡɑːstɪd/ *adj.* (*informal*) extremely surprised and/or shocked

flabby /ˈflæbi/ *adj.* (**flabbier**; **flabbiest**) (*informal*) having too much soft fat instead of muscle: *a flabby stomach*

flaccid /ˈflæsɪd/ *adj.* **1** (*formal*) soft and weak: *flaccid muscles* **2** (**BIOLOGY**) (used about parts of plants) not containing enough water

flag¹ ⓘ **B1** /flæɡ/ *noun* [C] a piece of cloth with a special design on it that may be the symbol of a country, club, etc. or may have a particular meaning. A flag can be tied to a POLE or held in the hand: *the French flag* ◊ *The train will leave when the guard waves his flag.*

flag² /flæɡ/ *verb* [I] (**-gg-**) to become tired or less strong
PHR V **flag sb/sth down** to wave to sb in a car to make them stop

flagrant /ˈfleɪɡrənt/ *adj.* [only before noun] (used about an action) shocking because it is done in a very obvious way and shows no respect for people, laws, etc.

flagship /ˈflæɡʃɪp/ *noun* [usually sing.] (in compounds) (**BUSINESS**) the most important product, service, building, etc. that an organization owns or produces: *The company is opening a new flagship store in London.*

flail /fleɪl/ *verb* [I, T] to wave or move (sth) about without control: *The insect's legs were flailing in the air.* ◊ *Don't flail your arms about like that — you might hurt somebody.*

flair /fleə(r)/ *noun* **1** [sing., U] **(a)** ~ **for sth** a natural ability to do sth well: *She has a flair for languages.* **SYN** **talent 2** [U] the quality of being interesting or having style: *That poster is designed with her usual flair.*

flak /flæk/ *noun* [U] (*informal*) criticism: *He'll get some flak for missing that goal.*

flake¹ /fleɪk/ *noun* [C] a small thin piece of sth: *snowflakes* ◊ *flakes of paint*

flake² /fleɪk/ *verb* [I] ~ (**off**) to come off in FLAKES: *This paint is very old — it's beginning to flake (off).*

flaky /ˈfleɪki/ *adj.* (**flakier**; **flakiest**) **1** tending to break into small, thin pieces: *dry flaky skin* **2** (especially *BrE*, *informal*) that does not work well **3** (*informal*) (used about a person) behaving in a strange way

flamboyant /flæmˈbɔɪənt/ *adj.* **1** (used about a person) acting in a loud, confident way that attracts attention: *a flamboyant gesture/style/personality* **2** bright and easily noticed: *flamboyant clothes* ▸ **flamboyance** /-əns/ *noun* [U] ▸ **flamboyantly** *adv.*

flame¹ ⓘ **B2** /fleɪm/ *noun* **1** [C, U] an area of bright burning gas that comes from sth that is on fire: *The flame of the candle flickered by the open window.* ◊ *The house was in flames when the fire engine arrived.* ◊ *The piece of paper burst into flames in the fire* (= suddenly began to burn strongly). ◊ *a sheet of flame* ⊃ picture at **laboratory** **2** [C] (*informal*) (**COMPUTING**) an angry or offensive message sent to sb by email or on the internet

flame² /fleɪm/ *verb* **1** [I] to burn with a bright flame: *The logs flamed on the hearth.* ◊ (*figurative*) *Hope flamed in her.* **2** [I, T] (*literary*) to become red as a result of a strong emotion; to make sth become red: *Her cheeks flamed with rage.* **3** [T] (*informal*) (**COMPUTING**) to send sb an angry or offensive message by email or on the internet

flamenco /fləˈmeŋkəʊ/ *noun* [U] (**ARTS AND MEDIA**, **MUSIC**) a traditional kind of dancing and music from Spain

flaming /ˈfleɪmɪŋ/ *adj.* [only before noun] **1** (used about anger, an argument, etc.) violent: *We had a flaming argument over the bills.* **2** burning brightly **3** (*informal*) used as a mild swear word: *I can't get in — I've lost the flaming key.* **4** (used about colours, especially red) very bright: *flaming red hair* ◊ *a flaming sunset*

flamingo /fləˈmɪŋɡəʊ/ *noun* [C] (*pl.* **-oes**, **-os**) a large pink bird that has long legs and lives near water

flammable /'flæməbl/ (also **inflammable** *especially in BrE*) *adj.* (**CHEMISTRY**) able to burn easily: *highly flammable liquids* **OPP** **non-flammable** ⊃ picture at **safety**

flan /flæn/ *noun* [C, U] a round open PIE (= a type of baked food) that is filled with eggs and cheese, fruit, etc.

flank¹ /flæŋk/ *noun* [C] **1** the side of an animal's body **2** the left or right side of an army during a battle, or a sports team during a game

flank² /flæŋk/ *verb* [T, usually passive] to be placed at the side or sides of: *The road was flanked by trees.*

flannel /'flænl/ *noun* **1** [U] a type of soft cloth made of wool **2** [C] = FACECLOTH

flap¹ /flæp/ *noun* [C] **1** a piece of material, paper, etc. that is fixed to sth at one side only, often covering an opening: *the flap of an envelope* **2** a part of the wing of an aircraft that can be moved up or down to control movement in either direction ⊃ picture at **airliner** **IDM** **be in/get into a flap** (*especially BrE, informal*) to be in/get into a state of worry or excitement

flap² /flæp/ *verb* (-pp-) **1** [I, T] to move (sth) up and down or from side to side, especially in the wind: *The sails were flapping in the wind.* ◇ *The bird flapped its wings and flew away.* **2** [I] (*informal*) to become worried or excited: *Stop flapping — it's all organized!*

flare¹ /fleə(r)/ *verb* [I] to burn for a short time with a sudden bright flame **PHR V** **flare up 1** (used about a fire) to suddenly burn more strongly **2** (used about violence, anger, a disease etc.) to start suddenly or to become suddenly worse

flare² /fleə(r)/ *noun* **1** [usually sing.] a sudden bright light or flame **2** [C] a thing that produces a bright light or flame, used especially as a signal: *The ship sent up distress flares as it started to sink.*

flared /fleəd/ *adj.* (used about trousers and skirts) becoming wider towards the bottom

flash¹ ⚡**B2** /flæʃ/ *verb* **1** [I, T] to produce or make sth produce a sudden bright light for a short time: *The neon sign above the door flashed on and off all night.* ◇ *That lorry driver's flashing his lights at us* (= in order to tell us sth). **2** [I] (used with an adverb or a preposition) to move very fast: *I saw something flash past the window.* ◇ (*figurative*) *Thoughts kept flashing through my mind and I couldn't sleep.* **3** [T] to show sth quickly: *The detective flashed his card and went straight in.* **4** [T] to send sth by radio, TV, etc: *The news of the disaster was flashed across the world.* **PHR V** **flash back** (used about a person's thoughts) to return suddenly to a time in the past: *Something he said made my mind flash back to my childhood.*

flash² ⚡**B2** /flæʃ/ *noun* **1** [C] a sudden bright light that comes and goes quickly: *a flash of lightning* **2** [C] ~ (**of sth**) a sudden strong feeling or idea: *a flash of inspiration* **3** [C, U] a bright light that you use with a camera for taking photos when it is dark; the device for producing this light: *a camera with a built-in flash* **IDM** **in/like a flash** very quickly: *The idea came to me in a flash.* **(as) quick as a flash** → QUICK¹

flashback /'flæʃbæk/ *noun* **1** [C, U] a part of a film, play, etc. that shows sth that happened before the main story: *The story is told in flashback.* **2** [C] a sudden, very vivid memory of sth that happened in the past that makes you feel that you are living through the experience again

flash drive (also **USB drive, pen drive**) (*AmE also* **thumb drive**) *noun* [C] (**COMPUTING**) a small device that you can carry around with you that is used for storing computer data and moving it onto another computer **SYN** **Memory Stick™**

flash flood *noun* [C] a sudden flood of water caused by heavy rain

flashlight /'flæʃlaɪt/ (*AmE*) = TORCH (1)

flash memory *noun* [U] (**COMPUTING**) computer memory that does not lose data when the power supply is lost

flash mob *noun* [C] a large group of people who arrange by SOCIAL MEDIA, mobile phone or email to gather together in a public place at exactly the same time, spend a short time doing sth there and then quickly all leave at the same time ▸ **flashmobbing** /'flæʃmɒbɪŋ/ *noun* [U]

flashy /'flæʃi/ *adj.* (*informal*) (**flashier; flashiest**) attracting attention by being very big, bright and expensive: *a flashy sports car*

flask /flɑːsk/ *noun* [C] **1** (*BrE*) (**SCIENCE**) a bottle with a narrow neck that is used for storing and mixing chemicals in scientific work ⊃ picture at **distillation, laboratory 2** = VACUUM FLASK

flat¹ ⚡**A1** /flæt/ *noun* **1** [C] (*BrE*) (also **apartment** *especially in AmE*) a set of rooms that is used as a home (usually in a large building): *Do you rent your flat or have you bought it?* ◇ *We live in a two-bedroom flat.* ❶ **Apartment** is the normal word in American English. In British English you say **apartment** when talking about a flat you are renting for a holiday, etc. rather than to live in: *We're renting an apartment in the South of France.* **2** [C] (*symb.* ♭) (**MUSIC**) a note that is half a note lower than the note with the same letter ⊃ look at **sharp³** ⊃ picture at **music 3** [sing.] **the ~ (of sth)** the flat part or side of sth: *the flat of your hand* **4** [C] (*especially AmE*) a tyre on a vehicle that has no air in it

flat² ⚡**A2** /flæt/ *adj.* (**flatter; flattest**)
- LEVEL **1** smooth and level, with no parts that are higher than the rest: *The countryside in Essex is quite flat* (= there are not many hills). ◇ *I need a flat surface to write this letter on.* ◇ *a flat roof*
- NOT HIGH **2** not high or deep: *You need flat shoes for walking.* ◇ *a flat dish*
- NOT EXCITING **3** without much interest or energy: *Things have been a bit flat since Alex left.*
- FIRM **4** [only before noun] (used about sth that you say or decide) that will not change; firm: *He answered our request with a flat 'No!'*
- IN MUSIC **5** half a note lower than the note with the same letter ⊃ look at **sharp¹** (9) **6** lower than the correct note: *That last note was flat. Can you sing it again?* ⊃ look at **sharp¹** (10)
- DRINK **7** (used about a drink) not fresh because it has lost its bubbles: *Open a new bottle. That lemonade has gone flat.*
- BATTERY **8** (*BrE*) (used about a battery) no longer producing electricity; not working: *We couldn't start the car because the battery was completely flat.*
- TYRE **9** (used about a tyre) without enough air in it: *This tyre looks flat — has it got a puncture?*
- COST **10** [only before noun] (used about the cost of sth) that is the same for everyone; that is fixed: *We charge a flat fee of £20, however long you stay.* ◇ *You will receive a flat rate of £62.50 for twelve weeks.*

flat³ /flæt/ *adv.* **1** spread out in a level, straight position: *She lay flat on her back in the sunshine.* **2** in a direct way: *I told him flat that I didn't want the car.* **3** lower than the correct note: *He always sings flat.* ⊃ look at **sharp²** (3) **IDM** **fall flat** (used about a joke, a story, an event, etc.) to fail to produce the effect that you wanted **fall flat on your face** to fall so that you are lying on your front **flat out** as fast as possible; without stopping: *He's been working flat out for two weeks and he needs a break.*

flatfish /'flætfɪʃ/ *noun* [C] (*pl.* **flatfish**) any sea fish with a flat body: *Plaice and turbot are flatfish.*

flatly /'flætli/ *adv.* **1** in a direct way; absolutely: *He flatly denied the allegations.* **2** in a way that shows no interest or emotion

flatmate /'flætmeɪt/ (*BrE*) (*AmE* **roommate**) *noun* [C] a person that you share a flat with

flat-screen *adj.* [only before noun] (used about a computer, TV, etc.) having a thin flat screen

flatten /'flætn/ *verb* [I, T] ~ (**sth**) (**out**) to become or make sth flat: *The countryside flattens out as you get nearer the sea.* ◊ *The storms have flattened crops all over the country.*

flatter /'flætə(r)/ *verb* [T] **1** to say nice things to sb, often in a way that is not sincere, because you want to please them or because you want to get an advantage for yourself **2** ~ **yourself (that)** to choose to believe sth good about yourself although other people may not think the same: *He flatters himself that he speaks fluent French.*
IDM **be/feel flattered** to be pleased because sb has made you feel important or special: *I felt very flattered when they gave me the job.* ◊ *He was flattered by her attention.*

flattering /'flætərɪŋ/ *adj.* making sb look or sound more attractive or important than they really are

flattery /'flætəri/ *noun* [U] saying good things about sb/ sth that you do not really mean

flatworm /'flætwɜːm/ *noun* [C] a very simple WORM (= a long thin creature with no bones or legs) with a flat body

flaunt /flɔːnt/ *verb* [T] to show sth that you are proud of so that other people will admire it: *She has received criticism for flaunting her wealth on social media.*

flautist /'flɔːtɪst/ (*BrE*) (*AmE* **flutist**) *noun* [C] (**MUSIC**) a person who plays the FLUTE (= a musical instrument that you blow into)

flavour¹ ʔ+ **B2** (*BrE*) (*AmE* **flavor**) /'fleɪvə(r)/ *noun* **1** [U, C] the taste (of food): *Do you think a little salt would improve the flavour?* ◊ *ten different flavours of yoghurt* ◊ *yogurt in ten different flavours* **2** [sing.] an idea of the particular quality or character of sth: *This video will give you a flavour of what the city is like.*

flavour² (*BrE*) (*AmE* **flavor**) /'fleɪvə(r)/ *verb* [T] to add sth to food or drink to give it more taste or a particular taste: *Add a little nutmeg to flavour the sauce.* ◊ *strawberry-flavoured milkshake*

flavouring (*BrE*) (*AmE* **flavoring**) /'fleɪvərɪŋ/ *noun* [U, C] something that you add to food or drink to give it a particular taste: *vanilla flavouring* ◊ *This orange juice contains no artificial flavourings.*

flaw ʔ+ **C1** /flɔː/ *noun* [C] **1** ~ (**in sth**) a mistake in sth that makes it not good enough, or means that it does not function as it should: *There are some flaws in her argument.* **2** a mark or CRACK in an object that means that it is not perfect **3** ~ (**in sb/sth**) a bad quality in sb's character ▸ **flawed** ʔ+ **C1** *adj.*: *I think your plan is flawed.*

flawless /'flɔːləs/ *adj.* perfect; with no faults or mistakes: *a flawless diamond* ◊ *a flawless complexion* **SYN** **perfect¹**

flax /flæks/ *noun* [U] a plant with blue flowers, grown for its STEM (= the main long thin part) that is used to make THREAD, and for its seeds that are used to make LINSEED OIL

flea /fliː/ *noun* [C] a very small jumping insect without wings that lives on animals, for example cats and dogs. Fleas bite people and animals and make them want to SCRATCH. ◘ picture at **animal**

flea market *noun* [C] (**BUSINESS**) a market, often in a street, that sells old and used goods

fleck /flek/ *noun* [C, usually pl.] a very small mark on sth; a very small piece of sth: *After painting the ceiling, her hair was covered with flecks of blue paint.*

fledgling (*BrE also* **fledgeling**) /'fledʒlɪŋ/ *noun* [C]
1 (**BIOLOGY**) a young bird that has just learnt to fly
2 (usually before another noun) a person, an organization or a system that is new and without experience: *fledgling democracies*

flee ʔ+ **C1** /fliː/ *verb* [I, T] (*pt, pp* **fled** /fled/) ~ (**to/into …**); ~ (**from**) **sb/sth** to run away or escape from sth: *The terrified animals fled into the forest.* ◊ *He fled from police in a stolen car.* ◊ *The robbers fled the country with £100 000.*

fleece¹ /fliːs/ *noun* **1** [C] the wool coat of a sheep ◘ picture at **sheep** **2** [U] a type of soft warm cloth that feels like sheep's wool **3** [C] a piece of clothing like a jacket, made of warm artificial material

fleece² /fliːs/ *verb* [T] (*informal*) to take a lot of money from sb by charging them too much **SYN** **rip sb off**

fleet ʔ+ **C1** /fliːt/ *noun* [C + sing./pl. verb] **1** a group of ships or boats that sail together: *a fishing fleet* **2** ~ (**of sth**) a group of vehicles (especially taxis, buses or aircraft) that are travelling together or owned by one person or organization

flesh ʔ+ **C1** /fleʃ/ *noun* [U] **1** the soft part of a human or animal body (between the bones and under the skin): *Tigers are flesh-eating animals.* **2** the part of a fruit or vegetable that is soft and can be eaten: *Mash up the flesh of the avocado.*
IDM **your (own) flesh and blood** a member of your family in the flesh in person, not on TV, in a photo, etc. **make your flesh creep** to make you feel afraid or full of horror: *The way he smiled made her flesh creep.*

flew /fluː/ *past tense of* **fly¹**

flex¹ /fleks/ (*BrE*) (*also* **cord** *especially in AmE*) *noun* [C, U] (a piece of) wire inside a plastic tube, used for carrying electricity to electrical equipment ❶ At the end of a flex there is a **plug** which you fit into a **socket** or a **power point**.

flex² /fleks/ *verb* [T] to bend or move a leg, an arm, a muscle, etc. in order to exercise it

flexible ʔ **B2** ◐ /'fleksəbl/ *adj.* **1** able to bend or move easily without breaking **2** able to change to suit new conditions or situations: *flexible working hours* ◊ *You need to be more flexible in your approach.*
OPP **inflexible** ▸ **flexibility** ʔ+ **C1** ◐ /ˌfleksə'bɪləti/ *noun* [U]

flexitime /'fleksitaɪm/ (*especially BrE*) (*AmE usually* **flextime** /'flekstaɪm/) *noun* [U] (**BUSINESS**) a system in which employees work a particular number of hours each week or month but can choose when they start and finish work each day: *She works flexitime.*

flexor /'fleksə(r)/ (*also* 'flexor **muscle**) *noun* [C] (**ANATOMY**) a muscle that allows you to bend part of your body ◘ look at **extensor**

flick /flɪk/ *verb* **1** [T] ~ **sth (away, off, onto, etc.)** to hit sth lightly and quickly with your finger or hand in order to move it: *She flicked the dust off her jacket.* ◊ *Please don't flick ash on the carpet.* **2** [I, T] ~ (**sth**) (**away, off, out, etc.**) to move, or to make sth move, with a quick sudden movement: *She flicked the switch and the light* came on. ◇ *The frog's tongue flicked out and caught the fly.* ► **flick** noun [C]

PHR V **flick/flip through sth** to turn over the pages of a book, magazine, etc. quickly without reading everything

flicker[1] /ˈflɪkə(r)/ verb [I] **1** (used about a light or a flame) to keep going on and off as it burns or shines: *The candle flickered and went out.* **2** (used about a feeling, thought, etc.) to appear for a short time: *A smile flickered across her face.* **3** to move lightly and quickly up and down: *His eyelids flickered for a second and then he lay still.*

flicker[2] /ˈflɪkə(r)/ noun [C, usually sing.] **1** a light that shines on and off quickly **2** a small, sudden movement of part of the body **3** a feeling of sth that only lasts for a short time: *a flicker of hope/interest/doubt*

flier /ˈflaɪə(r)/ = FLYER

flies /flaɪz/ noun [pl.] **1** plural of **fly**[2] **2** (*BrE*) = FLY[2] (2) **3** **the flies** (ARTS AND MEDIA) the space above the stage in a theatre, used for lights and for storing SCENERY (= the furniture, painted cloth, boards, etc. that are used on the stage)

flight 🔊 **A1** /flaɪt/ noun **1** [C] (TOURISM) a journey by air: *to book a flight* ◇ *a direct/scheduled/charter flight* ◇ *They met on a flight to Australia.* ◇ *a manned space flight to Mars* **2** [C] (TOURISM) an aircraft that takes you on a particular journey: *Flight number 340 to New York is boarding now* (= is ready for passengers to get on it). **3** [U] the act of flying: *It's unusual to see swans in flight* (= when they are flying). **4** [C] (ARCHITECTURE) a number of stairs or steps going up or down: *a flight of stairs* **5** [U, sing.] the action of running away or escaping from a dangerous or difficult situation: *the refugees' flight from the war zone*

flight attendant noun [C] (TOURISM) a person whose job is to serve and take care of passengers on an aircraft **SYN** **steward, stewardess**

flight crew noun [C] (TOURISM) the people who work on a plane during a flight

flight deck noun [C] **1** an area at the front of a large plane where the pilot sits to use the controls and fly the plane ⊃ picture at **airliner** **2** a long flat surface on top of an AIRCRAFT CARRIER (= a ship that carries aircraft) where they take off and land

flightless /ˈflaɪtləs/ adj. (used about birds and insects) not able to fly

flight path noun [C] the route taken by an aircraft through the air

flimsy /ˈflɪmzi/ adj. (flimsier; flimsiest) **1** not strong; easily broken or torn: *a flimsy bookcase* **2** weak; not making you believe that sth is true: *He gave a flimsy excuse for his absence.*

flinch /flɪntʃ/ verb [I] ~ **(at sth); ~ (away)** to make a sudden movement backwards because of sth painful or frightening **PHR V** **flinch from sth/doing sth** to avoid doing sth because it is unpleasant

fling[1] /flɪŋ/ verb [T] (*pt, pp* flung /flʌŋ/) to throw sb/sth/ yourself suddenly and carelessly or with great force: *He flung his coat on the floor.* ◇ *She flung her arms round my waist and hugged me.*

fling[2] /flɪŋ/ noun [C, usually sing.] a short period of fun and pleasure

flint /flɪnt/ noun **1** [U] (GEOLOGY) very hard grey stone that produces SPARKS (= small flames) when you hit it against steel **2** [C] a small piece of flint or metal that is

used to produce SPARKS (for example in a CIGARETTE LIGHTER)

flip /flɪp/ verb (-pp-) **1** [I, T] to turn (sth) over with a quick movement: *You can flip the phone over to mute a call.* **2** [T] to throw sth into the air and make it turn over: *Let's flip a coin to see who starts.* **3** [I] ~ **(out)** (*informal*) to become very angry or excited: *When his father saw the damage to the car he flipped.* **PHR V** **flick/flip through sth** → FLICK

flip chart noun [C] (BUSINESS) large sheets of paper fixed at the top to a stand so that they can be turned over, used for presenting information at a talk or meeting

flip-flop (*AmE also* thong) noun [C, usually pl.] a simple open shoe with a thin STRAP that goes between the big toe and the toe next to it

flippant /ˈflɪpənt/ (*also informal* flip) adj. not serious enough about things that are important

flipped classroom noun [C, usually sing.] (*also* flipped learning [U]) (EDUCATION) a method of teaching in which students study new material at home, for example over the internet, and then practise it with teachers in class ⊃ look at **blended learning**

flipper /ˈflɪpə(r)/ noun [C, usually pl.] **1** (BIOLOGY) a flat part like an arm on the body of some sea animals, which they use for swimming: *Seals have flippers.* ⊃ picture at **animal** **2** a rubber shoe shaped like an animal's flipper that people wear so that they can swim better, especially under water: *a pair of flippers*

flipping /ˈflɪpɪŋ/ adj., adv. (*informal*) used as a mild way of swearing: *When's the flipping bus coming?*

flirt[1] /flɜːt/ verb [I] ~ **(with sb)** to behave in a way that suggests you find sb attractive and are trying to attract them, without wanting a serious relationship: *Who was that boy Irene was flirting with at the party?* **PHR V** **flirt with sth 1** to think about doing sth (but not very seriously): *She had flirted with the idea of becoming a teacher for a while.* **2** to take risks or not worry about danger: *to flirt with death/danger/ disaster*

flirt[2] /flɜːt/ noun [C] a person who often FLIRTS with people

flirtatious /flɜːˈteɪʃəs/ adj. behaving in a way that shows a sexual attraction to sb that is not serious: *a flirtatious smile* ► **flirtatiously** adv.

flit /flɪt/ verb [I] (-tt-) ~ **(from A to B); ~ (between A and B)** to fly or move quickly from one place to another without staying anywhere for long

float[1] 🔊 **B2** /fləʊt/ verb **1** [I] to move slowly through air or on water: *The boats were floating gently down the river.* ◇ *The smell of freshly-baked bread floated in through the window.* **2** [I] ~ **(in/on sth)** to stay on the surface of a liquid and not sink: *Wood floats in water.* **3** [T] (BUSINESS) to sell shares in a company or business for the first time: *The company was floated on the stock market in 2017.* **4** [T, I] (ECONOMICS) if a government **floats** its country's money, or allows it to **float**, it allows its value to change freely according to the value of the money of other countries ⊃ note at **currency**

float[2] /fləʊt/ noun **1** [C] a large vehicle that is decorated and used in a celebration that travels through the streets: *a carnival float* **2** [C] a light object used in fishing that moves on the water when a fish has been caught **3** [C] a light object that floats in water and is held by sb who is learning to swim **4** [C, U] = FLOTATION (1)

floating /ˈfləʊtɪŋ/ adj. not fixed; not living permanently in one place: *London's floating population*

,floating 'voter (*BrE*) (*AmE* **swing voter**) *noun* [C] (**POLITICS**) a person who has not decided which party to vote for in an election or who does not always vote for the same party

flock[1] /flɒk/ *noun* [C + sing./pl. verb] **1** a group of sheep or birds ⊃ look at **herd**[1] **2** a large group of people, especially of the same type: *Flocks of tourists visit London every summer.*

flock[2] /flɒk/ *verb* [I] (used with an adverb or a preposition) (used about people) to go or meet somewhere in large numbers: *People are flocking to her latest exhibition.*

flog /flɒg/ *verb* [T] (-gg-) **1** [often passive] to hit sb hard many times with a stick or a WHIP (= a long thin piece of rope or leather) as a punishment **2** (*BrE, informal*) to sell sth

flogging /'flɒgɪŋ/ *noun* [C, U] the act of hitting sb many times with a stick or a WHIP (= a long thin piece of rope or leather) as a punishment

flood[1] 🔊 **B1** /flʌd/ *verb* **1** [T, I] (**GEOGRAPHY**) to fill a place with water; to be filled or covered with water: *I left the taps on and flooded the bathroom.* ◇ *The cellar floods whenever it rains heavily.* ⊃ note at **disaster** **2** [I, T] (**GEOGRAPHY**) (used about a river) to become so full that it spreads out onto the land around it: *The River Trent floods almost every year.* ◇ *The river flooded the valley.* **3** [I] ~**in/into/out of sth** to go somewhere in large numbers: *Since the TV programme was shown, phone calls have been flooding into the studio.* **4** [I, T] (used about a thought, feeling, etc.) to fill sb's mind suddenly: *At the end of the day all his worries came flooding back.*

flood[2] 🔊 **B1** /flʌd/ *noun* [C] **1** (**GEOGRAPHY**) a large amount of water covering an area that is usually dry: *Many people have been forced to leave their homes because of the floods.* ◇ *The region remains under a flood warning.* ⊃ look at **flash flood** ⊃ picture at **oxbow lake** **2** ~**(of sth)** a large number or amount: *She received a flood of letters after the accident.*

floodlight /'flʌdlaɪt/ *noun* [C, usually pl., U] a powerful light that is used for lighting places where sports are played, the outside of public buildings, etc.

floodlit /'flʌdlɪt/ *adj.* lit by FLOODLIGHTS: *a floodlit hockey match*

floodplain

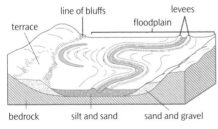

line of bluffs
levees
floodplain
terrace
bedrock   silt and sand   sand and gravel

floodplain /'flʌdpleɪn/ *noun* [C] (**GEOGRAPHY**) an area of flat land next to a river that often floods when there is too much water in the river

floor[1] 🔊 **A1** /flɔː(r)/ *noun* **1** [C, usually sing.] the flat surface that you walk on inside a building: *Don't come in — there's broken glass on the floor!* ◇ *a wooden/ concrete/marble floor* **2** [C] all the rooms that are on the same level of a building: *My office is on the second floor.* **3** [C, usually sing.] (**GEOGRAPHY**) the ground or surface at the bottom of the sea, a forest, etc: *the ocean/valley/cave/forest floor*

floor[2] /flɔː(r)/ *verb* [T] to surprise or confuse sb completely with a question or a problem: *Some of the questions I was asked in the interview completely floored me.*

floorboard /'flɔːbɔːd/ *noun* [C] one of the long wooden boards used to make a floor ⊃ picture at **joist**

'floor plan *noun* [C] (**ARCHITECTURE**) a drawing of the shape of a room or building, as seen from above, showing the position of the room or furniture, etc.

'floor show *noun* [C] (**ARTS AND MEDIA**) a series of performances by singers, dancers, etc. at a restaurant or club

flop[1] /flɒp/ *verb* [I] (-pp-) **1** ~**into/onto sth**; ~**(down/ back)** to sit or lie down in a sudden and careless way because you are very tired: *I was so tired that all I could do was flop onto the sofa and watch TV.* ◇ *He flopped down on the bed.* **2** ~**around, back, down, etc.** to move, hang or fall in a careless way without control: *I can't bear my hair flopping in my eyes.* **3** (*informal*) (**ARTS AND MEDIA**) (used about a book, film, record, etc.) to be a complete failure with the public

flop[2] /flɒp/ *noun* [C] (**ARTS AND MEDIA**) (used about a film, play, party, etc.) sth that is not a success; a failure: *a box-office flop* **OPP** **hit**[2]

floppy /'flɒpi/ *adj.* (**floppier; floppiest**) soft and hanging downwards; not hard and stiff: *a floppy hat*

,floppy 'disk (*also* **floppy,** *pl.* **-ies** /'flɒpiz/) *noun* [C] (**COMPUTING**) a flat disk inside a plastic cover, used in the past to store data from a computer ⊃ look at **hard disk**

flora /'flɔːrə/ *noun* [pl.] (**BIOLOGY**) all the plants growing in a particular area: *He's studying the flora and fauna* (= the plants and animals) *of South America.* ⊃ look at **fauna**

floral /'flɔːrəl/ *adj.* decorated with a pattern of flowers, or made with flowers

florist /'flɒrɪst/ *noun* [C] **1** a person who owns or works in a shop that sells flowers **2 florist's** (*pl.* **florists**) a shop that sells flowers

floss[1] /flɒs/ *noun* [U] = DENTAL FLOSS

floss[2] /flɒs/ *verb* [I, T] to clean between your teeth with DENTAL FLOSS (= a type of thin THREAD): *You should floss every day to avoid gum disease.*

flotation /fləʊ'teɪʃn/ *noun* **1** (*also* **float**) [C, U] (**BUSINESS**) the process of selling shares in a company to the public for the first time in order to make money: *plans for (a) flotation on the stock exchange* **2** [U] (*formal*) the act of floating on or in water

flounder /'flaʊndə(r)/ *verb* [I] **1** to find it difficult to speak or act (usually in a difficult or embarrassing situation): *The questions they asked her at the interview had her floundering helplessly.* **2** to struggle to move or get somewhere in water, mud, etc. **3** to have a lot of problems and be in danger of failing completely: *By the end of the year, the business was floundering.*

flour 🔊 **B1** /'flaʊə(r)/ *noun* [U] a very thin powder made from WHEAT or other grain and used for making bread, cakes, biscuits, etc: *plain/self-raising/wheat flour*

flourish[1] 🔊+ **C1** /'flʌrɪʃ/ *verb* **1** [I] to be strong and healthy; to develop in a successful way: *a flourishing business* **SYN** **thrive** **2** [T] to wave sth in the air so that people will notice it: *He proudly flourished two tickets for the concert.*

flourish² /ˈflʌrɪʃ/ *noun* [C, usually sing.] a movement that is done in a way that makes people notice: *He opened the door for her with a flourish.*

flout /flaʊt/ *verb* [T] to refuse to obey or accept sth: *to flout the rules of the organization* ◇ *They were willing to flout the law.*

flow¹ ʔ **B1** ⊙ /fləʊ/ *noun* [C, usually sing., U] ~ **(of sth/sb)** **1** a steady, continuous movement of sth/sb: *Press hard on the wound to stop the flow of blood.* ⊃ picture at **heart**, **income**, **switch¹ 2** a supply of sth: *the flow of information between the school and the parents* **3** the way in which words, ideas, etc. are joined together smoothly: *Once Charlie's in full flow, it's hard to stop him talking.* **IDM** the ebb and flow (of sth) → EBB

flow² ʔ **B1** ⊙ /fləʊ/ *verb* [I] **1** (often used with an adverb or a preposition) to move in a smooth and continuous way (like water): *This river flows south into the English Channel.* ◇ *a fast-flowing stream* ◇ *Traffic began to flow normally again after the accident.* ⊃ note at **river 2** (used about words, ideas, actions, etc.) to be joined together smoothly: *As soon as we sat down at the table, the conversation began to flow.* **3** (used about hair and clothes) to hang down in a loose way: *a long flowing dress*

ˈflow chart (*also* **ˈflow diagram**) *noun* [C] a diagram that shows the connections between different stages of a process or parts of a system ⊃ picture at **chart¹**

flower¹ ʔ **A1** /ˈflaʊə(r)/ *noun* [C] **1** (BIOLOGY) the coloured part of a plant or tree from which seeds or fruit grow **2** a plant that is grown for its flowers: *to grow flowers*

flower² /ˈflaʊə(r)/ *verb* [I] (BIOLOGY) to produce flowers: *This plant flowers in late summer.* **SYN** bloom²

ˈflower bed *noun* [C] a piece of ground in a garden or park where flowers are grown

flowerpot /ˈflaʊəpɒt/ *noun* [C] a pot in which a plant can be grown

flowery /ˈflaʊəri/ *adj.* **1** covered or decorated with flowers: *a flowery dress/hat/pattern* **2** (LITERATURE) (used about a style of speaking or writing) using long, difficult words when they are not necessary

flown /fləʊn/ past participle of **fly¹**

fl oz *abbr.* (in writing) (*pl.* **fl oz**) = FLUID OUNCE

flu ʔ **A2** /fluː/ (*often* the flu) (*also formal* **influenza**) *noun* [U] an illness caused by a virus that is like a bad cold but more serious. You usually feel very hot and your arms and legs hurt: *She's got flu.* ◇ *a flu vaccine*

fluctuate /ˈflʌktʃueɪt/ *verb* [I] ~ **(between A and B)** (used about prices and numbers, or people's feelings) to change many times from one thing to another: *The number of students fluctuates between 100 and 150.* ⊃ look at **vary** ▶ **fluctuation** /ˌflʌktʃuˈeɪʃn/ *noun* [C, U]

flue /fluː/ *noun* [C] a pipe or tube that takes smoke, gas or hot air away from a fire or an oven

fluent /ˈfluːənt/ *adj.* (LANGUAGE) **1** ~ **(in sth)** able to speak or write a foreign language easily and accurately: *After a year in France she was fluent in French.* ⊃ note at **language 2** (used about a language, especially a foreign language) expressed easily and well: *He speaks fluent German.* ▶ **fluency** /-ənsi/ *noun* [U]: *My knowledge of Japanese grammar is good but I need to work on my fluency.* ▶ **fluently** *adv.*

fluff /flʌf/ *noun* [U] **1** very small pieces of wool, cotton, etc. that form into balls and collect on clothes and other surfaces **2** the soft new fur on young animals or birds

fluffy /ˈflʌfi/ *adj.* (fluffier; fluffiest) **1** covered in soft fur: *a fluffy kitten* **2** that looks or feels very soft and light: *fluffy clouds/towels*

fluid¹ ʔ+ **C1** /ˈfluːɪd/ *noun* [C, U] (SCIENCE) a substance that can flow; a liquid: *The doctor told her to drink plenty of fluids.* ◇ *cleaning fluid*

fluid² /ˈfluːɪd/ *adj.* **1** able to flow smoothly like a liquid: (*figurative*) *I like her fluid style of dancing.* ◇ *The paint had a fluid consistency.* **2** (used about plans, etc.) able to change or likely to be changed

fluidize (*BrE also* **-ise**) /ˈfluːɪdaɪz/ *verb* [T] (CHEMISTRY) to make a solid substance act more like a liquid by passing a gas upwards through it ▶ **fluidization** (*BrE also* **-isation**) /ˌfluːɪdaɪˈzeɪʃn/ *noun* [U]

cross section of a flower

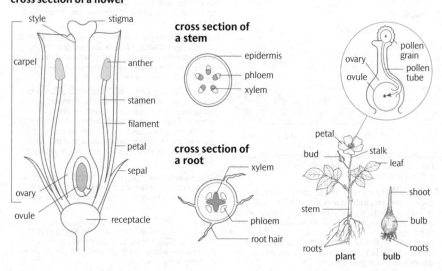

cross section of a stem

cross section of a root

plant

bulb

,**fluid 'ounce** *noun* [C] (*abbr.* **fl oz**) a measure of liquid equal to 0.028 of a LITRE in the UK and 0.03 of a LITRE in the US ❶ For more information about measurements, look at the **Reference Section** of this dictionary.

fluke /fluːk/ *noun* [C, usually sing.] (*informal*) a surprising and lucky result that happens by accident, not because of planning or skill

flung /flʌŋ/ past tense, past participle of **fling**¹

fluorescent /fləˈresnt/ *adj.* **1** (PHYSICS) producing a bright white light: *fluorescent lighting* **2** very bright; that can be seen in the dark: *fluorescent pink paint*

fluoride /ˈflɔːraɪd, ˈfluər-/ *noun* [U] (CHEMISTRY) a chemical that can be added to water or TOOTHPASTE (= a substance you use to clean your teeth) to help prevent bad teeth

fluorine /ˈflɔːriːn, ˈfluər-/ *noun* [U] (*symb.* F) (CHEMISTRY) a chemical element. Fluorine is poisonous, pale yellow gas. ❶ For more information on the periodic table of elements, look at the **Reference Section** of this dictionary.

fluorocarbon /ˈfluərəʊkɑːbən/ *noun* [C] (CHEMISTRY) a COMPOUND of FLUORINE and CARBON. Fluorocarbons are used in things such as cleaning products and fridges, and are harmful to the environment. ⸱ look at **chlorofluorocarbon**

flurry /ˈflʌri/ *noun* [C] (*pl.* -ies) **1** [usually sing.] a short time in which there is suddenly a lot of activity: *a flurry of excitement/activity* **2** a sudden short fall of snow or rain

flush¹ /flʌʃ/ *verb* **1** [I] (used about a person or their face) to go red: *Susan flushed and could not hide her embarrassment.* ⸱ look at **blush 2** [T, I] when a toilet **flushes** or you **flush** it, water passes through it to clean it after a handle, etc. has been pressed: *The toilet won't flush.* **3** [T] ~ **sth away, down, etc.** to get rid of sth in a flow of water: *You can't flush tea leaves down the sink — they'll block it.*

flush² /flʌʃ/ *noun* [C, usually sing.] **1** a hot feeling or red colour that you have in your face when you are embarrassed, excited, angry, etc: *The cold wind brought a flush to our cheeks.* ⸱ *a flush of anger* **2** the act of cleaning a toilet with a quick flow of water; the system for doing this

flushed /flʌʃt/ *adj.* with a hot red face: *You look very flushed. Are you sure you're all right?*

fluster /ˈflʌstə(r)/ *verb* [T, often passive] to make sb feel nervous and confused (because there is too much to do or not enough time): *Don't get flustered — there's plenty of time.* ▸ **fluster** *noun* [sing.]: *I always get **in a fluster** before exams.*

flute /fluːt/ *noun* [C] (MUSIC) a musical instrument like a pipe that you hold out from the side of your face and play by blowing over a hole at one side ⸱ picture at **instrument, orchestra**

flutist /ˈfluːtɪst/ (*AmE*) = FLAUTIST

flutter¹ /ˈflʌtə(r)/ *verb* **1** [I, T] to move or make sth move quickly and lightly, especially through the air: *The flags were fluttering in the wind.* ⸱ *The bird fluttered its wings and tried to fly.* **2** [I] (used about your heart or PULSE) to beat very quickly and not regularly

flutter² /ˈflʌtə(r)/ *noun* [C, usually sing.] a quick, light movement: *the flutter of wings/eyelids*

fluvial /ˈfluːviəl/ *adj.* (GEOGRAPHY) relating to rivers

flux /flʌks/ *noun* **1** [C, usually sing., U] (PHYSICS) a continuous movement: *a flux of neutrons* ⸱ *magnetic flux* **2** [U] continuous movement and change

fly¹ 🔑 **A1** /flaɪ/ *verb* (**flying; flies;** *pt* **flew** /fluː/; *pp* **flown** /fləʊn/)
• OF A BIRD, AN AIRCRAFT, ETC. **1** [I, T] (used about a bird, an insect, an aircraft, etc.) to move through the air: *This bird has a broken wing and can't fly.* ⸱ *I can hear a*

plane flying overhead. ⸱ *How long does it take to fly the Atlantic?*
• IN AN AIRCRAFT **2** [I, T] to travel or carry sth in an aircraft: *My daughter is flying (out) to Singapore next week.* ⸱ *Supplies of food were flown (in) to the starving people.* **3** [T, I] (used about a pilot) to control an aircraft: *You have to have special training to fly a jumbo jet.*
• MOVE QUICKLY **4** [I] (often used with an adverb or a preposition) to move quickly or suddenly, especially through the air: *A large stone came flying through the window.* ⸱ *I slipped and my shopping went flying everywhere.* ⸱ *Suddenly the door flew open and Mark came running in.* ⸱ (*figurative*) *The weekend has just flown by and now it's Monday again.*
• MOVE IN THE AIR **5** [I, T] to move about in the air; to make sth move about in the air: *The flags are flying.* ⸱ *to fly a flag/kite* ⸱ *noun* **flight**
IDM **as the crow flies** → CROW¹ **fly off the handle** (*informal*) to become very angry in an unreasonable way **let fly (at sb/sth) 1** to shout angrily at sb **2** to hit sb in anger: *She let fly at him with her fists.*

fly² 🔑 **A2** /flaɪ/ *noun* (*pl.* **flies**) **1** [C] a small insect with two wings: *Flies buzzed round the dead cow.* **2** [sing.] (*BrE also* **flies** [pl.]) an opening down the front of a pair of trousers that fastens with buttons or a ZIP (= a device for fastening clothes, with two rows of metal or plastic teeth) and is covered with a narrow piece of cloth ⸱ picture at **animal**
IDM **a fly on the wall** a person who watches others without being noticed **not harm/hurt a fly** to be kind and gentle and unwilling to cause unhappiness

,**fly-by** *noun* [C] (*pl.* **fly-bys**) (ASTRONOMY) the flight of a SPACECRAFT near a planet to record data

,**fly-drive** *adj.* [only before noun] (*BrE*) (TOURISM) organized by a travel company at a fixed price that includes your flight to a place, a car to drive while you are there and somewhere to stay: *a fly-drive break* ▸ **fly-drive** *noun* [C]: *a 14-night fly-drive to New Zealand*

flyer (*also* **flier**) /ˈflaɪə(r)/ *noun* [C] **1** (*informal*) a person who flies a plane (usually a small one, not a passenger plane) **2** (TOURISM) a person who travels in a plane as a passenger: *frequent flyers* **3** a thing, especially a bird or an insect, that flies in a particular way: *Ducks are strong flyers.* **4** a small sheet of paper that advertises a product or an event and is given to a large number of people

flying¹ 🔑 **A2** /ˈflaɪɪŋ/ *adj.* [only before noun] able to fly: *flying insects*
IDM **get off to a flying start** to begin sth well; to make a good start **with flying colours** with great success; very well: *Martin passed the exam with flying colours.*

flying² 🔑 **A2** /ˈflaɪɪŋ/ *noun* [U] travelling in or operating the controls of an aircraft: *I'm scared of flying.* ⸱ *flying lessons*

,**flying 'buttress** *noun* [C] (ARCHITECTURE) an ARCH (= curved structure) made of stone that supports the outside wall of a large building such as a church

,**flying 'saucer** *noun* [C] a round SPACECRAFT that some people say they have seen and that they believe comes from another planet ⸱ look at **UFO**

,**flying 'visit** *noun* [C] a very quick visit: *I can't stop. This is just a flying visit.*

flyover /ˈflaɪəʊvə(r)/ (*BrE*) (*AmE* **overpass**) *noun* [C] a type of bridge that carries a road over another road

flywheel /ˈflaɪwiːl/ *noun* [C] a heavy wheel in a machine or an engine that helps to keep it working smoothly and at a steady speed

FM /ˌef 'em/ *abbr.* (**PHYSICS**) one of the systems of sending out radio signals (the abbreviation for 'frequency modulation')

foal /fəʊl/ *noun* [C] a young horse

foam¹ /fəʊm/ *noun* [U] **1** (*also* ˌfoam 'rubber) a soft light rubber material that is used inside seats, CUSHIONS, etc: *a foam mattress* **2** a mass of small air bubbles that form on the surface of a liquid: *white foam on the tops of the waves* **3** a chemical substance made from very small bubbles, used for washing, SHAVING (= cutting hair from the skin), or putting out fires, for example: *shaving foam*

foam² /fəʊm/ *verb* [I] to produce FOAM: *We watched the foaming river below.*

fob /fɒb/ *verb* (-bb-)
PHR V **fob sb off (with sth)** **1** to try to stop sb asking questions or complaining by telling them sth that is not true: *Don't let them fob you off with any more excuses.* **2** to try to give sb sth that they do not want, or that is of worse quality than they want: *Don't try to fob me off with that old car — I want a new one.*

focal /'fəʊkl/ *adj.* [only before noun] central; very important; connected with or providing a focus

ˌfocal 'length *noun* [C] (**PHYSICS**) the distance between the centre of a mirror or a LENS and its FOCUS ⊃ picture at **lens**

'focal point *noun* [C] **1** the centre of interest or activity **2** (*also* focus) (**PHYSICS**) a point at which RAYS or waves of light, sound, etc. meet after REFLECTION or REFRACTION; the point from which RAYS or waves of light, sound, etc. seem to come ⊃ picture at **lens**

focus¹ ⭐ **A2** ⊙ /'fəʊkəs/ *verb* [I, T] (-s-, -ss-) ~ **(sth) (on sth)** **1** to give all your attention to sth: *to focus on a problem* ◊ *to focus attention on a problem* **2** (used about your eyes or a camera) to change or be changed so that things can be seen clearly: *Gradually his eyes focused.* ◊ *I focussed (the camera) on the person in the middle of the group.*

focus² ⭐ **A2** ⊙ /'fəʊkəs/ *noun* (*pl.* focuses, foci /'fəʊsaɪ, 'fəʊkaɪ/) **1** [C, usually sing.] the centre of interest or attention; special attention that is given to sb/sth: *The school used to be the focus of village life.* **2** [C] = FOCAL POINT (2)
IDM **in focus/out of focus** (used about a photo or sth in a photo) clear/not clear: *This picture is so badly out of focus (= the edges of what you can see are not clear or sharp) that I can't recognize anyone.*

focused (*also* **focussed**) /'fəʊkəst/ *adj.* with your attention directed to what you want to do; with very clear aims

'focus group *noun* [C] (**BUSINESS**, **POLITICS**) a small group of people who are asked to discuss a particular subject. The information obtained is used for research into people's choices and opinions.

fodder /'fɒdə(r)/ *noun* [U] (**AGRICULTURE**) food that is given to farm animals

foe /fəʊ/ *noun* [C] (*formal*) an enemy

foetal, foetus (*BrE*) = FETAL, FETUS

fog /fɒg/ *noun* [U, C] thick white cloud that forms close to the land or sea. Fog makes it difficult for us to see: *Patches of dense fog are making driving dangerous.* ◊ *Bad fogs are common in November.* ⊃ note at **weather¹**

foggy /'fɒgi/ *adj.* (foggier; foggiest) used to describe the weather when there is FOG
IDM **not have the faintest/foggiest (idea)** → FAINT¹

foil¹ /fɔɪl/ *noun* **1** (*also* tinfoil) [U] metal that has been made into very thin sheets, used for wrapping things, especially food: *aluminium foil* **2** [C] (**SPORT**) a long, thin, pointed weapon used in the sport of FENCING

foil² /fɔɪl/ *verb* [T, often passive] to prevent sb from succeeding, especially with a plan; to prevent a plan from succeeding: *The prisoners tried to escape but all their attempts were foiled.*

foist /fɔɪst/ *verb*
PHR V **foist sth on/upon sb** to force sb to accept sth that they do not want

fold¹ ⭐ **B1** /fəʊld/ *verb* **1** [T] ~ **sth (up)** to bend one part of sth over another part in order to make it smaller, tidier, etc: *He folded the letter into three before putting it into the envelope.* ◊ *Fold up your clothes neatly, please.* **OPP** unfold **2** [I] ~ **(up)** to be able to be made smaller in order to be carried or stored more easily: *This table folds up flat.* **3** [T] ~ **A in B**; ~ **sth around/ round/over sth** to put sth around sth else: *I folded the photos in a sheet of paper and put them away.* ◊ *She folded a blanket around the baby.* **4** [I] (used about a business, a play, etc.) to close because it is a failure
▸ **folding** ⭐ **B2** *adj.* [only before noun]: *a folding chair/ table/bike*
IDM **cross/fold your arms** → ARM¹

fold² ⭐ **B2** /fəʊld/ *noun* [C] **1** the mark or line where sth has been folded **2** a curved shape that is made when there is more material, etc. than is necessary to cover sth: *the folds of a dress/curtain* **3** (**AGRICULTURE**) a small area inside a fence where sheep are kept together in a field **4** (**GEOLOGY**) a curve or bend in the layers of rock under the earth's surface

-fold /fəʊld/ *suffix* (in adjectives and adverbs) multiplied by; having the number of parts mentioned: *to increase tenfold*

folder /'fəʊldə(r)/ *noun* [C] **1** a CARDBOARD (= very thick paper) or plastic cover that is used for holding papers, etc. **2** (**COMPUTING**) (in some computer systems) a way of organizing and storing computer files

foliage /'fəʊliɪdʒ/ *noun* [U] (*formal*) (**BIOLOGY**) all the leaves of a tree or plant

folic acid /ˌfɒlɪk 'æsɪd, ˌfəʊl-/ *noun* [U] (**HEALTH**) a natural substance that is found in green vegetables, and certain types of meat, for example LIVER and KIDNEYS. We must eat this substance so that our bodies can produce red blood cells.

folio /'fəʊliəʊ/ *noun* [C] (*pl.* -os) (**ARTS AND MEDIA**) **1** a book made with large sheets of paper, especially as used in early printing **2** a single sheet of paper from a book

folk¹ ⭐ **B1** /fəʊk/ *noun* **1** [C] (*also* folks especially in AmE [pl.]) (*informal*) people in general: *Some folk are never satisfied.* **2** [pl.] a particular type of people: *Old folk often don't like change.* ◊ *country folk* **3** folks [pl.] (*informal*) used as a friendly way of addressing more than one person: *What shall we do today, folks?* **4** folks [pl.] (*informal*) your parents or close relatives: *How are your folks?* **5** (*also* 'folk music) [U] (**MUSIC**) music in the traditional style of a country or community: *Do you like Irish folk?*

folk² ⭐ **B1** /fəʊk/ *adj.* [only before noun] traditional in a community; of a traditional style: *Robin Hood is an English folk hero.* ◊ *a folk song* ◊ *folk dancing*

folklore /'fəʊklɔː(r)/ *noun* [U] (**SOCIAL STUDIES**) traditional stories and beliefs

follicle /'fɒlɪkl/ *noun* [C] (**ANATOMY**) one of the very small holes in the skin that hairs grow from ⊃ picture at **skin¹**

follow 🔊 **A1** /ˈfɒləʊ/ *verb*

- **GO AFTER 1** [I, T] to come, go or happen after sb/sth: *You go first and I'll follow (on) later.* ◇ *The dog followed her (around) wherever she went.* ◇ *I'll have soup followed by spaghetti.* ◇ *He didn't notice that they were being followed.* ◇ *The news will be followed by a new drama serial.*
- **ROAD/PATH 2** [T] to go along a road, etc.; to go in the same direction as sth: *Follow this road for a mile and then turn right at the station.* ◇ *The road follows the river for a few miles.*
- **INSTRUCTIONS 3** [T] to do sth or to happen according to instructions, an example, what is usual, etc: *When lighting fireworks, it is important to **follow the instructions** carefully.* ◇ *The day's events followed the usual pattern.*
- **UNDERSTAND 4** [I, T] to understand the meaning of sth: *The children couldn't follow the plot of that film.*
- **KEEP WATCHING 5** [T] to keep watching or listening to sth as it happens or develops: *The film follows the career of a young dancer.* ◇ *Have you been following the tennis championships?* **6** [T] to regularly read the messages that sb writes on an internet site
- **BE THE RESULT OF STH 7** [I] **~ (on) (from sth)** to be the logical result of sth; to be the next logical step after sth: *Intermediate Book One follows on from Elementary Book Two.* ◇ *It doesn't follow that old people can't lead active lives.*

IDM **as follows** used for introducing a list: *The names of the successful candidates are as follows …* **follow sb's example/lead** to do what sb else has done or decided to do **follow in sb's footsteps** to do the same job as sb else who did it before you: *He followed in his father's footsteps and joined the army.* **follow your nose** to go straight forward **follow suit** to do the same thing that sb else has just done **a hard act to follow** → **HARD¹**

PHR V **follow sth through** to continue doing sth until it is finished **follow sth up 1** to take further action about sth: *You should follow up your email with a phone call.* **2** to find out more about sth: *We need to follow up the story about the school.*

follower /ˈfɒləʊə(r)/ *noun* [C] **1** (**RELIGION**) a person who follows or supports a person, belief, etc. ⊃ note at **religion 2** a person who regularly reads the messages that sb writes on an internet site

following¹ 🔊 **A2** **S** /ˈfɒləʊɪŋ/ *adj.* **1** next (in time): *He became ill on Sunday and died the following day.* **2** that are going to be mentioned next: *Please could you bring the following items to the meeting …*

following² 🔊 **B1** /ˈfɒləʊɪŋ/ *noun* **1** [C, usually sing.] a group of people who support or admire sth: *The Brazilian team has a large following all over the world.* **2 the following** [pl.] the person or thing (or people or things) that you will mention next: *The following are*

the winners of the competition … ◇ *The following is a summary of events.*

following³ 🔊 **B2** **S** /ˈfɒləʊɪŋ/ *prep.* after; as a result of: *Following the riots many students have been arrested.*

follow-up *noun* [C] something that is done as a second stage to continue or develop sth: *As a follow-up to the TV series, the BBC is publishing a book.* ◇ *follow-up treatment after an operation*

folly /ˈfɒli/ *noun* [C, U] (*pl.* **-ies**) (*formal*) an act that is not sensible and may have a bad result: *It would be folly to ignore their warnings.*

fond 🔊+ **B2** /fɒnd/ *adj.* **1** [not before noun] **~ of sb/sth**; **~ of doing sth** liking a person or thing, or liking doing sth: *Elephants are very fond of bananas.* ◇ *I'm not very fond of getting up early.* ◇ *Teachers often **grow fond** of their students.* **2** [only before noun] kind and loving: *I have **fond memories** of my grandmother.*

fondle /ˈfɒndl/ *verb* [T] to touch sb/sth gently in a loving or sexual way

fondly /ˈfɒndli/ *adv.* in a loving way: *Miss Murphy will be fondly remembered by all her former students.*

fondness /ˈfɒndnəs/ *noun* [U, sing.] **(a) ~ (for sb/sth)** a feeling of liking sb/sth: *I've always had a fondness for cats.* ◇ *My grandmother talks about her schooldays **with fondness**.*

font /fɒnt/ *noun* [C] **1** (**RELIGION**) a large stone bowl in a church that holds water for a BAPTISM (= a ceremony in which a person becomes a member of the Christian Church) **2** (**ARTS AND MEDIA, COMPUTING**) the particular size and style of a set of letters that are used in printing, on a computer screen, etc.

food 🔊 **A1** /fuːd/ *noun* **1** [U] things that people or animals eat: *Food and drink will be provided after the meeting.* ◇ *There is a shortage of food in some areas.* ⊃ picture at **digestive system 2** [U, C] a particular type of food that you eat: *My favourite food is pasta.* ◇ *Have you ever had Japanese food?* ◇ *baby food* ◇ *dog food* ◇ *health foods*

food bank *noun* [C] (**SOCIAL STUDIES**) (in the UK) a place where people in need can go to get free food ⊃ look at **food pantry**

food chain *noun* [C] (**BIOLOGY, ENVIRONMENT**) a series of living creatures in which each creature eats the one below it in the series ⊃ look at **food web**

foodie (*also* **foody**) /ˈfuːdi/ *noun* [C] (*pl.* **-ies**) (*informal*) a person who is very interested in cooking and eating different kinds of food

food insecurity *noun* [U] (**SOCIAL STUDIES**) the state of not being able to get enough healthy food

food mile *noun* [C] (**ENVIRONMENT**) a measurement of the distance food has to be transported from the

food chain

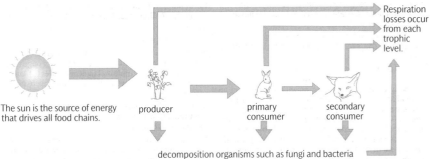

The sun is the source of energy that drives all food chains.

producer

primary consumer

secondary consumer

Respiration losses occur from each trophic level.

decomposition organisms such as fungi and bacteria

producer to the consumer and the fuel that this uses: *Keep food miles to a minimum by buying local produce.*

'food pantry *noun* [C] (*AmE*) (**SOCIAL STUDIES**) an organization that gives food to poor people who live in a particular area ⊃ look at **food bank**

'food poisoning *noun* [U] (**HEALTH**) an illness that is caused by eating food that contains harmful bacteria

'food processor *noun* [C] an electric machine that can mix food and also cut food into small pieces

'food se'curity *noun* [U] (**SOCIAL STUDIES**) 1 the state of being able to get enough healthy food 2 the fact of being able to produce enough food to feed the population of a country or region

foodstuff /'fuːdstʌf/ *noun* [C, usually pl.] a substance that is used as food: *There has been a sharp rise in the cost of basic foodstuffs.*

food web

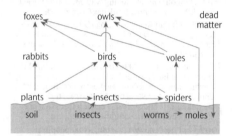

foxes owls dead matter
rabbits birds voles
plants insects spiders
soil insects worms moles

'food web *noun* [C] (**BIOLOGY**, **ENVIRONMENT**) a system of FOOD CHAINS that are connected and that depend on each other

fool¹ ႞+ **B2** /fuːl/ *noun* [C] a person who is silly or who acts in a silly way: *I felt such a fool when I realized my mistake.* **SYN idiot**
IDM **make a fool of sb/yourself** to make sb/yourself look FOOLISH or silly: *Barry forgot what he was going to say and made a complete fool of himself.*

fool² /fuːl/ *verb* [T] ~ **sb (into doing sth)** to trick sb: *Don't be fooled into believing everything that the salesman says.*
PHRV **fool around** (*BrE also* **fool about**) to behave in a silly way: *Stop fooling around with that knife or somebody will get hurt!*

foolhardy /'fuːlhɑːdi/ *adj.* taking unnecessary risks **SYN reckless**

foolish /'fuːlɪʃ/ *adj.* 1 silly; not sensible: *I was foolish enough to trust him.* ◇ *It was a foolish thing to do.* 2 looking silly or feeling embarrassed: *I felt a bit foolish when I couldn't remember the man's name.*
▶ **foolishly** *adv.*: *I foolishly agreed to lend him money.*
▶ **foolishness** *noun* [U]

foolproof /'fuːlpruːf/ *adj.* not capable of going wrong or being wrongly used: *Our security system is absolutely foolproof.*

foot¹ ႞ **A1** /fʊt/ *noun* (*pl.* feet /fiːt/)
• PART OF THE BODY **1** [C] (**ANATOMY**) the lowest part of the body, at the end of the leg, on which a person or an animal stands: *to get/rise **to your feet** (= stand up)* ◇ *I usually go to school **on foot** (= walking).* ◇ *I need to sit down — I've been **on my feet** all day.* ◇ *There's broken glass on the floor, so don't walk around **in bare feet** (= without shoes and socks).* ◇ *She sat by the fire and the dog sat at her feet.* ◇ *a foot brake/pedal/pump (= one that is operated by your foot)* ⊃ picture at

body 2 -footed (in adjectives and adverbs) having or using the type of foot or number of feet mentioned: *There are no left-footed players in the team.* ◇ *a four-footed creature*
• PART OF A SOCK **3** [C] the part of a sock, etc. that covers the foot
• BOTTOM **4** [sing.] **the ~ of sth** the bottom of sth: *There's a note at the foot of the page.* ◇ *the foot of the stairs* ◇ *the foot of the bed* **OPP top¹**
• MEASUREMENT **5** [C] (*abbr.* ft) a measure of length; 30.48 CENTIMETRES. There are 3 feet in a yard: *'How tall are you?' 'Five foot six (= 5 feet and 6 inches).'* ◇ *a 6-foot high wall* ❶ For more information about measurements, look at the **Reference Section** of this dictionary.
IDM **back on your feet** completely healthy again after an illness or a time of difficulty **be rushed/run off your feet** to be extremely busy; to have too many things to do: *Over Christmas we were rushed off our feet at work.* **fall/land on your feet** to be lucky in finding yourself in a good situation, or in getting out of a difficult situation **find your feet** → FIND¹ **get/have cold feet** → COLD¹ **get/start off on the right/wrong foot (with sb)** (*informal*) to start a relationship well/badly **have one foot in the grave** (*informal*) to be so old or ill that you are not likely to live much longer **put your feet up** to sit down and relax, especially with your feet off the floor and supported: *I'm so tired that I just want to go home and put my feet up.* **put your foot down** (*informal*) to say FIRMLY that sth must (not) happen: *I put my foot down and told Andy he couldn't use our car any more.* **put your foot in it** (*BrE, informal*) to say or do sth that makes sb embarrassed or upset **set foot in/on sth** to visit, enter or arrive at/in a place **stand on your own (two) feet** to take care of yourself without help; to be independent **under your feet** in the way; stopping you from working, etc: *Would somebody get these children out from under my feet and take them to the park?*

foot² /fʊt/ *verb*
IDM **foot the bill (for sth)** (*informal*) to pay (for sth)

footage ႞+ **C1** /'fʊtɪdʒ/ *noun* [U] (**ARTS AND MEDIA**) part of a film showing a particular event: *The documentary included footage of the assassination of Kennedy.*

foot-and-'mouth disease (*AmE also* **hoof-and-mouth disease**) *noun* [U] (**AGRICULTURE**) a disease of cows, sheep, etc. that causes painful places on the mouth and feet

football ႞ **A1** /'fʊtbɔːl/ *noun* (**SPORT**) **1** (*BrE*) (*also* **soccer** *AmE, BrE*) [U] a game that is played by two teams of eleven players who try to kick a round ball into a goal: *a football pitch/match* ◇ *Amy plays football every Saturday.* ❶ In the US **soccer** is the usual word for this game since Americans use the word **football** to refer to **American football**. **2** [U] (*AmE*) = AMERICAN FOOTBALL **3** [C] a large round or OVAL ball made of leather or plastic and filled with air ⊃ picture at **sport**

footballer /'fʊtbɔːlə(r)/ *noun* [C] (**SPORT**) a person who plays football, especially as a job: *a talented footballer*

footbridge /'fʊtbrɪdʒ/ *noun* [C] a narrow bridge used only by people who are walking

footer /'fʊtə(r)/ *noun* [C] (**COMPUTING**) **1** a line or block of text that appears at the bottom of every page that is printed from a computer ⊃ look at **header** (2) **2** a line at the bottom of a page on the internet: *a website footer*

foothill /'fʊthɪl/ *noun* [usually pl.] (**GEOGRAPHY**) a hill or low mountain at the base of a higher mountain or range of mountains

foothold /'fʊthəʊld/ *noun* [C] **1** a place where you can safely put your foot when you are climbing **2** a strong position in a business or profession from which sb can progress: *We need to get a foothold in the European market.*

footing /'fʊtɪŋ/ *noun* [sing.] **1** the position of your feet when they are safely on the ground or some other surface: *Climbers usually attach themselves to a rope in case they lose their footing* (= slip or lose their balance). **2** the basis on which sth is established or organized: *The company is now on a firm footing and should soon show a profit.* **3** the level or position of sb/sth (in relation to sb/sth else): *to be on an equal footing with somebody*

footnote /'fʊtnəʊt/ *noun* [C] an extra piece of information that is added at the bottom of a page in a book, below the main text

footpath /'fʊtpɑːθ/ *noun* [C] a path for people to walk on, especially in the country: *a public footpath*

footprint /'fʊtprɪnt/ *noun* [C] **1** a mark that is left on the ground by a foot or a shoe ➔ look at **track**[1] (4) **2** = ECOLOGICAL FOOTPRINT

footstep /'fʊtstep/ *noun* [C] the sound of sb walking: *I heard his footsteps in the hall.*
IDM **follow in sb's footsteps** → FOLLOW

footwear /'fʊtweə(r)/ *noun* [U] boots or shoes

for[1] ʔ+ **A1** /fə(r), *strong form* fɔː(r)/ *prep.* **1** showing the person that will use or have sth: *Here is a letter for you.* ◇ *He made lunch for them.* ◇ *It's a book for children.* **2** in order to do, have or get sth: *What's this gadget for?* ◇ *What did you do that for* (= why did you do that)? ◇ *She asked me for help.* ◇ *Phone now for information.* ◇ *to go for a walk/swim/drink* ◇ *Are you learning English for your job or for fun?* **3** in order to help sb/sth: *What can I do for you?* ◇ *You should take some medicine for your cold.* ◇ *Doctors are fighting for his life.* ◇ *shampoo for dry hair* **4** in support of (sb/sth): *Are you for or against the proposals for the new airport?* **5** meaning sth or representing sth/sb: *What's the 'C' for in 'BBC'?* ◇ *What's the Russian for 'window'?* **6** showing the place that sb/sth will go to: *Is this the train for Glasgow?* ◇ *They set off for the shops.* **7** (showing a reason) as a result of: *Ben didn't want to come for some reason.* ◇ *He was sent to prison for robbery.* ◇ *I couldn't speak for laughing.* **8** (showing the price or value of sth) in exchange for: *I bought this car for £2 000.* ◇ *You get one point for each correct answer.* ◇ *I want to exchange this sweater for a larger one.* ◇ *The officer was accused of giving secret information for cash.* **9** showing a length of time: *I'm going away for a few days.* ◇ *for a while/a long time/ ages* ◇ *They have left the town for good* (= they will not return). ◇ *She was in prison for 20 years* (= she is not in prison now). ◇ *She has been in prison for 20 years* (= she is still in prison). ➔ look at **forever** **10** showing how many times sth has happened: *I'm warning you for the last time.* ◇ *I met him for the second time yesterday.* **11** at a particular, fixed time: *What did they give you for your birthday?* ◇ *Shall we have eggs for breakfast?* ◇ *I'm going to my parents' for Christmas.* ◇ *The appointment is for 10.30.* **12** showing a distance: *He walked for 10 miles.* **13** (after an adjective) showing how usual, suitable, difficult, etc. sb/sth is in relation to sb/sth else: *She's tall for her age.* ◇ *It's quite warm for January.* ◇ *It's unusual for Alex to be late.* ◇ *I think Sandra is perfect for this job.*
IDM **for all** despite: *For all his money, he's a very lonely man.*

for[2] /fə(r), *strong form* fɔː(r)/ *conj.* (*formal*) because: *The children soon lost their way, for they had never been in the forest alone before.*

forage[1] /'fɒrɪdʒ/ *verb* [I] **~ (for sth)** (used about animals or people) to search for food: *His grandmother taught him to forage for mushrooms.*

forage[2] /'fɒrɪdʒ/ *noun* [U] (**AGRICULTURE**) plants that are grown as food for horses and cows

foray /'fɒreɪ/ *noun* [C] **~ (into sth)** **1** an attempt to become involved in a different activity or profession: *the company's first foray into the computer market* **2** a short sudden attack made by a group of soldiers

forbear[1] /fɔː'beə(r)/ *verb* [I, T] (*pt* **forbore** /-'bɔː(r)/; *pp* **forborne** /-'bɔːn/) **~ (from sth/doing sth)**; **~ (to do sth)** (*formal*) to stop yourself from saying or doing sth that you could or would like to say or do: *He wanted to answer back, but he forbore from doing so.* ◇ *She forbore to ask any further questions.*

forbear[2] /'fɔːbeə(r)/ *noun* [C] = FOREBEAR

forbid ʔ+ /fə'bɪd/ *verb* [T, often passive] (**forbidding**; *pt* **forbade** /-bæd, -beɪd/; *pp* **forbidden** /fə'bɪdn/) **~ sb to do sth**; **~ sb from doing sth** to order sb not to do sth; to not allow sb: *You cannot do that. I absolutely forbid it.* ◇ *My parents forbade me to see Tim again.* ◇ *He forbade them from mentioning the subject again.* ➔ look at **prohibit** **OPP** **allow**

forbidden /fə'bɪdn/ *adj.* not allowed: *Photography is strictly forbidden in the museum.*

forbidding /fə'bɪdɪŋ/ *adj.* looking unfriendly or frightening

force[1] ʔ **B1** ◉ /fɔːs/ *noun* **1** [U] physical strength or power: *The force of the explosion knocked them to the ground.* ◇ *The police used force to break up the demonstration.* **2** [U] power and influence: *the force of public opinion* **3** [C] a person or thing that has power or influence: *Britain is no longer a major force in international affairs.* ◇ *Julia has been the driving force behind the company's success.* **4** [C + sing./pl. verb] (in compounds) a group of people who are trained for a particular purpose: *a member of the sales force* ◇ *the police force* **5** [C + sing./pl. verb] the soldiers and weapons that an army, etc. has: *the armed forces* **6** [C, U] (**PHYSICS**) a power that can cause change or movement: *the force of gravity* ◇ *magnetic/centrifugal force* ➔ picture at **hydraulic**, **magnetism**[1] **7** [C, usually sing.] (**GEOGRAPHY**) a measure of wind strength: *a force 9 gale*
IDM **bring sth/come into force** to start using a new law, etc.; to start being used: *The government want to bring new anti-pollution legislation into force next year.* **force of habit** if you do sth from or out of **force of habit**, you do it in a particular way because you have always done it that way in the past **in force 1** (used about people) in large numbers: *The police were present in force at the football match.* **2** (used about a law, rule, etc.) being used: *The new speed limit is now in force.* **join forces (with sb)** to work together in order to achieve a shared goal

force[2] ʔ **B1** ◆ /fɔːs/ *verb* [T] **1** (often passive) **~ sb (to do sth)**; **~ sb (into sth/doing sth)** to make sb do sth that they do not want to do: *She forced herself to speak to him.* ◇ *The president was forced into resigning.* **2** to use physical strength to do sth or to move sth: *The window had been forced (open).* ◇ *We had to force our way through the crowd.* **3** to make sth happen when it will not happen naturally: *to force a smile/laugh* ◇ *To force the issue, I gave him until midday to decide.*
IDM **force sb's hand** to make sb do sth that they do not want to do, or make them do it sooner than intended

forced labour (*BrE*) (*AmE* **forced labor**) *noun* [U] (**LAW**) hard physical work that sb, often a prisoner or a slave, is forced to do

forceful /ˈfɔːsfl/ *adj.* having the power to persuade people: *He has a very forceful personality.* ◇ *a forceful speech*

forceps /ˈfɔːseps/ *noun* [pl.] (**MEDICINE**) an instrument used by doctors or scientists, with two long thin parts for picking up and holding things: *a pair of forceps*

forcible /ˈfɔːsəbl/ *adj.* [only before noun] done using (physical) force: *The police made a forcible entry into the building.* ▶ **forcibly** /-bli/ *adv.*: *The squatters were forcibly removed by the police.*

ford /fɔːd/ *noun* [C] (**GEOGRAPHY**) a place in a river where you can walk or drive across because the water is not deep

fore¹ /fɔː(r)/ *noun*
IDM **be/come to the fore** to be in or get into an important position so that you are noticed by people; to play an important part

fore² /fɔː(r)/ *adv., adj.* [only before noun] (*formal*) at, near or towards the front of a ship or an aircraft ➔ look at **aft**

fore- /fɔː(r)/ *prefix* **1** before; in advance: *foreword* ◇ *foretell* **2** in the front of: *the foreground of the picture*

forearm /ˈfɔːrɑːm/ *noun* [C] (**ANATOMY**) the lower part of the arm ➔ picture at **body**

forebear (*also* **forbear**) /ˈfɔːbeə(r)/ *noun* [C, usually pl.] (*formal*) a person in your family who lived a long time before you **SYN** **ancestor**

foreboding /fɔːˈbəʊdɪŋ/ *noun* [U, sing.] a strong feeling that danger or trouble is coming: *She was suddenly filled with a sense of foreboding.*

forecast ʔ+ **B2** /ˈfɔːkɑːst/ *verb* [T] (*pt, pp* **forecast**, **forecasted**) **~ (that)** ... to say (with the help of information) what will probably happen in the future: *The Chancellor did not forecast the sudden rise in inflation.* ◇ *Rain has been forecast for tomorrow.* ◇ *The report forecasts (that) prices will rise by 3 per cent next month.* ▶ **forecast** ʔ+ **B2** *noun* [C]: *a sales forecast for the coming year* ➔ look at **weather forecast**

forecourt /ˈfɔːkɔːt/ *noun* [C] (*BrE*) a large open area in front of a building such as a hotel or petrol station

forefinger /ˈfɔːfɪŋɡə(r)/ = INDEX FINGER

forefront /ˈfɔːfrʌnt/ *noun* [sing.] the leading position; the position at the front: *Our department is right at the forefront of scientific research.*

forego /fɔːˈɡəʊ/ *verb* [T] (*pt* **forewent** /-ˈwent/; *pp* **foregone** /-ˈɡɒn/) = FORGO

foregone /ˈfɔːɡɒn/ *adj.*
IDM **a foregone conclusion** a result that is or was certain to happen

foreground /ˈfɔːɡraʊnd/ *noun* **1** [C, usually sing.] (**ART**) the part of a view, picture, photo, etc. that appears closest to the person looking at it: *Notice the artist's use of colour in the foreground of the picture.* **OPP** **background 2** [sing.] a position where you will be noticed most: *He likes to be in the foreground at every meeting.* ➔ look at **background** (4)

forehand /ˈfɔːhænd/ *noun* [C, usually sing.] (**SPORT**) a way of hitting the ball in sports such as tennis that is made with the inside of your hand facing forward **OPP** **backhand**

forehead /ˈfɔːhed, ˈfɒrɪd/ (*also* **brow**) *noun* [C] (**ANATOMY**) the part of a person's face above the eyes and below the hair ➔ picture at **body**

foreign ʔ **A2** **S** /ˈfɒrən/ *adj.* **1** belonging to or connected with a country that is not your own: *a foreign country/coin/accent* ◇ *to learn a foreign language* **2** [only before noun] dealing with or involving other countries: *foreign policy* (= government decisions concerning other countries) ◇ *foreign affairs/news/trade* **3** (used about an object or a substance) not where it should be: *The X-ray showed up a foreign body* (= object) *in her stomach.*

the Foreign, Commonwealth and Development Office *noun* [sing. + sing./pl. verb] (*abbr.* **FCDO**) (**POLITICS**) the British government department that deals with relations with other countries **❶** Many people still refer to this department by its old name **the Foreign Office**.

foreigner ʔ+ **C1** /ˈfɒrənə(r)/ *noun* [C] a person who belongs to a country that is not your own

foreign exchange *noun* (**ECONOMICS**, **FINANCE**) **1** [C, U] the system of buying and selling money from a different country; the place where it is bought and sold **2** [U] money obtained using this system: *Most of the country's foreign exchange comes from oil.*

foreign minister *noun* [C] (**POLITICS**) a member of a government who is in charge of his or her country's relations with other countries: *the French foreign minister*

the Foreign Secretary *noun* [C] (**POLITICS**) the person in the British government who is responsible for dealing with foreign countries ➔ look at **Home Secretary**

foreleg /ˈfɔːleg/ *noun* [C] either of the two legs at the front of an animal that has four legs ➔ look at **hind**

foreman /ˈfɔːmən/ *noun* [C] (*pl.* **-men** /-mən/) **1** a male worker who is in charge of a group of other factory or building workers **2** (**LAW**) a man who acts as the leader of a JURY (= the group of people who decide if sb is guilty or not guilty) in court

foremost¹ /ˈfɔːməʊst/ *adj.* most famous or important; best: *Laurence Olivier was among the foremost actors of the last century.*

foremost² /ˈfɔːməʊst/ *adv.*
IDM **first and foremost** → FIRST²

forename /ˈfɔːneɪm/ *noun* [C] (*formal*) a first name, which is given to you when you are born, and that is not the name you share with the other members of your family

forensic /fəˈrenzɪk/ *adj.* [only before noun] (**LAW**, **SCIENCE**) connected with the scientific tests used by the police to find out about a crime: *The police are carrying out forensic tests to try and find out the cause of death.*

forensics /fəˈrenzɪks/ *noun* [pl.] (**LAW**, **SCIENCE**) scientific tests and techniques that are used to investigate a crime

forerunner /ˈfɔːrʌnə(r)/ *noun* [C] **~ (of sb/sth)** a person or thing that is an early example or a sign of sth that appears or develops later: *Country music was undoubtedly one of the forerunners of rock and roll.*

foresee /fɔːˈsiː/ *verb* [T] (*pt* **foresaw** /-ˈsɔː/; *pp* **foreseen** /-ˈsiːn/) **~ (that)** ... to know or guess that sth is going to happen in the future: *Nobody could have foreseen the result of the election.* ◇ *They foresaw that this could be dangerous.* ➔ look at **predict, unforeseen**

foreseeable /fɔːˈsiːəbl/ *adj.* that can be expected; that you can guess will happen: *These problems were foreseeable.* ◇ *The weather won't change in the foreseeable future* (= as far ahead as we can see).

foreshore /ˈfɔːʃɔː(r)/ *noun* [C, usually sing., U] (**GEOGRAPHY**) **1** (on a beach or by a river) the part of the SHORE (= the land at the edge of the water) between the highest and lowest levels reached by the water **2** the part of the SHORE (= the land at the edge of the water) between the highest level reached by the water and the area of land that has buildings, plants, etc. on it

foresight /ˈfɔːsaɪt/ *noun* [U] the ability to see what will probably happen in the future and to use this knowledge to make careful plans: *My neighbour had the foresight to move house before the new motorway was built.* ⊃ look at **hindsight**

foreskin /ˈfɔːskɪn/ *noun* [C] (**ANATOMY**) the piece of skin that covers the end of the PENIS (= male sexual organ)

forest ⬥ **A2** /ˈfɒrɪst/ *noun* [C, U] (**GEOGRAPHY**) a large area of land covered with trees: *the tropical rainforests of South America* ◇ *a forest fire* ⊃ picture at **carbon cycle**, **ecosystem ❶** A **forest** is larger than a **wood**. A **jungle** is a forest in a tropical part of the world.

forestall /fɔːˈstɔːl/ *verb* [T] (*formal*) to take action to prevent sth from doing sth or sth from happening

forester /ˈfɒrɪstə(r)/ *noun* [C] (**ENVIRONMENT**) a person whose job is planting and taking care of trees in forests

forestry /ˈfɒrɪstri/ *noun* [U] (**ENVIRONMENT**) the science or practice of planting and taking care of trees in forests

foretaste /ˈfɔːteɪst/ *noun* [sing.] **a ~ (of sth)** a small amount of a particular experience or situation that shows you what it will be like when the same thing happens on a larger scale in the future

forethought /ˈfɔːθɔːt/ *noun* [U] careful thought about, or preparation for, the future

forever ⬥ **B1** /fərˈevə(r)/ *adv.* **1** (*BrE also* **for ever**) for all time; permanently: *I wish the holidays would last forever!* ◇ *I realized that our relationship had finished forever.* **2** (only used in the progressive tenses) very often; in a way that is annoying: *Our neighbours are forever having noisy parties.*

forewent /fɔːˈwent/ past tense of **forgo**

forewoman /ˈfɔːwʊmən/ *noun* [C] (*pl.* **-women** /-wɪmɪn/) **1** a female worker who is in charge of a group of other factory or building workers **2** (**LAW**) a woman who acts as the leader of a JURY (= the group of people who decide if sb is guilty or not guilty) in court

foreword /ˈfɔːwɜːd/ *noun* [C] (**LITERATURE**) a piece of writing at the beginning of a book that introduces the book and/or its author

forfeit /ˈfɔːfɪt/ *verb* [T] to lose sth or have sth taken away from you, usually because you have done sth wrong: *Because of his violent behaviour he forfeited the right to visit his children.* ▸ **forfeit** *noun* [C]

forgave /fəˈɡeɪv/ past tense of **forgive**

forge¹ ⬥ **C1** /fɔːdʒ/ *verb* [T] **1** to make an illegal copy of sth: *to forge a signature/banknote/passport* ⊃ look at **counterfeit 2** to put a lot of effort into making sth strong and successful: *Our school has forged links with a school in Romania.*
PHRV **forge ahead** to go forward or make progress quickly

forge² /fɔːdʒ/ *noun* [C] a place where objects are made by heating and shaping metal

forgery /ˈfɔːdʒəri/ *noun* (*pl.* **-ies**) **1** [U] the crime of illegally copying a document, money, etc. **2** [C] something, for example a document, picture, etc., that is an illegal copy of the real one

forget ⬥ **A1** /fəˈɡet/ *verb* (*pt* **forgot** /-ˈɡɒt/; *pp* **forgotten** /-ˈɡɒtn/) **1** [T] **~ (doing) sth** to not be able to remember sth: *I've forgotten what I was going to say.* ◇ *I've forgotten her address.* ◇ *He forgot that he had invited her to the party.* ◇ *I'll never forget meeting my husband for the first time.* **2** [I, T] **~ (about) sth; ~ (to do sth)** to fail to remember to do sth that you ought to have done: *'Why didn't you come to the party?' 'Oh dear! I completely forgot about it!'* ◇ *'Did you feed the cat?' 'Sorry, I forgot.'* ◇ *Don't forget to do your homework!* **3** [T] to fail to bring sth with you: *When my father got to*

the airport he realized he'd forgotten his passport. **4** [I, T] **~ (about) sb/sth; ~ about doing sth** to make an effort to stop thinking about sb/sth; to stop thinking that sth is possible: *Forget about your work and enjoy yourself!* ◇ *Let's forget about cooking tonight and get a takeaway instead.* ◇ *'I'm sorry I shouted at you.' 'Forget it (= don't worry about it).'*

forgetful /fəˈɡetfl/ *adj.* often forgetting things: *My mother's nearly 80 and she's starting to get a bit forgetful.* **SYN** **absent-minded**

forgivable /fəˈɡɪvəbl/ *adj.* that can be forgiven

forgive ⬥ **B2** /fəˈɡɪv/ *verb* [T] (*pt* **forgave** /-ˈɡeɪv/; *pp* **forgiven** /-ˈɡɪvn/) **1 ~ sb/yourself (for sth/doing sth)** to stop being angry towards sb for sth that they have done wrong: *I can't forgive his behaviour last night.* ◇ *I can't forgive him for his behaviour last night.* ◇ *I can't forgive him for behaving like that last night.* ◇ *You'd never forgive yourself if you hurt someone.* **2 ~ me (for doing sth)** used to politely say sorry if what you are doing or saying seems rude or silly: *Forgive me for asking, but where did you get that dress?* ▸ **forgiveness** *noun* [U]: *He begged for forgiveness for what he had done.*

forgiving /fəˈɡɪvɪŋ/ *adj.* ready and able to forgive

forgo (*also* **forego**) /fɔːˈɡəʊ/ *verb* [T] (*pt* **forwent** /-ˈwent/; *pp* **forgone** /-ˈɡɒn/) (*formal*) to decide not to have or do sth that you want

forgot /fəˈɡɒt/ past tense of **forget**

forgotten /fəˈɡɒtn/ past participle of **forget**

fork¹ ⬥ **A2** /fɔːk/ *noun* [C] **1** a tool with a handle and three or four PRONGS (= sharp points) that you use for picking up and eating food: *a knife and fork* **2** a tool with a handle and three or more PRONGS (= sharp points) that you use for digging the ground: *a garden fork* ⊃ picture at **gardening 3** a place where a road, river, etc. divides into two parts; one of these parts: *After about 2 miles you'll come to a fork in the road.*

fork² /fɔːk/ *verb* [I] **1** (used about a road, river, etc.) to divide into two parts: *Bear right where the road forks at the top of the hill.* **2** to go along the left or right FORK of a road, etc: *Fork right up the hill.*
PHRV **fork out (for sth)** (*informal*) to pay for sth when you do not want to: *I forked out over £20 for that book.*

forked /fɔːkt/ *adj.* with one end divided into two parts, like the shape of the letter Y: *a bird with a forked tail* ◇ *the forked tongue of the snake* ⊃ picture at **animal**

forked ˈlightning *noun* [U] the type of LIGHTNING (= flashes of light in the sky when there is a storm) that is like a line that divides into smaller lines near the ground ⊃ look at **sheet lightning**

forklift ˈtruck (*also* **forklift** /ˈfɔːklɪft/) *noun* [C] a vehicle with special equipment on the front for moving and lifting heavy objects

forlorn /fəˈlɔːn/ *adj.* lonely and unhappy; not cared for

form¹ ⬥ **A1 ❶** /fɔːm/ *noun*
• TYPE **1** [C] a particular type or variety of sth or a way of doing sth: *Swimming is an excellent form of exercise.* ◇ *We never eat meat **in any form**.* **2** [C, U] the particular way sth is, seems, looks or is presented: *The articles will be published **in book form**.* ◇ *The disease can take several different forms.* ◇ *Help arrived **in the form of** two police officers.*
• DOCUMENT **3** [C] an official document with questions on it and spaces where you give answers and personal information: *an **entry form** for a competition* ◇ *Please fill in the **application form** on our website.*
• IN SCHOOL **4** [C] (*BrE, old-fashioned*) (**EDUCATION**) a class in a school

- OF A WORD **5** [C] (**GRAMMAR**) a way of spelling or changing a word in a sentence: *the irregular forms of the verbs* ◊ *The plural form of 'mouse' is 'mice'.*
- BEING FIT **6** [U] (**SPORT**) (used about a sports player, team, etc.) the state of being fit and strong: *to be in/out of form*
- PERFORMANCE **7** [U] how well sb/sth is performing at a particular time, for example in sport or business: *to be on/off form* ◊ *On present form the Italian team should win easily.*
  IDM true to form → TRUE

▼ CULTURE

In Britain, the years at secondary school used to be called **first/second/third**, etc. **form** but now they are called **Year 7** to **Year 13**. However, the last two years of school (for students aged between 16 and 18) are still also referred to as **the sixth form**. In the US, the years at elementary and high schools are called **grades**, from **first grade** to **twelfth grade**.

form² 🔒**A1** 🔊 /fɔːm/ *verb*
- START TO EXIST **1** [I, T] to begin to exist or to make sth exist: *These tracks were formed by rabbits.* ◊ *Storm clouds are forming on the horizon.* ᴐ note at **make¹**
  2 [T] to begin to have or think sth: *I haven't formed an opinion about the new boss yet.* ◊ *to form a friendship*
- MAKE **3** [T] to make or organize sth: *to form a government* ◊ *In English we usually form the past tense by adding '-ed'.* ᴐ note at **organization**
- MAKE A SHAPE **4** [T] to become or make a particular shape, or to produce sth in a particular way: *The police formed a circle around the house.* ◊ *to form a line/queue* ◊ *Rearrange the letters to form a new word.*
- FUNCTION **5** linking verb to be sth; to have a particular function: *Seminars form the main part of the course.* ◊ *The survey formed part of a larger programme of market research.*

formal 🔒**A2** 🔊 /ˈfɔːml/ *adj.* **1** (used about language or behaviour) used when you want to appear serious or official and in situations in which you do not know the other people very well: *'Yours faithfully' is a formal way of ending a letter.* ◊ *She has a very formal manner — she doesn't seem to be able to relax.* ◊ *a formal occasion* (= one where you must behave politely and wear the clothes that people think are suitable) **OPP** informal **2** official: *I shall make a formal complaint to the hospital about the way I was treated.* ◊ *a formal enquiry/announcement/request/ identification* **OPP** informal ▸ formally /-məli/ *adv.*: *'How do you do?' she said formally.*

formaldehyde /fɔːˈmældɪhaɪd/ *noun* [U] **1** (*symb.* **CH₂O**) (**CHEMISTRY**) a gas with a strong smell **2** (*also* formalin /ˈfɔːməlɪn/) (**CHEMISTRY**) a liquid made by mixing formaldehyde and water, used especially for keeping SPECIMENS (= examples) of animals, plants, etc. in a good condition for a long time so that they can be studied by experts or students

formalism /ˈfɔːməlɪzəm/ *noun* [U] (**ART**) a style or method in art that pays more attention to the correct arrangement of things than to meaning and feelings: *He found formalism boring and divorced from modern life.* ▸ formalist /-lɪst/ *noun* [C]: *formalist theory*

formality /fɔːˈmæləti/ *noun* (*pl.* -ies) **1** [C, usually pl.] an action that is necessary according to custom or law: *There are certain formalities to attend to before we can give you a visa.* **2** [C] a thing that you must do as part of an official process, but that has little meaning and will not affect what happens: *Michael already knows he has the job so the interview is just a*

formality. **3** [U] careful attention to rules of language and behaviour

format¹ 🔒**B2** /ˈfɔːmæt/ *noun* [C] the shape of sth or the way it is arranged or produced: *It's the same book but in a different format.*

format² /ˈfɔːmæt/ *verb* [T] (-tt-) to arrange text on a page or a screen: *to format a document*

formation 🔒**B2** 🔊 /fɔːˈmeɪʃn/ *noun* **1** [U] the act of making or developing sth: *the formation of a new government* **2** [C] (**GEOLOGY**) a thing that has been formed, especially in a particular way **3** [C, U] a particular arrangement or pattern: *A number of planes flew over in formation.* ◊ *The phone has three camera lenses arranged in a triangle formation.*

formative /ˈfɔːmətɪv/ *adj.* having an important and lasting influence (on sb's character and opinions): *A child's early years are thought to be the most formative ones.*

former 🔒**B2** /ˈfɔːmə(r)/ *adj.* [only before noun] of an earlier time; belonging to the past: *In former times people often had larger families.* ◊ *Barack Obama, the former American president*

the ˈformer *noun* [C] (*pl.* the former) the first of two people or things mentioned: *Of the two hospitals, the General and the Royal, the former* (= the General) *has the better reputation.* ◊ *Interrail and Eurail passes allow holders to travel across as many as 31 countries. The former are for European citizens.* ᴐ look at **latter**

formerly 🔒**B2** /ˈfɔːməli/ *adv.* in the past; before now: *The hotel was formerly a castle.* ◊ *Namibia, formerly known as South-West Africa* **SYN** previously

formidable /fəˈmɪdəbl, ˈfɔːmɪdəbl/ *adj.* **1** causing you to be quite frightened: *His mother is a rather formidable lady.* **2** difficult to deal with; needing a lot of effort: *Reforming the education system will be a formidable task.*

formula 🔒**C1** 🔊 /ˈfɔːmjələ/ *noun* [C] (*pl.* formulas, formulae /-liː/) **1** (**CHEMISTRY**, **MATHEMATICS**) a group of signs, letters or numbers used in science or mathematics to express a general law or fact: *What is the formula for converting miles to kilometres?* **2** (**CHEMISTRY**) a list of (often chemical) substances used for making sth; the instructions for making sth **3** ~ **for sth/doing sth** a plan of how to get or do sth: *What is her formula for success?* ◊ *Unfortunately, there's no magic formula for a perfect marriage.*

formulate 🔒**C1** 🔊 /ˈfɔːmjuleɪt/ *verb* [T] **1** to prepare and organize a plan or ideas for doing sth: *to formulate a plan* **2** to express sth (clearly and exactly): *He struggled to formulate a simple answer to her question.* ▸ formulation 🔊 /ˌfɔːmjuˈleɪʃn/ *noun* [U, C]

forsake /fəˈseɪk/ *verb* [T] (*pt* forsook /-ˈsʊk/; *pp* forsaken /-ˈseɪkən/) (*old-fashioned*) **1** to leave sb/sth, especially when you have a responsibility to stay **SYN** abandon **2** to stop doing sth, or leave sth, especially sth that you enjoy: *She forsook the glamour of the city and went to live in the wilds of Scotland.* **SYN** renounce

fort /fɔːt/ *noun* [C] a strong building that is used for military defence

forth 🔒**C1** /fɔːθ/ *adv.* away from a place; out: *They set forth at dawn.*
IDM and so forth and other things like those just mentioned: *The sort of job that you'll be doing is taking messages, making tea and so forth.* back and forth → BACK³

forthcoming 🔒**C1** /ˌfɔːθˈkʌmɪŋ/ *adj.* **1** [only before noun] that will happen or appear in the near future: *Look at our website for a list of forthcoming events.* **2** [not before noun] (*formal*) offered or given: *If no money is forthcoming, we shall not be able to continue the* project. **3** [not before noun] (used about a person) willng to give information about sth

forthright /'fɔːθraɪt/ *adj.* saying exactly what you think in a clear and direct way

forthwith /ˌfɔːθ'wɪθ, -'wɪð/ *adv.* (*formal*) immediately

fortieth /'fɔːtiəθ/ → FORTY

fortification /ˌfɔːtɪfɪ'keɪʃn/ *noun* [C, usually pl.] walls, towers, etc. built, especially in the past, to protect a place against attack

fortify /'fɔːtɪfaɪ/ *verb* [T] (fortifying; fortifies; *pt, pp* fortified) **1** to make a place stronger and more ready for an attack: *to fortify a city* **2** to make sb/yourself feel stronger, braver, etc.

fortnight /'fɔːtnaɪt/ *noun* [C, usually sing.] (*BrE*) two weeks: *We're going on holiday for a fortnight.* ◇ *School finishes in a fortnight/in a fortnight's time* (= two weeks from now).

fortnightly /'fɔːtnaɪtli/ *adj., adv.* (happening or appearing) once every two weeks: *This magazine is published fortnightly.*

fortress /'fɔːtrəs/ *noun* [C] a castle or other large strong building that it is not easy to attack

fortunate ʕ+ B2 /'fɔːtʃənət/ *adj.* ~ (to do sth) lucky: *You were fortunate to have such lovely weather for your holiday.* OPP **unfortunate**

fortunately ʕ A2 /'fɔːtʃənətli/ *adv.* by good luck: *Fortunately the traffic wasn't too bad so I managed to get to the meeting on time.* SYN **luckily**

fortune ʕ B2 /'fɔːtʃuːn/ *noun* **1** [C, U] a very large amount of money: *I always spend a fortune on presents at Christmas.* ◇ *She went to Hollywood in search of fame and fortune.* **2** [U] chance or luck, especially in the way it affects a person's life: *Fortune was not on our side that day* (= we were UNLUCKY). SYN **fate 3** [C, usually pl.] the things (both good and bad) that happen to a person, family, country, etc: *The country's fortunes depend on its industry being successful.* **4** [C] what is going to happen to a person in the future: *Show me your hand and I'll try to tell your fortune.* SYN **destiny, fate**
IDM **cost the earth/a fortune** → COST[2]

fortune teller *noun* [C] a person who tells people what will happen to them in the future

forty ʕ A1 /'fɔːti/ **1** *number* 40 **2** the forties *noun* [pl.] numbers, years or temperatures from 40 to 49
▶ **fortieth** *ordinal number, noun* [C]
IDM **forty winks** (*informal*) a short sleep, especially during the day **in your forties** between the ages of 40 and 49

forum ʕ+ B2 /'fɔːrəm/ *noun* [C] **1** ~ (for sth) a place or meeting where people can exchange and discuss ideas: *TV is still an important forum for political debate.* ◇ *an internet forum* ◇ *to hold an international forum on drug abuse* **2** (HISTORY) (in ancient Rome) a public place where meetings were held

forward[1] ʕ A2 /'fɔːwəd/ *adv.* **1** (also forwards) in the direction that is in front of you; towards the front, end or future: *Keep going forward and try not to look back.* ◇ *The series moves back and forward through time.* OPP **back**[3], **backwards 2** towards a good result: *The discovery of a new form of treatment is a big step forward in the fight against cancer.*
IDM **backward(s) and forward(s)** → BACKWARDS **put the clock/clocks forward/back** → CLOCK[1]

forward[2] ʕ B2 /'fɔːwəd/ *adj.* **1** [only before noun] towards the front or future: *forward planning* **2** behaving towards sb in a way that is too confident or too informal: *I hope you don't think I'm being too forward, asking you so many questions.*

forward[3] /'fɔːwəd/ *verb* [T] to send a letter, etc. received at one address to a new address

forward[4] /'fɔːwəd/ *noun* [C] (SPORT) an attacking player in a sport such as football

forwarding address *noun* [C] a new address to which letters, etc. should be sent: *The previous owners didn't leave a forwarding address.*

forward-looking *adj.* thinking about or planning for the future; having modern ideas

forwards /'fɔːwədz/ = FORWARD[1] (1)

forward slash *noun* [C] (COMPUTING) the symbol (/) used in computer commands and in internet addresses to separate the different parts ◯ look at **backslash**, **slash**[2] (3)

forwent /fɔː'went/ *past tense of* **forgo**

fossil B2 /'fɒsl/ *noun* [C] (BIOLOGY, GEOLOGY) (part of) an animal or a plant that lived thousands or millions of years ago and that has turned into rock

fossil fuel *noun* [C, U] (ENVIRONMENT) fuel such as coal or oil that was formed over millions of years from parts of dead animals or plants ◯ look at **alternative fuel** ◯ picture at **carbon cycle, energy**

fossilize (*BrE also* -ise) /'fɒsəlaɪz/ *verb* [I, T] **1** [usually passive] (GEOLOGY) to make an animal or a plant become a FOSSIL: *fossilized bones* **2** to become or make sb/sth become fixed and unable to change or develop

foster ʕ+ C1 /'fɒstə(r)/ *verb* [T] **1** (*especially BrE*) to take a child who needs a home into your family and to care for them without becoming their legal parent: *to foster a homeless child* ❶ The people who do this are foster parents. The child is a foster child. **2** to help or encourage the development of sth (especially feelings or ideas)

fought /fɔːt/ *past tense, past participle of* **fight**[1]

foul[1] /faʊl/ *adj.* **1** dirty or smelling bad: *a foul-smelling cigar* ◇ *This coffee tastes foul!* **2** (*especially BrE*) very bad or unpleasant: *Careful what you say — he's in a foul temper/mood.* ◇ *The foul weather prevented our plane from taking off.* **3** (used about language) very rude; full of swearing: *foul language*
IDM **fall foul of sb/sth** to get in trouble with sb/sth because you have done sth wrong: *At 16 she fell foul of the law for the first time.*

foul[2] /faʊl/ *verb* **1** [I, T] (SPORT) to do sth to another player that is against the rules of the game **2** [T] to make sth dirty (with rubbish, waste, etc.): *Do not allow your dog to foul the pavement.*
PHR V **foul sth up** (*informal*) to cause sth to fail: *The delay on the train fouled up my plans for the evening.*

foul[3] /faʊl/ *noun* [C] (SPORT) an action that is against the rules: *He was sent off for a foul on the goalkeeper.*

foul play *noun* [U] **1** (LAW) violence or crime that causes sb's death: *The police suspect foul play.* **2** (*BrE*) (SPORT) action that is against the rules of a sport

found[1] /faʊnd/ *past tense, past participle of* **find**[1]

found[2] ʕ B2 /faʊnd/ *verb* [T] **1** to start an organization, institution, etc: *This museum was founded in 1683.* ◯ note at **organization 2** (HISTORY) to be the first to start building and living in a town or country: *Liberia was founded by freed American slaves.* **3** [usually passive] **be founded (on sth)** to be based on sth: *The book was founded on real life.*

foundation ʕ+ B2 /faʊn'deɪʃn/ *noun* **1** foundations [pl.] (ARCHITECTURE) a layer of BRICKS, etc. under the surface of the ground that forms the solid base of a building **2** [C, U] the idea, principle or fact on which sth is based: *This coursebook aims to give students a* *solid foundation in grammar.* ◊ *That rumour is completely without foundation* (= it is not true). ⟳ note at **basis 3** [C] an organization that provides money for a special purpose: *the British Heart Foundation* **4** [U] the act of starting a new institution or organization: *The organization has grown enormously since its foundation in 1995.*

foun'dation course *noun* [C] (*BrE*) (**EDUCATION**) a general course at a college that prepares students for longer or more difficult courses: *an art foundation course*

foun'dation stone *noun* [C] (**ARCHITECTURE**) a large block of stone that is put at the base of an important new public building in a special ceremony

founder¹ ⓘ+ **B2** /'faʊndə(r)/ *noun* [C] a person who starts a new institution or organization

founder² /'faʊndə(r)/ *verb* [I] ~ **(on sth)** (*formal*) **1** to fail because of a particular problem or difficulty: *The project foundered after problems with funding.* ◊ *The talks foundered on disagreement about who would lead the government.* **2** to fill with water and sink: *Our boat foundered on a reef.*

founder 'member (*BrE*) (*AmE* ,founding 'member) *noun* [C] one of the original members of a club, organization, etc.

foundry /'faʊndri/ *noun* [C] (*pl.* -ies) a place where metal or glass is melted and shaped into objects ⟳ note at **factory**

fountain /'faʊntən/ *noun* [C] **1** (**ARCHITECTURE**) a decoration (in a garden or in a square in a town) that sends a flow of water into the air; the water that comes out of a fountain **2** ~ **(of sth)** a strong flow of liquid or another substance that is forced into the air: *a fountain of blood/sparks* **3** ~ **of sth** a person or thing that provides a large amount of sth: *Tourism is a fountain of wealth for the city.*

'fountain pen *noun* [C] a type of pen that you fill with INK (= coloured liquid for writing)

four ⓘ **A1** /fɔː(r)/ *number* 4
IDM **on all fours** bent over with your hands and knees on the ground: *The children went through the tunnel on all fours.*

,four-letter 'word *noun* [C] (**LANGUAGE**) a swear word that shocks or offends people (often with four letters)

'four-star *adj.* (**TOURISM**) having four stars in a system that measures quality. The highest quality is shown by either four or five stars: *a four-star hotel*

fourteen ⓘ **A1** /ˌfɔː'tiːn/ *number* 14 ▸ **fourteenth** /-'tiːnθ/ *ordinal number, noun* [C]

the ,Fourteenth A'mendment *noun* [sing.] (**HISTORY**) a change made to the US Constitution in 1866 that gave all Americans equal rights and allowed former slaves to become citizens

fourth ⓘ **A1** /fɔːθ/ *ordinal number* 4th

,four-wheel 'drive *noun* [U, C] a system that provides power to all four wheels of a vehicle, making it easier to control; a vehicle with this system: *a car with four-wheel drive* ◊ *We rented a four-wheel drive to get around the island.* ⟳ look at **ATV**

,four-'wheeler (*AmE*) = QUAD BIKE

fowl /faʊl/ *noun* [C] (*pl.* fowl, fowls) (**AGRICULTURE**) a bird, especially a chicken, that is kept on a farm

fox /fɒks/ *noun* [C] a wild animal like a small dog with red-brown fur, a pointed nose and a thick tail ⟳ picture at **food web**

foyer /'fɔɪeɪ/ *noun* [C] an entrance hall in a cinema, theatre, hotel, etc. where people can meet or wait

fracking /'frækɪŋ/ *noun* [U] (**ENVIRONMENT**, **GEOLOGY**) the process of forcing liquid at high pressure into rocks, etc. in order to take out oil or gas

fraction ⓘ+ **B2** /'frækʃn/ *noun* [C] **1** a small part or amount: *For a fraction of a second I thought the car was going to crash.* **HELP** If **fraction** is used with a plural noun, the verb is usually plural: *Only a fraction of cars in the UK use leaded petrol.* If it is used with a singular noun that represents a group of people, the verb can be singular or plural in British English, but is usually singular in North American English: *A tiny fraction of the population never vote/votes.* **2** (**MATHEMATICS**) a division of a number: *½ and ¼ are fractions.* ⟳ look at **integer, vulgar fraction**

fractional distillation /ˌfrækʃənl ˌdɪstɪ'leɪʃn/ *noun* [U] (**CHEMISTRY**) the process of separating the parts of a liquid mixture by heating it. As the temperature goes up, each part in turn becomes a gas, which then cools as it moves up a tube and can be collected as a liquid.

fractionally /'frækʃənəli/ *adv.* to a very small degree; slightly: *fractionally faster/taller/heavier*

fracture /'fræktʃə(r)/ *noun* [C, U] a break in a bone or other hard material ▸ **fracture** *verb* [I, T]: *A water pipe fractured and flooded the bathroom.* ◊ *She fell and fractured her ankle.*

fragile ⓘ+ **C1** /'frædʒaɪl/ *adj.* easily damaged or broken: *This bowl is very fragile. Please handle it carefully.* ◊ (*figurative*) *The economy remains extremely fragile.*

fragment¹ ⓘ+ **B2** /'frægmənt/ *noun* [C] a small piece that has broken off or that comes from sth larger: *The builders found fragments of Roman pottery on the site.* ◊ *I heard only a fragment of their conversation.*

fragment² /fræg'ment/ *verb* [I, T] (*formal*) to break or make sth break into small pieces: *The country is becoming increasingly fragmented by civil war.*

fragrance /'freɪgrəns/ *noun* [C, U] a pleasant smell **SYN** perfume, scent

fragrant /'freɪgrənt/ *adj.* having a pleasant smell

frail /freɪl/ *adj.* weak or not healthy: *My aunt is still very frail after her accident.*

frailty /'freɪlti/ *noun* [C, U] (*pl.* -ies) weakness of a person's body or character

frame¹ ⓘ **B1** /freɪm/ *noun* [C] **1** a border of wood, metal, etc. that goes around the outside of a door, picture, window, etc: *a window frame* **2** the basic strong structure of a piece of furniture, building, vehicle, etc. that gives it its shape: *the frame of a bicycle/an aircraft* **3** [usually pl.] a structure made of plastic or metal that holds the LENSES in a pair of glasses **4** [usually sing.] the basic shape of a human or animal body: *He has a large frame but he's not fat.* **5** (**COMPUTING**) one of the separate areas on an internet page that you can SCROLL through (= read by using the mouse to move the text up or down) **IDM** **frame of mind** a particular state or condition of your feelings; your mood: *I'm not in the right frame of mind for a party. I'd prefer to be on my own.*

frame² ⓘ **B1** /freɪm/ *verb* [T] **1** [usually passive] to put a border around sth (especially a picture or photo): *Let's have this photo framed.* **2** [usually passive] (**LAW**) to give false evidence against sb in order to make them seem guilty of a crime: *The man claimed that he had been framed by the police.* **3** (*formal*) to express sth in a particular way: *The question was very carefully framed.* ◊ *He framed the issue as a matter of national security.*

framework ⓘ+ **B2** ⊙ /'freɪmwɜːk/ *noun* [C] **1** the basic structure of sth that gives it shape and strength: *A greenhouse is made of glass panels fixed in a metal framework.* ◊ (*figurative*) *the basic framework of society* ⟳ note at **structure¹** **2** a system of rules or ideas that help you decide what to do: *The plan may be changed but it will provide a framework on which we can build.*

franc /fræŋk/ *noun* [C] (**ECONOMICS**) the unit of money in Switzerland and several other countries

franchise[1] ᵻ+ **C1** /'fræntʃaɪz/ *noun* **1** [C, U] (**BUSINESS**) formal permission to sell a company's goods or services in a particular area; formal permission given by a government to sb who wants to operate a public service as a business: *They have the franchise to sell this product in Cyprus.* ◇ *The company now runs six rail franchises across the UK.* **2** [C] a business or service run under franchise: *Most fast-food restaurants are franchises.* **3** [U] (*formal*) (**POLITICS**) the right to vote in elections **4** [C] (**ARTS AND MEDIA**) a set of films in which the same characters appear in related stories: *It's the most successful film franchise of all time.*

franchise[2] /'fræntʃaɪz/ *verb* [T, usually passive] (**BUSINESS**) to give or sell a FRANCHISE to sb: *Catering has been franchised (out) to a private company.* ◇ *franchised restaurants* ▸ **franchising** *noun* [U]

francium /'frænsiəm/ *noun* [U] (*symb.* Fr) (**CHEMISTRY**) a chemical element. Francium is a RADIOACTIVE metal. ❶ For more information on the periodic table of elements, look at the **Reference Section** of this dictionary.

frank /fræŋk/ *adj.* showing your thoughts and feelings clearly; saying what you mean: *To be perfectly frank with you, I don't think you'll pass your driving test.* ▸ **frankly** ᵻ+ **C1** *adv.*: *Please tell me frankly what you think about my idea.* ▸ **frankness** *noun* [U]

frankfurter /'fræŋkfɜːtə(r)/ (*AmE also* **wiener**) *noun* [C] a type of small SAUSAGE that has been SMOKED

frantic /'fræntɪk/ *adj.* **1** extremely worried or frightened: *frantic cries for help* ◇ *He became frantic when he couldn't find his child.* ◇ *She was frantic with worry about her daughters.* **2** very busy or done in a hurry: *We're not busy at work now, but things get frantic at Christmas.* ◇ *a frantic search for the keys* **SYN** hectic ▸ **frantically** /-kli/ *adv.*

fraternal /frə'tɜːnl/ *adj.* (*formal*) connected with the relationship that exists between brothers; like a brother: *fraternal love/rivalry*

fra‚ternal 'twin *noun* [C] (**BIOLOGY**) either of two children or animals born from the same mother at the same time but not from the same egg ⊃ look at **identical twin**

fraternity /frə'tɜːnəti/ *noun* (*pl.* -ies) **1** [C + sing./pl. verb] a group of people who share the same work or interests: *the medical fraternity* **2** (*also AmE, informal* **frat** /fræt/) [C] (**EDUCATION**) a club for a group of male students at an American college or university ⊃ look at **sorority** **3** [U] (*formal*) the feeling of friendship and support between people in the same group

fraud ᵻ+ **B2** /frɔːd/ *noun* **1** [U, C] (**LAW**) (an act of) cheating sb in order to get money, etc. illegally: *The accountant was sent to prison for fraud.* ◇ *Massive amounts of money are lost every year in credit card frauds.* **2** [C] a person who tricks sb by pretending to be sb else

'fraud squad *noun* [sing. + sing./pl. verb] (*BrE*) (**LAW**) part of a police force that investigates FRAUD: *The fraud squad was seeking to arrest him in relation to a major corruption case.*

fraudulent /'frɔːdʒələnt/ *adj.* (*formal*) done in order to cheat sb: *fraudulent insurance claims*

fraught /frɔːt/ *adj.* **1** ~ **with sth** filled with sth unpleasant: *a situation fraught with danger/difficulty* **2** (*especially BrE*) (used about people) worried and nervous; (used about a situation) very busy so that people become nervous: *Things are usually fraught at work on Mondays.*

fray /freɪ/ *verb* [I, T] **1** if cloth, etc. **frays** or sth **frays** it, some of the THREADS at the end start to come apart: *This shirt is beginning to fray at the cuffs.* ◇ *a frayed rope* **2** if sb's nerves, etc. **FRAY** or become **FRAYED**, they start to get annoyed: *Tempers began to fray towards the end of the match.*

fractional distillation

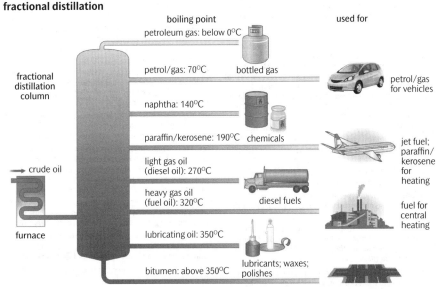

freak¹ /friːk/ *noun* [C] **1** (*informal*) a person who has a very strong interest in sth: *a fitness/computer freak* **SYN** **fanatic** **2** a very unusual and strange event, person, animal, etc: *The other kids think Ally's a freak because she doesn't have a phone.*

freak² /friːk/ *adj.* [only before noun] (used about an event or the weather) very unusual and unexpected: *a freak accident/storm/result*

freak³ /friːk/ *verb* [I, T] ~ **(sb) (out)** (*informal*) if sb **freaks** or sth **freaks** them, they react very strongly to sth that makes them suddenly feel shocked, surprised, frightened, etc: *She freaked out when she heard the news.* ◇ *The film 'Psycho' really freaked me out.*

freckle /ˈfrekl/ *noun* [C, usually pl.] a small brown spot on the skin: *A lot of people with red hair have got freckles.* ⊃ look at **mole** (2) ▸ **freckled** *adj.*

free¹ 🔊 **A1** 🔊 /friː/ *adj.*
• AVAILABLE **1** not busy or being used: *I'm afraid Mr Spencer is not free this afternoon.* ◇ *I don't get much free time.* ◇ *Is this seat free?*
• NO PAYMENT **2** costing nothing: *Admission is free/free of charge.*
• NOT CONTROLLED **3** ~ **(to do sth)** not controlled by the government, rules, etc: *There is free movement of people across the border.* ◇ *free speech/press* ◇ *You're free to do exactly what you want this afternoon.*
• NOT IN PRISON **4** not in prison, in a CAGE, etc.; not held or controlled: *a free man* ◇ *The government set six political prisoners free last year .*
• WITHOUT STH **5** ~ **from/of sth** not having sth dangerous, unpleasant, etc: *free of worries/responsibility* ◇ *free from pain*
IDM **feel free (to do sth)** → **FEEL¹** **for free** without payment: *You can't expect people to work for free.* **free and easy** informal or relaxed: *The atmosphere in our office is very free and easy.* **get, have, etc. a free hand** to get, have, etc. permission to make your own decisions about sth of your own free will because you want to, not because sb forces you

free² 🔊 **B2** /friː/ *verb* [T] **1** ~ **sb (from sth)** to let sb leave a place where they have been kept against their will: *to free a prisoner* **2** ~ **sb/sth (from sth)** to move sb/sth that is caught or fixed on sth: *The emergency services took three hours to free the man from the wreckage of his car.* **SYN** **release¹** **3** ~ **sb/sth of/from sth** to take away sth that is unpleasant from sb: *The medicine freed her from pain for a few hours.* **4** ~ **sb/sth (up) for sth; ~ sb/sth (up) to do sth** to make sth available so that it can be used; to put sb in a position in which they can do sth: *Cuts in defence spending would free up money to spend on education.* ◇ *If I cancel my trip, that will free me to see you on Friday.*

free³ 🔊 **A2** /friː/ *adv.* **1** (*also* **free of ˈcharge**) without payment: *Children under five travel free.* **2** away from or out of a position in which sb/sth is stuck or trapped: *The wagon broke free from the train.*

-free /friː/ *suffix* (in adjectives) without the thing mentioned: *fat-free yogurt* ◇ *tax-free earnings*

ˌfree ˈagent *noun* [C] a person who can do what they want because nobody else has the right to tell them what to do

freebie /ˈfriːbi/ *noun* [C] (*informal*) (**BUSINESS**) something that is given to sb without payment, usually by a company: *He took all the freebies that were on offer.* ◇ *a freebie holiday*

freedom 🔊 **B2** /ˈfriːdəm/ *noun* **1** [U] the state of not being held prisoner or controlled by sb else: *The opposition leader was given his freedom after 25 years.* **2** [C, U] ~ **(of sth); ~ (to do sth)** the right or ability to do or say what you want: *freedom of speech* ◇ *You have the freedom to come and go as you please.* ⊃ look at **liberty 3** [U] ~ **from sth** the state of not being affected by sth unpleasant: *freedom from fear/hunger/pain* **4** [U] **the ~ of sth** permission to use sth without limits: *You can have the freedom of the whole house while we're away.*

ˈfreedom fighter *noun* [C] (**POLITICS**) a person who takes part in a violent campaign to achieve greater political freedom

ˌfree ˈenterprise *noun* [U] (**BUSINESS, ECONOMICS**) the operation of private business without much government control **SYN** **private enterprise**

freegan /ˈfriːɡən/ *noun* [C] a person who only eats food that they can get for free and that otherwise would be thrown out or wasted

freehand /ˈfriːhænd/ *adj.* (**ART**) (used about a drawing) done by hand, without any instruments: *a freehand sketch* ▸ **freehand** *adv.*

freehold /ˈfriːhəʊld/ *noun* [C, U] (**LAW**) the fact of owning a building or piece of land for a period of time that is not limited: *Do you own the freehold of this house?* ▸ **freehold** *adj., adv.*: *a freehold property* ◇ *to buy a house freehold* ⊃ look at **leasehold**

ˌfree ˈkick *noun* [C] (**SPORT**) (in football or rugby) a situation in which a player of one team is allowed to kick the ball without any opposition because a member of the other team has broken a rule

freelance /ˈfriːlɑːns/ *adj., adv.* (**BUSINESS**) earning money by selling your services or work to different organizations rather than being employed by a single company: *a freelance journalist* ◇ *She works freelance.* ▸ **freelance** (*also* **freelancer**) *noun* [C] ▸ **freelance** *verb* [I]

freely 🔊 **B2** /ˈfriːli/ *adv.* **1** in a way that is not controlled or limited: *He is the country's first freely elected president for 40 years.* ◇ *There are no roadworks on the motorway and traffic is flowing freely.* **2** without trying to avoid the truth even though it might be embarrassing; in an honest way: *I freely admit that I made a mistake.*

freeman /ˈfriːmən/ *noun* [C] (*pl.* -men /-mən/) (**HISTORY**) (in past times) a person who is not a slave

ˌfree ˈmarket *noun* [C] (**ECONOMICS**) an economic system in which the price of goods and services is affected by supply and demand rather than controlled by the government

Freemason /ˈfriːmeɪsn/ (*also* **Mason**) *noun* [C] a man who belongs to an international secret society whose members help each other and who recognize each other by secret signs

ˌfree ˈport *noun* [C] (**ECONOMICS**) a port at which tax is not paid on goods that have been brought there for a short time before being sent to a different country

ˌfree ˈradical *noun* [C] (**CHEMISTRY, HEALTH**) an ATOM or a group of ATOMS that has an ELECTRON that is not part of a pair, causing it to take part easily in chemical reactions. Free radicals in the body are thought to be one of the causes of diseases such as cancer.

ˌfree-ˈrange *adj.* (**AGRICULTURE**) connected with a system of farming in which animals can move around freely: *free-range eggs/hens/turkeys* ⊃ look at **battery** (2)

ˌfree ˈrunning *noun* [U] (**SPORT**) the activity of moving through a city by running, jumping and climbing under, around and through things **SYN** **parkour**

ˌfree ˈspeech *noun* [U] the right to express any opinion in public

ˌfree-ˈstanding *adj.* not supported by or attached to anything: *a free-standing sculpture*

freestyle /ˈfriːstaɪl/ *noun* [U] (**SPORT**) **1** a swimming race in which people taking part can use any swimming style they want (usually CRAWL): *the men's 400 m freestyle* **2** (often used as an adjective) a sports competition in which people taking part can use any style that they want: *freestyle skiing*

ˌfree ˈtrade *noun* [U] (**ECONOMICS**, **POLITICS**) a system of international commercial activity in which there are no limits or taxes on imports and exports: *a free trade agreement/area*

ˌfree ˈverse *noun* [U] (**LITERATURE**) poetry without a regular rhythm or RHYME (= words that have the same sound) ➔ look at **blank verse**

freeware /ˈfriːweə(r)/ *noun* [U] (**COMPUTING**) computer software that is offered free for anyone to use ➔ look at **shareware**

freeway /ˈfriːweɪ/ (*AmE*) = MOTORWAY

freeze¹ 🔊 **B1** /friːz/ *verb* (*pt* froze /frəʊz/; *pp* frozen /ˈfrəʊzn/)

• BECOME ICE **1** [I, T] to become hard (and often change into ice) because of extreme cold; to make sth do this: *Water freezes at 0° Celsius.* ◇ *The ground was frozen solid for most of the winter.* ◇ *frozen peas/fish/food* ➔ note at **water¹** ➔ picture at **state¹, water cycle**

• OF WEATHER **2** [I] when **it freezes**, the weather is at or below 0° Celsius: *I think it's going to freeze tonight.*

• BE VERY COLD **3** [I, T] to be very cold or to die from cold: *It was so cold on the mountain that we thought we would freeze to death.* ◇ *Turn the heater up a bit — I'm frozen stiff.*

• STOP MOVING **4** [I] to stop moving suddenly and completely because you are frightened or in danger: *The terrible scream made her freeze with terror.* ◇ *Suddenly the man pulled out a gun and shouted 'Freeze!'* **5** [I] (**COMPUTING**) when a computer screen, etc. **freezes**, you cannot move any of the images, etc. on it, because there is a problem with the system

• PRICES, WAGES, ETC. **6** [T] (**ECONOMICS**) to keep prices, wages etc. at a fixed level for a certain period of time: *Spending on defence has been frozen for one year.* ➔ note at **price¹**

freeze² /friːz/ *noun* [C] **1** [usually sing.] a period of weather when the temperature stays below FREEZING POINT (= 0° Celsius) **2** (**ECONOMICS**) the fixing of wages, prices, etc. at one level for a certain period of time: *a wage/pay/price freeze*

ˈfreeze-dried *adj.* (used about food or drink) frozen and then dried very quickly, so that it can be kept for a long time

freezer /ˈfriːzə(r)/ (*BrE also* deep freeze) *noun* [C] a large piece of electrical equipment in which you can store food for a long time at a temperature below FREEZING POINT so that it stays frozen ➔ look at **fridge**

freezing /ˈfriːzɪŋ/ *adj.* (*informal*) very cold: *Can we turn the central heating on? I'm freezing.* ◇ *Put a coat on, it's absolutely freezing outside.* ➔ note at **cold¹**

ˈfreezing point *noun* (**CHEMISTRY**) **1** (*also* freezing) [U] 0° Celsius, the temperature at which water freezes: *Tonight temperatures will fall well below freezing (point).* **2** [C, usually sing.] the temperature at which a particular liquid freezes

freight /freɪt/ *noun* [U] goods that are carried from one place to another by ship, plane, train or lorry; the system for carrying goods in this way: *Your order will be sent by air freight.* ◇ *a freight train* ▸ freight *verb* [T] ~ *sth* (**to** …): *Donated goods are then freighted to the islands.*

ˈfreight car (*AmE*) = WAGON (1)

freighter /ˈfreɪtə(r)/ *noun* [C] a ship or an aircraft that carries only goods and not passengers

ˌFrench ˈbread /ˌfrentʃ ˈbred/ *noun* [U] white bread in the shape of a long thick stick

ˌFrench ˈdoor /ˌfrentʃ ˈdɔː(r)/ (*AmE*) = FRENCH WINDOW

ˌFrench ˈfry /ˈfrentʃ fraɪ/ (*especially AmE*) = CHIP¹ (1)

ˌFrench ˈhorn /ˌfrentʃ ˈhɔːn/ *noun* [C] (**MUSIC**) a BRASS musical instrument that consists of a long tube curved around in a circle with a wide opening at the end ➔ picture at **instrument**

ˌFrench ˈpress™ /ˌfrentʃ ˈpres/ (*AmE*) = CAFETIÈRE

ˌFrench ˈstick = BAGUETTE

ˌFrench ˈwindow /ˌfrentʃ ˈwɪndəʊ/ (*BrE*) (*AmE* French door) *noun* [C, usually pl.] one of a pair of glass doors that open onto a garden or BALCONY

frenetic /frəˈnetɪk/ *adj.* involving a lot of energy and activity in a way that is not organized: *a scene of frenetic activity* ▸ frenetically /-kli/ *adv.*

frenzied /ˈfrenzid/ *adj.* that is wild and out of control: *a frenzied attack* ◇ *frenzied activity*

frenzy /ˈfrenzi/ *noun* [sing., U] a state of great emotion or activity that is not under control

frequency 🔊 **B2** /ˈfriːkwənsi/ *noun* (*pl.* -ies) **1** [U, C] the number of times sth happens in a particular period: *Fatal accidents have decreased in frequency in recent years.* ◇ *locations with a high frequency of earthquakes* **2** [U] the fact that sth happens often: *The frequency of child deaths from cancer near the nuclear power station is being investigated.* **3** [C, U] (**PHYSICS**) the rate at which a sound wave or radio wave VIBRATES (= moves up and down): *high-frequency/low-frequency sounds* ➔ picture at **wavelength**

frequent¹ 🔊+ **B2** 🅦 /ˈfriːkwənt/ *adj.* happening often: *His visits became less frequent.* **OPP** infrequent

frequent² /friˈkwent/ *verb* [T] (*formal*) to go to a place often: *He spent most of his evenings in Paris frequenting bars and clubs.*

frequently 🔊 **B1** 🅦 /ˈfriːkwəntli/ *adv.* often: *Buses run frequently between the city and the airport.* ◇ *some of the most frequently asked questions about the internet* ➔ look at **FAQ**

fresco /ˈfreskəʊ/ *noun* [C, U] (*pl.* -oes, -os) (**ART**) a picture that is painted on a wall while the PLASTER (= a mixture of powder and water that becomes hard when it is dry) is still wet; the method of painting in this way

fresh 🔊 **A2** /freʃ/ *adj.*

• FOOD **1** (used especially about food) produced or picked very recently; not frozen or in a tin: *fresh bread/fruit/flowers* ➔ look at **stale** (1)

• NEW **2** left somewhere or experienced recently: *fresh blood/footprints* ◇ *Write a few notes while the lecture is still fresh in your mind.* **3** new and different: *They have decided to make a fresh start in a different town.* ◇ *I'm sure he'll have some fresh ideas on the subject.*

• WATER **4** (used about water) containing no salt

• CLEAN **5** pleasantly clean or bright: *Open the window and let some fresh air in.* ◇ *a collection of summer dresses in fresh colours*

• NOT TIRED **6** full of energy: *I'll think about the problem again in the morning when I'm fresh.*

• JUST FINISHED **7** ~ **from/out of** *sth* having just finished sth: *Life isn't easy for a young teacher fresh from university.*

▸ freshness *noun* [U]

IDM break fresh/new ground → GROUND¹

freshen /ˈfreʃn/ *verb* [T] ~ *sth* (**up**) to make sth cleaner or brighter

PHR V freshen up to wash and make yourself clean and tidy

fresher /ˈfreʃə(r)/ noun [C] (BrE, informal) (**EDUCATION**) a student who has just started his or her first term at a university

fresh-ˈfaced adj. having a young, healthy-looking face

freshly /ˈfreʃli/ adv. usually followed by a past participle showing that sth has been made, prepared, etc. recently: *freshly baked bread*

freshman /ˈfreʃmən/ noun [C] (pl. -men /-mən/) (AmE) (**EDUCATION**) a student who is in their first year at college, high school, university, etc.

freshwater /ˈfreʃwɔːtə(r)/ adj. [only before noun] **1** (**BIOLOGY**) living in water that is not the sea and does not contain salt: *freshwater fish* **2** (**GEOGRAPHY**) having water that does not contain salt: *freshwater lakes/pools* ➔ look at **saltwater**

fret¹ /fret/ verb [I] (-tt-) ~ (**about/at/over sth**) to be worried and unhappy (about sth): *I was awake for hours fretting about my exams.*

fret² /fret/ noun [C] (**MUSIC**) one of the bars across the long thin part of a guitar, etc. that show you where to put your fingers to produce a particular sound

fretwork /ˈfretwɜːk/ noun [U] (**ART**) patterns cut into wood, metal, etc. to decorate it; the process of making these patterns

Fri. abbr. (in writing) = FRIDAY

friar /ˈfraɪə(r)/ noun [C] (**RELIGION**) a member of one of several Roman Catholic religious groups of men who in the past travelled around teaching people about Christianity and lived by asking other people for food

fricative /ˈfrɪkətɪv/ noun [C] (**LANGUAGE**) a speech sound made by forcing breath out through a narrow space in the mouth with the lips, teeth or tongue in a particular position, for example /f/ and /ʃ/ in *fee* and *she* ▸ **fricative** adj.

friction /ˈfrɪkʃn/ noun [U] **1** (**PHYSICS**) the rubbing of one surface or thing against another: *You have to put oil in the engine to reduce friction between the moving parts.* **2** ~ (**between A and B**) a lack of friendship or agreement among people who have different opinions about sth: *There is a lot of friction between the older and younger members of staff.*

frictionless /ˈfrɪkʃnləs/ adj. (**PHYSICS**) with no RESISTANCE between a surface or substance and sth that is moving along or through it ➔ picture at **hydraulic**

Friday /ˈfraɪdeɪ, -di/ noun [C, U] (abbr. **Fri.**) the day of the week after Thursday

fridge /frɪdʒ/ (especially BrE) (AmE or formal **refrigerator**) noun [C] a piece of electrical equipment in which food, etc. is kept cold (but not frozen) so that it stays fresh ➔ look at **freezer**

fried² /fraɪd/ adj. (used about food) cooked in hot fat or oil: *a fried egg*

friend¹ /frend/ noun [C] **1** a person that you know and like (not a member of your family), and who likes you: *We're only inviting close friends and relatives to the wedding.* ◇ *Helen's my best friend.* ◇ *A friend of mine told me about this restaurant.* ◇ *One of my friends told me about this restaurant.* ◇ *Dalibor and I are old friends. We were at school together.* ➔ look at **boyfriend, false friend, girlfriend, penfriend 2** (**COMPUTING**) a person who is on your list of contacts on a SOCIAL MEDIA website: *She's got 150 friends on Facebook.* **3** ~ **of/to sth** a person who supports an organization, a charity, etc., especially by giving money; a person who supports a particular idea, etc.

IDM **be/make friends (with sb)** to be/become a friend (of sb): *Tony is rather shy and finds it hard to make friends.*

friend² /frend/ verb [T] to add sb to your list of contacts on a SOCIAL MEDIA website: *He friended me on Facebook.*

friendly¹ /ˈfrendli/ adj. (friendlier; friendliest) **1** ~ (**to/toward(s) sb**) behaving in a kind and open way: *Everyone here has been very friendly towards us.* **OPP** **unfriendly 2** showing that you are kind in a way that makes people feel happy and relaxed: *a friendly smile/atmosphere* **OPP** **unfriendly 3** ~ (**with sb**) treating sb as a friend: *Nick's become quite friendly with the boy next door.* ◇ *Are you on friendly terms with your neighbours?* **4** (also -friendly) (often in compounds) helpful to sb/sth; not harmful to sth: *ozone-friendly sprays* ◇ *This software is extremely user-friendly.* **5** in which people are not arguing or competing in a serious or unpleasant way: *a friendly argument* **6** [only before noun] (BrE) (**SPORT**) not part of an important competition: *I've organized a friendly match against my brother's team.* ▸ **friendliness** noun [U]

friendly² /ˈfrendli/ noun [C] (BrE) (pl. -ies) (**SPORT**) a sports match that is not part of an important competition

friendship /ˈfrendʃɪp/ noun **1** [C] ~ (**with sb**); ~ (**between A and B**) a relationship between people who are friends: *a close/lasting/lifelong friendship* ◇ *I have friendships with people from all over the world.* ◇ *The film will focus on a friendship between two young women.* **2** [U] the state of being friends: *Our relationship is based on friendship, not love.*

frieze /friːz/ noun [C] (**ARCHITECTURE**) a border that goes around the top of a room or building with pictures or CARVINGS (= designs that have been cut in wood or stone) on it

frigate /ˈfrɪɡət/ noun [C] a small fast ship in the NAVY that travels with other ships in order to protect them

fright /fraɪt/ noun [C, U] a sudden feeling of fear or shock: *I hope I didn't give you a fright when I shouted.* ◇ *The child cried out in fright.*

frighten /ˈfraɪtn/ verb [T] to make sb/sth afraid or shocked: *That programme about the rise in the crime rate really frightened me.*

PHR V **frighten sb/sth away/off** to cause a person or an animal to go away by frightening them or it: *Walk quietly so that you don't frighten the birds away.*

frightened /ˈfraɪtnd/ adj. ~ (**of sth/doing sth**); ~ (**to do sth**); ~ (**that**) … full of fear or worry, or afraid of a particular person, thing or situation: *Frightened children were calling for their mothers.* ◇ *When I was young I was frightened of spiders.* ◇ *I'm frightened of being in public places.* ◇ *I was too frightened to speak to her.* ◇ *I was frightened that the plane would crash.*

frightening /ˈfraɪtnɪŋ/ adj. making you feel afraid or shocked: *a frightening experience* ◇ *It's frightening how quickly time passes.* ◇ *It's frightening to think it could happen again.*

frigid /ˈfrɪdʒɪd/ adj. **1** (usually used about a woman) unable to enjoy sex **2** not showing any emotion

frill /frɪl/ noun [C] **1** a decoration for the edge of a dress, shirt, etc. that is made by forming many folds in a narrow piece of cloth **2** [usually pl.] something that is added for decoration but is not necessary: *We just want a plain simple meal — no frills.* ▸ **frilly** adj. (frillier; frilliest): *a frilly dress*

fringe¹ /frɪndʒ/ noun **1** [C, usually sing.] (BrE) (AmE **bangs** /bæŋz/ [pl.]) the part of your hair that is cut so that it hangs over your FOREHEAD: *Your hair looks better with a fringe.* **2** [C] a border for decoration on a piece of clothing, etc. that is made of hanging THREADS **3** [C] (BrE) the outer edge of an area or a group that is a long way from the centre or from what is usual: *Some* people **on the fringes of** the socialist party are opposed to the policy on Europe.

fringe² /frɪndʒ/ verb [T, usually passive] **be fringed (with sth)** to have sth as a border or around the edge: *The lake was fringed with pine trees.*

fringe benefit noun [C, usually pl.] (**BUSINESS**) something that an employer gives you as well as the money you earn

Frisbee™ /ˈfrɪzbi/ noun [C] a light plastic object, shaped like a plate, that is thrown from one player to another in a game

frisk /frɪsk/ verb **1** [T] to pass your hands over sb's body in order to search for hidden weapons, drugs, etc. **2** [I] (used about an animal or a child) to play and jump about happily and with a lot of energy

frisky /ˈfrɪski/ adj. (friskier; friskiest) full of life and wanting to play

fritter /ˈfrɪtə(r)/ verb
PHRV **fritter sth away (on sth)** to waste time or money on things that are not important

frivolity /frɪˈvɒləti/ noun [U, C] silly behaviour (especially when you should be serious)

frivolous /ˈfrɪvələs/ adj. not serious; silly (especially when you should be serious)

frizzy /ˈfrɪzi/ adj. (frizzier; frizziest) (informal) (used about hair) very curly

fro /frəʊ/ adv.
IDM **to and fro** → TO²

frock /frɒk/ noun [C] (especially BrE, old-fashioned) a dress: *a party frock*

frog ʔ **A2** /frɒg/ noun [C] a small animal with smooth skin and long back legs that it uses for jumping. Frogs live in or near water. ⊃ look at **amphibian** ⊃ picture at **animal**

frogman /ˈfrɒgmən/ noun [C] (pl. -men /-mən/) a person whose job is to work under the surface of water wearing special rubber clothes and using breathing equipment: *Police frogmen searched the river.*

frogspawn /ˈfrɒgspɔːn/ noun [U] (**BIOLOGY**) a clear substance that looks like JELLY and contains the eggs of a frog ⊃ picture at **animal**

from ʔ **A1** /frəm, strong form frɒm/ prep. **1** showing the place, direction or time that sth/sb starts or started: *She comes home from work at seven o'clock.* ◇ *a cold wind from the east* ◇ *Water was dripping from the tap.* ◇ *Peter's on holiday from next Friday.* ◇ *The supermarket is open from 8 a.m. till 8 p.m. every day.* **2** showing the person who sent or gave sth: *I borrowed this jacket from my sister.* ◇ *a phone call from my father* **3** showing the origin of sth/sb: *'Where do you come from?' 'I'm from Australia.'* ◇ *cheeses from France and Italy* ◇ *quotations from Shakespeare* **4** showing the material that is used to make sth: *Paper is* **made from** *wood.* ◇ *This sauce is made from cream and wine.* **5** showing the distance between two places: *The house is 5 miles from the town centre.* ◇ *I work not far from here.* **6** showing the range of sth: *Our prices start from £10 a bottle.* ◇ *Tickets cost from £3 to £11.* **7** showing the state of sb/sth before a change: *The time of the meeting has been changed from 7 to 8 o'clock.* ◇ *The article was translated from Russian* **into** *English.* ◇ *Things have gone from bad to worse.* **8** showing that sb/sth is taken away, removed or separated from sb/sth else: *Children don't like being separated from their parents for a long period.* ◇ *8 from 12 leaves 4.* **9** showing sth that you want to avoid: *There was no shelter from the wind.* ◇ *This game will stop you from getting bored.* **10** showing the cause of sth: *People in the camps are suffering from hunger and cold.* **11** showing the reason for making a judgement or forming an opinion: *You can tell quite a lot from a person's handwriting.* **12** showing the difference between two people, places or things: *Can you tell margarine from butter?* ◇ *Is Portuguese very different from Spanish?*
IDM **from … on** starting at a particular time and continuing for ever: *She never spoke to him again from that day on.* ◇ *From now on you must earn your own living.*

frond /frɒnd/ noun [C] (**BIOLOGY**) **1** a long leaf, often divided into parts along the edge, of some plants or trees: *the fronds of a palm tree* **2** a long piece of SEAWEED (= a plant that grows in the sea) that looks like one of these leaves

front¹ ʔ **A1** /frʌnt/ noun
• FORWARD PART/POSITION **1** (usually the front) [C, usually sing.] the side or surface of sth/sb that faces forward: *a dress with buttons down the front* ◇ *the front of a building* (= the front wall) ◇ *a card with flowers* **on the front** ◇ *She slipped on the stairs and spilt coffee all down her front.* **2** the front [sing.] the part of sth that is furthest forward; the area that is just outside of or before sb/sth: *Young children should not travel* **in the front** *of the car.* ◇ *There is a small garden* **at the front** *of the house.* ◇ *I turned round to face the front.*
• AREA OF ACTIVITY **3** [C] a particular area of activity: *Things are difficult* **on the** *domestic/political/economic* **front** *at the moment.* ◇ *Progress has been made* **on all fronts.**
• IN WAR **4** the front [sing.] the line or area where fighting takes place in a war: *to be sent to the front*
• HIDING FEELINGS **5** [C, usually sing.] a way of behaving that hides your true feelings: *His brave words were just a front. He was really feeling very nervous.*
• OF WEATHER **6** [C] (**GEOGRAPHY**) a line or an area where warm air and cold air meet: *A cold front is moving in from the north.* ⊃ picture at **cloud¹**
IDM **back to front** → BACK¹ **in front** further forward than sb/sth: *Some of the children ran on in front.* ◇ *After three laps the Kenyan runner was in front.* **SYN** **ahead** **in front of sb/sth 1** in a position further forward than but close to sb/sth: *The bus stops right in front of our house.* ◇ *He was standing in front of me in the line.* **2** in a position facing sb/sth: *The book was open in front of her on the desk.* ◇ *to perform in front of a big audience* **3** if you do sth in front of sb, you do it when that person is there in the same room or place as you: *I couldn't talk about that in front of my parents.* **up front** (informal) as payment before sth is done: *I want half the money up front and half when the job is finished.*

front² ʔ **A1** /frʌnt/ adj. [only before noun] of or at the front of sth: *the front door/garden/room* ◇ *to sit in the front row* ◇ *front teeth*

frontage /ˈfrʌntɪdʒ/ noun [C, U] (**ARCHITECTURE**) the front of a building, especially when this faces a road or river

frontal /ˈfrʌntl/ adj. [only before noun] from the front: *a frontal attack*

front desk noun [C] the desk inside the entrance of a hotel, an office building, etc. where guests or visitors go when they first arrive ⊃ look at **reception**

frontier /ˈfrʌntɪə(r)/ noun **1** [C] ~ (**between A and B**) the line where one country joins another: *the frontier between France and Spain* **SYN** **border¹** **2** the frontiers [pl.] the limit between what we do and do not know: *Scientific research is constantly* **pushing back the frontiers** *of our knowledge about the world.*

frontline (also **front-line**) /ˈfrʌntlaɪn/ adj. [only before noun] in the most important or dangerous position;

doing essential work that puts you at risk: *frontline troops* ◇ *frontline healthcare workers*

the ˌfront ˈline *noun* [sing.] **1** an area where the enemies are facing each other during a war and where fighting takes place: *Tanks have been deployed all along the front line.* **2** ~ **(of sth)** the most important position in a debate or an area of work: *women in the front line of the movement*

frontman /ˈfrʌntmæn/ *noun* [C] (*pl.* -men /-men/) **1** a person who represents an organization and tries to make its activities seem acceptable to the public, although in fact they may be illegal or dishonest **2** (MUSIC) a man who is the main singer in a pop or rock band

ˌfront of ˈhouse *noun* [U] (*BrE*) (TOURISM) the part of a hotel, restaurant or other business that involves dealing directly with customers: *I cooked and my wife did front of house.* ◇ *a front-of-house manager/worker*

ˌfront-ˈpage *adj.* interesting or important enough to appear on the front page of a newspaper: *front-page news/headlines*

frontwoman /ˈfrʌntwʊmən/ *noun* [C] (*pl.* -women /-wɪmɪn/) (MUSIC) a woman who is the main singer in a pop or rock band

frost¹ /frɒst/ *noun* [U, C] the weather condition when the temperature falls below FREEZING POINT (= 0° Celsius) and a thin layer of ice forms on the ground and other surfaces, especially at night: *There was a hard frost last night.* ◇ *It will be a chilly night with some ground frost.* ⊃ picture at **erosion**

frost² /frɒst/ *verb* [T] (*especially AmE*) = ICE²
PHRV frost over/up to become covered with a thin layer of ice: *The window has frosted over/up.* ⊃ look at **defrost** (1)

frostbite /ˈfrɒstbaɪt/ *noun* [U] (HEALTH) a serious medical condition of the fingers, toes, etc. that is caused by very low temperatures

frosted /ˈfrɒstɪd/ *adj.* (used about glass or a window) with a special surface so you cannot see through it

frosting /ˈfrɒstɪŋ/ (*especially AmE*) = ICING

frosty /ˈfrɒsti/ *adj.* (frostier; frostiest) **1** very cold, with FROST: *a cold and frosty morning* **2** cold and unfriendly: *a frosty welcome*

froth¹ /frɒθ/ *noun* [U] a mass of small white bubbles on the top of a liquid, etc. ▶ frothy *adj.* (frothier; frothiest): *frothy beer* ◇ *a frothy cappuccino*

froth² /frɒθ/ *verb* [I] to have or produce a mass of white bubbles: *The mad dog was frothing at the mouth.*

frown /fraʊn/ *verb* [I] to show you are angry, serious, etc. by making lines appear on your FOREHEAD (= the part of the face above the eyes) ▶ frown *noun* [C, usually sing.]
PHRV frown on/upon sth to think that sth is not good or suitable: *Smoking is very much frowned upon these days.*

froze /frəʊz/ past tense of **freeze¹**

frozen¹ /ˈfrəʊzn/ past participle of **freeze¹**

frozen² ⚡ **B1** /ˈfrəʊzn/ *adj.* **1** (used about food) stored at a very low temperature in order to keep it for a long time: *frozen meat/vegetables* **2** (*informal*) (used about people and parts of the body) very cold: *My feet are frozen!* ◇ *I was frozen stiff.* **SYN** freezing¹ **3** (used about water) with a layer of ice on the surface: *The pond is frozen. Let's go skating.*

fructose /ˈfrʌktəʊs, -təʊz/ *noun* [U] (BIOLOGY, CHEMISTRY) a type of natural sugar that is found in fruit juice and HONEY ⊃ look at **dextrose, glucose, lactose, sucrose**

frugal /ˈfruːgl/ *adj.* **1** using only as much money or food as is necessary: *a frugal existence/life* **OPP** extravagant **2** (used about meals) small, simple and not costing very much **SYN** meagre ▶ frugality /fruːˈgæləti/ *noun* [U] ▶ frugally /ˈfruːgəli/ *adv.*: *to live/eat frugally*

fruit ⚡ **A1** /fruːt/ *noun* **1** [C, U] (BIOLOGY) the part of a plant or tree that contains one or more seeds and that we eat: *Try and eat more fresh fruit and vegetables.* ◇ *Marmalade is made with citrus fruit* (= oranges, lemons, etc.). ◇ *fruit juice* ◇ *Is a tomato a fruit or a vegetable?* **2** [C] (BIOLOGY) the part of any plant in which the seed is formed
IDM bear fruit → BEAR¹ the fruit/fruits of sth the good results of an activity or a situation: *It will be years before we see the fruits of this research.*

ˈfruit fly *noun* [C] a small flying insect that eats plants that have died, especially fruit

fruitful /ˈfruːtfl/ *adj.* producing good results; useful: *fruitful discussions* **SYN** productive

fruition /fruˈɪʃn/ *noun* [U] (*formal*) the time when a plan, etc. starts to be successful: *After months of hard work, our efforts were coming to fruition.*

fruitless /ˈfruːtləs/ *adj.* producing poor or no results; not successful: *a fruitless search*

frustrate /frʌˈstreɪt/ *verb* [T] **1** to cause a person to feel annoyed or impatient because they cannot do or achieve what they want: *It's the lack of money that really frustrates him.* **2** (*formal*) to prevent sb from doing sth or sth from happening: *The rescue work has been frustrated by bad weather conditions.*
▶ frustrated ⚡ **C1** *adj.*: *He felt very frustrated at his lack of progress in learning Chinese.*
▶ frustrating ⚡ **C1** *adj.*

frustration ⚡+ **C1** /frʌˈstreɪʃn/ *noun* [U, C, usually pl.] a feeling of anger because you cannot get what you want; sth that causes you to feel like this: *She felt anger and frustration at no longer being able to see very well.* ◇ *Every job has its frustrations.*

fry¹ ⚡ **B1** /fraɪ/ *verb* [I, T] (frying; fries; *pt, pp* fried) to cook sth or to be cooked in hot fat or oil: *to fry an egg* ◇ *I could smell bacon frying in the kitchen.* ⊃ note at **cook¹, meat**

fry² /fraɪ/ *noun* [C] (*pl.* fries) (*especially AmE*) = CHIP¹ (1): *Would you like ketchup with your fries?*

ˈfrying pan (*AmE also* frypan /ˈfraɪpæn/, skillet) *noun* [C] a flat pan with a long handle that is used for frying food ⊃ note at **cook¹**

ft *abbr.* (in writing) (*pl.* ft) = FOOT¹ (5): *a room 10 ft by 6 ft*

FTP /ˌef tiː ˈpiː/ *abbr.* (COMPUTING) file transfer protocol (a set of rules for sending files from one computer to another on the internet)

the FTSE index™ /ðə ˈfʊtsi ɪndeks/ (*also* the FT index /ðɪ ˌef tiː ˈɪndeks/, the Financial Times index) *noun* [sing.] (FINANCE) a figure that shows the relative prices of shares on the London Stock Exchange

fudge /fʌdʒ/ *noun* [U] a type of soft brown sweet made from sugar, butter and milk

fuel¹ ⚡ **B1** /ˈfjuːəl/ *noun* **1** [U] material that is burned to produce heat or power: *What's the car's fuel consumption?* ◇ *The airline has become an industry leader in fuel efficiency.* ⊃ picture at **fractional distillation** **2** [C] a type of fuel: *I think gas is the best fuel for central heating.* ⊃ look at **alternative fuel, fossil fuel**

fuel² ⚡ **B2** /ˈfjuːəl/ *verb* [T] (-ll-, *AmE* -l-) **1** to make an emotion or an interest stronger: *Her interest in the Spanish language was fuelled by a visit to Spain.* **2** to put fuel into a vehicle **3** to supply sth with material that is burned to produce heat or power: *Uranium is used to fuel nuclear plants.*

'fuel cell *noun* [C] (**CHEMISTRY**, **ENGINEERING**) a device that produces electricity directly from a chemical reaction. Fuel cells are used to supply power to electric vehicles.

fugitive /'fjuːdʒətɪv/ *noun* [C] a person who is running away or escaping (for example from the police) ⇨ look at **refugee**

fugue /fjuːg/ *noun* [C] (**MUSIC**) a piece of music in which one or more tunes are introduced and then repeated in a complicated pattern

fulcrum /'fʊlkrəm, 'fʌl-/ *noun* [C, usually sing.] (**ENGINEERING**, **PHYSICS**) the point on which sth turns or is supported **SYN** **pivot¹** ⇨ picture at **lever**

fulfil ⓘ+ **B2** (*BrE*) (*AmE* **fulfill**) /fʊl'fɪl/ *verb* [T] (-ll-) **1** to make sth that you wish for happen; to achieve a goal: *She finally fulfilled her childhood dream of becoming a doctor.* ◇ *to fulfil your ambition/potential* **2** (*formal*) to do or have everything that you should or that is necessary: *to fulfil a duty/an obligation/a promise/a need* ◇ *The conditions of entry to university in this country are quite difficult to fulfil.* **3** to have a particular role or purpose: *Italy fulfils a very important role within the European Union.* **4** to make sb feel completely happy and satisfied: *I need a job that really fulfils me.* ▸ **fulfilled** *adj.*: *When I had my baby I felt totally fulfilled.* ▸ **fulfilling** *adj.*: *I found working abroad a very fulfilling experience.*

fulfilment (*BrE*) (*AmE* **fulfillment**) /fʊl'fɪlmənt/ *noun* [U] the act of achieving a goal; the feeling of SATISFACTION that you have when you have done sth: *the fulfilment of your dreams/hopes/ambitions* ◇ *to find personal/emotional fulfilment*

full¹ ⓘ **A1** /fʊl/ *adj.*
- WITH NO SPACE **1** holding or containing as much or as many as possible: *The bin needs emptying. It's **full up** (= completely full).* ◇ *a full bottle* ◇ *The bus was full so we had to wait for the next one.* ◇ (*figurative*) *We need a good night's sleep because we've got a full (= busy) day tomorrow.*
- HAVING A LOT **2** ~**of sb/sth** containing a lot of sb/sth: *The room was full of people.* ◇ *His work was full of mistakes.* ◇ *The children are full of energy.*
- WITH FOOD **3** ~(**up**) having had enough to eat and drink: *No more, thank you. I'm full (up).*
- COMPLETE **4** [only before noun] complete; not leaving anything out: *I should like a **full report** on the accident, please.* ◇ ***Full details** of today's TV programmes are on page 20.* ◇ *He took **full responsibility** for what had happened.* ◇ *Please give your **full name and address**.*
- MAXIMUM **5** [only before noun] the highest or greatest possible: *She got **full marks** in her French exam.* ◇ *The train was travelling at **full speed**.*
- TALKING A LOT **6** ~**of sb/sth** thinking or talking a lot about sb/sth/yourself: *When she got back from holiday she was full of everything they had seen.*
- FAT **7** round in shape: *She's got quite a **full figure**.* ◇ *He's quite **full in the face**.*
- CLOTHES **8** (used about clothes) made with plenty of cloth: *a full skirt*
IDM **at full stretch** working as hard as possible **full of beans/life** with a lot of energy and enthusiasm **full of yourself** very proud; thinking only of yourself: *He's **full of himself** (= thinks that he is very important) since he got that new job.* **have your hands full** → **HAND¹** **in full** with nothing missing; completely: *Your money will be refunded in full (= you will get all your money back).* ◇ *Please write your name in full.* **in full swing** at the stage when there is the most activity: *When we arrived the party was already in full swing.* **in full view (of sb/sth)** in a

place where you can easily be seen: *In full view of the guards, he tried to escape over the prison wall.* **to the full** as much as possible: *to enjoy life to the full*

full² /fʊl/ *adv.* ~**in/on (sth)** straight; directly: *John hit him full in the face.* ◇ *The two cars crashed full on.*

'full back *noun* [C] (**SPORT**) (in football, hockey, etc.) a defending player whose position is near the goal

full-'blown *adj.* fully developed: *Her anger turned into a full-blown tantrum.*

full 'board *noun* [U] (*BrE*) (**TOURISM**) a price for a room in a hotel, etc. that includes all meals ⇨ look at **bed and breakfast, half board** ⇨ note at **hotel**

full-fledged /ˌfʊl'fledʒd/ (*especially AmE*) = FULLY FLEDGED

full-'length *adj.* **1** (used about a picture, mirror, etc.) showing a person from head to foot **2** not made shorter: *a full-length film* **3** (used about a dress, skirt, etc.) reaching the feet

full 'moon *noun* [sing.] the moon when it appears as a complete circle ⇨ look at **new moon** ⇨ picture at **moon**

full-'scale *adj.* [only before noun] **1** using every person or thing that is available: *The police have started a full-scale murder investigation.* **2** (used about a plan, drawing, etc.) of the same size as the original object: *a full-scale plan/model*

full 'stop (*BrE*) (*AmE* **period**) *noun* [C] (**LANGUAGE**) a mark (.) that is used to show the end of a sentence

full-'time ⓘ+ **B2** *adj.*, *adv.* (**BUSINESS**) for all the hours in the week when people normally work: *He has a full-time job.* ◇ *He works full-time.* ◇ *We employ 800 full-time staff.* ⇨ look at **part-time** ⇨ note at **job**

fully ⓘ **B2** **W** /'fʊli/ *adv.* completely; to the highest possible degree: *I'm fully aware of the problem.* ◇ *All our engineers are fully trained.*

fully fledged /ˌfʊli'fledʒd/ (*BrE*) (*also* **full-fledged** *AmE*, *BrE*) *adj.* completely developed; with all the qualifications necessary for sth: *the emergence of a fully fledged market economy*

fumble /'fʌmbl/ *verb* [I] to try to find or take hold of sth with your hands in a nervous or careless way: *'It must be here somewhere', she said, fumbling in her pocket for her key.*

fume /fjuːm/ *verb* [I] to be very angry about sth

fumes /fjuːmz/ *noun* [pl.] smoke or gases that smell unpleasant and that can be dangerous to breathe in: *diesel/petrol/exhaust fumes*

fumigate /'fjuːmɪgeɪt/ *verb* [T] to use special chemicals, smoke or gas to destroy the harmful insects or bacteria in a place: *to fumigate a room* ▸ **fumigation** /ˌfjuːmɪ'geɪʃn/ *noun* [U]

fun¹ ⓘ **A1** /fʌn/ *noun* [U] the feeling of enjoying yourself; activities that you enjoy: *We had a lot of fun at the party last night.* ◇ *The party was great fun.* ◇ *Have fun (= enjoy yourself)!* ◇ *It's no fun having to get up at four o'clock every day.*
IDM **(just) for fun/for the fun of it** (just) for AMUSEMENT or pleasure; not seriously: *I don't need English for my work. I'm just learning it for fun.* **in fun** as a joke: *It was said in fun. They didn't mean to upset you.* **make fun of sb/sth** to laugh at sb/sth in an unkind way; to make other people do this: *The older children are always making fun of him because of his accent.* **poke fun at sb/sth** → POKE

fun² ⓘ **A2** /fʌn/ *adj.* that you enjoy: *to have a fun time/day out* ◇ *Brett's a fun guy.*

function¹ 🔊 **B1** ⊙ /'fʌŋkʃn/ noun **1** [C] the purpose or special duty of a person or thing: *The function of the heart is to pump blood through the body.* ◇ *to perform/ fulfil a function* **2** [U] the way in which sth works: *Vitamin E can support healthy brain function.* **3** [C] an important social event, ceremony, etc: *The princess attends hundreds of official functions every year.* **4** [C] (**MATHEMATICS**) a quantity whose value depends on the varying values of others. In the statement $2x=y$, y is a function of x.

function² 🔊 **B2** ⊙ /'fʌŋkʃn/ verb [I] to work correctly; to be in action: *Only one engine was still functioning.* **SYN** **operate**

functional 🔊+ **C1** **W** /'fʌŋkʃənl/ adj. **1** practical and useful rather than attractive: *cheap functional furniture* **2** working; being used: *The system is now fully functional.*

functionality /ˌfʌŋkʃə'næləti/ noun (pl. -ies) (**COMPUTING**) **1** [U, C] the set of functions that a computer or other electronic system can perform: *new software with additional functionality* **2** [U] the quality in sth of being very suitable for the purpose it was designed for **SYN** **practicality** **3** [U] the purpose that sth is designed for

function key noun [C] (**COMPUTING**) one of several keys on a computer, each marked with 'F' and a number, that can be used to perform a particular operation

fund¹ 🔊 **B2** **W** /fʌnd/ noun **1** [C] a sum of money that is collected for a particular purpose: *They contributed £300 to the disaster relief fund.* **2** funds [pl.] (**FINANCE**) money that is available and can be spent: *The hospital is trying to* **raise funds** *for a new kidney machine.*

fund² 🔊 **B2** **W** /fʌnd/ verb [T] to provide a project, school, charity etc. with money: *The entire project is funded by the government.* ➔ look at **finance²**

fundamental 🔊 **B2** ⊙ /ˌfʌndə'mentl/ adj. basic and important; from which everything else develops: *There will be fundamental changes in the way the school is run.* ◇ *There is a fundamental difference between your opinion and mine.* ➔ look at **essential** ▸ **fundamentally** 🔊+ **B2** **W** /-təli/ adv.: *The government's policy has changed fundamentally.*

fundamental force noun [C] (**PHYSICS**) any of the four forces that is a **PROPERTY** (= characteristic) of everything in the universe: *The theory describes the interactions of three of the four fundamental forces: electromagnetism and the strong and weak nuclear forces, but not gravity.*

fundamentalist /ˌfʌndə'mentəlɪst/ noun [C] (**RELIGION**) a person who follows the rules and teachings of their religion very strictly ▸ **fundamentalism** /-lɪzəm/ noun [U] ▸ **fundamentalist** adj.

fundamentals /ˌfʌndə'mentlz/ noun [pl.] basic facts or principles: *the fundamentals of physics*

funding 🔊 **B2** **W** /'fʌndɪŋ/ noun [U] (**FINANCE**) money for a particular purpose; the act of providing money for such a purpose: *There have been large cuts in government funding for scientific research.*

fundraiser /'fʌndreɪzə(r)/ noun [C] (**SOCIAL STUDIES**) a person whose job is to find ways of collecting money for a charity or an organization

fundraising 🔊+ **C1** /'fʌndreɪzɪŋ/ noun [U] (**FINANCE**) the activity of collecting money for a charity or an organization: *An online fundraising campaign has raised over £52 000.* ▸ **fundraise** /-dreɪz/ verb [I] ~ **(for sth)**: *We're looking at new ways to fundraise for the charity.*

funeral 🔊+ **C1** /'fjuːnərəl/ noun [C] a ceremony (usually religious) for burying or burning a dead person

funeral director = UNDERTAKER

funfair /'fʌnfeə(r)/ = FAIR³ (1)

fungicide /'fʌŋɡɪsaɪd, 'fʌndʒɪ-/ noun [C, U] (**AGRICULTURE**) a substance that kills FUNGUS

fungus /'fʌŋɡəs/ noun [C, U] (pl. fungi /'fʌŋɡiː, -ɡaɪ, 'fʌndʒaɪ/, funguses) (**BIOLOGY**) **1** a living thing similar to a plant without leaves, flowers or a green colour, such as a MUSHROOM. Some fungi can be harmful. ➔ look at **toadstool** ➔ picture at **food chain** **2** a substance like a wet powder that grows on old wood or food, walls, etc. ➔ look at **mould¹** (2) ▸ **fungal** /'fʌŋɡl/ adj.: *a fungal disease/infection/growth*

funky /'fʌŋki/ adj. (funkier; funkiest) (*informal*) fashionable and unusual: *She wears really funky clothes.*

fun-loving adj. (used about people) liking to enjoy themselves

funnel /'fʌnl/ noun [C] **1** an object that is wide at the top and narrow at the bottom, used for pouring liquid, powder, etc. into a small opening ➔ picture at **filtration, laboratory** **2** the metal pipe that takes smoke or STEAM out of a ship, an engine, etc.

funnily /'fʌnəli/ adv. in a strange or unusual way: *She's walking very funnily.* **IDM** **funnily enough** used for expressing surprise at sth strange that has happened: *Funnily enough, my parents weren't at all cross about it.*

funny 🔊 **A1** /'fʌni/ adj. (funnier; funniest) **1** that makes you smile or laugh: *a funny story* ◇ *He's an extremely funny person.* ◇ *That's the funniest thing I've heard in ages!* **2** strange or unusual; difficult to explain or understand: *Oh dear, the engine is making a funny noise.* ◇ *It's funny that they didn't phone to let us know they couldn't come.* ◇ ***That's funny*** — *he was here a moment ago and now he's gone.* ◇ (*informal*) *Can I sit down for a minute? I feel a bit* ***funny*** (= a bit ill). **SYN** **peculiar**

funny bone noun [C, usually sing.] (*informal*) the part of the ELBOW (= place where the arm bends) that hurts very much if you hit it against sth

fur 🔊 **B1** /fɜː(r)/ noun **1** [U] the soft thick hair that covers the bodies of some animals: *Sea otters rely on thick fur to keep warm.* **2** [U, C] the skin and hair of an animal that is used for making clothes, etc.; a piece of clothing that is made from this: *a fur coat*

furious 🔊+ **B2** /'fjʊəriəs/ adj. **1** ~ **(with sb)**; ~ **(at sth)** very angry: *She was furious with him for losing the car keys.* ◇ *He was furious at having to catch the train home.* ➔ noun **fury** **2** very strong; violent: *A furious row had broken out over the closure of the school.* ▸ **furiously** adv. **IDM** **fast and furious** → FAST¹

furnace /'fɜːnɪs/ noun [C] a large, very hot fire, surrounded on all sides by walls, that is used for melting metal, burning rubbish, etc. ➔ picture at **fractional distillation**

furnish /'fɜːnɪʃ/ verb [T] to put furniture in a room, house, etc: *The room was comfortably furnished.* ▸ **furnished** adj.: *She's renting a furnished room in Birmingham.*

furnishings /'fɜːnɪʃɪŋz/ noun [pl.] the furniture, carpets, curtains, etc. in a room, house, etc.

furniture 🔊 **A2** /'fɜːnɪtʃə(r)/ noun [U] the things that can be moved, for example tables, chairs, beds, etc. in a room, house or office: *modern/antique/second-hand furniture* ◇ *garden/office furniture*

furrow /ˈfʌrəʊ/ *noun* [C] **1** (**AGRICULTURE**) a line in a field that is made for planting seeds in by a PLOUGH (= a farming machine that turns the earth) **2** a deep line in the skin on a person's face, especially on the FOREHEAD ⊃ look at **wrinkle**[1]

furry /ˈfɜːri/ *adj.* (**furrier**; **furriest**) having fur: *a small furry animal*

further[1] ⚡ **A2** ⓦ /ˈfɜːðə(r)/ *adj.* more; additional: *Are there **any further questions**?* ◇ *Please let us know if you require any further information.* ◇ *The museum is closed **until further notice** (= until another announcement is made).*

further[2] **B1** /ˈfɜːðə(r)/ *adv.* **1** (*also* **farther**) (comparative of *far*) at or to a greater distance: *It's not safe to go any further.* ◇ *I can't remember any further back than 1970.* **2** to a greater degree: *Can I have time to consider the matter further?* ◇ *She was getting further and further into debt.*

further[3] /ˈfɜːðə(r)/ *verb* [T] (*formal*) to help sth to develop or be successful: *to further the cause of peace*

further eduˈcation *noun* [U] (*abbr.* FE) (*BrE*) (**EDUCATION**) education for people who have left school (but not at a university) ⊃ look at **higher education**

furthermore ⚡ **B2** ⓦ /ˌfɜːðəˈmɔː(r)/ *adv.* (*formal*) also; in addition: *We are donating £6 million to the disaster fund. Furthermore, we shall send medical supplies immediately.*

furthest /ˈfɜːðɪst/ = FARTHEST

furtive /ˈfɜːtɪv/ *adj.* secret; acting as though you are trying to hide sth because you feel guilty ▸ **furtively** *adv.*

fury /ˈfjʊəri/ *noun* [U] very great anger: *He was speechless with fury.* ⊃ adjective **furious**

fuse[1] /fjuːz/ *noun* [C] **1** a small piece of wire in an electrical system, machine, etc. that melts and breaks if there is too much power. This stops the flow of electricity and prevents fire or damage: *A fuse has blown — that's why the house is in darkness.* ◇ *That plug needs a 15-amp fuse.* ⊃ picture at **light bulb**, **plug**[1] **2** a piece of rope, string, etc. or a device that is used to make a bomb, etc. explode at a particular time

fuse[2] /fjuːz/ *verb* [I, T] **1** ~ (**together**); ~ (**sth**) (**into sth**) (used about two things) to join together to become one; to make two things do this: *As they heal, the bones will fuse together.* ◇ *The two companies have been fused into one large organization.* **2** to stop working because a FUSE has melted; to make a piece of electrical equipment do this: *The lights have fused.* ◇ *I've fused the lights.*

fuselage /ˈfjuːzəlɑːʒ/ *noun* [C] the main part of a plane (not the engines, wings or tail) ⊃ picture at **airliner**

fusion /ˈfjuːʒn/ *noun* **1** [U, sing.] the process or the result of joining different things together to form one: *the fusion of two political systems* **2** (*also* **nuclear fusion**) [U] (**PHYSICS**) the action or process of combining the NUCLEI (= central parts) of ATOMS to form a heavier NUCLEUS, with energy being created ⊃ look at **fission** (1)

fuss[1] /fʌs/ *noun* [sing., U] ~ (**over/about sth**) a time when people behave in an excited, nervous or angry way, especially about sth unimportant: *The waiter didn't **make a fuss** when I spilt my drink.* ◇ *What's all the fuss about?* ◇ *He does what he's told **without** any fuss.* **IDM** **make/kick up a fuss** (**about/over sth**) to complain strongly **make a fuss of sb** (*BrE*) (*also* **make a fuss over sb** *especially in AmE*) to pay a lot of attention to sb: *My grandmother used to make a big fuss of me when she visited.*

fuss[2] /fʌs/ *verb* [I] **1** to be worried or excited about small things: *Stop fussing. We're not going to be late.* **2** ~ (**over sb/sth**) to pay too much attention to sb/sth: *Stop fussing over all the details.* **IDM** **not be fussed** (**about sb/sth**) (*BrE*, *informal*) to not care very much: *'Where do you want to go for lunch?' 'I'm not fussed.'*

fussy /ˈfʌsi/ *adj.* (**fussier**; **fussiest**) **1** ~ (**about sth**) (used about people) giving too much attention to small details and therefore difficult to please: *He is very fussy about food* (= there are many things which he does not eat). ⊃ look at **particular** (4), **picky** **2** having too much detail or decoration: *I don't like that pattern. It's too fussy.*

futile /ˈfjuːtaɪl/ *adj.* (used about an action) having no chance of success: *They made a last futile attempt to make him change his mind.* ▸ **futility** /fjuːˈtɪləti/ *noun* [U]

futon /ˈfuːtɒn/ *noun* [C] a Japanese MATTRESS (= the soft part of a bed), often on a wooden frame, that can be used for sitting on or rolled out to make a bed

future ⚡ **A1** ⓦ /ˈfjuːtʃə(r)/ *noun* **1 the future** [sing.] the time that will come after the present: *Who knows what will happen **in the future**?* ◇ *in the near/distant future* (= soon/not soon) **2** [C] what will happen to sb/sth in the time after the present: *Our children's futures depend on a good education.* ◇ *The company's future does not look very hopeful.* **3** [sing., U] the possibility of being successful: *I could see no future in this country so I left to work abroad.* **4 futures** [pl.] (**BUSINESS**, **FINANCE**) goods or shares that are bought at agreed prices but that will be delivered and paid for at a later time: *oil futures* ◇ *the futures market* **5 the future** [sing.] (**GRAMMAR**) = FUTURE TENSE ▸ **future** ⚡ **A2** ⓦ *adj.* [only before noun]: *She met her future husband when she was still at school.* ◇ *You can keep that book **for future reference** (= to look at again later).* **IDM** **in future** from now on: *Please try to be more careful in future.*

the ˌfuture ˈperfect (*also* **the** ˌfuture ˈperfect tense) *noun* [sing.] (**GRAMMAR**) the form of a verb that expresses an action in the future that will be finished before the time mentioned. The future perfect is formed with the future tense of *have* and the past participle of the verb: *'We'll have been married for ten years next month' is **in the future perfect**.*

ˈfuture-proof[1] *adj.* designed to continue working or to be effective after changes that may happen in the future: *future-proof website design*

ˈfuture-proof[2] *verb* [T] to design sth so that it will continue working or be effective after changes that may happen in the future: *The firm claims that it future-proofs its software.*

the ˌfuture ˈtense (*also* **the future** /ðə ˈfjuːtʃə(r)/) *noun* [sing.] (**GRAMMAR**) the form of a verb that expresses what will happen after the present

Futurism /ˈfjuːtʃərɪzəm/ *noun* [U] (**ARTS AND MEDIA**) a movement in art and literature in the 1920s and 30s that did not try to show realistic figures and scenes but aimed to express confidence in the modern world, particularly in modern machines ▸ **Futurist** /-rɪst/ *noun* [C], *adj.*: *Futurist poets*

futuristic /ˌfjuːtʃəˈrɪstɪk/ *adj.* **1** extremely modern and unusual in appearance: *futuristic design* **2** (**LITERATURE**) imagining what the future will be like: *a futuristic novel*

fuzzy /ˈfʌzi/ *adj.* (**fuzzier; fuzziest**) not clear: *The photo was a bit fuzzy but I could just make out my mother in it.*

FYI /ˌef waɪ ˈaɪ/ *abbr.* **for your information** (written on documents that are sent to sb who needs to know the information in them but does not need to deal with them)

G g

G /dʒiː/ *noun* [C, U] (*pl.* **G's**) **1** (*also* **g**, *pl.* **g's**) the seventh letter of the English alphabet: *'Girl' begins with (a) 'G'.* **2** (**MUSIC**) the fifth note in the SCALE of C MAJOR

g *abbr.* (in writing) **1** (*pl.* **g**) = GRAM **2** GRAVITY or a measurement of the force with which sth moves faster through space because of GRAVITY: *g forces*

gable /ˈɡeɪbl/ *noun* [C] (**ARCHITECTURE**) the pointed part at the top of an outside end wall of a house between the two sloping sides of the roof

gadget /ˈɡædʒɪt/ *noun* [C] a small device, tool or machine that does sth useful

gadolinium /ˌɡædəˈlɪniəm/ *noun* [U] (*symb.* **Gd**) (**CHEMISTRY**) a chemical element. Gadolinium is a soft silver-white metal. ❶ For more information on the periodic table of elements, look at the **Reference Section** of this dictionary.

Gaelic *noun* [U] (**LANGUAGE**) **1** /ˈɡælɪk, ˈɡeɪl-/ the Celtic language of Scotland **2** /ˈɡeɪlɪk/ (*also* **Irish Gaelic**) the Celtic language of Ireland ▸ **Gaelic** *adj.*

gaffer /ˈɡæfə(r)/ *noun* [C] (**ARTS AND MEDIA**) the person who is in charge of the electrical work and the lights when a film or TV programme is being made

gag¹ /ɡæɡ/ *noun* [C] **1** a piece of cloth, etc. that is put in or over sb's mouth in order to stop them from talking **2** (*informal*) a joke

gag² /ɡæɡ/ *verb* [T] (-gg-) to put a GAG in or over sb's mouth

gage /ɡeɪdʒ/ (*AmE*) = GAUGE¹

gaiety /ˈɡeɪəti/ *noun* [U] (*old-fashioned*) a feeling of happiness and fun

gaily /ˈɡeɪli/ *adv.* **1** happily; cheerfully **2** in a bright and attractive way **3** without thinking or caring about the effect of your actions on other people: *She gaily announced that she was leaving.*

gain¹ ⓘ B2 ❍ /ɡeɪn/ *verb* **1** [T] to obtain or win sth, especially sth that you need or want: *They managed to gain access to secret information.* ◇ *The country gained its independence ten years ago.* **2** [T] to gradually get more of sth: *The train was gaining speed.* ◇ *to gain weight/confidence* OPP **lose** ⊃ note at **trend¹** **3** [I, T] ~ (**sth**) (**by/from sth/doing sth**) to get an advantage: *I've got nothing to gain by staying in this job.*
IDM **gain ground** to make progress; to become stronger or more popular
PHR V **gain in sth** to gradually get more of sth: *He's gained in confidence in the past year.* **gain on sb/sth** to get closer to sb/sth that you are trying to catch: *I saw the other runners were gaining on me so I increased my pace.*

gain² ⓘ B2 ❍ /ɡeɪn/ *noun* [C, U] an increase, improvement or advantage in sth: *We hope to make a gain (= more money) when we sell our house.* ◇ *a gain in weight of one kilo* OPP **loss**

gait /ɡeɪt/ *noun* [usually sing.] the way that sb/sth walks

gal. *abbr.* (in writing) (*pl.* **gal.**) = GALLON

gala /ˈɡɑːlə/ *noun* [C] a special social or sports event: *a swimming gala*

galactic /ɡəˈlæktɪk/ *adj.* (**ASTRONOMY**) relating to a GALAXY: *A galactic year is the time the galaxy takes to rotate once completely.*

galaxy /ˈɡæləksi/ *noun* (*pl.* -ies) (**ASTRONOMY**) **1** [C] any of the large systems of stars, etc. in outer space **2** (*also* **the Galaxy**) [sing.] the system of stars that contains our sun and its planets, seen as a bright band in the night sky ⊃ look at **Milky Way**

gale /ɡeɪl/ *noun* [C] a very strong wind: *Several trees blew down in the gale.* ◇ *Coastal areas are due to experience gale-force winds.*

gall¹ /ɡɔːl/ *noun* **1** [U] rude behaviour showing a lack of respect that is surprising because the person doing it is not embarrassed: *He arrived two hours late, then had the gall to complain about the food.* **2** [U] (*formal*) a bitter feeling full of hate SYN **resentment** **3** [C] (**BIOLOGY**) a SWELLING (= an area that is larger and rounder than normal) on plants and trees caused by insects, disease, etc. **4** [U] (*old-fashioned*) = BILE (2)

gall² /ɡɔːl/ *verb* [T] to make sb feel upset and angry, especially because sth is unfair: *It galls me to have to apologize to her.*

gallant /ˈɡælənt/ *adj.* (*formal*) **1** (*old-fashioned*) showing courage in a difficult situation: *gallant men/soldiers/ heroes* SYN **brave¹** **2** (used about men) polite to and showing respect for women

gallantry /ˈɡæləntri/ *noun* [C, U] (*pl.* -ies) (*formal*) **1** courage, especially in battle **2** polite behaviour towards women by men

gall bladder *noun* [C] (**ANATOMY**) an organ that is connected to the LIVER (= the organ that cleans the blood) where BILE (= a green-brown liquid that helps the body to deal with fats) is stored ⊃ picture at **digestive system**

gallery ⓘ A2 /ˈɡæləri/ *noun* [C] (*pl.* -ies) **1** (**ART**) a building or room where works of art are shown to the public: *an art gallery* ⊃ note at **art 2** (**ART**) a small private shop where you can see and buy works of art **3** an upstairs area at the back or sides of a large public hall or theatre where people can sit **4** (**ARTS AND MEDIA**) the highest level in a theatre where the cheapest seats are

galley /ˈɡæli/ *noun* [C] **1** (**HISTORY**) a long flat ship with sails, especially one used by the ancient Greeks or Romans in war, which was usually ROWED by criminals or slaves **2** the kitchen on a ship or plane

gallium /ˈɡæliəm/ *noun* [U] (*symb.* **Ga**) (**CHEMISTRY**) a chemical element. Gallium is a soft silver-white metal. ❶ For more information on the periodic table of elements, look at the **Reference Section** of this dictionary.

gallon ⓘ+ C1 /ˈɡælən/ *noun* [C] (*abbr.* **gal.**) a measure of liquid that is equal to about 4.5 LITRES in the UK and Canada, and about 3.8 LITRES in the US ⊃ note at **measure²**

gallop /ˈɡæləp/ *verb* [I] (used about a horse or a rider) to go at the fastest speed ⊃ look at **canter, trot¹** (1) ▸ **gallop** *noun* [sing.]

gallows /ˈɡæləʊz/ *noun* [C] (*pl.* **gallows**) (**HISTORY**) a wooden frame used for killing people by hanging

gallstone /ˈɡɔːlstəʊn/ *noun* [C] (**HEALTH**) a hard painful mass that can form in the GALL BLADDER

galore /ɡəˈlɔː(r)/ *adv.* (after a noun) (*informal*) in large numbers or amounts: *There will be prizes galore at our children's party on Saturday.*

galvanize (*BrE also* -ise) /ˈɡælvənaɪz/ *verb* [T] **1** ~ **sb (into sth/doing sth)** to make sb take action by shocking them or by making them excited: *The urgency of his voice galvanized them into action.* **2** to cover metal with ZINC (= a silver-grey metal) in order to protect it from being damaged by water

gamble¹ /ˈɡæmbl/ *verb* [I, T] ~ **(sth) (on sth)** to bet money on the result of a card game, horse race, etc: *She gambled all her money on the last race.* **SYN bet¹** ▸ **gambler** /-blə(r)/ *noun* [C]: *He's a compulsive gambler.*
PHRV gamble on sth/doing sth to act in the hope that sth will happen although it may not: *I wouldn't gamble on the weather staying fine.*

gamble² /ˈɡæmbl/ *noun* [C] something you do that is a risk: *Setting up this business was a bit of a gamble, but it paid off* (= was successful) *in the end.*

gambling ⓘ+ **C1** /ˈɡæmblɪŋ/ *noun* [U] the activity of playing games of chance for money and of betting on horses, etc: *heavy gambling debts* ◇ *These new regulations will tackle the issue of online gambling.*

game¹ ⓘ **A1** /ɡeɪm/ *noun* **1** [C] ~ **(of sth)** a form of play or sport with rules; a time when you play it: *Shall we play a game?* ◇ *Let's have a game of chess.* ◇ *a game of football/rugby/tennis* ◇ *'Monopoly' is a very popular board game.* ◇ *Tonight's game is between Holland and Italy.* ◇ *The game ended in a draw.* **2** [C] (in sports such as tennis) a section of a match that forms a unit in scoring **3** [C] an activity that you do to have fun: *Some children were playing a game of hide-and-seek.* **4** [C] (**SPORT**) how well sb plays a sport: *My new racket has really improved my game.* **5** games [pl.] (**SPORT**) an important sports competition: *Where were the last Olympic Games held?* **6** [C] (*informal*) a secret plan or trick: *Stop playing games with me and tell me where you've hidden my bag.* **7** [U] wild animals or birds that are killed for sport or food: *big game* (= lions, TIGERS, etc.) ⊃ picture at **animal**
IDM give the game away to tell a person sth that you are trying to keep secret: *It was the expression on her face that gave the game away.*

game² /ɡeɪm/ *adj.* (used about a person) ready to try sth new, unusual, difficult, etc: *I've never been sailing before but I'm game to try.*

ˈgame changer *noun* [C] an idea or event that completely changes the way a situation develops: *The election debate tonight could be a game-changer.*

gamekeeper /ˈɡeɪmkiːpə(r)/ *noun* [C] a person who is responsible for the birds and animals that are kept on private land for people to hunt

gamelan /ˈɡæməlæn/ *noun* [C] (**MUSIC**) a traditional group of Indonesian musicians, playing instruments such as XYLOPHONES and GONGS

ˈgame plan *noun* [C] a plan for success in the future, especially in sport, politics or business: *The team stuck rigidly to their game plan.*

gameplay /ˈɡeɪmpleɪ/ *noun* [U] (**COMPUTING**) the features of a computer game, such as its story or the way it is played, rather than the images or sounds it uses

gamer /ˈɡeɪmə(r)/ *noun* [C] (*informal*) a person who plays computer games

ˈgames console *noun* [C] an electronic device for playing computer games

ˈgame show *noun* [C] (**ARTS AND MEDIA**) a TV programme in which people play games or answer questions to win prizes ⊃ look at **quiz¹**

gamete /ˈɡæmiːt/ *noun* [C] (**BIOLOGY**) a male or female cell that joins with a cell of the opposite sex to form a ZYGOTE (= a single cell that develops into a person, an animal or a plant)

gaming ⓘ+ **B2** /ˈɡeɪmɪŋ/ *noun* [U] playing computer games

gamma /ˈɡæmə/ *noun* [C] (**LANGUAGE**) the third letter of the Greek alphabet (Γ, γ)

ˌgamma radiˈation *noun* [U] (*also* ˌgamma rays [pl.]) (**PHYSICS**) RAYS that are sent out by some RADIOACTIVE substances ⊃ look at **alpha radiation** ⊃ picture at **wavelength**

gammon /ˈɡæmən/ *noun* [U] (*BrE*) meat from the back leg or side of a pig that has been CURED (= treated with salt or smoke to make it last for a long time). Gammon is usually served in thick slices. ⊃ look at **bacon, ham, pork**

gander /ˈɡændə(r)/ *noun* [C] a male GOOSE (= a bird like a large duck)

gang¹ ⓘ **B2** /ɡæŋ/ *noun* [C + sing./pl. verb] **1** an organized group of criminals **2** a group of young people who cause trouble, fight other groups, etc: *The woman was robbed by a gang of youths.* ◇ *gang warfare/violence* ◇ *He was the leader of a notorious Chicago street gang.* **3** (*informal*) a group of friends who meet regularly

gang² /ɡæŋ/ *verb*
PHRV gang up on sb (*informal*) to join together with other people in order to act against sb: *He's upset because he says the other kids are ganging up on him.*

gangrene /ˈɡæŋɡriːn/ *noun* [U] (**HEALTH**) the DECAY (= a process of being destroyed) of a part of the body because the blood supply to it has been stopped as a result of disease or injury ▸ **gangrenous** /-ɡrɪnəs/ *adj.*

gangster /ˈɡæŋstə(r)/ *noun* [C] a member of a group of criminals

gangway /ˈɡæŋweɪ/ *noun* [C] **1** a passage between rows of seats in a cinema, an aircraft, etc. ⊃ look at **aisle 2** a bridge that people use for getting on or off a ship

gantry /ˈɡæntri/ *noun* [C] (*pl.* -ies) a tall metal frame like a bridge that is used to support signs over a road, lights over a stage, etc.

gaol, gaoler (*BrE*) = JAIL¹, JAILER

gap ⓘ **A2 W** /ɡæp/ *noun* [C] **1** ~ **(in/between sth)** an empty space in sth or between two things: *The sheep got out through a gap in the fence.* **2** a period of time when sth stops, or between two events: *I returned to teaching after a gap of about five years.* ◇ *a gap in the conversation* **3** a difference between people or their ideas: *The gap between the rich and the poor is getting wider.* **4** a part of sth that is missing: *In this exercise you have to fill (in) the gaps in the sentences.* ◇ *I think our new product should fill a gap in the market.*
IDM bridge the gap (between A and B) → BRIDGE²

gape /ɡeɪp/ *verb* [I] **1** ~ **(at sb/sth)** to look at sb/sth for a long time with your mouth open because you are surprised, shocked, etc: *Michael just stood there gaping at his father.* ◇ *We gaped in astonishment when we saw what Amy was wearing.* **2** ~ **(open)** to be or become wide open: *a gaping hole/wound* ◇ *Her mouth gaped open at my words.*

ˈgap year *noun* [C] (*BrE*) (**EDUCATION**) a year that a young person spends working and/or travelling, often between leaving school and starting university: *I'm planning to take a gap year and go backpacking in India.*

garage ⓘ **B1** /ˈɡærɑːʒ, -rɑːdʒ, -rɪdʒ/ *noun* **1** [C] a small building where a car, etc. is kept: *The house has a double garage* (= with space for two cars). **2** [C] a place where vehicles are repaired and/or petrol is sold: *a garage mechanic* ⊃ look at **petrol station 3** [U] (**MUSIC**) a type of fast electronic dance music: *His music is a mix of grime and garage.*

garbage /'gɑːbɪdʒ/ (*especially AmE*) = RUBBISH

'**garbage can** (*AmE*) = DUSTBIN

garbanzo /gɑːˈbænzəʊ/ (*pl.* -os) (*also* gar'banzo bean) (*AmE*) = CHICKPEA

garbled /'gɑːbld/ *adj.* (used about a message, story, etc.) difficult to understand because it is not clear

garden¹ 🔊 **A1** /'gɑːdn/ *noun* **1** (*BrE*) (*AmE* yard) [C] a piece of land next to a house where flowers and vegetables can be grown, usually with a LAWN (= an area of grass): *the back/front garden* ◇ *garden flowers* ◇ *garden chairs* (= for using in the garden) ◇ *Let's have lunch in the garden.* **2 gardens** [pl.] a public park: *the Botanical Gardens*

garden² /'gɑːdn/ *verb* [I] to work in a garden: *She's been gardening all afternoon.*

'**garden centre** (*BrE*) (*AmE* garden center) *noun* [C] a place where plants, seeds, garden equipment, etc. are sold

gardener /'gɑːdnə(r)/ *noun* [C] a person who works in a garden as a job or for pleasure

gardening equipment

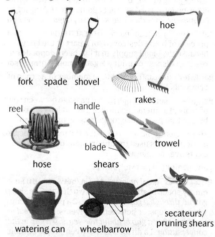

fork   spade   shovel   hoe   rakes   reel   handle   blade   trowel   hose   shears   watering can   wheelbarrow   secateurs/pruning shears

gardening /'gɑːdnɪŋ/ *noun* [U] the activity of working in a garden: *I'm going to do some gardening this afternoon.* ◇ *gardening tools/gloves*

'**garden party** *noun* [C] a formal social event that takes place outside, usually in a large garden in summer

gargle /'gɑːgl/ *verb* [I] to wash inside your mouth and throat using a liquid that you then SPIT out

gargoyle /'gɑːgɔɪl/ *noun* [C] (**ARCHITECTURE**) an ugly figure of a person or an animal that is made of stone and through which water is carried away from the roof of a building, especially a church

garish /'geərɪʃ/ *adj.* too bright or decorated and therefore unpleasant **SYN** **gaudy**

garlic /'gɑːlɪk/ *noun* [U] a plant of the onion family with a strong taste and smell that is used in cooking: *Chop two cloves of garlic and fry in oil.*

garment /'gɑːmənt/ *noun* [C] (*formal*) one piece of clothing ⊃ look at **clothes**

garnish /'gɑːnɪʃ/ *verb* [T] to decorate a dish of food with a small amount of another food ▶ **garnish** *noun* [C, U]

garrison /'gærɪsn/ *noun* [C + sing./pl. verb] a group of soldiers who are living in and guarding a town or building, or the building they live in

gas¹ 🔊 **A2** /gæs/ *noun* (*pl.* gases, gasses) **1** [C, U] (**CHEMISTRY**) a substance like air that is not a solid or a liquid: *Hydrogen and oxygen are gases.* ⊃ picture at **aerosol, energy, nitrogen cycle, state¹, water cycle** **2** [U] a particular type of gas or mixture of gases that is used for heating or cooking: *a gas cooker* ⊃ picture at **fractional distillation, generator** **3** [U] (*AmE*) = PETROL **4** [U] (*AmE*) = WIND¹ (2)

gas² /gæs/ *verb* [T] (-ss-) to poison or kill sb with gas

'**gas chamber** *noun* [C] a room that can be filled with poisonous gas in order to kill animals or people

gaseous /'gæsiəs, 'geɪs-/ *adj.* (**CHEMISTRY**) like gas or containing gas

gash /gæʃ/ *noun* [C] a long deep cut or wound: *He had a nasty gash in his arm.* ▶ **gash** *verb* [T]

gasket /'gæskɪt/ *noun* [C] a flat piece of rubber, etc. placed between two metal surfaces in a pipe or an engine to prevent STEAM, gas or oil from escaping: *The engine had blown a gasket* (= had allowed STEAM, etc. to escape). ◇ (*figurative*) *He blew a gasket* (= became very angry) *at the news.*

'**gas mask** *noun* [C] a piece of equipment that is worn over the face to protect against poisonous gas

'**gas meter** *noun* [C] an instrument that measures the amount of gas that you use in your home

gasoline /'gæsəliːn, ˌgæsəˈliːn/ (*also* gas) (*AmE*) = PETROL

gasp /gɑːsp/ *verb* [I] **1 ~ (at sth)** to take a sudden loud breath with your mouth open, usually because you are surprised or in pain **2** to have difficulty breathing: *I pulled the boy out of the pool and he lay there gasping for breath.* ▶ **gasp** *noun* [C]: *to give a gasp of surprise/pain/horror*

'**gas station** (*AmE*) = PETROL STATION

gastric /'gæstrɪk/ *adj.* [only before noun] (**ANATOMY**) relating to the stomach: *a gastric ulcer* ◇ *gastric juices* (= the ACIDS in your stomach that deal with the food you eat)

gastritis /gæˈstraɪtɪs/ *noun* [U] (**HEALTH**) an illness in which the inside of the stomach becomes larger than normal and painful

gastroenteritis /ˌgæstrəʊˌentəˈraɪtɪs/ *noun* [U] (**HEALTH**) an illness in which the inside of the stomach and the INTESTINE (= the tube that carries food out of the stomach) become larger than normal and painful

gastroenterology /ˌgæstrəʊˌentəˈrɒlədʒi/ *noun* [U] (**MEDICINE**) the study and treatment of diseases of the stomach and INTESTINES

gastrointestinal /ˌgæstrəʊɪnˈtestɪnl, -inteˈstaɪ-/ *adj.* (**HEALTH**) of or connected with the stomach and INTESTINES

gastronomic /ˌgæstrəˈnɒmɪk/ *adj.* [only before noun] connected with good food

gastropod /'gæstrəpɒd/ *noun* [C] (**BIOLOGY**) any of a CLASS of animals with a soft body and usually a shell that moves on one large foot: *Snails and slugs are gastropods.* ⊃ picture at **animal**

gate 🔊 **A2** /geɪt/ *noun* [C] **1** the part of a fence, wall, etc. like a door that can be opened to let people or vehicles through: *Please keep the garden gate closed.* **2** (*also* gateway) the space in a wall, fence, etc. where the gate is: *Drive through the gates and you'll find the car park on the right.* **3** (**TOURISM**) the place at an airport where you get on or off a plane: *Lufthansa Flight 139 to Geneva is now boarding at gate 16.*

gateau /'gætəʊ/ *noun* [C, U] (*pl.* gateaux /'gætəʊ/) a large cake that is usually decorated with cream, fruit, etc.

gatecrash /'geɪtkræʃ/ *verb* [T, I] to go to a private party without being invited ▶ **gatecrasher** *noun* [C]

gatehouse /'geɪthaʊs/ *noun* [C] (**ARCHITECTURE**) a house built at or over a gate, for example at the entrance to a park or castle

gatepost /'geɪtpəʊst/ *noun* [C] a post to which a gate is attached or against which it is closed

gateway /'geɪtweɪ/ *noun* **1** [C] = GATE (2) **2** [sing.] **the ~ to sth** the place that you must go through in order to get to somewhere else: *The port of Dover is England's gateway to Europe.*

gather ⓘ **B1** /'gæðə(r)/ *verb*
• COME/BRING TOGETHER **1** [I, T] **~ (round/around) (sb/sth); ~ sb/sth (round/around) (sb/sth)** (used about people) to come or be brought together in a group: *A crowd soon gathered at the scene of the accident.* ◇ *We all gathered round and listened to what the guide was saying.* ◇ *The children were gathered around the teacher's desk.* **2** [T] **~ sth (together/up)** to bring many things together: *He gathered up all his papers and put them away.* ◇ *They have gathered together a lot of information on the subject.* ⊃ note at **collect**
• COLLECT **3** [T] (*formal*) to pick wild flowers, fruit, etc. from a wide area: *to gather mushrooms*
• UNDERSTAND **4** [T, I] to understand or find out sth (from sb/sth): *I gather from your letter that you have several years' experience of this kind of work.* ◇ *'She's been very ill recently.' 'So I gather.'*
• INCREASE **5** [T] to increase: *I gathered speed as I cycled down the hill.* ◇ *The economy is gradually gathering strength.*

gathering ⓘ /'gæðərɪŋ/ *noun* [C] a time when people come together; a meeting: *a family gathering*

gaudy /'gɔːdi/ *adj.* (gaudier; gaudiest) too bright or decorated and therefore unpleasant **SYN** **garish**

gauge[1] (*AmE also* gage) /geɪdʒ/ *noun* [C] **1** an instrument for measuring the amount of sth: *a fuel/temperature/pressure gauge* **2** a measurement of how wide sth is or of the distance between two things: *a narrow-gauge railway* **3** [usually sing.] **~ (of sth)** a fact that you can use to judge a situation, sb's feelings, etc.

gauge[2] /geɪdʒ/ *verb* [T] **1** to make a judgement or to calculate sth by guessing: *It was difficult to gauge the mood of the audience.* **2** to measure sth accurately using a special instrument

gaunt /gɔːnt/ *adj.* (used about a person) very thin because of illness, worry or not having enough food

gauze /gɔːz/ *noun* **1** [U] light material that you can see through, usually made of cotton or silk **2** [U] thin material like a net that is used for covering an area of skin that you have hurt **3** [U, C] material like a net that is made of wire; a piece of this: *a wire gauze* ⊃ picture at **laboratory**

gave /geɪv/ past tense of **give**[1]

gawp /gɔːp/ *verb* [I] **~ (at sb/sth)** (*BrE, informal*) to look for a long time in a stupid way because you are surprised, shocked, etc: *Lots of drivers slowed down to gawp at the accident.*

gay[1] ⓘ **B2** /geɪ/ *adj.* **1** (used about people, especially men) sexually attracted to people of the same sex: *the gay community of New York* ◇ *a gay bar/club* (= for gay people) **SYN** **homosexual** **OPP** **straight**[1] ⊃ look at **lesbian** **2** (*old-fashioned*) happy and full of fun ⊃ noun **gaiety**

gay[2] /geɪ/ *noun* [C] a person, especially a man, who is sexually attracted to people of the same sex **SYN** **homosexual** ⊃ look at **lesbian**

gay 'pride *noun* [U] the feeling that GAY people should not be ashamed of telling people that they are GAY and should feel proud of themselves

gaze ⓘ+ **C1** /geɪz/ *verb* [I] (used with an adverb or a preposition) to look steadily for a long time: *She sat at the window gazing dreamily into space.* ▶ **gaze** ⓘ+ **C1** *noun* [sing.]

gazebo /gə'ziːbəʊ/ *noun* [C] (*pl.* -os) (**ARCHITECTURE**) a small building with open sides in a garden, especially one with a view

GB *abbr.* **1** /ˌdʒiː 'biː/ = GREAT BRITAIN **2** (in writing) (*pl.* GB) = GIGABYTE

Gb *abbr.* (in writing) (*pl.* Gb) = GIGABIT

GCSE /ˌdʒiː siː es 'iː/ *noun* [C, U] (**EDUCATION**) an exam that students in England, Wales and Northern Ireland take when they are about 16. They often take GCSEs in five or more subjects. (the abbreviation for 'General Certificate of Secondary Education') ⊃ look at **A level**

GDP /ˌdʒiː diː 'piː/ *abbr.* (**ECONOMICS**) **gross domestic product** (the total value of all the goods and services produced in a country in one year) ⊃ look at **GNP**

gear[1] ⓘ+ **C1** /gɪə(r)/ *noun* **1** [C, usually pl.] the equipment in a vehicle that turns engine power into a movement forwards or backwards: *Most cars have four or five forward gears and a reverse.* **2** [U, C] a particular position of the gears in a vehicle: *first/second/top/reverse gear* ◇ *to change gear* **3** [U] (*informal*) clothes **4** [U] equipment or clothing that you need for a particular activity, etc: *camping/fishing/sports gear* **5** [sing.] an instrument or part of a machine that is used for a particular purpose: *the landing gear of a plane*

gear[2] /gɪə(r)/ *verb*
PHR V **gear sth to/towards sb/sth** [often passive] to make sth suitable for a particular purpose or person: *There is a special course geared towards the older learner.* **gear up (for sb/sth) | gear sb/sth up (for sb/sth)** to get ready or to make sb/sth ready

gearbox /'gɪəbɒks/ *noun* [C] the metal case that contains the GEARS of a car, etc.

gearing /'gɪərɪŋ/ (*BrE*) (*also* **leverage** *AmE, BrE*) *noun* [U] (**FINANCE**) the relationship between the amount of money that a company owes and the value of its shares

'gear lever (*also* **gearstick** /'gɪəstɪk/) (*both BrE*) (*AmE* **gearshift** /'gɪəʃɪft/) *noun* [C] a handle that is used for changing GEAR in a vehicle

gecko /'gekəʊ/ *noun* [C] (*pl.* -os, -oes) a small LIZARD (= a type of REPTILE) that lives in warm countries

gee /dʒiː/ *exclamation* (*AmE, informal*) used for expressing surprise, pleasure, etc.

geek /giːk/ *noun* [C] (*informal*) a person who is not popular or fashionable: *a computer geek* **SYN** **nerd** ▶ **geeky** *adj.* (geekier; geekiest)

geese /giːs/ plural of **goose**

Geiger counter /'gaɪgə kaʊntə(r)/ *noun* [C] (**PHYSICS**) a machine used for finding and measuring the RAYS that are sent out by RADIOACTIVE substances

gel /dʒel/ *noun* [C, U] (often in compounds) a thick, clear, slightly sticky substance, especially one used in products for the hair or skin: *hair gel* ◇ *shower gel*

gelatin /'dʒelətɪn/ (*also* **gelatine** /'dʒelətiːn/) *noun* [U] a clear substance without any taste that is made from boiling animal bones and is used to make liquid food SET (= become firm or hard)

gelignite /'dʒelɪgnaɪt/ *noun* [U] (**CHEMISTRY**) a substance that is used for making explosions

gem /dʒem/ *noun* [C] **1** a rare and valuable stone that is used in jewellery **2** a person or thing that is especially good: *This picture is the gem* (= the best) *of the collection.*

Gemini /'dʒemɪnaɪ, -ni/ *noun* [U] the third sign of THE ZODIAC (= twelve signs that represent the positions of the sun, moon and planets), the Twins; a person born under this sign

Gen. *abbr.* (in writing) = GENERAL²

gender ᵀ+ **B2** ◐ /'dʒendə(r)/ *noun* [U, C] **1** (*formal*) the fact of being male or female, especially when considered with reference to social and cultural differences, not differences in biology ⊃ look at **sex** (1) **2** (GRAMMAR) (in some languages) the division of nouns, pronouns, etc. into MASCULINE, FEMININE and sometimes NEUTER; one of these three types

'**gender gap** *noun* [C] (SOCIAL STUDIES) the difference that separates men and women, especially in terms of attitudes and opportunities: *The organization is trying to narrow the gender gap in science, technology, engineering and maths.*

'**gender identity** *noun* [C, U] (BIOLOGY, SOCIAL STUDIES) the way sb considers their own GENDER (= whether they are male or female), which may be different from their BIOLOGICAL sex: *Different influences may help shape a child's gender identity.*

gene ᵀ+ **B2** /dʒiːn/ *noun* [C] (BIOLOGY) a unit inside a cell that controls a particular quality in a living thing. The information in genes is passed from parents to children: *A single gene may control the flower colour of some plants.* ⊃ look at **genetics**

'**gene editing** *noun* [U] (BIOLOGY) the scientific technique of changing GENES in order to cure or prevent diseases or faults: *Gene editing could provide a permanent cure for many diseases.*

'**gene pool** *noun* [C] (BIOLOGY) all of the GENES that exist within the population of a particular plant or animal: *The idea behind mating the tigers was to improve their gene pool.*

genera /'dʒenərə/ plural of **genus**

general¹ ᵀ **A2** ◐ /'dʒenrəl/ *adj.* **1** affecting all or most people, places, things, etc: *Fridges were once a luxury, but they are in general use.* ◊ *That is a matter of general interest.* ◊ *the general public* (= most ordinary people) **2** [only before noun] referring to or describing the main part of sth, not the details: *Your general health is very good.* ◊ *The introduction gives you a general idea of what the book is about.* ◊ *As a general rule, the most common verbs in English tend to be irregular.* **3** not limited to one subject, use or activity: *Children need a good general education.* ◊ *The quiz tests your general knowledge.* ◊ *a general hospital* **4** (often in compounds) with responsibility for the whole of an organization: *a general manager* IDM **in general** in most cases; usually: *In general, standards of hygiene are good.* **2** as a whole: *I'm interested in Spanish history in general, and the Civil War in particular.*

general² ⓦ /'dʒenrəl/ *noun* [C] (*abbr.* **Gen.**) an army officer in a very high position in the British or US armies

,**General Cer'tificate of ,Secondary Edu'cation** = GCSE

,**general e'lection** *noun* [C] (POLITICS) an election in which all the people of a country vote to choose a government ⊃ look at **by-election**

generalization ⓦ (*BrE also* -isation) /,dʒenrəlaɪ'zeɪʃn/ *noun* [C, U] a general statement that is based on only a few facts or examples; the act of making such a statement: *You can't make sweeping generalizations about French people if you've only been to France for a day!*

generalize ⓦ (*BrE also* -ise) /'dʒenrəlaɪz/ *verb* [I] ~ (**about sth**); ~ (**from sth**) to form an opinion or make a statement using only a small amount of information instead of looking at the details: *It is dangerous to generalize about the poor.* ◊ *We cannot generalize from these few examples.*

generally ᵀ **B1** ◐ /'dʒenrəli/ *adv.* **1** by or to most people: *He is generally considered to be a good doctor.* **2** usually: *She generally cycles to work.* **3** without discussing the details of sth: *Generally speaking, houses in America are bigger than houses in this country.*

,**general prac'titioner** (*especially BrE*) = GP

the ,general 'public *noun* [sing. + sing./pl. verb] ordinary people who are not members of a particular group or organization: *The general public was/were not aware of the risks.*

generate ᵀ **B2** ◐ /'dʒenəreɪt/ *verb* [T] to produce or create sth: *to generate heat/power/electricity* ◊ *Their work is already generating interest.* ⊃ note at **electricity, make¹** ⊃ picture at **energy**

generation ᵀ **B1** ◐ /,dʒenə'reɪʃn/ *noun* **1** [C + sing./pl. verb] (SOCIAL STUDIES) all the people in a family, group or country who were born at about the same time: *We should look after the planet for future generations.* ◊ *This photo shows three generations of my family* (= children, parents and grandparents). ⊃ look at **first generation 2** [C] (SOCIAL STUDIES) the average time that children take to grow up and have children of their own, usually considered to be about 30 years: *Many more people go to university now than a generation ago.* **3** [U] the production of sth, especially heat, power, etc.

the ,gene'ration gap *noun* [sing.] (SOCIAL STUDIES) the difference in behaviour, and the lack of understanding, between young people and older people

generator /'dʒenəreɪtə(r)/ *noun* [C] (ENGINEERING) a machine that produces electricity ⊃ note at **electricity**

generic ᵀ+ **C1** /dʒə'nerɪk/ *adj.* **1** shared by, including or typical of a whole group of things; not specific: '*Vine fruit' is the generic term for currants and raisins.* **2** (used about a product, especially a drug) not using the name of the company that made it ▸ **generically** /-kli/ *adv.*

generosity /,dʒenə'rɒsəti/ *noun* [U] the quality of being generous

generous ᵀ **B1** /'dʒenərəs/ *adj.* **1** happy to give more money, help, etc. than is usual or expected: *It was very generous of your parents to lend us all that money.* ◊ *He was extremely generous with his time.* **2** larger than usual: *a generous helping of pasta* ▸ **generously** *adv.*: *People gave very generously to our appeal for the homeless.*

genesis /'dʒenəsɪs/ *noun* [sing.] (*formal*) the beginning or origin of sth

'**gene therapy** *noun* [U] (MEDICINE) a treatment in which normal GENES are put into cells to replace ones that are missing or not normal

genetic ᵀ+ **B2** /dʒə'netɪk/ *adj.* (BIOLOGY) relating to GENES, or to GENETICS (= the study of GENES): *The disease is caused by a genetic defect.* ⊃ picture at **fertilization** ▸ **genetically** /-kli/ *adv.*

ge,netically 'modified *adj.* (*abbr.* **GM**) (AGRICULTURE, BIOLOGY) (used about food, plants, etc.) that has been grown from cells whose GENES have been changed in an artificial way

ge¦netic 'code noun [C] (**BIOLOGY**) the arrangement of GENES that controls how each living thing will develop

ge¦netic engi'neering noun [U] (**BIOLOGY**) the science of changing the way a human, an animal or a plant develops by changing the information in its GENES

ge¦netic 'fingerprinting = DNA FINGERPRINTING

genetics /dʒəˈnetɪks/ noun [U] (**BIOLOGY**) the scientific study of the ways in which different characteristics are passed from each generation of living things to the next ⊃ look at **gene** ▶ **geneticist** /-tɪsɪst/ noun [C]

genial /ˈdʒiːniəl/ adj. (used about a person) pleasant and friendly

genie /ˈdʒiːni/ noun [C] (in stories) a spirit with magic powers, especially one that lives in a bottle or lamp

genitals /ˈdʒenɪtlz/ (also genitalia /ˌdʒenɪˈteɪliə/) noun [pl.] (formal) (**ANATOMY**) the parts of a person's sex organs that are outside the body ▶ **genital** adj. [only before noun]

genitive /ˈdʒenətɪv/ noun [sing.] (**GRAMMAR**) (in some languages) the special form of a noun, a pronoun or an adjective that is used to show possession or close connection between two things ⊃ look at **accusative**, **dative**, **nominative**, **vocative** ▶ **genitive** adj.

genius ʔ+ **B2** /ˈdʒiːniəs/ noun **1** [U] very great and unusual intelligence or ability: *Her idea was a stroke of genius.* **2** [C] a person who has very great and unusual ability, especially in a particular subject: *Einstein was a mathematical genius.* ⊃ look at **prodigy 3** [sing.] **~ for sth/doing sth** a very good natural skill or ability: *Our teacher had a genius for explaining difficult things in a simple way.*

genocide ʔ+ **C1** /ˈdʒenəsaɪd/ noun [U] (**LAW**) the murder of a large group of people who belong to a particular human group, have a particular religion, etc.

genome /ˈdʒiːnəʊm/ noun [C] (**BIOLOGY**) the complete set of GENES (= the units that control particular qualities) in a cell or living thing: *the decoding of the human genome*

genotype /ˈdʒenətaɪp, ˈdʒiːn-/ noun [C] (**BIOLOGY**) the combination of GENES (= the units inside a cell that control particular qualities) that a particular living thing has ⊃ look at **phenotype**

genre ʔ **B2** /ˈʒɒrə, ˈʒɒnrə/ noun [C] (formal) (**ARTS AND MEDIA**) a particular type or style of literature, art, film or music that you can recognize because of its special characteristics

'genre painting noun [U, C] (**ART**) a style of painting showing scenes from ordinary life, especially associated with seventeenth-century Dutch and Flemish artists; a painting done in this style

genteel /dʒenˈtiːl/ adj. behaving in a very polite way, often in order to make people think that you are from a high social class ▶ **gentility** /-ˈtɪləti/ noun [U]

gentle ʔ **B1** /ˈdʒentl/ adj. (gentler /ˈdʒentlə(r)/; gentlest /-lɪst/) **1** (used about people) kind and calm; touching or treating people or things in a careful way so that they are not hurt: *'I'll try and be as gentle as I can,' said the dentist.* **2** not strong, violent or extreme: *gentle exercise ◇ a gentle slope/curve* ▶ **gentleness** noun [U]

gentleman ʔ **B1** /ˈdʒentlmən/ (pl. -men /-mən/) (also informal gent /dʒent/) noun [C] **1** a man who is polite and who behaves well towards other people **2** (formal) used when speaking to or about a man or men in a polite way: *Ladies and gentlemen* (= at the beginning of a speech) *◇ Mrs Flinn, there is a gentleman here to see you.* **3** (old-fashioned) a rich man with a high social position

gently /ˈdʒentli/ adv. **1** in a way that is soft and light, not strong, extreme or violent: *She held the baby gently.* *◇ Simmer the soup gently for 30 minutes. ◇ Massage the area gently but firmly.* **2** in a calm, kind and quiet way: *'You miss them, don't you?' he asked gently.* **3** Gently! (BrE) used to tell sb to be careful: *Gently! You'll hurt the poor thing! ◇ Don't go too fast — gently does it!*

genuine ʔ+ **B2** /ˈdʒenjuɪn/ adj. **1** real; true: *He thought that he had bought a genuine Rolex watch but it was a cheap fake.* ⊃ look at **imitation** (1) **2** sincere and honest; that can be trusted: *a very genuine person* ▶ **genuinely** ʔ+ **B2** adv.

genus /ˈdʒiːnəs/ noun [C] (pl. genera /ˈdʒenərə/) (**BIOLOGY**) a group into which animals, plants, etc. that have similar characteristics are divided, smaller than a family and larger than a species ⊃ look at **class¹** (4), **family¹** (3), **species** ⊃ picture at **animal**

generator

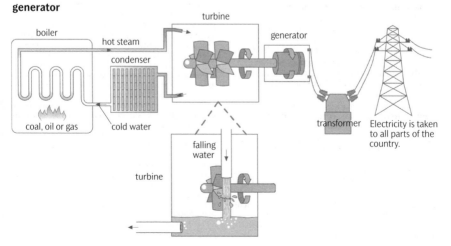

turbine

boiler

hot steam

condenser

generator

coal, oil or gas

cold water

transformer

Electricity is taken to all parts of the country.

falling water

turbine

geo- /dʒiːəʊ, dʒiːə, dʒiːɒ/ *prefix* (in nouns, adjectives and adverbs) of the earth: *geophysical* ◇ *geoscience*

geocentric /ˌdʒiːəʊˈsentrɪk/ *adj.* (ASTRONOMY) with the earth as the centre ⊃ look at **heliocentric**

geochemistry /ˌdʒiːəʊˈkemɪstri/ *noun* [U] (CHEMISTRY, GEOLOGY) the study of the different chemical substances that form the earth and its rocks and minerals ▸ **geochemical** /-mɪkl/ *adj.*: *Mining companies have been carrying out geochemical sampling.*

geodesic /ˌdʒiːəʊˈdesɪk, -ˈdiːs-/ *adj.* (GEOMETRY) relating to the shortest possible line between two points on a curved surface

geo desic 'dome *noun* [C] (ARCHITECTURE) a round building or structure in the shape of half a SPHERE that is built from pieces of glass, metal, etc. whose edges form GEODESIC lines

geodesic dome

geographer /dʒiˈɒɡrəfə(r)/ *noun* [C] (GEOGRAPHY) an expert in geography or a student of geography

geography ⚡ A1 /dʒiˈɒɡrəfi/ *noun* [U] **1** (EDUCATION) the study of the world's surface, physical qualities, climate, population, products, etc: *human/physical/economic geography* **2** the physical arrangement of a place: *We're studying the geography of Asia.* ▸ **geographical** ⓦ /dʒiːəˈɡræfɪkl/ (*also* **geographic** /-fɪk/) *adj.* ▸ **geographically** /-kli/ *adv.*

geolocation /ˌdʒiːəʊləʊˈkeɪʃn/ *noun* [U] (COMPUTING) the process or technique of finding the exact location of a person or device using the internet

geology /dʒiˈɒlədʒi/ *noun* [U] (EDUCATION) the study of rocks, and of the way they are formed ▸ **geological** /ˌdʒiːəˈlɒdʒɪkl/ *adj.* ▸ **geologist** /dʒiˈɒlədʒɪst/ *noun* [C]

geometric /ˌdʒiːəˈmetrɪk/ (*also* **geometrical** /ˌdʒiːəˈmetrɪkl/) *adj.* **1** (GEOMETRY) connected with GEOMETRY **2** consisting of regular shapes and lines: *a geometric design/pattern* ▸ **geometrically** /-kli/ *adv.*

geometric 'mean = MEAN³ (2)

geometric pro'gression *noun* [C] (MATHEMATICS) a series of numbers in which each is multiplied or divided by a fixed number to produce the next, for example 1, 3, 9, 27, 81 ⊃ look at **arithmetic progression**

geometry /dʒiˈɒmətri/ *noun* [U] (EDUCATION) the study in mathematics of lines, shapes, curves, etc.

geopolitics /ˌdʒiːəʊˈpɒlətɪks/ *noun* [U + sing./pl. verb] (POLITICS) the political relations between countries and groups of countries in the world; the study of these relations ▸ **geopolitical** /ˌdʒiːəʊpəˈlɪtɪkl/ *adj.*

Georgian /ˈdʒɔːdʒən/ *adj.* (ARCHITECTURE, HISTORY) (used especially about architecture and furniture) from the time of the British kings George I–IV (1714–1830): *a fine Georgian house*

geoscience /ˈdʒiːəʊsaɪəns/ *noun* [U] (geosciences [pl.]) (GEOGRAPHY) the sciences concerned with studying the earth, especially GEOLOGY

geothermal /ˌdʒiːəʊˈθɜːml/ *adj.* (GEOLOGY) connected with the natural heat of rock deep in the ground: *geothermal energy*

geriatrics /ˌdʒeriˈætrɪks/ *noun* [U] (MEDICINE) the area of medicine connected with the diseases and care of old people ▸ **geriatric** *adj.*

germ /dʒɜːm/ *noun* **1** [C] (BIOLOGY, HEALTH) a very small living thing that causes disease ⊃ look at **bacteria**, **virus** (1) **2** [sing.] **the ~ of sth** the beginning of sth that may develop: *the germ of an idea*

Germanic /dʒɜːˈmænɪk/ *adj.* **1** connected with or considered typical of Germany or its people: *She had an almost Germanic regard for order.* **2** (LANGUAGE) connected with the language family that includes German, English, Dutch and Swedish among others

germanium /dʒɜːˈmeɪniəm/ *noun* [U] (*symb.* Ge) (CHEMISTRY) a chemical element. Germanium is a shiny grey METALLOID (= has properties of both metals and other solid substances). ❶ For more information on the periodic table of elements, look at the **Reference Section** of this dictionary.

German measles /ˌdʒɜːmən ˈmiːzlz/ (*also* **rubella**) *noun* [U] (HEALTH) a mild disease that causes red spots all over the body. If a woman catches it when she is pregnant, it may harm the baby.

German shepherd /ˌdʒɜːmən ˈʃepəd/ (*BrE also* **Alsatian**) *noun* [C] a large dog, often trained to help the police or to guard buildings

germinate /ˈdʒɜːmɪneɪt/ *verb* [I, T] (BIOLOGY) (used about a seed) to start growing; to cause a seed to do this ▸ **germination** /ˌdʒɜːmɪˈneɪʃn/ *noun* [U]

germ 'warfare = BIOLOGICAL WARFARE

gerrymander /ˈdʒerimændə(r)/ *verb* [I, T] (POLITICS) to change the size and borders of an area for voting in order to give an unfair advantage to one party in an election ▸ **gerrymandering** *noun* [U]

gerund /ˈdʒerənd/ *noun* [C] (GRAMMAR) a noun, ending in *-ing*, that has been made from a verb: *In the sentence 'His hobby is collecting stamps', 'collecting' is a gerund.*

gestation /dʒeˈsteɪʃn/ *noun* [U, C] (BIOLOGY) the period of time that a baby human or animal develops inside its mother's body; the process of developing inside the mother's body: *The gestation period of a horse is about eleven months.*

gesticulate /dʒeˈstɪkjuleɪt/ *verb* [I] to make movements with your hands and arms in order to express sth

gesture¹ ⚡ B2 /ˈdʒestʃə(r)/ *noun* [C] **1** a movement of the hand, head, etc. that expresses sth: *I saw the boy make a rude gesture at the policeman before running off.* **2** something that you do that shows other people what you think or feel: *It would be a nice gesture to invite the neighbours in for a drink.* ⊃ note at **action¹**

gesture² /ˈdʒestʃə(r)/ *verb* [I, T] to point at sth; to make a sign to sb: *She asked them to leave and gestured towards the door.*

get ⚡ A1 /get/ *verb* (getting; *pt* got /gɒt/; *pp* got) HELP In spoken American English **gotten** is almost always used for the past participle.   **1** [T] to receive, obtain or buy sth: *I got a letter from my sister.* ◇ *Did you get a present for your mother?* ◇ *Did you get your mother a present?* ◇ *She got a job in a travel agency.* ◇ *Louise got 75 per cent in the maths exam.* ◇ *I'll come if I can get time off work.* ◇ *How much did you get for your old car* (= when you sold it)? ◇ *to get a shock/surprise* ◇ *Can I get a coffee please?* **2** [T] **have/has got sth** to have sth: *I've got a lot to do today.* ◇ *Lee's got blond hair.* ◇ *Have you got a spare pen?* **3** [T] to go to a place and bring sth back: *Go and get me a pen, please.* ◇ *Sam's gone to get his mother from the station.* SYN **fetch** **4** *linking verb* to become; to reach a particular state or condition: *It's getting dark.* ◇ *to get angry/bored/hungry/fat* ◇ *I can't get used to my new bed.* ◇ *to get dressed* ◇ *When did you get married?* ◇ *to get pregnant* ◇ *Just give me five minutes to get ready.* ◇ *He's always getting into trouble with the police.* ◇ *She's shy, but she's great fun once you get to know her.* **5** [I] (used with an adverb or a preposition) to arrive at or reach a place: *We should get to London at about ten.* ◇ *Can you tell me how to get to the hospital?* ◇ *What time do you usually get home?* ◇ *I got half way up the mountain then gave up.* ◇ *How far have you got with your book?* ⊃ look at **get in** (1)

6 [I, T] (often used with an adverb or a preposition) to move or go somewhere; to move or put sth somewhere: *I can't swim so I couldn't get across the river.* ◇ *My grandmother's 92 and she doesn't get out of the house much.* ◇ *We couldn't get the piano upstairs.* ◇ *My foot was swollen and I couldn't get my shoe off.* **7** [I] used instead of 'be' in the passive: *She got bitten by a dog.* ◇ *Don't leave your wallet on the table or it'll get stolen.* **8** [T] ~ **sth done** to cause sth to be done: *Let's get this work done, then we can go out.* ◇ *I'm going to get my hair cut.* **9** [T] ~ **sb/sth to do sth** to make or persuade sb/sth to do sth: *I got him to agree to the plan.* ◇ *I can't get the TV to work.* **10** [T] to catch or have an illness, pain, etc.: *I think I'm getting a cold.* ◇ *He gets really bad headaches.* **11** [T] to use a form of transport: *Shall we walk or get the bus?* **12** [T] to hit, hold or catch sb/sth: *He got me by the throat and threatened to kill me.* ◇ *A boy threw a stone at me but he didn't get me.* **13** [T] (*informal*) to hear or understand sth: *I'm sorry, I didn't get that. Could you repeat it?* ◇ *Did you get that joke that Karen told?* **14** [T] ~ **(sb) sth**; ~ **sth (for sb)** to prepare food: *Can I get you anything to eat?* ◇ *Joe's in the kitchen getting breakfast for everyone.* **15** [I] ~ **to do sth** to have the chance to do sth: *Did you get to see a musical when you were in London?* **16** [I] (used with verbs in the -*ing* form) to start doing sth: *I got talking to a woman on the bus.* ◇ *We'd better get going if we don't want to be late.*

IDM get somewhere/nowhere (with sb/sth) to make/not make progress: *I'm getting nowhere with my research.* what has got into sb? (*informal*) used to say that sb has suddenly started to behave in a strange or different way: *I wonder what's got into him — he isn't usually unfriendly.* ❶ For other idioms containing get, look at the entries for the nouns, adjectives, etc. For example, get rid of is at rid.

PHR V get about (*BrE*) = GET AROUND

get sth across (to sb) to succeed in making people understand sth: *The party failed to get its policies across to the voters.*

get ahead to progress and be successful in sth, especially a career

get along **1** (usually used in the progressive tenses) (*informal*) to leave a place: *I'd love to stay, but I should be getting along now.* **2** = GET ON/ALONG

get around (*BrE also* get about) **1** to move or travel from place to place: *My grandmother needs a stick to get around these days.* **2** (used about news, a story, etc.) to become known by many people get around sb (*especially AmE*) = GET ROUND SB get around sth (*especially AmE*) = GET ROUND STH get around to sth/doing sth (*especially AmE*) = GET ROUND TO STH/DOING STH

get at sb (usually used in the progressive tenses) to criticize sb a lot: *The teacher's always getting at me about my spelling.* get at sb/sth to be able to reach sb/sth; to have sth available for immediate use: *The files are locked away and I can't get at them.* get at sth (only used in the progressive tenses) to try to say sth without saying it in a direct way; to suggest: *I'm not quite sure what you're getting at — am I doing something wrong?*

get away (from ...) to succeed in leaving or escaping from sb or a place: *He kept talking to me and I couldn't get away from him.* ◇ *The thieves got away in a stolen car.* get away with sth/doing sth to do sth bad and not be punished for it: *He lied but he got away with it.*

get back to return to the place where you live or work: *When did you get back from Italy?* get sth back to be given sth that you had lost or lent: *Can I borrow this book? You'll get it back next week, I promise.* get back to sb to speak to, write to, email or phone sb later, especially in order to give an answer: *I'll get back to you on prices when I've got some more*

information. get back to sth to return to doing sth or talking about sth: *I woke up early and couldn't get back to sleep.* ◇ *Let's get back to the point you raised earlier.*

get behind (with sth) to fail to do, pay sth, etc. on time, and so have more to do, pay, etc. the next time: *to get behind with your work/rent*

get by (on/in/with sth) to manage to live or do sth with difficulty: *It's very hard to get by on such a low income.* ◇ *My Italian is good and I can get by in Spanish.*

get sb down (*informal*) to make sb unhappy get down to sth/doing sth to start working on sth: *We'd better stop chatting and get down to work.* ◇ *I must get down to answering these letters.*

get in | get into sth **1** to reach a place: *What time does your train get in?* ◇ *What time did you get in* (= arrive home) *last night?* **2** to climb into a car: *We all got in and Tim drove off.* **3** to be elected to a political position: *She got into Parliament in 2019.* get sb in to call sb to your house to do a job get sth in **1** to collect or bring sth inside; to buy a supply of sth: *It's going to rain — I'd better get the washing in from outside.* **2** to manage to find an opportunity to say or do sth: *He talked all the time and I couldn't get a word in.* get in on sth to become involved in an activity get into sth **1** to put on a piece of clothing with difficulty: *I've put on so much weight that I can't get into my trousers.* **2** to start a particular activity; to become involved in sth: *How did you first get into the music business?* ◇ *She has got into the habit of turning up late.* ◇ *We got into an argument about politics.* **3** (*informal*) to become more interested in or familiar with sth: *I've been getting into yoga recently.*

get off (sb/sth) used especially to tell sb to stop touching sb/sth: *Get off (me) or I'll call the police!* ◇ *Get off that money, it's mine!* get off (sth) **1** to leave a bus, train, etc.; to climb down from a bicycle, horse, etc. **2** to leave work with permission at a particular time: *I might be able to get off early today.* get off (with sth) to be lucky to receive no serious injuries or punishment: *to get off with just a warning* get on **1** to progress or become successful in life, in a career, etc. **2** (only used in the progressive tenses) to be getting old: *He's getting on — he's over 70, I'm sure.* **3** (only used in the progressive tenses) to be getting late: *Time's getting on — we don't want to be late.* get on/along to have a particular amount of success: *How are you getting on in your course?* ◇ *'How did you get on at your interview?' 'I got the job!'* get on/along with sb | get on/along (together) to have a friendly relationship with sb: *Do you get on well with your colleagues?* get on/along with sth **1** to make progress with sth that you are doing: *How are you getting on with that essay?* **2** to continue doing sth, especially after you have been interrupted: *Stop talking and get on with your work!* get on (sth)/onto sth to climb onto a bus, train, bicycle, horse, etc: *I got on just as the train was about to leave.* ◇ *He got onto his horse and rode off.* get on for (only used in the progressive tenses) to be getting near to a certain time or age: *I'm not sure how old he is but he must be getting on for 50.* get on to sb (about sth) to speak or write to sb about a particular matter: *Our rubbish still hasn't been collected — I'll get on to the council about it.*

get out (used about a piece of information) to become known, after being secret until now: *If this information gets out, do you know what will happen to me?* get sth out (of sth) to take sth from its container: *I got my keys out of my bag.* get out of sth/doing sth to avoid a duty or doing sth that you have

said you will do: *I said I'd go to their party and I can't get out of it now*. **get sth out of sb** to persuade or force sb to give you sth: *Her parents finally got the truth out of her*. **get sth out of sb/sth** to gain sth from sb/sth: *I get a lot of pleasure out of music*.
get over sth 1 to deal with a problem successfully: *We'll have to get over the problem of finding somewhere to live first*. **2** to feel normal again after being ill or having an unpleasant experience: *He still hasn't got over his wife's death*. **get sth over with** (*informal*) to do and complete sth unpleasant that has to be done: *I'll be glad to get my visit to the dentist's over with*.
get round sb (*BrE*) (*also* **get around sb** *especially in AmE*) (*informal*) to persuade sb to do sth or agree with sth: *My father says he won't lend me the money but I think I can get round him*. **get round sth** (*BrE*) (*also* **get around sth** *especially in AmE*) to find a way of avoiding or dealing with a problem **get round to sth/doing sth** (*BrE*) (*also* **get around to sth/doing sth** *especially in AmE*) to find the time to do sth, after a delay: *I've been meaning to read that book for ages but I haven't got round to it yet*.
get through sth to use or complete a certain amount or number of sth: *I got through a lot of money at the weekend*. ◇ *I got through an enormous amount of work today*. **get (sb) through (sth)** to manage to complete sth difficult or unpleasant; to help sb to do this: *She got through her final exams easily*.
get through (to sb) 1 to succeed in making sb understand sth: *They couldn't get through to him that he was completely wrong*. **2** to succeed in speaking to sb on the phone: *I couldn't get through to them but I left a message*.
get to sb (*informal*) to affect sb in a bad way: *Public criticism is beginning to get to the team manager*.
get sb/sth together to collect people or things in one place: *I'll just get my things together and then we'll go*. **get together (with sb)** to meet socially or in order to discuss or do sth: *Let's get together and talk about it*. ⊃ look at **meet up (with sb)** at **meet**
get up to stand up: *He got up to let an elderly woman sit down*. **get (sb) up** to get out of bed or make sb get out of bed: *What time do you have to get up in the morning?* ◇ *Could you get me up at six tomorrow?* **get up to sth 1** to reach a particular point or stage in sth: *We've got up to the last section of our grammar book*. **2** to be busy with sth, especially sth secret or bad: *I wonder what the children are getting up to?*

getaway /ˈɡetəweɪ/ *noun* [C] **1** an escape (after a crime): *to make a getaway* ◇ *a getaway car/driver* **2** (*informal*) (**TOURISM**) a short holiday; a place where you can go for a holiday: *They got engaged in March on a romantic weekend getaway*.

ˈget-together *noun* [C] (*informal*) an informal social meeting or party

geyser /ˈɡiːzə(r)/ *noun* [C] (**GEOGRAPHY**) **1** a place where hot water or **STEAM** is sent up naturally into the air from under the ground ⊃ look at **spring**[1] (2) ⊃ picture at **volcano 2** (*BrE*) a piece of equipment in a kitchen or bathroom that heats water, usually by gas

ghastly /ˈɡɑːstli/ *adj.* (**ghastlier; ghastliest**) extremely unpleasant or bad: *a ghastly accident* **SYN terrible**

gherkin /ˈɡɜːkɪn/ (*BrE*) (*AmE* **pickle**) *noun* [C] a small **CUCUMBER** that is stored in salt water or **VINEGAR** (= a liquid with a bitter taste) before being eaten

ghetto /ˈɡetəʊ/ *noun* [C] (*pl.* **-oes**) (**SOCIAL STUDIES**) a part of a town where many people who belong to the same human group, have the same religion, etc. live in poor conditions

ghost ⚗ **B1** /ɡəʊst/ *noun* [C] the spirit of a dead person that a living person believes they can see or hear: *I don't believe in ghosts*. ◇ *a ghost story* ⊃ look at **spectre** (2) ⊃ look at **apparition**

ghostly /ˈɡəʊstli/ *adj.* (**ghostlier; ghostliest**) looking or sounding like a ghost; full of ghosts: *ghostly noises*

ˈghost town *noun* [C] a town that used to be busy and have people living in it, but is now empty

ghostwriter /ˈɡəʊstraɪtə(r)/ *noun* [C] (**LITERATURE**) a person who writes a book, etc. for a famous person (whose name appears as the author)

giant ⚗ **B1** /ˈdʒaɪənt/ *noun* [C] **1** (in stories) an extremely large, strong person who is often cruel and stupid **2** a person or thing that is very large: *the multinational oil giants* (= very large companies) ▸ **giant** ⚗ **B1** *adj.*: *a giant new shopping centre*

gibberish /ˈdʒɪbərɪʃ/ *noun* [U] (*informal*) words that have no meaning or that are impossible to understand

gibbon /ˈɡɪbən/ *noun* [C] a small **APE** (= an animal like a monkey but without a tail) with long arms that is found in south-east Asia

giddy /ˈɡɪdi/ *adj.* (**giddier; giddiest**) having the feeling that everything is going round and that you are going to fall: *I feel giddy. I must sit down*. **SYN dizzy**

gift ⚗ **A2** /ɡɪft/ *noun* [C] **1** something that you give to sb: *This watch was a gift from my mother*. ◇ *This week's magazine contains a free gift of some make-up*. ◇ *The company made a gift of a computer to a local school*. **SYN present**[2] **2 ~(for sth/doing sth)** natural ability: *I'd love to have a gift for languages like Mike has*. **SYN talent**
IDM the gift of the gab (*BrE, informal*) the ability to speak easily and to persuade others with your words: *Your brother certainly has the gift of the gab*.

gifted /ˈɡɪftɪd/ *adj.* having natural ability or great intelligence

ˈgift-wrap *verb* [T] (**-pp-**) to put attractive paper round sth that has been bought as a present for sb, especially in a shop: *Would you like the chocolates gift-wrapped?*

gig ⚗+ **B2** /ɡɪɡ/ *noun* [C] **1** (**ARTS AND MEDIA**) an event where a musician, band or **COMEDIAN** is paid to perform **2** (*pl.* **gigs, gig**) (*informal*) = **GIGABYTE**

gigabit /ˈɡɪɡəbɪt/ *noun* [C] (*abbr.* **Gb**) (**COMPUTING**) a unit of computer memory or data, equal to 10^9 **BITS** (= the smallest units of information)

gigabyte /ˈɡɪɡəbaɪt/ (*also informal* **gig**) *noun* [C] (*abbr.* **GB**) (**COMPUTING**) a unit of computer memory or data, equal to 10^9 **BYTES** (= small units of information)

gigantic /dʒaɪˈɡæntɪk/ *adj.* extremely big **SYN enormous, huge**

ˈgig economy *noun* [C, usually sing.] (**ECONOMICS**) a way of working in which many short periods of work are available rather than permanent jobs

giggle /ˈɡɪɡl/ *verb* [I] to laugh in a silly way that you cannot control, because you are embarrassed or nervous or because you think sth is funny ▸ **giggle** *noun* [C]: *I've got the giggles* (= I can't stop laughing).

gild /ɡɪld/ *verb* [T] to cover sth with a thin layer of gold or gold paint

gill /ɡɪl/ *noun* [C, usually pl.] one of the parts on the side of a fish's head that it breathes through ⊃ picture at **animal**

gilt /ɡɪlt/ *noun* [U] a thin covering of gold, or sth like gold, that is used on a surface for decoration

gimmick /ˈɡɪmɪk/ *noun* [C] an unusual trick or idea for attracting customers or persuading people to buy sth: *New magazines often use free gifts or other gimmicks to get people to buy them*.

gin /dʒɪn/ *noun* [U, C] a strong alcoholic drink with no colour; a glass of this drink

ginger[1] /'dʒɪndʒə(r)/ *noun* [U] **1** a root that tastes hot and is used as a SPICE in cooking: *ground ginger* ◇ *ginger biscuits* **2** a light orange-brown colour

ginger[2] /'dʒɪndʒə(r)/ *adj.* light orange-brown in colour: *a ginger cat*

ginger 'ale *noun* [U] a clear FIZZY drink (= with bubbles) that does not contain alcohol and tastes of GINGER. It is often mixed with alcoholic drinks.

ginger 'beer *noun* [U, C] a FIZZY drink (= with bubbles) that tastes of GINGER. Some types of ginger beer contain a small amount of alcohol.

gingerbread /'dʒɪndʒəbred/ *noun* [U] a sweet cake or soft biscuit that is made with GINGER (= a powder made from the root of a plant with a hot taste)

gingerly /'dʒɪndʒəli/ *adv.* very slowly and carefully so as not to cause harm, make a noise, etc.

Gipsy /'dʒɪpsi/ = GYPSY

giraffe /dʒə'rɑːf/ *noun* [C] (*pl.* giraffe, giraffes) a large African animal with a very long neck and legs and big dark spots on its skin

girder /'ɡɜːdə(r)/ *noun* [C] a long heavy piece of iron or steel that is used in the building of bridges, large buildings, etc.

girl ʔ A1 /ɡɜːl/ *noun* **1** [C] a female child: *Is the baby a boy or a girl?* ◇ *There are more boys than girls in the class.* **2** [C] a daughter: *They have two boys and a girl.* **3** [C] a young woman: *The girl at the cash desk was very helpful.* ❶ Some people find this meaning of 'girl' offensive. **4** girls [pl.] a woman's female friends of any age, or the women in a group: *a night out with the girls*

girlfriend ʔ A1 /'ɡɜːlfrend/ *noun* [C] **1** a girl or woman with whom sb has a romantic and/or sexual relationship: *Have you got a girlfriend?* **2** a girl or woman's female friend

Girl 'Guide (*BrE, old-fashioned*) = GUIDE[1]

girlhood /'ɡɜːlhʊd/ *noun* [U] (*old-fashioned*) the time when sb is a girl

girlish /'ɡɜːlɪʃ/ *adj.* looking, sounding or behaving like a girl: *a girlish figure/giggle*

girth /ɡɜːθ/ *noun* **1** [U, C] the measurement around sth, especially the middle part of a person's body **2** [C] a leather or cloth STRAP that is fastened around the middle of a horse to keep the SADDLE (= seat) or a load in place

gist /dʒɪst/ *noun* [sing.] **the ~ (of sth)** the general meaning of sth rather than all the details: *I know a little Spanish so I was able to **get the gist** of what he said.*

give[1] ʔ A1 /ɡɪv/ *verb* (*pt* gave /ɡeɪv/; *pp* given /'ɡɪvn/) **1** [T] **~ sb sth; ~ sth to sb** to let sb have sth, especially sth that they want or need: *I gave Jackie a book for her birthday.* ◇ *Give me that book a minute — I just want to check something.* ◇ *I gave my bag to my friend to look after.* ◇ *I'll give you my phone number.* ◇ *He was thirsty so I gave him a drink.* **2** [T] **~ sb sth; ~ sth to sb** to make sb have sth, especially sth he/she does not want: *Playing chess gives me a headache.* ◇ *If you go to school with the flu, you'll give it to everyone.* **3** [T] to make sb have a particular feeling, idea, etc: *Swimming always gives me a good appetite.* ◇ *to give somebody a surprise/shock/fright* ◇ *What gives you the idea that he was lying?* **4** [T] **~ (sb) sth; ~ sth to sb** to let sb have your opinion, decision, judgement, etc: *My boss has given me permission to leave early.* ◇ *Can you give some advice to parents and teachers?* ◇ *The judge gave him five years in prison.* ◇ *She gave the assignment an A.* ⊃ note at **opinion 5** [T] **~ (sb) sth; ~ sth (to sb)** to speak to people in a formal situation: *She gave a talk to the History Club.* ◇ *The officer was called to give evidence in court.* ◇ *Stuart's going to give me a cooking lesson.* **6** [T] **~ sth for sth; ~ (sb) sth (to do sth)** to pay in order to have sth: *How much did you give him for fixing the car?* ◇ (*figurative*) *I'd give anything* (= I would love) *to be able to sing like that.* **7** [T] to spend time dealing with sb/sth: *We need to give some thought to this matter urgently.* **8** [T] **~ (sb/sth) sth** to do sth to sb/sth; to make a particular sound or movement: *to give somebody a kiss/push/hug* ◇ *to give something a clean/wash/polish* ◇ *Give me a call when you get home.* ◇ *He opened the door and gave a shout of horror.* **9** [T] to perform or organize sth for people: *The company gave a party to celebrate its 50th anniversary.* **10** [I] to bend or stretch under pressure: *The branch began to give under my weight.* ᴵᴰᴹ **give or take** more or less the number mentioned: *It took us two hours to get here, give or take five minutes.* ❶ For other idioms containing **give**, look at the entries for the nouns, adjectives, etc. For example, **give way** is at **way**. ᴾᴴᴿⱽ **give sth away** to give sth to sb without wanting money in return: *When she got older she gave all her toys away.* ◇ *We are giving away a free DVD with this month's issue.* **give sth/sb away** to show or tell the truth about sth/sb that was secret: *He smiled politely and didn't give away his real feelings.* **give sth back** to return sth to the person that you took or borrowed it from: *I lent her some books months ago and she still hasn't given them back to me.* **give sth in** (*BrE*) (*also* hand sth in *in BrE, AmE*) to give sth to the person who is collecting it: *I've got to give this essay in to my teacher by Friday.* ᴐ note at **study**[2] **give in (to sb/sth)** to stop fighting against sb/sth; to accept that you have been defeated: *give off* sth to send sth (for example smoke, a smell, heat, etc.) out into the air **give out** (used about a machine, a part of the body, etc.) to stop working: *His heart gave out and he died.* **give sth out** to give sth to a lot of people: *Could you give out these books to the class, please?* **give up** to stop trying to do sth; to accept that you cannot do sth: *They gave up once the other team had scored their third goal.* ◇ *I give up. What's the answer?* **give sb up | give up on sb** to stop expecting sb to arrive, succeed, improve, etc: *Her work was so poor that all her teachers gave up on her.* **give sth up | give up doing sth** to stop doing or having sth that you did or had regularly before: *I've tried many times to give up smoking.* ◇ *Don't give up hope. Things are bound to improve.* **give yourself/sb up (to sb)** to go to the police when they are trying to catch you; to tell the police where sb is **give sth up (to sb)** to give sth to sb who needs or asks for it: *He gave up his seat on the bus to an elderly woman.*

give[2] /ɡɪv/ *noun* [U] the quality of being able to bend or stretch a little: *The leather has plenty of give in it.* ᴵᴰᴹ **give and take** a situation in which two people, groups, etc. respect each other's rights and needs: *There has to be some give and take for a marriage to succeed.*

giveaway /'ɡɪvəweɪ/ *noun* [C] (*informal*) **1** a thing that is included free when you buy sth **2** something that makes you guess the truth about sb/sth: *She said she didn't know about the money but her face was **a dead giveaway**.*

given[1] ❺ /'ɡɪvn/ *adj.* [only before noun] already stated or decided: *At any given time, up to 200 people are using the library.*

given[2] /ɡɪvn/ *prep.* when you consider sth: *Given your interest in cookery, you might enjoy this article.*

'given name (*especially AmE*) = FIRST NAME

given that *conj.* when you consider sth: *Given that you had very little help, I think you did very well.*

gizzard /'gɪzəd/ *noun* [C] the part of a bird's stomach in which food is changed into smaller pieces before it can be DIGESTED

glacial /'gleɪʃl, 'gleɪsiəl/ *adj.* **1** (**GEOGRAPHY**, **GEOLOGY**) caused by ice or a GLACIER: *a glacial valley* **2** (*formal*) very cold: *glacial winds/temperatures* **SYN** *icy*

glaciation /ˌgleɪsi'eɪʃn/ *noun* [U] (**GEOGRAPHY**, **GEOLOGY**) the movement of a mass of ice over an area of land, and the things that are caused or created by this

glacier /'glæsiə(r)/ *noun* [C] (**GEOGRAPHY**, **GEOLOGY**) a large mass of ice that moves very slowly down a valley

glad 🔊 **B1** /glæd/ *adj.* **1** [not before noun] **~(about sth)**; **~ (to do sth/that)** … happy; pleased: *Are you glad about your new job?* ◊ *I'm glad to hear he's feeling better.* ◊ *I'm glad (that) he's feeling better.* ◊ *I'll be glad when these exams are over.* **2 ~(of sth)** grateful for sth: *If you are free, I'd be glad of some help.* ◊ *I'd be glad if you could help me.* **3** [only before noun] (*old-fashioned*) bringing happiness: *I want to be the first to tell her the glad news.* ▶ **gladness** *noun* [U]

gladden /'glædn/ *verb* [T] (*formal*) to make sb glad or happy

glade /gleɪd/ *noun* [C] (**GEOGRAPHY**) an open space in a forest or wood where there are no trees **SYN** *clearing*

gladiator /'glædieɪtə(r)/ *noun* [C] (**HISTORY**) (in ancient Rome) a man who fought against another man or a wild animal in a public show ▶ **gladiatorial** /ˌglædiə'tɔːriəl/ *adj.*: *gladiatorial combat*

gladly /'glædli/ *adv.* used for politely agreeing to a request or accepting an invitation: *'Could you help me carry these bags?' 'Gladly.'* ◊ *She gladly accepted the invitation to stay the night.*

glamorize (*BrE also* -ise) /'glæməraɪz/ *verb* [T] to make sth appear more attractive or exciting than it really is: *TV tends to glamorize violence.*

glamorous /'glæmərəs/ (*also informal* **glam** /glæm/) *adj.* very attractive and exciting, and different from ordinary things or people: *glamorous movie stars* ◊ *a glamorous job* ▶ **glamorously** *adv.*

glamour (*AmE also* **glamor**) /'glæmə(r)/ *noun* [U] the quality of seeming to be more exciting or attractive than ordinary things or people: *Young people are attracted by the glamour of city life.*

glance[1] 🔊 **C1** /glɑːns/ *verb* [I] (used with an adverb or a preposition) to look quickly at sb/sth: *She glanced round the room to see if they were there.* ◊ *He glanced at her and smiled.* ◊ *The receptionist glanced down the list of names.*
PHR V **glance off (sth)** to hit sth at an angle and move off again in another direction: *The ball glanced off his knee and into the net.*

glance[2] 🔊 **C1** /glɑːns/ *noun* [C] a quick look: *to take/have a glance at the newspaper headlines*
IDM **at first glance/sight** → FIRST[1] **at a (single) glance** with one look: *I could tell at a glance that something was wrong.*

gland /glænd/ *noun* [C] (**ANATOMY**) any of the organs inside the body that produce chemical substances for the body to use: *sweat glands* ⊃ picture at **skin**[1] ▶ **glandular** /'glændʒələ(r)/ *adj.*

glare[1] /gleə(r)/ *verb* [I] **1 ~(at sb/sth)** to look at sb in a very angry way: *They stood glaring at each other.* **SYN** **glower** **2** to shine with strong light that hurts your eyes

glare[2] /gleə(r)/ *noun* **1** [U] strong light that hurts your eyes: *the glare of the sun/a car's headlights* **2** [C] a very angry look

glaring /'gleərɪŋ/ *adj.* **1** (used about sth bad) very easy to see; shocking: *a glaring mistake/injustice* ⊃ look at **blatant** **2** (used about a light) too strong and bright **3** angry: *glaring eyes* ▶ **glaringly** *adv.*: *a glaringly obvious mistake*

glass 🔊 **A1** /glɑːs/ *noun* **1** [U] a hard substance that you can usually see through that is used for making windows, bottles, etc: *He cut himself on broken glass.* ◊ *a sheet/pane of glass* ◊ *a glass jar/dish/vase* ⊃ picture at **building** **2** [C] a drinking container made of glass; the amount of liquid it contains: *a wine glass* ◊ *Could I have a glass of water?* ◊ *He drank three glasses of milk.* **3 glasses** (*AmE also* **eyeglasses**) (*also old-fashioned or formal* **spectacles** /'spektəklz/) (*also informal* **specs** /speks/ *especially in BrE*) [pl.] two LENSES in a frame that a person wears in front of their eyes in order to be able to see better: *My sister has to **wear glasses**.* ◊ *I need a new pair of glasses.* ◊ *I need some new glasses.* ◊ *reading glasses* ◊ *dark glasses/sunglasses*

glass fibre (*BrE*) (*AmE* **glass fiber**) = FIBREGLASS

glacial features

pyramidal peak

cirque lake

hanging valley with waterfall

glacial U-shaped valley

ribbon lake

deposits of moraine

glacial movement

snow; avalanches; rock falls

accumulation zone

glacier movement

ablation zone

heat sediment

glacier movement

melting/ calving

glassful /ˈglɑːsfʊl/ *noun* [C] the amount of liquid that one glass holds

glasshouse /ˈglɑːshaʊs/ (*BrE*) = GREENHOUSE

glassy /ˈglɑːsi/ *adj.* (glassier; glassiest) **1** looking like glass **2** (used about the eyes) showing no interest or expression

glaucoma /glɔːˈkəʊmə, glɔːˈk-/ *noun* [U] (HEALTH) an eye disease that causes you to gradually lose your sight

glaze¹ /gleɪz/ *verb* [T] **1** if a person's eyes **glaze** or **glaze over**, the person begins to look bored or tired **2** to fit a sheet of glass into a window, etc. ⊃ look at **double glazing 3** ~ sth (with sth) to cover a pot, PIE, etc. with a thin clear liquid (before it is put into an oven): *Glaze the pie with beaten egg.*

glaze² /gleɪz/ *noun* [C, U] (a substance that gives) a clear shiny surface on a pot, PIE, etc.

glazed /gleɪzd/ *adj.* (used about the eyes, etc.) showing no interest or expression

glazier /ˈgleɪziə(r)/ *noun* [C] a person whose job is to fit glass into windows, etc.

gleam /gliːm/ *noun* [C, usually sing.] **1** a pale clear light, often reflected from sth: *the gleam of moonlight on the water* **2** a sudden expression of an emotion in sb's eyes: *I saw a gleam of amusement in his eyes.* **3** a small amount of sth: *a faint gleam of hope* ▸ **gleam** *verb* [I]: *gleaming white teeth* ◇ *Their eyes gleamed with enthusiasm.*

glean /gliːn/ *verb* [T] ~ sth (from sb/sth) to obtain information, knowledge, etc., sometimes with difficulty and often from various different places: *These figures have been gleaned from a number of studies.*

glee /gliː/ *noun* [U] a feeling of happiness, usually because sth good has happened to you or sth bad has happened to sb else: *She couldn't hide her glee when her rival came last in the race.* ▸ **gleeful** /ˈgliːfl/ *adj.* ▸ **gleefully** /-fəli/ *adv.*

glen /glen/ *noun* [C] (GEOGRAPHY) a deep narrow valley, especially in Scotland or Ireland

glib /glɪb/ *adj.* using words in a way that is clever and quick, but not sincere: *a glib salesman/politician* ◇ *a glib answer/excuse* ▸ **glibly** *adv.* ▸ **glibness** *noun* [U]

glide /glaɪd/ *verb* [I] (often used with an adverb or a preposition) **1** to move smoothly without noise or effort: *The dancers glided across the floor.* **2** (used about birds or aircraft) to fly using air currents, without the birds moving their wings or the aircraft using the engine: *I noticed a large bird gliding just above the rooftops.* ◇ *They saw the plane glide towards the water as it descended .*

glider /ˈglaɪdə(r)/ *noun* [C] a light aircraft without an engine that flies using air currents ⊃ look at **hang-glider**

gliding /ˈglaɪdɪŋ/ *noun* [U] the sport of flying in a GLIDER

glimmer /ˈglɪmə(r)/ *noun* [C] **1** a weak light that is not steady: *I could see a faint glimmer of light in one of the windows.* **2** a small sign of sth: *a glimmer of hope* ▸ **glimmer** *verb* [I]

glimpse /glɪmps/ *noun* [C, usually sing.] **1** ~ (at/of sth) a very quick and not complete view of sb/sth: *I just managed to catch a glimpse of the fox's tail as it ran down a hole.* **2** ~ (into/of sth) a short experience of sth that helps you understand it: *The programme gives us an interesting glimpse into the life of the cheetah.* ▸ **glimpse** *verb* [T]

glint /glɪnt/ *verb* [I] to shine with small bright flashes of light: *His eyes glinted at the thought of all that money.* ◇ *She thought the diamond was lost until she saw something glinting on the carpet.* ▸ **glint** *noun* [C]

glissando /glɪˈsændəʊ/ *noun* [C] (*pl.* glissandi /-diː/, glissandos) (MUSIC) a falling or rising series of notes that are played so as to give a continuous sliding sound

glisten /ˈglɪsn/ *verb* [I] (used about wet surfaces) to shine: *Her eyes glistened with tears.* ◇ *Tears glistened in her eyes.*

glitch /glɪtʃ/ *noun* a small problem or fault that stops sth from working successfully: *a technical glitch*

glitter /ˈglɪtə(r)/ *noun* [U] **1** a shiny appearance consisting of many small flashes of light: *the glitter of jewellery* **2** the exciting quality that sth appears to have: *the glitter of a career in show business* **3** very small shiny pieces of thin metal or paper, used as a decoration: *The children decorated their pictures with glitter.* ▸ **glitter** *verb* [I]

glittering /ˈglɪtərɪŋ/ *adj.* **1** very impressive or successful: *a glittering career/performance* **2** shining brightly with many small flashes of light

glitz /glɪts/ *noun* [U] the quality of appearing very attractive, exciting and impressive, in a way that is not always real ▸ **glitzy**

gloat /gləʊt/ *verb* [I] (often used with an adverb or a preposition) to show that you are happy about your own success or sb else's failure, in an unpleasant way

global /ˈgləʊbl/ *adj.* **1** affecting the whole world: *the global effects of pollution* **2** considering or including all parts: *We must take a global view of the problem.* ▸ **globally** /-bəli/ *adv.*

globalism /ˈgləʊbəlɪzəm/ *noun* [U] (POLITICS) the belief that events in one country affect those in all other countries, and that economic and foreign policy should be agreed in an international way ▸ **globalist** /-bəlɪst/ *noun* [C]

globalization (*BrE also* -isation) /ˌgləʊbəlaɪˈzeɪʃn/ *noun* [U] (ECONOMICS, SOCIAL STUDIES) the fact that different cultures and economic systems around the world are becoming connected and similar to each other because of the influence of large companies and of improved communication: *the globalization of world trade*

globalize (*BrE also* -ise) /ˈgləʊbəlaɪz/ *verb* [I, T] (ECONOMICS, SOCIAL STUDIES) if sth, for example a business company, **globalizes** or is **globalized**, it operates all around the world

global village *noun* [sing.] (SOCIAL STUDIES) the world considered as a single community connected by computers, phones, the internet, etc.

global warming *noun* [U] (ENVIRONMENT) the increase in the temperature of the earth's atmosphere, caused by the increase of certain gases ⊃ look at **greenhouse effect** ⊃ picture at **climate change**

globe /gləʊb/ *noun* **1** the globe [sing.] the world: *to travel all over the globe* **2** [C] a round object with a map of the world on it **3** [C] any object shaped like a ball

globe artichoke = ARTICHOKE

globetrotter /ˈgləʊbtrɒtə(r)/ *noun* [C] (*informal*) a person who travels to many countries

globule /ˈglɒbjuːl/ *noun* [C] a small drop or ball of a liquid, or of a solid that has melted: *There were globules of fat in the soup.*

glockenspiel /ˈglɒkənʃpiːl/ *noun* [C] (MUSIC) a musical instrument made of a row of metal bars of different lengths, that you hit with two small HAMMERS ⊃ look at **xylophone**

gloom /gluːm/ *noun* [U] **1** a feeling of being sad and without hope: *The news brought deep gloom to the village.* **2** a state when it is almost completely dark

gloomy /'gluːmi/ *adj.* (gloomier; gloomiest) **1** dark in way that makes you feel sad: *This dark paint makes the room very gloomy.* **2** sad and without much hope: *Don't be so gloomy — cheer up!* ▸ **gloomily** /-mɪli/ *adv.*

glorified /'glɔːrɪfaɪd/ *adj.* [only before noun] described in a way that makes sb/sth seem better, bigger, more important, etc. than they really are

glorify /'glɔːrɪfaɪ/ *verb* [T] (glorifying; glorifies; *pt, pp* glorified) to make sb/sth appear better or more important than they really are: *His biography does not attempt to glorify his early career.*

glorious ⓘ+ **C1** /'glɔːriəs/ *adj.* **1** (*formal*) deserving or bringing great success and making sb/sth famous: *a glorious victory* **2** very beautiful or impressive: *a glorious day/view* **SYN splendid** ▸ **gloriously** *adv.*

glory¹ ⓘ+ **C1** /'glɔːri/ *noun* [U] **1** great success that brings sb praise and honour and makes them famous: *The winning team was welcomed home **in a blaze of glory**.* **2** great beauty: *Autumn is the best time to see the forest in all its glory.*

glory² /'glɔːri/ *verb* (glorying; glories; *pt, pp* gloried) **PHR V glory in sth** to take (too much) pleasure in sth: *She gloried in her sporting successes.*

gloss¹ /glɒs/ *noun* [U, sing.] (a substance that gives sth) a smooth shiny surface: *gloss paint* ◇ *lip gloss* ⊃ look at **matt**

gloss² /glɒs/ *verb* **PHR V gloss over sth** to avoid talking about a problem, mistake, etc. in detail

glossary /'glɒsəri/ *noun* [C] (*pl.* -ies) a list of special or unusual words and their meanings, usually at the end of a text or book

glossy /'glɒsi/ *adj.* (glossier; glossiest) smooth and shiny: *glossy hair* ◇ *a glossy magazine* (= printed on shiny paper)

glottal stop /ˌglɒtl 'stɒp/ *noun* [C] (**LANGUAGE**) a speech sound made by closing and opening the GLOTTIS, which in English sometimes takes the place of a /t/, for example in *butter*

glottis /'glɒtɪs/ *noun* [C] (**ANATOMY**) the part of the LARYNX in the throat that contains the VOCAL CORDS (= muscles that move to produce the voice) and the narrow opening between them

glove ⓘ **B1** /glʌv/ *noun* [C] a piece of clothing that covers the hand and has five separate parts for the fingers: *I need a new **pair of gloves** for the winter.* ◇ *leather/woollen/rubber gloves* ⊃ look at **mitten**

'glove compartment (*also* glovebox /'glʌvbɒks/) *noun* [C] a small ENCLOSED space or shelf facing the front seats of a car, used for keeping small things in

glow /gləʊ/ *verb* [I] **1** to produce light and/or heat without smoke or flames: *A cigarette glowed in the dark.* **2** ~ (**with sth**) to be warm or red because of excitement, exercise, etc: *to glow with health/ enthusiasm/pride/pleasure* ▸ **glow** *noun* [sing.]: *the glow of the sky at sunset*

glower /'glaʊə(r)/ *verb* [I] ~ (**at sb/sth**) to look angrily (at sb/sth) **SYN glare**¹

glowing /'gləʊɪŋ/ *adj.* saying that sb/sth is very good: *His teacher wrote a glowing report about his work.* ▸ **glowingly** *adv.*

'glow-worm *noun* [C] a type of insect. The female has no wings and produces a green light at the end of her tail.

glucose /'gluːkəʊs, -kəʊz/ *noun* [U] (**BIOLOGY**) a simple type of sugar that is easily changed into energy by the human body ⊃ look at **dextrose, fructose, lactose, sucrose**

glue¹ /gluː/ *noun* [U, C] a thick sticky substance that is used for joining things together: *Stick the photo in with glue.*

glue² /gluː/ *verb* [T] (gluing) ~ **A** (**to/onto B**); ~ **A and B** (**together**) to join two things together with GLUE: *Do you think you can glue the handle back onto the teapot?* ◇ *Glue the pieces of card together.* **IDM glued to sth** (*informal*) giving all your attention to sth: *He just sits there every evening glued to the TV.*

glum /glʌm/ *adj.* sad and quiet ▸ **glumly** *adv.*

glut /glʌt/ *noun* [C, usually sing.] more of sth than is needed: *The glut of coffee has forced down the price.*

gluten /'gluːtn/ *noun* [U] a sticky substance that is found in plants that are made into flour, for example WHEAT: *We sell a range of **gluten-free** products* (= not containing gluten).

gluteus /'gluːtiəs/ (*pl.* glutei /-tiaɪ/) (*also* 'gluteus muscle) *noun* [C] (**ANATOMY**) any of the three muscles in each BUTTOCK (= either of the two round soft parts at the top of the legs) ▸ **gluteal** /-tiəl/ *adj.*: *the gluteal region*

glutton /'glʌtn/ *noun* [C] **1** a person who eats too much **2** ~ **for sth** (*informal*) a person who enjoys having or doing sth difficult, unpleasant, etc: *She's a glutton for hard work — she never stops.*

gluttony /'glʌtəni/ *noun* [U] the habit of eating and drinking too much

glycerine (*especially BrE*) (*AmE usually* glycerin) /'glɪsərɪn/ *noun* [U] (**CHEMISTRY**) an alternative name for GLYCEROL, frequently used in labels showing ingredients

glycerol /'glɪsərɒl/ *noun* [C] (**CHEMISTRY**) a thick sweet liquid made from fats and oils and used in medicines and EXPLOSIVES ⊃ look at **glycerine**

GM /ˌdʒiː 'em/ *abbr.* (*BrE*) = GENETICALLY MODIFIED

gm *abbr.* (in writing) (*pl.* gm, gms) = GRAM

GMO /ˌdʒiː em 'əʊ/ *noun* [C] (*pl.* GMOs) (**AGRICULTURE, BIOLOGY**) a plant, bacteria, etc. that has been grown from cells whose GENES (= the units that control particular qualities) have been changed artificially (the abbreviation for 'genetically modified organism'): *Our burgers contain no GMOs.*

GMT /ˌdʒiː em 'tiː/ *abbr.* **Greenwich Mean Time** (the time at Greenwich in England, used in the past for calculating the time everywhere in the world) **HELP** In the UK, people still refer to the time in the winter as **GMT**, even though it is actually UTC. ⊃ look at **BST**

gnarled /nɑːld/ *adj.* rough and having grown into a strange shape, because of old age or hard work: *The old man had gnarled fingers.* ◇ *a gnarled oak tree*

gnash /næʃ/ *verb* **IDM gnash your teeth** to feel very angry and upset about sth

gnat /næt/ *noun* [C] a type of very small fly that bites **SYN midge**

gnaw /nɔː/ *verb* **1** [I, T] ~ (**away**) (**at/on**) **sth** to keep biting sth: *The dog lay on the carpet gnawing away on its bone.* **2** [I] ~ (**away**) **at sb** to make sb feel worried or frightened over a long period of time: *Fear of the future gnawed away at her all the time.*

gneiss /naɪs/ *noun* [U] (**GEOLOGY**) a type of METAMORPHIC rock formed at high pressure and temperature deep in the ground

gnome /nəʊm/ *noun* [C] (in stories) a creature like a little old man with a BEARD (= hair on the sides and bottom part of his face) and a pointed hat, who lives under the ground

GNP /ˌdʒiː en 'piː/ *abbr.* (**ECONOMICS**) **gross national product** (the total value of all the goods and services produced by a country in one year, including the total amount of money that comes from foreign countries) ⊃ look at **GDP ❶ GNP = GDP + net foreign income**

GNVQ /ˌdʒiː en viː ˈkjuː/ *noun* [C] (**EDUCATION**) a qualification taken in British schools by students aged 15-18 to prepare them for university or work. (the abbreviation for 'General National Vocational Qualification'): *She's doing a GNVQ in Business Studies at the local college.*

go¹ ⚡ **A1** /gəʊ/ *verb* [I] (going; goes; *pt* went /went/; *pp* gone /gɒn/) **HELP** When sb has gone somewhere and come back, **been** is used for the past participle: *I've just been to Berlin. I got back this morning.* **1** (often used with an adverb or a preposition) to move or travel from one place to another: *She always goes home by bus.* ◇ *We're going to London tomorrow.* ◇ *He went to the cinema yesterday.* ◇ *We've still got 50 miles to go.* ◇ *How fast does this car go?* ◇ *I threw the ball and the dog went running after it.* **2** to travel to a place to take part in an activity or do sth: *Are you going to Dave's party?* ◇ *Shall we go swimming this afternoon?* ◇ *to go for a swim/drive/drink/walk/meal* ◇ *We went on a school trip to a museum.* ◇ *They've gone on holiday.* ◇ *We went to watch the match.* ◇ *I'll go and make the tea.* **3** to belong to or stay in an institution: *Which school does Ralph go to?* ◇ *to go to hospital/prison/college/university* **4** to leave a place: *I have to go now. It's nearly four o'clock.* ◇ *What time does the train go?* **5** to lead to or reach a place or time: *Where does this road go to?* **6** to be put or to fit in a particular place: *Where does this vase go?* ◇ *My clothes won't all go in one suitcase.* **7** to happen in a particular way; to develop: *How's the new job going?* **8** *linking verb* to become; to reach a particular state: *Her hair is going grey.* ◇ *to go blind/deaf/bald/mad* **9** to stay in the state mentioned: *Many mistakes go unnoticed.* **10** to be removed, lost, used, etc.; to disappear: *Has your headache gone yet?* ◇ *I like the furniture, but that carpet will have to go.* ◇ *About half my salary goes on rent.* ◇ *Jeans will never go out of fashion.* **11** to work correctly: *This clock doesn't go.* ◇ *Is your car going at the moment?* **12** to become worse or stop working correctly: *The brakes on the car have gone.* ◇ *His sight/voice/mind has gone.* **13** ~ (**with sth**); ~ (**together**) to look or taste good with sth else: *This sauce goes well with rice or pasta.* ◇ *These two colours don't really go (together).* **14** to have certain words or a certain tune: *How does that song go?* **15** (used about time) to pass: *The last hour went very slowly.* **16** to start an activity: *Everybody ready to sing? Let's go!* **17** to make a sound: *The bell went early today.* ◇ *Cats go 'miaow'.* **18** (*informal*) used in the present tense for saying what a person said: *I said, 'How are you, Jim?' and he goes, 'It's none of your business!'* **19** (*informal*) (only used in the progressive tenses) to be available: *Are there any jobs going in your department?* **20** (*informal*) used for saying that you do not want sb to do sth bad or stupid: *You can borrow my bike again, but don't go breaking it this time!* ◇ *I hope John doesn't go and tell everyone about our plan.*

IDM **as people, things, etc. go** compared to the average person or thing: *As action films go, it wasn't bad.* **be going to do sth 1** used for showing what you plan to do in the future: *We're going to sell our car.* **2** used for saying that you think sth will happen: *It's going to rain soon.* ◇ *Oh no! He's going to fall!* **go all out for sth | go all out to do sth** to make a great effort to do sth **go for it** (*informal*) to do sth after not being sure about it: *'Do you think we should buy it?' 'Yeah, let's go for it!'* **have a lot going for you** to have many advantages **Here goes!** said just before you start to do sth difficult or exciting **to go 1** that is/are left before sth ends: *How long (is there) to go before the end of the lesson?* **2** (*informal*) that you can take away

to eat or drink ❶ For other idioms containing **go**, look at the entries for the nouns, adjectives, etc. For example, **go astray** is at **astray**.

PHR V **go about** = GO AROUND/ABOUT **go about sth/ doing sth** to start trying to do sth difficult: *I wouldn't have any idea how to go about building a house.*
go after sb/sth to try to catch or get sb/sth
go against sb to not be in sb's favour or not be to sb's advantage: *The referee's decision went against her.*
go against sb/sth to do sth that sb/sth says you should not do: *She went against her parents' wishes and married him.*
go ahead 1 to take place after being delayed or in doubt: *Although several members were missing, the meeting went ahead without them.* **2** to travel in front of other people in your group and arrive before them **go ahead (with sth)** to do sth after not being sure that it was possible: *We decided to go ahead with the match in spite of the heavy rain.* ◇ *'Can I take this chair?' 'Sure, go ahead.'*
go along to continue; to progress: *The course gets more difficult as you go along.* **go along with sb/sth** to agree with sb/sth; to do what sb else has decided: *I'm happy to go along with whatever you suggest.*
go around (*also* **go round** *especially in BrE*) (especially after *enough*) to be shared among all the people: *In this area, there aren't enough jobs to go around.* **go around/about** (*also* **go round** *especially in BrE*) (used about a story, an illness, etc.) to pass from person to person: *There's a rumour going around that he's going to resign.* ◇ *There's a virus going round at work.* **go around (to …)** (*also* **go round (to …)** *especially in BrE*) to visit sb's home, usually a short distance away: *I'm going around to Jo's for dinner tonight.* **go around with sb** (*also* **go round with sb** *especially in BrE*) to spend time and go to places regularly with sb: *His parents don't like the people he has started going around with.*
go away 1 to disappear or leave: *I've got a headache that just won't go away.* ◇ *Just go away and leave me alone!* **2** to leave the place where you live for at least one night, especially for a holiday: *We're going away to the coast this weekend.*
go back (to sth) 1 to return to a place: *It's a wonderful city and I'd like to go back there one day.* ◇ *When her parents arrived they went back to her house.* **2** to return to an earlier matter or situation: *Let's go back to the subject we were discussing a few minutes ago.* **3** to have its origins in an earlier period of time: *A lot of the buildings in the village go back to the fifteenth century.* **go back on sth** to break a promise, an agreement, etc: *I promised to help them and I can't go back on my word.* **go back to sth/doing sth** to start doing again sth that you had stopped doing: *When the children got a bit older she went back to full-time work.* ◇ *He's decided to go back to teaching.*
go by 1 (used about time) to pass: *As time went by, her confidence grew.* **2** to pass a place: *He stood at the window watching people go by.* **go by sth** to use particular information, rules, etc. to help you decide your actions or opinions
go down 1 (used about a ship, etc.) to sink **2** (used about the sun) to disappear from the sky **3** to become lower in price, level, etc.; to fall: *The number of people out of work went down last month.* ⊃ note at **price¹, trend¹** **go down (with sb)** (used before an adverb, especially *well* or *badly*, or in questions beginning with *how*) to be received in a particular way by sb: *The film went down well with the critics.* **go down with sth** (*especially BrE*) to catch an illness; to become ill with sth: *Ten of our staff have gone down with flu.*

◇ *They went out together for five years before they got married.*

go over sth to look at, think about or discuss sth carefully from beginning to end: *Go over your work before you hand it in.* **go over to sth** to change to a different side, system, habit, etc: *I wore glasses until last year, then I went over to contact lenses.*

go round (*especially BrE*) = GO AROUND, GO AROUND/ABOUT **go round (to …)** (*especially BrE*) = GO AROUND (TO …) **go round with sb** (*especially BrE*) = GO AROUND WITH SB

go through to be completed successfully: *The deal went through as agreed.* **go through sth 1** to look in or at sth carefully, especially in order to find sth: *I went through all my pockets but I couldn't find my wallet.* **2** to look at, think about or discuss sth carefully from beginning to end: *We'll start the lesson by going through your homework.* **3** to have an unpleasant experience: *I'd hate to go through such a terrible ordeal again.* **go through with sth** to do sth unpleasant or difficult that you have decided, agreed or threatened to do: *Do you think she'll go through with her threat to leave him?*

go together 1 (used about two or more things) to belong to the same set or group **2** to look or taste good together

go towards sth to be used as part of the payment for sth: *The money I was given for my birthday went towards my new bike.*

go under 1 to sink below the surface of some water **2** (*informal*) (**BUSINESS**) (used about a company) to fail and close: *A lot of firms are going under in the recession.*

go up 1 to become higher in price, level, amount, etc.; to rise: *The birth rate has gone up by 10 per cent.* ⊃ note at **price**[1], **rise**[2], **trend**[1] **2** to start burning suddenly and strongly: *The car crashed into a wall and went up in flames.* **3** to be built: *New buildings are going up all over town.*

go with sth 1 to be included with sth; to happen as a result of sth: *Pressure goes with the job.* **2** to look or taste good with sth else: *What colour carpet would go with the walls?* **SYN match**[2]

go without (sth) to choose or be forced to not have sth: *They went without sleep night after night while the baby was ill.* ◇ *There wasn't time for breakfast, so I had to go without.*

go² **B1** /gəʊ/ *noun* [C] (*pl.* -oes) **1** (*BrE*) a turn to play in a game, etc: *Whose go is it?* ◇ *Hurry up — it's your go.* **SYN turn²** **2 ~ (at sth/doing sth)** (*informal*) an occasion when you try to do sth; an attempt: *Shall I have a go at fixing it for you?* ◇ *I've never played this game before, but I'll give it a go.* ◇ *Andrew passed his driving test first go.* ⊃ look at **attempt²** (1) **IDM be on the go** (*informal*) to be very active or busy: *I'm exhausted. I've been on the go all day.* **have a go at sb** (*informal*) to criticize sb/sth **make a go of sth** (*informal*) to be successful at sth

goad /gəʊd/ *verb* [T] **~ sb/sth (into sth/doing sth)** to cause sb to do sth by making them angry: *Don't let him goad you into fighting him.*

'go-ahead *adj.* enthusiastic to try new ways of doing things

the 'go-ahead *noun* [sing.] **~ (for sth)** (*informal*) permission to do sth: *It looks like the council are going to give us the go-ahead for the new building.*

goal **A2** **W** /gəʊl/ *noun* [C] **1** (**SPORT**) (in football, rugby, hockey, etc.) the area between two posts into which the ball must be kicked, hit, etc. for a point or points to be scored: *He crossed the ball in front of the goal.* **2** (**SPORT**) the act of kicking or hitting the ball into the goal area; a point or points that are scored for this: *Everton won by three goals to two.* ◇ *to score a*

---

go for sb to attack sb: *I was just stroking the dog and it went for me.* **go for sb/sth 1** to be true for a particular person or thing: *We've got financial problems but I suppose the same goes for a great many people.* **2** to choose sb/sth: *I think I'll go for the roast chicken.*

go in (used about the sun) to disappear behind a cloud **go in for sth** to enter or take part in an exam or competition **go in for sth/doing sth** to do or have sth as a hobby or interest: *He doesn't go in for sport much.*

go into sth 1 to hit sth while travelling in/on a vehicle: *I couldn't stop in time and went into the back of the car in front.* **2** to start working in a certain type of job: *When she left school she went into nursing.* **3** to look at or describe sth in detail: *I haven't got time to go into all the details now.*

go off 1 to explode: *A bomb has gone off in the city centre.* **2** to make a sudden loud noise: *I woke up when the alarm on my phone went off.* **3** (used about lights, heating, etc.) to stop working: *There was a power cut and all the lights went off.* **4** (*BrE*) (used about food and drink) to become too old to eat or drink; to go bad **5** (*BrE*) to become worse in quality: *I used to like that band but they've gone off recently.* **go off sb/sth** (*BrE, informal*) to stop liking or being interested in sb/sth: *I went off spicy food after I was ill last year.* **go off (with sb)** to leave with sb, or to leave your partner in order to have a relationship with sb else: *I don't know where Sid is — he went off with John an hour ago.* ◇ *He went off with his best friend's wife.* **go off with sth** to take sth that belongs to sb else: *Who's gone off with my cup?*

go on 1 (used about lights, heating, etc.) to start working: *I saw the lights go on in the house opposite.* **2** (used about time) to pass: *As time went on, she became more and more successful.* **3** (usually used in the progressive tenses) to happen or take place: *Can anybody tell me what's going on here?* **4** (used about a situation) to continue without changing: *This is a difficult period but it won't go on forever.* **5** to continue speaking after stopping for a moment: *Go on. What happened next?* **6** used for encouraging sb to do sth: *Oh go on, let me borrow your car. Just for tonight.* **go on sth** (usually used in negative sentences and questions) to use sth as information so that you can understand a situation: *There were no witnesses to the crime, so the police had very little to go on.* **go on (about sb/sth)** (*informal*) to talk about sb/sth for a long time in a boring or annoying way: *She went on and on about work.* **go on (at sb)** (*informal*) to keep complaining about sth: *Stop going on at me about that money.* **go on (doing sth)** to continue doing sth without stopping or changing: *We don't want to go on living here for the rest of our lives.* **go on (with sth)** to continue doing sth, perhaps after a break: *She ignored me and went on with her meal.* **go on to do sth** to do sth after completing sth else: *After retiring as a player, he went on to become a leading commentator.*

go out 1 to leave the place where you live or work for a short time, returning on the same day: *Let's go out for a meal tonight* (= to a restaurant). ◇ *I'm just going out for a walk. I won't be long.* ⊃ look at **socialize** (2) **2** to stop shining or burning: *Suddenly all the lights went out.* **3** to stop being fashionable or in use: *That kind of music went out in the seventies.* **4** (used about the sea) to move away from the land: *Is the tide coming in or going out?* **SYN ebb** ⊃ look at **tide**[1] **go out (with sb)** | **go out (together)** to spend time regularly with sb, having a romantic and/or sexual relationship: *Is Fiona going out with anyone?*

goal 3 your purpose or aim: *This year I should achieve my goal of visiting all the capital cities of Europe.* ⊃ note at **target**[1]

goalkeeper /ˈgəʊkiːpə(r)/ (*also informal* **goalie** /ˈgəʊli/, **keeper**) *noun* [C] (**SPORT**) (in football, hockey, etc.) the player who stands in front of the goal and tries to stop the other team from scoring: *The goalkeeper made a magnificent save.*

goalless /ˈgəʊlləs/ *adj.* (**SPORT**) with no goals scored: *a goalless draw* ◇ *The match finished goalless.*

'goal line *noun* [C] (**SPORT**) (in football, hockey, etc.) the line at either end of a sports field on which the goal stands or which the ball must cross to score a goal or TOUCHDOWN

goalpost /ˈgəʊlpəʊst/ *noun* [C] (**SPORT**) (in football, hockey, etc.) one of the two posts that form the sides of a goal. They are joined together by the CROSSBAR.

goat /gəʊt/ *noun* [C] a small animal with HORNS that lives in mountain areas or is kept on farms for its milk and meat

horn
bell
udder hoof
goat kid

goatee /gəʊˈtiː/ *noun* [C] a small pointed BEARD (= hair that grows on the face) on a man's CHIN (= the part of the face below the mouth)

gobble /ˈgɒbl/ *verb* [T] ~ **sth (up/down)** (*informal*) to eat sth quickly and noisily: *He'd gobbled down all his food before I'd started mine.*

gobbledegook (*also* **gobbledygook**) /ˈgɒbldiguːk/ *noun* [U] (*informal*) complicated language that is hard to understand

'go-between *noun* [C] a person who takes messages between two people or groups

goblin /ˈgɒblɪn/ *noun* [C] (in stories) a small ugly creature who tricks people

gobsmacked /ˈgɒbsmækt/ *adj.* (*informal*) so surprised that you cannot speak **SYN** **speechless**

go-cart, go-carting = GO-KART, GO-KARTING

god 🔒 **A2** /gɒd/ *noun* (**RELIGION**) **1** God [sing.] (not used with *the*) the being or spirit in Christianity, Islam and Judaism who people pray to and who people believe created the universe: *Do you believe in God?* ◇ *Muslims worship God in a mosque.* **HELP** God is used in a number of expressions. Some people think that it is wrong to use God's name in this way. **Oh my God!** expresses surprise or shock: *Oh my God! I've won the lottery!* **Thank God** is used when sb is happy and relieved about sth: *Thank God you've arrived — I was beginning to think you'd had an accident.* People use **for God's sake** when they are asking sb to do sth and want to make it sound more important or when they are angry with sb: *For God's sake, shut up!* **Heaven** or **goodness** are used in some of these expressions in order to avoid using the word **God**. **2** [sing.] (in some religions) a being or spirit that people believe has power over a particular part of nature or that represents a particular quality: *Mars was the Roman god of war and Venus was the goddess of love.*

godchild /ˈgɒdtʃaɪld/ *noun* [C] (*pl.* **godchildren** /-tʃɪldrən/) (**RELIGION**) a child that a GODPARENT at a Christian ceremony promises to help and to teach about the Christian religion

'god-daughter *noun* [C] (**RELIGION**) a female GODCHILD

goddess /ˈgɒdes, -dəs/ *noun* [C] (**RELIGION**) a female god

godfather /ˈgɒdfɑːðə(r)/ *noun* [C] (**RELIGION**) a male GODPARENT

godforsaken /ˈgɒdfəseɪkən/ *adj.* [only before noun] boring, depressing and ugly

godmother /ˈgɒdmʌðə(r)/ *noun* [C] (**RELIGION**) a female GODPARENT

godparent /ˈgɒdpeərənt/ *noun* [C] (**RELIGION**) a person chosen by a child's family who promises at a Christian ceremony to help the child and to teach them about the Christian religion

godsend /ˈgɒdsend/ *noun* [sing.] something unexpected that is very useful because it comes just when it is needed

godson /ˈgɒdsʌn/ *noun* [C] (**RELIGION**) a male GODCHILD

goes /gəʊz/ → GO[1]

goggles /ˈgɒglz/ *noun* [pl.] special glasses that you wear to protect your eyes from water, wind, dust, etc: *a pair of swimming/safety goggles* ⊃ look at **mask**[1]

going[1] /ˈgəʊɪŋ/ *noun* **1** [sing.] (*formal*) the act of leaving a place: *We were all saddened by his going.* ⊃ look at **departure** (1) **2** [U] the rate or speed of travel, progress, etc: *Three children in four years? That's not bad going!* **3** [U] how difficult it is to make progress: *The path up the mountain was rough going.* ◇ *It'll be hard going if we need to finish this by Friday!* **IDM** **get out, go, leave, etc. while the going is good** to leave a place or stop doing sth while it is still easy to do so

going[2] /ˈgəʊɪŋ/ *adj.* **IDM** **a going concern** (**BUSINESS**) a successful business **the going rate (for sth)** the usual cost (of sth): *What's the going rate for an office cleaner?*

-going /gəʊɪŋ/ *suffix* (in adjectives) going regularly to the place or event mentioned: *the theatre-going public*

,goings-'on *noun* [pl.] (*informal*) unusual things that are happening

'go-kart (*also* **go-cart**) *noun* [C] a vehicle like a very small car with no roof or doors, used for racing ▶ **go-karting** (*also* **go-carting**) *noun* [U]

gold 🔒 **A2** /gəʊld/ *noun* **1** [U] (*symb.* Au) (**CHEMISTRY**) a chemical element. Gold is a rare and valuable yellow metal used for making coins, jewellery, etc: *Is your bracelet made of solid gold?* ◇ *22 carat gold* ◇ *a gold chain/ring/watch* ❶ For more information on the periodic table of elements, look at the Reference Section of this dictionary. **2** [U, C] = GOLD MEDAL: *The team won Olympic gold.* ◇ *He won three golds and a bronze.* **3** [U, C] a bright yellow colour, like gold ▶ **gold** 🔒 **A2** *adj.*: *The invitation was written in gold letters.* ⊃ look at **golden** (1) **IDM** **(as) good as gold** → GOOD[1] **have a heart of gold** → HEART

golden 🔒+ **B2** /ˈgəʊldən/ *adj.* **1** made of gold or bright yellow in colour, like gold: *a golden crown* ◇ *golden hair/sand* **2** celebrating the 50th anniversary of sth: *The couple celebrated their golden wedding last year.* ⊃ look at **silver**[2] (2) **3** best, most important, favourite, etc: *a golden* (= wonderful) *opportunity* **IDM** **the golden rule (of sth)** the most important principle to follow when doing sth in order to be successful: *The golden rule is 'Keep your eye on the ball'.*

,golden 'wedding (*BrE*) (*AmE* **,golden anni'versary**) (*also* **,golden 'wedding anniversary** *BrE, AmE*) *noun* [C] the 50th anniversary of a wedding: *The couple celebrated their golden wedding in August.* ⊃ look at **diamond wedding, ruby wedding, silver wedding**

goldfish /ˈgəʊldfɪʃ/ *noun* [C] (*pl.* **goldfish**) a small orange fish that is often kept as a pet in a bowl or a POND (= a small artificial area of water)

gold 'medal *noun* [C] (*also* **gold** [U, C]) (**SPORT**) a medal that you get as a prize for coming first in a race or competition ⊃ look at **bronze medal, silver medal** ▸ ,gold 'medallist *noun* [C]

'gold mine *noun* [C] **1** a place where gold is taken from the ground **2** [usually sing.] a place, person or thing that provides a lot of sth: *This website is a gold mine of information.*

golf ੈ **A2** /gɒlf/ *noun* [U] (**SPORT**) a game that is played outdoors on a GOLF COURSE and in which you use a GOLF CLUB to hit a small hard ball into a series of HOLES (usually 18): *to play a round of golf*

'golf club (*also* **club**) *noun* [C] (**SPORT**) a long metal stick that is specially shaped at one end and used for hitting a ball when playing golf ⊃ look at **bat¹** (1), **racket** (3), **stick²** (3)

'golf course *noun* [C] (**SPORT**) a large area of land that is designed for playing golf on

golfer /'gɒlfə(r)/ *noun* [C] (**SPORT**) a person who plays golf

gondola /'gɒndələ/ *noun* [C] (**TOURISM**) a long boat with a flat bottom and high parts at each end, used on CANALS in Venice, Italy

gone¹ /gɒn/ past participle of **go¹**

gone² /gɒn/ *adj.* [not before noun] not present any longer; completely used or finished: *He stood at the door for a moment, and then he was gone.* ◇ *Can I have some more ice cream, please, or is it all gone?*

gone³ /gɒn/ *prep.* (*informal*) later than: *Hurry up! It's gone six already!*

gong /gɒŋ/ *noun* [C] a round piece of metal that hangs in a frame and makes a loud deep sound when it is hit with a stick. Gongs are used as musical instruments or to give signals, for example that a meal is ready.

gonna /'gənə/ (*informal*) a way of saying or writing 'going to' in informal speech, when it refers to the future: *'What's he gonna do now?' she asked.*

gonorrhoea (*BrE*) (*AmE* **gonorrhea**) /ˌgɒnə'rɪə/ *noun* [U] (**HEALTH**) a disease of the sexual organs, caught by having sex with a person who already has the disease

goo /guː/ *noun* [U] (*informal*) any sticky wet substance ⊃ look at **slime** ⊃ adjective **gooey**

good¹ ੈ **A1** /gʊd/ *adj.* (**better** /'betə(r)/; **best** /best/) **1** of a high quality or standard: *a good book/film/actor* ◇ *That's a really good idea! ◇ The hotel was pretty good, but not fantastic.* **2** ~ **at sth;** ~ **with sb/sth** able to do sth or deal with sb/sth well: *Jane's really good at science subjects but she's no good at languages.* ◇ *He's very good with children.* ◇ *Are you any good at drawing?* **3** pleasant; that you enjoy or want: *It's good to be home again.* ◇ *good news/weather* ◇ *Have a good time at the party!* **4** morally right or well behaved: *She was a very good person — she spent her whole life trying to help other people.* ◇ *Were the children good while we were out?* **5** ~ **(to sb);** ~ **of sb (to do sth)** kind; helpful: *They were good to me when I was ill.* ◇ *It was good of you to come.* **6** ~ **(for sb/sth)** having a positive effect on sb/sth's health or condition: *Green vegetables are very good for you.* ◇ *This cream is good for burns.* **7** ~ **(for sb/sth)** suitable or convenient: *This beach is very good for surfing.* ◇ *I think Paul would be a good person for the job.* ◇ *'When shall we meet?' 'Thursday would be a good day for me.'* **8** healthy or strong: *I don't feel too good today.* ◇ *'How are you?' 'I'm good.'* **9** (used about a reason, etc.) acceptable and easy to understand: *a good excuse/explanation/reason* ◇ *She has good reason to be pleased — she's just been promoted.* **10** ~ **(for sth)** that can be used or

can provide sth: *I've only got one good pair of shoes.* ◇ *This ticket's good for another three days.* **11** a good … more, larger, etc. than is usual or expected: *a good many/a good few people* (= a lot of people) ◇ *a good distance* (= a long way) ◇ *a good* (= at least) *ten minutes/a good 3 miles* ◇ *Take a good* (= long and careful) *look at this photo.* ◇ *What you need is a good rest.* ◇ *Give the fruit a good wash before you eat it.* **12** used when you are pleased about sth: *'Lisa's invited us to dinner next week.' 'Oh, good!'*

IDM as good as almost: *The project is as good as finished.* **SYN** **virtually** (as) good as gold (*informal*) very well behaved: *The children were as good as gold while you were out.* good for you, him, her, etc. (*informal*) used to show that you are pleased that sb has done sth clever: *'I passed my driving test!' 'Well done! Good for you!'* ❶ For other idioms containing **good**, look at the entries for the nouns, adjectives, etc. For example, **in good faith** is at **faith**.

good² ੈ **A2** /gʊd/ *noun* [U] behaviour that is morally right or acceptable: *the difference between good and evil* ◇ *I'm sure there's some good in everybody.*

IDM be no good (doing sth/to sb) to be of no use or value: *It's no good standing here in the cold. Let's go home.* ◇ *This sweater isn't any good. It's too small.* ◇ *This book is no good to me: I need the new edition.* do sb good to help or be useful to sb: *It'll do you good to meet some new people.* for good forever: *I hope they've gone for good this time!* for the good of sb/sth | for sb's/sth's good something that will help sb/sth; advantage: *She did it for the good of her country.* ◇ *I know you don't want to go into hospital, but it's for your own good.* What's the good of (= the advantage of) *learning French if you have no chance of using it?* not much good (*informal*) bad or not useful: *'How was the party?' 'Not much good.'* a/the world of good → **WORLD**

goodbye ੈ **A1** /ˌgʊd'baɪ/ *exclamation, noun* [C] said when sb goes or you go: *We said goodbye to Steven at the airport.* ◇ *Goodbye! See you tomorrow!* ◇ *We said our goodbyes and left.*

,Good 'Friday *noun* [U, C] (**RELIGION**) the Friday before Easter when Christians remember the death of Christ

,good-'humoured (*BrE*) (*AmE* **good-humored**) *adj.* pleasant and friendly

goodie /'gʊdi/ (*informal*) = **GOODY**

goodies /'gʊdiz/ *noun* [pl.] (*informal*) exciting things that are provided or given, especially nice things to eat: *There were lots of cakes and other goodies on the table.*

,good-'looking *adj.* (usually used about a person) attractive ⊃ look at **OPP ugly**

,good 'looks *noun* [pl.] the physical beauty of a person: *an actor famous for his rugged good looks*

,good-'natured *adj.* friendly or kind

goodness ੈ+ **B2** /'gʊdnəs/ *noun* [U] **1** the quality of being good: *They are taking advantage of your goodness.* ⊃ look at **virtue** (1) **HELP** **Goodness** is used in a number of expressions. You can say **Goodness (me)!** to show that you are surprised. **Thank goodness** expresses happiness and relief: *Thank goodness it's stopped raining!* You can say **For goodness' sake** when you are asking sb to do sth and want to make it sound more important or when you are angry with sb: *For goodness' sake, hurry up!* **2** the part of sth that has a good effect, especially on sb/sth's health: *Wholemeal bread has more goodness in it than white.*

goodnight /ˌgʊd'naɪt/ *exclamation* used when you are saying goodbye to sb late in the evening, before you go home or before you go to sleep

goods ⓘ **B1** /gʊdz/ *noun* [pl.] **1** (**BUSINESS**) things that are for sale: *a wide range of consumer goods* ◇ *electrical goods* ◇ *stolen goods* ⊃ picture at **income** ⊃ note at **product 2** things that are carried by train or lorry: *a goods train* ◇ *a heavy goods vehicle* ◇ *The road was closed both to passengers and goods.* ⊃ look at **freight**
IDM **come up with/deliver the goods** (*informal*) to do what you have promised to do

,good 'sense *noun* [U] good judgement or intelligence: *He had the good sense to refuse the offer.*

goodwill /ˌgʊd'wɪl/ *noun* [U] friendly, helpful feelings towards other people or countries: *The visit was designed to promote friendship and goodwill.*

goody (*also* **goodie**) /'gʊdi/ *noun* [C] (*pl.* -ies) (*informal*) a good person in a film, book, etc. **OPP** **baddy**

,goody-goody *noun* [C] (*informal*) (usually used in a critical way) a person who always behaves well to please people such as parents or teachers

gooey /'guːi/ *adj.* (**gooier; gooiest**) (*informal*) soft and sticky: *gooey cakes*

goof /guːf/ *verb* [I] (*especially AmE, informal*) to make a silly mistake

google /'guːgl/ *verb* [T, I] (**COMPUTING**) to type words into the SEARCH ENGINE Google™ in order to find information about sb/sth: *When I got home I googled the band's name.* ◇ *I tried googling but couldn't find anything useful.*

goose /guːs/ *noun* [C, U] (*pl.* **geese** /giːs/) a large bird with a long neck that lives on or near water; the meat of this bird. Geese live wild or are kept on farms for their meat and eggs.

gooseberry /'gʊzbəri/ *noun* [C] (*pl.* -ies) a small green fruit that is covered in small hairs and has a bitter sharp taste
IDM **play gooseberry** (*BrE, informal*) to be with two people who have a romantic relationship and who want to be alone together

goosebumps /'guːsbʌmps/ (*also* 'goose pimples *especially in BrE*) *noun* [pl.] raised spots that appear on your skin because you are cold or frightened

gore[1] /gɔː(r)/ *noun* [U] thick blood that comes from a wound ⊃ adjective **gory**

gore[2] /gɔː(r)/ *verb* [T] (used about an animal) to wound a person or another animal with a HORN, etc: *She was gored to death by a bull.*

gorge[1] /gɔːdʒ/ *noun* [C] (**GEOGRAPHY**) a deep narrow valley with steep sides ⊃ picture at **limestone**

gorge[2] /gɔːdʒ/ *verb* [T, I] ~ (**yourself**) (**on/with sth**) to eat a lot of food

gorgeous ⓘ+ **B2** /'gɔːdʒəs/ *adj.* (*informal*) extremely pleasant or attractive: *What gorgeous weather!* ◇ *You look gorgeous in that dress.* ▶ **gorgeously** *adv.*

gorilla /gə'rɪlə/ *noun* [C] a very large powerful African APE (= an animal like a large monkey but without a tail) with a body covered in black or brown hair

gory /'gɔːri/ *adj.* (**gorier; goriest**) (*informal*) full of violence and blood: *a gory film*

gosh /gɒʃ/ *exclamation* (*old-fashioned, informal*) used for expressing surprise, shock, etc.

gosling /'gɒzlɪŋ/ *noun* [C] a young GOOSE (= a bird like a large DUCK)

gospel /'gɒspl/ *noun* **1** Gospel [sing.] (**RELIGION**) one of the four books in the Bible that describe the life of Jesus Christ and the ideas that he taught: *St Matthew's/Mark's/Luke's/John's Gospel* **2** (*also* 'gospel music) [U] (**MUSIC**) a style of religious music developed by African Americans **3** (*also* ,gospel 'truth) [U] the truth: *You can't take what he says as gospel.*

gossip /'gɒsɪp/ *noun* **1** [U] informal talk about other people and their private lives that is often unkind or not true: *Matt phoned me up to tell me the latest gossip.* **2** [C, usually sing.] an informal conversation about other people and their private lives: *The two neighbours were having a good gossip over the fence.* **3** [C] a person who enjoys talking about other people's private lives ▶ **gossip** *verb* [I]

'gossip column *noun* [C] (**ARTS AND MEDIA**) a part of a newspaper or magazine where you can read about the private lives of famous people ⊃ note at **newspaper**

got /gɒt/ past tense, past participle of **get**

goth /gɒθ/ (*also* **Goth**) *noun* **1** [U] (**MUSIC**) a type of rock music that developed from PUNK music and expresses ideas about death and the end of the world **2** [C] a person who likes goth music and often wears black clothes and black and white MAKE-UP

Gothic /'gɒθɪk/ *adj.* **1** (**HISTORY**) connected with the Goths (= a Germanic people who fought against the Roman Empire) **2** (**ARCHITECTURE**) built in the style that was popular in western Europe from the twelfth to the sixteenth centuries, and which has pointed ARCHES and windows and tall thin PILLARS: *a Gothic church* **3** (**LITERATURE**) written in the style popular in the eighteenth and nineteenth centuries, which described romantic adventures in mysterious or frightening places or situations

go-to /'gəʊ tuː/ *adj.* [only before noun] used to refer to the person or place that sb goes to for help, advice or information: *He's the president's go-to guy on Asian politics.*

gotta /'gɒtə/ (*informal*) the written form of the word some people use to mean 'have) got to' or '(have) got a', which is not considered to be correct

gotten /'gɒtn/ (*AmE*) past participle of **get**

gouache /guˈɑːʃ, gwɑːʃ/ *noun* (**ART**) **1** [U] a method of painting using colours that are mixed with water and made thick with a type of GLUE (= a thick sticky substance); the paints used in this method **2** [C] a picture painted using this method

gouge /gaʊdʒ/ *verb* [T] to make a hole in a surface using a sharp object in a rough way
PHR V **gouge sth out** to remove or form sth by digging into a surface: *These deep valleys were gouged out by glaciers.*

goulash /'guːlæʃ/ *noun* [C, U] a hot Hungarian dish of meat that is cooked slowly in liquid with PAPRIKA (= a strong SPICE)

gourd /gʊəd, gɔːd/ *noun* [C] a type of large fruit, not normally eaten, with hard skin. Gourds are often dried and used as containers.

gourmand /'gʊəmənd/ *noun* [C] a person who enjoys eating and eats large amounts of food

gourmet /'gʊəmeɪ/ *noun* [C] a person who enjoys food and knows a lot about it

gout /gaʊt/ *noun* [U] (**HEALTH**) a disease that causes the JOINTS (= the places where two bones fit together), especially the toes, knees and fingers, to become painful and larger than normal

govern ⓘ **B2** ⓦ /'gʌvn/ *verb* **1** [T, I] (**POLITICS**) to legally control the public affairs of a country, city, etc: *Britain is governed by the prime minister and the Cabinet.* ◇ *He says that his rival is unfit to govern.* **2** [T, often passive] to influence or control sb/sth: *Our decision will be governed by the amount of money we have to spend.*

governance ʔ+ **C1** /ˈɡʌvənəns/ *noun* [U] (*formal*) (**POLITICS**) the activity of governing a country or controlling an organization; the way in which this is done: *Representatives of all ethnic groups will be included in the governance of the new state.* ◇ *high standards of corporate governance*

government ʔ **A2** **W** /ˈɡʌvənmənt/ *noun* (**POLITICS**) **1** (*often* the Government) [C + sing./pl. verb] (*abbr.* govt) the group of people who control a country: *He has resigned from the government.* ◇ *The foreign governments involved are meeting in Geneva.* ◇ *government policy/money/ministers* ⊃ look at **opposition** (3) **2** [U] the activity or method of controlling a country: *weak/strong/corrupt government* ◇ *Which party is in government?* ▸ **governmental** **W** /ˌɡʌvnˈmentl/ *adj.*: *a governmental department* ◇ *different governmental systems*

▼ VOCABULARY BUILDING

Different types of government include: **communist, conservative, democratic, liberal, reactionary** and **socialist**. A country or state may also have a **military, provisional, central, federal** or **coalition** government.

ˌgovernment ˈhealth warning *noun* [C] (**HEALTH**) (in the UK) a notice that must appear on the packages of some products, especially cigarettes, to warn people that the product is dangerous to their health

governor ʔ+ **B2** /ˈɡʌvənə(r)/ *noun* [C] **1** (*also* Governor) (**POLITICS**) a person who controls a region or state (especially in the US): *the Governor of New York State* **2** the leader or member of a group of people who control an organization: *the governor of the Bank of England* ◇ *school governors*

gown /ɡaʊn/ *noun* [C] **1** a long formal dress for a special occasion: *a ball gown* **2** a long loose piece of clothing that is worn over clothes by judges, doctors performing operations, etc.

GP /ˌdʒiː ˈpiː/ *noun* [C] (*especially BrE*) (**MEDICINE**) a doctor who treats all types of illnesses and works in the local community in a **PRACTICE**, not in a hospital (the abbreviation for 'general practitioner'): *Go and see your GP as soon as possible.* ◇ *There are four GPs in our local practice.* ⊃ note at **doctor**[1]

GPA /ˌdʒiː piː ˈeɪ/ *abbr.* (*AmE*) = GRADE POINT AVERAGE

GPS /ˌdʒiː piː ˈes/ *abbr.* **global positioning system** (a system by which signals are sent from satellites to a special device, used to show the position of a person or thing on the surface of the earth very accurately) ⊃ look at **satnav**

grab[1] ʔ **B2** /ɡræb/ *verb* (-bb-) **1** [T, I] ~ sth (from sb) to take sth with a sudden movement: *Helen grabbed the toy car from her little brother.* ◇ *Grab hold of his arm in case he tries to run!* ◇ *Somebody had arrived before us and grabbed all the seats.* ◇ (*figurative*) *He grabbed the opportunity of a free trip to America.* ◇ (*figurative*) *I'll try to grab the waitress's attention.* ◇ *Don't grab — there's plenty for everybody.* ⊃ look at **snatch**[1] (1) **2** [I] ~ at/for sth to try to get or catch sb/sth: *Jonathan grabbed at the ball but missed.* **3** [T] to get sth quickly because you are in a hurry: *I'll just grab something to eat and then we'll go.*

grab[2] /ɡræb/ *noun* **1** [usually sing.] ~ (at/for sb/sth) a sudden attempt to take or hold sb/sth: *She made a grab for the boy but she couldn't stop him falling.* ◇ *He made a grab for her bag.* **2** [C] (**COMPUTING**) a picture taken from a TV or video film, or from a computer screen, stored as an image on a computer: *a screen grab*

grace ʔ+ **C1** /ɡreɪs/ *noun* **1** [U] the ability to move in a smooth and controlled way **2** [U] extra time that is allowed for sth **3** [U] (**RELIGION**) the love that God shows to the human race **4** [U, C] (**RELIGION**) a short prayer of thanks to God before or after a meal **IDM** sb's fall from grace a situation in which sb loses the respect that people had for them by doing sth wrong or **IMMORAL** have the grace to do sth to be polite enough to do sth with good grace in a pleasant and reasonable way, without complaining: *He accepted the refusal with good grace.*

graceful /ˈɡreɪsfl/ *adj.* **1** moving in a smooth, attractive way or having a smooth, attractive form: *a graceful dancer* ◇ *graceful curves* ⊃ look at **gracious** (2) **2** polite and kind in a difficult situation ▸ **gracefully** /-fəli/ *adv.*: *The goalkeeper rose gracefully to catch the ball.* ◇ *She accepted the decision gracefully* (= without showing her DISAPPOINTMENT). ▸ **gracefulness** *noun* [U]

graceless /ˈɡreɪsləs/ *adj.* **1** not knowing how to be polite to people **2** (used about a movement or a shape) not pleasant or attractive to look at ▸ **gracelessly** *adv.*

gracious /ˈɡreɪʃəs/ *adj.* **1** (used about a person or their behaviour) kind, polite and generous: *a gracious smile* **2** [only before noun] showing the easy comfortable way of life that rich people can have: *gracious living* ⊃ look at **graceful** (1) ▸ **graciously** *adv.* ▸ **graciousness** *noun* [U] **IDM** good gracious! (*old-fashioned*) used for expressing surprise: *Good gracious! Is that the time?*

grade[1] ʔ **B1** /ɡreɪd/ *noun* [C] **1** the quality or the level of ability, importance, etc. that sb/sth has: *Which grade of petrol do you need?* ◇ *We need to use high-grade materials for this job.* ◇ *Staff on the lowest pay grade* (= level of pay) *will get an immediate pay rise.* **2** (**EDUCATION**) a mark that is given for school work, etc. or in an exam: *He got good/poor grades this term.* ◇ *Very few students pass the exam with a grade A.* ⊃ note at **study**[2] **3** (*AmE*) (**EDUCATION**) a class or classes in a school in which all the children are of a similar age: *My daughter is in the third grade.* ⊃ note at **form**[1] **IDM** make the grade (*informal*) to reach the expected standard; to succeed

grade[2] ʔ **B2** /ɡreɪd/ *verb* [T, often passive] to put things or people into groups according to their quality, ability, size, etc: *I've graded their work from 1 to 10.* ◇ *Eggs are graded by size.* ▸ **graded** *adj.*: *graded tests for language students*

ˈgrade point average *noun* [C, usually sing.] (*abbr.* GPA) (**EDUCATION**) the average of a student's marks over a period of time in the US education system

ˈgrade school = ELEMENTARY SCHOOL

gradient /ˈɡreɪdiənt/ *noun* [C] (**GEOGRAPHY, MATHEMATICS**) the degree at which a road, etc. goes up or down: *The hill has a gradient of 1 in 4* (= 25%). ◇ *a steep gradient*

ˈgrad school /ˈɡræd skuːl/ (*informal*) = GRADUATE SCHOOL

gradual /ˈɡrædʒuəl/ *adj.* happening slowly or over a long period of time; not sudden: *a gradual increase* **OPP** sudden

gradually ʔ **B2** /ˈɡrædʒuəli/ *adv.* slowly, over a long period of time: *After the war life gradually got back to normal.* ◇ *The weather gradually improved.*

graduate[1] ʔ **B1** /ˈɡrædʒuət/ *noun* [C] (**EDUCATION**) **1** ~ (in sth) a person who has a degree from a university, etc: *a law graduate/a graduate in law* ◇ *a graduate of London University/a London University graduate* ⊃ look at **bachelor** (2), **postgraduate, student, undergraduate** ⊃ note at **subject**[1] (*AmE*) person who has completed a course at a school, college, etc: *a high-school graduate*

graduate² 🔊 **B1** /ˈɡrædʒueɪt/ *verb* [I] **1 ~ (in sth) (from sth)** (**EDUCATION**) to get a degree from a university, etc., especially a first degree: *She graduated in history from Cambridge University.* **2 ~ (from sth)** (*AmE*) (**EDUCATION**) to complete a course at a school, college, etc: *He graduated from high school in 2010.* **3 ~ (from sth) to sth** to change (from sth) to sth more difficult, important, expensive, etc: *She's graduated from being a classroom assistant to becoming a teacher.*

ˈgraduate school (*also informal* **ˈgrad school**) (*both AmE*) *noun* [C] (**EDUCATION**) a part of a college or university where you can study for a second or further degree

graduation /ˌɡrædʒuˈeɪʃn/ *noun* (**EDUCATION**) **1** [U] the act of successfully completing a university degree or (in the US) studies at a high school **2** [U, C] a ceremony in which CERTIFICATES are given to people who have graduated

graffiti /ɡrəˈfiːti/ *noun* [U, pl.] pictures or writing on a wall, etc. in a public place: *Vandals had covered the walls in graffiti.*

graft /ɡrɑːft/ *noun* [C] **1** (**AGRICULTURE**) a piece of a living plant that is fixed onto another plant so that it will grow **2** (**MEDICINE**) a piece of living skin, bone, etc. that is fixed onto a damaged part of a body in an operation: *a skin graft* ▶ **graft** *verb* [T] **~ sth onto sth** (**MEDICINE**): *Skin from his leg was grafted onto the burnt area of his face.* ⊃ look at **transplant¹**

grain 🔊 **B1** /ɡreɪn/ *noun* **1** [U, C] (**AGRICULTURE**) the seeds of food plants such as rice, etc.; a single seed of such a plant: *The US is a major producer of grain.* ◇ *grain exports* ◇ *a few grains of rice* ⊃ picture at **cereal 2** [C] **~ of sth** a very small piece of sth: *a grain of sand/salt/sugar* ◇ (*figurative*) *There isn't **a grain of truth** in the rumour.* **3** [U] the natural pattern of lines that can be seen or felt in wood, rock, stone, etc. **IDM (be/go) against the grain** to be different from what is usual or natural

gram (*BrE also* **gramme**) /ɡræm/ *noun* [C] (*abbr.* **g, gm**) a measure of weight. There are 1 000 grams in a KILOGRAM. ❶ For more information about weights, look at the **Reference Section** of this dictionary.

grammar /ˈɡræmə(r)/ *noun* (**LANGUAGE**) **1** [U] the rules of a language, for example for forming words or joining words together in sentences: *Russian grammar can be difficult for foreign learners.* **2** [U] the way in which sb uses the rules of a language: *You have a good vocabulary, but your grammar needs improvement.* **3** [C] a book that describes and explains the rules of a language: *a French grammar*

ˈgrammar school *noun* [C] (**EDUCATION**) (in England, Wales and Northern Ireland, especially in the past) a type of secondary school for children between the ages of 11 and 18 who are good at academic subjects

grammatical /ɡrəˈmætɪkl/ *adj.* (**GRAMMAR**) **1** connected with grammar: *the grammatical rules for forming plurals* **2** following the rules of a language: *The sentence is not grammatical.* ▶ **grammatically** /-kli/ *adv.*

gramme /ɡræm/ (*BrE*) = GRAM

gran /ɡræn/ (*BrE, informal*) = GRANDMOTHER

Granary™ /ˈɡrænəri/ *adj.* (used about bread) containing whole grains of WHEAT

grand¹ 🔊 **B2** /ɡrænd/ *adj.* **1** impressive and large or important (also used in names): *Our house isn't very grand, but it has a big garden.* ◇ *She thinks she's very grand because she drives a Porsche.* ◇ *the Grand Canyon* ◇ *the Grand Hotel* ⊃ *noun* **grandeur 2** (*informal*) very good or pleasant: *You've done a grand job!* ▶ **grandly** *adv.* ▶ **grandness** *noun* [U]

grand² /ɡrænd/ *noun* [C] (*pl.* **grand**) (*slang*) 1 000 pounds or dollars

grandad (*also* **granddad** *especially in AmE*) /ˈɡrændæd/ (*informal*) = GRANDFATHER

grandchild /ˈɡræntʃaɪld/ *noun* [C] (*pl.* **grandchildren** /-tʃɪldrən/) a child of your son or daughter: *Her daughter and grandchildren live with her.*

granddaughter /ˈɡrændɔːtə(r)/ *noun* [C] a daughter of your son or daughter ⊃ look at **grandson**

grandeur /ˈɡrændʒə(r), -djə(r)/ *noun* [U] (*formal*) **1** the quality of being large and impressive: *the grandeur of the Swiss Alps* **2** the feeling of being important

grandfather 🔊 **A1** /ˈɡrænfɑːðə(r)/ *noun* [C] the father of your father or mother ⊃ look at **grandmother**

ˌgrandfather ˈclock *noun* [C] a clock that stands on the floor in a tall wooden case

grandiose /ˈɡrændiəʊs/ *adj.* bigger or more complicated than necessary

grandmother 🔊 **A1** /ˈɡrænmʌðə(r)/ (*also informal* **grandma** /ˈɡrænmɑː/) *noun* [C] the mother of your father or mother ⊃ look at **grandfather**

grandpa /ˈɡrænpɑː/ (*informal*) = GRANDFATHER

grandparent 🔊 **A1** /ˈɡrænpeərənt/ *noun* [C] the father or mother of your father or mother: *This is a picture of two of my great-grandparents* (= the parents of one of my grandparents).

ˌgrand piˈano *noun* [C] (**MUSIC**) a large piano in which the strings are HORIZONTAL

Grand Prix /ˌɡrɒ̃ ˈpriː/ *noun* [C] (*pl.* **Grands Prix** /ˌɡrɒ̃ ˈpriː/) (**SPORT**) one of a series of important international races for racing cars or motorcycles

ˌgrand ˈslam *noun* [C] (**SPORT**) the winning of all of a set of important matches or competitions in a particular sport in a single year, for example tennis or rugby

grandson /ˈɡrænsʌn/ *noun* [C] a son of your son or daughter ⊃ look at **granddaughter**

grandstand /ˈɡrænstænd/ *noun* [C] (**SPORT**) a structure with rows of seats, usually covered by a roof, from which you get a good view of a sports competition, etc.

ˌgrand ˈtotal *noun* [C] the amount that you get when you add several totals together

granite /ˈɡrænɪt/ *noun* [U] (**GEOLOGY**) a type of hard grey rock

granny /ˈɡræni/ *noun* [C] (*pl.* **-ies**) (*informal*) = GRANDMOTHER

grant¹ 🔊 **B2** /ɡrɑːnt/ *verb* [T, often passive] **1** (*formal*) to (officially) give sb what they have asked for: *He was granted permission to leave early.* **2 ~ (sb) (that)** … to agree (that sth is true): *I grant you that New York is an interesting place but I still wouldn't want to live there.* ⊃ note at **admit**
IDM take sb/sth for granted to be so used to sb/sth that you forget their true value and are not grateful: *In developed countries we take running water for granted.* **take it for granted** to accept sth as being true

grant² 🔊 **B2** /ɡrɑːnt/ *noun* [C] **~ (for sb) (to do sth); ~ (for sth)** money that is given by the government, etc. for a particular purpose: *She applied for a student grant* (= to help pay for university education). ◇ *The school has received a large grant to improve its buildings.* ◇ *They were awarded a grant for their research.*

granted /'grɑːntɪd/ *adv.* used for saying that sth is true, before you make a comment about it: *'We've never had any problems before.' 'Granted, but this year there are 200 more people coming.'*

granular /'grænjələ(r)/ *adj.* made of a mass of small hard pieces; looking or feeling like a mass of small hard pieces: *You can apply some granular fertilizer to the soil.*

granulated sugar /ˌgrænjuleɪtɪd 'ʃʊgə(r)/ *noun* [U] white sugar in the form of small grains

granule /'grænjuːl/ *noun* [C] a small hard piece of sth; a small grain: *instant coffee granules*

grape /greɪp/ *noun* [C] a small soft green or purple fruit that grows in bunches on a VINE (= a climbing plant) and that is used for making wine: *a bunch of grapes* **IDM** **sour grapes** → SOUR

grapefruit /'greɪpfruːt/ *noun* [C, U] (*pl.* **grapefruit**, **grapefruits**) a large round yellow fruit with a thick skin and a slightly sharp bitter taste

grapevine /'greɪpvaɪn/ *noun* [sing.] a climbing plant that produces GRAPES
IDM **on/through the grapevine** by talking in an informal way to other people: *I heard on/through the grapevine that you're moving.*

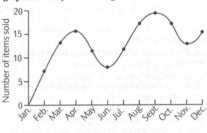

graph

graph /grɑːf/ *noun* [C] (**MATHEMATICS**) a diagram in which a line or curve shows the relationship between two quantities, measurements, etc: *a graph showing/ to show the number of cars sold each month* ⊃ look at **bar graph**

graphene /'græfiːn/ *noun* [U] (**CHEMISTRY**) a very strong, light form of CARBON: *Graphene is the thinnest, strongest material known to science.*

graphic ̊+ **B2** /'græfɪk/ *adj.* **1** [only before noun] connected with drawings, diagrams, etc: *graphic design* ◇ *a graphic artist* **2** (used about descriptions) clear and giving a lot of detail, especially about sth unpleasant: *She described the accident in graphic detail.* ► **graphically** /-kli/ *adv.*

ˌgraphic ˈnovel *noun* [C] (**LITERATURE**) a novel that is told mostly in a series of drawings, with some words

graphics ̊+ **B2** /'græfɪks/ *noun* (**ART**, **COMPUTING**) **1** [pl.] designs, diagrams, etc. that are used especially in the production of books, magazines, etc: *computer graphics* **2** [U] the production or use of these drawings, diagrams, etc.

graphite /'græfaɪt/ *noun* [U] (**CHEMISTRY**) a soft black substance (a form of CARBON) that is used in pencils

ˈgraph paper *noun* [U] (**MATHEMATICS**) paper with small squares of equal size printed on it, used for drawing GRAPHS and other diagrams

grapple /'græpl/ *verb* [I] **1** ~ (**with sb/sth**) to get hold of sb/sth and fight with or try to control them or it **2** ~ (**with sth/to do sth**) to try to find a solution to a problem: *We have been grappling with this problem all day.*

grasp¹ ̊+ **C1** /grɑːsp/ *verb* [T] **1** to take hold of sb/sth suddenly and FIRMLY: *Lisa grasped the child firmly by the hand before crossing the road.* ◇ (*figurative*) *to grasp an opportunity/a chance* **2** to understand sth completely: *I don't think you've grasped how serious the situation is.*
PHR V **grasp at sth** to try to take hold of sth

grasp² ̊+ **C1** /grɑːsp/ *noun* [C, usually sing.] **1** a firm hold of sb/sth: *Get a good grasp on the rope before pulling yourself up.* ◇ *I grabbed the boy, but he slipped from my grasp.* **2** a person's understanding of a subject or of difficult facts: *He has a good grasp of English grammar.* **3** the ability to get or achieve sth: *Finally their dream was within their grasp.*

grasping /'grɑːspɪŋ/ *adj.* wanting very much to have a lot more money, power, etc.

grass ̊ **A2** /grɑːs/ *noun* **1** [U] the common green plant with thin leaves that covers fields and parts of gardens. Cows, sheep, horses, etc. eat grass: *a blade (= one leaf) of grass* **2** (*usually* the grass) [sing., U] an area of ground covered with grass: *I must cut the grass at the weekend.* ◇ *Don't walk on the grass.* **3** [C] one type of grass: *an arrangement of dried flowers and grasses*

grasshopper /'grɑːshɒpə(r)/ *noun* [C] an insect with long back legs that can jump very high and that makes a sound with its legs ⊃ picture at **animal**

grassland /'grɑːslænd/ *noun* [U] (*also* **grasslands** [pl.]) (**GEOGRAPHY**) a large area of open land covered with wild grass ⊃ picture at **carbon cycle**, **ecosystem**

grassroots /ˌgrɑːsˈruːts/ *noun* [pl.] (**POLITICS**) ordinary people in society or in an organization, rather than the leaders or people who make decisions: *the grassroots of the party*

grassy /'grɑːsi/ *adj.* (**grassier**; **grassiest**) covered with grass

grate¹ /greɪt/ *verb* **1** [T] to rub food into small pieces using a GRATER: *grated cheese/carrot* **2** [I] ~ (**on sb**) to annoy sb: *It's her voice that grates on me.* **SYN** **irritate** **3** [I, T] ~ (**sth**) (**against/on sth**) when two hard surfaces **grate** as they rub together, they make a sharp unpleasant sound; somebody can also make one thing **grate** against another: *He grated his knife across the plate.*

grate² /greɪt/ *noun* [C] the metal frame that holds the wood, coal, etc. in a FIREPLACE (= the open place in a room where you light a fire)

grateful ̊ **B1** /'greɪtfl/ *adj.* ~ (**to sb**) (**for sth**); ~ (**that …**) feeling or showing thanks (to sb): *We are very grateful to you for all the help you have given us.* ◇ *He was very grateful that you did as he asked.* **OPP** **ungrateful** ► **gratefully** /-fəli/ *adv.*

WORD FAMILY
grateful *adj.*
(≠ ungrateful)
gratitude *noun*
(≠ ingratitude)

grater /'greɪtə(r)/ *noun* [C] a kitchen tool that is used for cutting food (for example cheese) into small pieces by rubbing it across its rough surface

gratify /'grætɪfaɪ/ *verb* [T, usually passive] (**gratifying**; **gratifies**; *pt, pp* **gratified**) (*formal*) to give sb pleasure and SATISFACTION: *I was gratified to hear that you enjoyed my book.* ► **gratifying** *adj.*

grating /'greɪtɪŋ/ *noun* [C] a frame made of metal bars that is fixed over a hole in the road, a window, etc.

gratitude /'grætɪtjuːd/ *noun* [U] ~ (**to sb**) (**for sth**) the feeling of being grateful or of wanting to give your thanks to sb: *We should like to express our gratitude to David for all his help.* **OPP** **ingratitude**

gratuity /grəˈtjuːəti/ *noun* [C] (*pl.* -ies) (*formal*) a small amount of extra money that you give to sb who serves you, for example in a restaurant **SYN** **tip**[1]

grave[1] ʔ+ **C1** /greɪv/ *noun* [C] the place where a dead body is buried: *I put some flowers on my grandmother's grave.* ⊃ look at **tomb**
IDM have one foot in the grave → FOOT[1]

grave[2] ʔ+ **C1** /greɪv/ *adj.* (*formal*) **1** bad or serious: *These events could have grave consequences for us all.* ◇ *The children were in grave danger.* **2** (used about people) sad or serious ⊃ noun **gravity** ▸ gravely *adv.*: *gravely ill*

grave[3] ʔ+ **C1** /grɑːv/ (*also* ˌgrave ˈaccent) *noun* [C] (**LANGUAGE**) a mark placed over a vowel in some languages to show how it should be pronounced, as over the *e* in the French word *père* ⊃ look at **acute accent, circumflex, tilde, umlaut**

gravel /ˈɡrævl/ *noun* [U] very small stones that are used for making roads, paths, etc. ⊃ picture at **floodplain, purification**

gravelly /ˈɡrævəli/ *adj.* **1** full of or containing many small stones: *Silt and gravelly deposits had been left by the tide.* **2** (used about a voice) deep and with a rough sound: *His gravelly voice is perfect for radio.*

gravestone /ˈɡreɪvstəʊn/ *noun* [C] a stone in the ground that shows the name, dates, etc. of the dead person who is buried there ⊃ look at **headstone, tombstone**

graveyard /ˈɡreɪvjɑːd/ *noun* [C] an area of land, often next to a church, where dead people are buried ⊃ look at **cemetery, churchyard**

gravitational /ˌɡrævɪˈteɪʃənl/ *adj.* (**PHYSICS**) connected with or caused by the force of GRAVITY: *a gravitational field* ◇ *the gravitational pull of the moon* ▸ gravitationally /-nəli/ *adv.*

gravity ʔ+ **C1** /ˈɡrævəti/ *noun* [U] **1** (**ASTRONOMY, PHYSICS**) the natural force that makes things fall to the ground when you drop them: *the force of gravity* ⊃ look at **electromagnetism, strong force, weak force** **2** (*formal*) importance, and a cause for worry: *Politicians are only now realizing the gravity of the situation.* ⊃ adjective **grave**

gravy /ˈɡreɪvi/ *noun* [U] a thin sauce that is made from the juices that come out of meat while it is cooking ⊃ look at **sauce**

gray /greɪ/ (*AmE*) = GREY[1], GREY[2]

grayish /ˈɡreɪʃ/ (*AmE*) = GREYISH

ˌgray ˈmarket (*AmE*) = GREY MARKET

graze[1] /greɪz/ *verb* **1** [I] (**AGRICULTURE**) (used about cows, sheep, etc.) to eat grass (that is growing in a field): *There were cows grazing by the river.* **2** [T] to break the surface of your skin by rubbing it against sth rough: *The child fell and grazed her knee.* **3** [T] to pass sth and touch it lightly: *The bullet grazed his shoulder.*

graze[2] /greɪz/ *noun* [C] a slight injury where the surface of the skin has been broken by being rubbed against sth rough

grazier /ˈɡreɪziə(r)/ *noun* [C] (**AGRICULTURE**) a farmer who keeps animals that eat grass

grease[1] /ɡriːs/ *noun* [U] **1** any thick substance containing oil, especially one that is used to make machines run smoothly: *engine grease* **2** animal fat that has been made soft by cooking: *You'll need very hot water to get all the grease off those pans.*

grease[2] /ɡriːs/ *verb* [T] to rub GREASE or fat on or in sth: *Grease the tin thoroughly to stop the cake from sticking.*

greaseproof paper /ˌɡriːspruːf ˈpeɪpə(r)/ (*BrE*) (*AmE* **wax paper**) *noun* [U] paper that does not let fat, oil etc. pass through it, used in cooking and for putting round food

greasy /ˈɡriːsi, ˈɡriːzi/ *adj.* (**greasier**; **greasiest**) covered with or containing a lot of GREASE: *greasy skin/hair* ◇ *greasy food*

great[1] ʔ **A1** /ɡreɪt/ *adj.*
- LARGE **1** large in amount, degree, size, etc: *The party was a great success.* ◇ *We had great difficulty in solving the problem.*
- IMPORTANT **2** particularly important; of unusually high quality: *Einstein was perhaps the greatest scientist of the century.*
- PLEASANT **3** (*informal*) good; wonderful: *We had a great time in Paris.* ◇ *It's great to see you again.* ◇ *You did a great job.*
- VERY **4** (*informal*) (used to emphasize adjectives of size, quantity, etc.) very; very good: *There was a great big dog in the garden.* ◇ *They were great friends.*
- FAMILY MEMBER **5** great- used before a noun to show a family relationship: *She's my great-grandmother.* (= the mother of one of my grandparents) ▸ greatness *noun* [U]
IDM ❶ For idioms containing **great**, look at the entries for the nouns, adjectives, etc. For example, **go to great lengths** is at **length**.

great[2] /ɡreɪt/ *noun* [C, usually pl.] (*informal*) a person of special ability or importance: *He is one of the all-time greats of the sport.*

ˌGreat ˈBritain *noun* [U] (*abbr.* GB) England, Scotland and Wales ⊃ note at **United Kingdom**

greatly ʔ+ **B2** /ˈɡreɪtli/ *adv.* (*formal*) very much: *Your help would be greatly appreciated.*

greed /ɡriːd/ *noun* [U] ~ (for sth) a strong desire for more food, money, power, etc. than you really need: *the companies' greed for profits*

greedy /ˈɡriːdi/ *adj.* (**greedier**; **greediest**) ~ (for sth) wanting more food, money, power, etc. than you really need: *Don't be so greedy — you've had three pieces of cake already.* ◇ *I was greedy for excitement and adventure.* ▸ greedily /-dɪli/ *adv.* ▸ greediness *noun* [U]

Greek /ɡriːk/ *noun* **1** [C] a person from modern or ancient Greece **2** [U] (**LANGUAGE**) the language of modern or ancient Greece

green[1] ʔ **A1** /ɡriːn/ *adj.* **1** having the colour of grass or leaves: *dark/light/pale green* **2** covered with grass or other plants: *green fields/pastures/hills* **3** (**ENVIRONMENT, POLITICS**) connected with protecting the environment or the natural world: *the Green Party* ◇ *green products* (= that do not damage the environment) **4** (*informal*) (used about a person) with little experience of life or a particular job **5** JEALOUS (wanting to have what sb else has got): *He was green with envy when he saw his neighbour's new car.* **SYN** jealous **6** (used about the skin) of a strange, pale colour (because you feel sick): *At the sight of all the blood he turned green and fainted.*
IDM give sb/get the green light (*informal*) to give sb/get permission to do sth have green fingers (*BrE*) | have a green thumb (*AmE*) to have the ability to make plants grow well

green[2] ʔ **A1** /ɡriːn/ *noun*
- COLOUR **1** [U, C] the colour of grass or leaves: *They were dressed in green.* ◇ *The room was decorated in greens and blues.*
- VEGETABLES **2** greens [pl.] green vegetables that are usually eaten cooked: *To have a healthy complexion you should eat more greens.*
- AREA OF GRASS **3** [C] (*BrE*) an area of grass in the centre of a village **4** [C] (**SPORT**) a flat area of very short grass used in games such as golf or BOWLS

• IN POLITICS **5** the Greens [pl.] the Green Party (= the party whose main aim is the protection of the environment)

'green belt noun [U, C, usually sing.] (BrE) (**ENVIRONMENT**) an area of open land around a city where building is not allowed

'green card noun [C] (**SOCIAL STUDIES**) a document that allows sb from another country to live and work legally in the US

greenery /'griːnəri/ noun [U] attractive green leaves and plants

greenfield /'griːnfiːld/ adj. [only before noun] (**GEOGRAPHY**) used to describe an area of land that has not yet had buildings on it, but for which building development may be planned: a greenfield site ⊃ look at **brownfield**

greenfly /'griːnflaɪ/ noun [U, C] (pl. greenflies, greenfly) a small flying insect that is harmful to plants

greengage /'griːnɡeɪdʒ/ noun [C] a small round yellow-green fruit that is a type of PLUM

greengrocer /'griːnɡrəʊsə(r)/ noun [C] (BrE) **1** a person who has a shop that sells fruit and vegetables ⊃ look at **grocer** (1) **2** greengrocer's (pl. greengrocers) a shop that sells fruit and vegetables

greenhouse ⏚+ **B2** /'griːnhaʊs/ (BrE also glasshouse) noun [C] (**AGRICULTURE**) a building made of glass in which plants are grown ⊃ look at **hothouse**

the 'greenhouse effect noun [sing.] (**ENVIRONMENT**) the warming of the earth's atmosphere as a result of harmful gases, etc. in the air: The destruction of forests is contributing to the greenhouse effect. ⊃ look at **global warming**

greenhouse 'gas noun [C] (**ENVIRONMENT**) any of the gases that are thought to cause THE GREENHOUSE EFFECT, especially CARBON DIOXIDE ⊃ picture at **climate change**

greening /'griːnɪŋ/ noun [U] (**ENVIRONMENT**) **1** the act of creating parks and other areas with trees and plants in a city: Urban greening could make the places we live resilient to climate change. **2** the act of making sb more aware of environmental issues, or of taking action to protect the environment: His work will contribute to the greening of our economy.

greenish /'griːnɪʃ/ adj. slightly green

green 'light noun [sing.] permission for a project, etc. to start or continue: The government has decided to **give the green light** to the plan. **SYN** go-ahead

green 'onion (AmE) = SPRING ONION

green 'pepper noun [C] a hollow green fruit that is eaten, raw or cooked, as a vegetable

'green roof noun [C] (**ENVIRONMENT**) a type of roof that has plants growing on it that help to keep the building cool in summer and warm in winter

green 'tea noun [U] a pale tea made from leaves that have been dried but that have not gone through FERMENTATION (= a natural chemical process)

greenwash /'griːnwɒʃ/ noun [U] (**BUSINESS, ENVIRONMENT**) activities by a company that are intended to make people think that it cares about the environment, even if its real business actually harms the environment

greet ⏚ **A2** /griːt/ verb [T] **1** ~ sb (with sth) to welcome sb when you meet them; to say hello to sb: He greeted me with a friendly smile. ◇ (figurative) As we entered the house we were greeted by the smell of cooking. **2** [often passive] ~ sb/sth (with sth); ~ sb/sth (as) sth to react to sb or receive sth in a particular way: The news was

greeted with a loud cheer. ◇ The team's win was greeted as a major triumph.

greeting /'griːtɪŋ/ noun [C, U] the first words you say when you meet sb or write to them: 'Hello' and 'Hi' are informal greetings. ◇ He raised his hand in greeting.

gregarious /ɡrɪˈɡeəriəs/ adj. liking to be with other people **SYN** sociable

Gregorian calendar /ɡrɪˌɡɔːriən ˈkælɪndə(r)/ noun [sing.] the system used since 1582 in Western countries of arranging the months in the year and the days in the months and of counting the years from the birth of Christ ⊃ look at **Julian calendar**

Gregorian chant /ɡrɪˌɡɔːriən ˈtʃɑːnt/ noun [U, C] (**MUSIC**) a type of church music for voices alone, used since the Middle Ages

grenade /ɡrəˈneɪd/ noun [C] a small bomb that is thrown by hand or fired from a gun

grew /ɡruː/ past tense of **grow**

grey¹ ⏚ **A1** (AmE usually gray) /ɡreɪ/ adj. **1** between black and white in colour: dark/light/pale grey ◇ He was wearing a grey suit. **2** having grey hair: He's going grey. **3** (used about the weather) full of cloud; not bright: grey skies ◇ a grey day **4** boring and sad; without interest or variety

grey² ⏚ **A1** (AmE usually gray) /ɡreɪ/ noun [U, C] the colour between black and white: dressed in grey

greyhound /'ɡreɪhaʊnd/ noun [C] a large thin dog that can run very fast and that is used for racing: greyhound racing

greyish (AmE usually grayish) /'ɡreɪɪʃ/ adj. slightly grey

grey 'market (AmE usually gray market) noun [C, usually sing.] (**BUSINESS**) **1** a system in which products are imported into a country and sold without the permission of the company that produced them **2** (BrE) old people, when they are thought of as customers for goods

grid ⏚+ **C1** /ɡrɪd/ noun [C] **1** a pattern of straight lines that cross each other to form squares: She drew a grid to show how the students had scored in each part of the test. **2** a frame of PARALLEL metal or wooden bars, usually covering a hole in sth **3** (**GEOGRAPHY**) a system of squares that are drawn on a map so that the position of any place can be described or found: a grid reference **4** the system of electricity wires, etc. taking power to all parts of a country: the National Grid

griddle /'ɡrɪdl/ noun [C] a flat iron plate that is heated on a cooker or over a fire and used for cooking

gridlock /'ɡrɪdlɒk/ noun [U, C] a situation in which there are so many cars in the streets of a town that the traffic cannot move at all ▶ gridlocked adj.

grief ⏚+ **C1** /ɡriːf/ noun [U] a very sad feeling (especially because of the death of sb you love) **IDM** good grief (informal) used for expressing surprise or shock: Good grief! Whatever happened to you?

grievance /'ɡriːvəns/ noun [C] ~ (against sb) something that you think is unfair and that you want to complain or protest about: They aired (= expressed) their grievances against the government.

grieve /ɡriːv/ verb **1** [I] ~ (for sb) to feel very sad (especially about the death of sb you love) **2** [T] (formal) to cause unhappiness

grill¹ /ɡrɪl/ noun [C] **1** (BrE) a part of a cooker where the food is cooked by heat from above ⊃ note at **cook¹ 2** a metal frame that you put food on to cook over an open fire **3** = GRILLE

grill² /ɡrɪl/ verb **1** (BrE) (AmE broil) [I, T] to cook under a GRILL or over a fire: grilled steak/chicken/fish ⊃ note at **cook¹, meat 2** [T] ~ sb (about sth) (informal) to question sb for a long time, often in an unpleasant way: *When she got home her parents grilled her about where she had been.*

grille (*also* **grill**) /grɪl/ *noun* [C] a metal frame that is placed over a window, machine, etc.

grim /grɪm/ *adj.* (**grimmer; grimmest**) **1** (used about a person) very serious; not smiling **2** (used about a situation, news, etc.) unpleasant or worrying: *The news is grim, I'm afraid.* **3** (used about a place) unpleasant to look at; not attractive: *a grim block of flats* **4** [not before noun] (*BrE, informal*) feeling ill: *I was feeling grim yesterday but I managed to get to work.* ▸ **grimly** *adv.*

grimace /'grɪməs, grɪ'meɪs/ *noun* [C] an ugly expression that you make by TWISTING your face to show pain, dislike, etc. or to make sb laugh: *a grimace of pain* ▸ **grimace** *verb* [I]: *She grimaced with pain.*

grime /graɪm/ *noun* [U] dirt in a thick layer

grimy /'graɪmi/ *adj.* (**grimier; grimiest**) very dirty ⊃ look at **filthy**

grin Ɂ+ **C1** /grɪn/ *verb* [I] (-nn-) ~ (**at sb**) to give a broad smile (so that you show your teeth): *She grinned at me as she came into the room.* ▸ **grin** Ɂ+ **C1** *noun* [C]

grind¹ Ɂ+ **C1** /graɪnd/ *verb* (*pt, pp* **ground** /graʊnd/) **1** [T] ~ **sth (down/up)**; ~ **sth (to/into sth)** to press and break sth into very small pieces or into a powder between two hard surfaces or in a special machine: *The machine grinds up the food waste.* ◇ *Wheat is ground into flour.* ◇ *ground pepper/coffee* **2** [T] to make sth sharp or smooth by rubbing it on a rough hard surface: *to grind a knife on a stone* **3** [T] ~ **sth in/into sth** to press or rub sth into a surface: *He ground his cigarette into the ashtray.* **4** [I, T] to rub together or make sth rub together, often producing an unpleasant noise: *Some people grind their teeth while they're asleep.* ◇ *Parts of the machine were grinding together noisily.* **IDM** **grind to a halt/standstill** to go slower and then stop

grind² /graɪnd/ *noun* [sing.] (*informal*) an activity that is boring or makes you tired and that takes a lot of time: *the daily grind of working life*

grinder /'graɪndə(r)/ *noun* [C] a machine for GRINDING a solid substance into a powder: *a coffee grinder*

grip¹ Ɂ+ **C1** /grɪp/ *verb* [I, T] (-pp-) **1** to hold sb/sth tightly: *She gripped my arm in fear.* **2** to interest sb very much; to hold sb's attention: *The book grips you from start to finish.* ⊃ adjective **gripping**

grip² Ɂ+ **C1** /grɪp/ *noun* **1** [C, usually sing.] ~ (**on sb/sth**) a firm hold (on sb/sth): *I relaxed my grip and he ran away.* ◇ *The climber slipped and lost his grip.* ◇ (*figurative*) *The teacher kept a firm grip on the class.* **2** [sing.] ~ (**on sth**) an understanding of sth **3** [C] (**ARTS AND MEDIA**) the person whose job it is to move the cameras while a film is being made **IDM** **come/get to grips with sth** to start to understand and deal with a problem **get/keep/take a grip/hold (on yourself)** (*informal*) to try to behave in a calmer or more sensible way; to control yourself **in the grip of sth** experiencing sth unpleasant that cannot be stopped: *a country in the grip of recession*

gripe /graɪp/ *noun* [C] (*informal*) a complaint about sb/sth **SYN** **complaint** ▸ **gripe** *verb* [I]

gripping /'grɪpɪŋ/ *adj.* exciting; holding your attention: *a gripping film/book*

grisly /'grɪzli/ *adj.* (**grislier; grisliest**) extremely unpleasant and frightening and usually connected with death and violence: *a grisly crime/death/murder* ⊃ look at **gruesome**

gristle /'grɪsl/ *noun* [U] a hard substance in a piece of meat that is unpleasant to eat ▸ **gristly** /-sli/ *adv.*

grit¹ /grɪt/ *noun* [U] **1** small pieces of stone or sand: *I've got some grit/a piece of grit in my shoe.* **2** (*informal*) courage and strength of mind that makes it possible for sb to continue doing sth difficult or unpleasant

grit² /grɪt/ *verb* [T] (-tt-) to spread small pieces of stone and sand or salt on a road that is covered with ice **IDM** **grit your teeth 1** to bite your teeth tightly together: *She gritted her teeth against the pain as the doctor examined her injured foot.* **2** to use your courage or strength of mind in a difficult situation

gritty /'grɪti/ *adj.* (**grittier; grittiest**) **1** containing or like GRIT: *a layer of gritty dust* **2** showing the courage to continue doing sth difficult or unpleasant: *gritty determination*

groan /grəʊn/ *verb* [I] (often used with an adverb or a preposition) to make a deep sad sound because you are in pain, or to show that you are unhappy about sth: *He groaned with pain.* ◇ *All the students were moaning and groaning* (= complaining) *about the amount of work they had to do.* ▸ **groan** *noun* [C]

grocer /'grəʊsə(r)/ *noun* [C] **1** a person who has a shop that sells food and other things for the home ⊃ look at **greengrocer** (1) **2** **grocer's** (*pl.* **grocers**) a shop that sells food and other things for the home

grocery Ɂ+ **B2** /'grəʊsəri/ *noun* **1** (*especially BrE*) (*AmE usually* **'grocery store**) [C] a shop that sells food and other things for the home **2** **groceries** [pl.] food and other things for the home that you buy regularly: *Can you help me unload the groceries from the car, please?*

groggy /'grɒgi/ *adj.* (**groggier; groggiest**) (*informal*) weak and unable to walk steadily because you feel ill, have not had enough sleep, etc.

groin /grɔɪn/ *noun* [C] **1** (**ANATOMY**) the part of the body where the legs join the main part of the body, including the area around the GENITALS (= sex organs) **2** (*AmE*) = **GROYNE**

groom¹ /gruːm/ *noun* [C] **1** (*also* **bridegroom**) a man on or just before his wedding day **2** a person who looks after horses, especially by cleaning and brushing them

groom² /gruːm/ *verb* [T] **1** to clean or look after an animal by brushing, etc: *to groom a horse/dog/cat* **2** [usually passive] **be groomed (for/as sth)** to be chosen and prepared for a particular career or job: *She is clearly being groomed for the top job.* **3** (used about a person who is sexually attracted to children) to prepare a child for a meeting, especially using SOCIAL MEDIA, with the intention of performing an illegal sexual act

groove /gruːv/ *noun* [C] a long deep line that is cut in the surface of sth

grope /grəʊp/ *verb* **1** [I] ~ (**about/around**) (**for sth**) to search for sth or find your way using your hands because you cannot see: *He groped around for the light switch.* **2** [T] (*informal*) to touch sb sexually, especially when they do not want you to

gross¹ Ɂ+ **C1** /grəʊs/ *adj.* **1** [only before noun] (**FINANCE**) being the total amount before anything is taken away: *gross income* (= before tax, etc. is taken away) ⊃ look at **net²** (1) ⊃ note at **income 2** [only before noun] (*formal*) very great or serious: *gross indecency/negligence/ misconduct* **3** very rude and unpleasant: *His behaviour was really gross.* **4** very fat and ugly **5** (*informal*) very unpleasant: *'She ate it with mustard.' 'Oh, gross!'* **SYN** **disgusting**

gross² /grəʊs/ *adv.* (**FINANCE**) in total, before anything is taken away: *She earns £25 000 a year gross.* ⊃ look at **net²**

gross³ /grəʊs/ verb [T] (BUSINESS, FINANCE) to earn a particular amount of money before tax has been taken off it: *The movie is grossing $25 million a day.*

,gross do,mestic 'product = GDP

grossly /'grəʊsli/ adv. very: *That is grossly unfair.*

,gross ,national 'product = GNP

grotesque /grəʊ'tesk/ adj. strange or ugly in a way that is not natural

grotto /'grɒtəʊ/ noun [C] (pl. -oes, -os) (ARCHITECTURE) a small CAVE (= a hole in the side of a hill or under the ground), especially one that has been made artificially, for example in a garden

grotty /'grɒti/ adj. (grottier; grottiest) (BrE, informal) unpleasant; of poor quality: *She lives in a grotty flat.*

ground¹ 🔊 A2 /graʊnd/ noun
• SURFACE OF EARTH 1 the ground [U] the solid surface of the earth: *We sat on the ground to eat our picnic.* ◇ *He slipped off the ladder and fell to the ground.* ◇ *waste ground* (= that is not being used)
• SOIL 2 [U] an area or type of soil: *solid/marshy/stony ground*
• AREA OF LAND 3 [C] a piece of land that is used for a particular purpose: *a sports ground* ◇ *a playground*
• GARDENS 4 grounds [pl.] land or gardens surrounding a large building: *the grounds of the palace*
• AREA OF INTEREST 5 [U] an area of interest, study, discussion, etc: *The lecture went over **the same old ground**/covered a lot of **new ground**.* ◇ *to be on dangerous ground* (= saying sth likely to cause anger)
• REASON 6 [C, usually pl.] ~ (for sth/doing sth) (formal) a reason for sth: *She retired on medical grounds.* ◇ *grounds for divorce* ⊃ note at **reason**¹
• WIRE 7 [C, usually sing.] (AmE) = EARTH¹ (4)
IDM **above/below ground** above/below the surface of the earth **break fresh/new ground** to make a discovery or introduce a new method or activity **gain ground** → GAIN¹ **get (sth) off the ground** (used about a business, project, etc.) to make a successful start; to make sth start successfully **give/lose ground (to sb/sth)** to allow sb to have an advantage; to lose an advantage for yourself: *Labour lost a lot of ground to the Liberal Democrats at the election.* **hold/stand your ground** to refuse to change your opinion or to be influenced by pressure from other people **thin on the ground** (BrE) difficult to find; not common

ground² /graʊnd/ verb [T] 1 [often passive] to force an aircraft, etc. to stay on the ground: *to be grounded by fog* 2 [usually passive] to punish a child by not allowing them to go out with friends for a period of time: *Jack was grounded for a whole week after he stayed out late without asking permission.* 3 (AmE) = EARTH²

ground³ /graʊnd/ past tense, past participle of **grind**¹: *ground almonds*

,ground 'beef (AmE) = MINCE

groundbreaking /'graʊndbreɪkɪŋ/ adj. [only before noun] making new discoveries; using new methods: *a groundbreaking piece of research*

'ground crew (also ground staff) noun [C + sing./pl. verb] the people in an airport whose job it is to look after an aircraft and its passengers while they are on the ground

,ground 'floor (BrE) (AmE first floor) noun [C] the floor of a building that is at ground level: *a ground-floor flat*

grounding /'graʊndɪŋ/ noun [sing.] a ~ (in sth) the teaching of the basic facts or principles of a subject

groundless /'graʊndləs/ adj. having no reason or cause: *Our fears were groundless.*

groundnut /'graʊndnʌt/ (BrE) = PEANUT (1)

'ground plan noun [C] (ARCHITECTURE) a plan of the ground floor of a building

groundsheet /'graʊndʃiːt/ noun [C] (BrE) a large piece of material that does not let water through that is placed on the ground inside a tent

'ground staff noun [C + sing./pl. verb] 1 (BrE) the people at a sports ground whose job it is to take care of the grass, equipment, etc. 2 = GROUND CREW

groundwater /'graʊndwɔːtə(r)/ noun [U] (GEOLOGY) water that is found under the ground in soil, rocks, etc. ⊃ picture at **water cycle**

groundwork /'graʊndwɜːk/ noun [U] work that is done in preparation for further work or study

,Ground 'Zero noun [U] the site of the Twin Towers in New York, destroyed on 11 September 2001

group¹ 🔊 A1 🔊 /gruːp/ noun [C] 1 [+ sing./pl. verb] a number of people or things that are together in the same place or that are connected in some way: *a group of girls/trees/houses* ◇ *Our discussion group is/are meeting this week.* ◇ *A group of us are planning to meet for lunch.* ◇ *Students were standing **in groups** waiting for their exam results.* ◇ *He is in the 40–50 **age group**.* ◇ *people of many different social groups* ◇ *a **pressure group*** (= a political group that tries to influence the government) ◇ *Which **blood group*** (= for example A, O, etc.) are you? ◇ *Divide the class into groups.* 2 (BUSINESS) a number of companies that are owned by the same person or organization 3 (old-fashioned) (MUSIC) a number of people who play music together, especially pop music: *a pop group* ⊃ look at **band**(1)

group² 🔊 /gruːp/ verb [I, T, often passive] ~ (sb/sth) (around/round sb/sth); ~ (sb/sth) (together) to gather into a group, or to make sb/sth form a group: *Most of the houses were grouped around the church.* ◇ *The books are grouped together by subject.* ◇ *Group these words according to their meaning.*

grouping /'gruːpɪŋ/ noun 1 [C] (POLITICS, SOCIAL STUDIES) a number of people or organizations that have the same interests, aims or characteristics and are often part of a larger group: *These small nations constitute an important grouping within the EU.* 2 [U] the act of forming sth into a group

,group 'therapy noun [U] (PSYCHOLOGY) a type of treatment for personal problems in which people with similar problems meet together to discuss them

grouse /graʊs/ noun [C, U] (pl. grouse) a fat brown bird with feathers on its legs that people shoot for sport and food; the meat of this bird

grove /grəʊv/ noun [C] (GEOGRAPHY) a small group of trees, especially of one particular type: *an olive grove* ⊃ note at **agriculture**

grovel /'grɒvl/ verb [I] (-ll-, AmE -l-) 1 ~ (to sb) (for sth) to try too hard to please sb who is more important than you or who can give you sth that you want: *to grovel for forgiveness* ◇ *I had to grovel to the receptionist to get an appointment with the doctor.* 2 ~ (around/about) (for sth) to move around on your hands and knees (usually when you are looking for sth) ▶ grovelling adj.: *I wrote a grovelling letter of apology.*

grow 🔊 A1 🔊 /grəʊ/ verb (pt grew /gruː/; pp grown /grəʊn/) 1 [I] ~ (in sth); ~ (into sth) to increase in size or number; to develop into an adult form: *a growing child* ◇ *She's growing in confidence all the time.* ◇ *You must invest if you want your business to grow.* ◇ *Plants grow from seeds.* ◇ *Kittens soon grow into cats.* ⊃ note at **rise**² 2 [I, T] (used about plants) to exist and develop in a particular place; to make plants grow by giving them water, etc: *Palm trees don't grow in cold climates.* ◇ *We grow vegetables in our garden.* 3 [T] to allow your hair or nails to grow: *Claire's growing her*

hair long. ◇ to grow a beard/moustache ⊃ note at
agriculture 4 linking verb to gradually change from one
state to another; to become: It began to grow dark. ◇ to
grow older/wiser/taller/bigger ⊃ The teacher was
growing more and more impatient. **SYN get**
PHR V grow into sth 1 to gradually develop into a
particular type of person: She has grown into a very
attractive young woman. **2** to become big enough to
fit into clothes, etc. that used to be too big: The coat is
too big for him, but he will soon grow into it. **grow on**
sb to become more pleasing: I didn't like ginger at
first, but it's a taste that grows on you. **grow out of sth**
to become too big or too old for sth: She's grown out
of that dress I made her last year. **grow up 1** to
develop into an adult: What do you want to be when
you grow up? (= what job do you want to do later?)
◇ She grew up (= spent her childhood) in Spain.
2 (used about a feeling, etc.) to develop or become
strong: A close friendship has grown up between
them.

grower /ˈɡrəʊə(r)/ noun [C] (**AGRICULTURE**) a person or
company that grows plants, fruit or vegetables to sell:
a tobacco grower ◇ All our vegetables are supplied by
local growers.

growing /ˈɡrəʊɪŋ/ adj. increasing: A growing number of
people are becoming vegetarian these days.

growl /ɡraʊl/ verb [I] ~ (at sb/sth) (used about dogs and
other animals) to make a low noise in the throat to
show anger or to give a warning ▶ growl noun [C]

grown /ɡrəʊn/ adj. [only before noun] physically an
adult: Grown men don't act so stupidly. ◇ a fully-grown
elephant

grown-up[1] adj. physically or mentally adult: He must
be at least 45 — he's got a grown-up daughter. ◇ She's
very grown-up for her age. **SYN mature**[1]

grown-up[2] noun [C] an adult person **SYN adult**

growth [B1] ⊙ /ɡrəʊθ/ noun **1** [U] the process of
growing and developing: A good diet is very important
for children's growth. **2** [U, sing.] an increase (in sth):
population growth **3** [U] (**ECONOMICS**) an increase in
economic activity: policies aimed at sustaining
economic growth ◇ an annual growth rate of 10% ◇ a
growth area/industry (= one that is growing) **4** [C]
(**HEALTH**) a mass of cells caused by a disease that
grows in a person's or an animal's body: a cancerous
growth **5** [U] something that has grown: several days'
growth of beard

growth mindset noun [C, usually sing.] (**EDUCATION**,
PSYCHOLOGY) the belief that you can develop your
natural abilities by working hard, listening to advice
from others, etc. ⊃ look at **fixed mindset**

groyne (BrE) (AmE **groin**) /ɡrɔɪn/ noun [C] (**ENVIRONMENT**)
a low wall built out into the sea to prevent it from
washing away sand and stones from the beach

grub /ɡrʌb/ noun **1** [C] (**BIOLOGY**) the first form that an
insect takes when it comes out of the egg. Grubs are
short, fat and white. **2** [U] (informal) food

grubby /ˈɡrʌbi/ adj. (grubbier; grubbiest) (informal) dirty
after being used and not washed

grudge[1] /ɡrʌdʒ/ noun [C] ~ (against sb) unfriendly
feelings towards sb, because you are angry about
what has happened in the past: to bear a grudge
against somebody

grudge[2] /ɡrʌdʒ/ verb [T] ~ sb sth; ~ doing sth to be
unhappy that sb has sth or that you have to do sth: I
don't grudge him his success — he deserves it. ◇ I
grudge having to pay so much tax. ⊃ look at **begrudge**

grudging /ˈɡrʌdʒɪŋ/ adj. given or done although you do
not want to: grudging thanks ▶ grudgingly adv.

gruelling (especially BrE) (AmE usually **grueling**) /ˈɡruːəlɪŋ/
adj. very long and making you very tired: a gruelling
nine-hour march

gruesome /ˈɡruːsəm/ adj. very unpleasant or shocking,
and usually connected with death or injury ⊃ look at
grisly

gruff /ɡrʌf/ adj. (used about a person or a voice) rough
and unfriendly ▶ gruffly adv.

grumble /ˈɡrʌmbl/ verb [I] (often used with an adverb or
a preposition) to complain about sb/sth, especially sth
that is not really very serious: The students were
always grumbling about the standard of the food.
⊃ look at **complain, moan** (2) ▶ grumble noun [C]

grumpy /ˈɡrʌmpi/ adj. (grumpier; grumpiest) (informal)
easily annoyed; in a bad mood ▶ grumpily /-pɪli/ adv.

grunge /ɡrʌndʒ/ noun [U] (**MUSIC**) (also ˌgrunge ˈrock) a
type of loud rock music, which was popular in the
early 1990s

grunt /ɡrʌnt/ verb [I, T] to make a short low sound in the
throat. People grunt when they do not like sth or are
not interested and do not want to talk: I tried to find out
her opinion but she just grunted when I asked her.
⊃ note at **pig**[1] ▶ grunt noun [C]

guanine /ˈɡwɑːniːn/ noun [U] (**BIOLOGY, CHEMISTRY**) one
of the four **COMPOUNDS** that make up DNA and RNA
⊃ picture at **DNA**

guano /ˈɡwɑːnəʊ/ noun [U] (**AGRICULTURE**) the waste
substance passed from the bodies of **SEABIRDS**, which
is used by farmers to make plants grow well

guarantee[1] [B2] /ˌɡærənˈtiː/ noun [C, U] **1** a firm
promise that sth will be done or that sth will happen:
The refugees are demanding guarantees about their
safety before they return home. **2** (**BUSINESS**) a written
promise by a company that it will repair or replace a
product if it breaks in a certain period of time: The
watch comes with a year's guarantee. ◇ Is the
computer still under guarantee? ⊃ look at **warranty**
3 something that makes sth else certain to happen:
Without a reservation there's no guarantee that you'll
get a seat on the train.

guarantee[2] [B2] /ˌɡærənˈtiː/ verb [T] **1** ~ (that) ... to
promise that sth will be done or will happen: They
have guaranteed delivery within one week. ◇ I can
guarantee that you will have a good time. **2** (**BUSINESS**)
to give a written promise to repair or replace a
product if anything is wrong with it: This washing
machine is guaranteed for three years. **3** to make sth
certain to happen: Tonight's win guarantees the team
a place in the final.

guarantor /ˌɡærənˈtɔː(r)/ noun [C] (formal) (**LAW**) a
person who agrees to be responsible for sb or for
making sure that sth happens or is done

guard[1] [B1] /ɡɑːd/ noun
• **PROTECTING 1** [C] a person who protects a place or
people, or who stops prisoners from escaping: a
security guard ⊃ look at **bodyguard, warder 2** [U] the
act or duty of protecting a place or people, or of
stopping prisoners from escaping: Soldiers keep
guard at the gate. ◇ Who is on guard? ◇ The prisoner
arrived under armed guard. ◇ a guard dog
• **SOLDIERS 3** [C + sing./pl. verb] a group of soldiers, police
officers, etc. who protect sb/sth: The president always
travels with an armed guard.
• **COVER 4** [C] (often in compounds) something that
covers sth dangerous or protects sth: a fireguard ◇ a
mudguard (= over the wheel of a bicycle)
• **IN SPORT 5** [U] a position that you take to defend
yourself, especially in sports such as **BOXING**
IDM off/on (your) guard not ready/ready for an
attack, a surprise, a mistake, etc: The question
caught me off (my) guard and I didn't know what to
say.

guard² ₹ **B1** /gɑːd/ *verb* [T] **1** to keep sb/sth safe from other people; protect: *The building was guarded by men with dogs.* ◇ (*figurative*) *a closely guarded secret* ◔ look at **protect 2** to be ready to stop prisoners from escaping
PHR V **guard against sth** to try to prevent sth or stop sth happening

guarded /'gɑːdɪd/ *adj.* (used about an answer, statement, etc.) careful; not giving much information or showing what you feel **OPP** **unguarded**
▶ **guardedly** *adv.*

guardian /'gɑːdiən/ *noun* [C] **1** a person or an institution that guards or protects sth: *The police are the guardians of law and order.* **2** (**LAW**) a person who is legally responsible for the care of another person, especially of a child whose parents are dead

guava /'gwɑːvə/ *noun* [C] the fruit of a tropical American tree that has yellow skin and is pink or yellow inside

guerrilla¹ ₹+ **C1** (*also* **guerilla**) /gə'rɪlə/ *noun* [C] a member of a small military group that is not part of an official army and that makes surprise attacks on official soldiers, usually to try and change the government

guerrilla² (*also* **guerilla**) /gə'rɪlə/ *adj.* [only before noun] done in an informal way and without official permission: *guerrilla film-making*

guess¹ ₹ **A1** **S** /ges/ *verb* **1** [I, T] ~ (**at sth**); ~ (**that**) ... to try to give an answer or make a judgement about sth without being sure of all the facts: *If you're not sure of an answer, guess.* ◇ *We can only guess at her reasons for leaving.* ◇ *I'd guess that he's about 45.*
2 [I, T] ~ (**that**) ... to give the correct answer when you are not sure about it; to guess correctly: *You'll never guess what Adam just told me!* ◇ *Did I guess right?* ◇ *I guessed the answer straightaway.* ◇ *She guessed that he would be at home, and he was.* **3** I guess [T] ~ (**that**) ... (*informal*) to imagine that sth is probably true or likely: *I guess (that) you're tired after your long journey.* **SYN** **suppose** **4** [T] used to show that you are going to say sth surprising or exciting: *Guess what! I'm getting married!*

guess² ₹ **A1** **S** /ges/ *noun* [C] an effort you make to imagine a possible answer or give an opinion when you cannot be sure if you are right: *My guess is that they've been delayed by the traffic.* ◇ *If you don't know the answer, then* **have a guess***!* ◇ *I don't know how far it is, but* **at a guess** *I'd say about 50 miles.* ◇ *I'd say it'll take about four hours, but that's just* **a rough guess***.*
IDM **anybody's/anyone's guess** (*informal*) something that nobody can be certain about: *What's going to happen next is anybody's guess.* **your guess is as good as mine** (*informal*) I do not know: *'Where's Ron?' 'Your guess is as good as mine.'*

guesswork /'geswɜːk/ *noun* [U] the process of trying to find an answer by guessing when you do not have enough information to be sure: *I arrived at the answer by pure guesswork.*

guest ₹ **A2** /gest/ *noun* [C] **1** a person who is invited to a place or to a special event: *wedding guests* ◇ *Who is the guest speaker at the conference?* **2** (**TOURISM**) a person who is staying at a hotel, etc: *This hotel has accommodation for 500 guests.*
IDM **be my guest** (*informal*) used to give sb permission to do sth that they have asked you to do: *'Do you mind if I have a look at your newspaper?' 'Be my guest!'*

guest house *noun* [C] (**TOURISM**) a small hotel, sometimes in a private house

GUI /'guːi, ˌdʒiː juː 'aɪ/ *abbr.* (**COMPUTING**) **graphical user interface** (a way of giving instructions to a computer using things that can be seen on the screen such as symbols and menus)

guidance ₹+ **C1** **W** /'gaɪdns/ *noun* [U] ~ (**on sth**) help or advice: *The centre offers guidance for unemployed people on how to find work.*

guide¹ ₹ **A2** /gaɪd/ *noun*
• **BOOK/MAGAZINE** **1** [C] a book, magazine, app, etc. that gives information or help on a subject: *A Guide to Family Health* ◇ *Have we got a TV guide for this week?* **2** (*also* **guidebook** /'gaɪdbʊk/) [C] (**TOURISM**) a book that gives information about a place for travellers and tourists
• **PERSON** **3** [C] (**TOURISM**) a person who shows tourists or people who are travelling where to go: *We found a guide who knew the mountains well.* ◇ *She works as a tour guide in Venice.*
• **STH THAT HELPS** **4** [C] something that helps you to judge or plan sth: *As a rough guide, use twice as much water as rice.*
• **ORGANIZATION FOR GIRLS** **5** the Guides [pl.] an organization for girls between the ages of 10 and 14 that trains them in practical skills and does a lot of activities with them **6** Guide [C] (*BrE*) a member of the Guides

guide² ₹ **A2** /gaɪd/ *verb* [T] **1** to help a person or a group of people to find the way to a place; to show sb a place that you know well: *He guided us through the busy streets to our hotel.* **2** to have an influence on sb/sth: *I was guided by your advice.* **3** to help sb deal with sth difficult or complicated: *The manual will guide you through every step of the procedure.* **4** to carefully move sb/sth or to help sb/sth to move in a particular direction: *A crane lifted the piano and two men carefully guided it through the window.*

guided /'gaɪdɪd/ *adj.* (**TOURISM**) led by a guide: *a guided tour/walk*

guide dog (*AmE also* **Seeing Eye dog™**) *noun* [C] a dog trained to guide a person who is unable to see

guideline ₹+ **B2** /'gaɪdlaɪn/ *noun* **1** guidelines [pl.] rules or instructions that are given by an official organization telling you how to do sth, especially sth difficult **2** [C] something that can be used to help you make a decision or form an opinion: *These figures are a useful guideline when buying a house.*

guild /gɪld/ *noun* [C + sing./pl. verb] **1** an organization of people who do the same job or who have the same interests or aims: *the Screen Actors' Guild* **2** (**HISTORY**) an association of SKILLED workers in the Middle Ages

guillotine /'gɪlətiːn/ *noun* [C] **1** a machine used for cutting paper **2** (**HISTORY**) a machine that was used in France in the past for cutting people's heads off
▶ **guillotine** *verb* [T]

guilt ₹+ **C1** /gɪlt/ *noun* [U] **1** ~ (**about/at sth**) the unhappy feelings that you have when you know or think that you have done sth bad: *I sometimes feel guilt about not spending more time with my children.* **2** (**LAW**) the fact of having broken a law: *We took his refusal to answer questions as an admission of guilt.* **OPP** **innocence** **3** the responsibility for doing sth wrong or for sth bad that has happened: *It's difficult to say whether the guilt lies with the parents or the children.* **SYN** **blame¹**

guilty ₹ **B1** /'gɪlti/ *adj.* (**guiltier; guiltiest**) **1** ~ (**of sth**) (**LAW**) having broken a law; being responsible for doing sth wrong: *She pleaded guilty/not guilty to the crime.* ◇ *to be guilty of murder* ◇ *The jury found him guilty of fraud.* **OPP** **innocent** ◔ note at **court¹**, **crime**
2 ~ (**about sth**) having an unpleasant feeling because you have done sth bad: *I feel really guilty about lying to Sam.* ◇ *Why has Mike got a guilty look on his face?* ◇ *It's*

hard to sleep with *a guilty conscience*. ▸ **guiltily** /-tɪli/ *adv.*

guinea pig /ˈgɪni pɪg/ *noun* [C] **1** a small animal with no tail that is often kept as a pet **2** (SCIENCE) a person who is used in an experiment: *I volunteered to act as a guinea pig in their research into dreams.*

guise /gaɪz/ *noun* [C] a way in which sb/sth appears, which is often different from usual or hides the truth: *The president was at the meeting in his guise as chairman of the charity.* ◇ *Her speech presented racist ideas under the guise of nationalism.*

guitar ⸙ A1 /gɪˈtɑː(r)/ *noun* [C] (MUSIC) a type of musical instrument with strings that you play with your fingers or with a PLECTRUM (= a small piece of plastic): *Can you play the guitar?* ⊃ picture at **instrument**

guitarist /gɪˈtɑːrɪst/ *noun* [C] (MUSIC) a person who plays the guitar

gulf /gʌlf/ *noun* **1** [C] (GEOGRAPHY) a part of the sea that is partly surrounded by land: *the Gulf of Mexico* **2** the Gulf [sing.] (*informal*) (GEOGRAPHY) a way of referring to the Persian Gulf (= the area of sea between Arabia and Iran) **3** [C, usually sing.] an important or serious difference between people in the way they live, think or feel: *the gulf between rich and poor*

the **ˈGulf Stream** *noun* [sing.] (GEOGRAPHY) a warm current of water flowing across the Atlantic Ocean from the Gulf of Mexico towards Europe ⊃ picture at **current²**

gull /gʌl/ (*also* **seagull**) *noun* [C] a white or grey bird that makes a loud noise and lives near the sea. There are several types of gull. ⊃ picture at **animal**

gullet /ˈgʌlɪt/ *noun* [C] (ANATOMY) the tube through which food passes from the mouth to the stomach **SYN** **oesophagus** ⊃ picture at **body, digestive system**

gullible /ˈgʌləbl/ *adj.* (used about a person) believing and trusting people too easily, and therefore easily tricked

gully /ˈgʌli/ *noun* [C] (*pl.* -ies) (GEOGRAPHY) a small, narrow passage or valley, usually formed by a stream or by rain ⊃ look at **ditch¹**

gulp¹ /gʌlp/ *verb* **1** [I, T] ~ sth (down) to SWALLOW large amounts of food, drink, etc. quickly: *He gulped down his breakfast and went out.* **2** [I] to make a SWALLOWING movement because you are afraid, surprised, etc. **3** [I, T] ~ (for) sth to breathe quickly and deeply, because you need more air: *She finally came to the surface, desperately gulping (for) air.*

gulp² /gʌlp/ *noun* [C] **1** ~ (of sth) an amount of sth that you SWALLOW quickly: *He took a gulp of coffee and rushed out.* **2** the act of breathing in or SWALLOWING sth: *I drank my coffee in one gulp and ran out of the door.*

gum /gʌm/ *noun* **1** [C] (ANATOMY) either of the firm pink parts of the mouth that hold the teeth ⊃ picture at **tooth 2** [U] a substance that you use to stick things together (especially pieces of paper) **3** [U] = CHEWING GUM

gun¹ ⸙ A2 /gʌn/ *noun* [C] **1** a weapon that is used for shooting: *The robber held a gun to the bank manager's head.* **2** a tool that uses pressure to send out a substance or an object: *a grease gun* ◇ *a staple gun* **IDM** jump the gun → JUMP¹

gun² /gʌn/ *verb* (-nn-)
PHR V **gun sb down** (*informal*) to shoot and kill or seriously injure sb

gunboat /ˈgʌnbəʊt/ *noun* [C] a small ship used in war that carries heavy guns

ˈgun control *noun* [U] (LAW) (especially in the US) laws that limit the sale and use of guns

gunfight /ˈgʌnfaɪt/ *noun* [C] a fight between people using guns ▸ **gunfighter** *noun* [C]

gunfire /ˈgʌnfaɪə(r)/ *noun* [U] the repeated firing of guns: *We could hear gunfire.*

gunman /ˈgʌnmən/ *noun* [C] (*pl.* -men /-mən/) a man who uses a gun to steal from or kill people

gunpoint /ˈgʌnpɔɪnt/ *noun*
IDM at gunpoint while threatening sb or being threatened with a gun: *He held the hostages at gunpoint.*

gunpowder /ˈgʌnpaʊdə(r)/ *noun* [U] a powder that can explode and is used in guns, bombs, FIREWORKS, etc.

gunshot /ˈgʌnʃɒt/ *noun* [C] the firing of a gun or the sound that it makes

gurgle /ˈgɜːgl/ *verb* [I] **1** to make a sound like water flowing quickly through a narrow space: *a gurgling stream* **2** if a baby **gurgles**, it makes a noise in its throat because it is happy ▸ **gurgle** *noun* [C]

guru /ˈgʊruː/ *noun* [C] **1** (RELIGION) a spiritual leader or teacher in the Hindu or Sikh religions **2** somebody whose opinions you admire and respect, and whose ideas you follow: *a management/fashion guru*

gush /gʌʃ/ *verb* **1** [I] ~ (out of/from/into sth); ~ out/in (used about a liquid) to flow out suddenly and in great quantities: *Blood gushed from the wound.* ◇ *I turned the tap on and water gushed out.* **2** [T] (used about a container, vehicle, etc.) to produce large amounts of a liquid: *The broken pipe was gushing water all over the road.* **3** [I, T] to express so much praise or emotion that it does not seem sincere: *'Oh you're so clever!' she gushed.* ▸ **gush** *noun* [C]: *a sudden gush of water*

gust /gʌst/ *noun* [C] a sudden strong wind ▸ **gust** *verb* [I]

gusto /ˈgʌstəʊ/ *noun*
IDM with gusto with great enthusiasm

gut¹ ⸙+ C1 /gʌt/ *noun* **1** [C] (ANATOMY) the tube in the body that food passes through when it leaves the stomach **SYN** **intestine 2** guts [pl.] (ANATOMY) the organs in and around the stomach, especially of an animal **3** guts [pl.] (*informal*) courage and strength of mind: *It takes guts to admit that you are wrong.* ◇ *I don't have the guts to tell my boss what he's doing wrong.* **4** [C] a person's fat stomach: *a beer gut* (= caused by drinking a lot of beer)
IDM sweat/work your guts out to work extremely hard

gut² /gʌt/ *verb* [T] (-tt-) **1** to remove the organs from inside an animal, fish, etc. **2** [usually passive] to destroy the inside of a building: *The warehouse was gutted by fire.*

gut³ /gʌt/ *adj.* [only before noun] based on feelings and emotions rather than thought and reason: *a gut feeling/reaction*

gutter /ˈgʌtə(r)/ *noun* **1** [C] a long piece of metal or plastic with a curved bottom that is fixed to the edge of a roof to carry away the water when it rains **2** [C] a lower part at the edge of a road along which the water flows away when it rains **3** the gutter [sing.] the very lowest level of society: *She rose from the gutter to become a great star.*

the ˌgutter ˈpress *noun* [sing.] (*BrE*) (**ARTS AND MEDIA**) newspapers that publish a lot of shocking stories about people's private lives rather than serious news

guy ⚡ A2 /gaɪ/ *noun* **1** [C] (*informal*) a man or boy: *He's a nice guy.* **2** guys [pl.] (*informal*) used when speaking to a group of people of either sex **3** [sing.] (*BrE*) a model of a man that is burned on 5 November during the celebrations for BONFIRE NIGHT ➔ note at **Bonfire Night**

guzzle /ˈɡʌzl/ *verb* [T, I] (*informal*) to drink sth too fast and in large amounts. In British English it also means to eat food in this way.

gym ⚡ A1 /dʒɪm/ *noun* **1** (*also formal* gymnasium /dʒɪmˈneɪziəm/, *pl.* gymnasiums /-əmz/, gymnasia /-ziə/) [C] (**SPORT**) a room or hall with equipment for doing physical exercise: *The school has built a new gym.* ➔ look at **fitness centre 2** (*also* health club) [C] (**HEALTH, SPORT**) a private club where people go to do physical exercise: *I just joined a gym.* ◊ *I work out at the gym twice a week.* **3** [U] (**SPORT**) physical exercises done in a gym, especially at school: *gym shoes*

gymnast /ˈdʒɪmnæst/ *noun* [C] (**SPORT**) a person who does GYMNASTICS

gymnastics /dʒɪmˈnæstɪks/ *noun* [U] (**SPORT**) physical exercises that are done inside a building, often using special equipment such as bars and ropes ▶ gymnastic *adj.*: *gymnastic ability*

gynaecology (*BrE*) (*AmE* gynecology) /ˌɡaɪnəˈkɒlədʒi/ *noun* [U] (**MEDICINE**) the study and treatment of the diseases and medical problems of women, especially those connected with sexual REPRODUCTION ▶ gynaecological (*BrE*) (*AmE* gynecological) /ˌɡaɪnəkəˈlɒdʒɪkl/ *adj.* ▶ gynaecologist (*BrE*) (*AmE* gynecologist) /ˌɡaɪnəˈkɒlədʒɪst/ *noun* [C]

gypsum /ˈdʒɪpsəm/ *noun* [U] a soft white rock like CHALK that is used in the building industry

Gypsy (*also* Gipsy) /ˈdʒɪpsi/ *noun* [C] (*pl.* -ies) a member of a human group who traditionally spend their lives travelling around from place to place, living in CARAVANS (= homes with wheels). Many people prefer to use the name Romani. ➔ look at **Romani, traveller** (2) ❶ Some people find the word **Gypsy** offensive.

gyroscope /ˈdʒaɪrəskəʊp/ (*also informal* gyro /ˈdʒaɪrəʊ/) *noun* [C] a device consisting of a wheel that turns very quickly inside a frame and does not change position when the frame is moved. Gyroscopes are often used to keep ships and aircraft steady

H h

H /eɪtʃ/ (*also* h) *noun* [C, U] (*pl.* H's, h's) the eighth letter of the English alphabet: '*Hat* begins with (an) '*H*'.

ha¹ /hɑː/ *exclamation* **1** used for showing that you are surprised or pleased: *Ha! I knew he was hiding something!* **2** ha! ha! /hɑː ˈhɑː/ used in written language to show that sb is laughing

ha² *abbr.* (in writing) (*pl.* ha) = HECTARE

habit ⚡ A2 /ˈhæbɪt/ *noun* **1** [C] ~ (of doing sth) something that you do often and almost without thinking, especially sth that is hard to stop doing: *He's got an annoying habit of coming round just as we're going out.* ◊ *I'm trying to get into the habit of hanging up my clothes every night.* ◊ *I'm trying to break the habit of staying up too late.* ➔ adjective **habitual 2** [U]

usual behaviour: *I sometimes think I only drink coffee out of habit now — I don't really enjoy it.* **IDM** force of habit → FORCE¹

habitable /ˈhæbɪtəbl/ *adj.* (used about buildings) suitable to be lived in **OPP** uninhabitable

habitat ⚡ B2 /ˈhæbɪtæt/ *noun* [C] (**BIOLOGY, ENVIRONMENT**) the natural home of a plant or an animal: *I've seen wolves in the zoo, but not in their natural habitat.*

habitation /ˌhæbɪˈteɪʃn/ *noun* [U] (*formal*) the act of living in a place: *These houses are not fit for human habitation.*

ˈhabit-forming *adj.* (**SOCIAL STUDIES**) a **habit-forming** activity or drug is one that makes you want to continue doing it or taking it

habitual /həˈbɪtʃuəl/ *adj.* **1** [only before noun] doing sth very often: *a habitual criminal/drinker/liar* **2** that you always have or do; usual: *He had his habitual nap after lunch.* ▶ habitually /-əli/ *adv.*

hack¹ /hæk/ *verb* [I, T] **1** ~ (away) (at) sth to cut sth in a rough way with a tool such as a large knife: *He hacked away at the bushes.* **2** ~ (into) (sth) (*informal*) (**COMPUTING**) to use a computer to look at and/or change information that is stored on another computer or mobile phone without permission: *She hacked into the bank's computer.* ◊ *They had hacked secret data.* ➔ look at **phone hacking**

hack² /hæk/ *noun* [C] **1** (**POLITICS**) a person who does the hard and often boring work for an organization, especially a politician or journalist: *a party hack* **2** (**COMPUTING**) a piece of computer code that provides a quick solution to a problem **3** (often in compounds) (*informal*) a strategy or technique that you use in order to do sth in a better way: *a clever parenting hack*

hacker /ˈhækə(r)/ *noun* [C] (*informal*) (**COMPUTING**) a person who uses a computer to look at and/or change information on another computer or a mobile phone without permission

hacking /ˈhækɪŋ/ *noun* [U] (**COMPUTING**) the activity of using computers to get access to sb else's computer or phone system without permission ➔ look at **phone hacking**

hacksaw /ˈhæksɔː/ *noun* [C] a tool with a narrow cutting edge in a frame, used for cutting metal

had /həd, əd, *strong form* hæd/ past tense, past participle of **have²**

haddock /ˈhædək/ *noun* [C, U] (*pl.* haddock) a sea fish like a COD but smaller that is white inside and used for food

hadn't /ˈhædnt/ *short form* had not

haematite (*BrE*) (*AmE* hematite) /ˈhiːmətaɪt/ *noun* [U] (**GEOLOGY**) a dark red rock from which we get iron

haematology (*BrE*) (*AmE* hematology) /ˌhiːməˈtɒlədʒi/ *noun* [U] (**MEDICINE**) the scientific study of the blood and its diseases ▶ haematologist (*AmE* hematologist) /-dʒɪst/ *noun* [C]

haemo- (*BrE*) (*AmE* hemo-) /hiːməʊ, hiːmə, hiːˈmɒ/ *prefix* (**BIOLOGY**) (in nouns and adjectives) connected with blood: *haemophilia*

haemoglobin (*BrE*) (*AmE* hemoglobin) /ˌhiːməˈɡləʊbɪn/ *noun* [U] (**BIOLOGY**) a red substance in the blood that carries OXYGEN (= the gas we need to live) and contains iron

haemophilia (*BrE*) (*AmE* hemophilia) /ˌhiːməˈfɪliə/ *noun* [U] (**HEALTH**) a disease that causes a person to lose a lot of blood even from very small injuries because the blood does not CLOT (= stop flowing)

haemophiliac (*BrE*) (*AmE* hemophiliac) /ˌhiːməˈfɪliæk/ *noun* [C] (**HEALTH**) a person who suffers from HAEMOPHILIA

haemorrhage (*BrE*) (*AmE* **hemorrhage**) /ˈhemərɪdʒ/ *noun* [C, U] (**HEALTH**) a medical condition in which there is severe loss of blood from damage inside sb's body
▸ **haemorrhage** (*AmE* **hemorrhage**) *verb* [I]

haemorrhoids (*BrE*) (*AmE* **hemorrhoids**) /ˈhemərɔɪdz/ (*also* **piles**) *noun* [pl.] (**HEALTH**) a medical condition in which the VEINS (= the tubes that carry blood) at or near the ANUS (= the place where solid waste leaves the body) become painful and larger than normal

hafnium /ˈhæfniəm/ *noun* [U] (*symb.* Hf) (**CHEMISTRY**) a chemical element. Hafnium is a hard RADIOACTIVE metal. ❶ For more information on the periodic table of elements, look at the **Reference Section** of this dictionary.

haggard /ˈhægəd/ *adj.* (used about a person) looking tired or worried

haggle /ˈhægl/ *verb* [I] ~ **(with sb) (over/about sth)** to argue with sb until you reach an agreement, especially about the price of sth: *In the market, some tourists were haggling over the price of a carpet.*

haiku /ˈhaɪkuː/ *noun* [C] (*pl.* **haiku, haikus**) (**LITERATURE**) a Japanese poem with three lines and usually 17 syllables

hail¹ ⚡+ 🄲 /heɪl/ *verb* **1** [T, usually passive] **be hailed as sth** to be praised in public as very good or very special: *A student who rescued a boy from a river is being hailed as a hero.* **2** [T] to call or wave to sb/sth: *to hail a taxi* **3** [I] when it **hails**, small balls of ice fall from the sky like rain

hail² /heɪl/ *noun* **1** [U] (*also* **hailstones** /ˈheɪlstəʊnz/ [pl.]) small balls of ice that fall from the sky like rain ⊃ note at **weather¹ 2** [sing.] ~ **of sth** a large amount of sth that is aimed at sb in order to harm them: *a hail of bullets/stones/abuse*

hair ⚡ 🄰 /heə(r)/ *noun* **1** [U, C] (**ANATOMY**) the mass of long thin things that grow on the head and body of people and animals; one of these things: *He has got short black hair.* ◇ *Dave's losing his hair* (= going BALD). ◇ *The dog left hairs all over the furniture.* ◇ *I'm having my hair cut today.* ⊃ picture at **body, skin¹ 2 -haired** (in adjectives) having the type of hair mentioned: *a dark-haired woman* ◇ *a long-haired dog* **3** [C] (**BIOLOGY**) a thing that looks like a very thin THREAD that grows on the surface of some plants: *The leaves and stem are covered in fine hairs.*
IDM keep your hair on (*informal*) (used to tell sb to stop shouting and become less angry) calm down **let your hair down** (*informal*) to relax and enjoy yourself after being formal **make sb's hair stand on end** (*informal*) to frighten or shock sb **not turn a hair** to not show any reaction to sth that many people would find surprising or shocking **split hairs** → SPLIT¹

hairbrush /ˈheəbrʌʃ/ *noun* [C] a brush that you use on your hair

haircut /ˈheəkʌt/ *noun* [C] **1** the act of sb cutting your hair: *You need (to have) a haircut.* **2** the style in which your hair has been cut: *That haircut really suits you.*

hairdo /ˈheəduː/ (*informal*) = HAIRSTYLE

hairdresser /ˈheədresə(r)/ *noun* **1** [C] a person whose job is to cut, shape, colour, etc. hair ⊃ look at **barber** (1) **2 the hairdresser's** [sing.] the place where you go to have your hair cut: *I've made an appointment at the hairdresser's for ten o'clock.*

hairdryer (*also* **hairdrier**) /ˈheədraɪə(r)/ *noun* [C] a machine that dries hair by blowing hot air through it

hairgrip /ˈheəɡrɪp/ *noun* [C] a small thin piece of metal or plastic that is folded in the middle and used for holding hair in place

hairless /ˈheələs/ *adj.* without hair ⊃ look at **bald**

hairline¹ /ˈheəlaɪn/ *noun* [C] (**ANATOMY**) the edge of sb's hair, especially at the front

hairline² /ˈheəlaɪn/ *adj.* (used about a CRACK in sth) very thin: *a hairline fracture of the leg*

hairpin /ˈheəpɪn/ *noun* [C] a small thin piece of wire that is folded in the middle, used for holding hair in place ⊃ look at **hairgrip**

hairpin ˈbend (*BrE*) (*AmE* ˌhairpin ˈturn) *noun* [C] a very sharp bend in a road, especially a mountain road

ˈhair-raising *adj.* that makes you very frightened: *a hair-raising experience*

hairspray /ˈheəspreɪ/ *noun* [U, C] a substance you SPRAY onto your hair to hold it in place

hairstyle /ˈheəstaɪl/ (*also informal* **hairdo**) *noun* [C] the style in which your hair has been cut or arranged

hairstylist /ˈheəstaɪlɪst/ (*also* **stylist**) *noun* [C] a person whose job is to cut and shape sb's hair

hairy /ˈheəri/ *adj.* (**hairier; hairiest**) **1** having a lot of hair **2** (*informal*) dangerous or worrying: *a hairy experience*

hajj (*also* **haj**) /hædʒ/ *noun* (*usually* **the Hajj**) *noun* [sing.] (**RELIGION**) the PILGRIMAGE (= religious journey) to Mecca that all Muslims try to make at least once in their lives

halal /həˈlæl, -ˈlɑːl/ *adj.* (**RELIGION**) (used about meat) from an animal that has been killed according to Muslim law

half¹ ⚡ 🄰 /hɑːf/ *det., pron., noun* [C] (*pl.* **halves** /hɑːvz/) one of two equal parts of sth; an amount equal to half of sb/sth: *three and a half kilos of potatoes* ◇ *Two halves make a whole.* ◇ *half an hour* ◇ *an hour and a half* ◇ *The second half of the book is more exciting.* ◇ *She scored in the first half* (= of a match). ◇ *Half of this money is yours.* ◇ *Half the people in the office leave at five.* ◇ *Out of 36 candidates, half passed.* ⊃ verb **halve**
IDM break, cut, etc. sth in half to break, etc. sth into two parts **do nothing/not do anything by halves** to do whatever you do completely and correctly **go half and half/go halves with sb** to share the cost of sth with sb **half past …** (in time) 30 minutes past an hour: *half past six* (= 6.30)

half² ⚡ 🄰 /hɑːf/ *adv.* not completely; to the amount of half: *half full* ◇ *The hotel was only half finished.* ◇ *He's half German* (= one of his parents is German).
IDM not half as much, many, good, bad, etc. much less: *This episode wasn't half as good as the last.*

ˌhalf-ˈbaked *adj.* (*informal*) not well planned or considered: *a half-baked idea/scheme*

ˌhalf ˈboard *noun* [U] (*BrE*) (**TOURISM**) a type of accommodation in a hotel, etc. that includes breakfast and an evening meal ⊃ look at **bed and breakfast, full board** ⊃ note at **hotel**

ˈhalf-brother *noun* [C] a person's **half-brother** is a boy or man who has either the same mother or the same father as them ⊃ look at **stepbrother**

ˌhalf-ˈhearted *adj.* without interest or enthusiasm
▸ **half-heartedly** *adv.*

ˈhalf-life *noun* [C] (**PHYSICS**) the time taken for the RADIOACTIVITY of a substance to fall to half its original value

ˌhalf-ˈmoon *noun* [C] the moon when only half of it can be seen from the earth ⊃ picture at **moon**

ˈhalf note (*AmE*) = MINIM

halfpipe /ˈhɑːfpaɪp/ *noun* [C] (**SPORT**) a structure or an area cut into snow, in the shape of a U, used for performing jumps and other complicated movements in SKATEBOARDING, ROLLERBLADING and SNOWBOARDING

half-'price adj. costing half the usual price: a half-price ticket ▶ half-price adv.: Children aged under 4 go half-price.

'half-sister noun [C] a person's **half-sister** is a girl or woman who has either the same mother or the same father as them ⊃ look at **stepsister**

'half step (AmE) = SEMITONE

half-'term noun [C] (BrE) (**EDUCATION**) a short holiday in the middle of each term

half-'time noun [U] (**SPORT**) the period of time between the two halves of a game

'half-tone (AmE) = SEMITONE

halfway ⅋+ **C1** /ˌhɑːfˈweɪ/ adj., adv. at an equal distance between two places; in the middle of a period of time: We arranged to meet at the halfway point. ◇ They have a break halfway through the morning. **SYN midway**

halibut /ˈhælɪbət/ noun [C, U] (pl. halibut) a large flat sea fish that is used for food

halitosis /ˌhælɪˈtəʊsɪs/ noun [U] (**HEALTH**) a condition in which the breath smells unpleasant

hall ⅋ **A2** /hɔːl/ noun [C] **1** (also **hallway** especially in BrE) a room or passage that is just inside the front entrance of a house or public building: Leave your coat in the hall. ◇ There is a reception desk in the **entrance hall** of this building. **2** a building or large room in which meetings, concerts, dances, etc. can be held: a concert hall ⊃ look at **town hall**

hallmark /ˈhɔːlmɑːk/ noun [C] **1** a characteristic that is typical of sb/sth: The ability to motivate students is the hallmark of a good teacher. **2** (in the UK) a mark that is put on objects made of valuable metals, giving information about the quality of the metal and when and where the object was made

hallo /həˈləʊ/ = HELLO

hall of 'residence (pl. halls of residence) (also **hall**) (both BrE) (AmE **dorm** /dɔːm/, **dormitory**) noun [C] (**EDUCATION**) (in colleges, universities, etc.) a building where students live

Halloween (also **Hallowe'en**) /ˌhæləʊˈiːn/ noun [U] the night of October 31st (before All Saints' Day)

▼ CULTURE

Halloween is the time when people say that witches and ghosts appear. Children now dress up as witches, etc. and go to people's houses. They say '**trick or treat**' and the people give them sweets.

hallucination /həˌluːsɪˈneɪʃn/ noun [C, U] seeing or hearing sth that is not really there (because you are ill or have taken a drug); something that is seen or heard when it is not really there

hallucinogen /həˈluːsɪnədʒən/ noun [C] (**HEALTH**) a drug that affects people's minds and makes them see and hear things that are not really there ▶ hallucinogenic /həˌluːsɪnəˈdʒenɪk/ adj.: hallucinogenic drugs

hallway /ˈhɔːlweɪ/ **1** (especially BrE) = HALL (1) **2** (AmE) = CORRIDOR

halo /ˈheɪləʊ/ noun [C] (pl. -os, -oes) (**RELIGION**) the circle of light that is drawn around the head of a holy person in a painting

halogen /ˈhælədʒən/ noun [C] (**CHEMISTRY**) any of five chemical elements that are not metals and that combine with HYDROGEN to form strong ACIDS from which simple SALTS can be made: the halogens fluorine, chlorine, bromine, iodine and astatine

halt ⅋+ **C1** /hɔːlt, hɒlt/ noun [sing.] a stop (that does not last very long): Work came to a halt when the machine broke down. ▶ halt ⅋+ **C1** verb [I, T] (formal): An accident halted the traffic in the town centre for half an hour. **IDM grind to a halt/standstill** → GRIND¹

halter /ˈhɔːltə(r), ˈhɒl-/ noun [C] **1** a rope or narrow piece of leather put around the head of a horse for leading it with **2** (usually used as an adjective) a narrow piece of cloth around the neck that holds a woman's dress or shirt in position, with the back and shoulders not covered

halve /hɑːv/ verb **1** [I, T] to reduce by a half; to make sth reduce by a half: Shares in the company have halved in value. ◇ We aim to halve the number of people on our waiting list in the next six months. **2** [T] to divide sth into two equal parts: First halve the peach and then remove the stone.

halves /hɑːvz/ plural of **half**¹

ham /hæm/ noun [U] meat from a pig's back leg that has been CURED (= treated with salt or smoke to keep it fresh): a slice of ham ◇ a ham sandwich ⊃ look at **bacon, gammon, pork** ⊃ note at **meat**

hamburger /ˈhæmbɜːgə(r)/ **1** = BURGER **2** (AmE) = MINCE

hamlet /ˈhæmlət/ noun [C] a very small village

hammer¹ /ˈhæmə(r)/ noun [C] **1** a tool with a heavy metal head that is used for hitting nails, etc. ⊃ picture at **tool 2** (**ANATOMY**) the first of three small bones in the MIDDLE EAR that carry sound to the INNER EAR **SYN malleus** ⊃ picture at **ear**

hammer² /ˈhæmə(r)/ verb [I, T] **1** ~ (sth) (in/into/onto sth) to hit sth with a HAMMER: She hammered the nail into the wall. ◇ I could hear somebody hammering next door. **2** to hit sth several times, making a loud noise: He hammered on the door until somebody opened it. **IDM hammer sth into sb** to force sb to remember sth by repeating it many times **hammer sth out** to succeed in making a plan or an agreement after a lot of discussion

hammering /ˈhæmərɪŋ/ noun **1** [U, sing.] the noise that is made by sb using a HAMMER or by sb hitting sth many times **2** [C] (BrE, informal) (**SPORT**) a very bad defeat

hammock /ˈhæmək/ noun [C] a bed made of rope or strong cloth that is hung up between two trees or POLES

hamper¹ /ˈhæmpə(r)/ verb [T] to make sth difficult: The building work was hampered by bad weather.

hamper² /ˈhæmpə(r)/ noun [C] a large BASKET with a LID that is used for carrying food

hamster /ˈhæmstə(r)/ noun [C] a small animal that is often kept as a pet. Hamsters are like mice but are fatter and do not have a tail. They store food in the sides of their mouths.

hamstring /ˈhæmstrɪŋ/ noun [C] (**ANATOMY**) one of the five TENDONS behind the knee that connect the muscles of the upper leg to the bones of the lower leg

hand¹ ⅋ **A1** /hænd/ noun
• PART OF THE BODY **1** [C] (**ANATOMY**) the part of the body at the end of the arm, including the fingers and THUMB: He took the child by the hand. ◇ She was on her hands and knees (= CRAWLING on the floor) looking for an earring. ◇ Put your hand up if you know the answer. ◇ He was holding a cup of coffee in his hand. ⊃ picture at **body 2** -handed (in adjectives) having, using or made for the type of hand(s) mentioned: heavy-handed (= CLUMSY and careless) ◇ right-handed/left-handed
• HELP **3** a hand [sing.] (informal) some help: I'll give you a hand with the washing up. ◇ Do you want/need a hand?

- ● ON A CLOCK **4** [C] the part of a clock or watch that points to the numbers: *the hour/minute/second hand*
- ● WORKER **5** [C] a person who does physical work on a farm, in a factory etc: *farmhands*
- ● IN CARD GAMES **6** [C] the set of PLAYING CARDS that sb has been given in a game of cards: *to be dealt a good/ bad hand*

IDM **(close/near) at hand** (*formal*) near in space or time: *Help is close at hand.* **be an old hand (at sth)** → OLD **by hand 1** done by a person and not by machine: *I had to do all the sewing by hand.* **2** not by post: *The letter was delivered by hand.* **catch sb red-handed** → CATCH¹ **change hands** → CHANGE¹ **a firm hand** → FIRM² **(at) first hand** by experiencing, seeing, etc. sth yourself rather than being told about it by sb else: *Did you get this information first hand?* ➷ look at **second-hand** (2) **force sb's hand** → FORCE² **get/lay your hands on sb/sth 1** to find or obtain sth: *I need to get my hands on that new game.* **2** (*informal*) to catch sb: *Just wait till I get my hands on that boy!* **get, have, etc. a free hand** → FREE¹ **get, have, etc. the upper hand** → UPPER **give sb a big hand** to CLAP (= hit) your hands together to show approval, enthusiasm, etc: *The audience gave the girl a big hand when she finished her song.* **hand in hand 1** holding each other's hands: *The couple walked hand in hand along the beach.* **2** usually happening together; closely connected: *Drought and famine usually go hand in hand.* **hands down** (*informal*) easily and without any doubt: *They won hands down.* **hands off (sb/sth)** (*informal*) used for ordering sb not to touch sb/sth **hands up 1** used in a school, etc. for asking people to lift one hand and give an answer: *Hands up, who'd like to go on the trip this afternoon?* **2** used by a person with a gun to tell other people to put their hands in the air **have sb eating out of your hand** → EAT **have a hand in sth** to take part in or share sth **have your hands full** to be very busy so that you cannot do anything else **have your hands tied** to be unable to do what you want to do because of rules, promises, etc: *I'd like to help but my hands are tied.* **a helping hand** → HELP¹ **hold sb's hand** to give sb support in a difficult situation: *I'll come to the dentist's with you to hold your hand.* **hold hands (with sb)** (used about two people) to hold each other's hands **in hand 1** being dealt with at the moment; under control: *The situation is in hand.* **OPP** **(get/be) out of hand 2** (used about money, time, etc.) not yet used: *If you have time in hand at the end of the exam, check what you have written.* **in your hands** in your possession, control or care: *The matter is in the hands of a solicitor.* **in safe hands** → SAFE¹ **keep your hand in** to do an activity from time to time so that you do not forget how to do it or lose the skill **lend (sb) a hand/lend a hand (to sb)** → LEND **off your hands** not your responsibility any more **on hand** available to help or to be used: *There is always an adult on hand to help when the children are playing outside.* **on your hands** being your responsibility: *We seem to have a problem on our hands.* **(on the one hand …) on the other (hand) …** used for showing opposite points of view: *On the one hand, of course, cars are very useful. On the other hand, they cause a huge amount of pollution.* **(get/be) out of hand** not under control: *Violence at football matches is getting out of hand.* **OPP** **in hand** **out of your hands** not in your control; not your responsibility: *I can't help you, I'm afraid. The matter is out of my hands.* **shake sb's hand/shake hands (with sb)/shake sb by the hand** to hand near or close to you: *I'm afraid I haven't got my diary to hand.* **try your hand at sth** → TRY¹ **turn your hand to sth** to have the ability to do sth: *She can turn her hand to all sorts of jobs.* **wash your hands of sb/sth** → WASH¹ **with your bare hands** → BARE

hand² 🔊 **B1** /hænd/ *verb* [T] **~ sb sth; ~ sth to sb** to give or pass sth to sb: *Please hand me the scissors.* ◇ *Please hand the scissors to me.*

IDM **have (got) to hand it to sb** (*informal*) used to say that sb deserves praise for sth: *You've got to hand it to Rita — she's a great cook.*

PHR V **hand sth around** (*also* **hand sth round** *especially in BrE*) to offer or pass sth, especially food and drinks, to all the people in a group **hand sth back (to sb)** to give or return sth to the person who owns it or to where it belongs **hand sth down (to sb) 1** to pass customs, traditions, etc. from older people to younger ones **2** to pass clothes, toys, etc. from older children to younger ones in the family **hand sth in (to sb)** to give sth to sb in authority, especially a piece of work or sth that is lost: *I found a wallet and handed it in to the police.* ➷ note at **job**, **study²** **hand sth on (to sb)** to send or give sth to another person: *When you have read the article, please hand it on to another student.* **hand sth out (to sb)** to give sth to many people in a group: *Food was handed out to the starving people.* **hand (sth/sb) over (to sb)** to give sth/sb officially or formally to another person **hand (sb) over to sb** (used at a meeting or on the TV, radio, phone, etc.) to let sb speak or listen to another person **hand sb/sth over (to sb)** to give sb/sth (to sb): *People were tricked into handing over large sums of money.* **hand sth round** (*especially BrE*) = HAND STH AROUND

handbag /'hændbæg/ (*AmE also* **purse**) *noun* [C] a small bag in which money, keys, etc. are carried, especially by women ▸ **shoulder bag**

'**hand baggage** (*especially AmE*) = HAND LUGGAGE

handball (**SPORT**) *noun* **1** /'hændbɔːl/ [U] a team game for two teams of seven players, usually played indoors, in which players try to score goals by throwing a ball with their hand **2** /ˌhænd'bɔːl/ [C, U] (in football) touching the ball with your hands, which is against the rules: *a penalty for handball*

handbook /'hændbʊk/ *noun* [C] a book that gives instructions on how to use sth or advice and information about a particular subject ➷ look at **manual¹**

handbrake /'hændbreɪk/ (*especially BrE*) (*AmE usually* **emergency brake**, **parking brake**) *noun* [C] a device that is operated by hand to stop a car from moving when it is parked

handcuffs /'hændkʌfs/ (*also informal* **cuffs**) *noun* [pl.] a pair of metal rings that are joined together by a chain, used for holding the WRISTS of a prisoner together: *She was led away in handcuffs.*

handful 🔊 **C1** /'hændfʊl/ *noun* **1** [C] **~ (of sth)** as much or as many of sth as you can hold in one hand: *a handful of sand* **2** [sing.] a small number (of sb/sth): *Only a handful of people came to the meeting.* **3** **a handful** [sing.] (*informal*) a person or an animal that is difficult to control

handgun /'hændɡʌn/ *noun* [C] a small gun that you can hold and fire with one hand

handheld¹ /ˌhænd'held/ *adj.* small enough to be held in the hand while being used: *handheld electronic devices*

handheld² /'hændheld/ *noun* [C] (**COMPUTING**) a small computer or electronic device that can be held in the hand while being used

handicap¹ /'hændikæp/ *noun* [C] **1** something that makes doing sth more difficult; a disadvantage: *Not speaking French is going to be a bit of a handicap in my new job.* **SYN** **obstacle 2** (*old-fashioned*) = DISABILITY **❶** This word is now considered offensive. **3** (**SPORT**) a disadvantage that is given to a strong competitor in a sports event, etc. so that the other competitors have more chance

handicap² /'hændikæp/ *verb* [T, usually passive] (-pp-) to give or be a disadvantage to sb: *They were handicapped by their lack of education.*

handicapped /'hændikæpt/ *(old-fashioned)* = DISABLED ❶ This word is now considered offensive.

handicraft /'hændikrɑːft/ *noun* (**ART**) **1** [C] an activity that needs skill with the hands as well as artistic ability **2** handicrafts [pl.] the objects that are produced by this activity

handiwork /'hændiwɜːk/ *noun* [U] **1** a thing that you have made or done, especially using your artistic skill: *We admired her exquisite handiwork.* **2** a thing done by a particular person or group, especially sth bad

handkerchief /'hæŋkətʃɪf, -tʃiːf/ *(pl. handkerchiefs, handkerchieves /'hæŋkətʃiːvz/) (also hanky, hankie) noun* [C] a square piece of cloth or soft thin paper that you use for blowing your nose

handle¹ 🔊 **B2** /'hændl/ *verb* [T] **1** to deal with or control sb/sth: *This port handles 100 million tons of cargo each year.* ◇ *I have a problem at work and I don't really know how to handle it.* ◇ *He should have been handling that dog better.* **2** to touch or hold sth with your hand(s): *Wash your hands before you handle food.*

handles

door handle · handle · handle

handle² 🔊 **B2** /'hændl/ *noun* [C] a part of sth that is used for holding or opening it: *She turned the handle and opened the door.* ◇ *He broke the handle off the cup by accident.*
IDM fly off the handle → FLY¹

handlebar /'hændlbɑː(r)/ *noun* [C, usually pl.] the metal bar with a handle at each end at the front of a bicycle or motorcycle that you hold when you are riding it

handler /'hændlə(r)/ *noun* [C] (especially in compounds) **1** a person who trains animals, especially dogs: *a dog handler* **2** a person who carries or deals with sth as part of their job: *airport baggage handlers*

handling 🔊 **C1** /'hændlɪŋ/ *noun* [U] **1** the way that sb deals with or controls a situation, a person, an animal, etc: *I was impressed by his handling of the affair.* **2** the action of touching or holding sth with your hands **3** the action of organizing or controlling sth: *data handling on a computer*

hand luggage *(especially BrE) (also carry-on baggage, hand baggage both especially AmE) noun* [U] (**TOURISM**) a small bag, etc. that you can keep with you on a plane

handmade /ˌhænd'meɪd/ *adj.* made by hand and of very good quality, not by machine

handout ❺ /'hændaʊt/ *noun* [C] **1** food, money, etc. given to people who need it badly **2** a free document that is given to a lot of people, to advertise sth or explain sth, for example in a class

hand-picked *adj.* carefully chosen for a special purpose

handprint /'hændprɪnt/ *noun* [C] a mark left by the flat part of sb's hand on a surface

handrail /'hændreɪl/ *noun* [C] a bar that you can hold to stop you from falling (on stairs, from a building, etc.)

handset /'hændset/ *noun* [C] **1** = RECEIVER (1) **2** a mobile phone, especially the main part of the phone not including the battery or SIM CARD **3** a device that you hold in your hand to control sth from a distance

hands-free *adj.* if a phone, etc. is **hands-free**, you can use it without needing to hold it in your hand

handshake /'hændʃeɪk/ *noun* [C] the act of shaking sb's right hand with your own, for example when you meet them

hands-off *adj.* dealing with people or a situation by not becoming involved and by allowing people to do what they want to: *a hands-off approach to staff management* ⊃ look at **hands-on**

handsome /'hænsəm/ *adj.* (handsomer; handsomest) **1** (used about a man) attractive **2** (used about money, an offer, etc.) large or generous: *a handsome profit* ▶ **handsomely** *adv.*: *Her efforts were handsomely rewarded.*

hands-on *adj.* learnt by doing sth yourself, not watching sb else do it: *She needs some hands-on computer experience.* ⊃ look at **hands-off**, **practical¹** (1)

handstand /'hændstænd/ *noun* [C] a movement in which you put your hands on the ground and lift your legs straight up in the air

handwriting /'hændraɪtɪŋ/ *noun* [U] a person's style of writing by hand

handwritten /ˌhænd'rɪtn/ *adj.* written by hand, not typed or printed

handy 🔊+ **C1** /'hændi/ *adj.* (handier; handiest) *(informal)* **1** useful; easy to use: *a handy tip* ◇ *a handy gadget* **SYN useful 2** ~ **(for sth/doing sth)** useful to sb/ sth; located near to or stored in a convenient place: *Our house is very handy for the shops.* ◇ *Always keep a first-aid kit handy.* **3** [not before noun] able to use your hands or tools to make or repair things well: *Jane is very handy around the house.*
IDM come in handy to be useful at some time: *Don't throw that box away. It may come in handy.*

handyman /'hændimæn/ *noun* [C] *(pl. -men /-men/)* a man who is good at doing practical jobs inside and outside the house, either as a hobby or as a job

hang¹ 🔊 **B1** /hæŋ/ *verb* (pt, pp hung /hʌŋ/) **HELP** In sense 3 **hanged** is used for the past tense and past participle. **1** [I, T] (used with an adverb or a preposition) to fasten sth or be fastened at the top so that the lower part is free or loose: *Hang your coat on the hook.* ◇ *I left the washing hanging on the line all day.* ◇ *She hung the picture over the fireplace.* **2** [I, T] (often used with an adverb or a preposition) to bend or let sth bend downwards: *Children hung over the gate.* ◇ *He hung his head in shame.* **3** [T] to kill sb/yourself by putting a rope around the neck and allowing the body to drop downwards: *He was hanged for murder.* **4** [I] ~ **(above/ over sb/sth)** to stay in the air in a way that is unpleasant or threatening: *Smog hung in the air over the city.*
IDM be/get hung up (about/on sb/sth) *(informal)* to think about sb/sth all the time in a way that is not healthy or good: *She's really hung up about her parents' divorce.* **hang (on) in there** *(informal)* to have courage and keep trying, even though a situation is difficult: *The worst part is over now. Just hang on in there and be patient.*
PHR V hang around *(BrE also hang about) (informal)* to stay in or near a place not doing very much **hang back 1** to not want to do or say sth, often because

you are shy or not sure of yourself **2** to stay in a place after other people have left it **hang on 1** (*informal*) to wait for a short time: *Hang on a minute. I'm nearly ready.* **2** to hold sth tightly: *Hang on, don't let go!* **hang on sth** to depend on sth **hang on to sth 1** (*informal*) to keep sth: *Let's hang on to the car for another year.* **2** to hold sth tightly: *He hung on to the child's hand as they crossed the street.* **hang out** (*informal*) to spend a lot of time in a place: *The local kids hang out at the park.* **hang sth out** to put washing, etc. on a clothes line so that it can dry **hang over sb** to be present or about to happen in a way that is unpleasant or threatening: *This essay has been hanging over me for days.* **hang sth up** to put sth on a nail, HOOK, etc: *Hang your coat up over there.* **hang up** to end a phone conversation ⊃ note at **phone¹ hang up on sb** (*informal*) to end a phone conversation without saying goodbye because you are angry

hang² /hæŋ/ *noun*
IDM **get the hang of sth/doing sth** (*informal*) to learn how to use or do sth: *It took me a long time to get the hang of the new system.*

hangar /ˈhæŋə(r)/ *noun* [C] a big building where planes are kept

hanger /ˈhæŋə(r)/ (*also* **coat hanger**, **clothes hanger**) *noun* [C] a metal, plastic or wooden object with a HOOK that is used for hanging up clothes in a cupboard

hanger-ˈon *noun* [C] (*pl.* **hangers-on**) a person who tries to be friendly with sb who is rich or important

ˈhang-glider *noun* [C] (**SPORT**) a type of frame covered with cloth that a person holds and flies through the air with as a sport ⊃ look at **glider** ▶ **hang-gliding** *noun* [U]

hanging /ˈhæŋɪŋ/ *noun* **1** [U, C] (**LAW**) the practice of killing sb as a punishment by putting a rope around their neck and hanging them from a high place; an occasion when this happens: *to sentence somebody to death by hanging* ◇ *public hangings* **2** [C, usually pl.] (**ART**) a large piece of material that is hung on a wall for decoration: *wall hangings*

ˈhanging ˈvalley *noun* [C] (**GEOGRAPHY**) a valley that joins a deeper valley, often with a WATERFALL where the two valleys join ⊃ picture at **glacial**

hangman *noun* **1** /ˈhæŋmən/ [C] (*pl.* -men /-mən/) (**LAW**) a person whose job is to kill criminals as a form of punishment by hanging them with a rope **2** /ˈhæŋmæn/ [U] a word game where the aim is to guess all the letters of a word before a picture of a person hanging is completed

hangover /ˈhæŋəʊvə(r)/ *noun* [C] the headache and sick feeling that you have if you have drunk too much alcohol the night before

ˈhang-up *noun* [C] ~ **(about sb/sth)** (*informal*) an emotional problem about sth that makes you embarrassed or worried: *He has a real hang-up about his height.*

hanker /ˈhæŋkə(r)/ *verb* [I] ~ **after/for sth** to want sth very much (often sth that you cannot easily have): *He hankered after fame.*

hanky (*also* **hankie**) /ˈhæŋki/ *noun* [C] (*pl.* -ies) (*informal*) = HANDKERCHIEF

Hanukkah /ˈhænʊkə, ˈxæ-/ *noun* [U] (**RELIGION**) an eight-day Jewish festival and holiday in November or December

haphazard /hæpˈhæzəd/ *adj.* with no particular order or plan; badly organized ▶ **haphazardly** *adv.*

haploid /ˈhæplɔɪd/ *adj.* (**BIOLOGY**) (used about a cell) containing the set of CHROMOSOMES from only one parent ⊃ look at **diploid**

happen ⚡ **A1** **S** /ˈhæpən/ *verb* [I] **1** (used about an event or a situation) to take place, usually without being planned first: *Can you describe to the police what happened after you left the party?* ◇ *How did the accident happen?* **2 ~ to do sth** to do sth by chance: *I happened to meet him in London yesterday.*
IDM **as it happens/happened** used when you say sth that is surprising, or sth connected with what sb else has just said: *I agree with you, as it happens.* **it (just) so happens** → **SO¹**
PHR V **happen to sb/sth** to be what sb/sth experiences: *What do you think has happened to Julie? She should have been here an hour ago.* ◇ *What will happen to the business when your father retires?*

happening /ˈhæpənɪŋ/ *noun* [C] **1** [usually pl.] an event; sth that happens, often sth unusual: *Strange happenings have been reported in that old hotel.* **2** (**ARTS AND MEDIA**) an artistic performance or event that is not planned

happily ⚡ **A2** /ˈhæpɪli/ *adv.* **1** in a happy way: *I would happily give up my job if I didn't need the money.* **2** it is lucky that: *The police found my handbag and, happily, nothing had been stolen.* **SYN** **fortunately 3** in a way that shows you are ready or pleased to do sth

happy ⚡ **A1** /ˈhæpi/ *adj.* (**happier**; **happiest**)
• FEELING/GIVING PLEASURE **1 ~ (to do sth); ~ (for sb); ~ (that)** … feeling or showing pleasure; pleased: *I was really happy to see Mark again yesterday.* ◇ *You look very happy today.* ◇ *Congratulations! I'm very happy for you.* ◇ *I'm happy (that) you could come.* **OPP** **sad, unhappy 2** giving or causing pleasure: *a happy marriage/memory/childhood* ◇ *The film is sad but it has a happy ending.*
• SATISFIED **3 ~ (with/about sb/sth)** satisfied that sth is good and right; not worried: *I'm not very happy with what you've done.* ◇ *She doesn't feel happy about the salary she's been offered.*
• WILLING **4** [not before noun] ~ **to do sth** ready to do sth; pleased: *I'll be more than happy to give you extra classes if you think you need them.*
• GREETING **5 Happy** used to wish sb a pleasant celebration: *Happy Birthday!*
• LUCKY **6** [only before noun] lucky **SYN** **fortunate OPP** **unhappy**
▶ **happiness** ⚡ **B1** *noun* [U]

ˌhappy-go-ˈlucky *adj.* not caring or worried about life and the future

ˈhappy hour *noun* [C, usually sing.] a time, usually in the evening, when a pub or bar sells alcoholic drinks at lower prices than usual

harass /ˈhærəs, həˈræs/ *verb* [T] to annoy or worry sb by doing unpleasant things to them, especially over a long time: *The court ordered him to stop harassing his ex-wife.* ▶ **harassment** ⚡+ **C1** *noun* [U] ⊃ look at **sexual harassment**

harassed /ˈhærəst, həˈræst/ *adj.* tired and worried because you have too much to do

harbinger /ˈhɑːbɪndʒə(r)/ *noun* [C] ~ **(of sth)** (*formal*) a sign that shows that sth is going to happen soon, often sth bad

harbour¹ ⚡+ **B2** (*BrE*) (*AmE* **harbor**) /ˈhɑːbə(r)/ *noun* [C, U] a place on the coast where ships can be tied up and protected by strong walls from the sea and bad weather

harbour² (*BrE*) (*AmE* **harbor**) /ˈhɑːbə(r)/ *verb* [T] **1** to keep feelings or thoughts secret in your mind for a long time: *She harboured a deep dislike of him for years.* ◇ *She began to **harbour doubts** about the decision.* **2** to hide or protect sb/sth that is bad: *They were accused of harbouring terrorists.*

hard¹ 🔊 **A1** /hɑːd/ *adj.*

• NOT SOFT **1** not soft to touch; not easy to break or bend: *The bed was so hard that I couldn't sleep.* ◇ *Diamonds are the hardest known mineral.* **OPP** soft

• NOT EASY **2** ~ **(for sb) (to do sth)** difficult to do or understand; not easy: *The first question in the exam was very hard.* ◇ *This book is hard to understand/It is a hard book to understand.* ◇ *It's hard for young people to find good jobs nowadays.* ◇ *I find his attitude very hard to take* (= difficult to accept). **SYN** tough **OPP** easy¹ ⊃ note at **difficult 3** (used about conditions) unpleasant or unhappy; full of difficulty: *He had a hard time when his parents died.* ◇ *to have a hard day/ life/childhood* **4** needing or using a lot of physical strength or mental effort: *It's a hard climb to the top of the hill.* ◇ *Hard work is said to be good for you.* ◇ *He's a hard worker.*

• NOT KIND **5** (used about a person) showing no kind feelings or sympathy; not gentle: *You have to be hard to succeed in business.* **OPP** lenient, soft

• OF WEATHER **6** (used about the weather) very cold: *The forecast is for a hard winter/frost.* **OPP** mild

• WATER **7** (used about water) containing particular minerals so that soap does not make many bubbles: *We live in a hard water area.* **OPP** soft

▶ hardness *noun* [U]

IDM be hard at it (*informal*) to be working very hard doing sth be hard on sb/sth **1** to treat sb/sth in a very strict or unkind way: *Don't be too hard on her — she's only a child.* **2** to be difficult for or unfair to sb/ sth give sb a hard time (*informal*) to make a situation unpleasant, embarrassing or difficult for sb a hard act to follow a person or a thing that it is difficult to do better than hard and fast (used about rules, etc.) that cannot be changed: *There are no hard and fast rules about this.* hard facts information that is true, not just people's opinions hard luck → LUCK hard of hearing unable to hear well hard to swallow difficult to believe the hard way through having unpleasant or difficult experiences, rather than learning from what you are told: *She won't listen to my advice so she'll just have to learn the hard way.* have a hard job doing sth/to do sth | have a hard time doing sth to do sth with great difficulty no hard feelings (*informal*) used to tell sb you do not feel angry after an argument, etc: '*No hard feelings, I hope,' he said, offering me his hand.* take a hard line (on sth) to deal with sth in a very serious way that you will not allow anyone to change: *The government has taken a hard line on people who drink and drive.*

hard² 🔊 **A1** /hɑːd/ *adv.* **1** with great effort, energy or attention: *He worked hard all his life.* ◇ *You'll have to try a bit harder than that.* ◇ *She should think hard about what she is doing.* **HELP** Do not confuse **hard** with **hardly.** Hardly is an adverb meaning 'almost not': *I hardly ever go to concerts.* ◇ *I can hardly wait for my birthday.* **2** with great force; heavily: *It was raining/snowing hard.* ◇ *He hit her hard across the face.*

IDM be hard pressed/pushed/put to do sth to find sth very difficult to do: *He was hard pressed to explain her sudden disappearance.* be hard up (for sth) to have too few or too little of sth, especially money: *We're too hard up to afford a holiday this year.* die hard → DIE¹ hard done by (*BrE, informal*) not fairly treated: *He felt very hard done by when he wasn't chosen for the team.*

hardback /'hɑːdbæk/ *noun* [C, U] (**LITERATURE**) a book that has a stiff cover: *This book is only available in hardback.* ⊃ look at **paperback**

hardboard /'hɑːdbɔːd/ *noun* [U] a type of wooden board made by pressing very small pieces of wood together into thin sheets

,hard-'boiled *adj.* (used about an egg) boiled until it is solid inside

,hard 'cash (*BrE*) (*AmE also* cold cash) *noun* [U] money, especially in the form of coins and notes, that you can spend

,hard 'copy *noun* [U, C] (**COMPUTING**) information from a computer that has been printed on paper

,hard 'core *noun* [sing. + sing./pl. verb] the members of a group who are the most active

,hard-'core *adj.* [only before noun] **1** having a belief or way of behaving that will not change: *hard-core party members* **2** showing or describing sexual acts in a detailed or violent way: *They sell hard-core pornography.*

,hard 'currency *noun* [U, C] (**ECONOMICS**) money belonging to a particular country that is easy to exchange and not likely to fall in value

'hard disk *noun* [C] (**COMPUTING**) a piece of hard plastic that is fixed inside or outside a computer and is used for storing data and programs permanently ⊃ look at **floppy disk**

'hard drive *noun* [C] (**COMPUTING**) a part of a computer that takes information from data on a HARD DISK

,hard 'drug *noun* [C, usually pl.] (**LAW, SOCIAL STUDIES**) a powerful and illegal drug that some people take for pleasure and can become ADDICTED to (= unable to stop taking or using it): *Heroin and cocaine are hard drugs.* **OPP** soft drug

harden /'hɑːdn/ *verb* **1** [I, T] to become or to make sth hard or less likely to change: *The concrete will harden in 24 hours.* ◇ *The firm has hardened its attitude on this question.* **2** [T, usually passive] ~ **sb (to sth/doing sth)** to make sb less kind or less easily shocked: *a hardened reporter/criminal* ◇ *Police officers get hardened to seeing dead bodies.* **3** [I] (used about a person's face, voice, etc.) to become serious and unfriendly

,hard-'headed *adj.* determined and not allowing yourself to be influenced by emotions: *a hard-headed businessman*

,hard-'hearted *adj.* not kind to other people and not considering their feelings **OPP** soft-hearted

,hard-'hitting *adj.* that talks about or criticizes sb/sth in an honest and very direct way: *a hard-hitting campaign/speech/report*

hardiness /'hɑːdinəs/ → HARDY

hardly 🔊 **B1** /'hɑːdli/ *adv.* **1** almost no; almost not; almost none: *There's hardly any coffee left.* ◇ *We hardly ever go out nowadays.* ◇ *I hardly spoke any English when I first came here.* ⊃ look at **almost, barely, scarcely 2** used especially after *can* and *could* and before the main verb to emphasize that sth is difficult to do: *Speak up — I can hardly hear you.* **3** (used to say that sth has just begun, happened, etc.) only just: *I'd hardly sat down when the phone rang.* ◇ *She'd hardly gone to sleep than it was time to get up again.* **4** (used to suggest that sth is unlikely or unreasonable) not really: *You can hardly expect me to believe that excuse!*

,hard-'nosed *adj.* not affected by feelings or emotions when trying to get what you want

hardship /'hɑːdʃip/ *noun* [U, C] a situation that is difficult or unpleasant because you do not have enough money, food, etc: *This new tax is going to cause a lot of hardship.*

hard 'shoulder (*BrE*) (*AmE* **breakdown lane**) *noun* [C] a narrow section of road at the side of major road such as a MOTORWAY where cars are allowed to stop in an emergency

hardware ℰ+ **C1** /'hɑːdweə(r)/ *noun* [U] **1** (**COMPUTING**) the machines and electronic parts of a computer system ⊃ look at **software 2** tools and equipment that are used in the house and garden: *a hardware shop*

hard-'wearing *adj.* (*BrE*) (used about materials, clothes, etc.) strong and able to last for a long time

hardwired /ˌhɑːd'waɪəd/ *adj.* **1** (**COMPUTING**) if a computer or a machine is **hardwired**, it works in a particular way because that was built into the permanent system and cannot be changed **2** if a person or an animal's behaviour is **hardwired**, they were born to behave that way and they cannot change what they do

hardwood /'hɑːdwʊd/ *noun* [U, C] hard heavy wood from DECIDUOUS trees (= trees that lose their leaves in winter): *tropical hardwoods* ⊃ look at **softwood**

hard-'working *adj.* working with effort and energy: *a hard-working man*

hardy /'hɑːdi/ *adj.* (**hardier**; **hardiest**) strong and able to survive difficult conditions and bad weather: *a hardy plant* ▸ **hardiness** *noun* [U]

hare /heə(r)/ *noun* [C] an animal like a RABBIT but bigger with longer ears and legs

harem /'hɑːriːm, -rəm/ *noun* [C] a number of women living with one man, especially in some Muslim societies in the past. The part of the building the women live in is also called a **harem**.

harm¹ ℰ **B2** ⓦ /hɑːm/ *noun* [U] damage or injury: *The scandal caused serious harm to the government.* ◇ *Peter ate some of those berries but they didn't **do him any harm**.* ◇ *Experienced staff watch over the children to make sure they don't **come to any harm**.* ⊃ look at **self-harm**
IDM **no harm done** (*informal*) used to tell sb that they have not upset anyone or caused any damage or injury: *'Sorry about what I said to you last night.' 'That's all right, Jack, no harm done!'* **out of harm's way** in a safe place: *Put the medicine out of harm's way where the children can't reach it.* **there is no harm in doing sth | it does no harm (for sb) to do sth** there's nothing wrong in doing sth (and sth good may result): *I'm sure he'll say no, but there's no harm in asking.*

harm² ℰ **B2** /hɑːm/ *verb* [T] to cause injury or damage: *Too much sun can harm your skin.* ⊃ look at **hurt¹** (1)

harmful ℰ **B2** ⓦ /'hɑːmfl/ *adj.* ~ (**to sb/sth**) causing harm: *Traffic fumes are harmful to the environment.* ⊃ picture at **safety**

harmless /'hɑːmləs/ *adj.* **1** not able or not likely to cause damage or injury; safe: *You needn't be frightened — these insects are completely harmless.* **2** not likely to upset people: *The children can watch that film — it's quite harmless.* ▸ **harmlessly** *adv.*

harmonic¹ /hɑː'mɒnɪk/ *adj.* (**MUSIC**) used to describe the way notes are played or sung together to make a pleasing sound

harmonic² /hɑː'mɒnɪk/ *noun* [C, usually pl.] (**MUSIC**) **1** a note that is played together with the main note and is higher and quieter than that note **2** a high quiet note that can be played on some instruments like the VIOLIN by touching the string very lightly

harmonica /hɑː'mɒnɪkə/ *noun* [C] (**MUSIC**) a small musical instrument that you play by moving it across your lips while you are blowing

harmonious /hɑː'məʊniəs/ *adj.* **1** friendly, peaceful and without any arguments **2** (used about musical notes, colours, etc.) producing a pleasant effect when heard or seen together ▸ **harmoniously** *adv.*

harmonize (*BrE* also **-ise**) /'hɑːmənaɪz/ *verb* [I] **1** ~ (**with sth**) (used about two or more things) to produce a pleasant effect when seen, heard, etc. together: *The new building doesn't harmonize with its surroundings.* **2** ~ (**with sb/sth**) (**MUSIC**) to sing or play music that sounds good combined with the main tune ▸ **harmonization** (*BrE* also **-isation**) /ˌhɑːmənaɪ'zeɪʃn/ *noun* [U, C]

harmony ℰ+ **C1** /'hɑːməni/ *noun* (*pl.* **-ies**) **1** [U] (**in**) ~ (**with sth**) a state of agreement or of living together in peace: *There is said to be a lack of harmony within the government.* ◇ *We need to live more in harmony with our environment.* **2** [U, C] (**MUSIC**) a pleasing combination of musical notes, colours, etc: *They sang in three-part harmony.* ◇ *There are some beautiful harmonies in that music.*

harness¹ /'hɑːnɪs/ *noun* [C] **1** a set of narrow pieces of leather that is put around the neck and body of an animal, especially a horse, so that it can pull sth **2** a set of narrow pieces of material for fastening sth to sb's body or for stopping sb from moving around, falling, etc: *a safety harness*

harness² /'hɑːnɪs/ *verb* [T] **1** ~ **sth** (**to sth**) to put a HARNESS on a horse, etc. or to tie a horse, etc. to sth using a HARNESS: *Two ponies were harnessed to the cart.* **2** to control the energy of sth in order to produce power or to achieve sth: *to harness the sun's rays as a source of energy*

harp /hɑːp/ *noun* [C] (**MUSIC**) a large musical instrument that has many strings stretching from the top to the bottom of a frame. You play the harp with your fingers. ⊃ picture at **instrument**, **orchestra** ▸ **harpist** *noun* [C]

harpoon /hɑː'puːn/ *noun* [C] a long thin weapon with a sharp pointed end and a rope tied to it that is used to catch WHALES (= very large sea animals) and large fish ▸ **harpoon** *verb* [T]

harrow /'hærəʊ/ *noun* [C] (**AGRICULTURE**) a piece of farming equipment that is pulled over land that has been PLOUGHED to break up the earth before planting

harrowing /'hærəʊɪŋ/ *adj.* making people feel very sad or upset: *a harrowing experience*

harsh ℰ+ **C1** /hɑːʃ/ *adj.* **1** very strict and unkind: *a harsh punishment/criticism* ◇ *The judge had some harsh words for the journalist's behaviour.* ⊃ look at **severe 2** unpleasant and difficult to live in, look at, listen to, etc: *She grew up in the harsh environment of New York City.* ◇ *a harsh winter/light/voice* **3** too strong or rough and likely to damage sth: *This soap is too harsh for a baby's skin.* ▸ **harshly** *adv.* ▸ **harshness** *noun* [U]

harvest ℰ+ **C1** /'hɑːvɪst/ *noun* (**AGRICULTURE**) **1** [C, U] the time of year when the grain, fruit, etc. is collected on a farm; the act of collecting the grain, fruit, etc: *Farmers always need extra help with the harvest.* ⊃ note at **agriculture 2** [C] the amount of grain, fruit, etc. that is collected: *This year's wheat harvest was very poor.* ▸ **harvest** ℰ+ **C1** *verb* [I, T] ⊃ look at **combine²**

has /həz, əz, *strong form* hæz/ → **HAVE²**

has-been /'hæz biːn/ *noun* [C] (*informal*) a person that is no longer as famous, successful or important as before

hash /hæʃ/ *noun* **1** [U] a hot dish of meat mixed together with potato and fried **2** (*also* **'hash sign** *both BrE*) (*also* **hashtag** *BrE, AmE*) [C] (**LANGUAGE**) the symbol (#), especially one on a phone or computer keyboard **3** [U] = HASHISH

IDM **make a hash of sth** (*informal*) to do sth badly

hashish /ˈhæʃiːʃ, ˈhæʃiːʃ/ (*also informal* **hash**) *noun* [U] a drug made from HEMP (= a type of plant) that some people smoke for pleasure and that is illegal in many countries **SYN** **cannabis**

hashtag /ˈhæʃtæg/ *noun* [C] **1** (COMPUTING) a word or phrase with the symbol (#) in front of it, that is used in messages sent on the internet to help people find the subjects that interest them **2** = HASH (2)

hasn't /ˈhæznt/ *short form* has not

hassle[1] /ˈhæsl/ *noun* (*informal*) **1** [C, U] a thing or situation that is annoying because it is complicated or involves a lot of effort: *It's going to be a hassle having to change trains with all this luggage.* ◊ *Let's walk — it's less hassle than waiting for the bus.* **2** [U] disagreeing or arguing: *I've decided what to do — please don't give me any hassle about it.*

hassle[2] /ˈhæsl/ *verb* [T] to annoy sb, especially by asking them to do sth many times **SYN** **bother**[1]

haste /heɪst/ *noun* [U] speed in doing sth, especially because you do not have enough time: *It was obvious that the email had been written in haste.*

hasten /ˈheɪsn/ *verb* (*formal*) **1** [I] ~ **to do sth** to be quick to do or say sth: *She hastened to apologize.* **2** [T] to make sth happen or be done earlier or more quickly

hasty /ˈheɪsti/ *adj.* (**hastier**; **hastiest**) **1** said or done too quickly: *He said a hasty 'goodbye' and left.* **2** ~ (**in doing sth**); ~ (**to do sth**) (used about a person) acting or deciding sth too quickly or without enough thought: *Maybe I was too hasty in rejecting her for the job.* ◊ *Don't be too hasty to judge him.* ▶ **hastily** /-stɪli/ *adv.*

hat ☂ **A1** /hæt/ *noun* [C] a covering that you wear on your head, usually when you are outside: *to wear a hat* ◊ *a sun hat* ◊ *a straw/woolly/cowboy hat*

IDM **at the drop of a hat** → DROP[2]

hatch[1] /hætʃ/ *verb* **1** [I] ~ (**out**) (BIOLOGY) (used about a baby bird, insect, fish, etc.) to come out of an egg: *Ten chicks hatched (out) this morning.* **2** [T] (BIOLOGY) to make a baby bird, etc. come out of an egg **3** [T] ~ **sth (up)** to think of a plan (usually to do sth bad): *He hatched a plan to avoid paying any income tax.*

hatch[2] /hætʃ/ *noun* [C] **1** an opening in the DECK (= the floor) of a ship or the bottom of an aircraft through which goods are passed **2** (ARCHITECTURE) an opening in the wall between a kitchen and another room that is used for passing food through **3** an opening or a door in a floor or ceiling: *a hatch to the attic*

hatchback /ˈhætʃbæk/ *noun* [C] a car with a large door at the back that opens upwards

hatchet /ˈhætʃɪt/ *noun* [C] a small AXE (= a tool with a short handle and a metal head with a sharp edge used for cutting wood) ⊃ picture at **axe**[1]

hate[1] ☂ **A1** /heɪt/ *verb* [T] **1** ~ (**doing sth**); ~ (**to do sth**) to have a very strong feeling of not liking sb/sth at all: *I hate grapefruit.* ◊ *I really hate him.* ◊ *He hates driving at night.* ◊ *I hate it when it's raining like this.* ◊ *I hate to see the countryside spoilt.* **2** used as a polite way of saying sorry for sth you would prefer not to have to say: *I hate to bother you, but did you pick up my keys by mistake?*

hate[2] ☂ **B1** /heɪt/ *noun* **1** [U] a very strong feeling of not liking sb/sth at all: *Do you feel any hate towards the kidnappers?* **SYN** **hatred** **2** [C] a thing that you do not like at all: *Plastic flowers are one of my pet hates* (= the things that I particularly dislike).

hate crime *noun* [U, C] (LAW) violent acts that are committed against people because of the human group they belong to, because they are GAY, etc.; a single act of this type: *Why has hate crime increased?*

hateful /ˈheɪtfl/ *adj.* ~ (**to sb**) extremely unpleasant: *Racism in any form was hateful to her.* ◊ *It was a hateful thing to say.* **SYN** **horrible**

hate speech *noun* [U] ~ (**against sb/sth**) (LAW) speech or writing that attacks or threatens a particular group of people, especially because of the human group they belong to, their religion or their sexual ORIENTATION

hatred ☂+ **C1** /ˈheɪtrɪd/ *noun* [U] ~ (**for/of sb/sth**) a very strong feeling of not liking sb/sth: *her hatred for her attackers* **SYN** **hate**[1]

hat-trick *noun* [C] (SPORT) three points, goals, etc. scored by one player in the same game; three successes achieved by one person: *to score a hat-trick*

haughty /ˈhɔːti/ *adj.* (**haughtier**; **haughtiest**) proud, and thinking that you are better than other people ▶ **haughtily** /-tɪli/ *adv.*

haul[1] /hɔːl/ *verb* [T] to pull sth with a lot of effort or difficulty: *A lorry hauled the car out of the mud.*

haul[2] /hɔːl/ *noun* **1** [C, usually sing.] ~ (**of sth**) a large amount of sth that has been stolen, caught, collected, etc: *The fishermen came back with a good haul of fish.* **2** [sing.] a distance to be travelled: *It seemed a long haul back home at night.*

haulage /ˈhɔːlɪdʒ/ *noun* [U] (BrE) the transport of goods by road, railway, etc.; the money charged for this

haunches /ˈhɔːntʃɪz/ *noun* [pl.] the back end of an animal, including the tops of its back legs; a person's bottom and the tops of his or her legs: *The lion rested on its haunches.*

haunt[1] ☂+ **C1** /hɔːnt/ *verb* [T] **1** [often passive] if a ghost **haunts** a place, people say that they have seen it there: *The castle is haunted by the ghost of a woman.* **2** (used about sth unpleasant or sad) to be always in your mind, or to continue to cause problems for sb: *His unhappy face has haunted me for years.*

haunt[2] /hɔːnt/ *noun* [C] a place that you visit regularly: *This cafe has always been a favourite haunt of mine.*

haunting /ˈhɔːntɪŋ/ *adj.* having a quality that stays in your mind: *a haunting song*

have[1] ☂ **A2** /həv, əv, *strong form* hæv/ *auxiliary verb* (*negative* **have not**; *short form* **haven't** /ˈhævnt/; *has* /həz, əz, *strong form* hæz/; *negative* **has not**; *short form* **hasn't** /ˈhæznt/; *pt* **had** /həd, əd, *strong form* hæd/; *negative* **had not**; *short form* **hadn't** /ˈhædnt/) used for forming the perfect tenses: *I've finished my work.* ◊ *Had they left before you got there?*

have[2] ☂ **A1** /*strong form* hæv/ *verb* [T] (*negative* **have not**; *short form* **haven't** /ˈhævnt/; *has* /həz, əz, *strong form* hæz/; *negative* **has not**; *short form* **hasn't** /ˈhæznt/; *pt, pp* **had** /həd, əd, *strong form* hæd/; *negative* **had not**; *short form* **hadn't** /ˈhædnt/)

• **OWN/HOLD** **1** (*also* **have got** /ˌhæv ˈɡɒt/) (not used in the progressive tenses) to own or to hold sth: *The flat has two bedrooms.* ◊ *He's got short dark hair.* ◊ *to have patience/enthusiasm/skill* ◊ *Have you got any brothers or sisters?* ◊ *Do you have time to check my work?* ◊ *They haven't got a car.* ⊃ look at **possess**

• **DO** **2** used with many nouns to talk about doing sth: *What time do you have breakfast?* ◊ *to have a drink/something to eat* ◊ *I'll just have a shower then we'll go.* ◊ *to have an argument/talk/chat*

• **EXPERIENCE** **3** to experience sth: *to have fun* ◊ *to have problems/difficulties* ◊ *to have an idea/an impression/a feeling* ◊ *to have an accident*

• **ILLNESS** **4** (*also* **have got**) (not used in the progressive tenses) to be ill with sth: *She's got a bad cold.* ◊ *to have flu/a headache/cancer/Aids*

- HAVE STH DONE **5 ~ sth done** (used with a past participle) to suffer the effect of what sb else does to you: *He had his driving licence taken away for six months.* **6 ~ sth done** (used with a past participle) to arrange for sb to do sth: *I have my hair cut every six weeks.* ◇ *You should have your eyes tested.*
- DUTY/PLAN **7** (*also* have got) (not used in the progressive tenses) to have a particular duty or plan: *Do you have any homework tonight?* ◇ *I've got a few things to do this morning, but I'm free later.*
- IN POSITION **8** (*also* have got) (not used in the progressive tenses) to hold sb/sth; to keep sth in a particular place: *The dog had me by the leg.* ◇ *We've got our TV on the wall.*
- CAUSE **9** to cause sb/sth to do sth or to be in a particular state: *The music soon had everyone dancing.* ◇ *I'll have dinner ready when you get home.*
- ENTERTAIN **10** to look after or entertain sb: *We're having some people to dinner tomorrow.*
  IDM **have had it** (*informal*) used about things that are completely broken, or dead: *This TV has had it. We'll have to buy a new one.* **❶** For other idioms containing **have**, look at the entries for the nouns, adjectives, etc. For example, **not have a clue** is at **clue**.
  PHR V **have sb on** (*informal*) to trick sb as a joke: *Don't listen to what Jimmy says — he's only having you on.* **have (got) sth on 1** to be wearing sth: *She's got a green jumper on.* **2** (*informal*) to have an arrangement to do sth: *I've got a lot on this week* (= I'm very busy). **have sth out** to allow part of your body to be removed: *to have a tooth/your appendix out*

haven /ˈheɪvn/ *noun* [C] **~ (of sth); ~ (for sb/sth)** a place where people or animals can be safe: *a haven of peace* ◇ *The lake is a haven for water birds.* ⊃ look at **tax haven**

haven't /ˈhævnt/ *short form* have not

have to ⚡**A1** /ˈhæv tə, ˈhæf/ (*also* have got to /həvˈgɒt tə/) *modal verb* used for saying that sb must do sth or that sth must happen: *I usually have to work on Saturday mornings.* ◇ *Do you have to have a visa to go to America?* ◇ *She's got to go to the bank this afternoon.* ◇ *We don't have to* (= it's not necessary to) *go to the party if you don't want to.* ◇ *We had to do lots of boring exercises.*

havoc /ˈhævək/ *noun* [U] a situation in which there is a lot of damage or CONFUSION: *The rail strikes will cause havoc all over the country.* ◇ *Heavy rain and flooding are playing havoc with the transport system.* ⊃ look at **wreak**

hawk[1] /hɔːk/ *noun* [C] a strong fast BIRD OF PREY (= a bird that kills other creatures for food). **❶** Hawks are a type of **bird of prey**.

hawk[2] /hɔːk/ *verb* [T] to try to sell things by going from place to place asking people to buy them ▸ **hawker** *noun* [C]

hay /heɪ/ *noun* [U] (**AGRICULTURE**) grass that has been cut and dried for use as animal food: *a bale of hay*

'hay fever *noun* [U] (**HEALTH**) an illness that affects the eyes, nose and throat and is caused by breathing in POLLEN (= the powder produced by some plants) ⊃ look at **allergy**

haywire /ˈheɪwaɪə(r)/ *adj.*
IDM **be/go haywire** (*informal*) to be or become out of control

hazard[1] ⚡+ **C1** /ˈhæzəd/ *noun* [C] a danger or risk: *hazard lights* (= flashing lights on a car that warn other drivers of possible danger) ◇ *Pollution is a serious health hazard.*

hazard[2] /ˈhæzəd/ *verb* [T] to make a guess or to suggest sth even though you know it may be wrong: *I don't know what he paid for the house but I could hazard a guess.*

hazardous /ˈhæzədəs/ *adj.* involving risk or danger **SYN** **risky**

haze /heɪz/ *noun* **1** [C, U] air that is difficult to see through because it contains very small drops of water, especially caused by hot weather: *a heat haze* ⊃ note at **weather**[1] **2** [sing.] air containing sth that makes it difficult to see through it: *a haze of smoke/dust/steam* **3** [sing.] a mental state in which you cannot think clearly

hazel[1] /ˈheɪzl/ *noun* **1** [C] a small tree or bush that produces nuts called HAZELNUTS **2** [U] a light brown colour

hazel[2] /ˈheɪzl/ *adj.* (used about eyes) light brown in colour

hazelnut /ˈheɪzlnʌt/ *noun* [C] the small brown nut of the HAZEL tree that we can eat

hazmat suit /ˈhæzmæt suːt/ *noun* [C] a special suit that protects a person's body when they are dealing with dangerous substances

hazy /ˈheɪzi/ *adj.* (hazier; haziest) **1** not clear, especially because of heat: *The fields were hazy in the early morning sun.* **2** difficult to remember or understand clearly: *a hazy memory* **3** (used about a person) uncertain, not expressing things clearly: *She's a bit hazy about the details of the trip.*

'H-bomb = HYDROGEN BOMB

HCF /ˌeɪtʃ siːˈef/ *abbr.* = HIGHEST COMMON FACTOR

HD /ˌeɪtʃ ˈdiː/ *abbr.* **high-definition** (used about TV, film or video images that are extremely high quality, with very clear details): *The film was shot in HD.*

HDI /ˌeɪtʃ diː ˈaɪ/ *abbr.* (**GEOGRAPHY, SOCIAL STUDIES**) **Human Development Index** (a measure that compares different countries each year based on their education, health, standards of living, etc.)

▼ VOCABULARY BUILDING

HDI is measured by comparing **life expectancy** (= the number of years an average person can expect to live for), **literacy** (= the ability to read), number of years of **education** and **standard of living** (GDP per capita). **HDI** is used to determine whether a country is **very developed**, **developed**, **developing** or **underdeveloped**.

HDMI /ˌeɪtʃ diː em ˈaɪ/ *abbr.* **high-definition multimedia interface** (a system for connecting AUDIO and video devices to electronic equipment such as a TV or computer, in one cable)

HDTV /ˌeɪtʃ diː tiː ˈviː/ *noun* [U] technology that produces extremely clear images on a TV screen (the abbreviation for 'high-definition television')

he[1] ⚡**A1** /hi, iː, i, *strong form* hiː/ *pron.* (the subject of a verb) the male person or animal mentioned earlier: *I spoke to John before he left.* ◇ *Look at that boy — he's going to fall in!*

he[2] /hiː/ *noun* [sing.] a male animal: *Is your cat a he or a she?*

head[1] ⚡**A1** /hed/ *noun*
- PART OF THE BODY **1** [C] (**ANATOMY**) the part of the body above the neck: *She turned her head to look at him.* ◇ *He's still suffering with serious head injuries after the crash.* ⊃ picture at **animal, body, circulation 2** a head [sing.] the height or length of one head: *She's a head taller than her sister.* **3** **-headed** (in adjectives) having the type of head mentioned: *a bald-headed man*

- MIND **4** [C] a person's mind, brain or mental ability: *Use your head!* (= think!) ◊ *A horrible thought entered my head.*
- TOP PART **5** [sing.] the top, front or most important part: *to sit at the head of the table* ◊ *the head of a nail* ◊ *the head of the queue* ⊃ picture at **bolt**¹
- PERSON IN CHARGE **6** [C] the person in charge of a group of people: *the head of the family* ◊ *the head waiter* ◊ *Several **heads of state** (= official leaders of countries) attended the funeral.* **7** (*also* head teacher) (*both BrE*) (*AmE* principal) [C] (**EDUCATION**) the teacher in charge of a school: *Who is going to be the new head?*
- SIDE OF A COIN **8** heads [U] the side of a coin with the head of a person on it: *Heads or tails? Heads I go first, tails you do.*
- BUBBLES IN BEER **9** [sing.] the white mass of small bubbles on the top of a glass of beer

IDM **bite sb's head off** → BITE¹ **can't make head nor/or tail of sth** (*informal*) to understand sth: *I can't make head or tail of this exercise.* **come to a head | bring sth to a head** if a situation comes to a head or if you bring it to a head, it suddenly becomes very bad and you have to deal with it immediately **do sb's head in** (*BrE, informal*) to make sb upset and confused **get sth into your head | put sth into sb's head** to start or to make sb start believing or thinking sth **get your head round sth** (*BrE, informal*) to be able to understand or accept sth: *She's dead. I can't get my head round it yet.* **go to sb's head 1** to make sb too proud: *If you keep telling him how clever he is, it will go to his head!* **2** to make sb drunk: *Wine always goes straight to my head.* **have a head for sth** to be able to deal with sth easily: *I haven't got a good head for heights* (= I feel nervous and think I am going to fall when I look down from a high place). ◊ *to have a head for business/figures* **a/per head** for each person: *How much will the meal cost a head?* **head first 1** with your head before the rest of your body: *Don't go down the slide head first.* **2** too quickly or suddenly: *Don't rush head first into a decision.* **head over heels** (in love) loving sb very much: *Jane's fallen head over heels in love with Andy.* **hit the nail on the head** → HIT¹ **keep your head** to stay calm **keep your head above water** to just manage to survive in a difficult situation, especially one in which you do not have enough money **keep your head down** to try not to be noticed **laugh, scream, etc. your head off** (*informal*) to laugh, shout, etc. very loudly and for a long time **lose your head** → LOSE **off the top of your head** → TOP¹ **out of/off your head** (*informal*) crazy, often because of the effects of drugs or alcohol **put/get your heads together** to make a plan with sb **a roof over your head** → ROOF **shake your head** → SHAKE¹ **take it into your head to do sth** to suddenly decide to do sth that other people consider strange: *I don't know why Kevin took it into his head to enter that marathon!*

head² ⏷ **B1** /hed/ *verb*
- MOVE TOWARDS **1** [I] (often used with an adverb or a preposition) to move in the direction mentioned: *The ship headed towards the harbour.* ◊ *Where are you heading?*
- BE IN CHARGE **2** [T] to be in charge of or to lead sth
- BE FIRST **3** [T] to be at the front of a line, top of a list, etc.
- WRITE A TITLE **4** [T, often passive] to give a title at the top of a piece of writing: *The report was headed 'The State of the Market'.*
- IN FOOTBALL **5** [T] (**SPORT**) to hit the ball with your head

PHRV **head for** to move towards a place: *It's getting late — I think it's time to head for home.*

headache ⏷ **A2** /ˈhedeɪk/ *noun* [C] **1** (**HEALTH**) a pain in the head: *I've got a splitting* (= very bad) *headache.* **2** a

person or thing that causes worry or difficulty: *Paying the bills is a constant headache.*

header /ˈhedə(r)/ *noun* [C] **1** (**SPORT**) an act of hitting the ball with your head **2** (**COMPUTING**) a line or block of text that appears at the top of every page in a book or document ⊃ look at **footer** (1)

headhunter /ˈhedhʌntə(r)/ *noun* [C] (**BUSINESS**) a person whose job is to find people to work for a particular company and to persuade them to join it

heading /ˈhedɪŋ/ *noun* [C] **1** a title printed at the top of a page or at the beginning of a section of a book: *The book has very unusual chapter headings.* **2** the subject of each section of a speech or piece of writing: *I've grouped our ideas under three main headings.*

headland /ˈhedlənd, -lænd/ *noun* [C] (**GEOGRAPHY**) a narrow piece of land that sticks out into the sea ⊃ picture at **erosion**

headlight /ˈhedlaɪt/ (*also* headlamp /ˈhedlæmp/) *noun* [C] one of the two large bright lights at the front of a vehicle

headline ⏷ **B1** /ˈhedlaɪn/ *noun* (**ARTS AND MEDIA**) **1** [C] the title of a newspaper article printed in large letters above the story or on the home page on a news website **2** the headlines [pl.] the main items of news read on TV or radio

headlong /ˈhedlɒŋ/ *adv., adj.* [only before noun] **1** with your head before the rest of your body: *I tripped and fell headlong into the road.* ◊ *He made a headlong dive for the ball.* **2** too quickly; without enough thought: *He rushed headlong into buying the business.*

headmaster /ˌhedˈmɑːstə(r)/ *noun* [C] (*BrE, old-fashioned*) (**EDUCATION**) the man who is in charge of a school, especially a private school

headmistress /ˌhedˈmɪstrəs/ *noun* [C] (*BrE, old-fashioned*) (**EDUCATION**) the woman who is in charge of a school

head ˈoffice (*AmE also* ˌhome ˈoffice) *noun* [C, U, + sing./pl. verb] (**BUSINESS**) the main office of a company; the managers who work there: *Their head office is in New York.* ◊ *Head office is/are sending someone to investigate.*

head of ˈstate *noun* [C] (*pl.* heads of state) (**POLITICS**) the official leader of a country who is sometimes also the leader of the government

head-ˈon *adj.* [only before noun], *adv.* with the front of one car, etc. hitting the front of another: *a head-on crash* ◊ *We hit the tree head-on* (= the front part of our car hit the tree).

headphones /ˈhedfəʊnz/ *noun* [pl.] (**MUSIC**) a piece of equipment worn over the ears that makes it possible to listen to music, the radio, etc. without other people hearing it ⊃ look at **earphones**

headquarters ⏷+ **B2** /ˌhedˈkwɔːtəz/ *noun* [U, + sing./pl. verb, C] (*abbr.* HQ) (**BUSINESS**) the place from where an organization is controlled; the people who work there: *Where is/are the firm's headquarters?*

headrest /ˈhedrest/ *noun* [C] the part of a seat or chair that supports a person's head, especially one attached to the front seat of a car

headroom /ˈhedruːm, -rʊm/ *noun* [U] **1** the amount of space between the top of a vehicle and an object, for example a bridge, that it drives under **2** the amount of space between the top of your head and the inside roof of a vehicle

headscarf /ˈhedskɑːf/ *noun* [C] (*pl.* headscarves /-skɑːvz/) a square piece of cloth worn by women to cover the head

headset /ˈhedset/ *noun* [C] a pair of HEADPHONES (= a piece of equipment for listening that you wear over or in your ears), especially one with a MICROPHONE (= a device for speaking into) fixed to it: *The pilot was talking into his headset.*

headstand /'hedstænd/ *noun* [C] a position in which a person has their head on the ground and their feet straight up in the air

head 'start *noun* [sing.] an advantage that you have from the beginning of a race or competition ⊃ look at **start**² (2)

headstone /'hedstəʊn/ *noun* [C] a large stone with writing on, used to mark where a dead person is buried ⊃ look at **gravestone, tombstone**

headstrong /'hedstrɒŋ/ *adj.* doing what you want, without listening to advice from other people

head 'teacher (*BrE*) = HEAD¹ (7)

head-to-'head *adj.* [only before noun] in which two people or groups face each other directly in order to decide the result of a competition or an argument: *a head-to-head battle/clash/contest*

headway /'hedweɪ/ *noun*
IDM **make headway** to go forward or make progress in a difficult situation

headwind /'hedwɪnd/ *noun* [C] a wind that is blowing towards a person or vehicle, so that it is blowing from the direction in which the person or vehicle is moving ⊃ look at **tailwind**

headword /'hedwɜːd/ *noun* [C] (**LANGUAGE**) the first word of an entry in a dictionary, which is followed by an explanation or a translation of its meaning

heal ⌃+ B2 /hiːl/ *verb* [I, T] ~ (**over/up**) to become healthy again; to make sth healthy again: *The cut will heal up in a few days.* ◇ (*figurative*) *Nothing he said could heal the damage done to their relationship.*

healer /'hiːlə(r)/ *noun* [C] a person who treats sick people using natural powers rather than medicine

health

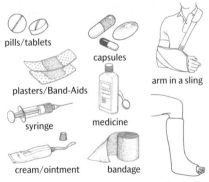

pills/tablets
capsules
arm in a sling
plasters/Band-Aids
syringe
medicine
cream/ointment
bandage
leg in plaster

health ⌃ A1 /helθ/ *noun* [U] **1** the condition of a person's body or mind: *Fresh fruit and vegetables are good for your health.* ◇ *in good/poor health* ◇ (*figurative*) *the health of your marriage/finances* ⊃ look at **mental health** **2** the state of being well and free from illness: *As long as you have your health, nothing else matters.* **3** the work of providing medical care: *health and safety regulations* ◇ *health insurance*

healthcare ⌃+ B2 /'helθkeə(r)/ *noun* [U] (**MEDICINE**) the service of providing medical care: *the costs of healthcare for the elderly* ◇ *health-care workers/professionals*

'health centre (*BrE*) (*AmE* **health center**) *noun* [C] (**MEDICINE**) a building where a group of doctors see their patients

'health club = GYM (2)

'health food *noun* [C, U] food that does not contain any artificial substances and is therefore thought to be good for your health

'health service *noun* [C] (**MEDICINE**) the organization of the medical services of a country ⊃ look at **National Health Service**

'health spa = SPA (2)

'health visitor *noun* [C] (in the UK) a trained nurse whose job is to visit people in their homes, for example new parents, and give them advice on some areas of medical care

healthy ⌃ A1 /'helθi/ *adj.* (**healthier; healthiest**) **1** (**HEALTH**) not often ill; strong and well: *a healthy child/animal/plant* OPP **unhealthy** **2** (**HEALTH**) showing good health (of body or mind): *healthy skin and hair* **3** (**HEALTH**) helping to produce good health: *a healthy climate/diet/lifestyle* OPP **unhealthy** **4** normal and sensible: *There was plenty of healthy competition between the brothers.* ▶ **healthily** /-θɪli/ *adv.*

heap¹ /hiːp/ *noun* [C] **1** ~ (**of sth**) an untidy pile of sth: *a heap of books/papers* ◇ *All his clothes are in a heap on the floor!* **2** [usually pl.] ~ (**of sth**) (*informal*) a large number or amount; plenty: *I've got a heap of work to do.* ◇ *There's heaps of time before the train leaves.* **IDM** **heaps better, more, older, etc.** (*informal*) much better, etc.

heap² /hiːp/ *verb* [T] **1** ~ **sth** (**up**) to put things in a pile: *I'm going to heap all the leaves up over there.* ◇ *Add six heaped tablespoons of flour* (= in a recipe). **2** ~ **A on/onto B; ~ B with A** to put a large amount of sth on sth/sb: *He heaped food onto his plate.* ◇ *The press heaped the team with praise.*

hear ⌃ A1 /hɪə(r)/ *verb* (*pt, pp* **heard** /hɜːd/) **1** [I, T] (not used in the progressive tenses) to receive sounds with your ears: *Can you speak a little louder — I can't hear very well.* ◇ *I didn't hear you go out this morning.* ◇ *Did you hear what I said?* ◇ *We went to hear him play in London.* **2** [T] (not used in the progressive tenses) to be told about sth: *I hear that you've been offered a job in Canada.* ◇ *I was sorry to hear about your mum's illness.* ◇ *'I passed my test!' 'So I've heard — well done!'* **3** [T] (**LAW**) (used about a judge, a court, etc.) to listen to the evidence in a trial in order to make a decision about it: *Your case will be heard this afternoon.*
IDM **hear! hear!** used for showing that you agree with what sb has just said, especially in a meeting **will/would not hear of sth** to refuse to allow sth: *I wanted to go to art school but my parents wouldn't hear of it.*
PHR V **hear from sb** to receive a letter, phone call, email etc. from sb **hear of sb/sth** to know about sb/sth because you have already been told about them/it: *Have you heard of the Bermuda Triangle?*

hearing ⌃ B2 /'hɪərɪŋ/ *noun* **1** [U] the ability to hear: *Her hearing isn't very good so you need to speak louder.* **2** [C] (**LAW**) an official meeting at which the facts about a crime, complaint, etc. are presented to the person or group of people who will have to decide what action to take: *a court/disciplinary hearing* **3** [sing.] a chance to give your opinion or explain your position: *to get/give somebody a fair hearing*
IDM **hard of hearing** → HARD¹ **in/within sb's hearing** near enough to sb so that they can hear what is being said

'hearing aid *noun* [C] (**HEALTH**) a small device for people who cannot hear well that fits inside the ear and makes sounds louder

hearsay /'hɪəseɪ/ *noun* [U] things you have heard another person or other people say, which may or may not be true

hearse /hɜːs/ *noun* [C] a long vehicle used for carrying a dead person to their FUNERAL

the heart

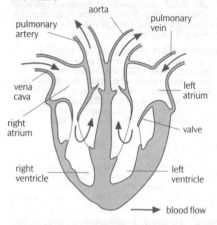

aorta
pulmonary artery
pulmonary vein
vena cava
left atrium
right atrium
valve
right ventricle
left ventricle
→ blood flow

heart ? **A2** /hɑːt/ *noun*

• PART OF THE BODY **1** [C] (**ANATOMY**) the organ inside the chest that sends blood round the body: *When you exercise your heart beats faster.* ◇ *heart disease/failure*

• FEELINGS/EMOTIONS **2** [C] the centre of a person's feelings and emotions: *In my heart I knew she was right.* ◇ *She has a kind heart* (= she is kind and gentle). ◇ *They say he died of a **broken heart*** (= unhappiness caused by sb he loved). **3** -hearted (in adjectives) having the type of feelings or character mentioned: *kind-hearted* ◇ *cold-hearted*

• CENTRE **4** [sing.] **the~ (of sth)** the most central or important part of sth; the middle: *Rare plants can be found **in the heart** of the forest.* ◇ *Let's get straight to **the heart of the matter**.*

• SYMBOL **5** [C] a symbol (♥) that is shaped like a heart, often red or pink and used to show love: *He sent her a card with a big red heart on it.*

• IN CARD GAMES **6** hearts [pl., U] one of the four SUITS (= sets) in a PACK of cards. The hearts are marked with red heart shapes: *the queen of hearts* **7** [C] one of the cards from this SUIT: *Play a heart, if you've got one.*

IDM **after your own heart** (used about people) similar to yourself or of the type you like best at heart really; in fact: *My father seems strict but he's a very kind man at heart.* **break sb's heart** to make sb very sad **by heart** (*BrE also* **off by heart**) by remembering exactly; from memory: *Learning lists of words off by heart isn't a good way to increase your vocabulary.* **a change of heart** → CHANGE² **close/dear/near to sb's heart** having a lot of importance and interest for sb **cross my heart** → CROSS² **from the (bottom of your) heart** in a way that is true and sincere: *I mean what I said from the bottom of my heart.* **have a heart of gold** to be a very kind person **have/with sb's (best) interests at heart** → INTEREST¹ **heart and soul** with a lot of energy and enthusiasm:

We put our heart and soul into winning this election. **sb's heart is not in sth** used to say that sb is not very interested in or enthusiastic about sth **sb's heart sinks** used to say that sb suddenly feels sad or depressed about sth: *My heart sank when I saw how much work there was left.* **in your heart (of hearts)** used to say that you know that sth is true although you do not want to admit or believe it: *She knew in her heart of hearts that she was making the wrong decision.* **lose heart** → LOSE **not have the heart (to do sth)** to be unable to do sth unkind: *I don't really have the time to help her, but I didn't have the heart to say no.* **pour your heart out (to sb)** → POUR **set your heart on sth** | **have your heart set on sth** to decide you want sth very much; to be determined to do or have sth **take heart (from sth)** to begin to feel positive and HOPEFUL about sth **take sth to heart** to be deeply affected or upset by sth **to your heart's content** as much as you want **with all your heart** | **with your whole heart** completely: *I hope with all my heart that things work out for you.* **young at heart** → YOUNG¹

heartache /'hɑːteɪk/ *noun* [U] a feeling of being very sad or worried

'heart attack *noun* [C] (**HEALTH**) a sudden serious medical condition in which the flow of blood to the heart is blocked, sometimes causing death: *She's had a heart attack.*

heartbeat /'hɑːtbiːt/ *noun* [C] (**BIOLOGY**) the regular movement or sound of the heart as it sends blood round the body

heartbreak /'hɑːtbreɪk/ *noun* [U] a feeling of being very sad

heartbreaking /'hɑːtbreɪkɪŋ/ *adj.* making you feel very sad

heartbroken /'hɑːtbrəʊkən/ (*also* **broken-hearted**) *adj.* extremely sad because of sth that has happened: *Mary was heartbroken when John left her.*

heartburn /'hɑːtbɜːn/ *noun* [U] (**HEALTH**) a pain that feels like sth burning in your chest and that you get when your stomach cannot deal with a particular food

hearten /'hɑːtn/ *verb* [T, usually passive] to encourage sb; to make sb feel happier **OPP** **dishearten**

heartening /'hɑːtnɪŋ/ *adj.* making you feel hope **SYN** **encouraging**

heartfelt /'hɑːtfelt/ *adj.* deeply felt; sincere: *a heartfelt apology*

hearth /hɑːθ/ *noun* [C] (**ARCHITECTURE**) the place where you have an open fire in the house or the area in front of it

heartily /'hɑːtɪli/ *adv.* **1** with obvious pleasure and enthusiasm: *He joined in heartily with the singing.* **2** very much; completely

heartland /'hɑːtlænd/ *noun* [C] (*also* **heartlands** [pl.]) the most central or important part of a country, an area, etc: *Germany's industrial heartland*

heartless /'hɑːtləs/ *adj.* unkind; cruel ► **heartlessly** *adv.* ► **heartlessness** *noun* [U]

'heart rate *noun* [C] (**HEALTH**) how fast your heart is beating

heart-rending /'hɑːt rendɪŋ/ *adj.* making you feel very sad

,heart-to-'heart *noun* [C, usually sing.] a conversation in which you say exactly what you really feel or think

hearty /'hɑːti/ *adj.* (**heartier; heartiest**) **1** showing warm and friendly feelings: *a hearty welcome* **2** loud, happy and full of energy: *a hearty laugh* **3** [only before noun] large; making you feel full: *a hearty appetite* ◇ *a hearty meal* **4** showing that you feel strongly about sth: *He nodded his head in hearty agreement.*

heat¹ ⨿ **A2** /hiːt/ noun
- BEING HOT **1** [U, sing.] the feeling of sth hot: *Too much heat from the sun is being trapped in the Earth's atmosphere.* ◇ *This fire doesn't give out much heat.* ◇ *Test the heat of the water before getting in.* ◇ *Dark surfaces absorb heat.* ⊃ picture at **energy 2** [sing.] (often used with *the*) hot weather: *I like the English climate because I can't stand the heat.* **3** [sing.] a thing that produces heat: *Remove the pan from the heat* (= the hot part of the cooker).
- STRONG FEELINGS **4** [U] a state or time of anger or excitement: *In the heat of the argument he said a lot of things he didn't mean.* ◇ **In the heat of the moment**, she threatened to resign.
- IN A RACE **5** [C] (**SPORT**) one of the first parts of a race or competition. The winners of the heats compete against other winners until the final result is decided.
IDM **be on heat** (*BrE*) (*AmE* **be in heat**) (used about some female animals) to be ready to have sex because it is the right time of the year

heat² ⨿ **A2** /hiːt/ verb [I, T] **~ (sth) (up)** to become or to make sth hot or warm: *Wait for the oven to heat up before you put the pie in.* ◇ *Old houses are more difficult to heat than modern ones.* ◇ *The meal is already cooked but it will need heating up.*

heated /'hiːtɪd/ adj. **1** (used about a person or discussion) angry or excited: *a heated argument/ debate* **2** (used about a room, building, etc.) made warmer using a HEATER: *a heated swimming pool* ▶ **heatedly** adv.

heater /'hiːtə(r)/ noun [C] a machine used for making water or the air in a room, car, etc. hotter: *an electric/ gas heater* ◇ *a water heater*

heath /hiːθ/ noun [C, U] (**GEOGRAPHY**) an area of open land that is not used for farming and that is often covered with rough grass and other wild plants

heathen /'hiːðn/ noun [C] (*old-fashioned*) (**HISTORY, RELIGION**) used by religious people to refer to sb who has no religion, or who does not believe in one of the world's main religions. Many people find this use offensive.

heather /'heðə(r)/ noun [U] a low wild plant that grows especially on hills and land that is not farmed and has small purple, pink or white flowers

heating ⨿ **B1** /'hiːtɪŋ/ (*especially BrE*) (*also* **heat** *especially in AmE*) noun [U] a system for making rooms and buildings warm: *Our heating goes off at 10 p.m. and comes on again in the morning.* ⊃ look at **central heating** ⊃ picture at **energy**

heatstroke /'hiːtstrəʊk/ noun [C] (**HEALTH**) a medical condition that you can get if you are in a hot place for too long

heatwave /'hiːtweɪv/ noun [C] a period of unusually hot weather

heave¹ /hiːv/ verb **1** [T, I] to lift, pull or throw sb/sth heavy with one big effort: *Take hold of this rope and heave!* ◇ *We heaved the cupboard up the stairs.* **2** [I] **~ (with sth)** to move up and down or in and out in a heavy but regular way: *His chest was heaving with the effort of carrying the cooker.* **3** [I] to experience the tight feeling you get in your stomach when you are just about to VOMIT (= bring up food through the mouth): *The sight of all that blood made her stomach heave.*
IDM **heave a sigh** to breathe out slowly and loudly: *He heaved a sigh of relief when he heard the good news.*

heave² /hiːv/ noun [C] a strong pull, push, throw, etc.

heaven ⨿ **B2** /'hevn/ noun **1** [U] (**RELIGION**) the place where, in some religions, it is believed that God lives and where good people go when they die: *to go to/be in*

heaven ⊃ look at **hell** (1) **2** [U, C] a place or a situation in which you are very happy: *It was heaven being away from work for a week.* **3** **the heavens** [pl.] (used in poetry and literature) the sky

heavenly /'hevnli/ adj. **1** [only before noun] (**ASTRONOMY, RELIGION**) connected with heaven or the sky: *heavenly bodies* (= the sun, moon, stars, etc.) **2** (*informal*) very pleasant; wonderful

heavily ⨿ **B1** /'hevɪli/ adv. **1** to a great degree; in large amounts: *It was raining heavily.* ◇ *to drink/smoke heavily* ◇ *heavily armed police* (= carrying a lot of weapons) ◇ *a heavily pregnant woman* (= one whose baby is nearly ready to be born) **2** with a lot of force or effort: *She fell heavily to the ground.* **3** **~ built** (used about a person) with a large, solid and strong body **4** slowly and loudly: *She was now breathing heavily.* **5** in a slow way that sounds as though you are worried or sad: *He sighed heavily.* **6** in a way that makes you feel uncomfortable or anxious: *The burden of guilt weighed heavily on his mind.* **7** **~ loaded/laden** full of or loaded with things: *a heavily loaded van*

heavy ⨿ **A2** /'hevi/ adj. (**heavier; heaviest**) **1** weighing a lot; difficult to lift or move: *This box is too heavy for me to carry.* **2** used when asking or stating how much sb/ sth weighs: *How heavy is your suitcase?* **3** larger, stronger or more than usual: *heavy rain* ◇ *heavy traffic* ◇ *a heavy smoker/drinker* (= a person who smokes/drinks a lot) ◇ *The sound of his heavy* (= loud and deep) *breathing told her that he was asleep.* ◇ *a heavy sleeper* (= somebody who is difficult to wake) ◇ *a heavy meal* **4** serious, difficult or boring: *His latest novel makes heavy reading.* ◇ *Things got a bit heavy when she started talking about her failed marriage.* **5** full of hard work; (too) busy: *a heavy day/ schedule/timetable* **6** (used about a material or substance) solid or thick: *heavy soil* ◇ *a heavy coat* **OPP** **light²** ▶ **heaviness** noun [U]
IDM **make heavy weather of sth** to make sth seem more difficult than it really is

,**heavy-'duty** adj. [only before noun] not easily damaged and therefore suitable for regular use or for hard physical work: *a heavy-duty carpet/tyre*

,**heavy-'handed** adj. **1** not showing much understanding of other people's feelings: *a heavy-handed approach* **2** using unnecessary force: *heavy-handed police methods*

,**heavy 'industry** noun [U, C] (**BUSINESS**) industry that uses large machines to produce metal, coal, vehicles, etc.

,**heavy 'metal** noun [U] (**MUSIC**) a style of very loud rock music that is played on electric instruments

heavyweight /'heviweɪt/ noun [C] (**SPORT**) a person who is in the heaviest weight group in certain fighting sports: *the world heavyweight boxing champion*

Hebrew /'hiːbruː/ noun **1** [C] a member of an ancient human group living in what is now Israel and Palestine. Their writings and traditions form the basis of the Jewish religion. **2** [U] the language traditionally used by the Hebrew people **3** [U] a modern form of the Hebrew language, which is now the official language of modern Israel ▶ **Hebrew** adj.

heckle /'hekl/ verb [I, T] to interrupt a speaker at a public meeting with difficult questions or rude comments ▶ **heckler** /-klə(r)/ noun [C]

hectare /'hekteə(r), -tɑː(r)/ noun [C] (*abbr.* **ha**) a measurement of land; 10 000 square metres

hectic /'hektɪk/ adj. very busy with a lot of things that you have to do quickly ▶ **hectically** /-kli/ adv.

he'd /hiːd/ *short form* he had; he would

hedge¹ /hedʒ/ *noun* [C] a row of bushes or small trees planted close together at the edge of a garden or field to separate one piece of land from another

hedge² /hedʒ/ *verb* [I] to avoid giving a direct answer to a question
IDM **hedge your bets** to protect yourself against losing or making a mistake by supporting more than one person or opinion

'hedge fund *noun* [C] (**FINANCE**) a way of investing money with other people, that involves taking high risks in order to try and make a lot of profit

hedgehog /'hedʒhɒg/ *noun* [C] a small brown European animal covered with SPINES (= sharp parts like needles)

hedgerow /'hedʒrəʊ/ *noun* [C] (especially in the UK) a row of bushes, etc. at the side of a country road or around a field

heed¹ /hiːd/ *verb* [T] (*formal*) to pay attention to advice, a warning, etc.

heed² /hiːd/ *noun* (*formal*)
IDM **take heed (of sb/sth)** | **pay heed (to sb/sth)** to pay careful attention to what sb says: *You should take heed of your doctor's advice.*

heel¹ 🔊 **B2** /hiːl/ *noun* [C] **1** (**ANATOMY**) the back part of the foot below the ankle ⊃ picture at **body 2** the part of a sock, etc. that covers the heel **3** the higher part of a shoe under the heel of the foot: *High heels* (= shoes with high heels) *are not practical for long walks.* **4** -heeled having the type of heel mentioned: *high-heeled/low-heeled shoes*
IDM **dig your heels in** → **DIG¹** **head over heels** → **HEAD¹**

hefty /'hefti/ *adj.* (**heftier**; **heftiest**) (*informal*) big and strong or heavy: *a hefty young man*

hegemony /hɪ'dʒeməni, 'hedʒɪməni/ *noun* [U, C] (*pl.* -ies) (*formal*) control by one country, organization, etc. over other countries, etc. within a particular group
▶ **hegemonic** /ˌhedʒɪ'mɒnɪk/ *adj.*

heifer /'hefə(r)/ *noun* [C] (**AGRICULTURE**) a young female cow, especially one that has not yet had a baby CALF (= a young cow)

height 🔊 **A2** /haɪt/ *noun* **1** [U, C] the measurement from the bottom to the top of a person or thing: *She's of medium height.* ◇ *The nurse is going to check your height and weight.* ◇ *We need a fence that's about 2 metres* **in height.** ⊃ picture at **dimension, wave¹** ⊃ adjective **high 2** [U] the fact that sb/sth is tall or high: *He looks older than he is because of his height.* **3** [C, U] the distance that sth is above the ground: *We are now flying at a height of 10 000 metres.* ❶ A plane **gains** or **loses** height. When talking about planes a more formal word for height is **altitude**. **4** [C, usually pl.] a high place or area: *I can't go up there. I'm afraid of heights.* **5** [U] the strongest or most important part of sth: *the height of summer* ◇ *The tourist season is at its height in July and August.*

heighten 🔊 **C1** /'haɪtn/ *verb* [I, T] to become or make sth greater or stronger

heir /eə(r)/ *noun* [C] ~ **(to sth)** (**LAW**) the person who has the legal right to INHERIT (= receive) sb's money, property or a title when that person dies: *He's the heir to a large fortune.*

heirloom /'eəluːm/ *noun* [C] something valuable that has belonged to the same family for many years

held /held/ *past tense, past participle of* **hold¹**

helicopter 🔊 **B1** /'helɪkɒptə(r)/ (*also informal* **chopper**) *noun* [C] a small aircraft that can go straight up into the air. Helicopters have BLADES (= long thin metal parts that go round very fast) on top.

heliocentric /ˌhiːliə'sentrɪk/ *adj.* (**ASTRONOMY**) with the sun as the centre: *the heliocentric model of the solar system* ⊃ look at **geocentric**

helium /'hiːliəm/ *noun* [U] (*symb.* **He**) (**CHEMISTRY**) A chemical element. Helium is a very light gas that does not burn and is often used to fill BALLOONS.
❶ **Helium** is a **noble gas.** ❶ For more information on the periodic table of elements, look at the **Reference Section** of this dictionary.

helix /'hiːlɪks/ *noun* [C] (*pl.* **helices** /-lɪsiːz/) a shape like a SPIRAL (= a long curved line that moves round and round away from a central point) or a line curved round a CYLINDER or CONE ⊃ look at **double helix**

helices

hell 🔊 **B2** /hel/ *noun* **1** (*also* **Hell**) [sing.] (**RELIGION**) (in some religions) the place where it is believed that the Devil lives and where bad people go to when they die: *to go to/be in hell* ⊃ look at **heaven** (1) **2** [U, sing.] (*informal*) a situation or place that is very unpleasant or painful: *He went through hell when his wife left him.* **3** [U] (*informal*) used as a swear word to show anger or surprise: *Oh hell, I've left my phone at home!* ◇ *Why the hell didn't you tell me this before?* **HELP** Be careful! Some people find meanings 3 and 4 of **hell** and the idioms offensive.
IDM **all hell broke loose** (*informal*) there was suddenly a lot of noise and CONFUSION **(just) for the hell of it** (*informal*) for fun **give sb hell** (*informal*) to speak to sb very angrily or to make life unpleasant for sb **a/one hell of a ...** (*informal*) used to make an expression stronger or to mean 'very': *He got into a hell of a fight* (= a terrible fight). **like hell** (*informal*) very much; with a lot of effort: *I'm working like hell at the moment.*

he'll /hiːl/ *short form* he will

hellish /'helɪʃ/ *adj.* (*especially BrE, informal*) terrible; very unpleasant: *a hellish experience*

hello 🔊 **A1** (*BrE also* **hallo**) /hə'ləʊ/ *exclamation, noun* [C] (*pl.* -os) used when you meet sb, for attracting sb's attention or when you are using the phone: *Hello John, how are you?* ◇ *Say hello to Liz for me.* ◇ *They exchanged hellos* (= said hello to each other).

helm /helm/ *noun* [C] a handle or a wheel used for controlling the direction in which a boat or ship moves
IDM **at the helm** in charge of an organization, group of people, etc.

helmet 🔊+ **B2** /'helmɪt/ *noun* [C] a type of hard hat that you wear to protect your head: *a crash helmet* ◇ *a cycle helmet* ⊃ picture at **sport**

help¹ 🔊 **A1** /help/ *verb* **1** [I, T] ~ **(sb) (with sth)**; ~ **(sb) (to) do sth** to do sth for sb in order to be useful or to make sth easier for them: *Can I help?* ◇ *My son's helping in our shop at the moment.* ◇ *Could you help me with the cooking?* ◇ *I helped her to organize the event.* **2** [I, T] to make sth better or easier: *If you apologize to him it might help.* ◇ *This medicine should help your headache.* **3** [T] (used with an adverb or a preposition) to help sb move or do some other action by letting them lean on you, guiding them, etc: *She helped her grandmother up the stairs* (= supported her as she climbed the stairs). **4** [T] ~ **yourself (to sth)** to take sth (especially food and drink) that is offered to you: '*Can I borrow your pen?*' '*Yes, help yourself.*' **5** [T] **~yourself to sth** to take sth without asking permission: *Don't just help yourself to my money!* ⊃ look at **steal** (1) **6** [I] used to get sb's attention when you are in danger or difficulty: *Help! I'm going to fall!*

IDM **can/can't/couldn't help sth** be able/not be able to stop or avoid doing sth: *It was so funny I couldn't stop laughing.* ◇ *I just couldn't help myself* (= couldn't stop myself) *— I had to laugh.* **a helping hand** some help: *My neighbour is always ready to give me a helping hand.*

PHRV **help (sb) out** to help sb in a difficult situation; to give money to help sb

help² ᴇ **A1** /help/ *noun* **1** [U] **~ (with sth)** the act of helping: *Do you need any help with that?* ◇ *This map isn't much help.* ◇ *'Run and get help — my son's fallen in the river!'* ◇ *He repaired his car with the help of his father.* **2** [sing.] **a ~ (to sb)** a person or thing that helps: *Your directions were a great help — we found the place easily.*

help desk *noun* [C] (**COMPUTING**) a service, usually in a business company, that gives people information and help, especially if they are having problems with a computer

helper /'helpə(r)/ *noun* [C] a person who helps (especially with work)

helpful ᴇ **A2** /'helpfl/ *adj.* **~ (to do sth)** giving help: *helpful advice* ◇ *You may find it helpful to read this.* **OPP** **unhelpful** ▸ **helpfully** /-fəli/ *adv.* ▸ **helpfulness** *noun* [U]

helping /'helpɪŋ/ *noun* [C] the amount of food that is put on a plate at one time: *After two helpings of pasta, I couldn't eat any more.* ⊃ look at **portion** (2)

helpless /'helpləs/ *adj.* unable to take care of yourself or do things without the help of other people: *a helpless baby* ▸ **helplessly** *adv.*: *They watched helplessly as their house went up in flames.* ▸ **helplessness** *noun* [U]

helpline /'helplaɪn/ *noun* [C] a phone or online service that provides advice and information about particular problems

hem¹ /hem/ *noun* [C] the edge at the bottom of a piece of cloth (especially on a skirt, dress or trousers) that has been turned up and SEWN

hem² /hem/ *verb* [T] (-mm-) to turn up and SEW the bottom of a piece of clothing or cloth **PHRV** **hem sb in** to surround sb and prevent them from moving away: *We were hemmed in by the crowd and could not leave.*

hematite /'hi:mətaɪt/ (*AmE*) = HAEMATITE

hematology, hematologist (*AmE*) = HAEMATOLOGY, HAEMATOLOGIST

hemisphere /'hemɪsfɪə(r)/ *noun* [C] **1** (**GEOGRAPHY**) one half of the earth: *the northern/southern/eastern/western hemisphere* ⊃ picture at **earth¹** **2** (**ANATOMY**) either half of the brain: *the left/right cerebral hemisphere* **3** (**GEOMETRY**) one half of a SPHERE (= a round solid object)

hemo-, hemoglobin, hemophilia, hemophiliac, hemorrhage, hemorrhoids (*AmE*) = HAEMO-, HAEMOGLOBIN, HAEMOPHILIA, HAEMOPHILIAC, HAEMORRHAGE, HAEMORRHOIDS

hemp /hemp/ *noun* [U] a plant that is used for making rope and rough cloth and for producing CANNABIS (= a drug that is illegal in many countries)

hen /hen/ *noun* [C] **1** a female bird that is kept for its eggs or its meat ⊃ note at **chicken¹** **2** the female of any type of bird: *a hen pheasant* ⊃ look at **cock¹**

hence ᴇ **B2** ⊙ /hens/ *adv.* (*formal*) for this reason: *Smartphones have got cheaper and hence more people can afford them.*

henceforth /ˌhens'fɔ:θ/ (*also* **henceforward** /ˌhens'fɔ:wəd/) *adv.* (*formal*) from now on; in future

henchman /'hentʃmən/ *noun* [C] (*pl.* **-men** /-mən/) a person who is employed by sb to protect them and who may do things that are illegal or violent

hendecagon /hen'dekəgən/ *noun* [C] (**GEOMETRY**) a flat shape with eleven straight sides and eleven angles

henna /'henə/ *noun* [U] a natural red-brown DYE (= a substance used to change the colour of sth), used especially on the hair and skin

hen party (*also* **hen night**) *noun* [C] (*BrE*) a party that a woman has with her female friends just before she gets married ⊃ look at **stag night**

hepatic /hɪ'pætɪk/ *adj.* (**ANATOMY**) relating to the LIVER (= the large organ in the body that cleans the blood)

hepatic portal vein = PORTAL VEIN

hepatitis /ˌhepə'taɪtɪs/ *noun* [U] (**HEALTH**) a serious disease of the LIVER (= one of the body's main organs)

hepta- /heptə, hep'tæ/ *prefix* (in nouns, adjectives and adverbs) seven; having seven: *heptathlon* (= an ATHLETICS competition, usually one for women, that consists of seven different events)

heptagon /'heptəgən/ *noun* [C] (**GEOMETRY**) a flat shape with seven straight sides ▸ **heptagonal** /hep'tægənl/ *adj.*

her¹ ᴇ **A1** /hə(r), ɜ:(r), ə(r), *strong form* hɜ:(r)/ *pron.* (the object of a verb or preposition) the woman or girl that was mentioned earlier: *He told Sue that he loved her.* ◇ *I've got a letter for your mother. Could you give it to her, please?* ⊃ look at **she**

her² ᴇ **A1** /hə(r), ɜ:(r), ə(r), *strong form* hɜ:(r)/ *det.* of or belonging to the woman or girl mentioned earlier: *That's her book. She left it there this morning.* ◇ *Fiona has broken her leg.* ⊃ look at **hers**

herald /'herəld/ *verb* [T] (*formal*) to be a sign that sth is going to happen soon: *The minister's speech heralded a change of policy.*

heraldry /'herəldri/ *noun* [U] (**HISTORY**) the study of the history of old and important families and their COATS OF ARMS (= a design that is used as a symbol of a family, etc.)

herb ᴇ **B2** /hɜ:b/ *noun* [C] a plant whose leaves, seeds, etc. are used in medicine or in cooking: *Add some herbs, such as rosemary and thyme.* ⊃ look at **spice¹** (1)

herbaceous /hɜ:'beɪʃəs/ *adj.* (**BIOLOGY**) connected with plants that have soft STEMS (= long central parts): *a herbaceous plant*

herbal /'hɜ:bl/ *adj.* made of or using HERBS: *herbal medicine/remedies*

herbalism /'hɜ:bəlɪzəm/ *noun* [U] (**MEDICINE**) the medical use of plants ▸ **herbalist** /-lɪst/ *noun* [C]

herbicide /'hɜ:bɪsaɪd/ *noun* [C, U] (**AGRICULTURE**) a chemical substance that farmers use to kill plants that are growing where they are not wanted ⊃ look at **insecticide, pesticide**

herbivore /'hɜ:bɪvɔ:(r)/ *noun* [C] (**BIOLOGY**) an animal that only eats plants ⊃ look at **carnivore, insectivore, omnivore** ▸ **herbivorous** /hɜ:'bɪvərəs/ *adj.*: *herbivorous dinosaurs*

herd¹ /hɜ:d/ *noun* [C + sing./pl. verb] a large number of animals that live and feed together: *a herd of cattle/deer/elephants* ⊃ look at **flock¹** (1) ⊃ note at **cow**

herd² /hɜːd/ *verb* [T] to move people or animals somewhere together in a group: *The prisoners were herded onto the train.*

herd im'munity *noun* [U] (**HEALTH**) protection from a disease that happens if a large percentage of the population is unable to catch it

herdsman /'hɜːdzmən/ *noun* [C] (*pl.* **-men** /-mən/) (**AGRICULTURE**) a person who looks after a group of animals

here¹ ⓘ **A1** **S** /hɪə(r)/ *adv.* **1** (after a verb or preposition) in, at or to the place where you are or that you are pointing to: *Come (over) here.* ◊ *The school is a mile from here.* ◊ *Please sign here.* **2** used at the beginning of a sentence to introduce or draw attention to sb/sth: *Here is the one o'clock news.* ◊ *Here comes the bus.* ◊ *Here we are* (= we've arrived). **3** (used for emphasizing a noun) **4** at this point in a discussion or a piece of writing: *Here the speaker stopped and looked around the room.* **IDM** **here and there** in various places **here goes** (*informal*) used to say that you are about to do sth exciting, dangerous, etc.: *I've never done a backward dive before, but here goes!* **here you are** | **here you go** (*informal*) used when you are giving sth to sb **here's to sb/sth** used when wishing for the health, success, etc. of sb/sth while holding a drink: *Here's to a great holiday!* **neither here nor there** not important: *My opinion is neither here nor there. If you like the dress then buy it.*

here² /hɪə(r)/ *exclamation* used for attracting sb's attention, when offering help or when giving sth to sb: *Here, let me help!*

hereabouts /ˌhɪərə'baʊts/ (*AmE also* **hereabout**) *adv.* near this place

hereafter /ˌhɪər'ɑːftə(r)/ *adv.* (*formal*) (used in legal documents, etc.) from now on

hereditary /hə'redɪtri/ *adj.* (**HEALTH**) passed on from parent to child: *a hereditary disease* ◊ *a hereditary title*

heredity /hə'redəti/ *noun* [U] (**BIOLOGY**) the process by which physical or mental qualities pass from parent to child

heresy /'herəsi/ *noun* [C, U] (*pl.* **-ies**) (**RELIGION**) a opinion or belief that is different from what is generally accepted to be true by a particular religion

heretic /'herətɪk/ *noun* [C] (**RELIGION**) a person whose religious beliefs do not agree with what is generally accepted ▸ **heretical** /hə'retɪkl/ *adj.*

herewith /ˌhɪə'wɪð, -'wɪθ/ *adv.* (*formal*) with this letter, etc: *Please fill in the form enclosed herewith.*

heritage ⓘ+ **C1** /'herɪtɪdʒ/ *noun* [C, usually sing.] (**HISTORY**) the traditions, qualities, buildings and objects of a country that have existed for a long time and that have great importance for the country

hermaphrodite /hɜː'mæfrədaɪt/ *noun* [C] (**BIOLOGY**) a person, an animal or a flower that has both male and female sexual organs or characteristics

hermit /'hɜːmɪt/ *noun* [C] a person who prefers to live alone, without contact with other people, often for religious reasons

hernia /'hɜːniə/ *noun* [C, U] (**HEALTH**) the medical condition in which an organ inside the body, for example the stomach, pushes through the wall of muscle that surrounds it

hero ⓘ **A2** /'hɪərəʊ/ *noun* [C] (*pl.* **-oes**) **1** a person who is admired, especially for having done sth difficult or good: *a war hero* ◊ *The team were given a hero's welcome on their return home.* **2** (**ARTS AND MEDIA**,

LITERATURE) the most important male character in a book, play, film, etc: *The hero of the film is a little boy.* ◊ look at **anti-hero, heroine** (2), **villain** (1)

heroic /hə'rəʊɪk/ *adj.* (used about people or their actions) having or showing a lot of courage: *a heroic effort* ▸ **heroically** /-kli/ *adv.*

heroin /'herəʊɪn/ *noun* [U] a powerful illegal drug that some people take for pleasure and then become ADDICTED to (= cannot stop taking)

heroine /'herəʊɪn/ *noun* [C] **1** a woman who is admired, especially for having done sth difficult or good **2** (**ARTS AND MEDIA, LITERATURE**) the most important female character in a book, play, film, etc. ◊ look at **hero** (2)

heroism /'herəʊɪzəm/ *noun* [U] great courage

heron /'herən/ *noun* [C] a large bird with a long neck and long legs, that lives near water

herpes /'hɜːpiːz/ *noun* [U] (**HEALTH**) a disease, caused by a virus, that causes painful spots on the skin, especially on the face and sexual organs

herring /'herɪŋ/ *noun* [C, U] (*pl.* **herring, herrings**) a fish that swims in very large groups and is used for food **IDM** **a red herring** → **RED¹**

herringbone /'herɪŋbəʊn/ *noun* [U] a pattern used in cloth consisting of lines of V shapes that are PARALLEL to each other

hers ⓘ **A2** /hɜːz, 3ːz/ *pron.* of or belonging to her: *I didn't have a pen but Helen lent me hers.*

herself ⓘ **A2** /hɜː'self, *weak form* hə's-/ *pron.* **1** used when the female who does an action is also affected by it: *She hurt herself quite badly when she fell downstairs.* ◊ *Irene looked at herself in the mirror.* **2** used to emphasize the female who did the action: *She told me the news herself.* ◊ *Has Rosy done this herself?* (= or did sb else do it for her?) **IDM** **(all) by herself** **1** alone: *She lives by herself.* **2** without help: *I don't think she needs any help — she can change a tyre by herself.* **(all) to herself** without having to share: *Julie has the bedroom to herself now her sister's left home.*

hertz /hɜːts/ *noun* [C] (*pl.* **hertz**) (*abbr.* **Hz**) (**PHYSICS**) a unit for measuring the FREQUENCY of sound waves ◊ picture at **wavelength**

he's /hiːz, hɪz, ɪz/ *short form* he is; he has

hesitant /'hezɪtənt/ *adj.* ~ **(to do sth)**; ~ **(about doing sth)** slow to speak or act because you are not sure if you should or not: *People are still hesitant to leave their homes for fear of infection.* ◊ *I'm very hesitant about criticizing him too much.* ▸ **hesitancy** /-zɪtənsi/ *noun* [U] ▸ **hesitantly** *adv.*

hesitate ⓘ **B2** /'hezɪteɪt/ *verb* [I] **1** ~ **(about/over sth)** to be slow to do sth or to take a decision, usually because you are uncertain or worried: *He hesitated before going into the room.* ◊ *She's still hesitating about whether to accept the job or not.* **2** ~ **(to do sth)** to not want to do sth because you are not sure that it is right: *Don't hesitate to phone if you have any problems.* ▸ **hesitation** /ˌhezɪ'teɪʃn/ *noun* [U, C]: *She agreed without a moment's hesitation.*

hessian /'hesiən/ (*especially BrE*) (*AmE usually* **burlap**) *noun* [U] a strong rough brown cloth, used especially for making SACKS (= large bags)

hetero- /hetərəʊ, hetərə, hetə'rɒ/ *prefix* (in nouns, adjectives and adverbs) other; different: *heterogeneous* ◊ *heterosexual* ◊ look at **homo-**

heterogeneous /ˌhetərə'dʒiːniəs/ *adj.* (*formal*) consisting of different kinds of people or things ◊ look at **homogeneous**

heterosexual /ˌhetərəˈsekʃuəl/ *adj.* sexually attracted to a person of the opposite sex ⊃ look at **bisexual**, **homosexual** ▸ heterosexual *noun* [C]

heterozygote /ˌhetərəˈzaɪɡəʊt/ *noun* [C] (**BIOLOGY**) a living thing that has two varying forms of a particular GENE (= a unit inside a cell that controls a particular quality), and whose young may therefore vary in a particular characteristic ▸ heterozygous /-ɡəs/ *adj.*

het up /ˌhet ˈʌp/ *adj.* [not before noun] ~ (**about/over sth**) (*informal*) worried or excited about sth

hexa- /heksə, hekˈsæ/ (*also* hex- /heks/) *prefix* (in nouns, adjectives and adverbs) six; having six: *hexagonal*

hexagon /ˈheksəɡən/ *noun* [C] (**GEOMETRY**) a shape with six sides ▸ hexagonal /hekˈsæɡənl/ *adj.*

hey ⚡**A1** /heɪ/ *exclamation* (*informal*) used to attract sb's attention or to show that you are surprised or interested: *Hey, what are you doing?*
IDM **hey presto** something that people say when they have done sth so quickly that it seems like magic

heyday /ˈheɪdeɪ/ *noun* [sing.] the period when sb/sth was most powerful, successful, rich, etc.

HGV /ˌeɪtʃ dʒiː ˈviː/ *noun* [C] (*BrE*) a large vehicle such as a lorry (the abbreviation for 'heavy goods vehicle')

hi ⚡**A1** /haɪ/ *exclamation* (*informal*) used to say hello

hiatus /haɪˈeɪtəs/ *noun* [sing.] (*formal*) a break in activity when nothing happens: *After a five-month hiatus, the talks resumed.*

hibernate /ˈhaɪbəneɪt/ *verb* [I] (**BIOLOGY**) (used about animals) to spend the winter in a state like deep sleep ▸ hibernation /ˌhaɪbəˈneɪʃn/ *noun* [U]

hiccup (*also* hiccough) /ˈhɪkʌp/ *noun* **1** [C] a sudden, usually repeated, sound that is made in the throat and that you cannot control **2** (the) hiccups [pl.] a series of hiccups: *Don't eat so fast or you'll get hiccups!* ◇ *If you have the hiccups, try holding your breath.* **3** [C] a small problem or difficulty ▸ hiccup (*also* hiccough) *verb* [I]

hidden ⚡+**B2** /ˈhɪdn/ *adj.* **1** something that is **hidden** is kept or located in a place where it cannot be seen: *Hidden dangers lurk in the ocean depths.* **2** secret: *She felt sure the letter had some hidden meaning.*

hide¹ ⚡**A2** /haɪd/ *verb* (*pt* hid /hɪd/; *pp* hidden /ˈhɪdn/) **1** [T] to put or keep sb/sth in a place where they or it cannot be seen; to cover sth so that it cannot be seen: *Where shall I hide the money?* ◇ *You couldn't see Bill in the photo — he was hidden behind John.* **2** [I] to be in or go into a place where you cannot be seen or found: *Quick, run and hide!* ◇ *The child was hiding under the bed.* **3** [T] ~ **sth (from sb)** to keep sth secret, especially your feelings: *She tried to hide her disappointment from them.*

hide² /haɪd/ *noun* **1** [C, U] the skin of a large animal, especially when it is used for leather ⊃ picture at **rhinoceros** **2** [C] a place from which people can watch wild animals, birds, etc. without being seen

hide-and-ˈseek *noun* [U] a children's game in which one person hides and the others try to find them

hideous /ˈhɪdiəs/ *adj.* very ugly or unpleasant: *a hideous sight* ◇ *a hideous crime* ▸ hideously *adv.*

hiding /ˈhaɪdɪŋ/ *noun* **1** [U] the state of being hidden: *The escaped prisoners are believed to be in hiding somewhere in London.* ◇ *to go into hiding* **2** [C, usually sing.] (*informal*) a punishment involving being hit hard many times: *You deserve a good hiding for what you've done.*

hierarchy ⚡+ **C1** 🌐 /ˈhaɪərɑːki/ *noun* [C] (*pl.* -ies) a system or an organization that has many levels from the lowest to the highest ▸ hierarchical 🌐 /ˌhaɪəˈrɑːkɪkl/ *adj.*

hieroglyph /ˈhaɪərəɡlɪf/ *noun* [C] (**LANGUAGE**) a picture or symbol of an object, representing a word, syllable or sound, especially as used in ancient Egyptian and other writing systems ▸ hieroglyphic /ˌhaɪərəˈɡlɪfɪk/ *adj.*

hieroglyphics /ˌhaɪərəˈɡlɪfɪks/ *noun* [pl.] (**HISTORY**, **LANGUAGE**) writing that uses HIEROGLYPHS

hi-fi /ˈhaɪ faɪ/ *noun* [C, U] equipment for playing recorded music that produces high-quality sound ▸ hi-fi *adj.*: *a hi-fi system*

higgledy-piggledy /ˌhɪɡldi ˈpɪɡldi/ *adv., adj.* (*informal*) not in any order; mixed up together

hieroglyph
hieroglyphics

high¹ ⚡**A1** 🔘 /haɪ/ *adj.*
• FROM BOTTOM TO TOP **1** (used about things) measuring a large distance between the bottom and the top: *high cliffs* ◇ *What's the highest mountain in the world?* ◇ *high heels* (= on shoes) ◇ *The garden wall was so high that we couldn't see over it.* **OPP** low¹ ⊃ *noun* **height** **2** having a particular height: *The hedge is one metre high.* ◇ *knee-high boots* ⊃ note at **measure²**
• FAR FROM GROUND **3** at a level that is a long way from the ground, or from sea level: *a high shelf* ◇ *The castle was built on high ground.* **OPP** low¹
• MORE THAN USUAL **4** above the usual or normal level or amount: *high prices* ◇ *at high speed* ◇ *a high level of unemployment* ◇ *He's got a high temperature.* ◇ *Oranges are high in vitamin C.* **OPP** low¹
• BETTER THAN USUAL **5** better than what is usual: *high-quality goods* ◇ *Her work is of a very high standard.* ◇ *He has a high opinion of you.* **OPP** low¹, poor
• IMPORTANT **6** having an important position: *Sam only joined the company three years ago, but she's already quite high up.*
• GOOD **7** morally good: *high ideals*
• SOUND **8** (used about a sound or voice) not deep or low: *Dogs can hear very high sounds.* ◇ *Women usually have higher voices than men.* **OPP** low¹
• ON DRUGS, ETC. **9** ~ (**on sth**) (*informal*) under the influence of drugs, alcohol, etc.
• IN A CAR **10** (used about a GEAR in a car) that allows a faster speed **OPP** low¹
IDM **be left high and dry** to be left without help in a difficult situation

high² ⚡**A2** /haɪ/ *adv.* **1** at or to a high position or level: *The sun was high in the sky.* ◇ *I can't jump any higher.* ◇ *The plane flew high overhead.* ⊃ *noun* **height** **2** (used about a sound) at a high level: *How high can you sing?* **OPP** low²
IDM **high and low** everywhere: *We've searched high and low for my wallet.* **run high** (used about the feelings of a group of people) to be especially strong: *Emotions are running high in the neighbourhood where the murders took place.*

high³ ⚡**B2** /haɪ/ *noun* [C] **1** a high level or point: *Profits reached an all-time high last year.* **OPP** low³ **2** (**GEOGRAPHY**) an area of high air pressure **OPP** low³ **3** (*informal*) a feeling of great pleasure or happiness that sb gets from doing sth exciting or being successful: *He was on a high after passing all his exams.* ◇ *She talked about the highs and lows of her* *career.* **OPP** low⁴ 4 (*informal*) a feeling of great pleasure or happiness that may be caused by a drug, alcohol, etc.

IDM on high (*formal*) (in) a high place, the sky or heaven: *The order came from on high.*

highbrow /'haɪbraʊ/ *adj.* interested in or concerned with matters that many people would find too serious to be interesting: *highbrow newspapers/TV programmes*

high chair *noun* [C] a special chair with long legs and a table, for a small child to sit in when eating

high-'class *adj.* of especially good quality: *a high-class restaurant*

High Com'missioner *noun* [C] 1 (**POLITICS**) a person who is sent by one Commonwealth country to live in another, to protect the interests of their own country 2 (**SOCIAL STUDIES**) a person who is head of an important international project: *the United Nations High Commissioner for Refugees*

high 'court *noun* (**LAW**) 1 [C] a court in England and Wales that deals with the most serious CIVIL cases (= not criminal cases) 2 (*also* Supreme Court) [sing.] the highest court in a country or state

high-defi'nition *adj.* = HD

high-'end *adj.* expensive and of high quality

higher edu'cation *noun* [U] (**EDUCATION**) education and training at a college or university, especially to degree level ⊃ look at **further education**

highest common 'factor *noun* [C] (*abbr.* HCF) (**MATHEMATICS**) the highest number that can be divided exactly into two or more numbers

high jump (*often* the high jump) *noun* [sing.] (**SPORT**) the sport in which people try to jump over a bar in order to find out who can jump the highest ⊃ look at **long jump**

highland /'haɪlənd/ *adj.* (**GEOGRAPHY**) 1 in or connected with an area of land that has mountains: *highland streams* ⊃ look at **lowland** 2 Highland connected with the Highlands (= the high mountain region of Scotland)

highlander /'haɪləndə(r)/ *noun* [C] (**SOCIAL STUDIES**) 1 a person who comes from an area where there are a lot of mountains ⊃ look at **lowlander** 2 Highlander a person who comes from the Scottish Highlands

high-'level *adj.* 1 involving important people: *high-level talks* 2 (**COMPUTING**) (used about a computer language) similar to an existing language such as English, making it fairly simple to use **OPP** low-level

highlight¹ ʔ⌄ **B1 W** /'haɪlaɪt/ *verb* [T] 1 to emphasize sth so that people give it special attention: *The report highlighted the need for improved safety at football grounds.* 2 to mark part of a text with a different colour or to mark an area on a computer screen so that people give it more attention 3 to make some parts of a person's hair a lighter colour: *Have you had your hair highlighted?*

highlight² ʔ⌄ **B1** /'haɪlaɪt/ *noun* 1 [C] the best or most interesting part of sth: *The highlights of the match will be shown on TV tonight.* 2 highlights [pl.] areas of lighter colour that are put in sb's hair

highlighter /'haɪlaɪtə(r)/ (*also* 'highlighter pen) *noun* [C] a special pen used for marking words in a text in bright colours

highly ʔ⌄ **B1 O** /'haɪli/ *adv.* 1 to a high degree; very: *highly trained/educated/developed* ◊ *a highly paid job* ◊ *It's highly unlikely that anyone will complain.* 2 with great respect or praise: *I think very highly of your work.*

highly 'strung *adj.* nervous and easily upset

Highness /'haɪnəs/ His/Her/Your Highness *noun* [C] a title used when speaking about or to a member of a royal family

high-per'formance *adj.* [only before noun] that can go very fast or do complicated things: *a high-performance car/computer*

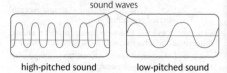

sound waves

high-pitched sound   low-pitched sound

high-'pitched *adj.* (used about sounds) very high: *a high-pitched voice/whistle* **OPP** low-pitched

high-'powered *adj.* 1 (used about things) having great power: *a high-powered engine* 2 (used about people) important and successful: *high-powered executives*

high-'profile ʔ⌄ **C1** *adj.* receiving a lot of attention in newspapers, etc: *a high-profile issue*

high-reso'lution (*also informal* high-res /ˌhaɪ 'rez/) *adj.* (used to talk about a photo or an image on a computer or TV screen) showing a lot of clear sharp detail

high-rise *adj.* [only before noun] (**ARCHITECTURE**) (used about a building) very tall and having a lot of floors

high-'risk *adj.* involving a lot of danger and the risk of injury, damage, etc: *a high-risk sport* ◊ *high-risk patients* (= who are very likely to get a particular illness)

high school *noun* [C, U] (**EDUCATION**) 1 (in the US and some other countries) a school for young people between the ages of 14 and 18 2 often used in England, Wales and Northern Ireland in the names of schools for young people between the ages of 11 and 18: *Edgbaston High School* ⊃ look at **secondary school**

high 'season *noun* [U, sing.] (*especially BrE*) (**TOURISM**) the time of year when a hotel or tourist area receives most visitors ⊃ look at **low season**

high-'speed *adj.* [only before noun] that travels, works or happens very fast: *a high-speed train*

high street *noun* [C] (*BrE*) (often used in names) the main street of a town: *The post office is in the High Street.*

high-'tech (*also* hi-tech) *adj.* 1 (**COMPUTING**) using the most modern methods and machines, especially electronic ones: *high-tech industries/hospitals* **OPP** low-tech 2 very modern in appearance; using modern materials: *a high-tech table made of glass and steel* ⊃ look at **low-tech**

high 'tide *noun* [U, C] (**GEOGRAPHY**) the time when the sea comes furthest onto the land **OPP** low tide ⊃ look at **ebb** ⊃ picture at **erosion**

highway ʔ⌄ **B2** /'haɪweɪ/ *noun* [C] (*especially AmE*) a main road (between towns): *The interstate highway was closed.* ⊃ look at **motorway**

hijab /hɪ'dʒɑːb/ *noun* [C] (**RELIGION**) a head covering worn in public by some Muslim women

hijack /'haɪdʒæk/ *verb* [T] 1 to take control of a plane, etc. by force, usually for political reasons: *The plane was hijacked on its flight to Sydney.* ⊃ look at **kidnap** 2 to take control of a meeting, an event, etc. in order to force people to pay attention to sth: *The rally was hijacked by right-wing extremists.* ▶ hijack *noun* [C]: *The hijack was ended by armed police.* ▶ hijacker *noun* [C] ▶ hijacking *noun* [C, U]

hike /haɪk/ *noun* [C] a long walk in the country: *We went on a ten-mile hike at the weekend.* ▶ hike *verb* [I] ▶ hiker *noun* [C]

hiking /'haɪkɪŋ/ noun [U] the activity of going for long walks in the country for pleasure

hilarious ₹+ **B2** /hɪ'leəriəs/ adj. extremely funny
▶ hilariously adv.

hilarity /hɪ'lærəti/ noun [U] the state of finding sth very funny

hill ₹ **A2** /hɪl/ noun [C] (GEOGRAPHY) **1** a high area of land that is not as high as a mountain: *We spent the day walking in the hills.* ○ look at **downhill**, **uphill** **2** a slope on a road: *Take care when driving down steep hills.*

hillock /'hɪlək/ noun [C] (GEOGRAPHY) a small hill

hillside /'hɪlsaɪd/ noun [C] (GEOGRAPHY) the side of a hill

hilltop /'hɪltɒp/ noun [C] (GEOGRAPHY) the top of a hill

hilly /'hɪli/ adj. (hillier; hilliest) (GEOGRAPHY) having a lot of hills: *The country's very hilly around here.*

hilt /hɪlt/ noun [C] the handle of a knife or SWORD ○ picture at **weapon**
IDM **to the hilt** to a high degree; completely: *I'll defend you to the hilt.*

him ₹ **A1** /hɪm, ɪm/ pron. (the object of a verb or preposition) the male person who was mentioned earlier: *Helen told Ian that she loved him.* ◇ *I've got a letter for your father — can you give it to him, please?*

himself ₹ **A2** /hɪm'self/ pron. **1** used when the male who does an action is also affected by it: *He cut himself when he was shaving.* ◇ *John looked at himself in the mirror.* **2** used to emphasize the male who does the action: *He told me the news himself.* ◇ *Did he write this himself?* (= or did sb else do it for him?)
IDM **(all) by himself 1** alone: *He lives by himself.* **2** without help: *He should be able to cook a meal by himself.* **(all) to himself** without having to share: *Charlie has the bedroom to himself now his brother's left home.*

hind /haɪnd/ adj. [only before noun] (used about an animal's legs, etc.) at the back

hinder /'hɪndə(r)/ verb [T] to make it more difficult for sb/sth to do sth: *A lot of scientific work is hindered by lack of money.*

Hindi /'hɪndi/ noun [U] (LANGUAGE) one of the official languages of India, spoken especially in North India
▶ Hindi adj.

hindquarters /ˌhaɪnd'kwɔːtəz/ noun [pl.] the back part of an animal that has four legs, including its two back legs

hindrance /'hɪndrəns/ noun [C, usually sing.] a person or thing that makes it difficult for you to do sth

hindsight /'haɪndsaɪt/ noun [U] the understanding that you have of a situation only after it has happened: *With hindsight, I wouldn't have lent him the money.* ○ look at **foresight**

Hindu /'hɪnduː/ noun [C] (RELIGION) a person whose religion is Hinduism ○ note at **religion** ▶ Hindu adj.: *Hindu beliefs*

Hinduism /'hɪnduːɪzəm/ noun [U] (RELIGION) the main religion of India and Nepal includes the WORSHIP of one or more gods and the belief that, after death, people will return to life in a different form. ○ note at **religion**

hinge¹ /hɪndʒ/ noun [C] a piece of metal or plastic that joins two sides of a box, door, etc. together and allows it to be opened or closed

hinge² /hɪndʒ/ verb (hingeing)

hinge

PHR V **hinge on sth** to depend on sth: *The future of the project hinges on the meeting today.*

hint¹ ₹+ **C1** /hɪnt/ noun [C] **1** something that you suggest in an indirect way: *If you keep mentioning parties, maybe they'll **take the hint** and invite you.* **2** something that suggests what will happen in the future: *The first half of the match **gave no hint** of the excitement to come.* **SYN** **sign¹** **3** [usually sing.] a small amount of sth: *There was a hint of sadness in his voice.* **SYN** **suggestion** **4** a piece of advice or information: *helpful hints* **SYN** **tip¹**

hint² ₹+ **C1** /hɪnt/ verb [I, T] ~ **(at sth)**; ~ **(that)** … to suggest sth in an indirect way: *They only hinted at their great disappointment.* ◇ *He hinted that he might be moving to Greece.*

hinterland /'hɪntəlænd/ noun [C] (GEOGRAPHY) the areas of a country that are away from the coast, from the banks of a large river or from the main cities: *the rural/agricultural hinterland*

hip¹ ₹+ **B2** /hɪp/ noun [C] (ANATOMY) the part on either side of the body above the legs and below the middle part of the body: *He stood there angrily with his hands on his hips.* ◇ *the hip bone* ○ picture at **body**

hip² /hɪp/ exclamation
IDM **hip, hip, hooray/hurrah** used by a group of people to show their approval of sb. One person in the group says 'hip, hip' and the others then shout 'hooray': *'Three cheers for David. He's done a great job. Hip, hip … ' 'Hooray!'*

ˈhip bone noun [C] (ANATOMY) the large bone that forms the main part of the PELVIS on each side of the body ○ picture at **body**

ˈhip-hop noun [U] (MUSIC) a type of dance music with spoken words and a steady beat played on electronic instruments

ˈhip joint noun [C] (ANATOMY) the JOINT (= place where two bones meet) that connects the leg to the body at the top of the leg

hippie (also hippy) /'hɪpi/ noun [C] (SOCIAL STUDIES) (pl. -ies) a person who rejects the way that most people live in Western society, often having long hair, wearing brightly coloured clothes and taking illegal drugs. The hippie movement was most popular in the 1960s.

the Hippocratic oath /ðə ˌhɪpəkrætɪk 'əʊθ/ noun [sing.] (MEDICINE) the promise that doctors make to keep to the principles of the medical profession

hippopotamus /ˌhɪpə'pɒtəməs/ (pl. hippopotamuses, hippopotami /-maɪ/) (also informal hippo /'hɪpəʊ/, pl. -os) noun [C] a large African animal with a large head, short legs and thick dark skin that lives in or near rivers ○ picture at **rhinoceros**

hire¹ ₹ **B1** /'haɪə(r)/ verb **1** [T, I] to give sb a job: *She was hired three years ago.* ○ note at **job 2** [T] to give sb a job for a short time: *We'll have to hire somebody to mend the roof.* **3** (especially BrE) (also **rent** especially in AmE) [T] ~ **sth (from sb)** to have the use of sth for a short time by paying for it
PHR V **hire sth out** to allow sb to use sth for a short fixed period in exchange for money: *We hire out our vans by the day.*

hire² ₹ **B2** /'haɪə(r)/ noun [U] (especially BrE) the act of paying to use sth for a short time: *Car hire is expensive in this country.* ◇ *Do you have bicycles **for hire**?*

ˌhire ˈpurchase noun [U] (BrE) (abbr. HP /ˌeɪtʃ 'piː/) (FINANCE) a way of buying goods. You do not pay the full price immediately, but pay by INSTALMENTS

(= regular small payments) until the full amount is paid: *a hire purchase agreement for a car*

his¹ ⓘ **A1** /hɪz, ɪz/ *det.* of or belonging to the man or boy who was mentioned earlier: *Matthew has hurt his shoulder.* ◇ *Have you met his sister?*

his² ⓘ **A2** /hɪz, ɪz/ *pron.* of or belonging to him: *This is my book so that one must be his.* ◇ *a friend of his*

Hispanic /hɪˈspænɪk/ *adj.* of or connected with Spain or Spanish-speaking countries, especially those of Latin America ▸ **Hispanic** *noun* [C] ⊃ look at **Latina, Latino**

hiss /hɪs/ *verb* 1 [I, T] to make a sound like a very long 's' to show that you are angry or do not like sth: *The cat hissed at me.* ◇ *The speech was hissed and booed.* 2 [T] to say sth in a quiet angry voice: '*Stay away from me!*' *she hissed.* ▸ **hiss** *noun* [C]

histamine /ˈhɪstəmiːn/ *noun* [U] (**BIOLOGY**) a chemical substance that is produced by the body if you are injured or have an ALLERGY (= a bad reaction to sth that you touch, eat or breathe) ⊃ look at **antihistamine**

historian ⓘ+ **B2** /hɪˈstɔːriən/ *noun* [C] (**HISTORY**) a person who studies or writes about history

historic ⓘ **B1** /hɪˈstɒrɪk/ *adj.* (**HISTORY**) famous or important in history: *The ending of apartheid was a historic event.* ⊃ look at **historical**

historical ⓘ **B1** /hɪˈstɒrɪkl/ *adj.* (**HISTORY**) 1 connected with the past: *stories based on historical fact* 2 connected with the study of history: *historical documents/records/research* ⊃ look at **historic** ▸ **historically** ⓦ /-kli/ *adv.*

hi‚storical lin‚guistics *noun* [U] (**LANGUAGE**) the study of the history and development of languages

historiography /hɪˌstɔːriˈɒɡrəfi/ *noun* [U] (**HISTORY**) the study of the way history is written about

history ⓘ **A1** ⊙ /ˈhɪstri/ *noun* (*pl.* -ies) 1 [U] all the events of the past: *an important moment in history* ⊃ look at **natural history** 2 [C, usually sing.] the series of events or facts that is connected with sb/sth: *He has a history of violence.* ◇ *a patient's medical history* 3 [U] (**EDUCATION**) the study of past events: *She has a degree in history.* ◇ *History was my favourite subject at school.* 4 [C] a written description of past events **IDM** **go down in/make history** to be or do sth so important that it will be recorded in history **the rest is history** used when you are telling a story to say that you are not going to tell the end of the story, because everyone knows it already

hit¹ ⓘ **A2** /hɪt/ *verb* (**hitting**; *pt, pp* **hit**) 1 to make sudden, violent contact with sb/sth: *The bus left the road and hit a tree.* ◇ *to hit somebody in the eye/across the face/on the nose* 2 ~ **sth (on/against sth)** to knock a part of your body, etc. against sth: *Peter hit his head on the low beam.* 3 to have a bad or unpleasant effect on sb/sth: *Inner-city areas have been badly hit by unemployment.* ◇ *Her father's death has hit her very hard.* 4 to experience sth unpleasant or difficult: *Things were going really well until we hit this problem.* 5 to reach a place or a level: *If you follow this road you should hit the motorway in about ten minutes.* ◇ *The price of oil hit a new high yesterday.* 6 to suddenly come into sb's mind; to make sb realize or understand sth: *I thought I recognized the man's face and then it hit me — he was my old maths teacher!* **IDM** **hit it off (with sb)** (*informal*) to like sb when you first meet them: *When I first met Tony's parents, we didn't really hit it off.* **hit the jackpot** to win a lot of money or have a big success **hit the nail on the head** to say sth that is exactly right **hit the roof** (*informal*) to suddenly become very angry

PHRV **hit back (at sb/sth)** to attack (with words) sb who has attacked you **hit on sth** to suddenly find sth by chance: *I finally hit on a solution to the problem.* **hit out (at sb/sth)** to attack sb/sth: *The newspapers hit out at the company for its poor safety record.*

hit² ⓘ **A2** /hɪt/ *noun* [C] 1 the act of hitting sth: *The ship took a* **direct hit** *and sank.* ◇ *She gave her brother a hard hit on the head.* ⊃ look at **miss²** (2) 2 a person or thing that is very popular or successful: *The series was a big hit.* **OPP** **flop²** 3 (**COMPUTING**) a result of a search on a computer, especially on the internet **IDM** **make a hit (with sb)** (*informal*) to make a good impression on sb

‚hit-and-ˈmiss (*also* **hit-or-miss**) *adj.* not done in a careful or planned way and therefore not likely to be successful

‚hit-and-ˈrun *adj.* (used about a road accident) caused by a driver who does not stop to help

hitch¹ /hɪtʃ/ *verb* 1 [I, T] (*informal*) to get a free ride in a person's car; to travel around in this way by waiting by the side of a road and trying to get passing cars to stop: *I managed to hitch to Paris in just six hours.* ◇ *We missed the bus so we had to* **hitch a lift**. **SYN** **hitchhike** 2 [T] to fasten sth to sth else: *to hitch a trailer to the back of a car*

hitch² /hɪtʃ/ *noun* [C] a small problem or difficulty: *a technical hitch*

hitchhike /ˈhɪtʃhaɪk/ *verb* [I] to travel by waiting by the side of a road and holding out your hand or a sign until a driver stops and takes you in the direction you want to go: *He hitchhiked across Europe.* ⊃ look at **hitch¹** (1) ▸ **hitchhiker** *noun* [C]

‚hi-ˈtech = HIGH-TECH

hitherto /ˌhɪðəˈtuː/ *adv.* (*formal*) until now

‚hit-or-ˈmiss = HIT-AND-MISS

HIV /ˌeɪtʃ aɪ ˈviː/ *noun* [U] the virus that can cause AIDS (the abbreviation for 'human immunodeficiency virus')

hive /haɪv/ = BEEHIVE

hiya /ˈhaɪjə/ *exclamation* (*informal*) used to say hello to sb in an informal way

HM *abbr.* (in writing) **His/Her Majesty('s)** (a title of respect used when referring to a king or queen, or sth that belongs to a king or queen): *HMS* (= Her Majesty's Ship) *Invincible*

hmm (*also* **hm**) /m, hm/ *exclamation* used when you are not sure or when you are thinking about sth

HMRC /ˌeɪtʃ em ɑː ˈsiː/ *abbr.* **HM Revenue and Customs** (the government department in the UK that collects taxes)

hoard¹ /hɔːd/ *noun* [C] a store (often secret) of money, food, etc.

hoard² /hɔːd/ *verb* [I, T] to collect and store large quantities of sth (often secretly)

hoarding /ˈhɔːdɪŋ/ (*BrE*) = BILLBOARD

hoarse /hɔːs/ *adj.* if a person or their voice is **hoarse**, their voice sounds rough and unpleasant, especially because of a SORE throat (= a painful throat because of an infection): *a hoarse whisper* ▸ **hoarsely** *adv.*

hoax /həʊks/ *noun* [C] a trick to make people believe sth that is not true, especially sth unpleasant

hob /hɒb/ *noun* [C] (*BrE*) (*AmE* **stovetop**) the surface on the top of a cooker or a kitchen unit that is used for boiling, frying, etc.

hobble /ˈhɒbl/ *verb* [I] to walk with difficulty, especially because your feet or legs hurt: *He hobbled home on his twisted ankle.*

hobby ⓣ **A1** /ˈhɒbi/ *noun* [C] (*pl.* -ies) something that you do regularly for pleasure in your free time: *Chloe's hobbies are gaming and mountain biking.* **SYN pastime**

hockey ⓣ **A2** /ˈhɒki/ *noun* [U] **1** (**SPORT**) a game that is played on a field by two teams of eleven players who try to hit a small hard ball into a goal with a curved wooden stick ➔ picture at **sport ❶** In the US hockey is usually called **field hockey** to show that it is not **ice hockey**. **2** (*AmE*) = ICE HOCKEY

hoe /həʊ/ *noun* [C] a garden tool with a long handle and a thin metal cutting edge that is used for turning the soil and for removing plants that you do not want ➔ picture at **gardening**

hog¹ /hɒɡ/ *noun* [C] a male pig that is kept for its meat **IDM go the whole hog** (*informal*) to do sth as completely as possible

hog² /hɒɡ/ *verb* [T] (-gg-) (*informal*) to take or keep too much or all of sth for yourself: *Don't hog the bathroom when everyone's getting ready to go out!*

Hogmanay /ˈhɒɡməneɪ, ˌhɒɡməˈneɪ/ *noun* [U, C] the Scottish name for New Year's Eve (31 December) and the celebrations that take place then

hoist /hɔɪst/ *verb* [T] to lift or pull sth up, often by using ropes, etc: *to hoist a flag/sail*

hold¹ ⓣ **A2** /həʊld/ *verb* (*pt, pp* held /held/)
• IN YOUR HANDS, ETC. **1** [T] to take sb/sth and keep them or it in your hand, arms, etc: *He held a book in his hand.* ◇ *The woman was holding a baby in her arms.* ◇ *Hold my hand. This is a busy road.*
• IN A POSITION **2** [T] to keep sth in a certain position: *Hold your head up straight.* ◇ *These two screws hold the shelf in place.*
• SUPPORT **3** [T] to take the weight of sb/sth: *Are you sure that branch is strong enough to hold you?*
• EVENT, MEETING, ETC. **4** [T] to organize an event; to have a meeting, an election, a concert, etc: *They're holding a party for his fortieth birthday.* ◇ *The Olympic Games are held every four years.*
• STAY THE SAME **5** [I] to stay the same or to remain strong: *I hope this weather holds till the weekend.* ◇ *What I said still holds — nothing has changed.* ◇ *They were afraid the dam wouldn't hold.*
• CONTAIN **6** [T] to contain or have space for a particular amount: *How much does this bottle hold?*
• PRISONER **7** [T] to keep a person in a position or place by force: *The terrorists are **holding** three men **hostage**.* ◇ *A man is being held at the police station.*
• OWN **8** [T] to have sth, usually in an official way: *She holds the world record in the 100 metres.*
• OPINION **9** [T] to have an opinion, etc: *They **hold the view** that we shouldn't spend any more money.* **10** [T] to believe that sth is true about a person: *I **hold** the parents **responsible** for the child's behaviour.*
• ON THE PHONE **11** [I, T] (used when you are phoning) to wait until the person you are calling is ready: *I'm afraid his phone is engaged. Will you **hold the line?***
• CONVERSATION **12** [T] to have a conversation: *It's impossible to **hold a conversation** with all this noise.* **IDM Hold it!** (*informal*) Stop! Don't move! ❶ For other idioms containing **hold**, look at the entries for the nouns, adjectives, etc. For example, **hold your own** is at **own**.
PHR V hold sth against sb to not forgive sb because of sth they have done **hold sb/sth back 1** to prevent sb from making progress: *Do you think that mixed-ability classes hold back the better students?* **2** to prevent sb/sth from moving forward **hold sth back 1** to refuse to give some of the information that you have **2** to control an emotion and stop yourself from showing what you really feel **hold off (sth/doing sth)** to not do sth immediately **hold on 1** (*informal*) used to tell sb to wait or stop for a moment: *Hold on. I'll be with you in a minute.* **2** to manage in a difficult or

dangerous situation: *They managed to hold on until a rescue party arrived.* **hold onto sb/sth** to hold sb/sth tightly: *The boy held onto his mother because he didn't want her to go.* **hold onto sth** to keep sth; to not give or sell sth: *They've offered me a lot of money for this painting, but I'm going to hold onto it.* **hold out** to last (in a difficult situation): *How long will our supply of water hold out?* **hold sth out** to offer sth to a person or an animal by moving it in your hand towards them/it: *He held out a carrot to the horse.* **hold out for sth** (*informal*) to cause a delay while you continue to ask for sth: *Union members are holding out for a better pay offer.* **hold sb/sth up** to make sb/sth late; to cause a delay: *We were held up by the traffic.* **hold up sth** to steal from a bank, shop, vehicle, etc. using a gun

hold² ⓣ **B2** /həʊld/ *noun* **1** [C] the act or manner of having sb/sth in your hand(s): *to have a firm hold on the rope* ◇ *judo/wrestling holds* **2** [sing.] **~(on/over sb/sth)** influence or control: *The new government has strengthened its hold on the country.* **3** [C] the part of a ship or an aircraft where goods are stored ➔ picture at **airliner**
IDM catch, get, grab, take, etc. hold (of sb/sth) 1 to take sb/sth in your hands: *I managed to catch hold of the dog before it ran out into the road.* **2** to take control of sb/sth; to start to have an effect on sb/sth: *Mass hysteria seemed to have taken hold of the crowd.* **get hold of sb** to find sb or make contact with sb: *I've been trying to get hold of the complaints department all morning.* **get hold of sth** to find sth that will be useful: *I must try and get hold of a good second-hand bike.* **on hold 1** delayed until a later time or date **2** if a person on the phone is put **on hold**, they have to wait until the person that they want to talk to is free

holdall /ˈhəʊldɔːl/ (*BrE*) (*AmE* **duffel bag**) *noun* [C] a large bag that is used for carrying clothes, etc. when you are travelling ➔ picture at **baggage**

holder /ˈhəʊldə(r)/ *noun* [C] (often in compounds) **1** a person who has or holds sth: *a season ticket holder* ◇ *the world record holder in the 100 metres* ◇ *holders of European passports* **2** something that contains or holds sth: *a toothbrush holder*

holding /ˈhəʊldɪŋ/ *noun* [C] **1 ~(in sth)** (**BUSINESS**) a number of shares that sb has in a company: *She has a 40% holding in the company.* **2** an amount of property that is owned by a person, museum, library, etc: *one of the most important private holdings of Indian art* **3** (**AGRICULTURE**) a piece of land that is rented by sb and used for farming ➔ look at **smallholding**

'holding company *noun* [C] (**BUSINESS**) a company that is formed to buy shares in other companies, which it then controls

'hold-up *noun* [C] **1** a situation when you have to wait for a short time: *'What's the hold-up?' 'There's been an accident ahead of us.'* **SYN delay²** **2** (**LAW**) the act of stealing from a bank, etc. using a gun: *The gang have carried out three hold-ups of high street banks.*

hole ⓣ **A2** /həʊl/ *noun* **1** [C] an opening; an empty space in sth solid: *The pavement is full of holes.* ◇ *There are holes in my socks.* ◇ *I've got a hole in my tooth.* **2** [C] the place where an animal lives in the ground or in a tree: *a mouse hole* **3** [C] (**SPORT**) (in golf) the hole in the ground that you must hit the ball into. Each section of a GOLF COURSE (= the land where you play) is also called a hole: *an eighteen-hole golf course* **4** [sing.] (*informal*) a small dark and unpleasant room, flat, etc: *This place is a hole — you can't live here!*

holiday 🔊 **A1** /'hɒlədeɪ, -di/ *noun* **1** (*also* **holidays** [pl.]) (*both BrE*) (*AmE* **vacation**) [C, U] (**TOURISM**) a period of rest from work or school (often when you go and stay away from home): *We're going to Italy for our summer holidays this year.* ◇ *How much holiday do you get a year in your new job?* ◇ *Mr Philips isn't here this week. He's away on holiday.* ◇ *I'm going to take a week's holiday in May and spend it at home.* ◇ *the school/Christmas/Easter/summer holidays* **2** [C] a day of rest when most people do not go to work, school, etc. often for religious or national celebrations: *Next Monday is a holiday.* ◇ *New Year's Day is a bank/ public holiday in Britain .*

holiday camp *noun* [C] (*BrE*) (**TOURISM**) a place that provides a place to stay and organized entertainment for people on holiday

holidaymaker /'hɒlədeɪmeɪkə(r), -dim-/ *noun* [C] (*BrE*) (**TOURISM**) a person who is away from home on holiday

holiness /'həʊlinəs/ → HOLY

holistic /həˈlɪstɪk/ *adj.* **1** considering a whole thing or being to be more than a collection of parts: *a holistic approach to life* **2** (**MEDICINE**) treating the whole person rather than just the symptoms of a disease: *holistic medicine* ▸ **holistically** /-kli/ *adv.*

hollow¹ 🔊 **B2** /'hɒləʊ/ *adj.* **1** with a hole or empty space inside: *a hollow tree* **2** (used about parts of the face) sinking deep into the face: *hollow cheeks* ◇ *hollow-eyed* **3** not sincere: *a hollow laugh/voice* ◇ *hollow promises/threats* **4** (used about a sound) seeming to come from a hollow place: *hollow footsteps*

hollow² /'hɒləʊ/ *verb*
PHR V **hollow sth out** to take out the inside part of sth

hollow³ /'hɒləʊ/ *noun* [C] (**GEOGRAPHY**) an area that is lower than the land around it

holly /'hɒli/ *noun* [U] a plant that has shiny, dark green leaves with sharp points and red BERRIES in the winter. It is often used as a Christmas decoration.

Hollywood /'hɒliwʊd/ *noun* [U] (**ARTS AND MEDIA**) the part of the city of Los Angeles that is the centre of the US film industry: *a Hollywood star*

holmium /'həʊlmiəm/ *noun* [U] (*symb.* Ho) (**CHEMISTRY**) a chemical element. Holmium is a soft silver-white metal. ❶ For more information on the periodic table of elements, look at the **Reference Section** of this dictionary.

holocaust /'hɒləkɔːst/ *noun* [C] a situation where a great many things are destroyed and a great many people die: *a nuclear holocaust*

hologram /'hɒləgræm/ *noun* [C] (**ART**) an image or picture that appears to stand out from the flat surface it is on when light falls on it

holster /'həʊlstə(r)/ *noun* [C] a leather case used for carrying a gun that is fixed to a belt or worn under the arm

holy 🔊 **B2** /'həʊli/ *adj.* (**holier**; **holiest**) (**RELIGION**) **1** connected with God or with religion and therefore very special or important: *the Holy Bible* ◇ *holy water* ◇ *The Koran is the holy book of Islam.* **2** (used about a person) good in a moral and religious way: *a holy life/ man* **3** (used about a person) serving God; pure ▸ **holiness** *noun* [U]

homage /'hɒmɪdʒ, ɒˈmɑːʒ/ *noun* [U, C, usually sing.] **~ (to sb/sth)** (*formal*) something that is said or done to show respect publicly for sb: *Thousands came to pay/do homage to the dead leader.*

home¹ 🔊 **A1** /həʊm/ *noun* **1** [C, U] the place where you live or where you feel that you belong: *She left home* (= left her parents' house and began an independent life) *at the age of 21.* ◇ *children from broken homes* (= whose parents are divorced or separated) ◇ *That old house would make an ideal family home.* ◇ *a holiday/summer home* ◇ *I often think about my friends back home.* ◇ *Stephen went abroad and made his home in Canada.* **2** [C] a place that provides care for a particular type of person or for animals: *a children's home* (= for children who have no parents to look after them) ◇ *an old people's home* **3** [sing.] **the ~ of sth** the place where sth began: *Greece is said to be the home of democracy.*
IDM **at home 1** in your house, flat, etc: *Is anybody at home?* ◇ *Tomorrow we're staying at home all day.* **2** comfortable, as if you were in your own home: *Please make yourself at home.* **3** (**SPORT**) if a sports team plays **at home**, it plays in the town, etc. that it comes from: *Manchester City are playing at home on Saturday.* **OPP** **away¹** **work from home** to do your job in your own home, especially a job that is usually done in an office

home² 🔊 **A2** /həʊm/ *adj.* [only before noun] **1** connected with the place where you live: *home cooking* ◇ *your home address/town* ◇ *a happy home life* (= with your family) **2** (*especially BrE*) connected with your own country, not with a foreign country: *The Home Secretary is responsible for home affairs.* **3** (**SPORT**) connected with a team's own sports ground: *The home team has a lot of support.* ◇ *a home game* **OPP** **away²**

home³ 🔊 **A1** /həʊm/ *adv.* at, in or to the place where you live: *We must be getting home soon.* ◇ *She'll be flying home for New Year.*
IDM **bring sth home to sb** to make sb understand sth fully: *Looking at those pictures of hungry children really brought home to me how lucky we are.* **drive sth home (to sb)** → DRIVE¹

home⁴ /həʊm/ *verb*
PHR V **home in on sb/sth** to move towards sb/sth: *The police homed in on the house where the thieves were hiding.*

homecoming /'həʊmkʌmɪŋ/ *noun* [C, U] the act of returning home, especially when you have been away for a long time

home-grown *adj.* (used about fruit and vegetables) grown in your own garden

homeland 🔊+ **C1** /'həʊmlænd/ *noun* [C, usually sing.] the country where you were born or that your parents came from, or to which you feel you belong: *Many refugees have been forced to leave their homeland.*

homeless 🔊+ **B2** /'həʊmləs/ *adj.* (**SOCIAL STUDIES**) **1** having no home **2** **the homeless** *noun* [pl.] people who have no home ▸ **homelessness** *noun* [U]

homely /'həʊmli/ *adj.* (**homelier**; **homeliest**) (*BrE*) (used about a place) simple but also pleasant or welcoming: *a homely atmosphere*

home-made *adj.* made at home; not bought in a shop: *home-made cakes*

homemaker /'həʊmmeɪkə(r)/ *noun* [C] (*especially AmE*) a person who does not have a job outside the home and takes care of the house and family ▸ **homemaking** *noun* [U]

the Home Office *noun* [sing.] (**POLITICS**) the British government department that deals with the law, the police and prisons, and with decisions about who can enter the country

homeopath (*BrE also* **homoeopath**) /'həʊmiəpæθ, 'hɒm-/ *noun* [C] (**MEDICINE**) a person who treats sick people using HOMEOPATHY

homeopathy (BrE also **homoeopathy**) /ˌhəʊmiˈɒpəθi, ˌhɒm-/ noun [U] (**MEDICINE**) the treatment of a disease by giving very small amounts of a drug that would cause the disease if given in large amounts
▶ **homeopathic** (BrE also **homoeopathic**) /ˌhəʊmiəˈpæθɪk, ˌhɒm-/ adj.: homeopathic medicine

homeostasis (BrE also **homoeostasis**) /ˌhəʊmiəˈsteɪsɪs, ˌhɒm-/ noun [U] (**BIOLOGY**) the process by which the body reacts to changes in order to keep conditions inside the body, for example temperature, the same

homeowner /ˈhəʊməʊnə(r)/ noun [C] a person who owns their house or flat

home page noun [C] (**COMPUTING**) the first of a number of pages of information on the internet that belongs to a person or an organization. A home page contains connections to other pages of information.

home rule noun [U] (**POLITICS**) the right of a country or region to govern itself, especially after another country or region has governed it

homeschooling /ˌhəʊmˈskuːlɪŋ/ noun [U] (**EDUCATION**) the practice of educating children at home, not in schools ▶ **homeschool** /-ˈskuːl/ verb [T]

Home Secretary noun [C] (**POLITICS**) the British government minister in charge of the Home Office ⊃ look at **Foreign Secretary**

homesick /ˈhəʊmsɪk/ adj. ~ (**for sb/sth**) sad because you are away from home and you miss your family and friends: She was very homesick for Canada.
▶ **homesickness** noun [U]

homestead /ˈhəʊmsted/ noun [C] (**AGRICULTURE**) a house with land and buildings around it, especially a farm: He grows tomatoes in a greenhouse at his rural homestead.

home town (BrE) (AmE **hometown**) noun [C] the place where you were born or lived as a child

homeward /ˈhəʊmwəd/ adj., adv. (going) towards home: the homeward journey ◇ to travel homeward

homework 🔊 **A1** /ˈhəʊmwɜːk/ noun [U] (**EDUCATION**) work that is given by teachers for students to do at home: Have we got any homework? ◇ I haven't **done my homework** yet. ⊃ note at **study²**

homey (also **homy**) /ˈhəʊmi/ adj. (**homier**; **homiest**) (AmE, informal) pleasant and comfortable, like home: The hotel had a nice, homey atmosphere.

homicidal /ˌhɒmɪˈsaɪdl/ adj. likely to kill another person: a homicidal maniac

homicide /ˈhɒmɪsaɪd/ noun [C, U] (especially AmE) (**LAW**) the crime of killing a person illegally and on purpose **SYN** **murder¹**

homo- /həʊməʊ, hɒmə, həˈmɒ/ prefix (in nouns, adjectives and adverbs) the same: homogeneous ◇ homosexual ⊃ look at **hetero-**

homoeopath, homoeopathy, homoeopathic, homoeostasis (BrE) = HOMEOPATH, HOMEOPATHY, HOMEOPATHIC, HOMEOSTASIS

homogeneous /ˌhɒməˈdʒiːniəs/ (also **homogenous** /həˈmɒdʒənəs/) adj. made up of things or people that are all of the same type ⊃ look at **heterogeneous**

homograph /ˈhɒməɡrɑːf/ noun [C] (**LANGUAGE**) a word that is spelt like another word but has a different meaning and may have a different pronunciation, for example bow /bəʊ/ and bow /baʊ/

homologous /həˈmɒləɡəs/ adj. ~ (**with sth**) (**BIOLOGY**) similar in position, structure, etc. to sth else: The seal's flipper is homologous with the human arm.

homonym /ˈhɒmənɪm/ noun [C] (**LANGUAGE**) a word that is spelt like another word (or pronounced like it) but that has a different meaning

homophobia /ˌhəʊməˈfəʊbiə, ˌhɒm-/ noun [U] (**SOCIAL STUDIES**) a strong and unreasonable dislike and fear of HOMOSEXUAL people ▶ **homophobic** /-bɪk/ adj.

homophone /ˈhɒməfəʊn/ noun [C] (**LANGUAGE**) a word that is pronounced the same as another word but that has a different spelling and meaning: 'Flower' and 'flour' are homophones.

Homo sapiens /ˌhəʊməʊ ˈsæpienz/ noun [U] (**BIOLOGY**) the kind or species of human being that exists now

homosexual /ˌhəʊməˈsekʃuəl, ˌhɒm-/ noun [C] sexually attracted to people of the same sex: a practising homosexual ▶ **homosexual** adj. ▶ **homosexuality** /ˌhəʊməˌsekʃuˈæləti, ˌhɒm-/ noun [U]

homozygote /ˌhɒməˈzaɪɡəʊt/ noun [C] (**BIOLOGY**) a living thing that has only one form of a particular GENE (= a unit inside a cell that controls a particular quality), and so whose young are more likely to share a particular characteristic ▶ **homozygous** /-ɡəs/ adj.

homy /ˈhəʊmi/ = HOMEY

Hon abbr. (in writing) **1** = HONORARY (2): Hon president **2** = HONOURABLE (2)

honest 🔊 **B1** /ˈɒnɪst/ adj. **1** (used about a person) telling the truth and never stealing or cheating: Just be honest — do you like this skirt or not? ◇ **To be honest**, I don't think that's a very good idea. **2** showing honest qualities: an honest face ◇ I'd like your honest opinion, please. **OPP** **dishonest**

honestly /ˈɒnɪstli/ adv. **1** in an honest way: He tried to answer the lawyer's questions honestly. **2** used for emphasizing that what you are saying is true: I honestly don't know where she has gone. **3** used to show that you think something is bad and are annoyed by it: Honestly! What a mess!

honesty 🔊+ **B2** /ˈɒnəsti/ noun [U] the quality of being honest: She answered all my questions with her usual honesty. ◇ His honesty is not in question.

honey /ˈhʌni/ noun **1** [U] the sweet sticky substance that is made by bees and that is spread on bread, etc. **2** [C] (informal) a person that you like or love; a way of speaking to sb that you like or love: He's a real honey — always ready to help. ◇ Honey, I'm home.

honeycomb /ˈhʌnikəʊm/ noun [C, U] a structure of shapes with six sides, in which bees keep their eggs and HONEY

honeymoon /ˈhʌnimuːn/ noun [C] (**TOURISM**) a holiday that is taken by two people who have just got married: We had our first argument while we were **on our honeymoon**. ▶ **honeymooner** noun [C]: The Seychelles is the perfect place for honeymooners.

honk /hɒŋk/ verb [I, T] to sound the HORN of a car; to make this sound

honorary /ˈɒnərəri/ adj. **1** given as an honour (without the person needing the usual CERTIFICATES, etc.): to be awarded an honorary degree **2** (abbr. Hon /ɒn/) not paid: He is the honorary president.

honour¹ 🔊 **B2** (BrE) (AmE **honor**) /ˈɒnə(r)/ noun **1** [U] the respect from other people that a person, country, etc. gets because of high standards of behaviour and moral character: the guest of honour (= the most important one) ⊃ look at **dishonour¹** **2** [sing.] (formal) something that you are very pleased or proud to do: It was a great honour to be asked to speak at the conference. **3** [U] the quality of doing what is morally right: I give you my word of honour. **4** **honours**, **honors** [pl.] (abbr. Hons) a university course that is of a higher level than a basic course: a First Class Honours degree **5** **honours**, **honors** [pl.] if you pass an exam with **honours**, you receive a special mark for having achieved a very high standard **6** [C] something that is given to a person officially, to show great respect: *He was buried with full military honours* (= with a military ceremony as a sign of respect). **IDM** **in honour of sb/sth** | **in sb/sth's honour** out of respect for sb/sth: *A party was given in honour of the guests from Bonn.*

honour² ⚡ **B2** (*BrE*) (*AmE* **honor**) /'ɒnə(r)/ *verb* [T] **1** [*often passive*] **~ sb/sth (with sth)** to show great (public) respect for sb/sth: *I am very honoured by the confidence you have shown in me.* **2** (*formal*) to do what you have agreed or promised: *They have failed to honour the peace agreement.*

honourable (*BrE*) (*AmE* **honorable**) /'ɒnərəbl/ *adj.* **1** acting in a way that makes people respect you; having or showing honour: *The only honourable thing to do was to resign.* **OPP** **dishonourable** **2** **the Honourable** (*abbr.* **Hon**) a title that is given to some high officials and (in the UK) to Members of Parliament when they are speaking to each other ▸ **honourably** (*AmE* **honorably**) /-bli/ *adv.*

Hons /ɒnz/ *abbr.* (**EDUCATION**) **Honours** (used after the name of a university degree): *John North BSc (Hons)*

hood /hʊd/ *noun* [C] **1** the part of a coat, etc. that you pull up to cover your head and neck in bad weather **2** a piece of cloth that covers sb's head so that they cannot be recognized or so that they cannot see **3** (*especially BrE*) a soft cover for a car that has no roof, or a folding cover on a baby's PRAM, which can be folded down in good weather **4** (*AmE*) = BONNET (1)

hooded /'hʊdɪd/ *adj.* having or wearing a HOOD: *a hooded jacket/figure*

hoody (*also* **hoodie**) /'hʊdi/ *noun* [C] (*pl.* **-ies**) (*BrE, informal*) a jacket or SWEATSHIRT with a HOOD

hoof /huːf/ *noun* [C] (*pl.* **hoofs, hooves** /huːvz/) the hard part of the foot of horses and some other animals ⊃ look at **paw¹** ⊃ picture at **animal, goat**

hoof-and-'mouth disease (*AmE*) = FOOT-AND-MOUTH DISEASE

hook¹ ⚡+ **B2** /hʊk/ *noun* [C] **1** a curved piece of metal, plastic, etc. that is used for hanging things on, catching fish with, etc: *Put your coat on the hook over there.* ◇ *a fish hook* **2** (**SPORT**) (used in BOXING) a way of hitting sb that is done with the arm bent: *a right hook* (= with the right arm) **IDM** **off the hook** (*informal*) having got free from a difficult situation or punishment: *My father paid the money I owed and got me off the hook.*

hook² ⚡+ **C1** /hʊk/ *verb* **1** [T, I] to fasten or catch sth with a HOOK; to be fastened in this way: *We hooked the trailer to the back of the car.* ◇ *The curtain simply hooks onto the rail.* **2** [T] to put sth around sth else so that you can hold on to it or move it: *Hook the rope through your belt.* **PHR V** **hook (sb/sth) up (to sth)** to connect sb/sth to a piece of electronic equipment or to a power supply

hooked /hʊkt/ *adj.* **1** shaped like a HOOK: *a hooked nose* **2** [*not before noun*] **~ (on sth)** (*informal*) needing sth that is bad for you, especially drugs: *to be hooked on gambling* **SYN** **addicted** **3** [*not before noun*] **~ (on sth)** (*informal*) enjoying sth very much, so that you want to do it, see it, etc. as much as possible: *Suzi is hooked on computer games.*

hooligan /'huːlɪɡən/ *noun* [C] a person who behaves in a violent and aggressive way in public places: *football hooligans* ⊃ look at **lout, yob** ▸ **hooliganism** *noun* [U]

hoop /huːp/ *noun* [C] a large metal or plastic ring

hooray /huˈreɪ/ (*also* **hurray, hurrah** /həˈrɑː/) *exclamation* used for expressing great pleasure, approval, etc. **IDM** **hip, hip, hooray/hurrah** → HIP²

hoot¹ /huːt/ *noun* **1** [C] (*especially BrE*) a short loud laugh or shout: *hoots of laughter* **2** [*sing.*] (*informal*) a situation or a person that is very funny: *Bob is a real hoot!* **3** [C] the loud sound that is made by the HORN of a vehicle **4** [C] the cry of an OWL (= a bird that hunts at night)

hoot² /huːt/ *verb* [I, T] **1** to make a loud noise: *They hooted with laughter at the suggestion.* **2** (*BrE*) if a car HORN **hoots** or you **hoot** the HORN, it makes a loud noise: *The driver hooted (his horn) at the dog but it wouldn't move.*

Hoover™ /'huːvə(r)/ (*BrE*) = VACUUM CLEANER

hoover /'huːvə(r)/ *verb* [T, I] (*BrE*) to clean a carpet, etc. with a machine that SUCKS up the dirt: *This carpet needs hoovering.* **SYN** **vacuum²**

hooves /huːvz/ plural of **hoof**

hop¹ /hɒp/ *verb* [I] (**-pp-**) **1** (often used with an adverb or a preposition) (used about a person) to jump on one leg: *I twisted my ankle so badly I had to hop all the way back to the car.* **2** (used with an adverb or a preposition) (used about an animal or a bird) to jump with both or all feet together **3 ~ (from sth to sth)** to change quickly from one activity or subject to another **4** (used with an adverb or a preposition) (*informal*) to go or move somewhere quickly or suddenly: *Hop in! I'll give you a lift to town.* **IDM** **hop it!** (*informal, old-fashioned*) Go away!

hop² /hɒp/ *noun* **1** [C] a short jump by a person on one leg or by a bird or animal with its feet together **2** [C] a tall climbing plant with flowers **3 hops** [*pl.*] the flowers of this plant that are used in making beer

hope¹ ⚡ **A1** /həʊp/ *verb* [I, T] **~ (that) … ; ~ (to do sth); ~ (for sth)** to want sth to happen or be true: *'Is it raining?' 'I hope not. I haven't got a coat with me.'* ◇ *'Are you coming to London with us?' 'I'm not sure yet but I hope so.'* ◇ *I hope that you feel better soon.* ◇ *Hoping to hear from you soon* (= at the end of a letter). ◇ *We are hoping for good weather on Sunday.*

hope² ⚡ **A2** /həʊp/ *noun* **1** [C, U] **~ (of/for sth); ~ of doing sth; ~ (that) …** the feeling of wanting sth to happen and thinking that it will: *What hope is there for the future?* ◇ *There is no hope of finding anybody else alive.* ◇ *David has high hopes of becoming a jockey* (= is very confident about it). ◇ *She never gave up hope that a cure for the disease would be found.* ◇ *I'll do what I can but don't get your hopes up* (= don't expect too much). **2** [*sing.*] a person, a thing or a situation that will help you get what you want: *Please can you help me? You're my last hope.* **IDM** **dash sb's hopes (of sth/doing sth)** → DASH² **in the hope of sth/that …** because you want sth to happen: *I came here in the hope that we could talk privately.* **pin (all) your hopes on sb/sth** → PIN² **a ray of hope** → RAY

hopeful¹ ⚡+ **C1** /'həʊpfl/ *adj.* **1 ~ (about sth); ~ (that) …** believing that sth that you want will happen: *He's very hopeful about the success of the business.* ◇ *The ministers seem hopeful that an agreement will be reached.* **SYN** **optimistic** **2** making you think that sth good will happen: *a hopeful sign* **SYN** **promising**

hopeful² /'həʊpfl/ *noun* [C] a person who wants to succeed at sth: *50 young hopefuls are trying for a place in the England team.*

hopefully ⚡+ **B2** **S** /'həʊpfəli/ *adv.* **1** used to say what you hope will happen: *Hopefully, we'll be finished by six o'clock.* **2** showing hope: *She smiled hopefully at me, waiting for my answer.*

hopeless /ˈhəʊpləs/ adj. **1** giving or feeling no hope that sth/sb will be successful or get better: *It's hopeless. There is nothing we can do.* **2** ~ (at sth) (*especially BrE*) (*informal*) (used about a person) often doing things wrong; very bad at doing sth: *I'm absolutely hopeless at tennis.* ▸ **hopelessly** adv.: *They were hopelessly lost.* ▸ **hopelessness** noun [U]

horde /hɔːd/ noun [C] a very large number of people

horizon ℝ+ **C1** /həˈraɪzn/ noun **1** [sing.] the line where the earth and sky appear to meet: *The ship appeared on/disappeared over the horizon.* **2** horizons [pl.] the limits of your knowledge or experience: *Foreign travel is a good way of expanding your horizons.* **IDM** on the horizon likely to happen soon: *There are further job cuts on the horizon.*

horizontal **W** /ˌhɒrɪˈzɒntl/ adj. (**GEOMETRY**) flat and level; going from side to side, not up and down: *horizontal lines* ⊃ look at **perpendicular** (1), **vertical** ⊃ picture at **line¹** ▸ **horizontally** /-təli/ adv.

horizontal ˈbar noun [C, sing.] (**SPORT**) a bar on two posts that is used by men for doing **GYMNASTIC** exercises

hormone /ˈhɔːməʊn/ noun [C] (**BIOLOGY**) a substance in the body that influences how you grow and develop and how some cells function ▸ **hormonal** /hɔːˈməʊnl/ adj.: *the hormonal changes occurring during pregnancy*

horn ℝ+ **C1** /hɔːn/ noun [C] **1** one of the hard pointed things that some animals have on their heads ⊃ picture at **goat, rhinoceros, sheep** **2** the thing in a car, etc. that gives a loud warning sound: *Don't sound your horn late at night.* **3** (**MUSIC**) one of the group of metal musical instruments that you play by blowing into them: *the French horn* ⊃ picture at **orchestra**

hornet /ˈhɔːnɪt/ noun [C] a black and yellow flying insect that has a very powerful **STING** ❶ A **hornet** is similar to but bigger than a **wasp**.

horoscope /ˈhɒrəskəʊp/ noun [C] a prediction about what is going to happen to a person in the future, based on the position of the stars and planets when they were born: *What does my horoscope for next week say?* **SYN** **star¹** ⊃ look at **astrology, zodiac**

horrendous /həˈrendəs/ adj. (*informal*) very bad or unpleasant ▸ **horrendously** adv.

horrible ℝ **B1** /ˈhɒrəbl/ adj. **1** (*informal*) bad or unpleasant: *This coffee tastes horrible!* ◇ *Don't be so horrible* (= unkind)! ◇ *I've got a horrible feeling that I've forgotten something.* **SYN** **awful** **2** shocking and/ or frightening: *a horrible murder/death/nightmare* **SYN** **horrific** ▸ **horribly** /-bli/ adv.

horrid /ˈhɒrɪd/ adj. (*informal or old-fashioned*) very unpleasant or unkind ◇ *I'm sorry that I was so horrid last night.* **SYN** **horrible**

horrific /həˈrɪfɪk/ adj. **1** extremely bad and shocking or frightening: *a horrific murder/accident/attack* **SYN** **horrible** **2** (*informal*) very bad or unpleasant: *We had a horrific journey — we were stuck in a traffic jam for two hours.* **SYN** **awful** ▸ **horrifically** /-kli/ adv.: *horrifically expensive*

horrify /ˈhɒrɪfaɪ/ verb [T] (**horrifying; horrifies;** pt, pp **horrified**) to make sb feel extremely shocked or frightened: *I was horrified by the conditions they were living in.* ▸ **horrifying** adj.

horror ℝ **B1** /ˈhɒrə(r)/ noun **1** [U, sing.] a feeling of great fear or shock: *They watched in horror as the building collapsed.* **2** [C, usually pl.] something that makes you feel frightened or shocked: *the horrors of war* ◇ *a horror film/story*

horse ℝ **A1** /hɔːs/ noun [C] **1** a large animal that is used for riding on or for pulling or carrying heavy loads ❶ A male horse is a **stallion**, a female horse is a **mare** and a young horse is a **foal**. **2** the horses [pl.] (*informal*) horse racing

horseback riding /ˈhɔːsbæk raɪdɪŋ/ (*AmE*) = **RIDING**

ˌhorse ˈchestnut noun [C] **1** a large tall tree with pink or white flowers, and nuts that grow inside cases that are covered with sharp points **2** (*informal*) the smooth brown nut from this tree **SYN** **conker**

horseman /ˈhɔːsmən/ noun [C] (pl. -**men** /-mən/) a **RIDER** on a horse; a person who can ride horses well: *an experienced horseman*

horsepower /ˈhɔːspaʊə(r)/ noun [C] (pl. **horsepower**) (*abbr.* h.p.) a measurement of the power of an engine: *a 10 horsepower engine*

ˈhorse racing (also **racing**) noun [U] (**SPORT**) the sport in which **JOCKEYS** ride horses in a race to win money

horseshoe /ˈhɔːsʃuː, ˈhɔːsʃuː/ (also **shoe**) noun [C] a piece of metal in the shape of a U that is fixed to the bottom of a horse's foot.

horsewoman /ˈhɔːswʊmən/ noun [C] (pl. -**women** /-wɪmɪn/) a female **RIDER** on a horse; a woman who can ride horses well

horticulture /ˈhɔːtɪkʌltʃə(r)/ noun [U] (**AGRICULTURE**) the study or practice of growing flowers, fruit and vegetables ▸ **horticultural** /ˌhɔːtɪˈkʌltʃərəl/ adj.

hose /həʊz/ (also **hosepipe** /ˈhəʊzpaɪp/) noun [C, U] a long rubber or plastic tube that water can flow through ⊃ picture at **gardening**

hospice /ˈhɒspɪs/ noun [C] (**MEDICINE**) a special hospital where people who are dying are cared for

hospitable /hɒˈspɪtəbl, ˈhɒspɪtəbl/ adj. (used about a person) friendly and kind to visitors **OPP** **inhospitable**

hospital ℝ **A1** /ˈhɒspɪtl/ noun [C] (**MEDICINE**) a place where ill or injured people are given medical treatment: *He was rushed to hospital in an ambulance.* ◇ *to be admitted to/discharged from hospital* ◇ *a psychiatric/mental hospital* ◇ *a hospital bed/ward/appointment* ⊃ note at **doctor¹** **HELP** If a person goes **to hospital** or is **in hospital** (without 'the' in British English), he/she is a patient receiving treatment there: *His mother's in hospital.* ◇ *She cut her hand and had to go to hospital.* **The hospital** refers to one particular hospital, or indicates that the person is only visiting the building temporarily: *He went to the hospital to visit Jana.*

▾ VOCABULARY BUILDING

hospital

If sb has an **accident**, they may need to go to **hospital** (**the hospital** in American English) for medical **treatment**. Dial *999* or *112* (or *911* in the US) and call an **ambulance**. They will be taken first to **A & E** (= the accident and emergency department). If you **cut** yourself very badly, you might need **stitches** (= small lines of thread used to sew your skin together). If your arm, ankle, etc. is **painful** and **swollen**, a doctor might take an **X-ray** to see if it is **broken**. A person who is being treated in a hospital by **doctors** and **nurses** is a **patient**. If people **have an operation/have surgery**, it is performed by a **surgeon** in an **operating theatre**. Patients sleep in a **ward** (= a room shared with other patients). The fixed times during the day when you are allowed to visit sb in hospital are called **visiting hours**.

---

hospitality /ˌhɒspɪˈtæləti/ noun [U] **1** looking after guests and being friendly and welcoming towards them: *Thank you for your kind hospitality.* **2** (**BUSINESS**) food, drink or services that are provided by an organization for guests, customers, etc: *We were* *entertained in the company's hospitality suite.* ◊ *the hospitality industry* (= hotels, restaurants, etc.)

hospitalize (*BrE also* -**ise**) /'hɒspɪtəlaɪz/ *verb* [T, usually passive] (**HEALTH**) to send sb to a hospital for treatment: *Eight people were hospitalized after receiving bullet wounds.*

host ⚆ **B1** /həʊst/ *noun* [C] **1** a person who invites guests to their house, etc. and provides them with food, drink, etc: *I'll be staying with a host family while I study English in the UK.* ➔ look at **hostess** (1) **2** a country, a city or an organization that holds and arranges a special event: *the host nation/country/city* ◊ *The college is playing host to a group of Russian scientists.* **3** (**ARTS AND MEDIA**) a person who introduces a TV or radio show and talks to the guests **4** ~ **of sth** a large number of people or things: *I've got a whole host of things I want to discuss with him.* **5** (**BIOLOGY**) an animal or a plant on which another animal or plant lives and feeds ▸ **host** ⚆ **B2** *verb* [T]: *The city is aiming to host the Olympic Games in ten years' time.*

hostage ⚆+ **C1** /'hɒstɪdʒ/ *noun* [C] a person who is caught and kept prisoner by a person or group. A hostage may be killed or injured if the person or group who is holding them does not get what they are asking for: *The robbers tried to take the staff hostage.* ◊ *The government is negotiating the release of the hostages.* ➔ look at **ransom**

hostel /'hɒstl/ *noun* [C] **1** (**TOURISM**) a place like a cheap hotel where people can stay when they are living away from home: *a youth hostel* ◊ *a student hostel* **2** a building where people who have no home can stay for a short time: (*BrE*) *a hostel for the homeless*

hostess /'həʊstəs, həʊ'stes/ *noun* [C] **1** a woman who invites guests to her house, etc. and provides them with food, drink, etc. ➔ look at **host** (1) **2** (**ARTS AND MEDIA**) a woman who introduces a TV or radio show and talks to the guests

hostile ⚆+ **C1** /'hɒstaɪl/ *adj.* ~ (**to/towards sb/sth**) having very strong feelings against sb/sth: *a hostile crowd* ◊ *They are very hostile to any change.*

hostility ⚆+ **C1** /hɒ'stɪləti/ *noun* **1** [U] ~ (**to/towards sth**) very strong feelings against sb/sth: *She didn't say anything but I could sense her hostility to us.* **SYN** animosity **2** hostilities [pl.] (*formal*) fighting in a war: *Negotiations have led to an end to hostilities.*

hot¹ ⚆ **A1** /hɒt/ *adj.* (**hotter; hottest**) **1** having a high temperature: *Can I open the window? I'm really hot.* ◊ *It was boiling hot on the beach.* ◊ *a hot meal* ◊ *Don't touch the plates — they're red hot!* ➔ look at **humid** ➔ note at **cold¹ 2** (used about food) spicy and causing a burning feeling in your mouth: *hot curry* **SYN** spicy **3** (*informal*) difficult or dangerous to deal with: *The defenders found the Italian strikers too hot to handle.* **4** (*informal*) (only before a noun) likely to be successful: *Brazil are hot favourites to win the competition.* **IDM** in hot pursuit following sb who is moving fast

hot² /hɒt/ *verb* (-tt-) **PHR V** hot up (*BrE, informal*) to become more exciting: *The election campaign has really hotted up in the past few days.*

hot-ˈair balloon = BALLOON

hot dog *noun* [C] a hot SAUSAGE in a soft bread roll

hotel ⚆ **A1** /həʊ'tel/ *noun* [C] (**TOURISM**) a place where you pay to stay when you are on holiday or travelling: *to stay in/at a hotel* ◊ *I've booked a double room at the Grand Hotel.* ◊ *a two-star hotel*

hotelier /həʊ'telɪə(r), həʊ'telɪeɪ/ *noun* [C] (**TOURISM**) a person who owns or manages a hotel

hothouse /'hɒthaʊs/ *noun* [C] a heated glass building where plants are grown ➔ look at **greenhouse**

hotline /'hɒtlaɪn/ *noun* [C] a special phone line to a business or an organization: *To enter the competition, phone our 24-hour hotline.*

hotly /'hɒtli/ *adv.* **1** in an angry or excited way: *They hotly denied the media reports.* **2** closely and with DETERMINATION (= the quality that makes you do something even when it is difficult): *The dog ran off, hotly pursued by its owner.*

hotspot (*also* hot spot) /'hɒtspɒt/ *noun* [C] (*informal*) **1** a place where there is a lot of activity or entertainment: *a tourist hot spot* **2** (**COMPUTING**) an area on a computer screen that you can click on to start an operation such as loading a file

houmous /'huməs, 'huːm-/ = HUMMUS

hound¹ /haʊnd/ *noun* [C] a type of dog that is used for hunting or racing: *a foxhound*

hound² /haʊnd/ *verb* [T] to keep following sb and not leave them alone, especially in order to get sth from them or to ask them questions: *Many famous people complain of being hounded by the press.*

hour ⚆ **A1** /'aʊə(r)/ *noun* **1** [C] (*abbr.* hr) a period of 60 minutes: *He studies for three hours most evenings.* ◊ *The programme lasts about half an hour.* ◊ *I'm going shopping now. I'll be back in about an hour.* ◊ *In two hours' time I'll be having lunch.* ◊ *a four-hour journey* ◊ *Japan is eight hours ahead of the UK.* ◊ *I get paid by the hour.* ◊ *How much do you get paid per/an hour?* ◊ *London is only two hours away.* **2** hours [pl.] the period of time when sb is working or a shop, etc. is open: *Employees are demanding shorter working hours.* ◊ *Office hours are usually from 9 a.m. to 5 p.m.* **3** [C] a period of about an hour when sth particular happens: *I'm going shopping in my lunch hour.* ◊ *The traffic is very bad in the rush hour.* **4** the [sing.] the time when a new hour starts (= one o'clock, two o'clock, etc.): *Buses are on the hour and at 20 past the hour.* **5** hours [pl.] a long time: *He went on speaking for hours and hours.* **IDM** at/till all hours at/until any time: *She stays out till all hours* (= very late). the early hours → EARLY¹

hourly /'aʊəli/ *adj., adv.* **1** done, happening, etc. every hour: *an hourly news bulletin* ◊ *Trains run hourly.* **2** for one hour: *What is your hourly rate of pay?*

house¹ ⚆ **A1** /haʊs/ *noun* (*pl.* houses /'haʊzɪz/)
• **BUILDING 1** [C] a building that is made for people to live in: *We live in a three-bedroom/three-bedroomed house.* ➔ look at **bungalow, cottage, flat¹** (1), **move¹** (3) **2** [C, usually sing.] all the people who live in one house: *Don't shout. You'll wake the whole house up.* **3** [C] a building that is used for a particular purpose: *a warehouse* ◊ *an opera house*
• **COMPANY 4** [C] (in compounds) (**BUSINESS**) a company involved in a particular kind of business: *a fashion/publishing house* ◊ *I work in house* (= in the offices of the company that I work for, not at home).

- RESTAURANT **5** [C] (in compounds) a restaurant, usually that sells one particular type of food: *a curry/ spaghetti house* ◇ *house wine* (= the cheapest wine on a restaurant's menu)
- PARLIAMENT **6** (*also* House) [C] (**POLITICS**) a group of people who meet to make a country's laws: *Legislation requires approval by both houses of parliament.* ⊃ look at **lower house, upper house**
7 the House [sing.] the House of Commons or the House of Lords in the UK; the House of Representatives in the US
- IN THEATRE, ETC. **8** [C, usually sing.] (**ARTS AND MEDIA**) the audience at a theatre or cinema, or the area where they sit: *There was a full house for the play this evening.*
- MUSIC **9** [U] = HOUSE MUSIC
IDM get on/along like a house on fire (*informal*) to immediately become good friends with sb on the house (*informal*) (used about drinks or meals) paid for by the pub, restaurant, etc. that you are visiting: *Your first drink is on the house.* **SYN** free[1]

house² 🔊 **B2** /haʊz/ *verb* [T] **1** to provide sb with a place to live: *The Council must house homeless families.* **2** to be the place where sth is kept or where sth operates from: *Her office is housed in a separate building.*

house ar'rest *noun* [U] (**LAW**) the state of being a prisoner in your own house rather than in a prison: *to be kept/held/placed under house arrest*

houseboat /'haʊsbəʊt/ *noun* [C] a boat on a river, etc. where sb lives and that usually stays in one place

housebound /'haʊsbaʊnd/ *adj.* unable to leave your house because you are old or ill

household 🔊 **B2** /'haʊshəʊld/ *noun* [C] (**SOCIAL STUDIES**) all the people who live in one house and the work, money, organization, etc. that is needed to look after them: *household expenses* ◇ *Most households now own at least one car.* ⊃ picture at **income**

householder /'haʊshəʊldə(r)/ *noun* [C] (*formal*) (**SOCIAL STUDIES**) a person who rents or owns the house that they live in

household 'name *noun* [C] a person, thing or name that has become very well known: *She became a household name in the 1980s.*

'house husband *noun* [C] a man who stays at home to cook, clean, take care of the children, etc. while his wife or partner goes out to work ⊃ look at **housewife**

housekeeper /'haʊskiːpə(r)/ *noun* [C] **1** a person, usually a woman, whose job is to manage the shopping, cooking, cleaning, etc. in a house or an institution **2** (**TOURISM**) a person whose job is to manage the cleaning of rooms in a hotel

housekeeping /'haʊskiːpɪŋ/ *noun* [U] **1** the work involved in taking care of a house, especially shopping and managing money **2** (**TOURISM**) the department in a hotel, a hospital, an office building, etc. that is responsible for cleaning the rooms, etc: *Call housekeeping and ask them to bring us some clean towels.* **3** (*also* 'housekeeping money *especially in BrE*) the money used to buy food, cleaning materials and other things needed for taking care of a house

'house music (*also* house /haʊs/) *noun* [U] (**MUSIC**) a type of popular dance music with a fast beat, played on electronic instruments

the ˌHouse of 'Commons *noun* [sing. + sing./pl. verb] (*also* the Commons [pl.]) (**POLITICS**) (in the UK and Canada) the part of Parliament whose members are elected by the people of the country ⊃ note at **parliament**

'house officer *noun* [C] (**MEDICINE**) (in the UK) a doctor who has finished medical school and who is working at a hospital to get further practical experience ⊃ look at **intern**[1]

the ˌHouse of 'Lords (*also* the Lords /ðə 'lɔːdz/) *noun* [sing. + sing./pl. verb] (**POLITICS**) (in the UK) the part of Parliament whose members are not elected by the people of the country ⊃ note at **parliament**

the ˌHouse of ˌRepreˈsentatives *noun* [sing. + sing./pl. verb] (**POLITICS**) the group of people who are elected to make new laws in the US ⊃ look at **congress** (2), **senate**

ˌhouse-to-'house *adj.* [only before noun] going to each house: *The police are making house-to-house enquiries.*

'house-warming *noun* [C] a party that you have when you have just moved into a new home

housewife /'haʊswaɪf/ *noun* [C] (*pl.* housewives /-waɪvz/) a woman who does not have a job outside the home and who spends her time cleaning the house, cooking, looking after her family, etc. ⊃ look at **house husband**

housework /'haʊswɜːk/ *noun* [U] the work that is needed to take care of a home and family, for example cleaning and cooking

housing 🔊 **B2** /'haʊzɪŋ/ *noun* [U] houses, flats, etc. for people to live in: *a housing shortage* ◇ *affordable housing*

'housing association *noun* [C] (**SOCIAL STUDIES**) (in the UK) an organization that owns houses, flats, etc. and helps people to rent or buy them at a low price

'housing estate *noun* [C] (*BrE*) (**SOCIAL STUDIES**) an area where there are a large number of similar houses that were built at the same time

hovel /'hɒvl/ *noun* [C] a house or room that is not suitable to live in because it is dirty or in very bad condition

hover /'hɒvə(r)/ *verb* [I] **1** (used about a bird, helicopter, etc.) to stay in the air in one place **2** (used about a person) to wait near sb/sth: *He hovered nervously outside the office.*

hovercraft /'hɒvəkrɑːft/ *noun* [C] (*pl.* hovercraft) a vehicle that can move over land or water, held up by air being forced downwards

how 🔊 **A1** /haʊ/ *adv.* **1** (often used in questions) in what way: *How do you spell your name?* ◇ *Can you show me how to use this machine?* ◇ *I can't remember how to get there.* **2** used when you are asking about sb's health or feelings: *'How is your mother?' 'She's much better, thank you.'* ◇ *How are you feeling today?* ◇ *How do you feel about your son joining the army?* ◇ *Hey, how are you doing?* **3** used when you are asking about sb's opinion of a thing or a situation: *How was the weather?* ◇ *How is your meal?* ◇ *How did the interview go?* **4** used in questions when you are asking about the degree, amount, age, etc. of sb/sth: *How old are you?* ◇ *How much is that?* **5** used for expressing surprise, pleasure, etc: *She's gone. How strange!* ◇ *I can't believe how expensive it is!*
IDM how/what about … ? → ABOUT² how come? → COME how do you do? (*formal*) used when meeting sb for the first time

however 🔊 **A1** 🔊 /haʊ'evə(r)/ *adv.* **1** (*formal*) (used for adding a comment to what you have just said) although sth is true: *Sales are poor this month. There may, however, be an increase before Christmas.* **2** how ever (used in questions for expressing surprise) in what way; how: *How ever did you manage to find me here?* **3** in whatever way: *However I sat I couldn't get*

comfortable. ◇ *You can dress however you like.*
4 (before an adjective or adverb) to whatever degree: *He won't wear a hat however cold it is.* ◇ *You can't catch her however fast you run.*

howl /haʊl/ *verb* [I] to make a long loud sound: *I couldn't sleep because there was a dog howling all night.* ◇ *Everyone howled with laughter when I fell off my chair.* ◇ *The child howled in pain.* ▶ **howl** *noun* [C]

h.p. *abbr.* **1** (in writing) = HORSEPOWER **2** (*also* HP /ˌeɪtʃ ˈpiː/) (*BrE*) = HIRE PURCHASE

HQ /ˌeɪtʃ ˈkjuː/ *abbr.* = HEADQUARTERS

HR /ˌeɪtʃ ˈɑː(r)/ *abbr.* = HUMAN RESOURCES

hr *abbr.* (in writing) (*pl.* hrs, hr) = HOUR (1): *3 hrs 15 min.*

HRH /ˌeɪtʃ ɑːr ˈeɪtʃ/ *abbr.* **His/Her Royal Highness** (a title of respect when talking about a member of the royal family who is not the queen or king)

HTML /ˌeɪtʃ tiː em ˈel/ *abbr.* (**COMPUTING**) **Hypertext Markup Language** (a system used to mark text for World Wide Web pages in order to obtain colours, style, pictures, etc.)

HTTP /ˌeɪtʃ tiː tiː ˈpiː/ (*also* http) *abbr.* (**COMPUTING**) the set of rules that control the way data is sent and received over the internet (the abbreviation for 'Hypertext Transfer Protocol')

hub /hʌb/ *noun* **1** [usually sing.] **the ~ (of sth)** the central and most important part of a place or an activity: *the commercial hub of the city* **2** [C] the central part of a wheel

hubbub /ˈhʌbʌb/ *noun* [sing., U] **1** the noise made by a lot of people talking at the same time: *I couldn't hear the announcement over the hubbub.* **2** a situation in which there is a lot of noise, excitement and activity

hubcap /ˈhʌbkæp/ *noun* [C] a round metal cover that fits over the HUB of a vehicle's wheel

hubris /ˈhjuːbrɪs/ *noun* [U] (**LITERATURE**) the fact of sb being too proud. A character with this quality usually dies or fails because they ignore warnings.

huddle¹ /ˈhʌdl/ *verb* [I] (often used with an adverb or a preposition) **1** to get close to other people because you are cold or frightened: *The campers huddled together around the fire.* **2** to make your body as small as possible because you are cold or frightened: *She huddled up in her sleeping bag and tried to get some sleep.* ▶ **huddled** *adj.*: *We found the children lying huddled together on the ground.*

huddle² /ˈhʌdl/ *noun* [C] a small group of people or things that are close together: *They all stood **in a huddle**, laughing and chatting.*

hue /hjuː/ *noun* [C] (*formal*) **1** a colour; a particular shade of a colour **2** a type of belief or opinion
IDM **hue and cry** strong public protest about sth

huff /hʌf/ *noun*
IDM **in a huff** (*informal*) in a bad mood because sb has annoyed or upset you: *Did you see Sam **go off in a huff** when he wasn't chosen for the team?*

hug /hʌg/ *verb* [T, I] (-gg-) **1** to put your arms around sb, especially to show that you love them: *They hugged each other.* ◇ *They put their arms around each other and hugged.* **2** to hold sth close to your body: *She hugged the parcel to her chest as she ran.* **3** (used about a ship, car, road, etc.) to stay close to sth: *to hug the coast* ▶ **hug** *noun* [C]: *Noel's crying—I'll go and **give him a hug**.*

huge 🔒A2 Ⓢ /hjuːdʒ/ *adj.* very big in size or amount: *a huge amount/quantity/sum/number* ◇ *a huge building* ◇ *The film was a huge success.* **SYN** **enormous**
▶ **hugely** *adv.*: *hugely successful/popular/expensive*

huh /hʌ/ *exclamation* (*informal*) used for expressing anger, surprise, etc. or for asking a question: *They've gone away, huh? They didn't tell me.* ◇ *Huh! Is that all you've done?*

hulk /hʌlk/ *noun* [C] the main part of an old vehicle or large structure that is no longer used

hull /hʌl/ *noun* [C] the main part of a ship

hullabaloo /ˌhʌləbəˈluː/ *noun* [sing.] (*informal*) a lot of loud noise, for example made by people shouting

hum /hʌm/ *verb* (-mm-) **1** [I] to make a continuous low noise: *The machine began to hum when I switched it on.* **2** [I, T] (**MUSIC**) to sing with your lips closed: *You can hum the tune if you don't know the words.* ▶ **hum** *noun* [sing.]: *the hum of machinery/distant traffic*

human¹ 🔒A2 Ⓞ /ˈhjuːmən/ *adj.* **1** [only before noun] connected with people, not with animals, machines or gods; typical of people: *the human body* **2** showing the typical weaknesses and hopes that people have, which means that other people should not criticize the person too much: *The disaster was caused by **human error**.* ◇ *It's only human to want the best for your children.* ▶ **humanly** *adv.*: *They did all that was humanly possible to rescue him* (= everything that a human being could possibly do).

human² 🔒A2 Ⓢ /ˈhjuːmən/ (*also* ˌhuman ˈbeing) *noun* [C] a person: *Dogs can hear much better than humans.*

humane /hjuːˈmeɪn/ *adj.* being kind or understanding, especially to a person or an animal that is suffering: *Animals must be kept in humane conditions.*
OPP **inhumane** ▶ **humanely** *adv.*

ˌhuman geˈography *noun* [U] (**GEOGRAPHY**) the scientific study of how human activity affects or is affected by the surface of the earth

humanism /ˈhjuːmənɪzəm/ *noun* [U] a system of thought that considers that solving human problems with the help of reason is more important than religious beliefs. It emphasizes the fact that the basic nature of humans is good. ▶ **humanistic** /ˌhjuːməˈnɪstɪk/ *adj.*: *humanistic ideals*

humanitarian 🔒+ **C1** /hjuːˌmænɪˈteəriən/ *adj.* (**SOCIAL STUDIES**) **1** concerned with trying to make people's lives better and reduce suffering: *Many countries have sent humanitarian aid to the earthquake victims.* **2** describing an event or a situation in which a lot of people are suffering and need help: *a humanitarian crisis*

humanity 🔒+ **C1** /hjuːˈmænəti/ *noun* **1** [U] all the people in the world, thought of as a group: *crimes against humanity* **SYN** **human race** **2** [U] the quality of being kind and understanding: *The prisoners were treated with humanity.* **OPP** **inhumanity** **3** (the) **humanities** [pl.] (**EDUCATION**) the subjects of study that are connected with the way people think and behave, for example literature, language, history and PHILOSOPHY

ˌhuman ˈnature *noun* [U] natural feelings, behaviour, etc. that all people have in common

the ˌhuman ˈrace *noun* [sing.] all the people in the world, thought of as a group: *Pollution is a threat to the survival of the human race.* **SYN** **humanity**

ˌhuman reˈsources *noun* [U + sing./pl. verb] (*abbr.* HR) (**BUSINESS**) the department in a company that deals with employing and training people: *the human resources director* **SYN** **personnel**

ˌhuman ˈright *noun* [C, usually pl.] (**SOCIAL STUDIES**) one of the basic rights that all people should have, for example the right to say what you think, to travel freely, etc.

humble¹ 🔒+ **C1** /ˈhʌmbl/ *adj.* (humbler /-blə(r)/; humblest /-blɪst/) **1** not thinking that you are better or more important than other people; not proud: *He* became very rich and famous but he always remained a very humble man. ⊃ look at **modest** (1) ⊃ noun **humility 2** not special or important: *She comes from a humble background.* ▶ humbly /-bli/ *adv.*: *He apologized very humbly for his behaviour.*

humble² /ˈhʌmbl/ *verb* [T] to make sb feel that they are not as good or important as they thought

humerus /ˈhjuːmərəs/ *noun* [C] (**ANATOMY**) the large bone in the top part of the arm between the shoulder and the ELBOW ⊃ picture at **body**

humid /ˈhjuːmɪd/ *adj.* (used about the air or climate) warm and feeling slightly wet: *Hong Kong is hot and humid in summer.* ▶ humidity /hjuːˈmɪdəti/ *noun* [U]

humiliate /hjuːˈmɪlieɪt/ *verb* [T] to make sb feel ashamed or stupid: *I felt humiliated when the teacher laughed at my work.* ▶ humiliating *adj.*: *a humiliating defeat* ▶ humiliation /hjuːˌmɪliˈeɪʃn/ *noun* [U, C]

humility /hjuːˈmɪləti/ *noun* [U] the quality of not thinking that you are better than other people ⊃ adjective **humble**

hummus (*also* **houmous**) /ˈhʊməs, ˈhuːm-/ *noun* [U] a type of food, originally from the Middle East, that is a soft mixture of CHICKPEAS, SESAME seeds, oil, lemon juice and GARLIC

humorous ？ **B2** /ˈhjuːmərəs/ *adj.* funny, showing a sense of humour: *He gave a humorous account of their trip to Spain.* ▶ humorously *adv.*

humour¹ ？ **B2** (*BrE*) (*AmE* **humor**) /ˈhjuːmə(r)/ *noun* [U] **1** the quality in sth that makes it funny; the ability to laugh at things that are funny: *It is sometimes hard to understand the humour* (= the jokes) *of another country.* ◇ *Rose has a good **sense of humour**.* **2** -humoured (*BrE*) (*AmE* -humored) (in adjectives) having or showing a particular mood: *good-humoured*

humour² (*BrE*) (*AmE* **humor**) /ˈhjuːmə(r)/ *verb* [T] to keep sb happy by doing what they want

humourless (*BrE*) (*AmE* **humorless**) /ˈhjuːmələs/ *adj.* having no sense of fun

hump /hʌmp/ *noun* [C] a large curved mass that sticks out above the surface of sth, for example on the back of a CAMEL (= an animal that lives in the desert)

humus /ˈhjuːməs/ *noun* [U] (**AGRICULTURE**) a substance made from dead leaves and plants that helps plants grow

hunch¹ /hʌntʃ/ *noun* [C] (*informal*) a thought or an idea that is based on a feeling rather than on facts or information: *I'm not sure, but I've got a hunch that she's got a new job.*

hunch² /hʌntʃ/ *verb* [I, T] to bend your back and shoulders forward into a round shape: *I found Ken hunched over his desk, writing.*

hunchback /ˈhʌntʃbæk/ *noun* [C] (*old-fashioned*) a person with a back that has a round LUMP on it. ❶ This word is now considered offensive.

hundred ？ **A1** /ˈhʌndrəd/ *number* **1** (*pl.* hundred) 100: *two hundred* ◇ *There were a/one hundred people in the room.* ◇ *She's a hundred today.* **HELP** When you say a number, for example 1420, put **and** after the word **hundred**: *one thousand four hundred **and** twenty.* Note that you use **hundred** without 's' when talking about more than one hundred: *two hundred people* **2** a hundred, hundreds (of) (*informal*) a lot; a large amount: *I've got hundreds of things to do today.* ❶ For more information about numbers, look at the **Reference Section** of this dictionary. ▶ hundredth /ˈhʌndrədθ, -drətθ/ *ordinal number, noun* [C]

hundredweight /ˈhʌndrədweɪt/ *noun* [C] (*pl.* hundredweight) (*abbr.* cwt) a unit for measuring weight equal to 112 pounds in the UK and 100 pounds

in the US. There are 20 hundredweight in a TON. ❶ For more information about weights, look at the **Reference Section** of this dictionary.

hung /hʌŋ/ past tense, past participle of **hang¹**

hunger¹ ？+ **B2** /ˈhʌŋɡə(r)/ *noun* **1** [U] (**SOCIAL STUDIES**) the state of not having enough food to eat, especially when this causes illness or death: *In some parts of the world many people die of hunger each year.* **SYN** starvation ⊃ look at **thirst** (1) **2** [U] the feeling caused by a need to eat: *Hunger is one reason why babies cry.* **3** [sing.] ~ (for sth) (*formal*) a strong desire for sth: *a hunger for knowledge/fame/success*

hunger² /ˈhʌŋɡə(r)/ *verb* (*formal*) **PHR V** hunger for/after sth to have a strong desire for sth

hunger strike *noun* [C, U] a time when sb (especially a prisoner) refuses to eat because they are protesting about sth: *to be/go **on hunger strike***

hungry ？ **A1** /ˈhʌŋɡri/ *adj.* (hungrier; hungriest) **1** wanting to eat: *I'm hungry. Let's eat soon.* ◇ *There were hungry children begging for food in the streets.* ⊃ look at **thirsty 2 ~for sth** wanting sth very much: *I'm hungry for some excitement tonight.* ▶ hungrily /-ɡrəli/ *adv.* **IDM** go hungry to not have any food

hunk /hʌŋk/ *noun* [C] **1** a large piece of sth: *a hunk of bread/cheese/meat* **2** (*informal*) a man who is big, strong and attractive

hunt¹ ？ **B1** /hʌnt/ *verb* [I, T] **1** to go after wild animals, etc. in order to catch or kill them either for sport or for food: *Owls hunt at night.* ◇ *Are tigers still being hunted in India?* **2** ~ (for) (sb/sth) to try to find sb/sth: *The police are still hunting the murderer.*

hunt² ？ **B2** /hʌnt/ *noun* [C] **1** the act of hunting wild animals, etc: *a fox hunt* **2** [usually sing.] ~ (for sb/sth) the act of looking for sb/sth that is difficult to find: *The police have launched a hunt for the missing child.*

hunter /ˈhʌntə(r)/ *noun* [C] a person that hunts wild animals for food or sport; an animal that hunts its food

hunter-gatherer /ˌhʌntə ˈɡæðərə(r)/ *noun* [C] (**SOCIAL STUDIES**) a member of a group of people who do not live in one place but move around and live by hunting, fishing and gathering plants

hunting ？ **B2** /ˈhʌntɪŋ/ *noun* [U] the act of following and killing wild animals or birds as a sport or for food ⊃ look at **shoot¹** (3)

hurdle¹ /ˈhɜːdl/ *noun* **1** [C] (**SPORT**) a type of light fence that a person or a horse jumps over in a race: *to clear a hurdle* (= to jump over it successfully) **2** hurdles [pl.] (**SPORT**) a race in which runners or horses have to jump over hurdles: *the 200 metres hurdles* **3** [C] a problem or difficulty that you must solve or deal with before you can achieve sth

hurdle² /ˈhɜːdl/ *verb* [I, T] ~ (over sth) to jump over sth while you are running

hurl /hɜːl/ *verb* [T] (used with an adverb or a preposition) to throw sth with great force

hurray /həˈreɪ/ = HOORAY

hurricane ？ **B1** /ˈhʌrɪkən/ *noun* [C] (**GEOGRAPHY**) a violent storm with very strong winds ⊃ note at **disaster, storm¹**

hurried /ˈhʌrid/ *adj.* done (too) quickly: *a hurried meal* ▶ hurriedly /-ɪdli/ *adv.*

hurry¹ ⚡ **B1** /'hʌri/ *noun* [U] the need or wish to do sth quickly: *In my hurry to leave, I forgot my passport.* ◇ *Take your time. There's no hurry.* **SYN** rush² **IDM** in a hurry quickly: *She got up late and left in a hurry.* in a hurry (to do sth) wanting to do sth soon; impatient: *They are in a hurry to get the job done before the winter.* in no hurry (to do sth) | not in any hurry (to do sth) **1** not needing or wishing to do sth quickly: *We weren't in any hurry so we stopped to admire the view.* **2** not wanting to do sth: *I am in no hurry to repeat that experience.*

hurry² ⚡ **B1** /'hʌri/ *verb* (hurrying; hurries; *pt, pp* hurried) **1** [I] to move or do sth quickly because there is not much time: *Don't hurry. There's plenty of time.* ◇ *They hurried back home after school.* ◇ *Several people hurried to help.* **2** [T] ~ sb (into sth/doing sth) to cause sb/sth to do sth, or sth to happen more quickly: *Don't hurry me. I'm going as fast as I can.* ◇ *He was hurried into a decision.* **3** [T, usually passive] to do sth too quickly **SYN** rush¹ **PHRV** hurry up (with sth) (*informal*) to move or do sth more quickly: *Hurry up or we'll miss the train.*

hurt¹ ⚡ **A2** /hɜːt/ *verb* (*pt, pp* hurt) **1** [T, I] (HEALTH) to cause sb/yourself physical pain or injury: *Did he hurt himself?* ◇ *I fell and hurt my arm.* ◇ *No one was seriously hurt in the accident.* ◇ *These shoes hurt; they're too tight.* ⊃ note at **injure 2** [I] (HEALTH) to feel painful: *My leg hurts.* ◇ **It hurts** when I lift my leg. ◇ *Where exactly does it hurt?* **3** [T, I] to make sb unhappy; to upset sb: *His unkind remarks hurt her deeply.* ◇ *I didn't want to **hurt** his feelings.* ◇ *It always hurts to lose, especially in the final.* **IDM** it won't/wouldn't hurt (sb/sth) (to do sth) (*informal*) used to say that sb should do sth: *It wouldn't hurt you to help with the housework occasionally.*

hurt² ⚡ **A2** /hɜːt/ *adj.* **1** injured physically: *None of the passengers were **badly/seriously hurt**.* **2** upset and offended by sth that sb has said or done: *She was **deeply hurt** that she had not been invited to the party.*

hurt³ ⚡ **B2** /hɜːt/ *noun* [U] a feeling of unhappiness because sb has been unkind or unfair to you

hurtful /'hɜːtfl/ *adj.* ~ (to sb) making sb feel upset and offended: *What he said was deeply hurtful to me.* **SYN** unkind

hurtle /'hɜːtl/ *verb* [I] (used with an adverb or a preposition) to move with great speed, perhaps causing danger: *Rocks hurtled down the mountainside.*

husband ⚡ **A1** /'hʌzbənd/ *noun* [C] a man that sb is married to: *Her ex-husband sees the children once a month.*

husbandry /'hʌzbəndri/ *noun* [U] (AGRICULTURE) farming; looking after animals and food crops

hush¹ /hʌʃ/ *verb* [I] used to tell sb to be quiet, to stop talking or crying: *Hush now and try to sleep.* **PHRV** hush sth up to hide information to stop people knowing about sth; to keep sth secret

hush² /hʌʃ/ *noun* [sing., U] no noise or sound at all

hush-'hush *adj.* (*informal*) very secret

husk /hʌsk/ *noun* [C] (BIOLOGY) the dry outside layer of nuts, fruits and seeds, especially of grain: *Brown rice has not had the husks removed.*

husky¹ /'hʌski/ *adj.* (huskier; huskiest) (used about a person or their voice) sounding rough and quiet

husky² /'hʌski/ *noun* [C] (*pl.* -ies) a strong dog with thick fur that is used in teams for pulling heavy loads over snow

hustle /'hʌsl/ *verb* [T] (used with an adverb or a preposition) to push or move sb in a way that is not gentle

hut /hʌt/ *noun* [C] a small simple building with one room: *a wooden/mud hut*

hutch /hʌtʃ/ *noun* [C] a wooden box with a front made of wire, that is used for keeping RABBITS or other small animals in

hyaena /haɪˈiːnə/ = HYENA

hybrid /'haɪbrɪd/ *noun* [C] **1** (BIOLOGY) an animal or a plant that has parents of two different species: *A mule is a hybrid of a male donkey and a female horse.* **2** ~ (between/of A and B) something that is the product of mixing two or more different things: *The music was a hybrid of Western pop and traditional folk song.* **SYN** mixture **3** a vehicle that uses two different types of power, such as petrol and electricity ▶ hybrid *adj.*: *a hybrid flower*

hydrant /'haɪdrənt/ *noun* [C] a pipe in a street from which water can be taken for stopping fires, cleaning the streets, etc.

hydrate /haɪˈdreɪt/ *verb* [T] (SCIENCE) to make sth/sb take in water ▶ hydration /-'dreɪʃn/ *noun* [U] ⊃ look at **dehydrate**

hydraulic jack

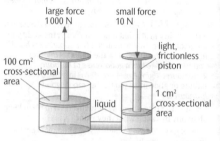

large force 1 000 N   small force 10 N

light, frictionless piston

100 cm² cross-sectional area

liquid

1 cm² cross-sectional area

hydraulic /haɪˈdrɒlɪk/ *adj.* (ENGINEERING) operated by water or another liquid moving through pipes, etc. under pressure: *hydraulic brakes* ◇ *a hydraulic jack* (= a device for lifting heavy objects)

hydraulics /haɪˈdrɒlɪks/ *noun* (ENGINEERING) **1** [pl.] machines that work by the use of liquid moving under pressure **2** [U] the science of the use of liquids moving under pressure

hydrocarbon /ˌhaɪdrəˈkɑːbən/ *noun* [C] (CHEMISTRY, ENVIRONMENT) a combination of HYDROGEN (= a very light gas) and CARBON (= a substance that is found in all living things). Hydrocarbons are found in petrol, coal and natural gas.

hydrochloric acid /ˌhaɪdrəˌklɒrɪk ˈæsɪd/ *noun* [U] (*symb.* HCl) (CHEMISTRY) an ACID containing HYDROGEN and CHLORINE

hydrocortisone /ˌhaɪdrəˈkɔːtɪzəʊn/ (*also* cortisol) *noun* [U] (MEDICINE) a HORMONE produced in the body that is used in drugs to help with diseases of the skin and muscles

hydroelectric /ˌhaɪdrəʊɪˈlektrɪk/ *adj.* (ENVIRONMENT, PHYSICS) using the power of water to produce electricity; produced by the power of water: *a hydroelectric dam* ◇ *hydroelectric power* ▶ hydroelectricity /ˌhaɪdrəʊɪlekˈtrɪsəti/ *noun* [U]

hydrofoil /'haɪdrəfɔɪl/ *noun* [C] a boat that rises above the surface of the water when it is travelling fast

hydrogen ⚡+ **C1** /'haɪdrədʒən/ *noun* [U] (*symb.* H) (CHEMISTRY) a chemical element. Hydrogen is a gas that is the lightest of all the elements. It combines with OXYGEN to form water. ❶ For more information on

ˈhydrogen bomb (*also* H-bomb) *noun* [C] (**PHYSICS**) a very powerful nuclear bomb

ˌhydrogen peˈroxide = PEROXIDE

hydrology /haɪˈdrɒlədʒi/ *noun* [U] (**GEOGRAPHY**, **SCIENCE**) the scientific study of the earth's water, especially its movement in relation to land

hydrolysis /haɪˈdrɒlɪsɪs/ *noun* [U] (**CHEMISTRY**) a chemical reaction with water that causes a COMPOUND to separate into its parts

hydroplane /ˈhaɪdrəpleɪn/ *noun* [C] **1** a light boat with an engine and a flat bottom, designed to travel fast over the surface of water **2** (*AmE*) = SEAPLANE

hydroponics /ˌhaɪdrəˈpɒnɪks/ *noun* [U] (**AGRICULTURE**) the process of growing plants in water or sand rather than in soil ⊃ look at **aeroponics**

hydrosphere /ˈhaɪdrəʊsfɪə(r)/ *noun* [C, usually sing.] (**GEOGRAPHY**) all of the water on or over the earth's surface

hydroxide /haɪˈdrɒksaɪd/ *noun* [C] (**CHEMISTRY**) a chemical COMPOUND consisting of a metal and a combination of OXYGEN (= a very light gas) and HYDROGEN (= a substance that is found in all living things)

hyena (*also* hyaena) /haɪˈiːnə/ *noun* [C] a wild animal from Africa or Asia that is like a dog and has a cry like a human laugh

hygiene /ˈhaɪdʒiːn/ *noun* [U] (**HEALTH**) (the rules of) keeping yourself and things around you clean, in order to prevent disease: *High standards of hygiene are essential when you are preparing food.* ◇ *personal hygiene*

hygienic /haɪˈdʒiːnɪk/ *adj.* (**HEALTH**) clean, without the bacteria that cause disease: *hygienic conditions* OPP **unhygienic** ▶ hygienically /-kli/ *adv.*

hymn /hɪm/ *noun* [C] (**MUSIC**, **RELIGION**) a religious song that Christians sing together in church, etc.

hyp- /haɪp/ → HYPO-

hype¹ /haɪp/ *noun* [U] (**ARTS AND MEDIA**) advertisements that tell you how good and important a new product, film, etc. is: *Don't believe all the hype — the book is rubbish!*

hype² /haɪp/ *verb* [T] ~ **sth (up)** to advertise something a lot and make its good qualities seem better than they actually are, in order to get a lot of public attention for it

hyper- /haɪpə(r)/ *prefix* (in adjectives and nouns) more than normal; too much: *hypercritical* ◇ *hypersensitive* ⊃ look at **hypo-**

hyperactive /ˌhaɪpərˈæktɪv/ *adj.* (used especially about children and their behaviour) too active and only able to keep quiet and still for short periods ▶ hyperactivity /ˌhaɪpərækˈtɪvəti/ *noun* [U]

hyperbola /haɪˈpɜːbələ/ *noun* [C] (**GEOMETRY**) a SYMMETRICAL open curve

hyperbole /haɪˈpɜːbəli/ *noun* [U, C, usually sing.] (**LANGUAGE**) a way of speaking or writing that makes sth sound better, more exciting, dangerous, etc. than it really is: *His latest movie is accompanied by the usual hyperbole.* SYN **exaggeration**

hyperlink /ˈhaɪpəlɪŋk/ *noun* [C] (**COMPUTING**) a place in an electronic document that is connected to another electronic document, or to another part of the same document: *Click on the hyperlink.*

hypermarket /ˈhaɪpəmɑːkɪt/ *noun* [C] (*BrE*) (**BUSINESS**) a very large shop outside a town that sells a wide variety of goods

hyperspace /ˈhaɪpəspeɪs/ *noun* [U] space that consists of more than three DIMENSIONS

hypertension /ˌhaɪpəˈtenʃn/ *noun* [U] (**HEALTH**) blood pressure that is higher than is normal

hypertext /ˈhaɪpətekst/ *noun* [U] (**COMPUTING**) text stored in a computer system that contains links that allow the user to move from one piece of text or document to another: *a hypertext link on the internet* ⊃ look at **HTML**

hyphen /ˈhaɪfn/ *noun* [C] (**LANGUAGE**) the mark (-) used for joining two words together (for example *left-handed*, *red-hot*) or to show that a word has been divided and continues on the next line ⊃ look at **dash**¹ (3)

hyphenate /ˈhaɪfəneɪt/ *verb* [T] (**LANGUAGE**) to join two words or two parts of a word together with a HYPHEN: *Is 'girlfriend' hyphenated or one word?* ▶ hyphenation /ˌhaɪfəˈneɪʃn/ *noun* [U]

hypnosis /hɪpˈnəʊsɪs/ *noun* [U] (**PSYCHOLOGY**) an unconscious state where sb's mind and actions can be controlled by another person; the practice of putting sb in this state: *She was questioned under hypnosis.*

hypnotherapy /ˌhɪpnəʊˈθerəpi/ *noun* [U] (**PSYCHOLOGY**) a kind of treatment that uses HYPNOSIS to help with physical or emotional problems: *Hypnotherapy could be the answer if you want to quit smoking.* ▶ hypnotherapist /-pɪst/ *noun* [C]

hypnotize (*BrE also* -ise) /ˈhɪpnətaɪz/ *verb* [T] (**PSYCHOLOGY**) to put sb into an unconscious state where the person's mind and actions can be controlled ▶ hypnotic /hɪpˈnɒtɪk/ *adj.* ▶ hypnotism /ˈhɪpnətɪzəm/ *noun* [U] ▶ hypnotist /-tɪst/ *noun* [C]

hypo- /haɪpəʊ, haɪpə, haɪˈpɒ/ (*also* hyp-) *prefix* (in adjectives and nouns) under; below normal: *hypodermic* ◇ *hypothermia* ⊃ look at **hyper-**

hypochondria /ˌhaɪpəˈkɒndriə/ *noun* [U] (**PSYCHOLOGY**) a mental condition in which sb believes that they are ill, even when there is nothing wrong

hypochondriac /ˌhaɪpəˈkɒndriæk/ *noun* [C] (**PSYCHOLOGY**) a person who is always worried about their health and believes they are ill, even when there is nothing wrong

hypocrisy /hɪˈpɒkrəsi/ *noun* [U] **1** behaviour in which sb pretends to have moral standards or opinions that they do not really have **2** behaviour in which sb does not act according to the moral standards that they claim to have

hypocrite /ˈhɪpəkrɪt/ *noun* [C] a person who pretends to have moral standards or opinions that they do not really have. Hypocrites say one thing and do another: *What a hypocrite! She says she's against the hunting of animals but she's wearing a fur coat.* ▶ hypocritical /ˌhɪpəˈkrɪtɪkl/ *adj.* ▶ hypocritically /-kli/ *adv.*

hypodermic /ˌhaɪpəˈdɜːmɪk/ (*also* ˌhypodermic syˈringe) *noun* [C] (**MEDICINE**) a medical instrument with a long hollow needle that is used for putting drugs, etc. into the body ▶ hypodermic *adj.*

hypotenuse /haɪˈpɒtənjuːz/ *noun* [C] (**GEOMETRY**) the side opposite the RIGHT ANGLE of a RIGHT-ANGLED TRIANGLE (= a shape with three sides and one angle of 90°)

hypothalamus /ˌhaɪpəˈθæləməs/ *noun* [C] (*pl.* hypothalami /-maɪ/) (**ANATOMY**) the part of the brain that controls body temperature, HUNGER, THIRST and other functions in the body ⊃ picture at **brain**

hypothermia /ˌhaɪpəˈθɜːmiə/ *noun* [U] (**HEALTH**) a medical condition in which the body temperature is much lower than normal

hypothesis 🔊+ **B2** ⊙ /haɪˈpɒθəsɪs/ *noun* [C] (*pl.* **hypotheses** /-θəsiːz/) (**SCIENCE**) an idea that is suggested as the possible explanation for sth but has not yet been found to be true or correct

hypothesize ⓦ (*BrE also* **-ise**) /haɪˈpɒθəsaɪz/ *verb* [I, T] (*formal*) to suggest a way of explaining sth when you do not definitely know about it; to form a HYPOTHESIS

hypothetical ⓦ /ˌhaɪpəˈθetɪkl/ *adj.* based on situations that have not yet happened, not on facts: *That's a hypothetical question because we don't know what the situation will be next year.* ▶ **hypothetically** /-kli/ *adv.*

hypoxia /haɪˈpɒksiə/ *noun* [U] (**HEALTH**) a condition in which not enough OXYGEN reaches the body's TISSUES (= groups of cells that form the different parts of the body)

hysteria /hɪˈstɪəriə/ *noun* [U] (**PSYCHOLOGY**) a state in which a person or a group of people cannot control their emotions, for example cannot stop laughing, crying, shouting, etc: *mass hysteria*

hysterical /hɪˈsterɪkl/ *adj.* **1** very excited and unable to control your emotions: *hysterical laughter* ◇ *She was hysterical with grief.* **2** (*informal*) very funny ▶ **hysterically** /-kli/ *adv.*

hysterics /hɪˈsterɪks/ *noun* [pl.] **1** an expression of extreme fear, excitement or anger that makes sb lose control of their emotions: *She went into hysterics when they told her the news.* ◇ (*informal*) *My father would have hysterics* (= be very angry) *if he knew I was with you.* **2** (*informal*) laughter that you cannot control: *The comedian had the audience in hysterics.*

Hz *abbr.* (in writing) (*pl.* **Hz**) = HERTZ

I i

I¹ /aɪ/ (*also* **i**) *noun* [C, U] (*pl.* **I's, i's**) the ninth letter of the English alphabet: *'Island' begins with (an) 'I'.*

I² 🔊 **A1** /aɪ/ *pron.* (the subject of a verb) the person who is speaking or writing: *I phoned and said that I was busy.* ◇ *I'm not going to fall, am I?*

i- /aɪ/ *prefix* (**COMPUTING**) INTERACTIVE (= involving direct communication both ways, between the computer and the person using it): *The i-Writer teaches you how to plan and write essays.*

iambic /aɪˈæmbɪk/ *adj.* (**LITERATURE**) (used about rhythm in poetry) having one short or weak syllable followed by one long or strong syllable: *a poem written in iambic pentameters* (= in lines of ten syllables, five short and five long)

IATA /aɪˈɑːtə/ *abbr.* (**TOURISM**) **International Air Transport Association** (the organization that most of the world's airlines belong to, which helps them to operate efficiently and sets standards for how tickets are sold, the safety of aircraft, etc.)

IB /ˌaɪ ˈbiː/ *abbr.* = INTERNATIONAL BACCALAUREATE™

IBS /ˌaɪ biː ˈes/ *noun* [U] (**HEALTH**) a condition of the BOWELS, often caused by stress and worry (the abbreviation for 'irritable bowel syndrome')

ice¹ 🔊 **A1** /aɪs/ *noun* [U] water that has frozen and become solid: *Do you want ice in your orange juice?* ◇ *I slipped on a patch of ice.* ◇ *black ice* (= ice on roads, that cannot be seen easily) ⊃ note at **water¹** **IDM** **break the ice** to say or do sth that makes people feel more relaxed, especially at the beginning of a party or meeting | **cut no ice (with sb)**

to have no influence or effect on sb | **on ice 1** (used about wine, etc.) kept cold by being surrounded by ice **2** (used about a plan, etc.) waiting to be dealt with later: *We've had to put our plans to go to Australia on ice for the time being.*

ice² /aɪs/ (*also* **frost** *especially in AmE*) *verb* [T] to decorate a cake by covering it with a mixture of sugar, butter, chocolate, etc. ⊃ look at **icing** **PHR V** **ice (sth) over/up** to cover sth or become covered with ice: *The windscreen of the car had iced over in the night.*

'ice age (*often* **the Ice Age**) *noun* [C] one of the long periods of time, thousands of years ago, when much of the earth's surface was covered in ice

iceberg /ˈaɪsbɜːɡ/ *noun* [C] (**GEOGRAPHY**) a very large block of ice that floats in the sea **IDM** **the tip of the iceberg** → TIP¹

'ice cap *noun* [C] (**GEOGRAPHY**) a layer of ice permanently covering parts of the earth, especially around the North and South Poles: *the polar ice caps*

ˌice-'cold *adj.* very cold: *ice-cold beer* ◇ *Your hands are ice-cold.*

'ice cream 🔊 **A1** *noun* **1** [U] a frozen sweet food that is made from cream **2** [C] an amount of ice cream that is served to sb, often in a CONE (= a container made of biscuit): *a strawberry ice cream*

'ice cube *noun* [C] a small block of ice that you put in a drink to make it cold

iced /aɪst/ *adj.* (used about drinks) very cold: *iced tea*

'ice floe /ˈaɪs fləʊ/ *noun* [C] (**GEOGRAPHY**) a large area of ice, floating in the sea

'ice hockey (*BrE*) (*AmE* **hockey**) *noun* [U] (**SPORT**) a game that is played on ice by two teams who try to hit a PUCK (= a small flat rubber object) into a goal with long wooden sticks

'ice lolly (*pl.* **-ies**) (*BrE*) (*AmE* **Popsicle™**) *noun* [C] a piece of ice with a sweet taste, served on a stick ⊃ look at **lollipop**

'ice rink (*also* **rink, skating rink**) *noun* [C] (**SPORT**) a large area of ice, or a building containing a large area of ice, where you can ICE-SKATE (= move on the ice wearing special boots)

'ice skate = SKATE¹ (1)

'ice-skate = SKATE² (1)

'ice skating = SKATING (1)

icicle /ˈaɪsɪkl/ *noun* [C] a pointed piece of ice that is formed by water freezing as it falls or runs down from sth

icing /ˈaɪsɪŋ/ (*especially BrE*) (*AmE usually* **frosting**) *noun* [U] a mixture of sugar, butter, chocolate, etc. that is used to decorate cakes

icon 🔊+ **B2** /ˈaɪkɒn/ *noun* [C] **1** (**COMPUTING**) a small picture or symbol on a computer or phone screen that represents a program: *Tap the app icon on your phone to open it.* **2** a person or thing that people admire and see as a symbol of sth: *Madonna and other pop icons of the 1980s* **3** (*also* **ikon**) (**RELIGION**) a painting or statue of a holy person that is also thought of as a holy object

iconic /aɪˈkɒnɪk/ *adj.* being a famous person or thing that people see as a symbol of a particular idea, way of life, etc: *This photo has become an iconic image of war.*

iconography /ˌaɪkəˈnɒɡrəfi/ *noun* [U] (**ART**) the use or study of images or symbols in art

ICT /ˌaɪ siː ˈtiː/ *noun* [U] (*BrE*) the study of the use of computer, the internet, video and other technology as a subject at school (the abbreviation for 'information and communications technology')

ICU /ˌaɪ siː ˈjuː/ noun [C] (**MEDICINE**) the department in a hospital that gives special care to patients who are very seriously ill or injured (the abbreviation for 'intensive care unit')

icy /ˈaɪsi/ adj. (icier; iciest) **1** very cold: icy winds/water/weather **SYN** freezing¹ **2** covered with ice: icy roads

ID ʔ+ **B2** /ˌaɪ ˈdiː/ noun [U, C] an official way of showing who you are, for example a document with your name, date of birth and often a photo on it (the abbreviation for 'identity' or 'identification'): You must carry ID at all times. ◇ an ID card

Id /iːd/ = EID

I'd /aɪd/ short form I had; I would

I'D card = IDENTITY CARD

idea ʔ **A1** **S** /aɪˈdɪə/ noun **1** [C] ~ (for sth); ~ (of sth/doing sth) a plan, thought or suggestion, especially about what to do in a particular situation: That's a good idea! ◇ He's got an idea for a new play. ◇ I had the bright idea of getting Jane to help me with my homework. ◇ Has anyone got any ideas of how to tackle this problem? ◇ It was your idea to invite so many people to the party. **2** [U, sing.] (an) ~ (of sth) a picture or impression in your mind: You have no idea (= you can't imagine) how difficult it was to find a time that suited everybody. ◇ The programme gave a good idea of what life was like before the war. ◇ Staying in to watch the football on TV is not my idea of a good time. **3** [C] ~ (about sth) an opinion or belief: She has her own ideas about how to bring up children. **4** the idea [sing.] the ~ (of sth/of doing sth) the aim or purpose of sth: The idea of the course is to teach the basics of car maintenance. ◇ note at **purpose** **IDM** get the idea to understand the aim or purpose of sth: Right! I think I've got the idea now. get the idea that … to get the feeling or impression that … : Where did you get the idea that I was paying for this meal? have an idea that … to feel or think that … : I'm not sure but I have an idea that they've gone on holiday. not have the faintest/foggiest (idea) → FAINT¹

ideal¹ ʔ **A2** **W** /aɪˈdiːəl/ adj. ~ (for sb/sth) the best possible; perfect: She's the ideal candidate for the job. ◇ In an ideal world there would be no poverty. ◇ It would be an ideal opportunity for you to practise your Spanish.

ideal² ʔ **B2** **W** /aɪˈdiːəl/ noun [C] **1** an idea or principle that seems perfect to you and that you want to achieve: She finds it hard to live up to her parents' high ideals. ◇ political/moral/social ideals **2** [usually sing.] ~ (of sth) a person or thing that you think is perfect: It's my ideal of what a family home should be.

idealism /aɪˈdiːəlɪzəm/ noun [U] the belief that a perfect life, situation, etc. can be achieved, even when this is not very likely: Young people are usually full of idealism. ◇ look at **realism** ▸ idealist /-lɪst/ noun [C] ▸ idealistic /ˌaɪdiəˈlɪstɪk/ adj.

idealize (BrE also -ise) /aɪˈdiːəlaɪz/ verb [T] to imagine or show sth/sb as being better than they really are: Old people often idealize the past.

ideally **W** /aɪˈdiːəli/ adv. **1** perfectly: They are ideally suited to each other. **2** in an ideal situation: Ideally, no class should be larger than 25.

identical ʔ+ **B2** **W** /aɪˈdentɪkl/ adj. **1** ~ (to/with sb/sth) exactly the same as; similar in every detail: That watch is identical to the one I lost yesterday. ◇ I can't see any difference between these two pens — they look identical to me. **2** the identical [only before noun] the same: This is the identical room we stayed in last year. ▸ identically /-kli/ adv.

identical twin noun [C] (**BIOLOGY**) either of two children born at the same time from the same mother who have developed from a single egg. Identical twins are of the same sex and look very similar. ◇ look at **fraternal twin**

identifiable /aɪˌdentɪˈfaɪəbl/ adj. that can be recognized: identifiable characteristics

identification ʔ+ **C1** **W** /aɪˌdentɪfɪˈkeɪʃn/ noun **1** [U, C] the process of showing, recognizing or giving proof of who or what sb/sth is: The identification of the bodies of those killed in the explosion was very difficult. ◇ The early identification of children with SEN is very important. **2** [U] = ID: Do you have any identification? **3** [U, C] ~ (with sb/sth) a strong feeling of understanding or sharing the same feelings as sb/sth: children's identification with TV heroes

identify ʔ **A2** **O** /aɪˈdentɪfaɪ/ verb [T] (identifying; identifies; pt, pp identified) ~ sb/sth (as sb/sth) to recognize or be able to say who or what sb/sth is: The police need somebody to identify the body. ◇ We must identify the cause of the problem before we look for solutions. ◇ The body was identified as that of the suspect. **PHRV** identify sth with sth to think or say that sth is the same as sth else: You can't identify nationalism with fascism. identify with sb to feel that you understand and share what sb else is feeling: I found it hard to identify with the woman in the film. identify (yourself) with sb/sth to support or be closely connected with sb/sth: He identified himself with the common people.

identity ʔ **B1** **O** /aɪˈdentəti/ noun [C, U] (pl. -ies) who or what a person or a thing is: There are few clues to the identity of the killer. ◇ Each region of Italy has its own cultural identity. ◇ The arrest was a case of mistaken identity (= the wrong person was arrested). ◇ look at **ID**

identity card (also **ID card**) noun [C] (**LAW**) a card with your name, photo, etc. on it that is proof of who you are

identity politics noun [U + sing./pl. verb] (**POLITICS**) political positions that are based on the social groups that people identify with, for example based on their religion or the human group they belong to, rather than on traditional political parties

identity theft noun [U, C] (**LAW**) the crime of using sb else's name and personal information in order, for example, to use their bank account or CREDIT CARDS

ideogram /ˈɪdiəgræm/ (also **ideograph** /ˈɪdiəgrɑːf/) noun [C] (**LANGUAGE**) a symbol that is used in a writing system, for example Chinese, to represent the idea of a thing, rather than the sounds of a word

ideology ʔ+ **C1** /ˌaɪdiˈɒlədʒi/ noun [C, U] (pl. -ies) (**POLITICS**) a set of ideas that a political or economic system is based on: Marxist ideology ▸ ideological ʔ+ **C1** /ˌaɪdiəˈlɒdʒɪkl/ adj.

idiolect /ˈɪdiəlekt/ noun [C] (**LANGUAGE**) the way that a particular person uses language ◇ look at **dialect**

idiom /ˈɪdiəm/ noun [C] (**LANGUAGE**) an expression whose meaning is different from the meanings of the individual words in it: The idiom 'bring something home to somebody' means 'make somebody understand something'.

idiomatic /ˌɪdiəˈmætɪk/ adj. (**LANGUAGE**) **1** containing expressions that are natural to sb who speaks that language as their first language: He speaks good idiomatic English. **2** containing an IDIOM: an idiomatic expression

idiosyncrasy /ˌɪdiəˈsɪŋkrəsi/ *noun* [C, U] (*pl.* -ies) a person's particular way of behaving, thinking, etc., especially when it is unusual; an unusual feature: *Eating garlic every morning is one of his idiosyncrasies.* **SYN** **eccentricity** ▸ idiosyncratic /ˌɪdiəsɪŋˈkrætɪk/ *adj.*: *His teaching methods are idiosyncratic but successful.*

idiot 🔑 **C1** /ˈɪdiət/ *noun* [C] (*informal*) a very stupid person: *I was an idiot to forget my passport.* ▸ idiotic /ˌɪdiˈɒtɪk/ *adj.* ▸ idiotically /-kli/ *adv.*

idle /ˈaɪdl/ *adj.* **1** not wanting to work hard: *He has the ability to succeed but he is just bone (= very) idle.* **SYN** **lazy 2** not doing anything; not being used: *She can't bear to be idle.* ◇ *The factory stood idle while the machines were being repaired.* **3** [only before noun] not to be taken seriously because it will not have any result: *an idle promise/threat* ◇ *idle chatter/curiosity* ▸ idleness *noun* [U] ▸ idly /ˈaɪdli/ *adv.*

idol /ˈaɪdl/ *noun* [C] **1** a person (such as a film star or pop musician) who is admired or loved: *a pop/football/teen/screen idol* **2** (**RELIGION**) a statue that people treat as a god

idolatry /aɪˈdɒlətri/ *noun* [U] (**RELIGION**) the practice of WORSHIPPING statues as gods

idolize (*BrE also* -ise) /ˈaɪdəlaɪz/ *verb* [T] to love or admire sb very much or too much: *He is an only child and his parents idolize him.*

idyllic /ɪˈdɪlɪk/ *adj.* very pleasant and peaceful; perfect: *an idyllic holiday*

i.e. /ˌaɪ ˈiː/ *abbr.* used to explain exactly what the previous thing that you have mentioned means (from Latin 'id est'): *deciduous trees, i.e. those which lose their leaves in autumn*

IED /ˌaɪ iː ˈdiː/ *noun* [C] a simple bomb made and used by people who are not members of an army (the abbreviation for 'improvised explosive device')

IELTS /ˈaɪelts/ *abbr.* (**EDUCATION**) **International English Language Testing System** (a test, set by the University of Cambridge, that measures a person's ability to speak and write English at the level that is necessary to go to university in the UK, Ireland, Australia, Canada, South Africa and New Zealand)

if 🔑 **A1** /ɪf/ *conj.* **1** used in sentences in which one thing only happens or is true when another thing happens or is true: *If you see him, give him this letter.* ◇ *We won't go to the beach if it rains.* ◇ *If I had more time, I would learn another language.* ◇ *I might see her tomorrow. If not, I'll see her at the weekend.* **2** when; every time: *If I try to phone her she just hangs up.* ◇ *If metal gets hot it expands.* **3** used after verbs such as ask, know, remember to introduce one of two or more possibilities: *They asked if we would like to go too.* ◇ *I can't remember if I posted the letter or not.* **4** used when you are asking sb to do sth or suggesting sth politely: *If you could just come this way, sir.* ◇ *If I might suggest something …* **IDM** as if → AS² even if → EVEN¹ if I were you used when you are giving sb advice: *If I were you, I'd leave now.* if it wasn't/weren't for sb/sth if a particular person or situation did not exist or was not there; without sb/sth: *If it wasn't for him, I wouldn't stay in this country.* if only used for expressing a strong wish: *If only I could drive.* ◇ *If only he'd write.*

IGCSE /ˌaɪ dʒiː siː ˈiː/ *noun* [C, U] (**EDUCATION**) an international exam in different subjects that students can take when they are between 14 and 16 (the abbreviation for 'International General Certificate of Secondary Education') ➔ look at **International Baccalaureate™**, **GCSE**

igloo /ˈɪɡluː/ *noun* [C] (*pl.* -oos) a small round house that is built from blocks of hard snow

igneous /ˈɪɡniəs/ *adj.* (**GEOLOGY**) (used about rocks) formed when MAGMA (= melted or liquid material from below the earth's surface) comes out of a VOLCANO and becomes solid ➔ look at **metamorphic**, **sedimentary** ➔ picture at **rock¹**

ignite /ɪɡˈnaɪt/ *verb* [I, T] (*formal*) to start burning or to make sth start burning: *A spark from the engine ignited the petrol.*

ignition /ɪɡˈnɪʃn/ *noun* **1** [C, usually sing.] the electrical system that starts the engine of a vehicle; the place in a vehicle where you start this system: *to turn the ignition on/off* ◇ *First of all, put the key in the ignition.* **2** [U] the action of starting to burn or making sth start to burn

ignominious /ˌɪɡnəˈmɪniəs/ *adj.* (*formal*) making you feel embarrassed and ashamed: *The team suffered an ignominious defeat.* ▸ ignominiously *adv.*

ignorance 🔑 **C1** /ˈɪɡnərəns/ *noun* [U] ~ (of/about sth) a lack of information or knowledge: *The workers were in complete ignorance of the management's plans.*

ignorant /ˈɪɡnərənt/ *adj.* **1** ~ (of/about sth) not knowing about sth; not educated: *Many people are ignorant of their rights.* ◇ *I'm very ignorant about modern technology, I'm afraid.* **2** (*informal*) having or showing bad manners: *an ignorant person/remark* ➔ look at **ignore**

ignore 🔑 **B1** /ɪɡˈnɔː(r)/ *verb* [T] to pay no attention to sb/sth: *I said hello to Debbie but she totally ignored me (= acted as though she hadn't seen me).* ◇ *Alison ignored her doctor's advice about getting more exercise.*

iguana /ɪˈɡwɑːnə/ *noun* [C] a large tropical American LIZARD (= a type of REPTILE)

ikon /ˈaɪkɒn/ = ICON (3)

il- /ɪl/ → IN-

ileum /ˈɪliəm/ *noun* [C] (*pl.* ilea /-liə/) (**ANATOMY**) one part of the INTESTINE (= the tube that carries food away from the stomach) ➔ picture at **digestive system**

ill¹ 🔑 **A2** /ɪl/ *adj.* **1** (*especially BrE*) (*AmE usually* sick) [not usually before noun] (**HEALTH**) not in good health; not well: *I can't drink milk because it makes me feel ill.* ◇ *My mother was taken ill suddenly last week.* ◇ *My grandfather is seriously ill in hospital.* ➔ note at **doctor¹** **2** [only before noun] bad or harmful: *He resigned because of ill health.* ◇ *I'm glad to say I suffered no ill effects from the experience.* ➔ noun **illness**

ill² /ɪl/ *adv.* **1** ill- (in adjectives) badly or wrongly: *You would be ill-advised (= not sensible) to drive until you have fully recovered.* **2** (*formal*) only with difficulty; not easily: *They could ill afford the extra money for better heating.* **IDM** augur well/ill for sb/sth → AUGUR bode well/ill (for sb/sth) → BODE

I'll /aɪl/ *short form* I will; I shall

illegal 🔑 **B1** /ɪˈliːɡl/ *adj.* (**LAW**) ~ (for sb) (to do sth) not allowed by the law: *It is illegal to drive a car without insurance.* ◇ *illegal drugs/immigrants/activities* ◇ *In the UK, it is illegal for anyone under 16 to get married.* **OPP** **legal** ➔ note at **crime** ▸ illegally /-ɡəli/ *adv.*

illegality /ˌɪliˈɡæləti/ *noun* (*pl.* -ies) (**LAW**) **1** [U] the state of being illegal: *No illegality is suspected.* ➔ look at **legality 2** [C] an illegal act

illegible /ɪˈledʒəbl/ *adj.* difficult or impossible to read: *Your handwriting is quite illegible.* **OPP** **legible** ▸ illegibly /-bli/ *adv.*

illegitimate /ˌɪləˈdʒɪtəmət/ adj. **1** (old-fashioned) (used about a child) born to parents who are not married to each other OPP **legitimate 2** (formal) (LAW) not allowed by law; against the rules: the illegitimate use of company money OPP **legitimate** ▸ illegitimacy /-məsi/ noun [U]

ill-fated adj. (formal) not lucky: the ill-fated ship, the Titanic

illicit /ɪˈlɪsɪt/ adj. (used about an activity or substance) not allowed by law or by the rules of society: the illicit trade in ivory ◇ They were having an illicit affair.

illiterate /ɪˈlɪtərət/ adj. **1** not able to read or write OPP **literate 2** (used about a piece of writing) very badly written **3** not knowing much about a particular subject: computer illiterate OPP **literate** ▸ illiteracy /-rəsi/ noun [U]: adult illiteracy

illness ⓘ A2 /ˈɪlnəs/ noun (HEALTH) **1** [U] the state of being physically or mentally ill: He's missed a lot of school through illness. ◇ There is a history of mental illness in the family. ➔ note at **disease 2** [C] a type or period of physical or mental ill health: a **minor/serious** illness ◇ May dad is just getting over his illness. ➔ note at **disease** ➔ adjective **ill**

illogical /ɪˈlɒdʒɪkl/ adj. not sensible or reasonable: It seems illogical to me to pay somebody to do work that you could do yourself. OPP **logical** ▸ illogicality /ɪˌlɒdʒɪˈkæləti/ noun [C, U] (pl. -ies) ▸ illogically /ɪˈlɒdʒɪkli/ adv.

ill-treat verb [T] to treat a person or an animal badly or in an unkind way ▸ ill-treatment noun [U]

illuminate /ɪˈluːmɪneɪt/ verb [T] (formal) **1** to shine light on sth or to decorate sth with lights: Floodlights illuminated the stadium. **2** (formal) to explain sth or make sth clear

illuminated /ɪˈluːmɪneɪtɪd/ adj. **1** lit with bright lights: the illuminated city at night **2** (ART) decorated with gold, silver and bright colours in a way that was done in the past, by hand: illuminated manuscripts

illuminating /ɪˈluːmɪneɪtɪŋ/ adj. helping to explain sth or make sth clear: an illuminating discussion

illumination /ɪˌluːmɪˈneɪʃn/ noun **1** [U, C] light or the place where a light comes from **2** illuminations [pl.] (BrE) coloured lights used to decorate a town or a building for a special occasion

illusion ⓘ+ B2 /ɪˈluːʒn/ noun **1** [C, U] a false idea, belief or impression: I **have no illusions** about the situation — I know it's serious. ◇ I think Peter's **under the illusion** that he'll be the new director. **2** [C] something that your eyes tell you is there or is true but in fact is not: That line looks longer, but in fact the lines are the same length. It's an **optical illusion**.

illusory /ɪˈluːsəri/ adj. (formal) not real, although seeming to be: The profits they had hoped for proved to be illusory.

illustrate ⓘ B2 ⊙ /ˈɪləstreɪt/ verb [T] **1** to explain or make sth clear by using examples, pictures or diagrams: These statistics **illustrate the point** that I was making very well. **2** to add pictures, diagrams, etc. to a book, etc: She illustrated her own books.

illustration ⓘ B2 /ˌɪləˈstreɪʃn/ noun **1** [C] a drawing, diagram or picture in a book, magazine, etc: colour illustrations **2** [U] (ART) the activity or art of illustrating **3** [C] an example that makes a point or an idea clear: Can you give me an illustration of what you mean? ➔ note at **example**

illustrative /ˈɪləstrətɪv, -streɪt-/ adj. (formal) helping to explain sth or show it more clearly **SYN** **explanatory**

illustrator /ˈɪləstreɪtə(r)/ noun [C] (ART) a person who draws or paints pictures for books, etc.

illustrious /ɪˈlʌstriəs/ adj. (formal) famous and successful

ILO /ˌaɪ el ˈəʊ/ abbr. (POLITICS) International Labour Organization (an organization within the United Nations concerned with work and working conditions)

IM /ˌaɪ ˈem/ noun [C] (pl. IMs) (informal) = INSTANT MESSAGE

im- /ɪm/ → IN-

I'm /aɪm/ short form I am

image ⓘ A2 ⊙ /ˈɪmɪdʒ/ noun [C] **1** a picture or description that appears in a book, film, painting, etc: horrific images of war ◇ We have more than 22 000 digital images on file. **2** a copy or picture of sb/sth seen in a mirror, through a camera, on a TV, etc: A perfect image of the building was reflected in the lake. ◇ (figurative) He's **the (spitting) image of** his father (= he looks exactly like him). ➔ picture at **reflection**, **short-sighted 3** the general impression that a person or an organization gives to the public: When you meet him, he's very different from his public image. **4** a mental picture or idea of sb/sth: I have an image of my childhood as always sunny and happy.

imagery ⓘ+ C1 /ˈɪmɪdʒəri/ noun [U] (LANGUAGE, LITERATURE) language that produces pictures in the minds of the people reading or listening: poetic imagery

imaginable /ɪˈmædʒɪnəbl/ adj. that you can imagine: Sophie made all the excuses imaginable when she was caught stealing. ◇ His house was equipped with every imaginable luxury.

imaginary ⓘ B1 /ɪˈmædʒɪnəri/ adj. existing only in the mind; not real: Many children have imaginary friends.

imagination ⓘ B2 /ɪˌmædʒɪˈneɪʃn/ noun [U, C] the ability to create mental pictures or new ideas; the part of the mind that uses this ability: She's very clever but she doesn't **have** much **imagination**. ◇ He has a lively imagination. ◇ If you **use** your **imagination**, you should be able to guess the answer.

imaginative /ɪˈmædʒɪnətɪv/ adj. having or showing new and exciting ideas: She's always full of imaginative ideas. ▸ imaginatively adv.

imagine ⓘ A1 /ɪˈmædʒɪn/ verb [T] **1** ~ that … ; ~ sb/sth (doing/as sth) to form a picture or idea in your mind of what sth/sb might be like: Imagine that you're lying on a beach. ◇ It's not easy to imagine your brother as a doctor. ◇ I can't imagine myself cycling 20 miles a day. **2** to see, hear or think sth that is not true or does not exist: She's always imagining that she's ill but she's fine really. ◇ I thought I heard somebody downstairs, but I must have been **imagining things**. **3** to think that sth is probably true: I imagine he'll be coming by car. **SYN** **suppose**

imaging /ˈɪmɪdʒɪŋ/ noun [U] (COMPUTING) the process of producing, storing and showing an image on a computer screen: imaging software ➔ look at **thermal imaging**

imam /ɪˈmɑːm/ noun [C] (RELIGION) (in Islam) a religious man who leads the prayers in a MOSQUE (= a religious building)

imbalance /ɪmˈbæləns/ noun [C] ~ (between A and B); ~ (in/of sth) a situation in which two or more things are not the same size or are not treated the same, in a way that is unfair or causes problems: an imbalance between our import and export trade ◇ an imbalance in the numbers of men and women teachers

imbecile /ˈɪmbəsiːl/ noun [C] a stupid person **SYN** **idiot**

IMF /ˌaɪ em ˈef/ *abbr.* (**ECONOMICS**) **International Monetary Fund** (the organization within the United Nations that is concerned with trade and economic development)

IMHO /ˌaɪ em eɪtʃ ˈəʊ/ (*informal*) = IMO

imitate /ˈɪmɪteɪt/ *verb* [T] **1** to copy sb/sth: *Small children learn by imitating their parents.* **2** to copy the speech or actions of sb/sth, often in order to make people laugh: *She could imitate her mother perfectly.*

imitation /ˌɪmɪˈteɪʃn/ *noun* **1** [C] a copy of sth real: *Some artificial flowers are good imitations of real ones.* ⊃ look at **genuine** (1) ⊃ note at **artificial 2** [U] the act of copying sb/sth: *Good pronunciation of a language is best learnt by imitation.* **3** [C] the act of copying the way sb talks and behaves, especially in order to make people laugh: *Can you do any imitations of politicians?* **SYN** **impression**

immaculate /ɪˈmækjələt/ *adj.* **1** perfectly clean and tidy: *immaculate white shirts* **2** without any mistakes: *His performance of 'Romeo' was immaculate.* **SYN** **perfect**[1] ▸ **immaculately** *adv.*

immaterial /ˌɪməˈtɪəriəl/ *adj.* ~ (**to sb/sth**) not important: *It's immaterial to me whether we go today or tomorrow.*

immature /ˌɪməˈtjʊə(r)/ *adj.* **1** not fully grown or developed: *an immature body* **OPP** **mature**[1] **2** (used about a person) behaving in a way that is not sensible and is typical of people who are much younger: *I think he's too immature to take his work seriously.* **OPP** **mature**[1]

immeasurable /ɪˈmeʒərəbl/ *adj.* (*formal*) too large, great, etc. to be measured: *to cause immeasurable harm* ◇ *Her contribution was of immeasurable importance.* ▸ **immeasurably** /-bli/ *adv.*: *Housing standards have improved immeasurably since the war.*

immediacy /ɪˈmiːdiəsi/ *noun* [U] (*formal*) the quality of being available or seeming to happen close to you and without delay: *Letters do not have the same immediacy as email.*

immediate B1 ⓦ /ɪˈmiːdiət/ *adj.* **1** happening or done without delay: *I'd like an immediate answer to my proposal.* ◇ *The government responded with immediate action.* **2** [only before noun] existing now and needing attention quickly: *Tell me what your immediate needs are.* **3** [only before noun] nearest in time, position or relationship: *They won't make any changes in the immediate future.* ◇ *He has left most of his money to his immediate family (= parents, children, brothers and sisters).*

immediately[1] A2 /ɪˈmiːdiətli/ *adv.* **1** without delay: *Can you come home immediately after work?* ◇ *I couldn't immediately see what he meant.* ◇ *She answered immediately.* **2** very closely; directly: *He wasn't immediately involved in the crime.* **3** nearest in time or position: *Who's the girl immediately in front of Simon?* ◇ *What did you do immediately after you left school?*

immediately[2] /ɪˈmiːdiətli/ *conj.* (*especially BrE*) as soon as: *I opened the package immediately I got home.*

immense + C1 /ɪˈmens/ *adj.* very big or great: *immense difficulties/importance/power* ◇ *She gets immense pleasure from her garden.* **SYN** **enormous**

immensely /ɪˈmensli/ *adv.* extremely; very much: *immensely enjoyable*

immensity /ɪˈmensəti/ *noun* [U] an extremely large size: *the immensity of the universe*

immerse /ɪˈmɜːs/ *verb* [T] **1** ~ **sb/sth (in sth)** to put sb/sth into a liquid so that it is covered: *Make sure the spaghetti is fully immersed in the boiling water.* **2** ~ **yourself (in sth)** to involve yourself completely in sth so that you give it all your attention: *Rachel's usually immersed in a book.*

immersion /ɪˈmɜːʃn/ *noun* [U] **1** ~ (**in sth**) the act of putting sb/sth into a liquid so that they are or it is completely covered; the state of being completely covered by a liquid: *Immersion in cold water resulted in rapid loss of heat.* **2** ~ (**in sth**) the state of being completely involved in sth: *a two-week immersion course in French* (= in which the student hears and uses only French)

immersive /ɪˈmɜːsɪv/ *adj.* (used about a game, performance, etc.) seeming to surround the player or viewer so they feel totally involved in the experience: *Immersive games can be used for training and education.*

immigrant B1 /ˈɪmɪɡrənt/ *noun* [C] (**SOCIAL STUDIES**) a person who has come into a foreign country to live there permanently: *The government plans to tighten controls to prevent illegal immigrants.* ◇ *London has a large immigrant population.* ⊃ look at **emigrant**

immigrate /ˈɪmɪɡreɪt/ *verb* [T] ~ (**to ...**) (**from ...**) (*especially AmE*) (**SOCIAL STUDIES**) to come and live permanently in a country after leaving your own country: *About 6.6 million people immigrated to the United States in the 1970s.* ⊃ look at **emigrate**

immigration + B2 /ˌɪmɪˈɡreɪʃn/ *noun* [U] **1** (**SOCIAL STUDIES**) the process of coming to live permanently in a country that is not your own; the number of people who do this: *There are greater controls on immigration than there used to be.* **2** (*also* immigration control) the control point at an airport, port, etc. where the official documents of people who want to come into a country are checked: *When you leave the plane you have to go through customs and immigration.* ⊃ look at **emigration**

imminent + C1 /ˈɪmɪnənt/ *adj.* (usually used about sth unpleasant) almost certain to happen very soon: *Heavy rainfall means that flooding is imminent.* ▸ **imminently** *adv.*

immiscible /ɪˈmɪsəbl/ *adj.* (**CHEMISTRY**) (used about liquids) that cannot be mixed together **OPP** **miscible**

immobile /ɪˈməʊbaɪl/ *adj.* not moving or not able to move ⊃ look at **mobile**[1] (2) ▸ **immobility** /ˌɪməˈbɪləti/ *noun* [U]

immobilize (*BrE also* -ise) /ɪˈməʊbəlaɪz/ *verb* [T] to prevent sb/sth from moving or working normally: *The railways have been completely immobilized by the strike.*

immobilizer (*BrE also* -iser) /ɪˈməʊbəlaɪzə(r)/ *noun* [C] a device in a vehicle that prevents thieves from starting the engine

immoral /ɪˈmɒrəl/ *adj.* (used about people or their behaviour) not considered to be honest by most people: *It's immoral to steal.* ⊃ look at **amoral, moral**[1] (2) ▸ **immorality** /ˌɪməˈræləti/ *noun* [U] ▸ **immorally** /ɪˈmɒrəli/ *adv.*

immortal /ɪˈmɔːtl/ *adj.* living or lasting for ever: *Nobody is immortal — we all have to die some time.* **OPP** **mortal**[1] ▸ **immortality** /ˌɪmɔːˈtæləti/ *noun* [U]

immortalize (*BrE also* -ise) /ɪˈmɔːtəlaɪz/ *verb* [T] to prevent sb/sth from being forgotten in the future, especially by mentioning them in literature, making films about them, painting them, etc: *He immortalized their relationship in a poem.*

immovable (*also* immoveable) /ɪˈmuːvəbl/ *adj.* that cannot be moved: *an immovable object* ◇ *immovable property* (= houses, land, etc.)

immune ₹+ B2 /ɪˈmjuːn/ *adj.* **1 ~ (to sth)** (**HEALTH**) having natural protection against a certain disease or illness: *You should be immune to measles if you've had it already.* **2 ~ (to sth)** not affected by sth: *You can say what you like — I'm immune to criticism!* **3 ~ (from sth)** (**LAW**) protected from a danger or punishment: *Young children are immune from prosecution.*

imˌmune deˈficiency = IMMUNODEFICIENCY

imˈmune response *noun* [C] (**HEALTH**) the reaction of the body to the presence of an ANTIGEN (= a substance that can cause disease)

imˈmune system *noun* [C] (**HEALTH**) the system in your body that produces substances to help it fight against infection and disease

immunity /ɪˈmjuːnəti/ *noun* [U] the ability to avoid or not be affected by disease, criticism, punishment by law, etc: *In many countries people have no immunity to diseases like measles.* ◇ *Ambassadors to other countries receive **diplomatic immunity** (= protection from PROSECUTION, etc.).*

immunize (*BrE also* -ise) /ˈɪmjunaɪz/ *verb* [T] (**MEDICINE**) to protect a person or an animal from a disease, usually by putting a VACCINE (= a substance that protects the body) into their blood: *Before visiting certain countries you will need to be immunized against cholera.* ⊃ look at **inoculate, vaccinate** ▸ **immunization** (*BrE also* -isation) /ˌɪmjunaɪˈzeɪʃn/ *noun* [U, C]

immunodeficiency /ˌɪmjuːnəʊdɪˈfɪʃnsi/ (*also* **immune deficiency**) *noun* [U] (**HEALTH**) a medical condition in which your body does not have the normal ability to resist infection: *human immunodeficiency virus or HIV*

IMO /ˌaɪ em ˈəʊ/ (*also* **IMHO**) *abbr.* (*informal*) used especially in text messages, on SOCIAL MEDIA, etc. when you give your opinion about sth (the abbreviation for 'in my opinion' or 'in my humble opinion')

imp /ɪmp/ *noun* [C] (in stories) a small creature like a little man, that has magic powers and behaves badly

impact¹ ₹ B1 ⊙ /ˈɪmpækt/ *noun* [C, usually sing., U] **1 ~ (on/upon sb/sth)** a powerful effect that sth has on sb/sth: *I hope this road safety campaign will **make/ have an impact** on drivers.* **2** the action or force of one object hitting another: *The impact of the crash threw the passengers out of their seats.* ◇ *The bomb exploded **on impact**.*

impact² ₹ B1 ⓦ /ɪmˈpækt/ *verb* [I, T] **~ (on/upon) sb/ sth** to have an effect on sb/sth: *Her father's death impacted greatly on her childhood years.* ◇ *The high cost of oil impacted the company's performance.* **SYN affect**

impair /ɪmˈpeə(r)/ *verb* [T] to damage sth or make it weaker: *Ear infections can result in impaired hearing.*

impairment /ɪmˈpeəmənt/ *noun* [U, C] (**HEALTH**) the state of having a physical or mental condition that means that part of your body or brain does not work correctly; a particular condition of this sort

impale /ɪmˈpeɪl/ *verb* [T] **~ sb/sth (on sth)** to push a sharp pointed object through sb/sth: *The boy fell out of the tree and impaled his leg on some railings.*

impart /ɪmˈpɑːt/ *verb* [T] (*formal*) **1 ~ sth (to sb)** to pass information, knowledge, etc. to other people: *He rushed home, eager to impart the good news to his mother.* **2 ~ sth (to sth)** to give a certain quality to sth: *The low lighting imparted a romantic atmosphere to the room.* **SYN lend**

impartial /ɪmˈpɑːʃl/ *adj.* not supporting one person or group more than another **SYN neutral¹** ▸ **impartiality** /ˌɪmˌpɑːʃiˈæləti/ *noun* [U] ▸ **impartially** /ɪmˈpɑːʃəli/ *adv.*

impassable /ɪmˈpɑːsəbl/ *adj.* (used about a road, area, etc.) impossible to travel on or through because it is in bad condition or it is blocked **OPP passable**

impasse /ˈɪmpæs/ *noun* [C, usually sing.] a difficult situation in which no progress can be made because the people involved cannot agree what to do: *to break/ end the impasse* ◇ *Negotiations have reached an impasse.* **SYN deadlock**

impassioned /ɪmˈpæʃnd/ *adj.* (usually used about speech) showing strong feelings about sth: *an impassioned defence/plea/speech*

impassive /ɪmˈpæsɪv/ *adj.* (used about a person) showing no emotion or reaction ▸ **impassively** *adv.*

impasto /ɪmˈpæstəʊ/ *noun* [U, C] (*pl.* -os) (**ART**) a painting technique in which the paint is put on so thickly that you can see the brush marks; a picture painted using this method

impatient ₹ B2 /ɪmˈpeɪʃnt/ *adj.* **1 ~ (at sth/with sb)** not able to stay calm and wait for sb/sth; easily annoyed by sb/sth that seems slow: *The passengers are getting impatient at the delay.* ◇ *It's no good being impatient with small children.* **OPP patient¹ 2 ~ for/to do sth** wanting sth to happen soon: *At the end of winter we are often impatient for spring to arrive.* ◇ *By the time they are sixteen many young people are impatient to leave school.* ▸ **impatience** /-ʃns/ *noun* [U]: *He began to explain for the third time with growing impatience.* ▸ **impatiently** *adv.*

impeach /ɪmˈpiːtʃ/ *verb* [T] **~ sb (for sth)** (**LAW**) (especially in the US) to officially accuse a public official of committing a serious crime ▸ **impeachment** *noun* [U, C]

impeccable /ɪmˈpekəbl/ *adj.* without any mistakes or faults ▸ **impeccably** /-bli/ *adv.*

impede /ɪmˈpiːd/ *verb* [T] (*formal*) to make it difficult for sb/sth to move or go forward

impediment /ɪmˈpedimənt/ *noun* [C] **1 ~ (to sth)** (*formal*) something that makes it difficult for a person or thing to move or progress **2** (**HEALTH**) a physical problem that makes it difficult to speak normally, hear easily, etc: *a speech impediment*

impel /ɪmˈpel/ *verb* [T] (-ll-) **~ sb (to do sth)** (*formal*) if an idea or a feeling **impels** you to do sth, you feel as if you are forced to do it: *He felt impelled to investigate further.* ◇ *There are various reasons that impel me to that conclusion.*

impending /ɪmˈpendɪŋ/ *adj.* [only before noun] (usually used about sth bad) that will happen soon: *There was a feeling of impending disaster in the air.*

impenetrable /ɪmˈpenɪtrəbl/ *adj.* **1** impossible to enter or go through: *The jungle was impenetrable.* **2** impossible to understand: *an impenetrable mystery*

imperative /ɪmˈperətɪv/ *adj.* (*formal*) very important or needing immediate action: *It's imperative that you see a doctor immediately.* **SYN vital**

the imˈperative *noun* [C] (**GRAMMAR**) the form of the verb that is used for giving orders: *In 'Shut the door!' the verb is in the imperative.*

imperceptible /ˌɪmpəˈseptəbl/ *adj.* (*formal*) too small to be seen or noticed: *The difference between the original painting and the copy was almost imperceptible.* **OPP perceptible** ▸ **imperceptibly** /-bli/ *adv.*: *Almost imperceptibly winter was turning into spring.*

imperfect /ɪmˈpɜːfɪkt/ *adj.* with mistakes or faults: *This is a very imperfect system.* **OPP perfect¹** ▸ **imperfectly** *adv.*

the im'perfect (*also* **the im,perfect 'tense**) *noun* [U] (**GRAMMAR**) used for expressing action in the past that is not completed: *In 'I was having a bath', the verb is in the imperfect.*

imperfection /ˌɪmpəˈfekʃn/ *noun* [C, U] a fault or weakness in sb/sth

imperial /ɪmˈpɪəriəl/ *adj.* **1** connected with an EMPIRE or its ruler: *the imperial palace* **2** connected with the system for measuring length, weight and volume using pounds, inches, etc. ⊃ look at **foot¹** (5), **gallon**, **inch¹**, **metric**, **ounce** (1), **pint** (1), **pound¹** (3), **yard** (4)

imperialism /ɪmˈpɪəriəlɪzəm/ *noun* [U] (**POLITICS**) a system in which one country controls other countries, often after defeating them in a war ▶ **imperialist** /-lɪst/ *adj., noun* [C]

impermeable /ɪmˈpɜːmiəbl/ *adj.* ~ (**to sth**) (**GEOLOGY**, **PHYSICS**) not allowing a liquid or gas to pass through: *impermeable rock* ◇ *The container is impermeable to water vapour.* **OPP permeable** ⊃ picture at **limestone**, **petroleum**

impersonal /ɪmˈpɜːsənl/ *adj.* **1** not showing friendly human feelings; cold in feeling or atmosphere: *The hotel room was very impersonal.* **2** not referring to any particular person: *Can we try to keep the discussion as impersonal as possible, please?*

impersonate /ɪmˈpɜːsəneɪt/ *verb* [T] to pretend to be sb in order to trick people or to entertain them: *a comedian who impersonates politicians* ◇ *He was arrested for impersonating a policeman.* ▶ **impersonation** /ɪmˌpɜːsəˈneɪʃn/ *noun* [C, U] ▶ **impersonator** *noun* [C]

impertinent /ɪmˈpɜːtɪnənt/ *adj.* (*formal*) not showing respect to sb who is older or more important **OPP polite, respectful** ⊃ look at **rude** (1) ▶ **impertinence** /-ˈpɜːtɪnəns/ *noun* [U] ▶ **impertinently** *adv.*

imperturbable /ˌɪmpəˈtɜːbəbl/ *adj.* (*formal*) not easily worried by a difficult situation

impervious /ɪmˈpɜːviəs/ *adj.* ~ (**to sth**) **1** not affected or influenced by sth: *She was impervious to criticism.* **2** (**GEOLOGY**, **PHYSICS**) not allowing water, etc. to pass through

impetigo /ˌɪmpɪˈtaɪɡəʊ/ *noun* [U] (**HEALTH**) a disease that causes painful areas on the skin

impetuous /ɪmˈpetʃuəs/ *adj.* acting or done quickly and without thinking: *Her impetuous behaviour often got her into trouble.* **SYN impulsive** ▶ **impetuously** *adv.*

impetus /ˈɪmpɪtəs/ *noun* [U, sing.] (**an**) ~ (**for sth**); (**an**) ~ (**to do sth**) something that encourages sth else to happen: *This scandal provided the main impetus for changes in the rules.* ◇ *I need (a) fresh impetus to start working on this essay again.*

impinge /ɪmˈpɪndʒ/ *verb* [I] ~ **on/upon sth/sb** (*formal*) to have a clear and definite effect on sth/sb, especially a bad one: *I'm not going to let my job impinge on my home life.*

implant¹ /ɪmˈplɑːnt/ *verb* [T] ~ (**sth**) (**in/into sth**) (**MEDICINE**) to put sth (often sth artificial) into a part of the body for medical purposes, usually by means of an operation: *an electrode implanted into the brain* ⊃ look at **transplant¹** (1) ▶ **implantation** /ˌɪmplɑːnˈteɪʃn/ *noun* [U]: *the implantation of the fertilized ovum* ⊃ picture at **fertilization**

implant² /ˈɪmplɑːnt/ *noun* [C] (**MEDICINE**) something that is put into a part of the body in a medical operation ⊃ look at **transplant²**

implausible /ɪmˈplɔːzəbl/ *adj.* not easy to believe: *an implausible excuse* **OPP plausible**

implement¹ /ˈɪmplɪmənt/ *noun* [C] (*formal*) (**AGRICULTURE**) a tool or instrument (especially for work outdoors): *farm implements* ⊃ note at **tool**

implement² ᴇ+ **B2 W** /ˈɪmplɪment/ *verb* [T] (*formal*) to start using a plan, system, etc: *Some teachers are finding it difficult to implement the government's educational reforms.* ▶ **implementation** ᴇ+ **C1 W** /ˌɪmplɪmenˈteɪʃn/ *noun* [U]

implicate /ˈɪmplɪkeɪt/ *verb* [T] ~ **sb (in sth)** to show or suggest that sb is involved in sth unpleasant, especially a crime: *His enemies tried to implicate him in the murder.*
IDM be implicated in sth to be involved in sth bad, especially a crime: *A well-known politician was implicated in the scandal.*

implication ᴇ+ **B2** /ˌɪmplɪˈkeɪʃn/ *noun* **1** [C, usually pl.] ~ (**of sth**) (**for sth**) the effect that sth might have on sth else in the future: *The new law will have serious implications for our work.* **2** [C, U] ~ (**of sth**) something that is suggested or said in a way that is not direct: *The implication of what she said was that we had made a bad mistake.* ⊃ verb **imply 3** [U] ~ (**in sth**) the fact of being involved, or of involving sb, in sth unpleasant, especially a crime: *The player's implication in this scandal could affect his career.* ⊃ verb **implicate**

implicit W /ɪmˈplɪsɪt/ *adj.* **1** not expressed in a direct way but understood by the people involved: *We had an implicit agreement that we would support each other.* ⊃ look at **explicit** (1) **2** complete; total: *I have implicit faith in your ability to do the job.* **SYN absolute** ▶ **implicitly W** *adv.*

implore /ɪmˈplɔː(r)/ *verb* [T] (*formal*) to ask sb with great emotion to do sth, because you are in a very serious situation: *She implored him not to leave her alone.* **SYN beg, beseech**

imply ᴇ **B2 O** /ɪmˈplaɪ/ *verb* [T] (**implying; implies;** *pt, pp* **implied**) ~ (**that**) … to suggest sth in an indirect way or without actually saying it: *He didn't say so — but he implied that I was lying.* ⊃ noun **implication**

impolite /ˌɪmpəˈlaɪt/ *adj.* rude: *I think it was impolite of him to ask you to leave.* **OPP polite** ▶ **impolitely** *adv.*

import¹ ᴇ **B1** /ˈɪmpɔːt/ *noun* (**ECONOMICS**) **1** [C, usually pl.] a product or service that is brought into one country from another: *What are your country's major imports?* **OPP export²** **2** [U] the act of bringing goods or services into a country: *new controls on the import of certain goods from abroad* **SYN importation**

import² ᴇ **B1** /ɪmˈpɔːt/ *verb* [I, T] **1** ~ **sth (from …)** (**ECONOMICS**) to buy goods, etc. from a foreign country and bring them into your own country: *Britain imports wine from Spain.* ◇ *imported goods* **OPP export¹** **2** (**COMPUTING**) to get data from another program in a form that the program you are using can read

importance ᴇ **B1 O** /ɪmˈpɔːtns/ *noun* [U] the quality of being important: *The decision was of great importance to the future of the business.*

important ᴇ **A1 O** /ɪmˈpɔːtnt/ *adj.* **1** ~ (**to sb**); ~ (**for sb/sth**) (**to do sth**); ~ (**that**) … having great value or influence; very necessary: *an important meeting/decision/factor* ◇ *This job is very important to me.* ◇ *It's important not to be late.* ◇ *It's important for people to see the results of what they do.* ◇ *It was important to me that you were there.* **2** (used about a person) having great influence or authority: *Milton was one of the most important writers of his time.* ▶ **importantly W** *adv.*

importation /ˌɪmpɔːˈteɪʃn/ *noun* [U] the act of bringing goods or services into a country **SYN import¹**

importer /ɪmˈpɔːtə(r)/ *noun* [C] a person, company, etc. that buys goods from another country in order to sell them in their own country **OPP** **exporter**

impose ⓘ **B2** ⓦ /ɪmˈpəʊz/ *verb* **1** [T] ~ sth (on/upon sb/sth) to make a law, a rule, an opinion, etc. be accepted by using your power or authority: *A new tax will be imposed on wine and spirits.* **2** [I] ~ (on/upon sb/ sth) to ask or expect sb to do sth that may cause extra work or trouble: *I hate to impose on you, but can you lend me some money?* ▸ **imposition** /ˌɪmpəˈzɪʃn/ *noun* [U, C]: *the imposition of military rule*

imposing /ɪmˈpəʊzɪŋ/ *adj.* big and important; impressive: *They lived in a large, imposing house near the park.*

impossible ⓘ **A2** /ɪmˈpɒsəbl/ *adj.* **1** ~ (for sb) (to do sth) not able to be done or to happen: *It's impossible for me to be there before 12.* ◇ *I find it almost impossible to get up in the morning!* ◇ *That's impossible!* (= I don't believe it!) **OPP** **possible** **2** very difficult to deal with: *This is an impossible situation!* ◇ *He's always been an impossible child.* ▸ **impossibility** /ɪmˌpɒsəˈbɪləti/ *noun* [C, U] (*pl.* -ies): *What you are suggesting is a complete impossibility!* ▸ the **impossible** *noun* [sing.]: *Don't attempt the impossible!*

impossibly /ɪmˈpɒsəbli/ *adv.* extremely: *impossibly complicated*

impostor (*BrE also* **imposter**) /ɪmˈpɒstə(r)/ *noun* [C] a person who pretends to be sb else in order to trick other people

impotent /ˈɪmpətənt/ *adj.* **1** without enough power to influence a situation or to change things **SYN** **powerless** **2** (**HEALTH**) (used about men) unable to achieve an ERECTION and therefore not able to have full sex ▸ **impotence** /-pətəns/ *noun* [U]

impound /ɪmˈpaʊnd/ *verb* [T] (**LAW**) (used about the police, courts, etc.) to take sth away from sb, so that they cannot use it: *The car was impounded by the police after the accident.*

impoverish /ɪmˈpɒvərɪʃ/ *verb* [T] (*formal*) (**SOCIAL STUDIES**) to make sb/sth poor or worse in quality: *A wave of price increases has impoverished the population.* ◇ *Intensive cultivation has impoverished the soil.* **OPP** **enrich**

impractical /ɪmˈpræktɪkl/ *adj.* **1** not sensible or realistic: *It would be impractical to take our bikes on the train.* **OPP** **practical**[1] **2** (used about a person) not good at doing ordinary things that involve using your hands; not good at organizing or planning things

imprecise /ˌɪmprɪˈsaɪs/ *adj.* not clear or exact: *imprecise instructions* **OPP** **precise**

impregnable /ɪmˈpregnəbl/ *adj.* **1** an **impregnable** building is so strongly built that it cannot be entered by force **2** strong and impossible to defeat or change **SYN** **invincible**

impregnate /ˈɪmpregneɪt/ *verb* [T] **1** [usually passive] to make a substance spread through an area so that the area is full of the substance: *The pad is impregnated with insecticide.* **2** (*formal*) (**BIOLOGY**) to make a woman or female animal pregnant

impress ⓘ **B2** /ɪmˈpres/ *verb* [T] **1** ~ sb (with sth); ~ sb that … if a person or thing impresses you, you admire them: *She's always trying to impress people with her new clothes.* ◇ *It impressed me that he understood immediately what I meant.* **2** ~ sth on/upon sb (*formal*) to make the importance of sth very clear to sb: *You should impress on John that he must pass these exams.*

impressed ⓘ **B2** /ɪmˈprest/ *adj.* ~ (by/with sb/sth) admiring sb/sth because you think they are particularly good, interesting, etc: *We were all impressed by her enthusiasm.*

impression ⓘ **B1** /ɪmˈpreʃn/ *noun* [C] **1** an idea, a feeling or an opinion that you get about sb/sth: *What's your first impression of the new director?* ◇ *I'm not sure but I have/get the impression that Jane's rather unhappy.* ◇ *I was under the impression* (= I believed, but I was wrong) *that you were married.* ⊃ note at **think**[1] **2** the effect that a person or thing produces on sb else: *She gives the impression of being older than she really is.* ◇ *Do you think I made a good impression on your parents?* **3** a clever or funny copy of the way a person acts or speaks: *My brother can do a good impression of the prime minister.* **SYN** **imitation** **SYN** **impersonation** **4** a mark that is left when an object has been pressed hard into a surface

impressionable /ɪmˈpreʃənəbl/ *adj.* easy to influence: *Sixteen is a very impressionable age.*

Impressionism /ɪmˈpreʃənɪzəm/ (*also* **impressionism**) *noun* [U] (**ART**) a style in painting developed in France in the late nineteenth century that uses colour to show the effects of light on things and to suggest atmosphere rather than showing exact details ▸ **Impressionist** (*also* **impressionist**) *adj.*: *Impressionist landscapes*

impressionist /ɪmˈpreʃənɪst/ *noun* [C] **1** (*usually* **Impressionist**) (**ART**) an artist who paints in the style of Impressionism: *Impressionists such as Monet and Pissarro* **2** a person who makes people laugh by copying the way a famous person speaks or behaves

impressive ⓘ **B1** /ɪmˈpresɪv/ *adj.* (used about things or people) making you admire them because of their importance, size, quality, etc: *an impressive building/ speech* ◇ *The way he handled the situation was most impressive.*

imprint /ˈɪmprɪnt/ *noun* [C] a mark made by pressing an object on a surface: *the imprint of a foot in the sand*

imprison ⓘ+ **C1** /ɪmˈprɪzn/ *verb* [T, often passive] (**LAW**) to put or keep sb in prison: *He was imprisoned for armed robbery.* **SYN** **jail** ▸ **imprisonment** ⓘ+ **C1** *noun* [U]: *She was sentenced to life imprisonment for murder.* ⊃ note at **crime**

improbable /ɪmˈprɒbəbl/ *adj.* not likely to be true or to happen: *an improbable explanation* ◇ *It is highly improbable that she will arrive tonight.* **SYN** **unlikely** **OPP** **probable** ▸ **improbability** /ɪmˌprɒbəˈbɪləti/ *noun* [U] ▸ **improbably** /ɪmˈprɒbəbli/ *adv.*

impromptu /ɪmˈprɒmptjuː/ *adj.* (done) without being prepared or organized: *an impromptu party*

improper /ɪmˈprɒpə(r)/ *adj.* **1** illegal or dishonest: *It seems that she had been involved in improper business deals.* **2** not suitable for the situation; rude in a sexual way: *It would be improper to say anything else at this stage.* ◇ *He lost his job for making improper suggestions to several of the women.* **OPP** **proper** ▸ **improperly** *adv.*

im,proper ˈfraction *noun* [C] (**MATHEMATICS**) a FRACTION in which the top number is greater than the bottom number, for example 7/6 ⊃ look at **proper fraction**

impropriety /ˌɪmprəˈpraɪəti/ *noun* [U, C] (*pl.* -ies) (*formal*) behaviour or actions that are morally wrong or not appropriate: *She was unaware of the impropriety of her remark.*

improve ⓘ **A1** ⓦ /ɪmˈpruːv/ *verb* [I, T] to become better or to make sth better: *Your work has greatly improved.* ◇ *I hope the weather will improve later on.* ◇ *Your vocabulary is excellent but you could improve your pronunciation.*

PHR V **improve on/upon sth** to produce sth that is better than sth else: *Nobody will be able to improve on that score* (= nobody will be able to make a higher score).

improvement 🔊 **B1** Ⓦ /ɪmˈpruːvmənt/ *noun* [U, C] ~ **(in sth)**; ~ **(on sth)** (a) change that makes the quality or condition of sb/sth better: *Your written work is in need of some improvement.* ◇ *a continuous/significant/marked improvement* ◇ *There's been a considerable improvement in your mother's condition.* ◇ *These marks are an improvement on your previous ones.*

improvise /ˈɪmprəvaɪz/ *verb* [I, T] **1** to make, do or manage sth without preparation, using what you have: *If you can't find the equipment you need, you'll have to improvise.* **2** (**MUSIC**) to play music, speak or act using your imagination instead of written or remembered material: *It was obvious that the actor had forgotten his lines and was trying to improvise.* ◇ *a brilliant improvised speech* ▶ **improvisation** /ˌɪmprəvaɪˈzeɪʃn/ *noun* [U, C]

impudent /ˈɪmpjədənt/ *adj.* (*formal*) very rude; lacking respect and not polite **SYN** **cheeky**, **impertinent** ▶ **impudence** /-dəns/ *noun* [U] ▶ **impudently** /-dntli/ *adv.*

impulse /ˈɪmpʌls/ *noun* [C] **1** [usually sing.] ~ **(to do sth)** a sudden desire to do sth without thinking about the results: *She felt a terrible impulse to rush out of the house and never come back.* **2** (**BIOLOGY**, **PHYSICS**) a force or movement of energy that causes a reaction: *nerve/electrical impulses* **IDM** **on (an) impulse** without thinking or planning and not considering the results

impulsive /ɪmˈpʌlsɪv/ *adj.* likely to act suddenly and without thinking; done without careful thought: *an impulsive character* ▶ **impulsively** *adv.* ▶ **impulsiveness** *noun* [U]

impure /ɪmˈpjʊə(r)/ *adj.* **1** not pure or clean; consisting of more than one substance mixed together (and therefore not of good quality): *impure metals* **OPP** **pure** **2** (*old-fashioned*) (used about thoughts and actions connected with sex) not moral; bad **OPP** **pure**

impurity /ɪmˈpjʊərəti/ *noun* (*pl.* -ies) **1** [C, usually pl.] a substance that is present in small amounts in another substance, making it dirty or of poor quality **2** [U] (*old-fashioned*) the state of being morally bad ⊃ look at **purity**

in¹ 🔊 **A1** /ɪn/ *adv., prep.* **1** (used to show place) inside or to a position inside a particular area or object: *a country in Africa* ◇ *an island in the Pacific* ◇ *in a box* ◇ *I read about it in the newspaper.* ◇ *He lay in bed.* ◇ *She put the keys in her pocket.* ◇ *His wife's in hospital.* ◇ *She opened the door and went in.* ◇ *My suitcase is full. I can't get any more in.* ◇ *When does the train get in* (= to the station)? **2** at home or at work: *She won't be in till late today.* ◇ *I knocked at the door, but he wasn't in.* **OPP** **out¹** **3** (showing time) during a period of time: *My birthday is in August.* ◇ *in spring/summer/autumn/winter* ◇ *He was born in 1980.* ◇ *You could walk there in about an hour* (= it would take that long to walk there). **4** (showing time) after a period of time: *I'll be finished in ten minutes.* **5** wearing sth: *They were all dressed in black for the funeral.* ◇ *I've never seen you in a suit before.* **6** showing the condition or state of sb/sth: *My father is in poor health.* ◇ *This room is in a mess!* ◇ *Richard's in love.* ◇ *He's in his mid-thirties.* **7** showing sb's job or the activity sb is involved in: *He's got a good job in advertising.* ◇ *All her family are in politics* (= they are politicians). ◇ *He's in the army.* **8** contained in; forming the whole or part of sth: *There are 31 days in*

January. ◇ *What's in this casserole?* **9** used for saying how things are arranged: *We sat in a circle.* ◇ *She had her hair in plaits.* **10** used for saying how sth is written or expressed: *Please write in pen.* ◇ *They were talking in Italian/French/Polish.* ◇ *to work in groups/teams* **11** used with feelings: *I watched in horror as the plane crashed to the ground.* ◇ *He was in such a rage I didn't dare to go near him.* **12** used for giving the rate of sth and for talking about numbers: *One family in ten owns a dishwasher.* **13** received by sb official: *All applications must be in by 20 March.* **14** (used about the sea) at the highest point, when the water is closest to the land: *The tide's coming in.* ❶ For special uses with many verbs and nouns, for example ▶ **in time**, **give in**, look at the verb and noun entries.

IDM **be in for it/sth** (*informal*) to be going to experience sth unpleasant: *He'll be in for a shock when he gets the bill.* ◇ *You'll be in for it when Mum sees what you've done.* **be/get in on sth** (*informal*) to be included or involved in sth: *I'd like to be in on the new project.* **have (got) it in for sb** (*informal*) to be unpleasant to sb because they have done sth to upset you: *The boss has had it in for me ever since I asked to be considered for the new post .*

in² /ɪn/ *noun* **IDM** **the ins and outs (of sth)** the details and difficulties (involved in sth): *Will somebody explain the ins and outs of the situation to me?*

in³ /ɪn/ *adj.* (*informal*) fashionable at the moment: *the in place to go* ◇ *The colour grey is very in this season.*

in. *abbr.* (in writing) (*pl.* in., ins.) = INCH¹

in- /ɪn/ *prefix* **1** (*also* il-, im-, ir-) (in nouns, adjectives and adverbs) not; the opposite of: *infinite* ◇ *illogical* ◇ *immorally* ◇ *irrelevance* **2** (*also* im-) (in verbs) to put into the condition mentioned: *inflame* ◇ *imperil*

inability 🔊+ **C1** Ⓦ /ˌɪnəˈbɪləti/ *noun* [U, sing.] ~ **(to do sth)** lack of ability, power or skill: *He has a complete inability to listen to other people's opinions.* **OPP** **ability** ⊃ adjective **unable**

inaccessible /ˌɪnækˈsesəbl/ *adj.* very difficult or impossible to reach, use or contact: *That beach is inaccessible by car.* **OPP** **accessible** ▶ **inaccessibility** /ˌɪnækˌsesəˈbɪləti/ *noun* [U]

inaccurate /ɪnˈækjərət/ *adj.* not correct or accurate; with mistakes: *an inaccurate report/description/statement* ⊃ look at **accurate** ▶ **inaccuracy** /-rəsi/ *noun* [C, U] (*pl.* -ies): *There are always some inaccuracies in newspaper reports.* ⊃ look at **accuracy** ▶ **inaccurately** *adv.*

inaction /ɪnˈækʃn/ *noun* [U] doing nothing; lack of action: *The crisis was blamed on the government's earlier inaction.* ⊃ look at **action¹** (1)

inactive /ɪnˈæktɪv/ *adj.* doing nothing; not active: *The virus remains inactive in the body.* **OPP** **active** ▶ **inactivity** /ˌɪnækˈtɪvəti/ *noun* [U]

inadequate 🔊+ **C1** Ⓦ /ɪnˈædɪkwət/ *adj.* ~ **(for sth/to do sth)** not enough; not good enough: *the problem of inadequate housing* ◇ *The building is inadequate for the needs of the community.* ◇ *The plan is inadequate to deal with climate change.* **OPP** **adequate** **2** (used about a person) not able to deal with a problem or situation; not confident: *There was so much to learn in the new job that for a while I felt totally inadequate.* ⊃ look at **incompetent** ▶ **inadequacy** /-kwəsi/ *noun* [C, U] (*pl.* -ies): *his inadequacy as a parent* ▶ **inadequately** *adv.*

inadmissible /ˌɪnədˈmɪsəbl/ *adj.* (*formal*) (**LAW**) that cannot be allowed or accepted, especially in a court of law: *inadmissible evidence* **OPP** **admissible**

inadvertently /ˌɪnədˈvɜːtntli/ *adv.* by accident, not on purpose: *She had inadvertently left the letter where he could find it.* **SYN** **unintentionally** ▸ **inadvertent** /ˌɪnədˈvɜːtnt/ *adj.*

inadvisable /ˌɪnədˈvaɪzəbl/ *adj.* (*formal*) not sensible; not showing good judgement: *It is inadvisable to go swimming after a meal.* **OPP** **advisable**

inalienable /ɪnˈeɪliənəbl/ (*also* **unalienable**) *adj.* (*formal*) that cannot be taken away from you: *Every citizen has an inalienable right to vote.*

inane /ɪˈneɪn/ *adj.* without any meaning; silly: *an inane remark* ▸ **inanely** *adv.*

inanimate /ɪnˈænɪmət/ *adj.* not alive in the way that people, animals and plants are: *A rock is an inanimate object.* **OPP** **animate**[1]

in-app *adj.* [only before noun] (used especially about sth you can buy) available from within a particular app on a device such as a smartphone or tablet

inappropriate ʔ+ **C1** **W** /ˌɪnəˈprəʊpriət/ *adj.* ~ **(for sb/sth) (to do sth)** not suitable: *Isn't that dress rather inappropriate for the occasion?* ◇ *It would be inappropriate for me to comment.* ◇ *inappropriate behaviour* **OPP** **appropriate**[1]

inarticulate /ˌɪnɑːˈtɪkjələt/ *adj.* **1** (used about a person) not able to express ideas and feelings clearly **OPP** **articulate**[1] **2** (used about speech) not clear or well expressed **OPP** **articulate**[1] ▸ **inarticulately** *adv.*

inasmuch as /ˌɪnəzˈmʌtʃ əz/ *conj.* (*formal*) because of the fact that: *We felt sorry for the boys inasmuch as they had not realized that what they were doing was wrong.*

inattention /ˌɪnəˈtenʃn/ *noun* [U] lack of attention: *a moment of inattention* ⊃ look at **attention**[1] (1)

inattentive /ˌɪnəˈtentɪv/ *adj.* not paying attention: *One inattentive student can disturb the whole class.* **OPP** **attentive**

inaudible /ɪnˈɔːdəbl/ *adj.* not loud enough to be heard **OPP** **audible** ▸ **inaudibly** /-bli/ *adv.*

inaugural /ɪˈnɔːɡjərəl/ *adj.* [only before noun] (used about an official speech, meeting, etc.) first, and marking the beginning of sth important: *the president's inaugural address*

inaugurate /ɪˈnɔːɡjəreɪt/ *verb* [T] **1** ~ **sb (as sth)** to introduce a new official, leader, etc. at a special formal ceremony: *He will be inaugurated as president next month.* **2** to start, introduce or open sth new (often at a special formal ceremony) ▸ **inauguration** /ɪˌnɔːɡjəˈreɪʃn/ *noun* [C, U]

inauspicious /ˌɪnɔːˈspɪʃəs/ *adj.* (*formal*) showing signs that the future will not be good or successful: *He made an inauspicious start* **OPP** **auspicious**

inborn /ˌɪnˈbɔːn/ *adj.* an **inborn** quality is one that you are born with **SYN** **innate**

inbound /ˈɪnbaʊnd/ *adj.* (*formal*) (**TOURISM**) travelling towards a place rather than leaving it: *inbound flights/passengers* **OPP** **outbound**

inbox /ˈɪnbɒks/ *noun* [C] (**COMPUTING**) **1** the place on a computer or phone where new emails, text messages, etc. are shown: *I have a stack of emails in my inbox.* **2** (*AmE*) = IN TRAY

inbred /ˌɪnˈbred/ *adj.* produced by BREEDING (= producing young) among closely related members of a group of animals, people or plants

inbreeding /ˈɪnbriːdɪŋ/ *noun* [U] BREEDING (= producing young) between closely related people or animals

Inc. /ɪŋk/ (*also* **inc.**) *abbr.* = INCORPORATED: *Manhattan Drugstores Inc.*

inc. (*BrE*) (*also* **incl.** *BrE, AmE*) *abbr.* (in writing) = INCLUDING, INCLUDED: *total £59.00 inc. tax*

incalculable /ɪnˈkælkjələbl/ *adj.* (*formal*) very great; too great to calculate: *an incalculable risk*

incapable /ɪnˈkeɪpəbl/ *adj.* **1** ~ **of sth/doing sth** not able to do sth: *She is incapable of hard work/working hard.* ◇ *He's quite incapable of unkindness* (= too nice to be unkind). **OPP** **capable** **2** not able to do, manage or organize anything well: *As a doctor, she's totally incapable.* **OPP** **capable**

incapacitate /ˌɪnkəˈpæsɪteɪt/ *verb* [T, usually passive] (*formal*) to make sb/sth unable to live or work normally

in-car *adj.* [only before noun] relating to sth that you have or use inside a car, for example a radio: *in-car entertainment*

incarcerate /ɪnˈkɑːsəreɪt/ *verb* [T, usually passive] (*formal*) (**LAW**) to put sb in prison or in another place from which they cannot escape **SYN** **imprison** ▸ **incarceration** /ɪnˌkɑːsəˈreɪʃn/ *noun* [U]

incarnation /ˌɪnkɑːˈneɪʃn/ *noun* [C] **1** a period of life in a particular form: *He believed he was a prince in a previous incarnation.* ⊃ look at **reincarnation** (2) **2** [usually sing.] **the ~ of sth** (a person that is) a perfect example of a particular quality: *She is the incarnation of goodness.*

incendiary /ɪnˈsendiəri/ *adj.* [only before noun] that causes a fire: *an incendiary bomb/device*

incense /ˈɪnsens/ *noun* [U] a substance that produces a sweet smell when burnt, used especially in religious ceremonies

incensed /ɪnˈsenst/ *adj.* ~ **(by/at sth)** very angry **SYN** **furious**

incentive ʔ+ **B2** /ɪnˈsentɪv/ *noun* [C, U] ~ **(for/to sb/sth) (to do sth)** something that encourages you (to do sth): *There's no incentive for young people to do well at school because there aren't any jobs when they leave.* ◇ *The company is offering cash incentives to staff to move to another area.*

incessant /ɪnˈsesnt/ *adj.* never stopping (and usually annoying): *incessant rain/noise/chatter* ⊃ look at **constant**[1] (1), **continual** ▸ **incessantly** *adv.*

incest /ˈɪnsest/ *noun* [U] (**LAW**) illegal sex between members of the same family who are very closely related, for example a brother and sister

incestuous /ɪnˈsestʃuəs/ *adj.* **1** involving illegal sex between members of the same family who are very closely related: *an incestuous relationship* **2** (used about a group of people and their relationships with each other) too close; not open to anyone outside the group: *Life in a small community can be very incestuous.*

inch[1] ʔ+ **B2** /ɪntʃ/ *noun* [C] (*abbr.* in.) a measure of length, equal to 2.54 CENTIMETRES. There are 12 inches in a foot: *He's 5 foot 10 inches tall.* ◇ *Three inches of rain fell last night.* ❶ For more information about measurements, look at the **Reference Section** of this dictionary.

inch[2] /ɪntʃ/ *verb* [I, T] (used with an adverb or a preposition) to move slowly and carefully in the direction mentioned: *He inched (his way) forward along the cliff edge.*

incidence ʔ+ **C1** /ˈɪnsɪdəns/ *noun* **1** [C, usually sing.] **an ~ of sth** (*formal*) the number of times sth (usually sth unpleasant) happens; the rate of sth: *a high incidence of crime/disease/unemployment* **2** [U] (**PHYSICS**) the way in which a RAY of light meets a surface: *the angle of incidence* ⊃ picture at **reflection** ▸ **incident** *adj.*: *the incident ray* (= the one that meets a surface) ◇ *the incident angle* (= at which a RAY of light meets a surface) ⊃ picture at **reflection**

incident¹ 🔊 **B2** /ˈɪnsɪdənt/ *noun* [C, U] (*formal*) something that happens (especially sth unusual or unpleasant): *There were a number of incidents after the football match.* ◇ *The demonstration passed off without incident.*

incident² /ˈɪnsɪdənt/ *adj.* (used about light, RADIATION, etc.) touching or hitting a surface ⊃ picture at **reflection** (2)

incidental /ˌɪnsɪˈdentl/ *adj.* ~ **(to sth)** happening as part of sth more important: *The book contains various themes that are incidental to the main plot.*

incidentally /ˌɪnsɪˈdentli/ *adv.* used to introduce extra news, information, etc. that the speaker has just thought of: *Incidentally, that new restaurant you told me about is excellent.* **SYN** **by the way**

ˈincident room *noun* [C] (LAW) a room where the police collect evidence and information about a crime or an accident that has taken place

incinerate /ɪnˈsɪnəreɪt/ *verb* [T] (*formal*) to destroy sth completely, especially waste material, by burning ▶ **incineration** /ɪnˌsɪnəˈreɪʃn/ *noun* [U]: *high-temperature incineration plants*

incinerator /ɪnˈsɪnəreɪtə(r)/ *noun* [C] a container or machine for burning rubbish, etc.

incipient /ɪnˈsɪpiənt/ *adj.* (*formal*) just beginning: *signs of incipient unrest*

incision /ɪnˈsɪʒn/ *noun* [C] (*formal*) a cut carefully made into sth (especially into a person's body as part of a medical operation)

incisive /ɪnˈsaɪsɪv/ *adj.* **1** showing clear thought and good understanding of what is important, and having the ability to express this: *incisive comments/criticism/analysis* ◇ *an incisive mind* **2** showing sb's ability to take decisions and act quickly and directly: *an incisive performance*

incisor /ɪnˈsaɪzə(r)/ *noun* [C] (ANATOMY) one of the sharp teeth at the front of the mouth that are used for biting. Humans have eight incisors. ⊃ look at **canine²**, **molar**, **premolar** ⊃ picture at **tooth**

incite /ɪnˈsaɪt/ *verb* [T] ~ **sb (to sth)** to encourage sb to do sth violent, illegal or unpleasant by making them very angry or excited: *He was accused of inciting the crowd to violence.* ▶ **incitement** *noun* [U, C]: *He was guilty of incitement to violence.*

inclination /ˌɪnklɪˈneɪʃn/ *noun* [U, C] ~ **(to do sth)**; ~ **(towards/for sth)** a feeling that makes sb want to behave in a particular way or make a particular choice: *He did not show the slightest inclination to help.* ◇ *She had no inclination for a career in teaching.*

incline¹ /ɪnˈklaɪn/ *verb* **1** [I] ~ **to/towards sth** (*formal*) to tend to behave in a particular way or make a particular choice **2** [T] ~ **your head** (*formal*) to bend your head forward: *They sat round the table, heads inclined, deep in discussion.*

incline² /ˈɪnklaɪn/ *noun* [C] (*formal*) (GEOGRAPHY) a slight hill: *a steep/slight incline* **SYN** **slope**

inclined 🔊 **C1** /ɪnˈklaɪnd/ *adj.* **1** [not before noun] ~ **(to do sth)** wanting to do sth in a particular way: *I know Amir well so I'm inclined to believe what he says.* **2** ~ **to do sth** tending to do sth; likely to do sth: *She's inclined to change her mind very easily.* **3** having a natural ability in the subject mentioned: *to be musically inclined*

include 🔊 **A1** 🌐 /ɪnˈkluːd/ *verb* [T] (not used in the progressive tenses) **1** to have as one part; to contain (among other things): *The price of the holiday includes the flight, the hotel and car hire.* ◇ *The crew included one woman.* **OPP** **exclude** **2** ~ **sb/sth (as/in/on sth)** to make sb/sth part (of another group, etc.): *The children immediately included the new girl in their games.*

included 🔊 **A2** /ɪnˈkluːdɪd/ *adj.* (after a noun) (*abbr.* incl., inc.) contained as part of sth: *Is breakfast included?* ◇ *Everyone was disappointed, myself included.*

including 🔊 **A2** 🌐 /ɪnˈkluːdɪŋ/ *prep.* (*abbr.* incl., inc.) having as a part: *It costs £17.99, including postage and packing.* **OPP** **excluding**

inclusion 🔊+ **C1** 🌐 /ɪnˈkluːʒn/ *noun* [U] **1** the fact of including sb/sth; the fact of being included: *The inclusion of all that violence in the film was unnecessary.* **2** (PSYCHOLOGY) the fact or policy of providing equal opportunities and resources for people who might otherwise not get them, for example people who are DISABLED or belong to minority groups: *As a society we are moving towards greater inclusion and equality for all people.*

inclusive /ɪnˈkluːsɪv/ *adj.* **1** ~ **(of sth)** (used about a price, etc.) including or containing everything; including the thing mentioned: *Is that an inclusive price or are there some extras?* ◇ *The rent is inclusive of electricity.* **OPP** **exclusive¹** **2** (after a noun) including the dates, numbers, etc. mentioned: *You are booked at the hotel from Monday to Friday inclusive* (= including Monday and Friday). **❶** When talking about time **through** is often used in American English instead of **inclusive**: *We'll be away from Friday through Sunday.*

incognito /ˌɪnkɒɡˈniːtəʊ/ *adv.* hiding your real name and identity (especially if you are famous and do not want to be recognized): *to travel incognito*

incoherent /ˌɪnkəʊˈhɪərənt/ *adj.* not clear, not well organized or easy to understand; not saying sth clearly **OPP** **coherent** ▶ **incoherence** /-rəns/ *noun* [U] ▶ **incoherently** *adv.*

circular flow of income

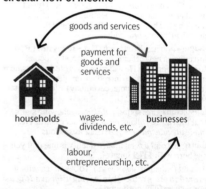

goods and services

payment for goods and services

households

businesses

wages, dividends, etc.

labour, entrepreneurship, etc.

income 🔊 **B2** /ˈɪnkʌm, -kəm/ *noun* [C, U] (FINANCE) the money that a person, a region, a country, etc. earns from work, from investing money, from business, etc: *It's often difficult for a family to live on one income.*

▼ **VOCABULARY BUILDING**

You can talk about a **monthly** or an **annual** income. An income may be **high** or **low**. Your **gross** income is the amount you earn before paying tax. Your **net** income is your income after tax. Look at the note at **pay²**.

ˈincome tax *noun* [U] (FINANCE) the amount of money you pay to the government according to how much you earn

incoming /ˈɪnkʌmɪŋ/ *adj.* [only before noun] **1** arriving or being received: *incoming flights/passengers* ◇ *incoming phone calls* **2** recently elected or chosen: *the incoming government*

incomparable /ɪnˈkɒmprəbl/ *adj.* so good or great that it does not have an equal: *incomparable beauty* ⊃ verb **compare**

incompatible /ˌɪnkəmˈpætəbl/ *adj.* ~ (with sb/sth) very different and therefore not able to live or work happily with sb or exist with sth: *The working hours of the job are incompatible with family life.* ◇ *Those two blood groups are incompatible.* **OPP compatible** ▸ incompatibility /ˌɪnkəmˌpætəˈbɪləti/ *noun* [U, C] (*pl.* -ies)

incompetent /ɪnˈkɒmpɪtənt/ *adj.* lacking the necessary skill to do sth well: *He is completely incompetent at his job.* ◇ *an incompetent teacher/manager* **OPP competent** ▸ incompetence /-pɪtəns/ *noun* [U] ▸ incompetent *noun* [C]: *He's a hopeless incompetent.* ▸ incompetently *adv.*

incomplete /ˌɪnkəmˈpliːt/ *adj.* having a part or parts missing; not finished or complete: *His happiness is incomplete without her.* ◇ *Unfortunately the jigsaw puzzle was incomplete.* **OPP complete**[1] ▸ incompletely *adv.*

incomprehensible /ɪnˌkɒmprɪˈhensəbl/ *adj.* (**LANGUAGE**) impossible to understand: *an incomprehensible explanation* ◇ *Her attitude is totally incomprehensible to the rest of us.* **OPP comprehensible, understandable** ▸ incomprehension /-ˈhenʃn/ *noun* [U]

inconceivable /ˌɪnkənˈsiːvəbl/ *adj.* impossible or very difficult to believe or imagine: *It's inconceivable that he would have stolen anything.* **SYN unthinkable OPP conceivable**

inconclusive /ˌɪnkənˈkluːsɪv/ *adj.* not leading to a definite decision or result: *an inconclusive discussion* ◇ *inconclusive evidence* (= that doesn't prove anything) **OPP conclusive** ▸ inconclusively *adv.*

incongruous /ɪnˈkɒŋɡruəs/ *adj.* strange and out of place; not suitable in a particular situation: *That huge table looks rather incongruous in such a small room.* ▸ incongruity /ˌɪnkənˈɡruːəti/ *noun* [U, C] ▸ incongruously *adv.*

inconsiderate /ˌɪnkənˈsɪdərət/ *adj.* (used about a person) not thinking or caring about the feelings or needs of other people **SYN thoughtless OPP considerate** ▸ inconsiderately *adv.* ▸ inconsiderateness *noun* [U]

inconsistent ⦿ /ˌɪnkənˈsɪstənt/ *adj.* **1** ~ (with sth) (used about statements, facts, etc.) not the same as sth else; not matching, so that one thing must be wrong or not true: *The witnesses' accounts of the event are inconsistent.* ◇ *These new facts are inconsistent with the earlier information.* **OPP consistent 2** (used about a person) likely to change (in attitude, behaviour, etc.) so that you cannot depend on them **OPP consistent** ▸ inconsistency /-stənsi/ *noun* [C, U] (*pl.* -ies): *There were a few inconsistencies in her argument.* ▸ inconsistently *adv.*

inconspicuous /ˌɪnkənˈspɪkjuəs/ *adj.* not easily noticed: *I tried to make myself as inconspicuous as possible so that no one would ask me a question.* **OPP conspicuous** ▸ inconspicuously *adv.*

incontinent /ɪnˈkɒntɪnənt/ *adj.* (**HEALTH**) unable to control the passing of URINE (= liquid waste) or FAECES (= solid waste) from the body ▸ incontinence /-ˈkɒntɪnəns/ *noun* [U]

inconvenience /ˌɪnkənˈviːniəns/ *noun* [U, C] trouble or difficulty, especially when it affects sth that you need to do; a person or thing that causes this: *We apologize for any inconvenience caused by the delays.* ◇ *The lack* of hot water is a minor inconvenience compared to the lack of light. ▸ inconvenience *verb* [T]

inconvenient /ˌɪnkənˈviːniənt/ *adj.* causing trouble or difficulty, especially when it affects sth that you need to do: *It's a bit inconvenient at the moment — could you phone again later?* **OPP convenient** ▸ inconveniently *adv.*

incorporate ⦿+ B2 Ⓦ /ɪnˈkɔːpəreɪt/ *verb* [T] ~ sth (in/ into/within sth) to make sth a part of sth else; to have sth as a part: *I'd like you to incorporate this information into your report.* ◇ *The new car incorporates all the most modern safety features.* **SYN include** ▸ incorporation /ɪnˌkɔːpəˈreɪʃn/ *noun* [U]

incorporated /ɪnˈkɔːpəreɪtɪd/ *adj.* (*abbr.* Inc., inc.) (**BUSINESS**) formed into a business company that is recognized by law

incorrect ⦿+ B2 /ˌɪnkəˈrekt/ *adj.* not right or true: *Incorrect answers should be marked with a cross.* **OPP correct**[1] ▸ incorrectly *adv.*

incorrigible /ɪnˈkɒrɪdʒəbl/ *adj.* (used about a person or their behaviour) very bad; too bad to be corrected or improved: *an incorrigible liar*

increase[1] ⦿ B2 A2 ⦿ /ɪnˈkriːs/ *verb* [I, T] ~ (sth) (from A) (to B); ~ (sth) (by sth) to become or to make sth larger in number or amount: *My employer would like me to increase my hours of work from 25 to 30.* ◇ *The rate of inflation has increased by 1% to 7%.* ◇ *She increased her speed to overtake the lorry.* **OPP decrease**[1], **reduce** ⊃ note at **price**[1], **rise**[2], **trend**[1]

increase[2] ⦿ A2 ⦿ /ˈɪnkriːs/ *noun* [C, U] ~ (in sth) a rise in the number, amount or level of sth: *There has been a sharp increase of nearly 50% on last year's figures.* ◇ *They are demanding a large wage increase.* ◇ *Doctors expect some further increase in the spread of the disease.* **OPP decrease**[2], **reduction** **IDM** on the increase becoming larger or more common; increasing: *Attacks by dogs on children are on the increase.*

increasingly ⦿ B2 ⦿ /ɪnˈkriːsɪŋli/ *adv.* more and more: *It's becoming increasingly dangerous to stay here.*

incredible ⦿ A2 /ɪnˈkredəbl/ *adj.* **1** impossible or very difficult to believe: *I found his account of the event incredible.* ◇ *It's just incredible that nobody was hurt.* **OPP credible** ⊃ look at **unbelievable 2** (*informal*) extremely good or big: *He earns an incredible salary.* ▸ incredibly ⦿ B1 /-bli/ *adv.*: *We have had some incredibly strong winds recently.*

increment /ˈɪŋkrəmənt/ *noun* [C] **1** (**FINANCE**) a regular increase in the amount of money that sb is paid for their job: *a salary with annual increments* **2** (*formal*) an increase in a number or an amount ▸ incremental /ˌɪŋkrəˈmentl/ *adj.*: *incremental costs* ▸ incrementally /-təli/ *adv.*

incriminate /ɪnˈkrɪmɪneɪt/ *verb* [T] (**LAW**) to provide evidence that sb is guilty of a crime: *The police searched the house but found nothing to incriminate the man.*

incubate /ˈɪŋkjubeɪt/ *verb* **1** [T] (**BIOLOGY**) to keep eggs, cells, bacteria, etc. at the right temperature so that they can develop **2** [I, T] (**HEALTH**) (used about a disease) to develop without showing signs; (used about a person or an animal) to have a disease developing inside you without showing signs: *Some viruses incubate for weeks.*

incubation /ˌɪŋkjuˈbeɪʃn/ *noun* **1** [U] (**BIOLOGY**) the process of INCUBATING eggs (= keeping them at the right temperature to develop) **2** (*also* ˌincuˈbation period) [C] (**HEALTH**) the period between catching a disease and the time when signs of it appear

incubator /'ɪŋkjubeɪtə(r)/ *noun* [C] **1** (**MEDICINE**) a heated machine used in hospitals for keeping small or weak babies alive **2** a machine for keeping eggs warm until the young birds are born

inculcate /'ɪnkʌlkeɪt/ *verb* [T] ~ sth (in/into sb); ~ sb with sth (*formal*) to cause sb to learn and remember ideas, moral principles, etc., especially by repeating them often: *to inculcate a sense of responsibility in somebody* ◇ *to inculcate somebody with a sense of responsibility*

incumbent /ɪn'kʌmbənt/ *noun* [C] a person who has an official position: *the **present incumbent** of the White House* ▸ **incumbent** *adj.*: *the incumbent president*

incur ⓘ+ /ɪn'kɜ:(r)/ *verb* [T] (-rr-) (*formal*) to suffer the unpleasant results of a situation that you have caused: *to incur debts/somebody's anger*

incurable /ɪn'kjʊərəbl/ *adj.* that cannot be cured or made better: *an incurable disease* **OPP** **curable** ▸ **incurably** /-bli/ *adv.*: *incurably ill*

incus /'ɪŋkəs/ *noun* [C] (*pl.* **incudes** /ɪn'kju:di:z/) (**ANATOMY**) the second of three small bones in the MIDDLE EAR that carry sound to the INNER EAR **SYN** anvil ⊃ picture at **ear**

Ind. *abbr.* (in writing) (*BrE*) = INDEPENDENT²: *G. Green (Ind.)*

indebted /ɪn'detɪd/ *adj.* ~ (to sb) (for sth) (*formal*) very grateful to sb: *I am deeply indebted to my family and friends for all their help.*

indecent /ɪn'di:snt/ *adj.* shocking to many people in society, especially because it involves sex or the body: *indecent photos/behaviour/language* ◇ *Those tiny swimming trunks are indecent!* ⊃ look at **decent** (3) ▸ **indecency** /-snsi/ *noun* [U, sing.] ▸ **indecently** *adv.*

indecision /ˌɪndɪ'sɪʒn/ (*also* **indecisiveness** /ˌɪndɪ-'saɪsɪvnəs/) *noun* [U] the state of being unable to decide: *This indecision about the future is really worrying.*

indecisive /ˌɪndɪ'saɪsɪv/ *adj.* not able to make decisions easily **OPP** **decisive** ▸ **indecisively** *adv.* ▸ **indecisiveness** *noun* [U]

indeed ⓘ Ⓑ❶ ⊙ /ɪn'di:d/ *adv.* **1** (used for emphasizing a positive statement or answer) really; certainly: *'Have you had a good holiday?' 'We have indeed.'* **2** used after *very* with an adjective or adverb to emphasize the quality mentioned: *Thank you very much indeed.* ◇ *She's very happy indeed.* **3** (used for adding information to a statement) in fact: *It's important that you come at once. Indeed, it's essential.* **4** used for showing interest, surprise, anger, etc.: *'They were talking about you last night.' 'Were they indeed!'*

indefensible /ˌɪndɪ'fensəbl/ *adj.* (used about behaviour, etc.) completely wrong; that cannot be defended or excused

indefinable /ˌɪndɪ'faɪnəbl/ *adj.* difficult or impossible to describe: *There was an indefinable atmosphere of hostility.* ▸ **indefinably** /-bli/ *adv.*

indefinite /ɪn'defɪnət/ *adj.* not fixed or clear: *Our plans are still rather indefinite.* **OPP** **definite**

in,definite 'article *noun* [C] (**GRAMMAR**) the words *a* and *an* in English, or a similar word in another language ⊃ look at **definite article**

indefinitely /ɪn'defɪnətli/ *adv.* for a period of time that has no fixed end: *The meeting was postponed indefinitely.*

indelible /ɪn'deləbl/ *adj.* that cannot be removed or washed out: *indelible ink* ◇ (*figurative*) *The experience made an indelible impression on me.* ▸ **indelibly** /-bli/ *adv.*

indemnify /ɪn'demnɪfaɪ/ *verb* [T] (**indemnifying**; **indemnifies**; *pt, pp* **indemnified**) (**LAW**) **1** ~ sb (against sth) to promise to pay sb an amount of money if they suffer any damage or loss: *The contract indemnifies them against loss of earnings.* **2** ~ sb (for sth) to pay sb an amount of money because of the damage or loss that they have suffered ▸ **indemnification** /ɪnˌdemnɪfɪ'keɪʃn/ *noun* [U]

indemnity /ɪn'demnəti/ *noun* (*pl.* -ies) (*formal*) (**LAW**) **1** [U] protection against damage or loss, especially in the form of a promise to pay for any that happens **2** [C] an amount of money that is given as payment for damage or loss

indent¹ /ɪn'dent/ *verb* [I, T] to start a line of print further away from the edge of the page than the other lines

indent² /'ɪndent/ *noun* [C] **1** ~ (for sth) (*especially BrE*) (**BUSINESS**) an official order for goods or equipment **2** = INDENTATION

indentation /ˌɪnden'teɪʃn/ (*also* **indent**) *noun* [C] a cut or mark on the edge or surface of sth

independence ⓘ+ Ⓑ❷ ⓦ /ˌɪndɪ'pendəns/ *noun* [U] ~ (from sb/sth) (used about a person, country, etc.) the state of being free and not controlled by another person, country, etc: *In 1947 India achieved independence from Britain.* ◇ *financial independence*

▼ CULTURE

On **Independence Day** (4 July) Americans celebrate the day in 1776 when America declared itself independent from Britain.

independent¹ ⓘ Ⓐ❷ ⓦ /ˌɪndɪ'pendənt/ *adj.* **1** ~ (of/from sb/sth) free from and not controlled by another person, country, etc: *The country became fully independent from France in 1960.* **2** ~ (of/from sb/sth) not needing or wanting help: *I got a part-time job because I wanted to be financially independent from my parents.* **OPP** **dependent** **3** not influenced by or connected with sb/sth: *Complaints against the police should be investigated by an independent body.* ◇ *Two independent opinion polls have obtained similar results.* **4** (**POLITICS**) not representing or belonging to a particular political party: *an independent candidate* ▸ **independently** ⓦ *adv.* ~ (of sb/sth): *Scientists working independently of each other have had very similar results in their experiments.*

independent² /ˌɪndɪ'pendənt/ *noun* [C] (*abbr.* **Ind.**) (**POLITICS**) a member of parliament, candidate, etc. who does not belong to a particular political party: *She's standing as an independent at the next election.*

inde,pendent 'school = PRIVATE SCHOOL

in-'depth *adj.* very detailed, careful and complete: *an in-depth discussion/study*

indescribable /ˌɪndɪ'skraɪbəbl/ *adj.* too good or bad to be described: *indescribable poverty/luxury/noise* ▸ **indescribably** /-'skraɪbəbli/ *adv.*

indestructible /ˌɪndɪ'strʌktəbl/ *adj.* that cannot be easily damaged or destroyed

index ⓘ+ Ⓑ❷ ⓦ /'ɪndeks/ *noun* [C] **1** (*pl.* **indexes**) a list in order from A to Z, usually at the end of a book, of the names or subjects that are referred to in the book: *If you want to find all the references to London, look it up in the index.* **2** (*pl.* **indexes**) (*BrE*) = CARD INDEX **3** (*pl.* **indexes, indices** /-dɪsi:z/) (**ECONOMICS**) a way of showing how the price, value, rate, etc. of sth has changed: *the cost-of-living index* ▸ **index** *verb* [T]: *The books in the library are indexed by subject and title.*

index card *noun* [C] a small card that you can write information on and keep with other cards in a box or file

index finger (*also* **forefinger**) *noun* [C] (**ANATOMY**) the finger next to the THUMB, which you use for pointing

Indian /ˈɪndiən/ *noun* [C], *adj.* **1** (a person) from the Republic of India, or whose family comes from India: *Indian food is hot and spicy.* **2** (*old-fashioned*) = NATIVE AMERICAN ❶ This word is now considered offensive. ▸ **Indian** *adj.*

indicate ⒤ 🄱🄵 Ⓦ /ˈɪndɪkeɪt/ *verb* **1** [T] ~ **that ...** to show that sth is probably true or exists: *Recent research indicates that children are getting too little exercise.* **2** [T] ~ **(that) ...** (*formal*) to say sth in an indirect way: *The spokesman indicated that an agreement was likely soon.* ⊃ note at **declare 3** [T] ~ **(that) ...** to make sb notice sth, especially by pointing to it: *The boy seemed to be indicating that I should follow him.* ◇ *The receptionist indicated where I should sign.* **4** [I, T] (*BrE*) to signal that your car, etc. is going to turn: *The lorry indicated left but turned right.* ⓈⓎⓃ **signal**

indication ⒤+ 🄱🄶 Ⓦ /ˌɪndɪˈkeɪʃn/ *noun* [C, U] ~ **(of sth/ doing sth)**; ~ **(that) ...** something that shows sth; a sign: *There was no indication of a struggle.* ◇ *There is every indication that he will make a full recovery.* ⊃ note at **sign¹**

indicative /ɪnˈdɪkətɪv/ *adj.* **1** ~ **(of sth)** (*formal*) showing or suggesting sth: *Is the unusual weather indicative of climatic changes?* **2** (**GRAMMAR**) stating a fact

the indicative *noun* [sing.] (**GRAMMAR**) the form of a verb that states a fact: *In 'Ben likes school', the verb 'like' is in the indicative.*

indicator ⒤+ 🄲🄵 Ⓦ /ˈɪndɪkeɪtə(r)/ *noun* [C] **1** something that gives information or shows sth; a sign: *The indicator showed that we had plenty of petrol.* ◇ *The unemployment rate is a reliable indicator of economic health.* ⊃ note at **sign¹ 2** (*BrE*) (*AmE* **turn signal**) the flashing light on a car, etc. that shows that it is going to turn right or left

indices /ˈɪndɪsiːz/ *plural of* **index** (3)

indict /ɪnˈdaɪt/ *verb* [T, usually passive] ~ **sb (for sb)** (*especially AmE*) (**LAW**) to officially charge sb with a crime: *The senator was indicted for murder.*

indictment ⒤+ 🄲🄵 /ɪnˈdaɪtmənt/ *noun* [C] **1** (*especially AmE*) (**LAW**) a written paper that officially accuses sb of a crime **2** ~ **(of sth)** something that shows how bad sth is: *The fact that many children leave school with no qualifications is an indictment of our education system.*

indie /ˈɪndi/ *adj.* [only before noun] (used about a company, person or product) not part of a large organization; independent: *an indie publisher* ◇ *indie music*

indifference /ɪnˈdɪfrəns/ *noun* [U, sing.] ~ **(to sb/sth)** a lack of interest or feeling towards sb/sth: *He has always shown indifference to the needs of others.*

indifferent /ɪnˈdɪfrənt/ *adj.* **1** ~ **(to sb/sth)** not interested in or caring about sb/sth: *The manager of the shop seemed indifferent to our complaints.* **2** not very good: *The standard of football in the World Cup was rather indifferent.* ▸ **indifferently** *adv.*

indigenous ⒤+ 🄲🄵 /ɪnˈdɪdʒənəs/ *adj.* ~ **(to ...)** (**BIOLOGY, SOCIAL STUDIES**) (used about people, animals or plants) living or growing in the place where they are from originally: *The kangaroo is indigenous to Australia.*

indigestible /ˌɪndɪˈdʒestəbl/ *adj.* (used about food) difficult or impossible for the stomach to deal with ⓄⓅⓅ **digestible**

indigestion /ˌɪndɪˈdʒestʃən/ *noun* [U] (**HEALTH**) pain that is caused by difficulty in dealing with food

indignant /ɪnˈdɪɡnənt/ *adj.* ~ **(about/at sth)**; ~ **that ...** shocked or angry because you think that you have been treated in an unfair way: *He was very indignant about the way she had been treated.* ◇ *They were indignant that they had to pay more for worse services.* ▸ **indignantly** *adv.*

indignation /ˌɪndɪɡˈneɪʃn/ *noun* [U] ~ **(at/about sth)**; ~ **that ...** a feeling of anger and surprise because sth seems unfair or not reasonable: *commuters' indignation at the rise in fares*

indignity /ɪnˈdɪɡnəti/ *noun* [U, C] (*pl.* **-ies**) ~ **(of sth/of doing sth)** a situation that makes you feel embarrassed because you are not treated with respect; an act that causes these feelings: *The chairman suffered the indignity of being refused admission to the meeting.* ◇ *the daily indignities of imprisonment* ⓈⓎⓃ **humiliation**

indigo /ˈɪndɪɡəʊ/ *adj.* very dark blue in colour ▸ **indigo** *noun* [U]

indirect ⒤ 🄱🄵 Ⓦ /ˌɪndəˈrekt, -daɪˈr-/ *adj.* **1** not being the direct cause of sth; not having a direct connection with sth: *The building collapsed as an indirect result of the heavy rain.* **2** that avoids saying sth in an obvious way: *She gave only an indirect answer to my question.* ⓄⓅⓅ **direct¹ 3** not going in a straight line or using the shortest route: *We came the indirect route to avoid driving through London.* ⓄⓅⓅ **direct¹** ▸ **indirectly** Ⓦ *adv.*

indirect cost *noun* [C, usually pl.] (**BUSINESS, FINANCE**) a cost that is not directly connected with making a particular product or providing a particular service, for example training, heating, rent, etc. ⓄⓅⓅ **direct cost**

indirect object *noun* [C] (**GRAMMAR**) a noun or phrase that refers to a person or thing that an action is done to or for: *In the sentence, 'I wrote him a letter', 'him' is the indirect object.* ⊃ look at **direct object**

indirect speech = REPORTED SPEECH

indiscreet /ˌɪndɪˈskriːt/ *adj.* not careful or polite in what you say or do ⓄⓅⓅ **discreet** ▸ **indiscreetly** *adv.*

indiscretion /ˌɪndɪˈskreʃn/ *noun* [C, U] behaviour that is not careful or polite, and that could be embarrassing or offensive

indiscriminate /ˌɪndɪˈskrɪmɪnət/ *adj.* done or acting without making sensible judgements or caring about the possible harmful effects: *He's indiscriminate in his choice of friends.* ▸ **indiscriminately** *adv.*

indispensable /ˌɪndɪˈspensəbl/ *adj.* very important, so that it is not possible to be without: *A car is indispensable nowadays if you live in the country.* ⓄⓅⓅ **dispensable** ⊃ note at **essential**

indisputable /ˌɪndɪˈspjuːtəbl/ *adj.* definitely true; that cannot be shown to be wrong ⓈⓎⓃ **undeniable**

indistinct /ˌɪndɪˈstɪŋkt/ *adj.* not clear: *indistinct figures/ sounds/memories* ⓄⓅⓅ **distinct** ▸ **indistinctly** *adv.*

indistinguishable /ˌɪndɪˈstɪŋɡwɪʃəbl/ *adj.* ~ **(from sth)** appearing to be the same: *From a distance the two colours are indistinguishable.* ◇ *The fake phones are virtually indistinguishable from the real thing.* ⓄⓅⓅ **distinguishable**

indium /ˈɪndiəm/ *noun* [U] (*symb.* **In**) (**CHEMISTRY**) a chemical element. Indium is a soft silver-white metal. ❶ For more information on the periodic table of elements, look at the **Reference Section** of this dictionary.

individual¹ 🔊 A2 ⊙ /ˌɪndɪˈvɪdʒuəl/ adj. **1** [only before noun] considered separately rather than as part of a group: *Each individual animal is weighed and measured before being set free.* **2** for or from one person: *an individual portion of butter* ◇ *Children need individual attention when they are learning to read.* **3** typical of one person in a way that is different from other people: *I like her individual style of dressing.*

individual² 🔊 A2 ⊙ /ˌɪndɪˈvɪdʒuəl/ noun [C] **1** one person, considered separately from others or a group: *Are the needs of society more important than the rights of the individual?* **2** (*informal*) a person of the type that is mentioned: *She's a strange individual.*

individualism /ˌɪndɪˈvɪdʒuəlɪzəm/ noun [U] **1** the quality of being different from other people and doing things in your own way: *She owes her success to her individualism and flair.* **2** the belief that individual people in society should have the right to make their own decisions, etc., rather than being controlled by the government ▸ **individualist** /-lɪst/ noun [C]: *He's a complete individualist in the way he paints.* ▸ **individualistic** /ˌɪndɪˌvɪdʒuəˈlɪstɪk/ (*also* **individualist**) adj.: *an individualistic culture* ◇ *Her music is highly individualistic and may not appeal to everyone.*

individuality /ˌɪndɪˌvɪdʒuˈæləti/ noun [U] the qualities that make sb/sth different from other people or things: *People often try to express their individuality by the way they dress.*

individually 🌐 /ˌɪndɪˈvɪdʒuəli/ adv. separately; one by one: *The teacher talked to each member of the class individually.*

indivisible /ˌɪndɪˈvɪzəbl/ adj. that cannot be divided or split into smaller pieces **OPP** **divisible**

indoctrinate /ɪnˈdɒktrɪneɪt/ verb [T] to force sb to accept particular beliefs without allowing them to consider others: *For 20 years the people have been indoctrinated by the government.* ▸ **indoctrination** /ɪnˌdɒktrɪˈneɪʃn/ noun [U]

Indo-European /ˌɪndəʊ jʊərəˈpiːən/ adj. (**LANGUAGE**) of or connected with the family of languages spoken in most of Europe and parts of western Asia (including English, French, Latin, Greek, Swedish, Russian and Hindi)

indoor 🔊 B1 /ˈɪndɔː(r)/ adj. [only before noun] done or used inside a building: *indoor games* ◇ *an indoor swimming pool* **OPP** **outdoor**

indoors 🔊 B1 /ˌɪnˈdɔːz/ adv. in or into a building: *Oh dear! I've left my sunglasses indoors.* ◇ *Let's go indoors.* **OPP** **out of doors, outdoors**

induce 🔊⁺ C1 🌐 /ɪnˈdjuːs/ verb [T] **1** (*formal*) to make or persuade sb to do sth: *Nothing could induce him to change his mind.* **2** (*formal*) to cause or produce: *herbal tea that induces sleep* ◇ *a drug-induced coma* **3** (**MEDICINE**) to make a woman start giving birth to her baby by giving her special drugs; to make a baby start being born by giving the mother special drugs

inducement /ɪnˈdjuːsmənt/ noun [C, U] something that is offered to sb to make them do sth: *The player was offered a car as an inducement to join the club.* ➔ look at **incentive**

induction 🌐 /ɪnˈdʌkʃn/ noun **1** [U, C] (**BUSINESS**) the process of introducing sb to a new job, skill, organization, etc.; an event at which this takes place: *an induction day for new students* **2** [U, C] (**MEDICINE**) the act of making a pregnant woman start giving birth, by giving her special drugs **3** [U] a method of discovering general rules and principles from particular facts and examples ➔ look at **deduction** (1)

4 [U] (**PHYSICS**) the process by which electricity or MAGNETISM passes from one object to another without them touching

inductive /ɪnˈdʌktɪv/ adj. **1** using particular facts and examples to form general rules and principles: *an inductive argument* ◇ *inductive reasoning* ➔ look at **deductive 2** (**PHYSICS**) connected with the INDUCTION of electricity

indulge 🔊⁺ C1 /ɪnˈdʌldʒ/ verb **1** [I, T] ~ (**yourself**) (**in sth**) to allow yourself to have or do sth for pleasure: *I'm going to indulge myself and go shopping for some new clothes.* ◇ *Maria never indulges in gossip.* **2** [T] to satisfy a particular desire, interest, etc. **3** [T] to allow sb to have or do whatever they like: *You shouldn't indulge that child. It will make him very selfish.* ◇ *At the weekends he indulges his passion for fishing.*

indulgence /ɪnˈdʌldʒəns/ noun **1** [U] the state of having or doing whatever you want, or of allowing sb to have or do whatever they want: *to lead a life of indulgence* ◇ *Over-indulgence in chocolate makes you fat.* **2** [C] something that you have or do because it gives you pleasure: *The holiday was an extravagant indulgence.*

indulgent /ɪnˈdʌldʒənt/ adj. allowing sb to have or do whatever they want: *indulgent parents* ▸ **indulgently** adv.

industrial 🔊 B2 /ɪnˈdʌstriəl/ adj. **1** [only before noun] (**BUSINESS**) connected with industry: *industrial development* ◇ *industrial workers* **2** (**GEOGRAPHY, SOCIAL STUDIES**) having a lot of factories, etc: *an industrial region/country/town*

inˌdustrial 'action noun [U] (*especially BrE*) (**BUSINESS, SOCIAL STUDIES**) action that workers take, especially stopping work, in order to protest about sth to their employers: *to threaten (to take) industrial action* **SYN** **strike¹**

industrialist /ɪnˈdʌstriəlɪst/ noun [C] (**BUSINESS**) a person who owns or manages a large industrial company

industrialize (*BrE also* -ise) /ɪnˈdʌstriəlaɪz/ verb [I, T] (**ECONOMICS**) to develop industries in a country: *Japan industrialized rapidly at the end of the nineteenth century.* ▸ **industrialization** (*BrE also* -isation) /ɪnˌdʌstriəlaɪˈzeɪʃn/ noun [U]

the Inˌdustrial Revoˈlution noun [sing.] (**HISTORY**) the period in the eighteenth and nineteenth centuries in Europe and the US when machines began to be used to do work, and industry grew rapidly

inˌdustrial triˈbunal = EMPLOYMENT TRIBUNAL

industrious /ɪnˈdʌstriəs/ adj. always working hard **SYN** **hard-working**

industry 🔊 A2 /ˈɪndəstri/ noun (*pl.* -ies) **1** [U] (**ECONOMICS**) the production of goods in factories: *Is British industry being threatened by foreign imports?* ◇ *heavy/light industry* **2** [C] (**BUSINESS**) the people and activities involved in producing sth, providing a service, etc: *the tourist/catering/entertainment industry*

inedible /ɪnˈedəbl/ adj. (*formal*) not suitable to be eaten **OPP** **edible**

ineffable /ɪnˈefəbl/ adj. (*formal*) too great or beautiful to describe in words ▸ **ineffably** /-bli/ adv.

ineffective /ˌɪnɪˈfektɪv/ adj. not producing the effect or result that you want **OPP** **effective**

inefficient /ˌɪnɪˈfɪʃnt/ adj. not working or producing results in the best way, so that time or money is wasted: *Our heating system is very old and extremely inefficient.* ◇ *an inefficient use of space* **OPP** **efficient** ▸ **inefficiency** /-ʃnsi/ noun [U, C] ▸ **inefficiently** adv.

ineligible /ɪnˈelɪdʒəbl/ adj. ~ (**for/to do sth**) without the necessary qualifications, etc. to do or get sth: *She was ineligible for the job because she wasn't a German*

inept /ɪˈnept/ adj. ~ (at sth) acting or done with no skill: *She is totally inept at dealing with people.* ◇ *He made some particularly inept remarks.* **OPP** **adept**

inequality **ʕ+ C1 W** /ˌɪnɪˈkwɒləti/ noun (pl. -ies) **1** [U, C] (SOCIAL STUDIES) the difference between groups in society, when one has more money, opportunities, etc. than the others: *There will be problems as long as inequality between the races exists.* **OPP** **equality** **2** [C] (MATHEMATICS) the relation between two expressions that are not equal, using a sign such as ≠ (not equal to), > (greater than) or < (less than) **3** [C] (MATHEMATICS) a symbol such as ≠ (not equal to), > (greater than) or < (less than) that shows that two quantities are not equal

inert /ɪˈnɜːt/ adj. **1** (formal) not able to move or act **2** (CHEMISTRY) (used about chemical elements) without active chemical or other PROPERTIES (= characteristics) **❶** Inert gases are also called **noble gases**. **Argon, helium, krypton** and **neon** are inert gases

inertia /ɪˈnɜːʃə/ noun [U] **1** a lack of energy; not being able or not wanting to move or change **2** (PHYSICS) the physical force that keeps things where they are or keeps them moving in the direction they are travelling

inescapable /ˌɪnɪˈskeɪpəbl/ adj. (formal) that cannot be avoided: *an inescapable conclusion* **SYN** **unavoidable**

inevitable **ʕ+ B2** /ɪnˈevɪtəbl/ adj. that cannot be avoided or prevented from happening: *With more cars on the road, traffic jams are inevitable.* **SYN** **unavoidable** ▶ inevitability /ɪnˌevɪtəˈbɪləti/ noun [U] ▶ the inevitable noun [sing.]: *They fought to save the firm from closure, but eventually had to accept the inevitable.*

inevitably **ʕ+ B2** /ɪnˈevɪtəbli/ adv. **1** as is certain to happen: *Flowers inevitably get broken or bent at the market.* **2** as you would expect: *Inevitably, it rained on the day of the wedding.*

inexcusable /ˌɪnɪkˈskjuːzəbl/ adj. that cannot be allowed or forgiven: *Their behaviour was quite inexcusable.* **SYN** **unforgivable** **OPP** **excusable**

inexhaustible /ˌɪnɪɡˈzɔːstəbl/ adj. that cannot be finished or used up completely: *Our energy supplies are not inexhaustible.*

inexpensive /ˌɪnɪkˈspensɪv/ adj. low in price **SYN** **cheap¹** **OPP** **expensive** ▶ inexpensively adv.

inexperience /ˌɪnɪkˈspɪəriəns/ noun [U] not knowing how to do sth because you have not done it before: *The mistakes were all due to inexperience.* **OPP** **experience¹** ▶ inexperienced adj.: *He's too young and inexperienced to be given such responsibility.*

inexplicable /ˌɪnɪkˈsplɪkəbl/ adj. that cannot be explained: *Her sudden disappearance is quite inexplicable.* **OPP** **explicable** ▶ inexplicably /-bli/ adv.

infallible /ɪnˈfæləbl/ adj. **1** (used about a person) never making mistakes or being wrong **2** always doing what you want it to do; never failing: *No computer is infallible.* **OPP** **fallible** ▶ infallibility /ɪnˌfæləˈbɪləti/ noun [U]

infamous **ʕ+ C1** /ˈɪnfəməs/ adj. ~ (for sth) (formal) famous for being bad: *The area is infamous for crime.* **SYN** **notorious** ⊃ look at famous

infancy /ˈɪnfənsi/ noun [U] the time when you are a baby or young child: (figurative) *Research in this field is still in its infancy.*

infant **ʕ+ C1** /ˈɪnfənt/ noun [C] **1** (formal) a baby or very young child: *There is a high rate of **infant mortality** (= many children die when they are still under the age of one year).* **2** (in England and Wales) a child at school between the ages of 4 and 7

infanticide /ɪnˈfæntɪsaɪd/ noun [U] (formal) (LAW) the crime of killing a baby, especially when a parent kills their own child

infantile /ˈɪnfəntaɪl/ adj. (used about behaviour) typical of a small child and therefore not appropriate for adults or older children: *infantile jokes* **SYN** **childish**

infantry /ˈɪnfəntri/ noun [U + sing./pl. verb] soldiers who fight on foot: *The infantry was/were supported by heavy gunfire.*

'infant school noun [C] (in England and Wales) a school for children between the ages of 4 and 7 ⊃ look at **primary school**

infarction /ɪnˈfɑːkʃn/ noun [C] (HEALTH) a condition in which the blood supply to an area of TISSUE is blocked and the TISSUE dies

infatuated /ɪnˈfætʃueɪtɪd/ adj. ~ (with sb/sth) having a very strong feeling of love or attraction for sb/sth that usually does not last long and makes you unable to think about anything else ▶ infatuation /ɪnˌfætʃuˈeɪʃn/ noun [C, U]

infect **ʕ+ C1** /ɪnˈfekt/ verb [T] **1** ~ sb/sth (with sth) (HEALTH) to cause sb/sth to have a disease or illness: *Many thousands of people have been infected with the virus.* **2** to make people share a particular feeling or emotion: *Paul's happiness infected the whole family.* **3** ~ sth (with sth) (COMPUTING) to make a computer virus spread to another computer or program

infected /ɪnˈfektɪd/ adj. **1** affected by harmful bacteria, a virus, etc. **2** (COMPUTING) affected by a computer virus: *an infected PC*

infection **ʕ B2** /ɪnˈfekʃn/ noun (HEALTH) **1** [U] the act or process of causing or getting a disease: *A dirty water supply can be a source of infection.* **2** [C] a disease or an illness that is caused by bacteria or a virus and that affects one part of the body: *She is suffering from a chest infection.* ◇ *an ear infection* ⊃ note at **disease** **❶** Infections can be caused by **bacteria** or **viruses**. An informal word for these is **germs**.

infectious /ɪnˈfekʃəs/ adj. (HEALTH) (used about a disease, an illness, etc.) that can be easily passed on to another person: *Flu is a highly infectious disease.* ◇ (figurative) *infectious laughter* ⊃ look at **contagious**

infer **ʕ+ B2 W** /ɪnˈfɜː(r)/ verb [T] (-rr-) ~ sth (from sth); ~ that … to form an opinion or decide that sth is true from the information you have: *I inferred from our conversation that he was unhappy with his job.* ▶ inference **W** /ˈɪnfərəns/ noun [C, U]

inferior /ɪnˈfɪəriə(r)/ adj. ~ (to sb/sth) low or lower in social position, importance, quality, etc: *This material is obviously inferior to that one.* ◇ *Don't let people make you **feel inferior**.* **OPP** **superior¹** ▶ inferior noun [C]: *She always treats me as her intellectual inferior.* ▶ inferiority /ɪnˌfɪəriˈɒrəti/ noun [U]

in,feri'ority complex noun [C] (PSYCHOLOGY) the state of feeling less important, clever, successful, etc. than other people

infertile /ɪnˈfɜːtaɪl/ adj. **1** (BIOLOGY) (used about a person or an animal) not able to have babies or produce young **OPP** **fertile 2** (AGRICULTURE) (used about land) not able to grow strong healthy plants **OPP** **fertile** ▶ infertility /ˌɪnfɜːˈtɪləti/ noun [U]: *infertility treatment*

infested /ɪnˈfestɪd/ adj. ~ (with sth) (used about a place) with large numbers of unpleasant animals or insects in it: *The warehouse was infested with rats.* ▶ infestation /ˌɪnfeˈsteɪʃn/ noun [C, U]: *an infestation of lice*

infidelity /ˌɪnfɪˈdeləti/ *noun* [U, C] (*pl.* -ies) the act of not being FAITHFUL to your wife, husband or partner, by having sex with sb else **SYN** **unfaithfulness**

infiltrate /ˈɪnfɪltreɪt/ *verb* [T] to enter an organization, etc. secretly so that you can find out what it is doing: *The police managed to infiltrate the gang of terrorists.* ▸ **infiltration** /ˌɪnfɪlˈtreɪʃn/ *noun* [U, C] ▸ **infiltrator** *noun* [C]

infinite /ˈɪnfɪnət/ *adj.* **1** very great: *You need infinite patience for this job.* **2** without limits; that never ends: *Supplies of oil are not infinite.* **OPP** **finite**

infinitely /ˈɪnfɪnətli/ *adv.* very much: *Your English is infinitely better than my German.*

infinitesimal /ˌɪnfɪnɪˈtesɪml/ *adj.* (*formal*) extremely small: *infinitesimal traces of poison* ◇ *an infinitesimal risk* ▸ **infinitesimally** /-məli/ *adv.*

infinitive /ɪnˈfɪnətɪv/ *noun* [C] (**GRAMMAR**) the basic form of a verb, such as *be/to be* or *run/to run*

infinity /ɪnˈfɪnəti/ *noun* **1** [U] space or time without end: *the infinity of space* ◇ *The ocean seemed to stretch over the horizon into infinity.* **2** [U, C] (*symb.* ∞) (**MATHEMATICS**) the number that is larger than any other

infirmary /ɪnˈfɜːməri/ *noun* [C] (*pl.* -ies) (**MEDICINE**) (used mainly in names) a hospital: *The Manchester Royal Infirmary*

inflamed /ɪnˈfleɪmd/ *adj.* (**HEALTH**) (used about a part of the body) red, larger than normal and painful because of an infection or injury

inflammable /ɪnˈflæməbl/ *adj.* (*especially BrE*) = FLAMMABLE

inflammation /ˌɪnfləˈmeɪʃn/ *noun* [U, C] (**HEALTH**) a condition in which a part of the body becomes red, painful and larger than normal because of infection or injury

inflammatory /ɪnˈflæmətri/ *adj.* **1** likely to cause very strong feelings of anger: *inflammatory remarks* **2** (**HEALTH**) causing or involving INFLAMMATION ⊃ look at **anti-inflammatory**

inflatable /ɪnˈfleɪtəbl/ *adj.* that must be filled with air before you can use it: *an inflatable dinghy/mattress*

inflate /ɪnˈfleɪt/ *verb* [T, I] (*formal*) **1** to fill sth with air; to become filled with air ⊃ look at **blow sth up** at **blow¹** (2) **OPP** **deflate 2** (**ECONOMICS**) to increase the price of sth; to increase in price: *The scheme has been criticized for inflating house prices.* ◇ *House prices have inflated at a surprising rate.* ⊃ look at **deflate** (3), **reflate** ▸ **inflationary** /-ˈfleɪʃənri/ *adj.*: *Inflationary pressure is expected to recede in second half of the year.*

inflation ⁊+ **B2** /ɪnˈfleɪʃn/ *noun* [U] (**ECONOMICS**) a general rise in prices; the rate at which prices rise: *the inflation rate/rate of inflation* ◇ *Inflation now stands at 3%.* ⊃ look at **deflation** (1)

inflect /ɪnˈflekt/ *verb* [I] (**GRAMMAR**) if a word **inflects**, its ending or spelling changes according to its function in the grammar of the sentence; if a language **inflects**, it has words that do this ▸ **inflected** *adj.*: *an inflected language/form/verb*

inflection (*also* **inflexion**) /ɪnˈflekʃn/ *noun* [C, U] **1** (**GRAMMAR**) a change in the form of a word, especially its ending, that changes its function in the grammar of the sentence, for example -ed, -est **2** the rise and fall of your voice when you are talking **SYN** **intonation**

inflexible /ɪnˈfleksəbl/ *adj.* **1** that cannot be changed or made more suitable for a particular situation: *He has a very inflexible attitude to change.* **SYN** **rigid** **OPP** **flexible 2** (used about people or organizations)

unwilling to change their opinions, decisions or the way in which they do things: *She's a good teacher, but she can be inflexible.* **OPP** **flexible 3** (used about a material) difficult or impossible to bend **SYN** **stiff¹** **OPP** **flexible** ▸ **inflexibility** /ɪnˌfleksəˈbɪləti/ *noun* [U] ▸ **inflexibly** /ɪnˈfleksəbli/ *adv.*

inflict ⁊+ **C1** /ɪnˈflɪkt/ *verb* [T] ~ **sth (on sb)** to force sb to have sth unpleasant or sth that they do not want: *Don't inflict your problems on me — I've got enough of my own.*
PHR V **inflict yourself/sb on sb** to force sb to spend time with you/sb, when they do not want to: *Sorry to inflict myself on you again like this!*

in-flight *adj.* [only before noun] (**TOURISM**) happening or provided during a journey on a plane: *in-flight entertainment*

inflow /ˈɪnfləʊ/ *noun* **1** [C, U] the movement of a lot of money, people or things into a place from somewhere else: *inflows of capital from abroad* **SYN** **influx 2** [sing., U] the movement of a liquid or of air into a place from somewhere else: *an inflow pipe*

influence¹ **B1** ⊙ /ˈɪnfluəns/ *noun* **1** [U, C] ~ **(on/upon sb/sth)** the power to affect, change or control sb/sth: *TV can have a strong influence on children.* ◇ *Nobody should drive while they are under the influence of alcohol.* **2** [C] ~ **(on sb/sth)** a person or thing that affects or changes sb/sth: *His new girlfriend has been a good influence on him.* ◇ *cultural/environmental influences*

influence² **B1** ⊙ /ˈɪnfluəns/ *verb* [T] to have an effect on or power over sb/sth so that the person or thing changes: *You must decide for yourself. Don't let anyone else influence you.* ◇ *Her style of painting has been influenced by Japanese art.*

influencer /ˈɪnfluənsə(r)/ *noun* [C] a person or thing that influences sb/sth, especially a person who is paid by companies to recommend products or services on SOCIAL MEDIA: *the social media feeds of fashion influencers*

influential ⁊+ **C1** /ˌɪnfluˈenʃl/ *adj.* ~ **(in sth/doing sth)** having power or influence: *an influential politician* ◇ *He was influential in getting the hostages set free.*

influenza /ˌɪnfluˈenzə/ (*formal*) = FLU

influx /ˈɪnflʌks/ *noun* [C, usually sing.] ~ **(of sb/sth) (into …)** the fact of large numbers of people or things arriving suddenly: *the summer influx of visitors from abroad*

info ⁊+ **B2** /ˈɪnfəʊ/ *noun* [U] (*informal*) = INFORMATION: *Have you had any more info about the job yet?* **2** info-/ɪnfəʊ, ɪnfə/ (in nouns) connected with information: *an infosheet* ◇ *Phone now for a free infopack.*

infographic /ˌɪnfəʊˈgræfɪk/ *noun* [C] information or data that is shown in a chart, diagram, etc. so that it is easy to understand

inform ⁊ **B2** ⊛ /ɪnˈfɔːm/ *verb* [T] ~ **sb (of/about sth)**; ~ **sb that …** to give sb information (about sth), especially in an official way: *You should inform the police of the accident.* ◇ *Do keep me informed of any changes.* ◇ *I was reliably informed that the robbery took place around 9 p.m.*
PHR V **inform on sb** to give information to the police, etc. about what sb has done wrong: *The wife of the killer informed on her husband.*

informal ⁊ **A2** /ɪnˈfɔːml/ *adj.* relaxed and friendly, or suitable for a relaxed occasion: *Don't get dressed up for the party — it'll be very informal.* ◇ *The two leaders had informal discussions before the conference began.* ◇ *I changed into more informal clothes.* **OPP** **formal** ▸ **informality** /ˌɪnfɔːˈmæləti/ *noun* [U]: *an atmosphere of informality* ▸ **informally** /ɪnˈfɔːməli/ *adv.*: *I was told* *informally* (= not officially) *that our plans had been accepted.*

informant /ɪnˈfɔːmənt/ *noun* [C] a person who gives secret knowledge or information about sb/sth to the police or a newspaper ⊃ look at **informer**

information 🔤 Ⓐ➊ Ⓞ /ˌɪnfəˈmeɪʃn/ (*also informal* info) *noun* [U] **~ (on/about sb/sth)** knowledge or facts: *For further information please see our website.* ◇ *Can you give me some information about evening classes in Italian, please?* ⊃ look at **FYI**

information tech'nology = IT

informative /ɪnˈfɔːmətɪv/ *adj.* giving useful knowledge or information

informed Ⓦ /ɪnˈfɔːmd/ *adj.* having knowledge or information about sth: *Do keep me informed of any changes.* ◇ *Consumers cannot make informed choices unless they are told all the facts.*

informer /ɪnˈfɔːmə(r)/ *noun* [C] (**LAW**) a person who gives the police information about other criminals ⊃ look at **informant**

infra- /ɪnfrə/ *prefix* (in adjectives) below a particular limit: *infrared* ⊃ look at **ultra-**

infrared /ˌɪnfrəˈred/ *adj.* (**PHYSICS**) having or using ELECTROMAGNETIC waves that are longer than those of red light in the SPECTRUM, and that cannot be seen ⊃ look at **ultraviolet** ⊃ picture at **climate change**, **wavelength**

infrasonic /ˌɪnfrəˈsɒnɪk/ *adj.* (**PHYSICS**) (used about sounds) lower than humans are able to hear ⊃ look at **ultrasonic**

infrastructure 🔤+ 🅱️2 /ˈɪnfrəstrʌktʃə(r)/ *noun* [C, U] (**ECONOMICS**, **SOCIAL STUDIES**) the basic systems and services that are necessary for a country or an organization, for example buildings, transport and water and power supplies: *economic/social/transport infrastructure* ▸ **infrastructural** /ˌɪnfrəˈstrʌktʃərəl/ *adj.*

infrequent /ɪnˈfriːkwənt/ *adj.* not happening often **OPP** **frequent**[1] ▸ **infrequently** *adv.*

infringe /ɪnˈfrɪndʒ/ *verb* (*formal*) **1** [T] (**LAW**) to break a rule, a law, an agreement, etc: *The material can be copied without infringing copyright.* **2** [I] **~ on/upon sth** to reduce or limit sb's rights, freedom, etc: *Use of the data might infringe on personal privacy.* ▸ **infringement** *noun* [U, C]

infuriate /ɪnˈfjʊərieɪt/ *verb* [T] to make sb very angry ▸ **infuriating** *adj.*: *an infuriating habit* ▸ **infuriatingly** *adv.*

infuse /ɪnˈfjuːz/ *verb* **1** [T] **~ A into B; ~ B with A** (*formal*) to make sb/sth have a particular quality: *He has infused confidence into the team.* ◇ *Her novels are infused with sadness.* **2** [T] (*formal*) to have an effect on all parts of sth: *Politics infuses all aspects of our lives.* **3** [I, T] if you **infuse** HERBS (= certain types of plant), etc. or they **infuse**, you put them in hot water until their taste has passed into the water

infusion /ɪnˈfjuːʒn/ *noun* **1** [C, U] **~ of sth (into sth)** (*formal*) the act of adding sth to sth else in order to make it stronger or more successful: *an infusion of new talent into teaching* ◇ *The company needs an infusion of new blood* (= new employees with new ideas). **2** [C] a drink or medicine made by putting HERBS (= plants whose leaves are used to give taste to sth or as medicine) in hot water **3** [C, U] (**MEDICINE**) the act of introducing a liquid substance into the body, especially into a VEIN

ingenious /ɪnˈdʒiːniəs/ *adj.* **1** (used about a thing or an idea) made or planned in a clever way: *an ingenious plan for making lots of money* ◇ *an ingenious device/ experiment/invention* **2** (used about a person) full of new ideas and clever at finding solutions to problems

or at inventing things ▸ **ingeniously** *adv.* ▸ **ingenuity** /ˌɪndʒəˈnjuːəti/ *noun* [U]

ingest /ɪnˈdʒest/ *verb* [T] (**BIOLOGY**) to take food, drugs, etc. into your body, usually by SWALLOWING ▸ **ingestion** /-ˈdʒestʃən/ *noun* [U]

ingot /ˈɪŋɡət/ *noun* [C] a solid piece of metal, especially gold or silver, usually shaped like a BRICK

ingrained /ɪnˈɡreɪnd/ *adj.* **~ (in sb/sth)** (used about a habit, an attitude, etc.) that has existed for a long time and is therefore difficult to change: *These beliefs are ingrained in us.*

ingratiate /ɪnˈɡreɪʃieɪt/ *verb* [T] **~ yourself (with sb)** (*formal*) to make yourself liked by doing or saying things that will please people, especially people who might be useful to you: *He was always trying to ingratiate himself with his teachers.* ▸ **ingratiating** *adj.*: *an ingratiating smile* ▸ **ingratiatingly** *adv.*

ingratitude /ɪnˈɡrætɪtjuːd/ *noun* [U] (*formal*) the state of not showing or feeling thanks for sth that has been done for you; not being grateful **OPP** **gratitude**

ingredient 🔤 🅱️1 /ɪnˈɡriːdiənt/ *noun* [C] **1** one of the things from which sth is made, especially one of the foods that are used together to make sth to eat: *Mix all the ingredients together in a bowl.* ◇ *80 per cent of the active ingredients in our medicines are made overseas.* **2** one of the qualities necessary to make sth successful: *The film has all the ingredients of success.*

inhabit /ɪnˈhæbɪt/ *verb* [T] to live in a place: *Are the Aran Islands inhabited* (= do people live there)?

inhabitable /ɪnˈhæbɪtəbl/ *adj.* that can be lived in: *The house was no longer inhabitable after the fire.* **OPP** **uninhabitable**

WORD FAMILY
inhabit *verb*
habitable *adj.*
(≠ **uninhabitable**)
uninhabited *adj.*
inhabitant *noun*
habitation *noun*

inhabitant 🔤+ 🅱️2 /ɪnˈhæbɪtənt/ *noun* [C, usually pl.] a person or an animal that lives in a place: *The local inhabitants protested at the plans for a new motorway.*

inhalant /ɪnˈheɪlənt/ *noun* [C] (**MEDICINE**) a drug or medicine that you breathe in

inhale /ɪnˈheɪl/ *verb* [I, T] (**BIOLOGY**) to breathe (sth) in: *Be careful not to inhale the fumes from the paint.* **OPP** **exhale** ▸ **inhalation** /ˌɪnhəˈleɪʃn/ *noun* [U]: *They were treated for the effects of smoke inhalation.*

inhaler /ɪnˈheɪlə(r)/ *noun* [C] (**MEDICINE**) a small device containing medicine that you breathe in through your mouth, used by people who have problems with breathing

inherent 🔤+ Ⓒ1 Ⓦ /ɪnˈherənt, -ˈhɪər-/ *adj.* **~ (in sb/sth)** that is a basic or permanent part of sb/sth and that cannot be removed: *The risk of collapse is inherent in any business.* **SYN** **intrinsic** ▸ **inherently** *adv.*: *No matter how safe we make them, cars are inherently dangerous.*

inherit 🔤+ 🅱️2 /ɪnˈherɪt/ *verb* [T] **~ sth (from sb)** **1** to receive property, money, etc. from sb who has died: *I inherited quite a lot of money from my mother.* ⊃ look at **disinherit, heir** **2** (**BIOLOGY**, **HEALTH**) to receive a quality, characteristic, etc. from your parents or family: *She has inherited her father's gift for languages.*

inheritable /ɪnˈherɪtəbl/ *adj.* (**BIOLOGY**) (used about a feature or disease) capable of being passed from a parent to a child in the GENES (= the units inside a cell that control particular qualities)

inheritance /ɪnˈherɪtəns/ noun [C, U] the act of INHERITING; the money, property, etc. that you INHERIT: *inheritance tax*

inhibit ᵉ⁺ **C1** /ɪnˈhɪbɪt/ verb [T] **1** to prevent sth or make sth happen more slowly: *a drug to inhibit the growth of tumours* **2** ~ sb (from sth/doing sth) to make sb nervous and embarrassed so that they are unable to do sth: *The fact that her boss was there inhibited her from saying what she really felt.*

inhibited /ɪnˈhɪbɪtɪd/ adj. unable to relax or express your feelings in a natural way: *The young man felt shy and inhibited in the presence of his boss.* **OPP** uninhibited

inhibition /ˌɪnhɪˈbɪʃn, ˌɪnɪ-/ noun [C, U] a shy or nervous feeling that stops you from saying or doing what you really want: *After the first day of the course, people started to lose their inhibitions.*

inhibitor /ɪnˈhɪbɪtə(r)/ noun [C] (**BIOLOGY, CHEMISTRY**) something that slows down or stops a process: *This is an important step towards developing effective inhibitors to fight tumour growth.*

inhospitable /ˌɪnhɒˈspɪtəbl/ adj. **1** (used about a place) not pleasant to live in, especially because of the weather: *the inhospitable Arctic regions* **2** (used about a person) not friendly or welcoming to guests **OPP** hospitable

in-ˈhouse adj. (**BUSINESS**) existing or happening within a company or an organization: *an in-house magazine* ◇ *in-house language training* ▶ in-house adv.: *This engine was designed in-house.*

inhuman /ɪnˈhjuːmən/ adj. **1** very cruel and without PITY: *inhuman treatment/conditions* **2** not seeming to be human and therefore frightening: *an inhuman noise*

inhumane /ˌɪnhjuːˈmeɪn/ adj. very cruel; not caring if people or animals suffer: *the inhumane conditions in which animals are kept on some large farms* **OPP** humane

inhumanity /ˌɪnhjuːˈmænəti/ noun [U] very cruel behaviour: *The twentieth century was full of examples of man's inhumanity to man.* **OPP** humanity

initial¹ ᵉ **B2** ⓞ /ɪˈnɪʃl/ adj. [only before noun] happening at the beginning; first: *My initial reaction was to refuse, but I later changed my mind.* ◇ *the initial stages of our survey*

initial² /ɪˈnɪʃl/ noun [C, usually pl.] the first letter of a name: *Alison Elizabeth Waters' initials are A.E.W.*

initial³ /ɪˈnɪʃl/ verb [T] (-ll-, AmE -l-) to mark or sign sth with your INITIALS: *Any changes made on the document should be initialled by you.*

initialize (BrE also -ise) /ɪˈnɪʃəlaɪz/ verb [T] (**COMPUTING**) to make a computer program or system ready for use or to FORMAT a disk ▶ initialization (BrE also -isation) /ɪˌnɪʃəlaɪˈzeɪʃn/ noun [U]

initially ᵉ **B2** ⓦ /ɪˈnɪʃəli/ adv. at the beginning; at first: *I liked the job initially but it soon got quite boring.*

initiate ᵉ⁺ **C1** ⓦ /ɪˈnɪʃieɪt/ verb [T] **1** (formal) to start sth: *to initiate peace talks* **2** ~ sb (into sth) to explain sth to sb or make them experience sth for the first time: *I wasn't initiated into the joys of skiing until I was 30.* **3** ~ sb (into sth) to bring sb into a group by means of a special ceremony: *to initiate somebody into a secret society* ▶ initiation ⓦ /ɪˌnɪʃiˈeɪʃn/ noun [U]: *All the new students had to go through a strange initiation ceremony.*

initiative ᵉ **B2** ⓦ /ɪˈnɪʃətɪv/ noun **1** [C] a new plan for solving a problem or improving a situation: *a new government initiative to help people start small businesses* **2** [U] the ability to see and do what is necessary without waiting for sb to tell you what to do: *Don't keep asking me how to do it. Use your initiative.* **3** the initiative [sing.] the power or opportunity to act and gain an advantage before other people do: *The enemy forces have lost the initiative.* **IDM** on your own initiative without being told by sb else what to do take the initiative to be first to act to influence a situation

initiator /ɪˈnɪʃieɪtə(r)/ noun [C] (formal) the person who starts sth

inject ᵉ⁺ **C1** /ɪnˈdʒekt/ verb [T] **1** ~ sth (into sb/sth); ~ sb/sth/yourself with sth (**MEDICINE**) to put a drug or other substance into a person's or an animal's body using a SYRINGE (= a medical instrument with a long hollow needle): *Something was injected into my arm and I soon fell asleep.* **2** ~ sth (into sth) to add sth: *They injected a lot of money into the business.*

injection ᵉ⁺ **C1** /ɪnˈdʒekʃn/ noun **1** [C, U] ~ (of sth) (into sb/sth) (**MEDICINE**) the act of putting a drug or other substance into a person's or an animal's body using a SYRINGE (= a medical instrument with a long hollow needle): *They gave him an injection of penicillin,* ◇ *a tetanus injection* ◇ *An anaesthetic was administered by injection.* ⊃ look at jab² (2) **2** [C] a large amount of sth that is added to sth to help it: *The theatre needs a huge cash injection if it is to stay open.* **3** [U, C] the act of forcing liquid into sth: *fuel injection*

injunction /ɪnˈdʒʌŋkʃn/ noun [C] ~ (against sb) (**LAW**) an official order from a court to do/not do sth: *The company obtained an injunction against the protesters.* ◇ *A court injunction prevented the programme from being shown on TV.* ⊃ look at restraining order

injure ᵉ **B1** /ˈɪndʒə(r)/ verb [T] to harm or hurt yourself or sb else physically, especially in an accident: *The goalkeeper seriously injured himself when he hit the goalpost.* ◇ *She fell and injured her back.*

▼ SYNONYMS

injure

wound ◆ hurt ◆ bruise ◆ maim ◆ sprain ◆ pull ◆ twist ◆ strain

These words all mean to harm yourself or sb else physically, especially in an accident.

injure *He was badly injured in a car crash.*

wound *Five people were seriously wounded in the attack.*

hurt *Did you hurt yourself?*

bruise *She had slipped and badly bruised her back.*

maim (formal) *She was maimed in the accident.*

sprain *He fell and sprained his wrist/ankle/knee.*

pull *He pulled a muscle playing hockey.*

twist *She twisted her ankle/wrist/knee.*

strain *Using a computer can strain your eyes.*

---

injured ᵉ **B1** /ˈɪndʒəd/ adj. **1** physically or mentally hurt: *an injured arm/leg* ◇ *injured pride* ◇ *A helicopter transported the seriously injured patient to hospital.* **2** the injured noun [pl.] people who have been hurt: *The injured were rushed to hospital.*

injury ᵉ **A2** /ˈɪndʒəri/ noun [C, U] (pl. -ies) ~ (to sb/sth) harm done to a person's or an animal's body, especially in an accident: *They escaped from the accident with only minor injuries.* ◇ *Injury to the head can be extremely dangerous.*

injury time *noun* [U] (*BrE*) (**SPORT**) time that is added to the end of a football, etc. match when there has been time lost because of injuries to players

injustice ⚑ **C1** /ɪnˈdʒʌstɪs/ *noun* [U, C] the fact of a situation being unfair; an unfair act: *racial/social injustice* ◇ *People are protesting about the injustice of the new tax.* ◇ *The court decided that he had suffered an injustice.*
IDM do sb an injustice to judge sb unfairly: *I'm afraid I've done you both an injustice.*

ink ⚑ **B2** /ɪŋk/ *noun* [U, C] coloured liquid that is used for writing, drawing, etc: *Please write in ink, not pencil.*

inkling /ˈɪŋklɪŋ/ *noun* [C, usually sing.] ~ **(of sth/that …)** a slight feeling (about sth): *I had an inkling that something was wrong.*

ink pad *noun* [C] a thick piece of soft material full of INK (= coloured liquid for writing), used with a rubber stamp

inky /ˈɪŋki/ *adj.* (**inkier**; **inkiest**) made dirty with INK; very dark: *inky fingers* ◇ *an inky night sky*

inlaid /ˌɪnˈleɪd/ *adj.* ~ **(with sth)** (**ART**) (used about furniture, floors, etc.) decorated with designs of wood, metal, etc. that are put into the surface: *a box inlaid with gold*

inland /ˈɪnlænd/ *adj.* (**GEOGRAPHY**) away from the coast or borders of a country: *inland areas* ▶ **inland** /ˌɪnˈlænd/ *adv.*: *The village lies 20 miles inland.*

in-laws *noun* [pl.] (*informal*) your relatives by marriage, especially your husband's or wife's parents: *My in-laws are coming to lunch on Sunday.*

inlay /ˌɪnˈleɪ/ *verb* [T] (**inlaying**; *pt, pp* **inlaid** /-ˈleɪd/) ~ **A (with B)**; ~ **B (in/into A)** (**ART**) to decorate the surface of sth by putting pieces of wood or metal into it in such a way that the surface remains smooth: *The lid of the box had been inlaid with silver.* ◇ *Silver had been inlaid into the lid of the box.* ▶ **inlay** /ˈɪnleɪ/ *noun* [C, U]: *The table was decorated with gold inlay.*

inlet /ˈɪnlet/ *noun* [C] **1** (**GEOGRAPHY**) a narrow area of water that stretches into the land from the sea or a lake, or between islands **2** an opening through which liquid, air or gas can enter a machine: *a fuel inlet* **OPP outlet** ➔ picture at **distillation**

inmate ⚑ **C1** /ˈɪnmeɪt/ *noun* [C] a person living in an institution such as a prison

inn /ɪn/ *noun* [C] (*BrE, old-fashioned*) a small hotel or old pub, usually in the country

innate /ɪˈneɪt/ *adj.* (used about an ability or quality) that you have when you are born: *the innate ability to learn* **SYN inborn**

inner ⚑ **B2** /ˈɪnə(r)/ *adj.* [only before noun] **1** inside; towards or close to the centre of a place: *an inner courtyard* **OPP outer 2** (used about a feeling, etc.) that you do not express or show to other people; private: *Everyone has inner doubts.*

inner city *noun* [C] the poor parts of a large city, near the centre, that often have a lot of social problems ▶ **inner-city** *adj.* [only before noun]: *inner-city schools*

inner ear *noun* [sing.] (**ANATOMY**) the part of the ear that consists of the organs that control balance and hearing ➔ look at **middle ear**, **outer ear** ➔ picture at **ear**

innermost /ˈɪnəməʊst/ *adj.* [only before noun] **1** (used about a feeling or thought) most secret or private: *She never told anyone her innermost thoughts.* **2** nearest to the centre or inside of sth: *the innermost shrine of the temple* **OPP outermost**

inner tube *noun* [C] a rubber tube filled with air inside a tyre

innings /ˈɪnɪŋz/ *noun* [C] (*pl.* **innings**) (**SPORT**) a period of time in a game of CRICKET when it is the turn of one player or team to BAT (= hit the ball)

innocence /ˈɪnəsns/ *noun* [U] **1** (**LAW**) the fact of not being guilty of a crime, etc: *The accused man protested his innocence throughout his trial.* **OPP guilt 2** lack of knowledge and experience of the world, especially of bad things: *the innocence of childhood*

innocent ⚑ **B1** /ˈɪnəsnt/ *adj.* **1** ~ **(of sth)** (**LAW**) not guilty of a crime: *An innocent man was arrested by mistake.* ◇ *She was found innocent of the murder.* **OPP guilty 2** [only before noun] being hurt or killed in a crime, war, etc. although not directly involved in it: *innocent victims of a bomb blast* ◇ *an innocent bystander* **3** not wanting to cause harm or upset sb: *He got very aggressive when I asked an innocent question about his past life.* **SYN harmless 4** not knowing the bad things in life; believing everything you are told: *She was so innocent as to believe that politicians never lie.* **SYN naive** ▶ **innocently** *adv.*: *'What are you doing here?' she asked innocently* (= pretending she did not know the answer).

innocuous /ɪˈnɒkjuəs/ *adj.* (*formal*) not meant to cause harm or upset sb: *I made an innocuous remark about teachers and she got really angry.* **SYN harmless** ▶ **innocuously** *adv.*

innovate /ˈɪnəveɪt/ *verb* [I] to introduce new things, ideas or ways of doing sth ▶ **innovation** ⚑ **B2** /ˌɪnəˈveɪʃn/ *noun* [U, C] ~ **(in sth)**: *technological innovations in industry* ▶ **innovative** ⚑ **B2** /ˈɪnəveɪtɪv, -vət-/ *adj.*: *innovative methods/designs/products* ▶ **innovator** *noun* [C]

innuendo /ˌɪnjuˈendəʊ/ *noun* [C, U] (*pl.* **-oes, -os**) (**LANGUAGE**) an indirect way of talking about sb/sth, usually suggesting sth bad or rude: *His speech was full of sexual innuendo.*

innumerable /ɪˈnjuːmərəbl/ *adj.* too many to be counted

inoculate /ɪˈnɒkjuleɪt/ *verb* [T] ~ **sb (against sth)** (**MEDICINE**) to protect a person or an animal from a disease by INJECTING them with a mild form of the disease (= putting it into their body through a needle): *The children have been inoculated against tetanus.* ➔ look at **immunize, vaccinate** ▶ **inoculation** /ɪˌnɒkjuˈleɪʃn/ *noun* [C, U]

inoffensive /ˌɪnəˈfensɪv/ *adj.* not likely to offend or upset anyone **SYN harmless OPP offensive¹**

inoperable /ɪnˈɒpərəbl/ *adj.* (**MEDICINE**) (used about a disease) that cannot be cured by a medical operation **OPP operable**

inopportune /ɪnˈɒpətjuːn/ *adj.* (*formal*) happening at a bad time **SYN inappropriate, inconvenient OPP opportune**

inordinate /ɪnˈɔːdɪnət/ *adj.* (*formal*) much greater than usual or expected: *They spent an inordinate amount of time and money on the production.* ▶ **inordinately** *adv.*

inorganic /ˌɪnɔːˈɡænɪk/ *adj.* (**CHEMISTRY**) not made of or coming from living things: *Rocks and metals are inorganic substances.* **OPP organic**

inorganic chemistry *noun* [U] (**CHEMISTRY**) the branch of chemistry that deals with substances that do not contain CARBON ➔ look at **organic chemistry**

inpatient /ˈɪnpeɪʃnt/ *noun* [C] (**MEDICINE**) a person who stays in a hospital while getting treatment ➔ look at **outpatient**

input¹ ⚑ **B2** ⊙ /ˈɪnpʊt/ *noun* **1** [C, U] ~ **(of sth) (into/to sth)** the time, knowledge, etc. that you put into sth to make it successful; the act of putting sth in: *Growing* *anything in this soil will require heavy inputs of nutrients.* ◇ *We need some input from teachers into this book.* **2** [U] (**COMPUTING**) the act of putting information into a computer, or the information that you put in: *The computer breakdown means we have lost the whole day's input.* **3** [C] a place or means for electricity, data, etc. to enter a machine or system: *an input lead* ⊃ look at **output**¹ (4)

input² /'ɪnpʊt/ *verb* [T] (**inputting**; *pt, pp* **input, inputted**) to put information into a computer

inquest /'ɪŋkwest/ *noun* [C] (**LAW**) an official investigation to find out how sb died: *to hold an inquest*

inquire, inquirer, inquiring, inquiry = ENQUIRE, ENQUIRER, ENQUIRING, ENQUIRY

inquisition /ˌɪŋkwɪ'zɪʃn/ *noun* **1 the Inquisition** [sing.] (**HISTORY**, **RELIGION**) the organization formed by the Roman Catholic Church to find and punish people who did not agree with its beliefs, especially from the fifteenth to the seventeenth century **2** [C] (*formal*) a series of questions that sb asks you, especially when they ask them in an unpleasant way

inquisitive /ɪn'kwɪzətɪv/ *adj.* **1** too interested in finding out about what other people are doing: *Don't be so inquisitive. It's none of your business.* **SYN nosy 2** interested in finding out about many different things: *You need an inquisitive mind to be a scientist.* **SYN curious** ▸ **inquisitively** *adv.* ▸ **inquisitiveness** *noun* [U]

insane /ɪn'seɪn/ *adj.* **1** (*informal*) very stupid: *You must be insane to leave such a great job.* **2** (*informal*) very annoyed; angry: *This situation is driving me insane.* **3** (*formal or old-fashioned*) seriously mentally ill ⊃ look at **sane** (1) ▸ **insanely** *adv.*: *insanely jealous* ▸ **insanity** /-'sænəti/ *noun* [U]

insanitary /ɪn'sænətri/ *adj.* (*formal*) (**HEALTH**) dirty and likely to cause disease: *The restaurant was closed because of the insanitary condition of the kitchen.* ⊃ look at **sanitary**

insatiable /ɪn'seɪʃəbl/ *adj.* that cannot be satisfied; very great: *an insatiable desire for knowledge* ◇ *an insatiable appetite*

inscribe /ɪn'skraɪb/ *verb* [T] ~ **A (on/in B)**; ~ **B (with A)** (*formal*) to write sth on sth or cut words into the surface of sth: *The names of all the previous champions are inscribed on the cup.* ◇ *The book was inscribed with the author's name.*

inscription /ɪn'skrɪpʃn/ *noun* [C] words that are written or cut on sth: *There was a Latin inscription on the tombstone.*

insect 🔒 **A2** /'ɪnsekt/ *noun* [C] (**BIOLOGY**) a small creature with six legs and a body that is divided into three parts. Insects usually also have wings: *Ants, flies, beetles, butterflies and mosquitoes are all insects.* ◇ *an insect bite/sting* ⊃ picture at **animal**, **food web**

insecticide /ɪn'sektɪsaɪd/ *noun* [C, U] (**AGRICULTURE**) a chemical that is used for killing insects ⊃ look at **herbicide**, **pesticide**

insectivore /ɪn'sektɪvɔː(r)/ *noun* [C] (**BIOLOGY**) any animal that eats insects ⊃ look at **carnivore**, **herbivore**, **omnivore**

insecure /ˌɪnsɪ'kjʊə(r)/ *adj.* **1** ~ **(about sb/sth)** not confident about yourself or your relationships with other people: *Many teenagers are insecure about their appearance.* **2** not safe or protected: *This ladder feels a bit insecure.* ◇ *Many people use insecure passwords.* **OPP secure**¹ ▸ **insecurely** *adv.* ▸ **insecurity** /-'kjʊərəti/

noun [U, C] (*pl.* **-ies**): *Their aggressive behaviour is really a sign of insecurity.*

insensitive /ɪn'sensətɪv/ *adj.* ~ **(to sth)** **1** not knowing or caring how another person feels and therefore likely to hurt or upset them: *an insensitive remark* ◇ *She's completely insensitive to my feelings.* **2** not able to feel or react to sth: *insensitive to pain/cold/criticism* **OPP sensitive** ▸ **insensitively** *adv.* ▸ **insensitivity** /ˌɪnˌsensə'tɪvəti/ *noun* [U]

inseparable /ɪn'seprəbl/ *adj.* that cannot be separated from sb/sth: *inseparable friends* ◇ *His reputation was inseparable from that of his family.* **OPP separable**

insert 🔒+ **B2** /ɪn'sɜːt/ *verb* [T] (*formal*) to put sth into sth or between two things: *I decided to insert an extra paragraph in the text.* ▸ **insertion** 🔒+ **C1** /-'sɜːʃn/ *noun* [C, U]

inshore /'ɪnʃɔː(r)/ *adj.* (**GEOGRAPHY**) in or towards the part of the sea that is close to the land: *inshore fishermen* ▸ **inshore** /ɪn'ʃɔː(r)/ *adv.*: *Sharks don't often come inshore.*

inside¹ 🔒 **A2** /ˌɪn'saɪd/ *prep., adv., adj.* **1** in, on or to the inner part or surface of sth: *Is there anything inside the box?* ◇ *It's safer to be inside the house in a thunderstorm.* ◇ *We'd better stay inside until the rain stops.* ◇ *It's getting cold. Let's go inside.* ◇ *the inside pages of a newspaper* **OPP outside**¹, **outside²** **2** (*formal*) (used about time) in less than; within: *Your prescription will be ready inside an hour.* **3** known or done by sb in a group or an organization: *The robbers seemed to have had some inside information about the bank's security system.* **4** (*informal*) in prison: *He was sentenced to three years inside.*

inside² 🔒 **A2** /ˌɪn'saɪd/ *noun* **1** [C] the inner part or surface of sth: *The door was locked from the inside.* ◇ *There's a label somewhere on the inside.* **OPP outside⁴ 2 insides** [pl.] (*informal*) the organs inside the body: *The coffee warmed his insides.* **IDM inside out** with the inner surface on the outside: *You've got your jumper on inside out.* **know sth inside out →** KNOW¹

insider 🔒+ **C1** /ɪn'saɪdə(r)/ *noun* [C] a person who knows a lot about a group or an organization because they are a part of it: *The book gives us an insider's view of how government works.* ⊃ look at **outsider** (1)

insidious /ɪn'sɪdiəs/ *adj.* (*formal*) spreading gradually or without being noticed, but causing serious harm: *the insidious effects of polluted water supplies* ▸ **insidiously** *adv.*

insight 🔒 **B2** 🌐 /'ɪnsaɪt/ *noun* [C, U] ~ **(into sth)** an understanding of what sb/sth is like: *The book gives a good insight into the lives of the poor.* ◇ *You need insight into human nature for this job.*

insightful /ɪn'saɪtfl/ *adj.* showing a clear understanding of a person or situation

insignia /ɪn'sɪɡniə/ *noun* [C + sing./pl. verb] (*pl.* **insignia**, **insignias**) the symbol or sign that shows sb's position, or that they are a member of a group or an organization: *His uniform bore the insignia of a captain.*

insignificant /ˌɪnsɪɡ'nɪfɪkənt/ *adj.* of little value or importance: *an insignificant detail* ◇ *Working in such a big company made her feel insignificant.* **OPP significant** ▸ **insignificance** /-kəns/ *noun* [U] ▸ **insignificantly** *adv.*

insincere /ˌɪnsɪn'sɪə(r)/ *adj.* saying or doing sth that you do not really believe: *My apology sounded insincere.* ◇ *an insincere smile* **OPP sincere** ▸ **insincerely** *adv.* ▸ **insincerity** /-'serəti/ *noun* [U]

insinuate /ɪn'sɪnjueɪt/ *verb* [T] ~ **(that…)** to suggest sth unpleasant in an indirect way: *She seemed to be insinuating that our work was below standard.*

insipid /ɪnˈsɪpɪd/ *adj.* **1** having almost no taste **2** not interesting or exciting

insist ⚡ B2 /ɪnˈsɪst/ *verb* [I, T] **1** ~ **(on sth/doing sth)**; ~ **that** … to say strongly that you must have or do sth, or that sb else must do sth: *He always insists on the best.* ◇ *Dan insisted on coming too.* ◇ *My parents insist that I come home by taxi.* ◇ '*Have another drink.' 'Oh all right, if you insist.'* ⊃ note at **demand**[2] **2** ~ **(on sth)**; ~ **(that)** … to say FIRMLY that sth is true (when sb does not believe you): *She insisted on her innocence.* ◇ *James insisted that the accident wasn't his fault.*
▶ **insistence** *noun* [U]

insistent /ɪnˈsɪstənt/ *adj.* **1** ~ **(on sth/doing sth)**; ~ **that** … saying strongly that you must have or do sth, or that sb else must do sth: *Doctors are insistent on the need for people to take more exercise.* ◇ *She was most insistent that we should all be there.* **2** continuing for a long time in a way that cannot be ignored: *the insistent ringing of the phone* ▶ **insistently** *adv.*

insolent /ˈɪnsələnt/ *adj.* (*formal*) lacking respect; rude: *insolent behaviour* ▶ **insolence** /-ləns/ *noun* [U]
▶ **insolently** *adv.*

insoluble /ɪnˈsɒljəbl/ *adj.* **1** that cannot be explained or solved: *We faced almost insoluble problems.* **OPP** **soluble** **2** (**CHEMISTRY**) that cannot be DISSOLVED in a liquid (= made to become part of the liquid) **OPP** **soluble**

insolvent /ɪnˈsɒlvənt/ *adj.* (*formal*) (**FINANCE**) not having enough money to pay what you owe: *The company has been declared insolvent.* **SYN** **bankrupt**[1]
▶ **insolvency** /-vənsi/ *noun* [U, C] (*pl.* -ies)

insomnia /ɪnˈsɒmniə/ *noun* [U] (**HEALTH**) the condition of being unable to sleep: *Do you ever suffer from insomnia?* ⊃ look at **sleepless**

insomniac /ɪnˈsɒmniæk/ *noun* [C] (**HEALTH**) a person who regularly finds it difficult to sleep

inspect ⚡+ C1 /ɪnˈspekt/ *verb* [T] **1** ~ **sb/sth (for sth)** to look at sth closely or in great detail: *The detective inspected the room for fingerprints.* **SYN** **examine** **2** to make an official visit to a place to make sure that rules are being obeyed, work is being done correctly, etc: *All food shops should be inspected regularly.*
▶ **inspection** ⚡+ C1 /-ˈspekʃn/ *noun* [C, U]: *The fire prevention service will carry out an inspection of the building next week.* ◇ *On inspection, the passport turned out to be false.*

inspector ⚡+ B2 /ɪnˈspektə(r)/ *noun* [C] **1** an official who visits schools, factories, etc. to make sure that rules are being obeyed, work is being done correctly, etc: *a health and safety inspector* **2** (*AmE*) = SURVEYOR (2) **3** (*BrE*) (**LAW**) a police officer with a fairly important position **4** a person whose job is to check passengers' tickets on buses or trains

inspiration ⚡+ C1 /ˌɪnspəˈreɪʃn/ *noun* **1** [C, U] ~ **(to/for sb)**; ~ **(to do/for sth)** a feeling, person or thing that makes you want to do sth or gives you exciting new ideas: *The beauty of the mountains was a great source of inspiration to the writer.* ◇ *What gave you the inspiration to become a dancer?* **2** [C, usually sing.] (*informal*) a sudden good idea: *I've had an inspiration — why don't we go to that new club?*

inspirational /ˌɪnspəˈreɪʃənl/ *adj.* providing exciting new ideas; making sb want to create sth: *an inspirational leader*

inspire ⚡ B2 /ɪnˈspaɪə(r)/ *verb* [T] **1** ~ **sth**; ~ **sb (to do sth)** to make sb want to do or create sth: *The attack was inspired by racial hatred.* ◇ *Nelson Mandela's autobiography inspired her to go into politics.* **2** ~ **sb (with sth)**; ~ **sth (in sb)** to make sb feel, think, etc. sth: *to*

be inspired with enthusiasm ◇ *The guide's nervous manner did not* **inspire** *much* **confidence** *in us.*
▶ **inspiring** *adj.*: *an inspiring speech*

inspired /ɪnˈspaɪəd/ *adj.* **1** having excellent qualities; influenced or helped by a particular feeling, thing or person: *The pianist gave an inspired performance.* **2** used with nouns, adjectives and adverbs to show how sth has been influenced: *a politically inspired killing*

instability ⓦ /ˌɪnstəˈbɪləti/ *noun* [U] the state of being likely to change: *There are growing signs of political instability.* **OPP** **stability** ⊃ adjective **unstable**

Instagram™ /ˈɪnstəɡræm/ (*also informal* **Insta**™ /ˈɪnstə/) *noun* (**COMPUTING**) a SOCIAL MEDIA website where people can share photos and short videos: *She shared photos on Instagram with her fans.* ◇ *Check out my Insta story if you haven't already.*

install ⚡ B2 (*BrE also* **instal**) /ɪnˈstɔːl/ *verb* [T] **1** to put a piece of equipment, etc. in place so that it is ready to be used: *We are waiting to have our new kitchen installed.* ◇ *to install a computer system* **SYN** **put sth in** **2** (**COMPUTING**) to put a new program into a computer: *I'll need some help installing the software.* **3** ~ **sb (as sth)** to put sb/sth or yourself in a position or place: *He was installed as president yesterday.*

installation ⚡+ B2 /ˌɪnstəˈleɪʃn/ *noun* **1** [U, C] the act of fixing equipment or furniture in position so that it can be used: *installation costs* **2** [C] a piece of equipment or a machine that has been fixed in position so that it can be used: *a heating installation* **3** [C] a place where specialist equipment is kept and used: *a military installation* **4** [C] (**ART**) a piece of modern sculpture that is made using sound, light, etc. as well as objects

instalment (*especially BrE*) (*AmE usually* **installment**) /ɪnˈstɔːlmənt/ *noun* [C] **1** (**FINANCE**) one of the regular payments that you make for sth until you have paid the full amount: *to pay for something* **in instalments** **2** one part of a story that is shown or published as a series: *Don't miss next week's exciting instalment of this new drama.*

instance ⚡ B2 ⓞ /ˈɪnstəns/ *noun* [C] ~ **(of sth)** (*formal*) an example or case (of sth): *There have been several instances of racial attacks in the area.* ◇ *In most instances the drug has no side effects.* ⊃ note at **example**
IDM **for instance** for example: *There are several interesting places to visit around here — Warwick, for instance.*

instant[1] ⚡+ B2 /ˈɪnstənt/ *adj.* **1** happening immediately: *The film was an instant success.* **SYN** **immediate** **2** [only before noun] (used about food) that can be prepared quickly and easily, usually by adding hot water: *instant coffee*

instant[2] /ˈɪnstənt/ *noun* [usually sing.] **1** a very short period of time: *Alex thought for an instant and then agreed.* **2** a particular point in time: *At that instant I realized I had been tricked.* ◇ *Stop doing that this instant* (= now)!

instantaneous /ˌɪnstənˈteɪniəs/ *adj.* happening immediately or extremely quickly ▶ **instantaneously** *adv.*

instantly ⚡+ B2 /ˈɪnstəntli/ *adv.* without delay; immediately: *I asked him a question and he replied instantly.*

instant messaging *noun* [U] (**COMPUTING**) a system on the internet that allows people to exchange written messages with each other very quickly ▶ **instant message** *noun* [C] (*abbr.* IM): *to send an instant message*

ˌinstant ˈreplay = ACTION REPLAY

instead ῗ **A2** /ɪnˈsted/ adv. in the place of sb/sth: *I couldn't go so my husband went instead.* ◊ *He didn't reply. Instead, he turned and left the room.*

inˈstead of prep. in the place of sb/sth: *You should play football instead of just watching it on TV.* ◊ *Instead of 7.30 could I come at 8.00?*

instigate /ˈɪnstɪɡeɪt/ verb [T] (formal) to make sth start to happen ▸ **instigation** /ˌɪnstɪˈɡeɪʃn/ noun [U]

instil (BrE) (AmE **instill**) /ɪnˈstɪl/ verb [T] (-ll-) ~ **sth (in/into sb)** to make sb think or feel sth: *Parents should try to instil a sense of responsibility into their children.*

instinct ῗ+ **C1** /ˈɪnstɪŋkt/ noun [U, C] (BIOLOGY) the natural quality that causes a person or an animal to behave in a particular way without thinking or learning about it: *Birds learn to fly by instinct.* ◊ *In a situation like that you don't have time to think — you just act on instinct.* ◊ *She did not seem to have any of the usual maternal instincts.* ▸ **instinctive** /ɪnˈstɪŋktɪv/ adj.: *Your instinctive reaction is to run from danger.* ▸ **instinctively** adv.

institute¹ ῗ **B2** /ˈɪnstɪtjuːt/ noun [C] an organization that has a particular purpose; the building used by this organization: *the Institute of Science and Technology* ◊ *institutes of higher education*

institute² /ˈɪnstɪtjuːt/ verb [T] (formal) to introduce a system, policy, etc., or start a process: *The government has instituted a new scheme for youth training.*

institution ῗ **B2** /ˌɪnstɪˈtjuːʃn/ noun **1** [C] a large important organization that has a particular purpose, such as a bank, a university, etc: *the financial institutions in the City of London* **2** [C] (MEDICINE) a building where certain people with special needs live and are looked after: *a mental institution* (= a hospital for the mentally ill) ◊ *She's been in institutions all her life.* **3** [C] (SOCIAL STUDIES) a social custom or habit that has existed for a long time: *the institution of marriage* **4** [U] the act of introducing a system, policy, etc., or of starting a process: *the institution of new safety procedures*

institutional ῗ+ **C1** /ˌɪnstɪˈtjuːʃənl/ adj. connected with an institution: *The old lady is in need of institutional care.*

institutionalized (BrE also -ised) /ˌɪnstɪˈtjuːʃənəlaɪzd/ adj. **1** that has happened or been done for so long that it is considered normal **2** (used about people) lacking the ability to live and think independently because they have spent so long in an institution: *institutionalized patients*

instruct ῗ+ **C1** /ɪnˈstrʌkt/ verb [T] (formal) **1** ~ **sb (to do sth)** to give an order to sb; to tell sb to do sth: *The soldiers were instructed to shoot above the heads of the crowd.* **2** ~ **sb (in sth)** to teach sb sth: *Children must be instructed in road safety before they are allowed to ride a bike on the road.*

instruction ῗ **A2** **⊚** /ɪnˈstrʌkʃn/ noun **1** instructions [pl.] detailed information on how you should use sth, do sth, etc: *Read the instructions on the back of the packet carefully.* ◊ *You should always follow the instructions.* **2** [C, usually pl.] ~ **(to do sth)** an order that tells you what to do or how to do sth: *The guard was under strict instructions not to let anyone in or out.* **3** [U] ~ **(in sth)** (formal) the act of teaching sth to sb: *The staff need instruction in the use of the new booking system.*

instructive /ɪnˈstrʌktɪv/ adj. giving useful information ▸ **instructively** adv.

instructor ῗ **A2** /ɪnˈstrʌktə(r)/ noun [C] (EDUCATION) a person whose job is to teach a practical skill or sport: *a driving/fitness/golf instructor*

instrument ῗ **A2** **⊚** /ˈɪnstrəmənt/ noun [C] **1** (MUSIC) something that is used for playing music: *'What instrument do you play?' 'The violin.'* **2** (SCIENCE) a tool that is used for doing a particular job or task: *surgical/optical/precision instruments* ⊃ note at **tool** **3** something that is used for measuring speed, distance, temperature, etc. in a vehicle or on a machine: *the instrument panel of a plane* **4** (formal) something that sb uses in order to achieve sth: *The press should be more than an instrument of the government.*

▼ VOCABULARY BUILDING

Musical instruments may be **stringed** (*violins, guitars, etc.*), **brass** (*horns, trumpets, etc.*), **woodwind** (*flutes, clarinets, etc.*) or **keyboard** (*piano, organ, synthesizer, etc.*). **Percussion** instruments include *drums* and *cymbals*.

---

instrumental ῗ+ **C1** /ˌɪnstrəˈmentl/ adj. **1** ~ **in doing sth** helping to make sth happen: *She was instrumental in getting him the job.* **2** (MUSIC) for musical instruments without voices: *instrumental music*

insubordinate /ˌɪnsəˈbɔːdɪnət/ adj. (formal) (used about a person or their behaviour) not obeying rules or orders ▸ **insubordination** /ˌɪnsəˌbɔːdɪˈneɪʃn/ noun [U]: *He was dismissed from the army for insubordination.*

insubstantial /ˌɪnsəbˈstænʃl/ adj. not large, solid or strong: *a hut built of insubstantial materials* **OPP** **substantial**

insufferable /ɪnˈsʌfrəbl/ adj. (formal) (used about a person or their behaviour) extremely unpleasant or annoying

insufficient ῗ+ **C1** **⊚** /ˌɪnsəˈfɪʃnt/ adj. ~ **(to do sth)** (formal) not enough: *insufficient time/funds* ◊ *The evidence was insufficient to prove that the defendant was guilty.* **OPP** **sufficient** ▸ **insufficiently** adv.

insular /ˈɪnsjələ(r)/ adj. only interested in your own country, ideas, etc. and not in those from outside **SYN** **narrow-minded** ▸ **insularity** /ˌɪnsjuˈlærəti/ noun [U]

insulate /ˈɪnsjuleɪt/ verb [T] ~ **sth (against/from sth)** (ENGINEERING) to protect sth with a material that prevents electricity, heat or sound from passing through: *The walls are insulated against noise.* ◊ (figurative) *This industry has been insulated from the effects of competition.* ▸ **insulation** /ˌɪnsjuˈleɪʃn/ noun [U]

insulating tape noun [U] a thin band of sticky material used for covering electrical wires to prevent the possibility of an electric shock

insulator /ˈɪnsjuleɪtə(r)/ noun [C] (ENGINEERING) a material or device used to prevent heat, electricity or sound from escaping from sth ⊃ picture at **light bulb**

insulin /ˈɪnsjəlɪn/ noun [U] (BIOLOGY, HEALTH) a substance, normally produced by the body itself, that controls the amount of sugar in the blood: *A diabetic relies on insulin injections.*

insult¹ ῗ+ **C1** /ɪnˈsʌlt/ verb [T] to say or do sth that offends sb: *I felt very insulted when I didn't even get an answer to my letter.* ◊ *He was thrown out of the hotel for insulting the manager.*

insult² ῗ+ **C1** /ˈɪnsʌlt/ noun [C] a rude comment or action that offends sb: *The drivers were standing in the road yelling insults at each other.*

insulting /ɪnˈsʌltɪŋ/ adj. ~ **(to sb/sth)** making sb feel offended: *insulting behaviour/remarks* ◊ *That poster is insulting to women.*

Musical instruments

strings

violin

viola

cello

double bass

other stringed instruments

harp

electric guitar

acoustic guitar

banjo

brass

French horn

tuba

trumpet

trombone

woodwind

saxophone

clarinet

oboe

flute

piccolo

bassoon

recorder

percussion

bass drum

xylophone

triangle

tambourine

cymbals

kettledrum

insuperable /ɪnˈsuːpərəbl/ *adj.* (*formal*) (used about a problem, etc.) impossible to solve **SYN** **insurmountable**

insurance 🔊 **B2** /ɪnˈʃʊərəns, -ˈʃɔːr-/ *noun* **1** [U] ~ **(against sth)** (**FINANCE**) an arrangement with a company in which you pay them regular amounts of money and they agree to pay the costs if, for example, you die or are ill, or if you lose or damage sth: *Builders should always have insurance against personal injury.* **2** [U] (**BUSINESS**) the business of providing insurance: *He works in insurance.* **3** [U, C] **(an)** ~ **(against sth)** something you do to protect yourself (against sth unpleasant): *Many people take vitamin pills as an insurance against illness.*

▼ **VOCABULARY BUILDING**

You **take out** an **insurance policy**. An **insurance premium** is the regular amount you pay to the insurance company. You can take out **life**, **health**, **car**, **travel** or **household insurance**.

---

insure /ɪnˈʃʊə(r), -ˈʃɔː(r)/ *verb* [T, I] **1** ~ **(sb/sth/yourself)** **(against/for sth)** (**FINANCE**) to buy or to provide insurance: *They insured the painting for £10 000 against damage or theft.* ◇ *We strongly recommend insuring against sickness or injury.* **2** (*especially AmE*) = ENSURE

insurer /ɪnˈʃʊərə(r), -ˈʃɔːr-/ *noun* [C] (**FINANCE**) a person or company that provides people with insurance

insurgency /ɪnˈsɜːdʒənsi/ *noun* [U, C] (*pl.* **-ies**) (**POLITICS**) an attempt to take control of a country by force **SYN** **rebellion**

insurgent /ɪnˈsɜːdʒənt/ *noun* [C, usually pl.] (*formal*) (**POLITICS**) a person fighting against the government or armed forces of their own country **SYN** **rebel¹** ▶ **insurgent** *adj.* **SYN** **rebellious**

insurmountable /ˌɪnsəˈmaʊntəbl/ *adj.* (*formal*) (used about a problem, etc.) impossible to solve **SYN** **insuperable**

insurrection /ˌɪnsəˈrekʃn/ *noun* [C, U] (*formal*) (**POLITICS**) violent action against the rulers of a country or the government **SYN** **uprising**

intact 🔊 **C1** /ɪnˈtækt/ *adj.* [not before noun] complete; not damaged: *Very few of the buildings remain intact following the earthquake.*

intake 🔊 **C1** /ˈɪnteɪk/ *noun* **1** [U, C] the amount of food, drink, etc. that you take into your body: *The doctor told me to cut down my alcohol intake.* **2** [C, + sing./pl. verb, U] the (number of) people who enter an organization or institution during a certain period: *This year's intake of students is down 10 per cent.* **3** [C, usually sing.] the act of taking sth into your body, especially breath **4** [C] a place where liquid, air, etc. enters a machine

intangible /ɪnˈtændʒəbl/ *adj.* difficult to describe, understand or measure: *The benefits of good customer relations are intangible.* **OPP** **tangible**

integer /ˈɪntɪdʒə(r)/ *noun* [C] (**GEOMETRY**) a whole number, such as 3 or 4 but not 3.5 ⊃ look at **fraction** (2)

integral 🔊 **C1** **W** /ˈɪntɪɡrəl, ɪnˈteɡrəl/ *adj.* **1** ~ **(to sth)** necessary in order to make sth complete: *Spending a year in France is **an integral part of** the university course.* ◇ *The illustrations are integral to the story.* **2** including sth as part of sth: *The car has an integral solar panel.*

integrate 🔊 **B2** **W** /ˈɪntɪɡreɪt/ *verb* **1** [T, I] ~ **(sth) (into/with sth)**; ~ **A and/with B** to join things so that they become one thing or work together: *The two small*

schools were integrated into one large one. ◇ *These programs can be integrated with your existing software.* **2** [I, T] ~ **(sb) (into/with sth)** (**SOCIAL STUDIES**) to join in and become part of a group or community, or to make sb do this: *It took Amir a while to integrate into his new school.* ◇ *They have made an effort to integrate with the local community.* ⊃ look at **segregate**

integrated 🔊+ **C1** **W** /ˈɪntɪɡreɪtɪd/ *adj.* **1** in which many different parts are closely connected and work successfully together: *an integrated transport system* (= including buses, trains, etc.) **2** including people from all human groups, religions, etc: *an integrated school*

integration **W** /ˌɪntɪˈɡreɪʃn/ *noun* **1** [U, C] ~ **(of A and/with B)** the act or process of combining two or more things so that they work together: *the integration of old and new technology* ⊃ look at **vertical integration** **2** [U] (**SOCIAL STUDIES**) the act or process of mixing people who have previously been separated, usually because of the human group they belong to, their religion, etc: *racial integration in schools* ⊃ look at **segregation**

integrity 🔊+ **C1** /ɪnˈteɡrəti/ *noun* [U] the quality of being honest and having strong moral principles: *He's a person **of great integrity** who can be relied on to tell the truth.*

intellect /ˈɪntəlekt/ *noun* **1** [U] the power of the mind to think and to learn: *a woman of considerable intellect* **2** [C] an extremely intelligent person: *He was one of the most brilliant intellects of his time.*

intellectual¹ 🔊+ **B2** /ˌɪntəˈlektʃuəl/ *adj.* **1** [only before noun] connected with a person's ability to think in a logical way and to understand things: *The boy's intellectual development was very advanced for his age.* **2** (used about a person) well educated and enjoying activities in which you have to think seriously about things ▶ **intellectually** /-əli/ *adv.*

intellectual² 🔊+ **C1** /ˌɪntəˈlektʃuəl/ *noun* [C] a person who is well educated and enjoys thinking deeply about things

intellectual ˈproperty *noun* [U] (**LAW**) an idea, a design, etc. that sb has created and that the law prevents other people from copying: *intellectual property rights*

intelligence 🔊 **B1** /ɪnˈtelɪdʒəns/ *noun* [U] **1** the ability to understand, learn and think: *a person of normal intelligence* ◇ *an intelligence test* **2** secret information that is collected, for example about a foreign country, especially one that is an enemy: *to receive intelligence about somebody* ◇ *the intelligence community* (= all the people that collect this information)

intelligent 🔊 **A2** /ɪnˈtelɪdʒənt/ *adj.* having or showing the ability to understand, learn and think: *All their children are very intelligent.* ◇ *an intelligent question* **SYN** **clever** ▶ **intelligently** *adv.*

intelligible /ɪnˈtelɪdʒəbl/ *adj.* possible or easy to understand **OPP** **unintelligible** ▶ **intelligibility** /ɪnˌtelɪdʒəˈbɪləti/ *noun* [U]

intend 🔊 **B1** **W** /ɪnˈtend/ *verb* **1** [T, I] ~ **to do sth;** ~ **doing sth** to plan or mean to do sth: *I'm afraid I spent more money than I had intended.* ◇ *I certainly don't intend to wait here all day!* ◇ *They had intended staying in Wales for two weeks but the weather was so bad that they left after one.* ⊃ noun **intention** **2** [T] ~ **sth for sb/ sth;** ~ **sb to do sth;** ~ **sth as sth** to plan, mean or make sth

WORD FAMILY
intend *verb*
intended *adj.*
(≠unintended)
intention *noun*
intentional *adj.*
(≠unintentional)

for a particular person or purpose: *You shouldn't have read that letter — it wasn't intended for you.* ◇ *I didn't intend you to have all the work.* ◇ *His comment was intended as a joke.*

intended ʔ **B2** /ɪnˈtendɪd/ *adj.* **1** [only before noun] that you are trying to achieve or reach: *the intended purpose* **2 ~ for sb/sth; ~ as sth; ~ to be/do sth** planned or designed for sb/sth: *The book is intended for children.* ◇ *The notes are intended as an introduction to the course.* ◇ *The lights are intended to be used in the garden.*

intense ʔ **B2** /ɪnˈtens/ *adj.* very great, strong or serious: *intense heat/cold/pressure* ◇ *intense anger/interest/desire* **SYN extreme** ▸ **intensely** *adv.*: *They obviously dislike each other intensely.*
▸ **intensity** ʔ+ **C1** **W** *noun* [U]: *I wasn't prepared for the intensity of his reaction to the news.*

intensifier /ɪnˈtensɪfaɪə(r)/ *noun* [C] (**GRAMMAR**) a word, especially an adjective or an adverb, for example 'so' or 'very', that makes the meaning of another word stronger ⊃ look at **modifier**

intensify ʔ+ **C1** /ɪnˈtensɪfaɪ/ *verb* [I, T] (intensifying; intensifies; *pt, pp* intensified) to become or to make sth greater or stronger: *Fighting in the region has intensified.* ◇ *The government has intensified its campaign against obesity.* ▸ **intensification** /ɪnˌtensɪfɪˈkeɪʃn/ *noun* [U]

intensive ʔ+ **C1** **W** /ɪnˈtensɪv/ *adj.* **1** involving a lot of work or care in a short period of time: *an intensive investigation/course* **2** (**AGRICULTURE**) (used about methods of farming) aimed at producing as much food as possible from the land or money available: *intensive agriculture* ⊃ look at **extensive** (2)
▸ **intensively** *adv.*

in,tensive 'care *noun* [U] (**MEDICINE**) special care in hospital for patients who are very seriously ill or injured; the department that gives this care: *She was in intensive care for a week after the crash.*

in,tensive 'care unit = ICU

intent¹ /ɪnˈtent/ *adj.* **1 ~ (on/upon sth)** showing great attention: *She was so intent upon her work that she didn't hear me come in.* **2 ~ on/upon sth/doing sth** determined to do sth: *He's always been intent on making a lot of money.* ▸ **intently** *adv.*

intent² ʔ+ **C1** /ɪnˈtent/ *noun* [U] **~ to do sth** (*formal*) (**LAW**) what sb intends to do: *He was charged with possession of a gun with intent to commit a robbery.* ◇ *to do something with evil/good intent*
IDM to/for all intents and purposes in the effects that sth has, if not in every respect: *When they scored their fourth goal the match was, to all intents and purposes, over.*

intention ʔ **B1** **W** /ɪnˈtenʃn/ *noun* [C, U] **~ (of doing sth); ~ (to do sth)** what sb intends or means to do; a plan or purpose: *I have no intention of staying indoors on a nice sunny day like this.* ◇ *I borrowed the money with the intention of paying it back the next day.* ◇ *Our intention was to leave early in the morning.* ⊃ note at **purpose**

intentional /ɪnˈtenʃənl/ *adj.* done deliberately, not by chance: *I'm sorry I took your jacket — it wasn't intentional.* **SYN deliberate¹** **OPP unintentional**
▸ **intentionally** /-ʃənəli/ *adv.*: *I can't believe the boys broke the window intentionally.*

inter- /ɪntə(r)/ *prefix* (in verbs, nouns, adjectives and adverbs) between; from one to another: *interface* ◇ *interaction* ◇ *international* ⊃ look at **intra-**

interact ʔ+ **B2** **O** /ˌɪntərˈækt/ *verb* [I] **1 ~ (with sb)** (used about people) to communicate or mix with sb, especially while you work, play or spend time together: *He is studying the way children interact with*

each other at different ages. **2** (used about two things) to have an effect on each other ▸ **interaction** ʔ+ **B2** **O** /-ˈækʃn/ *noun* [U, C] **~ (between/with sb/sth)**: *There is a need for greater interaction between the two departments.*

interactive ʔ+ **C1** /ˌɪntərˈæktɪv/ *adj.* **1** that involves people working together and having an influence on each other: *interactive language-learning techniques* **2** (**COMPUTING**) involving direct communication both ways, between the computer or other device and the person using it: *interactive TV/computer games*

interactive 'whiteboard *noun* [C] (**EDUCATION**) a piece of classroom equipment using a computer connected to a large screen that you can write on or use to control the computer by touching it with your finger or a pen

intercept /ˌɪntəˈsept/ *verb* [T] to stop or catch sb/sth that is moving from one place to another: *Detectives intercepted her at the airport.* ▸ **interception** /-ˈsepʃn/ *noun* [U, C]

interchange /ˈɪntətʃeɪndʒ/ *noun* **1** [C, U] the act of sharing or exchanging sth, especially ideas or information: *a continuous interchange of ideas* **2** [C] a place where a road joins a major road such as a MOTORWAY

interchangeable /ˌɪntəˈtʃeɪndʒəbl/ *adj.* **~ (with sth)** that can be exchanged without making any difference to the way sth works: *Are these two words interchangeable* (= do they have the same meaning)? ◇ *The V8 engines are all interchangeable with each other.* ▸ **interchangeably** /-bli/ *adv.*

intercity /ˌɪntəˈsɪti/ *adj.* (used especially about trains or buses) travelling between cities, usually with not many stops on the way: *an intercity rail service* ◇ *intercity travel*

intercom /ˈɪntəkɒm/ *noun* [C] a system of communication by radio or phone inside an office, plane, etc.; the device you press or switch on to start using this system

interconnect /ˌɪntəkəˈnekt/ *verb* [I, T] **~ (A) (with B); ~ A and B** to connect similar things; to be connected to similar things: *The tunnels were interconnected with one another.* ◇ *Bad housing, debt and poverty are interconnected.*

intercontinental /ˌɪntəˌkɒntɪˈnentl/ *adj.* (**GEOGRAPHY**) between continents: *intercontinental flights*

intercostal /ˌɪntəˈkɒstl/ *adj.* (**ANATOMY**) between the RIBS (= the curved bones that go around the chest): *intercostal muscles* ⊃ picture at **respiratory**

intercourse /ˈɪntəkɔːs/ (*formal*) = SEXUAL INTERCOURSE

interdependent /ˌɪntədɪˈpendənt/ *adj.* depending on each other: *Exercise and good health are generally interdependent.* ◇ *interdependent economies/organizations* ▸ **interdependence** /-dəns/ *noun* [U]

interdisciplinary /ˌɪntədɪsəˈplɪnəri/ *adj.* involving different areas of knowledge or study

interest¹ ʔ **A1** **O** /ˈɪntrəst, -trest/ *noun* **1** [U, sing.] **(an) ~ (in sb/sth)** a desire to learn or hear more about sb/sth or to be involved with sb/sth: *She's begun to show a great interest in politics.* ◇ *I wish he'd take more interest in his children.* ◇ *Don't lose interest now!* **2** [U] the quality that makes sth interesting: *I thought this article might be of interest to you.* ◇ *Computers hold no interest for me.* ◇ *places of historical interest* **3** [C, usually pl.] something that you enjoy doing or learning about: *What are your interests and hobbies?* **4** [U] **~ (on sth)** (**FINANCE**) the money that you pay for borrowing money from a bank, etc. or the money that you earn when you keep money in a bank, etc: *We pay 6 per cent interest on our mortgage at the moment.* ◇ *The* **interest rate** *has never been so high/low.* ⊃ look at **interest-free** ⊃ note at **mortgage**[1]

IDM **have/with sb's interests at heart** to want sb to be happy and successful, even though your actions may not show it in **sb's interest(s)** to sb's advantage: *Using less water is in the public interest.* **in the interest(s) of sth** in order to achieve or protect sth: *In the interest(s) of safety, please fasten your seat belts.*

interest² 🔊 **A1** /'ɪntrəst, -trest/ *verb* [T] to make sb want to learn or hear more about sth or to become involved in sth: *It might interest you to know that I didn't accept the job.* ◇ *The subject of the talk was one that interests me greatly.*

PHR V **interest sb in sth** to persuade sb to buy, have or do sth: *Can I interest you in our new brochure?*

interested 🔊 **A1** **S** /'ɪntrəstɪd, -tres-/ *adj.* **1** [not before noun] ~ **(in sth/sb)**; ~ **in doing sth**; ~ **to do sth** wanting to know or hear more about sth/sb; enjoying or liking sth/sb: *They weren't interested in my news at all!* ◇ *I'm really not interested in going to university.* ◇ *I was interested to hear that you've got a new job. Where is it?* **OPP** **uninterested** **2** [only before noun] involved in or affected by sth; in a position to gain from sth: *As an interested party* (= a person directly involved), *I was not allowed to vote.* **OPP** **disinterested**

interest-free *adj.* (**FINANCE**) with no interest charged on money borrowed: *an interest-free loan* ◇ *interest-free credit*

interest group *noun* [C + sing./pl. verb] (**POLITICS**) a group of people who work together to achieve sth that they are interested in, especially by trying to influence what the government does

interesting 🔊 **A1** **S** /'ɪntrəstɪŋ, -tres-/ *adj.* ~ **(to do sth)**; ~ **that…** special, exciting or unusual; holding your attention: *an interesting person/book/idea/job* ◇ *It's always interesting to hear about the customs of other societies.* ◇ *It's interesting that Luisa chose Peru for a holiday.* ▸ **interestingly** *adv.*

interface¹ 🔊 **C1** /'ɪntəfeɪs/ *noun* [C] **1** (**COMPUTING**) the way a computer program gives information to a user or receives information from a user, in particular the appearance of the screen: *the user interface* **2** (**COMPUTING**) an electrical CIRCUIT, connection or program that joins one device or system to another: *the interface between computer and printer* **3** ~ **(between A and B)** the point where two subjects, systems, etc. meet and affect each other: *the interface between manufacturing and sales*

interface² /'ɪntəfeɪs/ *verb* [I, T] ~ **(sth) (with sth)**; ~ **A and B** (**COMPUTING**) to be connected with sth using an INTERFACE; to connect sth in this way: *The new system interfaces with existing phone equipment.*

interfaith /'ɪntəfeɪθ/ *adj.* [only before noun] (**RELIGION**) between or connected with people of different religions: *The campus features interfaith prayer rooms.*

interfere 🔊 **C1** /ˌɪntə'fɪə(r)/ *verb* [I] **1** ~ **(in sth)** to get involved in a situation that does not involve you and where you are not wanted: *You shouldn't interfere in your children's lives — let them make their own decisions.* **2** ~ **(with sb/sth)** to prevent sth from succeeding or being done or happening as planned: *Every time the phone rings it interferes with my work.* **3** ~ **(with sth)** to touch or change sth without permission: *Many people feel that scientists shouldn't interfere with nature.* ▸ **interfering** *adj.*

interference 🔊 **C1** /ˌɪntə'fɪərəns/ *noun* [U] **1** ~ **(in sth)** the act of getting involved in a situation that does not involve you and where you are not wanted: *I left home because I couldn't stand my parents' interference in my affairs.* **2** (**PHYSICS**) extra noise (because of other signals or bad weather) that prevents you from receiving radio signals clearly **3** (**PHYSICS**) the combination of two or more wave movements to form a new wave, which may be bigger or smaller than the first

intergalactic /ˌɪntəgə'læktɪk/ *adj.* [only before noun] (**ASTRONOMY**) existing or happening between GALAXIES (= large systems of stars): *intergalactic travel*

intergovernmental /ˌɪntəˌgʌvn'mentl/ *adj.* [only before noun] (**POLITICS**) involving the governments of two or more countries: *The European Space Agency is an intergovernmental organization.*

interim¹ 🔊 **C1** /'ɪntərɪm/ *adj.* [only before noun] not final or lasting; temporary until sb/sth more permanent is found: *an interim arrangement* ◇ *The deputy head teacher took over in the* **interim period** *until a replacement could be found.*

interim² /'ɪntərɪm/ *noun*

IDM **in the interim** in the time between two things happening; until a particular event happens

interior 🔊 **C1** /ɪn'tɪəriə(r)/ *noun* **1** [C, usually sing.] the inside part of sth: *The interior of the hotel has been refurbished.* ◇ *the earth's interior* **OPP** **exterior²** **2** the interior [sing.] (**GEOGRAPHY**) the central part of a country or continent that is a long way from the coast **3** the Interior [sing.] (**POLITICS**) a country's own news and affairs that do not involve other countries: *the Department of the Interior* ▸ **interior** 🔊 **C1** *adj.*

interior angle *noun* [C] (**GEOMETRY**) an angle formed inside a shape where two sides of the shape meet ⊃ look at **exterior angle** ⊃ picture at **angle**[1]

interior design *noun* [U] the art or job of choosing colours, furniture, carpets, etc. to decorate the inside of a house ▸ **interior designer** *noun* [C]

interjection /ˌɪntə'dʒekʃn/ *noun* [C] (**GRAMMAR**) a word or phrase that is used to express surprise, pain, pleasure, etc. (for example *Oh!, Hurray!* or *Wow!*) **SYN** **exclamation**

interlude /'ɪntəluːd/ *noun* [C] a period of time between two events or activities during which sth different happens

intermediary /ˌɪntə'miːdiəri/ *noun* [C] (*pl.* **-ies**) an ~ **(between A and B)** a person or an organization that helps two people or groups to reach an agreement, by being a means of communication between them

intermediate 🔊 **C1** **S** /ˌɪntə'miːdiət/ *adj.* **1** located between two places, things, etc: *an intermediate step/stage in a process* **2** having more than a basic knowledge of sth but not yet advanced; suitable for sb who is at this level: *an intermediate student/book/level*

interminable /ɪn'tɜːmɪnəbl/ *adj.* lasting for a very long time and therefore boring or annoying: *an interminable delay/speech* **SYN** **endless** ▸ **interminably** /-bli/ *adv.*

intermission /ˌɪntə'mɪʃn/ *noun* [C, U] (*especially AmE*) (**ARTS AND MEDIA**) a short period of time separating the parts of a film, play, etc.

intermittent /ˌɪntə'mɪtənt/ *adj.* stopping for a short time and then starting again several times: *There will be intermittent showers.* ▸ **intermittently** *adv.*

intern¹ /ɪn'tɜːn/ *verb* [T, often passive] ~ **sb (in sth)** (*formal*) (**LAW**) to keep sb in prison for political reasons, especially during a war ▸ **internment** *noun* [U]

intern² /'ɪntɜːn/ *noun* [C] **1** (*AmE*) (**MEDICINE**) an advanced student of medicine whose training is nearly finished and who is working in a hospital to get further practical experience: *Interns and residents at the hospital are working 12-hour shifts.* ⊃ look at **house officer 2** (**EDUCATION**) a student or new graduate who is getting practical experience in a job, sometimes without pay, for example during the summer holiday: *a summer intern at a law firm* ⊃ look at **internship** (1)

internal 🔒**B2** ⊙ /ɪn'tɜːnl/ *adj.* **1** [only before noun] of or on the inside (of a place, person or object): *He was rushed to hospital with internal injuries.* **OPP external 2** happening or existing inside a particular organization: *an internal exam* (= one arranged and marked inside a particular school or college) ◇ *an internal police inquiry* **OPP external 3** [only before noun] (**ECONOMICS**, **POLITICS**) connected with a country's own affairs rather than those that involve other countries: *a country's internal affairs/trade/markets* ◇ *an internal flight* **OPP external** ▸ **internally** /-nəli/ *adv.*: *This medicine is not to be taken internally* (= not SWALLOWED).

in,ternal-com'bustion engine *noun* [C] (**ENGINEERING**) a type of engine used in cars that produces power by burning petrol or other fuel inside

internalize (*BrE also* **-ise**) /ɪn'tɜːnəlaɪz/ *verb* [I, T] (**PSYCHOLOGY**) to make a feeling, an attitude or a belief part of the way you think and behave ⊃ look at **externalize**

international 🔒**A2** ⊙ /ˌɪntə'næʃnəl/ *adj.* **1** involving two or more countries: *an international agreement/flight/football match* ◇ *international trade/law/sport* ⊃ look at **local¹**, **national¹**, **regional 2** used by people of many different countries: *large international hotels* ▸ **internationally** /-ʃəli/ *adv.*

the Inter,national Bacca'laureate™ *noun* [sing.] (*abbr.* IB) (**EDUCATION**) an exam that is taken by students in many different countries in the world around the age of 18 or 19, and that includes up to six subjects

the Inter,national 'Date Line (*also* **Date Line**) *noun* [sing.] (**GEOGRAPHY**) the imaginary line that goes from north to south through the Pacific Ocean. The date on the east side is one day earlier than that on the west side.

internationalism /ˌɪntə'næʃnəlɪzəm/ *noun* [U] (**POLITICS**) the belief that countries should work together in a friendly way

internet 🔒**A1** /'ɪntənet/ (*usually* **the internet**) (*also informal* **the 'net**) *noun* [sing.] (**COMPUTING**) an international computer network connecting other networks and computers that allows people to share information around the world: *I read about it on the internet.* ⊃ look at **intranet**, **ISP**, **Wi-Fi™**

'internet dating = ONLINE DATING

internship /'ɪntɜːnʃɪp/ *noun* [C] **1** (**EDUCATION**) a period of time during which a student or new graduate gets practical experience in a job, sometimes without payment, for example during the summer holiday: *an internship at a TV station* ⊃ look at **placement**, **work experience 2** (**MEDICINE**) a job that an advanced student of medicine, whose training is nearly finished, does in a hospital to get further practical experience

interplanetary /ˌɪntə'plænɪtri/ *adj.* [only before noun] (**ASTRONOMY**) between planets: *interplanetary travel*

interplay /'ɪntəpleɪ/ *noun* [U, sing.] **~ (between A and B)** the way in which two or more things or people affect each other: *the interplay between optimism and truth*

Interpol /'ɪntəpɒl/ *noun* [U + sing./pl. verb] (**LAW**) an international organization that makes it possible for the police forces of different countries to help each other to solve crimes

interpret 🔒**B2** ⊙ /ɪn'tɜːprət/ *verb* **1** [T] **~ sth (as sth)** to explain or understand the meaning of sth: *Your silence could be interpreted as rudeness.* ◇ *How would you interpret this part of the poem?* **OPP misinterpret 2** [I, T] **~ (for sb)** (**LANGUAGE**) to translate what sb is saying into another language as you hear it: *He can't speak much English so he'll need somebody to interpret for him.* ◇ *Interpreters must interpret everything that is said.*

interpretation 🔒**+ B2** ⊙ /ɪnˌtɜːprə'teɪʃn/ *noun* [C, U] **1** an explanation or understanding of sth: *What's your interpretation of these statistics?* ◇ *What he meant by that remark is open to interpretation* (= it can be explained in different ways). **2** (**ARTS AND MEDIA**) the way an actor or musician chooses to perform or understand a character or piece of music: *a modern interpretation of 'Hamlet'*

interpretative /ɪn'tɜːprətətɪv/ (*also* **interpretive** /ɪn'tɜːprətɪv/ *especially in AmE*) *adj.* connected with the particular way in which sth is understood, explained or performed; providing an INTERPRETATION: *an interpretative problem* ◇ *an interpretative exhibition*

interpreter /ɪn'tɜːprətə(r)/ *noun* [C] (**LANGUAGE**) a person whose job is to translate what sb is saying immediately into another language: *The president spoke to the crowd through an interpreter.* ◇ *a sign language interpreter* (= a person who translates what sb is saying into SIGN LANGUAGE) ⊃ look at **translator** ⊃ note at **language**

interracial /ˌɪntə'reɪʃl/ *adj.* [only before noun] (**SOCIAL STUDIES**) involving people who belong to different races: *interracial marriage*

interrelate /ˌɪntərɪ'leɪt/ *verb* [I, T, usually passive] (*formal*) (used about two or more things) to connect or be connected very closely so that each has an effect on the other ▸ **interrelated** *adj.*

interrogate /ɪn'terəgeɪt/ *verb* [T] **~ sb (about sth)** (**LAW**) to ask sb a lot of questions over a long period of time, especially in an aggressive way: *The prisoner was interrogated for six hours.* ▸ **interrogation** /ɪnˌterə'geɪʃn/ *noun* [U, C]: *The prisoner broke down under interrogation and confessed.* ▸ **interrogator** *noun* [C]

interrogative¹ /ˌɪntə'rɒgətɪv/ *adj.* **1** (*formal*) asking a question; having the form of a question: *an interrogative tone/gesture/remark* **2** (**GRAMMAR**) used in questions: *an interrogative sentence/pronoun/determiner/adverb*

interrogative² /ˌɪntə'rɒgətɪv/ *noun* [C] (**GRAMMAR**) a question word: *'Who', 'what' and 'where' are interrogatives.*

interrupt 🔒**B2** /ˌɪntə'rʌpt/ *verb* **1** [I, T] **~ (sb/sth) (with sth)** to say or do sth that makes sb stop what they are saying or doing: *Don't interrupt when I'm talking.* ◇ *He kept interrupting me with silly questions.* **2** [T] to stop the progress of sth for a short time: *The programme was interrupted by an important news flash.*

interruption /ˌɪntə'rʌpʃn/ *noun* [C, U] the act of interrupting sb/sth; the person or thing that interrupts sb/sth: *I need to work for a few hours without interruption.* ◇ *I've had so many interruptions this morning that I've done nothing!*

intersect /ˌɪntə'sekt/ *verb* [I, T] (used about roads, lines, etc.) to meet or cross each other: *The lines intersect at right angles.*

intersection /ˈɪntəsekʃn/ *noun* [C] the place where two or more roads, lines, etc. meet or cross each other

intersperse /ˌɪntəˈspɜːs/ *verb* [T, usually passive] **be interspersed with sth** to have things at various points in sth: *Lectures will be interspersed with practical demonstrations.*

interstate /ˈɪntəsteɪt/ (*also* ˌinterstate ˈhighway) *noun* [C] (in the US) a wide road, with at least two LANES in each direction, where traffic can travel fast for long distances across many states. You can only enter and leave interstates at special RAMPS. ⊃ look at **motorway**

interstellar /ˌɪntəˈstelə(r)/ *adj.* [only before noun] (**ASTRONOMY**) between the stars in the sky: *the vastness of interstellar space* ⊃ look at **stellar**

intertwine /ˌɪntəˈtwaɪn/ *verb* [I, T] if two things **intertwine** or **are intertwined**, they become very closely connected and difficult to separate

interval ?+ B2 Ⓦ /ˈɪntəvl/ *noun* [C] **1** a period of time between two events: *There was a long interval between sending the letter and getting a reply.* **2** (*BrE*) (**ARTS AND MEDIA**) a short break separating the different parts of a play, film, concert, etc. **3** [usually pl.] a short period during which sth different happens from what is happening for the rest of the time: *There'll be a few **sunny intervals** between the showers today.*
IDM **at(…) intervals** with time or spaces between: *I write home **at regular intervals.*** ◇ *Plant the trees at two-metre intervals.* ◇ *At intervals a bell rings and workers stop for a drink.*

intervene ?+ C1 Ⓦ /ˌɪntəˈviːn/ *verb* [I] **1 ~ (in sth)** to become involved in a situation in order to improve it: *She would have died if the neighbours hadn't intervened.* ◇ *to intervene in a dispute* **2** to interrupt sb who is speaking in order to say sth **3** (used about events, etc.) to happen in a way that delays sth or stops it from happening: *If no further problems intervene we should be able to finish in time.*

intervening /ˌɪntəˈviːnɪŋ/ *adj.* [only before noun] coming or existing between two events, dates, objects, etc: *the intervening years/days/months*

intervention Ⓦ /ˌɪntəˈvenʃn/ *noun* [U, C] **1** action taken to improve or help a situation: *There have been calls for government intervention to save the steel industry.* **2 ~ (in sth)** action by a country to become involved in the affairs of another country when they have not been asked to do so: *armed/military intervention* **3** (**MEDICINE**) action taken to improve a medical condition or an illness: *a medical/surgical intervention*

interventionism /ˌɪntəˈvenʃənɪzəm/ *noun* [U] (**POLITICS**) the policy or practice of a government influencing the economy of its own country, or of becoming involved in the affairs of other countries ▶ **interventionist** /-ʃənɪst/ *adj., noun* [C]: *interventionist policies*

interview¹ ? A1 Ⓦ /ˈɪntəvjuː/ *noun* [C] **1 ~ (for sth)** a meeting at which sb is asked questions to find out if they are suitable for a job, course of study, etc: *to attend an interview* ◇ *She has an interview next week for the manager's job.* **2 ~ (with sb)** (**ARTS AND MEDIA**) a meeting at which a journalist asks sb questions in order to find out their opinion, etc: *There was an interview with the prime minister on TV last night.* ◇ *The actor refused to **give an interview** (= answer questions).*

interview² ? A1 Ⓦ /ˈɪntəvjuː/ *verb* [T] **1 ~ sb (for sth)** to ask sb questions to find out if they are suitable for a job, course of study, etc: *How many applicants did you interview for the job?* **2 ~ sb (about sth)** (**ARTS AND MEDIA**) to ask sb questions about their opinions, private life, etc., especially on the radio or TV or for a newspaper, magazine, etc. **3 ~ sb (about sth)** to ask sb questions at a private meeting: *The police are waiting to interview the injured girl.* ◇ *Officers are interviewing witnesses about what happened.*

interviewee Ⓦ /ˌɪntəvjuːˈiː/ *noun* [C] a person who is questioned in an interview

interviewer Ⓦ /ˈɪntəvjuːə(r)/ *noun* [C] a person who asks the questions in an interview

intestine /ɪnˈtestɪn/ *noun* [C] (*also* intestines [pl.]) (**ANATOMY**) a long tube in the body between the stomach and the ANUS (= the place where solid waste leaves the body) SYN **gut**¹ ⊃ picture at **body**, **digestive system** ▶ **intestinal** /ɪnˈtestɪnl, ˌɪnteˈstaɪnl/ *adj.*

intimacy /ˈɪntɪməsi/ *noun* [U] the state of having a close personal relationship with sb: *Their intimacy grew over the years.*

intimate ?+ C1 /ˈɪntɪmət/ *adj.* **1** (used about people) having a very close relationship: *They're intimate friends.* **2** very private and personal: *They told each other their most intimate thoughts and secrets.* **3** (used about a place, an atmosphere, etc.) quiet and friendly: *I know an intimate little restaurant we could go to.* **4** very detailed: *He's lived here all his life and has an **intimate knowledge** of the area.* ▶ **intimately** *adv.*

intimation /ˌɪntɪˈmeɪʃn/ *noun* [C, U] (*formal*) the act of stating sth or of making it known, especially in an indirect way: *There was no intimation from his doctor that his condition was serious.*

intimidate /ɪnˈtɪmɪdeɪt/ *verb* [T] **~ sb (into sth/doing sth)** to frighten or threaten sb, often in order to make them do sth: *She refused to be intimidated by their threats.* ◇ *They were accused of intimidating people into voting for them.* ▶ **intimidating** *adj.*: *The teacher had rather an intimidating manner.* ▶ **intimidation** /ɪnˌtɪmɪˈdeɪʃn/ *noun* [U]: *The rebel troops controlled the area by intimidation.*

into ? A1 /ˈɪntə, *before vowels* -tu, *strong form* -tuː/ *prep.* **1** moving to a position inside or in sth: *Come into the house.* ◇ *I'm going into town.* **2** in the direction of sth: *Please speak into the microphone.* ◇ *At this point we were driving into the sun and had to shade our eyes.* **3** to a point at which you hit sth: *I backed the car into a wall.* ◇ *She walked into a glass door.* **4** showing a change from one thing to another: *We're turning the spare room into a study.* ◇ *She changed into her jeans.* ◇ *Translate the passage into German.* **5** concerning or involving sth: *an inquiry into safety procedures* **6** (**MATHEMATICS**) used when you are talking about dividing numbers: *7 into 28 is 4.*
IDM **be into sth** (*informal*) to be very interested in sth, for example as a hobby: *I'm really into canoeing.*

intolerable /ɪnˈtɒlərəbl/ *adj.* too bad, unpleasant or difficult to bear or accept: *The living conditions were intolerable.* ◇ *intolerable pain* SYN **unbearable** OPP **tolerable** ⊃ verb **tolerate** ▶ **intolerably** /-bli/ *adv.*

intolerant /ɪnˈtɒlərənt/ *adj.* **~ (of sb/sth)** not able to accept behaviour or opinions that are different from your own; finding sb/sth too unpleasant to bear: *They are intolerant of different viewpoints.* OPP **tolerant** ▶ **intolerance** /-rəns/ *noun* [U]: *religious intolerance* ▶ **intolerantly** *adv.*

intonation /ˌɪntəˈneɪʃn/ *noun* [C, U] (**LANGUAGE**) the rise and fall of your voice while you are speaking SYN **inflection**

intoxicated /ɪnˈtɒksɪkeɪtɪd/ *adj.* (*formal*) **1** having had too much alcohol to drink **SYN drunk**[1] **2** very excited and happy: *She was intoxicated by her success.*
▸ **intoxication** /ɪnˌtɒksɪˈkeɪʃn/ *noun* [U]

intra- /ˈɪntrə/ *prefix* (in adjectives and adverbs) inside; within: *intravenous* ◇ *intra-departmental* ⊃ look at **inter-**

intranet /ˈɪntrənet/ *noun* [C] (**COMPUTING**) a computer network that is private to a company, university, etc. often using the same software as ⊃ look at **internet**

intransitive /ɪnˈtrænzətɪv/ *adj.* (**GRAMMAR**) (used about a verb) used without a DIRECT OBJECT **OPP transitive**
▸ **intransitively** *adv.*

intrauterine /ˌɪntrəˈjuːtəraɪn/ *adj.* (**ANATOMY**) inside the UTERUS (= the part of a woman's body where a baby grows) ⊃ look at **IUD**

intravenous /ˌɪntrəˈviːnəs/ *adj.* (*abbr.* IV) (**MEDICINE**) (used about drugs or food) going into a VEIN (= a tube in the body that carries blood): *an intravenous injection* ▸ **intravenously** *adv.*: *The patient had to be fed intravenously.*

in tray (*especially BrE*) (*AmE also* **inbox**) *noun* [C] (in an office) a container on your desk for letters or documents that are waiting to be read or answered ⊃ look at **out tray**

intrepid /ɪnˈtrepɪd/ *adj.* (*formal*) without any fear of danger: *an intrepid climber* **SYN fearless**

intricacy /ˈɪntrɪkəsi/ *noun* **1** intricacies [pl.] the ~ of sth the complicated parts or details of sth: *It's difficult to understand all the intricacies of the situation.* **2** [U] the quality of having complicated parts, details or patterns

intricate /ˈɪntrɪkət/ *adj.* having many small parts or details put together in a complicated way: *an intricate pattern* ◇ *The story has an intricate plot.* ▸ **intricately** *adv.*

intrigue[1] /ɪnˈtriːg/ *verb* [T] to make sb very interested and want to know more: *I was intrigued by the way he seemed to know all about us already.*

intrigue[2] /ˈɪntriːg, ɪnˈtriːg/ *noun* [C, U] secret plans to do sth, especially sth bad: *The film is about political intrigues against the government.* ◇ *His new novel is full of intrigue and suspense.*

intriguing ʔ+ **C1** /ɪnˈtriːgɪŋ/ *adj.* very interesting because of being unusual or not having an obvious answer: *These discoveries raise intriguing questions.*
▸ **intriguingly** *adv.*: *The book is intriguingly titled, 'The Revenge of the Goldfish'.*

intrinsic **W** /ɪnˈtrɪnzɪk/ *adj.* [only before noun] belonging to sth as part of its nature: *The object is of no intrinsic value* (= the material it is made of is not worth anything). ▸ **intrinsically** /-kli/ *adv.*: *There's nothing intrinsically wrong with the idea, it's just that I don't think it will work in practice.*

introduce ʔ **A1 ⊙** /ˌɪntrəˈdjuːs/ *verb* [T]
• NEW PRODUCT/LAW **1** ~ **sth (in/into sth)** to bring in sth new, use sth, or take sth to a place for the first time: *The law was introduced in 2019.* ◇ *The company is introducing a new range of cars this summer.* ◇ *Goats were first introduced to the island in the seventeenth century.*
• PEOPLE **2** ~ **sb (to sb)** to tell two or more people who have not met before what each others' names are: *'Who's that girl over there?' 'Come with me and I'll introduce you to her.'* **3** ~ **yourself (to sb)** to tell sb you have met for the first time what your name is: *He just walked over and introduced himself to me.*
• NEW EXPERIENCE **4** ~ **sb to sth** to make sb begin to learn about sth or do sth for the first time: *This page will introduce you to the basic aims of the organization.*

• RADIO/TV PROGRAMME **5** (**ARTS AND MEDIA**) to be the main speaker on a radio or TV programme, who tells the audience who is going to speak, perform, etc: *May I introduce my first guest on the show tonight …*

introduction ʔ **A2 ⊙** /ˌɪntrəˈdʌkʃn/ *noun*
• NEW PRODUCT, ETC. **1** [U] ~ **of sth (into sth)** the act of bringing sth into use: *the introduction of new teaching methods into primary schools*
• PEOPLE **2** [C] the act of telling two or more people each other's names for the first time: *Once the introductions were over, we got straight down to business.*
• OF A BOOK/SPEECH **3** [C] the first part of a book, a piece of written work or a talk that gives a general idea of what is going to follow
• TO A SUBJECT **4** [C] ~ **(to sth)** (**EDUCATION**) a book for people who are beginning to study a subject: *'An Introduction to English Grammar'*
• FIRST EXPERIENCE **5** [sing.] **an~ to sth** a person's first experience of sth: *My first job — in a factory — was not a pleasant introduction to work.*

introductory /ˌɪntrəˈdʌktəri/ *adj.* **1** happening or said at the beginning in order to give a general idea of what will follow: *an introductory speech/chapter/remark* **SYN opening 2** intended as an introduction to a subject or an activity: *introductory courses* **3** offered for a short time only, when a product is first on sale: *an introductory price/offer*

introvert /ˈɪntrəvɜːt/ *noun* [C] (**PSYCHOLOGY**) a quiet, shy person who prefers to be alone than with other people **OPP extrovert** ▸ **introverted** *adj.*

intrude /ɪnˈtruːd/ *verb* [I] ~ **(on/upon sb/sth)** to enter a place or situation without permission or when you are not wanted: *I'm sorry to intrude on your Sunday lunch but …*

intruder /ɪnˈtruːdə(r)/ *noun* [C] a person who enters a place without permission and often secretly

intrusion /ɪnˈtruːʒn/ *noun* **1** [C, U] ~ **(on/upon/into sth)** something that affects a situation or people's lives in a way that they do not want: *This was another example of press intrusion into the affairs of the royals.* **2** [C] (**GEOLOGY**) a mass of hot liquid rock that has been forced up from below the earth's surface and cooled in between other layers of rock ▸ **intrusive** /-ˈtruːsɪv/ *adj.*

intuition /ˌɪntjuˈɪʃn/ *noun* [U, C] the feeling or understanding that makes you believe or know that sth is true without being able to explain why: *She knew, by intuition, about his illness, although he never mentioned it.* ▸ **intuitive** /ɪnˈtjuːɪtɪv/ *adj.* ▸ **intuitively** *adv.*: *Intuitively, he knew that she was lying.*

Inuit /ˈɪnjuɪt, ˈɪnu-/ *noun* [C] (*pl.* **Inuit, Inuits**) a human group from northern Canada and parts of Greenland and Alaska ⊃ look at **Eskimo**

inundate /ˈɪnʌndeɪt/ *verb* [T, often passive] **1** ~ **sb (with sth)** to give or send sb so many things that they cannot deal with them all: *We were inundated with applications for the job.* **SYN swamp 2** (*formal*) to cover an area of land with water: *After the heavy rains the fields were inundated.* **SYN flood**[1] ⊃ note at **disaster**

invade ʔ+ **B2** /ɪnˈveɪd/ *verb* **1** [I, T] to enter a country with an army in order to attack and take control of it: *When did the Romans invade Britain?* **2** [T] to enter in large numbers, especially in a way that causes damage or problems: *The whole area has been invaded by tourists.* ⊃ *noun* **invasion** ▸ **invader** *noun* [C]

invalid¹ /ɪnˈvælɪd/ adj. **1** not legally or officially acceptable: *I'm afraid your passport is invalid.* **OPP** valid **2** not correct according to reason; not based on all the facts: *an invalid argument* **OPP** valid **3** (COMPUTING) (used about an instruction, etc.) of a type that the computer cannot recognize: *an invalid command*

invalid² /ˈɪnvəlɪd/ noun [C] (HEALTH) a person who has been very ill for a long time and needs other people to take care of them

invalidate /ɪnˈvælɪdeɪt/ verb [T] **1** to prove that an idea, a story, an argument, etc. is wrong: *This new piece of evidence invalidates his version of events.* **OPP** validate **2** if you **invalidate** a document, a contract, an election, etc., you make it no longer legally or officially acceptable **OPP** validate ▸ invalidation /ɪnˌvælɪˈdeɪʃn/ noun [U]

invalidity /ˌɪnvəˈlɪdəti/ noun [U] **1** (BrE) (HEALTH) the state of being unable to take care of yourself because of illness or injury (formal) **2** the state of not being legally or officially acceptable ⊃ look at **validity**

invaluable /ɪnˈvæljuəbl/ adj. ~ (to/for sb/sth) extremely useful: *The book will be invaluable for students in higher education.* ◇ *invaluable help/information/support*

invariable /ɪnˈveəriəbl/ adj. not changing ⊃ look at **variable¹**

invariably /ɪnˈveəriəbli/ adv. always: *She invariably arrives late.*

invasion ʔ+ B2 /ɪnˈveɪʒn/ noun **1** [C, U] the action of entering another country with an army in order to take control of it: *the threat of invasion* **2** [C] an act that affects sb/sth in a way that is not wanted: *Such questions are an invasion of privacy.* ⊃ verb **invade**

invasive /ɪnˈveɪsɪv/ adj. (formal) **1** (HEALTH) (used especially about a disease) spreading very quickly and difficult to stop: *invasive cancer* **2** (MEDICINE) (used about medical treatment) involving cutting into the body: *invasive surgery* **OPP** non-invasive ⊃ look at **invade**

invent ʔ A2 🔊 /ɪnˈvent/ verb [T] **1** to think of or make sth for the first time: *When was the camera invented?* **2** to say or describe sth that is not true: *I realized that he had invented the whole story.* ▸ inventor noun [C]

invention ʔ A2 /ɪnˈvenʃn/ noun **1** [C] a thing that has been made or designed by sb for the first time: *The electric car is a useful invention.* **2** [U] the action or process of making or designing sth for the first time: *Books had to be written by hand before the invention of printing.* **3** [C, U] telling a story or giving an excuse that is not true: *It was obvious that her story about being robbed was (an) invention.*

inventive /ɪnˈventɪv/ adj. having clever and original ideas ▸ inventiveness noun [U]

inventory /ˈɪnvəntri/ noun [C] (pl. -ies) a detailed list, for example of all the furniture in a house: *The landlord is coming to make an inventory of the contents of the flat.*

inverse /ˌɪnˈvɜːs/ adj. [only before noun] opposite in amount or position to sth else: *A person's wealth is often in inverse proportion to their happiness* (= the more money they have, the less happy they are). ▸ inversely adv.

the inverse /ði ˈɪnvɜːs/ noun [sing.] the exact opposite of sth

inversion /ɪnˈvɜːʃn/ noun [U, C] the act of changing the position or order of sth to its opposite, or of turning sth into a position in which the top is where the bottom

normally is: *the inversion of normal word order* ◇ *an inversion of the truth*

invert /ɪnˈvɜːt/ verb [T] (formal) to put sth in the opposite order or position to the way it usually is

invertebrate /ɪnˈvɜːtɪbrət/ noun [C] (BIOLOGY) an animal without a BACKBONE (= a row of small bones along the middle of the body): *slugs, worms and other small invertebrates* **OPP** vertebrate

inverted commas noun [pl.] (BrE) = QUOTATION MARKS: *to put something in inverted commas*

invest ʔ B1 /ɪnˈvest/ verb ~ (sth) (in sth) **1** [I, T] (BUSINESS, FINANCE) to put money into a business, property, etc. in the hope that you will make a profit: *Many firms have invested heavily in this project.* ◇ *I've invested all my money in the company.* **2** [I, T] (BUSINESS, FINANCE) (used about an organization, a government, etc.) to spend money on sth in order to make it better or more successful: *The government has invested heavily in public transport.* **3** [T] to spend money, time or energy on sth that you think is good or useful: *I'm thinking of investing in a new guitar.* ◇ *You have to invest a lot of time if you really want to learn a language well.* ▸ investor ʔ+ B2 noun [C]: *small investors* (= private people)

investigate ʔ B1 🔊 /ɪnˈvestɪgeɪt/ verb [I, T] to try to find out all the facts about sth/sb: *A murder was reported and the police were sent to investigate.* ◇ *A group of experts are investigating the cause of the crash.* ⊃ note at **crime** ▸ investigator ʔ+ C1 🔊 noun [C]

investigation ʔ B2 🔊 /ɪnˌvestɪˈgeɪʃn/ noun [C, U] ~ (into sth) an official examination of the facts about a situation, crime, etc: *The airlines are going to carry out an investigation into security procedures at airports.* ◇ *The matter is still under investigation.*

investigative /ɪnˈvestɪgətɪv/ adj. trying to find out all the facts about sb/sth: *investigative journalism*

investment ʔ B2 /ɪnˈvestmənt/ noun **1** [U, C] ~ (in sth) (FINANCE) the act of putting money in a bank, business, property, etc.; the amount of money that you put in: *investment in local industry* ◇ *The company will have to make an enormous investment to update their computer systems.* ◇ *We got a good return on our original investment of £10 000.* **2** [C] (informal) a thing that is worth buying: *This coat has been a good investment — I've worn it for three years.*

investment bank (BrE also **merchant bank**) noun [C] (FINANCE) a bank that deals mainly with buying and selling shares and other investments ▸ investment banking noun [U]

invigilate /ɪnˈvɪdʒɪleɪt/ verb [I, T] (BrE) (EDUCATION) to watch the people taking an exam to make sure that nobody is cheating ▸ invigilator noun [C]

invigorate /ɪnˈvɪgəreɪt/ verb [I, T] to make sb feel healthy, fresh and full of energy: *I felt invigorated after my run.* ▸ invigorating adj.

invincible /ɪnˈvɪnsəbl/ adj. too strong or powerful to be defeated

invisible ʔ+ C1 /ɪnˈvɪzəbl/ adj. ~ (to sb/sth) that cannot be seen: *bacteria that are invisible to the naked eye* **OPP** visible ▸ invisibility /ɪnˌvɪzəˈbɪləti/ noun [U] ▸ invisibly /ɪnˈvɪzəbli/ adv.

invitation ʔ A2 /ˌɪnvɪˈteɪʃn/ noun **1** [U] the act of inviting sb or being invited: *Entry is by invitation only.* ◇ *a letter of invitation* **2** [C] ~ to sb/sth (to sth/to do sth) a written or spoken request to go somewhere or do sth: *Did you get an invitation to the conference?* ◇ *a wedding invitation*

invite ⚡**A2** /ɪnˈvaɪt/ *verb* [T] **1 ~ sb (to/for sth)** to ask sb to come somewhere or to do sth: *We invited all the family to the wedding.* ◇ *Selected applicants will be invited for interview next week.* **2** to make sth unpleasant likely to happen: *You're inviting trouble if you carry so much money around.*
PHR V **invite sb back 1** to ask sb to return with you to your home **2** to ask sb to come to your home or another place a second time, or after you have been a guest at their home **invite sb in** to ask sb to come into your home **invite sb out** to ask sb to go out somewhere with you: *We've been invited out to the theatre by my aunt and uncle.* **invite sb over/around** (*BrE* **invite sb round**) (*informal*) to ask sb to come to your home ❶ **Ask** can be used instead of **invite** in all meanings.

inviting /ɪnˈvaɪtɪŋ/ *adj.* attractive and pleasant: *The smell of cooking was very inviting.*

in vitro /ɪn ˈviːtrəʊ/ *adj., adv.* (**BIOLOGY**) (used about a process or reaction) taking place in a glass tube or dish, not inside a living body: *in vitro experiments* ◇ *an egg fertilized in vitro*

in vitro fertilization = IVF

invoice¹ /ˈɪnvɔɪs/ *noun* [C] (**BUSINESS, FINANCE**) an official list of goods or services that you have received saying how much you have to pay for them ⊃ note at **bill¹**

invoice² /ˈɪnvɔɪs/ *verb* [T] **~ sb (for sth); ~ sth (to sb/sth)** (**BUSINESS, FINANCE**) to write or send sb a bill for work you have done or goods you have provided: *You will be invoiced for these items at the end of the month.* ◇ *Invoice the goods to my account.*

invoke ⚡+ **C1** /ɪnˈvəʊk/ *verb* [T] (*formal*) **1 ~ sth (against sb)** to mention or use a law, rule, etc. as a reason for doing sth: *It is unlikely that libel laws will be invoked.* **2** to mention a person, a theory, an example, etc. to support your opinions or ideas, or as a reason for sth: *She invoked several eminent scholars to back up her argument.*

involuntary /ɪnˈvɒləntri/ *adj.* done without wanting or meaning to: *She gave an involuntary gasp of pain as the doctor inserted the needle.* **OPP** **voluntary** ▸ **involuntarily** /-trəli/ *adv.*

involve ⚡**A2 ⊘** /ɪnˈvɒlv/ *verb* [T] **1** (not used in the progressive tenses) to make sth necessary: *The job involves a lot of travelling.* **2** (not used in the progressive tenses) if a situation, an event or an activity **involves** sb/sth, they take part in it: *More than 100 people were involved in the project.* ◇ *The story involves a woman who cycled to India with her child.* **3 ~ sb/sth in sth/doing sth** to cause sb/sth to take part in or be concerned with sth: *Please don't involve me in your family arguments.*

involved ⚡**B1 ⑤** /ɪnˈvɒlvd/ *adj.* **1** [not before noun] **~ (in sth)** closely connected with sth; taking an active part in sth: *I'm very involved in local politics.* **2** [not before noun] **~ (with sb)** having a close personal relationship with sb: *She is involved with an older man.* **3** difficult to understand; complicated: *The book has a very involved plot.*

involvement ⚡+ **C1 ⓦ** /ɪnˈvɒlvmənt/ *noun* **1** [U] **~ (in/ with sth)** the act of taking part in sth: *US involvement in European wars* ◇ *The men deny any involvement in the robbery.* **2** [U, C] **~ (in/with sth)** the act of giving a lot of time and attention to sth you care about: *her growing involvement with contemporary music* **3** [C, U] **~ (with sb)** a romantic or sexual relationship with sb that you are not married to: *He spoke openly about his involvement with the singer.*

invulnerable /ɪnˈvʌlnərəbl/ *adj.* **~ (to sth)** that cannot be harmed or defeated: *The submarine is invulnerable to attack while at sea.* **OPP** **vulnerable** ▸ **invulnerability** /ɪnˌvʌlnərəˈbɪləti/ *noun* [U]

inward /ˈɪnwəd/ (*also* **inwards** *especially in BrE*) *adv.* **1** towards the inside or centre: *Stand in a circle facing inwards.* **2** towards yourself or your interests: *Her thoughts turned inward.* ▸ **inward** *adj.*: *my inward feelings* **OPP** **outward**

inwardly /ˈɪnwədli/ *adv.* in your mind; secretly: *He was inwardly relieved that they could not come to the party.*

iodide /ˈaɪədaɪd/ *noun* [C] (**CHEMISTRY**) a chemical COMPOUND consisting of IODINE and another chemical element

iodine /ˈaɪədiːn/ *noun* [U] (*symb.* I) (**CHEMISTRY**) a chemical element. Iodine is a substance found in sea water. A liquid containing iodine is sometimes used on wounds to prevent infection. ❶ For more information on the periodic table of elements, look at the **Reference Section** of this dictionary.

ion /ˈaɪən, ˈaɪɒn/ *noun* [C] (**CHEMISTRY, PHYSICS**) an ATOM or a MOLECULE that has gained or lost one or more of its ELECTRONS and so has a positive or negative electric CHARGE

ionic /aɪˈɒnɪk/ *adj.* **1** (**CHEMISTRY**) of or related to IONS **2** (**CHEMISTRY**) (used about the way chemicals join together) using the electrical pull between positive and negative IONS: *ionic bonds/compounds* **3** **Ionic** (**ARCHITECTURE**) used to describe a style of architecture in ancient Greece that uses a curved decoration in the shape of a SCROLL (= a roll of paper) ⊃ look at **Corinthian, Doric** ⊃ picture at **capital¹**

ionize (*BrE also* **-ise**) /ˈaɪənaɪz/ *verb* [T, I] (**CHEMISTRY**) (used about ATOMS and MOLECULES) to gain a positive or negative electric CHARGE by losing or gaining an ELECTRON

the ionosphere /ði aɪˈɒnəsfɪə(r)/ *noun* [sing.] (**ASTRONOMY, GEOGRAPHY**) the layer of the earth's atmosphere between about 80 and 1 000 kilometres above the surface of the earth that reflects some radio waves back towards the earth ⊃ look at **atmosphere**

IOU /ˌaɪ əʊ ˈjuː/ *noun* [C] (*informal*) a written promise that you will pay sb the money that you owe them (the abbreviation for 'I owe you')

IPA /ˌaɪ piː ˈeɪ/ *abbr.* (**LANGUAGE**) **International Phonetic Alphabet** (an alphabet that is used to show the pronunciation of words in any language)

iPad™ /ˈaɪpæd/ *noun* [C] (**COMPUTING**) a brand of tablet computer

IP address /ˌaɪ ˈpiː ədres/ *noun* [C] (**COMPUTING**) a series of numbers separated by DOTS (= small round marks) that identifies a particular computer connected to the internet

IPO /ˌaɪ piː ˈəʊ/ *abbr.* (**BUSINESS, FINANCE**) **initial public offering** (the act of selling shares in a company for the first time)

IQ /ˌaɪ ˈkjuː/ *noun* [C] (**EDUCATION**) a measure of how intelligent sb is (the abbreviation for 'intelligence quotient'): *to have a high/low IQ* ◇ *an IQ of 120*

ir- /ɪr/ → IN-

IRA /ˌaɪ ɑːr ˈeɪ/ *abbr.* (**POLITICS**) **Irish Republican Army**; (an organization that has fought for Northern Ireland to be united with the Republic of Ireland)

irate /aɪˈreɪt/ *adj.* (*formal*) very angry

iridescent /ˌɪrɪˈdesnt/ *adj.* (*formal*) showing many bright colours that seem to change in different lights ▸ **iridescence** /-sns/ *noun* [U]

iridium /ɪˈrɪdiəm/ *noun* [U] (*symb.* Ir) (**CHEMISTRY**) a chemical element. Iridium is a very hard yellow-white metal used especially in making ALLOYS. ❶ For more information on the periodic table of elements, look at the **Reference Section** of this dictionary.

iris /ˈaɪrɪs/ *noun* [C] (**ANATOMY**) the coloured part of the eye ⊃ look at **pupil** (3) ⊃ picture at **eye¹**

Irish /ˈaɪrɪʃ/ *adj.* of or connected with Ireland, its people or its language

Irish Gaelic /ˌaɪrɪʃ ˈɡeɪlɪk/ = GAELIC (2)

IRL /ˌaɪ ɑːr ˈel/ *abbr.* (*informal*) (**COMPUTING**) **in real life** (used in chat on the internet to talk about sth that does not happen on the internet): *I'm meeting him IRL next week.*

iron¹ 🔊 **B1** /ˈaɪən/ *noun* **1** [U] (*symb.* Fe) (**CHEMISTRY**) a chemical element. Iron is a hard strong metal used for making steel and found in small quantities in food and blood: *an iron bar* ◇ *iron ore* ◇ *The doctor gave me iron tablets.* ◇ (*figurative*) *The general has an iron* (= very strong) *will.* ⊃ look at **pig iron** ❶ For more information on the periodic table of elements, look at the **Reference Section** of this dictionary. **2** [C] an electrical instrument with a flat bottom that is heated and used to smooth clothes after you have washed and dried them: *a steam iron*

iron² 🔊 **B1** /ˈaɪən/ *verb* [T, I] to use an iron to make clothes, etc. smooth: *Could you iron this dress for me?* **PHRV** **iron sth out** to get rid of any problems or difficulties that are affecting sth

the ˌIron ˈAge *noun* [sing.] (**HISTORY**) the period in human history after the Bronze Age, about 3 000 years ago when people first used iron tools and weapons

the ˌIron ˈCurtain *noun* [U] (**HISTORY, POLITICS**) the name that people used for the border that used to exist between Western Europe and the COMMUNIST countries of Eastern Europe

ironic 🔊 **C1** /aɪˈrɒnɪk/ (*also* **ironical** /aɪˈrɒnɪkl/) *adj.* **1** meaning the opposite of what you say: *Jeff sometimes offends people with his ironic sense of humour.* ⊃ look at **sarcastic 2** (used about a situation) strange or funny because it is unusual or unexpected: *It is ironic that the busiest people are often the most willing to help.* ▸ **ironically** 🔊 **C1** /-kli/ *adv.*

ironing /ˈaɪənɪŋ/ *noun* [U] the task of pressing clothes, etc. with an iron to make them smooth: *to do the ironing*

ˈironing board *noun* [C] a long narrow board covered with cloth that you iron clothes on

irony 🔊 **C1** /ˈaɪrəni/ *noun* (*pl.* -ies) **1** [U, C] an unusual or unexpected part of a situation, etc. that seems strange or funny: *The irony was that when he finally got the job, he discovered that he didn't like it.* **2** [U] (**LANGUAGE**) a way of speaking that shows you are joking or that you mean the opposite of what you say: *'The English are such good cooks,' he said with heavy irony.*

irradiate /ɪˈreɪdieɪt/ *verb* [T] (**CHEMISTRY**) to treat food with GAMMA RADIATION in order to be able to keep it for a long time: *Irradiated food lasts longer, but some people think it is not safe.*

irrational /ɪˈræʃənl/ *adj.* not based on reason or clear thought: *an irrational fear of spiders* **OPP** **rational** ▸ **irrationality** /ɪˌræʃəˈnæləti/ *noun* [U] ▸ **irrationally** /ɪˈræʃnəli/ *adv.*

irˌrational ˈnumber (*also* **surd**) *noun* [C] (**MATHEMATICS**) a number, for example π, that cannot be expressed as the RATIO of two whole numbers ⊃ look at **rational number**

irreconcilable /ɪˌrekənˈsaɪləbl, ɪˈrekənsaɪləbl/ *adj.* (*formal*) (used about people or their ideas and beliefs) so different that they cannot be made to agree ▸ **irreconcilably** /-bli/ *adv.*

irregular /ɪˈreɡjələ(r)/ *adj.* **1** not having an even, smooth shape or pattern: *an irregular shape/outline* **OPP** **regular¹** **2** happening at times that you cannot predict: *His visits became more and more irregular.* **OPP** **regular¹** **3** not allowed according to the rules or social customs: *It is highly irregular for a doctor to give information about patients without their permission.* **4** (**GRAMMAR**) not following the usual rules of grammar: *irregular verbs* ◇ *'Caught' is an irregular past tense form.* **OPP** **regular¹** ▸ **irregularity** /ɪˌreɡjəˈlærəti/ *noun* [C, U] (*pl.* -ies) ▸ **irregularly** *adv.*

irrelevancy /ɪˈreləvənsi/ *noun* [C] (*pl.* -ies) something that is not important because it is not connected with sth else

irrelevant 🔊+ **C1** 🅦 /ɪˈreləvənt/ *adj.* not connected with sth or not important to it: *That's completely irrelevant to the subject under discussion.* **OPP** **relevant** ▸ **irrelevance** /-vəns/ *noun* [U, C] ▸ **irrelevantly** *adv.*

irreparable /ɪˈrepərəbl/ *adj.* that cannot be repaired or made right: *Irreparable damage has been done to the forests of Eastern Europe.* ▸ **irreparably** /-bli/ *adv.*

irreplaceable /ˌɪrɪˈpleɪsəbl/ *adj.* (used about sth very valuable or special) that cannot be replaced **OPP** **replaceable**

irrepressible /ˌɪrɪˈpresəbl/ *adj.* full of life and energy: *young people full of irrepressible good humour* ▸ **irrepressibly** /-bli/ *adv.*

irresistible /ˌɪrɪˈzɪstəbl/ *adj.* **1** so strong that it cannot be stopped or prevented: *an irresistible urge to laugh* **2** ~ **(to sb)** very attractive: *He seems to think he's irresistible to women.* ⊃ verb **resist** ▸ **irresistibly** /-bli/ *adv.*

irrespective of /ˌɪrɪˈspektɪv əv/ *prep.* not affected by: *Anybody can take part in the competition, irrespective of age.* **SYN** **regardless of**

irresponsible /ˌɪrɪˈspɒnsəbl/ *adj.* not thinking about the effect your actions will have; not sensible: *It is irresponsible to let small children go out alone.* **OPP** **responsible** ▸ **irresponsibility** /ˌɪrɪˌspɒnsəˈbɪləti/ *noun* [U] ▸ **irresponsibly** /ˌɪrɪˈspɒnsəbli/ *adv.*

irreverent /ɪˈrevərənt/ *adj.* not feeling or showing respect: *This comedy takes an irreverent look at the world of politics.* ▸ **irreverence** /-rəns/ *noun* [U] ▸ **irreverently** *adv.*

irreversible /ˌɪrɪˈvɜːsəbl/ *adj.* that cannot be stopped or changed: *The disease can do irreversible damage to the lungs.* ▸ **irreversibly** /-bli/ *adv.*

irrigate /ˈɪrɪɡeɪt/ *verb* [T] (**AGRICULTURE**) to supply water to an area of land so that crops will grow ▸ **irrigation** /ˌɪrɪˈɡeɪʃn/ *noun* [U]

irritable /ˈɪrɪtəbl/ *adj.* becoming angry easily: *to be/feel/get irritable* **SYN** **bad-tempered** ▸ **irritability** /ˌɪrɪtəˈbɪləti/ *noun* [U] ▸ **irritably** /ˈɪrɪtəbli/ *adv.*

ˌirritable ˈbowel syndrome = IBS

irritant /ˈɪrɪtənt/ *noun* [C] (**HEALTH**) a substance that makes part of your body painful ▸ **irritant** *adj.* ⊃ picture at **safety**

irritate /ˈɪrɪteɪt/ *verb* [T] **1** to make sb slightly angry: *It really irritates me the way he keeps repeating himself.* **SYN** **annoy 2** (**HEALTH**) to cause a part of the body to be painful: *I don't use soap because it irritates my skin.* ▸ **irritation** /ˌɪrɪˈteɪʃn/ *noun* [C, U]

irritated /ˈɪrɪteɪtɪd/ *adj.* ~ **(at/by/with sth)** annoyed or angry: *He was getting more and more irritated at her comments.*

is /ɪz/ → BE¹

ISDN /ˌaɪ es diː ˈen/ *abbr.* (**COMPUTING**) **integrated services digital network** (a system for carrying sound signals, images, etc. along wires at high speed): *an ISDN internet connection*

-ish /ɪʃ/ *suffix* (in adjectives) **1** from the country mentioned: *Turkish ◇ Irish* **2** having the nature of; like: *childish* **3** fairly; approximately: *reddish ◇ thirtyish* ▶ **-ishly** *suffix* (in adverbs): *foolishly*

Islam /ˈɪzlɑːm, ɪzˈlɑːm/ *noun* [U] (**RELIGION**) the religion of Muslim people. Islam teaches that there is only one God and that Muhammad is His Prophet. ➔ note at **religion** ▶ **Islamic** /ɪzˈlæmɪk, -ˈlɑːm-/ *adj.*: *Islamic law*

Islamist /ˈɪzləmɪst/ *noun* [C] (**RELIGION**) a person who believes in the teachings of ISLAM ▶ **islamist** *adj.*

island 🔊 **A1** /ˈaɪlənd/ *noun* [C] **1** (**GEOGRAPHY**) a piece of land that is surrounded by water: *the Greek islands* **2** = TRAFFIC ISLAND

islander /ˈaɪləndə(r)/ *noun* [C] a person who lives on a small island

island-hopping *noun* [U] (**TOURISM**) the activity of travelling from one island to another in an area that has lots of islands, especially as a tourist

isle /aɪl/ *noun* [C] (**GEOGRAPHY**) used especially in names to mean 'island': *the Isle of Wight ◇ the British Isles*

isn't /ˈɪznt/ *short form* is not

ISO /ˈaɪsəʊ, ˌaɪ es ˈəʊ/ *abbr.* (**BUSINESS**, **SCIENCE**) **International Organization for Standardization** (an organization established in 1946 to make the measurements used in science, industry and business standard throughout the world)

iso- /aɪsəʊ, aɪsə, aɪˈsɒ/ *prefix* (in nouns, adjectives and adverbs) equal: *isotope ◇ isometric*

isobar /ˈaɪsəbɑː(r)/ *noun* [C] (**GEOGRAPHY**) a line on a weather map that joins places that have the same air pressure at a particular time

isolate 🔊+ **B2** /ˈaɪsəleɪt/ *verb* [T] ~ **sb/sth (from sb/sth)** to put or keep sb/sth separate from other people or things: *Infected patients must be isolated from others.*

isolated 🔊+ **B2** **W** /ˈaɪsəleɪtɪd/ *adj.* **1** ~ **(from sb/sth)** alone or apart from other people or things: *an isolated village deep in the countryside ◇ I was kept isolated from the other patients.* **2** not connected with others; happening once: *Is this an isolated case or part of a general pattern?*

isolation 🔊+ **C1** **W** /ˌaɪsəˈleɪʃn/ *noun* [U] ~ **(from sb/sth)** the state of being separate and alone; the act of separating sb/sth: *He lived in complete isolation from the outside world. ◇ In isolation each problem does not seem bad, but together they are quite worrying.* ➔ look at **loneliness**, **solitude**

isolationism /ˌaɪsəˈleɪʃənɪzəm/ *noun* [U] (**POLITICS**) the policy of not becoming involved in the affairs of other countries or groups ▶ **isolationist** /-nɪst/ *adj., noun* [C]: *an isolationist foreign policy*

isosceles triangle /aɪˌsɒsəliːz ˈtraɪæŋgl/ *noun* [C] (**GEOMETRY**) a TRIANGLE with two of its three sides the same length ➔ picture at **triangle**

isotherm /ˈaɪsəθɜːm/ *noun* [C] (**GEOGRAPHY**) a line on a weather map that joins places that have the same temperature at a particular time

isotope /ˈaɪsətəʊp/ *noun* [C] (**CHEMISTRY**, **PHYSICS**) one of two or more forms of a chemical element that have different physical characteristics but the same chemical characteristics

---

▼ **VOCABULARY BUILDING**

Isotopes of the same element have the same number of **protons** in the **nucleus**, but a different number of **neutrons**.

ISP /ˌaɪ es ˈpiː/ *abbr.* (**COMPUTING**) **internet service provider** (a company that provides you with an internet connection and services such as email, etc.)

issue¹ 🔊 **B1** **O** /ˈɪʃuː/ *noun* **1** [C] (**SOCIAL STUDIES**) a problem or subject for discussion: *I want to raise the issue of overtime pay at the meeting. ◇ The government cannot avoid the issue of homelessness any longer.* **3** [U] note at **opinion** **2** [C] (**ARTS AND MEDIA**) one in a series of things that are published or produced: *Do you have last month's issue of this magazine?* **3** [U] the act of publishing or giving sth to people: *the issue of blankets to the refugees* **IDM** **make an issue (out) of sth** to give too much importance to a small problem **PHRV** **issue from sth** (*formal*) to come out of sth

issue² 🔊 **B2** /ˈɪʃuː/ *verb* **1** [T] to give or say sth to sb officially: *The new employees were issued with uniforms. ◇ to issue a visa ◇ The police will issue a statement later today.* **2** [T] to produce sth such as a magazine or an article: *We issue a monthly newsletter for students.* **3** [I] (*formal*) to come or go out: *An angry voice issued from the loudspeaker.*

isthmus /ˈɪsməs/ *noun* [C] (**GEOGRAPHY**) a narrow piece of land, with water on each side, that joins two larger pieces of land

IT 🔊 **A1** /ˌaɪ ˈtiː/ *noun* [U] (**COMPUTING**) the study or use of electronic equipment, especially computers, for collecting, storing and sending out information (the abbreviation for 'information technology')

it 🔊 **A1** /ɪt/ *pron.* **1** (used as the subject or object of a verb, or after a preposition) the thing or animal mentioned earlier: *Look at that car. It's going much too fast. ◇ The children went up to the dog and patted it.* **2** used for identifying a person: *It's your Mum on the phone. ◇ 'Who's that?' 'It's the postman.' ◇ It's me! ◇ It's him!* **3** used in the position of the subject or object of a verb when the real subject or object is at the end of the sentence: *It's hard for them to talk about their problems. ◇ I think it doesn't really matter what time we arrive.* **4** used in the position of the subject of a verb when you are talking about time, the date, distance, the weather, etc: *It's nearly half past eight. ◇ It's Tuesday today. ◇ It's about 100 kilometres from London. ◇ It was very cold at the weekend. ◇ It's raining.* **5** used when you are talking about a situation: *It gets very crowded here in the summer. ◇ I'll come at seven o'clock if it's convenient. ◇ It's a pity they can't come to the party. ◇ I like it here.* **6** used for emphasizing a part of a sentence: *It was Jerry who said it, not me. ◇ It's your health I'm worried about, not the cost.* **IDM** **that is it 1** that/this is the important point, reason, etc: *That's just it — he never really wanted to be famous.* **2** that/this is the end: *That's it — you can go home now.*

italics /ɪˈtælɪks/ *noun* [pl.] (*also* **italic** [sing.]) (**LANGUAGE**) letters that lean to the right: *All the example sentences in the dictionary are printed in italics.* ➔ look at **Roman** (2) ▶ **italic** *adj.*: *Use an italic font.*

itch /ɪtʃ/ *noun* [C, usually sing.] the feeling on your skin that makes you want to SCRATCH (= rub your skin with your nails): *My nose is itching.* ▶ **itch** *verb* [I]

itchy /ˈɪtʃi/ *adj.* (**itchier; itchiest**) having or producing an ITCH: *I feel itchy all over. ◇ This shirt is itchy.* ▶ **itchiness** *noun* [U]

it'd /ˈɪtəd/ *short form* it had; it would

item 🔊 **A2** **W** /ˈaɪtəm/ *noun* [C] **1** one single thing on a list or in a collection: *Some items arrived too late to be included in the catalogue. ◇ What is the first item on* the agenda? **2** one single article or object: *Can I pay for each item separately?* ◊ *an item of clothing* **3** (ARTS AND MEDIA) a single piece of news: *There was an interesting item about Spain in yesterday's news.*

itemize (*BrE also* -ise) /ˈaɪtəmaɪz/ *verb* [T] to make a list of all the separate items in sth: *an itemized phone bill*

iteration /ˌɪtəˈreɪʃn/ *noun* **1** [U, C] (COMPUTING, MATHEMATICS) the process of repeating a MATHEMATICAL or COMPUTING process again and again, each time starting with the result of the previous stage **2** [C] (COMPUTING) a new version of a piece of computer software

itinerant /aɪˈtɪnərənt/ *adj.* [only before noun] travelling from place to place: *an itinerant circus family*

itinerary /aɪˈtɪnərəri/ *noun* [C] (*pl.* -ies) (TOURISM) a plan of a journey, including the route and the places that you will visit

it'll /ˈɪtl/ *short form* it will

its ʔ A1 /ɪts/ *det.* of or belonging to a thing, an animal or a baby: *The club held its Annual General Meeting last night.*

it's /ɪts/ *short form* it is; it has

itself ʔ A2 /ɪtˈself/ *pron.* **1** used when the animal or thing that does an action is also affected by it: *The cat was washing itself.* ◊ *The company has got itself into financial difficulties.* **2** used to emphasize sth: *The building itself is beautiful, but it's in a very ugly part of town.*
IDM **(all) by itself 1** without being controlled by a person: *The central heating comes on by itself before we get up.* **2** alone: *The house stood all by itself on the hillside.*

ITV /ˌaɪ tiː ˈviː/ *abbr.* (ARTS AND MEDIA) **Independent Television** (a group of British companies that produce programmes that are paid for by advertising)

IUD /ˌaɪ juː ˈdiː/ *noun* [C] (MEDICINE) a small metal or plastic object that is placed inside the UTERUS (= the part of a woman's body where a baby grows) to stop her becoming pregnant (the abbreviation for 'intrauterine device')

IV¹ /ˌaɪ ˈviː/ *abbr.* = INTRAVENOUS, INTRAVENOUSLY

IV² /ˌaɪ ˈviː/ *noun* [C] (*especially AmE*) = DRIP² (3)

I've /aɪv/ *short form* I have

IVF /ˌaɪ viː ˈef/ *noun* [U] (MEDICINE) a process that FERTILIZES an egg from a woman outside her body. The egg is then put inside her body to develop. (the abbreviation for 'in vitro fertilization')

ivory /ˈaɪvəri/ *noun* [U] the hard white substance that the TUSKS (= long teeth) of an elephant are made of

ivy /ˈaɪvi/ *noun* [U] a climbing plant that has dark green leaves with five points

J j

J /dʒeɪ/ (*also* j) *noun* [C, U] (*pl.* J's, j's) the tenth letter of the English alphabet: *'Jam' begins with (a) 'J'.*

jab¹ /dʒæb/ *verb* [I, T] **~ (at sb/sth); ~ sb/sth (with sth); ~ sth into sb/sth** to push at sb/sth with a sudden, sharp movement, usually with sth sharp: *He kept jabbing at his potato with his fork.* ◊ *She jabbed me in the ribs with her elbow.* ◊ *The robber jabbed a gun into my back and ordered me to move.*

jab² /dʒæb/ *noun* [C] **1** a sudden rough push with sth sharp, or with a FIST (= tightly closed hand): *He gave me a jab in the ribs with the stick.* **2** (*BrE, informal*) (MEDICINE) an INJECTION (= putting a drug, etc. into the body through a needle) to help prevent you from catching a disease: *I'm going to the doctor's to have a flu jab today.* **SYN** **injection**

jack¹ /dʒæk/ *noun* [C] **1** a piece of equipment for lifting a car, etc. off the ground, for example in order to change its wheel **2** the card between the ten and the queen in a pack of cards
IDM **a jack of all trades** a person who can do many different types of work, but who perhaps does not do them very well

jack² /dʒæk/ *verb*
PHR V **jack sth in** (*informal*) to stop doing sth: *Jerry got fed up with his job and jacked it in.* **jack sth up** to lift a car, etc. using a JACK: *We jacked the car up to change the wheel.*

jackal /ˈdʒækl, -kɔːl/ *noun* [C] a wild animal like a dog that lives in Africa and Asia. Jackals eat the meat of animals that are already dead.

jacket ʔ A1 /ˈdʒækɪt/ *noun* [C] **1** a short light coat: *Do you have to wear a jacket and tie to work?* ➔ look at **life jacket** **2** an outer cover around a hot water pipe, etc. that stops heat from being lost

jacket potato (*BrE*) = BAKED POTATO

jackhammer /ˈdʒækhæmə(r)/ (*AmE*) = PNEUMATIC DRILL

jackknife /ˈdʒæknaɪf/ *verb* [I] (used about a lorry that is in two parts) to go out of control and bend suddenly in a dangerous way

jackpot /ˈdʒækpɒt/ *noun* [C] the largest money prize that you can win in a game of chance
IDM **hit the jackpot** → HIT¹

Jacuzzi™ /dʒəˈkuːzi/ *noun* [C] a large bath in which powerful movements of air make bubbles in the water

jade /dʒeɪd/ *noun* [U] **1** a hard stone that is usually green and is used in making jewellery **2** a bright green colour ▸ **jade** *adj.*

jaded /ˈdʒeɪdɪd/ *adj.* tired and bored after doing the same thing for a long time without a break

jagged /ˈdʒæɡɪd/ *adj.* rough with sharp points: *jagged rocks*

jaguar /ˈdʒæɡjuə(r)/ *noun* [C] a large wild cat with yellow-brown fur and black spots that comes from Central and South America

jail¹ ʔ+ B2 /dʒeɪl/ *noun* [U, C] a prison: *She was sent to jail for ten years.*

jail² ʔ+ B2 /dʒeɪl/ *verb* [T, usually passive] (LAW) to put sb in prison: *She was jailed for ten years.* **SYN** **imprison**

jailer /ˈdʒeɪlə(r)/ *noun* [C] (*old-fashioned*) (LAW) a person whose job is to guard prisoners

jam¹ ʔ A2 /dʒæm/ *noun* **1** [U, C] a sweet substance that you spread on bread, made by boiling fruit and sugar together: *a jar of raspberry jam* ➔ look at **jelly** (2) **2** [C] a situation in which you cannot move because there are too many people or vehicles: *a traffic jam* **3** [C] (*informal*) a difficult situation: *We're in a bit of jam without our passports or travel documents.* **4** [C] (*informal*) (MUSIC) the act of playing music together with other musicians in a way that has not been planned or prepared first: *a jam session*

jam² /dʒæm/ *verb* (-mm-) **1** [T] (used with an adverb or a preposition) to push or force sb/sth into a place where there is not much room: *She managed to jam everything into her suitcase.* **2** [I, T] **~ (sth) (up)** to become or to make sth unable to move so that it does not work: *Something is jamming (up) the machine.*

◇ *The paper keeps jamming in the photocopier.* ◇ *I can't open the door. The lock's jammed.* **3** [T, usually passive] **be jammed (up) (with sb/sth)** to be filled with too many people or things: *The cupboard was jammed full of old newspapers and magazines.* ◇ *The suitcase was jam-packed with* (= completely full of) *designer clothes.* ◇ *The switchboard was jammed with calls from unhappy customers.* **4** [T] to send out signals in order to stop radio programmes, etc. from being received or heard clearly **5** [I] (*informal*) (**MUSIC**) to play music with other musicians in an informal way without preparing or practising first: *They continued to jam together and write music and eventually they made their first record.*

PHR V jam on the brakes/jam the brakes on to stop a car suddenly by pushing hard on the BRAKE (= the device for making a vehicle stop) with your foot

jangle /ˈdʒæŋgl/ *verb* [I, T] to make a noise like metal hitting against metal; to move sth so that it makes this noise: *The baby smiles if you jangle your keys.* ▸ jangle *noun* [C, usually sing.]

janitor /ˈdʒænɪtə(r)/ (*AmE*) = CARETAKER

January ⚂ **A1** /ˈdʒænjuəri/ *noun* [U, C] (*abbr.* **Jan.**) the first month of the year, between December and Febuary: *We're going skiing in January.* ◇ *last/next January* ◇ *We first met on January 31st, 2009.* ◇ *Christine's birthday is (on) January 17.* ◇ *Our wedding anniversary is at the end of January.* ◇ *January mornings can be very dark in Britain.*

jar¹ /dʒɑː(r)/ *noun* [C] **1** a container with a LID, usually made of glass and used for keeping food, etc. in: *a jam jar* ◇ *a large storage jar for flour* **2** the food that a jar contains: *a jar of honey/jam/coffee*

jar² /dʒɑː(r)/ *verb* (**-rr-**) **1** [T] to hurt or damage sth as a result of a sharp knock: *He fell and jarred his back.* **2** [I] **~ (on sb/sth)** to have an unpleasant or annoying effect: *The dripping tap jarred on my nerves.*

jargon /ˈdʒɑːgən/ *noun* [U] (**LANGUAGE**) special or technical words that are used by a particular group of people or profession and that other people do not understand: *medical/scientific/legal/computer jargon*

jaundice /ˈdʒɔːndɪs/ *noun* [U] (**HEALTH**) a medical condition in which the skin and white parts of the eyes become yellow, caused by disease of the LIVER or the blood

jaundiced /ˈdʒɔːndɪst/ *adj.* **1** not expecting sb/sth to be good or useful, especially because of experiences that you have had in the past: *He had a jaundiced view of life.* **2** suffering from JAUNDICE

Java™ /ˈdʒɑːvə/ *noun* [U] (**COMPUTING**) a computer language that can be used to create programs that will run on any computer

javelin /ˈdʒævlɪn/ *noun* (**SPORT**) **1** [C] a long stick with a pointed end that is thrown in sports competitions **2 the javelin** [sing.] the event or sport of throwing the javelin as far as possible

jaw /dʒɔː/ *noun* **1** [C] (**ANATOMY**) either of the two bones in the face that contain the teeth: *the lower/upper jaw* ◇ picture at **body 2** jaws [pl.] the mouth (especially of a wild animal): *The lion came towards him with its jaws open.* **3** jaws [pl.] the parts of a tool or machine that are used to hold things tightly: *the jaws of a vice* ◇ picture at **workbench**

jawbone /ˈdʒɔːbəʊn/ *noun* [C] (**ANATOMY**) the bone that forms the lower JAW **SYN** mandible ◇ picture at **body, tooth**

jaw-dropping *adj.* (*informal*) so large or good that it surprises you very much: *a jaw-dropping 5 million dollars*

---

jersey J

jazz¹ ⚂ **A2** /dʒæz/ *noun* [U] (**MUSIC**) a style of music with a strong rhythm, originally of African American origin: *modern/traditional jazz* ◇ look at **classical** (3), **pop²** (1), **rock¹** (5)

jazz² /dʒæz/ *verb*
PHR V jazz sth up (*informal*) to make sth brighter, more interesting or more exciting

JCB™ /ˌdʒeɪ siː ˈbiː/ *noun* [C] (*BrE*) a powerful motor vehicle with a long arm for digging and moving earth

jealous /ˈdʒeləs/ *adj.* **1** feeling upset or angry because you think that sb you like or love is showing interest in sb else: *Tim seems to get jealous whenever Liz speaks to another boy!* **2 ~ (of sb/sth)** feeling angry or sad because you want to be like sb else or because you want what sb else has: *He's always been jealous of his older brother.* ◇ *I'm very jealous of your new car — how much did it cost?* **SYN** envious ▸ jealously *adv.* ▸ jealousy *noun* [U, C] (*pl.* -ies)

jeans ⚂ **A1** /dʒiːnz/ *noun* [pl.] trousers made of DENIM (= strong cotton cloth that is usually blue): *These jeans are a bit too tight.* ◇ *a pair of jeans*

Jeep™ /dʒiːp/ *noun* [C] a small strong vehicle suitable for travelling over rough ground

jeer /dʒɪə(r)/ *verb* [I, T] **~ (at) sb/sth** to laugh or shout rude comments at sb/sth to show your lack of respect for them or it: *The spectators booed and jeered at the losing team.* ▸ jeer *noun* [C, usually pl.]: *The prime minister was greeted with jeers in the House of Commons today.*

jelly /ˈdʒeli/ *noun* (*pl.* -ies) **1** (*BrE*) (*AmE* jello /ˈdʒeləʊ/) [U, C] a soft, solid, brightly coloured food that shakes when it is moved. Jelly is made from sugar, fruit juice and GELATIN and is eaten cold at the end of a meal, especially by children. **2** [U] a type of jam that does not contain any solid pieces of fruit
IDM be/feel like jelly (used especially about the legs or knees) to feel weak because you are nervous, afraid, etc. **turn to jelly** (used about the legs and knees) to suddenly become weak because of fear

jellyfish /ˈdʒelifɪʃ/ *noun* [C] (*pl.* jellyfish) a sea animal with a soft, almost clear body and long thin parts called TENTACLES that can give you a STING (= a painful wound on the skin)

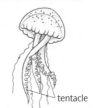
tentacle

jellyfish

jeopardize (*BrE also* -ise) /ˈdʒepədaɪz/ *verb* [T] to risk harming or destroying sth: *He would never do anything to jeopardize his career.*

jeopardy /ˈdʒepədi/ *noun*
IDM in jeopardy in a dangerous position and likely to be lost or harmed: *The future of the factory and 15 000 jobs are in jeopardy.*

jerk¹ /dʒɜːk/ *verb* [T, I] to move or make sb/sth move with a sudden sharp movement: *She jerked the door open.* ◇ *His head jerked back as the car suddenly set off.* ▸ jerkily /ˈdʒɜːkɪli/ *adv.* ▸ jerky *adj.* (jerkier; jerkiest)

jerk² /dʒɜːk/ *noun* [C] **1** a sudden sharp movement **2** (*especially AmE, informal*) a stupid or annoying person

jersey /ˈdʒɜːzi/ *noun* **1** [C] a piece of clothing for the upper part of the body, with long SLEEVES and no buttons, made by KNITTING wool or cotton **SYN** jumper, pullover, sweater **2** [C] a shirt worn by sb playing a sports game **3** [U] a type of soft fine

---

KNITTED cloth made of cotton or wool that is used for making clothes

Jesus /'dʒiːzəs/ (*also* ˌJesus 'Christ) = CHRIST

jet¹ ⸿+ B2 /dʒet/ *noun* [C] **1** a plane driven by JET ENGINES: *a jet plane/aircraft* **2** a fast, thin current of water, gas, etc. coming out of a small hole

jet² /dʒet/ *verb* [I] (used with an adverb or a preposition) (-tt-) (*informal*) to fly somewhere in a plane

ˌjet 'black *adj.* very dark black in colour ▸ jet black *noun* [U]

'jet engine *noun* [C] a powerful engine that makes planes fly by pushing out a current of hot air and gases at the back ⊃ picture at **airliner**

'jet lag *noun* [U] (TOURISM) the tired feeling that people often have after a long journey in a plane to a place where the local time is different ▸ 'jet-lagged *adj.*

the 'jet set *noun* [sing. + sing./pl. verb] the group of rich, successful and fashionable people (especially those who travel around the world a lot)

'Jet Ski™ *noun* [C] (SPORT) a vehicle with an engine, like a motorcycle, for riding across water ▸ 'jet-skiing *noun* [U]

jetty /'dʒeti/ (*pl.* -ies) (*AmE also* **dock**) *noun* [C] a stone wall or wooden platform built out into the sea or a river where boats are tied and where people can get on and off them

Jew /dʒuː/ *noun* [C] a member of the people and cultural community whose religion is Judaism ⊃ note at **religion** ▸ **Jewish** /'dʒuːɪʃ/ *adj.*: *He's Jewish.*

jewel /'dʒuːəl/ *noun* [C] **1** a valuable stone (for example a diamond) SYN **gem 2** [usually pl.] pieces of jewellery or beautiful objects that contain PRECIOUS (= rare and valuable) stones

jeweller (*BrE*) (*AmE* **jeweler**) /'dʒuːələ(r)/ *noun* [C] **1** a person whose job is to buy, sell, make or repair jewellery and watches **2** jeweller's (*pl.* jewellers) a shop where jewellery and watches are sold and repaired

jewellery ⸿ A2 (*BrE*) (*AmE* **jewelry**) /'dʒuːəlri/ *noun* [U] objects such as rings, etc. that are worn as personal decoration: *a piece of jewellery*

jig¹ /dʒɪg/ *noun* [C] (MUSIC) a type of quick dance with jumping movements; the music for this dance

jig² /dʒɪg/ *verb* [I] (-gg-) ~ **about/around** to move about in an excited or impatient way

jiggle /'dʒɪgl/ *verb* [T] (*informal*) to move sth quickly from side to side or up and down: *She jiggled her car keys to try to distract the baby.*

jigsaw /'dʒɪgsɔː/ *noun* [C] **1** (*also* 'jigsaw puzzle) a picture on CARDBOARD (= very thick paper) or wood that is cut into small pieces and has to be fitted together again **2** a SAW (= a type of tool) with a fine BLADE for cutting designs in thin pieces of wood or metal

jihad /dʒɪ'hɑːd/ *noun* [C, U] (RELIGION) **1** (in Islam) a spiritual struggle within yourself to stop yourself breaking religious or moral laws **2** a religious war that is fought by Muslims to defend Islam

jingle¹ /'dʒɪŋgl/ *noun* **1** [sing.] a ringing sound like small bells, made by metal objects gently hitting each other: *the jingle of coins* **2** [C] (ARTS AND MEDIA) a short simple tune or song that is easy to remember and is used in advertising on TV or radio

jingle² /'dʒɪŋgl/ *verb* [I, T] to make or cause sth to make a pleasant gentle sound like small bells ringing: *She jingled the coins in her pocket.*

jinx /dʒɪŋks/ *noun* [sing.] (*informal*) bad luck; a person or thing that people believe brings bad luck to sb/sth ▸ jinx *verb* [T] ▸ jinxed *adj.*: *After my third accident in a month, I began to think I was jinxed.*

JIT /dʒɪt/ *abbr.* (BUSINESS) **just-in-time** (used to describe a system in which parts or materials are only sent to a factory just before they are needed)

jitters /'dʒɪtəz/ (*often* the jitters) *noun* [pl.] (*informal*) feelings of fear or worry, especially before an important event or before having to do sth difficult: *Just thinking about the exam gives me the jitters!*

jittery /'dʒɪtəri/ *adj.* (*informal*) nervous or worried

Jnr *abbr.* (in writing) = JUNIOR¹ (2): *Samuel P Carson Jnr*

job ⸿ A1 /dʒɒb/ *noun* [C] **1** (BUSINESS) the work that you do regularly to earn money: *She took/got a job as a waitress.* ◇ *A lot of people will lose their jobs if the factory closes.* ⊃ note at **work²** **2** a task or a piece of work: *I always have a lot of jobs to do in the house at weekends.* ◇ *The garage has done a good/bad job on our car.* **3** [usually sing.] a duty or responsibility: *It's not his job to tell us what we can and can't do.* IDM **do the job/trick** (*informal*) to get the result that is wanted **have a hard job doing sth/to do sth** → HARD¹ **it's a good job** (*informal*) it is a good or lucky thing: *It's a good job you reminded me — I had completely forgotten!* **just the job/ticket** (*informal*) exactly what is needed in a particular situation **make a bad, good, etc. job of sth** to do sth badly, well, etc. **make the best of a bad job** → BEST³ **out of a job** without paid work SYN **unemployed**

▼ COLLOCATIONS

job

While you are learning, you **study/train to be** or **train as** a doctor, teacher, etc: *She trained as a painter and sculptor.* A **trainee** is sb who **starts work** while they are still **training**: *He started work as a trainee chef.* Somebody who has **completed their training** or passed their exams has **qualified**: *She qualified as a vet last year.* We say sb **is** or **works as** a writer, teacher, etc: *Tim worked as a bus driver for many years.* ◇ *Gerry is a cello teacher.* You **look for**, **apply for** or **find a job**: *He applied for 16 jobs before he found one.* A job can be **full-time** or **part-time**, **permanent** or **temporary**: *Many students find temporary jobs in hotels during the summer.* ◇ *I only worked part-time while Gloria was a baby.* **Job-sharing** can suit two people who want to work part-time: *Job-sharing allows employees to be parents as well as business people.* A company **engages (sb as)/hires (sb as)**, **recruits** or **takes on** a new employee: *They have taken on a new designer.* When an organization chooses sb for a high level position they **appoint sb (as)** or **make sb** president, chairman, head, etc: *She was appointed Professor of Law at Yale.* ◇ *At 35 he was made chairman of the board.* If you want to leave your job, you **resign** or **hand in** your **resignation**: *He resigned from his post as finance director in April.* If a company no longer needs an employee, it will **make** him/her **redundant**: *Hundreds of car workers were made redundant when the factory closed down.* If an employee's work is not good enough, the company can **dismiss/fire/sack** him/her: *Her boss fired her because she was always late for work.* ◇ *The manager of the company was sacked.* When you stop working because you have reached a certain age (often 67 in the UK), you **retire**: *After she retired from teaching, Maria taught herself to paint.* Some people **take early retirement**, especially if they **have a good pension**.

'job-hunt *verb* [I] (usually used in the progressive tenses) to try to find a job: *At that time I had been job-hunting for six months.*

jobless /'dʒɒbləs/ *adj.* (SOCIAL STUDIES) **1** (usually used about large numbers of people) without paid work SYN **unemployed 2** the jobless *noun* [pl.] people without paid work ▶ **joblessness** noun [U] **SYN** **unemployment**

job satis'faction noun [U] the good feeling that you get when you have a job that you enjoy

jobseeker (also **job seeker**) /'dʒɒbsiːkə(r)/ noun [C] (BrE) (**SOCIAL STUDIES**) a person without a job who is trying to find one

'**job-sharing** noun [U] (**BUSINESS**) an arrangement for two people to share the hours of work and the pay of one job ○ note at **job** ▶ '**job-share** noun [C], verb [I]: The company encourages job-shares and part-time working. ◇ She's looking for somebody to job-share with.

jockey /'dʒɒki/ noun [C] (**SPORT**) a person who rides horses in races, especially as a job ○ look at **DJ**

jocular /'dʒɒkjələ(r)/ adj. (formal) **1** funny; humorous: a jocular comment **2** (used about a person) enjoying making people laugh **SYN** **jolly** ▶ **jocularity** /ˌdʒɒkjə'lærəti/ noun [U]

jodhpurs /'dʒɒdpəz/ noun [pl.] (**SPORT**) special trousers that you wear for riding a horse

joey /'dʒəʊi/ noun [C] a young KANGAROO or WALLABY ○ picture at **animal**

jog¹ /dʒɒg/ verb (-gg-) **1** [I] (**SPORT**) to run slowly, especially as a form of exercise **2** [T] to push or knock sb/sth slightly: He jogged my arm and I spilled the milk. **SYN** **nudge**
IDM **jog sb's memory** to say or do sth that makes sb remember sth

jog² /dʒɒg/ noun [sing.] **1** (**SPORT**) a slow run as a form of exercise: She goes for a jog before breakfast. **2** a slight push or knock **SYN** **nudge**

jogger /'dʒɒgə(r)/ noun [C] (**SPORT**) a person who goes JOGGING for exercise

join¹ ʔ **A1** /dʒɔɪn/ verb
• **CONNECT 1** [T] **~ A to B; ~ A and B (together)** to fasten or connect one thing to another: The Channel Tunnel joins Britain to France. ◇ The two pieces of wood had been carefully joined together. ◇ We've knocked down the wall and joined the two rooms into one.
• **BECOME ONE 2** [I, T] **~ (with sb/sth)** if two things or groups **join**, or if one thing or group **joins** another, they come together to form one thing or group: Do the two rivers join at any point? ◇ Where does this road join the motorway? ◇ We'll join with the other class later.
• **CLUB 3** [T] to become a member of a club or an organization: I've joined an aerobics class. ◇ He joined the company three months ago. ○ note at **organization**
• **TAKE PART 4** [T] **~ sb (for sth); ~ sb (in doing sth)** to take part in sth that sb else is doing: Will you join us for lunch? ◇ Everybody here joins me in wishing you the best of luck in your new job.
IDM **join forces (with sb)** → FORCE¹
PHR V **join in (sth/doing sth)** to take part in an activity: Everyone started singing but Frank refused to join in. **join up** to become a member of the armed forces **SYN** **enlist**

join² /dʒɔɪn/ noun [C] a place where two things are fixed or connected: He glued the handle back on so cleverly that you couldn't see the join.

joiner /'dʒɔɪnə(r)/ noun [C] (BrE) a person whose job is to make the wooden parts of a building ○ look at **carpenter**

joinery /'dʒɔɪnəri/ noun [U] the work of a JOINER or things made by a JOINER

joint¹ ʔ+ **B2** /dʒɔɪnt/ noun [C] **1** (**ANATOMY**) a part of the body where two bones fit together and are able to bend ○ picture at **synovial 2** the place where two or more things are fastened or connected together, especially to form a corner **3** (BrE) a large piece of

meat that you cook whole in the oven: a joint of lamb ○ note at **meat**

joint² ʔ+ **B2** /dʒɔɪnt/ adj. [only before noun] shared or owned by two or more people: Have you and your husband got a joint account (= a shared bank account)? ◇ a joint decision ▶ **jointly** adv.

joint 'venture noun [C] (**BUSINESS**) a business project or activity that is begun by two or more companies, etc., which remain separate organizations

joist /dʒɔɪst/ noun [C] (**ARCHITECTURE**) a long thick piece of wood or metal that is used to support a floor or ceiling in a building ○ look at **beam¹**

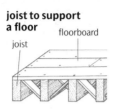
joist to support a floor
floorboard
joist

joke¹ ʔ **A2** /dʒəʊk/ noun **1** [C] something said or done to make you laugh, especially a funny story: to tell/crack jokes ◇ a dirty joke (= about sex) ◇ I'm sorry, I didn't **get the joke** (= understand it). ○ look at **practical joke 2** [sing.] (informal) a person, thing or situation that is silly and cannot be taken seriously: The salary he was offered was a joke!
IDM **play a joke/trick on sb** to trick sb because you think it is funny or in order to make other people laugh see the joke → SEE **take a joke** to be able to laugh at a joke against yourself: The trouble with Pete is he can't take a joke. **make a joke of sth** to laugh about sth that is serious or should be taken seriously

joke² ʔ **A2** /dʒəʊk/ verb [I] **1** **~ (with sb) (about sth)** to say sth to make people laugh; to tell a funny story: She spent the evening laughing and joking with her old friends. **2** **~ (about sth)** to say sth that is not true because you think it is funny: I never joke about religion. ◇ Don't get upset. I was **only joking**!
IDM **you must be joking** | **you're joking** (informal) (used to express great surprise) you cannot be serious

joker /'dʒəʊkə(r)/ noun [C] **1** a person who likes to tell jokes or play tricks **2** an extra card that can be used instead of any other one in some card games

jolly /'dʒɒli/ adj. (jollier; jolliest) happy and cheerful: a jolly crowd/face/mood

jolt¹ /dʒəʊlt/ verb [I, T] to move or make sb/sth move in a sudden rough way: The lorry jolted along the bumpy track. ◇ The crash jolted all the passengers forward.

jolt² /dʒəʊlt/ noun [C, usually sing.] **1** a sudden movement: The train stopped with a jolt. **2** a sudden surprise or shock: His sudden anger gave her quite a jolt.

jostle /'dʒɒsl/ verb [I, T] to push hard against sb in a crowd

jot /dʒɒt/ verb (-tt-)
PHR V **jot sth down** to make a quick short note of sth: Let me jot down your address.

joule /dʒuːl/ noun [C] (**PHYSICS**) a measurement of energy or work ○ look at **kilojoule**

journal ʔ **B1** **S1** /'dʒɜːnl/ noun [C] **1** (**ARTS AND MEDIA**) a newspaper or magazine, especially one in which all the articles are about a particular subject or profession: a medical/scientific/trade journal **2** a written record of the things you do, see, etc. each day: Have you read his journal of the years he spent in India? ○ look at **diary** (2)

journalism ₹+ B2 /ˈdʒɜːnəlɪzəm/ noun [U] (ARTS AND MEDIA) the work of collecting and writing news stories for newspapers, magazines, radio, TV or online news sites

journalist ₹ A2 /ˈdʒɜːnəlɪst/ noun [C] (ARTS AND MEDIA) a person whose job is to collect and write news stories for newspapers, magazines, radio, TV or online news sites: *a freelance journalist* ⊃ look at **reporter** ⊃ note at **newspaper**

journey ₹ A1 /ˈdʒɜːni/ noun [C] (TOURISM) the act of travelling from one place to another, especially when they are far apart: *Did you have a good journey?* ◇ *a two-hour journey* ◇ *The journey to work takes me 45 minutes.* ◇ *We'll have to **break the journey** (= stop for a rest).* ⊃ note at **travel²**

joust /dʒaʊst/ verb [I] (HISTORY) to fight on horses using a LANCE (= a long stick) to try to knock the other person off their horse, especially as part of a formal contest in the past ▸ **joust** noun [C] ▸ **jousting** noun [U]

jovial /ˈdʒəʊviəl/ adj. (used about a person) happy and friendly

joy ₹ B2 /dʒɔɪ/ noun 1 [U] a feeling of great happiness: *We'd like to wish you joy and success in your life together.* 2 [C] a person or thing that gives you great pleasure: *the joys of fatherhood* ◇ *That class is a joy to teach.* 3 [U] (BrE, informal) (in negative sentences and questions) success or SATISFACTION: '*I asked again if we could have seats with more legroom but **got no joy** from the check-in clerk.*'
IDM jump for joy → JUMP¹ sb's pride and joy → PRIDE¹

joyful /ˈdʒɔɪfl/ adj. very happy; causing people to be happy: *a joyful occasion* ▸ **joyfully** /-fəli/ adv. ▸ **joyfulness** noun [U]

joyless /ˈdʒɔɪləs/ adj. (formal) unhappy: *a joyless marriage*

joyous /ˈdʒɔɪəs/ adj. (formal) very happy; causing people to be happy SYN **joyful**

joystick /ˈdʒɔɪstɪk/ noun [C] 1 a stick with a handle used with some computer games to move images on the screen 2 a stick with a handle that is used to control direction or height in an aircraft

JP /ˌdʒeɪ ˈpiː/ = JUSTICE OF THE PEACE

JPEG /ˈdʒeɪpeg/ noun (COMPUTING) 1 [U] technology that reduces the size of files that contain images (the abbreviation for 'Joint Photographic Experts Group'): *JPEG files* 2 [C] an image created using this technology: *You can download the pictures as JPEGs.*

Jr (BrE) (also **Jr.** AmE, BrE) abbr. (in writing) (especially AmE) = JUNIOR¹ (2)

jubilant /ˈdʒuːbɪlənt/ adj. extremely happy, especially because of a success: *The football fans were jubilant at their team's victory in the cup.*

jubilation /ˌdʒuːbɪˈleɪʃn/ noun [U] great happiness because of a success

jubilee /ˈdʒuːbɪliː, ˌdʒuːbɪˈliː/ noun [C] a special anniversary of an event that took place a certain number of years ago, and the celebrations that go with it: *It's the company's **golden jubilee** this year (= it is 50 years since it was started).*

Judaism /ˈdʒuːdeɪɪzəm/ noun [U] (RELIGION) the religion of the Jewish people ⊃ note at **religion**

judge¹ ₹ B1 /dʒʌdʒ/ noun 1 (LAW) a person in a court whose job is to decide how criminals should be punished and to make legal decisions: *The judge sentenced the man to three years in prison.* ⊃ note at **court¹** 2 (SPORT) a person who decides who has won a

competition: *a panel of judges* 3 [usually sing.] **~ (of sth)** a person who has the ability or knowledge to give an opinion about sth: *You're a good judge of character — what do you think of him?*

judge² ₹ B1 /dʒʌdʒ/ verb 1 [I, T] **~ sb/sth (on sth)** to form or give an opinion about sb/sth based on the information you have: *Judging by what she said, her work is going well.* ◇ *The party was judged a great success by everybody.* ◇ *You shouldn't judge him on his appearance.* 2 [T] to guess the size, amount, etc. of sth: *It's difficult to judge how long the project will take.* 3 [T] to decide the result or winner of a competition: *The head teacher will judge the competition.* 4 [T] to give your opinion about sb, especially when you think they are bad: *Don't judge him too harshly — he's had a difficult time.* 5 [T] (LAW) to decide if sb is guilty or innocent in court: *She was judged not guilty and released immediately.*

judgement ₹ B2 ⊙ (also **judgment** especially in AmE) /ˈdʒʌdʒmənt/ noun 1 [U] the ability to form opinions or to make sensible decisions: *He always shows excellent judgement in his choice of staff.* ◇ *to have good/poor/sound judgement* 2 [C, U] an opinion that you form after carefully considering the information you have: *What, in your judgement, would be the best course of action?* 3 (usually judgment) [C, U] **~ (on sth)** (LAW) an official decision made by a judge or a court: *The man collapsed when the judgment was read out in court.* ◇ *I never **passed judgment** on her actions (= criticized them).*

Judgement Day (also **Judgment Day** especially in AmE) noun [sing.] (RELIGION) the day at the end of the world when, according to some religions, God will judge everyone who has ever lived

judicial ₹+ C1 /dʒuˈdɪʃl/ adj. (LAW) connected with a court, a judge or a legal judgment: *the judicial system* ◇ *a judicial review*

judiciary /dʒuˈdɪʃəri/ noun [C + sing./pl. verb] (pl. -ies) (LAW) the judges of a country or a state, when they are considered as a group ⊃ look at **executive¹**, **legislature**

judicious /dʒuˈdɪʃəs/ adj. (formal) (used about a decision or an action) sensible and careful; showing good judgement ▸ **judiciously** adv.

judo /ˈdʒuːdəʊ/ noun [U] (SPORT) a sport from Asia in which two people fight and try to throw each other to the ground ⊃ look at **martial art**

jug /dʒʌg/ (BrE) (AmE pitcher) noun [C] a container with a handle used for holding or pouring liquids; the amount of liquid contained in a jug: *a milk jug* ◇ *a jug of water*

juggle /ˈdʒʌgl/ verb [I, T] 1 **~ (with sth)** to keep three or more objects such as balls in the air at the same time by throwing them one at a time and catching them quickly 2 **~ sth (with sth)** to try to deal with two or more important jobs or activities at the same time: *Working parents have to juggle their workload with family life.*

juggler /ˈdʒʌglə(r)/ noun [C] a person who JUGGLES to entertain people

jugular /ˈdʒʌgjələ(r)/ (also **jugular vein**) noun [C] (ANATOMY) any of the three large VEINS (= tubes) in the neck that carry blood away from the head to the heart

juice ₹ A1 /dʒuːs/ noun 1 [U, C] the liquid that comes from fruit and vegetables: *carrot/grapefruit/lemon juice* ◇ *I'll have an orange juice, please.* 2 [C, usually pl., U] the liquid that comes from a piece of meat when it is cooked: *You can use the juices of the meat to make gravy.* 3 [C, usually pl.] the liquid in the stomach that helps you DIGEST the food you eat: *gastric/digestive juices*

juicer /ˈdʒuːsə(r)/ *noun* [C] a piece of electrical equipment for getting the juice out of fruit or vegetables

juicy /ˈdʒuːsi/ *adj.* (**juicier**; **juiciest**) **1** containing a lot of juice: *juicy oranges* **2** (*informal*) (used about information) interesting because it is shocking: *juicy gossip*

jukebox /ˈdʒuːkbɒks/ *noun* [C] (**MUSIC**) a machine in a bar, etc. that plays music when you pay with cash or a card

Julian calendar /ˌdʒuːliən ˈkælɪndə(r)/ *noun* [sing.] (**HISTORY**) the system of arranging days and months in the year introduced by Julius Caesar, and used in Western countries until the GREGORIAN CALENDAR replaced it

July A1 /dʒuˈlaɪ/ *noun* [U, C] (*abbr.* **Jul.**) the seventh month of the year, between June and August

jumble[1] /ˈdʒʌmbl/ *verb* [T, often passive] **~ sth (up/together)** to mix things together in a confused and untidy way

jumble[2] /ˈdʒʌmbl/ *noun* **1** [sing.] an untidy group of things: *a jumble of papers/ideas* **2** [U] (*BrE*) a collection of old things for a JUMBLE SALE: *Have you got any jumble you don't want?*

ˈ**jumble sale** (*BrE*) (*also* **rummage sale** *especially in AmE*) *noun* [C] a sale of old things that people do not want any more. Clubs, churches, schools and other organizations hold jumble sales to get money.

jumbo[1] /ˈdʒʌmbəʊ/ *adj.* [only before noun] (*informal*) very large: *a jumbo pack of cornflakes*

jumbo[2] /ˈdʒʌmbəʊ/ (*pl.* **-os**) (*also* ˈ**jumbo jet**) *noun* [C] a very large aircraft that can carry several hundred passengers

jump[1] A2 /dʒʌmp/ *verb*

- MOVE OFF THE GROUND **1** [I] (used with an adverb or a preposition) to move quickly into the air by pushing yourself up with your legs and feet, or by stepping off a high place: *to jump into the air/off a bridge/onto a chair* ◇ *How high can you jump?* ◇ *Jump up and down to keep warm.*
- MOVE QUICKLY **2** [I] (used with an adverb or a preposition) to move quickly and suddenly: *The doorbell rang and she jumped up to answer it.* ◇ *A taxi stopped and we jumped in.*
- GO OVER **3** [I, T] **~ (over) sth** to get over sth by jumping: *The dog jumped (over) the fence and ran off down the road.*
- FROM SURPRISE/FEAR **4** [I] to make a sudden movement because of surprise or fear: *'Oh, it's only you — you made me jump,' he said.*
- INCREASE **5** [I] **~ (from ...) (to ...)**; **~ (by ...)** to increase suddenly by a very large amount: *His salary jumped from £40 000 to £50 000 last year.* ◇ *Prices jumped by 50 per cent in the summer.* ➲ note at **trend**[1]
- CHANGE SUDDENLY **6** [I] **~ (from sth) to sth** to go suddenly from one point in a series, a story, etc. to another: *The book kept jumping from the present to the past.*

IDM climb/jump on the bandwagon → BANDWAGON **jump for joy** to be extremely happy about sth **jump the gun** to do sth too soon, before the proper time **jump the queue** (*BrE*) to go to the front of a line of people without waiting for your turn **jump to conclusions** to decide that sth is true without thinking about it carefully enough

PHR V jump at sth to accept an opportunity, offer, etc. with enthusiasm: *Of course I jumped at the chance to work in New York for a year.*

jump[2] A2 /dʒʌmp/ *noun* [C] **1** an act of jumping: *With a huge jump the horse cleared the hedge.* ◇ *to do a parachute jump* ➲ look at **high jump**, **long jump** **2 ~ (in sth)** a sudden increase in amount, price or value **3** a thing to be jumped over: *The horse fell at the first jump.*

jumper /ˈdʒʌmpə(r)/ *noun* [C] **1** (*BrE*) a KNITTED piece of clothing made of wool or cotton for the upper part of the body, with long SLEEVES and no buttons **SYN jersey, pullover, sweater** **2** a person or an animal that jumps

jumpy /ˈdʒʌmpi/ *adj.* (*informal*) (**jumpier**; **jumpiest**) nervous or worried

junction + C1 /ˈdʒʌŋkʃn/ *noun* [C] a place where roads, railway lines, etc. meet

June A1 /dʒuːn/ *noun* [U, C] (*abbr.* **Jun.**) the sixth month of the year, between May and July

jungle /ˈdʒʌŋgl/ *noun* [C, U] (**GEOGRAPHY**) a thick forest in a tropical country: *the jungles of Africa and South America* ➲ note at **forest**

junior[1] B2 /ˈdʒuːniə(r)/ *adj.* **1 ~ (to sb)** having a low or lower position (than sb) in an organization, etc: *a junior officer/doctor/employee* ◇ *She is junior to me.* **OPP senior**[1] **2 Junior** (*abbr.* **Jnr**, **Jr**, **Jr.**) (especially in the US) used after the name of a son who has the same first name as his father: *Sammy Davis, Junior* **3** [only before noun] of or for children below a particular age: *the junior athletics championships* ➲ look at **senior**[1] (3) **4** (*AmE*) (**EDUCATION**) connected with the year before the last year in a HIGH SCHOOL or college

junior[2] /ˈdʒuːniə(r)/ *noun* **1** [C] a young person below a particular age, rather than an adult: *At 16, he can still play for the juniors.* **2** [C] (*BrE*) (**EDUCATION**) a child who goes to JUNIOR SCHOOL: *The juniors are having an outing to a museum today.* **3** [C] (*AmE*) (**EDUCATION**) a student in the year before the last year in a HIGH SCHOOL or college ➲ look at **senior**[2] (3), **sophomore** (2) **4** [C] a person who has a low position in an organization, etc.

ˌ**junior** ˈ**college** *noun* [C] (**EDUCATION**) (in the US) a college that offers programmes that are two years long. Some students go to a university or a college offering four-year programmes after they have finished studying at a junior college.

ˌ**junior** ˈ**high school** (*also* ˌ**junior** ˈ**high**) *noun* [C, U] (**EDUCATION**) (in the US and Canada) a school for young people between the ages of 12 and 14 ➲ look at **senior high school**

ˈ**junior school** *noun* [C, U] (in England and Wales) a school for children between the ages of 7 and 11 ➲ look at **primary school**

junk /dʒʌŋk/ *noun* **1** [U] things that have no use or value: *There's an awful lot of junk up in the attic.* **2** = (*U*) JUNK FOOD **3** [C] a Chinese boat with a square sail and a flat bottom

ˈ**junk food** (*also* **junk**) *noun* [U] (*informal*) food that is not very good for you but that is ready to eat or quick to prepare

junkie /ˈdʒʌŋki/ *noun* [C] (*informal*) a person who is unable to stop taking dangerous drugs **SYN addict**

ˈ**junk mail** *noun* [U] (**BUSINESS**) advertising material that is sent to people who have not asked for it ➲ look at **spam**

junta /ˈdʒʌntə/ *noun* [C] a group, especially of military officers, who rule a country by force

Jupiter /ˈdʒuːpɪtə(r)/ *noun* [sing.] (**ASTRONOMY**) the planet in the SOLAR SYSTEM that is fifth in order of distance from the sun ➲ picture at **solar system**

Jurassic /dʒʊˈræsɪk/ *adj.* (**GEOLOGY**) connected with the period between around 208 to 146 million years ago, when DINOSAURS lived

jurisdiction ʒ+ **C1** /ˌdʒʊərɪsˈdɪkʃn/ noun [U] (**LAW**) legal power or authority; the area in which this power can be used: *That question is outside the jurisdiction of this council.*

jurisprudence /ˌdʒʊərɪsˈpruːdns/ noun [U] (**LAW**) the scientific study of law

juror /ˈdʒʊərə(r)/ noun [C] (**LAW**) a member of a JURY

jury ʒ+ **B2** /ˈdʒʊəri/ noun [C + sing./pl. verb] (pl. -ies) **1** (**LAW**) a group of members of the public in a court who listen to the facts about a crime and decide if sb is guilty or not guilty: *Has/have the jury reached a verdict?* ➷ note at **court**¹ **2** (**SPORT**) a group of people who decide who is the winner in a competition: *The jury is/are about to announce the winners.*

just¹ ʒ **A1** /dʒʌst/ adv. **1** a very short time before: *She's just been to the shops.* ◇ *He'd just returned from France when I saw him.* ◇ *They came here just before Easter.* **2** at exactly this/that moment, or immediately after: *He was **just about to** break the window when he noticed a policeman.* ◇ *I was **just going to** phone my mother when she arrived.* ◇ ***Just as** I was beginning to enjoy myself, John said it was time to go.* ◇ ***Just then** the door opened.* **3** exactly: *It's just eight o'clock.* ◇ *That's **just what** I meant.* ◇ *The room was too hot before, but now it's **just right**.* ◇ *He looks **just like** his father.* ◇ *My arm hurts **just here**.* **4** only; simply: *She's just a child.* ◇ *Just a minute! I'm nearly ready.* ◇ *It was just an ordinary day.* ◇ *I just don't want to go to the party.* **5** almost not: *I could **only just** hear what she was saying.* ◇ *We got to the station **just in time**.* **6** used in orders for getting attention, giving permission, etc.: *Just let me speak for a moment, will you?* ◇ *Just help yourself.* **7** used with **might**, **may** or **could** to express a slight possibility: *This might **just/just might** be the most important decision of your life.* **8** really; absolutely: *The whole day was just fantastic!* **IDM** **all/just the same** → SAME¹ **it is just as well (that …)** it is a good thing: *It's **just as well** you remembered to bring your umbrella!* **just about 1** almost: *I've **just about** finished.* **2** approximately: *Karen's plane should be taking off **just about** now.* **just in case** in order to be completely prepared or safe: *It might be hot in France — take your shorts **just in case**.* **just now 1** at this exact moment or during this exact period: *I can't come with you **just now** — can you wait 20 minutes?* **2** a very short time ago: *I saw Tony **just now**.* **just so** exactly right **not just yet** not now, but probably quite soon

just² ʒ+ **C1** /dʒʌst/ adj. fair and right; reasonable: *I don't think that was a very just decision.* ▸ **justly** adv.

justice ʒ **B2** /ˈdʒʌstɪs/ noun **1** [U] the fair treatment of people: *a struggle for justice* **2** [U] the quality of being fair or reasonable: *Everybody realized the justice of what he was saying.* **3** [U] (**LAW**) the law and the way it is used: *the criminal justice system* **4** [C] (*AmE*) (**LAW**) a judge in a court **IDM** **do justice to sb/sth | do sb/sth justice** to treat sb/sth fairly or to show the real quality of sb/sth: *I don't like her, but to do her justice, she's a very clever woman.* ◇ *The photo doesn't do him justice — he's actually very good-looking.* **a miscarriage of justice** → MISCARRIAGE

Justice of the Peace noun [C] (*abbr.* JP) (*formal*) (**LAW**) (in the UK) a person who judges less serious cases in court

justifiable /ˈdʒʌstɪfaɪəbl, ˌdʒʌstɪˈfaɪəbl/ adj. that you can accept because there is a good reason for it: *His action was entirely justifiable.* ▸ **justifiably** /-bli/ adv.

justification ʒ+ **C1** **W** /ˌdʒʌstɪfɪˈkeɪʃn/ noun [C, U] ~ (**for sth/doing sth**) (*formal*) (a) good reason: *I can't see any justification for cutting his salary.* ➷ note at **reason**¹

justified /ˈdʒʌstɪfaɪd/ adj. **1** ~ (**in doing sth**) having a good reason for doing sth: *She felt fully justified in asking for her money back.* **2** existing or done for a good reason: *His fears proved justified.* **OPP** **unjustified**

justify ʒ **B2** **W** /ˈdʒʌstɪfaɪ/ verb [T] (justifying; justifies; pt, pp justified) to give or be a good reason for sth: *Can you justify your decision?*

just-in-ˈtime adj. = JIT

jut /dʒʌt/ verb [I] (-tt-) ~ (**out**) (**from/into/over sth**) to stick out further than the surrounding surface, objects, etc.: *rocks that jut out into the sea*

jute /dʒuːt/ noun [U] thin THREADS from a plant that are used for making rope and rough cloth

juvenile /ˈdʒuːvənaɪl/ adj. **1** [only before noun] (*formal*) (**LAW**) of, for or involving young people who are not yet adults: *juvenile crime* ◇ *juvenile court* **2** silly and more typical of a child than an adult: *He's 20 but he is still quite juvenile.* ▸ **juvenile** noun [C]

juvenile deˈlinquent noun [C] (**LAW**) a young person who is guilty of committing a crime

juxtapose /ˌdʒʌkstəˈpəʊz/ verb [T] (*formal*) to put two people, things, etc. together, especially in order to show how they are different: *The artist achieves a special effect by juxtaposing light and dark.* ▸ **juxtaposition** /ˌdʒʌkstəpəˈzɪʃn/ noun [U, C]

K k

K¹ /keɪ/ (*also* k) noun [C, U] (pl. K's, k's) the eleventh letter of the English alphabet: *'Kate' begins with (a) 'K'.*

K² /keɪ/ abbr. (pl. K) **1** (*informal*) (used especially about quantities of money) a thousand: *She earns 22K (= £22 000) a year.* **2** (*informal*) = KILOMETRE **3** (in writing) = KELVIN **4** (in writing) = KILOBYTE

kaizen /ˈkaɪzen/ noun [U] (**BUSINESS**) the practice of continuously improving the way in which a company operates

kaleidoscope /kəˈlaɪdəskəʊp/ noun **1** [C] a toy that consists of a tube containing mirrors and small pieces of coloured glass. When you look into one end of the tube and turn it, you see changing patterns of colours. **2** [sing.] a situation, pattern, etc. containing a lot of different parts that are always changing

kanban /ˈkænbæn/ (*also* ˈkanban system) noun [U] (**BUSINESS**) a system for checking progress in producing goods through the use of instruction cards that accompany products as they move through the production process: *Kanban is a style of working that began in Japanese car manufacturing plants.* ◇ *A **kanban board** is a method of visually keeping track of the tasks.*

kangaroo /ˌkæŋɡəˈruː/ noun [C] (pl. -oos) a large Australian animal that moves by jumping on its strong back legs. The female kangaroo carries its young in a POUCH (= a pocket of skin) on the front of its body. ➷ picture at **animal**

kaolin /ˈkeɪəlɪn/ (*also* china clay) noun [U] (**GEOLOGY**, **MEDICINE**) a type of fine white CLAY that is used in some medicines and in making cups, plates, etc.

karaoke /ˌkæriˈəʊki/ noun [U] (**MUSIC**) a type of entertainment in which a machine plays only the music of popular songs so that people can sing the words themselves: *a karaoke machine/night/bar*

karat /ˈkærət/ (*AmE*) = CARAT

karate /kəˈrɑːti/ *noun* [U] (**SPORT**) a style of fighting originally from Japan in which the hands and feet are used as weapons ⊃ look at **martial art**

karma /ˈkɑːmə/ *noun* [U] (**RELIGION**) (in Buddhism and Hinduism) all of sb's good and bad actions in one of their lives that are believed to decide what will happen to them in the next life

kart /kɑːt/ = GO-KART

katabolism /kəˈtæbəlɪzəm/ = CATABOLISM

kayak /ˈkaɪæk/ *noun* [C] a light narrow boat for one person in which the part where you sit is covered over ⊃ picture at **canoe**

kayaking /ˈkaɪækɪŋ/ *noun* [U] (**SPORT**) the activity or sport of travelling in a KAYAK: *Guests can go kayaking on the lake.*

KB *abbr.* (in writing) (*pl.* KB) = KILOBYTE

Kb *abbr.* (in writing) (*pl.* Kb) = KILOBIT

KC /ˌkeɪ ˈsiː/ *noun* [C] (**LAW**) (used when there is a king in the UK) the highest level of BARRISTER (= a type of lawyer) who can speak for the government in court in the UK (the abbreviation for 'King's Counsel') ⊃ look at **QC** ⊃ note at **lawyer**

kebab /kɪˈbæb/ *noun* [C] small pieces of meat and vegetables that are cooked on a wooden or metal stick

keel¹ /kiːl/ *noun* [C] a long piece of wood or metal on the bottom of a boat that stops it falling over on its side in the water

keel² /kiːl/ *verb*
PHR V **keel over** to fall over

keen 🔊 **B1** /kiːn/ *adj.* **1** ~ **(to do sth); ~ (that …)** very interested in sth; wanting to do sth: *They are both keen gardeners.* ◊ *I failed the first time but I'm keen to try again.* ◊ *She was keen that we should all be there.* **2** ~ **(on sb/sth)** very interested in sth/sb; liking sb/sth very much: *He's very keen on jazz.* **3** (used about one of the senses, a feeling, etc.) good or strong: *Foxes have a keen sense of smell.* ▶ **keenly** *adv.* ▶ **keenness** *noun* [U]

keep¹ 🔊 **A1** /kiːp/ *verb* (*pt, pp* **kept** /kept/)
• NOT GIVE BACK/SAVE **1** [T] to continue to have sth; to save sth for sb: *You can keep that book — I don't need it any more.* ◊ *Can I keep the car until next week?* ◊ *Can you keep my seat for me till I get back?*
• PUT/STORE **2** [T] to have sth in a particular place: *Where do you keep the matches?* ◊ *Keep your passport in a safe place.*
• STAY **3** [I, T] to continue to be in a particular state or position; to make sb/sth do this: *Keep left along the wall.* ◊ *You must keep warm.* ◊ *That child can't keep still.* ◊ *Please keep this door closed.* ◊ *He kept his hands in his pockets.* ◊ *I'm sorry to keep you waiting.*
• CONTINUE **4** [I] ~ **doing sth** to continue doing sth or to repeat an action many times: *Keep going until you get to the church and then turn left.* ◊ *She keeps asking me silly questions.*
• PROMISE/ARRANGEMENT **5** [T] to do what you promised or arranged: *Can you keep a promise?* ◊ *She didn't keep her appointment at the dentist's.* ◊ *to keep a secret* (= not tell it to anyone)
• DIARY/RECORD **6** [T] to write down sth that you want to remember: *Keep a record of how much you spend.* ◊ *to keep a diary* ⊃ note at **meeting**
• ANIMALS **7** [T] to have and look after animals: *They keep ducks on their farm.*
• SUPPORT **8** [T] to support sb with your money: *You can't keep a family on the money I earn.*
• DELAY **9** [T] to delay sb/sth; to prevent sb from leaving: *Where's the doctor? What's keeping him?*
• FOOD **10** [I] (used about food) to stay fresh: *Eat up all the strawberries — they won't keep until tomorrow.*

IDM **keep going** to make an effort, especially when you are in a difficult situation: *You just have to keep yourself busy and keep going.* **keep it up** to continue doing sth as well as you are doing it now ❶ For other idioms containing **keep**, look at the entries for the nouns and adjectives. For example, **keep count** is at **count**.
PHR V **keep at it/sth** to continue to work on/at sth: *Keep at it — we should be finished soon.* **keep away from sb/sth** to not go near sb/sth: *Keep away from the town centre this weekend.* **keep sb/sth back** to prevent sb/sth from moving forwards: *The police tried to keep the crowd back.* **keep sth back (from sb)** to refuse to tell sb sth: *I know he's keeping something back; he knows much more than he says.* **keep sth down** to make sth stay at a low level; to stop sth increasing: *Keep your voice down.* **keep sb from sth/ doing sth** to prevent sb from doing sth **keep sth from sb** to refuse to tell sb sth **keep your mouth shut** → MOUTH¹ **keep off sth** to not go near or on sth: *Keep off the grass!* **keep sth off (sb/sth)** to stop sth touching or going on sth/sb: *I'm trying to keep the flies off the food.* **keep on (doing sth)** to continue doing sth or to repeat an action many times, especially in an annoying way: *He keeps on interrupting me.* **keep on (at sb) (about sth)** to continue talking to sb in an annoying or complaining way: *She kept on at me about my homework until I did it.* **keep (sb/sth) out (of sth)** to not enter sth; to stop sb/sth entering sth: *They put up a fence to keep people out of their garden.* **keep to sth** to not leave sth; to do sth in the usual, agreed or expected way: *Keep to the path!* ◊ *He didn't keep to our agreement.* **keep sth to/at sth** to not allow sth to rise above a particular level: *We're trying to keep costs to a minimum.* **keep sth up 1** to prevent sth from falling down **2** to make sth stay at a high level: *We want to keep up standards of education.* **3** to continue doing sth **keep up (with sb)** to do sth at the same speed as sb: *Can't you walk a bit slower? I can't keep up.* **keep up (with sth)** to know about what is happening: *You have to follow social media if you want to keep up.*

keep² /kiːp/ *noun* **1** [U] food, clothes and the other things that you need to live; the cost of these things: *to earn your keep* **2** [C] (**HISTORY**) a large strong tower, built as part of an old castle
IDM **for keeps** (*informal*) for always: *Take it. It's yours for keeps.*

keeper /ˈkiːpə(r)/ *noun* [C] **1** a person who guards or looks after sth: *a zookeeper* **2** (*informal*) = GOALKEEPER

keep-'fit *noun* [U] (*BrE*) physical exercises that you do, usually in a class with other people, in order to improve your strength and to stay healthy: *a keep-fit class*

keeping /ˈkiːpɪŋ/ *noun*
IDM **in/out of keeping (with sth) 1** that does/does not look good with sth: *That modern table is out of keeping with the style of the room.* **2** in/not in agreement with a rule, belief, etc: *The Council's decision is in keeping with government policy.*

keg /keg/ *noun* [C] a round metal or wooden container, used especially for storing beer

kelvin /ˈkelvɪn/ *noun* [C, U] (*abbr.* K) (**SCIENCE**) a unit for measuring temperature ❶ One degree **kelvin** is equal to one degree **Celsius**. Zero kelvin is **absolute zero**.

kennel /ˈkenl/ *noun* [C] a small house for a dog

kept /kept/ past tense, past participle of **keep¹**

keratin /ˈkerətɪn/ *noun* [U] (**BIOLOGY**) a PROTEIN that forms hair, feathers, HORNS, HOOFS, etc.

kerb (*BrE*) (*AmE* **curb**) /kɜːb/ *noun* [C] the edge of the raised path at the side of a road, usually made of long pieces of stone: *They stood on the kerb waiting to cross the road.*

kernel /'kɜːnl/ *noun* [C] **1** the inner part of a nut or seed **2** the most important part of an idea or a subject

kerosene /'kerəsiːn/ (*AmE*) = PARAFFIN

ketchup /'ketʃəp/ *noun* [U] a thick cold sauce made from tomatoes, usually sold in bottles

kettle /'ketl/ *noun* [C] a container with a LID, used for boiling water: *an electric kettle*

kettledrum /'ketldrʌm/ *noun* [C] (**MUSIC**) a large metal drum with a round bottom and a thin plastic top that can be made looser or tighter to produce different musical notes. A set of kettledrums is usually called TIMPANI. ➔ picture at **instrument**

key¹ ⚑ A1 ⑤ /kiː/ *noun* [C]
• TOOL FOR LOCKING **1** a metal object that is used for locking a door, starting a car, etc: *Have you seen my car keys anywhere?* ◇ *We need a spare key to the front door.* ◇ *a bunch of keys*
• MOST IMPORTANT PART **2** [usually sing.] **the ~ (to sth)** something that helps you achieve or understand sth: *A good education is the key to success.*
• ON A PIANO/COMPUTER **3** (**COMPUTING, MUSIC**) one of the parts of a piano, computer, etc. that you press with your fingers to make it work
• IN MUSIC **4** a set of musical notes that is based on one particular note: *The concerto is in the key of A minor.*
• ANSWERS **5** (**EDUCATION**) a set of answers to exercises or problems: *an answer key*
• ON A MAP **6** a list of the symbols and signs used in a map or book, showing what they mean
IDM **under lock and key** → LOCK²

key² ⚑ B1 /kiː/ *verb* [T] **~ sth (in)** to put information into a computer or give it an instruction by typing: *Have you keyed that report yet?* ◇ *First, key in your password.*

key³ ⚑ A1 ⑥ /kiː/ *adj.* very important: *Tourism is a key industry in Spain.* ➔ note at **main¹**

keyboard ⚑ B1 /'kiːbɔːd/ *noun* [C] **1** (**COMPUTING, MUSIC**) the set of keys on a piano, computer, etc. ➔ note at **instrument** ➔ picture at **piano 2** (**MUSIC**) an electrical musical instrument like a small piano ➔ picture at **piano**

keyhole /'kiːhəʊl/ *noun* [C] the hole in a lock where you put the key

keyhole surgery *noun* [U] (*especially BrE*) (**MEDICINE**) medical operations that involve only a very small cut being made in the patient's body

keynote /'kiːnəʊt/ *noun* [C] **1** [usually sing.] the main idea of a book, a speech, etc: *Choice is the keynote of the new education policy.* ◇ *a keynote speech/speaker* (= a very important one, introducing a meeting or its subject) **2** (**MUSIC**) the note on which the KEY (= a set of related notes) is based

keypad /'kiːpæd/ *noun* [C] (**COMPUTING**) a small set of buttons with numbers on that you press when you use a phone, TV, etc.

key ring *noun* [C] a ring on which you keep keys

key signature *noun* [C] (**MUSIC**) the set of marks at the beginning of a piece of music that are used to show what KEY the piece is in (= the particular set of notes that it uses) ➔ picture at **music**

keystone /'kiːstəʊn/ *noun* [C] **1** (**ARCHITECTURE**) the central stone at the top of an ARCH that keeps all the other stones in the right place **2** [usually sing.] the most

important part of a plan or argument that the other parts depend on: *Changes to the welfare system are the keystone of the government's reforms.*

keyword /'kiːwɜːd/ *noun* [C] **1** a word that tells you about the main idea or subject of sth: *When you're studying a language, the keyword is patience.* **2** (**COMPUTING**) a word or phrase that is used to give an instruction to or search for information on a computer

key worker *noun* [C] (*BrE*) a worker in one of the most important services such as health, education or the police

kg *abbr.* (in writing) (*pl.* kg) = KILOGRAM: *weight 10kg*

khaki /'kɑːki/ *adj.* yellow-brown in colour: *the khaki uniforms of the desert soldiers* ▸ **khaki** *noun* [U]

kHz *abbr.* (in writing) (*pl.* kHz) = KILOHERTZ

kibbutz /kɪˈbʊts/ *noun* [C] (*pl.* **kibbutzim** /ˌkɪbʊtˈsiːm/) (**SOCIAL STUDIES**) (in Israel) a type of farm or factory where a group of people live together and share all the work, decisions and income

kick¹ ⚑ A2 /kɪk/ *verb* **1** [T] to hit or move sb/sth with your foot: *He kicked the ball wide of the net.* ◇ *The police kicked the door down.* **2** [T, I] to move your foot or feet as if you were kicking sth: *You must kick harder if you want to swim faster.* **3** [T] **~ yourself** (*informal*) to be annoyed with yourself because you have done sth stupid, missed an opportunity, etc. **4** [T] (*informal*) to stop doing sth harmful that you have done for a long time: *I'd been a smoker for years and wanted to kick the habit.*
IDM **make, kick up, etc. a fuss** → FUSS¹
PHR V **kick off** (**SPORT**) to start a game of football **kick sb out (of sth)** (*informal*) to force sb to leave a place: *to be kicked out of university*

kick² ⚑ B1 /kɪk/ *noun* [C] **1** an act of kicking: *She gave the door a kick and it closed.* **2** (*informal*) a feeling of great pleasure, excitement, etc: *He seems to get a real kick out of driving fast.*

kick-off *noun* [C] (**SPORT**) the start of a game of football: *The kick-off is at 2.30.*

kick-start¹ *verb* [T] **1** to start a motorcycle by pushing down on one of the controls with your foot **2** to do sth to help a process or project start more quickly

kick-start² *noun* [C] **1** (*also* **kick-starter**) the part of a motorcycle that you push down with your foot in order to start it **2** a quick start that you give to sth by taking some action

kid¹ ⚑ A2 /kɪd/ *noun* **1** [C] (*informal*) a child or young person: *How are your kids?* **2** [C, U] a young GOAT (= a small animal with HORNS that lives in mountain areas) or its skin ➔ picture at **goat 3** [U] soft leather made from the skin of a young GOAT

kid² /kɪd/ *verb* [I, T] (**-dd-**) (*informal*) to trick sb/yourself by saying sth that is not true; to make a joke about sth: *I didn't mean it. I was only kidding.*

kiddie (*also* **kiddy**) /'kɪdi/ *noun* [C] (*pl.* **-ies**) (*informal*) a child

kidnap ⚑+ C1 /'kɪdnæp/ *verb* [T] (**-pp-**) (**LAW**) to take sb away by force and demand money for their safe return: *The child was kidnapped and a ransom of £50 000 was demanded for her release.* ➔ look at **hijack** (1) ▸ **kidnapper** *noun* [C]: *The kidnappers demanded £50 000.* ➔ note at **criminal¹** ▸ **kidnapping** *noun* [C, U]

kidney ⚑+ C1 /'kɪdni/ *noun* **1** [C] (**ANATOMY**) either of the two parts of the body that separate waste liquid from the blood ➔ picture at **body, circulation 2** [U, C] the kidneys of an animal when they are cooked and eaten as food: *steak and kidney pie* ➔ adjective **renal**

ˈ**kidney bean** *noun* [C] a type of red-brown bean shaped like a KIDNEY

kill¹ A2 /kɪl/ *verb* **1** [T, I] to make sb/sth die: *She was killed instantly in the crash.* ◇ *My mum will kill me* (= be very angry with me) *when she sees this mess.* ◇ *Smoking kills.* **2** [T] (*informal*) to cause sb pain; to hurt: *My feet are killing me.* **3** [T] to cause sth to end or fail: *The minister's opposition killed the idea stone dead.* **IDM** **kill time, an hour, etc.** to spend time doing sth that is not interesting or important while you are waiting for sth else to happen **kill two birds with one stone** to do one thing that will achieve two results **PHR V** **kill sth off** to cause sth to die or to not exist any more

▼ VOCABULARY BUILDING

Murder means to kill a person on purpose: *This was no accident. The old lady was murdered.* **Assassinate** means to kill for political reasons: *President Kennedy was assassinated.* **Slaughter** and **massacre** mean to kill a large number of people: *Hundreds of people were massacred when the army opened fire on the crowd.* **Slaughter** is also used about killing an animal for food.

kill² /kɪl/ *noun* [sing.] **1** the act of killing: *Lions often make a kill in the evening.* **2** an animal or animals that have been killed: *The eagle took the kill back to its young.*

killer /ˈkɪlə(r)/ *noun* [C] a person, an animal or a thing that kills: *a killer disease* ◇ *He's a dangerous killer who may strike again.*

ˈ**killer whale** *noun* [C] a black and white WHALE that eats meat

killing B1 /ˈkɪlɪŋ/ *noun* [C] an act of killing a person on purpose; a murder: *There have been a number of brutal killings in the area recently.* **IDM** **make a killing** to make a large profit quickly

ˈ**kill switch** *noun* [C] a switch that can quickly stop a machine working, especially if something goes wrong ➲ picture at **safety**

kiln /kɪln/ *noun* [C] a large oven for baking CLAY (= a type of earth used to make things) and BRICKS, drying wood and grain etc.

kilo /ˈkiːləʊ/ *noun* [C] (*pl.* **-os**) = KILOGRAM

kilo- /kɪləʊ, kɪlə, kɪˈlɒ/ *prefix* (in units of measurement) one thousand: *kilometre* ◇ *kilogram*

kilobit /ˈkɪləbɪt/ *noun* [C] (*abbr.* **Kb**) (**COMPUTING**) a unit of computer memory or data, equal to 1 000 BITS (= the smallest units of information)

kilobyte /ˈkɪləbaɪt/ *noun* [C] (*abbr.* **K, KB**) (**COMPUTING**) a unit of computer memory or data, equal to 1 000 BYTES (= small units of information)

kilogram (*also* **kilogramme**) /ˈkɪləɡræm/ (*also* **kilo**) *noun* [C] (*abbr.* **kg**) a measure of weight; 1 000 GRAMS ❶ For more information about weights, look at the **Reference Section** of this dictionary.

kilohertz /ˈkɪləhɜːts/ *noun* [C] (*pl.* **kilohertz**) (*abbr.* **kHz**) (**PHYSICS**) a unit for measuring radio waves

kilojoule /ˈkɪlədʒuːl/ *noun* [C] (*abbr.* **kJ**) (**PHYSICS**) a measurement of the energy that you get from food; 1 000 JOULES

kilometre A1 (*BrE*) (*AmE* **kilometer**) /kɪˈlɒmɪtə(r), ˈkɪləmiːtə(r)/ *noun* [C] (*abbr.* **km, k**) a measure of length; 1 000 metres

kilowatt /ˈkɪləwɒt/ *noun* [C] (*abbr.* **kW**) (**PHYSICS**) a unit for measuring electrical power; 1 000 WATTS

kilt /kɪlt/ *noun* [C] a skirt made of TARTAN cloth that is traditionally worn by Scottish men; a similar skirt worn by women ➲ look at **tartan**

kimono /kɪˈməʊnəʊ/ *noun* [C] (*pl.* **-os**) a traditional Japanese piece of clothing like a long dress with wide SLEEVES (= parts covering the arms), worn on formal occasions

kin /kɪn/ *noun* [C, pl.] (*old-fashioned or formal*) your family or your relatives ➲ look at **next of kin**

kind¹ A1 S /kaɪnd/ *noun* [C] **~ (of sb/sth)** a group of people or things that are the same in some way; a particular variety or type: *The concert attracted people* ***of all kinds***. ◇ *The concert attracted* ***all kinds*** *of people.* ◇ *What kind of car have you got?* ◇ *Many kinds of plant and animal are being lost every year.* ◇ *In the evenings I listen to music, catch up on social media, that* ***kind of thing***. **SYN** **sort¹, type¹**
IDM **a kind of** (*informal*) used for describing sth in a way that is not very clear: *I had a kind of feeling that something would go wrong.* **kind of** (*informal*) slightly; in some ways: *I'm kind of worried about the interview.* **of a kind** **1** the same: *The friends were two of a kind — very similar in so many ways.* **2** not as good as it could be: *You're making progress of a kind.*

kind² B1 /kaɪnd/ *adj.* **~ (to sb); ~ (of sb) (to do sth)** caring about others; friendly and generous: *Everyone's been so kind to us since we came here!* ◇ *It was kind of you to offer, but I don't need any help.* **OPP** **unkind**

kindergarten /ˈkɪndəɡɑːtn/ *noun* [C] (**EDUCATION**) **1** (*especially AmE*) a school or class to prepare children aged 5 for school **2** a school for children between the ages of about 2 and 5 ➲ look at **nursery school**

ˌ**kind-ˈhearted** *adj.* kind and generous

kindly /ˈkaɪndli/ *adv., adj.* **1** in a kind way: *The nurse smiled kindly.* **2** (*old-fashioned, informal*) (used for asking sb to do sth) please: *Would you kindly wait a moment?* **3** kind and friendly

kindness /ˈkaɪndnəs/ *noun* [U, C] the quality of being kind; a kind act: *Thank you very much for all your kindness.*

kinetic /kɪˈnetɪk, kaɪ-/ *adj.* (**PHYSICS**) of or produced by movement: *kinetic energy* ➲ picture at **energy**

kiˌnetic ˈart *noun* [U] (**ART**) art, especially sculpture, with parts that move

king A2 /kɪŋ/ *noun* [C] **1** (**POLITICS**) (the title of) a man who rules a country. A king is usually the son or close relative of the former ruler: *The new king was crowned in Westminster Abbey.* ◇ *King Edward VII* (= the seventh) ◇ (*figurative*) *The lion is the king of the jungle.* ➲ look at **prince, princess, queen** **2** one of the four PLAYING CARDS in a PACK, with a picture of a king: *the king of spades* **3** the most important piece in the game of CHESS that can move one square in any direction

kingdom + C1 /ˈkɪŋdəm/ *noun* [C] **1** (**POLITICS**) a country that is ruled by a king or queen: *the United Kingdom* **2** (**BIOLOGY**) one of the five major groups into which all living things are organized, larger than a CLASS or a PHYLUM: *the animal kingdom* ➲ picture at **animal**

kingfisher /ˈkɪŋfɪʃə(r)/ *noun* [C] a small bright blue bird with a long BEAK (= the hard pointed part of a bird's mouth) that catches fish in rivers

ˈ**king-size** (*also* **king-sized**) *adj.* bigger than usual: *a king-size bed*

kink /kɪŋk/ *noun* [C] a turn or bend in sth that should be straight

kiosk /ˈkiːɒsk/ *noun* [C] a very small building in the street where newspapers, sweets, cigarettes, etc. are sold

kip /kɪp/ *verb* [I] (**-pp-**) (*BrE, informal*) to sleep: *You could kip on the sofa if you like.* ▶ **kip** *noun* [sing., U]

kipper /'kɪpə(r)/ *noun* [C] a HERRING (= a type of fish) that has been kept for a long time in salt, and then SMOKED

kiss ⚡ **B1** /kɪs/ *verb* [I, T] ~ **(sb) (on sth)** to touch sb with your lips to show love or sexual desire, or when saying hello or goodbye: *Do people in Britain kiss when they meet?* ◇ *He kissed her on the cheek.* ▶ **kiss** ⚡ **B1** *noun* [C] ~ **(on sth)** : *a kiss on the lips/cheek*

kit¹ ⚡+ **B2** /kɪt/ *noun* **1** [C, U] a set of tools, equipment or clothes that you need for a particular purpose, sport or activity: *a tool kit* ◇ *a drum kit* ◇ *football/gym kit* **2** [C] a set of parts that you buy and put together in order to make sth: *a kit for a model aeroplane*

kit² /kɪt/ *verb* (**-tt-**)
PHR V **kit sb/yourself out (in/with sth)** to give sb all the necessary clothes, equipment, tools, etc. for sth

kitchen ⚡ **A1** /'kɪtʃɪn/ *noun* [C] a room where food is prepared and cooked: *the kitchen floor/table/sink*

kite /kaɪt/ *noun* [C] **1** a toy that consists of a light frame covered with paper or cloth. Kites are flown in the wind on the end of a long piece of string: *to fly a kite* **2** a BIRD OF PREY (= a bird that kills other creatures for food) of the HAWK family

kitesurfing /'kaɪtsɜːfɪŋ/ (*also* **kiteboarding** /'kaɪtbɔːdɪŋ/) *noun* [U] (**SPORT**) the sport of riding on water while standing on a short wide board and being pulled along by wind power, using a large KITE

kitsch /kɪtʃ/ *noun* [U] works of art or objects that are popular but that are considered to have no real artistic value and to be lacking in good taste, for example because they are SENTIMENTAL

kitten /'kɪtn/ *noun* [C] a young cat

kitty /'kɪti/ *noun* [C] (*pl.* **-ies**) **1** a sum of money that is collected from a group of people and used for a particular purpose: *All the students in the flat put £10 a week into the kitty.* **2** (*informal*) a way of calling or referring to a cat

kiwi fruit /'kiːwi fruːt/ (*also* **kiwi**, *pl.* **kiwis**) *noun* [C] a fruit with brown skin that is green inside with black seeds

kJ *abbr.* (in writing) (*pl.* **kJ**) = KILOJOULE

km *abbr.* (in writing) (*pl.* **km**) = KILOMETRE

knack /næk/ *noun* [sing.] **the ~ (of sth/doing sth)**; **~ (for sth/doing sth)** (*informal*) a special skill or ability that you have naturally or can learn: *Knitting isn't difficult once you've got the knack of it.* ◇ *He's got a real knack for making money.*

knead /niːd/ *verb* [T] to press and SQUEEZE DOUGH (= a mixture of flour, water, etc.) with your hands in order to make it ready to use

knee ⚡ **A2** /niː/ *noun* [C] **1** (**ANATOMY**) the place where the leg bends in the middle: *Angie fell and grazed her knee.* ◇ *She was on her hands and knees on the floor looking for her earrings.* ◇ *Come and sit on my knee.* ⊃ picture at **body** **2** the part of a pair of trousers, etc. that covers the knee
IDM **bring sth to its knees** to badly affect an organization, etc. so that it can no longer function: *The strikes brought the industry to its knees.*

kneecap /'niːkæp/ *noun* [C] (**ANATOMY**) the bone that covers the front of the knee **SYN** **patella** ⊃ picture at **body**

knee-deep *adj., adv.* up to your knees: *The water was knee-deep in places.* ◇ *I waded in knee-deep but the water was too cold to swim in.*

kneel /niːl/ *verb* [I] (*pt, pp* **knelt** /nelt/, **kneeled** *especially AmE*) ~ **(down)** to rest on one or both knees: *She knelt down to talk to the child.*

knew /njuː/ past tense of **know¹**

knickers /'nɪkəz/ (*BrE*) (*also* **panties** *AmE, BrE*) *noun* [pl.] a piece of underwear for women that covers the body from the middle part to the tops of the legs: *a pair of knickers*

knife¹ ⚡ **A2** /naɪf/ *noun* [C] (*pl.* **knives**) a sharp BLADE (= flat piece of metal) with a handle, used for cutting things or as a weapon: *The carving knife is very blunt/sharp.* ◇ *a knife and fork* ◇ *a penknife/pocket knife/flick knife*

knife² /naɪf/ *verb* [T] to deliberately injure or kill sb with a knife **SYN** **stab¹**

knight /naɪt/ *noun* [C] **1** (in the UK) a man who has been given a title of honour by the king or queen and who can use 'Sir' in front of his name **2** (**HISTORY**) a man of high social rank who fought on a horse for his king in the Middle Ages **3** a piece used in the game of CHESS that is shaped like a horse's head ▶ **knighthood** /'naɪthʊd/ *noun* [C, U]

knit /nɪt/ *verb* [T, I] (**-tt-**) ❶ In sense 2 **knit** is usually used for the past tense and past participle. **1** to make sth (for example a piece of clothing) with wool using two long needles or a special machine: *I'm knitting a sweater for my nephew.* ⊃ look at **crochet 2** to join people or things closely together; to be joined closely together: *a closely/tightly knit village community* (= one in which relationships are very close)

knitting /'nɪtɪŋ/ *noun* [U] **1** an item that is being KNITTED (= made with wool using two long needles or a machine): *Where's my knitting?* **2** the activity of KNITTING: *to do some knitting*

knitting needle = NEEDLE (2)

knitwear /'nɪtweə(r)/ *noun* [U] pieces of clothing that have been KNITTED (= made with wool using two long needles or a machine): *the knitwear department*

knives /naɪvz/ plural of **knife**

knob /nɒb/ *noun* [C] **1** a round switch on a machine (for example a radio) that you press or turn: *the volume control knob* ⊃ picture at **oscilloscope 2** a round handle on a door, DRAWER, etc.

knock¹ ⚡ **A2** /nɒk/ *verb* **1** [I] ~ **(at/on sth)** to make a noise by hitting sth firmly with your hand: *Somebody is knocking at the door.* **2** [T] ~ **sth (on/against sth)** to hit sth hard, often by accident: *Be careful not to knock your head on the shelf when you get up.* **3** [T] (*informal*) to say bad things about sb/sth; to criticize sb/sth
IDM **knock on wood** (*AmE*) → TOUCH¹
PHR V **knock around** (*BrE also* **knock about**) (*informal*) to be in a place; to travel and live in various places: *Is last week's newspaper still knocking about?* **knock sb down** to hit sb causing them to fall to the ground: *The old lady was knocked down by a cyclist.* **knock sth down** to destroy a building, etc: *They knocked down the old factory because it was unsafe.* **knock off (sth)** (*informal*) to stop working: *What time do you knock off?* **knock sth off** (*informal*) to reduce a price by a certain amount: *He agreed to knock £10 off the price.* **2** (*slang*) to steal sth **knock sb out 1** make sb go to sleep or become unconscious **2** (used about a drug, alcohol, etc.) to cause sb to sleep **knock sb out (of sth)** (**SPORT**) to beat a person or team in a competition so that they do not play any more games in it: *Belgium was knocked out of the European Cup by France.* **knock sb/sth over** to cause sb/sth to fall over: *Be careful not to knock over the drinks.*

knock² ⚡ **B1** /nɒk/ *noun* [C] a sharp hit from sth hard or the sound it makes: *a nasty knock on the head* ◇ *I thought I heard a knock at the door.* ◇ (*figurative*) *She has* *suffered some hard knocks* (= bad experiences) *in her life.*

knocker /ˈnɒkə(r)/ *noun* [C] a piece of metal fixed to the outside of a door that you hit against the door to attract attention

knock-ˈon *adj.* [only before noun] (*especially BrE*) causing other events to happen one after the other: *An increase in the price of oil has **a knock-on effect** on other goods.*

knockout /ˈnɒkaʊt/ *noun* [C] (**SPORT**) **1** (in BOXING) a hard hit that causes sb to become unconscious or to be unable to get up again for a while **2** (*especially BrE*) a competition in which the winner of each game goes on to the next part but the person or team that loses plays no more games

knot¹ /nɒt/ *noun* [C] **1** a place where two ends or pieces of rope, string, etc. have been tied together: *to tie/ untie a knot* **2** a measure of the speed of a ship; approximately 1.8 kilometres per hour **3** a hard round spot in a piece of wood where there was once a branch

knot² /nɒt/ *verb* [T] (-tt-) to fasten sth together with a KNOT

know¹ ᵻ **A1** /nəʊ/ *verb* (not used in the progressive tenses) (*pt* **knew** /njuː/; *pp* **known** /nəʊn/)

• HAVE INFORMATION **1** [I, T] ~ (**sth**) (**about sth**); ~ (**that**) … to have knowledge or information in your mind: *I don't know much about sport.* ◇ *Do you know where this bus stops?* ◇ *Do you know their phone number?* ◇ *'You've got a flat tyre.' 'I know.'* ◇ *Do you **know the way** to the restaurant?* ◇ *Did you know that she was coming?*

• BE FAMILIAR WITH **2** [T] to be familiar with a person or a place; to have met sb or been somewhere before: *We've known each other for years.* ◇ *I don't know this part of London well.* ◇ *Knowing Katie, she'll be out with her friends.*

• FEEL SURE **3** [T, I] to feel certain; to be sure of sth: *I just know you'll pass the exam!* ◇ *As far as I know* (= I think it is true but I am not absolutely sure), *the meeting is next Monday afternoon.*

• EXPERIENCE **4** [T] (only used in the perfect tenses) to have seen, heard or experienced sth: *I've known him go a whole day without eating.* ◇ *It's been known to snow in June.* **5** [T] to have personal experience of sth: *Many people in western countries don't know what it's like to be hungry.*

• BE ABLE TO DO **6** [T] to have learned sth and be able to do it: *Do you know how to make pancakes?*

• GIVE A NAME **7** [T, often passive] ~ **sb/sth as sth** to give sth a particular name; to recognize sb/sth as sth: *Istanbul was previously known as Constantinople.* **IDM** **God/goodness/Heaven knows 1** I do not know: *They've ordered a new car but goodness knows how they're going to pay for it.* **2** used for emphasizing sth: *I hope I get an answer soon. Goodness knows, I've waited long enough.* **know better (than that/than to do sth)** to have enough sense to realize that you should not do sth **know sth inside out | know sth like the back of your hand** (*informal*) to be very familiar with sth **know what you are talking about** (*informal*) to have knowledge of sth from your own experience **know what's what** (*informal*) to have all the important information about sth; to fully understand sth **let sb know** to tell sb; to inform sb about sth: *Could you let me know what time you're arriving?* **show sb/know/learn the ropes** → ROPE¹ **you know** used when the speaker is thinking of what to say next, or to remind sb of sth: *Well, you know, it's rather difficult to explain.* ◇ *I've just met Marta. You know — Jim's ex-wife.* **you never know** (*informal*) you cannot be certain: *Keep those empty boxes. You never know, they might come in handy one day.*

PHR V **know of sb/sth** to have information about or experience of sb/sth: *Do you know of any pubs around here that serve food?*

know² /nəʊ/ *noun* **IDM** **in the know** (*informal*) having information that other people do not

ˈknow-all (*BrE*) (*also* **know-it-all** *especially in AmE*) *noun* [C] an annoying person who behaves as if they know everything

ˈknow-how *noun* [U] (*informal*) practical knowledge of or skill in sth

knowing /ˈnəʊɪŋ/ *adj.* showing that you know about sth that is thought to be secret: *a knowing look*

knowingly /ˈnəʊɪŋli/ *adv.* **1** on purpose; deliberately: *I've never knowingly lied to you.* **2** in a way that shows that you know about sth that is thought to be secret: *He smiled knowingly at her.*

ˈknow-it-all = KNOW-ALL

knowledge ᵻ **A2** ⊘ /ˈnɒlɪdʒ/ *noun* **1** [U, sing.] ~ (**of/ about sth**) information, understanding and skills that you have gained through learning or experience: *I have a **working knowledge** of French* (= enough to be able to make myself understood). **2** [U] the state of knowing about a particular fact or situation: *She did it **without my knowledge*** (= I did not know about it). **3** [U] (usually before another noun) information, considered as a resource in industry, rather than producing goods: *a **knowledge economy*** ◇ **knowledge workers** **IDM** **be common/public knowledge** to be sth that everyone knows **to (the best of) your knowledge** from the information you have, although you may not know everything: *To my knowledge, they are still living there.*

knowledgeable /ˈnɒlɪdʒəbl/ *adj.* ~ (**about sth**) having a lot of knowledge: *She's very knowledgeable about history.* ▶ **knowledgeably** /-bli/ *adv.*

known /nəʊn/ past participle of **know**¹

knuckle /ˈnʌkl/ *noun* [C] (**ANATOMY**) the bones where the fingers join the rest of the hand ⊃ picture at **body**

koala /kəʊˈɑːlə/ *noun* [C] an Australian animal with thick grey fur that lives in trees and looks like a small bear ⊃ picture at **animal**

the Koran (*also* **the Qur'an**) /ðə kəˈrɑːn/ *noun* [sing.] (**RELIGION**) the holy book of the Islamic religion

kosher /ˈkəʊʃə(r)/ *adj.* (**RELIGION**) (used about food) prepared according to the rules of Jewish law

kph (*also* **kmph**) *abbr.* (in writing) kilometres per hour

krill /krɪl/ *noun* [pl.] very small SHELLFISH that live in the sea around the Antarctic and are eaten by WHALES

krypton /ˈkrɪptɒn/ *noun* [U] (*symb.* **Kr**) (**CHEMISTRY**) a chemical element. Krypton is a gas that does not react with anything and is used in FLUORESCENT lights. ❶ Krypton is a noble gas. For more information on the periodic table of elements, look at the **Reference Section** of this dictionary

kudos /ˈkjuːdɒs/ *noun* [U] the praise and honour that goes with a particular achievement or position: *the kudos of playing for such a famous team*

kung fu /ˌkʌŋ ˈfuː/ *noun* [U] (**SPORT**) a Chinese style of fighting using the feet and hands as weapons ⊃ look at **martial art**

kW *abbr.* (in writing) (*pl.* **kW**) = KILOWATT: *a 2kW electric heater*

L l

L¹ /el/ (*also* l) *noun* [C, U] (*pl.* L's, l's) the twelfth letter of the English alphabet: *'Lake' begins with (an) 'L'.* ⊃ look at **L-plate**

L² *abbr.* (in writing) (used for sizes of things, especially clothes) large

l *abbr.* (in writing) (*pl.* l) = LITRE

lab ⚡A2 /læb/ (*informal*) (**EDUCATION**, **SCIENCE**) = LABORATORY

label¹ ⚡B1 ⊙ /'leɪbl/ *noun* [C] **1** a piece of paper, etc. that is fixed to sth and that gives information about it: *There is a list of all the ingredients on the label.* **2** (*also* record label) (**MUSIC**) a company that produces and sells music

label² ⚡B1 ⊙ /'leɪbl/ *verb* [T] (-ll-, *AmE* -l-) **1** [usually passive] to fix a label or write information on sth **2** ~ sb/sth (as) (sth) to describe sb/sth in a particular way, especially unfairly: *The press had labelled him an extremist.*

laboratory ⚡B1 /lə'bɒrətri/ (*pl.* -ies) (*also informal* lab) *noun* [C] (**EDUCATION**, **SCIENCE**) a room or building that is used for scientific research, testing, experiments, etc. or for teaching about science: ◇ *a physics laboratory* ⊃ look at **language laboratory**

laborious /lə'bɔːriəs/ *adj.* needing a lot of time and effort: *a laborious task/process/job* ▶ **laboriously** *adv.*

labour¹ ⚡B2 (*BrE*) (*AmE* labor) /'leɪbə(r)/ *noun* **1** [U] work, usually of a hard, physical kind: *manual labour* (= work using your hands) ⊃ picture at **income** **2** [U] (**BUSINESS**, **ECONOMICS**) workers, when thought of as a group: *There is a shortage of skilled labour.* **3** [U, C, usually sing.] (**HEALTH**) the process of giving birth to a baby: *She went into labour in the early hours of this morning.* ◇ *She was in labour for ten hours.* **4** Labour [U + sing./pl. verb] = LABOUR PARTY

labour² (*BrE*) (*AmE* labor) /'leɪbə(r)/ *verb* [I] **1** ~ (away) to work hard at sth: *He spent all weekend labouring away on his essay* **2** to move or do sth with difficulty and effort

laboured (*BrE*) (*AmE* labored) /'leɪbəd/ *adj.* done slowly or with difficulty: *laboured breathing*

labourer (*BrE*) (*AmE* laborer) /'leɪbərə(r)/ *noun* [C] a person whose job involves hard physical work: *unskilled/farm labourers*

labour-in'tensive (*BrE*) (*AmE* labor-intensive) *adj.* (**BUSINESS**) (used about work) needing a lot of people to do it: *labour-intensive methods*

'labour market (*BrE*) (*AmE* labor market) *noun* [C] (**ECONOMICS**) the number of people who are available for work in relation to the number of jobs available: *young people about to enter the labour market*

the 'Labour Party *noun* [sing. + sing./pl. verb] (*also* Labour [U + sing./pl. verb]) (**POLITICS**) one of the main political parties in Britain. The Labour Party supports the interests of working people: *He has always voted Labour.* ⊃ look at **Conservative Party**, **Liberal Democrats** ⊃ note at **party**

'labour-saving (*BrE*) (*AmE* labor-saving) *adj.* reducing the amount of work needed to do sth: *labour-saving devices such as washing machines and dishwashers*

labyrinth /'læbərɪnθ/ *noun* [C] a complicated set of paths through which it is difficult to find your way: *a labyrinth of corridors* **SYN** maze

lace¹ /leɪs/ *noun* **1** [U] a DELICATE material that is made from very thin THREADS that that are made into a pattern with holes: *lace curtains* ◇ *a collar made of lace* ⊃ adjective **lacy** **2** [C] = SHOELACE: *Do up your laces or you'll trip over them.*

lace² /leɪs/ *verb* [T] ~ sth (up) to tie or fasten sth with a LACE: *She stopped to lace up her trainers.* ▶ **'lace-up** *adj.*, *noun* [C]: *lace-up shoes*

laboratory apparatus

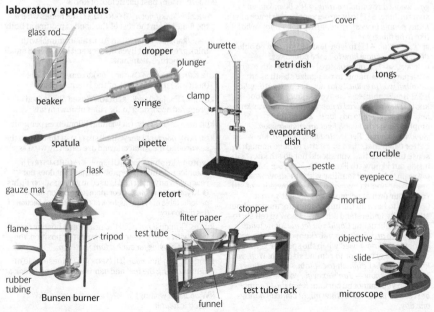

glass rod · dropper · burette · cover · Petri dish · tongs · plunger · clamp · beaker · syringe · spatula · pipette · evaporating dish · crucible · flask · pestle · eyepiece · gauze mat · retort · mortar · flame · stopper · filter paper · objective · test tube · slide · tripod · rubber tubing · Bunsen burner · funnel · test tube rack · microscope

lack¹ 🔊 **B1** 🌐 /læk/ *noun* [U, sing.] ~ **(of sth)** the state of not having sth or not having enough of sth: *A lack of food forced many people to leave their homes.*

lack² 🔊 **B1** 🌐 /læk/ *verb* [T] to have none or not enough of sth: *She seems to lack the will to succeed.*

lacking /ˈlækɪŋ/ *adj.* [not before noun] **1** ~ **in sth** not having enough of sth: *He's certainly not lacking in intelligence.* **2** not present or available: *I feel there is something lacking in my life.*

lacklustre (*BrE*) (*AmE* **lackluster**) /ˈlæklʌstə(r)/ *adj.* not interesting or exciting; not bright: *a lacklustre performance* **SYN** **dull¹**

laconic /ləˈkɒnɪk/ *adj.* (*formal*) using only a few words to say sth ▶ **laconically** /-kli/ *adv.*

lacquer /ˈlækə(r)/ *noun* [U] a liquid that is put on wood, metal, etc. to give it a hard, shiny surface ▶ **lacquer** *verb* [T]

lactate /lækˈteɪt/ *verb* [I] (**BIOLOGY**) (used about a woman or female animal) to produce milk from the body to feed a baby or young animal ▶ **lactation** /-ˈteɪʃn/ *noun* [U]: *the period of lactation*

lactic acid /ˌlæktɪk ˈæsɪd/ *noun* [U] (**BIOLOGY**) a substance that forms in milk that is no longer fresh and is also produced in the muscles during hard physical exercise

lactose /ˈlæktəʊs, -təʊz/ *noun* [U] (**BIOLOGY**) a type of sugar found in milk ⊃ look at **dextrose, fructose, glucose, sucrose**

lacy /ˈleɪsi/ *adj.* made of or looking like LACE (= material made of thin THREADS with small holes to form a pattern)

lad 🔊+ **C1** /læd/ *noun* [C] (*old-fashioned or informal*) a boy or young man: *School has changed since I was a lad.*

ladder¹ 🔊+ **B2** /ˈlædə(r)/ *noun* [C] **1** a piece of equipment that is used for climbing up sth. A ladder consists of two long pieces of metal, wood or rope with steps fixed between them: *to climb up a ladder* ⊃ look at **stepladder 2** (*BrE*) (*AmE* **run**) a long hole in TIGHTS or STOCKINGS (= thin pieces of clothing that women wear to cover their legs) where the THREADS have broken: *Oh no! I've got a ladder in my tights.*

ladder² /ˈlædə(r)/ *verb* [I, T] if TIGHTS or STOCKINGS (= the thin pieces of clothing that women wear to cover their legs) **ladder** or you **ladder** them, a long, thin hole appears in them: *Oh no! I've laddered my tights.*

laden /ˈleɪdn/ *adj.* [not before noun] ~ **(with sth)** having or carrying a lot of sth: *The orange trees were laden with fruit.*

ladle¹ /ˈleɪdl/ *noun* [C] a large deep spoon with a long handle, used especially for serving soup

ladle² /ˈleɪdl/ *verb* [T] to serve food with a LADLE

lady 🔊 **A2** /ˈleɪdi/ *noun* [C] (*pl.* **-ies**) **1** a polite way of saying 'woman', especially when you are referring to an older woman: *The old lady next door lives alone.* **2** (*formal*) used when speaking to or about a woman or women in a polite way: *Ladies and gentlemen!* (= at the beginning of a speech) ◇ *Mrs Flinn, there's a lady here to see you.* **3 Lady** (in the UK) a title that is used by a woman who has a very high position in society: *Lady Elizabeth Groves* ⊃ look at **lord** (2)

ladybird /ˈleɪdibɜːd/ (*BrE*) (*AmE* **ladybug** /ˈleɪdibʌg/) *noun* [C] a small insect that is usually red with black spots

lag¹ /læg/ *verb* [I] (-gg-) ~ **(behind)** **(sb/sth)** to move or develop more slowly than sb/sth: *I'm always lagging behind when we go walking in the mountains.*

lag² /læg/ (*also* **time lag**) *noun* [C] a period of time between two events; a delay ⊃ look at **jet lag**

lager /ˈlɑːgə(r)/ *noun* [U, C] (*BrE*) a type of light beer that is a gold colour: *a pint of lager*

lagoon /ləˈguːn/ *noun* [C] (**GEOGRAPHY**) a lake of salt water that is separated from the sea by sand or rock

laid /leɪd/ past tense, past participle of **lay¹**

laid-back *adj.* calm and relaxed; seeming not to worry about anything **SYN** **easy-going**

lain /leɪn/ past participle of **lie¹**

laissez-faire /ˌleseɪ ˈfeə(r)/ *noun* [U] (**POLITICS**) the policy of allowing private businesses to develop without government control ▶ **laissez-faire** *adj.*: *a laissez-faire economy*

lake 🔊 **A2** /leɪk/ *noun* [C] (**GEOGRAPHY**) a large area of water that is surrounded by land: *They've gone sailing on the lake.* ◇ *We all swam in the lake.* ◇ *Lake Constance* ⊃ note at **water¹** ⊃ picture at **glacial, water cycle**

lamb /læm/ *noun* **1** [C] a young sheep ⊃ note at **sheep** ⊃ picture at **sheep 2** [U] the meat of a lamb: *lamb chops* ⊃ note at **meat**

lame /leɪm/ *adj.* **1** (used mainly about animals) not able to walk properly because of an injury to the leg or foot **2** (used about an excuse, argument, etc.) not easily believed **SYN** **weak**

lament /ləˈment/ *noun* [C] (*formal*) (**LITERATURE, MUSIC**) a song, poem, etc. that expresses very sad feelings about sb who has died or about sth that has ended ▶ **lament** *verb* [T]

laminate /ˈlæmɪnət/ *noun* [U, C] a material that is made by sticking several thin layers together

laminated /ˈlæmɪneɪtɪd/ *adj.* **1** (used about wood, plastic, etc.) made by sticking several thin layers together: *laminated glass* **2** covered with thin clear plastic for protection

lamp 🔊 **A2** /læmp/ *noun* [C] a device that uses electricity, gas or oil to produce light: *a street lamp* ◇ *a table/desk lamp* ⊃ picture at **microscope**

lamp post *noun* [C] a tall POLE at the side of the road with a light on the top ⊃ look at **street light**

lampshade /ˈlæmpʃeɪd/ *noun* [C] a cover for a lamp that makes it look more attractive and makes the light softer

LAN /læn/ *noun* [C] (**COMPUTING**) a system for communicating by computer within a large building (the abbreviation for 'local area network') ⊃ look at **WAN**

lance¹ /lɑːns/ *noun* [C] (**HISTORY**) a weapon with a long wooden handle and pointed metal end that was used by people fighting on horses in the past

lance² /lɑːns/ *verb* [T] (**MEDICINE**) to cut open an INFECTED place on sb's body with a sharp knife in order to let out the PUS (= a yellow substance produced by infection): *to lance an abscess*

land¹ 🔊 **A1** /lænd/ *noun* **1** [U] the solid part of the surface of the earth that is not the sea: *Penguins can't move very fast on land.* **OPP** **sea** ⊃ note at **water¹** ⊃ picture at **convection 2** [U] (**GEOGRAPHY**) an area of ground: *The land rose to the east.* ◇ *She owns 500 acres of land in Scotland.* **3** [U] (**AGRICULTURE**) ground, soil or earth of a particular kind: *The land is rich and fertile.* ◇ *arid/barren land* ◇ *arable/agricultural/industrial land* **4** [C] a country or region: *She died far from her native land.* ◇ *to travel to distant lands* ⊃ note at **country**

land² 🔊 **A2** /lænd/ *verb* **1** [I, T] to come down from the air; to bring sth down to the ground: *The bird landed on the roof.* ◇ *He fell off the ladder and landed on his back.* ◇ *The pilot landed the plane safely.* ◇ *His flight is due to land at three o'clock.* **OPP** **take off 2** [I, T] to go

onto land or put sth onto land from a ship **3** [T] to succeed in getting sth, especially sth that a lot of people want: *The company has just landed a million-dollar contract.*
IDM fall/land on your feet → FOOT[1]
PHR V land up (in …) (*BrE, informal*) to finish in a certain position or situation: *He landed up in a prison cell for the night.* land sb with sb/sth (*informal*) to give sb sth unpleasant to do, especially because nobody else wants to do it: *I got landed with dealing with all the angry customers.*

landfill /'lændfɪl/ noun (**ENVIRONMENT**) **1** [C, U] an area of land where large amounts of waste material are buried **2** [U] waste material that will be buried; the burying of waste material

landform /'lændfɔːm/ noun [C] (**GEOGRAPHY**) a natural feature of the earth's surface

landholding /'lændhəʊldɪŋ/ noun [C, U] a piece of land that sb owns or rents; the fact of owning or renting land: *a map of tribal landholdings* ▶ landholder /-həʊldə(r)/ noun [C]

landing ʔ+ B2 /'lændɪŋ/ noun [C] **1** the act of bringing an aircraft or a SPACECRAFT down to the ground: *The plane made an emergency landing in a field.* ◇ *a crash landing* ◇ *a safe landing* **OPP** take-off **2** the area at the top of a set of stairs in a house, or between one set of stairs and another in a large building

landing card noun [C] (**TOURISM**) a card on which you have to write details about yourself when flying to a foreign country

landing gear = UNDERCARRIAGE

landing strip = AIRSTRIP

landlady /'lændleɪdi/ noun [C] (*pl.* -ies) **1** a woman who rents a house or room to people for money **2** a woman who owns or manages a pub, small hotel, etc. ▶ look at **landlord** (2)

landless /'lændləs/ adj. (**AGRICULTURE**) not owning land for farming; not allowed to own land

landline /'lændlaɪn/ noun [C] a phone connection that uses wires carried on POLES or under the ground, in contrast to a mobile phone: *I'll call you later on your landline.* ◯ look at **mobile phone** ◯ note at **phone**[1]

landlocked /'lændlɒkt/ adj. (**GEOGRAPHY**) completely surrounded by land

landlord ʔ+ C1 /'lændlɔːd/ noun [C] **1** a person who rents a house or room to people for money **2** a person who owns or manages a pub, small hotel, etc. ▶ look at **landlady** (2)

landmark ʔ+ B2 /'lændmɑːk/ noun [C] **1** an object (often a building) that can be seen easily from a distance and will help you to recognize where you are: *Big Ben is one of the landmarks on London's skyline.* ◯ look at **listed building 2 ~(in sth)** an important stage or change in the development of sth: *The Russian Revolution was a landmark in world history.* ◇ *a landmark decision*

land mass noun [C] (**GEOGRAPHY**) a large area of land, for example a continent

landmine /'lændmaɪn/ noun [C] a bomb placed on or under the ground, that explodes when vehicles or people move over it

landowner /'lændəʊnə(r)/ noun [C] (**SOCIAL STUDIES**) a person who owns land, especially a large area of land

landscape[1] ʔ B2 /'lændskeɪp/ noun **1** [C, usually sing.] everything you can see when you look across a large area of land: *an urban/industrial landscape* ◯ picture at **limestone 2** [C, U] (**ART**) a picture or a painting that

shows a view of the countryside; this style of painting ◯ look at **cityscape, townscape** ◯ note at **art 3** [U] (usually before another noun) (**COMPUTING**) the way of printing a document in which the top of the page is one of the longer sides: *Select the landscape option when printing the file.* ◯ look at **portrait** (3)

landscape[2] /'lændskeɪp/ verb [T] to improve the appearance of an area of land by changing its design and planting trees, flowers, etc.

landslide /'lændslaɪd/ noun [C] **1** (**GEOGRAPHY**) the sudden fall of a mass of earth, rocks, etc. down the side of a mountain ◯ picture at **erosion 2** (**POLITICS**) a great victory for one person or one political party in an election

lane ʔ+ B2 /leɪn/ noun [C] **1** a narrow road in the country: *winding country lanes* **2** used in the names of roads: *Crossley Lane* **3** a section of a wide road that is marked by painted white lines to keep lines of traffic separate: *a four-lane motorway* ◇ *the inside/middle/fast/outside lane* **4** (**SPORT**) a section of a sports track, swimming pool, etc. for one person to go along **5** a route or path that is regularly used by ships or aircraft: *the busy shipping lanes of the English Channel*

▼ SYNONYMS

language

vocabulary • terms • wording • terminology

These are all terms for the words and expressions people use when they speak or write, or for a particular style of speaking and writing.

language *Give your instructions in everyday language.*

vocabulary *to have a wide/limited vocabulary*

terms *I'll explain it in simple terms.*

wording *It was the standard form of wording for a letter of consent.*

terminology (*formal*) *medical terminology*

▼ COLLOCATIONS

language

Somebody who **is fluent in** a language speaks it without making any mistakes: *She was fluent in German, Urdu and Swahili.* ◇ *He speaks fluent Japanese.* Somebody who **masters** a language **has a good command** of that language (= can speak and understand it well): *I never really mastered Latin.* ◇ *She has a good command of Arabic.* Somebody who makes many mistakes speaks **bad/broken/poor** English, Spanish, Turkish, etc: *I got by with broken Chinese and sign language.* People often compare their use of **spoken** and **written** language: *My spoken Polish is better than my written Polish.* A **translator** is sb who **translates sth into** another language: *He translated her book into Korean.* An **interpreter** is sb who **translates** for sb else, usually when they are speaking: *The health service needs Gujarati interpreters.*

language ʔ A1 ◉ /'læŋgwɪdʒ/ noun
• **OF A COUNTRY 1** [C] the system of communication in speech and writing that is used by people of a particular country: *How many languages can you speak?* ◇ *They fell in love in spite of the language barrier* (= being unable to speak or understand each other's native language). ◇ *What is your first language* (= your mother tongue)?
• **COMMUNICATION 2** [U] the system of sounds and words that humans use to express their thoughts, ideas and feelings: *language teaching*
• **STYLE OF SPEAKING/WRITING 3** [U] words of a particular type or words that are used by a particular person or group: *written/spoken language* ◇ *bad* (= rude)

language ◊ legal language ◊ the language of Shakespeare

• SIGNS/SYMBOLS **4** [U, C] any system of signs, symbols, movements, etc. that is used to express sth: *sign language* (= using your hands, not speaking) ⊃ look at **body language**

• IN COMPUTING **5** [C, U] a system of symbols and rules that is used to operate a computer

'**language laboratory** *noun* [C] (**EDUCATION**) a room in a school or college that contains special equipment to help students to learn foreign languages by listening to recordings, watching videos, recording themselves, etc.

lanky /'læŋki/ *adj.* (lankier; lankiest) (used about a person) very tall and thin

lantern /'læntən/ *noun* [C] a type of light that can be carried, with a metal frame, glass sides and a light or CANDLE inside

lanthanum /'lænθənəm/ *noun* [U] (*symb.* La) (**CHEMISTRY**) a chemical element. Lanthanum is a silver-white metal. ❶ For more information on the periodic table of elements, look at the **Reference Section** of this dictionary.

lanyard /'lænjɑːd, -jəd/ *noun* [C] a string that you wear around your neck or WRIST for holding sth: *I carry my ID card on a lanyard round my neck.*

lap¹ ʔ+ **C1** /læp/ *noun* [C] **1** the flat area that is formed by the upper part of your legs when you are sitting down: *The child sat quietly on his mother's lap.* **2** (SPORT) one journey around a running track, etc: *There are three more laps to go in the race.* **3** one part of a long journey

lap² /læp/ *verb* (-pp-) **1** [I] (used about water) to make gentle sounds as it moves against sth: *The waves lapped against the side of the boat.* **2** [T] ~ **sth (up)** (usually used about an animal) to drink sth using the tongue: *The cat lapped up the cream.* **3** [T] (SPORT) to pass another runner in a race who has been round the track fewer times than you
PHR V lap sth up (*informal*) to accept sth with great pleasure, without stopping to think if it is good, true, etc.

laparotomy /ˌlæpəˈrɒtəmi/ *noun* [C] (*pl.* -ies) (**MEDICINE**) a cut in the ABDOMEN (= the part of the body below the chest) in order to perform an operation or an examination

lapel /ləˈpel/ *noun* [C] one of the two parts of the front of a coat or jacket that are folded back

lapse¹ /læps/ *noun* [C] **1** a short time when you cannot remember sth or you are not thinking about what you are doing: *a lapse of memory* ◊ *The crash was the result of a temporary lapse in concentration.* **2** a period of time between two things that happen: *She returned to work after a lapse of ten years bringing up her family.* ⊃ look at **elapse 3** a piece of bad behaviour from sb who usually behaves well

lapse² /læps/ *verb* [I] **1** (used about a contract, an agreement, etc.) to finish or stop, often by accident: *My membership has lapsed because I forgot to renew it.* **2** to become weaker or stop for a short time: *My concentration lapsed during the last part of the exam.*
PHR V lapse into sth 1 to gradually pass into a worse or less active state or condition: *to lapse into silence/ a coma* **2** to start speaking or behaving in a less acceptable way: *Eventually he lapsed back into crime.*

laptop ʔ **A2** /'læptɒp/ *noun* [C] (**COMPUTING**) a small computer that can work with a battery and be easily carried **SYN notebook** ⊃ look at **desktop** (3)

lard /lɑːd/ *noun* [U] a solid white substance made from melted fat that is used in cooking

larder /'lɑːdə(r)/ *noun* [C] a large cupboard or small room that is used for storing food **SYN pantry**

large ʔ **A1** ❻ /lɑːdʒ/ *adj.* greater in size, amount, etc. than usual; big: *a large area/house/family/appetite* ◊ *a large number of people* ◊ *I'd like a large coffee, please.* ◊ *We have this shirt in small, medium or large.*
IDM at large 1 as a whole; in general: *He is well known to scientists but not to the public at large.* **2** (used about a criminal, an animal, etc.) not caught; free **by and large** mostly; in general: *By and large the school is very efficient.*

largely ʔ **B2** ❻ /'lɑːdʒli/ *adv.* mostly: *His success was largely due to hard work.*

large-'scale ʔ+ **C1** *adj.* happening over a large area or affecting a lot of people: *large-scale production/ unemployment*

lark /lɑːk/ *noun* [C] a small brown bird with a pleasant song

larva /'lɑːvə/ *noun* [C] (*pl.* larvae /-viː/) (**BIOLOGY**) an insect at the stage when it has just come out of an egg and has a short fat soft body with no legs ⊃ look at **pupa** ⊃ picture at **animal**

laryngitis /ˌlærɪnˈdʒaɪtɪs/ *noun* [U] (**HEALTH**) a mild illness of the throat that makes it difficult to speak

larynx /'lærɪŋks/ *noun* [C] (**ANATOMY**) the area at the top of the throat that contains the VOCAL CORDS (= the muscles that move to produce the voice) **SYN voice box** ⊃ picture at **body**

laser ʔ+ **C1** /'leɪzə(r)/ *noun* [C] (**PHYSICS**) a device that produces a controlled line of very powerful light that can be used as a tool ⊃ picture at **safety**

'**laser printer** *noun* [C] (**COMPUTING**) a machine that produces very good quality printed material from a computer by using a controlled LASER BEAM

lash¹ /læʃ/ *verb* **1** [I, T] (used especially about wind, rain and storms) to hit sth with great force: *The rain lashed against the windows.* **2** [T] to hit sb with a piece of rope, leather, etc.; to move sth like a piece of rope, leather, etc. violently **3** [T] ~ **A to B**; ~ **A and B together** to tie two things together FIRMLY with rope, etc.
PHR V lash out (at/against sb/sth) to suddenly attack sb/sth (with words or by hitting them or it): *The actor lashed out at a photographer outside his house.*

lash² /læʃ/ *noun* [C] **1** = EYELASH **2** a hit with a piece of rope, leather, etc.

lass /læs/ (*also* lassie /'læsi/) *noun* [C] (*BrE, informal*) a girl or young woman

lasso /læˈsuː, ˈlæsəʊ/ *noun* [C] (*pl.* -os, -oes) a long rope tied in a circle at one end that is used for catching cows and horses ▸ **lasso** *verb* [T]

last¹ ʔ **A1** /lɑːst/ *det.* **1** happening or coming after all other similar things or people: *December is the last month of the year.* ◊ *Would the last person to leave please turn off the lights?* ◊ *Our house is the last one on the left.* ◊ *She lived alone for the last years of her life.* **2** [only before noun] most recent: *last night/week/ Saturday/summer* ◊ *We have been working on the book for the last six months.* ◊ *The last time I saw her was in London.* ◊ *We'll win this time, because they beat us last time.* **3** [only before noun] final: *This is my last chance to take the exam.* ◊ *Alison's retiring — tomorrow is her last day at work.* **4** [only before noun] not expected or not suitable: *He's the last person I thought would get the job.* ▸ **lastly** *adv.*: *Lastly, I would like to thank the band who played this evening.* **SYN finally**
IDM first/last thing → THING have the last laugh to be the person, team, etc. who is successful in the end **have, etc. the last word** to be the person who makes the final decision or the final comment

the last minute/moment the final minute/moment before sth happens: *We arrived at the last minute to catch the train.* ◇ *a last-minute change of plan* (as) a **last resort** when everything else has failed; the person or thing that helps when everything else has failed **the last/final straw** → STRAW

last² ℓ **A2** /lɑːst/ adv. **1** at the end; after all the others: *The British athlete came last in the race.* ◇ *They arrived last of all.* **2** most recently: *When did you last have your eyes checked?* ◇ *When I saw her last she seemed very happy.*
IDM **last but not least** (used before the final item in a list) just as important as all the other items

last³ ℓ **A2** /lɑːst/ **the last** noun [C] (*pl.* **the last**) **1** the person or thing that comes or happens after all other similar people or things: *Alex was the last to arrive.* **2** ~ **of sth** the only remaining part or items of sth: *We finished the last of the bread at breakfast so we'd better get some more.*
IDM **at (long) last** in the end; finally: *After months of separation they were together at last.* **next/second to last** (*BrE also* **last but one**) the one before the last one: *She finished second to last.*

last⁴ ℓ **B1** /lɑːst/ verb (not used in the progressive tenses) **1** [I] to continue for a period of time: *The exam lasts three hours.* ◇ *How long does a cricket match last?* ◇ *The flight seemed to last forever.* **2** [I, T] to continue to be good or to function: *Do you think this weather will last till the weekend?* ◇ *It's only a cheap radio but it'll probably last you a year or so.* **3** [I, T] to be enough for what sb needs: *The coffee won't last until next week.*

,last-'ditch adj. [only before noun] used to describe a final attempt to achieve something, when there is not much hope of succeeding

lasting /'lɑːstɪŋ/ adj. continuing for a long time: *The book left a **lasting impression** on me.*

,last-'minute adj. done, decided or organized just before sth happens or before it is too late: *a last-minute holiday*

'last name = SURNAME

latch¹ /lætʃ/ noun [C] **1** a small metal bar that is used for fastening a door or a gate. You have to lift the latch in order to open the door. **2** a type of lock for a door that you open with a key from the outside

latch² /lætʃ/ verb
PHR V **latch on (to sth)** (*informal*) to understand sth: *It took them a while to latch on to what she was talking about.*

late ℓ **A1** /leɪt/ adj., adv. **1** after the usual or expected time: *I'm sorry I'm late.* ◇ *She was ten minutes late for school.* ◇ *The ambulance arrived too late to save him.* ◇ *to be late with the rent* ◇ *The buses are running late today.* ◇ *to stay up late* **OPP** early¹ **2** near the end of a period of time: *in the late afternoon/summer/ twentieth century* ◇ *His mother's in her late fifties* (= between 55 and 60). ◇ *in late May/late in May* ◇ *We got back home late in the evening.* **OPP** early¹ **3** near the end of the day: *It's getting late. Let's go home.* **4** [only before noun] no longer alive; dead: *his late wife*
IDM **an early/a late night** → NIGHT **later on** at a later time: *Later on you'll probably wish that you'd worked harder at school.* ◇ *Bye — I'll see you a bit later on.* **sooner or later** → SOON

latecomer /'leɪtkʌmə(r)/ noun [C] a person who arrives or starts sth late

lately ℓ+ **B2** /'leɪtli/ adv. in the period of time up until now; recently: *What have you been doing lately?*

latent /'leɪtnt/ adj. existing, but not yet clear, active or well developed: *latent defects/disease* ◇ *latent talent* ▶ latency /'leɪtənsi/ noun [U] (*formal*)

later¹ **A1** ⑤ /'leɪtə(r)/ adv. at a time in the future; after the time you are talking about: *See you later.* ◇ *I met her again three years later.*

later² **A2** ⑤ /'leɪtə(r)/ adj. coming after sth else or at a time in the future: *The game has been postponed to a later date.*

lateral /'lætərəl/ adj. connected with the side of sth or with movement to the side: *the lateral branches of a tree* ◇ *lateral eye movements* ⊃ picture at **tooth** ▶ laterally /-rəli/ adv.

latest¹ ℓ **B1** /'leɪtɪst/ adj. [only before noun] very recent or new: *the latest fashions/news* ◇ *the terrorists' latest attack*

latest² ℓ **B2** /'leɪtɪst/ (*usually* **the latest**) noun [U] ~ (**in sth**) (*informal*) the most recent or the newest thing or piece of news: *It's the latest in mobile technology.* ◇ *Have you heard the latest?*
IDM **at the latest** no later than the time or the date mentioned: *You need to hand your projects in by Friday at the latest.*

latex /'leɪteks/ noun [U] **1** (BIOLOGY) a thick white liquid that is produced by some plants and trees, especially rubber trees **2** (CHEMISTRY) an artificial substance that is used to make paints, GLUES and materials

lathe /leɪð/ noun [C] a machine that shapes pieces of wood or metal by holding and turning them against a fixed cutting tool

lather /'lɑːðə(r)/ noun [U] a white mass of bubbles that are produced when you mix soap with water

Latin /'lætɪn/ noun [U] (LANGUAGE) the language that was used in ancient Rome ▶ Latin adj.: *Latin poetry* ◇ *Spanish, Italian and other Latin languages* (= that developed from Latin)

Latina /læˈtiːnə/ noun [C] a woman or girl, especially one who is living in the US, who is from Latin America, or whose family came from Latin America ⊃ look at **Hispanic**, **Latino** ▶ Latina adj.

Latin America /ˌlætɪn əˈmerɪkə/ noun [U] (GEOGRAPHY) Mexico and the parts of Central and South America in which Spanish or Portuguese is the main language

,Latin A'merican¹ adj. of or connected with Latin America: *Latin American music*

,Latin A'merican² noun [C] a person from Latin American

Latino /læˈtiːnəʊ/ noun [C] (*pl.* -os) a person, especially one who is living in the US, who is from Latin America, or whose family came from Latin America ⊃ look at **Hispanic**, **Latino** ▶ Latino adj.

latitude /'lætɪtjuːd/ noun [U] (GEOGRAPHY) the distance of a place north or south of the EQUATOR (= the imagined line around the middle of the earth) ⊃ look at **longitude** ❶ Latitude is measured in **degrees**.

latrine /ləˈtriːn/ noun [C] a type of toilet made by digging a hole in the ground

latter ℓ+ **C1** /'lætə(r)/ adj. [only before noun] nearer to the end of a period of time; later: *Interest rates should fall in the latter half of the year.* ▶ latterly adv.

the 'latter ℓ+ **C1** ⓦ noun [C] (*pl.* **the latter**) the second of two things or people that are mentioned: *She showed us two options. The latter seems much better.*

lattice /'lætɪs/ noun [U, C] (*also* latticework /'lætɪswɜːk/ [U]) a structure that is made of long narrow pieces of wood or metal that cross over each other with spaces shaped like a diamond between them; any structure or pattern like this: *a lattice of branches*

laugh¹ 🔊 **A1** /lɑːf/ *verb* [I] to make the sounds and movements of your face that show you think sth is funny or silly: *His jokes always make me laugh.* ◇ *to laugh out loud*
IDM die laughing → DIE¹
PHR V laugh at sb/sth **1** to show, by laughing, that you think sb/sth is funny: *The children laughed at the clown.* **2** to show that you think sb is silly: *Don't laugh at him. He can't help the way he speaks.*

laugh² 🔊 **A1** /lɑːf/ *noun* [C] the sound or act of laughing: *Her jokes got a lot of laughs.* ◇ *We all had a good laugh at what he'd written.* **2** a laugh [sing.] (*informal*) a person or thing that is good fun
IDM for a laugh as a joke have the last laugh → LAST¹

laughable /'lɑːfəbl/ *adj.* silly and not worth taking seriously

'laughing gas (*informal*) = NITROUS OXIDE

'laughing stock *noun* [C, usually sing.] **1** a person that other people laugh at because they have done sth stupid **2** a person or thing that other people laugh at (in an unpleasant way)

laughter 🔊 **A2** /'lɑːftə(r)/ *noun* [U] the sound or act of laughing: *Everyone roared with laughter.*

launch¹ 🔊 **B2** /lɔːntʃ/ *verb* [T] **1** to send a ship or boat into the water **2** to send sth such as a SPACECRAFT (= a vehicle that travels in space), weapon, etc. into space, into the sky or through the water: *to launch a missile* **3** to start sth new; to show sth for the first time: *to launch a new product onto the market* **4** (COMPUTING) to start a computer program

launch² 🔊 **B2** /lɔːntʃ/ *noun* [C] **1** [usually sing.] the act of launching a ship, SPACECRAFT, new product, etc. **2** a large boat with a motor

launder /'lɔːndə(r)/ *verb* [T] **1** (*formal*) to wash, dry and iron clothes, etc: *freshly laundered sheets* **2** (FINANCE, LAW) to move money that has been obtained illegally into foreign bank accounts or legal businesses so that it is difficult for other people to know where the money came from: *Most of the stolen money was laundered through Swiss bank accounts.*

launderette /ˌlɔːndə'ret/ (*BrE*) (*AmE* **Laundromat** /'lɔːndrəmæt/) *noun* [C] a type of shop where you pay to wash and dry your clothes in machines

laundry /'lɔːndri/ *noun* (*pl.* -ies) **1** [U] clothes, etc. that need washing or that are being washed: *dirty laundry* **2** [C] a business where you send sheets, clothes, etc. to be washed and dried

lava /'lɑːvə/ *noun* [U] (GEOLOGY) hot liquid rock that comes out of a VOLCANO ⊃ picture at **volcano**

lavatory /'lævətri/ *noun* [C] (*pl.* -ies) (*old-fashioned or formal*) **1** a toilet **2** a room that contains a toilet, a place to wash your hands, etc: *Where's the ladies' lavatory, please?*

lavender /'lævəndə(r)/ *noun* [U] a garden plant with purple flowers that smells very pleasant

lavish¹ /'lævɪʃ/ *adj.* **1** giving or spending a large amount of money: *She was always very lavish with her presents.* **2** large in amount or number: *a lavish meal*

lavish² /'lævɪʃ/ *verb*
PHR V lavish sth on sb/sth to give a lot of sth, often too much, to sb/sth

law 🔊 **A2** 🌐 /lɔː/ *noun* **1** [C] ~ (against sth/doing sth) an official rule of a country or state that says what people may or may not do: *There's a new law against discrimination in the workplace.* **2** the law [U] all the laws in a country or state: *Stealing is against the law.* ◇ *to break/obey the law* ⊃ look at **legal** ⊃ note at **crime** **3** [U] (EDUCATION) the law as a subject of study or as a profession: *My brother works for a law firm in Brighton.* ⊃ look at **legal 4** [C] (SCIENCE) a statement of

what always happens in certain situations or conditions: *the laws of physics*
IDM law and order a situation in which the law is obeyed

'law-abiding *adj.* (LAW) (used about a person) obeying the law: *law-abiding citizens*

lawbreaker /'lɔːbreɪkə(r)/ *noun* [C] (LAW) a person who does not obey the law; a criminal

'law court (*also* court of law) *noun* [C] (LAW) a place where legal cases are decided by a judge and often by a JURY (= a group of members of the public) ⊃ look at **defence** (6), **prosecution** (2), **witness¹** (2)

lawful /'lɔːfl/ *adj.* (LAW) allowed or recognized by law: *We shall use all lawful means to obtain our demands.* ⊃ look at **legal**, **legitimate** (2)

lawless /'lɔːləs/ *adj.* (LAW) (used about a person or their actions) breaking the law ▶ lawlessness *noun* [U]

lawn 🔊 **C1** /lɔːn/ *noun* [C, U] an area of grass in a garden or park that is regularly cut

lawnmower /'lɔːnməʊə(r)/ *noun* [C] a machine that is used for cutting the grass in a garden

lawrencium /lɒ'rensiəm/ *noun* [U] (*symb.* Lr) (CHEMISTRY) a chemical element. Lawrencium is a RADIOACTIVE metal. ❶ For more information on the periodic table of elements, look at the **Reference Section** of this dictionary.

lawsuit 🔊 **C1** /'lɔːsuːt/ *noun* [C] (LAW) a legal argument in court that is between two people or groups and not between the police and a criminal

lawyer 🔊 **A2** /'lɔːjə(r)/ *noun* [C] (LAW) a person who is trained and qualified to give people advice about the law and represent them in court: *a defence lawyer*

▼ VOCABULARY BUILDING

Lawyer is a general term for a person who is qualified to advise people about the law, to prepare legal documents for them and/or to represent them in court. In the UK, a **lawyer** who is qualified to speak in the higher courts of law is called a **barrister**. The highest level of **barrister** in the UK is called a **QC** or a **KC**. **Counsel** is the formal legal word used for a lawyer who is representing sb in court: *counsel for the prosecution/defence*. **Solicitor** is the term used in the UK for a lawyer who gives legal advice and prepares documents, for example when you are buying a house, and sometimes has the right to speak in court. In American English **attorney** is a more formal word used for a lawyer and is used especially in job titles: *the District Attorney*

---

lax /læks/ *adj.* not having high standards; not strict: *Their security checks are rather lax.* **SYN** careless

laxative /'læksətɪv/ *noun* [C] (MEDICINE) a medicine, food or drink that makes the body get rid of solid waste easily ▶ laxative *adj.*

lay¹ 🔊 **B1** /leɪ/ *verb* [T] (*pt, pp* laid /leɪd/)
• PUT DOWN **1** to put sb/sth carefully in a particular position or on a surface: *She laid a sheet over the dead body.* ◇ *He laid the child gently down on her bed.* ◇ *'Don't worry,' she said, laying her hand on my shoulder.* **2** to put sth in the correct position for a particular purpose: *They're laying new electricity cables in our street.*
• PREPARE **3** to prepare sth for use: *The police have laid a trap for him and I think they'll catch him this time.* ◇ *Can you lay the table, please (= put the knives, forks, plates, etc. on it)?*
• EGGS **4** (BIOLOGY) to produce eggs: *Hens lay eggs.*
• WITH A NOUN **5** (used with some nouns to give a similar meaning to a verb) to put: *They laid all the blame on*

him (= they blamed him). ◇ *to lay emphasis on something* (= emphasize it)

PHRV **lay sth down** to give sth as a rule: *It's all laid down in the rules of the club.* **lay into sb** (*informal*) to attack sb violently with blows or words: *She really laid into me for wasting so much money.* **lay off (sb)** (*informal*) to stop annoying sb: *Can't you lay off me for a bit?* **lay sb off** to stop giving work to sb: *They've laid off 500 workers at the car factory.* **lay sth on** (*informal*) to provide sth: *They're laying on a trip to London for everybody.* **lay sth out** **1** to spread out a number of things so that you can see them easily or so that they look nice: *All the food was laid out on a table in the garden.* **2** to arrange sth in a planned way: *The new shopping centre is so attractively laid out.*

lay² /leɪ/ *adj.* [only before noun] **1** (**RELIGION**) (used about a religious teacher) who has not been officially trained as a priest: *a lay preacher* **2** without special training in or knowledge of a particular subject

lay³ /leɪ/ past tense of **lie¹**

layabout /'leɪəbaʊt/ *noun* [C] (*BrE, informal*) a person who is lazy and does not do much work

lay-by *noun* [C] (*pl.* **-bys**) an area at the side of a road where vehicles can stop for a short time

layer ᵀ **B1** /'leɪə(r), leə(r)/ *noun* [C] **1** a quantity or sheet of sth that lies over a surface or between surfaces: *A thin layer of dust covered everything in the room.* ◇ *It's very cold. You'll need several layers of clothing.* ◇ *the top/bottom layer* ◇ *the inner/outer layer* ⊃ look at **ozone layer** ⊃ picture at **atmosphere, erosion** **2** a level or a part within a system or set of ideas: *There were too many layers of management in the company.* ◇ *the layers of meaning in the poem* ▶ **layer** *verb* [T]: *Layer the potatoes and onions in a dish.*

layman /'leɪmən/ (*pl.* **-men /-mən/**) (*also* **layperson,** /'leɪpɜːsn/, *pl.* **-persons, -people /-piːpl/**) *noun* [C] a person who does not have special training in or knowledge of a particular subject: *a medical reference book for the layman*

lay-off *noun* [C] **1** (**BUSINESS**) an act of making a person or people unemployed because there is no more work for them **2** a time when sb is not working or doing sth that they normally do regularly: *an eight-week lay-off with a broken leg*

layout ᵀ⁺ **C1** /'leɪaʊt/ *noun* [usually sing.] the way in which the parts of sth such as the page of a book, a garden or a building are arranged: *the layout of streets* ◇ *The magazine has a new page layout.* ⊃ picture at **orchestra**

laze /leɪz/ *verb* [I] ~ **(about/around)** to do very little; to rest or relax: *We just lazed around all afternoon.*

lazy ᵀ **A2** /'leɪzi/ *adj.* (**lazier; laziest**) **1** not wanting to work or be active: *Don't be lazy. Come and give me a hand.* **2** not involving much energy or activity: *a lazy summer's afternoon* ▶ **lazily** /-zɪli/ *adv.* ▶ **laziness** *noun* [U]

lb *abbr.* (in writing) (*pl.* **lb, lbs**) = **POUND¹** (3)

LCD¹ /ˌel siː 'diː/ *noun* [C] = **LOWEST COMMON DENOMINATOR**

LCD² /ˌel siː 'diː/ *abbr.* **liquid crystal display** (a way of showing information in electronic equipment. An electric current is passed through a special liquid and numbers and letters can be seen on a small screen.): *an LCD screen*

LEA /ˌel iː 'eɪ/ *noun* [C] (**EDUCATION**) a department responsible for education in British local government (the abbreviation for 'Local Education Authority')

leach /liːtʃ/ *verb* (**GEOLOGY**) **1** [I] ~ **(from sth) (into sth)** (used about chemicals, etc.) to be removed from soil by liquids passing through it: *Nitrates leach from the soil into rivers.* **2** [T] (used about liquids) to remove chemicals, etc. from soil by passing through it

lead¹ ᵀ **A2** ⓢ /liːd/ *verb* (*pt, pp* **led** /led/)

• SHOW THE WAY **1** [T, I] to go with or in front of a person or an animal to show the way or to make them or it go in the right direction: *The teacher led the children back to the classroom.* ◇ *She led the horse into its stable.* ◇ *The receptionist led the way to the boardroom.* ◇ *to lead somebody by the hand* ◇ *If you lead, I'll follow.*

• OF A ROAD/PATH **2** [I, T] (used about a road or path) to go to a place: *I don't think this path leads anywhere.*

• CAUSE **3** [I] ~ **to sth** to have sth as a result: *Eating too much sugar can lead to all sorts of health problems.* **4** [T] ~ **sb to do sth** to influence what sb does or thinks: *He led me to believe he really meant what he said.*

• BE BEST/FIRST **5** [I, T] to be winning or in first place in front of sb: *United are leading two goals to one.* ◇ *The champion is leading her rival by 18 seconds.*

• BE IN CONTROL **6** [T, I] to be in control or the leader of sth: *Who is going to lead the discussion?*

• LIFE **7** [T] to have a particular type of life: *They lead a very busy life.* ◇ *to lead a life of crime*

IDM **lead sb astray** to make sb start behaving or thinking in the wrong way

PHRV **lead up to sth** to be an introduction to or a cause of sth

lead² ᵀ **B1** /liːd/ *noun*

• FIRST PLACE **1** the first place or position in front of other people or organizations: *The French athlete has gone into the lead.* ◇ *Who is in the lead?* ◇ *Britain has taken the lead in developing computer software for that market.* **2** [sing.] the distance or amount by which sb/sth is in front of another person or thing: *The company has a lead of several years in the development of the new technology.*

• INFORMATION **3** [C] (**LAW**) a piece of information that may help to give the answer to a problem: *The police are following all possible leads to track down the killer.*

• ACTOR **4** [C] (**ARTS AND MEDIA**) the main part in a play, show or other situation: *Who's playing the lead in the new film?*

• FOR A DOG **5** [C] a long piece of leather, chain or rope that is used for controlling a dog. The lead is connected to a COLLAR (= a band that is put around the neck): *All dogs must be kept on a lead.*

• WIRE **6** [C] a piece of wire that carries electricity to a piece of equipment

IDM **follow sb's example/lead** → **FOLLOW**

lead³ /led/ *noun* **1** [U] (*symb.* **Pb**) (**CHEMISTRY**) a chemical element. Lead is a soft heavy grey metal used especially in the past for pipes, roofs, etc. ❶ For more information on the periodic table of elements, look at the **Reference Section** of this dictionary. **2** [C, U] the black substance inside a pencil that makes a mark when you write

leader ᵀ **A2** ⓦ /'liːdə(r)/ *noun* [C] **1** (**BUSINESS**) a person who is a manager or in charge of sth: *a weak/strong leader* ◇ *She is a natural leader* (= she knows how to tell other people what to do). **2** the person or thing that is best or in first place: *The leader has just finished the third lap.*

leadership ᵀ **B2** ⓦ /'liːdəʃɪp/ *noun* **1** [U] (**POLITICS**) the state or position of being a manager or the person in charge: *Who will take over the leadership of the party?* **2** [U] the qualities that a leader should have: *She's got good leadership skills.* **3** [C + sing./pl. verb] (**POLITICS**) the people who are in charge of a country, an organization, etc.

leading 🔊 B1 /'liːdɪŋ/ *adj.* [only before noun] **1** best or most important: *He's one of the leading experts in this field.* ◇ *She played a leading role in getting the business started.* **2** that tries to make sb give a particular answer: *The lawyer was warned not to ask the witness leading questions.*

lead story /ˌliːd 'stɔːri/ *noun* [C] (**ARTS AND MEDIA**) the most important piece of news in a newspaper or on a news programme

lead time /'liːd taɪm/ *noun* [C] (**BUSINESS**) the time between starting and completing a production process; the time between ordering and receiving an item: *This move will drastically shorten lead times and improve service.*

leaf¹ 🔊 B1 /liːf/ *noun* [C] (*pl.* leaves /liːvz/) (**BIOLOGY**) one of the thin, flat, usually green parts of a plant or tree: *The trees lose their leaves in autumn.* ◇ picture at **flower¹**, **photosynthesis**, **tree**

leaf² /liːf/ *verb*
PHR V **leaf through sth** to turn the pages of a book, etc. quickly and without looking at them carefully

leaflet 🔊 B2 /'liːflət/ *noun* [C] a printed piece of paper that gives information about sth. Leaflets are usually given free of charge: *I picked up a leaflet advertising a new club.*

leafy /'liːfi/ *adj.* (leafier; leafiest) **1** having many leaves **2** (used about a place) with many trees: *leafy suburbs*

league 🔊 B2 /liːg/ *noun* [C] **1** (**SPORT**) a group of sports clubs that compete with each other for a prize: *the football league* ◇ *Which team is top of the league at the moment?* ◇ look at **rugby** **2** (*informal*) a level of quality, ability, etc: *He is so much better than the others. They're just not in the same league.* **3** a group of people, countries, etc. that join together for a particular purpose: *the League of Nations*
IDM **in league (with sb)** having a secret agreement (with sb)

league table *noun* [C] (*BrE*) **1** (**SPORT**) a table that shows the position of sports teams and how successfully they are performing in a competition **2** a table that shows how well institutions such as schools or hospitals are performing in comparison with each other

leak¹ 🔊 C1 /liːk/ *verb* **1** [I, T] to allow liquid or gas to get through a hole or CRACK: *The boat was leaking badly.* ◇ *The tank had leaked a small amount of water.* **2** [I] (used about liquid or gas) to get out through a hole or CRACK: *Water is leaking in through the roof.* **3** [T] ~**sth (to sb)** to give secret information to sb: *The committee's findings were leaked to the press.*
PHR V **leak out** (used about secret information) to become known

leak² 🔊 C1 /liːk/ *noun* [C] **1** a small hole or CRACK that liquid or gas can get through: *There's a leak in the pipe.* ◇ *The roof has sprung a leak.* **2** the liquid or gas that gets through a hole: *a gas leak* **3** the act of giving away information that should be kept secret ▶ **leaky** *adj.* (leakier; leakiest)

leakage /'liːkɪdʒ/ *noun* [C, U] an amount of liquid or gas escaping through a hole in sth; an occasion when this happens: *a leakage of dangerous chemicals*

lean¹ 🔊 B2 /liːn/ *verb* (*pt, pp* leaned, *BrE also* leant /lent/) **1** [I] (used with an adverb or a preposition) to bend or move from a straight position to a sloping position: *He leaned across the table to pick up the phone.* ◇ *She leaned out of the window and waved.* ◇ *Just lean back and relax.* ◇ *That wardrobe leans to the right.* **2** [I, T] ~**(sth) against/on sth** to rest against sth so that it gives support; to put sth in this position: *She stopped and leant on the gate.* ◇ *Please don't lean bicycles against this window.*

---

lean² /liːn/ *adj.* **1** (used about a person or animal) thin and in good health **2** (used about meat) having little or no fat ⊃ note at **meat** **3** not producing much: *a lean harvest* **4** (**BUSINESS**) (used about organizations, etc.) avoiding spending more money or having more employees than is necessary: *The changes made the company leaner and more competitive.*

leap¹ 🔊 C1 /liːp/ *verb* (often used with an adverb or a preposition) (*pt, pp* leapt /lept/, leaped) **1** [I, T] (often used with an adverb or a preposition) to jump high or a long way: *A fish suddenly leapt out of the water.* ◇ *We all leapt into the air when they scored the goal.* ◇ (*figurative*) *Share prices leapt to a record high yesterday.* ◇ *The horse leapt a five-foot wall.* **2** [I] to move quickly: *I looked at the clock and leapt out of bed.* ◇ *She leapt back when the pan caught fire.*
PHR V **leap at sth** to accept a chance or an offer with enthusiasm: *She leapt at the chance to work in TV.*

leap² 🔊 C1 /liːp/ *noun* [C] **1** a big jump: *He took a flying leap at the wall but didn't get over it.* ◇ (*figurative*) *My heart gave a leap when I heard the news.* **2** a sudden large change or increase in sth: *The development of penicillin was a great leap forward in the field of medicine.*

leapfrog /'liːpfrɒg/ *noun* [U] a children's game in which one person bends over and another person jumps over their back

leap year *noun* [C] one year in every four, in which February has 29 days instead of 28

learn 🔊 A1 S /lɜːn/ *verb* (*pt, pp* learnt /lɜːnt/, learned) **1** [I, T] ~**(about sb/sth); ~(sth) (from sb/sth); ~(to do sth)** to get knowledge, a skill, etc. (from sb/sth): *I'm not very good at driving yet — I'm still learning.* ◇ *We're learning about China at school.* ◇ *I learned a lot from him.* ◇ *Debbie is learning to play the piano.* ◇ *to learn a foreign language/a musical instrument* ◇ *Where did you learn how to swim?* **2** [I] (**EDUCATION**) to study sth so that you can repeat it from memory: *I learned the poem by heart.* **3** [I] to understand or realize: *We should have learned by now that we can't rely on her.* ◇ *It's important to learn from your mistakes.* **4** [I] ~**(of/about) sth** to get some information about sth; to find out: *I was sorry to learn about your father's death.*
IDM **learn your lesson** to understand what you must do/not do in the future because you have had an unpleasant experience **show sb/know/learn the ropes** → ROPE¹

learned /'lɜːnɪd/ *adj.* having a lot of knowledge from studying; for people who have a lot of knowledge

learner /'lɜːnə(r)/ *noun* [C] a person who is learning: *a learner driver* ◇ *books for young learners*

learning 🔊 A2 O /'lɜːnɪŋ/ *noun* [U] (**EDUCATION**) **1** the process of learning sth: *new methods of language learning* **2** knowledge that you get from studying

learning curve *noun* [C] the rate at which you learn sth new: *She's on a steep learning curve* (= she has to learn a lot in a short time) *with this new job.*

learning difficulty (*BrE*) (*also* **learning disability** *AmE, BrE*) *noun* [C, usually pl.] (**EDUCATION, PSYCHOLOGY**) a mental problem that affects a person's ability to learn things: *There are more than 1.4 million people with learning difficulties in the UK.*

learnt /lɜːnt/ past tense, past participle of **learn**

lease /liːs/ *noun* [C] (**LAW**) a legal agreement that allows you to use a building or land for a fixed period of time in return for rent: *The lease on the flat runs out/ expires next year.* ▶ **lease** *verb* [T] ~**sth (from/to sb)**; ~**sb sth**: *They lease the land from a local farmer.* ◇ *A* *local farmer leased them the land.* ▸ **leasing** *noun* [U]: *car leasing*

leaseback /ˈliːsbæk/ *noun* [U] (**LAW**) the process of allowing the previous owner of a property to continue to use it if they pay rent to the new owner; an agreement to do this

leasehold /ˈliːshəʊld/ *adj.* (used about property or land) that you can pay to use for a limited period of time: *a leasehold property* ▸ **leasehold** *noun* [U] ⊃ look at **freehold**

least 🔊 **A2** /liːst/ *det., pron., adv.* **1** smallest in size, amount, degree, etc: *He's got the least experience of all of us.* ◊ *You've done the most work, and John has done the least.* **OPP** **most²** **2** less than anyone/ anything else; less than at any other time: *He's the person who needs help least.* ◊ *I bought the least expensive tickets.* ◊ *My uncle always appears when we're least expecting him.* **OPP** **most²**
IDM **at least 1** not less than, and probably more: *It'll take us at least two hours to get there.* ◊ *You could at least say you're sorry!* **2** used to add a positive comment about a negative situation: *It may not be beautiful but at least it's cheap.* **3** used for correcting sth that you have just said: *I saw him — at least I think I saw him.* **at the (very) least** not less and probably much more: *It'll take six months to build at the very least.* **last but not least** → LAST² **least of all** especially not: *Nobody should be worried, least of all you.* **not in the least (bit)** not at all: *It doesn't matter in the least.* ◊ *I'm not in the least bit worried.* **to say the least** → SAY¹

leather 🔊 **B1** /ˈleðə(r)/ *noun* [U] the skin of animals that has been specially treated. Leather is used to make shoes, bags, coats, etc: *a leather jacket*

leave¹ 🔊 **A1** /liːv/ *verb* (*pt, pp* left /left/)
• **GO AWAY 1** [I, T] to go away from sb/sth: *We should leave now if we're going to get there by eight o'clock.* ◊ *I felt sick in class so I left the room.* ◊ *At what age do most people leave school in your country?* ◊ *Hal left his wife for another woman.*
• **NOT BRING 2** [T] (often used with an adverb or a preposition) **~ sb/sth (behind)** to go away from a place without taking sth/sb with you: *I'm afraid I've left my homework at home. Can I give it to you tomorrow?* ◊ *I can't find my glasses. Maybe I left them behind at work.* ◊ *I left the children with my parents.*
• **SB/STH IN A PLACE/CONDITION 3** [T] to cause or allow sb/ sth to stay in a particular place or condition; to not deal with sth: *Leave the door open, please.* ◊ *Why do you always leave your homework till the last minute?* **4** [T] to make sth happen or stay as a result: *Don't put that cup on the table. It'll leave a mark.*
• **REMAIN 5** [T] to not use sth: *Leave some milk for me, please.* **6** be/have left [T] to remain to be used, sold, etc: *Is there any bread left?* ◊ *How much time do we have left?*
• **PUT 7** [T] to put sth somewhere: *Val left him a voicemail message.* ◊ *I left him a note.*
• **RESPONSIBILITY 8** [T] **~ (sth to sb)** to give the care of or responsibility for sb/sth to another person: *I'll leave it to you to organize all the food.*
• **AFTER DEATH 9** [T] to give sth to sb when you die: *In his will he left everything to his three sons.*
IDM **be left high and dry** → HIGH¹ **leave sb/sth alone** to not touch, annoy or speak to sb/sth **leave go (of sth)** to stop touching or holding sth: *Will you please leave go of my arm.* **leave sb in the lurch** to leave sb without help in a difficult situation **leave sth on one side** → SIDE¹

leave sb/sth out (of sth) to not include sb/sth: *This doesn't make sense. I think you've left out a word.* **be left over (from sth)** to remain when all that is needed has been used: *If there's any money left over, we'll have a cup of coffee.*

leave² 🔊 **B2** /liːv/ *noun* [U] a period of time when you do not go to work: *annual leave* ◊ *sick leave* ◊ *Molly's not working — she's on maternity leave.*

leaves /liːvz/ *plural of* **leaf¹**

lectern /ˈlektən/ *noun* [C] a stand for holding a book, notes, etc. when you are reading in church, giving a talk, etc.

lecture 🔊 **A2** 🔊 /ˈlektʃə(r)/ *noun* [C] **1 ~ (on/about sth)** (**EDUCATION**) a talk that is given to a group of people to teach them about a particular subject, especially as part of a university course: *The college has asked a journalist to come and give a lecture on the media.* ◊ *a course of lectures* ⊃ note at **subject¹ 2** a serious talk to sb that explains what they have done wrong or how they should behave: *They got a lecture from a policeman about playing near the railway.*
▸ **lecture** 🔊 **A2** *verb* [I, T]: *Alex lectures in European Studies at London University.* ◊ *The policeman lectured the boys about playing ball games in the road.*

lecturer 🔊 /ˈlektʃərə(r)/ *noun* [C] (**EDUCATION**) a person who gives talks to teach people about a subject, especially as a job in a university ⊃ note at **subject¹**

lecture theatre (*BrE*) (*AmE* **lecture theater**) *noun* [C] (**EDUCATION**) a large room with rows of seats on a slope, where lectures are given

LED /ˌel iː ˈdiː/ *noun* [C] (**PHYSICS**) a device that produces a light on electrical and electronic equipment (the abbreviation for 'light-emitting diode')

led /led/ *past tense, past participle of* **lead¹**

ledge /ledʒ/ *noun* [C] (**GEOGRAPHY**) a narrow shelf under a window; a narrow piece of rock that sticks out on the side of a CLIFF or mountain

lee /liː/ *noun* [sing.] the side or part of a hill, building, etc. that provides protection from the wind: *We built the house in the lee of the hill.* ⊃ look at **leeward, windward**

leech /liːtʃ/ *noun* [C] a small creature with a soft body and no legs that usually lives in water and that fastens itself to other creatures and drinks their blood

leek /liːk/ *noun* [C] a long thin vegetable that is white at one end with thin green leaves

leeward /ˈliːwəd, ˈluːəd/ *adj.* on the side of a hill, building, etc. that is protected from the wind **OPP** **windward** ▸ **leeward** *adv.*

left¹ /left/ *past tense, past participle of* **leave¹**

left² 🔊 **A1** /left/ *adj.* [only before noun] on the side where the heart is in the body: *I've broken my left arm.* **OPP** **right¹**

left³ 🔊 **A1** /left/ *adv.* to or towards the left: *Turn left just past the Post Office.* **OPP** **right²** ⊃ note at **direction**

left⁴ 🔊 **A1** /left/ *noun* **1** [U] the left side: *In Britain we drive on the left.* ◊ *Our house is just to/on the left of that tall building.* ◊ *If you look to your left you'll see one of the city's most famous landmarks.* **OPP** **right³** ⊃ note at **direction 2** the Left [+ sing./pl. verb] (**POLITICS**) political groups who support the ideas and beliefs of SOCIALISM (= the political idea that everyone is equal and that money should be equally divided) ⊃ look at **left wing** (1)

left-field *adj.* (*informal*) not following what is usually done; different, surprising and interesting: *a left-field comedy drama* ◊ *He was a left-field choice for the job.*

left-hand *adj.* [only before noun] of or on the left: *the left-hand side of the road* ◊ *a left-hand drive car* **OPP** **right-hand**

left-handed *adj., adv.* **1** using the left hand rather than the right hand: *Are you left-handed?* ◊ *I write left-handed.* **2** made for left-handed people to use: *left-handed scissors* **OPP** **right-handed**

leftist /ˈleftɪst/ *adj.* (POLITICS) supporting LEFT-WING political parties and their ideas: *They attack anyone who dares oppose leftist ideology.* ▶ **leftism** /ˈleftɪzəm/ *noun* [U] ▶ **leftist** *noun* [C]

left luggage office *noun* [C] (*BrE*) the place at a railway station, etc. where you can leave your LUGGAGE for a short time

leftovers /ˈleftəʊvəz/ *noun* [pl.] food that has not been eaten when a meal has finished

left-wing *adj.* (POLITICS) supporting the ideas of SOCIALISM: *They're both very left-wing.* ◊ *left-wing extremists* ⊃ look at **right-wing**

left wing *noun* **1** [sing. + sing./pl. verb] (POLITICS) the part of a political party whose members are most in favour of social change: *the left wing of the Labour Party* ⊃ look at **right wing** (1) **2** [C, U] (SPORT) an attacking player or position on the left side of the field in a sports game: *He plays on the left wing for Manchester United.* **OPP** **right wing**

leg 🔊 **A1** /leg/ *noun* [C] **1** (ANATOMY) one of the parts of the body on which a person or an animal stands or walks: *A spider has eight legs.* ◊ *She sat down and crossed her legs.* ⊃ picture at **animal, body, circulation** **2** one of the parts of a chair, table etc. on which it stands: *the leg of a chair/table* ◊ *a chair/table leg* **3** the part of a pair of trousers that covers the leg: *There's a hole in the leg of my trousers/my trouser leg.* **4** **-legged** /ˈlegɪd, legd/ (in adjectives) having the number or type of legs mentioned: *a three-legged stool* ◊ *a long-legged insect* **5** one part or section of a journey, competition, etc: *The band are in Germany on the first leg of their world tour.* **IDM** **pull sb's leg** → PULL[1] **stretch your legs** → STRETCH[1]

legacy 🔊 **C1** /ˈlegəsi/ *noun* [C] (*pl.* **-ies**) money or property that is given to you after sb dies, because they wanted you to have it

legal 🔊 **B1 🌐** /ˈliːgl/ *adj.* (LAW) **1** [only before noun] using or connected with the law: *legal advice* ◊ *to take legal action against somebody* ◊ *the legal profession* **2** allowed by law: *It is not legal to drive a car without insurance.* **OPP** **illegal** ⊃ look at **lawful, legitimate** (2) ▶ **legally 🌐** /-gəli/ *adv.*: *Schools are legally responsible for the safety of their pupils.*

legal action *noun* [U] (*also* **legal proceedings** [pl.]) (LAW) the act of using the legal system to solve an argument, etc: *Keep the letter in case you choose to* **take legal action** *against the company in the future.*

legality /lɪˈgæləti/ *noun* [U] (LAW) the state of being legal ⊃ look at **illegality** (1)

legalize (*BrE also* **-ise**) /ˈliːgəlaɪz/ *verb* [T] (LAW) to make sth legal ▶ **legalization** (*BrE also* **-isation**) /ˌliːgəlaɪˈzeɪʃn/ *noun* [U]

legal tender *noun* [U] (ECONOMICS) money that can be legally used to pay for things in a particular country

legato /lɪˈgɑːtəʊ/ *adj., adv.* (MUSIC) (to be played or sung) in a smooth manner **OPP** **staccato**

legend 🔊 **B2** /ˈledʒənd/ *noun* **1** [C, U] an old story about people and events that may or may not be true; this type of story: *the legend of Robin Hood* ◊ *According to legend, Robin Hood lived in Sherwood Forest.* **SYN** **myth** **2** [C] a famous person or event: *a movie/jazz/baseball legend* ⊃ look at **star**[1] (4) ▶ **legendary** 🔊 **C1** /ˈledʒəndri/ *adj.*: *the legendary*

heroes of Greek myths ◊ *Michael Jordan, the legendary basketball star*

leggings /ˈlegɪŋz/ *noun* [pl.] a piece of women's clothing that fits tightly over the legs, like a very thin pair of trousers

legible /ˈledʒəbl/ *adj.* that is clear enough to be read easily: *His writing is so small that it's barely legible.* **OPP** **illegible** ⊃ look at **readable** (2) ▶ **legibility** /ˌledʒəˈbɪləti/ *noun* [U] ▶ **legibly** /ˈledʒəbli/ *adv.*

legion /ˈliːdʒən/ *noun* [C] **1** a large group of soldiers that forms part of an army, especially the one that existed in ancient Rome: *the French Foreign Legion* **2** (*formal*) a large number of people of one particular type: *legions of photographers*

legislate /ˈledʒɪsleɪt/ *verb* [I] ~ **(for/against sth)** (LAW) to make a law or laws

legislation 🔊 **C1** /ˌledʒɪsˈleɪʃn/ *noun* [U] (LAW) **1** a group of laws: *The government is introducing new legislation to help small businesses.* **2** the process of making laws

legislative 🔊 **C1** /ˈledʒɪslətɪv/ *adj.* [only before noun] (*formal*) (LAW) connected with the act of making and passing laws: *a legislative assembly/body/council*

legislator /ˈledʒɪsleɪtə(r)/ *noun* [C] (*formal*) (LAW) a member of a group of people that has the power to make laws

legislature 🔊 **C1** /ˈledʒɪslətʃə(r)/ *noun* [C] (*formal*) (LAW) a group of people who have the power to make and change laws ⊃ look at **executive**[1]**, judiciary**

legitimate 🔊 **C1** /lɪˈdʒɪtɪmət/ *adj.* **1** reasonable or acceptable: *a legitimate excuse/question/concern* **2** (LAW) allowed by law: *Could he earn so much from legitimate business activities?* ⊃ look at **lawful, legal** (2) **3** (*old-fashioned*) (used about a child) having parents who are married to each other **OPP** **illegitimate** ▶ **legitimacy** /-məsi/ *noun* [U]: *I intend to challenge the legitimacy of his claim.* ▶ **legitimately** *adv.*

legitimize (*BrE also* **-ise**) /lɪˈdʒɪtəmaɪz/ *verb* [T] (LAW) to make sth legal or acceptable

legume /ˈlegjuːm, lɪˈgjuːm/ *noun* [C] any plant that has seeds in long PODS (= seed containers). PEAS and beans are legumes. ⊃ picture at **nitrogen cycle**

leisure 🔊 **B1** /ˈleʒə(r)/ *noun* [U] the time when you do not have to work; free time: *Shorter working hours mean that people have more leisure.* ◊ *leisure activities* **IDM** **at your leisure** (*formal*) when you have free time: *You can take the forms away and read them at your leisure.*

leisure centre *noun* [C] (*BrE*) a public building where you can do sports and other activities in your free time

leisurely /ˈleʒəli/ *adj.* without hurry: *a leisurely Sunday breakfast* ◊ *I always cycle at a leisurely pace.*

leitmotif (*also* **leitmotiv**) /ˈlaɪtməʊtiːf/ *noun* [C] **1** (MUSIC) a short tune in a piece of music that is often repeated and is connected with a particular person, thing or idea **2** (LITERATURE) an idea or a phrase that is repeated often in a book or work of art, and that is important in understanding the work: *The relationship between the two cousins is the leitmotif of the book.*

lemon 🔊 **A2** /ˈlemən/ *noun* [C, U] a yellow fruit with juice that has a bitter, sharp taste. Slices of lemon and lemon juice are used in cooking and drinks: *Add the juice of two lemons.* ◊ *a slice of lemon*

lemonade /ˌleməˈneɪd/ *noun* [C, U] **1** (*BrE*) a sweet FIZZY DRINK (= with bubbles) that tastes of lemon **2** a drink that is made from fresh lemon juice, sugar and water

lemur /ˈliːmə(r)/ *noun* [C] an animal like a monkey, with thick fur and a long tail, that lives in trees in Madagascar. There are many different types of lemur.

lend ʔ⚿ A2 /lend/ *verb* [T] (*pt, pp* **lent** /lent/) **1** ~ sb sth; ~ sth to sb (FINANCE) to allow sb to use sth for a short time; to give sb money that must be paid back after a certain period of time: *Could you lend me £30 until Friday?* ◇ *He lent me his bicycle.* ◇ *He lent his bike to me.* **OPP** **borrow 2** ~ sth (to sth) (*formal*) to give or add sth: *to lend support* ◇ *This evidence lends weight to our theory.*
IDM **lend (sb) a hand/lend a hand (to sb)** to help sb
PHR V **lend itself to sth** to be suitable for sth

lender /ˈlendə(r)/ *noun* [C] (FINANCE) a person or an organization that lends sth, especially money

lending /ˈlendɪŋ/ *noun* [U] (FINANCE) the act of lending money: *Lending by banks rose to $10 billion last year.*

length ʔ⚿ B1 /leŋkθ/ *noun*
• SIZE/MEASUREMENT **1** [U, C] the size of sth from one end to the other; how long sth is: *to measure the length of a room* ◇ *It took an hour to walk the length of Oxford Street.* ◇ *The tiny insect is only one millimetre in length.* ◇ *This snake can grow to a length of 2 metres.* ◯ look at **breadth** (1), **width** (1) ◯ note at **measure²** ◯ picture at **dimension** ◯ adjective **length**
• TIME **2** [U] the amount of time that sth lasts: *Many people complained about the length of time they had to wait.* ◇ *the length of a class/speech/film*
• OF A BOOK, ETC. **3** [U] the number of pages in a book, a letter, etc.
• OF A SWIMMING POOL **4** [C] (SPORT) the distance from one end of a swimming pool to the other: *I can swim a length in 30 seconds.*
• LONG THIN PIECE **5** [C] a piece of sth long and thin: *a length of material/rope/string*
IDM **at length** for a long time or in great detail: *We discussed the matter at great length.* **go to great lengths** to make more effort than usual in order to achieve sth **the length and breadth of sth** to or in all parts of sth: *They travelled the length and breadth of India.*

lengthen /ˈleŋkθən/ *verb* [I, T] to become longer; to make sth longer

lengthways /ˈleŋkθweɪz/ (*also* **lengthwise** /ˈleŋkθwaɪz/) *adv.* in the same direction as the longest side of sth: *Fold the paper lengthwise.*

lengthy ʔ⁺ C1 /ˈleŋkθi/ *adj.* very long

lenient /ˈliːniənt/ *adj.* (used about a punishment or person who punishes) not as strict as expected
▸ **lenience** /-əns/ (*also* **leniency** /-ənsi/) *noun* [U]
▸ **leniently** *adv.*

lens ʔ⁺ B2 /lenz/ *noun* [C] (*pl.* **lenses**) **1** (SCIENCE) a curved piece of glass that makes things look bigger, clearer, etc. when you look through it ◯ look at **zoom lens 2** = CONTACT LENS **3** (ANATOMY) the clear part of the eye, behind the PUPIL (= the round hole in the middle of the eye), that changes shape in order to direct light so that you can see clearly ◯ picture at **accommodation**, **eye¹**

Lent /lent/ *noun* [U] (RELIGION) a period of 40 days starting in February or March, when some Christians stop doing or eating certain things for religious reasons: *I'm giving up smoking for Lent.*

lent /lent/ past tense, past participle of **lend**

lentil /ˈlentl/ *noun* [C] a small brown, orange or green seed that can be dried and used in cooking: *lentil soup/stew*

Leo /ˈliːəʊ/ *noun* [U] the fifth sign of THE ZODIAC (= twelve signs that represent the positions of the sun, moon and planets), the Lion; a person born under this sign

leopard /ˈlepəd/ *noun* [C] a large wild animal of the cat family that has yellow fur with dark spots. Leopards live in Africa and Southern Asia. ◯ picture at **lion ❶** A female leopard is called a **leopardess** and a baby is called a **cub**.

leotard /ˈliːətɑːd/ *noun* [C] a piece of clothing that fits the body tightly from the neck down to the tops of the legs. Leotards are worn by dancers or women doing certain sports.

leper /ˈlepə(r)/ *noun* [C] (HEALTH) a person suffering from LEPROSY

leprosy /ˈleprəsi/ *noun* [U] (HEALTH) a disease that causes painful white areas on the skin and can destroy nerves, muscles, etc.

lesbian /ˈlezbiən/ *noun* [C] a woman who is sexually attracted to other women ◯ look at **gay¹** (1), **homosexual** ▸ **lesbian** ʔ⁺ C1 *adj.*: *a lesbian relationship* ▸ **lesbianism** *noun* [U]

lesion /ˈliːʒn/ *noun* [C] (HEALTH) an area of damage to the skin or part of the body caused by injury or by illness: *skin/brain lesions*

less¹ ʔ⚿ A2 ◉ /les/ *det., pron., adv.* **1** used with uncountable nouns to mean 'a smaller amount (of)': *It took less time than I thought.* ◇ *I'm too fat — I must try to eat less.* ◇ *It's not far — it'll take less than an hour to get there.* **OPP** **more¹**, **more² 2** not so much (as): *He's less intelligent than his brother.* ◇ *It rains less in London than in Manchester.* ◇ *People work less well when they're tired.* **OPP** **more²**
IDM **less and less** becoming smaller and smaller in amount or degree **more or less** → MORE²

lenses

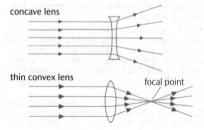

concave lens

thin convex lens

focal point

thick convex lens

focal point

main parts of a lens

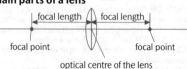

focal length focal length

focal point focal point

optical centre of the lens

less² /les/ *prep.* taking a certain number or amount away: *You'll earn £10 an hour, less tax.* **SYN minus¹**

lessee /leˈsiː/ *noun* [C] (**LAW**) a person who has a LEASE (= legal agreement) allowing them to use a building, an area of land, etc.

lessen /ˈlesn/ *verb* [I, T] to become less; to make sth less: *This medicine will lessen the pain.*

lesser ⨕+ **C1** /ˈlesə(r)/ *adj.* [only before noun], *adv.* not as great/much as: *He is guilty and so, **to a lesser extent**, is his wife.* ◇ *a lesser-known artist*
IDM the lesser of two evils the better of two bad things

lesson ⨕ **A1** /ˈlesn/ *noun* [C] **1** (**EDUCATION**) a period of time when you learn or teach sth: *She gives piano lessons.* ◇ *I want to take extra lessons in English conversation.* ◇ *a driving lesson* **2** something that is intended to be or should be learnt: *I'm sure we can all learn some lessons from this disaster.*
IDM learn your lesson → LEARN **teach sb a lesson** → TEACH

lessor /leˈsɔː(r)/ *noun* [C] (**LAW**) a person who gives sb the use of a building, an area of land, etc., having made a LEASE (= legal agreement)

let ⨕ **A1** /let/ *verb* [T] (**letting**; *pt, pp* **let**)
• MAKING SUGGESTIONS **1** used for making suggestions about what you and other people can do: *'Let's go to the cinema tonight.' 'Yes, let's.'*
• ALLOW **2 ~ sb/sth do sth** to allow sb/sth to do sth; to make sb/sth able to do sth: *My parents let me stay out till eleven o'clock.* ◇ *I wanted to borrow Dave's bike but he wouldn't let me.* ◇ *This ticket lets you travel anywhere in the city for a day.* **3** to allow sth to happen: *Don't let the fire go out.* **4** (used with an adverb or a preposition) to allow sb/sth to go somewhere: *Open the windows and let some fresh air in.* ◇ *She was let out of prison yesterday.*
• OFFERING HELP **5** used for offering help to sb: *Let me help you carry your bags.*
• HOUSE/ROOM **6 ~ sth (out) (to sb)** to allow sb to use a building, room, etc. in return for rent: *They let out two rooms to students.* ◇ *There's a flat to let in our block.*
IDM let sb/sth go | let go of sb/sth to stop holding sb/sth: *Let me go. You're hurting me!* ◇ *Hold the rope and don't let go of it.* **let yourself go 1** to relax without worrying what other people think **2** to allow yourself to become untidy, dirty, etc. ❶ For other idioms containing **let**, look at the entries for the nouns, adjectives, etc. For example, **let sth slip** is at **slip**.
PHRV let sb down to not do sth that you promised to do for sb or let sb on (about sth) (to sb) to tell sb a secret: *He didn't let on how much he'd paid for the vase.* **let sb off (with sth)** to not punish sb; to give them only a light punishment: *He expected to go to prison but they let him off with a fine.* **let sth out** to make a sound with your voice: *to let out a scream/sigh/groan/yell*

lethal ⨕+ **C1** /ˈliːθl/ *adj.* that can cause death or great damage: *a lethal weapon/drug* ▸ **lethally** /-θəli/ *adv.*

lethargy /ˈleθədʒi/ *noun* [U] the feeling of being very tired and not having any energy ▸ **lethargic** /ləˈθɑːdʒɪk/ *adj.*

letter ⨕ **A1** /ˈletə(r)/ *noun* [C] **1** a written or printed message that you send to sb: *I got a letter from Matthew this morning.* ◇ *I'm writing **a thank-you letter** to my uncle for the flowers he sent.* **2** (**LANGUAGE**) a written or printed sign that represents a sound in a language: *'Z' is the last letter of the English alphabet.*

letter bomb (*AmE also* **mail bomb**) *noun* [C] a small bomb that is sent to sb hidden in a letter that explodes when the ENVELOPE is opened

letter box *noun* [C] **1** a hole in a door or wall for putting letters, etc. through **2** (*AmE* **mailbox**) a small box near the main door of a building or by the road in which letters are left for the owner to collect

letterhead /ˈletəhed/ *noun* [C] the name and address of a person, a company or an organization printed at the top of their writing paper

lettuce /ˈletɪs/ *noun* [U, C] a plant with large green leaves that are eaten cold in salads: *a lettuce leaf*

leucocyte /ˈluːkəsaɪt/ *noun* [C] (**BIOLOGY**) a white blood cell

leukaemia (*BrE*) (*AmE* **leukemia**) /luːˈkiːmiə/ *noun* [U] (**HEALTH**) a serious disease of the blood that causes weakness and sometimes death

levee /ˈlevi/ *noun* [C] (**GEOGRAPHY**) **1** a raised area of sand, mud, etc. that is formed at the side of a river ⊃ picture at **floodplain 2** a low wall built at the side of a river to prevent it from flooding

level¹ ⨕ **A2** ⦿ /ˈlevl/ *noun* [C] **1** the amount, size or number of sth (compared to sth else): *a low level of unemployment* ◇ *high pollution levels* **2** the height, position, standard, etc. of sth: *He used to play tennis at a high level.* ◇ *an intermediate-level student* ◇ *top-level discussions* **3** a way of considering sth: *on a spiritual/personal/professional level* **4** a flat surface or layer: *a multi-level shopping centre* **5** = SPIRIT LEVEL

level² ⨕ **B1** /ˈlevl/ *adj.* **1** with no part higher than any other; flat: *Make sure the shelves are level before you fix them in position.* ◇ *Put the tent up on level ground.* ◇ *a level teaspoon of sugar* **2 ~ (with sb/sth)** at the same height, standard or position: *The boy's head was level with his father's shoulder.* ◇ *The teams are level on 34 points.*
IDM a level playing field a situation in which everyone has an equal chance of success

level³ ⨕ **B2** /ˈlevl/ *verb* [T] (**-ll-**, *AmE* **-l-**) to make sth flat, equal or level: *The ground needs levelling before we lay the patio.* ◇ *Juventus levelled the score with a late goal.* ◇ *Many buildings were levelled (= destroyed) in the earthquake.*
PHRV level sth at sb/sth to aim sth at sb/sth: *They levelled serious criticisms at the standard of teaching.* **level off/out** to become flat, equal or level

level crossing (*BrE*) (*AmE* **railroad crossing**) *noun* [C] a place where a railway crosses the surface of a road

level-headed *adj.* calm and sensible; able to make good decisions in a difficult situation

lever /ˈliːvə(r)/ *noun* [C] (**ENGINEERING**) **1** a handle that you pull or push in order to make a machine, etc. work: *Pull the lever towards you.* **2** a bar or tool that is used to lift or open sth when you put pressure or force on one end: *You need to get the tyre off with a tyre lever.* ⊃ picture on **page 436** ▸ **lever** *verb* [T]: *The police had to lever the door open.*

leverage /ˈliːvərɪdʒ/ *noun* [U] **1** (*formal*) the ability to influence what people do: *diplomatic leverage* **2** (**PHYSICS**) the act of using a LEVER to lift or open sth; the force needed to do this **3** (*AmE*) (**BUSINESS**) = GEARING

levitate /ˈlevɪteɪt/ *verb* [I, T] to rise and float in the air with no physical support, especially by means of magic or by using special mental powers; to make sth rise in this way ▸ **levitation** /ˌlevɪˈteɪʃn/ *noun* [U]

levy¹ /ˈlevi/ *noun* [C] (*pl.* **-ies**) (**POLITICS**) an extra amount of money that has to be paid, especially as a tax to the government: *to **impose a levy** on oil imports*

levy² /'levi/ *verb* [T] (levying; levies; *pt, pp* levied) **~ sth (on sb)** to officially demand and collect money, etc: *to levy a tax/fine*

lexical /'leksɪkl/ *adj.* connected with the words of a language: *lexical items* (= words and phrases) ▶ **lexically** /-kli/ *adv.*

lexicographer /ˌleksɪ'kɒgrəfə(r)/ *noun* [C] a person who writes and edits dictionaries

lexicography /ˌleksɪ'kɒgrəfi/ *noun* [U] the theory and practice of writing dictionaries

lexicon /'leksɪkən/ *noun* **1** *also* **the lexicon** [sing.] all the words and phrases used in a particular language or subject; all the words and phrases used and known by a particular person or group of people **2** [C] a list of words from A to Z on a particular subject or in a language: *a lexicon of technical scientific terms*

lexis /'leksɪs/ *noun* [U] all the words and phrases of a particular language **SYN vocabulary**

LGBT /ˌel dʒi: bi: 'ti:/ *abbr.* (**SOCIAL STUDIES**) **lesbian, gay, bisexual and transgender** (used to refer to people who are not HETEROSEXUAL)

liability /ˌlaɪə'bɪləti/ *noun* (*pl.* -ies) **1** [U] **~ (for sth)** (**LAW**) the state of being legally responsible for sth: *The company cannot accept liability for damage to cars in this car park.* **2** [C, usually sing.] (*informal*) a person or thing that can cause a lot of problems, cost a lot of money, etc. **3** [C, usually pl.] (**FINANCE**) the amount of money that a person or company owes: *The company is reported to have liabilities of nearly $90 000.* ⊃ look at **asset**

liable 🔑+ **C1** /'laɪəbl/ *adj.* [not before noun] **1 ~ (for sth)** (**LAW**) legally responsible for paying the cost of sth: *Is a wife liable for her husband's debts?* **2 ~ to do sth** likely to do sth: *We're all liable to have accidents when we are very tired.* **3 ~ to sth** likely to have or suffer from sth: *The area is liable to flooding.*

liaise /li'eɪz/ *verb* [I] **~ (with sb/sth)** to work closely with a person, group, etc. and give them regular information about what you are doing: *I've liaised with my manager on the matter.*

liaison /li'eɪzn/ *noun* **1** [U] **~ (between A and B)** communication between two or more people or groups that work together **2** [C] a secret sexual relationship

liar /'laɪə(r)/ *noun* [C] a person who does not tell the truth ⊃ look at **lie²** ⊃ Look at the verb and noun **lie**.

levers

libel /'laɪbl/ *noun* [U, C] (**LAW**) the act of printing a statement about sb that is not true and would give people a bad opinion of them: *The singer is suing the newspaper for libel.* ▶ **libel** *verb* [T] (-ll-, *AmE* -l-): *The actor claims he was libelled in the magazine article.*

liberal 🔑+ **C1** /'lɪbərəl/ *adj.* **1** accepting different opinions or kinds of behaviour, especially when they are different from your own: *He has very liberal parents.* **SYN tolerant 2** (**POLITICS**) believing in or based on principles of commercial freedom, freedom of choice, and avoiding extreme social and political change: *liberal policies/politicians* ⊃ note at **government 3 ~ (with sth)** generous; given in large amounts: *She is very liberal with her money.* ▶ **liberal** 🔑+ **C1** *noun* [C]: *He's always considered himself a liberal.* ▶ **liberalism** *noun* [U]

the Liberal Democrats *noun* [pl.] (**POLITICS**) a political party in Britain that represents views that are not extreme

liberalize (*BrE also* -ise) /'lɪbərəlaɪz/ *verb* [T] to make sth such as a law or a political or religious system less strict ▶ **liberalization** (*BrE also* -isation) /ˌlɪbərəlaɪ'zeɪʃn/ *noun* [U]

liberally /'lɪbərəli/ *adv.* freely or in large amounts: *Apply the suncream liberally.*

liberate /'lɪbəreɪt/ *verb* [T] **~ sb/sth (from sth)** to allow sb/sth to be free: *They were liberated from the concentration camp.* ▶ **liberation** 🔑+ **C1** /ˌlɪbə'reɪʃn/ *noun* [U]

liberated /'lɪbəreɪtɪd/ *adj.* free from the limits of traditional ideas about how you should behave

liberty 🔑+ **C1** /'lɪbəti/ *noun* [C, U] (*pl.* -ies) the freedom to go where you want, do what you want, etc: *We must defend our civil liberties at all costs.* ⊃ look at **freedom** (2)
IDM at liberty (to do sth) free or allowed to do sth: *You are at liberty to leave when you wish.*

Libra /'li:brə/ *noun* [U] the seventh sign of THE ZODIAC (= twelve signs that represent the positions of the sun, moon and planets), the Scales; a person born under this sign

librarian /laɪ'breəriən/ *noun* [C] a person who works in or is in charge of a library

library 🔑 **A1** /'laɪbrəri, -bri/ *noun* [C] (*pl.* -ies) **1** a room or building that contains a collection of books, etc. that can be looked at or borrowed: *My library books are due back tomorrow.* ⊃ look at **bookshop 2** a private collection of books, etc.

libretto /lɪ'bretəʊ/ *noun* [C] (*pl.* -os, libretti /-ti:/) (**MUSIC**) the words that are sung or spoken in an OPERA or a musical play

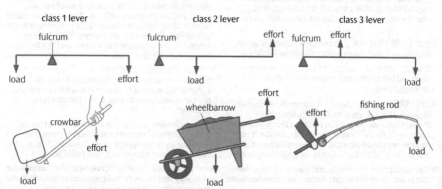

class 1 lever   class 2 lever   class 3 lever

licence ᵀ **B2** (*BrE*) (*AmE* license) /'laɪsns/ *noun* **1** [C]
~ **(for sth/to do sth)** (**LAW**) an official paper that shows
you are allowed to do or have sth: *You need a licence
for this software.* ◇ *The company has applied for a
licence to import goods into China.* ⊃ look at **driving
licence 2** [U] ~ **(to do sth)** (*formal*) permission or
freedom to do sth: *The soldiers were given licence to
kill if they were attacked.*

'**licence plate** (*AmE* **license plate**) = NUMBER PLATE

license ᵀ⁺ **C1** /'laɪsns/ *verb* [T] to give sb official
permission to do, own, or use sth: *The new drug has
not yet been licensed in the US.*

licensed /'laɪsnst/ *adj.* **1** having official permission
to sell alcoholic drinks: *a licensed restaurant* **2** that
you have official permission to own: *Is that gun
licensed?* **3** having official permission to do sth: *She is
licensed to fly solo.*

licensee /ˌlaɪsn'siː/ *noun* [C] a person who has a licence
to sell alcoholic drinks

'**license plate** (*AmE*) = NUMBER PLATE

'**licensing laws** *noun* [pl.] (*BrE*) (**LAW**) the laws that control
when and where alcoholic drinks can be sold

lichen /'laɪkən, 'lɪtʃən/ *noun* [U, C] (**BIOLOGY**) a very small
grey or yellow plant that spreads over the surface of
rocks, walls and trees and does not have any flowers

lick /lɪk/ *verb* [T] to move your tongue across sth: *The
child licked the spoon clean.* ◇ *I licked the envelope
and stuck it down.* ▶ **lick** *noun* [C]

licorice /'lɪkərɪʃ, -rɪs/ = LIQUORICE

lid /lɪd/ *noun* [C] **1** the top part of a box, pot, etc. that can
be lifted up or taken off ⊃ picture at **piano 2** = EYELID

lie¹ ᵀ **A1** /laɪ/ *verb* [I] (**lying; lies;** *pt* **lay** /leɪ/; *pp* **lain** /leɪn/)
1 to be in or move into a flat position (so that you are
not standing or sitting): *He lay on the sofa and went to
sleep.* ◇ *to lie on your back/side/front* ◇ *The book lay
open in front of her.* **2** to be or stay in a certain state or
position: *Snow lay thick on the ground.* ◇ *The hills lie to
the north of the town.* ◇ *They are young and their whole
lives **lie ahead** of them.* **3** ~ **(in sth)** to exist or to be
found somewhere: *The problem lies in deciding when
to stop.*
IDM **lie in wait (for sb)** to hide somewhere waiting
to attack, surprise or catch sb **lie low** to try not to
attract attention to yourself
PHR V **lie around** (*BrE also* **lie about**) to relax and do
nothing **lie back** to relax and do nothing while sb else
works, etc. **lie behind sth** to be the real hidden
reason for sth: *We may don't what lay behind his
decision to resign.* **lie down** (used about a person) to
be in or move into a flat position so that you can rest
lie in (*informal*) to stay in bed later than usual because
you do not have to get up ⊃ look at **oversleep lie with
sb (to do sth)** (*informal*) to be sb's responsibility to do
sth

lie² ᵀ **B1** /laɪ/ *verb* [I] (**lying; lies;** *pt, pp* **lied**) ~ **(to sb)
(about sth)** to say or write sth that you know is not
true: *He lied about his age in order to join the army.*
◇ *How could you lie to me?* ▶ **lie** ᵀ **B1** *noun* [C]: *to tell a
lie* ◇ *That story about his mother being ill was just **a
pack of lies**.*

'**lie detector** *noun* [C] a piece of equipment that can
show if a person is telling the truth or not

lieutenant /lef'tenənt/ *noun* [C] (*abbr.* **Lieut., Lt, Lt.**) an
officer at a middle level in the army, NAVY or AIR
FORCE: *Lieutenant Paul Fisher* ◇ *flight lieutenant*

life ᵀ **A1** /laɪf/ *noun* (*pl.* **lives** /laɪvz/)
• BEING ALIVE **1** [U] the quality that people, animals or
plants have when they are not dead: *Do you believe in
life after death?* ◇ *to bring somebody/come back to life*

2 [C, U] the state of being alive as a human being: *He
risked his **life** to protect the public.* ◇ *Doctors fought all
night to **save** her **life**.*
• LIVING THINGS **3** [U] (**BIOLOGY**) living things: *Life on
earth began in a very simple form.* ◇ *No life was found
on the moon.* ◇ *There was no sign of life in the deserted
house.* ◇ *plant life*
• PERIOD OF TIME **4** [C, U] the period during which sb/sth
is alive or exists: *I've lived in this town **all** my **life**.*
◇ *She took up tennis late in life.* ◇ *to have a short/long/
exciting life*
• EXPERIENCE/ACTIVITIES **5** [U] the things that you may
experience while you are alive: *Life can be hard for a
single parent.* ◇ *I'm not happy with the situation, but I
suppose **that's life**.* **6** [C, U] a way of living: *They went to
America to **start a new life**.* ◇ *They **lead a** busy **life**.*
◇ *married life*
• ENERGY **7** [U] energy; activity: *Young children are **full of**
life.* ◇ *These streets **come to life** in the evenings.*
• REALITY **8** [U] the experience and activities that are
typical of all people's lives: *the worries of everyday life*
◇ *I wonder what that actor's like **in real life**.*
IDM **a fact of life** → FACT **the facts of life** → FACT **full
of beans/life** → FULL¹ **get a life** (*informal*) used to tell
sb to stop being boring and do sth more interesting
have the time of your life → TIME¹ **lose your life**
→ LOSE **a matter of life and/or death** → MATTER¹ **take
your (own) life** to kill yourself **a walk of life** → WALK²
a/sb's way of life → WAY¹

ˌ**life-and-'death** (*also* **life-or-death**) *adj.* [only before noun]
very serious or dangerous: *a life-and-death struggle/
matter/decision*

lifebelt /'laɪfbelt/ (*also* **lifebuoy** /'laɪfbɔɪ/) *noun* [C] (*BrE*) a
ring made from light material that floats well. A
lifebelt is thrown to a person who has fallen into water
to stop them from sinking.

lifeboat /'laɪfbəʊt/ *noun* [C] **1** a small boat that is
carried on a large ship and that is used to escape from
the ship if it is in danger of sinking **2** a special boat
that is used for rescuing people who are in danger at
sea

'**life coach** *noun* [C] a person who is employed by sb to
give them advice about how to achieve the things
they want in their life and work

'**life cycle** *noun* [C] (**BIOLOGY**) the series of forms into
which a living thing changes as it develops: *the life
cycle of a frog*

'**life drawing** *noun* [U, C] (**ART**) the activity or skill of
drawing pictures of people who are present in front
of you, usually when they have no clothes on; a
drawing made in this way: *He teaches life drawing in
his studio.* ◇ *an exhibition of life drawings*

'**life expectancy** *noun* [U, C] (*pl.* **-ies**) (**SOCIAL STUDIES**) the
number of years that a person is likely to live ⊃ note
at **HDI**

lifeguard /'laɪfgɑːd/ *noun* [C] a person at a beach or
swimming pool whose job is to rescue people who are
in difficulty in the water

'**life insurance** *noun* [U] (**FINANCE**) a type of insurance in
which you make regular payments so that you
receive money when you are a particular age, or so
that your family will receive money when you die: *a
life insurance policy*

'**life jacket** (*also* **life vest** *especially in AmE*) *noun* [C] a plastic
or rubber jacket without arms that can be filled with
air. A life jacket is used to make sb float if they fall
into water. ⊃ picture at **canoe**

lifeless /'laɪfləs/ *adj.* **1** dead or appearing to be dead
2 not exciting or interesting **SYN** **dull¹**

lifelike /ˈlaɪflaɪk/ *adj.* looking like a real person or thing: *The flowers are made of silk but they are very lifelike.*

lifeline /ˈlaɪflaɪn/ *noun* [C] something that is very important for sb and that they depend on: *The extra payments are a lifeline for families on a low income.*

lifelong ̂+ **C1** /ˈlaɪflɒŋ/ *adj.* [only before noun] for all of your life: *a lifelong friend*

life-or-ˈdeath = LIFE-AND-DEATH

life ˈpeer *noun* [C] (**POLITICS**) (in the UK) a person who is given the title of PEER (= 'Lord' or 'Lady') but who cannot pass it on to their son or daughter

life science *noun* [C, usually pl., U] (**SCIENCE**) any of the sciences that involve the study of humans, animals or plants ⊃ look at **earth science, natural science**

life ˈsentence *noun* [C] (**LAW**) the punishment by which sb spends the rest of their life or a very long time in prison: *He's serving a life sentence for murder.*

life-size (*also* life-sized) *adj.* of the same size as the real person or thing: *a life-sized statue*

lifespan /ˈlaɪfspæn/ *noun* [C] the length of time that sth is likely to live, work, last, etc.: *A mosquito has a lifespan of only a few days.*

life story *noun* [C] (*pl.* -ies) the story of sb's life

lifestyle ̂ **A2** /ˈlaɪfstaɪl/ *noun* [C] (**SOCIAL STUDIES**) the way that you live: *a healthy lifestyle*

life supˈport *noun* [U] (**MEDICINE**) the fact of being kept alive by a special machine: *After the accident he was on life support for a week.*

life supˈport machine *noun* [C] (**MEDICINE**) a piece of equipment in a hospital that keeps sb alive when they cannot breathe without help

life-threatening *adj.* that is likely to kill sb: *life-threatening injuries* ◇ *His heart condition is not life-threatening.*

lifetime ̂+ **B2** /ˈlaɪftaɪm/ *noun* [C] the period of time that sb is alive

life vest (*AmE*) = LIFE JACKET

lift¹ ̂ **A2** /lɪft/ *verb*
- RAISE **1** [T] ~ **sb/sth (up)** to move sb/sth to a higher level or position: *He lifted the child up onto his shoulders.* ◇ *Lift your arm very gently and see if it hurts.* ◇ *It took two men to lift the piano.*
- MOVE **2** [T] to move sb/sth from one place or position to another: *She lifted the suitcase down from the rack.*
- REMOVE A LAW **3** [T] to end or remove a rule, law, etc.: *The ban on public meetings has been lifted.*
- MAKE SB HAPPY **4** [I, T] to become happier; to make sb happier: *His heart lifted at the sight of her.* ◇ *The news lifted our spirits.*
- OF CLOUDS, ETC. **5** [I] (used about clouds, FOG, etc.) to rise up or disappear: *The mist lifted towards the end of the morning.*
- COPY **6** [T] ~ **sth (from sb/sth)** (*informal*) to steal or copy sth: *Most of his essay was lifted straight from the textbook.* ⊃ look at **shoplifting**

PHR V lift off (used about a SPACECRAFT) to rise straight up from the ground ⊃ look at **lift-off**

lift² ̂ **A2** /lɪft/ *noun* **1** (*BrE*) (*AmE* elevator) [C] a machine in a large building that is used for carrying people or goods from one floor to another: *It's on the third floor so we'd better take the lift.* **2** [C] a free ride in a car, etc.: *Can you give me a lift to the station, please?* **3** [sing.] (*informal*) a feeling of being happier or more confident than before: *Her words of encouragement gave the whole team a lift.* **4** [U] (**ENGINEERING, PHYSICS**) the pressure of air moving upwards on an aircraft when flying ⊃ look at **drag²** (4)

IDM thumb a lift → THUMB²

ˈlift-off *noun* [C] the start of the flight of a SPACECRAFT when it leaves the ground

ligament /ˈlɪɡəmənt/ *noun* [C] (**ANATOMY**) a strong band in a person's or an animal's body that holds the bones, etc. together ⊃ look at **tendon** ⊃ picture at **synovial**

light¹ ̂ **A1** /laɪt/ *noun* **1** [U, C] the energy from the sun, a lamp, etc. that allows you to see things: *a beam/ray of light* ◇ *The light was too dim for us to read by.* ◇ *Strong light is bad for the eyes.* ◇ *We could see strange lights in the sky.* ⊃ picture at **energy, shadow¹, short-sighted, wavelength** **2** [C] something that produces light, for example an electric lamp: *Suddenly all the lights went out/came on.* ◇ *If the lights (= traffic lights) are red, stop!* ◇ *That car hasn't got its lights on.* **3** [sing.] something, for example a match, that can be used to light a cigarette: *Have you got a light?*

IDM bring sth/come to light to make sth known or to become known cast light on sth → CAST¹ give sb/get the green light → GREEN¹ in a good, bad, etc. light (used about the way that sth is seen or described by other people) well, badly, etc.: *The newspapers often portray his behaviour in a bad light.* in the light of because of; considering set light to sth to cause sth to start burning shed light on sth → SHED²

light² ̂ **A1** /laɪt/ *adj.*
- COLOUR **1** (used about a colour) pale: *a light-blue sweater* **OPP** dark
- FULL OF LIGHT **2** having a lot of light: *In summer it's still light at ten o'clock.* ◇ *a light room* **OPP** dark
- NOT HEAVY **3** not of great weight: *Carry this bag — it's the lightest.* ◇ *I've lost weight — I'm five kilos lighter than I used to be.* ◇ *light clothes* (= for summer) **OPP** heavy
- GENTLE **4** not using much force; gentle: *a light touch on the shoulder*
- EASY **5** easy to do; not making you tired: *light exercise* ◇ *light entertainment/reading*
- SMALL AMOUNT **6** not great in amount, degree, etc.: *Traffic in London is light on a Sunday.* ◇ *a light prison sentence* ◇ *a light wind* ◇ *a light breakfast*
- SLEEP **7** (used about sleep) not deep: *I'm a light sleeper, so the slightest noise wakes me.*
  ▶ **lightness** *noun* [U]

light³ ̂ **A2** /laɪt/ *verb* (*pt, pp* lit /lɪt/) **HELP** Lighted is also used for the past tense and past participle, especially before nouns: *The church was full of lighted candles.* **1** [I, T] to begin to burn; to make sth begin to burn: *The gas cooker won't light.* ◇ *to light a fire* **2** [T] to give light to sth: *The street is well/badly lit at night.* ◇ *We only had a small torch to light our way.*

PHR V light (sth) up **1** to make sth bright with light: *The fireworks lit up the whole sky.* **2** (used about sb's face, eyes, etc.) to become bright with happiness or excitement **3** to start smoking a cigarette

ˈlight bulb *noun* [C] the glass part of an electric lamp that gives out light: *a 60-watt light bulb*

lighten /ˈlaɪtn/ *verb* [I, T] to become or to make sth become lighter in colour

lighter /ˈlaɪtə(r)/ = CIGARETTE LIGHTER

ˌlight-ˈheaded *adj.* not in complete control of your thoughts and movements

ˌlight-ˈhearted *adj.* **1** intended to be fun rather than too serious **2** happy and without problems

lighthouse /ˈlaɪthaʊs/ *noun* [C] a tall building with a strong light at the top to warn and guide ships near the coast

lighting ̂+ **B2** /ˈlaɪtɪŋ/ *noun* [U] the quality or type of lights in a room, building, etc.

lightly /ˈlaɪtli/ adv. **1** gently; with very little force: *He touched her lightly on the arm.* **2** only a little; not much: *lightly cooked/spiced/whisked* **3** not seriously; without serious thought: *We do not take our customers' complaints lightly.*
IDM **get off/be let off lightly** to avoid serious punishment or trouble

lightning[1] /ˈlaɪtnɪŋ/ noun [U] a flash of very bright light that appears in the sky during a storm: *The tree was struck by lightning and burst into flames.* ◇ *a flash of lightning* ⊃ look at **thunder**[1] ⊃ note at **disaster**, **storm**[1] ⊃ picture at **nitrogen cycle**

lightning[2] /ˈlaɪtnɪŋ/ adj. [only before noun] very quick or sudden: *a lightning attack*

lightweight[1] /ˈlaɪtweɪt/ adj. made of thinner material and less heavy than usual: *a lightweight jacket*

lightweight[2] /ˈlaɪtweɪt/ noun [C] **1** (**SPORT**) a person who is in one of the lightest weight groups in certain fighting sports: *a lightweight boxing champion* **2** a person or thing that weighs less than usual

light year noun [C] (**ASTRONOMY**, **PHYSICS**) the distance that light travels in one year, 9.4607×10^{12} kilometres

lignite /ˈlɪɡnaɪt/ noun [U] (**GEOLOGY**) a soft brown type of coal

likable /ˈlaɪkəbl/ = LIKEABLE

like[1] ⚑ **A1** /laɪk/ prep. **1** similar to sb/sth: *You look very/just/exactly like your father.* ◇ *Those two singers sound like cats!* ◇ *Your house is nothing like how I imagined it.* **2** for example; such as: *They enjoy most team games, like football and rugby.* **3** typical of a particular person: *It was just like Maria to be late.*
IDM **sth like** about; approximately: *The cathedral took something like 200 years to build.* **like anything** (informal) very much, fast, hard, etc: *We had to pedal like anything to get up the hill.* **nothing like** → NOTHING **that's more like it** (used to say that sth is better than before): *The sun's coming out now — that's more like it!*

like[2] ⚑ **A1** /laɪk/ verb [T] **1** ~ sb/sth; ~ doing sth; ~ to do sth; ~ sth about sb/sth to find sb/sth pleasant; to enjoy sth: *He's nice. I like him a lot.* ◇ *Do you like their new flat?* ◇ *How do you like John's new girlfriend?* ◇ *I like my coffee strong.* ◇ *I like playing tennis.* ◇ *I don't like him borrowing my things without asking.* ◇ *I like to go to the cinema on Thursdays.* ◇ *What is it you like about Sarah?* ◇ *She didn't like it when I shouted at her.* ◇ *The job seems strange at first, but you'll get to like it.*
OPP **dislike**[1] **2** to want: *Do what you like. I don't care.* ◇ *We can go whenever you like.* ◇ *I didn't like to disturb you while you were eating.* **3** if you **like** a page on a website, you show that you agree with it or that you think it is good by clicking a special button
IDM **if you like** used for agreeing with sb or suggesting sth in a polite way: *'Shall we stop for a rest?' 'Yes, if you like.'* **I like that!** (BrE, informal) used

light bulb

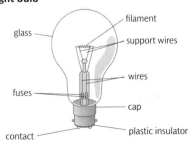

- filament
- glass
- support wires
- wires
- fuses
- cap
- contact
- plastic insulator

for saying that sth is not true or not fair **like the look/sound of sb/sth** to have a good impression of sb/sth after seeing or hearing about them or it

like[3] /laɪk/ conj. (informal) **1** in the same way as sb/sth: *Stop behaving like children.* ◇ *That's not right. Do it like this.* ◇ *She can't draw like her sister can.* **2** as if: *She behaves like she owns the place.*

like[4] ⚑ **B1** /laɪk/ noun **1** [sing.] a person or thing that is similar to sb/sth else: *I enjoy going round castles, old churches and the like.* ◇ *She was a great singer, and we may never see her like/the like of her again.* **2** likes [pl.] things that you like: *Tell me about some of your likes and dislikes.* **3** [C] if sth on SOCIAL MEDIA, a blog, etc. receives a **like**, it means that sb has shown that they agree with it or think it is good by clicking a special button

-like /laɪk/ suffix (in adjectives) similar to; typical of: *childlike* ◇ *shell-like*

likeable (also **likable**) /ˈlaɪkəbl/ adj. (used about a person) easy to like; pleasant

likelihood ⚑+ **C1** /ˈlaɪklihʊd/ noun [U] the chance of sth happening; how likely sth is to happen: *There seems very little likelihood of success.* **SYN** **probability**

likely[1] ⚑ **A2** ❷ /ˈlaɪkli/ adj. (likelier; likeliest) **1** ~ (to do sth); ~ (that ...) having a good chance of happening; PROBABLE or expected: *Do you think it's likely to rain?* ◇ *The boss is not likely to agree.* ◇ *It's not likely that the boss will agree.* **OPP** **unlikely** ⊃ note at **probable** **2** probably suitable: *a likely candidate for the job*

likely[2] ❷ /ˈlaɪkli/ adv.
IDM **as likely as not** | **most/very likely** very probably: *As likely as not she's forgotten all about it.* ◇ *The illness was caused, most likely, by a virus.* **not likely!** (informal) certainly not

like-ˈminded adj. having similar ideas and interests: *The course is a great way to meet like-minded people.*

liken /ˈlaɪkən/ verb [T] ~ sb/sth to sb/sth (formal) to compare one person or thing with another: *This young artist has been likened to Picasso.*

likeness /ˈlaɪknəs/ noun [C, U] the fact of being similar in appearance; an example of this: *The witness's drawing turned out to be a good likeness of the attacker.*

likewise ⚑+ **B2** /ˈlaɪkwaɪz/ adv. (formal) the same; in a similar way: *I intend to send a letter of apology and suggest that you do likewise.*

liking /ˈlaɪkɪŋ/ noun [sing.] ~ (for sb/sth) the feeling that you like sb/sth: *I have a liking for spicy food.*
IDM **too ... for your liking** that you do not like because he/she/it has too much of a particular quality: *The music was a bit too loud for my liking.*

lilac[1] /ˈlaɪlək/ noun **1** [U, C] a tree or large bush that has large purple or white flowers in spring **2** [U] a pale purple colour

lilac[2] /ˈlaɪlək/ adj. pale purple in colour

lilo (also **Li-lo**™) /ˈlaɪləʊ/ noun [C] (pl. -os) (BrE) a plastic or rubber bed that is filled with air and used when camping or for floating on water

lily /ˈlɪli/ noun [C] (pl. -ies) a type of plant that has large white or coloured flowers in the shape of a bell ⊃ look at **water lily**

limb ⚑+ **C1** /lɪm/ noun [C] **1** (**ANATOMY**) a leg or an arm of a person **2** one of the main branches of a tree
IDM **out on a limb** without the support of other people

lime /laɪm/ *noun* **1** [C] a fruit that looks like a small green lemon **2** [U] (**AGRICULTURE, CHEMISTRY**) a white substance that is used in building materials and to help plants grow

ˌlime-ˈgreen (*also* **lime**) *adj.* bright yellow-green in colour ▶ **ˌlime ˈgreen** (*also* **lime**) *noun* [U]

limelight /ˈlaɪmlaɪt/ (*usually* **the limelight**) *noun* [U] the centre of public attention: *to be **in the limelight*** ◇ *to **stay out of the limelight***

limerick /ˈlɪmərɪk/ *noun* [C] (**LITERATURE**) a humorous short poem, with two long lines that RHYME (= end with the same sound) with each other, followed by two short lines that RHYME with each other and ending with a long line that RHYMES with the first two

limestone /ˈlaɪmstəʊn/ *noun* [U] (**GEOLOGY**) a type of hard white SEDIMENTARY rock that is used for building or for making CEMENT

limit¹ 🔑 **B1** **O** /ˈlɪmɪt/ *noun* [C] **1** the greatest or smallest amount of sth that is allowed or possible: *an age/a time limit* ◇ *He was fined for exceeding the speed limit.* ◇ *There's a limit to the amount of time I'm prepared to spend on this.* **2** the outside edge of a place or an area: *the city limits* **3** (**MATHEMATICS**) a point or value that you aim for with a number or series of numbers, until they are as close to it as you want
IDM **within limits** only up to a reasonable point or amount

▼ **SYNONYMS**

limit

restriction • control • constraint • restraint • limitation

These are all words for sth that limits what you can do or what can happen.

limit *The EU has set strict limits on pollution levels.*

restriction *Speed restrictions are in place.*

control *international talks on arms control*

constraint *We have to work within severe time constraints.*

restraint (*formal*) *Wage restraints were imposed.*

limitation *He recognized the limitations of the medium.*

limestone landscape

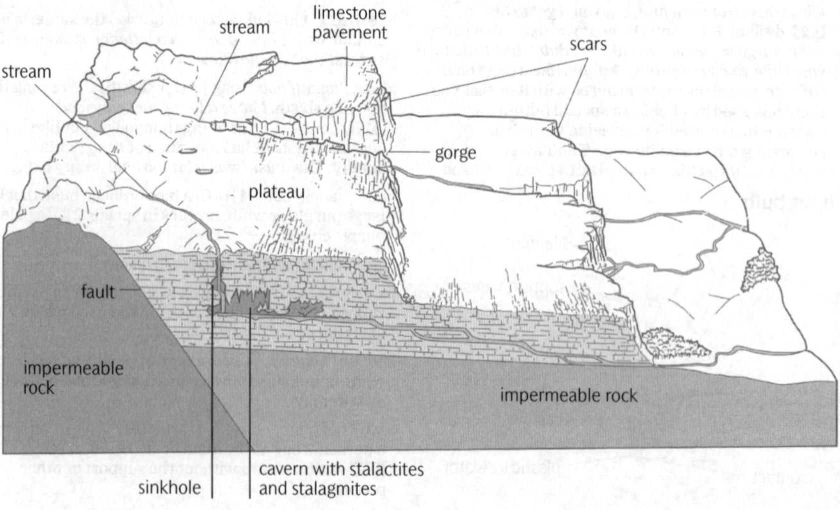
limestone pavement
stream
stream
scars
gorge
plateau
fault
impermeable rock
impermeable rock
sinkhole
cavern with stalactites and stalagmites

limit² 🔑 **B1** **O** /ˈlɪmɪt/ *verb* [T] **~ sb/sth (to sth)** to keep sb/sth within or below a certain amount, size, degree or area: *Try to limit the number of trips you make by plane.*

limitation 🔑+ **B2** **W** /ˌlɪmɪˈteɪʃn/ *noun* **1** [C, U] **~ (on sth)** the act of limiting or controlling sth; a condition that puts a limit on sth: *There are no limitations on what we can do.* **2** [C, usually pl.] things that you cannot do: *It is important to know your own limitations.* ➲ note at **limit¹**

limited 🔑 **B2** **O** /ˈlɪmɪtɪd/ *adj.* small in number, amount, etc: *Book early because there are only a limited number of seats available.* **OPP** **unlimited**

ˌlimited ˈcompany *noun* [C] (*abbr.* **Ltd**) (**BUSINESS**) (in the UK) a company whose owners only have to pay a limited amount of the money that they owe if the company fails

ˌlimited eˈdition *noun* [C] (**ART, LITERATURE**) a fixed, usually small, number of copies of a book, picture, etc. that is produced at one time: *The original limited edition prints will be for sale.*

limousine /ˈlɪməziːn, ˌlɪməˈziːn/ (*also informal* **limo** /ˈlɪməʊ/) *noun* [C] a large expensive car that usually has a sheet of glass between the driver and the passengers in the back

limp¹ /lɪmp/ *verb* [I] to walk with difficulty because you have hurt your leg or foot ▶ **limp** *noun* [sing.]: *to walk with a limp*

limp² /lɪmp/ *adj.* not firm or strong: *You should put those flowers in water before they go limp.*

limpet /ˈlɪmpɪt/ *noun* [C] a small SHELLFISH (= a creature with a shell that lives in water) that sticks very tightly to rocks: *She clung to her job like a limpet, refusing to resign.*

line¹ 🔑 **A1** **O** /laɪn/ *noun*

• LONG THIN MARK **1** [C] a long thin mark on the surface of sth or on the ground: *to draw a line* ◇ *a straight/wiggly/dotted line* ◇ *The ball was definitely over the line.* ◇ *the finishing line of a race*

• ROW **2** [C] a row of people, things, words on a page, etc: *There was a long line of people waiting at the Post Office.* ◇ *a five-line poem* ◇ *Start each paragraph on a new line.*

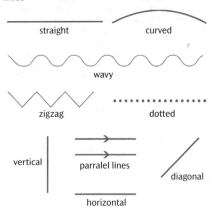

straight   curved

wavy

zigzag   dotted

vertical   parralel lines   diagonal

horizontal

- ON THE SKIN **3** [C] a mark like a line on sb's skin that people usually get as they get older: *He had fine lines around his eyes.*
- DIRECTION **4** [C] a direction or course of movement, thought or action: *The answer's not quite correct, but you're **on the right lines**.* ◇ *The two countries' economies are developing **along** similar **lines**.*
- STRING **5** [C] a piece of rope or string: *Hang out the clothes on the (washing) line, please.* ◇ *a fishing line*
- WIRE/CONNECTION **6** [C] a phone or electricity wire or connection: *I'm sorry — the line is engaged. Can you try again later?* ◇ *I'll just check for you. Can you **hold the line** (= wait)?*
- RAILWAY **7** [C] a section of railway track
- WORDS **8** lines [pl.] (**ARTS AND MEDIA**) the words that are spoken by an actor in a play, etc.
- TRANSPORT COMPANY **9** [C] a company that provides transport by air, ship, etc: *an airline*
- DIVISION **10** [C] a border or limit between one place or thing and another: *to cross state lines* ◇ *There's a thin line between showing interest and being nosy.*
- PRODUCT **11** [C] (**BUSINESS**) one type of goods in a shop, etc.
- IN WAR **12** [C] the place where an army is fighting: *There's renewed fighting on **the front line**.*
- SERIES **13** [C] a series of people in a family; things or events that follow each other in time: *He comes from **a long line** of musicians.*
- ACTIVITY **14** [C] ~ (**of sth**) something that you do as a job, do well, or enjoy doing: *What **line** of work are you in?* **IDM** **above the line 1** (**FINANCE**) connected with the money that a company earns and the costs it has to pay, which affect the profit it makes: *Raw materials are recorded as above-the-line costs.* ⊃ look at **below the line¹** (1) **2** (**BUSINESS**) connected with advertising in the MASS MEDIA (= newspapers, television and radio): *above-the-line promotion* ⊃ look at **below the line¹** (2) **below the line 1** (**FINANCE**) connected with unusual costs or money earned that are taken away or added after a company's profit has been calculated ⊃ look at **above the line¹** (1) **2** (**BUSINESS**) connected with advertising by means of DIRECT MAIL (= advertisements sent to people through the post), email, SOCIAL MEDIA, etc. ⊃ look at **above the line¹** (2) **draw the line at sth/doing sth →** DRAW¹ **drop sb a line →** DROP¹ **in line for sth** likely to get sth: *You could be in line for promotion if you keep working like this.* **in line with sth** similar to sth; in agreement with sth: *These changes will bring the industry in line with the new laws.* **out of line with sth** different from sth; not in agreement with sth: *London prices are out of line*

with the rest of the country. **overstep the mark/line →** OVERSTEP **somewhere along/down the line** at some time; sooner or later **take a hard line (on sth) →** HARD¹ **toe the (party) line →** TOE²

line² ʕ+ **B2** /laɪn/ *verb* [T] **1** [often passive] to cover the inside surface of sth with a different material **2** to form lines or rows along sth: *Crowds lined the streets to watch the race.* **PHR V** **line up (for sth)** stand in a line or a row **SYN** queue **line sth up** (*informal*) to arrange or organize sth: *She lined the bottles up on the shelf.*

linear ʕ+ **C1** /ˈlɪniə(r)/ *adj.* **1** of or in lines: *In his art he broke the laws of scientific linear perspective.* **2** going from one thing to another in a single series of stages: *Students do not always progress in a linear fashion.* **3** of length: *linear measurement* (= for example metres, feet, etc.) **4** (**MATHEMATICS**) able to be represented by a straight line on a GRAPH: *linear equations*

lined /laɪnd/ *adj.* **1** covered in lines: *a face lined with age* ◇ *lined paper* **2** -lined (in adjectives) having the object mentioned all along the side(s); having the inside surface covered with the material mentioned: *a tree-lined avenue* ◇ *fur-lined boots*

ˈline drawing *noun* [C] (**ART**) a drawing that consists only of lines

linen /ˈlɪnɪn/ *noun* [U] **1** a type of strong cloth that is made from FLAX (= a natural substance from a plant) **2** sheets and other types of cloth used in the house to cover beds, tables, etc: *bedlinen*

ˌline of ˈlatitude *noun* [C] (**GEOGRAPHY**) one of the lines drawn on a map of the world that is PARALLEL to the EQUATOR ⊃ picture at **earth¹**

ˌline of ˈlongitude *noun* [C] (**GEOGRAPHY**) one of the lines drawn from the North Pole to the South Pole on a map of the world **SYN** meridian ⊃ picture at **earth¹**

liner /ˈlaɪnə(r)/ *noun* [C] **1** (**TOURISM**) a large ship that carries people, etc. long distances **2** something that is put inside sth else to keep it clean or protect it. A liner is usually thrown away after it has been used: *a dustbin liner*

linesman /ˈlaɪnzmən/ *noun* [C] (*pl.* -men /-mən/) (**SPORT**) an official who helps the REFEREE in some games that are played on a field or court, especially in deciding whether or where a ball crosses one of the lines. Linesmen are now officially called REFEREE'S ASSISTANTS in football.

ˈline-up ʕ+ **C1** *noun* [C, usually sing.] **1** the people who are going to take part in a particular event: *an impressive line-up of speakers* **2** a set of events, etc. arranged to follow one another: *The final episode of the drama completes this evening's TV line-up.*

linger ʕ+ **C1** /ˈlɪŋɡə(r)/ *verb* [I] ~ (**on**) to stay somewhere or do sth for longer than usual: *The smell of her perfume lingered on long after she had left.*

lingerie /ˈlɒ̃ʒəri/ *noun* [U] (used in shops, etc.) women's underwear

lingua franca /ˌlɪŋɡwə ˈfræŋkə/ *noun* [usually sing.] (**LANGUAGE**) a shared language of communication used between people whose main languages are different: *English has become a lingua franca in many parts of the world.*

linguist /ˈlɪŋɡwɪst/ *noun* [C] (**LANGUAGE**) **1** a person who knows several foreign languages well **2** a person who studies or languages **3** a person who studies languages or LINGUISTICS

linguistic /lɪŋˈgwɪstɪk/ *adj.* (**LANGUAGE**) connected with language or the study of language

linguistics /lɪŋˈgwɪstɪks/ *noun* [U] (**EDUCATION, LANGUAGE**) the scientific study of language

lining /ˈlaɪnɪŋ/ *noun* [C] material that covers the inside surface of sth: *I've torn the lining of my coat.*
IDM **every cloud has a silver lining** → CLOUD¹

link¹ ⚡ **A2** ⊙ /lɪŋk/ *noun* [C] **1** ~ (**between A and B**); ~ (**with sb/sth**) a connection or relationship between two or more people or things: *There is a strong link between obesity and heart disease.* ◊ *to establish/ maintain/break trading links with a country* **2** one ring of a chain **3** a means of travelling or communicating between two places: *For more details, click on the links at the bottom of the page.*

link² ⚡ **A2** ⊙ /lɪŋk/ *verb* [T] ~ **A to/with B**; ~ **A and B** (**together**) to make a connection between two or more people or things: *The new bridge will link the island to the mainland.* ◊ *The computers are linked together in a network.* ◊ *These two factors are directly linked.*
PHRV **link up (with sb/sth)** to join together (with sb/sth): *The bands have linked up for a charity concert.*

linkage /ˈlɪŋkɪdʒ/ *noun* **1** [U, C] ~ (**between A and B**) the act of linking things; a link or system of links **SYN** **connection 2** [C] a device that links two or more things

linking verb *noun* [C] (**GRAMMAR**) a verb such as *be* or *become* that connects a subject with the adjective or noun that describes it: *In 'She became angry', the verb 'became' is a linking verb.*

link-up *noun* [C] the joining together or connection of two or more things

linocut /ˈlaɪnəʊkʌt/ *noun* [C] (**ART**) a design or shape cut in a piece of LINOLEUM, used to make a print; a print made in this way

linoleum /lɪˈnəʊliəm/ (*BrE, informal* **lino** /ˈlaɪnəʊ/) *noun* [U] a type of strong material with a hard shiny surface, used for covering floors

linseed oil /ˈlɪnsiːd ɔɪl/ *noun* [U] an oil made from FLAX seeds, used in paint or to protect wood, etc.

lint /lɪnt/ *noun* [U] **1** soft cotton cloth used for covering and protecting injuries **2** (*especially AmE*) small soft pieces of wool, cotton, etc. that stick on the surface of clothes, etc.

lintel /ˈlɪntl/ *noun* [C] (**ARCHITECTURE**) a piece of wood or stone over a door or window

Linux™ /ˈlɪnəks, ˈlaɪ-/ *noun* [U] (**COMPUTING**) a computer OPERATING SYSTEM that you do not have to pay to use

lion ⚡ **A1** /ˈlaɪən/ *noun* [C] a large animal of the cat family that lives in Africa and parts of southern Asia. Male lions have a MANE (= long, thick hair around their head and neck). ❶ A female lion is called a **lioness** and a young lion is called a **cub**. The noise a lion makes is a **roar**.
IDM **the lion's share (of sth)** the largest or best part of sth when it is divided

lioness /ˈlaɪənes/ *noun* [C] a female lion

lip ⚡ **B1** /lɪp/ *noun* [C] **1** (**ANATOMY**) either of the two soft edges at the opening of the mouth: *to kiss somebody on the lips* ◊ *top/upper lip* ◊ *bottom/lower lip* ◲ picture at **body 2** -**lipped** (in adjectives) having the type of lips mentioned: *thin-lipped* **3** the edge of a cup or sth that is shaped like a cup
IDM **purse your lips** → PURSE²

lipase /ˈlaɪpeɪz, ˈlɪ-/ *noun* [U] (**BIOLOGY**) an ENZYME (= a substance that helps a chemical change take place) that makes fats change into ACIDS and alcohol

lip gloss *noun* [U, C] a substance that you put on your lips to make them look shiny

lipid /ˈlɪpɪd/ *noun* [C] (**BIOLOGY**) any of a group of natural substances that do not DISSOLVE (= become liquid) in water, including plant oils and STEROIDS (= chemical substances produced naturally in the body)

lip-read /ˈlɪp riːd/ *verb* [I, T] (*pt, pp* **lip-read** /- red/) to understand what sb is saying by looking at the movements of their lips

lip service *noun* [U] if sb pays **lip service** to sth, they say that they approve of it or support it, without proving their support by what they actually do: *All the political parties pay lip service to environmental issues.*

lipstick /ˈlɪpstɪk/ *noun* [U, C] a substance that is used for giving colour to your lips: *to put on some lipstick* ◊ *a new lipstick*

liquefy /ˈlɪkwɪfaɪ/ *verb* [I, T] (**liquefying**; **liquefies**; *pt, pp* **liquefied**) (*formal*) to become liquid; to make sth liquid

liqueur /lɪˈkjʊə(r)/ *noun* [U, C] a strong sweet alcoholic drink that is often drunk in small quantities after a meal

liquid¹ ⚡ **B1** /ˈlɪkwɪd/ *noun* [C, U] (**PHYSICS**) a substance, for example water, that is not solid or a gas and that can flow or be poured: *the transition from liquid to vapour* ◲ picture at **state¹**, **water cycle**

liquid² ⚡ **B1** /ˈlɪkwɪd/ *adj.* **1** in the form of a liquid; not a solid or a gas: *liquid soap* ◊ *liquid nitrogen* ◲ picture at **aerosol 2** (**BUSINESS**) that can easily be changed into cash: *liquid assets*

liquidate /ˈlɪkwɪdeɪt/ *verb* [I, T] (**BUSINESS**) to close a business because it has no money left **2** [T] (**FINANCE**) to sell sth in order to get money: *to liquidate assets* **3** [T] (**FINANCE**) to pay a debt **4** [T] to destroy or remove sb/sth that causes problems ▶ **liquidation** /ˌlɪkwɪˈdeɪʃn/ *noun* [U]: *If the company doesn't receive a big order soon, it will have to go into liquidation.*

liquidity /lɪˈkwɪdəti/ *noun* [U] (**ECONOMICS**) the state of owning things of value that can be exchanged for cash

lioness

mane

whiskers   cub

lion

claws

leopard   paw   tiger

cheetah   panther

liquidize (*BrE also* -ise) /ˈlɪkwɪdaɪz/ *verb* [T] to cause sth to become liquid

liquidizer (*also* -iser) /ˈlɪkwɪdaɪzə(r)/ = BLENDER

liquor /ˈlɪkə(r)/ *noun* [U] (*AmE*) strong alcoholic drinks; spirits

liquorice (*especially BrE*) (*also* **licorice** *especially in AmE*) /ˈlɪkərɪʃ, -rɪs/ *noun* [U] a black substance, made from a plant, that is used in some sweets

ˈliquor store (*AmE*) = OFF-LICENCE

lisp /lɪsp/ *noun* [C] a speech fault in which 's' is pronounced as 'th': *He speaks with a slight lisp.* ▶ **lisp** *verb* [I, T]

list ⚡ **A1** ⊙ /lɪst/ *noun* [C] a series of names, figures, items, etc. that are written, printed or said one after another: *a waiting list* ◇ *Your name is third on the list.* ▶ **list** ⚡ **A1** ⊙ *verb* [T]: *to list items in alphabetical order*

ˌlisted ˈbuilding *noun* [C] (*BrE*) (**ARCHITECTURE**) a building that is officially protected because it has artistic or historical value ⊃ look at **landmark** (1)

listen ⚡ **A1** /ˈlɪsn/ *verb* [I] **1 ~(to sb/sth)** to pay attention to sb/sth in order to hear them or it: *Now please listen carefully to what I have to say.* ◇ *to listen to music/the radio* **2 ~to sb/sth** to take notice of or believe what sb says: *You should listen to your parents' advice.* ▶ **listen** *noun* [sing.] (*informal*): *Have a listen and see if you can hear anything.*
PHR V **listen (out) for sth** to wait to hear sth: *to listen (out) for a knock on the door* **listen in (on/to sth)** to listen to sb else's private conversation: *Have you been listening in on my phone calls?*

listener ⚡ **A2** /ˈlɪsnə(r)/ *noun* [C] a person who listens: *When I'm unhappy I always phone Charlie — he's such a good listener.* ◇ *The new radio show has attracted a record number of listeners.*

listeria /lɪˈstɪəriə/ *noun* [U] (**BIOLOGY**, **HEALTH**) a type of bacteria that makes people ill if they eat food that contains it

listing ⚡+ /ˈlɪstɪŋ/ *noun* **1** [C] an official list of people or things, often arranged in alphabetical order: *a complete listing of approved medications* **2** listings [pl.] information online or in a newspaper, etc. about which films, plays, etc. are being shown in a particular place

listless /ˈlɪstləs/ *adj.* tired and without energy ▶ **listlessly** *adv.*

lit /lɪt/ past tense, past participle of **light**³

liter /ˈliːtə(r)/ (*AmE*) = LITRE

literacy ⚡+ **C1** /ˈlɪtərəsi/ *noun* [U] (**EDUCATION**) **1** the ability to read and write **OPP** **illiteracy** ⊃ look at **numeracy** ⊃ note at **HDI** **2** (in compounds) knowledge or skills in a specific area: *computer/digital literacy*

literal /ˈlɪtərəl/ *adj.* (**LANGUAGE**) **1** (used about the meaning of a word or phrase) original or basic: *The adjective 'big-headed' is hardly ever used in its literal sense.* ⊃ look at **figurative** (1), **metaphor** **2** (used when translating, etc.) dealing with each word separately without looking at the general meaning

literally ⚡+ **B2** /ˈlɪtərəli/ *adv.* **1** according to the basic or original meaning of the word, etc: *You can't translate these idioms literally.* **2** (*informal*) used for emphasizing sth: *We were literally frozen to death* (= we were very cold).

literary ⚡+ **B2** /ˈlɪtərəri/ *adj.* [only before noun] (**LITERATURE**) of or concerned with literature: *literary criticism* ◇ *a literary journal*

literate /ˈlɪtərət/ *adj.* **1** (**EDUCATION**) able to read and write **OPP** **illiterate** ⊃ look at **numerate** ⊃ noun **literacy** **2** having skills or knowledge in a particular area **3** well educated

the literati /ðə ˌlɪtəˈrɑːti/ *noun* [pl.] (*formal*) educated and intelligent people who enjoy literature: *He was underrated as a writer by the literati.*

literature ⚡ **B1** ⊙ /ˈlɪtrətʃə(r)/ *noun* [U] **1** writing that is considered to be a work of art, especially novels, plays and poems: *French literature* **2 ~(on sth)** printed material about a particular subject

lithium /ˈlɪθiəm/ *noun* [U] (*symb.* Li) (**CHEMISTRY**) a chemical element. Lithium is a soft, very light, silver-white metal used in batteries. ❶ For more information on the periodic table of elements, look at the **Reference Section** of this dictionary.

lithography /lɪˈθɒɡrəfi/ (*also informal* **litho** /ˈlaɪθəʊ/) *noun* [U] (**ART**) the process of printing from a smooth surface, for example a metal plate, that has been specially prepared so that INK only sticks to the design to be printed ▶ **lithograph** /ˈlɪθəɡrɑːf/ *noun* [C]

lithosphere /ˈlɪθəsfɪə(r)/ *noun* [sing.] (**GEOLOGY**) the layer of rock that forms the outer part of the earth

litigant /ˈlɪtɪɡənt/ *noun* [C] (**LAW**) a person who is making or defending a claim in court

litigate /ˈlɪtɪɡeɪt/ *verb* [I, T] (**LAW**) to take a claim or DISAGREEMENT to court ▶ **litigator** *noun* [C]

litigation /ˌlɪtɪˈɡeɪʃn/ *noun* [U] (**LAW**) the process of making or defending a claim in court

litmus /ˈlɪtməs/ *noun* [U] (**CHEMISTRY**) a substance that turns red when it touches an ACID and blue when it touches an ALKALI

litotes /laɪˈtəʊtiːz/ *noun* [U] (**LANGUAGE**) the use of a negative or weak statement to emphasize a positive meaning, for example 'he wasn't slow to accept the offer' (= he was quick to accept the offer) ⊃ look at **understatement** (2)

litre ⚡+ **B2** (*BrE*) (*AmE* **liter**) /ˈliːtə(r)/ *noun* [C] (*abbr.* l) a measure of liquid: *10 litres of petrol* ◇ *a litre bottle of wine* ⊃ note at **measure²**

litter¹ ⚡+ **B2** /ˈlɪtə(r)/ *noun* **1** [U] pieces of paper, rubbish, etc. that are left in a public place **2** [C] all the young animals that are born to one mother at the same time: *a litter of six puppies* ▶ **litter** *verb* [T]: *The streets were littered with rubbish.*

litter² /ˈlɪtə(r)/ *verb* **1** [T] to be spread around a place, making it look untidy: *Rubbish littered the streets.* **2** [T, usually passive, U] **be littered (with sth)** (used about rubbish, etc.) to be left in a place, making it look untidy: *The streets were littered with rubbish.* ◇ *He was fined for littering.*

ˈlitter bin (*BrE*) (*AmE* **trash can**) *noun* [C] a container to put rubbish in, in the street or a public building

little¹ ⚡ **A1** /ˈlɪtl/ *adj.* **1** not big; small: *a little bag of sweets* ◇ *Do you want the big one or the little one?* ◇ *a little mistake/problem* **2** (used about distance or time) short: *Do you mind waiting a little while?* ◇ *We only live a little way from here.* ◇ *It's only a little further.* **3** young: *a little girl/boy* ◇ *my little brother* ◇ *I was very naughty when I was little.*

little² ⚡ **A1** /ˈlɪtl/ *pron., det.* (**less** /les/; **least** /liːst/) **1** a little used with uncountable nouns to mean 'a small amount': *I like a little sugar in my tea.* ◇ *Could I have a little help, please?* **2** used with uncountable nouns to mean 'not much': *They have very little money.* ⊃ look at **least, less¹**
IDM **little by little** slowly: *After the accident her strength returned little by little.*

little³ ⚡ **A2** /ˈlɪtl/ *adv.* (**less** /les/; **least** /liːst/) **1** a little to a small degree: *This skirt is a little too tight.* ◇ *These days I'm a little more relaxed.* **2** not much; only slightly: *I slept very little last night.* ◊ *He is little known as an artist.* ➔ look at **least**, **less¹**

little 'finger *noun* [C] (**ANATOMY**) the smallest finger of the hand

littoral /ˈlɪtərəl/ *noun* [C] (**GEOGRAPHY**) the part of a country that is near the coast: *the Hawaiian littoral*

live¹ 🔊 **A1** /lɪv/ *verb* **1** [I] to have your home in a particular place: *Where do you live?* ◊ *He still lives with his parents.* **2** [I] to be or stay alive: *She hasn't got long to live.* ◊ *to live to a great age* **3** [I, T] to pass or spend your life in a certain way: *to live a quiet life* ◊ *to live in comfort/poverty* **4** [I] to enjoy all the opportunities of life fully: *I want to live a bit before settling down.*
IDM **live/sleep rough** → **ROUGH³**
PHRV **live by sth** to follow a particular belief or set of principles **live by doing sth** to get the money, food, etc. you need by doing a particular activity: *They live by hunting and fishing.* **not live sth down** to be unable to make people forget sth bad or embarrassing that you have done **live for sb/sth** to consider sb/sth to be the most important thing in your life: *He felt he had nothing to live for after his wife died.* **live off sb/sth** to depend on sb/sth in order to live: *Barry lives off tinned food.* ◊ *She could easily get a job but she still lives off her parents.* **live on** to continue to live or exist: *Mozart is dead but his music lives on.* **live on sth 1** to have sth as your only food: *to live on bread and water* **2** to manage to buy what you need to live: *I don't know how they live on so little money!* **live out sth 1** to actually do sth that you only imagined doing before: *to live out your dreams/fantasies* **2** to spend the rest of your life in a particular way: *He lived out his days alone.* **live through sth** to survive an unpleasant experience: *She lived through two wars.* **live together** (*also* **live with sb**) **1** to live in the same house, flat, etc: *Rhoda and I lived together when we were students.* **2** to live in the same house, etc. as sb and have a sexual relationship with them **3** to share a home and have a sexual relationship, but without being married **live it up** to enjoy yourself in an exciting way, usually spending a lot of money **live up to sth** to be as good as expected: *Children sometimes find it hard to live up to their parents' expectations.* **live with sb** = **LIVE TOGETHER** **live with sth** to accept sth unpleasant that you cannot change: *It can be hard to live with the fact that you are getting older.*

live² 🔊 **B1** /laɪv/ *adj.*
• NOT DEAD **1** having life; not dead: *Have you ever touched a **real live** snake?*
• RADIO/TV PROGRAMME **2** (**ARTS AND MEDIA**) (used about a TV programme, etc.) sent out while the event is actually happening: *live coverage of the Olympic Games*
• PERFORMANCE **3** (**ARTS AND MEDIA**) (used about a performance) given or made while people are watching: *The cafe has live music on Saturdays.*
• BOMB, ETC. **4** (used about a bomb, bullet, etc.) that has not yet exploded
• WIRE, ETC. **5** (**ENGINEERING**) (used about a wire, etc.) carrying electricity ➔ picture at **plug¹**

live³ 🔊 **B1** /laɪv/ *adv.* broadcast at the time of an actual event; played or recorded at an actual performance: *This programme is coming live from Wembley Stadium.* ◊ *to go out live on TV*

livelihood /ˈlaɪvlihʊd/ *noun* [C, usually sing.] the way that you earn money: *When the factory closed he lost his livelihood.*

lively 🔊 **B2** /ˈlaɪvli/ *adj.* (livelier; liveliest) full of energy, interest, excitement, etc: *lively children* ◊ *The town is quite lively at night.*

liven /ˈlaɪvn/ *verb*
PHRV **liven (sb/sth) up** to become more interesting and exciting; to make sb/sth become more interesting and exciting: *Once the band began to play the party livened up.*

liver 🔊 **C1** /ˈlɪvə(r)/ *noun* **1** [C] (**ANATOMY**) the part of the body that cleans the blood ➔ picture at **body**, **circulation**, **digestive system 2** [U] the liver of an animal when it is cooked and eaten as food

lives /laɪvz/ plural of **life**

livestock /ˈlaɪvstɒk/ *noun* [U] (**AGRICULTURE**) animals that are kept on a farm, such as cows, pigs, sheep, etc.

livid /ˈlɪvɪd/ *adj.* extremely angry **SYN** **furious**

living¹ 🔊 **B1** /ˈlɪvɪŋ/ *adj.* **1** alive now: *He has no living relatives.* **OPP** **dead¹ 2** still used or practised now: *living languages/traditions* **OPP** **dead¹**

living² 🔊 **B1** /ˈlɪvɪŋ/ *noun* **1** [C, usually sing.] money to buy things that you need in life: *What do you do for a living?* **2** [U] your way or quality of life: *The cost of living has risen in recent years.* ◊ *The standard of living is very high in that country.*

'living room (*BrE also* **sitting room**) *noun* [C] a room in a house where people sit together, relax, watch TV, etc.

lizard /ˈlɪzəd/ *noun* [C] a small REPTILE with four legs, rough skin and a long body and tail

lizard

load¹ 🔊 **B2** /ləʊd/ *noun*
1 [C] something (heavy) that is being or is waiting to be carried: *a truck carrying a load of sand* ➔ picture at **lever 2** [C] (often in compounds) the quantity of sth that can be carried: *busloads of tourists* **3** **loads (of sth)** [pl.] (*informal*) a lot (of sth): *There are loads of things to do in London in the evenings.*
IDM **a load of rubbish, etc.** (*informal*) used to emphasize that something is wrong, stupid, bad, etc.

load² 🔊 **B2** /ləʊd/ *verb* **1** [T, I] ~ (**sth/sb**) (**up**) (**with sth**); ~ (**sth/sb**) (**into/onto sth**) to put a large quantity of sth into or onto sb/sth: *They loaded the plane (up) with supplies.* ◊ *Load the washing into the machine.* **2** [I] to receive a load: *The ship is still loading.* **3** [T, I] (**COMPUTING**) to put data or a program into the memory of a computer: *The program is now loading.* ◊ *Have you loaded the software?* **4** [T] to put sth into a machine, a weapon, etc. so that it can be used: *to load a new cartridge into the camera* ◊ *to load a gun* **OPP** **unload** ➔ note at **gun¹**

loaded /ˈləʊdɪd/ *adj.* **1** ~ (**with sth**) carrying a load; full and heavy **2** (used especially about a gun or a camera) containing a bullet, a film, etc. **3** giving an advantage: *The system is loaded in their favour.* **4** [not before noun] (*informal*) having a lot of money; rich

loaf /ləʊf/ *noun* [C] (*pl.* **loaves** /ləʊvz/) bread baked in one piece: *a loaf of bread*

loam /ləʊm/ *noun* [U] (**AGRICULTURE**) good quality soil containing sand, CLAY and dead plants

loan 🔊 **B2** /ləʊn/ *noun* **1** [C] (**FINANCE**) money, etc. that sb/sth lends you: *to take out a bank loan* ◊ *to pay off a loan* ➔ look at **borrow** (1) ➔ note at **mortgage¹ 2** [U] the act of lending sth or the state of being lent: *The books are on loan from the library.* ▶ **loan** *verb* [T] ~ **sth (to sb)** (*formal*): *The painting was loaned to the gallery by the artist's family.* ❶ In American English **loan** is less formal and more common.

'loan translation = **CALQUE**

loath (*also* **loth**) /ləʊθ/ *adj.* ~ **to do sth** (*formal*) not willing to do sth: *He was loath to admit his mistake.*

loathe /ləʊð/ *verb* [T] (not used in the progressive tenses) to hate sb/sth **SYN** detest ▸ **loathing** *noun* [sing., U] (*formal*) ▸ **loathsome** /ˈləʊðsəm/ *adj.* (*formal*)

loaves /ləʊvz/ plural of **loaf**

lob /lɒb/ *verb* [T] (-bb-) (**SPORT**) to hit, kick or throw a ball high into the air, so that it lands behind your opponent ▸ **lob** *noun* [C]

lobby[1] ʔ+ **C1** /ˈlɒbi/ *noun* [C] (*pl.* -ies) **1** (**ARCHITECTURE**) the area that is just inside a large building, where people can meet and wait: *a hotel lobby* **2** [+ sing./pl. verb] (**POLITICS**) a group of people who try to influence politicians to do or not do sth: *the anti-smoking lobby*

lobby[2] ʔ+ **C1** /ˈlɒbi/ *verb* [T, I] (lobbying; lobbies; *pt, pp* lobbied) (**POLITICS**) to try to influence a politician or the government to do or not do sth: *Farmers will lobby Congress for higher subsidies.* ▸ **lobbyist** *noun* [C]: *political lobbyists*

lobe /ləʊb/ *noun* [C] **1** = EARLOBE **2** (**ANATOMY**) one part of an organ of the body, especially the brain or lungs

lobster /ˈlɒbstə(r)/ *noun* **1** [C] a sea creature with a hard shell, eight legs and two CLAWS (= curved and pointed arms). Its shell is black but it turns red when it is cooked. **2** [U] cooked lobster eaten as food

local[1] ʔ **A1** /ˈləʊkl/ *adj.* of a particular place (near you): *local newspapers/radio* ◇ *the local doctor/police* ⊃ look at **international** (1), **national**[1], **regional** ▸ **locally** **W** /-kəli/ *adv.*: *I do most of my shopping locally.*

local[2] ʔ **B1** /ˈləʊkl/ *noun* [C] **1** [usually pl.] a person who lives in a particular place: *The locals seem very friendly.* **2** (*BrE, informal*) a pub that is near your home where you often go to drink

local government *noun* [U] (**POLITICS**) the system of government of a town or an area by people who have been elected by the people who live there

localized **W** (*BrE also* -ised) /ˈləʊkəlaɪzd/ *adj.* (*formal*) happening within one small area: *localized pain/problems*

local time *noun* [U] the time at a particular place in the world: *We arrive in Singapore at two o'clock p.m., local time.*

locate ʔ **B1** /ləʊˈkeɪt/ *verb* [T] **1** to find the exact position of sb/sth: *The damaged ship has been located 2 miles off the coast.* **2** to put or build sth in a particular place

located ʔ **B1** **W** /ləʊˈkeɪtɪd/ *adj.* if sth is **located** in a particular place, it exists there or has been put there: *a small town located 30 miles south of Chicago* ◇ *The offices are located a few minutes from the station.*

location ʔ **B1** **W** /ləʊˈkeɪʃn/ *noun* **1** [C] a place or position: *Several locations have been suggested for the new office block.* **2** [C, U] (**ARTS AND MEDIA**) a place outside a studio where scenes of a film or a TV programme are made: *The series was filmed on location in Thailand.* **3** [U] the action of finding where sb/sth is

loch /lɒk, lɒx/ *noun* [C] (**GEOGRAPHY**) the Scottish word for a lake: *the Loch Ness monster*

lock[1] ʔ **A2** /lɒk/ *verb* **1** [T, I] to close or fasten (sth) so that it can only be opened with a key: *Have you locked the car?* ◇ *The door won't lock.* **OPP** unlock **2** [T] to put sb/sth in a safe place and lock it: *Lock your passport in a safe place.* **3** [T] **be locked in sth** to be involved in an angry argument, etc. with sth; to be holding sb very tightly: *The two sides were locked in a bitter dispute.* ◇ *They were locked in a passionate embrace.* **PHR V** **lock sth away** to keep sth in a safe or secret place that is locked **lock sb in/out** to lock a door so that a person cannot get in/out: *I locked myself out of the house and had to climb in through the window.*

lock (sth) up to lock all the doors, windows, etc. of a building: *Make sure that you lock up before you leave.* **lock sb up** to put sb in prison

lock[2] ʔ **A2** /lɒk/ *noun* [C] **1** something that is used for fastening a door, LID, etc. so that you need a key to open it again: *to turn the key in the lock* ⊃ look at **padlock** **2** a device that prevents a vehicle, machine, etc. from being used **3** a part of a river or a CANAL where the level of water changes. Locks have gates at each end and are used to allow boats to move to a higher or lower part of the CANAL or river. **IDM** **pick a lock** → PICK[1] **under lock and key** in a locked place

lockdown /ˈlɒkdaʊn/ *noun* [C, U] an official order to control the movement of people or vehicles because of a dangerous situation: *The city schools were in lockdown.*

locker /ˈlɒkə(r)/ *noun* [C] a small cupboard that can be locked in a school or sports centre, where you can leave your clothes, books, etc.

locker room *noun* [C] a room with LOCKERS in it, especially one where people can change their clothes

locket /ˈlɒkɪt/ *noun* [C] a piece of jewellery that you wear on a chain around your neck and that opens so that you can put a picture, etc. inside

locksmith /ˈlɒksmɪθ/ *noun* [C] a person who makes and repairs locks

locomotion /ˌləʊkəˈməʊʃn/ *noun* [U] (*formal*) movement or the ability to move

locomotive /ˌləʊkəˈməʊtɪv/ = ENGINE (2)

locus /ˈləʊkəs/ *noun* [C] (*pl.* loci /ˈləʊkaɪ, ˈləʊsaɪ/) (*formal*) the exact place where sth happens or that is thought to be the centre of sth

locust /ˈləʊkəst/ *noun* [C] a flying insect from Africa and Asia that moves in very large groups, eating and destroying large quantities of plants ⊃ picture at **animal**

lode /ləʊd/ *noun* [C] (**GEOLOGY**) a line of metal in the ground or in rocks

lodge[1] /lɒdʒ/ *verb* **1** [T] ~ sth (with sb) (against sb/sth) (*formal*) to make a formal statement complaining about sth to a public organization or authority: *He lodged a complaint with the police* ◇ *They lodged a compensation claim against the factory.* **2** [I] to pay to live in sb's house with them: *He lodged with a family for his first term at university.* **3** [I, T] to become FIRMLY fixed or to make sth do this

lodge[2] /lɒdʒ/ *noun* [C] **1** a small house in the country **2** a room at the main entrance to a building for the person whose job is to see who enters and leaves the building

lodger /ˈlɒdʒə(r)/ *noun* [C] a person who pays rent to live in sb's house ⊃ look at **boarder** (2)

lodging /ˈlɒdʒɪŋ/ *noun* **1** [U] a place where you can stay: *The family offered full board and lodging* (= a room and all meals) *in exchange for English lessons.* **2 lodgings** [pl.] (*old-fashioned*) a room or rooms in sb's house where you can pay to stay

loft /lɒft/ *noun* [C] the room or space under the roof of a house or other building ⊃ look at **attic**

lofty /ˈlɒfti/ *adj.* (loftier; loftiest) (*formal*) **1** (used about buildings, mountains, etc.) very high and impressive: *lofty ceilings/rooms/towers* **2** (used about a thought, goal, etc.) deserving praise because of its high moral quality: *lofty ambitions/ideals/principles*

log¹ ₤+ **C1** /lɒg/ *noun* [C] **1** a thick piece of wood that has fallen or been cut from a tree ⊃ picture at **tree** **2** (*also* logbook /'lɒgbʊk/) the official written record of a ship's or an aircraft's journey: *to keep a log* **3** (*informal*) = LOGARITHM

log² ₤+ **C1** /lɒg/ *verb* [T] (-gg-) to keep an official written record of sth
PHR V log in/on (COMPUTING) to perform the actions that allow you to start using a computer system: *You need to key in your password to log on.* log off/out (COMPUTING) to perform the actions that allow you to finish using a computer system

logarithm /'lɒgərɪðəm/ (*also informal* log) *noun* [C] (MATHEMATICS) any of a series of numbers arranged in lists that make it possible to solve problems in mathematics by adding or taking away numbers instead of multiplying or dividing ▸ logarithmic /ˌlɒgə'rɪðmɪk/ *adj.*

log 'cabin *noun* [C] a small house built of LOGS (= a thick piece of wood that has been cut from a tree)

loggerheads /'lɒgəhedz/ *noun* [pl.]
IDM at loggerheads (with sb) strongly disagreeing (with sb)

logging /'lɒgɪŋ/ *noun* [U] (AGRICULTURE) the work of cutting down trees for their wood

logic ₤+ **C1** **W** /'lɒdʒɪk/ *noun* [U] **1** a sensible reason or way of thinking: *There is no logic in your argument.* **2** the science of using reason

logical ₤ **B2** **W** /'lɒdʒɪkl/ *adj.* **1** seeming natural, reasonable or sensible: *As I see it, there is only one logical conclusion.* **OPP** illogical **2** thinking in a sensible way: *a logical mind* ▸ logically /-kli/ *adv.*

login /'lɒgɪn/ (*also* logon) *noun* (COMPUTING) **1** [U] the act of starting to use a computer system or online account, usually by typing a name or word that you choose to use: *If you've forgotten your login ID, click this link.* **2** [C] the name that you use to enter a computer system: *Now enter your login and password.*

logistics /lə'dʒɪstɪks/ *noun* [U + sing./pl. verb] ~ (of sth) the practical organization that is needed to make a complicated plan successful when a lot of people and equipment is involved: *the logistics of moving the company to a new building* ▸ logistic (*also* logistical /-'dʒɪstɪkl/) *adj.*: *huge logistical problems* ▸ logistically /-kli/ *adv.*

logjam /'lɒgdʒæm/ *noun* [C] **1** a mass of LOGS (= large pieces of wood cut from trees) that are floating on a river and blocking it **2** a difficult situation in which you cannot make progress easily because there are too many things to do

logo ₤+ **B2** /'ləʊgəʊ/ *noun* [C] (pl. -os) (ART, BUSINESS) a printed symbol or design that a company or an organization uses as its special sign

logoff /'lɒgɒf/ (*also* logout /'lɒgaʊt/) *noun* [U] (COMPUTING) the act of finishing using a computer system

logon /'lɒgɒn/ = LOGIN

loiter /'lɔɪtə(r)/ *verb* [I] to stand or walk around somewhere for no obvious reason

LOL /lɒl, ˌel əʊ 'el/ (*also* lol) *abbr.* (*informal*) **laugh out loud** (used in emails, on SOCIAL MEDIA, etc. to show that you think sth is funny)

lollipop /'lɒlipɒp/ (*also* lolly /'lɒli/, pl. -ies) *noun* [C] a sweet on a stick ⊃ look at **ice lolly**

lone /ləʊn/ *adj.* [only before noun] **1** without any other people; alone: *a lone swimmer* **SYN** solitary **2** (used about a parent) single; without a partner: *a support group for lone parents*

lonely ₤ **B1** /'ləʊnli/ *adj.* (lonelier; loneliest) **1** unhappy because you are not with other people: *to feel sad and lonely* **2** (used about a situation or a period of time) sad and spent alone **3** [only before noun] far from other people and places where people live ▸ loneliness *noun* [U] ⊃ look at **isolation, solitude**

loner /'ləʊnə(r)/ *noun* [C] (*informal*) a person who prefers being alone to being with other people

long¹ ₤ **A1** /lɒŋ/ *adj.* (longer /'lɒŋgə(r)/; longest /-gɪst/) **1** measuring or covering a great distance or length: *She has lovely long hair.* ◇ *a very long journey/book/corridor* ◇ *I walked a long way today.* **OPP** short¹ ⊃ note at **direction** **2** used for asking or talking about how much sth measures in length, distance or time: *How long is the film?* ◇ *The insect was only 2 millimetres long.* ◇ *a five-mile-long traffic jam* **OPP** short¹ ⊃ note at **measure²** ⊃ noun **length** **3** lasting or taking a great amount of time or more time than usual: *We had to wait a long time.* ◇ *Nurses work very long hours* (= more hours in the day than is usual).
IDM at (long) last → LAST³ at the longest not longer than the stated time: *It will take a week at the longest.* go a long way (used about money, food, etc.) to be used for buying a lot of things, feeding a lot of people, etc. have a long way to go to need to make a lot more progress before sth can be achieved in the long run over a long period of time; in the end in the long/short term → TERM¹ a long shot a person or thing that probably will not succeed, win, etc.

long² ₤ **A1** /lɒŋ/ *adv.* (longer /'lɒŋgə(r)/; longest /-gɪst/) **1** for a long time: *She didn't stay long.* ◇ *This shouldn't take long.* ◇ *I hope we don't have to wait much longer.* ◇ *They won't be gone for long.* ◇ *Just wait here — I won't be long.* ◇ 'How long will it take to get there?' 'Not long.' **2** a long time before or after a particular time or event: *We got married long before we moved here.* ◇ *Don't worry — they'll be here before long.* ◇ *All that happened long ago.* **3** for the whole of the time that is mentioned: *The baby cried all night long.*
IDM as/so long as only if: *As long as no problems arise we should get the job finished by Friday.* **SYN** provided no/not any longer not any more: *They no longer live here.* ◇ *They don't live here any longer.*

long³ /lɒŋ/ *verb* [I] ~ for sb/sth; ~ (for sb) to do sth to want sb/sth very much, especially sth that is not likely: *He longed for someone to talk to.* ◇ *She longed to return to Greece.* **SYN** yearn ▸ longing *noun* [C, U]: *a longing for peace* ▸ longingly *adv.*

long-'distance *adj., adv.* (used about travel or communication) between places that are far from each other: *a long-distance lorry driver*

long di'vision *noun* [U] (MATHEMATICS) a method of dividing one large number by another in which all the stages are written down

longevity /lɒn'dʒevəti/ *noun* [U] (*formal*) long life; the fact of lasting a long time: *He prides himself on the longevity of the company.*

longhand /'lɒŋhænd/ *noun* [U] ordinary writing that is not typed and does not use any special signs or short forms ⊃ look at **shorthand**

'long-haul *adj.* [only before noun] connected with the transport of people or goods over long distances: *a long-haul flight*

longitude /ˈlɒŋgɪtjuːd, ˈlɒndʒɪ-/ *noun* [U] (**GEOGRAPHY**) the distance of a place east or west of a line from the North Pole to the South Pole that passes through Greenwich in London. Longitude is measured in degrees. ➔ look at **latitude** ➔ picture at **earth**[1]

longitudinal wave /ˌlɒŋgɪˌtjuːdənl ˈweɪv, ˌlɒndʒɪ-/ *noun* [C] (**PHYSICS**) a wave that VIBRATES (= makes very small, fast movements from side to side) in the direction that it is moving ➔ look at **transverse wave**

ˈ**long jump** (*often* **the long jump**) *noun* [sing.] (**SPORT**) the sport in which people try to jump forward as far as possible ➔ look at **high jump**

ˌ**long-ˈlife** *adj.* made to last for a long time: *a long-life battery* ◊ *long-life milk*

ˌ**long-ˈlived** *adj.* that has lived or lasted for a long time: *a long-lived dispute*

ˌ**long-ˈrange** *adj.* **1** of or for a long period of time starting from the present: *the long-range weather forecast* **2** that can go or be sent over long distances: *long-range nuclear missiles*

ˈ**long-running** *adj.* [only before noun] that has been continuing for a long time: *a long-running dispute* ◊ *a long-running TV series*

longshore drift

land
backwash
Sand, etc. is carried along the beach.
backwash
swash
sea
direction of the current
direction of the prevailing wind

longshore drift /ˌlɒŋʃɔː ˈdrɪft/ *noun* [U] (**GEOGRAPHY**) the movement of sand, etc. along a beach caused by waves hitting the beach at an angle and going back in a straight line

ˌ**long-ˈsighted** (*BrE*) (*AmE* **far-sighted**) *adj.* able to see things clearly only when they are quite far away **OPP** **short-sighted** ➔ picture at **short-sighted**

ˌ**long-ˈstanding** ⟨ᵏ+⟩ **C1** *adj.* that has lasted for a long time: *a long-standing arrangement*

ˌ**long-ˈsuffering** *adj.* (used about a person) having a lot of troubles but not complaining

ˌ**long-ˈterm** ⟨ᵏ⟩ **B2** *adj., adv.* of or for a long period of time: *long-term planning* ◊ *It is unclear if this change will benefit us long-term.*

ˈ**long-time** ⟨ᵏ+⟩ **C1** *adj.* [only before noun] having been the thing mentioned for a long time: *her long-time friend*

ˈ**long wave** *noun* [U] (*abbr.* **LW**) (**PHYSICS**) the system of sending radio signals using sound waves of 1 000 metres or more ➔ look at **medium wave, short wave** ➔ picture at **wavelength**

long-winded /ˌlɒŋ ˈwɪndɪd/ *adj.* (used about sth that is written or spoken) boring because it is too long

loo /luː/ *noun* [C] (*pl.* **loos**) (*BrE, informal*) a toilet

look[1] ⟨ᵏ⟩ **A1** **S** /lʊk/ *verb*

• USE THE EYES **1** [I, T] (often used with an adverb or a preposition) ~ (**at sb/sth**) to turn your eyes in a particular direction (in order to pay attention to sb/sth): *Sorry, I wasn't looking. Can you show me again?* ◊ *Look carefully at this picture.* ◊ *to look out of the window* ◊ *She blushed and looked away.* ◊ *Look who's come to see us.* ◊ *Look where you're going!*

• SEARCH **2** [I] ~ (**for sb/sth**) to try to find (sb/sth): *We've been looking for you everywhere. Where have you been?* ◊ *to look for work* ◊ *'I can't find my shoes.' 'Have you looked under the bed?'* ➔ note at **job**

• SEEM **3** *linking verb* ~ (**like sb/sth**) (**to sb**) to seem or appear: *You look very smart in that shirt.* ◊ *to look tired/ill/sad/well/happy* ◊ *The boy looks like his father.* ◊ *You look (to me) as if/as though you need some sleep.*

• LISTEN **4** [I] used for asking sb to listen to what you are saying: *Look, Will, I know you are busy but could you give me a hand?*

• FACE A DIRECTION **5** [I] to face a particular direction: *This room looks south so it gets the sun all day.* ➔ note at **compass**

IDM **be looking to do something** to try to find ways of doing something: *We are looking to double our profits over the next five years.* **look bad** | **not look good** to be considered bad manners: *It'll look bad if we get there an hour late.* **look good** to seem to be encouraging: *This year's sales figures are looking good.* **look sb in the eye** to look straight at sb without feeling embarrassed or afraid **look on the bright side (of sth)** to be positive about a bad situation, thinking of the advantages and not the disadvantages **(not) look yourself** to (not) look as well or healthy as usual **never/not look back** to become and continue being successful

PHR V **look after sb/sth/yourself** to be responsible for or take care of sb/sth/yourself: *I want to go back to work if I can find somebody to look after the children.* ◊ *The old lady's son looked after all her financial affairs.* **look ahead** to think about or plan for the future **look around** (*also* **look round** *especially in BrE*) **1** to turn your head in order to see sb/sth **2** to look at many things (before buying sth): *She looked round but couldn't find anything she liked.* **look around sth** (*also* **look round sth** *especially in BrE*) to walk around a place looking at things: *to look round a town/shop/museum* **look at sth 1** to examine or study sth: *My tooth aches. I think a dentist should look at it.* ◊ *The government is looking at ways of reducing unemployment.* **2** to read sth: *Could I look at the newspaper when you've finished with it?* **3** to consider sth: *Different races and nationalities look at life differently.* **look back (on sth)** to think about sth in your past **look down on sb/sth** to think that you are better than sb/sth **look forward to sth/doing sth** to wait with pleasure for sth to happen: *I'm really looking forward to the weekend.* **look into sth** to study or try to find out sth: *A committee was set up to look into the causes of the accident.* **look on** to watch sth happening without taking any action: *All we could do was look on as the house burned.* **look on sb/sth as sth** | **look on sb with sth** to think of sb/sth in a particular way: *They seem to look on me as somebody who can advise them.* **look out** to be careful or to pay attention to sth dangerous: *Look out! There's a bike coming.* **look out (for sb/sth)** to pay attention in order to see, find or avoid sb/sth: *Look out for thieves!* **look round** = LOOK AROUND **look round sth** (*especially BrE*) = LOOK AROUND **look through sth** to read sth quickly **look to sb for sth** | **look to sb to do sth** to expect sb to do or to provide sth: *He always looked to his father for advice.* **look up 1** (*informal*) to improve: *Business is looking up.* **2** to move your eyes upwards to look at sb/sth: *She looked up and smiled.* **look sth up** to search for information in a book or using a computer: *to look up* *a word in a dictionary* **look up to sb** to respect and admire sb

look² 🔊 **A2** /lʊk/ *noun*
• USING THE EYES **1** [C, usually sing.] the act of looking: *Have a look at this article.* ◇ *Take a close look at the contract before you sign it.*
• SEARCH **2** [C, usually sing.] **a ~ (for sb/sth)** a search: *I'll have a good look for that book later.*
• EXPRESSION **3** [C] the expression on sb's face: *He had a worried look on his face.*
• APPEARANCE **4** looks [pl.] a person's appearance, especially when the person is attractive: *He's lucky — he's got good looks and intelligence.*
• FASHION **5** [C] a fashion or style: *The shop has a new look to appeal to younger customers.*
IDM **by/from the look of sb/sth** judging by the appearance of sb/sth: *It's going to be a fine day by the look of it.* **like the look/sound of sb/sth** → LIKE²

look-in *noun*
IDM **(not) give sb a look-in** | **(not) get/have a look-in** (*BrE, informal*) to (not) give sb, or to (not) have a chance to do sth

lookout /ˈlʊkaʊt/ *noun* [C] a person who has the responsibility of watching to see if danger is coming; the place this person watches from: *One of the gang acted as lookout.*
IDM **be on the lookout for sb/sth** | **keep a lookout for sb/sth** to pay attention in order to see, find or avoid sb/sth: *Police are on the lookout for two men who robbed a bank yesterday.*

loom¹ /luːm/ *noun* [C] a piece of equipment that is used for WEAVING (= making cloth by passing pieces of THREAD over and under other pieces)

loom² 🔊+ **C1** /luːm/ *verb* [I] (often used with an adverb or a preposition) to appear as a shape that is not clear and in a way that seems frightening: *The mountain loomed (up) in the distance.*

the warp
the weft
loom

loony /ˈluːni/ *noun* [C] (*pl.* -ies) (*slang*) a person who is crazy ▸ **loony** *adj.*

loop 🔊+ **C1** /luːp/ *noun* [C] a curved or round shape made by a line curving round and joining or crossing itself: *a loop in a rope* ◇ *The road goes around the lake in a loop.* ▸ **loop** *verb* [T, I]: *He was trying to loop a rope over the horse's head.*
IDM **in the loop/out of the loop** (*informal*) part of a group of people that is dealing with sth important/ not part of this group

loophole /ˈluːphəʊl/ *noun* [C] a way of avoiding sth because the words of a rule or law are badly chosen

loose¹ 🔊 **B2** /luːs/ *adj.*
• NOT TIED/FIXED **1** not tied up or shut in sth; free: *The horse managed to get loose and escape.* ◇ *I take the dog to the woods and let him loose.* ◇ *She wore her long hair loose.* **2** not FIRMLY fixed: *a loose tooth* **3** not contained in sth; joined together: *loose change* (= coins) ◇ *some loose sheets of paper*
• CLOTHES **4** not fitting closely; not tight: *These trousers don't fit. They're much too loose round the waist.* **OPP** **tight¹**
• NOT EXACT **5** not completely accurate or the same as sth: *a loose translation*

IDM **all hell broke loose** → HELL **at a loose end** having nothing to do and feeling bored

loose² /luːs/ *noun*
IDM **on the loose** escaped and dangerous: *a lion on the loose from a zoo*

loose ˈcannon *noun* [C] a person, usually a public figure, who often behaves in a way that nobody can predict

loose-ˈleaf *adj.* (used about a book, file, etc.) with pages that can be removed or added separately

loosely /ˈluːsli/ *adv.* **1** in a way that is not firm or tight: *She fastened the belt loosely around her waist.* **2** in a way that is not exact: *The play is loosely based on his childhood in Russia.*

loosen /ˈluːsn/ *verb* [T, I] to become less tight; to make sth less tight: *to loosen your tie/belt* ◇ *Don't loosen your grip on the rope or you'll fall.*
PHR V **loosen (sb/sth) up** to relax or move more easily: *These exercises will help you to loosen up.*

loot¹ /luːt/ *verb* [T, I] (LAW) to steal things from shops or buildings after a RIOT (= a period of fighting), fire, etc. ▸ **looting** *noun* [U]

loot² /luːt/ *noun* [U] **1** money and valuable objects taken by soldiers from the enemy after winning a battle **2** (*informal*) money and valuable objects that have been stolen by thieves

lop /lɒp/ *verb* [T] (-pp-) to cut branches off a tree
PHR V **lop sth off/away** to cut sth off/away

lopsided /ˌlɒpˈsaɪdɪd/ *adj.* with one side lower or smaller than the other: *a lopsided smile*

lord 🔊 **B2** /lɔːd/ *noun* **1** [C] (in the UK) a man with a very high position in society: *She's married to a lord.* **2** Lord [C] (in the UK) the title used by a lord: *the Lord Mayor of London* ◇ *Lord and Lady Derby* **3** (*usually the Lord*) [sing.] (RELIGION) God; Christ **4** the Lords [sing. + sing./pl. verb] = HOUSE OF LORDS: *The Lords has/ have voted against the bill.*

lorry 🔊 **A2** /ˈlɒri/ (*pl.* -ies) (*BrE*) (*also* truck *especially in AmE*) *noun* [C] a large strong motor vehicle that is used for carrying goods by road ⊃ picture at **vehicle**

lose 🔊 **A1** /luːz/ *verb* (*pt, pp* lost /lɒst/) **1** [T] to become unable to find sth: *I've lost my purse. I can't find it anywhere.* **2** [T] to no longer have sb/sth: *She lost a leg in the accident.* ◇ *He lost his wife last year* (= she died). ◇ *to lose your job* **3** [T] to have less of sth: *to lose weight/ interest/patience* ◇ *The company is losing money all the time.* **OPP** **gain¹** ⊃ note at **trend¹** **4** [T, I] to not win; to be defeated: *We played well but we lost 2–1.* ◇ *to lose a court case/an argument* ◇ *Parma lost to Milan in the final.* **5** [T] to waste time, a chance, etc.: *Hurry up! There's no time to lose.* **6** [T, I] to fail to keep sth you want or need, especially money: *The company lost on the deal.* **7** [T] (*informal*) to cause sb not to understand sth: *You've totally lost me! Please explain again.*
IDM **give/lose ground (to sb/sth)** → GROUND¹ **keep/lose your cool** → COOL **keep/lose count (of sth)** → COUNT² **keep/lose your temper** → TEMPER **keep/lose track of sb/sth** → TRACK¹ **lose face** to lose the respect of other people **lose your head** to become confused or very excited **lose heart** to stop believing that you will be successful in sth you are trying to do **lose it** to go crazy or suddenly become unable to control your emotions **lose your life** to be killed **lose sight of sb/sth** to no longer be able to see sb/sth: *We eventually lost sight of the animal in some trees.* ◇ (*figurative*) *We mustn't lose sight of our original aim.* **lose your touch** to lose a special skill or ability **lose touch (with sb/sth)** to no longer have contact (with sb/sth): *I've lost touch with a lot of my old school friends.* **a losing battle** a competition, fight, etc. in which it seems that you will not be successful **win/ lose the toss** → TOSS²

PHR V **lose out** (**on sth/to sb**) (*informal*) to be at a disadvantage: *If a teacher pays too much attention to the bright students, the others lose out.*

loser /'luːzə(r)/ *noun* [C] **1** a person who is defeated: *He is a bad loser. He always gets angry if I beat him.* **2** (*informal*) a person who is rarely successful, especially when you have a low opinion of them **3** a person who suffers because of a particular situation, decision, etc.

loss ⚡ **B1** ⊙ /lɒs/ *noun* **1** [U, C] ~ (**of sth**) the state of no longer having sth or not having as much as before; the act of losing sth: *loss of blood/sleep* ◇ *weight/hair loss* ◇ *Have you reported the loss of your wallet?* ◇ *The plane crashed with great loss of life.* **2** [C] ~ (**of sth**) (**FINANCE**) the amount of money that is lost by a business: *The firm made a loss of £5 million.* ⊃ look at **profit**² **3** [sing.] ~ (**to sb**) the disadvantage that is caused when sb/sth leaves or is taken away; the person or thing that causes this disadvantage: *If she leaves, it/she will be a big loss to the school.* **IDM** **at a loss** not knowing what to do or say **cut your losses** to stop wasting time or money on sth that is not successful

'**loss-leader** *noun* [C] (**BUSINESS**) an item that a shop sells at a very low price to attract customers

lost¹ /lɒst/ past tense, past participle of **lose**

lost² **A2** /lɒst/ *adj.* **1** unable to find your way; not knowing where you are: *This isn't the right road — we're completely lost!* ◇ *If you get lost, stop and ask somebody the way.* **2** that cannot be found or that no longer exists: *The letter must have got lost in the post.* **3** [only before noun] unable to deal with a situation; unable to understand sth: *Sorry, I'm lost. Could you explain the last part again?* **IDM** **be lost on sb** to not be noticed or understood by sb: *The humour of the situation was completely lost on Joe.* **get lost** (*slang*) used to rudely tell sb to go away **a lost cause** a goal or an aim that cannot be achieved **lost for words** not knowing what to say

lost 'property *noun* [U] things that people have lost or left in a public place and that are kept in a special office for the owners to collect; the office where these things are kept

lot¹ ⚡ **A1** /lɒt/ **a lot (of)** /ə 'lɒt əv/ (*also informal* **lots (of)** /'lɒts əv/) *pron., det.* a large number or amount (of things or people): *'How many do you need?' 'A lot.'* ◇ *I've got a lot to do today.* ◇ *Have some more cake. There's lots left.* ◇ *An awful lot of* (= very many) *people will be disappointed if the concert is cancelled.* ◇ *There seem to be quite a lot of new shops opening.* ◇ *Sit here — there's lots of room.* ◇ *Lots of love from Jane* (= words at the end of a letter).

lot² ⚡ **A1** /lɒt/ *adv.* (*informal*) **1 a lot** used with verbs to mean 'a great amount': *Thanks a lot — that's very kind.* ◇ *It generally rains a lot at this time of year.* **2 a lot, lots** used with adjectives and adverbs to mean 'much': *a lot bigger/better/faster* ◇ *They see lots more of each other than before.*

lot³ /lɒt/ *noun* **1** [sing. + sing./pl. verb] (*informal*) all of sth; the whole of a group of things or people: *When we opened the bag of potatoes the whole lot was/were bad.* ◇ *The manager has just sacked the lot of them!* ◇ *Just one more suitcase and that's the lot!* ◇ *'How many of these books shall we take?' 'The lot.'* ◇ *You count those kids and I'll count this lot.* **2** [C] an object or group of objects that are being sold at an AUCTION (= a public sale): *Lot 27 is six chairs.* **3** [sing.] the quality or state of your life; your FATE: *I'm quite happy with my lot in life.* **IDM** **draw lots** → **DRAW¹**

,lo-'tech = LOW-TECH

loth /ləʊθ/ = LOATH

lotion /'ləʊʃn/ *noun* [C, U] liquid that you use on your hair or skin: *suntan lotion*

lottery ⚡⁺ **B2** /'lɒtəri/ *noun* [C] (*pl.* -ies) a way of raising money for a government, charity, etc. by selling tickets that have different numbers on them that people have chosen. Numbers are then chosen by chance and the people who have those numbers on their tickets win prizes.

loud¹ ⚡ **A2** /laʊd/ *adj.* **1** making a lot of noise: *Can you turn the TV down? It's too loud.* **OPP** **quiet¹, soft** **2** (used about clothes or colours) too bright: *a loud shirt* ▶ **loudly** ⚡ **A2** *adv.* **SYN** **loud²** ▶ **loudness** *noun* [U] **IDM** **out loud** so that people can hear it: *Shall I read this bit out loud to you?*

loud² **A2** /laʊd/ *adv.* in a way that makes a lot of noise or can be easily heard: *Do you have to play that music so loud?* ◇ *You'll have to speak louder — the people at the back can't hear.* **SYN** **loudly**

loudspeaker /ˌlaʊd'spiːkə(r)/ *noun* [C] a piece of electrical equipment that is used in public places for announcing things, playing music, etc. to a lot of people

lounge¹ /laʊndʒ/ *noun* [C] **1** a comfortable room in a house or hotel where you can sit and relax **2** (**TOURISM**) the part of an airport where passengers wait: *the departure lounge*

lounge² /laʊndʒ/ *verb* [I] ~ (**about/around**) to sit, stand or lie in a lazy way: *Stop lounging about and do something useful!*

louse /laʊs/ *noun* [C] (*pl.* **lice** /laɪs/) a small insect that lives on the bodies of animals and people: *head lice*

lousy /'laʊzi/ *adj.* (lousier; lousiest) (*informal*) very bad: *We had lousy weather on holiday.*

lout /laʊt/ *noun* [C] a man or boy who behaves in a rude, rough or stupid way ⊃ look at **hooligan, yob**

lovable (*also* **loveable**) /'lʌvəbl/ *adj.* having qualities that people find easy to love: *a lovable little boy*

love¹ ⚡ **A1** /lʌv/ *noun*
• LIKING AND CARING **1** [U] a very strong feeling of liking and caring for sb/sth: *a mother's love for her children* **2** [U] a strong feeling of romantic attraction for sb: *to fall in love with somebody* ◇ *It was love at first sight* (= they were attracted to each other the first time they met). ◇ *He's madly in love with her.* ◇ *a love song/story*
• ENJOYMENT **3** [U, sing.] the strong feeling of pleasure that sth gives you: *a love of adventure/nature/sport*
• SB/STH YOU LIKE **4** [C] a person, a thing or an activity that you like very much: *His great love was always music.* ◇ *Who was your first love?*
• FRIENDLY NAME **5** [C] (*BrE, informal*) used as a friendly way of speaking to sb, often sb you do not know: *'Hello, love. What can I do for you?'*
• IN TENNIS **6** [U] (**SPORT**) (used in tennis) a score of zero: *The score is 40-love.*
IDM **give/send sb your love** to give/send sb a friendly message: *Give Maria my love when you next see her.* (**lots of**) **love (from)** used at the end of a letter to a friend or a member of your family: *See you soon. Love, Richard* **make love (to sb)** to have sex

love² ⚡ **A1** /lʌv/ *verb* [T] **1** to like sb/sth in the strongest possible way: *I split up with my girlfriend last year, but I still love her.* ◇ *She loves her children.* **2** to like or enjoy sth very much: *I love the summer!* ◇ *I really love swimming in the sea.* ◇ *'What do you think of this music?' 'I love it!'* **3** **would ~ sth; would ~ (sb/sth) to do sth** used to say that you would very much like sth/to do sth

sth: *'Would you like to come?' 'I'd love to.'* ◇ *'What about a drink?' 'I'd love one.'* ◇ *We'd love you to come and stay with us.*

love affair *noun* [C] **1** ~ (with sb) a romantic and/or sexual relationship between two people who are in love and not married to each other: *She had a love affair with her tennis coach.* **2** ~ with sth a great enthusiasm for sth: *His love affair with motor cars began when he was a boy.*

love life *noun* [C] the part of your life that involves your romantic and sexual relationships

lovely 🔒 A2 /'lʌvli/ *adj.* (lovelier; loveliest) **1** beautiful or attractive: *a lovely room/voice/expression* ◇ *You look lovely with your hair short.* **2** ENJOYABLE or pleasant; very nice: *We had a lovely holiday.*
▶ **loveliness** *noun* [U]
IDM lovely and warm, peaceful, fresh, etc. used for emphasizing how good sth is because of the quality mentioned: *These blankets are lovely and soft.*

lover /'lʌvə(r)/ *noun* [C] **1** a partner in a sexual relationship with sb they are not married to: *He discovered that his wife had a lover.* **2** a person who likes or enjoys the thing mentioned: *a music lover* ◇ *an animal lover*

loving /'lʌvɪŋ/ *adj.* **1** feeling or showing love or care: *She's very loving towards her brother.*
SYN affectionate **2** -loving /lʌvɪŋ/ (in adjectives) loving the thing or activity mentioned: *a fun-loving girl* ▶ **lovingly** *adv.*

low¹ 🔒 A2 ⊙ /ləʊ/ *adj.*
• NOT HIGH/TALL **1** not high or tall; close to the ground or to the bottom of sth: *a low wall/building/table* ◇ *Hang that picture a bit higher, it's much too low!*
• LEVEL/VALUE **2** below the usual or normal level or amount: *Temperatures were very low last winter.* ◇ *The price of fruit is lower in the summer.* ◇ *low wages* ◇ *low-fat yogurt* **3** below what is normal or acceptable in quality, importance or development: *a low standard of living* ◇ *low status*
• SOUND/VOICE **4** (used about a sound or voice) deep or quiet: *His voice is already lower than his father's.* ◇ *A group of people in the library were speaking in low voices.*
• UNHAPPY **5** not happy and lacking energy: *He's been feeling a bit low since his illness.*
• LIGHT/HEAT **6** (used about a light, an oven, etc.) producing only a little light or heat: *Cook the rice on a low heat for 20 minutes.* ◇ *The low lighting adds to the restaurant's atmosphere.*
• IN A CAR **7** (used about a GEAR in a car) that allows a slower speed **OPP** high¹
IDM run low (on sth) to start to have less of sth than you need; to start to be less than is needed: *We're running low on coffee — shall I go and buy some?*

low² 🔒 A2 /ləʊ/ *adv.* **1** in or to a low position, not far above the ground: *to crouch/bend low* ◇ *That plane is flying very low.* ◇ *The sun sank lower towards the horizon.* **2** at a level below what is usual or expected: *low-priced goods* ◇ *a very low-scoring game* **3** not high; not loudly: *Turn the music lower or you'll wake the baby.*
IDM high and low → HIGH² lie low → LIE¹

low³ 🔒 B2 /ləʊ/ *noun* [C] a low point, level, figure, etc: *Unemployment has fallen to a new low.* **OPP** high³

low-down *noun* (*informal*)
IDM give sb/get the low-down (on sb/sth) to tell sb/be told the true facts or secret information (about sb/sth)

lower¹ ⑤ /'ləʊə(r)/ *adj.* [only before noun] below sth or at the bottom of sth: *She bit her lower lip.* ◇ *the lower deck of a ship* **OPP** upper

lower² 🔒 B2 /'ləʊə(r)/ *verb* [T] **1** to make or let sb/sth go down: *They lowered the boat into the water.* ◇ *to lower your head/eyes* **2** to make sth less in amount, quality, etc: *The virus lowers resistance to other diseases.* ◇ *Could you lower your voice slightly? I'm trying to sleep.* **OPP** raise¹

lower case *noun* [U] (LANGUAGE) letters that are written or printed in their small form; not in capital letters: *The text is all in lower case.* ◇ *lower-case letters* **OPP** upper case

lower house (*also* lower chamber) *noun* [sing.] (POLITICS) the larger group of people who make laws in a country, usually consisting of elected representatives, such as the House of Commons in Britain or the House of Representatives in the US ⊃ look at upper house

lowest common denominator *noun* [C] (*abbr.* LCD) (MATHEMATICS) the smallest number that the bottom numbers of a group of FRACTIONS can be divided into exactly

lowest common multiple *noun* [C] (MATHEMATICS) the smallest number that a group of numbers can be divided into exactly

low-key *adj.* quiet and not wanting to attract a lot of attention: *The wedding will be very low-key. We're only inviting ten people.*

lowland /'ləʊlənd/ *noun* [C, usually pl.] (GEOGRAPHY) a flat area of land at about sea level: *the lowlands near the coast* ◇ *lowland areas*

lowlander /'ləʊləndə(r)/ *noun* [C] a person who comes from an area that is flat and low ⊃ look at highlander (1)

low-level *adj.* **1** close to the ground: *low-level bombing attacks* **2** of low rank; involving people who do not have a high position in an organization: *a low-level job* ◇ *low-level negotiations* **3** (COMPUTING) (used about a computer language) similar to MACHINE CODE **OPP** high-level

low-lying *adj.* (GEOGRAPHY) (used about land) near to sea level; not high

low-pitched *adj.* (used about sounds) deep; low: *a low-pitched voice* **OPP** high-pitched ⊃ picture at high-pitched

low season *noun* [U, sing.] (*especially BrE*) (TOURISM) the time of year when a hotel or tourist area receives fewest visitors **SYN** off season ⊃ look at high season

low-tech (*also* lo-tech) *adj.* (*informal*) not using the most modern technology or methods **OPP** high-tech

low tide *noun* [U] (GEOGRAPHY) the time when the sea is at its lowest level: *At low tide you can walk out to the island.* **OPP** high tide ⊃ picture at erosion

loyal 🔒 B2 /'lɔɪəl/ *adj.* (used about a person) not changing in your friendship or beliefs: *a loyal friend/ supporter* **SYN** faithful **OPP** disloyal ▶ **loyally** /-əli/ *adv.* ▶ **loyalty** 🔒 C1 /-əlti/ *noun* [U, C] (*pl.* -ies)

loyalty card *noun* [C] (*BrE*) (BUSINESS) a card given to customers by a shop/store to encourage them to shop there regularly. Each time they buy sth they collect points that will allow them to have an amount of money taken off goods they buy in the future.

lozenge /'lɒzɪndʒ/ *noun* [C] **1** (GEOMETRY) a figure with four sides in the shape of a diamond that has two opposite angles more than 90° and the other two less than 90° **2** (MEDICINE) a sweet that you SUCK if you have a COUGH or if your throat hurts

ᴸL-plate *noun* [C] (in the UK and some other countries) a sign with a large red letter L (for 'ʟᴇᴀʀɴᴇʀ') on it, that you put on a car when you are learning to drive

Lt (*BrE*) (*AmE* **Lt.**) *abbr.* (in writing) = ʟɪᴇᴜᴛᴇɴᴀɴᴛ

Ltd *abbr.* (in writing) (*BrE*) (**BUSINESS**) **Limited** (used after the name of a British company or business): *Pierce and Co. Ltd*

lubricant /ˈluːbrɪkənt/ *noun* [U, C] a substance, for example oil, that makes the parts of a machine work easily and smoothly ➔ picture at **fractional distillation**

lubricate /ˈluːbrɪkeɪt/ *verb* [T] to put oil, etc. onto or into sth so that it works smoothly ▸ **lubrication** /ˌluːbrɪˈkeɪʃn/ *noun* [U]

lucid /ˈluːsɪd/ *adj.* (*formal*) **1** (used about sth that is said or written) clear and easy to understand: *a lucid style/ description* **2** (**HEALTH**) (used about a person's mind) not confused; clear and normal ▸ **lucidity** /luːˈsɪdəti/ *noun* [U] ▸ **lucidly** *adv.*

luck 🔒 A2 /lʌk/ *noun* [U] **1** success or good things that happen by chance: *We'd like to wish you lots of luck in your new career.* ◇ *He says this necklace will bring you luck.* ◇ *I could hardly believe my luck when they offered me the job.* ◇ *With a bit of luck, we'll finish this job today.* **2** chance; the force that people believe makes things happen: *There's no skill in this game — it's all luck.* ◇ *to have good/bad luck*
IDM **bad luck!** | **hard luck!** used to show ᴘɪᴛʏ for sb: *'Bad luck. Maybe you'll win next time.'* **be in/out of luck** to be lucky/not be lucky: *I was in luck — they only had one ticket left!* **good luck (to sb)** used to wish that sb is successful: *Good luck! I'm sure you'll get the job.* → ᴡᴏʀsᴇ¹

lucky 🔒 A2 /ˈlʌki/ *adj.* (**luckier**; **luckiest**) **1** (used about a person) having good luck: *He's lucky to be alive after an accident like that.* ◇ *With so much unemployment, I count myself lucky that I've got a job.* ◇ *'I'm off on holiday next week.' 'Lucky you!'* **2** (used about a situation, an event, etc.) having a good result: *It's lucky I got here before the rain started.* ◇ *a lucky escape* **3** (used about a thing) bringing success or good luck: *a lucky number* ◇ *It was not my lucky day.* **OPP** **unlucky** ▸ **luckily** /-kɪli/ *adv.*: *Luckily, I remembered to bring some money.*
IDM **you'll be lucky** used to tell sb that sth they are expecting will probably not happen: *You're hoping for a ticket for Sunday's match? You'll be lucky!*

lucrative /ˈluːkrətɪv/ *adj.* allowing sb to earn a lot of money: *a lucrative contract/business/market* ➔ note at **successful**

ludicrous /ˈluːdɪkrəs/ *adj.* very silly: *What a ludicrous idea!* **SYN** **ridiculous** ▸ **ludicrously** *adv.*

lug /lʌg/ *verb* [T] (**-gg-**) (*informal*) to carry or pull sth very heavy with great difficulty

luge /luːʒ, luːdʒ/ *noun* **1** [C] a type of sʟᴇᴅɢᴇ (= a vehicle for sliding over ice) for racing, used by one person lying on their back with their feet pointing forwards **2 the luge** [sing.] (**SPORT**) the event or sport of racing down a track of ice on a luge

luggage /ˈlʌgɪdʒ/ *noun* [U] (**TOURISM**) bags, cases, etc. that contain somebody's clothes and things when they are travelling: *'How much luggage are you taking with you?' 'Only one suitcase.'* ◇ *You're only allowed one piece of hand luggage* (= a bag that you carry with you on the plane). **SYN** **baggage** ➔ picture at **baggage**

ᴸluggage rack *noun* [C] (**TOURISM**) a shelf above the seats in a train or bus for putting your bags, etc. on

lukewarm /ˌluːkˈwɔːm/ *adj.* **1** (used about liquids) only slightly warm **2** ~ (**about sb/sth**) not interested or enthusiastic: *The committee is lukewarm about the idea.*

lull¹ /lʌl/ *noun* [C, usually sing.] ~ (**in sth**) a short period of quiet between times of activity: *When she entered the room there was a lull in the conversation.*

lull² /lʌl/ *verb* [T] **1** to make sb relaxed and calm: *She sang a song to lull the children to sleep.* **2** ~ **sb into sth/ doing sth** to make sb feel safe, and not expecting anything bad to happen: *Our first success lulled us into a false sense of security.*

lullaby /ˈlʌləbaɪ/ *noun* [C] (*pl.* **-ies**) (**MUSIC**) a gentle song that you sing to help a child to go to sleep

lumber¹ /ˈlʌmbə(r)/ *noun* [U] (*especially AmE*) = ᴛɪᴍʙᴇʀ (1)

lumber² /ˈlʌmbə(r)/ *verb* **1** [I] (used with an adverb or a preposition) to move in a slow, heavy way: *A family of elephants lumbered past.* **2** [T, usually passive] ~ **sb (with sb/sth)** (*informal*) to give sb a responsibility or job that they do not want

luminous /ˈluːmɪnəs/ *adj.* that shines in the dark: *a luminous watch*

lump¹ /lʌmp/ *noun* [C] **1** a piece of sth solid of any size or shape: *a lump of coal/cheese/wood* **2** (**HEALTH**) a sᴡᴇʟʟɪɴɢ under the skin: *You'll have a bit of a lump on your head where you banged it.*
IDM **have/feel a lump in your throat** to feel pressure in the throat because you are about to cry

lump² /lʌmp/ *verb* [T] ~ **A and B together**; ~ **A (in) with B**; ~ **sth into sth** to put or consider different people or things together in the same group: *Sales and marketing are often lumped together.* ◇ *You can't lump beginners in with advanced students!* ◇ *Whales can be broadly lumped into two main groups.*
IDM **lump it** (*informal*) to accept sth unpleasant because you have no choice: *That's the deal — like it or lump it.*

ˌlump 'sum *noun* [C] (**FINANCE**) an amount of money paid all at once rather than in several smaller amounts

lumpy /ˈlʌmpi/ *adj.* (**lumpier**; **lumpiest**) full of or covered with ʟᴜᴍᴘs (= pieces of sth hard or solid): *This bed is very lumpy.* **OPP** **smooth¹**

lunacy /ˈluːnəsi/ *noun* [U] very stupid behaviour: *It was lunacy to drive so fast in that terrible weather.* **SYN** **madness**

lunar /ˈluːnə(r)/ *adj.* (**ASTRONOMY**) connected with the moon: *a lunar spacecraft/eclipse/landscape*

lunatic¹ /ˈluːnətɪk/ *noun* [C] (*informal*) a person who behaves in a stupid way doing crazy and often dangerous things **SYN** **maniac**

lunatic² /ˈluːnətɪk/ *adj.* stupid; crazy: *a lunatic idea*

lunch 🔒 A1 /lʌntʃ/ *noun* [U, C] a meal that you have in the middle of the day: *Hot and cold lunches are served between twelve and two.* ◇ *What would you like for lunch?* ▸ **lunch** *verb* [I] (*formal*)

ᴸlunch hour *noun* [C, usually sing.] the time around the middle of the day when you stop work or school to have lunch: *I went to the shops in my lunch hour.*

lunchtime /ˈlʌntʃtaɪm/ *noun* [U, C] the time around the middle of the day when lunch is eaten: *I'll meet you at lunchtime.*

lung 🔒 B2 /lʌŋ/ *noun* [C] (**ANATOMY**) one of the two organs of the body that are inside the chest and are used for breathing ➔ picture at **respiratory**

lunge /lʌndʒ/ *noun* [C, usually sing.] ~ (**at sb**); ~ (**for sb/ sth**) a sudden powerful forward movement of the body, especially when trying to attack sb/sth: *She made a lunge for the ball.* ◇ *He made a sudden lunge at her.* ▸ **lunge** *verb* [I]: *He lunged towards me with a knife.*

lurch /lɜːtʃ/ *noun* [C, usually sing.] a sudden movement forward or to one side ▸ **lurch** *verb* [I]

IDM leave sb in the lurch → LEAVE¹

lure¹ /lʊə(r)/ *verb* [T] (often used with an adverb or a preposition) to persuade or trick sb to go somewhere or do sth, usually by offering them sth nice: *Young people are lured to the city by the prospect of a good job.*

lure² /lʊə(r)/ *noun* [C, usually sing.] **~ of sth** the attractive qualities of sth: *the lure of money/fame/adventure*

lurid /ˈlʊərɪd/ *adj.* **1** having colours that are too bright, in a way that is not attractive: *a lurid purple and orange dress* **2** (used about a story or a piece of writing) deliberately shocking, especially because of violent or unpleasant detail ▸ **luridly** *adv.*

lurk /lɜːk/ *verb* [I] to wait somewhere secretly especially in order to do sth bad or illegal: *I thought I saw somebody lurking among the trees.*

luscious /ˈlʌʃəs/ *adj.* (used about food) tasting very good: *luscious fruit*

lush /lʌʃ/ *adj.* (used about plants, gardens, etc.) growing well, with a lot of healthy grass and plants

lust¹ /lʌst/ *noun* **1** [U] **~ (for sb)** very strong sexual desire **2** [C, usually sing., U] **~ (for sth)** very strong desire to have or get sth: *a lust for power* ◇ *(a) lust for life* (= ENJOYMENT of life)

lust² /lʌst/ *verb* [I] **~ (after sb)**; **~ (after/for sth)** to feel a very strong desire for sb/sth: *to lust for power/success/fame*

lustful /ˈlʌstfl/ *adj.* full of sexual desire: *lustful thoughts* ▸ **lustfully** /-fəli/ *adv.*

lustre (*BrE*) (*AmE* **luster**) /ˈlʌstə(r)/ *noun* [U] the shining quality of a surface: *Her hair had lost its lustre.*

lute /luːt/ *noun* [C] (MUSIC) an early type of musical instrument with strings, played like a guitar

lutetium /luːˈtiːtiəm, -ˈtiːsi-/ *noun* [U] (*symb.* Lu) (CHEMISTRY) a chemical element. Lutetium is a rare silver-white metal used in the nuclear industry. ❶ For more information on the periodic table of elements, look at the **Reference Section** of this dictionary.

lyre

lute

luxurious /lʌɡˈʒʊəriəs/ *adj.* very comfortable; full of expensive and beautiful things: *a luxurious hotel* ▸ **luxuriously** *adv.*

luxury¹ /ˈlʌkʃəri/ *noun* (*pl.* **-ies**) **1** [U] the fact of enjoying special and expensive things that you do not really need: *They are said to be living in luxury in Barbados.* ◇ *to lead a life of luxury* **2** [C] something that is expensive and pleasant, but that you do not really need: *luxuries such as wine and chocolates* **3** [U, sing.] a pleasure that you do not often have: *It was (an) absolute luxury to do nothing all weekend.*

luxury² /ˈlʌkʃəri/ *adj.* expensive and of very high quality: *a luxury hotel/car/yacht* ◇ *luxury goods*

LW *abbr.* (in writing) = LONG WAVE

lychee /ˈlaɪtʃi/ *noun* [C] a small Chinese fruit with thick rough red skin, that is white inside and has a large stone

lying /ˈlaɪɪŋ/ present participle of LIE¹, LIE²

lymph /lɪmf/ *noun* [U] (BIOLOGY) a clear liquid containing white blood cells that cleans the inside of the body and helps to prevent infections from

spreading ▸ **lymphatic** /lɪmˈfætɪk/ *adj.* [only before noun]: *the lymphatic system*

ˈlymph node (*also* **ˈlymph gland**) *noun* [C] (ANATOMY) a small hard mass in the body through which LYMPH passes

lymphocyte /ˈlɪmfəsaɪt/ *noun* [C] (BIOLOGY) a type of LEUCOCYTE (= a small white blood cell)

lymphoma /lɪmˈfəʊmə/ *noun* [U, C] (HEALTH) cancer of the LYMPH NODES

lynch /lɪntʃ/ *verb* [T] (used about a crowd of people) to kill sb who is thought to be guilty of a crime, usually by hanging them, without a legal trial in court

lyre /ˈlaɪə(r)/ *noun* [C] (MUSIC) an ancient musical instrument with strings fastened in a frame that is like a U in shape ⊃ picture at **lute**

lyric¹ /ˈlɪrɪk/ *adj.* **1** (LITERATURE) (used about poetry) expressing a person's personal feelings and thoughts **2** (MUSIC) connected with, or written for, singing

lyric² /ˈlɪrɪk/ *noun* **1 lyrics** [pl.] (MUSIC) the words of a song: *music and lyrics by Rodgers and Hart* **2** [C] (LITERATURE) a LYRIC poem ⊃ look at **epic¹** (1)

lyrical /ˈlɪrɪkl/ *adj.* like a song or a poem, expressing strong personal feelings

M m

M¹ /em/ (*also* **m**) *noun* [C, U] (*pl.* **M's, m's**) the 13th letter of the English alphabet: *'Miranda' begins with (an) 'M'.*

M² *abbr.* (in writing) **1** (*also* **med.**) (used for sizes of things, especially clothes) medium **2** (used in the UK before a number) MOTORWAY: *heavy traffic on the M25*

m *abbr.* (in writing) **1** = MALE (2) **2** (*pl.* **m**) = METRE (1) **3** (*pl.* **m**) = MILLION (1) **4** = MASCULINE

MA (*BrE*) (*AmE* **M.A.**) /ˌem ˈeɪ/ *noun* [C] (EDUCATION) a second university degree in an arts subject, or, in Scotland, a first university degree in an arts subject (the abbreviation for 'Master of Arts') ⊃ look at **BA, MSc**

mac /mæk/ (*also* **mackintosh**) *noun* [C] (*BrE*) a coat that is made to keep out the rain

macabre /məˈkɑːbrə/ *adj.* unpleasant and frightening because it is connected with death: *a macabre tale/joke/ritual*

macaroni /ˌmækəˈrəʊni/ *noun* [U] a type of PASTA (= Italian food made from flour, eggs and water) in the shape of short tubes

Mace™ /meɪs/ *noun* [U] a chemical that hurts your eyes and skin, that some people, including police officers, carry in SPRAY cans so that they can defend themselves against people attacking them

mace /meɪs/ *noun* **1** [C] a special stick, carried as a sign of authority by an official such as a MAYOR (= the person who manages the affairs of a town or city) **2** [C] a large heavy stick that has a head with metal points on it, used in the past as a weapon **3** [U] the dried outer covering of NUTMEGS (= the hard nuts of an East Indian tree), used in cooking as a SPICE

Mach /mɑːk, mæk/ *noun* [U] (ENGINEERING, PHYSICS) (often before a number) a measurement of speed, used especially for aircraft. Mach 1 is the speed of sound.

machete /məˈʃeti/ *noun* [C] a broad heavy knife used as a cutting tool and as a weapon

machine /məˈʃiːn/ *noun* [C] **1** (often in compounds) a piece of equipment with moving parts that is designed to do a particular job. A machine usually needs electricity, gas, STEAM, etc. in order to work: *a washing/sewing/knitting machine* ◇ *a machine for making pasta* ➔ note at **tool** **2** (COMPUTING) a computer: *Switch off your machine before you leave the office.* ◇ *machine translation* (= using software to translate from one language to another)

ma'chine code *noun* [U] (COMPUTING) a language used for computer programs in which instructions are written in the form of numbers so that a computer can understand and act on them

ma'chine gun *noun* [C] a gun that fires bullets very quickly and continuously ➔ note at **gun**[1]

ma,chine 'learning *noun* [U] (COMPUTING) a process in which computers use huge amounts of data to learn how to do tasks without people programming them ➔ look at **AI**

ma,chine-'readable *adj.* (COMPUTING) (used about data) in a form that a computer can understand

machinery ʔ+ **C1** /məˈʃiːnəri/ *noun* [U] (ENGINEERING) machines in general, especially large ones; the moving parts of a machine: *farm/agricultural/industrial machinery*

ma'chine tool *noun* [C] (ENGINEERING) a tool for cutting or shaping metal, wood, etc., driven by a machine

machinist /məˈʃiːnɪst/ *noun* [C] **1** a person whose job is operating a machine, especially machines used in industry for cutting and shaping things, or a SEWING machine **2** a person whose job is to make or repair machines

macho /ˈmætʃəʊ/ *adj.* male in an aggressive way: *He's too macho to ever admit he was wrong.* ◇ *macho pride*

mackerel /ˈmækrəl/ *noun* [C, U] (*pl.* mackerel) a sea fish with blue-green bands on its body, that is used for food

mackintosh /ˈmækɪntɒʃ/ = MAC

macramé /məˈkrɑːmi/ *noun* [U] (ART) the art of tying KNOTS in string in an attractive pattern, to make items for decoration

macro /ˈmækrəʊ/ *noun* [C] (*pl.* -os) (COMPUTING) a single instruction that a computer reads as a set of instructions necessary to do a particular task

macro- /ˈmækrəʊ/ *prefix* (in nouns, adjectives and adverbs) large; on a large scale: *macroeconomics* **OPP** micro-

macrobiotic /ˌmækrəʊbaɪˈɒtɪk/ *adj.* (used about food) that is grown without using chemicals and is thought to make us live longer

macrocosm /ˈmækrəʊkɒzəm/ *noun* [C] any large complete structure that contains smaller structures, for example the universe ➔ look at **microcosm**

mad ʔ **B1** /mæd/ *adj.*
• ILL **1** (*especially BrE*) (PSYCHOLOGY) having a mind that does not work normally; mentally ill **HELP** Mentally ill is the polite way of describing a person who is not mentally normal. You can also say that sb **has mental health issues**.
• STUPID **2** (*especially BrE*) not at all sensible; stupid: *You must be mad to drive in this weather.*
• ANGRY **3** [not before noun] **~ (at/with sb) (for doing sth)** (*especially AmE, informal*) very angry: *Don't get mad at me.* ◇ *She's mad at me for forgetting her birthday.* ◇ (*BrE*) *His laziness drives me mad!*
• VERY INTERESTED **4** **~ about/on sb/sth** (*informal*) liking sb/sth very much: *He's mad on computer games at the moment.* ◇ *Steve's mad about Jane.*
• WILD **5** not controlled; wild or very excited: *The audience was cheering and clapping like mad* (= very hard). ◇ (*BrE*) *The team won and the fans went mad.*

madam /ˈmædəm/ *noun* [sing.] (*formal*) **1** used as a polite way of speaking to a woman whose name you do not know, for example in a shop or restaurant, or to show respect: *Can I help you, madam?* ➔ look at **sir** (1) **2** Dear Madam used at the beginning of a formal letter to a woman when you do not know her name: *Dear Madam, I am writing in reply …* ➔ look at **sir** (2)

,mad 'cow disease *noun* [U] (*informal*) = BSE

maddening /ˈmædnɪŋ/ *adj.* that makes you very angry or annoyed: *She has some really maddening habits.* ▸ maddeningly *adv.*

made /meɪd/ past tense, past participle of **make**[1] **IDM** made to measure → MEASURE[2]

madly /ˈmædli/ *adv.* **1** in a wild or crazy way: *They were rushing about madly.* **2** (*informal*) very; extremely: *They're madly in love.*

madman /ˈmædmən/ *noun* [C] (*pl.* -men /-mən/) a man who has a serious mental illness

madness /ˈmædnəs/ *noun* [U] crazy or stupid behaviour that could be dangerous: *It would be madness to take a boat out in such rough weather.*

madonna /məˈdɒnə/ *noun* **1** the Madonna [sing.] (RELIGION) the Virgin Mary, mother of Jesus Christ **2** [C] (ART) a statue or picture of the Virgin Mary: *a madonna and child*

madrigal /ˈmædrɪɡl/ *noun* [C] (MUSIC) a song for several singers, usually without musical instruments, popular in the sixteenth century

madwoman /ˈmædwʊmən/ *noun* [C] (*pl.* -women /-wɪmɪn/) a woman who has a serious mental illness

the Mafia /ðə ˈmæfiə/ *noun* [sing. + sing./pl. verb] a secret organization of criminals, that is active especially in Sicily, Italy and the US: *a cocaine-smuggling network run by the Mafia*

magazine ʔ **A1** /ˌmæɡəˈziːn/ (*also informal* mag /mæɡ/) *noun* [C] (ARTS AND MEDIA) a type of large thin book with a paper cover that you can buy every week or month containing articles, photos, etc. often on a particular topic; a similar collection of articles, etc. that appears regularly online: *a woman's/computer/gardening magazine*

magenta /məˈdʒentə/ *adj.* red-purple in colour ▸ magenta *noun* [U]

maggot /ˈmæɡət/ *noun* [C] a young insect before it grows wings and legs and becomes a fly

magic[1] ʔ **B1** /ˈmædʒɪk/ *noun* [U] **1** the secret power that some people believe can make strange or impossible things happen if you say special words or do special things ➔ look at **black magic 2** the art of doing tricks that seem impossible in order to entertain people **3** a special quality that makes sth seem wonderful: *I'll never forget the magic of that moment.*

magic[2] ʔ **B1** /ˈmædʒɪk/ *adj.* **1** used in or using magic: *a magic spell/potion/charm/trick* **2** having a special quality that makes sth seem wonderful: *Respect is the magic ingredient in our relationship.* ▸ magically /-kli/ *adv.*

magical ʔ+ **C1** /ˈmædʒɪkl/ *adj.* **1** that seems to use magic: *a herb with magical powers to heal* **2** wonderful and exciting: *Our holiday was absolutely magical.*

magician /məˈdʒɪʃn/ *noun* [C] **1** a person who performs magic tricks to entertain people ➔ look at **conjuror 2** (in stories) a person who has magic powers ➔ look at **wizard** (1)

magistrate ᵻ+ **C1** /'mædʒɪstreɪt/ *noun* [C] (**LAW**) an official who acts as a judge in cases involving less serious crimes

magma /'mægmə/ *noun* [U] (**GEOLOGY**) very hot liquid rock found below the earth's surface ⊃ picture at **rock¹**, **volcano**

magnanimous /mæg'nænɪməs/ *adj.* kind, generous and forgiving (especially towards an enemy or a competitor that you have beaten)

magnate /'mægneɪt/ *noun* [C] a person who is rich, powerful and successful, especially in business: *a media/property/shipping magnate*

magnesium /mæg'niːziəm/ *noun* [U] (*symb.* Mg) (**CHEMISTRY**) a chemical element. Magnesium is a light silver-white metal that burns with a bright white flame. **❶** For more information on the periodic table of elements, look at the **Reference Section** of this dictionary.

magnet /'mægnət/ *noun* [C] (**PHYSICS**) a piece of iron, steel, etc. that can attract and pick up other metal objects ⊃ picture at **magnetism**

magnetic ᵻ+ **C1** /mæg'netɪk/ *adj.* **1** (**PHYSICS**) having the ability to attract metal objects: *Steel is magnetic.* **2** having a quality that strongly attracts people: *a magnetic personality*

mag,netic 'field *noun* [C] (**PHYSICS**) an area around a MAGNET or materials that behave like a MAGNET, where there is a force that will attract some metals towards it ⊃ picture at **magnetism**

mag,netic 'north *noun* [U] (**GEOGRAPHY**) the direction that is approximately north as it is shown on a COMPASS (= an instrument that shows direction) ⊃ look at **true north**

magnetism

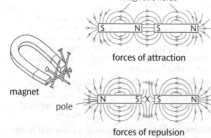

magnetic fields

forces of attraction

magnet

pole

forces of repulsion

magnetism /'mægnətɪzəm/ *noun* [U] **1** (**PHYSICS**) a characteristic of some metals such as iron, produced by electric currents, that causes forces between objects, either pulling them towards each other or pushing them apart **2** qualities that strongly attract people: *Nobody could resist his magnetism.*

magnetize (*BrE also* **-ise**) /'mægnətaɪz/ *verb* [T] **1** (**PHYSICS**) to make sth metal behave like a MAGNET **2** to strongly attract sb

magnificent ᵻ+ **B2** /mæg'nɪfɪsnt/ *adj.* extremely impressive and attractive **SYN** splendid ▸ **magnificence** /-sns/ *noun* [U] ▸ **magnificently** *adv.*

magnify /'mægnɪfaɪ/ *verb* [T] (**magnifying; magnifies;** *pt, pp* **magnified**) **1** (**PHYSICS**) to make sth look bigger than it is, usually using a special piece of equipment: *to magnify something under a microscope* **SYN** enlarge **2** to make sth seem more important than it really is: *to magnify a problem* **SYN** exaggerate ▸ **magnification** /,mægnɪfɪ'keɪʃn/ *noun* [U]

magnifying glass *noun* [C] a round piece of glass, usually with a handle, that is used for making things look bigger than they are

magnifying glass

magnitude ᵻ+ **C1** /'mægnɪtjuːd/ *noun* [U] **1** (*formal*) the great size or importance of sth **2** (**GEOLOGY**) the size of an earthquake: *An earthquake of magnitude 6.5 hit the island on Thursday.*

mahogany /mə'hɒɡəni/ *noun* [U] hard dark red-brown wood (from a tropical tree) that is used for making furniture

maid /meɪd/ *noun* [C] a woman whose job is to clean in a hotel or large house ⊃ look at **chambermaid**

maiden name /'meɪdn neɪm/ *noun* [C] a woman's family name before marriage ⊃ look at **née**

maiden voyage /,meɪdn 'vɔɪdʒ/ *noun* [C] the first journey of a new ship

mail¹ ᵻ **A2** /meɪl/ (*BrE also* **post**) *noun* **1** [U] the system for collecting and sending letters and packages: *to send a parcel by airmail/surface mail* **2** [U] the letters, etc. that you receive: *junk mail* (= letters, usually advertising sth, that are sent to people although they have not asked for them) **3** [C, U] = EMAIL (2)

mail² ᵻ **A2** /meɪl/ (*BrE also* **post**) *verb* [T] **1** ~ **sth (to sb/ sth); ~ (sb) sth** (*especially AmE*) to send sth to sb using the POSTAL system: *Don't forget to mail that letter to your mother.* ◊ *Don't forget to mail your mother that letter.* **2** ~ **sb (sth); ~ sth (to sb/sth)** to send a message to sb by email: *Can you mail me that document you mentioned?* ◊ *Can you mail it to me?*

'mail bomb (*AmE*) = LETTER BOMB

mailbox /'meɪlbɒks/ *noun* [C] **1** (*AmE*) = LETTER BOX (2) **2** (*AmE*) = POSTBOX **3** a computer program that receives and stores emails

'mailing list *noun* [C] a list of the names and addresses of people to whom advertising material or information is regularly sent by a business or an organization

mailman /'meɪlmæn/ *noun* [C] (*pl.* **-men** /-men/) (*AmE*) = POSTMAN

'mail order *noun* [U] a method of shopping. You choose what you want from a CATALOGUE (= a book or internet site showing goods for sale) and the goods are sent to you by post.

mailshot /'meɪlʃɒt/ *noun* [C] (**BUSINESS**) advertising or information that is sent to a large number of people at the same time by mail or email

maim /meɪm/ *verb* [T] (*formal*) to hurt sb so badly that part of their body can no longer be used ⊃ note at **injure**

main¹ ᵻ **A1 ●** /meɪn/ *adj.* [only before noun] most important: *My main reason for wanting to learn English is to get a better job.* ◊ *a busy main road* ◊ *He doesn't earn very much but he's happy, and that's the main thing.* **SYN** chief¹ **IDM in the main** (*formal*) generally; mostly: *We found English people very friendly in the main.*

main² /meɪn/ *noun* **1** [C] a large pipe or wire that carries water, gas or electricity between buildings: *The water main has burst.* **2 the mains, mains** [pl.] (*BrE*) the place where the supply of gas, water or electricity to a building starts; the system of providing these services to a building: *Turn the water off at the mains.* ◊ *mains gas/water/electricity*

mainframe /'meɪnfreɪm/ (*also* ,mainframe com'puter) *noun* [C] (**COMPUTING**) a large powerful computer, usually the centre of a network and shared by many users ⊃ look at **PC¹** (1)

the **ˈmainland** ʔ+ **C1** *noun* [sing.] (**GEOGRAPHY**) the main part of a country or continent, not including the islands around it: *They took the ferry back from the Isle of Skye to the mainland.* ▸ mainland /ˈmeɪnlənd, -lænd/ *adj.*: *mainland Greece*

mainly ʔ **B1** /ˈmeɪnli/ *adv.* mostly: *The students here are mainly from Japan.*

mainsail /ˈmeɪnseɪl, -sl/ *noun* [C] the largest and most important sail on a boat or ship

mainstay /ˈmeɪnsteɪ/ *noun* [C] a person or thing that is the most important part of sth and makes it possible for it to exist or to be successful: *Cocoa is the mainstay of the country's economy.*

the **mainstream** ʔ+ **C1** /ðə ˈmeɪnstriːm/ *noun* [sing.] the ideas and opinions that are considered normal because they are shared by most people; the people who hold these opinions and beliefs: *The new party is not **in the mainstream** of British politics.* ▸ mainstream **C1** *adj.*

maintain ʔ **B2** ⊙ /meɪnˈteɪn/ *verb* [T] **1** to make sth continue at the same level, standard, etc: *We need to maintain the quality of our goods.* ◊ *to maintain law and order* **2** to keep sth in good condition by checking and repairing it regularly: *to maintain a road/building/machine* ◊ *The house is large and expensive to maintain.* **3** to support sb with your own money: *He has to maintain two children from his previous marriage.* **4** to keep saying that sth is true even when others disagree or do not believe it: *I still maintain that I was right to sack him.* ◊ *She has always maintained her innocence.*

maintenance ʔ+ **C1** /ˈmeɪntənəns/ *noun* [U] **1** keeping sth in good condition: *car maintenance* **2** (*BrE*) (**FINANCE, LAW**) money that sb must pay regularly to a former wife, husband or partner, especially when they have had children together

maisonette /ˌmeɪzəˈnet/ *noun* [C] (*BrE*) a flat on two floors that is part of a larger building

maître d' /ˌmeɪtrə ˈdiː/ (*pl.* maître d's) (*also formal* maître d'hôtel, *pl.* maîtres d'hôtel /ˌmeɪtrə dəʊˈtel/) *noun* [C] (*from French*) **1** a head waiter **2** a man who manages a hotel

maize /meɪz/ (*BrE*) (*AmE* corn) *noun* [U] a tall plant that produces yellow grains in a **COB** ꙮ picture at **cereal** ❶ The yellow grains from **maize** that people eat as a vegetable are called **sweetcorn** or **corn**.

Maj. *abbr.* (in writing) = MAJOR² (1)

majestic /məˈdʒestɪk/ *adj.* impressive because of its size or beauty: *a majestic mountain landscape* ▸ majestically /-kli/ *adv.*

majesty /ˈmædʒəsti/ *noun* (*pl.* -ies) **1** [U] the impressive and attractive quality that sth has: *the splendour and majesty of the palace and its gardens* **2** His/Her/Your

---

Majesty [C] (*formal*) used when speaking to or about a king or queen: *Her Majesty, the Queen*

major¹ ʔ **A2** ⊙ /ˈmeɪdʒə(r)/ *adj.* **1** very large, important or serious: *The patient needs major heart surgery.* ◊ *There haven't been any major problems.* **OPP minor¹** ꙮ note at **main¹ 2** (**MUSIC**) of one of the two types of KEY in which music is usually written: *the key of D major* ꙮ look at **minor¹** (2)

major² /ˈmeɪdʒə(r)/ *noun* **1** (*abbr.* Maj.) [C] an officer of a middle level in the army or the US AIR FORCE **2** [C] (*AmE*) (**EDUCATION**) the main subject or course of a student at college or university; the student who studies it: *She's a French major.*

major³ /ˈmeɪdʒə(r)/ *verb* **PHR V** major in sth (*AmE*) (**EDUCATION**) to study sth as your main subject at college or university

ˌmajor ˈgeneral *noun* [C] an officer of a high level in the army

majority ʔ **B2** ⊙ /məˈdʒɒrəti/ *noun* (*pl.* -ies) **1** [sing. + sing./pl. verb] ~ (**of sb/sth**) the largest number or part of a group of people or things: *The majority was/were in favour of the ban.* ◊ *This treatment is not available in the **vast majority** of hospitals.* **OPP minority 2** [C, usually sing.] ~ (**over sb**) (**POLITICS**) (in an election) the difference in the number of votes for the person/party who came first and the person/party who came second: *He was elected **by/with a majority** of almost 5 000 votes.* ◊ *Labour had a huge majority over the Conservatives.* ꙮ look at **absolute majority, overall majority**

IDM be in the/a majority to form the largest number or part of sth: *Women are in the majority in the teaching profession.*

maˌjority ˈverdict *noun* [C] (**LAW**) a decision made by a JURY (= a group of members of the public) in a court case that most, but not all of them, agree with

make¹ ʔ **A1** /meɪk/ *verb* (*pt, pp* made /meɪd/)
- CREATE **1** [T] (often used with an adverb or a preposition) **be made (of/from/out of sth)** to produce or create sth: *to make bread* ◊ *This model is made of steel, and that one is made out of used matches.* ◊ *Cheese is made from milk.* ◊ *Those cars are made in Slovakia.* ◊ *Shall I make you a sandwich/make a sandwich for you?* ◊ *to make a law/rule* ◊ *to make a hole in something* ◊ *to make a scratch/mark/stain on something*
- CAUSE TO HAPPEN, BECOME, ETC. **2** [T] to cause a particular effect, feeling, situation, etc: *The film made me cry.* ◊ *Flying makes him nervous.* ◊ *Her remarks made the situation worse.* ◊ *I'll **make it clear** to him that we won't pay.* ◊ ***Make sure** you lock the car.* ◊ *You don't need to know much of a language to make **yourself understood**.* ◊ *to make trouble/a mess/a noise* **3** *linking verb* to make sb/sth become sth; to have the right qualities to become sth: *She was made (= given the job of) president.* ◊ *You can borrow some money this time, but don't **make a habit of** it.* ◊ *Karen explains things very clearly — she'd make a good teacher.* ꙮ note at **job 4** *linking verb* to become sth; to achieve sth: *I'm hoping to make head of department by the time I'm 30.*
- PERFORM AN ACTION **5** [T] (used with nouns) to perform a certain action: *to make a mistake* ◊ *to make a guess/comment/statement/suggestion* ◊ *to make progress* ◊ *I've made an appointment to see the doctor.*
- FORCE **6** [T] ~ **sb do sth** to force sb/sth to do sth: *You can't make her come with us if she doesn't want to.*
- MONEY/NUMBERS/TIME **7** [T] used with money, numbers and time: *How much do you think he makes (= earns) a*

month? ◇ *to make a lot of money* ◇ *5 and 7 make 12 (5+7=12).* ◇ *'What's the time?' 'I make it 6.45.'*
• **GET TO 8** [T] to manage to reach a place or go somewhere: *We should make Bristol by about ten.* ◇ *I can't make the meeting next week.*
IDM **make do with sth** to use sth that is not good enough because nothing better is available: *If we can't get limes, we'll have to make do with lemons.* **make it (as sth)** to manage to do sth; to succeed: *She'll never make it as an actress.* ◇ *He's badly injured — it looks like he might not make it (= survive).* **make the most of sth** to get as much pleasure, profit, etc. as possible from sth: *You won't get another chance — make the most of it!* ❶ For other idioms containing **make**, look at the nouns, adjectives, etc. For example, **make amends** is at **amends**.
PHRV **be made for sb/each other** to be well suited to sb/each other: *Jim and Alice seem made for each other.* **make for sb/sth** to move towards sb/sth **make for sth** to help or allow sth to happen: *Arguing all the time doesn't make for a happy marriage.* **make sb/sth into sth** to change sb/sth into sth/sb: *She made her spare room into an office.* **make sth of sb/sth** to understand the meaning or nature of sb/sth: *What do you make of Colin's letter?* **make off (with sth)** to leave or escape in a hurry, for example after stealing sth: *Somebody's made off with my wallet!* **make sb/sth out 1** to understand sb/sth: *I just can't make him out.* **2** to be able to see or hear sb/sth; to manage to read sth: *I could just make out her signature.* **make out that …** | **make yourself out to be** sth to say that sth is true and try to make people believe it: *He made out that he was a millionaire.* ◇ *She's not as clever as she makes herself out to be.* **make sth up 1** to form sth: *the different groups that make up our society* **2** to invent sth, often sth that is not true: *to make up an excuse* **3** to make a number or an amount complete; to replace sth that has been lost: *We need one more person to make up our team.* **make yourself/sb up** to put powder, colour, etc. on your/sb's face to make it look attractive **make up for sth** to do sth that corrects a bad situation: *Her enthusiasm makes up for her lack of experience.* **make it up to sb** to do sth that shows that you are sorry for what you have done to sb or that you are grateful for what they have done for you: *You've done me a big favour. How can I make it up to you?* **make (it) up (with sb)** to become friends again after an argument: *Has she made it up with him yet?*

make

create ♦ **develop** ♦ **produce** ♦ **generate** ♦ **form**

These words all mean to make sth from parts or materials, or to cause sth to exist or happen.

make *She makes her own clothes.*

create *How was the universe created?*

develop *to develop new software*

produce *a factory that produces microchips*

generate *to generate electricity* ◇ *Brainstorming is a good way of generating new ideas.*

form *Rearrange the letters to form a new word.*

make² 🔉 **B2** /meɪk/ *noun* [C] (**BUSINESS**) the name of the company that produces sth: *What make is your TV?*
IDM **on the make** always trying to make money for yourself, especially in a dishonest way

'make-believe *noun* [U] things that sb imagines or invents that are not real

makeover /'meɪkəʊvə(r)/ *noun* [C, U] the process of improving the appearance of a person or a place, or of changing the impression that sth gives

maker /'meɪkə(r)/ *noun* [C] a person, company or machine that makes sth: *a film-maker* ◇ *an ice cream maker*

makerspace /'meɪkəspeɪs/ *noun* [C] (**EDUCATION**) a place where people who are interested in similar things can come together to work and share ideas and equipment: *We want to open our own makerspace, where we can hold events, lectures and workshops.*

makeshift /'meɪkʃɪft/ *adj.* made to be used for only a short time until there is sth better: *makeshift shelters of old cardboard boxes*

'make-up 🔉+ **B2** *noun* **1** [U] powder, cream, etc. that you put on your face to make yourself more attractive. Actors use make-up to change their appearance when they are acting: *to put on/take off make-up* ⊃ look at **cosmetic¹** ⊃ verb **make(yourself/somebody)up 2** [sing.] a person's character: *He can't help his temper. It's part of his make-up.* **3** [sing.] the different things, people, etc. that combine to form sth: *the make-up of a TV audience* ⊃ note at **structure¹**

making 🔉+ **B2** /'meɪkɪŋ/ *noun* [sing.] the act of doing or producing sth; the process of being made: *breadmaking* ◇ *This movie has been three years in the making.*
IDM **be the making of sb** to be the reason that sb is successful: *University was the making of Gina.* **have the makings of sth** to have the necessary qualities for sth: *The book has the makings of a good film.*

mal- /mæl/ *prefix* (in nouns, verbs and adjectives) bad or badly; not correct or correctly: *malnutrition* ◇ *malfunction*

maladjusted /ˌmælə'dʒʌstɪd/ *adj.* (used about a person) not able to behave well with other people

malapropism /'mæləprɒpɪzəm/ *noun* [C] (**LANGUAGE**) a mistake that sb makes when they use a word that sounds similar to the word they wanted to use, but means something different and sounds funny

malaria /mə'leəriə/ *noun* [U] (**HEALTH**) a serious disease in hot countries that you get from the bite of a MOSQUITO (= a small flying insect) ▶ **malarial** /-riəl/ *adj.*: *a malarial region*   *malaise*

male 🔉 **A2** ❶ /meɪl/ *adj.* (**BIOLOGY**) **1** being a man or a boy: *a male friend* ◇ *The two main characters in the book are male.* **2** (*abbr.* m) belonging to the sex that does not give birth to babies or produce eggs: *a male bird* ◇ *a male model/nurse* ⊃ look at **masculine**(1) ⊃ picture at **fertilization 3** (used about plants and flowers) producing POLLEN ▶ **male** 🔉 **A2** ❶ *noun* [C]: *The male of the species has a white tail.*

male 'chauvinism = **CHAUVINISM**

malformation /ˌmælfɔː'meɪʃn/ *noun* **1** [C] (**HEALTH**) a part of the body that is not formed correctly: *foetal malformations* **2** [U] the state of not being correctly formed

malice /'mælɪs/ *noun* [U] a wish to hurt other people ▶ **malicious** /mə'lɪʃəs/ *adj.* ▶ **maliciously** *adv.*
IDM **with malice aforethought** with the deliberate intention of committing a crime or harming sb

malignant /mə'lɪɡnənt/ *adj.* (**HEALTH**) (used about a serious disease or a TUMOUR) likely to cause death if not controlled: *He has a malignant brain tumour.*
OPP **benign, non-malignant**

mall 🔉 **B1** /mɔːl, mæl/ (*also* **shopping mall**) *noun* [C] (*both especially AmE*) a large area or covered area that has many shops, restaurants, etc. inside it

malleable /'mæliəbl/ *adj.* **1** (used about metals, etc.) that can be hit or pressed into shape easily without breaking or CRACKING (= starting to split) **2** (used about metal or plastic) that can be hit or pressed into different shapes easily without breaking **3** (used about people, ideas, etc.) easily influenced or changed ▸ **malleability** /ˌmæliə'bɪləti/ *noun* [U]

mallet /'mælɪt/ *noun* [C] a heavy wooden HAMMER ⊃ picture at **tool**

malleus /'mæliəs/ *noun* [C] (*pl.* mallei /-liaɪ/) (ANATOMY) the first of three small bones in the MIDDLE EAR that carry sound to the INNER EAR **SYN hammer**[1] ⊃ picture at **ear**

malnutrition /ˌmælnju'trɪʃn/ *noun* [U] (SOCIAL STUDIES) bad health that is the result of not having enough food or enough of the right kind of food ▸ **malnourished** /ˌmæl'nʌrɪʃt/ *adj.*: *The children were badly malnourished.*

malpractice /ˌmæl'præktɪs/ *noun* [U, C] (LAW) careless, wrong or illegal behaviour while in a professional job: *medical malpractice* ◊ *He is standing trial for alleged malpractices.*

malt /mɔːlt, mɒlt/ *noun* [U] (AGRICULTURE) grain that is used for making beer and WHISKY (= a strong alcoholic drink)

maltose /'mɔːltəʊz, -təʊs/ *noun* [U] (BIOLOGY) a sugar that chemicals in the body make from STARCH (= a food substance found in flour, rice, potatoes, etc.)

maltreat /ˌmæl'triːt/ *verb* [T] to treat a person or an animal in a cruel or unkind way ▸ **maltreatment** *noun* [U]

malware /'mælweə(r)/ *noun* [U] (COMPUTING) computer programs, especially viruses, that are designed to damage your computer

mammal /'mæml/ *noun* [C] (BIOLOGY) an animal of the type that gives birth to live babies, not eggs, and feeds its young on milk from its own body: *Whales, dogs and humans are mammals.* ⊃ picture at **animal**

mammary /'mæməri/ *adj.* [only before noun] (ANATOMY) connected with the breasts: *mammary glands* (= parts of the breast that produce milk)

mammogram /'mæməgræm/ *noun* [C] (MEDICINE) an examination of a breast using X-RAYS to check for cancer

mammoth /'mæməθ/ *adj.* very big

man[1] 🔊 **A1** /mæn/ *noun* (*pl.* men /men/) **1** [C] an adult male person **2** [C] a person of either sex, male or female: *All men are equal.* ◊ *No man could survive long in such conditions.* **3** [U] humans as a group, both male and female: *Early man lived by hunting.* ◊ *the damage man has caused to the environment* **4** [C] (in compounds) a man who comes from a particular place; a man who has a particular job or interest: *a Frenchman* ◊ *a businessman* ◊ *sportsmen and women* **IDM the man in the street** (*BrE*) an ordinary man or woman **the odd man/one out** → ODD

man[2] /mæn/ *verb* [T] (-nn-) to operate sth; to provide people to operate sth: *The telephones are manned 24 hours a day.*

manage 🔊 **A2** /'mænɪdʒ/ *verb* **1** [T, I] ~ **(to do sth)** to succeed in doing or dealing with sth difficult; to be able to do sth: *However did you manage to find us here?* ◊ *I can't manage this suitcase. It's too heavy.* ◊ *Paula can't manage next Tuesday* (= she can't come then) *so we'll meet another day.* **2** [T] to be in charge or control of sth: *She manages a small advertising business.* ◊ *You need to manage your time more efficiently.* ⊃ note at **organization 3** [I] ~ **(without/with sb/sth); ~ (on sth)** to deal with a difficult situation; to continue despite difficulties: *My grandmother couldn't manage without her neighbours.* ◊ *Can you*

manage with just one assistant? ◊ *It's hard for a family to manage on just one income.*

manageable /'mænɪdʒəbl/ *adj.* not too big or too difficult to deal with **OPP unmanageable**

management 🔊 **B1** /'mænɪdʒmənt/ *noun* **1** [U] the control or organization of sth: *Good classroom management is vital with large groups of children.* **2** [C + sing./pl. verb, U] (BUSINESS) the people who control a business or company: *The management is/are considering closing the factory.* ◊ *The hotel is now under new management.*

manager 🔊 **A2** /'mænɪdʒə(r)/ *noun* [C] **1** (BUSINESS) a person who controls an organization or part of an organization: *a bank manager* **2** (ARTS AND MEDIA) a person who looks after the business affairs of a singer, an actor, etc. **3** (SPORT) a person who is in charge of a sports team: *the England manager*

managerial /ˌmænə'dʒɪəriəl/ *adj.* (BUSINESS) connected with the work of a manager: *Do you have any managerial experience?*

managing di'rector *noun* [C] (*abbr.* MD) (BUSINESS) a person who controls a business or company

'man bag *noun* [C] a bag designed for men to carry money, keys, a mobile phone, etc.

mandarin /'mændərɪn/ *noun* **1** [C] (HISTORY) a government official of high rank in China in the past **2** Mandarin [U] (LANGUAGE) the standard form of Chinese, which is the official language of China **3** (*also* ˌmandarin 'orange) [C] a type of small orange with loose skin that comes off easily

mandate 🔊+ **C1** /'mændeɪt/ *noun* [C, usually sing.] ~ **(to do sth)** (POLITICS) the power that is officially given to a group of people to do sth, especially after they have won an election: *The union leaders had a clear mandate to call a strike.*

mandatory 🔊+ **C1** /'mændətəri, mæn'deɪtəri/ *adj.* (*formal*) that you must do, have, obey, etc: *The crime carries a mandatory life sentence.* **SYN obligatory OPP optional**

mandible /'mændɪbl/ *noun* [C] **1** (ANATOMY) the bone that forms the lower JAW **SYN jawbone** ⊃ picture at **body 2** either of the two parts that are at the front and on either side of an insect's mouth, used especially for biting and CRUSHING food (= pressing so that it breaks into small pieces) ⊃ picture at **animal**

mandolin /ˌmændə'lɪn, 'mændəlɪn/ *noun* [C] (MUSIC) a musical instrument with four pairs of metal strings, that looks like a guitar with a curved back

mane /meɪn/ *noun* [C] the long hair on the neck of a horse or a lion ⊃ picture at **animal, lion**

maneuver /mə'nuːvə(r)/ (*AmE*) = MANOEUVRE[1], MANOEUVRE[2]

manganese /'mæŋɡəniːz/ *noun* [U] (*symb.* Mn) (CHEMISTRY) a chemical element. Manganese is a grey-white metal that breaks easily. ❶ For more information on the periodic table of elements, look at the **Reference Section** of this dictionary.

mangle /'mæŋɡl/ *verb* [T, usually passive] to damage sth so badly that it is difficult to see what it looked like originally: *The motorway was covered with the mangled wreckage of cars.*

mango /'mæŋɡəʊ/ *noun* [C] (*pl.* -oes) a tropical fruit that usually has a yellow, red or green skin and is orange inside

mangrove /'mæŋɡrəʊv/ *noun* [C] a tropical tree that grows in wet ground or at the edge of rivers and has some roots that are above ground

manhole /ˈmænhəʊl/ *noun* [C] a hole in the street that has a LID over it, used when sb needs to go down to look at the pipes, etc. below the street

manhood /ˈmænhʊd/ *noun* [U] the state of being a man rather than a boy

mania /ˈmeɪniə/ *noun* **1** [C, usually sing., U] (*informal*) a great enthusiasm for sth: *World Cup mania is sweeping the country.* **2** [U] (HEALTH, PSYCHOLOGY) a serious mental illness that may cause sb to be very excited or violent

maniac /ˈmeɪniæk/ *noun* [C] **1** a person who behaves in a wild and stupid way: *to drive like a maniac* **SYN lunatic¹ 2** a person who has a stronger love of sth than is normal: *a football/sex maniac*

manic /ˈmænɪk/ *adj.* **1** full of nervous energy or excited activity; behaving in a busy, anxious way: *Things are manic* (= very busy) *at work at the moment.* **2** connected with MANIA: *His behaviour became more manic as he began to feel stressed.*

manicure /ˈmænɪkjʊə(r)/ *noun* [C] treatment to make your hands and nails look attractive

manifest 🔑+ C1 /ˈmænɪfest/ *verb* [I, T] ~ sth/itself (in sth) (*formal*) to show sth clearly; to be shown clearly: *Mental illness can manifest itself in many forms.* ▶ **manifest** *adj.*: *manifest failure/anger* ▶ **manifestly** *adv.*

manifestation /ˌmænɪfeˈsteɪʃn/ *noun* [C, U] (*formal*) a sign that sth is happening

manifesto /ˌmænɪˈfestəʊ/ *noun* [C] (*pl.* -os) (POLITICS) a written statement by a political party that explains what it hopes to do if it becomes the government in the future

manifold¹ /ˈmænɪfəʊld/ *adj.* (*formal*) many; of many different types

manifold² /ˈmænɪfəʊld/ *noun* [C] a pipe or an ENCLOSED space with several openings for taking gases in and out of a car engine

manioc /ˈmæniɒk/ = CASSAVA

manipulate 🔑+ C1 /məˈnɪpjuleɪt/ *verb* [T] **1** to influence sb so that they do or think what you want: *Clever politicians know how to manipulate public opinion.* **2** to use, move or control sth with skill: *The doctor manipulated the bone back into place.* ▶ **manipulation** 🔑+ C1 /məˌnɪpjuˈleɪʃn/ *noun* [U, C]

manipulative /məˈnɪpjələtɪv/ *adj.* **1** showing skill at influencing sb or forcing sb to do what you want, often in an unfair way: *manipulative behaviour* **2** connected with the ability to handle objects with skill: *manipulative skills such as typing and knitting*

mankind /mænˈkaɪnd/ *noun* [U] all the people in the world: *A nuclear war would be a threat to all mankind.*

manly /ˈmænli/ *adj.* (manlier; manliest) typical of or suitable for a man: *a deep manly voice* ▶ **manliness** *noun* [U]

man-ˈmade *adj.* made by people; not natural: *man-made fabrics such as nylon and polyester* ⊃ note at **artificial**

manner 🔑 A2 /ˈmænə(r)/ *noun* **1** [sing.] the way that you do sth or that sth happens: *Stop arguing! Let's try to act in a civilized manner.* **2** [sing.] the way that sb behaves towards other people: *to have an aggressive/a relaxed/a professional manner* **3** manners [pl.] a way of behaving that is considered acceptable in your country or culture: *In some countries it is bad manners to show the soles of your feet.* ◊ *Their children have no manners.*

IDM **all manner of …** every kind of …: *You meet all manner of people in my job.*

mannerism /ˈmænərɪzəm/ *noun* **1** [C] somebody's particular way of speaking or a particular movement they often do **2** Mannerism [U] (ART) a style in sixteenth-century Italian art that did not show things in a natural way but made them look strange or out of their usual shape

manoeuvre¹ (*BrE*) (*AmE* maneuver) /məˈnuːvə(r)/ *noun* **1** [C] a movement that needs care or skill: *Parking the car in such a small space would be a tricky manoeuvre.* **2** [C, U] something clever that you do in order to trick sb, etc: *political manoeuvre(s)* **SYN move¹ 3** manoeuvres [pl.] a way of training soldiers when large numbers of them practise fighting in battles: *large-scale military manoeuvres*

manoeuvre² (*BrE*) (*AmE* maneuver) /məˈnuːvə(r)/ *verb* [I, T] to move (sth) to a different position using skill: *There was very little room to manoeuvre.*

manor /ˈmænə(r)/ (*also* ˈmanor house) *noun* [C] a large house in the country that has land around it

manpower /ˈmænpaʊə(r)/ *noun* [U] the people that you need to do a particular job: *a shortage of skilled manpower*

mansion /ˈmænʃn/ *noun* [C] a very large house

manslaughter /ˈmænslɔːtə(r)/ *noun* [U] (LAW) the crime of killing sb without intending to do so ⊃ look at **murder¹** (1)

mantelpiece /ˈmæntlpiːs/ *noun* [C] a narrow shelf above the space in a room where a fire goes

mantle /ˈmæntl/ *noun* [sing.] (GEOLOGY) the part of the earth between the surface and the centre ⊃ picture at **rock¹, seismic**

mantra /ˈmæntrə/ *noun* [C] (RELIGION) a word, phrase or sound that is repeated again and again, especially during prayer or MEDITATION: *a Buddhist mantra*

manual¹ /ˈmænjuəl/ *adj.* using your hands; operated by hand: *manual work/labour* ◊ *a manual worker* ◊ *Does your car have a manual or an automatic gearbox?* ▶ **manually** /-əli/ *adv.*

manual² /ˈmænjuəl/ *noun* [C] a book that explains how to do or operate sth: *a training manual* ◊ *a car manual*

manufacture 🔑+ B2 /ˌmænjuˈfæktʃə(r)/ *verb* [T] to make sth in large quantities using machines: *a local factory that manufactures furniture* **SYN produce¹** ▶ **manufacture** *noun* [U]: *the manufacture of cars*

manufacturer /ˌmænjuˈfæktʃərə(r)/ *noun* [C] a person or company that makes sth: *a car manufacturer*

manufacturing 🔑+ B2 /ˌmænjuˈfæktʃərɪŋ/ *noun* [U] (BUSINESS) the business or industry of producing goods in large quantities in factories, etc: *Many jobs in manufacturing were lost during the recession.*

manure /məˈnjʊə(r)/ *noun* [U] (AGRICULTURE) the waste matter from animals that is put on the ground in order to make plants grow better ⊃ look at **fertilizer**

manuscript 🔑+ C1 /ˈmænjuskrɪpt/ *noun* [C] (LITERATURE) **1** a copy of a book, piece of music, etc. before it has been printed **2** a very old book or document that was written by hand

many 🔑 A1 ⊙ /ˈmeni/ *det., pron.* **1** used with plural nouns and verbs, especially in negative sentences or in more formal English, to mean 'a large number of': *Have you made many friends at school yet?* ◊ *Not many of my friends drive.* ◊ *Many of the mistakes are just careless.* ◊ *There are too many mistakes in this essay.* ◊ *a many-sided shape* **2** used to ask about the number of people or things, or to refer to a known number: *How many children have you got?* ◊ *How many came to the meeting?* ◊ *I don't work as many hours as you.* ◊ *There are half/twice as many boys as*

girls in the class. **3 many a** (*formal*) used with a singular noun and verb to mean 'a large number of': *I've heard him say that many a time.*
IDM a good/great many very many

Maori /ˈmaʊri/ *noun* [C] (*pl.* Maori, Maoris) a member of the human group who were the original people to live in New Zealand ▸ **Maori** *adj.*

map 🔊 **A1** /mæp/ *noun* [C] a drawing or plan of (part of) the surface of the earth that shows countries, rivers, mountains, roads, etc: *a map of the world* ◇ *a road/ street map* ◇ *I can't find Cambridge on the map.* ◇ *to read a map* ⊃ look at **atlas** ▸ **map** 🔊 **B2** *verb* [T] (-pp-): *The region is so remote it has not yet been mapped.*

maple /ˈmeɪpl/ *noun* [C] a tall tree with leaves that have five points and turn bright red or yellow in the autumn

maple ˈsyrup *noun* [U] a sweet, sticky sauce made with liquid obtained from some types of MAPLE tree, often eaten with PANCAKES

mapping /ˈmæpɪŋ/ *noun* [C] **1** (**GEOGRAPHY**) the process of making a map of an area **2** the process of discovering or giving information about something, especially the way it is arranged or organized: *gene mapping*

Mar. *abbr.* (in writing) = MARCH

mar /mɑː(r)/ *verb* [T] (-rr-) to damage sth or make sth less good or successful: *The game was marred by the behaviour of drunken fans.* **SYN blight**[1] ⊃ look at **ruin**[1]

marathon 🔊 **B2** /ˈmærəθən/ *noun* [C] **1** (**SPORT**) a long running race of about 42 kilometres or 26 miles **2** an activity that lasts much longer than expected: *The interview was a real marathon.*

marauding /məˈrɔːdɪŋ/ *adj.* [only before noun] (used about people or animals) going around a place in search of things to steal or people to attack: *marauding wolves*

marble /ˈmɑːbl/ *noun* **1** [U] (**GEOLOGY**) a hard attractive stone that is used to make statues and parts of buildings ⊃ note at **art** **2** [C] a small ball of coloured glass that children play with **3 marbles** [U] the children's game that you play by rolling marbles along the ground trying to hit other marbles

March 🔊 **A1** /mɑːtʃ/ *noun* [U, C] (*abbr.* Mar.) the third month of the year, between February and April

march[1] 🔊 **C1** /mɑːtʃ/ *verb* **1** [I] to walk with regular steps (like a soldier): *The president saluted as the troops marched past.* **2** [I] to walk in a determined way: *She marched up to the manager and demanded an apology.* **3** [I] (**SOCIAL STUDIES**) to walk in a large group to protest about sth: *The demonstrators marched through the centre of town.* **4** [T] to make sb walk or march somewhere: *The prisoner was marched away.*

march[2] 🔊 **C1** /mɑːtʃ/ *noun* [C] **1** (**SOCIAL STUDIES**) an organized walk by a large group of people who are protesting about sth: *a peace march* ⊃ look at **demonstration** **2** a journey made by MARCHING: *The soldiers were tired after their long march.*

mare /meə(r)/ *noun* [C] a female horse

margarine /ˌmɑːdʒəˈriːn/ *noun* [U] a food that is similar to butter, made of animal or vegetable fats

margin 🔊 **B2** 🔊 /ˈmɑːdʒɪn/ *noun* [C] **1** the empty space at the side of a page in a book, etc. **2** [usually sing.] the amount of space, time, votes, etc. by which you win sth: *He won by a wide/narrow/comfortable margin.* **3** = PROFIT MARGIN: *a gross margin of 45%* **4** the area around the edge of sth: *the margins of the Pacific Ocean* **5** [usually sing.] an amount of space, time, etc. that is more than you need: *The schedule left no margin for error.*

marginal 🔊 **C1** /ˈmɑːdʒɪnl/ *adj.* **1** small in size or importance: *The differences are marginal.* **2** (*especially BrE*) (**POLITICS**) won or lost by a very small number of votes: *The number of marginal seats meant it was difficult to predict the result of the election.*
▸ **marginally** /-nəli/ *adv.*: *In most cases costs will increase only marginally.*

marginalize (*BrE also* -ise) /ˈmɑːdʒɪnəlaɪz/ *verb* [T] (**SOCIAL STUDIES**) to make sb feel as if they are not important; to put sb in a position in which they have no power

marijuana /ˌmærəˈwɑːnə/ *noun* [U] a drug that is smoked and is illegal in many countries

marina /məˈriːnə/ *noun* [C] (**GEOGRAPHY**) a HARBOUR (= a small area of water) designed for pleasure boats

marinade /ˌmærɪˈneɪd/ *noun* [C, U] a mixture of oil, wine, SPICES, etc. in which food is left before it is cooked in order to make it softer or to give it a particular taste

marinate /ˈmærɪneɪt/ (*also* **marinade**) *verb* [T, I] if you **marinate** food or it **marinates**, you leave it in a MARINADE before cooking it

marine[1] 🔊 **C1** /məˈriːn/ *adj.* [only before noun] **1** connected with the sea: *the study of marine life* **2** connected with ships or sailing: *marine insurance*

marine[2] /məˈriːn/ *noun* [C] a soldier who has been trained to fight on land or at sea

marital /ˈmærɪtl/ *adj.* [only before noun] connected with marriage: *marital problems*

marital ˈstatus *noun* [U] (*formal*) (used on official documents) if you are married, single, divorced, etc.

maritime /ˈmærɪtaɪm/ *adj.* [only before noun] connected with the sea or ships

mark[1] 🔊 **A2** /mɑːk/ *noun* [C]

• SPOT/DIRT **1** a spot or line that makes sth look less good: *There's a dirty mark on the front of your shirt.* ◇ *If you put a hot cup down on the table it will leave a mark.* ⊃ look at **birthmark** **2** something that shows who or what sb/sth is, especially by making them or it different from others: *My horse is the one with the white mark on its face.*

• SYMBOL **3** (**LANGUAGE**) a written or printed symbol that is a sign of sth: *a question/a punctuation/an exclamation mark*

• SIGN **4** a sign of a quality or feeling: *They stood in silence for two minutes as a mark of respect.*

• GRADE **5** (**EDUCATION**) a number or letter you get for school work that tells you how good your work was; a point given for a correct answer in an exam or competition: *She got very good marks in the exam.* ◇ *The pass mark is 60 out of 100.* ◇ *to get full marks* (= everything correct) ⊃ note at **study**[2]

• LEVEL **6** the level or point that sth/sb has reached: *The race is almost at the half-way mark.*

• EFFECT **7** an effect that people notice and will remember: *The time he spent in prison left its mark on him.* ◇ *He was only 18 when he first made his mark in politics.*

• MODEL/TYPE **8** a particular model or type of sth: *the new SL S3 Mark III*

• TARGET **9** (*formal*) a person or an object towards which sth is directed; a target: *The arrow hit/missed its mark.* ◇ *His judgement of the situation was wide of the mark* (= wrong). **SYN target**[1]
IDM on your marks, get set, go! (**SPORT**) used at the start of a sports race **overstep the mark/line**
→ OVERSTEP **quick, slow, etc. off the mark** quick, slow, etc. in reacting to a situation

mark² ⚡ **A2** /mɑːk/ *verb* [T]

- WRITE **1** to put a sign on sth: *We marked the price on all items in the sale.* ◇ *I'll mark all the boxes I want you to move.*
- SPOIL **2** to damage sth or make it look less good by making a mark on it: *The white walls were dirty and marked.*
- SHOW A POSITION **3** to show where sth is or where sth happened: *The route is marked in red.* ◇ *Flowers mark the spot where he died.*
- CELEBRATE **4** to celebrate or officially remember an important event: *The ceremony marked the fiftieth anniversary of the opening of the school.*
- SHOW A CHANGE **5** to be a sign that sth new is going to happen: *This decision marks a change in government policy.*
- GIVE A GRADE **6** (EDUCATION) to look at a student's work, show where there are mistakes and give it a number or letter to show how good it is: *Why did you mark that answer wrong?* ◇ *He has 100 exam papers to mark.*
- IN SPORT **7** to stay close to a player of the opposite team so that they cannot play easily

PHR V **mark sb down** (*BrE*) to reduce the mark given to sb in an exam, etc: *She was marked down because of poor grammar.* **mark sb/sth down as/for sth** to decide that sb/sth is of a particular type or suitable for a particular use: *From the first day of school, the teachers marked Fred down as a troublemaker.* **mark sth out** to draw lines to show the position of sth: *Spaces for each car were marked out in the car park.* **mark sth up/down** (BUSINESS) to increase/decrease the price of sth that you are selling: *All goods have been marked down by 15%.*

marked /mɑːkt/ *adj.* clear; easy to see: *There has been a marked increase in vandalism in recent years.*
▶ **markedly** /'mɑːkɪdli/ *adv.*: *This year's sales have risen markedly.*

marker ⚡+ **B2** /'mɑːkə(r)/ *noun* [C] something that shows the position of sth: *He placed a marker where the ball had landed.*

market¹ ⚡ **A1** /'mɑːkɪt/ *noun* (BUSINESS) **1** [C] a place where people go to buy and sell things: *a market stall/trader/town* ◇ *a cattle/fish/meat market* ⊃ look at **flea market, hypermarket, supermarket 2** [C] business or commercial activity; the amount of buying or selling of a particular type of goods: *The company currently has a 5% share of the market.* ◇ *the property/job market* **3** [C, U] ~ (for sth) a country, an area or a group of people that buys sth; the number of people who buy sth: *The company is hoping to expand into the European market.* ◇ *There's no market for very large cars when petrol is so expensive.* ⊃ look at **black market, stock market 4** [C] = STOCK MARKET
IDM **on the market** available to buy: *This is one of the best cameras on the market.*

market² ⚡ **B1** /'mɑːkɪt/ *verb* [T] (BUSINESS) to sell sth with the help of advertising

marketable /'mɑːkɪtəbl/ *adj.* (BUSINESS) that can be sold easily because people want it

market e'conomy *noun* [C] (ECONOMICS) an economic system in which salaries and prices are based on the balance between supply and demand rather than being controlled by the state

market 'garden *noun* [C] (AGRICULTURE) a type of farm where vegetables and fruit are grown for sale

market 'gardening (*BrE*) (*AmE* **truck farming**) *noun* [U] (AGRICULTURE) the business of growing vegetables and fruit for sale on a farm

marketing ⚡ **B1** /'mɑːkɪtɪŋ/ *noun* [U] (BUSINESS) the activity of showing and advertising a company's products in the best possible way: *Effective marketing will lead to increased sales.* ◇ *the marketing department*

'marketing mix *noun* [C, usually sing.] (BUSINESS) the combination of things that a company decides to try in order to persuade people to buy a product

market 'leader *noun* [C] (BUSINESS) **1** the company that sells the largest quantity of a particular kind of product **2** a product that is the most successful of its kind

marketplace ⚡+ **C1** /'mɑːkɪtpleɪs/ *noun* **1** the marketplace [sing.] (BUSINESS) the activity of competing with other companies to buy and sell goods, services, etc. **2** [C] the place in a town where a market is held

market 'price *noun* [C] (BUSINESS) the price that people in general will pay for sth at a particular time

market re'search *noun* [U] (BUSINESS) the study of what people want to buy and why: *to carry out/do market research*

market segmen'tation *noun* [U, C] (BUSINESS, FINANCE) the act of dividing existing and potential customers into groups according to their age, sex, class, income, etc.

market 'share *noun* [U, sing.] (BUSINESS) the amount that a company sells of its products or services compared with other companies selling the same things: *They claim to have a 40% worldwide market share.*

'market town *noun* [C] a town that has a regular market, or that had one in the past

market 'value *noun* [U, C] (FINANCE) what sth would be worth if it were sold: *The property cost a lot more when they bought it than its current market value.*

marking /'mɑːkɪŋ/ *noun* [C, usually pl.] shapes, lines and patterns of colour on an animal or a bird, or painted on a road, vehicle, etc.

marksman /'mɑːksmən/ *noun* [C] (*pl.* -men /-mən/) a person who can shoot very well with a gun

markup /'mɑːkʌp/ *noun* [C, usually sing.] (BUSINESS) the difference between the cost of producing sth and the price it is sold at

marmalade /'mɑːməleɪd/ *noun* [U] a type of jam that is made from oranges or lemons

marmoset /'mɑːməset, -məzet/ *noun* [C] a small monkey with a long thick tail that lives in Central and South America

maroon /mə'ruːn/ *adj.* dark red-brown in colour
▶ **maroon** *noun* [U]

marooned /mə'ruːnd/ *adj.* in a place that you cannot leave: *The sailors were marooned on a desert island.*

marquee /mɑː'kiː/ *noun* [C] a very large tent that is used for parties, shows, etc.

marriage ⚡ **B1** /'mærɪdʒ/ *noun* **1** [C, U] the state of being married: *They are getting divorced after five years of marriage.* ◇ *a happy marriage* **2** [C] a wedding ceremony: *The marriage took place at a registry office.* ⊃ verb **get married (to somebody)** or **marry (somebody)**

'marriage certificate (*BrE*) (*AmE* **'marriage license**) *noun* [C] (LAW) a legal document that proves two people are married

'marriage counselling (*AmE* **marriage counseling**) (*BrE* **marriage 'guidance**) *noun* [U] (PSYCHOLOGY) advice that is given by trained people to couples with problems in their relationship

married 🔊 **A1** /ˈmærɪd/ *adj.* **1 ~ (to sb)** having a husband or wife: *a married man/woman/couple* ◇ *Sasha's married to Mark.* ◇ *They're planning to get married in the summer.* **OPP** **single¹, unmarried** **2** [only before noun] connected with marriage: *How do you like married life?*

marrow /ˈmærəʊ/ *noun* **1** [C, U] a large vegetable with green skin that is white inside **2** [U] = BONE MARROW

marry 🔊 **A2** /ˈmæri/ *verb* (marrying; marries; *pt, pp* married) **1** [T, I] to become sb's husband or wife; to get married to sb: *When did Rick ask you to marry him?* ◇ *They married when they were very young.* ➔ look at **divorce²** (1) **2** [T] to join two people together in marriage: *We asked the local vicar to marry us.* ➔ noun **marriage**

WORD FAMILY
marry *verb*
marriage *noun*
married *adj.*
(≠**unmarried**)

Mars /mɑːz/ *noun* [sing.] (ASTRONOMY) the planet in the SOLAR SYSTEM that is fourth in order of distance from the sun ➔ picture at **solar system**

marsh /mɑːʃ/ *noun* [C, U] (GEOGRAPHY) an area of soft wet land ▸ **marshy** *adj.*

marshal /ˈmɑːʃl/ *noun* [C] **1** a person who helps to organize or control a large public event: *Marshals are directing traffic in the car park.* **2** (*AmE*) an officer of a high level in the police or fire department or in a court

marsupial /mɑːˈsuːpiəl/ *noun* [C] (BIOLOGY) any animal that carries its young in a POUCH (= a pocket of skin) on the mother's stomach: *Kangaroos and koalas are marsupials.* ➔ picture at **animal** ▸ **marsupial** *adj.*

martial 🔊 **B2** /ˈmɑːʃl/ *adj.* [only before noun] (*formal*) connected with fighting or war

martial art *noun* [C, usually pl.] (SPORT) any of the fighting sports that include KARATE and JUDO

martial law *noun* [U] (POLITICS) a situation in which the army of a country instead of the police controls an area during a time of trouble: *The city remains under martial law.*

Martian /ˈmɑːʃn/ *noun* [C] (in stories) a creature that comes from the planet Mars

martyr /ˈmɑːtə(r)/ *noun* [C] **1** a person who is killed because of what they believe **2** a person who tries to make people feel sorry for them: *Don't be such a martyr! You don't have to do all the housework.* ▸ **martyrdom** /-tədəm/ *noun* [U]

marvel /ˈmɑːvl/ *noun* [C] a person or thing that is wonderful or that surprises you: *the marvels of modern technology* ▸ **marvel** *verb* [I] (-ll-, *AmE* -l-) **~ (at sth)**: *We marvelled at how much they had managed to do.*

marvellous (*BrE*) (*AmE* **marvelous**) /ˈmɑːvələs/ *adj.* very good; wonderful: *a marvellous opportunity* **SYN** **fantastic** ▸ **marvellously** (*AmE* **marvelously**) *adv.*

Marxism /ˈmɑːksɪzəm/ *noun* [U] (POLITICS) the political and economic thought of Karl Marx ➔ look at **capitalism, communism, socialism** ▸ **Marxist** /-sɪst/ *noun* [C], *adj.*: *Marxist ideology*

marzipan /ˈmɑːzɪpæn/ *noun* [U] a food that is made of sugar, egg and ALMONDS (= a type of nut). Marzipan is used to make sweets or to cover cakes.

mascara /mæˈskɑːrə/ *noun* [U] a beauty product that is used to make the EYELASHES (= the hairs around the eyes) dark and attractive

mascot /ˈmæskət/ *noun* [C] a person, an animal or a thing that is thought to bring good luck

masculine /ˈmæskjəlɪn/ *adj.* **1** typical of or looking like a man; connected with men: *a deep, masculine voice* ◇ *Her short hair makes her look quite masculine.* ➔ look at **feminine** (1) **2** (*abbr.* m) (GRAMMAR) belonging

to a class of words that refer to male people or animals and often have a special form: *'He' is a masculine pronoun.* **3** (*abbr.* m) (GRAMMAR) (in the grammar of some languages) belonging to a certain class of nouns, pronouns or adjectives: *The French word for 'sun' is masculine.* ➔ look at **feminine** (3), **neuter¹** ▸ **masculinity** /ˌmæskjəˈlɪnəti/ *noun* [U]

mash /mæʃ/ *verb* [T] to make food into a soft mass: *mashed banana*

mashed potato (*also* **mash**) *noun* [U] (*both especially BrE*) (*also* **mashed potatoes** [pl.] *BrE, AmE*) potatoes that have been boiled and made into a soft mass, often with butter and milk

mash-up *noun* [C] (ARTS AND MEDIA, MUSIC) a combination of elements from different sources used to create a new song, film, etc.

mask¹ 🔊+ **C1** /mɑːsk/ *noun* [C] something that you wear that covers your face or part of your face. People wear masks in order to hide or protect their faces or to make themselves look different: *a surgical/Halloween mask* ➔ look at **gas mask**

mask² /mɑːsk/ *verb* [T] **1** to cover or hide your face with a mask: *a masked gunman* **2 ~ sth (with sth)** to hide a feeling, smell, fact, etc: *He masked his anger with a smile.*

masked /mɑːskt/ *adj.* wearing a MASK: *a masked gunman*

masochism /ˈmæsəkɪzəm/ *noun* [U] pleasure in sth that most people would find unpleasant or painful: *He swims in the sea even in winter — that's sheer masochism!* ➔ look at **sadism** ▸ **masochist** /-kɪst/ *noun* [C] ▸ **masochistic** /ˌmæsəˈkɪstɪk/ *adj.*

mason /ˈmeɪsn/ *noun* [C] **1** a person who makes things from stone **2 Mason** = FREEMASON

masonry /ˈmeɪsənri/ *noun* [U] (ARCHITECTURE) the parts of a building that are made of stone

masquerade /ˌmæskəˈreɪd, ˌmɑːs-/ *noun* [C] (*formal*) a way of behaving that hides the truth or sb's true feelings ▸ **masquerade** *verb* [I] **~ as sth**: *Two people, masquerading as doctors, knocked at the door and asked to see the child.*

mass¹ 🔊 **B2** /mæs/ *noun* **1** [C] **~ (of sth)** a large amount or number of sth: *a dense mass of smoke* ◇ (*informal*) *There were masses of people at the market today.* **2 the masses** [pl.] (SOCIAL STUDIES) ordinary people when considered as a political group **3** [U] (PHYSICS) the quantity of material that sth contains **4** Mass [U, C] (RELIGION) the ceremony in some Christian churches when people eat bread and drink wine in order to remember the last meal that Christ had before he died: *to go to Mass*

mass² 🔊 **B2** /mæs/ *adj.* [only before noun] involving a large number of people or things: *mass unemployment* ◇ *mass production*

mass³ /mæs/ *verb* [I, T] to come together or bring people or things together in large numbers: *The students massed in the square.*

massacre 🔊+ **C1** /ˈmæsəkə(r)/ *noun* [C] the killing of a large number of people or animals ▸ **massacre** *verb* [T] ➔ note at **kill¹**

massage /ˈmæsɑːʒ/ *noun* [C, U] the act of rubbing and pressing sb's body in order to reduce pain or to help them relax: *to give somebody a massage* ▸ **massage** *verb* [T]

massive 🔊 **B2** /ˈmæsɪv/ *adj.* very big: *a massive increase in prices* **SYN** **huge** ▸ **massively** *adv.*

,mass-'market *adj.* [only before noun] (**BUSINESS**) produced for very large numbers of people

the ,mass 'media *noun* [pl., + sing./pl. verb] (**ARTS AND MEDIA**) newspapers, TV and radio that reach a large number of people

'mass number *noun* [C] (**CHEMISTRY, PHYSICS**) the total number of NEUTRONS in an ATOM

,mass-pro'duce *verb* [T] (**BUSINESS**) to make large numbers of similar things by machine in a factory: *mass-produced goods* ◇ ,mass pro'duction *noun* [U]

mast /mɑːst/ *noun* [C] **1** a tall wooden or metal POLE for holding a ship's sails **2** a tall metal tower that is used for sending out radio or TV signals

master¹ ⓘ **B2** /'mɑːstə(r)/ *noun* [C] **1** (*old-fashioned*) a man who has people working for him, often as servants in his home: *They lived in fear of their master.* **2** a person who has great skill at doing sth: *a master builder* **3** (*BrE, old-fashioned*) (**EDUCATION**) a male teacher (usually in a private school): *the chemistry master* **4** master's (*also* 'master's degree) (**EDUCATION**) a second university degree, or, in Scotland, a first university degree, such as an MA **5** (*usually* Master) (**EDUCATION**) a person who has a master's: *a Master of Arts/Science* **6** (**ART**) a famous painter who lived in the past: *an exhibition of work by the French master, Monet* ⊃ look at **old master** **7** a version of a recording from which copies are made: *the master copy*

master² ⓘ **B2** /'mɑːstə(r)/ *verb* [T] **1** to learn how to do sth well: *It takes a long time to master a foreign language.* ⊃ note at **language** **2** to control sth: *to master a situation*

mastermind /'mɑːstəmaɪnd/ *noun* [C] a very clever person who has planned or organized sth: *a criminal mastermind* ▸ mastermind *verb* [T]: *The police failed to catch the man who masterminded the robbery.*

,master of 'ceremonies (*also* MC) *noun* [C] a person who introduces guests or ENTERTAINERS at a formal occasion

masterpiece /'mɑːstəpiːs/ *noun* [C] (**ARTS AND MEDIA, LITERATURE**) a work of art, music, literature, etc. that is of the highest quality ⊃ note at **art**

'master's degree (*also* master's /'mɑːstəz/) *noun* [C] a second or higher university degree. You usually get a master's degree by studying for one or two years after your first degree: *Master of Arts (MA)* ◇ *Master of Science (MSc)* ⊃ look at **bachelor** (2)

mastery /'mɑːstəri/ *noun* [U] **1** ~ (of sth) great skill at doing sth: *His mastery of the violin was quite exceptional for a child.* **2** ~ (of/over sb/sth) control over sb/sth: *The battle was fought for mastery of the seas.*

masthead /'mɑːsthed/ *noun* [C] **1** the top of a MAST on a ship **2** (**ARTS AND MEDIA**) the name of a newspaper at the top of the front page

masturbate /'mæstəbeɪt/ *verb* [I, T] to make yourself or sb else feel sexually excited by touching and rubbing the sex organs ▸ masturbation /,mæstə'beɪʃn/ *noun* [U]

mat /mæt/ *noun* [C] **1** a piece of carpet or other thick material that you put on the floor: *a doormat* ⊃ look at **rug** (1) **2** a small piece of material that you put under sth on a table: *a table mat* ◇ *a beer mat* ◇ *a mouse mat*

match¹ ⓘ **A1** /mætʃ/ *noun* **1** [C] (**SPORT**) an organized game or sports event: *a tennis/football match* **2** [sing.] a/no ~ for sb; sb's ~ a person or thing that is as good as or better than sb/sth else: *Anna is no match for her mother when it comes to cooking* (= she doesn't cook as well as her mother). ◇ *I was his match at tennis.* ◇ *I think you've met your match in Dave — you won't beat*

him. **3** [sing.] a person or thing that combines well with sb/sth else: *Tim and Ella are a perfect match for each other.* ◇ *The curtains and carpet are a very good match.* **4** [C] a small stick of wood, CARDBOARD (= very thick paper), etc. that you use for starting a fire, lighting a cigarette, etc: *to light/strike a match* ◇ *a box of matches*

match² ⓘ **A1** /mætʃ/ *verb* **1** [T] to find sb/sth that goes together with another person or thing: *In this exercise, match the words with the pictures.* **2** [T, I] if two things match or if one thing matches another, they are the same or very similar: *The two sets of figures don't match.* **3** [T, I] to have the same colour or pattern as sth else; to look good with sth else: *That shirt doesn't match your jacket.* ◇ *Your shirt and jacket don't match.* **4** [T] to be as good as or better than sb/sth else: *The two teams are very evenly matched.* ◇ *Vietnam produces the goods at a price that Europe cannot match.*

PHR V match up to be the same: *The statements of the two witnesses don't match up.* match sth up (with sth) to fit or put sth together (with sth else): *What you have to do is match up each star with his or her pet.* match up to sb/sth to be as good as sb/sth: *The film didn't match up to my expectations*

matchbox /'mætʃbɒks/ *noun* [C] a small box for matches

matching ⓘ **B2** /'mætʃɪŋ/ *adj.* [only before noun] (used about clothes, objects, etc.) having the same colour, pattern, style, etc. and therefore looking attractive together: *a pine table with four matching chairs*

matchstick /'mætʃstɪk/ *noun* [C] the thin wooden part of a match

mate¹ ⓘ+ **B2** /meɪt/ *noun* [C] **1** (*informal*) a friend or sb you live, work or do an activity with: *He's an old mate of mine.* ◇ *a flatmate/classmate/teammate/playmate* **2** (*BrE, informal*) used when speaking to a man: *Can you give me a hand, mate?* **3** (**BIOLOGY**) one of a male and female pair of animals, birds, etc: *The female sits on the eggs while her mate hunts for food.* **4** an officer on a ship

mate² ⓘ+ **B2** /meɪt/ *verb* **1** [I] (**BIOLOGY**) (used about animals and birds) to have sex and produce young: *Pandas rarely mate in zoos.* **2** [T] to bring two animals together so that they can mate **SYN** breed¹

material¹ ⓘ **A2** ◉ /mə'tɪəriəl/ *noun* **1** [C, U] a substance that can be used for making or doing sth: *raw materials* ◇ *writing/teaching/building materials* ◇ *This new material is strong but it is also very light.* **2** [U, C] cloth (for making clothes, etc.): *Is there enough material for a dress?* **3** [U] (**ARTS AND MEDIA**) facts or information that you collect before you write a book, article, etc.

material² ⓘ **B2** ⓦ /mə'tɪəriəl/ *adj.* [only before noun] **1** connected with real or physical things rather than the spirit or emotions: *material possessions* ⊃ look at **spiritual¹** (1) **2** important and needing to be considered: *material evidence* ⊃ look at **immaterial** ▸ materially /-riəli/ *adv.*

materialism /mə'tɪəriəlɪzəm/ *noun* [U] the belief that money and possessions are the most important things in life ▸ materialist /-lɪst/ *noun* [C] ▸ materialistic /mə,tɪəriə'lɪstɪk/ *adj.*

materialize (*BrE also* -ise) /mə'tɪəriəlaɪz/ *verb* [I] to become real; to happen: *The pay rise that they had promised never materialized.*

maternal /mə'tɜːnl/ *adj.* **1** behaving as a mother would behave; connected with being a mother: *maternal love/instincts* **2** [only before noun] related through your mother's side of the family: *your maternal grandfather* ⊃ look at **paternal** (2)

maternity /mə'tɜːnəti/ *adj.* connected with women who are going to have or have just had a baby: *maternity clothes* ◊ *the hospital's maternity ward* ⊃ look at **paternity**

ma'ternity leave *noun* [U] a period of time when a woman is allowed to be away from work before and after having a baby

mathematician /ˌmæθəmə'tɪʃn/ *noun* [C] (**MATHEMATICS**) a person who studies or is an expert in mathematics

mathematics ⓘ **A2** /ˌmæθə'mætɪks/ (*BrE also* **maths** /mæθs/) (*AmE also* **math**) *noun* [U] (**EDUCATION, MATHEMATICS**) the science or study of numbers, quantities or shapes ⊃ look at **algebra**, **arithmetic**, **geometry** ▸ **mathematical** ⓘ+ **C1** /ˌmæθə'mætɪkl/ *adj.*: *mathematical calculations* ▸ **mathematically** /-kli/ *adv.*

matinee (*also* **matinée**) /'mætɪneɪ/ *noun* [C] an afternoon performance of a play, film, etc.

matriarch /'meɪtriɑːk/ *noun* [C] (**SOCIAL STUDIES**) a woman who is the head of a family or social group ⊃ look at **patriarch**

matriarchal /ˌmeɪtri'ɑːkl/ *adj.* (**SOCIAL STUDIES**) (used about a society or system) controlled by women rather than men; passing power, property, etc. from mother to daughter rather than from father to son ⊃ look at **patriarchal**

matriarchy /'meɪtriɑːki/ *noun* [C, U] (*pl.* -ies) (**SOCIAL STUDIES**) a social system that gives power and control to women rather than men ⊃ look at **patriarchy**

matricide /'mætrɪsaɪd/ *noun* [U] (*formal*) (**LAW**) the crime of killing your mother ⊃ look at **patricide**

matrimony /'mætrɪməni/ *noun* [U] (*formal*) the state of being married ▸ **matrimonial** /ˌmætrɪ'məʊniəl/ *adj.*

matrix /'meɪtrɪks/ *noun* [C] (*pl.* **matrices** /-trɪsiːz/) **1** (**MATHEMATICS**) an arrangement of numbers, symbols, etc. in rows and columns, treated as a single quantity **2** (*formal*) (**SOCIAL STUDIES**) the social, political, etc. situation from which a society or person grows and develops: *the European cultural matrix* **3** (*formal*) a system of lines, roads, etc. that cross each other, forming a series of squares or shapes in between: *a matrix of paths* **SYN** **network**[1] **4** (**GEOLOGY**) a mass of rock in which minerals, PRECIOUS stones, etc. are found in the ground

matron /'meɪtrən/ *noun* [C] (*BrE*) (**MEDICINE**) **1** (*BrE also* **senior nursing officer**) a nurse who is in charge of the other nurses in a hospital **2** a woman who works as a nurse in a BOARDING SCHOOL

matt (*BrE*) (*AmE also* **mat**) (*also* **matte** *AmE, BrE*) /mæt/ *adj.* not shiny: *This paint gives a matt finish.* ⊃ look at **gloss**[1]

matted /'mætɪd/ *adj.* (used especially about hair) forming a thick mass, especially because it is wet and/or dirty

matter[1] ⓘ **A2** **ⓦ** /'mætə(r)/ *noun* **1** [sing.] **the~(with sb/sth)** the reason sb/sth has a problem or is not good: *She looks sad. What's the matter with her?* ◊ *There seems to be something the matter with the car.* ◊ *Eat that food! There's nothing the matter with it.* **2** [C] a subject or situation that you must think about and give your attention to: *It's a personal matter and I don't want to discuss it with you.* ◊ *Finding a job will be no easy matter.* ◊ *to simplify/complicate matters* **3** [U] (**CHEMISTRY**) a substance of a particular kind: *waste matter* **4** [U] (**PHYSICS**) physical substance that everything in the world is made of; not mind or spirit: *Scientists compare the properties of matter and antimatter.* ⊃ look at **antimatter**, **dark matter** **5** [U] the contents of a book, film, etc.: *I don't think the subject matter of this programme is suitable for children.*

IDM **as a matter of fact** to tell the truth; in reality: *I like him very much, as a matter of fact.* **be another/a different matter** to be very different: *I can speak a little Japanese, but reading it is quite another matter.* **for that matter** in addition; now that I think about it: *Mick is really fed up with his course. I am too, for that matter.* **a matter of course** something that you always do; the usual thing to do: *Goods leaving the factory are checked as a matter of course.* **a matter of hours, miles, etc.** used to say that sth is not very long, far, expensive, etc: *The fight lasted a matter of seconds.* **a matter of life and/or death** extremely important or serious **a matter of opinion** a subject on which people do not agree: '*I think the government is doing a good job.' 'That's a matter of opinion.'* **(be) a matter of sth/doing sth** a situation in which sth is needed: *Learning a language is largely a matter of practice.* **no matter who, what, where, etc.** it is not important who, what, where, etc: *They never listen no matter what you say.* **to make matters/things worse** → **WORSE**[1]

matter[2] ⓘ **A2** /'mætə(r)/ *verb* [I] **~(to sb)** (not used in the progressive tenses) to be important: *It doesn't really matter how much it costs.* ◊ *Nobody's hurt, and that's all that matters.* ◊ *It doesn't matter to me what he does in his free time.*

ˌmatter-of-'fact *adj.* said or done without showing any emotion, especially when it would seem more normal to express your feelings: *He was very matter-of-fact about his illness.*

mattress /'mætrəs/ *noun* [C] the soft part of a bed, that you lie on

maturation /ˌmætʃu'reɪʃn/ *noun* [U] (*formal*) **1** the process of becoming or being made MATURE (= ready to eat or drink after being left for a period of time) **2** (**BIOLOGY**) the process of becoming adult

mature[1] ⓘ+ **C1** /mə'tʃʊə(r), -'tjʊə(r)/ *adj.* **1** fully grown or fully developed: *a mature tree/bird/animal* **OPP** **immature** **2** behaving in a sensible adult way: *Is she mature enough for such responsibility?* **OPP** **immature** ▸ **maturity** *noun* [U]

mature[2] ⓘ+ **C1** /mə'tʃʊə(r), -'tjʊə(r)/ *verb* [I] **1** to become fully grown or developed: *This particular breed of cattle matures early.* ◊ *Technology in this field has matured considerably over the last decade.* **2** to develop emotionally and start to behave like a sensible adult: *He has matured a great deal over the past year.* **3** (**FINANCE**) to reach the date when it must be paid: *She has a number of investments that mature at the end of the year.*

maul /mɔːl/ *verb* [T] (usually used about a wild animal) to attack and injure sb: *He was mauled to death by a lion.*

mausoleum /ˌmɔːzə'liːəm/ *noun* [C] (**ARCHITECTURE**) a special building made to hold the dead body of an important person or the dead bodies of a family: *the royal mausoleum*

mauve /məʊv/ *adj.* pale purple in colour ▸ **mauve** *noun* [U]

maverick /'mævərɪk/ *noun* [C] a person who does not behave or think like everyone else, but who has independent, unusual opinions ▸ **maverick** *adj.* [only before noun]

maxim /'mæksɪm/ *noun* [C] a few words that express a rule for good or sensible behaviour: *Our maxim is: 'If a job's worth doing, it's worth doing well.'*

maximize ⓘ+ **C1** **ⓦ** (*BrE also* -**ise**) /'mæksɪmaɪz/ *verb* [T] to increase sth as much as possible: *to maximize profits* **OPP** **minimize**

maximum¹ 🔒 B2 ◎ /'mæksıməm/ *adj.* [only before noun] (*abbr.* max /mæks/) as large, fast, etc. as is possible, allowed, etc: *a maximum speed of 120 miles per hour* **OPP** **minimum¹** ▸ maximum *adv.*: *The table has a length of four feet maximum.*

maximum² 🔒 B2 ◎ /'mæksıməm/ *noun* [sing.] (*abbr.* max /mæks/) the greatest amount or level of sth that is possible, allowed, etc: *The bus can carry a maximum of 40 people.* ◇ *That is the maximum we can afford.* **OPP** **minimum²**

May 🔒 A1 /meı/ *noun* [U, C] the fifth month of the year, between April and June

may 🔒 A2 ◎ /meı/ *modal verb* (*negative* may not) **1** used for saying that sth is possible: '*Where's Sue?' 'She may be in the garden.'* ◇ *You may be right.* ◇ *I may be going to China next year.* ◇ *They may have forgotten the meeting.* **2** (*formal*) used as a polite way of asking for and giving permission: *May I use your phone?* ◇ *You may not take photos in the museum.* **3** used for contrasting two facts: *He may be very clever but he can't do anything practical.* **4** (*formal*) used for expressing wishes and hopes: *May you both be very happy.*
IDM may/might as well (do sth) → WELL¹

maybe 🔒 A1 /'meıbi/ *adv.* perhaps; possibly: '*Are you going to come?' 'Maybe.'* ◇ *There were three, maybe four armed men.* ◇ *Maybe I'll accept the invitation and maybe I won't.*

'May Day *noun* [C] 1 May

mayfly /'meıflaı/ *noun* [C] (*pl.* -ies) a small insect that lives near water and only lives for a very short time

mayhem /'meıhem/ *noun* [U] a situation in which there is fear and a great lack of order: *There was absolute mayhem when everyone tried to get out at once.* ◇ *It only takes a few stupid people to create mayhem in a crowd.*

mayonnaise /ˌmeıə'neız/ *noun* [U] a thick, cold white sauce made with eggs and oil

mayor 🔒+ B2 /meə(r)/ *noun* [C] (**POLITICS**) **1** the head of government of a town, city, etc., elected by the public **2** (in England, Wales and Northern Ireland) a person who is elected to be the leader of a council

mayoress /meə'res/ *noun* [C] (**POLITICS**) a woman MAYOR, or a woman who is married to or helps a MAYOR

maypole /'meıpəʊl/ *noun* [C] a decorated POLE that people dance around in traditional celebrations on MAY DAY

maze /meız/ *noun* [C] a system of paths that is designed to confuse you so that it is difficult to find your way out: (*figurative*) *a maze of winding streets*
SYN labyrinth

MB *abbr.* (in writing) (*pl.* MB) = MEGABYTE

Mb *abbr.* (in writing) (*pl.* Mb) = MEGABIT

MBA /ˌem biː 'eı/ *noun* [C] (**BUSINESS, EDUCATION**) an advanced university degree in business (the abbreviation for 'Masters of Business Administration')

MBE /ˌem biː 'iː/ *noun* [C] an award given to some people in the UK because they have achieved sth special (the abbreviation for 'Member of the Order of the British Empire'): *She was made an MBE in 2001.*

MC /ˌem 'siː/ *noun* [C] **1** = MASTER OF CEREMONIES **2** (*also* M.C.) (**POLITICS**) a person who has been elected to represent the people of a particular area in Congress (the abbreviation for 'Member of Congress') **3** (**MUSIC**) a person who provides entertainment at a club or party by giving instructions to the DJ and performing RAP music

MD /ˌem 'diː/ *noun* [C] **1** (**MEDICINE**) an advanced university degree needed to work as a doctor of medicine (the abbreviation for 'Doctor of Medicine') **2** = MANAGING DIRECTOR

me 🔒 A1 /mi, *strong form* miː/ *pron.* (used as an object) the person who is speaking or writing: *He telephoned me yesterday.* ◇ *She wrote to me last week.* ◇ *Hello, is that Frank? It's me, Sadiq.*

meadow /'medəʊ/ *noun* [C] a field of grass

meagre (*BrE*) (*AmE* meager) /'miːgə(r)/ *adj.* too small in amount: *a meagre salary*

meal 🔒 A1 /miːl/ *noun* [C] the time when you eat or the food that is eaten at that time: *Shall we go out for a meal on Friday?* ◇ *a heavy/light meal*
IDM a square meal → SQUARE¹

mealtime /'miːltaım/ *noun* [C] the time at which a meal is usually eaten

mean¹ 🔒 A1 /miːn/ *verb* [T] (*pt, pp* meant /ment/)
• HAVE AS A MEANING **1** (not used in the progressive tenses) to express, show or have as a meaning: *What does this word mean?* ◇ *The bell means that the lesson has ended.* ◇ *Does the name 'Michael Potter' mean anything to you?*
• WANT TO SAY **2** (not used in the progressive tenses) to want or intend to say sth; to refer to sb/sth: *Well, she said 'yes' but I think she really meant 'no'.* ◇ *What do you mean by 'a lot of money'?* ◇ *I only meant that I couldn't come tomorrow — any other day would be fine.* ◇ *I see what you mean, but I'm afraid it's not possible.*
• INTEND TO DO **3** [often passive] ~ (sb) to do sth; ~ sth (as/for sth/sb); ~ sb/sth to be sth to intend sth; to be supposed to be/do sth: *I'm sure she didn't mean to upset you.* ◇ *I didn't mean you to cook the whole meal!* ◇ *She meant the present to be for both of us.* ◇ *It was only meant as a joke.* ◇ *What's this picture meant to be?*
• CAUSE **4** to make sth likely; to cause: *The shortage of teachers means that classes are larger.*
• BE IMPORTANT **5** ~ sth (to sb) to be important to sb: *This job means a lot to me.*
• BE SERIOUS **6** to be serious or sincere about sth: *He said he loved me but I don't think he meant it!*
IDM be meant to be sth to be considered or said to be sth: *That restaurant is meant to be excellent.* mean well to want to be kind and helpful but usually without success: *My mother means well but I wish she'd stop treating me like a child.*

mean² /miːn/ *adj.* **1** ~ (with sth) wanting to keep money, etc. for yourself rather than let other people have it: *It's no good asking him for any money — he's much too mean.* ◇ *They're mean with the food in the canteen.* **OPP** generous **2** ~ (to sb) (used about people or their behaviour) unkind: *Don't be so mean to her!* ◇ *It was mean of him not to invite you too.* **3** [only before noun] (**MATHEMATICS**) average: *What is the mean annual temperature in California?* ▸ meanness *noun* [U]

mean³ /miːn/ *noun* [C] (**MATHEMATICS**) **1** (*also* arithmetic mean) the value found by adding together all the numbers in a group, and dividing the total by the number of numbers **2** (*also* geometric mean) a value that can be calculated by multiplying a series of numbers together and then finding the ROOT of the number of numbers that have been multiplied, for example the CUBE ROOT of three numbers

meander /mi'ændə(r)/ *verb* [I] **1** (used about a river, road, etc.) to have a lot of curves and bends **2** (used about a person or an animal) to walk or travel slowly or without any definite direction ▶ **meander** *noun* [C] (**GEOGRAPHY**): *the meanders of a river* ⊃ picture at **oxbow lake**

meaning ⟨ **A1** ⓦ /'mi:nɪŋ/ *noun* **1** [C, U] the thing or idea that sth represents; what sb is trying to communicate: *This word has two different meanings in English.* ◇ *What's the meaning of the last line of the poem?* **2** [U] the purpose or importance of an experience: *Having a child gave new meaning to their lives.*

meaningful ⟨+ **C1** ⓦ /'mi:nɪŋfl/ *adj.* **1** useful, important or interesting: *Most people need a meaningful relationship with another person.* **2** (used about a look, an expression, etc.) trying to express a certain feeling or idea: *They kept giving each other meaningful glances across the table.* ▶ **meaningfully** /-fəli/ *adv.*

meaningless /'mi:nɪŋləs/ *adj.* without meaning, reason or sense: *The figures are meaningless if we have nothing to compare them with.*

means ⟨ **B2** ⦿ /mi:nz/ *noun* (*pl.* means) **1** [C] ~ (**of doing sth**) a method of doing sth: *Do you have any means of transport* (= a car, bicycle, etc.)? ◇ *Is there any means of contacting your husband?* **2** [pl.] (*formal*) (**FINANCE**) all the money that sb has: *If you don't live within your means you'll get into serious debt.* **IDM** **by all means** used to say that you are happy for sb to have or do sth: *'Can I borrow your newspaper?' 'By all means.'* **by means of** by using: *We got out of the hotel by means of the fire escape.* **by no means** | **not by any means** (used to emphasize sth) not at all: *I'm by no means sure that this is the right thing to do.* **a means to an end** an action or a thing that is not important in itself but is a way of achieving sth else: *I don't enjoy my job, but it's a means to an end.*

meant /ment/ past tense, past participle of **mean¹**

meantime ⟨+ **C1** /'mi:ntaɪm/ *noun* **IDM** **in the meantime** in the time between two things happening: *Our house isn't finished so in the meantime we're living with my mother.*

meanwhile ⟨ **B1** /'mi:nwaɪl/ *adv.* during the same time or during the time between two things happening: *Peter was at home studying. Omar, meanwhile, was out with his friends.*

measles /'mi:zlz/ *noun* [U] (**HEALTH**) a disease, especially of children, that causes a high temperature and small red spots that cover the whole body

measly /'mi:zli/ *adj.* (*informal*) much too small in size, amount or value: *All that work for this measly amount of money!*

measurable /'meʒərəbl/ *adj.* **1** that can be measured **2** large enough to be noticed or to have a clear and definite effect: *measurable improvements* ▶ **measurably** /-bli/ *adv.*: *Working conditions have changed measurably in the last ten years.*

measure¹ ⟨ **B1** ⦿ /'meʒə(r)/ *verb* **1** [T] to find the size, weight, quantity, etc. of sb/sth in standard units by using an instrument: *to measure the height/width/length/depth of something* ◇ *Could you measure the table to see if it will fit into our room?* **2** *linking verb* to be a certain height, length, amount, etc: *The room measures 5 metres across.* **3** [T] ~ **sth (against sth)** to judge the value or effect of sth: *Our sales do not look good when measured against those of our competitors.*

PHR V **measure up (to sth)** to be as good as you need to be or as sb expects you to be: *Did the holiday measure up to your expectations?*

measure² ⟨ **B1** ⦿ /'meʒə(r)/ *noun* **1** [C, usually pl.] an official action that is done for a special reason: *The government is to take new measures to reduce inflation.* ◇ *As a temporary measure, the road will have to be closed.* **2** [C] a way of describing the size, amount, etc. of sth: *A metre is a measure of length.* ⊃ look at **tape measure 3** [sing.] ~ **of sth** (*formal*) a certain amount of sth; some: *The play achieved a measure of success.* **4** [sing.] a way of understanding or judging sth: *The school's popularity is a measure of the teachers' success.* **5** [C] (*AmE*) = BAR¹ (8) **6** [C] (*AmE*) (**POLITICS**) a written suggestion for a new law that people can vote for or against in an election **IDM** **for good measure** in addition to sth, especially to make sure that there is enough: *He made a few extra sandwiches for good measure.* **made to measure** specially made or perfectly suitable for a particular person, use, etc: *I'm getting a suit made to measure for the wedding.*

▼ COLLOCATIONS

measure

Liquids are measured in **litres/liters** in most countries: *a litre of milk* ◇ *half a litre of beer* ◇ *a quarter of a litre of water* ◇ *How many centilitres are there in a litre?* ◇ *One litre is equivalent to 1 000 cubic centimetres.* In the past, people in Britain used **pints** and **gallons** to measure liquids, rather than **litres/liters**. Nowadays, most people use and understand both: *My grandfather liked a pint of beer with his lunch.* ◇ *Our old car used gallons of petrol.* People in the US still use **pints** and **gallons** (but note that an American **pint** = 0.47 litres). You can use **about/approximately/around** to convert measurements roughly: *A pint is about half a litre.* ◇ *One foot is approximately 0.3 metres.* You can say how **long/wide/high/tall/deep** something is when you measure in just one direction: *The garden was 10 metres long and 6 wide.* ◇ *The fence is 2 metres high to keep out the animals.* ◇ *He's 1.89 m tall.* ◇ *The snow was 25 cm deep in places.* **Area** (= the size of a surface) is calculated by multiplying the **length** by the **width** and is expressed as a **square** measurement: *The floor is about 15 square metres* (= 3x5 metres). We use **be** or **weigh** with measures of weight: *I'm just under 10 stone.* ◇ *Jo's baby weighed just over 3 kilos.*

measured /'meʒəd/ *adj.* slow and careful; showing control: *She replied in a calm, measured tone.* ◇ *He walked down the corridor with measured steps.*

measurement ⟨ **B2** /'meʒəmənt/ *noun* **1** [C] a size, an amount, etc. that is found by measuring: *What are the exact measurements of the room?* (= how wide, long, etc. is it?) **2** [U] the act or process of measuring sth: *the metric system of measurement*

'measuring tape = TAPE MEASURE

meat ⟨ **A1** /mi:t/ *noun* [U] the parts of animals or birds that people eat: *She doesn't eat meat — she's a vegetarian.* ◇ *meat-eating animals* ⊃ note on **page 466**

meatball /'mi:tbɔ:l/ *noun* [C] a small round ball of meat, usually eaten hot with a sauce

meaty /'mi:ti/ *adj.* (**meatier, meatiest**) **1** like meat, or containing a lot of meat: *meaty sausages* **2** large and fat: *meaty tomatoes* **3** containing a lot of important or good ideas: *a meaty topic for discussion*

Mecca /'mekə/ *noun* **1** [sing.] (**RELIGION**) the city in Saudi Arabia where the Prophet Muhammad was born, which is the centre of Islam **2** mecca [C, usually sing.]

Some types of meat have different names from the animals they come from. **Pork**, **ham** or **bacon** comes from a pig, **beef** from a cow and **veal** from a calf. **Mutton** comes from a sheep, but you get **lamb** from a lamb. For birds and fish there is not a different word. Meat that is dark brown when it is cooked is called **red meat**. Meat that is pale in colour when it has been cooked is called **white meat**. You can **fry**, **grill**, **roast** or **stew** meat. You **carve** a **joint** of meat (= cut it up when it is cooked). Meat can be described as **tough** or **tender**, **lean** or **fatty**. Uncooked meat is **raw**. The **butcher's** is a shop that sells meat. A person who does not eat meat is a **vegetarian**.

~ for sb a place that many people wish to visit because of a particular interest: *Italy is a mecca for art lovers.*

mechanic ℛ+ **B2** /məˈkænɪk/ *noun* **1** [C] a person whose job is to repair and work with machines: *a car mechanic* **2 mechanics** [U] (**PHYSICS**) the science of how machines work **3 the mechanics** [pl.] the way in which sth works or is done: *Don't ask me — I don't understand the mechanics of the legal system.*

mechanical ℛ+ **B2** /məˈkænɪkl/ *adj.* **1** connected with or produced by machines: *a mechanical pump* ◇ *mechanical engineering* ◇ *mechanical problems* **2** (used about a person's behaviour) done like a machine, as if you are not thinking about what you are doing: *He played the piano in a dull and mechanical way.* ▸ **mechanically** /-kli/ *adv.*

mechanism ℛ+ **B2** **O** /ˈmekənɪzəm/ *noun* [C] **1** a set of moving parts in a machine that does a certain task: *Our car has an automatic locking mechanism.* **2** the way in which sth works or is done: *I'm afraid there is no mechanism for dealing with your complaint.*

mechanize (*BrE also* -ise) /ˈmekənaɪz/ *verb* [T] to use machines instead of people to do work: *We have mechanized the entire production process.* ▸ **mechanization** (*BrE also* -isation) /ˌmekənaɪˈzeɪʃn/ *noun* [U]

the Med /ðə ˈmed/ (*informal*) = MEDITERRANEAN

med. (in writing) = M² (1)

medal ℛ+ **B2** /ˈmedl/ *noun* [C] a small flat piece of metal, usually with a design and words on it, that is given to sb who has shown courage or as a prize in a sport: *to win a gold/silver/bronze medal in the Olympics*

medallion /məˈdæliən/ *noun* [C] a small round piece of metal on a chain that is worn as jewellery around the neck

medallist (*BrE*) (*AmE* **medalist**) /ˈmedəlɪst/ *noun* [C] (**SPORT**) a person who has won a MEDAL, especially in sport: *an Olympic gold medallist*

meddle /ˈmedl/ *verb* [I] **1 ~ (in/with sth)** to take too much interest in sth that should not really involve you: *The group must stop meddling in the affairs of other countries.* **2 ~ (with sth)** to touch sth that does not belong to you: *Somebody's been meddling with the papers on my desk.*

media ℛ **A2** **W** /ˈmiːdiə/ *noun* (**ARTS AND MEDIA**) **1 the media** [C + sing./pl. verb] TV, radio, newspapers and the internet used as a means of communication: *The reports in the media have been greatly exaggerated.* ⊃ look at **mass media**, **press**¹ (1) **2** plural of **medium**²

mediaeval /ˌmediˈiːvl/ = MEDIEVAL

median¹ /ˈmiːdiən/ *adj.* [only before noun] **1** (**MATHEMATICS**) having a value in the middle of a series of values: *the median age/price* **2** located in or passing through the middle: *a median point/line*

median² /ˈmiːdiən/ *noun* [C] **1** (**MATHEMATICS**) the middle value of a series of numbers arranged in order of size **2** a straight line passing from a point of a TRIANGLE to the centre of the opposite side **3** (*AmE*) = CENTRAL RESERVATION

media-savvy *adj.* (*informal*) (**ARTS AND MEDIA**) having a good understanding of the internet, newspapers, TV, etc. and how they influence people: *Interviewing media-savvy politicians is a very difficult task.*

media studies *noun* [U + sing./pl. verb] (**ARTS AND MEDIA**, **EDUCATION**) the study of newspapers, TV, radio, etc., especially as an academic subject

mediate **W** /ˈmiːdieɪt/ *verb* [I] **~ (in sth)**; **~ (between A and B)** to try to end a situation between two or more people or groups who disagree by talking to them and trying to find things that everyone can agree on: *to mediate in a dispute* ◇ *As a supervisor she had to mediate between her colleagues and the management.* ▸ **mediation** /ˌmiːdiˈeɪʃn/ *noun* [U] ▸ **mediator** *noun* [C]

Medicaid /ˈmedɪkeɪd/ *noun* [U] (**MEDICINE**) (in the US) the insurance system that provides medical care for poor people

medical¹ ℛ **A2** **W** /ˈmedɪkl/ *adj.* (**MEDICINE**) connected with medicine and the treatment of illness: *medical treatment/care* ◇ *the medical profession* ▸ **medically** /-kli/ *adv.*

medical

Medical practitioners **practise as** (= work as) dentists, doctors, opticians, etc: *She practises as a clinical psychologist.* ◇ *Not many doctors practise from home these days.* If you are ill, you **consult** or **see a doctor**: *She ought to see a doctor with that rash.* A doctor **prescribes treatment** or gives **the patient** (= the person consulting him/her) a **prescription**: *The psychiatrist prescribed antidepressants.* ◇ *The doctor gave her patient a prescription for antibiotics.* You can **be treated by** sb or **be treated for/have treatment for** sth: *He is being treated by a physiotherapist.* ◇ *She was treated for malaria at St James' Hospital.* Sometimes one doctor **refers sb to** a specialist or another type of doctor: *The clinic referred her to a cardiologist.*

medical² /ˈmedɪkl/ *noun* [C] (**MEDICINE**) an examination of your body by a doctor to check your state of health: *to have a medical*

medical school *noun* [C] (**EDUCATION**) a college where students study for a degree in medicine

Medicare /ˈmedɪkeə(r)/ *noun* [U] (**MEDICINE**) **1** (in the US) the FEDERAL insurance system that provides medical care for people over 65 **2** (in Australia and Canada) the national medical care system for all people that is paid for by taxes (spelt 'medicare' in Canada)

medication ℛ+ **B2** /ˌmedɪˈkeɪʃn/ *noun* [U, C] (**MEDICINE**) medicine that a doctor has given to you: *Are you on any medication?*

medicinal /məˈdɪsɪnl/ *adj.* (**MEDICINE**) useful for curing illness or infection: *medicinal plants*

medicine ℛ **A2** /ˈmedsn, ˈmedɪsn/ *noun* (**MEDICINE**) **1** [U] the science of preventing and treating illness: *to study medicine* **2** [C, U] a substance, especially a liquid, that you take in order to cure an illness: *Take this medicine three times a day.* ◇ *cough medicine* ⊃ note at **doctor**¹ ⊃ picture at **health**

medieval ℛ+ **C1** (*also* **mediaeval**) /ˌmediˈiːvl/ *adj.* (**HISTORY**) connected with THE MIDDLE AGES (= the period in history between about 1000 AD and 1450 AD): *medieval art/architecture/castles*

mediocre /ˌmiːdiˈəʊkə(r)/ adj. of not very high quality: *He gave a mediocre performance* ▶ **mediocrity** /-ˈɒkrəti/ noun [U]

meditate /ˈmedɪteɪt/ verb [I] **1** (RELIGION) to focus your mind, especially for religious reasons or to make your mind calm: *I've been meditating on what you said last week.* **2 ~ (on/upon sth)** (*formal*) to think deeply about sth ▶ **meditation** ⁺ CI /ˌmedɪˈteɪʃn/ noun [U]

the Mediterranean /ðə ˌmedɪtəˈreɪniən/ (*also informal* **the Med**) noun [sing.] (GEOGRAPHY) the Mediterranean Sea or the countries around it ▶ **Mediterranean** adj.: *Mediterranean cookery* ⊃ picture at **ecosystem**

medium¹ ⁺ B1 /ˈmiːdiəm/ adj. **1** in the middle between two sizes, lengths, temperatures, etc.; average: *She was of medium height.* ◇ *Would you like the small, medium or large packet?* ◇ *a medium-sized car/town/dog* **2** (used about meat) cooked until it is brown almost all the way through ⊃ look at **rare** (2), **well done**

medium² ⁺ B2 ⓦ /ˈmiːdiəm/ noun [C] **1** (*pl.* **media** /-diə/, **mediums**) a means you can use to express or communicate sth: *the medium of radio/TV* ◇ *English is the medium of instruction in the school.* ⊃ look at **mass media**, **media 2** (*pl.* **media**, **mediums**) (ARTS AND MEDIA) the material or the form that an artist, a writer or a musician uses: *the medium of paint/poetry/drama* ◇ *Watercolour is his favourite medium.* **3** (*pl.* **media**, **mediums**) (BIOLOGY) a substance that sth exists or grows in or that it travels through: *The bacteria were growing in a sugar medium.* **4** (*pl.* **mediums**) a person who says that they can speak to the spirits of dead people

medium wave noun [U] (*abbr.* **MW**) (PHYSICS) the system of sending out radio signals using sound waves between 100 and 1 000 metres ⊃ look at **long wave**, **short wave** ⊃ picture at **wavelength**

medley /ˈmedli/ noun [C] **1** (MUSIC) a piece of music consisting of several tunes or songs played one after the other without a break **2** a mixture of different things: *a medley of styles/flavours*

medulla oblongata /meˌdʌlə ˌɒblɒŋˈgɑːtə/ noun [C] (*pl.* **medullae oblongatae** /meˌdʌli ˌɒblɒŋˈgɑːti/) (ANATOMY) the part of the brain that controls the way the heart and lungs work ⊃ picture at **brain**

meek /miːk/ adj. (used about people) quiet, and doing what other people say without asking questions: *meek and mild* ▶ **meekly** adv. ▶ **meekness** noun [U]

meet ⁺ A1 /miːt/ verb (*pt, pp* **met** /met/)
• COME TOGETHER **1** [I, T] to come together by chance or because you have arranged it: *What time shall we meet for lunch?* ◇ *I just met Kareem on the train.* **2** [T] to go to a place and wait for sb/sth to arrive: *I'll come and meet you at the station.*
• FOR THE FIRST TIME **3** [I, T] to see and know sb for the first time: *Have you two met before?* ◇ *Where did you first meet your husband?*
• IN A COMPETITION **4** [I, T] (SPORT) to play, fight, etc. together as opponents in a sports competition: *These two teams met in last year's final.* ◇ *Yamada will meet Suzuki in the second round.*
• EXPERIENCE **5** [T] to experience sth, often sth unpleasant: *We will never know how he met his death.*
• JOIN **6** [I, T] to touch, join or make contact with: *The two roads meet not far from here.* ◇ *His eyes met hers.*
• BE ENOUGH **7** [T] to be enough for sth; to be able to deal with sth: *The money that I earn is enough to meet our basic needs.* ◇ *to meet a challenge*
IDM **make ends meet** → **END¹** **there is more to sb/ sth than meets the eye** somebody/something is more interesting or complicated than you might think at first: *Do you think there's more to their relationship than meets the eye?*

PHR V **meet up (with sb)** to meet sb, especially after a period of being apart: *I have a few things I need to do now, but let's meet up later.* ⊃ look at **get together (with sb)** at **get meet with sb** to meet sb, especially for discussion: *The president met with his advisers early this morning.* **meet with sth** to get a particular answer, reaction or result: *to meet with success/ failure/opposition*

meet-and-greet adj. (BUSINESS) arranged so that sb, especially a famous person, can meet and talk to people: *His publishers had arranged a signing and meet-and-greet session.* ▶ **meet and greet** noun [C]

meeting ⁺ A1 /ˈmiːtɪŋ/ noun **1** [C] an organized occasion when a number of people come together in order to discuss or decide sth: *to go to/attend a meeting* ◇ *The group* **hold** *regular* **meetings** *all year.* ◇ *We need to* **have a meeting** *to discuss these matters.* **2** [sing.] the people at a meeting: *The meeting was in favour of the new proposals.* **3** [C] the coming together of two or more people: *Christmas is a time of family meetings and reunions.*

▼ COLLOCATIONS

meeting

Somebody can **call/convene**, **arrange** or **organize a meeting**: *She convened a meeting for the following morning.* Before a meeting, that person will **draw up** and **circulate the agenda** (= a list of items to be discussed): *The manager drew up and then circulated the agenda.* It is sometimes necessary to **cancel/call off** or **postpone** a meeting: *The meeting has been postponed until next week.* ◇ *The committee meeting had to be cancelled due to illness.* The **chairperson** (or **chair**) **opens/closes** the meeting: *Mrs Green opened the meeting on Friday.* ◇ *The chairperson thanked everybody for coming, and closed the meeting.* A **secretary keeps/takes the minutes** (= a summary of what is said or decided at a formal meeting): *Sam offered to take the minutes.* At the beginning of a meeting, the **minutes** of the last meeting are **approved** and an **agenda is agreed on**: *Can we approve the minutes of the last meeting?* ◇ *The agenda was agreed on.* At the end of the meeting the chairperson asks if there is **any other business**: *If there is no other business then I declare this meeting closed.*

mega- /ˈmegə/ *prefix* **1** (in nouns) very large or great: *a megastore* **2** (in units of measurement) one million: *a megawatt* **3** (in units of measurement) (COMPUTING) 220, or 1 048 576: *megabyte*

megabit /ˈmegəbɪt/ noun [C] (*abbr.* **Mb**) (COMPUTING) a unit of computer memory or data, equal to 10⁶ BITS (= the smallest units of information)

megabyte /ˈmegəbaɪt/ (*also informal* **meg** /meg/, *pl.* **megs**, **meg**) noun [C] (*abbr.* **MB**) (COMPUTING) a unit of computer memory or data, equal to 10⁶ BYTES (= small units of information)

megahertz /ˈmegəhɜːts/ noun [C] (*pl.* **megahertz**) (*abbr.* **MHz**) (COMPUTING) a unit for measuring radio waves and the speed at which a computer operates; 1 000 000 HERTZ

megaphone /ˈmegəfəʊn/ noun [C] a piece of equipment that you speak through to make your voice sound louder when speaking to a crowd

megapixel /ˈmegəpɪksl/ noun [C] (COMPUTING) a million PIXELS (= very small individual areas on a computer screen), used

megaphone

to measure the quality of a digital screen or image: *a 32 megapixel camera*

megastore /ˈmeɡəstɔː(r)/ *noun* [C] (**BUSINESS**) a very large shop that sells a wide variety of one particular type of goods, for example computers

megathermal /ˌmeɡəˈθɜːməl/ *adj.* (**GEOGRAPHY**) (used about a climate) hot and wet **SYN** **tropical** ⟳ look at **mesothermal, microthermal**

megawatt /ˈmeɡəwɒt/ *noun* [C] (*abbr.* MW) a unit for measuring electrical power; one million WATTS

meiosis /maɪˈəʊsɪs/ *noun* [U] (**BIOLOGY**) the division of a cell in two stages that results in four cells, each with half the number of CHROMOSOMES of the original cell ⟳ look at **mitosis**

melancholy /ˈmelənkəli, -kɒli/ *noun* [U] (*formal*) a very sad feeling that lasts for a long time ▶ **melancholy** *adj.*

melanin /ˈmelənɪn/ *noun* [U] (**BIOLOGY**) a dark substance in the skin and hair that causes the skin to change colour in the sun's light

melanoma /ˌmeləˈnəʊmə/ *noun* [C, U] (**HEALTH**) a type of cancer that appears as a dark spot or TUMOUR on the skin

melee /ˈmeleɪ/ *noun* [sing.] a situation in which a crowd of people are in a hurry or pushing each other in a confused way

melisma /məˈlɪzmə/ *noun* [C] (*pl.* melismas, melismata /-tə/) (**MUSIC**) a group of notes sung to one syllable of text

mellow /ˈmeləʊ/ *adj.* **1** (used about colours or sounds) soft and pleasant **2** (used about people) calm and relaxed: *My dad's grown mellower as he's got older.* ▶ **mellow** *verb* [I, T]: *She had mellowed a lot over the years.*

melodious /məˈləʊdiəs/ (*also* melodic /məˈlɒdɪk/) *adj.* pleasant to listen to, like music: *a rich melodious voice*

melodrama /ˈmelədrɑːmə/ *noun* [U, C] (**ARTS AND MEDIA, LITERATURE**) a story, play or film in which a lot of exciting things happen and in which people's emotions are stronger than in real life

melodramatic /ˌmelədrəˈmætɪk/ *adj.* (used about a person's behaviour) making things seem more exciting or serious than they really are: *Don't be so melodramatic, Simon — of course you're not going to die!*

melody /ˈmelədi/ *noun* [C] (*pl.* -ies) (**MUSIC**) a song or tune; the main tune of a piece of music

melon /ˈmelən/ *noun* [C, U] a large round fruit with a thick yellow or green skin and a lot of seeds

melt /melt/ *verb* [I, T] **1** to change or make sth change from a solid to a liquid by means of heat: *Ice melts as the temperature rises.* ◇ *First melt the butter in a saucepan.* ⟳ look at **thaw** ⟳ picture at **glacial, rock¹, state¹, water cycle 2** (used about sb's feelings, etc.) to become softer or less strong: *My heart melted when I saw the baby.*
IDM melt in your mouth (used about food) to be soft and very good to eat
PHR V melt away to disappear: *The crowd slowly melted away when the speaker had finished.* **melt sth down** to heat a metal or glass object until it becomes liquid

meltdown /ˈmeltdaʊn/ *noun* [U, C] **1** a serious accident in which the central part of a NUCLEAR REACTOR (= a large machine producing nuclear energy) melts, causing harmful substances to escape **2** (**ECONOMICS**) a situation where sth fails or becomes weaker in a

sudden or dramatic way: *The country is in economic meltdown.*

melting point *noun* [U, C] (**PHYSICS**) the temperature at which a substance will melt

melting pot *noun* [C, usually sing.] a place where a lot of different cultures, ideas, etc. come together: *New York is a melting pot of different cultures.*

meltwater /ˈmeltwɔːtə(r)/ *noun* [U] (*also* meltwaters [pl.]) (**GEOGRAPHY**) water formed by the melting of snow and ice, especially from a GLACIER (= a large moving mass of ice)

member /ˈmembə(r)/ *noun* [C] a person, an animal or a thing that belongs to a group, a club, an organization, etc: *All the members of the family were there.* ◇ *to become a member of a club* ◇ *a member of staff* ⟳ note at **organization**

Member of Parliament = MP

membership /ˈmembəʃɪp/ *noun* **1** [U, C] the state of being a member of a group, an organization, etc: *To apply for membership, please fill in the enclosed form.* ◇ *a membership card/fee* **2** [C + sing./pl. verb] the people who belong to a group, an organization, etc: *Membership has fallen in the past year* (= the number of members).

membrane /ˈmembreɪn/ *noun* [C] **1** (**ANATOMY**) a thin layer of skin or TISSUE that connects or covers parts inside the body ⟳ look at **mucous membrane** ⟳ picture at **fertilization, respiratory, synovial 2** a very thin layer found in the structure of cells in plants ⟳ picture at **cell 3** a thin layer of material used to prevent air, liquid, etc. from entering a particular part of sth: *a waterproof membrane*

meme /miːm/ *noun* [C] (**COMPUTING**) **1** an image or a video that is passed between people using the internet and becomes very popular **2** a type of behaviour that is passed from one member of a group to another, not in the GENES (= the units inside a cell that control particular qualities) but by another means such as people copying it

memento /məˈmentəʊ/ *noun* [C] (*pl.* -oes, -os) something that you keep to remind you of sb/sth **SYN** **souvenir**

memo /ˈmeməʊ/ *noun* [C] (*pl.* -os) (*also formal* memorandum) (**BUSINESS**) a note sent from one person or office to another within an organization

memoir /ˈmemwɑː(r)/ *noun* (**LITERATURE**) **1 memoirs** [pl.] a person's written account of their own life and experiences **SYN** **autobiography 2** [C] (*formal*) a written account of sb's life, a place or an event, written by sb who knows it well: *her memoir of her father's life*

memorabilia /ˌmemərəˈbɪliə/ *noun* [U] things that people buy because they are connected with a famous person, event, etc: *Beatles/war memorabilia*

memorable /ˈmemərəbl/ *adj.* worth remembering or easy to remember **SYN** **unforgettable** ▶ **memorably** /-bli/ *adv.*

memorandum /ˌmeməˈrændəm/ *noun* [C] (*pl.* memoranda /-də/) (*formal*) = MEMO

memorial /məˈmɔːriəl/ *noun* [C] ~ (to sb/sth) something that is built or done to remind people of an event or a person: *a memorial to the victims of the bombing* ◇ *a war memorial* ◇ *a memorial service*

memorize (*BrE also* -ise) /ˈmeməraɪz/ *verb* [T] to learn sth so that you can remember it exactly: *Actors have to memorize their lines.*

memory /ˈmeməri/ *noun* (*pl.* -ies) **1** [C, U] ~ (for sth) a person's ability to remember things: *to have a good/bad memory* ◇ *A teacher needs to have a good memory for names.* ◇ *Are you going to do your speech from memory, or are you going to use notes?* **2** [U] the

period of time that a person or group of people is able to remember events: *This hasn't happened **within living memory*** (= nobody alive can now remember it happening). **3** [C] something that you remember: *That is one of my happiest memories.* ◇ *childhood memories* **4** [C, U] (**COMPUTING**) the part of a computer where information is stored: *This computer has a 6GB memory/6GB of memory.*
IDM **in memory of sb** in order to remind people of sb who has died: *A service was held in memory of the dead.* **jog sb's memory** → JOG¹ **refresh your memory** → REFRESH

'**memory card** *noun* [C] (**COMPUTING**) an electronic device that can be used to store data, used especially with digital cameras, mobile phones, etc.

'**Memory Stick**™ *noun* [C] (*especially BrE*) (**COMPUTING**) a small device that you can carry around with you that is used for storing computer data and moving it onto another computer **SYN** **flash drive**

men /men/ plural of **man**¹

menace /'menəs/ *noun* **1** [C, usually sing.] ~ **(to sb/sth)** a danger or threat: *The new road is a menace to everyone's safety.* **2** [U] a quality, feeling, etc. that is threatening or frightening: *He spoke with menace in his voice.* **3** [C] a person or thing that causes trouble ▸ **menace** *verb* [T] ▸ **menacing** *adj.*

mend¹ /mend/ *verb* [T] to repair sth that is damaged or broken: *Can you mend the hole in this jumper for me?* **SYN** **repair**¹

mend² /mend/ *noun*
IDM **be on the mend** (*informal*) to be getting better after an illness or injury

mendelevium /ˌmendə'liːviəm, -'leɪv-/ *noun* [U] (*symb.* Md) (**CHEMISTRY**) a chemical element. Mendelevium is a RADIOACTIVE element that is produced artificially. ❶ For more information on the periodic table of elements, look at the **Reference Section** in this dictionary.

menial /'miːniəl/ *adj.* (used about work) not SKILLED or important: *a menial job*

meninges /mə'nɪndʒiːz/ *noun* [pl.] (**BIOLOGY**) the three thin layers of material that surround the brain and the SPINAL CORD ➔ picture at **brain**

meningitis /ˌmenɪn'dʒaɪtɪs/ *noun* [U] (**HEALTH**) a dangerous illness that affects the brain and the SPINAL CORD (= the inside of the bones in the back)

menopause /'menəpɔːz/ *noun* [U] (*often* the menopause [sing.]) (**HEALTH**) the period of time during which a woman stops MENSTRUATING, usually at around the age of 50: *to reach (the) menopause* ◇ *Women experience many emotional and physical changes during the menopause.*

menstrual /'menstruəl/ *adj.* (**HEALTH**) connected with the time when a woman MENSTRUATES each month: *a woman's **menstrual cycle***

menstruate /'menstrueɪt/ *verb* [I] (*formal*) (**BIOLOGY, HEALTH**) (used about women) to lose blood once a month from the WOMB (= the part of the body where a baby can develop) **HELP** A less formal way of saying this is to **have a period.** ▸ **menstruation** /ˌmenstru'eɪʃn/ *noun* [U]

mental ⓘ **B1** ⓞ /'mentl/ *adj.* (**PSYCHOLOGY**)
1 connected with or happening in the mind; involving the process of thinking: *It's fascinating to watch a child's mental development.* **2** connected with illness of the mind: *a mental disorder/illness*

ˌ**mental aˈrithmetic** *noun* [U] (**MATHEMATICS**) adding, multiplying, etc. numbers in your mind without writing anything down or using a CALCULATOR

ˌmental 'health *noun* [U] (**PSYCHOLOGY**) the state of health of sb's mind: *to have **mental health issues/ problems***

mentality /men'tæləti/ *noun* [C, usually sing.] (*pl.* -ies) a type of mind or way of thinking: *I just can't understand his mentality!* ◇ *the criminal mentality*

mentally /'mentəli/ *adv.* connected with or happening in the mind: *She's mentally ill.* ◇ *Mentally, I began making a list of things I had to do.*

mention ⓘ **A2** ⓢ /'menʃn/ *verb* [T] ~ **(sth/sb) (to sb)**; ~ **(that …)** to say or write sth about sth/sth without giving much information: *Did she mention what time the film starts?* ◇ *He mentioned (to me) that he might be late.* ▸ **mention** ⓘ **B1** *noun* [C, U]: *It was odd that there wasn't even a mention of the riots in the newspaper.*
IDM **don't mention it** used as a polite reply when sb thanks you for sth: '*Thank you for all your help.*' '*Don't mention it.*' **not to mention** (used to emphasize sth) and also; as well as: *This is a great habitat for birds, not to mention other wildlife.*

▼ SYNONYMS

mention

refer to ♦ cite ♦ quote ♦ allude to

These words all mean to write or speak about sb/sth, often in order to give an example or prove sth.

mention *I didn't like to mention it.*

refer to *He referred to an earlier matter.*

cite (*formal*) *She cited her heavy workload as the reason for her breakdown.*

quote *He quoted two instances of violence suffered.*

allude to (*formal*) *She alluded briefly to the problem.*

mentor ⓘ+ **C1** /'mentɔː(r)/ *noun* [C] an experienced person who advises and helps sb with less experience over a period of time ▸ **mentoring** /-tərɪŋ/ *noun* [U]: *a mentoring programme*

menu ⓘ **A1** /'menjuː/ *noun* [C] **1** a list of the food that you can choose at a restaurant: *I hope there's soup **on the menu**.* ◇ *They do a special lunchtime menu here.* **2** (**COMPUTING**) a list of choices in a computer program that is shown on the screen: *a pull-down menu*

'**menu bar** *noun* [C] (**COMPUTING**) a bar at the top of a computer screen that contains DROP-DOWN MENUS (= lists of possible choices) such as 'File', 'Edit' and 'Help'

MEP /ˌem iː 'piː/ *noun* [C] (**POLITICS**) a person elected as the representative at the European Parliament of any of the CONSTITUENCIES of countries in the European Union (the abbreviation for 'Member of the European Parliament')

mercantile /'mɜːkəntaɪl/ *adj.* (*formal*) (**BUSINESS**) connected with trade and commercial affairs

mercantilism /mɜː'kæntɪlɪzəm/ *noun* [U] (**BUSINESS**) the economic theory that trade increases wealth

mercenary¹ /'mɜːsənəri/ *adj.* interested only in making money: *Her motives are entirely mercenary.*

mercenary² /'mɜːsənəri/ *noun* [C] (*pl.* -ies) a soldier who fights for any group or country that will pay them

merchandise¹ /'mɜːtʃəndaɪs, -daɪz/ *noun* [U] (*formal*) (**BUSINESS**) goods that are for sale ➔ note at **product**

merchandise² /'mɜːtʃəndaɪz/ *verb* [T] to sell sth using advertising, etc: *The movie is being merchandised like any big blockbuster release.*

merchandising /ˈmɜːtʃəndaɪzɪŋ/ *noun* [U] **1** (**BUSINESS**) the activity of selling goods, or of trying to sell them, by advertising or showing them **2** products connected with a popular film, person or event; the process of selling these goods: *millions of dollars' worth of Batman merchandising*

merchant ʔ+ **C1** /ˈmɜːtʃənt/ *noun* [C] (**BUSINESS**) a person whose job is to buy and sell goods, usually of one particular type, in large amounts

merchant ˈbank = INVESTMENT BANK

merchant ˈnavy *noun* [C + sing./pl. verb] a country's commercial ships and the people who work on them

merciful /ˈmɜːsɪfl/ *adj.* (used about an event) seeming to be lucky, especially because it brings an end to sb's problems or pain: *His death was a merciful release from pain.* ▸ **mercifully** /-fəli/ *adv.*: *The chairman's speech was mercifully short.*

merciless /ˈmɜːsɪləs/ *adj.* showing no MERCY ▸ **mercilessly** *adv.*

Mercury /ˈmɜːkjəri/ *noun* [sing.] (**ASTRONOMY**) the planet in the SOLAR SYSTEM that is nearest to the sun ⊃ picture at **solar system**

mercury /ˈmɜːkjəri/ *noun* [U] (*symb.* Hg) (**CHEMISTRY**) a chemical element. Mercury is a poisonous silver liquid metal. **❶** For more information on the periodic table of elements, look at the **Reference Section** of this dictionary.

mercy ʔ+ **C1** /ˈmɜːsi/ *noun* [U] forgiving or having a kind attitude towards sb that you have the power to harm or the right to punish: *The rebels were shown no mercy. They were taken out and shot.*
IDM **at the mercy of sb/sth** having no power against sb/sth that is strong: *The climbers spent the night on the mountain at the mercy of the wind and rain.*

mere ʔ+ **C1** /mɪə(r)/ *adj.* [only before noun] **1** (used for emphasizing how small or unimportant sth is) nothing more than: *90% of the country's land is owned by a mere 2% of the population.* **2** used to say that just the fact that sb/sth is present in a situation is enough to have an influence: *The mere thought of giving a speech makes me feel sick.* ◊ *The merest* (= the slightest) *smell of the fish market made her feel ill.*

merely ʔ+ **C1** /ˈmɪəli/ *adv.* (*formal*) only; just: *I don't want to place an order. I am merely making an enquiry.*

merge ʔ+ **C1** /mɜːdʒ/ *verb* **1** [I] ~ (**with/into sth**); ~ (**together**) to become part of sth larger: *This stream merges with the river a few miles downstream.* ◊ *Fact and fiction merge together in his latest thriller.* **2** [T] to join things together so that they become one: *We have merged the two classes into one.* **SYN** **amalgamate**

merger ʔ+ **C1** /ˈmɜːdʒə(r)/ *noun* [C, U] ~ (**with sb/sth**); ~ (**between/of A and B**) (**BUSINESS**) the act of joining two or more companies together

meridian /məˈrɪdiən/ *noun* [C] (**GEOGRAPHY**) one of the lines that is drawn from the North Pole to the South Pole on a map of the world: *the Greenwich meridian* **SYN** **line of longitude** ⊃ picture at **earth**[1]

meringue /məˈræŋ/ *noun* [U, C] a mixture of sugar and egg whites that is cooked in the oven; a cake made from this

merit[1] ʔ+ **C1** /ˈmerɪt/ *noun* **1** [U] the quality of being good: *He got the job on merit, not because he's the manager's son.* **2** [C, usually pl.] an advantage or a good quality of sb/sth: *Each case must be judged separately on its own merits* (= not according to general principles).

merit[2] /ˈmerɪt/ *verb* [T] (*formal*) to be good enough for sth; to deserve: *This suggestion merits further discussion.*

meritocracy /ˌmerɪˈtɒkrəsi/ *noun* (**SOCIAL STUDIES**) (*pl.* -ies) **1** [C, U] a country or social system where people get power or money on the basis of their ability **2** the meritocracy [sing.] the group of people with power in this kind of social system

mermaid /ˈmɜːmeɪd/ *noun* [C] (in stories) a woman who has the tail of a fish instead of legs and who lives in the sea

merriment /ˈmerimənt/ *noun* [U] (*formal*) happiness, fun and the sound of people laughing **SYN** **mirth**

merry /ˈmeri/ *adj.* (**merrier; merriest**) **1** happy: *merry laughter* ◊ **Merry Christmas** (= used to say you hope sb has a happy holiday) **2** (*informal*) slightly drunk ▸ **merrily** /-rəli/ *adv.*

ˈmerry-go-round (*BrE also* **roundabout**) (*also* **carousel** *especially in AmE*) *noun* [C] a big round platform that turns round and round and has model animals, etc. on it for children to ride on

mesh /meʃ/ *noun* [U, C] material that is like a net (= made of plastic, wire or rope THREADS with holes in between): *a fence made of wire mesh*

mesmerize (*BrE also* **-ise**) /ˈmezməraɪz/ *verb* [T] to hold sb's attention completely: *The audience seemed to be mesmerized by the speaker's voice.*

mesophyll /ˈmezəfɪl, ˈmiːz-/ *noun* [U] (**BIOLOGY**) the material that the inside of a leaf is made of

the mesosphere /ðə ˈmezəsfɪə(r), ˈmiːz-/ *noun* [sing.] (**ASTRONOMY**, **GEOGRAPHY**) the region of the earth's atmosphere between about 50 and 80 kilometres above the surface of the earth, above the STRATOSPHERE and below the THERMOSPHERE ⊃ picture at **atmosphere**

mesothermal /ˌmezəʊˈθɜːməl, ˌmiːz-/ *adj.* (**GEOGRAPHY**) (used about a climate) not very hot and not very cold **SYN** **temperate** ⊃ look at **megathermal**, **microthermal**

mess[1] ʔ **B1** /mes/ *noun* **1** [C, usually sing.] the state of being dirty or untidy; a person or thing that is dirty or untidy: *The kitchen's in a terrible mess!* ◊ *My hair is a mess.* ◊ *You can paint the door, but don't make a mess!* **2** [sing.] the state of having problems or troubles: *The company is in a financial mess.* ◊ *to make a mess of your life*

mess[2] /mes/ *verb* [T] (*AmE, informal*) to make sth dirty or untidy: *Don't mess your hands.*
PHR V **mess around** (*BrE also* **mess about**) **1** to behave in a silly and annoying way **2** to spend your time in a relaxed way without any real purpose: *We spent Sunday just messing around at home.* **mess sb around** (*BrE also* **mess sb about**) to treat sb in a way that is not fair or reasonable, for example by changing your plans without telling them: *The builders really messed us around. They never turned up when they promised to.* **mess around with sth** (*BrE also* **mess about with sth**) to touch or use sth in a careless way: *It is dangerous to mess around with fireworks.* **mess up 1** to make sth dirty or untidy **2** to fail at sth or do it badly: *I really messed up the last question in the exam.* **mess with sb/sth** to deal or behave with sb/sth in a way that you should not: *You shouldn't mess with people's feelings.*

message ʔ **A1** /ˈmesɪdʒ/ *noun* [C] **1** a written or spoken piece of information that you send to or leave for a person when you cannot speak to them: *Mr Khan is not here at the moment. Can I take a message?* ◊ *Could you give a message to Kate, please?* ◊ *If he's not in I'll leave a message on his voicemail.* **2** a piece of information that is sent in electronic form: *There* were six messages in my inbox. **3** [usually sing.] an important idea that a book, speech, etc. is trying to communicate: *The advertising campaign is trying to* **get the message across** *that recycling is important.* **IDM** **get the message** (*informal*) to understand what sb means even if it is not clearly stated: *He finally got the message and went home.*

'**message board** *noun* [C] (**COMPUTING**) a place on a website where a user can write or read messages: *I posted a question on the message board.*

messenger /'mesɪndʒə(r)/ *noun* [C] a person who carries a message

messiah /mə'saɪə/ *noun* (**RELIGION**) **1 the Messiah** [sing.] (in Christianity) Jesus Christ, who was sent by God into the world to save people from evil **2** [C] a leader who people believe will solve the problems of a country or the world

messy /'mesi/ *adj.* (**messier; messiest**) **1** dirty or untidy: *a messy room* **2** that makes sb/sth dirty: *Painting the ceiling is a messy job.* **3** having or causing problems or trouble: *a messy divorce*

met /met/ past tense of **meet**

meta- /metə, mə'tæ/ *prefix* (in verbs, nouns and adjectives) **1** connected with a change of position or state: *metamorphosis* ◇ *metabolism* **2** higher; beyond: *metaphysics*

metabolism /mə'tæbəlɪzəm/ *noun* [U, C] (**BIOLOGY**) the chemical processes in plants or animals that change food into energy and help them grow: *An athlete has a faster metabolism than most ordinary people.* ▶ **metabolic** /ˌmetə'bɒlɪk/ *adj.*: *a high/low metabolic rate*

metacarpal /ˌmetə'kɑːpl/ *noun* [C] (**ANATOMY**) any of the five bones in the hand between the WRIST and the fingers ⊃ picture at **body**

metadata /'metədeɪtə, -daːtə/ *noun* [U] information that describes other information in order to help you understand or use it: *In the metadata she found the author and location of the file.*

metal 🔑 **A2** /'metl/ *noun* [C, U] (**CHEMISTRY**) a type of solid substance that is usually hard and shiny and that heat and electricity can travel through: *metals such as tin, iron, gold and steel* ◇ *to recycle scrap metal* ◇ *a metal bar/pipe*

metallic /mə'tælɪk/ *adj.* **1** connected with metal or metals: *metallic alloys* **2** looking like metal; making a noise like one piece of metal hitting another: *a metallic blue car* ◇ *harsh metallic sounds*

metalloid /'metlɔɪd/ *noun* [C] (**CHEMISTRY**) a chemical element that has properties both of metals and of other solid substances

metallurgy /mə'tælədʒi/ *noun* [U] (**CHEMISTRY**) the scientific study of metals and their uses ▶ **metallurgist** /-dʒɪst/ *noun* [C]

metamorphic /ˌmetə'mɔːfɪk/ *adj.* (**GEOLOGY**) (used about rocks) that have been changed by heat or pressure ⊃ look at **igneous, sedimentary** ⊃ picture at **rock**[1]

metamorphosis /ˌmetə'mɔːfəsɪs/ *noun* [C] (*pl.* **metamorphoses** /-fəsiːz/) ~ (**of sth**) (**into sth**) (**BIOLOGY**) a complete change of form (as part of natural development): *the metamorphosis of a tadpole into a frog*

metaphor 🔑+ **B2** /'metəfə(r), -fɔː(r)/ *noun* [C, U] (**LANGUAGE, LITERATURE**) a word or phrase that is used in an **IMAGINATIVE** way to show that sb/sth has the same qualities as another thing. 'Her words were a knife in his heart' is a metaphor. ⊃ look at **figurative** (1), **literal** (1), **simile** ▶ **metaphorical** /ˌmetə'fɒrɪkl/ ▶ **metaphorically** /-kli/ *adv.*

metaˌphysical 'poets *noun* [pl.] (**LITERATURE**) a group of seventeenth-century English poets who explored the nature of the world and human life, and who used images that were surprising at that time

metaphysics /ˌmetə'fɪzɪks/ *noun* [U] (**SOCIAL STUDIES**) the area of philosophy that deals with the nature of existence, truth and knowledge ▶ **metaphysical** /-zɪkl/ *adj.*: *metaphysical problems/speculation*

metastasis /mə'tæstəsɪs/ *noun* [U, C] (*pl.* **metastases** /-'tæstəsiːz/) (**HEALTH**) the development of TUMOURS in different parts of the body resulting from cancer that has started in another part of the body; one of these TUMOURS

metatarsal /ˌmetə'tɑːsl/ *noun* [C] (**ANATOMY**) any of the bones in the part of the foot between the ankle and the toes ⊃ picture at **body**

mete /miːt/ *verb* **PHR V** **mete sth out (to sb)** (*formal*) to give sb a punishment; to make sb suffer bad treatment: *Severe penalties were meted out by the court.*

meteor /'miːtiə(r), -tiːɔː(r)/ *noun* [C] (**ASTRONOMY**) a small piece of rock, etc. from space that enters the earth's atmosphere and makes a bright line in the night sky

meteoric /ˌmiːti'ɒrɪk/ *adj.* very fast or successful: *a meteoric rise to fame*

meteorite /'miːtiəraɪt/ *noun* [C] (**ASTRONOMY**) a piece of rock from space that hits the earth's surface

meteoroid /'miːtiərɔɪd/ *noun* [C] (**ASTRONOMY**) a small piece of rock in space that would become a METEOR if it entered the earth's atmosphere

meteorology /ˌmiːti'rɒlədʒi/ *noun* [U] (**SCIENCE**) the scientific study of the weather ▶ **meteorological** /ˌmiːtiərə'lɒdʒɪkl/ *adj.* ▶ **meteorologist** /ˌmiːtiə'rɒlədʒɪst/ *noun* [C]

meter /'miːtə(r)/ *noun* [C] **1** (**ENGINEERING**) a piece of equipment that measures the amount of gas, water, electricity, etc. you have used: *a parking meter* **2** (*AmE*) = **METRE** ▶ **meter** *verb* [T]: *Is your water metered?*

methane /'miːθeɪn/ *noun* [U] (*symb.* CH_4) (**CHEMISTRY**) a gas without colour or smell, that burns easily and is used as fuel

methanol /'meθənɒl/ *noun* [U] (*symb.* CH_3OH) (**CHEMISTRY**) a poisonous form of alcohol formed when METHANE reacts with OXYGEN

method 🔑 **A2** ⊙ /'meθəd/ *noun* [C] a way of doing sth: *modern teaching methods* ◇ *What method of payment do you prefer? Cash, credit or debit card?*

methodical /mə'θɒdɪkl/ *adj.* (used about a person) doing sth in a careful and logical way: *Paul is a very methodical worker.* ▶ **methodically** /-kli/ *adv.*

Methodist /'meθədɪst/ *noun* [C] (**RELIGION**) a member of a Protestant Church that was started by John Wesley in the eighteenth century ▶ **Methodist** *adj.*

methodology 🔑+ **C1** **W** /ˌmeθə'dɒlədʒi/ *noun* [C, U] (*pl.* **-ies**) a way of doing sth based on particular principles and methods: *language teaching methodologies* ▶ **methodological** **W** /ˌmeθədə'lɒdʒɪkl/ *adj.*

methylated spirits /ˌmeθəleɪtɪd 'spɪrɪts/ (*also informal* **meths** /meθs/) *noun* [U] a type of alcohol that you cannot drink, used as a fuel for lighting and heating and for cleaning off dirty marks

meticulous /mə'tɪkjələs/ *adj.* giving or showing great attention to detail; very careful ▶ **meticulously** *adv.*

metonymy /mə'tɒnəmi/ *noun* [U] (**LANGUAGE**) the act of referring to sth by the name of sth else that is closely connected with it, for example using *the White House* for *the US president*

metre 🔊 **A1** (*BrE*) (*AmE* **meter**) /'miːtə(r)/ *noun* **1** [C] (*abbr.* m) a measure of length; 100 CENTIMETRES: *a two-metre high wall* **2** metres [C, U] (**SPORT**) used in the name of races: *She came second in the 100 metres.* **3** [U, C] (**LITERATURE**) the arrangement of strong and weak stresses in lines of poetry that produces the rhythm; a particular example of this

metric /'metrik/ *adj.* using THE METRIC SYSTEM ⊃ look at **imperial** (2)

the 'metric system *noun* [sing.] the system of measurement that uses the metre, the KILOGRAM and the LITRE as basic units

metric 'ton = TONNE

metronome /'metrənəʊm/ *noun* [C] (**MUSIC**) a device that makes a regular sound like a clock and is used by musicians to help them keep the correct rhythm when playing a piece of music

metropolis /mə'trɒpəlɪs/ *noun* [C] a very large city ▶ **metropolitan** /ˌmetrə'pɒlɪtən/ *adj.*

metrosexual /ˌmetrə'sekʃuəl/ *noun* [C] (*informal*) a HETEROSEXUAL man (= one who is

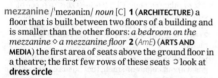
metronome

sexually attracted to women) who lives in a city and is interested in things like fashion and shopping ▶ **metrosexual** *adj.*

mezzanine /'mezəniːn/ *noun* [C] **1** (**ARCHITECTURE**) a floor that is built between two floors of a building and is smaller than the other floors: *a bedroom on the mezzanine* ◇ *a mezzanine floor* (*AmE*) (**ARTS AND MEDIA**) the first area of seats above the ground floor in a theatre; the first few rows of these seats ⊃ look at **dress circle**

mg *abbr.* (in writing) (*pl.* mg) = MILLIGRAM

MHz *abbr.* (in writing) (*pl.* MHz) = MEGAHERTZ

miaow /mi'aʊ/ *noun* [C] the sound that a cat makes ▶ **miaow** *verb* [I] ⊃ look at **purr**

mice /maɪs/ plural of **mouse¹**

micro- /'maɪkrəʊ, maɪkrə, maɪ'krɒ/ *prefix* (in nouns, adjectives and adverbs) small; on a small scale: *microchip* ◇ *micro-organism* **OPP** **macro-**

microbe /'maɪkrəʊb/ *noun* [C] (**BIOLOGY**) an extremely small living thing that you can only see under a MICROSCOPE (= a piece of equipment that makes small objects look bigger) and that may cause disease ▶ **microbial** /maɪ'krəʊbiəl/ *adj.*: *Cool soil temperatures slow down microbial activity.*

microbiology /ˌmaɪkrəʊbaɪ'ɒlədʒi/ *noun* [U] (**BIOLOGY**) the scientific study of very small living things ▶ **microbiologist** /-dʒɪst/ *noun* [C]

microblogging /'maɪkrəʊblɒɡɪŋ/ *noun* [U] (**COMPUTING**) the activity of sending regular short messages, pictures or videos over the internet as a way of letting people know about your activities and thoughts ⊃ look at **Twitter™**

microchip /'maɪkrəʊtʃɪp/ (*also* **chip**) *noun* [C] (**COMPUTING**) a very small piece of a special material that is used inside a computer, etc. to make it work

microcomputer /'maɪkrəʊkəmpjuːtə(r)/ *noun* [C] (**COMPUTING**) a small computer that contains a MICROPROCESSOR

microcosm /'maɪkrəʊkɒzəm/ *noun* [C] something that is a small example of sth larger: *Our little village is a microcosm of society as a whole.* ⊃ look at **macrocosm**

microelectronics /ˌmaɪkrəʊɪˌlek'trɒnɪks/ *noun* [U] (**ENGINEERING**, **PHYSICS**) the design, production and use of very small electronic CIRCUITS (= paths that electric currents can flow around)

microfiche /'maɪkrəʊfiːʃ/ *noun* [C, U] a piece of film on which information is stored in very small print

microfilm /'maɪkrəʊfɪlm/ *noun* [U, C] film used for storing written information on in print of very small size

microgram /'maɪkrəʊɡræm/ *noun* [C] (*symb.* μg) a unit for measuring weight. There are one million micrograms in one GRAM.

micrometre (*BrE*) (*AmE* **micrometer**) /'maɪkrəʊmiːtə(r)/ *noun* [C] (*symb.* μm) a unit for measuring length. There are one million micrometres in one metre.

microorganism /ˌmaɪkrəʊ'ɔːɡənɪzəm/ *noun* [C] (**BIOLOGY**) a very small living thing that you can only see with a MICROSCOPE (= a piece of equipment that makes small objects look bigger)

microphone /'maɪkrəfəʊn/ (*also informal* **mike**) *noun* [C] a piece of electrical equipment that is used for making sounds louder or for recording them: *Speak into the microphone so that everyone can hear you.*

microplastic /'maɪkrəʊplæstɪk/ *noun* [U] (*also* microplastics [pl.]) (**ENVIRONMENT**) extremely small pieces of plastic waste that are found in the environment: *Studies have found microplastics in seafood, soil, Arctic ice and the air.*

microprocessor /ˌmaɪkrəʊ'prəʊsesə(r)/ *noun* [C] (**COMPUTING**) a small unit of a computer that contains all the functions of the CENTRAL PROCESSING UNIT (= the part of the computer that controls all the other parts of the system)

microscope

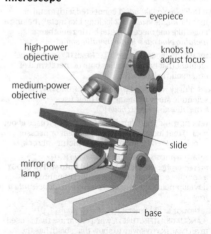

eyepiece

high-power objective

knobs to adjust focus

medium-power objective

slide

mirror or lamp

base

microscope /'maɪkrəskəʊp/ *noun* [C] (**SCIENCE**) a piece of equipment that makes very small objects look big enough for you to be able to see them: *to examine something under a microscope*

microscopic /ˌmaɪkrə'skɒpɪk/ adj. too small to be seen without a MICROSCOPE

microscopy /maɪ'krɒskəpi/ noun [U] (**SCIENCE**) the use of MICROSCOPES to look at very small things

microsurgery /'maɪkrəʊsɜːdʒəri/ noun [U] (**MEDICINE**) the use of extremely small instruments and MICROSCOPES in order to perform very detailed and complicated medical operations

microthermal /ˌmaɪkrəʊ'θɜːməl/ adj. (**GEOGRAPHY**) (used about a climate) having cold winters and short summers ⊃ look at **megathermal**, **mesothermal**

microwave /'maɪkrəweɪv/ noun **1** (also ˌmicrowave 'oven) a type of oven that cooks or heats food very quickly using microwaves ⊃ picture at **wavelength** **2** (**PHYSICS**) a short electric wave that is used for sending radio messages and for cooking food ▸ **microwave** verb [T] ⊃ note at **cook¹**

mid /mɪd/ adj. [only before noun] the middle of: *I'm away from mid June.* ◇ *the mid 1990s*

mid- /mɪd/ prefix (in nouns and adjectives) in the middle of: *mid-afternoon* ◇ *a mid-air collision*

midday /ˌmɪd'deɪ/ noun [U] at or around twelve o'clock in the middle of the day: *We arranged to meet at midday.* ◇ *the heat of the midday sun* **SYN** **noon** ⊃ look at **midnight**

middle¹ ⚡ **A2 ⑤** /'mɪdl/ noun **1** [sing.] **the ~ (of sth)** the part, point or position that is at about the same distance from the two ends or sides of sth: *the white line in the middle of the road* ◇ *Here's a photo of me with my two brothers. I'm the one in the middle.* **2** [C, usually sing.] (*informal*) the WAIST: *I want to lose weight around my middle.*
IDM **be in the middle of sth/doing sth** to be busy doing sth: *Can you call back in five minutes — I'm in the middle of feeding the baby.* **in the middle of nowhere** a long way from any town

middle² ⚡ **A2** /'mɪdl/ adj. [only before noun] in the middle: *I wear my ring on my middle finger.*

ˌmiddle 'age noun [U] the time when you are about 40 to 60 years old: *in early/late middle age* ▸ ˌmiddle-'aged adj.: *a middle-aged man*

the ˌMiddle 'Ages noun [pl.] (**HISTORY**) the period of European history from about 1100 to 1500 AD

ˌmiddle 'class noun [sing. + sing./pl. verb] (**SOCIAL STUDIES**) the group of people in society whose members are neither very rich nor very poor and that includes professional and business people: *the upper/lower middle class* ◇ *the growth of the middle classes* ⊃ look at **upper class**, **working class** ▸ ˌmiddle-'class adj.: *a middle-class background*

ˌmiddle-'distance adj. [only before noun] (in sport) connected with running a race over a distance that is neither very short nor very long: *a middle-distance runner* (= for example, sb who runs 800 or 1500 metre races)

ˌmiddle 'ear noun [sing.] (**ANATOMY**) the central part of the ear behind the EARDRUM (= the thin piece of skin that allows you to hear sound) ⊃ look at **inner ear**, **outer ear** ⊃ picture at **ear**

the ˌMiddle 'East noun [sing.] (**GEOGRAPHY**) an area that covers south-west Asia and north-east Africa ⊃ look at **Far East** ▸ ˌMiddle 'Eastern adj.

ˌmiddle 'finger noun [C] (**ANATOMY**) the longest finger in the middle of each hand

middleman /'mɪdlmæn/ noun [C] (*pl.* -men /-men/) **1** (**BUSINESS**) a person or company who buys goods from the company that makes them and then sells them to sb else **2** a person who helps to arrange things between two people who do not want to meet each other

ˌmiddle 'management noun [U + sing./pl. verb] (**BUSINESS**) the people who are in charge of small groups of people and departments within an organization: *She is working on ways to improve the number of women in middle management.* ▸ ˌmiddle 'manager noun [C]

ˌmiddle 'name noun [C] a name that comes after your first name and before your family name

ˌmiddle-of-the-'road adj. (used about people, policies, etc.) not extreme; acceptable to most people

ˌmiddle school noun [C] (**EDUCATION**) (in the UK) a school for children aged between the ages of 9 and 13

midfield /'mɪdfiːld, ˌmɪd'fiːld/ noun [U, C, sing.] (**SPORT**) the central part of a sports field; the group of players in this position: *He plays (in) midfield.* ◇ *a midfield player* ▸ **midfielder** /ˌmɪd'fiːldə(r)/ noun [C]

midge /mɪdʒ/ noun [C] a very small flying insect that can bite people **SYN** **gnat**

midget /'mɪdʒɪt/ noun [C] a very small person or animal ❶ Many people find this word offensive.

MIDI /'mɪdi/ noun [U] (**MUSIC**) a connection or program that connects electronic musical instruments and computers (the abbreviation for 'Musical Instrument Digital Interface')

the **Midlands** /ðə 'mɪdləndz/ noun [sing. + sing./pl. verb] (**GEOGRAPHY**) the central part of England around Birmingham and Nottingham

midlife /mɪd'laɪf/ noun [U] the middle part of your life when you are neither young nor old: *We both started new careers in midlife.* ◇ *a midlife crisis* (= disappointed feelings that a person may have in the middle part of their life)

midnight ⚡ **A1** /'mɪdnaɪt/ noun [U] twelve o'clock at night: *They left the party at midnight.* ◇ *The clock struck midnight.* ⊃ look at **midday**

midpoint /'mɪdpɔɪnt/ noun [C, usually sing.] (**MATHEMATICS**) the point that is at an equal distance between the beginning and the end of sth; the point that is at an equal distance between two things: *the mid-point between the first number and the last*

mid-'range adj. [only before noun] (used especially about products for sale) neither the best nor the worst that is available: *a mid-range computer*

midriff /'mɪdrɪf/ noun [C] (**ANATOMY**) the part of the body between the chest and the WAIST

midst ⚡ **C1** /mɪdst/ noun [U] **~ (of sth)** the middle of sth; among a group of people or things: *The country is in the midst of a recession.* ◇ *They realized with a shock that there was an enemy in their midst.*

midsummer /ˌmɪd'sʌmə(r)/ noun [U] the time around the middle of summer: *a beautiful midsummer's evening*

midway /ˌmɪd'weɪ/ adj., adv. in the middle of a period of time or between two places: *I began to feel ill midway through the exam.* **SYN** **halfway**

midweek /ˌmɪd'wiːk/ noun [U] the middle of the week (= Tuesday, Wednesday and Thursday) ▸ **midweek** adv.: *If you travel midweek it will be less crowded.*

the **Midwest** /ðə ˌmɪd'west/ noun [sing.] (**GEOGRAPHY**) the northern central part of the US

midwife /'mɪdwaɪf/ noun [C] (*pl.* midwives /-waɪvz/) (**MEDICINE**) a person who is trained to help women give birth to babies

midwifery /ˌmɪd'wɪfəri/ noun [U] (**MEDICINE**) the profession and work of a MIDWIFE

midwinter /ˌmɪdˈwɪntə(r)/ *noun* [U] the time around the middle of winter

might[1] ⚑ **A2** ⊙ /maɪt/ *modal verb* (*negative* **might not** /ˈmaɪt nɒt/; *short form* **mightn't** /ˈmaɪtnt/) **1** used for saying that sth is possible: *'Where's Vinay?' 'He might be upstairs.'* ◇ *I think I might have forgotten the tickets.* ◇ *She might not come if she's very busy.* **2** used as the form of *may* when you report what sb has said: *He said he might be late* (= his words were, 'I may be late'). **3** (*BrE, formal*) used to ask for sth or suggest sth very politely: *I wonder if I might go home half an hour early today?* **4** used when you are angry to say what sb could or should have done: *You might tell me if you're going to be late.* **5** used for saying that you are not surprised that sth has happened: *I might have known he wouldn't help.*
IDM **may/might as well (do sth)** → **WELL**[1]

might[2] /maɪt/ *noun* [U] (*formal*) great strength or power: *I pushed with all my might, but the rock did not move.*

mighty[1] /ˈmaɪti/ *adj.* (**mightier; mightiest**) very strong or powerful

mighty[2] /ˈmaɪti/ *adv.* (*AmE, informal*) very: *That's mighty kind of you.*

migraine /ˈmaɪɡreɪn, ˈmiːɡ-/ *noun* [C, U] (**HEALTH**) a very bad headache that often makes a person feel sick

migrant /ˈmaɪɡrənt/ *noun* [C] **1** (**SOCIAL STUDIES**) a person who goes from one place to another, especially in order to find work or better living conditions: *skilled migrants looking for work* **2** (**BIOLOGY**) a bird or an animal that moves from one place to another according to the season

migrate ⊙ /maɪˈɡreɪt/ *verb* [I] **1** (**BIOLOGY**) (used about animals and birds) to travel from one part of the world to another at the same time every year **2** (**SOCIAL STUDIES**) (used about a large number of people) to go and live and work in another place: *Many people who lived in the country were forced to migrate to the cities to look for work.* ⊃ look at **emigrate** ▸ **migration** ⚑ **C1** ⊙ /-ˈɡreɪʃn/ *noun* [U, C]: *the migration routes of birds*

migratory /ˈmaɪɡrətri, maɪˈɡreɪtəri/ *adj.* (**BIOLOGY**) (used about animals) travelling from one part of the world to another at the same time every year

mike /maɪk/ (*informal*) = **MICROPHONE**

milage /ˈmaɪlɪdʒ/ = **MILEAGE**

mild ⚑ **B1** /maɪld/ *adj.* **1** not strong; not very bad: *a mild soap* ◇ *a mild winter* ◇ *a mild punishment* **2** (used about food) not having a strong taste: *mild cheese* **3** kind and gentle: *He's a very mild man — you never see him get angry.* ▸ **mildness** *noun* [U]

mildew /ˈmɪldjuː/ *noun* [U] (**BIOLOGY**) a living white substance that grows on walls, plants, food, etc. in warm wet conditions

mildly /ˈmaɪldli/ *adv.* **1** not very; slightly: *mildly surprised* **2** in a gentle way: *He spoke mildly to the child.*

mile ⚑ **A1** /maɪl/ *noun* **1** [C] a measure of length; 1.6 kilometres. There are 1 760 yards in a mile: *The nearest beach is 7 miles away.* ◇ *It's a 7-mile drive to the beach.* ◇ (*figurative, informal*) *He missed the target by a mile.* ❶ For more information about measurements, look at the **Reference Section** of this dictionary. **2 miles** [pl.] a long way: *How much further is it? We've walked miles already.* ◇ *From the top of the hill you can see for miles.*
IDM **see, hear, tell, spot, etc. sb/sth a mile off** (*informal*) used to say that sb/sth is very obvious: *He's lying — you can tell that a mile off.*

mileage (*also* **milage**) /ˈmaɪlɪdʒ/ *noun* **1** [U, C, usually sing.] the distance that has been travelled, measured in miles: *The car is five years old but it has a low mileage.* **2** [U] (*informal*) the amount of use that you get from sth: *The newspapers got a lot of mileage out of the scandal.*

mileometer /maɪˈlɒmɪtə(r)/ = **MILOMETER**

milestone /ˈmaɪlstəʊn/ *noun* [C] **~ (in sth)** a very important event: *The concert was a milestone in the band's history.*

militant[1] ⚑ **C1** /ˈmɪlɪtənt/ *adj.* ready to use force or strong pressure to get what you want: *The workers were in a very militant mood.* ▸ **militancy** /-lɪtənsi/ *noun* [U] ▸ **militant**[2] ⚑ **C1** *noun* [C]

militarism /ˈmɪlɪtərɪzəm/ *noun* [U] (**POLITICS**) the belief that a country should have great military strength in order to be powerful ▸ **militaristic** /ˌmɪlɪtəˈrɪstɪk/ *adj.*

military[1] ⚑ **B2** /ˈmɪlətri/ *adj.* [only before noun] connected with soldiers or the army, NAVY, etc: *to do two years' military service* ◇ *to take military action* ⊃ note at **government**

military[2] ⚑ **B2** /ˈmɪlətri/ (*usually* **the military**) *noun* [C + sing./pl. verb] (*pl.* **-ies**) soldiers; the armed forces: *The military was/were called in to deal with the riot.*

militia ⚑ **C1** /məˈlɪʃə/ *noun* [C + sing./pl. verb] a group of people who are not professional soldiers but who have had military training

milk[1] ⚑ **A1** /mɪlk/ *noun* [U] (**BIOLOGY**) **1** a white liquid that is produced by some animals as food for their young. People drink milk and use it to make butter and cheese: *skimmed/long-life/low-fat milk* ◇ *a bottle/carton of milk* **2** a white liquid that is produced by women and female animals to feed their babies **3** the juice of some plants or trees that looks like milk: *coconut milk*

milk[2] /mɪlk/ *verb* [T] **1** (**AGRICULTURE**) to take milk from a cow, GOAT, etc. **2** to get as much money, advantage, etc. for yourself from sb/sth as you can, without caring about others

milkman /ˈmɪlkmən/ *noun* [C] (*pl.* **-men** /-mən/) (especially in the UK) a person who takes milk to people's houses every day

milkshake /ˈmɪlkʃeɪk/ *noun* [C, U] a drink made of milk with the added taste of fruit or chocolate

milk tooth *noun* [C] (**ANATOMY**) any of the first set of teeth in young children that fall out and are replaced by others

milky /ˈmɪlki/ *adj.* (**milkier; milkiest**) like milk, or made with milk: *milky white skin* ◇ *milky coffee*

the Milky Way *noun* [sing.] a band of light across the night sky, made up of the stars that form a large part of the GALAXY that contains our sun and its planets

mill[1] ⚑ **C1** /mɪl/ *noun* [C] **1** (**BUSINESS**) a factory that is used for making certain kinds of material: *a cotton/paper/steel mill* ⊃ note at **factory 2** a building that contains a large machine that was used in the past for making grain into flour: *a windmill* ⊃ look at **windmill 3** a kitchen tool that is used for making sth into powder: *a pepper mill*

mill[2] /mɪl/ *verb* [T] to produce sth in a MILL
PHR V **mill about/around** (used about a large number of people or animals) to move around in a place with no real purpose

millennial /mɪˈleniəl/ *noun* [C, usually pl.] (**SOCIAL STUDIES**) a person who belongs to the generation who became adults in the early twenty-first century: *Millennials are willing to take risks and see career change as normal.*

millennium /mɪˈleniəm/ *noun* [C] (*pl.* millennia /-niə/, millenniums) a period of 1 000 years: *the start of a new millennium*

miller /ˈmɪlə(r)/ *noun* [C] a person who owns or works in a MILL for making flour

millet /ˈmɪlɪt/ *noun* [U] (**AGRICULTURE**) a plant with a lot of small seeds that are used as food for people and birds ⊃ picture at **cereal**

milli- /mɪli/ *prefix* (in units of measurement) one THOUSANDTH: *millisecond* ◊ *millimetre*

millibar /ˈmɪlibɑː(r)/ *noun* [C] (**PHYSICS**) a unit for measuring the pressure of the atmosphere. 1 000 millibars are equal to one BAR.

milligram (*also* **milligramme**) /ˈmɪligræm/ *noun* [C] (*abbr.* mg) a measure of weight. There are 1 000 milligrams in a GRAM.

millilitre (*BrE*) (*AmE* **milliliter**) /ˈmɪliliːtə(r)/ *noun* [C] (*abbr.* ml) a measure of liquid. There are 1 000 millilitres in a LITRE.

millimetre (*BrE*) (*AmE* **millimeter**) /ˈmɪlimiːtə(r)/ *noun* [C] (*abbr.* mm) a measure of length. There are 1 000 millimetres in a metre.

millinery /ˈmɪlɪnəri/ *noun* [U] (**BUSINESS**) the business of making or selling women's hats

million 🔑 **A1** /ˈmɪljən/ *number* **1** 1 000 000: *Over 60 million people live in Britain.* ◊ *Millions of people are at risk from the disease.* **HELP** Note that when you are counting you use **million** without 's': *six million people* **2** a million, millions (of) (*informal*) a very large amount: *I still have a million things to do.* ◊ *There are millions of reasons why you shouldn't go.* ❶ For more information about numbers, look at the **Reference Section** of this dictionary. ▸ **millionth** /-jənθ/ *ordinal number, noun* [C]

millionaire /ˌmɪljəˈneə(r)/ *noun* [C] a person who has a million pounds, dollars, etc.; a very rich person

millipede /ˈmɪlipiːd/ *noun* [C] a small creature like an insect, with a long thin body divided into many sections, each with two pairs of legs

millstone /ˈmɪlstəʊn/ *noun*
IDM a millstone around/round your neck a difficult problem or responsibility that it seems impossible to solve: *My debts are a millstone around my neck.*

milometer (*also* **mileometer**) /maɪˈlɒmɪtə(r)/ (*both BrE*) (*AmE* **odometer**) *noun* [C] an instrument in a vehicle that measures the number of miles it has travelled

mime /maɪm/ (*AmE also* **pantomime**) *noun* [U, C] (**ARTS AND MEDIA**) the use of movements of your hands and body and the expression on your face to tell a story or to act sth without speaking; a performance using this method of acting: *The performance consisted of dance, music and mime.* ▸ **mime** *verb* [I, T]

mimic¹ /ˈmɪmɪk/ *verb* [T] (-ck-) to copy sb's behaviour, movements, voice, etc. in a way that makes people laugh

mimic² /ˈmɪmɪk/ *noun* [C] a person who can copy sb's behaviour, movements, voice, etc. in a way that makes people laugh ▸ **mimicry** /-mɪkri/ *noun* [U]

min. *abbr.* (in writing) **1** = MINIMUM¹: *min. temp tomorrow: 2°* **2** (*pl.* min.) = MINUTE¹ (1): *fastest time: 6 min.*

minaret /ˌmɪnəˈret/ *noun* [C] (**RELIGION**) a tall thin tower, usually part of a MOSQUE (= a religious building), from which Muslims are called to come and say prayers

muezzin's platform

minaret

mince /mɪns/ (*BrE*) (*AmE* **ground beef, hamburger**) *noun* [U] meat that has been cut into very small pieces with a special machine ▸ **mince** *verb* [T]

mincemeat /ˈmɪnsmiːt/ *noun* [U] a mixture of dried fruit, nuts, sugar, etc. (but no meat) that is used as a filling for sweet dishes, especially MINCE PIES

mince 'pie *noun* [C] a small round PASTRY (= a mixture of flour, fat and water) filled with MINCEMEAT (= a mixture of dried fruit, sugar, etc.), traditionally eaten in the UK at Christmas time

mind¹ 🔑 **A2** /maɪnd/ *noun* [C, U] the part of the brain that thinks and remembers; your thoughts, feelings and intelligence: *He has a brilliant mind.* ◊ *My mind wandered as the teacher went on talking.*
IDM at/in the back of your mind → BACK¹ be in two minds (about sth/doing sth) (*BrE*) (*AmE* be of two minds (about sth/doing sth)) to not feel sure of sth: *I'm in two minds about leaving Will alone in the house while we're away.* be/go out of your mind to be or become crazy or very worried: *I was going out of my mind when Tina didn't come home on time.* bear in mind (that) | bear/keep sth in mind to remember or consider (that); to remember sb/sth: *We'll bear/keep your suggestion in mind for the future.* bring/call sb/sth to mind to be reminded of sb/sth; to remember sb/sth cast your mind back → CAST¹ change your mind → CHANGE¹ come/spring to mind if sth comes/springs to mind, you suddenly remember or think of it cross your mind → CROSS² ease sb's mind → EASE² frame of mind → FRAME¹ give sb a piece of your mind → PIECE¹ go clean out of your mind → CLEAN³ have a good mind/half a mind to do sth used to threaten to do sth, although you probably will not: *I've a good mind to write and tell your parents about it.* have sb/sth in mind (for sth) to be considering sb/sth as suitable for sth; to have a plan: *We have some projects in mind that will affect everybody here.* have/keep an open mind → OPEN¹ keep your mind on sth to continue to pay attention to sth: *Keep your mind on the road while you're driving!* make up your mind to decide: *I can't make up my mind which sweater to buy.* on your mind worrying you: *Don't bother her with that. She's got enough on her mind already.* prey on sb's mind → PREY² put/set sb's mind at rest to make sb stop worrying: *The results of the blood test set his mind at rest.* slip your mind → SLIP¹ speak your mind → SPEAK state of mind → STATE¹ take your mind off sth to help sb not to think or worry about sth to my mind in my opinion: *To my mind, this is a complete waste of time!*

mind² 🔑 **A2** /maɪnd/ *verb* **1** [I, T] (especially in negative sentences and questions) to feel annoyed, upset or uncomfortable about sth/sb: *I'm sure Simon won't mind if you don't invite him.* ◊ *I don't mind what you do — it's your decision.* ◊ *Do you mind having to travel so far to work every day?* ◊ *Are you sure your parents won't mind me coming?* ◊ *'Would you like tea or coffee?' 'I don't mind.'* (= I'm happy to have either).' ◊ *I wouldn't mind a break right now* (= I would like one). **2** [I, T] ~(sb) (doing sth) (used in a question as a polite way of asking sb to do sth or for permission to do sth) could you ... ?; may I ... ?: *Do you mind if I close the window?* ◊ *Do you mind driving? I'm feeling rather tired.* ◊ *Are you married, if you don't mind me asking?* **3** [T] used to tell sb to be careful of sth or to pay attention to sb/sth: *It's a very low doorway so mind your head.* ◊ *Mind that step!* ◊ *Don't mind me! I won't disturb you.* **4** [T] (*especially BrE*) to look after or watch sb/

sth for a short time: *Could you mind my bag while I go and get us some drinks?*
IDM I wouldn't mind something/doing something used to say politely that you would very much like something/to do something: *I wouldn't mind a cup of tea.* **mind you** used for attracting attention to a point you are making or for giving more information: *Paul seems very tired. Mind you, he has been working very hard recently.* **mind your own business** to pay attention to your own affairs, not other people's: *Stop asking me personal questions and mind your own business!* **never mind** don't worry; it doesn't matter: *'I forgot to post your letter.' 'Never mind, I'll do it later.'*
PHR V mind out (*BrE, informal*) used to tell sb to move so that you can pass: *Mind out! There's a car coming.*

ˈmind-boggling *adj.* (*informal*) difficult to imagine, understand or believe: *Mind-boggling amounts of money were being discussed.*

-minded /ˈmaɪndɪd/ *adj.* **1** (used with adjectives to form compound adjectives) having the way of thinking, attitude, etc. mentioned: *a strong-minded/open-minded/narrow-minded person* **2** (used with nouns to form compound adjectives) interested in or able to understand the thing mentioned: *money-minded*

minder /ˈmaɪndə(r)/ *noun* [C] a person whose job is to look after and protect sb/sth: *a star surrounded by her minders*

mindful /ˈmaɪndfl/ *adj.* **~ of sb/sth; ~ that ...** (*formal*) **1** remembering sb/sth and considering them or it when you do sth: *mindful of our responsibilities* ◇ *We are mindful that this is a nationwide problem.* **SYN conscious 2** (**PSYCHOLOGY**) focusing on the present moment, especially as part of a technique to help you relax

mindfulness /ˈmaɪndflnəs/ *noun* [U] (**PSYCHOLOGY**) a mental state that involves concentrating on the present moment, while accepting the feelings that come to you, used as a technique to help you relax: *Pupils practise mindfulness at school to help them deal with the pressures of the modern world.*

mindless /ˈmaɪndləs/ *adj.* **1** done or acting without thought and for no particular reason: *mindless violence* **2** not needing thought or intelligence: *a mindless and repetitive task*

mindset /ˈmaɪndset/ *noun* [C] (**PSYCHOLOGY**) a set of attitudes or ideas that sb has: *a positive mindset* ➲ look at **mentality**

mine¹ 🔑 **A2** /maɪn/ *pron.* of or belonging to me: *'Whose is this jacket?' 'It's mine.'* ◇ *Don't take your car — you can come in mine.* ◇ *May I introduce a friend of mine* (= one of my friends)? ➲ look at **my**

mine² 🔑 **B1** /maɪn/ *noun* [C] **1** (**GEOLOGY**) a deep hole, or a system of passages under the ground where minerals such as coal, tin, gold, etc. are dug: *a coal/salt/gold mine* ➲ look at **quarry¹** (1) **2** a bomb that is hidden under the ground or in the sea and explodes when sb/sth touches it: *The car went over a mine and blew up.*

mine³ /maɪn/ *verb* **1** [T, I] (**GEOLOGY**) to dig in the ground for minerals such as coal, tin, gold, etc: *Diamonds are mined in South Africa.* ➲ look at **mining 2** [T] to put mines in an area of land or sea

minefield /ˈmaɪnfiːld/ *noun* [C] **1** an area of land or sea where mines have been hidden **2** a situation that is full of hidden dangers or difficulties: *a political minefield*

miner 🔑+ **B2** /ˈmaɪnə(r)/ *noun* [C] a person whose job is to work in a mine to get coal, salt, tin, etc.

mineral 🔑 **B2** /ˈmɪnərəl/ *noun* [C] (**GEOLOGY, HEALTH**) a natural substance such as coal, salt, oil, etc., especially one that is found in the ground. Some minerals are also present in food and drink and are very important for good health: *a country rich in minerals* ◇ *the recommended daily intake of vitamins and minerals* ➲ picture at **erosion**

ˈmineral water *noun* [U] water from a spring that contains mineral SALTS or gases

mingle /ˈmɪŋgl/ *verb* [I, T] **~ (together); ~ (A) (with B)** to combine; to make one thing combine with another: *The colours slowly mingled together to make a muddy brown.* ◇ *His excitement was mingled with fear.*

mini /ˈmɪni/ = MINISKIRT

mini- /mɪni/ *prefix* (in nouns) very small: *a miniskirt* ◇ *minigolf*

miniature /ˈmɪnətʃə(r)/ *noun* [C] a small copy of sth that is much larger ▶ **miniature** *adj.*: *miniature roses*
IDM in miniature exactly the same as sb/sth else but in a very small form

minibar /ˈmɪnibɑː(r)/ *noun* [C] a small fridge in a hotel room, with drinks in it for guests to use

minibeast /ˈmɪnibiːst/ *noun* [C] (*BrE*) (used especially in schools) any small animal that does not have a BACKBONE (= the row of bones in the middle of the back): *minibeasts such as worms, snails, centipedes, ants and spiders*

minibreak /ˈmɪnibreɪk/ *noun* [C] (**TOURISM**) a short holiday, usually of only two or three days

minibus /ˈmɪnibʌs/ *noun* [C] (*especially BrE*) a small bus with seats for about twelve people

minim /ˈmɪnɪm/ (*BrE*) (*AmE* **half note**) *noun* [C] (**MUSIC**) a note that lasts twice as long as a CROTCHET ➲ note at **crotchet** ➲ picture at **music**

minimal 🔑+ **C1** **W** /ˈmɪnɪml/ *adj.* very small in amount, size or level; as little as possible: *The project must be carried out at minimal cost.*

minimalist /ˈmɪnɪməlɪst/ *noun* [C] (**ARTS AND MEDIA**) an artist, a musician, etc. who uses very simple ideas or a very small number of simple things in their work ▶ **minimalism** /-lɪzəm/ *noun* [U] ▶ **minimalist** *adj.*

minimize 🔑+ **C1** **W** (*BrE also* **-ise**) /ˈmɪnɪmaɪz/ *verb* [T] **1** to make sth as small as possible (in amount or level): *We shall try to **minimize the risks** to the public.* **OPP maximize 2** to try to make sth seem less important than it really is **3** (**COMPUTING**) to make sth small on a computer screen

minimum¹ 🔑 **B2** **W** /ˈmɪnɪməm/ *adj.* [only before noun] (*abbr.* **min.**) the smallest that is possible or allowed; extremely small: *to introduce a national **minimum wage*** (= the lowest wage that an employer is legally allowed to pay) **OPP maximum¹** ▶ **minimum** *adv.*: *We'll need £200 minimum for expenses.*

minimum² 🔑 **B2** **W** /ˈmɪnɪməm/ *noun* [sing.] the smallest amount or level that is possible or allowed: *I need a minimum of seven hours' sleep.* ◇ *We will try and **keep** the cost of the tickets **to a minimum**.* **OPP maximum²**

ˌminimum ˈwage *noun* [sing., U] (**FINANCE**) the lowest wage that an employer is allowed to pay by law: *to introduce a national minimum wage* ◇ *workers on minimum wage*

mining 🔑+ **C1** /ˈmaɪnɪŋ/ *noun* [U] (**GEOLOGY**) the process or industry of getting minerals, metals, etc. out of the ground by digging: *coal/tin/gold mining*

miniskirt /ˈmɪniskɜːt/ *noun* [C] a very short skirt

minister 🔑 **B2** /ˈmɪnɪstə(r)/ *noun* [C] **1** (*often* **Minister**) (*AmE* **Secretary**) (**POLITICS**) a member of the government, often the head of a government

department: *the Minister for Education* ᗡ look at **cabinet**(1), **prime minister** 2 (RELIGION) a priest in some Protestant churches ᗡ look at **vicar**

ministerial /ˌmɪnɪˈstɪəriəl/ *adj.* (POLITICS) connected with a government minister or department: *a ministerial decision*

ministry ⟨+ **C1** /ˈmɪnɪstri/ (*pl.* -ies) (*also* department) *noun* [C] (POLITICS) a government department that has a particular area of responsibility: *the Ministry of Defence* ❶ **Department** is the only word used in American English.

minivan /ˈmɪnivæn/ (*AmE*) = PEOPLE CARRIER

mink /mɪŋk/ *noun* [C] a small wild animal that is kept for its thick brown fur, which is used to make expensive coats

minor¹ ⟨ **B2** ⓦ /ˈmaɪnə(r)/ *adj.* **1** not very big, serious or important (when compared with others): *It's only a minor problem. Don't worry.* ◇ *She's gone into hospital for a minor operation.* **OPP major¹** **2** (MUSIC) of one of the two types of KEY in which music is usually written: *a symphony in F minor* ᗡ look at **major¹** (2)

minor² /ˈmaɪnə(r)/ *noun* [C] (LAW) a person who is under the age at which you legally become an adult and are responsible for your actions: *It is an offence to serve alcohol to minors.*

minority ⟨ **B2** ⓦ /maɪˈnɒrəti/ *noun* [C] (*pl.* -ies) **1** [usually sing. + sing./pl. verb] the smaller number or part of a group; less than half: *Only a minority of teenagers become/becomes involved in crime.* **OPP majority** **2** (SOCIAL STUDIES) a small group of people who belong to a different human group or have a different religion from most of the people in the community or country where they live: *the rights of ethnic minorities*
IDM **be in a/the minority** to be the smaller of two groups: *Men are in the minority in the teaching profession.*

mi,nority 'government *noun* [C, U] (POLITICS) a government that has fewer seats in parliament than the total number held by all the other parties

minster /ˈmɪnstə(r)/ *noun* [C] (BrE) (RELIGION) a large or important church: *York Minster*

mint /mɪnt/ *noun* **1** [U] a plant whose leaves have a fresh smell and taste that are added to food and drinks and TOOTHPASTE and used in cooking as a HERB: *lamb with mint sauce* **2** [C] a type of sweet that tastes of PEPPERMINT **3** [sing.] the place where money in the form of coins and notes is made by the government
▸ **mint** *verb* [T]: *freshly minted coins*

minuet /ˌmɪnjuˈet/ *noun* [C] (MUSIC) a slow formal dance that was popular in the seventeenth and eighteenth centuries; a piece of music for this dance

minus¹ /ˈmaɪnəs/ *prep.* **1** (MATHEMATICS) (used in sums) less; SUBTRACT; take away: *6 minus 2 is 4 (6–2=4).* **OPP plus¹** ᗡ look at **subtract** **2** (MATHEMATICS) (used about a number) below zero: *The temperature will fall to minus 10.* **3** (*informal*) without sth that was there before: *We're going to be minus a car for a while.*

minus² /ˈmaɪnəs/ *noun* [C] **1** (*also* 'minus sign) (MATHEMATICS) the symbol (–), used in mathematics to show that a number is below zero or that you should take the second number away from the first **OPP plus³** **2** (*also* 'minus point) (*informal*) a negative quality; a disadvantage: *Let's consider the pluses and minuses of moving out of the city.* **OPP plus³**

minus³ /ˈmaɪnəs/ *adj.* **1** [only before noun] (MATHEMATICS) lower than zero: *a minus figure* **2** [not before noun] (EDUCATION) (used in a system of marks given for school work) slightly lower than: *I got A minus (A–) for my essay.* **OPP plus²**

minuscule /ˈmɪnəskjuːl/ *adj.* extremely small

minute¹ ⟨ **A1** /ˈmɪnɪt/ *noun* **1** [C] (*abbr.* min.) one of the 60 parts that make up one hour; 60 seconds: *It's twelve minutes to nine.* ◇ *He phoned ten minutes ago.* ◇ *The programme lasts for about 50 minutes.* **2** [sing.] (*informal*) a very short time; a moment: *Just/Wait a minute* (= wait)*! You've forgotten your notes.* ◇ *Have you got a minute? — I'd like to talk to you.* ◇ *I'll be with you in a minute.* **3** the minutes [pl.] (BUSINESS) a written record of what is said and decided at a meeting ᗡ note at **meeting** **4** [C] each of the 60 equal parts of a degree, used in measuring angles: *37 degrees 30 minutes (37° 30')*
IDM **(at) any minute/moment (now)** (*informal*) very soon: *The plane should be landing any minute now.* **the last minute/moment** → **LAST¹** **the minute/moment (that)** as soon as: *I'll tell him you rang the minute (that) he gets here.* **this minute** immediately; now: *I don't know what I'm going to do yet — I've just this minute found out.* **up to the minute** (*informal*) having the most recent information: *For up-to-the-minute information on flight times, phone this number…*

minute² /ˈmɪnɪt/ *verb* [T, often passive] (BUSINESS) to write sth that is said in a meeting in the official record: *I'd like that last remark to be minuted.*

minute³ ⟨+ **C1** /maɪˈnjuːt/ *adj.* (minuter; minutest) **1** very small: *I couldn't read his writing. It was minute!* **SYN tiny** **2** very exact or accurate: *She was able to describe the man in minute detail/the minutest detail.*

miracle ⟨+ **C1** /ˈmɪrəkl/ *noun* **1** [C] (RELIGION) a wonderful event that seems impossible and that is believed to be caused by God or a god **2** [sing.] a lucky thing that happens that you did not expect or think was possible: *It's a miracle (that) nobody was killed in the crash.*
IDM **work/perform miracles** to achieve very good results: *The new diet and exercise programme have worked miracles for her.*

miraculous /mɪˈrækjələs/ *adj.* completely unexpected and very lucky: *She's made a miraculous recovery.*
▸ **miraculously** *adv.*

mirage /ˈmɪrɑːʒ, ˈmɪrɑːʒ/ *noun* [C] something that you think you see in very hot weather, for example water in a desert, which is not really there

mirror ⟨ **A2** /ˈmɪrə(r)/ *noun* [C] a piece of special flat glass that you can look into in order to see yourself or what is behind you: *to look in the mirror* ◇ *a rear-view mirror* (= in a car, so that the driver can see what is behind) ◇ *a mirror image* ᗡ picture at **microscope, periscope, reflection** ❶ A mirror **reflects** images. What you see in a mirror is a **reflection**. ▸ **mirror** *verb* [T]: *The trees were mirrored in the lake.*

'mirror site (*also* mirror) *noun* [C] (COMPUTING) a copy of a busy website that is created to reduce the number of people visiting the main website

mirth /mɜːθ/ *noun* [U] happiness, fun and the sound of people laughing **SYN merriment**

mis- /mɪs/ *prefix* (in verbs and nouns) bad or wrong; badly or wrongly: *misunderstand* ◇ *misbehave*

misapprehension /ˌmɪsæprɪˈhenʃn/ *noun* [U, C] (*formal*) a wrong idea about sth, or sth you believe to be true that is not true: *I was under the misapprehension that this course was for beginners.*

misbehave /ˌmɪsbɪˈheɪv/ *verb* [I] to behave badly **OPP behave** ▸ **misbehaviour** (*BrE*) (*AmE* misbehavior) /-jə(r)/ *noun* [U]

misc. *abbr.* (in writing) = MISCELLANEOUS

miscalculate /ˌmɪsˈkælkjuleɪt/ *verb* [I, T] to make a mistake in calculating or judging a situation, an amount, etc. ▸ **miscalculation** /ˌmɪskælkjuˈleɪʃn/ *noun* [C, U]

miscarriage /ˈmɪskærɪdʒ, ˌmɪsˈkærɪdʒ/ *noun* [C, U] (**HEALTH**) giving birth to a baby a long time before it is ready to be born, with the result that it cannot live ⊃ look at **abortion**
IDM **a miscarriage of justice** an occasion when sb is punished for a crime that they did not do

miscarry /ˌmɪsˈkæri/ *verb* [I, I] (miscarrying; miscarries; *pt, pp* miscarried) (**HEALTH**) to give birth to a baby before it is ready to be born, with the result that it cannot live

miscellaneous /ˌmɪsəˈleɪniəs/ *adj.* (*abbr.* misc.) consisting of many different types or things: *a box of miscellaneous items for sale*

mischief /ˈmɪstʃɪf/ *noun* [U] bad behaviour (usually of children) that is not very serious: *The children are always getting into mischief.*

mischievous /ˈmɪstʃɪvəs/ *adj.* (usually used about children) liking to behave badly and embarrassing or annoying people ▸ **mischievously** *adv.*

miscible /ˈmɪsəbl/ *adj.* (**CHEMISTRY**) (used about liquids) that can be mixed together **OPP** **immiscible**

misconception /ˌmɪskənˈsepʃn/ *noun* [C, U] a wrong idea or understanding of sth: *It is a popular misconception* (= many people wrongly believe) *that people need meat to be healthy.*

misconduct /ˌmɪsˈkɒndʌkt/ *noun* [U] (*formal*) unacceptable behaviour, especially by a professional person: *The doctor was dismissed for gross* (= very serious) *misconduct.*

misconstrue /ˌmɪskənˈstruː/ *verb* [T] ~ **sth (as sth)** (*formal*) to understand sb's words or actions wrongly ⊃ look at **construe**

misdemeanour (*AmE* misdemeanor) /ˌmɪsdɪˈmiːnə(r)/ *noun* [C] **1** something slightly bad or wrong that a person does **2** (*AmE*) (**LAW**) a crime that is not very serious = FELONY

miser /ˈmaɪzə(r)/ *noun* [C] a person who loves having a lot of money but hates spending it ▸ **miserly** *adj.*

miserable ⓘ+ 🄱🄲 /ˈmɪzrəbl/ *adj.* **1** very unhappy: *Oh dear, you look miserable. What's wrong?* **2** unpleasant; making you feel unhappy: *What miserable weather!* (= grey, cold and wet) **SYN** **dismal** **3** too small or of bad quality: *I was offered a miserable salary so I didn't take the job.* ▸ **miserably** /-bli/ *adv.*: *I stared miserably out of the window.* ◇ *He failed miserably as an actor.*

misery ⓘ+ 🄲🄸 /ˈmɪzəri/ *noun* [U, C] (*pl.* -ies) great unhappiness or suffering: *I couldn't bear to see him in such misery.* ◇ *the miseries of war*
IDM **put sb out of his/her misery** (*informal*) to stop sb worrying about sth by telling the person what they want to know: *Put me out of my misery — did I pass or not?* **put sth out of its misery** to kill an animal because it has an illness or injury that cannot be treated

misfire /ˌmɪsˈfaɪə(r)/ *verb* [I] to fail to have the intended result or effect: *The plan misfired.*

misfit /ˈmɪsfɪt/ *noun* [C] a person who is not accepted by other people, especially because their behaviour or ideas are very different

misfortune /ˌmɪsˈfɔːtʃuːn/ *noun* [U, C] (*formal*) (an event, accident, etc. that brings) bad luck or disaster: *I hope I don't ever have the misfortune to meet him again.*

misgiving /ˌmɪsˈɡɪvɪŋ/ *noun* [C, usually pl., U] ~ **(about sth/doing sth)** a feeling of doubt or worry about what might happen: *I had serious misgivings about leaving him on his own.*

misguided /ˌmɪsˈɡaɪdɪd/ *adj.* wrong because you have understood or judged a situation badly: *a misguided attempt to help*

mishap /ˈmɪshæp/ *noun* [C, U] a small accident or piece of bad luck that does not have serious results: *to have a slight mishap*

misinform /ˌmɪsɪnˈfɔːm/ *verb* [T, often passive] to give sb the wrong information: *I think you've been misinformed — no one is going to lose their job.*

misinterpret /ˌmɪsɪnˈtɜːprət/ *verb* [T] ~ **sth (as sth)** to understand sth wrongly: *His comments were misinterpreted as a criticism of the project.* **OPP** **interpret** ▸ **misinterpretation** /ˌmɪsɪntɜːprəˈteɪʃn/ *noun* [U, C]: *Parts of the speech were open to misinterpretation* (= easy to understand wrongly).

misjudge /ˌmɪsˈdʒʌdʒ/ *verb* [T, I] **1** to form a wrong opinion of sb/sth, usually in a way that is unfair to them or it **2** to guess time, distance, etc. wrongly: *He completely misjudged the speed of the other car and almost crashed.* ▸ **misjudgement** (*also* misjudgment) *noun* [C, U]

mislay /ˌmɪsˈleɪ/ *verb* [T] (*pt, pp* mislaid /-ˈleɪd/) (*formal*) to lose sth, usually for a short time, because you cannot remember where you put it

mislead /ˌmɪsˈliːd/ *verb* [T, I] (*pt, pp* misled /-ˈled/) to make sb have the wrong idea or opinion about sb/sth ▸ **misleading** ⓘ+ 🄲🄸 *adj.*: *a misleading advertisement*

mismanage /ˌmɪsˈmænɪdʒ/ *verb* [T] to manage or organize sth badly ▸ **mismanagement** *noun* [U]

misogynist /mɪˈsɒdʒɪnɪst/ *noun* [C] (*formal*) a person who hates women ▸ **misogynistic** /mɪˌsɒdʒɪˈnɪstɪk/ (*also* misogynist) *adj.* ▸ **misogyny** /mɪˈsɒdʒɪni/ *noun* [U]

misplaced /ˌmɪsˈpleɪst/ *adj.* given to sb/sth that is not suitable or good enough to have it: *misplaced loyalty*

misprint /ˈmɪsprɪnt/ *noun* [C] a mistake that is made when a book, etc. is printed

mispronounce /ˌmɪsprəˈnaʊns/ *verb* [T] to say a word or letter wrongly: *People always mispronounce my surname.* ▸ **mispronunciation** /ˌmɪsprənʌnsiˈeɪʃn/ *noun* [C, U]

misread /ˌmɪsˈriːd/ *verb* [T] (*pt, pp* misread /-ˈred/) ~ **sth (as sth)** **1** to understand sth wrongly: *He misread my silence as a refusal.* **2** to read something wrongly: *I misread the timetable and missed the last bus home.* ◇ *I misread 'Ms' as 'Mr'.*

misrepresent /ˌmɪsˌreprɪˈzent/ *verb* [T, often passive] ~ **sb/sth (as sb/sth)** (*formal*) to give a wrong description of sb/sth: *In the newspaper article they were misrepresented as uncaring parents.* ▸ **misrepresentation** /ˌmɪsˌreprɪzenˈteɪʃn/ *noun* [C, U]

miss¹ 🄰🄰 /mɪs/ *verb*
• NOT GO **1** [T] to arrive too late for sth; to fail to go to or do sth: *Hurry up or you'll miss the plane!* ◇ *Of course I'm coming to your wedding. I wouldn't miss it for the world* (= used to emphasize that you really want to go to sth).
• NOT HIT/CATCH **2** [T, I] to fail to hit, catch, etc. sth: *The bullet narrowly missed his heart.* ◇ *She tried to catch the ball but she missed.*
• NOT SEE/HEAR **3** [T] to not see, hear, understand, etc. sb/sth: *The house is on the corner so you can't miss it.* ◇ *They completely missed the point of what I was saying.* ◇ *My Mum will know there's something wrong. She doesn't miss much.*
• FEEL SAD **4** [T] to feel sad because sb is not with you any more, or because you have not got or cannot do sth that you once had or did: *I'll miss you terribly when*

you go away. ◇ *What did you miss most when you lived abroad?*

• NOTICE SB/STH NOT THERE **5** [T] to notice that sb/sth is not where they or it should be: *When did you first miss your handbag?*

• AVOID STH BAD **6** [T] to avoid sth unpleasant: *If we leave now, we'll miss the rush-hour traffic.*

PHR V **miss sb/sth out** to not include sb/sth: *You've missed out several important points in your report.*

miss out (on sth) to not have a chance to have or do sth: *You'll miss out on all the fun if you stay at home.*

miss² /mɪs/ *noun* [C] **1** Miss a title that comes before the name of a woman who is not married **2** a failure to hit, catch or reach sth: *After several misses he finally managed to hit the target.*

IDM **give sth a miss** (*especially BrE, informal*) to decide not to do or have sth: *I think I'll give aerobics a miss tonight.* **a near miss** → NEAR¹

▼ CULTURE

Miss, Mrs, Ms and **Mr** are all titles that are used in front of sb's family name, NOT his/her first name, unless it is included with the family name: *Is there a Miss (Emma) Hudson here?* NOT: ~~Miss Emma~~

missile ʔ⁺ **C1** /'mɪsaɪl/ *noun* [C] **1** a powerful exploding weapon that can be sent long distances through the air: *nuclear missiles* **2** an object that is thrown at sb in order to hurt them: *The rioters threw missiles such as bottles and stones.*

missing ʔ **A2** /'mɪsɪŋ/ *adj.* **1** lost, or not in the right or usual place: *a missing person* ◇ *Two files have gone missing from my office.* **2** (used about a person) not present after a battle, an accident, etc. but not known to have been killed: *Many soldiers were listed as missing in action.* **3** not included, often when it should have been: *Fill in the missing words in the text.*

mission ʔ **B2** /'mɪʃn/ *noun* [C]

• OFFICIAL JOB/GROUP **1** an important official job that sb is sent somewhere to do, especially to another country: *Your mission is to send back information about the enemy's movements.* **2** a group of people who are sent to a foreign country to perform a special task: *a British trade mission to China*

• JOURNEY **3** a special journey made by a SPACECRAFT or military aircraft: *a mission to the moon*

• PLACE **4** (**RELIGION**) a place where people are taught about the Christian religion, given medical help, etc. by MISSIONARIES

• DUTY **5** a particular task that you feel it is your duty to do: *Her work with the poor was more than just a job — it was her mission in life.*

missionary /'mɪʃənri/ *noun* [C] (*pl.* -ies) (**RELIGION**) a person who is sent to a foreign country to teach about the Christian religion

mission statement *noun* [C] (**BUSINESS**) an official statement of the aims of a company or an organization

misspell /ˌmɪs'spel/ *verb* [T] (*pt, pp* misspelled, misspelt /-'spelt/) to spell sth wrongly

mist¹ /mɪst/ *noun* [U, C] a cloud made of very small drops of water in the air just above the ground, that makes it difficult to see: *The fields were covered in mist.* ◯ note at **weather¹** ▶ misty *adj.*: *a misty morning* ◯ look at **foggy**

mist² /mɪst/ *verb*

PHR V **mist (sth) up/over** to cover or be covered with very small drops of water that make it difficult to see: *My glasses keep misting up.*

mistake¹ ʔ **A1** /mɪ'steɪk/ *noun* [C] **~ (of doing sth); (it is a) ~ (to do sth)** something that you think or do that is wrong: *Try not to make any mistakes in your essays.*

◇ *a spelling mistake* ◇ *I made the mistake of leaving money on my desk.* ◇ *It was a big mistake to trust her.* ◯ note at **error**

IDM **by mistake** as a result of being careless: *The terrorists shot the wrong man by mistake.*

mistake² ʔ **B2** /mɪ'steɪk/ *verb* [T] (*pt* mistook /-'stʊk/; *pp* mistaken /-'steɪkən/) to be wrong about sth: *I think you've mistaken my meaning.*

PHR V **mistake sb/sth for sb/sth** to think wrongly that sb/sth is sb/sth else: *I'm sorry, I mistook you for a friend of mine.*

mistaken /mɪ'steɪkən/ *adj.* wrong; not correct: *a case of mistaken identity* ◇ *a mistaken belief/idea* ▶ mistakenly *adv.*

Mister /'mɪstə(r)/ *noun* [C] (not often in writing) = MR

mistletoe /'mɪsltəʊ, 'mɪzl-/ *noun* [U] a plant with white BERRIES that grows on other trees and is often used as a decoration at Christmas: *the tradition of kissing under the mistletoe*

mistook /mɪ'stʊk/ past tense of **mistake¹**

mistreat /ˌmɪs'triːt/ *verb* [T] to be cruel to a person or animal: *The owner of the zoo was accused of mistreating the animals.* ▶ mistreatment *noun* [U]

mistress /'mɪstrəs/ *noun* [C] **1** a man's (usually a married man's) mistress is a woman that he is having a regular sexual relationship with and who is not his wife **2** (*formal*) a woman who is in authority or control

mistrust /ˌmɪs'trʌst/ *verb* [T] to have no confidence in sb/sth because you think they or it may be harmful: *I always mistrust politicians who smile too much.* ◯ look at **distrust** ▶ mistrust *noun* [U, sing.]: *She has a deep mistrust of strangers.* ◯ look at **distrust**

misty /'mɪsti/ *adj.* with a lot of MIST

misunderstand /ˌmɪsʌndə'stænd/ *verb* [T, I] (*pt, pp* misunderstood /-'stʊd/) to understand sb/sth wrongly: *I misunderstood the instructions and answered too many questions.*

misunderstanding /ˌmɪsʌndə'stændɪŋ/ *noun* **1** [C, U] a situation in which sb/sth is not understood correctly: *The contract is written in both languages to avoid any misunderstanding.* **2** [C] a slight DISAGREEMENT or argument

misuse /ˌmɪs'juːz/ *verb* [T] (*formal*) to use sth in the wrong way or for the wrong purpose: *These chemicals can be dangerous if misused.* ▶ misuse /-'juːs/ *noun* [U, C, usually sing.]

mite /maɪt/ *noun* [C] a very small creature like a spider that lives on plants and animals and in carpets, etc.

mitigate /'mɪtɪgeɪt/ *verb* [T] (*formal*) to make sth less serious, painful, unpleasant, etc.

mitigating /'mɪtɪgeɪtɪŋ/ *adj.* (*formal*) [only before noun] providing a reason that explains sb's actions or why they committed a crime, which makes it easier to understand so that the punishment may be less HARSH: *mitigating circumstances/factors*

mitigation /ˌmɪtɪ'geɪʃn/ *noun* [U] (*formal*) a reduction in how unpleasant, serious, etc. sth is

IDM **in mitigation** (**LAW**) with the aim of making a crime seem less serious: *In mitigation, the defence lawyer said his client was seriously depressed at the time of the assault.*

mitochondrion /ˌmaɪtəʊ'kɒndrɪən/ *noun* [C] (*pl.* mitochondria /-drɪə/) (**BIOLOGY**) a small part found in most cells, in which the energy in food is released ◯ picture at **cell, fertilization**

mitosis /maɪˈtəʊsɪs/ *noun* [U] (**BIOLOGY**) the division of a cell of the body that results in two cells, each with the same number of CHROMOSOMES as the original cell ⊃ look at **meiosis**

mitre (*BrE*) (*AmE* **miter**) /ˈmaɪtə(r)/ *noun* [C] **1** (**RELIGION**) a tall pointed hat worn by BISHOPS (= Christian priests with a high position in the church) at special ceremonies as a symbol of their position and authority **2** (*also* **'mitre joint**) a corner JOINT, formed by two pieces of wood each cut at an angle, as in a picture frame ⊃ picture at **dovetail²**

mitten /ˈmɪtn/ *noun* [C] a type of glove that has one part for the THUMB and another part for all four fingers ⊃ look at **glove**

mix¹ ⚹ **B1** ⓦ /mɪks/ *verb* **1** [I, T] ~ (**A**) (**with B**); ~ (**A and B**) (**together**) if two or more substances mix or if you mix them, they combine to form a new substance: *Oil and water don't mix.* ◇ *If you mix yellow with blue you get green.* ◇ *Mix all the ingredients together in a bowl.* ◇ *to mix cement* (= to make CEMENT by mixing other substances) **2** [T] to combine different recordings of voices and/or instruments to produce a single piece of music **3** [I] ~ (**with sb**) to be with and talk to other people: *He mixes with all types of people at work.* **IDM** **be/get mixed up in sth** to be/become involved in sth bad or unpleasant **PHR V** **mix sth up** to put sth in the wrong order: *He was so nervous that he dropped his speech and got the pages all mixed up.* **mix sb/sth up** (**with sb/sth**) to confuse sb/sth with sb/sth else: *I always get him mixed up with his brother.*

mix² ⚹ **B1** /mɪks/ *noun* **1** [C, usually sing.] a group of different types of people or things: *The school has a good social and ethnic mix.* **2** [C, U] a special powder that contains all the substances needed to make sth. You add water or another liquid to this powder: *cake mix*

mixed ⚹ **B2** /mɪkst/ *adj.* **1** being both good and bad: *I have mixed feelings about leaving my job.* **2** made or consisting of different types of person or thing: *Was your school mixed or single-sex?* ◇ *a mixed salad*

mixed 'farming *noun* [U] (**AGRICULTURE**) a system of farming in which farmers both grow crops and keep animals

mixed 'media *noun* [U] (**ART**) the use of various methods or materials in art

mixed 'number *noun* [C] (**MATHEMATICS**) a number consisting of a whole number and a PROPER FRACTION, for example 3¼

mixed-'race *adj.* (*also* **biracial** *especially in AmE*) involving people who belong to two different human groups: *a mixed-race child* (= with parents of different races)

mixed 'up *adj.* (*informal*) confused because of emotional problems: *He has been very mixed up since his parents' divorce.*

mixer /ˈmɪksə(r)/ *noun* [C] a machine that is used for mixing sth: *a food/cement mixer*

mixture ⚹ **B1** /ˈmɪkstʃə(r)/ *noun* **1** [C, usually sing.] a combination of different things: *Monkeys eat a mixture of leaves and fruit.* **2** [C, U] a substance that is made by mixing other substances together: *cake mixture* ◇ *a mixture of eggs, flour and milk* ⊃ picture at **filtration** **3** [C] (**CHEMISTRY**) a combination of two or more substances that mix together without any chemical reaction taking place ⊃ look at **compound¹** (2)

'mix-up *noun* [C] (*informal*) a mistake in the planning or organization of sth: *There was a mix-up and we were given the wrong ticket.*

ml *abbr.* (in writing) (*pl.* **ml, mls**) = MILLILITRE: *contents 75ml*

mm *abbr.* (in writing) (*pl.* **mm**) = MILLIMETRE: *a 35mm camera*

moan /məʊn/ *verb* [I] **1** ~ (**in/with sth**) to make a low sound because you are in pain, very sad, etc: *to moan with pain* **2** ~ (**about sth**) (*informal*) to keep saying what is wrong about sth; to complain: *The English are always moaning about the weather.* ▸ **moan** *noun* [C]

moat /məʊt/ *noun* [C] (**HISTORY**) a hole that was dug around a castle and filled with water to make it difficult for enemies to attack ⊃ picture at **drawbridge**

mob¹ ⚹+ **C1** /mɒb/ *noun* [C + sing./pl. verb] a large crowd of people that may become violent or cause trouble

mob² /mɒb/ *verb* [T] (-bb-) to form a large crowd around sb, for example in order to see or touch them: *The band was mobbed by fans as they left the hotel.*

mobile¹ ⚹ **A2** ⓦ /ˈməʊbaɪl/ *adj.* **1** connected with mobile phones, tablets, etc: *What's your mobile number?* ◇ *mobile devices/apps* **2** able to move or be moved easily: *Lifts make it easier for less mobile people to access the platforms.* **OPP** **immobile** ▸ **mobility** ⚹+ **C1** ⓦ /məʊˈbɪləti/ *noun* [U]

mobile² ⚹ **A2** /ˈməʊbaɪl/ *noun* [C] **1** = MOBILE PHONE **2** a decoration that you hang from the ceiling and that moves when the air around it moves

mobile de'vice *noun* [C] (**COMPUTING**) any small electronic device that will fit into your pocket, such as a smartphone

mobile 'home *noun* [C] **1** (*BrE*) (*AmE* **trailer**) a large CARAVAN that can be moved, sometimes with wheels, that is usually parked in one place and used for living in **2** (*especially AmE*) (*AmE also* **trailer**) a small building for people to live in that is made in a factory and moved to a permanent place

mobile 'phone (*also* **mobile**) (*both BrE*) (*also* **cell phone**, *informal* **cell** *especially in AmE*) *noun* [C] a phone that you can carry around with you

mobilize ⚹+ **C1** ⓦ (*BrE also* **-ise**) /ˈməʊbəlaɪz/ *verb* **1** [T] to organize people or things to do sth: *They mobilized the local residents to oppose the new development.* **2** [T, I] (used about the army, NAVY, etc.) to get ready for war **OPP** **immobilize**

Möbius strip (*also* **Moebius strip**) /ˈmɜːbiəs strɪp/ *noun* [C] (**MATHEMATICS**) a surface with one continuous side, formed by joining the ends of a STRIP of material after turning one end through 180 degrees

Möbius strip

moccasin /ˈmɒkəsɪn/ *noun* [C] a flat shoe that is made from soft leather and has large STITCHES around the front, of a type originally worn by Native Americans

mock¹ /mɒk/ *verb* [T, I] (*formal*) to laugh at sb/sth in an unkind way or to make other people laugh at them or it

mock² /mɒk/ *adj.* [only before noun] not real or sincere: *mock surprise.* ◇ *a mock* (= practice) *exam*

mock³ /mɒk/ *noun* [C, usually pl.] (**EDUCATION**) (in the UK) a practice exam that you do before the official one

mockery /ˈmɒkəri/ *noun* (*pl.* -ies) **1** [U, C] comments or actions that are intended to make sb/sth look silly or stupid: *She couldn't stand any more of their mockery.* **SYN** ridicule **2** [C, usually sing.] an action, a decision, etc. that is a failure and that is not as it should be: *It was a mockery of a trial.*
IDM make a mockery of sth to make sth seem silly or without effect: *The trial made a mockery of justice* (= the trial was not fair).

'**mock-up** *noun* [C] a model of sth that shows what it will look like or how it will work

modal /ˈməʊdl/ (*also* ˌmodal ˈverb*) *noun* [C] (**GRAMMAR**) a verb, for example *might*, *can* or *must*, that is used with another verb for expressing possibility, permission, intention, etc.

mode ʔ+ **B2** ⑩ /məʊd/ *noun* [C] **1** a type of sth or way of doing sth: *a mode of transport/life* **2** one of the ways in which a machine can work: *Switch the camera to automatic mode.* **3** (**MUSIC**) a particular arrangement of notes in music, for example the musical SCALE system: *major/minor mode* **4** (**MATHEMATICS**) the most common number or value in a group of numbers

model[1] ʔ **A1** ⑩ /ˈmɒdl/ *noun* [C]
• COPY **1** a copy of sth that is usually smaller than the real thing: *a model aeroplane*
• MACHINE **2** one of the machines, vehicles, etc. that is made by a particular company: *The latest models are on display at the show.*
• GOOD EXAMPLE **3** a person or thing that is a good example to copy: *a model student* ◇ *Children often use older brothers or sisters as **role models*** (= copy the way they behave).
• FASHION **4** a person who is employed to wear clothes at a fashion show or for magazine photos
• FOR AN ARTIST **5** (**ART**) a person who is painted, drawn or photographed by an artist

model[2] ʔ **B1** ⑩ /ˈmɒdl/ *verb* (-ll-, *AmE* -l-) **1** [T] to create a copy or description of an activity, a situation, etc. before dealing with the real thing: *We can accurately model the development process.* **2** [T] to shape a material in order to make sth: *This clay is difficult to model.* **3** [I, T] to wear and show clothes at a fashion show or for photos: *to model swimsuits*
PHR V model sth/yourself on sb/sth to make sth/ yourself similar to sth/sb else: *The house is modelled on a Roman villa.*

modelling ⑩ (*BrE*) (*AmE* modeling) /ˈmɒdlɪŋ/ *noun* [U] the work of a fashion model

modem /ˈməʊdem/ *noun* [C] (**COMPUTING**) a piece of equipment that connects two or more computers together by means of a phone line so that information can go from one to the other

moderate[1] ʔ+ /ˈmɒdərət/ *adj.* **1** being, having, using, etc. neither too much nor too little of sth: *a moderate speed* ◇ *We've had a moderate amount of success.* **2** having or showing opinions, especially about politics, that are not extreme: *moderate policies/views* ◇ look at **extreme** (2), **radical**[1] (2)
▶ moderately *adv.*: *His career has been moderately successful.*

moderate[2] /ˈmɒdəreɪt/ *verb* **1** [I, T] to become less strong or extreme; to make sth less strong or extreme: *The union moderated its original demands.* **2** [T, I] to be in charge of a discussion and make sure it is fair: *Each discussion was moderated by a subject expert.* **3** [T] (**COMPUTING**) to be responsible for making sure that offensive material is not published on a website; to remove offensive material from a website: *to moderate an online forum* ◇ *Comments on this article will be moderated.*

moderate[3] /ˈmɒdərət/ *noun* [C] (**POLITICS**) a person whose opinions, especially about politics, are not extreme ◇ look at **extremist**

moderation /ˌmɒdəˈreɪʃn/ *noun* [U] **1** the quality of being reasonable and not being extreme: *Alcohol can harm unborn babies even if it's taken **in moderation***. **2** (**EDUCATION**) the process of making sure that the same standards are used by different people in marking exams, etc.

moderator /ˈmɒdəreɪtə(r)/ *noun* [C] **1** (**EDUCATION**) a person whose job is to make sure that the same standards are used by different people in marking exams, etc. **2** a person who prevents offensive material from being published on a website **3** a person whose job is to make sure that contributions to a discussion are fair, especially on the internet

modern ʔ **A1** ⑩ /ˈmɒdn/ *adj.* **1** [only before noun] of the present or recent times: *Pollution is one of the major problems in the modern world.* ◇ *modern history* **2** [only before noun] (**ARTS AND MEDIA**) (used about styles of art, music, etc.) new and different from traditional styles: *modern jazz/architecture/art* **3** using all the newest methods, equipment, designs, etc: *It is one of the most modern hospitals in the country.* **SYN** up to date ◇ look at **old-fashioned** (1)

ˌmodern-ˈday *adj.* [only before noun] **1** of the present time: *modern-day America* **SYN** contemporary[1] **2** used to describe a modern form of sb/sth, usually sb/ sth bad or unpleasant, that existed in the past: *It has been called modern-day slavery.*

modernism /ˈmɒdənɪzəm/ *noun* [U] **1** modern ideas or methods **2** (**ARCHITECTURE**, **ARTS AND MEDIA**) a style and movement in art, architecture and literature popular in the middle of the twentieth century in which modern ideas, methods and materials were used rather than traditional ones ◇ look at **postmodernism**
▶ modernist /-nɪst/ *noun* [C], *adj.* [only before noun]: *modernist art*

modernity ⑩ /məˈdɜːnəti/ *noun* [U] the condition of being new and modern

modernize (*BrE also* -ise) /ˈmɒdənaɪz/ *verb* [T] to make sth suitable for today using new methods, styles, etc. ▶ modernization ⑩ (*BrE also* -isation) /ˌmɒdənaɪˈzeɪʃn/ *noun* [U]: *The house is large but is in need of modernization.*

ˌmodern ˈlanguage *noun* [pl.] a language that is spoken now and that you study at school or college

modest ʔ+ **B2** /ˈmɒdɪst/ *adj.* **1** not talking too much about your own abilities, good qualities, etc: *She got the best results in the exam but she was too modest to tell anyone.* ◇ look at **humble**[1] (1), **proud** (2) **2** not very large, expensive, etc: *a modest pay increase* **3** (used about a woman's clothes) not showing much of the body ▶ modestly *adv.* ▶ modesty /-dəsti/ *noun* [U]

modifier /ˈmɒdɪfaɪə(r)/ *noun* [C] (**GRAMMAR**) a word, such as an adjective or adverb, that describes another word, or changes its meaning in some way ◇ look at **intensifier**

modify ʔ **B2** ⑩ /ˈmɒdɪfaɪ/ *verb* [T] (modifying; modifies; *pt, pp* modified) to change sth slightly
▶ modification ʔ+ **C1** /ˌmɒdɪfɪˈkeɪʃn/ *noun* [C, U]

modular /ˈmɒdjələ(r)/ *adj.* **1** (**EDUCATION**) (used about a course of study, especially at a British university or college) consisting of separate units from which students may choose several: *a modular course* **2** (used about machines, buildings, etc.) consisting of separate parts or units that can be joined together

module **⑤** /ˈmɒdjuːl/ *noun* [C] **1** (**EDUCATION**) a unit that can form part of a course of study, especially at a college or university in the UK: *You must complete three modules* (= courses that you study) *in your first year.* **2** (**COMPUTING**) a unit of a computer system or program that has a particular function **3** one of a set of separate parts or units that can be joined together to make a machine, a piece of furniture, a building, etc. **4** a unit of a SPACECRAFT that can function independently of the main part: *The lunar module separated from the spacecraft to land on the moon.*

Moebius strip /ˈmɜːbiəs strɪp/ = MÖBIUS STRIP

mohair /ˈməʊheə(r)/ *noun* [U] very soft wool that comes from a type of GOAT

Mohammed /məˈhæmɪd/ = MUHAMMAD

moist /mɔɪst/ *adj.* slightly wet: *Her eyes were moist with tears.* ◇ *Keep the soil moist or the plant will die.* ▶ moisten /ˈmɔɪsn/ *verb* [T, I]

moisture /ˈmɔɪstʃə(r)/ *noun* [U] water in small drops on a surface, in the air, etc.

moisturize (*BrE also* -ise) /ˈmɔɪstʃəraɪz/ *verb* [I, T] to put special cream on your skin to make it less dry

moisturizer (*BrE also* -iser) /ˈmɔɪstʃəraɪzə(r)/ *noun* [C, U] a special cream that you put on your skin to make it less dry

molar /ˈməʊlə(r)/ *noun* [C] (**ANATOMY**) one of the large teeth at the back of the mouth ◌ look at **canine²**, **incisor, premolar** ◌ picture at **tooth**

molasses /məˈlæsɪz/ (*AmE*) = TREACLE

mold /məʊld/ (*AmE*) = MOULD¹

molding /ˈməʊldɪŋ/ = MOULDING

moldy /ˈməʊldi/ (*AmE*) = MOULDY

mole /məʊl/ *noun* [C] **1** a small animal with dark fur that lives underground and is almost blind ◌ picture at **food web 2** a small dark spot on sb's skin that never goes away ◌ look at **freckle 3** (*informal*) a person who works in one organization and gives secret information to another organization **SYN spy¹** **4** (**CHEMISTRY**) a unit for measuring the amount of a substance

molecule /ˈmɒlɪkjuːl/ *noun* [C] (**CHEMISTRY**) the smallest unit into which a substance can be divided without changing its chemical nature ◌ look at **atom** ▶ molecular /məˈlekjələ(r)/ *adj.* [only before noun]

molest /məˈlest/ *verb* [T] (**LAW**) to attack sb, especially a child, in a sexual way

mollify /ˈmɒlɪfaɪ/ *verb* [T] (mollifying; mollifies; *pt, pp* mollified) (*formal*) to make sb feel less angry or upset: *His explanation failed to mollify her.*

mollusc (*BrE*) (*AmE* mollusk) /ˈmɒləsk/ *noun* [C] (**BIOLOGY**) any creature with a soft body that is not divided into different sections, and usually with a hard outer shell. Molluscs can live either on land or in water: *Snails, slugs and mussels are molluscs.* ◌ look at **shellfish**

molt /məʊlt/ (*AmE*) = MOULT

molten /ˈməʊltən/ *adj.* (used about metal, rock or glass) made liquid by very great heat ◌ picture at **rock¹**

molybdenum /məˈlɪbdənəm/ *noun* [U] (*symb.* Mo) (**CHEMISTRY**) a chemical element. Molybdenum is a silver-grey metal that breaks easily. **❶** For more information on the periodic table of elements, look at the **Reference Section** of this dictionary.

mom /mɒm/ (*AmE*) = MUM

moment **Ĩ A1 ⑤** /ˈməʊmənt/ *noun* **1** [C] a very short period of time: *One moment, please* (= please wait). ◇ *Joe left just a few moments ago.* **2** [sing.] a particular

point in time: *Just at that moment my mother arrived.* ◇ *the moment of birth/death*

IDM (**at**) **any minute/moment** (**now**) → MINUTE¹ **at the moment** now: *I'm afraid she's busy at the moment. Can I take a message?* **for the moment/ present** for a short time; for now: *I'm not very happy at work but I'll stay there for the moment.* **in a moment** very soon: *Just wait here. I'll be back in a moment.* **the last minute/moment** → LAST¹ **the minute/moment** (**that**) → MINUTE¹ **on the spur of the moment** → SPUR¹

momentary /ˈməʊməntri/ *adj.* lasting for a very short time **SYN brief¹** ▶ momentarily /-trəli/ *adv.*

momentous /məˈmentəs/ *adj.* very important: *a momentous decision/event/change*

momentum **Ĩ+ C1** /məˈmentəm/ *noun* [U] (**PHYSICS**) the ability to keep increasing or developing; the force that makes sth move faster and faster: *The environmental movement is gathering momentum.*

mommy /ˈmɒmi/ *noun* [C] (*pl.* -ies) (*AmE*) = MUMMY

Mon. *abbr.* (in writing) = MONDAY

monarch /ˈmɒnək/ *noun* [C] (**POLITICS**) a king or queen

monarchy /ˈmɒnəki/ *noun* (*pl.* -ies) (**POLITICS**) **1** [sing., U] the system of government or rule by a king or queen **2** [C] a country that is governed by a king or queen ◌ look at **republic**

monastery /ˈmɒnəstri/ *noun* [C] (*pl.* -ies) (**RELIGION**) a place where MONKS (= members of a religious group of men) live together ◌ look at **convent**

Monday **Ĩ A1** /ˈmʌndeɪ, -di/ *noun* [C, U] (*abbr.* Mon.) the day of the week after Sunday: *I'm going to see her on Monday.* ◇ (*informal*) *I'll see you Monday.* ◇ *I finish work a bit later on Mondays/on a Monday.* ◇ *Monday morning/afternoon/evening/night* ◇ *last/next Monday* ◇ *a week on Monday/Monday week* (= not next Monday, but the Monday after that) ◇ *The museum is open Monday to Friday, 10.00 till 4.30.* ◇ *Did you see that article about Italy in Monday's paper?*

monetarism /ˈmʌnɪtərɪzəm/ *noun* [U] (**ECONOMICS**) the policy of controlling the amount of money available in a country as a way of keeping the economy strong

monetary /ˈmʌnɪtri/ *adj.* [only before noun] (*formal*) connected with money: *the government's monetary policy* ◌ note at **economic**

monetize (*BrE also* -ise) /ˈmʌnɪtaɪz/ *verb* [T] (**FINANCE**) to earn money from sth, especially a business or sth that a business owns: *Game companies might have to find new ways to monetize their content.* ▶ monetization /ˌmʌnɪtaɪˈzeɪʃn/ *noun* [U]

money **Ĩ A1** /ˈmʌni/ *noun* [U] (**FINANCE**) **1** what you earn by working or selling things, and use to buy things: *Will you earn more money in your new job?* ◇ *The new road will cost a lot of money.* ◇ *If we do the work ourselves we will save money.* ◇ *The government make a huge amount of money out of tobacco tax.* ◌ look at **pocket money 2** coins or paper notes: *I counted the money carefully.*

IDM **be rolling in money/in it** → ROLL² **get your money's worth** to get full value for the money you have spent **put money on sth** to bet money on sth **SYN bet¹**

mongoose /ˈmɒŋguːs/ *noun* [C] (*pl.* mongooses) a small animal with fur that lives in hot countries and kills snakes, RATS, etc.

mongrel /ˈmʌŋɡrəl/ *noun* [C] a dog that has parents of different BREEDS ◌ look at **pedigree¹ (1)**

monitor **Ĩ+ B2** /ˈmɒnɪtə(r)/ *noun* [C] **1** (**COMPUTING**) a machine that shows information or pictures on a screen like a TV; a screen that shows information

monitor² 🔊 **B2** Ⓦ /ˈmɒnɪtə(r)/ *verb* [T] to check, record or test sth regularly for a period of time: *Pollution levels in the lake are closely monitored.*

monk 🔊+ **C1** /mʌŋk/ *noun* [C] (**RELIGION**) a member of a religious group of men who live in a MONASTERY (= a special building) and do not get married or have possessions ➔ look at **nun**

monkey 🔊 **A2** /ˈmʌŋki/ *noun* [C] an animal with a long tail that lives in hot countries and can climb trees ➔ look at **ape¹** ➔ picture at **animal ❶** Chimpanzees and gorillas are apes, although people sometimes call them **monkeys.**
IDM **monkey business** (*informal*) silly or dishonest behaviour

monkey wrench = ADJUSTABLE SPANNER

mono /ˈmɒnəʊ/ *adj.* (used about recorded music or a system for playing it) having the sound coming from one direction only ➔ look at **stereo** (1)

mono- /mɒnəʊ, mɒnə, məˈnɒ/ *prefix* (in nouns and adjectives) one; single: *monorail* ◇ *monogamy* ◇ *monolingual*

monochrome /ˈmɒnəkrəʊm/ *adj.* (used about a photo or picture) using only black, white and shades of grey

monoculture /ˈmɒnəkʌltʃə(r)/ *noun* [U] (**AGRICULTURE**) the practice of growing only one type of crop on a certain area of land

monogamy /məˈnɒɡəmi/ *noun* [U] (**SOCIAL STUDIES**) the fact or custom of being married to, or having a sexual relationship with, only one person at a particular time ➔ look at **bigamy, polygamy** ▸ **monogamous** /-məs/ *adj.*: *a monogamous society*

monolingual /ˌmɒnəˈlɪŋɡwəl/ *adj.* (**LANGUAGE**) speaking or using only one language: *This is a monolingual dictionary.* ➔ look at **bilingual** (1), **multilingual**

monolith /ˈmɒnəlɪθ/ *noun* [C] (**HISTORY**) a large single standing block of stone, especially one that was put there by people living in ancient times ▸ **monolithic** /ˌmɒnəˈlɪθɪk/ *adj.*

monologue (*AmE also* **monolog**) /ˈmɒnəlɒɡ/ *noun* [C] (**ARTS AND MEDIA, LITERATURE**) a long speech by one person, for example in a play ➔ look at **soliloquy**

monomer /ˈmɒnəmə(r)/ *noun* [C] (**CHEMISTRY**) MOLECULES that can join together in a repeating pattern to form a POLYMER ➔ look at **polymer**

monopolize (*BrE also* **-ise**) /məˈnɒpəlaɪz/ *verb* [T] to control sth so that other people cannot share it: *She completely monopolized the conversation. I couldn't get a word in.*

monopoly 🔊+ **C1** /məˈnɒpəli/ *noun* [C] (*pl.* **-ies**) ~ **(on/in sth)** **1** (**BUSINESS**) the control of an industry or a service by only one company; a type of goods or a service that is controlled in this way: *The company has a monopoly on broadcasting international football.* ➔ look at **oligopoly 2** the complete control, possession or use of sth; sth that belongs to only one person or group and is not shared

monorail /ˈmɒnəʊreɪl/ *noun* [C] a railway in which the train runs on a single track, usually high above the ground

monosodium glutamate /ˌmɒnəˌsəʊdiəm ˈɡluːtəmeɪt/ *noun* [U] (*abbr.* MSG) a chemical COMPOUND that is sometimes added to food to improve its taste

monosyllabic /ˌmɒnəsɪˈlæbɪk/ *adj.* **1** (**LANGUAGE**) having only one syllable **2** (used about a person or their way of speaking) saying very little, in a way that appears rude to other people: *He gave monosyllabic replies to everything I asked him.*

monosyllable /ˈmɒnəsɪləbl/ *noun* [C] (**LANGUAGE**) a short word, such as *leg*, that has only one syllable

monotheism /ˈmɒnəʊθiɪzəm/ *noun* [U] (**RELIGION**) the belief that there is only one God ➔ look at **polytheism** ▸ **monotheistic** /ˌmɒnəʊθiˈɪstɪk/ *adj.*

monotonous /məˈnɒtənəs/ *adj.* never changing and therefore boring: *monotonous work* ◇ *a monotonous voice* ▸ **monotonously** *adv.*

monotony /məˈnɒtəni/ *noun* [U] the state of being always the same and therefore boring: *the monotony of working on a production line*

monsoon /ˌmɒnˈsuːn/ *noun* [C] (**GEOGRAPHY**) the season when it rains a lot in Southern Asia; the rain that falls during this period

monster 🔊+ **B2** /ˈmɒnstə(r)/ *noun* [C] (in stories) a creature that is large, ugly and frightening: *a monster with three heads* ◇ (*figurative*) *The murderer was described as a dangerous monster.*

monstrosity /mɒnˈstrɒsəti/ *noun* [C] (*pl.* **-ies**) something that is very large and ugly, especially a building

monstrous /ˈmɒnstrəs/ *adj.* **1** that people think is shocking and unacceptable because it is morally wrong or unfair: *It's monstrous that she earns less than he does for the same job!* **2** very large (and often ugly or frightening): *a monstrous spider/wave/ creature*

montage /ˌmɒnˈtɑːʒ, ˈmɒntɑːʒ/ *noun* [C] (**ARTS AND MEDIA**) a picture, film or piece of music or writing that consists of many separate items put together, especially in an interesting or unusual combination: *a photographic montage*

month 🔊 **A1** /mʌnθ/ *noun* [C] **1** one of the twelve periods of time into which the year is divided: *They are starting work next month.* ◇ *Have you seen this month's 'Vogue'?* **2** the period of about 30 days from a certain date in one month to the same date in the next, for example 13 May to 13 June: *'How long will you be away?' 'For about a month.'* ◇ *a six-month course*

monthly¹ 🔊+ **B2** /ˈmʌnθli/ *adj.* **1** happening or produced once every month: *a monthly meeting/ magazine/visit* **2** paid, calculated or legally acceptable for one month: *a monthly season ticket* ➔ note at **income**

monthly² /ˈmʌnθli/ *adv.* every month or once a month: *Are you paid weekly or monthly?*

monthly³ /ˈmʌnθli/ *noun* [C] (*pl.* **-ies**) (**ARTS AND MEDIA**) a magazine that is published once a month

monument 🔊+ **B2** /ˈmɒnjumənt/ *noun* [C] ~ **(to sb/sth)** (**ARCHITECTURE**) **1** a building or statue that is built to remind people of a famous person or event: *a monument to the founder of the city* **2** an old building or other place that is of historical importance

monumental /ˌmɒnjuˈmentl/ *adj.* very great, large or important: *a monumental success/task/achievement*

moo /muː/ *noun* [C] (*pl.* **moos**) the sound that a cow makes ➔ note at **cow** ▸ **moo** *verb* [I] (mooing; moos; *pt, pp* mooed)

mood 🔊 **B1** /muːd/ *noun* **1** [C, U] **(in the) ~ (for sth/ doing sth); (in the) ~ (to do sth)** the way that you are feeling at a particular time: *She had a sudden change of mood.* ◇ *to be in a good mood* (= happy) ◇ *Turn that music down a bit — I'm not in the mood for it.* ◇ *Are you in the mood to go and see a film tonight?* **2** [C] a time when you are angry or impatient: *Becky's in one of her moods again.* **SYN** **temper 3** [sing.] the way that a group of people feel about sth: *The mood of the crowd suddenly changed and violence broke out.*

moody /'mu:di/ *adj.* (moodier; moodiest) **1** often changing moods in a way that people cannot predict: *You never know where you are with Andy because he's so moody.* **2** angry or unhappy, often for no particular reason ▸ **moodily** /-dɪli/ *adv.* ▸ **moodiness** *noun* [U]

phases of the moon

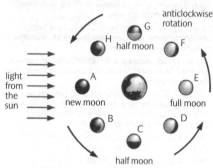

anticlockwise rotation

G

H F

half moon

A

light
from
the
sun
new moon

E

B

C D

full moon

half moon

moon ⚓ 🔤 /mu:n/ *noun* **1 the moon** [sing.] the object that shines in the sky at night and that moves around the earth once every 28 days ⟳ adjective **lunar ❶** The moon as it appears at its different stages can be called a **new moon**, a **full moon**, a **half-moon** or a **crescent moon**. **2** [C] an object like the moon that moves around another planet: *How many moons does Neptune have?* **IDM once in a blue moon** → ONCE¹ **over the moon** (*especially BrE, informal*) extremely happy and excited about sth

moonlight /'mu:nlaɪt/ *noun* [U] light that comes from the moon: *The lake looked beautiful in the moonlight.*

moonlit /'mu:nlɪt/ *adj.* lit by the moon

Moor /mɔ:(r), mʊə(r)/ *noun* [C] (**HISTORY**) a member of a Muslim people of north-west Africa who ruled part of Spain until the fifteenth century ▸ **Moorish** /'mɔ:rɪʃ, 'mʊər-/ *adj.*: *the Moorish architecture of Granada*

moor¹ /mɔ:(r), mʊə(r)/ (*also* **moorland** /'mɔ:lənd, 'mʊəl-/) *noun* [C, usually pl., U] (**GEOGRAPHY**) a wild open area of high land that is covered with grass and HEATHER: *We walked across the moors.* ⟳ look at **heath**

moor² /mɔ:(r), mʊə(r)/ *verb* [I, T] ~ (**sth to sth**) to fasten a boat to the land or to an object in the water with a rope or chain

mooring /'mɔ:rɪŋ, 'mʊər-/ *noun* [C, usually pl.] a place where a boat is tied; the ropes, chains, etc. used to fasten a boat

moose /mu:s/ *noun* [C] (*pl.* **moose**) (*especially AmE*) = ELK

mop¹ /mɒp/ *noun* [C] a tool for washing floors that has a long handle with a bunch of thick strings or soft material at the end

mop² /mɒp/ *verb* [T] (-pp-) **1** to clean a floor with water and a MOP **2** to remove liquid from sth using a dry cloth: *to mop your forehead with a handkerchief* **PHR V mop sth up** to get rid of liquid from a surface with a MOP or dry cloth

mope /məʊp/ *verb* [I] ~ (**about/around**) to spend your time doing nothing and feeling sorry for yourself because you are unhappy

moped /'məʊped/ *noun* [C] a type of small, not very powerful motorcycle

moraine /mə'reɪn, mɒ'r-/ *noun* [U] (**GEOGRAPHY**) earth, stones, etc., that have been carried along by a GLACIER (= a large moving mass of ice) and left when it melted ⟳ picture at **glacial**

moral¹ ⚓ 🔤 /'mɒrəl/ *adj.* **1** [only before noun] concerned with what is right and wrong: *Some people refuse to eat meat on moral grounds* (= because they believe it to be wrong). ◇ *a moral dilemma/issue/question* **2** having a high standard of behaviour that is considered good and right by most people: *She has always led a very moral life.* **OPP immoral** ⟳ look at **amoral**

IDM moral support the act of helping sb by showing your approval and interest, rather than by giving financial or practical support: *I went to the dentist's with him just to give him some moral support.*

moral² ⚓ 🔤 /'mɒrəl/ *noun* **1 morals** [pl.] standards of good behaviour: *These people appear to have no morals.* **2** [C] a lesson in the right way to behave that can be learnt from a story or an experience: *The moral of the play is that friendship is more important than money.*

morale /mə'rɑ:l/ *noun* [U] how happy, sad, confident, etc. a group of people feels at a particular time: *The team's morale was low/high before the match* (= they felt worried/confident). ◇ *to boost/raise/improve morale*

moralistic /ˌmɒrə'lɪstɪk/ *adj.* (*formal*) having or showing very fixed ideas about what is right and wrong, especially when this causes you to judge other people's behaviour

morality ⚓+ 🔤 /mə'ræləti/ *noun* [U] principles concerning what is good and bad or right and wrong behaviour: *a debate about the morality of abortion* **OPP immorality**

moralize (*BrE also* -ise) /'mɒrəlaɪz/ *verb* [I] ~ (**about/on sth**) to tell other people what the right or wrong way to behave is

morally /'mɒrəli/ *adv.* connected with standards of what is right or wrong

moratorium /ˌmɒrə'tɔ:riəm/ *noun* [C] (*pl.* -toriums, -toria /-riə/) ~ (**on sth**) a temporary stopping of an activity, especially by official agreement: *The convention called for a two-year moratorium on commercial whaling.*

morbid /'mɔ:bɪd/ *adj.* showing interest in unpleasant things, for example disease and death

more¹ ⚓ 🔤 /mɔ:(r)/ *det., pron.* ~ (**of sb/sth**); ~ (**sth**) (**than…**) a larger number or amount of people or things; sth extra as well as what you have: *We had more time than we thought.* ◇ *I can't spend much more of this.* ◇ *There were more people than 20 people at the meeting.* ◇ *There's room for three more people.* ◇ *I couldn't eat any more.* ◇ *Tell me more about your job.* **OPP few, less¹**

IDM more and more an increasing amount or number: *There are more and more cars on the road.* **what's more** (used for adding another fact) also; in addition: *The hotel was awful and what's more, it was miles from the beach.*

more² ⚓ 🔤 /mɔ:(r)/ *adv.* ~ (**than…**) **1** used to form the comparative of many adjectives and adverbs: *She was far more intelligent than her sister.* ◇ *a course for more advanced students* ◇ *Please write more carefully.* **OPP less¹** **2** to a greater degree than usual or than sth else: *I like him much more than his wife.* **OPP less¹**

IDM more or less approximately; almost: *We are more or less the same age.* **the more, less, etc…, the more, less, etc…** used to show that two things change to the same degree: *The more she thought about it, the more depressed she became.* **not any more** not any longer: *She doesn't live here any more.*

moreover ⚓+ 🔤 **W** /mɔ:r'əʊvə(r)/ *adv.* (*formal*) (used for adding another fact) also; in addition: *This firm did the work very well. Moreover, the cost was not too high.*

morgue /mɔːg/ *noun* [C] a building where dead bodies are kept until they are buried or CREMATED (= burned as part of a FUNERAL service) ⊃ look at **mortuary**

morning ʔ A1 /ˈmɔːnɪŋ/ *noun* [C, U] **1** the early part of the day between the time when the sun rises and the middle of the day: *Pat's going to London tomorrow morning.* ◇ *Bye, see you in the morning* (= tomorrow morning). ◇ *I've been studying hard all morning.* ◇ *Dave makes breakfast every morning.* ◇ *She only works in the mornings.* **2** the part of the night that is after midnight: *I was woken by a strange noise in the early hours of the morning.* ◇ *He didn't come home until three in the morning.*
IDM Good morning used when you see sb for the first time in the morning

ˈmorning suit *noun* [C] (*also* ˈmorning dress [U]) a suit worn by men on very formal occasions, for example a wedding

moron /ˈmɔːrɒn/ *noun* [C] (*informal*) a rude way of referring to sb who you think is very stupid ▶ moronic /məˈrɒnɪk/ *adj.*

morose /məˈrəʊs/ *adj.* unhappy, in a bad mood and not talking very much ▶ morosely *adv.*

morpheme /ˈmɔːfiːm/ *noun* [C] (**GRAMMAR**) the smallest unit of meaning that a word can be divided into: *The word 'like' contains one morpheme but 'un-like-ly' contains three.*

morphine /ˈmɔːfiːn/ *noun* [U] (**MEDICINE**) a powerful drug that is used for reducing pain

morphology /mɔːˈfɒlədʒi/ *noun* [U] **1** (**BIOLOGY**) the form and structure of animals and plants, studied as a science **2** the form of words, studied as a branch of LINGUISTICS ⊃ look at **grammar** ▶ morphological /ˌmɔːfəˈlɒdʒɪkl/ *adj.*

Morse code /ˌmɔːs ˈkəʊd/ *noun* [U] a system for sending messages, using combinations of long and short sounds or flashes of light to represent letters of the alphabet and numbers

morsel /ˈmɔːsl/ *noun* [C] a very small piece of sth, usually food

mortal¹ /ˈmɔːtl/ *adj.* **1** that cannot live for ever and must die: *We are all mortal.* **OPP** immortal **2** that will result in death: *a mortal wound/blow* ◇ *to be in mortal danger* ⊃ look at **fatal** (1) **3** [only before noun] (*formal*) very great or extreme: *They were in mortal fear of the enemy.* ▶ mortally /-təli/ *adv.*

mortal² /ˈmɔːtl/ *noun* [C] a human being

mortality /mɔːˈtæləti/ *noun* [U] **1** the fact that nobody can live for ever: *He didn't like to think about his own mortality.* **2** (**SOCIAL STUDIES**) the number of deaths in one period of time or in one place: *the infant mortality rate* (= the number of babies that die at or just after birth)

mortar /ˈmɔːtə(r)/ *noun* **1** [U] a mixture of CEMENT, sand and water used in building for holding BRICKS and stones together **2** [C] (**SCIENCE**) a small hard bowl in which you CRUSH (= press hard and break up) some foods or substances into powder with a PESTLE (= a heavy tool with a round end) ⊃ picture at **laboratory 3** [C] a type of heavy gun that fires a type of bomb high into the air; the bombs that are fired by this gun

mortgage¹ ʔ+ B2 /ˈmɔːgɪdʒ/ *noun* [C] (**FINANCE**) money that you borrow in order to buy a house or flat: *We took out a £150 000 mortgage.*

mortgage² /ˈmɔːgɪdʒ/ *verb* [T] (**FINANCE**) to give a bank, etc. the legal right to own your house, land, etc. if you do not pay the money back that you have borrowed from the bank to buy the house or land: *He had to mortgage his house to pay his legal costs.*

mortician /mɔːˈtɪʃn/ (*AmE*) = UNDERTAKER

mortify /ˈmɔːtɪfaɪ/ *verb* [T, usually passive] (**mortifying; mortifies;** *pt, pp* **mortified**) be mortified (to do sth) to be made to feel very embarrassed: *She was mortified to realize he had heard every word she said.* ▶ mortification /ˌmɔːtɪfɪˈkeɪʃn/ *noun* [U] ▶ mortifying *adj.*: *How mortifying to have to apologize to him!*

mortise (*also* **mortice**) /ˈmɔːtɪs/ *noun* [C] a hole cut in a piece of wood, etc. to receive the end of another piece of wood, so that the two are held together

mortuary /ˈmɔːtʃəri/ *noun* [C] (*pl.* -ies) (**MEDICINE**) a room, usually in a hospital, where dead bodies are kept before they are buried or CREMATED (= burned as part of a FUNERAL service) ⊃ look at **morgue**

mosaic /məʊˈzeɪɪk/ *noun* [C, U] (**ART**) a picture or pattern that is made by placing together small coloured stones, pieces of glass, etc.

Moslem /ˈmɒzləm/ = MUSLIM

mosque ʔ+ B2 /mɒsk/ *noun* [C] (**RELIGION**) a building where Muslims meet and WORSHIP

mosquito /məˈskiːtəʊ, mɒˈs-/ *noun* [C] (*pl.* -oes) a small flying insect that lives in warm countries and bites people or animals to drink their blood. Some types of mosquito spread MALARIA (= a very serious disease). ⊃ picture at **animal**

moss /mɒs/ *noun* [U, C] (**BIOLOGY**) a small soft green plant, with no flowers, that grows in wet places, especially on rocks or trees ▶ mossy *adj.*

most¹ ʔ A1 ⓦ /məʊst/ *det., pron.* **1** (superlative of *many* and *much*) greatest in number or amount: *Who got the most points?* ◇ *The children had the most fun.* ◇ *We all worked hard but I did the most.* **OPP** least **2** nearly all of a group of people or things: *Most people in this country have a TV.* ◇ *I like most Italian food.*
IDM at (the) most not more than a certain number, and probably less: *There were 20 people there, at the most.* make the most of sth → MAKE¹

most² ʔ A1 /məʊst/ *adv.* **1** used to form the superlative of most adjectives and adverbs of two or more syllables: *It's the most beautiful house I've ever seen.* ◇ *I work most efficiently in the morning.* **OPP** least **2** more than anyone/anything else: *What do you miss most when you're abroad?* **OPP** least **3** (*formal*) very: *We heard a most interesting talk about Japan.*

mostly ʔ A2 /ˈməʊstli/ *adv.* in almost every case; almost all the time: *Our students come mostly from Europe.*

MOT /ˌem əʊ ˈtiː/ (*also* MOˈT test) *noun* [C] a test in the UK to make sure that vehicles over a certain age are safe to drive (the abbreviation for 'Ministry of Transport'): *My car failed its MOT.*

motel /məʊˈtel/ *noun* [C] (**TOURISM**) a hotel near a main road for people who are travelling by car ⊃ note at **hotel**

moth /mɒθ/ *noun* [C] an insect with wings that usually flies at night. Some moths eat cloth and leave small holes in your clothes. ⊃ picture at **animal**

mothball /ˈmɒθbɔːl/ *noun* [C] a small ball made of a chemical substance that protects clothes in cupboards from MOTHS

mother[1] 🔊 **A1** /'mʌðə(r)/ noun [C] the female parent of a person or an animal ⊃ look at **mum**, **mummy**, **stepmother**

mother[2] /'mʌðə(r)/ verb [T] to look after sb as a mother does: *Stop mothering me — I can look after myself!*

motherboard /'mʌðəbɔːd/ noun [C] (**COMPUTING**) the main board of a computer, containing all the CIRCUITS

motherhood /'mʌðəhʊd/ noun [U] the state of being a mother

mother-in-law noun [C] (pl. **mothers-in-law**) your husband's or wife's mother

motherland /'mʌðəlænd/ noun [C] (formal) the country where you or your family were born and that you feel a strong emotional connection with

motherly /'mʌðəli/ adj. having the qualities of a good mother: *motherly love*

Mother's Day noun [C] a day when mothers receive cards and gifts from their children, celebrated in the UK in February or March and in the US on the second Sunday in May

mother tongue noun [C] (**LANGUAGE**) the first language that you learnt to speak as a child

motif /məʊ'tiːf/ noun [C] a picture or pattern on sth

motion[1] 🔊+ **B2** /'məʊʃn/ noun 1 [U, C] movement or a way of moving: *The motion of the ship made us all feel sick.* ◇ *Pull the lever to set the machine in motion* (= make it start moving). ◇ *She made a chopping motion with her hand.* ⊃ look at **slow motion 2** [C] a formal suggestion at a meeting that you discuss and vote on: *The motion was carried/rejected by a majority of eight votes.*

motion[2] /'məʊʃn/ verb [I, T] **~ to sb (to do sth); ~ (for) sb (to do sth)** to make a movement, usually with your hand, that tells sb what to do: *I motioned to the waiter.* ◇ *The manager motioned for me to sit down.*

motionless /'məʊʃnləs/ adj. not moving

motivate 🔊+ **B2** 🅦 /'məʊtɪveɪt/ verb [T] **1** [usually passive] to cause sb to act in a particular way: *Her reaction was motivated by fear.* **2 ~ sb (to do sth)** to make sb want to do sth, especially sth that involves hard work and effort: *Our new teacher certainly knows how to motivate his classes.* ▶ **motivated** adj.: *highly motivated students* ▶ **motivation** 🔊+ **B2** 🅞 /ˌməʊtɪ'veɪʃn/ noun [C, U]: *What is the motivation behind this change?* ◇ *He's clever enough, but he lacks motivation.*

motive[1] 🔊+ **C1** /'məʊtɪv/ noun [C] **~ (for sth/doing sth)** a reason for doing sth, often sth bad: *The police couldn't discover a motive for the murder.* ⊃ note at **reason**[1]

motive[2] /'məʊtɪv/ adj. [only before noun] (**PHYSICS**) causing movement or action: *motive power/force* (= for example, electricity, to operate MACHINERY)

motor[1] 🔊 **B2** /'məʊtə(r)/ noun [C] (**ENGINEERING**) a device that uses petrol, gas, electricity, etc. to produce movement and makes a machine, etc. work: *The washing machine doesn't work. I think something is wrong with the motor.*

motor[2] 🔊 **B2** /'məʊtə(r)/ adj. [only before noun] **1** having or using the power of an engine or a motor: *a motor vehicle* **2** (especially BrE) connected with vehicles that have engines, especially cars: *the motor industry* ◇ *motor racing* **3** (**ANATOMY**) connected with movement of the body that is produced by muscles; connected with the nerves that control movement: *uncoordinated motor activity* ◇ *Both motor and sensory functions are affected.*

motorboat /'məʊtəbəʊt/ noun [C] a small fast boat that has a motor

motor car (BrE, formal) = CAR (1)

motorcycle 🔊 **A2** /'məʊtəsaɪkl/ (also motorbike /'məʊtəbaɪk/ especially in BrE) noun [C] a vehicle that has two wheels and an engine

motorcyclist /'məʊtəsaɪklɪst/ noun [C] a person who rides a motorcycle

motorhome /'məʊtəhəʊm/ = CAMPER (2)

motoring /'məʊtərɪŋ/ noun [U] driving in a car: *a motoring holiday*

motorist 🔊+ **C1** /'məʊtərɪst/ noun [C] a person who drives a car ⊃ look at **pedestrian**

motorized (BrE also -ised) /'məʊtəraɪzd/ adj. [only before noun] that has an engine: *a motorized wheelchair*

motor neuron noun [C] (**ANATOMY**) a nerve cell that sends signals to a muscle or GLAND

motor neuron disease noun [U] (**HEALTH**) a disease in which the nerves and muscles become gradually weaker until the person dies

motorsport /'məʊtəspɔːt/ noun [U] (especially BrE) (AmE usually motorsports [pl.]) (**SPORT**) the sport of racing fast cars or motorcycles on a special track

motorway /'məʊtəweɪ/ (BrE) (AmE expressway, freeway) noun [C] (abbr. M) a wide road where traffic can travel fast for long distances between large towns

motte /mɒt/ noun [C] (**HISTORY**) the small hill on which the FORT (= a strong building used for military defence) is built in a MOTTE-AND-BAILEY CASTLE

motte-and-bailey castle noun [C] (**HISTORY**) an old type of castle that consists of a FORT (= a strong building used for military defence) on a small hill surrounded by an outer wall

mottled /'mɒtld/ adj. marked with shapes of different colours without a regular pattern: *the mottled skin of a snake*

motto /'mɒtəʊ/ noun [C] (pl. -oes, -os) a short sentence or phrase that expresses the aims and beliefs of a person, a group, an organization, etc: '*Live and let live*' — *that's my motto.*

mould[1] (BrE) (AmE mold) /məʊld/ noun **1** [C] a container that you pour a liquid or substance into. The liquid then becomes solid in the same shape as the container, for example after it has cooled or cooked. **2** [U, C] (**BIOLOGY**) a soft green or black substance like fur that grows in wet places or on old food ⊃ look at **fungus** (2) **3** [C, usually sing.] a particular type: *She doesn't fit into the usual mould of sales directors.* ▶ **mouldy** (AmE moldy) adj.: *The cheese had gone mouldy.*

mould[2] (BrE) (AmE mold) /məʊld/ verb [T] **~ A (into B); ~ B (from/out of A)** to make sth into a particular shape or form by pressing it, or by putting it into a MOULD: *First mould the dough into a ball.* ◇ *a bowl moulded from clay*

moulding (BrE) (AmE molding) /'məʊldɪŋ/ noun [C] (**ARCHITECTURE**) a narrow STRIP of plastic, stone, wood, etc. around the top edge of a wall, on a door, etc., usually for decoration: *There were elaborate plaster mouldings around the ceiling.*

moult (BrE) (AmE molt) /məʊlt/ verb [I] (**BIOLOGY**) (used about an animal or a bird) to lose hairs or feathers before growing new ones

mound /maʊnd/ noun [C] **1** (**GEOGRAPHY**) a large pile of earth or stones; a small hill **2 ~ (of sth)** (informal) a pile or a large amount of sth: *I've got a mound of work to do.*

mount[1] 🔊 **B2** /maʊnt/ verb **1** [T] to organize sth: *to mount a protest/a campaign/an exhibition/an attack* **2** [I] to increase gradually in level or amount: *The*

tension mounted as the end of the match approached.
3 [T] (*formal*) to go up sth or up on to sth: *He mounted the platform and began to speak.* **4** [I, T] to get on a horse or bicycle **OPP** **dismount** **5** [T] ~ **sth (on/onto/in sth)** to fix sth FIRMLY on sth else: *The gas boiler was mounted on the wall.*
PHR V mount up to increase (often more than you want): *When you're buying food for six people the cost soon mounts up.*

mount² /maʊnt/ *noun* [C] (*abbr.* Mt) (used in names) a mountain: *Mt Vesuvius/Fuji*

mountain ℝ **A1** /ˈmaʊntən/ *noun* [C] **1** (GEOGRAPHY) a very high hill: *Which is the highest mountain in the world?* ◇ *mountain roads/scenery/villages* ◇ *a mountain range* ◑ picture at **ecosystem** **2** ~ **(of sth)** a large amount of sth: *I've got a mountain of work to do.* ◇ *We made mountains of sandwiches.*

ˈmountain bike *noun* [C] a bicycle with a strong frame, wide tyres and many different GEARS, designed for riding on rough ground

ˈmountain biking *noun* [U] (SPORT) the sport or activity of riding a MOUNTAIN BIKE: *Shall we go mountain biking at the weekend?*

mountaineering /ˌmaʊntəˈnɪərɪŋ/ *noun* [U] (SPORT) the sport of climbing mountains ▸ mountaineer /-ˈnɪə(r)/ *noun* [C]

ˈmountain lion (*AmE*) = PUMA

mountainous /ˈmaʊntənəs/ *adj.* **1** (GEOGRAPHY) having many mountains: *a mountainous region* **2** very large in size or amount: *The mountainous waves made sailing impossible.* **SYN** **huge**

mountainside /ˈmaʊntənsaɪd/ *noun* [C] (GEOGRAPHY) the land on the side of a mountain

mounted /ˈmaʊntɪd/ *adj.* [only before noun] riding a horse: *mounted police*

mounting /ˈmaʊntɪŋ/ *adj.* [only before noun] increasing: *mounting unemployment/tension*

mourn /mɔːn/ *verb* [I, T] ~ **(for/over) sb/sth** to feel and show that you are sad, especially because sb has died: *He is still mourning (for) his wife.* ▸ mourning *noun* [U]: *He wore a black armband to show he was in mourning.*

mourner /ˈmɔːnə(r)/ *noun* [C] a person who goes to a FUNERAL as a friend or relative of the person who has died

mournful /ˈmɔːnfl/ *adj.* very sad: *a mournful song* ▸ mournfully /-fəli/ *adv.*

mouse¹ ℝ **A1** /maʊs/ *noun* [C] **1** (*pl.* mice /maɪs/) a very small animal with fur and a long thin tail **2** (*pl.* mice, mouses) (COMPUTING) a small device that is moved by hand across a surface to control the movement of the CURSOR on a computer screen: *Use the mouse to drag the icon to a new position.*

mouse² /maʊs/ *verb*
PHR V mouse over sth (COMPUTING) to use the mouse to move over sth on a computer screen: *Mouse over the link in the original message.*

ˈmouse mat (*BrE*) (*also* ˈmouse pad *especially in AmE*) *noun* [C] (COMPUTING) a small piece of material that is the best kind of surface on which to use a computer mouse

mousse /muːs/ *noun* [C, U] **1** a cold DESSERT (= a sweet food) made with cream and egg whites and with fruit, chocolate, etc. to give it a sweet taste; a similar dish made with fish, vegetables, etc: *a chocolate/ strawberry mousse* ◇ *salmon mousse* **2** a light substance containing a lot of bubbles that you use to make your hair stay in a particular style

moustache (*BrE*) (*AmE* mustache) /məˈstɑːʃ, məˈstɑːʃ/ *noun* [C] hair that grows on a man's top lip, between the mouth and nose

mouth¹ ℝ **A1** /maʊθ/ *noun* [C] (*pl.* mouths /maʊðz/) **1** (ANATOMY) the part of the face that you use for eating and speaking: *to open/close your mouth* ◑ picture at **body**, **digestive system**, **respiratory** **2** -mouthed /maʊðd/ (in adjectives) having a particular type of mouth or a particular way of speaking: *We stared open-mouthed in surprise.* ◇ *He's a loud-mouthed bully.* **3** (GEOGRAPHY) the place where a river enters the sea ◑ note at **river**
IDM keep your mouth shut (*informal*) to not say sth to sb because it is a secret or because it will upset or annoy them

mouth² /maʊð/ *verb* [T] to move your mouth as if you were speaking but without making any sound: *Vinay was outside the window, mouthing something to us.*

mouthful /ˈmaʊθfl/ *noun* **1** [C] the amount of food or drink that you can put in your mouth at one time **2** [sing.] a word or phrase that is long or difficult to say: *Her name is a bit of a mouthful.*

mouthpiece /ˈmaʊθpiːs/ *noun* [C] **1** (MUSIC) the part of a phone, musical instrument, etc. that you put near your mouth or between your lips **2** a person, newspaper, etc. that a particular group uses to express its opinions

mouthwash /ˈmaʊθwɒʃ/ *noun* [U, C] (MEDICINE) a liquid used to make the mouth fresh and healthy

ˈmouth-watering *adj.* (used about food) that looks or smells very good

movable (*also* moveable) /ˈmuːvəbl/ *adj.* **1** that can be moved from one place or position to another: *a doll with a movable head* **OPP** **fixed** ◑ look at **mobile¹** (2), **portable** **2** (LAW) (used about property) able to be taken from one house, etc. to another

move¹ ℝ **A1** **S** /muːv/ *verb*
• CHANGE POSITION **1** [I, T] to change position or to put sth in a different position: *The station is so crowded you can hardly move.* ◇ *Please move your car. It's blocking the road.* ◇ *The meeting has been moved to Thursday.* **2** [I, T] (used with an adverb or a preposition) to move (sth) further in a particular direction in order to make space for sb/sth else: *If we move up a bit, Rob can sit here too.* ◇ *Move your head down — I can't see the screen.*
• CHANGE HOUSE, JOB, ETC. **3** [I, T] to change the place where you live, work, study, etc: *Our neighbours are moving to York next week.* ◇ *Yuka's moved down to the beginners' class.* ◇ *They're going to move house.*
• MAKE PROGRESS **4** [I] ~ **(on/ahead)** to make progress: *When the new team of builders arrived things started moving ahead very quickly.*
• TAKE ACTION **5** [I] to take action: *Unless we move quickly lives will be lost.*
• CAUSE STRONG FEELINGS **6** [T] to cause sb to have strong feelings, especially of sympathy or of being sad: *Many people were moved to tears by reports of the massacre.*
IDM get moving to go, leave or do sth quickly get sth moving to cause sth to make progress
PHR V move in (with sb) to start living in a new home (with sb) move on (to sth) to start doing or discussing sth new move off (used about a vehicle) to start a journey; to leave move out to leave your old home

move² ℝ **B1** /muːv/ *noun* [C] **1** a change of place or position: *She was watching every move I made.* ◑ note at **action¹** **2** a change in the place where you live or work: *a move to a bigger house* **3** an action that you take because you want to achieve a particular result: *Both sides want to negotiate but neither is prepared to make the first move.* ◇ *Asking him to help me was a* good move. **4** (in CHESS and other games) a change in the position of a piece: *It's your move.*

IDM be on the move to be going somewhere get a move on (*informal*) to hurry: *I'm late. I'll have to get a move on.* make a move (*BrE, informal*) to start to go somewhere: *It's time to go home. Let's make a move.*

movement ?⃝ **A2** ⊙ /ˈmuːvmənt/ *noun*

• CHANGING POSITION **1** [C, U] an act of moving: *The dancer's movements were smooth and controlled.* ◇ *The seat belt doesn't allow much freedom of movement.* ◇ *I could see some movement (=somebody/something moving) in the trees.* **2** [C, U] an act of moving or being moved from one place to another: *the slow movement of the clouds across the sky*

• GROUP OF PEOPLE **3** [C] (**SOCIAL STUDIES**) a group of people who have the same aims or ideas: *I support the Animal Rights movement.*

• SB'S ACTIVITIES **4** movements [pl.] a person's actions or plans during a period of time: *Detectives have been watching the man's movements for several weeks.*

• CHANGE OF IDEAS/BEHAVIOUR **5** [sing.] **~ (away from/towards sth)** a general change in the way people think or behave: *There's been a movement away from the materialism of the 1980s.*

• IN MUSIC **6** [C] one of the main parts of a long piece of music

movie ?⃝ **A1** /ˈmuːvi/ *noun* (*especially AmE*) **1** [C] = FILM¹ (1): *Shall we go and see a movie?* ◇ *a science fiction/horror movie* ◇ *a movie director/star* ◇ *a movie theater* (= cinema) **2** the movies [pl.] = CINEMA (2): *Let's go to the movies.*

moving ?⃝+ **B2** /ˈmuːvɪŋ/ *adj.* **1** causing strong feelings, especially sad feelings: *a deeply moving speech/story* **2** [only before noun] that moves: *It's a computerized machine with few moving parts.*

mow /məʊ/ *verb* [T, I] (*pt* mowed; *pp* mown /məʊn/, mowed) to cut grass using a MOWER: *to mow the lawn* **PHR V** mow sb down to kill sb with a gun or a car

mower /ˈməʊə(r)/ *noun* [C] a machine for cutting grass: *a lawnmower* ◇ *an electric mower*

MP /ˌem ˈpiː/ *noun* [C] (**POLITICS**) a person who has been elected to represent people from a particular area in Parliament (the abbreviation for 'Member of Parliament'): *I'm going to write to my local MP about the problem.*

MP3 /ˌem piː ˈθriː/ *noun* [U, C] (**COMPUTING**) a method of reducing the size of a computer file containing sound; a file that is reduced in size in this way

mpg /ˌem piː ˈdʒiː/ *abbr.* **miles per gallon** (used for saying how much petrol a vehicle uses): *This car does 40 mpg (= you can drive 40 miles on one GALLON of fuel).*

mph /ˌem piː ˈeɪtʃ/ *abbr.* miles per hour: *a 70 mph speed limit*

MPV /ˌem piː ˈviː/ *noun* [C] a large car like a van (the abbreviation for 'multipurpose vehicle') **SYN** people carrier

Mr (*BrE*) (*also* **Mr.** *AmE, BrE*) /ˈmɪstə(r)/ *abbr.* **Mister** (a title that comes before the name of a man): *Mr (Matthew) Botham* ⊃ note at **miss²**

MRI /ˌem ɑːr ˈaɪ/ *noun* [U, C] (**MEDICINE**) a method of producing an image of the inside of a person's body using a strong MAGNETIC FIELD (the abbreviation for 'magnetic resonance imaging'): *an MRI scan*

Mrs (*BrE*) (*also* **Mrs.** *AmE, BrE*) /ˈmɪsɪz/ *abbr.* a title that comes before the name of a married woman: *Mrs (Sylvia) Allen* ⊃ note at **miss²**

MRSA /ˌem ɑːr es ˈeɪ/ *noun* [U] (**HEALTH**) a type of bacteria that cannot be killed by ANTIBIOTICS (the abbreviation for 'methicillin-resistant Staphylococcus aureus'): *rising rates of MRSA infections in hospitals* ⊃ look at **superbug**

MS /ˌem ˈes/ *abbr.* = MULTIPLE SCLEROSIS

Ms (*BrE*) (*also* **Ms.** *AmE, BrE*) /mɪz, məz/ *abbr.* a title that comes before the name of a woman who may or may not be married: *Ms (Keiko) Harada* ◇ *Dear Ms Harada, …* ⊃ note at **miss²**

MSc /ˌem es ˈsiː/ (*BrE*) (*AmE* M.S. /ˌem ˈes/) *noun* [C] (**EDUCATION**) a second university degree in science (the abbreviation for 'Master of Science') ⊃ look at **BSc, MA**

MSG /ˌem es ˈdʒiː/ *abbr.* = MONOSODIUM GLUTAMATE

much ?⃝ **A1** /mʌtʃ/ *det., pron., adv.* **1** used with uncountable nouns, especially in negative sentences, to mean 'a large amount of sth', or after 'how' to ask about the amount of sth. It is also used with 'as', 'so' and 'too': *I haven't got much money.* ◇ *Did she say much?* ◇ *You've given me too much food.* ◇ *How much time have you got?* ◇ *I can't carry that much!* ◇ *Eat as much as you can.* **2** to a great degree: *I don't like her very much.* ◇ *Do you see Sashi much? (= very often)* ◇ *Do you see much of Sashi?* ◇ *much taller/prettier/harder* ◇ *much more interesting/unusual* ◇ *much more quickly/happily* ◇ *You ate much more than me.* **3** (before past participles used as adjectives) very: *She was much loved by all her friends.* ◇ *a much-needed rest*

IDM much the same very similar: *Softball is much the same as baseball.* not much good (at sth) not SKILLED (at sth): *I'm not much good at singing.* not much of a … not a good … : *She's not much of a cook.* not up to much → UP¹ nothing much → NOTHING

muck¹ /mʌk/ *noun* [U] **1** (**AGRICULTURE**) the waste from farm animals, used to make plants grow better **SYN** manure **2** (*informal*) dirt or mud

muck² /mʌk/ *verb* **PHR V** muck about/around (*BrE, informal*) to behave in a silly way; to waste time: *Stop mucking around and come and help me!* muck sth up (*especially BrE, informal*) to do sth badly; to cause sth to fail: *I was so nervous that I completely mucked up my interview.*

mucky /ˈmʌki/ *adj.* (muckier; muckiest) (*especially BrE, informal*) dirty: *mucky hands*

mucous membrane *noun* [C] (**ANATOMY**) a thin layer of skin that covers the inside of the nose and mouth and the outside of other organs in the body, producing MUCUS to stop these parts from becoming dry

mucus /ˈmjuːkəs/ *noun* [U] (**BIOLOGY**) a sticky substance that is produced in some parts of the body, especially the nose ▶ **mucous** /ˈmjuːkəs/ *adj.*: *mucous glands*

mud ?⃝ **B1** /mʌd/ *noun* [U] soft, wet earth: *He came home from the football match covered in mud.*

muddle /ˈmʌdl/ *verb* [T] **1 ~ sth up** to put things in the wrong place or order or to make them untidy: *Try not to muddle up those papers.* **2** (often passive) **~ sb (up)** to confuse sb: *Slow down a little — you're muddling me.* **3 ~ sb/sth (up); ~ A (up) with B** to confuse one person or thing with another: *I muddled the dates and arrived a week early.* ◇ *She had muddled him up with another student.* ▶ **muddle** *noun* [C, usually sing., U]: *If you get in a muddle, I'll help you.* ▶ **muddled** *adj.*

muddy /ˈmʌdi/ *adj.* (muddier; muddiest) full of or covered with mud: *muddy boots* ◇ *It's very muddy down by the river.*

mudflat /ˈmʌdflæt/ *noun* [C] (*also* **mudflats** [pl.]) (**GEOGRAPHY**) an area of flat wet land that is covered by the sea when it is at its highest level

mudguard /'mʌdgɑːd/ *noun* [C] a curved cover over the wheel of a bicycle or motorcycle

mudslide /'mʌdslaɪd/ *noun* [C] (**GEOGRAPHY**) a large amount of mud sliding down a mountain, often destroying buildings and injuring or killing people below

muesli /'mjuːzli/ *noun* [U] food made of grains, nuts, dried fruit, etc. that you eat with milk for breakfast

muezzin /muːˈezɪn, mjuː-/ *noun* [C] (**RELIGION**) a man who calls Muslims to come to a MOSQUE (= a religious building) to pray ⊃ picture at **minaret**

muffin /'mʌfɪn/ *noun* [C] **1** a type of small cake **2** (*BrE*) (*AmE* **English muffin**) a type of bread roll often eaten hot with butter

muffle /'mʌfl/ *verb* [T] to make a sound quieter and more difficult to hear: *He put his hand over his mouth to muffle his laughter.* ▶ **muffled** *adj.*: *I heard muffled voices outside.*

muffler /'mʌflə(r)/ (*AmE*) = SILENCER

mug¹ /mʌg/ *noun* [C] **1** a large cup with straight sides and a handle: *a coffee mug* ◇ *a mug of tea* **2** (*informal*) a person who seems stupid

mug² /mʌg/ *verb* [T] (-gg-) (**LAW**) to attack and steal from sb in the street: *Keep your wallet out of sight or you'll get mugged.* ▶ **mugger** *noun* [C] ⊃ note at **criminal¹** ▶ **mugging** *noun* [C, U]: *The mugging took place around midnight.*

muggy /'mʌgi/ *adj.* (**muggier; muggiest**) (used about the weather) warm and slightly wet in an unpleasant way **SYN** **humid**

mugshot /'mʌgʃɒt/ *noun* [C] (*informal*) (**LAW**) a photo of sb's face kept by the police in their records

Muhammad (*also* **Mohammed**) /məˈhæmɪd/ *noun* (**RELIGION**) the PROPHET (= a person who is sent by God to teach and give people messages from God) who started the religion of Islam

mulch /mʌltʃ/ *noun* [U, C] (**AGRICULTURE**) material, for example dead leaves, that you put around a plant to protect its base and its roots, to improve the soil or to stop WEEDS (= wild plants) from growing ▶ **mulch** *verb* [T]

mule /mjuːl/ *noun* [C] **1** an animal that is used for carrying heavy loads and whose parents are a horse and a DONKEY **2** (*slang*) a person who is paid to take drugs illegally from one country to another

mull /mʌl/ *verb*
PHR V **mull sth over** to think about sth carefully and for a long time: *Don't ask me for a decision right now. I'll have to mull it over.*

multi- /mʌlti/ *prefix* (in nouns and adjectives) more than one; many: *multicoloured* ◇ *a multimillionaire*

multicellular /ˌmʌltiˈseljələ(r)/ *adj.* (**BIOLOGY**) having or consisting of many cells: *a multicellular organism*

multicultural /ˌmʌltiˈkʌltʃərəl/ *adj.* (**SOCIAL STUDIES**) for or including people who belong to different human groups and have different, languages, religions and traditions: *a multicultural society*

multiculturalism /ˌmʌltiˈkʌltʃərəlɪzəm/ *noun* [U] (**SOCIAL STUDIES**) the practice of giving importance to all cultures in a society

multidisciplinary /ˌmʌltidɪsəˈplɪnəri/ *adj.* involving several different subjects of study: *The team took a multidisciplinary approach, involving maths, genetics and physics.*

multifaith /ˌmʌltiˈfeɪθ/ *adj.* [only before noun] (**RELIGION**) involving two or more religions

multilateral /ˌmʌltiˈlætərəl/ *adj.* involving more than two groups of people, countries, etc. ⊃ look at **unilateral** ⊃ look at **bilateral** (1)

multilateralism /ˌmʌltiˈlætərəlɪzəm/ *noun* [U] (**POLITICS**) the policy of trying to make agreements that involve several different countries or organizations

multilingual /ˌmʌltiˈlɪŋgwəl/ *adj.* (**LANGUAGE**) speaking or using several different languages: *a multilingual classroom* ⊃ look at **bilingual** (2), **monolingual**

multimedia /ˌmʌltiˈmiːdiə/ *adj.* [only before noun] (**COMPUTING**) using sound, pictures and film in addition to text on a screen: *multimedia systems/products*

multinational¹ /ˌmʌltiˈnæʃnəl/ *adj.* existing in or involving many countries: *multinational companies*

multinational² /ˌmʌltiˈnæʃnəl/ *noun* [C] a large and powerful company that operates in several different countries: *The company is owned by Ford, the US multinational.*

multiple¹ ? **B2** **W** /'mʌltɪpl/ *adj.* [only before noun] involving many people or things or having many parts: *a multiple pile-up* (= a crash involving many vehicles)

multiple² /'mʌltɪpl/ *noun* [C] (**MATHEMATICS**) a number that contains another number an exact number of times: *12, 18 and 24 are multiples of 6.*

multiple-'choice *adj.* (**EDUCATION**) (used about exam questions) showing several different answers from which you have to choose the right one

multiple sclerosis /ˌmʌltɪpl skləˈrəʊsɪs/ *noun* [U] (*abbr.* **MS**) (**HEALTH**) a serious disease that causes you to slowly lose control of your body and become less able to move

multiplex /'mʌltɪpleks/ (*BrE also* ˌmultiplex 'cinema) *noun* [C] (**ARTS AND MEDIA**) a large cinema with several separate rooms with screens

multipli'cation table (*also* **table**) *noun* [C] (**MATHEMATICS**) a list showing the results when a number is multiplied by a set of other numbers, especially 1 to 12, in turn

multiply ? **B2** /'mʌltɪplaɪ/ *verb* [I, T] (**multiplying; multiplies;** *pt, pp* **multiplied**) **1 ~ A by B** (**MATHEMATICS**) to increase a number by the number of times mentioned: *2 multiplied by 4 makes 8 (2×4=8).* **OPP** **divide¹** **2** to increase by a very large amount; to make sth increase by a very large amount: *We've multiplied our profits over the last two years.* ▶ **multiplication** /ˌmʌltɪplɪˈkeɪʃn/ *noun* [U] ⊃ look at **addition** (1), **division** (2), **subtraction**

multi-'purpose *adj.* that can be used for several different purposes: *a multi-purpose tool/machine*

multiracial /ˌmʌltiˈreɪʃl/ *adj.* (**SOCIAL STUDIES**) including or involving several different human groups: *a multiracial society*

multi-storey 'car park (*also* ˌmulti 'storey) (*both BrE*) (*AmE* **parking garage**) *noun* [C] a large building with several floors for parking cars in

multitask /ˌmʌltiˈtɑːsk/ *verb* [I] **1** (**COMPUTING**) (used about a computer) to operate several programs at the same time **2** to do several things at the same time ▶ **multitasking** *noun* [U]

multitude /'mʌltɪtjuːd/ *noun* [C] (*formal*) a very large number of people or things

multi-'user *adj.* [only before noun] (**COMPUTING**) able to be used by more than one person at the same time: *a multi-user software licence*

mum ? **A1** /mʌm/ (*BrE*) (*AmE* **mom**) *noun* [C] (*informal*) used often as a name to mean 'mother': *Is that your mum?* ◇ *Can I have a drink, Mum?* ⊃ look at **mummy**

mumble /'mʌmbl/ *verb* [I, T] to speak quietly without opening your mouth properly, so that people cannot hear the words: *I can't hear if you mumble.* ᴐ look at **mutter**

mummified /'mʌmɪfaɪd/ *adj.* (used about the dead body of a person or an animal) preserved by rubbing it with special oils and covering it in cloth: *the mummified bodies of Egyptian pharaohs*

mummy /'mʌmi/ *noun* [C] (*pl.* -ies) **1** (*BrE*) (*AmE* **mommy**) (*informal*) used especially by and to young children, and often as a name, to mean 'mother': *Here comes your mummy now.* **2** (**HISTORY**) the dead body of a person or an animal that has been kept by rubbing it with special oils and covering it in cloth: *an Egyptian mummy*

mumps /mʌmps/ *noun* [U] (**HEALTH**) a disease, especially of children, that causes areas at the sides of the neck to become larger than normal: *to have/catch (the) mumps*

munch /mʌntʃ/ *verb* [I, T] ~ (**on sth**) to bite and eat sth noisily: *He sat there munching (on) an apple.*

mundane /mʌn'deɪn/ *adj.* ordinary; not interesting or exciting: *a mundane job*

municipal ʔ+ **C1** /mjuː'nɪsɪpl/ *adj.* (**POLITICS**) connected with a town or city that has its own local government: *municipal buildings* (= the town hall, public library, etc.)

munitions /mjuː'nɪʃnz/ *noun* [pl.] military supplies, especially bombs and guns

mural /'mjʊərəl/ *noun* [C] (**ART**) a large picture painted on a wall

murder¹ ʔ **B1** /'mɜːdə(r)/ *noun* **1** [U, C] (**LAW**) the crime of killing a person illegally and on purpose: *to commit murder* ◇ *a vicious murder* ◇ *the murder victim/weapon* ᴐ look at **manslaughter** ᴐ note at **criminal¹** **2** [U] (*informal*) a very difficult or unpleasant experience: *It's murder trying to work when it's so hot.* **IDM** **get away with murder** to do whatever you want without being stopped or punished: *He lets his students get away with murder.*

murder² ʔ **B1** /'mɜːdə(r)/ *verb* [T] (**LAW**) to kill sb deliberately and illegally: *He denies murdering his ex-wife's lover.* ᴐ note at **kill¹** ▸ **murderer** /-dərə(r)/ *noun* [C]

murderous /'mɜːdərəs/ *adj.* intending or likely to murder

murky /'mɜːki/ *adj.* (**murkier; murkiest**) dark and unpleasant or dirty: *The water in the river looked very murky.* ◇ (*figurative*) *According to rumours, the new boss had a murky past.*

murmur /'mɜːmə(r)/ *verb* [T, I] to say sth in a low quiet voice: *He murmured a name in his sleep.* ▸ **murmur** *noun* [C]

muscle ʔ **B1** /'mʌsl/ *noun* [C, U] (**ANATOMY**) one of the parts inside the body that you can make tight or relax in order to produce movement: *leg/arm muscles* ◇ *Lifting weights builds muscle.*

muscular /'mʌskjələ(r)/ *adj.* **1** (**ANATOMY**) connected with the muscles: *muscular pain/tissue* **2** having large strong muscles: *a muscular body*

muse¹ /mjuːz/ *verb* [I] (*formal*) **1** ~ (**about/on/over/upon sth**) to think carefully about sth for a time, without noticing what is happening around you: *She looked out to sea, musing on what he had said.* **2** to say sth, usually to yourself, in a way that shows you are thinking carefully about it: *'I wonder if I should tell him?' she mused.*

muse² /mjuːz/ *noun* [C] (**ARTS AND MEDIA**) a person or spirit that gives a writer, painter, musician, etc. ideas and the desire to create things: *He felt that his muse had deserted him* (= that he could no longer write, paint, etc.).

museum ʔ **A1** /mjuː'ziːəm/ *noun* [C] a building where collections of valuable and interesting objects are kept and shown to the public: *Have you been to the Science Museum in London?* ᴐ look at **gallery** (1)

mushroom /'mʌʃrʊm, -ruːm/ *noun* [C] a type of plant that grows very quickly and has a flat or round top **❶** A mushroom is a type of **fungus**. Some, but not all, **fungi** can be eaten. **Toadstool** is the name for some types of poisonous fungi.

musical notation

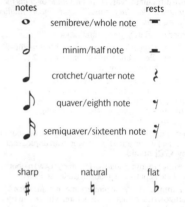

notes · rests

semibreve/whole note

minim/half note

crotchet/quarter note

quaver/eighth note

semiquaver/sixteenth note

sharp · natural · flat

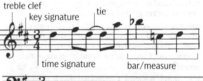

treble clef · key signature · tie

time signature · bar/measure

bass clef · stave

music ʔ **A1** /'mjuːzɪk/ *noun* [U] **1** an arrangement of sounds in patterns to be sung or played on instruments: *What sort of music do you like?* ◇ *classical/pop/rock music* ◇ *to write/compose music* ◇ *a music lesson/teacher* **2** the written signs that represent the sounds of music: *Can you read music?*

musical¹ ʔ **A2** /'mjuːzɪkl/ *adj.* (**MUSIC**) **1** [only before noun] connected with music: *Can you play a musical instrument* (= the piano, the VIOLIN, etc.)? **2** interested in or good at music: *He's very musical.* **3** having a pleasant sound like music: *a musical voice* ▸ **musically** /-kli/ *adv.*

musical² ʔ **B1** /'mjuːzɪkl/ *noun* [C] (**ARTS AND MEDIA**) a play or film that has singing and dancing in it ᴐ look at **opera** ᴐ note at **performing arts**

musician ʔ **A2** /mjuː'zɪʃn/ *noun* [C] (**MUSIC**) a person who plays a musical instrument or writes music, especially as a job

'music video = VIDEO (3)

musket /'mʌskɪt/ *noun* [C] a type of long gun that was used by soldiers in the past

Muslim /'mʊzlɪm, 'mʌz-, 'mʊslɪm/ (*also* **Moslem**) *noun* [C] (**RELIGION**) a person whose religion is Islam ᴐ note at **religion** ▸ **Muslim** (*also* **Moslem**) *adj.*: *Muslim beliefs*

muslin /ˈmʌzlɪn/ *noun* [U] thin cotton cloth that you can almost see through, used, especially in the past, for making clothes and curtains

mussel /ˈmʌsl/ *noun* [C] a SHELLFISH (= a creature with a shell that lives in water) that can be eaten, with a black shell in two parts

must¹ ⓘ **A1** ⓦ /məst, *strong form* mʌst/ *modal verb* (*negative* must not /mʌst ˈnɒt/; *short form* mustn't /ˈmʌsnt/) **1** used for saying that it is necessary that sth happens: *I must remember to go to the bank today.* ◊ *You mustn't take photos in here. It's forbidden.* **2** used for saying that you feel sure that sth is true: *Have something to eat. You must be hungry.* ◊ *I can't find my phone. I must have left it at home.* **3** used for giving sb advice: *You really must see that film. It's wonderful.*

must² /mʌst/ *noun* [C, usually sing.] a thing that you strongly recommend: *This book is a must for all science fiction fans.*

mustache /ˈmʌstæʃ, məˈstæʃ/ (*AmE*) = MOUSTACHE

mustard /ˈmʌstəd/ *noun* [U] a cold yellow or brown sauce that tastes hot and is eaten in small amounts with meat

muster /ˈmʌstə(r)/ *verb* **1** [T] to find as much support, courage, etc. as you can: *We mustered all the support we could for the project.* **SYN summon 2** [I, T] to come together, or bring people, especially soldiers, together, for some purpose, especially for military action: *The troops mustered.* ◊ *to muster an army*

musty /ˈmʌsti/ *adj.* having an unpleasant wet smell because of a lack of fresh air: *The rooms in the old house were dark and musty.*

mutant /ˈmjuːtənt/ *noun* [C] (**BIOLOGY**) a living thing that is different from other living things of the same type because of a change in its GENETIC structure

mutate /mjuːˈteɪt/ *verb* ~ (**into sth**) **1** [I, T] (**BIOLOGY**) to develop or make sth develop a new form or structure, because of a GENETIC change: *the ability of the virus to mutate into new forms* ◊ *mutated genes* **2** [I] (*formal*) to change into a new form: *Rhythm and blues mutated into rock and roll.*

mutation /mjuːˈteɪʃn/ *noun* [U, C] (**BIOLOGY**) a change in the GENETIC structure of a living or developing thing; an example of such a change: *mutations caused by radiation*

mute /mjuːt/ *adj.* **1** not speaking: *a look of mute appeal* ◊ *The child sat mute in the corner of the room.* **SYN silent 2** (*old-fashioned*) (used about a person) unable to speak **SYN dumb**

muted /ˈmjuːtɪd/ *adj.* **1** (used about colours or sounds) not bright or loud; soft **2** (used about a feeling or reaction) not strongly expressed: *muted criticism* ◊ *a muted response*

mutilate /ˈmjuːtɪleɪt/ *verb* [T, usually passive] to damage sb's body very badly, often by cutting off parts ▸ **mutilation** /ˌmjuːtɪˈleɪʃn/ *noun* [U, C]

mutiny /ˈmjuːtəni/ *noun* [U, C] (*pl.* **-ies**) an act of a group of people, especially sailors or soldiers, refusing to obey the person who is in command ▸ **mutiny** *verb* [I] (**mutinying; mutinies;** *pt, pp* **mutinied**)

mutter /ˈmʌtə(r)/ *verb* [T, I] to speak in a low, quiet and often angry voice that is difficult to hear: *He muttered something about being late and left the room.* ⊃ look at **mumble**

mutton /ˈmʌtn/ *noun* [U] the meat from an adult sheep ⊃ note at **meat, sheep**

mutual ⓘ+ **C1** /ˈmjuːtʃuəl/ *adj.* **1** (used about a feeling or an action) felt or done equally by both people involved: *We have a mutual agreement* (= we both agree) *to help each other out when necessary.* ◊ *I just* can't stand her and I'm sure **the feeling is mutual** (= she doesn't like me either). **2** [only before noun] shared by two or more people: *mutual interests* ◊ *It seems that Jane is a mutual friend of ours.* ▸ **mutually** /-əli/ *adv.*

mutual fund = UNIT TRUST

muzzle¹ /ˈmʌzl/ *noun* [C] **1** the nose and mouth of an animal, especially a dog or a horse ⊃ picture at **animal 2** a cover made of leather or wire that is put over an animal's nose and mouth so that it cannot bite **3** the open end of a gun where the bullets come out

muzzle² /ˈmʌzl/ *verb* [T, usually passive] to put a MUZZLE over the head of an animal, especially a dog, so that it cannot bite: *Dogs must be kept muzzled.*

MW *abbr.* (in writing) **1** = MEDIUM WAVE **2** (*pl.* MW) = MEGAWATT

my ⓘ **A1** /maɪ/ *det.* of or belonging to me: *This is my husband, Jim.* ◊ *My favourite colour is blue.* ⊃ look at **mine¹**

myelin /ˈmaɪəlɪn/ *noun* [U] (**BIOLOGY**) a substance that forms a covering over most of the nerves in the body, increasing the speed at which messages travel

myocardial /ˌmaɪəʊˈkɑːdiəl/ *adj.* [only before noun] (**HEALTH**) relating to the TISSUE (= cells) that forms the heart muscle

myopia /maɪˈəʊpiə/ *noun* [U] (**HEALTH**) the condition of not being able to see things clearly when they are far away **SYN short-sightedness** ▸ **myopic** /-ˈɒpɪk/ *adj.* **SYN short-sighted**

myriad /ˈmɪriəd, -riæd/ *noun* [C] an extremely large number of sth ▸ **myriad** *adj.*

myself ⓘ **A2** /maɪˈself/ *pron.* **1** used when the person who does an action is also affected by it: *I felt rather pleased with myself.* ◊ *I looked at myself in the mirror.* **2** used to emphasize the person who does the action: *I'll speak to her myself.* ◊ *I'll do it myself* (= if you don't want to do it for me). **IDM (all) by myself 1** alone: *I live by myself.* **2** without help: *I painted the house all by myself.*

mysterious ⓘ **B2** /mɪˈstɪəriəs/ *adj.* **1** that you do not understand or cannot explain; strange: *Several people reported seeing mysterious lights in the sky.* **2** (used about a person) keeping sth secret or refusing to explain sth: *They're being very mysterious about where they're going this evening.* ▸ **mysteriously** *adv.*

mystery ⓘ **B1** /ˈmɪstri/ *noun* (*pl.* **-ies**) **1** [C] a thing that you cannot understand or explain: *The cause of the accident is a complete mystery.* ◊ *It's a mystery to me what my sister sees in her boyfriend.* **2** [U] the quality of being strange and secret and full of things that are difficult to explain: *There's a lot of mystery surrounding this case.* **3** [C] (**ARTS AND MEDIA**) a story, film or play in which crimes or strange events are only explained at the end

mystery shopper *noun* [C] (**BUSINESS**) a person whose job is to visit or phone a shop or other business, or to use their website, pretending to be a customer, in order to get information on the quality of the service, the facilities, etc. ▸ **mystery shopping** *noun* [U]

mystic /ˈmɪstɪk/ *noun* [C] (**RELIGION**) a person who spends their life developing their spirit and communicating with God or a god

mystical /ˈmɪstɪkl/ (*also* **mystic**) *adj.* connected with the spirit; strange and wonderful: *Watching the sun set over the island was an almost mystical experience.*

mysticism /'mɪstɪsɪzəm/ noun [U] (RELIGION) the belief that you can reach complete truth and knowledge of God or gods by prayer, thought and development of the spirit

mystify /'mɪstɪfaɪ/ verb [T, often passive] (mystifying; mystifies; pt, pp mystified) to make sb confused because they cannot understand sth: I was mystified by the strange note he'd left behind.

mystique /mɪ'stiːk/ noun [U, sing.] the quality of being mysterious or secret that makes sb/sth seem interesting or attractive

myth ʔ+ B2 /mɪθ/ noun [C] 1 (LITERATURE) a story from past times, especially one about gods and men of courage. Myths often explain natural or historical events. SYN legend 2 an idea or a story that many people believe but that does not exist or is false: The idea that money makes you happy is a myth.

mythical /'mɪθɪkl/ adj. 1 existing only in MYTHS: mythical beasts/heroes 2 not real or true; existing only in the imagination

mythology /mɪ'θɒlədʒi/ noun [U] very old stories and the beliefs contained in them: Greek and Roman mythology ▶ mythological /ˌmɪθə'lɒdʒɪkl/ adj.: mythological beasts/figures/stories

N n

N¹ /en/ (also n) noun [C, U] (pl. N's, n's) the 14th letter of the English alphabet: 'Nicholas' begins with (an) 'N'.

N² abbr. (in writing) 1 = NORTH¹, NORTHERN: N Yorkshire 2 (pl. N) = NEWTON

naan /nɑːn/ = NAN²

nadir /'neɪdɪə(r)/ noun [sing.] (formal) the worst moment of a particular situation: the nadir of her career OPP zenith

naff /næf/ adj. (BrE, informal) lacking style, taste or quality: There was a naff band playing.

nag /næg/ verb [I, T] (-gg-) ~ (at) sb 1 to continuously complain to sb about their behaviour or to ask them to do sth many times: My parents are always nagging (at) me to work harder. 2 to worry sb or cause sb pain continuously: a nagging doubt/headache

nail¹ ʔ B1 /neɪl/ noun [C] 1 (ANATOMY) the thin hard layer that covers the ends of the fingers and toes: fingernails/toenails 2 a small thin piece of metal that is used for holding pieces of wood together, hanging pictures on, etc: to hammer in a nail ⊃ picture at bolt¹ ▶ nail verb [T]
IDM hit the nail on the head → HIT¹

nail² /neɪl/ verb [T] to fasten sth to sth with a nail or nails
PHR V nail sb down (to sth) to make a person say clearly what they want or intend to do: She says she'll visit us in the summer but I can't nail her down to a definite date.

'nail-biting adj. making you feel very excited or anxious because you do not know what is going to happen: a nail-biting finish to the race

'nail brush noun [C] a small brush for cleaning your nails

'nail file noun [C] a small metal tool with a rough surface that you use for shaping your nails

'nail polish (BrE also **'nail varnish**) noun [U] a liquid that people paint on their nails to give them colour

naive (also **naïve**) /naɪ'iːv/ adj. 1 without enough experience of life and too ready to believe or trust other people: I was too naive to realize what was happening. ◇ a naive remark/question/view SYN innocent 2 (ART) in a style that is deliberately very simple, often uses bright colours and is similar to that produced by a child ▶ naively (also naïvely) adv.: She naively accepted the first price he offered. ▶ naivety (also naïvety) /-'iːvəti/ noun [U]

naked ʔ+ B2 /'neɪkɪd/ adj. 1 not wearing any clothes: He came to the door naked except for a towel. ◇ naked shoulders/arms ⊃ look at bare (1), nude¹ 2 [only before noun] (used about sth that is usually covered) not covered: a naked flame/bulb 3 [only before noun] clearly shown or expressed in a way that is often shocking: naked aggression/ambition/fear
IDM the naked eye the normal power of your eyes without the help of glasses, a machine, etc: Bacteria are too small to be seen with the naked eye.

name¹ ʔ A1 /neɪm/ noun 1 [C] a word or words by which sb/sth is known: What's your name, please? ◇ Do you know the name of this flower? 2 [sing.] an opinion that people have of a person or thing: That area of London has rather a bad name. SYN reputation 3 [C] a famous person: All the big names in show business were invited to the party.
IDM by name using the name of sb/sth: It's a big school but the head teacher knows all the children by name. call sb names → CALL¹ enter sb's/your name (for sth) | put sb's/your name down (for sth) to ask for a place at a school, in a competition, etc. for sb or yourself: Have you entered your name for the quiz yet? in the name of sb | in sb's name for sb; officially belonging to sb: The contract is in my name. in the name of sth used to give a reason or an excuse for an action, even when what you are doing might be wrong: They acted in the name of democracy. make a name for yourself (as sth) | make your name (as sth) to become well known and respected: She made a name for herself as a journalist.

name² ʔ A1 /neɪm/ verb [T] 1 [often passive] ~ sb/sth (after sb) to give sb/sth a name: He was named James after his father (= James was his father's name). 2 to say what the name of sb/sth is: The journalist refused to name the person who had given her the information. ◇ Can you name all the planets? 3 to state sth exactly: Name your price — we'll pay it!

nameless /'neɪmləs/ adj. 1 without a name or with a name that you do not know 2 whose name is kept a secret: a well-known public figure who shall remain nameless SYN anonymous

namely ʔ+ C1 W /'neɪmli/ adv. (used for giving more detail about what you are saying) that is to say: We need to concentrate on our target audience, namely women aged between 20 and 30.

namesake /'neɪmseɪk/ noun [C] a person who has the same name as another person

nan¹ /næn/ noun [C] (used by children) grandmother

nan² (also **naan**) /nɑːn/ noun [C, U] a type of flat Indian bread

nanny /'næni/ noun [C] (pl. -ies) a woman whose job is to look after a family's children and who usually lives in the family home

'nanny goat noun [C] a female GOAT (= an animal like a sheep that lives wild in mountain areas or is kept on farms)

nano- /nænəʊ/ prefix (especially in units of measurement) one billionth: a nanosecond

nanometre (BrE) (AmE **nanometer**) /'nænəʊmiːtə(r)/ noun [C] (abbr. nm) one thousand millionth of a metre

nanoscience /ˈnænəʊsaɪəns/ *noun* [U] (**PHYSICS**) the scientific study of objects that are less than 100 NANOMETRES long

nanotechnology /ˌnænəʊtekˈnɒlədʒi/ *noun* [U] (**ENGINEERING, SCIENCE**) the branch of technology that deals with structures that are less than 100 NANOMETRES long. Scientists often build these structures using individual MOLECULES of substances.

nap /næp/ *noun* [C] a short sleep that you have during the day ⊃ look at **snooze** ▶ **nap** *verb* [I] (-pp-)

nape /neɪp/ *noun* [sing.] (**ANATOMY**) the back part of the neck

naphtha /ˈnæfθə, ˈnæpθə/ *noun* [U] (**CHEMISTRY**) a type of oil that starts burning very easily, used as fuel or in making chemicals ⊃ picture at **fractional distillation**

napkin /ˈnæpkɪn/ *noun* [C] a piece of cloth or paper that you use when you are eating to protect your clothes or for cleaning your hands and mouth: *a paper napkin* **SYN serviette**

nappy /ˈnæpi/ (*pl.* -ies) (*BrE*) (*AmE* diaper) *noun* [C] a piece of soft thick cloth or paper that a baby or very young child wears around its bottom and between its legs: *Does his nappy need changing?* ◇ *disposable nappies* (= that you throw away when they have been used)

narcotic /nɑːˈkɒtɪk/ *noun* [C] **1** (**LAW**) a powerful illegal drug that affects your mind in a harmful way **2** (**MEDICINE**) a substance or drug that relaxes you, stops pain, or makes you sleep ▶ **narcotic** *adj.*

narrate /nəˈreɪt/ *verb* [T] (*formal*) to tell a story ▶ **narration** /nəˈreɪʃn, næˈr-/ *noun* [U, C]

narrative ʔ **B1** /ˈnærətɪv/ *noun* [C, U] (*formal*) (**LITERATURE**) the description of events in a story ▶ **narrative** ʔ **B1** *adj.* [only before noun]: *narrative fiction*

narrator /nəˈreɪtə(r)/ *noun* [C] (**LITERATURE**) the person who tells a story or explains what is happening in a play, film, etc.

narrow¹ ʔ **A2** /ˈnærəʊ/ *adj.* **1** having only a short distance from side to side: *The bridge is too narrow for two cars to pass.* **OPP broad, wide**¹ **2** by a small amount: *That was a very narrow escape. You were lucky.* ◇ *a narrow defeat/victory* **3** not large; limited: *a narrow circle of friends* ▶ **narrowness** *noun* [U]

narrow² ʔ **B2** /ˈnærəʊ/ *verb* [I, T] to become or make sth narrower: *The road narrows in 50 metres.* ◇ *He narrowed his eyes at her.*
PHR V narrow sth down to make a list of things smaller: *The police have narrowed down their list of suspects to three.*

narrowboat /ˈnærəʊbəʊt/ *noun* [C] (*BrE*) a long narrow boat, used on CANALS (= artificial rivers)

narrowly /ˈnærəʊli/ *adv.* only by a small amount

narrow-ˈminded *adj.* not willing to listen to new ideas or to the opinions of other people **SYN insular OPP broad-minded, open-minded**

narthex /ˈnɑːθeks/ *noun* [C] (**ARCHITECTURE**) a small room or area at the western entrance of some Christian churches

NASA /ˈnæsə/ *abbr.* **National Aeronautics and Space Administration** a US government organization that does research into space and organizes space travel)

nasal /ˈneɪzl/ *adj.* **1** (**ANATOMY**) connected with the nose ⊃ picture at **respiratory 2** (used about sb's voice) produced partly through the nose: *a nasal voice* **3** (**LANGUAGE**) (used about a speech sound) produced by allowing air to flow through the nose but not the mouth, for example /m/ and /ŋ/ in *sum* and *sung*

nasty ʔ+ **B2** /ˈnɑːsti/ *adj.* (nastier; nastiest) very bad or unpleasant: *a nasty accident* ◇ *I had a nasty feeling he would follow me.* ◇ *When she was asked to leave she **got/turned nasty**.* ◇ *a nasty bend in the road* ◇ *What's that nasty smell?* ▶ **nastily** /-stɪli/ *adv.* ▶ **nastiness** *noun* [U]

nation ʔ **B1** /ˈneɪʃn/ *noun* [C] (**POLITICS**) a country or all the people in a country: *a summit of the leaders of seven nations* ⊃ note at **country**

national¹ ʔ **A2** ◐ /ˈnæʃnəl/ *adj.* connected with all of a country; typical of a particular country: *Here is today's national and international news.* ◇ *a national newspaper* ◇ *national identity* ⊃ look at **international** (1), **local**¹, **regional** ▶ **nationally** /-əli/ *adv.*

national² ʔ **B2** ◐ /ˈnæʃnəl/ *noun* [C] (**POLITICS**) a citizen of a particular country

ˌnational ˈanthem *noun* [C] (**MUSIC**) the official song of a country that is played at public events

the ˌnational curˈriculum *noun* [sing.] (**EDUCATION**) (in England and Wales) a programme of study in all the main subjects that children aged 5 to 16 in state schools must follow

ˌnational ˈdebt *noun* [usually sing.] (**FINANCE**) the total amount of money that the government of a country owes

the ˌNational ˈHealth Service *noun* [sing.] = NHS

ˌNational Inˈsurance *noun* [U] (*abbr.* NI) (in the UK) the system of payments that have to be made by employers and employees to the government to help people who are ill, unemployed, old, etc: *to pay National Insurance contributions*

nationalism /ˈnæʃnəlɪzəm/ *noun* [U] **1** (**POLITICS**) the desire of a group of people who belong to the same human group or have the same culture, language, etc. to form an independent country **2** a feeling of loving your country and being very proud of it; a feeling that your country is better than any other country

nationalist /ˈnæʃnəlɪst/ *noun* [C] (**POLITICS**) **1** a person who wants their country or region to become independent: *a Welsh nationalist* **2** a person who loves their country and is very proud of it; a person who feels that their country is better than any other country ▶ **nationalist** *adj.*

nationalistic /ˌnæʃnəˈlɪstɪk/ *adj.* loving your country and being very proud of it, so that you think it is better than any other

nationality /ˌnæʃəˈnæləti/ *noun* [U, C] (*pl.* -ies) (**POLITICS**) the state of being a legal citizen of a particular country: *to have French nationality* ◇ *students of many nationalities* ◇ *to have **dual nationality** (= of two countries)*

nationalize (*BrE also* -ise) /ˈnæʃnəlaɪz/ *verb* [T] (**POLITICS**) to put a company or an organization under the control of the government **OPP privatize** ▶ **nationalization** (*BrE also* -isation) /ˌnæʃnəlaɪˈzeɪʃn/ *noun* [U]

ˌnational ˈpark *noun* [C] a large area of beautiful land that is protected by the government so that the public can enjoy it

ˌNational Qualifiˈcation *noun* [C] = NQ

nationwide ʔ+ **C1** /ˌneɪʃnˈwaɪd/ *adj., adv.* over the whole of a country: *The police launched a nationwide hunt for the killer.*

native¹ ʔ **B1** /ˈneɪtɪv/ *adj.* **1** [only before noun] connected with the place where you were born or where you have always lived: *your native language/country/city* ◇ *native Londoners* **2** [only before noun] connected with the people who originally lived in a country before other people, especially white people, came to live there: *native art/dance* **HELP** Be careful. This meaning of **native** is sometimes considered offensive. **3 ~(to …)** (used about an animal or a plant) living or growing naturally in a particular place: *This plant is native to South America.* ◇ *a native species/habitat*

native² ʔ **B1** /ˈneɪtɪv/ *noun* [C] **1** a person who was born in a particular place: *a native of New York* **2** [usually pl.] (*old-fashioned*) the people who were living in Africa, America, etc. originally, before the Europeans arrived there **HELP** Be careful. This meaning of **native** is now considered offensive.

‚Native A'merican (*also* American Indian) *noun* [C] a member of any of the human groups who were the original people to live in America ▶ Native American (*also* American Indian) *adj.*

‚native 'speaker *noun* [C] (**LANGUAGE**) a person who speaks a language as their first language and has not learned it as a foreign language: *All our Spanish teachers are native speakers.*

NATO /ˈneɪtəʊ/ (*also* Nato) *abbr.* (**POLITICS**) **North Atlantic Treaty Organization** (a group of European countries, Canada and the US, who agree to give each other military help if necessary)

natter /ˈnætə(r)/ *verb* [I] (*BrE, informal*) to talk a lot about things that are not important **SYN** chat¹ ▶ natter *noun* [sing.]: *to have a natter*

natural¹ ʔ **A1** ◉ /ˈnætʃrəl/ *adj.* **1** [only before noun] existing in nature; not made or caused by humans: *I prefer to see animals in their natural habitat rather than in zoos.* ◇ *Britain's natural resources include coal, oil and gas.* ◇ *She died of natural causes* (= of old age or illness). **2** usual or normal: *It's natural to feel nervous before an interview.* **OPP** unnatural **3** that you had from birth or that was easy for you to learn: *a natural gift for languages* **4** [only before noun] (used about parents or their children) related by blood: *She's his stepmother, not his natural mother.* **5** (**MUSIC**) used after the name of a note to show that the note is neither SHARP (= half a note higher) nor FLAT (= half a note lower).

natural² /ˈnætʃrəl/ *noun* [C] (**MUSIC**) a that is neither SHARP (= half a note higher) nor FLAT (= half a note lower). ◯ picture at **music**

‚natural 'gas *noun* [U] (**CHEMISTRY**) gas that is found under the ground or the sea, and that we burn for light and heat ◯ picture at **petroleum**

‚natural 'history *noun* [U] the study of plants and animals

naturalist /ˈnætʃrəlɪst/ *noun* [C] a person who studies plants and animals

naturalize (*BrE also* -ise) /ˈnætʃrəlaɪz/ *verb* [T, usually passive] (**POLITICS**, **SOCIAL STUDIES**) to make sb a citizen of a country where they were not born ▶ naturalization (*BrE also* -isation) /ˌnætʃrəlaɪˈzeɪʃn/ *noun* [U]

‚natural 'language *noun* [C, U] (**LANGUAGE**) a language that has developed in a natural way and is not designed by humans

naturally ʔ **B1** ◍ /ˈnætʃrəli/ *adv.* **1** of course; as you would expect: *The team was naturally upset about its defeat.* **2** in a natural way; not forced or artificial: *naturally wavy hair* ◇ *He is naturally a very cheerful person.* **3** in a way that is relaxed and normal: *Don't try and impress people. Just act naturally.*

‚natural 'science *noun* [C, usually pl., U] (**SCIENCE**) the sciences that involve studying the physical world. Chemistry, biology and physics are all natural sciences. ◯ look at **earth science**, **life science**

‚natural se'lection *noun* [U] (**BIOLOGY**) the process by which plants, animals, etc. that can adapt to their environment survive and produce young, while the others disappear

nature ʔ **A2** ◉ /ˈneɪtʃə(r)/ *noun* **1** [U] all the plants, animals, etc. in the universe and all the things that happen in it that are not made or caused by people: *the forces of nature* (= for example VOLCANOES, hurricanes, etc.) ◇ *the wonders/beauties of nature* **2** [C, U] the qualities or character of a person or thing: *It's not in his nature to be unkind.* ◇ *It's human nature never to be completely satisfied.* ◇ *She's basically honest by nature.* **3** [sing.] a type or kind of sth: *I'm not very interested in things of that nature.* ◇ *books of a scientific nature* **4** -natured /ˈneɪtʃəd/ (in adjectives) having a particular quality or type of character: *a kind-natured man*
IDM second nature → SECOND¹

naturopathy /ˌneɪtʃəˈrɒpəθi/ *noun* [U] (**MEDICINE**) a system for treating illness using natural foods, HERBS (= special plants) and other techniques, rather than drugs ▶ naturopathic /ˌneɪtʃərəˈpæθɪk/ *adj.*: *Naturopathic doctors have successfully used plant-based compounds to treat pain.*

naughty /ˈnɔːti/ *adj.* (naughtier; naughtiest) (*especially BrE*) (used when you are talking to or about a child) badly behaved; not obeying: *It was very naughty of you to wander off on your own.* ▶ naughtily /-təli/ *adv.* ▶ naughtiness *noun* [U]

nausea /ˈnɔːziə/ *noun* [U] (**HEALTH**) the feeling that you are going to VOMIT (= bring up food from the stomach) ◯ look at **sick¹** (3)

nauseate /ˈnɔːzieɪt/ *verb* [T] to cause sb to feel sick or full of horror ▶ nauseating *adj.*

nautical /ˈnɔːtɪkl/ *adj.* connected with ships, sailors or sailing

‚nautical 'mile *noun* [C] a unit for measuring distance at sea; 1 852 metres

naval ʔ+ **C1** /ˈneɪvl/ *adj.* connected with the NAVY: *a naval base/officer/battle*

nave /neɪv/ *noun* [C] (**ARCHITECTURE**) the long central part of a church where most of the seats are ◯ look at **transept**

navel /ˈneɪvl/ (*also informal* belly button) *noun* [C] (**ANATOMY**) the small hole or raised part in the middle of the stomach

navigable /ˈnævɪɡəbl/ *adj.* (used about a river or narrow area of sea) that boats can sail along

navigate /ˈnævɪɡeɪt/ *verb* **1** [I] to use a map, etc. to find your way to somewhere: *If you drive, I'll navigate.* ◯ look at **satnav 2** [I, T] (**COMPUTING**) to find your way around on the internet or on a website **3** [T] to sail a boat along a river or across a sea ▶ navigation ʔ+ **B2** /ˌnævɪˈɡeɪʃn/ *noun* [U] ▶ navigator *noun* [C]

navy /ˈneɪvi/ *noun* (*pl.* -ies) **1** [C + sing./pl. verb] the part of a country's armed forces that fights at sea in times of war: *to join the navy* ◇ *Their son is in the Navy.* ◯ look at **air force**, **army** (1), **merchant navy** ◯ adjective **naval 2** [U] = NAVY BLUE

‚navy 'blue (*also* navy) *adj.* very dark blue in colour ▶ navy blue (*also* navy) *noun* [U]

Nazi /ˈnɑːtsi/ *noun* [C] **1** (**HISTORY**, **POLITICS**) a member of the National Socialist party that controlled Germany from 1933 to 1945 **2** a person who uses their power in a cruel way; a person with extreme and unreasonable views about people who belong to different human groups ▶ Nazi *adj.* ▶ Nazism /-sɪzəm/ *noun* [U]

NB (*also* N.B.) /ˌen ˈbiː/ *abbr.* used in writing to make sb take notice of a particular piece of information (from Latin 'nota bene')

NCT /ˌen siː ˈtiː/ *noun* [C] (**EDUCATION**) (in England) a test taken by children at the ages of 7 and 11, also called SAT (the abbreviation for 'National Curriculum Test')

NE *abbr.* (in writing) = NORTH-EAST¹, NORTH-EASTERN: *NE Scotland*

Neanderthal /niˈændətɑːl/ *noun* [C] **1** (**HISTORY**) a type of human being who used stone tools and lived in Europe during the early period of human history **2** a man who is unpleasant and rude and does not behave in a socially acceptable way ▶ Neanderthal *adj.*

near¹ ? **A1** **W** /nɪə(r)/ *adj., adv., prep.* **1** not far away in time or distance; close: *Let's walk to the library. It's quite near.* ◇ *We're hoping to move to Wales in the near future* (= very soon). ◇ *Where's the nearest Post Office?* ◇ *The day of the interview was getting nearer.* ◇ note at **direction** **2** (*usually* nearest /ˈnɪərɪst/) similar; most similar ◇ look at **o.n.o.** **3** near- (in adjectives) almost: *a near-perfect performance*
IDM **close/dear/near to sb's heart** → HEART **a near miss** a situation where sth nearly hits you or where sth bad nearly happens **a near thing** a situation in which you are successful, but which could also have ended badly **nowhere near** far from; not at all **to the nearest…** followed by a number when you are calculating or measuring approximately

near² /nɪə(r)/ *verb* [T, I] to get closer to sth in time or distance: *At last we were nearing the end of the project.*

nearby ? + **B2** /ˌnɪəˈbaɪ/ *adj., adv.* not far away in distance: *A new restaurant has opened nearby.* ◇ *We went out to a nearby restaurant.* ◇ note at **direction**

nearly ? **A2** /ˈnɪəli/ *adv.* almost; not completely or exactly: *It's nearly five years since I've seen him.* ◇ *Linda was so badly hurt she very nearly died.* ◇ *It's not far now. We're nearly there.*
IDM **not nearly** much less than; not at all: *It's not nearly as warm as it was yesterday.*

nearside /ˈnɪəsaɪd/ *adj.* [only before noun] (*BrE*) (used about a part of a vehicle) on the side that is nearest the edge of the road: *the car's nearside doors*
SYN **offside**

nearsighted /ˌnɪəˈsaɪtɪd/ (*AmE*) = SHORT-SIGHTED (1)

neat ? **B2** /niːt/ *adj.* **1** arranged or done carefully; tidy and in order: *Please keep your room neat and tidy.* ◇ *neat rows of figures* **2** (used about a person) liking to keep things tidy and in order: *By nature he's very clean and neat.* **3** simple but clever: *a neat solution/ explanation/idea/trick* **4** (*AmE, informal*) good; nice: *That's a really neat car!* **5** (*BrE*) (*also* straight *especially in AmE*) (used about an alcoholic drink) on its own, without ice, water or any other liquid: *a neat whisky* ▶ neatly *adv.*: *neatly folded clothes* ▶ neatness *noun* [U]

nebula /ˈnebjələ/ *noun* [C] (*pl.* nebulae /-liː/) (**ASTRONOMY**) a bright area in the night sky that is caused by a mass of dust or gas, or by a large cloud of stars that are far away

necessarily ? **B1** **O** /ˌnesəˈserəli, ˈnesəsərəli/ *adv.* used to say that sth cannot be avoided or has to happen: *The number of tickets available is necessarily limited.*
IDM **not necessarily** used to say that sth might be true but is not definitely or always true

necessary ? **A2** **W** /ˈnesəsəri/ *adj.* ~ (for sb/sth) (to do sth) that is needed for a purpose or a reason: *A good diet is necessary for a healthy life.* ◇ *It's not necessary for you all to come.* ◇ *If necessary I can take you to work that day.* **SYN** essential **OPP** unnecessary

necessitate /nəˈsesɪteɪt/ *verb* [T] (*formal*) to make sth necessary

necessity ? + **B2** **W** /nəˈsesəti/ *noun* (*pl.* -ies) **1** [U] ~ (for sth/to do sth) the need for sth; the fact that sth must be done or must happen: *Is there any necessity for change?* ◇ *There's no necessity to write every single name down.* ◇ *They sold the car out of necessity* (= because they had to). **2** [C] something that you must have: *Clean water is an absolute necessity.*

neck ? **A2** /nek/ *noun* **1** [C] (**ANATOMY**) the part of the body that joins the head to the shoulders: *She wrapped a scarf around her neck.* ◇ *Giraffes have long necks.* ◇ picture at **body** **2** [C] the part of a piece of clothing that goes round your neck: *a polo-neck/ V-neck sweater* ◇ *The neck on this shirt is too tight.* **3** -necked (in adjectives) having the type of neck mentioned: *a round-necked sweater* **4** [C] the long narrow part of sth: *the neck of a bottle*
IDM **by the scruff (of the/your neck)** → SCRUFF **neck and neck (with sb/sth)** equal or level with sb in a race or competition **up to your neck in sth** having a lot of sth to deal with: *We're up to our necks in work at the moment.*

necklace /ˈnekləs/ *noun* [C] a piece of jewellery that you wear around your neck

neckline /ˈneklaɪn/ *noun* [C] the edge of a piece of clothing, especially a woman's, that fits around or below the neck: *a dress with a low/round neckline*

necktie /ˈnektaɪ/ (*AmE*) = TIE¹ (1)

necrosis /neˈkrəʊsɪs/ *noun* [U] (**HEALTH**) the death of cells in part of the body, caused by injury, disease or a loss of blood supply

nectar /ˈnektə(r)/ *noun* [U] **1** a sweet liquid that is produced by flowers and collected by bees to make HONEY (= a sweet substance that is spread on bread, etc.) **2** the thick juice of some fruit, used as a drink: *apricot nectar*

nectarine /ˈnektəriːn/ *noun* [C] a soft round red and yellow fruit that looks like a PEACH with smooth skin

née /neɪ/ *adj.* used in front of the family name that a woman had before she got married: *Louise Mitchell, née Greenan* ◇ look at **maiden name**

need¹ ? **A1** **S** /niːd/ *verb* [T] (not usually used in the progressive tenses) **1** ~ sth/sb; ~ (sb) to do sth; sth needs doing to require sth/sb because they are essential or very important: *All living things need water.* ◇ *I need to find a doctor.* ◇ *I need you to go to the shop for me.* ◇ *This jumper needs washing.* **2** ~ to do sth used to show what you should or have to do: *Do we need to buy the tickets in advance?*

need² ? **B1** /niːd/ *modal verb* used to state that sth is not necessary or to ask if something is necessary: *Need we pay the whole amount now?* ◇ *You needn't come to the meeting if you're too busy.* ◇ *I hardly need remind you* (= you already know) *that this is very serious.*

need³ ? **A2** **W** /niːd/ *noun* **1** [U, sing.] ~ (for sth); ~ (for sb/sth) to do sth a situation in which you must have or do sth: *There's no need for you to come if you don't want to.* ◇ *Do phone me if you feel the need to talk to somebody.* ◇ *We are all in need of a rest.* ◇ *There is a growing need for new books in schools.* ◇ note at **reason¹** **2** [C, usually pl.] the things that you must h

He doesn't earn enough to pay for his basic needs. ◇ *Parents must consider their children's emotional as well as their physical needs.* **3** [U] the state of not having enough food, money or support: *a campaign to help families* **in need**

needle 🔒 **B1** /'niːdl/ *noun* [C]
• FOR SEWING **1** a small thin piece of metal with a point at one end and an EYE (= a hole) at the other, used for SEWING: *to thread a needle with cotton* ⊃ look at **pins and needles**
• FOR KNITTING **2** (*also* **knitting needle**) one of two long thin pieces of metal or plastic with a point at one end that are used for KNITTING
• FOR DRUGS **3** the sharp metal part of a SYRINGE (= a device used for putting a drug, etc. into the body and for taking blood out)
• ON AN INSTRUMENT **4** a thin metal part on a scientific instrument that moves to point to the correct measurement or direction
• ON A TREE **5** the thin, hard pointed leaf of certain trees that stay green all year: *pine needles* ⊃ picture at **tree**

needlepoint /'niːdlpɔɪnt/ *noun* [U] (**ART**) a type of SEWING in which you use very small STITCHES to make a picture on strong cloth

needless /'niːdləs/ *adj.* that is not necessary and that you can easily avoid: *Banning smoking would save needless deaths.* **SYN** **unnecessary** ▶ **needlessly** *adv.*: *Many soldiers died needlessly.*

needlework /'niːdlwɜːk/ *noun* [U] something that you SEW by hand, especially for decoration; the activity of making things by SEWING

needy /'niːdi/ *adj.* (**needier**; **neediest**) **1** not having enough money, food, clothes, etc. **2 the needy** *noun* [pl.] people who do not have enough money, food, clothes, etc.

negate /nɪ'ɡeɪt/ *verb* [T] (*formal*) **1** to stop sth from having any effect: *Alcohol negates the effects of the drug.* **2** to state that sth does not exist

negative¹ 🔒 **A1** ⊙ /'neɡətɪv/ *adj.* **1** bad or harmful: *The effects of the new rule have been rather negative.* **OPP** **positive¹** **2** only thinking about the bad qualities of sb/sth: *I'm feeling very negative about my job — in fact I'm thinking of leaving.* ◇ *If you go into the match with a negative attitude, you'll never win.* **OPP** **positive¹** **3** (used about a word, phrase or sentence) meaning 'no' or 'not': *a negative sentence* ◇ *His reply was negative/He gave a negative reply* (= he said 'no'). **OPP** **affirmative¹** **4** (*abbr.* **neg.**) (used about a medical or scientific test) showing that sth has not happened or has not been found: *The results of the pregnancy test were negative.* **OPP** **positive¹** **5** (**PHYSICS**) containing or producing the type of electricity that is carried by an ELECTRON **OPP** **positive¹** ⊃ picture at **dry cell 6** (**MATHEMATICS**) (used about a number) less than zero **OPP** **positive¹** ▶ **negatively** 🔒 *adv.*

negative² 🔒 **B2** ⑤ /'neɡətɪv/ *noun* [C] **1** a word, phrase or sentence that says or means 'no' or 'not': *Aisha answered* **in the negative** (= she said no). ◇ *'Never', 'neither' and 'nobody' are all negatives.* **OPP** **affirmative¹ 2** a piece of film that can be used to m̶ ̶ ̶a photo. The light areas of a negative are dark ̶ ̶ ̶ ̶ ̶al photo and the dark areas are light.

̶ ̶ ̶ ̶uity *noun* [U] (**FINANCE**) the situation in ̶ ̶ ̶ ̶ue of sb's house is less than the amount ̶ ̶ ̶ ̶s still owed to a MORTGAGE company,

negativity /ˌneɡə'tɪvəti/ *noun* [U] (*formal*) the fact of usually considering only the bad side of sth/sb; a lack of enthusiasm or hope

neglect 🔒 **C1** /nɪ'ɡlekt/ *verb* [T] **1** to give too little or no attention or care to sb/sth: *Don't neglect your health.* ◇ *The old house had stood neglected for years.* **2 ~ to do sth** (*formal*) to fail or forget to do sth: *He neglected to mention that he had spent some time in prison.* ▶ **neglect** 🔒 **C1** *noun* [U]: *The garden was like a jungle after years of neglect.* ▶ **neglected** *adj.*: *neglected children*

negligence /'neɡlɪdʒəns/ *noun* [U] (*formal*) (**LAW**) the failure to give sb/sth enough care or attention: *The accident was a result of negligence.* ▶ **negligent** /-dʒənt/ *adj.* ▶ **negligently** *adv.*

negligible /'neɡlɪdʒəbl/ *adj.* very small and therefore not important

negotiable /nɪ'ɡəʊʃiəbl/ *adj.* that can be decided or changed by discussion: *The price is not negotiable/non-negotiable.*

negotiate 🔒 **B2** /nɪ'ɡəʊʃieɪt/ *verb* **1** [I] **~ (with sb) (for/about sth)** (**BUSINESS**) to talk to sb in order to decide or agree about sth: *The unions are still negotiating with management about this year's pay claim.* **2** [T] (**BUSINESS**) to decide or agree sth by talking about it: *to negotiate an agreement/a deal/a settlement* **3** [T] to get over, past or through sth difficult: *To escape, prisoners would have to negotiate a five-metre wall.* ▶ **negotiator** *noun* [C]

negotiation 🔒 **B2** /nɪˌɡəʊʃi'eɪʃn/ *noun* [C, usually pl., U] (**BUSINESS**) discussions at which people try to decide or agree sth: *to enter into/break off negotiations* ◇ *The pay rise is still* **under negotiation**.

Negro /'niːɡrəʊ/ *noun* [C] (*pl.* **-oes**) (*old-fashioned*) a member of a human group with dark skin who originally came from Africa ❶ This word is now considered offensive.

neigh /neɪ/ *noun* [C] the long high sound that a horse makes ▶ **neigh** *verb* [I]

neighbour 🔒 **A1** (*BrE*) (*AmE* **neighbor**) /'neɪbə(r)/ *noun* [C] **1** a person who lives near you: *My neighbours are very friendly.* ◇ *our* **next-door neighbours 2** a person or thing that is near or next to another: *Britain's nearest neighbour is France.* ◇ *Try not to look at what your neighbour is writing.*

neighbourhood 🔒 **B1** (*BrE*) (*AmE* **neighborhood**) /'neɪbəhʊd/ *noun* [C] a particular part of a town and the people who live there

neighbouring 🔒 **C1** (*BrE*) (*AmE* **neighboring**) /'neɪbərɪŋ/ *adj.* [only before noun] near or next to: *neighbouring villages*

neighbourly (*BrE*) (*AmE* **neighborly**) /'neɪbəli/ *adj.* friendly and helpful

neither¹ 🔒 **A2** /'naɪðə(r), 'niːð-/ *det., pron.* (used about two people or things) not one and not the other: *Neither team played very well.* ◇ *Neither of the teams played very well.* ◇ *'Would you like tea or juice?' 'Neither, thank you. I'm not thirsty.'*

neither² 🔒 **B1** /'naɪðə(r), 'niːð-/ *adv.* **1** also not; not either: *I don't like fish.' 'Neither do I.'* ◇ (*informal*) *'I don't like fish.' 'Me neither.'* **HELP** In this meaning **nor** can be used in the same way: *'I don't like fish.' 'Nor do I.'* When you use **not … either**, the order of words is different: *I don't eat meat and Carlos doesn't either.* ◇ *'I haven't seen that film.' 'I haven't either.'* **2** neither … nor … not … and not … : *Neither Carlos nor I eat meat.* ⊃ look at **either¹**

nemesis /'neməsɪs/ *noun* [U, sing.] (*formal*) a punishment or defeat that sb deserves and cannot avoid

neo- /ˈniːəʊ, niːə, niˈɒ/ *prefix* (in nouns and adjectives) new; in a later form: *neo-Georgian* ◊ *neo-fascist*

neoclassical /ˌniːəʊˈklæsɪkl/ *adj.* (**ARCHITECTURE, ART**) used to describe art and architecture that is based on the style of ancient Greece or Rome, or music, literature, etc. that uses traditional ideas or styles

neoconservative /ˌniːəʊkənˈsɜːvətɪv/ *adj.* (**POLITICS**) relating to political, economic, religious, etc. beliefs that return to traditional conservative views in a slightly changed form ▸ **neoconservative** (*also* **neocon** /ˈniːəʊkɒn/) *noun* [C]

neodymium /ˌniːəʊˈdɪmiəm/ *noun* [U] (*symb.* **Nd**) (**CHEMISTRY**) a chemical element. Neodymium is a silver-white metal. ❶ For more information on the periodic table of elements, look at the **Reference Section** of this dictionary.

Neolithic /ˌniːəˈlɪθɪk/ *adj.* (**HISTORY**) from or connected with the later part of the Stone Age (= the very early period of human history): *Neolithic stone axes* ◊ look at **Palaeolithic**

neologism /niˈɒlədʒɪzəm/ *noun* [C] (*formal*) (**LANGUAGE**) a new word or expression or a new meaning of a word

neon /ˈniːɒn/ *noun* [U] (*symb.* **Ne**) (**CHEMISTRY**) a chemical element. Neon is a gas that does not react with anything and shines with a bright light when electricity is passed through it. ❶ **Neon** is a **noble gas**. ❶ For more information on the periodic table of elements, look at the **Reference Section** of this dictionary.

neonatal /ˌniːəʊˈneɪtl/ *adj.* (**HEALTH**) connected with a child that has just been born: *neonatal care*

nephew /ˈnefjuː, ˈnevjuː/ *noun* [C] your brother's or sister's son; the son of your husband's or wife's brother or sister ◊ look at **niece**

nephron /ˈnefrɒn/ *noun* [C] (**ANATOMY**) one of the tiny tubes in the **KIDNEYS** that **FILTER** the blood

nepotism /ˈnepətɪzəm/ *noun* [U] giving unfair advantages to your own family if you are in a position of power, especially by giving them jobs

Neptune /ˈneptjuːn/ *noun* [sing.] (**ASTRONOMY**) the planet in the **SOLAR SYSTEM** that is eighth in order of distance from the sun ◊ picture at **solar system**

neptunium /nepˈtjuːniəm/ *noun* [U] (*symb.* **Np**) (**CHEMISTRY**) a chemical element. Neptunium is a **RADIOACTIVE** metal. ❶ For more information on the periodic table of elements, look at the **Reference Section** of this dictionary.

nerd /nɜːd/ *noun* [C] (*informal*) a person who spends a lot of time on a particular interest and who is not always popular or fashionable **SYN** **geek** ▸ **nerdy** *adj.* (**nerdier; nerdiest**)

nerve 🔊 **B2** /nɜːv/ *noun* **1** [C] (**ANATOMY, BIOLOGY**) one of the long thin **THREADS** in the body that carry feelings or other messages to and from the brain ◊ picture at **ear, eye**[1]**, tooth** **2** **nerves** [pl.] worried, nervous feelings: *Breathing deeply should help to* ***calm/steady*** *your* ***nerves***. ◊ *I was* ***a bag of nerves*** *before my interview.* **3** [U] the courage that you need to do sth difficult or dangerous: *Racing drivers need a lot of nerve.* ◊ *He didn't* ***have the nerve*** *to ask Maria to go out with him.* ◊ *Some pilots* ***lose their nerve*** *and can't fly any more.* **4** [sing.] a way of behaving that people think is not acceptable: *You've got a nerve, calling me lazy!*
IDM ***get on sb's nerves*** (*informal*) to annoy sb or make sb angry

ˈnerve cell *noun* [C] (**ANATOMY**) a cell that carries information between the brain and the other parts of the body **SYN** **neuron**

ˈnerve-racking *adj.* making you very nervous or worried

nervous 🔊 **A2** /ˈnɜːvəs/ *adj.* **1** ~ (**about/of sth/doing sth**) worried or afraid: *I'm a bit nervous about travelling on my own.* ◊ *She was nervous of giving the wrong answer.* ◊ *I always* ***get nervous*** *just before a match.* ◊ *a nervous laugh/smile/voice* **OPP** **confident** **2** connected with the nerves of the body: *a nervous disorder* ▸ **nervously** *adv.* ▸ **nervousness** *noun* [U]

ˌnervous ˈbreakdown (*also* **breakdown**) *noun* [C] (**PSYCHOLOGY**) a time when sb suddenly becomes so unhappy that they cannot continue living and working normally: *to have a nervous breakdown*

ˈnervous system *noun* [C] (**BIOLOGY**) the brain and all the nerves in the body

nest 🔊 **C1** /nest/ *noun* [C] **1** a structure that a bird builds to keep its eggs and babies in ◊ picture at **animal** **2** the home of certain animals or insects: *a wasps' nest* ▸ **nest** *verb* [I]

ˈnest egg *noun* [C] (*informal*) an amount of money that you save to use in the future

nestle /ˈnesl/ *verb* [I, T] (used with an adverb or a preposition) to be or go into a position where you are comfortable, protected or hidden: *The baby nestled her head on her mother's shoulder.*

net[1] 🔊 **A2** /net/ *noun* **1** [U] material that has spaces between the **THREADS** **2** [C] a piece of net that is used for a particular purpose: *a tennis/fishing/mosquito net* ◊ look at **safety net** **3** **the net** [sing.] = **INTERNET**: *I spent most of the evening* ***surfing the net***.

net[2] 🔊 **C1** 🔊 (*BrE also* **nett**) /net/ *adj.* **1** (**FINANCE**) a net amount of money is the amount that remains when nothing more is to be taken away: *a net profit of £500* ◊ ***net income/earnings*** ◊ look at **gross**[1] (1) ◊ note at **income** **2** the net weight of sth is the weight without its container or the material it is wrapped in: *450 gms net weight* ◊ look at **gross**[1] (1) **3** final, after all the important facts have been included: *The net result is that small shopkeepers are being forced out of business.* ▸ **net** *adv.: a salary of $50 000 net*

net[3] /net/ *verb* [T] (**-tt-**) **1** (**FINANCE**) to earn an amount of money as a profit after you have paid tax on it: *The sale of land netted £2 million.* **2** (*especially BrE*) (**SPORT**) to kick or hit a ball into the goal **SYN** **score**[1]

netball /ˈnetbɔːl/ *noun* [U] (**SPORT**) a game that is played by two teams of seven players, usually women. Players score by throwing the ball through a high net hanging from a ring.

netbook /ˈnetbʊk/ *noun* [C] (**COMPUTING**) a small laptop computer, designed especially for using the internet and email

netiquette /ˈnetɪkət, -ket/ *noun* [U] (*informal*) (**COMPUTING**) the rules of correct or polite behaviour among people using the internet

netizen /ˈnetɪzn/ *noun* [C] (*informal*) (**COMPUTING**) a person who uses the internet a lot

netting /ˈnetɪŋ/ *noun* [U] material that is made of long pieces of string, **THREAD**, wire, etc. that are tied together with spaces between them

nettle /ˈnetl/ *noun* [C] a wild plant with leaves that make your skin red and painful if you touch them

network[1] 🔊 **A2** 🔊 /ˈnetwɜːk/ *noun* [C] **1** a system of roads, railway lines, nerves, etc. that are connected to each other: *an underground railway network* **2** (**BUSINESS**) a group of people or companies that work closely together: *We have a network of agents who sell our goods all over the country.* **3** (**COMPUTING**) a number of computers that are connected together so that information can be shared **4** (**ARTS AND MEDIA**) a group of TV or radio companies that are connected and that send out the same programmes at the same time in different parts of a country

network² /ˈnetwɜːk/ verb 1 [T] (COMPUTING) to connect a number of computers and other devices together so that equipment and information can be shared: *networked computer systems* 2 [I] (BUSINESS) to try to meet and talk to people who may be useful to you in your work: *Conferences are a good place to network.*

networking /ˈnetwɜːkɪŋ/ noun [U] (BUSINESS) a system of trying to meet and talk to other people who may be useful to you in your work

neural /ˈnjʊərəl/ adj. (BIOLOGY) connected with a nerve or the NERVOUS SYSTEM: *neural processes*

neuro- /njʊərəʊ, njʊərə, njʊəˈrɒ/ prefix (BIOLOGY) (in nouns, adjectives and adverbs) connected with the nerves: *neuroscience ◇ a neurosurgeon*

neurodiversity /ˌnjʊərəʊdaɪˈvɜːsəti/ noun [U] (PSYCHOLOGY) the idea that people with brains that work differently are part of the normal range in humans ▸ neurodiverse /-ˈvɜːs/ adj.: *The play is designed for children with autism, and for other neurodiverse audiences.*

neurologist /njʊəˈrɒlədʒɪst/ noun [C] (MEDICINE) a doctor who studies and treats diseases of the nerves

neurology /njʊəˈrɒlədʒi/ noun [U] (MEDICINE) the scientific study of nerves and their diseases ▸ neurological /ˌnjʊərəˈlɒdʒɪkl/ adj.: *neurological damage/diseases* ▸ neurologist noun [C]

neuron /ˈnjʊərɒn/ (*also* neurone /ˈnjʊərəʊn/) noun [C] (BIOLOGY) a cell that carries information within the brain and between the brain and other parts of the body; a nerve cell. ❶ A less technical term is nerve cell.

neuroscience /ˈnjʊərəʊsaɪəns/ noun [U] (BIOLOGY) the science that deals with the structure and function of the brain and the NERVOUS SYSTEM

neurosis /njʊəˈrəʊsɪs/ noun [C] (pl. neuroses /-ˈrəʊsiːz/) a mental illness that causes strong feelings of fear and worry

neurotic /njʊəˈrɒtɪk/ adj. 1 worried about things in a way that is not normal 2 suffering from a NEUROSIS

neuter¹ /ˈnjuːtə(r)/ adj. (GRAMMAR) (used about a word in some languages) not MASCULINE or FEMININE according to the rules of grammar

neuter² /ˈnjuːtə(r)/ verb [T] to remove the sexual parts of an animal ⊃ look at castrate

neutral¹ ?+ B2 W /ˈnjuːtrəl/ adj. 1 not supporting or belonging to either side in an argument, a war, etc: *I don't take sides when my brothers argue — I remain neutral.* ◇ *The two sides agreed to meet on neutral ground.* 2 having or showing no strong qualities, emotions or colour: *neutral colours ◇ a neutral tone of voice* 3 (PHYSICS) having neither a positive nor a negative charge ⊃ picture at plug¹ 4 (CHEMISTRY) neither ACID nor ALKALINE ⊃ picture at pH

neutral² /ˈnjuːtrəl/ noun [U] the position of the GEARS (= a part of the equipment in a vehicle) when no power is sent from the engine to the wheels

neutrality /njuːˈtræləti/ noun [U] the state of not supporting either side in an argument, a war, etc.

neutralize (BrE also -ise) /ˈnjuːtrəlaɪz/ verb [T] 1 to take away the effect of sth: *to neutralize a threat* 2 (CHEMISTRY) to have an effect on a substance so that it becomes neither an ACID nor an ALKALI 3 to make a country or an area NEUTRAL (= not belonging to or supporting any of the countries in a war) ▸ neutralization (BrE also -isation) /ˌnjuːtrəlaɪˈzeɪʃn/ noun [U]

neutron /ˈnjuːtrɒn/ noun [C] (CHEMISTRY, PHYSICS) one of the three types of PARTICLES that form the NUCLEUS (= central part) of an ATOM. Neutrons have no electric CHARGE. ⊃ look at electron, proton ⊃ note at isotope

never ?A1 /ˈnevə(r)/ adv. 1 at no time; not ever: *I've never been to Portugal.* ◇ *He never ever eats meat.* ◇ (formal) *Never before has such a high standard been achieved.* 2 used for emphasizing a negative statement instead of 'not': *I never realized she was so unhappy.* ◇ *Roy never so much as looked at us* (= he didn't even look at us). ◇ '*I got the job!*' '*Never!*' (= expressing surprise)
IDM never mind → MIND² you never know → KNOW¹

nevertheless ?B2 ❶ /ˌnevəðəˈles/ adv. despite that: *It was a cold, rainy day. Nevertheless, more people came than we had expected.* SYN nonetheless

new ?A1 ❶ /njuː/ adj. 1 that has recently been built, made, discovered, etc: *a new design/film/hospital ◇ a new method of treating mental illness ◇ new evidence* OPP old 2 different or changed from what was before: *I've just started reading a new book.* ◇ *to make new friends* OPP old 3 ~ (to sb) that you have not seen, learnt, etc. before: *This type of machine is new to me.* ◇ *to learn a new language* 4 ~ (to sth) having just started being or doing sth: *a new parent ◇ She's new to the job and needs a lot of help.* ▸ newness noun [U]
IDM break fresh/new ground → GROUND¹

New Age adj. connected with a way of life that rejects modern Western values and is based on spiritual ideas and beliefs: *a New Age festival ◇ New Age travellers* (= people in Britain who reject the values of modern society and travel from place to place living in their vehicles)

newbie /ˈnjuːbi/ noun [C] (informal) a person who is new and has little experience in doing sth

newborn /ˈnjuːbɔːn/ adj. [only before noun] (HEALTH) (used about a baby) that has been born very recently ▸ newborn noun [C]

new build noun [C] a house, etc. that has been built very recently or that is to be built soon

newcomer /ˈnjuːkʌmə(r)/ noun [C] a person who has just arrived in a place

newfangled /ˌnjuːˈfæŋgld/ adj. new or modern in a way that the speaker does not like

newly ?+ B2 /ˈnjuːli/ adv. (usually before a past participle) recently: *the newly appointed Minister for Health*

newly-wed /ˈnjuːli wed/ noun [C, usually pl.] a person who has recently got married: *The newly-weds went to Venice for their honeymoon.*

new moon noun [sing.] the moon when it appears as a thin curved line ⊃ look at full moon

news ?A1 /njuːz/ noun 1 [U] information about sth that has happened recently: *Write and tell me all your news.* ◇ *Have you had any news from Nadia recently?* ◇ *That's news to me* (= I didn't know that). ◇ *News is coming in of a plane crash.* 2 the news [sing.] (ARTS AND MEDIA) a regular programme giving the latest news on the radio or TV: *We always watch the ten o'clock news on TV.* ◇ *I heard about the accident on the news.*
IDM break the news (to sb) to be the first to tell sb about sth important that has happened

newsagent /ˈnjuːzeɪdʒənt/ (BrE) (AmE newsdealer /ˈnjuːzdiːlə(r)/) noun [C] 1 a person who owns or works in a shop that sells newspapers and magazines, etc. 2 newsagent's (pl. newsagents) a shop that sells newspapers, magazines, etc.

news conference (especially AmE) = PRESS CONFERENCE

newsfeed /'nju:zfi:d/ *noun* [C] a service that provides regular news to be broadcast or distributed on the internet ⊃ look at **feed²** (3)

newsflash /'nju:zflæʃ/ *noun* [C] (**ARTS AND MEDIA**) a short report on TV or radio that interrupts the normal programme to give information about an important event that has just happened

newsgroup /'nju:zgru:p/ *noun* [C] (**COMPUTING**) a place in a computer network, especially the internet, where people can discuss a particular subject and exchange information about it

newsletter ʕ+ **C1** /'nju:zletə(r)/ *noun* [C] a report about a club or an organization that is sent regularly to members and other people who may be interested

newspaper ʕ **A1** /'nju:zpeɪpə(r)/ *noun* **1** (*also* paper) [C] (**ARTS AND MEDIA**) a set of large printed sheets of paper, or a website, containing news, articles, advertisements, etc. and published every day or every week; the organization responsible for producing this: *a daily/weekly/Sunday newspaper* ◊ *a newspaper article* ◊ *I read about it in the newspaper.* ◊ *Which newspaper does he work for?* **2** [U] the paper on which newspapers are printed: *We wrapped the glasses in newspaper.*

▼ **VOCABULARY BUILDING**

Newspapers and the **journalists/reporters** who write articles for them are called **the press**. The **editor** decides what is printed. **Quality** newspapers deal with the news in a serious way. **Tabloids** are smaller in size and some of them have **sensational** (= shocking) stories and **gossip columns** (= unkind reports about famous people). Photographers who follow famous people in order to take photos of them are called **paparazzi**.

newsreader /'nju:zri:də(r)/ *noun* [C] (*BrE*) (**ARTS AND MEDIA**) a person who reads the news on the radio or TV

newsstand /'nju:z stænd/ (*AmE*) = BOOKSTALL

newsworthy /'nju:zwɜ:ði/ *adj.* (**ARTS AND MEDIA**) interesting and important enough to be in the news: *a newsworthy event*

the New Testament *noun* [sing.] (**RELIGION**) the second part of the Bible, that describes the life and teachings of Jesus Christ ⊃ look at **Old Testament**

newton /'nju:tən/ *noun* [C] (*abbr.* N) (**PHYSICS**) a unit of force. One newton is equal to the force that would give a mass of one KILOGRAM an ACCELERATION (= an increase in speed) of one metre per second.

new town *noun* [C] one of the towns that were planned by the government as complete units and built in the UK after 1946

new year (*also* New Year) *noun* [sing.] the first few days of January: *Happy New Year!* ◊ *We'll get in touch in the new year.* ◊ *New Year's Eve* (= 31 December) ◊ *New Year's Day* (= 1 January)

next¹ ʕ **A1** /nekst/ *adj.* [only before noun], *adv.* **1** (usually used with *the*) coming immediately after sth in order, space or time; closest: *The next bus leaves in 20 minutes.* ◊ *The next name on the list is Paulo.* **2** (used without *the* before days of the week, months, seasons, years, etc.) the one immediately following the present one: *See you again next Monday.* ◊ *next summer/year/Christmas* **3** after this or after that; then: *I wonder what will happen next.* ◊ *I know Joe arrived first, but who came next?* ◊ *It was ten years until I next saw her.*

next² ʕ **B1** /nekst/ (*usually the next*) *noun* [sing.] the person or thing that is next: *If we miss this train we'll have to wait two hours for the next.*

next door *adj.*, *adv.* in or into the next house or building: *our next-door neighbours* ◊ *Who lives next door?* ◊ *The school is next door to an old people's home.* ◊ *He's gone next door.*

next of kin *noun* [C] (*pl.* next of kin) your closest living relative or relatives: *My husband is my next of kin.*

next to ʕ **A1** *prep.* **1** at the side of sb/sth; right by sb/sth: *He sat down next to Gita.* ◊ *There's a cafe next to the cinema.* **2** in a position after sth: *Next to English my favourite subject is maths.*
IDM next to nothing almost nothing: *We took plenty of money but we've got next to nothing left.*

NGO /ˌen dʒiː 'əʊ/ *noun* [C] (*pl.* NGOs) (**SOCIAL STUDIES**) a charity, an association, etc. that is independent of government and business (the abbreviation for 'non-governmental organization')

NHS /ˌen eɪtʃ 'es/ *abbr.* (**MEDICINE**) **National Health Service** (the system that provides free or cheap medical care for everyone in Britain and that is paid for by taxes): *Can you get glasses on the NHS?* ⊃ look at **health service**

NI /ˌen 'aɪ/ *abbr.* = NATIONAL INSURANCE

nib /nɪb/ *noun* [C] the metal point of a pen

nibble /'nɪbl/ *verb* [T, I] to eat sth by taking small bites: *The bread had been nibbled by mice.* ▸ **nibble** *noun* [C]

nice ʕ **A1** /naɪs/ *adj.* **1** pleasant or attractive: *a nice place/feeling/smile* ◊ *It would be nice to spend more time at home.* ◊ *I'm not eating this — it doesn't taste very nice.* ◊ *'Hi, I'm Tony.' 'I'm Ray — nice to meet you.'* **2** ~ (to sb); ~ (of sb) (to do sth); ~ (about sth) kind; friendly: *What a nice girl!* ◊ *Everyone was very nice to me when I felt ill.* ◊ *It was really nice of Donna to help us.* ◊ *The neighbours were very nice about it when I hit their car.* **OPP** nasty **3** (*informal*) used before adjectives and adverbs to emphasize how pleasant or suitable sth is: *It's nice and warm by the fire.* ◊ *a nice long chat* ◊ *Everyone arrived nice and early.* ▸ **niceness** *noun* [U]

nicely /'naɪsli/ *adv.* **1** in an attractive or acceptable way; well: *The room was nicely furnished.* ◊ *The plants are coming along nicely* (= growing well). **2** in a kind, friendly or polite way: *If you ask her nicely she might say yes.* **3** (*formal*) carefully; exactly: *His novels nicely describe life in France between the wars.*
IDM do nicely **1** to be making good progress: *Her new business is doing very nicely.* **2** to be acceptable: *Tomorrow at ten will do nicely* (= will be a good time).

niche ʕ+ **C1** /niːʃ, nɪtʃ/ *noun* [C] **1** a job, position, etc. that is suitable for you: *to find your niche in life* **2** (**BUSINESS**) a small section of the market for a particular kind of product or service: *the development of niche marketing* (= aiming products at particular groups) **3** (**ARCHITECTURE**) a place in a wall that is further back, where a statue, etc. can be put **4** (**BIOLOGY**) the conditions of its environment within which a particular type of living thing can live successfully: *Within each niche, similar animals avoid competing with each other.*

nick¹ /nɪk/ *noun* [C] a small cut in sth
IDM in good/bad nick (*BrE*, *informal*) in a good/bad state or condition in the nick of time only just in time

nick² /nɪk/ *verb* [T] **1** to make a very small cut in sb/sth **2** (*BrE*, *informal*) to steal sth **3** (*BrE*, *informal*) to arrest sb

nickel /'nɪkl/ *noun* **1** [U] (*symb.* Ni) (**CHEMISTRY**) a chemical element. Nickel is a hard silver-white metal used in making some ALLOYS. ❶ For more information on the periodic table of elements, look at the **Reference Section**

of this dictionary. **2** [C] an American or Canadian coin that is worth five cents

nickname /'nɪkneɪm/ *noun* [C] an informal name that is used instead of your real name, usually by your family or friends ▶ **nickname** *verb* [T]

nicotine /'nɪkətiːn/ *noun* [U] the poisonous substance in TOBACCO (= the dried leaves used for making cigarettes)

niece /niːs/ *noun* [C] your brother's or sister's daughter; the daughter of your husband's or wife's brother or sister ⊃ look at **nephew**

nifty /'nɪfti/ *adj.* (niftier; niftiest) (*informal*) **1** accurate and showing skill: *There's some nifty guitar work on his latest album.* **2** practical; working well: *a nifty gadget* **SYN** **handy**

niggle /'nɪgl/ *verb* **1** [I, T] ~ **(at) sb** to annoy or worry sb: *His untidy habits really niggled her.* **2** [I] ~ **(about/over sth)** to complain or argue about things that are not important: *It's not worth niggling over such a small amount of money.* ▶ **niggle** *noun* [C]

niggling /'nɪglɪŋ/ *adj.* [only before noun] not very serious (but that does not go away): *niggling doubts* ◇ *a niggling injury*

night ᴀ1 /naɪt/ *noun* [C, U] **1** the part of the day when it is dark and when most people sleep: *I had a strange dream last night.* ◇ *The baby cried all night.* ◇ *It's a long way home. Why don't you stay the night?* ◇ *We will be away for a few nights.* **2** the time between late afternoon and when you go to bed: *Let's go out on Saturday night.* ◇ *He doesn't get home until eight o'clock at night.* ◇ *I went out with Kate the other night* (= a few nights ago). **IDM** **an early/a late night** an evening when you go to bed earlier/later than usual **good night** said in the evening, before you go home or before you go to sleep **in the dead of night** → DEAD **a night out** an evening that you spend out of the house enjoying yourself

nightclub /'naɪtklʌb/ *noun* [C] a place that is open late in the evening where people can go to dance, drink, etc.

nightdress /'naɪtdres/ (*also informal* nightie /'naɪti/) *noun* [C] a loose dress that a girl or woman wears in bed

nightingale /'naɪtɪŋɡeɪl/ *noun* [C] a small brown bird, the male of which has a beautiful song

nightlife /'naɪtlaɪf/ *noun* [U] the entertainment that is available in the evenings in a particular place: *It's a small town with very little nightlife.*

nightly /'naɪtli/ *adj., adv.* happening every night: *a nightly news bulletin* ◇ *The programme is broadcast nightly.*

nightmare ᴮ2 /'naɪtmeə(r)/ *noun* [C] **1** a frightening or unpleasant dream: *I had a terrible nightmare about being stuck in a lift last night.* **2** (*informal*) an experience that is very unpleasant or frightening: *Travelling in the rush hour can be a real nightmare.*

night-time *noun* [U] the time when it is dark

nightwatchman /naɪt'wɒtʃmən/ *noun* [C] (*pl.* -men /-mən/) a person who guards a building such as a factory at night

nil /nɪl/ *noun* [U] the number 0 (especially as the score in some games): *We won by two goals to nil.* ◇ *They lost two-nil.*

nimble /'nɪmbl/ *adj.* (nimbler /-blə(r)/; nimblest /-blɪst/) able to move quickly and lightly ▶ **nimbly** /-bli/ *adv.*

nimbostratus /ˌnɪmbəʊ'strɑːtəs/ *noun* [U] (GEOGRAPHY) a type of cloud that forms a thick grey layer at a low level, from which rain or snow often falls ⊃ picture at **cloud**¹

nimbus /'nɪmbəs/ *noun* [C, usually sing.] (GEOGRAPHY) a large grey rain cloud

nine ᴀ1 /naɪn/ *number* 9
IDM **nine to five** the hours that you work in most offices: *a nine-to-five job*

nineteen ᴀ1 /ˌnaɪn'tiːn/ *number* 19 ▶ **nineteenth** /-'tiːnθ/ *ordinal number, noun* [C]

ninety ᴀ1 /'naɪnti/ **1** *number* 90 **2 the nineties** *noun* [pl.] numbers, years or temperatures from 90 to 99 ▶ **ninetieth** /-əθ/ *ordinal number, noun* [C]
IDM **in your nineties** between the ages of 90 and 99

ninth¹ /naɪnθ/ *ordinal number* 9th

ninth² /naɪnθ/ *noun* [C] one of nine equal parts of sth

niobium /naɪ'əʊbiəm/ *noun* [U] (*symb.* Nb) (CHEMISTRY) a chemical element. Niobium is a silver-grey metal used in steel ALLOYS. ❶ For more information on the periodic table of elements, look at the **Reference Section** of this dictionary.

nip /nɪp/ *verb* (-pp-) **1** [T, I] to give sb/sth a quick bite or to quickly SQUEEZE a piece of sb's skin between your THUMB and finger: *She nipped him on the arm.* **2** [I] (used with an adverb or a preposition) (*BrE*, *informal*) to go somewhere quickly and/or for a short time ▶ **nip** *noun* [C]
IDM **nip sth in the bud** to stop sth bad before it develops or gets worse

nipple /'nɪpl/ *noun* [C] **1** (ANATOMY) either of the two small dark circles on either side of the chest. A baby can drink milk from its mother's breasts through the nipples. **2** (*AmE*) = TEAT

niqab /nɪ'kɑːb/ *noun* [C] a piece of cloth that covers the face but not usually the eyes, worn in public by some Muslim women

nit /nɪt/ *noun* [C] the egg of a small insect that lives in the hair of people or animals

nit-picking *noun* [U] the habit of finding small mistakes in sb's work or paying too much attention to small details that are not important ▶ **nit-picking** *adj.* [only before noun]

nitrate /'naɪtreɪt/ *noun* [U, C] (AGRICULTURE, BIOLOGY, CHEMISTRY) a COMPOUND containing NITROGEN. Nitrates are often used to improve the quality of soil. ⊃ picture at **nitrogen cycle**

nitric acid /ˌnaɪtrɪk 'æsɪd/ *noun* [U] (*symb.* HNO₃) (CHEMISTRY) a powerful clear substance that can destroy most substances and is used to make EXPLOSIVE substances and other chemical products

nitrify /'naɪtrɪfaɪ/ *verb* [T] (nitrifying; nitrifies; *pt, pp* nitrified) (CHEMISTRY) to change a substance into a COMPOUND that contains NITROGEN ⊃ look at **nitrate**

nitrite /'naɪtraɪt/ *noun* [U, C] (CHEMISTRY) a chemical COMPOUND containing NITROGEN and OXYGEN. There are several different nitrites.

nitrogen /'naɪtrədʒən/ *noun* [U] (*symb.* N) (CHEMISTRY) a chemical element. Nitrogen is a gas found in large quantities in the earth's atmosphere. ❶ For more information on the periodic table of elements, look at the **Reference Section** of this dictionary. ▶ **nitrogenous** /naɪ'trɒdʒənəs/ *adj.*: *nitrogenous fertilizers*

nitrogen cycle *noun* [C, U] (AGRICULTURE, BIOLOGY) the processes by which NITROGEN is passed from one part of the environment to another, for example when plants DECAY (= become destroyed by natural processes)

nitrogen di'oxide *noun* [U] (**CHEMISTRY**) a brown poisonous gas. Nitrogen dioxide is formed when some metals DISSOLVE (= become liquid) in NITRIC ACID. ➔ picture at **diffusion**

nitrogen fixation *noun* [U] (**BIOLOGY, CHEMISTRY**) the chemical process by which NITROGEN from the atmosphere is changed by bacteria into COMPOUNDS in the soil that plants and other living things can use, especially as part of the NITROGEN CYCLE ▶ **nitrogen-fixing** *adj.: nitrogen-fixing bacteria*

nitrous oxide /ˌnaɪtrəs ˈɒksaɪd/ (*also informal* **laughing gas**) *noun* [U] (**MEDICINE**) a gas used in the past especially by dentists to prevent you from feeling pain

the nitty-gritty /ðə ˌnɪti ˈɡrɪti/ *noun* [sing.] (*informal*) the most important facts, not the small or unimportant details

nm *abbr.* (in writing) (*pl.* nm, nms) = NANOMETRE

NNE *abbr.* (in writing) = NORTH-NORTH-EAST

NNW *abbr.* (in writing) = NORTH-NORTH-WEST

No. (*also* no.) *abbr.* (in writing) (*pl.* Nos, nos) = NUMBER[1] (4): *No. 10 Downing Street* ◇ *tel. no. 512364*

no[1] ⚡**A1** /nəʊ/ *exclamation* **1** used for giving a negative reply: *'Are you ready?' 'No, I'm not.'* ◇ *'Would you like something to eat?' 'No, thank you.'* ◇ *'Can I borrow the car?' 'No, you can't.'* **OPP** **yes** **2** used for expressing surprise or shock: *'Mike's had an accident.' 'Oh, no!'*

no[2] ⚡**A1** /nəʊ/ *det.* **1** not any; not a: *I have no time to talk now.* ◇ *No visitors may enter without a ticket.* ◇ *He's no friend of mine.* **2** used for saying that sth is not allowed: *No smoking.* ◇ *No flash photography.* ◇ *No parking.*

no[3] /nəʊ/ *adv.* used before adjectives and adverbs to mean 'not': *Alice is feeling no better this morning.*

Noah's ark /ˌnəʊəz ˈɑːk/ = ARK

nobelium /nəʊˈbiːliəm, -ˈbel-/ *noun* [U] (*symb.* **No**) (**CHEMISTRY**) a chemical element. Nobelium is a RADIOACTIVE metal produced artificially from CURIUM. ❶ For more information on the periodic table of elements, look at the **Reference Section** of this dictionary.

Nobel Prize /ˌnəʊbel ˈpraɪz/ *noun* [C] an international prize given each year for achievements in physics, chemistry, PHYSIOLOGY, ECONOMICS, medicine, literature and peace

nobility /nəʊˈbɪləti/ *noun* **1** the nobility [sing. + sing./pl. verb] people of high social position who have titles such as Duke or Duchess **SYN** **aristocracy 2** [U] (*formal*) the quality of having courage and honour

noble[1] ⚡+ **C1** /ˈnəʊbl/ *adj.* (**nobler** /-blə(r)/; **noblest** /-blɪst/) **1** honest; full of courage and care for others: *a noble leader* ◇ *noble ideas/actions* **2** belonging to the highest social class: *a man of noble birth* ▶ **nobly** /-bli/ *adv.*

noble[2] /ˈnəʊbl/ *noun* [C] a person who comes from a family of high social rank; a member of the NOBILITY

noble 'gas *noun* [C] (**CHEMISTRY**) any of a group of gases that do not react with other chemicals ❶ Noble gases are also called **inert gases** and include **argon, helium, krypton** and **neon**.

nobleman /ˈnəʊblmən/ *noun* [C] (*pl.* -men /-mən/) a man from a family of high social rank; a member of the NOBILITY (= the group of people who belong to the highest social class) **SYN** **aristocrat**

noble 'metal *noun* [C] (**CHEMISTRY**) a metal, such as gold or silver, that does not react easily with air or ACID

noblewoman /ˈnəʊblwʊmən/ *noun* [C] (*pl.* -women /-wɪmɪn/) a woman from a family of high social rank; a member of the NOBILITY (= the group of people who belong to the highest social class) **SYN** **aristocrat**

the nitrogen cycle

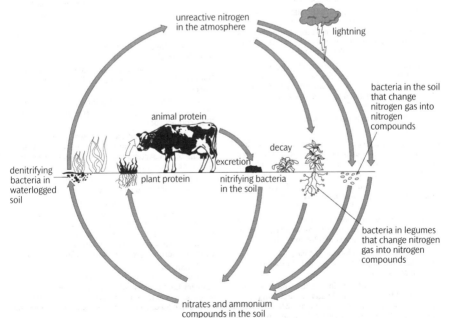

unreactive nitrogen in the atmosphere

lightning

bacteria in the soil that change nitrogen gas into nitrogen compounds

animal protein

decay

denitrifying bacteria in waterlogged soil

excretion

plant protein

nitrifying bacteria in the soil

bacteria in legumes that change nitrogen gas into nitrogen compounds

nitrates and ammonium compounds in the soil

nobody¹ ⓘ A1 /ˈnəʊbədi/ (*also* **no one**) *pron.* no person; not anyone: *He screamed but nobody came to help him.* ◇ *No one else was around.* ◇ *There was nobody at home.*

nobody² /ˈnəʊbədi/ *noun* [C] (*pl.* **-ies**) a person who is not important or famous: *She rose from being a nobody to a superstar.*

no-ˈbrainer *noun* [C, usually sing.] (*informal*) a decision that you do not need to think about much because it is obvious what you should do

nocturnal /nɒkˈtɜːnl/ *adj.* **1** (used about animals and birds) active at night and asleep during the day: *Owls are nocturnal birds.* OPP **diurnal 2** (*formal*) happening in the night: *a nocturnal adventure*

nod ⓘ C1 /nɒd/ *verb* [I, T] (-dd-) to move your head up and down as a way of saying 'yes' or as a sign to sb to do sth: *Everybody at the meeting nodded in agreement.* ◇ *Nod your head if you understand what I'm saying and shake it if you don't.* ▸ **nod** *noun* [C] PHR V **nod off** (*informal*) to fall asleep for a short time

node /nəʊd/ *noun* [C] **1** (BIOLOGY) a place on the STEM (= long thin part) of a plant from which a branch or leaf grows **2** (MATHEMATICS) a point at which two lines or systems meet or cross **3** (ANATOMY) a small hard mass, especially near a JOINT (= the place where two bones meet) in the human body ⊃ look at **lymph node**

nodule /ˈnɒdjuːl/ *noun* [C] (BIOLOGY) a small round mass of cells or SWELLING, especially on a plant

no-ˈfrills *adj.* [only before noun] including only the basic features, without anything that is unnecessary, especially things added to make sth more attractive or comfortable: *a no-frills airline*

no-ˈgo area *noun* [C] a place, especially part of a city, where it is very dangerous to go because there is a lot of violence or crime

Noh /nəʊ/ *noun* [U] (ARTS AND MEDIA) traditional Japanese theatre in which songs, dance, and MIME are performed by people wearing MASKS

noir /nwɑː(r)/ *noun* [U, C] (ARTS AND MEDIA) a type of film, fiction or drama in which there are strong feelings of fear or danger, or a film, etc. made in this way: *This film is not classic noir.* ◇ *the stylish detective noir Blade Runner* ⊃ look at **film noir**

noise ⓘ A2 /nɔɪz/ *noun* [C, U] a sound, especially one that is loud or unpleasant: *Did you hear a noise downstairs?* ◇ *Try not to **make a noise** if you come home late.* ◇ *What an awful noise! Why is the engine making so much noise?*

noiseless /ˈnɔɪzləs/ *adj.* (*formal*) making no sound ▸ **noiselessly** *adv.*

noisy ⓘ A2 /ˈnɔɪzi/ *adj.* (**noisier**; **noisiest**) making a lot of or too much noise; full of noise: *The clock was so noisy that it kept me awake.* ◇ *noisy children/traffic/crowds* ◇ *The classroom was very noisy.* ▸ **noisily** /-zɪli/ *adv.*

nomad /ˈnəʊmæd/ *noun* [C] a member of a community that moves with its animals from place to place ▸ **nomadic** /nəʊˈmædɪk/ *adj.*: *nomadic tribes*

ˈno-man's-land *noun* [U, sing.] an area of land between the borders of two countries or between two armies during a war, that is not controlled by either

nomenclature /nəˈmeŋklətʃə(r)/ *noun* [U, C] (*formal*) a system of naming things, especially in science: *zoological nomenclature*

nominal /ˈnɒmɪnl/ *adj.* **1** being sth in name only, and not in reality: *the nominal leader of the country* (= somebody else is really in control) **2** (used about a price, sum of money, etc.) very small; much less than

normal: *Because we are friends he only charges me a **nominal rent.*** ▸ **nominally** /-nəli/ *adv.*

nominate ⓘ C1 /ˈnɒmɪneɪt/ *verb* [T] ~ **sb/sth (for/as sth)** to formally suggest that sb/sth should be given a job, role, prize, etc: *I would like to nominate Ana as chairperson.* ◇ *The novel has been nominated for the Booker prize.* ◇ *You may nominate a representative to speak for you.* ▸ **nomination** ⓘ C1 /ˌnɒmɪˈneɪʃn/ *noun* [C, U]

nominative /ˈnɒmɪnətɪv/ *noun* [sing.] (GRAMMAR) (in some languages) the form of a noun, a pronoun or an adjective when it is the subject of a verb ▸ **nominative** *adj.*: *nominative pronouns* ⊃ look at **accusative, dative, genitive, vocative**

nominee ⓘ /ˌnɒmɪˈniː/ *noun* [C] a person who is suggested for an important job, prize, etc.

non- /nɒn/ *prefix* (in nouns, adjectives and adverbs) not: *non-biodegradable* ◇ *non-flammable*

nona- /ˈnɒnə, ˈnəʊnə/ *prefix* (in nouns and adjectives) nine; having nine: *nonagenarian* (= a person who is between 90 and 99 years old)

non-acaˈdemic *adj.* connected with technical or practical subjects rather than subjects of interest to the mind

nonagon /ˈnɒnəgən/ *noun* [C] (GEOMETRY) a flat shape with nine straight sides and nine angles

non-alcoˈholic *adj.* (used about drinks) not containing any alcohol: *non-alcoholic drinks*

non-aˈligned *adj.* (POLITICS) (used about a country) not providing support for or receiving support from any of the powerful countries in the world

non-biodeˈgradable *adj.* (ENVIRONMENT) a substance or chemical that is **non-biodegradable** cannot be changed by bacteria to a state that does not harm the environment OPP **biodegradable**

nonchalant /ˈnɒnʃələnt/ *adj.* behaving in a calm and relaxed way and not appearing to be worried or excited ▸ **nonchalance** /-ləns/ *noun* [U] ▸ **nonchalantly** *adv.*

non-coˈmmittal *adj.* not saying or showing exactly what your opinion is or which side of an argument you agree with

nonconformist /ˌnɒnkənˈfɔːmɪst/ *noun* [C] a person who behaves or thinks differently from most other people in society OPP **conformist** ▸ **nonconformist** *adj.*

nonconformity /ˌnɒnkənˈfɔːməti/ *noun* [U] behaving or thinking differently from most other people in society

non-ˈcontact sport *noun* [C] (SPORT) a sport in which players do not have physical contact with each other OPP **contact sport**

non-deˈfining *adj.* (used about clauses) giving extra information about a noun phrase, inside COMMAS in writing or in a particular INTONATION (= the rise and fall of the voice) in speech

nondescript /ˈnɒndɪskrɪpt/ *adj.* not having any interesting or unusual qualities

none¹ ⓘ A2 /nʌn/ *pron.* ~ **(of sb/sth)** not any, not one (of a group of three or more): *They gave me a lot of information but none of it was very helpful.* ◇ *I've got four brothers but none of them live/lives nearby.* ◇ *'Have you brought any books to read?' 'No, none.'* ◇ *I went to several shops but none had what I wanted.*

none² /nʌn/ *adv.* IDM **none too happy, clean, pleased, etc.** (*informal*) not very happy, clean, pleased, etc. **none the wiser/ worse** knowing no more than before; no worse than before: *We talked for a long time but I'm still **none the wiser**.*

non-es'sential adj. not completely necessary: *a ban on non-essential travel*

nonetheless ʔ+ **C1** /ˌnʌnðəˈles/ adv. (*formal*) despite this fact: *It won't be easy but they're going to try nonetheless.* **SYN** nevertheless

non-e'xistent adj. not existing or not available

non-'fiction noun [U] (**LITERATURE**) writing that is about real people, events and facts: *You'll find biographies in the non-fiction section of the library.* **OPP** fiction

non-'flammable adj. not likely to burn easily

non-ma'lignant adj. (**HEALTH**) (used about a TUMOUR (= a growing mass of cells)) not caused by cancer and not likely to be dangerous **SYN** benign **OPP** malignant

nonplussed /ˌnɒnˈplʌst/ adj. confused; not able to understand

non-'profit ʔ+ **C1** (*especially BrE*) (*also* **not-for-profit** *BrE, AmE*) adj. (**BUSINESS**) (used about an organization) without the aim of making a profit: *The centre is run on a non-profit basis.*

non-refoulement /ˌnɒn rəˈfuːlmɒ̃/ noun [U] (**LAW**) the practice of not forcing REFUGEES (= people who have had to leave their country) to return to a country where they would be in danger **OPP** refoulement

non-re'newable adj. (**ENVIRONMENT**) (used about natural sources of energy such as gas or oil) that cannot be replaced after use

nonsense ʔ+ **C1** /ˈnɒnsns/ noun [U] **1** ideas, statements or beliefs that you think are silly or not true: *Don't talk nonsense!* **SYN** rubbish **2** silly or unacceptable behaviour: *The head teacher won't stand for any nonsense.*

nonsensical /ˌnɒnˈsensɪkl/ adj. silly; with no meaning

non-'smoker noun [C] a person who does not smoke cigarettes, etc. **OPP** smoker ▶ **non-'smoking** adj.: *Would you like a table in the smoking or the non-smoking section?*

non-'starter noun [C] (*informal*) a person, a plan or an idea that has no chance of success

non-'stick adj. (used about a pan, etc.) covered with a substance that prevents food from sticking to it

non-'stop adj., adv. without a stop or a rest: *a non-stop flight to Delhi* ◇ *He talked non-stop for two hours about his holiday.*

non-'verbal adj. not involving words or speech: *non-verbal communication*

non-'violence noun [U] fighting for political or social change without using force, for example by not obeying laws ▶ **non-'violent** adj.

non-'white adj. (**SOCIAL STUDIES**) belonging to a human group that does not have white skin: *Non-white voters represented over half of those who turned out.* ▶ **non-white** noun [C]

noodle /ˈnuːdl/ noun [C, usually pl.] long thin pieces of food made of flour, egg and water that are cooked in boiling water or used in soups

nook /nʊk/ noun [C] a small quiet place or corner (in a house, garden, etc.) **IDM** every nook and cranny (*informal*) every part of a place

noon ʔ+ **C1** /nuːn/ noun [U] twelve o'clock in the middle of the day: *At noon the sun is at its highest point in the sky.* **SYN** midday ◇ look at **midnight**

'no one ʔ **A1** = NOBODY¹

noose /nuːs/ noun [C] a circle that is tied in the end of a rope and that gets smaller as one end of the rope is pulled

'no place adv. (*especially AmE*) = NOWHERE: *I have no place else to go.*

nor ʔ **B1** /nɔː(r)/ conj., adv. **1 neither … nor …** and not: *She seemed neither surprised nor worried.* **2** (used before a positive verb to agree with sth negative that has just been said) also not; neither: *'I don't like football.' 'Nor do I.'* ◇ *'We haven't been to America.' 'Nor have we.'* **HELP** In this meaning **neither** can be used in the same way: *'I won't be here tomorrow.' 'Nor/Neither will I.'* **3** (used after a negative statement to add some more information) also not: *Michael never forgot her birthday. Nor their wedding anniversary for that matter.*

Nordic /ˈnɔːdɪk/ adj. **1** connected with Scandinavia, Finland and Iceland **2** typical of a member of a European human group who are tall and have blue eyes and fair hair: *Nordic features*

Nordic 'skiing noun [U] (**SPORT**) the sport of skiing across the countryside ◇ look at **Alpine skiing**

norm ʔ+ **B2** **W** /nɔːm/ noun [C] (often used with *the*) a situation or way of behaving that is usual or expected

normal¹ ʔ **A2** **O** /ˈnɔːml/ adj. typical, usual or ordinary; what you expect: *I'll meet you at the normal time.* ◇ *It's quite normal to feel angry in a situation like this.* **OPP** abnormal

normal² ʔ **B1** /ˈnɔːml/ noun [U] the usual or average state, level or standard: *temperatures above/below normal* ◇ *Things are back to normal at work now.*

normality /nɔːˈmæləti/ (*also* **normalcy** /ˈnɔːmlsi/ *especially in AmE*) noun [U] the state of being normal

normalize (*BrE also* -**ise**) /ˈnɔːməlaɪz/ verb [T, I] (*formal*) to become normal again; to make sth normal again or return to how it was before: *The two countries agreed to normalize relations* (= return to a normal, friendly relationship, for example after an argument or a war).

normally ʔ **A2** **W** /ˈnɔːməli/ adv. **1** usually: *I normally leave the house at eight o'clock.* ◇ *Normally he takes the bus.* **2** in the usual or ordinary way: *His heart is beating normally.*

Norman /ˈnɔːmən/ adj. **1** (**ARCHITECTURE**) used to describe the style of architecture in Britain in the eleventh and twelfth centuries that developed from the ROMANESQUE style: *a Norman church/castle* **2** (**HISTORY**) connected with the Normans (= the people from northern Europe who defeated the English in 1066 and then ruled the country): *the Norman Conquest*

Norse¹ /nɔːs/ noun [U] (**LANGUAGE**) the Norwegian language, especially in an ancient form, or the Scandinavian language group

Norse² /nɔːs/ adj. (**HISTORY**) relating to Norway or Scandinavia in the ancient past

north¹ ʔ **A1** /nɔːθ/ noun [U, sing.] (*abbr.* N) (**GEOGRAPHY**) **1** (*usually* **the north**) ~(**of …**) the direction that is on your left when you watch the sun rise; one of the points of the COMPASS (= the four main directions that we give names to): *cold winds from the north* ◇ *Which way is north?* ◇ *I live to the north of Belfast.* ◇ look at **east¹** (1), **magnetic north**, **south¹** (1), **true north**, **west¹** (1) ◇ note at **compass** ◇ picture at **compass 2 the north, the North** the northern part of a country, a city, a region or the world: *Houses are less expensive in the North of England than in the South.* ◇ *I live in the north of Athens.*

north² ʔ **A1** /nɔːθ/ adj., adv. (**GEOGRAPHY**) **1** in or towards the north: *The new offices will be in North London.* ◇ *The north wing of the hospital was destroyed in a fire.* ◇ *We got onto the motorway going north instead of south.* ◇ *The house faces north.* **2** ~(**of …**)

nearer to the north than sth: *Is Leeds north of Manchester?* **3** (used about a wind) coming from the north

the North Atlantic Drift /ðə ˌnɔːθ ətˌlæntɪk ˈdrɪft/ *noun* [sing.] (**GEOGRAPHY**) a current of warm water in the Atlantic Ocean, that has the effect of making the climate of north-west Europe warmer ➔ picture at **current²**

northbound /ˈnɔːθbaʊnd/ *adj.* travelling or leading towards the north: *northbound traffic*

ˌnorth-ˈeast¹ (*usually* the North-East) *noun* [sing.] (*abbr.* NE) (**GEOGRAPHY**) the direction or a region that is an equal distance between north and east ➔ picture at **compass**

ˌnorth-ˈeast² *adj., adv.* (**GEOGRAPHY**) in, from or to the north-east of a place or country: *the north-east coast of Australia* ◇ *If you look north-east you can see the sea.*

ˌnorth-ˈeasterly *adj.* (**GEOGRAPHY**) **1** [only before noun] towards the north-east: *in a north-easterly direction* **2** (used about a wind) coming from the north-east

ˌnorth-ˈeastern *adj.* [only before noun] (*abbr.* NE) (**GEOGRAPHY**) connected with the north-east of a place or country

ˌnorth-ˈeastwards (*also* north-eastward) *adv.* (**GEOGRAPHY**) towards the north-east: *Follow the road north-eastwards.*

northerly /ˈnɔːðəli/ *adj.* (**GEOGRAPHY**) **1** [only before noun] to, towards or in the north: *Keep going in a northerly direction.* **2** (used about a wind) coming from the north

northern ⚡ **B1** /ˈnɔːðən/ (*also* Northern) *adj.* (*abbr.* N) (**GEOGRAPHY**) of, in or from the north of a place: *She has a northern accent.* ◇ *in northern Australia*

northerner /ˈnɔːðənə(r)/ (*also* Northerner) *noun* [C] a person who was born in or who lives in the northern part of a country **OPP southerner**

the ˌNorthern ˈLights *noun* [pl.] (*also* aurora borealis [sing.]) (**ASTRONOMY**) bands of coloured light, mainly green and red, that are sometimes seen in the sky at night in the most northern countries of the world

northernmost /ˈnɔːðənməʊst/ *adj.* (**GEOGRAPHY**) furthest north: *the northernmost island of Japan*

ˌnorth-north-ˈeast *noun* [sing.] (*abbr.* NNE) (**GEOGRAPHY**) the direction that is an equal distance between north and north-east

ˌnorth-north-ˈwest *noun* [sing.] (*abbr.* NNW) (**GEOGRAPHY**) the direction that is an equal distance between north and north-west

the ˌNorth ˈPole *noun* [sing.] (**GEOGRAPHY**) the point on the Earth's surface that is furthest north ➔ picture at **earth¹**

ˌnorth-ˈsouth (*also* North-South) *adj.* (**GEOGRAPHY**) extending between or relating to the north and the south of a place: *The main north-south highway was closed because of heavy snow.* ◇ *A new report reveals a growing north-south divide between UK cities.*

northwards /ˈnɔːθwədz/ (*also* northward /ˈnɔːθwəd/) *adv.* towards the north: *Continue northwards out of the city for about 5 miles.* ▸ **northward** *adj.*: *in a northward direction*

ˌnorth-ˈwest¹ (*usually* the North-West) *noun* [sing.] (*abbr.* NW) (**GEOGRAPHY**) the direction or a region that is an equal distance between north and west ➔ picture at **compass**

ˌnorth-ˈwest² *adj., adv.* (**GEOGRAPHY**) in, from or to the north-west of a place or country: *the north-west coast of Scotland* ◇ *Our house faces north-west.*

ˌnorth-ˈwesterly *adj.* (**GEOGRAPHY**) **1** [only before noun] towards the north-west: *in a north-westerly direction* **2** (used about a wind) coming from the north-west

ˌnorth-ˈwestern *adj.* [only before noun] (*abbr.* NW) (**GEOGRAPHY**) connected with the north-west of a place or country

ˌnorth-ˈwestwards (*also* north-westward) *adv.* (**GEOGRAPHY**) towards the north-west: *Follow the road north-westwards for ten kilometres.*

nose¹ ⚡ **A1** /nəʊz/ *noun* [C] **1** (**ANATOMY**) the part of the face, above the mouth, that is used for breathing and smelling ➔ picture at **body 2** the front part of a plane, etc. ➔ picture at **airliner 3** -nosed (in adjectives) having the type of nose mentioned: *red-nosed* ◇ *big-nosed*

IDM blow your nose → BLOW¹ **follow your nose** → FOLLOW **look down your nose at sb/sth** (*especially BrE, informal*) to think that you are better than sb else; to think that sth is not good enough for you **poke/ stick your nose into sth** (*informal*) to be interested in or try to become involved in sth that does not concern you **turn your nose up at sth** (*informal*) to refuse sth because you do not think it is good enough for you

nose² /nəʊz/ *verb* [I, T] (used with an adverb or a preposition) (used about a vehicle) to move forward slowly and carefully

PHR V nose around (*also* nose about *especially in BrE*) to look for sth, especially private information about sb

nosebleed /ˈnəʊzbliːd/ *noun* [C] (**HEALTH**) a sudden flow of blood that comes from the nose

nosedive /ˈnəʊzdaɪv/ *noun* [C] a sudden sharp fall or drop: *Oil prices took a nosedive in the crisis.* ▸ **nosedive** *verb* [I]

nostalgia /nɒˈstældʒə/ *noun* [U] a feeling of pleasure, mixed with SADNESS, when you think of happy times in the past: *She was suddenly filled with nostalgia for her university days.* ▸ **nostalgic** /-dʒɪk/ *adj.* ▸ **nostalgically** /-kli/ *adv.*

nostril /ˈnɒstrəl/ *noun* [C] (**ANATOMY**) one of the two openings at the end of the nose, that you breathe through ➔ picture at **body**

nosy (*also* nosey) /ˈnəʊzi/ *adj.* (nosier; nosiest) too interested in other people's personal affairs: *a nosy neighbour*

not ⚡ **A1** /nɒt/ *adv.* **1** used with the verbs 'be', 'do' and 'have' to form the negative of verbs; used to form the negative of modal verbs such as 'can', 'must' and 'will': *It's not/it isn't raining now.* ◇ *I cannot/can't see from here.* ◇ *He didn't invite me.* ◇ *Don't you like spaghetti?* ◇ *I hope she will not/won't be late.* ◇ *You're German, aren't you?* **2** used to give the following word or phrase a negative meaning: *He told me not to phone.* ◇ *She accused me of not telling the truth.* ◇ *Not one person replied to my advertisement.* ◇ *It's not easy.* ◇ *He's not very tall.* **3** used to give a short negative reply: *'Do you think they'll get divorced?' 'I hope not.'* (= I hope that they will not.) ◇ *'Can I borrow £20?' 'Certainly not!'* ◇ *'Whose turn is it to do the shopping?' 'Not mine.'* **4** used with the word *or* to give a negative possibility: *Shall we tell her or not?*

IDM not at all 1 used as a way of replying when sb has thanked you: *'Thanks for the present.' 'Not at all, don't mention it.'* **2** used as a way of saying 'no' or 'definitely not': *'Do you mind if I come too?' 'Not at all.'* ◇ *The instructions are not at all clear.* **not only ... (but) also** used for emphasizing the fact that there is sth more to add: *They not only have two houses in London, they also have one in France.*

notable ʔ+ **C1** /ˈnəʊtəbl/ *adj.* ~ (for sth) interesting or important enough to receive attention: *The area is notable for its wildlife.*

notably ʔ+ **C1** /ˈnəʊtəbli/ *adv.* used for giving an especially important example of what you are talking about: *Several politicians, most notably the prime minister and the Home Secretary, have given the proposal their full support.*

notary /ˈnəʊtəri/ (*pl.* -ies) (*also* ˌnotary ˈpublic, *pl.* ˌnotaries ˈpublic) *noun* [C] (**LAW**) a person, especially a lawyer, with official authority to be a witness when sb signs a document and to make this document legally acceptable

notation /nəʊˈteɪʃn/ *noun* [U, C] a system of signs or symbols used to represent information, especially in mathematics, science and music ⊃ picture at **music**

notch¹ /nɒtʃ/ *noun* [C] **1** a level on a scale of quality: *This meal is certainly a notch above the last one we had here.* **2** a cut in an edge or a surface in the shape of a V or a circle, sometimes used to help you count sth

notch² /nɒtʃ/ *verb*
PHR V notch sth up to score or achieve sth: *He notched up his best ever time in the 100 metres.*

note¹ ʔ **A1** **S** /nəʊt/ *noun*
- TO REMIND YOU **1** [C] some words that you write down quickly to help you remember sth: *I'd better make a note of your name and address.* ◇ *Keep a note of who has paid and who hasn't.* ◇ *The lecturer advised the students to take notes while she was speaking.*
- SHORT LETTER **2** [C] a short letter: *This is just a note to thank you for having us to dinner.* ◇ *If Mark's not at home we'll leave a note for him.* ◇ *a sick note from your doctor*
- IN A BOOK **3** [C] a short explanation or an extra piece of information that is given at the back of a book, etc. or at the bottom or side of a page: *See note 5, page 340.* ⊃ look at **footnote**
- MONEY **4** [C] (*BrE*) (*also* banknote *especially in BrE*) (*AmE usually* bill) (**FINANCE**) a piece of paper money: *I'd like the money in £10 notes, please.*
- IN MUSIC **5** [C] a single musical sound made by a voice or an instrument; a written sign that represents a musical sound: *I can only remember the first few notes of the song.* ⊃ picture at **music**
- QUALITY **6** [sing.] something that shows a certain quality or feeling: *The meeting ended on a rather unpleasant note.*
IDM compare notes (with sb) → COMPARE take note (of sth) to pay attention to sth and be sure to remember it

note² ʔ **B1** **O** /nəʊt/ *verb* [T] **1** to notice or pay careful attention to sth: *He noted a slight change in her attitude towards him.* ◇ *Please note that this office is closed on Tuesdays.* **2** (*formal*) to mention sth: *I'd like to note that the project has so far been extremely successful.* ⊃ note at **comment²**
PHR V note sth down to write sth down so that you remember it

notebook ʔ+ **B2** /ˈnəʊtbʊk/ *noun* [C] **1** a small book in which you write things that you want to remember **2** (*also* ˌnotebook comˈputer) (**COMPUTING**) a small computer that can work with a battery and be easily carried **SYN** laptop ⊃ look at **desktop** (3) **3** (*AmE*) = EXERCISE BOOK

noted /ˈnəʊtɪd/ *adj.* ~ (for/as sth) (*formal*) well known; famous: *The hotel is noted for its food.*

notepad /ˈnəʊtpæd/ *noun* [C] sheets of paper in a block that are used for writing things on

notepaper /ˈnəʊtpeɪpə(r)/ *noun* [U] paper that you write letters on

noteworthy /ˈnəʊtwɜːði/ *adj.* interesting or important; that is worth noticing

ˌnot-for-ˈprofit *adj.* = NON-PROFIT: *The scheme provides grants of up to £10 000 for not-for-profit organizations.*

nothing ʔ **A1** /ˈnʌθɪŋ/ *pron.* not anything; no thing: *There's nothing in this suitcase.* ◇ *I'm bored — there's nothing to do here.* ◇ *There was nothing else to say.* ◇ *'What's the matter?' 'Oh, nothing.'* ◇ *'Thank you so much for all your help.' 'It was nothing.'* ◇ *The doctor said there's nothing wrong with me.*
IDM be/have nothing to do with sb/sth to have no connection with sb/sth: *That question has nothing to do with what we're discussing.* ◇ *Keep out of this — it's nothing to do with you.* come to nothing → COME for nothing **1** for no good reason or with no good result: *His hard work was all for nothing.* **2** for no payment; free: *Children under four are allowed in for nothing.* nothing but only: *He does nothing but sit around watching TV all day.* nothing like (*informal*) **1** not at all like: *She looks nothing like either of her parents.* **2** not at all; not nearly: *There's nothing like enough food for all of us.* nothing much not a lot of sth; nothing of importance: *It's a nice town but there's nothing much to do in the evenings.* ◇ *'What did you do at the weekend?' 'Nothing much.'* (there's) nothing to it (it's) very easy: *You'll soon learn — there's nothing to it really.* there is/was nothing (else) for it (but to do sth) there is/was no other action possible: *There was nothing for it but to resign.*

notice¹ ʔ **A2** /ˈnəʊtɪs/ *noun* **1** [C] a piece of paper or a sign giving information, a warning, etc. that is put where everyone can read it: *There's a notice on the board saying that the meeting has been cancelled.* ◇ *The notice said 'No dogs allowed'.* **2** [U] the act of paying attention to sth or knowing about sth: *The protests are finally making the government take notice.* ◇ *Take no notice of what he said — he was just being silly.* ◇ *Some people don't take any notice of* (= choose to ignore) *speed limits.* ◇ *It has come to my notice that you have missed a lot of classes.* **3** [U] a warning that sth is going to happen: *I can't produce a meal at such short notice!* ◇ *I wish you'd give me more notice when you're going to be off work.* ◇ *The swimming pool is closed until further notice* (= until we are told that it will open again).
IDM at short notice not long in advance

notice² ʔ **A2** /ˈnəʊtɪs/ *verb* [I, T] (not usually used in the progressive tenses) to see and become conscious of sth: *'What kind of car was the man driving?' 'I'm afraid I didn't notice.'* ◇ *I noticed (that) he was carrying a black briefcase.* ◇ *Did you notice which direction she went in?* ◇ *We didn't notice him leave/him leaving.*

noticeable /ˈnəʊtɪsəbl/ *adj.* easy to see or notice: *The scar from the accident was hardly noticeable.*
▶ **noticeably** /-bli/ *adv.*

noticeboard /ˈnəʊtɪsbɔːd/ (*BrE*) (*AmE* bulletin board) *noun* [C] a board on a wall for putting written information where everyone can read it

notify ʔ+ **C1** /ˈnəʊtɪfaɪ/ *verb* [T] (notifying; notifies; *pt, pp* notified) ~ sb (of sth) (*formal*) to tell sb about sth officially: *The police should be notified of the theft.*
▶ **notification** /ˌnəʊtɪfɪˈkeɪʃn/ *noun* [U, C]

notion ʔ **B2** **O** /ˈnəʊʃn/ *noun* [C] ~ (that ... /of sth) an idea, a belief or an understanding of sth: *I had a vague notion that I had seen her before.*

notional /ˈnəʊʃənl/ *adj.* existing only in the mind; not based on facts or reality

notoriety /ˌnəʊtəˈraɪəti/ *noun* [U] the state of being well known for sth bad

notorious ℓ+ **C1** /nəʊˈtɔːriəs/ *adj.* ~ **(for/as sth)** well known for sth bad: *This road is notorious for the number of accidents on it.* ◇ *a notorious criminal* **SYN** **infamous** ▸ notoriously *adv.*

notwithstanding /ˌnɒtwɪθˈstændɪŋ, -wɪð's-/ *prep., adv.* (formal) despite sth

nougat /ˈnuːɡɑː/ *noun* [U] a hard pink or white sweet containing nuts

nought /nɔːt/ *noun* [C] (BrE) = ZERO¹ (1): *A million is written with six noughts.* ◇ *nought point one* (= written 0.1)

noughts and ˈcrosses (BrE) (AmE tic-tac-toe) *noun* [U] a game for two players in which each person tries to win by writing three 0s or three Xs in a line.

noun /naʊn/ *noun* [C] (**GRAMMAR**) a word that is the name of a thing, an idea, a place or a person: *'Water', 'happiness', 'James' and 'France' are all nouns.* ➔ look at **abstract noun, countable, proper noun, uncountable**

nourish /ˈnʌrɪʃ/ *verb* [T] **1** to give sb/sth the right kind of food so that they can grow and be healthy **2** (formal) to allow a feeling, an idea, etc. to grow stronger ▸ nourishment *noun* [U]

Nov. *abbr.* (in writing) = NOVEMBER

nova /ˈnəʊvə/ *noun* [C] (pl. novae /-viː/, novas) (**ASTRONOMY**) a star that suddenly becomes much brighter for a short period ➔ look at **supernova**

novel¹ ℓ **A2** /ˈnɒvl/ *noun* [C] (**LITERATURE**) a book that tells a story about people and events that are not real: *a romantic/historical/detective novel*

novel² ℓ+ **C1** **W** /ˈnɒvl/ *adj.* new and different: *That's a novel idea! Let's try it.*

novelist ℓ+ **B2** /ˈnɒvəlɪst/ *noun* [C] (**LITERATURE**) a person who writes novels

novella /nəˈvelə/ *noun* [C] (**LITERATURE**) a short novel

novelty /ˈnɒvlti/ *noun* (pl. -ies) **1** [U] the quality of being new and different: *The novelty of her new job soon wore off.* **2** [C] something new and unusual: *It was quite a novelty not to have to get up early.* **3** [C] a small, cheap object that is sold as a toy or decoration

November ℓ **A1** /nəʊˈvembə(r)/ *noun* [U, C] (abbr. Nov.) the eleventh month of the year, between October and December

novice /ˈnɒvɪs/ *noun* [C] a person who is new and without experience in a job, situation, etc. **SYN** **beginner**

now¹ ℓ **A1** /naʊ/ *adv.* **1** (at) the present time: *We can't go for a walk now — it's raining.* ◇ *Where are you living now?* ◇ *From now on I'm going to work harder.* ◇ *Up till now we haven't been able to afford a house of our own.* ◇ *He will be on his way home by now.* ◇ *I can manage for now but I might need some help later.* **2** immediately: *Go now before anyone sees you.* ◇ *You must go to the doctor right now.* **3** used to introduce or to emphasize what you are saying, or while stopping to think: *Now listen to what he's saying.* ◇ *What does he want now?* ◇ *Now, let me think.* **IDM** **any moment/second/minute/day (now)** → ANY¹ **just now** → JUST¹ **(every) now and again/then** from time to time; occasionally: *We see each other now and then, but not very often.* **now what?** **1** used when you are annoyed because sb keeps interrupting you **2** used to say that you do not know what to do next in a particular situation **right now** → RIGHT²

now² ℓ **B1** /naʊ/ *conj.* ~ **(that)** ... because of the fact that: *Now (that) the children have left home we can move to a smaller house.*

nowadays ℓ+ **B2** /ˈnaʊədeɪz/ *adv.* at the present time (when compared with the past): *I don't travel much nowadays* (= but I did in the past). **SYN** **today**

nowhere ℓ **A2** /ˈnəʊweə(r)/ (also informal **no place** especially in AmE) *adv.* not in or to any place; not anywhere: *I'm afraid there's nowhere to stay in this village.* ◇ *I don't like it here, but there's nowhere else for us to sit.* **IDM** **get nowhere (with sth)** to not make any progress with sth **in the middle of nowhere** → MIDDLE¹ **nowhere near** → NEAR¹

noxious /ˈnɒkʃəs/ *adj.* (formal) harmful or poisonous: *noxious gases*

nozzle /ˈnɒzl/ *noun* [C] a narrow tube that is put on the end of a pipe to control the liquid or gas coming out ➔ picture at **aerosol**

NQ /ˌen ˈkjuː/ *noun* [C] (**EDUCATION**) (in Scotland) one of a range of courses and exams that are taken in a number of different subjects and at different levels between the ages of approximately 15 and 18 (the abbreviation for 'National Qualification')

nr *abbr.* (in writing) (used, for example, in the address of a small village) near: *Masham, nr Ripon*

nuance /ˈnjuːɑːns/ *noun* [C, U] a very small difference in meaning, feeling, sound, etc.

nuclear ℓ **B1** /ˈnjuːkliə(r)/ *adj.* **1** (**PHYSICS**) using, producing or resulting from the energy that is produced when the NUCLEUS (= central part) of an ATOM is split: *nuclear energy* ◇ *a nuclear power station* ◇ *nuclear war/weapons* ➔ look at **atomic** (2) **2** (**PHYSICS**) connected with the NUCLEUS (= central part) of an ATOM: *nuclear physics* ➔ look at **atomic** (1) **3** (**BIOLOGY**) connected with the NUCLEUS (= central part) of a cell ➔ picture at **cell**

nuclear ˈenergy (also **nuclear power, atomic energy**) *noun* [U] (**PHYSICS**) a powerful form of energy produced by splitting the NUCLEI (= central parts) of ATOMS. Nuclear power is used to produce electricity.

nuclear ˈfamily *noun* [C] (**SOCIAL STUDIES**) a family that consists of father, mother and children, when it is thought of as a unit in society: *Not everybody nowadays lives in the conventional nuclear family.* ➔ look at **extended family**

nuclear ˈfission = FISSION (1)

nuclear ˈfusion = FUSION (2)

nuclear ˈphysics *noun* [U] (**PHYSICS**) the scientific study of the NUCLEI (= central parts) of ATOMS, especially of how energy can be produced from them

nuclear ˈpower = NUCLEAR ENERGY

nuclear reˈactor (also **reactor**) *noun* [C] (**PHYSICS**) a very large machine that produces nuclear energy

nucleic acid /njuːˌkliːɪk ˈæsɪd, -ˌkleɪk/ *noun* [U, C] (**BIOLOGY**) either of two substances, DNA or RNA, that are present in all living cells ➔ picture at **virus**

nucleotide /ˈnjuːkliətaɪd/ *noun* [C] (**BIOLOGY**) one of the many small MOLECULES that combine to form DNA and RNA

nucleus /ˈnjuːkliəs/ *noun* [C] (pl. nuclei /-kliaɪ/) **1** (**BIOLOGY, PHYSICS**) the central part of an ATOM or of some cells ➔ note at **isotope** ➔ picture at **cell, fertilization 2** the central or most important part of sth

nude¹ /njuːd/ *adj.* not wearing any clothes ➔ look at **bare** (1), **naked** (1) ▸ nudity *noun* [U]: *This film contains scenes of nudity.*

nude[2] /njuːd/ *noun* [C] (**ART**) a picture or photo of a person who is not wearing any clothes
IDM in the nude not wearing any clothes

nudge /nʌdʒ/ *verb* [T] to touch or push sb/sth in a gentle way, especially with your arm ▶ nudge *noun* [C]: *to give somebody a nudge*

nudist /'njuːdɪst/ *noun* [C] a person who does not wear any clothes because they believe this is more natural and healthy: *a nudist beach/camp*

nugget /'nʌgɪt/ *noun* [C] a small piece of a valuable metal or mineral, especially gold, that is found in the earth

nuisance /'njuːsns/ *noun* [C, usually sing.] a person, thing or situation that annoys you or causes you trouble: *It's a nuisance having to queue for everything.*

null /nʌl/ *adj.*
IDM null and void (**LAW**) having no legal force

numb /nʌm/ *adj.* not able to feel anything; not able to move: *My fingers were numb with cold.* ◇ *I'll give you an injection and the tooth will go numb.* ▶ numb *verb* [T]: *We were numbed by the dreadful news.*
▶ numbness *noun* [U]

number[1] ⓘ **A1** ⊙ /'nʌmbə(r)/ *noun*
• WORD/SYMBOL **1** [C] (**MATHEMATICS**) a word or symbol that indicates a quantity: *Choose a number between 10 and 20.* ◇ *even numbers* (= 2, 4, 6, etc.) ◇ *odd numbers* (= 1, 3, 5, etc.) ◇ *a three-figure number* (= from 100 to 999)
• GROUP OF NUMBERS **2** [C] a group of numbers that is used to identify sb/sth: *a phone number* ◇ *an account number*
• QUANTITY **3** [C, U] **~ (of sth)** a quantity of people or things: *a large number of visitors* ◇ *We must reduce the number of accidents on the roads.* ◇ *Pupils in the school have doubled in number in recent years.* ◇ *There are a number of* (= several) *things I don't understand.*
• POSITION **4** [C] (*abbr.* No., no.) (*symb.* #) used before a number to show the position of sth in a series: *We live in Hazel Road, at number 21.* ◇ *room No. 347*
• SONG **5** [C] (*informal*) a song or dance
• IN GRAMMAR **6** [U] the form of a word, showing whether one or more than one person or thing is being talked about
IDM any number of very many: *There could be any number of reasons why she isn't here.* in round figures/numbers → ROUND[1] your opposite number → OPPOSITE

number[2] ⓘ **A2** /'nʌmbə(r)/ *verb* [T] **1** to give a number to sth: *The houses are numbered from 1 to 52.* **2** used for saying how many people or things there are: *Our forces number 40 000.*

'number plate (*BrE*) (*AmE* license plate) *noun* [C] the sign on the front and back of a vehicle that shows the REGISTRATION NUMBER (= the particular combination of numbers and letters belonging to that vehicle)

numeracy /'njuːmərəsi/ *noun* [U] (**MATHEMATICS**) a good basic knowledge of mathematics; the ability to understand and work with numbers: *standards of literacy and numeracy* ⊃ look at **literacy** (1)

numeral /'njuːmərəl/ *noun* [C] (**MATHEMATICS**) a sign or symbol that represents a quantity: *Roman numerals* (= I, II, III, IV, etc.)

numerate /'njuːmərət/ *adj.* (**EDUCATION**) having a good basic knowledge of mathematics ⊃ look at **literate** (1)

numerator /'njuːməreɪtə(r)/ *noun* [C] (**MATHEMATICS**) the number above the line in a FRACTION, for example the 3 in ¾ ⊃ look at **denominator**

numerical /njuː'merɪkl/ *adj.* of or shown by numbers: *to put something in numerical order*

numerous ⓘ **B2** /'njuːmərəs/ *adj.* (*formal*) existing in large numbers; many

numinous /'njuːmɪnəs/ *adj.* (*formal*) (**RELIGION**) having a strong religious quality that makes you feel that God is present

nun /nʌn/ *noun* [C] (**RELIGION**) a member of a religious group of women who live together in a CONVENT (= a special building) and do not marry or have possessions ⊃ look at **monk**

nurse[1] ⓘ **A1** /nɜːs/ *noun* [C] (**MEDICINE**) a person who is trained to look after sick or injured people: *a psychiatric nurse* (= one who works in a hospital for people with mental illnesses) ◇ *a qualified/registered nurse* ⊃ note at **hospital**

nurse[2] /nɜːs/ *verb* **1** [T] (**MEDICINE**) to take care of sb who is sick or injured: *She nursed her mother back to health.* **2** [T] (**MEDICINE**) to take care of an injury, especially by resting: *Ahmed is still nursing a back injury.* **3** [T] to hold sb/sth in a loving way: *He nursed the child in his arms.* **4** [T] (*formal*) to have a strong feeling or idea in your mind for a long time: *Tim had long nursed the hope that Sharon would marry him.* **5** [I, T] to feed a baby or young animal with milk from the breast; to drink milk from the mother's breast

nursery ⓘ+ **C1** /'nɜːsəri/ *noun* [C] (*pl.* -ies) **1** a place where small children and babies are looked after so that their parents can go to work ⊃ look at **crèche** **2** (**AGRICULTURE**) a place where young plants are grown and sold

'nursery rhyme *noun* [C] a traditional poem or song for young children

'nursery school *noun* [C] (**EDUCATION**) a school for children between the ages of about 2 and 5 **SYN** preschool ⊃ look at **playgroup**

nursing ⓘ+ **B2** /'nɜːsɪŋ/ *noun* [U] (**MEDICINE**) the job of being a nurse

'nursing home *noun* [C] (**MEDICINE**) a small private hospital, usually for old people

nurture[1] /'nɜːtʃə(r)/ *verb* [T] **1** (*formal*) to care for and protect sb/sth while they are growing and developing **2** to help sth to develop and be successful: *This is a talent which should be nurtured.*

nurture[2] /'nɜːtʃə(r)/ *noun* [U] (*formal*) care and support for sb/sth while they are growing and developing

nut ⓘ **A2** /nʌt/ *noun* [C] **1** a dry fruit that consists of a hard shell with a seed inside. Many types of nut can be eaten. **2** a small piece of metal with a round hole in the middle through which you put a BOLT (= long round piece of metal) to fasten things together ⊃ picture at **bolt**[1]

nutcracker /'nʌtkrækə(r)/ *noun* [C] (*BrE also* nutcrackers [pl.]) a tool that you use for breaking open the shell of a nut

nutmeg /'nʌtmeg/ *noun* [C, U] a type of hard seed that is often made into powder and used as a SPICE in cooking

nutrient /'njuːtriənt/ *noun* [C] (**BIOLOGY**) a substance that is needed to keep a living thing alive and to help it grow: *Plants get minerals and other nutrients from the soil.*

nutrition ⓘ+ **B2** /nju'trɪʃn/ *noun* [U] (**HEALTH**) the food that you eat and the way that it affects your health ▶ nutritional /-ʃənl/ *adj.*

nutritionist /nju'trɪʃənɪst/ *noun* [C] (**HEALTH**) a person who is an expert on the relationship between food and health ⊃ look at **dietician**

nutritious /nju'trɪʃəs/ *adj.* (used about food) very good for you

nuts /nʌts/ *adj.* [not before noun] (*informal*) crazy: *He's driving me nuts with his stupid questions.*

nutshell /'nʌtʃel/ *noun*
IDM **in a nutshell** using few words

nutty /'nʌti/ *adj.* (**nuttier; nuttiest**) containing or tasting of nuts

nuzzle /'nʌzl/ *verb* [I, T] to press or rub sb/sth gently with the nose

NVQ /ˌen viː 'kjuː/ *noun* [C] (**EDUCATION**) a British qualification that shows that you have reached a particular standard in the work that you do (the abbreviation for 'National Vocational Qualification')

NW *abbr.* (in writing) = NORTH-WEST[1], NORTH-WESTERN: *NW Australia*

nylon /'naɪlɒn/ *noun* [U] a very strong artificial material that is used for making clothes, rope, brushes, etc.

nymph /nɪmf/ *noun* [C] (**LITERATURE**) (in ancient Greek and Roman stories) a spirit of nature in the form of a young woman that lives in rivers, woods, etc.

O o

O /əʊ/ (*also* **o**) *noun* [C, U] (*pl.* **O's, o's**) **1** the 15th letter of the English alphabet: *'Orange' begins with (an) 'O'.* **2** used to mean 'zero' when saying phone numbers, etc: *My number is five O nine double four* (= 50944).

oak /əʊk/ *noun* **1** (*also* **oak tree**) [C] a type of large tree with hard wood that is common in many northern parts of the world ❶ The fruit of the **oak** is an **acorn**. **2** [U] the wood from the oak tree: *a solid oak table* ⊃ look at **acorn**

oar /ɔː(r)/ *noun* [C] a long POLE with a flat end that you use for ROWING (= moving a boat through water) ⊃ look at **paddle**[1]

oasis /əʊ'eɪsɪs/ *noun* [C] (*pl.* **oases** /-'eɪsiːz/) (**GEOGRAPHY**) a place in the desert where there is water and where plants grow

oath /əʊθ/ *noun* [C] **1** a formal promise: *They have to swear/take an oath of loyalty.* **2** (*old-fashioned*) = SWEAR WORD
IDM **be on/under oath** to have made a formal promise to tell the truth in court

oatmeal[1] /'əʊtmiːl/ *noun* [U] **1** flour made from OATS that is used to make biscuits, cakes, etc. **2** a pale brown colour

oatmeal[2] /'əʊtmiːl/ *adj.* pale brown in colour

oats /əʊts/ *noun* [pl.] a type of grain that is used as food for animals and for making flour, etc. ⊃ picture at **cereal**

obbligato /ˌɒblɪ'ɡɑːtəʊ/ *noun* [C] (*pl.* **-os**) (**MUSIC**) an important part for an instrument in a piece of music, that cannot be left out

OBE /ˌəʊ biː 'iː/ *noun* [C] an award given to some people in the UK because they have achieved sth special (the abbreviation for 'Officer of the Order of the British Empire')

obedient /ə'biːdiənt/ *adj.* ~ **(to sb/sth)** doing what you are told to do: *As a child he was always obedient to his parents.* **OPP** **disobedient** ▶ **obedience** /-əns/ *noun* [U] ▶ **obediently** *adv.*

obelisk /'ɒbəlɪsk/ *noun* [C] (**ARCHITECTURE**) a tall pointed stone column with four sides, put up in memory of a person or an event

obelisk

obese /əʊ'biːs/ *adj.* (**HEALTH**) (used about people) very fat, in a way that is not healthy ▶ **obesity** ʔ+ **B2** *noun* [U]

obey ʔ **B2** ❷ /ə'beɪ/ *verb* [T, I] to do what you are told to do: *Soldiers are trained to obey orders.* **OPP** **disobey**

obituary /ə'bɪtʃuəri/ *noun* [C] (*pl.* **-ies**) a piece of writing about sb's life that is printed in a newspaper soon after they have died

object[1] ʔ **A1** ❷ /'ɒbdʒɪkt, -dʒekt/ *noun* [C] **1** a thing that can be seen and touched, but is not alive: *The shelves were filled with objects of all shapes and sizes.* ◇ *everyday/household objects* **2** an aim or a purpose: *Making money is his sole object in life.* ⊃ note at **target**[1] **3** ~ **of sth** a person or thing that causes a feeling, an interest, a thought, etc: *the object of his desire/affections/interest* **4** (**GRAMMAR**) the noun or phrase describing the person or thing that is affected by the action of a verb ⊃ look at **subject**[1] (4)
IDM **money is no object** money is not important or is no problem: *They always want the best. Money is no object.*

object[2] ʔ **B2** /əb'dʒekt/ *verb* **1** [I] ~ **(to sb/sth)**; ~ **(to doing sth)**; ~ **(to sb doing sth)** to not like or to be against sb/sth: *Many people object to the new tax.* ◇ *They objected to working at weekends.* ◇ *I object to companies trying to sell me things over the phone.* **2** [T] to say a reason why you think sth is wrong: *'I think that's unfair,' he objected.* ▶ **objector** *noun* [C]

objection ʔ+ **C1** /əb'dʒekʃn/ *noun* [C] ~ **(to sb/sth)**; ~ **(to doing sth)**; ~ **(to sb doing sth)** a reason why you do not like or are against sb/sth: *We listed our objections to the proposed new road.* ◇ *Ten families raised objections to moving out of the old flats.* ◇ *I have no objection to you using my desk while I'm away.* ⊃ note at **opinion**

objectionable /əb'dʒekʃənəbl/ *adj.* very unpleasant

objective[1] ʔ **B2** ❷ /əb'dʒektɪv/ *noun* [C] **1** something that you are trying to achieve; an aim: *Our objective is to finish by the end of the year.* ◇ *to achieve your objective* **SYN** **goal** ⊃ note at **target**[1] **2** (*also* **objective 'lens**) (**SCIENCE**) the LENS that is nearest to the object being looked at in a MICROSCOPE (= an instrument that makes very small objects look bigger) ⊃ picture at **laboratory, microscope**

objective[2] ʔ **B2** ❷ /əb'dʒektɪv/ *adj.* not influenced by your own personal feelings; considering only facts: *Please try and give an objective report of what happened.* ◇ *It's hard to be objective about your own family.* **OPP** **subjective** ▶ **objectively** *adv.* ▶ **objectivity** /ˌɒbdʒek'tɪvəti/ *noun* [U]

obligation ʔ **B2** /ˌɒblɪ'ɡeɪʃn/ *noun* [U, C] ~ **(to sb) (to do sth)** the state of having to do sth because it is a law or duty, or because you have promised; sth you have promised to do: *The shop is under no obligation to give you your money back.* ◇ *We have an obligation to help people who are in need.*

obligatory /ə'blɪɡətri/ *adj.* (*formal*) that you must do: *It is obligatory to get insurance before you drive a car.* **SYN** **compulsory** **OPP** **optional**

oblige ʔ+ **C1** /əˈblaɪdʒ/ *verb* **1** [T, usually passive] to force sb to do sth: *Parents are obliged by law to send their children to school.* **2** [I, T] (*formal*) to do what sb asks; to be helpful: *If you ever need any help, I'd be happy to oblige.* ▸ **obliged** *adj.*: *Thanks for your help. I'm* **much obliged** *to you.* ▸ **obliging** *adj.* [not before noun]: *I asked my neighbour for advice and he was very obliging.*

oblique[1] /əˈbliːk/ *adj.* **1** not expressed or done in a direct way **SYN** **indirect** **2** (used about a line) at an angle; sloping **3** (GEOMETRY) used to describe an angle that is not an angle of 90°: *The extension was built at an oblique angle to the house.* ▸ **obliquely** *adv.*

oblique[2] /əˈbliːk/ *noun* [C] (*BrE*) = SLASH[2] (3)

obliterate /əˈblɪtəreɪt/ *verb* [T, often passive] to remove all signs of sth by destroying or covering it completely

oblivion /əˈblɪviən/ *noun* [U] **1** a state in which you do not realize what is happening around you, usually because you are unconscious or asleep: *I was in a state of complete oblivion.* **2** the state in which sb/sth has been forgotten and is no longer famous or important: *His work* **faded into oblivion** *after his death.*

oblivious /əˈblɪviəs/ *adj.* ~ **(to/of sb/sth)** not noticing or realizing what is happening around you: *She was completely oblivious to all the trouble she had caused.*

oblong /ˈɒblɒŋ/ *adj.* (GEOMETRY) an **oblong** shape has two long sides, two short sides and four RIGHT ANGLES (= angles of 90°) **SYN** **rectangle** ▸ **oblong** *noun* [C]

obnoxious /əbˈnɒkʃəs/ *adj.* extremely unpleasant, especially in a way that offends people

oboe /ˈəʊbəʊ/ *noun* [C] (MUSIC) a musical instrument made of wood that you play by blowing through it ⊃ picture at **instrument**, **orchestra**

obscene /əbˈsiːn/ *adj.* **1** connected with sex in a way that most people find offensive: *obscene books/ gestures/language* **2** very large in size or amount in a way that some people find unacceptable: *He earns an obscene amount of money.*

obscenity /əbˈsenəti/ *noun* (*pl.* -ies) **1** [U] sexual language or behaviour, especially in books, plays, etc., that shocks people and causes offence **2** [C, usually pl.] a word or an act that shocks people or causes offence: *He shouted a string of obscenities out of the car window.*

obscure[1] /əbˈskjʊə(r)/ *adj.* **1** not well known: *an obscure Spanish poet* **2** not easy to see or understand: *For some obscure reason, he decided to give up his well-paid job to become a writer.* ▸ **obscurity** /-ˈskjʊərəti/ *noun* [U]

obscure[2] /əbˈskjʊə(r)/ *verb* [T] to make sth difficult to see or understand

observance /əbˈzɜːvəns/ *noun* [U, sing.] ~ **(of sth)** the practice of obeying or following a law, custom, etc.

observant /əbˈzɜːvənt/ *adj.* good at noticing things around you: *An observant passer-by gave the police a full description of the men.*

observation ʔ **B2** ⊙ /ˌɒbzəˈveɪʃn/ *noun* **1** [U] the act of watching sb/sth carefully, especially to learn sth: *My research involves the observation of animals in their natural surroundings.* ◇ *The patient is being kept* **under observation.** **2** [U] the ability to notice things: *Scientists need good* **powers of observation.** **3** [C] ~ **(about/on sth)** (*formal*) something that you say or write about sth: *He began by making a few general observations about the sales figures.* ⊃ note at **statement** ▸ **observational** /-ʃənl/ *adj.*: *observational skills*

observatory /əbˈzɜːvətri/ *noun* [C] (*pl.* -ies) a building from which scientists can watch the stars, the weather, etc.

observe ʔ **B2** ⊙ /əbˈzɜːv/ *verb* [T] (*formal*) **1** to watch sb/sth carefully, especially to learn more about them or it: *We observed the birds throughout the breeding season.* **2** to see or notice sb/sth: *A man and a woman were observed leaving by the back door.* **3** to make a comment: *'We're late,' she observed.* ⊃ note at **comment**[2] **4** to obey a law, rule, etc: *to observe the speed limit*

observer ʔ+ **B2** **W** /əbˈzɜːvə(r)/ *noun* [C] **1** a person who watches sb/sth: *According to observers, the plane exploded shortly after take-off.* **2** a person who attends a meeting, lesson, etc. to watch and listen but who does not take part

obsess ʔ+ **C1** /əbˈses/ *verb* [T, usually passive] **be obsessed (about/with sb/sth)** to completely fill your mind so that you cannot think of anything else: *He was obsessed with getting his revenge.*

obsession ʔ+ **C1** /əbˈseʃn/ *noun* ~ **(with sb/sth)** **1** [U] the state in which you can only think about one person or thing so that you cannot think of anything else: *the tabloid press's obsession with celebrities* **2** [C] a person or thing that you think about too much

obsessive /əbˈsesɪv/ *adj.* thinking too much about one particular person or thing; behaving in a way that shows this: *He's obsessive about not being late.* ◇ *obsessive cleanliness*

ob,sessive com'pulsive disorder = OCD

obsolete /ˈɒbsəliːt/ *adj.* no longer used because sth new has been invented ▸ **obsolescence** /ˌɒbsəˈlesns/ *noun* [U] (*formal*)

obstacle ʔ+ **B2** /ˈɒbstəkl/ *noun* [C] ~ **(to sth/doing sth)** **1** something that makes it difficult for you to do sth: *Not speaking a foreign language was a major obstacle to her career.* **2** an object that is in your way and that makes it difficult for you to move forward

'obstacle course *noun* [C] **1** (*BrE*) a series of objects that people taking part in a race have to climb over, under, through, etc. **2** a series of difficulties that people have to deal with in order to achieve a particular aim **3** (*AmE*) = ASSAULT COURSE

obstetrician /ˌɒbstəˈtrɪʃn/ *noun* [C] (MEDICINE) a hospital doctor who looks after women who are pregnant

obstetrics /əbˈstetrɪks/ *noun* [U] (MEDICINE) the area of medicine connected with the birth of children

obstinate /ˈɒbstɪnət/ *adj.* refusing to change your opinions, way of behaving, etc. when other people try to persuade you to change: *an obstinate refusal to apologize* **SYN** **stubborn** ▸ **obstinacy** /-nəsi/ *noun* [U] ▸ **obstinately** *adv.*

obstruct /əbˈstrʌkt/ *verb* [T] (*formal*) to stop sth from happening or sb/sth from moving, either by accident or deliberately: *You'll obstruct the traffic if you park there.*

obstruction /əbˈstrʌkʃn/ *noun* **1** [U] the act of stopping sth from happening or moving **2** [C] a thing that stops sb/sth from moving or doing sth: *This car is* **causing an obstruction.**

obstructive /əbˈstrʌktɪv/ *adj.* trying to stop sb/sth from moving or doing sth

obtain ʔ **B2** **W** /əbˈteɪn/ *verb* [T] (*formal*) to get sth: *to obtain advice/information/permission*

obtainable /əbˈteɪnəbl/ *adj.* that you can get: *That make of vacuum cleaner is no longer obtainable.* **SYN** **available**

obtuse /əb'tju:s/ *adj.* (*formal*) slow to understand sth; not wanting to understand sth ▸ **obtuseness** *noun* [U]

ob.tuse 'angle *noun* [C] (**GEOMETRY**) an angle between 90° and 180° ◯ look at **acute angle, reflex angle, right angle** ◯ picture at **angle**[1]

obvious ᵻ+ **B1** **S** /'ɒbviəs/ *adj.* ~ (**to sb**) easily seen or understood; clear: *His disappointment was obvious to everyone.* ◇ *For obvious reasons, I'd prefer not to give my name.* ◯ note at **clear**[1]

obviously ᵻ **B1** **S** /'ɒbviəsli/ *adv.* **1** used when giving information that you expect other people to know already or agree with: *Obviously, we don't want to spend too much money.* **2** used to say that a particular situation or fact is easy to see or understand: *They're obviously not coming.*

occasion ᵻ **B1** /ə'keɪʒn/ *noun* **1** [C] a particular time when sth happens: *I have met Bill on two occasions.* **2** [C] a special event, ceremony, etc: *Their wedding was a memorable occasion.* **3** [sing.] the suitable or right time (for sth): *I shall tell her what I think if the occasion arises* (= if I get the chance). **IDM** **on occasion(s)** sometimes, but not often

occasional ᵻ+ **C1** /ə'keɪʒənl/ *adj.* [only before noun] done or happening from time to time but not very often: *We have the occasional argument but most of the time we get on.*

occasionally ᵻ **B2** /ə'keɪʒnəli/ *adv.* sometimes but not often: *We see each other occasionally.* ◇ *We occasionally meet for a drink after work.*

occlusion /ə'klu:ʒn/ *noun* **1** [U] (**HEALTH**) the closing or blocking of a BLOOD VESSEL (= a narrow tube through which blood passes) or an organ of the body **2** [C] (**GEOMETRY**) a process by which, when a band of cold air meets and passes a band of warm air in the atmosphere, the warm air is pushed upwards off the earth's surface

occult /'ɒkʌlt, ə'kʌlt/ *adj.* **1** [only before noun] connected with magic powers and things that cannot be explained by reason or science **2** **the occult** *noun* [sing.] magic powers, ceremonies, etc.

occupancy /'ɒkjəpənsi/ *noun* [U] (*formal*) the act of living in or using a building, room, piece of land, etc: *Prices are based on full occupancy of an apartment.*

occupant /'ɒkjəpənt/ *noun* [C] a person who is in a building, car, etc. at a particular time

occupation ᵻ+ **B2** **W** /ˌɒkju'peɪʃn/ *noun* **1** [C] a job or profession; the way in which you spend your time: *Please state your occupation on the form.* ◯ note at **work**[2] **2** [U] the act of the army of one country taking control of another country; the period of time that this situation lasts: *the Roman occupation of Britain* **3** [U] the act of living in or using a room, building, etc.

occupational /ˌɒkju'peɪʃənl/ *adj.* [only before noun] connected with your work: *Accidents are an occupational hazard* (= a risk connected with a particular job) *on building sites.*

occu.pational 'therapy *noun* [U] (**MEDICINE**) a way of helping people to get better after illness or injury by giving them special activities to do ▸ **occu.pational 'therapist** *noun* [C]

occupied /'ɒkjupaɪd/ *adj.* **1** [not before noun] being used by sb: *Is this seat occupied?* **2** [not before noun] busy doing sth: *Looking after the children keeps me fully occupied.* ◯ look at **preoccupied** **3** (used about a country or a piece of land) under the control of another country

occupier /'ɒkjupaɪə(r)/ *noun* [C] (*formal*) a person who owns, lives in or uses a house, piece of land, etc.

occupy ᵻ+ **B2** **W** /'ɒkjupaɪ/ *verb* [T] (occupying; occupies; *pt, pp* occupied) **1** to fill a space or period of time: *The large table occupied most of the room.* **SYN** **take up sth** **2** (*formal*) to live in or use a house, piece of land, etc. **3** to enter a place in a large group and take control of it, especially by military force: *The capital has been occupied by the rebel army.* **4** ~ **sb/(yourself)** to keep sb/yourself busy

occur ᵻ **B1** **O** /ə'kɜ:(r)/ *verb* [I] (-rr-) **1** (*formal*) to happen, especially in a way that has not been planned: *The accident occurred late last night.* **2** (used with an adverb or a preposition) to exist or be found somewhere: *The virus occurs more frequently in children.* **PHR V** **occur to sb** (used about an idea or a thought) to come into your mind: *It never occurred to John that his wife might be unhappy.*

occurrence ᵻ+ **C1** **W** /ə'kʌrəns/ *noun* [C] something that happens or exists

OCD /ˌəʊ si: 'di:/ *noun* [U] (**PSYCHOLOGY**) a mental DISORDER in which sb feels that they have to repeat certain actions to get rid of fears or unpleasant thoughts (the abbreviation for 'obsessive compulsive disorder')

ocean ᵻ **A2** /'əʊʃn/ *noun* (**GEOGRAPHY**) **1** [U] (*especially AmE*) the mass of salt water that covers most of the surface of the earth: *Two thirds of the earth's surface is covered by ocean.* **2** (also Ocean) [C] one of the five main areas into which this water is divided: *the Atlantic/Indian/Pacific Ocean* ◯ look at **sea** (2) ◯ picture at **current**[2] **IDM** **a drop in the ocean** → DROP[2]

oceanic /ˌəʊʃi'ænɪk/ *adj.* (**GEOGRAPHY**) connected with the oceans

oceanography /ˌəʊʃə'nɒɡrəfi/ *noun* [U] (**BIOLOGY, GEOGRAPHY**) the scientific study of the oceans

ocean 'trench = TRENCH (3)

ochre (*AmE also* **ocher**) /'əʊkə(r)/ *adj.* a pale yellow-brown colour ▸ **ochre** *noun* [U]

o'clock ᵻ **A1** /ə'klɒk/ *adv.* used after the numbers one to twelve for saying what the time is: *Lunch is at twelve o'clock.*

Oct. *abbr.* (in writing) = OCTOBER

octa- /ɒktə, ɒk'tæ/ *prefix* (in nouns, adjectives and adverbs) eight; having eight: *octagon* ◇ *octagonal*

octagon /'ɒktəɡən/ *noun* [C] (**GEOMETRY**) a shape that has eight straight sides ▸ **octagonal** /ɒk'tæɡənl/ *adj.*

octahedron /ˌɒktə'hi:drən/ *noun* [C] (**GEOMETRY**) a solid figure with eight flat sides, especially one whose sides are eight equal TRIANGLES ◯ picture at **solid**[2]

octane /'ɒkteɪn/ *noun* [U] (**CHEMISTRY**) a substance in petrol that is used for measuring its quality: *high-octane fuel*

octave /'ɒktɪv/ *noun* [C] (**MUSIC**) the set of eight musical notes that western music is based on

octet /ɒk'tet/ *noun* [C] (**MUSIC**) **1** a group of eight singers or musicians **2** a piece of music for eight singers or musicians

octo- /ɒktəʊ, ɒktə/ *prefix* (in nouns, adjectives and adverbs) eight; having eight: *octogenarian*

October ᵻ **A1** /ɒk'təʊbə(r)/ *noun* [U, C] (*abbr.* Oct.) the tenth month of the year, between September and November

octopus /'ɒktəpəs/ *noun* [C] a sea animal with a soft body and eight TENTACLES (= long thin parts like arms) ◯ picture at **animal**

odd ᵻ **B1** /ɒd/ *adj.*
• STRANGE **1** strange; unusual: *There's something odd about him.* ◇ *It's a bit odd that she didn't phone to say*

she couldn't come. **SYN** peculiar 2 odd- (in adjectives) strange or unusual in the way mentioned: *an odd-sounding name*

- NOT REGULAR 3 [only before noun] not regular or fixed; happening sometimes: *He makes the odd mistake, but nothing very serious.*
- VARIOUS 4 [only before noun] that is left after other similar things have been used: *He made the bookshelves out of a few odd bits of wood.*
- NOT MATCHING 5 not with the pair or set it belongs to; not matching: *You're wearing odd socks.*
- NUMBER 6 (**MATHEMATICS**) (used about a number) that cannot be divided by two: *1, 3, 5 and 7 are all odd numbers.* **OPP** even²
- APPROXIMATELY 7 (used after a number) a little more than: *'How old do you think he is?' 'Well, he must be thirty-odd, I suppose.'*
  ▶ oddness *noun* [U]

IDM the odd man/one out one that is different from all the others in a group: *Her brothers and sisters were much older than she was. She was always the odd one out.*

oddity /ˈɒdəti/ *noun* [C] (*pl.* -ies) a person or thing that is unusual

ˌodd ˈjobs *noun* [pl.] small jobs or tasks of various types

oddly /ˈɒdli/ *adv.* 1 in a strange or unusual way: *She's been behaving very oddly lately.* 2 used to show that sth is surprising: *Oddly enough, the most expensive tickets sold fastest.*

odds ʔ+ **C1** /ɒdz/ (*usually* the odds) *noun* [pl.] ~ **(on sb doing sth)** the degree to which sth is likely to happen: *The odds on him surviving are very slim* (= he will probably die). ◇ *The odds are against you* (= you are not likely to succeed). ◇ *The odds are in your favour* (= you are likely to succeed). ◇ *What are the odds* (= how likely is it) *that Barcelona will win?*

IDM against (all) the odds happening although it seemed impossible be at odds (with sb) (over sth) to disagree with sb about sth be at odds (with sth) to be different from sth, when the two things should be the same odds and ends (*BrE, informal*) small things of little value or importance

ode /əʊd/ *noun* [C] (**LITERATURE**) a poem that is written to or about a person or thing or to celebrate a special event: *Keats's 'Ode to a Nightingale'*

odious /ˈəʊdiəs/ *adj.* (*formal*) extremely unpleasant **SYN** horrible

odometer /əʊˈdɒmɪtə(r)/ (*AmE*) = MILOMETER

odour (*BrE*) (*AmE* odor) /ˈəʊdə(r)/ *noun* [C] (*formal*) a smell (often an unpleasant one)

odourless (*BrE*) (*AmE* odorless) /ˈəʊdələs/ *adj.* without a smell

odyssey /ˈɒdəsi/ *noun* [sing.] a long journey full of experiences

oedema (*BrE*) (*AmE* edema) /ɪˈdiːmə/ *noun* [U] (**HEALTH**) a condition in which liquid collects in the spaces inside the body and makes it SWELL (= become larger or rounder than normal)

oesophagus (*BrE*) (*AmE* esophagus) /iˈsɒfəgəs/ *noun* [C] (*pl.* oesophaguses, oesophagi /-gaɪ/) (**ANATOMY**) the tube through which food passes from the mouth to the stomach **SYN** gullet ⊃ picture at **body**

oestrogen (*BrE*) (*AmE* estrogen) /ˈiːstrədʒən/ *noun* [U] (**BIOLOGY**) the chemical HORMONE produced in a woman's body that makes her develop female physical and sexual characteristics and that causes the body to prepare to become pregnant ⊃ look at **progesterone, testosterone**

of ʔ **A1** /əv, *strong form* ɒv/ *prep.* 1 belonging to sb; relating to sb: *a friend of mine* (= one of my friends) ◇ *the role of the teacher* ◇ *the poems of Milton*

2 belonging to sth; being part of sth; relating to sth: *the roof of the house* ◇ *the result of the exam* ◇ *the back of the book* ◇ *the leader of the party* 3 showing sb/sth: *a map of York* ◇ *a photo of my parents* 4 used to say what sb/sth is, consists of or contains: *a woman of intelligence* ◇ *the city of Paris* ◇ *a glass of milk* ◇ *a crowd of people* ◇ *It's made of silver.* ◇ *a feeling of anger* 5 used with measurements, directions and expressions of time and age: *a litre of milk* ◇ *the fourth of July* ◇ *a girl of 12* ◇ *an increase of 2.5%* ◇ *ten kilometres north of Lisbon* 6 used for showing that sb/sth is part of a larger group: *some of the people* ◇ *three of the houses* 7 used after a noun describing an action to show either who did the action or who it happened to: *the arrival of the president* (= he arrives) ◇ *the murder of the president* (= he is murdered) 8 used after some verbs: *This perfume smells of roses.* ◇ *Think of a number.* ◇ *It reminds me of you.* 9 used after some adjectives: *I'm proud of you.* ◇ *He's jealous of her.*

off¹ ʔ **A1** /ɒf/ *adv., prep.* 1 down or away from a place or a position on sth: *to fall off a ladder/motorbike/wall* ◇ *We got off the bus.* ◇ *I shouted to him but he just walked off.* ◇ *I must be off* (= I must leave here). *It's getting late.* ◇ *When are you off to Spain?* ◇ (*figurative*) *We've got off the subject.* 2 used to say that sth has been removed: *She took her coat off.* ◇ *He shook the rain off his umbrella.* **OPP** on 3 joined to and leading away from: *My street is off the Cowley Road.* 4 at some distance from sth: *The Isle of Wight is just off the south coast of England.* ◇ *Christmas is still a long way off* (= it is a long time till then). 5 (used about a machine, a light, etc.) not connected, working or being used: *Please make sure the TV/light/heating is off.* **OPP** on 6 not present at work, school, etc: *She's off work/off sick with a cold.* ◇ *I'm having a day off* (= a day's holiday) *next week.* 7 (used about a plan or an arrangement) not going to happen; cancelled: *The meeting/wedding/trip is off.* **OPP** on 8 cheaper; less by a certain amount: *cars with £400 off* ◇ *£400 off the price of a car* 9 not eating or using sth: *The baby's off his food.*

IDM off and on | on and off sometimes; starting and stopping: *It rained on and off all day.* off the top of your head → TOP¹

off² /ɒf/ *adj.* [not before noun] 1 (used about food or drink) no longer fresh enough to eat or drink: *The milk's off.* 2 ~ **(with sb)** (*informal*) unfriendly: *My neighbour was rather off with me today.*

off- /ɒf/ *prefix* (in verbs, nouns, adjectives and adverbs) not on; away from: *offstage* ◇ *offload*

offal /ˈɒfl/ *noun* [U] the heart and other organs of an animal, used as food

ˈoff day *noun* [C] (*informal*) a day when things go badly or you do not work well: *Even the best players have off days occasionally.*

ˌoff-ˈduty *adj.* not at work

offence ʔ **B2** (*BrE*) (*AmE* offense) /əˈfens/ *noun* 1 [C] (*formal*) (**LAW**) a crime; an illegal action: *to commit an offence* ◇ *a criminal/minor/serious/sexual offence* 2 [U] the feeling of being upset or angry at sth that sb has said or done: *I didn't mean to cause you any offence.* **IDM** take offence (at sth) to feel upset or hurt by sb/sth

offend ʔ **B2** /əˈfend/ *verb* 1 [T, often passive] to hurt sb's feelings; to upset sb: *I hope they won't be offended if I don't come.* ◇ *He felt offended that she hadn't called for so long.* 2 [I] (*formal*) (**LAW**) to do sth illegal; to commit a crime: *The prisoner had offended again within days of his release from jail.*

offender ʔ+ **B2** /əˈfendə(r)/ *noun* [C] **1** (**LAW**) a person who breaks the law or commits a crime: *young offenders* ◇ *a first offender* (= somebody who has committed a crime for the first time) **2** a person or thing that does sth wrong

offensive¹ ʔ **B2** /əˈfensɪv/ *adj.* **1** ~ (**to sb**) rude in a way that causes sb to feel upset or annoyed because it shows a lack of respect: *offensive behaviour/language/remarks* ◇ *His comments were offensive to many viewers.* **OPP** **inoffensive** **2** [only before noun] used for or connected with attacking: *offensive weapons* **OPP** **defensive¹** ▶ **offensively** *adv.*

offensive² /əˈfensɪv/ *noun* [C] a military attack **IDM** **be on the offensive** to be the first to attack sb/sth, rather than waiting for them to attack you

offer¹ ʔ **A2** **W** /ˈɒfə(r)/ *verb* **1** ~ **sth (to sb) (for sth); ~ (sb) sth** to ask if sb would like sth or to give sb the chance to have sth: *He offered his seat on the bus to an old lady.* ◇ *I've been offered a job in London.* ◇ *He offered (me) £2 000 for the car and I accepted.* **2** [I] ~ (**to do sth**) to say or show that you will do sth for sb if they want: *My brother's offered to help me paint the house.* **3** [T] to make sth available or to provide the opportunity for sth: *The job offers plenty of opportunity for travel.*

offer² ʔ **A2** /ˈɒfə(r)/ *noun* [C] **1** ~ (**of sth); ~ (to do sth)** a statement offering to do sth or give sth to sb: *She accepted my offer of help.* ◇ *Thank you for your kind offer to help.* ◇ *to accept/refuse/decline an offer* **2** ~ (**of sth) (for sth)** an amount of money that you say you will give for sth: *They've made an offer for the house.* ◇ *We've turned down* (= refused) *an offer of £150 000.* ○ look at **o.n.o.** **3** a low price for sth in a shop, usually for a short time: *See below for details of our special holiday offer.* **IDM** **on offer** **1** for sale or available: *The college has a wide range of courses on offer.* **2** (*especially BrE*) for sale at a lower price than usual for a certain time: *This cheese is on offer until next week.*

offering ʔ+ **C1** /ˈɒfərɪŋ/ *noun* [C] something that is given or produced for other people to watch, enjoy, etc.

offhand¹ /ˌɒfˈhænd/ *adj.* (used about behaviour) not showing any interest in sb/sth in a way that seems rude: *an offhand manner/voice*

offhand² /ˌɒfˈhænd/ *adv.* without having time to think; immediately: *I can't tell you what it's worth offhand.*

office ʔ **A1** /ˈɒfɪs/ *noun* **1** [C] a room, set of rooms or a building where people work, usually sitting at desks: *I usually get to the office at about nine o'clock.* ◇ *The firm's head office* (= the main branch of the company) *is in Glasgow.* ◇ *Please phone again during office hours.* ❶ In the US doctors and dentists have **offices**. In the UK they have **surgeries**. **2** [C] (often in compounds) a room or building that is used for a particular purpose, especially for providing a service: *the tax/ticket/tourist office* ○ look at **booking office, box office, post office 3** Office [sing.] (**POLITICS**) a government department, including the people who work there and the work they do: *the Foreign/Home Office* **4** [U] (**POLITICS**) an official position, often as part of a government or other organization: *The Labour Party was in office from 1997 to 2010.*

office block *noun* [C] (**ARCHITECTURE**) a large building that contains offices, usually belonging to more than one company

officer ʔ **A2** /ˈɒfɪsə(r)/ *noun* [C] **1** a person who is in a position of authority in the armed forces: *an army/air-force officer* **2** a person who is in a position of authority in the government or a large organization: *a prison/customs/welfare officer* **3** = POLICE OFFICER

official¹ ʔ **B1** /əˈfɪʃl/ *adj.* **1** [only before noun] connected with the position of sb in authority: *official duties/responsibilities* **2** accepted and approved by the government or some other authority: *The scheme has not yet received official approval.* ◇ *The country's official language is Spanish.* **3** that is told to the public but may or may not be true: *The official reason for his resignation was that he wanted to spend more time with his family.* **OPP** **unofficial**

official² ʔ **B2** /əˈfɪʃl/ *noun* [C] a person who has a position of authority: *The reception was attended by MPs and high-ranking officials.*

officialdom /əˈfɪʃldəm/ *noun* [U] groups of people in positions of authority in large organizations who seem more interested in following the rules than in being helpful

officially /əˈfɪʃəli/ *adv.* **1** in a public way and by sb in a position of authority: *The new school was officially opened last week.* **2** according to a particular set of laws, rules, etc: *Officially we don't accept children under six, but we'll make an exception in this case.*

officious /əˈfɪʃəs/ *adj.* too ready to tell other people what to do and use the power you have to give orders

offing /ˈɒfɪŋ/ *noun* **IDM** **in the offing** (*informal*) likely to appear or happen soon

off-licence (*BrE*) (*AmE* **liquor store**) *noun* [C] a shop that sells alcoholic drinks in bottles and cans

off-limits /ˌɒf ˈlɪmɪts/ *adj.* (used about a place) where people are not allowed to go ○ look at **out of bounds (to sb) at bounds**

offline /ˌɒfˈlaɪn/ *adj., adv.* (**COMPUTING**) not directly controlled by or connected to a computer or to the internet ○ look at **online¹**

offload /ˌɒfˈləʊd/ *verb* [T] ~ **sth (on/onto sb)** to give away sth that you do not want to sb else: *She was able to offload some of her work onto a colleague.*

off-peak *adj.* [only before noun], *adv.* (**TOURISM**) available, used or done at a less popular or busy time: *an off-peak train ticket/bus pass/phone call* ◇ *It's cheaper to travel off-peak.* ○ look at **peak¹** (1)

off-putting *adj.* (*especially BrE, informal*) unpleasant in a way that stops you from liking sb/sth

off season *noun* [sing.] (**TOURISM**) the time of the year that is less busy in business and travel: *We don't get many tourists in the off season.* **SYN** **low season** **OPP** **high season** ▶ off-season *adj., adv.*: *off-season prices* ◇ *We prefer to travel off-season.*

offset¹ /ˈɒfset/ *verb* [T] (**offsetting;** *pt, pp* **offset**) to use one cost, payment or situation in order to cancel or reduce the effect of another: *The disadvantages of the scheme are more than offset by the advantages.*

offset² /ˈɒfset/ *adj.* [only before noun] used to describe a method of printing in which INK is put onto a metal plate, then onto a rubber surface and only then onto the paper

offshoot /ˈɒfʃuːt/ *noun* [C] a thing that develops from sth else, especially a small organization that develops from a larger one

offshore /ˌɒfˈʃɔː(r)/ *adj.* (**GEOGRAPHY**) **1** in the sea but not very far from the land: *an offshore oil rig* ○ look at **onshore** (1) **2** (used about winds) blowing from the land towards the sea ○ look at **onshore** (2) ○ picture at **convection**

offside adj. **1** /ˌɒfˈsaɪd/ (**SPORT**) (used about a player in football) in a position that is not allowed by the rules of the game **2** /ˈɒfsaɪd/ [only before noun] (*BrE*) (used about a part of a vehicle) on the side that is furthest away from the edge of the road **SYN** **nearside**

offspring ʔ+ **C1** /ˈɒfsprɪŋ/ *noun* [C] (*pl.* offspring) (*formal*) a child or children; the young of an animal: *to produce/ raise offspring*

offstage /ˌɒfˈsteɪdʒ/ *adj., adv.* (**ARTS AND MEDIA**) not on the stage in a theatre; not where the audience can see: *offstage sound effects* ◇ *The hero dies offstage.* ↪ look at **onstage**

off-ˈwhite *adj.* not pure white

OFSTED /ˈɒfstɛd/ *abbr.* (**EDUCATION**) **the Office for Standards in Education** (the British government department that is responsible for checking that standards in schools are acceptable)

often ʔ **A1** ⊙ /ˈɒfn, ˈɒftən/ *adv.* **1** many times: *We often go swimming at the weekend.* ◇ *I'm sorry I didn't call very often.* ◇ *How often should you go to the dentist?* **SYN** **frequently 2** in many cases: *Old houses are often damp.* **SYN** **commonly**
IDM **every so often** sometimes; from time to time **more often than not** usually

ogre /ˈəʊɡə(r)/ *noun* [C] **1** (in children's stories) a very large, cruel and frightening creature that eats people **2** a person who is unpleasant and frightening

oh ʔ **A1** /əʊ/ *exclamation* **1** used for reacting to sth that sb has said, for emphasizing what you are saying, or when you are thinking of what to say next: *'I'm a teacher.' 'Oh? Where? Where?'* **2** used to express surprise, fear, joy, etc: *'Oh no!' she cried as she began to read the email.*

ohm /əʊm/ *noun* [C] (*symb.* Ω) (**PHYSICS**) a unit for measuring electrical RESISTANCE (= the fact of not allowing heat or electricity to pass through) ↪ picture at **resistor**

ˈoh well = WELL³ (2)

oil ʔ **A2** /ɔɪl/ *noun* **1** [U] (**CHEMISTRY**, **GEOLOGY**) a thick dark liquid that comes from under the ground and is used as a fuel or to make machines work smoothly ↪ picture at **energy, fractional distillation, generator 2** [U, C] (**BIOLOGY**) a thick liquid that comes from animals or plants and is used in cooking: *cooking/ vegetable/sunflower/olive oil* ▶ **oil** *verb* [T]

oilfield /ˈɔɪlfiːld/ *noun* [C] (**GEOLOGY**) an area where there is oil under the ground or under the sea

ˈoil paint (*also* ˈoil colour) *noun* [U, C] (**ART**) a type of paint that contains oil

ˈoil painting *noun* [C] (**ART**) a picture that has been painted using paint made with oil ↪ note at **art**

ˈoil rig (*also* rig) *noun* [C] a large platform in the sea with equipment for getting oil out from under the sea

oilseed rape /ˌɔɪlsiːd ˈreɪp/ = RAPE² (3)

ˈoil slick (*also* slick) *noun* [C] (**ENVIRONMENT**) an area of oil that floats on the sea, usually after a ship carrying oil has crashed

ˈoil well (*also* well) *noun* [C] a hole that is made deep in the ground or under the sea in order to obtain oil

oily /ˈɔɪli/ *adj.* (oilier; oiliest) covered with or containing oil, or like oil: *oily food* ◇ *Mechanics always have oily hands.*

ointment /ˈɔɪntmənt/ *noun* [U, C] (**MEDICINE**) a smooth substance that you put on painful skin or on an injury to help it get better **SYN** **cream¹** ↪ picture at **health**

OK¹ ʔ **A1** **S** (*also* okay) /əʊˈkeɪ/ *adj., adv., exclamation* (*informal*) **1** all right; good or well enough: *'Did you have a nice day?' 'Well, it was OK, I suppose.'* ◇ *Is it okay if I come at about seven?* **2** safe and well: *Are you*

OK? **SYN** **all right¹ 3** yes; all right: *'Do you want to come with us?' 'OK.'* **4** used to check that sb agrees or understands: *I'll pick you up on the way to the shop, OK?* **SYN** **all right²**

OK² (*also* okay) /əʊˈkeɪ/ *noun* [sing.] permission: *As soon as my parents **give me the OK**, I'll come and stay with you.*

OK³ (*also* okay) /əʊˈkeɪ/ *verb* [T] (OK'ing, okaying /-ˈkeɪɪŋ/; OK's, okays /-ˈkeɪz/; *pt, pp* OK'd, okayed /-ˈkeɪd/) ~ sth (with sb) (*informal*) to officially agree to sth or allow it to happen: *She filled in an expenses claim and her manager OK'd it.*

okra /ˈəʊkrə, ˈɒk-/ *noun* [U] the green seed cases of the okra plant, eaten as a vegetable

old ʔ **A1** /əʊld/ *adj.*

• AGE **1** of a particular age: *That building is 500 years old.* ◇ *The book is aimed at eight- to ten-year-olds.* ◇ *How old are you?*

• NOT YOUNG **2** having lived for a long time: *My mother wasn't very old when she died.* ◇ *He's only 50 but he looks older.* ◇ *to get/grow old* **OPP** **young¹ 3** the old *noun* [pl.] old people ↪ look at **elderly** (2)

• NOT NEW **4** having existed for a long time; connected with past times: *This house is quite old.* ◇ *old ideas/ traditions* ◇ *In the old days, people generally had larger families than nowadays.* **OPP** **modern, new 5** having been used a lot: *I got rid of all my old clothes.* **OPP** **new** ↪ look at **second-hand** (1) **6** [only before noun] known for a long time: *She's a very old friend of mine. We knew each other at school.*

• PREVIOUS **7** [only before noun] former: *I earn more now than I did in my old job.* **SYN** **previous**
IDM **any old …** (*informal*) used for emphasizing that sth has little importance or value: *I write any old rubbish in my diary.* **be an old hand (at sth)** to be good at sth because you have done it often before

ˌold ˈage *noun* [U] the part of your life when you are old: *He's enjoying life **in his old age**.* ↪ look at **youth** (1)

ˌOld ˈEnglish = ANGLO-SAXON

ˌold-ˈfashioned ʔ **B1** *adj.* **1** usual in the past but not now: *old-fashioned clothes/ideas* **2** (used about people) believing in old ideas, customs, etc: *My parents are quite old-fashioned about some things.* ↪ look at **modern** (3), **unfashionable**

ˌold ˈmaster *noun* [C] (**ART**) **1** a famous painter, especially of the thirteenth to seventeenth centuries in Europe **2** a picture painted by an old master

ˌOld ˈNorse *noun* [U] (**LANGUAGE**) the language of Norway, Iceland, Denmark and Sweden until the fourteenth century

the ˌOld ˈTestament *noun* [sing.] (**RELIGION**) the first part of the Bible that tells the history of the Jewish people before the birth of Christ ↪ look at **New Testament**

OLED /ˈəʊlɛd, ˌəʊ el iː ˈdiː/ *noun* [C] a device containing a light-producing material that is used in the screens of TVs, mobile phones, etc. (the abbreviation for 'organic light-emitting diode')

ˈO level (*also* ordinary level) *noun* [C, U] (**EDUCATION**) an exam in a particular subject, at a lower level than A LEVEL, usually taken at the age of 16. In 1988, it was replaced in England and Wales by the GCSE, but it is still taken in some other countries.

oligarch /ˈɒlɪɡɑːk/ *noun* [C] **1** a member of a government in which only a small group of people hold all the power **2** (**BUSINESS**) an extremely rich and powerful person

oligopoly /ˌɒlɪˈɡɒpəli/ *noun* [C] (*pl.* -ies) (**BUSINESS**) a market in which there are only a few companies producing or selling a product or service. This can result in less competition and higher prices for customers: *The company operates in a near oligopoly in western markets.* ⊃ look at **monopoly** (1)

olive[1] /ˈɒlɪv/ *noun* **1** [C] a small green or black fruit with a bitter taste, used for food and oil: *Fry the onions in a little olive oil.* **2** (*also* ˌolive ˈgreen) [U] a grey-green colour

olive[2] /ˈɒlɪv/ (*also* ˌolive ˈgreen) *adj.* **1** grey-green in colour **2** (used about sb's skin) yellow-brown in colour

ˌolive ˈoil *noun* [U] oil produced from OLIVES, used in cooking and on salad ⊃ look at **extra virgin**

Olympian /əˈlɪmpiən/ *noun* [C] (**SPORT**) a person who takes part in the Olympic Games

the Oˌlympic ˈGames (*also* **the Olympics**) *noun* [pl.] (**SPORT**) an international sports competition that is organized every four years in a different country: *to win a medal at/in the Olympics* ▶ Olympic /əˈlɪmpɪk/ *adj.* [only before noun]: *Who holds the Olympic record for the 1500 metres?*

ombudsman /ˈɒmbʊdzmən/ *noun* [C] (*pl.* -men /-mən/) (**POLITICS**) an official whose job is to examine and report on complaints made by ordinary people about public organizations

omega /ˈəʊmɪɡə/ *noun* [C] the last letter of the Greek alphabet (Ω, ω)

Omega-3 /ˌəʊmɪɡə ˈθriː/ *noun* [C] (**HEALTH**) a kind of fat that is found mainly in fish oils and is good for your health

omelette (*also* omelet) /ˈɒmlət/ *noun* [C] a dish made of eggs that have been mixed together and fried

omen /ˈəʊmən/ *noun* [C] a sign of sth that will happen in the future: *a good/bad omen for the future*

OMG /ˌəʊ em ˈdʒiː/ *abbr.* (*informal*) **oh my God** (used to express surprise, excitement, etc., especially in text messages, etc.): *OMG! If my parents find out they will go mad!*

ominous /ˈɒmɪnəs/ *adj.* suggesting that sth bad is going to happen: *Those black clouds look ominous.*

omission /əˈmɪʃn/ *noun* [C, U] something that has not been included; the act of not including sb/sth: *There were several omissions on the list of names.*

omit /əˈmɪt/ *verb* [T] (-tt-) (*formal*) **1** to not include sth; to leave sth out: *Several verses of the song can be omitted.* **2** ~ **to do sth** to forget or choose not to do sth

omni- /ɒmni/ *prefix* (in nouns, adjectives and adverbs) of all things; in all ways or places: *omnivore*

omniscient /ɒmˈnɪsiənt/ *adj.* (*formal*) knowing everything: *The novel has an omniscient narrator.* ▶ omniscience /-əns/ *noun* [U]

omnivore /ˈɒmnɪvɔː(r)/ *noun* [C] (**BIOLOGY**) an animal that eats both plants and meat ⊃ look at **carnivore**, **herbivore**, **insectivore** ▶ omnivorous /ɒmˈnɪvərəs/ *adj.*: *an omnivorous diet*

on /ɒn/ *adv., prep.* **1** (*also formal* upon) supported by, fixed to or touching sth, especially a surface: *on the table/ceiling/wall* ◇ *We sat on the beach/grass/floor.* ◇ *She was carrying the baby on her back.* ◇ *Write it down on a piece of paper.* ◇ *The ball hit me on the head.* **2** in a place or position: *on a farm/housing estate/campsite* ◇ *a house on the river/seafront/border* ◇ *I live on the other side of town.* **3** showing direction: *on the right/left* ◇ *on the way to school* **4** used with ways of travelling and types of travel: *on the bus/train/plane*

◇ *We came on foot* (= we walked). ◇ *Eddie went past on his bike.* ◇ *to go on a trip/a journey/an excursion* **5** with expressions of time: *on 19 August* ◇ *on Monday* ◇ *on Christmas Day* ◇ *on your birthday* **6** working; being used: *All the lights were on.* ◇ *Switch the TV on.* **OPP** off[1] **7** wearing sth; carrying sth in your pocket or bag: *What did she have on?* ◇ *to put your shoes/coat/hat/make-up on* ◇ *I've got no money on me.* ◇ *You should carry ID on you at all times.* **8** about sth: *We've got a test on irregular verbs tomorrow.* ◇ *a talk/a book/an article on Japan* **9** happening or arranged to happen: *What's on at the cinema?* ◇ *Is the meeting still on, or has it been cancelled?* **10** using sth; by means of sth: *I was (talking) on the phone to Laura.* ◇ *I saw it on TV.* ◇ *I cut my hand on some glass.* ◇ *Dave spends most evenings on the internet.* **11** showing the thing or person that is affected by an action or is the object of an action: *Divorce can have a bad effect on children.* ◇ *He spends a lot on clothes.* ◇ *Don't waste your time on that.* **12** using drugs or medicine; using a particular kind of food or fuel: *to be on medication/antibiotics* ◇ *Gorillas live on leaves and fruit.* ◇ *Does this car run on petrol or diesel?* **13** receiving a certain amount of money: *What will you be on* (= how much will you earn) *in your new job?* ◇ *He's been (living) on unemployment benefit since he lost his job.* **14** showing that sth continues: *The man shouted at us but we walked on.* ◇ *The speeches went on and on until everyone was bored.* **15** (*also formal* upon) showing the reason or basis for sth: *She doesn't eat meat on principle.* ◇ *The film is based on a true story.* **16** compared to: *Sales are up 10% on last year.* **17** (*also formal* upon) immediately; soon after: *He phoned her on his return from New York.* **18** paid for by sb: *The drinks are on me!* **IDM** from now/then **on** starting from this/that time and continuing: *From then on she never spoke to him again.* not **on** (*informal*) not acceptable: *No, you can't stay out that late. It's just not on.* off and on | on and off → OFF[1]

ˌon-ˈboard *adj.* [only before noun] on a ship, an aircraft or a vehicle: *an on-board motor*

onboard /ˈɒnbɔːd/ *verb* [T] (**BUSINESS**) to make a new employee or customer familiar with an organization or its products or services: *We're onboarding new administrators, as well as around 60 new teachers.* ▶ onboarding *noun* [U]

once[1] /wʌns/ *adv.* **1** one time only; on one occasion: *I've only been to France once.* ◇ *once a week/month/year* ◇ *I visit them about once every six months.* **2** at some time in the past: *This house was once the village school.* **SYN** formerly **IDM** all at once all at the same time or suddenly: *People began talking all at once.* ◇ *All at once she got up and left the room.* at once **1** immediately; now: *Come here at once!* **2** at the same time: *I can't understand if you all speak at once.* just this once | (just) for once on this occasion only: *Just this once, I'll help you with your homework.* once again | once more one more time; another time: *Once again the train was late.* ◇ *Let's listen to that track once more.* once and for all now and for the last time: *You've got to make a decision once and for all.* once in a blue moon (*informal*) very rarely; almost never once in a while sometimes but not often once upon a time (used at the beginning of a children's story) a long time ago; in the past: *Once upon a time there was a princess …*

once[2] /wʌns/ *conj.* as soon as; when: *Once you've practised a bit you'll find that it's quite easy.*

oncology /ɒŋˈkɒlədʒi/ *noun* [U] (**MEDICINE**) the scientific study of and treatment of TUMOURS (= cells caused by disease) in the body ▶ oncologist /-dʒɪst/ *noun* [C]

oncoming /ˈɒnkʌmɪŋ/ adj. [only before noun] coming towards you: *oncoming traffic*

on-de'mand adj. [only before noun] (ARTS AND MEDIA) done or happening whenever sb asks: *an on-demand music streaming service* ⊃ look at **demand**[1]

one[1] ʔ A1 /wʌn/ number, det. **1** the number 1: *There's only one biscuit left.* ◇ *The journey takes one hour.* ◇ *If you take one from ten it leaves nine.* ⊃ look at **first**[1] **2** used for emphasizing that there is only one of sth: *She's the one person I trust.* ◇ *His one concern was for his job.* **3** used when you are talking about a time in the past or the future, without actually saying which one: *He came to see me one evening last week.* ◇ *We must go and visit them one day.* ◇ *I'll come over one evening.*
IDM (all) in one all together or combined: *It's a printer and scanner all in one.* one after another/the other first one, then the next, etc: *One after another the winners went up to get their prizes.* one by one separately: *One by one, people began to arrive at the meeting.* one or two a few: *I've bought one or two books from that shop.*

one[2] ʔ A1 /wʌn/ pron. **1** used instead of repeating a noun: *I think I'll have an apple. Would you like one?* ◇ *'Which dress do you like?' 'This one.'* ◇ *'Can I borrow some books of yours?' 'Yes. Which ones?'* ◇ *'That coat's a bit small. You need a bigger one.'* ◇ *'That idea is a very good one.* **2** the one/the ones used before a group of words that show which person or thing you are talking about: *My house is the one after the post office.* ◇ *If you find some questions difficult, leave out the ones you don't understand.* **3** ~ of sb/sth a member (of a certain group): *He's staying with one of his friends.* ◇ *One of the children is crying.* **4** (formal) used for referring to people in general, including the speaker or writer: *One must be sure of one's facts before criticizing other people.*
IDM the odd man/one out → ODD

one a'nother pron. used when you are saying that each member of a group does sth to or for the other people in the group: *We exchanged news with one another.*

one-'off adj. made or happening only once and not regularly: *a one-off payment/opportunity* ▸ **one-off** noun [C]: *It was a one-off—it won't happen again.*

one-on-'one (AmE) = ONE-TO-ONE

onerous /ˈəʊnərəs/ adj. (formal) needing great effort; causing trouble or worry SYN **taxing**

oneself /wʌnˈself/ pron. (formal) **1** used when the person who does an action is also affected by it: *One can teach oneself to play the piano but it is easier to have lessons.* **2** used to emphasize the person who does the action: *One could easily arrange it all oneself.*
IDM (all) by oneself **1** alone **2** without help

one-'sided adj. **1** (used about an opinion, an argument, etc.) showing only one point of view; not balanced: *Some newspapers give a very one-sided view of politics.* **2** (used about a relationship or a competition) not equal: *The match was very one-sided—we lost 12-1.*

one-'star adj. (TOURISM) having one star in a system that measures quality. The highest standard is usually represented by four or five stars: *a one-star hotel*

one-time adj. [only before noun] **1** used to describe sth that used to happen or was true in the past: *her one-time best friend, Anna* **2** that will not be repeated: *a one-time fee of $500*

one-to-'one adj., adv. **1** (also one-on-one) between only two people: *one-to-one English lessons* (= one teacher to one student) **2** (MATHEMATICS) in which each member of one set is associated with one member of another

one-'way adj. **1** (used about roads) that you can only drive along in one direction: *a one-way street* **2** (TOURISM) (used about a ticket) that you can use to travel somewhere but not back again: *a one-way ticket* SYN **single**[1] OPP **return**[2]

ongoing ʔ+ B2 W /ˈɒngəʊɪŋ/ adj. continuing to exist now: *It's an ongoing problem.*

onion ʔ A1 /ˈʌnjən/ noun [C, U] a white or red vegetable with many layers. Onions are often used in cooking and have a strong smell: *a kilo of onions* ◇ *onion soup*

online[1] ʔ A1 W /ˈɒnlaɪn/ adj. (COMPUTING) controlled by or connected to a computer or to the internet: *online shopping/dating/banking* ◇ *You can see which of your friends are online and send them messages.* ⊃ look at **offline**

online[2] ʔ A1 /ˌɒnˈlaɪn/ adv. (COMPUTING) onto the internet; using the internet: *Many childern would rather go online than watch TV.* ◇ *I'm studying French online.* ⊃ look at **offline**

online 'dating (also internet dating) noun [U] using the internet to arrange to meet sb and possibly begin a romantic relationship with them: *an online dating service/site*

onlooker /ˈɒnlʊkə(r)/ noun [C] a person who watches sth happening without taking part in it

only[1] ʔ A1 /ˈəʊnli/ adj. [only before noun], adv. **1** with no others existing or present: *I was the only woman in the room.* ◇ *This is the only dress we have in your size.* **2** and nobody or nothing else; no more than: *She only likes pop music.* ◇ *I've only asked a few friends to the party.* ◇ *It's only one o'clock.* **3** the most suitable or the best: *It's so cold that the only thing to do is to sit by the fire.*
IDM if only → IF not only … but also both … and: *He not only did the shopping but he also cooked the meal.* only just **1** not long ago: *I've only just started this job.* **2** almost not: *We only just had enough money to pay for the meal.* SYN **hardly**

only[2] /ˈəʊnli/ conj. (informal) except that; but: *The film was very good, only it was a bit too long.*

only 'child noun [C] a child who has no brothers or sisters

o.n.o. (also ono) abbr. (in writing) (BrE) or near/nearest offer (used in small advertisements to show that sth may be sold at a lower price than the price that has been asked): *Motorbike for sale. £750 o.n.o.*

onomatopoeia /ˌɒnə mætəˈpiːə/ noun [U] (LANGUAGE, LITERATURE) the fact of words containing sounds similar to the noises they describe, for example *hiss* or *thud*; the use of words like this in a piece of writing ▸ **onomatopoeic** /-ˈpiːɪk/ adj.

on-'screen adj. [only before noun] (ARTS AND MEDIA) appearing or written on the screen of a computer, TV or cinema: *Follow the on-screen instructions.* ◇ *her on-screen husband* (= in a TV programme)

onset /ˈɒnset/ noun [sing.] the ~ (of sth) the beginning (often of sth unpleasant): *the onset of winter/a headache*

onshore /ˈɒnʃɔː(r)/ adj. (GEOGRAPHY) **1** on or towards land ⊃ look at **offshore** (1) **2** (used about winds) blowing from the sea towards the land ⊃ look at **offshore** (2) ⊃ picture at **convection**

onslaught /ˈɒnslɔːt/ noun [C] ~ (on/against sb/sth) a violent or strong attack: *the enemy onslaught on our military forces*

onstage /ˌɒnˈsteɪdʒ/ *adj., adv.* (**ARTS AND MEDIA**) on the stage in a theatre; in front of an audience: *onstage fights* ◊ *He ran onstage and bowed to the audience.* ⊃ look at **offstage**

onto ⓔ **A2** (*also* on to) /ˈɒntə, *before vowels* -tu/ *prep.* to a position on sth: *The cat jumped onto the sofa.* ◊ *The bottle fell off the table onto the floor.* ◊ *The crowd ran onto the pitch.*
IDM **be onto sb** (*informal*) to have found out about sth illegal that sb is doing: *The police were onto the car thieves.* **be onto sth** to have some information, etc. that could lead to an important discovery

onwards /ˈɒnwədz/ (*also* **onward** /ˈɒnwəd/) *adv.*
1 from … ~ continuing from a particular time: *From September onwards it usually begins to get colder.*
2 (*formal*) forward: *The road stretched onwards into the distance.*

oops /ʊps, uːps/ *exclamation* used when you have, or nearly have, a small accident or do sth embarrassing: *Oops! I almost spilled the wine.*

ooze /uːz/ *verb* [I, T] ~ **from/out of sth**; ~ **(with) sth** to flow slowly out or to allow sth to flow slowly out: *Blood oozed from the cut on his head.* ◊ *The fruit was oozing with juice.* ◊ *The wound was oozing blood.*

op /ɒp/ (*BrE, informal*) = OPERATION (1)

opaque /əʊˈpeɪk/ *adj.* **1** that you cannot see through: *opaque glass in the door* **OPP** **transparent** ⊃ picture at **shadow**¹ **2** difficult to understand; not clear

op art *noun* [U] (**ART**) a style of modern art that uses patterns and colours in a way that makes the images seem to move as you look at them

OPEC /ˈəʊpek/ *abbr.* **Organization of Petroleum Exporting Countries** (an organization of countries that produce and sell oil)

open¹ ⓔ **A1** /ˈəʊpən/ *adj.*
• NOT CLOSED **1** not closed or covered: *Don't leave the door open.* ◊ *an open window* ◊ *I can't get this bottle of wine open.* ◊ *She stared at me with her eyes wide open.* ◊ *The diary was lying open on her desk.* ◊ *The curtains were open so that we could see into the room.* ◊ *His shirt was open at the neck.*
• LAND/SEA **2** [only before noun] (used about an area of land) away from towns and buildings; (used about an area of sea) at a distance from the land: *open country* ◊ *Once we were out in the open sea, the wind got stronger.*
• FOR VISITORS/CUSTOMERS **3** ~ **(for sth)**; ~ **(to sb/sth)** available for people to enter, visit, use, etc.; not closed to the public: *The bank isn't open till 9.30.* ◊ *The new shopping centre will soon be open.* ◊ *The hotel damaged by the bomb is now open for business again.* ◊ *The competition is open to everyone.* ◊ *The gardens are open to the public in the summer.* **OPP** **closed**, **shut²**
• OF CHARACTER **4** not keeping feelings and thoughts hidden: *Elena doesn't mind talking about her feelings — she's a very open person.* ◊ *He looked at him with open dislike.*
• NOT DECIDED **5** [not before noun] not finally decided; still being considered: *Let's leave the details open.*
IDM **have/keep an open mind (about/on sth)** to be ready to listen to or consider new ideas and suggestions **in the open air** outside; not in a building: *Somehow, food eaten in the open air tastes much better.* **keep an eye open/out (for sb/sth)** → EYE¹ **open to sth** willing to receive sth: *I'm always open to suggestions.* **with your eyes open** → EYE¹ **with open arms** in a friendly way that shows that you are pleased to see sb or have sth: *The unions welcomed the government's decision with open arms.*

open² ⓔ **A1** /ˈəʊpən/ *verb* **1** [T, I] to move sth or part of sth so that it is no longer closed; to move so as to be no longer closed: *Open the curtains, will you?* ◊ *to open your eyes/hand/mouth* ◊ *to open a bag/letter/box* ◊ *This window won't open — it's stuck.* ◊ *The parachute failed to open and he was killed.* ◊ *The book opened at the very page I needed.* **OPP** **close¹**, **shut²** **2** [T] to start a computer program or file so that you can use it on the screen **3** [I, T] to make it possible for people to enter a place: *Does that shop open on Sundays?* ◊ *The museum opens at ten.* ◊ *The company are opening two new branches soon.* ◊ *Police finally opened the road six hours after the accident.* **OPP** **close¹**, **shut²** **4** [T] to start: *The chairman opened the meeting by welcoming everybody.* ◊ *I'd like to open a bank account.* **OPP** **close¹** ⊃ note at **meeting**
IDM **open fire (at/on sb/sth)** to start shooting: *He ordered his men to open fire.*
PHR V **open into/onto sth** to lead to another room, area or place: *This door opens onto the garden.* **open out** to become wider **open up 1** to talk about what you feel and think **2** to open a door **open (sth) up 1** to become available or to make sth available: *When I left school all sorts of opportunities opened up for me.* **2** (**BUSINESS**) to start a business: *The restaurant opened up last year.*

the ˈopen *noun* [sing.] outside or in the countryside: *After working in an office all week, I like to be out in the open at weekends.*
IDM **bring sth out into the open | come out into the open** to make sth known publicly; to be known publicly: *I'm glad our secret has come out into the open at last.*

open-ˈair *adj.* [only before noun] not inside a building: *an open-air swimming pool*

opencast /ˈəʊpənkɑːst/ *adj.* in **opencast** mines, coal is taken out of the ground near the surface

ˈopen day *noun* [C] a day when the public can visit a place that they cannot usually go into: *The college is having an open day next month.*

opener /ˈəʊpənə(r)/ *noun* [C] (usually in compounds) a thing that takes the LID, etc. off sth: *a tin-opener* ◊ *a bottle-opener*

opening ⓔ **B2** /ˈəʊpənɪŋ/ *noun* [C]
• SPACE/HOLE **1** a space or hole that sb/sth can go through: *We were able to get through an opening in the hedge.*
• BEGINNING **2** the beginning or first part of sth: *The film is famous for its dramatic opening.*
• CEREMONY **3** a ceremony to celebrate the first time a public building, road, etc. is used: *the opening of the new hospital*
• JOB **4** a job that is available: *We have an opening for a sales manager at the moment.*
• OPPORTUNITY **5** a good opportunity: *I'm sure she'll be a great journalist — all she needs is an opening.*
▶ **opening** *adj.* [only before noun]: *the opening chapter of a book* ◊ *the opening ceremony of the Olympic Games*

open-ˈjaw *adj.* [only before noun] (**TOURISM**) allowing sb to fly to one place and fly back from another place

openly ⓔ+ **B2** /ˈəʊpənli/ *adv.* honestly; not keeping anything secret: *I think you should discuss your feelings openly with each other.*

open-ˈminded *adj.* ready to consider new ideas and opinions **OPP** **narrow-minded**

openness /ˈəʊpənnəs/ *noun* [U] the quality of being honest and ready to talk about your feelings

,open-'plan *adj.* (used about a large area indoors) not divided into separate rooms: *an open-plan office*

,open-'source *adj.* (**COMPUTING**) used to describe software for which the original SOURCE CODE is made available to anyone

the ,Open Uni'versity *noun* [sing.] (*BrE*) (**EDUCATION**) a British university providing degree courses that students can take at home

opera ʕ+ B2 /'ɒprə/ *noun* [C, U] (**ARTS AND MEDIA**) a dramatic work in which all or most of the words are sung to music; works of this kind performed as entertainment: *an opera by Wagner* ◊ *a comic opera* ◊ *Do you like opera?* ➔ look at **soap opera** ➔ note at **performing arts**

operable /'ɒpərəbl/ *adj.* (**MEDICINE**) (used about a disease) that can be cured by a medical operation **OPP** inoperable

'opera house *noun* [C] (**ARCHITECTURE**) a theatre where OPERAS are performed

operate ʕ B2 ⊙ /'ɒpəreɪt/ *verb* 1 [I, T] to work; to make sth work: *I don't understand how this machine operates.* ◊ *These switches here operate the central heating.* **SYN** function¹ 2 [T, I] (**BUSINESS**) to manage sth; to do business: *The firm operates from its central office in Delhi.* 3 [I] to act; to have an effect: *Several factors were operating to our advantage.* 4 [I] ~(on sb/ sth) (for sth) (**MEDICINE**) to cut open sb's body in hospital in order to deal with a part that is damaged by an injury or disease, etc: *The surgeon is going to operate on her in the morning.* ◊ *He was operated on for appendicitis.*

operatic /ˌɒpəˈrætɪk/ *adj.* (**ARTS AND MEDIA**) connected with OPERA: *operatic music*

'operating system *noun* [C] (**COMPUTING**) a computer program that organizes a number of other programs at the same time

'operating theatre (*also* theatre) (*BrE*) (*AmE* 'operating room) *noun* [C] (**MEDICINE**) a room in a hospital where medical operations are performed ➔ note at **hospital**

operation ʕ B1 ⊙ /ˌɒpəˈreɪʃn/ *noun*
• MEDICAL PROCESS 1 (*also informal* op) [C] (**MEDICINE**) the process of cutting open a patient's body in order to deal with a part inside: *He had an operation to remove his appendix.* ➔ note at **hospital**
• ACTIVITY 2 [C] an organized activity that involves many people doing different things: *A rescue operation was mounted to find the missing children.*
• BUSINESS 3 [C] a business or company involving many parts
• IN COMPUTING 4 [C] an act performed by a machine, especially a computer
• OF A MACHINE/SYSTEM 5 [U] the way in which you make sth work: *The operation of these machines is extremely simple.*
• IN MATHEMATICS 6 [C] a process in which a number or quantity is changed by adding, multiplying, etc. **IDM** be in operation | come into operation to be/ start working or having an effect: *The new tax system will come into operation in the spring.*

operational ʕ+ C1 W /ˌɒpəˈreɪʃənl/ *adj.* 1 connected with the way a business, machine, system, etc. works: *operational costs* 2 ready for use: *The new factory is now fully operational.* 3 [only before noun] connected with military operations

operative /'ɒpərətɪv/ *adj.* 1 working, able to be used; in use: *The new law will be operative from 1 May.* 2 (**MEDICINE**) connected with a medical operation

operator ʕ+ B2 /'ɒpəreɪtə(r)/ *noun* [C] 1 a person whose job is to work a particular machine or piece of equipment: *a computer operator* 2 (**BUSINESS**) a person or company that does certain types of business: *a tour*

operator 3 a person whose job is to connect phone calls, for the public or in a particular building: *Dial 100 for the operator.* ◊ *a switchboard operator*

ophthalmology /ˌɒfθælˈmɒlədʒi, ˌɒpθ-/ *noun* [U] (**MEDICINE**) the scientific study of the eye and its diseases

opiate /'əʊpiət/ *noun* [C] (**MEDICINE**) a drug containing OPIUM

opinion ʕ A1 /əˈpɪnjən/ *noun* 1 [C] ~(of sb/sth); ~(on/ about sth) what you think about sb/sth: *She asked me for my opinion of her new hairstyle and I told her.* ◊ *He has very strong opinions on almost everything.* ◊ *In my opinion, you're making a terrible mistake.* 2 [U] what people in general think about sth: *Public opinion is in favour of a change in the law.* **IDM** be of the opinion that … (*formal*) to think or believe that … ➔ note at **think**¹ have a good/high opinion of sb/sth | have a bad/low/poor opinion of sb/sth to think that sb/sth is good/bad a matter of opinion → MATTER¹

▼ COLLOCATIONS

opinion

You can **give/state a view/an opinion**: *You will have an opportunity to state your view.* ◊ *He invited the committee members to give their opinions.* You can **make a suggestion, proposal** or **point**: *I'd like to make a suggestion to the chairman.* ◊ *He made an interesting point.* ◊ *Could I make a proposal?* You can **raise an objection, an issue** or **a point**: *The workers raised an objection to longer working hours.* ◊ *I'm glad you've raised that issue/point.*

opinionated /əˈpɪnjəneɪtɪd/ (*also* self-opinionated) *adj.* having very strong opinions that you are not willing to change

o'pinion poll = POLL¹ (1)

opium /'əʊpiəm/ *noun* [U] a powerful drug that is made from the juice of a type of POPPY (= a type of flower)

opponent ʕ B2 /əˈpəʊnənt/ *noun* [C] 1 (**SPORT**) (in sport or competitions) a person who plays against sb: *They are the toughest opponents we've played against.* 2 ~(of sth) a person who disagrees with sb's actions, plans or beliefs and tries to stop or change them: *He is an outspoken opponent of nuclear power.*

opportune /'ɒpətjuːn/ *adj.* (*formal*) 1 (used about a time) suitable for doing a particular thing, so that it is likely to be successful: *I waited for an opportune moment to ask him.* **SYN** favourable 2 done or happening at the right time to be successful: *the opportune visit of the managing director* **OPP** inopportune

opportunism /ˌɒpəˈtjuːnɪzəm/ *noun* [U] the practice of using situations unfairly to get an advantage for yourself without thinking about how your actions will affect other people: *political opportunism*

opportunist /ˌɒpəˈtjuːnɪst/ (*also* opportunistic) *adj.* making use of an opportunity, especially to get an advantage for yourself; not done in a planned way: *an opportunist crime* ▶ opportunist *noun* [C]: *80% of burglaries are committed by casual opportunists.*

opportunistic /ˌɒpətjuːˈnɪstɪk/ *adj.* 1 = OPPORTUNIST 2 [only before noun] (**HEALTH**) harmful to people whose IMMUNE SYSTEM (= the system in the body that produces substances to fight infection) has been made weak by disease or drugs: *an opportunistic infection*

opportunity ʕ A2 W /ˌɒpəˈtjuːnəti/ *noun* [C, U] (*pl.* -ies) ~(for sth/to do sth) a chance to do sth that you would like to do; a situation or a time in which it is possible to do sth: *I have a **golden opportunity** to go to America now that my sister lives there.* ◇ *When we're finally alone, I'll **take the opportunity** to ask him a few personal questions.* ◇ *I'll give Steve your message if I **get the opportunity**.* ◇ *There will be plenty of opportunity for asking questions later.* **SYN** chance[1]

oppose ʰ **B2** /əˈpəʊz/ *verb* [T] to disagree with sb's beliefs, actions or plans and to try to change or stop them: *They opposed the plan to build a new road.*

opposed ʰ **B2** /əˈpəʊzd/ *adj.* ~ **to sth** disagreeing with a plan, an action, etc.; believing that sth is wrong: *She has always been strongly opposed to experiments on animals.*
IDM **as opposed to** (used to emphasize the difference between two things) rather than; and not: *Your work will be judged by quality, as opposed to quantity.*

opposing /əˈpəʊzɪŋ/ *adj.* [only before noun] **1** playing, fighting, working, etc. against each other: *a player from the opposing side* ◇ *It is time for opposing factions to unite and work towards a common goal.* **2** very different from each other

opposite ʰ **A1** /ˈɒpəzɪt/ *adj., adv., prep.* **1** in a position on the other side of sb/sth; facing: *The old town and the new town are on opposite sides of the river.* ◇ *You sit there and I'll sit opposite.* **2** completely different: *I can't walk with you because I'm going in the opposite direction.* ◇ *the opposite sex* (= the other sex)
▶ **opposite** ʰ **A1** *noun* [C] **the ~ (of sth)**: *'Hot' is the opposite of 'cold'.*
IDM **your opposite number** a person who does the same job or has the same position as you in a different company, organization, team, etc: *The prime minister met his Italian opposite number.*

opposition ʰ **B2** /ˌɒpəˈzɪʃn/ *noun* **1** [U] **~ (to sb/sth)** the feeling of disagreeing with sth and the act of trying to change it: *He expressed strong opposition to the plan.* **2** **the opposition** [sing. + sing./pl. verb] the person or team who you compete against in sport, business, etc: *We need to find out what the opposition is/are doing.* **3** **the Opposition** [sing. + sing./pl. verb] (**POLITICS**) the politicians or the political parties that are in a parliament but not in the government: *the leader of the Opposition* ◇ *Opposition MPs*

oppress /əˈpres/ *verb* [T] to treat a group of people in a cruel and unfair way by not allowing them the same freedom and rights as others ▶ **oppressed** *adj.*: *an oppressed minority* ▶ **oppression** /əˈpreʃn/ *noun* [U]: *a struggle against oppression*

oppressive /əˈpresɪv/ *adj.* **1** allowing no freedom; controlling by force **2** (used especially about heat or the atmosphere) causing you to feel very uncomfortable

opt ʰ+ **C1** /ɒpt/ *verb* [I] **~ to do sth/for sth** to choose to do or have sth after thinking about it: *She opted for a career in music.*
PHR V **opt in (to sth)** to choose to be part of a system or an agreement **opt out (of sth)** to choose not to take part in sth

optic /ˈɒptɪk/ *adj.* (**ANATOMY**) connected with the eye or the sense of sight: *the optic nerve* (= from the eye to the brain) ⊃ picture at **eye**[1]

optical ʰ+ **C1** /ˈɒptɪkl/ *adj.* (**BIOLOGY**) connected with the sense of sight: *optical effects*

optical fibre (*BrE*) (*AmE* **optical fiber**) *noun* [C, U] (**PHYSICS**) (a) thin glass THREAD for sending information in the form of light signals

optical illusion *noun* [C] an image that tricks the eye and makes you think you can see sth that you cannot see

optician /ɒpˈtɪʃn/ *noun* [C] a person whose job is to test eyes, sell glasses, etc: *I have to go to the optician's* (= the shop) *for an eye test.*

optics /ˈɒptɪks/ *noun* [U] (**PHYSICS**) the scientific study of sight and light

optimal /ˈɒptɪməl/ = OPTIMUM (1)

optimism ʰ+ **C1** /ˈɒptɪmɪzəm/ *noun* [U] a feeling that good things will happen and that sth will be successful: *There is considerable optimism that the economy will improve.* **OPP** pessimism
▶ **optimistic** ʰ+ **B2** /ˌɒptɪˈmɪstɪk/ *adj.* ▶ **optimistically** /-kli/ *adv.*

optimist /ˈɒptɪmɪst/ *noun* [C] a person who always thinks that good things will happen **OPP** pessimist

optimize (*BrE* also -ise) /ˈɒptɪmaɪz/ *verb* [T] **1** to make sth as good as it can be; to use sth in the best possible way: *to optimize the use of resources* **2** (**COMPUTING**) to change data, software, etc. in order to make it work better or to make it suitable for a particular purpose: *It is important that websites are optimized for mobile devices.*

optimum /ˈɒptɪməm/ *adj.* [only before noun] **1** (*also* **optimal**) the best possible; producing the best possible results ◇ **the optimum** *noun* [sing.] the best possible result or the best set of conditions to get good results

option ʰ **A2** ◉ /ˈɒpʃn/ *noun* **1** [C, U] something that you can choose to do; the freedom to choose: *She looked carefully at all the options before deciding on a career.* ◇ *Students **have the option** of studying part-time or full-time.* ◇ *If you're late again, you will give us **no option but** to dismiss you.* **SYN** choice[1] **2** [C] (**EDUCATION**) a subject that a student can choose to study, but that they do not have to do: *The course offers options in design and computing.* **3** [C] **~ (on sth)**; **~ (to do sth)** (**BUSINESS**) the right to buy or sell sth at some time in the future: *We have an option on the house.* ◇ *The property is for rent with an option to buy.* ◇ *share options* (= the right to buy shares in a company) **4** [C] (**COMPUTING**) one of the choices you can make when using a computer program: *Choose the 'Cut' option from the Edit menu.*

optional /ˈɒpʃənl/ *adj.* that you can choose or not choose: *an optional subject at school*
OPP compulsory, obligatory

optometry /ɒpˈtɒmətri/ *noun* [U] the job of testing eyes and providing treatment ▶ **optometrist** /-trɪst/ *noun* [C]

or ʰ **A1** /ɔː(r)/ *conj.* **1** used in a list of possibilities or choices: *Would you like to sit here or next to the window?* ◇ *Are you interested or not?* ◇ *For the main course, you can have lamb, beef or fish.* ◇ look at **either**[1], **either**[3] **2** if not; otherwise: *Don't drive so fast or you'll have an accident!* **SYN** or else **3** used in negative sentences when mentioning two or more things: *I've never been either to Italy or Spain.* ◇ *Alexi hasn't phoned or messaged me for weeks.* ◇ look at **neither**[1], **neither**[2] (2) **4** used between two numbers to show approximately how many: *I've been there five or six times.* **5** used before a word or phrase that explains or comments on what has been said before: *20% of the population, or one in five*
IDM **or else** ⇒ ELSE **or so** about; approximately: *You should feel better in three days or so.* **or somebody/something/somewhere | somebody/something/somewhere or other** used for showing that you are not sure, cannot remember or do not know which person, thing or place: *She's a computer programmer or something.* ◇ *He muttered something or other about having no time, and disappeared.*

oracle /'ɒrəkl/ *noun* [C] **1** (**HISTORY**) (in ancient Greece) a place where people could go to ask the gods for advice and information about the future; the priest through whom the gods were thought to give their message: *They consulted the oracle at Delphi.* **2** (**HISTORY**) (in ancient Greece) the advice or information that the gods gave, which often had a hidden meaning **3** [usually sing.] a person or book that gives valuable advice or information: *My sister's the oracle on financial matters.*

oral¹ ⟨̣+⟩ **C1** /'ɔːrəl/ *adj.* **1** (**LANGUAGE**) spoken, not written: *an oral test* **2** [only before noun] (**ANATOMY**) concerning or used in the mouth: *oral hygiene* ⊃ look at **aural** ▶ **orally** /-rəli/ *adv.*: *You can ask the questions orally or in writing.* ◊ *This medicine is taken orally* (= is SWALLOWED).

oral² /'ɔːrəl/ *noun* [C] (**EDUCATION**) a spoken exam: *I've got my German oral next week.*

orange¹ ⟨̣+⟩ **A1** /'ɒrɪndʒ/ *noun* **1** [C, U] a round fruit with a thick skin that is divided into SEGMENTS (= sections) inside and is a colour between red and yellow: *orange juice/peel* ◊ *an orange tree* **2** [U, C] a drink made from oranges or with the taste of oranges; a glass of this drink **3** [U, C] a bright colour between red and yellow

orange² ⟨̣+⟩ **A1** /'ɒrɪndʒ/ *adj.* between red and yellow in colour: *orange paint*

orange 'squash *noun* [U, C] (*BrE*) a drink made by adding water to a liquid that tastes of orange

orangutan /ə'ræŋətæn/ *noun* [C] a large APE (= an animal like a large monkey with no tail) with long arms and red-brown hair, that lives in Borneo and Sumatra

orator /'ɒrətə(r)/ *noun* [C] (*formal*) a person who is good at making public speeches

oratorio /ˌɒrə'tɔːriəʊ/ *noun* [C] (*pl.* -os) (**MUSIC**) a long piece of music for singers and an ORCHESTRA, usually based on a religious story

orbit /'ɔːbɪt/ *noun* [C, U] (**ASTRONOMY**) a curved path taken by a planet or another object as it moves around another planet, star, moon, etc. ⊃ picture at **season¹** ▶ **orbit** *verb* [I, T]

orbital /'ɔːbɪtl/ *adj.* [only before noun] **1** (used about a road) built around the outside of a city or town to reduce the amount of traffic travelling through the centre **2** (**ASTRONOMY**) connected with the ORBIT of a planet or another object in space ▶ **orbital** *noun* [C]

orbiter /'ɔːbɪtə(r)/ *noun* [C] (**ASTRONOMY**) a SPACECRAFT designed to move around a planet or moon rather than to land on it

orchard /'ɔːtʃəd/ *noun* [C] (**AGRICULTURE**) a piece of land on which fruit trees are grown: *a cherry orchard* ⊃ note at **agriculture**

orchestra ⟨̣+⟩ **B2** /'ɔːkɪstrə/ *noun* [C] (**MUSIC**) a large group of musicians who play various musical instruments together, led by a CONDUCTOR: *a symphony orchestra* ▶ **orchestral** /ɔː'kestrəl/ *adj.*

orchestra pit (*also* **pit**) *noun* [C] (**ARTS AND MEDIA**) the place in a theatre just in front of the stage where the ORCHESTRA sits and plays for an OPERA, a BALLET, etc.

orchestration /ˌɔːkɪ'streɪʃn/ *noun* [U] **1** (**MUSIC**) the way that a piece of music is written so that an ORCHESTRA can play it **2** the careful organization of a complicated plan or event, done secretly

orchid /'ɔːkɪd/ *noun* [C] a plant with brightly coloured flowers of unusual shapes. There are many different types of orchid and some of them are very rare.

ordain /ɔː'deɪn/ *verb* [T, usually passive] **~ sb (as) (sth)** (**RELIGION**) to make sb a priest or minister: *He was ordained (as) a priest last year.* ⊃ noun **ordination**

ordeal /ɔː'diːl, 'ɔːdiːl/ *noun* [C, usually sing.] a very unpleasant or difficult experience

order¹ ⟨̣+⟩ **A1** ⊙ /'ɔːdə(r)/ *noun*
• ARRANGEMENT **1** [U, C] the way in which people or things are arranged in relation to each other: *a list of names*

layout of an orchestra

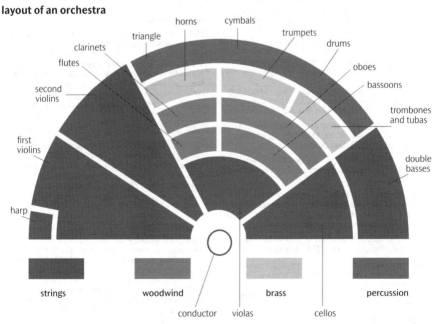

- horns
- cymbals
- triangle
- trumpets
- clarinets
- drums
- flutes
- oboes
- second violins
- bassoons
- first violins
- trombones and tubas
- harp
- double basses
- strings
- woodwind
- brass
- percussion
- conductor
- violas
- cellos

in **alphabetical order** ◇ *Try to put the things you have to do* **in order of importance.** ◇ *What's the order of events today?* **2** [U] an organized state, where everything is in its right place: *I really must* **put my notes in order,** *because I can never find what I'm looking for.* **OPP** **disorder**

• CONTROLLED STATE **3** [U] the situation in which laws, rules, authority, etc. are obeyed: *Following last week's riots, order has now been restored.* ⊃ look at **disorder** (2)

• INSTRUCTION **4** [C] **~ (for sb) (to do sth)** something that you are told to do by sb in a position of authority: *In the army, you have to* **obey orders** *at all times.* ◇ *She* **gave the order** *for the work to be started.*

• FOOD/DRINKS **5** [C] a request for food or drinks in a hotel, restaurant, etc.; the food or drinks you asked for: *Can I* **take your order** *now, sir?*

• GOODS **6** [C, U] **~ (for sth) (BUSINESS)** a request asking for sth to be made, supplied or sent: *The book I need is* **on order** (= they are waiting for it to arrive). ◇ *She* placed an **order** for ten copies of the book.

• IN BIOLOGY **7** [C] a group into which animals, plants, etc. that have similar characteristics are divided, smaller than a CLASS and larger than a FAMILY: *the order of primates* ⊃ picture at **animal**
IDM **in order to do sth** with the purpose or intention of doing sth; so that sth can be done: *We left early in order to avoid the traffic.* **in/into reverse order** → REVERSE[2] **in working order** (used about machines, etc.) working properly, not broken **law and order** → LAW **out of order 1** (used about a machine, etc.) not working properly or not working at all: *I had to walk up to the tenth floor because the lift was out of order.* **2** (*informal*) (used about a person's behaviour) unacceptable, because it is rude, etc: *That comment was completely out of order!*

order[2] ₤ **A1** **S** /ˈɔːdə(r)/ *verb* **1** [T] **~ sb (to do sth)** to use your position of authority to tell sb to do sth or to say that sth must happen: *I'm not asking you to do your homework, I'm ordering you!* ◇ *The company was ordered to pay compensation to its former employees.* **2** [T] to ask for sth to be made, supplied or sent somewhere: *The shop didn't have the book I wanted so I ordered it.* **3** [I, T] **~ (sb) (sth); ~ (sth) (for sb) (TOURISM)** to ask for food or drinks in a restaurant, hotel, etc: *Are you ready to order yet, madam?* ◇ *Can you order me a sandwich while I make a phone call?* ◇ *Could you order a sandwich for me?*
PHRV **order sb around** (*also* **order sb about** *especially in BrE*) to keep telling sb what to do and how to do it: *Stop ordering me about! You're not my father.*

orderly[1] /ˈɔːdəli/ *adj.* **1** arranged or organized in a tidy way: *an orderly office/desk* **SYN** **tidy[1]** **2** peaceful; behaving well **OPP** **disorderly**

orderly[2] /ˈɔːdəli/ *noun* [C] (*pl.* -ies) (**MEDICINE**) a worker in a hospital, usually doing jobs that do not need special training

ordinal /ˈɔːdɪnl/ (*also* **ordinal 'number**) *noun* [C] (**GRAMMAR**, **MATHEMATICS**) a number that shows the order or position of sth in a series: *'First', 'second', and 'third' are ordinals.* ⊃ look at **cardinal** (2)

ordinarily /ˈɔːdnrəli/ *adv.* usually; generally: *Ordinarily, I don't work as late as this.* **SYN** **normally**

ordinary ₤ **A2** **W** /ˈɔːdnri/ *adj.* normal; not unusual or different from others: *It's interesting to see how ordinary people live in other countries.*
IDM **out of the ordinary** unusual; different from normal

'ordinary level *noun* [C, U] = O LEVEL

ordination /ˌɔːdɪˈneɪʃn/ *noun* [U, C] (**RELIGION**) the act or ceremony of making sb a priest, etc. ⊃ verb **ordain**

ore /ɔː(r)/ *noun* [U, C] (**CHEMISTRY**, **GEOLOGY**) rock or earth from which metal can be taken: *iron ore*

oregano /ˌɒrɪˈgɑːnəʊ/ *noun* [U] a plant with leaves that have a sweet smell and are used in cooking as a HERB

organ ₤ **B2** /ˈɔːgən/ *noun* [C] **1** (**ANATOMY**) one of the parts inside the body that have a particular function: **vital organs** (= those such as the heart and LIVER which help to keep you alive) ◇ *sexual/reproductive organs* ⊃ picture at **body** **2** (**MUSIC**) a large musical instrument like a piano with pipes through which air is forced. Organs are often found in churches: *organ music* ▶ **organist** *noun* [C]

organic ₤+ **B2** /ɔːˈgænɪk/ *adj.* **1** (**AGRICULTURE**) (used about food or farming methods) produced by or using natural materials, without artificial chemicals: *organic vegetables* ◇ *organic farming* **2** (**BIOLOGY**, **CHEMISTRY**) produced by or from living things: *organic compounds/molecules* **OPP** **inorganic** ▶ **organically** /-kli/ *adv.*: *organically produced*

or'ganic 'chemistry *noun* [U] (**CHEMISTRY**) the branch of chemistry that deals with substances that contain CARBON ⊃ look at **inorganic chemistry**

organism /ˈɔːgənɪzəm/ *noun* [C] (**BIOLOGY**) a living thing, especially one that is so small that you can only see it with a MICROSCOPE (= a piece of equipment that makes small objects look bigger)

organization ₤ **A2** **O** (*BrE also* -isation) /ˌɔːgənaɪˈzeɪʃn/ *noun* **1** [C] a group of people who form a business, club, etc. together in order to achieve a particular aim: *She works for a voluntary organization helping homeless people.* **2** [U] the activity of making preparations or arrangements for sth: *An enormous amount of organization went into the festival.* **3** [U] the way in which sth is organized, arranged or prepared **OPP** **disorganization** ▶ **organizational** ₤+ **C1** (*BrE also* -isational) /-ʃənl/ *adj.*: *The job requires a high level of organizational ability.*

▼ COLLOCATIONS

organization

You can **create**, **establish**, **form**, **found**, **set up** or **start an organization**, a **company**, etc: *an association created to promote local industry* ◇ *The company was founded in 1991.* You can **dissolve a company** or **partnership**: *a court order to have the partnership dissolved.* You can **run/manage a firm**, **company**, etc: *He runs an accountancy firm.* ◇ *The executive committee manages the group on a day-to-day basis.* You can **join** or **be/become a member of a society** or **an organization**: *She became a member of the Society of Arts.* ◇ *She joined Greenpeace in 2006.*

---

organize ₤ **A2** **W** (*BrE also* -ise) /ˈɔːgənaɪz/ *verb* **1** [T] to plan or arrange an event, activity, etc: *The school organizes trips to various places of interest.* ⊃ note at **meeting** **2** [T, I] to put or arrange things into a system or logical order: *You need to organize your work more carefully.* ◇ *Can you decide what needs doing? I'm hopeless at organizing.* ▶ **organizer** ₤ **B1** (*BrE also* -iser) *noun* [C]: *The organizers of the concert said that it had been a great success.*

organized ₤ **B1** (*BrE also* -ised) /ˈɔːgənaɪzd/ *adj.* **1** arranged or planned in the way mentioned: *a carefully/badly/well organized trip* **OPP** **disorganized** **2** (used about a person) able to plan your work, life, etc. well: *I wish I were as organized as you!* **OPP** **disorganized** **3** [only before noun] involving a large number of people working together to do sth in a way that has been carefully planned: *an organized campaign against cruelty to animals* ◇ *organized* *crime* (= done by a large group of professional criminals)

orgasm /ˈɔːgæzəm/ *noun* [U, C] the point of greatest sexual pleasure: *to have an orgasm*

orgy /ˈɔːdʒi/ *noun* [C] (*pl.* -ies) **1** a party involving a lot of eating, drinking and sexual activity **2 ~ (of sth)** a period of doing sth in a wild way, without control: *The gang went on an orgy of destruction.*

the Orient /ði ˈɔːriənt/ *noun* [sing.] (*old-fashioned, formal*) (**GEOGRAPHY**) the eastern part of the world, especially China and Japan

orient ⓦ /ˈɔːrient/ (*BrE also* **orientate** /ˈɔːrienteɪt/) *verb* [T] **~ yourself** to find out where you are; to become familiar with a place ⊃ look at **disorientate**

oriental /ˌɔːriˈentl/ (*also* **Oriental**) *adj.* (*old-fashioned*) coming from or belonging to the East or Far East: *oriental languages* **HELP** Be careful. If it refers to a person, this word is offensive.

orientation ⭐+ 🅲1 ⓦ /ˌɔːriənˈteɪʃn/ *noun* **1** [U, C] **~ (to/towards sth)** the type of aims or interests that a person or an organization has; the act of directing your aims towards a particular thing **2** [U, C] a person's basic beliefs or feelings about a particular subject: *religious/political orientation* **3** [C] the direction in which an object faces: *The orientation of the planet's orbit is changing continuously.*

-oriented /ˈɔːrientɪd/ (*BrE also* **-orientated** /ˈɔːrienteɪtɪd/) *adj.* (after a noun) for or interested in a particular type of person or thing: *She's very career orientated.* ◊ *a company selling male-oriented products*

orienteering /ˌɔːriənˈtɪərɪŋ/ *noun* [U] (**SPORT**) a sport in which you find your way across country on foot, as quickly as possible, using a map and a **COMPASS** (= an instrument that shows direction)

orifice /ˈɒrɪfɪs/ *noun* [C] (*formal*) a hole or an opening, especially in the body

origami /ˌɒrɪˈgɑːmi/ *noun* [U] the Japanese art of folding paper into attractive shapes

origin ⭐ 🅱2 ⓞ /ˈɒrɪdʒɪn/ *noun* [C, U] **1** the point from which sth starts; the cause of sth: *This particular tradition* **has its origins** *in India.* ◊ *Many English words are* **of** *Latin* **origin.** **2** a person's social and family background: *people of African origin* ◊ *children of various ethnic origins*

original¹ ⭐ 🅰2 ⓦ /əˈrɪdʒənl/ *adj.* **1** [only before noun] first; earliest (before any changes or developments): *The original meaning of this word is different from the meaning it has nowadays.* **2** new and interesting; different from others of its type: *There are no original ideas in his work.* **3** made or created first, before copies: '*Is that the original painting?*' '*No, it's a copy.*'

original² ⭐ 🅱1 /əˈrɪdʒənl/ *noun* [C] the first document, painting, etc. that was made; not a copy: *Could you make a photocopy of my birth certificate and give the original back to me?*

originality /əˌrɪdʒəˈnæləti/ *noun* [U] the quality of being new and interesting

originally ⭐ 🅱1 ⓦ /əˈrɪdʒənəli/ *adv.* in the beginning, before any changes or developments: *I'm from London originally, but I left there when I was very young.*

originate ⭐+ 🅲1 /əˈrɪdʒɪneɪt/ *verb* [I] (*formal*) to happen or appear for the first time in a particular place or situation

ornament /ˈɔːnəmənt/ *noun* [C] an object that you have because it is attractive, not because it is useful. Ornaments are used to decorate rooms, etc.

ornamental /ˌɔːnəˈmentl/ *adj.* made or put somewhere in order to look attractive, not for any practical use

ornate /ɔːˈneɪt/ *adj.* covered with a lot of small, complicated designs as decoration

ornithology /ˌɔːnɪˈθɒlədʒi/ *noun* [U] (**BIOLOGY**) the study of birds ▸ **ornithologist** /-dʒɪst/ *noun* [C]

orographic /ˌɒrəˈɡræfɪk/ *adj.* (**GEOGRAPHY**) connected with mountains, especially with their position and shape

orphan /ˈɔːfn/ *noun* [C] a child whose parents are dead ▸ **orphan** *verb* [T, usually passive]: *She was orphaned when she was three and went to live with her grandparents.*

orphanage /ˈɔːfənɪdʒ/ *noun* [C] a home for children whose parents are dead

ortho- /ˈɔːθəʊ, ɔːθə, ɔːˈθɒ/ *prefix* (in nouns, adjectives and adverbs) correct; standard: *orthography* ◊ *orthodox*

orthodontics /ˌɔːθəˈdɒntɪks/ *noun* [U] (**MEDICINE**) the treatment of problems concerning the position of the teeth and JAWS (= the two bones in the face that contain the teeth) ▸ **orthodontic** *adj.*: *orthodontic treatment* ▸ **orthodontist** /-tɪst/ *noun* [C]

orthodox /ˈɔːθədɒks/ *adj.* **1** that most people believe, do or accept; usual: *orthodox opinions/methods* **OPP** **unorthodox** **2** (**RELIGION**) closely following the old, traditional beliefs, ceremonies, etc: *an orthodox Jew* ◊ *the Greek Orthodox Church*

orthography /ɔːˈθɒɡrəfi/ *noun* [U] (*formal*) (**LANGUAGE**) the system of spelling in a language ▸ **orthographic** /ˌɔːθəˈɡræfɪk/ *adj.*

orthopaedics (*BrE*) (*AmE* **orthopedics**) /ˌɔːθəˈpiːdɪks/ *noun* [U] (**MEDICINE**) the area of medicine connected with injuries and diseases of the bones or muscles ▸ **orthopaedic** (*AmE* **orthopedic**) *adj.*

oscillate /ˈɒsɪleɪt/ *verb* [I] **~ (between A and B)** (*formal*) **1** to keep changing from one extreme of feeling or behaviour to another, and back again: *Her moods oscillated between joy and despair.* **2** to keep moving from one position to another and back again: *Watch how the needle oscillates as the current changes.* **3** (**PHYSICS**) (used about an electric current, radio waves, etc.) to change in strength or direction at regular times ▸ **oscillation** /ˌɒsɪˈleɪʃn/ *noun* [U, C]

oscillator /ˈɒsɪleɪtə(r)/ *noun* [C] (**PHYSICS**) a piece of equipment for producing OSCILLATING electric currents

oscilloscope /əˈsɪləskəʊp/ *noun* [C] (**PHYSICS**) a piece of equipment that shows changes in electrical current as waves in a line on a screen

osmium /ˈɒzmiəm/ *noun* [U] (*symb.* **Os**) (**CHEMISTRY**) a chemical element. Osmium is a hard silver-white metal. ❶ For more information on the periodic table of elements, look at the **Reference Section** of this dictionary.

screen   control knobs
oscilloscope

osmosis /ɒzˈməʊsɪs/ *noun* [U] (**BIOLOGY, CHEMISTRY**) the slow, steady passing of a liquid through a MEMBRANE (= a thin layer of material): *Water passes into the roots of a plant* **by** *osmosis.*

ossicle /ˈɒsɪkl/ *noun* [C] (**ANATOMY**) any of the three very small bones in the MIDDLE EAR

ostentatious /ˌɒstenˈteɪʃəs/ *adj.* **1** showing your wealth or status in a way that is intended to impress people: *ostentatious gold jewellery* **2** (used about an action) done in a very obvious way so that people will notice it ▸ **ostentatiously** *adv.*

ostensibly

osteo- /ˈɒstiəʊ, ɒstiə, ɒstiˈɒ/ *prefix* (in nouns and adjectives) (**ANATOMY**) connected with bones: *osteopathy*

osteopath /ˈɒstiəpæθ/ *noun* [C] (**MEDICINE**) a person whose job involves treating some diseases and physical problems by pressing and moving the bones and muscles ⊃ look at **chiropractor**

osteopathy /ˌɒstiˈɒpəθi/ *noun* [U] the treatment of some diseases and physical problems by pressing and moving the bones and muscles

osteoporosis /ˌɒstiəʊpəˈrəʊsɪs/ *noun* [U] (**HEALTH**) a medical condition in which the bones become weak and are easily broken

ostracize (*BrE also* -ise) /ˈɒstrəsaɪz/ *verb* [T, usually passive] (*formal*) to refuse to allow sb to be a member of a social group; to refuse to meet or talk to sb

ostrich /ˈɒstrɪtʃ/ *noun* [C] a very large African bird with a long neck and long legs, that can run very fast but cannot fly

other 🔑 **A1** 🅦 /ˈʌðə(r)/ *adj., pron.* **1** in addition to or different from the one or ones that have already been mentioned: *I hadn't got any other plans that evening so I accepted their invitation.* ◇ *If you're busy now, I'll come back some other time.* ◇ *She doesn't care what other people think.* ◇ *I like this jumper but not the colour. Have you got any others?* ◇ *All my friends went to university, others didn't.* **2** the, my, your, etc. other used to refer to the second of two people or things, when the first has already been mentioned: *I can only find one sock. Have you seen the other one?* **3** the, my, your, etc. other/others used to refer to the rest of a group or number of people or things: *Their youngest son still lives with them but their other children have left home.* ◇ *I'll have to wear this shirt because all my others are dirty.* ◇ *Mick and I got a taxi there, the others walked.* **IDM** every other → **EVERY** in other words used for saying sth in a different way: *My boss said she would have to let me go. In other words, she fired me.* one after another/the other → **ONE**[1] other than (usually in negative sentences) apart from; except (for): *The plane was a little late, but other than that the journey was fine.* the other day/morning/week recently, not long ago: *An old friend rang me the other day.* the other way round → **ROUND**[2] somebody/something/somewhere or other → **OR**

otherwise 🔑 **B2** 🅦 /ˈʌðəwaɪz/ *adv.* **1** (used for stating what will happen if you do not do sth or if sth does not happen) if not: *You have to press the red button, otherwise it won't work.* **2** apart from that: *I'm a bit tired but otherwise I feel fine.* **3** in a different way to the way mentioned; differently

otitis /əʊˈtaɪtɪs/ *noun* [U] (**HEALTH**) a painful **SWELLING** of the ear, caused by an infection

OTT /ˌəʊ tiː ˈtiː/ *abbr.* = **OVER THE TOP**

otter /ˈɒtə(r)/ *noun* [C] a river animal with brown fur that eats fish

ouch /aʊtʃ/ *exclamation* used when reacting to a sudden feeling of pain

oud /uːd/ *noun* [C] (**MUSIC**) a musical instrument similar to a **LUTE** played mainly in Arab countries

ought to 🔑 **B1** /ˈɔːt tə, *before vowels and finally* tu/ *modal verb* (*negative* ought not to; *short form* oughtn't to /ˈɔːtnt tə, *before vowels and finally* tu/) **1** used to say what sb should do: *You ought to visit your parents more often.* ◇ *She oughtn't to make private phone calls in work time.* ◇ *He oughtn't to have been driving so fast.* **2** used to say what should happen or what you expect: *She*

ought to pass her test. ◇ *They ought to be here by now. They left at six.* ◇ *There ought to be more buses in the rush hour.* **3** used for asking for and giving advice about what to do: *You ought to read this book. It's really interesting.*

ounce /aʊns/ *noun* **1** [C] (*abbr.* oz) a measure of weight; 28.35 **GRAMS**. There are 16 ounces in a pound: *For this recipe you need four ounces of flour.* ❶ For more information about weights, look at the **Reference Section** of this dictionary. **2** [sing.] **an ~ of sth** (usually in negative sentences) a very small amount of sth: *He hasn't got an ounce of imagination.*

our 🔑 **A1** /ɑː(r), ˈaʊə(r)/ *det.* of or belonging to us: *Our house is at the bottom of the road.* ◇ *This is our first visit to Morocco.*

ours 🔑 **B1** /ɑːz, ˈaʊəz/ *pron.* the one or ones belonging to us: *Their garden is quite nice but I prefer ours.*

ourselves 🔑 **A2** /ɑːˈselvz, ˌaʊəˈselvz/ *pron.* **1** used when you and another person or other people together cause and are affected by an action: *Let's relax and enjoy ourselves.* ◇ *They asked us to wait so we sat down and made ourselves comfortable.* **2** used to emphasize the people who do the action: *Do you think we should paint the flat ourselves? (= or should we ask sb else to do it for us?)* **IDM** (all) by ourselves **1** alone: *Now that we're by ourselves, could I ask you a personal question?* **2** without help: *We managed to move all our furniture into the new flat by ourselves.*

oust /aʊst/ *verb* [T] **~ sb (from/as sth)** to force sb out of a job or position of power, especially in order to take their place: *He was ousted as chairman.*

out[1] 🔑 **A1** /aʊt/ *adv., prep.* **1 ~ (of sth)** away from the inside of a place or thing: *He opened the drawer and took a fork out.* ◇ *She opened the window and put her head out.* ◇ *Can you show me the way out?* ◇ *to get out of bed* **2** not at home or in your place of work: *The manager was out when she called.* ◇ *I'd love a night out — I'm bored with staying at home.* **3 ~ of sth** used to show where sth comes from: *I copied the recipe out of a book.* ◇ *I paid for it out of the money I earned last month.* **4 ~ of sth** used to show what sth is made from: *to be made out of wood/metal/plastic/gold* **5 ~ of sth** used for saying that you no longer have sth: *to be out of milk/sugar/tea* ◇ *He's been out of work for months.* **6 ~ of sth** used to show that sb/sth is not or is no longer in a particular state or condition: *Keep that present out of sight!* ◇ *The doctors say she's out of danger.* **7 ~ of sth** from among a number or set: *Nine out of ten people prefer this model.* **8** in a loud voice; clearly: *She cried out in pain.* **9** a long or a particular distance away from a place or from land: *We live a long way out of London.* ◇ *The current is quite strong so don't swim too far out.* **10** made available to the public; published: *There'll be a lot of controversy when her book comes out next year.* **11 ~ of sth** used for saying which feeling causes you to do sth: *I was only asking out of curiosity.* **12** (used about the sea) when the water is furthest away from the land: *Don't swim when the tide is on the way out.* **13** (used about flowers) fully open: *I love the spring when all the flowers are out.* **14** (used about a player in a game or sport) not allowed to continue playing: *If you get three answers wrong, you're out.* **15** (**SPORT**) (used about a ball, etc.) not inside the playing area and therefore not allowed **16** (used when you are calculating sth) making or containing a mistake; wrong: *My guess was only out by a few centimetres.* **17** not possible or acceptable: *I'm afraid Friday is out. I've got a meeting that day.* **18** not in fashion: *Short skirts are out this season.* **19** (used about a light or a fire) not on; not burning: *The lights are out. They must be in bed.* ◇ *Once the fire was* completely out, experts were sent in to inspect the damage.

IDM be out for sth | be out to do sth to try hard to get or do sth: *I'm not out for revenge.* down and out → DOWN¹ out-and-out complete: *It was out-and-out war between us.* out of bounds (*especially BrE*) → BOUNDS out of it lonely and unhappy because you are not included in sth: *I don't speak French so I felt rather out of it at the meeting.* out loud in a voice that other people can hear ⊃ look at **aloud** out of order → ORDER¹

out² /aʊt/ *verb* [T] to say publicly that sb is a HOMOSEXUAL, especially when they would rather keep it a secret: *The politician was eventually outed by a tabloid newspaper.*

out³ /aʊt/ *adj.* (*informal*) having told other people that you are GAY or LESBIAN: *an out gay man* ◇ *I had been out since I was 17.*

out- /aʊt/ *prefix* **1** (in verbs) greater, better, further, longer, etc: *outdo* ◇ *outrun* **2** (in nouns and adjectives) outside; away from: *outbuildings* ◇ *outlying*

outage /ˈaʊtɪdʒ/ *noun* [C] (*especially AmE*) a period of time when the supply of electricity, etc. is not working: *a power outage* ⊃ look at **power cut**

the outback /ðiˈaʊtbæk/ *noun* [sing.] (**GEOGRAPHY**) the part of Australia that is a long way from the coast and towns, where few people live

outboard motor /ˌaʊtbɔːd ˈməʊtə(r)/ *noun* [C] an engine that can be fixed to a boat

outbound /ˈaʊtbaʊnd/ *adj.* (**TOURISM**) travelling from a place rather than arriving in it: *outbound flights/passengers* **OPP** inbound

'out box (*AmE*) = OUT TRAY

outbox /ˈaʊtbɒks/ *noun* [C] (**COMPUTING**) the place on a computer where new email messages that you write are stored before you send them ⊃ look at **inbox** (1)

outbreak ʔ+ **C1** /ˈaʊtbreɪk/ *noun* [C] the sudden start of sth unpleasant (especially a disease or violence): *an outbreak of cholera/fighting*

outbuilding /ˈaʊtbɪldɪŋ/ *noun* [C] a building such as a SHED or stable that is built near to, but separate from, a large building: *a large farmhouse with several outbuildings*

outburst /ˈaʊtbɜːst/ *noun* [C] a sudden expression of a strong feeling, especially anger: *Afterwards, she apologized for her outburst.*

outcast /ˈaʊtkɑːst/ *noun* [C] a person who is no longer accepted by society or by a group of people: *a social outcast*

outclass /ˌaʊtˈklɑːs/ *verb* [T, often passive] to be much better than sb/sth, especially in a game or competition

outcome ʔ **B2** ◉ /ˈaʊtkʌm/ *noun* [C] the result or effect of an action or event ⊃ note at **effect¹**

outcrop /ˈaʊtkrɒp/ *noun* [C] (**GEOGRAPHY**) a large mass of rock that stands above the surface of the ground

outcry /ˈaʊtkraɪ/ *noun* [C, usually sing.] (*pl.* -ies) a strong protest by a large number of people because they disagree with sth: *The public outcry forced the government to change its mind about the new tax.*

outdated /ˌaʊtˈdeɪtɪd/ *adj.* not useful or common any more; old-fashioned: *A lot of the computer equipment is getting outdated.*

outdo /ˌaʊtˈduː/ *verb* [T] (outdoing; outdoes /-ˈdʌz/; *pt* outdid /-ˈdɪd/; *pp* outdone /-ˈdʌn/) to do sth better than another person: *Not to be outdone* (= not wanting anyone else to do better), *she tried again.*

outdoor ʔ **B1** /ˈaʊtdɔː(r)/ *adj.* [only before noun] happening, done, or used outside, not in a building: *an outdoor swimming pool* ◇ *outdoor clothing/activities* **OPP** indoor

outdoors ʔ **B1** /ˌaʊtˈdɔːz/ *adv.* outside a building: *It's a very warm evening so why don't we eat outdoors?* **SYN** out of doors **OPP** indoors ⊃ look at **outside¹**

outer ʔ **B2** /ˈaʊtə(r)/ *adj.* [only before noun] **1** on the outside of sth: *the outer layer of skin on an onion* **2** far from the inside or the centre of sth: *the outer suburbs of a city* **OPP** inner

outer 'ear *noun* [sing.] (**ANATOMY**) the part of the ear that is on the outside of the body and the part that leads to the EARDRUM (= the thin piece of skin that allows you to hear sound) ⊃ look at **inner ear**, **middle ear** ⊃ picture at **ear**

outermost /ˈaʊtəməʊst/ *adj.* [only before noun] furthest from the inside or centre **OPP** innermost

outer 'space = SPACE¹ (1)

outfit ʔ+ **B2** /ˈaʊtfɪt/ *noun* [C] a set of clothes that are worn together for a particular occasion or purpose: *I'm going to buy a whole new outfit for the party.*

outflow /ˈaʊtfləʊ/ *noun* [C, usually sing.] ~ (of sth/sb) (from sth) the movement of a large amount of money, liquid, people, etc. out of a place: *a steady outflow of oil from the tank*

outgoing /ˈaʊtɡəʊɪŋ/ *adj.* **1** friendly and interested in other people and new experiences **SYN** sociable **2** [only before noun] leaving a job or a place: *the outgoing president/government* ◇ *Put all the outgoing mail in a pile on that table.* **OPP** incoming

outgoings /ˈaʊtɡəʊɪŋz/ *noun* [pl.] (*BrE*) (**FINANCE**) an amount of money that you spend regularly, for example every week or month **OPP** income

outgrow /ˌaʊtˈɡrəʊ/ *verb* [T] (*pt* outgrew /-ˈɡruː/; *pp* outgrown /-ˈɡrəʊn/) to become too old or too big for sth

outing ʔ+ **C1** /ˈaʊtɪŋ/ *noun* [C] a short trip for pleasure: *to go on an outing to the zoo*

outlandish /aʊtˈlændɪʃ/ *adj.* very strange or unusual: *outlandish clothes*

outlast /ˌaʊtˈlɑːst/ *verb* [T] to continue to exist or to do sth for a longer time than sb/sth

outlaw¹ /ˈaʊtlɔː/ *verb* [T] (**LAW**) to make sth illegal

outlaw² /ˈaʊtlɔː/ *noun* [C] (**HISTORY**) (used in past times) a person who has done sth illegal and is hiding to avoid being caught

outlay /ˈaʊtleɪ/ *noun* [C, U] ~ (on sth) (**BUSINESS**, **FINANCE**) money that is spent, especially in order to start a business or project

outlet ʔ+ **C1** /ˈaʊtlet/ *noun* [C] **1** (**BUSINESS**) a shop, business, etc. that sells goods made by a particular company or of a particular type: *fast food/retail outlets* **2** ~ (for sth) a way of expressing and making good use of strong feelings, ideas or energy: *Gary found an outlet for his aggression in boxing.* **3** a pipe through which a gas or liquid can escape **OPP** inlet ⊃ picture at **distillation**

outline¹ ʔ **B2** ⓦ /ˈaʊtlaɪn/ *verb* [T] ~ sth (to sb) to give the most important facts or ideas about sth: *We outlined our proposals to the committee.*

outline² ʔ **B2** /ˈaʊtlaɪn/ *noun* [C] **1** a description of the most important facts or ideas about sth: *a brief outline of Indian history* **2** a line that shows the shape or outside edge of sb/sth: *She could see the outline of a person through the mist.*

outlive /ˌaʊtˈlɪv/ *verb* [T] to live or exist longer than sb/sth **SYN** **survive**

outlook ⚡+ **C1** /ˈaʊtlʊk/ *noun* [C] **1** ~ (on sth) your attitude to or feeling about life and the world: *an optimistic outlook on life* **2** ~ (for sth) what will probably happen: *The outlook for the economy is not good.*

outlying /ˈaʊtlaɪŋ/ *adj.* [only before noun] far away from the centre of a town or city: *outlying villages*

outmoded /ˌaʊtˈməʊdɪd/ *adj.* [only before noun] no longer common or fashionable

outnumber /ˌaʊtˈnʌmbə(r)/ *verb* [T, often passive] to be greater in number than an enemy, another team, etc: *The demonstrators were heavily outnumbered by the police.* ◇ *The enemy troops outnumbered us by three to one.*

ˌout of ˈdate *adj.* **1** old-fashioned: *Her ideas were out of date.* ◇ *out-of-date fashions* **2** no longer legally acceptable: *an out-of-date driving licence* ⊃ look at **up to date**

ˌout-of-ˈwork *adj.* unable to find a job; unemployed: *an out-of-work actor*

outpace /ˌaʊtˈpeɪs/ *verb* [T] to go, rise, improve, etc. faster than sb/sth: *He easily outpaced the other runners.*

outpatient /ˈaʊtpeɪʃnt/ *noun* [C] (**MEDICINE**) a person who goes to a hospital for treatment but who does not stay there during the night ⊃ look at **inpatient**

outperform /ˌaʊtpəˈfɔːm/ *verb* [T] to achieve better results than sb/sth: *The company has consistently outperformed its larger rivals.*

outplay /ˌaʊtˈpleɪ/ *verb* [T] (**SPORT**) to play much better than sb you are competing against: *We were totally outplayed and lost 106–74.*

outpost /ˈaʊtpəʊst/ *noun* [C] **1** a small military camp away from the main army, used for watching an enemy's movements, etc. **2** a small town or group of buildings in a lonely part of a country

output¹ ⚡+ **B2** ⊙ /ˈaʊtpʊt/ *noun* [U, sing.] **1** the amount that a person or machine produces **2** (**COMPUTING**) the information that a computer produces ⊃ look at **input¹** (2) **3** (**PHYSICS**) the power, energy, etc. produced by a piece of equipment: *an output of 100 watts* **4** (**PHYSICS**) the place where power, energy, etc. leaves a system

output² /ˈaʊtpʊt/ *verb* [T] (**outputting**; *pt, pp* **output**) (**COMPUTING**) to supply or produce information, results, etc: *Computers can now output data much more quickly.* ⊃ look at **input²**

outrage ⚡+ **C1** /ˈaʊtreɪdʒ/ *noun* **1** [C] something that is very bad or wrong and that causes you to feel great anger: *It's an outrage that such poverty should exist in the twenty-first century.* **2** [U] great anger: *a feeling of outrage* ▸ **outrage** ⚡+ **C1** *verb* [T]

outrageous /aʊtˈreɪdʒəs/ *adj.* that makes you very angry or shocked: *outrageous behaviour/prices* ▸ **outrageously** *adv.*

outreach /ˈaʊtriːtʃ/ *noun* [U] the activity of providing a service or advice to people in the community, especially those who cannot come to an office, a hospital, etc. for help: *an outreach and education programme*

outright /ˈaʊtraɪt/ *adj., adv.* **1** open and direct; in an open and direct way: *She told them outright what she thought about it.* **2** complete and clear; completely and clearly: *an outright victory* ◇ *to win outright* **3** not gradually; immediately: *They were able to buy the house outright.*

outrun /ˌaʊtˈrʌn/ *verb* [T] (**outrunning**; *pt* **outran** /-ˈræn/; *pp* **outrun**) to run faster or further than sb/sth: *He couldn't outrun his pursuers.*

outset /ˈaʊtset/ *noun* **IDM** **at/from the outset (of sth)** at/from the beginning (of sth)

outside¹ ⚡ **A1** /ˌaʊtˈsaɪd/ *adv.* not in a room or a building but on or to the outside of it: *Please wait outside for a few minutes.* ◇ *It's warm enough to eat outside.*

outside² ⚡ **A2** /ˌaʊtˈsaɪd/ *prep.* **1** on or to a place on the outside of sth: *Leave your muddy boots outside the door.* **2** (also **outˈside of** *especially in AmE*) not in; away from: *You may do as you wish outside office hours.* ◇ *a small village just outside Stratford*

outside³ ⚡ **A2** /ˈaʊtsaɪd/ *adj.* [only before noun] **1** of or on the outer side or surface of a building **SYN** **external 2** not part of the main building: *an outside toilet* **3** not connected with or belonging to a particular group or organization: *We can't do all the work by ourselves. We'll need outside help.* **4** (used about a chance or possibility) very small: *He has an outside chance of winning.* **IDM** **the outside world** people, places, activities, etc. that are away from the area where you live and your own experience of life

outside⁴ ⚡ **A2** /ˌaʊtˈsaɪd/ *noun* **1** [C, usually sing.] the outer side or surface of sth: *There is a list of all the ingredients on the outside of the packet.* **2** [sing.] the area that is near or round a building, etc: *We've only seen the church from the outside.* **3** [sing.] the part of a road, a track, etc. that is away from the side that you usually drive on, run on, etc: *The other runners all overtook him on the outside.* **OPP** **inside²** **IDM** **at the outside** at the most: *It will take us three days at the outside.*

outsider ⚡+ **C1** /ˌaʊtˈsaɪdə(r)/ *noun* [C] **1** a person who is not accepted as a member of a particular group ⊃ look at **insider 2** (**SPORT**) a person or an animal in a race or competition that is not expected to win **OPP** **favourite²**

outsize /ˈaʊtsaɪz/ *adj.* (often used about clothes) larger than usual

outskirts /ˈaʊtskɜːts/ *noun* [pl.] (**GEOGRAPHY**) the parts of a town or city that are furthest from the centre: *They live on the outskirts of Athens.*

outsource /ˈaʊtsɔːs/ *verb* [T, I] (**BUSINESS**) to arrange for sb outside a company to do work or provide goods for that company: *We outsource all our computing work.* ▸ **outsourcing** *noun* [U]

outspoken /aʊtˈspəʊkən/ *adj.* ~ (in sth) saying exactly what you think or feel although you may shock or upset other people: *Linda is very outspoken in her criticism.*

outstanding ⚡+ **B2** /aʊtˈstændɪŋ/ *adj.* **1** extremely good; excellent: *The results in the exams were outstanding.* ◇ *an area of outstanding natural beauty* **2** not yet paid, done or dealt with: *outstanding debts/issues* ◇ *Some of the work is still outstanding.*

outstandingly /aʊtˈstændɪŋli/ *adv.* extremely; very well: *outstandingly good*

outstretched /ˌaʊtˈstretʃt/ *adj.* reaching as far as possible: *He came towards her with his arms outstretched.*

ˈout tray (*BrE*) (*AmE* **out box**) *noun* [C] (in an office) a container on your desk for letters or documents that are waiting to be sent out or passed to sb else ⊃ look at **in tray**

outward /'aʊtwəd/ adj. [only before noun] **1** connected with the way things seem to be rather than what is actually true: *Despite her cheerful outward appearance, she was in fact very unhappy.* **OPP inward 2 (TOURISM)** (used about a journey) going away from the place that you will return to later **OPP return²** **3** away from the centre or from a particular point: *outward movement/pressure* **OPP inward** ▶ **outwardly** adv.: *He remained outwardly calm so as not to frighten the children.*

outwards /'aʊtwədz/ (BrE) (also **outward** AmE, BrE) adv. towards the outside; away from the place where you are: *This door opens outwards.*

outweigh /ˌaʊt'weɪ/ verb [T] to be more in amount or importance than sth: *The advantages outweigh the disadvantages.*

outwit /ˌaʊt'wɪt/ verb [T] (-tt-) to gain an advantage over sb by doing sth clever

oval /'əʊvl/ adj. shaped like an egg ▶ **oval** noun [C]

oval 'window noun [C] (**ANATOMY**) the first of two openings covered by a MEMBRANE (= a thin layer of skin) between the MIDDLE EAR and the INNER EAR ⊃ look at **round window** ⊃ picture at **ear**

ovary /'əʊvəri/ noun [C] (pl. -ies) **1** (**ANATOMY**) one of the two parts of the female body that produce eggs ⊃ picture at **fertilization 2** (**BIOLOGY**) the part of a plant that produces seeds ⊃ picture at **flower¹**

ovation /əʊ'veɪʃn/ noun [C] an enthusiastic reaction given by an audience when it likes sb/sth very much. The people in the audience CLAP (= make a noise with their hands) and CHEER (= shout) and often stand up: *The dancers got a standing ovation at the end of the performance.*

oven 🔊 **A2** /'ʌvn/ noun [C] the part of a cooker that has a door. You put food inside an oven to cook or heat it: *Cook in a hot oven for 50 minutes.* ◇ *a microwave oven* ⊃ note at **cook¹**

over¹ 🔊 **A1** /'əʊvə(r)/ adv., prep. **1** straight above sth, but not touching it: *There's a painting over the bookcase.* ◇ *We watched the plane fly over.* ⊃ look at **above¹** (1) **2** covering sth: *He was holding a towel over the cut.* ◇ *She hung her coat over the back of the chair.* **3** across to the other side of sth: *The horse jumped over the fence.* ◇ *a bridge over the river* **4** on or to the other side: *The student turned the paper over and read the first question.* **5** falling or bending down or towards the side: *He leaned over to speak to the woman next to him.* ◇ *I fell over in the street this morning.* **6** above or more than a number, price, etc: *She lived in Athens for over ten years.* ◇ *suitable for children aged 10 and over* **7** used for expressing distance: *He's over in America at the moment.* ◇ *Sit down over there.* ◇ *Come over here, please.* **8** not used: *There are a lot of cakes left over from the party.* **9** all 'over everywhere: *There was blood all over the place.* ◇ *I can't find my glasses. I've looked all over for them.* **10** used for saying that sth is repeated: *You'll have to start all over again* (= from the beginning). ◇ *She kept saying the same thing over and over again.* **11** about; on the subject of: *We quarrelled over money.* **12** during: *We met several times over the Christmas holiday.*

over² /'əʊvə(r)/ adj. finished: *The exams are all over now.*

over- /əʊvə(r)/ prefix (in nouns, verbs, adjectives and adverbs) **1** more than usual; too much: *to oversleep/ overeat* ◇ *overcrowded* **2** completely: *overjoyed* **3** upper; outer; extra: *overcoat* ◇ *overtime* **4** over; above: *overcast* ◇ *overhang*

overall¹ 🔊 **B2** 🔊 /ˌəʊvər'ɔːl/ adv., adj. **1** including everything; total: *What will the overall cost of the work be?* **2** generally; when you consider everything: *Overall, I can say that we are pleased with the year's work.*

overall² /'əʊvərɔːl/ noun **1** [C] a piece of clothing like a coat that you wear over your clothes to keep them clean when you are working **2 overalls** (AmE **coveralls**) [pl.] a piece of clothing that covers the arms, legs and body that you wear over your clothes to keep them clean when you are working **3 overalls** [pl.] (AmE) = DUNGAREES

overall ma'jority noun [C, usually sing.] more than half of the total number of votes in an election **SYN absolute majority**

overawe /ˌəʊvər'ɔː/ verb [T, usually passive] to impress sb so much that they feel nervous or frightened

overbalance /ˌəʊvə'bæləns/ verb [I] to lose your balance and fall

overbearing /ˌəʊvə'beərɪŋ/ adj. trying to control other people in an unpleasant way **SYN domineering**

overblown /ˌəʊvə'bləʊn/ adj. that is made to seem larger, more impressive or more important than it really is

overboard /'əʊvəbɔːd/ adv. over the side of a boat or ship into the water **IDM go overboard (on/about/for sb/sth)** (informal) to be too excited or enthusiastic about sb/sth

overbook /ˌəʊvə'bʊk/ verb [T, I] (**TOURISM**) to sell more tickets on a plane or reserve more rooms in a hotel than there are places available: *Most scheduled airlines overbook flights.*

overcame /ˌəʊvə'keɪm/ past tense of **overcome**

overcast /ˌəʊvə'kɑːst/ adj. (used about the sky) covered with cloud

overcharge /ˌəʊvə'tʃɑːdʒ/ verb [T, I] to ask sb to pay too much money for sth: *The taxi driver overcharged me.* ⊃ look at **charge²** (1)

overcoat /'əʊvəkəʊt/ noun [C] a long thick coat that you wear in cold weather

overcome 🔊+ **B2** /ˌəʊvə'kʌm/ verb [T] (pt **overcame** /-'keɪm/; pp **overcome**) **1** to manage to control or defeat sb/sth: *She tried hard to overcome her fear of flying.* **2** [usually passive] **be ~ with sth** to be extremely strongly affected by sth: *He was overcome with emotion.*

overcook /ˌəʊvə'kʊk/ verb [T] to cook food for too long **OPP undercook**

overcrowded /ˌəʊvə'kraʊdɪd/ adj. (used about a place) with too many people inside

overdo /ˌəʊvə'duː/ verb [T] (pt **overdid** /-'dɪd/; pp **overdone** /-'dʌn/) **1** to use or do too much of sth **2** to cook sth for too long: *The meat was overdone.* **IDM overdo it/things** to work too hard: *Exercise is fine but don't overdo it.*

overdose /'əʊvədəʊs/ noun [C] (**HEALTH**) an amount of a drug or medicine that is too large and so is not safe: *to take an overdose* ⊃ look at **dose¹** (1)

overdraft /'əʊvədrɑːft/ noun [C] (**FINANCE**) an amount of money that you have spent that is greater than the amount you have in your bank account; an arrangement with your bank that allows you to spend more money than you have

overdrawn /ˌəʊvə'drɔːn/ adj. (**FINANCE**) having spent more money than you have in your bank account: *I checked my balance and discovered I was overdrawn.*

overdue /ˌəʊvə'dju:/ adj. late in arriving, happening, being paid, returned, etc: an overdue library book ◇ Her baby is a week overdue.

overeat /ˌəʊvər'i:t/ verb [I] to eat more than is necessary or healthy

overestimate /ˌəʊvər'estɪmeɪt/ verb [T] to guess that sb/ sth is bigger, better, more important, etc. than they really are: I overestimated how much we could paint in a day. **OPP underestimate** ▸ overestimate /-mət/ noun [C]

overfishing /ˌəʊvə'fɪʃɪŋ/ noun [U] (**ENVIRONMENT**) the process of taking so many fish from the sea, a river, etc. that the number of fish in it becomes very low

overflow /ˌəʊvə'fləʊ/ verb **1** [I, T] ~ **(with sth)** to be so full that there is no more space: His bag was overflowing with clothes. **2** [I, T] to be so full that the contents go over the sides: The tap was left on and the bath overflowed. **3** [I] ~ **(into sth)** to be forced out of a place or a container that is too full: The crowd overflowed into the street.

overgeneralize (BrE also -ise) /ˌəʊvə'dʒenrəlaɪz/ verb [I] to make a statement that is not accurate because it is too general ▸ overgeneralization (BrE also -isation) /ˌəʊvədʒenrəlaɪ'zeɪʃn/ noun [C, U]

overgrazing /ˌəʊvə'ɡreɪzɪŋ/ noun [U] (**AGRICULTURE**, **ENVIRONMENT**) the practice of allowing animals such as cows to eat the plants on an area of land for too long so that the plants disappear completely

overgrown /ˌəʊvə'ɡrəʊn/ adj. covered with plants that have grown too big and untidy

overhang /ˌəʊvə'hæŋ/ verb [T, I] (pt, pp overhung /-'hʌŋ/) to stick out, over and above sth else: The overhanging trees kept the sun off us.

overhaul /ˌəʊvə'hɔ:l/ verb [T] to look at sth carefully and change or repair it if necessary: to overhaul an engine ▸ overhaul /'əʊvəhɔ:l/ noun [C]

overhead /ˌəʊvə'hed/ adv. adj. above your head: A helicopter flew overhead. ◇ overhead electricity cables

overheads /'əʊvəhedz/ noun [pl.] (**BUSINESS**) money that a company must spend on things like heat, light, rent, etc.

overhear /ˌəʊvə'hɪə(r)/ verb [T] (pt, pp overheard /-'hɜ:d/) to hear what sb is saying by accident, when they are speaking to sb else and not to you

overhung /ˌəʊvə'hʌŋ/ past tense, past participle of **overhang**

overjoyed /ˌəʊvə'dʒɔɪd/ adj. [not before noun] ~ **(at sth)**; ~ **(to do sth)** very happy: They were overjoyed at her success. ◇ We were overjoyed to hear the news.

overland /'əʊvəlænd/ adj., adv. not by sea or by air: an overland journey ◇ We travelled overland to India.

overlap ⓦ /ˌəʊvə'læp/ verb (-pp-) **1** [T, I] when two things **overlap**, part of one covers part of the other: Make sure that the two pieces of material overlap. **2** [I, T] to be partly the same as sth: Our jobs overlap to some extent. ▸ overlap ⓦ /'əʊvəlæp/ noun [C, U]

overlapping tiles

overleaf /ˌəʊvə'li:f/ adv. on the other side of the page: Full details are given overleaf.

overload /ˌəʊvə'ləʊd/ verb [T] **1** [often passive] to put too many people or things into or onto sth: an overloaded vehicle **2** ~ **sb (with sth)** to give sb too much of sth: to be overloaded with work/information **3** to put too much electricity through sth: If you use too many electrical appliances at one time you may overload the system.

overlook ʳ+ **C1** /ˌəʊvə'lʊk/ verb [T] **1** to fail to see or notice sth: to overlook a spelling mistake ◇ She felt that her opinion had been completely overlooked. **2** to see sth that is wrong or bad but decide to forget it: I will overlook your behaviour this time but don't let it happen again. **3** to have a view over sth: My room overlooks the sea.

overly ʳ+ **C1** /'əʊvəli/ adv. too; very: We think you are being overly optimistic.

overnight¹ ʳ+ **B2** /ˌəʊvə'naɪt/ adv. **1** during or for the night: We stayed overnight in Hamburg. **2** suddenly or quickly: She became a star overnight.

overnight² /ˌəʊvə'naɪt/ adj. **1** happening during the night; for a night: an overnight flight ◇ an overnight bag **2** happening suddenly or quickly: an overnight success

overpass /'əʊvəpɑ:s/ (AmE) = FLYOVER

overpay /ˌəʊvə'peɪ/ verb [T, usually passive] (pt, pp overpaid /-'peɪd/) to pay sb too much; to pay sb more than their job is worth: He is grossly overpaid for what he does. **OPP underpay**

overpopulated /ˌəʊvə'pɒpjuleɪtɪd/ adj. (used about a country or city) with too many people living in it ▸ overpopulation /ˌəʊvəˌpɒpju'leɪʃn/ noun [U]

overpower /ˌəʊvə'paʊə(r)/ verb [T] to be too strong for sb: The fireman was overpowered by the heat and smoke. ▸ overpowering adj.: an overpowering smell

overpriced /ˌəʊvə'praɪst/ adj. too expensive; costing more than it is worth

overproduce /ˌəʊvəprə'dju:s/ verb [T, I] (**BUSINESS**) to produce more of sth than is wanted or needed ▸ overproduction /-'dʌkʃn/ noun [U]

overprotective /ˌəʊvəprə'tektɪv/ adj. too anxious to protect sb from being hurt, in a way that limits their freedom: overprotective parents

overran /ˌəʊvə'ræn/ past tense of **overrun**

overrate /ˌəʊvə'reɪt/ verb [T, often passive] to think that sb/sth is better than they really are **OPP underrate**

overreact /ˌəʊvəri'ækt/ verb [I] ~ **(to sth)** to react too strongly, especially to sth unpleasant: I thought she overreacted to my comment. ▸ overreaction /-'ækʃn/ noun [sing., U]

override /ˌəʊvə'raɪd/ verb [T] (pt overrode /-'rəʊd/; pp overridden /-'rɪdn/) **1** to use your authority to reject sb's decision, order, etc: They overrode my protest and continued with the meeting. **2** to be more important than sth: Safety overrides all other design considerations. **3** to stop sth that usually works by itself in order to control it yourself: You need a password to override the safety lock.

overriding /ˌəʊvə'raɪdɪŋ/ adj. [only before noun] more important than anything else: Our overriding concern is safety.

overrule /ˌəʊvə'ru:l/ verb [T] (**LAW**) to use your authority to change what sb else has already decided or done: The Appeal Court overruled the judge's decision.

overrun /ˌəʊvə'rʌn/ verb (pt overran /-'ræn/; pp overrun) **1** [T, often passive] to spread all over an area in great numbers: The city was completely overrun by rats. **2** [I, T] to use more time or money than expected: The meeting overran by 30 minutes.

overseas¹ ʳ+ **B2** /ˌəʊvə'si:z/ adj. connected with other countries, especially those that you have to cross the sea to get to: overseas students studying in Britain

overseas² ʔ+ **B2** /ˌəʊvəˈsiːz/ adv. to or in another country, especially one that you have to cross the sea to get to: *Frank was working overseas.*

oversee ʔ+ **C1** /ˌəʊvəˈsiː/ verb [T] (pt **oversaw** /-ˈsɔː/; pp **overseen** /-ˈsiːn/) to watch sth to make sure that it is done properly

overshadow /ˌəʊvəˈʃædəʊ/ verb [T, often passive] **1** to cause sb/sth to seem less important or successful: *Connor always seemed to be overshadowed by his sister.* **2** to make an event less pleasant than it should be

oversight /ˈəʊvəsaɪt/ noun [C, U] something that you do not notice or do that you should have noticed or done

oversimplify /ˌəʊvəˈsɪmplɪfaɪ/ verb [T, I] (**oversimplifying**; **oversimplifies**; pt, pp **oversimplified**) to explain sth in such a simple way that its real meaning is lost

oversleep /ˌəʊvəˈsliːp/ verb [I] (pt, pp **overslept** /-ˈslept/) to sleep longer than you should have done: *He overslept and was late for school.* ⊃ look at **lie in** at **lie¹**, **sleep in** at **sleep²**

overstate /ˌəʊvəˈsteɪt/ verb [T] to say sth in a way that makes it seem more important than it really is **OPP** **understate** ▸ **overstatement** /ˈəʊvəsteɪtmənt/ noun [C, U]: *It is not an overstatement to say a crisis is imminent.*

overstep /ˌəʊvəˈstep/ verb [T] (-pp-) to go further than what is normal or allowed **IDM** **overstep the mark/line** to behave in a way that people think is not acceptable

overt /əʊˈvɜːt, ˈəʊvɜːt/ adj. (formal) done in an open way and not secretly **OPP** **covert** ▸ **overtly** adv.

overtake /ˌəʊvəˈteɪk/ verb [T, I] (pt **overtook** /-ˈtʊk/; pp **overtaken** /-ˈteɪkən/) **1** to go past another person, car, etc. because you are moving faster: *The lorry overtook me on the bend.* **2** to become greater in number, amount or importance than sth else

overthrow /ˌəʊvəˈθrəʊ/ verb [T] (pt **overthrew** /-ˈθruː/; pp **overthrown** /-ˈθrəʊn/) (POLITICS) to remove a leader or government from power, by using force ▸ **overthrow** /ˈəʊvəθrəʊ/ noun [sing.]

overtime /ˈəʊvətaɪm/ noun [U] (BUSINESS) time that you spend at work after your usual working hours; the money that you are paid for this: *She did ten hours' overtime last week.* ▸ **overtime** adv.: *I have been working overtime for weeks.*

overtone /ˈəʊvətəʊn/ noun [C, usually pl.] something that is suggested but not expressed in an obvious way: *People claimed there were political overtones in the advertisement.*

overtook /ˌəʊvəˈtʊk/ past tense of **overtake**

overture /ˈəʊvətʃʊə(r)/ noun **1** [C] (MUSIC) a piece of music that is the introduction to a musical play (such as an OPERA or a BALLET) **2** [C, usually pl.] (formal) an act of being friendly towards sb, especially because you want to be friends, to start a business relationship, etc.

overturn ʔ+ **C1** /ˌəʊvəˈtɜːn/ verb **1** [I, T] to turn over so that the top is at the bottom: *The car overturned but the driver escaped unhurt.* **2** [T] to officially decide that a decision is wrong and change it

overview W /ˈəʊvəvjuː/ noun [C] a general description that gives the most important facts about sth

overweight /ˌəʊvəˈweɪt/ adj. too heavy or fat: *I'm a bit overweight — I think I might go on a diet.* **OPP** **underweight**

overwhelm ʔ+ **C1** /ˌəʊvəˈwelm/ verb [T, usually passive] **1** to cause sb to feel such a strong emotion that they do not know how to react: *The new world champion was overwhelmed by all the publicity.* **2** to be so powerful, big, etc., that sb cannot deal with it: *The TV company was overwhelmed by complaints.* ◇ *He overwhelmed his opponent with his superb technique.*

overwhelming ʔ+ **C1** /ˌəʊvəˈwelmɪŋ/ adj. extremely great or strong: *Anna had an overwhelming desire to return home.* ▸ **overwhelmingly** adv.

overwork /ˌəʊvəˈwɜːk/ verb [T, I] to make sb work too hard: *The staff are overworked and underpaid.* ▸ **overwork** noun [U]

overwrought /ˌəʊvəˈrɔːt/ adj. very worried and upset; excited in a nervous way **SYN** **distraught**

oviparous /əʊˈvɪpərəs/ adj. (BIOLOGY) (used about animals) producing eggs rather than live babies ⊃ look at **viviparous**

ovulate /ˈɒvjuleɪt/ verb [I] (BIOLOGY) (used about a woman or female animal) to produce an egg from the OVARY ▸ **ovulation** /ˌɒvjuˈleɪʃn/ noun [U] ⊃ picture at **fertilization**

ovule /ˈɒvjuːl, ˈəʊv-/ noun [C] (BIOLOGY) (in plants that produce seeds) the part of the OVARY that contains the female cell that becomes the seed ⊃ picture at **flower¹**

ovum /ˈəʊvəm/ noun [C] (pl. **ova** /-və/) (BIOLOGY) an egg produced by a woman or female animal ⊃ picture at **fertilization**

ow /aʊ/ exclamation used when reacting to a sudden feeling of pain

owe ʔ **B2** /əʊ/ verb [T] **1** ~ sth (to sb); ~ sb for sth to have to pay money to sb for sth that they have done or given: *I owe a lot of money to Katrina.* ◇ *I owe Katrina a lot of money.* ◇ *I still owe you for that bread you bought yesterday.* ⊃ look at **debt 2** to feel that you should do sth for sb or give sth to sb, especially because they have done sth for you: *Claudia owes me an explanation.* ◇ *I owe you an apology.* **3** ~ sth to sb/sth to have sth for the reason given: *She said she owes her success to hard work and determination.*

owing /ˈəʊɪŋ/ adj. [not before noun] ~ (to sb) not yet paid: *How much is still owing to you?*

owing to prep. because of: *The match was cancelled owing to bad weather.*

owl /aʊl/ noun [C] a BIRD OF PREY (= a bird that kills other creatures for food) with large eyes that hunts at night ⊃ picture at **animal**, **food web**

own¹ **A1** /əʊn/ adj., pron. **1** used to emphasize that sth belongs to a particular person: *I saw him do it with my own eyes.* ◇ *This is his own house.* ◇ *This house is his own.* ◇ *Rachel would like her own room/a room of her own.* **2** used to show that sth is done or made without help from another person: *The children are old enough to get their own breakfast.* **IDM** **come into your own** to have the opportunity to show your special qualities **hold your own (against sb/sth)** to be as strong, good, etc. as sb/sth else **(all) on your own 1** alone: *John lives all on his own.* **2** without help: *I managed to repair the car all on my own.* **get/have your own back (on sb)** (informal) to hurt sb who has hurt you

own² **A2** /əʊn/ verb [T] to have sth belonging to you: *We don't own the house. We just rent it.* ◇ *a privately owned company* **PHRV** **own up (to sth)** to tell sb that you have done sth wrong: *None of the children owned up to breaking the window.*

owner ʔ **A2** /ˈəʊnə(r)/ noun [C] a person who owns sth: *a house/dog owner*

ownership ʔ+ **B2** /ˈəʊnəʃɪp/ noun [U] the state of owning sth: *in private/public ownership*

ox /ɒks/ noun [C] (pl. oxen /ˈɒksn/) a BULL (= an adult male cow) that has been CASTRATED (= had part of its sex organs removed) and is used for pulling or carrying heavy loads ⊃ look at bull (1) ⊃ note at cow

oxbow /ˈɒksbəʊ/ noun [C] (GEOGRAPHY) 1 a bend in a river that almost forms a full circle 2 = OXBOW LAKE

formation of an oxbow lake

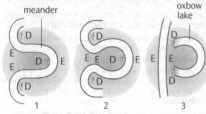

1 Erosion (E) and deposition (D) occur around a meander.

2 Increased erosion during flood conditions makes the meander become exaggerated, forming an oxbow.

3 The river breaks through during a flood. Further deposition causes the old meander to become an oxbow lake.

oxbow 'lake (also oxbow) noun [C] (GEOGRAPHY) a lake that forms when a bend in a river is separated from the river

oxide /ˈɒksaɪd/ noun [U, C] (CHEMISTRY) a combination of OXYGEN and another chemical element: iron oxide

oxidize (BrE also -ise) /ˈɒksɪdaɪz/ verb [T, I] (CHEMISTRY) to remove one or more ELECTRONS from a substance, or to combine or make sth combine with OXYGEN, especially when this causes metal to become covered with RUST ⊃ look at reduce (2) ⊃ picture at safety ▸ oxidation /ˌɒksɪˈdeɪʃn/ noun [U] ⊃ look at reduction (3)

oxygen ʔ+ B2 /ˈɒksɪdʒən/ noun [U] (symb. O) (CHEMISTRY) a chemical element. Oxygen is a gas that is present in air and water and is necessary for people, animals and plants to live. ⊃ picture at photosynthesis ❶ For more information on the periodic table of elements, look at the Reference Section of this dictionary.

oxygenate /ˈɒksɪdʒəneɪt/ verb [T] (BIOLOGY) to add OXYGEN to sth: oxygenated blood

oxymoron /ˌɒksɪˈmɔːrɒn/ noun [C] (LANGUAGE, LITERATURE) a phrase that combines two words that seem to be the opposite of each other, such as a deafening silence

oyster /ˈɔɪstə(r)/ noun [C] a type of SHELLFISH (= a creature with a shell that lives in water). Some types of oysters can be eaten and others produce PEARLS (= small hard shiny white balls that are used to make jewellery).

oz abbr. (in writing) (pl. oz) = OUNCE (1): Add 4oz flour.

ozone /ˈəʊzəʊn/ noun [U] (CHEMISTRY) a poisonous gas that is a form of OXYGEN

ozone-'friendly adj. (ENVIRONMENT) (used about cleaning products, etc.) not containing chemicals that could harm THE OZONE LAYER

the 'ozone layer noun [sing.] (ENVIRONMENT) the layer of OZONE high up in the atmosphere that helps to protect the earth from the harmful effects of the sun: a hole in the ozone layer ⊃ look at CFC ⊃ picture at atmosphere

P p

P /piː/ (also p) noun [C, U] (pl. P's, p's) the 16th letter of the English alphabet: 'Pencil' begins with (a) 'P'.

p abbr. 1 (in writing) (pl. pp.) page: See p94. ◇ pp. 63-96 2 /piː/ (pl. p) (BrE, informal) = PENNY (1): an 87p stamp

PA /ˌpiː ˈeɪ/ noun [C] (especially BrE) (BUSINESS) = PERSONAL ASSISTANT: She's the Managing Director's PA.

Pa abbr. (in writing) (pl. Pa) = PASCAL (1)

p.a. abbr. (in writing) = PER ANNUM: salary: £25 000 p.a.

PAC /pæk/ abbr. = POLITICAL ACTION COMMITTEE

pace¹ ʔ B2 /peɪs/ noun 1 [sing., U] ~ (of sth) the speed at which you walk, run, etc. or at which sth happens: to run at a steady/gentle pace ◇ Students are encouraged to work at their own pace (= as fast or as slowly as they like). ◇ The traffic was moving at walking pace. 2 [C] the distance that you move when you take one step: Take two paces forward and then stop. SYN step¹ IDM keep pace (with sb/sth) to move or do sth at the same speed as sb/sth else; to change as quickly as sth else is changing: Wages are not keeping pace with inflation. set the pace to move or do sth at the speed that others must follow: The gold medallist set the pace for the first three miles.

pace² ʔ B2 /peɪs/ verb [I, T] (used with an adverb or a preposition) to walk up and down in the same area many times, especially because you are nervous or angry

pacemaker /ˈpeɪsmeɪkə(r)/ noun [C] 1 (MEDICINE) a machine that helps to make sb's heart beat regularly or more strongly 2 (SPORT) a person in a race who sets the speed that the others try to follow

pachyderm /ˈpækɪdɜːm/ noun [C] (BIOLOGY) a type of animal with a very thick skin, for example an elephant

pacifier /ˈpæsɪfaɪə(r)/ (AmE) = DUMMY (3)

pacifism /ˈpæsɪfɪzəm/ noun [U] (POLITICS) the belief that all wars are wrong and that you should not fight in them ▸ pacifist /-fɪst/ noun [C]

pacify /ˈpæsɪfaɪ/ verb [T] (pacifying; pacifies; pt, pp pacified) to make sb who is angry or upset be calm or quiet

pack¹ A2 /pæk/ verb 1 [I, T] (TOURISM) to put your things into a bag, etc. before you go away or go on holiday: I'll have to pack in the morning. ◇ Have you packed your toothbrush? OPP unpack 2 [T, I] to put things into containers so they can be stored, transported or sold: I packed all my books into boxes. ◇ Have you finished packing for the move? OPP unpack 3 [T, I, often passive] be packed (with sb/sth) (informal) to be filled with people or things until crowded or full: The train was absolutely packed. ◇ The book is packed with useful information. ◇ People packed the pavements, waiting for the president to arrive. PHR V pack sth in (informal) to stop doing sth: I've packed in my job. ◇ I've had enough of you boys arguing — just pack it in! pack sth in/into sth to do a lot in a short time: They packed a lot into their three days in Rome. pack sth out [usually passive] to fill sth with people: The restaurants are packed out every night. pack up (informal) 1 to finish working or doing sth: There was nothing else to do so we packed up and went home. 2 (used about a machine, an engine, etc.) to stop working: My old car packed up last week so now I cycle to work.

pack² 🔊 B1 /pæk/ *noun*
- CONTAINER **1** [C] (*especially AmE*) a container, usually made of paper, that holds a number of the same thing or an amount of something: *These batteries are sold in packs of four.* ○ look at **package** (2), **packet** (1)
- SET OF THINGS **2** [C] a set of things that are supplied together for a particular purpose: *an information pack* ◇ (*figurative*) *Everything she told me was **a pack of lies**.*
- LARGE BAG **3** [C] a large bag that you carry on your back ○ look at **rucksack**
- OF ANIMALS **4** [C + sing./pl. verb] a group of wild animals that hunt together: *a pack of dogs/wolves*
- OF PEOPLE **5** [C + sing./pl. verb] a large group of similar people or things, especially one that you do not like or approve of: *a pack of journalists*
- OF PLAYING CARDS **6** (*especially BrE*) (*also* **deck** *especially in AmE*) [C] a complete set of PLAYING CARDS

package 🔊 B1 /'pækɪdʒ/ *noun* [C] **1** = PARCEL **2** (*AmE*) a box, bag, etc. in which things are wrapped or packed; the contents of a box, etc: *a package of hamburger buns* ○ look at **pack²** (1), **packet** (1) **3** a number of things that must be bought or accepted together: *a word-processing package* ◇ *a financial aid package* ▶ **package** 🔊 B2 *verb* [T]: *Goods that are attractively packaged sell more quickly.*

'package holiday (*BrE*) (*also* **'package tour** *especially in AmE*) *noun* [C] (**TOURISM**) a holiday that is organized by a company for a fixed price that includes the cost of travel, hotels, etc.

packaging /'pækɪdʒɪŋ/ *noun* [U] all the materials (boxes, bags, paper, etc.) that are used to cover or protect goods before they are sold

packed /pækt/ *adj.* **1** extremely full of people **SYN crowded 2** ~ (**with sth**) containing a lot of a particular thing: *a book packed with information*

packed 'lunch *noun* [C] food that you prepare at home and take with you to eat at work or school

packer /'pækə(r)/ *noun* [C] a person, company or machine that puts products, especially food, into boxes, plastic, paper, etc. to be sold

packet 🔊 B2 /'pækɪt/ *noun* **1** [C] (*BrE*) a small box, bag, etc. in which things are packed to be sold in a shop: *a packet of sweets/biscuits/crisps* ◇ *a cigarette packet* ○ look at **pack²** (1), **package** (2) **2** [sing.] (*BrE, informal*) a large amount of money: *That new kitchen must have cost them a packet.* **3** [C] (**COMPUTING**) an amount of data that is sent through a computer network

packing /'pækɪŋ/ *noun* [U] **1** (**TOURISM**) the act of putting your clothes, possessions, etc. into boxes or cases in order to take or send them somewhere: *We're going on holiday tomorrow so I'll **do my packing** tonight.* **2** soft material that you use to stop things from being damaged or broken when you are sending them somewhere

'packing case *noun* [C] a wooden box that you put things in before they are sent somewhere or stored

pact /pækt/ *noun* [C] a formal agreement between two or more people, groups or countries

pad¹ 🔊 B2 /pæd/ *noun* [C] **1** a thick piece of soft material, used for cleaning or protecting sth or to make sth a different shape: *Remove eye make-up with cleanser and a cotton wool pad.* ◇ *a jacket with shoulder pads* ◇ *knee/shin pads* **2** a number of pieces of paper that are fastened together at one end: *a notepad* **3** the place where a SPACECRAFT takes off: *a launch pad* **4** the soft part on the bottom of the feet of some animals, for example dogs and cats

pad² /pæd/ *verb* (-dd-) **1** [T, usually passive] ~ **sth (with sth)** to fill or cover sth with soft material in order to protect it, make it larger or more comfortable, etc: *All the sharp corners were padded with foam.* **2** [I]

(used with an adverb or a preposition) to walk quietly, especially because you are not wearing shoes: *He got up and padded into the bathroom.*
PHR V pad sth out to make a book, speech, etc. longer by adding things that are not necessary

padding /'pædɪŋ/ *noun* [U] soft material that is put inside sth to protect it or to make it larger, more comfortable, etc.

paddle¹ /'pædl/ *noun* [C] a short POLE that is flat and wide at one or both ends and that you use for moving a small boat through water ○ look at **oar** ○ picture at **canoe**

paddle² /'pædl/ *verb* **1** [I, T] to move a small boat through water using a short POLE that is flat and wide at one or both ends: *We paddled down the river.* ○ look at **row¹ 2** [I] to walk in water that is not very deep: *We paddled in the stream.*

paddleboarding /'pædlbɔːdɪŋ/ *noun* [U] (**SPORT**) the sport of moving on the water while lying, sitting or standing on a board, using your arms or a PADDLE to move yourself along ▶ **paddleboard** /-bɔːd/ *noun* [C]

'paddle steamer (*BrE*) (*AmE, BrE* **'paddle boat**) *noun* [C] an old-fashioned type of boat driven by STEAM and moved forward by a large wheel or wheels at the side

paddock /'pædək/ *noun* [C] a small field where horses are kept

paddy /'pædi/ (*pl.* -**ies**) (*also* **'paddy field**) *noun* [C] (**AGRICULTURE**) a field in which rice is grown

padlock /'pædlɒk/ *noun* [C] a type of lock that you can use for fastening gates, bicycles, etc. ▶ **padlock** *verb* [T] ~ **sth (to sth)**: *I padlocked my bike to a post.*

paed- (*AmE* **ped-**) /piːd, ped/ *prefix* (in nouns and adjectives) connected with children: *paediatrics*

paediatrician (*BrE*) (*AmE* **pediatrician**) /ˌpiːdiə'trɪʃn/ *noun* [C] (**MEDICINE**) a doctor who deals with the diseases of children

paediatrics (*BrE*) (*AmE* **pediatrics**) /ˌpiːdi'ætrɪks/ *noun* [U] (**MEDICINE**) the area of medicine connected with the diseases of children ▶ **paediatric** (*AmE* **pediatric**) *adj.*

paedophile (*BrE*) (*AmE* **pedophile**) /'piːdəfaɪl/ *noun* [C] a person who is sexually attracted to children

paedophilia (*BrE*) (*AmE* **pedophilia**) /ˌpiːdə'fɪliə/ *noun* [U] the condition of being sexually attracted to children; sexual activity with children

paella /paɪ'elə/ *noun* [U, C] a Spanish dish made with rice, meat, fish and vegetables

pagan /'peɪɡən/ *adj.* (**RELIGION**) having religious beliefs that do not belong to any of the main religions ▶ **pagan** *noun* [C]

page 🔊 A1 /peɪdʒ/ *noun* [C] **1** (*abbr.* **p**) one or both sides of a piece of paper in a book, magazine, etc: *The letter was three pages long.* ◇ *Turn over the page.* ◇ *Turn to page 12 of your book.* ◇ *the front page of a newspaper* **2** (**COMPUTING**) a section of data or information that can be shown on a computer screen at any one time ○ look at **home page**

pageant /'pædʒənt/ *noun* [C] **1** (**HISTORY**) a type of public entertainment at which people dress in clothes from past times and give outdoor performances of scenes from history **2** (*AmE*) a competition for young women in which their beauty, personal qualities and skills are judged ○ look at **beauty contest**

pageantry /'pædʒəntri/ *noun* [U] impressive public events or ceremonies with many people wearing special clothes: *Millions enjoyed the pageantry of the Olympic opening ceremony.*

'page-turner *noun* [C] (*informal*) (**LITERATURE**) a book that is very exciting

pagoda /pə'ɡəʊdə/ *noun* [C] (**RELIGION**) a religious building in South or East Asia in the form of a tall tower with several levels, each with a roof

pagoda

paid¹ /peɪd/ past tense, past participle of **pay¹**

paid² /peɪd/ *adj.* **1** for which people receive money: *Neither of them is currently in paid employment.* ◇ *a well-paid job* **2** receiving money for doing work: *Men still outnumber women in the paid workforce.* **OPP** **unpaid**

paid-'up *adj.* [only before noun] having paid all the money that you owe, for example to become a member of a club: *He's a fully paid-up member of Friends of the Earth.*

pail /peɪl/ (*AmE, old-fashioned*) = BUCKET (1)

pain¹ 🔊 **A2** /peɪn/ *noun* **1** [U, C] the unpleasant feeling that you have when a part of your body has been hurt or when you are ill: *to be in pain* ◇ *He screamed with pain.* ◇ *chest pains* ⊃ note at **doctor¹** **2** [U] sad feelings that you have because sth bad has happened: *the pain of losing a parent*
IDM **a pain (in the neck)** (*informal*) a person, thing or situation that makes you angry or annoyed

pain² /peɪn/ *verb* [T] (*formal*) to make sb feel sad or upset: *It pains me that she won't visit us.* **SYN** **hurt¹**

pained /peɪnd/ *adj.* showing that you are sad or upset: *a pained expression*

painful 🔊 **B1** /'peɪnfl/ *adj.* ~ **(for sb) (to do sth)** **1** that causes pain: *It was painful for him to move his arm.* ⊃ note at **hospital** **2** making you feel upset or embarrassed: *The memories were too painful for her to bear.* ▶ **painfully** /-fəli/ *adv.*

painkiller /'peɪnkɪlə(r)/ *noun* [C] (**MEDICINE**) a drug that is used for reducing pain

painless /'peɪnləs/ *adj.* that does not cause pain: *The animals' death is quick and painless.* ▶ **painlessly** *adv.*

pains /peɪnz/ *noun*
IDM **be at/take pains to do sth** | **take pains (with/over sth)** to make a special effort to do sth well: *He was at pains to hide his true feelings.*

painstaking /'peɪnzteɪkɪŋ/ *adj.* very careful and taking a long time: *The painstaking search of the wreckage gave us clues as to the cause of the crash.* **SYN** **thorough** ▶ **painstakingly** *adv.*

paint¹ 🔊 **A1** /peɪnt/ *noun* **1** [U] coloured liquid that you put onto a surface to decorate or protect it: *green/orange/yellow paint* ◇ *The door will need another coat of paint.* **2** [U] (**ART**) coloured liquid that you can use to make a picture: *oil paint* ◇ *watercolour paint* **3** **paints** [pl.] (**ART**) a collection of tubes or blocks of paint that an artist uses for painting pictures

paint² 🔊 **A1** /peɪnt/ *verb* **1** [T] to put paint onto a surface or an object: *We painted the fence.* ◇ *The walls were painted pink.* **2** [T, I] (**ART**) to make a picture of sb/sth using paints: *We painted some animals on the wall.*

paintbox /'peɪntbɒks/ *noun* [C] (**ART**) a box that contains blocks or tubes of paint of many colours

paintbrush /'peɪntbrʌʃ/ *noun* [C] (**ART**) a brush that you use for painting with

painter 🔊 **A2** /'peɪntə(r)/ *noun* [C] **1** a person whose job is to paint buildings, walls, etc. **2** (**ART**) a person who paints pictures ⊃ note at **art**

painterly /'peɪntəli/ *adj.* (**ART**) typical of artists or painting: *a painterly style of photography*

painting 🔊 **A1** /'peɪntɪŋ/ *noun* (**ART**) **1** [C] a picture that sb has painted: *a famous painting by Van Gogh* ❶ A **drawing** is similar to a **painting**, but is done using pencils, pens or crayons instead of paints. **2** [U] the act or art of painting pictures or buildings: *Her hobbies include music and painting.*

paintwork /'peɪntwɜːk/ *noun* [U] a painted surface of a door, wall, car, etc.

pair¹ 🔊 **A1** /peə(r)/ *noun* [C] **1** two things of the same type that are used or worn together: *a pair of shoes/gloves/earrings* **2** a thing that consists of two parts that are joined together: *a pair of scissors/glasses/trousers* **3** two people or animals that are doing sth together: *These boxers have fought several times, and tonight the pair meet again.*
IDM **in pairs** two at a time: *These earrings are only sold in pairs.* ◇ *The students were working in pairs.*

pair² /peə(r)/ *verb*
PHR V **pair (sb/sth) off (with sb)** to come together, especially to form a romantic relationship; to bring two people together for this purpose: *She's always trying to pair me off with her brother.* **pair up (with sb)** to join together with another person or group to work, play a game, etc: *I paired up with another student and we did the project together.*

pairing /'peərɪŋ/ *noun* **1** [C] two people or things that work together or are placed together; the act of placing them together: *Tonight they take on a Chinese pairing in their bid to reach the final tomorrow.* **2** [U] (**POLITICS**) (in the British Parliament) the practice of an MP agreeing with an MP of a different party that neither of them will vote in a debate so that they do not need to attend the debate

paisley /'peɪzli/ *noun* [U] a detailed pattern of curved shapes that look like feathers: *a paisley tie*

pajamas /pə'dʒɑːməz/ (*AmE*) = PYJAMAS

palace 🔊 **A2** /'pæləs/ *noun* [C] a large house that is or was the home of a king or queen

Palaeolithic (*especially BrE*) (*AmE usually* **Paleolithic**) /ˌpæliə'lɪθɪk, ˌpeɪl-/ *adj.* (**HISTORY**) from or connected with the early part of the Stone Age (= the very early period of human history) ⊃ look at **Neolithic**

palaeontology (*especially BrE*) (*AmE usually* **paleontology**) /ˌpælɪɒn'tɒlədʒi, ˌpeɪl-/ *noun* [U] (**GEOLOGY, HISTORY**) the scientific study of FOSSILS (= the very old parts of dead animals or plants in rocks) ▶ **palaeontologist** (*especially BrE*) (*AmE usually* **paleontologist**) /-dʒɪst/ *noun* [C]

palatable /'pælətəbl/ *adj.* **1** (used about food or drink) having a pleasant or an acceptable taste **2** ~ **(to sb)** pleasant or acceptable to sb

palatal /'pælətl/ *noun* [C] (**LANGUAGE**) a speech sound made by placing the tongue against or near the hard PALATE of the mouth, for example /j/ in *yes* ▶ **palatal** *adj.*

palate /'pælət/ *noun* [C] (**ANATOMY**) the top part of the inside of the mouth ⊃ picture at **digestive system**

pale 🔊 **B1** /peɪl/ *adj.* **1** (used about a person or their face) having skin that is light in colour, often because of fear or illness: *She has a pale complexion.* ◇ *I felt myself go/turn pale with fear.* ⊃ look at **pallid** ▶ *noun* **pallor** **2** not bright or strong in colour: *a pale yellow dress* **OPP** **dark** ▶ **pale** *verb* [I]

Paleolithic, paleontology, paleontologist (*especially AmE*) = PALAEOLITHIC, PALAEONTOLOGY, PALAEONTOLOGIST

palette /ˈpælət/ *noun* [C] (**ART**) a thin board with a hole in it for the THUMB to go through, used by an artist for mixing colours when painting

palisade /ˌpælɪˈseɪd/ *noun* [C] (**HISTORY**) (in past times) a fence made of strong wooden or metal posts that are pointed at the top, especially used to protect a building

pall /pɔːl/ *verb* [I] to become less interesting or important: *After a few months, the excitement of his new job began to pall.*

palladium /pəˈleɪdiəm/ *noun* [U] (*symb.* Pd) (**CHEMISTRY**) a chemical element. Palladium is a rare silver-white metal that looks like PLATINUM. ❶ For more information on the periodic table of elements, look at the **Reference Section** of this dictionary.

palliative /ˈpæliətɪv/ *adj.* **1** (**MEDICINE**) (used about a medicine or medical treatment) reducing pain without curing its cause: *palliative care/treatment* **2** (*formal*) (used about an action, a decision, etc.) designed to make a difficult situation seem better without actually solving the cause of the problems ▶ **palliative** *noun* [C]

pallid /ˈpælɪd/ *adj.* (used about a person or their face) light in colour, especially because of illness: *His pallid complexion made him look unhealthy.* ⊃ look at **pale** (1)

pallor /ˈpælə(r)/ *noun* [U] a pale colour of the face, especially because of illness or fear

palm¹ ℂ+ B2 /pɑːm/ *noun* [C] **1** (**ANATOMY**) the flat, inner surface of the hand: *She held the coins tightly in the palm of her hand.* ⊃ picture at **body 2** (*also* ˈpalm tree) a tall straight type of tree that grows in hot countries. Palms have a lot of large leaves at the top but no branches.

palm² /pɑːm/ *verb*
PHRV **palm sb off (with sth)** (*informal*) to persuade sb to believe sth that is not true in order to stop them asking questions or complaining **palm sth off (on sb)** (*informal*) to persuade sb to accept sth that they do not want: *She's always palming off the worst jobs on her assistant.*

ˈpalm oil *noun* [U] oil that we get from the fruit of a PALM tree that is used in cooking and in making soap, CANDLES, etc.

palpable /ˈpælpəbl/ *adj.* easily noticed by the mind or the senses: *a palpable sense of relief* ◇ *The tension in the room was almost palpable.* ◇ *His statement is palpable nonsense.*

palpate /pælˈpeɪt/ *verb* [T] (**MEDICINE**) to examine part of the body by touching it

paltry /ˈpɔːltri/ *adj.* too small to be considered important or useful: *a paltry sum of money*

pampas /ˈpæmpəs/ (*usually* the pampas) *noun* [sing.] (**GEOGRAPHY**) the large area of land in South America that has no trees and is covered in grass

pamper /ˈpæmpə(r)/ *verb* [T] to take care of sb very well and make them feel as comfortable as possible

pamphlet /ˈpæmflət/ *noun* [C] a very thin book with a paper cover containing information about a particular subject

pan¹ ℂ B1 /pæn/ *noun* [C] **1** a metal container with a handle or handles that is used for cooking food in; the contents of a pan: *Cook the spaghetti in a large pan of boiling water.* ⊃ look at **frying pan, saucepan 2** either of the dishes on a pair of scales that you put things into in order to weigh them

pan² /pæn/ *verb* (-nn-) (**ARTS AND MEDIA**) **1** [T, usually passive] (*informal*) to severely criticize sth such as a play or a film **2** [I, T] (used with an adverb or a preposition) if a television or video camera **pans** somewhere, or a person **pans**, the camera moves in a particular direction to follow an object or to film a wide area: *The camera panned back to the audience.*

pan- /pæn/ *prefix* (in nouns and adjectives) including all of sth; connected with the whole of sth: *pan-African* ◇ *a global pandemic*

pancake /ˈpænkeɪk/ *noun* [C] a type of very thin round cake that is made by frying a mixture of flour, milk and eggs

ˈPancake Day *noun* [U, C] (*informal*) a Tuesday in February when people traditionally eat PANCAKES **SYN** **Shrove Tuesday** ❶ Pancake Day is the day before the period of LENT begins.

pancreas /ˈpæŋkriəs/ *noun* [C] (**ANATOMY**) an organ near the stomach that produces INSULIN (= the substance that controls the amount of sugar in the blood) and that helps the body to DIGEST the food you eat ⊃ picture at **body, digestive system** ▶ **pancreatic** /ˌpæŋkriˈætɪk/ *adj.*

panda /ˈpændə/ *noun* [C] a large black and white animal like a bear that comes from China

pandemic /pænˈdemɪk/ *noun* [C] (**HEALTH**) a disease that spreads over a whole country or the whole world ▶ **pandemic** *adj.* ⊃ look at **endemic, epidemic**

pandemonium /ˌpændəˈməʊniəm/ *noun* [U] a state of great noise and CONFUSION **SYN** **chaos**

pander /ˈpændə(r)/ *verb*
PHRV **pander to sb/sth** to do or say exactly what sb wants, especially when this is not reasonable: *He refuses to pander to his boss's demands.*

p. and p. (*also* **p. & p.**) /ˌpiː ən ˈpiː/ *abbr.* (*BrE*) **postage and packaging** (the cost of packing something and sending it by post): *price: £29 incl. p. and p.*

pane /peɪn/ *noun* [C] a piece of glass in a window, etc: *a pane of glass*

panel ℂ B2 /ˈpænl/ *noun* [C] **1** a square or long thin piece of wood, metal or glass that forms part of a door or wall **2** [+ sing./pl. verb] (**ARTS AND MEDIA**) a group of people who give their advice or opinions about sth; a group of people who discuss topics of interest on TV or radio: *a panel of judges* (= in a competition) ◇ *a panel game* (= a television game show with teams) **3** a flat surface that contains the equipment for controlling a vehicle, machine, etc: *a control/display panel*

panelling (*BrE*) (*AmE* **paneling**) /ˈpænəlɪŋ/ *noun* [U] large flat pieces of wood used to cover and decorate walls, ceilings, etc.

panellist (*BrE*) (*AmE* **panelist**) /ˈpænəlɪst/ *noun* [C] (**ARTS AND MEDIA**) a person who is a member of a panel answering questions during a discussion

pang /pæŋ/ *noun* [C] a sudden strong feeling of emotional or physical pain: *hunger pangs* ◇ *a pang of jealousy*

panic ℂ+ B2 /ˈpænɪk/ *noun* [U, C, usually sing.] a sudden feeling of fear that cannot be controlled and stops you from thinking clearly: *People fled in panic as the fire spread.* ◇ *There was a mad panic when the alarm went off.* ▶ **panic** *verb* [I, T] (-ck-): *Stay calm and don't panic.*

panicky /ˈpænɪki/ *adj.* (*informal*) anxious about sth; feeling or showing PANIC

panic-stricken /ˈpænɪk strɪkən/ *adj.* very frightened in a way that stops you from thinking clearly

panini /pəˈniːni/ (*pl.* paninis) (*also* panino /pəˈniːnəʊ/, *pl.* panini) *noun* [C] a sandwich made with Italian bread, usually heated

panorama /ˌpænəˈrɑːmə/ noun [C] a view over a wide area of land ▸ **panoramic** /-ˈræmɪk/ adj.

pant /pænt/ verb [I, T] to breathe quickly, for example after running or because it is very hot ▸ **pant** noun [C]

panther /ˈpænθə(r)/ noun [C] a large wild animal of the cat family with black fur ⊃ picture at **lion**

panties /ˈpæntiz/ (especially AmE) = KNICKERS

pantomime /ˈpæntəmaɪm/ noun [C, U] **1** (ARTS AND MEDIA) (also informal **panto** /ˈpæntəʊ/) (BrE) a type of play for children, with music, dancing and jokes, that is usually performed at Christmas. Pantomimes are based on FAIRY TALES (= traditional children's stories). **2** (AmE) = MIME

pantry /ˈpæntri/ noun [C] (pl. -ies) a small room where food is kept **SYN** **larder**

pants **A2** /pænts/ noun [pl.] **1** (BrE) = UNDERPANTS: a pair of pants **2** (especially AmE) = TROUSERS: She wore black pants and a white T-shirt.

pantyhose /ˈpæntihəʊz/ (AmE) = TIGHTS

paparazzi /ˌpæpəˈrætsi/ noun [pl.] photographers who follow famous people around in order to get pictures of them to sell to a newspaper or magazine ⊃ note at **newspaper**

papaya /pəˈpaɪə/ (also **pawpaw**) noun [C] a large tropical fruit that is sweet and orange inside and has small black seeds

paper **A1** /ˈpeɪpə(r)/ noun
• FOR WRITING, ETC. **1** [U] a material made in thin sheets that you use for writing or drawing on, covering things, etc: a piece/sheet of paper ◇ a paper napkin
• NEWSPAPER **2** [C] = NEWSPAPER (1): the local paper
• DOCUMENTS **3** papers [pl.] important letters or pieces of paper that have information written on them: The document you want is somewhere in the pile of papers on her desk.
• EXAM **4** [C] (EDUCATION) a set of exam questions; the answers that people write to the questions: The history exam is divided into three papers.
• PIECE OF WRITING **5** [C] (EDUCATION) a piece of writing on a particular subject that is written for specialists: At the conference, the Professor presented a paper on Sri Lankan poetry.
IDM **on paper** **1** in writing: I've had nothing on paper to say that I've been accepted. **2** as an idea, but not in a real situation: The scheme seems fine on paper, but would it work in practice? **SYN** **in theory**

paperback /ˈpeɪpəbæk/ noun [C, U] (LITERATURE) a book that has a paper cover: The novel is available in paperback. ⊃ look at **hardback**

'paper boy noun [C] a boy who takes newspapers to people's houses

'paper clip noun [C] a small piece of bent wire that is used for holding pieces of paper together

'paper girl noun [C] a girl who takes newspapers to people's houses

paperless /ˈpeɪpələs/ adj. using computers, telephones, etc. rather than paper to exchange information: the paperless office

paperweight /ˈpeɪpəweɪt/ noun [C] a small heavy object that you put on top of loose papers to keep them in place

paperwork /ˈpeɪpəwɜːk/ noun [U] (BUSINESS) **1** the written work that is part of a job, such as writing letters and reports and filling in forms, etc: I hate doing paperwork. **2** documents that need to be prepared, collected, etc. in order for a piece of

business to be completed: Some of the paperwork is missing from this file.

papier mâché /ˌpæpieɪ ˈmæʃeɪ/ noun [U] (ART) paper mixed with GLUE (= a thick sticky substance) or flour and water, that is used to make attractive objects

paprika /pəˈpriːkə, ˈpæprɪkə/ noun [U] a red powder made from a sweet red pepper that you can use in cooking

papyrus /pəˈpaɪrəs/ noun (pl. papyri /-riː/) **1** [U, C] a tall plant with a thick STEM (= the main central part of the plant) that grows in water **2** [U] (HISTORY) paper made from the STEMS of the papyrus plant; a piece of this paper

par /pɑː(r)/ noun [U] (in golf) the standard number of times a good player should hit the ball in order to complete a particular HOLE or series of HOLES
IDM **below par** (informal) not as good or as well as usual **on a par with sb/sth** of an equal level, standard, etc. to sb/sth else

par. (also **para.**) abbr. (in writing) = PARAGRAPH

para- /pærə/ prefix (in nouns and adjectives) **1** beyond: paranormal **2** similar to but not official or not fully qualified: a paramedic ◇ paramilitary

parable /ˈpærəbl/ noun [C] (RELIGION) a short story that teaches a lesson, especially one told by Jesus in the Bible

parabola /pəˈræbələ/ noun [C] (GEOMETRY) a curve like the path of an object that is thrown through the air and falls back to earth ⊃ picture at **conic section** ▸ **parabolic** /ˌpærəˈbɒlɪk/ adj.: parabolic curves

parachute /ˈpærəʃuːt/ noun [C] a piece of equipment made of thin cloth, that opens and lets a person fall to the ground slowly when they jump from a plane ▸ **parachute** verb [I, T]

parade **B2** /pəˈreɪd/ noun [C] a celebration of a special day or event, usually with bands in the streets and decorated vehicles: a military parade ◇ the Lord Mayor's parade

paradigm /ˈpærədaɪm/ noun [C] **1** (formal) a typical example or pattern of sth: a paradigm for students to copy ◇ The war was a paradigm of the destructive side of human nature. **2** (GRAMMAR) a set of all the different forms of a word: verb paradigms

paradise /ˈpærədaɪs/ noun **1** (often Paradise) [U] the perfect place where some people think that good people go after they die **SYN** **heaven** **2** [C] a perfect place: This beach is a paradise for windsurfers.

paradox /ˈpærədɒks/ noun [C] (LANGUAGE) a situation or statement with two or more parts that seem strange or impossible together: It's a paradox that some countries produce too much food while in other countries people are starving. ▸ **paradoxical** /ˌpærəˈdɒksɪkl/ adj. ▸ **paradoxically** /-kli/ adv.

paraffin /ˈpærəfɪn/ (BrE) (AmE **kerosene**) noun [U] (CHEMISTRY) a type of oil that is burned to produce heat or light ⊃ picture at **fractional distillation**

paragliding /ˈpærəɡlaɪdɪŋ/ noun [U] (SPORT) a sport in which you wear a special structure like a PARACHUTE (= a piece of equipment that opens and lets you fall to the ground slowly), jump from a high place and are carried along by the wind before coming down to earth: to go paragliding

paragraph **A1** /ˈpærəɡrɑːf/ noun [C] (abbr. par., para.) (LANGUAGE) a part of a piece of writing that usually consists of several sentences. A paragraph always starts on a new line.

paragraphing /ˈpærəɡrɑːfɪŋ/ noun [U] (LANGUAGE) the way that a piece of writing is divided into paragraphs: Your paragraphing could be improved.

paralegal /ˌpærə'liːgl/ noun [C] (AmE) (LAW) a person who is trained to help a lawyer ▸ **paralegal** adj.

parallel¹ ₹+ B2 Ⓦ /'pærəlel/ adj. **1** (GEOMETRY) two lines, etc. that are **parallel** to each other have the same distance between them for all their length: *parallel lines* ⊃ picture at **line¹** **2** similar and happening at the same time: *The two brothers followed parallel careers in different companies.* ▸ **parallel** adv.: *The railway runs parallel to the road.*

parallel² ₹+ B2 Ⓞ /'pærəlel/ noun [C, U] a person, thing or situation that is similar to another one in a different situation, place or time: *The government's huge election victory is without parallel this century.*

parallel³ /'pærəlel/ verb [T] **1** to be similar to sth; to happen at the same time as sth: *Their legal system parallels our own.* **2** to be as good as sth: *a level of achievement that has never been paralleled* **SYN** equal²

parallel 'bars noun [pl.] two bars on posts of the same height that are used for doing GYMNASTIC exercises ⊃ picture at **asymmetric bars**

parallel 'circuit noun [C] (PHYSICS) an electrical CIRCUIT in which the current divides into more than one path and then meets again ⊃ look at **series circuit**

parallelograms

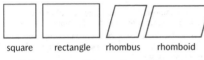

square   rectangle   rhombus   rhomboid

parallelogram /ˌpærə'leləgræm/ noun [C] (GEOMETRY) a flat shape with four straight sides, the opposite sides being PARALLEL and equal to each other

the Paralympics /ðə ˌpærə'lɪmpɪks/ noun [pl.] (SPORT) an international ATHLETICS competition for people who are DISABLED (= unable to use a part of the body completely or easily)

paralyse (BrE) (AmE **paralyze**) /'pærəlaɪz/ verb [T, often passive] **1** (HEALTH) to make a person unable to move their body or a part of it: *Miriam is paralysed from the waist down.* **2** to make sb/sth unable to work in a normal way ▸ **paralysis** /pə'ræləsɪs/ noun [U]: *The disease can cause paralysis or even death.* ◇ *There has been complete paralysis of the railway system.*

paramedic /ˌpærə'medɪk/ noun [C] (MEDICINE) a person who has had special training in treating people who are hurt or ill, but who is not a doctor or nurse ⊃ look at **first responder**

parameter ₹+ C1 /pə'ræmɪtə(r)/ noun [C, usually pl.] (formal) something that decides or limits the way in which sth can be done: *to set/define the parameters* ◇ *We had to work within the parameters that had already been established.*

paramilitary /ˌpærə'mɪlətri/ adj. organized in the same way as, but not belonging to, an official army: *a paramilitary group*

paramount /'pærəmaʊnt/ adj. most important: *Safety is paramount in car design.*

paranoia /ˌpærə'nɔɪə/ noun [U] **1** (PSYCHOLOGY) a type of mental illness in which you wrongly believe that other people want to harm you **2** (informal) a feeling of fear of other people when there is no evidence or reason for this

paranoid /'pærənɔɪd/ adj. wrongly believing that other people are trying to harm you or are saying bad things about you

paranormal /ˌpærə'nɔːml/ adj. **1** that cannot be explained by science and that seems to involve mysterious forces **2** the paranormal noun [sing.] events or subjects that are PARANORMAL

paraphernalia /ˌpærəfə'neɪliə/ noun [U] a large number of different objects that you need for a particular purpose

paraphrase /'pærəfreɪz/ verb [T, I] (LANGUAGE) to express sth again using different words so that it is easier to understand ▸ **paraphrase** noun [C]

paraplegia /ˌpærə'pliːdʒə/ noun [U] (HEALTH) PARALYSIS (= loss of control or feeling) in the legs and lower body

paraplegic /ˌpærə'pliːdʒɪk/ noun [C] (HEALTH) a person who suffers from PARAPLEGIA

parasite /'pærəsaɪt/ noun [C] (BIOLOGY) a plant or an animal that lives in or on another plant or animal and gets its food from it. Parasites sometimes cause disease. ▸ **parasitic** /ˌpærə'sɪtɪk/ adj.

parasol /'pærəsɒl/ noun [C] an umbrella that you use to protect yourself from the sun

paratroops /'pærətruːps/ noun [pl.] soldiers who are trained to jump from a plane with a PARACHUTE (= a piece of equipment on their backs that opens and allows them to fall slowly)

parcel /'pɑːsl/ (especially BrE) (also **package** BrE, AmE) noun [C] something that is covered in paper or put into a thick ENVELOPE and sent or given to sb

parched /pɑːtʃt/ adj. **1** very hot and dry **2** (informal) very thirsty: *Can I have a drink? I'm parched!*

parchment /'pɑːtʃmənt/ noun [U] **1** (HISTORY) material made from the skin of a sheep or GOAT, used in the past for writing on: *parchment scrolls* **2** a thick type of paper

pardon¹ /'pɑːdn/ (also ˌpardon 'me) exclamation **1** used for asking sb to repeat what they have just said because you did not hear or understand it **2** used by some people to mean 'sorry' or 'excuse me'

pardon² /'pɑːdn/ noun [C] (LAW) an official decision not to punish sb for a crime ▸ **pardon** verb [T] ~ **sb (for sth/ doing sth)**

pare /peə(r)/ verb [T] **1** ~ **sth (off/away)** to remove the thin outer layer of sth: *First, pare the rind off the lemon.* ◇ *She pared the apple.* **2** ~ **sth (back/down)** to gradually reduce the size or amount of sth: *The training budget has been pared back to a minimum.* ◇ *The workforce has been pared to the bone* (= reduced to the lowest possible level). **3** (especially BrE) to cut away the edges of sth, especially your nails, in order to make them smooth

parent ₹ A1 /'peərənt/ noun [C] **1** a person's mother or father ⊃ picture at **fertilization** ❶ A **single parent** is a mother or father who is bringing up his/her child or children alone, without the other parent. A **foster parent** is a person who looks after a child who is not legally his/her own. **2** a company that owns smaller companies of the same type: *a parent company*

parentage /'peərəntɪdʒ/ noun [U] (formal) the origin of a person's parents and who they are: *a young American of German parentage*

parental ₹+ C1 /pə'rentl/ adj. [only before noun] of a parent or parents: *parental support/responsibility*

paˌrental 'leave noun [U] time that a parent is allowed to have away from work to care for a child

parenthesis /pə'renθəsɪs/ noun [C] (pl. **parentheses** /-θəsiːz/) **1** a word, sentence, etc. that is added to a speech or piece of writing, especially in order to give extra information. In writing, it is separated from the rest of the text using BRACKETS, COMMAS or DASHES. **2** (*AmE, formal*) = BRACKET¹ (1): *Irregular forms are given in parentheses.*

parenthood /'peərənthʊd/ *noun* [U] the state of being a parent

parenting /'peərəntɪŋ/ *noun* [U] the process of caring for your child or children

parent-'teacher association *noun* [C] = PTA

parish ʔ+ **C1** /'pærɪʃ/ *noun* [C] (**RELIGION**) an area or a district that has its own church; the people who live in this area: *the parish church* ▸ **parishioner** /pə'rɪʃənə(r)/ *noun* [C]

parish 'council *noun* [C + sing./pl. verb] (**POLITICS**) a division of local government that looks after the interests of a very small area, especially a village

parity /'pærəti/ *noun* [U] ~ (**with sb/sth**); ~ (**between A and B**) **1** (*formal*) the state of being equal, especially the state of having equal pay or position: *Prison officers are demanding pay parity with the police force.* ◇ *There is a lack of parity between men and women in many areas of life.* **2** (**ECONOMICS**) the fact of the units of money of two different countries being equal: *to achieve parity with the dollar*

park¹ ʔ **A1** /pɑːk/ *noun* [C] **1** an open area in a town, often with grass or trees, where people can go to walk, play, etc: *Let's go for a walk in the park.* **2** (in compounds) a large area of land that is used for a special purpose: *a national park* ◇ *a business park* ◇ *a theme park*

park² ʔ **A1** /pɑːk/ *verb* [I, T] to leave the vehicle that you are driving somewhere for a period of time: *You can't park in the centre of town.* ◇ *Somebody's parked their car in front of the exit.*

parka /'pɑːkə/ *noun* [C] a warm jacket or coat, with a HOOD (= a part that covers your head) that often has fur inside

park and 'ride *noun* [C] a system designed to reduce traffic in towns in which people park their cars on the edge of a town and then take a special bus or train to the town centre; the area where people park their cars before taking the bus: *Use the park and ride.* ◇ *I've left my car in the park and ride.*

parking ʔ **A2** /'pɑːkɪŋ/ *noun* [U] **1** the act of leaving a car, lorry, etc. somewhere for a time: *The sign said 'No Parking'.* **2** a space or an area for leaving cars, lorries, etc.

parking brake (*AmE*) = HANDBRAKE

parking garage (*AmE*) = MULTI-STOREY CAR PARK

parking lot (*AmE*) = CAR PARK

parking meter *noun* [C] a machine next to the road that you put money into when you park your car next to it

parking ticket *noun* [C] a piece of paper that orders you to pay money as a punishment for parking your car where it is not allowed

Parkinson's disease /'pɑːkɪnsnz dɪziːz/ *noun* [U] (**HEALTH**) a disease that gets worse over a period of time and causes the muscles to become weak and the arms and legs to shake

parkour /pɑː'kɔː(r)/ *noun* [U] (**SPORT**) the activity of moving through a city by running, jumping and climbing under, around and through things **SYN** free running

parliament ʔ **B2** /'pɑːləmənt/ *noun* (**LAW, POLITICS**) **1** [C + sing./pl. verb] the group of people who are elected to make and change the laws of a country

2 Parliament [sing.] the parliament of the United Kingdom: *a Member of Parliament*

▼ CULTURE

The UK Parliament consists of **the House of Lords**, whose members have been appointed rather than elected, and **the House of Commons**, whose members have been elected by the people to represent areas of the country (called **constituencies**).

parliamentarian /ˌpɑːləmən'teəriən/ *noun* [C] (**POLITICS**) a member of a parliament, especially one with a lot of skill and experience

parliamentary ʔ+ **C1** /ˌpɑːlə'mentri/ *adj.* [only before noun] (**POLITICS**) connected with a parliament

parody /'pærədi/ *noun* [C, U] (*pl.* -ies) (**LITERATURE**) a piece of writing, speech or music that copies the style of sb/sth in a funny way: *a parody of a spy novel* ▸ **parody** *verb* [T] (parodying; parodies; *pt, pp* parodied)

parole /pə'rəʊl/ *noun* [U] (**LAW**) permission that is given to a prisoner to leave prison early on the condition that they behave well: *He's going to be released on parole.*

parrot /'pærət/ *noun* [C] a tropical bird with a curved BEAK (= the hard pointed part of a bird's mouth). There are several types of parrot, most of which have very bright feathers. Some are kept as pets and can be trained to copy what people say.

parrot-fashion *adv.* without understanding the meaning of sth: *to learn something parrot-fashion*

parsley /'pɑːsli/ *noun* [U] a HERB (= a type of plant) with small curly leaves that are used in cooking or for decorating food

parsnip /'pɑːsnɪp/ *noun* [C] a long thin white vegetable, that grows under the ground

part¹ ʔ **A1** ⊙ /pɑːt/ *noun*
- PIECE **1** [C, U] (a) ~ (of sth) one of the pieces, areas, periods, things, etc. that together with others forms the whole of sth; some, but not all of sth: *Which part of Spain do you come from?* ◇ *The film is good in parts.* ◇ *spare parts for a car* ◇ *a part of the body* ◇ *Part of the problem is lack of information.* ◇ *I enjoy being part of a team.*
- REGION **2** parts [pl.] a region or an area: *Are you from these parts?*
- OF A BOOK/SERIES **3** [C] (**ARTS AND MEDIA**) a section of a book, TV series, etc: *You can see part 2 of this programme at the same time next week.*
- IN A FILM/PLAY **4** [C] (**ARTS AND MEDIA**) a role or character in a play, film, etc: *He played the part of Macbeth.* ◇ *I had a small part in the school play.*
- EQUAL AMOUNT **5** [C] an amount or a quantity (of a liquid or substance): *Use one part cleaning fluid to ten parts water.*
- IN HAIR **6** [C] (*AmE*) = PARTING (2)
IDM the best/better part of sth most of sth, especially a period of time; more than half of sth: *They've lived here for the best part of 40 years.* for the most part usually or mostly for my/his/their, etc. part speaking for myself, himself, etc.; personally have/play a part (in sth) to be involved in sth in part not completely: *The accident was, in part, the fault of the driver.* on the part of sb/on sb's part made, done or felt by sb: *There is concern on the part of the teachers that class sizes will increase.* ◇ *I'm sorry. It was a mistake on my part.* take part (in sth) to join with other people in an activity: *Everybody took part in the discussion.*

part² ʔ **B2** /pɑːt/ *verb* **1** [I, T] ~ (sb) (from sb) (*formal*) to leave or go away from sb; to separate people or things: *We exchanged phone numbers when we parted.* ◇ *He hates being parted from his children for long.* **2** [I, T] to move apart; to make things or people move apart: *Her lips were slightly parted.* **3** [T] to separate the hair on your head so as to make a clear line that goes from the back of your head to the front: *She parts her hair in the middle.* ⊃ look at **parting**

IDM **part company (with sb/sth)** to go different ways or to separate after being together

PHR V **part with sth** to give or sell sth to sb: *When we went to live in Italy, we had to part with our horses.*

part³ /pɑːt/ *adv.* not completely one thing and not completely another: *She's part Russian and part Chinese.*

part ex'change *noun* [U] a way of buying sth, such as a car, in which you give your old one as some of the payment for a more expensive one

partial 𝄫+ **C1** **W** /ˈpɑːʃl/ *adj.* **1** not complete: *The project was only a partial success.* **2 ~ to sth** (*old-fashioned*) liking sth very much: *He's very partial to ice cream.*
▶ **partially** 𝄫+ **C1** **W** /-ʃəli/ *adv.*

partiality /ˌpɑːʃiˈæləti/ *noun* [U] (*formal*) unfair support for one person, team, etc. above another: *The referee was accused of partiality towards the home team.*
OPP **impartiality**

participant 𝄫 **B2** **W** /pɑːˈtɪsɪpənt/ *noun* [C] a person who takes part in sth

participate 𝄫 **B1** **W** /pɑːˈtɪsɪpeɪt/ *verb* [I] **~ (in sth)** to take part or become involved in sth: *Students are encouraged to participate in sporting activities.*
▶ **participation** 𝄫+ **B2** **W** /pɑːˌtɪsɪˈpeɪʃn/ *noun* [U]
▶ **participatory** /-ˈpeɪtəri/ *adj.*: *Ordinary people had no participatory role in the government.*

participle /ˈpɑːtɪsɪpl/ *noun* [C] (**GRAMMAR**) a word that is formed from a verb and that ends in *-ing* (present participle) or *-ed*, *-en*, etc. (past participle). Participles are used to form tenses of the verb, or as adjectives: *'Hurrying' and 'hurried' are the present and past participles of 'hurry'.*

particle /ˈpɑːtɪkl/ *noun* [C] **1** a very small piece: *dust particles* **2** (**PHYSICS**) a very small piece of MATTER, such as an ELECTRON or a PROTON, that is part of an ATOM ⊃ look at **alpha particle, elementary particle** ⊃ picture at **state¹** **3** (**GRAMMAR**) a small word that is not as important as a noun, a verb or an adjective: *In the phrasal verb 'break down', 'down' is an adverbial particle.*

particle physics *noun* [U] (**PHYSICS**) the scientific study of very small pieces of MATTER that are parts of an ATOM

particular 𝄫 **A2** **O** /pəˈtɪkjələ(r)/ *adj.* **1** [only before noun] used to emphasize that you are talking about one person, thing, time, etc. and not about others: *Is there any particular dish you enjoy making?* **2** [only before noun] greater than usual; special: *This article is of particular interest to me.* **3** connected with one person or thing and not with others: *Everybody has their own particular problems.* **4** [not before noun] **~ (about/over sth)** difficult to please: *Some people are extremely particular about what they eat.* ⊃ look at **fussy** (1)

IDM **in particular** especially: *Is there anything in particular you'd like to do this weekend?*

particularly 𝄫 **B1** **O** /pəˈtɪkjələli/ *adv.* especially; more than usual or more than others: *I'm particularly interested in Indian history.* ◊ *The match was excellent, particularly the second half.*

particulars **W** /pəˈtɪkjələz/ *noun* [pl.] (*formal*) facts or details about sb/sth: *The police took down all the particulars about the missing child.*

parting /ˈpɑːtɪŋ/ *noun* **1** [C, U] saying goodbye to, or being separated from, another person (usually for quite a long time) **2** (*BrE*) (*AmE* **part**) [C] the line in sb's

hair where it is divided in two with a COMB (= a flat piece of metal or plastic with teeth): *a side/centre parting*

partisan¹ /ˈpɑːtɪzæn, ˌpɑːtɪˈzæn/ *adj.* showing too much support for one person, group or idea, especially without considering it carefully: *Most newspapers are politically partisan.* **SYN** **one-sided**
▶ **partisanship** /ˈpɑːtɪzænʃɪp/ *noun* [U]

partisan² /ˈpɑːtɪzæn, ˌpɑːtɪˈzæn/ *noun* [C] (**POLITICS**) **1** a person who strongly supports a particular leader, group or idea **SYN** **follower** **2** a member of an armed group that is fighting secretly against enemy soldiers who have taken control of its country

partition /pɑːˈtɪʃn/ *noun* **1** [C] something that divides a room, an office etc. into two or more parts, especially a thin or temporary wall **2** [U] (**POLITICS**) the division of a country into two or more countries ▶ **partition** *verb* [T]: *to partition a country/room*

partly 𝄫 **B2** **O** /ˈpɑːtli/ *adv.* not completely: *She was only partly responsible for the mistake.*

partner 𝄫 **A1** /ˈpɑːtnə(r)/ *noun* [C] **1** a person that you are doing an activity with as a team, for example dancing or playing a game **2** the person that you are married to or live with as if you are married **3** (**BUSINESS**) one of the people who owns a business: *business partners* **4** (**POLITICS**) a country or an organization that has an agreement with another ▶ **partner** *verb* [T]: *Hales partnered his brother in the doubles, and they won the gold medal.*

partnership 𝄫+ **B2** /ˈpɑːtnəʃɪp/ *noun* **1** [U] **~ (with sb)** (**BUSINESS**) the state of being a partner in business: *Simona went into partnership with her sister and opened a shop in Rome.* **2** [C] a relationship between two people, organizations, etc: *Marriage is a partnership for life.* **3** [C] (**BUSINESS**) a business owned by two or more people ⊃ note at **organization**

part of 'speech *noun* [C] (**GRAMMAR**) one of the groups that words are divided into, for example noun, verb, adjective, etc. **SYN** **word class**

partridge /ˈpɑːtrɪdʒ/ *noun* [C, U] (*pl.* **partridges**, **partridge**) a brown bird with a round body and a short tail, that people hunt for sport or food; the meat of this bird

part-'time 𝄫+ **B2** *adj.*, *adv.* for only a part of the working day or week: *She's got a part-time job.* ◊ *I work part-time.* ⊃ look at **full-time** ⊃ note at **job**

party 𝄫 **A1** /ˈpɑːti/ *noun* [C] (*pl.* **-ies**) **1** a social occasion to which people are invited in order to eat, drink and enjoy themselves: *When we've moved into our new house we're going to have a party.* ◊ *a birthday/dinner party* **2** (*also* **Party**) [+ sing./pl. verb] (**POLITICS**) a group of people who have the same political aims and ideas and who are trying to win elections to parliament, etc. **3** [+ sing./pl. verb] (often in compounds) a group of people who are working, travelling, etc. together: *a party of tourists* **4** (*formal*) (**LAW**) one of the people or groups of people involved in a legal case: *the guilty/innocent party* ⊃ look at **third party**

▼ CULTURE

The two main political parties in the UK are the **Labour Party** (left-wing) and the **Conservative** (or **Tory**) Party (right-wing). There is also a centre party called the **Liberal Democrats** and some other smaller parties. The main party in Scotland is the **Scottish National Party**. In the United States the main political parties are the **Republican Party** and the **Democratic Party**.

,party 'politics *noun* [U + sing./pl. verb] (**POLITICS**) political activity that involves political parties: *The president should stand above party politics.* ◇ *Many people think that party politics should not enter into local government.*

pascal *noun* **1** /'pæskl/ (*abbr.* Pa) [C] (**PHYSICS**) the standard unit for measuring pressure **2** Pascal, PASCAL /pæ'skæl/ [U] (**COMPUTING**) a language used for writing programs for computer systems

pass¹ ⚡ **A2** /pɑːs/ *verb*
• EXAM **1** [I, T] (**EDUCATION**) to achieve the necessary standard in an exam, a test, etc: *Good luck in the exam! I'm sure you'll pass.* **OPP** fail¹ ➔ note at study² **2** [T] (**EDUCATION**) to test sb/sth and say that they are good enough: *The examiner passed most of the students.* **OPP** fail¹
• MOVE **3** [I, T] to move past or to the other side of sb/sth: *The street was crowded and the two buses couldn't pass.* ◇ *I passed him in the street but he didn't say hello.* **4** [I, T] (used with an adverb or a preposition) to go or move, or make sth move, in the direction mentioned: *A plane passed overhead.* ◇ *We'll have to pass the wire through the window.*
• GIVE **5** [T] ~ sth (to sb); ~ (sb) sth to give sth to sb: *Could you pass a message to my father?* ◇ *Could you pass (me) the salt, please?*
• BALL **6** [I, T] ~ (sth) (to sb) (**SPORT**) (in some sports) to kick, hit or throw the ball to sb on your own team: *He passed (the ball) to Sterling.*
• TIME **7** [I] (used about time) to go by: *At least a year has passed since I last saw them.* ◇ *It was a long journey but the time passed very quickly.* **8** [T] to spend time, especially when you are bored or waiting for sth: *I'll have to think of something to do to **pass the time** in hospital.*
• LAW **9** [T] to officially approve a law, etc. by voting: *One of the functions of Parliament is to **pass** new laws.*
• OPINION, JUDGEMENT, ETC. **10** [T] ~ sth (on sb/sth) to give an opinion, a judgement, etc: *The judge **passed sentence** on the young man* (= said what his punishment would be).
• BE ALLOWED **11** [I] to be allowed or accepted: *I didn't like what they were saying but I let it pass.* **IDM** pass water (*formal*) (**HEALTH**) to get rid of waste liquid from the body
PHR V pass away used as a polite way of saying 'die' pass by (sb/sth) to go past: *I pass by your house on the way to work.* pass sth down to give or teach sth to people who will live after you have died pass for sb/ sth to be accepted as sb/sth that you are not: *His mother looks so young she'd pass for his sister.* pass sb/sth off (as sb/sth) to say that a person or a thing is sth that he/she/it is not: *He tried to pass the work off as his own.* pass sth on (to sb) to give sth to sb else, especially after you have been given it or used it yourself: *Could you pass the message on to Mr Roberts?* pass out (**HEALTH**) to become unconscious **SYN** faint² **OPP** come around

pass² ⚡ **B1** /pɑːs/ *noun* [C] **1** an official piece of paper that gives you permission to enter or leave a building, travel on a bus or train, etc: *Show your student pass when you buy a ticket.* **2** (**EDUCATION**) a successful result in an exam: *The pass mark is 50%.* ◇ *Grades A, B and C are passes.* **OPP** fail² **3** (**SPORT**) the act of kicking, hitting or throwing the ball to sb on your own team in some sports **4** a road or way over or through mountains: *a mountain pass*

passable /'pɑːsəbl/ *adj.* **1** good enough but not very good: *My French is not brilliant but it's passable.* **2** [not before noun] (used about roads, rivers, etc.) possible to use or cross; not blocked **OPP** impassable

passage ⚡ **B2** /'pæsɪdʒ/ *noun* **1** (*also* passageway /'pæsɪdʒweɪ/) [C] a long, narrow way with walls on either side that connects one place with another: *a secret underground passage* **2** [C] (**BIOLOGY**) a tube in the body through which air, liquid, etc. can pass: *the nasal passages* ➔ picture at **respiratory 3** [C] (**ARTS AND MEDIA**) a short part of a book, a speech or a piece of music: *The students were given a passage from the novel to study.* **4** [sing.] the process of passing: *His painful memories faded with the **passage of time**.*

passenger ⚡ **A2** /'pæsɪndʒə(r)/ *noun* [C] a person who is travelling in a car, bus, train, plane, etc. but who is not driving it or working on it

,passer-'by *noun* [C] (*pl.* passers-by) a person who is walking past sb/sth

passing¹ /'pɑːsɪŋ/ *adj.* [only before noun] **1** lasting for only a short time: *a passing phase/thought/interest* **SYN** brief¹ **2** going past: *I stopped a passing car and asked for help.*

passing² ⚡+ **C1** /'pɑːsɪŋ/ *noun* [U] the process of going by: *the passing of time* **IDM** in passing done or said quickly, while you are thinking or talking about sth else: *He mentioned the house in passing but he didn't give any details.*

passion ⚡ **B1** /'pæʃn/ *noun* **1** [U, C] (a) very strong feeling, especially of love, hate or anger: *He was a violent man, controlled by his passions.* **2** [sing.] ~ (for sth) a very strong liking for or interest in sth: *She has a passion for history.* **3** [sing.] ~ (for sb) very strong sexual love or attraction: *He longed to tell Sashi of his passion for her.*

passionate ⚡+ **B2** /'pæʃənət/ *adj.* **1** showing or caused by very strong feelings: *The president gave a passionate speech about crime.* **2** showing or feeling very strong love or sexual attraction: *a passionate kiss* ▸ passionately *adv.*: *He believes passionately in democracy.*

'passion fruit *noun* [C, U] (*pl.* passion fruit) a small tropical fruit with a thick purple skin and many seeds inside

passive¹ ⚡+ **C1** /'pæsɪv/ *adj.* **1** showing no reaction, feeling or interest; not active: *Some people prefer to play a passive role in meetings.* **2** (**GRAMMAR**) used about the form of a verb or a sentence when the subject of the sentence is affected by the action of the verb: *In the sentence 'He was bitten by a dog', the verb is passive.* ➔ look at **active (5)** ▸ passively *adv.*

passive² /'pæsɪv/ (*also* ,passive 'voice) *noun* [sing.] (**GRAMMAR**) the form of a verb used when the subject is affected by the action of the verb ➔ look at **active (5)**

,passive 'smoking *noun* [U] (**HEALTH, SOCIAL STUDIES**) the act of breathing in smoke from other people's cigarettes

Passover /'pɑːsəʊvə(r)/ *noun* [U, C] (**RELIGION**) the Jewish religious festival and holiday in memory of the escape of the Jews from Egypt

passport ⚡ **A1** /'pɑːspɔːt/ *noun* [C] **1** (**TOURISM**) an official document that identifies you as a citizen of a particular country and that you have to show when you enter or leave a country: *a valid passport* ◇ *a South African passport* ◇ *You have to go through **passport control** (= where passports are checked) at the airport.* ❶ You **apply for** or **renew** your passport at the **passport office**. This office **issues** new passports. **2** ~ to/into sth a thing that makes it possible to achieve sth: *a passport to success*

password ⚡+ **B2** /'pɑːswɜːd/ *noun* [C] **1** (**COMPUTING**) a series of letters or numbers that you must type into a computer or computer system in order to be able to use it: *Please enter your password.* **2** a secret word or phrase that you need to know in order to be allowed into a place

past¹ 🔊 **A1** /pɑːst/ *adj.* **1** already gone; belonging to a time before the present: *in past centuries/times* ◊ *I'd rather forget some of my past mistakes.* **2** [only before noun] just finished; last: *He's had to work very hard during the past year.*

past² 🔊 **A1** /pɑːst/ *noun* **1** the past [sing.] the time that has gone by; things that happened in an earlier time: *in the recent/distant past* ◊ *Writing letters seems to be a thing of the past.* **2** [C] a person's life and career before now **3** the past [sing.] = PAST TENSE: *The past of 'take' is 'took'.*

past³ 🔊 **A1** /pɑːst/ *prep.* **1** (used when telling the time) after; later than: *It's ten (minutes) past three.* ◊ *It was past midnight when we got home.* **2** on or to the other side of sb/sth **3** above or further than a certain point, limit or age: *Unemployment is now past the 2 million mark.* ◊ *I'm so tired that I'm **past caring** (= I don't care any more) what we eat.*
IDM **not put it past sb** to think sb is capable of doing sth bad: *I wouldn't put it past him to do a thing like that.* **past it** (*BrE, informal*) too old

past⁴ 🔊 **A2** /pɑːst/ *adv.* **1** from one side to the other of sb/sth: *She looked right past me without realizing who I was.* ◊ *He smiled as he walked past.* **2** used to describe time passing: *A week went past and nothing had changed.*

pasta /ˈpæstə/ *noun* [U] an Italian food made from flour, water and sometimes eggs, formed into different shapes, cooked, and usually served with a sauce

paste¹ /peɪst/ *noun* **1** [U, sing.] a soft, wet mixture, usually made of a powder and a liquid and sometimes used for sticking things: *wallpaper paste* ◊ *Mix the flour and milk into a paste.* **2** [U] (usually in compounds) a soft mixture of food that you can spread onto bread, etc: *fish paste*

paste² /peɪst/ *verb* [T] **1** to stick sth to sth else using PASTE or a similar substance: *He pasted the picture into his book.* **2** (**COMPUTING**) to copy or move text into a document from somewhere else: *This function allows you to **cut and paste** text.*

pastel /ˈpæstl/ *noun* **1** [U] (**ART**) soft coloured CHALK, used for drawing pictures: *drawings in pastel* **2** pastels [pl.] (**ART**) small sticks of CHALK: *a box of pastels* **3** [C] (**ART**) a picture drawn with pastels **4** [C] a pale DELICATE colour: *The whole house was painted in soft pastels.*

pasteurized (*BrE also* -ised) /ˈpɑːstʃəraɪzd/ *adj.* (used about milk or cream) free from bacteria because it has been heated and then cooled ▶ **pasteurization** (*BrE also* -isation) /ˌpɑːstʃəraɪˈzeɪʃn/ *noun* [U]

pastiche /pæˈstiːʃ/ *noun* **1** [C, U] (**ART, LITERATURE**) a work of art, piece of writing, etc. that is created by deliberately copying the style of sb/sth else: *a pastiche of the classic detective story* ◊ *She's an expert in the art of pastiche.* **2** [C] (**ART**) a work of art, etc. that consists of a variety of different styles

pastime /ˈpɑːstaɪm/ *noun* [C] something that you enjoy doing when you are not working **SYN** **hobby**

pastor 🔊 **C1** /ˈpɑːstə(r)/ *noun* [C] (**RELIGION**) a priest in charge of some types of Christian church or group

pastoral /ˈpɑːstərəl/ *adj.* **1** (connected with the work of a priest or a teacher) giving help and advice on personal matters rather than on matters of religion or education **2** connected with pleasant country life

past participle *noun* [C] (**GRAMMAR**) the form of the verb that ends in -ed, -en, etc. ➔ look at **participle**

the past perfect (*also* **the past perfect tense**, **the pluperfect**) *noun* [sing.] (**GRAMMAR**) the form of a verb that describes an action that was finished before another event happened

pastry /ˈpeɪstri/ *noun* (*pl.* -ies) **1** [U] a mixture of flour, fat and water that is rolled out flat and cooked as a base or covering for PIES, etc. **2** [C] a small cake made with pastry

the past tense (*also* **the past** /ðə ˈpɑːst/) *noun* [sing.] (**GRAMMAR**) the form of a verb used to describe actions in the past: *The past (tense) of the verb 'come' is 'came'.*

pasture /ˈpɑːstʃə(r)/ *noun* [C, U] (**AGRICULTURE**) a field or land covered with grass, where cows, etc. can feed

pasty /ˈpæsti/ *noun* [C] (*pl.* -ies) (*BrE*) a small PIE containing meat and/or vegetables

PA system *noun* [C] = PUBLIC ADDRESS SYSTEM: *Announcements were made over the PA system.*

pat¹ /pæt/ *verb* [T] (-tt-) to touch sb/sth gently with a flat hand, especially as a sign of friendship, care, etc.

pat² /pæt/ *noun* [C] a gentle friendly touch with a flat hand: *He gave the dog's head an affectionate pat.*
IDM **a pat on the back** (**for sth/doing sth**) approval for sth good that a person has done: *She deserves a pat on the back for all her hard work.*

pat³ /pæt/ *adj., adv.* (used about an answer, comment, etc.) said in a quick or simple way that does not sound natural or realistic: *The ending of the book is a little pat.*

patch¹ 🔊+ **C1** /pætʃ/ *noun* [C] **1** ~ (**of sth**) a part of a surface that is different in some way from the area around it: *Drive carefully. There are patches of ice on the roads.* ◊ *a bald patch* **2** a small piece of material that you use to cover a hole in clothes, etc: *I sewed patches on the knees of my jeans.* **3** a small piece of material that you wear over one eye, usually because the eye is damaged **4** a small piece of land, especially for growing vegetables or fruit: *a vegetable patch*
IDM **go through a bad patch** (*especially BrE, informal*) to experience a difficult or unhappy period of time **not a patch on sb/sth** (*especially BrE, informal*) not nearly as good as sb/sth: *Her new book isn't a patch on her others.*

patch² /pætʃ/ *verb* [T] to cover a hole in clothes, etc. with a piece of material in order to repair it: *patched jeans*
PHR V **patch sth up 1** to repair sth, especially in a temporary way by adding a new piece of material **2** to stop arguing with sb and be friends again: *Have you tried to patch things up with her?*

patchwork /ˈpætʃwɜːk/ *noun* [U] (**ART**) a type of SEWING in which small pieces of cloth of different colours and patterns are SEWN together

patchy /ˈpætʃi/ *adj.* (patchier; patchiest) **1** existing or happening in some places but not others: *patchy fog/clouds/rain* **2** not complete; good in some parts but not in others: *My knowledge of German is rather patchy.*

pâté /ˈpæteɪ/ *noun* [U] food that is made by making meat, fish or vegetables into a smooth, thick mixture that is served cold and spread on bread, etc: *liver pâté*

patella /pəˈtelə/ *noun* [C] (**ANATOMY**) the bone that covers the front of the knee ➔ picture at **body**

patent¹ /ˈpeɪtnt/ *adj.* [only before noun] (*formal*) clear; obvious: *a patent lie* ▶ **patently** *adv.*

patent² ɪ̆+ **C1** /'pætnt, 'peɪt-/ *noun* [C, U] (**BUSINESS**) **1** the official right to be the only person to make, use or sell a product or an invention **2** the document that proves this ▶ **patent** *verb* [T]

patent ˈleather *noun* [U] a type of leather with a hard, shiny surface, used especially for making shoes and bags

paternal /pə'tɜːnl/ *adj.* [only before noun] **1** behaving as a father would behave; connected with being a father: *paternal advice* **2** related through the father's side of the family: *my paternal grandparents* ⊃ look at **maternal** (2)

paternalism /pə'tɜːnəlɪzəm/ *noun* [U] the system in which a government or an employer protects the people who are governed or employed by providing them with what they need, but does not give them any responsibility or freedom of choice ▶ **paternalistic** /pə,tɜːnə'lɪstɪk/ (*also* **paternalist** /pə'tɜːnəlɪst/) *adj.*: *a paternalistic employer/state*

paternity /pə'tɜːnəti/ *noun* [U] the fact of being the father of a child: *paternity leave* (= time that the father of a new baby is allowed to have away from work) ⊃ look at **maternity**

path ɪ̆ **B1** /pɑːθ/ *noun* [C] **1** a way across a piece of land that is made by or used by people walking: *the garden path* ◇ *There was a narrow path leading down the cliff.* ⊃ look at **footpath 2** (*also* **pathway**) ~ **(to sth)** a plan of action or a way of achieving something: *His best friend followed a different career path.* ◇ *This course will help you on your path to success.* **3** the line along which sb/sth moves; the space in front of sb/sth as they move: *He fell into the path of an oncoming vehicle.* ⊃ look at **flight path**

pathetic /pə'θetɪk/ *adj.* **1** making you feel sad: *the pathetic cries of the hungry children* **2** (*informal*) very bad, weak or not successful: *What a pathetic performance! The team deserved to lose.* ▶ **pathetically** /-kli/ *adv.*

paˌthetic ˈfallacy *noun* [U, sing.] (**LITERATURE**) the act of describing animals and things as having human feelings

patho- /pæθəʊ, pæθə, pə'θɒ/ *prefix* (in nouns, adjectives and adverbs) (**BIOLOGY**) connected with disease: *pathology*

pathogen /'pæθədʒən/ *noun* [C] (**HEALTH**) a thing that causes disease

pathogenesis /,pæθə'dʒenɪsɪs/ *noun* [C] (*pl.* **pathogeneses** /-nɪsiz/) (**HEALTH**) the way in which a disease develops

pathological /,pæθə'lɒdʒɪkl/ *adj.* **1** caused by feelings that you cannot control; not reasonable or sensible: *He's a pathological liar* (= he cannot stop lying). ◇ *pathological fear/hatred/violence* **2** (**HEALTH**) caused by or connected with disease or illness: *pathological depression* **3** (**MEDICINE**) connected with PATHOLOGY ▶ **pathologically** /-kli/ *adv.*

pathologist /pə'θɒlədʒɪst/ *noun* [C] (**MEDICINE**) a doctor who is an expert in PATHOLOGY, and examines dead bodies to find out why people have died

pathology /pə'θɒlədʒi/ *noun* [U] (**MEDICINE**) the scientific study of diseases of the body

pathos /'peɪθɒs/ *noun* [U] (**LITERATURE**) (in writing, speech and plays) the power of a performance, description, etc. to make you feel PITY or be sad

pathway ɪ̆+ **C1** /'pɑːθweɪ/ *noun* [C] **1** a track that serves as a path **2** = PATH (2) **3** (**BIOLOGY**) a route formed by a chain of nerve cells along which electrical signals travel from one part of the body to another: *neural pathways*

patience ɪ̆ **B2** /'peɪʃns/ *noun* [U] **1** ~ **(with sb/sth)** the quality of being able to stay calm and not get angry, especially when there is a difficulty or you have to wait a long time: *I've got no patience with people who don't even try.* ◇ *to lose patience with somebody* **OPP impatience 2** (*BrE*) (*AmE* **solitaire**) a card game for only one player

patient¹ ɪ̆ **B2** /'peɪʃnt/ *adj.* ~ **(with sb/sth)** able to stay calm and not get angry, especially when there is a difficulty or you have to wait a long time: *She's very patient with young children.* **OPP impatient** ▶ **patiently** *adv.*: *to wait patiently*

patient² ɪ̆ **A2** /'peɪʃnt/ *noun* [C] (**MEDICINE**) a person who is receiving medical treatment: *a hospital patient* ◇ *He's one of Dr Waters' patients.* ⊃ note at **hospital, medical¹**

patio /'pætiəʊ/ *noun* [C] (*pl.* **-os**) a flat, hard area, usually behind a house, where people can sit, eat, etc. outside ⊃ look at **balcony** (1), **terrace** (2), **veranda**

patois /'pætwɑː/ *noun* [C] (*pl.* **patois** /-wɑːz/) (**LANGUAGE**) a form of a language, spoken by people in a particular area, that is different from the standard language of the country

patriarch /'peɪtriɑːk/ *noun* [C] a man who is the head of a family or social group ⊃ look at **matriarch**

patriarchal /,peɪtri'ɑːkl/ *adj.* (**SOCIAL STUDIES**) (used about a society or system) controlled by men rather than women; passing power, property, etc. from father to son rather than from mother to daughter ⊃ look at **matriarchal**

patriarchy /'peɪtriɑːki/ *noun* [C, U] (*pl.* **-ies**) (**SOCIAL STUDIES**) a social system that gives power and control to men rather than women ⊃ look at **matriarchy**

patricide /'pætrɪsaɪd/ *noun* [U, C] (*formal*) (**LAW**) the crime of killing your father ⊃ look at **matricide**

patrimony /'pætrɪməni/ *noun* [sing.] (*formal*) (**LAW**) **1** property that is given to sb when their father dies **SYN inheritance 2** the works of art and TREASURES of a nation, church, etc. **SYN heritage**

patriot /'pætriət, 'peɪt-/ *noun* [C] a person who loves their country and is ready to defend it against an enemy ▶ **patriotism** *noun* [U]

patriotic /,pætri'ɒtɪk, ,peɪt-/ *adj.* having or showing great love for your country ▶ **patriotically** /-kli/ *adv.*

patrol¹ ɪ̆+ **C1** /pə'trəʊl/ *verb* [I, T] (**-ll-**) to go round an area, a building, etc. at regular times to make sure that it is safe and that nothing is wrong

patrol² ɪ̆+ **C1** /pə'trəʊl/ *noun* **1** [C, U] the act of going round an area, a building, etc. at regular times to make sure that it is safe and that nothing is wrong: *a police car on patrol in the area* **2** [C] a group of soldiers, vehicles, etc. that PATROL sth: *a naval/police patrol* ◇ *a patrol car/boat*

patron ɪ̆+ **C1** /'peɪtrən/ *noun* [C] **1** (**ARTS AND MEDIA**) a person who gives money and support to artists, writers and musicians: *a patron of the arts* ◇ a famous person who supports an organization such as a charity and whose name is used in advertising it ⊃ look at **sponsor** (1) **3** (*formal*) a person who uses a particular shop, theatre, restaurant, etc: *This car park is for patrons only.*

patronage /'pætrənɪdʒ, 'peɪt-/ *noun* [U] (*formal*) **1** the support, especially financial, that is given to a person or an organization by a PATRON: *Patronage of the arts comes mainly from businesses and private individuals.* **2** the system by which an important person gives help or a job to sb in return for their support **3** (*especially AmE*) the support that a person gives a shop, restaurant, etc. by spending money there

patronize (BrE also -ise) /'pætrənaɪz/ verb [T] **1** to treat sb in a way that shows that you think you are better, more intelligent, experienced, etc. than they are **2** (formal) to be a regular customer of a shop, restaurant, etc.

patronizing (BrE also -ising) /'pætrənaɪzɪŋ/ adj. showing that you think you are better, more intelligent, experienced, etc. than sb else: a patronizing smile ▸ **patronizingly** (BrE also -isingly) adv.

patron 'saint noun [C] (**RELIGION**) a religious being who is believed by Christians to protect a particular place or people doing a particular activity

patter /'pætə(r)/ noun **1** [sing.] the sound of many quick light steps or knocks on a surface: just before the children's feet on the stairs **2** [U, sing.] fast continuous talk by sb who is trying to sell you sth or entertain you: sales patter ▸ **patter** verb [I]

pattern 🔤 **A2 ❶** /'pætn/ noun [C] **1** the regular way in which sth happens, develops, or is done: Her days all seemed to follow the same pattern. ◇ changing patterns of behaviour/work/weather **2** (**ART**) a regular arrangement of lines, shapes, colours, etc. as a design: a shirt with a floral pattern on it **SYN** design[1] **3** a design, a set of instructions or a shape to cut around that you use in order to make sth

patterned /'pætənd/ adj. decorated with a pattern

pause[1] 🔤+ **B2** /pɔːz/ noun **1** [C] ~ (in sth) a short period of time during which sb stops talking or stops what they are doing: There was an awkward pause in the conversation when Amy came in. **2** (also 'pause button) [U] a control that allows you to stop playing or recording a video, etc. for a short time

pause[2] 🔤+ **B2** /pɔːz/ verb [I] to stop talking or doing sth for a short time before continuing

pave /peɪv/ verb [T, often passive] ~ sth (with sth) to cover an area of ground with large flat stones

pavement /'peɪvmənt/ noun [C] **1** (BrE) (AmE **sidewalk**) a hard flat area at the side of a road for people to walk on **2** (**GEOLOGY**) a large flat area of rock with nothing growing on it ⊃ picture at **limestone**

pavilion /pə'vɪliən/ noun [C] (BrE) **1** a building at a sports ground where players can change their clothes **2** a temporary building used at public events and exhibitions

'paving stone noun [C] a flat piece of stone that is used for covering the ground

paw[1] /pɔː/ noun [C] (**BIOLOGY**) the foot of an animal such as a dog, cat, bear, etc. ⊃ picture at **animal, lion**

paw[2] /pɔː/ verb [I, T] ~ (at) sth (used about an animal) to touch or **SCRATCH** sb/sth several times with a **PAW**: The dog pawed at my sleeve.

pawn[1] /pɔːn/ noun [C] **1** (in the game of **CHESS**) one of the eight pieces that are of least value and importance **2** a person who is used or controlled by other more powerful people

pawn[2] /pɔːn/ verb [T] to leave a valuable object with a **PAWNBROKER** in return for money. If you cannot pay back the money after a certain period, the object can be sold or kept.

pawnbroker /'pɔːnbrəʊkə(r)/ noun [C] a person who lends money to people when they leave sth of value with them

pawpaw /'pɔːpɔː/ = PAPAYA

pay[1] 🔤 **A1** /peɪ/ verb (pt, pp **paid** /peɪd/) **1** [I, T] ~ (sb) (for sth); ~ (sb) sth (for sth) (**FINANCE**) to give sb money for work, goods, services, etc: She is very **well paid**. ◇ The work's finished but we haven't paid for it yet. ◇ We paid the dealer £3 000 for the car. **2** [T] ~ sth (to sb); ~ (sb) sth

(**FINANCE**) to give the money that you owe for sth: to pay a bill/fine ◇ Have you paid her the rent yet? **3** [I, T] (**FINANCE**) to make a profit; to be worth doing: It's hard to make farming pay. **4** [I] ~ (**for sth**) to suffer or be punished because of your beliefs or actions: You'll pay for that remark!

IDM **pay attention (to sb/sth)** to listen carefully to or to take notice of sb/sth **pay sb a compliment** | **pay a compliment to sb** to say that you like sth about sb **pay your respects (to sb)** (formal) to visit sb or to send a message of good wishes as a sign of respect for them: Hundreds came to pay their last respects to her (= came to her **FUNERAL**). **put paid to sth** to destroy or finish sth: The bad weather put paid to our picnic.

PHR V **pay sb back (sth)** | **pay sth back (to sb)** to give money back to sb that you borrowed from them: Can you lend me £5? I'll pay you back on Friday. ◇ You can pay the loan back over three years. **pay sb back (for sth)** to punish sb for making you or sb else suffer: What a mean trick! I'll pay you back one day. **pay off** (informal) to be successful: All her hard work has paid off! She passed her exam. **pay sth off** to pay all the money that you owe for sth: to pay off a debt/mortgage **pay up** to pay the money that you owe: If you don't pay up, we'll take you to court.

pay[2] 🔤 **A2** /peɪ/ noun [U] (**FINANCE**) money that you get regularly for work that you have done

▼ **VOCABULARY BUILDING**

Pay is the general word for money that you **earn** (= get regularly for work that you have done). **Wages** are paid weekly or daily in cash. A **salary** is paid monthly, directly into a bank account. When your wages or salary are increased, you get a **pay rise**. Your **earnings** are all the money you earn by working. Your **income** is all the money you get regularly, both for work you have done, and as interest on money you have saved. **Payment** is money for work that you do once or not regularly. You pay a **fee** for professional services, for example to a doctor, lawyer, etc. The money that you have to pay to the government is called **tax**.

payable /'peɪəbl/ adj. [not before noun] ~ (to sb/sth) that should or must be paid: A 10% deposit is payable in advance. ◇ Make the cheque payable to Emily Nolan.

pay-as-you-'go adj. connected with a system of paying for a service just before you use it rather than paying for it later: pay-as-you-go phones

'pay channel noun [C] (**ARTS AND MEDIA**) a TV station that you must pay for separately in order to watch it

payday lender /ˌpeɪdeɪ 'lendə(r)/ noun [C] (**FINANCE**) a business that lends small amounts of money to people for a short time at a very high rate of interest

payday loan /ˌpeɪdeɪ 'ləʊn/ noun [C] (**FINANCE**) a small amount of money that sb borrows for a short time at a very high rate of interest

PAYE /ˌpiː eɪ waɪ 'iː/ abbr. **pay as you earn** (a British system of paying tax in which money is taken from the money you earn by your employer and paid to the government)

payee /ˌpeɪ'iː/ noun [C] a person that money, especially a **CHEQUE**, is paid to

payment 🔤 **B1** /'peɪmənt/ noun ~ (**for sth**) **1** [U] the act of paying sb or of being paid: I did the work last month but I haven't had any payment for it yet. ⊃ picture at **income** ⊃ note at **pay**[2] **2** [C] an amount of money that you must pay: They asked for a payment of £100 as a deposit.

payout /'peɪaʊt/ noun [C] a large amount of money that is given to sb: *an insurance payout* ◊ *a lottery payout*

pay-per-view noun [U] (**ARTS AND MEDIA**) a system of TV BROADCASTING in which you pay an extra sum of money to watch a particular programme, such as a film or a sports event

payphone /'peɪfəʊn/ noun [C] a phone, usually in a public place, that is operated using coins or a card

payroll /'peɪrəʊl/ noun **1** [C] a list of people employed by a company showing the amount of money to be paid to each of them: *There are 70 people on the payroll.* **2** [C, usually sing.] the total amount paid by a company to its employees

payslip /'peɪslɪp/ noun [C] (*BrE*) a piece of paper that your employer gives you each month to show how much money you have been paid and how much tax, etc. has been taken off

PC¹ /ˌpiː 'siː/ noun [C] **1** (**COMPUTING**) a computer that is designed for one person to use at work or at home (the abbreviation for 'personal computer') ⊃ look at **mainframe 2** (*BrE*) = POLICE CONSTABLE

PC² /ˌpiː 'siː/ abbr. = POLITICALLY CORRECT

PDF /ˌpiː diː 'ef/ (*also* ˌPD'F file) noun [C] (**COMPUTING**) a file FORMAT that allows a document to be sent electronically and look exactly the same when viewed on different computer systems (the abbreviation for 'Portable Document Format'): *I'll send it to you as a PDF.*

PE /ˌpiː 'iː/ noun [U] (**EDUCATION**) sport and exercise that is taught in schools (the abbreviation for 'physical education'): *a PE lesson*

pea /piː/ noun [C] a small round green seed that is eaten as a vegetable. A number of peas grow together in a POD (= a long thin case).

peace 🔒 **A2** /piːs/ noun [U] **1** a situation or a period of time in which there is no war or violence in a country or an area: *The two communities now manage to live in peace together.* ◊ *UN forces have been sent in to keep the peace.* **2** the state of being calm or quiet: *He longed to escape from the city to the peace and quiet of the countryside.*
IDM **make (your) peace with sb** to end an argument with sb, usually by saying you are sorry

peaceful 🔒 **B1** /'piːsfl/ adj. **1** not wanting or involving war, violence or argument: *a peaceful protest/ demonstration/solution* **2** calm and quiet: *a peaceful village* ▶ **peacefully** /-fəli/ adv.: *The siege ended peacefully.* ▶ **peacefulness** noun [U]

peacekeeping /'piːskiːpɪŋ/ adj. [only before noun] (**POLITICS**) intended to help keep the peace and prevent war or violence in a place where this is likely: *a United Nations peacekeeping force*

peacemaker /'piːsmeɪkə(r)/ noun [C] (**POLITICS**) a person who tries to persuade people or countries to stop arguing or fighting and to make peace

peacetime /'piːstaɪm/ noun [U] a period when a country is not at war

peach¹ /piːtʃ/ noun **1** [C] a soft round fruit with a red and yellow skin and a large stone in the centre **2** [U] a colour between pink and orange

peach² /piːtʃ/ adj. between pink and orange in colour

peacock /'piːkɒk/ noun [C] a large male bird with long blue and green tail feathers that it can lift up and spread out

peak¹ 🔒 **C1** /piːk/ noun [C] **1** the point at which sth is the highest, best, strongest, etc: *a man at the peak of his career* **2** (*BrE*) (*AmE* bill) the stiff front part of a cap

that sticks out above your eyes **3** (**GEOGRAPHY**) the pointed top of a mountain: *snow-covered peaks* ⊃ picture at **glacial**

peak² /piːk/ verb [I] to reach the highest point or value: *Sales peak just before Christmas.* ◊ *Unemployment peaked at 17%.*

peak³ /piːk/ adj. [only before noun] (**TOURISM**) used to describe the highest level of sth, or a time when the greatest number of people are doing or using sth: *Summer is the peak period for most hotels.* ◊ *The athletes are all in peak condition.* ◊ *We need extra help during the peak season.* ⊃ look at **off-peak**

peal /piːl/ noun [C] **~ (of sth) 1** a loud sound or series of sounds: *peals of laughter* **2** the loud ringing of a bell or bells ▶ **peal** verb [I]

peanut /'piːnʌt/ noun **1** (*BrE also* groundnut) [C] a nut that grows underground in a thin shell **2** peanuts [pl.] (*informal*) a very small amount of money: *We get paid peanuts for doing this job.*

peanut 'butter noun [U] a thick soft substance made from PEANUTS, usually eaten spread on bread

pear /peə(r)/ noun [C] a fruit that has a yellow or green skin and is white inside. Pears are wider at the bottom than at the top.

pearl /pɜːl/ noun [C] a small hard shiny white ball that is used as jewellery. Pearls grow inside the shells of OYSTERS (= sea creatures with large flat shells): *pearl earrings*

peasant 🔒+ **C1** /'peznt/ noun [C] (used especially in past times) a person who owns or rents a small piece of land on which they grow food and keep animals in order to feed their family

peat /piːt/ noun [U] (**AGRICULTURE**) a soft black or brown natural substance that is formed from dead plants just under the surface of the ground in cool, wet places. It can be burned as a fuel or used in the garden to make plants grow better.

pebble /'pebl/ noun [C] a small smooth round stone that is found in or near water

pecan /'piːkən, pɪ'kæn/ noun [C] a type of nut with a smooth pink-brown shell

peck /pek/ verb **1** [I, T] **~ (at) sth** (used about a bird) to eat or bite sth with its BEAK (= the hard pointed part of a bird's mouth) **2** [T] **~ sb on sth; ~ sth** (*informal*) to kiss sb quickly and lightly: *She pecked him on the cheek and then left.* ◊ *He pecked her cheek.* ▶ **peck** noun [C]
IDM **a/the pecking order** (*informal*) the order of importance in relation to one another among the members of a group: *A number of players are ahead of him in the pecking order.*

peckish /'pekɪʃ/ adj. (*BrE, informal*) hungry

pectoral /'pektərəl/ adj. (**BIOLOGY**) on or connected with the chest or breast of a fish or an animal: *pectoral fins* ⊃ look at **dorsal**, **ventral**

pectorals /'pektərəlz/ (*also informal* pecs /peks/) noun [pl.] (**ANATOMY**) the muscles of the chest

peculiar 🔒+ **C1** /pɪ'kjuːliə(r)/ adj. **1** unusual or strange: *There's a very peculiar smell in here.* **SYN** funny, odd **2** **~ to sb/sth** only belonging to one person or found in one place: *a species of bird peculiar to south-east Asia*

peculiarity /pɪˌkjuːli'ærəti/ noun (*pl.* -ies) **1** [C] a strange or unusual characteristic, quality or habit: *There are some peculiarities in her behaviour.* **2** [C] a characteristic or a quality that only belongs to one particular person, thing or place: *the cultural peculiarities of the English* **3** [U] the quality of being strange or unusual

peculiarly /pɪ'kjuːliəli/ adv. **1** especially; very: *Some people's laughs can be peculiarly annoying.* **2** in a way that is especially typical of one person, thing or place:

a peculiarly French custom **3** in a strange and unusual way: *Luke is behaving very peculiarly.*

ped- /piːd/ (*AmE*) = PAED-

pedagogic /ˌpedəˈɡɒdʒɪk/ (*also* **pedagogical** /ˌpedəˈɡɒdʒɪkl/) *adj.* (**EDUCATION**) connected with ways of teaching

pedagogy /ˈpedəɡɒdʒi/ *noun* [U] (**EDUCATION**) the study of teaching methods

pedal¹ /ˈpedl/ *noun* [C] the part of a bicycle, car or other machine that you push with your foot in order to make it move or work ➔ picture at **piano**

pedal² /ˈpedl/ *verb* [I, T] (often used with an adverb or a preposition) (-ll-, *AmE* -l-) **1** to ride a bicycle somewhere: *She jumped on her bike and pedalled off.* ◇ *He pedalled his bike along the track.* **2** to turn or press the PEDALS on a bicycle: *She had to pedal hard to get up the hill.*

pedantic /pɪˈdæntɪk/ *adj.* too worried about rules or details ▸ **pedantically** /-kli/ *adv.*

pedestal /ˈpedɪstl/ *noun* [C] the base on which a column, statue, etc. stands

pedestrian /pəˈdestriən/ *noun* [C] a person who is walking in the street (not travelling in a vehicle) ➔ look at **motorist**

pe,destrian ˈcrossing (*BrE*) (*AmE* **crosswalk**) *noun* [C] a place where vehicles must stop to allow people to cross the road ➔ look at **zebra crossing**

pedestrianize (*BrE also* -ise) /pəˈdestriənaɪz/ *verb* [T] to make a street or part of a town into an area that is only for people who are walking, not for vehicles: *Most of the city streets have been pedestrianized.*

pediatrician, pediatrics, pediatric (*AmE*) = PAEDIATRICIAN, PAEDIATRICS, PAEDIATRIC

pedigree¹ /ˈpedɪɡriː/ *noun* [C] **1** an official record of the parents, grandfather, etc. of an animal ➔ look at **mongrel 2** a person's family history, especially when this is impressive

pedigree² /ˈpedɪɡriː/ *adj.* [only before noun] (used about an animal) of high quality because the parents, grandfather, grandmother, etc. are all of the same BREED (= variety) and specifically chosen

pediment /ˈpedɪmənt/ *noun* [C] (**ARCHITECTURE**) the part in the shape of a TRIANGLE above the entrance of a building in the ancient Greek style

pedophile, pedophilia (*AmE*) = PAEDOPHILE, PAEDOPHILIA

pee /piː/ *verb* [I] (*informal*) to get rid of waste water from the body **SYN** **urinate** ▸ **pee** *noun* [U, sing.]

peek /piːk/ *verb* [I] ~ **(at sth)** to look at sth quickly and secretly because you should not be looking at it: *No peeking at your presents before your birthday!* ▸ **peek** *noun* [sing.]: *to have a quick peek*

peel¹ /piːl/ *verb* **1** [T] to take the skin off a piece of fruit or a vegetable: *Could you peel the potatoes, please?* **2** [T, I] ~ **(sth) (off/away/back)** to come off or to take sth off a surface in one piece or in small pieces: *I peeled off the price label before handing her the book.* **IDM** **keep your eyes peeled/skinned (for sb/sth)** → EYE¹

peel² /piːl/ *noun* [U] the skin of fruit or vegetables: *apple/potato peel* ➔ look at **rind, skin¹** (4)

peeler /ˈpiːlə(r)/ *noun* [C] a special knife for taking the skin off fruit and vegetables: *a potato peeler*

peep¹ /piːp/ *verb* [I] **1** (often used with an adverb or a preposition) to look to sth quickly and secretly, especially through a small opening: *Could I just peep inside?* **2** to be just able to be seen: *The moon peeped out from behind the clouds.*

peep² /piːp/ *noun* [sing.] **1** a quick look: *Have a peep in the bedroom and see if the baby is asleep.* **2** a sound: *There hasn't been a peep out of the children for hours.*

peer¹ ʔ+ B2 /pɪə(r)/ *noun* [C] (**SOCIAL STUDIES**) **1** a person who is of the same age or position in society as you: *Children hate to look stupid in front of their peers.* **2** (in the UK) a member of the NOBILITY (= people of the highest social class, who have special titles)

peer² /pɪə(r)/ *verb* [I] (used with an adverb or a preposition) to look closely or carefully at sb/sth, for example because you cannot see very well: *He peered at the photo, but it was blurred.* ◇ *She went to the window and peered out.*

peerage /ˈpɪərɪdʒ/ *noun* **1** [sing.] all the PEERS as a group **2** [C] the rank (= social position) of a PEER

ˈpeer group *noun* [C] (**SOCIAL STUDIES**) a group of people who are all of the same age and social position

ˌpeer reˈview *noun* [U, C] a judgement on a piece of scientific or other professional work by others working in the same area: *All research proposals are subject to peer review before selection.* ▸ **peer-reviewed** *adj.*: *peer-reviewed journals*

ˌpeer-to-ˈpeer *adj.* [only before noun] (**COMPUTING**) in which each computer can act as a SERVER for the others, allowing data to be shared without the need for a central SERVER

peeved /piːvd/ *adj.* ~ **(about sth)** (*informal*) quite angry or annoyed

peevish /ˈpiːvɪʃ/ *adj.* annoyed by things that are not important ▸ **peevishly** *adv.*

peg¹ /peɡ/ *noun* [C] **1** a piece of wood, metal, etc. on a wall or door that you hang your coat on **2** (*also* **tent peg**) a piece of metal that you push into the ground to keep one of the ropes of a tent in place **3** (*BrE*) (*AmE* **clothespin**) a type of small wooden or plastic object used for fastening wet clothes to a clothes line

peg² /peɡ/ *verb* [T] (-gg-) **1** ~ **sth (out)** to fasten sth with a PEG **2** ~ **sth (at/to sth)** to fix or keep sth at a certain level: *Wage increases were pegged at 5%.*

pelican /ˈpelɪkən/ *noun* [C] a large bird that lives near water. A pelican has a large BEAK (= the hard pointed part of a bird's mouth) that it uses for catching and holding fish.

pellet /ˈpelɪt/ *noun* [C] **1** a small hard ball of any substance, often of soft material that has become hard **2** a very small metal ball that is fired from a gun: *shotgun pellets*

pelt /pelt/ *verb* **1** [T] ~ **sb (with sth)** to attack sb/sth by throwing things: *The speaker was pelted with tomatoes.* **2** [I] ~ **(down)** (used about rain) to fall very heavily: *It's absolutely pelting down.* **3** [I] (used with an adverb or a preposition) (*informal*) to run very fast: *Some kids pelted past us.*

pelvis /ˈpelvɪs/ *noun* [C] (*pl.* **pelvises**) (**ANATOMY**) the set of wide bones at the bottom of the back, to which the leg bones are joined ➔ picture at **body** ▸ **pelvic** /-vɪk/ *adj.* [only before noun]

pen ʔ A1 /pen/ *noun* [C] **1** an object that you use for writing in INK: *a ballpoint/felt-tip/marker/fountain pen* **2** (**AGRICULTURE**) a small piece of ground with a fence around it that is used for keeping animals in

penal /ˈpiːnl/ *adj.* [only before noun] (**LAW**) connected with punishment by law: *the penal system*

penalize (*BrE also* -ise) /ˈpiːnəlaɪz/ *verb* [T] **1** (**LAW**) to punish sb for breaking a law or rule **2** to cause sb to have a disadvantage: *Children should not be penalized because their parents cannot afford to pay.*

penalty ℰ+ **B2** /ˈpenəlti/ *noun* [C] (*pl.* -ies) **1** (**LAW**) a punishment for breaking a law, rule or contract: *the death penalty* ◇ *What's the maximum penalty for using your mobile phone while driving?* **2** a disadvantage or sth unpleasant that happens as the result of sth: *I didn't work hard enough and I paid the penalty: I failed all my exams.* **3** (**SPORT**) a punishment for one team and an advantage for the other team because a rule has been broken: *The referee awarded a penalty to the home team.*

penalty area (*BrE also* **penalty box**) *noun* [C] (**SPORT**) the marked area in front of the goal in football

penalty box *noun* [C] (**SPORT**) **1** (*BrE*) = PENALTY AREA **2** (in ICE HOCKEY) an area next to the ice where a player who has broken the rules must wait for a short time

penalty ˈshoot-out *noun* [C] (**SPORT**) (in football) a way of deciding who wins when both teams have the same score at the end of a game. Each team has a number of chances to kick the ball into the goal and the team that scores the most goals wins.

penance /ˈpenəns/ *noun* [C, usually sing., U] a punishment that you give yourself to show you are sorry for doing sth wrong

pence /pens/ plural of **penny**

pencil¹ ℰ **A1** /ˈpensl/ *noun* [C, U] an object that you use for writing or drawing. Pencils are usually made of wood and contain a thin stick of a black or coloured substance: *Bring a pencil and paper with you.* ◇ *Write in pencil, not ink.* ⊃ picture at **refraction**

pencil² /ˈpensl/ *verb* [T] (-ll-, *AmE* -l-) to write or draw sth with a pencil
PHR V **pencil sth/sb in** to write down the details of an arrangement that might have to be changed later: *Shall we pencil the next meeting in for 14 May?*

pencil case *noun* [C] a small bag or box that you keep pens, pencils, etc. in

pencil sharpener *noun* [C] a small device that you use for making pencils sharp

pendant /ˈpendənt/ *noun* [C] a piece of jewellery that you wear around your neck on a chain

pending /ˈpendɪŋ/ *adj., prep.* (*formal*) **1** waiting to be done or decided: *The judge's decision is still pending.* **2** until sth happens: *He took over the leadership pending the elections.*

pen drive = FLASH DRIVE

pendulum /ˈpendʒələm/ *noun* [C] a chain or stick with a heavy weight at the bottom that moves regularly from side to side to work a clock: (*figurative*) *Since last year's election, the pendulum of public opinion has swung against the government.*

penetrate /ˈpenətreɪt/ *verb* **1** [T, I] to go or get into or through sth, especially when this is difficult: *The knife penetrated her arm.* ◇ *They managed to penetrate airport security.* ◇ *The car's headlamps could not penetrate the thick fog.* **2** [T] to manage to understand sth difficult: *Scientists have still not penetrated the workings of the brain.* **3** [I, T] to be understood or realized: *I was back at home when the meaning of her words finally penetrated.* ▸ **penetration** /ˌpenəˈtreɪʃn/ *noun* [U]

penetrating /ˈpenətreɪtɪŋ/ *adj.* **1** (used about sb's eyes or of a way of looking) making you feel uncomfortable because it seems sb knows what you are thinking: *a penetrating look/stare/gaze* ◇ *penetrating blue eyes* **2** loud and hard **3** spreading deeply or widely **4** showing that you have understood sth completely and quickly: *a penetrating question/comment*

penfriend /ˈpenfrend/ (*BrE*) (*also* **pen pal** *especially in AmE*) *noun* [C] a person that you become friendly with by exchanging letters or emails, often a person that you have never met

penguin /ˈpeŋgwɪn/ *noun* [C] a black and white bird that cannot fly and that lives in the Antarctic. There are several types of penguin.

penicillin /ˌpenɪˈsɪlɪn/ *noun* [U] (**MEDICINE**) a substance that is used as a drug for preventing and treating infections caused by bacteria

peninsula /pəˈnɪnsjələ/ *noun* [C] (**GEOGRAPHY**) an area of land that is almost surrounded by water

penis /ˈpiːnɪs/ *noun* [C] (**ANATOMY**) the male sex organ that is used for getting rid of waste liquid and having sex

penitent /ˈpenɪtənt/ *adj.* sorry for having done sth wrong **SYN** **remorseful**

penitentiary /ˌpenɪˈtenʃəri/ *noun* [C] (*pl.* -ies) (*AmE*) a prison

penknife /ˈpennaɪf/ *noun* [C] (*pl.* -knives /ˈpennaɪvz/) a small knife with one or more BLADES (= parts used for cutting) that fold down into the handle

penniless /ˈpeniləs/ *adj.* having no money; poor

penny ℰ **A2** /ˈpeni/ *noun* [C] (*pl.* **pence** /pens/, **pennies**) **1** (*abbr.* p) a small British coin and unit of money. There are 100 pence in a pound: *a 50-pence piece/coin* **2** (*AmE*) a cent

pen pal /ˈpen pæl/ (*especially AmE*) = PENFRIEND

pension¹ ℰ **B2** /ˈpenʃn/ *noun* [C] money that is paid regularly by a government or company to sb who has stopped working because they have reached a particular age or because they are ill ⊃ note at **job** ▸ **pensioner** /-ʃənə(r)/ *noun* [C] ⊃ look at **senior citizen**

pension² /ˈpenʃn/ *verb*
PHR V **pension sb off** (*especially BrE*) to allow or force sb to retire and to pay them a pension: *He was pensioned off and his job given to a younger man.*

penta- /ˈpentə, penˈtæ/ *prefix* (in nouns, adjectives and adverbs) five; having five: *pentathlon*

pentagon /ˈpentəgən/ *noun* **1** [C] (**GEOMETRY**) a shape that has five straight and equal sides **2 the Pentagon** [sing.] (**POLITICS**) a large government building near Washington DC in the US that contains the main offices of the US Department of Defense; the military officials who work there

pentameter /penˈtæmɪtə(r)/ *noun* [C, U] (**LITERATURE**) a line of poetry with five stressed syllables; the rhythm of poetry with five stressed syllables to a line

pentathlon /penˈtæθlən/ *noun* [C] (**SPORT**) a sports competition in which you have to take part in five different events ⊃ look at **biathlon, decathlon, triathlon**

pentatonic /ˌpentəˈtɒnɪk/ *adj.* (**MUSIC**) related to or based on a SCALE (= a series) of five notes

penthouse /ˈpenthaʊs/ *noun* [C] an expensive flat at the top of a tall building

pent-up /ˌpent ˈʌp/ *adj.* [only before noun] (used about feelings) that you hold inside and do not express: *pent-up anger*

penultimate /pəˈnʌltɪmət/ *adj.* (in a series) the one before the last one: *'Y' is the penultimate letter of the alphabet.*

penumbra /pəˈnʌmbrə/ *noun* [C] (*pl.* **penumbras**, **penumbrae** /-briː/) **1** the outer part of a shadow, which is less dark than the central part **2** (**ASTRONOMY**) a dark area on the earth caused by the moon, or a dark area on the moon caused by the earth, during a PARTIAL ECLIPSE (= a time when the moon comes between the earth and the sun, or when the earth comes between the moon and the sun) ⊃ look at umbra (2) ⊃ picture at **shadow**[1]

people 🔒**A1** /ˈpiːpl/ noun **1** [pl.] more than one person: *How many people are coming to the party?* **2** [C] (*pl.* **peoples**) (*formal*) all the men, women and children who belong to a particular place or human group: *The president addressed the American people.* ◇ *the French-speaking peoples of the world* **3** [pl.] men and women who work in a particular activity: *business/ sports people* **4** the people [pl.] the ordinary citizens of a country: *The president was popular because he listened to the people.*

people carrier (*BrE*) (*also* **minivan** *especially in AmE*) *noun* [C] a large car, like a van, designed to carry up to eight people **SYN** **MPV**

pepper[1] 🔒**A1** /ˈpepə(r)/ *noun* **1** [U] a black or white powder with a hot taste that is used to give a hot, spicy taste to food: *salt and pepper* **2** [C, U] (*BrE*) (*AmE* **bell pepper** [C]) a green, red or yellow vegetable that is almost empty inside

pepper[2] /ˈpepə(r)/ *verb* [T, usually passive] ~ **sb/sth with sth** to hit sb/sth with a series of small objects, especially bullets: *The wall had been peppered with bullets.*

peppercorn /ˈpepəkɔːn/ *noun* [C] a dried BERRY from a tropical plant, that is pressed into small pieces or powder to make pepper

peppermint /ˈpepəmɪnt/ *noun* **1** [U] a plant with a strong fresh taste that is used in sweets and medicines ⊃ look at **spearmint** **2** [C] a sweet made with peppermint oil

pepperoni /ˌpepəˈrəʊni/ *noun* [U] a type of Italian SAUSAGE with a strong hot taste: *a pepperoni pizza*

pepsin /ˈpepsɪn/ *noun* [U] (**BIOLOGY**) the main ENZYME (= a substance that helps a chemical change take place) in the stomach that breaks down PROTEIN

pep talk /ˈpep tɔːk/ *noun* [C] (*informal*) a speech that is given to encourage people or to make them work harder

peptide /ˈpeptaɪd/ *noun* [C] (**CHEMISTRY**) a chemical consisting of two or more AMINO ACIDS joined together

per 🔒**A2** ⊙ /pə(r), *strong form* pɜː(r)/ *prep.* for each: *The speed limit is 110 kilometres per hour.*

per annum /pər ˈænəm/ *adv.* (*abbr.* **p.a.**) for each year: *earning £30 000 per annum*

per capita /pə ˈkæpɪtə/ *adj., adv.* (**BUSINESS**) for each person: *Per capita income rose sharply last year.* ◇ *average earnings per capita*

perceive 🔒+ **B2** ⊙ /pəˈsiːv/ *verb* [T] (*formal*) **1** ~ **sb/ sth/yourself (as sth)** to understand or think of sb/ sth in a particular way: *I perceived his comments as a criticism.* **SYN** **see** ⊃ note at **regard**[1] ⊃ noun **perception** **2** to notice or realize sth: *Scientists failed to perceive how dangerous the level of pollution had become.*

WORD FAMILY
perceive *verb*
perception *noun*
perceptive *adj.*
perceptible *adj.*
(≠imperceptible)

per cent[1] 🔒**A2** ⊙ (*especially BrE*) (*AmE usually* **percent**) *noun* [C + sing./pl. verb] (*pl.* **per cent, percent**) (*symb.* **%**) ~ **(of sth)** one part in every hundred: *You get 10 per cent off if you pay cash.* ◇ *90 per cent of the population owns/own a TV.* ◇ *The price of bread has gone up by 50 per cent in two years.*

per cent[2] 🔒**A2** ⊙ (*especially BrE*) (*AmE usually* **percent**) *adj., adv.* (*symb.* **%**) (**MATHEMATICS**) by, in or for every hundred: *House prices dropped 8 per cent last year.*

percentage 🔒**B1** ⊙ /pəˈsentɪdʒ/ *noun* [C + sing./pl. verb] (**MATHEMATICS**) the number, amount, rate, etc. of sth, expressed as if it is part of a total that is 100; a part or share of a whole: *What percentage of people voted in the last election?*

percentile /pəˈsentaɪl/ *noun* [C] (**MATHEMATICS**) one of the 100 equal groups that a larger group of people can be divided into in order to compare sth, for example weight or test results: *Overall these students rank in the 21st percentile on the tests — that is, they did worse than 79 per cent of all children taking the test.*

perceptible /pəˈseptəbl/ *adj.* (*formal*) that can be seen or felt: *a barely perceptible change in colour* **OPP** **imperceptible** ▸ **perceptibly** /-bli/ *adv.*

perception 🔒+ **B2** ⊙ /pəˈsepʃn/ *noun* **1** [C] a particular way of looking at or understanding sth; an opinion: *What is your perception of the situation?* ⊃ verb **perceive** **2** [U] (*formal*) the ability to notice or understand sth

perceptive /pəˈseptɪv/ *adj.* quick to notice or understand things ▸ **perceptively** *adv.*

perch[1] /pɜːtʃ/ *verb* ~ **(on sth)** **1** [I] (used about a bird) to sit on a branch, etc: *The robin was perching on a fence.* **2** [I, T] to sit or be put on the edge of sth: *The house was perched on the edge of a cliff.*

perch[2] /pɜːtʃ/ *noun* [C] a place where a bird sits, especially a branch or a bar in a CAGE

percolate /ˈpɜːkəleɪt/ *verb* **1** [I] (often used with an adverb or a preposition) (used about a liquid, gas, etc.) to move gradually through a surface that has very small holes or spaces in it: *Water had percolated down through the rocks.* **2** [I] to gradually become known or spread through a group or society **3** [T, I] to make coffee in a PERCOLATOR; to be made in this way ▸ **percolation** /ˌpɜːkəˈleɪʃn/ *noun* [U]

percolator /ˈpɜːkəleɪtə(r)/ *noun* [C] a pot for making coffee, in which boiling water is forced up a central tube and then comes down again through the coffee ⊃ look at **cafetière**

percussion /pəˈkʌʃn/ *noun* [U] (**MUSIC**) drums and other instruments that you play by hitting them ▸ note at **instrument** ⊃ picture at **instrument, orchestra**

percussionist /pəˈkʌʃənɪst/ *noun* [C] (**MUSIC**) a person who plays PERCUSSION instruments, for example drums

perennial[1] /pəˈreniəl/ *adj.* **1** that happens often or that lasts for a very long time: *a perennial problem* **2** (**BIOLOGY**) (used about plants) living for two years or more

perennial[2] /pəˈreniəl/ *noun* [C] (**BIOLOGY**) any plant that lives for more than two years ⊃ look at **annual**[2] (2), **biennial**[2]

perfect[1] 🔒**A1** /ˈpɜːfɪkt/ *adj.* **1** completely good; without faults or weaknesses: *The car is two years old but it is still in perfect condition.* **OPP** **imperfect** **2** ~ **(for sb/sth)** exactly suitable or right: *Ken would be perfect for the job.* **3** [only before noun] complete; total: *What he was saying made perfect sense to me.* ◇ *a perfect stranger* **4** (**GRAMMAR**) used to describe the form of a verb that consists of the verb *have* and the past participle of the main verb ▸ **perfectly** 🔒**B1** ⊙ *adv.*: *He played the piece of music perfectly.*

perfect[2] /pəˈfekt/ *verb* [T] to make sth perfect: *He's spending a year in France to perfect his French.*

the perfect (*also the* **perfect tense**) *noun* [sing.] (**GRAMMAR**) the form of a verb that is formed with *has/ have/had* and the past participle: '*I've finished*' *is in the present perfect tense.*

perfection /pə'fekʃn/ *noun* [U] the state of being perfect or without fault: *The steak was cooked to perfection.*

perfectionist /pə'fekʃənɪst/ *noun* [C] a person who always does things as well as he/she possibly can and who expects others to do the same ▸ **perfectionism** /-nɪzəm/ *noun* [U]

perforate /'pɜːfəreɪt/ *verb* [T] to make a hole or holes in sth

perforation /ˌpɜːfə'reɪʃn/ *noun* **1** [C] a series of small holes in paper, etc. that make it easy for you to tear **2** [U] the process of making a hole or holes in sth

perform 🔑 **A2 ⊙** /pə'fɔːm/ *verb* **1** [T] to do a piece of work or sth that you have been ordered to do: *to perform an operation/an experiment/a task* **2** [I, T] (**ARTS AND MEDIA**) to take part in a play or to sing, dance, etc. in front of an audience: *She is currently performing at the National Theatre.* ⊃ note at **performing arts** [I] ~ **(well/badly/poorly)** to work or function well or badly: *The company has not been performing well recently.*
IDM work/perform miracles → MIRACLE

performance 🔑 **B1 ⓦ** /pə'fɔːməns/ *noun* **1** [C] the act of performing sth in front of an audience; sth that you perform: *What time does the performance start?* **2** [U, C] (**ARTS AND MEDIA**) the way a person performs in a play, concert, etc: *His moving performance in the film won him an Oscar.* **3** [U] the way in which you do sth, especially how successful you are: *The company's performance was disappointing last year.* **4** [U] (used about a machine, etc.) how well or badly sth works: *This car has a high performance engine.* **5** [U, sing.] (*formal*) the act or process of doing a task, an action, etc: *the performance of your duties*

per'formance art *noun* [U] (**ART**) an art form in which an artist gives a performance, rather than producing a physical work of art

performer /pə'fɔːmə(r)/ *noun* [C] **1** (**ARTS AND MEDIA**) a person who performs for an audience **2** a person or thing that behaves or works in the way mentioned: *Diana is a poor performer in exams.*

the per forming 'arts *noun* [pl.] (**ARTS AND MEDIA**) arts such as music, dance and drama, which are performed for an audience

---

▼ COLLOCATIONS

the performing arts

A **composer** writes a **song/a musical/an opera.** A **playwright** or **dramatist** writes **plays:** *He's written a new musical.* A group **presents/performs/produces/puts on/ stages** a play, show, etc: *The drama group is putting on a show at the local school.* ◇ *We are proud to present Arthur Miller's 'The Crucible'.* A **director directs** a play, show, etc: *The theatre has got a new director.* ◇ *She is directing Mozart's 'Figaro' at La Scala.* A performer, an actor, etc. **acts/ appears/performs/sings/stars** in a play, show, etc: *She's appearing in 'The Seagull' at the New Theatre.* ◇ *He starred in the musical 'Guys and Dolls'.* A performer, an actor, etc. **rehearses (for)** a play, show, etc: *She had three weeks to rehearse for the concert.*

---

perfume /'pɜːfjuːm/ *noun* [C, U] **1** a liquid with a sweet smell that you put on your body to make yourself smell nice: *Are you wearing perfume?* **SYN** **scent 2** a pleasant, often sweet, smell **SYN** **fragrance, scent**

perhaps 🔑 **A2 ⓢ** /pə'hæps, præps/ *adv.* (used when you are not sure about sth) possibly; maybe: *Perhaps he's forgotten.* ◇ *She was, perhaps, one of the most famous writers of the time.* **SYN** **maybe**

---

pericardium /ˌperi'kɑːdiəm/ *noun* [C] (*pl.* pericardia /-diə/) (**ANATOMY**) the MEMBRANE (= thin layer) that surrounds the heart

peril /'perəl/ *noun* (*formal*) **1** [U] great danger: *A lack of trained nurses is putting patients' lives in peril.* **2** [C] something that is very dangerous: *the perils of drug abuse* ▸ **perilous** /-rələs/ *adj.*

perimeter /pə'rɪmɪtə(r)/ *noun* [C] the outside edge or limit of an area of land: *the perimeter fence of the army camp*

period 🔑 **A1 ⊙** /'pɪəriəd/ *noun* [C] **1** (**HISTORY**) a length of time: *The scheme will be introduced for a six-month trial period.* ◇ *Her son is going through a difficult period at the moment.* ◇ *What period of history are you most interested in?* **2** (**EDUCATION**) a lesson in school: *We have five periods of English a week.* **3** (**HEALTH**) the time every month when a woman loses blood from her body **4** (*AmE*) = **FULL STOP**

periodic /ˌpɪəri'ɒdɪk/ (*also* **periodical**) *adj.* happening regularly and fairly often: *We have periodic meetings to check on progress.* ▸ **periodically** /-kli/ *adv.*: *All machines need to be checked periodically.*

periodical /ˌpɪəri'ɒdɪkl/ *noun* [C] (**ARTS AND MEDIA**) a magazine that is produced regularly, especially one that is about an academic subject

the ˌperiodic 'table *noun* [sing.] (**CHEMISTRY**) a list of all the chemical elements, arranged according to the number of PROTONS that they each have in their NUCLEUS (= central part) **❶** For more information on the periodic table of elements, look at the **Reference Section** of this dictionary.

peripheral¹ /pə'rɪfərəl/ *adj.* **1** ~ **(to sth)** (*formal*) not as important as the main aim, part, etc. of sth **2** connected with the outer edge of a particular area: *the peripheral nervous system* ◇ *peripheral vision* **3** (**COMPUTING**) (used about equipment) connected to a computer: *a peripheral device* ▸ **peripherally** /-rəli/ *adv.*

peripheral² /pə'rɪfərəl/ *noun* [C] (**COMPUTING**) a piece of equipment that is connected to a computer

periphery /pə'rɪfəri/ *noun* [C, usually sing.] (*pl.* -ies) (*formal*) **1** the outer edge of a particular area: *an industrial development on the periphery of town* **2** the less important part of sth, for example of a particular activity or of a social or political group: *minor parties on the periphery of American politics*

periscope /'perɪskəʊp/ *noun* [C] a device like a long tube, containing mirrors that allow you to see over the top of sth, used especially in a SUBMARINE (= a ship that can travel UNDERWATER) to see above the surface of the water

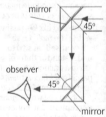
periscope

perish /'perɪʃ/ *verb* [I] (*formal*) to die or be destroyed: *Thousands perished in the war.*

perishable /'perɪʃəbl/ *adj.* (used about food) that will go bad quickly

peristalsis /ˌperi'stælsɪs/ *noun* [U] (**BIOLOGY**) the wave-like movements of the large tubes inside the body when the muscles pull tight and relax to push sth out or along

perjury /'pɜːdʒəri/ *noun* [U] (**LAW**) the act of telling a lie in court ▸ **perjure** /-dʒə(r)/ *verb* [T] ~ **yourself**: *She admitted that she had perjured herself while giving evidence.*

perk¹ /pɜːk/ *verb*

PHRV **perk (sb/sth) up** to become or make sb become happier and have more energy

perk² /pɜːk/ *noun* [C, usually pl.] something extra that you get from your employer in addition to money: *Travelling abroad is one of the perks of the job.*

perm /pɜːm/ *noun* [C] the treatment of hair with special chemicals in order to make it curly ⊃ look at **wave¹** (6) ▸ **perm** *verb* [T]: *She has had her hair permed.*

permaculture /ˈpɜːməkʌltʃə(r)/ *noun* [U] (**AGRICULTURE**) a way of living and growing food that copies the way things happen in nature in order to cause less damage to the environment: *The farm's mission is to create food security through permaculture and organic farming.*

permafrost /ˈpɜːməfrɒst/ *noun* [U] (**GEOGRAPHY**) a layer of soil that is permanently frozen, in very cold regions of the world

permanent 🔒 **B2** /ˈpɜːmənənt/ *adj.* lasting for a long time or for ever; that will not change: *The accident left him with a permanent scar.* ◇ *Are you looking for a permanent or a temporary job?* ⊃ note at **job** ▸ **permanence** /-mənəns/ *noun* [U] ▸ **permanently** 🔒+ **B2** *adv.*: *Has she left permanently?*

permeable /ˈpɜːmiəbl/ *adj.* ~ **(to sth)** allowing a liquid or gas to pass through: *A frog's skin is permeable to water.* **OPP** **impermeable** ⊃ picture at **petroleum** ▸ **permeability** /ˌpɜːmiəˈbɪləti/ *noun* [U]

permissible /pəˈmɪsəbl/ *adj.* ~ **(for sb) (to do sth)** (*formal*) that is allowed by law or by a set of rules: *It is not permissible for banks to release their customers' personal details.*

permission 🔒 **A2** /pəˈmɪʃn/ *noun* [U] ~ **(for sth)**; ~ **(for sb/sth) (to do sth)** the act of allowing sb to do sth, especially when this is done by sb in a position of authority: *You must ask permission for all major expenditure.* ◇ *His parents gave permission for him to take part.* ◇ *I'm afraid you can't leave without permission.*

permissive /pəˈmɪsɪv/ *adj.* having, allowing or showing a lot of freedom that many people do not approve of, especially in sexual matters

permit¹ 🔒 **B2** 🌐 /pəˈmɪt/ *verb* (-tt-) **1** [T, often passive] ~ **(sb to do sth)** to allow sb to do sth; to allow sth to happen: *His visa does not permit him to work.* ◇ *You are not permitted to use mobile phones in school.* **2** [I, T] to make sth possible: *Let's have a barbecue at the weekend, weather permitting.*

permit² 🔒 **B2** /ˈpɜːmɪt/ *noun* [C] an official document that says you are allowed to do sth, especially for a limited period of time: *Next month I'll have to apply for a new work permit.*

peroxide /pəˈrɒksaɪd/ (*also* **hydrogen peroxide**) *noun* [U] (**CHEMISTRY**) a clear liquid that is used to kill bacteria or to make hair a lighter colour

perpendicular /ˌpɜːpənˈdɪkjələ(r)/ *adj.* **1** ~ **(to sth)** (**GEOMETRY**) at an angle of 90° to sth: *Are the lines perpendicular to each other?* ⊃ look at **horizontal**, **vertical 2** pointing straight up: *The path was almost perpendicular* (= it was very steep).

perpetrate /ˈpɜːpətreɪt/ *verb* [T] ~ **sth (against/upon/on sb)** (*formal*) (**LAW**) to commit a crime or do sth wrong or evil: *to perpetrate a crime/fraud/massacre* ◇ *violence perpetrated against women and children* ▸ **perpetration** /ˌpɜːpəˈtreɪʃn/ *noun* [U]

perpetrator /ˈpɜːpətreɪtə(r)/ *noun* [C] (**LAW**) a person who commits a crime or does sth that is wrong: *the perpetrator of the crime* ◇ *We will do everything in our power to bring the perpetrators to justice.*

perpetual /pəˈpetʃuəl/ *adj.* **1** continuing for a long period of time without stopping: *They lived in perpetual fear of losing their jobs.* **2** frequently repeated in a way that is annoying: *How can I work with these perpetual interruptions?* ▸ **perpetually** /-əli/ *adv.*

perpetuate /pəˈpetʃueɪt/ *verb* [T] (*formal*) to cause sth to continue for a long time: *to perpetuate an argument*

perplexed /pəˈplekst/ *adj.* not understanding sth; confused

persecute /ˈpɜːsɪkjuːt/ *verb* [T] **1** (often passive) ~ **sb (for sth)** (**SOCIAL STUDIES**) to treat sb in a cruel and unfair way, especially because of the human group they belong to, their religion or their political beliefs **2** to deliberately annoy sb and make their life unpleasant ▸ **persecution** /ˌpɜːsɪˈkjuːʃn/ *noun* [U, C]: *the persecution of minorities* ▸ **persecutor** *noun* [C]

persevere /ˌpɜːsəˈvɪə(r)/ *verb* [I] ~ **(at/in/with sth)** to continue trying to do or achieve sth that is difficult: *The treatment is painful but I'm going to persevere with it.* ▸ **perseverance** /-ˈvɪərəns/ *noun* [U]

persist 🔒+ **C1** /pəˈsɪst/ *verb* [I] **1** ~ **(in sth/doing sth)** to continue doing sth even though other people say that you are wrong or that you should not do it: *If you persist in making so much noise, I shall call the police.* **2** to continue to exist: *If your symptoms persist you should consult your doctor.* ▸ **persistence** *noun* [U]: *Finally her persistence was rewarded and she got what she wanted.*

persistent 🔒+ **C1** /pəˈsɪstənt/ *adj.* **1** determined to continue doing sth even though people say that you are wrong or that you should not do it: *Some salesmen can be very persistent.* **2** lasting for a long time or happening often: *a persistent cough* ▸ **persistently** *adv.*

person 🔒 **A1** /ˈpɜːsn/ *noun* [C] (*pl.* **people** /ˈpiːpl/, **persons**) **1** a man or woman; a human being: *I would like to speak to the person in charge.* **2** -person /pɜːsn/ (in nouns) a person doing the job mentioned: *a salesperson/spokesperson* **3** (**GRAMMAR**) one of the three types of pronoun in grammar. *I/we* are the first person, *you* is the second person and *he/she/it/they* are the third person.

IDM **in person** if you do sth **in person**, you go somewhere and do it yourself, instead of doing it by email, asking sb else to do it, etc.

persona /pəˈsəʊnə/ *noun* [C] (*pl.* **personae** /-naɪ/, **personas**) (*formal*) the parts of a person's character that they show to other people, especially when their real character is different: *His public persona is quite different from the quiet man described in the book.*

personal 🔒 **A1** 🌐 /ˈpɜːsnl/ *adj.*

• YOUR OWN **1** [only before noun] of or belonging to one particular person: *personal belongings* ◇ *Judges should not let their personal feelings influence their decisions.*

• FEELINGS, ETC. **2** connected with your feelings, health or relationships with other people: *I'd like to speak to you in private. I have something personal to discuss.* ◇ *Do you mind if I ask you a personal question?*

• NOT OFFICIAL **3** not connected with a person's job or official position: *Please keep personal phone calls to a minimum.* ◇ *I try not to let work interfere with my personal life.*

• DONE BY A PERSON **4** [only before noun] done by a particular person rather than by sb who is acting for them: *The prime minister made a personal visit to the victims in hospital.*

• FOR EACH PERSON **5** [only before noun] made or done for one particular person rather than for a large group of people or people in general: *We offer a personal service to all our customers.*

• OFFENSIVE **6** speaking about sb's appearance or character in an unpleasant or unfriendly way: *It started as a general discussion but then people started to get personal and an argument began.*

• HYGIENE, APPEARANCE, ETC. **7** [only before noun] connected with the body: *personal hygiene* ◇ *She's always worrying about her personal appearance.*

,personal as'sistant *noun* [C] (*abbr.* PA) (**BUSINESS**) a person who works as a secretary or an assistant for one person

,personal com'puter = PC¹ (1)

personality ʔ **A2** /ˌpɜːsəˈnæləti/ *noun* (*pl.* -ies) **1** [C, U] the qualities of a person's character that make them different from other people: *Joe has a kind personality.* **2** [U] the quality of having a strong, interesting and attractive character: *A good entertainer needs a lot of personality.* **3** [C] (**ARTS AND MEDIA**) a famous person (especially in sport, on TV, etc.): *a TV personality* **SYN** celebrity

,perso'nality disorder *noun* [C] (**PSYCHOLOGY**) a serious mental condition in which sb's behaviour makes it difficult for them to have normal relationships with other people

personalize (*BrE also* -ise) /ˈpɜːsənəlaɪz/ *verb* [T, usually passive] to mark sth in some way to show that it belongs to you: *a car with a personalized number plate*

personally ʔ **B1** /ˈpɜːsənəli/ *adv.* **1** used to show that you are expressing your own opinion: *Personally, I think that nurses deserve more money.* **2** done by you yourself, not by sb else acting for you: *I will deal with this matter personally.* **3** in a way that is connected with one particular person rather than a group of people: *I wasn't talking about you personally — I meant all teachers.* **4** in a way that is intended to offend: *Please don't take it personally, but I would just rather be alone this evening.* **5** in a way that is connected with sb's private life, rather than their job: *Have you had any dealings with any of the suspects, either personally or professionally?*

,personal 'pronoun *noun* [C] (**GRAMMAR**) any of the pronouns *I, me, she, her, he, him, we, us, you, they, them*

,personal pro,tective e'quipment *noun* [U] (*abbr.* PPE) (**MEDICINE**) clothing and equipment that is worn or used to protect people against infection or injury

,personal 'trainer *noun* [C] (**SPORT**) a person who is paid by sb to help them exercise, especially by deciding what types of exercise are best for them

persona non grata /pɜːˌsəʊnə nɒn ˈɡrɑːtə, ˌnəʊn/ *noun* [U] (**POLITICS**) a person who is not welcome in a particular place because of sth they have said or done, especially one who is told to leave a country by the government

personification /pəˌsɒnɪfɪˈkeɪʃn/ *noun* **1** [C, usually sing.] ~ of sth a person who has a lot of a particular quality or characteristic: *She was the personification of elegance.* **SYN** epitome **2** [U, C] (**ART, LITERATURE**) the practice of representing objects, qualities, etc. as humans; an object, a quality, etc. that is represented in this way: *the personification of autumn in Keats's poem*

personify /pəˈsɒnɪfaɪ/ *verb* [T] (personifying; personifies; *pt, pp* personified) **1** to be an example in human form of a particular quality: *She is kindness personified.* **2** (**LITERATURE**) to describe an object or a feeling as if it were a person, for example in a poem

personnel ʔ+ **C1** /ˌpɜːsəˈnel/ *noun* **1** [pl.] the people who work for a large organization or one of the armed forces: *sales/medical/technical personnel* **2** (*also* ,person'nel department) [U + sing./pl. verb] (**BUSINESS**) the department of a large company or organization that deals with employing and training people: *Personnel is/are currently reviewing pay scales.* **SYN** human resources

perspective ʔ **B2** ⊙ /pəˈspektɪv/ *noun* **1** [C] your opinion or attitude towards sth: *Try and look at this from my perspective.* **2** [U] the ability to think about problems and decisions in a reasonable way without making them seem more important than they are: *Hearing about others' experiences often helps to put your own problems into perspective* (= makes them seem less important than you thought). ◇ *Try to keep these issues in perspective* (= do not EXAGGERATE them). **3** [U] (**ART**) the art of drawing on a flat surface so that some objects appear to be further away than others

Perspex™ /ˈpɜːspeks/ *noun* [U] a strong clear plastic material that is often used instead of glass

perspire /pəˈspaɪə(r)/ *verb* [I] (*formal*) (**BIOLOGY**) to lose liquid through your skin when you are hot **SYN** sweat ▸ perspiration /ˌpɜːspəˈreɪʃn/ *noun* [U] **SYN** sweat

persuade ʔ **B1** /pəˈsweɪd/ *verb* [T] **1** ~ sb (to do sth); ~ sb (into sth/doing sth) to make sb do sth by giving them good reasons: *It was difficult to persuade Louise to change her mind.* ◇ *We eventually persuaded Sanjay into coming with us.* **OPP** dissuade **2** ~ sb that … ; ~ sb (of sth) (*formal*) to make sb believe sth: *She had persuaded herself that she was going to fail.* ◇ *The jury was not persuaded of his innocence.* ⊃ look at convince

persuasion /pəˈsweɪʒn/ *noun* **1** [U] the act of persuading sb to do sth or to believe sth: *It took a lot of persuasion to get Alan to agree.* **2** [C, U] a religious or political belief: *politicians of all persuasions*

persuasive /pəˈsweɪsɪv/ *adj.* able to persuade sb to do or believe sth: *the persuasive power of advertising* ▸ persuasively *adv.* ▸ persuasiveness *noun* [U]

pertinent /ˈpɜːtɪnənt/ *adj.* (*formal*) closely connected with the subject being discussed: *to ask a pertinent question* **SYN** relevant

perturb /pəˈtɜːb/ *verb* [T] (*formal*) to make sb worried or upset ▸ perturbed *adj.*

peruse /pəˈruːz/ *verb* [T] (*formal*) to read sth, especially in a careful way ▸ perusal /-ˈruːzl/ *noun* [U, sing.]: *The agreement was signed after careful perusal.*

pervade /pəˈveɪd/ *verb* [T] (*formal*) to spread through and be easy to notice in every part of sth: *A sadness pervades most of her novels.*

pervasive /pəˈveɪsɪv/ *adj.* that is present in all parts of sth: *a pervasive mood of pessimism*

perverse /pəˈvɜːs/ *adj.* liking to behave in a way that is not acceptable or reasonable or that most people think is wrong: *David gets perverse pleasure from shocking his parents.* ▸ perversely *adv.* ▸ perversity *noun* [U]

perversion /pəˈvɜːʃn/ *noun* [U, C] **1** sexual behaviour that is not considered normal or acceptable by most people **2** the act of changing sth from right to wrong or from good to bad: *That statement is a perversion of the truth.*

pervert¹ /pəˈvɜːt/ *verb* [T] **1** to change a system, process, etc. in a bad way: *to pervert the course of justice* (= to deliberately prevent the police from finding out the truth about a crime) **2** to cause sb to think or behave in a way that is not moral or acceptable

pervert[2] /'pɜːvɜːt/ noun [C] a person whose sexual behaviour is not thought to be natural or normal by most people

pessimism /'pesɪmɪzəm/ noun [U] ~ **(about/over sth)** a feeling that bad things will happen and that sth will not be successful: *There is a mood of pessimism in the company about future job prospects.* **OPP optimism** ▶ pessimistic /ˌpesɪ'mɪstɪk/ adj. ▶ **pessimistically** /-kli/ adv.

pessimist /'pesɪmɪst/ noun [C] a person who always thinks that bad things will happen **OPP optimist**

pest /pest/ noun [C] **1** (**AGRICULTURE, BIOLOGY**) an insect or animal that destroys plants, food, etc. **2** (informal) a person or thing that annoys you: *That child is such a pest!*

PEST analysis noun [C, U] (**BUSINESS**) an examination of a situation to see how it is affecting a company and its products **HELP PEST** is formed from the first letters of 'political', 'economic', 'social' and 'technological'.

pester /'pestə(r)/ verb [T] ~ **sb (for sth)**; ~ **sb (to do sth)** to annoy sb, for example by asking them sth many times: *to pester somebody for money ◇ The kids kept pestering me to take them to the park.*

pesticide /'pestɪsaɪd/ noun [C, U] (**AGRICULTURE**) a chemical substance that is used for killing insects and other creatures that eat food crops ◔ look at **herbicide, insecticide**

pestle /'pesl/ noun [C] (**SCIENCE**) a small heavy tool with a round end used for pressing some foods or other substances into powder in a MORTAR (= a hard bowl) ◔ picture at **laboratory**

pet 🔊 **A2** /pet/ noun [C] **1** an animal or a bird that you keep in your home for pleasure rather than for food or work: *a pet dog/cat/hamster ◇ a pet shop* **2** a person who is treated better because they are liked more than any others: *She's the teacher's pet.*

petal /'petl/ noun [C] (**BIOLOGY**) one of the thin soft coloured parts of a flower ◔ picture at **flower**[1]

peter /'piːtə(r)/ verb
PHRV peter out to slowly become smaller, quieter, etc. and then stop

pet 'hate noun [C] something that you particularly do not like: *Filling in forms is one of my pet hates.*

petition 🔊+ **C1** /pə'tɪʃn/ noun [C] (**POLITICS**) a document, signed by many people, that asks a government, etc. to do or change sth: *More than 50 000 people signed the petition protesting about the new road.* ▶ **petition** verb [I, T]

Petri dish /'petri dɪʃ, 'piːt-/ noun [C] (**SCIENCE**) a covered dish that is not very deep, used for growing bacteria, etc. in ◔ picture at **laboratory**

petrified /'petrɪfaɪd/ adj. ~ **(of sb/sth)** very frightened: *She's petrified of spiders.*

petro- /petrəʊ, petrə, pə'trɒ/ prefix (in nouns, adjectives and adverbs) **1** (**GEOLOGY**) connected with rocks: *petrology* **2** connected with petrol: *petrochemical*

petrochemical /ˌpetrəʊ'kemɪkl/ noun [C] (**CHEMISTRY**) any chemical substance obtained from petrol or natural gas

petrol 🔊 **A2** /'petrəl/ (BrE) (AmE **gas, gasoline**) noun [U] liquid that is used as fuel for vehicles such as cars and motorcycles ◔ look at **diesel** (1) ◔ picture at **fractional distillation**

petroleum /pə'trəʊliəm/ noun [U] (**CHEMISTRY**) mineral oil that is found under the ground or sea and is used to make petrol, plastic and other types of chemical substances

'petrol station (BrE) (AmE **gas station**) noun [C] a place where you can buy petrol and other things for your car ◔ look at **garage** (2)

petticoat /'petɪkəʊt/ noun [C] (old-fashioned) a piece of women's underwear like a thin dress or skirt, worn under a dress or skirt

petty /'peti/ adj. (**pettier; pettiest**) **1** small and unimportant: *He didn't want to get involved with the petty details. ◇ petty crime/theft* (= that is not very serious) **SYN minor**[1] **2** unkind or unpleasant to other people (for a reason that does not seem very important): *petty jealousy/revenge ◇ Don't be so petty!*

ˌpetty 'cash noun [U] a small amount of money kept in an office for small payments

pew /pjuː/ noun [C] (**RELIGION**) a long wooden seat in a church

pewter /'pjuːtə(r)/ noun [U] a grey metal made by mixing tin with LEAD (= a soft heavy metal), used especially in the past for making cups, dishes, etc.; objects made from this metal

PG /ˌpiː 'dʒiː/ abbr. (BrE) (**ARTS AND MEDIA**) **parental guidance** (the label of a film in which some scenes may not be suitable for young children) ◔ look at **U**[2]

PGCE /ˌpiː dʒiː siː 'iː/ noun [C] (**EDUCATION**) a British teaching qualification taken by people who have a university degree (the abbreviation for 'Postgraduate Certificate in Education')

pH /ˌpiː 'eɪtʃ/ noun [sing.] (**CHEMISTRY**) a measurement of the level of ACID or ALKALI in a substance ❶ A pH value of below 7 shows an acid and a value of above 7 shows an alkali. ◔ picture on **page 548**

phagocyte /'fægəsaɪt/ noun [C] (**BIOLOGY**) a type of cell in the body that can surround smaller cells or small pieces of material and take them into itself

petroleum formation

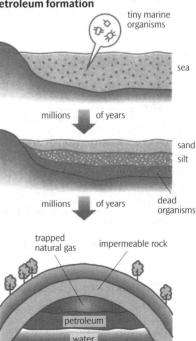

tiny marine organisms

sea

millions of years

sand
silt

millions of years

dead organisms

trapped natural gas

impermeable rock

petroleum

water

permeable sandstone

phalanx /ˈfælæŋks/ noun [C] **1** (pl. phalanxes) (formal) a group of people or things standing very close together **2** (pl. phalanges /fəˈlændʒiz/) (ANATOMY) a bone of the finger or toe

phantom /ˈfæntəm/ noun [C] **1** the spirit of a dead person that is seen or heard by sb who is still living **SYN** ghost **2** something that you think exists, but that is not real: phantom fears/illnesses

pharaoh /ˈfeərəʊ/ noun [C] (HISTORY) a ruler of ancient Egypt

pharma /ˈfɑːmə/ (also Pharma) noun [U] (informal) (MEDICINE) PHARMACEUTICAL companies as an industry

pharmaceutical /ˌfɑːməˈsuːtɪkl, -ˈsjuː-/ adj. [only before noun] (CHEMISTRY, MEDICINE) connected with the production of medicines and drugs: pharmaceutical companies

pharmacist /ˈfɑːməsɪst/ = CHEMIST

pharmacology /ˌfɑːməˈkɒlədʒi/ noun [U] (CHEMISTRY, MEDICINE) the scientific study of drugs and their use in medicine ▸ pharmacological /ˌfɑːməkəˈlɒdʒɪkl/ adj.: pharmacological research ▸ pharmacologist /ˌfɑːməˈkɒlədʒɪst/ noun [C]

pharmacy /ˈfɑːməsi/ noun (pl. -ies) (MEDICINE) **1** [C] a shop or part of a shop where medicines and drugs are prepared and sold ❶ A shop that sells medicine is also called a chemist's (shop) in British English or a drugstore in American English.   **2** [U] the preparation of medicines and drugs

pharming /ˈfɑːmɪŋ/ noun [U] **1** (COMPUTING, LAW) the practice of secretly changing computer files so that visitors to a website are sent to a different website instead, where their personal details are stolen and used to steal money from them ⊃ look at phishing **2** pharming™ (BIOLOGY) the process of changing the GENES (= the units inside a cell that control particular qualities) of an animal or a plant so that it produces large quantities of a substance, especially for use in medicine

pharynx /ˈfærɪŋks/ noun [C] (pl. pharynges /fəˈrɪndʒiːz/) (ANATOMY) the soft area at the top of the throat where the passages to the nose and mouth connect with the throat ⊃ picture at body

phase¹ ⓔ B2 ⊙ /feɪz/ noun [C] a stage in the development of sth: Julie went through a difficult phase when she started school.

phase² /feɪz/ verb [T, usually passive] to arrange to do sth gradually in stages over a period of time: Closure of the hospitals was phased over a three-year period. **PHR V** phase sth in to introduce or start using sth gradually in stages over a period of time: The tax system was phased in over two years. phase sth out to stop using sth gradually in stages over a period of time: The older machines are gradually being phased out and replaced by new ones.

PhD (BrE) (also Ph.D. especially in AmE) /ˌpiː eɪtʃ ˈdiː/ noun [C] (EDUCATION) an advanced university degree that you receive when you complete a piece of research into a special subject (the abbreviation for 'Doctor of Philosophy')

pheasant /ˈfeznt/ noun [C] (pl. pheasants, pheasant) a type of bird with a long tail. The males have brightly coloured feathers. Pheasants are often shot for sport and eaten. ⊃ picture at animal

phenomenal /fəˈnɒmɪnl/ adj. very great or impressive: phenomenal success ▸ phenomenally /-nəli/ adv.

phenomenon ⓔ B2 ⊙ /fəˈnɒmɪnən/ noun [C] (pl. phenomena /-mɪnə/) a fact or an event in nature or society, especially one that is not fully understood: Acid rain is not a natural phenomenon. It is caused by pollution.

phenotype /ˈfiːnətaɪp/ noun [C] (BIOLOGY) the set of characteristics of a living thing, resulting from its combination of GENES (= the units inside a cell that control particular qualities) and the effect of its environment ⊃ look at genotype

phew /fjuː/ exclamation a sound that you make to show that you are hot, tired or happy that sth bad did not happen or has finished: Phew, it's hot! ◇ Phew, I'm glad that interview's over!

philanthropy /fɪˈlænθrəpi/ noun [U] (SOCIAL STUDIES) the practice of helping the poor and those in need, especially by giving money ▸ philanthropic /ˌfɪlənˈθrɒpɪk/ adj.: philanthropic work ▸ philanthropically /-kli/ adv. ▸ philanthropist /fɪˈlænθrəpɪst/ noun [C]

-phile /faɪl/ suffix (in nouns and adjectives) liking a particular thing; a person who likes a particular thing or particular people: technophile (= a person who is enthusiastic about new technology) ⊃ look at -phobe

philo- /ˈfɪlə, fəˈlɒ/ (also phil- /fɪl, fəˈl/) prefix (in verbs, nouns, adjectives and adverbs) liking: philanthropist

philosopher ⓔ+ C1 /fəˈlɒsəfə(r)/ noun [C] a person who has developed a set of ideas and beliefs about the meaning of life

philosophical ⓔ+ C1 /ˌfɪləˈsɒfɪkl/ (also philosophic /ˌfɪləˈsɒfɪk/) adj. **1** connected with philosophy: a philosophical debate **2** ~ (about sth) staying calm and not getting upset or worried about sth bad that happens: He is quite philosophical about failing the exam and says he will try again next year. ▸ philosophically /-kli/ adv.

philosophize (BrE also -ise) /fəˈlɒsəfaɪz/ verb [I] ~ (about/ on sth) to talk about sth in a serious way, especially when other people think this is boring: He spent hours philosophizing on the meaning of life.

philosophy ⓔ B2 /fəˈlɒsəfi/ noun (pl. -ies) **1** [U] (EDUCATION) the study of ideas and beliefs about the meaning of life **2** [C] a set of beliefs that tries to explain the meaning of life or give rules about how to behave: Her philosophy is 'If a job's worth doing, it's worth doing well'.

phishing /ˈfɪʃɪŋ/ noun [U] (COMPUTING, LAW) the activity of tricking people by getting them to give their identity, bank account number, etc. over the internet

pH

| acidic | | | | | | | | | | | | | | alkaline |

pH	0	1	2	3	4	5	6	7	8	9	10	11	12	13	14
		strong acids		weak acids			neutral solutions			weak bases				strong bases	
			red		yellow				green				blue		violet

colour of universal indicator

or by email, and then using these to steal money from them ➔ look at **pharming** (1)

phlegm /flem/ *noun* [U] (**HEALTH**) the thick substance that is produced in the nose and throat, especially when you have a cold

phlegmatic /fleg'mætɪk/ *adj.* not easily made angry or upset; calm

phloem /'fləʊem/ *noun* [U] (**BIOLOGY**) the material in a plant containing very small tubes that carry SUGARS and other substances down from the leaves ➔ look at **xylem** ➔ picture at **flower**[1]

-phobe /fəʊb/ *suffix* (in nouns) a person who dislikes or is afraid of a particular thing or particular people: *Anglophobe* (= a person who dislikes the English) ◇ *xenophobe* (= a person who dislikes FOREIGNERS) ➔ look at **-phile**

phobia /'fəʊbiə/ *noun* [C] (often in compounds) (**PSYCHOLOGY**) a very strong fear that you cannot explain: *She has a phobia about flying.* ◇ *arachnophobia* (= fear of spiders)

phoenix /'fiːnɪks/ *noun* [C] (in stories) a magic bird that lives for several hundred years before burning itself and then being born again from its ASHES: *to rise like a phoenix from the ashes* (= to be powerful or successful again)

phon- /fəʊn, fə'n/ → PHONO-

phone[1] 🔵 **A1** /fəʊn/ (*also formal* **telephone**) *noun* **1** [C] the piece of equipment that you use when you talk to sb by phone: *The phone is ringing — could you answer it?* ➔ look at **mobile phone 2** [U] an electrical system for talking to sb in another place by speaking into a special piece of equipment: *a phone conversation* ◇ *You can book the tickets over the phone.* ◇ *He contacted me by phone.*
IDM on the phone/telephone using the phone

▼ **VOCABULARY BUILDING**

When you make a phone call, you first **dial** the number. The phone **rings** and the person at the other end **answers** it. If they are already using the phone, it is **engaged**. Introduce yourself by saying: *It's …* or: *This is …* (NOT: *Here is …*). When you finish speaking you **hang up** or **put the phone down**. The number that you dial before the phone number if you are phoning a different area or country is called the **code**: *What's the code for Spain?*

---

phone[2] 🔵 **A1** /fəʊn/ (*also formal* **telephone**) *verb* [I, T] to speak to sb by phone: *Did anybody phone while I was out?* ◇ *Could you phone the restaurant and book a table?* **SYN call**[1], **ring**[2]

phone call = CALL[2] (1)

phone hacking *noun* [U] the practice of looking at or listening to information on sb else's mobile phone without their permission

phone-in *noun* [C] (**ARTS AND MEDIA**) a radio or TV programme during which you can ask a question or give your opinion by phone

phoneme /'fəʊniːm/ *noun* [C] (**LANGUAGE**) any one of the set of smallest units of sound in a language that make the difference between one word and another. In English, the /s/ sound in *sip* and the /z/ sound in *zip* represent two different phonemes. ▸ **phonemic** /fə'niːmɪk/ *adj.*

phonetic /fə'netɪk/ *adj.* (**LANGUAGE**) **1** connected with the sounds of human speech; using special symbols to represent these sounds: *the phonetic alphabet* ➔ look at **transcribe** (2) **2** (used about spelling) having a close relationship with the sounds represented: *Spanish spelling is phonetic, unlike English spelling.* ▸ **phonetically** /-kli/ *adv.*

phonetics /fə'netɪks/ *noun* [U] (**LANGUAGE**) the study of the sounds of human speech

phoney (*also* **phony**) /'fəʊni/ *adj.* (**phonier**; **phoniest**) not real: *She spoke with a phoney Russian accent.* **SYN fake** ▸ **phoney** (*also* **phony**) *noun* [C] (*pl.* **-eys, -ies**)

phono- /fəʊnəʊ, fəʊnə, fə'nɒ/ (*also* **phon-**) *prefix* (in nouns, adjectives and adverbs) (**LANGUAGE**) connected with sound or sounds: *phonetic* ◇ *phonics*

phonology /fə'nɒlədʒi/ *noun* [U] the speech sounds of a particular language; the study of these sounds

phosphate /'fɒsfeɪt/ *noun* [C, U] (**AGRICULTURE**, **CHEMISTRY**) any SALT or COMPOUND containing PHOSPHORUS, used in industry or for helping plants to grow ➔ picture at **DNA**

phosphorus /'fɒsfərəs/ *noun* [U] (*symb.* P) (**CHEMISTRY**) a chemical element. Phosphorus is found in several different forms, including as a poisonous, pale yellow substance that shines in the dark and starts to burn as soon as it is placed in air. ❶ For more information on the periodic table of elements, look at the **Reference Section** of this dictionary.

photo- /fəʊtəʊ, fə'tɒ/ *prefix* (in verbs, nouns, adjectives and adverbs) **1** connected with light: *photosynthesis* **2** connected with photography: *photocopier*

photo 🔵 **A1** /'fəʊtəʊ/ (*pl.* **-os**) (*also* **photograph**) *noun* [C] a picture that is taken with a camera: *Shall I take your photo?* ◇ *to post/share a photo on Instagram*

photocell /'fəʊtəʊsel/ = PHOTOELECTRIC CELL

photochemical /ˌfəʊtəʊ'kemɪkl/ *adj.* (**CHEMISTRY**) caused by or relating to the chemical action of light

photocopier /'fəʊtəʊkɒpiə(r)/ *noun* [C] a machine that makes copies of documents by taking photos of them

photocopy /'fəʊtəʊkɒpi/ *noun* [C] (*pl.* **-ies**) a copy of a document, a page in a book, etc. that is made by a PHOTOCOPIER ➔ look at **copy**[1] (1) ▸ **photocopy** *verb* [T, I] (photocopying; photocopies; *pt, pp* photocopied)

photoelectric /ˌfəʊtəʊɪ'lektrɪk/ *adj.* (**PHYSICS**) using an electric current that is controlled by light

photoelectric 'cell (*also* **photocell**) *noun* [C] (**PHYSICS**) an electric device that uses a stream of light. When the stream is broken, it shows that sb/sth is present, and can be used to control alarms, machines, etc.

photo 'finish *noun* [C] (**SPORT**) the end of a race in which the competitors are so close together that only a photo of them passing the finishing line can show who has won: *The marathon ended in a photo finish.*

photograph 🔵 **A1** /'fəʊtəgrɑːf/ (*also* **photo**) *noun* [C] a picture that is taken with a camera: *to take a photograph* ◇ *She looks younger in real life than she does in the photograph.* ▸ **photograph** 🔵 **A2** *verb* [T]

photographer 🔵 **B1** /fə'tɒgrəfə(r)/ *noun* [C] a person who takes photos ➔ look at **cameraman**

photographic /ˌfəʊtə'græfɪk/ *adj.* connected with photos or photography

photography 🔵 **B1** /fə'tɒgrəfi/ *noun* [U] the skill or process of taking photos

photomontage /ˌfəʊtəʊmɒn'tɑːʒ/ *noun* [C, U] (**ART**) a picture that is made up of different photos put together; the technique of producing these pictures

photon /'fəʊtɒn/ *noun* [C] (**PHYSICS**) a unit of ELECTROMAGNETIC energy, for example light

photorealism /ˌfəʊtəʊ'riːəlɪzəm, -'rɪə-/ *noun* [U] (**ART**) an artistic style that represents a subject in an accurate and detailed way, like a photo

photo shoot noun [C] (**ARTS AND MEDIA**) an occasion when a photographer takes pictures of sb, for example a famous person, fashion model, etc. for use in a magazine, etc: *I went on a photo shoot to Rio with him.*

photoshop /ˈfəʊtəʊʃɒp/ verb [T] (-pp-) (**COMPUTING**) to change a picture or photo using a computer: *I'm sure this picture has been photoshopped.*

photosynthesis

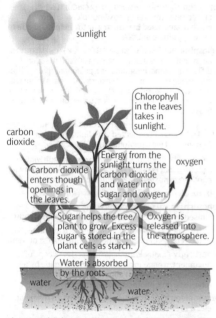

sunlight

Chlorophyll in the leaves takes in sunlight.

carbon dioxide

Carbon dioxide enters though openings in the leaves.

Energy from the sunlight turns the carbon dioxide and water into sugar and oxygen.

oxygen

Sugar helps the tree/ plant to grow. Excess sugar is stored in the plant cells as starch.

Oxygen is released into the atmosphere.

Water is absorbed by the roots.

water

water

photosynthesis /ˌfəʊtəʊˈsɪnθəsɪs/ noun [U] (**BIOLOGY**) the process by which green plants turn CARBON DIOXIDE (= a gas) and water into food using energy obtained from light from the sun

phototropism /ˌfəʊtəʊˈtrəʊpɪzəm/ noun [U] (**BIOLOGY**) the action of a plant turning towards or away from light ▶ **phototropic** /-ˈtrɒpɪk/ adj.

phrasal verb /ˌfreɪzl ˈvɜːb/ noun [C] (**GRAMMAR**) a verb that is combined with an adverb or a preposition, or sometimes both, to give a new meaning, such as 'look after' or 'put sb off' ⊃ look at **verb**

phrase¹ ⁊ **A1** /freɪz/ noun [C] (**GRAMMAR**) a group of words that are used together. A phrase does not contain a full verb: *'First of all' and 'a bar of chocolate' are phrases.* ⊃ look at **sentence¹** (1)

phrase² /freɪz/ verb [T] to express sth in a particular way: *The statement was phrased so that it would offend no one.*

phrase book noun [C] (**TOURISM**) a book that gives common words and useful phrases in a foreign language. People often use phrase books when they travel to another country whose language they do not know.

phylum /ˈfaɪləm/ noun [C] (pl. phyla /-lə/) (**BIOLOGY**) a group into which animals, plants, etc. are divided, smaller than a KINGDOM and larger than a CLASS ⊃ picture at **animal**

physical ⁊ **A2** ❂ /ˈfɪzɪkl/ adj. **1** connected with the body rather than the mind: *physical fitness/strength/disabilities* **2** [only before noun] connected with real things that you can touch, or with the laws of nature: *physical geography* (= the natural features on the face of the earth) **3** [only before noun] (**PHYSICS**) connected with the study of physics and things that are not alive

physical edu'cation noun [U] = PE

physically /ˈfɪzɪkli/ adv. **1** in a way that is connected with a person's body rather than their mind: *to be physically fit* ◊ *I don't find him physically attractive.* **2** according to the laws of nature or what is likely: *It's physically impossible to finish by the end of the week.*

physical 'therapy (AmE) = PHYSIOTHERAPY

physician ⁊+ **C1** /fɪˈzɪʃn/ noun [C] (especially AmE) a doctor, especially one who is a specialist in general medicine

physics ⁊ **A2** /ˈfɪzɪks/ noun [U] (**SCIENCE**) the scientific study of natural forces such as light, sound, heat, electricity, pressure, etc. ▶ **physicist** /-zɪsɪst/ noun [C]

physio- /fɪziəʊ, fɪziə, fɪziˈɒ/ prefix (in nouns, adjectives and adverbs) **1** connected with nature **2** (**BIOLOGY**) connected with PHYSIOLOGY

physiology /ˌfɪziˈɒlədʒi/ noun [U] (**BIOLOGY**) **1** the scientific study of the normal functions of living things **2** the way in which a particular living thing functions ▶ **physiologist** /-dʒɪst/ noun [C]

physiotherapy /ˌfɪziəʊˈθerəpi/ (BrE) (AmE physical therapy) noun [U] (**MEDICINE**) the treatment of disease or injury by exercise, light, heat, MASSAGE, etc. ▶ **physiotherapist** /-pɪst/ noun [C]

physique /fɪˈziːk/ noun [C] the size and shape of a person's body: *a strong muscular physique* **SYN** build¹

pi /paɪ/ noun [sing.] (**MATHEMATICS**) the symbol (π) used to show the relation between the CIRCUMFERENCE of a circle (= the distance around it) and its DIAMETER (= the distance across it) that is about 3.14159

pianist /ˈpɪənɪst/ noun [C] (**MUSIC**) a person who plays the piano

piano ⁊ **A1** /piˈænəʊ/ noun [C] (pl. -os) (**MUSIC**) a large musical instrument that you play by pressing down black and white keys: *an upright piano* ◊ *a grand piano*

lid

keyboard

pedals

piano stool

piano

piccolo /ˈpɪkələʊ/ noun [C] (pl. -os) (**MUSIC**) a musical instrument like a small FLUTE (= an instrument like a pipe that you play by blowing over a hole at one side) that plays high notes ⊃ picture at **instrument**

keyboard

pick¹ ⁊ **A2** /pɪk/ verb [T] **1** to choose sb/sth from a group of people or things: *I was upset not to be picked for the team.* ◊ *Have I picked a bad time to visit?* ⊃ look at **select¹** **2** to take a flower, fruit or vegetable from the place where it is growing: *to pick flowers/grapes/cotton* **3** to remove a small piece or pieces of sth with your fingers: *Don't pick your nose!* ◊ *She picked a hair off her jacket.* **IDM** have a bone to pick with sb → BONE¹ **pick and choose** to choose only the things that you like or want very much **pick a fight (with sb)** to start a fight with sb deliberately **pick a lock** to open a lock without using a key **pick sb's pocket** to steal money, etc. from sb's pocket or bag **pick up speed** to get

faster **pick your way across, over, etc. sth** to walk carefully, choosing the best places to put your feet: *She picked her way over the rough ground.*
PHR V **pick at sth** 1 to eat only small amounts of food because you are not hungry 2 to touch sth many times with your fingers **pick on sb** to behave unfairly or in a cruel way towards sb **pick sb/sth out** to choose or recognize sb/sth from a number of people or things: *I immediately picked Jean out in the photo.* **SYN** **identify** **pick up** to become better; to improve **pick sb up** to collect sb: *We've ordered a taxi to pick us up at ten.* **pick sb/sth up** to take hold of and lift sb/sth: *Lucy picked up the child and gave him a cuddle.* **pick sth up** 1 to learn sth without formal lessons: *Joe picked up a few words of Spanish on holiday.* 2 to receive an electronic signal, sound or picture: *We were able to pick up the BBC World Service in Delhi.* 3 to get or find sth: *I picked up this book at the market.* 4 to go and get sth; to collect sth: *I have to pick up my jacket from the cleaner's.*

pick² 🔊 **B2** /pɪk/ *noun* 1 [sing.] the one that you choose; your choice: *You can have whichever cake you like. Take your pick.* 2 [sing.] **the ~ of sth** the best of a group: *You can see the pick of the new films at this year's festival.*

pickaxe (*AmE also* **pickax**) /ˈpɪkæks/ (*also* **pick**) *noun* [C] a tool that consists of a curved iron bar with sharp points at both ends, fixed onto a wooden handle. Pickaxes are used for breaking stones or hard ground. ⊃ picture at **axe¹**

picket /ˈpɪkɪt/ *noun* [C] (**SOCIAL STUDIES**) a worker or group of workers who stand outside the entrance to a building to protest about sth, especially in order to stop people entering a factory, etc. during a strike ▶ **picket** *verb* [I, T]

pickle /ˈpɪkl/ *noun* 1 [C, usually pl.] (*BrE*) a vegetable that is cooked and put in salt water or **VINEGAR** (= a liquid with a bitter taste), served cold with meat, salads, etc. 2 [U] a cold thick sauce with a strong taste made from fruit and vegetables that have been boiled. Pickle is served with meat, cheese, etc. 3 [U, C] (*AmE*) = **GHERKIN** ▶ **pickle** *verb* [T]: *pickled onions*

pickpocket /ˈpɪkpɒkɪt/ *noun* [C] (**LAW**) a person who steals things from other people's pockets or bags in public places ▶ **pickpocketing** *noun* [U]: *crimes such as pickpocketing*

pickup /ˈpɪkʌp/ (*also* **pickup truck**) *noun* [C] a type of vehicle that has an open part with low sides at the back

picky /ˈpɪki/ *adj.* (**pickier**; **pickiest**) (*informal*) (used about a person) liking only certain things and difficult to please ⊃ look at **fussy** (1)

picnic /ˈpɪknɪk/ *noun* [C] a meal that you take with you to eat outdoors: *We had a picnic on the beach.* ▶ **picnic** *verb* [I] (-ck-)

Pict /pɪkt/ *noun* [C] (**HISTORY**) a member of an ancient human group that lived in northern Scotland in Roman times ▶ **Pictish** /ˈpɪktɪʃ/ *adj.*

pictograph /ˈpɪktəɡrɑːf/ (*also* **pictogram** /ˈpɪktəɡræm/) *noun* [C] 1 (**LANGUAGE**) a picture representing a word or phrase 2 a diagram that uses pictures to represent amounts or numbers of a particular thing ⊃ picture at **chart¹**

pictorial /pɪkˈtɔːriəl/ *adj.* expressed in pictures: *pictorial representations of objects*

picture¹ 🔊 **A1** **S** /ˈpɪktʃə(r)/ *noun* [C] 1 (**ART**) a painting, drawing or photo: *Who painted the picture in the hall?* ◇ *The teacher asked us to draw a picture of our families.* ⊃ note at **art** 2 an image on a TV screen: *They showed pictures of the crash on the news.*
3 a description of sth that gives you a good idea of what it is like: *The police are trying to build up a picture of exactly what happened.*

picture² 🔊 **B2** /ˈpɪktʃə(r)/ *verb* [T] 1 **~ sb/sth (as sth)** to imagine sth in your mind: *I can't picture Ivan as a father.* 2 [usually passive] to show sb/sth in a photo or picture: *She is pictured here with her parents.*

picturesque /ˌpɪktʃəˈresk/ *adj.* (usually used about an old building or a place) attractive: *a picturesque fishing village*

pidgin /ˈpɪdʒɪn/ *noun* [U] (**LANGUAGE**) a simple form of a language, especially English, Portuguese or Dutch, with a limited number of words, that are used together with words from a local language. It is used when people who do not speak the same language need to talk to each other.

pie /paɪ/ *noun* [C, U] meat, vegetables or fruit baked in a dish with **PASTRY** (= a mixture of flour, fat and water) on the bottom, sides and top: *apple pie* ◇ *meat pie*

piece¹ 🔊 **A1** /piːs/ *noun* [C]
• SEPARATE AMOUNT 1 **~ (of sth)** an amount or example of sth: *a piece of paper* ◇ *a piece of furniture* ◇ *a good piece of work* ◇ *a piece of advice/information/news*
• PART OF STH 2 one of the parts that sth is made of: *We'll have to take the engine to pieces to find the problem.* 3 one of the parts into which sth breaks: *The plate fell to the floor and smashed to pieces.* ◇ *The vase lay in pieces on the floor.*
• NEWS ARTICLE 4 **~ (on/about sb/sth)** an article in a newspaper or magazine: *There's a good piece on China in today's paper.*
• OF ART, MUSIC, ETC. 5 a single work of art, music, etc: *He played a piece by Chopin.*
• IN A GAME 6 one of the small objects that you use when you are playing games such as **CHESS**
• COIN 7 a coin of the value mentioned: *a 50-pence piece*
IDM **bits and pieces** → **BIT¹** **give sb a piece of your mind** to speak to sb angrily because of sth they have done **go to pieces** to be no longer able to work or behave normally because of a difficult situation **in one piece** not broken or injured: *I've only been on a motorbike once, and I was just glad to get home in one piece.* **a piece of cake** (*informal*) something that is very easy

piece² /piːs/ *verb*
PHR V **piece sth together** 1 to discover the truth about sth from different pieces of information: *Detectives are trying to piece together the last few days of the man's life.* 2 to put sth together from several pieces

piecemeal /ˈpiːsmiːl/ *adj., adv.* done or happening a little at a time

piece rate *noun* [C] an amount of money paid for each thing or amount of sth that a worker produces

pie chart *noun* [C] (**MATHEMATICS**) a diagram consisting of a circle divided into parts to show the size of particular parts in relation to the whole ⊃ picture at **chart¹**

pier /pɪə(r)/ *noun* [C] 1 a large wooden or metal structure that is built out into the sea from the land. Boats can stop at piers so that people or goods can be taken on or off. 2 (in the UK) a large wooden or metal structure that is built out into the sea in holiday towns, where people can walk

pierce /pɪəs/ *verb* 1 [T] to make a hole in sth with a sharp point: *I'm going to have my ears pierced.* 2 [T, I] **~ (through/into) sth** to manage to go through or into sth: *A scream pierced the air.*

piercing¹ /ˈpɪəsɪŋ/ *adj.* **1** (used about the wind, pain, a loud noise, etc.) strong and unpleasant **2** (used about sb's eyes or a look) seeming to know what you are thinking

piercing² /ˈpɪəsɪŋ/ *noun* [U, C] the act of making holes in parts of the body as a decoration; a hole that is made

piety /ˈpaɪəti/ *noun* [U] (**RELIGION**) a way of behaving that shows a deep respect for God and religion ⊃ adjective **pious**

pig¹ ⚡ **A1** /pɪg/ *noun* [C] **1** an animal with pink, black or brown skin, short legs, a wide nose and a curly tail, and that is kept on farms for PORK (= its meat) **2** (*informal*) an unpleasant person or a person who eats too much

▼ **VOCABULARY BUILDING**

A male pig is a **boar**, a female pig is a **sow** and a young pig is a **piglet**. When they make a noise, pigs **grunt** and piglets **squeal**.

pig² /pɪg/ *verb* [T] (-gg-) ~ **sth**; ~ **yourself (on sth)** (*informal*) to eat too much of sth
PHR V **pig out (on sth)** (*informal*) to eat too much of sth

pigeon /ˈpɪdʒɪn/ *noun* [C] a fat grey and white bird with short legs that is common in cities

pigeonhole /ˈpɪdʒɪnhəʊl/ *noun* [C] one of a set of small open boxes that are used for putting papers or letters in

piggyback /ˈpɪgibæk/ *noun* [C] the way of carrying sb, especially a child, on your back: *to give somebody a piggyback*

piggy bank /ˈpɪgi bæŋk/ *noun* [C] a small box, often shaped like a pig, that children save money in

pig-ˈheaded *adj.* not prepared to change your mind or say that you are wrong ⊃ look at **obstinate**, **stubborn**

pig iron *noun* [U] (**CHEMISTRY**) a form of iron that is not pure

piglet /ˈpɪglət/ *noun* [C] a young pig ⊃ note at **pig¹**

pigment /ˈpɪgmənt/ *noun* [C, U] (**ART**, **BIOLOGY**) a substance that gives colour to things

pigmy /ˈpɪgmi/ **1** = PYGMY¹ **2** = PYGMY²

pigsty /ˈpɪgstaɪ/ (*pl.* -ies) (*also* sty) (*AmE also* pigpen /ˈpɪgpen/) *noun* [C] (**AGRICULTURE**) a small building where pigs are kept

pigtail /ˈpɪgteɪl/ *noun* [C] (*BrE*) hair that is tied together in one or two lengths made by PLAITING (= crossing three pieces of hair over and under each other) ⊃ look at **plait**

pilchard /ˈpɪltʃəd/ *noun* [C] a small sea fish that is used for food

pile¹ ⚡ **B2** /paɪl/ *noun* [C] **1** a number of things lying on top of each other; an amount of sth lying in a mass: *a pile of books/sand* ◇ *He put the coins in neat piles.* ◇ *She threw the clothes in a pile on the floor.* **2** [usually pl.] ~ **of sth** (*informal*) a lot of sth: *I've got piles of work to do this evening.*

pile² ⚡ **B2** /paɪl/ *verb* [T] **1** ~ **sth (up)** to put things one on top of the other to form a pile: *We piled the boxes in the corner.* **2** ~ **A on(to) B**; ~ **B with A** to put a lot of sth on top of sth: *She piled the papers on the desk.* ◇ *The desk was piled with papers.* **3** (used with an adverb or a preposition) (used about a number of people) to go somewhere quickly and all at the same time: *The children piled onto the bus.*
PHR V **pile up** (used about sth bad) to increase in quantity: *Our problems are really piling up.*

piles /paɪlz/ = HAEMORRHOIDS

ˈpile-up *noun* [C] a crash that involves several cars, etc: *a multiple pile-up on the motorway*

pilgrim /ˈpɪlgrɪm/ *noun* [C] **1** (**RELIGION**) a person who travels a long way to visit a religious place: *Many pilgrims visit Mecca every year.* **2** Pilgrim (**HISTORY**) a member of the group of English people (the Pilgrim Fathers) who sailed to America on a ship (the Mayflower) in 1620 and started a COLONY in Massachusetts

pilgrimage /ˈpɪlgrɪmɪdʒ/ *noun* [C, U] (**RELIGION**) a long journey that a person makes to visit a religious place

pill ⚡+ **B2** /pɪl/ *noun* (**MEDICINE**) **1** [C] a small round piece of medicine that you SWALLOW without biting it: *Take one pill, three times a day after meals.* ◇ *a sleeping pill* **SYN** **tablet** ⊃ picture at **health** **2** **the pill** [sing.] a pill that some women take regularly so that they do not become pregnant: *She is on the pill.*

pillar /ˈpɪlə(r)/ *noun* [C] **1** (**ARCHITECTURE**) a column of stone, wood or metal that is used for supporting part of a building **2** a person who has a strong character and is important to sb/sth: *Dave was a pillar of strength to his sister when she was ill.*

pillion /ˈpɪliən/ *noun* [C] a seat for a passenger behind the driver on a motorcycle ▸ **pillion** *adv.*: *to ride pillion on a motorbike*

pillow /ˈpɪləʊ/ *noun* [C] a large cloth bag filled with soft material that you put under your head when you are in bed

pillowcase /ˈpɪləʊkeɪs/ *noun* [C] a thin soft cloth cover for a PILLOW

pilot¹ ⚡ **A2** /ˈpaɪlət/ *noun* [C] a person who flies an aircraft: *an airline pilot*

pilot² /ˈpaɪlət/ *verb* [T] **1** to fly an aircraft or guide a ship: *The plane was piloted by the instructor.* **2** to lead sb/sth through a difficult situation: *The booklet pilots you through the process of starting your own business.* **3** to test a new product, idea, etc. that will be used by everyone: *The new exam is being piloted in schools in Italy.*

pilot³ /ˈpaɪlət/ *adj.* [only before noun] done as an experiment or to test sth that will be used by everyone: *The pilot scheme will run for six months.*

pimple /ˈpɪmpl/ *noun* [C] a small spot on the skin

PIN /pɪn/ (*also* ˈPIN number) *noun* [C, usually sing.] (**FINANCE**) a number given to you, for example by a bank, so that you can use a plastic card to take out money from a CASH MACHINE (= a special machine in or outside a bank) (the abbreviation for 'personal identification number')

pin¹ ⚡ **B1** /pɪn/ *noun* [C] **1** a short thin piece of metal with a round head at one end and a sharp point at the other. Pins are used for fastening together pieces of cloth, paper, etc. **2** a thin piece of wood or metal that is used for a particular purpose: *a hairpin* ◇ *a two-pin plug* ⊃ picture at **plug¹**

pin² ⚡ **B1** /pɪn/ *verb* [T] (-nn-) **1** ~ **sth to/on sth**; ~ **sth together** to fasten sth with a pin or pins: *Could you pin this notice on the board, please?* ◇ *The dress is just pinned together. I've not sewn it yet.* **2** to make sb/sth unable to move by holding or pressing down on them or it (used with an adverb or a preposition): *He caught his brother and pinned him to the floor.* ◇ *He was pinned under the fallen tree.*
IDM **pin (all) your hopes on sb/sth** to believe completely that sb/sth will help you or you will succeed
PHR V **pin sb down 1** to hold sb so they cannot move **2** to force sb to decide sth or to say exactly what they are going to do **pin sth down** to describe or explain exactly what sth is

pinafore /ˈpɪnəfɔː(r)/ *noun* [C] (*old-fashioned*) **1** a loose dress with no SLEEVES (= parts that cover the arms), usually worn over other clothes **2** a piece of clothing or a dress that a woman can wear over her normal clothes to keep them clean when she is cooking or doing dirty jobs ⊃ look at **apron**

pinball /ˈpɪnbɔːl/ *noun* [U] a game played on a pinball machine, in which a player sends a small metal ball along a board and scores points as it hits against objects. The player tries to prevent the ball from reaching the bottom of the machine by pressing two buttons at the side.

pincer /ˈpɪnsə(r)/ *noun* **1** pincers [pl.] a tool made of two crossed pieces of metal that is used for holding things, pulling nails out of wood, etc. **2** [C] one of the two sharp, curved front legs of some SHELLFISH (= creatures with shells that live in water) that are used for holding things

pinch¹ /pɪntʃ/ *verb* **1** [T] to hold a piece of sb's skin tightly between your THUMB and first finger, especially in order to hurt them: *Paul pinched his brother and made him cry.* **2** [I, T] to hold sth too tight, often causing pain: *I've got a pinched nerve in my neck.* **3** [T] (*informal*) to steal: *Who's pinched my pen?*

pinch² /pɪntʃ/ *noun* [C] **1** the holding of sb's skin tightly between your finger and THUMB: *She gave him a little pinch on the arm.* **2** the amount of sth that you can pick up with your THUMB and first finger: *a pinch of salt*
IDM **at a pinch** used to say that sth can be done if it is really necessary: *We really need three cars but we could manage with two at a pinch.* **take sth with a pinch of salt** to think that sth is probably not true or accurate

pinched /pɪntʃt/ *adj.* (used about sb's face) thin and pale because of illness or cold

pine¹ /paɪn/ *noun* **1** (*also* pine tree) [C] a tall tree that has NEEDLES (= thin pointed leaves) **2** [U] the wood from pine trees, which is often used for making furniture: *a pine table*

pine² /paɪn/ *verb* [I] ~ (for sb/sth) to be very unhappy because sb has died or gone away: *The dog sat outside, pining for its owner.*

pineapple /ˈpaɪnæpl/ *noun* [C, U] a large sweet fruit that is yellow inside and has a thick brown skin with sharp points. Pineapples grow in hot countries.

pine nut (*BrE also* **pine kernel**) *noun* [C] the white seed of some PINE trees, used in cooking

pine tree = PINE¹ (1)

ping¹ /pɪŋ/ *noun* [C] a short high noise that is made by a small bell or by a metal object hitting against sth: *The lift went ping and the doors opened.*

ping² /pɪŋ/ *verb* **1** [I] to make a short high noise **2** [T] (**COMPUTING**) to test whether an internet connection is working by sending a signal to a computer and waiting for a reply **3** [T] ~ sth (to sb); ~ sb sth; ~ sb (with sth) (**COMPUTING**) (*informal*) to send an email or a TEXT MESSAGE to sb: *I'll ping it to you later.* ◇ *Can you ping me it now?* ◇ *My sister pinged me with a question.*

ping-pong (*BrE, informal*) (*AmE* **Ping-Pong™**) = TABLE TENNIS

pink ⌇**A1** /pɪŋk/ *adj.* pale red in colour ▸ **pink** ⌇ **A1** *noun* [U, C]

pinna /ˈpɪnə/ *noun* [C] (*pl.* pinnae /-niː/) (**ANATOMY**) the part of the ear that is on the outside of the body ⊃ picture at **ear**

pinnacle /ˈpɪnəkl/ *noun* [C] **1** the most important or successful part of sth: *Celia is at the pinnacle of her career.* **2** (**GEOGRAPHY**) a high pointed rock on a mountain

pinpoint /ˈpɪnpɔɪnt/ *verb* [T] **1** to find the exact position of sth: *to pinpoint a place on the map* **2** to describe or explain exactly what sth is: *First we have to pinpoint the cause of the failure.*

pins and ˈneedles *noun* [pl.] a strange, sometimes painful feeling that you get in a part of your body after it has been in one position for too long and when the blood is returning to it

pinstripe /ˈpɪnstraɪp/ *noun* **1** [C] one of the white VERTICAL lines printed on dark material that is used especially for making business suits **2** [U] dark material with white VERTICAL lines printed on it: *a pinstripe suit*

pint /paɪnt/ *noun* [C] **1** (*abbr.* pt) a measure of liquid; 0.57 of a LITRE. There are 8 pints in a GALLON: *a pint of milk* ⊃ note at **measure²** ❶ An American pint is 0.47 of a litre. ❶ For more information about measurements, look at the **Reference Section** of this dictionary. **2** (*BrE*) a pint of beer

pin-up *noun* [C] a picture of an attractive person, made to be put on a wall; a person who appears in these pictures

pioneer ⌇+ **C1** /ˌpaɪəˈnɪə(r)/ *noun* [C] **1** ~ (in/of sth) a person who is one of the first to develop an area of human knowledge, culture, etc: *Yuri Gagarin was one of the pioneers of space exploration.* **2** a person who is one of the first to go and live in a particular area: *the pioneers of the American West* ▸ **pioneer** ⌇ **C1** *verb* [T]: *a technique pioneered in the US*

pious /ˈpaɪəs/ *adj.* (**RELIGION**) having or showing a deep belief in religion ▸ **piously** *adv.* ⊃ noun **piety**

pip /pɪp/ *noun* [C] (*BrE*) the small seed of an apple, a lemon, an orange, etc.

pipe¹ ⌇ **B1** /paɪp/ *noun* [C] **1** a tube that carries gas or liquid: *Waste water is carried away down the drainpipe.* ⊃ picture at **purification** **2** a tube with a small bowl at one end that is used for smoking TOBACCO: *to smoke a pipe* **3** (**MUSIC**) a simple musical instrument that consists of a tube with holes in it. You blow into it to play it.

pipe² /paɪp/ *verb* [T] to carry liquid or gas in pipes: *Water is piped to all the houses in the village.* **PHR V** **pipe up** (*informal*) to suddenly say sth: *Suddenly Shirin piped up with a question.*

pipeline ⌇+ **C1** /ˈpaɪplaɪn/ *noun* [C] a series of pipes that are used for carrying liquid or gas over a long distance
IDM **in the pipeline** being planned or prepared

piper /ˈpaɪpə(r)/ *noun* [C] (**MUSIC**) a person who plays music on a pipe, or who plays the BAGPIPES (= a musical instrument that is typical in Scotland)

pipette /pɪˈpet/ *noun* [C] (**SCIENCE**) a narrow tube used in a laboratory for measuring or moving small amounts of liquids ⊃ picture at **laboratory**

piracy /ˈpaɪrəsi/ *noun* [U] **1** (**LAW**) the crime of attacking ships in order to steal from them **2** the illegal copying of books, computer programs, etc.

piranha /pɪˈrɑːnə/ *noun* [C] a small South American fish that attacks and eats live animals

pirate¹ ⌇+ **C1** /ˈpaɪrət/ *noun* [C] **1** (especially in the past or in stories) a criminal who attacks ships in order to steal from them **2** (**LAW**) a person who copies books, DVDs, computer programs, etc. in order to sell them illegally

pirate² /ˈpaɪrət/ *verb* [T] (**LAW**) to make an illegal copy of a book, DVD, etc. in order to sell it

Pisces /ˈpaɪsiːz/ *noun* [U] the twelfth sign of THE ZODIAC (= twelve signs that represent the positions of the sun, moon and planets), the Fishes; a person born under this sign

pistachio /pɪˈstæʃiəʊ, -ˈstɑːʃ-/ (*pl.* -os) (*also* piˈstachio nut) *noun* [C] the small green nut of an Asian tree

pistil /ˈpɪstɪl/ *noun* [C] (**BIOLOGY**) the female organs of a flower, which receive the POLLEN and produce seeds

pistol /ˈpɪstl/ *noun* [C] a small gun that you hold in one hand ⊃ note at **gun¹**

piston /ˈpɪstən/ *noun* [C] (**ENGINEERING**) a piece of metal in an engine, etc. that fits tightly inside a CYLINDER (= metal tube). The piston is moved up and down inside the tube and causes other parts of the engine to move. ⊃ picture at **hydraulic**

pit¹ ⁊+ **C1** /pɪt/ *noun* **1** [C] a large hole that is made in the ground: *They dug a large pit to bury the dead animals.* **2** [C] = COAL MINE **3** [C] (*AmE*) = STONE (4) **4** the pits [pl.] (*BrE*) (*AmE usually* the pit [C]) the place on a motor racing track where cars stop for fuel, new tyres, etc. during a race **5** [C] = ORCHESTRA PIT
IDM be the pits (*informal*) to be very bad: *The food in that restaurant is the pits!*

pit² /pɪt/ *verb* [T] (-tt-) to make small holes in the surface of sth: *Acne scars had pitted his face.*
PHR V pit A against B to test one person or thing against another in a fight or competition: *The two teams were pitted against each other in the final.*

pita /ˈpiːtə, ˈpɪtə/ = PITTA

pitch¹ ⁊ **B2** /pɪtʃ/ *noun* **1** [C] (*BrE*) (**SPORT**) a special area of ground where you play certain sports: *a football/hockey/cricket pitch* ⊃ look at **court¹** (3), **field¹** (3) **2** [U] (**MUSIC**) how high or low a sound is, especially a note **3** [sing.] the strength or level of feelings, activity, etc: *The children's excitement almost reached fever pitch.* **4** [C] talk or arguments used by sb who is trying to sell sth or persuade sb to do sth: *a sales pitch* ◇ *to make a pitch for something*

pitch² /pɪtʃ/ *verb* **1** [I, T] to throw sth/sb; to be thrown: *Doug pitched his empty can into the bushes.* **2** [T] to set sth at a particular level: *The talk was pitched at people with far more experience than me.* **3** [T] to put up a tent or tents: *They pitched their tents in the valley.* **4** [T] ~ **sth (at sb)** to try to sell a product to a particular group of people or in a particular way: *This new breakfast cereal is being pitched at kids.*
PHR V pitch in (*informal*) to join in and work together with other people: *Everybody pitched in to clear up the flood damage.*

pitch-ˈblack *adj.* completely dark; with no light at all

pitched /pɪtʃt/ *adj.* (**ARCHITECTURE**) (used about a roof) sloping; not flat: *steeply pitched roofs*

pitcher /ˈpɪtʃə(r)/ *noun* [C] **1** a large container for holding and pouring liquids **2** (*AmE*) = JUG **3** (**SPORT**) (in baseball) the player who PITCHES (= throws) the ball to a player from the other team, who tries to hit it

pitchfork /ˈpɪtʃfɔːk/ *noun* [C] (**AGRICULTURE**) a farm tool like a fork with a long handle and two or three sharp metal points. It is used for lifting and moving HAY (= dried cut grass).

piteous /ˈpɪtiəs/ *adj.* (*formal*) that makes you feel PITY ▸ **piteously** *adv.*

pitfall /ˈpɪtfɔːl/ *noun* [C] a danger or difficulty, especially one that is hidden or not obvious

pith /pɪθ/ *noun* [U] (**BIOLOGY**) the white substance inside the skin of an orange, a lemon, etc.

pithy /ˈpɪθi/ *adj.* (pithier; pithiest) (used about a comment, piece of writing, etc.) short but expressed in a clear, direct way: *a pithy comment*

pitiable /ˈpɪtiəbl/ *adj.* (*formal*) **1** deserving PITY or causing you to feel PITY: *The refugees were in a pitiable state.* **2** not deserving respect: *a pitiable lack of talent* ▸ **pitiably** /-bli/ *adv.*

pitiful /ˈpɪtɪfl/ *adj.* causing you to feel PITY: *the pitiful groans of the wounded soldiers* ▸ **pitifully** /-fəli/ *adv.*

pitiless /ˈpɪtiləs/ *adj.* having or showing no PITY for other people's suffering ▸ **pitilessly** *adv.*

pitta (*BrE*) (*AmE* pita) /ˈpiːtə, ˈpɪtə/ *noun* [U, C] a type of flat bread in the shape of an OVAL that can be split open and filled

pituitary /pɪˈtjuːɪtəri/ (*pl.* -ies) (*also* piˈtuitary gland) *noun* [C] a small organ at the base of the brain that produces HORMONES (= substances that affect growth and sexual development) ⊃ picture at **brain**

pity¹ ⁊+ **B2** /ˈpɪti/ *noun*
1 [U] ~ **(for sb)** a sad feeling caused because sb is suffering or in trouble: *The situation is his fault so I don't feel any pity for him.* **2** [sing.] something that makes you feel a little sad or disappointed: *'You're too late. Emily left five minutes ago.' 'Oh, **what a pity!**'* ◇ *It's a pity that Bina couldn't come.* **SYN shame¹**
IDM take pity on sb to help sb who is suffering or in trouble because you feel sorry for them

WORD FAMILY
pity *noun, verb*
pitiful *adj.*
pitiless *adj.*
pitiable *adj.*
piteous *adj.*

pity² /ˈpɪti/ *verb* [T] (pitying; pities; *pt, pp* pitied) to feel PITY or SADNESS for sb who is suffering or in trouble

pivot¹ /ˈpɪvət/ *noun* [C] **1** (**ENGINEERING**, **PHYSICS**) the central point on which sth turns or balances **SYN fulcrum 2** the central or most important person or thing: *West Africa was the pivot of the cocoa trade.*

pivot² /ˈpɪvət/ *verb* [I] to turn or balance on a central point

pivotal /ˈpɪvətl/ *adj.* very important because other things depend on it: *a pivotal role in European affairs* ◇ *The competition proved pivotal in her career.*

pixel /ˈpɪksl/ *noun* [C] (**COMPUTING**) any of the very small individual areas on a computer, TV or camera screen, which together form the whole image

pixelate (*also* pixellate) /ˈpɪksəleɪt/ *verb* [T]
1 (**COMPUTING**) to divide an image into PIXELS **2** (**ARTS AND MEDIA**) to show an image on TV as a small number of large PIXELS, especially in order to hide sb's identity

pixie /ˈpɪksi/ *noun* [C] (in children's stories) a creature like a small person with pointed ears that has magic powers

pizza /ˈpiːtsə/ *noun* [C, U] an Italian dish consisting of a flat round bread base with vegetables, cheese, meat, etc. on top, which is cooked in an oven

pizzicato /ˌpɪtsɪˈkɑːtəʊ/ *adj., adv.* (**MUSIC**) using the fingers to pull the strings of a musical instrument, for example a VIOLIN, that you usually play with a BOW (= a long thin piece of wood with strings stretched tightly across it)

pl. *abbr.* (in writing) = PLURAL

placard /ˈplækɑːd/ *noun* [C] a large written or printed notice that is put in a public place or carried on a stick in a protest march

placate /pləˈkeɪt/ *verb* [T] to make sb feel less angry about sth

place¹ ⁊ **A1** /pleɪs/ *noun*
• POSITION/AREA **1** [C] a particular position or area: *Show me the exact place where it happened.* ◇ *This would be a good place to sit down and have a rest.* ◇ *The wall*

was damaged in several places. **2** [C] a building or an area that is used for a particular purpose: *The square is a popular **meeting place** for young people.* ◇ *The town is full of inexpensive eating places.*

• TOWN/BUILDING **3** [C] a particular village, town, country, etc: *Which places did you go to in Italy?* ◇ *Vienna is a very beautiful place.*

• CORRECT POSITION **4** [C] the usual or correct position or occasion for sth: *The room was tidy. Everything had been put away **in its place**.* ◇ *A funeral is not the place to discuss business.*

• SEAT **5** [C] a seat or position that can be used by sb/sth: *They went into the classroom and sat down in their places.* ◇ *Go on ahead and **save** me **a place** in the queue.*

• IN A COLLEGE/TEAM **6** [C] an opportunity to study at a college, play for a team, etc: *Abina has got a place to study law at Oxford University.* ◇ *Laila is now sure of a place on the team.*

• IN A COMPETITION **7** [C, usually sing.] the position that you have at the end of a race, competition, etc: *Cara finished **in second place**.*

• ROLE **8** [sing.] your position in society; your role: *I feel **it is not my place** to criticize my boss.*

• SB'S HOME **9** [sing.] (*informal*) a person's home: *Her parents have got a place on the coast.*

• IN A NUMBER **10** [C] (**MATHEMATICS**) the position of a number after the DECIMAL POINT: *Your answer should be correct to three decimal places.*

IDM **all over the place** everywhere **change/swap places (with sb)** to take sb's seat, position, etc. and let them have yours **fall/slot into place** (used about sth that is complicated or difficult to understand) to become organized or clear in your mind: *After two weeks in my new job, everything suddenly started to fall into place.* **in the first, second, etc. place** used when you are giving a list of reasons for sth or explaining sth; firstly, secondly, etc. **in place** **1** in the correct or usual position: *Use tape to hold the picture in place.* **2** (used about plans or preparations) finished and ready to be used **in my, your, etc. place/shoes** in my, your, etc. situation or position: *If I were in your place, I would wait a year before getting married.* **in place of sb/sth | in sb/sth's place** instead of sb/sth **out of place** **1** not suitable for a particular situation: *I felt very out of place among all those clever people.* **2** not in the correct or usual place **put sb in his/her place** to show that sb is not as clever, important, etc. as they believe: *It really put her in her place when she failed to qualify for the race.* **put yourself in sb's place** to imagine that you are in the same situation as sb else **take place** (used about a meeting, an event, etc.) to happen: *The ceremony took place in glorious sunshine.*

place[2] 🔑 B1 /pleɪs/ *verb* [T]

• IN A POSITION **1** (used with an adverb or a preposition) to put sth carefully or deliberately in a particular position: *The chairs had all been placed in neat rows.* ◇ *The parking areas are strategically placed.*

• ATTITUDE **2** **~ sth on sb/sth** used to express the attitude that sb has to sb/sth: *The blame for the disaster was placed firmly on the company.* ◇ *They place a high value on education.*

• ORDER, BET, ETC. **3** to give instructions about sth or to ask for sth to happen: *to place a bet/an order* ◇ *They placed an advertisement for a cleaner in the local paper.*

• IN A POSITION/SITUATION **4** **~ sb (in sth)** to put sb in a particular position or situation: *His behaviour placed me in a difficult situation.* ◇ *Rhoda was placed third in the competition.*

• RECOGNIZE **5** (usually in negative sentences) to recognize sb/sth and be able to identify them or it: *Her face is familiar but I just can't place her.*

placebo /pləˈsiːbəʊ/ *noun* [C] (*pl.* **-os**) (**MEDICINE**) a substance that has no physical effects, given to patients who do not need medicine but think that they do, or used when testing new drugs: *the **placebo effect*** (= the effect of taking a placebo and feeling better)

ˈplace mat *noun* [C] a MAT on a table on which a person's plate is put

placement 🔑+ B2 /ˈpleɪsmənt/ (*also* **work placement**) *noun* [C, U] (**EDUCATION**) a job, often as part of a course of study, where you get some experience of a particular kind of work: *The third year is spent **on placement** in selected companies.* ➲ look at **internship** (1)

ˈplace name *noun* [C] the name of a city, town, etc.

placenta /pləˈsentə/ *noun* [C] (**ANATOMY**) the material inside the WOMB (= the part of a woman's body where a baby grows) that protects the baby and supplies food through the UMBILICAL CORD ➲ picture at **fertilization**

placid /ˈplæsɪd/ *adj.* (used about a person or an animal) calm and not easily excited ▶ **placidly** *adv.*

plagiarism /ˈpleɪdʒərɪzəm/ *noun* [U, C] the act of copying another person's ideas, words or work and pretending that they are your own; sth that has been copied in this way

plagiarize (*BrE also* **-ise**) /ˈpleɪdʒəraɪz/ *verb* [T, I] to copy another person's ideas, words or work and pretend that they are your own ▶ **plagiarism** *noun* [U, C]

plague[1] /pleɪg/ *noun* **1** **the plague** [U] a disease spread by RATS (= animals like large mice) that makes large spots form on the body, causes a very high temperature and often results in death **2** [C] (**HEALTH**) any disease that spreads quickly and kills many people **3** [C] **~ of sth** a large number of unpleasant animals or insects that come into an area at one time: *a plague of ants/locusts*

plague[2] /pleɪg/ *verb* [T] to cause sb/sth a lot of trouble: *The project was plagued by a series of disasters.*

plain[1] 🔑 B2 /pleɪn/ *adj.* **1** simple in style; not decorated or complicated: *My father likes plain English cooking.* **2** [only before noun] all one colour; without a pattern on it: *a plain blue jumper* **3** easy to see, hear or understand; clear: ***It was plain that** he didn't want to talk about it.* ◇ *She **made it plain that** she didn't want to see me again.* ➲ note at **clear**[1] **4** (used about people, thoughts, actions, etc.) saying what you think; direct and honest: *I'll be plain with you. I don't like the idea.* **5** (used especially about a woman or girl) not beautiful or attractive: *She's a rather plain child.*

plain[2] /pleɪn/ *noun* [C] (**GEOGRAPHY**) a large area of flat land with few trees

plain[3] /pleɪn/ *adv.* (*informal*) completely: *That's plain silly.*

ˌplain-ˈclothes *adj.* (**LAW**) (used about a police officer) wearing ordinary clothes; not in uniform: *a plain-clothes detective* ▶ **ˌplain ˈclothes** *noun* [pl.]: *officers **in plain clothes***

ˌplain ˈflour *noun* [U] flour that does not contain BAKING POWDER (= powder that makes cakes, etc. rise) ➲ look at **self-raising flour**

plainly /ˈpleɪnli/ *adv.* **1** in a way that is easy to see, hear, understand or believe: *He was plainly very upset.* **SYN** **clearly** **2** using simple words to say sth in a direct and honest way: *She told him plainly that he was not doing his job properly.* **3** in a simple way, without decoration: *She was plainly dressed and wore no make-up.*

plaintiff /ˈpleɪntɪf/ (*also* **complainant**) *noun* [C] (**LAW**) a person who starts a legal action against sb in court ➔ look at **defendant**

plaintive /ˈpleɪntɪv/ *adj.* sounding sad, especially in a weak complaining way ▸ **plaintively** *adv.*

plait /plæt/ (*BrE*) (*also* **braid** *especially in AmE*) *noun* [C] a long piece of something, especially hair, that is divided into three parts and TWISTED together ➔ look at **pigtail** ▸ **plait** (*BrE*) (*also* **braid** *especially in AmE*) *verb* [T]

plan¹ ⓘ **A1** /plæn/ *noun* **1** ~ (**for sth/to do sth**) an idea or arrangement for doing or achieving sth in the future: *We usually* **make our plans** *for the summer in January.* ◇ *The firm has no plans to employ more people.* ◇ *There has been a* **change of plan** *— we're meeting at the restaurant.* ◇ *If everything* **goes according to plan** (= happens as we planned) *we should be home by midnight.* ➔ note at **purpose 2** a set of things to do in order to achieve something: *an action plan* ◇ *Before you start writing an essay, it's a good idea to* **make a brief plan. 3** a detailed map of a building, town, etc: *a street plan of Berlin* **4** [usually pl.] detailed drawings of a building, machine, road, etc. that show its size, shape and measurements: *We're getting an architect to* **draw up** *some* **plans** *for a new kitchen.* **5** a diagram that shows how sth is to be organized or arranged: *a seating plan* (= showing where each person will sit, for example at a dinner)

plan² ⓘ **A1** /plæn/ *verb* (-nn-) **1** [T, I] ~ (**sth**) (**for sth**) to decide, organize or prepare for sth you want to do in the future: *You need to plan your work more carefully.* ◇ *to plan for the future* ◇ *We're planning a surprise for Gwen's 50th birthday.* **2** [I, T] ~ (**on sth/doing sth**); ~ (**to do sth**) to intend or expect to do sth: *I'm planning on having a holiday in July.* ◇ *We plan to arrive at about four o'clock.* **3** [T] to make a diagram or a design of sth: *The new shopping centre is very badly planned.* ◇ *You need an expert to help you plan the garden.*

plane¹ ⓘ **A1** /pleɪn/ (*BrE also* **aeroplane**) (*also* **airplane** *especially in AmE*) *noun* [C] **1** a vehicle that can fly through the air, with wings and one or more engines: *Has her plane landed yet?* ➔ picture at **speed¹ 2** (**GEOMETRY**) any flat or level surface, or an imaginary flat surface through or joining material objects: *the* **horizontal/vertical plane 3** a tool used for making the surface of wood smooth by taking very thin pieces off it ➔ picture at **tool**

plane² /pleɪn/ *verb* [T] to make the surface of a piece of wood flat and smooth using a PLANE

plane³ /pleɪn/ *adj.* [only before noun] completely flat; level: *a plane mirror* ➔ picture at **reflection**

planet ⓘ **A2** /ˈplænɪt/ *noun* **1** [C] (**ASTRONOMY**) a very large round object in space that moves around the sun or another star: *the planets of our solar system* **2** **the planet** [sing.] (**ENVIRONMENT**) the world we live in; the Earth, especially when talking about the environment: *the battle to save the planet*

planetarium /ˌplænɪˈteəriəm/ *noun* [C] (*pl.* -**tariums**) (**ASTRONOMY**) a building with a curved ceiling that represents the sky at night. It is used for showing the positions and movements of the planets and stars for education and entertainment.

planetary /ˈplænətri/ *adj.* [only before noun] relating to a planet or planets: *a planetary system*

plank /plæŋk/ *noun* [C] a long flat thin piece of wood that is used for building or making things ➔ picture at **workbench**

plankton /ˈplæŋktən/ *noun* [U + sing./pl. verb] very small forms of plant and animal life that live in water

planned e'conomy (*also* **command economy**) *noun* [C] (**ECONOMICS**) an economy in which levels of pay, prices, production, etc. are decided by the government

planner /ˈplænə(r)/ *noun* [C] **1** (*also* **town planner**) a person whose job is to plan the growth and development of a town **2** a person who makes plans for a particular area of activity: *curriculum planners* **3** a book, computer program, etc. that contains dates and is used for recording information, arranging meetings, etc.

planning ⓘ **B1** /ˈplænɪŋ/ *noun* [U] **1** the act or process of making plans for sth: *financial planning* ◇ *The project requires careful planning.* **2** = TOWN PLANNING

plant¹ ⓘ **A1** /plɑːnt/ *noun* [C] **1** (**BIOLOGY**) a living thing that grows in the ground and usually has leaves, a STEM (= the central part) and roots: *a tomato plant* ◇ *a plant pot* (= a container for plants) ➔ picture at **energy, flower¹, food web 2** a factory or place where power is produced or an industrial process takes place: *a car plant* ◇ *a nuclear reprocessing plant* ➔ note at **factory** ➔ picture at **purification**

plant² ⓘ **A2** /plɑːnt/ *verb* [T] **1** to put plants, seeds, etc. in the ground to grow **2** ~ **sth** (**with sth**) to cover or supply a garden, an area of land, etc. with plants: *The field's been planted with wheat this year.* **3** (used with an adverb or a preposition) to put yourself/sth in a particular place or position: *He planted himself in the best seat.* **4** ~ **sth** (**on sb**) to hide sth, especially sth illegal, in sb's clothing, property, etc., in order to make them seem guilty of a crime: *The women claimed that the drugs had been planted on them.* **5** to hide sth such as a bomb in a place where it will not be found: *The police think that terrorists may have* **planted the bomb.**

plantain /ˈplæntɪn, -teɪn/ *noun* [C, U] a fruit similar to a banana, but larger and less sweet, that is cooked and eaten as a vegetable

plantation /plɑːnˈteɪʃn/ *noun* [C] **1** (**AGRICULTURE**) a large area of land, especially in a hot country, where tea, cotton, TOBACCO, etc. are grown: *a coffee plantation* ➔ note at **agriculture 2** an area of land where trees are grown to produce wood

plaque /plæk, plɑːk/ *noun* **1** [C] a flat piece of stone or metal, usually with names and dates on it, that is fixed on a wall in memory of a famous person or an event **2** [U] (**HEALTH**) a harmful substance that forms on the teeth

plasma /ˈplæzmə/ (*also* **plasm** /ˈplæzəm/) *noun* [U] (**BIOLOGY**) the clear liquid part of blood, in which the blood cells, etc. float

'plasma screen *noun* [C] (**ARTS AND MEDIA**) a type of TV or computer screen that is larger and thinner than most screens and produces a very clear image

plaster¹ /ˈplɑːstə(r)/ *noun* **1** [U] a mixture of a special powder and water that becomes hard when it is dry. Plaster is put on walls and ceilings to form a smooth surface. **2** (*both BrE*) (*AmE* **Band-Aid™**) [C] (**MEDICINE**) a small piece of sticky material that is used to cover a cut, etc. on the body **3** (*also* **plaster of Paris** /ˌplɑːstər əv ˈpærɪs/) [U] (**MEDICINE**) a white powder that is mixed with water and becomes hard when dry. It is then used especially for making copies of statues or for holding broken bones in place: *When Alan broke his leg it was* **in plaster** *for six weeks.* ➔ picture at **health**

plaster² /ˈplɑːstə(r)/ *verb* [T] **1** to cover a wall, etc. with PLASTER to make the surface smooth **2** ~ **sb/sth** (**in/ with sth**) to cover sb/sth with a large amount of sth: *He plastered his walls with posters.*

plaster cast *noun* [C] **1** (**MEDICINE**) a case made of PLASTER that covers a broken bone and protects it **2** a copy of sth, made using PLASTER: *They took a plaster cast of the teeth for identification purposes.*

plastic¹ ⚡**A2** /ˈplæstɪk/ *noun* [U, C, usually pl.] (**CHEMISTRY**) a light, strong material that is made with chemicals and is used for making many different kinds of objects: *recycled plastic* ◇ *single-use plastics*

plastic² ⚡**A2** /ˈplæstɪk/ *adj.* made of plastic: *plastic cups* ◇ *a plastic bag*

plastic surgery *noun* [U] (**MEDICINE**) a medical operation to repair or replace damaged skin or to improve the appearance of a person's face or body ➔ look at **facelift, surgery** (1)

plate¹ ⚡**A2** /pleɪt/ *noun* **1** [C] a flat, usually round, dish for eating or serving food from: *a plastic/paper/china plate* ◇ *a plate of food* **2** [C] a thin flat piece of metal or glass: *a steel/metal plate* **3** [C] a flat piece of metal with sth written on it: *The brass plate beside the door said 'Dr Temple'.* **4** [U] metal that has a thin covering of gold or silver: *gold/silver plate* **5** [C] (**GEOLOGY**) one of the sheets of rock that cover the earth's surface: *Where two continental plates collide, mountain ranges are created such as the Himalayas.* ➔ picture at **plate tectonics**

plate² /pleɪt/ *verb* [T, usually passive] **be plated (with sth)** **1** (used about a metal) to be covered with a thin layer of another metal, especially gold or silver: *a silver ring plated with gold* **2** to be covered with sheets of metal or another hard substance: *The walls of the vault were plated with steel.*

plateau /ˈplætəʊ/ *noun* [C] (*pl.* plateaus, plateaux /-təʊz/) **1** (**GEOGRAPHY**) a large high area of flat land ➔ picture at **limestone** **2** a state where there is little development or change: *House prices seem to have reached a plateau.*

plateful /ˈpleɪtfʊl/ *noun* [C] the amount of food that a plate can hold

platelet /ˈpleɪtlət/ *noun* [C] (**ANATOMY, BIOLOGY**) a very small blood cell, shaped like a disc. Platelets make the blood become thicker so that it CLOTS (= stops flowing) when you cut yourself.

plate tectonics *noun* [U] (**GEOLOGY**) the movements of the large PLATES (= sheets of rock) that form the earth's surface; the scientific study of these movements ➔ look at **continental drift** ➔ picture on **page 558**

platform ⚡**A2** /ˈplætfɔːm/ *noun* [C] **1** the place where you get on or off trains at a railway station: *Which platform does the train to York leave from?* **2** a flat surface, higher than the level of the floor or ground, on which people stand when they are speaking or performing, so that the audience can see them ➔ picture at **minaret** **3** (**COMPUTING**) the type of computer system or the software that is used: *an IBM platform* ◇ *a multimedia platform* **4** [usually sing.] (**POLITICS**) the ideas and aims of a political party that wants to be elected: *They fought the election on an anti-immigration platform.*

platinum /ˈplætɪnəm/ *noun* [U] (*symb.* Pt) (**CHEMISTRY**) a chemical element. Platinum is a valuable silver-grey metal used in making expensive jewellery: *a platinum wedding ring* ❶ For more information on the periodic table of elements, look at the **Reference Section** of this dictionary.

platonic /pləˈtɒnɪk/ *adj.* (used about a relationship between two people) friendly but not sexual

platoon /pləˈtuːn/ *noun* [C] a small group of soldiers

plausible /ˈplɔːzəbl/ *adj.* that you can believe; reasonable: *a plausible excuse* **OPP** **implausible**

play¹ ⚡**A1** /pleɪ/ *verb*
- HAVE FUN **1** [I] ~ (**with sb/sth**) to do sth to enjoy yourself; to have fun: *The children have been playing on the beach all day.* ◇ *Emma's found a new friend to play with.*
- GAMES/SPORTS **2** [T, I] to take part in a game or sport: *to play football/tennis/hockey* ◇ *I usually play against Bill.* ◇ *She played him at table tennis and won.* ◇ *Do you know how to play chess?* ◇ *Who's Brazil playing next in the World Cup?*
- MUSIC **3** [T, I] ~ (**sth**) (**on sth**) to make music with a musical instrument: *to play the piano/guitar/trumpet* ◇ *My son's learning the piano. He plays very well.* ◇ *She played a few notes on the violin.*
- VIDEO, SONG, ETC. **4** [I, T] (used about a video or DVD) to start working; to make a video or DVD start working: *I tried to play the DVD, but nothing happened.* ◇ *These videos won't play.* **5** [T] to use a STEREO, mobile phone, etc. to make it possible to hear a song, an album, etc: *I asked the DJ to play my favourite song.*
- ACT/PERFORM **6** [T, I] (**ARTS AND MEDIA**) to act in a play, film, TV programme, etc.; to act the role of sb: *Richard is going to play Romeo.* **7** [T] ~ **a part/role in sth** to have an effect on sth: *The media played an important part in the last election.* ◇ *John played a key role in organizing the protest.*
- OF LIGHT **8** [I] to move quickly and lightly: *Sunlight played on the surface of the sea.*
IDM **what is sb playing at?** used to ask in an angry way about what sb is doing: *What is that driver playing at?* ❶ For other idioms containing **play**, look at the entries for the nouns, adjectives, etc. For example, **play it by ear** is at **ear**.
PHRV **play sth back (to sb)** to turn on and watch or listen to a film, music, etc. that you have recorded: *Play that last scene back to me again.* **play sth down** to make sth seem less important than it really is: *to play down a crisis* **play A off against B** to make people compete or argue with each other, especially for your own advantage: *I think she enjoys playing one friend off against another.* **play on sth** to use and take advantage of sb's fears or weaknesses: *This advertising campaign plays on people's fears of illness.* **play (sb) up** (*informal*) to cause sb trouble or pain: *The car always plays up in wet weather.*

play² ⚡**A1** /pleɪ/ *noun* **1** [C] (**ARTS AND MEDIA**) a piece of writing performed by actors in the theatre, or on TV or radio: *Would you like to see a play while you're in London?* ◇ *a radio/TV play* ➔ note at **performing arts** **2** [U] (**SPORT**) the playing of a game or sport: *Bad weather stopped play yesterday.* **3** [U] things that people, especially children, do for pleasure rather than as work: *Young children learn through play.* ◇ *the happy sound of children at play*
IDM **fair play** → FAIR¹

playback /ˈpleɪbæk/ *noun* [U, C, usually sing.] the act of playing music, showing a film or listening to a phone message that has been recorded before; a recording that you listen to or watch again

playbook /ˈpleɪbʊk/ *noun* [C] a set of rules or way of doing sth: *The competition took their sales approach right out of our playbook.*

playboy /ˈpleɪbɔɪ/ *noun* [C] a rich man who spends his time enjoying himself

player ⚡**A1** /ˈpleɪə(r)/ *noun* [C] **1** (**SPORT**) a person who plays a game or sport: *a game for four players* ◇ *She's an excellent tennis player.* **2** (in compounds) a machine for producing sound or pictures that have been recorded: *a DVD player* **3** (**MUSIC**) a person who plays a musical instrument: *a piano player*

Plate tectonics

continental plates

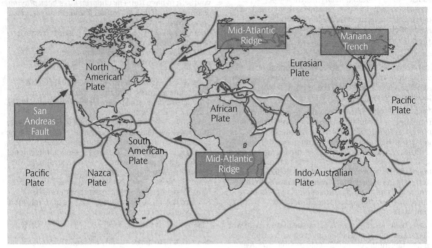

plate boundaries

The point where two plates meet is called a **plate boundary**. Earthquakes are most likely to occur either on or near plate boundaries. There are three types of plate boundary:

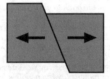

divergent boundary

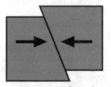

convergent boundary

At a **divergent boundary** the plates move apart. Divergent boundaries produce **rift valleys**, caused when a crack develops in the earth's surface and spreads to form a steep-sided valley as the plates move apart from each other. Volcanoes are often found along or near rift valleys. The Great Rift Valley in the Middle East and Africa is the most famous system of rift valleys.

At a **convergent boundary** the plates move towards each other and one plate is usually pushed up over the other plate. The earth's biggest earthquakes, some measuring over 9 on the Richter scale, occur at convergent boundaries and may cause tsunamis if the earthquake occurs underwater, as in the Asian tsunami disaster in December 2004.

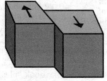

transform boundary

At a **transform boundary** plates slide and rub against each other along a transform fault. Most transform boundaries are found on the ocean floor. However, the most famous are found on land, for example the San Andreas Fault in California.

playful /'pleɪfl/ adj. **1** done or said in fun; not serious: a playful remark **2** full of fun; wanting to play: a playful puppy

playground /'pleɪgraʊnd/ noun [C] an area of land where children can play: the school playground

playgroup /'pleɪgruːp/ (also **playschool**) noun [C] (BrE) a place where very young children go to play and learn ⊃ look at **nursery school, preschool**

playhouse /'pleɪhaʊs/ noun **1** [sing.] (**ARTS AND MEDIA**) used in the name of some theatres: the Liverpool Playhouse **2** [C] a model of a house for children to play in

playing card = CARD (7)

playing field noun [C] (**SPORT**) a large field used for sports
IDM a level playing field → LEVEL²

playlist /'pleɪlɪst/ noun [C] (**MUSIC**) **1** a list of songs and pieces of music that you create to play on a music app, computer, etc: You can compile a playlist of your favourite songs. **2** a list of all the songs and pieces of music that are played by a radio station

play-off noun [C] (**SPORT**) a match between two teams or players who have equal scores to decide the winner

playschool /'pleɪskuːl/ = PLAYGROUP

playtime /'pleɪtaɪm/ noun [U, C] a period of time between lessons when children at school can go outside to play

playwright /'pleɪraɪt/ noun [C] (**ARTS AND MEDIA**) a person who writes plays for the theatre, TV or radio **SYN** **dramatist** ⊃ note at **performing arts**

plc /ˌpiː el 'siː/ (also **PLC**) abbr. (BrE) = PUBLIC COMPANY

plea ✸+ **C1** /pliː/ noun [C] **1** ~ (for sth) (formal) an important and emotional request: a plea for help **2** ~ (of sth) (**LAW**) a statement made by or for sb in court: a plea of guilty/not guilty

plead ✸+ **C1** /pliːd/ verb (pt, pp **pleaded**, AmE also **pled** /pled/) **1** [I] ~ (with sb) (to do/for sth) to ask sb for sth in a very strong and serious way: She pleaded with him not to leave her. ◇ He pleaded for mercy. ⊃ look at **beg** (1) **2** [I, T] (**LAW**) to state in court that you did or did not do a crime: The defendant pleaded not guilty to the charge of theft. ⊃ note at **crime 3** [T, I] ~ sth (for sb/sth) (**LAW**) (used especially about a lawyer in court) to support sb's case: He needs the very best lawyer to plead (his case) for him. **4** [T] ~ sth (for sth) to give sth as an excuse or explanation for sth: He pleaded family problems for his lack of concentration.

pleasant ✸ **B1** /'pleznt/ adj. fun, attractive or friendly: a pleasant evening/climate/place/view ◇ a pleasant smile/voice/manner **OPP** **unpleasant** ▶ **pleasantly** adv.

please¹ ✸ **A1** /pliːz/ exclamation used as a polite way of asking for sth or telling sb to do sth: Come in, please. ◇ Please don't spend too much money. ◇ Sit down, please. ◇ Two cups of coffee, please.
IDM **yes, please** used when you are accepting an offer of sth politely: 'Sugar?' 'Yes, please.' **OPP** **no¹**

please² ✸ **A2** /pliːz/ verb [I, T] to make sb happy: There's just no pleasing some people (= some people are impossible to please). **SYN** **satisfy**
OPP **displease 2** [I] often used after as or what, where, etc. to mean 'to want', 'to choose' or 'to like' to do something: You can't always do as you please. ◇ She has so much money she can buy anything she pleases.
IDM **please yourself** to be able to do whatever you want: Without anyone else to cook for, I can please myself what I eat.

pleased ✸ **A2** /pliːzd/ adj. [not before noun] ~ (with sb/ sth); ~ to do sth; ~ that … happy or satisfied about sth: John seems very pleased with his new car. ◇ Aren't you

pleased to see me? ◇ We're **only too pleased** (= very happy) to help. ◇ I'm so pleased that you've decided to stay another week. **OPP** **displeased**

pleasing /'pliːzɪŋ/ adj. giving you pleasure and SATISFACTION: The exam results are very pleasing this year.

pleasurable /'pleʒərəbl/ adj. (formal) giving pleasure: a pleasurable experience

pleasure ✸ **B1** /'pleʒə(r)/ noun **1** [U] the feeling of being happy or satisfied: Parents **get a lot of pleasure out of** watching their children grow up. ◇ **It gives me great pleasure** to introduce our next speaker. **2** [U] the activity of enjoying yourself, especially in contrast to working: What brings you to Paris — business or pleasure? **3** [C] an event or activity that you enjoy or that makes you happy: It's been a pleasure to work with you. ◇ 'Thanks for your help.' '**It's a pleasure.**'
IDM **take (no) pleasure in sth/doing sth** to (not) enjoy (doing) sth **with pleasure** used as a polite way of saying that you are happy to do sth: 'Could you give me a lift into town?' 'Yes, with pleasure.'

pleat /pliːt/ noun [C] a permanent fold that is SEWN or pressed into a piece of cloth: a skirt with pleats at the front

plebiscite /'plebɪsaɪt, -sɪt/ noun [C] ~ (on sth) (**POLITICS**) a vote by the people of a country or a region on a question that is very important: to hold a plebiscite on the country's future system of government
SYN **referendum**

plectrum /'plektrəm/ noun [C] (**MUSIC**) a small piece of plastic, metal, etc., that you use to play the strings of a guitar or similar musical instrument

pled /pled/ (AmE) past tense, past participle of **plead**

pledge ✸+ **C1** /pledʒ/ noun [C] ~ (to do sth); ~ (of sth) a formal promise or agreement: The government **made a pledge** to bring down interest rates. ◇ a pledge of support ▶ **pledge** ✸+ **C1** verb [T] ~ (sth) (to sb/sth): The footballers pledged £250 000 to the emergency fund.

the Pledge of Allegiance noun [sing.] a formal promise to respect and support the US, which Americans make standing in front of the flag with their right hand on their heart

plenary /'pliːnəri/ adj. (used about meetings, etc.) to be attended by everyone who has the right to attend: The new committee holds its first **plenary session** this week. ▶ **plenary** noun [C] (pl. -ies): the opening/final plenary of the conference

plentiful /'plentɪfl/ adj. available in large amounts or numbers: Fruit is plentiful at this time of year.
OPP **scarce**

plenty¹ ✸ **B1** /'plenti/ pron. ~ (of sb/sth) a large amount; as much or as many of sth as you need: 'Shall I get some more coffee?' 'No, we've still got plenty.' ◇ There's still plenty of time to get there. ◇ Have you brought plenty to drink?

plenty² /'plenti/ adv. **1** ~ **more (of) (sth)** a lot: There's plenty more ice cream. **2** ~ **big, long, etc. enough** (informal) more than big, long, etc. enough: 'This shirt's too small.' 'Well, it looks plenty big enough to me.'

plethora /'pleθərə/ noun [sing.] (formal) an amount that is greater than is needed or can be used: The report contained a plethora of detail.

pleura /'plʊərə/ noun [C] (pl. **pleurae** /-riː/) (**ANATOMY**) one of the two MEMBRANES (= thin layers) that surround the lungs

pleurisy /'plʊərəsi/ noun [U] (**HEALTH**) a serious illness that affects the inner covering of the chest and lungs, causing severe pain in the chest or sides

pliable /ˈplaɪəbl/ (*also* **pliant** /ˈplaɪənt/) *adj.* **1** easy to bend or shape **2** (used about a person) easy to influence

pliers /ˈplaɪəz/ *noun* [pl.] a metal tool with handles, that is used for holding things FIRMLY and for cutting wire: *a pair of pliers* ⊃ picture at **tool**

plight /plaɪt/ *noun* [sing.] a bad or difficult state or situation

plimsoll /ˈplɪmsəl, -səʊl/ (*also* **pump** *both BrE*) *noun* [C] a light sports shoe made of CANVAS (= strong cotton cloth) with a rubber SOLE: *The children changed into their plimsolls for PE.* ⊃ look at **trainer** (1)

plinth /plɪnθ/ *noun* [C] a block of stone on which a column or statue stands

plod /plɒd/ *verb* [I] (-dd-) ~ (along/on) to walk slowly and in a heavy or tired way: *We plodded on through the rain for nearly an hour.*
PHR V **plod along/on** to make slow progress, especially with difficult or boring work

plonk¹ /plɒŋk/ *verb* [T] (*informal*) **1** ~ sth (down) to put sth down on sth, especially noisily or carelessly: *Just plonk your bag down anywhere.* **2** ~ (yourself) (down) to sit down heavily and carelessly: *He just plonked himself down in front of the TV.*

plonk² /plɒŋk/ *noun* [U] (*BrE, informal*) cheap wine: *Let's open a bottle of plonk!*

plop¹ /plɒp/ *noun* [C, usually sing.] a sound like that of a small object dropping into water

plop² /plɒp/ *verb* [I] (used with an adverb or a preposition) (-pp-) to fall making a PLOP: *The frog plopped back into the water.*

plosive /ˈpləʊsɪv/ *noun* [C] (**LANGUAGE**) a speech sound made by stopping the flow of air coming out of the mouth and then suddenly releasing it, for example /t/ and /p/ in *top* ▸ **plosive** *adj.*

plot¹ ⟨B1⟩ /plɒt/ *noun* [C] **1** (**LITERATURE**) the series of events that form the story of a novel, film, etc: *The play had a very weak plot.* ◇ *I can't follow the plot of this novel.* **SYN** **storyline** **2** ~ (to do sth) a secret plan made by a group of people to do sth wrong or illegal: *a plot to kill the president* **3** (**AGRICULTURE**) a small piece of land, used for a special purpose: *a vegetable plot*

plot² ⟨B2⟩ /plɒt/ *verb* (-tt-) **1** [I, T] ~ (with sb) (against sb) to make a secret plan to do sth wrong or illegal: *They were accused of plotting against the government.* ◇ *The terrorists had been plotting this campaign for years.* **2** [T] to mark sth on a map, diagram, etc: *to plot the figures on a graph*

plough (*BrE*) (*AmE* **plow**) /plaʊ/ *noun* [C] (**AGRICULTURE**) a large piece of farming equipment that is pulled by a TRACTOR (= a large vehicle that is used on farms) or by an animal. A plough turns the soil over ready for seeds to be planted. ⊃ look at **snowplough** ▸ **plough** (*BrE*) (*AmE* **plow**) *verb* [T, I]: *(figurative) The book was long and boring but I managed to plough through it (= read it with difficulty).*

tractor pulling a plough

plough

tractor

ploy /plɔɪ/ *noun* [C] ~ (to do sth) something that you say or do in order to get what you want or to persuade sb to do sth

pluck¹ /plʌk/ *verb* [T] **1** ~ sth/sb (from sth); ~ sth/sb (out) to remove or take sth/sb from a place: *He plucked the letter from my hands.* ◇ *She plucked out a grey hair.* **2** (**MUSIC**) to play a musical instrument by pulling the strings with your fingers **3** to pull the feathers out of a dead bird in order to prepare it for cooking
IDM **pluck up courage** to try to get enough courage to do sth
PHR V **pluck at sth** to pull sth gently several times

pluck² /plʌk/ *noun* [U] (*informal*) the quality of being brave and wanting to continue even when sth is difficult ▸ **plucky** *adj.* (**pluckier; pluckiest**)

plug¹ ⟨+ C1⟩ /plʌg/ *noun* [C] **1** a plastic or rubber object with two or three metal pins that connects a piece of electrical equipment to the electricity supply **2** (*especially BrE, informal*) a place in a wall where a piece of electrical equipment can be connected to the electricity supply **SYN** **socket 3** a round piece of rubber or plastic that you use to block the hole in a bath, etc. **4** (*informal*) a mention that sb makes of a new book, film, etc. in order to encourage people to buy or see it

plugs

earth/ground (yellow/green stripes)
fuse
live (brown)
neutral (blue)
cable
socket
pin
plug

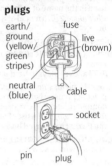

plug² ⟨+ C1⟩ /plʌg/ *verb* [T] (-gg-) **1** to fill or block a hole with sth that fits tightly into it: *He managed to plug the leak in the pipe.* **2** (*informal*) to say good things about a new book, film, etc. in order to encourage people to buy or see it: *They're really plugging that song on the radio at the moment.*
PHR V **plug sth in** to connect a piece of electrical equipment to the electricity supply or to another piece of equipment: *Is the microphone plugged in?* **OPP** **unplug**

plughole /ˈplʌɡhəʊl/ *noun* [C] (*BrE*) a hole in a bath, etc. where the water flows away

plug-in¹ *adj.* **1** able to be connected using a PLUG: *a plug-in kettle* **2** (**COMPUTING**) able to be added to a computer system so that it can do more things: *a plug-in graphics card*

plug-in² *noun* [C] (**COMPUTING**) a piece of computer software that can be added to a system so that it can do more things

plum /plʌm/ *noun* [C] a soft, round fruit with red or yellow skin and a stone in the middle

plumage /ˈpluːmɪdʒ/ *noun* [U] the feathers covering a bird's body

plumber /ˈplʌmə(r)/ *noun* [C] a person whose job is to put in or repair water pipes, baths, toilets, etc.

plumbing /ˈplʌmɪŋ/ *noun* [U] **1** all the pipes, etc. that supply water to a building **2** the work of a PLUMBER

plume /pluːm/ *noun* [C] **1** a narrow cloud of smoke, etc. that rises in the air **2** a large feather or group of feathers, often worn as a decoration

plummet /ˈplʌmɪt/ *verb* [I] to fall suddenly and quickly from a high level or position: *Share prices plummeted to an all-time low.* ◇ *The jet plummeted into a row of houses.* **SYN** **plunge**¹ ⊃ note at **trend**¹

plump¹ /plʌmp/ *adj.* (used about a person or an animal) pleasantly fat: *the baby's plump cheeks*

plump² /plʌmp/ *verb*
PHR V **plump (yourself/sb/sth) down** to sit down heavily; to put sb/sth down heavily: *She plumped herself down by the fire.* **plump for sb/sth** (*informal*) to choose or decide to have sb/sth: *I think I'll plump for the roast chicken, after all.*

plunder /'plʌndə(r)/ *noun* [U] the act of stealing from people or places, especially during war or fighting; the goods that are stolen ▸ **plunder** *verb* [I, T]

plunge¹ ⓘ+ 🄒🄵 /plʌndʒ/ *verb* **1** [I, T] to move or make sb/ sth move suddenly forwards and/or downwards **2** [I] to decrease suddenly and quickly: *Share prices plunged overnight.* ⊃ note at **trend¹**
🄿🄷🅁🅅 **plunge in** | **plunge into sth 1** to jump into sth, especially with force: *He ran to the river and plunged in.* **2** to start doing sth with energy and enthusiasm **plunge sth in** | **plunge sth into sth** to push sth suddenly and with force into sth: *He plunged the knife into the table in anger.* **plunge sb/sth into sth** to cause sb/sth to suddenly be in the state mentioned: *The country has been plunged into chaos by the floods.*

plunge² /plʌndʒ/ *noun* [C] **~ (in sth)** a sudden jump, drop or fall: *the plunge in house prices*
🄸🄳🄼 **take the plunge** (*informal*) to decide to do sth difficult after thinking about it for quite a long time: *After going out together for five years, they took the plunge and got married.*

plunge pool *noun* [C] **1** a small deep artificial pool filled with cold water **2** (**GEOGRAPHY**) a deep pool at the bottom of a WATERFALL

plunger /'plʌndʒə(r)/ *noun* [C] **1** a part of a piece of equipment that can be pushed down, for example in a SYRINGE (= a device used for putting a drug, etc. into the body and for taking blood out) **2** a piece of equipment used for clearing kitchen and bathroom pipes

the pluperfect /ðə ‚pluː'pɜːfɪkt/ = PAST PERFECT

plural /'plʊərəl/ *noun* [C] (*abbr.* **pl.**) (**GRAMMAR**) the form of a noun, verb, etc. that refers to more than one person or thing: *The plural of 'boat' is 'boats'.* ◊ *The verb should be **in the plural**.* ▸ **plural** *adj.* ⊃ look at **singular** (1)

pluralism /'plʊərəlɪzəm/ *noun* [U] (*formal*) (**SOCIAL STUDIES**) **1** the existence of many different groups of people in one society, for example people who belong to different human groups or have different political or religious beliefs: *cultural pluralism* **2** the belief that it is possible and good for different groups of people to live together in peace in one society

plus¹ ⓘ 🄑🄓 /plʌs/ *prep.* **1** (**MATHEMATICS**) and; added to: *Two plus two is four (2+2=4).* 🄾🄿🄿 **minus¹ 2** in addition to; and also: *You have to work five days a week plus every other weekend.*

plus² ⓘ 🄑🄓 /plʌs/ *adj.* (after a noun) **1** or more: *I'd say there were 30 000 plus at the match.* **2** (**EDUCATION**) (used for marking work done by students) slightly above: *I got a B plus (= B+) for my homework.* 🄾🄿🄿 **minus³**

plus³ ⓘ 🄑🄓 /plʌs/ *noun* [C] **1** (**MATHEMATICS**) the symbol (+) used in mathematics 🄾🄿🄿 **minus² 2** an advantage; a good thing: *Knowledge of French is a plus in this job.* 🄾🄿🄿 **minus²**

plus⁴ ⓘ 🄑🄓 /plʌs/ *conj.* (*informal*) used to add more information: *I'm very busy at work. Plus my mother is not well.*

plush /plʌʃ/ *adj.* comfortable and expensive: *a plush hotel*

Pluto /'pluːtəʊ/ *noun* [sing.] (**ASTRONOMY**) one of the large round objects in space that are not as large as planets but which go around the sun

plutonium /pluː'təʊniəm/ *noun* [U] (*symb.* **Pu**) (**CHEMISTRY**) a chemical element. Plutonium is RADIOACTIVE and is used in nuclear weapons and in producing nuclear energy. ❶ For more information on the periodic table of elements, look at the **Reference Section** of this dictionary.

ply /plaɪ/ *verb* [I, T] (**plying; plies;** *pt, pp* **plied**) to try to sell services or goods to people, especially on the street: *Boat owners were **plying** their **trade** to passing tourists.* ◊ *to ply for business*
🄿🄷🅁🅅 **ply sb with sth** to keep giving sb food and drink; to keep asking sb questions: *They plied us with food from the moment we arrived.*

plywood /'plaɪwʊd/ *noun* [U] board made by sticking several thin layers of wood together

PM /‚piː 'em/ *abbr.* = PRIME MINISTER

p.m. /‚piː 'em/ *abbr.* after twelve o'clock in the middle of the day (from Latin 'post meridiem'): *2 p.m.* (= two o'clock in the afternoon) ◊ *11.30 p.m.* (= 11.30 in the evening) ⊃ look at **a.m.**

PMS /‚piː em 'es/ (*also* **PMT** /‚piː em 'tiː/) *noun* [U] physical and emotional problems such as pain and feeling unhappy that many women experience before their PERIOD (= flow of blood) each month (the abbreviation for 'premenstrual syndrome/tension')

pneumatic /njuː'mætɪk/ *adj.* **1** filled with air: *a pneumatic tyre* **2** worked by air under pressure: *pneumatic tools*

pneu‚matic 'drill (*BrE*) (*AmE* **jackhammer**) *noun* [C] a large powerful tool, worked by air pressure, used especially for breaking up road surfaces

pneumonia /njuː'məʊniə/ *noun* [U] (**HEALTH**) a serious illness of the lungs that makes breathing difficult

PO /‚piː 'əʊ/ *abbr.* THE POST OFFICE: *a PO box*

poach /pəʊtʃ/ *verb* **1** [T] to cook food (especially fish or eggs) gently in a small amount of liquid **2** [T, I] to hunt animals illegally on sb else's land **3** [T] to take and use sth/sth that belongs to sb/sth else, especially in a secret or unfair way: *She accused him of poaching her ideas.*

poacher /'pəʊtʃə(r)/ *noun* [C] a person who hunts animals illegally on sb else's land

PO box *noun* [C] a place in a post office where letters, packages, etc. are kept until they are collected by the person they were sent to: *The address is PO Box 4287, Nairobi, Kenya.*

pocket¹ ⓘ 🄐🄞 /'pɒkɪt/ *noun* [C] **1** a piece of material like a small bag that is SEWN inside or on a piece of clothing and is used for carrying things in: *He always walks with his hands in his trouser pockets.* ◊ *a pocket dictionary/calculator* (= one small enough to fit in your pocket) **2** a small bag or container that is fixed to the inside of a car door, bag, etc. and used for putting things in: *There are safety instructions in the pocket of the seat in front of you.* **3** used to talk about the amount of money that you have to spend: *They sell cars to suit every pocket.* ◊ *He had no intention of paying for the meal **out of his own pocket**.* **4** a small area or group that is different from everything around it: *pockets of warm water* ⊃ look at **air pocket**
🄸🄳🄼 **pick sb's pocket** → PICK¹

pocket² /'pɒkɪt/ *verb* [T] **1** to put sth in your pocket: *He took the letter and pocketed it quickly.* **2** to steal or win money

▼ **CULTURE**

In August 2006, the International Astronomical Union declared that **Pluto** was to be called a **dwarf planet** because it has different characteristics from the other planets (**Mercury, Mars, Venus,** etc.) in our **solar system.** From 1930, when it was first discovered, until 2006, **Pluto** was known as the ninth planet in the **solar system** because of its position furthest from the sun.

'pocket money (*especially BrE*) (*also* **allowance** *especially in AmE*) *noun* [U] an amount of money that parents give a child to spend, usually every week

pod /pɒd/ *noun* [C] (**BIOLOGY**) the long, green part of some plants, such as PEAS and beans, that contains the seeds

podcast /'pɒdkɑːst/ *noun* [C] (**COMPUTING**) a recording of sth such as a radio programme that you can copy from the internet and play on your computer, mobile phone, etc: *Click here to subscribe, and receive podcasts automatically each week.*

podiatrist /pə'daɪətrɪst/ = CHIROPODIST

podiatry /pə'daɪətri/ (*especially AmE*) = CHIROPODY

podium /'pəʊdiəm/ *noun* [C] a small platform for people to stand on when they are speaking, performing, etc. in public

poem ? **B1** /'pəʊɪm/ *noun* [C] (**LITERATURE**) a piece of writing arranged in short lines. Poems try to express thoughts and feelings with the help of sound and rhythm.

poet ? **B1** /'pəʊɪt/ *noun* [C] (**LITERATURE**) a person who writes poems

poetic /pəʊ'etɪk/ (*also* **poetical** /pəʊ'etɪkl/) *adj.* (**LITERATURE**) connected with poetry or like a poem ▶ **poetically** /-kli/ *adv.*

IDM **poetic licence** (**LITERATURE**) the freedom to change facts, the normal rules of language, etc. in a special piece of writing or speech in order to achieve a particular effect

Poet Laureate /ˌpəʊɪt 'lɒriət/ *noun* [C] (*pl.* **Poets Laureate**) (**LITERATURE**) **1** (especially in the UK) a person who has been officially chosen to write poetry for the country's important occasions **2** (*especially AmE*) a person whose poetry is considered to be the best or most typical of their country or region.

poetry ? **B1** /'pəʊətri/ *noun* [U] (**LITERATURE**) a collection of poems; poems in general: *Shakespeare's poetry and plays* ◇ *Do you like poetry?* ⊃ look at **prose**

pogo stick /'pəʊɡəʊ stɪk/ *noun* [C] a POLE with a bar to stand on and a spring at the bottom, that you jump around on for fun

poignant /'pɔɪnjənt/ *adj.* having a strong effect on your feelings, especially making you feel sad: *a poignant memory* ▶ **poignancy** /'pɔɪnjənsi/ *noun* [U] ▶ **poignantly** *adv.*

point¹ ? **A1** ◉ /pɔɪnt/ *noun*

• FACT/OPINION **1** [C] a particular fact, idea or opinion that sb expresses: *You make some interesting points in your essay.* ◇ *I see your point but I don't agree with you.* ⊃ note at **opinion** ❶ You can **bring up**, **raise**, **argue**, **emphasize** or **illustrate** a point.

• DIRECTION **2** [C] one of the marks of direction around a COMPASS (= a device for finding direction)

• IMPORTANT IDEA **3** **the point** [sing.] the most important part of what is being said; the main piece of information: *She always talks and talks and takes ages to get to the point.* ◇ *The point is we don't have any money!* **4** [C] an important idea or thought that needs to be considered: '*Have you checked what time the last bus back is?*' '*That's a point — no I haven't.*'

• QUALITY **5** [C] a detail, characteristic or quality of sb/sth: *Make a list of your strong points and your weak points* (= good and bad qualities).

• PURPOSE **6** [sing.] **the ~ (of/in sth/doing sth)** the meaning, reason or purpose of sth: *She's said no, so what's the point of telephoning her again?* ◇ *There's no point in talking to my parents — they never listen.* ⊃ note at **purpose**

• PLACE/TIME **7** [C] (often in compounds) a particular place, position or moment: *The library is a good starting point for that sort of information.* ◇ *He has reached the high point of his career.* ◇ *the boiling/freezing point of water* ◇ *He waved to the crowd and it was at that point that the shot was fired.* ◇ *At one point I thought I was going to laugh.*

• SHARP END **8** [C] the thin sharp end of sth: *the point of a pin/needle/pencil*

• IN A NUMBER **9** [C] a small round mark used when writing parts of numbers: *She ran the race in 11.2 (eleven point two) seconds.*

• IN A GAME, SPORT, ETC. **10** [C] (*abbr.* **pt**) a single mark in some games, sports, etc. that you add to others to get the score: *to score a point* ◇ *He needs two more points to win the match.*

• MEASUREMENT **11** [C] a unit of measurement for certain things: *The value of the dollar has fallen by a few points.*

IDM **be beside the point** → BESIDE **be on the point of doing sth** just going to do sth: *I was on the point of going out when the phone rang.* **have your, etc. (good) points** to have some good qualities: *Bill has his good points, but he's very unreliable.* **make a point of doing sth** to make sure you do sth because it is important or necessary: *I made a point of locking all the doors and windows before leaving the house.* **point of view** a way of looking at a situation; an opinion: *From my point of view it would be better to wait a little longer.* **SYN** **standpoint**, **viewpoint** a **sore point** → SORE¹ **sb's strong point** → STRONG **take sb's point** to understand and accept what sb is saying **to the point** connected with what is being discussed: *His speech was short and to the point.* **SYN** **relevant up to a point** partly: *I agree with you up to a point.*

point² ? **B1** **S** /pɔɪnt/ *verb* **1** [I] **~ (at/to sb/sth)** to show where sth is or to draw attention to sth using your finger, a stick, etc: '*I'll have that one,' she said, pointing to a chocolate cake.* **2** [I, T] **~ (sth) (at/towards sb/sth)** to aim (sth) in the direction of sb/sth: *She pointed the gun at the target and fired.* ⊃ note at **gun¹** **3** [I] (used with an adverb or a preposition) to face in a particular direction; to show that sth is in a particular direction: *Turn round until you're pointing north.* ◇ *The sign pointed towards the motorway.* **4** [I] **~ to sth** to show that sth is likely to exist, happen or be true: *Research points to a connection between diet and cancer.*

PHR V **point sth out (to sb)** to make sb look at sth; to make sth clear to sb: *The guide pointed out all the places of interest to us on the way.* ◇ *I'd like to point out that we haven't got much time left.*

ˌpoint-'blank *adj., adv.* **1** (used about a shot) from a very close position: *He was shot in the leg at point-blank range.* **2** (used about sth that is said) very direct and not polite; not allowing any discussion: *He told her point-blank to get out of the house and never come back.*

pointed ? **B2** /'pɔɪntɪd/ *adj.* **1** having a sharp end: *a pointed stick/nose* **2** said in a critical way: *She made a pointed comment about people who are always late.* ▶ **pointedly** *adv.*

pointer /'pɔɪntə(r)/ *noun* [C] **1** a piece of helpful advice or information: *Could you give me some pointers on how best to tackle the problem?* **2** a stick that is used to point to things on a map, etc. **3** (**COMPUTING**) a small ARROW on a computer screen that you move by moving the mouse

pointillism /'pɔɪntɪlɪzəm, 'pwæn-/ *noun* [U] (**ART**) a style of painting that was developed in France in the late nineteenth century in which very small DOTS (= round marks) of colour are used to build up the picture ▶ **pointillist** /'pɔɪntɪlɪst/ *adj., noun* [C]

pointless /ˈpɔɪntləs/ adj. without any use or purpose: *It's pointless to try and make him agree.* ▸ **pointlessly** adv. ▸ **pointlessness** noun [U]

,**point of 'sale** noun [sing.] (**BUSINESS**) the place where a product is sold: *More information on healthy foods should be provided at the point of sale.*

pointy /ˈpɔɪnti/ adj. (**pointier; pointiest**) (*informal*) with a point at one end: *pointy ears* **SYN pointed**

poise /pɔɪz/ noun [U] a calm, confident way of behaving

poised /pɔɪzd/ adj. **1** not moving but ready to move: *'Shall I call the doctor or not?' he asked, his hand poised above the phone.* **2** ~ (**to do sth**) ready to act; about to do sth: *The government is poised to take action if the crisis continues.* **3** calm and confident

poison¹ ? **B1** /ˈpɔɪzn/ noun [C, U] a substance that kills or harms you if you eat or drink it: *rat poison* ◇ *poison gas*

poison² ? **B1** /ˈpɔɪzn/ verb [T] **1** to kill, harm or damage sb/sth with poison **2** to put poison in sth: *The cup of coffee had been poisoned.* **3** to have a bad effect on sth: *The quarrel had poisoned their relationship.* ▸ **poisoned** adj.: *a poisoned drink*

poisoning /ˈpɔɪzənɪŋ/ noun [U] (**HEALTH**) the giving or taking of poison or a dangerous substance: *He got food poisoning from eating fish that wasn't fresh.*

poisonous ? **B1** /ˈpɔɪzənəs/ adj. **1** causing death or illness if you eat or drink it **2** (used about animals, etc.) producing and using poison to attack its enemies: *He was bitten by a poisonous snake.* **3** very unpleasant and intended to upset sb: *She wrote him a poisonous letter criticizing his behaviour.*

poke /pəʊk/ verb **1** [T] to push sb/sth with a finger, stick or other long, thin object: *Be careful you don't poke yourself in the eye with that stick!* **2** [T, I] (used with an adverb or a preposition) to move or to push sth quickly into sth or in a certain direction: *He poked the stick down the hole to see how deep it was.* ◇ *A child's head poked up from behind the wall.* ▸ **poke** noun [C] **IDM poke fun at sb/sth** to make jokes about sb/sth, often in an unkind way **poke/stick your nose into sth** → NOSE¹

poker /ˈpəʊkə(r)/ noun **1** [U] a type of card game usually played to win money **2** [C] a metal stick for moving the coal or wood in a fire

poky /ˈpəʊki/ adj. (**pokier; pokiest**) (*especially BrE, informal*) (used about a house, room, etc.) too small: *a poky little office*

polar /ˈpəʊlə(r)/ adj. [only before noun] (**GEOGRAPHY**) of or near the North or South Pole: *the polar regions*

,**polar bear** noun [C] a large white bear that lives in the area near the North Pole

polarize (*BrE also* -**ise**) /ˈpəʊləraɪz/ verb **1** [I, T] to separate or make people separate into two groups with completely opposite opinions: *Public opinion has polarized on this issue.* **2** [T] (**PHYSICS**) to make waves of light, etc. VIBRATE (= move up and down with very small continuous movements) in a single direction **3** [T] (**PHYSICS**) to make sth have two POLES with opposite qualities: *to polarize a magnet* ▸ **polarization** (*BrE also* -**isation**) /ˌpəʊləraɪˈzeɪʃn/ noun [U]

pole ?⁺ **C1** /pəʊl/ noun [C] **1** a long, thin piece of wood or metal, used especially to hold sth up: *a flagpole* ◇ *a tent pole* **2** (**GEOGRAPHY**) either of the two points at the exact top and bottom of the earth: *the North/South Pole* **3** (**PHYSICS**) either of the two ends of a MAGNET, or the positive or negative points of an electric battery ◇ *picture at* **magnetism 4** either of two opposite or very different extremes: *Their opinions were at opposite poles of the debate.*

the ,**'pole vault** noun [sing.] (**SPORT**) a sporting event in which people try to jump over a high bar, using a long POLE to push themselves off the ground

police¹ ? **A1** /pəˈliːs/ noun [pl.] (**LAW**) the official organization whose job is to make sure that people obey the law, and to prevent and solve crime; the people who work for this organization: *Dial 999 if you need to call the police.* ◇ *a police car* ◇ *the local police station*

police² /pəˈliːs/ verb [T] to keep control in a place by using the police or a similar official group: *The cost of policing football games is extremely high.*

po,**lice 'constable** (*also* **constable**) noun [C] (*BrE*) (*abbr.* **PC**) (**LAW**) (in the UK) a police officer of the lowest rank

po'**lice force** noun [C] (**LAW**) the police organization of a country, district or town: *Kamal wants to join the police force when he finishes school.*

policeman ? **A1** /pəˈliːsmən/ noun [C] (*pl.* -**men** /-mən/) a male police officer

po'**lice officer** (*also* **officer**) noun [C] (**LAW**) a member of the police

po'**lice state** noun [C] (**POLITICS**) a country where people's freedom, especially to travel and to express political opinions, is controlled by the government, with the help of the police

policewoman /pəˈliːswʊmən/ noun [C] (*pl.* -**women** /-wɪmɪn/) a female police officer

policy ? **B1 ⓦ** /ˈpɒləsi/ noun (*pl.* -**ies**) **1** [C, U] ~ (**on sth**); ~ (**to do sth**) a plan of action agreed or chosen by a government, a company, etc: *Labour has a new set of policies on health.* ◇ *It is company policy not to allow children on the premises.* **2** [C, U] (*formal*) a way of behaving that you think is best in a particular situation: *It's my policy only to do business with people I like.* **3** [C] a document that shows an agreement that you have made with an insurance company: *an insurance policy* ◇ *note at* **insurance**

policymaker /ˈpɒləsimeɪkə(r)/ noun [C] (**POLITICS**) a person who is involved in developing plans for a political party, business, etc: *Policymakers need to decide what services the government should provide.*

polio /ˈpəʊliəʊ/ noun [U] (**HEALTH**) a serious disease that can cause loss of control or feeling in part or most of the body

polish¹ /ˈpɒlɪʃ/ verb [T] to make sth shine by rubbing it and often by putting a special cream or liquid on it: *to polish your shoes/a table* **PHR V polish sth off** (*informal*) to finish sth, especially food, quickly: *The two of them polished off a whole chicken for dinner!*

polish² /ˈpɒlɪʃ/ noun **1** [U] a cream, liquid, etc. that you put on sth to clean it and make it shine: *a tin of shoe polish* **2** [sing.] the act of POLISHING sth: *I'll give the glasses a polish before the guests arrive.*

polished /ˈpɒlɪʃt/ adj. **1** shiny because it has been rubbed clean: *polished wood floors* **2** (used about a performance, etc.) of a high standard: *Most of the actors gave a polished performance.*

politburo /ˈpɒlɪtbjʊərəʊ/ noun [C] (*pl.* -**os**) (**POLITICS**) the most important committee of a Communist party, with the power to decide on policy

polite ? **A2** /pəˈlaɪt/ adj. (**politer; politest**) having good manners and showing respect for others: *The assistants in that shop are always very helpful and polite.* ◇ *He gave me a polite smile.* **OPP impertinent, impolite** ▸ **politely** adv. ▸ **politeness** noun [U]

political ﹖ **B1** /pəˈlɪtɪkl/ *adj.* **1** (**POLITICS**) connected with politics and government: *a political leader/debate/party* ◇ *She has very strong political opinions.* **2** (**POLITICS**) (used about people) interested in politics **3** concerned with the competition for power inside an organization: *I suspect he was dismissed for political reasons.*

po,litical ˈaction committee *noun* [C] (*abbr.* **PAC**) (**POLITICS**) (in the US) a group of people who collect money to support the candidates and policies that will help them achieve their political and social aims

po,litical aˈsylum (*formal*) = ASYLUM (1)

politically /pəˈlɪtɪkli/ *adv.* (**POLITICS**) in a way that is connected with politics: *a politically sensitive issue* ◇ *It makes sense politically as well as economically.*

po,litically corˈrect *adj.* (*abbr.* **PC**) (**SOCIAL STUDIES**) used to describe language or behaviour that carefully avoids offending particular groups of people
▶ po,litical corˈrectness *noun* [U]

politician ﹖ **B1** /ˌpɒləˈtɪʃn/ *noun* [C] (**POLITICS**) a person whose job is in politics, especially one who is a member of parliament or of the government: *Politicians of all parties supported the war.*

politics ﹖ **B1** /ˈpɒlətɪks/ *noun* **1** [U + sing./pl. verb] the work and ideas that are connected with governing a country, a town, etc: *to go into politics* ◇ *Politics has/have never been of great interest to me.* **2** [pl.] a person's political opinions and beliefs: *His politics are extreme.* **3** [U + sing./pl. verb] matters concerned with competition for power between people in an organization: *I never get involved in office politics.* **4** (*also* Po,litical ˈScience) [U] (**EDUCATION**) the scientific study of government: *a degree in Politics*

polka dot /ˈpɒlkə dɒt/ *noun* [C] one of many DOTS (= round marks) that together form a pattern, especially on material: *a blue scarf with white polka dots*

poll[1] ﹖+ **C1** /pəʊl/ *noun* [C] **1** (*also* opinion poll) a way of finding out public opinion by asking a number of people their views on sth: *This was voted best drama series in a viewers' poll.* **2** (**POLITICS**) the process of voting in a political election; the number of votes given: *The country will go to the polls* (= vote) *in June.*

poll[2] /pəʊl/ *verb* [T] **1** (**POLITICS**) to receive a certain number of votes in an election: *The Liberal Democrat candidate polled over 3 000 votes.* **2** to ask members of the public their opinion on a subject: *Of those polled, only 20 per cent were in favour of changing the law.*

pollen /ˈpɒlən/ *noun* [U] (**BIOLOGY**) a fine, usually yellow, powder that is formed in flowers. It makes other flowers of the same type produce seeds when it is carried to them by the wind, insects, etc. ⊃ picture at **flower**[1]

ˈpollen count *noun* [C, usually sing.] (**ENVIRONMENT**) a number that shows how much POLLEN is in the air

ˈpollen tube *noun* [C] (**BIOLOGY**) a tube that grows when POLLEN lands on the top of the STIGMA (= the female part in the middle of a flower) to carry the male cell to the OVULE (= the part that contains the female cell) ⊃ picture at **flower**[1]

pollinate /ˈpɒləneɪt/ *verb* [T] (**BIOLOGY**) to put POLLEN into a flower or plant so that it produces seeds
▶ pollination /ˌpɒləˈneɪʃn/ *noun* [U]

polling /ˈpəʊlɪŋ/ *noun* [U] **1** (**POLITICS**) the activity of voting in an election: *Polling has been heavy since eight o'clock this morning.* **2** the act of asking questions in order to find out public opinion

ˈpolling booth (*especially BrE*) (*AmE usually* **voting booth**) *noun* [C] (**POLITICS**) a small space, separated from the surrounding area, where you stand to mark your card in order to vote in an election

ˈpolling day *noun* [U, C] (*BrE*) (**POLITICS**) a day on which people vote in an election

ˈpolling station *noun* [C] (*especially BrE*) (**POLITICS**) a building where you go to vote in an election

pollutant /pəˈluːtənt/ *noun* [C] (**ENVIRONMENT**) a substance that POLLUTES air, rivers, etc.

pollute /pəˈluːt/ *verb* [T] (**ENVIRONMENT**) to make air, rivers, etc. dirty and dangerous: *Traffic fumes are polluting our cities.* ◇ *The beach had been polluted with oil.*

polluter /pəˈluːtə(r)/ *noun* [C] (**ENVIRONMENT**) a person, company, country, etc. that causes pollution

pollution ﹖ **A2** /pəˈluːʃn/ *noun* [U] (**ENVIRONMENT**) **1** the process of making the air, water, etc. dirty and dangerous: *Major steps are being taken to control the pollution of beaches.* **2** substances that POLLUTE: *The rivers are full of pollution.*

polo /ˈpəʊləʊ/ *noun* [U] (**SPORT**) a game for two teams of players riding horses. The players try to score goals by hitting a ball with MALLETS (= long wooden HAMMERS).

ˈpolo neck (*BrE*) (*AmE* **turtleneck**) *noun* [C] a high round COLLAR (= the part around the neck) on a piece of clothing that is rolled over and that covers most of your neck; a piece of clothing with a polo neck

polonium /pəˈləʊniəm/ *noun* [U] (*symb.* **Po**) (**CHEMISTRY**) a chemical element. Polonium is a RADIOACTIVE metal that is present in nature when URANIUM DECAYS. **❶** For more information on the periodic table of elements, look at the **Reference Section** of this dictionary.

poly /ˈpɒli/ *noun* [C] (*pl.* polys) (*informal*) = POLYTECHNIC

poly- /ˈpɒli, pəˈlɪ/ *prefix* (in nouns, adjectives and adverbs) many: *polygamy*

polyester /ˌpɒliˈestə(r)/ *noun* [U] an artificial material that is used for making clothes, etc.

polyethylene /ˌpɒliˈeθəliːn/ (*AmE*) = POLYTHENE

polygamy /pəˈlɪɡəmi/ *noun* [U] the custom of having more than one wife or husband at the same time ⊃ look at **bigamy**, **monogamy** ▶ polygamous /-məs/ *adj.*: *a polygamous society*

polygon /ˈpɒlɪɡən/ *noun* [C] (**GEOMETRY**) a flat shape with at least three, and usually five or more, angles and straight sides ▶ polygonal /pəˈlɪɡənl/ *adj.*

polyhedron /ˌpɒliˈhiːdrən/ *noun* [C] (*pl.* polyhedra /-drə/, polyhedrons) (**GEOMETRY**) a solid shape with many flat sides, usually more than six

polymer /ˈpɒlɪmə(r)/ *noun* [C] (**CHEMISTRY**) a substance consisting of large MOLECULES that are made from combinations of small simple MOLECULES ⊃ look at **biopolymer**, **monomer**

polymerize (*BrE also* **-ise**) /ˈpɒlɪmaraɪz/ *verb* [I, T] (**CHEMISTRY**) to combine, or to make units of a chemical combine, to make a POLYMER: *The substance polymerizes to form a hard plastic.* ▶ polymerization (*BrE also* **-isation**) /ˌpɒlɪmaraɪˈzeɪʃn/ *noun* [U]

polyp /ˈpɒlɪp/ *noun* [C] **1** (**HEALTH**) a small mass of cells that grows inside the body, especially in the nose. It is caused by disease but is not usually harmful. **2** (**BIOLOGY**) a small and very simple sea creature with a body shaped like a tube

polypropylene /ˌpɒliˈprəʊpəliːn/ *noun* [U] a strong plastic often used for objects such as toys or chairs that are made in a MOULD (= a shaped container)

polystyrene /ˌpɒliˈstaɪriːn/ *noun* [U] a light firm plastic substance that is usually white and is used for packing things so that they do not get broken

polytechnic /ˌpɒliˈteknɪk/ (*also informal* **poly**) *noun* [C] (**EDUCATION**) (in some countries) a college for higher education, especially in scientific and technical subjects

polytheism /ˈpɒliθiːɪzəm/ *noun* [U] (**RELIGION**) the belief that there is more than one god ⊃ look at **monotheism** ▸ **polytheistic** /ˌpɒliθiˈɪstɪk/ *adj.*

polythene /ˈpɒliθiːn/ (*BrE*) (*AmE* **polyethylene**) *noun* [U] a type of very thin plastic material often used to make bags for food, etc. or to keep things dry

polytunnel /ˈpɒlitʌnl/ *noun* [C] (**AGRICULTURE**) a long low structure covered with plastic, used for growing seeds or young plants outdoors

polyunsaturated fat /ˌpɒliʌnˌsætʃəreɪtɪd ˈfæt/ *noun* [C, U] (**HEALTH**) a type of fat found, for example, in seeds and vegetable oils, that is considered to be healthier in the diet than other types of fat: *polyunsaturated margarine* ⊃ look at **saturated fat, unsaturated fat**

pomegranate /ˈpɒmɪɡrænɪt/ *noun* [C] a round fruit with thick smooth skin that is red inside and full of large seeds that are eaten

pommel /ˈpɒml/ *noun* [C] **1** the higher front part of a SADDLE (= a leather seat) on a horse **2** the round part on the end of the handle of a SWORD (= a long sharp metal weapon)

pommel horse *noun* [C] (**SPORT**) a large object on legs with two handles on top, that GYMNASTS put their hands on and SWING their body and legs around

pommel horse

pomp /pɒmp/ *noun* [U] the impressive nature of a large official occasion or ceremony

pompous /ˈpɒmpəs/ *adj.* showing that you think you are more important than other people, for example by using long words that sound impressive

pond ⚡+ **C1** /pɒnd/ *noun* [C] a small area of still water

ponder /ˈpɒndə(r)/ *verb* [I, T] ~ **(on/over) sth** to think about sth carefully or for a long time: *The teacher gave us a question to ponder over before the next class.*

pong /pɒŋ/ *noun* [C] (*BrE, informal*) a strong unpleasant smell ▸ **pong** *verb* [I]

pony /ˈpəʊni/ *noun* [C] (*pl.* -ies) a small horse

ponytail /ˈpəʊniteɪl/ *noun* [C] long hair that is tied at the back of the head and that hangs down in one piece

pony-trekking *noun* [U] the activity of riding horses for pleasure in the country

poo /puː/ *noun* [C, U] (*pl.* poos) (*BrE, informal*) a child's word for the solid waste matter that you get rid of from the body when you go to the toilet ▸ **poo** *verb* [I] (pooing; poos; *pt, pp* pooed)

poodle /ˈpuːdl/ *noun* [C] a type of dog with thick curly fur that is sometimes cut into a special pattern

pooh /puː/ *exclamation* (*BrE*) said when you smell sth unpleasant

pool¹ ⚡ **A1** /puːl/ *noun*
• OF LIQUID/LIGHT **1** [C] = SWIMMING POOL: *She swam ten lengths of the pool.* **2** [C] a small amount of liquid or light lying on a surface: *There's a huge pool of water on the kitchen floor.* ◇ *a pool of light* **3** [C] a small amount of water, especially one that has formed naturally

• GAME **4** [U] a game for two people played with 16 balls on a table. Players use CUES (= long sticks) to try to hit the balls into pockets at the edge of the table. ⊃ look at **billiards, snooker** ⊃ picture at **sport**
• GROUP OF THINGS/PEOPLE **5** [C] a quantity of money, goods, etc. that is shared between a group of people: *There is a pool of cars that anyone in the company can use.*

pool² /puːl/ *verb* [T] to collect money, ideas, etc. together from a number of people: *If we pool our ideas we should come up with a good plan.*

poor ⚡ **A1** /pɔː(r), pʊə(r)/ *adj.* **1** not having enough money to have a comfortable life: *The family was too poor to buy new clothes.* ◇ *Richer countries could do more to help poorer countries.* **OPP** **rich 2** the poor *noun* [pl.] people who do not have enough money to have a comfortable life **3** of low quality or in a bad condition: *Paul is in very poor health.* ◇ *The industry has a poor safety record.* **4** [only before noun] used when you are showing that you feel sorry for sb: *Poor Dan! He's very upset!*

poorly¹ /ˈpɔːli, ˈpʊəli/ *adv.* not well; badly: *a poorly paid job*

poorly² /ˈpɔːli, ˈpʊəli/ *adj.* (*BrE, informal*) not well; ill: *I'm feeling a bit poorly.*

pop¹ ⚡ **C1** /pɒp/ *verb* (-pp-) **1** [I, T] to make a short sudden sound like a small explosion; to cause sth to do this: *The balloon popped.* ◇ *He popped the balloon.* **2** [I] (used with an adverb or a preposition) (*informal*) to come or go somewhere quickly or suddenly: *I'm just popping out to the shops.* ◇ *Why don't you pop in* (= visit us) *for a cup of tea?* **3** [T] (*especially BrE, informal*) (used with an adverb or a preposition) to put or take sth somewhere quickly or suddenly: *She popped the note into her bag.* **4** [I] (used with an adverb or a preposition) to suddenly appear, especially when not expected: *A window opened and a man's head popped out.*

pop² ⚡ **A2** /pɒp/ *noun* **1** (*also* **pop music**) [U] (**MUSIC**) modern music that is most popular among young people: *a pop song* ⊃ look at **classical** (3), **jazz¹, rock¹** (5) **2** [C] a short sudden sound like a small explosion: *There was a loud pop as the champagne cork came out of the bottle.* ▸ **pop** ⚡ **A2** *adj.* [only before noun]: *a pop song/band/concert*

pop. *abbr.* (in writing) = POPULATION (1): *pop. 12m*

pop art (*also* **Pop Art**) *noun* [U] (**ART**) a style of art, developed in the 1960s, that was based on popular culture and used material such as advertisements, film images, etc.

popcorn /ˈpɒpkɔːn/ *noun* [U] a type of food made from MAIZE (= a tall plant with yellow grains) that is heated until it expands and forms light white balls that are eaten with salt or sugar on them

pope /pəʊp/ (*often* **the pope**) *noun* [C] (**RELIGION**) the head of the Roman Catholic Church

poplar /ˈpɒplə(r)/ *noun* [C] a tall thin straight tree with soft wood

pop music = POP² (1)

popper /ˈpɒpə(r)/ (*also* **press stud**) (*BrE*) (*AmE* **snap**) *noun* [C] two round pieces of metal or plastic that you press together in order to fasten a piece of clothing

poppy /ˈpɒpi/ *noun* [C] (*pl.* -ies) a bright red wild flower that has small black seeds

Popsicle™ /ˈpɒpsɪkl/ (*AmE*) = ICE LOLLY

popular ⚡ **A1** ⑤ /ˈpɒpjələ(r)/ *adj.* **1** ~ **(with sb)** liked by many people or by most people in a group: *a popular holiday resort* ◇ *That teacher has always been* *very popular with his pupils.* **OPP** **unpopular** **2** made for the tastes and knowledge of ordinary people: *The popular newspapers seem more interested in scandal than news.* **3** [only before noun] of or for a lot of people: *The programme is being repeated by popular demand.*

popularity ⌐**B2** /ˌpɒpjuˈlærəti/ *noun* [U] the quality or state of being liked by many people: *The band's popularity is growing.*

popularize (*BrE also -ise*) /ˈpɒpjələraɪz/ *verb* [T] to make a lot of or most people like sth: *The film did a lot to popularize her novels.*

popularly /ˈpɒpjələli/ *adv.* by many people; generally: *The Conservatives are popularly known as the Tories.*

ˌpopular ˈvote *noun* (**POLITICS**) **1** [U, C] the act of voting by the people in a country or an area: *He was democratically elected by popular vote.* **2** the popular vote [C, usually sing.] the choice made in an election by the majority of people who vote: *A candidate could win the popular vote but still lose the election.*

populate /ˈpɒpjuleɪt/ *verb* [T, usually passive] (**GEOGRAPHY**) to fill a particular area with people: *Parts of the country are very thinly populated.*

population ⌐**A2** ⊙ /ˌpɒpjuˈleɪʃn/ *noun* **1** [C, + sing./pl. verb, U] (*abbr.* **pop.**) (**GEOGRAPHY**) the number of people who live in a particular area, city or country: *What is the population of your country?* ◇ *an increase/a fall in population* **2** [C + sing./pl. verb] all the people who live in a particular place or all the people or animals of a particular type that live somewhere: *the local population* ◇ *the male/female population* ◇ *The prison population has increased in recent years.*

ˌpopuˈlation exploˌsion *noun* [C] (**GEOGRAPHY**) a sudden large increase in the number of people in an area

populism /ˈpɒpjəlɪzəm/ *noun* [U] (**POLITICS**) a type of politics that claims to represent the opinions and wishes of ordinary people ▸ **populist** /-lɪst/ *adj., noun* [C]: *a populist leader*

ˈpop-up *adj.* **1** (**COMPUTING**) (used about a computer menu, etc.) that can be brought to the screen quickly while you are working on another document: *Select an item from the pop-up dialog box.* **2** a **pop-up** shop, restaurant, etc. is a business that opens quickly somewhere and is designed to only use that location for a short period of time **3** (used about a book, etc.) containing a picture that stands up when the pages are opened ▸ **pop-up** *noun* [C]: *The software automatically blocks annoying pop-ups.*

porcelain /ˈpɔːsəlɪn/ *noun* [U] a hard white substance that is used for making expensive cups, plates, etc.

porch /pɔːtʃ/ *noun* [C] **1** (*BrE*) a small covered area at the entrance to a house or church **2** (*AmE*) = **VERANDA**

porcupine /ˈpɔːkjupaɪn/ *noun* [C] an animal covered with QUILLS (= long thin sharp points), which it can lift up to protect itself when it is attacked

pore¹ /pɔː(r)/ *noun* [C] one of the small holes in the skin through which SWEAT can pass

pore² /pɔː(r)/ *verb*
PHR V **pore over sth** to study or read sth very carefully

pork /pɔːk/ *noun* [U] meat from a pig ⊃ look at **bacon, gammon, ham** ⊃ note at **meat**

pornography /pɔːˈnɒɡrəfi/ (*also informal* **porn** /pɔːn/) *noun* [U] magazines, films, websites, etc. that describe or show sexual acts in order to cause sexual excitement ▸ **pornographic** /ˌpɔːnəˈɡræfɪk/ *adj.*

porous /ˈpɔːrəs/ *adj.* having many small holes that allow water or air to pass through slowly: *porous rock*

porpoise /ˈpɔːpəs/ *noun* [C] a sea animal that looks like a large fish with a pointed mouth. Porpoises are similar to DOLPHINS but smaller. ⊃ look at **dolphin**

porridge /ˈpɒrɪdʒ/ *noun* [U] a soft, thick, white food that is made from OATS (= a type of grain) boiled with milk or water and eaten hot, especially for breakfast

port¹ ⌐**B1** /pɔːt/ *noun* **1** [C, U] an area where ships stop to let goods and passengers on and off: *a fishing port* ◇ *The damaged ship reached port safely.* **2** [C] a town or city that has a large area of water where ships load goods, etc: *Hamburg is a major port.* **3** [U] a strong sweet red wine **4** [U] the side of a ship that is on your left when you are facing towards the front of the ship **OPP** **starboard** **5** [C] (**COMPUTING**) a place on a computer where you can attach another piece of equipment, often using a cable: *the modem port* ◇ *a USB port*

port² /pɔːt/ *verb* [T] (**COMPUTING**) to copy software from one system or machine to another: *The software can be ported to multiple platforms.*

portable /ˈpɔːtəbl/ *adj.* that can be moved or carried easily: *a portable TV* ⊃ look at **mobile¹** (2), **movable** (1)

portal /ˈpɔːtl/ *noun* [C] (**COMPUTING**) a website that is used as a point of entry to the internet, where information has been collected that will be useful to a person interested in particular kinds of things: *a business/health/children's portal*

ˈportal vein (*also* **hepatic portal vein**) *noun* [C] (**ANATOMY**) a VEIN that takes blood from the stomach and other organs near the stomach to the LIVER (= the large organ in the body that cleans the blood) ⊃ picture at **circulation**

portcullis /pɔːtˈkʌlɪs/ *noun* [C] (*pl.* **portcullises**) a strong, heavy iron gate that can be raised or let down at the entrance to a castle

porter /ˈpɔːtə(r)/ *noun* [C] **1** (*BrE*) a person whose job is to carry bags, cases, etc. at a railway station, an airport, etc. **2** a person whose job is to be in charge of the entrance of a hotel or other large building

portfolio ⌐+ **C1** /pɔːtˈfəʊliəʊ/ *noun* [C] (*pl.* **-os**) **1** a thin flat case used for carrying documents, drawings, etc. **2** (**ART**) a collection of photos, drawings, etc. that you use as an example of your work, especially when applying for a job **3** (**BUSINESS**) a set of shares owned by a particular person or organization: *an investment/a share portfolio*

porthole /ˈpɔːthəʊl/ *noun* [C] a small round window in a ship

portico /ˈpɔːtɪkəʊ/ *noun* [C] (*pl.* **-oes, -os**) (*formal*) (**ARCHITECTURE**) a roof that is supported by columns, especially one that forms the entrance to a large building

portico on a large building

portico

portion ⌐+ **B2** /ˈpɔːʃn/ *noun* [C] **~ (of sth)** **1** a part or share of sth: *What portion of your salary goes on tax?* ◇ *We must both accept a portion of the blame.* **2** an amount of food for one person (especially in a restaurant): *Could we have two extra portions of chips, please?* ⊃ look at **helping**

portrait ⌐**B1** /ˈpɔːtreɪt, -trət/ *noun* **1** [C] (**ART**) a picture, painting or photo of a person: *to paint somebody's portrait* ⊃ note at **art** **2** [C] a description of sb/sth in words **3** [U] (**COMPUTING**) (used especially before another noun) the way of printing a document in which the top of the page is one of the shorter sides ⊃ look at **landscape¹** (3)

portray ʔ+ **C1** /pɔːˈtreɪ/ *verb* [T] **1** (ART) to show sb/sth in a picture: *The painting portrays the artist's wife.* **2** ~ sb/sth (as sth) to describe sb/sth in a particular way: *In many of his novels life is portrayed as being hard.* **3** (ARTS AND MEDIA) to act the part of sb in a play or film: *In this film she portrays a very old woman.* ▶ **portrayal** /-əl/ *noun* [C]

pose¹ ʔ **B2** Ⓦ /pəʊz/ *verb* **1** [T] to create a threat, problem, etc., that sb has to deal with: *to pose a problem/threat/challenge/risk* ◊ *to pose* (= ask) *a question* **2** [I] ~ (for sb/sth) to sit or stand in a particular position for a painting, photo, etc: *After the wedding we all posed for photos.* **3** [I] ~ as sb/sth to pretend to be sb/sth: *The robbers got into the house by posing as phone engineers.* **4** [I] to behave in a way that is intended to impress people who see you: *They hardly swam at all. They just sat posing at the side of the pool.*

pose² /pəʊz/ *noun* [C] **1** a position in which sb stands, sits, etc. especially in order to be painted or photographed **2** a way of behaving that is intended to impress people who see you

posh /pɒʃ/ *adj.* (*informal*) **1** attractive and expensive: *We went for a meal in a really posh hotel.* **SYN** stylish **2** (*BrE*) (used about people) belonging to or typical of a high social class

position¹ ʔ **A2** Ⓞ /pəˈzɪʃn/ *noun*
• PLACE **1** [C, U] the place where sb/sth is or should be: *Are you happy with the position of the chairs?* ◊ *All the dancers were in position waiting for the music to begin.*
• WAY SB/STH IS PLACED **2** [C, U] the way in which sb is sitting or standing; the direction that sth is pointing in: *My leg hurts when I change position.* ◊ *Turn the switch to the off position.*
• SITUATION **3** [C, usually sing.] the state or situation that sb/sth is in: *I'm in a very difficult position.* ◊ *I'm sorry, I'm not in a position to help you financially.* ⊃ note at **situation**
• OPINION **4** [C] ~ (on sth) what you think about sth; your opinion: *What is your position on school uniform?*
• LEVEL OF IMPORTANCE **5** [C, U] the place or level of a person, company, team, etc. compared to others: *the position of women in society* ◊ *Max finished the race in second position.* ◊ *Wealth and position are very important to some people.*
• JOB **6** [C] (*formal*) a job: *There have been over 100 applications for the position of Sales Manager.* **SYN** post¹
• IN SPORT **7** [C] the part you play in a team game: *Maya can play any position except goalkeeper.*

position² ʔ **B2** Ⓦ /pəˈzɪʃn/ *verb* [T] to put sb/sth in a particular place or position: *Mary positioned herself near the door so she could get out quickly.*

positive¹ ʔ **A1** Ⓞ /ˈpɒzətɪv/ *adj.*
• EFFECTIVE/USEFUL **1** good or useful: *a positive influence/effect* **OPP** negative¹ **2** expressing agreement or support: *The book has had a lot of positive reviews.* ◊ *We had a very positive response to the idea.* **OPP** negative¹
• CONFIDENT **3** thinking about what is good in a situation; feeling confident and sure that sth good will happen: *I feel very positive about our team's chances this season.* ◊ *Positive thinking will help you to succeed.* **OPP** negative¹
• SCIENTIFIC TEST **4** (MEDICINE) (used about a medical or scientific test) showing that sth has happened or is present: *The result of the pregnancy test was positive.* ◊ *Two athletes tested positive for steroids.* **OPP** negative¹
• CERTAIN/DEFINITE **5** [not before noun] ~ (that) ... (*informal*) certain; sure: *Are you positive (that) this is*

the woman you saw? ⊃ note at **sure**¹ **6** clear; definite: *There is no positive evidence that he is guilty.*
• NUMBER **7** (MATHEMATICS) (used about a number) more than zero **OPP** negative¹
• ELECTRICITY **8** (PHYSICS) containing or producing the type of electricity that is carried by a PROTON **OPP** negative¹ ⊃ picture at **dry cell**

positive² ʔ **B2** Ⓢ /ˈpɒzətɪv/ *noun* **1** [C, U] a good or useful quality: *What are the positives and negatives of working from home?* **2** [C] the result of a test that shows that sth is present: *The result was a false positive — she wasn't pregnant after all.*

positive dis‧crimin‧ation (*BrE*) (*AmE* affirmative action) *noun* [U] (SOCIAL STUDIES) the practice or policy of making sure that a particular number of jobs, etc. are given to people from groups that are often treated unfairly because of the human group they belong to, their sex, etc. ⊃ look at **reverse discrimination**

positively Ⓦ /ˈpɒzətɪvli/ *adv.* **1** (used for emphasizing sth) really; extremely: *He wasn't just annoyed — he was positively furious!* **2** in a way that shows you are thinking about the good things in a situation, not the bad: *Thinking positively helps many people deal with stress.* **3** in a way that shows you approve of or agree with sb/sth: *Investors reacted positively to news of the takeover.* **4** in a way that leaves no possibility of doubt: *The attacker was positively identified by police.*

possess ʔ **B2** /pəˈzes/ *verb* [T] (not used in the progressive tenses) **1** (*formal*) to have or own sth: *They lost everything they possessed in the fire.* ◊ *Paola possesses a natural ability to make people laugh.* **2** to influence sb or to make sb do sth: *What possessed you to say a thing like that!*

possession ʔ **A2** /pəˈzeʃn/ *noun* **1** [U] the state of having or owning sth: *The gang were caught in possession of stolen goods.* ◊ *Enemy forces managed to take possession of the town.* **2** [C, usually pl.] something that you have or own: *Bud packed all his possessions and left.*

possessive¹ /pəˈzesɪv/ *adj.* **1** ~ (of/about sb/sth) not wanting to share sb/sth: *Dan is so possessive about his toys — he won't let other children play with them.* **2** (GRAMMAR) used to describe words that show who or what a person or thing belongs to: *'My', 'your' and 'his' are possessive adjectives.*

possessive² /pəˈzesɪv/ *noun* (GRAMMAR) **1** [C] a pronoun or a form of a word that shows that sth belongs to sb/sth: *'Ours' and 'their' are possessives.* **2** the possessive [sing.] the special form of a word that expresses belonging

possessor /pəˈzesə(r)/ *noun* [C] (*formal*) a person who has or owns sth

possibility ʔ **A2** Ⓞ /ˌpɒsəˈbɪləti/ *noun* (*pl.* -ies) **1** [C, U] ~ (of sth/doing sth); ~ that ... the fact that sth might exist or happen, but is not likely to: *There's not much possibility of the letter reaching you before Saturday.* ◊ *There is a strong possibility that the fire was started deliberately.* **2** [C] one of the different things that you can do in a particular situation or in order to achieve sth: *There is a wide range of possibilities open to us.*

possible ʔ **A1** Ⓞ /ˈpɒsəbl/ *adj.* **1** that can happen or be done: *Could you give me your answer today, if possible?* ◊ *The doctors did everything possible to save his life.* ◊ *You were warned of all the possible dangers.* **OPP** impossible **2** that might exist or happen but is not certain to **3** reasonable or acceptable in a particular situation: *There are four possible candidates for the job.* ⊃ look at **probable 4** used after adjectives to emphasize that sth is the best, worst,

etc. of its type: *Alone and with no job or money, I was in the worst possible situation.*
PHR V **as quickly, much, soon, etc. as possible** as quickly, much, soon, etc. as you can: *I'll phone you back as soon as possible.*

possibly ⚡**B1** /ˈpɒsəbli/ *adv.* **1** perhaps; maybe: *'Will you be free on Sunday?' 'Possibly.'* **2** (used for emphasizing sth) according to what is possible: *I will leave as soon as I possibly can.*

post¹ ⚡**A1** /pəʊst/ *noun*
• LETTERS, PACKAGES, ETC. **1** (*BrE*) (*also* mail *AmE, BrE*) [U] the system or organization for collecting and dealing with letters, packages, etc: *The document is too valuable to send by post.* ◇ *If you hurry you might catch the post* (= post it before everything is collected). **2** (*BrE*) (*also* mail *AmE, BrE*) [U] letters, packages, etc. that are collected or brought to your house: *Has the post come yet this morning?* ◇ *There wasn't any post for you.*
• ON THE INTERNET **3** (*also* posting) [C] (COMPUTING) a message sent to a discussion group on the internet; a piece of writing that forms part of a blog
• JOB **4** [C] a job: *The post was advertised in the local newspaper.* **SYN** position¹
• FOR A SOLDIER/GUARD **5** [C] a place where sb is on duty or is guarding sth: *The soldiers had to remain at their posts all night.*
• PIECE OF METAL/WOOD **6** [C] a piece of metal or wood that is put in the ground pointing upwards to mark a position or to support sth: *a goalpost* ◇ *Can you see a signpost anywhere?*
IDM **by return (of post)** → RETURN²

post² ⚡**A1** /pəʊst/ *verb* **1** (*BrE*) (*also* mail *especially in AmE*) [T] to send a letter, package, etc. by post: *This letter was posted in Edinburgh yesterday.* **2** [T, I] ~ **(sth) (on sth)** (COMPUTING) to put information or pictures on a website: *The winners' names will be posted on our website.* ◇ *The photos have been provided by fans who post on the message board.* **3** [T, usually passive] to send sb to go and work somewhere: *After two years in London, Rosa was posted to the Tokyo office.* **4** [T, usually passive] to put sb on guard or on duty in a particular place: *Policemen were posted outside the building.* **5** [T, usually passive] to put a notice where everyone can see it: *The exam results will be posted on the main noticeboard.*

post- /pəʊst/ *prefix* (in verbs, nouns and adjectives) after: *postgraduate* ◇ *post-war* ⊃ look at **ante-, pre-**

postage /ˈpəʊstɪdʒ/ *noun* [U] the amount that you must pay to send a letter, package etc.

postage stamp = STAMP¹ (1)

postal /ˈpəʊstl/ *adj.* connected with the sending and collecting of letters, packages, etc.

postal order *noun* [C] a piece of paper that you can buy at a post office that represents a certain amount of money. A postal order is a safe way of sending money by post.

postal vote (*BrE*) (*AmE* absentee ballot) *noun* [C] (POLITICS) a vote in an election that you can send by mail when you cannot be present

postbox /ˈpəʊstbɒks/ (*BrE*) (*AmE* mailbox) *noun* [C] a box in a public place where you put letters, etc. that you want to send

postcard /ˈpəʊstkɑːd/ *noun* [C] (TOURISM) a card that you write a message on and send to sb. Postcards have a picture on one side and are usually sent without an ENVELOPE.

postcode /ˈpəʊstkəʊd/ (*BrE*) (*AmE* zip code) *noun* [C] a group of letters and/or numbers that you put at the end of an address

poster ⚡**A2** /ˈpəʊstə(r)/ *noun* [C] **1** a large printed picture or a notice in a public place, often used to advertise sth **2** a large picture printed on paper that is put on a wall for decoration

posterity /pɒˈsterəti/ *noun* [U] (*formal*) the future and the people who will be alive then: *We should look after our environment for the sake of posterity.*

postgraduate /ˌpəʊstˈɡrædʒuət/ *noun* [C] (EDUCATION) a person who is doing further studies at a university after taking their first degree ⊃ look at **graduate¹** (1), **undergraduate** ⊃ note at **subject¹**

posthumous /ˈpɒstʃəməs/ *adj.* given or happening after sb has died: *a posthumous medal for bravery*
▶ **posthumously** *adv.*

post-Im'pressionism *noun* [U] (ART) the work or style of a group of artists in the late nineteenth century and early twentieth century that came after and reacted against IMPRESSIONISM (= a style of painting developed in France in the late nineteenth century)
▶ **post-Im'pressionist** *noun* [C], *adj.*

posting /ˈpəʊstɪŋ/ *noun* [C] **1** (*especially BrE*) an act of sending sb to a particular place to do their job, especially for a limited period of time **2** = POST¹ (3)

Post-it™ (*also* **Post-it note**) *noun* [C] a small piece of coloured, sticky paper that you use for writing a note on, and that can be easily removed

postman /ˈpəʊstmən/ (*pl.* **-men** /-mən/) (*BrE*) (*AmE* mailman) *noun* [C] a person whose job is to collect letters, packages, etc. and take them to people's houses

postmark /ˈpəʊstmɑːk/ *noun* [C] an official mark over a stamp on a letter, package, etc. that says when and where it was posted

postmodernism /ˌpəʊstˈmɒdənɪzəm/ *noun* [U] (ARCHITECTURE, ARTS AND MEDIA) a style and movement in art, architecture, literature, etc. in the late twentieth century that reacted against modern styles, for example by mixing features from traditional and modern styles ⊃ look at **modernism**
▶ **postmodern** /-dn/ *adj.*: *postmodern architecture*
▶ **postmodernist** /-dənɪst/ *noun* [C], *adj.*

post-mortem /ˌpəʊst ˈmɔːtəm/ *noun* [C] (LAW, MEDICINE) a medical examination of a dead body to find out how the person died

postnatal /ˌpəʊstˈneɪtl/ *adj.* [only before noun] (MEDICINE) connected with the period after the birth of a baby ⊃ look at **antenatal**

postnatal de'pression (*BrE*) (*AmE* post-partum depression /ˌpəʊst ˌpɑːtəm dɪˈpreʃn/) *noun* [U] (PSYCHOLOGY) a medical condition in which a woman feels very sad and anxious in the period after her baby is born

post office *noun* [C] **1** a place where you can buy stamps, post packages, etc. **2 the Post Office** (*abbr.* PO) the national organization that is responsible for collecting and dealing with letters, packages, etc.

post-'operative (*also informal* ˌpost-'op) *adj.* [only before noun] (MEDICINE) connected with the period after a medical operation

postpone ⚡+**C1** /pəˈspəʊn/ *verb* [T] to arrange that sth will happen at a later time than the time you had planned: *The match was postponed because of water on the pitch.* **SYN** delay¹ ⊃ look at **cancel** (1) ⊃ note at **meeting** ▶ **postponement** *noun* [C, U]

postscript /ˈpəʊstskrɪpt/ *noun* [C] = PS

post-trau matic 'stress disorder = PTSD

posture /ˈpɒstʃə(r)/ noun [U, C] the way that a person sits, stands, walks, etc: *Poor posture can lead to backache.*

post-war ⁺ **C1** adj. (**HISTORY**) existing or happening in the period after the end of a war, especially the Second World War

pot¹ ⁺ **B1** /pɒt/ noun [C] **1** a round container that is used for cooking food in **2** a container that you use for a particular purpose: *a flowerpot* ◇ *a pot of paint* **3** the amount that a pot contains: *We drank two pots of tea.*

pot² /pɒt/ verb [T] (-tt-) **1** to put a plant into a pot filled with soil **2** (**SPORT**) to hit a ball into one of the POCKETS in the table in the games of POOL, BILLIARDS and SNOOKER

potable /ˈpəʊtəbl/ adj. (formal) (used about water) safe to drink

potassium /pəˈtæsiəm/ noun [U] (symb. K) (**CHEMISTRY**) a chemical element. Potassium is a soft silver-white metal that exists mainly in COMPOUNDS used in industry and farming. ❶ For more information on the periodic table of elements, look at the **Reference Section** of this dictionary.

potato ⁺ **A1** /pəˈteɪtəʊ/ noun [C, U] (pl. -oes) a round vegetable that grows under the ground with a brown, yellow or red skin. Potatoes are white or yellow inside: *to peel potatoes* ◇ *mashed potato*

poˈtato ˈcrisp (AmE poˈtato chip) = CRISP¹

potent /ˈpəʊtnt/ adj. strong or powerful: *a potent drug/ drink* ▸ potency /ˈpəʊtnsi/ noun [U]

potential¹ ⁺ **B2** ❶ /pəˈtenʃl/ adj. [only before noun] that may possibly become sth, happen, be used, etc: *a potential threat* ◇ *potential customers* **SYN** possible ▸ potentially ⁺ **B2** ❶ /-ʃəli/ adv.

potential² ⁺ **B2** ❶ /pəˈtenʃl/ noun **1** [U] the qualities or abilities that sb/sth has but that may not be fully developed yet: *That boy **has great potential** as an athlete.* **2** [U, C] (**PHYSICS**) the difference in VOLTAGE between two points in an electric FIELD or circuit

poˌtential ˈenergy noun [U] (**PHYSICS**) the form of energy that an object gains as it is lifted ⊃ picture at **energy**

pothole /ˈpɒthəʊl/ noun [C] **1** a hole in the surface of a road that is formed by traffic and bad weather **2** (**GEOLOGY**) a deep hole in rock that is formed by water over thousands of years

potholing /ˈpɒthəʊlɪŋ/ noun [U] (BrE) (AmE spelunking) (**SPORT**) the sport of climbing down inside POTHOLES, walking through underground tunnels, etc: *to go potholing*

potion /ˈpəʊʃn/ noun [C] a drink of medicine or poison; (in stories) a liquid with magic powers: *a magic/love potion*

ˈpot plant noun [C] (BrE) a plant that you grow in a pot and keep indoors

potter¹ /ˈpɒtə(r)/ (BrE) (AmE putter) verb [I] ~ (about/ around) to spend your time doing small jobs or things that you enjoy without hurrying

potter² /ˈpɒtə(r)/ noun [C] a person who makes POTTERY

pottery /ˈpɒtəri/ noun (pl. -ies) **1** [U] pots, dishes, etc. that are made from baked CLAY (= a type of heavy, sticky earth) **2** [U] the activity or skill of making dishes, etc. from CLAY: *a pottery class* ⊃ look at **ceramic** (2) **3** [C] a place where CLAY pots and dishes are made

potty¹ /ˈpɒti/ adj. (pottier; pottiest) (BrE, informal) **1** crazy or silly **2** ~ **about sb/sth** liking sb/sth very much: *Penny's potty about horses.*

potty² /ˈpɒti/ noun [C] (pl. -ies) a plastic bowl that young children use when they are too small to use a toilet

pouch /paʊtʃ/ noun [C] **1** a small leather bag **2** a pocket of skin on the stomach of some female animals, for example KANGAROOS, in which they carry their babies ⊃ picture at **animal**

poultice /ˈpəʊltɪs/ noun [C] (**MEDICINE**) a soft substance that you spread on a cloth and put on the skin to reduce pain or SWELLING

poultry /ˈpəʊltri/ noun **1** [pl.] (**AGRICULTURE**) birds, for example chickens, DUCKS, etc. that are kept for their eggs or their meat ⊃ picture at **animal 2** [U] the meat from these birds

pounce /paʊns/ verb [I] ~ **(on sb/sth)** to attack sb/sth by jumping suddenly on them or it: *(figurative) He was quick to pounce on any mistakes I made.*

pound¹ ⁺ **A1** /paʊnd/ noun **1** (also ˌpound ˈsterling) [C] (**ECONOMICS**) (symb. £) the unit of money in the UK; 100 pence: *Melissa earns £26 000 a year.* ◇ *Can you change a ten-pound note?* ◇ *a pound coin* **2** the pound [sing.] (**ECONOMICS**) the value of the UK pound on international money markets: *The pound has fallen against the dollar.* ◇ *How many yen are there to the pound?* **3** [C] (abbr. lb) a measurement of weight, equal to 0.454 of a KILOGRAM: *Half a pound of mushrooms, please.* ◇ *The carrots cost 45p a pound.* ❶ For more information about weights, look at the **Reference Section** of this dictionary. **4** [C] (**LAW**) a place where vehicles that have been parked illegally are kept until their owners pay to get them back **5** [C] a place where dogs that have been found in the street without their owners are kept until their owners claim them

pound² /paʊnd/ verb **1** [I, T] ~ **(at/against/on sth)** to hit sth hard many times making a lot of noise: *She pounded on the door with her fists.* **2** [I] (used with an adverb or a preposition) to walk with heavy, noisy steps in a particular direction: *Jason went pounding up the stairs three at a time.* **3** [I] (used about the heart, blood, etc.) to beat quickly and loudly: *Her heart was pounding with fear.* **4** [T] to hit sth many times to break it into smaller pieces

pour ⁺ **B1** /pɔː(r)/ verb **1** [T] to make a liquid or other substance flow steadily out of or into a container: *Pour the sugar into a bowl.* **2** [I] (used with an adverb or a preposition) (used about a liquid, smoke, light, etc.) to flow out of or into sth quickly and steadily, and in large quantities: *Tears were pouring down her cheeks.* ◇ *She opened the curtains and sunlight poured into the room.* **3** [T] ~ **sth (out)** to serve a drink to sb by letting it flow from a container into a cup or glass: *Have you poured out the tea?* **4** [I] ~ **(down) (with rain)** to rain heavily: *I'm not going out. It's pouring with rain.* ◇ *The rain poured down all day long.* ⊃ note at **weather¹ 5** [I] (used with an adverb or a preposition) to come or go somewhere continuously in large numbers: *People were pouring out of the station.*

IDM **pour your heart out (to sb)** to tell sb all your personal problems, feelings, etc.

PHR V **pour sth out** to speak freely about what you think or feel about sth that has happened to you: *to pour out all your troubles*

pout /paʊt/ verb [I] to push your lips, or your bottom lip, forward to show that you are annoyed about sth or to look sexually attractive ▸ pout noun [C]

poverty ⁺ **B1** ❿ /ˈpɒvəti/ noun [U] (**SOCIAL STUDIES**) the state of being poor: *There are millions of people in this country who are living **in poverty.***

the 'poverty line (*also* the 'poverty level *especially in AmE*) *noun* [sing.] (**FINANCE**) the official level of income that is necessary to be able to buy the basic things you need such as food and clothes and to pay for somewhere to live: *A third of the population is living below the poverty line.*

poverty-stricken /'pɒvəti strɪkən/ *adj.* (**SOCIAL STUDIES**) very poor

'poverty trap *noun* [C, usually sing.] (**SOCIAL STUDIES**) a situation in which a person stays poor even when they get a job because the money they receive from the government is reduced

POW /ˌpiː əʊ 'dʌbljuː/ *abbr.* = PRISONER OF WAR

powder ⁇ B1 /'paʊdə(r)/ *noun* [U, C] a dry substance that is in the form of very small grains: *washing powder* ◇ *Grind the spices into a fine powder.*
▶ powder *verb* [T]

powdered /'paʊdəd/ *adj.* (used about a substance that is usually liquid) dried and made into powder: *powdered milk/soup*

power¹ ⁇ A2 ⊙ /'paʊə(r)/ *noun*
• CONTROL 1 [U] ~ (over sb/sth); ~ (to do sth) the ability to control people or things; the ability to do sth: *The aim is to give people more power over their own lives.* ◇ *It's not in my power* (= I am unable) *to help you.* ◇ *to have somebody in your power* 2 [U] (**POLITICS**) political control of a country or an area: *When did this government come to power?* ◇ *to take/seize power*
• ENERGY 3 [U] the energy or strength that sb/sth has: *The ship was helpless against the power of the storm.* ◇ *I've lost all power in my right arm.* 4 [U] energy that can be collected and used for operating machines, making electricity, etc: *nuclear/wind/solar power* ◇ *This car has power steering.*
• ABILITY 5 powers [pl.] a particular ability of the body or mind: *He has great powers of observation.* ◇ *She had to use all her powers of persuasion on him.*
• AUTHORITY 6 [C] ~ (to do sth) the right or authority to do sth: *Do the police have the power to stop cars without good reason?*
• COUNTRY 7 [C] a country with a lot of influence in world affairs or that has great military strength: *a military/economic power* ⊃ look at **superpower**, **world power**
• IN MATHEMATICS 8 [C, usually sing.] (to the) ~ (of sth) the number of times that an amount is to be multiplied by itself: *4 to the power of 3 is 4³ (4×4×4=64).*
• OF A LENS 9 [U] (**PHYSICS**) the amount by which a LENS can make objects appear larger: *the power of a microscope/telescope*

power² ⁇ B2 /'paʊə(r)/ *verb* [T] to supply energy to sth to make it work: *What powers the motor in this machine?* ▶ -powered *adj.*: *a solar-powered calculator* ◇ *a high-powered engine*

'power cut *noun* [C] a time when the supply of electricity stops, for example during a storm ⊃ look at **outage**

powerful ⁇ B1 ⊙ /'paʊəfl/ *adj.* 1 having a lot of control or influence over other people: *a powerful nation* ◇ *He's one of the most powerful directors in Hollywood.* 2 having great strength or force: *a powerful car/engine/telescope* ◇ *a powerful swimmer* 3 having a strong effect on your mind or body: *The prime minister made a powerful speech.* ◇ *a powerful drug* ▶ powerfully /-fəli/ *adv.*

powerless /'paʊələs/ *adj.* 1 without strength, influence or control 2 [not before noun] ~ to do sth completely unable to do sth: *I stood and watched him struggle, powerless to help.*

power of at'torney *noun* [U, C] (*pl.* powers of attorney) (**LAW**) the right to act as the representative of sb in business or financial matters; a document that gives sb this right

'power point (*BrE*) = SOCKET (1)

'power station (*BrE*) (*also* 'power plant *especially in AmE*) *noun* [C] a place where electricity is produced ⊃ note at **electricity**

pp (*also* p.p.) /ˌpiː 'piː/ *abbr.* (*especially BrE*) used in front of a person's name when sb signs a business letter for that person (from Latin 'per procurationem'): *pp Mark Dilks* (= from Mark Dilks, but signed by sb else because Mark Dilks is away)

pp. *abbr.* (in writing) plural of **p** (1): See *pp. 100–178.*

PPE /ˌpiː piː 'iː/ *abbr.* = PERSONAL PROTECTIVE EQUIPMENT

PR /ˌpiː 'ɑː(r)/ *noun* [U] 1 (**BUSINESS**) the business of giving the public information about a particular organization or person in order to create a good impression (the abbreviation for 'public relations'): *a PR campaign* 2 = PROPORTIONAL REPRESENTATION

practicable /'præktɪkəbl/ *adj.* (used about an idea, a plan or a suggestion) able to be done successfully: *The scheme is just not practicable.*

practical¹ ⁇ B1 ⊙ /'præktɪkl/ *adj.*
• CONNECTED WITH REAL THINGS 1 concerned with actually doing sth rather than with ideas or thought: *Have you got any practical experience of working on a farm?* ⊃ look at **theoretical** (1)
• LIKELY TO WORK 2 that is likely to succeed; right or sensible: *We need to find a practical solution to the problem.* OPP **impractical**
• USEFUL 3 very suitable for a particular purpose; useful: *a practical little car, ideal for the city* OPP **impractical**
• PERSON 4 (used about a person) making sensible decisions and good at dealing with problems: *We must be practical. It's no good buying a house we cannot afford.* OPP **impractical** 5 (used about a person) good at making and repairing things

practical² ⊙ /'præktɪkl/ *noun* [C] (*BrE, informal*) (**EDUCATION**) a lesson or an exam where you do or make sth rather than just writing: *He passed the theory paper but failed the practical.*

practicality /ˌpræktɪˈkæləti/ *noun* 1 [U] the quality of being suitable and realistic, or likely to succeed: *I am not convinced of the practicality of the scheme.* 2 practicalities [pl.] the real facts rather than ideas or thoughts: *Let's look at the practicalities of the situation.*

practical 'joke *noun* [C] a trick that you play on sb that makes them look silly and makes other people laugh

practically /'præktɪkli/ *adv.* 1 almost; very nearly: *My essay is practically finished now.* 2 in a realistic or sensible way

practice¹ ⁇ A1 ⊙ /'præktɪs/ *noun*
• FOR IMPROVING SKILL 1 [U, C] (a period of) doing an activity many times or training regularly so that you become good at it: *piano/football practice* ◇ *His accent should improve with practice.*
• ACTION NOT IDEAS 2 [U] action rather than ideas or thought: *the theory and practice of language teaching* ◇ *I can't wait to put what I've learnt into practice.* ⊃ look at **theory**
• WAY OF DOING STH 3 [U, C] the usual or expected way of doing sth in a particular organization or situation; a habit or custom: *It is standard practice not to pay bills until the end of the month.*
• OF A DOCTOR/LAWYER 4 [U, C] the work or business of a doctor, dentist or lawyer; the place where they work:

*Dr Roberts doesn't work in a hospital. He's in **general practice** (= he's a family doctor).*

IDM **be/get out of practice** to find it difficult to do sth because you have not done it for a long time: *I'm not playing very well at the moment. I'm really out of practice.* **in practice** in reality: *Prisoners have legal rights, but in practice these rights are not always respected.*

practise 🔊 **A1** (*BrE*) (*AmE* **practice**) /ˈpræktɪs/ *verb* [I, T]
1 ~ **(sth) (on sb)** to do an activity or train regularly so that you become very good at sth: *If you want to play a musical instrument well, you must practise every day.* ◇ *He always wants to **practise** his English **on** me.*
2 ~ **(sth/as sth)** to work as a doctor or lawyer: *She's practising as a barrister in Leeds.* ◇ *He was banned from practising medicine.* ⊃ note at **medical**[1], **professional**[2] **3** to do sth or take part in sth regularly or publicly: *a practising Catholic/Jew/Muslim*

practised (*BrE*) (*AmE* **practiced**) /ˈpræktɪst/ *adj.* ~ **(in sth)** very good at sth, because you have done it a lot or often: *He was practised in the art of inventing excuses.*

practitioner 🔊+ **C1** 🌐 /prækˈtɪʃənə(r)/ *noun* [C] (*formal*)
1 a person who works in a profession, especially medicine or law ⊃ look at **GP 2** a person who regularly does a particular activity, especially one that requires skill: *one of the greatest practitioners of science fiction*

pragmatic /prægˈmætɪk/ *adj.* dealing with problems in a practical way rather than by following ideas or principles

pragmatism /ˈprægmətɪzəm/ *noun* [U] (*formal*) thinking about solving problems in a practical and sensible way rather than by having fixed ideas ▶ **pragmatist** /-tɪst/ *noun* [C]: *Most successful teachers are pragmatists and realists.*

prairie /ˈpreəri/ *noun* [C] (**GEOGRAPHY**) a very large area of flat land in North America, covered in grass with few trees

praise[1] 🔊 **B2** /preɪz/ *verb* [T] ~ **sb/sth (for sth)** to say that sb/sth is good and should be admired: *The firefighters were praised for their courage.*

praise[2] 🔊 **B2** /preɪz/ *noun* [U] ~ **(for sth/sb)** words that show that you approve of and admire sb/sth: *The survivors were full of praise for the paramedics.*

praiseworthy /ˈpreɪzwɜːði/ *adj.* (*formal*) that should be admired and recognized as good

pram /præm/ (*BrE*) (*AmE* **baby carriage**) *noun* [C] a small vehicle on four wheels for a young baby, pushed by a person on foot

prance /prɑːns/ *verb* [I] (often used with an adverb or a preposition) to move about with quick, high steps, often because you feel proud or pleased with yourself

prank /præŋk/ *noun* [C] a trick that is played on sb as a joke: *a childish prank*

praseodymium /ˌpreɪziəʊˈdɪmiəm/ *noun* [U] (*symb.* Pr) (**CHEMISTRY**) a chemical element. Praseodymium is a soft silver-white metal used in ALLOYS and to colour glass. **❶** For more information on the periodic table of elements, look at the **Reference Section** of this dictionary.

prat /præt/ *noun* [C] (*BrE, informal*) a stupid person: *What a prat!*

prawn /prɔːn/ (*especially BrE*) (*AmE usually* **shrimp**) *noun* [C, U] a small SHELLFISH (= a creature with a shell that lives in water) that can be eaten and that turns pink when cooked ⊃ look at **shrimp** (1) ⊃ picture at **animal**

pray 🔊 **B1** /preɪ/ *verb* [I, T] ~ **(to sb)** **(for sb/sth)**; ~ **(that)** ... **1** (**RELIGION**) to speak to God or a god in order to give thanks or to ask for help: *They prayed for peace.* ◇ *They prayed (that) the war would end soon.*
2 to hope very much that sth will happen: *We're praying for good weather on Saturday.* ◇ *I prayed (that) nobody would notice my mistake.*

prayer 🔊 **B1** /preə(r)/ *noun* (**RELIGION**) **1** [C] ~ **(for sb/sth)** the words that you use when you speak to God or a god: *Let's say a prayer for all the people who are ill.* ◇ *a prayer book* **2** [U] the act of speaking to God or a god: *to kneel in prayer*

prayer rug (*also* **prayer mat**) *noun* [C] (**RELIGION**) a small carpet on which Muslims rest their knees when they are saying prayers

pre- /priː/ *prefix* (in verbs, nouns and adjectives) before: *prepay* ◇ *preview* ◇ *pre-war* ⊃ look at **ante-, post-**

preach 🔊+ **C1** /priːtʃ/ *verb* [I, T] **1** (**RELIGION**) to give a SERMON (= a talk on a religious subject), especially in a church ⊃ note at **religion 2** [T] to say that sth is good and persuade other people to accept it: *I always preach caution in situations like this.* **3** [I] to give sb advice on moral behaviour, in a way that they find boring or annoying: *I'm sorry, I didn't mean to preach.*

preacher /ˈpriːtʃə(r)/ *noun* [C] (**RELIGION**) a person who gives SERMONS (= talks on religious subjects), for example in a church

preamble /ˈpriːæmbl/ *noun* [C, U] (*formal*) an introduction to a book or a written document, or to sth you say: *Her sister called us and broke the news without preamble.*

precarious /prɪˈkeəriəs/ *adj.* not safe or certain; dangerous ▶ **precariously** *adv.*

precaution /prɪˈkɔːʃn/ *noun* [C] ~ **(against sth)** something that you do now in order to avoid danger or problems in the future: *precautions against fire/theft* ◇ *You should always take the precaution of locking your valuables in the hotel safe.* ▶ **precautionary** /-ʃənəri/ *adj.*

precede 🔊+ **B2** 🌐 /prɪˈsiːd/ *verb* [I, T] (*formal*) to happen, come or go before sb/sth: *Look at the table on the preceding page.*

precedence /ˈpresɪdəns/ *noun* [U] ~ **(over sb/sth)** the right that sb/sth has to come before sb/sth else because they or it are more important: *In business, making a profit seems to take precedence over everything else.*

precedent 🔊+ **C1** /ˈpresɪdənt/ *noun* [C, U] an official action or decision that has happened in the past and that is considered as an example or a rule to follow in the same situation later: *We don't want to set a precedent by allowing one person to come in late or they'll all want to do it.* ◇ *Such protests are without precedent in recent history.* ⊃ look at **unprecedented**

preceding /prɪˈsiːdɪŋ/ *adj.* [only before noun] happening before sth; coming before sth/sb in order: *See the preceding chapter.* ◇ *It had happened during the preceding year.*

precinct /ˈpriːsɪŋkt/ *noun* **1** [C] (*BrE*) a special area of shops in a town where cars are not allowed: *a shopping precinct* **2** [C] (*AmE*) one of the parts into which a town or city is divided **3** [C] (*AmE*) a part of a town that has its own police station **4** **precincts** [pl.] (*formal*) the area near or around a building: *the cathedral and its precincts*

precious 🔊+ **B2** /ˈpreʃəs/ *adj.* **1** worth a lot of money, usually because it is rare or difficult to find: *In overcrowded Hong Kong, every small piece of land is precious.* **2** loved very much: *The painting was very precious to her.*

precious metal *noun* [C] a metal that is very rare and valuable and often used in jewellery: *Gold and silver are precious metals.*

ˌprecious ˈstone (*also* **stone**) *noun* [C] a stone that is very rare and valuable and often used in jewellery: *diamonds and other precious stones*

precipice /ˈpresəpɪs/ *noun* [C] (**GEOGRAPHY**) a very steep side of a high mountain or rock

precipitate[1] /prɪˈsɪpɪteɪt/ *verb* [T] (*formal*) **1** to make sth, especially sth bad, happen suddenly or sooner than it should **2 ~ sb/sth into sth** to suddenly force sb/sth into a particular state or condition: *The president's assassination precipitated the country into war.*

precipitate[2] /prɪˈsɪpɪtət/ *adj.* (*formal*) (used about an action or a decision) happening very quickly or suddenly and usually without enough care and thought ▸ **precipitately** *adv.*

precipitate[3] /prɪˈsɪpɪteɪt/ *noun* [C] (**CHEMISTRY**) a solid substance that has been separated from a solution in a chemical process

precipitation /prɪˌsɪpɪˈteɪʃn/ *noun* **1** [U] (**GEOGRAPHY**) rain, snow, etc. that falls; the amount of this that falls **2** [U, C] (**CHEMISTRY**) a chemical process in which solid material is separated from a liquid

precis /ˈpreɪsiː/ *noun* [C, U] (*pl.* **precis** /-siːz/) a short version of a speech or a piece of writing that gives the main points or ideas **SYN summary**[1]

precise 🔑+ B2 W /prɪˈsaɪs/ *adj.* **1** clear and accurate: *precise details/instructions/measurements* ◇ *He's in his forties — well, 44, **to be precise**.* ◇ *She couldn't be very precise about what her attacker was wearing.* **OPP imprecise** ➲ note at **true 2** [only before noun] exact; particular: *I'm sorry. I can't come just **at this precise moment**.* **3** (used about a person) taking care to get small details right: *He's very precise about his work.* **SYN meticulous**

precisely 🔑+ B2 O /prɪˈsaɪsli/ *adv.* **1** exactly: *The time is 10.03 precisely.* **SYN exactly 2** used to emphasize that sth is very true or obvious: *It's precisely because I care about you that I got so angry when you stayed out late.* **3** (used for agreeing with a statement) yes, that is right: *'So, if we don't book now, we probably won't get a flight?' 'Precisely.'* **SYN exactly**

precision 🔑+ C1 W /prɪˈsɪʒn/ *noun* [U] the quality of being clear or exact: *The plans were drawn with great precision.* ◇ *precision instruments/tools*

preclude /prɪˈkluːd/ *verb* [T] **~ sth; ~ sb from doing sth** (*formal*) to prevent sth from happening or sb from doing sth; to make sth impossible: *Lack of time precludes any further discussion.* ◇ *The rules preclude us from naming the individuals.*

precocious /prɪˈkəʊʃəs/ *adj.* (used about children) having developed certain abilities and ways of behaving at a much younger age than usual: *a precocious child who started her acting career at the age of 5*

preconceived /ˌpriːkənˈsiːvd/ *adj.* [only before noun] (used about an idea or opinion) formed before you have enough information or experience

preconception /ˌpriːkənˈsepʃn/ *noun* [C] an idea or opinion that you have formed about sb/sth before you have enough information or experience

precondition /ˌpriːkənˈdɪʃn/ *noun* [C] **~ (for/of sth)** something that must happen or exist before sth else can exist or be done **SYN prerequisite**

precursor /priˈkɜːsə(r)/ *noun* [C] **~ (of/to sth)** (*formal*) a person or thing that comes before sb/sth similar and that leads to or influences its development

predator 🔑+ C1 /ˈpredətə(r)/ *noun* [C] (**BIOLOGY**) an animal that kills and eats other animals

predatory /ˈpredətri/ *adj.* **1** (**BIOLOGY**) (used about an animal) living by killing and eating other animals **2** (used about a person) using weaker people for their own financial or sexual advantage

predecessor 🔑+ C1 /ˈpriːdəsesə(r)/ *noun* [C] **1** the person who was in the job or position before the person who is in it now **2** a thing such as a machine, that has been followed or replaced by sth else ➲ look at **successor**

predestined /ˌpriːˈdestɪnd/ *adj.* **~ (to do sth)** already decided or planned by God or by FATE: *She seemed almost predestined to win a gold medal.*

predicament /prɪˈdɪkəmənt/ *noun* [C] an unpleasant and difficult situation that is hard to get out of

predicative /prɪˈdɪkətɪv/ *adj.* (**GRAMMAR**) (used about an adjective) not used before a noun: *You cannot say 'an asleep child' because 'asleep' is a predicative adjective.* ▸ **predicatively** *adv.*: *'Asleep' can only be used predicatively.*

▼ VOCABULARY BUILDING

An adjective that *can* be used before a noun is called **attributive**. Many adjectives, for example *big*, can be either **predicative** or **attributive**: *The house is big.* ◇ *It's a big house.*

predict 🔑 A2 O /prɪˈdɪkt/ *verb* [T] to say that sth will happen in the future: *Scientists still cannot predict exactly when earthquakes will happen.*

predictable 🔑+ B2 /prɪˈdɪktəbl/ *adj.* **1** that was or could be expected to happen: *The match had a predictable result.* **2** (used about a person) always behaving in a way that you would expect and therefore rather boring: *I knew you were going to say that — you're so predictable.* ▸ **predictably** /-bli/ *adv.*

prediction 🔑 B1 W /prɪˈdɪkʃn/ *noun* [C, U] saying what will happen; what sb thinks will happen: *The exam results confirmed my predictions.*

predictive /prɪˈdɪktɪv/ *adj.* **1** (*formal*) connected with the ability to show what will happen in the future **2** (**COMPUTING**) (used about a computer program) allowing you to enter text on a computer or a mobile phone more quickly by using the first few letters of each word to predict what you want to say: ***predictive text***

predilection /ˌpriːdɪˈlekʃn/ *noun* [usually sing.] **~ (for sth)** (*formal*) if you have a **predilection** for sth, you like it very much **SYN liking, preference**

predispose /ˌpriːdɪˈspəʊz/ *verb* [T] (*formal*) **1 ~ sb to sth/to do sth** to influence sb so that they are likely to think or behave in a particular way: *He believes that some people are predisposed to criminal behaviour.* **2 ~ sb to sth** (**HEALTH**) to make it likely that you will suffer from a particular illness: *Stress can predispose people to heart attacks.*

predisposition /ˌpriːdɪspəˈzɪʃn/ *noun* [C, U] **~ (to/towards sth)** (*formal*) (**HEALTH**) a condition that makes sb/sth likely to behave in a particular way or to suffer from a particular disease: *a genetic predisposition to liver disease*

predominance /prɪˈdɒmɪnəns/ *noun* [sing.] the state of being more important or greater in number than other people or things: *There is a predominance of Japanese tourists in Hawaii.*

predominant /prɪˈdɒmɪnənt/ *adj.* easiest to notice or most powerful or important: *The predominant colour was blue.*

predominantly 🔑+ C1 W /prɪˈdɒmɪnəntli/ *adv.* mostly; mainly: *The population of the island is predominantly Spanish.*

predominate /prɪˈdɒmɪneɪt/ *verb* [I] ~ **(over sb/sth)** to be most important or greatest in number: *Private interest was not allowed to predominate over public good.*

pre-empt /ˌpriːˈempt/ *verb* [T] **1** to prevent sth from happening by taking action to stop it: *Her departure pre-empted any further questions.* ◇ *A good training course will pre-empt many problems.* **2** to do or say sth before sb else does: *She was just about to apologize when he pre-empted her.*

pre-emptive /ˌpriːˈemptɪv/ *adj.* done to stop sb taking action, especially action that will be harmful to you

pre-e'xist *verb* [I] to exist from an earlier time: *a pre-existing medical condition*

preface /ˈprefəs/ *noun* [C] (**LITERATURE**) a written introduction to a book that explains what it is about or why it was written

prefect /ˈpriːfekt/ *noun* [C] (*BrE*) (**EDUCATION**) (in some British schools) a student who has special duties and responsibilities. Prefects often help to make sure that the younger students behave properly.

prefer 🔊 **A1** **S** /prɪˈfɜː(r)/ *verb* [T] (-rr-) ~ **sth (to sth)**; ~ **(sb/sth) to do sth**; ~ **doing sth** (not used in the progressive tenses) to choose sth rather than sth else; to like sth better: *Would you prefer tea or coffee?* ◇ *Marianne prefers not to walk home on her own at night.* ◇ *My parents would prefer me to study law at university.* ◇ *I prefer playing in defence.*

preferable /ˈprefrəbl/ *adj.* ~ **(to sth/doing sth)** better or more suitable: *Going anywhere is preferable to staying at home for the weekend.*

preferably /ˈprefrəbli/ *adv.* used to show which person or thing would be better or preferred, if you are given a choice: *Give me a ring tonight — preferably after seven o'clock.*

preference 🔊 **B2** **W** /ˈprefrəns/ *noun* [U, sing.] ~ **(for sth)** an interest in or a desire for one thing more than another: *Most people expressed a preference for Option B.* ◇ *What you wear is entirely a matter of personal preference.* ◇ *Please list your choices in order of preference* (= put the things you want most first on the list).

IDM **give (a) preference to sb/sth** to give special treatment to one person or group rather than to others: *When allocating accommodation, we will give preference to families with young children.*

preferential /ˌprefəˈrenʃl/ *adj.* [only before noun] giving or showing special treatment to one person or group rather than to others: *I don't see why he should get preferential treatment — I've worked here just as long as he has!*

prefix /ˈpriːfɪks/ *noun* [C] (**GRAMMAR**) a letter or group of letters that you put at the beginning of a word to change its meaning, such as *un-* in *unhappy* ⊃ look at **affix²**, **suffix**

pregnancy 🔊 **C1** /ˈpregnənsi/ *noun* [U, C] (*pl.* -ies) (**HEALTH**) the state of being pregnant

pregnant 🔊 **B2** /ˈpregnənt/ *adj.* (**HEALTH**) (used about a woman or female animal) having a baby developing in her body: *Liz is five months pregnant.* ◇ *to get pregnant*

prehensile /prɪˈhensaɪl/ *adj.* (**BIOLOGY**) (used about a part of an animal's body) able to hold things: *the monkey's prehensile tail* ⊃ picture at **animal**

prehistoric /ˌpriːhɪˈstɒrɪk/ *adj.* (**HISTORY**) from the time in history before events were written down

prehistory /ˌpriːˈhɪstri/ *noun* [U] (**HISTORY**) the period of time in history before information was written down

prejudice¹ 🔊 **C1** /ˈpredʒədɪs/ *noun* [U, C] ~ **(against sb/sth)** (**SOCIAL STUDIES**) a strong unreasonable feeling of not liking or trusting a person, group, etc., especially when it is based on the human group they belong to, their religion or their sex: *a victim of racial prejudice* ◇ *He has a prejudice against women doctors.*

prejudice² /ˈpredʒədɪs/ *verb* [T] **1** ~ **sb (against sb/sth)** to influence sb so that they have an unreasonable or unfair opinion about sb/sth: *The newspaper stories had prejudiced the jury against him.* **2** to have a harmful effect on sb/sth: *Living with her violent father will prejudice the child's welfare.*

prejudiced /ˈpredʒədɪst/ *adj.* (**SOCIAL STUDIES**) not liking or trusting sb/sth for no other reason than the human group they belong to, their religion or their sex

preliminary¹ 🔊 **C1** /prɪˈlɪmɪnəri/ *adj.* coming or happening before sth else that is more important

preliminary² /prɪˈlɪmɪnəri/ *noun* [C, usually pl.] (*pl.* -ies) an action or event that is done before and in preparation for another event

prelude /ˈpreljuːd/ *noun* [C] **1** (**MUSIC**) a short piece of music, especially an introduction to a longer piece **2** ~ **(to sth)** an action or event that happens before sth else or that forms an introduction to sth

premature /ˈpremətʃə(r)/ *adj.* **1** happening before the normal or expected time: *Her baby was premature* (= born before the expected time). **2** acting or happening too soon: *I think our decision was premature. We should have thought about it for longer.* ▸ **prematurely** /ˈpremətʃʊəli/ *adv.*

premeditated /ˌpriːˈmedɪteɪtɪd/ *adj.* (**LAW**) (used about a crime) planned in advance

premier¹ 🔊 **C1** /ˈpremiə(r)/ *adj.* [only before noun] most important; best: *a premier chef* ◇ *the Premier Division/League* (= in football)

premier² /ˈpremiə(r)/ *noun* [C] (**POLITICS**) (used especially in newspapers) the leader of the government of a country **SYN** **prime minister**

premiere /ˈpremieə(r)/ *noun* [C] (**ARTS AND MEDIA**) the first public performance of a play, film, etc.

premise 🔊 **C1** /ˈpremɪs/ *noun* [C] (*formal*) a statement or an idea that a line of argument is based on: *His argument is based on the premise that all people are capable of both good and evil.*

premises /ˈpremɪsɪz/ *noun* [pl.] (**BUSINESS**) the building and the land around it that a business owns or uses: *Smoking is not allowed on the premises.* ⊃ note at **building**

premium 🔊 **C1** /ˈpriːmiəm/ *noun* [C] **1** an amount of money that you pay regularly to a company for insurance against accidents, damage, etc: *a monthly premium of £25* ⊃ note at **insurance** **2** an extra payment: *You must pay a premium for express delivery.*

premolar /ˌpriːˈməʊlə(r)/ *noun* [C] (**ANATOMY**) one of the eight teeth near the back of the mouth between the MOLARS and the CANINES ⊃ look at **canine²**, **incisor**, **molar** ⊃ picture at **tooth**

premonition /ˌpreməˈnɪʃn, ˌpriːm-/ *noun* [C] ~ **(of sth)** a feeling that sth unpleasant is going to happen in the future: *a premonition of disaster*

prenatal /ˌpriːˈneɪtl/ (*especially AmE*) = ANTENATAL

preoccupation /priˌɒkjuˈpeɪʃn/ *noun* [U, C] ~ **(with sth)** the state of thinking and/or worrying continuously about sth: *She was irritated by his preoccupation with money.*

preoccupied /pri'ɒkjupaɪd/ adj. ~ (with sth) not paying attention to sb/sth because you are thinking or worrying about sb/sth else ⊃ look at **occupied** (2)

preoccupy /pri'ɒkjupaɪ/ verb [T] (preoccupying; preoccupies; pt, pp preoccupied) to fill sb's mind so that they do not think about anything else; to worry

pre-'packed (also ,pre-'packaged) adj. (used about goods, especially food) put into packages before being sent to shops to be sold: pre-packed sandwiches

prepaid /ˌpriː'peɪd/ adj. paid for in advance: A prepaid envelope is enclosed (= so you do not have to pay the cost of sending a letter).

preparation ⟨B2⟩ /ˌprepə'reɪʃn/ noun 1 [U] ~ (for sth) getting sb/sth ready: The team has been training hard in preparation for the big game. ◇ exam preparation 2 [C, usually pl.] ~ (for sth/to do sth) something that you do to get ready for sth: We started to make preparations for the wedding six months ago.

preparatory /pri'pærətri/ adj. (formal) done in order to get ready for sth

pre'paratory school (also prep school) noun [C] (EDUCATION) 1 (in the UK) a private school for children between the ages of 7 and 13 ⊃ look at **public school** (1) 2 (in the US) a school, usually a private one, that prepares students for college

prepare ⟨A1⟩ /pri'peə(r)/ verb [I, T] ~ (sb/sth) (for sb/sth) to get ready; to make sb/sth ready: Bo helped me prepare for the exam. ◇ The course prepares foreign students for studying at university. ◇ to prepare a meal

prepared ⟨B1⟩ /pri'peəd/ adj. 1 [not before noun] ~ (for sth) ready for sth, especially sth difficult or unpleasant: We'll be better prepared next time. ◇ In this job you have to be prepared for anything. 2 [not before noun] ~ to do sth ready and happy to do sth: How much are you prepared to pay? 3 done in advance: The police officer read out a prepared statement.

preponderance /pri'pɒndərəns/ noun [sing.] (formal) if there is a **preponderance** of one type of people or things in a group, there are more of them than others **SYN** predominance

preponderant /pri'pɒndərənt/ adj. (formal) larger in number or more important than other people or things in a group

preposition /ˌprepə'zɪʃn/ noun [C] (GRAMMAR) a word or phrase that is used before a noun or pronoun to show place, time, direction, etc: 'In', 'for', 'to' and 'out of' are all prepositions.

preposterous /pri'pɒstərəs/ adj. (formal) silly; not to be taken seriously **SYN** outrageous

prep school /'prep skuːl/ = PREPARATORY SCHOOL

prerequisite /ˌpriː'rekwəzɪt/ noun [C] ~ (for/of sth) something that is necessary for sth else to happen or exist ⊃ look at **requisite**

prerogative /pri'rɒgətɪv/ noun [C] (formal) a special right that sb/sth has: It is the prime minister's prerogative to fix the date of the election.

preschool /'priːskuːl/ noun [C] (EDUCATION) a school for children between the ages of about 2 and 5 **SYN** nursery school ⊃ look at **playgroup**

prescribe ⟨C1⟩ /pri'skraɪb/ verb [T] 1 ~ (sb) sth (for sth) (MEDICINE) to say what medicine or treatment sb should have: Can you prescribe (me) something for my cough please, doctor? ⊃ note at **doctor**¹, **medical**¹ 2 ~ (that …) (formal) (used about a person or an organization with authority) to say that sth must be

done: The law prescribes that the document must be signed in the presence of two witnesses.

prescription ⟨C1⟩ /pri'skrɪpʃn/ noun (MEDICINE) 1 [C, U] a paper on which a doctor has written the name of the medicine that you need. You take your prescription to the CHEMIST'S and get the medicine there: a prescription for sleeping pills ◇ Some medicines are only available on prescription (= with a prescription from a doctor). ⊃ note at **doctor**¹, **medical**¹ 2 [C] medicine that your doctor has ordered for you: I have to pick up my prescription from the chemist's.

presence ⟨B2⟩ ⊙ /'prezns/ noun 1 [U] the fact of being in a particular place: an experiment to test for the presence of oxygen **OPP** absence 2 [sing.] a group of people, especially soldiers or police officers, who are in a place for a special reason: There was a huge police presence at the demonstration.
IDM in the presence of sb | in sb's presence with sb in the same place: He apologized to her in the presence of the whole family.

present¹ ⟨A1⟩ ⟨w⟩ /'preznt/ adj. 1 [only before noun] existing or happening now: We hope to overcome our present difficulties very soon. 2 [not before noun] being in a particular place: There were 200 people present at the meeting. **OPP** absent

present² ⟨A1⟩ ⟨w⟩ /'preznt/ noun 1 [C] ~ (for sb) something that you give to sb or receive from sb: a birthday/wedding/leaving/Christmas present ◇ I bought the book as a present for my sister. **SYN** gift 2 (usually the present) [sing.] the time now: We live in the present but we must learn from the past. ◇ I'm rather busy at present. Can I call you back later?
IDM for the moment/present → MOMENT

present³ ⟨A2⟩ ⟨w⟩ /pri'zent/ verb [T] 1 ~ sth (to sb) to show sth that you have prepared to people: Good teachers try to present their material in an interesting way. 2 ~ sb with sth; ~ sth (to sb) to give sth to sb, especially at a formal ceremony: All the dancers were presented with flowers. ◇ Flowers were presented to all the dancers. 3 ~ sb with sth; ~ sth (to sb) to give sb sth that has to be dealt with: The manager presented us with a bill for the broken chair. ◇ Learning English presented no problem to him. 4 (ARTS AND MEDIA) to introduce a TV or radio programme 5 (ARTS AND MEDIA) to show a play, etc. to the public: The Theatre Royal is presenting a new production of 'Ghosts'. ⊃ note at **performing arts** 6 ~ sb (to sb) to introduce sb to a person in a formal ceremony: The teams were presented to the president before the game.

presentable /pri'zentəbl/ adj. clean and attractive and good enough to be seen by people you do not know well

presentation ⟨B1⟩ ⟨w⟩ /ˌprezn'teɪʃn/ noun 1 [C] a meeting at which sth, especially a new product or idea, or piece of work, is shown or explained to a group of people: Each student has to give a short presentation on a subject of his/her choice. 2 [U] the act of giving or showing sth to sb: The presentation of prizes began after the speeches. 3 [U] the way in which sth is shown, explained, offered, etc. to people: Untidy presentation of your work may lose you marks. 4 [C] a formal ceremony at which a prize, etc. is given to sb

the ,present 'day noun [sing.] the situation that exists in the world now, rather than in the past or the future: a study of European drama, from Ibsen to the present day ▸ **present-day** adj. [only before noun]: present-day fashions ◇ present-day America

presenter /pri'zentə(r)/ noun [C] (ARTS AND MEDIA) a person who introduces a TV or radio programme

presently ʔ+ **C1** /ˈprezntli/ *adv.* **1** (*especially AmE*) now: *The management are presently discussing the matter.* **SYN** **currently 2** soon: *I'll be finished presently.* **SYN** **shortly 3** after a short time: *Presently, I heard the car door shut.*

ˌpresent parˈticiple *noun* [C] (**GRAMMAR**) the form of the verb that ends in *-ing*

the ˌpresent ˈperfect *noun* [sing.] (**GRAMMAR**) the form of a verb that expresses an action done in a time period from the past to the present, formed with the present tense of *have* and the past participle of the verb: *'I've finished', 'She hasn't arrived'* and *'I've been studying'* are all *in the present perfect.*

the ˌpresent ˈtense (*also* the present /ðə ˈpreznt/) *noun* [C, usually sing.] (**GRAMMAR**) the form of a verb that you use when you are talking about what is happening or what exists now

preservative /prɪˈzɜːvətɪv/ *noun* [C, U] a substance that is used for keeping food, etc. in good condition

preserve ʔ **B2** /prɪˈzɜːv/ *verb* [T] to keep sth safe or in good condition: *They've managed to preserve most of the wall paintings in the caves.* ▸ preservation ʔ+ **C1** /ˌprezəˈveɪʃn/ *noun* [U]

preside ʔ+ **C1** /prɪˈzaɪd/ *verb* [I] to be in charge of a discussion, meeting, etc.
PHR V **preside over sth** to be in control of or responsible for sth

presidency ʔ+ **C1** /ˈprezɪdənsi/ *noun* (*pl.* -ies) **1** the presidency [sing.] (**POLITICS**) the position of being president **2** [C] the period of time that sb is president

president ʔ **A2** /ˈprezɪdənt/ *noun* [C] **1** (*also* President) (**POLITICS**) the leader of a REPUBLIC: *the president of France* ◇ *the US president* **2** the person with the highest position in some organizations ▸ presidential ʔ+ **C1** /ˌprezɪˈdenʃl/ *adj.*: *presidential elections*

press¹ ʔ **B1** /pres/ *noun*
• NEWSPAPERS **1** (*often* the press) [sing. + sing./pl. verb] (**ARTS AND MEDIA**) newspapers and the journalists who work for them: *The story has been reported on TV and* **in the press**. ◇ *the local/national press* ◇ *The press support/supports government policy.* ⊃ note at **newspaper 2** [sing., U] (**ARTS AND MEDIA**) the type or amount of reports that newspapers write about sb/ sth: *This company has had* **a bad press** *recently.* ◇ *The strike got very little press.*
• PRINTING MACHINE **3** [C, U] a machine for printing books, newspapers, etc.; the process of printing them: *All details were correct at the time of* **going to press**.
• BUSINESS **4** [C] a business that prints books, etc: *Oxford University Press*
• ACT OF PUSHING **5** [C] an act of pushing sth FIRMLY: *Give that button* **a press** *and see what happens.*

press² ʔ **B1** /pres/ *verb*
• PUSH/SQUEEZE **1** [T, I] to push sth FIRMLY: *Just press that button and the door will open.* ◇ *He pressed the lid firmly shut.* **2** [T, I] ~ to push sth closely against sth; to be pushed in this way: *She pressed the photo to her chest.* **3** [I] (used with an adverb or a preposition) (used about people) to move in a particular direction by pushing: *The crowd pressed against the line of policemen.*
• TRY TO PERSUADE **4** [I, T] ~ **(sb) (for sth)**; ~ **(sb) (to do sth)** to try to persuade or force sb to do sth: *to press somebody for an answer* ◇ *I pressed them to stay for dinner.* **SYN** **urge**¹
• MAKE FLAT/SMOOTH **5** [T] to make something flat by using force or putting something heavy on top: *to press wild flowers between the pages of a book* **6** [T] to make a piece of clothing smooth by using an iron: *This shirt needs pressing.*

• SAY/REPEAT **7** [T] to express or repeat sth with force: *I don't want to press the point, but you still owe me money.*
IDM **be hard pressed/pushed/put to do sth** → HARD² **bring/press charges (against sb)** → CHARGE¹
PHR V **press ahead/forward/on (with sth)** to continue doing sth even though it is difficult or hard work: *They pressed on with the building work in spite of the bad weather.*

ˈpress conference *noun* [C] (**ARTS AND MEDIA**) a meeting when a famous or important person answers questions from newspaper and TV journalists: *to hold a press conference*

pressed /prest/ *adj.* [not before noun] ~ **(for sth)** not having enough of something, especially time or money: *I must hurry. I'm really pressed for time.*

pressing /ˈpresɪŋ/ *adj.* that must be dealt with immediately **SYN** **urgent**

ˈpress release *noun* [C] (**ARTS AND MEDIA**) an official statement made to journalists by a large organization, a political party or a government department: *The company issued a press release to end speculation about its future.*

ˈpress stud = POPPER

ˈpress-up (*BrE*) (*AmE* push-up) *noun* [C] (**SPORT**) a type of exercise in which you lie on your front on the floor and push your body up with your arms: *I do 50 press-ups every morning.* ⊃ picture at **sit-up**

pressure¹ ʔ **B1** **●**
/ˈpreʃə(r)/ *noun* **1** [U]
~ **(on sb) (to do sth)**;
~ **(from sb/sth)** the act of
trying to persuade or to
force sb to do sth: *There
was tremendous
pressure on her to take
the job.* ◇ *pressure from
environmental groups*
2 [C, U] (*also* pressures [pl.])
worries or difficulties
that you have because
you have too much to
deal with: *financial
pressures* ◇ *I find it
difficult to cope with
pressure at work.*
SYN **stress**¹ **3** [U] the
force that is produced
when you press on or against sth: *Apply pressure to the cut and it will stop bleeding.* ◇ *The pressure of the water caused the dam to crack.* **4** [U] (**PHYSICS**) the force that a gas or liquid has when it is contained inside sth: *high/low blood pressure* ◇ *You should check your tyre pressures regularly.* **5** [U] ~ **(on sth)** the effect that sth has on the way a situation develops, especially when this causes problems: *This puts upward pressure on prices.* ⊃ note at **currency**
IDM **put pressure on sb (to do sth)** to force sb to do sth: *His boss is putting pressure on him to resign.* **under pressure 1** being forced to do sth: *Anna was under pressure from her parents to leave school and get a job.* **2** worried or in difficulty because you have too much to deal with: *I perform poorly under pressure, so I hate exams.* **3** (used about liquid or gas) contained inside sth or sent somewhere using force: *Water is forced out through the hose under pressure.*

pressure² /ˈpreʃə(r)/ *verb* [T] = PRESSURIZE

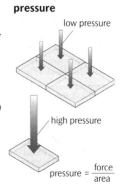

pressure

low pressure

high pressure

$$pressure = \frac{force}{area}$$

pressure cooker *noun* [C] a strong metal pot with a tight LID, that cooks food quickly using STEAM under high pressure

pressure group *noun* [C + sing./pl. verb] (**POLITICS**) a group of people who are trying to influence what a government or other organization does

pressurize (*BrE also* -ise) /ˈpreʃəraɪz/ *verb* [T] **1** (*BrE*) (*also* **pressure** *AmE, BrE*) ~ **sb** (**into sth/doing sth**) to use force or influence to make sb do sth: *Some workers were pressurized into taking early retirement.* **2** [usually passive] to keep the air pressure in a SUBMARINE, an aircraft, etc. the same as it is on earth

prestige /preˈstiːʒ/ *noun* [U] the respect and value that sb/sth has because of their social position, or what they have done ▶ **prestigious** ɪ+ **C1** /-ˈstɪdʒəs/ *adj.*: *a prestigious prize/school/job*

presumably ɪ+ **C1** /prɪˈzjuːməbli/ *adv.* I imagine; I suppose: *Presumably this rain means the match will be cancelled?*

presume ɪ+ **C1** /prɪˈzjuːm/ *verb* [T] to think that sth is true even if you do not know for sure: *The house looks empty so I presume they are away on holiday.* **SYN** **assume** ▶ **presumption** /-ˈzʌmpʃn/ *noun* [C]

presumptuous /prɪˈzʌmptʃuəs/ *adj.* confident that sth will happen or that sb will do sth without making sure first, in a way that annoys people

presuppose /ˌpriːsəˈpəʊz/ *verb* [T] (*formal*) **1** to accept sth as true or existing and act on that basis, before it has been proved to be true: *Teachers sometimes presuppose a fairly high level of knowledge by the students.* **SYN** **presume** **2** to depend on sth in order to exist or be true: *His argument presupposes that it does not matter who is in power.*

pre-teen /ˌpriː ˈtiːn/ *noun* [C] (**SOCIAL STUDIES**) a young person of about 11 or 12 years of age ▶ **pre-teen** *adj.*

pretence (*BrE*) (*AmE* **pretense**) /prɪˈtens/ *noun* [U, sing.] an action that makes people believe sth that is not true: *She was unable to keep up the pretence that she loved him.*
IDM **on/under false pretences** → **FALSE**

pretend ɪ **B1** /prɪˈtend/ *verb* [I, T] ~ **(that)** … ; ~ **(to do sth)** **1** to behave in a particular way in order to make other people believe sth that is not true: *You can't just pretend (that) the problem doesn't exist.* ◇ *Paul's not really asleep. He's just pretending.* **2** (used especially about children) to imagine that sth is true as part of a game: *The kids were under the bed pretending to be snakes.*

pretentious /prɪˈtenʃəs/ *adj.* trying to appear more serious or important than you really are

pretext /ˈpriːtekst/ *noun* [C] (**as a)~ (for doing sth**); (**on the)~ (of doing sth**) (*formal*) a reason that you give for doing sth that is not the real reason: *It was feared that the leader's words would be used as a pretext for violence.* ◇ *Tariq left on the pretext of having an appointment at the dentist's.* ⊃ note at **reason¹**

pretty¹ ɪ **A1** /ˈprɪti/ *adj.* (**prettier; prettiest**) attractive and pleasant to look at or hear: *a pretty girl/smile/dress/garden/name* ▶ **prettily** /-ɪli/ *adv.*: *The room is prettily decorated.* ▶ **prettiness** *noun* [U]

pretty² ɪ **A1** /ˈprɪti/ *adv.* (*informal*) quite; fairly: *The film was pretty good but not fantastic.* ◇ *I'm pretty certain that Alex will agree.* ⊃ note at **rather**
IDM **pretty much/nearly/well** almost; very nearly: *I won't be long. I've pretty well finished.*

prevail ɪ+ **C1** /prɪˈveɪl/ *verb* [I] **1** (*formal*) to exist or be common in a particular place or at a particular time **2** ~ (**against/over sb/sth**) to win or be accepted, especially after a fight or discussion: *Good prevailed over evil.*

prevailing /prɪˈveɪlɪŋ/ *adj.* [only before noun] **1** existing or most common at a particular time: *the prevailing climate of opinion* **2** (**GEOGRAPHY**) (used about the wind) most common in a particular area: *The prevailing wind is from the south-west.* ⊃ picture at **longshore drift**

prevalent /ˈprevələnt/ *adj.* (*formal*) most common in a particular place or at a particular time: *The prevalent atmosphere was one of fear.* ▶ **prevalence** ɪ+ **C1** /-ləns/ *noun* [U]

prevent ɪ **A2** **⊙** /prɪˈvent/ *verb* ~ **sb/sth (from) (doing sth)** to stop sth happening or to stop sb doing sth: *This accident could have been prevented.* ◇ *Her parents tried to prevent her from going.* ▶ **prevention** ɪ+ **C1** **W** /-ˈvenʃn/ *noun* [U]: *accident/crime prevention*

preventable /prɪˈventəbl/ *adj.* that can be prevented: *Many accidents are preventable.*

preventive /prɪˈventɪv/ (*also* **preventative** /prɪˈventətɪv/) *adj.* [only before noun] intended to stop or prevent sth from happening: *preventative medicine*

preview /ˈpriːvjuː/ *noun* [C] (**ARTS AND MEDIA**) a chance to see a play, film, etc. before it is shown to the general public

previous ɪ **B1** **⊙** /ˈpriːviəs/ *adj.* coming or happening before or earlier: *Do you have previous experience of this type of work?* ▶ **previously** ɪ **B1** **W** *adv.*: *Before I moved to Spain I had previously worked in Italy.*

prey¹ ɪ+ **C1** /preɪ/ *noun* [U] an animal or a bird that is killed and eaten by another animal or bird: *The eagle is a bird of prey* (= it kills and eats other birds or small animals).

prey² /preɪ/ *verb*
IDM **prey on sb's mind** to cause sb to worry or think about sth: *The thought that he was responsible for the accident preyed on the train driver's mind.*
PHR V **prey on sth** (used about an animal or a bird) to kill and eat other animals or birds: *Owls prey on mice and other small animals.*

price¹ ɪ **A1** /praɪs/ *noun* **1** [C] the amount of money that you must pay in order to buy sth: *What's the price of petrol now?* ◇ *We can't afford to buy the car at that price.* ◇ *There's no price on* (= written on) *this jar of coffee.* **2** [sing.] unpleasant things that you have to experience in order to achieve sth or as a result of sth: *Sleepless nights are a small price to pay for having a baby.*
IDM **at a price** costing a lot of money or involving sth unpleasant: *Food is available, at a price.* **at any price** even if the cost is very high or if it will have unpleasant results: *Richard was determined to succeed at any price.* **not at any price** never; not for any reason

---

▼ **COLLOCATIONS**

price

A **charge** is the amount of money that you must pay for using sth: *Is there a charge for parking here?* ◇ *admission charges.* You use **cost** when you are talking about paying for services or about prices in general without mentioning an actual sum of money: *The cost of electricity is going up.* ◇ *a steady rise in the cost of living.* The **price** of sth is the amount of money that you must pay in order to buy it. A shop may **raise/increase**, **reduce/bring down** or **freeze** its prices. The prices **rise/go up** or **fall/go down**.

price² 🔊 **B2** /praɪs/ *verb* [T] to fix the price of sth or to write the price on sth: *The books were all priced at between £5 and £10.* ▸ **pricing** *noun* [U]: *competitive pricing* ◇ *pricing policy*

price-fixing *noun* [U] (**FINANCE**) an agreement between companies not to sell goods below a particular price, usually in a way that is illegal

priceless /'praɪsləs/ *adj.* of very great value: *priceless jewels and antiques* ⊃ look at **invaluable**, **valuable** (1), **worthless** (1)

price list *noun* [C] a list of the prices of the goods that are on sale

price tag *noun* [C] a label on sth that shows how much you must pay

pricey /'praɪsi/ *adj.* (pricier; priciest) (*informal*) expensive

prick¹ /prɪk/ *verb* [T] to make a small hole in sth; to cause sb pain with a sharp point: *She pricked her finger on a needle.*
IDM **prick up your ears** (used about an animal) to hold up the ears in order to listen carefully to sth: (*figurative*) *Mike pricked up his ears when he heard Emma's name mentioned.*

prick² /prɪk/ *noun* [C] the sudden pain that you feel when sth sharp goes into your skin

prickle¹ /'prɪkl/ *noun* [C] one of the sharp points on some plants and animals: *Hedgehogs are covered in prickles.* ⊃ look at **spine** (2)

prickle² /'prɪkl/ *verb* [I, T] to have or make sb/sth have an uncomfortable feeling on the skin: *His skin prickled with fear.*

prickly /'prɪkli/ *adj.* (pricklier; prickliest) **1** covered with sharp points: *a prickly bush* **2** causing an uncomfortable feeling on the skin **3** (*informal*) (used about a person) easily made angry

pride¹ 🔊+ **B2** /praɪd/ *noun* **1** [U, sing.] **~ (in sth/doing sth)** the feeling of pleasure that you have when you or people who are close to you do sth good or own sth good: *I take great pride in my work.* ◇ *You should feel pride in your achievement.* ◇ *Jane's parents watched with pride as she went up to collect her prize.* **2** [U] the respect that you have for yourself: *You'll hurt his pride if you refuse to accept the present.* ⊃ look at **gay pride** **3** [U] the feeling that you are better than other people **4** [sing.] **the ~ of sth/sb** a person or thing that is very important or of great value to sth/sb: *The new stadium was the pride of the whole town.* ⊃ adjective **proud**
IDM **sb's pride and joy** a thing or person that gives sb great pleasure or SATISFACTION

pride² /praɪd/ *verb*
PHR V **pride yourself on sth/doing sth** to feel pleased about sth good or clever that you can do: *Fabio prides himself on his ability to cook.*

priest 🔊 **B1** /priːst/ *noun* [C] (**RELIGION**) a person who performs religious ceremonies in some religions

prim /prɪm/ *adj.* (used about a person) always behaving in a careful or formal way and easily shocked by anything that is rude ▸ **primly** *adv.*

primacy /'praɪməsi/ *noun* (pl. -ies) (*formal*) **1** [U] the fact of being the most important person or thing: *a belief in the primacy of the family* **2** [C] (**RELIGION**) the position of an ARCHBISHOP

prima donna /ˌpriːmə 'dɒnə/ *noun* [C] **1** (**ARTS AND MEDIA**) the main woman singer in an OPERA performance or an OPERA company **2** a person who thinks they are very important because they are good at sth, and who behaves badly when they do not get what they want

primaeval /praɪ'miːvl/ = PRIMEVAL

primal /'praɪml/ *adj.* [only before noun] (*formal*) connected with the earliest origins of life; very basic: *the primal hunter-gatherer* **SYN** **primeval**

primarily 🔊+ **B2** **W** /praɪ'merəli, 'praɪmərəli/ *adv.* more than anything else; mainly: *The course is aimed primarily at beginners.*

primary¹ 🔊 **B1** 🅾 /'praɪməri/ *adj.* **1** most important; main: *Smoking is one of the primary causes of lung cancer.* **2** (*especially BrE*) (**EDUCATION**) connected with the education of children between about five and eleven years old: *primary teachers* ⊃ look at **primary school**

primary² /'praɪməri/ (pl. -ies) (*also* ˌprimary e'lection) *noun* [C] (*AmE*) (**POLITICS**) an election in which people from a particular area vote to choose a person who will represent the party for a future important election

ˌprimary 'care (*also* ˌprimary 'health care) *noun* [U] (**MEDICINE**) the medical treatment that you receive first when you are ill, for example from your family doctor

ˌprimary 'colour *noun* [C] any of the colours red, yellow or blue. You can make any other colour by mixing primary colours in different ways.

primary school *noun* [C] (*BrE*) (**EDUCATION**) a school for children between the ages of 4 and 11 ⊃ look at **secondary school**

ˌprimary 'source *noun* [C] a document, etc. that contains information obtained by research or observation, not taken from other books, etc. ⊃ look at **secondary source**

ˌprimary 'stress *noun* [C, U] (**LANGUAGE**) the strongest stress that is put on a syllable in a word or a phrase when it is spoken ⊃ look at **secondary stress**

primate /'praɪmeɪt/ *noun* [C] (**BIOLOGY**) any animal that belongs to the group that includes humans and monkeys ⊃ picture at **animal**

prime¹ 🔊 **B2** /praɪm/ *adj.* [only before noun] **1** main; the first example of sth that sb would think of or choose: *She is a prime candidate for the next team captain.* ⊃ note at **main¹** **2** of very good quality; best: *prime pieces of beef* **3** having all the typical qualities: *That's a prime example of what I was talking about.*

prime² /praɪm/ *noun* [sing.] the time when sb is strongest, most beautiful, most successful, etc: *Several of the team are past their prime.* ◇ *In his prime he was a fine actor.* ◇ *to be in the prime of life*

prime³ /praɪm/ *verb* [T] **~ sb (for/with sth)** to give sb information in order to prepare them for sth: *The politician had been well primed with all the facts before the interview.*

ˌprime 'minister (*also* Prime Minister) *noun* [C] (*abbr.* PM) (**POLITICS**) the main minister and leader of the government in some countries ⊃ look at **minister** (1)

ˌprime 'number *noun* [C] (**MATHEMATICS**) a number that can be divided exactly only by itself and 1, for example 7, 17 and 41

prime time *noun* [U] (**ARTS AND MEDIA**) the time when the greatest number of people are watching TV

primeval (*also* primaeval) /praɪ'miːvl/ *adj.* (**HISTORY**) from the earliest period of the history of the world, very ancient

primitive /'prɪmətɪv/ *adj.* **1** very simple and not developed: *The washing facilities in the camp were very primitive.* **2** [only before noun] (**HISTORY**) connected with a very early stage in the development of humans or animals: *Primitive man lived in caves and hunted wild animals.*

primitivism /ˈprɪmɪtɪvɪzəm/ *noun* [U] (**ARTS AND MEDIA**) a belief that simple forms and ideas are the most valuable, expressed as a philosophy or in art or literature

primrose /ˈprɪmrəʊz/ *noun* [C] a yellow spring flower

prince ⓔ **B1** /prɪns/ *noun* [C] **1** a son or other close male relative of a king or queen **2** (**POLITICS**) the male ruler of a small country

princess ⓔ **B1** /ˌprɪnˈses, ˈprɪnses/ *noun* [C] **1** a daughter or other close female relative of a king or queen **2** the wife of a prince

principal[1] ⓔ+ **B2** /ˈprɪnsəpl/ *adj.* [only before noun] most important; main: *the principal characters in a play* ↄ note at **main**[1] ▶ **principally** /-pli/ *adv.*: *Our products are designed principally for the European market.*

principal[2] ⓔ+ **C1** /ˈprɪnsəpl/ *noun* [C] (*AmE*) = **HEAD**[1] (7)

principality /ˌprɪnsɪˈpæləti/ *noun* [C] (*pl.* -ies) (**GEOGRAPHY**) a country that is ruled by a prince: *the principality of Andorra*

principle ⓔ **B2** ⓞ /ˈprɪnsəpl/ *noun* **1** [C, U] a rule for good behaviour, based on what a person believes is right: *He doesn't eat meat **on principle**. ◇ She refuses to wear fur. It's **a matter of principle** with her.* **2** [C] ~ (**that …**) a basic general law, rule or idea: *The system works **on the principle** that heat rises. ◇ The course teaches the basic principles of car maintenance.*
IDM **in principle** in general, but possibly not in detail: *His proposal sounds fine in principle, but there are a few points I'm not happy about.*

principled /ˈprɪnsəpld/ *adj.* **1** having strong beliefs about what is right and wrong; based on strong beliefs: *a principled woman* **OPP** **unprincipled** **2** based on rules or **TRUTHS**: *a principled approach to language teaching*

print[1] ⓔ **A2** /prɪnt/ *verb*
• WORDS, PICTURES, ETC. **1** [T, I] to put words, pictures, etc. onto paper using a special machine: *How much did it cost to print the posters?* **2** [T] to make a photo from a digital image or a piece of film
• BOOKS, ETC. **3** [T] to produce books, newspapers, etc. in this way: *50 000 copies of the textbook were printed.*
• PUBLISH **4** [T] to include sth in a book, newspaper, etc: *The newspaper should not have printed the photos of the crash.*
• WRITE **5** [T, I] to write with letters that are not joined together: *Please print your name clearly at the top of the paper.*
• MAKE A DESIGN **6** [T] to put a pattern onto cloth, paper, etc.
PHR V **print (sth) out** to print information from a computer onto paper: *I'll just print out this file.*

print[2] ⓔ **B2** /prɪnt/ *noun*
• LETTERS, WORDS, ETC. **1** [U] the letters, words, etc. in a book, newspaper, etc: *The print is too small for me to read without my glasses.*
• BOOKS, ETC. **2** [U] used to refer to the business of producing books, newspapers, etc: *the print unions/ workers*
• MARK **3** [C] a mark that is made by sth pressing onto sth else: *His prints were found at the scene of the crime. ◇ footprints in the snow* ↄ look at **fingerprint**, **footprint** (1)
• PICTURE **4** [C] a picture that was made by printing **IDM** **in print 1** (used about a book) still available from the company that published it **2** (used about a

person's work) published in a book, newspaper, etc. **out of print** (used about a book) no longer available from the company that published it; not being printed any more

printer ⓔ **A2** /ˈprɪntə(r)/ *noun* [C] **1** (**COMPUTING**) a machine that prints out information from a computer onto paper: *a laser printer* **2** a person or company that prints books, newspapers, etc.

printing ⓔ **B1** /ˈprɪntɪŋ/ *noun* **1** [U] the act of producing letters, pictures, patterns, etc. on sth by pressing a surface covered with **INK** against it: *colour printing ◇ the invention of printing by Gutenberg* **2** [C] the act of printing a number of copies of a book at one time: *The book is in its sixth printing.* **3** [U] a type of writing when you write all the letters separately and do not join them together

printing press *noun* [C] a machine that is used for printing books, newspapers, etc.

printmaking /ˈprɪntmeɪkɪŋ/ *noun* [U] (**ART**) the art of making pictures or designs by pressing a surface covered with **INK** onto paper or other material ▶ **printmaker** /-kə(r)/ *noun*

printout /ˈprɪntaʊt/ *noun* [C, U] (**COMPUTING**) information from a computer that is printed onto paper

prior ⓔ+ **B2** ⓦ /ˈpraɪə(r)/ *adj.* **1** [only before noun] existing before or earlier **2** ~ **to sth** before sth: *Passengers are asked to report to the check-in desk prior to departure.*

prioritize (*BrE also* -ise) /praɪˈɒrətaɪz/ *verb* **1** [T, I] to put tasks, problems, etc. in order of importance, so that you can deal with the most important first: *You should make a list of all the jobs you have to do and prioritize them.* **2** [T] (*formal*) to treat sth as being more important than other things: *The organization was formed to prioritize the needs of older people.*

priority ⓔ **B2** ⓦ /praɪˈɒrəti/ *noun* (*pl.* -ies) **1** [U] ~ (**over sb/sth**) the state of being more important than sb/sth or of coming before sb/sth else: *Emergency cases **take priority** over other patients in hospital. ◇ We give priority to families with small children.* **2** [C] something that is most important or that you must do before anything else: *Our **top priority** is to get food and water to the refugee camps. ◇ I'll **make it my priority** to sort out your problem.*

prise (*especially BrE*) (*AmE* **prize**) /praɪz/ (*also* **pry** *especially in AmE*) *verb* [T] (often used with an adverb or a preposition) to use force to open sth, remove a **LID**, etc: *I used a knife to prise the lid off.*

prism /ˈprɪzəm/ *noun* [C] **1** (**GEOMETRY**) a solid figure with ends that are **PARALLEL** (= the same distance apart at every point) and of the same size and shape, and with sides whose opposite edges are equal and **PARALLEL** ↄ picture at **solid**[2] **2** (**PHYSICS**) a clear glass or plastic object that separates light that passes through it into the seven different colours

prison ⓔ **A2** /ˈprɪzn/ *noun* [C, U] (**LAW**) a building where criminals are kept as a punishment: *The terrorists were **sent to prison** for 25 years. ◇ He will be **released from prison** next month.* **SYN** **jail**[1] ↄ note at **court**[1]

prisoner ⓔ **B1** /ˈprɪznə(r)/ *noun* [C] (**LAW**) a person who is being kept in prison: *a political prisoner* **IDM** **hold/take sb captive/prisoner** → **CAPTIVE**[1]

prisoner of ˈwar *noun* [C] (*pl.* **prisoners of war**) (*abbr.* **POW**) a soldier, etc. who is caught by the enemy during a war and who is kept in prison until the end of the war

pristine /ˈprɪstiːn/ *adj.* fresh and clean, as if new: *The car is **in pristine condition**.* **SYN** **immaculate**

privacy ʔ B2 /ˈprɪvəsi/ *noun* [U] **1** the state of being alone and not watched or interrupted by other people: *There is not much privacy in large hospital wards.* **2** the state of being free from the attention of the public: *The actress claimed that the photos were an invasion of privacy.*

private¹ ʔ B1 ⓦ /ˈpraɪvət/ *adj.* **1** belonging to or intended for one particular person or group and not to be shared by others: *This is private property. You may not park here.* ◇ *a private letter/conversation* **2** with nobody else present: *I would like a private interview with HR manager.* **3** owned, done or organized by a person or company, and not by the government: *a private hospital/school* (= you pay to go there) ◇ *a private detective* (= one who is not in the police) ➔ look at **public¹** (2) **4** (used about classes, lessons, etc.) given to one student or a small group for payment: *Claire gives private English lessons at her house.* **5** not connected with work or business: *He never discusses his private life with his colleagues at work.* **6** not wanting to share thoughts and feelings with other people: *He's a very private person.*
▸ **privately** *adv.*

private² /ˈpraɪvət/ *noun* [C] a soldier of the lowest level
IDM **in private** with nobody else present: *May I speak to you in private?*

ˌprivate ˈenterprise *noun* [U] (**BUSINESS, ECONOMICS**) the economic system in which industry or business is owned by independent companies or private people and is not controlled by the government **SYN** **free enterprise**

ˌprivate ˈequity *noun* [U] (**FINANCE**) investment made in a company, usually a small one, whose shares are not bought and sold by the public

ˌprivate ˈschool (*also* independent school) *noun* [C] (**EDUCATION**) a school that receives no money from the government and where the education of the students is paid for by their parents ➔ look at **public school** (1), **state school** (1)

the ˌprivate ˈsector *noun* [sing.] (**ECONOMICS**) the part of the economy of a country that is not under the direct control of the government: *to work in the private sector* ➔ look at **public sector**

prisms

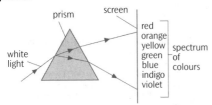

White light can be split into its components using a prism.

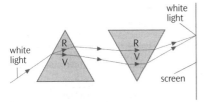

The colours in white light can be split and combined again using prisms.

R = red   V = violet

privatize (*BrE also* -ise) /ˈpraɪvətaɪz/ *verb* [T] (**BUSINESS**) to sell a business or an industry that was owned by the government to a private company: *The water industry has been privatized.* **OPP** **nationalize**
▸ **privatization** ʔ+ C1 (*BrE also* -isation) /ˌpraɪvətaɪˈzeɪʃn/ *noun* [U]

privilege ʔ+ C1 /ˈprɪvəlɪdʒ/ *noun* **1** [C, U] a special right or advantage that only one person or group can have: *Prisoners who behave well enjoy special privileges.* **2** [sing.] a special advantage or opportunity that gives you great pleasure: *It was a great privilege to hear her sing.*

privileged /ˈprɪvəlɪdʒd/ *adj.* having an advantage or opportunity that most people do not have: *Only a privileged few are allowed to enter this room.* ◇ *I feel very privileged to be playing for the national team.* **OPP** **underprivileged**

prize¹ ʔ A2 /praɪz/ *noun* [C] something of value that is given to sb who is successful in a race, competition, game, etc: *She won first prize in the competition.*

prize² /praɪz/ *adj.* [only before noun] winning, or good enough to win, a prize: *a prize flower display*

prize³ /praɪz/ *verb* [T] **1** to consider sth to be very valuable: *This picture is one of my most prized possessions.* **2** (*AmE*) = PRISE

pro /prəʊ/ *noun* [C] (*pl.* pros) (*informal*) **1** (**SPORT**) a person who plays or teaches a sport for money: *a golf pro* **SYN** **professional²** **2** a person who has a lot of skill and experience **SYN** **professional²**
IDM **the pros and cons** the reasons for and against doing sth: *We should consider all the pros and cons before reaching a decision.* ➔ look at **advantage** (2)

pro- /prəʊ/ *prefix* (in adjectives) in favour of; supporting: *pro-democracy* ◇ *pro-European* ➔ look at **anti-** (1)

proactive /ˌprəʊˈæktɪv/ *adj.* controlling a situation by making things happen rather than waiting for things to happen and then reacting to them ➔ look at **reactive** (1) ▸ **proactively** *adv.*

probability ʔ+ B2 ⓞ /ˌprɒbəˈbɪləti/ *noun* (*pl.* -ies) **1** [U, C] how likely sth is to happen: *At that time there seemed little probability of success.* **2** [C] something that is likely to happen: *Closure of the factory now seems a probability.* **3** [C, U] (**MATHEMATICS**) a RATIO (= the relation between two numbers that shows how much bigger one quantity is than another) showing the chances that a particular thing will happen: *There is a 60% probability that the population will be infected with the disease.*

probable ʔ+ B2 /ˈprɒbəbl/ *adj.* that you expect to happen or to be true; likely **OPP** **improbable** ➔ look at **possible**

▼ SYNONYMS

Note that **probable** and **likely** mean the same but are used differently: *It's probable that he will be late.* ◇ *He is likely to be late.*

probably ʔ A1 /ˈprɒbəbli/ *adv.* almost certainly: *I will phone next week, probably on Wednesday.*

probation /prəˈbeɪʃn/ *noun* [U] **1** (**LAW**) a system that allows sb who has committed a crime not to go to prison if they go to see an official regularly for a fixed period of time: *Jamie is on probation for two years.* **2** a period of time at the start of a new job when you are tested to see if you are suitable: *a three-month probation period*

probe¹ ͡ɪ+ **C1** /prəʊb/ *verb* **1** [I, T] ~ **(into sth)** to ask questions in order to find out secret or hidden information: *The newspapers are now probing into the president's past.* **2** [T] to examine or look for sth, especially with a long thin instrument: *The doctor probed the cut for pieces of broken glass.* ▶ **probing** *adj.*: *to ask probing questions*

probe² ͡ɪ+ **C1** /prəʊb/ *noun* [C] **1** ~ **(into sth)** the process of asking questions, collecting facts, etc. in order to find out hidden information about sth: *a police probe into illegal financial dealing* **2** (*also* **space probe**) (**ASTRONOMY**) a SPACECRAFT without people on board that obtains information and sends it back to earth **3** (**MEDICINE**) a long thin metal tool used by doctors for examining inside the body **4** (**SCIENCE**) a small device put inside sth and used by scientists to test sth or record information

problem ͡ɪ **A1** ⊙ /'prɒbləm/ *noun* [C] **1** ~ **(with sth)** a thing that is difficult to deal with or to understand: *I can't play because I've got a problem with my knee.* ◇ *social/family/financial/technical problems* ◇ *You won't **solve the problem** if you ignore it.* ◇ *The company will **face problems** from unions if it sacks workers.* ◇ *It's going to **cause problems** if Donna brings her husband.* ◇ *'Can you fix this for me?' 'No problem.'* ◇ *It's a great painting — **the problem** is I've got nowhere to put it.* **2** a question that you have to solve by thinking about it: *a maths/logic problem*

problematic ͡ɪ+ **C1** ⓦ /ˌprɒbləˈmætɪk/ (*also* **problematical** /ˌprɒbləˈmætɪkl/) *adj.* difficult to deal with or to understand; full of problems; not certain to be successful: *Finding replacement parts for such an old car could be problematic.*

pro bono /ˌprəʊ ˈbəʊnəʊ/ *adj.* (**FINANCE, LAW**) (used especially about legal work) done without asking for payment ▶ **pro bono** *adv.*

procaryote, procaryotic = PROKARYOTE, PROKARYOTIC

procedure ͡ɪ **B2** ⊙ /prəˈsiːdʒə(r)/ *noun* **1** [C, U] the usual or correct way of doing sth: *What's the procedure for making a complaint?* **2** [C] (**MEDICINE**) a medical operation: *to perform a routine surgical procedure* ▶ **procedural** ⓦ /-dʒərəl/ *adj.* (*formal*): *procedural rules*

proceed ͡ɪ+ **B2** /prəˈsiːd/ *verb* [I] **1** ~ **(with sth)** to continue doing sth; to continue being done: *We're not sure whether we still want to proceed with the sale.* **2** ~ **to do sth** to do sth next, after having done sth else first: *Once he had calmed down he proceeded to tell us what had happened.*

proceeding ͡ɪ+ **C1** /prəˈsiːdɪŋ/ *noun* (*formal*) **1** [C, usually pl.] ~ **(against sb/for sth)** (**LAW**) the process of using a court to settle an argument or to deal with a complaint: *to start divorce proceedings* ◇ *to bring **legal proceedings** against somebody* **2** **proceedings** [pl.] an event or a series of actions: *The Mayor will open the proceedings at the City Hall tomorrow.*

proceeds ͡ɪ+ **C1** /'prəʊsiːdz/ *noun* [pl.] ~ **(of/from sth)** money that you get when you sell sth: *The proceeds from the sale will go to charity.*

process¹ ͡ɪ **A2** ⊙ /'prəʊses/ *noun* [C] **1** a series of actions that you do for a particular purpose: *We've just begun the complicated process of selling the house.* **2** a series of changes that happen naturally: *Mistakes are part of the learning process.* **IDM in the process** while you are doing sth else: *We washed the dog yesterday — and we all got very wet*

in the process. **in the process of sth/doing sth** in the middle of doing sth: *They are in the process of moving house.*

process² ͡ɪ **B2** ⓦ /'prəʊses/ *verb* [T] **1** to treat sth, for example with chemicals, in order to preserve it, change it, etc: *Cheese is processed so that it lasts longer.* **2** (**COMPUTING**) to deal with information, for example on a computer: *It will take about ten days to process your application.* ▶ **processing** ͡ɪ+ **C1** *noun* [U]: *the food processing industry* ◇ *data processing*

procession /prəˈseʃn/ *noun* [C, U] a number of people, vehicles, etc. that move slowly in a line, especially as part of a ceremony: *a funeral procession* ◇ *to walk **in procession***

processor ͡ɪ+ **C1** /'prəʊsesə(r)/ *noun* [C] **1** a machine or a person that processes things ⊃ look at **food processor, word processor 2** (**COMPUTING**) a part of a computer that controls all the other parts of the system

proclaim ͡ɪ+ **C1** /prəˈkleɪm/ *verb* [T] (*formal*) to make sth known officially or publicly: *The day was proclaimed a national holiday.* ⊃ note at **religion** ▶ **proclamation** /ˌprɒkləˈmeɪʃn/ *noun* [C, U]: *to make a proclamation of war*

procrastinate /prəˈkræstɪneɪt/ *verb* [I] (*formal*) to delay doing sth that you should do, usually because you do not want to do it ▶ **procrastination** /prəˌkræstɪˈneɪʃn/ *noun* [U]

procreate /'prəʊkrieɪt/ *verb* [I, T] (*formal*) (**BIOLOGY**) to produce children or baby animals **SYN** reproduce ▶ **procreation** /ˌprəʊkriˈeɪʃn/ *noun* [U]

procure /prəˈkjʊə(r)/ *verb* [T] ~ **sth (for sb)** (*formal*) to obtain sth, especially with difficulty: *They procured a copy of the report for us.*

procurement /prəˈkjʊəmənt/ *noun* [U] (*formal*) the process of getting supplies of sth, especially for a government or an organization: *She is responsible for the procurement of equipment in the company.*

prod /prɒd/ *verb* [T, I] (**-dd-**) to push or press sb/sth with your finger or a pointed object: *She prodded him in the ribs to wake him up.* ▶ **prod** *noun* [C]: *to give the fire a prod with a stick* ▶ **prodding** *noun* [U]

prodigious /prəˈdɪdʒəs/ *adj.* very large or powerful and surprising: *He seemed to have a prodigious amount of energy.*

prodigy /'prɒdədʒi/ *noun* [C] (*pl.* **-ies**) a child who is unusually good at sth: *Mozart was a **child prodigy**.* ⊃ look at **genius** (2)

produce¹ ͡ɪ **A2** ⊙ /prəˈdjuːs/ *verb* [T]
- GOODS **1** to make sth to be sold, especially in large quantities: *The factory produces 20 000 cars a year.* **SYN** manufacture ⊃ note at **make¹**
- MAKE NATURALLY **2** to make sth by a natural process; to grow sth: *This region produces most of the country's wheat.* ◇ (*figurative*) *He's the greatest athlete this country has produced.* ⊃ note at **agriculture**
- MAKE WITH SKILL **3** to create sth using skill: *The children have produced some beautiful pictures for the exhibition.*
- EFFECT/RESULT **4** to cause a particular effect or result: *Her remarks produced roars of laughter.*
- SHOW **5** to show sth so that sb else can look at or examine it: *to produce evidence in court*
- FILM/PLAY **6** (**ARTS AND MEDIA**) to be in charge of preparing a film, play, etc. so that it can be shown to

WORD FAMILY
produce *verb*
produce *noun*
producer *noun*
production *noun*
productive *adj.*
(≠ unproductive)

the public: *She is producing 'Romeo and Juliet' at the local theatre.* ➔ note at **performing arts**

produce² ʔ **B2** ⑤ /ˈprɒdjuːs/ *noun* [U] (**AGRICULTURE**) food, etc. that is grown on a farm and sold: *fresh farm produce* ➔ note at **product**

producer ʔ **B1** /prəˈdjuːsə(r)/ *noun* [C]
1 (**AGRICULTURE**) a person, company or country that makes or grows sth: *Brazil is a major producer of coffee.* **2** (**ARTS AND MEDIA**) a person who deals with the business side of organizing a play, film, etc. **3** (**ARTS AND MEDIA**) a person who arranges for sb to make a programme for TV or radio, or to record an album, etc. **4** (**BIOLOGY**) a living thing such as a green plant that makes its own food by PHOTOSYNTHESIS and is itself eaten as food by other living things ➔ picture at **food chain**

product ʔ **A1** ⓞ /ˈprɒdʌkt/ *noun* [C] **1** (**BUSINESS**) something that is made in a factory or that is formed naturally: *dairy/meat/pharmaceutical/software products* ◇ *Carbon dioxide is one of the waste products of this process.* ➔ picture at **aerosol 2 ~ of sth** the result of sth: *The industry's problems are the product of government policy.* **3** (**MATHEMATICS**) the amount that you get if you multiply one number by another: *The product of 3 and 5 is 15 (= 3×5=15).*

▼ SYNONYMS

product

goods ✦ commodity ✦ merchandise ✦ produce

These are all words for things that are produced to be sold.

product *to create/develop/launch a new product*

goods *electrical/leather goods*

commodity *rice, flour and other basic commodities*

merchandise *official Olympic merchandise*

produce *fresh local produce*

production ʔ **B1** ⓞ /prəˈdʌkʃn/ *noun* **1** [U] (**BUSINESS**) the making or growing of sth, especially in large quantities: *The latest model will be in production from April.* ◇ *This farm specializes in the production of organic vegetables.* ◇ *mass production* **2** [U] the amount of sth that is made or grown: *a rise/fall in production* ◇ *a high level of production* **3** [C] (**ARTS AND MEDIA**) a play, film or programme that has been made for the public

IDM on production of sth when you show sth: *You can get a 10 per cent discount on production of your membership card.*

productive ʔ+ **C1** Ⓦ /prəˈdʌktɪv/ *adj.* **1** that makes or grows sth, especially in large quantities: *The company wants to sell off its less productive factories.* **2** useful (because results come from it): *a productive discussion* **SYN fruitful** ▸ **productivity** ʔ+ **C1** /ˌprɒdʌkˈtɪvəti/ *noun* [U]

,**product 'placement** *noun* [U, C] (**ARTS AND MEDIA**, **BUSINESS**) the use of particular products in films or TV programmes in order to advertise them

Prof. /prɒf/ *abbr.* (in writing) = PROFESSOR

profess /prəˈfes/ *verb* [T] (*formal*) **1** to say that sth is true or correct, even when it is not: *Marianne professed to know nothing at all about it, but I did not believe her.* **2** to state OPENLY (= in an honest way) that you have a particular belief, feeling, etc: *He professed his hatred of war.*

profession ʔ **B1** /prəˈfeʃn/ *noun* [C] **1** a job that needs a high level of training and/or education: *the medical/legal/teaching profession* ◇ *She's thinking of entering the nursing profession.* ➔ note at **work² 2** the ... **profession** [+ sing./pl. verb] all the people who work in a

particular profession: *The legal profession is trying to resist the reforms.*

IDM by profession as your job: *George is an accountant by profession.*

professional¹ ʔ **A2** ⓞ /prəˈfeʃənl/ *adj.* **1** [only before noun] connected with a job that needs a high level of training and/or education: *Get professional advice from your lawyer before you take any action.* **2** doing sth in a way that shows skill, training or care: *The police are trained to deal with every situation in a calm and professional manner.* ◇ *Her application was neatly typed and looked very professional.* **OPP unprofessional 3** doing a sport, etc. for money; (used about a sport, etc.) done by people who are paid: *He's planning to turn professional after the Olympics.* ◇ *professional football* **OPP amateur²**

professional² ʔ **B2** ⓞ /prəˈfeʃənl/ *noun* [C] **1** a person who works in a job that needs a high level of training and/or education **2** (*also informal* pro) (**SPORT**) a person who plays or teaches a sport, etc. for money: *a top golf professional* **3** (*also informal* pro) a person who has a lot of skill and experience

▼ COLLOCATIONS

professional

If you work in law or architecture or one of the medical professions, you **practise** your profession or you **practise as** a lawyer, an architect, etc: *He's a practising child psychiatrist.* ◇ *She practised as a barrister for years.* If you want a professional to work for you, you **appoint** or **engage** them: *A lawyer was appointed to represent the child.* ◇ *He engaged a sports psychologist to motivate his team.* When you need help, you can **consult/get advice from/see** a professional: *She consulted her financial adviser.* ◇ *We were advised to seek legal advice.* ◇ *You ought to see a doctor about that cough.* A solicitor or lawyer can **act for/defend** or **represent** sb: *a lawyer acting for a major company*

pro,fessional 'foul *noun* [C] (*BrE*) (**SPORT**) (in sport, especially football) a rule that sb breaks deliberately so that their team can gain an advantage, especially to prevent a player from the other team from scoring a goal

professionalism /prəˈfeʃənəlɪzəm/ *noun* [U] a way of doing a job that shows great skill and experience: *We were impressed by the professionalism of the staff.*

professionally /prəˈfeʃənəli/ *adv.* **1** in a way that shows great skill and experience **2** for money; by a professional person: *Rob plays the saxophone professionally.*

professor ʔ **A2** /prəˈfesə(r)/ *noun* [C] (*abbr.* Prof.) (**EDUCATION**) **1** (*BrE*) a university teacher of the highest level: *She's professor of English at Bristol University.* ➔ note at **subject¹ 2** (*AmE*) a teacher at a college or university

proficient /prəˈfɪʃnt/ *adj.* ~ (in/at sth/doing sth) able to do a particular thing well; SKILLED: *We are looking for somebody who is proficient in French.* ▸ **proficiency** /-ʃnsi/ *noun* [U] ~ (in sth/doing sth): *a certificate of proficiency in English*

profile¹ ʔ **A2** Ⓦ /ˈprəʊfaɪl/ *noun* [C] **1** a short description of sb/sth that gives useful information: *We're building up a profile of our average customer.* **2** a person's face or head seen from the side, not the front: *I did a sketch of him in profile.*

IDM a high/low profile a way of behaving that attracts/does not attract other people's attention: *I don't know much about the subject — I'm going to keep a low profile at the meeting tomorrow.*

profile² /ˈprəʊfaɪl/ *verb* [T] to give or write a description of sb/sth that gives the most important information: *His career is profiled in this month's journal.*

profiling /ˈprəʊfaɪlɪŋ/ *noun* [U] the act of collecting useful information about sb/sth so that you can give a description of them or it: *customer profiling*

profit¹ 🔊 **B1** /ˈprɒfɪt/ *noun* [C, U] ~ **(on sth)** (**ECONOMICS**) the money that you make when you sell sth for more than it cost you: *Did you **make a profit** on your house when you sold it?* ◇ *I'm hoping to sell my shares at a profit.* ◇ *There is little profit in the restaurant business.* ⊃ look at **loss** (2)

profit² /ˈprɒfɪt/ *verb* [I, T] ~ **(from/by sth)** (*formal*) to get an advantage from sth; to give sb an advantage: *Who will profit most from the tax reforms?*

profitable 🔊+ **C1** /ˈprɒfɪtəbl/ *adj.* **1** that makes money: *a profitable business* ⊃ note at **successful 2** helpful or useful: *We had a very profitable discussion yesterday.* ▶ **profitability** /ˌprɒfɪtəˈbɪləti/ *noun* [U] ▶ **profitably** /ˈprɒfɪtəbli/ *adv.*: *to spend your time profitably*

ˌprofit and ˈloss account *noun* [C] (**FINANCE**) a written record of the amounts of money that a business or an organization earns and spends in a particular period

profiterole /prəˈfɪtərəʊl/ *noun* [C] a small cake in the shape of a ball, made of light PASTRY, filled with cream and usually with chocolate on top

ˈprofit margin (*also* **margin**) *noun* [C] (**FINANCE**) the difference between the cost of buying or producing sth and the price that it is sold for: *a profit margin of 20%*

profligate /ˈprɒflɪɡət/ *adj.* (*formal*) using money, time, materials, etc. in a careless way: *profligate spending* **SYN** **wasteful**

pro forma /ˌprəʊ ˈfɔːmə/ *adj.* **1** (used especially about a document) prepared in order to show the usual way of doing sth or to provide a standard method: *a pro forma letter* ◇ *pro forma instructions* **2** (used about a document) sent in advance: *a pro forma invoice* (= a document that gives details of the goods being sent to a customer) ▶ **pro forma** *noun* [C]: *I enclose a pro forma for you to complete, sign and return.*

profound 🔊+ **C1** /prəˈfaʊnd/ *adj.* **1** very great; that you feel very strongly: *The experience had a profound influence on her.* **2** needing or showing a lot of knowledge or thought: *He's always making profound statements about the meaning of life.* **SYN** **deep¹** ▶ **profoundly** *adv.*: *I was profoundly relieved to hear the news.*

profuse /prəˈfjuːs/ *adj.* given or produced in great quantity: *profuse apologies* ▶ **profusely** *adv.*: *She apologized profusely for being late.*

profusion /prəˈfjuːʒn/ *noun* [sing. + sing./pl. verb, U] (*formal*) a very large quantity of sth: *a profusion of colours/flowers* ◇ *Roses grew **in profusion** against the old wall.* **SYN** **abundance**

progesterone /prəˈdʒestərəʊn/ *noun* [U] (**BIOLOGY**) a HORMONE produced in the bodies of women and female animals that prepares the body to become pregnant ⊃ look at **oestrogen, testosterone**

prognosis /prɒɡˈnəʊsɪs/ *noun* [C] (*pl.* **prognoses** /-ˈnəʊsiːz/) **1** (**MEDICINE**) an opinion, based on medical experience, of the likely development of a disease or an illness **2** (*formal*) a judgement about how sth is likely to develop in the future: *The prognosis is for more people to work part-time in the future.*

program¹ 🔊 **A2** /ˈprəʊɡræm/ *noun* [C] **1** (**COMPUTING**) a set of instructions that you give to a computer so

that it will do a particular task: *to write a program* **2** (*AmE*) = **PROGRAMME¹**

program² 🔊 **B1** /ˈprəʊɡræm/ *verb* (**-mm-**) **1** [I, T] (**COMPUTING**) to give a set of instructions to a computer, etc. to make it perform a particular task **2** [T, usually passive] (*AmE*) = **PROGRAMME²**

programme¹ 🔊 **A1** 🅦 (*BrE*) (*AmE* **program**) /ˈprəʊɡræm/ *noun* [C] **1** ~ **(on/about sth)** (**ARTS AND MEDIA**) a show or other item that is sent out on the radio or TV: *a TV/radio programme* ◇ *We've just missed an interesting programme on elephants.* **2** ~ **(for sb)**; ~ **(of sth)** a plan of things to do; a scheme: *a training programme for new staff* ◇ *The leaflet outlines the government's programme of educational reforms.* **3** (*AmE*) (**EDUCATION**) a course of study: *a school programme* **4** a little book or piece of paper that gives you information about a play, concert, etc.

programme² (*BrE*) (*AmE* **program**) /ˈprəʊɡræm/ *verb* [T, usually passive] (**-mm-**) **1** to plan for sth to happen at a particular time: *The road is programmed for completion next May.* **2** to give a machine instructions to do a particular task: *The lights are programmed to come on as soon as it gets dark.*

programmer /ˈprəʊɡræmə(r)/ *noun* [C] (**COMPUTING**) a person whose job is to write programs for a computer

programming 🔊+ **B2** /ˈprəʊɡræmɪŋ/ *noun* [U] **1** (**COMPUTING**) the process of writing and testing programs for computers: *a high-level programming language* **2** (**ARTS AND MEDIA**) the planning of which TV or radio programmes to broadcast: *politically balanced programming*

progress¹ 🔊 **A2** 🅞 /ˈprəʊɡres/ *noun* [U] **1** the process of improving or developing sth, or of getting nearer to achieving sth: *Anna's **making progress** at school.* ◇ *to make slow/steady/rapid/good progress* ◇ *scientific progress* **2** movement forwards or towards a place: *We made slow progress in the heavy traffic.* **IDM** **in progress** happening now: *Silence! Examination in progress.*

progress² 🔊 **B2** /prəˈɡres/ *verb* [I] **1** to become better; to develop (well): *Medical knowledge has progressed rapidly in the last 20 years.* **SYN** **advance¹ 2** to move forward; to continue: *I got more and more tired as the evening progressed.* **SYN** **go on**

progression 🅦 /prəˈɡreʃn/ *noun* [U, C] ~ **(from sth) (to sth)** movement forward or a development from one stage to another: *You've made the progression from beginner to intermediate level.*

progressive 🔊+ **B1** 🅦 /prəˈɡresɪv/ *adj.* **1** using modern methods and ideas: *a progressive school* **2** happening or developing steadily: *a progressive reduction in the number of staff* **3** (*also* **continuous**) (**GRAMMAR**) connected with the form of a verb that is made from a part of the verb *be* and the present participle, for example 'I am waiting'. Progressive forms are used to express an action that continues for a period of time.

progressively /prəˈɡresɪvli/ *adv.* steadily; a little at a time: *The situation became progressively worse.*

prohibit 🔊+ **B2** /prəˈhɪbɪt/ *verb* [T] ~ **sb/sth (from doing sth)** (*formal*) (**LAW**) to say that sth is not allowed by law: *Soviet citizens were prohibited from travelling abroad.* **SYN** **forbid, prevent**

prohibition /ˌprəʊɪˈbɪʃn/ *noun* (**LAW**) **1** [U] the act of stopping sth being done or used, especially by law: *the prohibition of alcohol in the 1920s* **2** [C] ~ **(on/against sth)** a law or rule that stops sth being done or used: *There is a prohibition on the carrying of knives.*

prohibitive /prəˈhɪbətɪv/ *adj.* (used about a price or cost) so high that it prevents people from buying sth

project¹ 🔊 **A1** 🔊 /ˈprɒdʒekt/ *noun* [C] **1** ~ **(on sth)** (EDUCATION) a piece of school work in which the student has to collect information about a certain subject and then write about it: *Our group chose to do a project on rainforests.* **2** ~ **(to do sth)** a piece of work, often involving many people, that is planned and organized carefully: *a major project to reduce pollution in our rivers*

project² 🔊 **B2** 🔊 /prəˈdʒekt/ *verb*
• GUESS **1** [T, usually passive] to guess or calculate the size, cost or amount of sth: *a projected increase of 10%* **SYN** forecast
• PLAN **2** [T, usually passive] to plan sth that will happen in the future: *The projected development should go ahead next year.*
• LIGHT/IMAGE **3** [T] ~ **sth (on/onto sth)** to make light, a picture from a film, etc. appear on a flat surface or screen: *Images are projected onto the retina of the eye.*
• STICK OUT **4** [I] to stick out: *The balcony projects one metre out from the wall.*
• PRESENT YOURSELF **5** [T] to show or represent sb/sth/ yourself in a certain way: *The government is trying to project a more caring image.*
• SEND UP/AWAY **6** [T] to send or throw sth upwards or away from you: *Actors have to learn to project their voice.*

projectile /prəˈdʒektaɪl/ *noun* [C] (*formal*) **1** an object, such as a bullet, that is fired from a gun or other weapon **2** any object that is thrown as a weapon

projection 🔊+ **C1** 🔊 /prəˈdʒekʃn/ *noun* **1** [C] a guess about a future amount, situation, etc. based on the present situation: *sales projections for the next five years* **2** [U, C] the act of making light, a picture from a film, a computer image, etc. appear on a surface

projector /prəˈdʒektə(r)/ *noun* [C] a piece of equipment that PROJECTS images, pictures or films onto a screen or wall

prokaryote (*also* procaryote) /ˌprəʊˈkæriəʊt/ *noun* [C] (BIOLOGY) an ORGANISM (= living thing) consisting of just one cell that does not have a clear NUCLEUS (= central part). Most prokaryotes are bacteria. ⊃ look at eukaryote ▶ prokaryotic (*also* procaryotic) /ˌprəʊkæriˈɒtɪk/ *adj.*

proliferate /prəˈlɪfəreɪt/ *verb* [I] to increase quickly in number: *Time passed and animal life proliferated.* ▶ proliferation /prəˌlɪfəˈreɪʃn/ *noun* [U]

prolific /prəˈlɪfɪk/ *adj.* (used especially about a writer, an artist, etc.) producing a lot: *a prolific author*

prologue /ˈprəʊlɒg/ *noun* [C] (LITERATURE) a piece of writing or a speech that introduces a play, poem, etc. ⊃ look at epilogue

prolong /prəˈlɒŋ/ *verb* [T] to make sth last longer: *to prolong somebody's life*

prolonged /prəˈlɒŋd/ *adj.* continuing for a long time: *There was a prolonged silence before anybody spoke.*

prom /prɒm/ *noun* [C] **1** a formal dance, especially one that is held at a school for students who are in their final year: *the senior prom* **2** (*BrE*) (MUSIC) a concert at which many of the audience stand up or sit on the floor: *the last night of the proms* **3** (*BrE, old-fashioned, informal*) = PROMENADE

promenade /ˌprɒməˈnɑːd/ (*also informal* prom) *noun* [C] (*BrE, old-fashioned*) a public place for walking, usually a wide path next to the sea

promethium /prəˈmiːθiəm/ *noun* [U] (*symb.* Pm) (CHEMISTRY) a chemical element. Promethium is a RADIOACTIVE metal that is produced artificially and is found in small amounts in nature. ❶ For more information on the periodic table of elements, look at the Reference Section of this dictionary.

prominent 🔊+ **C1** /ˈprɒmɪnənt/ *adj.* **1** important or famous: *a prominent political figure* **2** easy to see: *The church is the most prominent feature of the village.* ▶ prominence /-mɪnəns/ *noun* [U]: *The newspaper gave the affair great prominence.* ▶ prominently *adv.*

promiscuous /prəˈmɪskjuəs/ *adj.* having sexual relations with many people ▶ promiscuity /ˌprɒmɪsˈkjuːəti/ *noun* [U]

promise¹ 🔊 **A2** /ˈprɒmɪs/ *verb* **1** [I, T] ~ **(to do sth)**; ~ **(sb) that …** to say definitely that you will do or not do sth or that sth will happen: *She promised to phone every week.* ◇ *She promised (me) that she would write every week.* **2** [T] ~ **sth (to sb)**; ~ **sb sth** to say definitely that you will give sth to sb: *Can you promise your support?* ◇ *You have to give him the money if you promised it to him.* ◇ *My dad has promised me a bike.* **3** [T] to show signs of sth, so that you expect it to happen: *It promises to be an exciting occasion.*

promise² 🔊 **A2** /ˈprɒmɪs/ *noun* **1** [C] ~ **(to do sth/ that …)** a written or spoken statement or agreement that you will or will not do sth: *I want you to make a promise that you won't do that again.* ◇ *Make sure you keep your promise to always do your homework.* ◇ *You should never break a promise.* ◇ *I give you my promise that I won't tell anyone.* **2** [U] signs that you will be able to do sth well or be successful: *He showed great promise as a musician.*

promising 🔊+ **B2** /ˈprɒmɪsɪŋ/ *adj.* showing signs of being very good or successful: *a promising young writer*

promontory /ˈprɒməntri/ *noun* [C] (*pl.* -ies) (GEOGRAPHY) a long narrow area of high land that goes out into the sea: *a rocky promontory*

promote 🔊 **B1** 🔊 /prəˈməʊt/ *verb* [T] **1** ~ **sth (as sth)** (BUSINESS) to advertise sth in order to increase its sales or make it popular: *The new face cream is being promoted as a miracle cure for wrinkles.* **2** to encourage sth; to help sth to happen or develop: *to promote good relations between countries* **3** [often passive] ~ **sb (from sth) (to sth)** (BUSINESS) to give sb a higher position or more important job: *He's been promoted from assistant manager to manager.* **OPP** demote

promoter /prəˈməʊtə(r)/ *noun* [C] a person who organizes or provides the money for an event

promotion 🔊+ **B2** 🔊 /prəˈməʊʃn/ *noun* **1** [C, U] ~ **(to sth)** (BUSINESS) a move to a higher position or more important job: *The new job is a promotion for him.* **OPP** demotion **2** [U, C] (BUSINESS) things that you do in order to advertise a product and increase its sales: *It's all part of a special promotion of the new book.* ⊃ note at advertisement **3** [U] ~ **(of sth)** (*formal*) the activity of trying to make sth develop or become accepted by people: *We need to work on the promotion of health, not the treatment of disease.*

promotional /prəˈməʊʃənl/ *adj.* connected with advertising: *promotional material*

prompt¹ /prɒmpt/ *adj.* **1** immediate; done without delay: *We need a prompt decision on this matter.* **2** [not before noun] ~ **(in doing sth)**; ~ **(to do sth)** (used about a person) quick; acting without delay: *We are always prompt in paying our bills.* ◇ *She was prompt to point out my mistake.*

prompt² 🔊+ **B2** /prɒmpt/ *verb* **1** [T] to cause sth to happen; to make sb decide to do sth: *What prompted you to give up your job?* **2** [T, I] to encourage sb to speak by asking questions; to remind an actor of their words in a play: *The speaker had to be prompted several times.* ▶ prompting *noun* [U]: *He apologized without any prompting.*

prompt³ /prɒmpt/ *noun* [C] **1** (**ARTS AND MEDIA**) a word or words said to an actor to remind them of what to say next: *When she forgot her lines I had to give her a prompt.* **2** (**COMPUTING**) a sign on a computer screen that shows that the computer has finished what it was doing and is ready for more instructions: *Wait for the prompt to come up then type in your password.*

promptly /ˈprɒmptli/ *adv.* **1** immediately; without delay: *I invited her to dinner and she promptly accepted.* **2** (*also* **prompt**) at exactly the time that you have arranged: *We arrived promptly at twelve o'clock.* ◇ *I'll pick you up at seven o'clock prompt.* **SYN** **punctually**

prone /prəʊn/ *adj.* **~ to sth/to do sth** likely to suffer from sth or to do sth bad: *prone to infection/injury/heart attacks* ◇ *to be accident-prone* (= to have a lot of accidents)

prong /prɒŋ/ *noun* [C] **1** each of the two or more long pointed parts of a fork **2** each of the separate parts of an attack, argument, etc. that sb uses to achieve sth **3** -**pronged** (in adjectives) having the number or type of prongs mentioned: *a three-pronged attack*

pronoun /ˈprəʊnaʊn/ *noun* [C] (**GRAMMAR**) a word that is used in place of a noun or a phrase that contains a noun: *'He', 'it', 'hers', 'me', 'them', etc. are all pronouns.* ⊃ look at **personal pronoun**

pronounce 🔒 **A2** /prəˈnaʊns/ *verb* **1** [T] (**LANGUAGE**) to make the sound of a word or letter in a particular way: *You don't pronounce the 'b' at the end of 'comb'.* ◇ *How do you pronounce your surname?* ⊃ noun **pronunciation** **2** [T, I] (*formal*) to give a judgement or statement formally, officially or publicly: *The judge will pronounce sentence today.* ◇ *He was pronounced dead on arrival at the hospital.*

> **WORD FAMILY**
> **pronounce** *verb*
> **pronunciation** *noun*
> **unpronounceable** *adj.*
> **mispronounce** *verb*

pronounced 🔒+ **C1** /prəˈnaʊnst/ *adj.* very obvious, easy to notice or strongly expressed: *His English is excellent although he speaks with a pronounced French accent.*

pronunciation /prəˌnʌnsiˈeɪʃn/ *noun* **1** [U, C] (**LANGUAGE**) the way in which a language or a particular word or sound is said: *American pronunciation* ⊃ verb **pronounce** **2** [U, sing.] a person's way of speaking a language: *His grammar is good but his pronunciation is awful!*

proof 🔒 **B2** /pruːf/ *noun* **1** [U] **~ (of sth); ~ that …** information, documents, etc. that show that sth is true: *'We need some proof of identity,' the shop assistant said.* ◇ *You've got no proof that John took the money.* ⊃ look at **evidence** (1) ⊃ note at **court¹** ⊃ verb **prove** **2** [C, usually pl.] a first copy of printed material that is produced so that mistakes can be corrected

-**proof** /pruːf/ *suffix* (in adjectives) able to protect against the thing mentioned: *a soundproof room* ◇ *a waterproof/windproof jacket* ◇ *bulletproof glass*

proofread /ˈpruːfriːd/ *verb* [T, I] (*pt, pp* **proofread** /-red/) (**LITERATURE**) to read and correct a piece of written or printed work: *You'd better proofread the script before you send it in.* ◇ *Remember to proofread before submitting.* ▶ **proofreader** /-riːdə(r)/ *noun* [C]: *She works as a proofreader.*

prop¹ /prɒp/ *verb* [T] (-pp-) to support sb/sth or keep sb/sth in position by putting them or it against or on sth: *I'll use this book to prop the window open.* ◇ *He propped his bike against the wall.*

PHR V **prop sth up** to support sth that would otherwise fall or fail

prop² /prɒp/ *noun* [C] **1** a stick or other object that you use to support sth or to keep sth in position: *Rescuers used props to stop the roof of the tunnel collapsing.* **2** [usually pl.] (**ARTS AND MEDIA**) an object that is used in a play, film, etc: *He's responsible for all the stage props, machinery and lighting.*

propaganda 🔒+ **C1** /ˌprɒpəˈɡændə/ *noun* [U] (**POLITICS**) ideas or statements that may be false or present only one side of an argument that are used in order to gain support for a political leader, party, etc.

propagate /ˈprɒpəɡeɪt/ *verb* [T, I] (**AGRICULTURE**) **1** to produce new plants from a parent plant **2** [T] (*formal*) to spread an idea, a belief or a piece of information among many people ▶ **propagation** /ˌprɒpəˈɡeɪʃn/ *noun* [U]

propane /ˈprəʊpeɪn/ *noun* [U] (**CHEMISTRY**) a gas that is found in natural gas and petrol and that we use as a fuel for cooking and heating

propel /prəˈpel/ *verb* [T] (used with an adverb or a preposition) (-ll-) to move, drive or push sb/sth forward or in a particular direction

propellant /prəˈpelənt/ *noun* [C, U] a gas that forces out the contents of an AEROSOL ⊃ picture at **aerosol**

propeller /prəˈpelə(r)/ *noun* [C] a device with several BLADES (= flat metal parts) that turn round very fast in order to make a ship or a plane move

propensity /prəˈpensəti/ *noun* [C] (*pl.* -ies) **~ (for sth/doing sth); ~ (to do sth)** (*formal*) a habit of behaving in a particular way: *He showed a propensity for violence.* ◇ *She has a propensity to exaggerate.* **SYN** **inclination**

proper 🔒 **B1** /ˈprɒpə(r)/ *adj.* **1** [only before noun] (*especially BrE*) right, suitable or correct: *If you're going skiing you must have the proper clothes.* ◇ *I've got to get these pieces of paper in the proper order.* **2** [only before noun] (*BrE, informal*) that you consider to be real or good enough: *I didn't see much of the flat yesterday. I'm going to go today and have a proper look.* **3** (*formal*) socially and morally acceptable: *I think it would be only proper for you to apologize.* **OPP** **improper** **4** (after a noun) real or main: *We travelled through miles of suburbs before we got to the city proper.*

ˌproper ˈfraction *noun* [C] (**MATHEMATICS**) a FRACTION that is less than one, with the bottom number greater than the top number, for example ¼ or ⅝ ⊃ look at **improper fraction**

properly 🔒 **B1** /ˈprɒpəli/ *adv.* **1** (*especially BrE*) correctly; in an acceptable way: *The teacher said I hadn't done my homework properly.* ◇ *These shoes don't fit properly.* **2** in a way that is socially and morally acceptable: *If you two children can't behave properly then we'll have to go home.* **OPP** **improperly**

ˌproper ˈnoun (*also* ˌproper ˈname) *noun* [C] (**GRAMMAR**) a word that is the name of a particular person or place and begins with a capital letter: *'Mary' and 'Rome' are proper nouns.*

property 🔒 **B1** /ˈprɒpəti/ *noun* (*pl.* -ies) **1** [U] a thing or things that belong to sb: *The sack contained stolen property.* ◇ *Is this bag your property?* ◇ *This file is government property.* ◇ *lost property* **2** [U] land and buildings: *Property prices vary enormously from area to area.* ⊃ note at **building** **3** [C] (*formal*) one building and the land around it: *There are a lot of empty properties in the area.* ⊃ note at **building** **4** [C, usually pl.] (*formal*) a special quality or characteristic that a substance, etc. has: *Some plants have healing properties.* ◇ *Compare the physical properties of the two substances.*

ˈproperty developer = DEVELOPER (1)

prophecy /'prɒfəsi/ *noun* [C] (*pl.* **-ies**) (**RELIGION**) a statement about what is going to happen in the future, especially one made by sb with religious powers: *to fulfil a prophecy* (= to make it come true)

prophesy /'prɒfəsaɪ/ *verb* [T] (prophesying; prophesies; *pt, pp* prophesied) to say what you think will happen in the future: *to prophesy disaster/war*

prophet /'prɒfɪt/ *noun* **1** [C] (**RELIGION**) (in the Christian, Jewish and Muslim religions) a person who is sent by God to teach the people and give them messages: *the prophets of the Old Testament* **2** the Prophet [sing.] Muhammad, who founded the religion of Islam **3** [C] a person who claims to know what will happen in the future ▶ **prophetic** /prə'fetɪk/ *adj.*

prophylactic¹ /ˌprɒfə'læktɪk/ *adj.* (**MEDICINE**) done or used in order to prevent a disease: *prophylactic treatment*

prophylactic² /ˌprɒfə'læktɪk/ *noun* [C] (**MEDICINE**) a medicine, device or course of action that prevents disease

proponent /prə'pəʊnənt/ *noun* [C] (*formal*) a person who supports an idea or course of action

proportion ℃+ **B2** ⊙ /prə'pɔːʃn/ *noun* **1** [C] ~ **(of sth)** (**MATHEMATICS**) a part or share of a whole: *A large proportion of the earth's surface is covered by sea.* **2** [U] ~ **(of sth to sth)**; **in ~ (to sth)** the relationship between the size or amount of two things: *The proportion of men to women in the college has changed dramatically over the years.* ◇ *The room is very long in proportion to its width.* **3** [U, C, usually pl.] **(in)** ~ **(to sth)**; **(out of)** ~ **(with sth)** the correct relationship in size, degree, importance, etc. between one thing and another: *Political unrest is reaching alarming proportions.* ◇ *to draw something in proportion* ◇ *Salaries have not risen in proportion to inflation.* ◇ *The head is out of proportion with the body.* **IDM** **keep sth in proportion** to not think that sth is worse or more serious than it really is: *He's so upset that it's hard for him to keep the problem in proportion.* **out of (all) proportion (to sth)** too great, serious, important, etc. in relation to sth: *His reaction was completely out of proportion to the situation.*

proportional ⊙ /prə'pɔːʃənl/ *adj.* ~ **(to sth)** of the right size, amount or degree compared with sth else: *Salary is proportional to years of experience.* ▶ **proportionally** /-ʃənli/ *adv.*

pro,portional ,represen'tation *noun* [U] (*abbr.* **PR**) (**POLITICS**) a system that gives each political party in an election a number of seats in a parliament in direct relation to the number of votes it receives ⊃ look at **representation** (2)

proportionate /prə'pɔːʃənət/ *adj.* ~ **(to sth)** (*formal*) increasing or decreasing in size, amount or degree according to changes in sth else: *The number of accidents is proportionate to the increased volume of traffic.* **SYN** **proportional** **OPP** **disproportionate**

proposal ℃ **B2** ⊙ /prə'pəʊzl/ *noun* [C] **1** ~ **(for/to do sth)**; ~ **(that …)** (**BUSINESS**) a plan that is formally suggested: *a new proposal for raising money* ◇ *a proposal to build more student accommodation* ◇ *May I make a proposal that we all give an equal amount?* ⊃ note at **opinion** **2** an act of formally asking sb to marry you

propose ℃ **B2** ⊙ /prə'pəʊz/ *verb* **1** [T] (*formal*) to suggest sth as a possible plan or action: *At the meeting a new advertising campaign was proposed.* **2** [T] ~ **do sth** to intend to do sth; to have sth as a plan: *What do you propose to do now?* **3** [I, T] ~ **(to sb)** to ask sb to marry you: *He proposed to me on the plane flying to Italy.* ◇ *to propose marriage* **4** [T] ~ **sb (for/as sth)** to

suggest sb for an official position: *I'd like to propose Anna Marsland as chairperson.*

proposition ℃+ **C1** ⊙ /ˌprɒpə'zɪʃn/ *noun* [C] **1** (**BUSINESS**) an idea, a plan or an offer, especially in business; a suggestion: *I'd like to put a business proposition to you.* ◇ *She was trying to make it look like an attractive proposition.* **2** Proposition (**POLITICS**) (in the US) a suggested change to the law that people can vote on: *How did you vote on Proposition 8?* **3** (*formal*) an idea or opinion that sb expresses about sth: *That's a very interesting proposition. Are you sure you can prove it?* **4** (**MATHEMATICS**) a statement of a THEOREM (= a rule or principle in mathematics that can be shown to be true), and an explanation of how it can be proved

proprietor /prə'praɪətə(r)/ *noun* [C] (**BUSINESS**) the owner of a business, a hotel, etc.

propulsion /prə'pʌlʃn/ *noun* [U] (**ENGINEERING**, **PHYSICS**) the force that drives sth forward: *wind/steam/jet propulsion* ⊃ look at **propel**

pro rata /ˌprəʊ 'rɑːtə/ *adj.* (*formal*) (**FINANCE**) calculated according to how much of sth has been used, the amount of work done, etc: *If costs go up, there will be a pro rata increase in prices.* ▶ **pro rata** *adv.*: *Prices will increase pro rata.*

proscenium /prə'siːniəm/ *noun* [C] (**ARTS AND MEDIA**) the part of the stage in a theatre that is in front of the curtain: *a traditional theatre with a proscenium arch* (= one that forms a frame for the stage where the curtain is opened)

prose /prəʊz/ *noun* [U] (**LITERATURE**) written language that is not poetry: *to write in prose* ⊃ look at **poetry**

prosecute ℃+ **C1** /'prɒsɪkjuːt/ *verb* [T, I] ~ **(sb) (for sth)** (**LAW**) to officially charge sb with a crime and try to show that they are guilty in court: *He was prosecuted for theft.* ◇ *the prosecuting counsel/lawyer/attorney* ⊃ look at **defend**

prosecution ℃+ **C1** /ˌprɒsɪ'kjuːʃn/ *noun* (**LAW**) **1** [U, C] the process of officially charging sb with a crime and of trying to show that they are guilty in court: *Failure to pay your parking fine will result in prosecution.* ◇ *to bring a prosecution against somebody* **2** the prosecution [sing. + sing./pl. verb] a person or group of people who try to show that sb is guilty of a crime in court: *The prosecution claim/claims that Lloyd was driving at 100 miles per hour.* ⊃ look at **defence** (6) ⊃ note at **court¹**

prosecutor ℃+ **C1** /'prɒsɪkjuːtə(r)/ *noun* [C] (**LAW**) **1** a public official who charges sb with a crime and PROSECUTES them in court: *the public/state prosecutor* **2** a lawyer who leads the case against the person who is accused of a crime

prosody /'prɒsədi/ *noun* [U] (**LITERATURE**) the patterns of sounds and rhythms in poetry and speech; the study of this

prospect ℃ **B2** /'prɒspekt/ *noun* **1** [U, sing.] ~ **(of sth/ doing sth)** the possibility that sth will happen: *There's little prospect of better weather before next week.* **2** [sing.] ~ **(of sth/doing sth)** a thought about what may or will happen in the future: *The prospect of becoming a father filled James with horror.* **3** prospects [pl.] chances of being successful in the future: *good job/career/promotion prospects*

prospective ℃+ **C1** /prə'spektɪv/ *adj.* likely to be or to happen: *They are worried about prospective changes in the law.*

prospectus /prə'spektəs/ *noun* [C] (**BUSINESS**, **EDUCATION**) a small book that gives information about a school, college or business in order to advertise it

prosper /ˈprɒspə(r)/ *verb* [I] to develop in a successful way; to be successful, especially with money

prosperity ↗+ C1 /prɒˈsperəti/ *noun* [U] the state of being successful, especially with money: *Tourism has brought prosperity to many parts of Spain.*

prosperous /ˈprɒspərəs/ *adj.* rich and successful

prostate /ˈprɒsteɪt/ (*also* **prostate gland**) *noun* [C] (ANATOMY) a small organ in a man's body near the BLADDER (= the organ where waste liquid collects), that produces a liquid in which SPERM is carried

prostitute /ˈprɒstɪtjuːt/ *noun* [C] a person, especially a woman, who earns money by having sex with people

prostitution /ˌprɒstɪˈtjuːʃn/ *noun* [U] the work of a PROSTITUTE

prostrate /ˈprɒstreɪt/ *adj.* lying flat on the ground, facing downwards

protactinium /ˌprəʊtækˈtɪniəm/ *noun* [U] (*symb.* Pa) (CHEMISTRY) a chemical element. Protactinium is a RADIOACTIVE metal found naturally when URANIUM DECAYS. ❶ For more information on the periodic table of elements, look at the **Reference Section** of this dictionary.

protagonist /prəˈtæɡənɪst/ *noun* [C] (*formal*) (LITERATURE) the main character in a play, film or book ⊃ look at **hero** (2)

protease /ˈprəʊtieɪz/ *noun* [U] (BIOLOGY) an ENZYME (= a substance that helps a chemical change take place) that breaks down PROTEIN

protect ↗ A2 W /prəˈtekt/ *verb* [T] ~ sb/sth (against/ from sth) to keep sb/sth safe; to defend sb/sth: *Parents try to protect their children from danger as far as possible.* ◇ *These bats are a protected species* (= they must not be killed).

protection ↗ B2 W /prəˈtekʃn/ *noun* [U] ~ (against/ from sth) the act of keeping sb/sth safe so that they or it are not harmed or damaged: *Vaccination gives protection against diseases.* ◇ *After the attack he was put under police protection.*

protectionism /prəˈtekʃənɪzəm/ *noun* [U] (ECONOMICS) the principle or practice of protecting a country's own industry by taxing foreign goods ▶ **protectionist** /-nɪst/ *adj.*: *protectionist measures/policies*

protective ↗+ C1 /prəˈtektɪv/ *adj.* **1** [only before noun] that prevents sb/sth from being damaged or harmed: *In certain jobs workers need to wear protective clothing.* **2** ~ (of/towards sb/sth) wanting to keep sb/ sth safe: *Female animals are very protective of their young.*

protector /prəˈtektə(r)/ *noun* [C] a person, an organization or a thing that protects sb/sth: *I regarded him as my friend and protector.* ◇ *Hard hats and ear protectors are provided.*

protectorate /prəˈtektərət/ *noun* [C] (POLITICS) a country that is controlled and protected by a more powerful country

protein ↗+ B2 /ˈprəʊtiːn/ *noun* [C, U] (BIOLOGY) a substance, found within all living things, that forms the structure of muscles, organs, etc. ⊃ picture at **nitrogen cycle**, **virus**

protest¹ ↗ B1 /ˈprəʊtest/ *noun* [U, C] ~ (against sth) a statement or an action that shows that you do not like or approve of sth: *He resigned in protest against the decision.* ◇ *The union organized a protest against the redundancies.*

IDM **under protest** not happily and after expressing the fact that you do not agree: *Fiona agreed to pay in the end but only under protest.*

protest² ↗ B1 /prəˈtest/ *verb* **1** [I, T] ~ (about/against/ at sth) to say or show that you do not approve of or agree with sth, especially publicly: *Students have been protesting against the government's decision.* ❶ In American English **protest** is used without a preposition: *They protested the government's handling of the situation.* **2** [T] to say sth FIRMLY, especially when others do not believe you: *She has always protested her innocence.* ▶ **protester** ↗+ B2 /prəˈtestə(r), ˈprəʊtestə(r)/ *noun* [C]: *Protesters blocked the road outside the factory.*

Protestant /ˈprɒtɪstənt/ *noun* [C] (RELIGION) a member of the Christian church that separated from the Catholic church in the sixteenth century ▶ **Protestant** *adj.*: *a Protestant church* ⊃ look at **Roman Catholic**

protest vote *noun* (POLITICS) **1** [C] a vote for a person or party that you make to prevent another person or party from succeeding **2** [sing.] the total number of protest votes in an election: *The size of the protest vote has shocked the party.*

proto- /ˈprəʊtəʊ, prəʊtə/ *prefix* (in nouns and adjectives) original; from which others develop: *prototype*

protocol ↗+ C1 W /ˈprəʊtəkɒl/ *noun* **1** [U] (POLITICS) a system of fixed rules and formal behaviour used at official meetings, usually between governments: *a breach of protocol* ◇ *the protocol of diplomatic visits* **2** [C] (POLITICS) the first or original version of a written agreement, especially one between countries; an extra part added to a written agreement: *the first Geneva Protocol* ◇ *It is set out in a legally binding protocol which forms part of the treaty.* **3** [C] (COMPUTING) a set of rules that control the way information is sent between computers **4** [C] (MEDICINE) a plan for carrying out a scientific experiment or medical treatment

proton /ˈprəʊtɒn/ *noun* [C] (CHEMISTRY, PHYSICS) one of the three types of PARTICLES that form the NUCLEUS (= central part) of an ATOM. Protons have a positive electric CHARGE. ⊃ look at **electron**, **neutron** ⊃ note at **isotope**

protoplasm /ˈprəʊtəplæzəm/ *noun* [U] (BIOLOGY) a clear substance like JELLY that forms the living part of an animal or plant cell ⊃ look at **cytoplasm**

prototype /ˈprəʊtətaɪp/ *noun* [C] (ENGINEERING) the first model or design of sth from which other forms will be developed

protozoan /ˌprəʊtəˈzəʊən/ *noun* [C] (*pl.* protozoans, protozoa /-ˈzəʊə/) (BIOLOGY) a very small living thing, usually with only one cell, that can only be seen using a MICROSCOPE (= an instrument that makes things look bigger)

protractor /prəˈtræktə(r)/ *noun* [C] (GEOMETRY) an instrument for measuring and drawing angles, usually made from a HALF-CIRCLE of clear plastic with degrees (0° to 180°) marked on it

protrude /prəˈtruːd/ *verb* [I] ~ (from sth) to stick out from a place or surface: *The nail was protruding from the wall.* ◇ *protruding eyes/teeth*

protrusion /prəˈtruːʒn/ *noun* [C, U] (*formal*) a thing that sticks out from a place or surface; the fact of doing this: *a protrusion on the rock face*

protuberance /prəˈtjuːbərəns/ *noun* [C] (*formal*) a round part that sticks out from a surface: *The diseased trees have protuberances on their trunks.*

proud ↗ B1 /praʊd/ *adj.* **1** ~ (of sb/sth); ~ (to do sth); ~ (that) … feeling pleased and satisfied about sth that you own or have done: *They are very proud of their new house.* ◇ *I feel very proud to be part of such a successful organization.* ◇ *You should feel very proud that you have been chosen.* **2** feeling that you are better and more important than other people: *Now she's at university she'll be much too proud to talk to us!*

3 having respect for yourself and not wanting to lose the respect of others: *He was too proud to ask for help.* ⊃ noun **pride**

proudly /ˈpraʊdli/ *adv.* in a way that shows that sb is proud of sth: *'I did all the work myself,' he said proudly.*

prove ⓘ B1 /pruːv/ *verb* (*pp* proved, proven /ˈpruːvn, ˈprəʊvn/ *especially AmE*) **1** [T] ~ (sth to sb); ~ (that) … to use facts and evidence to show that sth is true: *She tried to prove her innocence to the court.* ◇ *It will be difficult to prove that she was lying.* ◇ *He felt he needed to prove a point* (= show other people that he was right). ⊃ noun **proof 2** *linking verb* to show a particular quality over a period of time: *The job proved more difficult than we'd expected.* **3** [T] ~ yourself (to sb) to show other people how good you are at doing sth and/or that you are capable of doing sth: *He constantly feels that he has to prove himself to others.*

> **WORD FAMILY**
> **prove** *verb* (≠ **disprove**)
> **proof** *noun*
> **proven** *adj.*
> (≠ **unproven**)

proven /ˈpruːvn, ˈprəʊvn/ *adj.* [only before noun] that has been shown to be true: *a proven fact*

proverb /ˈprɒvɜːb/ *noun* [C] (**LANGUAGE**) a short well-known sentence or phrase that gives advice or says that sth is generally true in life: *'Too many cooks spoil the broth' is a proverb.* ⊃ look at **saying**

proverbial /prəˈvɜːbiəl/ *adj.* **1** [only before noun] used to show you are referring to a PROVERB (= a well-known phrase): *Let's not count our proverbial chickens.* **2** well known and talked about by a lot of people

provide ⓘ A2 Ⓦ /prəˈvaɪd/ *verb* [T] ~ sb (with sth); ~ sth (for sb) to give sth to sb; to make sth available for sb to use; to supply sth: *This book will provide you with all the information you need.* ◇ *We are able to provide accommodation for two students.* ⊃ noun **provision** PHRV **provide for sb** to give sb all that they need to live, for example food and clothing **provide for sth** to make preparations to deal with sth that might happen in the future: *We did not provide for such a large increase in prices.*

provided /prəˈvaɪdɪd/ (*also* providing /prəˈvaɪdɪŋ/) *conj.* ~ (that) … only if; on condition that: *She agreed to go and work abroad provided (that) her family could go with her.*

providence /ˈprɒvɪdəns/ *noun* [U] (**RELIGION**) God, or a force that some people believe controls the things that happen to us ⊃ look at **fate** (1)

provider /prəˈvaɪdə(r)/ *noun* [C] (**BUSINESS**) a person or an organization that supplies sb with sth they need or want: *training providers* ◇ *The eldest son is the family's sole provider* (= the only person who earns money). ⊃ look at **service provider**

province ⓘ C1 /ˈprɒvɪns/ *noun* **1** [C] (**POLITICS**) one of the areas that some countries are divided into with its own local government: *Canada has ten provinces.* ⊃ look at **county**, **state**[1] (5) **2** the provinces [pl.] (**GEOGRAPHY**) all the parts of a country except the capital city

provincial ⓘ C1 /prəˈvɪnʃl/ *adj.* **1** [only before noun] (**POLITICS**) connected with one of the areas that some countries are divided into with its own local government: *provincial governments/elections* **2** (**GEOGRAPHY**) connected with the parts of a country that do not include its capital city: *a provincial town/ newspaper* **3** (used about a person or their ideas) not wanting to consider new or different ideas or things: *provincial attitudes*

provision ⓘ C1 /prəˈvɪʒn/ *noun* **1** [U] the giving or supplying of sth to sb; the act of making sth available for sb to use: *The council is responsible for the provision of education and social services.* **2** [U] ~ for sb/sth preparations that you make to deal with sth that might happen in the future: *She made provision for* (= planned for the financial future of) *her children in the event of her death.* **3** provisions [pl.] supplies of food and drink, especially for a long journey ⊃ verb **provide**

provisional /prəˈvɪʒənl/ *adj.* only for the present time, that is likely to be changed in the future: *The provisional date for the next meeting is 18 November.* ◇ *a provisional driving licence* (= that you use when you are learning to drive) **SYN** temporary ⊃ note at **government** ▸ provisionally /-nəli/ *adv.*: *The meeting has been provisionally arranged for next Monday.*

proviso /prəˈvaɪzəʊ/ *noun* [C] (*pl.* -os) (on/with the) ~ (that …) a condition that must be accepted before an agreement can be made: *He agreed to the visit with the proviso that they should stay no longer than a week.*

provocation /ˌprɒvəˈkeɪʃn/ *noun* [U, C] the act of doing or saying sth deliberately to try to make sb angry or upset; sth that is said or done to cause this: *You should never hit children, even under extreme provocation.* ⊃ verb **provoke**

provocative /prəˈvɒkətɪv/ *adj.* **1** intended to make sb angry or upset or to cause an argument: *He made a provocative remark about a woman's place being in the home.* **2** intended to cause sexual excitement ▸ provocatively *adv.*

provoke ⓘ C1 /prəˈvəʊk/ *verb* [T] **1** to cause a particular feeling or reaction: *an article intended to provoke discussion* **2** ~ sb (into sth/doing sth) to say or do sth that you know will make a person angry or upset: *The lawyer claimed his client was provoked into acts of violence.* ⊃ noun **provocation**

prow /praʊ/ *noun* [C] the pointed front part of a ship or boat ⊃ look at **stern**[1]

prowess /ˈpraʊəs/ *noun* [U] (*formal*) great skill at doing sth: *academic/sporting prowess*

prowl /praʊl/ *verb* [I, T] ~ (about/around) (used about an animal that is hunting or a person who is waiting for a chance to steal sth or do sth bad) to move around an area quietly so that you are not seen or heard: *I could hear somebody prowling around outside so I called the police.* ▸ prowler *noun* [C]: *The police arrested a prowler outside the hospital.*

proximal /ˈprɒksɪməl/ *adj.* (**ANATOMY**) located towards the centre of the body ⊃ look at **distal**

proximity /prɒkˈsɪməti/ *noun* [U] ~ (of sb/sth) (to sb/ sth) (*formal*) the state of being near to sb/sth in distance or time: *The proximity of the new offices to the airport is a great advantage.*

proxy /ˈprɒksi/ *noun* [U] the authority that you give to sb to act for you if you cannot do sth yourself: *to vote by proxy*

prude /pruːd/ *noun* [C] a person who is easily shocked by anything connected with sex ▸ prudish /ˈpruːdɪʃ/ *adj.*

prudent /ˈpruːdnt/ *adj.* (*formal*) sensible and careful when making judgements and decisions; avoiding unnecessary risks: *It would be prudent to get some more advice before you invest your money.* ▸ prudence /-dns/ *noun* [U] ⊃ note at **care**[1] ▸ prudently *adv.*

prune[1] /pruːn/ *noun* [C] a dried PLUM (= a small soft fruit that grows on trees)

prune² /pruːn/ *verb* [T] (**AGRICULTURE**) to cut branches or parts of branches off a tree or bush so that it will grow better or stronger

'pruning shears = SECATEURS

pry /praɪ/ *verb* (**prying; pries;** *pt, pp* **pried**) **1** [I] ~ **(into sth)** to try to find out about other people's private affairs: *I'm sick of you prying into my private life.* **2** [T] (*especially AmE*) = PRISE

PS /ˌpiː ˈes/ *abbr.* **postscript** (used at the end of an email, a message, etc. to introduce some more information or sth that you have forgotten): *Love Tessa. PS I'll bring the car.*

psalm /sɑːm/ *noun* [C] (**RELIGION**) a song, poem or prayer that praises God, especially one in the Bible

pseudo- /suːdəʊ, sjuːdəʊ/ *prefix* (in nouns, adjectives and adverbs) not what sb says it is; false or pretended: *pseudonym* ◇ *pseudo-scientific*

pseudonym /ˈsuːdənɪm, ˈsjuː-/ *noun* [C] a name used by sb, especially a writer, instead of their real name

PSHE /ˌpiː es eɪtʃ ˈiː/ *noun* [U] (**EDUCATION**) a subject taught in British schools that deals with a person's emotional and social development (the abbreviation for 'personal, social and health education')

psych /saɪk/ *verb*
PHR V **psych yourself up** (*informal*) to prepare yourself in your mind for sth difficult: *I've got to psych myself up for this interview.*

psych- /saɪk/ → PSYCHO-

psyche /ˈsaɪki/ *noun* [C] (*formal*) (**PSYCHOLOGY**) the mind; your deepest feelings and attitudes: *the human/ female/national psyche*

psychedelic /ˌsaɪkəˈdelɪk/ *adj.* (used about art, music, clothes, etc.) having bright colours or patterns or strange sounds

psychiatry /saɪˈkaɪətri/ *noun* [U] (**PSYCHOLOGY**) the study and treatment of mental illness ⊃ look at **psychology** (1) ▶ **psychiatric** ⚑+ **C1** /ˌsaɪkiˈætrɪk/ *adj.*: *a psychiatric hospital/unit/nurse* ▶ **psychiatrist** /saɪˈkaɪətrɪst/ *noun* [C]

psychic /ˈsaɪkɪk/ *adj.* (used about a person or their mind) seeming to have unusual powers that cannot be explained, for example knowing what sb else is thinking or being able to see into the future

psycho /ˈsaɪkəʊ/ *noun* [C] (*pl.* **-os**) (*informal*) = PSYCHOPATH

psycho- /saɪkəʊ, saɪkə, saɪˈkɒ/ (*also* **psych-**) *prefix* (in nouns, adjectives and adverbs) connected with the mind: *psychological* ◇ *psychiatrist*

psychoanalysis /ˌsaɪkəʊəˈnæləsɪs/ (*also* **analysis**) *noun* [U] (**PSYCHOLOGY**) a method of treating sb with a mental illness by asking about their past experiences, feelings, dreams, etc. in order to find out what is making them ill ▶ **psychoanalyse** (*BrE*) (*AmE* **psychoanalyze**) /ˌsaɪkəʊˈænəlaɪz/ *verb* [T] ▶ **psychoanalyst** /-lɪst/ *noun* [C]

psycholinguistics /ˌsaɪkəʊlɪŋˈɡwɪstɪks/ *noun* [U] the study of how the mind processes and produces language ▶ **psycholinguistic** *adj.*

psychological ⚑+ **B2** ⓦ /ˌsaɪkəˈlɒdʒɪkl/ *adj.* (**PSYCHOLOGY**) **1** connected a person's mind and the way in which it works: *Has her ordeal caused her long-term psychological damage?* **2** connected with the study of PSYCHOLOGY ▶ **psychologically** /-kli/ *adv.*: *Psychologically, it was a bad time to be starting a new job.*

psychologist ⚑ **B2** /saɪˈkɒlədʒɪst/ *noun* [C] (**PSYCHOLOGY**) a scientist who studies the mind and the way that people behave

psychology ⚑ **B2** /saɪˈkɒlədʒi/ *noun* **1** [U] (**EDUCATION**) the scientific study of the mind and the way that people behave: *child psychology* ⊃ look at **psychiatry 2** [sing.] the type of mind that a person has, that makes them think or behave in a particular way: *If we understand the psychology of the killer we would have a better chance of catching him.*

psychopath /ˈsaɪkəpæθ/ (*also informal* **psycho**) *noun* [C] (**PSYCHOLOGY**) a person who has a serious mental illness that may cause them to hurt or kill other people

psychosis /saɪˈkəʊsɪs/ *noun* [C, U] (*pl.* **psychoses** /-ˈkəʊsiːz/) (**PSYCHOLOGY**) a very serious mental illness that affects your whole personality ▶ **psychotic** /-ˈkɒtɪk/ *adj., noun* [C]: *a psychotic patient/individual*

psychosomatic /ˌsaɪkəʊsəˈmætɪk/ *adj.* (**PSYCHOLOGY**) (used about an illness) caused by mental problems rather than physical problems

psychotherapy /ˌsaɪkəʊˈθerəpi/ (*also* **therapy**) *noun* [U] (**MEDICINE, PSYCHOLOGY**) the treatment of mental illness by discussing sb's problems with them rather than by giving them drugs ▶ **psychotherapist** /-pɪst/ (*also* **therapist** /ˈθerəpɪst/) *noun* [C]

PT /ˌpiː ˈtiː/ *abbr.* (*BrE*) **physical training** (sport and physical exercise that is taught in the army, etc.)

pt *abbr.* (in writing) **1** (*pl.* **pt, pts**) = PINT (1): *2 pts milk* **2** (*pl.* **pts**) = POINT¹ (10): *Laura 5 pts, Arthur 4 pts*

PTA /ˌpiː tiː ˈeɪ/ *abbr.* (**EDUCATION**) **parent-teacher association** (a group run by parents and teachers in a school that organizes social events and helps the school to raise money)

PTO /ˌpiː tiː ˈəʊ/ *abbr.* (*BrE*) **please turn over** (written at the bottom of a page to show that there is more on the other side)

PTSD /ˌpiː tiː es ˈdiː/ *noun* [U] (**PSYCHOLOGY**) a mental illness in which a person suffers problems caused by experiencing sth that shocked them very much, such as a war (the abbreviation for 'post-traumatic stress disorder'): *Many survivors of the hurricane are experiencing PTSD.*

pub ⚑ **A2** /pʌb/ (*also formal* **public house**) (*both BrE*) *noun* [C] a place where people go to buy and drink alcohol. Pubs also often serve food.

puberty /ˈpjuːbəti/ *noun* [U] (**BIOLOGY**) the time when a child's body is changing and becoming physically like that of an adult **SYN** **adolescence**

pubic /ˈpjuːbɪk/ *adj.* (**BIOLOGY**) of the area around the sexual organs: *pubic hair*

public¹ ⚑ **A2** ⓦ /ˈpʌblɪk/ *adj.* **1** [only before noun] connected with ordinary people in general: *Public opinion was in favour of the war.* ◇ *How much public support is there for the government's policy?* **2** provided for the use of people in general; not private: *a public library* ◇ *public spending* (= money that the government spends on education, health care, etc.) ⊃ look at **private¹** (3) **3** known, seen or heard by many people: *We're going to make the news public soon.* ▶ **publicly** *adv.*: *The company refused to admit publicly that it had acted wrongly.*
IDM **be common/public knowledge** → KNOWLEDGE **go public 1** to tell people about sth that is a secret: *The sacked employee went public with his stories of corruption inside the company.* **2** (used about a company) to start selling shares to the public **in the public eye** often appearing on TV, in magazines, on the internet, etc.

public² ? A2 Ⓦ /ˈpʌblɪk/ *noun* [sing. + sing./pl. verb] **1** the public people in general: *The university swimming pool is* **open to the public** *in the evenings.* ◇ *The police have asked for help from* **members of the public.** ◇ *The public is/are generally in favour of the new law.* **2** a group of people who are all interested in sth or who have sth in common: *the theatre-going public*

IDM **in public** when other people are present: *This is the first time that Miss Potter has spoken about her experience in public.*

,public ad'dress system *noun* [C] (*abbr.* **PA system**) an electronic system that uses MICROPHONES and LOUDSPEAKERS to make music, voices, etc. louder so that they can be heard by everyone in a particular place or building

publican /ˈpʌblɪkən/ *noun* [C] a person who owns or manages a pub

publication ? B2 /ˌpʌblɪˈkeɪʃn/ *noun* **1** [U, C] (**LITERATURE**) the act of printing a book, magazine, etc. and making it available to the public; a book, magazine, etc. that has been published: *His latest book has just been accepted for publication.* ◇ *specialist publications* **2** [U] the act of making sth known to the public: *the publication of exam results*

,public 'company (*also* **public limited company**) *noun* [C] (*abbr.* **plc, PLC** /ˌpiː el ˈsiː/) (*BrE*) (**BUSINESS**) a large company that sells shares in itself to the public

,public con'venience *noun* [C] (*BrE*) a toilet in a public place that anyone can use

,public 'holiday *noun* [C] a day on which most of the shops, businesses and schools in a country are closed, often to celebrate a particular event ◇ look at **bank holiday**

,public 'house (*formal*) = PUB

publicist /ˈpʌblɪsɪst/ *noun* [C] a person whose job is to make sth known to the public, for example a new product, an actor, etc.

publicity ?+ B2 /pʌbˈlɪsəti/ *noun* [U] **1** (**ARTS AND MEDIA**) notice or attention from the newspapers, TV, etc: *to seek/avoid publicity* **2** the business of attracting people's attention to sth/sb; advertising: *There has been a lot of publicity for this film.*

publicize (*BrE also* **-ise**) /ˈpʌblɪsaɪz/ *verb* [T] to attract people's attention to sth: *The event has been well publicized and should attract a lot of people.*

,public ,limited 'company = PUBLIC COMPANY

,public o'pinion *noun* [U] the opinions that people in society have about an issue: *The media has a powerful influence on public opinion.*

,public re'lations *noun* **1** [U] = PR (1) **2** (1) [pl.] the state of the relationship between an organization and the public: *Giving money to local charities is good for public relations.*

,public 'school *noun* [C] (**EDUCATION**) **1** (in Britain, especially in England) a private school for children aged between 13 and 18, whose parents pay for their education. The children often live at the school while they are studying. ◇ look at **preparatory school** (1), **private school 2** (in the US, Australia, New Zealand and other countries) a free local school paid for by the government ◇ look at **state school** (1)

the ,public 'sector *noun* [sing.] (**ECONOMICS**) the part of the economy of a country that is owned or controlled by the government ◇ look at **private sector**

,public-'spirited *adj.* always ready to help other people and the public in general

,public 'transport *noun* [U] (the system of) buses, trains, etc. that run according to a series of planned times and that anyone can use: *to travel by/on public transport*

publish ? A2 Ⓢ /ˈpʌblɪʃ/ *verb* [T] **1** (**ARTS AND MEDIA**) to prepare a book, magazine, etc. and make it available to the public in print or on the internet: *This dictionary was published by Oxford University Press.* **2** (**ARTS AND MEDIA**) (used about a writer, etc.) to have your work put in a book, magazine, etc: *Dr Wreth has published several articles on the subject.* **3** to make sth known to the public: *Large companies must publish their accounts every year.*

publisher /ˈpʌblɪʃə(r)/ *noun* [C] (**ARTS AND MEDIA**) a person or company that publishes books, magazines, etc.

publishing ?+ B2 /ˈpʌblɪʃɪŋ/ *noun* [U] the business of preparing books, magazines, etc. to be sold in print or on the internet: *She's aiming for a career in publishing.*

puck /pʌk/ *noun* [C] (**SPORT**) a hard flat rubber disc that is used as a ball in ICE HOCKEY

pudding /ˈpʊdɪŋ/ *noun* [C, U] (*BrE*) **1** any sweet food that is eaten at the end of a meal: *What's for pudding today?* ◇ look at **sweet²** (2) **2** a type of sweet food that is made from bread, flour or rice with eggs, milk, etc: *rice pudding*

puddle /ˈpʌdl/ *noun* [C] a small pool of water or other liquid, especially rain, that has formed on the ground

puff¹ /pʌf/ *verb* **1** [I, T] **~ (on sth)** to smoke a cigarette, pipe, etc: *to puff on a cigarette* **2** [T, I] **~ (sth) (out)** (used about air, smoke, wind, etc.) to blow or come out in clouds: *Smoke was puffing out of the chimney.* **3** [I] (*informal*) to breathe loudly or quickly, for example when you are running: *He was puffing hard as he ran up the hill.* **4** [I] (used with an adverb or a preposition) to move in a particular direction with loud breaths or small clouds of smoke: *The train puffed into the station.*

PHR V **puff sth out/up** to cause sth to become larger by filling it with air: *The trumpet player was puffing out his cheeks.* **puff up** (used about part of the body) to become larger and rounder than normal: *Her arm puffed up when she was stung by a wasp.*

puff² /pʌf/ *noun* [C] **1** one breath that you take when you are smoking a cigarette or pipe: *to take/have a puff on a cigarette* **2** a small amount of air, smoke, wind, etc. that is blown or sent out: *a puff of smoke*

puffed /pʌft/ (*also* **,puffed 'out**) *adj.* [not before noun] finding it difficult to breathe, for example because you have been running

puffin /ˈpʌfɪn/ *noun* [C] a black and white bird with a large, brightly coloured BEAK (= the hard pointed part of a bird's mouth) that lives near the sea, common in the North Atlantic ◇ picture at **animal**

puffy /ˈpʌfi/ *adj.* (**puffier; puffiest**) (used about a part of a person's body) looking soft and SWOLLEN (= larger or rounder than normal): *Your eyes look a bit puffy. Have you been crying?*

puke /pjuːk/ *verb* [I, T] (*informal*) (**HEALTH**) to be sick **SYN** **vomit** ◇ **puke** *noun* [U]

pull¹ ? A2 /pʊl/ *verb* **1** [I, T] to use force to move sb/sth towards yourself: *I pulled on the rope to make sure that it was secure.* ◇ *to pull the trigger of a gun* ◇ *I felt somebody pull at my sleeve and turned round.* ◇ *They managed to pull the child out of the water just in time.* **2** [T] (used with an adverb or a preposition) to move sth in the direction that is described: *She pulled her sweater on/She pulled on her sweater.* ◇ *He pulled up* his trousers/He pulled his trousers up. ◇ I switched off the TV and pulled out the plug. **3** [T] to hold or be fastened to sth and move it along behind you in the direction that you are going: *That cart is too heavy for one horse to pull.* **4** [I, T] to move your body or a part of your body away with force: *She pulled away as he tried to kiss her.* ◇ *I pulled back my fingers just as the door slammed.* **5** [T] (**HEALTH**) to damage a muscle, etc. by using too much force: *I've **pulled a muscle** in my thigh.* ➔ note at **injure 6** [T] to open or close curtains, etc: *It's dark — pull the curtains* (= close them). **SYN draw¹**

IDM make/pull faces/a face (at sb) → FACE¹ pull sb's leg (*informal*) to play a joke on sb by trying to make them believe sth that is not true pull out all the stops (*informal*) to make the greatest possible effort to achieve sth pull your punches (*informal*) (usually in negative sentences) to be careful what you say or do in order not to shock or upset anyone: *The film pulls no punches in its portrayal of urban violence.* pull strings (*informal*) to use your influence to gain an advantage pull your weight to do your fair share of the work

PHR V pull away (from sb/sth) to start moving forward, leaving sb/sth behind: *We waved as the bus pulled away.* pull sth down to destroy a building pull in (to sth) | pull into sth **1** (used about a train) to enter a station **2** (used about a car, etc.) to move to the side of the road and stop pull sth off (*informal*) to succeed in sth: *to pull off a business deal* pull out (used about a car, etc.) to move away from the side of the road: *I braked as a car suddenly pulled out in front of me.* pull out (of sth) (used about a train) to leave a station pull (sb/sth) out (of sth) (to cause sb/sth) to leave sth: *The Americans have pulled their forces out of the area.* ◇ *We've pulled out of the deal.* pull sth out to take sth out of a place suddenly or with force: *She walked into the bank and pulled out a gun.* pull over (used about a vehicle or its driver) to slow down and move to the side of the road: *I pulled over to let the ambulance past.* pull sb/sth over (used about the police) to make a driver or vehicle move to the side of the road and stop pull through (sth) to survive a dangerous illness or a difficult time pull together to do sth or work together with other people in an organized way and without fighting pull yourself together to control your feelings and behave in a calm way: *Pull yourself together and stop crying.* pull up (to cause a car, etc.) to stop

pull² ʕ+ **B1** /pʊl/ *noun* **1** [C] ~ (at/on sth) the act of moving sb/sth towards you using force: *I gave a pull on the rope to check it was secure.* **2** [sing.] a physical force or an attraction that makes sb/sth move in a particular direction: *the earth's gravitational pull* ◇ *He couldn't resist the pull of the city.* **3** [sing.] the act of taking a breath of smoke from a cigarette

pulley /'pʊli/ *noun* [C] a piece of equipment, consisting of a wheel and a rope, that is used for lifting heavy things

pullover /'pʊləʊvə(r)/ *noun* [C] (*especially BrE*) a KNITTED piece of clothing made of wool or cotton for the upper part of the body,

effort

pulley

with long SLEEVES and no buttons **SYN** jersey, jumper, sweater

'**pull tab** (*AmE*) = RING PULL

pulmonary /'pʌlmənəri/ *adj.* [only before noun] (**ANATOMY**) connected with the lungs: *the pulmonary artery* ➔ picture at **heart**

pulp /pʌlp/ *noun* **1** [sing., U] a soft substance that is made especially by pressing sth: *Mash the beans to a pulp.* ➔ look at **wood pulp 2** [U] the soft inner part of some fruits or vegetables **3** [U] (**ANATOMY**) the soft, sensitive TISSUE in the inside of a tooth

'**pulp cavity** *noun* [C] (**ANATOMY**) the area inside a tooth where the PULP is ➔ picture at **tooth**

pulpit /'pʊlpɪt/ *noun* [C] (**RELIGION**) a raised platform in a church where the priest stands when he or she is speaking

pulsar /'pʌlsɑː(r)/ *noun* [C] (**ASTRONOMY**) a star that cannot be seen but that sends out fast regular radio signals ➔ look at **quasar**

pulsate /pʌl'seɪt/ *verb* [I] to move or shake with strong regular movements: *a pulsating rhythm*

pulse¹ ʕ+ **C1** /pʌls/ *noun* **1** [C, usually sing.] (**BIOLOGY**) the regular beating in the body as blood is pushed around it by the heart. You can feel your pulse at your WRIST, neck, etc: *Your pulse rate increases after exercise.* ◇ *to feel/take somebody's pulse* (= to count how many times it beats in one minute) **2** [C] a single short increase in the amount of light, sound or electricity produced by a machine, etc. **3** pulses [pl.] the seeds of some plants such as beans and PEAS that are cooked and eaten as food

pulse² /pʌls/ *verb* [I] to move, beat or flow with strong regular movements

pulverize (*BrE also* -ise) /'pʌlvəraɪz/ *verb* [T] (*formal*) **1** to make sth into a fine powder by pressing it very hard: *pulverized bones* **2** (*especially BrE, informal*) to defeat or destroy sb/sth completely

puma /'pjuːmə/ (*especially BrE*) (*AmE usually* cougar) (*AmE also* mountain lion) *noun* [C] a large American wild animal of the cat family, with yellow-brown or grey fur

pumice /'pʌmɪs/ (*also* 'pumice stone) *noun* [U] a type of grey stone that is very light in weight. It is used as a powder for cleaning and POLISHING, and in larger pieces for rubbing on the skin to make it softer.

pump¹ ʕ+ **C1** /pʌmp/ *verb* **1** [T] (**ENGINEERING**) to force a gas or liquid to go in a particular direction: *Your heart pumps blood around your body.* **2** [I] (used about a liquid) to flow in a particular direction as if forced by a PUMP: *Blood was pumping out of the wound.* **3** [I, T] to be moved or to move sth very quickly up and down or in and out: *He pumped his arms up and down to keep warm.*

PHR V pump sth into sth/sb to put a lot of sth into sth/sb: *He pumped all his savings into the business.* pump sth up to fill sth with air, for example using a PUMP: *to pump up a car tyre*

pump² ʕ+ **C1** /pʌmp/ *noun* [C] **1** (**ENGINEERING**) a machine that is used for forcing a gas or liquid in a particular direction: *Have you got a bicycle pump?* ◇ *a petrol pump* **2** (*BrE*) = PLIMSOLL **3** (*especially AmE*) a woman's formal shoe that is plain and does not cover the top part of the foot: *ballet pumps*

'**pump-action** *adj.* [only before noun] (used about a machine or device) that you operate using a PUMPING action of your hand or arm: *a pump-action spray/shotgun*

pumped /pʌmpt/ (*also* ,pumped 'up) *adj.* ~ (for sth) (*informal*) filled with enthusiasm or excitement: *We're really pumped for the match tonight.*

pumpkin /ˈpʌmpkɪn/ *noun* [C, U] a very large round vegetable with thick orange skin

pun /pʌn/ *noun* [C] (**LANGUAGE**) a clever and funny use of a word that can have two meanings; a clever and funny use of different words that sound the same

punch¹ ʔ+ **C1** /pʌntʃ/ *verb* [T] **1 ~ sb (in/on sth)** to hit sb/ sth hard with your FIST (= closed hand): *to punch somebody on the nose* ◇ *He punched the air when he heard the good news.* **2** to make a hole in sth with a PUNCH: *He punched a hole in the ticket.*

punch² ʔ+ **C1** /pʌntʃ/ *noun* **1** [C] a hard hit with your FIST (= closed hand) **2** [C] a machine or tool that you use for making holes in sth: *a hole punch* **3** [U] a drink made from wine, fruit juice and sugar
IDM **pull your punches** → PULL¹

punchline /ˈpʌntʃlaɪn/ *noun* [C] the last and most important words of a joke or story

ˈ**punch-up** *noun* [C] (*BrE, informal*) a fight in which people hit each other

punctual /ˈpʌŋktʃuəl/ *adj.* doing sth or happening at the right time; not late: *It is important to be punctual for your classes.* ▶ **punctuality** /ˌpʌŋktʃuˈæləti/ *noun* [U]: *Japanese trains are famous for their punctuality.* ▶ **punctually** /ˈpʌŋktʃuəli/ *adv.*

punctuate /ˈpʌŋktʃueɪt/ *verb* **1** [T] **~ sth (with sth)** to interrupt sth many times: *Her speech was punctuated with bursts of applause.* **2** [I, T] (**LANGUAGE**) to divide writing into sentences and phrases by adding full stops, question marks, etc.

punctuation /ˌpʌŋktʃuˈeɪʃn/ *noun* [U] the use of marks to divide writing into sentences and phrases, or the marks themselves: *spelling and punctuation errors*

ˌ**punctuˈation mark** *noun* [C] (**LANGUAGE**) a sign or mark used in writing to divide sentences and phrases: *Punctuation marks include full stops, commas and question marks.*

puncture /ˈpʌŋktʃə(r)/ *noun* [C] a small hole made by a sharp point, especially in a bicycle or car tyre ▶ **puncture** *verb* [I, T]

pungent /ˈpʌndʒənt/ *adj.* (used about a smell) very strong

punish ʔ **B1** /ˈpʌnɪʃ/ *verb* [T] **~ sb (for sth/for doing sth)** to make sb suffer because they have done sth bad or wrong: *The children were severely punished for telling lies.*

punishable /ˈpʌnɪʃəbl/ *adj.* **~ (by sth)** (**LAW**) (used about a crime, etc.) that you can be punished for doing: *a punishable offence* ◇ *In some countries drug smuggling is punishable by death.*

punishing /ˈpʌnɪʃɪŋ/ *adj.* that makes you very tired or weak: *The prime minister had a punishing schedule, visiting five countries in five days.*

punishment ʔ **B1** /ˈpʌnɪʃmənt/ *noun* [U, C] the action or way of punishing sb: *capital punishment* (= punishment by death) ◇ *He was excluded from school for a week as a punishment.*

punitive /ˈpjuːnətɪv/ *adj.* (*formal*) **1** (**LAW**) intended as a punishment: *to take punitive measures against somebody* **2** (used about taxes, etc.) very severe and that people find very difficult to pay: *punitive taxation*

punk ʔ+ **B2** /pʌŋk/ *noun* **1** [U] (**MUSIC**) a type of loud music that was popular in the late 1970s and early 1980s. Punk musicians deliberately tried to offend people with traditional opinions. **2** [C] a person who likes punk music and often has brightly coloured hair and unusual clothes

punt /pʌnt/ *noun* [C] a long narrow boat with a flat bottom and square ends, that is moved by pushing a long POLE against the bottom of a river ▶ **punt** *verb* [I, T]: *to go punting*

puny /ˈpjuːni/ *adj.* (**punier; puniest**) very small and weak

pup /pʌp/ *noun* [C] **1** = PUPPY **2** the young of some animals such as SEALS and WOLVES

pupa /ˈpjuːpə/ *noun* [C] (*pl.* **pupae** /-piː/) (**BIOLOGY**) an insect in the stage of development before it becomes an adult insect ⊃ look at **larva** ❶ The pupa of a butterfly or moth is called a **chrysalis**.

pupil ʔ **B2** /ˈpjuːpl/ *noun* [C] **1** (**EDUCATION**) a child in school: *There are 28 pupils in my class.* ⊃ look at **student 2** (**ARTS AND MEDIA**) a person who is taught artistic, musical, etc. skills by an expert: *He was a pupil of Liszt.* **3** (**ANATOMY**) the round black hole in the middle of the eye ⊃ picture at **eye¹**

puppet /ˈpʌpɪt/ *noun* [C] (**ARTS AND MEDIA**) a model of a person or an animal that you can move by pulling the strings, which are tied to it, or by putting your hand inside it and moving your fingers **2** a person or an organization that is controlled by sb else: *The occupying forces set up a puppet government.*

puppetry /ˈpʌpɪtri/ *noun* [U] (**ARTS AND MEDIA**) the art and skill of making and using PUPPETS

puppy ʔ /ˈpʌpi/ (*pl.* **-ies**) (*also* **pup**) *noun* [C] a young dog

purchase ʔ **B2** /ˈpɜːtʃəs/ *noun* (*formal*) **1** [U, C] the act of buying sth: *to take out a loan for the purchase of a car* **2** [C] something that you buy: *These shoes were a poor purchase — they're falling apart already.* ◇ *to make a purchase* ▶ **purchase** ʔ **B2** *verb* [T]: *Many employees have the opportunity to purchase shares in the company they work for.*

purchaser /ˈpɜːtʃəsə(r)/ *noun* [C] (*formal*) a person who buys sth: *The purchaser of the house agrees to pay a deposit of 10%.* ⊃ look at **vendor**

pure ʔ **B2** ❺ /pjʊə(r)/ *adj.*
- NOT MIXED **1** not mixed with anything else: *pure orange juice/silk/alcohol*
- CLEAN **2** clean and not containing any harmful substances: *pure air/water* **OPP** **impure**
- COMPLETE **3** [only before noun] complete and total: *We met by pure chance.*
- SUBJECT **4** [only before noun] (used about an area of learning) concerned only with increasing your knowledge rather than having practical uses: *pure mathematics* **OPP** **applied**
- SOUND/COLOUR/LIGHT **5** (used about a sound, colour or light) very clear; perfect: *She was dressed in pure white.*
- MORALLY GOOD **6** not doing or knowing anything evil or anything that is connected with sex: *a young girl still pure in mind and body* **OPP** **impure**

purée /ˈpjʊəreɪ/ *noun* [U, C] a food that you make by cooking a fruit or vegetable and then pressing and mixing it until it is smooth and liquid: *apple/tomato purée*

purely ʔ+ **B2** /ˈpjʊəli/ *adv.* only or completely: *It's not purely a question of money.*

purge /pɜːdʒ/ *verb* [T] **~ sth (of sb); ~ sb (from sth)** to remove people that you do not want from a political party or other organization ▶ **purge** *noun* [C]: *The General carried out a purge of his political enemies.*

purify /ˈpjʊərɪfaɪ/ *verb* [T] (**purifying; purifies;** *pt, pp* **purified**) to remove dirty or harmful substances from sth: *purified water* ▶ **purification** /ˌpjʊərɪfɪˈkeɪʃn/ *noun* [U] ⊃ picture on **page 592**

puritan /ˈpjʊərɪtən/ *noun* [C] a person who thinks that it is wrong to enjoy yourself ▶ **puritan** (*also* **puritanical** /ˌpjʊərɪˈtænɪkl/) *adj.*: *a puritan attitude to life*

purity /ˈpjʊərəti/ *noun* [U] the state of being pure: *to test the purity of the air* ⊃ look at **impurity (2)**

water purification

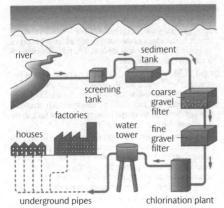

river

sediment tank

screening tank

coarse gravel filter

factories

water tower

fine gravel filter

houses

underground pipes

chlorination plant

purl /pɜːl/ *noun* [U] a simple STITCH used in KNITTING (= making sth with wool and two long needles or a machine)

purple ⚡ A1 /ˈpɜːpl/ *adj.* having the colour of blue and red mixed together: *His face was purple with rage.* ▶ **purple** ⚡ A1 *noun* [U, C]

purport /pəˈpɔːt/ *verb* [I] — **to be/have sth** (*formal*) to give the impression of being sth or of having done sth, when this may not be true: *The book does not purport to be a true history of the period.*

purpose ⚡ A2 ⊙ /ˈpɜːpəs/ *noun* **1** [C] the aim or intention of sth: *The main purpose of this meeting is to decide what we should do next.* **2 purposes** [pl.] what is needed in a particular situation: *For the purposes of this demonstration, I will use model cars.* ◇ *You may only use the phone for business purposes.* **3** [U] a meaning or reason that is important to you: *A good leader inspires people with a sense of purpose.* **4** [U] the ability to plan sth and work hard to achieve it: *I was impressed by his strength of purpose.*
IDM **to/for all intents and purposes** → INTENT² **on purpose** not by accident; with a particular intention: *'You've torn a page out of my book!' 'I'm sorry, I didn't do it on purpose.'* **SYN** **deliberately**

▼ SYNONYMS

purpose

aim • intention • plan • point • idea

These are all words for talking about what sb/sth intends to do or achieve.

purpose *Our purpose is to raise money.*

aim *Her aim was to find a job in London.*

intention *I have no intention of going to the party.*

plan *There are plans to build new offices.*

point *What's the point of all this violence?*

idea *The idea was to meet her new boyfriend.*

purposeful /ˈpɜːpəsfl/ *adj.* having a definite aim or plan: *Greg strode off down the street looking purposeful.* ▶ **purposefully** /-fəli/ *adv.*

purposely /ˈpɜːpəsli/ *adv.* with a particular intention: *I purposely waited till everyone had gone so that I could speak to you in private.* **SYN** **deliberately**

purr /pɜː(r)/ *verb* [I] (used about a cat) to make a continuous low sound that shows pleasure ⊃ look at **miaow**

purse¹ /pɜːs/ *noun* [C] **1** a small bag made of leather, etc., for carrying money and bank cards, used especially by women ⊃ look at **wallet 2** (*AmE*) = HANDBAG

purse² /pɜːs/ *verb*
IDM **purse your lips** to press your lips together to show that you do not like sth

purser /ˈpɜːsə(r)/ *noun* [C] the person on a ship who looks after the accounts and deals with passengers' problems

pursue ⚡ B2 /pəˈsjuː/ *verb* [T] (*formal*) **1** to follow sb/sth in order to catch them or it: *The robber ran off pursued by two policemen.* **SYN** **chase¹ 2** to try to achieve sth or to continue to do sth over a period of time: *to pursue a career in banking* ◇ *She didn't seem to want to pursue the discussion so I changed the subject.*

pursuer /pəˈsjuːə(r)/ *noun* [C] a person who is following and trying to catch sb/sth

pursuit ⚡+ B2 /pəˈsjuːt/ *noun* **1** [U] the act of trying to achieve or get sth: *the pursuit of pleasure* **2** [U] the act of following or going after sb **3** [C] an activity that you do either for work or for pleasure: *outdoor/leisure pursuits*
IDM **in hot pursuit** → HOT¹ **in pursuit (of sb/sth)** trying to catch or get sb/sth: *He neglected his family in pursuit of his own personal ambitions.*

pus /pʌs/ *noun* [U] (**HEALTH**) a thick yellow liquid that may form in a part of the body that has been hurt

push¹ ⚡ A2 /pʊʃ/ *verb*
• MOVE **1** [I, T] to use force to move sb/sth forward or away from you: *She pushed him into the water.* ◇ *to push a pram* ◇ *She pushed the door shut with her foot.* **2** [I, T] to move forward by pushing sb/sth: *John pushed his way through the crowd.* ◇ *to push past somebody* ◇ *People were pushing and shoving to try to get to the front.*
• SWITCH/BUTTON **3** [I, T] to press a switch, button, etc., for example in order to start a machine: *Push the red button if you want the bus to stop.*
• PERSUADE/FORCE **4** [T] ~ **sb (to do sth/into doing sth)**; ~ **sb (for sth)** to try to make sb do sth that they do not want to do: *My friend pushed me into entering the competition.* ◇ *to push somebody for an answer*
• NEW PRODUCT **5** [T] (*informal*) to try to make sth seem attractive, for example so that people will buy it: *They are launching a major publicity campaign to push their new product.*
IDM **be hard pressed/pushed/put to do sth** → HARD² **push your luck | push it/things** (*informal*) to take a risk because you have successfully avoided problems in the past: *You didn't get caught last time, but don't push your luck!*
PHR V **push sb around** (*BrE also* **push sb about**) to give orders to sb in a rude and unpleasant way: *Don't let your boss push you around.* **push ahead/forward (with sth)** to continue with sth **push for sth** to try hard to get sth: *Jim is pushing for a pay rise.* **push in** to join a line of people waiting for sth by standing in front of others who were there before you **push on** to continue a journey: *Although it was getting dark, we decided to push on.* **push sb/sth over** to make sb/sth fall down by pushing them or it

push² ⚡ B1 /pʊʃ/ *noun* [C] an act of pushing: *Can you help me give the car a push to get it started?* ◇ *The car windows opened at the push of a button.*
IDM **at a push** (*BrE, informal*) if it is really necessary (but only with difficulty): *We can get ten people*

round the table at a push. **give sb the push** (*BrE*, *informal*) to tell sb you no longer want them in a relationship, or in a job

ˈpush-button *adj.* [only before noun] (used about a machine, etc.) that you work by pressing a button: *a radio with push-button controls*

pushchair /ˈpʊʃtʃeə(r)/ (*BrE*) (*AmE* **stroller**) (*also* **buggy** *BrE*, *AmE*) *noun* [C] a chair on wheels that you use for pushing a young child in

pushed /pʊʃt/ *adj.* [not before noun] **~ (for sth)** not having enough of sth: *Hurry up. We're really **pushed for time**.*

pusher /ˈpʊʃə(r)/ *noun* [C] (*informal*) a person who sells illegal drugs

pushover /ˈpʊʃəʊvə(r)/ *noun* [C] (*informal*) **1** something that is easy to do or win **2** a person who is easy to persuade to do sth

ˈpush technology *noun* [U] (**COMPUTING**) a service that allows internet users to keep receiving a particular type of information that they want without having to request it each time

ˈpush-up (*AmE*) = PRESS-UP

pushy /ˈpʊʃi/ *adj.* (**pushier**; **pushiest**) (*informal*) (used about a person) trying hard to get what you want, in a way that seems rude

put 🔊 **A1** /pʊt/ *verb* [T] (**putting**; *pt, pp* **put**)
- IN PLACE/POSITION **1** to move sb/sth into a particular place or position: *She put the book on the table.* ◊ *Did you put sugar in my tea?* ◊ *When do you put the children to bed?*
- FIX **2** to fix sth to or in sth else: *Can you put a button on this shirt?* ◊ *We're going to put a picture on this wall.*
- WRITE **3** to write sth: *12.30 on Friday? I'll put it in my diary.* ◊ *What did you put for question 2?*
- INTO A STATE/CONDITION **4 ~ sb/sth in/into sth** to bring sb/sth into the state or condition mentioned: *This sort of weather always puts me in a bad mood.* ◊ *I was **put in charge** of the project.* ◊ *It was time to **put** our ideas **into** practice.*
- AFFECT **5** to make sb/sth feel sth or be affected by sth: *This will **put pressure on** them to finish the job quickly.* ◊ *Don't **put the blame on** me! ◊ The new teacher soon **put a stop to** cheating in tests.*
- EXPRESS **6** to say or express sth: *I don't know exactly how to put this, but … ◊ **To put it another way**, you're sacked. ◊ **Put simply**, he just wasn't good enough.*
- GIVE VALUE TO **7** to give or fix a particular value or importance to sb/sth: *We'll have to **put a limit on** how much we spend.* ◊ *I'd put him in my top five favourite writers.*

IDM **put it to sb that …** (*formal*) to suggest to sb that sth is true: *I put it to you that this man is innocent.* **put together** used when comparing sb/sth with a group of other people or things to mean 'combined' or 'in total': *You got more presents than the rest of the family put together.* **❶** For other idioms containing **put**, look at the entries for the nouns, adjectives, etc. For example, **put an end to something** is at **end**.

PHR V **put sth/yourself across/over** to say what you want to say clearly, so that people can understand it: *He didn't put his ideas across very well at the meeting.*

put sth aside 1 to save sth, especially money, to use later **2** to ignore or forget sth: *We agreed to put aside our differences and work together.*

put sb away (*informal*) to send sb to prison **put sth away 1** to put sth where you usually keep it because you have finished using it: *Put the tools away if you've finished with them.* **2** to save money to spend later

put sth back 1 to return sth to its place: *I put the books back on the shelf.* **2** to move sth to a later time: *The meeting's been put back until next week.* **OPP** **bring sth forward 3** to change the time shown on a clock to an earlier time: *We have to put the clocks back tonight.* **OPP** **put sth forward**

put sb/sth before/above sb/sth to treat sb/sth as more important than sb/sth else: *He puts his children before anything else.*

put sth by to save money to use later: *Her grandparents had put some money by for her education.*

put sb down 1 (*informal*) to say things to make sb seem stupid **2** to put a baby to bed **put sth down 1** to stop holding sth and put it on the floor, a table, etc: *The policeman persuaded him to put the gun down.* **2** to write sth: *I'll put that down in my diary.* **3** to pay part of the cost of sth: *We put down a 10% deposit on a car.* **4** (used about a government, an army or the police) to stop sb by force: *to put down a rebellion* **5** to kill an animal because it is old, sick or dangerous: *The dog was put down after it attacked a child.* **put sth down to sth** to believe that sth is caused by sth: *I put his bad exam results down to laziness rather than a lack of ability.*

put yourself/sb forward to suggest that you or another person should be considered for a job, etc: *His name was put forward for the position of chairman.* **put sth forward 1** to change the time shown on a clock to a later time: *We put the clocks forward in spring.* **OPP** **put sth back 2** to move sth to an earlier time or date **3** to suggest sth: *She put forward a plan to help the homeless.*

put sth in 1 to fix equipment or furniture in position so that it can be used: *We're having a shower put in.* **SYN** **install 2** to include a piece of information, etc. in sth that you write **3** to ask for sth officially: *to put in an invoice/a request* **put sth in | put sth into sth/doing sth** to spend time, etc. on sth: *She puts all her time and energy into her business.*

put sb off (sb/sth/doing sth) 1 to make sb not like sb/sth or not want to do sth: *The accident put me off driving for a long time.* **2** to say to a person that you can no longer do what you had agreed: *They were coming to stay last weekend but I had to put them off at the last moment.* **3** to make sb unable to give their attention to sth: *Don't stare at me — you're putting me off!* **put sth off** to turn or switch a light off: *She put off the light and went to sleep.* **OPP** **put sth on put sth off | put off doing sth** to move sth to a later time: *She put off writing her essay until the last minute.* **SYN** **delay¹**

put sth on 1 to dress yourself in sth: *Put on your coat! ◊ I'll have to put my glasses on.* **OPP** **take sth off 2** to cover an area of your skin with sth: *You'd better put some sun cream on.* **3** to switch on a piece of electrical equipment: *It's too early to put the lights on yet.* **OPP** **put sth off, put sth out 4** to make recorded music, a video, etc. begin to play: *Let's put some music on.* **5** to become heavier, especially by the amount mentioned: *I put on weight very easily.* **OPP** **lose 6** to organize or prepare sth for people to see or use: *The school is putting on 'Macbeth'.* ◊ *They put on extra trains in the summer.* ⊃ note at **performing arts 7** to pretend to be feeling sth; to pretend to have sth: *He's not angry with you really; he's just putting it on.* **put sth on sth 1** to add an amount of money, etc. to the cost or value of sth: *The government want to put more tax on the price of a packet of cigarettes.* **2** to bet money on sth: *He put all his money on a horse.* **SYN** **bet¹**

put sb out 1 to give sb trouble or extra work: *He put his hosts out by arriving very late.* **SYN** inconvenience **2** to make sb upset or angry: *I was quite put out by their selfish behaviour.* **put sth out 1** to make sth stop burning: *to put out a fire* **SYN** extinguish **2** to switch off a piece of electrical equipment: *They put out the lights and locked the door.* **OPP** put sth on **3** to take sth out of your house and leave it: *to put the rubbish out* **4** to give or tell the public sth, often on the TV or radio or in newspapers: *The police put out a warning about the escaped prisoner.* **put yourself out** (*informal*) to do sth for sb, even though it brings you trouble or extra work: *'I'll give you a lift home.' 'I don't want you to put yourself out. I'll take a taxi.'*
put sth/yourself over = PUT STH/YOURSELF ACROSS/OVER
put sb through sth to make sb experience sth unpleasant **put sb/sth through** to make a phone connection that allows sb to speak to sb: *Could you put me through to Jeanne, please?*
put sth to sb to suggest sth to sb; to ask sb sth: *I put the question to her.*
put sth together to build or repair sth by joining its parts together: *The furniture comes with instructions on how to put it together.* ⊃ note at **build**[1]
put sth towards sth to give money to pay part of the cost of sth: *We all put a pound towards a leaving present for Joe.*
put sb up to give sb food and a place to stay: *She had missed the last train home, so I offered to put her up for the night.* **put sth up 1** to lift or hold sth up: *Put your hand up if you know the answer.* **2** to build sth: *to put up a fence/tent* ⊃ note at **build**[1] **3** to fix sth to a wall, etc. so that everyone can see it: *to put up a notice* **4** to increase sth: *Some shops put up their prices just before Christmas.* **put up sth** to show a particular level of skill, DETERMINATION (= not wanting to give up), etc. in a fight: *The shop assistant put up a struggle against the attacker.* **put up with sb/sth** to suffer sb/sth unpleasant and not complain about it: *I don't know how they put up with this noise.*

putrid /ˈpjuːtrɪd/ *adj.* **1** (used about dead animals and plants) smelling bad after being dead for some time **SYN** foul[1] **2** (*informal*) very unpleasant: *The food there was putrid.*

putt /pʌt/ *verb* [I, T] (SPORT) (used in golf) to hit the ball gently when it is near the HOLE

putter /ˈpʌtə(r)/ (*AmE*) = POTTER[1]

putty /ˈpʌti/ *noun* [U] a soft substance that is used for fixing glass into windows that becomes hard when dry

puzzle[1] ?+ B2 /ˈpʌzl/ *noun* [C] **1** a game or toy that makes you think a lot: *a crossword/jigsaw puzzle* ◇ *I like to **do puzzles**.* **2** [usually sing.] something that is difficult to understand or explain; a mystery: *The reasons for his actions have remained a puzzle to historians.*

puzzle[2] /ˈpʌzl/ *verb* [T] to make sb feel confused because they do not understand sth: *Her strange illness puzzled all the experts.*
PHR V puzzle sth out to find the answer to sth by thinking hard **puzzle over sth** to think hard about sth in order to understand or explain it: *to puzzle over a mathematical problem*

puzzled /ˈpʌzld/ *adj.* not able to understand or explain sth: *a puzzled expression*

PVC /ˌpiː viː ˈsiː/ *noun* [U] (CHEMISTRY) a strong plastic material used to make a wide variety of products, such as clothing, pipes, floor COVERINGS, etc. (the abbreviation for 'polyvinyl chloride')

pygmy[1] (*also* pigmy) /ˈpɪɡmi/ *noun* [C] (*pl.* -ies) **1** Pygmy a member of a human group who are very short and live in parts of Africa and South East Asia **2** a very small person or thing or one that is weak in some way

pygmy[2] (*also* pigmy) /ˈpɪɡmi/ *adj.* [only before noun] (BIOLOGY) used to describe a plant or a type of animal that is much smaller than other similar kinds: *a pygmy shrew*

pyjamas (*BrE*) (*AmE* pajamas) /pəˈdʒɑːməz/ *noun* [pl.] loose trousers and a loose jacket or T-shirt that you wear in bed

pylon /ˈpaɪlən/ *noun* [C] a tall metal tower that supports heavy electrical wires

pyramid /ˈpɪrəmɪd/ *noun* [C] **1** (GEOMETRY) a shape with a flat base in the shape of a square or a TRIANGLE (= a shape with three straight sides) and three or four sloping sides that meet in a point at the top ⊃ picture at **solid**[2] **2** (HISTORY) a large building in the shape of a pyramid. The ancient Egyptians built stone pyramids as places to bury their kings and queens. ▶ pyramidal /-ˈmɪdl/ *adj.*

Pythagoras' theorem /paɪˌθæɡərəsɪz ˈθɪərəm/ *noun* [sing.] (GEOMETRY) the rule that, in a RIGHT-ANGLED TRIANGLE, the SQUARE (= the number that you get when you multiply another number by itself) of the HYPOTENUSE (= the side opposite the right angle) is equal to the SQUARES of the other two sides added together

python /ˈpaɪθən/ *noun* [C] a large snake that kills animals by wrapping its long body tightly around them

Q q

Q[1] /kjuː/ (*also* q) *noun* [C, U] (*pl.* Q's, q's) the 17th letter of the English alphabet: *'Queen' begins with (a) 'Q'.*

Q[2] *abbr.* (in writing) = QUESTION[1] (1): *Qs 1-5 are compulsory.*

QC /ˌkjuː ˈsiː/ *noun* [C] (LAW) (used when there is a queen in the UK) the highest level of BARRISTER (= a type of lawyer) who can speak for the government in a court of law in the UK (the abbreviation for 'Queen's Counsel') ⊃ look at **KC** ⊃ note at **lawyer**

QE /ˌkjuː ˈiː/ *abbr.* = QUANTITATIVE EASING

QR code /ˌkjuː ˈɑː kəʊd/ *noun* [C] a pattern of black and white squares that contains information, often a link to a website, that can be read by the camera on a smartphone

qt *abbr.* (in writing) (*pl.* qt) = QUART

quack /kwæk/ *noun* [C] the sound that a DUCK (= a bird that lives on or near water) makes ▶ quack *verb* [I]

quad /kwɒd/ **1** = QUADRANGLE **2** = QUADRUPLET

quad- /kwɒd, kwɒˈd/ *prefix* (in verbs, nouns, adjectives and adverbs) four; having four: *quadruple*

quad bike (*BrE*) (*AmE* four-wheeler) *noun* [C] a motorcycle with four large wheels, used for riding over rough ground, often for fun ⊃ look at **ATV**

quadrangle /ˈkwɒdræŋgl/ (*also* quad) *noun* [C] a square open area with buildings round it in a school, college, etc.

quadrant /ˈkwɒdrənt/ *noun* [C] **1** (GEOMETRY) a quarter of a circle or of its CIRCUMFERENCE (= the distance around it) ⊃ picture at **circle¹ 2** an instrument for measuring angles, especially to check your position at sea or to look at stars

quadratic /kwɒˈdrætɪk/ *adj.* (MATHEMATICS) involving an unknown quantity that is multiplied by itself once only: *a quadratic equation*

quadri- /ˈkwɒdrɪ, kwɒˈdrɪ/ *prefix* (in verbs, nouns, adjectives and adverbs) four; having four: *quadrilateral*

quadriceps /ˈkwɒdrɪseps/ *noun* [C] (*pl.* quadriceps) (ANATOMY) the large muscle at the front of the THIGH (= the top part of the leg)

quadrilateral /ˌkwɒdrɪˈlætərəl/ *noun* [C] (GEOMETRY) a flat shape with four straight sides ▸ quadrilateral *adj.*

quadruped /ˈkwɒdruped/ *noun* [C] (BIOLOGY) any creature with four feet ⊃ look at **biped**

quadruple /ˈkwɒdrʊpl/ *verb* [I, T] (MATHEMATICS) to multiply by four; to be multiplied by four

quadruplet /ˈkwɒdrʊplət/ (*also* quad) *noun* [C] (BIOLOGY) one of four children or animals that are born to one mother at the same time

quail /kweɪl/ *noun* [C, U] a small brown bird whose meat and eggs are used for food; the meat of this bird

quaint /kweɪnt/ *adj.* attractive or unusual because it seems to belong to the past

quake¹ /kweɪk/ *verb* [I] (used about a person) to shake: *to quake with fear*

quake² /kweɪk/ *noun* [C] (*informal*) = EARTHQUAKE

qualification ♀ B1 /ˌkwɒlɪfɪˈkeɪʃn/ *noun* **1** [C] (*BrE*) (EDUCATION) an exam that you have passed or a course of study that you have completed: *to have a teaching/nursing qualification* ◇ *She left school at 16 with no formal qualifications.* **2** [C] a skill or quality that you need to do a particular job: *What qualifications are required for this job?* **3** [C, U] something that limits the meaning of a general statement or makes it weaker: *I can recommend him for the job without qualification.* ◇ *She accepted the proposal with only a few qualifications.* **4** [U] the fact of doing what is necessary in order to be able to do a job, play in a competition, etc.

qualified ♀ B1 /ˈkwɒlɪfaɪd/ *adj.* **1** ~ (for sth/to do sth) having passed an exam or having the knowledge, experience, etc. in order to be able to do sth: *a fully qualified doctor* ◇ *Edward is well qualified for this job.* ◇ *I don't feel qualified to comment — I know nothing about the subject.* ⊃ note at **job 2** not complete; limited: *My boss gave only qualified approval to the plan.* **OPP** unqualified

qualify ♀ B1 /ˈkwɒlɪfaɪ/ *verb* (qualifying; qualifies; *pt, pp* qualified) **1** [I] ~ (as sth) to pass the exam that is necessary to do a particular job; to have the qualities that are necessary for sth: *It takes five years to qualify as a vet.* ◇ *A cup of coffee and a sandwich doesn't really qualify as a meal.* ⊃ note at **job 2** [I, T] ~ (sb) (for sth/to do sth) to have or give sb the right to have or do sth: *How many years must you work to qualify for a pension?* ◇ *This exam will qualify me to teach music.* **3** [I] ~ (for sth) (SPORT) to win the right to enter a competition or continue to the next part: *Our team has qualified for the final.* **4** [T] to limit the meaning of a general statement or make it weaker

qualitative ♥ /ˈkwɒlɪtətɪv/ *adj.* connected with how good sth is, rather than with how much of it there is: *qualitative analysis/research* ◇ *There are qualitative differences between the two products.* ⊃ look at **quantitative**

quality¹ ♀ A2 ♥ /ˈkwɒləti/ *noun* (*pl.* -ies) **1** [U, sing.] how good or bad sth is: *This paper isn't very good quality.* ◇ *to be of good/poor/top quality* ◇ *goods of a high quality* ◇ *high-quality goods* ◇ *the quality of life in our cities* **2** [U] a high standard or level: *Aim for quality rather than quantity in your writing.* **3** [C] a thing that is part of a person's character, especially sth good: *Vicky has all the qualities of a good manager.*

quality² /ˈkwɒləti/ *adj.* [only before noun] used especially by people trying to sell goods or services to say that sth is of a high quality: *quality service at a competitive price*

quality conˈtrol *noun* [U] (BUSINESS) the practice of checking goods as they are being produced, to make sure that they are of a high standard

quality of ˈlife *noun* [U] the level of health, comfort and happiness that a particular person or group has: *Their quality of life improved dramatically when they moved to the country.*

qualm /kwɑːm, kwɔːm/ *noun* [C, usually pl.] a feeling of doubt or worry that what you are doing may not be morally right: *I don't have any qualms about asking them to lend us some money.*

quandary /ˈkwɒndəri/ *noun* [C, usually sing.] (*pl.* -ies) a state of not being able to decide what to do; a difficult situation: *I'm in a quandary — should I ask her or not?*

quango /ˈkwæŋɡəʊ/ *noun* [C] (*pl.* -os) (POLITICS) (in the UK) an organization dealing with public matters, started by the government, but working independently and with its own legal powers

quantify ♥ /ˈkwɒntɪfaɪ/ *verb* [T] (quantifying; quantifies; *pt, pp* quantified) to describe or express sth as an amount or a number ▸ quantifiable /ˈkwɒntɪfaɪəbl, ˌkwɒntɪˈfaɪəbl/ *adj.* ▸ quantification /ˌkwɒntɪfɪˈkeɪʃn/ *noun* [U]

quantitative ♥ /ˈkwɒntɪtətɪv/ *adj.* connected with the amount or number of sth rather than how good it is: *quantitative analysis/research* ◇ *There is no difference between the two in quantitative terms.* ⊃ look at **qualitative**

quantitative ˈeasing *noun* [U] (*abbr.* QE) (FINANCE) the introduction of new money into a country's money supply by a central bank

quantity ♀ A2 ♥ /ˈkwɒntəti/ *noun* [C, U] (*pl.* -ies) **1** a number or an amount of sth: *Add a small quantity of salt.* ◇ *It's cheaper to buy goods in large quantities.* **2** a large number or amount of sth: *It's cheaper to buy goods in quantity.*

IDM an unknown quantity → UNKNOWN¹

ˈquantity surveyor *noun* [C] (*BrE*) a person whose job is to calculate the quantity of materials needed for building sth, how much it will cost and how long it will take

quantum /ˈkwɒntəm/ *noun* [C] (*pl.* quanta /-tə/) (PHYSICS) a very small quantity of ELECTROMAGNETIC energy

ˈquantum physics *noun* [U] (PHYSICS) the area of science that investigates QUANTUM THEORY to understand the behaviour of PARTICLES

ˈquantum theory *noun* [U] (PHYSICS) a theory based on the idea that energy exists in units that cannot be divided

quarantine /ˈkwɒrəntiːn/ *noun* [U] (MEDICINE) a period of time when a person or an animal that has or may have a disease must be kept away from other people or animals in order to prevent the disease from spreading ▸ quarantine *verb* [T, I]

quarantine Q

quark /kwɑːk/ *noun* [C] a very small part of MATTER. There are several types of quark and it is thought that PROTONS, NEUTRONS, etc. are formed from them.

quarrel[1] /ˈkwɒrəl/ *noun* [C] **1** ~ (about/over sth) an angry argument: *We sometimes have a quarrel about who should do the washing-up.* ◇ look at **argument** (1), **fight**[2] (3) **2** ~ with sb/sth a reason for complaining about or disagreeing with sb/sth: *I have no quarrel with what has just been said.*

quarrel[2] /ˈkwɒrəl/ *verb* [I] (-ll-, *AmE* -l-) ~ (with sb) (about/over sth) to have an angry argument: *The children are always quarrelling!* ◇ *I don't want to quarrel with you about it.* ◇ look at **argue** (1), **fight**[1] (3)
PHR V quarrel with sb/sth to disagree with sb/sth: *I wouldn't quarrel with Moira's description of what happened.*

quarrelsome /ˈkwɒrəlsəm/ *adj.* (used about a person) liking to argue with other people
SYN argumentative

quarry[1] /ˈkwɒri/ *noun* (*pl.* -ies) **1** [C] a place where large amounts of stone, sand, etc. are dug out of the ground ◇ look at **mine**[2] (1) **2** [sing.] a person or an animal that is being hunted

quarry[2] /ˈkwɒri/ *verb* [I, T] (quarrying; quarries; *pt, pp* quarried) to dig stone, sand, etc. out of the ground: *to quarry for marble*

quart /kwɔːt/ *noun* [C] (*abbr.* qt) a measure of liquid that is equal to about 1.14 LITRES in the UK and Canada. There are 2 PINTS in a quart. ➊ An American quart is 0.95 of a litre.

quarter ʔ 🄐🄰 /ˈkwɔːtə(r)/ *noun*
• ONE OF FOUR PARTS **1** [C] one of four equal parts of sth: *The programme lasts for three quarters of an hour.* ◇ *a mile and a quarter* ◇ *to cut an apple into quarters*
• 15 MINUTES **2** [sing.] 15 minutes before or after every hour: *I'll meet you at (a) quarter past six.* ◇ *It's (a) quarter to three.* ➊ In American English you say '(a) quarter after' and '(a) quarter of': *I'll meet you at (a) quarter after six.* ◇ *It's a quarter of three.*
• THREE MONTHS **3** [C] a period of three months: *You get a gas bill every quarter.*
• PART OF A TOWN **4** [C, usually sing.] a part of a town, especially a part where a particular group of people live: *the Chinese quarter* ◇ *the historic quarter of the city*
• PERSON/GROUP **5** [C] a person or group of people who may give help or information or who have certain opinions: *The news was greeted with dismay in some quarters.*
• 25 CENTS **6** [C] (in the US or Canada) a coin that is worth 25 cents (¼ dollar)
• PLACE TO LIVE **7** quarters [pl.] a place that is provided for people, especially soldiers, to live in
• MEASUREMENT **8** [C] a unit for measuring weight, equal to four OUNCES; a quarter of a pound: *a quarter of mushrooms*
IDM at close quarters → CLOSE[3]

quarter-ˈfinal *noun* [C] one of the four matches between the eight players or teams left in a competition ◇ look at **semi-final**

quarterly /ˈkwɔːtəli/ *adj., adv.* (produced or happening) once every three months: *a quarterly magazine*

quarter note (*AmE*) = CROTCHET

quartet /kwɔːˈtet/ *noun* [C] (MUSIC) **1** [+ sing./pl. verb] four people who sing or play music together **2** a piece of music for four people to sing or play together

quartz /kwɔːts/ *noun* [U] (GEOLOGY) a type of hard rock that is used in making very accurate clocks or watches

quasar /ˈkweɪzɑː(r)/ *noun* [C] (ASTRONOMY) a large object like a star, that is far away and that shines very brightly and sometimes sends out strong radio signals ◇ look at **pulsar**

quash /kwɒʃ/ *verb* [T] **1** (LAW) to say that an official decision is no longer true or legal **2** to stop or defeat sth by force: *to quash a rebellion*

quasi- /ˈkweɪzaɪ, kweɪsaɪ, kwɑːzi/ *prefix* (in nouns and adjectives) **1** that appears to be sth but is not really so: *a quasi-scientific explanation* **2** partly; almost: *a quasi-official body*

quatrain /ˈkwɒtreɪn/ *noun* [C] (LITERATURE) a poem or VERSE of a poem that has four lines

quaver[1] /ˈkweɪvə(r)/ *verb* [I] if sb's voice **quavers**, it shakes, usually because the person is nervous or afraid

quaver[2] /ˈkweɪvə(r)/ (*BrE*) (*AmE* eighth note) *noun* [C] (MUSIC) a note that lasts half as long as a CROTCHET ◇ note at **crotchet** ◇ picture at **music**

quay /kiː/ *noun* [C] a platform where goods and passengers are loaded on and off boats

quayside /ˈkiːsaɪd/ *noun* [sing.] the area of land that is near a QUAY

queasy /ˈkwiːzi/ *adj.* (queasier; queasiest) feeling sick; wanting to VOMIT (= bring up food from the stomach)

queen ʔ 🄰🄐 ➋ /kwiːn/ *noun* [C] **1** (*also* Queen) (POLITICS) the female ruler of a country: *Queen Elizabeth II* (= the second) ◇ look at **king** (1), **prince**, **princess** **2** (*also* Queen) the wife of a king **3** (in CHESS) the most powerful piece, that can move any distance and in all directions **4** one of the four PLAYING CARDS in a PACK, with a picture of a queen: *the queen of hearts* **5** (BIOLOGY) the largest and most important female in a group of insects: *the queen bee*

queer /kwɪə(r)/ *adj.* (*old-fashioned*) strange or unusual: *His face was a queer pink colour.* **SYN odd**

quell /kwel/ *verb* [T] (*formal*) to end sth

quench /kwentʃ/ *verb* [T] to drink so that you no longer feel thirsty: *He drank some juice to quench his thirst.*

query[1]+ 🄒🄵 /ˈkwɪəri/ *noun* [C] (*pl.* -ies) a question, especially one asking for information or expressing a doubt about sth: *Does anyone have any queries?*
▶ **query** *verb* [T] (querying; queries; *pt, pp* queried): *We queried the bill but were told it was correct.* ◇ note at **ask**

quest ʔ+ 🄒🄵 /kwest/ *noun* [C] ~ (for sth) (*formal*) a long search for sth that is difficult to find: *the quest for happiness/knowledge/truth*

question[1] ʔ 🄐🄵 ➊ /ˈkwestʃən/ *noun* **1** [C] (*abbr.* Q) ~ (about/on sth) a sentence or phrase that asks for an answer: *Put up your hand if you want to ask a question.* ◇ *In the examination, you must answer five questions in one hour.* ◇ *Are there any questions on what I've just said?* ◇ *What's the answer to Question 5?* **2** [C] a problem or difficulty that needs to be discussed or dealt with: *The resignations raise the question of who will take over.* ◇ *The question is, how are we going to raise the money?* **3** [U] doubt or not being certain about sth: *There is no question about Brenda's enthusiasm for the job.* ◇ *His honesty is beyond question.* ◇ *The results of the report were accepted without question.*
IDM in question that is being considered or talked about: *The lawyer asked where she was on the night in question.* **no question of** no possibility of: *There is no question of him leaving hospital yet.* **out of the question** impossible: *A new car is out of the question.*

It's just too expensive. **a question of sth/doing sth** used to say that sth is not difficult to predict, explain, do, etc: *It's not difficult — it's just a question of finding the time to do it.*

question² 🔊 **A2** **S** /ˈkwestʃən/ *verb* [T] **1 ~ sb (about/ on sth)** to ask sb a question or questions: *The interviewers questioned me on my past experience.* **2** to express or feel doubt about sth: *She told me she was from the council so I didn't question her right to be there.* ◇ *to question somebody's sincerity/honesty*

questionable /ˈkwestʃənəbl/ *adj.* **1** that you have doubts about; not certain: *It's questionable whether we'll be able to finish in time.* **OPP** **unquestionable 2** likely to be dishonest or morally wrong: *questionable motives*

ˈ**question mark** *noun* [C] (**LANGUAGE**) the mark (**?**) that you use when you write a question

questionnaire 🔊+ **B2** /ˌkwestʃəˈneə(r)/ *noun* [C] a list of questions that are answered by many people. A questionnaire is used to collect information about a particular subject: *to complete/fill in a questionnaire*

ˈ**question tag** (*also* **tag question**) *noun* [C] (**GRAMMAR**) a short phrase such as *isn't it?* or *did you?* at the end of a sentence that changes it into a question and is often used to ask sb to agree with you

queue 🔊 **B1** /kjuː/ (*BrE*) (*AmE* **line**) *noun* [C] a line of people, cars, etc. that are waiting for sth or to do sth: *We had to **wait in a queue** for hours to get tickets.* ◇ *to **join the end of a queue*** ◇ *We were told to **form a queue** outside the doors.* ▸ **queue** 🔊 **B1** *verb* [I] **~ (up) (for sth):** *to queue for a bus* **IDM** **jump the queue** → JUMP¹

quiche /kiːʃ/ *noun* [C, U] a type of food made of PASTRY (= a mixture of flour, fat and water) filled with egg and milk with cheese, onion, etc. and cooked in the oven. You can eat quiche hot or cold.

quick¹ 🔊 **A1** /kwɪk/ *adj.* **1** done with speed; taking or lasting a short time: *May I make a quick phone call?* ◇ *This dish is quick and easy to make.* ◇ *His quick thinking saved her life.* ◇ *We need to make a quick decision.* **2 ~ (to do sth)** doing sth at speed or in a short time: *It's quicker to travel by train.* ◇ *Nicola is a quick worker.* ◇ *She was quick to point out all the mistakes I had made.* **3** used to form compound adjectives: *quick-thinking* ◇ *quick-drying paint* **IDM** **(as) quick as a flash** very quickly **quick/slow on the uptake** → UPTAKE

quick² /kwɪk/ *adv.* (*informal*) quickly: *Come over here quick!*

quicken /ˈkwɪkən/ *verb* [I, T] (*formal*) **1** to become quicker or make sth quicker: *She felt her heartbeat quicken as he approached.* ◇ *He quickened his pace to catch up with them.* **2** to become more active; to make sth more active: *His interest quickened as he heard more about the plan.*

quickly 🔊 **A1** **S** /ˈkwɪkli/ *adv.* fast; in a short time: *He quickly undressed and got into bed.* ◇ *I'd like you to get here as quickly as possible.*

quicksand /ˈkwɪksænd/ *noun* [U] (*also* **quicksands** [pl.]) deep wet sand that you sink into if you walk on it

quid /kwɪd/ *noun* [C] (*pl.* **quid**) (*BrE, informal*) a pound (in money); £1: *Can you lend me a couple of quid until tomorrow?*

quid pro quo /ˌkwɪd prəʊ ˈkwəʊ/ *noun* [sing.] a thing given in return for sth else

quiet¹ 🔊 **A1** /ˈkwaɪət/ *adj.* **1** with very little or no noise: *Be quiet!* ◇ *His voice was quiet but firm.* ◇ *Go into the library if you want to work. It's much quieter in there.* **OPP** **loud¹ 2** without much activity or many people: *The streets are very quiet on Sundays.* ◇ *Business is*

quiet at this time of year. ◇ *a quiet country village* ◇ *We lead a quiet life.* **3** (used about a person) not talking very much: *You're very quiet today. Is anything wrong?* ◇ *He's very quiet and shy.* ▸ **quietly** 🔊 **A2** *adv.*: *Try and shut the door quietly!* ▸ **quietness** *noun* [U] **IDM** **keep quiet about sth | keep sth quiet** to say nothing about sth

quiet² /ˈkwaɪət/ *noun* [U] the state of being calm and without much noise or activity: *the **peace and quiet** of the countryside* **IDM** **on the quiet** secretly

quieten /ˈkwaɪətn/ *verb* [T] to make sb/sth quiet **PHR V** **quieten (sb/sth) down** to become quiet or to make sb/sth quiet: *When you've quietened down, I'll tell you what happened.*

quill /kwɪl/ *noun* [C] **1** (*also* ˈ**quill feather**) a large feather from the wing or tail of a bird **2** (*also* ˈ**quill pen**) a pen made from a quill feather **3** one of the long, thin, sharp points on the body of a PORCUPINE

quilt /kwɪlt/ *noun* [C] a cover for a bed that has a thick warm material, for example feathers, inside it ➔ look at **duvet**

quinoa /ˈkiːnwɑː, kiˈnəʊə/ *noun* [U] the seeds of a South American plant that are used as food and to make alcoholic drinks

quintessential /ˌkwɪntɪˈsenʃl/ *adj.* (*formal*) being the perfect example of sth: *He was the quintessential tough guy.* ▸ **quintessence** /kwɪnˈtesns/ *noun* [sing.]: *It was the quintessence of an English manor house.* ▸ **quintessentially** /ˌkwɪntɪˈsenʃəli/ *adv.*: *a sense of humour that is quintessentially British*

quintet /kwɪnˈtet/ *noun* [C] (**MUSIC**) **1** a group of five people who sing or play music together **2** a piece of music for five people to sing or play together

quintuplet /ˈkwɪntʊplət/ *noun* [C] (**BIOLOGY**) one of five children or animals that are born to one mother at the same time

quirk /kwɜːk/ *noun* [C] **1** an aspect of sb's character or behaviour that is strange: *You'll soon get used to the boss's little quirks.* **2** a strange thing that happens by chance: *By a **strange quirk of fate** they met again several years later.* ▸ **quirky** *adj.* (**quirkier; quirkiest**): *Some people don't like his quirky sense of humour.*

quit 🔊 **B1** /kwɪt/ *verb* (**quitting**; *pt, pp* **quit, quitted**) **1** [I, T] **~ (as sth)** to leave a job, etc. or to go away from a place: *She quit as manager of the volleyball team.* **2** [T] (*especially AmE, informal*) to stop doing sth: *to quit smoking* **3** [I, T] (**COMPUTING**) to close a computer program

quite 🔊 **A1** /kwaɪt/ *adv.* **1** not very; to a certain degree; rather: *The film's quite good.* ◇ *It's quite a good film.* ◇ *I quite enjoy cooking.* ◇ *They had to wait quite a long time.* ◇ *It's quite cold today.* ◇ *We still meet up quite often.* ➔ note at **rather 2** (used for emphasizing sth) completely; very: *Are you quite sure you don't mind?* ◇ *I quite agree.* ◇ *You're quite right.* ◇ *To my surprise, the room was quite empty.* ◇ *Life in Japan is quite different from here.* **SYN** **absolutely 3** used for showing that you agree with or understand sth: *'He'll find it difficult.' 'Well, quite (= I agree).'* **IDM** **not quite** used for showing that there is almost enough of sth, or that it is almost suitable: *There's not quite enough bread for breakfast.* ◇ *These shoes don't quite fit.* **quite a sth** used for showing that sth is unusual: *It's quite a climb to the top of the hill.* **quite enough** used for emphasizing that no more of sth is wanted or needed: *I've had quite enough of listening to you two arguing!* ◇ *That's quite enough wine,* thanks. **quite a few | quite a lot (of)** a fairly large amount or number: *We've received quite a few enquiries.*

quits /kwɪts/ *adj.*
IDM **be quits (with sb)** (*informal*) if two people are quits, it means that neither of them owes the other anything: *You buy me a drink and then we're quits.*

quiver /ˈkwɪvə(r)/ *verb* [I] to shake slightly: *to quiver with rage/excitement/fear* **SYN** **tremble**

quiz¹ /kwɪz/ *noun* [C] (*pl.* **quizzes**) a game or competition in which you have to answer questions: *a quiz show on TV* ◇ *a general knowledge quiz*

quiz² /kwɪz/ *verb* [T] (**-zz-**) to ask sb a lot of questions in order to get information

quizzical /ˈkwɪzɪkl/ *adj.* (used about a look, smile, etc.) seeming to ask a question ▶ **quizzically** /-kli/ *adv.*

quorum /ˈkwɔːrəm/ *noun* [sing.] the smallest number of people that must be at a meeting before it can make official decisions

quota ⒤+ **C1** /ˈkwəʊtə/ *noun* [C] the number or amount of sth that is allowed or that you must do: *We have a fixed quota of work to get through each day.*

quotation ⒤ **B1** /kwəʊˈteɪʃn/ *noun* [C] (*formal*) **1** = QUOTE² (1) **2** (*also informal* **quote**) (**BUSINESS**) a statement that says how much a piece of work will cost: *You should get quotations from three different builders.* ◯ look at **estimate¹** (2)

quoˈtation marks (*also* **speech marks**) (*also informal* **quotes** /kwəʊts/) (*BrE also* **inverted commas**) *noun* [pl.] (**LANGUAGE**) the signs ' … ' or " … " that you put around a word, a sentence, etc. to show that it is what sb said or wrote, that it is a title, or that you are using it in a special way

quote¹ ⒤ **B1** Ⓢ /kwəʊt/ *verb* **1** [T, I] ~ **(sth) (from sb/ sth)** to repeat exactly sth that sb else has said or written before: *She quoted a line from a poem.* ◇ *The minister asked the newspaper not to quote him.* **2** [T] to give sth as an example to support what you are saying ◯ note at **mention 3** [T, I] (**BUSINESS**) to say what the cost of a piece of work, etc. will be

quote² ⒤ **B1** Ⓢ /kwəʊt/ (*also formal* **quotation**) *noun* **1** [C] ~ **(from sth/sb)** (**LITERATURE**) a phrase from a book, speech, play, etc. that sb repeats because it is interesting or useful: *a quote from Shakespeare* **2** [C] (**BUSINESS**) = QUOTATION (2) **3 quotes** [pl.] (*informal*) (**LANGUAGE**) = QUOTATION MARKS: *If you take text from other sources, place it in* **quotes**.

quotient /ˈkwəʊʃnt/ *noun* [C] (**MATHEMATICS**) a number that is the result when one number is divided by another ◯ look at **IQ**

the Qurˈan /ðə kəˈrɑːn/ = KORAN

R r

R /ɑː(r)/ (*also* **r**) *noun* [C, U] (*pl.* **R's, r's**) the 18th letter of the English alphabet: *'Rabbit' begins with an 'R'.*

rabbi /ˈræbaɪ/ *noun* [C] (*pl.* **rabbis**) (**RELIGION**) a Jewish religious leader and teacher of Jewish law

rabbit /ˈræbɪt/ *noun* [C] a small animal with long ears: *a wild rabbit* ◇ *a rabbit hutch* (= a CAGE for rabbits) ◯ picture at **food web**

ˈrabbit warren *noun* [C] **1** a system of holes and underground tunnels where wild RABBITS live **2** a building or part of a city with many narrow passages or streets

rabble /ˈræbl/ *noun* [C] a noisy crowd of people who are or may become violent

rabies /ˈreɪbiːz/ *noun* [U] (**HEALTH**) a very dangerous disease that a person can get if they are bitten by an animal that has the disease

race¹ ⒤ **A2** Ⓦ /reɪs/ *noun* **1** [C] ~ **(against/with sb/sth)**; ~ **for sth/to do sth** a competition between people, animals, cars, etc. to see which is the fastest or to see which can achieve sth first: *to run/win/lose a race* ◇ *to come first/second/last* **in a race** ◇ *Rescuing victims of the earthquake is now* **a race against time**. ◇ *the race for the presidency* **2 the races** [pl.] (*BrE*) (**SPORT**) an occasion when a number of horse races are held in one place **3** [C, U] (**SOCIAL STUDIES**) one of the groups into which people can be divided according to their physical differences, for example the colour of their skin ◯ look at **human race 4** [C] (**SOCIAL STUDIES**) a group of people who have the same language, customs, history, etc.
IDM **the rat race** → RAT

race² ⒤ **A2** /reɪs/ *verb* **1** [I, T] ~ **(against/with sb/sth)**; ~ **sb/sth** to have a competition with sb/sth to find out who is the fastest or to see who can do sth first: *Who will he be racing against in the next round?* ◇ *I'll race you home.* **2** [I, T] (often used with an adverb or a preposition) to go very fast or to move sb/sth very fast: *We raced up the stairs.* ◇ *The child had to be raced to hospital.* **3** [T] (**SPORT**) to make an animal or a vehicle take part in a race

racecourse /ˈreɪskɔːs/ (*BrE*) (*AmE* **racetrack**) *noun* [C] (**SPORT**) a place where horse races take place

racehorse /ˈreɪshɔːs/ *noun* [C] (**SPORT**) a horse that is trained to run in races

racer /ˈreɪsə(r)/ *noun* [C] (**SPORT**) a person or an animal that competes in races; a vehicle designed for racing

ˌrace reˈlations *noun* [pl.] the relationships between people belonging to different human groups who live in the same town, area, etc.

racetrack /ˈreɪstræk/ *noun* [C] **1** (**SPORT**) a track for races between runners, cars, bicycles, etc. **2** (*AmE*) = RACECOURSE

racial ⒤+ **B2** /ˈreɪʃl/ *adj.* [only before noun] connected with the human groups that people belong to; happening between people who belong to different human groups: *racial tension/discrimination* ▶ **racially** /-ʃəli/ *adv.*: *a racially mixed school*

racing ⒤ **B1** /ˈreɪsɪŋ/ *noun* [U] **1** = HORSE RACING **2** (**SPORT**) the sport of taking part in races: *motor racing* ◇ *a racing driver/car*

racism ⒤+ **B2** /ˈreɪsɪzəm/ *noun* [U] (**SOCIAL STUDIES**) the belief that some human groups are better than others; unfair ways of treating people that show this belief: *to take measures to combat racism* ▶ **racist** ⒤+ **B2** /-sɪst/ *noun* [C], *adj.*: *He's a racist.* ◇ *racist beliefs/views/remarks*

rack¹ /ræk/ *noun* [C] (often in compounds) a piece of equipment, usually made of bars, that you can put things in or on: *I got on the train and put my bags up in the luggage rack.* ◇ *a wine/plate/toast rack* ◯ picture at **laboratory**
IDM **go to rack and ruin** to be in or get into a bad state because of a lack of care

rack² /ræk/ *verb*
IDM **rack your brains** to try hard to think of sth or remember sth

racket /ˈrækɪt/ *noun* **1** [sing.] (*informal*) a loud noise: *Stop making that terrible racket!* **2** [C] (*informal*) (**LAW**) an illegal way of making money: *a drugs racket* **3** (*also* **racquet** /ˈrækɪt/) [C] (**SPORT**) a piece of sports equipment that you use to hit the ball with in sports such as tennis and BADMINTON ⊃ picture at **sport**

racy /ˈreɪsi/ *adj.* (**racier**; **raciest**) (used especially about speech and writing) having a style that is exciting and fun, sometimes in a way that is connected with sex: *a racy novel*

radar ⚓+ 🔵 /ˈreɪdɑː(r)/ *noun* [U] a system that uses radio waves for finding the position of moving objects, for example ships and planes: *This plane is hard to detect by radar.* ⊃ look at **sonar**

ˈradar trap = SPEED TRAP

radial /ˈreɪdiəl/ *adj.* having a pattern of lines, etc. that go out from a central point towards the edge of a circle

radiant /ˈreɪdiənt/ *adj.* **1** showing great happiness: *a radiant smile* **2** sending out light or heat from a central point: *the radiant heat/energy of the sun* ⊃ picture at **energy**

radiate /ˈreɪdieɪt/ *verb* **1** [T, I] ~ **(from sb)** (used about people) to clearly show a particular quality or emotion in your appearance or behaviour: *She radiated self-confidence in the interview.* ◇ *the energy that seemed to radiate from her* **2** [T, I] (**PHYSICS**) to send out light or heat **3** [I] ~ **(from sth)** to go out in all directions from a central point: *Narrow streets radiate from the village square.*

radiation ⚓+ 🔵🔵 /ˌreɪdiˈeɪʃn/ *noun* [U] **1** (**CHEMISTRY, PHYSICS**) powerful and very dangerous RAYS that are sent out from certain substances. You cannot see or feel radiation, but it can cause serious illness or death. ⊃ look at **radioactive 2** (**PHYSICS**) heat, light or energy that is sent out from sth: *solar radiation* ⊃ picture at **climate change 3** (**MEDICINE**) (*also* ˌradiation ˈtherapy) the treatment of cancer and other diseases using radiation ⊃ look at **chemotherapy, radiotherapy**

radiator /ˈreɪdieɪtə(r)/ *noun* [C] **1** a piece of equipment that is usually fixed to the wall and is used for heating a room. Radiators are made of metal and filled with hot water. **2** a piece of equipment that is used for keeping a vehicle engine cool

radical¹ ⚓+ 🔵 /ˈrædɪkl/ *adj.* **1** (used about changes in sth) very great; complete: *The tax system needs radical reform.* ◇ *radical change* **2** wanting great social or political change: *to have radical views* ⊃ look at **moderate¹** (2) ⊃ look at **extreme** (3) ▶ **radically** /-kli/ *adv.*: *The First World War radically altered the political map of Europe.*

radical² /ˈrædɪkl/ *noun* [C] a person who wants great social or political change ⊃ look at **extremist, moderate³**

radicalism /ˈrædɪkəlɪzəm/ *noun* [U] (**POLITICS**) belief that extreme and complete political and social change is necessary ▶ **radicalist** /-lɪst/ *adj.*

radii /ˈreɪdiaɪ/ plural of **radius**

radio ⚓ 🔵 /ˈreɪdiəʊ/ *noun* (*pl.* -os) **1** (*often* the radio) [U, sing.] (**ARTS AND MEDIA**) the activity of sending out programmes for people to listen to; the programmes that are sent out: *I always listen to the radio in the car.* ◇ *I heard an interesting report on the radio this morning.* ◇ *a radio station/programme* ◇ *national/local radio* ⊃ look at **media** (1) **2** [C] a piece of equipment that is used for receiving and/or sending radio messages or programmes (on a ship, plane, etc. or in your house) **3** [U] the sending or receiving of messages through the air by electrical signals: *to keep in radio contact* ◇ *radio signals/waves* ▶ **radio** *verb* [I, T] (**radioing**; **radioes**; *pt, pp* **radioed**)

radio- /ˈreɪdiəʊ, ˌreɪdiˈɒ/ *prefix* (in nouns, adjectives and adverbs) **1** connected with radio waves or BROADCASTING: *a radio-controlled car* **2** (**PHYSICS**) connected with RADIOACTIVITY: *radiographer*

radioactive /ˌreɪdiəʊˈæktɪv/ *adj.* (**CHEMISTRY, PHYSICS**) sending out powerful and very dangerous energy that is produced when ATOMS are broken up. This energy cannot be seen or felt but can cause serious illness or death: *the problem of the disposal of radioactive waste from power stations* ⊃ look at **radiation** (1) ▶ **radioactivity** /ˌreɪdiəʊækˈtɪvəti/ *noun* [U]

radiocarbon dating /ˌreɪdiəʊkɑːbən ˈdeɪtɪŋ/ = CARBON DATING

radiographer /ˌreɪdiˈɒɡrəfə(r)/ *noun* [C] (**MEDICINE**) a person in a hospital who is trained to take X-RAYS (= pictures of the inside of the body) or to use X-RAYS for the treatment of certain illnesses

radiology /ˌreɪdiˈɒlədʒi/ *noun* [U] (**MEDICINE**) the study and use of different types of RADIATION in medicine, for example to treat diseases

radiotherapy /ˌreɪdiəʊˈθerəpi/ *noun* [U] (**MEDICINE**) the treatment of disease by RADIATION (= powerful and very dangerous energy that comes from some substances when they start to break down): *a course of radiotherapy* ⊃ look at **chemotherapy** ▶ **radiotherapist** /-pɪst/ *noun* [C]

ˈradio wave *noun* [C] (**PHYSICS**) a low-energy ELECTROMAGNETIC wave, used especially for LONG-DISTANCE communication ⊃ picture at **wavelength**

radish /ˈrædɪʃ/ *noun* [C] a small red vegetable that is white inside with a strong taste. You eat radishes in salads.

radium /ˈreɪdiəm/ *noun* [U] (*symb.* Ra) (**CHEMISTRY**) a chemical element. Radium is a white RADIOACTIVE metal used in the treatment of some serious diseases. ❶ For more information on the periodic table of elements, look at the **Reference Section** of this dictionary.

radius /ˈreɪdiəs/ *noun* [C] (*pl.* radii /-diaɪ/) **1** (**GEOMETRY**) the distance from the centre of a circle to the outside edge ⊃ look at **circumference, diameter** ⊃ picture at **circle¹** **2** a round area that is measured from a point in its centre: *The wreckage of the plane was scattered over a radius of several miles.* **3** (**ANATOMY**) the shorter bone of the two bones in the lower part of the arm between the WRIST and the ELBOW ⊃ look at **ulna** ⊃ picture at **body**

radon /ˈreɪdɒn/ *noun* [U] (*symb.* Rn) (**CHEMISTRY**) a chemical element. Radon is a RADIOACTIVE gas used in the treatment of diseases such as cancer. ❶ For more information on the periodic table of elements, look at the **Reference Section** of this dictionary.

RAF /ˌɑːr eɪ ˈef, ræf/ *abbr.* (*BrE*) **Royal Air Force** (the part of Britain's armed forces that fights using aircraft)

raffle /ˈræfl/ *noun* [C] a way of making money for a charity or a project by selling tickets with numbers on them. Later some numbers are chosen and the tickets with these numbers on them win prizes.

raft /rɑːft/ *noun* [C] **1** a flat structure made of pieces of wood tied together and used as a boat or a floating platform **2** a small boat made of rubber or plastic that is filled with air: *an inflatable raft*

rafter /ˈrɑːftə(r)/ *noun* [C] one of the long pieces of wood that support a roof

rafting /ˈrɑːftɪŋ/ *noun* [U] (**SPORT**) the sport or activity of travelling down a river on a RAFT: *We went white-water rafting on the Colorado River.*

rag /ræg/ *noun* **1** [C, U] a small piece of old cloth that you use for cleaning **2** rags [pl.] clothes that are very old and torn

raga /ˈrɑːɡə/ *noun* [C] (**MUSIC**) a traditional pattern of notes used in Indian music; a piece of music based on one of these patterns

rage¹ ⬥+ **C1** /reɪdʒ/ *noun* [U, C] a feeling of violent anger that is difficult to control: *He was trembling with rage.* ◊ *to fly into a rage*

rage² /reɪdʒ/ *verb* [I] **1** ~ (at/against/about sb/sth) to show great anger about sth, especially by shouting: *He raged against the injustice of it all.* **2** (used about a battle, disease, storm, etc.) to continue with great force: *The battle raged for several days.* ➔ note at **disaster** ▸ **raging** *adj.* [only before noun]: *a raging headache*

ragged /ˈræɡɪd/ *adj.* **1** (used about clothes) old and torn **2** not straight; untidy: *a ragged edge/coastline*

ragtime /ˈræɡtaɪm/ *noun* [U] (**MUSIC**) an early form of jazz, especially for the piano, first played by African American musicians in the early 1900s

raid ⬥+ **C1** /reɪd/ *noun* [C] ~ (on sth) **1** a short surprise attack on an enemy by soldiers, ships or aircraft: *an air raid on London* **2** (**LAW**) a surprise visit by the police looking for criminals or illegal goods: *Drugs were found during a police raid on the nightclub.* **3** a surprise attack on a building in order to steal sth: *a bank raid* ◊ *Two customers foiled a raid on a local post office.* ▸ **raid** ⬥+ **C1** *verb* [T]: *Police raided the club at dawn this morning.*

rail ⬥+ **B2** /reɪl/ *noun* **1** [C] a wooden or metal bar placed round sth to stop you falling **2** [C] a bar fixed to a wall for hanging things on: *a towel/curtain/picture rail* **3** [C, usually pl.] each of the two metal bars that form the track that trains run on **4** [U] the railway system; trains as a means of transport: *rail travel/services/fares*

railcard /ˈreɪlkɑːd/ *noun* [C] (*BrE*) a special card that allows you to buy train tickets at a lower price if you are an old person, a student, etc.

railing /ˈreɪlɪŋ/ *noun* [C, usually pl.] a fence (around a park, garden, etc.) made of metal bars that go straight upwards

railroad crossing (*AmE*) = LEVEL CROSSING

railway ⬥ **A2** /ˈreɪlweɪ/ (*BrE*) (*AmE* **railroad** /ˈreɪlrəʊd/) *noun* [C] **1** (*BrE also* **railway line**) the metal lines on which trains travel between one place and another **2** the whole system of tracks, the trains and the organization and people needed to operate them: *He works on the railways.* ◊ *a railway engine/company*

railway station = STATION¹ (1)

rain¹ ⬥ **A1** /reɪn/ *noun* **1** [U] the water that falls from the sky: *Take your umbrella, it looks like rain* (= as if it is going to rain). ◊ *It's pouring with rain* (= the rain is very heavy). ➔ look at **acid rain, shower¹** (3) ➔ note at **water¹, weather¹** ➔ picture at **erosion, water cycle** **2** rains [pl.] (in tropical countries) the time of the year when there is a lot of rain: *The rains come in July.* **IDM (come) rain or shine** even if the weather is bad or the conditions are difficult; whatever happens **(as) right as rain** → RIGHT¹

rain² ⬥ **A1** /reɪn/ *verb* **1** [I] when it rains, water falls from the sky in drops: *Oh no! It's raining again! ◊ Is it raining hard?* ◊ *We'll go out when it stops raining.* **2** [I, T] ~ (sth) (down) (on sb/sth) to fall or make sth fall on sb/sth in large quantities: *Bombs rained down on the city.*

PHR V be rained off to be cancelled or to have to stop because it is raining

rainbow /ˈreɪnbəʊ/ *noun* [C] a curved band of many colours that sometimes appears in the sky when the sun shines through rain

rain check *noun* (*especially AmE*) **IDM take a rain check on sth** (*informal*) to refuse an invitation or offer but say that you might accept it later

raincoat /ˈreɪnkəʊt/ *noun* [C] a long light coat that keeps you dry in the rain

raindrop /ˈreɪndrɒp/ *noun* [C] a single drop of rain

rainfall /ˈreɪnfɔːl/ *noun* [U, C] (**GEOGRAPHY**) the total amount of rain that falls in a particular place during a month, year, etc.

rainforest /ˈreɪnfɒrɪst/ *noun* [C] (**GEOGRAPHY**) a thick forest in tropical parts of the world that have a lot of rain: *the Amazon rainforest* ➔ picture at **ecosystem**

rainwater /ˈreɪnwɔːtə(r)/ *noun* [U] water that has fallen as rain

rainy /ˈreɪni/ *adj.* (rainier; rainiest) having or bringing a lot of rain: *a rainy day* ◊ *floods during the rainy season* **IDM keep/save sth for a rainy day** to save sth, especially money, for a time when you really need it

raise¹ ⬥ **A2** /reɪz/ *verb* [T]
• MOVE UPWARDS **1** to lift sth/sb/yourself up: *If you want to leave the room raise your hand.* ◊ *He raised himself up on one elbow.* **OPP lower²**
• INCREASE **2** ~ sth (to sth) to increase the level of sth or to make sth better or stronger: *to raise taxes/salaries/prices* ◊ *The hotel needs to raise its standards.* ◊ *They raised their offer to £900.* **OPP lower²** ➔ note at **price¹**
• COLLECT MONEY **3** to get money from people for a particular purpose: *We are doing a sponsored walk to raise money for charity.* ◊ *a fund-raising event*
• INTRODUCE A TOPIC **4** to introduce a subject that needs to be talked about or dealt with: *I would like to raise the subject of money.* ◊ *This raises the question of why nothing was done before.* ➔ note at **opinion**
• CAUSE **5** to cause a particular reaction or emotion: *The neighbours raised the alarm* (= told everybody there was a fire/an emergency) *when they saw smoke.* ◊ *to raise doubts/fears/suspicions in people's minds*
• CHILD/ANIMAL **6** to look after a child or an animal until they are an adult: *You can't raise a family on what I earn.* ➔ look at **bring sb up** at **bring 7** to BREED (= keep and produce young from) animals or grow a particular plant for a special purpose **IDM raise the bar** to set a new, higher standard of quality or performance: *The factory has raised the bar on productivity.* **raise your eyebrows** to show that you are surprised or that you do not approve of sth

raise² /reɪz/ *noun* [C] (*AmE*) = RISE¹ (2)

raisin /ˈreɪzn/ *noun* [C] a dried GRAPE, used in cakes, etc. ➔ look at **sultana**

the Raj /ðə ˈrɑːdʒ, ˈrɑːʒ/ *noun* [sing.] (**HISTORY**) British rule in India before 1947

rake¹ /reɪk/ *noun* [C] (**AGRICULTURE**) a garden tool with a long handle and a row of metal teeth, used for collecting leaves or making the earth smooth ➔ picture at **gardening**

rake² /reɪk/ *verb* [T] to pull a RAKE over a surface in order to make it level or to remove sth: *to rake up the leaves* **PHR V rake sth in** (*informal*) to earn a lot of money, especially when it is done easily: *She's been raking it in since she got promoted.* **rake sth up** to start talking about sth that it would be better to forget: *Don't rake up all those old stories again.*

rallentando /ˌrælən'tændəʊ/ noun [C, U] (pl. -os) (MUSIC) a time in a piece of music when it gradually slows down

rally¹ ℃+ **C1** /'ræli/ noun (pl. -ies) **1** [C] (POLITICS) a large public meeting, especially one held to support a political idea **2** [C] (SPORT) a race for cars or motorcycles on public roads **3** [C] (SPORT) (used in tennis and similar sports) a series of hits of the ball before a point is won **4** [sing.] (BUSINESS, SPORT) an act of returning to a strong position after a period of difficulty or weakness: *After a furious late rally, they finally scored.* ◇ *a rally in shares on the stock market* **SYN** **recovery**

rally² ℃+ **C1** /'ræli/ verb (rallying; rallies; pt, pp rallied) **1** [I, T] ~ (sb/sth) (around/behind/to sb) to come together or to bring people together in order to help or support sb/sth: *The cabinet rallied behind the prime minister.* **2** [I] to get stronger, healthier, etc. after an illness or a period of weakness **SYN** **recover** **PHR V** **rally around | rally around sb** (*also* rally round, rally round sb *especially in BrE*) to come together to help sb: *When I was in trouble my family all rallied round.*

RAM /ræm/ abbr. (COMPUTING) **random-access memory** (computer memory in which data can be changed or removed and can be looked at in any order): *32 megabytes of RAM* ➔ look at **ROM**

ram¹ /ræm/ noun [C] a male sheep ➔ note at **sheep** ➔ picture at **sheep**

ram² /ræm/ verb [T] (-mm-) to crash into sth or push sth with great force

Ramadan /'ræmədæn/ noun [U, C] (RELIGION) the ninth month of the Muslim year, when Muslims do not eat or drink anything from when light first appears in the sky in the morning to when the sun goes down in the evening ➔ look at **Eid**

ramble¹ /'ræmbl/ verb [I] **1** (*especially BrE*) to walk in the countryside for pleasure: *to go rambling* **2** ~ (on) (about sth) to talk for a long time in a confused way: *What is she rambling on about now?*

ramble² /'ræmbl/ noun [C] (*especially BrE*) a long walk in the country for pleasure

rambler /'ræmblə(r)/ noun [C] **1** (*especially BrE*) a person who walks in the countryside for pleasure, especially as part of an organized group **2** a plant that grows up walls, fences, etc.

rambling /'ræmblɪŋ/ adj. **1** (used about a building) spreading in many directions: *a rambling old house* **2** (used about speech or writing) very long and confused

ramp /ræmp/ noun [C] **1** a slope that joins two parts of a road, path, building, etc. when one is higher than the other: *There are ramps at both entrances for wheelchair access.* **2** (*AmE*) = SLIP ROAD: *a freeway exit ramp*

rampage¹ /ræm'peɪdʒ, 'ræmpeɪdʒ/ verb [I] to move through a place in a violent group, usually breaking things and attacking people: *The football fans rampaged through the town.*

rampage² /'ræmpeɪdʒ/ noun **IDM** **be/go on the rampage** to move through a place in a violent group, usually breaking things and attacking people

rampant /'ræmpənt/ adj. (used about sth bad) existing or spreading everywhere in a way that is very difficult to control: *Car theft is rampant in this town.*

ramshackle /'ræmʃækl/ adj. (usually used about a building) old and needing repair

ran /ræn/ past tense of **run¹**

ranch /rɑːntʃ/ noun [C] (AGRICULTURE) a large farm, especially in the US or Australia, where cows, horses, sheep, etc. are kept

rancid /'rænsɪd/ adj. if food containing fat is **rancid**, it tastes or smells unpleasant because it is no longer fresh: *rancid butter*

R & B /ˌɑːr ən 'biː/ abbr. = RHYTHM AND BLUES

R & D /ˌɑːr ən 'diː/ abbr. = RESEARCH AND DEVELOPMENT

random ℃+ **B2** ◐ /'rændəm/ adj. **1** happening or chosen by chance: *For the opinion poll they interviewed a random selection of people in the street.* **2** (*informal*) a thing or a person that is **random** is strange and does not make sense, often in a way that makes you laugh or interests you **3** [only before noun] (*informal*) not known or not identified: *Some random guy came up and started talking to me.* ▸ **randomly** ◓ adv. **IDM** **at random** without thinking or deciding in advance what is going to happen: *The competitors were chosen at random from the audience.*

random-access memory = RAM

randomize ◓ (*BrE also* -ise) /'rændəmaɪz/ verb [T] (SCIENCE) to use a method in an experiment or a piece of research that gives every item an equal chance of being considered; to put things in an order that is chosen by chance

rang /ræŋ/ past tense of **ring²**

range¹ **B1** ◐ /reɪndʒ/ noun **1** [C, usually sing.] ~ (of sth) a variety of things that belong to the same group: *The course will cover a whole range of topics.* ◇ *This shop has a very wide range of clothes.* **2** [C] the limits between which sth can vary: *That car is outside my price range.* ◇ *I don't think this game is suitable for all age ranges.* **3** [C, U] the distance that it is possible for sb/sth to travel, see, hear, etc: *The gunman shot the policeman at close range.* ◇ *They can pick up signals at a range of 400 metres.* ◇ *Keep out of range of the cameras.* **4** [C] (GEOGRAPHY) a line of mountains or hills **5** [C] (MATHEMATICS) the difference between the largest and smallest number in a set. To find the range, take away the lowest number from the highest number in the set. **6** [C] (*AmE*) = COOKER

range² **B2** ◒ /reɪndʒ/ verb [I] **1** ~ between A and B; ~ from A to B to vary between two amounts, sizes, etc., including all those between them: *Estimates range between £1m and £2m.* ◇ *The ages of the students range from 15 to 50.* **2** ~ (from A to B) to include a variety of things in addition to those mentioned: *She's had a number of different jobs, ranging from chef to swimming instructor.*

ranger /'reɪndʒə(r)/ noun [C] a person whose job is to take care of a park, a forest or an area of the countryside

rank¹ **B2** /ræŋk/ noun **1** [U, C] the position, especially a high position, that sb has in an organization such as the army, or in society: *General is one of the highest ranks in the army.* ◇ *She's much higher in rank than I am.* **2** the ranks [pl.] the ordinary soldiers in the army; the members of any large group: *At the age of 43, he was forced to join the ranks of the unemployed.* **3** [C] a group or line of things or people: *a taxi rank* **IDM** **the rank and file** the ordinary soldiers in the army; the ordinary members of an organization

rank² ℃ **B2** /ræŋk/ verb [I, T] ~ (sb/sth) (as sth) (not used in the progressive tenses) to give sb/sth a particular position on a scale according to importance, quality, success, etc.; to have a position of this kind: *She's ranked as one of the world's top*

players. ◇ *a high-ranking police officer*
▶ **ranking** Ⓔ+ **C1** *noun* [C]: *She has retained her No.1 world ranking.*

ransack /'rænsæk/ *verb* [T] to make a mess in a place, causing damage, because you are looking for sth: *The house had been ransacked by burglars.*

ransom /'rænsəm/ *noun* [C, U] the money that you must pay to free sb who has been captured illegally and who is being kept as a prisoner: *The kidnappers demanded a ransom of $500 000 for the boy's release.*
IDM **hold sb to ransom** (**LAW**) to keep sb as a prisoner and say that you will not free them until you have received a certain amount of money ⊃ look at **hostage** ⊃ note at **criminal**[1]

rant /rænt/ *verb* [I] ~ **(on) (about sth)** to speak or complain about sth in a loud or angry way ▶ **rant** *noun* [C]

rap[1] /ræp/ *noun* **1** [C] a quick, sharp hit or knock on a door, window, etc: *There was a sharp rap on the door.* **2** [U, C] (**MUSIC**) a style or a piece of music with a fast strong rhythm, in which the words are spoken fast, not sung ⊃ look at **rapper**

rap[2] /ræp/ *verb* (-pp-) **1** [I, T] to hit a hard object or surface several times quickly and lightly, making a noise: *She rapped angrily on/at the door.* **2** [T] (used mainly in newspaper headlines) to criticize sb strongly: *Minister raps police over rise in crime* **3** [I] (**MUSIC**) to speak the words of a RAP

rape[1] Ⓔ+ **C1** /reɪp/ *verb* [T] (**LAW**) to force a person to have sex when they do not want to, using threats or violence

rape[2] Ⓔ+ **C1** /reɪp/ *noun* **1** [U, C] (**LAW**) the crime of forcing sb to have sex when they do not want to: *to commit rape* **2** [sing.] ~ **(of sth)** (*formal*) the act of destroying sth beautiful: *the rape of the countryside* **3** (*also* oilseed rape) [U] (**AGRICULTURE**) a plant with bright yellow flowers, that farmers grow as food for farm animals and for its seeds that are used to make oil: *a field of rape* ◇ *rape oil/seed*

rapeseed /'reɪpsiːd/ *noun* [U] seeds of the RAPE plant, used mainly for cooking oil

rapid Ⓔ **B2** Ⓦ /'ræpɪd/ *adj.* happening very quickly or moving with great speed: *She made rapid progress and was soon the best in the class.* ▶ **rapidity** /rə'pɪdəti/ *noun* [U] (*formal*): *The rapidity of change has astonished most people.* ▶ **rapidly** Ⓔ **B2** Ⓞ *adv.*

rapids /'ræpɪdz/ *noun* [pl.] (**GEOGRAPHY**) a part of a river where the water flows very fast over rocks

rapist /'reɪpɪst/ *noun* [C] (**LAW**) a person who forces sb to have sex when they do not want to ⊃ look at **rape**[1]

rappel /ræ'pel/ (*AmE*) = ABSEIL

rapper /'ræpə(r)/ *noun* [C] a person who performs a RAP (= a piece of music with a strong fast rhythm, in which the words are spoken, not sung)

rapport /ræ'pɔː(r)/ *noun* [sing., U] **(a)** ~ **(with sb)**; **(a)** ~ **(between A and B)** a friendly relationship in which people understand each other very well: *She has established a close rapport with clients.* ◇ *Honesty is essential if there is to be good rapport between patient and therapist.*

rapt /ræpt/ *adj.* (*formal*) so interested in one particular thing that you do not notice anything else: *a rapt audience* ◇ *She listened to the speaker with rapt attention.*

rapture /'ræptʃə(r)/ *noun* [U] a feeling of extreme happiness

IDM **go into raptures (about/over sb/sth)** to feel and show that you think that sb/sth is very good: *I didn't like the film much but my boyfriend went into raptures about it.*

rapturous /'ræptʃərəs/ *adj.* expressing extreme pleasure or enthusiasm for sb/sth: *rapturous applause*

rare Ⓔ **B1** /reə(r)/ *adj.* **1** ~ **(for sb/sth to do sth)**; ~ **(to do sth)** not done, seen, happening, etc. very often: *a rare bird/flower/plant* ◇ *It was rare for her to go out alone.* ◇ *It's rare to find such loyalty these days.* **2** (used about meat) not cooked for very long so that the inside is still red: *a rare steak* ⊃ look at **medium**[1] (2), **well done**

rarefied /'reərɪfaɪd/ *adj.* **1** understood or experienced by only a very small group of people who share a particular area of knowledge or activity **2** (**ENVIRONMENT**) (used about air) containing less OXYGEN than usual: *Climbers may experience difficulty breathing in the rarefied air at high altitudes.*

rarely Ⓔ **B1** /'reəli/ *adv.* not very often: *People rarely live to be 100 years old.* ◇ *She is rarely seen in public nowadays.*

raring /'reərɪŋ/ *adj.* ~ **to do sth** wanting to start doing sth very much: *They were raring to try out the new computer.*

rarity /'reərəti/ *noun* (*pl.* -ies) **1** [C] a thing or a person that is unusual and is therefore often valuable or interesting: *His collection of plants contains many rarities.* **2** [U] the quality of being rare: *The rarity of this stamp increases its value a lot.*

rascal /'rɑːskl/ *noun* [C] a person, especially a child or man, who shows a lack of respect for other people and enjoys playing tricks on them

rash[1] /ræʃ/ *noun* **1** [C, usually sing.] (**HEALTH**) an area of small red spots that appear on the skin when you are ill or have a reaction to sth: *He came out in a rash where the plant had touched him.* **2** [sing.] ~ **(of sth)** a series of unpleasant events of the same kind happening over a short period of time

rash[2] /ræʃ/ *adj.* (used about people) doing things that might be dangerous or bad without thinking about the possible results first; (used about actions) done in this way: *a rash decision/promise* ▶ **rashly** *adv.*

rasher /'ræʃə(r)/ *noun* [C] (*especially BrE*) a slice of BACON (= meat from a pig)

raspberry /'rɑːzbəri/ *noun* [C] (*pl.* -ies) a small, soft, red fruit that grows on bushes: *raspberry jam*

rasterize (*BrE also* -ise) /'ræstəraɪz/ (*also* rip) *verb* [T] (**COMPUTING**) to change text or images into a form in which they can be displayed on a screen or printed

rat Ⓔ+ **B2** /ræt/ *noun* [C] an animal like a large mouse
IDM **rat race** the way of life in which everyone is only interested in being better or more successful than everyone else

ratatouille /ˌrætə'tuːi, -'twiː/ *noun* [U, C] a dish of onions, peppers, AUBERGINES, COURGETTES and tomatoes cooked together

ratchet /'rætʃɪt/ *noun* [C] a wheel or bar with teeth along the edge and a metal piece that fits between the teeth, allowing movement in one direction only

ratchet

rate[1] Ⓔ **A2** Ⓞ /reɪt/ *noun* [C] **1** ~ **(of sth)** a measurement of the speed at which sth happens or the number of times sth happens or exists during a particular

period: *the rate of inflation* ◇ *The population is increasing at the rate of less than 0.5% a year.* ◇ *The birth rate* (= the number of children born each year) *is falling.* ◇ *The death rate from lung cancer is far higher among smokers.* ◇ *an exchange rate of one pound to 1.5 dollars* **2** (**FINANCE**) a fixed amount of money that sth costs or that sb is paid: *The basic rate of pay is £10 an hour.* ◇ *We offer special reduced rates for students.* ⊃ look at **first-rate, second-rate** ⊃ note at **mortgage**[1]
IDM **at any rate** (*informal*) **1** whatever else might happen: *Well, that's one good piece of news at any rate.* **2** used when you are giving more exact information about sth: *He said that they would be here by ten. At any rate, I think that's what he said.* **the going rate (for sth)** → GOING[2]

rate[2] 🔒 **B2** 🔊 /reɪt/ *verb* (not used in the progressive tenses) **1** [T, I] **~ (sb/sth) (as) (sth)** to say how good you think sb/sth is: *She's among the best tennis players of all time.* ◇ *The match rated as one of their worst defeats.* **2** [T] to be good, important, etc. enough to be treated in a particular way: *The accident wasn't very serious — it didn't rate a mention in the local newspaper.*

rather 🔒 **A2** 🔊 /ˈrɑːðə(r)/ *adv.* quite; to some extent: *It was a rather nice day.* ◇ *It was rather a nice day.* ◇ *It cost rather a lot of money.* ◇ *I was rather hoping that you'd be free on Friday.*
IDM **or rather** used as a way of correcting sth you have said, or making it more exact: *She lives in London, or rather she lives in a suburb of London.* **rather than** instead of; in place of: *I think I'll just have a sandwich rather than a full meal.* **would rather … (than)** would prefer to: *I'd rather go to the cinema than watch TV.*

▼ SYNONYMS

rather

fairly • quite • pretty

These words can all mean 'to some extent'. **Rather** and **pretty** (*informal*) are the strongest and **fairly** is the weakest.

Fairly and **quite** are mostly used with words that are positive.

Rather is used with a negative word when you are criticizing sb/sth. If you use **rather** with a positive word, it sounds as if you are surprised and pleased

rather *This room's rather untidy.* ◇ *The new teacher is actually rather nice, though he doesn't look very friendly.*

fairly *The car was fairly clean.*

quite *He plays the guitar quite well.*

pretty *The game was pretty good.*

ratify /ˈrætɪfaɪ/ *verb* [T] (**ratifying; ratifies;** *pt, pp* **ratified**) to make an agreement officially acceptable by voting for or signing it ▸ **ratification** /ˌrætɪfɪˈkeɪʃn/ *noun* [U]: *The agreement is subject to ratification by the Senate.*

rating 🔒 **B2** 🔊 /ˈreɪtɪŋ/ *noun* [C] **1** a measurement of how popular, important, good, etc. sth is **2** **the ratings** [pl.] a set of figures showing the number of people who watch a particular TV programme, etc., used to show how popular the programme is

ratio 🔒 **C1** 🔊 /ˈreɪʃiəʊ/ *noun* [C] (*pl.* -os) **~ (of A to B)** (**MATHEMATICS**) the relation between two numbers that shows how much bigger one quantity is than another: *The ratio of boys to girls in this class is three to one* (= there are three times as many boys as girls).

ration /ˈræʃn/ *noun* [C] a limited amount of food, petrol, etc. that you are allowed to have when there is not enough for everyone to have as much as they want
▸ **ration** *verb* [T]: *In the desert water is strictly rationed.*
▸ **rationing** /-ʃənɪŋ/ *noun* [U]

rational 🔒+ **C1** 🔊 /ˈræʃnəl/ *adj.* **1** (used about a person) able to use logical thought rather than emotions to make decisions **SYN** **reasonable** **2** based on reason; sensible or logical: *There must be a rational explanation for why he's behaving like this.*
OPP **irrational** ▸ **rationality** 🔊 /ˌræʃəˈnæləti/ *noun* [U]: *the rationality of his argument* ▸ **rationally** /ˈræʃnəli/ *adv.*

rationale 🔊 /ˌræʃəˈnɑːl/ *noun* [C] **~ (behind/for/of sth)** (*formal*) the principles or reasons that explain a particular decision, plan, belief, etc: *What is the rationale behind these new exams?* **SYN** **reasoning**

rationalism /ˈræʃnəlɪzəm/ *noun* [U] the belief that all behaviour, opinions, etc. should be based on reason rather than on emotions or religious beliefs

rationalize (*BrE also* -ise) /ˈræʃnəlaɪz/ *verb* [T, I] **1** to find reasons that explain why you have done sth (perhaps because you do not like the real reason) **2** (*BrE*) to make a business or a system better organized
▸ **rationalization** (*BrE also* -isation) /ˌræʃnəlaɪˈzeɪʃn/ *noun* [U, C]

rational number *noun* [C] (**MATHEMATICS**) a number that can be expressed as the RATIO of two whole numbers ⊃ look at **irrational number**

rattle[1] /ˈrætl/ *verb* [I, T] to make a noise like hard things hitting each other; to shake sth so that it makes this noise: *The windows were rattling all night in the wind.* ◇ *He rattled the money in the tin.* **2** [T] (*informal*) to make sb suddenly become worried: *The news of his arrival really rattled her.*
PHR V **rattle sth off** to say a list of things you have learned very quickly: *She rattled off the names of every player in the team.*

rattle[2] /ˈrætl/ *noun* [C] **1** a noise made by hard things hitting each other **2** a toy that a baby can shake to make a noise

rattlesnake /ˈrætlsneɪk/ *noun* [C] a poisonous American snake that makes a noise by moving the end of its tail quickly when it is angry or afraid

raucous /ˈrɔːkəs/ *adj.* (used about people's voices) loud and unpleasant

ravage /ˈrævɪdʒ/ *verb* [T] to damage sth very badly; to destroy sth

rave[1] /reɪv/ *verb* [I, T] **1** **~ (about sb/sth)** to say very good things about sb/sth: *Everyone's raving about her latest album!* **2** to speak angrily or in a wild way

rave[2] /reɪv/ *noun* [C] (*BrE*) (**MUSIC**) (in the UK) a large party held outside or in an empty building, at which people dance to fast electronic music

raven /ˈreɪvn/ *noun* [C] a large black bird of the CROW family that makes an unpleasant sound

ravenous /ˈrævənəs/ *adj.* very hungry ▸ **ravenously** *adv.*

rave review *noun* [C] (**ARTS AND MEDIA**) an article in a newspaper, etc. that says very good things about a new book, film, play, etc.

ravine /rəˈviːn/ *noun* [C] (**GEOGRAPHY**) a narrow deep valley with steep sides

raving /ˈreɪvɪŋ/ *adj.* [only before noun], *adv.* (used about a person) talking or behaving in a way that shows they are crazy: *The man's a raving lunatic.* ◇ *Have you gone raving mad?*

raw 🔒 **B2** 🔊 /rɔː/ *adj.* **1** not cooked: *Raw vegetables are good for your teeth.* ⊃ note at **meat** **2** in its natural state; not yet changed, used or made into sth else: *raw sugar* **3** (**HEALTH**) used about an injury where the skin has come off from being rubbed

raw ma'terial noun [C, U] (BUSINESS) a basic material that is used to make a product: *We have had problems with the supply of raw materials to the factory.* ◇ *These trees provide the raw material for high-quality paper.*

ray ⁱ+ **C1** /reɪ/ noun [C] (PHYSICS) a line of light, heat or energy: *the sun's rays* ◇ *ultraviolet rays* ⊃ look at **X-ray** ⊃ picture at **reflection, short-sighted**
IDM **a ray of hope** a small chance that things will get better

razor /'reɪzə(r)/ noun [C] a sharp instrument that people use to SHAVE (= cut off hair from their skin): *an electric razor* ◇ *a disposable razor*

'razor blade noun [C] the thin sharp piece of metal that you put in a RAZOR

Rd abbr. (in writing) = ROAD (2): *21 Hazel Rd*

RE /ɑːr 'iː/ noun [U] (EDUCATION, RELIGION) a school subject in which students learn about different religions (the abbreviation for 'religious education'): *an RE teacher*

re /riː/ prep. used at the beginning of a business letter, email, etc. to introduce the subject that it is about: *Re: travel expenses*

re- /riː/ prefix (in verbs, nouns, adjectives and adverbs) again: *rebuild* ◇ *reappearance*

reach¹ ⁱ **A2** **S** /riːtʃ/ verb **1** [T] to arrive at a place or condition that you have been going towards: *We won't reach home before twelve.* ◇ *The two sides hope to reach an agreement sometime today.* ◇ *Sometimes the temperature reaches 45°C.* ◇ *The team reached the semi-final last year.* ◇ *to reach a decision/conclusion/compromise* ⊃ note at **trend¹** **2** [I, T] (often used with an adverb or a preposition) to stretch out your arm to try and touch or get sth: *The child reached out for her mother.* ◇ *She reached into her bag for her purse.* **3** [I, T] to be able to touch sth: *Can you get me that book off the top shelf? I can't reach.* ◇ *I need a longer ladder. This one won't reach.* ◇ *He couldn't reach the light switch.* **4** [T] to communicate with sb, especially by phone; contact: *You can reach me on this number.*

reach² ⁱ **B2** /riːtʃ/ noun [U] the distance that you can stretch your arm
IDM **beyond/out of (sb's) reach 1** outside the distance that you can stretch your arm: *Keep this medicine out of the reach of children.* **2** not able to be got or done by sb: *A job like that is beyond his reach.* **within (sb's) reach 1** inside the distance that you can stretch your arm **2** able to be achieved by sb: *We were one goal ahead with ten minutes left and so could sense that victory was within our reach.* **within (easy) reach of sth** not far from sth

react ⁱ **A2** **S** /riˈækt/ verb [I] **1** ~ (to sth) (by doing sth) to do or say sth because of sth that has happened or been said: *He reacted to the news by jumping up and down and shouting.* ◇ *The players reacted angrily to the decision.* **2** ~ (to sth) (HEALTH) to become ill after eating, breathing, etc. a particular substance: *He reacted badly to the drug and had to go to hospital.* **3** ~ (with sth/together) (CHEMISTRY) (used about a chemical substance) to change after coming into contact with another substance: *Iron reacts with water and air to produce rust.*
PHRV **react against sb/sth** to behave or talk in a way that shows that you do not like the influence of sb/sth (for example authority, your family, etc.)

reactant /riˈæktənt/ noun [C] (CHEMISTRY) a substance that takes part in and is changed by a chemical reaction

reaction ⁱ **B1** **O** /riˈækʃn/ noun
• TO AN EVENT **1** [C, U] ~ (to sb/sth) something that you do or say because of sth that has happened: *Could we have your reaction to the latest news, Prime Minister?* ◇ *I shook him to try and wake him up but there was no reaction.*
• TO AN INFLUENCE **2** [C, U] ~ (against sb/sth) behaviour that shows that you do not like the influence of sb/sth (for example authority, your family, etc.): *Her strange clothes are a reaction against the conservative way she was brought up.*
• TO FOOD, DRUGS, ETC. **3** [C] ~ (to sth) (HEALTH) a bad effect that the body experiences because of sth that you have eaten, touched or breathed: *She had an allergic reaction to something in the food.*
• TO DANGER **4** [C, usually pl.] the physical ability to act quickly when sth happens: *If the other driver's reactions hadn't been so good, there would have been an accident.*
• IN CHEMISTRY **5** [C, U] a chemical change produced by two or more substances coming into contact with each other

reactionary /riˈækʃənri/ noun [C] (pl. -ies) (POLITICS, SOCIAL STUDIES) a person who tries to prevent political or social change ▸ **reactionary** adj.: *reactionary views/politics* ⊃ note at **government**

reactivate /riˈæktɪveɪt/ verb [T] to make sth start working or happening again after a period of time

reactive /riˈæktɪv/ adj. **1** (formal) showing a reaction or response ⊃ look at **proactive 2** (CHEMISTRY) having chemical characteristics that change when mixed with another substance **OPP** **unreactive**

reactivity /ˌriːækˈtɪvəti/ noun [U] (CHEMISTRY) the degree to which a substance shows chemical change when mixed with another substance

reactor /riˈæktə(r)/ = NUCLEAR REACTOR

read¹ ⁱ **A1** **S** /riːd/ verb (pt, pp read /red/) **1** [I, T] to look at words or symbols and understand them: *He never learnt to read and write.* ◇ *Have you read any good books lately?* ◇ *Can you read music?* **2** [I, T] to discover or find out about sb/sth by reading **3** [I, T] ~ (sb) (sth); ~ sth (to sb) to say written words to sb: *My father used to read me stories when I was a child.* ◇ *Read that sentence to me again, I didn't understand it.* ◇ *I hate reading out loud.* **4** [T] to be able to understand sth from what you can see: *A man came to read the gas meter.* ◇ *I've no idea what he'll say — I can't read his mind!* ◇ *Profoundly deaf people often learn to read lips.* **5** [T] to show words or a sign of sth: *The sign read 'Keep Left'.* **6** [T] (formal) (EDUCATION) to study a subject at university: *She read Modern Languages at Cambridge.*
PHRV **read sth into sth** to think that there is a meaning in sth that may not really be there **read on** to continue reading; to read the next part of sth **read sth out** to read sth to other people **read sth through** to read sth to check details or to look for mistakes: *I read my essay through a few times before handing it in.* **read up on sth** to find out a lot about a subject

read² /riːd/ noun [sing.] (informal) a period or the act of reading: *I generally have a quick read of the news headlines over breakfast.*

readable /'riːdəbl/ adj. **1** easy or interesting to read **2** able to be read: *machine-readable data* ⊃ look at **legible**

reader ⁱ **A1** /'riːdə(r)/ noun [C] **1** (often after an adjective) a person who reads a lot or in a particular way: *a fast/slow reader* ◇ *She's an avid reader of science fiction.* **2** a person who reads a particular newspaper, magazine, etc. **3** (EDUCATION) a book for practising reading

readership /'riːdəʃɪp/ *noun* [sing.] the number of people who regularly read a particular newspaper, magazine, etc: *The newspaper has a readership of 200 000.*

readily ⁀+ **C1** **W** /'redɪli/ *adv.* **1** easily, without difficulty: *Most vegetables are **readily available** at this time of year.* **2** in a way that shows you do not object to sth: *He readily admitted that he was wrong.* **SYN** **willingly**

readiness /'redinəs/ *noun* [U] **1** ~ **(for sth)** the state of being ready or prepared: *I'm having doubts about my readiness for parenthood.* **2** ~ **(to do sth)** the state of being prepared to do sth without arguing or complaining: *The bank have indicated their readiness to lend him the money.*

reading ⁀ **A1** **S** /'riːdɪŋ/ *noun* **1** [U] what you do when you read: *I haven't had time to do much reading lately.* ◇ *Her hobbies include painting and reading.* **2** [U] **(ARTS AND MEDIA, LITERATURE)** books, articles, etc. that are intended to be read: *The information office gave me a pile of **reading matter** to take away.* **3** [C] the particular way in which sb understands sth: *What's your reading of the situation?* **4** [C] the number or measurement that is shown on an instrument: *a reading of 20°*

readjust /ˌriːə'dʒʌst/ *verb* **1** [I] ~ **(to sth/doing sth)** to get used to a different or new situation: *After her divorce, it took her a long time to readjust to being single again.* **2** [T] to change or move sth slightly ▸ **readjustment** *noun* [C, U]

read-only 'memory = ROM

ready¹ ⁀ **A1** /'redi/ *adj.* **1** ~ **(for sb/sth)**; ~ **(to do sth)** prepared and able to do sth or to be used: *The car will be ready for you to collect on Friday.* ◇ *He isn't ready to take his driving test — he hasn't had enough lessons.* ◇ *I'm meeting him at seven, so I don't have long to **get ready**.* ◇ *I'll go and **get the dinner ready**.* ◇ **Have** *your money **ready** before you get on the bus.* **2** ~ **(to do sth)**; ~ **(for sth)**; ~ **(with sth)** prepared and happy to do sth: *You know me — I'm always ready to help.* ◇ *I know it's early, but I'm ready for bed.* ◇ *Charlie's always ready with advice.*

ready² /'redi/ *adv.* (used before a past participle; especially in compounds) already made or done: *ready-prepared meals* ◇ *ready-made pastry*

'ready meal *noun* [C] (*BrE*) a meal that you buy already prepared and which only needs to be heated

reagent /ri'eɪdʒənt/ *noun* [C] **(CHEMISTRY)** a substance used to cause a chemical reaction, especially in order to find out if another substance is present

real¹ ⁀ **A1** **S** /'riːəl, rɪəl/ *adj.*
• NOT IMAGINED **1** actually existing, not imagined: *The film is based on **real life**.* *This isn't a real word, I made it up.* ◇ *We have a **real chance** of winning.* ◇ *Closure of the factory is a very real danger.*
• NATURAL **2** natural, not false or artificial: *This shirt is real silk.*
• TRUE **3** actually true; not only what people think is true: *The name he gave to the police wasn't his real name.*
• GENUINE **4** [only before noun] having all, not just some, of the qualities necessary to really be sth: *She was my first real girlfriend.*
• BIG **5** [only before noun] (used to emphasize a state, feeling or quality) strong or big: *Money is a real problem for us at the moment.* ◇ *He made a real effort to be polite.*
IDM **for real** what sb says it is or serious: *Her tears weren't for real.* ◇ *Was he for real when he offered you the job?* **the real thing** actually what sb claims sth is, not a copy: *She's had boyfriends before but this time she says it's the real thing (= real love).*

real² /'riːəl, rɪəl/ *adv.* (*AmE, informal*) very; really

'real estate *noun* [U] property in the form of land and buildings

'real estate agent (*AmE*) = ESTATE AGENT

realise /'riːəlaɪz, 'rɪə-/ = REALIZE

realism /'riːəlɪzəm, 'rɪə-/ *noun* [U] **1** behaviour that shows that you accept the facts of a situation and are not influenced by your feelings ◯ look at **idealism** **2** **(ARTS AND MEDIA)** (used about films, paintings, etc.) showing things as they really are

realist /'riːəlɪst, 'rɪə-/ *noun* [C] **1** a person who accepts the facts of a situation, and does not try to pretend that it is different: *I'm a realist — I don't expect the impossible.* **2** **(ART, LITERATURE)** an artist or a writer who shows things as they really are

realistic ⁀ **B2** /ˌriːə'lɪstɪk, ˌrɪə-/ *adj.* **1** sensible and understanding what it is possible to achieve in a particular situation: *We have to be realistic about our chances of winning.* **2** showing things as they are in real life: *a realistic drawing/description* ▸ **realistically** /-kli/ *adv.*

reality ⁀ **B1** **O** /ri'æləti/ *noun* (*pl.* -ies) **1** [U] the way life really is, not the way it may appear to be or how you would like it to be: *I enjoyed my holiday, but now it's back to reality.* ◇ *We have to **face reality** and accept that we've failed.* **2** [C] a thing that is actually experienced, not just imagined: *Films portray war as heroic and exciting, but the reality is very different.* **3** [U] (usually before another noun) a form of TV entertainment that uses real people in real situations: *a reality show/series* **IDM** **in reality** in fact, really (not the way sth appears or has been described): *People say this is an exciting city but in reality it's rather boring.*

re'ality check *noun* [sing.] (*informal*) an occasion when you are reminded of how things are in the real world, rather than how you would like things to be

re,ality 'TV *noun* [U] **(ARTS AND MEDIA)** TV shows that use real people in real situations, presented as entertainment

realize ⁀ **A2** (*BrE also* -ise) /'riːəlaɪz, 'rɪə-/ *verb* **1** [T, I] (not used in the progressive tenses) to understand or become aware of a particular fact or situation: *I'm sorry I mentioned it, I didn't realize how much it upset you.* ◇ *When I got home, I realized (that) I had left my keys at the office.* ◇ *They left without anybody realizing.* **2** [T] to make sth that you imagined become reality: *His worst fears were realized when he saw the damage caused by the fire.* ▸ **realization** ⁀+ **C1** (*BrE also* -isation) /ˌriːəlaɪ'zeɪʃn, ˌrɪə-/ *noun* [U, sing.]

real-'life *adj.* [only before noun] actually happening or existing in life, not in books, stories or films: *a novel based on real-life events* ◇ *a real-life Romeo and Juliet* **OPP** **fictional**

really ⁀ **A1** /'riːəli, 'rɪə-/ *adv.* **1** very; very much: *I'm really tired.* ◇ *Are you really sure?* ◇ *I really hope you enjoy yourself.* ◇ *I really tried but I couldn't do it.* **2** actually; in fact: *I couldn't believe it was really happening.* ◇ *He said he was sorry but I don't think he really meant it.* ◇ *She wasn't really angry, she was only pretending.* ◇ *Is it really true?* **3** used as a question for expressing surprise, interest, doubt, etc: *'She's left her husband.' 'Really? When did that happen?'* **4** used in negative sentences to make what you are saying less strong: *I don't really agree with that.* **5** used in questions when you are expecting sb to answer 'No': *You don't really expect me to believe that, do you?*

realm ʔ+ **C1** /relm/ noun [C] **1** an area of activity, interest or knowledge: *The final chapters of the book move into the realms of fantasy.* **2** (*formal*) a country ruled by a king or queen: *the defence of the realm*

ˌreal ˈtime noun [U] (**COMPUTING**) the fact that there is only a very short time between a computer system receiving information and dealing with it: *To make the training realistic the simulation operates in real time.* ◊ *real-time missile guidance systems*

Realtor™ /ˈriːəltə(r)/ (*AmE*) = ESTATE AGENT

ˈreal-world adj. [only before noun] existing in the real world and not invented only for a particular purpose: *Teachers need to prepare their students to deal with real-world situations outside the classroom.*

reap /riːp/ verb [T] **1** to obtain sth, especially sth good, as a direct result of sth that you have done: *If you work hard now, you'll reap the benefits later on.* **2** (**AGRICULTURE**) to cut and collect a crop, especially CORN, WHEAT (= types of plant grown for their grain), etc., from a field

reappear /ˌriːəˈpɪə(r)/ verb [I] to appear again or be seen again ▸ reappearance noun [U, sing.]

reappraisal /ˌriːəˈpreɪzl/ noun [C, usually sing., U] the new examination of a situation, way of doing sth, etc. in order to decide if any changes are necessary

rear¹ ʔ+ **C1** /rɪə(r)/ noun [sing.] **1 the rear** the back part: *There are toilets at the rear of the plane.* **2** (*informal*) the part of the body that you sit on ▸ rear ʔ+ **C1** adj.: *the rear window/lights of a car*
IDM bring up the rear to be the last one in a race, a line of people, etc.

rear² /rɪə(r)/ verb **1** [T] to care for young children or animals until they are fully grown: *This generation of children will be reared without fear of war.* **2** [T] (**AGRICULTURE**) to BREED (= produce young from) and look after animals on a farm, etc: *to rear cattle/poultry* **3** [I] ~ (**up**) (used about animals, especially horses) to stand only on the back legs

rearm /riˈɑːm/ verb [I, T] to obtain, or supply sb with, new or better weapons, armies, etc: *The country was forbidden to rearm under the terms of the treaty.* ◊ *Rebel troops were being rearmed.* ▸ rearmament /-ˈɑːməmənt/ noun [U]

rearrange /ˌriːəˈreɪndʒ/ verb [T] **1** to change the position or order of things **2** to change a plan, meeting, etc. that has been fixed: *The match has been rearranged for next Wednesday.*

ˌrear-view ˈmirror noun [C] a mirror in which a driver can see the traffic behind

reason¹ ʔ+ **A1** ⊙ /ˈriːzn/ noun **1** [C] ~ (**for sth/doing sth**); ~ (**that**) … a cause or an explanation for sth that has happened or for sth that sb has done: *What's your reason for being so late?* ◊ *He said he couldn't come but he didn't give a reason.* ◊ *The reason (that) I'm phoning you is to ask a favour.* ◊ *For some reason* (= one that I do not know) *they can't give us an answer until next week.* ◊ *She left the job for personal reasons.* **2** [U] ~ (**to do sth**); ~ (**for sth/doing sth**) something that shows that it is right or fair to do sth: *I have reason to believe that you've been lying.* ◊ *You have every reason* (= you are completely right) *to be angry, considering how badly you've been treated.* ◊ *I think we have reason for complaint.* **3** [U] the ability to think and to make sensible decisions: *Only human beings are capable of reason.* **4** [U] what is right or acceptable: *I tried to persuade him not to drive but he just wouldn't listen to reason.* ◊ *I'll pay anything within reason for a ticket.*

IDM it stands to reason (*informal*) it is obvious if you think about it

▼ SYNONYMS

reason

grounds ✦ excuse ✦ motive ✦ need ✦ justification ✦ cause ✦ pretext

These are all words for a cause or an explanation for sth that has happened or that sb has done.

reason *What's your reason for being so late?*

grounds (*formal*) *He had no grounds for complaint.*

excuse *The rain gave her an excuse to take the car.*

motive *There didn't seem to be any motive for the murder.*

need *There's no need to ask permission.*

justification (*formal*) *There's no justification for the tax rises.*

cause *There's no cause for alarm.*

pretext (*formal*) *He left the party early on the pretext of having to finish some work.*

reason² /ˈriːzn/ verb [T, I] to form a judgement or an opinion, after thinking about sth in a logical way
PHRV reason with sb to talk to sb in order to persuade them to behave or think in a more reasonable way

reasonable ʔ **B2** Ⓦ /ˈriːznəbl/ adj. **1** fair, practical and sensible: *I think it's reasonable to expect people to keep their promises.* ◊ *I tried to be reasonable even though I was very angry.* **OPP unreasonable** **2** acceptable and appropriate in a particular situation: *You must submit your claim within a reasonable time.* **OPP unreasonable** **3** (used about prices) not too expensive: *We sell good quality food at reasonable prices.* **4** quite good, high, big, etc. but not very: *His work is of a reasonable standard.*

reasonably ʔ+ **B2** Ⓦ /ˈriːznəbli/ adv. **1** fairly or quite (but not very): *The weather was reasonably good but not brilliant.* **2** in a sensible and fair way: *We discussed the matter calmly and reasonably.*

reasoning ʔ+ **C1** Ⓦ /ˈriːznɪŋ/ noun [U] the process of thinking about sth and making a judgement or decision: *What's the reasoning behind his sudden decision to leave?*

reassemble /ˌriːəˈsembl/ verb [T] to fit the parts of sth together again after it has been taken apart

reassess /ˌriːəˈses/ verb [T] to think again about sth to decide if you need to change your opinion of it

reassurance /ˌriːəˈʃʊərəns, -ˈʃɔːr-/ noun [U, C] advice or help that you give to sb to stop them worrying or being afraid: *I need some reassurance that I'm doing things the right way.*

reassure ʔ+ **C1** /ˌriːəˈʃʊə(r), -ˈʃɔː(r)/ verb [T] to say or do sth in order to stop sb worrying or being afraid: *The mechanic reassured her that the engine was fine.* ▸ reassuring adj. ▸ reassuringly adv.

rebate /ˈriːbeɪt/ noun [C] (**FINANCE**) a sum of money that is given back to you because you have paid too much: *to get a tax rebate*

rebel¹ ʔ+ **C1** /ˈrebl/ noun [C] **1** (**POLITICS**) a person who fights against their country's government because they want things to change **SYN insurgent** **2** a person who refuses to obey people in authority or to accept rules: *At school he had a reputation as a rebel.*

rebel² /rɪˈbel/ verb [I] (-ll-) ~ (**against sb/sth**) to fight against authority, society, a law, etc: *As a teenager, she rebelled against her parents.*

rebellion ʔ+ **C1** /rɪˈbeljən/ noun [U, C] **1** (**POLITICS**) an occasion when some of the people in a country try to change the government, using violence **2** the act of fighting against authority or refusing to accept rules: *Voting against the leader of the party was an act of open rebellion.*

rebellious /rɪ'beljəs/ *adj.* not doing what authority, society, etc. wants you to do: *rebellious teenagers*

rebirth /ˌriː'bɜːθ/ *noun* [U, sing.] a period of new life, growth or activity: *the seasonal cycle of death and rebirth*

reboot /ˌriː'buːt/ *verb* [T, I] (**COMPUTING**) if you **reboot** a computer or if it **reboots**, you turn it off and then turn it on again immediately

rebound /rɪ'baʊnd/ *verb* [I] ~ **(from/off sth)** to hit sth/sb and then go in a different direction: *The ball rebounded off a defender and went into the goal.* ▸ **rebound** /'riːbaʊnd/ *noun* [C]

rebrand /ˌriː'brænd/ *verb* [T] (**BUSINESS**) to change the image of a company or an organization or one of its products or services, for example by changing its name or by advertising it in a different way: *In the 1990s the Labour Party rebranded itself as New Labour.* ▸ **rebranding** *noun* [sing., U]: *a rebranding exercise* ◇ *a £5 million rebranding*

rebuff /rɪ'bʌf/ *noun* [C] (*formal*) an unkind REFUSAL of an offer or a suggestion ▸ **rebuff** *verb* [T]

rebuild 🔊+ B2 /ˌriː'bɪld/ *verb* [T] (*pt, pp* **rebuilt** /-'bɪlt/) (**ARCHITECTURE**) to build sth again: *Following the storm, a great many houses will have to be rebuilt.*

rebuke /rɪ'bjuːk/ *verb* [T] (*formal*) to speak angrily to sb because they have done sth wrong ▸ **rebuke** *noun* [C, U]

recall 🔊 B2 /rɪ'kɔːl/ *verb* [T] 1 ~ **(doing sth)** to remember sth (a fact, an event, an action, etc.) from the past: *She couldn't recall meeting him before.* 2 to order sb to return; to ask for sth to be returned: *The company has recalled all the fridges that have this fault.*

recap /'riːkæp/ (-pp-) (*also formal* **recapitulate** /ˌriːkə'pɪtʃuleɪt/) *verb* [I, T] to repeat or look again at the main points of sth to make sure that they have been understood: *Let's quickly recap what we've done in today's lesson.* ▸ **recap** *noun* [C, U]

recapture /ˌriː'kæptʃə(r)/ *verb* [T] 1 to win back sth that was taken from you by an enemy or a competitor: *Government troops have recaptured the city.* 2 to catch a person or an animal that has escaped 3 to create or experience again sth from the past: *The film brilliantly recaptures life in the 1930s.*

recede /rɪ'siːd/ *verb* [I] 1 to move away and begin to disappear: *The coast began to recede into the distance.* 2 (used about a hope, fear, chance, etc.) to become smaller or less strong 3 (used about a man's hair) to fall out and stop growing at the front of the head: *He's got a receding hairline.*

receipt 🔊 B1 /rɪ'siːt/ *noun* 1 [C] ~ **(for sth)** a piece of paper that is given to show that you have paid for sth: *Keep the receipt for the shirt in case you want to exchange it.* 2 [U] ~ **(of sth)** (*formal*) the act of receiving sth: *You will get a message confirming receipt of your email.*

receive 🔊 A2 /rɪ'siːv/ *verb* [T] 1 ~ **sth (from sb)** to get or accept sth that sb sends or gives to you: *I received a letter from an old friend last week.* ◇ *to receive a phone call/a prize* 2 ~ **sth (from sb)** to experience a particular kind of treatment or injury: *We received a warm welcome from our hosts.* ◇ *He received several cuts and bruises.* 3 [often passive] to react to sth new in a particular way: *The film has been well received by the critics.*

re,ceived pro,nunci'ation *noun* [U] = RP

receiver 🔊+ B2 /rɪ'siːvə(r)/ *noun* [C] 1 (*also* **handset**) the part of a phone that is used for listening and speaking 2 a piece of TV or radio equipment that changes electronic signals into sounds or pictures 3 (**LAW**) a person who is chosen by a court to be in charge of a company that is BANKRUPT (= does not have enough money to pay its debts): *to call in the receivers*

receivership /rɪ'siːvəʃɪp/ *noun* [U] (**LAW**) the state of a business being controlled by an official RECEIVER because it has no money: *500 jobs were lost last year when the company went into receivership.*

recent 🔊 A2 🌐 /'riːsnt/ *adj.* that happened or began only a short time ago: *In recent years there have been many changes.* ◇ *This is a recent photo of my daughter.*

recently 🔊 A2 🌐 /'riːsntli/ *adv.* not long ago: *She worked here until quite recently.* ◇ *Have you seen Paul recently?*

receptacle /rɪ'septəkl/ *noun* [C] 1 ~ **(for sth)** (*formal*) a container for putting sth in 2 (**BIOLOGY**) the ROUNDED area at the top of a STEM that supports the head of a flower ⊃ picture at **flower**[1]

reception 🔊 A2 /rɪ'sepʃn/ *noun* 1 [U] the place inside the entrance of a hotel or an office building where guests or visitors go when they first arrive: *Leave your key at/in reception if you go out, please.* ◇ *the reception desk* ⊃ note at **hotel** 2 [C] a formal party to celebrate sth or to welcome an important person: *Their wedding reception was held at a local hotel.* ◇ *There will be an official reception at the embassy for the visiting ambassador.* 3 [sing.] the way people react to sth: *The play got a mixed reception (= some people liked it, some people didn't).* 4 [U] the quality of radio, mobile phone or TV signals: *TV reception is very poor where we live.*

receptionist /rɪ'sepʃənɪst/ *noun* [C] a person who works in a hotel, a doctor's surgery, an office, etc. answering the phone and dealing with visitors and guests when they arrive: *a hotel receptionist*

receptive /rɪ'septɪv/ *adj.* ~ **(to sth)** ready to listen to new ideas, suggestions, etc.

receptor /rɪ'septə(r)/ *noun* [C] (**ANATOMY**) a sense organ or nerve ending in the body that reacts to changes such as heat or cold and makes the body react in a particular way ⊃ picture at **skin**[1]

recess /'riːses, rɪ'ses/ *noun* 1 [C, U] a period of time when parliament, committees, etc. do not meet 2 [U] (**LAW**) a short break during a trial in a court 3 [U] (*AmE*) = BREAK[2] (3) 4 [C] part of a wall that is further back than the rest, forming a space 5 [C, usually pl.] a part of a room that receives very little light

recession 🔊+ B2 /rɪ'seʃn/ *noun* [C, U] (**ECONOMICS**) a period when the business and industry of a country is not successful: *The country is now in recession.* ◇ *How long will the recession last?*

recessive /rɪ'sesɪv/ *adj.* (**BIOLOGY**) a **recessive** physical characteristic only appears in a child if they have two GENES (= units inside a cell that control particular qualities) for this characteristic, one from each parent ⊃ look at **dominant** (2)

recharge /ˌriː'tʃɑːdʒ/ *verb* [T, I] (**PHYSICS**) to fill a battery with electrical power; to fill up with electrical power: *He plugged the drill in to recharge it.* ⊃ look at **charge**[2] (4) ▸ **rechargeable** *adj.*: *rechargeable batteries*

recipe 🔊 A2 /'resəpi/ *noun* [C] 1 ~ **(for sth)** the instructions for cooking or preparing sth to eat. A **recipe** tells you the ingredients and what to do: *a recipe for chocolate cake* 2 ~ **for sth** the way to get or produce sth: *Putting Dave in charge of the project is a recipe for disaster*.

recipient ⚓+ **C1** /rɪˈsɪpiənt/ *noun* [C] (*formal*) a person who receives sth

reciprocal /rɪˈsɪprəkl/ *adj.* involving two or more people or groups who agree to help each other or to behave in the same way towards each other: *The arrangement is reciprocal. They help us and we help them.*

reciprocate /rɪˈsɪprəkeɪt/ *verb* **1** [T, I] ~ (sth) (with sth) to behave or feel towards sb in the same way as they behave or feel towards you: *Her passion for him was not reciprocated.* **2** [I] to move backwards and forwards in a straight line: *a reciprocating action/ movement* ▸ **reciprocation** /rɪˌsɪprəˈkeɪʃn/ *noun* [U]

recital /rɪˈsaɪtl/ *noun* [C] (**LITERATURE, MUSIC**) a formal public performance of music or poetry: *a piano recital* ⊃ look at **concert**

recitative /ˌresɪtəˈtiːv/ *noun* [C, U] (**MUSIC**) a passage in an OPERA or ORATORIO that is sung in the rhythm of ordinary speech with many words on the same note

recite /rɪˈsaɪt/ *verb* [T, I] (**LITERATURE**) to say a poem, piece of literature, etc. that you have learned, especially to an audience

reckless /ˈrekləs/ *adj.* not thinking about possible bad or dangerous results that could come from your actions: *reckless driving* ▸ **recklessly** *adv.*

reckon ⚓+ **B2** /ˈrekən/ *verb* **1** [T, I] (*especially BrE, informal*) to think; to have an opinion about sth: *She's very late now. I reckon (that) she isn't coming.* ◇ *I think she's forgotten. What do you reckon?* **2** [T] to calculate sth approximately: *I reckon the journey will take about half an hour.* **3** [T] ~ to do sth (*BrE, informal*) to expect to do sth: *I wasn't reckoning to pay so much.*
PHR V **reckon on sth** to expect sth to happen and therefore to base a plan or an action on it: *I didn't book in advance because I wasn't reckoning on tickets being so scarce.* **reckon (sth) up** to calculate the total amount or number of sth **reckon with sb/ sth** to think about sb/sth as a possible problem

reckoning /ˈrekənɪŋ/ *noun* **1** [U, C] the act of calculating sth, especially in a way that is not very exact **2** [C, usually sing., U] a time when sb's actions will be judged to be right or wrong and they may be punished: *In the final reckoning truth is rewarded.* ◇ *Officials concerned with environmental policy predict that a day of reckoning will come.*
IDM **in/into/out of the reckoning** (*especially BrE*) (especially in sport) among/not among those who are likely to win or be successful: *Greene is fit again and should come into the reckoning.*

reclaim /rɪˈkleɪm/ *verb* [T] **1** ~ sth (from sb/sth) to get back sth that has been lost or taken away: *Reclaim your luggage after you have been through passport control.* **2** (**ENVIRONMENT**) to make wet land suitable for use **3** to get back useful materials from waste products ▸ **reclamation** /ˌrekləˈmeɪʃn/ *noun* [U]

recline /rɪˈklaɪn/ *verb* [I] (*formal*) **1** to sit or lie back in a relaxed and comfortable way **2** when a seat **reclines** or when you **recline** a seat, the back of it moves into a comfortable, sloping position: *a reclining chair*

recluse /rɪˈkluːs/ *noun* [C] a person who lives alone and likes to avoid other people ▸ **reclusive** /-ˈkluːsɪv/ *adj.*: *a reclusive millionaire*

recognition ⚓+ **B2** ⊙ /ˌrekəɡˈnɪʃn/ *noun* **1** [U] the fact that you can identify sb/sth that you see: *She looked at me with no sign of recognition on her face.* **2** [U, sing.] the act of accepting that sth exists, is true or is official: *There is a growing recognition that older people are important in the workplace.* **3** [U] a public

show of respect for sb's work or actions: *She has received public recognition for her services to charity.* ◇ *Please accept this gift in recognition of the work you have done.*

recognizable (*BrE also* -**isable**) /ˈrekəɡnaɪzəbl, ˌrekəɡˈnaɪzəbl/ *adj.* ~ (as sb/sth) that can be identified as sb/sth: *The building is easily recognizable as a prison.* ▸ **recognizably** (*BrE also* -**isably**) /-bli/ *adv.*

recognize ⚓ **A2** ⊙ (*BrE also* -**ise**) /ˈrekəɡnaɪz/ *verb* [T] **1** to know again sb/sth that you have seen or heard before: *I recognized him but I couldn't remember his name.* **2** to accept that sth exists or is true: *I recognize that some of my ideas are unrealistic.* **3** to accept sth officially: *My qualifications are not recognized in other countries.* **4** to show officially that you think sth that sb has done is good

recoil /rɪˈkɔɪl/ *verb* [I] to quickly move away from sb/sth unpleasant: *She recoiled in horror at the sight of the rat.*

recollect /ˌrekəˈlekt/ *verb* [T, I] (not used in the progressive tenses) to remember sth, especially by making an effort: *I don't recollect exactly when it happened.*

recollection /ˌrekəˈlekʃn/ *noun* **1** [U] ~ (of sth/doing sth) the ability to remember: *I have no recollection of promising to lend you money.* **2** [C] something that you remember: *I have only vague recollections of the town where I spent my early years.*

recommend ⚓ **A2** ⓦ /ˌrekəˈmend/ *verb* [T] **1** ~ sb/sth (to sb) (for/as sth) to say that sb/sth is good and that sb should try or use them or it: *Which film would you recommend?* ◇ *We hope that you'll recommend this restaurant to all your friends.* ◇ *Doctors don't always recommend drugs as the best treatment for every illness.* ◇ *Could you recommend me a good hotel?* ⊃ look at **suggest** (3) **2** to tell sb what you strongly believe they should do: *I recommend that you get some legal advice.* ◇ *I wouldn't recommend (your) travelling on your own. It could be dangerous.*

▼ SYNONYMS

recommend

advise • advocate • urge

These words all mean to tell sb what you think they should do in a particular situation.

recommend *Early booking is recommended.*

advise *I'd advise you not to tell him.*

advocate (*formal*) *The group does not advocate the use of violence.*

urge *The UN is urging caution in this dangerous situation.*

recommendation ⚓ **B1** /ˌrekəmenˈdeɪʃn/ *noun* **1** [C] a statement about what should be done in a particular situation: *In their report on the crash, the committee make several recommendations on how safety could be improved.* **2** [C, U] saying that sth is good and should be tried or used: *I visited Seville on their recommendation and I really enjoyed it.*

recompense /ˈrekəmpens/ *verb* [T] ~ sb (for sth) (*formal*) to give money, etc. to sb for special efforts or work or because you are responsible for a loss they have suffered: *The airline has agreed to recompense us for the damage to our luggage.* ▸ **recompense** *noun* [U] ~ (for sth): *Please accept this cheque in recompense for our poor service.*

reconcile /ˈrekənsaɪl/ *verb* [T] (*formal*) **1** ~ sth (with sth) to find a way of dealing with two ideas, situations, statements, etc. that seem to be opposite to each other: *She finds it difficult to reconcile her career ambitions with her responsibilities to her children.*

2 [often passive] ~ *sb* (**with** *sb*) to make people become friends again after an argument: *He has recently been reconciled with his wife.* **3** ~ **yourself to sth** to accept an unpleasant situation because there is nothing you can do to change it: *He could not reconcile himself to the prospect of losing her.* ▸ **reconciliation** /ˌrekənsɪliˈeɪʃn/ *noun* [sing., U]: *The negotiators are hoping to bring about a reconciliation between the two sides.*

reconnaissance /rɪˈkɒnɪsns/ *noun* [C, U] the study of an area for military reasons: *The plane was shot down while on a reconnaissance mission over enemy territory.*

reconsider /ˌriːkənˈsɪdə(r)/ *verb* [T, I] to think again about sth, especially because you may want to change your mind

reconstruct 𝗪 /ˌriːkənˈstrʌkt/ *verb* [T] **1** (**ARCHITECTURE**) to build again sth that has been destroyed or damaged **2** to get a full description or picture of sth using the facts that are known: *The police are trying to reconstruct the victim's movements on the day of the murder.*

reconstruction ϙ+ C1 𝗪 /ˌriːkənˈstrʌkʃn/ *noun* [C, U] **1** the activity of building again sth that has been damaged or destroyed **2** a short film showing events that are known to have happened, made in order to try and get more information or better understanding: *a reconstruction of the crime using actors*

record¹ ϙ A2 𝗪 /ˈrekɔːd/ *noun* **1** [C] ~ (**of sth**) a written account of what has happened, been done, etc.: *The teachers keep records of the children's progress.* ◇ *medical records* **2** [C] the best performance or the highest or lowest level, etc. ever reached in sth, especially in sport: *Who holds the world record for high jump?* ◇ *She's hoping to break the record for the 100 metres.* ◇ *He did it in record time* (= very fast). **3** [C] (**MUSIC**) a thin, round piece of plastic on which music is recorded **4** [sing.] the facts, events, etc. that are known (and sometimes written down) about sb/sth: *The police said that the man had a criminal record* (= he had been found guilty of crimes in the past). ◇ *This airline has a bad safety record.*
IDM **be/go on (the) record (as saying …)** to say sth publicly or officially so that it may be written down and repeated: *He didn't want to go on the record as either praising or criticizing the proposal.* **off the record** if you tell sb sth off the record, it is not yet official and you do not want them to repeat it publicly: *She told me off the record that she was going to resign.* **put/set the record straight** to correct a mistake by telling sb the true facts

record² ϙ A2 𝗪 /rɪˈkɔːd/ *verb* **1** [T] to write down or film facts or events so that they can be referred to later and will be remembered: *He recorded everything in his diary.* ◇ *At the inquest the coroner recorded a verdict of accidental death.* **2** [I, T] to make a copy of music, a film, etc: *Quiet, please! We're recording.* ◇ *The band has recently recorded a new album.*

ˈrecord-breaker *noun* [C] (**SPORT**) a person or thing that achieves a better result or higher level than has ever been achieved before

ˈrecord-breaking *adj.* [only before noun] the best, fastest, highest, etc. ever: *He won the race in record-breaking time.*

recorder /rɪˈkɔːdə(r)/ *noun* [C] **1** a machine for recording sound and/or pictures: *a DVD recorder* **2** (**MUSIC**) a type of musical instrument that is often played by children. You play it by blowing through it and covering the holes in it with your fingers. ⊃ picture at **instrument**

ˈrecord holder *noun* [C] (**SPORT**) a person who has achieved the best result that has ever been achieved in a sport

recording ϙ A2 𝗪 /rɪˈkɔːdɪŋ/ *noun* **1** [C] sound or pictures that have been put onto computer files or on a CD, video, etc: *the Berlin Philharmonic's recording of Mahler's sixth symphony* **2** [U] the process of recording sound or a performance: *a recording session/studio*

ˈrecord label = LABEL¹

ˈrecord player *noun* [C] a machine that you use for playing records in order to listen to music, etc. on them

recount¹ ϙ+ C1 /rɪˈkaʊnt/ *verb* [T] ~ **sth (to** *sb*) to tell a story or describe an event: *He recounted the story to us in vivid detail.*

recount² /ˌriːˈkaʊnt/ *verb* [T] to count sth again, especially votes

recourse /rɪˈkɔːs/ *noun* [U] ~ (**to** *sth*) (*formal*) the fact of having to use sth or ask sb for help in a difficult situation: *She made a complete recovery without recourse to surgery.*

recover ϙ B2 /rɪˈkʌvə(r)/ *verb* **1** [I] ~ (**from** *sth*) to become well again after you have been ill: *It took him two months to recover from the operation.* **2** [I] ~ (**from sth**) to get back to normal again after a bad experience, etc: *The old lady never really recovered from the shock of being mugged.* **3** [T] ~ **sth (from** *sb*/*sth*) to find or get back sth that was lost or stolen: *Police recovered the stolen goods from a warehouse in South London.* **4** [T] to get back the use of your senses, control of your emotions, etc.

recovery ϙ+ B2 𝗪 /rɪˈkʌvəri/ *noun* (*pl.* -ies) **1** [U, C, usually sing.] ~ (**from sth**) a return to good health after an illness or to a normal state after a difficult period of time: *He made a full recovery from the operation.* ◇ *a good/quick/speedy/slow recovery* ◇ *She's on the road to recovery* (= getting better all the time) now. ◇ *the prospects of economic recovery* **2** [U] ~ (**of sth/sb**) getting back sth that was lost, stolen or missing: *He offered a reward for the recovery of the paintings.*

reˈcovery position *noun* [sing.] (**MEDICINE**) a position lying on the side, with the arms and legs carefully placed, that helps a person who is not conscious to breathe

recreate /ˌriːkriˈeɪt/ *verb* [T] to make sth that existed in the past exist or seem to exist again: *The movie recreates the glamour of 1940s Hollywood.*

recreation /ˌrekriˈeɪʃn/ *noun* [U, C] the fact of enjoying yourself and relaxing when you are not working; a way of doing this: *the need to improve facilities for leisure and recreation* ▸ **recreational** /-ʃənl/ *adj.*: *recreational activities*

recreˌational ˈvehicle (*AmE*) = RV

recrimination /rɪˌkrɪmɪˈneɪʃn/ *noun* [C, usually pl., U] an angry statement accusing sb of sth, especially in answer to a similar statement from them: *bitter recriminations*

recruit¹ ϙ+ B2 /rɪˈkruːt/ *noun* [C] a person who has just joined the army or another organization

recruit² ϙ+ B2 /rɪˈkruːt/ *verb* [T, I] ~ **sb (to sth)** to find new people to join a company, an organization, the armed forces, etc: *to recruit young people to the teaching profession* ⊃ note at **job** ▸ **recruitment ϙ+ B2** *noun* [U]

rectal /ˈrektəl/ *adj.* (**ANATOMY**) relating to the RECTUM (= that place where food waste collects before leaving the body)

rectangle /'rektæŋgl/ *noun* [C] (**GEOMETRY**) a shape with four straight sides and four RIGHT ANGLES (= angles of 90°). Two of the sides are longer than the other two. **SYN** oblong ⊃ picture at **parallelogram** ▸ **rectangular** /rek'tæŋgjələ(r)/ *adj.*

rectify /'rektɪfaɪ/ *verb* [T] (rectifying; rectifies; *pt, pp* rectified) (*formal*) to correct sth that is wrong

rectum /'rektəm/ *noun* [C] (**ANATOMY**) the end section of the tube where solid food waste collects before leaving the body ⊃ picture at **body**, **digestive system**

recuperate /rɪ'ku:pəreɪt/ *verb* [I] ~ (**from sth**) (*formal*) (**HEALTH**) to get well again after an illness or injury ▸ **recuperation** /rɪ,ku:pə'reɪʃn/ *noun* [U]

recur /rɪ'kɜ:(r)/ *verb* [I] (-rr-) to happen again or many times: *a recurring problem/illness/nightmare* ▸ **recurrence** /-'kʌrəns/ *noun* [C, usually sing., U] ▸ **recurrent** /-rənt/ *adj.*

re,curring 'decimal *noun* [C] (**MATHEMATICS**) a DECIMAL in which the same figure or group of figures is repeated for ever, for example 3.999…: *The recurring decimal 3.999… is also described as 3.9 recurring.*

recycle 🔊 A2 /,ri:'saɪkl/ *verb* [T] (**ENVIRONMENT**) 1 to put used objects and materials through a process so that they can be used again: *recycled paper ◇ Aluminium cans can be recycled.* 2 to keep used objects and materials and use them again: *Don't throw away your plastic carrier bags — recycle them!* ▸ **recyclable** *adj.*: *Most plastics are recyclable.* ▸ **recycling** *noun* [U]: *the recycling of glass ◇ a recycling plant*

red¹ 🔊 A1 /red/ *adj.* (redder; reddest) 1 having the colour of blood: *red wine ◇ She's wearing a bright red dress.* ⊃ look at **crimson**, **maroon**, **scarlet** 2 (used about a person's hair or an animal's fur) red-brown in colour: *She's got red hair and freckles.* 3 (used about the face) bright red or pink, especially because you are embarrassed, angry, shy, etc: *He went bright red when she spoke to him. ◇ to turn/be/go red in the face* **IDM** catch sb red-handed → CATCH¹ a red herring an idea or a subject that takes people's attention away from what is really important

red² 🔊 A1 /red/ *noun* [U, C] the colour of blood: *She was dressed in red.* **IDM** be in the red (**FINANCE**) to have spent more money than you have in the bank, etc: *I'm £500 in the red at the moment.* **OPP** be in the black see red → SEE

redact /rɪ'dækt/ *verb* [T] ~ **sth (from sth)** to remove information from a document because you do not want the public to see it: *All sensitive personal information has been redacted from the report.*

red 'card *noun* [C] (**SPORT**) (in football and some other games) a card that is shown to a player who is being sent off the field for doing sth wrong ⊃ look at **yellow card**

red 'carpet (*usually* the red carpet) *noun* [sing.] a piece of red carpet that is put on the ground to receive an important visitor; a special welcome for an important visitor: *I didn't expect to be given **the red carpet treatment!***

the **Red 'Cross** *noun* [sing.] (**MEDICINE**, **POLITICS**) an international organization that takes care of people who are suffering because of war or natural DISASTERS. Its full name is 'the International Movement of the Red Cross and the Red Crescent'.

redcurrant /'redkʌrənt/ *noun* [C] a small round red fruit: *redcurrant jelly*

redden /'redn/ *verb* [I, T] to become red; to make sth red

reddish /'redɪʃ/ *adj.* fairly red in colour

redecorate /,ri:'dekəreɪt/ *verb* [I, T] to put new paint and/or paper on the walls of a room or house

redeem /rɪ'di:m/ *verb* [T] 1 to prevent sth from being completely bad: *The redeeming feature of the job is the good salary.* 2 ~ **yourself** to do sth to improve people's opinion of you, especially after you have done sth bad

redefine /,ri:dɪ'faɪn/ *verb* [T] to change the nature or limits of sth; to make people consider sth in a new way: *The new constitution redefined the powers of the president. ◇ We need to redefine what success means to us.*

redemption /rɪ'dempʃn/ *noun* [U] (*formal*) (**RELIGION**) the act of being saved from evil **IDM** beyond redemption too bad to be saved or improved

redesign /,ri:dɪ'zaɪn/ *verb* [T] to design sth again, in a different way

redevelop /,ri:dɪ'veləp/ *verb* [T] (**ARCHITECTURE**) to build or arrange an area, a town, a building, etc. in a different and more modern way: *They're redeveloping the city centre.* ▸ **redevelopment** *noun* [U, C]

redhead /'redhed/ *noun* [C] a person who has red hair

red-'hot *adj.* (used about a metal) so hot that it turns red

redial /,ri:'daɪəl/ *verb* [I, T] (-ll-, *AmE* -l-) to call the same phone number again

redid /,ri:'dɪd/ past tense of **redo**

redistribute /,ri:dɪ'strɪbju:t, ,ri:dɪstrɪ-/ *verb* [T] to share sth out among people in a different way from before ▸ **redistribution** /,ri:dɪstrɪ'bju:ʃn/ *noun* [U, sing.]

red-'letter day *noun* [C] an important day, or a day that you will remember, because of sth good that happened then

red-'light district *noun* [C] a part of a town where there are a lot of PROSTITUTES (= people who earn money by having sex with people)

redo /,ri:'du:/ *verb* [T] (redoes /-'dʌz/; *pt* redid /-'dɪd/; *pp* redone /-'dʌn/) to do sth again or differently: *A whole day's work had to be redone. ◇ We've just redone the bathroom (= decorated it differently).*

red 'pepper = PEPPER¹ (2)

redress¹ /rɪ'dres/ *verb* [T] (*formal*) to correct sth that is unfair or wrong: *to redress an injustice*

redress² /rɪ'dres/ *noun* [U] ~ (**for/against sth**) (*formal*) (**LAW**) payment, etc. that you should get for sth wrong that has happened to you or harm that you have suffered: *to seek legal redress for unfair dismissal* **SYN** compensation

red 'tape *noun* [U] official rules that seem unnecessary and often prevent things from being done quickly

red-top *noun* [C] (*BrE*, *informal*) (**ARTS AND MEDIA**) a British TABLOID newspaper (= a newspaper with small pages, a lot of pictures and stories about famous people, often thought of as less serious than other newspapers), whose name is in red at the top of the front page

reduce 🔊 A2 ⊙ /rɪ'dju:s/ *verb* [T] 1 ~ **sth (from sth) (to sth)**; ~ **sth (by sth)** to make sth less or smaller in quantity, price, size, etc: *The number of employees was reduced from 40 to 25. ◇ Costs were reduced by 20%.* **OPP** increase¹ ⊃ note at **price¹** 2 (**CHEMISTRY**) to add one or more ELECTRONS to a substance or to remove OXYGEN from a substance ⊃ look at **oxidize** **PHR V** reduce sb/sth (from sth) to sth [often passive] to force sb/sth into a particular state or condition, usually a bad one: *One of the older boys **reduced** the small child **to tears**.*

reduction ⓘ B2 Ⓦ /rɪˈdʌkʃn/ noun **1** [C, U] ~ (in sth) the act of becoming or making sth less or smaller: *a sharp reduction in the number of students* **2** [C] the amount by which sth is made smaller, especially in price: *There were massive reductions in the June sales.* **3** [U, C] (**CHEMISTRY**) the fact of adding one or more ELECTRONS to a substance or of removing OXYGEN from a substance ⊃ look at **oxidation**

redundant /rɪˈdʌndənt/ adj. **1** (used about employees) no longer needed for a job and therefore out of work: *When the factory closed 800 people were **made redundant**.* ⊃ note at **job** **2** not necessary or wanted ▸ **redundancy** /-dənsi/ noun [U, C] (pl. -ies): *redundancy payments*

reed /riːd/ noun [C] **1** a tall plant, like grass, that grows in or near water **2** (**MUSIC**) a thin piece of wood, metal or plastic at the end of some musical instruments that produces a sound when you blow through it

reef /riːf/ noun [C] (**GEOGRAPHY**) a long line of rocks, plants, etc. just below or above the surface of the sea: *a coral reef*

reek /riːk/ verb [I] ~ (of sth) to smell strongly of sth unpleasant: *His breath reeked of tobacco.* ▸ **reek** noun [sing.]

reel¹ /riːl/ noun [C] a round object that THREAD, wire, film for cameras, etc. is put around: *a cotton reel* ◇ *a reel of film* ⊃ look at **spool** ⊃ picture at **gardening**

reel² /riːl/ verb **1** [I] to walk without being able to control your legs, for example because you are drunk or you have been hit **2** [I] ~ (at/from sth) to feel very shocked or upset about sth: *His mind was still reeling from the shock of seeing her again.*
PHR V **reel sth in/out** to pull sth towards you or move it away from you by turning a REEL: *to reel in a fish* **reel sth off** to say or repeat sth from memory quickly and without having to think about it: *She reeled off a long list of names.*

re-ˈentry noun [U] **1** ~ (into sth) the act of returning to a place or an area of activity that you used to be in: *She feared she would not be granted re-entry into Britain.* **2** (**ASTRONOMY**) the return of a SPACECRAFT into the earth's atmosphere: *The capsule gets very hot on re-entry.*

ref /ref/ (informal) = REFEREE (1)

ref. /ref/ abbr. (used especially in business as a way of identifying something such as a document) reference: *ref. no. 3456*

refectory /rɪˈfektəri/ noun [C] (pl. -ies) a large room in which meals are served, especially in a religious institution and in some schools and colleges in the UK

refer ⓘ A2 Ⓞ /rɪˈfɜː(r)/ verb [T] (-rr-) ~ (sb/sth to sb/sth) to send sb/sth to sb/sth for help, advice or a decision: *The doctor has referred me to a specialist.* ⊃ note at **medical¹**
PHR V **refer to sb/sth (as sth)** to mention or talk about sb/sth: *When he said 'some students', do you think he was referring to us?* ◇ *She always referred to Ben as 'that nice man'.* ⊃ note at **mention** **refer to sb/sth 1** to describe or be connected with sb/sth: *The term 'adolescent' refers to young people between the ages of 12 and 17.* ◇ *The figures in brackets refer to holidays in July.* **2** to find out information by asking sb or by looking in a book, etc: *If you don't understand a word you may refer to your dictionaries.*

referee ⓘ+ B2 /ˌrefəˈriː/ noun [C] **1** (also informal ref) (**SPORT**) the official person in sports such as football who controls the match and prevents players from breaking the rules ⊃ look at **umpire 2** (BrE) a person who gives information about your character and ability, usually in a letter, for example when you are hoping to be chosen for a job: *Her teacher agreed to act as her referee.* ▸ **referee** verb [I, T]

ˌrefereeˈs asˈsistant noun [C] (**SPORT**) (in football) the official name for a LINESMAN (= an official who helps the REFEREE)

reference ⓘ B1 Ⓞ /ˈrefrəns/ noun
• MENTIONING SB/STH **1** [C, U] ~ (to sb/sth) a written or spoken comment that mentions sb/sth: *The article **made a** direct **reference** to a certain member of the royal family.*
• LOOKING FOR INFORMATION **2** [U] looking at sth for information: *The guidebook might be useful **for future reference**.*
• IN BUSINESS **3** [C] (abbr. ref.) a number, word or symbol that shows where sth is on a map, or where you can find a piece of information: *accurate grid references* ◇ *Please quote our reference when replying.*
• FOR NEW JOB **4** [C] a statement or letter describing a person's character and ability that is given to a possible future employer: *My boss gave me a good reference.*
• IN A BOOK **5** [C] (**LITERATURE**) a note, especially in a book, that tells you where certain information came from or can be found
IDM **in/with reference to sb/sth** (formal) about or concerning sb/sth: *I am writing with reference to your email of 10 April ...*

ˈreference book noun [C] a book that you use to find a piece of information: *dictionaries, encyclopedias and other reference books*

referendum ⓘ+ C1 /ˌrefəˈrendəm/ noun [C, U] (pl. referendums, referenda /-də/) (**POLITICS**) an occasion when all the people of a country can vote on a particular political question: *The government will hold a referendum on the issue.*

referral /rɪˈfɜːrəl/ noun [U, C] ~ (to sb/sth) the act of sending sb who needs professional help to a person or place that can provide it: *illnesses requiring referral to hospitals* ◇ *to make a referral*

refill /ˌriːˈfɪl/ verb [T] to fill sth again: *Can I refill your glass?* ▸ **refill** /ˈriːfɪl/ noun [C]: *a refill for a pen*

refine /rɪˈfaɪn/ verb [T] **1** to make a substance pure and free from other substances: *to refine sugar/oil* **2** to improve sth by changing little details: *to refine a theory*

refined /rɪˈfaɪnd/ adj. **1** (used about a substance) that has been made pure by having other substances taken out of it: *refined sugar/oil/flour* **2** (used about a person) polite; having very good manners

refinement /rɪˈfaɪnmənt/ noun **1** [C] a small change that improves sth: *The new model has electric windows and other refinements.* **2** [U] good manners and polite behaviour

refinery /rɪˈfaɪnəri/ noun [C] (pl. -ies) a factory where a substance is made pure by having other substances taken out of it: *an oil/a sugar refinery*

reflate /ˌriːˈfleɪt/ verb [T, I] (**ECONOMICS**) to increase the amount of money that is used in a country, usually in order to increase the demand for goods ⊃ look at **deflate** (3), **inflate** (2) ▸ **reflation** /-ˈfleɪʃn/ noun [U] ⊃ look at **deflation** (1), **inflation** ▸ **reflationary** /-ri/ adj.

reflect ⓘ B1 Ⓞ /rɪˈflekt/ verb **1** [T, usually passive] ~ sb/sth (in sth) to show an image of sb/sth on the surface of sth such as a mirror, water or glass: *She caught sight of herself reflected in the shop window.* **2** [T] (**PHYSICS**) to send back light, heat or sound from a surface: *The windows reflected the bright morning sunlight.* ⊃ picture at **reflection 3** [T] to show or express sth: *His music reflects his interest in African culture.* **4** [I, T]

~ **(on/upon sth)** to think, especially deeply and carefully, about sth: *I really need some time to reflect on what you've said.*

PHR V reflect **(well, badly, etc.) on sb/sth** to give a particular impression of sb/sth: *It reflects badly on the whole school if some of its pupils misbehave in public.*

reflection

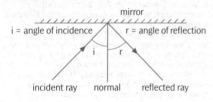

mirror

i = angle of incidence   r = angle of reflection

incident ray   normal   reflected ray

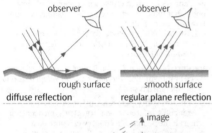

observer   observer

rough surface   smooth surface
diffuse reflection   regular plane reflection

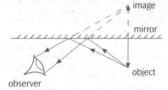

image

mirror

object

observer

reflection ʔ+ **C1** **O** (*BrE also* **reflexion**) /rɪˈflekʃn/ *noun*
1 [C] an image that you see in a mirror, in water or on a shiny surface: *He admired his reflection in the mirror.* **2** [U] (**PHYSICS**) the sending back of light, heat or sound from a surface **3** [C] ~ **(on sb/sth)** a sign that shows what sb/sth is like: *The increase in crime is a reflection on* (= shows sth bad about) *our society today.* ◇ *Your clothes are a reflection of your personality.* **4** [C, usually pl.] ~ **(on sth)** careful thought about sth: *a book of his reflections on fatherhood*
IDM **on reflection** after thinking again: *I think, on reflection, that we were wrong.*

reflective /rɪˈflektɪv/ *adj.* **1** (*formal*) (used about a person, mood, etc.) thinking deeply about things: *a reflective expression* **2** (used about a surface) sending back light or heat: *Wear reflective strips when you're cycling at night.* ◇ *a reflective vest* **3** ~ **(of sth)** showing what sth is like

reflector /rɪˈflektə(r)/ *noun* [C] **1** a surface that reflects light, heat or sound that hits it **2** a small piece of glass or plastic on a bicycle or on clothing that can be seen at night when light shines on it

reflex /ˈriːfleks/ *noun* [C] (**BIOLOGY**) an action or a movement of your body that happens naturally in response to sth and that you cannot control; sth that you do without thinking: *The doctor tested his reflexes.* ◇ *She put her hands out as a reflex action to stop her fall.* ◇ *A good tennis player needs to have excellent reflexes.*

reflex 'angle *noun* [C] (**GEOMETRY**) an angle of more than 180° ◇ look at **acute angle, obtuse angle, right angle** ◇ picture at **angle¹**

reflexion /rɪˈflekʃn/ (*BrE*) = REFLECTION

reflexive /rɪˈfleksɪv/ *adj.* (**GRAMMAR**) (used about a word or verb form) showing that the person who performs an action is also affected by it: *In 'He cut himself', 'cut' is a reflexive verb and 'himself' is a reflexive pronoun.*

reflexology /ˌriːfleksˈɒlədʒi/ *noun* [U] (**MEDICINE**) a type of treatment in which sb's feet are rubbed in a particular way in order to cure a health problem in another part of their body or to make them feel relaxed ► **reflexologist** /-dʒɪst/ *noun* [C]

reflux /ˈriːflʌks/ *noun* [U] **1** (**CHEMISTRY**) the process of boiling a liquid so that any VAPOUR (= very small drops of liquid in the air) that rises up from it is changed to liquid again and falls back down into the bottle or container **2** (**HEALTH**) the flowing back of a liquid inside the body, such as ACID from the stomach into the OESOPHAGUS: *acid reflux*

reform ʔ+ **C1** /rɪˈfɔːm/ *verb* **1** [T] to change a system, the law, etc. in order to make it better **2** [I, T] to improve your behaviour; to make sb do this: *Our prisons aim to reform criminals, not simply to punish them.*
► **reform** ʔ+ **C1** *noun* [U, C]

reformation /ˌrefəˈmeɪʃn/ *noun* **1** [U] (*formal*) the act of improving or changing sb/sth **2 the Reformation** [sing.] (**HISTORY, RELIGION**) new ideas in religion in sixteenth-century Europe that led to changes in the Roman Catholic Church and the forming of the Protestant Churches; the period in history when these changes were taking place

reformer /rɪˈfɔːmə(r)/ *noun* [C] (**SOCIAL STUDIES**) a person who tries to change society and make it better

reformist /rɪˈfɔːmɪst/ *adj.* (**POLITICS**) wanting or trying to change political or social situations ► **reformist** *noun* [C]

refoulement /rəˈfuːlmõ/ *noun* [U] (**LAW**) the practice of forcing REFUGEES (= people who have had to leave their country) to return to a country where they would be in danger **OPP** **non-refoulement**

refract /rɪˈfrækt/ *verb* [T] (**PHYSICS**) (used about water, glass, etc.) to make a wave of light, sound or energy change direction when it goes through an angle ► **refraction** /-ˈfrækʃn/ *noun* [U]

refraction

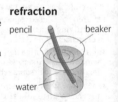

pencil   beaker

water

re,fractive 'index *noun* [C] (**PHYSICS**) a measurement of how much an object or a substance REFRACTS light

refrain¹ /rɪˈfreɪn/ *verb* [I] ~ **(from sth/doing sth)** to stop yourself doing sth; to not do sth: *Please refrain from eating in the classroom.*

refrain² /rɪˈfreɪn/ *noun* [C] (*formal*) (**MUSIC**) a part of a song that is repeated, usually at the end of each VERSE **SYN** **chorus¹**

refresh /rɪˈfreʃ/ *verb* **1** [T] to make sb/sth feel less tired or less hot and full of energy again: *He looked refreshed after a good night's sleep.* **2** [T, I] (**COMPUTING**) to make the most recent information show, for example on an internet page: *Click here to refresh this document.* ◇ *The page refreshes automatically.*
IDM **refresh your memory (about sb/sth)** to remind yourself about sb/sth: *Could you refresh my memory about what we said on this point last week?*

refreshing /rɪˈfreʃɪŋ/ *adj.* **1** pleasantly new or different: *It makes a refreshing change to meet somebody who is so enthusiastic.* **2** making you feel less tired or hot: *a refreshing swim/shower/drink*

refreshment /rɪˈfreʃmənt/ *noun* **1** refreshments [pl.] light food and drinks that are available at a cinema, theatre or other public place **2** [U] (*formal*) the fact of making sb feel stronger and less tired or hot

refrigerant /rɪˈfrɪdʒərənt/ *noun* [C, U] (CHEMISTRY) a chemical substance used in the REFRIGERATION process

refrigerate /rɪˈfrɪdʒəreɪt/ *verb* [T] to make or keep food, etc. cold in order to keep it fresh ▸ refrigeration /rɪˌfrɪdʒəˈreɪʃn/ *noun* [U]

refrigerator /rɪˈfrɪdʒəreɪtə(r)/ (*AmE or formal*) = FRIDGE

refuge ʔ+ **C1** /ˈrefjuːdʒ/ *noun* [U, C] ~ **(from sb/sth)** protection from danger, trouble, etc.; a place that is safe: *a refuge for the homeless* ◇ *We had to take refuge from the rain under a tree.* **SYN** shelter[1]

refugee ʔ+ **B2** /ˌrefjuˈdʒiː/ *noun* [C] (POLITICS, SOCIAL STUDIES) a person who has been forced to leave their country for political or religious reasons, or because there is a war, not enough food, etc: *a refugee camp* ➔ look at **economic migrant**, **exile** (2), **fugitive**

refund /ˈriːfʌnd/ *noun* [C] (FINANCE) a sum of money that is paid back to you, especially because you have paid too much or you are not happy with sth you have bought: *to claim/demand/get a refund* ▸ refund /rɪˈfʌnd/ *verb* [T] ▸ refundable /rɪˈfʌndəbl/ *adj.*: *The deposit is not refundable.*

refurbish /ˌriːˈfɜːbɪʃ/ *verb* [T] to clean and decorate a room, building, etc. in order to make it more attractive, more useful, etc. ▸ refurbishment *noun* [U, C]: *The hotel is now closed for refurbishment.*

refusal ʔ+ **C1** /rɪˈfjuːzl/ *noun* [U, C] ~ **(to do sth)** the act of saying or showing that you will not do, give or accept sth: *I can't understand her refusal to see me.*

refuse[1] ʔ **A2** /rɪˈfjuːz/ *verb* [I, T] ~ **(to do sth)**; ~ **sb sth** to say or show that you do not want to do, give, or accept sth: *He refused to listen to what I was saying.* ◇ *My application for a grant has been refused.*

refuse[2] /ˈrefjuːs/ *noun* [U] (*formal*) things that you throw away; rubbish: *the refuse collection* (= when DUSTBINS are emptied)

regain ʔ+ **C1** /rɪˈɡeɪn/ *verb* [T] to get sth back that you had lost: *to regain consciousness*

regal /ˈriːɡl/ *adj.* very impressive; typical of or suitable for a king or queen

regard[1] ʔ **B2** ⓦ /rɪˈɡɑːd/ *verb* [T] **1** ~ **sb/sth/yourself (as sth)**; ~ **sb/sth (with sth)** to think of sb/sth (in the way mentioned): *Do you regard this issue as important?* ◇ *In some villages newcomers are regarded with suspicion.* **2** (often used with an adverb or a preposition) (*formal*) to look at sb/sth for a while: *She regarded us warily.*
IDM **as regards sb/sth** (*formal*) in connection with sb/ sth: *What are your views as regards this proposal?*

▼ SYNONYMS

regard

consider ◆ see ◆ view ◆ perceive

These words all mean to think about sb/sth in a particular way.

regard *He seems to regard the whole thing as a joke.*

consider *Who do you consider responsible?*

see *Try to see things from her point of view.*

view *How do you view your position here?*

perceive (*formal*) *The discovery was perceived as a major breakthrough in scientific research.*

regard[2] ʔ **B2** ⓦ /rɪˈɡɑːd/ *noun* **1** [U] ~ **(for sb/sth)** (*formal*) attention to or care for sb/sth: *He shows little regard for other people's feelings.* **2** [U, sing.] ~ **(for sb/ sth)** (*formal*) respect for sb/sth: *She obviously has great regard for your ability.* **3** regards [pl.] (used especially to end a letter or an email politely) kind thoughts; best wishes: *Please give my regards to your parents.*
IDM **in/with regard to sb/sth** | **in this/that/one regard** (*formal*) about sb/sth; connected with sb/sth: *With regard to the details — these will be finalized later.*

regarding /rɪˈɡɑːdɪŋ/ *prep.* (*formal*) about or in connection with: *Please write if you require further information regarding this matter.*

regardless ʔ+ **C1** /rɪˈɡɑːdləs/ *adv.* paying no attention to sb/sth; treating problems and difficulties as unimportant: *I suggested she should stop but she carried on regardless.*

re'gardless of ⓦ *prep.* paying no attention to sb/sth; treating sb/sth as not being important: *Everybody will receive the same amount, regardless of how long they've worked here.*

regatta /rɪˈɡætə/ *noun* [C] (SPORT) an event at which there are boat races

regenerate /rɪˈdʒenəreɪt/ *verb* **1** [T] (BUSINESS) to make an area, institution, etc. develop and grow strong again: *The money will be used to regenerate the commercial heart of the town.* **2** [I, T] (BIOLOGY) to grow again; to make sth grow again: *Once destroyed, brain cells do not regenerate.* ◇ *If the woodland is left alone, it will regenerate itself in a few years.* ▸ regeneration /rɪˌdʒenəˈreɪʃn/ *noun* [U]: *economic regeneration* ◇ *the regeneration of cells in the body* ▸ regenerative /rɪˈdʒenərətɪv/ *adj.*: *the regenerative powers of nature*

reggae /ˈreɡeɪ/ *noun* [U] (MUSIC) a type of West Indian music with a strong rhythm

regicide /ˈredʒɪsaɪd/ *noun* [U] (*formal*) the crime of killing a king or queen

regime ʔ+ **C1** ⓦ /reɪˈʒiːm/ *noun* [C] (POLITICS) a method or system of government, especially one that has not been elected in a fair way: *a military/fascist regime*

re'gime change *noun* [U, C, usually sing.] (POLITICS) the situation when one government is replaced by another, especially by force: *He told the government he was not seeking regime change.*

regiment /ˈredʒɪmənt/ *noun* [C + sing./pl. verb] a group of soldiers in the army who are commanded by a COLONEL (= an officer of a high level) ▸ regimental /ˌredʒɪˈmentl/ *adj.*

regimented /ˈredʒɪmentɪd/ *adj.* (too) strictly controlled

region ʔ **A2** ⓦ /ˈriːdʒən/ *noun* [C] **1** (GEOGRAPHY) a part of the country or the world; a large area of land: *desert/tropical/polar regions* ◇ *This region of France is very mountainous.* **2** an area of the body
IDM **in the region of sth** about or approximately: *There were somewhere in the region of 30 000 people at the rally.*

regional ʔ **B2** ⓦ /ˈriːdʒənl/ *adj.* (GEOGRAPHY) connected with a particular region: *regional accents* ➔ look at **international** (1), **local**[1], **national**[1]

register[1] ʔ **B2** /ˈredʒɪstə(r)/ *verb*
• PUT A NAME ON A LIST **1** [T, I] ~ **(for sth)** to put a name on an official list: *You should register with a doctor nearby.* ◇ *All births, deaths and marriages must be registered.* ➔ note at **hotel**
• MEASURE **2** [I, T] to show sth or to be shown on a measuring instrument: *The thermometer registered 32°C.* ◇ *The earthquake registered 6.4 on the Richter scale.*

- SHOW FEELINGS, ETC. **3** [T] to show feelings, opinions, etc: *Her face registered intense dislike.*
- NOTICE STH **4** [I, T] (often in negative sentences) to notice sth and remember it; to be noticed and remembered: *He told me his name but it didn't register.*
- LETTER/PACKAGE **5** [T] to send a letter or package by REGISTERED MAIL

register² 🔒 **B2** /ˈredʒɪstə(r)/ *noun* **1** [C] an official list of names, etc. or a book that contains this kind of list: *The teacher calls the register first thing in the morning.* ◇ *the electoral register* (= of people who are able to vote in an election) **2** [C, U] (**LANGUAGE**) the type of language (formal or informal) that is used in a piece of writing or speech

ˌregistered ˈmail (*BrE also* ˌregistered ˈpost) *noun* [U] a method of sending a letter or package in which the person sending it can claim money if it arrives late or if it is lost or damaged

ˌregistered ˈtrademark *noun* [C] (*symb.* ®) (**BUSINESS**) the sign or name of a product, etc. that is officially recorded and protected so that nobody else can use it

ˈregister office = REGISTRY OFFICE

registrar /ˌredʒɪˈstrɑː(r)/ *noun* [C] **1** a person whose job is to keep official lists, especially of births, marriages and deaths **2** (**EDUCATION**) a person who is responsible for keeping information about the students at a college or university

registration 🔒+ **B2** /ˌredʒɪˈstreɪʃn/ *noun* [U] putting sb/ sth's name on an official list: *Registration for evening classes will take place on 8 September.*

ˌregiˈstration number *noun* [C] (*BrE*) the numbers and letters on the front and back of a vehicle that are used to identify it

registry /ˈredʒɪstri/ *noun* [C] (*pl.* -ies) a place where official lists are kept

ˈregistry office (*also* ˈregister office) *noun* [C] an office where a marriage can take place and where births, marriages and deaths are officially written down

regress /rɪˈgres/ *verb* [I] ~ **(to sth)** (*formal*) (**PSYCHOLOGY**) to return to an earlier or less advanced form or way of behaving ▶ regression /-ˈgreʃn/ *noun* [U, C]: *He began to show signs of regression to his childhood.*

regressive /rɪˈgresɪv/ *adj.* becoming or making sth less advanced: *The policy has been condemned as a regressive step.*

regret¹ 🔒 **B2** /rɪˈgret/ *verb* [T] (-tt-) **1** ~ **(doing sth)** to feel sorry that you did sth or that you did not do sth: *I hope you won't regret your decision later.* ◇ *Do you regret not taking the job?* **2** ~ **to do sth** (*formal*) used as a way of saying that you are sorry for sth: *I regret to inform you that your application has been unsuccessful.*

regret² 🔒 **B2** /rɪˈgret/ *noun* [U, C] a sad feeling about sth that cannot now be changed: *Do you have any regrets that you didn't go to university?* ▶ regretful /-fl/ *adj.*: *a regretful look/smile* ▶ regretfully /-fəli/ *adv.*

regrettable /rɪˈgretəbl/ *adj.* that you should feel sorry or sad about: *It is deeply regrettable that we were not informed sooner.* ▶ regrettably /-bli/ *adv.*

regular¹ 🔒 **A2** /ˈregjələ(r)/ *adj.*
- FOLLOWING A PATTERN **1** having the same amount of space or time between each thing or part: *a regular heartbeat* ◇ *Nurses checked her blood pressure at regular intervals.* ◇ *The fire alarms are tested on a regular basis.* ◇ *We have regular meetings every Thursday.* **OPP** irregular

- FREQUENT **2** done or happening often: *The doctor advised me to take regular exercise.* ◇ *Accidents are a regular occurrence on this road.* **3** going somewhere or doing sth often: *a regular customer* ◇ *We're regular visitors to Britain.*
- IN GRAMMAR **4** (used about a noun, verb, etc.) having the usual or expected plural, verb form, etc: *'Walk' is a regular verb.* **OPP** irregular
- USUAL **5** [only before noun] normal or usual: *Who is your regular dentist?*
- SAME SHAPE **6** not having any individual part that is different from the rest: *regular teeth/features* ◇ *a regular pattern* **OPP** irregular
- ORDINARY **7** (*especially AmE*) standard, average or normal: *Regular or large fries?*
- PERMANENT **8** fixed or permanent: *a regular income/job* ◇ *a regular soldier/army*
▶ regularity /ˌregjuˈlærəti/ *noun* [U, C] (*pl.* -ies): *Aircraft passed overhead with monotonous regularity.*

regular² /ˈregjələ(r)/ *noun* [C] **1** a person who goes to a particular shop, bar, restaurant, etc. very often **2** a person who often does a particular activity or sport **3** a permanent member of the army, NAVY, etc.

regularly 🔒 **B1** /ˈregjələli/ *adv.* **1** at regular INTERVALS or times: *We meet regularly to discuss the progress of the project.* **2** often: *I go there quite regularly.* **3** in an even or balanced way: *The plants were spaced regularly, about 50 cm apart.*

regulate 🔒+ **B2** /ˈregjuleɪt/ *verb* [T] **1** to control sth by using laws or rules **2** to control a machine, piece of equipment, etc: *You can regulate the temperature in the car with this dial.*

regulation 🔒 **B2** 🌐 /ˌregjuˈleɪʃn/ *noun* **1** [C, usually pl.] an official rule that controls how sth is done: *to observe/obey the safety regulations* ◇ *The plans must comply with EU regulations.* **2** [U] the control of sth by using rules: *state regulation of imports and exports*

regulator 🔒+ **C1** /ˈregjuleɪtə(r)/ *noun* [C] **1** (**BUSINESS**) a person or an organization that officially controls an area of business or industry and makes sure that it is operating fairly **2** (**ENGINEERING**) a device that controls sth such as speed, temperature or pressure

regulatory 🔒+ **C1** /ˈregjələtəri/ *adj.* having the power to control an area of business or industry and make sure that it is operating fairly: *regulatory authorities/bodies*

regurgitate /rɪˈgɜːdʒɪteɪt/ *verb* [T] **1** (*formal*) (**BIOLOGY**) to bring food that has been SWALLOWED back up into the mouth again: *The bird regurgitates half-digested fish to feed its young.* **2** to repeat sth you have heard or read without really thinking about it or understanding it: *He's just regurgitating what his father says.* ▶ regurgitation /rɪˌgɜːdʒɪˈteɪʃn/ *noun* [U]

rehabilitate /ˌriːəˈbɪlɪteɪt/ *verb* [T] to help sb to live a normal life again after an illness, being in prison, etc. ▶ rehabilitation 🔒+ **C1** /ˌriːəˌbɪlɪˈteɪʃn/ *noun* [U]: *a rehabilitation centre for drug addicts*

rehearsal /rɪˈhɜːsl/ *noun* [C, U] (**ARTS AND MEDIA, MUSIC**) the time when you practise a play, dance, piece of music, etc. before you perform it to other people: *a dress rehearsal* (= when all the actors wear their stage clothes) ▶ rehearse /-ˈhɜːs/ *verb* [I, T] ⊃ note at **performing arts**

rehouse /ˌriːˈhaʊz/ *verb* [T] to provide sb with a different home to live in: *Thousands of earthquake victims are still waiting to be rehoused.*

reign 🔒+ **C1** /reɪn/ *verb* [I] **1** ~ **(over sb/sth)** (**POLITICS**) (used about a king or queen) to rule a country **2** to be the best or most important in a particular situation: *Mary, Queen of Scots, reigned over Scotland from 1542 to 1567.* ◇ (*figurative*) *the reigning world champion*

3 ~ **(over sb/sth)** to be in charge of a business or an organization **4** to be present as the most important quality of a particular situation: *Chaos reigned after the first snow of the winter.* ▶ reign ∑+ **C1** *noun* [C]

reign of 'terror *noun* [C] (*pl.* reigns of terror) (**HISTORY**) a period during which there is a lot of violence and many people are killed by the people in power

reiki /'reɪki/ *noun* [U] (**MEDICINE**) a way of treating illness based on the idea that energy can be directed into a person's body by touch

reimburse /ˌriːɪm'bɜːs/ *verb* [T] ~ **sth; ~ sb (for sth)** (*formal*) (**FINANCE**) to pay money back to sb: *The company will reimburse you in full for your travelling expenses.*

rein /reɪn/ *noun* [C, usually pl.] a long narrow leather band that is attached to a metal bar in a horse's mouth and is held by the rider in order to control the horse

reincarnation /ˌriːɪnkɑː'neɪʃn/ *noun* (**RELIGION**) **1** [U] the belief that people who have died can live again in a different body: *Do you believe in reincarnation?* **2** [C, usually sing.] a person or an animal whose body is believed to contain the soul of a dead person: *He believes he is the reincarnation of an Egyptian princess.* ⊃ look at **incarnation** (1)

reindeer /'reɪndɪə(r)/ *noun* [C] (*pl.* reindeer) a type of large brown wild animal with ANTLERS (= hard parts on the head that are like branches), that lives in cold northern regions

reinforce ∑+ **B2** /ˌriːɪn'fɔːs/ *verb* [T] to make sth stronger: *Concrete can be reinforced with steel bars.*

reinforcement /ˌriːɪn'fɔːsmənt/ *noun* **1** reinforcements [pl.] extra people who are sent to make an army, a NAVY, etc. stronger **2** [U, sing.] the act of making sth stronger: *The sea wall is weak in places and needs reinforcement.*

reinstate /ˌriːɪn'steɪt/ *verb* [T] **1** ~ **sb (in/as sth)** to give back a job or position that was taken from sb: *He was cleared of the charge of theft and reinstated as Head of Security.* **2** to return sth to its former position or role ▶ reinstatement *noun* [U]

reinvest /ˌriːɪn'vest/ *verb* [T, I] (**FINANCE**) to put profits that have been made on an investment back into the same investment or into a new one

reissue /ˌriː'ɪʃuː/ *verb* [T] ~ **sth (as sth)** to publish or produce again a book, record, etc. that has not been available for some time: *old jazz recordings reissued as digital downloads*

reiterate /ri'ɪtəreɪt/ *verb* [T] (*formal*) ~ **(that …)** to repeat sth that you have already said, especially to make it very clear: *to reiterate an argument/a demand/an offer* ◇ *Let me reiterate that there are no plans to close the centre.*

reject¹ ∑ **B1** ◑ /rɪ'dʒekt/ *verb* [T] to refuse to accept sb/sth: *I've rejected all the candidates for the job except one.* ◇ *The plan was rejected as being impractical.* ▶ rejection ∑+ **C1** **W** /-'dʒekʃn/ *noun* [C, U]: *Gargi got a rejection from Leeds University.* ◇ *There has been total rejection of the new policy.*

reject² /'riːdʒekt/ *noun* [C] a person or thing that is not accepted because they are not good enough: *Rejects are sold at half price.*

rejoice /rɪ'dʒɔɪs/ *verb* [I, T] ~ **(at/over sth)** (*formal*) to feel or show great happiness: *The people rejoiced at the news of the victory.* ▶ rejoicing *noun* [U]: *There were scenes of rejoicing when the war ended.*

rejoin /ˌriː'dʒɔɪn/ *verb* [T, I] to join sb/sth again after leaving them or it

rejuvenate /rɪ'dʒuːvəneɪt/ *verb* [T, often passive] to make sb/sth feel or look younger ▶ rejuvenation /rɪ,dʒuːvə'neɪʃn/ *noun* [U]

relapse /rɪ'læps/ *verb* [I] ~ **(into sth)** to become worse again after an improvement: *He relapsed into his old bad habits.* ▶ relapse /'riːlæps/ *noun* [C]: *The patient had a relapse and then died.*

relate ∑ **B1** **W** /rɪ'leɪt/ *verb* [T] **1** ~ **A to/with B** to show or make a connection between two or more things: *The report relates heart disease to high levels of stress.* **2** ~ **sth (to sb)** (*formal*) to tell a story to sb: *He related his side of the story to a journalist.* **PHRV** relate to sb/sth **1** to be concerned or involved with sth **2** to be able to understand how sb feels: *Some teenagers find it hard to relate to their parents.*

related ∑ **B1** ◑ /rɪ'leɪtɪd/ *adj.* ~ **(to sb/sth)** **1** connected with sb/sth: *The rise in the cost of living is directly related to the price of oil.* **2** in the same family: *We are related by marriage.*

relation ∑ **B1** ◑ /rɪ'leɪʃn/ *noun* **1** relations [pl.] ~ **(with sb); ~ (between A and B)** the way that people, groups, countries, etc. feel about or behave towards each other: *The police officer stressed that good relations with the community were essential.* ◇ *Relations between the two countries are under strain.* **2** [U] ~ **(between sth and sth); ~ (to sth)** the connection between two or more things: *There seems to be little relation between the cost of the houses and their size.* ◇ *Their salaries **bear no relation** to the number of hours they work.* **3** [C] a member of your family: *a near/close/distant relation* **SYN** relative¹ **IDM** in/with relation to sb/sth **1** concerning sb/sth: *Many questions were asked, particularly in relation to the cost of the new buildings.* **2** compared with: *Prices are low in relation to those in other parts of Europe.*

relationship ∑ **A2** ◑ /rɪ'leɪʃnʃɪp/ *noun* **1** [C] ~ **(with sb/sth); ~ (between A and B)** the way that people, groups, countries, etc. feel about or behave towards each other: *The police have a poor relationship with the local people.* ◇ *The relationship between the parents and the school has improved greatly.* **2** [C] ~ **(with sb); ~ (between A and B)** a friendly or loving connection between people: *to **have a relationship** with somebody* ◇ *The film describes the relationship between a young man and an older woman.* ◇ *He'd never been **in a** serious **relationship** before he got married.* ◇ *Do you have a close relationship with your brother?* **3** [C, U] ~ **(to sth); ~ (between A and B)** the way in which two or more things are connected: *the relationship of art to reality* ◇ *Is there a relationship between violence on TV and the increase in crime?* **4** [C, U] ~ **(to sb); ~ (between A and B)** a family connection: *'What is your relationship to Bruce?' 'He's married to my cousin.'*

relative¹ ∑ **B1** **W** /'relətɪv/ *adj.* **1** ~ **(to sth)** when compared to sb/sth else: *the position of the earth relative to the sun* ◇ *They live in relative luxury.* **2** (**LANGUAGE**) referring to an earlier noun, sentence or part of a sentence: *In the phrase 'the lady who lives next door', 'who' is a **relative pronoun** and 'who lives next door' is a **relative clause**.*

relative² ∑ **B1** **W** /'relətɪv/ *noun* [C] a member of your family: *a close/distant relative* **SYN** relation

relatively ∑ **B2** ◑ /'relətɪvli/ *adv.* to quite a large degree, especially when compared to others: *Spanish is a relatively easy language to learn.*

relativity /ˌrelə'tɪvəti/ *noun* [U] (**PHYSICS**) Einstein's belief that all movement is affected by space, light, time and GRAVITY (= the force that makes things fall to the ground)

relax 🔊 **A1** /rɪˈlæks/ *verb* **1** [I, T] to rest while you are doing sth that you enjoy, especially after work or effort: *This holiday will give you a chance to relax.* ◇ *They spent the evening relaxing in front of the TV.* **SYN** **unwind 2** [I] to become or make sb become calmer and less worried: *Relax — everything's going to be OK!* ◇ *A hot bath will relax you after a hard day's work.* **3** [I, T] to become or make sth become less hard or tight: *Don't relax your grip on the rope!* **4** [T] to make rules or laws less strict

relaxation /ˌriːlækˈseɪʃn/ *noun* **1** [U, C] a way or ways to rest and enjoy yourself, especially after work or effort: *Everyone needs time for rest and relaxation.* **2** [U] the state of feeling calm and not worried: *relaxation techniques* **3** [U] making sth less strict, tight or strong

relaxed 🔊 **B1** /rɪˈlækst/ *adj.* calm and not worried: *The relaxed atmosphere made everyone feel at ease.* **SYN** **calm¹** ◇ look at **stressed** (1)

relaxing 🔊 **B1** /rɪˈlæksɪŋ/ *adj.* pleasant, helping you to rest and become less worried: *a quiet, relaxing holiday*

relay¹ /ˈriːleɪ, rɪˈleɪ/ *verb* [T] **1** to receive and then pass on a signal or message: *Instructions were relayed to us by phone.* **2** (*BrE*) to send out a programme on the radio or TV

relay² /ˈriːleɪ/ (*also* ˈrelay race) *noun* [C] (**SPORT**) a race in which each member of a team runs, swims, etc. one part of the race

release¹ 🔊 **B1** /rɪˈliːs/ *verb* [T]
- SET FREE **1 ~ sb/sth (from sth)** to allow sb/sth to be free: *He's been released from prison.* ◇ (*figurative*) *His firm released him for two days a week to go on a training course.*
- STOP HOLDING STH **2** to stop holding sth so that it can move, fly, fall, etc. freely: *1 000 balloons were released at the ceremony.* ◇ (*figurative*) *Crying is a good way to release pent-up emotions.*
- MOVE STH **3** to move sth from a fixed position: *He released the handbrake and drove off.*
- MAKE PUBLIC **4** to allow sth to be known by the public: *The identity of the victim has not been released.* **5** to make a film, record, etc. available so the public can see or hear it: *Their new album is due to be released next week.*

release² 🔊 **B1** **W** /rɪˈliːs/ *noun* [U, C] **1 ~ (of sb/sth) (from sth)** the freeing of sb/sth or the state of being freed: *The release of the hostages took place this morning.* ◇ *I had a great feeling of release when my exams were finished.* **2** (**ARTS AND MEDIA, LITERATURE**) a book, film, music recording, piece of news, etc. that has been made available to the public; the act of making sth available to the public: *a press release* ◇ *The band played their latest release.* ◇ *The film won't be/go on release until March.*

relegate /ˈrelɪɡeɪt/ *verb* [T] **~ sb/sth (to sth)** to put sb/sth into a lower level or position: *She was relegated to the role of assistant.* ▶ **relegation** /ˌrelɪˈɡeɪʃn/ *noun* [U]

relent /rɪˈlent/ *verb* [I] **1** to finally agree to sth that you had refused: *Her parents finally relented and allowed her to go to the concert.* **2** to become less determined, strong, etc: *The heavy rain finally relented and we went out.*

relentless /rɪˈlentləs/ *adj.* not stopping or changing: *the relentless fight against crime* ▶ **relentlessly** *adv.*: *The sun beat down relentlessly.*

relevant 🔊 **B2** **O** /ˈreləvənt/ *adj.* **~ (to sb/sth)** **1** connected with what is happening or being talked about: *Much of what was said was not directly relevant to my case.* **2** important and useful: *Many people feel that poetry is no longer relevant in today's world.* **OPP** **irrelevant** ▶ **relevance** 🔊+ **C1** **W** /-vəns/ *noun* [U]: *I honestly can't see the relevance of what he said.*

reliable 🔊 **B1** /rɪˈlaɪəbl/ *adj.* that you can trust: *Japanese cars are usually very reliable.* ◇ *Is he a reliable witness?* **OPP** **unreliable** ◇ verb **rely** ▶ **reliability** 🔊+ **C1** **W** /rɪˌlaɪəˈbɪləti/ *noun* [U] ▶ **reliably** /rɪˈlaɪəbli/ *adv.*: *I have been reliably informed that there will be no trains tomorrow.*

reliance **W** /rɪˈlaɪəns/ *noun* [U] **~ on sb/sth 1** the state of not being able to survive, be successful, etc. without sb/sth: *the country's reliance on imported oil* **SYN** **dependence 2** the fact of being able to trust sb/sth: *Don't place too much reliance on her promises.* ◇ verb **rely**

reliant /rɪˈlaɪənt/ *adj.* **~ on sb/sth** not able to live or work without sb/sth: *They are totally reliant on the state for financial support.* **SYN** **dependent** ◇ look at **self-reliant** ◇ verb **rely**

relic /ˈrelɪk/ *noun* [C] (**HISTORY**) an object, a tradition, etc. from the past that still survives today

relief 🔊 **B2** /rɪˈliːf/ *noun* **1** [U, sing.] the feeling that you have when sth unpleasant stops or becomes less strong: *What a relief! That awful noise has stopped.* ◇ *It was a great relief to know they were safe.* ◇ *to breathe a sigh of relief* ◇ *To my relief, he didn't argue with my suggestion at all.* **2** [U] **~ (from sth)** the act of removing or reducing pain, worry, etc: *The drugs brought him some relief from the pain.* **3** [U] (**POLITICS**) money or food that is given to help people who are in trouble or difficulty: *disaster relief for the flood victims* **SYN** **aid¹** ◇ note at **disaster 4** [U] (**FINANCE**) a reduction in the amount of tax you have to pay **5** [U, C] (**ART**) a way of decorating wood, stone, etc. by cutting designs into the surface of it so that some parts stick out more than others; a design that is made in this way: *The column was decorated in high relief* (= with designs that stick out a lot) *with scenes from Greek mythology.* ◇ look at **bas-relief**

reˈlief map *noun* [C] (**GEOGRAPHY**) a map that uses different colours to show the different heights of hills, valleys, etc.

relieve 🔊+ **B2** /rɪˈliːv/ *verb* [T] to make an unpleasant feeling or situation stop or get better: *This injection should relieve the pain.* ◇ *We played cards to relieve the boredom.* **PHR V** **relieve sb of sth** to take sth away from sb: *to relieve somebody of responsibility*

relieved 🔊+ **B2** /rɪˈliːvd/ *adj.* pleased because your fear or worry has been taken away: *I was very relieved to hear that you weren't seriously hurt.*

religion 🔊 **B1** /rɪˈlɪdʒən/ *noun* **1** [U] the belief in a god or gods and the activities connected with this **2** [C] one of the systems of beliefs that is based on a belief in a god or gods: *Representatives of all the major world religions were present at the talks.*

religious 🔊 **B1** /rɪˈlɪdʒəs/ *adj.* (**RELIGION**) **1** connected with religion: *religious faith* **2** having a strong belief in a religion: *a deeply religious person*

religiously /rɪˈlɪdʒəsli/ *adv.* **1** very carefully or regularly: *She stuck to the diet religiously.* **2** (**RELIGION**) in a religious way

relinquish /rɪˈlɪŋkwɪʃ/ *verb* [T] (*formal*) to stop having or doing sth **SYN** **give up**

relish¹ /ˈrelɪʃ/ *verb* [T] to enjoy sth or to look forward to sth very much: *I don't relish the prospect of getting up early tomorrow.*

relish² /ˈrelɪʃ/ *noun* **1** [U] great pleasure: *She accepted the award with obvious relish.* **2** [U, C] a thick, cold sauce made from fruit and vegetables

relive /ˌriːˈlɪv/ *verb* [T] to remember sth and imagine that it is happening again

reload /ˌriːˈləʊd/ *verb* [I, T] to put sth into a machine again: *to reload a gun* ◇ *to reload a computer program*

relocate /ˌriːləʊˈkeɪt/ *verb* [I, T] (**BUSINESS**) (used especially about a company or workers) to move or to move sb/sth to a new place to work or operate: *The firm may be forced to relocate from New York to Stanford.* ▸ **relocation** /-ˈkeɪʃn/ *noun* [U]: *relocation costs*

reluctant ⓘ+ 🄲🄻 /rɪˈlʌktənt/ *adj.* ~ (to do sth) not wanting to do sth because you are not sure it is the right thing to do: *They were reluctant to reveal the names.* ▸ **reluctance** /-ˈlʌktəns/ *noun* [U]: *Tony left with obvious reluctance.* ▸ **reluctantly** *adv.*

rely ⓘ 🄱🄸 ⊙ /rɪˈlaɪ/ *verb* (relying; relies; *pt, pp* relied)

PHR V **rely on/upon sb/ sth (to do sth)** **1** to need sb/sth and not be able to live or work properly without them or it: *The old lady had to rely on other people to do her shopping for her.* **2** to trust sb/ sth to work or behave well: *Can I rely on you to keep a secret?* ◌ look at **reliable**, **reliant** ◌ note at **trust²** ◌ noun **reliance**

WORD FAMILY
rely *verb*
reliable *adj.*
(≠**unreliable**)
reliability *noun*
(≠**unreliability**)
reliance *noun*

remade /ˌriːˈmeɪd/ past tense, past participle of **remake²**

remain ⓘ 🄱🄸 /rɪˈmeɪn/ *verb* **1** linking verb to stay or continue in the same place or condition: *to remain silent/standing/seated* ◌ note at **trend¹** **2** [I] to be left after other people or things have gone: *Josef went to live in America but his family remained behind in Europe.* **3** [I] to still need to be done, said or dealt with: *It remains to be seen* (= we do not know yet) *whether we've made the right decision.* ◇ *Although he seems very pleasant, the fact remains that I don't trust him.*

remainder ⓘ+ 🄲🄻 /rɪˈmeɪndə(r)/ (*usually* the remainder) *noun* [sing. + sing./pl. verb] the people, things, etc. that are left after the others have gone away or been dealt with; the rest

remaining /rɪˈmeɪnɪŋ/ *adj.* [only before noun] still needing to be done or dealt with: *They spent the remaining two days of their holiday relaxing on the beach.* ◇ *Any remaining tickets for the concert will be sold on the door.*

remains ⓘ+ 🄲🄻 /rɪˈmeɪnz/ *noun* [pl.] **1** (**ARCHITECTURE**) what is left behind after other parts have been used or taken away: *The builders found the remains of a Roman mosaic floor.* **2** (*formal*) a dead body (sometimes one that has been found somewhere a

long time after death): *Human remains were discovered in the wood.*

remake¹ /ˈriːmeɪk/ *noun* [C] (**ARTS AND MEDIA**) a new or different version of sth such as an old film or song

remake² /ˌriːˈmeɪk/ *verb* [T] (*pt, pp* remade /-ˈmeɪd/) to make a new or different version of sth such as an old film or song; to make sth again

remand /rɪˈmɑːnd/ *noun* [U] (**LAW**) the time before a prisoner's trial takes place: *a remand prisoner* ▸ **remand** *verb* [T]: *The man was **remanded in custody** (= sent to prison until the trial).* **IDM** **on remand** (used about a prisoner) waiting for the trial to take place

remark¹ ⓘ 🄱🄸 /rɪˈmɑːk/ *verb* [I, T] ~ (on/upon sb/sth) to say or write sth; to comment: *A lot of people have remarked on the similarity between them.* ◌ look at **observation** (3) ◌ note at **comment²**

remark² ⓘ 🄱🄸 /rɪˈmɑːk/ *noun* [C] something that you say or write about sb/sth ◌ note at **statement**

remarkable ⓘ+ 🄱🄸 /rɪˈmɑːkəbl/ *adj.* unusual and surprising in a way that people notice: *That is a remarkable achievement for somebody so young.* **SYN** **astonishing** ▸ **remarkably** ⓘ+ 🄱🄸 /-bli/ *adv.*

remedial /rɪˈmiːdiəl/ *adj.* [only before noun] **1** aimed at improving or correcting a situation **2** (**EDUCATION**) helping people who are slower at learning than others: *remedial English classes*

remedy¹ ⓘ+ 🄲🄻 /ˈremədi/ *noun* [C] (*pl.* -ies) **1** ~ (for sth) a way of solving a problem: *There is no easy remedy for unemployment.* **SYN** **solution** **2** ~ (for sth) (**MEDICINE**) something that makes you better when you are ill or in pain: *Hot lemon with honey is a good remedy for colds.* **3** ~ (against sth) (**LAW**) a way of dealing with a problem, using the processes of the law: *Holding copyright provides the only legal remedy against unauthorized copying.* **SYN** **redress²**

remedy² /ˈremədi/ *verb* [T] (remedying; remedies; *pt, pp* remedied) to change or improve sth that is wrong or bad

remember ⓘ 🄰🄸 /rɪˈmembə(r)/ *verb* **1** [T, I] ~ (doing sth) to have an image of an event, a person, etc. in your memory: *Do you remember the night we first met?* ◇ *Do you remember meeting him for the first time?* ◇ *As far as I can remember, I haven't seen him before.* **2** [T, I] ~ (that) … to bring a fact, piece of information, etc. back into your mind: *I'm sorry. I don't remember your name.* ◇ *Remember (that) we're having visitors tonight.* ◇ *We arranged to go out tonight — remember?* **3** [T] ~ (to do sth) to not forget to do what you have to do: *I remembered to buy the coffee.* ◇ *Did you remember your camera?* **4** [T] to think about and show respect for sb who is dead **5** [T] to give money, etc. to sb/sth: *to remember somebody in your will* **IDM** **remember me to sb** used when you want to send good wishes to a person you have not seen for a long time: *Please remember me to your wife.*

remembrance /rɪˈmembrəns/ *noun* [U] (in) ~ (of sb/sth) thinking about and showing respect for sb who is dead: *a service in remembrance of those killed in the war* ◇ *a remembrance service*

remind ⓘ 🄱🄸 /rɪˈmaɪnd/ *verb* [T] ~ sb (about/of sth); ~ sb (to do sth/that …) to help sb to remember sth, especially sth important that they have to do: *Can you remind me of your address?* ◇ *He reminded the children to wash their hands.* ◇ *Remind me what we're supposed to be doing tomorrow.*

▼ COLLOCATIONS

religion

Six of the main world **religions** or **faiths** are **Buddhism**, **Christianity**, **Hinduism**, **Islam**, **Judaism** and **Sikhism**: *He's a follower of Sikhism.* **Followers** of these religions are called **Buddhists**, **Christians**, **Hindus**, **Muslims**, **Jews** and **Sikhs**: *She's a Hindu.* ◇ *He's a Muslim.* You can **turn to/embrace** religion: *Elly turned to religion after her father's death.* You can **convert to/reject** a faith: *He converted to Judaism when he got married.* A follower of a religion **preaches**, **teaches** or **proclaims** its **beliefs**: *Buddha came to preach his first sermon near Varanasi.* You can talk about the **rise/ spread** of religion: *He described the rise of Christianity in the first century.* ◇ *Islam spread rapidly through North Africa.*

PHR V **remind sb of sb/sth** to cause sb to remember sb/sth: *That smell reminds me of school.* ◇ *You remind me of your father.*

reminder 🔑+ **C1** /rɪˈmaɪndə(r)/ *noun* [C] something that makes you remember sth: *We received a reminder that we hadn't paid the electricity bill.*

reminisce /ˌremɪˈnɪs/ *verb* [I] **~ (about sb/sth)** to talk about pleasant things that happened in the past

reminiscent /ˌremɪˈnɪsnt/ *adj.* [not before noun] **~ of sb/sth** that makes you remember sb/sth; similar to: *His suit was reminiscent of an old army uniform.*

remission /rɪˈmɪʃn/ *noun* [U, C] **1** (**HEALTH**) a period during which a serious illness improves for a time and the patient seems to get better: *The patient has been* ***in remission*** *for the past six months.* **2** (*BrE*) (**LAW**) a reduction in the amount of time sb spends in prison, usually because they have behaved well: *With remission for good behaviour, he could be out by June.* **3** (*formal*) (**FINANCE**) an act of reducing or cancelling the amount of money that sb has to pay: *There is a partial remission of fees for overseas students.*

remit¹ /ˈriːmɪt, rɪˈmɪt/ *noun* [C, usually sing.] **~ (of sb/sth); ~ (to do sth)** (*BrE*) the area of activity over which a particular person or group has authority, control or influence: *Such decisions are* ***outside the remit*** *of this committee.* ◇ *The committee had a remit to report on medical services.*

remit² /rɪˈmɪt/ *verb* [T] (-tt-) (*formal*) **1 ~ sth (to sb)** (**FINANCE**) to send money, etc. to a person or place: *to remit funds* ◇ *Payment will be remitted to you in full.* **2** (**LAW**) to cancel or free sb from a debt, duty, punishment, etc: *to remit a fine* ◇ *to remit a prison sentence* **SYN** **cancel**

PHR V **remit sth to sb** (**LAW**) to send a matter to an authority so that a decision can be made: *The case was remitted to the Court of Appeal.*

remnant /ˈremnənt/ *noun* [C, usually pl.] a piece of sth that is left after the rest has gone: *These few trees are the remnants of a huge forest.*

remorse /rɪˈmɔːs/ *noun* [U] **~ (for sth/doing sth)** the feeling of being very sorry for sth wrong that you have done: *She was filled with remorse for what she had done.* ➲ look at **guilt** (1) ▸ **remorseful** /-fl/ *adj.*

remorseless /rɪˈmɔːsləs/ *adj.* **1** not stopping or becoming less strong: *a remorseless attack on somebody* **2** showing no PITY ▸ **remorselessly** *adv.*

remote 🔑 **B1** /rɪˈməʊt/ *adj.* (**remoter; remotest**) **1 ~ (from sth)** far away from where other people live: *a remote island in the Pacific* ◇ (*figurative*) *The film star's lifestyle was very remote from that of most ordinary people.* **2** [only before noun] far away in time: *the remote past/future* **3** not very friendly or interested in other people: *He seemed rather remote.* **4** (**COMPUTING**) that you can connect to from far away, using an electronic link: *Staff working from home have remote access to the company's network.* ◇ *remote working* **5** not very great: *I haven't* ***the remotest*** *idea who could have done such a thing.* ◇ *a remote possibility* ▸ **remoteness** *noun* [U]

reˌmote conˈtrol *noun* **1** [U] a system for controlling sth from a distance: *The doors can be opened by remote control.* **2** (*also informal* **remote**) [C] a piece of equipment for controlling sth from a distance

remotely /rɪˈməʊtli/ *adv.* **1** (used in negative sentences) to a very small degree; at all: *I'm not remotely interested in your problems.* **2** from a distance: *Offices were closed and staff worked remotely.* ◇ *remotely operated vehicles*

removable /rɪˈmuːvəbl/ *adj.* that can be taken off or out of sth **SYN** **detachable**

removal 🔑+ **C1** **W** /rɪˈmuːvl/ *noun* **1** [U] the act of taking sb/sth away: *the removal of restrictions/regulations/rights* **2** [C, U] the activity of moving from one house to live in another: *a removal van*

remove¹ 🔑 **A2** **W** /rɪˈmuːv/ *verb* [T] **1 ~ sb/sth (from sth)** to take sb/sth off or away: *Remove the saucepan from the heat.* ◇ *This washing powder will remove most stains.* ◇ *to remove doubts/fears/problems* ◇ *I would like you to remove my name from your mailing list.* ◇ *He had an operation to remove the tumour.* **2 ~ sb (from sth)** to make sb leave their job or position: *The elections removed the government from power.*

remove² /rɪˈmuːv/ *noun* [U, C] (*formal*) an amount by which two things are separated: *Jane seemed to be living* ***at one remove*** *from reality.*

removed /rɪˈmuːvd/ *adj.* [not before noun] far or different from sth: *Hospitals today are* ***far removed from*** *what they were 50 years ago.*

remover /rɪˈmuːvə(r)/ *noun* [C, U] a substance that cleans off paint, dirty marks, etc: *make-up remover*

remuneration /rɪˌmjuːnəˈreɪʃn/ *noun* [U, C] (*formal*) an amount of money that is paid to sb for the work they have done: *a generous* ***remuneration package***

the Renaissance /ðə ˌrɪˈneɪsns/ *noun* [sing.] (**ARTS AND MEDIA, HISTORY**) the period in Europe during the fourteenth, fifteenth and sixteenth centuries when people became interested in the ideas and culture of ancient Greece and Rome, and used these influences in their own art, literature, etc: *Renaissance art/drama*

renal /ˈriːnl/ *adj.* (**ANATOMY**) involving or connected to the KIDNEYS (= the two organs in the body that separate waste liquid from the blood): *renal failure*

rename /ˌriːˈneɪm/ *verb* [T] to give sb/sth a new name: *to rename a street* ◇ *Leningrad was renamed St Petersburg.*

render 🔑+ **C1** /ˈrendə(r)/ *verb* [T] (*formal*) **1** to cause sb/sth to be in a certain condition: *She was rendered speechless by the criticism.* **2** to give help, etc. to sb: *to render somebody a service/render a service to somebody*

rendezvous /ˈrɒndɪvuː, -deɪ-/ *noun* [C] (*pl.* **rendezvous** /-vuːz/) **1** a meeting that you have arranged with sb: *He had a secret rendezvous with Daniela.* **2** a place where people often meet: *The cafe is a popular rendezvous for students.*

rendition /renˈdɪʃn/ *noun* [C] the performance of sth, especially a song or piece of music; the particular way in which it is performed

renegade /ˈrenɪɡeɪd/ *noun* [C] (*formal*) **1** (often used as an adjective) a person who leaves one political, religious, etc. group to join another that has very different views **2** a person who decides to live outside a group or society because they have different opinions: *teenage renegades*

renew 🔑+ **C1** /rɪˈnjuː/ *verb* [T] **1** to start sth again: *renewed outbreaks of violence* ◇ *to renew a friendship* **2** to make sth legally acceptable for a further period of time: *to renew a contract/passport/library book* ▸ **renewal** /-əl/ *noun* [U, C]: *When is your passport due for renewal?*

renewable /rɪˈnjuːəbl/ *adj.* **1** (**ENVIRONMENT**) (used about sources of energy) that can be replaced naturally: *renewable resources such as wind and solar power* **OPP** **non-renewable** **2** that can be continued or replaced with a new one for another period of time: *The work permit is not renewable.*

renewables /rɪˈnjuːəblz/ *noun* [pl.] (*also* reˌnewable ˈenergy* [U]) (**ENVIRONMENT**) types of energy that can be replaced naturally such as energy from wind or water

renewed /rɪˈnjuːd/ *adj.* happening again with increased interest or strength: *renewed enthusiasm*

renounce /rɪˈnaʊns/ *verb* [T] (*formal*) to say formally that you no longer want to have sth or to be connected with sth ⊃ *noun* **renunciation**

renovate /ˈrenəveɪt/ *verb* [T] (**ARCHITECTURE**) to repair an old building, etc. and put it back into good condition ▶ renovation /ˌrenəˈveɪʃn/ *noun* [U, C, usually pl.]: *The house is in need of complete renovation* .

renown /rɪˈnaʊn/ *noun* [U] (*formal*) the state of being famous and receiving respect because of sth you have done that people admire ▶ renowned ⟨+ **C1** *adj.* ~ (**for/as sth**): *The region is renowned for its food.*

rent¹ ⟨ **B1** /rent/ *noun* [U, C] (**FINANCE**) money that you pay regularly for the use of land, a house or a building: *a high/low rent* ◇ *She was allowed to live there rent-free until she found a job.* ◇ *Is this house for rent* (= available to rent)?

rent² ⟨ **B1** /rent/ *verb* **1** [T, I] ~ (**sth**) (**from sb**) to pay money for the use of land, a building, a machine, etc: *Do you own or rent your flat?* ◇ *to rent a car* ⊃ look at **hire¹** (3) **2** [T] ~ **sth** (**out**) (**to sb**) to allow sb to use land, a building, a machine, etc. for money: *We could rent out the small bedroom to a student.* **3** [T] (*especially AmE*) = HIRE¹ (3)

rental ⟨+ **C1** /ˈrentl/ *noun* **1** [U, C, usually sing.] the amount of money that you pay to use sth for a particular period of time: *Phone charges include line rental.* **2** [U] the act of renting sth; an arrangement to rent sth: *the world's largest car rental company* ◇ *video rental* ⊃ look at **hire¹** 3 **3** [C] (*especially AmE*) a house, car, or piece of equipment that you can rent: *'Is this your own car?' 'No, it's a rental.'*

renunciation /rɪˌnʌnsiˈeɪʃn/ *noun* [U, C] (*formal*) saying that you no longer want sth or believe in sth ⊃ *verb* **renounce**

reorganize (*BrE also* -ise) /riˈɔːɡənaɪz/ *verb* [T, I] to organize sth again or in a new way ▶ reorganization (*BrE also* -isation) /riˌɔːɡənaɪˈzeɪʃn/ *noun* [U, C]

Rep. *abbr.* (in writing) **1** = REPRESENTATIVE² (3) **2** = REPUBLICAN (2)

rep /rep/ (*informal*) = REPRESENTATIVE² (2)

repaid /rɪˈpeɪd/ past tense, past participle of **repay**

repair¹ ⟨ **A2** /rɪˈpeə(r)/ *verb* [T] **1** to put sth old or damaged back into good condition: *These cars can be expensive to repair.* ◇ *How much will it cost to have the washing machine repaired?* **SYN** **fix¹**, **mend¹** ⊃ look at **irreparable 2** to say or do sth to improve a bad or an unpleasant situation: *It is difficult to see how relations between the two countries can be repaired.*

repair² ⟨ **B1** /rɪˈpeə(r)/ *noun* [C, U] something that you do to fix sth that is damaged: *The school is closed for repairs to the roof.* ◇ *The road is in need of repair.* ◇ *The bridge is under repair.* ◇ *The bike was damaged beyond repair so I threw it away.*
IDM **in good, bad, etc. repair** in a good, bad, etc. condition

reparation /ˌrepəˈreɪʃn/ *noun* (*formal*) **1** [pl.] (**POLITICS**) money that is paid by a country that has lost a war, for the damage, injuries, etc. that it has caused **2** [U] (**LAW**) the act of giving sth to sb or doing sth for them in order to show that you are sorry for suffering that you have caused: *Offenders should be forced to make reparation to the community.*

repatriate /ˌriːˈpætrieɪt/ *verb* [T] (**POLITICS**) to send or bring sb back to their own country ▶ repatriation /ˌriːˌpætriˈeɪʃn/ *noun* [U, C]

repay /rɪˈpeɪ/ *verb* [T] (*pt, pp* repaid /-ˈpeɪd/) **1** ~ **sth** (**to sb**); ~ (**sb**) **sth** to pay back money that you owe to sb: *to repay a debt/loan* ◇ *When will you repay the money to them?* ◇ *When will you repay them the money?* **2** ~ **sb** (**for sth**) to give sth to sb in return for sth kind or helpful that they have done for you: *How can I ever repay you for all you have done for me?*

repayable /rɪˈpeɪəbl/ *adj.* (**FINANCE**) that you can or must pay back: *The loan is repayable over three years.*

repayment /rɪˈpeɪmənt/ *noun* **1** [U] paying sth back: *the repayment of a loan* **2** [C, usually pl.] money that you must pay back to sb/sth regularly: *I make monthly repayments on my loan.*

repeal /rɪˈpiːl/ *verb* [T] (*formal*) (**LAW**) to officially make a law no longer have any legal force

repeat¹ ⟨ **A1** /rɪˈpiːt/ *verb*
1 [T, I] ~ (**sth/yourself**) to say, write or do sth again or more than once: *Could you repeat what you just said?* ◇ *The essay is quite good, but you repeat yourself several times.* ◇ *Raise and lower your left leg ten times, then repeat with the right.* ◇ *Don't repeat the same mistake again.* **2** [T] ~ **sth** (**to sb**) to say or write sth that sb else has said or written or that you have learnt: *Please don't repeat what you've heard here to anyone.* ◇ *Repeat each sentence after me.* ⊃ *noun* **repetition**

WORD FAMILY
repeat *verb, noun*
repeatable *adj.*
(≠ **unrepeatable**)
repeated *adj.*
repetition *noun*
repetitive *adj.*
repetitious *adj.*

repeat² ⟨ **B1** /rɪˈpiːt/ *noun* [C] something that is done, shown, given, etc. again: *I think I've seen this programme before — it must be a repeat.*

repeatable /rɪˈpiːtəbl/ *adj.* **1** (usually in negative sentences) (used about a comment, etc.) polite and not offensive: *His reply was not repeatable.* **2** that can be repeated **OPP** **unrepeatable**

repeated ⟨ **B1** /rɪˈpiːtɪd/ *adj.* [only before noun] done or happening many times: *There have been repeated accidents on this stretch of road.* ▶ repeatedly *adv.*: *I've asked him repeatedly not to leave his bike there.*

repel /rɪˈpel/ *verb* [T] (-ll-) **1** to send or push sb/sth back or away **2** to make sb feel horror or DISGUST: *The dirt and smell repelled her.* **3** (**PHYSICS**) if one thing **repels** another, or if two things **repel** each other, an electrical or MAGNETIC force pushes them apart: *Like poles repel each other.* **OPP** **attract** ⊃ *noun* **repulsion**

repellent¹ /rɪˈpelənt/ *noun* [U, C] a chemical substance that is used to keep insects, etc. away

repellent² /rɪˈpelənt/ *adj.* very unpleasant, causing strong dislike: *a repellent smell*

repent /rɪˈpent/ *verb* [I, T] ~ (**of sth**) (*formal*) to feel and show that you are sorry about sth bad that you have done: *to repent of your sins* ◇ *He repented his hasty decision.* ▶ repentance *noun* [U] ▶ repentant *adj.*

repercussion /ˌriːpəˈkʌʃn/ *noun* [C, usually pl.] an unpleasant effect or result of sth you do: *His resignation will have serious repercussions.* ⊃ note at **effect¹**

repertoire /ˈrepətwɑː(r)/ *noun* [C] **1** (**ARTS AND MEDIA, MUSIC**) all the plays or music that an actor or a musician knows and can perform: *He must have sung every song in his repertoire last night.* **2** all the things that a person is able to do

repetition /ˌrepəˈtɪʃn/ *noun* [U, C] the fact of doing sth again; sth that you do or that happens again: *to learn by repetition* ◇ *Let's try to avoid a repetition of what happened last Friday.* ➔ *verb* **repeat**

repetitious /ˌrepəˈtɪʃəs/ *adj.* involving sth that is often repeated: *a long and repetitious speech* ▸ **repetitiously** *adv.* ▸ **repetitiousness** *noun* [U]

repetitive /rɪˈpetətɪv/ *adj.* not interesting because the same thing is repeated many times

rephrase /ˌriːˈfreɪz/ *verb* [T] to say or write sth using different words in order to make the meaning clearer

replace ⓘ A2 Ⓦ /rɪˈpleɪs/ *verb* [T] 1 ~ sb/sth (as/with sb/sth) to take the place of sb/sth; to use sb/sth in place of another person or thing: *Teachers will never be replaced by computers in the classroom.* 2 ~ sth (with sb/sth) to exchange sth/sth for sb/sth that is better or newer: *I replaced the old battery with a new one.* ◇ *We will replace any goods that are damaged.* 3 to put sth back in the place where it was before: *Please replace the books on the shelves when you have finished with them.*

replaceable /rɪˈpleɪsəbl/ *adj.* that can be replaced **OPP** **irreplaceable**

replacement ⓘ+ C1 Ⓦ /rɪˈpleɪsmənt/ *noun* 1 [U] exchanging sb/sth for sb/sth that is better or newer: *The carpets are in need of replacement.* 2 [C] ~ (for sb/sth) a person or thing that will take the place of sb/sth

replay[1] /ˈriːpleɪ/ *noun* [C] 1 (SPORT) a sports match that is played again because neither team won the first time 2 a short section of a recording that you watch or listen to again: *Now let's see an action replay of that tremendous goal!*

replay[2] /ˌriːˈpleɪ/ *verb* [T] 1 (usually passive) (SPORT) to play a sports match, etc. again because neither team won the first time: *The match will be replayed on Thursday.* 2 to play again a video, music recording or video game: *They kept replaying the goal over and over again.*

replenish /rɪˈplenɪʃ/ *verb* [T] ~ sth (with sth) (*formal*) to make sth full again by replacing what has been used: *to replenish food and water supplies*

replete /rɪˈpliːt/ *adj.* [not before noun] ~ (with sth) (*formal*) filled with sth; with a full supply of sth: *literature replete with drama and excitement*

replica /ˈreplɪkə/ *noun* [C] ~ (of sth) an exact copy of sth

replicate /ˈreplɪkeɪt/ *verb* [T] (*formal*) to copy sth exactly **SYN** **duplicate**[1] ▸ **replication** /ˌreplɪˈkeɪʃn/ *noun* [U, C]

replicator /ˈreplɪkeɪtə(r)/ *noun* [C] (BIOLOGY) a GENE (= a unit inside a cell that controls a particular quality in a living thing) that is able to make a section of DNA copy itself

reply ⓘ A2 /rɪˈplaɪ/ *verb* [I, T] (replying; replies; *pt, pp* replied) ~ (to sb/sth) (with sth) to say, write or do sth as an answer to sb/sth: *I wrote to Sue but she hasn't replied.* ◇ *'Yes, I will,' she replied.* ◇ *to reply to a question* ◇ *Brazil replied to Chile's early goal with a penalty.* ▸ **reply** ⓘ A2 *noun* [C, U] (*pl.* -ies) ~ (to sth): *Al nodded in reply to my question.*

report[1] ⓘ A2 Ⓦ /rɪˈpɔːt/ *verb* 1 [T, I] ~ (on sth/sb) (to sb); ~ (doing sth); ~ (that) ... to give people information about what you have seen, heard, done, etc: *The company reported huge profits last year.* ◇ *The research team will report to the committee on their findings next month.* ◇ *Several people reported seeing the boy.* ◇ *Several people reported (that) they had seen the boy.* 2 [T, I] ~ (on sth) (in a newspaper or on the TV or radio) to write or speak about sth that has happened: *The paper sent a journalist to report on the*

events. 3 be reported [T] **be reported (to do sth); be reported (as doing sth)** used to say that you have heard sth said, but you are not sure if it is true: *The 70-year-old actor is reported to be/as being comfortable in hospital.* 4 [T] ~ sth (to sb); ~ sb (to sb) (for doing sth) (LAW) to tell a person in authority about an accident, a crime, etc. or about sth wrong that sb has done: *All accidents must be reported to the police.* ◇ *Somebody reported her to the head teacher for cheating.* 5 [I] ~ (to sb/sth) (for sth) to tell sb that you have arrived: *On your arrival, please report to the reception desk.* ◇ *to report for duty*

PHR V **report back (on sth) (to sb)** to give information to sb about sth that they have asked you to find out about: *One person in each group will report back to the class on what you've decided.*
report to sb to have sb as your manager in the company or organization that you work for

report[2] ⓘ A1 Ⓦ /rɪˈpɔːt/ *noun* [C] 1 ~ (on sth); ~ (of sth) a written or spoken description of what you have seen, heard, done, studied, etc: *newspaper reports* ◇ *a report on the company's finances* ◇ *a first-hand report* (= from the person who saw what happened) *of the event* 2 (EDUCATION) a written statement about the work of a student at school, college, etc: *to get a good/bad report*

reportedly ⓘ+ C1 /rɪˈpɔːtɪdli/ *adv.* according to what some people say: *The band have reportedly decided to split up.*

re,ported 'speech (*also* indirect speech) *noun* [U] (GRAMMAR) a report of what sb has said that does not use their exact words. If sb says 'I'll phone again later', this becomes *She said that she would phone again later* in reported speech. ➔ look at **direct speech**

reporter ⓘ A2 /rɪˈpɔːtə(r)/ *noun* [C] (ARTS AND MEDIA) a person who writes about the news in a newspaper or speaks about it on the TV or radio ➔ look at **journalist** ➔ note at **newspaper**

reporting ⓘ+ B2 Ⓦ /rɪˈpɔːtɪŋ/ *noun* [U] the presenting of and writing about news on television and radio, and in newspapers, etc: *accurate/objective reporting*

represent ⓘ B1 Ⓞ /ˌreprɪˈzent/ *verb* 1 [T] (LAW) to act or speak in the place of sb else; to be the representative of a group or country: *You will need a lawyer to represent you in court.* ◇ *It's an honour for an athlete to represent his or her country.* ➔ note at **professional**[2] 2 [T] to be a picture, a sign, an example, etc. of sb/sth: *The yellow lines on the map represent minor roads.* 3 *linking verb* (not used in the progressive tenses) to be equal to sth; to be sth: *These results represent a major breakthrough in our understanding of cancer.* 4 [T] ~ sb/sth as sb/sth (*formal*) to present or describe sb/sth in a particular way: *The film represents women as victims.*

representation ⓘ+ C1 Ⓞ /ˌreprɪzenˈteɪʃn/ *noun* 1 [U, C] the way that sb/sth is shown or described; sth that shows or describes sth: *The show offers a realistic representation of life in rural Spain.* 2 [U] having sb to speak for you ➔ look at **proportional representation**

representative[1] ⓘ B2 Ⓦ /ˌreprɪˈzentətɪv/ *adj.* ~ (of sb/sth) typical of a larger group to which sb/sth belongs: *Tonight's audience is not representative of national opinion.*

representative[2] ⓘ B2 Ⓦ /ˌreprɪˈzentətɪv/ *noun* [C] 1 a person who has been chosen to act or speak for sb else or for a group 2 (*also informal* rep) (BUSINESS) a person who works for a company and travels around selling its products: *a sales representative* ◇ *She's our representative in France.* 3 Representative (*abbr.* Rep.) (POLITICS) (in the US) a member of the House of Representatives, the Lower House of Congress; a

repress /rɪˈpres/ *verb* [T] **1** to control an emotion or to try to prevent it from being shown or felt: *She tried to repress her anger.* **2** (**POLITICS**) to limit the freedom of a group of people ▸ **repression** /-ˈpreʃn/ *noun* [U]: *protests against government repression*

repressed /rɪˈprest/ *adj.* **1** (used about a person) having emotions and desires that they do not show or express **2** (used about an emotion) that you do not show: *repressed anger/desire*

repressive /rɪˈpresɪv/ *adj.* (**POLITICS**) that limits people's freedom: *a repressive government*

reprieve /rɪˈpriːv/ *verb* [T] (**LAW**) **1** to stop or delay the punishment of a prisoner who was going to be punished by death **2** to officially cancel or delay plans to close sth or end sth ▸ **reprieve** *noun* [C]: *The judge granted him a last-minute reprieve.*

reprimand /ˈreprɪmɑːnd/ *verb* [T] ~ **sb (for sth)** to tell sb officially that they have done sth wrong: *The manager reprimanded a waiter for having dirty nails.* ▸ **reprimand** *noun* [C]: *a severe reprimand*

reprisal /rɪˈpraɪzl/ *noun* [C, U] a violent or an aggressive act towards sb because of sth bad that they have done towards you: *The army carried out reprisals on the village that had sheltered the rebels.* ◇ *Ten villagers were shot in reprisal for the attack.*

reproach /rɪˈprəʊtʃ/ *verb* [T] ~ **sb (for/with sth)** to tell sb that they are responsible for sth bad that has happened: *You've nothing to reproach yourself for. It wasn't your fault.* **SYN** **blame**[1] ▸ **reproach** *noun* [U, C]: *His behaviour is beyond reproach* (= cannot be criticized). ◇ *Alison felt his reproaches were unjustified.* ▸ **reproachful** /-fl/ *adj.*: *a reproachful look* ▸ **reproachfully** /-fəli/ *adv.*

reprocess /riːˈprəʊses/ *verb* [T] (**ENVIRONMENT**) to treat waste material so that it can be used again: *to reprocess nuclear fuel*

reproduce ℂ⁺ **C1** /ˌriːprəˈdjuːs/ *verb* **1** [T] to produce a copy of sth: *It is very hard to reproduce a natural environment in the laboratory.* **2** [I] (**BIOLOGY**) (used about people, animals and plants) to produce young

reproduction ℂ⁺ **C1** /ˌriːprəˈdʌkʃn/ *noun* **1** [U] (**BIOLOGY**) the process of producing babies or young: *sexual reproduction* **2** [U] the production of copies of sth: *Digital recording gives excellent sound reproduction.* **3** [C] (**ART**) a copy of a painting, etc.

reproductive /ˌriːprəˈdʌktɪv/ *adj.* (**BIOLOGY**) connected with the production of young animals, plants, etc: *the male reproductive organs*

reproof /rɪˈpruːf/ *noun* [U, C] (*formal*) something that you say to sb when you do not approve of what they have done

reptile /ˈreptaɪl/ *noun* [C] an animal that has cold blood and a skin covered in scales, and whose young come out of eggs: *Crocodiles, turtles and snakes are all reptiles.* ◇ look at **amphibian** ◇ picture at **animal**

republic ℂ⁺ **C1** /rɪˈpʌblɪk/ *noun* [C] (**POLITICS**) a country that has an elected government and a president: *the Republic of Ireland* ◇ look at **monarchy** (2)

republican /rɪˈpʌblɪkən/ *noun* [C] (**POLITICS**) **1** a person who supports the system of an elected government with no king or queen **2** Republican (*abbr.* **Rep.**) a member of the Republican Party of the US ◇ look at **democrat** (2) ▸ **republican** *adj.*

the Re·publican Party *noun* [sing.] (**POLITICS**) one of the two main political parties of the US ◇ note at **party** ❶ The other party is **the Democratic Party**, whose members are called **Democrats**.

repudiate /rɪˈpjuːdieɪt/ *verb* [T] (*formal*) to say that you refuse to accept or believe sth: *to repudiate a suggestion/an accusation* ▸ **repudiation** /rɪˌpjuːdiˈeɪʃn/ *noun* [U]

repugnant /rɪˈpʌɡnənt/ *adj.* ~ **(to sb)** (*formal*) making you feel strong dislike: *The idea of eating meat was repugnant to her.* **SYN** **repulsive**

repulsion /rɪˈpʌlʃn/ *noun* [U] **1** a strong feeling of not liking sth that you find extremely unpleasant **2** (**PHYSICS**) the force by which objects push each other away: *the forces of attraction and repulsion* ◇ picture at **magnetism** ◇ verb **repel**

repulsive /rɪˈpʌlsɪv/ *adj.* that causes a strong feeling of dislike; very unpleasant ◇ verb **repel**

reputable /ˈrepjətəbl/ *adj.* honest and providing a good service **OPP** **disreputable**

reputation ℂ **B2** /ˌrepjuˈteɪʃn/ *noun* [C] ~ **(for/as sth)** the opinion that people in general have about what sb/ sth is like: *to have a good/bad reputation* ◇ *Adam has a reputation for being late.* **SYN** **name**[1]

repute /rɪˈpjuːt/ *noun* [U] (*formal*) the opinion that people have of sb/sth: *I know him only by repute.* ◇ *She's a writer of international repute* (= having a good reputation in many countries). **SYN** **reputation**

reputed /rɪˈpjuːtɪd/ *adj.* ~ **(to be sth)** generally said to be sth, although it is not certain: *He's reputed to be the highest-paid sportsman in the world.* ▸ **reputedly** *adv.*

request[1] ℂ **A2** /rɪˈkwest/ *noun* [C, U] ~ **(to do sth)**; ~ **(for sth)** an act of asking for sth: *She submitted a request to attend the conference.* ◇ *a request for help* ◇ *I'm going to make a request for a larger desk.* ◇ *to grant/ refuse a request*

request[2] ℂ **B1** /rɪˈkwest/ *verb* [T] ~ **sth (from/of sb)** (*formal*) to ask for sth: *to request a loan from the bank* ◇ *Passengers are requested not to bring hot drinks onto the coach.*

require ℂ **B1** ◐ /rɪˈkwaɪə(r)/ *verb* [T] **1** to need sth: *a situation that requires tact and diplomacy* **2** [often passive] to officially demand or order sth: *Passengers are required by law to wear seat belts.* ◇ note at **demand**[2]

requirement ℂ **B2** ◑ /rɪˈkwaɪəmənt/ *noun* [C] something that you need or that you must do or have: *university entrance requirements*

requisite /ˈrekwɪzɪt/ *adj.* [only before noun] (*formal*) necessary for a particular purpose: *She lacks the requisite experience for the job.* ▸ **requisite** *noun* [C] ~ **(for/of sth)**: *toilet requisites* (= soap, TOOTHPASTE, etc.) ◇ *A university degree has become a requisite for entry into most professions.* ◇ look at **prerequisite**

reschedule /ˌriːˈʃedjuːl/ *verb* [T] **1** ~ **sth (for/to sth)** to change the time at which sth has been arranged to happen, especially so that it takes place later: *The meeting has been rescheduled for next week.* **2** (**FINANCE**) to arrange for sb to pay back money that they have borrowed at a later date than was originally agreed: *to reschedule a loan*

rescind /rɪˈsɪnd/ *verb* [T] (*formal*) (**LAW**) to officially state that a law, contract, decision, etc. no longer has any legal force

rescue ℂ **B2** /ˈreskjuː/ *verb* [T] ~ **sb/sth (from sb/sth)** to save sb/sth from a situation that is dangerous or unpleasant: *He rescued a child from drowning.* ▸ **rescue** ℂ **B2** *noun* [U, C]: *Blow the whistle if you're in danger, and somebody should come to your rescue.* ◇ *rescue workers/boats/helicopters* ◇ *Ten fishermen were saved in a daring sea rescue.* ▸ **rescuer** *noun* [C]

research ⓵ A2 ⓞ /rɪˈsɜːtʃ, ˈriːsɜːtʃ/ *noun* [U] ~ (into/on sth) (SCIENCE) a detailed and careful study of sth to find out more information about it: *to do research into something* ◇ *scientific/medical/historical research* ◇ *We are carrying out market research to find out who our typical customer is.* ▸ **research** ⓵ A2 ⓢ /rɪˈsɜːtʃ/ *verb* [I, T] ~ (into/in/on sth): *They're researching into ways of reducing traffic in the city centre.*

re,search and de'velopment *noun* [U] (*abbr.* R & D) (BUSINESS) (in industry, etc.) work that tries to find new products and processes or to improve existing ones

researcher ⓵ A2 ⓦ /rɪˈsɜːtʃə(r), ˈriːsɜːtʃə(r)/ *noun* [C] a person who does research

resemble ⓵+ C1 /rɪˈzembl/ *verb* [T] to be or look like sb/ sth else: *Laura resembles her brother.* ▸ **resemblance** /-bləns/ *noun* [C, U] ~ (to sb/sth): *a family resemblance* ◇ *The boys bear no resemblance to their father.*

resent /rɪˈzent/ *verb* [T] to feel angry about sth because you think it is unfair: *I resent his criticism.* ◇ *Louise bitterly resented being treated differently from the others.* ▸ **resentful** /-fl/ *adj.* ▸ **resentment** *noun* [U, sing.]: *to feel resentment towards somebody/something*

reservation ⓵ B1 /ˌrezəˈveɪʃn/ *noun* 1 [C] (TOURISM) a seat, table, room, etc. that you have booked: *We have reservations in the name of Petrovic.* ◇ *I'll phone the restaurant to make a reservation.* ⊃ note at **hotel** 2 (*also* reserve) [C] an area of land in the US that is kept separate for Native Americans to live in 3 [C, U] a feeling of doubt about sth (such as a plan or an idea): *I have some reservations about letting Julie go out alone.*

reserve¹ ⓵ B2 /rɪˈzɜːv/ *verb* [T] ~ sth (for sb/sth) 1 to ask for a seat, table, room, etc. to be available at a future time: *I'd like to reserve a table for this evening.* SYN **book²** 2 to keep sth for a special reason or to use at a later time: *The car park is reserved for hotel guests only.*

reserve² ⓵ B2 /rɪˈzɜːv/ *noun* 1 [C, usually pl.] something that you keep for a special reason or to use at a later date: *The US has huge oil reserves.* 2 [C] (ENVIRONMENT) an area of land where the plants, animals, etc. are protected by law: *a nature reserve* ◇ *He works as a warden on a game reserve in Kenya.* 3 [U] the quality of being shy or keeping your feelings hidden: *It took a long time to break down her reserve and get her to relax.* 4 [C] (SPORT) a person who will play in a game if one of the usual members of the team cannot play 5 [C] = RESERVATION (2) IDM **in reserve** that you keep and use only if you need to: *Keep some money in reserve for emergencies.*

reserved /rɪˈzɜːvd/ *adj.* shy and keeping your feelings hidden

reservoir /ˈrezəvwɑː(r)/ *noun* [C] (GEOGRAPHY) a large lake where water is stored to be used by a particular area, city, etc.

reshuffle /ˌriːˈʃʌfl/ *verb* [T, I] to change around the jobs that a group of people do, for example in the British government ▸ **reshuffle** /ˈriːʃʌfl/ *noun* [C]: *a Cabinet reshuffle*

reside ⓵+ C1 /rɪˈzaɪd/ *verb* [I] (*formal*) (used with an adverb or a preposition) to have your home in or at a particular place

residence ⓵+ C1 /ˈrezɪdəns/ *noun* 1 [C] (*formal*) a house, especially an impressive or important one 2 [U] the state of having your home in a particular place: *a hall of residence for college students* ◇ *Some birds have*

taken up residence in our roof. 3 (*also* residency) [U] permission to live in a country that is not your own: *The family applied for permanent residence in the United States.*

residency /ˈrezɪdənsi/ *noun* (*pl.* -ies) (*formal*) 1 [U, C] (ARTS AND MEDIA) the period of time that an artist, a writer or a musician spends working for a particular institution 2 [U, C] (*especially AmE*) (MEDICINE) the period of time when a doctor working in a hospital receives special advanced training 3 [U] = RESIDENCE (3)

resident ⓵ B2 ⓦ /ˈrezɪdənt/ *noun* [C] 1 a person who lives in a place: *local residents* 2 (TOURISM) a person who is staying in a hotel: *The hotel bar is open only to residents.* 3 (MEDICINE) a doctor working in a hospital in the US who is receiving special advanced training ▸ **resident** ⓵ B2 *adj.*

residential ⓵+ C1 /ˌrezɪˈdenʃl/ *adj.* 1 (used about a place or an area) that has houses rather than offices, large shops or factories: *They live in a quiet residential area.* 2 that provides a place for sb to live: *This home provides residential care for the elderly.*

residual /rɪˈzɪdjuəl/ *adj.* [only before noun] (*formal*) left at the end of a process: *There are still a few residual problems with the computer program.*

residue ⓵+ C1 /ˈrezɪdjuː/ *noun* [C] what is left after the main part of sth is taken or used: *The washing powder left a white residue on the clothes.* ⊃ picture at **filtration**

resign ⓵+ B2 /rɪˈzaɪn/ *verb* [I, T] ~ (as) (sth); ~ (from) (sth) to leave your job or position: *He's resigned as chairman of the committee.* ◇ *I'm resigning from the board.* ⊃ note at **job** PHR V **resign yourself to sth/doing sth** to accept sth that is unpleasant but that you cannot change: *Jamie resigned himself to the fact that she was not coming back to him.*

resignation ⓵+ C1 /ˌrezɪɡˈneɪʃn/ *noun* 1 [U, C] the act of giving up your job or position; the occasion when you do this: *a letter of resignation* ◇ *to hand in your resignation* (= to say that you are giving up your job) ⊃ note at **job** 2 [U] the state of accepting sth unpleasant that you cannot change

resigned /rɪˈzaɪnd/ *adj.* ~ (to sth/doing sth) accepting sth that is unpleasant but that you cannot change: *Ben was resigned to the fact that he would never be an athlete.*

resilient /rɪˈzɪliənt/ *adj.* strong enough to deal with illness, a shock, change, etc. ▸ **resilience** /-əns/ *noun* [U]

resin /ˈrezɪn/ *noun* [U, C] 1 a sticky substance that is produced by some trees and is used in making VARNISH (= a liquid that you paint onto hard surfaces to protect them), medicine, etc. 2 an artificial substance that is used in making plastics

resist ⓵ B2 /rɪˈzɪst/ *verb* 1 [T, I] to try to stop sth happening or to stop sb from doing sth; to fight back against sth/sb: *The government are resisting pressure to change the law.* ◇ *to resist arrest* SYN **oppose** 2 [T] (usually in negative sentences) to stop yourself from having or doing sth that you want to have or do: *I couldn't resist telling Nadia what we'd bought for her.*

resistance ⓵+ C1 ⓦ /rɪˈzɪstəns/ *noun* 1 [U, sing.] ~ (to sb/ sth) trying to stop sth from happening or to stop sb from doing sth; fighting back against sb/sth: *There has been a lot of resistance to this new law.* 2 [U, sing.] ~ (to sth) (HEALTH) the power in a person's body not to be affected by disease 3 [U, C] (*symb.* R) (PHYSICS) the fact of a substance not CONDUCTING heat or electricity (= not allowing heat or electricity to flow through it); a measurement of this ⊃ picture at **resistor**

resistant ⓦ /rɪˈzɪstənt/ *adj.* ~ **(to sth)** **1** not harmed or affected by sth: *This watch is water-resistant.* **2** not wanting sth and trying to prevent it from happening: *resistant to change*

resistor

Resistance is measured in ohms (Ω). A resistor of 100 Ω is a much greater obstacle to the flow of current than a resistor of 10 Ω.

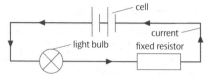

Variable resistors have values that can be altered so it is possible to adjust the current flowing in the circuit.

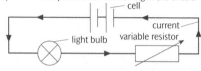

resistor /rɪˈzɪstə(r)/ *noun* [C] (**PHYSICS**) a device that does not allow electric current to flow through it freely in a CIRCUIT

resolute /ˈrezəluːt/ *adj.* having or showing great DETERMINATION (= not giving up): *a resolute refusal to change* **SYN** determined ▸ **resolutely** *adv.*

resolution ʔ+ B2 ⓦ /ˌrezəˈluːʃn/ *noun* **1** [C] a firm decision to do or not to do sth **2** [U] the quality of being firm and determined **3** [C] (**POLITICS**) a formal decision that is taken after a vote by a group of people: *The UN resolution condemned the invasion.* **4** [U, sing.] solving or settling a problem, an argument, etc. **5** [U, sing.] (**COMPUTING**) the power of a computer screen, printer, etc. to give a clear image, depending on the size of the DOTS (= small round marks) that make up the image: *high-resolution graphics*

resolve¹ ʔ B2 ⓦ /rɪˈzɒlv/ *verb* (formal) **1** [T] to find an answer to a problem: *Most of the difficulties have been resolved.* **SYN** settle **2** [T, I] ~ **(to do sth)** to decide sth and be determined not to change your mind: *He resolved never to repeat the experience.*

resolve² /rɪˈzɒlv/ *noun* [U] ~ **(to do sth)** (formal) a strong desire to achieve sth and not give up: *The difficulties in her way merely strengthened her resolve to find out the truth.*

resonance /ˈrezənəns/ *noun* **1** [U] (formal) (used about sound) the quality of being RESONANT: *the strange and thrilling resonance of her voice* **2** [C, U] (**PHYSICS**) the sound produced in an object by sound of a similar FREQUENCY from another object **3** [U, C] (formal) (**ARTS AND MEDIA, LITERATURE, MUSIC**) (in a piece of writing, music, etc.) the power to bring images, feelings, etc. into the mind of the person reading or listening; the images, etc. produced in this way

resonant /ˈrezənənt/ *adj.* **1** (used about a sound) deep, clear and continuing for a long time: *a deep, resonant voice* **2** causing sounds to continue for a long time: *resonant frequencies* **3** having the power to bring images, feelings, memories, etc. into your mind: *a poem filled with resonant imagery*

resonate /ˈrezəneɪt/ *verb* [I] (formal) **1** (used about a voice, an instrument, etc.) to make a deep, clear sound that continues for a long time: *Her voice resonated through the theatre.* **2** ~ **(with sth)** (**MUSIC**) (used about a place) to be filled with sound; to make a sound continue longer: *The room resonated with the*

chatter of 100 people. **3** ~ **(with sb/sth)** to remind sb of sth; to be similar to what sb thinks or believes: *These issues resonated with the voters.*

resort¹ ʔ B2 /rɪˈzɔːt/ *noun* [C] (**TOURISM**) a place where a lot of people go on holiday: *a seaside/ski resort* **IDM** **(as) a last resort** → LAST¹

resort² /rɪˈzɔːt/ *verb* **PHR V** **resort to sth/doing sth** to do or use sth bad or unpleasant because you feel you have no choice: *After not sleeping for three nights, I finally resorted to sleeping pills.*

resounding /rɪˈzaʊndɪŋ/ *adj.* [only before noun] **1** very great: *a resounding victory/win/defeat/success* **2** very loud: *resounding cheers*

resource¹ ʔ B1 ⓞ /rɪˈsɔːs, -ˈzɔːs/ *noun* [C, usually pl.] a supply of sth, a piece of equipment, etc. that is available for sb to use: *Russia is rich in **natural resources** such as oil and minerals.*

resource² /rɪˈsɔːs, -ˈzɔːs/ *verb* [T] to provide sth with the money or equipment that is needed: *Schools in the area are still inadequately resourced.*

resourceful /rɪˈsɔːsfl, -ˈzɔːs-/ *adj.* good at finding ways of doing things and solving problems, etc. ▸ **resourcefully** /-fəli/ *adv.*

resourcefulness /rɪˈsɔːsflnəs, -ˈzɔːs-/ *noun* [U] an ability to find ways of doing things and solve problems, etc.

respect¹ ʔ B1 ⓦ /rɪˈspekt/ *noun* **1** [U, sing.] ~ **(for sb/sth)** the feeling that you have when you admire or have a high opinion of sb/sth: *I have little respect for people who are arrogant.* ◇ *to win/lose somebody's respect* ⊃ look at **self-respect** **2** [U, sing.] ~ **(for sb/sth)** polite behaviour or care towards sb/sth that you think is important: *We should all treat older people with more respect.* **OPP** disrespect **3** [C] a detail or point: *In what respects do you think things have changed in the last ten years?* ◇ *Her performance was brilliant in every respect.* **IDM** **pay your respects** → PAY¹ **with respect to sth** (formal) about or concerning sth

respect² ʔ B1 /rɪˈspekt/ *verb* [T] **1** ~ **sb/sth (for sth)** to admire or have a high opinion of sb/sth: *I respect him for his honesty.* **2** to show care for or pay attention to sb/sth: *We should respect other people's cultures and values.* ▸ **respectful** /-fl/ *adj.*: *The crowd listened in respectful silence.* **OPP** disrespectful ▸ **respectfully** /-fəli/ *adv.*

respectable /rɪˈspektəbl/ *adj.* **1** considered by society to be good, proper or correct: *a respectable family* ◇ *He combed his hair and tried to look respectable for the interview.* **2** quite good or large: *a respectable salary* ▸ **respectability** /rɪˌspektəˈbɪləti/ *noun* [U]

respective ʔ+ C1 /rɪˈspektɪv/ *adj.* [only before noun] belonging separately to each of the people who have been mentioned: *They all left for their respective destinations.*

respectively ʔ+ C1 ⓦ /rɪˈspektɪvli/ *adv.* in the same order as sb/sth that was mentioned: *Rhoda Jones and Robbie Vaccaro, aged 17 and 19 respectively*

respiration /ˌrespəˈreɪʃn/ *noun* [U] **1** (formal) (**HEALTH**) the act of breathing **2** (**BIOLOGY**) a process by which living things produce energy from food. Respiration usually needs OXYGEN.

respirator /ˈrespəreɪtə(r)/ *noun* [C] **1** (**MEDICINE**) a piece of equipment that makes it possible for sb to breathe over a long period when they are unable to do so naturally: *She was put on a respirator.* **2** a device worn over the nose and mouth to allow sb to breathe in a place where there is a lot of smoke, gas, etc.

respiratory /rəˈspɪrətri, ˈrespərətri/ adj. (HEALTH) connected with breathing: *the respiratory system* ◊ *respiratory diseases*

respire /rɪˈspaɪə(r)/ verb [I] (BIOLOGY) to breathe

respite /ˈrespaɪt/ noun [sing., U] ~ (from sth) a short period of rest from sth that is difficult or unpleasant: *There was a brief respite from the fighting.*

respond ⓘ A2 ⊙ /rɪˈspɒnd/ verb 1 [I, T] ~ (to sb/sth) (with/by sth) (formal) to say or do sth as an answer or a reaction to sth: *He responded to my question with a nod.* **SYN** reply 2 [I] ~ (to sb/sth) to do sth as a quick reaction to sb/sth: *The patient did not respond well to the new treatment.*

respondent /rɪˈspɒndənt/ noun [C] 1 a person who answers questions, especially in a survey: *60% of the respondents agreed with the suggestion.* 2 (LAW) a person who is accused of sth

response ⓘ A2 ⊙ /rɪˈspɒns/ noun [C, U] ~ (to sb/sth) an answer or a reaction to sb/sth: *I've sent out 20 letters of enquiry but I've had no responses yet.* ◊ *The government acted in response to economic pressure.*

responsibility ⓘ B1 Ⓦ /rɪˌspɒnsəˈbɪləti/ noun (pl. -ies) 1 [U, C] ~ (for sb/sth); ~ (to do sth) a duty to deal with

sth so that it is your fault if sth goes wrong: *Who has responsibility for the new students?* ◊ *I refuse to take responsibility if anything goes wrong.* ◊ *I feel that I have a responsibility to help them — after all, they did help me.* 2 [U] ~ (for sth/doing sth) the fact of sth being your fault: *No group has yet admitted responsibility for planting the bomb.* **SYN** blame[1]
IDM shift the blame/responsibility (for sth) (onto sb) → SHIFT[1]

responsible ⓘ B1 Ⓦ /rɪˈspɒnsəbl/ adj.
• HAVING A DUTY 1 [not before noun] ~ (for sb/sth); ~ (for doing sth) having the job or duty of dealing with sb/sth, so that it is your fault if sth goes wrong: *The school is responsible for the safety of the children in school hours.* ◊ *The manager is responsible for making sure the shop is run properly.*
• CAUSING STH 2 [not before noun] ~ (for sth) being the thing or person that caused sth to happen: *Who was responsible for the accident?*
• RELIABLE 3 (used about a person) that you can trust to behave well and in a sensible way: *Marisa is responsible enough to take her little sister to school.* **OPP** irresponsible
• JOB 4 (used about a job) that is important and that should be done by a person who can be trusted
• REPORTING TO SB 5 [not before noun] ~ (to sb/sth) having to report to sb/sth with authority, or to sb who you are working for, about what you are doing: *Members of Parliament are responsible to the electors.*

the respiratory system

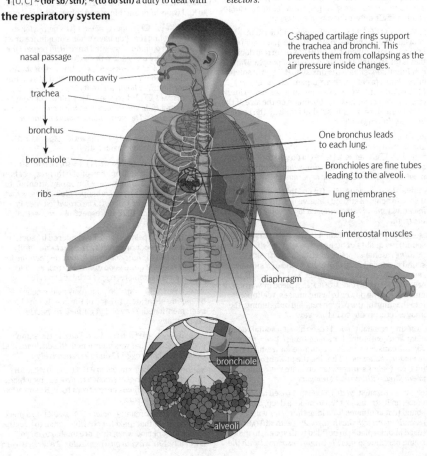

nasal passage

mouth cavity

trachea

bronchus

bronchiole

ribs

C-shaped cartilage rings support the trachea and bronchi. This prevents them from collapsing as the air pressure inside changes.

One bronchus leads to each lung.

Bronchioles are fine tubes leading to the alveoli.

lung membranes

lung

intercostal muscles

diaphragm

bronchiole

alveoli

responsibly /rɪˈspɒnsəbli/ *adv.* in a sensible way that shows that you can be trusted: *They can be relied on to act responsibly.*

responsive /rɪˈspɒnsɪv/ *adj.* ~(to sb/sth) **1** paying attention to sb/sth and reacting in a suitable or positive way: *By being responsive to changes in the market, the company has had great success.* **2** (**COMPUTING**) used to describe a website, etc. that changes to suit the kind of device you are using, for example by changing the size of the text or the way that items are arranged on the screen **OPP** unresponsive

rest¹ /rest/ *verb* **1** [I] to relax, sleep or stop after a period of activity or because of illness: *We've been walking for hours. Let's rest here for a while.* **2** [T] to not use a part of your body for a period of time: *Your knee will get better as long as you rest it as much as you can.* **3** [T, I] ~(sth) on/against sth to place sth in a position where it is supported by sth else; to be in such a position: *She rested her head on his shoulder and went to sleep.* **IDM** let sth rest to not talk about sth any longer **PHR V** rest on sth/sb to depend on sth/sb or be based on sth: *The whole theory rests on a very simple idea.*

rest² /rest/ *noun* **1** [sing., pl.] the ~(of sb/sth) the part that is left; the ones that are left: *Help yourself to more cake. The rest is in the tin.* ◇ *We had lunch and spent the rest of the day on the beach.* ◇ *They were the first people to arrive. The rest came later.* ◇ *The rest of our bags are still in the car.* **2** [C, U] a period of relaxing, sleeping or doing nothing: *I can't walk any further! I need a rest.* ◇ *I'm going upstairs to have a rest before we go out.* ◇ *Try not to worry now. Get some rest and think about it again tomorrow.* ◇ *I sat down to give my bad leg a rest.* **3** [C, U] (**MUSIC**) a period of silence between notes; a sign for this ⊃ picture at **music** **IDM** at rest not moving: *At rest the insect looks like a dead leaf.* come to rest to stop moving: *The car crashed through a wall and came to rest in a field.* put/set your/sb's mind at rest → **MIND¹**

restart /ˌriːˈstɑːt/ *verb* [I, T] to start again or make sth start again after it has stopped

restate /ˌriːˈsteɪt/ *verb* [T] (*formal*) to say sth again or in a different way, especially so that it is more clearly or strongly expressed

restaurant /ˈrestrɒnt/ *noun* [C] a place where you can buy and eat a meal: *a fast food/hamburger restaurant* ◇ *a Chinese/an Italian/a Thai restaurant* ⊃ look at **cafe, takeaway**

restful /ˈrestfl/ *adj.* giving a relaxed, peaceful feeling: *I find this piece of music very restful.*

restitution /ˌrestɪˈtjuːʃn/ *noun* [U] ~(of sth) (to sb/sth) **1** (*formal*) the act of giving back sth that was lost or stolen to its owner **2** (**LAW**) payment, usually money, for some harm or wrong that sb has suffered

restless /ˈrestləs/ *adj.* **1** unable to relax or be still because you are bored, nervous or impatient: *The children always get restless on long journeys.* **2** (used about a period of time) without good sleep or rest: *a restless night* ▸ **restlessly** *adv.*

restoration /ˌrestəˈreɪʃn/ *noun* **1** [U, C] the return of sth to its original condition; the things that are done to achieve this: *The house is in need of restoration.* **2** [U] the return of sth to its original owner: *the restoration of stolen property to its owner*

restore /rɪˈstɔː(r)/ *verb* [T] **1** ~sb/sth (to sb/sth) to put sb/sth back into their former condition or position: *She restores old furniture as a hobby.* ◇ *In the recent elections, the former president was restored to power.* **2** ~sth to sb (*formal*) to give sth that was lost or stolen back to sb

restrain /rɪˈstreɪn/ *verb* [T] ~sb/sth (from sth/doing sth) to keep sb/sth under control; to prevent sb/sth from doing sth: *I had to restrain myself from saying something rude.*

restrained /rɪˈstreɪnd/ *adj.* not showing strong feelings

restraining order *noun* [C] ~(against sb) (**LAW**) an official order given by a judge that stops sb from doing sth for a particular period of time ⊃ look at **injunction**

restraint /rɪˈstreɪnt/ *noun* **1** [U] the quality of behaving in a calm or controlled way: *It took a lot of restraint on my part not to hit him.* ◇ *Soldiers have to exercise self-restraint even when provoked.* **SYN** self-control **2** [C] (*formal*) ~(on sb/sth) a limit or control on sb/sth: *Are there any restraints on what the newspapers are allowed to publish?* ⊃ note at **limit¹**

restrict /rɪˈstrɪkt/ *verb* [T] ~sb/sth/yourself (to sth/doing sth) to put a limit on sb/sth: *I restrict myself to one cup of coffee per day.*

restricted /rɪˈstrɪktɪd/ *adj.* ~(to sb/sth) controlled or limited: *There is only restricted parking available.*

restriction /rɪˈstrɪkʃn/ *noun* ~(on sth) **1** [C] something (sometimes a rule or law) that limits the number, amount, size, freedom, etc. of sb/sth: *parking restrictions in the city centre* ◇ *The government is to impose tighter restrictions on the number of immigrants permitted to settle in this country.* ⊃ note at **limit¹** **2** [U] the act of limiting the freedom of sb/sth: *This ticket permits you to travel anywhere, without restriction.*

restrictive /rɪˈstrɪktɪv/ *adj.* limiting; preventing people from doing what they want

restroom /ˈrestruːm, -rʊm/ *noun* [C] (*AmE*) a room with a toilet in a public place such as a hotel, shop, etc.

restructure /ˌriːˈstrʌktʃə(r)/ *verb* [T, I] (**BUSINESS**) to organize sth such as a system or a company in a new and different way ▸ **restructuring** *noun* [U, C, usually sing.]: *The company is undergoing a major restructuring.*

result¹ /rɪˈzʌlt/ *noun*
- CAUSED BY STH **1** [C] something that happens because of sth else; the final situation at the end of a series of actions: *The traffic was very heavy and as a result I arrived late.* ◇ *This wasn't really the result that I was expecting.* ⊃ note at **effect¹**
- SUCCESS **2** [C] a good effect of an action: *The treatment is beginning to show results.*
- OF A COMPETITION **3** [C] the score at the end of a game, a competition or an election: *Have you heard today's football results?* ◇ *The results of this week's competition will be published next week.* ◇ *The result of the by-election was a win for the Liberal Democrats.*
- OF AN EXAM **4** [C, usually pl.] (**EDUCATION**) the mark given for an exam or a test: *When do you get your exam results?* ⊃ note at **study²**
- OF A MEDICAL TEST **5** [C] (**MEDICINE**) something that is discovered by a medical test: *I'm still waiting for the result of my X-ray.* ◇ *The result of the test was negative.*

result² /rɪˈzʌlt/ *verb* [I] ~(from sth) to happen or exist because of sth: *90 per cent of the deaths resulted from injuries to the head.* **PHR V** result in sth to cause sth to happen; to produce sth as an effect: *There has been an accident on the motorway, resulting in long delays.*

resume /rɪˈzjuːm/ *verb* [T, I] (*formal*) if you resume an activity, or if it resumes, it begins again or continues after being interrupted: *Normal service* will resume as soon as possible. ▸ **resumption** /-ˈzʌmpʃn/ noun [sing., U]

résumé /ˈrezjuːmeɪ/ (AmE) = CV

resurgence /rɪˈsɜːdʒəns/ noun [C, usually sing.] the return and growth of an activity that had stopped: a resurgence of interest in the artist's work

resurrect /ˌrezəˈrekt/ verb [T] to bring back sth that has not been used or has not existed for a long time

resurrection /ˌrezəˈrekʃn/ noun **1** the Resurrection [sing.] (RELIGION) (in Christianity) the return to life of Jesus Christ **2** [U] the action of bringing back sth that has not existed or not been used for a long time

resuscitate /rɪˈsʌsɪteɪt/ verb [T] (MEDICINE) to make sb start breathing again after they have almost died: Unfortunately, all efforts to resuscitate the patient failed. ▸ **resuscitation** /rɪˌsʌsɪˈteɪʃn/ noun [U]: mouth-to-mouth resuscitation

retail¹ ⚡+ B2 /ˈriːteɪl/ noun [U] (BUSINESS) the selling of goods to the public in shops, etc. ⊃ look at **wholesale** (1) ▸ **retail** adv.: to buy/sell retail (= in a shop)

retail² /ˈriːteɪl/ verb (BUSINESS) **1** [T] to sell goods to the public, usually through shops: The firm manufactures and retails its own range of sportswear. **2** [I] ~ **at/for sth** to be sold at a particular price: The book retails at £14.95. ▸ **retailing** noun [U]: career opportunities in retailing

retailer /ˈriːteɪlə(r)/ noun [C] a person or company that sells goods to the public ⊃ look at **wholesaler**

retain ⚡ B2 /rɪˈteɪn/ verb [T] (formal) to keep or continue to have sth; not to lose: Despite all her problems, she has managed to retain a sense of humour. ⊃ noun **retention**

retainer /rɪˈteɪnə(r)/ noun [C] **1** (FINANCE) a sum of money that is paid to sb to make sure they will be available to do work when they are needed **2** (BrE) (FINANCE) a small amount of rent that you pay for a room, etc. when you are not there in order to keep it available for your use **3** (old-fashioned) a servant, especially one who has been with a family for a long time

retaliate /rɪˈtælieɪt/ verb [I] ~ **(against sb/sth)** to react to sth unpleasant that sb does to you by doing sth unpleasant in return ▸ **retaliation** /rɪˌtæliˈeɪʃn/ noun [U] ~ **(against sb/sth) (for sth)**: The terrorist group said that the shooting was in retaliation for the murder of one of its members.

retch /retʃ/ verb [I] (HEALTH) to make sounds and movements as if you are VOMITING (= bringing up food from the stomach) although you do not actually do so

retell /ˌriːˈtel/ verb [T] (pt, pp retold /-ˈtəʊld/) to tell a story again, often in a different way

retention /rɪˈtenʃn/ noun [U] (formal) the act of keeping sth or of being kept; the ability to remember things ⊃ verb **retain**

retentive /rɪˈtentɪv/ adj. (used about the memory) able to store facts and remember things easily

rethink /ˌriːˈθɪŋk/ verb [T, I] (pt, pp rethought /-ˈθɔːt/) to think about sth again because you probably need to change it: The government has been forced to rethink its economic policy.

reticent /ˈretɪsnt/ adj. ~ **(about sth)** not wanting to tell people about things: He is extremely reticent about his personal life. ▸ **reticence** /-sns/ noun [U]

retina /ˈretɪnə/ noun [C] (ANATOMY) the area at the back of the eye that is sensitive to light and sends signals to the brain about what is seen ⊃ picture at **eye**¹ ▸ **retinal** /-nl/ adj.

retinol /ˈretɪnɒl/ (also vitamin A) noun [U] (HEALTH) a vitamin found in cheese, eggs, fish oils and milk that is essential for healthy growth and sight

retire ⚡ B1 /rɪˈtaɪə(r)/ verb [I] **1** ~ **(from sth)** to leave your job and stop working, usually because you have reached a certain age: Most people in the company retire at 67. ◇ Injury forced her to retire from professional athletics. ⊃ note at **job** 2 (formal) to leave and go to a quiet or private place

retired ⚡ B1 /rɪˈtaɪəd/ adj. having stopped work permanently: a retired teacher

retirement ⚡+ B2 /rɪˈtaɪəmənt/ noun **1** [U, C] the act of stopping working permanently: She has decided to take early retirement. ◇ The former world champion has announced his retirement from the sport. ⊃ note at **job** 2 [U, sing.] the situation or period after retiring from work: We all wish you a long and happy retirement. ⊃ look at **senior citizen**

retiring /rɪˈtaɪərɪŋ/ adj. (used about a person) shy and quiet

retold /ˌriːˈtəʊld/ past tense, past participle of **retell**

retort¹ /rɪˈtɔːt/ verb [T] to reply quickly to what sb says, in an angry or a funny way: 'Who asked you for your opinion?' she retorted.

retort² /rɪˈtɔːt/ noun [C] **1** a quick, angry or funny reply: an angry retort **2** (CHEMISTRY) a closed bottle with a long narrow bent SPOUT (= a tube through which liquid comes out) that is used in a laboratory for heating chemicals ⊃ picture at **laboratory**

retrace /rɪˈtreɪs/ verb [T] to repeat a past journey, series of events, etc: If you retrace your steps, you might see where you dropped the ticket.

retract /rɪˈtrækt/ verb [T] (formal) to say that sth you have said is not true: When he appeared in court, he retracted the confession he had made to the police.

retreat¹ ⚡+ C1 /rɪˈtriːt/ verb [I] **1** (used about an army, etc.) to move backwards in order to leave a battle or in order not to become involved in a battle: The order was given to retreat. **OPP** advance¹ **2** to move backwards; to go to a safe or private place: (figurative) She seems to retreat into a world of her own sometimes.

retreat² ⚡+ C1 /rɪˈtriːt/ noun **1** [C, usually sing., U] the act of moving backwards, away from a difficult or dangerous situation: The invading forces are now in retreat. **OPP** advance² **2** [C] a private place where you can go when you want to be quiet or to rest: a country retreat

retrial /ˈriːtraɪəl/ noun [C, usually sing.] (LAW) a new trial for a person whose criminal offence has already been judged once in a court: The judge ordered a retrial because new evidence had appeared.

retribution /ˌretrɪˈbjuːʃn/ noun [U] ~ **(for sth)** (formal) (LAW) punishment for a crime

retrieve ⚡+ C1 /rɪˈtriːv/ verb [T] **1** ~ **sth (from sb/sth)** (formal) to get sth back from the place where it was left or lost: Police divers retrieved the body from the canal. **2** (COMPUTING) to find information that has been stored on a computer: The computer can retrieve all the data about a particular customer. **3** to make a bad situation or a mistake better; to put sth right: The team was losing 2–0 at half-time but they managed to retrieve the situation in the second half. ▸ **retrieval** /-ˈtriːvl/ noun [U]

retro /ˈretrəʊ/ adj. using styles or fashions from the recent past: the current Seventies retro trend

retrograde /ˈretrəɡreɪd/ *adj.* (*formal*) (used about an action) making a situation worse or returning to how sth was in the past: *The closure of the factory is a* **retrograde step.**

retrospect /ˈretrəspekt/ *noun*
IDM **in retrospect** thinking about sth that happened in the past, often seeing it differently from the way you saw it at the time: *In retrospect, I can see what a stupid mistake it was.*

retrospective /ˌretrəˈspektɪv/ *adj.* **1** looking again at the past: *a retrospective analysis of historical events* **2** (used about laws, decisions, payments, etc.) intended to take effect from a date in the past: *Is this new tax law retrospective?* ▶ **retrospectively** *adv.*

return¹ ⚡ **A1** /rɪˈtɜːn/ *verb*
• GO/COME BACK **1** [I] ~ **(to/from ...)** to come or go back to a place: *I leave on 10 July and return on 6 August.* ◇ *I shall be returning to this country in six months.* ◇ *When did you return from Italy?*
• GIVE BACK **2** [T] ~ **sth (to sb/sth)** to give, send, put or take sth back: *I've stopped lending him things because he never returns them.* ◇ *Application forms must be returned to this address by 14 March.*
• HAPPEN AGAIN **3** [I] to come back; to happen again: *If the pain returns, make another appointment to see me.*
• TO AN EARLIER STATE **4** [I] ~ **(to sth/doing sth)** to go back to the former or usual activity, situation, condition, etc: *The strike is over and they will* **return to work** *on Monday.* ◇ *It is hoped that train services will* **return to normal** *soon.*
• DO THE SAME **5** [T] to react to sth that sb does, says or feels by doing, saying or feeling sth similar: *I've phoned them several times and left messages but they haven't returned any of my calls.* ◇ *We'll be happy to return your hospitality if you ever come to our country.*
• IN TENNIS **6** [T] (**SPORT**) (in tennis) to hit or throw the ball back

return² ⚡ **A1** /rɪˈtɜːn/ *noun*
• COMING BACK **1** [sing.] ~ **(to/from ...)** coming or going back to a place or to a former activity, situation or condition: *I'll contact you* **on** *my* **return** *from holiday.* ◇ *He has recently made a return to form* (= started playing well again).
• GIVING BACK **2** [U, sing.] giving, sending, putting or taking sth back: *I demand the immediate return of my passport.*
• PROFIT **3** [U, C] ~ **(on sth)** (**BUSINESS**) the profit from a business, etc: *This account offers high rates of return on all investments.*
• TICKET **4** (*also* reˌturn ˈticket) (*both BrE*) (*AmE* ˌround trip ˈticket) [C] a ticket to travel to a place and back again: *A day return to Oxford, please.* ◇ *Is the* **return fare** *cheaper than two singles?* **OPP** **one-way**, **single²**
• ON A COMPUTER **5** [U] (*also* reˈturn key [C]) (**COMPUTING**) the button on a computer that you press when you reach the end of a line or of an instruction
• IN TENNIS **6** [C] (**SPORT**) (in tennis) the act of hitting or throwing the ball back: *She hit a brilliant return.*
IDM **by return (of post)** (*BrE*) immediately; by the next post **in return (for sth)** as payment or in exchange (for sth); as a reaction to sth: *Please accept this present in return for all your help.*

returnable /rɪˈtɜːnəbl/ *adj.* that can or must be given or taken back: *a non-returnable deposit*

retweet /ˌriːˈtwiːt/ *verb* [I, T] if you **retweet** a message written by another user on the Twitter SOCIAL MEDIA service, the message can be seen by all the people who regularly receive messages from you.

reunion /riːˈjuːniən/ *noun* **1** [C] a social occasion or party attended by a group of people who have not seen each other for a long time: *The college holds an annual reunion for former students.* **2** [C, U] ~ **(with sb)**; ~ **(between A and B)** coming together again after being apart: *The released hostages had an emotional reunion with their families at the airport.*

reunite /ˌriːjuˈnaɪt/ *verb* [I, T, usually passive] **be reunited (with sb)** to join two or more people, groups, etc. together again; to come together again: *The missing child was found by the police and reunited with his parents.*

reusable /ˌriːˈjuːzəbl/ *adj.* that can be used again: *reusable plastic bottles*

reuse /ˌriːˈjuːz/ *verb* [T] to use sth again: *Please reuse your plastic bags.* ▶ **reuse** /-ˈjuːs/ *noun* [U]

Rev. /rev/ *abbr.* = REVEREND

rev¹ /rev/ *verb* [T, I] (-vv-) ~ **(sth) (up)** if you **rev** an engine or it **revs**, it runs quickly and loudly

rev² /rev/ *noun* [C] (*informal*) (used when talking about an engine's speed) one complete turn: *4 000 revs per minute* ⊃ look at **revolution** (3)

revalue /ˌriːˈvæljuː/ *verb* [T] (**ECONOMICS**) to increase the value of the money of a country when it is exchanged for the money of another country ⊃ note at **currency** ▶ **revaluation** /ˌriːvæljuˈeɪʃn/ *noun* [U, C]

revamp /ˌriːˈvæmp/ *verb* [T] to make changes to the form of sth, usually to improve its appearance

reveal ⚡ **B2** **W** /rɪˈviːl/ *verb* [T] **1** ~ **sth (to sb)** to make sth known that was secret or unknown before: *He refused to reveal any names to the police.* **2** to show sth that was hidden before: *The X-ray revealed a tiny fracture in her right hand.*

revealing /rɪˈviːlɪŋ/ *adj.* **1** allowing sth to be known that was secret or unknown before: *This book provides a revealing insight into the world of politics.* **2** allowing sth to be seen that is usually hidden, especially sb's body: *a very revealing swimsuit*

revel /ˈrevl/ *verb* (-ll-, *AmE* -l-)
PHR V **revel in sth/doing sth** to enjoy sth very much: *He likes being famous and revels in the attention he gets.*

revelation ⚡+ **C1** /ˌrevəˈleɪʃn/ *noun* **1** [C] something that is made known, that was secret or unknown before, especially sth surprising: *This magazine is full of revelations about the private lives of the stars.* **2** [sing.] a thing or a person that surprises you and makes you change your opinion about sb/sth

revenge¹ ⚡+ **C1** /rɪˈvendʒ/ *noun* [U] ~ **(on sb) (for sth)** something that you do to punish sb who has hurt you, made you suffer, etc: *He made a fool of me and now I want to* **get** *my* **revenge.** ◇ *He wants to* **take revenge** *on the judge who sent him to prison.* ◇ *The shooting was in revenge for an attack by the nationalists.* ⊃ look at **vengeance**

revenge² /rɪˈvendʒ/ *verb*
PHR V **revenge yourself on sb** to punish or hurt sb because they have made you suffer: *She revenged herself on her enemy.*

revenue ⚡+ **B2** /ˈrevənjuː/ *noun* [U] (*also* **revenues** [pl.]) ~ **(from sth)** (**ECONOMICS, FINANCE**) money regularly received by a government, company, etc: *Revenue from income tax rose last year.*

reverberate /rɪˈvɜːbəreɪt/ *verb* [I] **1** (used about a sound) to be repeated several times as it hits and is sent back from different surfaces: *Her voice reverberated around the hall.* **SYN** **echo²** **2** ~ **(with/to sth)** (used about a place) to seem to shake because of a loud noise: *The hall reverberated with the sound of music and dancing.*

revere /rɪ'vɪə(r)/ *verb* [T, usually passive] **~ sb/sth (as sth)** (*formal*) to admire and respect sb/sth very much: *He is revered as one of the greatest musicians of his generation.*

reverence /'revərəns/ *noun* [U] **~ (for sb/sth)** (*formal*) a feeling of great respect

reverend /'revərənd/ (*also* Reverend) *adj.* [only before noun] (*abbr.* Rev.) (**RELIGION**) the title of a Christian priest

reverent /'revərənt/ *adj.* (*formal*) showing great respect

reversal /rɪ'vɜːsl/ *noun* [C, U] the act of changing sth to the opposite of what it was before; an occasion when this happens: *The decision taken yesterday was a complete reversal of last week's decision.* ◇ *The government insists that there will be no reversal of policy.*

reverse¹ ʔ+ **C1** /rɪ'vɜːs/ *verb* **1** [T] to put sth in the opposite position to normal or to how it was before: *Today's results have reversed the order of the top two teams.* **2** [T] to exchange the positions or functions of two things or people: *Jane and her husband have reversed roles — he stays at home now and she goes to work.* **3** [I, T] to go backwards in a vehicle; to make a vehicle go backwards: *It might be easier to reverse into that parking space.* ◇ *He reversed his brand new car into a wall.*

reverse² ʔ+ **C1** /rɪ'vɜːs/ *noun* **1** [sing.] **the ~ (of sth)** the complete opposite of what was just said before, or of what is expected: *Of course I don't dislike you — quite the reverse* (= I like you very much). ◇ *This course is the exact reverse of what I was expecting.* **2** (*also* re,verse 'gear) [U] the control in a car, etc. that allows it to move backwards: *Leave the car in reverse while it's parked on this hill.* ◇ *Where's reverse in this car?* **IDM** **in reverse** in the opposite order, starting at the end and going backwards to the beginning **SYN** backwards

reverse³ ʔ+ **C1** /rɪ'vɜːs/ *adj.* [only before noun] opposite to what is expected or has just been described: *The results will be announced in reverse order* (= the person in the lowest place will be announced first).

re,verse dis,crimin'ation *noun* [U] (**SOCIAL STUDIES**) (often used in a critical way) the practice or policy of making sure that a particular number of jobs, etc. are given to people from groups that are often treated unfairly because of the human group they belong to, their sex, etc. ◯ look at **positive discrimination**

reversible /rɪ'vɜːsəbl/ *adj.* **1** (used about clothes) that can be worn with either side on the outside: *a reversible coat* **2** (used about a process, an action or a disease) that can be changed so that sth returns to its original state or situation **OPP** irreversible

revert /rɪ'vɜːt/ *verb* [I] **~ (to sth)** to return to a former state or activity: *The land will soon revert to jungle if it is not farmed.* ◇ *If the experiment is unsuccessful we will revert to the old system.*

review¹ ʔ **A2** ⓦ /rɪ'vjuː/ *noun* [C, U] **1** (**ARTS AND MEDIA**) a report in a newspaper or magazine, or on the internet, television or radio, in which sb gives an opinion on a book, film, play, product, etc: *The film got bad reviews.* **2** the examining or considering again of sth in order to decide if changes are necessary: *There will be a review of your contract after the first six months.* ◇ *The system is in need of review.* **3** a look back at sth in order to check, remember or be clear about sth: *a review of the major events of the year*

review² ʔ **A2** /rɪ'vjuː/ *verb* [T] **1** (**ARTS AND MEDIA**) to write a report of a book, film, product, etc. in which you give your opinion of it: *In this week's edition our film critic reviews the latest films.* **2** to examine or consider sth again in order to decide if changes are necessary: *Your salary will be reviewed after one year.* ◯ note at **examine** **3** to look at or think about sth again to make sure that you understand it: *Let's review what we've done in class this week.*

reviewer /rɪ'vjuːə(r)/ *noun* [C] (**ARTS AND MEDIA**) a person who writes reviews of books, films, etc.

revise ʔ **B1** /rɪ'vaɪz/ *verb* **1** [T] to make changes to sth in order to correct or improve it: *The book has been revised for this new edition.* ◇ *I revised my opinion of him when I found out that he had lied.* **2** [I, T] **~ (sth) (for sth)** (*BrE*) (**EDUCATION**) to read or study again sth that you have learnt, especially when preparing for an exam: *I can't come out tonight. I'm revising for my exam.* ◇ *None of the things I had revised came up in the exam.* ◯ note at **study²**

revision ʔ+ **B2** /rɪ'vɪʒn/ *noun* **1** [U, C] the changing of sth in order to correct or improve it: *It has been suggested that the whole system is in need of revision.* **2** [U] (*BrE*) (**EDUCATION**) the work of reading or studying again sth you have learnt, especially when preparing for an exam: *I'm going to have to do a lot of revision for my French exam.*

revitalize (*BrE also* -ise) /ˌriː'vaɪtəlaɪz/ *verb* [T] to make sth stronger, more active or more healthy: *measures to revitalize the inner cities*

revival ʔ+ **C1** /rɪ'vaɪvl/ *noun* **1** [U, C] the act of becoming or making sth strong or popular again: *economic revival* ◇ *a revival of interest in traditional farming methods* **2** [C] (**ARTS AND MEDIA**) a new performance of a play that has not been performed for some time: *a revival of the musical 'The Sound of Music'*

revive ʔ+ **C1** /rɪ'vaɪv/ *verb* [I, T] to become strong, healthy or conscious again; to make sb/sth become strong, healthy or conscious again: *Hopes have revived for an early end to the fighting.* ◇ *I'm very tired but I'm sure a cup of coffee will revive me.* ◇ *Attempts were made to revive him but he was already dead.* **2** [T] to begin to do or use sth again: *to revive an old custom*

revoke /rɪ'vəʊk/ *verb* [T] (*formal*) to officially cancel sth so that it is no longer legally acceptable

revolt /rɪ'vəʊlt/ *verb* **1** [I] **~ (against sb/sth)** to protest in a group, often violently, against the person or people in power: *A group of generals revolted against the government.* **2** [I] to behave in a way that is the opposite of what sb expects of you **3** [T] to make sb feel horror: *The sight and smell of the meat revolted him.* ◯ *noun* **revulsion** ► **revolt** *noun* [C, U]: *The people rose in revolt against the corrupt government.*

revolting /rɪ'vəʊltɪŋ/ *adj.* extremely unpleasant **SYN** disgusting

revolution ʔ **B2** /ˌrevə'luːʃn/ *noun* **1** [C, U] (**POLITICS**) action taken by a large group of people to try to change the government of a country, especially by violent action: *the French Revolution of 1789* ◇ *a country on the brink of revolution* **2** [C] **~ (in sth)** a complete change in methods, opinions, etc., often as a result of progress: *the Industrial Revolution* ◇ *a revolution in the treatment of cancer* **3** [C, U] a movement around sth; one complete turn around a central point (for example in a car engine): *400 revolutions per minute* ◯ look at **rev²**

revolutionary¹ ʔ+ **C1** /ˌrevə'luːʃənəri/ *adj.* **1** (**POLITICS**) connected with or supporting political revolution: *the revolutionary leaders* **2** producing great changes; very new and different: *a revolutionary new scheme to ban cars from the city centre*

revolutionary² /ˌrevəˈluːʃənəri/ *noun* [C] (*pl.* -ies) (**POLITICS**) a person who starts or supports action to try to change the government of a country, especially by using violent action

revolutionize (*BrE also* -ise) /ˌrevəˈluːʃənaɪz/ *verb* [T] to change sth completely, usually improving it: *a discovery that could revolutionize the treatment of mental illness*

revolve /rɪˈvɒlv/ *verb* [I] to move in a circle around a central point: *The earth revolves around the sun.* **PHR V** **revolve around sb/sth** (*also* **revolve round sb/sth** *especially in BrE*) to have sb/sth as the most important part: *His life revolves around the family.*

revolver /rɪˈvɒlvə(r)/ *noun* [C] a type of small gun with a container for bullets that turns around ⊃ note at **gun¹**

revolving /rɪˈvɒlvɪŋ/ *adj.* that goes round in a circle: *revolving doors*

revulsion /rɪˈvʌlʃn/ *noun* [U] (*formal*) a strong feeling of horror (because sth is extremely unpleasant) ⊃ verb **revolt**

reward¹ ⓧ **B2** /rɪˈwɔːd/ *noun* **1** [C, U] ~ **(for sth/doing sth)** something that you are given because you have done sth good, worked hard, etc: *Winning the match was **just reward** for all the effort.* **2** [C] ~ **(for sth)** an amount of money that is given in exchange for helping the police, returning sth that was lost, etc: *Police are offering a reward for information leading to a conviction.*

reward² ⓧ **B2** /rɪˈwɔːd/ *verb* [T, often passive] ~ **sb (for sth/doing sth)** to give sth to sb because they have done sth good, worked hard, etc: *She was rewarded for her efforts with a cash bonus.*

rewarding /rɪˈwɔːdɪŋ/ *adj.* (used about an activity, a job, etc.) giving **SATISFACTION**; making you happy because you think it is important, useful, etc.

rewilding /ˌriːˈwaɪldɪŋ/ *noun* [U] (**ENVIRONMENT**) the return of an environment to its natural state, for example by putting back particular animals, plants, etc. that once lived there

rewind /ˌriːˈwaɪnd/ *verb* [T, I] (*pt, pp* rewound /-ˈwaʊnd/) to make a film, recording, etc. go back to the beginning or to an earlier point: *Rewind the video and watch it more closely.* ▶ **rewind** *noun* [U]: *Press rewind to go back to the beginning.*

rewritable /ˌriːˈraɪtəbl/ *adj.* (**COMPUTING**) able to be used again for different data: *a rewritable CD*

rewrite /ˌriːˈraɪt/ *verb* [T] (*pt* rewrote /-ˈrəʊt/; *pp* rewritten /-ˈrɪtn/) to write sth again in a different or better way

rhenium /ˈriːniəm/ *noun* [U] (*symb.* Re) (**CHEMISTRY**) a chemical element. Rhenium is a rare silver-white metal found with **MOLYBDENUM** and some other metals. ❶ For more information on the periodic table of elements, look at the **Reference Section** of this dictionary.

rhetoric ⓧ⁺ **C1** /ˈretərɪk/ *noun* [U] (*formal*) (**LANGUAGE**) a way of speaking or writing that is intended to impress or influence people but is not always sincere ▶ **rhetorical** /rɪˈtɒrɪkl/ *adj.* ▶ **rhetorically** /-kli/ *adv.*

rhe₍torical ˈquestion *noun* [C] (**LANGUAGE**) a question that is asked only to make a statement or to produce an effect rather than to get an answer

rheumatism /ˈruːmətɪzəm/ *noun* [U] (**HEALTH**) an illness that causes pain in the muscles and **JOINTS** (= where the bones are connected) ▶ **rheumatic** /ruˈmætɪk/ *adj.*

rheumatology /ˌruːməˈtɒlədʒi/ *noun* [U] (**MEDICINE**) the study of the diseases of **JOINTS** and muscles, such as **RHEUMATISM** and **ARTHRITIS**

rhinoceros /raɪˈnɒsərəs/ (*pl.* rhinoceros, rhinoceroses) (*also informal* **rhino** /ˈraɪnəʊ/, *pl.* -os) *noun* [C] a large animal from Africa or Asia, with a thick skin and with one or two **HORNS** (= hard pointed parts) on its nose

rhodium /ˈrəʊdiəm/ *noun* [U] (*symb.* Rh) (**CHEMISTRY**) a chemical element. Rhodium is a hard silver-white metal, usually found with **PLATINUM**. ❶ For more information on the periodic table of elements, look at the **Reference Section** of this dictionary.

rhomboid /ˈrɒmbɔɪd/ *noun* [C] (**GEOMETRY**) a flat shape with four straight sides, with only the opposite sides and angles equal to each other ⊃ picture at **parallelogram**

rhombus /ˈrɒmbəs/ *noun* [C] (**GEOMETRY**) a flat shape with four equal sides and four angles that are not 90° ⊃ picture at **parallelogram**

rhubarb /ˈruːbɑːb/ *noun* [U] a plant with red **STALKS** (= the long thin parts) that can be cooked and eaten as fruit

rhyme¹ /raɪm/ *noun* **1** [C] a word that has the same sound as another **2** [C] a short piece of writing, or sth spoken, in which the word at the end of each line sounds the same as the word at the end of the line before it ⊃ look at **nursery rhyme** **3** [U] the use of words in a poem or song that have the same sound, especially at the ends of lines: *All of his poetry was written **in rhyme**.*

rhyme² /raɪm/ *verb* **1** [I] ~ **(with sth)** to have the same sound as another word; to contain lines that end with words that sound the same: *'Tough' rhymes with 'stuff'.* **2** [T] ~ **sth (with sth)** to put together words that have the same sound

rhythm ⓧ **B2** /ˈrɪðəm/ *noun* [C, U] (**MUSIC**) a regular repeated pattern of sound or movement: *I'm not keen on the tune but I love the rhythm.* ◇ *He's a terrible dancer because he has no **sense of rhythm**.* ◇ *He tapped his foot **in rhythm** with the music.* ▶ **rhythmic** /ˈrɪðmɪk/ (*also* **rhythmical** /-mɪkl/) *adj.*: *the rhythmic qualities of African music* ▶ **rhythmically** /-kli/ *adv.*

ˌrhythm and ˈblues *noun* [U] (*abbr.* R & B) (**MUSIC**) a type of music that is a mixture of **BLUES** and jazz and has a strong rhythm

ria /ˈriːə/ *noun* [C] (**GEOGRAPHY**) a long narrow area of water formed when a river valley floods

rib /rɪb/ *noun* [C] (**ANATOMY**) one of the curved bones that go round the chest: *He's so thin that you can see his ribs.* ⊃ picture at **respiratory**

ribbon /ˈrɪbən/ *noun* [C, U] a long, thin piece of material that is used for tying or decorating sth

ˈribbon lake *noun* [C] (**GEOGRAPHY**) a long narrow lake ⊃ picture at **glacial**

ribcage /ˈrɪbkeɪdʒ/ *noun* [C] (**ANATOMY**) the structure of **RIBS** (= curved bones that surround the chest) ⊃ picture at **body**

rice ⓧ **A1** /raɪs/ *noun* [U] short, thin, white or brown grain from a plant that grows on wet land in hot countries. We cook and eat rice: *boiled/fried/steamed rice* ⊃ picture at **cereal**

rich ⓧ **A1** /rɪtʃ/ *adj.*

• WITH A LOT OF MONEY **1** having a lot of money or property: *a rich family/country* ◇ *one of the richest women in the world* **OPP** **poor** ⊃ look at **wealthy** **2** the rich *noun* [pl.] people with a lot of money or property

horn

rhinoceros

• FULL OF STH **3** ~ **(in sth)** containing a lot of sth: *Oranges are rich in vitamin C.* **4** very

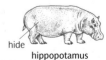

hide

hippopotamus

interesting and full of variety
- FOOD **5** (used about food) containing a lot of fat, oil, sugar or cream and making you feel full quickly: *a rich chocolate cake*
- SOIL **6** (used about soil) containing the substances that make it good for growing plants in
- COLOUR/SOUND/SMELL **7** (used about colours, sounds or smells) strong and deep
  ▶ **richness** *noun* [U]

riches /ˈrɪtʃɪz/ *noun* [pl.] a lot of money or property **SYN** **wealth**

richly /ˈrɪtʃli/ *adv.* **1** in a beautiful and expensive manner: *a richly decorated room* **2** in a generous way: *She was richly rewarded for her hard work.* **3** in a way that people think is right: *His promotion was richly deserved.*

the Richter scale /ðə ˈrɪktə skeɪl/ *noun* [sing.] (GEOGRAPHY, GEOLOGY) a system for measuring earthquakes: *an earthquake measuring 7 on the Richter scale* ⊃ picture at **plate tectonics**

rickets /ˈrɪkɪts/ *noun* [U] (HEALTH) a disease of children caused by a lack of good food that makes the bones become soft and badly formed, especially in the legs

rickety /ˈrɪkəti/ *adj.* likely to break; not strongly made: *a rickety old fence ◇ rickety furniture*

rickshaw /ˈrɪkʃɔː/ *noun* [C] (TOURISM) a small light vehicle with two wheels, used especially in some Asian countries to carry passengers. The rickshaw is pulled by a person walking or riding a bicycle.

ricochet /ˈrɪkəʃeɪ, -ʃet/ *verb* [I] ~ **(off sth)** (used about a moving object) to fly away from a surface after hitting it: *The bullet ricocheted off the wall and grazed his shoulder.*

rid ⁊ **B2** /rɪd/ *verb* (**ridding**; *pt, pp* **rid**)
IDM **be rid of sb/sth** (*formal*) to be free of sb/sth that is annoying you or that you do not want **get rid of sb/sth** to make yourself free of sb/sth that is annoying you or that you do not want; to throw sth away: *Let's get rid of that old chair and buy a new one.*
PHRV **rid yourself/sb/sth of sb/sth** (*formal*) to make yourself/sb/sth free from sb/sth that is unpleasant or not wanted: *He was unable to rid himself of his fears and suspicions.*

riddance /ˈrɪdns/ *noun*
IDM **good riddance (to sb/sth)** used for expressing pleasure or SATISFACTION that sb/sth that you do not like has gone

ridden¹ /ˈrɪdn/ past participle of **ride¹**

ridden² /ˈrɪdn/ *adj.* (usually in compounds) ~ **(with sth)** full of: *She was guilt-ridden. ◇ She was ridden with guilt.*

riddle /ˈrɪdl/ *noun* [C] **1** a difficult question that you ask people for fun that has a clever or funny answer **2** an event, a thing or a person that you cannot understand or explain

riddled /ˈrɪdld/ *adj.* ~ **with sth** full of sth, especially sth unpleasant: *This essay is riddled with mistakes.*

ride¹ ⁊ **A1** /raɪd/ *verb* (*pt* rode /rəʊd/; *pp* ridden /ˈrɪdn/)
1 [I, T] (SPORT) to sit on a horse, etc. and control it as it moves: *We rode through the woods and over the moor. ◇ to ride a horse/pony/donkey/camel* **2** [I, T] to sit on a bicycle, motorcycle, etc. and control it as it moves: *She jumped onto her bike and rode off* (= went away). *◇ Can John ride a bike yet?* **3** [I] (*especially AmE*) (TOURISM) to travel as a passenger in a bus, car, etc: *She rode the bus to school every day.*

ride² ⁊ **A2** /raɪd/ *noun* [C] **1** a short journey on a horse or bicycle, or in a car, bus, etc: *It's only a short bus/train ride into Warwick. ◇ We went for a bike ride on Saturday.* **2** used to describe what a journey or trip is like: *a smooth/bumpy/comfortable ride* **3** a large moving machine that you pay to go on for fun or excitement; an occasion when you go on one of these: *My favourite fairground ride is the roller coaster.*
IDM **take sb for a ride** (*informal*) to cheat or trick sb

rider /ˈraɪdə(r)/ *noun* [C] **1** a person who rides a horse, bicycle or motorcycle: *She's an experienced rider. ◇ a motorcycle dispatch rider* **2** ~ **(to sth)** (LAW) an extra piece of information that is added to an official document

ridge /rɪdʒ/ *noun* [C] **1** (GEOGRAPHY) a long narrow piece of high land along the top of a line of hills or mountains ⊃ picture at **plate tectonics** **2** (GEOMETRY) a line where two surfaces meet at an angle

ridicule /ˈrɪdɪkjuːl/ *noun* [U] cruel behaviour or comments that make sb/sth look silly: *He had become an object of ridicule.* ▶ **ridicule** *verb* [T]: *The idea was ridiculed by everybody present.*

ridiculous ⁊⁺ **B2** /rɪˈdɪkjələs/ *adj.* very silly or unreasonable: *They're asking a ridiculous* (= very high) *price for that house.* **SYN** **absurd** ▶ **ridiculously** *adv.*

riding /ˈraɪdɪŋ/ (*AmE also* **horseback riding**) *noun* [U] (SPORT) the sport or hobby of riding a horse: *riding boots ◇ a riding school*

rife /raɪf/ *adj.* [not before noun] (used about bad things) very common: *Rumours are rife that his wife has left him.*

rifle¹ ⁊⁺ **C1** /ˈraɪfl/ *noun* [C] a long gun that you hold against your shoulder to shoot with ⊃ note at **gun¹**

rifle² /ˈraɪfl/ *verb* [I, T] ~ **(through sth)** to search sth, usually in order to steal from it: *I caught him rifling through the papers on my desk.*

rift /rɪft/ *noun* [C] **1** a serious break in the relationship between people or organizations: *a growing rift between the brothers* **2** (GEOGRAPHY, GEOLOGY) a very large CRACK or opening in the ground, a rock, etc.

rift valley *noun* [C] (GEOGRAPHY) a valley with steep sides formed when TECTONIC PLATES move apart from each other ⊃ picture at **plate tectonics**

rig¹ /rɪg/ *verb* [T, usually passive] (**-gg-**) to arrange or control an event, etc. in an unfair way, in order to get the result you want: *They claimed that the competition had been rigged.*
PHRV **rig sth up** to make sth quickly, using any materials you can find: *We tried to rig up a shelter using our coats.*

rig² /rɪg/ *noun* [C] = OIL RIG

rigging /ˈrɪgɪŋ/ *noun* [U] the ropes, etc. that support a ship's sails

right¹ ⁊ **A1** /raɪt/ *adj.*
- CORRECT **1** correct; true: *I'm afraid that's not the right answer. ◇ Have you got the right time? ◇ You're quite right — the film does start at seven o'clock. ◇ You were right about the weather — it did rain. ◇ 'You're Chinese, aren't you?' 'Yes, that's right.'* **OPP** **wrong¹** ⊃ note at **true**
- MOST SUITABLE **2** ~ **(for sb/sth)** best; most suitable: *I hope I've made the right decision. ◇ I am sure we've chosen the right person for the job. ◇ I would help you to wash the car, but I'm not wearing the right clothes.* **OPP** **wrong¹**
- MORALLY GOOD **3** (used about behaviour, actions, etc.) fair; morally and socially correct: *It's not right to pay people so badly. ◇ What do you think is the right thing to do?* **OPP** **wrong¹**

• NORMAL **4** healthy or normal; as it should be: *The car exhaust doesn't sound right — it's making a funny noise.* ◇ *I don't feel quite right today* (= I feel ill). ◇ *If only I could have helped put matters right.* **OPP** wrong¹

• NOT LEFT **5** on or of the side of the body that faces east when a person is facing north: *Most people write with their right hand.* ◇ *He's blind in his right eye.* **OPP** left²

• COMPLETE **6** [only before noun] (*BrE, informal*) (used for emphasizing sth bad) real or complete: *I'll look a right idiot in that hat!*
▶ **rightness** *noun* [U]
IDM **get/start off on the right/wrong foot (with sb)** → FOOT¹ **get on the right/wrong side of sb** → SIDE¹ **on the right/wrong track** → TRACK¹ (as) **right as rain** completely healthy and normal

right² ⚡ A1 /raɪt/ *adv.*

• NOT LEFT **1** to the right side: *Turn right at the traffic lights.* **OPP** left³ ○ note at **direction**

• EXACTLY **2** exactly; directly: *The train was right on time.* ◇ *He was sitting right beside me.*

• COMPLETELY **3** all the way; completely: *Did you watch the film right to the end?* ◇ *There's a high wall that goes right round the house.*

• IMMEDIATELY **4** immediately: *Wait here a minute — I'll be right back.*

• CORRECTLY **5** correctly; in the way that it should happen or should be done: *Have I spelt your name right?* ◇ *Nothing seems to be going right for me at the moment.* **OPP** wrong²
IDM **right/straight away** → AWAY¹ **right now** at this moment; immediately now: *We can't discuss this right now.* **serve sb right** → SERVE¹

right³ ⚡ A1 Ⓦ /raɪt/ *noun* **1** [sing.] the right side or direction: *We live in the first house on the right.* ◇ *Take the first right and then the second left.* **OPP** left⁴ ○ note at **direction 2** [C, U] ~ **(to sth/to do sth)** (LAW) a thing that you are allowed to do according to the law; a moral authority to do sth: *Freedom of speech is one of the basic human rights.* ◇ *civil rights* (= the rights each person has to political and religious freedom, etc.) ◇ *animal rights campaigners* ◇ *Everyone has the right to a fair trial.* ◇ *You have no right to tell me what to do.* **3** [U, C] what is morally good and fair: *Does a child of four really understand the difference between right and wrong?* ◇ *You did right to tell me what happened.* **OPP** wrong³ **4** the **Right** [sing. + sing./pl. verb] (POLITICS) the people or political parties who are against social change and who believe in individual responsibility rather than state support ○ look at **right wing**
IDM **be in the right** to be doing what is correct and fair: *You don't need to apologize. You were in the right and he was in the wrong.* **by rights** according to what is fair or correct: *By rights, half the profit should be mine.* **in your own right** because of what you are yourself and not because of other people **within your rights (to do sth)** acting in a reasonable or legal way: *You are quite within your rights to demand to see your lawyer.*

right⁴ /raɪt/ *verb* [T] to put sb/sth/yourself back into a normal position: *The boat tipped over and then righted itself again.*
IDM **right a wrong** to do sth to correct an unfair situation or sth bad that you have done

'right angle *noun* [C] (GEOMETRY) an angle of 90°: *A square has four right angles.* ○ look at **acute angle, obtuse angle, reflex angle** ○ picture at **angle**¹ ▶ right-angled *adj.*

right-angled 'triangle (*especially BrE*) (*AmE usually* right triangle) *noun* [C] (GEOMETRY) a TRIANGLE with a RIGHT ANGLE: *a right-angled triangle* ○ picture at **triangle**

right-'click *verb* [T, I] ~ **(on sth)** (COMPUTING) to press the button on a mouse that is on the right side, in order to choose a particular function on a computer screen: *Right-click on the 'My Computer' icon.*

righteous /'raɪtʃəs/ *adj.* (*formal*) that you think is morally good or fair: *righteous anger/indignation* ○ look at **self-righteous**

rightful /'raɪtfl/ *adj.* [only before noun] (*formal*) legally or morally correct; fair ▶ rightfully /-fəli/ *adv.*

'right-hand *adj.* [only before noun] of or on the right of sb/sth: *The postbox is on the right-hand side of the road.* ◇ *in the top right-hand corner of the screen* **OPP** left-hand

right-hand 'man *noun* [sing.] the person you depend on most to help and support you in your work: *the president's right-hand man*

the ,Right 'Honourable *adj.* [only before noun] (*abbr.* Rt Hon) a title of respect used when talking to or about a person of high social rank, especially a lord

rightly /'raɪtli/ *adv.* correctly or fairly: *He's been sacked and quite rightly, I believe.*

,right of 'way *noun* (*pl.* rights of way) **1** [U, C] (*especially BrE*) (LAW) legal permission to go into or through another person's land; a path across private land that the public may use: *Walkers have right of way through the farmer's field.* **2** [U] (used in road traffic) the fact that a vehicle in a particular position is allowed to drive into or across a road before another vehicle in a different position: *He should have stopped — I had the right of way.*

,right 'triangle (*AmE*) = RIGHT-ANGLED TRIANGLE

,right-'wing *adj.* (POLITICS) supporting the ideas of CAPITALISM: *right-wing policies* ○ look at **left-wing**

,right 'wing *noun* **1** [sing. + sing./pl. verb] (POLITICS) the part of a political party whose members are least in favour of social change ○ look at **left wing**(1) **2** [C, U] (SPORT) an attacking player or a position on the right side of the field in a sports game **OPP** left wing

rigid /'rɪdʒɪd/ *adj.* **1** not able or not wanting to change or be changed **SYN** inflexible **2** difficult to bend; stiff: *a rucksack with a rigid frame* ◇ *She was rigid with fear.* ▶ rigidity /rɪ'dʒɪdəti/ *noun* [U] ▶ rigidly *adv.*: *The speed limit must be rigidly enforced.*

rigor mortis /,rɪɡə 'mɔːtɪs/ *noun* [U] (HEALTH) the process by which the body becomes difficult to bend or move after death

rigorous /'rɪɡərəs/ *adj.* done very carefully and with great attention to detail: *Rigorous tests are carried out on the drinking water.* ▶ rigorously *adv.*

rigour (*BrE*) (*AmE* rigor) /'rɪɡə(r)/ *noun* **1** [U] doing sth carefully and with great attention to detail: *The tests were carried out with rigour.* **2** [U] (*formal*) the quality of being strict: *the full rigour of the law* **3** [pl.] the **rigours of sth** difficult conditions: *the rigours of a harsh winter*

rim /rɪm/ *noun* [C] an edge at the top or outside of sth that is round: *the rim of a cup*

rind /raɪnd/ *noun* [C, U] the thick hard skin on the outside of some fruits, some types of cheese, meat, etc.

ring¹ ⚡ A2 /rɪŋ/ *noun*

• JEWELLERY **1** [C] a piece of jewellery that you wear on your finger: *a gold/diamond/wedding ring* ◇ *an engagement ring*

• CIRCLE **2** [C] (usually in compounds) a round object of any material with a hole in the middle: *curtain rings* ◇ *a key ring* (= for holding keys) **3** [C] a round mark or

shape: *The coffee cup left a ring on the table top.*
◇ *Stand in a ring and hold hands.*
• FOR PERFORMANCE, ETC. **4** [C] the space with seats all around it where a performance, etc. takes place: *a circus/boxing ring*
• FOR COOKING **5** [C] (*especially BrE*) a small flat place on a cooker that is heated and is used for cooking on
• GROUP OF PEOPLE **6** [C] a number of people who are involved in sth that is secret or not legal: *a spy/drugs ring*
• OF A BELL **7** [C] the sound made by a bell; the act of ringing a bell: *There was a ring at the door.*
• QUALITY **8** [sing.] **~ of sth** a particular quality that words or sounds have: *What the man said had a ring of truth about it* (= sounded true).
IDM **give sb a ring** (*BrE, informal*) to phone sb: *I'll give you a ring in the morning.*

ring² 🔊 **A2** /rɪŋ/ *verb* (*pt* **rang** /ræŋ/; *pp* **rung** /rʌŋ/) ❶ In senses 6 and 7 **ringed** is used for the past tense and past participle.
• PHONE **1** [T, I] (*BrE*) to phone sb/sth: *What time will you ring tomorrow?* ◇ *I rang up yesterday and booked the hotel.* ◇ *Ring the theatre and ask if there are any tickets available.* **SYN** **call¹, phone²**
• BELL **2** [I, T] to make a sound like a bell or to cause sth to make this sound: *Is that the phone ringing?* ◇ *We rang the door bell but nobody answered.* ➔ note at **phone¹** **3** [I] **~ (for sb/sth)** to ring a bell in order to call sb, ask for sth, etc: *Ring for the nurse if you need help.*
• FILLED WITH SOUNDS **4** [I] **~ (with sth)** to be filled with loud sounds: *The room was ringing with laughter.*
• WITH A QUALITY **5** [I] (used about words or sounds) to have a certain effect when you hear them: *Her words didn't ring true* (= you felt that you could not believe what she said).
• SURROUND **6** [T, often passive] **~ sb/sth (with sth)** to surround sb/sth: *The whole area was ringed with police.*
• DRAW A CIRCLE **7** [T] (*especially BrE*) to draw a circle around sth **SYN** **circle²**
IDM **ring a bell** to sound familiar or to remind you, not very clearly, of sb/sth: *'Do you know Chris Oliver?' 'Well, the name rings a bell.'*
PHR V **ring (sb) back** (*BrE*) to phone sb again or to phone sb who has phoned you: *I can't talk now — can I ring you back?* **ring in** (*BrE*) to phone a TV or radio show, or the place where you work: *Mandy rang in sick this morning.* **ring off** (*BrE*) to put down the phone, because you have finished speaking **ring out** to sound loudly and clearly

'ring binder *noun* [C] a file for holding papers, in which metal rings go through the edges of the pages, holding them in place

'ring finger *noun* [C] (**ANATOMY**) the finger next to the smallest one, especially on the left hand, on which people sometimes wear a ring to show that they are married

ringleader /'rɪŋliːdə(r)/ *noun* [C] a person who leads others in crime or in causing trouble: *The ringleaders were jailed for 15 years.*

'ring pull (*BrE*) (*AmE* **pull tab**) *noun* [C] a small piece of metal with a ring attached that is pulled to open cans of food, drink, etc.

'ring road *noun* [C] (*BrE*) a road that is built all around a town so that traffic does not have to go into the town centre ➔ look at **bypass¹ (1)**

ringtone /'rɪŋtəʊn/ *noun* [C] the sound that your phone (especially a mobile phone) makes when sb is calling you. Ringtones are often short tunes.

ringworm /'rɪŋwɜːm/ *noun* [U] (**HEALTH**) a skin disease that produces round red areas, especially on the head or the feet

rink /rɪŋk/ = SKATING RINK

rinse /rɪns/ *verb* [T] to wash sth in water in order to remove soap or dirt: *Rinse your hair thoroughly after each shampoo.* ▸ **rinse** *noun* [C]

riot 🔊+ **C1** /'raɪət/ *noun* [C] (**SOCIAL STUDIES**) a situation in which a group of people behave in a violent way in a public place, often as a protest ▸ **riot** *verb* [I]: *There is a danger that the prisoners will riot if conditions do not improve.* ▸ **rioter** *noun* [C]
IDM **run riot** **1** to behave in a wild way without any control: *At the end of the football match, the crowd ran riot.* **2** if your imagination, a feeling, etc. **runs riot**, you allow it to develop and continue without trying to control it

riotous /'raɪətəs/ *adj.* **1** wild or violent; lacking in control **2** wild and full of fun

'riot police *noun* [U] (**LAW**) police who are trained to deal with groups of people who are behaving in a violent way in a public place

'riot shield = SHIELD¹ (2)

RIP /ɑːr aɪ 'piː/ *abbr.* **rest in peace** (often written on GRAVES)

rip 🔊+ **C1** /rɪp/ *verb* (-pp-) **1** [T, I] to tear or be torn quickly and suddenly: *Oh no! My dress has ripped!* ◇ *He ripped the letter in half/two and threw it in the bin.* ◇ *The blast of the bomb ripped the house apart.* **2** [T] (used with an adverb or a preposition) to remove sth quickly and violently, often by pulling it: *He ripped the poster from the wall.* **3** [T] (**COMPUTING**) to copy sound or video files from a website or CD on to a computer **4** [T] = RASTERIZE
PHR V **rip sb off** (*informal*) to cheat sb by charging too much money for sth **rip through sth** to move very quickly and violently through sth: *The house was badly damaged when fire ripped through the first floor.* **rip sth up** to tear sth into small pieces

rip² /rɪp/ *noun* [C] a long tear (in material, etc.)

ripe /raɪp/ *adj.* **1** (**AGRICULTURE**) (used about fruit, grain, etc.) ready to be picked and eaten ➔ note at **agriculture 2 ~ (for sth)** ready for sth or in a suitable state for sth: *The land is ripe for development.* ▸ **ripen** /'raɪpən/ *verb* [I, T]

'rip-off *noun* [C, usually sing.] (*informal*) something that costs a lot more than it should

ripped /rɪpt/ *adj.* **1** (used about clothes or cloth) badly torn: *ripped blue jeans* **2** (*informal*) having strong muscles that you can see clearly: *I'm not trying to get ripped. I just want to stay fit.*

ripple /'rɪpl/ *noun* [C] **1** a very small wave or movement on the surface of water **2** [usually sing.] **~ (of sth)** a sound that gradually becomes louder and then quieter again; a feeling that gradually spreads through a person or a group of people: *a ripple of laughter* ▸ **ripple** *verb* [I, T]

rise¹ 🔊 **B1** **W** /raɪz/ *noun* **1** [C] **~ (in sth)** an increase in an amount, a number or a level: *There has been a sharp rise in the number of people out of work.* **OPP** **drop², fall²** **2** [C] (*BrE*) (*AmE* **raise**) (**FINANCE**) an increase in the money you are paid for the work you do: *I'm hoping to get a rise next April.* ◇ *a 10% pay rise* ➔ note at **pay²** **3** [sing.] **~ (of sth)** the process of becoming more powerful or important: *the rise of fascism in Europe* ◇ *her meteoric rise to fame/power* ➔ note at **religion**
IDM **give rise to sth** (*formal*) to cause sth to happen or exist

rise² ĩ **A2** /raɪz/ *verb* [I] (*pt* **rose** /rəʊz/; *pp* **risen** /'rɪzn/)

• MOVE UPWARDS **1** to move upwards, to become higher, stronger or to increase: *Smoke was rising from the chimney.* ◇ *The temperature has risen by nearly 40°.* **OPP fall¹** ⊃ note at **price¹, trend¹**

• OF THE SUN/MOON **2** (used about the sun or moon) to appear above the HORIZON: *The sun rises in the east and sets in the west.* **OPP set¹**

• BECOME POWERFUL **3** to become more successful, powerful, important, etc: *He rose through the ranks to become managing director.* ◇ *She rose to power in the 90s.*

• GET UP **4** (*formal*) to get up from a chair, bed, etc: *The audience rose and applauded the singers.*

• COME FROM **5** to come from: *Shouts of protest rose from the crowd.*

• FIGHT **6** ~ **(up) (against sb/sth)** (*formal*) to start fighting against your ruler, government, etc: *The people were afraid to rise up against the dictator.*

• BE SEEN **7** (*formal*) to be seen above or higher than sth else

▶ **rising** *adj.*: *the rising cost of living* ◇ *a rising young rock star*

IDM **rise to the occasion, challenge, task, etc.** to show that you are able to deal with a problem, etc. successfully

rise

grow ◆ increase ◆ climb ◆ go up ◆ escalate

These are all words that can be used when the amount, level or number of sth gets bigger or higher.

rise *We are all concerned by rising divorce rates.*

grow *There is growing opposition to the latest proposals.*

increase *The population has increased from 1.2 million to 1.8 million.*

climb *The temperature has been climbing all week.*

go up *The price of bread has gone up again.*

escalate (*formal*) *The fighting escalated into a full-scale war.*

risk¹ ĩ **B1** ⊙ /rɪsk/ *noun* **1** [C, U] ~ **(of sth/that …); ~ (to sb/sth)** a possibility of sth dangerous or unpleasant happening; a situation that could be dangerous or have a bad result: *If we don't leave early enough we run the risk of missing the plane.* ◇ *Scientists say these pesticides pose a risk to wildlife.* ◇ *Don't take any risks when you're driving.* ◇ *You could drive a car without insurance, but it's not worth the risk.* ◇ *Small children are most at risk from the disease.* **2** [sing.] a person or thing that might cause danger: *If he knows your real name he's a security risk.*

IDM **at your own risk** having the responsibility for whatever may happen: *This building is in a dangerous condition — enter at your own risk.* **at the risk of sth/doing sth** even though there could be a bad effect: *At the risk of showing my ignorance, how exactly does this gadget work?*

risk² ĩ **B1** /rɪsk/ *verb* [T] **1** to put sth or yourself in a dangerous position: *The man risked his life to save the little boy.* **2 ~ (doing sth)** to do sth that may mean that you get into a situation that is unpleasant for you: *If you don't work hard now you risk failing your exams.*

risky ĩ+ **B2** /'rɪski/ *adj.* (**riskier; riskiest**) involving the possibility of sth bad happening; dangerous

rite /raɪt/ *noun* [C] (**RELIGION**) a ceremony performed by a particular group of people, often for religious purposes

ritual ĩ+ **C1** /'rɪtʃuəl/ *noun* [C, U] (**RELIGION**) a series of actions that is always done in the same way: (*a*) *religious ritual* ▶ **ritual** *adj.* ▶ **ritually** /-əli/ *adv.*

rival¹ ĩ+ **B2** /'raɪvl/ *noun* [C] a person, company, or thing that competes with another in sport, business, etc: *It seems that we're rivals for the sales manager's job.* ◇ *The two teams have always been rivals.* ▶ **rival** ĩ+ **B2** *adj.*: *a rival bid/claim*

rival² /'raɪvl/ *verb* [T] (**-ll-**, *AmE* **-l-**) ~ **sb/sth (for/in sth)** to be as good as sb/sth: *Nothing rivals skiing for sheer excitement.*

rivalry /'raɪvlri/ *noun* [C, U] (*pl.* **-ies**) ~ **(with sb); ~ (between A and B)** competition between people, groups, etc: *There was a lot of rivalry between the sisters.*

river ĩ **A1** /'rɪvə(r)/ *noun* [C] (**GEOGRAPHY**) a large, natural flow of water that goes across land and into the sea: *the River Nile* ◇ *He sat down on the bank of the river to fish.* ⊃ note at **water¹** ⊃ picture at **oxbow lake, purification, water cycle**

A river **flows** into the sea. Where it joins the sea is the river **mouth**. A boat sails **on** the river. You walk, sail, etc. **up** or **down river**. The ground by the side of a river is the **bank**

riverbank /'rɪvəbæŋk/ *noun* [C] (**GEOGRAPHY**) the ground at the side of a river: *on the riverbank*

river bed *noun* [C] (**GEOGRAPHY**) the area of ground over which a river usually flows: *a dried-up river bed*

riverside /'rɪvəsaɪd/ *noun* [sing.] (**GEOGRAPHY**) the land next to a river: *a riverside hotel*

rivet¹ /'rɪvɪt/ *noun* [C] a metal pin for fastening two pieces of metal together

rivet² /'rɪvɪt/ *verb* [T] **1** [usually passive] to keep sb very interested: *I was riveted by her story.* **2** to fasten sth with RIVETS: *The steel plates were riveted together.*

RNA /ˌɑːr en 'eɪ/ *noun* [U] (**BIOLOGY**) a chemical present in all living cells. Like DNA, it is a type of NUCLEIC ACID. (the abbreviation for 'ribonucleic acid')

roach /rəʊtʃ/ (*AmE*) = COCKROACH

road ĩ **A1** /rəʊd/ *noun* **1** [C] a hard surface built for vehicles to travel on: *Turn left off the main road.* ◇ *road signs* ⊃ note at **direction 2 Road** (*abbr.* **Rd**) [sing.] used in names of roads, especially in towns: *60 Marylebone Road, London*

IDM **by road** in a car, bus, etc: *It's going to be a terrible journey by road — let's take the train.* **on the road** travelling: *We were on the road for 14 hours.*

roadblock /'rəʊdblɒk/ *noun* [C] a barrier put across a road by the police or army to stop traffic

road rage *noun* [U] a situation in which a driver becomes extremely angry or violent with the driver of another car because of the way they are driving

roadside /'rəʊdsaɪd/ *noun* [sing.] the edge of a road: *a roadside cafe*

road sign *noun* [C] a sign near a road giving information or instructions to drivers

road tax *noun* [U] (*BrE*) a tax that the owner of a vehicle has to pay to be allowed to drive it on public roads

roadway /'rəʊdweɪ/ *noun* [C, U] a road or the part of a road used by vehicles

roadworks /'rəʊdwɜːks/ *noun* [pl.] work that involves repairing or building roads

roadworthy /'rəʊdwɜːði/ *adj.* (used about a vehicle) in good enough condition to be driven on the road ▶ **roadworthiness** *noun* [U]

roam /rəʊm/ *verb* [I, T] to walk or travel with no particular plan or aim: *Gangs of youths were roaming the streets looking for trouble.*

roaming /'rəʊmɪŋ/ *noun* [U] using a mobile phone by connecting to a different company's network, for example when you are in a different country: *international roaming charges*

roar /rɔː(r)/ *verb* **1** [I] to make a loud, deep sound: *She* **roared with laughter** *at the joke.* ◇ *The lion opened its huge mouth and roared.* **2** [I, T] to shout sth very loudly **3** [I] (used with an adverb or a preposition) to move in the direction mentioned, making a loud, deep sound: *A motorbike roared past us.* ▶ roar *noun* [C]: *the roar of heavy traffic on the motorway* ◇ *roars of laughter*

roaring /'rɔːrɪŋ/ *adj.* **1** making a very loud noise **2** (used about a fire) burning very well **3** very great: *a roaring success*

roast¹ /rəʊst/ *verb* **1** [T, I] to cook or be cooked in an oven or over a fire: *a smell of roasting meat* ◇ *to roast a chicken* ➔ note at **cook¹**, **meat 2** [T] to heat and dry sth: *roasted peanuts* ▶ roast *adj.* [only before noun]: *roast beef/potatoes/chestnuts*

roast² /rəʊst/ *noun* [C] **1** a piece of meat that has been cooked in an oven **2** (*especially AmE*) an outdoor meal at which food is cooked over a fire ➔ look at **barbecue** (2)

rob ᵻ+ **B2** /rɒb/ *verb* [T] (-bb-) ~ **sb/sth (of sth)** (**LAW**) to take money, property, etc. from a person or place illegally: *to rob a bank* ◇ *Several people on the train were robbed of their money and jewellery.* ➔ note at **criminal¹**
PHRV rob sb/sth (of sth) to take sth away from sb/sth that they should have: *His illness robbed him of the chance to play for his country.*

robber /'rɒbə(r)/ *noun* [C] (**LAW**) a person who steals from a place or a person, especially using violence or threats ➔ note at **criminal¹**

robbery ᵻ+ **B2** /'rɒbəri/ *noun* [U, C] (*pl.* -ies) (**LAW**) the crime of stealing from a place or a person, especially using violence or threats: *They were found guilty of* **armed robbery** (= using a weapon). ➔ note at **criminal¹**

robe /rəʊb/ *noun* [C] **1** a long, loose piece of clothing, especially one worn at ceremonies **2** (*AmE*) = DRESSING GOWN

robin /'rɒbɪn/ *noun* [C] a small brown bird with a bright red chest

robot ᵻ **B1** /'rəʊbɒt/ *noun* [C] a machine that can perform a complicated series of tasks by itself: *These cars are built by robots.*

robotic /rəʊ'bɒtɪk/ *adj.* **1** connected with robots: *a robotic arm* **2** like a robot, making stiff movements, speaking without feeling or expression, etc.

robotics /rəʊ'bɒtɪks/ *noun* [U] (**ENGINEERING**) the science of designing and using robots

robust ᵻ+ **C1** /rəʊ'bʌst/ *adj.* strong and healthy

rock¹ ᵻ **A2** /rɒk/ *noun*
• HARD MATERIAL **1** [U, C] (**GEOLOGY**) the hard, solid material that forms part of the surface of the earth: *layers of rock formed over millions of years* **2** [C] (**GEOGRAPHY**) a large mass of rock that sticks out of the sea or the ground: *The ship hit the rocks and started to sink.* **3** [C] a single large piece of rock: *The beach was covered with rocks that had broken away from the cliffs.*
• STONE **4** [C] (*AmE*) a small piece of rock that can be picked up; a stone: *The boy threw a rock at the dog.*
• MUSIC **5** (*also* **rock music**) [U] a type of music with a very strong beat, played on musical instruments such as electric guitars, drums, etc: *I prefer jazz to rock.* ◇ *a rock singer/band* ➔ look at **classical** (3), **jazz¹**, **pop²** (1)
• SWEET **6** [U] (*BrE*) a type of hard sweet made in long, round sticks
IDM on the rocks **1** (used about a marriage, business, etc.) having problems and likely to fail **2** (used about drinks) served with ice but no water: *whisky on the rocks*

rock² ᵻ+ **C1** /rɒk/ *verb* **1** [I, T] to move backwards and forwards or from side to side; to make sb/sth do this: *boats rocking gently on the waves* ◇ *He rocked the baby in his arms to get her to sleep.* **2** [T] to shock sb **3** [T, often passive] to shake sth violently: *The city was rocked by a bomb blast.*
IDM rock the boat to do sth that causes problems or upsets people

the rock cycle

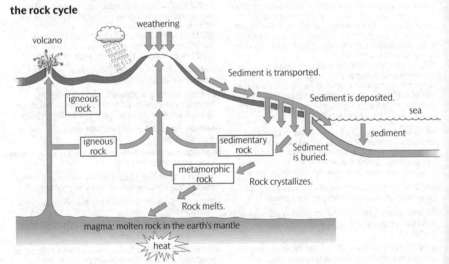

rock and 'roll (*also* rock 'n' roll) *noun* [U] (**MUSIC**) a type of music with a strong beat that was most popular in the 1950s

rock 'bottom *noun* [U] the lowest point: *He hit rock bottom when he lost his job and his wife left him.* ◇ *rock-bottom prices*

'rock climbing *noun* [U] (**SPORT**) the sport of climbing rocks and mountains with ropes, etc.

rocket¹ ⚓+ **B2** /'rɒkɪt/ *noun* **1** [C] (**ASTRONOMY**) a vehicle that is used for travel into space: *a space rocket* ◇ *to launch a rocket* **2** [C] a weapon that travels through the air and that carries a bomb **SYN** missile **3** [C] a type of FIREWORK (= an object that explodes in a beautiful way when you light it with a flame) that shoots high into the air **4** (*BrE*) (*AmE* arugula) a plant with long green leaves that have a strong taste and are eaten raw in salads

rocket² /'rɒkɪt/ *verb* [I] to increase or rise very quickly: *Prices have rocketed recently.* ⊃ note at **trend¹**

'rock face *noun* [C] (**GEOLOGY**) a surface of rock that goes straight upwards, especially on a mountain

'rock music = ROCK¹ (5)

rock 'n' 'roll = ROCK AND ROLL

rocky /'rɒki/ *adj.* (**rockier; rockiest**) covered with or made of rocks: *a rocky road/coastline*

rococo /rə'kəʊkəʊ/ (*also* Rococo) *adj.* (**ARCHITECTURE, ARTS AND MEDIA**) used to describe a style of architecture, furniture, etc. that has a lot of decoration, especially in curved round shapes; used to describe a style of literature or music that has a lot of detail and decoration. The rococo style was popular in the eighteenth century.

rod ⚓+ **C1** /rɒd/ *noun* [C] (often in compounds) a thin straight piece of wood, metal, etc: *a fishing rod* ⊃ picture at **dry cell, laboratory**

rode /rəʊd/ past tense of **ride¹**

rodent /'rəʊdnt/ *noun* [C] a type of small animal, with strong sharp front teeth. ⊃ picture at **animal**

rodeo /'rəʊdiəʊ, rəʊ'deɪəʊ/ *noun* [C] (*pl.* -os) a competition or performance in which people show their skill in riding wild horses, catching cows, etc.

roe /rəʊ/ *noun* [U, C] the mass of eggs inside a female fish, used as food

rogue /rəʊg/ *adj.* [only before noun] behaving differently from other similar people or things, often causing damage: *a rogue gene/program*

role ⚓ **A2** ⊙ /rəʊl/ *noun* [C] **1** ~ (of sb) a person's part in a play, film, etc: *She was chosen to play the role of Cleopatra.* ◇ *a leading role in the film* **2** ~ (in sth) the position or function of sb/sth in a particular situation: *Parents play a vital role in their children's education.*

'role model *noun* [C] a person that people admire and try to copy

'role-play *noun* [U, C] an activity, used especially in teaching, in which a person acts a part

roll¹ ⚓ **B1** /rəʊl/ *noun* [C]
- **BREAD 1** bread baked in a round shape for one person to eat: *a cheese roll* (= filled with cheese)
- **OF PAPER, ETC. 2** something made into the shape of a tube by turning it round and round itself: *a roll of fabric/wallpaper*
- **MOVEMENT 3** an act of moving or making sth move by turning over and over: *Everything depended on one roll of the dice.* **4** a movement from side to side
- **LIST OF NAMES 5** an official list of names: *the electoral roll* (= the list of people who can vote in an election)
- **SOUND 6** a long, low sound: *a roll of drums*

roll² ⚓ **B1** /rəʊl/ *verb*
- **TURN OVER 1** [I, T] to move by turning over and over; to make sth move in this way: *The apples fell out of the bag and rolled everywhere.* ◇ *Delivery men were rolling barrels across the yard.* **2** [I, T] to turn over to face a different direction; to make sb/sth do this: *The car rolled over in the crash.* ◇ *We rolled the log over to see what was underneath.* **3** [I, T] ~ (sth) (over) to turn over and over; to make sth do this: *The horse was rolling in the dirt.* ◇ *I rolled over onto my stomach.*
- **MOVE SMOOTHLY 4** [I] to move smoothly, often on wheels: *The car began to roll back down the hill.* ◇ *Tears were rolling down her cheeks.*
- **MAKE A BALL/TUBE 5** [I, T] ~ (sth) (up) to make sth into the shape of a ball or tube: *He was rolling a cigarette.* ◇ *The insect rolled up when I touched it.* **OPP** unroll
- **MAKE FLAT 6** [T] ~ sth (out) to make sth become flat by moving sth heavy over it: *Roll out the pastry thinly.*
- **OF A SHIP, ETC. 7** [I] (used about a ship, etc.) to move from side to side: *The ship began to roll in the storm.*
- **MAKE A SOUND 8** [I, T] to make a long continuous sound: *Thunder rolled.* ◇ *You have to roll your r's* (= by letting your tongue VIBRATE with each 'r' sound) *when you speak Spanish.*

IDM be rolling in money/in it (*slang*) to have a lot of money

PHR V roll in (*informal*) to arrive in large numbers or amounts: *Offers of help have been rolling in.* roll up (*informal*) (used about a person or a vehicle) to arrive, especially late

roller /'rəʊlə(r)/ *noun* [C] **1** a piece of equipment or part of a machine that is shaped like a tube and used, for example, to help sth move or to make sth flat: *a roller blind on a window* ◇ *A roller is used to flatten the grass.* **2** [usually pl.] a small plastic tube that hair is rolled around to make it curly

Rollerblade™ /'rəʊləbleɪd/ *noun* [C] a boot with one row of narrow wheels on the bottom: *a pair of Rollerblades* ▶ **rollerblade** *verb* [I] ▶ **rollerblading** *noun* [U]

'roller coaster *noun* [C] a narrow metal track that goes up and down and round tight bends, and that people ride on in a small train for fun and excitement

'roller skate (*also* skate) *noun* [C] a type of boot with two pairs of small wheels on the bottom: *a pair of roller skates* ▶ **roller skate** *verb* [I] ▶ **roller skating** *noun* [U]

rolling /'rəʊlɪŋ/ *adj.* [only before noun] **1** (used about hills or the countryside) having gentle slopes **2** done in regular stages or at regular INTERVALS over a period of time: *a rolling programme of reform*

'rolling pin *noun* [C] a piece of wood, etc. in the shape of a tube, that you use for making PASTRY flat and thin before cooking

ROM /rɒm/ *noun* [U] (**COMPUTING**) computer memory that contains instructions or data that cannot be changed or removed (the abbreviation for 'read-only memory') ⊃ look at **CD-ROM, RAM**

the Roma /ðə 'rəʊmə/ *noun* [pl.] the ROMANI people: *the Roma population of eastern Europe*

Roman /'rəʊmən/ *adj.* **1** (**HISTORY**) connected with ancient Rome or the Roman Empire: *Roman coins* ◇ *the Roman invasion of Britain* **2** roman ordinary printing type that does not lean forward: *Definitions in this dictionary are printed in roman type.* ⊃ look at **italics 3** connected with the modern city of Rome ▶ **Roman** *noun* [C]

the Roman 'alphabet *noun* [sing.] (**LANGUAGE**) the letters A to Z, used in most western European languages

Roman ˈCatholic (*also* **Catholic**) *noun* [C] (**RELIGION**) a member of the Christian Church that has the Pope as its head: *She's (a) Roman Catholic.* ⊃ look at **Protestant** ▶ Roman Catholic (*also* **Catholic**) *adj.* ▶ Roman Caˈtholicism (*also* **Catholicism**) *noun* [U]

Romance /rəʊˈmæns/ *adj.* (**LANGUAGE**) **Romance** languages, such as French, Italian and Spanish, are languages that developed from Latin

romance ⭐+ **B2** /rəʊˈmæns, ˈrəʊmæns/ *noun* **1** [C] a relationship between two people who are in love with each other: *The film was about a teenage romance.* **2** [U] a feeling or an atmosphere of love or of sth new, special and exciting **3** [C] (**LITERATURE**) a novel about a love affair: *historical romances*

Romanesque /ˌrəʊməˈnesk/ *adj.* (**ARCHITECTURE**) used to describe a style of building that was popular in western Europe from the tenth to the twelfth centuries and that had round ARCHES, thick walls and tall PILLARS ⊃ look at **Norman**

Romani (*also* Romany) /ˈrəʊməni, ˈrɒm-/ *noun* (*pl.* -ies) **1** [C] a member of a human group who traditionally spend their lives travelling around from place to place, living in CARAVANS (= homes with wheels) ⊃ look at **Gypsy, traveller** (2) **2** [U] the language of Romani people

Roman ˈnumeral *noun* [C] (**HISTORY, MATHEMATICS**) one of the letters used by the ancient Romans to represent numbers and still used today, in some situations. In this system I=1, V=5, X=10, L=50, C=100, D=500, M=1000 and these letters are used in combinations to form other numbers: *Henry VIII*

romantic¹ ⭐ **B1** /rəʊˈmæntɪk/ *adj.* **1** having a quality that strongly affects your emotions or makes you think about love; showing feelings of love: *a romantic candlelit dinner* ◇ *He isn't very romantic — he never says he loves me.* **2** connected with a relationship between two people who are in love with each other: *Reports of a romantic relationship between the two film stars have been strongly denied.* **3** having or showing ideas about life that are emotional rather than real or practical: *He has a romantic idea that he'd like to live on a farm in Scotland.* ▶ romantically /-kli/ *adv.*

romantic² /rəʊˈmæntɪk/ *noun* [C] a person who has ideas that are not based on real life or that are not very practical

romanticism /rəʊˈmæntɪsɪzəm/ (*also* Romanticism) *noun* [U] (**ARTS AND MEDIA**) a style and movement in art, music and literature in the late eighteenth and early nineteenth century, in which strong feelings, imagination and a return to nature were more important than reason, order and INTELLECTUAL ideas ⊃ look at **realism** (2)

romanticize (*BrE also* -ise) /rəʊˈmæntɪsaɪz/ *verb* [T, I] to make sth seem more interesting, exciting, etc. than it really is

romp /rɒmp/ *verb* [I] (used about children and animals) to play in a happy and noisy way ▶ romp *noun* [C]

rondo /ˈrɒndəʊ/ *noun* [C] (*pl.* -os) (**MUSIC**) a piece of music in which the main tune is repeated several times, sometimes forming part of a longer piece

roof ⭐ **A2** /ruːf/ *noun* [C] (*pl.* roofs) **1** (**ARCHITECTURE**) the part of a building, vehicle, etc. that covers the top of it: *a flat/sloping/tiled roof* ◇ *the roof of a car* ◇ *The library and the sports hall are under one roof* (= in the same building). **2** the highest part of the inside of sth: *The roof of the cave had collapsed.* **3** ~ **of your mouth** (**ANATOMY**) the top of the inside of the mouth: *The soup burned the roof of my mouth.*

IDM a roof over your head somewhere to live: *I might not have any money, but at least I've got a roof over my head.*

ˈroof rack *noun* [C] a structure that you fix to the roof of a car and use for carrying LUGGAGE or other large objects

rooftop /ˈruːftɒp/ *noun* [C, usually pl.] the outside of the roof of a building: *From the tower we looked down over the rooftops of the city.*

rookie /ˈrʊki/ *noun* [C] (*informal*) **1** (*especially AmE*) a person who has just started a job or an activity and has very little experience **2** (*AmE*) (**SPORT**) a member of a sports team in his or her first full year of playing that sport

room ⭐ **A1** /ruːm, rʊm/ *noun* **1** [C] a part of a house or building that has its own walls, floor and ceiling: *a sitting/dining/living room* ◇ *I sat down in the waiting room until the doctor called me.* ◇ *I'd like to book a double room for two nights.* **2** [U] ~ **(for sb/sth); ~ (to do sth)** space; enough space: *These chairs take up too much room.* ◇ *How can we make room for all the furniture?* ◇ *There were so many people that there wasn't any room to move.* ⊃ look at **space¹** (2) **3** [U] ~ **for sth** the opportunity or need for sth: *There's room for improvement in your work* (= it could be much better). ◇ *The lack of time gives us very little room for manoeuvre.*

roomful /ˈruːmfʊl, ˈrʊm-/ *noun* [C] a large number of people or things in a room

roommate /ˈruːmmeɪt, ˈrʊm-/ *noun* [C] **1** a person that you share a room with, especially at a college or university **2** (*AmE*) a person that you share a flat/an apartment with ⊃ look at **flatmate**

ˈroom service *noun* [U] (**TOURISM**) a service provided in a hotel, by which guests can order food and drink to be brought to their rooms: *He ordered coffee from room service.*

ˈroom temperature *noun* [U] the normal temperature inside a building: *Serve the wine at room temperature.*

roomy /ˈruːmi, ˈrʊmi/ *adj.* (roomier; roomiest) having plenty of space: *a roomy house/car* **SYN** spacious

roost /ruːst/ *noun* [C] a place where birds rest or sleep ▶ roost *verb* [I]

rooster /ˈruːstə(r)/ = COCK¹ (1)

root¹ ⭐ **B2** ⓦ /ruːt/ *noun* **1** [C] the part of a plant that grows under the ground and takes in water and food from the soil: *tree roots* ◇ *root vegetables* such as carrots and parsnips ⊃ picture at **flower¹, photosynthesis, tree 2** [C] (**ANATOMY**) the part of a hair or tooth that is under the skin and that holds it in place on the body ⊃ picture at **skin¹, tooth 3** [C] the basic cause or origin of sth: *Let's try and get to the root of the problem.* **4** roots [pl.] the feelings or connections that you have with a place because you have lived there or your family came from there: *She's proud of her Italian roots.* **5** [C] (**MATHEMATICS**) a quantity which, when multiplied by itself a particular number of times, produces another quantity ⊃ look at **cube root, square root**

root² /ruːt/ *verb*
PHR V root about/around (for sth) to search for sth by moving things: *What are you rooting around in my desk for?* root for sb to give support to sb who is in a competition, etc. root sth out to find sth bad and destroy it completely

rope¹ ⭐ **B1** /rəʊp/ *noun* [C, U] very thick, strong string that is used for tying or lifting heavy things, climbing up, etc: *We need some rope to tie up the boat with.* **IDM** show sb/know/learn the ropes to show sb/ know/learn how a job should be done

rope² /rəʊp/ *verb* [T] ~ **A to B**; ~ **A and B together** to tie sb/sth with a rope: *The climbers were roped together when they crossed the glacier.*
PHR V **rope sb in (to do sth)** (*informal*) to persuade sb to help in an activity, especially when they do not want to **rope sth off** to put ropes round or across an area in order to keep people out of it

rosary /ˈrəʊzəri/ *noun* [C] (*pl.* -ies) (**RELIGION**) a string of small round pieces of wood, etc. used by some Roman Catholics for counting prayers

rose¹ /rəʊz/ past tense of **rise²**

rose² ᵎ+ **B2** /rəʊz/ *noun* [C] a flower with a sweet smell, that grows on a bush that usually has THORNS (= sharp points) growing on it

rosé /ˈrəʊzeɪ/ *noun* [U] pink wine

rosebud /ˈrəʊzbʌd/ *noun* [C] the flower of a ROSE before it is open

rosemary /ˈrəʊzməri/ *noun* [U] a HERB (= a type of plant) with small narrow leaves that smell sweet and are used in cooking

rosette /rəʊˈzet/ *noun* [C] a round decoration made from RIBBONS (= long pieces of coloured cloth) that you wear on your clothes. Rosettes are given as prizes or worn to show that sb supports a particular political party.

roster /ˈrɒstə(r)/ (*especially AmE*) = ROTA

rostrum /ˈrɒstrəm/ *noun* [C] (*pl.* rostrums, rostra /-strə/) a platform that sb stands on to make a public speech, etc.

rosy /ˈrəʊzi/ *adj.* (rosier; rosiest) **1** pink and pleasant in appearance: *rosy cheeks* **2** likely to be good or successful: *The future was looking rosy.*

rotate ᵎ+ **C1** /rəʊˈteɪt/ *verb* [I, T] **1** to turn in circles round a central point; to make sth do this: *The earth rotates on its axis.* **2** to happen in turn or in a particular order; to make sth do this: *We rotate the duties so that nobody is stuck with a job they don't like.*

rotation ᵎ+ **C1** /rəʊˈteɪʃn/ *noun* [U, C] **1** movement in circles around a central point; one complete movement in a circle around a central point: *one rotation every 24 hours* ⊃ picture at **axis 2** the act of regularly changing the thing that is being used in a particular situation, or of changing the person who does a particular job: *crop rotation* (= changing the type of crop that is grown on an area of land in order to protect the soil) ◇ *job rotation* ◇ *The company is chaired by all the members in rotation.*

rotor /ˈrəʊtə(r)/ *noun* [C] a part of a machine that turns around a central point: *rotor blades on a helicopter*

rotten /ˈrɒtn/ *adj.* **1** (used about food and other substances) old and not fresh enough or good enough to use: *rotten vegetables* **2** (*informal*) very unpleasant: *That was a rotten thing to say!* **3** (*informal*) used to emphasize that you are angry: *You can keep your rotten job!*

rouge /ruːʒ/ *noun* [U] (*old-fashioned*) a red powder or cream used for giving more colour to the CHEEKS (= the sides of the face) ⊃ look at **blusher**

rough¹ ᵎ **B1** /rʌf/ *adj.* **1** not smooth, soft or level: *rough ground* **OPP** **smooth¹ 2** made or done quickly or without much care; not exact: *a rough estimate* ◇ *Can*

you give me a rough idea of what time you'll be arriving? **SYN** **approximate¹ 3** violent; not calm or gentle: *You can hold the baby, but don't be rough with him.* ◇ *The sea was rough and half the people on the boat were seasick.* **4** difficult and unpleasant **SYN** **tough 5** (*informal*) looking or feeling ill: *You look a bit rough — are you feeling OK?* ▸ **roughness** *noun* [U]
IDM **be rough (on sb)** be unpleasant or bad luck for sb

rough² /rʌf/ *noun*
IDM **in rough** (used about a piece of work or drawing) done quickly without worrying about mistakes, as a preparation for the finished piece of work or drawing **take the rough with the smooth** to accept difficult or unpleasant things in addition to pleasant things

rough³ /rʌf/ *adv.* using force or violence: *One of the boys was told off for playing rough.*
IDM **live/sleep rough** to live or sleep outdoors, usually because you have no home or money

rough⁴ /rʌf/ *verb*
IDM **rough it** to live without all the comfortable things that you usually have: *You have to rough it a bit when you go camping.*

roughage /ˈrʌfɪdʒ/ *noun* [U] the part of food that helps food and waste products to pass through the body **SYN** **fibre**

roughen /ˈrʌfn/ *verb* [T] to make sth less smooth or soft

roughly ᵎ+ **B2** **●** /ˈrʌfli/ *adv.* **1** not exactly; approximately: *It took roughly three hours, I suppose.* **2** in a violent way; not gently: *He grabbed her roughly by her arm.*

roulette /ruːˈlet/ *noun* [U] a game in which a ball is dropped onto a moving wheel that has holes with numbers on them. The players bet on which hole the ball will be in when the wheel stops.

round¹ ᵎ **A2** /raʊnd/ *adj.* having the shape of a circle or a ball: *a round table*
IDM **in round figures/numbers** given to the nearest 10, 100, 1 000, etc.; not given in exact numbers

round² ᵎ **A2** /raʊnd/ (*especially BrE*) (*AmE usually* **around**) *adv., prep.* **1** (moving) in a circle: *The wheels spun round and round but the car wouldn't move.* ◇ *The earth moves round the sun.* **2** surrounding sb/sth; on all sides of sth: *He had a bandage right round his head.* ◇ *A large crowd had gathered round to watch.* ◇ *We sat round the table, talking late into the night.* **3** on, to or from the other side of sb/sth: *Our house is just round the corner.* ◇ *The bus came round the bend.* (*figurative*) *There must be a way round the problem.* **4** turning to look or go in the opposite direction: *Don't look round but the teacher's just come in.* ◇ *She turned the car round and drove off.* **5** from one place, person, etc. to another: *Pass the photos round for everyone to see.* ◇ *I've been rushing round all day.* **6** in or to many places: *Let me show you round the house.* ◇ *He spent six months travelling round Europe.* ◇ *People stood round waiting for something to happen.* **7** (*informal*) in or to a particular area or place: *Do you live round here?* ◇ *I'll come round to see you at about eight o'clock.*
IDM **the other way round** in the opposite way or order: *My appointment's at three and Lella's at 3.15 — or was it the other way round?* **round about (sth) 1** approximately: *We hope to arrive round about six.* **2** in the area near a place

round³ ᵎ **B2** /raʊnd/ *noun* [C]
• EVENTS **1** a number or series of events, etc: *a further round of talks with other European countries*

- REGULAR ACTIVITIES **2** a regular series of visits, etc., often as part of a job: *The postman's round takes him about three hours.* ◊ *Dr Adamou is on his daily round of the wards.*
- DRINKS **3** a number of drinks (one for all the people in a group): *It's my round* (= it's my turn to buy the drinks).
- IN SPORT **4** one part of a game or competition: *Parma will play Real Madrid in the next round.* **5** (in golf) one game, usually of 18 HOLES: *to play a round of golf*
- SHOT **6** a bullet or a number of bullets, fired from a gun: *He fired several rounds at us.*
- APPLAUSE **7** a short, sudden period of loud noise: *The last speaker got the biggest* **round of applause**.
- IN MUSIC **8** a song for two or more voices in which each sings the same tune but starts at a different time

round⁴ /raʊnd/ *verb* [T] to go round sth: *The police car rounded the corner at high speed.*
PHR V **round sth off** to do sth that completes a job or an activity: *We rounded off the meal with coffee and chocolates.* **round sb/sth up** to bring sb/sth together in one place: *The teacher rounded up the children.*
round sth up/down to increase/decrease a number, price, etc. to the nearest whole number

roundabout¹ /'raʊndəbaʊt/ *noun* [C] **1** a circle where several roads meet, that all the traffic has to go round in the same direction **2** a round platform made for children to play on. They sit or stand on it and sb pushes it round. **3** (*BrE*) = MERRY-GO-ROUND

roundabout² /'raʊndəbaʊt/ *adj.* longer than is necessary or usual; not direct: *We got lost and came by a rather roundabout route.* ◊ *She told us in a roundabout way that we had to work harder.*

rounded /'raʊndɪd/ *adj.* **1** having a round shape **2** having a wide variety of qualities that combine to produce sth pleasant and complete

rounders /'raʊndəz/ *noun* [U] (SPORT) a British game played especially in schools by two teams using a BAT and ball. Each player tries to hit the ball and then run around the four sides of a square before the other team can return the ball. ⊃ look at **baseball**

round 'trip *noun* [C] a journey to a place and back again: *It's a four-mile round trip to the centre of town.*

round-trip 'ticket = RETURN² (4)

round 'window *noun* [C] (ANATOMY) the second of two openings covered by a MEMBRANE (= a thin layer of skin) between the MIDDLE EAR and the INNER EAR ⊃ look at **oval window** ⊃ picture at **ear**

roundworm /'raʊndwɜːm/ *noun* [C] a WORM (= a small creature with a soft body and no legs) that lives inside the bodies of pigs, humans and some other animals

rouse /raʊz/ *verb* [T] **1** (*formal*) to make sb wake up: *She was sleeping so soundly that I couldn't rouse her.* **2** [usually passive] to make sb/sth very angry, excited, interested, etc.

rousing /'raʊzɪŋ/ *adj.* exciting and powerful: *a rousing speech*

rout /raʊt/ *verb* [T] to defeat sb completely ▸ **rout** *noun* [C]

route ʔ **A2** /ruːt/ *noun* [C] **1** ~ **(from A) (to B)** a way from one place to another: *What is the most direct route from Bordeaux to Lyon?* ◊ *I got a leaflet about the bus routes from the information office.* **2** ~ **to sth** a way of achieving sth: *Hard work is the only route to success.* **3** used before the number of a main road in the US: *Route 66* ▸ **route** *verb* [T] (*routing, routeing*): *Satellites route data all over the globe.*

router /'ruːtə(r)/ *noun* [C] (COMPUTING) a device that sends data to the appropriate parts of a computer network

routine¹ ʔ **A1** /ruːˈtiːn/ *noun* **1** [C, U] the usual order and way in which you regularly do things: *Make exercise part of your daily routine.* **2** [U] tasks that have to be done again and again and so are boring: *She needed a break from the routine.* **3** [C] a series of movements, jokes, etc. that are part of a performance: *a dance/comedy routine* **4** [C] (COMPUTING) a list of instructions that make a computer able to perform a particular task

routine² **B2** /ruːˈtiːn/ *adj.* **1** normal and regular; not unusual or special: *The police would like to ask you some* **routine questions**. **2** boring; not exciting: *It's a very routine job, really.*

routinely /ruːˈtiːnli/ *adv.* regularly; as part of a routine: *The machines are routinely checked every two months.*

row¹ ʔ **B1** /rəʊ/ *noun* [C] **1** a line of people or things: *a row of books* ◊ *The children were all standing* **in a row** *at the front of the class.* **2** a line of seats in a theatre, cinema, etc: *Our seats were in the back row.* ◊ *a front-row seat*
IDM **in a row** one after another; without a break: *It rained solidly for four days in a row.*

row² /rəʊ/ *verb* **1** [I, T] (SPORT) to move a boat through the water using OARS (= POLES with flat ends): *We often go rowing on the lake.* **2** [T] to carry sb/sth in a boat that you row: *Could you row us over to the island?* ⊃ look at **paddle²** (1) ▸ **row** *noun* [sing.]

row³ **B1** /raʊ/ *noun* (*especially BrE, informal*) **1** [C] ~ **(about/over sth)** a serious or noisy argument between two or more people, groups, etc: *When I have a row with my girlfriend, I always try to make up as soon as possible.* ◊ *A row has broken out between the main parties over education.* **2** [sing.] a loud noise: *What a row! Could you be a bit quieter?* ▸ **row** *verb* [I] ~ **(with sb) (about/over sth)**: *Pete and I are always rowing about money!*

rowdy /'raʊdi/ *adj.* (*rowdier; rowdiest*) noisy and likely to cause trouble: *a rowdy group of football fans* ◊ *rowdy behaviour* ▸ **rowdily** /-dəli/ *adv.* ▸ **rowdiness** *noun* [U]

rowing boat /'rəʊɪŋ bəʊt/ (*BrE*) (*AmE* **rowboat** /'rəʊbəʊt/) *noun* [C] a small boat that you move through the water using OARS (= POLES with flat ends)

royal ʔ **B1** /'rɔɪəl/ *adj.* (POLITICS) **1** connected with a king or queen or a member of their family: *the royal family* **2** (used in the names of organizations) supported by a member of the royal family ▸ **royal** *noun* [C, usually pl.] (*informal*): *the Queen, the Princes and other royals*

Royal 'Highness *noun* [C] His/Her/Your Royal Highness used when you are speaking to or about a member of the royal family

royalty /'rɔɪəlti/ *noun* (*pl. -ies*) **1** [U] members of the royal family **2** [C] (ARTS AND MEDIA) an amount of money that is paid to the person who wrote a book, piece of music, etc. every time their work is sold or performed: *The author earns a 2% royalty on each copy sold.*

RP /ˌɑː ˈpiː/ *abbr.* (LANGUAGE) received pronunciation (a widely recognized ACCENT (= way of pronouncing words) of British English, associated with education, broadcasting and the South of England)

rpm /ˌɑː piː ˈem/ *abbr.* (ENGINEERING) revolutions per minute (a measurement of the speed of an engine, a computer HARD DRIVE, etc.): *an engine speed of 2 500 rpm*

RSI /ˌɑːr es ˈaɪ/ noun [U] (**HEALTH**) pain and SWELLING (= being larger and rounder than normal), especially in the WRISTS and hands, caused by doing the same movement many times in a job or an activity (the abbreviation for 'repetitive strain/stress injury')

RSS /ˌɑːr es ˈes/ abbr. (**COMPUTING**) a standard system for sending news and information from a website to people using the internet (the abbreviation for 'Really Simple Syndication')

RSVP /ˌɑːr es viː ˈpiː/ abbr. used on invitations to mean 'please reply' (from French 'répondez s'il vous plaît')

Rt Hon abbr. (in writing) (BrE) = RIGHT HONOURABLE

rub 🔒 B2 /rʌb/ verb (-bb-) **1** [T, I] (often used with an adverb or a preposition) to move your hand, a cloth, etc. backwards and forwards on the surface of sth while pressing FIRMLY: Ralph rubbed his hands together to keep them warm. ◇ The cat rubbed against my leg. **2** [I, T] ~ (on/against sth) to press on/against sth, often causing pain or damage: These new shoes are really rubbing. ◇ The wheel is rubbing on the mudguard. **3** [T] ~ sth in (to sth) to put a cream, liquid, etc. onto a surface by rubbing: Apply a little of the lotion and rub it into the skin. ▸ rub noun [C]
IDM rub salt into the wound/sb's wounds **1** to make a situation that makes sb feel bad even worse **2** to make sb who feels bad feel even worse rub shoulders with sb to meet and spend time with famous people: As a journalist you rub shoulders with the rich and famous.
PHRV rub it/sth in to keep reminding sb of sth embarrassing that they want to forget: I know it was a stupid mistake, but there's no need to rub it in! rub off (on/onto sb) (used about a good quality) to be passed from one person to another: Let's hope some of her enthusiasm rubs off onto her brother. rub sth off (sth) to remove sth from a surface by rubbing: He rubbed the dirt off his boots. rub sth out to remove the marks made by a pencil, etc. using a rubber, etc: That answer is wrong. Rub it out.

rubber 🔒 B2 /ˈrʌbə(r)/ noun **1** [U] a strong substance that can be stretched and does not allow water to pass through it, used for making tyres, boots, etc. Rubber is made from the SAP of a tropical tree or is produced using chemicals: a rubber tree/plantation ◇ foam rubber **2** [C] (BrE) (also eraser AmE, BrE) a small piece of rubber that you use for removing pencil marks from paper; a piece of soft material used for removing CHALK (= soft stone that you use for writing or drawing) marks or pen marks from a board **3** [C] (especially AmE, informal) = CONDOM ▸ rubber 🔒 B2 adj.: rubber gloves ◇ a rubber ball

‚rubber ˈband (BrE also elastic band) noun [C] a thin round piece of rubber that is used for holding things together: Her hair was tied back with a rubber band.

‚rubber ˈstamp noun [C] **1** a small tool that you hold in your hand and use for printing the date, the name of an organization, etc. on a document **2** a person or group who gives official approval to sth without thinking about it first ▸ ‚rubber-ˈstamp verb [T]: The committee have no real power — they just rubber-stamp the chairman's ideas.

rubbery /ˈrʌbəri/ adj. like rubber: This meat is rubbery.

rubbish 🔒 A2 /ˈrʌbɪʃ/ (especially BrE) (AmE garbage, trash) noun [U] **1** things that you do not want any more; waste material: The dustmen collect the rubbish every Monday. ◇ a rubbish bin ◇ It's only rubbish — throw it away. ⊃ look at waste² (3) **2** something that you think is bad, silly or wrong: I thought that film was absolute rubbish. ◇ Don't talk such rubbish. **SYN** nonsense

ˈrubbish tip = TIP¹ (4)

rubble /ˈrʌbl/ noun [U] pieces of broken BRICK, stone, etc., especially from a damaged building

rubella /ruːˈbelə/ = GERMAN MEASLES

rubidium /ruːˈbɪdiəm/ noun [U] (symb. Rb) (**CHEMISTRY**) a chemical element. Rubidium is a rare soft silver-coloured metal that reacts strongly with water and burns when it is brought into contact with air. ❶ For more information on the periodic table of elements, look at the **Reference Section** of this dictionary.

rubric /ˈruːbrɪk/ noun [C] (formal) a title or set of instructions written in a book, an exam paper, etc.

ruby /ˈruːbi/ noun [C] (pl. -ies) a red PRECIOUS STONE (= one that is rare and valuable)

‚ruby ˈwedding noun [C] the 40th anniversary of a wedding ⊃ look at diamond wedding, golden wedding, silver wedding

rucksack /ˈrʌksæk/ (BrE) (also backpack AmE, BrE) noun [C] a bag that you use for carrying things on your back ⊃ look at pack² (3) ⊃ picture at baggage

rudder /ˈrʌdə(r)/ noun [C] a piece of wood or metal that is used for controlling the direction of a boat or plane ⊃ picture at airliner

rude 🔒 A2 /ruːd/ adj. **1** ~ (to sb) (about sb/sth); ~ (of sb) (to do sth) not polite: She was very rude to me about my new jacket. ◇ It's rude to interrupt when people are speaking. ◇ I think it was rude of them not to phone and say that they weren't coming. **SYN** impolite **2** connected with sex, using the toilet, etc. in a way that might offend people: a rude joke/word/gesture **SYN** offensive¹ **3** [only before noun] (formal) sudden and unpleasant: If you're expecting any help from him, you're in for a rude shock. ▸ rudeness noun [U]

rudely /ˈruːdli/ adv. **1** in a way that shows a lack of respect for other people and their feelings: They brushed rudely past us. ◇ 'What do you want?' she asked rudely. **2** in a way that is sudden, unpleasant and unexpected: I was rudely awakened by the phone ringing.

rudimentary /ˌruːdɪˈmentri/ adj. (formal) very basic or simple

rudiments /ˈruːdɪmənts/ noun [pl.] the ~ (of sth) (formal) the most basic or important facts of a particular subject, skill, etc.

ruffle /ˈrʌfl/ verb [T] **1** ~ sth (up) to make sth untidy or no longer smooth: to ruffle somebody's hair **2** [often passive] to make sb annoyed or confused

rug /rʌɡ/ noun [C] **1** a piece of thick material that covers a small part of a floor ⊃ look at carpet (1), mat (1) **2** (BrE) a large piece of thick cloth that you put over your legs to keep warm

rugby 🔒 B1 /ˈrʌɡbi/ noun [U] (**SPORT**) a game that is played by two teams of 13 or 15 players with a ball shaped like an egg that can be carried, kicked or thrown ⊃ picture at sport ❶ Rugby League is played with 13 players in a team, Rugby Union with 15 players.

rugged /ˈrʌɡɪd/ adj. **1** (used about land) rough, with a lot of rocks and not many plants **2** (used about a man) strong and attractive **3** (used about equipment, clothes, etc.) strong and made for difficult conditions

ruin¹ 🔒+ B2 /ˈruːɪn/ verb [T] **1** to damage sth so badly that it loses all its value, pleasure, etc: The bad news ruined my week. ◇ That one mistake ruined my chances of getting the job. **2** to cause sb to lose all their money, hope of being successful, etc: The cost of the court case nearly ruined them.

ruin² ℞+ **B2** /'ruːɪn/ *noun* **1** [U] the state of being destroyed or very badly damaged: *The city was in a state of ruin.* **2** [U] the fact of having no money, of having lost your job, position, etc: *Many small companies are facing financial ruin.* **3** [sing.] something that causes a person, company, etc. to lose all their money, job, position, etc. **4** [C] (*also* ruins [pl.]) the parts of a building that are left standing after it has been destroyed or badly damaged: *the ruins of the ancient city of Pompeii*
IDM go to rack and ruin → RACK¹ in ruins badly damaged or destroyed: *After the accident her life seemed to be in ruins.*

ruined /'ruːɪnd/ *adj.* [only before noun] destroyed or severely damaged so that only parts remain

ruinous /'ruːɪnəs/ *adj.* (*formal*) causing serious problems, especially with money

rule¹ ℞ **A1** ⊙ /ruːl/ *noun*
• OF AN ACTIVITY/A GAME **1** [C] an official statement that tells you what you must or must not do in a particular situation or when playing a game: *to obey/break a rule* ◊ *Do you know the rules of chess?* ◊ *It's against the rules to talk during the exam.* ◊ *The company have strict rules and regulations governing employees' dress.*
• IN GRAMMAR **2** [C] a description of what is usual or correct: *What is the rule for forming the past tense?*
• ADVICE **3** [C] a piece of advice about what you should do in a particular situation: *When you run a marathon, the golden rule is: don't start too fast.*
• NORMAL SITUATION **4** [sing.] what is usual: *Large families are the exception rather than the rule nowadays.* ◊ *As a general rule, women live longer than men.* ◊ *I don't read much as a rule.*
• GOVERNMENT **5** [U] government; control: *The country is under military rule.*
IDM bend the rules → BEND¹ the golden rule (of sth) → GOLDEN a rule of thumb a simple piece of practical advice, not involving exact details or figures work to rule to follow the rules of your job in a very strict way in order to cause delay, as a form of protest against your employer or your working conditions ⊃ look at **work-to-rule**

rule² ℞ **B1** /ruːl/ *verb* [I, T] **1** ~ (over sb/sth) (POLITICS) to have the power over a country, group of people, etc: *Julius Caesar ruled over a vast empire.* ◊ *The Congress Party ruled India for almost 40 years.* ◊ (*figurative*) *His whole life was ruled by his ambition to become president.* **2** ~ (on sth); ~ (in favour of/against sb/sth); ~ (that …) to make an official decision: *The judge will rule on whether or not the case can go ahead.* ◊ *The court ruled in favour of the defendant.* ◊ *The committee ruled that Waters did not break the rules.*
PHRV rule sb/sth out to say that sb/sth is not possible, cannot do sth, etc.; to prevent sth: *The government has ruled out further increases in train fares next year.*

ruler /'ruːlə(r)/ *noun* [C] **1** (POLITICS) a person who rules a country, etc. **2** (MATHEMATICS) a straight piece of wood, plastic, etc. marked in CENTIMETRES or inches, used for measuring sth or for drawing straight lines

ruling¹ /'ruːlɪŋ/ *adj.* [only before noun] with the most power in an organization, a country, etc: *the ruling political party*

ruling² ℞+ **C1** /'ruːlɪŋ/ *noun* [C] an official decision

rum /rʌm/ *noun* [U, C] a strong alcoholic drink that is made from the juice of SUGAR CANE (= a plant from which sugar is made)

rumble /'rʌmbl/ *verb* [I] to make a long deep sound: *I was so hungry that my stomach was rumbling.*
▶ rumble *noun* [sing.]: *a rumble of thunder*

ruminant /'ruːmɪnənt/ *noun* [C] (BIOLOGY) any animal that brings back food from its stomach and CHEWS it (= breaks it up in its mouth with its teeth) again: *Cows and sheep are both ruminants.* ▶ ruminant *adj.*

rummage /'rʌmɪdʒ/ *verb* [I] to move things and make them untidy while you are looking for sth: *Nina rummaged through the drawer looking for the tin-opener.*

'rummage sale (*AmE*) = JUMBLE SALE

rumour ℞+ **C1** (*BrE*) (*AmE* rumor) /'ruːmə(r)/ *noun* [C, U] ~ (about sb/sth); ~ (of sb/sth) (a piece of) news or information that many people are talking about but that is possibly not true: *I didn't start the rumour about Barry's operation.* ◊ *There are rumours of a strike going round the factory.* ◊ *Rumour has it* (= people are saying) *that Lena has resigned.* ◊ *to confirm/deny a rumour* (= to say that it is true/not true)

rumour² (*BrE*) (*AmE* rumored) /'ruːmə(r)/ be rumoured *verb* [T] be rumoured that … ; be rumoured to do sth … to be reported as a RUMOUR and possibly not true: *It's widely rumoured that they are getting divorced.* ◊ *They are rumoured to be getting divorced.*

rumoured (*BrE*) (*AmE* rumored) /'ruːməd/ *adj.* [only before noun] reported or said, but perhaps not true: *He denied the rumoured love affair.*

rump /rʌmp/ *noun* [C] the back end of an animal: *rump steak* (= meat from the rump)

run¹ ℞ **A1** /rʌn/ *verb* (running; *pt* ran /ræn/; *pp* run)
• ON FOOT **1** [I, T] (often used with an adverb or a preposition) to move using your legs, going faster than a walk: *I had to run to catch the bus.* ◊ *I often go running in the evenings* (= as a hobby). ◊ *I ran nearly 10 kilometres this morning.* ◊ *to run a marathon* ◊ *The dog ran off as soon as we appeared.*
• MOVE SOMEWHERE **2** [I, T] (used with an adverb or a preposition) to move, or move sth, quickly in a particular direction: *I've been running around after the kids all day.* ◊ *The car ran off the road and hit a tree.* ◊ *She ran her finger down the list of passengers.*
• ORGANIZE **3** [T] to organize or be in charge of sth; to provide a service: *She runs a restaurant.* ◊ *They run English courses all the year round.* ⊃ note at **organization**
• OF A MACHINE/VEHICLE **4** [I, T] to operate or function; to make sth do this: *There are too many programs running on your computer.* ◊ *When I tried to run the application, I got an error message.* ◊ *The engine is running very smoothly now.* **5** [T] to use and pay for a vehicle: *It costs a lot to run a car.*
• LEAD/STRETCH **6** [I] (*BrE*) to lead or stretch from one place to another; to be in a particular position: *The road runs along the side of a lake.*
• OF LIQUID **7** [I, T] (used about water or other liquid) to flow; to make water flow: *When it's really cold, my nose runs.* ◊ *I can hear a tap running somewhere.* ◊ *to run a bath/a tap* **8** [I] ~ with sth to be covered with flowing water: *My face was running with sweat.*
• OF COLOUR **9** [I] (used about the colour in material, etc.) to come out and spread, for example when the material is washed: *Don't put that red shirt in the washing machine. It might run.*
• CONTINUE **10** [I] to continue for a time: *My contract has two months left to run.* ◊ *The play ran for nearly two years in a London theatre.*
• HAPPEN **11** [I] (used with an adverb or a preposition) to operate at a particular time: *All the trains are running late this morning.* ◊ *We'd better hurry up — we're running behind schedule.*
• IN AN ELECTION **12** [I] (*especially AmE*) = STAND¹ (9): *He's running for president.*

- IN A NEWSPAPER **13** [T] (**ARTS AND MEDIA**) to publish sth in a newspaper or magazine: *'The Times' is running a series of articles on pollution.*
- TEST **14** [T] ~ **a test/check (on sth)** to do a test or check on sth: *They're running checks on the power supply to see what the problem is.*

IDM **be running at** to be at a certain level **run for it** to run in order to escape ❶ For other idioms containing **run**, look at the entries for the nouns, adjectives, etc. For example, **run in the family** is at **family**.

PHR V **run across sb/sth** to meet or find sb/sth by chance **run after sb/sth** to try to catch sb/sth **run away** to escape from somewhere: *He's run away from home.* **run sb/sth down** **1** to hit a person or an animal with your vehicle: *She was run down by a bus.* **2** to criticize sb/sth: *He's always running her down in front of other people.* **run (sth) down** to stop functioning gradually; to make sth do this: *Turn the lights off or you'll run the battery down.* **run into sb** to meet sb by chance **run into sth** to have difficulties or a problem: *If you run into any problems, just let me know.* **run (sth) into sth** to hit sb/sth with a car, etc: *He ran his car into a brick wall.* **run sth off** to copy sth, using a machine **run off with sth** to take or steal sth **run out (of sth)** to finish your supply of sth; to come to an end: *We've run out of coffee.* ◇ *Time is running out.* ◇ *My passport runs out next month.* **run sb/sth over** to hit a person or an animal with your vehicle: *The child was run over as he was crossing the road.* **run through sth** to discuss or read sth quickly: *She ran through the names on the list.*

run² 🔒 A2 /rʌn/ *noun*

- ON FOOT **1** [C] (**SPORT**) an act of running on foot: *I go for a three-mile run every morning.* ◇ *The prisoner tried to make a run for it* (= to escape on foot).
- IN A CAR, ETC. **2** [C] a journey by car, train, etc: *The bus driver was picking up kids on the school run.*
- OF SUCCESS/FAILURE **3** [C] a series of similar events or sth that continues for a very long time: *We've had a run of bad luck recently.*
- SUDDEN DEMAND **4** [sing.] ~ **on sth** a sudden great demand for sth
- IN SPORT **5** [C] a point scored in the games of baseball and CRICKET
- IN CLOTHING **6** [C] (*AmE*) = LADDER¹ (2)

IDM **in the long run** → LONG¹ **on the run** hiding or trying to escape from sb/sth: *The escaped prisoner is still on the run.*

runaway¹ /'rʌnəweɪ/ *adj.* [only before noun] **1** out of control: *a runaway horse/car/train* **2** happening very easily: *a runaway victory*

runaway² /'rʌnəweɪ/ *noun* [C] a person, especially a child, who has left or escaped from somewhere

run-down *adj.* **1** (used about a building or place) in bad condition: *a run-down block of flats* **2** [not before noun] (used about a person) very tired and not healthy

rung¹ /rʌŋ/ *noun* [C] one of the bars that form the steps of a LADDER

rung² /rʌŋ/ past participle of **ring²**

runner 🔒 A2 /'rʌnə(r)/ *noun* [C] **1** (**SPORT**) a person or an animal that runs, especially in a race: *a long-distance runner* **2** (**LAW**) a person who takes guns, drugs, etc. illegally from one country to another

runner-up *noun* [C] (*pl.* **runners-up**) the person or team that finished second in a race or competition

running¹ 🔒 A2 /'rʌnɪŋ/ *noun* [U] **1** the action or sport of running: *How often do you go running?* ◇ *running shoes* **2** the process of managing a business or other organization: *She's not involved in the day-to-day running of the office.* ◇ *the running costs of a car* (= petrol, insurance, repairs, etc.)

IDM **in/out of the running (for sth)** (*informal*) having/not having a good chance of getting or winning sth

running² /'rʌnɪŋ/ *adj.* **1** used after a number and a noun to say that sth has happened a number of times in the same way without a change: *Our school has won the competition for four years running.* **2** [only before noun] (used about water) flowing or available from a TAP: *There is no running water in the cottage.* **3** [only before noun] not stopping; continuous: *a running battle between two rival gangs*

running commentary *noun* [C] a spoken description of sth while it is happening

running mate *noun* [C] (**POLITICS**) (in the US) a person who is chosen by a person who wants to be elected in an election, especially an election for a president, to support them and to have the next highest political position if they win

runny /'rʌni/ *adj.* (*informal*) (**runnier**; **runniest**) **1** (used about your eyes or nose) producing too much liquid: *Their children always seem to have runny noses.* **2** containing more liquid than is usual or than you expected: *runny jam* ▶ **runniness** *noun* [U]

run-of-the-mill *adj.* ordinary, with no special or interesting characteristics: *a run-of-the-mill job*

run-up *noun* [sing.] **1** the period of time before a certain event: *the run-up to the election* **2** (in sport) a run that people do in order to be going fast enough to do an action, such as jumping or throwing

runway /'rʌnweɪ/ *noun* [C] **1** a long piece of ground with a hard surface where aircraft take off and land at an airport **2** (*AmE*) = CATWALK

rupee /ruː'piː/ *noun* [C] (**ECONOMICS**) the unit of money in India, Pakistan and some other countries

rupture /'rʌptʃə(r)/ *noun* [C, U] **1** a sudden BURSTING or breaking **2** (*formal*) the sudden ending of good relations between two people or groups ▶ **rupture** *verb* [I, T]: *Her appendix ruptured and she had to have emergency surgery.*

rural 🔒 B2 ⓦ /'rʊərəl/ *adj.* (**GEOGRAPHY**) connected with the country, not the town ⊃ look at **rustic**, **urban** (1)

ruse /ruːz/ *noun* [C] a trick or clever plan

rush¹ 🔒 B2 /rʌʃ/ *verb* **1** [I, T] to move or do sth with great speed, often too fast: *I rushed back home when I got the news.* ◇ *Don't rush off — I want to talk to you.* ◇ *We had to rush our meal.* ◇ *The public rushed to buy shares in the new company.* **2** [T] to take sb/sth to a place very quickly: *He suffered a heart attack and was rushed to hospital.* **3** [I, T] ~ **(sb) (into sth/doing sth)** to do sth or make sb do sth without thinking about it first: *We don't want to rush into having a baby.* ◇ *Don't let yourself be rushed into marriage.* ◇ *Don't rush me — I'm thinking!*

IDM **be rushed/run off your feet** → FOOT¹

rush² 🔒 B2 /rʌʃ/ *noun*

- HURRY **1** [sing.] a sudden quick movement: *At the end of the match there was a rush for the exits.* ◇ *I was so nervous, all my words came out in a rush.* **2** [sing., U] a situation in which you are in a hurry and need to do things quickly: *I can't stop now. I'm in a terrible rush.* ◇ *Don't hurry your meal. There's no rush.*
- BUSY SITUATION **3** [sing.] a time when there is a lot of activity and people are very busy: *We'll leave early to avoid the rush.*
- SUDDEN DEMAND **4** [sing.] ~ **(on sth)** a time when many people try to get sth: *There's always a rush on umbrellas when it rains.*

• PLANT **5** [C] a type of tall grass that grows near water

'**rush hour** noun [C] the times each day when there is a lot of traffic because people are travelling to or from work: *Try to avoid travelling in the rush hour.*

rust /rʌst/ noun [U] (**CHEMISTRY**) a red-brown substance that forms on the surface of iron, etc., caused by the action of air and water ▸ **rust** verb [I, T]: *Some parts of the car had rusted.*

rustic /'rʌstɪk/ adj. typical of the country or of country people; simple: *The whole area is full of rustic charm.* ⊃ look at **rural, urban** (1)

rustle /'rʌsl/ verb [I, T] to make a sound like dry leaves or paper moving: *There was a rustling noise in the bushes.* ▸ **rustle** noun [sing.]
PHR V **rustle sth up (for sb)** (*informal*) to make or find sth quickly for sb and without planning: *Shall I rustle something up for our lunch?*

rusty /'rʌsti/ adj. (**rustier; rustiest**) **1** (used about metal objects) covered with RUST: *rusty tins* **2** (used about a skill) not as good as it was because you have not used it for a long time: *My French is rather rusty.*

rut /rʌt/ noun [C] **1** a deep track that a wheel makes in soft ground **2** a boring way of life that is difficult to change

rutabaga /'ru:təbeɪɡə/ (*AmE*) = SWEDE

ruthenium /ru:'θi:niəm/ noun [U] (*symb.* **Ru**) (**CHEMISTRY**) a chemical element. Ruthenium is a hard silver-white metal that breaks easily and is found with PLATINUM. ❶ For more information on the periodic table of elements, look at the **Reference Section** of this dictionary.

ruthless /'ru:θləs/ adj. (used about people and their behaviour) hard and cruel; determined to get what you want and showing no PITY to others: *a ruthless dictator* ▸ **ruthlessly** adv. ▸ **ruthlessness** noun [U]

RV /ˌɑː 'viː/ noun [C] (*AmE*) a large vehicle in which you can sleep, cook, etc. when you are on holiday (the abbreviation for 'recreational vehicle') ⊃ picture at **camper**

rye /raɪ/ noun [U] (**AGRICULTURE**) a plant that is grown in colder countries for its grain, which is used to make flour and also WHISKY (= a strong alcoholic drink) ⊃ picture at **cereal**

S s

S¹ /es/ (*also* s) noun [C, U] (*pl.* **S's, s's**) the 19th letter of the English alphabet: *'School' begins with (an) 'S'.*

S² abbr. (in writing) **1** (used for sizes of things, especially clothes) small **2** = SOUTH¹, SOUTHERN: *S Yorkshire*

sabbath /'sæbəθ/ (*often* the Sabbath) noun [sing.] (**RELIGION**) the day of the week for rest and prayer in certain religions. For Jews this day is Saturday and for Christians it is Sunday.

sabotage /'sæbətɑːʒ/ noun [U] damage that is done on purpose and secretly in order to prevent an enemy from being successful, for example by destroying machines, roads, bridges, etc: *industrial/economic/military sabotage* ▸ **sabotage** verb [T]

sabre (*BrE*) (*AmE* **saber**) /'seɪbə(r)/ noun [C] **1** a heavy SWORD with a curved BLADE (= metal cutting edge) **2** (**SPORT**) a light SWORD with a thin BLADE used in the sport of FENCING

saccharin /'sækərɪn/ noun [U] (**CHEMISTRY**) a very sweet chemical substance that can be used instead of sugar

sachet /'sæʃeɪ/ noun [C] a closed plastic or paper package that contains a very small amount of liquid or powder: *a sachet of shampoo/sugar/coffee*

sack¹ /sæk/ noun [C] a large bag made from a rough heavy material, paper or plastic, used for carrying or storing things: *sacks of flour/potatoes*
IDM **get the sack** (*BrE, informal*) to be told by your employer that you can no longer continue working for them (usually because you have done sth wrong): *Tony got the sack for poor work.* **give sb the sack** (*BrE*) to tell an employee that they can no longer continue working for you (because of bad work, behaviour, etc.): *Tony's work wasn't good enough and he was given the sack.*

sack² ʔ+ **C1** /sæk/ verb [T] (*especially BrE, informal*) to tell an employee that they can no longer work for you (because of bad work, bad behaviour, etc.): *Her boss has threatened to sack her if she's late again.* **SYN** **fire²** ⊃ note at **job**

sackcloth /'sækklɒθ/ (*also* **sacking** /'sækɪŋ/) noun [U] a rough cloth that is used for making SACKS

sacred ʔ+ **C1** /'seɪkrɪd/ adj. **1** (**RELIGION**) connected with God, a god or religion: *The Koran is the sacred book of Muslims.* **2** too important and special to be changed or harmed: *a sacred tradition*

sacrifice¹ ʔ+ **C1** /'sækrɪfaɪs/ noun [U, C] **1** the act of giving up sth that is important or valuable to you in order to get or do sth that seems more important; sth that you give up in this way: *If we're going to have a holiday this year, we'll have to make some sacrifices.* **2** ~ **(to sb)** the act of offering sth to a god, especially an animal that has been killed in a special way; an animal, etc. that is offered in this way

sacrifice² ʔ+ **C1** /'sækrɪfaɪs/ verb **1** [T] ~ **sth (for sb/sth)** to give up sth that is important or valuable to you in order to get or do sth that seems more important: *to sacrifice your life for your country* **2** [T, I] (**RELIGION**) to kill an animal and offer it to a god, in order to please the god

sacrilege /'sækrəlɪdʒ/ noun [U, sing.] (**RELIGION**) treating a religious object or place without the respect that it deserves ▸ **sacrilegious** /ˌsækrə'lɪdʒəs/ adj.

sacrum /'seɪkrəm, 'sæk-/ noun [C] (*pl.* **sacra** /-krə/, **sacrums**) (**ANATOMY**) a bone in the lower part of the back

SAD /sæd/ = SEASONAL AFFECTIVE DISORDER

sad ʔ **A1** /sæd/ adj. (**sadder; saddest**) **1** ~ **(to do sth)**; ~ **(that …)** unhappy or causing sb to feel unhappy: *We are very sad to hear that you are leaving.* ◇ *I'm very sad that you don't trust me.* ◇ *That's one of the saddest stories I've ever heard!* ◇ *a sad poem/song/film* **2** bad or unacceptable: *It's a sad state of affairs when your best friend doesn't trust you.* ▸ **sadden** /'sædn/ verb [T, often passive] (*formal*): *The news of your father's death saddened me greatly.*

saddle¹ /'sædl/ noun [C] **1** a seat, usually made of leather, that you put on a horse so that you can ride it **2** a seat on a bicycle or motorcycle

saddle² /'sædl/ verb [T] to put a SADDLE on a horse
PHR V **saddle sb with sth** to give sb a responsibility or task that they do not want

saddlebag /'sædlbæɡ/ noun [C] **1** one of a pair of bags put over the back of a horse **2** a bag attached to the back of a bicycle or motorcycle

sadism /'seɪdɪzəm/ noun [U] getting pleasure, especially sexual pleasure, from hurting other people ⊃ look at **masochism**

sadist /'seɪdɪst/ noun [C] a person who gets pleasure, especially sexual pleasure, from hurting other people ▸ **sadistic** /sə'dɪstɪk/ adj. ▸ **sadistically** /-kli/ adv.

sadly ʔ A2 /'sædli/ adv. **1** in a way that shows unhappiness **2** unfortunately: *Sadly, after eight years of marriage they had grown apart.* **3** very much and in a way that makes you sad: *If you think that I've forgotten what you did, you're **sadly mistaken**.*

sadness /'sædnəs/ noun **1** [U, sing.] the feeling of being sad: *memories tinged with sadness* ◇ *I felt a deep sadness.* **2** [C, usually pl.] something that makes you sad: *our joys and sadnesses*

sae /ˌes eɪ 'iː/ (BrE) = STAMPED ADDRESSED ENVELOPE: *Please enclose an sae.*

safari /sə'fɑːri/ noun [U, C] (pl. safaris) a trip to see or hunt wild animals, especially in east or southern Africa: *to be/go **on safari***

safe¹ ʔ A2 /seɪf/ adj. **1** [not before noun] ~ (from sb/sth) free from danger; not able to be hurt: *She didn't feel safe in the house on her own.* ◇ *Do you think my car will be safe in this street?* ◇ *Keep the papers where they will be safe from fire.* **2** ~ (to do sth); ~ (for sb) not likely to cause danger, harm or risk: *Don't sit on that chair — it isn't safe.* ◇ *I left my suitcase in a **safe place** and went for a cup of coffee.* ◇ *She's a very safe driver.* ◇ *Is this drug safe for children?* ◇ *Is it safe to drink the water here?* ◇ *I think **it's safe to say** that the situation is unlikely to change for some time.* **3** [not before noun] not hurt, damaged or lost: *After the accident he checked that all the passengers were safe.* ◇ *After five days the child was found, **safe and sound**.* **4** (LAW) based on good evidence: *a safe verdict*
IDM **in safe hands** with sb who will take good care of you **on the safe side** not taking risks; being very careful: *I took some extra cash just to be **on the safe side**.*

safe² /seɪf/ noun [C] a strong metal box or cupboard with a special lock that is used for keeping money, jewellery, documents, etc. in

safeguard /'seɪfgɑːd/ noun [C] ~ (against sb/sth) something that protects against possible dangers ▸ **safeguard** verb [T]: *to safeguard somebody's interests/rights/privacy*

safely /'seɪfli/ adv. **1** without being harmed, damaged or lost: *The plane landed safely.* ◇ *I rang my parents to tell them I had arrived safely.* **2** in a way that does not cause harm or that protects sb/sth from harm: *The bomb has been safely disposed of.* ◇ *The money is safely locked in a drawer.* **3** without much possibility of being wrong: *We can safely say that he will accept the job.*

safe mode noun [U] (COMPUTING) a way of starting a computer that makes it easier to find a problem without the risk of losing data

safety ʔ B1 W /'seɪfti/ noun [U] the state of being safe; not being dangerous or in danger: *road safety* (= the prevention of road accidents) ◇ *New safety measures have been introduced on trains.* ◇ *In the interests of safety, please stay behind the yellow line.*

safety belt = SEAT BELT

safety net noun [C] **1** an arrangement that helps to prevent disaster (usually with money) if sth goes wrong **2** a net that is placed to catch sb who is performing high above the ground if they fall

safety pin noun [C] a metal pin with a point that is bent back towards the head, that is covered so that it cannot be dangerous.

safety valve noun [C] a device in a machine that allows STEAM, gas, etc. to escape if the pressure becomes too great

saffron¹ /'sæfrən/ noun [U] **1** a bright yellow powder from a CROCUS (= a flower), that is used in cooking to give colour to food **2** a bright orange-yellow colour

saffron² /'sæfrən/ adj. bright orange-yellow in colour

sag /sæg/ verb [I] (-gg-) to hang or to bend down, especially in the middle

saga /'sɑːgə/ noun [C] (LITERATURE) a very long story; a long series of events

sage /seɪdʒ/ noun [U] a HERB (= a type of plant) with flat, light green leaves that have a strong smell and are used in cooking: *duck with sage and onion stuffing*

Sagittarius /ˌsædʒɪ'teəriəs/ noun [U] the ninth sign of THE ZODIAC (= twelve signs that represent the positions of the sun, moon and planets), the Archer; a person born under this sign

sago /'seɪgəʊ/ noun [U] hard white grains made from the soft inside of a PALM tree, often cooked with milk to make a sweet dish: *sago pudding*

said¹ /sed/ past tense, past participle of **say¹**

said² /sed/ adj. = AFOREMENTIONED

sail¹ ʔ A2 /seɪl/ verb **1** [I] (used about a boat or ship or the people on it) to travel on water using sails or an engine: *I stood at the window and watched the ships sailing by.* ◇ *They sailed around the world.* **2** [I, T] (SPORT) to travel in and control a boat with sails, especially as a sport: *My father is teaching me to sail.* ◇ *I've never sailed this kind of yacht before.* **3** [I] to begin a journey on water: *When does the ship sail?* ◇ *We sail for Santander at six o'clock tomorrow morning.* **4** [I] to move somewhere quickly in a smooth or proud way: *The ball sailed over the fence and into the neighbour's garden.* ◇ *Mary sailed into the room, completely ignoring all of us.*
IDM **sail through (sth)** to pass a test or exam easily

sail² ʔ B1 /seɪl/ noun **1** [C] a large piece of strong cloth that is fixed onto a ship or boat. The wind blows against the sail and moves the ship along. **2** [C] a set of boards that the wind moves round that are fixed to a WINDMILL (= a building used for making flour from grain) or WIND TURBINE (= a machine used to make electricity) ⊃ picture at **windmill** **3** [sing.] a trip on water in a ship or boat with a sail

safety symbols

 harmful

 kill switch

 toxic

 first aid

 oxidizing

 danger

 irritant

 electric shock: 230 V

 corrosive

 laser

highly flammable

IDM **set sail** to begin a journey by sea: *Columbus set sail for India.*

sailboard /ˈseɪlbɔːd/ = WINDSURFER (1)

sailing A2 /ˈseɪlɪŋ/ *noun* [U] (**SPORT**) the sport of being in, and controlling, small boats with sails

ˈ**sailing boat** (*BrE*) (*AmE* **sailboat** /ˈseɪlbəʊt/) *noun* [C] a boat with a sail or sails

sailor B1 /ˈseɪlə(r)/ *noun* [C] a person who works on a ship or a person who sails a boat

saint + C1 /seɪnt/ *noun* [C] **1** (**RELIGION**) a very good or religious person who is given special respect after death by the Christian church **2** a very good, kind person

sake + C1 /seɪk/ *noun*

IDM **for goodness'/Heaven's/pity's, etc. sake** used to emphasize that it is important to do sth or to show that you are annoyed: *For goodness' sake, hurry up!* ◇ *Why have you taken so long, for pity's sake?* **for the sake of sb/sth | for sb's/sth's sake** in order to help sb/sth: *Don't go to any trouble for my sake.* ◇ *They only stayed together for the sake of their children/for their children's sake.* **for the sake of sth/doing sth** in order to get or keep sth; for the purpose of sth: *She gave up her job for the sake of her health.*

salad A1 /ˈsæləd/ *noun* [U, C] a mixture of vegetables, usually not cooked, that you often eat together with other foods: *All main courses are served with salad.*

salamander /ˈsæləmændə(r)/ *noun* [C] a small thin AMPHIBIAN (= an animal that lives on land and in water) with four legs and a long tail. Salamanders often have bright colours on their skin. ➲ look at **lizard** ➲ picture at **animal**

salami /səˈlɑːmi/ *noun* [U, C] (*pl.* **salamis**) a type of large spicy SAUSAGE (= meat that is made into a long thin shape) served cold in thin slices

salary A2 /ˈsæləri/ *noun* [C] (*pl.* **-ies**) (**BUSINESS**) the money that a person receives (usually every month) for the work they have done: *My salary is paid directly into my bank account.* ◇ *a high/low salary* ➲ note at **pay**²

sale A2 /seɪl/ *noun* **1** [U, C] the act of selling or being sold; the occasion when sth is sold: *The sale of alcohol to anyone under the age of 18 is forbidden.* ◇ *a sale of used toys* **2 sales** [pl.] the number of items sold: *The company reported excellent sales figures.* ◇ *Sales of electric cars have increased rapidly.* **3 sales** [U] (*also* ˈ**sales department** [C]) (**BUSINESS**) the part of a company that deals with selling its products: *Jodie works in sales/in the sales department.* ◇ *a sales representative/sales rep* **4** [C] a time when shops sell things at prices that are lower than usual: *The sale starts on December 28th.* ◇ *I got several bargains* ***in the sales.*** ➲ look at **car boot sale, jumble sale**

IDM **for sale** offered for sb to buy: *This painting is not for sale.* ◇ *I see our neighbours have* ***put*** *their house* ***up for sale.*** **on sale 1** available for sb to buy, especially in shops: *This week's edition is on sale now at your local newsagents.* **2** (*AmE*) offered at a lower price than usual

ˈ**sales clerk** (*AmE*) = SHOP ASSISTANT

salesman /ˈseɪlzmən/ *noun* [C] (*pl.* **-men** /-mən/) a man whose job is selling things to people

salesperson /ˈseɪlzpɜːsn/ *noun* [C] (*pl.* **-people** /-piːpl/) a SALESMAN or SALESWOMAN

ˈ**sales rep** (*also formal* ˈ**sales representative**) *noun* [C] (**BUSINESS**) an employee of a company who travels around a particular area selling the company's goods to shops, etc.

saleswoman /ˈseɪlzwʊmən/ *noun* [C] (*pl.* **-women** /-wɪmɪn/) a woman whose job is selling things to people

salient /ˈseɪliənt/ *adj.* [only before noun] most important or easy to notice: *I noted down the* ***salient points*** *of her speech.*

saline /ˈseɪlaɪn/ *adj.* (**CHEMISTRY**) containing salt: *a saline solution*

saliva /səˈlaɪvə/ *noun* [U] (**BIOLOGY**) the liquid that is produced in the mouth ➲ look at **spit**² (1) ➲ picture at **digestive system**

salivary /səˈlaɪvəri, ˈsælɪvəri/ *adj.* (**ANATOMY**) of or producing SALIVA: *salivary glands* ➲ picture at **digestive system**

salivate /ˈsælɪveɪt/ *verb* [I] (*formal*) (**BIOLOGY**) to produce more SALIVA in your mouth than usual, especially when you see or smell food

sallow /ˈsæləʊ/ *adj.* (**HEALTH**) (used about a person's skin or face) having a slightly yellow colour that does not look healthy

salmon /ˈsæmən/ *noun* [C, U] (*pl.* **salmon**) a large fish with silver skin that is pink inside and is used for food: *smoked salmon*

salmonella /ˌsælməˈnelə/ *noun* [U] (**HEALTH**) a type of bacteria that makes people sick if they eat food that contains it; an illness caused by this bacteria

salon /ˈsælɒn/ *noun* [C] **1** a shop where you can have beauty or hair treatment or where you can buy expensive clothes **2** (*old-fashioned*) a room in a large house that is used for receiving guests **3** (in the past) a regular meeting of writers, artists and other guests at the house of a famous or important person

saloon /səˈluːn/ (*BrE*) (*AmE* **sedan**) *noun* [C] a car with a fixed roof and a BOOT (= a space in the back for bags, cases, etc.)

salsa /ˈsælsə/ *noun* **1** [U, C] (**MUSIC**) a type of Latin American dance music; a dance performed to this music **2** [U] a spicy tomato sauce eaten with Mexican food

salt¹ A1 /sɔːlt, sɒlt/ *noun* **1** [U] a common white substance that is found in sea water and the earth. Salt is used in cooking to make food taste better: *Season with* ***salt and pepper.*** ◇ *Add a pinch* (= a small amount) *of salt.* ➲ picture at **erosion 2** [C] (**CHEMISTRY**) a chemical mixture of a metal and an ACID ▶ **salt** *adj.*: *salt water*

IDM **rub salt into the wound/sb's wounds** → RUB **take sth with a pinch of salt** → PINCH²

salt² /sɔːlt, sɒlt/ *verb* [T, usually passive] to put salt on or in sth: *salted peanuts*

ˈ**salt cellar** (*BrE*) (*AmE also* ˈ**salt shaker**) *noun* [C] a small container for salt, usually with one hole in the top, that is used at the table

saltwater /ˈsɔːltwɔːtə(r), ˈsɒlt-/ *adj.* [only before noun] living in or connected with the sea: *a saltwater fish* ➲ look at **freshwater**

salty /ˈsɔːlti, ˈsɒl-/ *adj.* (**saltier**; **saltiest**) having the taste of or containing salt: *I didn't like the soup; it was too salty.*

salutation /ˌsæljuˈteɪʃn/ *noun* **1** [C, U] (*formal*) something that you say to welcome or say hello to sb; the action of welcoming or saying hello to sb: *He raised his hand in salutation.* **2** [C] the words that are used in a letter to address the person you are writing to, for example 'Dear Sir'

salute /səˈluːt/ *noun* [C] **1** an action that a soldier, etc. does to show respect, by touching the side of their head with the right hand: *to give a salute* **2** ~ **(to sth)** something that shows respect for sb: *The next programme is a salute to one of the world's greatest film stars.* ▸ **salute** *verb* [I, T]: *The soldiers saluted as they marched past the general.*

salvage¹ /ˈsælvɪdʒ/ *noun* [U] the action of saving things that have been or are likely to be lost or damaged, especially in an accident or a disaster; the things that are saved: *a salvage operation/company/team*

salvage² /ˈsælvɪdʒ/ *verb* [T] ~ **sth (from sth)** to manage to rescue sth from being lost or damaged; to rescue sth or a situation from disaster: *They salvaged as much as they could from the house after the fire.*

salvation /sælˈveɪʃn/ *noun* **1** [U] (**RELIGION**) (in Christianity) being saved from the power of evil **2** [U, sing.] a thing or person that rescues sb/sth from danger, disaster, etc.

samarium /səˈmeəriəm/ *noun* [U] (*symb.* Sm) (**CHEMISTRY**) a chemical element. Samarium is a hard silver-white metal used in making strong MAGNETS. ❶ For more information on the periodic table of elements, look at the **Reference Section** of this dictionary.

same¹ 🔒 **A1** 🟢 /seɪm/ *adj.*, *pron.* **1** the ~ … **(as sb/sth)**; the ~ … that … not different, not another or other; exactly the one or ones that you have mentioned before: *My brother and I had the same teacher at school.* ◇ *They both said the same thing.* ◇ *I'm going to wear the same clothes as/that I wore yesterday.* ◇ *This one looks exactly the same as that one.* **2** the ~ … **(as sb/sth); the ~ … that …** exactly like the one already mentioned: *I wouldn't buy the same car again* (= the same model of car). ◇ *I had the same experience as you some time ago.*

IDM **all/just the same** despite this/that; anyway: *I understand what you're saying. All the same, I don't agree with you.* ◇ *I don't want to borrow any money but thanks all the same for offering.* **at the same time** **1** together; at one time: *I can't think about more than one thing at the same time.* **2** on the other hand; however: *It's a very good idea but at the same time it's rather risky.* **much the same** → MUCH **on the same wavelength** able to understand sb because you have similar ideas and opinions **(the) same again** (*informal*) a request to be served or given the same drink as before **same here** (*informal*) the same thing is also true for me: *'I'm bored.' 'Same here.'* **(the) same to you** (*informal*) used as an answer when sb says sth rude to you or wishes you sth: *'You idiot!' 'Same to you!'* ◇ *'Have a good weekend.' 'The same to you.'*

same² 🔒 **A1** /seɪm/ (*usually* **the same**) *adv.* in the same way: *We treat all the children in the class the same.*

ˈsame-sex *adj.* [only before noun] of the same sex; involving people of the same sex: *a same-sex relationship* ◇ *same-sex parents*

sample 🔒 **B1** ⊕ /ˈsɑːmpl/ *noun* [C] **1** a number of people or things taken from a larger group and used in tests to provide information about the group: *The interviews were given to a random sample of shoppers.* **2** (**SCIENCE**) a small amount of a substance taken from a larger amount and tested in order to obtain information about the substance: *to take a blood sample* ◇ *Samples of the water contained pesticide.* ○ look at **specimen** (1) **3** a small amount or example of sth that can be looked at or tried to see what it is like: *a free sample of shampoo* **4** (**MUSIC**) a piece of recorded music or sound that is used in a new piece of music ▸ **sample** 🔒 **B2** ⊛ *verb* [T]: *You are welcome to sample any of our wines before making a purchase.*

sampling 🟢 /ˈsɑːmplɪŋ/ *noun* [U] **1** the process of taking a sample: *statistical sampling* **2** (**MUSIC**) the process of copying and recording parts of a piece of music in an electronic form so that they can be used in a different piece of music

sanatorium /ˌsænəˈtɔːriəm/ (*pl.* -toriums, -toria /-riə/) (*AmE also* **sanitarium**) *noun* [C] (**MEDICINE**) a type of hospital where patients who need a long period of treatment for an illness can stay

sanction¹ 🔒+ **C1** /ˈsæŋkʃn/ *noun* **1** [C, usually pl.] ~ **(against sb)** (**LAW**, **POLITICS**) an official order that limits business, contact, etc. with a particular country, in order to make it do sth, such as obeying international law: *Economic sanctions were imposed on any country that refused to sign the agreement.* ◇ *The sanctions against those countries have now been lifted.* **2** [U] (*formal*) official permission to do or change sth **3** [C] a punishment for breaking a rule or law

sanction² /ˈsæŋkʃn/ *verb* [T] to give official permission for sth

sanctuary /ˈsæŋktʃuəri/ *noun* (*pl.* -ies) **1** [C] a place where birds or animals are protected and encouraged to produce young: *a wildlife sanctuary* **2** [U] safety and protection, especially for people who are in danger of being attacked or captured: *to take sanctuary in a place* **3** [C] a safe place, especially one where people who are being in danger of being attacked or captured can stay and be protected **4** [C] a holy building or the part of it that is considered the most holy

sand 🔒 **B1** /sænd/ *noun* (**GEOGRAPHY**) **1** [U] a powder consisting of very small grains of rock, found in deserts and on beaches: *a grain of sand* ◇ *Concrete is a mixture of sand and cement.* ○ picture at **building**, **erosion**, **floodplain**, **longshore drift**, **petroleum** **2** [U, C, usually pl.] a large area of sand on a beach: *We went for a walk along the sand.* ◇ *children playing on the sand* ◇ *miles of golden sands*

sandal /ˈsændl/ *noun* [C] a type of light, open shoe that people wear when the weather is warm

sandalwood /ˈsændlwʊd/ *noun* [U] a type of oil with a sweet smell that comes from a hard tropical wood and is used to make PERFUME (= liquid that makes you smell nice)

sandbank /ˈsændbæŋk/ *noun* [C] (**GEOGRAPHY**) an area of sand that is higher than the sand around it in a river or the sea

sandbar /ˈsændbɑː(r)/ *noun* [C] (**GEOGRAPHY**) a long mass of sand at the point where a river meets the sea that is formed by the movement of the water

sandcastle /ˈsændkɑːsl/ *noun* [C] a pile of sand that looks like a castle, made by children playing on a beach

ˈsand dune = DUNE

sandpaper /ˈsændpeɪpə(r)/ *noun* [U] strong paper with a rough surface on it that is used for rubbing surfaces in order to make them smooth

sandstone /ˈsændstəʊn/ *noun* [U] (**GEOLOGY**) a type of stone that is formed of grains of sand tightly pressed together and that is used in building ○ picture at **petroleum**

sandstorm /ˈsændstɔːm/ *noun* [C] a storm in a desert in which sand is blown into the air by strong winds

sandwich¹ 🔒 **A1** /ˈsænwɪtʃ, -wɪdʒ/ *noun* [C] two slices of bread with food between them: *a ham/cheese sandwich*

sandwich² /ˈsænwɪtʃ, -wɪdʒ/ *verb*
PHR V **sandwich sb/sth between sb/sth** to place sb/sth in a very narrow space between two other things or people

'sandwich course *noun* [C] (*BrE*) (**EDUCATION**) a course of study that includes periods of working in business or industry

sandy /ˈsændi/ *adj.* (**sandier; sandiest**) covered with or full of sand

sane /seɪn/ *adj.* **1** (used about a person) having a normal healthy mind; not mentally ill: *No sane person would do anything like that.* **2** sensible and reasonable: *the sane way to solve the problem* **OPP insane** ➲ noun **sanity**

sang /sæŋ/ past tense of **sing**

sanitarium /ˌsænəˈteəriəm/ *noun* [C] (*pl.* **-tariums, -taria** /-riə/) (*AmE*) = SANATORIUM

sanitary /ˈsænətri/ *adj.* connected with the protection of health, for example how human waste is removed: *Sanitary conditions in the refugee camps were terrible.* ➲ look at **insanitary**

'sanitary towel (*BrE*) (*AmE* **'sanitary napkin**) *noun* [C] a thick piece of soft material that women use to take in and hold blood lost during their period ➲ look at **tampon**

sanitation /ˌsænɪˈteɪʃn/ *noun* [U] the equipment and systems that keep places clean, especially by removing human waste

sanitize (*BrE also* **-ise**) /ˈsænɪtaɪz/ *verb* [T] to clean sth completely using chemicals to remove bacteria

sanity /ˈsænəti/ *noun* [U] **1** the state of having a normal healthy mind **2** the state of being sensible and reasonable **OPP insanity** ➲ adjective **sane**

sank /sæŋk/ past tense of **sink¹**

Santa Claus /ˈsæntə klɔːz/ = FATHER CHRISTMAS

sap¹ /sæp/ *noun* [U] (**BIOLOGY**) the liquid in a plant or a tree

sap² /sæp/ *verb* [T] (**-pp-**) **~ (sb of) sth** to make sb/sth weaker; to destroy sth gradually: *Years of failure have sapped (him of) his confidence.*

sapling /ˈsæplɪŋ/ *noun* [C] (**BIOLOGY**) a young tree ➲ picture at **tree**

sapphire /ˈsæfaɪə(r)/ *noun* [C, U] a bright blue PRECIOUS STONE

sarcasm /ˈsɑːkæzəm/ *noun* [U] (**LANGUAGE**) the use of words or expressions to mean the opposite of what they actually say. People use sarcasm in order to criticize other people or to make them look silly. ➲ look at **irony** (2) ▶ **sarcastic** /sɑːˈkæstɪk/ *adj.*: *a sarcastic comment* ▶ **sarcastically** /-kli/ *adv.*

sardine /sɑːˈdiːn/ *noun* [C] a small young sea fish (for example, a PILCHARD) that is used for food: *a tin of sardines*

sari /ˈsɑːri/ *noun* [C] a dress that consists of a long piece of cloth that women, particularly Indian women, wear around their bodies

sarong /səˈrɒŋ/ *noun* [C] a long piece of cloth wrapped around the body from the middle part or the chest, worn especially by Indonesian and Malaysian men and women

SARS /sɑːz/ *noun* [U] (**HEALTH**) an illness that is easily spread from person to person, which affects the lungs and can sometimes cause death (the abbreviation for 'severe acute respiratory syndrome'): *No new SARS cases have been reported in the region.*

sash /sæʃ/ *noun* [C] a long piece of material that is worn round the the middle part of the body or over the shoulder, often as part of a uniform

sassy /ˈsæsi/ *adj.* (**sassier; sassiest**) (*especially AmE, informal*) **1** rude; showing a lack of respect **2** fashionable and confident: *his sassy, streetwise daughter*

SAT *noun* [C] (**EDUCATION**) **1** /ˌes eɪ ˈtiː/ **SAT™** (in the US) a test taken by HIGH SCHOOL students who want to go to a college or university (the abbreviation for 'Scholastic Aptitude Test'): *to take the SAT* ◇ *I scored 1050 on the SAT.* ◇ *an SAT score* **2** /sæt/ (in England) a test taken by children at the ages of 7 and 11, now officially called NCT (the abbreviation for 'Standard Assessment Task')

Sat. *abbr.* (in writing) = SATURDAY

sat /sæt/ past tense, past participle of **sit**

Satan /ˈseɪtn/ *noun* (**RELIGION**) a name for the Devil ➲ look at **devil** (1)

satchel /ˈsætʃəl/ *noun* [C] a bag, often carried over the shoulder, used by children for taking books to and from school

satellite 🔤**B2** /ˈsætəlaɪt/ *noun* [C] **1** an electronic device that is sent into space and moves around the earth or another planet for a particular purpose: *a weather/communications satellite* **2** (**ASTRONOMY**) a natural object that moves round a bigger object in space

'satellite dish (*also* **dish**) *noun* [C] a large, round piece of equipment that people have on the outside of their houses so that they can receive SATELLITE TV

,satellite T'V (*also* **satellite 'television**) *noun* [U] TV programmes that are sent out using a satellite

satin /ˈsætɪn/ *noun* [U] a type of cloth that is smooth and shiny: *a satin dress/ribbon*

satire /ˈsætaɪə(r)/ *noun* **1** [U] the use of humour to attack a person, an organization, an idea, etc. that you think is bad or silly **2** [C] **~ (on sb/sth)** (**ARTS AND MEDIA, LITERATURE**) a piece of writing or a play, film, etc. that uses satire: *a satire on political life* ▶ **satirical** /səˈtɪrɪkl/ *adj.*: *a satirical magazine* ▶ **satirically** /-kli/ *adv.*

satirize (*BrE also* **-ise**) /ˈsætəraɪz/ *verb* [T] to use SATIRE to show the faults in a person, an organization, a system, etc.

satisfaction 🔤**+** **B2** **W** /ˌsætɪsˈfækʃn/ *noun* [U, C] the feeling of pleasure that you have when you have done, got, or achieved what you wanted; sth that gives you this feeling: *Roshni stood back and looked at her work with a sense of satisfaction.* ◇ *We finally found a solution that was to everyone's satisfaction.* ◇ *She was about to have the satisfaction of seeing her book in print.* **OPP dissatisfaction**

satisfactory /ˌsætɪsˈfæktəri/ *adj.* good enough for a particular purpose; acceptable: *This piece of work is not satisfactory. Please do it again.* **OPP unsatisfactory** ▶ **satisfactorily** /-rəli/ *adv.*: *Work is progressing satisfactorily.*

satisfied 🔤**B2** /ˈsætɪsfaɪd/ *adj.* **~ (with sb/sth)** pleased because you have achieved sth or because sth that you wanted to happen has happened: *a satisfied customer* ◇ *She's never satisfied with what she's got.* **OPP dissatisfied**

satisfy 🔤**B2** **W** /ˈsætɪsfaɪ/ *verb* [T] (**satisfying; satisfies;** *pt, pp* **satisfied**) **1** to make sb pleased by doing or giving them what they want: *Nothing satisfies him — he's always complaining.* **2** to have or do what is necessary for sth: *Make sure you satisfy the entry requirements before you apply to the university.* ◇ *I had a quick look inside the parcel just to satisfy my curiosity.* **3 ~ sb (that …)** (*formal*) to show or give proof to sb that sth is true or has been done: *Once the police were satisfied* *that they were telling the truth, they were allowed to go.*

satisfying /ˈsætɪsfaɪɪŋ/ *adj.* pleasing; giving SATISFACTION: *I find it satisfying to see people enjoying something I've cooked.*

satnav /ˈsætnæv/ *noun* [U, C] a computer system that uses information obtained from satellites to guide the driver of a vehicle (the abbreviation for 'satellite navigation')

satsuma /sætˈsuːmə/ *noun* [C] a type of small orange

saturate /ˈsætʃəreɪt/ *verb* [T] **1** to make sth extremely wet **2** [often passive] ~ **sth (with sth)** to fill sth so completely that it is impossible to add any more: *The market is saturated with cheap imports.* ▸ **saturation** /ˌsætʃəˈreɪʃn/ *noun* [U]

saturated /ˈsætʃəreɪtɪd/ *adj.* completely wet

saturated ˈfat *noun* [C, U] (HEALTH) a type of fat found, for example, in butter and fried food, that is considered to be less healthy in the diet than other types of fat ⊃ look at **polyunsaturated fat**, **unsaturated fat**

satuˈration point *noun* [U, sing.] **1** the stage at which no more of sth can be accepted or added because there is already too much of it or too many of them: *The market for mobile phones is reaching saturation point.* **2** (CHEMISTRY) the stage at which no more of a substance can be ABSORBED by a liquid or VAPOUR

Saturday ⚡ **A1** /ˈsætədeɪ, -di/ *noun* [C, U] (*abbr.* Sat.) the day of the week after Friday

Saturn /ˈsætɜːn, -tən/ *noun* [sing.] (ASTRONOMY) the planet in the SOLAR SYSTEM that is sixth in order of distance from the sun ⊃ picture at **solar system**

sauce ⚡ **A2** /sɔːs/ *noun* [C, U] a thick hot or cold liquid that you eat on or with food: *The chicken was served in a delicious sauce.* ◊ *ice cream with chocolate sauce* ⊃ look at **gravy**

saucepan /ˈsɔːspən/ *noun* [C] a round metal pot with a handle that is used for cooking things on top of a cooker ⊃ note at **cook**[1]

saucer /ˈsɔːsə(r)/ *noun* [C] a small round plate that a cup stands on

sauna /ˈsɔːnə, ˈsaʊnə/ *noun* [C] a period of time in which you sit or lie in a small room (also called a sauna) which has been heated to a very high temperature by burning coal or wood. Some saunas involve the use of STEAM: *to have a sauna* ◊ *a hotel with a swimming pool and sauna*

saunter /ˈsɔːntə(r)/ *verb* [I] to walk without hurrying

sausage /ˈsɒsɪdʒ/ *noun* [C, U] a mixture of meat cut into very small pieces and pepper, etc. that is made into a long thin shape. Some sausage is eaten cold in slices; other types are cooked and then served whole: *We had sausages and chips for lunch.* ◊ *garlic/liver sausage*

savage[1] /ˈsævɪdʒ/ *adj.* very cruel or violent: *He was the victim of a savage attack.* ◊ *The book received savage criticism.* ▸ **savagely** *adv.* ▸ **savagery** /-ri/ *noun* [U]

savage[2] /ˈsævɪdʒ/ *verb* [T] (used about an animal) to attack sb violently, causing serious injury: *The boy died after being savaged by a dog.*

savannah (*also* **savanna**) /səˈvænə/ *noun* [U] (GEOGRAPHY) a wide flat open area of land, especially in Africa, that is covered with grass but has few trees ⊃ picture at **ecosystem**

save[1] ⚡ **A2** /seɪv/ *verb*
• KEEP SAFE **1** [T] ~ **sb/sth (from sth/from doing sth)** to keep sb/sth safe from death, harm, loss, etc: *to save somebody's life* ◊ *We are trying to save the school from closure.* ◊ *to save somebody from drowning*

• MONEY **2** [I, T] ~ **(sth) (up) (for sth)** to keep or not spend money so that you can use it later: *I'm saving up for a new bike.* ◊ *Do you manage to save any of your wages?*

• FOR THE FUTURE **3** [T] to keep sth for future use: *I'll be home late so please save me some dinner.* ◊ *Save that box. It might come in useful.* ◊ *If you get there first, please save me a seat.*

• NOT WASTE **4** [I, T] ~ **(sb) (sth) (on sth)** to avoid wasting time, money, etc: *It will save you 20 minutes on the journey if you take the express train.* ◊ *You can save on petrol by getting a smaller car.* ◊ *This car will save you a lot on petrol.*

• AVOID STH BAD **5** [T] ~ **(sb) sth/doing sth** to avoid, or make sb able to avoid, doing sth unpleasant or difficult: *If you make an appointment it will save you waiting.*

• IN COMPUTING **6** [T] (COMPUTING) to store information in a computer by giving a special instruction: *Don't forget to save the file before you close it.*

• IN SPORT **7** [T, I] (SPORT) (in football, etc.) to prevent an opponent's shot from going in the goal

IDM keep/save sth for a rainy day → RAINY **save face** to prevent yourself losing the respect of other people

save[2] /seɪv/ *noun* [C] (SPORT) (in football, etc.) the act of preventing a goal from being scored: *The goalkeeper made a great save.*

saver /ˈseɪvə(r)/ *noun* [C] **1** a person who saves money for future use: *The rise in interest rates is good news for savers.* **2** (often in compounds) a thing that helps you save time, money, or the thing mentioned: *a great time saver*

saving ⚡ **B2** /ˈseɪvɪŋ/ *noun* **1** [C] ~ **(of sth) (on sth)** an amount of time, money, etc. that you do not have to use or spend: *The sale price represents a saving of 25% on the usual price.* **2** **savings** [pl.] money that you have saved for future use: *All our savings are in the bank.*

saviour (*BrE*) (*AmE* **savior**) /ˈseɪvjə(r)/ *noun* **1** [C, usually sing.] a person who rescues sb/sth from a dangerous or difficult situation **2** **the Saviour** [sing.] (RELIGION) used in the Christian religion as another name for Jesus Christ

savoury (*BrE*) (*AmE* **savory**) /ˈseɪvəri/ *adj.* (used about food) tasting of salt, not sweet ⊃ look at **sweet**[1] (1)

savvy /ˈsævi/ *noun* [U] (*informal*) practical knowledge or understanding of sth: *political savvy* ▸ **savvy** *adj.* (**savvier**; **savviest**): *savvy shoppers* ◊ *my computer-savvy brother*

saw[1] /sɔː/ past tense of **see**

saw[2] /sɔː/ *noun* [C] a tool that is used for cutting wood, etc. A saw has a BLADE (= metal cutting part) with sharp teeth on it, and a handle at one or both ends. ⊃ picture at **tool**

saw[3] /sɔː/ *verb* [I, T] (*pt* **sawed**; *pp* **sawn** /sɔːn/, *AmE also* **sawed**) to use a SAW to cut sth: *to saw through the trunk of a tree* ◊ *He sawed the log up into small pieces.*

sawdust /ˈsɔːdʌst/ *noun* [U] very small pieces of wood that fall like powder when you are cutting a large piece of wood

sawmill /ˈsɔːmɪl/ *noun* [C] a factory in which wood is cut into boards using machines

saxophone /ˈsæksəfəʊn/ (*also informal* **sax** /sæks/) *noun* [C] (MUSIC) a metal musical instrument that you play by blowing into it. Saxophones are especially used for playing modern music, for example jazz. ⊃ picture at **instrument**

saxophonist /ˈsæksəfənɪst/ *noun* [C] (**MUSIC**) a person who plays the SAXOPHONE

say¹ ⟁ **A1** /seɪ/ *verb* (says /sez/; *pt, pp* said /sed/)
• SPEAK **1** [I, T] ~ **(sth to sb)**; ~ **(that)** … ; ~ **(sth about sb)** to speak or tell sb sth, using words: *'Please come back,' she said.* ◇ *We can ask him, but I'm sure he'll say no.* ◇ *I said goodbye to her at the station.* ◇ *The teacher said (that) we should hand in our essays on Friday.* ◇ *He said to his mother that he would phone back later.* ◇ *She said nothing to me about it.* ◇ *'This isn't going to be easy,' she said to herself* (= she thought). ◇ *'What time is she coming?' 'I don't know — she didn't say.'* ◇ **It is said that** *cats can sense the presence of ghosts.*
• WRITTEN INFORMATION **2** [T] ~ **(that)** … (used about a book, notice, etc.) to give information: *What time does it say on that clock?* ◇ *The map says (that) the hotel is just past the railway bridge.* ◇ *The sign clearly says 'No dogs'.*
• EXPRESS AN OPINION **3** [T, I] to express an opinion on sth: *I wouldn't say she's unfriendly — just shy.* ◇ *What is the artist trying to say in this painting?* ◇ *Well,* **what do you say?** *Do you think it's a good idea?* ◇ *It's* **hard to say** *what I like about the book.* ◇ *'When will it be finished?' 'I couldn't say* (= I don't know)*.'*
• SHOW FEELINGS **4** [T] ~ **sth (about sb/sth)** to show a feeling, a situation, etc. without using words: *His angry look said everything about the way he felt.*
• IMAGINE **5** [T] ~ **(that)** … to imagine or guess sth about a situation; to suppose: *We will need, say, £5 000 for a new car.* ◇ *Say (that) you don't get a place at university, what will you do then?*
IDM **go without saying** to be clear, so that you do not need to say it: *It goes without saying that the children will be well looked after at all times.* **have a lot, nothing, etc. to say for yourself** to have a lot, nothing, etc. to say in a particular situation: *Late again! What have you got to say for yourself?* **I dare say → DARE¹** **I must say** (*informal*) used to emphasize your opinion: *I must say, I didn't believe him at first.* **I wouldn't say no** (*informal*) used to say that you would like sth: *'Coffee?' 'I wouldn't say no.'* **let's say** for example: *You could work two mornings a week, let's say Tuesday and Friday.* **say no (to sth)** to refuse an offer, a suggestion, etc. **Say when** used to tell sb to say when you have poured enough drink in their glass or put enough food on their plate **that is to say** in other words: *We're leaving on Friday, that's to say in a week's time.* **to say the least** used to say that sth is in fact much worse, more serious, etc. than you are saying: *Adam's going to be annoyed, to say the least, when he sees his car.*

say² ⟁ **C1** /seɪ/ *noun* [sing., U] **(a)** ~ **(in sth)** the authority or right to decide sth: *I'd like to have some say in the arrangements for the party.*
IDM **have your say** to express your opinion: *Thank you for your comments. Now let somebody else have their say.*

saying /ˈseɪɪŋ/ *noun* [C] a well-known phrase that gives advice about sth or says sth that many people believe is true: *'Love is blind' is an old saying.* ◇ look at **proverb**

scab /skæb/ *noun* [C] (**HEALTH**) a mass of dried blood that forms over a part of the body where the skin has been cut or broken ◇ look at **scar** (1)

scabies /ˈskeɪbiːz/ *noun* [U] (**HEALTH**) a skin disease that causes small red spots and makes the skin feel uncomfortable so that you want to rub or SCRATCH it

scaffold /ˈskæfəʊld/ *noun* [C] a platform on which criminals were killed in past times by hanging

scaffolding /ˈskæfəldɪŋ/ *noun* [U] long metal POLES and wooden boards that form a structure that is put next to a building so that people who are building, painting, etc. can stand and work on it

scalable (*BrE also* **scaleable**) /ˈskeɪləbl/ *adj.* (**COMPUTING**) used to describe a computer, a network, software, etc. that can be changed to meet greater needs: *A business database needs to be scalable.*

scalar /ˈskeɪlə(r)/ *adj.* (**MATHEMATICS**) (used about a measurement or quantity) having size but no direction ▸ **scalar** *noun* [C] ◇ note at **vector**

scald /skɔːld/ *verb* [T] to burn sb/sth with very hot liquid: *I scalded my arm badly when I was cooking.* ▸ **scald** *noun* [C]

scalding /ˈskɔːldɪŋ/ *adj.* hot enough to SCALD: *scalding water*

scale¹ ⟁ **B2** ✪ /skeɪl/ *noun*
• SIZE **1** [C, U] the size of sth, especially when compared to other things: *We shall be making the product on a large scale next year.* ◇ *At this stage it is impossible to estimate the full scale of the disaster.*
• FOR MEASURING **2** [C] a series of numbers, amounts, etc. that are used for measuring or fixing the level of sth: *the new pay scale for nurses* ◇ look at **Beaufort scale**, **Richter scale** **3** [C] (**MATHEMATICS**) a series of marks on a tool or piece of equipment that you use for measuring sth: *The ruler has one scale in centimetres and one scale in inches.*
• FOR WEIGHING **4** **scales** [pl.] a piece of equipment that is used for weighing sb/sth: *I weighed it on the kitchen scales.*
• OF A MAP/DRAWING **5** [C] (**GEOGRAPHY**, **MATHEMATICS**) the relationship between the actual size of sth and its size on a map or plan: *The map has a scale of one centimetre to a kilometre.* ◇ *a scale of 1:50 000* (= one to 50 thousand) ◇ *We need a map with a larger scale.* ◇ *a scale model*
• IN MUSIC **6** [C] (**MUSIC**) a series of musical notes that go up or down in a fixed order. People play or sing scales to improve their technical ability: *the scale of C major*
• ON FISH **7** [C] (**BIOLOGY**) one of the small flat pieces of hard material that cover the body of some fish and animals: *the scales of a snake* ◇ picture at **animal**

scale² ⟁ /skeɪl/ *verb* [T] to climb to the top of sth very high and steep
PHR V **scale sth up/down** to increase/decrease the size, number, importance, etc. of sth: *Police have scaled up their search for the missing boy.*

scalene triangle /ˌskeɪliːn ˈtraɪæŋgl/ *noun* [C] (**GEOMETRY**) a TRIANGLE whose sides are all of different lengths ◇ picture at **triangle**

scallop /ˈskɒləp/ *noun* [C] a SHELLFISH (= a creature with a shell that lives in water) that can be eaten, with two flat round shells that fit together

scalp /skælp/ *noun* [C] (**ANATOMY**) the skin on the head that is under the hair

scalpel /ˈskælpəl/ *noun* [C] (**MEDICINE**) a small knife that is used by SURGEONS (= doctors who perform medical operations) when they are doing operations

scaly /ˈskeɪli/ *adj.* (**scalier; scaliest**) covered with SCALES, or hard and dry, with small pieces that come off

scam /skæm/ *noun* [C] (*informal*) a clever and dishonest plan for making money ▸ **scammer** *noun* [C]

scamper /ˈskæmpə(r)/ *verb* [I] (used especially about a child or small animal) to run quickly

scan¹ ⟁ **B1** /skæn/ *verb* [T] (-nn-) **1** to look at or read every part of sth quickly until you find what you are looking for: *Vic scanned the list until he found his own name.* **2** (used about a machine) to examine what is inside a person's body or inside an object such as a bag: *Machines scan all the luggage for bombs and guns.* **3** ~ **sth (into sth)**; ~ **sth (in)** (**COMPUTING**) to pass light over a picture or document using a SCANNER (= an electronic machine) in order to copy it and put it in the memory of a computer: *Text and pictures can be scanned into the computer.*

scan² /skæn/ *noun* **1** [C] (**MEDICINE**) a medical test in which a machine produces a picture of the inside of a person's body, or a baby inside its mother's body, on a computer screen: *to do/have a brain scan ◇ The scan showed the baby was in the normal position.* **2** [sing.] the act of looking quickly through sth written or printed, usually in order to find sth: *a scan of the newspapers*

scandal ↾+ **B2** /'skændl/ *noun* **1** [C, U] an action, a situation or behaviour that shocks people; the public feeling that is caused by such behaviour: *The chairman resigned after being involved in a financial scandal. ◇ The poor state of school buildings is a real scandal. ◇ There was no suggestion of scandal in his private life.* **2** [U] talk about sth bad or wrong that sb has done or may have done: *to spread scandal about somebody*

scandalize (*BrE also* -**ise**) /'skændəlaɪz/ *verb* [T] to cause sb to feel shocked, by doing sth that they think is bad or wrong

scandalous /'skændələs/ *adj.* very shocking or wrong: *It is scandalous that so much money is wasted.*

Scandinavia /ˌskændɪ'neɪviə/ *noun* [sing.] (**GEOGRAPHY**) the group of countries in northern Europe that consists of Denmark, Norway and Sweden. Sometimes Finland and Iceland are also said to be part of Scandinavia. ▶ **Scandinavian** /-ən/ *adj., noun* [C]

scandium /'skændiəm/ *noun* [U] (*symb.* **Sc**) (**CHEMISTRY**) a chemical element. Scandium is a silver-white metal found in various minerals. ❶ For more information on the periodic table of elements, look at the **Reference Section** of this dictionary.

scanner /'skænə(r)/ *noun* [C] **1** an electronic machine that can look at, record or send images or electronic information: *The scanner can detect cancer at an early stage.* **2** (**COMPUTING**) a device that copies pictures and documents so that they can be stored on a computer: *I used the scanner to send the document by email.*

scant /skænt/ *adj.* [only before noun] not very much; not as much as necessary

scanty /'skænti/ *adj.* (**scantier**; **scantiest**) **1** too little in amount for what is needed: *Details of his life are scanty.* **2** (used about clothes) very small and not covering much of your body: *a scanty bikini* ▶ **scantily** /-təli/ *adv.*: *scantily dressed models*

scapegoat /'skeɪpgəʊt/ *noun* [C] a person who is blamed for sth bad that sb else has done or for some failure: *When Alison was sacked she felt she had been **made a scapegoat** for all of the company's problems.*

scapula /'skæpjələ/ *noun* [C] (**ANATOMY**) either of the two large flat bones on each side of the back, below the shoulders **SYN** **shoulder blade** ⊃ picture at **body**

scar /skɑː(r)/ *noun* [C] **1** ~ **(on sth)** (**HEALTH**) a mark on the skin that is left after a wound has got better: *The operation didn't leave a very big scar. ◇* (*figurative*) *These bitter experiences left a deep scar on her mind.* ⊃ look at **scab 2** (**GEOGRAPHY**) an area of a hill or CLIFF where there is rock with nothing covering it and no grass: *a mile-long limestone scar* ⊃ picture at **limestone** ▶ **scar** *verb* [T, usually passive] (-**rr**-): *William's face was scarred for life in the accident.*

scarce /skeəs/ *adj.* not existing in large quantities; hard to find: *Food for birds and animals is scarce in the winter.* **OPP** **plentiful** ▶ **scarcity** *noun* [U, C] (*pl.* -**ies**): (*a*) *scarcity of food/jobs/resources*

scarcely /'skeəsli/ *adv.* **1** only just; almost not: *There was scarcely a car in sight. ◇ She's not a friend of mine. I scarcely know her.* ⊃ look at **hardly** (1) **2** used to suggest that sth is not reasonable or likely: *You can scarcely expect me to believe that after all you said before.*

scare¹ ↾+ **B2** /skeə(r)/ *verb* **1** [T] to make a person or an animal frightened: *The sudden noise scared us all. ◇ It scares me to think what might happen.* **2** [I] to become frightened: *I don't scare easily, but when I saw the snake I was terrified.*
PHR V **scare sb/sth away/off** to make a person or animal leave or stay away by frightening them

scare² ↾+ **B2** /skeə(r)/ *noun* **1** [C] a situation where many people are afraid or worried about sth: *Last night there was a **bomb scare** in the city centre.* **2** [sing.] a feeling of being frightened: *It wasn't a serious heart attack but it gave him a scare.*

scarecrow /'skeəkrəʊ/ *noun* [C] (**AGRICULTURE**) a very simple model of a person that is put in a field to frighten away the birds

scared ↾ **A2** /skeəd/ *adj.* ~ **(of sb/sth)**; ~ **(of doing sth)**; ~ **(to do sth)** frightened: *Are you scared of the dark? ◇ She's scared of walking home alone. ◇ Everyone was too scared to move.*

scarf /skɑːf/ *noun* [C] (*pl.* **scarves** /skɑːvz/, **scarfs**) a piece of cloth that is worn around the neck, for example to keep warm or for decoration. Women also wear scarves over their shoulders or hair.

scarlet /'skɑːlət/ *adj.* bright red in colour ▶ **scarlet** *noun* [U]

scarlet 'fever *noun* [U] (**HEALTH**) a serious disease that is passed from one person to another and that makes sb very hot and get red marks on the skin

scarp /skɑːp/ *noun* [C] (**GEOGRAPHY**) a very steep piece of land

scary ↾ **A2** /'skeəri/ *adj.* (**scarier**; **scariest**) (*informal*) frightening: *a scary ghost story ◇ It was a bit scary driving in the mountains at night.*

scat /skæt/ *noun* [U] (**MUSIC**) a style of jazz singing in which the voice is made to sound like a musical instrument

scathing /'skeɪðɪŋ/ *adj.* expressing a very strong negative opinion about sb/sth; very critical: *a scathing attack on the new leader ◇ scathing criticism*

scatter /'skætə(r)/ *verb* **1** [T] to drop or throw things in different directions over a wide area: *The wind scattered the papers all over the room.* **2** [I, T] (used about a group of people or animals) to move away quickly in different directions

scatter diagram (*also* **scattergram** /'skætəgræm/) *noun* [C] (**MATHEMATICS**) a diagram that shows the relationship between two VARIABLES by creating a pattern of DOTS (= small round marks) ⊃ picture at **chart¹**

scattered ↾+ **C1** /'skætəd/ *adj.* spread over a large area or happening several times during a period of time: *There will be sunny intervals with scattered showers today.*

scavenge /'skævɪndʒ/ *verb* [I, T] to look for food, etc. among waste and rubbish ▶ **scavenger** *noun* [C]: *Scavengers steal the food that the lion has killed.*

scenario ʔ+ B2 W /səˈnɑːriəʊ/ *noun* [C] (*pl.* -os) **1** one way that things may happen in the future: *A likely scenario is that the company will get rid of some staff.* **2** (ARTS AND MEDIA) a description of what happens in a play or film

scene ʔ A2 /siːn/ *noun*
- PLACE **1** [C] the place where sth happened: *the scene of a crime/an accident* ◇ *An ambulance was on the scene in minutes.*
- IN A PLAY, FILM, ETC. **2** [C] (ARTS AND MEDIA, LITERATURE) one part of a book, play, film, etc. in which the events happen in one place: *The first scene of 'Hamlet' takes place on the castle walls.*
- VIEW **3** [C, U] what you see around you in a particular place: *a delightful rural scene* ◇ *They went abroad for a change of scene* (= to see and experience new SURROUNDINGS).
- AREA OF ACTIVITY **4** the scene [sing.] the way of life or the present situation in a particular area of activity: *the fashion scene* ◇ *The political scene in that part of the world is very confused.*
- ARGUMENT **5** [C] an occasion when sb expresses great anger or another strong emotion in public: *There was quite a scene when she refused to pay the bill.*
IDM **behind the scenes 1** (ARTS AND MEDIA) in the part of a theatre, etc. that the public does not usually see: *The students were able to go behind the scenes to see how programmes are made.* **2** in a way that people in general are not aware of: *A lot of negotiating has been going on behind the scenes.* ◇ *behind-the-scenes work* **set the scene (for sth) 1** to create a situation in which sth can easily happen or develop: *His arrival set the scene for another argument.* **2** to give sb the information and details that they need in order to understand what comes next: *The first part of the programme was just setting the scene.*

scenery /ˈsiːnəri/ *noun* [U] **1** the natural beauty that you see around you in the country: *The scenery is superb in the mountains.* **2** (ARTS AND MEDIA) the furniture, painted cloth, boards, etc. that are used on the stage in a theatre: *The scenery is changed during the interval.*

scenic /ˈsiːnɪk/ *adj.* having beautiful SCENERY

scent /sent/ *noun* **1** [C, U] a pleasant smell: *This flower has no scent.* **SYN** **fragrance, perfume 2** [C, U] the smell that an animal leaves behind and that some other animals can follow **3** [U] (*especially BrE*) a liquid with a pleasant smell that you wear on your skin to make it smell nice **SYN** **perfume 4** [sing.] the feeling that sth is going to happen: *The scent of victory was in the air.* ▶ **scent** *verb* [T]: *The dog scented a rabbit and shot off.* ▶ **scented** *adj.*

sceptic (*BrE*) (*AmE* **skeptic**) /ˈskeptɪk/ *noun* [C] a person who doubts that sth is true, right, etc.
▶ **sceptical** ʔ+ C1 (*BrE*) (*AmE* **skeptical**) /-tɪkl/ *adj.* ~ (**of/about sth**): *Many doctors are sceptical about the value of alternative medicine.* ▶ **scepticism** (*BrE*) (*AmE* **skepticism**) /-tɪsɪzəm/ *noun* [U]

schedule¹ ʔ A2 /ˈʃedjuːl/ *noun* [C, U] a plan of things that will happen or of work that must be done: *Max has a busy schedule for the next few days.* ◇ *to be ahead of/behind schedule* (= to have done more/less than was planned) **2** [C] (*AmE*) = TIMETABLE

schedule² ʔ B2 /ˈʃedjuːl/ *verb* [T] ~ **sth (for sth)** (BUSINESS) to arrange for sth to happen or be done at a particular time: *We've scheduled the meeting for Monday morning.* ◇ *The train was scheduled to arrive at 10.07.*

ˈscheduled flight *noun* [C] (TOURISM) a plane service that leaves at a regular time each day or week ⊃ look at **charter flight**

schematic /skiːˈmætɪk/ *adj.* **1** (used about a diagram) showing the main features or relationships but not the details: *a schematic diagram* **2** according to a fixed plan or pattern: *The play has a very schematic plot.*

scheme¹ ʔ B2 W /skiːm/ *noun* [C] **1** ~ (**to do sth**); ~ (**for doing sth**) an official plan or system for doing or organizing sth: *a new scheme to provide houses in the area* ◇ *a local scheme for recycling newspapers* **2** a clever plan to do sth: *He's thought of a new scheme for making money fast.* ⊃ look at **colour scheme**

scheme² /skiːm/ *verb* [I, T] to make a secret or dishonest plan: *She felt that everyone was scheming to get rid of her.*

scherzo /ˈskeətsəʊ/ *noun* [C] (*pl.* -os) (MUSIC) a short, lively piece of music that is often part of a longer piece

schist /ʃɪst/ *noun* [U] (GEOLOGY) a type of rock formed of layers of different minerals, that breaks naturally into thin flat pieces

schizophrenia /ˌskɪtsəˈfriːniə/ *noun* [U] (PSYCHOLOGY) a serious mental illness in which a person confuses the real world and the world of the imagination and often behaves in strange and unexpected ways
▶ **schizophrenic** /-ˈfrenɪk/ *adj., noun* [C]

scholar ʔ+ B2 /ˈskɒlə(r)/ *noun* [C] (EDUCATION) **1** a person who studies and has a lot of knowledge about a particular subject **2** a person who has passed an exam or won a competition and has been given a SCHOLARSHIP to help pay for their studies: *He has come here as a British Council scholar.* ⊃ look at **student**

scholarly /ˈskɒləli/ *adj.* (EDUCATION) **1** (used about a person) spending a lot of time studying and having a lot of knowledge about an academic subject ⊃ look at **studious 2** connected with academic study **SYN** **academic¹**

scholarship ʔ+ B2 /ˈskɒləʃɪp/ *noun* (EDUCATION) **1** [C] an amount of money that is given to a person who has passed an exam or won a competition, in order to help pay for their studies: *to win a scholarship to Yale* **2** [U] serious study of an academic subject

school ʔ A1 /skuːl/ *noun*
- FOR CHILDREN **1** [C] (EDUCATION) the place where children go to be educated: *They're building a new school in our area.* ◇ *Was your school co-educational* (= for boys and girls) *or single-sex?* **2** [U] (EDUCATION) the time you spend at a school; the process of being educated in a school: *Where did you go to school?* ◇ *Their children are still at school.* ◇ *Children start school at 5 years old in Britain and can leave school at 16.* ◇ *School starts at nine o'clock and finishes at about 3.30.* ◇ *After school we usually have homework to do.*
HELP You say **school** (without 'the') when you are talking about going there for the usual reasons (that is, as a student or teacher): *Where do your children go to school?* ◇ *I enjoyed being at school.* ◇ *Do you walk to school?* You say **the school** if you are talking about going there for a different reason (for example, as a parent): *I have to go to the school on Thursday to talk to John's teacher.* You must also use **a** or **the** when more information about the school is given: *Rahul goes to the school in the next village.* ◇ *She teaches at a special school for children with learning difficulties.* **3** [sing. + sing./pl. verb] (EDUCATION) all the students and teachers in a school: *The whole school cheered the winner.* **4** [U] (in compounds) (EDUCATION) connected with school: *Do you have to wear school uniform?* ◇ *children of school age* ◇ *It is getting increasingly difficult for school-*

leavers to find jobs. ◇ *I don't have many good memories of my* **schooldays**.

- FOR A PARTICULAR SKILL **5** [C] (**EDUCATION**) a place where you go to learn a particular subject: *a language/driving/drama/business school*
- COLLEGE/UNIVERSITY **6** [C] (*AmE*) (**EDUCATION**) a college or university **7** [C] (**EDUCATION**) a department of a university that teaches a particular subject: *the School of Geography at Leeds University*
- ARTISTS **8** [C] (**ART**, **LITERATURE**) a group of writers, artists, etc. who have the same ideas or style: *the Flemish school of painting*
- OF FISH **9** [C] a large group of fish or other sea animals swimming together

IDM **a school of thought** the ideas or opinions that one group of people share: *There are various schools of thought on this matter.*

schoolboy /'sku:lbɔɪ/ *noun* [C] (**EDUCATION**) a boy who goes to school

schoolchild /'sku:ltʃaɪld/ *noun* [C] (*pl.* **schoolchildren** /-tʃɪldrən/) (**EDUCATION**) a child who goes to school: *The bus was full of schoolchildren.*

schoolgirl /'sku:lgɜ:l/ *noun* [C] (**EDUCATION**) a girl who goes to school

schooling /'sku:lɪŋ/ *noun* [U] (**EDUCATION**) the time that you spend at school; your education

'school-leaver *noun* [C] (*BrE*) a person who has just left school, especially when they are looking for a job

schoolmaster /'sku:lmɑːstə(r)/ *noun* [C] (*especially BrE, old-fashioned*) (**EDUCATION**) a male teacher in a school, especially a private school ⊃ look at **master**[1] (3)

schoolmistress /'sku:lmɪstrəs/ *noun* [C] (*especially BrE, old-fashioned*) (**EDUCATION**) a male teacher in a school, especially a private school

schoolteacher /'sku:lti:tʃə(r)/ *noun* [C] (**EDUCATION**) a person whose job is teaching in a school: *Schoolteachers have been awarded a 2% pay rise.*

schoolwork /'sku:lwɜ:k/ *noun* [U] (**EDUCATION**) work that students do at school or for school: *She is struggling to keep up with her schoolwork.*

schooner /'sku:nə(r)/ *noun* [C] **1** a sailing ship with two or more MASTS (= posts that support the sails) **2** a tall glass for beer or SHERRY (= a type of strong wine)

schwa /ʃwɑː/ *noun* [C] (**LANGUAGE**) a vowel sound in parts of words that are not stressed, for example the 'a' in *about* or the 'e' in *moment*; the symbol that represents this sound, /ə/

science 🔑 **A1** ◉ /'saɪəns/ *noun* **1** [U] the study of and knowledge about the physical world and natural laws: *Modern science has discovered a lot about the origin of life.* ◇ *Fewer young people are studying science at university.* **2** [C] (**EDUCATION**) one of the subjects into which science can be divided: *Biology, chemistry and physics are all sciences.* ⊃ look at **art** (4), **social science**

science 'fiction (*also* **sci-fi**) *noun* [U] (**ARTS AND MEDIA**, **LITERATURE**) books, films, etc. about imaginary events that take place in the future, often involving travel in space

scientific 🔑 **B1** ◉ /ˌsaɪən'tɪfɪk/ *adj.* **1** (**SCIENCE**) connected with or involving science: *We need more funding for scientific research.* ◇ *scientific instruments* **2** (used about a way of thinking or of doing sth) careful and logical: *a scientific study of the way people use language* ▶ **scientifically** /-kli/ *adv.*: *scientifically proven facts* ◇ *Sorting out the files won't take long if we do it scientifically.*

scientist 🔑 **A1** /'saɪəntɪst/ *noun* [C] (**SCIENCE**) a person who studies or teaches science, especially biology, chemistry or physics

Scientology™ /ˌsaɪən'tɒlədʒi/ *noun* [U] (**RELIGION**) a religious system based on getting knowledge of yourself through courses of study and training ▶ **scientologist** /-dʒɪst/ *noun* [C]

sci-fi /'saɪ faɪ/ (*informal*) = SCIENCE FICTION

scintillating /'sɪntɪleɪtɪŋ/ *adj.* very clever, funny and interesting: *The lead actor gave a scintillating performance.*

scissors /'sɪzəz/ *noun* [pl.] a tool for cutting paper or cloth, that has two sharp BLADES (= cutting edges) with handles, joined together in the middle: *a pair of scissors*

sclera /'sklɪərə/ *noun* [C] (*pl.* **-rae** /-riː/, **-ras**) (**ANATOMY**) the white part of the eye

scoff /skɒf/ *verb* **1** [I] ~ **(at sb/sth)** to speak about sb/sth in a way that shows you think that they are stupid or silly **2** [T] (*BrE, informal*) to eat a lot of sth quickly

scold /skəʊld/ *verb* [T] ~ **sb (for sth/doing sth)** to speak angrily to sb because they have done sth bad or wrong: *The teacher scolded her for being late.*

scone /skɒn, skəʊn/ *noun* [C] a small round cake that you cut in half and eat with butter, cream and jam on it

scoop[1] /sku:p/ *noun* [C] **1** a tool like a spoon used for picking up ice cream, flour, grain, etc. **2** the amount that one scoop contains **3** an exciting piece of news that is reported by one newspaper, TV or radio station before it is reported anywhere else

scoop[2] /sku:p/ *verb* [T] **1** ~ **sth (out/up)** to move or lift sth with a SCOOP or sth like a SCOOP: *Scoop out the middle of the pineapple.* **2** ~ **sb/sth (up)** to move or lift sb/sth using a continuous action: *He scooped up the child and ran.* **3** to win a big or important prize: *The film has scooped all the awards this year.* **4** (**ARTS AND MEDIA**) to get a story before all other newspapers, TV stations, etc.

scooter /'sku:tə(r)/ *noun* [C] **1** a light motorcycle with a small engine **2** a vehicle, used especially by children, with two or three small wheels attached to a narrow board with a handle that rises straight up at the front. The RIDER holds the handle, puts one foot on the board and pushes against the ground with the other.

scope 🔑+ **C1** 🔴 /skəʊp/ *noun* **1** [U] ~ **(for sth/to do sth)** the chance or opportunity to do sth: *The job offers plenty of scope for creativity.* **2** [sing.] the variety of subjects that are being discussed or considered: *The government was unwilling to extend the scope of the inquiry.*

scorch /skɔːtʃ/ *verb* [T] to burn sth so that its colour changes but it is not destroyed: *I scorched my blouse when I was ironing it.*

scorching /'skɔːtʃɪŋ/ *adj.* very hot: *It was absolutely scorching on Tuesday.*

score[1] 🔑 **A2** /skɔː(r)/ *noun* **1** [C] the number of points, goals, etc. that sb/sth gets in a game, competition, exam, etc: *What was the final score?* ◇ *The score is 3-2 to Liverpool.* ◇ *The top score in the test was 80%.* ⊃ note at **study[2]** **2** [C] (**MUSIC**) the written form of a piece of music **3** [C] (*pl.* **score**) a set or group of 20 or approximately 20 **4** **scores** [pl.] very many: *Scores of people have written to offer their support.*

IDM **on that score** as far as that is concerned: *Alan will be well looked after. Don't worry on that score.*

score[2] 🔑 **A2** /skɔː(r)/ *verb* [I, T] (**SPORT**) to get points, goals, etc. in a game, a competition, an exam, etc: *The team still hadn't scored by half-time.* ◇ *Louise scored the highest marks in the exam.*

scoreboard /'skɔːbɔːd/ *noun* [C] (**SPORT**) a large board that shows the score during a game, competition, etc.

scorer /'skɔːrə(r)/ *noun* [C] (**SPORT**) **1** a player who scores points, goals, etc. in a game: *United's top scorer* **2** a person who keeps a record of the score during a game, competition, etc.

scorn[1] /skɔːn/ *noun* [U] ~ (**for sb/sth**) the strong feeling that you have when you do not respect sb/sth: *He had nothing but scorn for his colleagues.*

scorn[2] /skɔːn/ *verb* [T] **1** to feel or show a complete lack of respect for sb/sth: *The president scorned his critics.* **2** (*formal*) to refuse to accept help or advice, especially because you are too proud: *The old lady scorned all offers of help.* ▶ **scornful** /'skɔːnfl/ *adj.: a scornful look/smile/remark* ▶ **scornfully** /-fəli/ *adv.*

Scorpio /'skɔːpiəʊ/ *noun* [U] the eighth sign of the THE ZODIAC (= twelve signs that represent the positions of the sun, moon and planets), the Scorpion; a person born under this sign

scorpion /'skɔːpiən/ *noun* [C] a creature that looks like a large insect and lives in hot countries. A scorpion has a long curved tail with a poisonous STING in it ⊃ picture at **animal**

Scotch /skɒtʃ/ *noun* [U, C] a type of WHISKY (= a strong alcoholic drink) that is made in Scotland; a glass of this

'**Scotch tape**™ (*AmE*) = SELLOTAPE™

Scots /skɒts/ *adj.* of or connected with people from Scotland

Scottish /'skɒtɪʃ/ *adj.* of or connected with Scotland or its people

the **Scottish National Party** *noun* [sing. + sing./pl. verb] (*abbr.* the SNP) (**POLITICS**) a Scottish political party that wants Scotland to be an independent nation ⊃ note at **party**

scoundrel /'skaʊndrəl/ *noun* [C] (*old-fashioned*) a man who behaves very badly towards other people, especially by being dishonest

scour /'skaʊə(r)/ *verb* [T] **1** to clean sth by rubbing it hard with sth rough: *to scour a dirty pan* **2** to search a place very carefully because you are looking for sb/sth

scourge /skɜːdʒ/ *noun* [C] a person or thing that causes a lot of trouble or suffering: *The Green Party sees the car as a scourge on society.*

scout /skaʊt/ *noun* **1** the Scouts [sing. + sing./pl. verb] an organization, originally for boys, that trains young people in practical skills and does a lot of activities with them: *to join the Scouts* **2** [C] (*BrE*) a member of the Scouts ⊃ look at **guide**[1] (6) **3** [C] a soldier who is sent on in front of the rest of the group to find out where the enemy is or which is the best route to take

scowl /skaʊl/ *noun* [C] a look on your face that shows you are angry or in a bad mood ⊃ look at **frown** ▶ **scowl** *verb* [I]

scrabble /'skræbl/ *verb* [I] to move your fingers or feet around quickly, trying to find sth or get hold of sth: *She scrabbled about in her purse for some coins.*

scramble /'skræmbl/ *verb* [I] **1** (used with an adverb or a preposition) to climb quickly up or over sth using your hands to help you; to move somewhere quickly: *He scrambled up the hill and over the wall.* ◇ *He scrambled to his feet* (= off the ground) *and ran off into the trees.* ◇ *The children scrambled into the car.* **2** ~ (**for sth/to do sth**) to fight or move quickly to get sth that a lot of people want: *People stood up and began scrambling for the exits.* ◇ *Everyone was scrambling to get the best bargains.* ▶ **scramble** *noun* [sing.]

scrambled 'egg *noun* [U] (*also* **scrambled eggs** [pl.]) eggs mixed together with milk and then cooked in a pan

scrap[1] /skræp/ *noun* **1** [C] a small piece of sth: *a scrap of paper/cloth* ◇ *scraps of food* **SYN** **bit**[1] **2** [U] something that you do not want any more but that is made of material that can be used again: *The old car was sold for scrap.* ◇ *scrap paper* **3** [C] (*informal*) a short fight or argument

scrap[2] /skræp/ *verb* [T] (-pp-) to get rid of sth that you do not want any more: *I think we should scrap that idea.*

scrapbook /'skræpbʊk/ *noun* [C] a large book with empty pages that you can stick pictures, newspaper articles, etc. in

scrape[1] /skreɪp/ *verb* **1** [T] (used with an adverb or a preposition) to remove sth from a surface by moving a sharp edge across it: *Scrape all the mud off your boots before you come in.* ◇ *They had scraped their plates clean.* **2** [T] (used with an adverb or a preposition) to damage or hurt sth by rubbing it against sth rough or hard: *Mark fell and scraped his knee.* ◇ *Sunita scraped the car against the wall.* **3** [I, T] (used with an adverb or a preposition) to make a sharp unpleasant noise by rubbing against sth; to make sth do this: *The branches scraped against the window.* **4** [T] to manage to get or win sth with difficulty: *I just scraped a pass in the maths exam.* **PHR V** **scrape by** to manage to live on the money you have, but with difficulty: *We can just scrape by on my salary.* **scrape through (sth)** to succeed in doing sth with difficulty: *to scrape through an exam* (= just manage to pass it) **scrape sth together/up** to get or collect sth together with difficulty

scrape[2] /skreɪp/ *noun* [C] **1** the action or unpleasant sound of one thing rubbing against another **2** damage or an injury caused by rubbing against sth rough: *I got a nasty scrape on my knee.* **3** (*informal*) a difficult situation that was caused by your own stupid behaviour: *to get into a scrape*

scrapheap /'skræphiːp/ *noun* [C] a large pile of objects, especially metal, that are no longer wanted **IDM** **on the scrapheap** (*informal*) not wanted any more: *Many unemployed people feel that they are on the scrapheap.*

scrappy /'skræpi/ *adj.* (**scrappier**; **scrappiest**) not organized or tidy and so not pleasant to see: *a scrappy essay/football match*

scratch[1] 🔧+ **B2** /skrætʃ/ *verb* **1** [T, I] ~ (**at sth**) to rub your skin with your nails: *Could you scratch my back for me?* ◇ *Don't scratch at your insect bites or they'll get worse.* **2** [T, I] to make a mark on a surface or a slight cut on a person's skin with sth sharp: *The cat will scratch if you annoy it.* ◇ *The table was badly scratched.* **3** [T] to use sth sharp to make or remove a mark: *He scratched his name on the top of his desk.* ◇ *I tried to scratch the paint off the table.* **4** [I] to make a sound by rubbing a surface with sth sharp: *The dog was scratching at the door to go outside.*

scratch[2] 🔧+ **B2** /skrætʃ/ *noun* **1** [C] a cut, mark or sound that was made by sb/sth sharp rubbing a surface: *There's a scratch on the car door.* **2** [sing.] an act of SCRATCHING part of the body: *The dog had a good scratch.* **IDM** **from scratch** from the very beginning: *I'm learning Spanish from scratch.* **(be/come) up to scratch** (*informal*) (to be/become) good enough

scrawl /skrɔːl/ *verb* [T, I] to write sth quickly in an untidy and careless way: *He scrawled his name across the top of the paper.* **SYN** **scribble** ▶ **scrawl** *noun* [sing.]: *Her signature was just a scrawl.*

scrawny /'skrɔːni/ *adj.* (**scrawnier**; **scrawniest**) very thin in a way that is not attractive

scream¹ ɛ **B2** /skriːm/ *verb* [I, T] **~ (sth) (out) (at sb)** to cry out loudly in a high voice because you are afraid, excited, angry, in pain, etc: *She saw a rat and screamed out.* ◇ *'Don't touch that,' he screamed.* ◇ *She screamed at the children to stop.* ◇ *He screamed with pain.* ◇ *He clung to the edge of the cliff, screaming for help.* ᗈ look at **shout**

scream² ɛ **B2** /skriːm/ *noun* **1** [C] a loud cry in a high voice: *a scream of pain* **2** [sing.] (*informal*) a person or thing that is very funny: (*informal, old-fashioned*) *Mel's a real scream.*

scree /skriː/ *noun* [U, C] (**GEOGRAPHY**) a steep area of small loose stones, especially on a mountain

screech /skriːtʃ/ *verb* [I, T] to make an unpleasant loud, high sound: *'Get out of here,' she screeched at him.* ᗈ look at **shriek** ▶ **screech** *noun* [sing.]: *the screech of brakes*

screen¹ ɛ **A2** /skriːn/ *noun* **1** [C] (**ARTS AND MEDIA**, **COMPUTING**) the surface of a TV or computer where the picture or information appears ᗈ picture at **oscilloscope 2** [C] (**ARTS AND MEDIA**) the large flat surface on which films are shown; one of the rooms in a cinema where films are shown **3** [sing., U] (**ARTS AND MEDIA**) films or TV in general: *Some actors look better in real life than on screen.* ◇ *It's on in Screen 3.* **4** [C] (**COMPUTING**) the data or images shown on a computer screen: *Press the F1 key to display a help screen.* **5** [C] a flat VERTICAL surface that is used for dividing a room or keeping sb/sth out of sight: *The nurse pulled the screen round the bed.*

screen² ɛ **B2** /skriːn/ *verb* [T] **1** [usually passive] (**ARTS AND MEDIA**) to show sth on TV or in a cinema **2 ~ sb (for sth)** (**MEDICINE**) to examine or test sb to find out if they have a particular disease or if they are suitable for a particular job: *All women over 50 should be screened for breast cancer.* ◇ *The Ministry of Defence screens all job applicants.* **3** to check sth to see if it is suitable or if you want it: *I use my voicemail to screen my calls.* ᗈ picture at **purification 4 ~ sb/sth (off) (from sb/sth)** to hide or protect sb/sth from sb/sth else: *The bed was screened off while the doctor examined him.* ◇ *to screen your eyes from the sun*

screening ɛ+ **B2** /ˈskriːnɪŋ/ *noun* [C] (**ARTS AND MEDIA**) the act of showing a film or TV programme: *This will be the movie's first screening in this country.*

screenplay /ˈskriːnpleɪ/ *noun* [C] (**ARTS AND MEDIA**) the words that are written for a film, together with instructions for how it is to be acted and made into a film

ˈ**screen-print** *verb* [T, I] (**ART**) to produce a picture by forcing INK or metal onto a surface through a screen of silk or artificial material ▶ ˈ**screen print** *noun* [C]

ˈ**screen saver** *noun* [C] (**COMPUTING**) a computer program that replaces what is on the screen with a moving image if the computer is not used for a certain amount of time

screenshot /ˈskriːnʃɒt/ *noun* [C] (**COMPUTING**) an image of the display on a screen

ˈ**screen time** *noun* [U] (**ARTS AND MEDIA**) **1** the amount of time that is given to sb/sth on film or TV: *They never actually shared any screen time on the series together.* **2** time spent using a device such as a computer, TV or tablet: *Experts recommend limiting screen time for children.*

screenwriter /ˈskriːnraɪtə(r)/ *noun* [C] (**ARTS AND MEDIA**) a person who writes instructions about what happens in a film and the words the actors say

screw¹ ɛ+ **C1** /skruː/ *noun* [C] (**ENGINEERING**) a thin pointed piece of metal used for fixing two things, for example pieces of wood, together. You turn a screw

with a SCREWDRIVER (= a special tool). ᗈ picture at **bolt¹**, **workbench**

screw² ɛ+ **C1** /skruː/ *verb* [T] **1** (**ENGINEERING**) (used with an adverb or a preposition) to fasten sth with a SCREW or SCREWS: *The bookcase is screwed to the wall.* ◇ *The lid is screwed down so you can't remove it.* **2** [I, T] to fasten sth, or to be fastened, by turning: *The legs screw into holes in the underside of the seat.* ◇ *Make sure that you screw the top of the jar on tightly.* **3** [T] **~ sth (up) (into sth)** to SQUEEZE sth, especially a piece of paper, into a tight ball: *He screwed the letter up into a ball and threw it away.*

PHR V **screw (sth) up** (*slang*) to make a mistake and cause sth to fail: *You'd better not screw up this deal.* **screw your eyes, face, etc. up** to change the expression on your face by nearly closing your eyes, because you are in pain or because the light is strong

screwdriver /ˈskruːdraɪvə(r)/ *noun* [C] a tool that you use for turning SCREWS (= pointed pieces of metal used for fastening things together) ᗈ picture at **tool**

scribble /ˈskrɪbl/ *verb* [T, I] **1** to write sth quickly and carelessly: *to scribble a note down on a pad* **SYN** **scrawl 2** to make marks with a pen or pencil that are not letters or pictures: *The children had scribbled all over the walls.* ▶ **scribble** *noun* [U, C]

script ɛ **B1** /skrɪpt/ *noun* **1** [C] (**ARTS AND MEDIA**, **LITERATURE**) the written form of a play, film, speech, etc: *Who wrote the script for the movie?* **2** [C, U] (**LANGUAGE**) a system of writing: *Arabic/Cyrillic/ Roman script* **3** [U, C] (**COMPUTING**) a series of instructions for a computer, carried out in a particular order, for example when a link in a website is clicked

Scripture /ˈskrɪptʃə(r)/ *noun* (**RELIGION**) **1** [U] (*also* the Scriptures [pl.]) the Bible **2 scriptures** [pl.] the holy books of a particular religion

scroll¹ /skrəʊl/ *noun* [C] **1** (**LITERATURE**) a long roll of paper with writing on it **2** (**ARCHITECTURE**) a decoration cut in stone or wood with a curved shape like a roll of paper

scroll² /skrəʊl/ *verb* [I, T] **~ (sth) (up/down)** (**COMPUTING**) to move text on a computer screen up or down or from side to side so that you can read different parts of it: *Scroll down to the bottom of the page.*

ˈ**scroll bar** *noun* [C] (**COMPUTING**) a narrow area at the edge of a computer screen that you use to move the text up and down or left and right

scrotum /ˈskrəʊtəm/ *noun* [C] (*pl.* scrotums, scrota /-tə/) (**ANATOMY**) the bag of skin that contains the TESTICLES (= male sex organs)

scrounge /skraʊndʒ/ *verb* [I, T] **~ (sth) (from/off sb)** (*informal*) to get sth by asking another person to give it to you instead of making an effort to get it for yourself: *Lucy is always scrounging money off her friends.*

scrub¹ /skrʌb/ *verb* [T, I] (-bb-) **1 ~ (sth) (down/out)** to clean sth with soap and water by rubbing it hard, often with a brush: *to scrub (down) the floor/walls* **2 ~ (sth) (off/out); ~ (sth) (off sth/out of sth)** to remove sth or be removed by scrubbing: *I hope these coffee stains will scrub out.* ◇ *to scrub the dirt off the walls*

scrub² /skrʌb/ *noun* **1** [sing.] an act of cleaning sth by rubbing it hard, often with a brush: *This floor needs a good scrub.* **2** [U] (**GEOGRAPHY**) small trees and bushes that grow in an area that has very little rain **3** (*also* **scrubland** /ˈskrʌblənd/) [U] (**GEOGRAPHY**) an area of dry land covered with small bushes and trees ᗈ picture at **ecosystem**

scruff /skrʌf/ noun
IDM **by the scruff (of the/your neck)** roughly holding the back of an animal's or a person's neck

scruffy /'skrʌfi/ adj. (scruffier; scruffiest) dirty and untidy: He always looks so scruffy. ◇ scruffy jeans

scrum /skrʌm/ noun [C] (**SPORT**) the part of a game of rugby when several players put their heads down in a circle and push against each other to try to get the ball

scruples /'skru:plz/ noun [pl.] a feeling that stops you from doing sth that you think is morally wrong: I've got no scruples about asking them for money (= I don't think it's wrong).

scrupulous /'skru:pjələs/ adj. **1** very careful or paying great attention to detail: a scrupulous investigation into the causes of the disaster **2** careful to do what is right or honest **OPP** **unscrupulous** ▶ **scrupulously** adv.: scrupulously clean/honest

scrutinize (BrE also -ise) /'skru:tənaɪz/ verb [T] to look at or examine sth carefully: The immigration official scrutinized every page of my passport.
▶ **scrutiny** ℝ+ **C1** /-ni/ noun [U]: These claims do not stand up to close scrutiny (= are not credible when you look carefully).

scuba diving /'sku:bə daɪvɪŋ/ noun [U] (**SPORT**) the activity of swimming UNDERWATER using special equipment for breathing: to go scuba-diving

scuff /skʌf/ verb [T] to make a mark on your shoes or with your shoes, for example by kicking sth or by rubbing your feet along the ground

scuffle /'skʌfl/ noun [C] a short, not very violent fight

sculptor /'skʌlptə(r)/ noun [C] (**ART**) a person who makes sculptures

sculpture ℝ **B1** /'skʌlptʃə(r)/ noun (**ART**) **1** [C, U] a work of art that is a figure or an object made from stone, wood, metal, etc. ◇ note at **art** **2** [U] the art of making sculptures

scum /skʌm/ noun [U] **1** a dirty or unpleasant substance on the surface of a liquid **2** (slang) an offensive word for people that you have no respect for: Drug dealers are scum.

scurry /'skʌri/ verb [I] (scurrying; scurries; pt, pp scurried) to run quickly with short steps; to hurry

scurvy /'skɜ:vi/ noun [U] (**HEALTH**) a disease caused by a lack of VITAMIN C

scuttle /'skʌtl/ verb [I] to run quickly with short steps: The spider scuttled away when I tried to catch it.

scythe /saɪð/ noun [C] (**AGRICULTURE**) a tool with a long handle and a long, curved BLADE (= a piece of metal with a very sharp edge). You use a scythe to cut long grass, CORN, etc.

SD card /ˌes 'di: kɑːd/ noun [C] a type of MEMORY CARD, used with digital cameras, mobile phones, etc.

SE abbr. (in writing) = SOUTH-EAST[1], SOUTH-EASTERN: SE Asia

sea ℝ **A1** /si:/ noun **1** (often the sea) [U] (**GEOGRAPHY**) the salt water that covers large parts of the surface of the earth: The sea is quite calm/rough today. ◇ Do you live by the sea? ◇ to travel by sea ◇ There were several people swimming in the sea. ◇ note at **water**[1] ◇ picture at **convection**, **longshore drift**, **petroleum** **2** (often Sea) [C] (**GEOGRAPHY**) a particular large area of salt water. A sea may be part of the ocean or may be surrounded by land: the Mediterranean Sea ◇ the Black Sea ◇ look at **ocean** (1) **3** [C] (also seas [pl.]) (**GEOGRAPHY**) the state or movement of the waves of the sea: The boat sank in heavy (= rough) seas off the Scottish coast. **4** [sing.] ~ (of sth) a large amount of sb/

sth close together: The pavement was just a sea of people.
IDM **at sea** **1** sailing in a ship: They spent about three weeks at sea. **2** not understanding or not knowing what to do: When I first started this job, I was completely at sea.

'sea anemone noun [C] a small, brightly coloured sea creature that lives on rocks and looks like a flower ◇ look at **anemone**

the seabed /ðə ˈsiːbed/ noun [sing.] (**GEOGRAPHY**) the floor of the sea ◇ picture at **wave**[1]

seabird /'si:bɜːd/ noun [C] any bird that lives close to the sea and gets its food from it ◇ look at **waterbird** ◇ picture at **animal**

seafood /'si:fu:d/ noun [U] fish and sea creatures that can be eaten, especially SHELLFISH

seafront /'si:frʌnt/ (often the seafront) noun [sing.] the part of a town facing the sea: The hotel is right on the seafront. ◇ to walk along the seafront

seagull /'si:gʌl/ = GULL

seal[1] ℝ+ **C1** /si:l/ noun [C] **1** an official design or mark that is put on a document, a letter, etc. to show that it is really from the person or organization that sent it **2** something that stops air or liquid from getting in or out of sth: The seal has worn and oil is escaping. **3** a small piece of paper, metal, plastic, etc. on a PACKET, bottle, etc. that you must break before you can open it **4** a grey animal with short fur that lives in and near the sea and that eats fish. Seals have no legs and swim with the help of FLIPPERS (= short flat arms).

seal[2] ℝ+ **C1** /si:l/ verb [T] **1** ~ sth (up/down) to close or fasten a package, letter, etc: The parcel was sealed with tape. ◇ to seal (down) an envelope **2** ~ sth (up) to fill a hole or cover sth so that air or liquid does not get in or out: The food is packed in sealed bags to keep it fresh. **3** to make sth sure, so that it cannot be changed or argued about: to seal an agreement
PHR V **seal sth off** to stop any person or thing from entering or leaving an area or a building: The building was sealed off by the police.

'sea level noun [U] (**GEOGRAPHY**) the average level of the sea, used for measuring the height of places on land: The town is 500 metres above sea level.

'sea lion noun [C] a large SEAL that lives by the Pacific Ocean

seam /si:m/ noun [C] **1** the line where two pieces of cloth are SEWN together **2** (**GEOLOGY**) a layer of coal or other material under the ground

seaman /'si:mən/ noun [C] (pl. -men /-mən/) a sailor

seamless /'si:mləs/ adj. with no spaces or breaks between one part and the next: a seamless flow of talk ▶ **seamlessly** adv.

seance (also séance) /'seɪɒs/ noun [C] a meeting at which people try to talk to the spirits of dead people

seaplane /'si:pleɪn/ (AmE also hydroplane) noun [C] a plane that can take off from and land on water

search[1] ℝ **A2** /sɜːtʃ/ verb [I, T] ~ (sb/sth) (for sb/sth); ~ (through sth) (for sth) to examine sb/sth carefully because you are looking for sb/sth; to look for sb/sth that is missing: The men were arrested and searched for drugs. ◇ Were your bags searched at the airport? ◇ They are still searching for the missing child. ◇ She searched through the papers on the desk, looking for the letter.

search[2] ℝ **A2** /sɜːtʃ/ noun **1** [C, U] an act of trying to find sb/sth, especially by looking carefully for them or it: the search for the missing boy ◇ She walked round for hours in search of (= looking for) her missing dog. **2** [C] (**COMPUTING**) an act of looking for information: to do a search on the internet '**search engine** *noun* [C] (**COMPUTING**) a computer program that searches the internet for information

searcher /'sɜːtʃə(r)/ *noun* [C] a person who is looking for sb/sth

searching /'sɜːtʃɪŋ/ *adj.* (used about a look, question, etc.) trying to find out the truth: *The customs officers asked a lot of searching questions about our trip.*

searchlight /'sɜːtʃlaɪt/ *noun* [C] a powerful lamp that can be turned in any direction, used, for example, for finding people or vehicles at night

'**search party** *noun* [C + sing./pl. verb] an organized group of people who are looking for sb/sth that is lost or missing

'**search warrant** *noun* [C] an official piece of paper that gives the police the right to search a building, etc.

seascape /'siːskeɪp/ *noun* [C] (**ART**) a picture or view of the sea: *a vast, sweeping seascape of sky, waves and sand* ⊃ look at **landscape**[1] (1)

'**sea shanty** (*BrE*) = SHANTY

seashell /'siːʃel/ *noun* [C] the empty shell of a small animal that lives in the sea

seashore /'siːʃɔː(r)/ (*usually* the seashore) *noun* [sing.] (**GEOGRAPHY**) the part of the land that is next to the sea: *We were looking for shells on the seashore.*

seasick /'siːsɪk/ *adj.* (**HEALTH**) feeling sick or VOMITING because of the movement of a boat or ship: *to feel/get/be seasick* ⊃ look at **airsick, carsick, travel-sick**

seaside /'siːsaɪd/ (*often* the seaside) *noun* [sing.] (**GEOGRAPHY, TOURISM**) an area on the coast, especially one where people go on holiday: *to go to the seaside* ◇ *a seaside town*

season[1] ⟨A2⟩ /'siːzn/ *noun* [C] **1** one of the four main periods of the year: *In cool countries the four seasons are spring, summer, autumn and winter.* **2** the period of the year when sth is common or popular or when sth usually happens or is done: *the holiday/football season* ◇ *the dry/rainy season* ⊃ look at **high season, low season, off season**

IDM **in season 1** (used about fresh foods) available in large quantities because it is the right time of the year **2** (**BIOLOGY**) (used about a female animal) ready to have sex **out of season 1** (used about fresh foods)

not available in large quantities because it is the wrong time of the year **2** (**TOURISM**) at the times of year when few people go on holiday

season[2] /'siːzn/ *verb* [T] to add salt, pepper etc. to food in order to make it taste better ▶ **seasoning** /-zənɪŋ/ *noun* [U, C]: *Add seasoning to the soup and serve with bread.*

seasonal /'siːzənl/ *adj.* happening or existing at a particular time of the year: *There are a lot of seasonal jobs in the summer.*

'**seasonal af fective disorder** *noun* [U] (*abbr.* **SAD**) (**PSYCHOLOGY**) a medical condition in which a person feels sad and tired during late autumn and winter when there is not much light from the sun

seasoned /'siːznd/ *adj.* having a lot of experience of sth: *a seasoned traveller*

'**season ticket** *noun* [C] a ticket that allows you to make a particular journey by bus, train, etc. or to go to a theatre or watch a sports team as often as you like for a fixed period of time

seat[1] ⟨A2⟩ /siːt/ *noun* [C] **1** something that you sit on: *the back/driving/passenger seat of a car* ◇ *Please take a seat* (= sit down). **2** the part of a chair, etc. that you sit on **3** a place in a theatre, on a plane, etc. where you pay to sit: *There are no seats left on that flight.* **4** an official position as a member of a parliament, etc: *to win/lose a seat*

IDM **be in the driving seat** to be the person, group, etc. that has the most powerful position in a particular situation **take a back seat** → BACK[2]

seat[2] ⟨B2⟩ /siːt/ *verb* [T] **1** [often passive] (*formal*) to give sb a place to sit; to sit down in a place: *Please be seated.* **2** to have seats or chairs for a particular number of people: *The theatre seats 750 people.*

'**seat belt** (*also* safety belt) *noun* [C] a long narrow piece of cloth that is fixed to the seat in a car or plane and that you wear around your body, so that you are not thrown forward if there is an accident: *to fasten/unfasten your seat belt* ⊃ look at **belt**[1] (1)

the seasons

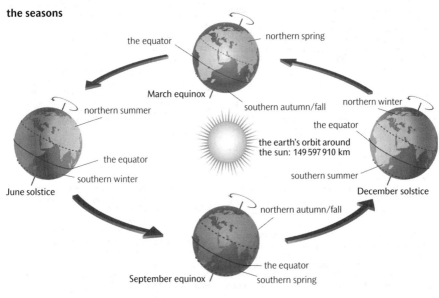

seating /'siːtɪŋ/ *noun* [U] the seats or chairs in a place or the way that they are arranged: *The conference hall has seating for 500 people.*

'sea turtle (*AmE*) = TURTLE (1)

seaweed /'siːwiːd/ *noun* [U] a plant that grows in the sea. There are many different types of seaweed.

seaworthy /'siːwɜːði/ *adj.* (used about a ship) in a suitable condition to sail ▶ **seaworthiness** *noun* [U]

sebaceous /sɪ'beɪʃəs/ *adj.* (**HEALTH**) producing a substance like oil in the body: *the sebaceous glands in the skin* ⊃ picture at **skin**[1]

sec /sek/ *noun* [sing.] (*informal*) = SECOND[3] (2)

sec. /sek/ *abbr.* (in writing) = SECOND[3] (1)

secateurs /ˌsekə'tɜːz/ (*BrE*) (*AmE* **pruning shears**) *noun* [pl.] a garden tool like a pair of strong SCISSORS, used for cutting plants and small branches: *a pair of secateurs* ⊃ picture at **gardening**

secede /sɪ'siːd/ *verb* [I] ~ **(from sth)** (*formal*) (**POLITICS**) (used about a state, country, etc.) to officially leave an organization of states, countries, etc. and become independent: *The Republic of Panama seceded from Colombia in 1903.*

secession /sɪ'seʃn/ *noun* [U, C] ~ **(from sth)** (**POLITICS**) the fact of an area or group becoming independent from the country or larger group that it belongs to

secluded /sɪ'kluːdɪd/ *adj.* far away from other people, roads, etc.; very quiet: *a secluded beach/garden* ▶ **seclusion** /-'kluːʒn/ *noun* [U]

second[1] {A1} /'sekənd/ *det., ordinal number*
1 happening or coming next after the first in a series; 2nd: *We are going on holiday in the second week in July.* ◇ *He was the second to arrive.* ◇ *Queen Elizabeth the Second* ◇ **the second of** January ◇ January **the second** **2** next in order of size, importance, etc. to one other person or thing: *Birmingham is the second largest city in Britain after London.* **3** [only before noun] another: *They have a second home in France.*
IDM **second nature (to sb)** something that has become a habit or that you can do easily because you have done it so many times: *With practice, typing becomes second nature.* **second thoughts** a change of mind or opinion about sth; doubts that you have when you are not sure if you have made the right decision: **On second thoughts**, *let's go today, not tomorrow.* ◇ *I'm starting to* **have second thoughts** *about accepting their offer.*

second[2] {A1} /'sekənd/ *adv.* after one other person or thing in order or importance: *Our team finished second.* ◇ *I came second in the competition.*

second[3] {A1} /'sekənd/ *noun*
• SHORT TIME **1** [C] one of the 60 parts into which a minute is divided **2** (*also informal* a **sec**) [C] a short time: *Wait a second, please.* **SYN** **moment**
• PRODUCT **3** [C] something that has a small fault and that is sold at a lower price: *The clothes are all seconds.*
• UNIVERSITY **4** [C] ~ **(in sth)** (*formal*) (**EDUCATION**) the second highest level of degree given by a British university: *to get an upper/a lower second in physics*

second[4] /'sekənd/ *verb* [T] to support sb's suggestion or idea at a meeting so that it can then be discussed or voted on

second[5] /sɪ'kɒnd/ *verb* [T, usually passive] **be seconded (from sth) (to sth)** (**BUSINESS**) (used about an employee) to be sent to another department, office, etc., in order to do a different job for a short period of time: *Our teacher has been seconded to another school for a year.* ▶ **secondment** *noun* [U, C]: *to be on secondment*

secondary {B1} {W} /'sekəndri/ *adj.* **1** less important than sth else: *Other people's opinions are secondary — it's my opinion that counts.* ⊃ picture at **seismic** **2** caused by or developing from sth else **3** [only before noun] (*BrE*) (**EDUCATION**) at, or connected with SECONDARY SCHOOL: *secondary students*

'secondary colour *noun* [C] a colour made by mixing two primary colours

'secondary school *noun* [C] (*especially BrE*) (**EDUCATION**) a school for children between the ages of 11 and 18

'secondary source *noun* [C] a book or other source of information where the writer has taken the information from some other source and not collected it himself or herself ⊃ look at **primary source**

ˌsecondary 'stress *noun* [C, U] (**LANGUAGE**) the second strongest stress that is put on a syllable in a word or a phrase when it is spoken ⊃ look at **primary stress**

ˌsecond 'best[1] *adj.* not quite the best but the next one after the best: *the second-best time in the 100 metres race* ⊃ look at **best**[1]

ˌsecond 'best[2] *noun* [U] something that is not as good as the best, or not as good as you would like: *I'm not prepared to accept second best.*

ˌsecond 'chamber (*especially BrE*) = UPPER HOUSE

ˌsecond-'class *adj.* **1** less important than other people: *Old people should not be treated as* **second-class citizens**. **2** of a lower standard or quality than the best: *a second-class education* **3** [only before noun] = STANDARD-CLASS: *second-class carriages/compartments/passengers* **4** [only before noun] (in the UK) connected with letters, packages, etc. that you pay less to send and that are delivered less quickly: *second-class letters/stamps* **5** (in the US) connected with the system of sending newspapers and magazines by mail **6** [only before noun] (**EDUCATION**) used to describe a university degree from a British university, that is good but not of the highest class: *a second-class honours degree in geography* ▶ **second class** *adv.*: *to travel second class* ◇ *to send a letter second class*

ˌsecond 'class *noun* [U] **1** = STANDARD CLASS **2** (in the UK) the way of sending letters, etc. that is cheaper but that takes longer than FIRST CLASS **3** (in the US) the system of sending newspapers and magazines by mail

ˌsecond 'cousin *noun* [C] the child of your mother's or father's cousin

ˌsecond-de'gree *adj.* [only before noun] **1** (*especially AmE*) (**LAW**) (used about murder and some other crimes) not of the most serious kind **2** (**HEALTH**) (used about burns) of the second most serious of three kinds, causing the skin to form BLISTERS (= bubbles containing clear liquid) but not leaving any permanent marks ⊃ look at **first-degree** (2), **third-degree** (1)

ˌsecond 'floor *noun* [C] the floor in a building that is two floors above the lowest floor: *I live on the second floor.* ◇ *a second-floor flat* ❶ In American English the second floor is next above the lowest.

ˌsecond-'hand *adj., adv.* **1** already used or owned by sb else: *a second-hand car* ◇ *I bought this camera second-hand.* ⊃ look at **old** (5) **2** (used about news or information) that you heard from sb else, and did not see or experience yourself ⊃ look at **first-hand**

'second hand *noun* [C] the hand on some clocks and watches that shows seconds

ˌsecond 'language *noun* [C] (**LANGUAGE**) a language that sb learns to speak well and that they use for work or at school, but that is not the language they learned first:

secondly ⚏ **A2** **◉** /'sekəndli/ *adv.* (used when you are giving your second reason or opinion) also: *Firstly, I think it's too expensive and secondly, we don't really need it.*

'**second name** *noun* [C] (*especially BrE*) **1** = SURNAME **2** a second personal name: *His second name is Prabhakar, after his father.*

the ˌsecond ˈperson *noun* [sing.] (**GRAMMAR**) the set of pronouns and verb forms that you use when you talk to sb: *In the phrase 'you are', the verb 'are' is in the second person and the word 'you' is a second-person pronoun.* ➔ look at **first person** (1), **third person** (1)

ˌsecond-ˈrate *adj.* of poor quality: *a second-rate poet*

secrecy /'si:krəsi/ *noun* [U] the fact of being secret or keeping sth secret: *I must stress the importance of secrecy in this matter.*

secret¹ ⚏ **A2** /'si:krət/ *noun* **1** [C] something that is not or must not be known by other people: *to keep a secret* ◇ *to let somebody in on/tell somebody a secret* ◇ *I can't tell you where we're going — it's a secret.* ◇ *It's no secret that they don't like each other* (= everybody knows). **2** [sing.] ~ **(of/to sth/doing sth)** the only way or the best way of doing or achieving sth: *What is the secret of your success* (= how did you become so successful)?
IDM **in secret** without other people knowing: *to meet in secret*

secret² ⚏ **A2** /'si:krət/ *adj.* **1** ~ **(from sb)** that is not or must not be known by other people: *We have to keep the party secret from Carmen.* ◇ *a secret address* ◇ *a secret love affair* **2** [only before noun] used to describe actions that you do not tell anyone about: *a secret drinker* ◇ *She's got a secret admirer.* ▶ **secretly** *adv.*: *The government secretly agreed to pay the kidnappers.*

ˌsecret ˈagent (*also* agent) *noun* [C] a person who tries to find out secret information, especially about the government of another country ➔ look at **spy¹**

secretarial /ˌsekrə'teəriəl/ *adj.* involving or connected with the work that a secretary does: *secretarial skills/work*

secretariat /ˌsekrə'teəriət, -riæt/ *noun* [C] (**POLITICS**) the department of a large international or political organization that is responsible for managing it

secretary ⚏ **A2** /'sekrətri/ *noun* [C] (*pl.* -ies) **1** a person who works in an office. A secretary types letters, answers the phone, keeps records, etc: *the director's personal secretary* **❶** This meaning of **secretary** is starting to become old-fashioned. It is now more usual to call sb an **assistant** or **PA** (= personal assistant): *Please contact my assistant to make an appointment.* **2** an official of a club or society who is responsible for keeping records, writing letters, etc. ➔ note at **meeting** **3** Secretary (*AmE*) (**POLITICS**) the head of a government department, chosen by the president ➔ look at **minister** (1) **4** Secretary = SECRETARY OF STATE (1)

ˌSecretary ˈGeneral *noun* [C] the person who is in charge of the department that runs a large international or political organization

ˌSecretary of ˈState *noun* [C] (**POLITICS**) **1** (*also* Secretary) (in the UK) the head of one of the main government departments: *the Secretary of State for Defence* **2** (in the US) the head of the government department that deals with foreign affairs

secrete /sɪ'kri:t/ *verb* [T] **1** (used about a part of a plant, an animal or a person) to produce a liquid **2** (*formal*) to hide sth in a secret place

secretion /sɪ'kri:ʃn/ *noun* [C, U] (*formal*) a liquid that is produced by a plant or an animal; the process by which the liquid is produced: *The frog covers itself in a poisonous secretion for protection.*

secretive /'si:krətɪv/ *adj.* liking to keep things secret from other people: *Wendy is very secretive about her private life.* ▶ **secretively** *adv.* ▶ **secretiveness** *noun* [U]

ˌsecret po'lice *noun* [C + sing./pl. verb] (**POLITICS**) a police force that works secretly to make sure that people behave as their government wants

ˌsecret ˈservice *noun* [usually sing.] (**POLITICS**) the government department that tries to find out secret information about other countries and governments

sect /sekt/ *noun* [C] (**POLITICS, RELIGION**) a group of people who have a particular set of religious or political beliefs. A sect has often broken away from a larger group.

sectarian /sek'teəriən/ *adj.* (**RELIGION**) connected with the differences that exist between groups of people who have different religious views: *sectarian attacks/violence* ▶ **sectarianism** *noun* [U]

section¹ ⚏ **A1** **◉** /'sekʃn/ *noun* [C] **1** one of the parts into which sth is divided: *the string section of an orchestra* ◇ *the financial section of a newspaper* ◇ *The library has an excellent reference section.* **2** a drawing or diagram of sth as it would look if it were cut from top to bottom or from one side to the other: *The illustration shows a section through a leaf.* **3** (**MEDICINE**) the act of cutting or separating sth in an operation: *The surgeon performed a section* (= made a cut) *on the vein.* ➔ look at **caesarean**

section² /'sekʃn/ *verb* [T] **1** (**MEDICINE**) to divide body TISSUE by cutting **2** (**BIOLOGY**) to cut animal or plant TISSUE into thin slices in order to look at it under a MICROSCOPE **3** (*BrE*) (**MEDICINE**) to officially order a mentally ill person to go and receive treatment in a PSYCHIATRIC hospital, using a law that can force them to stay there until they are successfully treated

sector ⚏ **B2** **◍** /'sektə(r)/ *noun* [C] **1** a part of the business activity of a country: *The manufacturing sector has declined in recent years.* ➔ look at **private sector, public sector** **2** a part of a particular area, especially an area under military control: *the occupied sector of the city* ➔ picture at **cloud¹** **3** (**GEOMETRY**) a part of a circle that is between two straight lines drawn from the centre to the edge ➔ picture at **circle¹**

secular ⚏+ **C1** /'sekjələ(r)/ *adj.* (**RELIGION**) not concerned with religion or the church

secure¹ ⚏ **B1** /sɪ'kjʊə(r)/ *adj.* **1** not likely to be lost; safe: *Business is good so his job is secure.* ◇ *a secure investment* **2** free from worry or doubt; confident: *Children need to feel secure.* ◇ *to be financially secure* **OPP** insecure **3** ~ **(against/from sth)** well locked or protected: *Check that the house is secure against intruders.* **4** not likely to move, fall down, etc: *That ladder doesn't look very secure.* **SYN** **stable¹** ▶ **securely** *adv.*: *All doors and windows must be securely fastened.*

secure² ⚏ **B2** /sɪ'kjʊə(r)/ *verb* [T] **1** to obtain or achieve sth, especially by having to make a big effort: *The company has secured a contract to build ten planes.* **2** ~ **sth (against/from sth)** to make sth safe: *The sea wall needs strengthening to secure the town against flooding.* **3** ~ **sth (to sth)** to fix or lock sth FIRMLY: *The load was secured with ropes.* ◇ *Secure the rope to a tree or a rock.*

security 🔉 **B1** 🌐 /sɪ'kjʊərəti/ *noun* (*pl.* -ies) **1** [U] things that you do to protect sb/sth from attack, danger, thieves, etc: *Security was tightened at the airport before the president arrived.* ◇ *The robbers were caught on the bank's security cameras.* **2** [U] (**BUSINESS**) the section of a large company or organization that deals with the protection of buildings, equipment and staff: *If you see a suspicious bag, contact airport security immediately.* **3** [U] the state of feeling safe and being free from worry; protection against the difficulties of life: *Children need the security of a stable home environment.* ◇ *financial/job security* **OPP** **insecurity** **4** [C, U] (**FINANCE**) something of value that you use when you borrow money. If you cannot pay the money back then you lose the thing you gave as security. **5** securities [pl.] (**BUSINESS**) documents proving that sb is the owner of shares, etc. in a particular company: *government securities*

se'curity forces *noun* [pl.] soldiers and police who are responsible for security in a city, region, etc: *Two terrorists were killed in a gun battle with the security forces.*

sedan /sɪ'dæn/ (*AmE*) = SALOON

sedate¹ /sɪ'deɪt/ *adj.* quiet, calm and well behaved

sedate² /sɪ'deɪt/ *verb* [T] (**MEDICINE**) to give a person or animal a drug to make them feel calm or want to sleep: *The lion was sedated and treated by a vet.* ▶ sedation /-'deɪʃn/ *noun* [U]: *The doctor put her under sedation.*

sedative /'sedətɪv/ *noun* [C] (**MEDICINE**) a drug that makes you feel calm or want to sleep ᵓ look at tranquillizer

sedentary /'sedntri/ *adj.* involving a lot of sitting down; not active: *a sedentary lifestyle/job*

sediment /'sedɪmənt/ *noun* [U, C] **1** (**CHEMISTRY**) the thick substance that forms at the bottom of a liquid **2** (**GEOLOGY**) sand, stones, mud, etc. carried by water or wind and left, for example, on the bottom of a lake, river, etc. ᵓ picture at **glacial**, **rock**¹

sedimentary /ˌsedɪ'mentri/ *adj.* (**GEOLOGY**) (used about rocks) formed from the sand, stones, mud, etc. that are at the bottom of lakes, rivers, etc. ᵓ look at **igneous**, **metamorphic** ᵓ picture at **rock**¹

sedimentation /ˌsedɪmen'teɪʃn/ *noun* [U] (**GEOLOGY**) the process of leaving SEDIMENT, for example on the bottom of a lake, river, etc. ᵓ picture at **purification**

sedition /sɪ'dɪʃn/ *noun* [U] (*formal*) (**POLITICS**) the use of words or actions that are intended to encourage people to be or act against a government ▶ seditious /-'ʃəs/ *adj.*

seduce /sɪ'djuːs/ *verb* [T] **1** to persuade sb to have sex with you **2** ~ sb (into sth/doing sth) to persuade sb to do sth they would not usually agree to do: *Special offers seduce customers into spending their money.* ▶ seduction /-'dʌkʃn/ *noun* [U, C]

seductive /sɪ'dʌktɪv/ *adj.* **1** sexually attractive: *a seductive smile* **2** attractive in a way that makes you want to have or do sth: *a seductive argument/opinion* (= one which you want to agree with)

see 🔉 **A1** /siː/ *verb* (*pt* saw /sɔː/; *pp* seen /siːn/)
• USE YOUR EYES **1** [T, I] to become conscious of sth, using your eyes; to use the power of sight: *Have you seen my wallet anywhere?* ◇ *He couldn't see her in the crowd.* ◇ *It was so dark that we couldn't see.* ◇ *On a clear day you can see for miles.*
• FILM, TV PROGRAMME, ETC. **2** [T] to look at or watch a film, TV programme, etc: *Did you see that programme on*

sharks last night? ◇ *Have you seen Spielberg's latest film?*
• VISIT **3** [T] to spend time with sb; to visit sb: *I saw Alan at the weekend; we had dinner together.* ◇ *You should see a doctor about that cough.* ᵓ note at **medical**¹, **professional**²
• HAVE A RELATIONSHIP **4** [T] to have a romantic relationship with sb: *Is Frank seeing anybody at the moment?*
• UNDERSTAND **5** [I, T] to understand sth; to realize sth: *'You have to key in your password first.' 'Oh, I see.'* ◇ *Do you see what I mean?* ◇ *She doesn't see the point in spending so much money on a car.* ᵓ note at **regard**¹
• HAVE AN OPINION **6** [T] to have an opinion about sth: *How do you see the situation developing?*
• IMAGINE **7** [T] to imagine sth as a future possibility: *I can't see her changing her mind.*
• FIND OUT **8** [I, T] to find out sth by looking, asking or waiting: *Go and see if the postman has been yet.* ◇ *We'll wait and see what happens before making any decisions.* ◇ *I saw in the paper that they're building a new theatre.* ◇ *'Can we go swimming today, Dad?' 'We'll see.'*
• MAKE SURE **9** [T] to do what is necessary in a situation; to make sure that sb does sth: *I'll see that he gets the letter.*
• HAPPEN **10** [T] to be the time when an event happens: *Last year saw huge changes in the education system.*
• HELP **11** [T] to go with sb, for example to help or protect them: *He asked me if he could see me home, but I said no.* ◇ *I'll see you to the door.*
IDM as far as the eye can see → FAR² let me see | let's see used when you are thinking or trying to remember sth: *Where did I put the car keys? Let's see. I think I left them in the kitchen.* see eye to eye (with sb) to agree with sb; to have the same opinion as sb: *We don't always see eye to eye on political matters.* see if … to try to do sth: *I'll see if I can find time to do it.* ◇ *See if you can undo this knot.* see the joke to understand what is funny about a joke or trick see red (*informal*) to become very angry see you (later) used for saying goodbye to sb you expect to see soon or later that day see you around (*informal*) used for saying goodbye to sb you have made no arrangement to see again wait and see → WAIT¹ you see used for giving a reason: *She's very unhappy. He was her first real boyfriend, you see.*
PHR V see about sth/doing sth to deal with sth: *I've got to go to the bank to see about my new account.* see sb off to go with sb to the railway station, the airport, etc. in order to say goodbye to them see through sb/sth to be able to see that sb/sth is not what he/she/it appears: *The police immediately saw through his story.* see to sb/sth to do what is necessary in a situation; to deal with sb/sth: *I'll see to the travel arrangements and you book the hotel.*

seed 🔉 **B1** /siːd/ *noun* **1** [C, U] (**BIOLOGY**) the small hard part of a plant from which a new plant of the same kind can grow: *a packet of sunflower seeds* **2** [C] the start of a feeling or event that continues to grow: *Her answer planted the seed of doubt in my mind.* **3** [C] a player in a sports competition, especially tennis, who is expected to finish in a high position

seeded /'siːdɪd/ *adj.* (**SPORT**) (used about a player or a team) expected to finish in a high position

seedless /'siːdləs/ *adj.* (used about fruit) having no seeds: *seedless grapes*

seedling /'siːdlɪŋ/ *noun* [C] (**BIOLOGY**) a very young plant or tree that has grown from a seed

seedy /'siːdi/ *adj.* (seedier; seediest) dirty and unpleasant; possibly connected with illegal or IMMORAL activities: *a seedy hotel/neighbourhood*

seeing /ˈsiːɪŋ/ (also ˈseeing that, ˈseeing as) *conj.* (*informal*) because; as: *Seeing as we're going the same way, I'll give you a lift.*

ˌSeeing ˈEye dog™ (*AmE*) = GUIDE DOG

seek ᵻ **B2** **W** /siːk/ *verb* [T] (*pt, pp* sought /sɔːt/) (*formal*) **1** to try to find or get sth: *Politicians are still seeking a peaceful solution.* **2** ~ **sth (from sb)** to ask sb for sth: *You should seek advice from a solicitor about what to do next.* **3** ~ **to do sth** to try to do sth: *They are still seeking to find a peaceful solution to the conflict.* **SYN** **attempt**[1] **4** -seeking (in adjectives) looking for or trying to get the thing mentioned: *a heat-seeking missile* ◇ *attention-seeking behaviour*

seeker ᵻ **B2** /ˈsiːkə(r)/ *noun* [C] (often in compounds) a person who is trying to find or get the thing mentioned: *an attention seeker* ◇ *asylum seekers*

seem ᵻ **A2** /siːm/ *linking verb* ~ **(to be) sth**; ~ **(like) sth** (not used in the progressive tenses) to give the impression of being or doing sth; to appear: *Emma seems to be a very nice girl.* ◇ *It seems to me that we have no choice.* ◇ *You seem happy today.* ◇ *This machine doesn't seem to work.* ◇ *Emma seems (like) a very nice girl.* **SYN** **appear**

seeming /ˈsiːmɪŋ/ *adj.* [only before noun] appearing to be sth: *Despite her seeming enthusiasm, Sandra didn't really help much.* **SYN** **apparent** ▸ seemingly ᵻ+ **C1** *adv.*: *a seemingly endless list of complaints*

seen /siːn/ past participle of **see**

seep /siːp/ *verb* [I] (used about a liquid) to flow very slowly through sth: *Water started seeping in through small cracks.*

ˈsee-saw *noun* [C] an outdoor toy for children that consists of a long piece of wood that is balanced in the middle. One child sits on each end of the see-saw and one goes up while the other goes down.

seethe /siːð/ *verb* [I] ~ **(with sth)** **1** to be very angry but to try not to show it: *She seethed silently in the corner.* **2** to be very crowded: *The streets were seething with people.*

segment ᵻ+ **C1** **W** /ˈseɡmənt/ *noun* [C] **1** a section or part of sth: *I've divided the sheet of paper into three segments.* ◇ *a segment of the population* ◷ picture at **circle**[1] **2** one of the sections of an orange, a lemon, etc. **3** (GEOMETRY) a part of a circle separated from the rest by a single line ▸ segment /seɡˈment/ *verb* [T]: *Market researchers often segment the population on the basis of age and social class.*

segmentation /ˌseɡmenˈteɪʃn/ *noun* [U, C] the act of dividing sth into different parts; one of these parts: *the segmentation of social classes* ◷ look at **market segmentation**

segregate /ˈseɡrɪɡeɪt/ *verb* [T] ~ **sb/sth (from sb/sth)** (SOCIAL STUDIES) to separate one group of people or things from the rest: *The two groups of football fans were segregated to avoid trouble.* ◷ look at **integrate** (2) ▸ segregation /ˌseɡrɪˈɡeɪʃn/ *noun* [U]: *racial segregation* (= separating people of different human groups)

segregationist /ˌseɡrɪˈɡeɪʃənɪst/ *adj.* (POLITICS, SOCIAL STUDIES) believing that people should be separated according to the human group they belong to, their sex or their religion: *segregationist policies* ▸ segregationist *noun* [C]

seismic /ˈsaɪzmɪk/ *adj.* (GEOLOGY) connected with or caused by earthquakes

seismograph /ˈsaɪzməɡrɑːf/ *noun* [C] (GEOLOGY) an instrument that measures and records information about earthquakes

seismology /saɪzˈmɒlədʒi/ *noun* [U] (GEOLOGY) the scientific study of earthquakes

seize ᵻ+ **C1** /siːz/ *verb* [T] **1** to take hold of sb/sth suddenly and with force: *The thief seized her handbag and ran off with it.* ◇ (*figurative*) *to seize a chance/an opportunity* **SYN** **grab**[1] **2** (LAW) to take control or possession of sb/sth: *The police seized 50 kilos of illegal drugs.* **3** [usually passive] (used about an emotion) to affect sb suddenly and very strongly: *I felt myself seized by panic.*
PHR V seize (on/upon) sth to make use of a good and unexpected chance **seize up** (used about a machine) to stop working because it is too hot, does not have enough oil, etc.

seizure /ˈsiːʒə(r)/ *noun* [U] using force or legal authority to take control or possession of sth: *the seizure of 30 kilos of heroin by police*

seldom ᵻ+ **C1** /ˈseldəm/ *adv.* not often: *There is seldom snow in Athens.* ◇ *I very seldom go to the theatre.* **SYN** **rarely**

select[1] ᵻ **B2** **W** /sɪˈlekt/ *verb* [T] **1** ~ sb/sth (for sth) (from sth) to choose sb/sth from a number of similar things: *The best candidates will be selected for interview.* **HELP** Select is more formal than **choose** and suggests that a lot of care is taken when making the decision. **2** (COMPUTING) to mark sth on a computer screen; to choose sth, especially from a menu

select[2] /sɪˈlekt/ *adj.* (*formal*) **1** [only before noun] carefully chosen as the best of a group: *A university education is no longer the privilege of a select few.* **2** used or owned by rich people

selection ᵻ **B2** **W** /sɪˈlekʃn/ *noun* **1** [U] the process of choosing or being chosen: *The manager is responsible for team selection.* **2** [C] a number of people or things that have been chosen: *a selection of hits from the fifties and sixties* **3** [C] a number of things from which you can choose: *This shop has a very good selection of toys.* **SYN** **choice**[1], **range**[1]

selective ᵻ+ **C1** **W** /sɪˈlektɪv/ *adj.* **1** affecting or concerned with only a small number of people or things from a larger group: *the selective breeding of cattle* **2** ~ **(about/in sth)** being careful about what or who you choose: *She's very selective about who she*

paths of seismic waves through the earth

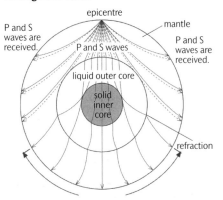

epicentre

P and S waves are received.

mantle

P and S waves

P and S waves are received.

liquid outer core

solid inner core

refraction

Only P waves are received because S waves cannot travel through the liquid core.

P waves = primary waves ───────
S waves = secondary waves - - - - -

invites to her parties. ◇ *a selective school* (= one that chooses which children to admit, especially according to ability) ▸ **selectively** *adv.*

selector /sɪˈlektə(r)/ *noun* [C] **1** (*BrE*) (**SPORT**) a person who chooses the members of a particular sports team **2** a device in an engine, a machine, etc. that allows you to choose a particular function

selenium /səˈliːniəm/ *noun* [U] (*symb.* Se) (**CHEMISTRY**) a chemical element. Selenium is a grey substance used in making electrical equipment and coloured glass. ❶ For more information on the periodic table of elements, look at the **Reference Section** of this dictionary.

self ⛿ **B2** /self/ *noun* [C] (*pl.* selves /selvz/) a person's own nature or qualities: *It's good to see you back to* **your old self** *again* (= feeling well or happy again). ◇ *Her spiteful remark revealed her* **true self** (= what she was really like).

self- /self/ *prefix* (in nouns and adjectives) of, to, or by yourself or itself: *self-control* ◇ *self-addressed* ◇ *self-taught*

self-ˈaccess *noun* [U] (**EDUCATION**) a method of learning in which students choose their materials and use them to study on their own: *a* **self-access** *centre/library*

self-asˈsurance = ASSURANCE (2)

self-asˈsured = ASSURED

self-ˈcare *noun* [U] (**PSYCHOLOGY**) the act of caring for yourself, for example by eating and sleeping well, taking exercise and getting help so that you do not become ill

self-ˈcatering *adj.* (*BrE*) (**TOURISM**) (used about a holiday or a place to stay) where meals are not provided for you so you cook them yourself

self-ˈcentred (*BrE*) (*AmE* **self-centered**) *adj.* thinking only about yourself and not about other people ⊃ look at **selfish**

self-conˈfessed *adj.* [only before noun] admitting that you are sth or do sth that most people consider to be bad: *a self-confessed chocolate addict*

self-ˈconfident *adj.* feeling sure about your own value and abilities ⊃ look at **confident** (1) ▸ **self-ˈconfidence** *noun* [U]: *Many women lack the self-confidence to apply for senior jobs.*

self-ˈconscious *adj.* too worried about what other people think about you ▸ **self-consciously** *adv.* ▸ **self-consciousness** *noun* [U]

self-conˈtained *adj.* (*BrE*) **1** (used about a flat, etc.) having its own private entrance, kitchen and bathroom (*BrE*) **2** not needing or depending on other people

self-conˈtrol *noun* [U] the ability to control your emotions and appear calm even when you are angry, afraid, excited, etc: *to lose/keep your self-control*

self-deˈfence (*BrE*) (*AmE* **self-defense**) *noun* [U] the use of force to protect yourself or your property: *Lee is learning karate for self-defence.* ◇ *to shoot somebody* **in self-defence** (= because they are going to attack you)

self-deˈstruct *verb* [I] (used especially about a machine, etc.) to destroy itself, usually by exploding

self-deˈstruction *noun* [U] the act of doing things to deliberately harm yourself ▸ **self-deˈstructive** *adj.*

self-deˌtermiˈnation *noun* [U] (**POLITICS**, **SOCIAL STUDIES**) the right of a country and its people to be independent and to choose their own government and political system **SYN** independence

self-ˈdiscipline *noun* [U] the ability to make yourself do sth difficult or unpleasant: *It takes a lot of self-discipline to train for a marathon.*

self-ˈdrive *adj.* [only before noun] (*BrE*) (**TOURISM**) **1** a **self-drive** car is one that you hire and drive yourself **2** a **self-drive** holiday is one on which you use your own car or a car you hire to travel to the holiday area

self-ˈdriving = DRIVERLESS

self-emˈployed *adj.* working for yourself and earning money from your own business

self-esˈteem *noun* [U] (**PSYCHOLOGY**) a good opinion of your own character and abilities: *a man with high/low self-esteem*

self-ˈevident *adj.* that does not need any proof or explanation; clear

self-exˈplanatory *adj.* clear and easy to understand; not needing to be explained: *The book's title is self-explanatory.*

self-ˈharm *noun* [U] (**PSYCHOLOGY**) the practice of deliberately hurting yourself, for example by cutting yourself, because you have serious emotional or mental problems ▸ **self-harm** *verb* [I]

self-ˈhelp *adj.* [only before noun] (**PSYCHOLOGY**) designed to help people solve their problems for themselves, rather than depending on other people for help: *It's a self-help book for anyone dealing with grief.* ▸ **self-help** *noun* [U]

selfie /ˈselfi/ *noun* [C] (*informal*) a photo of yourself that you take, usually with a smartphone or WEBCAM, and often put on SOCIAL MEDIA

self-imˈportant *adj.* thinking that you are more important than other people **SYN** arrogant ▸ **self-imˈportance** *noun* [U] ▸ **self-importantly** *adv.*

self-imˈprovement *noun* [U] the process by which a person improves their knowledge, character, etc. by their own efforts

self-inˈdulgent *adj.* allowing yourself to have or do things that you like, especially when you do this too much or too often ▸ **self-inˈdulgence** *noun* [U]

self-ˈinterest *noun* [U] thinking about what is best for you rather than for other people

selfish /ˈselfɪʃ/ *adj.* thinking only about your own needs or wishes and not about other people's: *a selfish attitude* ◇ *I'm sick of your selfish behaviour!* **OPP** selfless, unselfish ⊃ look at **self-centred** ▸ **selfishly** *adv.* ▸ **selfishness** *noun* [U]

self-ˈisolate *verb* [I] (**HEALTH**) to avoid contact with other people in order to prevent the spread of infection ▸ **self-isoˈlation** *noun* [U]

selfless /ˈselfləs/ *adj.* thinking more about other people's needs or wishes than your own **OPP** selfish ⊃ look at **unselfish**

self-ˈmade *adj.* having become rich or successful by your own efforts: *a self-made millionaire*

self-oˈpinionated = OPINIONATED

self-ˈpity *noun* [U] the state of thinking too much about your own problems or troubles and feeling sorry for yourself

self-ˈportrait *noun* [C] (**ART**) a picture that you draw or paint of yourself

self-raising ˈflour (*BrE*) (*AmE* **self-rising flour**) *noun* [U] flour that contains BAKING POWDER (= a powder that makes cakes, etc. rise during cooking) ⊃ look at **plain flour**

self-reˈliant *adj.* not depending on help from anyone else ⊃ look at **reliant**

self-reˈspect *noun* [U] a feeling of being proud of yourself and that what you do, say, etc. is right and good: *Old people need to keep their dignity and self-*

respect. ⊃ look at **respect**[1] (1) ▶ **self-respecting** adj.
[only before noun] (often in negative sentences): No self-respecting language student (= nobody who is serious about learning a language) should be without this book .

,self-re'straint noun [U] the ability to stop yourself doing or saying sth, because you know it is better not to do or say it: She **exercised** all her **self-restraint** and kept quiet.

,self-'righteous adj. believing that you are always right and other people are wrong, so that you are better than other people ⊃ look at **righteous** ▶ self-righteously adv. ▶ self-righteousness noun [U]

,self-rising 'flour (AmE) = SELF-RAISING FLOUR

,self-'sacrifice noun [U] giving up what you need or want, in order to help others

,self-'satisfied adj. too pleased with yourself or with what you have done **SYN** smug

,self-'service adj. (used about a shop, petrol station, restaurant, etc.) where you serve yourself and then pay for the goods

,self-'study noun [U] (EDUCATION) the activity of learning about sth without a teacher to help you ▶ self-study adj.

,self-'styled adj. [only before noun] using a name or title that you have given yourself, especially when you do not have the right to do it: the self-styled king of fashion

,self-suf'ficient adj. able to produce or provide everything that you need without help from other people or having to buy from other people

sell ৰ **A1** /sel/ verb (pt, pp sold /səʊld/)
• EXCHANGE FOR MONEY **1** [T, I] ~ **(sb) (sth) (at/for sth)**; ~ **(sth) (to sb) (at/for sth)** to give sth to sb who pays for it and is then the owner of it: We are going to sell our car. ◊ Would you sell me your ticket? ◊ I sold my guitar to my neighbour for £200. ◊ I offered them a lot of money but they wouldn't sell. **2** [T] to offer sth for people to buy: Excuse me, do you sell stamps? ◊ to sell insurance/advertising space
• BE BOUGHT **3** [I, T] ~ **(for/at sth)** to be bought by people in the way or in the numbers mentioned; to be offered at the price mentioned: These watches sell at £1 000 each in the shops but you can have this one for £500. ◊ Her books sell well abroad. ◊ This newspaper sells over a million copies a day.
• PERSUADE **4** [T] to make people want to buy sth: They rely on advertising to sell their products. ⊃ noun for senses 1 to 4 is **sale 5** [T] ~ **sth/yourself to sb** to persuade sb to accept sth; to persuade sb that you are the right person for a job, position, etc: Now we have to try and sell the idea to the management.
IDM be sold on sth (informal) to be very enthusiastic about sth
PHR V sell sth off to sell sth in order to get rid of it, often at a low price: The shops sell their remaining winter clothes off in the spring sales. sell out | be sold out (used about tickets for a concert, football game, etc.) to be all sold sell out (of sth) | be sold out (of sth) to sell all of sth so that no more is available to be bought: I'm afraid we've sold out of bread. sell up to sell everything you own, especially your house, your business, etc. (in order to start a new life, move to another country, etc.)

'sell-by date noun [C] (BrE) the date printed on food packages after which the food should not be sold: This milk is past its sell-by date.

seller /'selə(r)/ noun [C] **1** (often in compounds) a person or business that sells: a bookseller ◊ a flower seller **OPP** buyer **2** something that is sold, especially in the amount or way mentioned: This magazine is a big seller in the 25-40 age group. ⊃ look at **bestseller**

'selling price noun [C] (FINANCE) the price at which sth is sold ⊃ look at **asking price**, **cost price**

Sellotape™ /'seləteɪp/ (also sticky tape) (BrE) (AmE Scotch tape™) noun [U] a type of clear sticky tape that is sold in rolls and used for sticking things ⊃ look at **tape**[1] (1) ▶ sellotape verb [T]

'sell-out noun [C, usually sing.] **1** a play, concert, etc. for which all the tickets have been sold: Next week's final is likely to be a sell-out. ◊ The band are on a sell-out tour. **2** a situation in which sb does sth that fails to support a person or group that trusted them: The workers see the deal as a union sell-out to management.

selves /selvz/ plural of **self**

semantic /sɪ'mæntɪk/ adj. (LANGUAGE) connected with the meaning of words and sentences ▶ semantically /-kli/ adv.

semantics /sɪ'mæntɪks/ noun [U] (LANGUAGE) **1** the study of the meanings of words and phrases **2** the meaning of words and phrases: the semantics of the language

semblance /'semblans/ noun [sing., U] ~ **of sth** (formal) the appearance of being sth or of having a certain quality

semen /'siːmən/ noun [U] (BIOLOGY) the liquid that is produced by the male sex organs containing SPERM (= the seed necessary for making babies)

semester /sɪ'mestə(r)/ noun [C] (EDUCATION) (especially in North America) one of the two periods that the school or college year is divided into: the spring/fall semester ⊃ look at **term**[1] (2), **trimester** (2)

semi /'semi/ noun [C] (pl. semis) (BrE, informal) a house that is joined to another house with a shared wall on one side ⊃ look at **semi-detached**

semi- /'semi/ prefix (in nouns and adjectives) half; partly: semicircular ◊ semi-final

,semi-'arid adj. (GEOGRAPHY) (used about land or climate) dry; with little rain

semibreve /'semibriːv/ (BrE) (AmE whole note) noun [C] (MUSIC) a note that lasts as long as four CROTCHETS ⊃ note at **crotchet** ⊃ picture at **music**

semicircle /'semisɜːkl/ noun [C] one half of a circle; sth that is arranged in this shape: I want you all to sit **in a** semicircle. ⊃ picture at **circle**[1] ▶ semicircular /,semi'sɜːkjələ(r)/ adj.

,semi,circular ca'nals noun [pl.] (ANATOMY) three SEMICIRCULAR tubes in the INNER EAR, that are filled with liquid and are connected together. The semicircular canals are important for the body's balance. ⊃ picture at **ear**

semicolon /,semi'kəʊlən, -lɒn/ noun [C] (LANGUAGE) a mark (;) used for separating parts of a sentence or items in a list

semiconductor /,semikən'dʌktə(r)/ noun [C] (PHYSICS) a solid substance that allows heat or electricity to pass through it or along it in particular conditions ⊃ look at **conductor** (3)

,semi-de'tached adj. (used about a house) joined to another house with a shared wall on one side ⊃ look at **semi**

,semi-'final noun [C] (SPORT) one of the two games in a sports competition that decide which players or teams will play each other in the final ⊃ look at **final**[2] (1), **quarter-final** ▶ semi-'finalist noun [C]

seminar ৰ+ **B2** **S** /'semɪnɑː(r)/ noun [C] **1** (EDUCATION) a class at a university, college, etc. in which a small group of students discuss or study a subject with a teacher: *Teaching is by lectures and seminars.* ◇ *a graduate seminar* ◇ *a seminar room* ⊃ note at **subject**[1] **2 (BUSINESS)** a meeting for business people in which working methods, etc. are taught or discussed: *a one-day management seminar*

,semi-'precious *adj.* (used about a JEWEL) less valuable than the most valuable types of JEWELS

semiquaver /'semikweɪvə(r)/ (*BrE*) (*AmE* **sixteenth note**) *noun* [C] (**MUSIC**) a note that lasts half as long as a QUAVER ⊃ note at **crotchet** ⊃ picture at **music**

,semi-'skilled *adj.* (used about workers) having some special training or qualifications, but less than SKILLED people

semitone /'semitəʊn/ (*BrE*) (*AmE* **half step, half-tone**) *noun* [C] (**MUSIC**) the shortest step between notes in a musical scale, for example between C♯ and D, or B♭ and B ⊃ look at **tone**[1] (5)

semolina /,semə'li:nə/ *noun* [U] large hard grains of WHEAT used for making sweet dishes and PASTA

SEN /,es iː 'en/ (*also* **SEND** /send/) *abbr.* (*BrE*) (**EDUCATION**) the educational needs of children who have physical problems or difficulty learning (the abbreviation for 'special educational needs' or 'special educational needs and disability'): *The government should do more to support pupils with SEN.*

senate /'senət/ (*usually* **the Senate**) *noun* [sing.] (**POLITICS**) one of the two groups of elected politicians who make laws in the government in some countries, for example the US ⊃ look at **congress** (2), **House of Representatives**

senator 🔒+ **C1** /'senətə(r)/ (*often* **Senator**) *noun* [C] (*abbr.* **Sen.**) (**POLITICS**) a member of a SENATE: *Senator McCarthy*

send 🔒 **A1** /send/ *verb* [T] (*pt, pp* **sent** /sent/) **1 ~ sth (to sb/sth); ~ (sb) sth** to make sth go or be taken somewhere, especially by post, radio, email etc: *to send a letter/parcel/message to somebody* ◇ *Don't forget to send me a postcard.* **2** to tell sb to go somewhere or to do sth; to arrange for sb to go somewhere: *My company is sending me on a training course next month.* ◇ *She sent the children to bed early.* ◇ *to send somebody to prison* ◇ *I'll send somebody round to collect you at 10.00.* **3** to cause sb/sth to move in a particular direction, often quickly or as a reaction that cannot be prevented: *I accidentally pushed the table and sent all the drinks flying.* **4 ~ sb (to/into sth)** to make sb have a particular feeling or enter a particular state: *The movement of the train sent me to sleep.*
IDM give/send sb your love → LOVE[1]
PHRV send for sb/sth to ask for sb to come to you; to ask for sth to be brought or sent to you: *Quick! Send for an ambulance!* send sb in to order sb to go to a place to deal with a difficult situation: *Troops were sent in to restore order.* send sth in to send sth to a place where it will be officially dealt with: *I sent my application in three weeks ago but I still haven't had a reply.* send off (for sth) | send away (to sb) (for sth) to write to sb and ask for sth to be sent to you: *I sent off for a free sample.* send sb off (**SPORT**) to order a player who has broken a rule to leave the field and not to return send sth off to post sth: *I'll send the information off today.* send sth out **1** to send sth to a lot of different people or places: *We sent out the invitations two months before the wedding.* **2** to produce sth, for example light, heat, sound, etc. send sb/sth up (*BrE, informal*) to make people laugh at sb/sth by copying them in a funny way

sender /'sendə(r)/ *noun* [C] a person who sends sth: *The sender's name appears at the top of the email.*

senile /'si:naɪl/ *adj.* (**PSYCHOLOGY**) behaving in a confused and strange way, and unable to remember things because of old age: *I think she's going senile.* ▸ **senility** /sə'nɪləti/ *noun* [U]

senior[1] 🔒 **B2** /'si:niə(r)/ *adj.* **1 ~ (to sb)** having a high or higher position in a company, organization, etc: *a senior lecturer/officer/manager* ◇ *senior management* ◇ *He's senior to me.* **OPP** **junior**[1] **2 Senior** (*abbr.* **Snr, Sr, Sr.**) used after the name of a man who has the same name as his son, to avoid CONFUSION **OPP** **junior**[1] **3** (*BrE*) (**EDUCATION**) (used in schools) for children over the age of 11 or 13 **4** (*AmE*) (**EDUCATION**) connected with the final year in a HIGH SCHOOL or college ⊃ look at **junior**[1] (4)

senior[2] /'si:niə(r)/ *noun* [C] **1** somebody who is older or of a higher position (than one or more other people): *My oldest sister is ten years my senior.* ◇ *She felt undervalued, both by her colleagues and her seniors.* **OPP** **junior**[2] **2** (**EDUCATION**) one of the older students at a school **3** (*AmE*) (**EDUCATION**) a student in the final year of school, college or university: *high school seniors* ⊃ look at **junior**[2] (3)

,senior 'citizen *noun* [C] an older person, especially sb who has retired from work ⊃ look at **pensioner**

,senior 'high school (*also* ,senior 'high) *noun* [C, U] (**EDUCATION**) (in the US and Canada) a school for young people between the ages of 14 and 18 ⊃ look at **junior high school**

seniority /,si:ni'ɒrəti/ *noun* [U] the position or importance that a person has in a company, organization, etc. in relation to others: *The names are listed below in order of seniority.*

,senior 'nursing officer *noun* [C] (*BrE*) = MATRON (1)

sensation 🔒+ **C1** /sen'seɪʃn/ *noun* **1** [C] a feeling that is caused by sth affecting your body or part of your body: *a pleasant/unpleasant/tingling sensation* **SYN** **feeling 2** [U] the ability to feel when touching or being touched: *For some time after the accident he had no sensation in his legs.* **SYN** **feeling 3** [C, usually sing.] a general feeling or impression that is difficult to explain: *I had the peculiar sensation that I was floating in the air.* **SYN** **feeling 4** [C, usually sing.] great excitement, surprise or interest among a group of people; sb/sth that causes this excitement: *The young American caused a sensation by beating the top player.*

sensational /sen'seɪʃənl/ *adj.* **1** causing, or trying to cause, a feeling of great excitement, surprise or interest among people: *This magazine specializes in sensational stories about the rich and famous.* ⊃ note at **newspaper 2** (*informal*) extremely good or beautiful; very exciting **SYN** **fantastic** ▸ **sensationally** /-nəli/ *adv.*

sensationalism /sen'seɪʃənəlɪzəm/ *noun* [U] a way of getting people's interest by using shocking words or by presenting facts and events as worse or more shocking than they really are ▸ **sensationalist** /-lɪst/ *adj.*: *sensationalist headlines*

sense[1] 🔒 **A2** 🅾 /sens/ *noun*
• UNDERSTANDING/JUDGEMENT **1** [U, sing.] the ability to understand sth; the ability to recognize what sth is or what its value is: *She seems to have lost all sense of reality.* ◇ *I like him — he's got a great sense of humour.* ◇ *I'm always getting lost. I've got absolutely no sense of direction.* ◇ *Good business sense made her a millionaire.* ◇ *He's got absolutely no dress sense* (= he dresses very badly). **2** [U] **~ (in sth/doing sth)** the ability to think or act in a reasonable or sensible way;

good judgement: *I think there's a lot of sense in what you're saying.* ◇ *There's no sense in going any further — we're obviously lost.* ◇ *What's the sense in making things more difficult for yourself?* ◇ *At least he had the sense to stop when he realized he was making a mistake.* ◄ look at **common sense**

• MEANING **3** [C] (**LANGUAGE**) (used about a word, phrase, etc.) a meaning: *This word has two senses.*

• SIGHT, HEARING, ETC. **4** [C] (**BIOLOGY**) one of the five natural physical powers of sight, hearing, smell, taste and touch, that people and animals have: *I've got a cold and I've lost my sense of smell.* ◇ *Dogs have an acute sense of hearing.*

• FEELING **5** [sing.] a feeling of sth: *I felt a tremendous sense of relief when the exams were finally over.* ◇ *She only visits her family out of a sense of duty.* ◇ *the sense organs* (= eyes, ears, etc.) ◄ picture at **skin¹**

IDM **come to your senses** to finally realize that you should do sth because it is the most sensible thing to do **in a sense** in one particular way but not in other ways; partly: *In a sense you're right, but there's more to the matter than that.* **make sense** **1** to be possible to understand; to have a clear meaning: *What does this sentence mean? It doesn't make sense to me.* **2** (used about an action) to be sensible or logical: *I think it would make sense to wait for a while before making a decision.* **make sense of sth** to manage to understand sth that is not clear or is difficult to understand: *I can't make sense of these instructions.*

sense² ⁊ **B2** /sens/ *verb* [T] (not used in the progressive tenses) to realize or become conscious of sth; to get a feeling about sth even though you cannot see it, hear it, etc: *He sensed her unease.* ◇ *I sensed that something was wrong as soon as I went in.*

senseless /'sensləs/ *adj.* **1** having no meaning or purpose **2** unconscious: *He was beaten senseless.*

sensibility /ˌsensə'bɪləti/ *noun* (*pl.* -ies) **1** [U, C] the ability to understand and experience deep feelings, for example in art, literature, etc. **2** sensibilities [pl.] a person's feelings, especially when they are easily offended

sensible ⁊ **B1** /'sensəbl/ *adj.* (used about people and their behaviour) able to make good judgements based on reason and experience; practical: *a sensible person/decision/precaution* ◇ *Stop joking and give me a sensible answer.* ◇ *I think it would be sensible to leave early, in case there's a lot of traffic.* **OPP** **foolish**, **silly** ▶ **sensibly** /-bli/ *adv.*: *Let's sit down and discuss the matter sensibly.*

sensitive ⁊ **B2** **W** /'sensɪtɪv/ *adj.*

• THINKING OF FEELINGS **1** ~ (**to sth**) showing that you are conscious of and able to understand people's feelings, problems, etc: *to be sensitive to somebody's feelings/wishes* ◇ *It wasn't very sensitive of you to keep mentioning her boyfriend. You know they've just split up.* **OPP** **insensitive**

• TO PAIN, COLD, ETC. **2** ~ (**to sth**) easily hurt or damaged; painful, especially if touched: *a new cream for sensitive skin* ◇ *My teeth are very sensitive to hot or cold food.*

• EASILY UPSET **3** ~ (**about/to sth**) easily upset, offended or annoyed, especially about a particular subject: *She's still a bit sensitive about her divorce.* ◇ *He's very sensitive to criticism.* **OPP** **insensitive**

• SUBJECT/SITUATION **4** (used about a subject, a situation, etc.) needing to be dealt with carefully because it is likely to cause anger or trouble: *This is a sensitive period in the negotiations between the two countries.*

• SCIENTIFIC INSTRUMENT **5** (used about a scientific instrument, a piece of equipment, etc.) able to measure very small changes
▶ **sensitively** *adv.*: *The investigation will need to be handled sensitively.* ▶ **sensitivity** ⁊+ **C1** /ˌsensə'tɪvəti/

noun [U]: *I think your comments showed a complete lack of sensitivity.*

sensor /'sensə(r)/ *noun* [C] (**PHYSICS**) a device that can react to light, heat, pressure, etc. in order to make a machine, etc. do sth or show sth: *security lights with an infrared sensor* (= that come on when a person is near them)

sensory **W** /'sensəri/ *adj.* (**BIOLOGY**) connected with your physical senses: *sensory organs* ◇ *sensory deprivation*

sensual /'senʃuəl/ *adj.* connected with physical or sexual pleasure: *the sensual rhythms of Latin music* ▶ **sensuality** /ˌsenʃu'æləti/ *noun* [U]

sensuous /'senʃuəs/ *adj.* giving pleasure to the mind or body through the senses: *the sensuous feel of pure silk* ▶ **sensuously** *adv.* ▶ **sensuousness** *noun* [U]

sent /sent/ *past tense, past participle of* **send**

sentence¹ ⁊ **A1** /'sentəns/ *noun* [C] **1** (**GRAMMAR**) a group of words containing a subject and a verb, that expresses a statement, a question, etc. When a sentence is written, it begins with a capital letter and ends with a full stop. ◄ look at **phrase¹ 2** (**LAW**) the punishment given by a judge to sb who has been found guilty of a crime: *20 years in prison was a very harsh sentence.* ◄ note at **court¹**

sentence² ⁊ **B2** /'sentəns/ *verb* [T] ~ **sb** (**to sth**) (**LAW**) (used about a judge) to tell sb who has been found guilty of a crime what the punishment will be: *The judge sentenced her to three months in prison for shoplifting.* ◄ note at **crime**

sentiment ⁊+ **C1** /'sentɪmənt/ *noun* **1** [C, U] (*formal*) an attitude or opinion that is often caused or influenced by emotion: *Public sentiment is against any change to the law.* **2** [U] feelings such as sympathy, romantic love, being sad, etc. that influence sb's action or behaviour (sometimes in situations where this is not appropriate): *There's no room for sentiment in business.*

sentimental /ˌsentɪ'mentl/ *adj.* **1** producing emotions such as sympathy, romantic love, or being sad, which may be too strong or not appropriate; feeling these emotions too much: *How can you be sentimental about an old car!* ◇ *a sentimental love song* **2** connected with happy memories or feelings of love rather than having any financial value: *The jewellery wasn't worth much but it had great sentimental value to me.* ▶ **sentimentality** /ˌsentɪmen'tæləti/ *noun* [U] ▶ **sentimentally** /ˌsentɪ'mentəli/ *adv.*

sentry /'sentri/ *noun* [C] (*pl.* -ies) a soldier who stands outside a building and guards it

SEO /ˌes i: 'əʊ/ *abbr.* the process of making a website appear high on a list of results given by a SEARCH ENGINE (the abbreviation for 'search engine optimization')

sepal /'sepl/ *noun* [C] (**BIOLOGY**) a part of a flower, like a leaf, that lies under and supports the PETALS (= the coloured parts that make up the head of the flower) ◄ look at **calyx** ◄ picture at **flower¹**

separable /'sepərəbl/ *adj.* able to be separated **OPP** **inseparable**

separate¹ ⁊ **A2** **W** /'seprət/ *adj.* **1** ~ (**from sth/sb**) apart; not together: *You should always keep your cash separate from your credit cards.* **2** different; not connected: *It happened on three separate occasions.*

separate² ⁊ **B1** **W** /'sepəreɪt/ *verb* **1** [I, T] ~ (**sb/sth**) (**from sb/sth**) to stop being together; to cause people or things to stop being together: *I think we should separate into two groups.* ◇ *The friends separated at* the airport. ◇ *I got separated from my friends in the crowd.* **2** [T] **~ sb/sth (from sb/sth)** to keep people or things apart; to be between people or things with the result that they are apart: *The two sides of the city are separated by the river.* ◇ *The girls are separated from the boys.* ⊃ look at **divide¹** (4) **3** [I] to stop living together as a couple with your wife, husband or partner: *His parents separated when he was young.*

separated /'separeɪtɪd/ *adj.* not living together as a couple any more: *My wife and I are separated.*

separately ⓦ /'seprətli/ *adv.* apart; not together: *Shall we pay separately or all together?*

separation 🔑+Ⓒ❶ ⓦ /,sepə'reɪʃn/ *noun* **1** [U, C] **~ (from sb/sth)** the act of separating or being separated; a situation or period of being apart **2** [C] an agreement where a couple decide not to live together any more: *a trial separation*

separatist /'seprətɪst/ *noun* [C] (**POLITICS**) a member of a group of people within a country who want to separate from the rest of the country and form their own government ▸ **separatism** /-prətɪzəm/ *noun* [U] ▸ **separatist** *adj.*

sepsis /'sepsɪs/ *noun* [U] (**HEALTH**) a serious infection of the blood or part of the body

sept- /sept, sep't/ *prefix* (in nouns, adjectives and adverbs) seven; having seven: *septet* ◇ *septennial*

September ⒶⒷ /sep'tembə(r)/ *noun* [U, C] (*abbr.* Sept.) the ninth month of the year, between August and October

septet /sep'tet/ *noun* [C] (**MUSIC**) **1** a group of seven musicians or singers **2** a piece of music for seven musicians or singers

septic /'septɪk/ *adj.* (**HEALTH**) (used about a wound or part of the body) containing harmful bacteria that cause infection: *The wound went septic.*

septicaemia (*BrE*) (*AmE* **septicemia**) /,septɪ'si:miə/ *noun* [U] (**HEALTH**) infection of the blood by poisoning bacteria ⓈⓎⓃ **blood poisoning**

septum /'septəm/ *noun* [C] (*pl.* **septa** /-tə/) (**ANATOMY**) a thin part that separates two hollow areas in the body, for example the part of the nose between the NOSTRILS (= the openings in the nose)

sequel /'si:kwəl/ *noun* [C] **~ (to sth)** **1** (**ARTS AND MEDIA**, **LITERATURE**) a book, film, etc. that continues the story of the one before **2** something that happens after, or is the result of, an earlier event

sequence¹ 🔑 ⒷⒶ ❶ /'si:kwəns/ *noun* **1** [C] (**MATHEMATICS**) a number of things (actions, events, etc.) that happen or come one after another: *Complete the following sequence: 1, 4, 8, 13, …* **2** [U] the order in which a number of things happen or are arranged: *The photos are in sequence.*

sequence² /'si:kwəns/ *verb* [T] **1** to arrange things into a sequence **2** (**BIOLOGY**) to order in which a set of GENES (= the units inside a cell that control particular qualities in a living thing) or parts of MOLECULES are arranged: *The human genome has now been sequenced.* ▸ **sequencing** *noun* [U]: *a gene sequencing project*

sequential /sɪ'kwenʃl/ *adj.* (*formal*) following in order of time or place: *sequential data processing* ▸ **sequentially** /-ʃəli/ *adv.*: *data stored sequentially on the computer*

sequin /'si:kwɪn/ *noun* [C] a small shiny round piece of metal or plastic that is attached to clothing as decoration ▸ **sequinned** *adj.*

serenade /,serə'neɪd/ *noun* [C] (**MUSIC**) **1** a song or tune played or sung at night by a lover outside the window of the woman he loves **2** a gentle piece of music in several parts, usually for a small group of instruments ▸ **serenade** *verb* [T]: *We were serenaded by a string quartet.*

serene /sə'ri:n/ *adj.* calm and peaceful: *a serene smile* ▸ **serenely** *adv.* ▸ **serenity** /-'renəti/ *noun* [U]

serf /sɜ:f/ *noun* [C] (**HISTORY**) a person in the past who lived and worked on land that they did not own, and who had to obey the owner of the land

sergeant /'sa:dʒənt/ *noun* [C] (*abbr.* Sgt) **1** a member of one of the middle ranks in the army and the AIR FORCE **2** an officer with a middle position in the police force

serial¹ 🔑+Ⓒ /'sɪəriəl/ *adj.* [only before noun] **1** doing the same thing in the same way several times; done in the same way several times: *a serial rapist* **2** (used about a story, etc.) published in several parts: *Dickens' serial novels*

serial² /'sɪəriəl/ *noun* [C] (**ARTS AND MEDIA**) a story in a magazine or on television or radio that is told in a number of parts over a period of time: *the first part of a six-part drama serial*

serial killer *noun* [C] (**LAW**) a person who murders several people one after the other in a similar way

serial number *noun* [C] the number put on sth in order to identify it

series 🔑 ⒶⒷ ❶ /'sɪəri:z/ *noun* [C] (*pl.* **-ies**) **1** (**ARTS AND MEDIA**) a set of television or radio programmes or PODCASTS that deal with the same subject or that have the same characters **2** a number of things that happen one after another and are of the same type or connected: *a series of events* ◇ *There has been a series of burglaries in this district recently.*

series circuit *noun* [C] (**PHYSICS**) a electrical CIRCUIT in which the current follows one path ⊃ look at **parallel circuit**

serious 🔑 ⒶⒷ /'sɪəriəs/ *adj.* **1** bad or dangerous: *a serious accident/illness/offence* ◇ *Pollution is a very serious problem.* ◇ *Her condition is serious and she's likely to be in hospital for some time.* **2** needing to be treated as important; not just for fun: *Don't laugh! It's a serious matter.* ◇ *a serious discussion* **3** **~ (about sth/doing sth)** (used about a person) not joking; thinking about things in a careful and sensible way: *Are you serious about starting your own business* (= are you really going to do it)? ◇ *He's terribly serious. I don't think I've ever seen him laugh.* ◇ *You're looking very serious. Was it bad news?* ▸ **seriousness** *noun* [U]

seriously 🔑 ⒷⒶ /'sɪəriəsli/ *adv.* **1** in a serious way: *Three people were seriously injured in the accident.* ◇ *My mother is seriously ill.* ◇ *It's time you started to think seriously about the future.* **2** used at the beginning of a sentence to show that you are not joking or that you really mean what you are saying: *Seriously, I do appreciate all your help.* ◇ *Seriously, you've got nothing to worry about.* **3** (*informal*) very; extremely: *They're seriously rich.*
ⒾⒹⓂ **take sb/sth seriously** to treat sb/sth as important: *You take everything too seriously! Relax and enjoy yourself.*

sermon /'sɜ:mən/ *noun* [C] (**RELIGION**) a speech on a religious or moral subject that is usually given by a religious leader as part of a service in church

serotonin /,serə'təʊnɪn/ *noun* [U] (**BIOLOGY**, **CHEMISTRY**) a chemical in the brain that affects how messages are sent from the brain to the body, and also affects how a person feels

serpent /ˈsɜːpənt/ *noun* [C] (*formal*) a snake, especially a large one

serrated /səˈreɪtɪd/ *adj.* having a row of sharp points along the edge: *a knife with a serrated edge*

serum /ˈsɪərəm/ *noun* (*pl.* **sera** /-rə/, **serums**) **1** [U] (**BIOLOGY**) the thin liquid that is left after blood has CLOTTED (= formed thick masses) **2** [U, C] (**MEDICINE**) a liquid that is taken from the blood of an animal and given to people to protect them from disease, poison, etc.

servant 🔊 **B1** /ˈsɜːvənt/ *noun* [C] a person who is paid to work in sb's house, doing work such as cooking, cleaning, etc. ⊃ look at **civil servant**

serve 🔊 **A2** /sɜːv/ *verb*
- FOOD/DRINK **1** [T] to give food or drink to sb during a meal; to take an order and then bring food or drink to sb in a restaurant, bar, etc: *Breakfast is served from 7.30 to 9.00 a.m.* **2** [T] (used about an amount of food) to be enough for a certain number of people: *According to the recipe, this dish serves four.*
- IN A SHOP **3** [T, I] to take a customer's order; to give help, sell goods, etc: *There was a long queue of people waiting to be served.*
- BE USEFUL **4** [I, T] to be useful or suitable for a particular purpose: *The judge said the punishment would serve as a warning to others.* ◊ *It's an old car but it will serve our purpose for a few months.*
- PERFORM A DUTY **5** [I, T] to perform a duty or provide a service for the public or for an organization: *During the war, he served in the Army.* ◊ *She became a nurse because she wanted to serve the community.*
- IN PRISON **6** [T] (**LAW**) to spend a period of time in prison as a punishment: *He is currently serving a ten-year sentence for fraud.*
- IN TENNIS, ETC. **7** [I, T] (**SPORT**) to start play by hitting the ball
  IDM **first come, first served** → **FIRST²** **serve sb right** used when sth unpleasant happens to sb and you do not feel sorry for them because you think it is their own fault: *'I feel sick.' 'It serves you right for eating so much.'*

server /ˈsɜːvə(r)/ *noun* [C] (**COMPUTING**) a computer that stores information that a number of computers can share ⊃ look at **client**

service¹ 🔊 **A2** **w** /ˈsɜːvɪs/ *noun*
- PROVIDING STH **1** [C] a system or organization that provides the public with sth that it needs; the job that an organization does: *There is a regular bus service to the airport.* ◊ *the postal service* ◊ *the National Health Service* ⊃ look at **civil service** ⊃ picture at **income** **2** [C, U] (**BUSINESS**) a business whose work involves doing sth for customers but not producing goods; the work that such a service does: *financial/banking/insurance services* ◊ *the service sector* (= the part of the economy involved in this type of business) ⊃ look at **service industry**
- IN A RESTAURANT, HOTEL, ETC. **3** [U] (**BUSINESS**) the work or the quality of work done by sb when serving a customer: *I enjoyed the meal but the service was terrible.* ◊ *Is service included in the bill?* ⊃ look at **service charge**
- WORK/HELP **4** [U, C] work done for sb; help given to sb: *He left the police force after 30 years' service.* ◊ *He offered his services as a driver.*
- ARMY, NAVY, ETC. **5** [C, usually pl., U] (**POLITICS**) the army, the NAVY and the AIR FORCE; the work done by the people in them: *They both joined the services when they left school.* ◊ *Do you have to do military service in your country?*
- OF A VEHICLE/MACHINE **6** [C] (**ENGINEERING**) the checks, repairs, etc. that are necessary to make sure that a machine is working properly: *We take our car for a service every six months.*
- RELIGIOUS CEREMONY **7** [C] (**RELIGION**) a religious ceremony, usually including prayers, singing, etc: *a funeral service*
- IN TENNIS, ETC. **8** [sing.] (*also* **serve** [C]) (**SPORT**) an act of hitting the ball in order to start playing; the way that you hit it; a player's turn to SERVE
- BESIDE A ROAD **9** **services** [sing. + sing./pl. verb] (*also* **service station** [C]) (*both BrE*) a place at the side of a MOTORWAY where there is a petrol station, a shop, a restaurant, etc.

service² /ˈsɜːvɪs/ *verb* [T] (**ENGINEERING**) to examine and, if necessary, repair a car, machine, etc: *All cars should be serviced at regular intervals.*

ˈ**service charge** *noun* [C] **1** (**BUSINESS**) an amount of money that is added to a bill, as an extra charge for a service: *That will be $50, plus a service charge of $2.50.* **2** (*BrE*) (**BUSINESS**) an amount of money that is added to a bill in a restaurant, for example 10% of the total, that goes to pay for the work of the staff **3** an amount of money that is paid to the owner of an apartment building for services such as putting out rubbish, cleaning the stairs, etc.

ˈ**service industry** = TERTIARY INDUSTRY

serviceman /ˈsɜːvɪsmən/ *noun* [C] (*pl.* **-men** /-mən/) a man who is a member of the armed forces

ˈ**service provider** *noun* [C] (**BUSINESS**, **COMPUTING**) a business company that provides a service to customers, especially one that connects customers to the internet: *an internet service provider*

ˈ**service station** = SERVICE¹ (9)

servicewoman /ˈsɜːvɪswʊmən/ *noun* [C] (*pl.* **-women** /-wɪmɪn/) a woman who is a member of the armed forces

serviette /ˌsɜːviˈet/ *noun* [C] a square of cloth or paper that you use when you are eating to keep your clothes clean and to clean your mouth or hands on **SYN** **napkin**

sesame /ˈsesəmi/ *noun* [U] a tropical plant grown for its seeds and their oil, which are used in cooking

session 🔊 **B2** **S** /ˈseʃn/ *noun* **1** [C] a period of doing a particular activity: *She has a session at the gym every week.* ◊ *The whole album was recorded in one session.* **2** [C, U] (**LAW**, **POLITICS**) a formal meeting or series of meetings of a court, parliament, etc.

ˈ**session musician** *noun* [C] a musician who is paid to play on recordings but is not a permanent member of a band

set¹ 🔊 **B1** **S** /set/ *verb* (setting; *pt, pp* set)
- PREPARE/ARRANGE **1** [T] (often used with an adverb or a preposition) to prepare or arrange sth for a particular purpose: *I set my alarm for 6.30.* ◊ *to set the table* (= put the plates, knives, forks, etc. on it)
- EXAMPLE/STANDARD **2** [T] to do sth good that people have to try to copy or achieve: *Try to set a good example to the younger children.* ◊ *He has set a new world record.* ◊ *They set high standards of customer service.*
- WORK/TASK **3** [T] to give sb a piece of work or a task: *We've been set a lot of homework this weekend.* ◊ *I've set myself a target of four hours' study every evening.*
- ARRANGE **4** [T] to decide or arrange sth: *Can we set a limit of two hours for the meeting?* ◊ *They haven't set the date for their wedding yet.*
- PLAY/BOOK/FILM **5** [T, often passive] (used with an adverb or a preposition) (**ARTS AND MEDIA**, **LITERATURE**) (used about the action of a book, play, film, etc.) to be placed in a particular time, situation, etc: *The film is set in sixteenth-century Spain.*

- BE LOCATED **6** [T, often passive] (used with an adverb or a preposition) to be located in a particular place: *The hotel is set in beautiful grounds.*
- PUT/START **7** [T] (used with an adverb or a preposition) to put sth/sb in a particular place or position: *I set the box down carefully on the floor.* **8** [T] (often used with an adverb or a preposition) to cause sb/sth to be in a particular state; to start sth happening: *The rioters set a number of cars on fire.* ◇ *The new government set the prisoners free.*
- SUN/MOON **9** [I] (used about the sun) to go below the HORIZON in the evening **OPP** rise²
- IN JEWELLERY **10** [T, usually passive] **be set (in sth)** (used about a PRECIOUS STONE) to be fixed in a piece of jewellery
- BECOME HARD **11** [I] to become firm or hard: *The concrete will set solid/hard in just a few hours.*
- BONE **12** [T] (MEDICINE) to fix a broken bone in the correct position so that it can get better: *The doctor set her broken leg.*

IDM ❶ For idioms containing **set**, look at the entries for the nouns, adjectives, etc. For example, **set the scene** is at **scene**. **PHR V** **set about sth** to start doing sth, especially dealing with a problem or task: *How would you set about tackling this problem?* **set sth aside** to keep sth to use later: *I try to set aside part of my wages every week.* **set sb/sth back** to delay sb/sth: *The bad weather has set our plans back six weeks.* **set forth** (*formal*) to start a journey **set sth forth** (*formal*) to show or tell sth to sb; to make sth known **set in** to arrive and stay or continue for a period of time: *I'm afraid that the bad weather has set in.* **set off** to leave on a journey: *We set off at three o'clock this morning.* **set sth off** to do sth that starts a reaction: *When this door is opened, it sets off an alarm.* **set on/upon sb** to attack sb suddenly: *He was set upon by a gang of youths on his way home.* **set out** to leave on a journey **set out to do sth** to decide to achieve sth: *He set out to prove that his theory was right.* **set (sth) up** to start a business, an organization, a system, etc. ⊃ note at **organization**

set² 🔒 **B1** ❶ /set/ *noun* [C] **1** ~ **(of sth)** a number of things that belong together: *a set of kitchen knives* ◇ *a spare set of keys* ◇ *a chess set* ◇ *In the first set of questions, you have to fill in the gaps.* **2** [+ sing./pl. verb] a group of people who have similar interests and spend a lot of time together socially ⊃ look at **jet set** **3** (ARTS AND MEDIA) a piece of equipment for receiving TV or radio signals: *a TV set* **4** (ARTS AND MEDIA) the furniture, painted cloth, boards, etc. that are made to be used in a play or film: *a set designer* **5** (SPORT) one section of a match in games such as tennis or VOLLEYBALL: *She won in straight sets* (= without losing a set). **6** (MATHEMATICS) a group of things that have a shared quality **7** (*BrE*) (EDUCATION) a group of school students with a similar ability who are taught together in a particular subject

set³ /set/ *adj.* **1** placed in a particular position: *deep-set eyes* ◇ *Our house is quite set back from the road.* **2** planned or fixed and not changing: *There are no set hours in my job.* **3** [only before noun] (used about a meal in a restaurant) having a fixed price and a limited choice of dishes: *a set dinner/lunch/meal* ◇ *Shall we have the set menu?* **4** ~ **(for sth)**; ~ **(to do sth)** ready, prepared or likely to do sth: *Okay, I'm set — let's go!* ◇ *The Swiss team look set for victory.* ◇ *I was all set to leave when the phone rang.*

IDM **be set against sth/doing sth** to be determined that sth will not happen or that you will not do sth **be set on sth/doing sth** to be determined to do sth: *She's set on a career in acting.*

setback /'setbæk/ *noun* [C] a difficulty or problem that stops you progressing as fast as you would like: *She suffered a major setback when she missed the exams through illness.*

'set square (*BrE*) (*AmE* **triangle**) *noun* [C] (GEOMETRY) an instrument for drawing straight lines and angles, made from a flat piece of plastic or metal in the shape of a TRIANGLE with one angle of 90°

settee /se'ti:/ *noun* [C] (*BrE*) a long soft seat with a back and arms that more than one person can sit on **SYN** sofa

,set 'text *noun* [C] (*BrE*) (EDUCATION) a book that students must study for a particular exam

setting 🔒 **B1** /'setɪŋ/ *noun* [C] **1** ~ **(for sth)** the position sth is in; the place and time in which sth happens: *The hotel is in a beautiful setting, close to the sea.* **2** one of the positions of the controls of a machine: *Cook it in the oven on a low setting.*

settle 🔒 **B2** /'setl/ *verb*
- END AN ARGUMENT **1** [T, I] to put an end to an argument: *They settled the dispute without going to court.* ◇ *We didn't speak to each other for years, but we've settled our differences now.* ◇ *They settled out of court.*
- DECIDE/ARRANGE **2** [T] to decide or arrange sth finally: *Everything's settled. We leave on the nine o'clock flight on Friday.*
- PERMANENT HOME **3** [I] to go and live permanently in a new country, area, town, etc: *A great many immigrants have settled in this country.*
- BECOME COMFORTABLE **4** [I, T] to put yourself or sb else into a comfortable position: *I settled in front of the TV for the evening.* ◇ *She settled herself beside him on the sofa.* **5** [I, T] to become calm or relaxed; to make sb/sth calm or relaxed: *The baby wouldn't settle.*
- COME TO REST **6** [I] to land on a surface and stop moving: *A flock of birds settled on the roof.*
- PAY MONEY **7** [T] to pay money that you owe: *to settle a bill/a debt*

PHR V **settle down 1** to get into a comfortable position, sitting or lying **2** to start having a quieter way of life, especially by staying in the same place or getting married: *She had a number of jobs abroad before she eventually settled down.* **3** to become calm and quiet: *Settle down! It's time to start the lesson.* **settle down to sth** to start doing sth that involves all your attention: *Before you settle down to your work, could I ask you something?* **settle for sth** to accept sth that is not as good as what you wanted: *We're going to have to settle for the second prize.* **settle in/into sth** to start feeling comfortable in a new home, job, etc: *How are the children settling in at their new school?* **settle on sth** to choose or decide sth after considering many different things **settle up (with sb)** to pay money that you owe to sb

settled /'setld/ *adj.* **1** not changing or not likely to change: *More settled weather is forecast for the next few days.* **2** comfortable; feeling that you belong (in a home, a job, a way of life, etc.): *We feel very settled here.*

settlement 🔒 **C1** /'setlmənt/ *noun* [C, U] **1** (LAW) an official agreement that ends an argument; the act of reaching an agreement: *a divorce settlement* ◇ *the settlement of a dispute* **2** (GEOGRAPHY) a place that a group of people have built and live in, where few or no people lived before; the process of people starting to live in a place: *There is believed to have been a prehistoric settlement on this site.* ◇ *the settlement of the American West*

settler 🔒+ **B2** /'setlə(r)/ *noun* [C] (GEOGRAPHY) a person who goes to live permanently in a place where not many people live: *the first white settlers in Australia*

set-top box noun [C] a device that changes a digital TV signal into a form that can be seen on an ordinary TV

set-up ?+ **C1** noun [C, usually sing.] (*informal*) **1** a way of organizing sth; a system: *I've only been here a couple of weeks and I don't really know the set-up.* **2** a situation in which sb tricks you or makes it seem as if you have done sth wrong: *He didn't steal the goods. It was a set-up.*

seven ? **A1** /'sevn/ number 7

seventeen ? **A1** /ˌsevnˈtiːn/ number 17 ▶ **seventeenth** /-ˈtiːnθ/ ordinal number, noun [C]

seventh¹ /'sevnθ/ ordinal number 7th

seventh² /'sevnθ/ noun [C] one of seven equal parts of sth

seventy ? **A1** /'sevnti/ **1** number 70 **2** the seventies noun [pl.] numbers, years or temperatures from 70 to 79 ▶ **seventieth** /-əθ/ ordinal number, noun [C]
IDM **in your seventies** between the ages of 70 and 79

sever /'sevə(r)/ verb [T] (*formal*) **1** to cut sth into two pieces; to cut sth off: *The builders accidentally severed a water pipe.* ◇ *His hand was almost severed in the accident.* **2** to end a relationship or communication with sb: *He has severed all links with his former friends.*

several ? **A2** /'sevrəl/ det., pron. more than two but not very many: *It took her several days to recover from the shock.* ◇ *There were lots of applications for the job — several of them from very well-qualified people.* ◇ *I don't think it's a good idea for several reasons.*

severance /'sevərəns/ noun [sing., U] (*formal*) **1** the act of ending a connection or relationship: *the severance of diplomatic relations* **2** (**BUSINESS**) the act of ending sb's work contract: *severance pay/terms*

severe ? **B2** /sɪˈvɪə(r)/ adj. (severer; severest)
HELP **more severe** and **most severe** are more common.
1 extremely bad or serious: *The company is in severe financial difficulty.* ◇ *He suffered severe injuries in the fall.* ◇ *severe weather conditions* **2** punishing sb in an extreme way when they break rules: *Such terrible crimes deserve the severest punishment.* **3** not kind or showing sympathy, not smiling or showing approval: *I think your criticism of her work was too severe.*
▶ **severely** ? **B2** adv.: *The roof was severely damaged in the storm.* ◇ *The report severely criticizes the Health Service.* ▶ **severity** /-'verəti/ noun [U]: *I don't think you realize the severity of the problem.*

sew /səu/ verb [I, T] (*pt* sewed; *pp* sewn /səun/, sewed)
~ (sth) (on) to join pieces of cloth, or to join sth to cloth, using a needle and THREAD and forming STITCHES: *I can't sew.* ◇ *A button's come off my shirt — I'll have to sew it back on.*
PHRV **sew sth up 1** to join two things by sewing; to repair sth by sewing two things together: *The surgeon sewed up the wound.* **2** [usually passive] (*informal*) to arrange sth so that it is certain to happen or be successful: *I think we've got the deal sewn up.*

sewage /'suːɪdʒ/ noun [U] the waste material from people's bodies that is carried away from their homes through SEWERS (= special pipes)

sewer /'suːə(r)/ noun [C] an underground pipe that carries human waste to a place where it can be treated

sewing /'səuɪŋ/ noun [U] **1** using a needle and THREAD to make or repair things: *I'm hopeless at sewing.* ◇ *a sewing machine* **2** something that is being SEWN: *Where's my sewing?*

sewn /səun/ past participle of **sew**

sex ? **B1** ⓦ /seks/ noun **1** [U] (**BIOLOGY**) the state of being either male or female: *Applications are welcome from anyone, regardless of sex or race.* ◇ *Do you mind what sex your baby is?* **SYN** **gender 2** [C] (**SOCIAL STUDIES**) one of the two groups consisting of all male people or all female people: *the male/female sex* ◇ *He's always found it difficult to get on with the opposite sex* (= women). **3** [U] (**BIOLOGY**) physical activity between two people in which they touch each other's sexual organs, and which may include SEXUAL INTERCOURSE: *to have sex with somebody* ◇ *sex education in schools*

sexism /'seksɪzəm/ noun [U] (**SOCIAL STUDIES**) the unfair treatment of people, especially women, because of their sex; the attitude that causes this ▶ **sexist** /-sɪst/ adj.: *a sexist attitude to women* ◇ *sexist jokes*

sex life noun [C] a person's sexual activities: *ways to improve your sex life*

sextet /seks'tet/ noun [C] (**MUSIC**) **1** a group of six musicians or singers who play or sing together **2** a piece of music for six musicians or singers

sextuplet /'sekstjuplət/ noun [C] one of six children or animals that are born to one mother at the same time

sexual ? **B1** ⓞ /'sekʃuəl/ adj. connected with sex: *sexual problems* ◇ *the sexual organs* ◇ *sexual reproduction* ◇ *a campaign for sexual equality* (= to get fair and equal treatment for both men and women)
⊃ look at **sexy** ▶ **sexually** /-ʃəli/ adv.: *to be sexually attracted to somebody*

sexual harassment noun [U] physical contact, comments about sex, etc. that a person finds annoying and offensive: *She accused her boss of sexual harassment.*

sexual intercourse (*also* intercourse, coitus) noun [U] (*formal*) the physical activity of sex, usually describing the act of a man putting his PENIS inside a woman's VAGINA

sexuality ?+ **C1** ⓦ /ˌsekʃuˈæləti/ noun [U] the nature of sb's sexual activities or desires

sexy ?+ **B2** /'seksi/ adj. (sexier; sexiest) sexually attractive or exciting: *Do you find the lead singer sexy?* ◇ *a sexy dress*

SFX /ˌes ef 'eks/ abbr. = SPECIAL EFFECTS

Sgt abbr. (in writing) = SERGEANT

sh /ʃ/ exclamation used to tell sb to stop making noise: *Sh! People are trying to sleep in here.*

shabby /'ʃæbi/ adj. (shabbier; shabbiest) **1** in bad condition because of having been used or worn too much: *a shabby suit* **2** (used about people) dressed in an untidy way; wearing clothes that are in bad condition **3** (used about the way that sb is treated) unfair; not generous ▶ **shabbily** /-bɪli/ adv.: *a shabbily-dressed man* ◇ *She felt she'd been treated shabbily by her employers.*

shack /ʃæk/ noun [C] a small building, usually made of wood or metal, that has not been built well

shade¹ ? **B2** /ʃeɪd/ noun
• OUT OF THE SUN **1** [U] an area that is out of the direct light of the sun and is darker and cooler than areas in the sun: *It was so hot that I had to go and sit in the shade.*
• IN A PICTURE **2** [C] the dark areas in a picture, especially the use of these to produce variety
• ON A LAMP, ETC. **3** [C] something that keeps out light or makes it less bright: *a lampshade*
• COLOUR **4** [C] ~ (of sth) a type of a particular colour: *a shade of green*

- OF OPINION, FEELING, ETC. **5** [C] a different kind of opinion, feeling, etc: *a word with various shades of meaning*
- SLIGHTLY **6** [sing.] **a ~** a little bit
- FOR THE EYES **7** shades [pl.] (*informal*) = SUNGLASSES

shade² /ʃeɪd/ *verb* [T] **1** to protect sth from direct light; to give shade to sth: *The sun was so bright that I had to shade my eyes.* **2 ~ sth (in)** to make an area of a drawing darker, for example with a pencil: *The trees will look more realistic once you've shaded them in.*

types of shadow

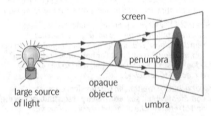

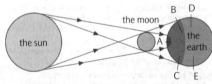

A	umbra: total eclipse
B + C	penumbra: partial eclipse
D + E	no shadow: no eclipse

shadow¹ ⚡**B2** /ˈʃædəʊ/ *noun* **1** [C] a dark shape on a surface that is caused by sth being between the light and that surface: *The dog was chasing its own shadow.* ◇ *The shadows lengthened as the sun went down.* ⊃ look at **penumbra** (2), **umbra** (2) **2** [U] an area that is dark because sth prevents direct light from reaching it: *His face was **in shadow**.* **3** [sing.] a very small amount of sth: *I know without a **shadow of doubt** that he's lying.*
IDM **cast a shadow (across/over sth)** → CAST¹

shadow² /ˈʃædəʊ/ *verb* [T] **1** to follow and watch sb: *The police shadowed the suspect for three days.* **2** to be with sb who is doing a particular job, so that you can learn about it

shadow³ /ˈʃædəʊ/ *adj.* [only before noun] (*BrE*) (**POLITICS**) belonging to the biggest political party that is not in power, with special responsibility for a particular subject, for example education or defence. Shadow ministers would probably become government ministers if their party won the next election: *the shadow Cabinet*

shadowy /ˈʃædəʊi/ *adj.* **1** dark and full of shadows: *a shadowy forest* **2** that not much is known about

SYN **mysterious 3** difficult to see because there is not much light: *A shadowy figure was coming towards me.*

shady /ˈʃeɪdi/ *adj.* (**shadier; shadiest**) **1** giving shade; giving protection from the sun: *I found a shady spot under the trees and sat down.* **2** (*informal*) not completely honest or legal

shaft /ʃɑːft/ *noun* [C] **1** a long, narrow hole in which sth can go up and down or enter or leave: *a lift shaft* ◇ *a mine shaft* **2** a bar that connects parts of a machine so that power can pass between them

shaggy /ˈʃægi/ *adj.* (**shaggier; shaggiest**) **1** (used about hair, material, etc.) long, thick and untidy **2** covered with long, thick, untidy hair: *a shaggy dog*

shake¹ ⚡**A2** /ʃeɪk/ *verb* (*pt* shook /ʃʊk/; *pp* shaken /ˈʃeɪkən/) **1** [I, T] to move or make sb/sth move from side to side or up and down with short, quick movements: *I was so nervous that I was shaking.* ◇ *The whole building shakes when big lorries go past.* ◇ (*figurative*) *His voice shook with emotion as he described the accident.* ◇ *Shake the bottle before taking the medicine.* ◇ *She shook him to wake him up.* **2** [T] to shock or upset sb/sth: *The scandal has shaken the whole country.* **3** [T] to cause sth to be less certain; to cause doubt about sth: *Nothing seems to shake her belief that she was right.*
IDM **shake sb's hand/shake hands (with sb)** | **shake sb by the hand** to take sb's hand and move it up and down, as a greeting or sign of agreement **shake your head** to move your head from side to side, as a way of saying no
PHR V **shake sb/sth off** to get rid of sb/sth; to remove sth by shaking: *I don't seem to be able to shake off this cold.* ◇ *Shake the crumbs off the tablecloth.*

shake² ⚡**B1** /ʃeɪk/ *noun* [C] [usually sing.] the act of shaking sth or being shaken

shaker /ˈʃeɪkə(r)/ *noun* [C] (often in compounds) a container that is used for shaking things: *a salt shaker* ◇ *a cocktail shaker*

ˈshake-up *noun* [C] a complete change in the structure or organization of sth

shaky /ˈʃeɪki/ *adj.* (**shakier; shakiest**) **1** shaking or feeling weak because you are frightened or ill **2** not firm; weak or not very good: *The table's a bit shaky so don't put anything heavy on it.* ◇ *They've had a **shaky start** to the season, losing most of their games.* ▸ **shakily** /-kɪli/ *adv.*

shale /ʃeɪl/ *noun* [U] (**GEOLOGY**) a type of soft stone that splits easily into thin flat layers

ˌshale ˈgas *noun* [U] (**GEOLOGY**) gas that is found in SHALE (= a type of soft stone): *the extraction of shale gas by fracking*

shall ⚡**A2** /ʃəl, *strong form* ʃæl/ *modal verb* (*negative* ˈshall not; *short form* shan't /ʃɑːnt/) (*especially BrE*) **1** used in questions with *I* and *we* for asking advice: *What time shall I come?* ◇ *Where shall we go for our holiday?* **2** used in questions with *I* and *we* for offering to do sth: *Shall I help you carry that box?* ◇ *Shall we drive you home?* **3** used in questions with *we* for suggesting that you do sth with the person or people that you are talking to: *Shall we go out for a meal this evening?* **4** used with *I* and *we* for talking about or predicting the future: *I shall be very happy to see him again.* ◇ *We shan't be arriving until ten o'clock.* ◇ *At the end of this year, I shall have been working here for five years.* **5** (*formal*) used for saying that sth must happen or will definitely happen: *In the rules it says that a player shall be sent off for using bad language.* ⊃ look at **should**

shallot /ʃəˈlɒt/ *noun* [C] a vegetable like a small onion with a very strong taste

shallow ʔ B2 /ˈʃæləʊ/ adj. **1** not deep; with not much distance between top and bottom: *The sea is very shallow here.* ◇ *a shallow dish* **2** not having or showing serious or deep thought: *a shallow person/book* OPP **deep¹** ▶ shallowness noun [U]

shame¹ ʔ B2 /ʃeɪm/ noun **1** [U] the unpleasant feelings of being embarrassed, guilty or sad that you get when you have done sth stupid or wrong; the ability to have these feelings: *She was filled with shame at the thought of how she had lied to her mother.* ◇ *His actions have brought shame on his whole family.* ◇ *He doesn't care how he behaves in public. He's got no shame!* ➲ adjective **ashamed** **2** a shame [sing.] a fact or situation that makes you feel disappointed: *It's a shame about Adam failing his exams, isn't it?* ◇ *What a shame you have to leave so soon.* ◇ *It would be a shame to miss an opportunity like this.*

shame² /ʃeɪm/ verb [T] to make sb feel shame for sth bad that they have done

shameful /ˈʃeɪmfl/ adj. that sb should feel bad about; shocking: *a shameful waste of public money* ▶ shamefully /-fəli/ adv.

shameless /ˈʃeɪmləs/ adj. not feeling embarrassed about doing sth bad; having no shame: *a shameless display of greed and bad manners* ▶ shamelessly adv.

shampoo /ʃæmˈpuː/ noun (pl. -oos) **1** [C, U] a liquid that you use for washing your hair; a similar liquid for cleaning carpets, cars, etc: *shampoo for greasy/dry/normal hair* **2** [C, usually sing.] the act of washing your hair using shampoo ▶ shampoo verb [T] (shampooing; shampoos; pt, pp shampooed)

shamrock /ˈʃæmrɒk/ noun [C, U] a plant with three leaves, which is the national symbol of Ireland

shandy /ˈʃændi/ noun [U, C] (pl. -ies) a drink that is a mixture of beer and LEMONADE

shan't /ʃɑːnt/ short form shall not

shanty /ˈʃænti/ noun [C] (pl. -ies) **1** a small house, built of pieces of wood, metal and CARDBOARD (= very thick paper), where very poor people live, especially on the edge of a big city **2** (also sea shanty) (both BrE) (AmE chantey) (MUSIC) a song that sailors traditionally used to sing while pulling ropes, etc.

ˈshanty town noun [C] an area, usually on the edge of a big city, where poor people live in bad conditions in buildings that they have made themselves

shape¹ ʔ A2 ◐ /ʃeɪp/ noun **1** [C, U] the form of the outer edges or surfaces of sth; an example of sth that has a particular form: *a round/square/rectangular shape* ◇ *a cake in the shape of a heart* ◇ *clothes to fit people of all shapes and sizes* ◇ *I could just make out a dark shape in the distance.* ◇ *The country is roughly square in shape.* **2** [U] (HEALTH) the physical condition of sb/sth; the good or bad state of sb/sth: *She was in such bad shape (= so ill) that she had to be taken to hospital.* ◇ *I go swimming regularly to keep in shape.* **3** [sing.] the ~ of sth the organization, form or structure of sth: *Recent developments have changed the shape of the company.* IDM out of shape **1** not in the usual or correct shape: *My sweater's gone out of shape now that I've washed it.* **2** (HEALTH) not physically fit: *You're out of shape. You should get more exercise.* take shape to start to develop well: *Plans to expand the company are beginning to take shape.*

shape² ʔ B2 ◐ /ʃeɪp/ verb [T] **1** ~ sth (into sth) to make sth into a particular form: *Shape the mixture into small balls.* **2** to influence the way in which sth develops; to cause sth to have a particular form or nature: *His political ideas were shaped by his upbringing.*

shaped ʔ+ B2 /ʃeɪpt/ adj. having the type of shape mentioned: *a huge balloon shaped like a cow* ◇ *almond-shaped eyes* ◇ *an L-shaped room*

shapeless /ˈʃeɪpləs/ adj. not having a clear shape: *a shapeless dress*

share¹ ʔ A1 Ⓦ /ʃeə(r)/ verb **1** [T] ~ sth (out) to divide sth between two or more people: *We shared the pizza out between the four of us.* **2** [I, T] ~ (sth) (with sb) to have, use, do or pay sth together with another person or other people: *Children should learn to share.* ◇ *I share a flat with four other people.* ◇ *We share the same interests.* **3** [T] ~ sth (with sb) to tell sb about sth; to allow sb to know sth: *Sometimes it helps to share your problems with a friend.* **4** [T] ~ sth (with sb) (COMPUTING) to post a message on SOCIAL MEDIA so that other people can see it: *She has been sharing photos with her followers since December.*

share² ʔ B1 Ⓦ /ʃeə(r)/ noun **1** [sing.] ~ (of sth) a part or an amount of sth that has been divided between several people: *We each pay a share of the household bills.* ◇ *I'm willing to take my share of the blame.* **2** [C, usually pl.] ~ (in sth) (BUSINESS, ECONOMICS) one of many equal parts into which the value of a company is divided, that can be sold to people who want to own part of the company: *He sold his shares in the company.* **3** [C] (COMPUTING) the action of sending a message on SOCIAL MEDIA for other people to see: *The video has received thousands of shares on Twitter.* IDM (more than) your fair share of sth → FAIR¹ the lion's share (of sth) → LION

sharecropper /ˈʃeəkrɒpə(r)/ noun [C] (especially AmE) (AGRICULTURE) a farmer who gives part of his or her crop as rent to the owner of the land

shareholder ʔ+ C1 /ˈʃeəhəʊldə(r)/ noun [C] (BUSINESS, ECONOMICS) an owner of shares in a company

shareware /ˈʃeəweə(r)/ noun [U] (COMPUTING) software that is available free for a user to test, after which they must pay if they want to continue using it ➲ look at **freeware**

sharia (also shariah) /ʃəˈriːə/ noun [U] (RELIGION) the system of religious laws that Muslims follow

shark /ʃɑːk/ noun [C] a large sea fish with very sharp teeth and a pointed fin on its back. Some types of shark can attack people swimming.

sharp¹ ʔ B1 /ʃɑːp/ adj.
- EDGE/POINT **1** having a very thin but strong edge or point; able to cut or make a hole in sth easily: *a sharp knife* ◇ *sharp teeth* OPP **blunt**
- SUDDEN **2** (used especially about a change in sth) quick, sudden and large: *a sharp rise/fall in inflation*
- CLEAR **3** clear and definite: *the sharp outline of the hills* ◇ *a sharp contrast between the lives of the rich and the poor*
- MIND, EYES, ETC. **4** able to think, act, understand, see or hear quickly: *a sharp mind* ◇ *You must have sharp eyes if you can read that sign from here.*
- WORDS/COMMENTS **5** (used about words, comments, etc.) said in an angry way; intended to upset sb or be critical
- PAIN **6** (used about pain or an emotion) very strong and sudden: *a sharp pain in the chest* OPP **dull¹**
- CURVES **7** changing direction suddenly: *This is a sharp bend so slow down.*
- TASTE/FEELING **8** (used about sth that affects the senses) strong; not mild or gentle, often causing an unpleasant feeling: *a sharp taste* ◇ *a sharp wind*
- IN MUSIC **9** (symb. ♯) half a note higher than the note with the same letter: *in the key of C sharp minor* ➲ look at **flat²** (5) **10** slightly higher than the correct

note: *That last note was sharp. Can you sing it again?* ⊃ look at **flat²** (6)
▶ **sharpness** *noun* [U]

sharp² /ʃɑːp/ *adv.* **1** (used about a time) exactly: *Be here at three o'clock sharp.* **SYN punctually 2** turning suddenly: *Go to the traffic lights and turn sharp right.* **3** (MUSIC) higher than the correct note ⊃ look at **flat³** (3)

sharp³ /ʃɑːp/ *noun* [C] (*symb.* ♯) (MUSIC) a note that is half a note higher than the note with the same letter ⊃ look at **flat¹** (2) ⊃ picture at **music**

sharpen /ˈʃɑːpən/ *verb* [T, I] to become sharp or sharper; to make sth sharp or sharper: *to sharpen a knife* ◇ *The outline of the trees sharpened as it grew lighter.*

sharpener /ˈʃɑːpnə(r)/ *noun* [C] an object or a tool that is used for making sth sharp: *a pencil/knife sharpener*

sharply /ˈʃɑːpli/ *adv.* **1** in a critical, rough or severe way: *'Is there a problem?' he asked sharply.* **2** suddenly and by a large amount: *The road bends sharply to the left.* ◇ *Share prices fell sharply this morning.* **3** in a way that clearly shows the differences between two things: *Their experiences contrast sharply with those of other children.* **4** quickly and suddenly or loudly: *She rapped sharply on the window.*

shatter ʔ+ **C1** /ˈʃætə(r)/ *verb* **1** [I, T] (used about glass, etc.) to break or make sth break into very small pieces: *I dropped the glass and it shattered on the floor.* ◇ *The force of the explosion shattered the windows.* **2** [T] to destroy sth completely: *Her hopes were shattered by the news.*

shattered /ˈʃætəd/ *adj.* **1** very shocked and upset **2** (*informal*) very tired: *I'm absolutely shattered.*

shave¹ /ʃeɪv/ *verb* [I, T] **~ (sth) (off)** to remove hair from the face or another part of the body with a RAZOR (= a very sharp piece of metal): *I cut myself shaving this morning.* ◇ *When did you shave off your moustache?* ◇ *to shave your legs*
PHR V **shave sth off (sth)** to cut a very small amount from sth

shave² /ʃeɪv/ *noun* [C, usually sing.] an act of SHAVING: *to have a shave* ◇ *I need a shave.*
IDM a close shave/thing → CLOSE³

shaven /ˈʃeɪvn/ *adj.* having been SHAVED: *clean-shaven* (= not having a BEARD or MOUSTACHE)

shaver /ˈʃeɪvə(r)/ (*also* electric razor) *noun* [C] an electric tool that is used for removing hair from the face or another part of the body

shavings /ˈʃeɪvɪŋz/ *noun* [pl.] thin pieces cut from a piece of wood, etc. using a sharp tool, especially a PLANE (= a tool used for making the surface of wood smooth): *wood shavings*

shawl /ʃɔːl/ *noun* [C] a large piece of cloth that is worn by a woman round her shoulders or head or that is put round a baby

she ʔ **A1** /ʃi, *strong form* ʃiː/ *pron.* (LANGUAGE) (the subject of a verb) the female person who has already been mentioned: *'What does your sister do?' 'She's a dentist.'* ◇ *I asked her a question but she didn't answer.*

shear /ʃɪə(r)/ *verb* [T] (*pt* sheared; *pp* shorn /ʃɔːn/, sheared) (AGRICULTURE) to cut the wool off a sheep

shears /ʃɪəz/ *noun* [pl.] a tool that is like a very large pair of SCISSORS and that is used for cutting things in the garden: *a pair of shears* ⊃ picture at **gardening**

sheath /ʃiːθ/ *noun* [C] (*pl.* sheaths /ʃiːðz/) a cover for a knife or other sharp weapon ⊃ picture at **weapon**

shed¹ /ʃed/ *noun* [C] a small building that is used for keeping things or animals in: *a garden shed* ◇ *a bicycle shed* ◇ *a cattle shed*

shed² ʔ+ **C1** /ʃed/ *verb* [T] (shedding; *pt, pp* shed) **1** to lose sth because it falls off: *This snake sheds its skin every year.* ◇ *Autumn is coming and the trees are beginning to shed their leaves.* **2** to get rid of or remove sth that is not wanted
IDM shed blood to kill or injure people **shed light on sth** to make sth clear and easy to understand **shed tears** to cry

she'd /ʃiːd/ *short form* she had; she would

sheep

ram   fleece   lamb   ewe   horn

sheep ʔ **A1** /ʃiːp/ *noun* [C] (*pl.* sheep) an animal that is kept on farms and used for its wool or meat

▼ VOCABULARY BUILDING

A male sheep is a **ram**, a female sheep is a **ewe** and a young sheep is a **lamb**. When sheep make a noise, they **bleat**. This is written as **baa**. The meat from sheep is called **lamb** or **mutton**.

sheepdog /ˈʃiːpdɒg/ *noun* [C] (AGRICULTURE) a dog that has been trained to control sheep

sheepish /ˈʃiːpɪʃ/ *adj.* looking or feeling embarrassed because you have done something silly or wrong: *a sheepish grin* ▶ **sheepishly** *adv.*

sheepskin /ˈʃiːpskɪn/ *noun* [U, C] the skin of a sheep, including the wool, from which coats, etc. are made: *a sheepskin rug/jacket*

sheer ʔ+ **C1** /ʃɪə(r)/ *adj.* **1** [only before noun] used to emphasize the size, degree or amount of sth: *I was impressed by the sheer size of the cathedral.* **2** [only before noun] complete and not mixed with anything else: *It was sheer luck that I happened to be in the right place at the right time.* ◇ *I only agreed out of sheer desperation.* **3** very steep; almost VERTICAL: *Don't walk near the edge. It's a sheer drop to the sea.*

sheet ʔ **A2** **S** /ʃiːt/ *noun* [C] **1** a large piece of cloth used on a bed **2** a piece of paper that is used for writing, printing, etc. on: *a sheet of notepaper* ◇ *Write each answer on a separate sheet.* ⊃ look at **balance sheet 3** a flat, thin piece of any material, especially a square or RECTANGULAR one: *a sheet of metal/glass* **4** a wide, flat area of sth: *The road was covered with a sheet of ice.*

sheet 'lightning *noun* [U] LIGHTNING (= flashes of light in the sky when there is a storm) that appears as a broad area of light in the sky ⊃ look at **forked lightning**

'sheet music *noun* [U] (MUSIC) music printed on separate pieces of paper rather than in a book

sheikh /ʃeɪk, ʃiːk/ *noun* [C] (POLITICS) an Arab prince or leader

sheikhdom /ˈʃeɪkdəm, ˈʃiːk-/ *noun* [C] (POLITICS) an area of land ruled by a SHEIKH

shelf ʔ **B1** /ʃelf/ *noun* [C] (*pl.* shelves /ʃelvz/) a long flat piece of wood, glass, etc. that is fixed to a wall or in a cupboard, used for putting things on: *I put up a shelf in*

'shelf life *noun* [C] [usually sing.] the length of time that food, etc. can be kept before it is too old to be sold or used

shell¹ ₹ **B1** /ʃel/ *noun* **1** [C, U] a hard covering that protects eggs, nuts and some animals: *Some children were collecting shells on the beach.* ◇ *a piece of eggshell* ◇ *Tortoises have a hard shell.* ⊃ picture at **animal 2** [C] a metal container that explodes when it is fired from a large gun **3** [C] the walls or hard outer structure of sth: *The body shell of the car is made in another factory.*
IDM **come out of your shell** to become less shy and more confident when talking to other people **go, retreat, etc. into your shell** to suddenly become shy and stop talking

shell² /ʃel/ *verb* [T] **1** to fire SHELLS from a large gun **2** to take the shell off a nut or other kind of food: *to shell peas*

she'll /ʃiːl/ *short form* she will

shellfish /'ʃelfɪʃ/ *noun* (*pl.* shellfish) **1** [C] a type of animal that lives in water and has a shell **2** [U] these animals eaten as food

shelter¹ ₹ **B1** /'ʃeltə(r)/ *noun* **1** [U] the fact of having a place to live or stay: *to give somebody food and shelter* **2** [U] ~ (from sth) protection from danger or bad weather: *We looked around for somewhere to take shelter from the storm.* **3** [C] a small building that gives protection, for example from bad weather or attack: *a bus shelter* ◇ *an air-raid shelter* **4** [C] a building, usually owned by a charity, where people or animals can stay if they do not have a home, or have been badly treated **SYN** refuge

shelter² ₹ **B2** /'ʃeltə(r)/ *verb* **1** [I] ~ (from sth) to find protection or a safe place: *Let's shelter from the rain under that tree.* **2** [T] ~ sb/sth (from sb/sth) to protect sb/sth; to provide a safe place away from harm or danger: *The trees shelter the house from the wind.*

sheltered /'ʃeltəd/ *adj.* **1** (used about a place) protected from bad weather **2** protected from unpleasant things in your life: *We had a sheltered childhood, living in the country.*

shelve /ʃelv/ *verb* [T] to decide not to continue with a plan, either for a short time or permanently: *Plans for a new motorway have been shelved.*

shelves /ʃelvz/ plural of **shelf**

shelving /'ʃelvɪŋ/ *noun* [U] a set of shelves

shepherd¹ /'ʃepəd/ *noun* [C] (AGRICULTURE) a person whose job is to look after sheep

shepherd² /'ʃepəd/ *verb* [T] to guide and look after people so that they do not get lost

sherbet /'ʃɜːbət/ *noun* [U] (*BrE*) a powder that tastes of fruit and that makes bubbles when you put it in your mouth. It is eaten as a sweet.

sheriff /'ʃerɪf/ *noun* [C] (LAW) (in the US) an officer of the law who is responsible for a particular town or part of a state

sherry /'ʃeri/ *noun* [U, C] (*pl.* -ies) a type of strong Spanish wine; a glass of this wine

she's /ʃiːz, ʃiz/ *short form* she is; she has

Shia /'ʃiːə/ *noun* (*pl.* Shia, Shias) (RELIGION) **1** [U] one of the two main groups of the religion of ISLAM ⊃ look at **Sunni** (1) **2** (*also* Shiite, Shi˙ite /'ʃiːaɪt/) [C] a member of the Shia religious group ⊃ look at **Sunni** (2) ▶ Shiite (*also* Shi˙ite) *adj.*

shied /ʃaɪd/ past tense, past participle of **shy²**

shield¹ /ʃiːld/ *noun* [C] **1** (in past times) a large piece of metal or wood that soldiers carried to protect themselves **2** (*also* riot shield) a piece of equipment made of strong plastic, that the police use to protect themselves from angry crowds **3** a person or thing that is used to protect sb/sth especially by forming a barrier: *The metal door acted as a shield against the explosion.* **4** an object or a drawing in the shape of a shield, sometimes used as a prize in a sports competition

shield² /ʃiːld/ *verb* ~ sb/sth (against/from sb/sth) **1** [T] to protect sb/sth from danger or damage: *I shielded my eyes from the bright light with my hand.* **2** [I] (*BrE*) to keep yourself away from other people for a period of time because you are particularly at risk from a disease

shift¹ ₹ **B2** **S** /ʃɪft/ *verb* [I, T] **1** to move or move sth from one position or place to another: *She shifted uncomfortably in her chair.* ◇ *He shifted his desk closer to the window.* **2** to change your opinion of or attitude towards sth: *Public attitudes towards marriage have shifted over the years.*
IDM **shift the blame/responsibility (for sth) (onto sb)** to make sb else responsible for sth you should do or for sth bad you have done

shift² ₹ **B1** **O** /ʃɪft/ *noun* **1** [C] (in a factory, etc.) one of the periods that the working day is divided into: *to work in shifts* ◇ *shift work/workers* ◇ *to be on the day/night shift* **2** [C + sing./pl. verb] the workers who work a particular shift: *The night shift has/have just gone off duty.* **3** [C] ~ (in sth) a change in your opinion of or attitude towards sth: *There has been a shift in public opinion away from war.* **4** [U] (COMPUTING) one of the keys on a computer keyboard that allows you to write a capital letter: *the shift key*

ˌshifting culti'vation *noun* [U] (AGRICULTURE) a way of farming in some tropical countries in which farmers use an area of land until it cannot be used for growing plants any more, then move on to a new area of land

shifty /'ʃɪfti/ *adj.* (shiftier; shiftiest) (used about a person or their appearance) seeming to be dishonest; looking guilty about sth: *shifty eyes*

Shiite (*also* Shi˙ite) /'ʃiːaɪt/ = SHIA (2)

shimmer /'ʃɪmə(r)/ *verb* [I] to shine with a soft light that seems to be moving: *Moonlight shimmered on the sea.*

shin /ʃɪn/ *noun* [C] (ANATOMY) the front part of the leg from the knee to the foot ⊃ picture at **body**

'shin bone *noun* [C] the inner and larger bone of the two bones in the lower part of the leg between the knee and foot **SYN** tibia ⊃ picture at **body**

shine¹ ₹ **B1** /ʃaɪn/ *verb* (*pt, pp* shone /ʃɒn/) **1** [I] to send out or reflect light; to be bright: *I could see a light shining in the distance.* ◇ *The sea shone in the light of the moon.* **2** [T] to direct a light at sb/sth: *The policeman shone a torch on the stranger's face.* **3** [I] ~ (at/in sth) to be very good at a school subject, a sport, etc: *She has always shone at languages.*

shine² /ʃaɪn/ *noun* [sing.] **1** the bright quality that something has when light is reflected on it **2** the act of cleaning and rubbing sth so that it shines
IDM **(come) rain or shine** → RAIN¹

shingle /'ʃɪŋgl/ *noun* [U] (GEOGRAPHY, GEOLOGY) small pieces of stone lying in a mass on a beach

shingles /'ʃɪŋglz/ *noun* [U] (HEALTH) a disease that affects the nerves and produces a band of painful spots on the skin

'**shin guard** (BrE also '**shin pad**) noun [C] (**SPORT**) a thick piece of material used to protect the lower front part of the leg when playing some sports

shiny 🔊 **B1** /'ʃaɪni/ adj. (shinier; shiniest) causing a bright effect when in light: The shampoo leaves your hair soft and shiny. ◇ a shiny new car

ship[1] 🔊 **A2** /ʃɪp/ noun [C] a large boat used for carrying passengers or goods by sea: Groceries are brought to the island **by ship**. ◇ a cargo/cruise ship

ship[2] 🔊 **B2** /ʃɪp/ verb [T] (-pp-) to send or carry sth by ship or by another type of transport

shipbuilder /'ʃɪpbɪldə(r)/ noun [C] a person or company who makes or builds ships ▸ **shipbuilding** noun [U]

shipment /'ʃɪpmənt/ noun **1** [U] the carrying of goods from one place to another **2** [C] a quantity of goods that are sent from one place to another

shipping 🔊 **C1** /'ʃɪpɪŋ/ noun [U] **1** ships in general or considered as a group **2** the carrying of goods from one place to another: a shipping company

shipwreck /'ʃɪprek/ noun [C, U] an accident at sea in which a ship is destroyed by a storm, rocks, etc. and sinks ❶ A person or a ship that has suffered such an accident has been **shipwrecked**.

shipyard /'ʃɪpjɑːd/ noun [C] a place where ships are repaired or built

shirk /ʃɜːk/ verb [T, I] to avoid doing sth that is difficult or unpleasant, especially because you are too lazy: to shirk your responsibilities ◇ The boss knows who works hard and who shirks.

shirt 🔊 **A1** /ʃɜːt/ noun [C] a piece of clothing made of cotton, etc., worn on the upper part of the body

shiver /'ʃɪvə(r)/ verb [I] ~ **(with sth)** to shake slightly, especially because you are cold or frightened: shivering with cold/fright ▸ **shiver** noun [C]: The thought sent a shiver down my spine.

shoal /ʃəʊl/ noun [C] a large group of fish that feed and swim together

shock[1] 🔊 **B2** /ʃɒk/ noun **1** [C, U] the feeling that you get when sth unpleasant happens suddenly; the situation that causes this feeling: The sudden noise **gave him a shock**. ◇ The bad news **came as a shock** to her. ◇ I'm still suffering **from shock** at the news. ◇ His mother is **in a state of shock**. **2** [U] (**HEALTH**) a serious medical condition of extreme weakness caused by damage to the body: He was **in/went into shock** after the accident. **3** [C] a violent shaking movement (caused by a crash, an explosion, etc.) **4** [C] = ELECTRIC SHOCK

shock[2] 🔊 **B2** /ʃɒk/ verb **1** [T] to cause an unpleasant feeling of surprise in sb: We were shocked by his death. ◇ I'm sorry, I didn't mean to shock you when I came in. **2** [I, T] to make sb feel offended or full of horror: These films deliberately set out to shock. ▸ **shocked** 🔊 **B2** adj.: a shocked expression/look

'**shock absorber** noun [C] a device that is fitted to each wheel of a vehicle in order to reduce the effects of travelling over rough ground, so that passengers can be more comfortable

shocking 🔊 **B2** /'ʃɒkɪŋ/ adj. **1** that offends or upsets people; that is morally wrong: a shocking accident ◇ shocking behaviour/news **2** (especially BrE, informal) very bad (BrE, informal)

'**shock wave** noun [C] (**GEOLOGY**) a movement of very high air pressure that is caused by an explosion, an earthquake, etc. ⊃ picture at **erosion**

shoddy /'ʃɒdi/ adj. (shoddier; shoddiest) **1** made carelessly or with poor quality materials: shoddy goods **2** dishonest or unfair ▸ **shoddily** /-dəli/ adv.

shoe[1] 🔊 **A1** /ʃuː/ noun [C] **1** a type of covering for the foot, usually made of leather or plastic: a pair of shoes ◇ running shoes ◇ What size are your shoes/What is your shoe size? ◇ I tried on a nice pair of shoes but they didn't fit. **2** = HORSESHOE
IDM in my, your, etc. place/shoes → PLACE[1]

shoe[2] /ʃuː/ verb [T] (pt, pp shod /ʃɒd/) to fit a HORSESHOE (= a piece of metal in the shape of a U) on a horse

shoehorn /'ʃuːhɔːn/ noun [C] a curved piece of plastic or metal that you use to help the back of your foot go into your shoe

shoelace /'ʃuːleɪs/ (also lace) (AmE also shoestring) noun [C] a long thin piece of material like string used to fasten a shoe: to tie/untie a shoelace

shoestring /'ʃuːstrɪŋ/ noun [C] (AmE) = SHOELACE
IDM on a shoestring (informal) using very little money: They were living on a shoestring.

shone /ʃɒn/ past tense, past participle of **shine**[1]

shoo[1] /ʃuː/ verb [T] (used with an adverb or a preposition) (shooing; shoos; pt, pp shooed) to make sb/ sth go away by saying 'shoo' and waving your hands: She shooed the children out of the kitchen.

shoo[2] /ʃuː/ exclamation used to tell a child or an animal to go away

shook /ʃʊk/ past tense of **shake**[1]

shoot[1] 🔊 **B1** /ʃuːt/ verb (pt, pp shot /ʃɒt/)
• WITH A GUN **1** [I, T] ~ **(sth) (at sb/sth)** to fire a gun or another weapon: Don't shoot! ◇ She shot an arrow at the target, but missed it. **2** [T, often passive] ~ **sb/sth/ yourself (in sth)** to injure or kill a person or an animal with a gun: The policeman was shot in the arm. ◇ The soldier was **shot dead**. **3** [I, T] (**SPORT**) to hunt and kill birds and animals with a gun as a sport: He goes shooting at the weekends. ⊃ look at **hunting**
• FILM/PHOTO **4** [I, T] (**ARTS AND MEDIA**) to make a film or photo of sth: They shot the scene ten times.
• MOVE FAST **5** [I, T] (used with an adverb or a preposition) to move somewhere quickly and suddenly; to make sth move in this way: The car shot past me at 100 miles per hour.
• PAIN **6** [I] (**HEALTH**) (used about pain) to go very suddenly along part of your body: The pain shot up my leg. ◇ shooting pains in the chest
• IN SPORT **7** [I] ~ **(at sth)** to try to kick, hit or throw the ball into the goal: He should have shot (at goal) instead of passing. ⊃ noun **shot**
PHR V shoot sb/sth down to make sb/sth fall to the ground by shooting them or it: The helicopter was shot down by a missile. shoot up to increase by a large amount; to grow very quickly: Prices have shot up in the past year. ⊃ note at **trend**[1]

shoot[2] 🔊 **C1** /ʃuːt/ noun [C] (**BIOLOGY**) a new part of a plant or tree ⊃ picture at **flower**[1]

shooting 🔊 **B2** /'ʃuːtɪŋ/ noun **1** [C] a situation in which sb is shot with a gun: Two people were injured in a gang-related shooting last night. **2** [U] the sport of shooting animals and birds with guns **3** [U] the process of filming a film

,**shooting** '**star** noun [C] (**ASTRONOMY**) a small METEOR (= a piece of rock in space) that travels very fast and burns with a bright light as it enters the earth's atmosphere

shop[1] 🔊 **A1** /ʃɒp/ (especially BrE) noun [C] a building or part of a building where things are bought and sold: to **open/close a shop** ◇ a cake/shoe shop ◇ When do the shops open?
IDM talk shop → TALK[1]

shop² ɭ **A1** /ʃɒp/ *verb* [I] (-pp-) ~ **(for sth)** to go to a shop or shops in order to buy things: *He's shopping for some new clothes.* ▸ **shopper** *noun* [C]
PHR V **shop around (for sth)** to look at the price and quality of an item in different shops before you decide where to buy it

shopaholic /ˌʃɒpə'hɒlɪk/ *noun* [C] (*informal*) a person who enjoys shopping very much and spends too much time or money doing it

'**shop assistant** (*also* **assistant**) (*both BrE*) (*AmE* **sales clerk, clerk**) *noun* [C] a person whose job is to serve customers in a shop

ˌ**shop 'floor** *noun* [sing.] (*BrE*) **1** an area of a factory where the goods are made by the workers: *to work on the shop floor* **2** the workers in a factory, not the managers

shopkeeper /'ʃɒpkiːpə(r)/ (*also* **storekeeper** *especially in AmE*) *noun* [C] a person who owns or manages a small shop

shoplifting /'ʃɒplɪftɪŋ/ *noun* [U] (**LAW**) the crime of stealing goods from a shop while pretending to be a customer: *He was arrested for shoplifting.* ⊃ look at **lift¹** (6) ▸ **shoplifter** /-tə(r)/ *noun* [C] ⊃ note at **criminal¹**

shopping ɭ **A1** /'ʃɒpɪŋ/ *noun* [U] **1** the activity of going to the shops and buying things: *We always do the shopping on a Friday night.* ◇ *a shopping basket/bag/trolley* **2** (*especially BrE*) the things that you have bought in a shop

'**shopping arcade** = ARCADE (4)

'**shopping centre** *noun* [C] a place where there are many shops, either outside or in a covered building ⊃ look at **mall**

'**shopping mall** (*especially AmE*) = MALL

shore¹ ɭ+ **B2** /ʃɔː(r)/ *noun* [C, U] (**GEOGRAPHY**) the land at the edge of a sea or lake: *The sailors went on shore* (= on land). ⊃ look at **ashore**

shore² /ʃɔː(r)/ *verb*
PHR V **shore sth up 1** to support part of a building or other large structure by placing large pieces of wood or metal against or under it so that it does not fall down **2** to help support sth that is weak or going to fail: *The measures were aimed at shoring up the economy.*

shoreline /'ʃɔːlaɪn/ *noun* [C, usually sing.] (**GEOGRAPHY**) the edge of the sea, the ocean or a lake: *a rocky shoreline*

shorn /ʃɔːn/ *past participle of* **shear**

short¹ ɭ **A1** /ʃɔːt/ *adj.*
• LENGTH/DISTANCE **1** not measuring much from one end to the other: *a short line/distance/dress* ◇ *This essay is rather short.* ◇ *short hair* **OPP** **long** ⊃ *verb* **shorten**
• HEIGHT **2** less than the average height: *a short, fat man* **OPP** **tall**
• TIME **3** not lasting a long time; brief: *a short visit/film* ◇ *She left a short time ago.* ◇ *to have a short memory* (= to only remember things that have happened recently) **OPP** **long** ⊃ *verb* **shorten**
• NOT ENOUGH **4** ~ **(of sth)** not having enough of sth: *We're a bit short of money at the moment.* ⊃ *noun* **shortage** **5** ~ **(on sth)** not having enough of a particular quality: *Your essay is a bit short on detail.* ⊃ *noun* **shortage**
• NAME/WORD **6** ~ **for sth** used as a shorter way of saying sth: *'Bill' is short for 'William'.*
• IMPATIENT **7** ~ **(with sb)** (used about a person) speaking in an impatient and angry way to sb
▸ **shortness** *noun* [U]: *She suffered from shortness of breath.*
IDM **at short notice** → NOTICE¹ **in the long/short term** → TERM¹

short² /ʃɔːt/ *adv.* **1** if you **go short of** or **run short of** sth, you do not have enough of it: *He made sure his family never went short of food.* ◇ *We're running short of coffee.* **2** before the time expected; suddenly: *She stopped short when she saw the accident.* ◇ *His career was cut short by injury.*
IDM **fall short (of sth)** to not be enough; to not reach sth: *The pay rise fell short of the workers' demands.* **short of sth/doing sth** apart from; except for: *Nothing short of a miracle will save the business now.* **stop short of sth/doing sth** → STOP¹

short³ /ʃɔːt/ *noun* [C] **1** (*especially BrE*) a small strong alcoholic drink: *I prefer wine to shorts.* **2** (*informal*) = SHORT CIRCUIT
IDM **in short** in a few words

shortage ɭ+ **B2** /'ʃɔːtɪdʒ/ *noun* [C] a situation where there is not enough of sth: *a food/housing/water shortage* ◇ *a shortage of trained teachers*

shortbread /'ʃɔːtbred/ *noun* [U] a sweet biscuit made with sugar, flour and butter

ˌ**short 'circuit** (*also informal* **short**) *noun* [C] (**PHYSICS**) a bad electrical connection that causes a machine to stop working ▸ **short-'circuit** *verb* [I, T]: *The lights short-circuited.*

shortcoming /'ʃɔːtkʌmɪŋ/ *noun* [C, usually pl.] a fault or weakness

shortcut /'ʃɔːt kʌt/ *noun* [C] a quicker, easier or more direct way to get somewhere or to do sth: *He took a shortcut to school through the park.*

shorten /'ʃɔːtn/ *verb* [T, I] to make sth shorter or to become shorter **OPP** **lengthen**

shortfall /'ʃɔːtfɔːl/ *noun* [C] ~ **(in sth)** the amount by which sth is less than you need or expect: *a shortfall of £50 000 in the annual budget*

shorthand /'ʃɔːthænd/ *noun* [U] (**LANGUAGE**) a method of writing quickly that uses signs or short forms of words: *to write in shorthand* ◇ *a shorthand typist* ⊃ look at **longhand**

'**short-haul** *adj.* (**TOURISM**) that involves transporting people or goods over short distances, especially by plane: *short-haul flights* **OPP** **long-haul**

shortlist /'ʃɔːtlɪst/ *noun* [C, usually sing.] a list of the best people for a job, etc. who have been chosen from all the people who want the job: *She's one of the four people on the shortlist.* ▸ **shortlist** *verb* [T, usually passive]: *Six candidates were shortlisted for the post.*

ˌ**short-'lived** *adj.* lasting only for a short time

shortly ɭ+ **B2** /'ʃɔːtli/ *adv.* **1** soon; not long: *The manager will see you shortly.* **2** in an impatient, angry way

shorts /ʃɔːts/ *noun* [pl.] **1** a type of short trousers ending above the knee that you wear in hot weather, while playing sports, etc. **2** (*AmE*) = BOXER SHORTS

ˌ**short-'sighted** *adj.* **1** (*especially BrE*) (*AmE usually* **nearsighted** /ˌnɪə 'saɪtɪd/) (**HEALTH**) able to see things clearly only when they are very close to you: *I have to wear glasses because I'm short-sighted.* **SYN** **myopic** **OPP** **long-sighted** ⊃ picture on **page 674 2** not considering what will probably happen in the future: *a short-sighted attitude/policy* ▸ **short-sightedness** *noun* [U]

ˌ**short-'staffed** *adj.* (used about an office, a shop, etc.) not having enough people to do the work

ˌ**short 'story** *noun* [C] (**LITERATURE**) a piece of writing that is shorter than a novel

ˌ**short-'tempered** *adj.* if you are **short-tempered**, you get angry very quickly and easily

ˌ**short-'term** ɭ+ **B2** *adj.* lasting for a short period of time from the present: *short-term plans/memory*

'short wave *noun* [C, U] (*abbr.* SW) (**ARTS AND MEDIA, PHYSICS**) a system for sending radio signals: *Short wave is a radio wave of frequency greater than 3 MHz.* ⊃ look at **long wave, medium wave** ⊃ picture at **wavelength**

shot¹ ⓘ **B2** /ʃɒt/ *noun*
- WITH A GUN **1** [C] ~ **(at sb/sth)** an act of firing a gun, etc., or the noise that this makes: *to take a shot at the target* ◊ *The policeman fired a warning shot into the air.*
- IN SPORT **2** [C] the act of kicking, throwing or hitting a ball in order to score a point or a goal: *She scored with a low shot into the corner of the net.* ◊ *Good shot!* **3** (*often* the shot) [sing.] the heavy ball that is used in the sports competition called the SHOT-PUT
- PHOTO **4** [C] (**ARTS AND MEDIA**) a photo or a scene in a film: *I got some good shots of the runners as they crossed the line.*
- TRY **5** [C, usually sing.] ~ **(at sth/doing sth)** (*informal*) an attempt at doing sth: *Let me have a shot at it* (= let me try to do it). ◊ *Just give it your best shot* (= try as hard as you can). **SYN attempt²**
- DRUG **6** [C] (*especially AmE, informal*) (**MEDICINE**) a small amount of a drug that is INJECTED into the body (= put into the body through a needle)
IDM call the shots/tune → CALL¹ like a shot (*informal*) very quickly; without stopping to think about it: *If somebody invited me on a free holiday, I'd go like a shot.* **a long shot → LONG¹**

shot² /ʃɒt/ past tense, past participle of **shoot¹**

shotgun /'ʃɒtɡʌn/ *noun* [C] a long gun that is used for shooting small animals and birds ⊃ note at **gun¹**

'shot-put (*often* the shot-put) *noun* [sing.] (**SPORT**) the event or sport of throwing a heavy metal ball as far as possible

should ⓘ **A1** ⓦ /ʃəd, *strong form* ʃʊd/ *modal verb* (*negative* should not; *short form* shouldn't /'ʃʊdnt/)
1 (used for saying that it is right or appropriate for sb to do sth, or for sth to happen) ought to: *The police should do something about street crime in this area.* ◊ *Children shouldn't be left on their own.* ◊ *I'm tired. I shouldn't have gone to bed so late/I should have gone to bed earlier.* **2** used for giving or for asking for advice: *You should try that new restaurant.* ◊ *Do you think I should phone him?* ◊ *What should I do?* **3** used for saying that you expect sth is true or will happen: *It's 4.30. They should be in New York by now.* ◊ *It should stop raining soon.* **4** (*BrE, formal*) used with I/we instead of *would* in *if* sentences: *I should be most grateful if you could send me …* **5** (*formal*) used to refer to a possible event or situation: *In case/If you should decide to accept, please phone us.* ◊ *Should you decide to accept, please phone us.* **6** used as the past tense of *shall* when we report what sb says: *He asked me if he should come today* (= he asked 'Shall I come today?'). **7** I~imagine, say, think, etc. used to give opinions that you are not certain about

shoulder¹ ⓘ **A2** /'ʃəʊldə(r)/ *noun* **1** (**ANATOMY**) the part of the body between the neck and the top of the arm: *I asked him why he'd done it but he just shrugged his shoulders* (= raised his shoulders to show that he did not know or care). ◊ *She fell asleep with her head on his shoulder.* ⊃ picture at **body 2** -shouldered /ʃəʊldəd/ (in adjectives) having the type of shoulders mentioned: *a broad-shouldered man* **3** [C] a part of a dress, coat, etc. that covers the shoulders
IDM have a chip on your shoulder → CHIP¹ rub shoulders with sb → RUB a shoulder to cry on used to describe a person who listens to your problems and understands how you feel

shoulder² /'ʃəʊldə(r)/ *verb* **1** [T] to accept the responsibility for sth: *to shoulder the blame/responsibility for something* **2** [T, I] to push sb/sth with your shoulder

'shoulder bag *noun* [C] a type of bag that you carry over one shoulder with a long STRAP (= a narrow piece of cloth, leather, etc.)

'shoulder blade *noun* [C] (**ANATOMY**) either of the two large flat bones on each side of the back, below the shoulders **SYN scapula** ⊃ picture at **body**

'shoulder strap *noun* [C] **1** a narrow piece of material on a dress or other piece of clothing that goes over your shoulder from the front to the back **2** a long narrow piece of material, leather, etc. that is part of a bag so that you can carry it over your shoulder

shout ⓘ **A2** /ʃaʊt/ *verb* **1** [I] ~ **(at/to sb)**; ~ **(out)** to speak or cry out in a very loud voice: *There's no need to shout — I can hear you.* ◊ *The teacher shouted angrily at the boys.* ◊ *to shout out in pain/excitement* **2** [T] ~ **sth (at/to sb)**; ~ **sth (out)** to say sth in a loud voice: *'Careful,' she shouted.* ◊ *The captain shouted instructions to his team.* ⊃ look at **scream¹**
▶ **shout** ⓘ **A2** *noun* [C]
PHR V shout sb down to shout so that sb who is speaking cannot be heard: *The speaker was shouted down by a group of protesters.* **shout sth out** to say sth in a loud voice: *The students kept shouting out the answers, so we stopped playing in the end.*

shove /ʃʌv/ *verb* [I, T] (*informal*) to push with a sudden, rough movement: *Everybody in the crowd was pushing and shoving.* ◊ *The policeman shoved the thief*

short-sighted/nearsighted

long-sighted/far-sighted

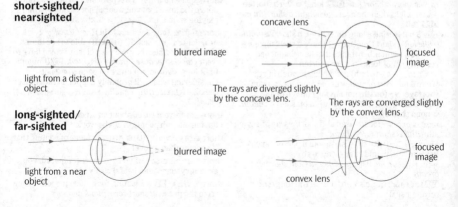

light from a distant object — blurred image

light from a near object — blurred image

concave lens — focused image

The rays are diverged slightly by the concave lens.

The rays are converged slightly by the convex lens.

convex lens — focused image

shovel /ˈʃʌvl/ noun [C] a tool used for picking up and moving earth, snow, sand, etc. ⊃ look at **spade** (1) ⊃ picture at **gardening** ▸ **shovel** verb [I, T] (-ll-, AmE -l-)

show¹ ⚡ **A1** ◉ /ʃəʊ/ verb (pt showed; pp shown /ʃəʊn/)

• MAKE CLEAR **1** [T] to make sth clear; to give information about sth: Research shows that most people get too little exercise. ◇ This graph shows how prices have gone up in the last few years.

• LET SB SEE **2** [T] ~ sb/sth (to sb); ~ sb (sth); ~ sb/sth (doing sth) to let sb see sb/sth: I showed the letter to him. ◇ I showed him the letter. ◇ She showed me what she had bought. ◇ They're showing his latest film at our local cinema. ◇ She was showing signs of stress. ◇ This white T-shirt really shows the dirt. ◇ The picture showed him arguing with a photographer.

• TEACH **3** [T] to help sb to do sth by doing it yourself; to explain sth: Can you show me how to make pancakes?

• GUIDE **4** [T] (often used with an adverb or a preposition) to lead sb to or round a place; to explain how to go to a place: I'll come with you and show you the way. ◇ Shall I show you to your room? ◇ A guide showed us round the museum.

• BE SEEN **5** [I] to be able to be seen; to appear: I tried not to let my disappointment show.

PHR V **show (sth) off** (informal) to try to impress people by showing them how clever you are or by showing them sth that you are proud of: John was showing off by driving his new car very fast. ⊃ noun **show-off** **show up** (informal) to arrive, especially when sb is expecting you: Where have you been? I thought you'd never show up. **show (sth) up** to be seen or to allow sth to be seen: The sunlight shows up those dirty marks on the window. **show sb up** (informal) to make sb embarrassed by your behaviour or appearance: Her criticisms showed him up in front of the boss.

show² ⚡ **A1** /ʃəʊ/ noun **1** [C] (ARTS AND MEDIA) a type of entertainment performed for an audience: a TV comedy show ◇ a quiz show **2** [C, U] an occasion when a collection of things is brought together for people to look at: a dog show ◇ a fashion show ◇ Paintings by local children will be **on show** at the town hall next week. ⊃ note at **art 3** [sing.] an occasion when you let sb see sth: a show of emotion/gratitude/temper **4** [U, sing.] something that a person does or has in order to make people believe sth that is not true: His bravery is **all show** (= he is not as brave as he pretends to be). ◇ Although she hated him, she **put on a show of** politeness.

show business (also informal **showbiz** /ˈʃəʊbɪz/) noun [U] (ARTS AND MEDIA) the business of entertaining people, in the theatre, in films, on TV, etc: He's been **in show business** since he was five years old.

showcase /ˈʃəʊkeɪs/ noun [C, usually sing.] ~ (for sb/sth) an event that presents sb's abilities or the good qualities of sth in an attractive way: The festival was a showcase for young musicians. ▸ **showcase** verb [T]: Jack found a film role that showcased all his talents.

showdown /ˈʃəʊdaʊn/ noun [C] a final argument, meeting or fight at the end of a long DISAGREEMENT: The management are preparing for a showdown with the union.

shower¹ ⚡ **A1** /ˈʃaʊə(r)/ noun [C] **1** a piece of equipment that produces a flow of water in small drops that you stand under to wash; the small room or part of a room that contains a shower: The shower doesn't work. ◇ She's in the shower. ◇ I'd like a room with a shower, please. **2** an act of washing yourself by standing under a shower: I'll just **have a** quick **shower** then we can go out. **3** a short period of rain ⊃ look at **acid rain, rain¹** (1) **4** a lot of very small objects that fall

or fly through the air together: a shower of sparks/broken glass

shower² /ˈʃaʊə(r)/ verb **1** [I] to wash yourself under a shower: I came back from my run, showered and got changed. **2** [I, T] ~ **down (on sb/sth)**; ~ **sb with sth** to cover sb/sth with a lot of small falling objects: Ash from the volcano showered down on the town. ◇ People suffered cuts after being showered with broken glass.

showing /ˈʃəʊɪŋ/ noun [C] **1** (ARTS AND MEDIA) an act of showing a film, etc: The second showing of the film begins at eight o'clock. **2** [usually sing.] how sb/sth behaves; how successful sb/sth is: On its present showing, the party should win the election.

showjumping /ˈʃəʊdʒʌmpɪŋ/ noun [U] (SPORT) a competition in which a person rides a horse over a series of fences

shown /ʃəʊn/ past participle of **show¹**

show-off noun [C] a person who tries to impress others by showing them how clever they are, or by showing them sth they are proud of: She's such a show-off, always boasting about how good she is at this and that.

showroom /ˈʃəʊruːm, -rʊm/ noun [C] a type of large shop where customers can look at goods such as cars, furniture and electrical items that are on sale

shrank /ʃræŋk/ past tense of **shrink**

shrapnel /ˈʃræpnəl/ noun [U] small pieces of metal that fly around when a bomb explodes

shred¹ /ʃred/ noun **1** [C, usually pl.] a small thin piece of material that has been cut or torn off: His clothes were torn to shreds by the rose bushes. **2** [sing.] ~ **of sth** (in negative sentences) a very small amount of sth: There wasn't a shred of truth in her story.

shred² /ʃred/ verb [T] (-dd-) to tear or cut sth into SHREDS: shredded cabbage

shrew /ʃruː/ noun [C] **1** a small animal like a mouse with a long nose **2** (old-fashioned) an angry unpleasant woman

shrewd /ʃruːd/ adj. able to make good decisions because you understand a situation well: a shrewd thinker/decision ▸ **shrewdly** adv.

shriek /ʃriːk/ verb **1** [I] ~ **(with sth)** to make a short, loud, noise in a high voice: She shrieked in fright. ◇ The children were shrieking with laughter. **2** [T] to say sth loudly in a high voice: 'Stop it!' she shrieked. ⊃ look at **screech** ▸ **shriek** noun [C]

shrill /ʃrɪl/ adj. (used about a sound) high and unpleasant: a shrill cry

shrimp /ʃrɪmp/ noun [C] (pl. shrimps, shrimp) **1** a small SHELLFISH (= a creature with a shell that lives in water) that can be eaten and that turns pink when cooked. Shrimps are similar to PRAWNS but smaller. **2** (AmE) = PRAWN

shrine /ʃraɪn/ noun [C] (RELIGION) a place that is important to a particular person or group of people for religious reasons or because it is connected with a special person

shrink ⚡+ **C1** /ʃrɪŋk/ verb (pt shrank /ʃræŋk/, shrunk /ʃrʌŋk/; pp shrunk) **1** [I, T] to become smaller; to make sth smaller: My T-shirt shrank in the wash. ◇ TV has shrunk the world. ◇ The rate of inflation has shrunk to 4%. **2** [I] (used with an adverb or a preposition) to move back because you are frightened or shocked: We shrank back against the wall when the dog appeared.

PHR V **shrink from sth/doing sth** to not want to do sth because you find it unpleasant

'shrink-wrapped *adj.* covered tightly in a thin sheet of plastic: *The books are shrink-wrapped so you can't open them in the shop.*

shrivel /ˈʃrɪvl/ *verb* [I, T] (-ll-, *AmE* -l-) ~ **(sth) (up)** to become smaller or to make sth smaller, especially because of dry conditions: *The plants shrivelled up and died in the hot weather.*

shroud¹ /ʃraʊd/ *noun* [C] a cloth or sheet that is put round a dead body before it is buried

shroud² /ʃraʊd/ *verb* [T, usually passive] **be ~ (in sth)** to cover or hide sth: *The tops of the mountains were shrouded in mist.*

Shrove Tuesday /ˌʃraʊv ˈtjuːzdeɪ, -di/ *noun* [C] (**RELIGION**) (in the Christian Church) the day before the beginning of Lent ⊃ look at **Pancake Day**

shrub /ʃrʌb/ *noun* [C] a small bush

shrubbery /ˈʃrʌbəri/ *noun* [C] (*pl.* -ies) an area where a lot of small bushes have been planted

shrug ⚡+ **C1** /ʃrʌɡ/ *verb* [I, T] (-gg-) to lift your shoulders as a way of showing that you do not know sth or are not interested: *'Who knows?' he said and shrugged.* ◇ *'It doesn't matter to me,' he said, **shrugging his shoulders**.* ▶ shrug *noun* [C, usually sing.]: *I asked him if he was sorry and he just answered with a shrug.*
PHR V **shrug sth off** to not allow sth to affect you in a bad way: *An actor has to learn to shrug off criticism.*

shrunk /ʃrʌŋk/ past tense, past participle of **shrink**

shrunken /ˈʃrʌŋkən/ *adj.* that has become smaller (and less attractive)

shudder /ˈʃʌdə(r)/ *verb* [I] to suddenly shake hard, especially because of an unpleasant feeling or thought: *Just thinking about the accident makes me shudder.* ◇ *The engine shuddered violently and then stopped.* ▶ shudder *noun* [C, usually sing.]

shuffle¹ /ˈʃʌfl/ *verb* **1** [I] to walk by sliding your feet along instead of lifting them off the ground **2** [T, I] to move your body or feet around because you are uncomfortable or nervous: *The audience were so bored that they began to shuffle in their seats.* **3** [I, T] to mix a PACK of PLAYING CARDS before a game: *It's your turn to shuffle.* ◇ *She shuffled the cards carefully.*

shuffle² /ˈʃʌfl/ *noun* [C, usually sing.] **1** a way of walking without lifting your feet off the ground **2** an act of SHUFFLING cards

shun /ʃʌn/ *verb* [T] (-nn-) to avoid sb/sth; to keep away from sb/sth: *They were shunned by their families when they married.*

shunt /ʃʌnt/ *verb* [T] **1** to push a train from one track to another **2** (used with an adverb or a preposition) to move sb/sth to a different place, especially a less important one: *He was shunted around from one hospital to another.*

shush /ʃʊʃ/ *exclamation* used to tell sb to stop making a noise: *Shush! I'm trying to work.*

shut¹ ⚡ **A2** /ʃʌt/ *verb* (shutting; *pt, pp* shut) **1** [T, I] to make sth close; to become closed: *Could you shut the door, please?* ◇ *I can't shut my suitcase.* ◇ *Shut your books, please.* ◇ *He shut his eyes and tried to go to sleep.* ◇ *This window won't shut properly.* ◇ *The doors open and shut automatically.* **2** [I, T] (*BrE*) (used about a shop, restaurant, etc.) to stop doing business for the day; to close: *What time do the shops shut on Saturday?*
PHR V **shut sb/sth away** to keep sb/sth in a place where people cannot find or see them or it **shut (sth) down** (used about a factory, etc.) to close for a long time or for ever: *Financial problems forced the business to shut down.* **shut sb/yourself in (sth)** to put

sb in a room and keep them there; to go to a room and stay there **shut sth in sth** to trap sth by closing a door etc. on it **shut sth off (from sth)** to keep sb/sth apart from sth: *He shuts himself off from the rest of the world.* **shut sb/sth out (of sth) 1** to prevent sb/sth from entering a place: *She shut her sister out of the bedroom.* **2** to stop yourself from having particular feelings: *He tried to shut out all thoughts of the accident.* **shut up** (*informal*) to stop talking; to be quiet: *I wish you'd shut up!* **shut sb up** (*informal*) to make sb stop talking **shut sb/sth up (in sth)** to put sb/sth somewhere and stop them or it leaving: *He was shut up in prison for nearly ten years.*

shut² ⚡ **A2** /ʃʌt/ *adj.* [not before noun] **1** in a closed position: *Make sure the door is shut properly before you leave.* **2** not open to the public: *The restaurant was shut so we went to one round the corner.*
IDM **keep your mouth shut** → MOUTH¹

shutter /ˈʃʌtə(r)/ *noun* [C] **1** a wooden or metal cover that is fixed outside a window and that can be opened or shut. A shop's shutter usually slides down from the top of the shop window. **2** the part at the front of a camera that opens for a very short time to let light in so that a photo can be taken

shuttle /ˈʃʌtl/ *noun* [C] **1** a plane, bus or train that travels regularly between two places: *There is a **shuttle service** between the station and the airport.* **2** a pointed tool used in WEAVING (= making cloth) to pull a THREAD between the other THREADS that pass along the length of the cloth

shuttlecock /ˈʃʌtlkɒk/ *noun* [C] (**SPORT**) (in the sport of BADMINTON) the small, light object that is hit over the net ⊃ picture at **sport**

shy¹ ⚡ **B1** /ʃaɪ/ *adj.* **1** nervous and uncomfortable about meeting and speaking to people; showing that sb feels like this: *She's very shy with strangers.* ◇ *a shy smile* **2** ~ **(of/about sth/doing sth)** frightened to do sth or to become involved in sth: *She's not shy of telling people what she thinks.* ▶ shyly *adv.* ▶ shyness *noun* [U]

shy² /ʃaɪ/ *verb* [I] (shying; shies; *pt, pp* shied) (used about a horse) to suddenly move away in fear
PHR V **shy away from sth/doing sth** to avoid doing sth because you are afraid

SI /ˌes ˈaɪ/ *abbr.* used to describe units of measurement (from French 'Système International'): *SI units* ❶ For more information about **SI units**, look at the **Reference Section** of this dictionary.

sibling ⚡+ **B2** /ˈsɪblɪŋ/ *noun* [C] (*formal*) a brother or a sister

sic /sɪk/ *adv.* (**GRAMMAR**) written after a word that you have copied from somewhere, to show that you know that the word is wrongly spelled or wrong in some other way: *In the letter to parents it said: 'The school is proud of it's [sic] record of excellence'.*

sick¹ ⚡ **A1** /sɪk/ *adj.*
• ILL **1** (**HEALTH**) not well; ill: *a sick child* ◇ *Do you get paid for days when you're off sick* (= from work)? ◇ *You're too ill to work today — you should phone in sick.* **2** the sick *noun* [pl.] (**HEALTH**) people who are ill
• WANTING TO VOMIT **3** (**HEALTH**) feeling ill in the stomach so that you may VOMIT (= bring up food through the mouth): *I feel sick — I think it was that fish I ate.* ◇ *Don't eat any more or you'll make yourself sick.* ⊃ look at **airsick, carsick, nausea, seasick, travel-sick**
• BORED/ANGRY **4** ~ **of sb/sth; ~ of doing sth** feeling bored or annoyed because you have had too much of sb/sth: *I'm sick of my job.* ◇ *I'm sick of tidying up your mess!* **5** ~ **(at/about sth)** very annoyed or DISGUSTED by sth: *He felt sick at the sight of so much waste.*
• CRUEL **6** (*informal*) (especially of humour) dealing with physical or mental pain, disease or death in a cruel

way that some people think is offensive: *He offended everyone with a sick joke about blind people.*
IDM be sick (HEALTH) to bring up food from the stomach **SYN** vomit make sb sick to make sb very angry: *Oh, stop complaining. You make me sick!* sick to death of sb/sth feeling tired of or annoyed by sb/sth: *I'm sick to death of his grumbling.*

sick² /sɪk/ *noun* [U] (HEALTH) food that sb has brought up from their stomach: *There was sick all over the car seat.* **SYN** vomit

,sick 'building syndrome *noun* [U] (HEALTH) a condition that affects people who work in large offices, making them feel tired and causing headaches, painful eyes and breathing problems, thought to be caused by, for example, the lack of fresh air or by chemicals in the air

sicken /'sɪkən/ *verb* [T] to make sb feel very shocked and angry: *The sight of people fighting sickens me.*
▸ sickening *adj.*

sickle /'sɪkl/ *noun* [C] (AGRICULTURE) a tool with a short handle and a long, curved BLADE (= a metal part with a sharp edge) that is used for cutting long grass etc.

'sick leave *noun* [U] (BUSINESS) a period spent away from work, etc. because of illness: *Mike's been off on sick leave since March.*

,sickle cell a'naemia (*BrE*) (*AmE* sickle cell anemia) (*also* 'sickle cell disease) *noun* [U] (HEALTH) a serious medical condition in which the red blood cells are damaged and change shape

sickly /'sɪkli/ *adj.* (sicklier; sickliest) **1** (used about a person) weak and often ill: *a sickly child* **2** unpleasant; causing you to feel ill: *the sickly smell of rotten fruit*

sickness /'sɪknəs/ *noun* (HEALTH) **1** [U] the state of being ill: *A lot of workers are absent because of sickness.* **2** [U, C] a particular type of illness: *pills for seasickness* ⊃ look at sleeping sickness **3** [U] a feeling in the stomach that may make you VOMIT (= bring up food through the mouth): *Symptoms of the disease include sickness and diarrhoea.*

'sick pay *noun* [U] (BUSINESS, HEALTH) pay given to an employee who is away from work because of illness

side¹ ⭐ **A2** /saɪd/ *noun* [C]
• SURFACE **1** one of the flat outer surfaces of sth: *A cube has six sides.* **2** -sided (in adjectives) having the number of sides mentioned: *a six-sided coin*
• NEAR TO SB/STH **3** a place or position very near to sb/sth
• NOT TOP OR BOTTOM **4** one of the surfaces of sth except the top, bottom, front or back: *I went round to the side of the building.* ◊ *The side of the car was damaged.*
• EDGE **5** the edge of sth, away from the middle: *Make sure you stay at the side of the road when you're cycling.* ◊ *We moved to one side to let the doctor get past.*
• LEFT/RIGHT **6** the area to the left or right of sth; the area in front of or behind sth: *We live (on) the other side of the main road.* ◊ *It's more expensive to live on the north side of town.* ◊ *In Japan they drive on the left-hand side of the road.* ◊ *She sat at the side of his bed/at his bedside.*
• OF STH FLAT/THIN **7** either of the two flat surfaces of sth thin: *Write on both sides of the paper.*
• OF THE BODY **8** the right or the left part of the body, especially from under the arm to the top of the leg: *She lay on her side.* ◊ *The soldier stood with his hands by his sides.*
• IN A FIGHT/COMPETITION **9** either of two or more people or groups who are fighting, playing, arguing, etc. against each other: *The two sides agreed to stop fighting.* ◊ *the winning/losing side* ◊ *Whose side are you on?* (= Who do you want to win?)

• OF A STORY **10** what is said by one person or group that is different from what is said by another: *I don't know whose side of the story to believe.*
• OF YOUR FAMILY **11** your mother's or your father's family: *There is no history of illness on his mother's side.*
IDM get on the right/wrong side of sb to please/annoy sb: *He tried to get on the right side of his new boss.* look on the bright side → LOOK¹ on/from all sides | on/from every side in/from all directions on the big, small, high, etc. side (*informal*) slightly too big, small, high, etc. on the safe side → SAFE¹ put sth on/to one side | leave sth on one side to leave or keep sth so that you can use it or deal with it later: *You should put some money to one side for the future.* side by side next to each other; close together: *They walked side by side along the road.* take sides (with sb) to show that you support one person rather than another in an argument: *Parents should never take sides when their children are quarrelling.*

side² /saɪd/ *verb*
PHR V side with sb (against sb) to support sb in an argument

sideboard /'saɪdbɔːd/ *noun* [C] a type of low cupboard about as high as a table, that is used for storing plates, etc. in a DINING ROOM (= a room that is used for eating in)

sideburns /'saɪdbɜːnz/ *noun* [pl.] hair that grows down a man's face in front of his ears

'side dish *noun* [C] a small amount of food, for example a salad, served with the main course of a meal

'side effect *noun* [C] **1** (MEDICINE) the unpleasant effect that a drug may have in addition to its useful effects: *Side effects of the drug include nausea and dizziness.* **2** an unexpected effect of sth that happens in addition to the intended effect: *One of the side effects when the chemical factory closed was that fish returned to the river.* ⊃ look at after-effect, effect¹ (1)

sideline /'saɪdlaɪn/ *noun* **1** [C] something that you do in addition to your regular job, especially to earn extra money: *He's an engineer, but he repairs cars as a sideline.* **2** sidelines [pl.] the lines that mark the two long sides of the area used for playing sports such as football, tennis, etc.; the area behind this
IDM on the sidelines not involved in an activity; not taking part in sth

sidelong /'saɪdlɒŋ/ *adj.* [only before noun] directed from the side; out of the corner of your eye: *a sidelong glance*

'side order *noun* [C] a small amount of food ordered in a restaurant to go with the main dish, but served separately: *a side order of fries* ⊃ look at side dish

'side road *noun* [C] a small road that joins a bigger main road

sidestep /'saɪdstep/ *verb* (-pp-) **1** [T] to avoid answering a question or dealing with a problem: *Did you notice how she neatly sidestepped the question?* **2** [T, I] to avoid sth, for example being hit, by stepping to one side

'side street *noun* [C] a narrow or less important street near a main street

sidetrack /'saɪdtræk/ *verb* [T, usually passive] to make sb forget what they are doing or talking about and start doing or talking about sth less important

sidewalk /'saɪdwɔːk/ (*AmE*) = PAVEMENT (1)

sideways /'saɪdweɪz/ *adv., adj.* **1** to, towards or from one side: *He jumped sideways to avoid being hit.* **2** with one of the sides at the top: *We'll have to turn the sofa sideways to get it through the door.*

siding /'saɪdɪŋ/ *noun* [C, usually pl.] a short track next to a main railway line, where trains can stand when they are not being used

sidle /'saɪdl/ *verb* [I] ~ **up/over (to sb/sth)** to move towards sb/sth in a nervous way, as if you do not want anyone to notice you

siege /siːdʒ/ *noun* [C, U] a situation in which an army surrounds a town for a long time or the police surround a building so that nobody can get in or out: *The house was under siege for several hours, until the man released his hostages.*
IDM **lay siege to sth** **1** to begin a siege of a town, building, etc: *The crusaders laid siege to Lisbon.* **2** to surround a building, especially in order to speak to or question the person or people living or working there

siesta /si'estə/ *noun* [C] a short sleep or rest that people take in the afternoon, especially in hot countries

sieve /sɪv/ *noun* [C] a type of kitchen tool that has a metal or plastic net, used for separating solids from liquids or very small pieces of food from large pieces: *Pour the soup through a sieve to get rid of any lumps.*
▶ **sieve** *verb* [T]: *to sieve flour*

sift /sɪft/ *verb* **1** [T] to pass flour, sugar or a similar substance through a SIEVE in order to remove any LUMPS (= solid parts): *to sift flour/sugar* **2** [I, T] ~ **(through) sth** to examine sth very carefully: *It took weeks to sift through all the evidence.*

sigh ☕+ **C1** /saɪ/ *verb* **1** [I] ~ **(with sth)** to let out a long, deep breath that shows you are tired, sad, disappointed, etc: *She sighed with disappointment at the news.* **2** [I] to make a long sound like a sigh **3** [T] to say sth with a sigh: *'I'm so tired,' he sighed.*
▶ **sigh** ☕+ **C1** *noun* [C]
IDM **heave a sigh** → HEAVE¹

sight¹ ☕ **B1** /saɪt/ *noun*
- ABILITY TO SEE **1** [U] (**HEALTH**) the ability to see: *He lost his sight in the war* (= he became blind). ◇ *My grandmother has very poor sight.* **2** -sighted (in adjectives) able to see in the way mentioned: *a partially sighted child* ⊃ look at **long-sighted, short-sighted** (1)
- ACT OF SEEING **3** [U] ~ **of sb/sth** the act of seeing sb/sth: *I feel ill at the sight of blood.* ◇ *She caught sight of a car in the distance.* ◇ *We flew over Paris and had our first sight of the Eiffel Tower.*
- HOW FAR YOU CAN SEE **4** [U] a position where sb/sth can be seen: *They waited until the plane was in/within sight and then fired.* ◇ *When we get over this hill the town should come into sight.* ◇ *She didn't let the kids out of her sight.*
- WHAT YOU CAN SEE **5** [C] something that you see: *The burned-out building was a terrible sight.*
- INTERESTING PLACES **6** sights [pl.] (**TOURISM**) places of interest that are often visited by tourists: *When you come to New York I'll show you the sights.*
- PERSON/THING **7** a sight [sing.] (*especially BrE, informal*) a person or thing that looks strange or funny: *She looks a sight in that hat!*
- ON A GUN **8** [C, usually pl.] the part of a gun that you look through in order to aim it
IDM **at first glance/sight** → FIRST¹ **in sight** likely to happen or come soon: *A peace settlement is in sight.* **lose sight of sb/sth** → LOSE **on sight** as soon as you see sb/sth: *The soldiers were ordered to shoot the enemy on sight.*

sight² /saɪt/ *verb* [T] to see sb/sth, especially after looking out for them or it

sighting /'saɪtɪŋ/ *noun* [C] an occasion when sb/sth is seen: *the first sighting of a new star*

sightseeing /'saɪtsiːɪŋ/ *noun* [U] (**TOURISM**) visiting the sights of a city, etc. as a tourist: *We did some sightseeing in Rome.*

sightseer /'saɪtsiːə(r)/ *noun* [C] (**TOURISM**) a person who visits the sights of a city, etc. as a tourist ⊃ look at **tourist**

sign¹ ☕ **A2** **S** /saɪn/ *noun* [C]
- SHOWING STH **1** ~ **(of sth)** something that shows that sb/sth is present, exists or may happen: *The patient was showing some signs of improvement.* ◇ *As we drove into the village there was no sign of life anywhere* (= we couldn't see anyone).
- FOR INFORMATION/WARNING **2** a piece of wood, paper, metal, etc. that has writing or a picture on it that gives you a piece of information, an instruction or a warning: *What does that sign say?* ◇ *a road sign* ◇ *Follow the signs to Banbury.*
- MOVEMENT **3** a movement that you make with your head, hands or arms that has a particular meaning: *I made a sign for him to follow me.* ◇ *I'll give you a sign when it's time for you to speak.*
- SYMBOL **4** a type of shape, mark or symbol that has a particular meaning: *In mathematics, a cross is a plus sign.* **5** (*informal*) = STAR SIGN

▼ SYNONYMS

sign

indication ◆ symptom ◆ symbol ◆ indicator ◆ signal

These are all words for an event, action or fact that shows that sth exists, is happening or may happen in the future.

sign *Headaches may be a sign of stress.*

indication *She gave no indication of being tired.*

symptom *Symptoms include a sore throat.*

symbol *The dove is a symbol of peace.*

indicator (*formal*) *early economic indicators*

signal *The rise in inflation is a clear signal that the government's policies are not working.*

sign² ☕ **A2** **S** /saɪn/ *verb* **1** [I, T] to write your name on a letter, document, etc. to show that you have written it or that you agree with what it says: *'Could you sign here, please?'* ◇ *I forgot to sign the cheque.* ◇ *The two presidents signed the treaty.* ⊃ noun **signature 2** [T] ~ **sb (up)** to get sb to sign a contract to work for you: *Real Madrid have signed two new players.* **3** [I] (**LANGUAGE**) to communicate using sign language
PHR V **sign in/out** to write your name to show you have arrived at or left a hotel, club, etc. **sign up (for sth)** to agree formally to do sth: *I've signed up for evening classes.*

signal ☕ **B1** /'sɪgnəl/ *noun* [C] **1** ~ **(to do sth)** a sign, an action or a sound that sends a particular message: *When I give (you) the signal, run!* **2** a set of lights used to give information to drivers **3** an event, action or a fact that shows that sth exists or is likely to happen: *The fall in unemployment is a clear signal that the economy is improving.* ⊃ note at **sign¹ 4** a series of radio waves, etc. that are sent out or received: *a signal from a satellite* ▶ **signal** ☕ **B1** *verb* [I, T] (-ll-, *AmE* -l-): *She was signalling wildly that something was wrong.*

signatory /'sɪgnətri/ *noun* [C] (*pl.* -ies) ~ **(to sth)** one of the people or countries that sign an agreement, etc.

signature ☕+ **B2** /'sɪgnətʃə(r)/ *noun* [C] a person's name, written by that person and always written in the same way ⊃ verb **sign**

significance ₹+ B2 ○ /sɪɡ'nɪfɪkəns/ *noun* [U] the importance or meaning of sth: *Few people realized the significance of the discovery.*

significant ₹ B2 ○ /sɪɡ'nɪfɪkənt/ *adj.* **1** important or large enough to be noticed or to have an effect: *Police said that the time of the murder was extremely significant.* ◇ *There has been a significant improvement in your work.* **2** having a particular meaning: *It could be significant that he took out life insurance shortly before he died.*

significantly ₹ B2 ○ /sɪɡ'nɪfɪkəntli/ *adv.* **1** in a way that is large or important enough to have an effect on sth or to be noticed: *Profits have increased significantly over the past few years.* ◇ *Attitudes have changed significantly since the 1960s.* **2** in a way that has a particular meaning: *Significantly, he did not deny that there might be an election.* **3** in a way that has a special or secret meaning: *She paused significantly before she answered.*

signify /'sɪɡnɪfaɪ/ *verb* [T] (signifying; signifies; pt, pp signified) (formal) **1** to be a sign of sth; to mean: *What do those lights signify?* **2** to express or indicate sth: *They signified their agreement by raising their hands.*

sign language *noun* [U] (LANGUAGE) a language used especially by people who cannot hear or speak, using the hands to make signs instead of spoken words

signpost /'saɪnpəʊst/ *noun* [C] a sign at the side of a road that gives information about directions and distances to towns

Sikh /siːk/ *noun* [C] (RELIGION) a member of a religion (called Sikhism) that developed in Punjab in the late fifteenth century and is based on a belief that there is only one god) ➷ note at **religion** ▸ Sikh *adj.* ▸ Sikhism *noun* [U]

silage /'saɪlɪdʒ/ *noun* [U] (AGRICULTURE) grass or other green plants that are stored without being dried and are used to feed farm animals in winter

silence ₹ B2 /'saɪləns/ *noun* **1** [U] no noise or sound at all: *There must be silence during examinations.* **SYN quiet²** **2** [C, U] a period when nobody speaks or makes a noise: *My question was met with an awkward silence.* ◇ *We ate in silence.* **3** [U] not making any comments about sth ▸ silence *verb* [T]

silencer /'saɪlənsə(r)/ (BrE) (AmE muffler) *noun* [C] **1** a device that is fixed to the EXHAUST PIPE (= the long tube under a vehicle) to reduce the noise made by the engine **2** a device that is fixed to a gun to reduce the noise that it makes when it is fired

silent ₹ B1 /'saɪlənt/ *adj.* **1** where there is no noise; making no noise; very quiet: *The house was empty and silent.* **2** ~ (on/about sth) not speaking; refusing to speak about sth: *The policeman told her she had the right to remain silent.* ◇ *He has remained silent on the issue.* **3** [only before noun] not using spoken words: *a silent prayer/protest* **4** (used about a letter) not pronounced: *The 'b' in 'comb' is silent.* ▸ silently *adv.*

silent partner (AmE) = SLEEPING PARTNER

silhouette /ˌsɪlu'et/ *noun* [C] the dark solid shape of sb/sth seen against a light background ▸ silhouetted *adj.*

silica /'sɪlɪkə/ *noun* [U] (symb. SiO_2) (CHEMISTRY) a chemical containing SILICON found in sand and in rocks such as QUARTZ, used in making glass and CEMENT

silicon /'sɪlɪkən/ *noun* [U] (symb. Si) (CHEMISTRY) a chemical element. Silicon exists as a grey solid or a brown powder, and is found in rocks and sand. It is used in making glass and electronic equipment. ❶ For more information on the periodic table of elements, look at the **Reference Section** of this dictionary.

silicon chip *noun* [C] (COMPUTING) a very small piece of SILICON that is used to carry a complicated electronic CIRCUIT

silicone /'sɪlɪkəʊn/ *noun* [U] (CHEMISTRY) a chemical containing SILICON. There are several different types of silicone, used to make paint, artificial rubber, etc: *a silicone breast implant*

Silicon Valley *noun* [U] (COMPUTING) the area in California where there are many companies connected with the computer and ELECTRONICS industries

silk ₹ B2 /sɪlk/ *noun* [U] the soft smooth cloth that is made from THREADS produced by a SILKWORM: *a silk shirt/dress*

silkworm /'sɪlkwɜːm/ *noun* [C] a CATERPILLAR (= a small animal like a WORM with legs) that produces silk

silky /'sɪlki/ *adj.* (silkier; silkiest) smooth, soft and shiny; like silk: *silky hair*

sill /sɪl/ = WINDOWSILL

silly ₹ B1 /'sɪli/ *adj.* (sillier; silliest) **1** not showing thought or understanding; stupid: *a silly mistake* ◇ *Don't be so silly!* **SYN foolish OPP sensible** **2** stupid or embarrassing, especially in a way that is more typical of a child than an adult: *I'm not wearing that hat — I'd look silly in it.* ▸ silliness *noun* [U]

silo /'saɪləʊ/ *noun* [C] (pl. -os) (AGRICULTURE) **1** a tall tower on a farm used for storing grain, etc. **2** an underground place where grass or other green plants are made into SILAGE (= a substance that is stored until winter to feed the farm animals)

silt /sɪlt/ *noun* [U] (GEOGRAPHY) sand, soil or mud that collects at the sides or on the bottom of a river ➷ picture at **floodplain, petroleum**

silver¹ ₹ A2 /'sɪlvə(r)/ *noun* **1** (symb. Ag) [U] (CHEMISTRY) a valuable shiny grey-white metal that is used for making jewellery, coins, etc: *a silver spoon/necklace* ◇ *That's a nice ring. Is it silver?* ❶ For more information on the periodic table of elements, look at the **Reference Section** of this dictionary. **2** [U] a shiny grey-white colour **3** [U] (FINANCE) coins made from silver or sth that looks like silver **4** [U] objects that are made of silver, for example knives, forks, spoons, dishes: *The thieves stole some jewellery and some valuable silver.* **5** [U, C] (SPORT) = SILVER MEDAL
IDM every cloud has a silver lining → CLOUD¹

silver² ₹ A2 /'sɪlvə(r)/ *adj.* **1** shiny grey-white in colour: *a silver sports car* **2** celebrating the 25th anniversary of sth ➷ look at **diamond wedding, golden** (2)

silver medal *noun* [C] (also silver [U, C]) (SPORT) a medal that you get as a prize for coming second in a race or competition: *to win a silver medal at the Olympic Games* ➷ look at **bronze medal, gold medal** ▸ silver medallist *noun* [C]

silver service *noun* [U] a style of serving food at formal meals in which the person serving uses a silver fork and spoon

silverware /'sɪlvəweə(r)/ *noun* [U] **1** objects that are made of or covered with silver, especially knives, forks, dishes, etc. that are used for eating and serving food: *a piece of silverware* **2** (AmE) = CUTLERY **3** (BrE, informal) (SPORT) silver cups, etc. that you get for winning sports competitions: *The team has won silverware every season he has been in charge.*

silver wedding *noun* [C] the 25th anniversary of a wedding ➷ look at **diamond wedding, golden wedding**

silvery /ˈsɪlvəri/ *adj.* having the appearance or colour of silver: *an old lady with silvery hair*

SIM card /ˈsɪm kɑːd/ *noun* [C] a plastic card inside a mobile phone that stores personal information about the person using the phone

similar ⚡**A1** ◑ /ˈsɪmələ(r)/ *adj.* ~ **(to sb/sth);** ~ **(in sth)** like sb/sth but not exactly the same: *Your handwriting is very similar to mine.* ◊ *Our houses are very similar in size.* **OPP different, dissimilar**

similarity ⚡**B1** Ⓦ /ˌsɪməˈlærəti/ *noun* (*pl.* -ies) **1** [U, sing.] ~ **(to sb/sth);** ~ **(in sth)** the state of being like sb/sth but not exactly the same: *She bears a remarkable/striking similarity to her mother.* ◊ *I noticed the similarity in the way the two sisters thought and spoke.* **2** [C] ~ **(between A and B);** ~ **(in/of sth)** a characteristic that people or things have that makes them similar: *Although there are some similarities between the two towns, there are a lot of differences too.* ◊ *similarities in/of style*

similarly ⚡**B1** Ⓦ /ˈsɪmələli/ *adv.* **1** in almost the same way: *Husband and wife were similarly successful in their chosen careers.* **2** used to say that two facts, actions, statements, etc. are like each other: *The plural of 'shelf' is 'shelves'. Similarly, the plural of 'wolf' is 'wolves'.*

simile /ˈsɪməli/ *noun* [C, U] (**LANGUAGE, LITERATURE**) a word or phrase that compares sth to sth else, using the words *as* or *like*, for example *a face like a mask* or *as white as snow*; the use of such words and phrases ○ look at **metaphor**

simmer /ˈsɪmə(r)/ *verb* [T, I] to cook sth gently in a liquid that is almost boiling; to be cooked in this way

simple ⚡**A2** ◑ /ˈsɪmpl/ *adj.* (simpler /-plə(r)/; simplest /-plɪst/) **1** easy to understand, do or use; not difficult or complicated: *This dictionary is written in simple English.* ◊ *a simple task/method/solution* ◊ *I can't just leave the job. It's not as simple as that.* **SYN easy**[1] **2** without decoration or unnecessary extra things; plain and basic: *a simple black dress* ◊ *The food is simple but perfectly cooked.* **OPP fancy**[2] **3** used for saying that the thing you are talking about is the only thing that is important or true: *I'm not going to buy it for the simple reason that* (= only because) *I haven't got enough money.* **4** (used about a person or a way of life) ordinary; not special: *a simple life in the country* **5** (*old-fashioned*) not intelligent; slow to understand **6** (**GRAMMAR**) used to describe the present or past tense of a verb that is formed without using an auxiliary verb, as in 'She loves him' (= the simple present tense) and 'He arrived late' (= the simple past tense).

simple ˈinterest *noun* [U] (**FINANCE**) interest that is paid only on the original amount of money that you invested, and not on any interest that it has earned ○ look at **compound interest**

simplicity /sɪmˈplɪsəti/ *noun* [U] **1** the quality of being easy to understand, do or use: *We all admired the simplicity of the plan.* **2** the quality of having no decoration or unnecessary extra things; being natural and not complicated: *I like the simplicity of her paintings.*

simplify Ⓦ /ˈsɪmplɪfaɪ/ *verb* [T] (simplifying; simplifies; *pt, pp* simplified) to make sth easier to do or understand; to make sth less complicated: *The process of applying for visas has been simplified.* ▶ **simplification** /ˌsɪmplɪfɪˈkeɪʃn/ *noun* [U, C]

simplistic /sɪmˈplɪstɪk/ *adj.* making a problem, situation, etc. seem less difficult and complicated than it really is

simply ⚡**B1** ◑ /ˈsɪmpli/ *adv.* **1** used to emphasize how easy or basic sth is: *Simply add hot water and stir.* **2** in a way that makes sth easy to understand: *Could you explain it more simply?* **3** in a simple, basic way; without decoration or unnecessary extra things: *They live simply, with very few luxuries.* **4** (used to emphasize an adjective) completely: *That meal was simply excellent.* **SYN absolutely 5** only; just: *There's no need to get angry. The whole problem is simply a misunderstanding.*

simulate ⚡+ **C1** /ˈsɪmjuleɪt/ *verb* [T] to create certain conditions that exist in real life using computers, models, etc., usually for study or training purposes: *The astronauts trained in a machine that simulates conditions in space.* ▶ **simulation** ⚡+ **C1** /ˌsɪmjuˈleɪʃn/ *noun* [C, U]: *a computer simulation of a nuclear attack*

simulator /ˈsɪmjuleɪtə(r)/ *noun* [C] a piece of equipment that creates certain conditions using computers, models, etc., in order to train sb to deal with a situation that they may experience in reality: *a flight simulator*

simultaneous ◑ /ˌsɪmlˈteɪniəs/ *adj.* happening or done at exactly the same time as sth else ▶ **simultaneously** ⚡+ **C1** Ⓦ *adv.*

sin[1] ⚡+ **C1** /sɪn/ *noun* [C, U] (**RELIGION**) an action or a way of behaving that is not allowed by a religion: *He believes it is a sin for two people to live together without being married.* ▶ **sin** *verb* [I] (-nn-) ▶ **sinner** *noun* [C]

sin[2] /sɪn/ *abbr.* = SINE

since[1] ⚡**A2** /sɪns/ *conj., prep.* **1** from a particular time in the past until a later time in the past or until now: *I've been working in a bank since I left school.* ◊ *It was the first time they'd won since 1974.* ◊ *I haven't seen him since last Tuesday.* ◊ *She has had a number of jobs since leaving university.* **2** because; as: *Since they've obviously forgotten to phone me, I'll have to phone them.*

since[2] ⚡**B1** /sɪns/ *adv.* **1** from a particular time in the past until a later time in the past or until now: *My parents bought this house in 1990 and we've been living here ever since.* **2** at a time after a particular time in the past: *We were divorced two years ago and she has since married somebody else.*

sincere ⚡**B2** /sɪnˈsɪə(r)/ *adj.* (superlative sincerest) **1** (used about a person's feelings, beliefs or behaviour) true; showing what you really mean or feel: *Please accept our sincere thanks/apologies.* **SYN genuine OPP insincere 2** (used about a person) really meaning or believing what you say; not pretending: *Do you think she was being sincere when she said she admired me?* **SYN honest** ▶ **sincerity** /-ˈserəti/ *noun* [U]

sincerely /sɪnˈsɪəli/ *adv.* in a way that shows what you really feel or think about sb/sth: *I am sincerely grateful to you for all your help.* ◊ *'I won't let you down.' 'I sincerely hope not.'*
IDM Yours sincerely (*AmE*) **| Sincerely (yours)** used at the end of a formal letter before you sign your name, when you have addressed sb by their name: *Yours sincerely, …*

sine /saɪn/ *noun* [C] (*abbr.* sin) (**MATHEMATICS**) the RATIO of the length of the side opposite one of the angles in a RIGHT-ANGLED TRIANGLE (= a shape with three sides and one angle of 90°) to the length of the longest side ○ look at **cosine, tangent** (2)

sinew /ˈsɪnjuː/ *noun* [C, U] (**ANATOMY**) a strong band of substance that joins a muscle to a bone

sinful /ˈsɪnfl/ *adj.* (**RELIGION**) breaking a religious law **SYN immoral**

sing 🔊 **A1** /sɪŋ/ *verb* [I, T] (*pt* sang /sæŋ/; *pp* sung /sʌŋ/) (**MUSIC**) to make musical sounds with your voice: *He always sings when he's in the bath.* ◇ *The birds were singing outside my window.* ◇ *She sang all her most popular songs at the concert.* ⊃ note at **performing arts**

singe /sɪndʒ/ *verb* [I, T] (**singeing**) to burn the surface of sth slightly, usually by accident; to be burned in this way

singer 🔊 **A1** /ˈsɪŋə(r)/ *noun* [C] (**MUSIC**) a person who sings, or whose job is singing, especially in public: *an opera singer*

singing 🔊 **A2** /ˈsɪŋɪŋ/ *noun* [U] (**MUSIC**) the activity of making musical sounds with your voice: *There was singing and dancing all night.* ◇ *singing lessons*

single¹ 🔊 **A2** ⊙ /ˈsɪŋɡl/ *adj.*
• ONE **1** [only before noun] only one: *He gave her a single red rose.* ◇ *I managed to finish the whole job in a single afternoon.*
• FOR EMPHASIS **2** [only before noun] used to emphasize that you are talking about each individual item of a group or series: *You answered every single question correctly. Well done!*
• NOT MARRIED **3** not married or in a relationship: *Are you married or single?* ◇ *a single man/woman*
• FOR ONE PERSON **4** [only before noun] for the use of only one person: *I'd like to book a single room, please.* ⊃ note at **hotel**
• TICKET **5** [only before noun] (*BrE*) (*also* **one-way** *especially in AmE*) (used about a ticket or the price of a ticket) for a journey to a particular place, but not back again: *How much is the single fare to Rome?* ⊃ look at **return²** (4)
IDM in single file → FILE¹

single² 🔊 **A2** /ˈsɪŋɡl/ *noun*
• TICKET **1** [C] a ticket for a journey to a particular place, but not back again: *Two singles to Hull, please.* ⊃ look at **return²** (4)
• ROOM **2** [C] a bedroom for one person in a hotel, etc. ⊃ look at **double⁵** (4)
• UNMARRIED PEOPLE **3** singles [pl.] people who are not married and do not have a romantic relationship with sb else
• IN MUSIC **4** [C] a piece of recorded music, usually popular music, that consists of one song; a CD that a single is recorded on: *Adele's best-selling single* ⊃ look at **album** (1)
• IN SPORT **5** singles [pl.] (in sports such as tennis) a game in which one player plays against one other player ⊃ look at **double⁵** (5)

single³ /ˈsɪŋɡl/ *verb*
PHRV single sb/sth out (for sth) to give special attention or treatment to one person or thing from a group: *She was singled out for criticism.*

single-ˈbreasted *adj.* (used about a jacket or a coat) having only one row of buttons that fasten in the middle ⊃ look at **double-breasted**

single-ˈdecker *noun* [C] a bus with only one level

single-ˈhanded *adv.* on your own with nobody helping you: *to sail round the world single-handed* ▸ single-handed *adj.* ▸ single-handedly *adv.*

single ˈmarket *noun* [C, usually sing.] (**ECONOMICS**) a group of countries that have few or no controls or limits on the movement of goods, money and people between the members of the group

single-ˈminded *adj.* having one clear aim or goal, which you are determined to achieve ▸ single-mindedness *noun* [U]

single ˈparent *noun* [C] a person who looks after their child or children without a husband, wife or partner: *a single-parent family*

singlet /ˈsɪŋɡlət/ *noun* [C] a piece of clothing without SLEEVES (= parts that cover the arms), worn under or instead of a shirt, often worn by runners, etc.

singly /ˈsɪŋɡli/ *adv.* one at a time; alone: *You can buy the pens either singly or in packs of three.*
SYN individually

singular /ˈsɪŋɡjələ(r)/ *adj.* **1** (**GRAMMAR**) in the form that is used for talking about one person or thing only: *'Table' is a singular noun; 'tables' is a plural noun.* ⊃ look at **plural 2** (*formal*) unusual ▸ singular *noun* [sing.] (**GRAMMAR**): *The word 'clothes' has no singular.* ◇ *What's the singular of 'people'?*

singularly /ˈsɪŋɡjələli/ *adv.* (*formal*) very; in an unusual way: *The government has been singularly unsuccessful in its policy against terrorism.*

sinister /ˈsɪnɪstə(r)/ *adj.* seeming evil or dangerous; making you feel that sth bad will happen: *There's something sinister about him. He frightens me.*

sink¹ 🔊 **B1** /sɪŋk/ *verb* (*pt* sank /sæŋk/; *pp* sunk /sʌŋk/)
1 [I, T] to go down or make sth go down under the surface of liquid or a soft substance: *If you throw a stone into water, it sinks.* ◇ *My feet sank into the mud.* ◇ *The ship was sunk by a torpedo.* **2** [I] (used with an adverb or a preposition) (used about a person) to move downwards, usually by falling or sitting down: *I came home and sank into a chair, exhausted.* **3** [I] to get lower; to fall to a lower position or level: *We watched the sun sink slowly below the horizon.* **4** [I] to decrease in value, number, amount, strength, etc.
IDM your heart sinks → HEART
PHRV sink in (used about information, an event, an experience, etc.) to be completely understood or realized: *It took a long time for the terrible news to sink in.* sink in | sink into sth (used about a liquid) to go down into another substance through the surface

sink² /sɪŋk/ *noun* [C] a large open container in a kitchen, with TAPS to supply water, where you wash things ⊃ look at **washbasin**

sinkhole /ˈsɪŋkhəʊl/ (*also* swallow hole) *noun* [C] (**GEOGRAPHY**) a large hole in the ground created over a long period of time by water that has fallen as rain ⊃ picture at **limestone**

sinus /ˈsaɪnəs/ *noun* [C] (**ANATOMY**) one of the spaces in the bones of the face that are connected to the nose: *I've got a terrible cold and my sinuses are blocked.* ◇ *a sinus infection*

sip /sɪp/ *verb* [I, T] (-pp-) ~ (at sth) to drink, taking only a very small amount of liquid into your mouth at a time: *She sipped at the hot tea.* ◇ *We sat in the sun, sipping lemonade.* ▸ sip *noun* [C]: *a sip of water*

siphon (*also* syphon) /ˈsaɪfn/ *verb* [T] (used with an adverb or a preposition) **1** (**CHEMISTRY**) to remove a liquid from a container, often into another container, through a tube: *I siphoned the petrol out of the car into a can.* **2** (**LAW**) to take money from a company illegally over a period of time: *He was accused of siphoning off thousands for his own use.*

sir 🔊 **A2** /sɜː(r)/ *noun* **1** [sing.] used as a polite way of speaking to a man whose name you do not know, for example in a shop or restaurant, or to show respect: *I'm afraid we haven't got your size, sir.* ⊃ look at **madam** (1) **2** Dear Sir/Sirs [C] used at the beginning of a formal letter when you do not know the name of the man or people you are dealing with ⊃ look at **madam** (2) **3** /sɜː; sə(r)/ [sing.] the title that is used in front of the name of a man who has received one of the highest British honours

siren /'saɪrən/ *noun* [C] **1** a device that makes a long, loud sound as a warning or signal: *an air-raid siren* ◇ *Three fire engines raced past, sirens wailing.* **2** (LITERATURE) (in ancient Greek stories) any of a group of sea creatures that were part woman and part bird, or part woman and part fish, whose beautiful singing made sailors sail towards them into rocks or dangerous waters

sirloin /'sɜːlɔɪn/ (*also* ˌsirloin 'steak) *noun* [U, C] good quality meat that is cut from a cow's back

sirocco /sɪ'rɒkəʊ/ *noun* [C] (*pl.* -os) a hot wind that blows from Africa into Southern Europe

sisal /'saɪsl/ *noun* [U] strong thin THREADS made from the leaves of a tropical plant and used for making rope, floor COVERINGS, etc.

sister 🔊 **A1** /'sɪstə(r)/ *noun* [C] **1** a girl or woman who has the same parents as another person: *I've got one brother and two sisters.* ◇ *We're sisters.* ⊃ look at **half-sister, stepsister 2** a woman who you feel close to because she is a member of the same society, group, etc. as you **3** Sister (RELIGION) a member of a religious group of women **4** Sister (*BrE*) (MEDICINE) a female nurse who has responsibility for part of a hospital **5** (usually used as an adjective) a thing that belongs to the same type or group as sth else: *We have a sister company in Japan.*

'sister-in-law *noun* [C] (*pl.* sisters-in-law) your husband's or wife's sister; your sister's or brother's wife

sit 🔊 **A1** /sɪt/ *verb* (sitting; *pt, pp* sat /sæt/)
• ON A CHAIR, ETC. **1** [I] to rest your weight on your bottom, for example in a chair: *We sat in the garden all afternoon.* ◇ *She was sitting on the sofa, talking to her mother.* **2** [T] ~ **sb (down)** to put sb into a sitting position; make sb sit down: *He picked up his daughter and sat her on a chair.* ◇ *She sat me down and offered me a cup of tea.*
• OF THINGS **3** [I] to be in a particular place or position: *The letter sat on the table for several days before anybody opened it.*
• EXAM **4** [T] (*BrE, formal*) (EDUCATION) to take an exam: *If I fail, will I be able to sit the exam again?* ⊃ note at **study²**
• OF PARLIAMENT, ETC. **5** [I] (used about an official group of people) to have a meeting or series of meetings **IDM** **sit on the fence** to avoid saying which side of an argument you support
PHR V **sit about/around** (*informal*) to spend time doing nothing active or useful: *We just sat around chatting all afternoon.* **sit back** to relax and not take an active part in what other people are doing: *Sit back and take it easy while I make dinner.* **sit down** to lower your body into a sitting position: *He sat down in an armchair.* **sit sth out 1** to stay in a place and wait for sth unpleasant or boring to finish **2** to not take part in a dance, game, etc. **sit through sth** to stay in your seat until sth boring or long has finished **sit up 1** to move into a sitting position when you have been lying down or to make your back straight: *Sit up straight and concentrate!* **2** to not go to bed although it is very late: *We sat up all night talking.*

sitar /sɪ'tɑː(r), 'sɪtɑː(r)/ *noun* [C] (MUSIC) a musical instrument from India like a guitar, with a long neck and two sets of metal strings

sitcom /'sɪtkɒm/ *noun* (*also formal* situation comedy) *noun* [C, U] (ARTS AND MEDIA) a programme on TV that makes people laugh, that shows the same characters in different funny situations

site¹ 🔊 **A2** 🌐 /saɪt/ *noun* [C] **1** a piece of land where a building was, is or will be located: *a building/construction site* ◇ *The company is looking for a site for its new offices.* **2** a place where sth has happened or that is used for sth: *the site of a famous battle* ◇ *a caravan site* **3** (COMPUTING) a place on the internet where a company, an organization, a university, etc. puts information ⊃ look at **website**

site² /saɪt/ *verb* [T, usually passive] to build or place sth in a particular position: *The hotel was sited by the lake.*

sitting /'sɪtɪŋ/ *noun* [C] **1** (LAW) a period of time during which a court of law or a parliament meets and does its work **2** a time when a meal is served in a school, hotel, etc. to a number of people at the same time: *Dinner will be in two sittings.*

'sitting room (*BrE*) = LIVING ROOM

situate /'sɪtʃueɪt/ *verb* [T] **1** to build or place sth in a particular position **2** to consider how an idea, event, etc. is related to other things that influence your view of it: *Let me try and situate the events in their historical context.*

situated 🔊+ **C1** /'sɪtʃueɪtɪd/ *adj.* in a particular place or position: *The hotel is conveniently situated close to the beach.* ◇ *a conveniently situated hotel*

situation 🔊 **A1** 🌐 /ˌsɪtʃu'eɪʃn/ *noun* [C] **1** the things that are happening in a particular place or at a particular time: *The situation in the north of the country is extremely serious.* ◇ *Tim is in a difficult situation at the moment.* ◇ *the economic/financial/political situation* **2** (formal) the position of a building, town, etc. in relation to the area around it **3** (old-fashioned or formal) a job: *Situations Vacant* (= the part of a newspaper where jobs are advertised)

▼ SYNONYMS

situation

circumstances ◆ position ◆ conditions

These are all words for the conditions and facts that are connected with and affect the way things are.

situation *the present economic situation*

circumstances *The ship sank in mysterious circumstances.*

position *She was in a position of power.*

conditions *They had to work outside in freezing conditions.*

ˌsituation 'comedy (*formal*) = SITCOM

sit-up   press-up/push-up

'sit-up *noun* [C] an exercise for the stomach muscles in which you lie on your back with your legs bent, then lift the top half of your body from the floor: *to do sit-ups*

six 🔊 **A1** /sɪks/ *number* 6 **HELP** Note how numbers are used in sentences: *The answers are on page six.* ◇ *There are six of us for dinner tonight.* ◇ *They have six cats.* ◇ *My son is six (years old) next month.* ◇ *She lives at 6 Elm Drive.* ◇ *a birthday card with a big 6 on it*

'six-pack *noun* [C] **1** a set of six bottles or cans sold together, especially of beer **2** (*informal*) stomach muscles that are very strong and can be seen clearly across sb's stomach

sixteen 🔊 **A1** /ˌsɪks'tiːn/ *number* 16 ► sixteenth /-'tiːnθ/ *ordinal number, noun* [C]

ˌsix'teenth note (*AmE*) = SEMIQUAVER

sixth[1] /sɪksθ/ *ordinal number* 6th **HELP** Note how ordinal numbers are used in sentences: *Today is the sixth of March.* ◇ *Today is March the sixth.* ◇ *My office is on the sixth floor.* ◇ *This is the sixth time I've tried to phone him.* ◇ *It was Olivia's sixth birthday.* ❶ For more information about numbers in dates, measurements, prices, etc., look at the **Reference Section** of this dictionary.

sixth[2] /sɪksθ/ *noun* [C] one of six equal parts of sth

ˈ**sixth form** *noun* [C, usually sing., + sing./pl. verb] (*BrE*) (**EDUCATION**) the final two years at secondary school for students from the age of 16 to 18 who are studying for A level exams ➲ note at **form**¹ ▶ ˈ**sixth-former** *noun* [C]

ˈ**sixth-form college** *noun* [C] (**EDUCATION**) (in England, Wales and Northern Ireland) a school for students over the age of 16

sixty 🔑 A1 /ˈsɪksti/ **1** *number* 60 **HELP** Note how numbers are used in sentences: *Sixty people went to the meeting.* ◇ *There are sixty pages in the book.* ◇ *He retired* ***at sixty***. **2 the sixties** *noun* [pl.] the numbers, years or temperatures between 60 and 69: *I don't know the exact number of members, but it's in the sixties.* ◇ *The most famous pop group of the sixties was The Beatles.* ◇ *The temperature tomorrow will be in the high sixties.* ▶ **sixtieth** /-əθ/ *ordinal number, noun* [C]
IDM **in your sixties** between the ages of 60 and 69: *I'm not sure how old she is but I should think she's in her sixties.* ◇ *in your* ***early/mid/late sixties*** ❶ For more information about numbers in dates, measurements, prices, etc., look at the **Reference Section** of this dictionary.

size[1] 🔑 A2 Ⓦ /saɪz/ *noun* **1** [U, C] how big or small sth is: *I was surprised at the size of the hotel. It was enormous!* ◇ *The planet Uranus is about four times the size of* (= as big as) *Earth.* **2** [C] one of a number of fixed measurements in which sth is made: *Have you got this dress* ***in a*** *bigger* ***size***? ◇ *I'm a size 12.* ◇ *What size pizza would you like? Medium or large?* **3 -sized** (*also* **-size**) (in adjectives) of the size mentioned: *a medium-sized flat* ◇ *a king-size bed*

size[2] /saɪz/ *verb*
PHR V **size sb/sth up** to form an opinion or judgement about sb/sth

sizeable (*also* **sizable**) /ˈsaɪzəbl/ *adj.* quite large: *a sizeable sum of money*

sizzle /ˈsɪzl/ *verb* [I] to make the sound of food frying in hot fat

skate[1] /skeɪt/ *noun* [C] **1** (*also* **ice skate**) (**SPORT**) a boot with a thin sharp metal part on the bottom that is used for moving on ice **2** = ROLLER SKATE

skate[2] /skeɪt/ *verb* [I] **1** (*also* **ice-skate**) to move on ice wearing SKATES: *Can you skate?* ◇ *They skated across the frozen lake.* **2** = ROLLER SKATE ▶ **skater** *noun* [C]

skateboard /ˈskeɪtbɔːd/ *noun* [C] a short narrow board with small wheels at each end that you can stand on and ride as a sport ▶ **skateboarder** *noun* [C] ▶ **skateboarding** *noun* [U]: *When we were children we used to* ***go skateboarding*** *in the park.*

skating /ˈskeɪtɪŋ/ *noun* [U] (**SPORT**) **1** (*also* **ice skating**) the activity or sport of moving on ice wearing special boots: *Would you like to* ***go skating*** *this weekend?* **2** = ROLLER SKATING

ˈ**skating rink** (*also* **rink**) *noun* [C] (**SPORT**) **1** = ICE RINK **2** an area or a building where you can ROLLER SKATE (= move using a type of shoe with wheels on the bottom)

skeletal /ˈskelətl/ *adj.* **1** (**ANATOMY**) connected with the SKELETON of a person or an animal: *Skeletal remains of the earliest dinosaurs are rare.* **2** looking like a SKELETON; very thin

skeleton[1] /ˈskelɪtn/ *noun* [C] (**ANATOMY**) the structure formed by all the bones in a human or an animal body: *the human skeleton* ◇ *a dinosaur skeleton* ➲ picture at **body**

skeleton[2] /ˈskelɪtn/ *adj.* (used about an organization, a service, etc.) having the smallest number of people that is necessary for it to operate

skeptic, skeptical, skepticism (*AmE*) = SCEPTIC, SCEPTICAL, SCEPTICISM

sketch 🔑+ B2 /sketʃ/ *noun* [C] **1** (**ART**) a simple, quick drawing without many details: *He drew a* ***rough sketch*** *of the new building on the back of an envelope.* **2** (**ARTS AND MEDIA**) a short funny scene on TV, in the theatre, etc: *The drama group did a sketch about a couple buying a new house.* **3** a short description without any details ▶ **sketch** *verb* [T, I]: *I sat on the grass and sketched the castle.*

sketchy /ˈsketʃi/ *adj.* (**sketchier**; **sketchiest**) not having many or enough details

skewer /ˈskjuːə(r)/ *noun* [C] a long thin pointed piece of metal or wood that is pushed through pieces of meat, vegetables, etc. to hold them together while they are cooking or to check that they are completely cooked ▶ **skewer** *verb* [T]

ski[1] 🔑 A2 /skiː/ *verb* [I] (**skiing**; *pt, pp* **skied**) to move over snow on skis: *When did you learn to ski?* ◇ *They* ***go skiing*** *every year.* ▶ **ski** 🔑 A2 *adj.*: *a ski resort/instructor/slope/suit* ▶ **skiing** 🔑 A2 *noun* [U]: *Alpine/downhill/cross-country skiing*

ski[2] 🔑 A2 /skiː/ *noun* [C] one of a pair of long, flat, narrow pieces of wood or plastic that are fastened to boots and used for sliding over snow: *a pair of skis*

skid /skɪd/ *verb* [I] (**-dd-**) (usually used about a vehicle) to suddenly slide forwards or to one side without any control: *I skidded on a patch of ice and hit a tree.* ▶ **skid** *noun* [C]: *The car went into a skid and came off the road.*

skier /ˈskiːə(r)/ *noun* [C] a person who skis

ˈ**ski jumping** *noun* [U] (**SPORT**) a sport in which people ski down a very steep slope, jump off the end and try to travel as far as they can through the air before landing ▶ ˈ**ski jumper** *noun* [C]

skilful (*BrE*) (*AmE* **skillful**) /ˈskɪlfl/ *adj.* **1** (used about a person) very good at doing sth: *a skilful painter/politician* ◇ *He's very skilful with his hands.* **2** done very well: *skilful guitar playing* ▶ **skilfully** (*AmE* **skillfully**) /-fəli/ *adv.*

skill 🔑 A1 Ⓞ /skɪl/ *noun* **1** [U] the ability to do sth well, especially because of training, practice, etc: *It takes great skill to make such beautiful jewellery.* ◇ *This is an easy game to play. No skill is required.* **2** [C] an ability that you need in order to do a job, an activity, etc. well: *The course will help you to develop your reading and listening skills.* ◇ *management skills* ◇ *Typing is a skill I have never mastered.*

skilled 🔑+ B2 /skɪld/ *adj.* **1** (used about a person) having enough ability, experience and knowledge to be able to do something well: *a skilled worker* **2** (used about work, a job, etc.) needing skill or skills; done by people who have been trained: *a highly skilled job* ◇ *Skilled work is difficult to find in this area.*
OPP **unskilled**

skillet /ˈskɪlɪt/ (*AmE*) = FRYING PAN

skillful, skillfully (*AmE*) = SKILFUL, SKILFULLY

skim /skɪm/ *verb* (**-mm-**) **1** [T] **~ sth (off/from sth)** to remove sth from the surface of a liquid: *to skim the cream off the milk* **2** [I, T] to move quickly over or past sth, almost touching it or touching it slightly: *The* *plane flew very low, skimming the tops of the buildings.* **3** [I, T] ~ **(through/over)** sth to read sth quickly in order to get the main idea, without paying attention to the details and without reading every word: *I usually just skim through the newspaper in the morning.*

skimmed ˈmilk *noun* [U] milk from which the cream has been removed

skimp /skɪmp/ *verb* [I] ~ **(on sth)** to use or provide less of sth than is necessary: *I don't think we should skimp on books. The students must have one each.*

skimpy /ˈskɪmpi/ *adj.* **(skimpier; skimpiest)** using or having less than is necessary; too small or few

skin¹ ⚓ **A2** /skɪn/ *noun* [U, C]
• ON THE BODY **1** (**ANATOMY**) the natural outer covering of a human or an animal body: *to have (a) fair/dark/sensitive skin ◇ skin cancer* **2** -skinned (in adjectives) having the type of skin mentioned: *My sister's very dark-skinned.*
• OF A DEAD ANIMAL **3** (often in compounds) the skin of a dead animal, with or without its fur, used for making things: *a sheepskin jacket ◇ a bag made of crocodile skin*
• OF A FRUIT/VEGETABLE **4** the natural outer covering of some fruits or vegetables; the outer covering of a SAUSAGE: *(a) banana/tomato skin*
• ON A LIQUID **5** the thin solid layer that can form on the surface of a liquid: *A skin had formed on top of the milk.*
IDM by the skin of your teeth (*informal*) (used to show that sb almost failed to do sth) only just: *I ran into the airport and caught the plane by the skin of my teeth.* have a thick skin → THICK¹

skin² /skɪn/ *verb* [T] (-nn-) to remove the skin from sth
IDM keep your eyes peeled/skinned (for sb/sth) → EYE¹

ˌskin-ˈdeep *adj.* (used about a feeling or an attitude) not as important or as strongly felt as it appears to be
SYN superficial

structure of the skin

skinhead /ˈskɪnhed/ *noun* [C] a young person with very short hair, especially one who is violent, aggressive and RACIST

skinny /ˈskɪni/ *adj.* **(skinnier; skinniest)** (used about a person) too thin

skint /skɪnt/ *adj.* (*BrE, informal*) having no money

skintight /ˌskɪnˈtaɪt/ *adj.* (used about a piece of clothing) fitting very tightly and showing the shape of the body

skip¹ ⚓+ **C1** /skɪp/ *verb* (-pp-) **1** [I] (often used with an adverb or a preposition) to move along quickly and lightly in a way that is similar to dancing, with little jumps and steps, from one foot to the other: *A little girl came skipping along the road. ◇ Lambs were skipping about in the field.* **2** [I] to jump over a rope that you or two other people hold at each end, turning it round and round over the head and under the feet: *Some girls were skipping in the playground.* **3** [T] to not do sth that you usually do or should do: *I got up rather late, so I skipped breakfast.* **4** [T] to miss the next thing that you would normally read, do, etc: *I accidentally skipped one of the questions in the test.*

skip² /skɪp/ *noun* [C] **1** a small jumping movement **2** (*BrE*) a large, open metal container for rubbish, often used during building work

skipper /ˈskɪpə(r)/ *noun* [C] (*informal*) the captain of a boat or ship, or of a sports team

skirmish /ˈskɜːmɪʃ/ *noun* [C] a short fight between groups of people

skirt¹ ⚓ **A1** /skɜːt/ *noun* [C] **1** a piece of clothing that is worn by women and girls and that hangs down from the the middle part of the body ⊃ look at **culottes 2** an outer covering or PROTECTIVE part for the base of a vehicle or machine: *the rubber skirt around the bottom of a hovercraft*

skirt² /skɜːt/ *verb* [I, T] to go around the edge of sth
PHR V skirt around/round sth to avoid talking about sth in a direct way: *The manager skirted round the subject of our pay increase.*

ˈskirting board (*also* skirting /ˈskɜːtɪŋ/) (*BrE*) (*AmE* baseboard) *noun* [C, U] a narrow piece of wood that is fixed along the bottom of the walls in a house

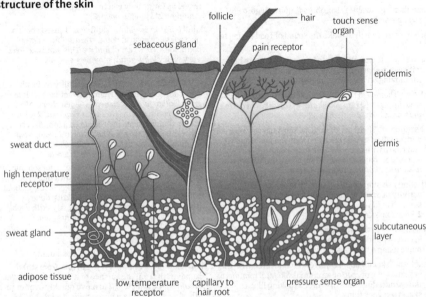

skittle /ˈskɪtl/ *noun* **1** [C] an object shaped like a bottle which players try to knock over with a ball in the game of skittles **2 skittles** [U] (in Britain) a game in which players roll a ball at nine skittles and try to knock over as many of them as possible

skulk /skʌlk/ *verb* [I] (used with an adverb or a preposition) to stay somewhere quietly and secretly, hoping that nobody will notice you, especially because you are planning to do sth bad

skull ɪ̃+ **B2** /skʌl/ *noun* [C] (**ANATOMY**) the bone that forms the head and surrounds the brain: *She suffered a fractured skull in the fall.* **SYN cranium** ➔ picture at **body**

sky ɪ̃ **A2** /skaɪ/ *noun* [C, U] (*pl.* skies) the space that you can see when you look up from the earth, and where you can see the sun, moon and stars: *a cloudless/clear blue sky* ◇ *I saw a bit of blue sky between the clouds.* ◇ *I saw a plane high up in the sky.*

skydiving /ˈskaɪdaɪvɪŋ/ *noun* [U] (**SPORT**) a sport in which you jump from a plane and fall for as long as you safely can before opening your PARACHUTE (= a piece of thin cloth that opens and lets you fall to the ground slowly): *to go skydiving* ▶ **skydiver** /-və(r)/ *noun* [C]

sky-ˈhigh *adj., adv.* very high

skylight /ˈskaɪlaɪt/ *noun* [C] a small window in a roof

skyline /ˈskaɪlaɪn/ *noun* [C] the shape that is made by tall buildings, etc. against the sky: *the Manhattan skyline*

Skype™ /skaɪp/ *noun* [U] (**COMPUTING**) a phone system that allows people to make calls on their computers over the internet ▶ **Skype™** *verb* [T, I]: *I Skyped him.*

skyrocket /ˈskaɪrɒkɪt/ *verb* [I] (used about prices, etc.) to rise quickly to a very high level: *House prices skyrocketed as the city's population grew.*

skyscraper /ˈskaɪskreɪpə(r)/ *noun* [C] (**ARCHITECTURE**) an extremely tall building

SLA /ˌes el ˈeɪ/ *abbr.* (**LANGUAGE**) **second language acquisition** (the learning of a second language)

slab /slæb/ *noun* [C] a thick, flat piece of sth: *huge concrete slabs*

slack /slæk/ *adj.* **1** loose; not tightly stretched: *Leave the rope slack.* **2** (used about a period of business) not busy; not having many customers: *Trade is very slack here in winter.* **3** not carefully or properly done: *Slack security made terrorist attacks possible.* **4** (used about a person) not doing sth carefully or properly: *You've been rather slack about your homework lately.*

slacken /ˈslækən/ *verb* [I, T] **1** to become less tight; to make sth less tight: *The rope slackened and he pulled his hand free.* **2 ~ (sth) (off)** to become slower or less active; to make sth slower or less active: *He slackened off his pace towards the end of the race.*

slacks /slæks/ *noun* [pl.] (*old-fashioned or AmE, formal*) trousers (especially not very formal ones): *a pair of slacks*

slag¹ /slæɡ/ *verb* (-gg-)
PHRV slag sb off (*informal*) to say cruel or critical things about sb

slag² /slæɡ/ *noun* [U] the waste material that is left after metal has been removed from rock

slain /sleɪn/ past participle of **slay**

slalom /ˈslɑːləm/ *noun* [C] (in skiing, CANOEING, etc.) a race along a course on which competitors have to move from side to side between POLES

slam ɪ̃+ **C1** /slæm/ *verb* (-mm-) **1** [I, T] to shut or make sth shut very loudly and with great force: *I heard the front door slam.* ◇ *She slammed her book shut and rushed out of the room.* **2** [T] to put sth somewhere very quickly and with great force: *He slammed the

plate down on the table and stormed out.* ➔ look at **grand slam**

slam dunk /ˌslæm ˈdʌŋk/ *noun* [C] (**SPORT**) (in basketball) the act of jumping up and putting the ball through the net with a lot of force ▶ **slam-dunk** *verb* [T, I]

slander /ˈslɑːndə(r)/ *noun* [C, U] (**LAW**) a spoken statement about sb that is not true and that is intended to damage the good opinion that other people have of them; the legal offence of making this kind of statement ▶ **slander** *verb* [T] ▶ **slanderous** /-dərəs/ *adj.*

slang /slæŋ/ *noun* [U] (**LANGUAGE**) very informal words and expressions that are more common in spoken than written language. Slang is sometimes used only by a particular group of people (for example students, young people or criminals) and often stays in fashion for a short time. Some slang is not polite: *'Wicked' is slang for 'very good'.*

slant¹ /slɑːnt/ *verb* **1** [I, T] to slope in a particular direction or at a particular angle; to make sth slope in this way: *My handwriting slants backwards.* **2** [T, usually passive] to describe information, events, etc. in a way that supports a particular group or opinion ▶ **slanting** *adj.*: *slanting eyes/rain/rays*

slant² /slɑːnt/ *noun* [C, usually sing.] **1** a sloping position: *The sunlight fell on the table at a slant.* **2** a way of thinking, writing, etc. about sth, that sees things from a particular point of view

slap¹ ɪ̃+ **C1** /slæp/ *verb* [T] (-pp-) **1** to hit sb/sth with the inside of your hand when it is flat: *She slapped him across the face.* ◇ *People slapped him on the back and congratulated him on winning.* **2** (used with an adverb or a preposition) to put sth onto a surface quickly and carelessly ▶ **slap** *noun* [C]: *I gave him a slap across the face.*

slap² /slæp/ (*also* **slap ˈbang**) *adv.* (*informal*) **1** straight, and with great force: *I hurried round the corner and walked slap into somebody coming the other way.* **2** exactly

slapdash /ˈslæpdæʃ/ *adj.* careless, or done quickly and carelessly: *slapdash building methods* ◇ *He's a bit slapdash about doing his homework on time.*

slapstick /ˈslæpstɪk/ *noun* [U] a type of humour that is based on simple physical jokes, for example people falling over or hitting each other

slash¹ ɪ̃+ **C1** /slæʃ/ *verb* **1** [I, T] **~ (at) sb/sth** to make or try to make a long cut in sth with a violent movement: *He slashed wildly at me with a knife.* **2** [T] (*informal*) to reduce an amount of money, etc. very much: *The price of coffee has been slashed by 20%.*

slash² /slæʃ/ *noun* [C] **1** a sharp movement made with a knife, etc. in order to cut sb/sth **2** a long narrow wound or cut **3** (*BrE also* **oblique**) (**LANGUAGE**) the symbol (/) used to show alternatives, as in *lunch and/ or dinner*, in FRACTIONS, as in ¾, and in internet addresses to separate the different parts of the address ➔ look at **backslash, forward slash**

ˌslash-and-ˈburn *adj.* **1** (**AGRICULTURE**) relating to a method of farming in which existing plants, crops, etc. are cut down and burned before new seeds are planted: *slash-and-burn agriculture* **2** aggressive and causing a lot of harm or damage: *a slash-and-burn takeover*

slat /slæt/ *noun* [C] one of a series of long, narrow pieces of wood, metal or plastic, used in furniture, fences, etc.

slate /sleɪt/ *noun* **1** [U] (**GEOLOGY**) a type of dark grey rock that can easily be split into thin flat pieces **2** [C] one of the thin flat pieces of slate that are used for covering roofs

slaughter /ˈslɔːtə(r)/ *verb* [T] **1** to kill an animal, usually for food **2** to kill a large number of people at one time, especially in a cruel way: *Men, women and children were slaughtered and whole villages destroyed.* ⊃ note at **kill**[1] ▸ **slaughter** *noun* [U]

slaughterhouse /ˈslɔːtəhaʊs/ (*BrE also* **abattoir**) *noun* [C] a place where animals are killed for food

slave[1] 🔒 **B2** /sleɪv/ *noun* [C] (**SOCIAL STUDIES**) a person who is owned by another person and has to work for them ▸ **slavery** 🔒+ **C1** /ˈsleɪvəri/ *noun* [U]: *the abolition of slavery in America*

slave[2] /sleɪv/ *verb* [I] ~ (**away**) to work very hard

slay /sleɪ/ *verb* [T] (*pt* **slew** /sluː/; *pp* **slain** /sleɪn/) (*old-fashioned*) to kill violently; to murder

sleazy /ˈsliːzi/ *adj.* (**sleazier**; **sleaziest**) (used about a place or a person) unpleasant and probably connected with activities that are not moral: *a sleazy nightclub*

sledge /sledʒ/ (*BrE*) (*also* **sled** /sled/ *especially in AmE*) *noun* [C] a vehicle without wheels that is used for travelling on snow. Large sledges are often pulled by dogs, and smaller ones are used for going down hills, for fun or as a sport. ⊃ look at **bobsleigh**, **toboggan** ▸ **sledge** *verb* [I]

sledgehammer /ˈsledʒhæmə(r)/ *noun* [C] a large heavy HAMMER with a long handle

sleek /sliːk/ *adj.* **1** (used about hair or fur) smooth and shiny because it is healthy **2** (used about a vehicle) having an attractive, smooth shape: *a sleek new sports car*

sleep[1] 🔒 **A2** /sliːp/ *noun* **1** [U] the natural condition of rest when your eyes are closed and your mind and body are not active or conscious: *Most people need at least seven hours' sleep every night.* ◇ *I didn't get much sleep last night.* ◇ *Do you ever talk in your sleep?* ◇ *I couldn't **get to sleep** last night.* **2** [sing.] a period of sleep: *You'll feel better after a good night's sleep.* ◇ *I sometimes have a short sleep in the afternoon.* **3** [U] (*informal*) the substance that sometimes forms in the corners of your eyes after you have been sleeping **IDM go to sleep** **1** to start sleeping: *He got into bed and soon went to sleep.* **2** (used about an arm, a leg, etc.) to lose the sense of feeling in a part of your body **put (an animal) to sleep** to kill an animal that is ill or injured because you want to stop it suffering

sleep[2] 🔒 **A1** /sliːp/ *verb* (*pt, pp* **slept** /slept/) **1** [I] to rest with your eyes closed and your mind and body not active: *Did you sleep well?* ◇ *I only slept for a couple of hours last night.* ◇ *I slept solidly from ten last night till eleven this morning.* **2** [T] (used about a place) to have enough beds for a particular number of people: *The apartment sleeps five.*
IDM sleep/live rough → **ROUGH**[3]
PHR V sleep in to sleep until later than usual in the morning ⊃ look at **oversleep** **sleep together** | **sleep with sb** to have sex with sb (usually when you are not married to or living with that person)

sleeper /ˈsliːpə(r)/ *noun* [C] **1** (after an adjective) a person who sleeps in a particular way: *a light/heavy sleeper* **2** a bed on a train; a train with beds

sleeping bag *noun* [C] a large soft bag that you use for sleeping in when you go camping, etc.

sleeping partner (*BrE*) (*AmE* **silent partner**) *noun* [C] (**BUSINESS**) a person who has put money into a business but who is not involved in running it

sleeping pill *noun* [C] (**MEDICINE**) a medicine in solid form that you take to help you sleep

sleeping sickness *noun* [U] (**HEALTH**) a tropical disease carried by a TSETSE FLY that makes you want to go to sleep and usually causes death

sleepless /ˈsliːpləs/ *adj.* (used about a period, usually the night) without sleep ▸ **sleeplessness** *noun* [U] ⊃ look at **insomnia**

sleepover /ˈsliːpəʊvə(r)/ (*AmE also* **slumber party**) *noun* [C] a party for children or young people when a group of them spend the night at one house

sleepwalk /ˈsliːpwɔːk/ *verb* [I] to walk around while you are asleep

sleepy /ˈsliːpi/ *adj.* (**sleepier**; **sleepiest**) **1** tired and ready to go to sleep: *These pills might make you feel a bit sleepy.* **2** (used about a place) very quiet and not having much activity ▸ **sleepily** /-pɪli/ *adv.*

sleet /sliːt/ *noun* [U] a mixture of rain and snow ⊃ note at **weather**[1]

sleeve /sliːv/ *noun* [C] **1** one of the two parts of a piece of clothing that cover the arms or part of the arms: *a blouse with long sleeves* **2** -**sleeved** (in adjectives) with sleeves of a particular kind: *a short-sleeved shirt*

sleeveless /ˈsliːvləs/ *adj.* (used about clothes) without any part covering your arms: *a sleeveless top*

sleigh /sleɪ/ *noun* [C] a vehicle without wheels that is used for travelling on snow and that is usually pulled by horses ⊃ look at **bobsleigh**

sleight of hand /ˌslaɪt əv ˈhænd/ *noun* [U] movements of your hand that are done with skill so that other people cannot see them: *The trick is done simply by sleight of hand.*

slender /ˈslendə(r)/ *adj.* **1** (used about a person or part of sb's body) thin in an attractive way: *long slender fingers* **2** smaller in amount or size than you would like: *My chances of winning are very slender.*

slept /slept/ *past tense, past participle of* **sleep**[1]

slew /sluː/ *past tense of* **slay**

slice[1] 🔒 **B1** /slaɪs/ *noun* [C] **1** a flat piece of food that is cut from a larger piece: *a thick/thin slice of bread* ◇ *Cut the meat into thin slices.* **2** a part of sth: *The directors have taken a large slice of the profits.*

slice[2] 🔒 **B1** /slaɪs/ *verb* **1** [T] to cut sth into thin flat pieces: *Peel and slice the apples.* ◇ *a loaf of sliced bread* **2** [I, T] to cut sth easily with sth sharp: *He sliced through the rope with a knife.* ◇ *The glass sliced her hand.* **3** [T] (in ball sports) to hit the ball on the bottom or side so that it does not travel in a straight line

slick[1] /slɪk/ *adj.* **1** done smoothly and well, and seeming to be done without any effort **2** clever at persuading people but perhaps not completely honest

slick[2] /slɪk/ *noun* [C] = **OIL SLICK**

slide[1] 🔒 **B2** /slaɪd/ *verb* (*pt, pp* **slid** /slɪd/) **1** [I, T] to move or make sth move smoothly along a surface: *She fell over and slid along the ice.* ◇ *The doors slide open automatically.* **2** [I, T] to move or make sth move quietly without being noticed: *I slid out of the room when nobody was looking.* ◇ *She slid her hand into her pocket and took out a sweet.* **3** [I] (used about prices, values, etc.) to go down slowly and continuously: *Share prices slid to a new low.* **4** [I] to move gradually towards a worse situation: *The company slid into debt and eventually closed.*

slide[2] 🔒 **B2** ⑤ /slaɪd/ *noun* [C] **1** one page of an electronic presentation that is usually viewed on a computer screen or projected onto a larger screen

2 (SCIENCE) a small piece of glass that you put sth on when you want to examine it under a MICROSCOPE (= a piece of equipment that makes things appear much bigger) ⊃ picture at **laboratory**, **microscope 3** a large toy consisting of steps and a long piece of metal, plastic, etc. Children climb up the steps then slide down the other part. **4** a continuous slow fall, for example of prices, values, levels, etc.

'slide show noun [C] (COMPUTING) a piece of software that shows a number of images on a computer screen in a particular order

'sliding 'scale noun [C] a system in which the rate at which sth is paid varies according to particular conditions: *Fees are calculated on a sliding scale according to income* (= richer people pay more).

slight ⚡ B2 /slaɪt/ adj. **1** very small; not important or serious: *I've got a slight problem, but it's nothing to get worried about.* ◊ *a slight change/difference/increase/ improvement* ◊ *I haven't the slightest idea* (= no idea at all) *what you're talking about.* **2** (used about a person's body) thin and light: *His slight frame is perfect for a long-distance runner.*
IDM **not in the slightest** not at all: *'Are you angry with me?' 'Not in the slightest.'*

slightly ⚡ B1 ⑤ /'slaɪtli/ adv. **1** a little: *I'm slightly older than her.* **2** a **slightly-built** person is small and thin

slim¹ /slɪm/ adj. (slimmer; slimmest) **1** thin in an attractive way: *a tall, slim woman* **2** not as big as you would like: *Her chances of success are very slim.*

slim² /slɪm/ verb [I] (-mm-) to become or try to become thinner and lighter by eating less food, taking exercise, etc. ⊃ look at **diet¹**

slime /slaɪm/ noun [U] a thick unpleasant liquid: *The pond was covered with slime and had a horrible smell.* ⊃ look at **sludge**

slimy /'slaɪmi/ adj. (slimier; slimiest) **1** covered with SLIME **2** (used about a person) pretending to be friendly, in a way that you do not trust or like

sling¹ /slɪŋ/ noun [C] (MEDICINE) a piece of cloth that is tied around a person's neck and used to support a broken or injured arm: *She had her arm in a sling.* ⊃ picture at **health 2** a device consisting of a band, ropes, etc. for holding and lifting heavy objects: *The engine was lifted in a sling of steel rope.* **3** a device like a bag for carrying a baby on your back or in front of you **4** (in the past) a simple weapon made from a band of leather, etc., used for throwing stones
SYN **catapult¹**

sling² /slɪŋ/ verb [T] (used with an adverb or a preposition) (pt, pp slung /slʌŋ/) **1** to put or throw sth somewhere in a rough or careless way **2** [often passive] to put sth into a position where it hangs in a loose way: *She was carrying her bag slung over her shoulder.*

slingback /'slɪŋbæk/ noun [C] a woman's shoe that is open at the back with a STRAP around the heel

slingshot /'slɪŋʃɒt/ (AmE) = CATAPULT¹

slink /slɪŋk/ verb [I] (used with an adverb or a preposition) (pt, pp slunk /slʌŋk/) to move somewhere slowly and quietly because you do not want anyone to see you, often when you feel guilty or embarrassed

slip¹ ⚡ B2 /slɪp/ verb (-pp-)
• SLIDE/FALL **1** [I] ~ (over); ~ (on sth) to slide a short distance by accident and fall or nearly fall: *She slipped over on the wet floor.* ◊ *I slipped on the ice and twisted my ankle.*
• OUT OF POSITION **2** [I] (often used with an adverb or a preposition) to slide out of the correct position or out of your hand: *This hat's too big. It keeps slipping down over my eyes.* ◊ *The glass slipped out of my hand and smashed on the floor.*

• GO/PUT QUIETLY **3** [I] (used with an adverb or a preposition) to move or go somewhere quietly, quickly, and often without being noticed: *While everyone was dancing we slipped away and went home.* **4** [T] ~ sth (to sb); ~ (sb) sth to put sth somewhere or give sth to sb quietly and often without being noticed: *She picked up the money and slipped it into her pocket.* ◊ *He slipped her a note under the table.*
• BECOME WORSE **5** [I] to fall a little in value, level, etc.
• CLOTHES **6** [I, T] ~ into/out of sth; ~ sth on/off to put on or take off a piece of clothing quickly and easily: *She slipped into her silk jacket.* ◊ *I slipped off my shoes.*
IDM **let sth slip** to give sb information that you should keep secret **slip your mind** if sth **slips your mind**, you forget it or forget to do it: *I'm sorry, the meeting completely slipped my mind.*
PHRV **slip out** when sth **slips out**, you say it without really intending to: *It just slipped out.* **slip up** (informal) to make a mistake

slip² /slɪp/ noun [C] **1** a small mistake, usually made by being careless or not paying attention: *to make a slip* **2** a small piece of paper: *I made a note of her name on a slip of paper.* ⊃ look at **payslip 3** an act of sliding and falling or nearly falling **4** a thin piece of clothing that is worn by a woman under a dress or skirt
IDM **give sb the slip** (informal) to escape from sb who is following or trying to catch you **a slip of the tongue** something that you say that you did not mean to say

slipped 'disc noun [C] (HEALTH) a painful injury caused when one of the DISCS in the SPINE (= the bones of the back) moves out of its correct position

slipper /'slɪpə(r)/ noun [C] a light soft shoe that is worn inside the house: *a pair of slippers*

slippery /'slɪpəri/ (also informal slippy /'slɪpi/) adj. (slipperier; slippiest) (used about a surface or an object) difficult to walk on or hold because it is smooth, wet, etc: *a slippery floor*

'slip road (BrE) (AmE ramp) noun [C] a road that leads onto or off a large road such as a MOTORWAY

slipway /'slɪpweɪ/ noun [C] a track leading down to water, on which ships are built or pulled up out of the water for repairs, or from which they are launched

slit¹ /slɪt/ noun [C] a long narrow cut or opening: *a long skirt with a slit up the back*

slit² /slɪt/ verb [T] (slitting; pt, pp slit) to make a long narrow cut in sth: *She slit the envelope open with a knife.*

slither /'slɪðə(r)/ verb [I] to move by sliding from side to side along the ground like a snake: *I saw a snake slithering down a rock.*

slob /slɒb/ noun [C] (informal) (used in a critical way) a very lazy or untidy person

slog¹ /slɒg/ verb [I] (-gg-) **1** ~ (away) (at sth); ~ (through sth) (informal) to work hard for a long period at sth difficult or boring: *I've been slogging away at this homework for hours.* **2** (used with an adverb or a preposition) to walk or move in a certain direction with a lot of effort

slog² /slɒg/ noun [sing.] a period of long, hard, boring work; a long journey that makes you tired

slogan ⚡+ B2 /'sləʊgən/ noun [C] (POLITICS) a short phrase that is easy to remember and that is used in politics or advertising: *Anti-government slogans had been painted all over the walls.* ◊ *an advertising slogan*

sloop /sluːp/ noun [C] a small sailing ship with one MAST (= a post to support the sails)

slop /slɒp/ *verb* [I, T] (-pp-) (used about a liquid) to pour over the edge of its container; to make a liquid do this: *He filled his glass too full and beer slopped onto the table.*

slope 🔑 B2 /sləʊp/ *noun* **1** [C] a surface or piece of land that goes up or down: *The village is built on a slope.* ◊ *The best ski slopes are in the Alps.* **2** [sing.] the amount by which a surface is not level; the fact of not being level: *a steep/gentle slope* ▶ **slope** 🔑 B2 *verb* [I]: *The road slopes down to the river.* ◊ *a sloping roof*

sloppy /ˈslɒpi/ *adj.* (sloppier; sloppiest) **1** that shows lack of care, thought or effort; untidy: *a sloppy worker/writer/dresser* ◊ *a sloppy piece of work* **2** (used about clothes) not tight and without much shape **3** (*BrE, informal*) showing emotions in a silly embarrassing way: *I can't stand sloppy love songs.* SYN **sentimental**

slosh /slɒʃ/ *verb* (used with an adverb or a preposition) (*informal*) **1** [I] (used about a liquid) to move around noisily inside a container **2** [T] to pour or drop liquid somewhere in a careless way

slot¹ 🔑 C1 /slɒt/ *noun* [C] **1** a straight narrow opening in a machine, etc: *Put your money into the slot and take the ticket.* **2** a place in a list, a system, an organization, etc: *He has a regular slot on the late-night programme.*

slot² /slɒt/ *verb* [T, I] (used with an adverb or a preposition) (-tt-) to put sth into a particular space that is designed for it; to fit into such a space: *Slot the tubes into the correct holes.* ◊ *The dishwasher slots neatly between the cupboards.*
IDM **fall/slot into place** → PLACE¹

slot machine *noun* [C] a machine with an opening for coins that sells drinks, cigarettes, etc. or on which you can play games

slouch /slaʊtʃ/ *verb* [I] to sit, stand or walk in a lazy way, with your head and shoulders hanging down

slovenly /ˈslʌvnli/ *adj.* (*old-fashioned*) lazy, careless and untidy

slow¹ 🔑 A1 /sləʊ/ *adj.*
- NOT FAST **1** moving, doing sth or happening without much speed; not fast: *The traffic is always very slow in the city centre.* ◊ *Haven't you finished your homework yet? You're being very slow!* ◊ *Progress was slower than expected.* ◊ *a slow driver/walker/reader* OPP **fast¹**
- WITH DELAY **2** ~ **to do sth; ~ (in/about) doing sth** not doing sth immediately: *She was rather slow to realize what was going on.* ◊ *They've been rather slow in replying to my letter!*
- NOT CLEVER **3** not quick to learn or understand: *He's the slowest student in the class.*
- NOT BUSY **4** not very busy; with little action: *Business is very slow at the moment.*
- WATCH/CLOCK **5** [not before noun] (used about watches and clocks) showing a time that is earlier than the real time: *That clock is five minutes slow* (= it says it is 8.55 when the correct time is 9.00). OPP **fast¹**
▶ **slowness** *noun* [U]
IDM **quick/slow on the uptake** → UPTAKE

slow² 🔑 B1 /sləʊ/ *verb* [I, T] to start to move, do sth or happen at a slower speed; to cause sth to do this: *Economic growth has slowed this year.* ◊ *He slowed his pace a little.*
PHR V **slow (sb/sth) down/up** to start to move, do sth or happen at a slower speed; to cause sb/sth to do this: *Can't you slow down a bit? You're driving much too fast.* ◊ *These problems have slowed up the whole process.*

slow³ /sləʊ/ *adv.* (used especially in the comparative and superlative forms, or in compounds) at a slow speed: *Could you go a little slower?* ◊ *slow-moving traffic* SYN **slowly**

slowdown /ˈsləʊdaʊn/ *noun* [C] (BUSINESS) a reduction in speed or activity: *a slowdown in economic growth*

slowly 🔑 A2 /ˈsləʊli/ *adv.* at a slow speed; not quickly: *He walked slowly along the street.*

slow 'motion *noun* [U] (ARTS AND MEDIA) (in a film or on TV) a method of making action appear much slower than in real life: *They showed the winning goal again, this time in slow motion.*

sludge /slʌdʒ/ *noun* [U] thick, soft, wet mud or a substance that looks like it ⊃ look at **slime**

slug /slʌɡ/ *noun* [C] a small black or brown creature with a soft body and no legs, that moves slowly along the ground and eats garden plants ⊃ picture at **animal**

sluggish /ˈslʌɡɪʃ/ *adj.* moving or working more slowly than normal in a way that seems lazy

sluice /sluːs/ (*also* **sluice gate**) *noun* [C] a type of gate that you can open or close to control the flow of water out of or into a CANAL, etc.

slum /slʌm/ *noun* [C] (GEOGRAPHY, SOCIAL STUDIES) an area of a city where living conditions are extremely bad, and where the buildings are dirty and have not been repaired for a long time

slumber¹ /ˈslʌmbə(r)/ *verb* [I] (*formal*) to be deeply asleep

slumber² /ˈslʌmbə(r)/ *noun* [U, C, usually pl.] (*formal*) sleep; a time when sb is asleep ▶ **slumber** *verb* [I]

'slumber party (*AmE*) = SLEEPOVER

slump¹ /slʌmp/ *verb* [I] **1** ~ **(to sth); ~ (by sth)** (ECONOMICS) (used about economic activity, prices, etc.) to fall suddenly and by a large amount: *Shares in the bank slumped 33p to 181p yesterday.* ◊ *The newspaper's circulation has slumped by 30%.* SYN **drop¹** ⊃ note at **fall¹, trend¹** **2** (used with an adverb or a preposition) to fall or sit down suddenly when your body feels heavy and weak, usually because you are tired or ill

slump² /slʌmp/ *noun* [C] **1** ~ **(in sth)** a sudden large fall in sales, prices, the value of sth, etc: *a slump in house prices* SYN **decline²** **2** (ECONOMICS) a period when a country's economy is doing very badly and a lot of people do not have jobs ⊃ look at **boom¹ (1)**

slung /slʌŋ/ *past tense, past participle of* **sling²**

slunk /slʌŋk/ *past tense, past participle of* **slink**

slur¹ /slɜː(r)/ *verb* [T] (-rr-) to pronounce words in a way that is not clear, often because you are drunk

slur² /slɜː(r)/ *noun* [C] ~ **(on sb/sth)** an unfair comment about sb/sth that could damage people's opinion of them: *a racial slur* SYN **insult²**

slurp /slɜːp/ *verb* [T, I] (*informal*) to drink noisily

slurry /ˈslʌri/ *noun* [U] (AGRICULTURE) a thick liquid consisting of water mixed with animal waste that farmers use on their fields to make plants grow better

slush /slʌʃ/ *noun* [U] **1** partly melted snow that is usually dirty **2** (*informal*) films, books, feelings, etc. that are considered to be silly because they are too romantic and emotional ▶ **slushy** *adj.* (slushier; slushiest)

'slush fund *noun* [C] (POLITICS) an amount of money that is kept to pay people illegally to do things, especially in politics

sly /slaɪ/ *adj.* **1** (used about a person) acting or done in a secret or dishonest way, often intending to trick people SYN **cunning** **2** (used about an action) suggesting that you know sth secret: *a sly smile/look* ► **slyly** *adv.*

smack /smæk/ *verb* [T] to hit sb with the inside of your hand when it is flat, especially as a punishment: *I never smack my children.* ◊ *You're going to get a smack if you don't do as I say!*
PHR V **smack of sth** to make you think that sb/sth has an unpleasant attitude or quality

small ⓣ **A1** Ⓢ /smɔːl/ *adj.* **1** not large in size, number, amount, etc: *a small car/flat/town* ◊ *a small group of people* ◊ *a small amount of money* ◊ *That dress is too small for you.* **2** young: *He has a wife and three small children.* ◊ *When I was small we lived in a big old house.* **3** not important or serious; slight: *Don't worry. It's only a small problem.* ► **small** *adv.*: *She's painted the picture far too small.*
IDM **in a big/small way** → WAY¹ **the early/small hours** → EARLY¹

'**small ad** (*BrE, informal*) = CLASSIFIED ADVERTISEMENT

'**small arms** *noun* [pl.] small light weapons that you can carry in your hands

,**small 'change** *noun* [U] (**FINANCE**) coins that have a low value

smallholding /'smɔːlhəʊldɪŋ/ *noun* [C] (**AGRICULTURE**) a small piece of land that is used for farming ► **smallholder** /-də(r)/ *noun* [C]

smallpox /'smɔːlpɒks/ *noun* [U] (**HEALTH**) a serious disease that causes a high temperature and leaves marks on the skin. In past times many people died from smallpox.

the 'small print (*BrE*) (*AmE* **the fine print**) *noun* [U] (**LAW**) the important details of a legal document, contract, etc. that are usually printed in small type and are therefore easy to miss: *Make sure you read the small print before you sign anything.*

,**small-'scale** *adj.* (used about an organization or activity) not large; limited in what it does

'**small talk** *noun* [U] polite conversation, for example at a party, about unimportant things: *We had to **make small talk** for half an hour.*

smart¹ ⓣ **B1** /smɑːt/ *adj.* **1** (*especially BrE*) (used about a person) having a clean and tidy appearance: *You look smart. Are you going somewhere special?* **2** (*especially BrE*) (used about a piece of clothing, etc.) good enough to wear on a formal occasion: *a smart suit* **3** (*especially AmE*) clever; intelligent: *He's not smart enough to be a politician.* **4** (**COMPUTING**) (used about a device) controlled by a computer, so that it appears to act in an intelligent way: *smart bombs* **5** (*especially BrE*) fashionable and usually expensive: *a smart restaurant/hotel* **6** (used about a movement or an action) quick and usually done with force: *We set off at a smart pace.* ► **smartly** *adv.*: *She's always smartly dressed.*

smart² /smɑːt/ *verb* [I] **1** ~ (**from sth**) to feel a sharp pain in your body: *Her cheek smarted from the blow.* **2** ~ (**from/over sth**) to feel upset or offended because of a criticism, failure, etc: *He was still smarting from her insult.*

'**smart card** *noun* [C] (**COMPUTING**) a small plastic card on which information can be stored in electronic form

smarten /'smɑːtn/ *verb*
PHR V **smarten (yourself/sb/sth) up** (*especially BrE*) to make yourself/sb/sth look tidy and more attractive

smartphone ⓣ **A2** /'smɑːtfəʊn/ *noun* [C] (**COMPUTING**) a mobile phone that also has some of the functions of a computer

smartwatch /'smɑːtwɒtʃ/ *noun* [C] (**COMPUTING**) a device like a watch that has many of the features of a computer or a smartphone

smash¹ ⓣ+ **C1** /smæʃ/ *verb* **1** [T, I] to break sth, or to be broken violently and noisily into many pieces: *The glass smashed into a thousand pieces.* ◊ *The police had to smash the door open.* **2** [I, T] (used with an adverb or a preposition) to move with great force in a particular direction; to hit sth very hard: *The car smashed into a tree.* ◊ *He smashed his fist through the window.* **3** [T] ~ **sth (up)** to crash a vehicle, usually causing a lot of damage **4** [T] (**SPORT**) (in tennis) to hit a ball that is high in the air downwards very hard over the net

smash² /smæʃ/ *noun* **1** [sing.] the action or the noise of sth breaking violently **2** [C] (**SPORT**) (in tennis, etc.) a way of hitting a ball that is high in the air downwards and very hard over the net **3** (*also* ,**smash 'hit**) [C] (*informal*) (**ARTS AND MEDIA**) a song, play, film, etc. that is very successful

smashing /'smæʃɪŋ/ *adj.* (*BrE, informal*) very good or pleasant

smear¹ /smɪə(r)/ *verb* [T] ~ **sth on/over sth/sb**; ~ **sth/sb with sth** to spread a sticky substance across sth/sb: *The child had smeared chocolate over his clothes.* ◊ *Her face was smeared with blood.*

smear² /smɪə(r)/ *noun* [C] **1** a dirty mark made by spreading a substance across sth **2** something that is not true that is said or written about an important person and that is intended to damage people's opinion about them, especially in politics: *He was the victim of a **smear campaign**.*

smell¹ ⓣ **A2** /smel/ *verb* (*pt, pp* **smelt** /smelt/, *BrE also* **smelled**) **1** [I] ~ (**of sth**) to have a particular smell: *Dinner smells good!* ◊ *This perfume smells of roses.* ◊ *His breath smelt of whisky.* **2** [T, no passive] (not used in the progressive tenses) to notice or recognize sb/sth by using your nose: *He could smell something burning.* ◊ *Can you smell gas?* ◊ *I could still smell her perfume in the room.* **3** [I] to be able to smell: *I can't smell properly because I've got a cold.* **4** [T] to put your nose near sth and breathe in so that you can discover or identify its smell: *I smelt the milk to see if it had gone off.* **5** [I] to have a bad smell: *Your feet smell.*

smell² ⓣ **A2** /smel/ *noun* **1** [C] the impression that you get of sth by using your nose; the thing that you smell: *What's that smell?* ◊ *a sweet/musty/fresh/sickly smell* ◊ *a strong/faint smell of garlic* **2** [sing.] an unpleasant smell: *Ugh! What a smell!* **3** [U] the ability to sense things with the nose: *Dogs have a very good **sense of smell**.* **4** [C] the act of putting your nose near sth to smell it: *Have a smell of this milk; is it all right?*

smelly /'smeli/ *adj.* (*informal*) (**smellier; smelliest**) having a bad smell: *smelly feet*

smelt¹ /smelt/ *verb* [T] to heat and melt rock containing ORE in order to get the metal out

smelt² /smelt/ past tense, past participle of **smell¹**

smile¹ ⓣ **A2** /smaɪl/ *noun* [C] an expression on your face in which the corners of your mouth turn up, showing happiness, pleasure, etc: *to have a smile on your face* ◊ *'It's nice to see you,' he said with a smile.* ⊃ look at **beam¹**, **grin**, **smirk**

smile² ⓣ **A2** /smaɪl/ *verb* **1** [I] ~ (**at sb/sth**) to make a smile appear on your face: *to smile sweetly/faintly/broadly* ◊ *She smiled at the camera.* **2** [T] to say or express sth with a smile: *I smiled a greeting to them.*

smiley /'smaɪli/ *noun* [C] **1** a simple picture of a smiling face that is drawn as a circle with two eyes and a curved mouth **2** (**COMPUTING**) a simple picture or series of keyboard symbols :-) that represents a smiling face. The symbols are used, for example, in email or text messages to show that the person sending the message is pleased or joking. ⊃ look at **emoticon**

smirk /smɜːk/ noun [C] an unpleasant smile that shows that you are pleased with yourself, think you are very clever, etc. ▶ **smirk** verb [I]

smock /smɒk/ noun [C] **1** a loose comfortable piece of clothing like a long shirt, worn especially by women **2** a long loose piece of clothing worn over other clothes to protect them from dirt, etc: *an artist's smock*

smog /smɒg/ noun [U] (**ENVIRONMENT**) dirty, poisonous air that can cover a whole city ⊃ note at **weather¹**

smoke¹ 🔑 **A2** /sməʊk/ noun **1** [U] the grey, white or black gas that you can see in the air when sth is burning: *Thick smoke poured from the chimney.* ◇ *a room full of cigarette smoke* **2** [C, usually sing.] an action of smoking a cigarette, etc: *He went outside for a quick smoke.*

smoke² 🔑 **A2** /sməʊk/ verb **1** [I, T] to breathe in smoke through a cigarette, etc. and let it out again; to use cigarettes, etc. in this way, as a habit: *Do you mind if I smoke?* ◇ *I used to smoke 20 cigarettes a day.* **2** [I] to send out smoke: *The oil in the pan started to smoke.* ▶ **smoker** noun [C]: *She's a **chain smoker** (= she finishes one cigarette and then immediately lights another).* **OPP** **non-smoker**

smoked /sməʊkt/ adj. (used of certain types of food) given a special taste by being hung for a period of time in smoke from wood fires: *smoked salmon/ham/cheese*

smoking 🔑 **A2** /ˈsməʊkɪŋ/ noun [U] (**HEALTH**) the activity or habit of smoking cigarettes, etc: *No Smoking* (= for example, on a notice) ◇ *He's trying to give up smoking.*

smoky /ˈsməʊki/ adj. (smokier; smokiest) **1** full of smoke; producing a lot of smoke: *a smoky room/fire* **2** with the smell, taste or appearance of smoke

smolder /ˈsməʊldə(r)/ (*AmE*) = SMOULDER

smooth¹ 🔑 **B1** /smuːð/ adj. **1** having a completely flat surface without any rough areas or holes: *smooth skin* ◇ *a smooth piece of wood* **OPP** **rough¹** **2** (of a liquid mixture) without any solid pieces: *Stir the sauce until it is smooth.* **OPP** **lumpy** **3** without difficulties: *The transition from the old method to the new has been very smooth.* **4** (used about a journey in a car, etc.) with an even, comfortable movement: *You get a very smooth ride in this car.* **OPP** **bumpy** **5** too pleasant or polite to be trusted ▶ **smoothness** noun [U] **IDM** **take the rough with the smooth** → ROUGH²

smooth² /smuːð/ verb [T] (used with an adverb or a preposition) to move your hands in the direction mentioned over a surface to make it smooth: *She smoothed her hair away from her face.* ◇ *I smoothed the tablecloth out.*

smoothie /ˈsmuːði/ noun [C] **1** a drink made of fruit or fruit juice, sometimes mixed with milk or ice cream **2** (*informal*) a man who dresses well and talks very politely in a confident way, but who is often not honest or sincere

smoothly /ˈsmuːðli/ adv. without any difficulty: *My work has been going quite smoothly.*

smother /ˈsmʌðə(r)/ verb [T] **1** ~ **sb (with sth)** to kill sb by covering their face so that they cannot breathe: *She was smothered with a pillow.* **2** ~ **sth/sb in/with sth** to cover sth/sb with too much of sth: *a dessert smothered in cream* **3** to stop a feeling, etc. from

being expressed **4** to stop sth burning by covering it: *to smother the flames with a blanket*

smoulder (*BrE*) (*AmE* **smolder**) /ˈsməʊldə(r)/ verb [I] ~ **(with sth)** to burn slowly without a flame: *The bonfire was still smouldering the next day.*

SMS /ˌes em ˈes/ noun **1** [U] a system for sending short written messages from one mobile phone to another (the abbreviation for 'short message service') **2** [C] a message sent by SMS **SYN** **text¹** ▶ **SMS** verb [I, T]

smudge /smʌdʒ/ verb **1** [T] to make sth dirty or untidy by touching it: *Leave your painting to dry or you'll smudge it.* **2** [I] to become untidy, without a clean line around it: *Her lipstick smudged when she kissed him.* ▶ **smudge** noun [C]

smug /smʌg/ adj. too pleased with yourself: *Don't look so smug.* ▶ **smugly** adv.: *He smiled smugly as the results were announced.* ▶ **smugness** noun [U]

smuggle /ˈsmʌgl/ verb [T] (**LAW**) to take things into or out of a country secretly in a way that is not allowed by the law; to take a person or a thing secretly into or out of a place: *The drugs had been smuggled through customs.* ▶ **smuggler** /-glə(r)/ noun [C]: *a drug smuggler*

snack /snæk/ noun [C] food that you eat quickly between main meals: *I had a snack on the train.* ▶ **snack** verb [I] ~ **on sth** (*informal*): *I snacked on a chocolate bar instead of having lunch.*

'snack bar noun [C] a type of small cafe where you can buy a small quick meal like a sandwich

snag¹ /snæg/ noun [C] a small difficulty or disadvantage that is often unexpected or hidden: *His offer is very generous — are you sure there isn't a snag?*

snag² /snæg/ verb [T] (-gg-) ~ **sth (on/in sth)** to catch a piece of clothing, etc. on sth sharp and tear it

snail /sneɪl/ noun [C] a type of animal with no legs and a soft body that is covered by a shell. Snails move very slowly. ⊃ picture at **animal**

'snail mail noun [U] (*informal*) used to describe the system of sending letters by ordinary post, contrasted with the speed of sending email

snake¹ 🔑 **A1** /sneɪk/ noun [C] a type of long thin animal with no legs that slides along the ground by moving its body from side to side

snake² /sneɪk/ verb [I, T] to move like a snake in long curves from side to side

snakes and 'ladders noun [U] a children's game played on a special board with pictures of snakes and LADDERS on it

snap¹ 🔑 **C1** /snæp/ verb (-pp-)
• BREAK **1** [T, I] to break or be broken suddenly, usually with a sharp noise: *He snapped a twig off a bush.* ◇ *The top has snapped off my pen.* ◇ *The branch snapped.*
• TAKE A PHOTO **2** [I, T] (*informal*) to take a quick photo of sb/sth: *A tourist snapped the plane as it crashed.*
• MOVE INTO POSITION **3** [I, T] to move or be moved into a particular position, especially with a sharp noise: *She snapped the bag shut and walked out.*
• SPEAK ANGRILY **4** [I, T] ~ **(sth) (at sb)** to speak or say sth in a quick angry way: *Why do you always snap at me?*
• OF AN ANIMAL **5** [I] ~ **(at sb/sth)** to try to bite sb/sth: *The dog snapped at the child's hand.*
• LOSE CONTROL **6** [I] to suddenly be unable to control your feelings any longer: *Suddenly something just snapped and I lost my temper.*
IDM **snap your fingers** to make a sharp noise by moving your middle finger quickly against your THUMB, especially when you want to attract sb's attention
PHR V **snap sth up** to buy or take sth quickly, especially because it is very cheap

snap[2] /snæp/ *noun* **1** [C] a sudden sharp sound of sth breaking **2** [C] (*AmE*) = POPPER **3** [C] = SNAPSHOT **4** Snap [U] (*BrE*) a card game where players call out 'snap' when two cards that are the same are put down by different players

snap[3] /snæp/ *adj.* [only before noun] (*informal*) done quickly and suddenly, often without any careful thought: *a snap decision/judgement*

Snapchat™ /ˈsnæptʃæt/ *noun* [U] (**COMPUTING**) a SOCIAL MEDIA website where people can send or share photos, short videos and messages. Photos, etc. sent or shared using Snapchat™ are only available for a short time.

snapshot /ˈsnæpʃɒt/ *noun* [C] **1** a photo, especially one taken quickly: *snapshots of the children* **2** [usually sing.] a short description or a small amount of information that gives you an idea of what something is like: *The play offers a snapshot of life in Britain under the Romans.*

snare /sneə(r)/ *noun* [C] a piece of equipment used to catch birds or small animals **SYN** trap[1] ▶ snare *verb* [T]

snarl /snɑːl/ *verb* ~ (at sb) **1** [I] (used about an animal) to make an angry sound while showing the teeth: *The dog snarled at the stranger.* **2** [T, I] to speak in a rough, angry voice: *'Get out of here!' he snarled.* ▶ snarl *noun* [C, usually sing.]

snatch[1] /snætʃ/ *verb* **1** [T, I] to take sth with a quick rough movement: *A boy snatched her handbag and ran off.* **SYN** grab[1] **2** [T] to take or get sth quickly using the only time or chance that you have: *I managed to snatch some sleep on the train.* **PHR V** snatch at sth to try to take hold of sth suddenly: *The man snatched at my wallet but I didn't let go of it.*

snatch[2] /snætʃ/ *noun* **1** [C] a short part or period of sth: *I heard snatches of conversation from the next room.* **2** [sing.] a sudden movement that sb makes when trying to take hold of sth

sneak[1] /sniːk/ *verb* (*pt, pp* sneaked) **HELP** Snuck is almost always used for the past tense and past participle in spoken American English and some people use it in British English too. **1** [I] (used with an adverb or a preposition) to go very quietly in the direction mentioned, so that nobody can see or hear you: *The prisoner sneaked past the guards.* ◇ *Instead of working, he sneaked out to play football.* **2** [T] to do or take sth secretly: *I tried to sneak a look at the test results in the teacher's bag.* **PHR V** sneak up (on sb/sth) to go near sb very quietly, especially so that you can surprise them

sneak[2] /sniːk/ *noun* [C] (*old-fashioned*) (used in a critical way) a person, especially a child, who tells sb about the bad things sb else has done

sneaker /ˈsniːkə(r)/ (*AmE*) = TRAINER (1)

sneaking /ˈsniːkɪŋ/ *adj.* [only before noun] (used about feelings) not expressed; secret: *I've a sneaking suspicion that he's lying.*

sneer /snɪə(r)/ *verb* [I, T] ~ (at sb/sth) to show that you have no respect for sb/sth by the expression on your face or the way that you speak: *She sneered at his attempts to speak French.* ▶ sneer *noun* [C, usually sing.]

sneeze /sniːz/ *verb* [I] (**HEALTH**) to make air come out of your nose suddenly and noisily in a way that you cannot control, for example because you have a cold: *Dust makes me sneeze.* ▶ sneeze *noun* [C]

snide /snaɪd/ *adj.* (used about an expression or comment) critical in an unpleasant way

sniff /snɪf/ *verb* **1** [I] to breathe air in through the nose in a way that makes a sound, especially when you have a cold or you are crying: *Stop sniffing and blow your nose.* **2** [T, I] ~ (at) sth to smell sth by sniffing: '*I*

can smell gas,' he said, sniffing the air. ◇ *The dog sniffed at the bone.* ▶ sniff *noun* [C]: *Have a sniff of this milk and tell me if it's still OK.*

sniffle /ˈsnɪfl/ *verb* [I] to make noises by breathing air suddenly up your nose, especially because you have a cold or you are crying

snigger /ˈsnɪɡə(r)/ *verb* [I, T] ~ (at sb/sth) to laugh quietly and secretly in an unpleasant way ▶ snigger *noun* [C]

snip[1] /snɪp/ *verb* [T, I] (-pp-) ~ (at/through) sth to cut using SCISSORS, with a short quick action: *to snip a hole in something* ◇ *I snipped at the loose threads.* **PHR V** snip sth off to remove sth by cutting it with SCISSORS in short quick movements: *He sewed on the button and snipped off the ends of the cotton.*

snip[2] /snɪp/ *noun* **1** [C] a small cut made with SCISSORS **2** [sing.] (*BrE, informal*) something that is much cheaper than expected

sniper /ˈsnaɪpə(r)/ *noun* [C] a person who shoots at sb from a hidden position

snippet /ˈsnɪpɪt/ *noun* [C] a small piece of sth, especially information or news

snivel /ˈsnɪvl/ *verb* [I] (-ll-, *AmE* -l-) to keep crying quietly in a way that is annoying

snob /snɒb/ *noun* [C] a person who thinks they are better than sb of a lower social class and who admires people who have a high social position ▶ snobbish /ˈsnɒbɪʃ/ *adj.* ▶ snobbishly *adv.* ▶ snobbishness *noun* [U]

snobbery /ˈsnɒbəri/ *noun* [U] behaviour or attitudes typical of people who think they are better than other people in society, for example because they have more money, better education, etc.

snog /snɒɡ/ *verb* [I, T] (-gg-) (*BrE, informal*) (used about a couple) to kiss each other for a long period of time ▶ snog *noun* [sing.]

snooker /ˈsnuːkə(r)/ *noun* [U] a game in which two players try to hit a number of coloured balls into pockets at the edges of a large table using a CUE (= a long thin stick): *to play snooker* ◇ look at **billiards**, **pool**[1] (4) ◇ picture at **sport**

snoop /snuːp/ *verb* [I] ~ (around); ~ (around sth); ~ (on sb) to look around secretly and without permission in order to find out information, etc: *Someone's been snooping around my flat.* ◇ *She suspected that her neighbours visited just to snoop on her.* ▶ snoop *noun* [sing.]: *He had a snoop around her office.*

snooty /ˈsnuːti/ *adj.* (snootier; snootiest) acting in a rude way because you think you are better than other people

snooze /snuːz/ *verb* [I] (*informal*) to have a short sleep, especially during the day ▶ snooze *noun* [C, usually sing.]: *I had a bit of a snooze on the train.* ◇ look at **nap**

snore /snɔː(r)/ *verb* [I] to breathe noisily through your nose and mouth while you are asleep ▶ snore *noun* [C]: *He's got the loudest snore I've ever heard.*

snorkel /ˈsnɔːkl/ *noun* [C] a tube that you can breathe air through when you are swimming under the surface of the water

snorkelling (*BrE*) (*AmE* snorkeling) /ˈsnɔːkəlɪŋ/ *noun* [U] the sport or activity of swimming UNDERWATER with a SNORKEL: *to go snorkelling*

snort /snɔːt/ *verb* **1** [I] (used about animals) to make a noise by blowing air through the nose and mouth **2** [I, T] (used about people) to blow out air noisily as a way of showing that you do not like sth, or that you are impatient ▶ snort *noun* [C]: *to give a snort*

snot /snɒt/ *noun* [U] (*informal*) (**HEALTH**) the liquid produced by the nose

snout /snaʊt/ *noun* [C] (**BIOLOGY**) the long nose of certain animals: *a pig's snout* ➒ picture at **animal**

snow¹ ⚡ **A1** /snəʊ/ *noun* [U] small, soft, white pieces of frozen water that fall from the sky in cold weather: *Three centimetres of snow fell during the night.* ◊ *The snow melted before it could settle* (= stay on the ground). ➒ note at **water¹**, **weather¹** ➒ picture at **water cycle**

snow² ⚡ **A1** /snəʊ/ *verb* [I] when it snows, snow falls from the sky: *It snowed all night.*

snowball¹ /ˈsnəʊbɔːl/ *noun* [C] a ball that you make out of snow to throw at sb/sth in a game

snowball² /ˈsnəʊbɔːl/ *verb* [I] to quickly grow bigger and bigger or more and more important

snowboard /ˈsnəʊbɔːd/ *noun* [C] (**SPORT**) a type of board that you fasten to both your feet and use for moving down mountains that are covered with snow
▶ **snowboarder** *noun* [C] ▶ **snowboarding** *noun* [U]: *Have you ever been snowboarding?*

snowdrift /ˈsnəʊdrɪft/ *noun* [C] a deep pile of snow that has been made by the wind: *The car got stuck in a snowdrift.*

snowdrop /ˈsnəʊdrɒp/ *noun* [C] a type of small white flower that appears at the end of winter

snowed 'in *adj.* [not before noun] not able to leave home or travel because the snow is too deep

snowed 'under *adj.* [not before noun] **~ (with sth)** with more work, etc. than you can deal with

snowfall /ˈsnəʊfɔːl/ *noun* **1** [C] the snow that falls on one occasion: *heavy snowfalls* **2** [U] the amount of snow that falls in a particular place

snowflake /ˈsnəʊfleɪk/ *noun* [C] one of the small, soft, white pieces of frozen water that fall together as snow

snowman /ˈsnəʊmæn/ *noun* [C] (*pl.* **-men** /-men/) the figure of a person made out of snow

snowplough (*BrE*) (*AmE* **snowplow**) /ˈsnəʊplaʊ/ *noun* [C] a vehicle that is used to clear snow away from roads or railways ➒ look at **plough**

snowstorm /ˈsnəʊstɔːm/ *noun* [C] a very heavy fall of snow, usually with a strong wind ➒ note at **storm¹**

snowy /ˈsnəʊi/ *adj.* (**snowier**; **snowiest**) with a lot of snow: *snowy weather* ◊ *a snowy scene*

the SNP /ˌði es en ˈpiː/ *abbr.* = SCOTTISH NATIONAL PARTY

Snr (*BrE*) *abbr.* (in writing) = SENIOR¹ (2)

snub /snʌb/ *verb* [T] (**-bb-**) to treat sb rudely, for example by refusing to look at or speak to them
▶ **snub** *noun* [C]

snuck /snʌk/ (*especially AmE, informal*) past tense, past participle of **sneak¹**

snuff /snʌf/ *noun* [U] (especially in past times) TOBACCO (= the dried leaves used for making cigarettes) in the form of a powder that people breathe up into their noses

snuffle /ˈsnʌfl/ *verb* [I] (used about people and animals) to make a noise through your nose

snug /snʌg/ *adj.* **1** warm and comfortable: *a snug little room* ◊ *The children were snug in bed.* **2** fitting sb/sth closely: *Adjust the safety belt to give a snug fit.*
▶ **snugly** *adv.*

snuggle /ˈsnʌgl/ *verb* [I] **~ (up to sb)**; **~ (up/down)** to get into a position that makes you feel safe, warm and comfortable, especially next to another person: *She snuggled up to her mother.* ◊ *I snuggled down under the blanket to get warm.*

so¹ ⚡ **A1** /səʊ/ *adv.* **1** used to emphasize an adjective or adverb, especially when this produces a particular result: *She's so ill (that) she can't get out of bed.* ◊ *He was driving so fast that he couldn't stop.* ◊ *You've been so kind. How can I thank you?* **2** used in negative sentences for comparing people or things: *She's not so clever as we thought.* **3** used in place of sth that has been said already, to avoid repeating it: *Are you coming by plane? If so,* (= if you are coming by plane) *I can meet you at the airport.* ◊ *'I failed, didn't I?' 'I'm afraid so.'* **4** (in positive sentences) also, too: *He's a teacher and so is his wife.* ◊ *'I've been to New York.' 'So have I.'* ◊ *I like singing and so does Helen.* ➒ look at **neither¹** (1) **5** used to show that you agree that sth is true, especially when you are surprised: *'It's getting late.' 'So it is. We'd better go.'* **6** (used when you are showing sb sth) in this way; like this: *It was a black insect, about so big* (= using your hands to show the size). ◊ *Fold the paper in two diagonally, like so.*
IDM **and so on** (**and so forth**) used at the end of a list to show that it continues in the same way: *They sell pens, pencils, paper and so on.* **I told you so** I warned you that this would happen: *'I missed the bus.' 'I told you so. I said you needed to leave earlier.'* **it (just) so happens** (used to introduce a surprising fact) by chance: *It just so happened that we were going the same way, so he gave me a lift.* **just so** → JUST¹ **or so** (used to show that a number, time, etc. is not exact) approximately; about: *100 or so people came to the meeting.* **so as to do sth** with the intention of doing sth; in order to do sth **so much for** used for saying that sth was not helpful or successful: *So much for that diet! I didn't lose any weight at all.* **that is so** (*formal*) that is true

so² ⚡ **A1** ⑤ /səʊ/ *conj.* **1** with the result that; therefore: *She felt very tired so she went to bed early.* **2 ~ (that)** with the purpose that; in order that: *She wore dark glasses so (that) nobody would recognize her.* **3** used to show how one part of a story follows another: *So what happened next?*
IDM **so what?** (*informal*) (showing that you think sth is not important) Who cares?: *'It's late.' 'So what? We don't have to go to school tomorrow.'*

soak ⚡+ **C1** /səʊk/ *verb* **1** [T, I] to make sth completely wet; to become completely wet: *The dog came out of the river and shook itself, soaking everyone.* ◊ *Leave the dishes to soak for a while.* **2** [I] **~ into/through sth**; **~ in** (used about a liquid) to pass into or through sth: *Blood had soaked through the bandage.* ◊ *Pour the juice over the cake and allow it to soak in.*
PHR V **soak sth up** to take sth in (especially a liquid): *I soaked the water up with a cloth.*

soaked /səʊkt/ *adj.* [not before noun] extremely wet: *I got soaked waiting for my bus in the rain.*

soaking /ˈsəʊkɪŋ/ (*also* ˌsoaking ˈwet) *adj.* extremely wet

'so-and-so *noun* [C] (*pl.* **-os**) (*informal*) **1** a person who is not named: *Imagine a Mrs So-and-so telephones. What would you say?* **2** a person that you do not like: *He's a bad-tempered old so-and-so.*

soap ⚡ **A2** /səʊp/ *noun* **1** [U] a substance that you use for washing and cleaning: *He washed his hands with soap.* ◊ *a bar of soap* ◊ *soap powder* (= for washing clothes) **2** [C] (*informal*) = SOAP OPERA ▶ **soapy** *adj.* (**soapier**; **soapiest**)

a story about the lives and problems of a group of people that continues several times a week on TV or radio ➲ look at **opera**

soar ʔ+ **C1** /sɔː(r)/ *verb* [I] **1** to fly high in the air **2** to rise very fast: *Prices are soaring because of inflation.* ➲ note at **trend¹**

soaraway /ˈsɔːrəweɪ/ *adj.* [only before noun] (*BrE*) (used especially about success) very great; growing very quickly

sob /sɒb/ *verb* [I] (-bb-) to cry while taking in sudden, sharp breaths; to speak while you are crying: *The child was sobbing because he'd lost his toy.* ▸ **sob** *noun* [C]: *It was heartbreaking to listen to her sobs.*

sober¹ /ˈsəʊbə(r)/ *adj.* **1** (of a person) not affected by alcohol: *He'd been drunk the first time he'd met her, but this time he was stone-cold sober.* **2** not funny; serious: *a sober expression* ◊ *Her death is a sober reminder of just how dangerous extreme sports can be.* **3** (used about a colour) not bright or likely to be noticed: *a sober grey suit*

sober² /ˈsəʊbə(r)/ *verb*
PHR V **sober (sb) up** to become or make sb become normal again after being affected by alcohol: *I need a cup of black coffee to sober me up.* ◊ *There's no point talking to him until he's sobered up.*

sobering /ˈsəʊbərɪŋ/ *adj.* making you feel serious: *It is a sobering thought that over 25 million people have been killed in car accidents.*

Soc. *abbr.* (in writing) = SOCIETY (2): *Amateur Dramatic Soc.*

so-called ʔ+ **B2** ◉ *adj.* **1** [only before noun] used to show that the words you describe sb/sth with are not correct: *Her so-called friends only wanted her money.* **2** used to show that a special name has been given to sb/sth

soccer ʔ **A2** /ˈsɒkə(r)/ (*especially AmE*) = FOOTBALL (1)

sociable /ˈsəʊʃəbl/ *adj.* enjoying being with other people; friendly

social ʔ **A2** ◉ /ˈsəʊʃl/ *adj.* **1** connected with meeting people and enjoying yourself: *He has a busy social life.* ◊ *a social club* ◊ *Children have to develop their social skills when they start school.* **2** (**SOCIAL STUDIES**) connected with society and the way it is organized: *social problems/issues/reforms* **3** (**SOCIAL STUDIES**) connected with the position of people in society: *We share the same social background.* **4** (used about animals) living in groups ▸ **socially** ◉ /-ʃəli/ *adv.*: *We work together but I don't know him socially.*

social conscience *noun* [sing., U] (**SOCIAL STUDIES**) if you have a **social conscience**, you know about the problems that affect a lot of people in society, and want to do sth to help these people

social democracy *noun* [U, C] (**POLITICS**) a political system that combines the principles of SOCIALISM with the greater personal freedom of DEMOCRACY; a country that has this political system of government ▸ **social democrat** *noun* [C]

social distancing *noun* [U] (**HEALTH**) the practice of keeping a safe distance between yourself and other people in order to prevent the spread of disease

social enterprise *noun* [C, U] (**BUSINESS**, **SOCIAL STUDIES**) a business that uses its profits to try and help the community or for another social purpose: *It's a social enterprise aiming to help ex-offenders find work.*

socialism /ˈsəʊʃəlɪzəm/ *noun* [U] (**POLITICS**) the political idea that is based on the belief that everyone has an equal right to a share of a country's wealth and that the government should own and control the main industries ➲ look at **capitalism**, **communism**,

Marxism ▸ **socialist** ʔ+ **C1** /-lɪst/ *noun* [C], *adj.*: *Tony was a socialist when he was younger.* ◊ *socialist beliefs/policies/writers* ➲ note at **government**

socialist realism *noun* [U] (**ARTS AND MEDIA**) a theory that was put into practice in some COMMUNIST countries, especially in the Soviet Union under Stalin, that art, music and literature should be used to show people the principles of a SOCIALIST society and encourage them to support it

socialization (*BrE also* **-isation**) /ˌsəʊʃəlaɪˈzeɪʃn/ *noun* [U] (*formal*) (**SOCIAL STUDIES**) the process by which sb, especially a child, learns to behave in a way that is acceptable in their society

socialize (*BrE also* **-ise**) /ˈsəʊʃəlaɪz/ *verb* **1** [I] ~ **(with sb)** to meet and spend time with people in a friendly way, in order to enjoy yourself: *I enjoy socializing with the other students.* ➲ look at **go out** at **go¹** (1) **2** [T] (*formal*) (**SOCIAL STUDIES**) to teach people to behave in ways that are acceptable to their society

social media *noun* [U, pl.] (**COMPUTING**) websites and software programs used for SOCIAL NETWORKING: *images posted on social media* ◊ *social media sites such as Facebook and Twitter*

social networking *noun* [U] (**COMPUTING**) communication with people who share your interests using a website or other service on the internet: *a social networking site*

social science *noun* [U, C] (**EDUCATION**, **SOCIAL STUDIES**) the study of people in society

social security (*BrE*) (*also* **welfare** *especially in AmE*) *noun* [U] (**FINANCE**, **POLITICS**, **SOCIAL STUDIES**) money paid regularly by the government to people who are poor, old, ill, or who have no job: *to live on social security*

social services *noun* [pl.] (**POLITICS**, **SOCIAL STUDIES**) a group of services organized by local government to help people who have money or family problems

social work *noun* [U] (**SOCIAL STUDIES**) paid work that involves giving help and advice to people living in the community who have financial or family problems

social worker *noun* [C] (**SOCIAL STUDIES**) a person whose job is SOCIAL WORK

societal ◉ /səˈsaɪətl/ *adj.* [only before noun] connected with society and the way it is organized: *societal structure/values*

society ʔ **A2** ◉ /səˈsaɪəti/ *noun* (*pl.* -ies) **1** [C, U] (**SOCIAL STUDIES**) the people in a country or an area, thought of as a group, who have shared customs and laws: *a civilized society* ◊ *Society's attitude to women has changed considerably.* ◊ *The role of men in society is changing.* **2** [C] (*abbr.* **Soc.**) an organization of people who share a particular interest or purpose; a club: *a drama society* ➲ note at **organization**

socio- /ˈsəʊsiəʊ, ˈsəʊsiˈɒ/ *prefix* (in nouns, adjectives and adverbs) (**SOCIAL STUDIES**) connected with society or the study of society: *socio-economic* ◊ *sociolinguistics*

socio-economic *adj.* (**SOCIAL STUDIES**) relating to both social class and economic matters: *people from different socio-economic backgrounds*

sociolinguistics /ˌsəʊsiəʊlɪŋˈɡwɪstɪks/ *noun* [U] the study of the way language is affected by differences in social class, region, sex, etc. ▸ **sociolinguistic** *adj.*

sociology /ˌsəʊsiˈɒlədʒi/ *noun* [U] (**EDUCATION**, **SOCIAL STUDIES**) the study of human societies and social behaviour ▸ **sociological** /ˌsəʊsiəˈlɒdʒɪkl/ *adj.* ▸ **sociologist** /ˌsəʊsiˈɒlədʒɪst/ *noun* [C]

sociopolitical /ˌsəʊsiəʊpəˈlɪtɪkl/ *adj.* (**SOCIAL STUDIES**) relating to society and politics

sock ʔ **A2** /sɒk/ *noun* [C] a piece of clothing that is worn on the foot and lower leg, inside a shoe: *a pair of socks*
IDM **pull your socks up** (*BrE*) to start working harder or better than before

socket /'sɒkɪt/ *noun* [C] **1** (*also* **power point**) a place in a wall where a piece of electrical equipment can be connected to the electricity supply ⊃ picture at **plug**[1] **2** a hole in a piece of electrical equipment where another piece of equipment can be connected **3** a hole that sth fits into: *your eye socket*

soda /'səʊdə/ *noun* **1** (*also* 'soda water) [U] water that has bubbles in it and is usually used for mixing with other drinks: *a whisky and soda* **2** [U, C] (*AmE*) = FIZZY DRINK

sodium /'səʊdiəm/ *noun* [U] (*symb.* Na) (**CHEMISTRY**) a chemical element. Sodium is a soft, silver-white metal that is found naturally only in COMPOUNDS, such as salt. ❶ For more information on the periodic table of elements, look at the **Reference Section** of this dictionary.

sodium bi'carbonate (*also* bicarbonate of soda, baking soda) *noun* [U] (*symb.* NaHCO₃) (**CHEMISTRY**) a chemical in the form of a white powder that is used in baking to make cakes, etc. rise and become light

sodium 'carbonate (*also* 'washing soda) *noun* [U] (*symb.* Na₂CO₃) (**CHEMISTRY**) a chemical in the form of white CRYSTALS or powder that is used in making glass, soap and paper, and for making water soft

sodium 'chloride *noun* [U] (*symb.* NaCl) (**CHEMISTRY**) common salt (a chemical made up of SODIUM and CHLORINE)

sofa /'səʊfə/ *noun* [C] a comfortable seat with a back and arms for two or more people to sit on: *a sofa bed* (= a sofa that you can open out to make a bed) **SYN** **settee**

soft ʔ **A2** /sɒft/ *adj.*
• NOT HARD **1** not hard or firm: *a soft bed/seat* ◊ *The ground is very soft after all that rain.* **OPP** **hard**[1]
• NOT ROUGH **2** not rough and pleasant to touch: *soft skin/hands* ◊ *a soft towel* **OPP** **rough**[1]
• NOT LOUD **3** (used about sounds, voices, words, etc.) quiet or gentle; not loud or angry: *She spoke in a soft whisper.* **OPP** **harsh, loud**[1]
• LIGHT/COLOURS **4** (used about light, colours, etc.) gentle and pleasant: *The room was decorated in soft pinks and greens.* **OPP** **bright**
• NOT STRICT **5** (used about people) kind and gentle, sometimes too much so: *A good manager can't afford to be too soft.* **OPP** **hard**[1], **strict**
• WATER **6** (used about water) not containing mineral salts and therefore good for washing as soap will make a lot of bubbles **OPP** **hard**[1]
▶ **softness** *noun* [U]
IDM **have a soft spot for sb/sth** (*informal*) to like sb/sth

softball /'sɒftbɔːl/ *noun* [U] (**SPORT**) a team game that is similar to baseball but played on a smaller field with a larger, softer ball

soft 'drink *noun* [C] a cold drink that contains no alcohol ⊃ look at **alcoholic**[1]

soft 'drug *noun* [C] (**LAW**) an illegal drug, such as CANNABIS, that some people take for pleasure, that is not considered very harmful ⊃ look at **hard drug**

soften /'sɒfn/ *verb* **1** [I, T] to become softer or gentler; to make sb/sth softer or gentler: *Fry the onions until they soften.* ◊ *a lotion to soften the skin* **2** [T] to make sth less strong and unpleasant: *Her letter sounded too angry so she softened the language.* ◊ *The airbag softened the impact of the crash.*

soft 'fruit *noun* [C, U] small fruits without a large seed inside or hard skin: *raspberries, strawberries and other soft fruits*

soft-'hearted *adj.* kind and good at understanding other people's feelings **OPP** **hard-hearted**

'soft launch *noun* [C] (**BUSINESS**) the activity or occasion of making a product or service available in a limited way, before it becomes fully available: *A soft launch of the site in August was followed by an official launch in November.* ▶ 'soft-launch *verb* [T]

softly /'sɒftli/ *adv.* in a soft way: *She closed the door softly behind her.* ◊ *'I missed you,' he said softly.*

soft 'option *noun* [C] the easier thing to do of two or more possibilities, but not the best one: *The government has taken the soft option of agreeing to their demands.*

soft-'spoken *adj.* having a gentle, quiet voice: *He was a kind, soft-spoken man.*

software ʔ **B1** **W** /'sɒftweə(r)/ *noun* [U] (**COMPUTING**) the programs and other operating information used by a computer: *There's a lot of new educational software available now.* ⊃ look at **hardware** (1)

softwood /'sɒftwʊd/ *noun* [U, C] wood that is cheap to produce and can be cut easily: *Pine is a softwood.* ⊃ look at **hardwood**

soggy /'sɒgi/ *adj.* (soggier; soggiest) very wet and soft in a way that is unpleasant

soil[1] ʔ **B1** /sɔɪl/ *noun* **1** [C, U] (**AGRICULTURE, GEOLOGY**) the substance that plants, trees, etc. grow in; earth: *poor/dry/acid/sandy soil* ⊃ picture at **erosion, food web, nitrogen cycle** **2** [U] (*formal*) the land that is part of a country: *to set foot on British soil* (= to arrive in Britain)

soil[2] /sɔɪl/ *verb* [T, often passive] (*formal*) to make sth dirty

solace /'sɒləs/ *noun* [U, sing.] (*formal*) a feeling of comfort when you are sad or disappointed; a person or thing that gives you this feeling: *to find/seek solace in somebody/something* **SYN** **comfort**[1]

solar ʔ **B2** /'səʊlə(r)/ *adj.* [only before noun]
1 (**ASTRONOMY**) connected with the sun: *a solar eclipse* (= when the sun is blocked by the moon)
2 (**ENVIRONMENT**) using the sun's energy: *solar heating/power* ⊃ picture at **climate change, water cycle**

solar 'cell *noun* [C] (**ENGINEERING, ENVIRONMENT**) a device that converts light and heat energy from the sun into electricity ⊃ picture at **energy**

solar 'energy *noun* [U] **1** energy given out by the sun in the form of heat and light **2** (**ENVIRONMENT, PHYSICS**)

solarium /sə'leəriəm/ *noun* [C] a room whose walls are mainly made of glass, or that has special lamps, where people go to get a SUNTAN (= make their skin go brown) using light from the sun or artificial light

solar 'panel *noun* [C] (**ENVIRONMENT, PHYSICS**) a piece of equipment on a roof that uses light and heat energy from the sun to produce hot water and electricity ⊃ picture at **energy**

solar plexus /ˌsəʊlə 'pleksəs/ *noun* [sing.] (**ANATOMY**) a system of nerves at the base of the stomach

'solar system *noun* (**ASTRONOMY**) **1** the solar system [sing.] the sun and all the planets that move around it ⊃ note at **Pluto** **2** [C] any group of planets that all move around the same star

solar 'year *noun* [C] (**ASTRONOMY**) the time it takes the earth to go around the sun once, approximately 365¼ days

sold /səʊld/ past tense, past participle of **sell**

solder¹ /ˈsəʊldə(r), ˈsɒl-/ *noun* [U] a mixture of metals that is heated and melted, and then used to join pieces of metal or wire together

solder² /ˈsəʊldə(r), ˈsɒl-/ *verb* [T] ~ sth (to/onto sth); ~ (A and B together) to join pieces of metal or wire together using a mixture of metals that is heated and melted ➲ look at **weld**

ˈsoldering iron *noun* [C] a tool that is heated and used for joining metals and wires by SOLDERING them

soldier 🔤 **A2** /ˈsəʊldʒə(r)/ *noun* [C] a member of an army: *The soldiers marched past.*

sole¹ 🔤 **C1** /səʊl/ *adj.* [only before noun] **1** only; single: *His sole interest is football.* **2** belonging to one person only; not shared ▶ **solely** 🔤 **C1** *adv.*: *I agreed to come solely because of your mother.*

sole² /səʊl/ *noun* **1** [C] (ANATOMY) the bottom surface of the foot ➲ picture at **body** **2** [C] the part of a shoe or sock that covers the bottom surface of the foot **3** [C, U] (*pl.* sole) a flat sea fish that is used for food

solemn /ˈsɒləm/ *adj.* **1** (used about a person) very serious; not happy or smiling: *Her solemn face told them that the news was bad.* **OPP** **cheerful** **2** sincere; done or said in a formal way: *to make a solemn promise* **SYN** **serious** ▶ **solemnity** /səˈlemnəti/ *noun* [U] ▶ **solemnly** *adv.*: *'I have something very important to tell you,'* she began solemnly.

solicit /səˈlɪsɪt/ *verb* **1** [T] (*formal*) to ask sb for money, help, support, etc: *They tried to solicit support for the proposal.* **2** [I, T] (used about a person who has sex for money) to go to sb, especially in a public place, and offer sex in return for money

solicitor 🔤 **C1** /səˈlɪsɪtə(r)/ *noun* [C] (*BrE*) (LAW) a lawyer whose job is to give legal advice, prepare legal documents and arrange the buying and selling of land, etc. ➲ note at **lawyer**

solid¹ 🔤 **B1** /ˈsɒlɪd/ *adj.*

• NOT LIQUID/GAS **1** (CHEMISTRY) hard and firm; not in the form of liquid or gas: *It was so cold that the village pond had frozen solid.* ➲ picture at **state¹, water cycle**

• WITHOUT HOLES **2** having no holes or empty spaces inside; not hollow: *a solid mass of rock*

• STRONG **3** strong, firm and well made: *a solid little car* ◊ (*figurative*) *They built up a solid friendship over the years.*

• MATERIAL **4** [only before noun] made completely of one substance, both on the inside and outside: *a solid gold chain*

• THAT YOU CAN TRUST **5** of good enough quality; that you can trust: *The police cannot make an arrest without solid evidence.*

• PERIOD OF TIME **6** (*informal*) without a break, continuous: *I was so tired that I slept for twelve solid hours/twelve hours solid.*
▶ **solidity** /səˈlɪdəti/ *noun* [U]

solids

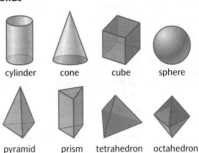

cylinder   cone   cube   sphere

pyramid   prism   tetrahedron   octahedron

solid² 🔤 **B1** /ˈsɒlɪd/ *noun* [C] **1** a substance or an object that is hard; not a liquid or gas: *Liquids become solids when frozen.* ◊ *The baby is not yet on solids* (= solid food). **2** (GEOMETRY) an object that has length, WIDTH and height, not a flat shape: *A cube is a solid.*

solidarity 🔤 **C1** /ˌsɒlɪˈdærəti/ *noun* [U] ~ (with sb) the support of one group of people for another, because they agree with their aims: *Many local people expressed solidarity with the strikers.*

solidify /səˈlɪdɪfaɪ/ *verb* [I] (solidifying; solidifies; *pt, pp* solidified) (CHEMISTRY) to become hard or solid

solidly /ˈsɒlɪdli/ *adv.* **1** strongly: *a solidly built house* **2** without stopping: *It rained solidly all day.*

soliloquy /səˈlɪləkwi/ *noun* [C, U] (*pl.* -ies) (ARTS AND MEDIA, LITERATURE) a speech in a play in which a character, who is alone on the stage, speaks their thoughts; the act of speaking thoughts in this way: *Hamlet's famous soliloquy, 'To be or not to be ...'* ➲ look at **monologue** ▶ **soliloquize** (*BrE also* -ise) /-kwaɪz/ *verb* [I]

solitaire /ˌsɒləˈteə(r)/ *noun* [U] **1** a game for one person in which you remove pieces from a special board by moving other pieces over them until you have only one piece left **2** (*AmE*) = PATIENCE (2)

solitary /ˈsɒlətri/ *adj.* **1** done alone, without other people: *Writing novels is a solitary occupation.* **2** (used about a person or an animal) enjoying being alone; often spending time alone: *She was always a solitary*

the solar system

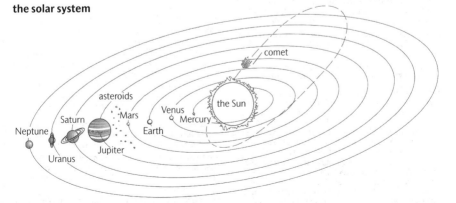

child. **3** [only before noun] alone; with no others around: *a solitary figure walking up the hillside* **SYN** **lone** **4** [only before noun] (usually in negative sentences and questions) only one; single: *I can't think of a solitary example* (= not even one).

,solitary con'finement *noun* [U] (**LAW**) a punishment in which a person in prison is kept completely alone in a separate cell away from the other prisoners

solitude /'sɒlətjuːd/ *noun* [U] the state of being alone, especially when you find this pleasant: *She longed for peace and solitude.* ➔ look at **isolation**, **loneliness**

solo¹ ഽ+ **C1** /'səʊləʊ/ *adj.* **1** alone, without anybody helping you: *a solo flight* **2** connected with or played as a musical SOLO: *a solo artist* (= a singer who is not part of a group) ▶ **solo** *adv.*: *to fly solo* ◇ *The singer decided to go solo when the band split up.*

solo² ഽ+ **C1** /'səʊləʊ/ *noun* [C] (*pl.* -os) (**MUSIC**) a piece of music for only one person to play or sing ➔ look at **duet** ▶ **soloist** *noun* [C]

solstice /'sɒlstɪs/ *noun* [C] (**ASTRONOMY**) either of the two times of the year at which the sun reaches its highest or lowest point in the sky at MIDDAY, marked by the longest and shortest days: *the summer/winter solstice* ➔ look at **equinox** ➔ picture at **season¹**

soluble /'sɒljəbl/ *adj.* **1** ~ (in sth) (**CHEMISTRY**) that will DISSOLVE (= become liquid) in liquid: *These tablets are soluble in water.* **OPP** **insoluble** **2** (*formal*) (used about a problem, etc.) that has an answer; that can be solved **OPP** **insoluble**

solute /'sɒljuːt, sɒ'ljuːt/ *noun* [C] (**CHEMISTRY**) a substance that has been DISSOLVED in a liquid (= made to become part of the liquid) so that together they form a SOLUTION

solution ഽ **A2** **O** /sə'luːʃn/ *noun* **1** ~ (to sth) a way of solving a problem, dealing with a difficult situation, etc: *a solution to the problem of unemployment* **2** [C] ~ (to sth) the answer (to a game, competition, etc.): *The solution to the quiz will be published next week.* **3** [C, U] (**CHEMISTRY**) a liquid in which sth solid has been DISSOLVED (= made liquid): *saline solution* ➔ picture at **pH** **4** [U] (**CHEMISTRY**) the process of DISSOLVING a solid or gas in a liquid (= making it become part of the liquid): *the solution of glucose in water* ➔ picture at **carbon cycle**, **water cycle**

solve ഽ **A2** **W** /sɒlv/ *verb* [T] **1** to find a way of dealing with a problem or difficult situation: *The government is trying to solve the problem of inflation.* ◇ *The police have not managed to solve the crime.* ◇ *to solve a mystery* **2** (**MATHEMATICS**) to find the correct answer or explanation for sth: *to solve a puzzle/equation/ riddle* ➔ noun **solution** ➔ adjective **soluble**

solvent /'sɒlvənt/ *noun* [U, C] (**CHEMISTRY**) a liquid that can DISSOLVE another substance (= make it become part of the liquid)

sombre (*BrE*) (*AmE* somber) /'sɒmbə(r)/ *adj.* **1** dark in colour **SYN** **dull¹** **2** sad and serious ▶ **sombrely** *adv.*

some ഽ **A1** /səm, *strong form* sʌm/ *det., pron.* **1** used with uncountable nouns or plural countable nouns to mean 'an amount of' or 'a number of': *We need some butter and some potatoes.* ◇ *I don't want any more money — I've still got some.* **HELP** In negative sentences and in most questions you use **any** instead of **some**: *I need some more money. I haven't got any.* ◇ *Do we need any butter?* Look at sense **2** for examples of questions where **some** is used. **2** used in questions when you expect or want the answer 'yes': *Would you like some more cake?* ◇ *Can I take some paper from here?* **3** ~ (of sb/ sth) used when you are referring to certain members

of a group or certain types of a thing, but not all of them: *Some pupils enjoy this kind of work, some don't.* ◇ *Some of his books are very exciting.* ◇ *Some of us are going to the park.* **4** used with singular nouns for talking about a person or thing without saying any details: *I'll see you again some time, I expect.* ◇ *There must be some mistake.* ◇ *I read about it in some newspaper or other.*

somebody ഽ **A1** /'sʌmbədi/ (*also* someone) *pron.* a person who is not known or not mentioned by name: *How are you? Somebody said that you'd been ill.* ◇ *She's getting married to somebody she met at work.* ◇ *I think you should talk to somebody else* (= another person) *about this problem.*

'some day (*also* someday) *adv.* at a time in the future that is not yet known: *I hope you'll come and visit me some day.*

somehow ഽ+ **B2** **S** /'sʌmhaʊ/ *adv.* **1** in a way that is not known or certain: *The car's broken down but I'll get to work somehow.* ◇ *Somehow we had got completely lost.* **2** for a reason you do not know or understand: *I somehow get the feeling that I've been here before.*

someone ഽ **A1** /'sʌmwʌn/ = SOMEBODY

someplace /'sʌmpleɪs/ (*AmE*) = SOMEWHERE

somersault /'sʌməsɔːlt/ *noun* [C] a movement in which you roll right over with your feet going over your head

something ഽ **A1** /'sʌmθɪŋ/ *pron.* **1** a thing that is not known or not named: *I've got something in my eye.* ◇ *Wait a minute — I've forgotten something.* ◇ *Would you like something else* (= another thing) *to drink?* **2** a thing that is important, useful or worth considering: *There's something in what your mother says.* ◇ *I think you've got something there — I like that idea.* **3** (*informal*) used to show that a description, an amount, etc. is not exact: *a new comedy series aimed at thirty-somethings* (= people between 30 and 40 years old) **IDM** **or something** (*informal*) used for showing that you are not sure about what you have just said: *'What's his job?' 'I think he's a plumber, or something.'* **something like** similar to: *A loganberry is something like a raspberry.* **something to do with** connected with or involved with: *The programme's something to do with the environment.*

sometime ഽ+ **B2** (*also* some time) /'sʌmtaɪm/ *adv.* at a time that you do not know exactly or have not yet decided: *I'll phone you sometime this evening.* ◇ *I must go and see her sometime.*

sometimes ഽ **A1** **S** /'sʌmtaɪmz/ *adv.* on some occasions; now and then: *Sometimes I drive to work and sometimes I go by bus.* ◇ *I sometimes watch TV in the evenings.*

somewhat ഽ **B2** /'sʌmwɒt/ *adv.* (*formal*) rather; to some degree: *We missed the train, which was somewhat unfortunate.*

somewhere ഽ **A2** /'sʌmweə(r)/ (*AmE also* someplace) *adv., pron.* (at, in, or to) a place that you do not know or do not mention by name: *I saw your glasses somewhere downstairs.* ◇ *'Have they gone to France?' 'No, I think they've gone somewhere else* (= to another place) *this year.'* ◇ *They are looking for somewhere to live.* ◇ *I know somewhere we can go.* **IDM** **somewhere around** used when you do not know an exact time, number, etc: *Your ideal weight should probably be somewhere around 70 kilos.*

sommelier /sə'melɪeɪ, 'sɒməljeɪ/ *noun* [C] (**TOURISM**) a person who works in a restaurant serving wine and helping customers to decide which wine to choose **SYN** **wine waiter**

son ഽ **A1** /sʌn/ *noun* [C] a male child ➔ look at **daughter**

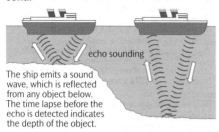

echo sounding

The ship emits a sound wave, which is reflected from any object below. The time lapse before the echo is detected indicates the depth of the object.

sonar /ˈsəʊnɑː(r)/ *noun* [U] (**PHYSICS**) equipment or a system for finding objects under water using sound waves ⊃ look at **radar**

sonata /səˈnɑːtə/ *noun* [C] (**MUSIC**) a piece of music written for the piano, or for another instrument together with the piano

song ʔ **A1** /sɒŋ/ *noun* **1** [C] (**MUSIC**) a piece of music with words that you sing: *a folk/love/pop song* ⊃ note at **performing arts 2** [U] (**MUSIC**) songs in general; music for singing: *to burst/break into song* (= to suddenly start singing) **3** [U, C] the musical sounds that birds make: *birdsong*

songbird /ˈsɒŋbɜːd/ *noun* [C] a bird that has a musical call, for example a BLACKBIRD or a THRUSH

songwriter /ˈsɒŋraɪtə(r)/ *noun* [C] (**MUSIC**) a person who writes songs

sonic /ˈsɒnɪk/ *adj.* (**PHYSICS**) connected with sound waves

son-in-law *noun* [C] (*pl.* **sons-in-law**) your daughter's or son's husband

sonnet /ˈsɒnɪt/ *noun* [C] (**LITERATURE**) a type of poem that has 14 lines that RHYME (= end with the same sound) in a fixed pattern

soon ʔ **A1** /suːn/ *adv.* **1** in a short time from now; a short time after sth else has happened: *It will soon be dark.* ◇ *He left soon after me.* ◇ *We should arrive at your house soon after twelve.* ◇ *See you soon.* **2** early; quickly: *Don't leave so soon. Stay for tea.* ◇ *How soon can you get here?*
IDM **as soon as** at the moment (that); when: *Phone me as soon as you hear some news.* ◇ *I'd like your reply as soon as possible* (= at the earliest possible moment). **no sooner … than** immediately when or after: *No sooner had I shut the door than I realized I'd left my keys inside.* **the sooner the better** very soon; as soon as possible **sooner or later** at some time in the future; one day

soot /sʊt/ *noun* [U] black powder that is produced when wood, coal, etc. is burnt

soothe /suːð/ *verb* [T] **1** to make sb calmer or less upset **SYN** **comfort**[2] **2** to make a part of the body or a feeling less painful: *The doctor gave me some skin cream to soothe the irritation.* ▶ **soothing** *adj.*: *soothing music* ◇ *a soothing massage* ▶ **soothingly** *adv.*

sophisticated ʔ+ **B2** /səˈfɪstɪkeɪtɪd/ *adj.* **1** (used about machines, systems, etc.) advanced and complicated **2** having or showing a lot of experience of the world and social situations; knowing about fashion, culture, etc. **3** able to understand difficult or complicated things: *Voters are much more sophisticated these days.* ▶ **sophistication** /səˌfɪstɪˈkeɪʃn/ *noun* [U]

sophomore /ˈsɒfəmɔː(r)/ *noun* [C] (*AmE*) (**EDUCATION**) **1** a student in the second year of a course of study at a college or university **2** a HIGH SCHOOL student in the tenth grade ⊃ look at **freshman, junior**[2] (3), **senior**[2] (3)

soppy /ˈsɒpi/ *adj.* (*informal*) (**soppier; soppiest**) full of unnecessary emotion; silly: *a soppy romantic film*

soprano /səˈprɑːnəʊ/ *noun* [C] (*pl.* -os) (**MUSIC**) the highest singing voice; a woman, girl, or boy with this voice ⊃ look at **alto, treble**[2]

sordid /ˈsɔːdɪd/ *adj.* **1** unpleasant; not honest or moral: *We discovered the truth about his sordid past.* **2** very dirty and unpleasant

sore[1] /sɔː(r)/ *adj.* (**HEALTH**) (used about a part of the body) painful and often red: *to have a sore throat* ◇ *My feet were sore from walking so far.* ▶ **soreness** *noun* [U]: *a cream to reduce soreness and swelling*
IDM **a sore point** a subject that is likely to make sb upset or angry when mentioned **stand/stick out like a sore thumb** to be extremely obvious, especially in a negative way: *A big new office block would stand out like a sore thumb in the old part of town.*

sore[2] /sɔː(r)/ *noun* [C] (**HEALTH**) a painful, often red place on your body where there is a wound or an infection ⊃ look at **cold sore**

sorely /ˈsɔːli/ *adv.* very much; seriously: *You'll be sorely missed when you leave.*

sorority /səˈrɒrəti/ *noun* [C] (*pl.* -ies) (**EDUCATION**) a club for a group of women students at an American college or university ⊃ look at **fraternity** (2)

sorrow /ˈsɒrəʊ/ *noun* **1** [U] a feeling of being very sad because sth bad has happened **2** [C] a very sad event or situation ▶ **sorrowful** /-fl/ *adj.* ▶ **sorrowfully** /-fəli/ *adv.*

sorry[1] ʔ **A1** /ˈsɒri/ *adj.* (**sorrier; sorriest**) **1** [not before noun] **~ (to see, hear, etc.) (that)** sad or disappointed: *I was sorry to hear that you've been ill.* ◇ *I am sorry that we have to leave so soon.* ◇ *'Simon's mother died last week.' 'Oh, I am sorry.'* **2** [not before noun] **~ (for/about sth); ~ (to do sth/that …)** used for excusing yourself for sth that you have done: *I'm awfully sorry for spilling that coffee.* ◇ *I'm sorry I've kept you all waiting.* ◇ *I'm sorry to disturb you so late in the evening, but I wonder if you can help me.* **3** [only before noun] very bad: *The house was in a sorry state when we first moved in.* ◇ *They were a sorry sight when they finally got home.*
IDM **be/feel sorry for sb** to be sad or feel sympathy for sb: *I feel very sorry for the families of the victims.* ◇ *Stop feeling sorry for yourself!* **I'm sorry** used for saying 'no' to sth, disagreeing with sth or introducing bad news in a polite way: *'Would you like to come to dinner on Friday?' 'I'm sorry, I'm busy that evening.'* ◇ *I'm sorry, I don't agree with you. I think we should accept the offer.* ◇ *I'm sorry to tell you that your application has been unsuccessful.*

sorry[2] ʔ **A1** /ˈsɒri/ *exclamation* **1** used for making excuses, apologizing, etc: *Sorry, I didn't see you standing behind me.* ◇ *Sorry I'm late — the bus didn't come on time.* ◇ *He didn't even say sorry* (= apologize)! **2** (*especially BrE*) (used for asking sb to repeat sth that you have not heard correctly): *'My name's Dave Harries.' 'Sorry? Dave who?'* **3** (used for correcting yourself when you have said sth wrong): *Take the second turning, sorry, the third turning on the right.*

sort[1] ʔ **A2** **S** /sɔːt/ *noun* **1** [C] **~ (of sb/sth)** a group of people or things that are the same in some way: *What sort of music do you like?* ◇ *She's got all sorts of problems at the moment.* ◇ *There were snacks — peanuts, olives, that sort of thing.* **2** [sing.] (*especially BrE*) a particular type of character; a person: *He wouldn't lie; he's not that sort.* **SYN** **kind**[1]
IDM **a sort of sth** (*informal*) used for describing sth in a way that is not very exact: *Can you hear a sort of*

ticking noise? **sort of** (*informal*) rather; in a way: *'Do you see what I mean?' 'Sort of.'* ◇ *I'd sort of like to go, but I'm not sure.*

sort² ⟟ **B1** ⑤ /sɔːt/ *verb* [T] **1** ~ **sth (into sth)** to put things into different groups or places, according to their type, etc.; to separate things of one type from others: *I'm just sorting these papers into the correct files.* **2** [often passive] (*especially BrE, informal*) to find an answer to a problem or difficult situation; to organize sth/sb: *I'll have more time when I've got things sorted at home.*
PHR V **sort sth out 1** to find an answer to a problem; to organize sth: *I haven't found a flat yet but I hope to sort something out soon.* **2** to tidy or organize sth: *The toy cupboard needs sorting out.* **sort through sth** to look through a number of things, in order to find sth that you are looking for or to put them in order

so-'so *adj., adv.* (*informal*) all right but not particularly good/well: *'How are you feeling today?' 'So-so.'*

soufflé /'suːfleɪ/ *noun* [C, U] a type of food made mainly from egg whites, flour and milk, beaten together and baked until it rises

sought /sɔːt/ past tense, past participle of **seek**

'sought after *adj.* that people want very much, because it is of high quality or rare

soul ⟟ **B2** /səʊl/ *noun*
- SPIRIT OF A PERSON **1** [C] (**RELIGION**) the spiritual part of a person that is believed to continue to exist after the body is dead
- INNER CHARACTER **2** [C, U] the inner part of a person containing their deepest thoughts and feelings: *There was a feeling of restlessness deep in her soul.* ➲ look at **spirit**¹ (1)
- PERSON **3** [sing.] (in negative sentences) a person: *There wasn't a soul in sight* (= there was nobody). ◇ *Promise me you won't tell a soul.*
- MUSIC **4** (*also* 'soul music) [U] a type of music made popular by African American musicians: *a soul singer*
IDM **heart and soul** → HEART

soulful /'səʊlfl/ *adj.* having or showing deep feeling: *a soulful expression*

soulless /'səʊlləs/ *adj.* without feeling or interest: *soulless industrial towns* **SYN** **depressing**

sound¹ ⟟ **A1** /saʊnd/ *noun* **1** [C, U] something that you hear or that can be heard: *the sound of voices* ◇ *a clicking/buzzing/scratching sound* ◇ *After that, he didn't make a sound.* ◇ *She opened the door without a sound.* ◇ *Light travels faster than sound.* ◇ *sound waves* **SYN** **noise** ➲ picture at **high-pitched**, **sound wave 2** [U] what you can hear coming from a TV, radio, etc: *Can you turn the sound up/down?*
IDM **by the sound of it/things** judging from what sb has said or what you have read about sb/sth: *She's an interesting person, by the sound of it.*

sound² ⟟ **A1** /saʊnd/ *verb* **1** *linking verb* (not usually in the progressive tenses) to give a particular impression when heard or read about; to seem: *That sounds like a child crying.* ◇ *She sounded upset and angry on the phone.* ◇ *You sound like your father when you say things like that!* ◇ *He sounds a very nice person from his letter.* ◇ *Does she sound like the right person for the job?* ◇ *It doesn't sound as if/though he's very reliable.* **2** -sounding (in adjectives) seeming to be of the type mentioned, from what you have heard or read: *a Spanish-sounding surname* **3** [T] to cause sth to make a sound; to give a signal by making a sound: *to sound the horn of your car* ◇ *A student on one of the upper floors sounded the alarm.* **4** [T, I] to measure the

depth of the sea or a lake by using a line with a weight on it, or an electronic instrument
PHR V **sound sb out (about sth)** to ask sb questions in order to find out what they think or intend

sound³ ⟟+ **C1** /saʊnd/ *adj.* **1** sensible; that you can depend on and that will probably give good results: *sound advice* ◇ *a sound investment* **2** healthy and strong; in good condition: *The structure of the bridge is basically sound.* **OPP** **unsound** ▸ **soundness** *noun* [U]

sound⁴ /saʊnd/ *adv.*
IDM **be sound asleep** to be deeply asleep

the 'sound barrier *noun* [sing.] (**PHYSICS**) the point at which an aircraft's speed is the same as the speed of sound: *to break the sound barrier* (= to travel faster than the speed of sound)

'sound bite *noun* [C] (**POLITICS**) a short phrase or sentence taken from a longer speech, especially a speech made by a politician, that is particularly effective or appropriate

'sound effect *noun* [C, usually pl.] (**ARTS AND MEDIA**) a sound that is made artificially, for example the sound of the wind, and used in a play, film or computer game to make it more realistic

soundly /'saʊndli/ *adv.* completely or deeply: *The children were sleeping soundly.*

soundproof /'saʊndpruːf/ *adj.* made so that no sound can get in or out: *a soundproof room*

soundtrack /'saʊndtræk/ *noun* [C] (**ARTS AND MEDIA**, **MUSIC**) the recorded sound and music from a film or computer game ➲ look at **track**¹ (5)

sound waves

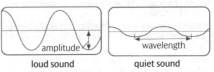

loud sound   quiet sound

'sound wave *noun* [C] (**PHYSICS**) a movement in the air, in water, etc. that we hear as sound

soup ⟟ **A1** /suːp/ *noun* [U, C] liquid food made by cooking meat, vegetables, etc. in water: *a tin of chicken soup* ➲ picture at **vacuum flask**

sour /'saʊə(r)/ *adj.* **1** having a sharp taste like that of a lemon: *This sauce is quite sour.* ➲ look at **bitter**¹ (4), **sweet**¹ (1) **2** (used especially about milk) tasting or smelling unpleasant because it is no longer fresh: *This cream has gone sour.* **3** (used about people) angry and unpleasant: *a sour expression* ◇ *a sour-faced old woman* ▸ **sour** *verb* [T] (*formal*): *The disagreement over trade tariffs has soured relations between the two countries.* ▸ **sourly** *adv.* ▸ **sourness** *noun* [U]
IDM **go/turn sour** to stop being pleasant or friendly: *Their relationship turned sour after a few months.* **sour grapes** pretending to not want sth that in fact you secretly want, because you cannot have it: *He said he didn't want the job anyway, but that's just sour grapes.*

source¹ ⟟ **A2** ⊙ /sɔːs/ *noun* [C] ~ **(of sth)** a place, person or thing where sth comes or starts from or where sth is obtained: *Britain's oil reserves are an important source of income.* ◇ *This word has its source in Greek.* ◇ *The TV is a great source of entertainment.* ◇ *Police have refused to reveal the source of their information.* ◇ *the source of the Nile* ➲ picture at **shadow**¹

source² /sɔːs/ *verb* [T] ~ **sth (from …)** (**BUSINESS**) to get sth from a particular place: *We source all the meat sold in our stores from British farms.*

source code *noun* [U] (**COMPUTING**) a computer program written in text form that must be translated into MACHINE CODE before it can run on a computer

sous-chef /'suː ʃef/ *noun* [C] a person who is the second most senior cook in a restaurant ⊃ look at **chef**, **commis**

south¹ ᵻ **A1** /saʊθ/ *noun* [U, sing.] (*abbr.* S) (**GEOGRAPHY**) **1** (*usually* the south) ~ (of …) the direction that is on your right when you watch the sun rise; one of the points of the COMPASS (= the four main directions that we give names to): *warm winds from the south* ◊ *Which way is south?* ◊ *We live to the south of London.* ⊃ look at **east**¹ (1), **north**¹ (1), **west**¹ (1) ⊃ note at **compass** ⊃ picture at **compass 2** the south, the South the southern part of a country, a city, a region or the world: *Nice is in the South of France.*

south² ᵻ **A1** /saʊθ/ *adj., adv.* (**GEOGRAPHY**) **1** in or towards the south: *the south coast of Cornwall* ◊ *The house faces south.* **2** ~ (of …) nearer to the south than sth: *We live just south of Birmingham.* **3** (used about a wind) coming from the south

southbound /'saʊθbaʊnd/ *adj.* (**GEOGRAPHY**) travelling or leading towards the south

south-'east¹ (*also* the South-East) *noun* [sing.] (*abbr.* SE) (**GEOGRAPHY**) the direction or a region that is an equal distance between south and east ⊃ picture at **compass**

south-'east² *adj., adv.* (**GEOGRAPHY**) in, from or to the south-east of a place or country: *the south-east coast of Spain*

south-'easterly *adj.* (**GEOGRAPHY**) **1** [only before noun] towards the south-east: *in a south-easterly direction* **2** (used about a wind) coming from the south-east

south-'eastern *adj.* [only before noun] (*abbr.* SE) (**GEOGRAPHY**) connected with the south-east of a place or country: *the south-eastern states of the US*

south-'eastwards (*also* south-eastward) *adv.* (**GEOGRAPHY**) towards the south-east: *Follow the A423 south-eastward.*

southerly /'sʌðəli/ *adj.* (**GEOGRAPHY**) **1** to, towards or in the south: *Keep going in a southerly direction.* **2** (used about a wind) coming from the south

southern ᵻ **B1** /'sʌðən/ (*also* Southern) *adj.* (*abbr.* S) (**GEOGRAPHY**) of, in or from the south of a place: *a man with a southern accent* ◊ *Greece is in Southern Europe.*

southerner /'sʌðənə(r)/ (*also* Southerner) *noun* [C] a person who was born in or lives in the southern part of a country **OPP** northerner

the Southern 'Lights *noun* [pl.] (*also* aurora australis [sing.]) (**ASTRONOMY**) bands of coloured light that are sometimes seen in the sky at night in the most southern countries of the world

the South 'Pole *noun* [sing.] (**GEOGRAPHY**) the point on the earth's surface that is furthest south ⊃ picture at **earth**¹

south-south-'east *noun* [sing.] (*abbr.* SSE) (**GEOGRAPHY**) the direction that is at an equal distance between south and south-east

south-south-'west *noun* [sing.] (*abbr.* SSW) (**GEOGRAPHY**) the direction that is at an equal distance between south and south-west

southwards /'saʊθwədz/ (*also* southward /'saʊθwəd/) *adv.* (**GEOGRAPHY**) towards the south ▶ southward *adj.*: *in a southward direction*

south-'west¹ (*also* the South-West) *noun* [sing.] (*abbr.* SW) (**GEOGRAPHY**) the direction or a region that is an equal distance between south and west ⊃ picture at **compass**

south-'west² *adj., adv.* (**GEOGRAPHY**) in, from or to the south-west of a place or country: *the south-west coast of France* ◊ *Our garden faces south-west.*

south-'westerly *adj.* (**GEOGRAPHY**) **1** [only before noun] towards the south-west: *in a south-westerly direction* **2** (used about a wind) coming from the south-west

south-'western *adj.* [only before noun] (*abbr.* SW) (**GEOGRAPHY**) connected with the south-west of a place or country

south-'westwards (*also* south-westward) *adv.* (**GEOGRAPHY**) towards the south-west: *Follow the B409 south-westwards for 20 miles.*

souvenir /ˌsuːvə'nɪə(r)/ *noun* [C] (**TOURISM**) something that you buy or keep to remind you of somewhere you have been on holiday or of a special event: *I brought back a menu as a souvenir of my trip.* **SYN** memento

sovereign¹ /'sɒvrɪn/ *noun* [C] (*formal*) (**POLITICS**) a king or queen

sovereign² /'sɒvrɪn/ *adj.* **1** [only before noun] (**POLITICS**) (used about a country) not controlled by any other country; independent **2** having the highest possible authority

sovereignty ᵻ⁺ **C1** /'sɒvrənti/ *noun* [U] (*formal*) (**POLITICS**) the power that a country has to control its own government

Soviet /'səʊviət, 'sɒv-/ *adj.* connected with the former USSR

sow¹ /saʊ/ *noun* [C] (**AGRICULTURE**) an adult female pig ⊃ note at **pig**¹

sow² /səʊ/ *verb* [T] (*pt* sowed; *pp* sown /səʊn/, sowed) ~ **A (in B); ~ B (with A)** (**AGRICULTURE**) to plant seeds in the ground: *to sow seeds in pots* ◊ *to sow a field with wheat*

soya /'sɔɪə/ (*BrE*) (*AmE* soy /sɔɪ/) *noun* [U] a plant on which SOYA BEANS grow; the food obtained from those beans: *soya flour/milk/oil*

soya bean (*BrE*) (*AmE* 'soy bean) *noun* [C] a type of bean that is used in a variety of foods, especially instead of meat

soy 'sauce (*also* ˌsoya 'sauce) *noun* [U] a thin dark brown sauce that is made from SOYA BEANS and tastes of salt, used in Chinese and Japanese cooking

spa /spɑː/ *noun* [C] **1** a place where mineral water comes out of the ground and where people go to drink this water because it is considered to be healthy **2** (*also* health spa) a place where people can relax and improve their health or receive beauty treatments

space¹ ᵻ **A1** ⊙ /speɪs/ *noun* **1** (*also* outer space) [U] (**ASTRONOMY**) the area that surrounds the planet Earth and the other planets and stars: *space travel* ◊ *a spaceman/spacewoman* (= a person who travels in space) **2** [C, U] ~ (**for sb/sth**) (**to do sth**) a place or an area that is empty or not used: *There's a space here for you to write your name.* ◊ *Leave a space after the comma.* ◊ *Is there enough space for me to park the car there?* ◊ *Shelves would take up less space than a cupboard.* ◊ *a parking space* ◊ *We're a bit short of space.* ⊃ look at **room** (2) **3** [C, usually sing.] a period of time: *Priti had been ill three times in/within the space of four months.* ◊ *He's achieved a lot in a short space of time.* **4** [U] time and freedom to think and do what you want: *I need some space to think.*

space² /speɪs/ *verb* [T] ~ **sth (out)** to arrange things so that there are empty spaces between them

space bar *noun* [sing.] (**COMPUTING**) a bar on the keyboard of a computer that you press to make spaces between words

spacecraft /'speɪskrɑːft/ *noun* [C] (*pl.* **spacecraft**) (**ASTRONOMY**) a vehicle that travels in space

,spaced 'out *adj.* (*informal*) not completely conscious of what is happening around you, often because of taking drugs

'space probe = PROBE² (2)

spaceship /'speɪsʃɪp/ *noun* [C] (**ASTRONOMY**) a vehicle that travels in space, carrying people

'space shuttle *noun* [C] (**ASTRONOMY**) a vehicle that can travel into space and land like a plane when it returns to Earth

'space station *noun* [C] (**ASTRONOMY**) a large structure that is sent into space for a long time as a base for scientists working in space

spacesuit /'speɪssuːt/ *noun* [C] (**ASTRONOMY**) a special suit that covers the whole body and has a supply of air, allowing sb to survive and move around in space

spacewalk /'speɪswɔːk/ *noun* [C] (**ASTRONOMY**) a period of time that an ASTRONAUT spends in space outside a SPACECRAFT

spacious /'speɪʃəs/ *adj.* having a lot of space; large in size **SYN** **roomy** ▸ **spaciousness** *noun* [U]

spade /speɪd/ *noun* **1** [C] a tool that you use for digging ⊃ look at **shovel** ⊃ picture at **gardening** **2 spades** [pl.] one of the four SUITS (= sets) in a PACK of cards. The spades have shapes like pointed black leaves on them: *the king of spades* **3** [C] one of the cards from this SUIT: *Have you got a spade?*

spaghetti /spə'geti/ *noun* [U] a type of PASTA (= Italian food made from flour, eggs and water) that looks like long strings: *How long does spaghetti take to cook?*

spam ᵂ⁺ **C1** /spæm/ *noun* [U] (*informal*) (**COMPUTING**) advertising material sent by email to people who have not asked for it: *There are filters to block spam from your inbox.* ⊃ look at **junk mail** ▸ **spam** *verb* [T] (-mm-) ▸ **spamming** *noun* [U]

span¹ ᵂ⁺ **C1** /spæn/ *noun* [C] **1** the length of time that sth lasts or continues: *Young children have a short attention span.* **2** the length of sth from one end to the other: *the wingspan of a bird*

span² ᵂ⁺ **C1** /spæn/ *verb* [T] (-nn-) **1** to form a bridge over sth **2** to last or continue for a particular period of time

spank /spæŋk/ *verb* [T] to hit sb, especially a child, several times on their bottom with an open hand as a punishment

spanner /'spænə(r)/ (*BrE*) (*AmE* **wrench**) *noun* [C] a metal tool with an end shaped for turning NUTS (= small metal rings) and BOLTS (= pins that are used for holding things together) ⊃ look at **adjustable spanner** ⊃ picture at **tool**

spare¹ ᵂ⁺ **B2** /speə(r)/ *adj.* **1** not used for work: *What do you do in your spare time?* **2** not being used; free: *There were no seats spare so we had to stand.* **3** not needed now but kept because it may be needed in the future: *The spare tyre is kept in the boot.* ◇ *a spare room* ▸ **spare** *noun* [C]: *The fuse has blown. Where do you keep your spares?*

spare² ᵂ⁺ **C1** /speə(r)/ *verb* [T] **1** ~ **sth (for sb)**; ~ **(sb) sth** to be able to give sth to sb: *We can only spare one room for you.* ◇ *I suppose I can spare you a few minutes.* **2** ~ **sb (from) sth/doing sth** to save sb from having an unpleasant experience: *I told him what happened but spared him all the details.* **3** ~ **sb/sth (from sth)** (*figurative*) to not hurt or damage sb/sth: *The soldiers killed the man but spared the child's life.* **4** ~ **no effort, expense, etc.** to do sth as well as possible without limiting the money, time, etc. involved: *No expense*

was spared at the wedding. ◇ *He spared no effort in trying to find a job.*
IDM **to spare** more than is needed: *There's no time to spare. We must leave straight away.*

,spare 'part *noun* [C] (**ENGINEERING**) a part for a machine, an engine, etc. that you can use to replace an old part that is damaged or broken

,spare 'rib *noun* [C] a RIB (= a bone) of PORK (= meat from a pig) with most of the meat cut off

sparing /'speərɪŋ/ *adj.* ~ **(with sth)** using only a little of sth; careful ▸ **sparingly** *adv.*

spark¹ /spɑːk/ *noun* **1** [C] a very small bright piece of burning material: *A spark set fire to the carpet.* **2** [C] a flash of light that is caused by electricity: *A spark ignites the fuel in a car engine.* **3** [U, sing.] an exciting quality that sb/sth has

spark² /spɑːk/ *verb* [T] ~ **sth (off)** to cause sth, especially suddenly: *Eric's comments sparked off a tremendous argument.*

sparkle /'spɑːkl/ *verb* [I] ~ **(with sth)** to shine with many small points of light: *The river sparkled in the sunlight.* ▸ **sparkle** *noun* [C, U]

sparkler /'spɑːklə(r)/ *noun* [C] a type of small FIREWORK (= a small object that burns or explodes with coloured lights and loud sounds) that you hold in your hand and light. It burns with many bright flashes of light.

sparkling /'spɑːklɪŋ/ *adj.* **1** shining with many small points of light: *sparkling blue eyes* **2** (used about a drink) containing bubbles of gas: *sparkling wine/ mineral water* **SYN** **fizzy**

'spark plug *noun* [C] a small piece of equipment in an engine that produces a SPARK (= a flash of electricity) to make the fuel burn and start the engine

sparrow /'spærəʊ/ *noun* [C] a small brown and grey bird that is common in many parts of the world

sparse /spɑːs/ *adj.* small in quantity or amount: *a sparse crowd* ◇ *He just had a few sparse hairs on his head.* ▸ **sparsely** *adv.*: *a sparsely populated area* ▸ **sparseness** *noun* [U]

spartan /'spɑːtn/ *adj.* (*formal*) very simple and not comfortable: *spartan living conditions*

spasm /'spæzəm/ *noun* [C, U] (**HEALTH**) a sudden movement of a muscle that you cannot control: *He had painful spasms in his leg.*

spat /spæt/ past tense, past participle of **spit¹**

spate /speɪt/ *noun* [sing.] ~ **of sth** (*formal*) a large number or amount of sth happening at one time: *There has been a spate of burglaries in the area recently.*

spatial ᵂ /'speɪʃl/ *adj.* (*formal*) connected with the size or position of sth

spatter /'spætə(r)/ *verb* [T] ~ **sb/sth (with sth)**; ~ **sth (on sb/sth)** to cover sb/sth with small drops of sth wet

spatula /'spætʃələ/ *noun* [C] a tool with a wide flat part, used for mixing and spreading things, especially in cooking ⊃ picture at **laboratory**

speak ᵂ **A1** /spiːk/ *verb* (*pt* **spoke** /spəʊk/; *pp* **spoken** /'spəʊkən/) **1** [I] ~ **(to sb) (about sb/sth)** to talk or say things: *I'd like to speak to the manager, please.* ◇ *I need to speak to you about something important.* ◇ *Could you speak more slowly?* ◇ *I was so angry I could hardly speak.* **2** [T] (not used in the progressive tenses) to know and be able to use a language: *Does anyone here speak German?* ◇ *She speaks (in) Greek to her parents.* ◇ *a French-speaking guide* **3** [I] ~ **(on/ about sth)** to make a speech to a group of people **IDM** **be on speaking terms (with sb)** | **be speaking (to sb)** to be friendly with sb again after an argument: *Thankfully they are back on speaking terms again.* **so to speak** used when you are describing sth in a way that sounds strange: *She* turned green, so to speak, after watching a TV programme about the environment. **speak for itself** to be very clear so that no other explanation is needed: *The statistics speak for themselves.* **speak/talk of the devil** → DEVIL **speak your mind** to say exactly what you think, even though you might offend sb

PHR V **speak for sb** to express the thoughts or opinions of sb else **speak out (against sth)** to say publicly that you think sth is bad or wrong **speak up** to speak louder

-speak /spiːk/ *suffix* (**LANGUAGE**) (in nouns) the language used by a particular group of people: *management-speak*

speaker 🔒 **A2** /'spiːkə(r)/ *noun* [C] **1** a person who makes a speech to a group of people: *Tonight's speaker is a well-known writer and journalist.* **2** the part of a radio, computer or piece of musical equipment that the sound comes out of **3** a person who speaks a particular language: *She's a fluent Russian speaker.*

spear /spɪə(r)/ *noun* [C] a long POLE with a sharp point at one end, used for hunting or fighting ➔ picture at **weapon**

spearhead /'spɪəhed/ *noun* [C, usually sing.] a person or group that begins or leads an attack ▶ **spearhead** *verb* [T]

spearmint /'spɪəmɪnt/ *noun* [U] a type of leaf that has a strong fresh taste that is used in sweets, etc: *spearmint chewing gum* ➔ look at **peppermint** (1)

special¹ 🔒 **A1** /'speʃl/ *adj.* **1** not usual or ordinary; important for some particular reason: *a special occasion* ◊ *Please take special care of it.* ◊ *Are you doing anything special tonight?* **2** [only before noun] for a particular purpose: *Andy goes to a special school for the deaf.* ◊ *There's a special tool for doing that.*

special² /'speʃl/ *noun* [C] something that is not of the usual or ordinary type: *an all-night election special on TV* ◊ *I'm going to cook one of my specials tonight.*

special effects (*also* **SFX**) *noun* [pl.] (**ARTS AND MEDIA**) unusual or exciting pieces of action in films or TV programmes, that are created by computers or clever photography to show things that do not normally exist or happen

specialist¹ 🔒 **B2** ⓦ /'speʃəlɪst/ *noun* [C] ~ (**in sth**) a person with special knowledge of a particular subject: *She's a specialist in diseases of cattle.* ◊ *I have to see a heart specialist.*

specialist² 🔒 **B2** /'speʃəlɪst/ *adj.* [only before noun] having or involving special knowledge of a particular area of work, study or medicine: *specialist knowledge/training/skills* ◊ *a specialist nurse/doctor* ◊ *to give specialist advice*

speciality /ˌspeʃiˈæləti/ (*pl.* -ies) (*BrE*) (*also* **specialty** *especially in AmE,* *pl.* -ies /'speʃəlti/) *noun* [C] **1** something made by a person, place, business, etc. that is very good and that they or it are known for: *The cheese is a speciality of the region.* **2** (**EDUCATION**) an area of study or a subject that you know a lot about

specialize 🔒+ **B2** (*BrE also* -ise) /'speʃəlaɪz/ *verb* [I] ~ (**in sth**) to give most of your attention to one subject, type of product, etc: *This shop specializes in clothes for taller men.* ▶ **specialization** (*BrE also* -isation) /ˌspeʃəlaɪˈzeɪʃn/ *noun* [U]

specialized 🔒+ **C1** ⓦ (*BrE also* -ised) /'speʃəlaɪzd/ *adj.* **1** to be used for a particular purpose: *a specialized system* **2** having or needing deep or special knowledge of a particular subject: *We have specialized staff to help you with any problems.*

specially /'speʃəli/ *adv.* **1** for a particular purpose or reason: *I made this specially for you.* **2** (*informal*) more than usual; more than other things: *The restaurant*

has a great atmosphere but the food is not specially good. ◊ *It's not a specially difficult exam.*

special 'needs *noun* [pl.] (*especially BrE*) (**EDUCATION, HEALTH, PSYCHOLOGY**) needs that a person has because of mental or physical problems: *She teaches children with special needs.*

special 'offer *noun* [C, U] (**BUSINESS**) a product that is sold at less than its usual price, especially in order to persuade people to buy it; the act of offering goods in this way: *French wine is on special offer this week.*

specialty /'speʃəlti/ (*AmE*) = SPECIALITY

species 🔒 **B2** /'spiːʃiːz/ *noun* [C] (*pl.* species) (**BIOLOGY**) a group of plants or animals that are all similar and that can produce young together: *This conservation group aims to protect endangered species.* ◊ *a rare species of frog* ➔ picture at **animal**

specific 🔒 **A2** ⓞ /spəˈsɪfɪk/ *adj.* **1** particular; not general: *Everyone has been given a specific job to do.* **2** ~ (**about sth**) detailed or exact: *Can you be more specific about what the man was wearing?*

specifically 🔒 **B1** ⓦ /spəˈsɪfɪkli/ *adv.* **1** connected with or intended for one particular thing only: *a play written specifically for radio* **2** in a detailed and exact way: *I specifically told you not to go near the water!*

specification 🔒+ **C1** ⓦ /ˌspesɪfɪˈkeɪʃn/ *noun* [C, U] detailed information about how sth is or should be built or made

specify 🔒+ **B2** ⓦ /'spesɪfaɪ/ *verb* [T] (**specifying; specifies;** *pt, pp* **specified**) to say or name sth clearly or in detail: *The fire regulations specify the maximum number of people allowed in.*

specimen 🔒+ **C1** /'spesɪmən/ *noun* [C] **1** (**MEDICINE**) a small amount of sth that is tested for medical or scientific purposes: *Specimens of the patient's blood were tested in the hospital laboratory.* **2** (**SCIENCE**) an example of a particular type of thing, especially intended to be studied by experts or scientists ➔ note at **example**

speck /spek/ *noun* [C] a very small spot or mark: *a speck of dust/dirt*

spectacle 🔒+ **C1** /'spektəkl/ *noun* **1** spectacles (*formal*) (*also informal* **specs** /speks/ *especially in BrE*) [pl.] = GLASS (3) **2** [C] something that is impressive or shocking to look at

spectacular 🔒+ **B2** /spekˈtækjələ(r)/ *adj.* very impressive to see: *The view from the top of the hill is quite spectacular.* ▶ **spectacularly** *adv.*

spectator 🔒+ **B2** /spekˈteɪtə(r)/ *noun* [C] (**SPORT**) a person who is watching an event, especially a sports event

spec'tator sport *noun* [C] (**SPORT**) a sport that many people watch; a sport that is interesting to watch

spectre (*AmE* **specter**) /'spektə(r)/ *noun* [C] **1** ~ (**of sth**) something unpleasant that people are afraid might happen in the future: *the spectre of unemployment* **2** (*old-fashioned*) = GHOST

spectroscopy /spekˈtrɒskəpi/ *noun* [U] (**CHEMISTRY, PHYSICS**) the study of forming and looking at SPECTRA

spectrum 🔒+ **C1** /'spektrəm/ *noun* [C, usually sing.] (*pl.* spectra /-trə/) **1** (**PHYSICS**) the set of seven colours into which white light can be separated: *You can see the colours of the spectrum in a rainbow.* ➔ picture at **prism** **2** (**PHYSICS**) a range of sound waves or several other types of wave: *the electromagnetic/radio/sound spectrum* **3** all the possible varieties of sth: *The speakers represented the whole spectrum of political opinions.*

IDM **on the spectrum** having an ASD

speculate ʔ+ **B2** /'spekjuleɪt/ *verb* **1** [I, T] ~ **(about/on sth)**; ~ **that ...** to make a guess about sth: *to speculate about the result of the next election* ◇ *We can only speculate that this vase was made in the tenth century.* **2** [I] (**BUSINESS**) to buy and sell with the aim of making money but with the risk of losing it: *to speculate on the stock market* ▶ **speculator** *noun* [C]

speculation ʔ+ **B2** /ˌspekju'leɪʃn/ *noun* [U, C]
1 ~ **(that ...)**; ~ **(about/over sth)** the act of forming opinions about what has happened or what might happen without knowing all the facts: *There was widespread speculation that she was going to resign.* ◇ *The president's absence led to speculation over his health.* **2** ~ **(in sth)** (**BUSINESS**) the activity of buying and selling goods or shares in a company in the hope of making a profit, but with the risk of losing money: *speculation in oil*

speculative /'spekjələtɪv/ *adj.* **1** based on guessing or on opinions that have been formed without knowing all the facts: *a speculative look/glance* **2** (**BUSINESS**) (used in business) done in the hope of making money, but involving the risk of losing it: *speculative investment*

speculum /'spekjələm/ *noun* [C] (**MEDICINE**) a metal instrument that is used to make a hole or tube in the body wider so it can be examined

sped /sped/ past tense, past participle of **speed**¹

speech ʔ **A2** /spiːtʃ/ *noun* **1** [C] a formal talk that you give to a group of people: *The Chancellor is going to make a speech to city businessmen.* **2** [U] the ability to speak: *He lost the power of speech after the accident.* ◇ *freedom of speech* (= being allowed to express your opinions openly) **3** [U] the particular way of speaking of a person or group of people: *She's doing a study of children's speech.* **4** [C] (**ARTS AND MEDIA**, **LITERATURE**) a group of words that an actor speaks in a play

'speech community *noun* [C] (**LANGUAGE**) all the people who speak a particular language or variety of a language

speechless /'spiːtʃləs/ *adj.* not able to speak, for example because you are shocked, angry, etc.

'speech marks = QUOTATION MARKS

speed¹ ʔ **A2** /spiːd/ *noun* **1** [C, U] (**PHYSICS**) the rate at which sb/sth moves or travels: *The car was travelling at a speed of 140 kilometres an hour.* ◇ *to travel at top/ high/full/maximum speed* ◇ *The bus was travelling at speed when it hit the wall.* **2** [U] fast movement: *The bus began to pick up speed down the hill.*

speed² ʔ **B2** /spiːd/ *verb* [I] (*pt, pp* speeded) **HELP** In sense 1 **sped** is also used for the past tense and past participle. **1** (used with an adverb or a preposition) to go or move very quickly: *He sped round the corner on his bike.* **2** (usually used in the progressive tenses) to drive a car, etc. faster than the legal speed limit: *The police said she had been speeding.*
PHR V **speed (sth) up** (*pt, pp* speeded) to go or make sth go faster: *The new computer system should speed up production in the factory.*

speedboat /'spiːdbəʊt/ *noun* [C] a small fast boat with an engine

'speed bump (*BrE also* **'speed hump**) *noun* [C] a raised area across a road that is put there to make traffic go slower

'speed camera *noun* [C] (*BrE*) (**LAW**) a machine that takes pictures of vehicles that are being driven too fast. The pictures are then used as evidence so that the drivers can be punished.

'speed dating *noun* [U] meeting people at an event organized for single people who want to begin a

$$speed = \frac{distance\ travelled}{time\ taken}$$

This arrow travels 50 m each second it is in flight. Its speed is 50 m per second.

This plane travels 1 000 km each hour it is in flight. Its speed is 1 000 km per hour.

romantic relationship, where you spend only a few minutes talking to one person before you have to move on to meet the next person

speedily /'spiːdəli/ → SPEEDY

speeding /'spiːdɪŋ/ *noun* [U] (**LAW**) driving a car, etc. faster than the legal speed limit

'speed limit *noun* [C, usually sing.] (**LAW**) the highest speed that you are allowed to drive without breaking the law on a particular road: *He was going way over the speed limit when the police stopped him.*

speedometer /spiː'dɒmɪtə(r)/ *noun* [C] a piece of equipment in a vehicle that tells you how fast you are travelling

'speed skating *noun* [U] (**SPORT**) the sport of SKATING on ice as fast as possible ⊃ look at **figure skating**

'speed trap (*BrE also* **radar trap**) *noun* [C] (**LAW**) a place on a road where police use special equipment to catch drivers who are going too fast

speedway /'spiːdweɪ/ *noun* [U] the sport of racing cars or motorcycles around a special track

speedy /'spiːdi/ *adj.* (speedier; speediest) fast; quick: *a speedy response/reply* ▶ **speedily** *adv.*

spell¹ ʔ **A1** /spel/ *verb* (*pt, pp* spelt /spelt/, spelled)
1 [I, T] (**LANGUAGE**) to write or say the letters of a word in the correct order: *I could never spell very well at school.* ◇ *How do you spell your surname?* ◇ *His name is spelt P-H-I-L-I-P.* **2** [T] (used about a set of letters) to form a particular word: *If you add an 'e' to 'car' it spells 'care'.* **3** [T] to mean sth; to have sth as a result: *Another poor harvest would spell disaster for the region.*
PHR V **spell sth out** **1** to write or say the letters of a word or name in the correct order: *I have an unusual name, so I always have to spell it out to people.* **2** to express sth in a very clear and direct way

spell² ʔ+ **C1** /spel/ *noun* [C] **1** a short period of time: *a spell of cold weather* **2** (especially in stories) magic words that cause sb to be in a particular state or condition

spellcheck /'speltʃek/ *verb* [T] (**COMPUTING**) to use a computer program to check your writing to see if your spelling is correct ▶ **spellcheck** *noun* [C]

spellchecker /'speltʃekə(r)/ (*also* **spellcheck**) *noun* [C] (**COMPUTING**) a computer program that checks your writing to see if your spelling is correct

spelling ʔ **A1** /'spelɪŋ/ *noun* **1** [U] the ability to write the letters of a word correctly: *Roger is very poor at spelling.* **2** [C] (**LANGUAGE**) the way that letters are arranged to make a word: *'Center'* is the American spelling of *'centre'*.

spelt /spelt/ past tense, past participle of **spell**¹

spelunking /spə'lʌŋkɪŋ/ = POTHOLING

spend 🔊 **A1** /spend/ *verb* (*pt, pp* **spent** /spent/) **1** [T, I] ~ **(sth) (on sth)** to give or pay money for sth: *How much do you spend on food each week?* ◇ *You shouldn't go on spending like that.* **2** [T] ~ **sth (on sth/doing sth)** to pass time: *I spent the whole evening chatting with my friends.* ◇ *I'm spending the weekend at my parents' house.* ◇ *He spent two years in Rome.* ◇ *I don't want to spend too much time on this project.*

spending 🔊 **B1** /'spendɪŋ/ *noun* [U] ~ **(on sth)** (FINANCE) the amount of money that is spent by a government or an organization

sperm /spɜːm/ *noun* (*pl.* **sperm**, **sperms**) (BIOLOGY) **1** [C] a cell that is produced in the sex organs of a male and that can join with a female egg to produce young ◯ picture at **fertilization 2** [U] the liquid that contains these cells **SYN** **semen**

SPF /ˌes piː 'ef/ *abbr.* **sun protection factor**; (a number that tells you how much protection a particular cream or liquid gives you from the harmful effects of the sun)

sphere 🔊+ **C1** **W** /sfɪə(r)/ *noun* [C] **1** (GEOMETRY) any round object shaped like a ball ◯ picture at **solid**² **2** an area of interest or activity ▶ **spherical** /'sferɪkl/ *adj.*

spheroid /'sfɪərɔɪd/ *noun* [C] (GEOMETRY) a solid object that is approximately the same shape as a SPHERE

sphincter /'sfɪŋktə(r)/ *noun* [C] (ANATOMY) a ring of muscle that surrounds an opening in the body and that can become tighter in order to close the opening: *the anal sphincter*

sphinx /sfɪŋks/ *noun* [C] (HISTORY) an ancient Egyptian stone statue of a creature with a human head and the body of a lion lying down

spice¹ 🔊+ **B2** /spaɪs/ *noun* **1** [C, U] a substance, especially a powder, that is made from a plant and used in cooking. Spices have a strong taste and smell: *I use a lot of herbs and spices in my cooking.* ◯ look at **herb 2** [U] excitement and interest: *to add spice to a situation*

spice² /spaɪs/ *verb* [T] ~ **sth (up) (with sth) 1** to add SPICE to food: *He always spices his cooking with lots of chilli powder.* **2** to add excitement to sth

spicy 🔊 **B1** /'spaɪsi/ *adj.* (**spicier**; **spiciest**) **1** (used about food) having a strong taste because SPICES have been added to it: *Do you like spicy food?* **2** (*informal*) (used about a story, piece of news, etc.) exciting and slightly shocking

spider 🔊 **A2** /'spaɪdə(r)/ *noun* [C] a small creature with eight thin legs. Spiders SPIN webs to catch insects for food. ◯ picture at **food web**

spike¹ /spaɪk/ *noun* [C] a piece of metal, wood, etc. that has a sharp point at one end

spike² /spaɪk/ *verb* [T] **1** to push a sharp piece of metal, wood, etc. into sb/sth; to injure sth on a sharp point ◯ look at **stab**¹ **2** ~ **sth (with sth)** to add alcohol, poison or a drug to sb's drink or food without them knowing

spill 🔊+ **B2** /spɪl/ *verb* (*pt, pp* **spilled**, **spilt** /spɪlt/) **1** [I, T] (used especially about a liquid) to come out of a container by accident; to make a liquid, etc. do this: *The bag split, and sugar spilled everywhere.* ◇ *Some water had spilled out of the bucket onto the floor.* ◇ *I've spilt some coffee on the desk.* **2** [I] (used with an adverb or a preposition) to come out of a place suddenly and go in different directions: *The train stopped and everyone spilled out.* ▶ **spill** *noun* [C]: *Many seabirds died as a result of the oil spill.*

IDM **spill the beans** (*informal*) to tell a person about sth that should be a secret

spin¹ 🔊+ **C1** /spɪn/ *verb* (**spinning**; *pt, pp* **spun** /spʌn/) **1** [I, T] ~ **(sth) (round)** to turn or to make sth turn round quickly: *Mary spun round when she heard somebody call her name.* ◇ *to spin a ball/coin/wheel* **2** [I, T] to make THREAD from a mass of wool, cotton, etc: *A spider spins a web.* **3** [T] to remove water from clothes that have just been washed by turning them round and round very fast in a machine

PHR V **spin sth out** to make sth last as long as possible

spin² 🔊+ **C1** /spɪn/ *noun* **1** [C, U] an act of making sth SPIN: *She put a lot of spin on the ball.* **2** [sing., U] (*informal*) (POLITICS) a way of talking publicly about a difficult situation, a mistake, etc. that makes it sound positive for you

IDM **go/take sb for a spin** to go/take sb out in a car or other vehicle

spinach /'spɪnɪtʃ, -nɪdʒ/ *noun* [U] a plant with large, dark green leaves that can be cooked or eaten in salads

spinal /'spaɪnl/ *adj.* (ANATOMY) connected with the SPINE (= the bones of the back)

spinal column = SPINE (1)

spinal cord *noun* [C] (ANATOMY) the mass of nerves inside the SPINE that connects all parts of the body to the brain ◯ picture at **body**, **brain**

spindle /'spɪndl/ *noun* [C] **1** (ENGINEERING) a ROD that turns in a machine, or that another part of the machine turns around **2** a thin pointed ROD used for SPINNING wool into THREAD by hand

spin doctor *noun* [C] (POLITICS) a person who finds ways of talking about difficult situations, mistakes, etc. in a positive way

spin dryer *noun* [C] (*BrE*) a machine that removes water from wet clothes by turning them round and round very fast ◯ look at **tumble dryer** ▶ **spin-dry** *verb* [T]

spine 🔊+ **C1** /spaɪn/ *noun* [C] **1** (ANATOMY) the row of small bones that are connected together down the middle of the back **SYN** **backbone** ◯ picture at **body 2** one of the sharp points like needles, on some plants and animals: *Porcupines use their spines to protect themselves.* ◯ look at **prickle**¹ **3** the narrow part of the cover of a book that you can see when it is on a shelf

spineless /'spaɪnləs/ *adj.* weak and easily frightened

spinnaker /'spɪnəkə(r)/ *noun* [C] a large extra sail on a racing YACHT that you use when the wind is coming from behind

spinning /'spɪnɪŋ/ *noun* [U] **1** the art or the process of making THREAD from a mass of wool, cotton, etc. **2** Spinning™ (SPORT) a type of exercise performed on an EXERCISE BIKE (= a bicycle that does not move and that is used for exercise), usually in a class

spin-off *noun* [C] ~ **(from/of sth)** something unexpected and useful that develops from sth else

spinster /'spɪnstə(r)/ *noun* [C] (*old-fashioned*) a woman, especially an older woman, who has never been married ◯ look at **bachelor** (1)

spiral /'spaɪrəl/ *noun* [C] a long curved line that moves round and round away from a central point ▶ **spiral** *adj.*: *a spiral staircase* ▶ **spiral** *verb* [I] (-ll-, *AmE* -l-)

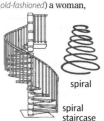

spiral

spiral staircase

spire /ˈspaɪə(r)/ *noun* [C] (**ARCHITECTURE**) a tall pointed structure on the top of a building, especially a church

spirit¹ 🔑 **B1** /ˈspɪrɪt/ *noun*
- MIND/FEELINGS **1** [U, C] the part of a person that is not physical; your thoughts and feelings, not your body: *the power of the human spirit to overcome difficulties*
- SOUL **2** [C] (**RELIGION**) the part of a person that many people believe still exists after their body is dead; a ghost or a being without a body: *It was believed that people could be possessed by evil spirits.* ⊃ look at **ghost**, **soul** (1)
- ATTITUDE **3** [sing.] (*also* **spirits** [pl.]) the mood, attitude or state of mind of sb/sth: *Everyone entered into the spirit of the party* (= joined in with enthusiasm). ◊ *to be in high/low spirits* (= in a happy/sad mood) **4** -spirited /ˈspɪrɪtɪd/ (in adjectives) having the mood or attitude of mind mentioned: *a group of high-spirited teenagers*
- DETERMINATION **5** [U] energy, strength of mind or DETERMINATION (= not giving up): *The group had plenty of team spirit.*
- QUALITY **6** [sing.] the typical or most important quality of sth: *The painting perfectly captures the spirit of the times.*
- ALCOHOL **7** spirits [pl.] (*especially BrE*) strong alcoholic drinks

spirit² /ˈspɪrɪt/ *verb*
PHR V **spirit sb/sth away/off** to take sb/sth away secretly

spirited /ˈspɪrɪtɪd/ *adj.* full of energy, courage, and strength of mind

spirit level

ˈspirit level (*also* **level**) *noun* [C] a glass tube partly filled with liquid, with a bubble of air inside. Spirit levels are used to test whether a surface is level, by the position of the bubble.

spiritual¹ 🔑 **B2** /ˈspɪrɪtʃuəl/ *adj.* **1** connected with deep thoughts, feelings or emotions rather than the body or physical things: *spiritual development/growth/needs* ⊃ look at **material¹ 2** (**RELIGION**) connected with religion: *a spiritual leader* ▶ **spiritually** /-əli/ *adv.*

spiritual² /ˈspɪrɪtʃuəl/ *noun* [C] (**MUSIC**, **RELIGION**) a religious song of the type originally sung by black slaves in America

spiritualism /ˈspɪrɪtʃuəlɪzəm/ *noun* [U] (**RELIGION**) the belief that people who have died can send messages to living people, usually through a MEDIUM (= a person who has special powers) ▶ **spiritualist** /-lɪst/ *noun* [C]

spit¹ /spɪt/ *verb* [I, T] (spitting; *pt, pp* spat /spæt/, spit *especially AmE*) ~ (at/on/in sb/sth); ~ (sth) (out) to force liquid, food, etc. out from your mouth: *She spat in his face and ran away.* ◊ *He took one sip of the wine and spat it out.*

spit² /spɪt/ *noun* **1** [U] the liquid in your mouth ⊃ look at **saliva 2** [C] (**GEOGRAPHY**) a long, thin piece of land that sticks out into the sea, a lake, etc. **3** [C] a long thin metal stick that you put through meat to hold it when you cook it over a fire: *chicken roasted on a spit*

spite 🔑+ **B2** /spaɪt/ *noun* [U] the desire to hurt or annoy sb: *He stole her letters out of spite.* ▶ **spite** *verb* [T]

IDM **in spite of** used to show that sth happened although you did not expect it: *In spite of all her hard work, Sue failed her exam.* **SYN** **despite**

spiteful /ˈspaɪtfl/ *adj.* behaving in a cruel or unkind way in order to hurt or upset sb: *He's been saying a lot of spiteful things about his ex-girlfriend.* ▶ **spitefully** /-fəli/ *adv.*

splash¹ /splæʃ/ *verb* [I, T] (used about a liquid) to fall or to make liquid fall noisily or fly in drops onto a person or thing: *Rain splashed against the windows.* ◊ *The children were splashing each other with water.* ◊ *Be careful not to splash paint onto the floor.*
PHR V **splash out (on sth)** (*BrE, informal*) to spend money on sth that is expensive and that you do not really need

splash² /splæʃ/ *noun* [C] **1** the sound of liquid hitting sth or of sth hitting liquid: *Paul jumped into the pool with a big splash.* **2** a small amount of liquid that falls onto sth: *splashes of oil on the cooker* **3** a small bright area of colour: *Flowers add a splash of colour to a room.*

splatter /ˈsplætə(r)/ *verb* [I, T] (used about a liquid) to fly about in large drops and hit sb/sth noisily; to throw or drop water, paint, etc. on sb/sth in large drops: *Heavy rain splattered on the roof.* ◊ *The paint was splattered all over the floor.*

splay /spleɪ/ *verb* [T, I] ~ (sth) (out) to make sth spread out or to be spread out wide apart at one end: *splayed fingers*

spleen /spliːn/ *noun* **1** [C] (**ANATOMY**) a small organ near the stomach that controls the quality of the blood: *a ruptured spleen* ⊃ picture at **body 2** [U] (*formal*) anger: *He vented his spleen on the assembled crowd* (= shouted in an angry way at them).

splendid /ˈsplendɪd/ *adj.* **1** very good; excellent: *What a splendid idea!* **SYN** **great¹ 2** very impressive: *the splendid royal palace* **SYN** **glorious** ▶ **splendidly** *adv.*

splendour (*BrE*) (*AmE* **splendor**) /ˈsplendə(r)/ *noun* [U] very impressive beauty

splint /splɪnt/ *noun* [C] (**MEDICINE**) a piece of wood or metal that is tied to a broken arm or leg to keep it in the right position

splinter /ˈsplɪntə(r)/ *noun* [C] a small thin sharp piece of wood, metal or glass that has broken off a larger piece: *I've got a splinter in my finger.* ▶ **splinter** *verb* [I, T]

split¹ 🔑 **B2** 🅢 /splɪt/ *verb* (splitting; *pt, pp* split) **1** [I, T] ~ (sb) (up) (into sth) to divide or to make a group of people into smaller groups: *Let's split into two groups.* ◊ *The teacher had to split the two brothers up because they were always arguing.* **2** [T] ~ sth (between sb/sth); ~ sth (with sb) to divide or share sth: *We split the cost of the meal between the six of us.* ◊ *I split the cost with Jo.* **3** [I, T] ~ (sth) (open) to break or make sth break along a straight line: *My jeans have split.* ◊ *He split the bag open and the flour went everywhere.*
IDM **split the difference** (used when agreeing on a price) to agree on an amount or a figure that is HALFWAY between the two amounts or figures already mentioned **split hairs** to pay too much attention in an argument to details that are very small and not important
PHR V **split up (with sb)** to end a marriage or relationship: *He's split up with his girlfriend.*

split² 🔑 **B2** /splɪt/ *noun* [C] **1** an argument that divides a group of people **2** a division between two or more things **3** a long cut or hole in sth

ˌsplit ˈsecond *noun* [C] a very short period of time

split 'shift *noun* [C] (**BUSINESS**) two separate periods of time that you spend working in a single day, with several hours between them: *I work split shifts in a busy restaurant.*

splutter /ˈsplʌtə(r)/ *verb* **1** [T, I] to speak with difficulty, for example because you are very angry or embarrassed **2** [I] to make a series of sounds like a person COUGHING (= sending air out of your throat with a loud noise) ▸ **splutter** *noun* [C]

spoil ᵻ+ **B2** /spɔɪl/ *verb* [T] (*pt, pp* **spoiled**, *BrE also* **spoilt** /spɔɪlt/) **1** to change sth good into sth bad, unpleasant, etc: *The new office block will spoil the view.* ◇ *Our holiday was spoilt by bad weather.* ◇ *Eating between meals will* **spoil** *your* **appetite.** **2** to do too much for sb, especially a child, so that you have a bad effect on their character: *a spoilt child* **3** ~ (**sb/yourself**) to do sth special or nice to make sb/yourself happy

spoiler /ˈspɔɪlə(r)/ *noun* [C] **1** a part of an aircraft's wing that can be raised in order to interrupt the flow of air over it and so slow the aircraft's speed ◯ picture at **airliner** **2** a raised part on a fast car that prevents it from being lifted off the road when travelling very fast **3** (*especially AmE*) (**POLITICS**) a candidate for a political office who is unlikely to win but who may get enough votes to prevent one of the main candidates from winning **4** (**ARTS AND MEDIA**) information that you are given about what is going to happen in a film, TV series, etc. before it is shown to the public

spoils /spɔɪlz/ *noun* [pl.] (*formal*) things that have been stolen by thieves, or taken in a war or battle: *the spoils of war*

spoilsport /ˈspɔɪlspɔːt/ *noun* [C] (*informal*) a person who tries to stop other people enjoying themselves, for example by not taking part in an activity

spoilt /spɔɪlt/ past tense, past participle of **spoil**

spoke¹ /spəʊk/ *noun* [C] one of the thin pieces of metal that connect the centre of a wheel to the outside edge

spoke² /spəʊk/ past tense of **speak**

spoken¹ /ˈspəʊkən/ past participle of **speak**

spoken² ᵻ **B1** /ˈspəʊkən/ *adj.* involving speaking rather than writing; expressed in speech rather than in writing ◯ look at **written**² ◯ note at **language**

spokesman ᵻ+ **B2** /ˈspəʊksmən/ *noun* [C] (*pl.* -men /-mən/) a person who is chosen to speak for a group or an organization

spokesperson ᵻ+ **B2** /ˈspəʊkspɜːsn/ (*pl.* -persons, -people /ˈspəʊkspiːpl/) *noun* [C] a SPOKESMAN or SPOKESWOMAN

spokeswoman ᵻ+ **B2** /ˈspəʊkswʊmən/ *noun* [C] (*pl.* -women /-wɪmɪn/) a woman who is chosen to speak for a group or an organization

sponge¹ /spʌndʒ/ *noun* [C, U] **1** a piece of artificial or natural material that is soft and light and full of holes and can hold water easily, used for washing yourself or cleaning sth; this kind of material used for filling furniture, CUSHIONS, etc. **2** = SPONGE CAKE

sponge² /spʌndʒ/ *verb* [T] **1** to remove or clean sth with a wet SPONGE or cloth **2** ~ **off/on sb** (*informal*) to get money, food, etc. from sb without paying or doing anything in return: *It's about time you stopped sponging off your parents!*

'sponge cake (*also* **sponge**) *noun* [C, U] a light cake made from eggs, flour and sugar, with or without fat

spongy /ˈspʌndʒi/ *adj.* (**spongier**; **spongiest**) soft and able to ABSORB (= take in and hold) water easily like a SPONGE: *The ground was soft and spongy.* ◇ *The bread had a spongy texture.*

sponsor ᵻ **B2** /ˈspɒnsə(r)/ *noun* [C] **1** (**BUSINESS**, **SPORT**) a person or an organization that helps to pay for a special sports event, etc. (usually so that it can advertise its products) ◯ look at **patron** (2) **2** a person who agrees to pay money to a charity if sb else completes a particular activity ▸ **sponsor** ᵻ **B2** *verb* [T] (**BUSINESS**): *a sponsored walk to raise money for children in need* ▸ **sponsorship** ᵻ+ **B2** *noun* [U] (**BUSINESS**): *Many theatres depend on industry for sponsorship.*

spontaneous /spɒnˈteɪniəs/ *adj.* done or happening suddenly; not planned: *a spontaneous burst of applause* ▸ **spontaneity** /ˌspɒntəˈneɪəti/ *noun* [U] ▸ **spontaneously** *adv.*

spoof /spuːf/ *noun* [C] ~ (**on sth**) (**ARTS AND MEDIA**) a funny copy of a film, TV programme, etc. that EXAGGERATES (= shows them in a much stronger way) its typical characteristics: *It's a spoof on horror movies.*

spooky /ˈspuːki/ *adj.* (*informal*) (**spookier**; **spookiest**) strange and frightening: *It's spooky being in the house alone at night.* **SYN** **creepy**

spool /spuːl/ *noun* [C] a round object around which film, wire, etc. is wound ◯ look at **reel**¹

spoon ᵻ **A2** /spuːn/ *noun* [C] an object with a round end and a long handle that you use for eating, mixing or serving food: *Give each person a knife, fork and spoon.* ◇ *a wooden spoon for cooking* ◯ look at **cutlery** ▸ **spoon** *verb* [T]

spoonerism /ˈspuːnərɪzəm/ *noun* [C] (**LANGUAGE**) a mistake in which you change around the first sounds of two words when saying them, often with a funny result, for example 'shake a tower' for 'take a shower'

spoonful /ˈspuːnfʊl/ *noun* [C] the amount that one spoon can hold: *Add two spoonfuls of sugar.*

sporadic /spəˈrædɪk/ *adj.* not done or happening regularly ▸ **sporadically** /-kli/ *adv.*

spore /spɔː(r)/ *noun* [C] (**BIOLOGY**) one of the very small cells like seeds that are produced by some plants and that develop into new plants

sport ᵻ **A1** /spɔːt/ *noun* **1** [U] (*BrE*) (*AmE* **sports** [pl.]) physical games or activity that you do for exercise or because you enjoy it: *John did a lot of sport when he was at school.* ◇ *Do you like sport?* **2** [C] a particular game or type of sport: *What's your favourite sport?* ◇ **winter sports** (= skiing, SKATING, etc.) ◯ picture on **page 706** ▸ **sporting** ᵻ+ **B2** *adj.* [only before noun]: *a major sporting event*

'sports car *noun* [C] a low, fast car often with a roof that you can open

sportsman /ˈspɔːtsmən/ *noun* [C] (*pl.* -men /-mən/) (*especially BrE*) (**SPORT**) a man who does a lot of sport or who is good at sport: *a keen sportsman*

sportsmanlike /ˈspɔːtsmənlaɪk/ *adj.* behaving in a fair, generous and polite way when you are playing a game or doing sport

sportsmanship /ˈspɔːtsmənʃɪp/ *noun* [U] (**SPORT**) the quality of being fair, generous and polite when you are playing a game or doing sport

sportswear /ˈspɔːtsweə(r)/ *noun* [U] clothes that are worn for playing sports or in informal situations

sportswoman /ˈspɔːtswʊmən/ *noun* [C] (*pl.* -women /-wɪmɪn/) (*especially BrE*) (**SPORT**) a woman who does a lot of sport or who is good at sport

'sport u'tility vehicle = SUV

sporty /ˈspɔːti/ *adj.* (**sportier**; **sportiest**) (*especially BrE, informal*) (**SPORT**) liking or good at sport: *I'm not very sporty.*

spot¹ ᵻ **B1** /spɒt/ *noun* [C]
• SMALL MARK **1** a small round mark on a surface: *Leopards have dark spots.* ◇ *a blue skirt with red spots*

on it ⊃ adjective **spotted** **2** a small dirty mark on sth: *grease/rust spots*
- ON THE SKIN **3** (**HEALTH**) a small red or yellow mark that appears on the skin: *Many teenagers get spots.* ⊃ adjective **spotty**
- PLACE **4** a particular place or area: *a quiet/lonely/ secluded spot*
- SMALL AMOUNT **5** [usually sing.] **~ of sth** (*BrE, informal*) a small amount of sth: *Can you help me? I'm having a spot of trouble.*
- LIGHT **6** → SPOTLIGHT (1)

IDM have a soft spot for sb/sth → SOFT **on the spot 1** immediately: *Paul was caught stealing money and was dismissed on the spot.* **2** at the place where sth happened or where sb/sth is needed: *The fire brigade were on the spot within five minutes.* **put sb on the spot** to make sb answer a difficult question or make a difficult decision without having much time to think

spot² 🔒 **B2** /spɒt/ *verb* [T] (-tt-) (not used in the progressive tenses) to see or notice sb/sth, especially suddenly or when it is not easy to do: *I've spotted a couple of spelling mistakes.*

'**spot check** *noun* [C] a check that is made suddenly and without warning on a few things or people chosen from a group

spotless /'spɒtləs/ *adj.* perfectly clean

spotlight 🔒 **C1** /'spɒtlaɪt/ *noun* **1** (*also* spot) [C] (**ARTS AND MEDIA**) a lamp that can send a single line of bright light onto a small area. Spotlights are often used in theatres. **2** the spotlight [sing.] the centre of public attention or interest: *to be in the spotlight*

,**spot 'on** *adj.* [not before noun] (*BrE, informal*) exactly right: *Your estimate was spot on.*

spotted /'spɒtɪd/ *adj.* (used about clothes, cloth, etc.) having a regular pattern of round DOTS (= small round marks) on it: *a red spotted blouse*

spotty /'spɒti/ *adj.* (**HEALTH**) (spottier; spottiest) having a lot of spots on the skin: *a spotty teenager/adolescent*

spouse 🔒+ **C1** /spaʊs, spaʊz/ *noun* [C] (*formal*) your husband or wife

spout¹ /spaʊt/ *noun* [C] a tube or pipe through which liquid comes out: *the spout of a teapot*

spout² /spaʊt/ *verb* [I, T] **1 ~ (sth) (out) (from sth)** to send out a liquid with great force; to come out of sth in this way **2 ~ (on/off) (about sth)** (*informal*) to say sth, using a lot of words, in a way that is boring or annoying

sprain /spreɪn/ *verb* [T] (**HEALTH**) to injure part of your body, especially your WRIST or your ankle by suddenly bending or turning it ⊃ note at **injure**
▶ **sprain** *noun* [C]

sprang /spræŋ/ past tense of **spring²**

sprawl /sprɔːl/ *verb* [I] **1** (used with an adverb or a preposition) to sit or lie with your arms and legs spread out in an untidy way: *People lay sprawled out in the sun.* **2** to cover a large area of land ▶ **sprawling** *adj.* [only before noun]: *the sprawling city suburbs*

spray¹ /spreɪ/ *noun* **1** [U] liquid in very small drops that is sent through the air: *clouds of spray from the waves* **2** [U, C] liquid in an AEROSOL (= a special container) that is forced out under pressure when you push a button: *hairspray* ⊃ picture at **aerosol**

spray² /spreɪ/ *verb* [T, I] **~ sb/sth (with sth)** to send a liquid through the air in very small drops; to be forced out of a container or sent through the air in this way: *The crops are regularly sprayed with pesticide.*

spread¹ 🔒 **B1** **S** /spred/ *verb* (*pt, pp* spread) **1** [I, T] to affect a larger area or a bigger group of people; to make sth do this: *The fire spread rapidly because of the strong wind.* ◇ *Rats and flies spread disease.* ◇ *to spread rumours about somebody* **2** [T] **~ A on/over B; ~ B with A** to cover a surface with a layer of a soft substance: *to spread jam on bread* ◇ *to spread bread with jam* **3** [T] **~ sth (out) (on/over sth)** to open sth that has been folded so that it covers a larger area; to move things so that they cover a larger area: *Spread the map out on the table so we can all see it!* **4** [T] **~ sth (out) (over sth)** to separate sth into parts and divide them between different times or people: *You can spread your repayments over a period of three years.*
PHR V spread (sb/yourself) out to move away from other people in a group in order to cover a larger area: *The police spread out to search the whole area.*

spread² 🔒 **B2** **S** /spred/ *noun* **1** [U] an increase in the amount or number of sth that there is, or in the area that is affected by sth: *Dirty drinking water encourages the spread of disease.* ⊃ note at **religion** **2** [C] a range or variety of people or things: *a broad spread of opinions* **3** [C, U] a soft food that you put on bread: *4* [C] (**ARTS AND MEDIA**) a newspaper or magazine article that covers one or more pages: *a double-page spread*

spreadsheet /'spredʃiːt/ *noun* [C] (**COMPUTING**) a computer program for working with rows and columns of data, for example, for doing financial or project planning

spree /spriː/ *noun* [C] a short time that you spend doing sth you enjoy, often doing too much of it: *to go on a shopping/spending spree*

sprig /sprɪg/ *noun* [C] a small piece of a plant with leaves on it

spring¹ 🔒 **A1** /sprɪŋ/ *noun* **1** [U, C] the season of the year between winter and summer, when plants begin to grow and the weather gets warmer: *Daffodils bloom in (the) spring.* ◇ *spring flowers* ◇ *She was born in the spring of 1999.* ⊃ picture at **season¹** **2** [C]

sports equipment

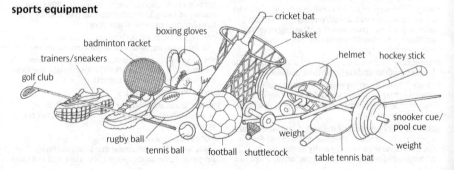

cricket bat
boxing gloves
basket
badminton racket
trainers/sneakers
helmet
hockey stick
golf club
snooker cue/ pool cue
rugby ball
weight
weight
tennis ball
football
shuttlecock
table tennis bat

spring

(**GEOGRAPHY**) a place where water comes up naturally from under the ground: *a hot spring* **3** [C] a long piece of thin metal or wire that is bent round and round. After you push or pull a spring it goes back to its original shape and size: *bed springs* **4** [C] a sudden jump upwards or forwards

spring[2] ʔ **B2** /sprɪŋ/ *verb* [I] (*pt* sprang /spræŋ/; *pp* sprung /sprʌŋ/) **1** (used with an adverb or a preposition) to jump or move quickly: *When the alarm went off, Ray sprang out of bed.* ◊ *to spring to your feet* (= stand up suddenly) ◊ (*figurative*) *to spring to somebody's defence/assistance* (= to quickly defend or help sb) **2** (used about an object) to move suddenly and violently: *The branch sprang back and hit him in the face.* **3** to appear or come somewhere suddenly: *Tears sprang to her eyes.* ◊ *Where did you just spring from?*
IDM come/spring to mind → MIND[1]
PHR V spring from sth (*formal*) to be the result of: *The idea for the book sprang from an experience she had while travelling in India.* spring sth on sb (*informal*) to do or say sth that sb is not expecting spring up to appear or develop quickly or suddenly

spring balance *noun* [C] (*BrE*) a device that uses a HOOK (= a curved piece of metal) on a SPRING to measure the weight of things

springboard /ˈsprɪŋbɔːd/ *noun* [C] **1** a low board that bends and that helps you jump higher, for example before you jump into a swimming pool **2** ~ (**for/to sth**) something that helps you start an activity, especially by giving you ideas

spring-ˈclean *verb* [T] to clean a house, room, etc. very well, including the parts that you do not usually clean

spring ˈonion (*BrE*) (*AmE* green onion) *noun* [C, U] a type of small onion with a long green central part and leaves

springtime /ˈsprɪŋtaɪm/ *noun* [U] the season of spring

springy /ˈsprɪŋi/ *adj.* (springier; springiest) going quickly back to its original shape or size after being pushed, pulled, etc: *soft springy grass*

sprinkle /ˈsprɪŋkl/ *verb* [T] ~ **A** (**on/onto/over B**); ~ **B** (**with A**) to throw drops of liquid or small pieces of sth over a surface: *to sprinkle sugar on a cake* ◊ *to sprinkle a cake with sugar*

sprinkler /ˈsprɪŋklə(r)/ *noun* [C] a device with holes in it that sends out water in small drops. Sprinklers are used in gardens to keep the grass green, and in buildings to stop fires from spreading.

sprint /sprɪnt/ *verb* [I, T] (**SPORT**) to run a short distance as fast as you can ▸ sprint *noun* [C] ▸ sprinter *noun* [C]

sprocket /ˈsprɒkɪt/ *noun* [C] **1** one of the teeth on a SPROCKET WHEEL ⊃ picture at **cogwheel 2** = SPROCKET WHEEL

ˈsprocket wheel (*also* sprocket) *noun* [C] a wheel with a row of teeth around the edge that connect with the holes of a bicycle chain or with holes in a film, etc. in order to turn it ⊃ picture at **cogwheel**

sprout[1] /spraʊt/ *verb* [I, T] (**BIOLOGY**) (used about a plant) to begin to grow or to produce new leaves: *The seeds are sprouting.*

sprout[2] /spraʊt/ *noun* [C] **1** = BRUSSELS SPROUT **2** a new part that has grown on a plant

spruce /spruːs/ *verb*
PHR V spruce (sb/yourself) up to make sb/yourself clean and tidy

sprung /sprʌŋ/ past participle of **spring**[2]

spud /spʌd/ *noun* [C] (*informal*) a potato

spun /spʌn/ past tense, past participle of **spin**[1]

spur[1] /spɜː(r)/ *noun* [C] **1** a piece of metal that some riders wear on the back of their boots to encourage their horses to go faster **2** ~ (**to sth**) something that encourages you to do sth or that makes sth happen more quickly: *My poor exam results acted as a spur to make me study harder.* **3** (**GEOGRAPHY**) a part of a hill that sticks out from the rest, often with lower ground around it
IDM on the spur of the moment without planning; suddenly

spur[2] /spɜː(r)/ *verb* [T] (-rr-) ~ **sb/sth (on/into sth)** to encourage sb or make them work harder or faster: *The letter spurred me into action.* ◊ *We were spurred on by the positive feedback from customers.*

spurn /spɜːn/ *verb* [T] (*formal*) to refuse sth that sb has offered to you: *She spurned his offer of friendship.*

spurt /spɜːt/ *verb* **1** [I, T] ~ (**from sth**) (used about a liquid) to come out quickly with great force; to make a liquid do this: *Blood spurted from the wound.* **2** [I] (used with an adverb or a preposition) to suddenly increase your speed or effort ▸ spurt *noun* [C]

spy[1] ʔ+ **C1** /spaɪ/ *noun* [C] (*pl.* spies) a person who tries to get secret information about another country, person or organization

spy[2] ʔ+ **C1** /spaɪ/ *verb* (spying; spies; *pt, pp* spied) **1** [I] to try to get secret information about sb/sth ⊃ look at **espionage 2** [T] (*formal*) to suddenly see or notice sb/sth
IDM spy on sb/sth to watch sb/sth secretly: *The man next door is spying on us.*

spyhole /ˈspaɪhəʊl/ *noun* [C] a small hole in a door for looking at the person on the other side before deciding to let them in

Sq. *abbr.* (in writing) = SQUARE[2] (2): *6 Hanover Sq.*

sq *abbr.* (in writing) = SQUARE[1] (3): *10 sq cm*

squabble /ˈskwɒbl/ *verb* [I] ~ (**over/about sth**) to argue in a noisy way about sth that is not very important ▸ squabble *noun* [C]

squad ʔ+ **C1** /skwɒd/ *noun* [C + sing./pl. verb] a group of people who work as a team: *He's a policeman with the bomb squad.* ◊ *The squad is/are setting off for a training camp in Italy.*

squadron /ˈskwɒdrən/ *noun* [C + sing./pl. verb] a group of military aircraft or ships

squalid /ˈskwɒlɪd/ *adj.* very dirty, untidy and unpleasant: *squalid housing conditions*

squall /skwɔːl/ *noun* [C] a sudden storm with strong winds

squalor /ˈskwɒlə(r)/ *noun* [U] the state of being very dirty, untidy or unpleasant: *to live in squalor*

squander /ˈskwɒndə(r)/ *verb* [T] ~ **sth (on sth)** to waste time, money, etc: *He squanders his time on TV and computer games.*

square¹ ⚡ A2 /skweə(r)/ *adj.*

- SHAPE **1** (GEOMETRY) having four straight sides of the same length and four RIGHT ANGLES (= angles of 90°): *a square tablecloth* **2** shaped like a square or forming an angle of about 90°: *a square face* ◇ *square shoulders*
- MEASUREMENT **3** (*abbr.* sq) (GEOMETRY) used for talking about the area of sth: *If a room is 5 metres long and 4 metres wide, its area is 20 square metres.* ⊃ note at **measure²** **4** (GEOMETRY) (used about sth that is square in shape) having sides of a particular length: *The picture is 20 centimetres square* (= each side is 20 CENTIMETRES long).
- WITH MONEY **5** [not before noun] not owing any money: *Here is the money I owe you. Now we're (all) square.*
- IN SPORT **6** [not before noun] having equal points (in a game, etc.): *The teams were all square at half-time.*
- HONEST **7** fair or honest, especially in business matters: *a square deal*
  IDM **a square meal** a good meal that makes you feel satisfied

square² ⚡ A2 /skweə(r)/ *noun* [C] **1** (GEOMETRY) a shape that has four straight sides of the same length and four RIGHT ANGLES (= angles of 90°): *There are 64 squares on a chess board.* ⊃ picture at **parallelogram** **2** (*also* Square) (*abbr.* Sq.) an open space in a town or city that has buildings all around it: *Protesters gathered in the town square.* ◇ *Trafalgar Square* **3** (MATHEMATICS) the number that you get when you multiply another number by itself: *4 is the square of 2.* ⊃ look at **square root**

square³ /skweə(r)/ *verb* [I, T] **~ (sth) with sb/sth 1** to agree with sth; to make sure that sth/sth agrees with sth: *Your conclusion doesn't really square with the facts.* ◇ *If you want time off you'll have to square it with the boss.* **2** [usually passive] (MATHEMATICS) to multiply a number by itself: *4 squared (4²) is 16 (4×4=16).* ⊃ look at **square root**
PHR V **square up (to sb)** to face sb as if you are going to fight them

square⁴ /skweə(r)/ (*also* **squarely**) *adv.* (after a verb) directly: *I looked her square in the face.*

,square 'number *noun* [C] (MATHEMATICS) a number that is the result of multiplying any whole number by itself. For example, nine is a square number.

,square 'root *noun* [C] (MATHEMATICS) a number that produces another particular number when it is multiplied by itself: *The square root of 16 (√16) is 4.* ⊃ look at **cube root**, **square²** (3), **square³** (2)

squash¹ /skwɒʃ/ *verb* **1** [T] to press sth so that it is damaged, changes shape or becomes flat: *The fruit at the bottom of the bag will get squashed.* ◇ *Move up — you're squashing me!* **2** [I, T] (used with an adverb or a preposition) to go into a place, or move sb/sth to a place, where there is not much space: *We all squashed into the back of the car.* **3** [T] to destroy sth because it is a problem: *to squash somebody's suggestion/plan/idea*

squash² /skwɒʃ/ *noun* **1** [U] (SPORT) a game for two people, played in an area surrounded by four walls using RACKETS and a small rubber ball: *a squash racket* **2** [U, C] (*BrE*) a drink that is made from fruit juice and sugar. You add water to squash before you drink it: *orange squash* **3** [C, U] (*pl.* squash, squashes) a type of vegetable that grows on the ground and has hard yellow, orange or green skin **4** [sing.] (*informal*) a lot of people in a small space: *We can get ten people around the table, but it's a bit of a squash.*

squat¹ /skwɒt/ *verb* [I] (-tt-) **1 ~ (down)** to rest with your weight on your feet, your legs bent and your bottom just above the ground **2** to go and live in an empty building without permission from the owner

squat² /skwɒt/ *adj.* short and fat or thick: *a squat ugly building*

squatter /ˈskwɒtə(r)/ *noun* [C] a person who is living in an empty building without the owner's permission

squawk /skwɔːk/ *verb* [I] (used especially about a bird) to make a loud unpleasant noise ▸ **squawk** *noun* [C]

squeak /skwiːk/ *noun* [C] a short high noise that is not very loud: *the squeak of a mouse* ◇ *She gave a little squeak of surprise.* ▸ **squeak** *verb* [I, T] ▸ **squeaky** *adj.* (squeakier; squeakiest): *a squeaky floorboard* ◇ *a squeaky voice*

squeal /skwiːl/ *verb* [I, T] to make a loud high noise because of pain, fear or pleasure: *The baby squealed in delight at the new toy.* ⊃ note at **pig¹** ▸ **squeal** *noun* [C]

squeamish /ˈskwiːmɪʃ/ *adj.* easily upset by unpleasant sights, especially blood

squeeze¹ ⚡ C1 /skwiːz/ *verb* **1** [T] to press sth hard for a particular purpose: *She squeezed his hand as a sign of affection.* ◇ *to squeeze a tube of toothpaste* **2** [T] **~ sth (out)**; **~ sth (from/out of sth)** to get liquid out of sth by pressing it hard: *He took off his wet clothes and squeezed the water out.* ◇ *I squeezed the water out of the cloth.* ◇ *Squeeze a lemon/the juice of a lemon into a glass.* **3** [I, T] (used with an adverb or a preposition) to force sb/sth into or through a small space: *We can squeeze another person into the back of the car.* ◇ *There was just room for the bus to squeeze past.*

squeeze² /skwiːz/ *noun* **1** [C, usually sing.] an act of pressing sth FIRMLY: *He gave her hand a squeeze and told her he loved her.* **2** [C] a small amount of liquid that is produced by pressing sth: *a squeeze of lemon juice* **3** [sing.] a situation where there is not much space: *It was a tight squeeze to get everybody around the table.* **4** [C, usually sing.] a reduction in the amount of money, jobs, etc. available; a difficult situation caused by this

squelch /skweltʃ/ *verb* [I] to make the sound your feet make when you are walking in deep wet mud

squid /skwɪd/ *noun* [C, U] (*pl.* squid, squids) a sea animal with a long soft body, eight arms and two TENTACLES (= long thin parts like arms)

squid

squiggle /ˈskwɪɡl/ *noun* [C] a quickly drawn line that goes in all directions

squint /skwɪnt/ *verb* [I] **1 ~ (at sth)** to look at sth with your eyes almost closed: *He squinted at the letter in his hand.* **2** to have eyes that appear to look in different directions at the same time ▸ **squint** *noun* [C, usually sing.]

squirm /skwɜːm/ *verb* [I] to move around a lot because you are nervous, uncomfortable, etc.

squirrel /ˈskwɪrəl/ *noun* [C] a small animal with a long thick tail and red, grey or black fur, that lives in trees and eats nuts ⊃ picture at **animal**

squirt /skwɜːt/ *verb* [I, T] **~ (sb/sth) (with sth); ~ (sth) (at/on sb/sth)** if a liquid **squirts** or if you **squirt** it, it is suddenly forced out of sth in a particular direction: *I cut the orange and juice squirted out.* ◇ *He squirted me with water.* ◇ *She squirted water on the flames.* ▸ **squirt** *noun* [C]: *a squirt of lemon juice*

Sr (*BrE*) (*also* **Sr.** *AmE, BrE*) *abbr.* (in writing) = SENIOR¹ (2)

SSE *abbr.* (in writing) = SOUTH-SOUTH-EAST

SSRI /ˌes es ɑːr ˈaɪ/ *noun* [C] (**PSYCHOLOGY**) any of a group of drugs used mainly to treat mental illness and DEPRESSION (the abbreviation for 'selective serotonin reuptake inhibitor')

SSW *abbr.* (in writing) = SOUTH-SOUTH-WEST

St *abbr.* (in writing) **1** = SAINT (1): *St Peter* **2** (*BrE*) (*also* St. *AmE, BrE*) = STREET (1): *20 Swan St*

st (*BrE*) (*also* st. *AmE, BrE*) *abbr.* (in writing) (*pl.* st, st.) = STONE (5)

stab¹ ʕ+ **C1** /stæb/ *verb* [T] (-bb-) to push a knife or other pointed object into sb/sth: *The man had been stabbed in the back.* ◇ *He stabbed a potato with his fork.*

stab² /stæb/ *noun* [C] **1** an injury that was caused by a knife, etc: *He received stab wounds to his neck and back.* **2 ~ of sth** (**HEALTH**) a sudden sharp pain: *a sudden stab of pain* ◇ *a stab of guilt* **IDM** **have a stab at sth/doing sth** (*informal*) to try to do sth

stabbing¹ /ˈstæbɪŋ/ *noun* [C] an occasion when sb is injured or killed with a knife or other sharp object

stabbing² /ˈstæbɪŋ/ *adj.* [only before noun] (used about a pain) sudden and strong

stability ʕ+ **C1** **W** /stəˈbɪləti/ *noun* [U] the state or quality of being steady and not changing: *After so much change we now need a period of stability.* ◇ *The ladder is slightly wider at the bottom for greater stability.* **OPP** **instability** ◇ adjective **stable**

stabilize ʕ+ **C1** **W** (*BrE also* -ise) /ˈsteɪbəlaɪz/ *verb* [I, T] to become firm, steady and unlikely to change; to make sth firm, steady and unlikely to change: *The patient's condition has stabilized.* ◇ look at **destabilize**

stabilizer (*BrE also* -iser) /ˈsteɪbəlaɪzə(r)/ *noun* [C] **1** a device that keeps sth steady, especially one that stops an aircraft or a ship from rolling to one side **2** a chemical that is sometimes added to food or paint to stop the various substances in it from becoming separate

stable¹ ʕ **B2** **O** /ˈsteɪbl/ *adj.* steady, firm and unlikely to change: *This ladder doesn't seem very stable.* ◇ *The patient is in a stable condition.* **OPP** **unstable** ◇ noun **stability**

WORD FAMILY
stable *adj.* (≠ **unstable**)
stability *noun* (≠ **instability**)
stabilize *verb*

stable² /ˈsteɪbl/ *noun* [C] (**AGRICULTURE**) a building where horses are kept

staccato /stəˈkɑːtəʊ/ *adj., adv.* (**MUSIC**) with each note played separately in order to produce short, sharp sounds **OPP** **legato**

stack¹ /stæk/ *noun* [C] **1 ~ (of sth)** a tidy pile of sth: *a stack of plates/books/chairs* **2 ~ (of sth)** (*informal*) a lot of sth: *I've still got stacks of work to do.* **3** (**GEOLOGY**) a tall thin part of a CLIFF that has been separated from the land and stands on its own in the sea ◇ picture at **erosion**

stack² /stæk/ *verb* [T] **~ sth (up)** to put sth into a tidy pile: *Could you stack those chairs for me?*

stacked /stækt/ *adj.* **~ with sth** full of piles of things: *The room was stacked high with books.*

stadium ʕ **B1** /ˈsteɪdiəm/ *noun* [C] (*pl.* stadiums, stadia /-diə/) (**SPORT**) a large structure, usually with no roof, where people can sit and watch sport

staff ʕ **B1** /stɑːf/ *noun* [C, usually sing., U] **1** the group of people who work for a particular organization: *hotel/library/medical staff* ◇ *Two members of staff will accompany the students on the school trip.* ◇ *The hotel has over 200 people on its staff.* ◇ *full-time/part-time staff* **HELP** Staff is usually used in the singular but with a plural verb: *The staff are all English.* **2** (*AmE*) = STAVE¹ (2)

▸ **staff** *verb* [T, usually passive]: *The office is staffed 24 hours a day.*

staffroom /ˈstɑːfruːm, -rʊm/ *noun* [C] (*BrE*) (**EDUCATION**) a room in a school where teachers can go when they are not teaching

stag /stæɡ/ *noun* [C] a male DEER (= a large wild animal) with ANTLERS (= hard parts on the head that are like branches) ◇ note at **deer** ◇ picture at **animal, deer**

stage¹ ʕ **A2** **O** /steɪdʒ/ *noun* **1** [C] one part of the progress or development of sth: *The first stage of the course lasts for three weeks.* ◇ *I suggest we do the journey in two stages.* ◇ *At this stage it's too early to say what will happen.* **2** [C] (**ARTS AND MEDIA**) a platform in a theatre, concert hall, etc. on which actors, musicians, etc. perform **3** [sing., U] (**ARTS AND MEDIA**) the world of theatre; the profession of acting: *Her parents didn't want her to go on the stage.* ◇ *an actor of stage and screen*

stage² ʕ **B2** /steɪdʒ/ *verb* [T] **1** (**ARTS AND MEDIA**) to organize a performance of a play, concert, etc. for the public ◇ note at **performing arts 2** to organize an event: *They have decided to stage a 24-hour strike.*

stagehand /ˈsteɪdʒhænd/ *noun* [C] (**ARTS AND MEDIA**) a person whose job is to help move furniture, SCENERY, etc. in a theatre, to prepare the stage for the next play or the next part of a play

ˌstage ˈmanager *noun* [C] (**ARTS AND MEDIA**) the person who is responsible for the stage, lights, etc. during a theatre performance

stagflation /stæɡˈfleɪʃn/ *noun* [U] (**ECONOMICS**) an economic situation where there is high INFLATION (= prices rising) but no increase in the jobs that are available or in business activity

stagger /ˈstæɡə(r)/ *verb* [I] to walk with short steps as if you could fall at any moment, for example because you are ill, drunk or carrying sth heavy: *He staggered across the finishing line and collapsed.*

staggered /ˈstæɡəd/ *adj.* **1** [not before noun] (*informal*) very surprised: *I was absolutely staggered when I heard the news.* **2** (used about a set of times, payments, etc.) arranged so that they do not all happen at the same time: *staggered working hours* (= when people start and finish work at different times)

staggering /ˈstæɡərɪŋ/ *adj.* that you find difficult to believe ▸ **staggeringly** *adv.*

stagnant /ˈstæɡnənt/ *adj.* **1** (used about water) not flowing and therefore dirty and having an unpleasant smell **2** (**BUSINESS**) not active; not developing: *a stagnant economy*

stagnate /stæɡˈneɪt/ *verb* [I] **1** to stop developing, changing or being active: *a stagnating economy* **2** (used about water) to be or become STAGNANT ▸ **stagnation** /-ˈneɪʃn/ *noun* [U]

ˈstag night (*also* ˈstag party) *noun* [C] a party for men only that is given for a man just before his wedding day ◇ look at **hen party**

staid /steɪd/ *adj.* serious, old-fashioned and rather boring

stain /steɪn/ *verb* [T, I] to leave a mark that is difficult to remove: *Don't spill any of that juice — it'll stain the carpet.* ▸ **stain** *noun* [C]: *The blood had left a stain on his shirt.*

ˌstained ˈglass *noun* [U] (**ARCHITECTURE**) pieces of coloured glass that are put together to make windows, especially in churches: *a magnificent medieval stained glass window*

stainless steel /ˌsteɪnləs ˈstiːl/ *noun* [U] a type of steel that does not RUST (= change colour or get damaged by water): *a stainless steel pan*

stair ⚹ A2 /steə(r)/ *noun* 1 stairs [pl.] a series of steps inside a building that lead from one level to another: *a flight of stairs* ◇ *I heard somebody coming down the stairs.* ◇ *She ran up the stairs.* ⊃ look at **downstairs**[1], **upstairs** 2 [C] (**ARCHITECTURE**) one of the steps in a series inside a building

staircase /ˈsteəkeɪs/ (*also* stairway /ˈsteəweɪ/) *noun* [C] a set of stairs inside a building including the posts and bars at the side that you can hold on to ⊃ look at **escalator** ⊃ picture at **spiral**

stairlift /ˈsteəlɪft/ *noun* [C] a piece of equipment in the form of a seat that sb can sit on to be moved up and down stairs, used by people who find it difficult to walk up and down stairs without help

stake[1] ⚹+ C1 /steɪk/ *noun* 1 [C] (**BUSINESS**) a part of a company, etc. that you own, usually because you have put money into it: *Foreign investors now have a 20% stake in the company.* 2 [C] something, especially money, that you might win or lose in a game or in a particular situation: *We play cards for money, but never for very high stakes.* 3 [C] a wooden or metal POLE with a point at one end that you push into the ground
IDM **at stake** in danger of being lost; at risk: *He thought very carefully about the decision because he knew his future was at stake.*

stake[2] /steɪk/ *verb* [T] ~ **sth (on sth)** to put your future, etc. in danger by doing sth, because you hope that it will bring you a good result: *He is staking his political reputation on this issue.* **SYN** **bet**[1]
IDM **stake (out) a/your claim (to/for/on sth)** to say or show that you have a right to have sth
PHRV **stake sth out** 1 to clearly mark the limits of sth that you claim is yours 2 to make your position, opinion, etc. clear to everyone: *In his speech, the president staked out his position on tax reform.* 3 (**LAW**) to watch a place secretly for a period of time: *The police had been staking out the house for months.*

stakeholder /ˈsteɪkhəʊldə(r)/ *noun* [C] (**BUSINESS**) a person or company that is interested in the success of a particular organization or project, especially because they have invested money in it: *All our employees are stakeholders in the company.*

stalactite /ˈstæləktaɪt/ *noun* [C] (**GEOLOGY**) a long thin piece of rock hanging down from the roof of a CAVE ⊃ picture at **limestone**

stalagmite /ˈstæləgmaɪt/ *noun* [C] (**GEOLOGY**) a thin piece of rock pointing upwards from the floor of a CAVE ⊃ picture at **limestone**

stale /steɪl/ *adj.* 1 (used about food or air) old and not fresh any more: *The bread will go stale if you don't put it away.* ⊃ look at **fresh** (1) 2 not interesting or exciting any more

stalemate /ˈsteɪlmeɪt/ *noun* [U, sing.] 1 a situation in an argument in which neither side can win or make any progress 2 (in CHESS) a position in which a game ends without a winner because neither side can move

stalk[1] /stɔːk/ *noun* [C] (**BIOLOGY**) a thin STEM that joins a leaf, flower or fruit to another part of the plant or tree; the main STEM of a plant ⊃ picture at **flower**[1], **tree**

stalk[2] /stɔːk/ *verb* 1 [T] to move slowly and quietly towards an animal in order to catch or kill it: *a lion stalking its prey* 2 [T] to follow sb or use the internet, etc. to contact them repeatedly over a period of time in a frightening or annoying way: *The actress claimed*

the man had been stalking her for two years. 3 [I] (used with an adverb or a preposition) to walk in an angry way

stalker /ˈstɔːkə(r)/ *noun* [C] a person who follows sb or uses the internet, etc. to contact them repeatedly over a period of time in a way that is frightening or annoying

stall[1] ⚹+ B2 /stɔːl/ *noun* 1 [C] a small shop with an open front or a table with things for sale: *a market stall* ◇ *a bookstall at the station* 2 stalls [pl.] (**ARTS AND MEDIA**) the seats nearest the front in a theatre or cinema 3 [C, usually sing.] a situation in which a vehicle's engine suddenly stops because it is not receiving enough power: *The plane went into a stall and almost crashed.*

stall[2] /stɔːl/ *verb* [I, T] 1 (used about a vehicle) to stop suddenly because the engine is not receiving enough power; to make a vehicle or engine do this: *The bus often stalls on this hill.* ◇ *I kept stalling the car.* 2 to avoid doing sth or to try to stop sth happening until a later time

stallion /ˈstæliən/ *noun* [C] an adult male horse, especially one that is kept for BREEDING (= producing young)

stalwart /ˈstɔːlwət/ *adj.* constant in your support of the same organization, team, etc: *a stalwart supporter of the club* ▸ **stalwart** *noun* [C]

stamen /ˈsteɪmən/ *noun* [C] (**BIOLOGY**) a small thin male part in the middle of a flower that produces POLLEN (= a fine yellow powder) ⊃ picture at **flower**[1]

stamina /ˈstæmɪnə/ *noun* [U] the ability to do sth that involves a lot of physical or mental effort for a long time: *You need a lot of stamina to run long distances.*

stammer /ˈstæmə(r)/ *verb* [I, T] to speak with difficulty, repeating sounds or words and often stopping, before saying things correctly: *He stammered an apology and left quickly.* ▸ **stammer** *noun* [sing.]: *to have a stammer*

stamp[1] ⚹ A2 /stæmp/ *noun* 1 (*also formal* postage stamp) [C] a small piece of paper that you stick onto a letter or package to show that you have paid for it to be posted: *a first-class/second-class stamp* ⊃ look at **first class** 2 [C] a small object that prints some words, a design, the date, etc. when you press it onto a surface: *a date stamp* 3 [C] the mark made by STAMPING sth onto a surface: *Have you got any visa stamps in your passport?* ◇ (*figurative*) *The government has given the project its stamp of approval.* 4 [sing.] **the ~ of sth** something that shows a particular quality or that sth was done by a particular person: *Her novels have the stamp of genius.*

stamp[2] /stæmp/ *verb* 1 [I, T] ~ **(on sth)** to put your foot down very heavily and noisily: *He stamped on the spider and squashed it.* ◇ *It was so cold that I had to stamp my feet to keep warm.* ◇ *She stamped her foot in anger.* 2 [I] to walk with loud heavy steps: *She stamped around the room, shouting angrily.* 3 [T] ~ **A (on B)**; ~ **B (with A)** to print some words, a design, the date, etc. by pressing a STAMP onto a surface: *She stamped the date on the receipt.* ◇ *She stamped the receipt with the date.*
PHRV **stamp sth out** to put an end to sth completely: *The police are trying to stamp out this kind of crime.*

stamp duty *noun* [U] (**FINANCE**, **LAW**) a tax in the UK on some legal documents

stamped addressed envelope *noun* [C] (*abbr.* sae) (*BrE*) an empty ENVELOPE with your own name and address and a stamp on it that you send to a company, etc. when you want sth sent back to you

stampede /stæmˈpiːd/ *noun* [C] a situation in which a large number of animals or people start running in the same direction, for example because they are frightened or excited ▶ **stampede** *verb* [I]

stance 🔑+ B2 /stæns, stɑːns/ *noun* [C, usually sing.] **1 ~ (on sth)** the opinions that sb expresses publicly about sth: *the prime minister's stance on foreign affairs* **2** the position in which sb stands, especially when playing a sport

stand¹ 🔑 A1 /stænd/ *verb* (*pt, pp* **stood** /stʊd/)
• ON YOUR FEET **1** [I] to be on your feet, not sitting or lying down; to be in a VERTICAL position: *He was standing near the window.* ◇ ***Stand still*** *— I'm trying to take a photo of you!* ◇ *Only a few houses were left standing after the earthquake.* **2** [I] to rise to your feet from another position: *He stood when I entered the room.*
• IN A POSITION **3** [T] to put sb/sth in a particular place or position: *We stood the mirror against the wall while we decided where to hang it.* **4** [I] to be or to stay in a particular position or situation: *The castle stands on a hill.* ◇ *The house has stood empty for ten years.*
• STAY THE SAME **5** [I] (used about an offer, a decision, etc.) to stay the same as before, without being changed: *Does your decision still stand?* ◇ *The world record has stood for ten years.*
• AT A HEIGHT, LEVEL, ETC. **6** [I] **~ (at) sth** to be of a particular height, level, amount, etc: *The world record stands at 6.59 metres.* ◇ *The building stands nearly 60 metres high.* ➲ note at **trend¹**
• HAVE AN OPINION **7** [I] **~ (on sth)** to have an opinion or a view about sth: *Where do you stand on euthanasia?*
• BE LIKELY TO **8** [I] **~ to do sth** to be in a situation where you are likely to do sth: *If he has to sell the company, he stands to lose a lot of money.*
• IN AN ELECTION **9** (*especially BrE*) (*AmE usually* **run**) [I] **~ (for/as sth)** to be one of the people hoping to be chosen in an election: *She's standing for the European Parliament.*
• NOT LIKE **10** [T] (not used in the progressive tenses) used especially after *can/could* in negative sentences and questions to emphasize that you do not like sth/sb: *I **can't stand** that woman — she's so rude.* ◇ *I couldn't **stand the thought of** waiting another two hours so I went home.* **SYN** **bear¹**
• SURVIVE **11** [T] (especially after *can/could* or *will*) to be able to survive difficult conditions: *Camels can stand extremely hot and cold temperatures.* **SYN** **bear¹**, **take**

IDM ℹ For idioms containing **stand**, look at the entries for the nouns, adjectives, etc. For example, **it stands to reason** is at **reason**.

PHR V **stand around** to stand somewhere not doing anything: *A lot of people were just standing around outside.* **stand aside** to move to one side: *People stood aside to let the police pass.* **stand back** to move back: *The policeman told everybody to stand back.* **stand by** **1** to be present, but do nothing in a situation: *How can you stand by and let them treat their animals like that?* **2** to be ready to act: *The police are standing by in case there's trouble.* **stand by sb** to help sb or be friends with them, even in difficult times **stand for sth** **1** to be a short form of sth: *What does BBC stand for?* **2** to support sth (such as an idea or opinion): *I hate everything that the party stands for.* **stand in (for sb)** to take sb's place for a short time **stand out** to be easily seen or noticed **stand up** to be or become VERTICAL: *You'll look taller if you stand up straight.* **stand sb up** (*informal*) to not appear when you have arranged to meet sb, especially a boyfriend or girlfriend **stand up for sb/sth** to support or defend sb/sth: *I admire him. He really stands up for his rights.* **stand up to sb/sth** to defend yourself against sb/sth who is stronger or more powerful

stand² 🔑 B2 /stænd/ *noun* [C] **1** [usually sing.] **~ (on/against sth)** a strong effort to defend yourself or sth that you have a strong opinion about: *The workers have decided to **take/make a stand** against further job losses.* **2** a table or an object that holds or supports sth, often so that people can buy it or look at it: *a newspaper/hamburger stand* ◇ *a company stand at a trade fair* ➲ picture at **laboratory** **3** a large structure with rows where people sit or stand to watch a sports event **4** = WITNESS BOX: *He **took the stand** as the first witness.*

ˈstand-alone *adj.* (**COMPUTING**) (used especially about a computer) able to be operated on its own without being connected to a larger system

standard¹ 🔑 B1 ⓪ /ˈstændəd/ *noun* **1** [C, U] a level of quality, especially one that people think is acceptable: *We complained about the low standard of service in the hotel.* ◇ *This work is not **up to** your usual **standard**.* **2** [C] a level of quality that you compare sth else with: ***By** European **standards** this is a very expensive city.* ◇ *He is a brilliant player **by any standard**.* **3** [C, usually pl.] a level of behaviour that is morally acceptable: *Many people are worried about falling standards in modern society.* **4** [C] a flag that is used during official ceremonies, especially one connected with a particular military group

standard² 🔑 B1 ⓪ /ˈstændəd/ *adj.* **1** normal or average; not special or unusual: *He's got long arms, so standard sizes of shirt don't fit him.* **2** that people generally accept as normal and correct: *standard English*

ˈstandard-class (*BrE also* **second-class**) *adj.* connected with the less expensive way of travelling by train, ship, etc: *standard-class carriages/passengers*

ˈstandard class (*BrE also* **second class**) *noun* [U] a way of travelling on a train or ship that costs less and is less comfortable than first class. In the UK, this used to be called second class.

ˌstandard deviˈation *noun* [C] (**MATHEMATICS**) the amount by which measurements in a set vary from the average for the set

standardize (*BrE also* **-ise**) /ˈstændədaɪz/ *verb* [T] to make things that are different the same: *Safety tests on old cars have been standardized throughout Europe.* ▶ **standardization** (*BrE also* **-isation**) /ˌstændədaɪˈzeɪʃn/ *noun* [U]

ˌstandard of ˈliving *noun* [C] (**SOCIAL STUDIES**) the amount of money and level of comfort that a particular person or group has: *There is a higher standard of living in the north than in the south.* ➲ note at **HDI**

standby /ˈstændbaɪ/ *noun* (*pl.* **standbys**) **1** [C] a thing or person that can be used if needed, for example if sb/sth is not available or in an emergency **2** [U] the state of being ready to do sth immediately if needed or if a ticket becomes available: *Ambulances were **on standby** along the route of the marathon.* ◇ *We were **put on standby** for the flight to Rome.* ▶ **standby** *adj.* [only before noun]: *a standby ticket/passenger*

ˈstand-in *noun* [C] **1** a person who does sb's job for a short time when they are not available **2** a person who replaces an actor in some scenes in a film, especially dangerous ones

standing¹ /ˈstændɪŋ/ *noun* [U] **1** the position that sb/sth has, or how people think of them or it: *The agreement has no legal standing.* **SYN** **status** **2** the amount of time during which sth has continued to exist: *a friendship of many years' standing*

standing² 🔑+ C1 /ˈstændɪŋ/ *adj.* [only before noun] that always exists; permanent

standing 'order *noun* [C] (**FINANCE**) an instruction to your bank to make a regular payment to sb from your account

standout /ˈstændaʊt/ *adj.* [only before noun] (*informal*) very easy to notice because of being better, more impressive, etc. than others in a group: *the standout track on this album*

standpoint /ˈstændpɔɪnt/ *noun* [C] a particular way of thinking about sth **SYN** **point of view**

standstill /ˈstændstɪl/ *noun* [sing.] a situation when there is no movement, progress or activity: *The traffic is at/ has come to a complete standstill.*
IDM grind to a halt/standstill → GRIND¹

stank /stæŋk/ past tense of **stink**

stanza /ˈstænzə/ *noun* [C] (**LITERATURE**) a group of lines in a repeated pattern that form a unit in some types of poem **SYN** **verse**

stapes /ˈsteɪpiːz/ *noun* [C] (*pl.* **stapes**) (**ANATOMY**) the third of three small bones in the MIDDLE EAR that carry sound to the INNER EAR **SYN** **stirrup** ⊃ picture at **ear**

staple /ˈsteɪpl/ *noun* [C] a small thin piece of bent wire that you push through pieces of paper using a STAPLER (= a special tool) to fasten them together ▸ **staple** *verb* [T]: *Staple the letter to the application form.* ▸ **stapler** /-plə(r)/ *noun* [C]

staple 'diet *noun* [C, usually sing.] the main food that a person or an animal normally eats: *a staple diet of rice and fish*

star¹ ⁅ **A1** /stɑː(r)/ *noun*
• IN THE SKY **1** [C] (**ASTRONOMY**) a large ball of burning gas in space that you see as a small point of light in the sky at night: *It was a clear night and the stars were shining brightly.*
• SHAPE **2** [C] a shape, decoration, mark, etc. with five or six points sticking out in a regular pattern: *I've marked the possible candidates on the list with a star.*
• BEST IN A GROUP **3** [C] a person or thing that is the best
• PERSON **4** [C] (**ARTS AND MEDIA**, **MUSIC**, **SPORT**) a famous person in acting, music or sport: *a pop/rock/film/ movie star* ◊ *a football/tennis star* **5** [C] a person who has the main part, or one of the main parts in a film, play etc.
• FOR A HOTEL, ETC. **6** [C] (**TOURISM**) a mark that represents a star that is used for telling you how good sth is, especially a hotel or restaurant: *a five-star hotel*
• PREDICTION **7** stars [pl.] a prediction about what is going to happen to a person in the future, based on the position of the stars and planets when they were born **SYN** **horoscope**

star² ⁅ **A2** /stɑː(r)/ *verb* (-rr-) **1** [I] ~ **(in sth)** (**ARTS AND MEDIA**) to be one of the main actors in a play, film, etc: *Anne Hathaway is to star in a new romantic comedy.* ⊃ note at **performing arts 2** [T] ~ **sb (as sb/sth)** (**ARTS AND MEDIA**) to have sb as a star: *The film starred Kate Winslet.*

starboard /ˈstɑːbəd/ *noun* [U] the side of a ship that is on the right when you are facing towards the front of it **OPP** **port**¹

starch /stɑːtʃ/ *noun* **1** [U, C] (**BIOLOGY**, **CHEMISTRY**) a white substance that is found in foods such as potatoes, rice and bread ⊃ picture at **photosynthesis 2** [U] a substance that is used for making cloth stiff

stardom /ˈstɑːdəm/ *noun* [U] the state of being a famous person in acting, music or sport: *She shot to stardom in a Broadway musical.*

stare ⁅ **B2** /steə(r)/ *verb* [I] ~ **(at sb/sth)** to look at sb/ sth for a long time because you are surprised, shocked, etc: *Everybody stared at his hat.* ◊ *He didn't reply — he just stared into the distance.*

starfish /ˈstɑːfɪʃ/ *noun* [C] (*pl.* **starfish**) a flat sea animal in the shape of a star with five or more arms

'star fruit *noun* [C] (*pl.* **star fruit**) a green or yellow tropical fruit with a shape like a star when sliced

stark¹ ⁅ **C1** /stɑːk/ *adj.* **1** unpleasant and impossible to avoid: *He now faces the stark reality of life in prison.* **2** very different to sth in a way that is easy to see: *stark differences* **3** very empty and without decoration and therefore not attractive: *a stark landscape*

stark² /stɑːk/ *adv.* completely; extremely: *stark naked* ◊ *Have you gone stark raving mad?*

starlight /ˈstɑːlaɪt/ *noun* [U] (**ASTRONOMY**) the light that is sent out by stars in the sky

starling /ˈstɑːlɪŋ/ *noun* [C] a common bird with dark shiny feathers and a noisy call

starry /ˈstɑːri/ *adj.* (**ASTRONOMY**) full of stars: *a starry night*

'star sign (*also informal* **sign**) *noun* [C] one of the twelve divisions of THE ZODIAC (= symbols that represent the positions of the sun, moon and planets)

start¹ ⁅ **A1** /stɑːt/ *verb*
• BEGIN **1** [I, T] ~ **(sth/to do sth/doing sth)** to begin doing sth: *Turn over your exam papers and start now.* ◊ *We'll have to start (=leave) early if we want to be in Dover by 10.00* ◊ *Prices start at £5.* ◊ *What time do you have to start work in the morning?* ◊ *After waiting for an hour, the customers started to complain.* ◊ *She started playing the piano when she was six.* **2** [I, T] to begin to happen; to make sth begin to happen: *What time does the concert start?* ◊ *I'd like to start the meeting now.* ◊ *The police think a young woman may have started the fire.*
• MACHINE/VEHICLE **3** [I, T] ~ **(sth) (up)** (used about a machine, etc.) to begin to work; to make an engine, a car, etc. begin to work: *The car won't start.* ◊ *We heard an engine starting up in the street.* ◊ *He got onto his motorbike, started the engine and rode away.*
• ORGANIZATION **4** [I, T] ~ **(sth) (up)** (**BUSINESS**) to create a company, an organization, etc.; to begin to exist: *They've decided to start their own business.* ◊ *There are a lot of new companies starting up in that area now.* ⊃ note at **organization**
• MOVE SUDDENLY **5** [I] to make a sudden, quick movement because you are surprised or afraid: *A loud noise outside made me start.*
IDM get/start off on the right/wrong foot (with sb) → FOOT¹ to start (off) with **1** used for giving your first reason for sth: *'Why are you so angry?' 'Well, to start off with, you're late, and secondly you've lied to me.'* **2** in the beginning; at first set/start the ball rolling → BALL
PHR V start off to begin in a particular way: *I'd like to start off by welcoming you all to Leeds.* start on sth to begin doing sth that needs to be done start out to begin to do sth, especially in business or work: *She started out as a teacher in Glasgow.* start out to do sth to have a particular intention when you begin sth start over (AmE) to begin again

start² ⁅ **A2** /stɑːt/ *noun*
• BEGINNING **1** [C, usually sing.] the point at which sth begins: *The chairman made a short speech at the start of the meeting.* ◊ *I told you it was a bad idea from the start.* **2** [C, usually sing.] the action or process of starting: *to make a fresh start* (= do sth again in a different way)
• IN A RACE **3** the start [sing.] (**SPORT**) the place where a race begins: *The athletes are now lining up at the*

start. **4** [C, usually sing.] an amount of time or distance that you give to a weaker person at the beginning of a race, game, etc. ⊃ look at **head start**
• SUDDEN MOVEMENT **5** [C, usually sing.] a sudden quick movement that your body makes because you are surprised or afraid: *She woke up with a start.*
IDM **for a start** (*informal*) (used to emphasize your first reason for sth): *'Why can't we go on holiday?' 'Well, for a start, we can't afford it…'* **get off to a good, bad, etc. start** to start well, badly, etc. **get off to a flying start** → FLYING¹

starter /ˈstɑːtə(r)/ (*especially BrE*) (*also* **appetizer** *AmE, BrE*) *noun* [C] a small amount of food that is served before the main course of a meal

starting point *noun* [C] **1** an idea or a topic that you use to begin a discussion with **2** the place where you begin a journey

startle /ˈstɑːtl/ *verb* [T] to surprise sb/sth in a way that slightly shocks or frightens them or it: *The noise startled the horses.* ▶ **startled** *adj.* ▶ **startling** *adj.*

start-up *noun* (**BUSINESS**) **1** [C] a new company: *This region has the highest level of start-ups in the country.* **2** [U] the action or process of making sth start: *They announced the start-up of a new pension scheme.* ◇ *On start-up, the computer asks for a password.* ▶ **start-up** *adj.* [only before noun]: *The venture failed because of high start-up costs.* ◇ *a start-up company*

starvation /stɑːˈveɪʃn/ *noun* [U] (**HEALTH, SOCIAL STUDIES**) suffering or death because there is not enough food: *to die of starvation*

starve 🔊+ **B2** /stɑːv/ *verb* [I, T] (**HEALTH, SOCIAL STUDIES**) to suffer or die because you do not have enough food to eat; to make sb/sth suffer or die in this way: *Millions of people are starving in the poorer countries of the world.* ◇ *That winter many animals starved to death.*
IDM **be starved of sth** to suffer because you are not getting enough of sth that you need: *The children had been starved of love and affection for years.* **be starving** (*informal*) to be extremely hungry

state¹ 🔊 **A2** 🅞 /steɪt/ *noun*
• CONDITION **1** [C] the mental, emotional or physical condition that sb/sth is in at a particular time: *the state of the economy* ◇ *He is in a state of shock.* ◇ *The house is in a terrible state.* **2** [C] (**CHEMISTRY**) the physical condition of sth according to its internal or MOLECULAR structure: *water in a liquid state* ◇ *the three states of matter* (= liquid, solid and gas)

• COUNTRY **3** (*also* State) [C] (**POLITICS**) a country considered as an organized political community controlled by one government: *Pakistan has been an independent state since 1947.* ⊃ note at **country**
• GOVERNMENT **4** the State [U, sing.] (**POLITICS**) the government of a country: *affairs/matters of state* ◇ *the relationship between the Church and the State* ◇ *a state-owned company* ◇ *heads of State* (= government leaders)
• PART OF A COUNTRY **5** (*also* State) [C] (**POLITICS**) an organized political community forming part of a country: *the southern States of the US* ⊃ look at **county, province** (1)
• THE US **6** the States [pl.] (*informal*) the United States of America: *We lived in the States for about five years.*
IDM **be in/get into a state** (*especially BrE, informal*) **1** to be or become very nervous or upset: *Now don't get into a state! I'm sure everything will be all right.* **2** (*informal*) to be or become dirty or untidy **state of affairs** a situation: *This state of affairs must not be allowed to continue.* **state of mind** mental condition: *She's in a very confused state of mind.*

state² 🔊 **B1** 🅞 /steɪt/ *verb* [T] (*formal*) to say or write sth, especially formally: *Your letter states that you sent the goods on 31 March, but we have not received them.* ⊃ note at **declare, opinion**

state³ 🔊 **B1** /steɪt/ *adj.* [only before noun] **1** provided or controlled by the government of a country: *She went to a state school.* **2** connected with the leader of a country attending an official ceremony: *The Queen is on a state visit to Moscow.* **3** connected with a particular state of a country, especially in the US: *a state prison/hospital/university*

stateless /ˈsteɪtləs/ *adj.* (**LAW, SOCIAL STUDIES**) not officially a citizen of any country: *The children of illegal immigrants will in many cases be born stateless.*

stately /ˈsteɪtli/ *adj.* formal and impressive: *a stately old building*

stately home *noun* [C] (*BrE*) a large old house that has historical interest, especially one that can be visited by the public

statement 🔊 **A1** 🅦 /ˈsteɪtmənt/ *noun* [C] **1** (**LAW**) something that you say or write, especially formally: *The prime minister will make a statement about the defence cuts today.* ▶ note on **page 714 2** a printed

states of matter

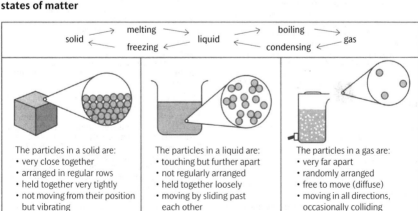

The particles in a solid are:	The particles in a liquid are:	The particles in a gas are:
• very close together	• touching but further apart	• very far apart
• arranged in regular rows	• not regularly arranged	• randomly arranged
• held together very tightly	• held together loosely	• free to move (diffuse)
• not moving from their position but vibrating	• moving by sliding past each other	• moving in all directions, occasionally colliding

record of money paid, received or owed ⊃ look at **bank statement** ⊃ note at **bill**¹

▼ SYNONYMS

statement

comment ♦ announcement ♦ remark ♦ declaration ♦ observation

These are all words for sth that you say or write, especially sth that gives information or an opinion.

statement *The police issued a statement.*

comment *She made helpful comments on his work.*

announcement *the announcement of a peace agreement*

remark *He made rude remarks about her cooking.*

declaration (*formal*) *a declaration of war*

observation (*formal*) *He began with a few general observations about the report.*

,state of the 'art *adj.* using the most modern or advanced methods; as good as it can be at the present time: *The system was state of the art.* ◇ *a state-of-the-art system*

'state school *noun* [C] (**EDUCATION**) **1** (*BrE*) a school that is paid for by the government and provides free education ⊃ look at **private school**, **public school** **2** (*AmE*) = STATE UNIVERSITY

statesman /'steɪtsmən/ *noun* [C] (*pl.* -men /-mən/) (**POLITICS**) a man who is a wise, experienced and respected political leader

stateswoman /'steɪtswʊmən/ *noun* [C] (*pl.* -women /-wɪmɪn/) (**POLITICS**) a woman who is a wise, experienced and respected political leader

,state uni'versity (*also* state school) *noun* [C] (*AmE*) (**EDUCATION**) a university that is managed by a state of the US

static¹ /'stætɪk/ *adj.* **1** not moving, changing or developing: *House prices are static.* **2** (**PHYSICS**) (used about a force) acting as a weight but not producing movement: *static pressure* **OPP** **dynamic**¹

static² /'stætɪk/ *noun* [U] **1** noise or other effects that interrupt radio or television signals and are caused by particular conditions in the atmosphere **2** (*also* ,static elec'tricity) (**PHYSICS**) electricity that collects on a surface: *My hair gets full of static when I brush it.*

station¹ ⓘ **A1** /'steɪʃn/ *noun* [C] **1** (*also* railway station) a building on a railway line where trains stop so that passengers can get on and off: *I get off at the next station.* ◇ *the main station* ◇ *a train station* **2** (usually in compounds) a building from which buses begin and end journeys **3** (usually in compounds) a building where a particular service or activity is based: *a police/fire station* ◇ *a petrol station* ◇ *a power station* (= where electricity is generated) **4** (often in compounds) (**ARTS AND MEDIA**) a radio or TV company and the programmes it sends out: *a local radio/TV station* ◇ *He tuned in to another station.* ⊃ look at **channel**¹ (1)

station² /'steɪʃn/ *verb* [T] [often passive] to send sb, especially a member of the armed forces, to work in a place for a period of time

stationary /'steɪʃənri/ *adj.* not moving: *He crashed into the back of a stationary vehicle.*

stationer's /'steɪʃənəz/ *noun* [C] (*pl.* stationers) a shop that sells writing equipment, such as paper, pens, ENVELOPES, etc.

stationery /'steɪʃənri/ *noun* [U] writing equipment, for example pens, pencils, paper and ENVELOPES

'station wagon (*AmE*) = ESTATE CAR

statistic ⓘ **B1** ⓦ /stə'tɪstɪk/ *noun* **1** statistics (*also informal* stats /stæts/) [pl.] a collection of information shown in numbers: *Statistics indicate that 90% of homes in this country have a broadband connection.* ◇ *crime statistics* **2** statistics (*also informal* stats) [U] (**MATHEMATICS**) the science of collecting and studying these numbers: *There is a compulsory course in statistics.* **3** [C] a piece of information shown in numbers: *I felt I was no longer being treated as a person but as a statistic.* ▶ statistical ⓘ+ **C1** /stə'tɪstɪkl/ *adj.*: *statistical analysis* ▶ statistically ⓦ /-kli/ *adv.*

statistician /,stætɪ'stɪʃn/ *noun* [C] a person who studies or works with statistics

statue ⓘ **B1** /'stætʃuː/ *noun* [C] (**ART**) a figure of a person or an animal that is made of stone or metal and usually put in a public place

statuette /,stætʃu'et/ *noun* [C] (**ART**) a small statue

stature /'stætʃə(r)/ *noun* [U] (*formal*) **1** the importance and respect that sb has because people have a high opinion of their skill or of what they have done **2** the height of a person: *He's quite small in stature.*

status ⓘ **B2** ⓦ /'steɪtəs/ *noun* **1** [U, C, usually sing.] the legal position of a person, group or country: *Please indicate your name, age and marital status* (= whether you are married or single). ◇ *They were granted refugee status.* **2** [U, C, usually sing.] your social or professional position in relation to other people: *Teachers don't have a very high status in this country.* **SYN** **standing**¹ **3** [U] a high social position: *The new job gave him much more status.* **4** [C] (**COMPUTING**) a piece of information that sb publishes on SOCIAL MEDIA, showing what they are doing or what situation they are in: *He updated his relationship status to indicate they were no longer together.*

status quo /,steɪtəs 'kwəʊ/ *noun* [sing.] the situation as it is now, or as it was before a recent change: *conservatives who want to maintain the status quo*

'status symbol *noun* [C] (**SOCIAL STUDIES**) something that a person owns that shows that they have a high position in society and a lot of money

statute /'stætʃuːt/ *noun* [C] (*formal*) (**LAW**) a law or a rule

'statute law *noun* [U] (**LAW**) all the written laws of a parliament, etc. ⊃ look at **case law**, **common law**

statutory /'stætʃətri/ *adj.* (**LAW**) decided by law: *a statutory right*

staunch /stɔːntʃ/ *adj.* always showing strong support in your opinions and attitude **SYN** **loyal**

stave¹ /steɪv/ *noun* [C] **1** a strong stick or POLE: *fence staves* **2** (*also* staff) (**MUSIC**) a set of five lines on which music is written ⊃ picture at **music**

stave² /steɪv/ *verb*

PHRV stave sth off to stop sth unpleasant from happening now, although it may happen at a later time; to delay sth: *to stave off hunger/illness/inflation/bankruptcy*

stay¹ ⓘ **A1** /steɪ/ *verb* [I] **1** to continue to be somewhere and not go away: *Patrick stayed in bed until eleven o'clock.* ◇ *I can't stay long.* ◇ *Stay on this road until you get to Wells.* ◇ *Pete's staying late at the office tonight.* **2** to live in a place temporarily as a visitor or guest: *We stayed with friends in France.* ◇ *Which hotel are you staying at?* ◇ *Can you stay for lunch?* ◇ *Why don't you stay the night?* **3** to continue to be in a particular state or situation without change: *I can't stay awake any longer.* ◇ *I don't know why they stay together* (= continue to be married or in a relationship). **IDM** stay put (*informal*) to continue in one place; to not leave

PHR V **stay behind** to not leave a place after other people have gone: *I'll stay behind and help you wash up.* **stay in** to remain at home and not go out: *I'm going to stay in and watch TV.* **stay on** to continue studying, working, etc. somewhere for longer than expected or after other people have left **stay out** to continue to be away from your house, especially late at night **stay out of sth** to avoid or not become involved in sth **stay up** to go to bed later than usual: *I'm going to stay up to watch this film.*

stay² **🔊 A2** /steɪ/ *noun* [C] a period of time that you spend somewhere as a visitor or guest: *Did you enjoy your stay in Crete?*

staycation /ˌsteɪˈkeɪʃn/ *noun* [C] a holiday that you spend at or near your home

STD /ˌes tiː ˈdiː/ *noun* [C] **(HEALTH)** any disease that is spread through having sex (the abbreviation for 'sexually transmitted disease')

steady¹ **B2** /ˈstedi/ *adj.* (**steadier; steadiest**) **1** developing, growing or happening gradually and at a regular rate: *a steady increase/decline* **2** staying the same; not changing and therefore safe: *a steady job/income* **3** fixed, supported or balanced; not shaking or likely to fall down: *You need **a steady hand** to take good photos.* ◊ *He held the ladder steady as she climbed up it.* ▸ **steadily** **🔊 B2** /-dəli/ *adv.*: *Unemployment has risen steadily for the last two years.*

steady² /ˈstedi/ *verb* [T, I] (**steadying; steadies;** *pt, pp* **steadied**) to stop yourself/sb/sth from moving, shaking or falling; to stop moving, shaking or falling: *She thought she was going to fall, so she put out a hand to steady herself.* ◊ *He had to **steady** his **nerves/voice** before beginning his speech.*

steak /steɪk/ *noun* [C, U] a thick flat piece of meat or fish: *a cod/salmon steak* ◊ *a piece of steak* ⊃ look at **chop¹**

steal **🔊 A2** /stiːl/ *verb* (*pt* **stole** /stəʊl/; *pp* **stolen** /ˈstəʊlən/) **1** [I, T] **~ (sth) (from sb/sth)** **(LAW)** to take sth from a person, shop, etc. without permission and without intending to return it or pay for it: *We found out she had been stealing from us for years.* ◊ *The terrorists were driving a stolen car.* ⊃ note at **criminal¹** **2** [I] (used with an adverb or a preposition) to move somewhere secretly and quietly: *She stole out of the room.*

stealth¹ /stelθ/ *noun* [U] behaviour that is secret or quiet ▸ **stealthily** /ˈstelθɪli/ *adv.* ▸ **stealthy** *adj.* (**stealthier; stealthiest**): *a stealthy approach/movement*

stealth² /stelθ/ *adj.* [only before noun] designed in a way that makes it difficult to be discovered by RADAR (= a system that uses radio waves for finding the position of moving objects): *a stealth bomber*

STEAM /stiːm/ *abbr.* **(EDUCATION)** **science, technology, engineeing, arts and mathematics** (used to refer to these subjects as a group when talking about education and jobs): *There's a big focus in schools on STEAM subjects.*

steam¹ **🔊 B2** /stiːm/ *noun* [U] **(PHYSICS)** the hot gas that water changes into when it boils: *Steam was rising from the coffee.* ◊ *a **steam engine** (= that uses the power of steam)* ⊃ note at **water¹** ⊃ picture at **generator**
IDM **let off steam** (*informal*) to get rid of energy or express strong feeling by behaving in a noisy or wild way **run out of steam** (*informal*) to gradually lose energy or enthusiasm

steam² /stiːm/ *verb* **1** [I] to send out STEAM: *a bowl of steaming hot soup* **2** [T, I] to place food over boiling water so that it cooks in the STEAM; to cook in this way: *steamed vegetables/fish* ◊ *Leave the potatoes to steam for 30 minutes.* ⊃ note at **cook¹**

IDM **be/get steamed up** (*informal*) to be or become very angry or worried about sth
PHR V **steam (sth) up** to cover sth with STEAM; to become covered with STEAM: *The windows have steamed up.*

steamer /ˈstiːmə(r)/ *noun* [C] **1** a boat or ship driven by STEAM power **2** a metal container with small holes in it, that is placed over a pan of boiling water in order to cook food in the steam

steamroller /ˈstiːmrəʊlə(r)/ *noun* [C] a big heavy vehicle with wide heavy wheels that is used for making the surface of a road flat

steel¹ **🔊 B2** /stiːl/ *noun* [U] **(CHEMISTRY)** a very strong metal that is made from iron mixed with CARBON. Steel is used for making knives, tools, machines, etc.

steel² /stiːl/ *verb* [T] **~ yourself** to prepare yourself to deal with sth difficult or unpleasant: *Steel yourself for a shock.*

steel ˈband *noun* [C] **(MUSIC)** a group of musicians who play music on drums that are made from empty metal oil containers. Steel bands originally came from the Caribbean.

steel ˈdrum (*also* **steel ˈpan**) *noun* [C] **(MUSIC)** a musical instrument used in Caribbean music, made from a metal oil container, that is hit in different places with two sticks to produce different notes

steel ˈwool (*also* **wire wool**) *noun* [U] a mass of fine steel THREADS that you use for cleaning pots and pans, making surfaces smooth, etc.

steelworks /ˈstiːlwɜːks/ *noun* [C + sing./pl. verb] (*pl.* **steelworks**) a factory where steel is made

steep **🔊 B2** /stiːp/ *adj.* **1** (used about a hill, mountain, street, etc.) rising or falling quickly; at a sharp angle: *I don't think I can cycle up that hill. It's too steep.* **2** (used about an increase or a fall in sth) very big: *a steep rise in unemployment* **3** (*informal*) too expensive ▸ **steeply** *adv.*: *House prices have risen steeply this year.* ▸ **steepness** *noun* [U]

steeped /stiːpt/ *adj.* [not before noun] **~ in sth** having a lot of; full of sth: *a city steeped in history*

steeple /ˈstiːpl/ *noun* [C] **(ARCHITECTURE)** a tower on the roof of a church, often with a SPIRE (= a tall pointed top)

steer **🔊 C1** /stɪə(r)/ *verb* **1** [T, I] to control the direction that a vehicle is going in: *to steer a boat/ship/bike/motorbike* ◊ *Can you push the car while I steer?* **2** [T] (used with an adverb or a preposition) to take control of a situation and try to influence the way it develops: *She tried to steer the conversation away from the subject of money.*
IDM **keep/stay/steer clear (of sb/sth)** → **CLEAR²**

steering /ˈstɪərɪŋ/ *noun* [U] the parts of a vehicle that control the direction that it moves in: *a car with power steering*

ˈsteering wheel (*also* **wheel**) *noun* [C] the wheel that the driver turns in a vehicle to control the direction that it moves in

stellar /ˈstelə(r)/ *adj.* [only before noun] **(ASTRONOMY)** connected with the stars ⊃ look at **interstellar**

STEM /stem/ *abbr.* **(EDUCATION)** **science, technology, engineering and mathematics** (used to refer to these subjects as a group when talking about education and jobs): *The team's mission is to promote STEM education.*

stem¹ **🔊 C1** /stem/ *noun* [C] **1** **(BIOLOGY)** the main long thin part of a plant above the ground from which the leaves or flowers grow **2** **(GRAMMAR)** the main part of a word onto which other parts are added: '*Writ-*' *is the stem of the words* '*write*', '*writing*', '*written*' *and* '*writer*'.

stem² ℝ+ **C1** /stem/ *verb* [T] (-mm-) to stop sth that is increasing or spreading: *He bandaged the cut to stem the bleeding.*
PHR V **stem from sth** (not used in the progressive tenses) to be the result of sth

stem cell *noun* [C] (**BIOLOGY**) a basic type of cell that can divide and develop into cells with particular functions. All the different kinds of cells in the human body develop from stem cells: *Stem cell research is the essential first step for cloning.*

stench /stentʃ/ *noun* [sing.] a very unpleasant smell

stencil /'stensl/ *noun* [C] (**ART**) a thin piece of metal, plastic or card with a design cut out of it, that you put onto a surface and paint over, so that the design is left on the surface; the pattern or design that is produced in this way ▶ **stencil** *verb* [T] (-ll-, *AmE* -l-)

stent /stent/ *noun* [C] (**MEDICINE**) a small support that is put inside a BLOOD VESSEL (= tube) in the body, in order to keep the tube open enough for blood to flow through

step¹ ℝ **A2** /step/ *noun* [C] **1** the act of lifting one foot and putting it down in a different place: *Nick took a step forward and then stopped.* ◇ *I heard steps outside the window.* ◇ *We were obviously lost so we decided to retrace our steps* (= go back the way we had come). **2** one action in a series of actions that you take in order to achieve sth: *This will not solve the problem completely, but it is a step in the right direction.* **3** a surface that you put your foot on in order to walk to a higher or lower level, especially one of a series: *on the top/bottom step* ◇ *We walked down some stone steps to the beach.*
IDM **in/out of step (with sb/sth)** moving/not moving your feet at the same time as other people when you are MARCHING, dancing, etc. **step by step** (used for talking about a series of actions) moving slowly and gradually from one action or stage to the next: *clear step-by-step instructions* **take steps to do sth** to take action in order to achieve sth **watch your step 1** to be careful about where you are walking **2** to be careful about how you behave

step² ℝ **B2** /step/ *verb* [I] (-pp-) (used with an adverb or a preposition) to lift one foot and put it down in a different place when you are walking: *Be careful! Don't step in the mud.* ◇ *to step forward/back* ◇ *Ouch! You stepped on my foot!* ◇ *Could you step out of the car please, sir?* ◇ *I stepped outside for a minute to get some air.*
PHR V **step down** to leave an important job or position and let sb else take your place **step in** to help sb in a difficult situation or to become involved in an argument **step sth up** to increase the amount, speed, etc. of sth: *The Army has decided to step up its security arrangements.*

step- /step/ *prefix* (in nouns) related as a result of one parent marrying again

stepbrother /'stepbrʌðə(r)/ *noun* [C] a son that your STEPFATHER or STEPMOTHER has from an earlier marriage ⊃ look at **half-brother**

stepchild /'steptʃaɪld/ *noun* [C] (*pl.* **stepchildren** /'steptʃɪldrən/) a child that your husband or wife has from an earlier marriage

stepdaughter /'stepdɔ:tə(r)/ *noun* [C] a daughter that your husband or wife has from an earlier marriage

stepfather /'stepfɑ:ðə(r)/ *noun* [C] the man who is married to your mother but who is not your real father

stepladder /'steplædə(r)/ *noun* [C] a short LADDER with two parts, one with steps, that are joined together at the top so that it can stand on its own and be folded up when you are not using it

stepmother /'stepmʌðə(r)/ *noun* [C] the woman who is married to your father but who is not your real mother

steppe /step/ *noun* [C, usually pl., U] (**GEOGRAPHY**) a large area of land with grass but few trees, especially in south-east Europe and Siberia

stepping stone *noun* [C] **1** one of a line of flat stones that you can step on in order to cross a river **2** something that allows you to make progress or helps you to achieve sth

stepsister /'stepsɪstə(r)/ *noun* [C] a daughter that your STEPFATHER or STEPMOTHER has from an earlier marriage ⊃ look at **half-sister**

stepson /'stepsʌn/ *noun* [C] a son that your husband or wife has from an earlier marriage

stereo /'steriəʊ/ *noun* (*pl.* -os) **1** [U] the system for playing recorded music, speech etc. in which the sound is divided in two parts: *This programme is broadcast in stereo.* ⊃ look at **mono** (*also* 'stereo system) [C] a machine that plays CDs, etc., sometimes with a radio, that has two separate speakers so that you hear sounds from each: *a car stereo* ▶ **stereo** *adj.* [only before noun]: *stereo sound*

stereotype ℝ+ **C1** /'steriətaɪp/ *noun* [C] a fixed idea about a particular type of person or thing, which is often not true in reality: *cultural/gender/racial stereotypes* ▶ **stereotype** *verb* [T, often passive] ~**sb (as sth)**: *In advertisements, women were often stereotyped as housewives.* ▶ **stereotypical** /ˌsteriə'tɪpɪkl/ *adj.*: *the stereotypical image of a car salesman*

sterile /'steraɪl/ *adj.* **1** (**HEALTH**) not able to produce young animals or babies **2** (**HEALTH**) completely clean and free from bacteria: *All equipment used during a medical operation must be sterile.* **3** not producing any useful result: *a sterile discussion/argument* ▶ **sterility** /stə'rɪləti/ *noun* [U]

sterilize (*BrE also* -ise) /'sterəlaɪz/ *verb* [T] (**MEDICINE**) **1** to make sb/sth completely clean and free from bacteria **2** [usually passive] to perform an operation on a person or an animal so that they or it cannot have babies ▶ **sterilization** (*BrE also* -isation) /ˌsterəlaɪ'zeɪʃn/ *noun* [U]

sterling¹ /'stɜːlɪŋ/ *noun* [U] (**ECONOMICS**, **FINANCE**) the system of money used in the UK, that uses the pound as its basic unit

sterling² /'stɜːlɪŋ/ *adj.* of very high quality: *sterling work*

stern¹ /stɜːn/ *adj.* very serious; not smiling: *a stern expression/warning* ▶ **sternly** *adv.*

stern² /stɜːn/ *noun* [C] the back end of a ship or boat ⊃ look at **bow²** (2)

sternum /'stɜːnəm/ *noun* [C] (**ANATOMY**) the long flat bone in the middle of the chest that the seven top pairs of RIBS (= curved bones that surround the chest) are connected to **SYN** **breastbone** ⊃ picture at **body**

steroid /'sterɔɪd, 'stɪər-/ *noun* [C] (**MEDICINE**) a chemical substance produced naturally in the body. There are several different types of steroids. They can be used to treat various diseases and are also sometimes used illegally by people playing sports to improve their performance. ⊃ look at **anabolic steroid**

stethoscope /'steθəskəʊp/ *noun* [C] (**MEDICINE**) the piece of equipment that a doctor uses for listening to your breathing and heart

stew /stjuː/ *noun* [U, C] a type of food that you make by cooking meat and/or vegetables in liquid for a long time ▸ **stew** *verb* [I, T] ⊃ note at **meat**

steward /ˈstjuːəd/ *noun* [C] **1** a man whose job is to look after passengers on an aircraft, a ship or a train **2** a person who helps to organize a large public event, for example a race

stewardess /ˌstjuːəˈdes, ˈstjuːədes/ *noun* [C] **1** (*old-fashioned*) a woman whose job is to look after passengers on an aircraft **2** a woman who looks after the passengers on a ship or train

stick¹ ⓘ **B1** /stɪk/ *verb* (*pt, pp* **stuck** /stʌk/)
• PUSH STH IN **1** [T, I] ~ **(sth) in/into (sth)** to push a pointed object into sth; to be pushed into sth: *Stick a fork into the meat to see if it's ready.*
• FIX **2** [T, I] to fix sth to sth else by using a sticky substance; to become fixed to sth else: *I stuck a stamp on an envelope.* ◇ *Can we stick the broken pieces together?*
• PUT **3** [T] (used with an adverb or a preposition) (*informal*) to put sth somewhere, especially quickly or carelessly: *Stick your bags in the bedroom.* ◇ *Just at that moment James stuck his head round the door.*
• BECOME FIXED **4** [I] ~ **(in sth)** (used about sth that can usually be moved) to become fixed in one position so that it cannot be moved: *The car was stuck in the mud.* ◇ *This drawer keeps sticking.*
• DIFFICULT SITUATION **5** [T] (*informal*) (often in negative sentences and questions) to stay in a difficult or unpleasant situation: *I can't stick this job much longer.* **SYN** **stand**¹
IDM **poke/stick your nose into sth** → NOSE¹ **stick/ put your tongue out** → TONGUE
PHR V **stick around** (*informal*) to stay somewhere, waiting for sth to happen or for sb to arrive **stick at sth** to continue working at sth even when it is difficult **stick by sb** to continue to give sb help and support even in difficult times **stick out** to be easily seen or noticed: *The new office block really sticks out from the older buildings around it.* **stick (sth) out** to be further out than sth else; to push sth further out than sth else: *The boy's head was sticking out of the window.* ◇ *Don't stick your tongue out.* **stick it/sth out** (*informal*) to stay in a difficult or an unpleasant situation until the end **stick to sth** to continue with sth and not change to anything else **stick together** (*informal*) (used about a group of people) to stay together and support each other **stick up** to point upwards: *You look funny. Your hair's sticking up!* **stick up for yourself/sb/sth** (*informal*) to support or defend yourself/sb/sth: *Don't worry. I'll stick up for you if there's any trouble.*

stick² ⓘ **A2** /stɪk/ *noun* [C] **1** a small thin piece of wood from a tree **2** (*especially BrE*) = WALKING STICK **3** (in hockey and some other sports) a long thin piece of wood that you use for hitting the ball: *a hockey stick* ⊃ look at **bat**¹ (1), **club**¹ (4), **racket** (3) ⊃ picture at **sport 4** a long thin piece of sth: *a stick of celery/ dynamite*

sticker /ˈstɪkə(r)/ *noun* [C] a piece of paper with writing or a picture on one side that you can stick onto sth

sticky ⓘ **B2** /ˈstɪki/ *adj.* (**stickier; stickiest**) **1** used for describing a substance that easily becomes joined to things that it touches, or sth that is covered with this kind of substance: *These sweets are very sticky.* ◇ *sticky tape* **2** (*informal*) (used about a situation) difficult or unpleasant

ˈsticky tape = SELLOTAPE™

stiff¹ ⓘ **B2** /stɪf/ *adj.*
• DIFFICULT TO BEND **1** (used about material, paper, etc.) firm and difficult to bend or move: *My new shoes feel rather stiff.* ◇ *The door handle is stiff and I can't turn it.*

• OF A PART OF THE BODY **2** if a person or a part of their body is stiff, their muscles hurt when they move them: *My arm feels really stiff after playing tennis yesterday.*
• LIQUID **3** (used about a liquid) very thick; almost solid: *Beat the egg whites until they are stiff.*
• DIFFICULT/STRONG **4** more difficult or stronger than usual: *The firm faces stiff competition from its rivals.* ◇ *a stiff breeze/wind*
• BEHAVIOUR **5** (used about sb's behaviour) not relaxed or friendly; formal
• ALCOHOLIC DRINK **6** (used about an alcoholic drink) strong: *a stiff whisky*
▸ **stiffness** *noun* [U]

stiff² /stɪf/ *adv.* (*informal*) extremely: *to be bored/frozen/ scared/worried stiff*

stiffen /ˈstɪfn/ *verb* **1** [I] (used about a person) to suddenly stop moving and hold your body very straight, usually because you are afraid or angry **2** [T] to make sth become difficult to bend or move

stiffly /ˈstɪfli/ *adv.* in an unfriendly formal way: *He smiled stiffly.*

stifle /ˈstaɪfl/ *verb* **1** [T] to stop sth happening, developing or continuing: *Her strict education had stifled her natural creativity.* ◇ *to stifle a yawn/cry/ giggle* **2** [I, T] to be or to make sb unable to breathe because it is very hot and/or there is no fresh air: *Richard was almost stifled by the smoke.* ▸ **stifling** *adj.*: *The heat was stifling.*

stigma /ˈstɪɡmə/ *noun* **1** [U, C, usually sing.] bad and often unfair feelings that people in general have about a particular illness, way of behaving, etc: *There is still a lot of stigma attached to being unemployed.* **2** [C] (**BIOLOGY**) the top of the CARPEL (= the female part in the middle of a flower) where POLLEN is received ⊃ picture at **flower**¹

stile   turnstile

stile /staɪl/ *noun* [C] a set of steps that help people climb over a fence or gate in a field, etc.

stiletto /stɪˈletəʊ/ (*pl.* -**os**, -**oes**) (*also* ˌstiletto ˈheel) *noun* [C] a woman's shoe with a very high narrow heel; the heel on such a shoe

still¹ ⓘ **A1** /stɪl/ *adv.* **1** continuing until now or until the time you are talking about and not finishing: *Do you still live in London?* ◇ *It's still raining.* ◇ *I've eaten all the food but I'm still hungry.* ◇ *In 1997 Zoran was still a student.* ◇ *There are still ten days to go until my holiday.* **2** despite what has just been said: *He had a bad headache but he still went to the party.* **3** used for making a comparison stronger: *It was very cold yesterday, but today it's colder still.* **4** ~ **more/another** even more: *There was still more bad news to come.*

still² ⓘ **B1** /stɪl/ *adj.* **1** not moving: *Stand still! I want to take a photo!* ◇ *Children find it hard to keep/stay still for long periods.* **2** quiet or calm: *The water was perfectly still.* **3** (used about a drink) not containing gas: *still mineral water* ⊃ look at **fizzy**, **sparkling** (2)

still³ /stɪl/ *noun* [C] (**ARTS AND MEDIA**) a single photo that is taken from a film or video

stillborn /ˈstɪlbɔːn/ *adj.* (**HEALTH**) (used about a baby) dead when it is born

still ˈlife *noun* [U, C] (*pl.* still lifes) (**ART**) the art of painting or drawing arrangements of objects such as flowers, fruit, etc.; a painting, etc. like this: *a still life in oils*

stillness /ˈstɪlnəs/ *noun* [U] the quality of being quiet and not moving

stilt /stɪlt/ *noun* [C, usually pl.] **1** one of two long pieces of wood, with places to rest your feet on, on which you can walk above the ground: *Have you tried walking on stilts?* **2** one of a set of POLES that supports a building above the ground or water

stilted /ˈstɪltɪd/ *adj.* (used about a way of speaking or writing) not natural or relaxed; too formal

stimulant /ˈstɪmjələnt/ *noun* [C] a drug or medicine that makes you feel more active

stimulate ⟨+ B2 ⟩ /ˈstɪmjuleɪt/ *verb* [T] **1** to make sth active or more active: *Exercise stimulates the blood circulation.* ◇ *The government has decided to cut taxes in order to stimulate the economy.* **2** to make sb feel interested and excited about sth: *The lessons don't really stimulate him.* ▸ **stimulation** ⟨ ⟩ /ˌstɪmjuˈleɪʃn/ *noun* [U]

stimulating /ˈstɪmjuleɪtɪŋ/ *adj.* interesting and exciting: *a stimulating discussion*

stimulus ⟨+ C1 ⟩ /ˈstɪmjələs/ *noun* [C] (*pl.* stimuli /-laɪ/) ~ (for sth) something that causes activity, development or interest: *Books provide children with ideas and a stimulus for play.*

sting¹ /stɪŋ/ *verb* (*pt, pp* stung /stʌŋ/) **1** [I, T] (**HEALTH**) (used about an insect, a plant, etc.) to make a person or an animal feel a sudden pain by pushing sth sharp into their skin and sending poison into them: *Ow! I've been stung by a bee!* ◇ *Be careful. Those plants sting.* ◯ look at **bite¹** **2** [I, T] to make sb/sth feel a sudden, sharp pain: *Soap stings if it gets in your eyes.* **3** [T] to make sb feel very hurt and upset because of sth you say

sting² /stɪŋ/ *noun* [C] **1** the sharp pointed part of some insects and animals that is used for pushing into the skin of a person or an animal and putting in poison ◯ picture at **animal** **2** a wound that is made when an animal or insect pushes its sting into you: *I got a wasp sting on the leg.* **3** (**HEALTH**) a sharp pain that feels like a sting

stink /stɪŋk/ *verb* [I] (*pt* stank /stæŋk/, stunk /stʌŋk/; *pp* stunk) ~ (of sth) (*informal*) **1** to have a very strong and unpleasant smell: *It stinks in here — open a window!* ◇ *to stink of fish* **2** to seem to be very bad, unpleasant or dishonest: *The whole business stinks of corruption.* ▸ **stink** *noun* [C, usually sing.]

stint /stɪnt/ *noun* [C] a fixed period of time that you spend doing sth: *He did a brief stint in the army after leaving school.*

stipulate /ˈstɪpjuleɪt/ *verb* [T] (*formal*) to say exactly and officially what must be done: *The law stipulates that all schools must be inspected every three years.* ▸ **stipulation** /ˌstɪpjuˈleɪʃn/ *noun* [C, U]

stir¹ ⟨+ C1 ⟩ /stɜː(r)/ *verb* (-rr-) **1** [T] to move a liquid, etc. round and round, using a spoon, etc: *She stirred her coffee with a teaspoon.* **2** [I, T] to move slightly; to make sb/sth move slightly: *She heard the baby stir in the next room.* **3** [T] to make sb feel a strong emotion: *The story stirred Carol's imagination.* ◇ *a stirring speech*

PHR V **stir sth up** to cause problems, or to make people feel strong emotions: *He's always trying to stir up trouble.* ◇ *The article stirred up a lot of anger among local residents.*

stir² /stɜː(r)/ *noun* **1** [sing.] excitement, anger or shock that is felt by a number of people **2** [C, usually sing.] the act of STIRRING: *Give the soup a stir.*

ˈstir-fry¹ *verb* [T] to cook thin STRIPS of vegetables or meat quickly in a small amount of very hot oil: *stir-fried chicken*

ˈstir-fry² *noun* [C] a hot dish made by STIR-FRYING small pieces of meat, fish and/or vegetables

stirring /ˈstɜːrɪŋ/ *adj.* causing strong feelings; exciting: *a stirring performance*

stirrup /ˈstɪrəp/ *noun* [C] **1** one of the two metal objects that you put your feet in when you are riding a horse **2** (**ANATOMY**) the third of three small bones in the MIDDLE EAR that carry sound to the INNER EAR **SYN** **stapes** ◯ picture at **ear**

stitch¹ /stɪtʃ/ *noun* [C] **1** one of the small lines of THREAD that you can see on a piece of cloth after it has been SEWN **2** one of the small circles of wool that you put round a needle when you are KNITTING **3** (**MEDICINE**) one of the small pieces of THREAD that a doctor uses to SEW your skin together if you cut yourself very badly, or after an operation: *How many stitches did you have in your leg?* ◯ note at **hospital** **4** [usually sing.] (**HEALTH**) a sudden pain that you get in the side of your body when you are running

IDM **in stitches** (*informal*) laughing so much that you cannot stop

stitch² /stɪtʃ/ *verb* [I, T] to use a needle and THREAD to repair, join or decorate pieces of cloth **SYN** **sew**

stock¹ ⟨+ B2 ⟩ /stɒk/ *noun* **1** [U, C] the supply of things that a shop, etc. has for sale: *We'll have to order extra stock if we sell a lot more this week.* ◇ *I'm afraid that book's out of stock at the moment. Shall I order it for you?* ◇ *I'll see if we have your size in stock.* **2** [C, U] an amount of sth that has been kept ready to be used: *Food stocks in the village were very low.* **3** [C, usually pl., U] (**BUSINESS, FINANCE**) a share that sb has bought in a company; the value of a company's shares: *to invest in stocks and shares* **4** [U, C] a liquid that is made by boiling meat, bones, vegetables, etc. in water, used especially for making soups and sauces

IDM **take stock (of sth)** to think about sth very carefully before deciding what to do next ◯ note at **examine**

stock² /stɒk/ *verb* [T] **1** (usually used about a shop) to have a supply of sth: *They stock food from all over the world.* **2** [often passive] to fill a place with sth: *a well-stocked library*

PHR V **stock up (on/with sth)** to collect a large supply of sth for future use: *to stock up with food for the winter*

stock³ /stɒk/ *adj.* [only before noun] (used for describing sth that sb says) used so often that it does not have much meaning: *He always gives the same stock answers.*

stockbroker /ˈstɒkbrəʊkə(r)/ (*also* broker) *noun* [C] a person whose job it is to buy and sell shares in companies for other people

ˈstock exchange (*also* stock market, market) *noun* [C, usually sing.] (**FINANCE**) a place where shares in companies are bought and sold; all of the business activity involved in doing this: *the Tokyo Stock Exchange* ◇ *to lose money on the stock exchange*

stocking /ˈstɒkɪŋ/ *noun* [C] one of a pair of thin pieces of clothing that fit tightly over a woman's feet and legs: *a pair of stockings* ◯ look at **tights**

stockist /'stɒkɪst/ *noun* [C] a shop that sells a particular product or type of goods

stockman /'stɒkmən/ *noun* [C] (*pl.* -men /-mən/) (**AGRICULTURE**) a man whose job is to take care of farm animals

stock market (*also* **market**) *noun* [C] the business of buying and selling shares in companies and the place where this happens; a STOCK EXCHANGE: *to make money on the stock market* ◇ *a stock market crash* (= when prices of shares fall suddenly and people lose money)

stockpile¹ /'stɒkpaɪl/ *noun* [C] a large supply of sth that is kept to be used in the future if necessary: *a stockpile of weapons*

stockpile² /'stɒkpaɪl/ *verb* [T] to collect and keep a large supply of sth

stocktaking /'stɒkteɪkɪŋ/ *noun* [U] the activity of counting the total supply of things that a shop or business has at a particular time: *They close for an hour a month to do the stocktaking.*

stocky /'stɒki/ *adj.* (**stockier; stockiest**) (used about a person's body) short but strong and heavy

stoic /'stəʊɪk/ (*also* **stoical** /'stəʊɪkl/) *adj.* suffering pain or difficulty without complaining ▸ **stoically** /-kli/ *adv.* ▸ **stoicism** /-ɪsɪzəm/ *noun* [U]

stoke /stəʊk/ *verb* [T] **1 ~ sth (up) (with sth)** to add fuel to a fire, etc: *to stoke up a fire with more coal* **2 ~ sth (up)** to make people feel sth more strongly: *to stoke anger/envy* ◇ *The publicity was intended to stoke up interest in her music.*
PHR V **stoke up (on/with sth)** (*informal*) to eat or drink a lot of sth, especially so that you do not feel hungry later: *Stoke up for the day on a good breakfast.*

stole /stəʊl/ past tense of **steal**

stolen /'stəʊlən/ past participle of **steal**

stolid /'stɒlɪd/ *adj.* (used about a person) showing very little emotion or excitement ▸ **stolidly** *adv.*

stoma /'stəʊmə/ *noun* [C] (*pl.* **stomas, stomata** /-mətə/) **1** (**BIOLOGY**) any of the very small holes in the surface of a leaf or the STEM (= the main long thin part) of a plant that allow gases to pass in and out **2** (**BIOLOGY**) a small opening like a mouth in some simple creatures **3** (**MEDICINE**) an opening made in an organ of the body, especially in the COLON or TRACHEA

stomach¹ ⓘ **A2** /'stʌmək/ (*also informal* **tummy**) *noun* [C] **1** (**ANATOMY**) the organ in the body where food goes after you have eaten it: *He went to the doctor with stomach pains.* ⊃ picture at **body**, **digestive system 2** the front part of the body below the chest and above the legs: *She turned over onto her stomach.* ⊃ picture at **body**

stomach² /'stʌmək/ *verb* [T] (usually in negative sentences and questions) to be able to watch, listen to, accept, etc. sth that you think is unpleasant: *I can't stomach too much violence in films.*

stomach ache *noun* [C, U] (**HEALTH**) a pain in the stomach: *I've got terrible stomach ache.*

stomata /'stəʊmətə/ plural of **stoma**

stomp /stɒmp/ *verb* [I] (*informal*) to walk with heavy steps

stone ⓘ **A2** /stəʊn/ *noun*
• HARD SUBSTANCE **1** [U] a hard solid substance that is found in the ground: *The house was built of grey stone.* ◇ *a stone wall* ⊃ look at **cornerstone, foundation stone 2** [C] a small piece of rock: *The boy picked up a stone and threw it into the river.* **3** [C] = PRECIOUS STONE
• IN A FRUIT **4** (*AmE* **pit**) [C] the hard seed inside some types of fruit

• MEASUREMENT **5** [C] (*pl.* **stone**) (*abbr.* **st, st.**) a measure of weight; 6.35 KILOGRAMS. There are 14 pounds in a stone: *I weigh 11 stone.*

the 'Stone Age *noun* [sing.] (**HISTORY**) the very early period of human history when tools and weapons were made of stone

stoned /stəʊnd/ *adj.* (*informal*) not behaving or thinking normally because of drugs or alcohol

stonemason /'stəʊnmeɪsn/ *noun* [C] a person whose job is cutting and preparing stone for buildings

stonework /'stəʊnwɜːk/ *noun* [U] (**ARCHITECTURE**) the parts of a building that are made of stone

stony /'stəʊni/ *adj.* (**stonier; stoniest**) **1** (used about the ground) having a lot of stones in it, or covered with stones **2** not friendly: *There was a stony silence as he walked into the room.*

stood /stʊd/ past tense, past participle of **stand**¹

stool /stuːl/ *noun* [C] **1** a seat that does not have a back or arms: *a piano stool* ⊃ picture at **piano 2** (**MEDICINE**) a piece of solid waste from the body

stoop /stuːp/ *verb* [I] to bend your head and shoulders forwards and downwards: *He had to stoop to get through the low doorway.* ▸ **stoop** *noun* [sing.]: *to walk with a stoop*
PHR V **stoop to sth/doing sth** to do sth bad or wrong that you would normally not do

stop¹ **A1** /stɒp/ *verb* (-pp-) **1** [I, T] to finish moving; to make sth finish moving: *He walked along the road for a bit, and then stopped.* ◇ *Does this train stop at Didcot?* ◇ *My watch has stopped.* ◇ *I stopped somebody in the street to ask the way to the station.* **2** [I, T] to no longer continue; to make sth not continue: *I think the rain has stopped.* ◇ *It's stopped raining now.* ◇ *Stop making that terrible noise!* ◇ *The bus service stops at midnight.* ◇ *We tied a bandage round his arm to stop the bleeding.* **3** [T] **~ sb/sth (from) doing sth** to make sb/sth end or finish an activity; to prevent sb/sth from doing sth: *They've built a fence to stop the dog getting out.* ◇ *I'm going to go and you can't stop me.* **4** [I, T] **~ (sth) (for sth); ~ (and do/to do sth)** to end an activity for a short time in order to do sth: *Shall we stop for lunch now?* ◇ *Let's stop and look at the map.* ◇ *We stopped work for half an hour to have a cup of coffee.*
IDM **stop at nothing** to do anything to get what you want, even if it is wrong or dangerous **stop short of sth/doing sth** to almost do sth, but then decide not to do it at the last minute
PHR V **stop off (at/in ...)** to stop during a journey to do sth **stop over (at/in ...)** to stay somewhere for a short time during a long journey

stop² **A1** /stɒp/ *noun* [C] **1** the place where a bus, train, etc. stops so that people can get on and off: *a bus stop* ◇ *I'm getting off at the next stop.* ◇ *Our first stop will be Edinburgh.* **2** an act of stopping or state of being stopped: *Production at the factory will come to a stop at midnight tonight.* ◇ *I managed to bring the car to a stop just in time.*
IDM **pull out all the stops** → PULL¹ **put a stop to sth** to prevent sth bad or unpleasant from continuing

stopgap /'stɒpgæp/ *noun* [C] a person or a thing that does a job for a short time until sb/sth permanent can be found

stopover /'stɒpəʊvə(r)/ *noun* [C] a short stay between two parts of a journey

stoppage /ˈstɒpɪdʒ/ *noun* [C] **1** a situation in which people stop working as part of a protest **2** (in sport) a situation in which a game is interrupted for a particular reason

stopper /ˈstɒpə(r)/ *noun* [C] an object that you put into the top of a bottle in order to close it ⊃ picture at **laboratory**, **vacuum flask**

stopwatch /ˈstɒpwɒtʃ/ *noun* [C] a watch that can be started and stopped by pressing a button, so that you can measure exactly how long sth takes

storage 🔑+ **C1** /ˈstɔːrɪdʒ/ *noun* [U] **1** the process of keeping things until they are needed; the space where they are kept: *This room is being used for storage at the moment.* ⊃ look at **cold storage 2** (COMPUTING) the process of keeping information, etc. on a computer or other electronic device; the way it is kept: *With free cloud storage, you won't have to worry about paying a monthly fee.*

store¹ 🔑 **A2** /stɔː(r)/ *noun* [C] **1** a large shop: *She's a sales assistant in a large department store.* ◇ *a furniture store* ⊃ look at **chain store 2** (*AmE*) = SHOP¹ **3** a supply of sth that you keep for future use; the place where it is kept: *a good store of food for the winter* ◇ *Police discovered a weapons store in the house.*

IDM in store (for sb/sth) going to happen in the future: *There's a surprise in store for you when you get home!* **set … store by sth** to consider sth to be important: *Nick sets great store by his mother's opinion.*

store² 🔑 **B1** **W** /stɔː(r)/ *verb* [T] **1** to put sth somwhere and keep it there to use later **2** to keep information or facts in a computer or in your brain: *to store information on a computer*

storekeeper /ˈstɔːkiːpə(r)/ (*AmE*) = SHOPKEEPER

storeroom /ˈstɔːruːm, -rʊm/ *noun* [C] a room where things are kept until they are needed

storey (*BrE*) (*AmE* **story**) /ˈstɔːri/ *noun* [C] (ARCHITECTURE) one floor or level of a building: *The building will be five storeys high.* ◇ *a two-storey house* ◇ *a multi-storey car park*

stork /stɔːk/ *noun* [C] a large black and white bird with a long BEAK (= the hard pointed part of a bird's mouth), neck and legs. Storks live near water and often make their NESTS (= homes) on the top of buildings.

storm¹ 🔑 **A2** /stɔːm/ *noun* [C] very bad weather with strong winds and rain: *Look at those black clouds. I think there's going to be a storm.* ◇ *a snowstorm/ thunderstorm* ◇ *a sandstorm* (= a storm in the desert when sand is blown into the air) ◇ *a hailstorm* (= a storm when HAIL falls from the sky)

▼ VOCABULARY BUILDING

During a **thunderstorm** you hear **thunder** and see flashes of **lightning** in the sky. A **cyclone** is a large, violent tropical storm with very strong winds. A cyclone in the western Atlantic ocean is called a **hurricane**. In the Indian or western Pacific ocean it is called a **typhoon**. A storm with a very strong circular wind is called a **tornado**. A **blizzard** is a very bad **snowstorm**.

storm² /stɔːm/ *verb* **1** [T] to attack a building, town, etc. suddenly and violently in order to take control of it **2** [I] (used with an adverb or a preposition) to enter or leave somewhere in a very angry and noisy way: *He threw down the book and stormed out of the room.*

storm surge *noun* [C, U] (GEOGRAPHY) an unusual rise in the level of the sea near the coast, caused by wind from a violent storm

stormy /ˈstɔːmi/ *adj.* (stormier; stormiest) **1** used for talking about very bad weather, with strong winds, heavy rain, etc: *a stormy night* ◇ *stormy weather* **2** involving a lot of angry argument and strong feeling: *a stormy relationship*

story 🔑 **A1** **S** /ˈstɔːri/ *noun* [C] (*pl.* -ies) **1** ~ (about sb/ sth) (ARTS AND MEDIA, LITERATURE) a description of people and events that are not real: *I'll tell you a story about the animals that live in that forest.* ◇ *I always read the children a bedtime story.* ◇ *a detective/fairy/ ghost/love story* **2** a description of true events that happened in the past: *He's writing his life story.* **3** an account, especially a spoken one, of sth that has happened: *The police didn't believe his story.* **4** (ARTS AND MEDIA) an article or a report in a newspaper or magazine: *The plane crash was the front-page story in most newspapers.* **5** (*AmE*) = STOREY

storyboard /ˈstɔːribɔːd/ *noun* [C] (ARTS AND MEDIA) a series of drawings or pictures that show the plan for the story of a film, etc. ▶ **storyboard** *verb* [T]: *They started storyboarding various scenes for the film.*

storyline /ˈstɔːrilaɪn/ *noun* [C] (ARTS AND MEDIA, LITERATURE) the basic story in a book, play, film, etc: *The film is entertaining and has an interesting storyline.* **SYN plot¹**

stout /staʊt/ *adj.* **1** (used about a person) rather fat **2** strong and thick: *stout walking boots*

stove /stəʊv/ *noun* [C] **1** a piece of equipment that can burn various fuels and is used for heating rooms: *a gas/wood-burning stove* **2** (especially *AmE*) = COOKER: *She put a pan of water on the stove.*

stovetop /ˈstəʊvtɒp/ (*AmE*) = HOB

stow /stəʊ/ *verb* [T] ~ sth (away) to put sth away in a particular place until it is needed

stowaway /ˈstəʊəweɪ/ *noun* [C] a person who hides in a ship or plane so that they can travel without paying

straddle /ˈstrædl/ *verb* [T] **1** (used about a person) to sit or stand with your legs on each side of sb/sth: *to straddle a chair* **2** (used about a building, bridge, etc.) to cross, or exist on both sides of, a river, a road or an area of land

straggle /ˈstrægl/ *verb* [I] (used with an adverb or a preposition) **1** to walk, etc. more slowly than the rest of the group: *The children straggled along behind their parents.* **2** to grow, spread or move in an untidy way or in different directions: *Her wet hair straggled across her forehead.* ▶ **straggler** /-glə(r)/ *noun* [C] ▶ **straggly** /-gli/ *adj.*: *long straggly hair*

straight¹ 🔑 **A2** /streɪt/ *adj.*

• WITHOUT BENDS **1** with no bends or curves; going in one direction only: *a straight line* ◇ *He's got dark, straight hair.* ◇ *Keep your back straight!* ◇ *He was so tired he couldn't walk in a straight line.* ⊃ picture at **line¹**

• IN A LEVEL POSITION **2** in an exactly level or VERTICAL position: *That picture isn't straight.*

• HONEST **3** honest and direct: *Politicians never give a straight answer.* ◇ *Are you being straight with me?*

• TIDY **4** tidy or organized as it should be: *It took ages to put the room straight after we'd decorated it.*

• ALCOHOL **5** (*AmE*) = NEAT (5)

• PERSON **6** (*informal*) sexually attracted to people of the opposite sex **SYN heterosexual OPP gay¹ 7** (*informal*) used to describe a person who you think is too serious and boring

IDM get sth straight to make sure that you understand sth completely **keep a straight face** to stop yourself from smiling or laughing **put/set the record straight** → RECORD¹

straight² ⌕ **A2** /streɪt/ adv. **1** not in a curve or at an angle; in a straight line: Go **straight on** for about 2 miles until you come to some traffic lights. ◇ He was looking **straight ahead**. ◇ to sit up straight (= with a straight back) ᴐ note at **direction 2** without stopping; directly: I took the children straight home after school. ◇ to walk straight past somebody/something ◇ I'm going straight to bed when I get home. ◇ He joined the army straight from school. **3** in an honest and direct way: Tell me straight, doctor — is it serious?
IDM **go straight** (informal) to become honest after being a criminal **right/straight away** → AWAY¹ **straight out** in an honest and direct way: I told Asif straight out that I didn't want to see him any more.

ˈstraight angle noun [C] (**GEOMETRY**) an angle of 180° ᴐ picture at **angle¹**

straighten /'streɪtn/ verb [I, T] ~ (sth) (out); ~ (sth) (up) to become straight or to make sth straight: The road straightens out at the bottom of the hill. ◇ to straighten your tie ◇ I straightened up my back.
PHR V **straighten sth out** to remove the CONFUSION or difficulties from a situation **straighten up** to make your body straight and VERTICAL

straightforward ⌕⁺ **C1** **S** /ˌstreɪtˈfɔːwəd/ adj. **1** easy to do or understand; simple: straightforward instructions **2** honest and open: a straightforward person

straightjacket /'streɪtdʒækɪt/ = STRAITJACKET

strain¹ ⌕⁺ **C1** /streɪn/ noun
• PRESSURE **1** [U, C] pressure that is put on sth when it is pulled or pushed by a physical force: Running downhill puts strain on the knees. ◇ The rope finally broke **under the strain**.
• WORRY **2** [C, U] worry or mental pressure caused by having too much to deal with; sth that causes this pressure: to be **under** a lot of **strain** at work ◇ Mum's illness has **put a strain on** the whole family. ◇ I always find exams a terrible strain.
• INJURY **3** [C, U] (**HEALTH**) an injury to part of your body that is caused by using it too much
• TYPE OF ANIMAL, ETC. **4** [C] (**BIOLOGY**) a particular type of animal, plant or disease

strain² /streɪn/ verb **1** [T] (**HEALTH**) to injure a part of your body by using it too much: Don't read in the dark. You'll strain your eyes. ◇ I think I've strained a muscle in my neck. ᴐ note at **injure 2** [T, I] ~ (sth) (to do sth) to make a great mental or physical effort to do sth: I was straining to see what was happening. ◇ She strained her ears (= listened very hard) to catch what they were saying. ◇ Bend down as far as you can without straining. **3** [T] to put a lot of pressure on sth: Money problems have strained their relationship. **4** [T] to separate a solid and a liquid by pouring them into a special container with small holes in it: to strain tea/ vegetables/spaghetti

strained /streɪnd/ adj. **1** worried because of having too much to deal with: Martin looked tired and strained. **2** not natural or friendly: Relations between the two countries are strained.

strait /streɪt/ noun **1** [C, usually pl.] (**GEOGRAPHY**) a narrow piece of sea that joins two larger seas: the straits of Gibraltar **2** straits [pl.] a very difficult situation, especially one caused by having no money: The business is **in dire straits** financially and may go bankrupt.

straitjacket (also **straightjacket**) /'streɪtdʒækɪt/ noun [C] a piece of clothing like a jacket, with long arms that are tied to stop the person wearing it from behaving violently

strand ⌕⁺ **C1** /strænd/ noun [C] **1** a single piece of cotton, wool, hair, etc. **2** one part of a story, a situation or an idea

stranded /'strændɪd/ adj. left in a place that you cannot get away from: We were left stranded when our car broke down in the mountains.

strange ⌕ **A2** /streɪndʒ/ adj. **1** unusual or unexpected: A very strange thing happened to me on the way home. ◇ a strange noise **2** that you have not seen, visited, met, etc. before: a strange town ◇ My mother told me not to talk to strange men. ▶ **strangeness** noun [U]

strangely /'streɪndʒli/ adv. in an unusual or surprising way: She's been acting very strangely lately. ◇ **Strangely enough**, I don't feel at all nervous.

stranger ⌕ **B1** /'streɪndʒə(r)/ noun [C] **1** a person that you do not know: I had to ask a **complete stranger** to help me with my suitcase. **2** ~ (to ...) a person who is in a place that they do not know: I'm a stranger to this part of the country.

strangle /'stræŋgl/ verb [T] **1** to kill sb by pressing their throat and neck hard, especially with your fingers **SYN** **throttle¹** ᴐ look at **choke¹** (1) **2** to prevent sth from developing

strap /stræp/ noun [C] a long narrow piece of leather, cloth, plastic, etc. that you use for carrying sth or for keeping sth in position: a leather watch strap ▶ **strap** verb [T] (-pp-) (used with an adverb or a preposition): The racing driver was securely strapped into the car.

strapping /'stræpɪŋ/ noun [U] (**MEDICINE**) sticky material that is wrapped round a part of the body that is injured

strata /'strɑːtə/ plural of **stratum**

strategic ⌕⁺ **C1** /strə'tiːdʒɪk/ (also **strategical** /strə'tiːdʒɪkl/) adj. **1** helping you to achieve a plan; giving you an advantage: They made a strategic decision to sell off part of the company. **2** connected with a country's plans to achieve success in a war or in its defence system **3** (used about bombs and other weapons) intended to be fired at an enemy's country rather than be used in battle ▶ **strategically** /-kli/ adv.: The island is strategically important.

strategist /'strætədʒɪst/ noun [C] a person who is SKILLED at planning things, especially military activities

strategy ⌕ **A2** **O** /'strætədʒi/ noun (pl. -ies) (**BUSINESS**) **1** [C] a plan that you use in order to achieve sth **2** [U] the process of planning how to do or achieve sth: military strategy

stratification /ˌstrætɪfɪˈkeɪʃn/ noun [U] the division of sth into different layers or groups: social stratification

the stratosphere /ðə ˈstrætəsfɪə(r)/ noun [sing.] (**ASTRONOMY**, **GEOGRAPHY**) the layer of the earth's atmosphere between about 10 and 50 kilometres above the surface of the earth ᴐ picture at **atmosphere** ▶ **stratospheric** /ˌstrætəˈsferɪk/ adj.: stratospheric clouds/ozone

stratum /'strɑːtəm/ noun [C] (pl. strata /'strɑːtə/) (**GEOLOGY**) a layer or set of layers of rock, earth, etc. in the ground

stratus /'strɑːtəs/ noun [U] (**GEOGRAPHY**) a type of cloud that forms a continuous grey sheet covering the sky ᴐ picture at **cloud¹**

straw /strɔː/ noun **1** [U] (**AGRICULTURE**) the STEMS (= long thin parts) of some plants, for example WHEAT (= a plant grown for its grain) that are dried and then used for animals to sleep on or for making hats, covering a roof, etc: a straw hat **2** [C] one piece of straw **3** [C] a long plastic or paper tube that you can use for drinking through
IDM **the last/final straw** the last in a series of bad things that happen to you that makes you decide that you cannot accept the situation any longer

strawberry /ˈstrɔːbəri/ *noun* [C] (*pl.* -ies) a small soft red fruit with small white seeds on it: *strawberries and cream*

stray[1] /streɪ/ *verb* [I] **1** to go away from the place where you should be: *The sheep had strayed onto the road.* **2** to not keep to the subject you should be thinking about or discussing: *My thoughts strayed for a few moments.*

stray[2] /streɪ/ *noun* [C] a dog, cat, etc. that does not have a home ▸ **stray** *adj.* [only before noun]: *a stray dog*

streak[1] /striːk/ *noun* [C] **1** ~ (of sth) a thin line or mark: *The cat had brown fur with streaks of white in it.* **2** a part of a person's character that sometimes shows in the way they behave: *Vesna's a very caring girl, but she does have a selfish streak.* **3** a continuous period of bad or good luck in a game of sport: *The team is on a losing/winning streak at the moment.*

streak[2] /striːk/ *verb* [I] (used with an adverb or a preposition) to move fast: *A police car streaked by.*

streaked /striːkt/ *adj.* ~ (with sth) having lines of a different colour: *black hair streaked with grey*

stream[1] ? **B2** /striːm/ *noun* [C] **1** (GEOGRAPHY) a small river: *I waded across the shallow stream.* ⊃ note at **water**[1] ⊃ picture at **limestone 2** the continuous movement of a liquid, gas or light: *a stream of blood* **3** a continuous movement of people or things: *a stream of traffic* **4** a large number of things that happen one after another: *a stream of letters/phone calls/questions*

stream[2] /striːm/ *verb* **1** [I] (used with an adverb or a preposition) (used about a liquid, gas or light) to flow in large amounts: *Tears were streaming down his face.* ◇ *Sunlight was streaming in through the windows.* **2** [T] to play video or sound on a computer by receiving it as a continuous stream, from the internet for example **3** [I] (used with an adverb or a preposition) (used about people or things) to move somewhere in a continuous flow: *People were streaming out of the station.*

streamer /ˈstriːmə(r)/ *noun* [C] a long piece of coloured paper that you use for decorating a room before a party, etc.

streaming /ˈstriːmɪŋ/ *noun* [U] (COMPUTING) a method of sending or receiving data, especially video, over a computer network

streamline /ˈstriːmlaɪn/ *verb* [T] **1** to give a vehicle, etc. a long smooth shape so that it will move easily through air or water **2** to make an organization, a process, etc. work better by making it simpler ▸ **streamlined** *adj.*

ˌstream of ˈconsciousness *noun* [U] (LITERATURE) a continuous flow of ideas, thoughts and feelings, as they are experienced by a person; a style of writing that expresses this without using the usual methods of description and conversation

street ? **A1** /striːt/ *noun* **1** [C] (*abbr.* St, St.) a public road in a city or town that has houses and buildings on one side or both sides: *to walk along/down the street* ◇ *to cross the street* ◇ *I met Karen in the street this morning.* ◇ *a narrow street* ◇ *a street map of Oporto* ◇ *64 High Street* ◇ *The post office is in Sheep Street.* **2** [sing.] the ideas and opinions of ordinary people, especially people who live in cities: *The word on the street is that it's not going to happen.*

IDM the man in the street → **MAN**[1] **(out) on/onto the streets/street** (*informal*) without a home; outside, not in a house or other building: *young people living on the streets* **streets ahead (of sb/sth)** (*BrE, informal*) much better than sb/sth **(right) up your street**

(*informal*) (used about an activity, a subject, etc.) exactly right for you because you know a lot about it, like it very much, etc.

streetcar /ˈstriːtkɑː(r)/ (*AmE*) = TRAM

street cred /ˈstriːt kred/ *noun* [U] (*informal*) a way of behaving and dressing that is acceptable to young people, especially those who live in cities: *Those clothes do nothing for your street cred.*

ˈstreet light (*BrE also* ˈstreet lamp) *noun* [C] a light at the top of a tall post in the street ⊃ look at **lamp post**

streetwise /ˈstriːtwaɪz/ (*AmE also* ˈstreet-smart) *adj.* (*informal*) having the knowledge and experience that is needed to deal with the difficulties and dangers of life in a big city

strength ? **B1** ◉ /streŋkθ/ *noun*

• PHYSICAL POWER **1** [U] the quality of being physically strong; the amount of this quality that you have: *He pulled with all his strength but the rock would not move.* ◇ *I didn't have the strength to walk any further.* **2** [U] the ability of an object to hold heavy weights or not to break or be damaged easily: *All our suitcases are tested for strength before they leave the factory.*

• INFLUENCE **3** [U] the power and influence that sb has: *Germany's economic strength*

• OF A FEELING/AN OPINION **4** [U] how strong a feeling or an opinion is: *the strength of public opinion*

• GOOD QUALITY **5** [C, U] a good quality or ability that sb/sth has: *His greatest strength is his ability to communicate with people.* ◇ *the strengths and weaknesses of a plan* **OPP weakness**

IDM at full strength (used about a group) having all the people it needs or usually has: *Nobody is injured, so the team will be at full strength for the game.* **below strength** (used about a group) not having the number of people it needs or usually has **on the strength of** as a result of information, advice, etc.

strengthen ? **B2** ◉ /ˈstreŋkθn/ *verb* [I, T] to become stronger; to make sth stronger: *exercises to strengthen your muscles* **OPP weaken** ⊃ note at **currency**

strenuous /ˈstrenjuəs/ *adj.* needing or using a lot of effort or energy: *Don't do strenuous exercise after eating.* ◇ *She's making a strenuous effort to be on time every day.* ▸ **strenuously** *adv.*

streptococcus /ˌstreptəˈkɒkəs/ *noun* [C] (*pl.* streptococci /-kaɪ/) (BIOLOGY, HEALTH) a type of bacteria, some types of which can cause serious infections and illnesses

stress[1] ? **A2** ◉ /stres/ *noun* **1** [U, C] (PSYCHOLOGY) worry and pressure that is caused by problems and by having too much to deal with: *He's been under a lot of stress since his wife went into hospital.* ◇ *stress-related illnesses* ⊃ look at **trauma 2** [U, C] ~ (on sth) physical pressure put on sth that can damage it or make it lose its shape: *Heavy lorries put too much stress on this bridge.* ◇ *a stress fracture of the foot* (= one caused by such pressure) ◇ *They are studying how this metal behaves under stress.* **3** [U] ~ (on sth) the special attention that you give to sth because you think it is important: *We should put more stress on preventing crime.* **4** [C, U] ~ (on sth) (LANGUAGE) the force that you put on a particular word or part of a word when you speak: *In the word 'dictionary' the stress is on the first syllable, 'dic'.*

stress[2] ? **A2** ◉ /stres/ *verb* [T] to give sth special force or attention because it is important: *The minister stressed the need for a peaceful solution.* ◇ *Which syllable is stressed in this word?* **SYN emphasize**

stressed /strest/ *adj.* **1** (*also informal* ˌstressed ˈout) [not before noun] too anxious and tired to be able to relax: *He was feeling very stressed and tired.* **2** (LANGUAGE) (used about a syllable) pronounced with emphasis of physical pressure put on it: *stressed metal*

stressful /ˈstresfl/ *adj.* causing worry and pressure: *a stressful job*

ˈ**stress mark** *noun* [C] (**LANGUAGE**) a mark used to show which part of a particular word or syllable is pronounced with more force than others

stretch¹ ⚡ **B2** /stretʃ/ *verb* **1** [T, I] to pull sth so that it becomes longer or wider; to become longer or wider in this way: *The artist stretched the canvas tightly over the frame.* ◇ *My T-shirt stretched when I washed it.* **2** [I, T] ~ **(sth) (out)** to push out your arms, legs, etc. as far as possible: *He switched off the alarm clock, yawned and stretched.* ◇ *She stretched out on the sofa and fell asleep.* ◇ *She stretched out her arm to take the book.* **3** [I] ~ **(out)** to cover a large area of land or a long period of time: *The long white beaches stretch for miles along the coast.* **4** [T] to make use of all the money, ability, time, etc. that sb has available for use: *The test has been designed to really stretch students' knowledge.*
IDM **stretch your legs** to go for a walk after sitting down for a long time

stretch² ⚡ **B2** /stretʃ/ *noun* [C] **1** ~ **(of sth)** an area of land or water: *a dangerous stretch of road* **2** [usually sing.] the act of making the muscles in your arms, legs, back, etc. as long as possible: *Stand up, everybody, and have a good stretch.*
IDM **at a stretch** without stopping: *We travelled for six hours at a stretch.* **at full stretch** → FULL¹

stretcher /ˈstretʃə(r)/ *noun* [C] (**MEDICINE**) a piece of cloth supported by two POLES that is used for carrying a person who has been injured

stretchy /ˈstretʃi/ *adj.* (**stretchier; stretchiest**) that can easily be made longer or wider without tearing or breaking: *stretchy fabric*

strict ⚡ **B2** /strɪkt/ *adj.* **1** not allowing people to break rules or behave badly: *Samir's very strict with his children.* ◇ *I went to a very strict school.* **2** obeying the rules of a particular religion or belief exactly **3** that must be obeyed completely: *I gave her strict instructions to be home before 9.00.* **4** very exact: *a strict interpretation of the law*

strictly ⚡+ **B2** /ˈstrɪktli/ *adv.* **1** used to emphasize that sth happens or must happen in all circumstances: *Chewing gum is strictly forbidden in the classroom.* **2** with a lot of control and rules that must be obeyed
IDM **strictly speaking** to be exactly correct or accurate: *Strictly speaking, the tomato is not a vegetable. It's a fruit.*

stride¹ /straɪd/ *verb* [I] (used with an adverb or a preposition; not used in the perfect tenses) (*pt* **strode** /strəʊd/) to walk with long steps, often because you feel very confident or determined: *He strode up to the house and knocked on the door.*

stride² /straɪd/ *noun* [C] a long step
IDM **get into your stride** to start to do sth in a confident way and well after an uncertain beginning **make great strides** to make very quick progress **take sth in your stride** to deal with a new or difficult situation easily and without worrying

strident /ˈstraɪdnt/ *adj.* (used about a voice or a sound) loud and unpleasant

strife /straɪf/ *noun* [U] (*formal*) trouble or fighting between people or groups

strike¹ ⚡ **B2** /straɪk/ *noun* [C] **1** (**SOCIAL STUDIES**) a period of time when people refuse to go to work, usually because they want more money or better working conditions: *a one-day strike* ◇ *Union*

members voted to **go on strike**. **2** a sudden military attack, especially by aircraft

strike² ⚡ **B2** /straɪk/ *verb* (*pt, pp* **struck** /strʌk/)
• HIT **1** [T, I] (*formal*) to hit sb/sth: *The stone struck her on the head.* ◇ *The boat struck a rock and began to sink.*
• ATTACK **2** [I, T] to attack and harm sb/sth suddenly: *The building had been struck by lightning.* ◇ *The enemy aircraft struck just after 2 a.m.* ⊃ note at **disaster**
• GIVE AN IMPRESSION **3** [T] ~ **sb (as sth)** to give sb a particular impression: *Does anything here strike you as unusual?* ◇ *He strikes me as a very caring man.*
• OF A THOUGHT/IDEA **4** [T] (not used in the progressive tenses) (used about a thought or an idea) to come suddenly into sb's mind: *It suddenly struck me that she would be the ideal person for the job.*
• OF WORKERS **5** [I] (**SOCIAL STUDIES**) to stop work as a protest: *The workers voted to strike for more money.*
• MAKE FIRE **6** [T] to produce fire by rubbing sth, especially a match, on a surface: *She struck a match and lit the candle.*
• OF A CLOCK **7** [I, T] (used about a clock) to ring a bell so that people know what time it is: *The clock struck eight* (= eight o'clock).
• GOLD, OIL, ETC. **8** [T] to discover gold, oil, etc. in the ground
IDM **strike a balance (between A and B)** to find a middle way between two extremes **strike a bargain (with sb)** to make an agreement with sb **within striking distance** near enough to be reached or attacked easily
PHR V **strike back** to attack sb/sth that has attacked you **strike up sth (with sb)** to start a conversation or friendship with sb

striker /ˈstraɪkə(r)/ *noun* [C] **1** (**SOCIAL STUDIES**) a person who has stopped working as a protest **2** (**SPORT**) (in football) a player whose job is to score goals

striking ⚡+ **C1** /ˈstraɪkɪŋ/ *adj.* interesting and unusual enough to attract attention: *There was a striking similarity between the two men.* ▸ **strikingly** *adv.*

string¹ ⚡ **B1** /strɪŋ/ *noun*
• FOR TYING THINGS **1** [U, C] a piece of long, strong material like very thin rope, that you use for tying things: *a ball/piece/length of string* ◇ *The key is hanging on a string.*
• LINE OF THINGS **2** [C] ~ **of sth** a line of things that are joined together on the same piece of THREAD: *a string of beads*
• SERIES **3** [C] ~ **of sth** a series of people, things or events that follow one after another: *a string of visitors*
• IN COMPUTING **4** [C] a series of letters, numbers, words, etc.
• MUSICAL INSTRUMENTS **5** [C] (**MUSIC**) one of the pieces of thin wire, etc. that produce the sound on some musical instruments: *A guitar has six strings.* **6** the strings [pl.] (**MUSIC**) the instruments in an ORCHESTRA that have strings ⊃ picture at **instrument, orchestra**
• IN TENNIS **7** [C] one of the pieces of thin material that are stretched across a RACKET (= the thing you use to hit the ball in some sports such as tennis)
IDM **(with) no strings attached | without strings** with no special conditions **pull strings** → PULL¹

string² /strɪŋ/ *verb* [T] (*pt, pp* **strung** /strʌŋ/) ~ **sth (up)** to hang or tie sth in place, especially as a decoration: *Coloured lights were strung up along the front of the hotel.*
PHR V **string sth out** to make sth last longer than expected or necessary **string sth together** to put words or phrases together to make a sentence, speech, etc.

stringed instrument /ˈstrɪŋd ɪnstrəmənt/ *noun* [C] (**MUSIC**) any musical instrument with strings that you play with your fingers or with a BOW ⊃ note at **instrument** ⊃ picture at **instrument**

stringent /ˈstrɪndʒənt/ *adj.* (used about a law, rule, etc.) very strict

strip¹ **C1** /strɪp/ *noun* [C] **1** a long narrow piece of sth: *a strip of paper* **2** (*BrE*) (**SPORT**) the uniform that is worn by the members of a sports team when they are playing: *the team's **away strip** (= that they use when playing games away from home)*

strip² **C1** /strɪp/ *verb* (-pp-) **1** [I, T] ~ (**sth**) (**off**) to take off your clothes; to take off sb else's clothes: *The doctor asked him to strip to the waist.* ◇ *I was stripped and searched at the airport by two customs officers.* **2** [T] ~ **sth** (**off**) to remove sth that is covering a surface: *to strip the paint off a door* ◇ *to strip wallpaper* **3** [T] ~ **sb/sth** (**of sth**) to take sth away from sb/sth: *They stripped the house of all its furniture.*

stripe /straɪp/ *noun* [C] a long narrow line of colour: *Zebras have black and white stripes.*

striped /straɪpt/ (*also BrE, informal* **stripy** /ˈstraɪpi/) *adj.* marked with a pattern of STRIPES: *a red and white striped dress*

stripper /ˈstrɪpə(r)/ *noun* [C] a person whose job is to take off their clothes in order to entertain people

striptease /ˈstrɪptiːz/ *noun* [C, U] entertainment in which sb takes off their clothes, usually to music

strive **C1** /straɪv/ *verb* [I] (*pt* **strove** /strəʊv/, **strived**; *pp* **striven** /ˈstrɪvn/, **strived**) ~ (**for sth/to do sth**) (*formal*) to try very hard to do or get sth: *to strive for perfection*

strode /strəʊd/ past tense of **stride¹**

stroke¹ **B2** /strəʊk/ *noun*
- IN SPORT **1** [C] an act of hitting a ball, for example with a BAT or a RACKET **2** [C] one of the movements that you make when you are swimming, ROWING (= in a boat), etc. **3** [C, U] (in compounds) one of the styles of swimming: *Butterfly is the only stroke I can't do.* ⊃ look at **backstroke**, **breaststroke**, **crawl¹**
- ILLNESS **4** [C] (**HEALTH**) a sudden illness that attacks the brain and can leave a person unable to move part of their body, speak clearly, etc: *to **have a stroke***
- LUCK **5** [sing.] ~ **of sth** a single successful action or event: *It was **a stroke of luck** finding your ring on the beach, wasn't it?*
- WITH A PEN/BRUSH **6** [C] (**ART**) one of the movements that you make when you are writing or painting: *a brush stroke*
- OF A CLOCK, ETC. **7** [C] each of the sounds made by a clock or bell giving the hours: *At the first stroke it will be nine o'clock exactly.* ◇ *on the **stroke** of three* (= at three o'clock exactly)

IDM **at a/one stroke** with a single action **not do a stroke (of work)** to not do any work at all

stroke² /strəʊk/ *verb* [T] **1** to move your hand gently over sb/sth: *She stroked his hair affectionately.* ◇ *to stroke a dog* **2** to move sth somewhere with a gentle movement: *She stroked away his tears.*

stroll /strəʊl/ *noun* [C] a slow walk for pleasure: *to **go for a stroll** along the beach* ▶ **stroll** *verb* [I]

stroller /ˈstrəʊlə(r)/ (*AmE*) = PUSHCHAIR

strong **A1** /strɒŋ/ *adj.*
- POWERFUL **1** (used about a person) having physical power; able to lift or carry heavy things: *I need somebody strong to help me move this bookcase.* ◇ *to have strong arms/muscles* **2** (used about a natural force) powerful: *strong winds/currents/sunlight*
- NOT EASILY BROKEN **3** (used about an object) not easily broken or damaged: *That chair isn't strong enough for you to stand on.* ⊃ look at **fragile**
- HAVING A BIG EFFECT **4** having a big effect on the mind, body or senses: *a **strong smell** of garlic* ◇ *strong coffee* ◇ *a strong drink* (= with a lot of alcohol in it) ◇ *I have the **strong impression** that they don't like us.*
- OPINION/BELIEF **5** (used about opinions and beliefs) very powerful; difficult to fight against: *There was **strong opposition** to the idea.* ◇ *strong support for the government's plan* **SYN** **firm²**
- LIKELY TO SUCCEED **6** powerful and likely to succeed: *She's a strong candidate for the job.* ◇ *a strong team* **OPP** **weak**
- ECONOMY **7** (used about prices, the economy, etc.) having a value that is high or increasing: *strong economic growth* ◇ *The euro is getting stronger against the dollar.* **OPP** **weak** ⊃ note at **currency**
- NUMBER **8** great in number: *Sales were surprisingly strong last year.* **9** (after a number) having a particular number of people: *The army was 50 000 strong.* ⊃ noun **strength** for senses 1 to 9
- IN PHONETICS **10** (**LANGUAGE**) used to describe the way some words are pronounced when they are emphasized. For example, the strong form of *and* is /ænd/.

▶ **strongly** **B1** **W** *adv.*: *The directors are strongly opposed to the idea.* ◇ *to feel very strongly about something*

IDM **going strong** (*informal*) continuing, even after a long time: *The company was formed in 1851 and is still going strong.* **sb's strong point** something that a person is good at: *Maths is not my strong point.*

ˈstrong force *noun* [C] (**PHYSICS**) the natural force that holds the parts of an ATOM together ⊃ look at **electromagnetism**, **gravity** (1), **weak force**

stronghold /ˈstrɒŋhəʊld/ *noun* [C] **1** (**POLITICS**) an area in which there is a lot of support for a particular belief or group of people, especially a political party: *a Republican stronghold/a stronghold of Republicanism* **2** (**HISTORY**) a castle or a place that is strongly built and difficult to attack **3** an area where there are a large number of a particular type of animal: *This valley is one of the last strongholds of the Siberian tiger.*

ˌstrong-ˈminded *adj.* having firm ideas or beliefs **SYN** **determined**

strontium /ˈstrɒntiəm, ˈstrɒnʃi-/ *noun* [U] (*symb.* Sr) (**CHEMISTRY**) a chemical element. Strontium is a soft silver-white metal. ❶ For more information on the periodic table of elements, look at the **Reference Section** of this dictionary.

stroppy /ˈstrɒpi/ *adj.* (*BrE, slang*) (**stroppier**; **stroppiest**) (*informal*) (used about a person) easily annoyed and difficult to deal with

strove /strəʊv/ past tense of **strive**

struck /strʌk/ past tense, past participle of **strike¹**

structure¹ **A2** **O** /ˈstrʌktʃə(r)/ *noun* **1** [C, U] the way that the parts of sth are put together or organized: *the political and social structure of a country* ◇ *the grammatical structures of a language* **2** [C, U] the state of being well organized or planned; a careful plan: *Your essay needs (a) structure.* **3** [C] (**ARCHITECTURE**) a building or sth that has been built or made from a number of parts: *The old office block had been replaced by a modern glass structure.* ⊃ note at **building** ▶ **structural** **C1** **O** /ˈstrʌktʃərəl/ *adj.*

structure² ⏣ B2 ⊙ /'strʌktʃə(r)/ *verb* [T] to arrange sth in an organized way: *a carefully-structured English course*

struggle¹ ⏣ B2 /'strʌgl/ *verb* [I] **1** ~ **(with sth/for sth/to do sth)** to try very hard to do sth, especially when it is difficult: *We struggled up the stairs with our heavy suitcases.* ◇ *Maria was struggling with her English homework.* ◇ *The country is struggling for independence.* **2** ~ **(with sb/sth)**; ~ **(against sth)** to fight in order to prevent sth or to escape from sb: *He shouted and struggled but he couldn't get free.* ◇ *A passer-by was struggling with one of the robbers on the ground.* ◇ *He has been struggling against cancer for years.*
PHR V **struggle on** to continue to do sth although it is difficult: *I felt terrible but managed to struggle on to the end of the day.*

struggle² ⏣ B2 /'strʌgl/ *noun* [C] **1** ~ **(for/against sth)** a fight in which sb tries to do or get sth when this is difficult: *a struggle for independence* ◇ *They took up the struggle against racism.* ◇ *He will not give up the presidency without a struggle.* ⊃ note at **campaign**¹ **2** [usually sing.] something that is difficult to achieve: *It will be a struggle to get there on time.* **SYN** **effort**

strum /strʌm/ *verb* [I, T] (-mm-) (MUSIC) to play a guitar by moving your hand up and down over the strings

strung /strʌŋ/ past tense, past participle of **string**²

strut /strʌt/ *verb* [I] (-tt-) to walk in a proud way

strychnine /'strɪkniːn/ *noun* [U] (MEDICINE) a poisonous substance that can be used in very small amounts as a medicine

stub /stʌb/ *noun* [C] the short piece of a cigarette or pencil that is left after the rest of it has been used

stubble /'stʌbl/ *noun* [U] **1** (AGRICULTURE) the short parts of crops such as WHEAT (= a plant grown for its grain) that are left standing after the rest has been cut **2** the short hairs that grow on a man's face when he has not SHAVED for some time

stubborn /'stʌbən/ *adj.* not wanting to do what other people want you to do; refusing to change your plans or decisions: *She's too stubborn to apologize.* **SYN** **obstinate** ⊃ look at **pig-headed** ▶ **stubbornly** *adv.*: *He stubbornly refused to apologize.* ▶ **stubbornness** *noun* [U]

stuck¹ /stʌk/ past tense, past participle of **stick**¹

stuck² /stʌk/ *adj.* **1** not able to move: *This drawer's stuck. I can't open it at all.* ◇ *We were stuck in traffic for over two hours.* **2** not able to continue with an exercise, etc. because it is too difficult: *If you get stuck, ask your teacher for help.*

stud /stʌd/ *noun* **1** [C] a small, round, solid piece of metal that you wear through a hole in your ear or other part of the body **2** [C] a small piece of metal that sticks out from the rest of the surface that it is fixed

to: *a black leather jacket with studs all over it* **3** [C] one of the pieces of plastic or metal that stick out from the bottom of football, etc. boots and that help you stand up on wet ground **4** [C, U] (AGRICULTURE) a number of high quality horses or other animals that are kept for producing young animals; the place where these horses, etc. are kept: *a stud farm*

studded /'stʌdɪd/ *adj.* **1** covered or decorated with small pieces of metal **2** ~ **(with sth)** containing a lot of sth

student ⏣ A1 ⓢ /'stjuːdnt/ *noun* [C] (EDUCATION) a person who is studying at a school, college or university: *Paola is a medical student at Bristol University.* ◇ *a full-time/part-time student* ◇ *a postgraduate/research student* ⊃ look at **graduate**¹, **pupil** (1), **scholar** (2), **undergraduate**

studied /'stʌdid/ *adj.* [only before noun] (*formal*) carefully planned or done, especially when you are trying to give a particular impression

studio ⏣ B1 /'stjuːdiəʊ/ *noun* [C] (*pl.* -os) **1** (ARTS AND MEDIA, MUSIC) a room or building where films or TV programmes are made, or where music, radio programmes, etc. are recorded: *a film/TV/recording studio* **2** (ART) a room where an artist or a photographer works ⊃ note at **art 3** (*BrE also* 'studio flat) (*AmE also* 'studio apartment) a small flat with one main room for living and sleeping in and usually a kitchen and bathroom

studious /'stjuːdiəs/ *adj.* (used about a person) spending a lot of time studying

studiously /'stjuːdiəsli/ *adv.* with great care

study¹ ⏣ A1 ⊙ /'stʌdi/ *noun* (*pl.* -ies) **1** [U] (EDUCATION) the activity of learning about sth: *One hour every afternoon is left free for individual study.* ◇ *Physiology is the study of how living things work.* **2** studies [pl.] (EDUCATION) the subjects that you study; used in the name of some subjects: *to continue your studies* ◇ *business/media/Japanese studies* **3** [C] (EDUCATION) a piece of research that examines a question or a subject in detail: *They are doing a study of the causes of heart disease.* **4** [C] a room in a house where you go to read or write

study

When you study a subject, you need to **do your homework**, and then **give/hand it in**: *Have you done your physics homework?* ◇ *Hand in your essays on Friday.* You **revise/study for a test** or an **exam**: *He revised for four hours a day for his chemistry exam.* You **have/take a test** or **take/sit an exam** to see how well you know sth: *They have a vocabulary test every Monday.* ◇ *He took the TOEFL exam last week.* The **results** tell you your **marks/grades** or **scores**: *Have you had your results yet?* ◇ *He was thrilled when he got top/full marks for history.* ◇ *She got good grades for all five subjects.* ◇ *They achieved the necessary IELTS scores.* If you have been successful, you have **passed**. If you have been unsuccessful, you have **failed**: *She was delighted when she passed her maths exam.* ◇ *He failed his driving test twice.* The **pass mark** (= the number of marks that you need to pass an exam) is usually given as a percentage: *The pass mark is 65%.*

study² ⏣ A1 ⊙ /'stʌdi/ *verb* (studying; studies; *pt, pp* studied) **1** [T, I] ~ **(sth/for sth)** (EDUCATION) to spend time learning about sth: *to study French at university* ◇ *Leon has been studying hard for his exams.* ⊃ note at **job**, **subject**¹ **2** [T] to look at sth very carefully: *to study a map* ⊃ note at **examine**

structure

framework ♦ composition ♦ construction ♦ fabric ♦ make-up

These are all words for the way the different parts of sth combine together or the way that sth has been made.

structure *the structure of the human body*

framework *The report provides a framework for further research.*

composition *changes in the composition of the workforce*

construction *ships of steel construction*

fabric *the fabric of society*

make-up *the genetic make-up of plants*

stuff¹ 🔑 **B1** /stʌf/ *noun* [U] (*informal*) **1** used to refer to sth without using its name: *What's that green stuff at the bottom of the bottle?* ◇ *The shop was burgled and a lot of stuff was stolen.* ◇ *They sell stationery and stuff (like that).* ◇ *I'll put the swimming stuff in this bag.* **2** used to refer in general to things that people do, say, think, etc: *I've got lots of stuff to do tomorrow so I'm going to get up early.* ◇ *I don't believe all that stuff about him being robbed.* ◇ *I like reading and stuff.*

stuff² 🔑 **B2** /stʌf/ *verb* **1** [T] ~ **sth (with sth)** to fill sth with sth: *The pillow was stuffed with feathers.* ◇ *red peppers stuffed with rice* **2** [T] ~ **sth into sth** to put sth into sth else quickly or carelessly: *He quickly stuffed a few clothes into a suitcase.* **3** [T] ~ **sb/yourself (with sth)** (*informal*) to eat too much of sth; to give sb too much to eat: *Barry just sat there stuffing himself with sandwiches.* ◇ *Don't stuff the kids with chocolate before their dinner.* **4** [T, usually passive] to fill the body of a dead bird or animal with special material so that it looks as if it is alive: *They've got a stuffed crocodile in the museum.*

stuffing /'stʌfɪŋ/ *noun* [U] **1** a mixture of small pieces of food that you put inside a chicken, vegetable, etc. before you cook it **2** the material that you put inside CUSHIONS, soft toys, etc.

stuffy /'stʌfi/ *adj.* (**stuffier**; **stuffiest**) **1** (used about a room) too warm and having no fresh air **2** (*informal*) (used about a person) formal and old-fashioned

stumble 🔑+ **C1** /'stʌmbl/ *verb* [I] **1** ~ **(over/on sth)** to hit your foot against sth when you are walking or running and almost fall over **SYN** **trip²** **2** ~ **(over/through sth)** (LANGUAGE, MUSIC) to make a mistake when you are speaking, playing music, etc: *The newsreader stumbled over the name of the Russian tennis player.*
PHR V **stumble across/on sb/sth** to meet or find sb/sth by chance

'stumbling block *noun* [C] something that causes trouble or a problem, so that you cannot achieve what you want: *Money is still the stumbling block to settling the dispute.*

stump¹ /stʌmp/ *noun* [C] **1** the bottom part of a tree left in the ground after the rest has fallen or been cut down **2** the end of sth or the part that is left after the main part has been cut, broken off or worn away: *the stump of a pencil* ⊃ picture at **erosion** **3** (HEALTH) the short part of sb's leg or arm that is left after the rest has been cut off **4** [usually pl.] (SPORT) (in the game of CRICKET) one of the set of three VERTICAL wooden sticks that form the WICKET: *The ball went past the batsman and hit the stumps.*

stump² /stʌmp/ *verb* [T, usually passive] (*informal*) to cause sb to be unable to answer a question or find a solution for a problem: *I was completely stumped by question 14.*

stun 🔑+ **C1** /stʌn/ *verb* [T] (-nn-) **1** to make a person or an animal unconscious or confused, especially by hitting them or it on the head **2** to make a person very surprised by telling them some unexpected news: *His sudden death stunned his friends and colleagues.*
SYN **astound** ▸ **stunned** *adj.*

stung /stʌŋ/ past tense, past participle of **sting¹**

stunk /stʌŋk/ past participle of **stink**

stunning 🔑+ **B2** /'stʌnɪŋ/ *adj.* (*informal*) very attractive, impressive or surprising: *a stunning view*

stunt¹ /stʌnt/ *noun* [C] **1** (ARTS AND MEDIA) a very difficult or dangerous thing that sb does to entertain people or as part of a film: *Some actors do their own stunts, others use a stuntman.* **2** something that you do to get people's attention: *a publicity stunt*

stunt² /stʌnt/ *verb* [T] to stop sb/sth growing or developing properly: *A poor diet can stunt a child's growth.*

stuntman /'stʌntmæn/ *noun* [C] (*pl.* **-men** /-men/) (ARTS AND MEDIA) a man whose job is to do dangerous things in place of an actor in a film, etc.; a person who does dangerous things in order to entertain people

stuntwoman /'stʌntwʊmən/ *noun* [C] (*pl.* **-women** /-wɪmɪn/) (ARTS AND MEDIA) a woman whose job is to do dangerous things in place of an actor in a film, etc.; a person who does dangerous things in order to entertain people

stupendous /stju:'pendəs/ *adj.* very large or impressive: *a stupendous achievement*

stupid 🔑 **A2** /'stju:pɪd/ *adj.* **1** not intelligent or sensible: *Don't be so stupid — of course I'll help you!* ◇ *He was stupid to trust her.* ◇ *a stupid mistake/suggestion/question* **SYN** **silly** **2** [only before noun] (*informal*) used to show that you are angry or do not like sb/sth: *I'm tired of hearing about his stupid car.* ▸ **stupidity** /stju:'pɪdəti/ *noun* [U] ▸ **stupidly** *adv.*

stupor /'stju:pə(r)/ *noun* [sing., U] the state of being nearly unconscious or being unable to think properly

sturdy /'stɜ:di/ *adj.* (**sturdier**; **sturdiest**) strong and healthy; that will not break easily: *sturdy legs* ◇ *sturdy shoes* ▸ **sturdily** /-dɪli/ *adv.* ▸ **sturdiness** *noun* [U]

stutter /'stʌtə(r)/ *verb* [T, I] (LANGUAGE) to have difficulty when you speak, so that you keep repeating the first sound of a word ▸ **stutter** *noun* [sing.]: *to have a stutter*

sty /staɪ/ *noun* [C] (*pl.* **sties**) **1** = PIGSTY **2** (*also* **stye** /staɪ/) (HEALTH) a painful spot on the EYELID (= the skin that covers the eye)

style¹ 🔑 **A1** **S** /staɪl/ *noun* **1** [C, U] the way that sth is done, built, etc: *a new style of architecture* ◇ *The writer's style is very clear and simple.* ◇ *an American-style education system* **2** [C] the fashion, shape or design of sth: *We stock all the latest styles.* ◇ *I like your new hairstyle.* ⊃ look at **hairstyle** **3** [U] the ability to do things in a way that other people admire: *He's got no sense of style.* **4** [C] (BIOLOGY) the long thin part of the CARPEL (= the female part in the middle of a flower) that supports the STIGMA ⊃ picture at **flower¹**

style² /staɪl/ *verb* [T] to design, make or shape sth in a particular way: *He'd had his hair styled at an expensive salon.*
PHR V **style sth/yourself on sth/sb** to copy the style, manner or appearance of sb/sth: *a coffee bar styled on a Parisian cafe* **SYN** **model¹**

stylish /'staɪlɪʃ/ *adj.* fashionable and attractive: *She's a stylish dresser.*

stylist /'staɪlɪst/ *noun* [C] a person whose job is cutting and shaping people's hair

stylistic /staɪ'lɪstɪk/ *adj.* (ART) connected with the style an artist uses in a particular piece of art, writing or music: *stylistic analysis* ◇ *stylistic features* ▸ **stylistically** /-kli/ *adv.*

stylized (*BrE also* **-ised**) /'staɪlaɪzd/ *adj.* (ART, LITERATURE) drawn, written, etc. in a way that is not natural or realistic: *a stylized drawing of a house*

stylus /'staɪləs/ *noun* [C] (*pl.* **styluses**, **styli** /-laɪ/) **1** a device on a RECORD PLAYER that looks like a small needle and is placed on the record in order to play it **2** (COMPUTING) a special pen used to write text or draw an image on a special computer screen

stymie /ˈstaɪmi/ *verb* [T] (stymieing, stymying; stymies; *pt, pp* stymied) to prevent sb from doing sth that they have planned or want to do; to prevent sth from happening **SYN** foil[1]

suave /swɑːv/ *adj.* (usually used about a man) confident, attractive and polite, sometimes in a way that does not seem sincere

sub /sʌb/ *noun* [C] (*informal*) **1** = SUBMARINE **2** (**SPORT**) a SUBSTITUTE who replaces another player in a team

sub- /sʌb/ *prefix* **1** (in nouns and adjectives) below; less than: *sub-zero temperatures* ◇ *a subtropical* (= almost tropical) *climate* **2** (in nouns and adjectives) under: *subway* ◇ *submarine* **3** (in verbs and nouns) making a smaller part of sth: *subdivide* ◇ *subset*

subarctic /ˌsʌbˈɑːktɪk/ *adj.* (**GEOGRAPHY**) connected with the region just south of the Arctic Circle

the subconscious /ðə ˌsʌbˈkɒnʃəs/ *noun* [sing.] (**PSYCHOLOGY**) the hidden part of your mind that can affect the way you behave without you realizing ⊃ look at **unconscious** ▸ subconscious *adj.*: *the subconscious mind* ◇ *Many advertisements work at a subconscious level.* ▸ subconsciously *adv.*

subcontinent /ˌsʌbˈkɒntɪnənt/ *noun* [sing.] (**GEOGRAPHY**) a large land mass that forms part of a continent, especially the part of Asia that includes India, Pakistan and Bangladesh

subcontract /ˌsʌbkənˈtrækt/ *verb* [T] ~ **sth (to sb)** (**BUSINESS**) to pay a person or company to do some of the work that you have been given a contract to do

subculture /ˈsʌbkʌltʃə(r)/ *noun* [C] (**SOCIAL STUDIES**) the behaviour and beliefs of a particular group of people in society that are different from those of most people: *the criminal/drug/youth subculture*

subcutaneous /ˌsʌbkjuˈteɪniəs/ *adj.* (**ANATOMY**) under the skin: *a subcutaneous injection* ⊃ picture at **skin**[1]

subdivide /ˈsʌbdɪvaɪd, ˌsʌbdɪˈvaɪd/ *verb* [I, T] to divide into smaller parts; to be divided into smaller parts ▸ subdivision /ˈsʌbdɪvɪʒn/ *noun* [U, C]

subdue /səbˈdjuː/ *verb* [T] to defeat sb/sth or bring sb/sth under control

subdued /səbˈdjuːd/ *adj.* **1** (used about a person) quieter and with less energy than usual **2** not very loud or bright: *subdued laughter/lighting*

subject[1] ᴵ ᴬ¹ Ⓞ /ˈsʌbdʒɪkt, -dʒekt/ *noun* [C] **1** a person or thing that is being considered, shown or talked about: *What subject is the lecture on?* ◇ *What are your views on this subject?* ◇ *I've tried several times to bring up/raise the subject of money.*
2 (**EDUCATION**) an area of knowledge that you study at school, university, etc: *My favourite subjects at school are biology and French.* **3** (**ART**) a person or thing that is the main feature of a picture or photo, or that a work of art is based on: *Focus the camera on the subject.* ◇ *Classical landscapes were a popular subject with many eighteenth-century painters.*
4 (**GRAMMAR**) the person or thing that does the action described by the verb in a sentence: *In the sentence 'The cat sat on the mat', 'the cat' is the subject.* ⊃ look at **object**[1] (4) **5** (**POLITICS**) a person from a particular country, especially one with a king or queen; a citizen: *a British subject*
IDM change the subject → CHANGE[1]

subject[2] Ⓦ /səbˈdʒekt/ *verb* [T] ~ **sth (to sth)** to bring a country or group of people under your control, especially by using force: *The Roman Empire subjected most of Europe to its rule.*
PHRV subject sb/sth to sth to make sb/sth experience sth unpleasant: *He was subjected to verbal and physical abuse from the other boys.*

subject[3] ᴵ ᴮ² Ⓞ /ˈsʌbdʒɪkt, -dʒekt/ *adj.* **1** ~ **to sth** likely to be affected by sth: *The area is subject to regular flooding.* ◇ *People who eat a lot of fatty foods are more subject to heart attacks.* **2** ~ **to sth** depending on sth as a condition: *The plan for new housing is still subject to approval by the minister.* **3** ~ **to sb/sth** controlled by or having to obey sb/sth: *Everyone is subject to the law.*

subjective Ⓦ /səbˈdʒektɪv/ *adj.* based on your own tastes and opinions instead of on facts **OPP** objective[2] ▸ subjectively *adv.*

subject matter *noun* [U] (**ART**, **ARTS AND MEDIA**, **LITERATURE**) the ideas or information contained in a book, speech, painting, etc.

subjunctive /səbˈdʒʌŋktɪv/ *noun* [sing.] (**GRAMMAR**) the form of a verb in certain languages that expresses doubt, possibility, a wish, etc. ▸ subjunctive *adj.*

sublet /ˌsʌbˈlet/ *verb* [T, I] (subletting; *pt, pp* sublet) ~ **(sth) (to sb)** (**FINANCE**) to rent to sb else all or part of a property that you rent from the owner

sublime[1] /səˈblaɪm/ *adj.* of extremely high quality that makes you admire sth very much ▸ sublimely *adv.*

sublime[2] /səˈblaɪm/ (*also* sublimate /ˈsʌblɪmeɪt/) *verb* [I] (**CHEMISTRY**) (used about a solid substance) to change into a gas when heated and back into a solid after cooling, without first becoming a liquid ▸ sublimation /ˌsʌblɪˈmeɪʃn/ *noun* [U]

subliminal /ˌsʌbˈlɪmɪnl/ *adj.* affecting your mind even though you are not aware of it: *subliminal advertising* ▸ subliminally /-nəli/ *adv.*

submarine /ˌsʌbməˈriːn, ˈsʌbməriːn/ *noun* [C] a type of ship that can travel under the water as well as on the surface

submerge /səbˈmɜːdʒ/ *verb* [I, T] to go under the surface of water or liquidr; to make sth go under the surface of water or liquid: *The fields were submerged by the floods.* ▸ submerged *adj.*

submersible[1] /səbˈmɜːsəbl/ (*AmE also* submergible /səbˈmɜːdʒəbl/) *adj.* that can be used UNDERWATER: *a submersible camera*

submersible[2] /səbˈmɜːsəbl/ *noun* [C] a SUBMARINE that goes under the water for short periods

---

▼ COLLOCATIONS

subject

A student can **do/study** a **course/subject** at college or university: *Rhodri did history at Exeter University.* ◇ *Lucy did a course in art and design.* ◇ *She's studying health and psychology at Witney College.* ◇ (BrE, formal) He read Classics at Cambridge. A **lecturer/tutor** teaches in a **department** of a college or university: *She's an economics lecturer.* ◇ *Dr Scragg was my history tutor at university.* ◇ *The anthropology department is expanding.* A **professor** is a **lecturer** at the highest level in a university: *He's professor of linguistics at Bangor University.* A student **attends/goes to lectures, seminars** and **tutorials**: *She went to a seminar on Wittgenstein with Professor Brown.* ◇ *The genetics lectures are on a different campus.* At the end of a course a student is awarded a **degree** or a **diploma**: *a sociology degree* ◇ *a diploma in food hygiene* An **undergraduate** is a student studying for their first degree, a **graduate** is sb who has got a university degree and a **postgraduate** already holds a first degree and is doing further study or research: *Good science graduates are always in demand.* ◇ *She completed a postgraduate course in journalism.*

submission ⓘ+ **C1** /səbˈmɪʃn/ *noun* **1** [U] the accepting of sb else's power or control because they have defeated you **2** [U, C] the act of giving a plan, document, etc. to an official organization so that it can be studied and considered; the plan, document, etc. that you send

submissive /səbˈmɪsɪv/ *adj.* ready to obey other people and do whatever they want

submit ⓘ **B2** /səbˈmɪt/ *verb* (-tt-) **1** [T] ~ **sth (to sb/sth)** to give a plan, document, etc. to an official organization so that it can be studied and considered: *to submit an application/complaint/claim* **2** [I] ~ **(to sb/sth)** (*formal*) to accept sb/sth's power or control because they have defeated you: *After a bitter struggle the rebels were forced to submit to government troops.*

subordinate¹ /səˈbɔːdɪnət/ *adj.* ~ **(to sb/sth)** having less power or authority than sb else; less important than sth else ▶ **subordinate** *noun* [C]: *the relationship between superiors and their subordinates*

subordinate² /səˈbɔːdɪneɪt/ *verb* [T] to treat one person or thing as less important than another

su‚bordinate ˈclause *noun* [C] (**GRAMMAR**) a group of words that is not a sentence but that adds information to the main part of the sentence: *In the sentence 'We left early because it was raining', 'because it was raining' is the subordinate clause.*

subplot /ˈsʌbplɒt/ *noun* [C] (**LITERATURE**) a series of events in a play, novel, etc. that is separate from but linked to the main story

subpoena /səˈpiːnə/ *noun* [C, U] (**LAW**) a written order to attend court to give evidence: *She is appearing today under subpoena* (= she has been given a subpoena to appear in court). ▶ **subpoena** *verb* [T]: *The court subpoenaed her to appear as a witness.*

‚sub-ˈprime (*BrE*) (*AmE* **subprime**) *adj.* (**FINANCE**) connected with the practice of lending money to people who may not be able to pay the money back: *sub-prime mortgages/loans* ◇ *sub-prime lenders/ borrowers*

sub-Saharan /‚sʌb səˈhɑːrən/ *adj.* [only before noun] (**GEOGRAPHY**) from or connected with areas in Africa that are south of the Sahara Desert: *sub-Saharan Africa*

subscribe /səbˈskraɪb/ *verb* [I] ~ **(to sth)** **1** (**ARTS AND MEDIA**) to pay an amount of money regularly in order to receive or use sth: *Do you subscribe to 'Marie Claire'?* ◇ *We subscribe to several sports channels* (= on TV). **2** to pay money regularly to be a member of an organization or to support a charity ▶ **subscriber** ⓘ+ **C1** *noun* [C] ~ **(to sth)**: *subscribers to satellite and cable TV* **PHRV** **subscribe to sth** to agree with an idea, a belief, etc: *I don't subscribe to the view that all war is wrong.*

subscription ⓘ+ **C1** /səbˈskrɪpʃn/ *noun* [C, U] ~ **(to sth)** (**ARTS AND MEDIA**) an amount of money that you pay regularly to receive or use sth, be a member of a club, or support a charity. etc; the act of paying this money: *a subscription to Netflix*

subsequent ⓘ+ **B2** ⓦ /ˈsʌbsɪkwənt/ *adj.* [only before noun] (*formal*) coming after or later: *I thought that was the end of the matter but subsequent events proved me wrong.* ▶ **subsequently** ⓘ+ **B2** *adv.*: *The rumours were subsequently found to be untrue.*

subservient /səbˈsɜːviənt/ *adj.* **1** ~ **(to sb/sth)** too ready to obey other people **2** ~ **(to sth)** (*formal*) considered to be less important than sth else ▶ **subservience** /-əns/ *noun* [U]

subset /ˈsʌbset/ *noun* [C] a smaller group of people or things formed from the members of a larger group

subside /səbˈsaɪd/ *verb* [I] **1** to become calmer or quieter: *The storm seems to be subsiding.* **2** (used about land, a building, etc.) to sink down into the ground ▶ **subsidence** /səbˈsaɪdns, ˈsʌbsɪdns/ *noun* [U]

subsidiarity /səbˌsɪdiˈærəti, ‚sʌbsɪ-/ *noun* [U] (**POLITICS**) the principle that a central authority should not be very powerful, and should only control things that cannot be controlled by local organizations

subsidiary¹ /səbˈsɪdiəri/ *adj.* connected with sth but less important than it

subsidiary² /səbˈsɪdiəri/ *noun* [C] (*pl.* -ies) a business company that belongs to and is controlled by another larger company

subsidize (*BrE also* -ise) /ˈsʌbsɪdaɪz/ *verb* [T] (**ECONOMICS**) (used about a government, etc.) to give money to sb or an organization to help pay for sth: *Public transport should be subsidized.*

subsidy ⓘ+ **C1** /ˈsʌbsədi/ *noun* [C, U] (*pl.* -ies) (**ECONOMICS**) money that the government, etc. pays to help an organization or to keep the cost of a service low: *agricultural/state/housing subsidies*

subsist /səbˈsɪst/ *verb* [I] ~ **(on sth)** to manage to live with very little food or money: *Old people often subsist on very small incomes.*

subsistence /səbˈsɪstəns/ *noun* [U] (**AGRICULTURE**) the state of having just enough money or food to stay alive: *to live at subsistence level* (= having the smallest amount of food or money necessary to stay alive) ◇ *subsistence farming* (= growing enough only to live on, not to sell) ◇ *subsistence crops* ⊃ look at **cash crop**

subsoil /ˈsʌbsɔɪl/ *noun* [U] (**GEOLOGY**) the layer of soil between the surface of the ground and the hard rock below it ⊃ look at **topsoil**

substance ⓘ **B1** ⓦ /ˈsʌbstəns/ *noun* **1** [C] (**CHEMISTRY**) a solid or liquid material: *poisonous substances* ◇ *The cloth is coated in a new waterproof substance.* **2** [U] importance, value or truth: *The manager's report gives substance to these allegations.* **3** [U] the most important or main part of sth: *What was the substance of his argument?*

substandard /‚sʌbˈstændəd/ *adj.* of poor quality; not as good as usual or as it should be

substantial ⓘ+ **C1** ⓦ /səbˈstænʃl/ *adj.* **1** large in amount: *The storms caused substantial damage.* ◇ *a substantial sum of money* **2** large and/or strongly built **OPP** **insubstantial**

substantially ⓘ+ **C1** ⓦ /səbˈstænʃəli/ *adv.* **1** very much: *House prices have fallen substantially.* **SYN** **greatly** **2** generally; in most points: *What she says is substantially true.*

substantiate /səbˈstænʃieɪt/ *verb* [T] (*formal*) to provide information or evidence to prove that sth is true: *The accusations could not be substantiated.*

substantive ⓦ /səbˈstæntɪv, ˈsʌbstəntɪv/ *adj.* (*formal*) dealing with real, important or serious things: *substantive issues*

substitute ⓘ+ **C1** /ˈsʌbstɪtjuːt/ *noun* [C] ~ **(for sb/sth)** a person or thing that takes the place of sb/sth else: *The bus was a poor substitute for their car.* ▶ **substitute** ⓘ+ **C1** ⓦ *verb* [T] ~ **sb/sth (for sb/sth)**: *You can substitute margarine for butter.* ▶ **substitution** ⓘ+ **C1** ⓦ /‚sʌbstɪˈtjuːʃn/ *noun* [U, C]

‚substitute ˈteacher (*AmE*) = **SUPPLY TEACHER**

substrate /'sʌbstreɪt/ *noun* [C] (**BIOLOGY**) a substance or layer which is under sth or on which sth happens, for example the surface on which a living thing grows and feeds

substructure /'sʌbstrʌktʃə(r)/ *noun* [C] (**ARCHITECTURE**) a base or structure that is below another structure and that supports it ➔ look at **superstructure**

subterranean /ˌsʌbtə'reɪniən/ *adj.* (*formal*) (**GEOGRAPHY**) under the ground: *a subterranean cave/passage/ tunnel*

subtitle /'sʌbtaɪtl/ *noun* [C, usually pl.] (**ARTS AND MEDIA**) words at the bottom of the picture on TV or at the cinema. Subtitles translate the words of a foreign film or programme, or show the words that are spoken to help people with hearing problems: *a Polish film with English subtitles* ➔ look at **dub** (2) ▸ **subtitle** *verb* [T, usually passive]: *a Spanish film subtitled in English*

subtle 𝔹+ **C1** /'sʌtl/ *adj.* (**subtler** /-tələ(r)/; **subtlest** /-tlɪst/) **1** not very easy to notice; not very strong or bright: *subtle colours* ◇ *I noticed a subtle difference in her.* **2** very clever; and using indirect methods to achieve sth: *Advertisements persuade us to buy things in very subtle ways.* ▸ **subtlety** /-tlti/ *noun* [U, C] (*pl.* **-ies**) ▸ **subtly** /-təli/ *adv.*

subtotal /'sʌbtəʊtl/ *noun* [C] (**MATHEMATICS**) the total of a set of numbers, which is then added to other totals to give a final number

subtract /səb'trækt/ *verb* [T] ~ **sth (from sth)** (**MATHEMATICS**) to take one number or quantity away from another: *If you subtract five from nine you get four.* **OPP** **add** ▸ **subtraction** /-'trækʃn/ *noun* [U, C]

subtropical /ˌsʌb'trɒpɪkl/ *adj.* (**GEOGRAPHY**) in or connected with regions that are near tropical parts of the world: *subtropical forests*

suburb 𝔹+ **B2** /'sʌbɜːb/ *noun* [C] (**GEOGRAPHY**) an area where people live that is outside the central part of a town or city: *Most people live **in the suburbs** and work in the centre of town.* ▸ **suburban** 𝔹+ **C1** /sə'bɜːbən/ *adj.* ❶ People often think of life in the suburbs as dull, so **suburban** sometimes means 'dull and uninteresting'. ▸ **suburbia** /-biə/ *noun* [U]

subversive /səb'vɜːsɪv/ *adj.* trying to destroy or damage a government, religion or political system by attacking it secretly and in an indirect way ▸ **subversion** /-'vɜːʃn/ *noun* [U] ▸ **subversive** *noun* [C]: *She was a known political subversive.*

subvert /səb'vɜːt/ *verb* [T] to try to destroy or damage a government, religion or political system by attacking it secretly and in an indirect way

subway /'sʌbweɪ/ *noun* [C] **1** (*BrE*) a tunnel under a busy road or railway that people can walk through to cross to the other side **2** (*AmE*) = UNDERGROUND³

succeed 𝔹 **A2** /sək'siːd/ *verb* **1** [I] ~ **(in sth/doing sth)** to manage to achieve what you want; to do well: *Our plan succeeded.* ◇ *A good education will help you succeed in life.* ◇ *to succeed in passing an exam* **OPP** **fail¹** ➔ *noun* **success** **2** [T, I] ~ **sb (as sth)**; ~ **(to sth)** to have a job or an important position after sb else: *Who succeeded Kennedy as president?* ◇ *She succeeded to the throne* (= became queen) *in 1558.* ➔ *noun* **succession**

success 𝔹 **A1** /sək'ses/ *noun* **1** [U] the fact that you have achieved what you want; doing well and becoming famous, rich, etc: *Hard work is **the key to success**.* ◇ *Her attempts to get a job for the summer have not **met with** much success* (= she hasn't managed to do it). ◇ *What's the secret of your success?* **OPP** **failure 2** [C] the thing that you achieve; sth that becomes very popular: *He really tried to **make a success** of the business.* **OPP** **failure**

successful 𝔹 **A2** 🌐 /sək'sesfl/ *adj.* having achieved what you wanted; having become popular, rich, etc: *a successful attempt to climb Mount Everest* ◇ *a successful actor* **OPP** **unsuccessful** ▸ **successfully** 𝔹 **B1** 🌐 /-fəli/ *adv.*

▼ SYNONYMS

successful

profitable ◆ commercial ◆ lucrative ◆ economic
These words all describe sb/sth that is making or is likely to make money.

successful *The company has had another successful year.*

profitable *a highly profitable business*

commercial *The film was not a commercial success* (= made no profit).

lucrative *They do a lot of business in lucrative overseas markets.*

economic *Local shops stop being economic when supermarkets open.*

succession 𝔹+ **C1** /sək'seʃn/ *noun* **1** [C, usually sing.] a number of people or things that follow each other in time or order; a series: *a succession of events/ problems/visitors* **2** [U] the act of taking over an official position or title; the right to take over an official position or title, especially to become the king or queen of a country: *Prince William is second in order of succession to the throne.* ➔ *verb* **succeed** **IDM** **in succession** following one after another: *There have been three deaths in the family in quick succession.*

successive 𝔹+ **C1** /sək'sesɪv/ *adj.* [only before noun] following immediately one after the other: *This was their fourth successive win.* **SYN** **consecutive** ▸ **successively** *adv.*

successor 𝔹+ **C1** /sək'sesə(r)/ *noun* [C] a person or thing that comes after sb/sth else and takes their/its place ➔ look at **predecessor**

succinct /sək'sɪŋkt/ *adj.* said clearly, in a few words ▸ **succinctly** *adv.*

succulent /'sʌkjələnt/ *adj.* (used about fruit, vegetables and meat) containing a lot of juice and tasting very good

succumb /sə'kʌm/ *verb* [I] ~ **(to sth)** to not be able to fight an attack, an illness, etc: *He succumbed to temptation and stole the wallet.*

such 𝔹 **A2** 🌐 /sʌtʃ/ *det., pron.* **1** used for emphasizing the degree of sth: *It was such a fascinating book that I couldn't put it down.* **2** (used for referring to sth/sth that you mentioned earlier) of this or that type: *I don't believe in ghosts. There's **no such thing**.* ◇ *The economic situation is such that we all have less money to spend.* **3** used to describe the result of sth: *The statement was worded **in such a way that** it did not upset anyone.* **IDM** **as such** as the word is usually understood; exactly: *It's not a promotion as such, but it will mean more money.* **such as** for example: *Fatty foods such as chips are bad for you.*

suck 𝔹+ **C1** /sʌk/ *verb* **1** [T] to pull a liquid into your mouth: *to suck milk up through a straw* **2** [I, T] ~ **(at/on) sth** to have sth in your mouth and keep touching it with your tongue: *He was noisily sucking (on) a sweet.* **3** [T] (used with an adverb or a preposition) to pull sth in a particular direction, using force: *Vacuum cleaners suck up the dirt.*

sucker /ˈsʌkə(r)/ *noun* [C] **1** (*informal*) a person who believes everything that you tell them and who is easy to trick or persuade to do sth **2** a part of some animals or insects that is used for helping them stick onto a surface ⊃ picture at **animal**

sucrose /ˈsuːkrəʊz, -krəʊs/ *noun* [U] the form of sugar that comes from SUGAR CANE and SUGAR BEET, and that is used to make food sweet ⊃ look at **dextrose, fructose, glucose, lactose**

suction /ˈsʌkʃn/ *noun* [U] the act of removing air or liquid from a space or container so that sth else can be pulled into it or so that two surfaces can stick together: *A vacuum cleaner works by suction.*

sudden ⟨² B1⟩ /ˈsʌdn/ *adj.* done or happening quickly, or when you do not expect it: *a sudden decision/change* ▶ **suddenness** *noun* [U]
IDM **all of a sudden** quickly and unexpectedly: *All of a sudden the lights went out.* **sudden death** (**SPORT**) a way of deciding who wins a game where the score is equal by playing one more point or game

suddenly ⟨² A2⟩ /ˈsʌdənli/ *adv.* quickly and unexpectedly: *I suddenly realized what I had to do.* ◇ *It all happened so suddenly.*

sudoku /suˈdəʊkuː, -ˈdɒku:/ *noun* [U, C] a number PUZZLE (= a game) with nine squares, each containing nine smaller squares in which you have to write the numbers 1 to 9 in a particular pattern

suds /sʌdz/ *noun* [pl.] the bubbles that you get when you mix soap and water

sue ⟨²+ C1⟩ /su:/ *verb* [I, T] ~ (**sb**) (**for sth**) (**LAW**) to go to court and ask for money from sb because they have done sth bad to you, or said sth bad about you: *to sue somebody for libel/breach of contract/damages*

suede /sweɪd/ *noun* [U] a type of soft leather that does not have a smooth surface and feels a little like cloth

suet /ˈsuːɪt/ *noun* [U] a type of hard animal fat that is used in cooking

suffer ⟨² B1⟩ /ˈsʌfə(r)/ *verb* **1** [I, T] ~ (**from sth**); ~ (**for sth**); ~ (**sth**) to experience sth unpleasant, for example pain, bad feelings, difficulty, etc: *Mary often suffers from severe headaches.* ◇ *He made a rash decision and now he's suffering for it.* ◇ *Our troops suffered heavy losses.* **2** [I] to become worse in quality: *My work is suffering as a result of problems at home.* ⊃ note at **trend**[1] ▶ **sufferer** /-fərə(r)/ *noun* [C]: *asthma sufferers*

suffering ⟨²+ B2⟩ /ˈsʌfərɪŋ/ *noun* **1** [U] physical or mental pain: *Death finally brought an end to her suffering.* ◇ *This war has caused widespread human suffering.* **2 sufferings** [pl.] feelings of pain and unhappiness: *The hospice aims to ease the sufferings of the dying.*

sufficiency /səˈfɪʃnsi/ *noun* [sing.] ~ (**of sth**) (*formal*) an amount of sth that is enough for a particular purpose

sufficient ⟨²+ B2 W⟩ /səˈfɪʃnt/ *adj.* (*formal*) as much as is necessary; enough: *We have sufficient oil reserves to last for three months.* **OPP** **insufficient** ▶ **sufficiently** ⟨²+ B2 W⟩ *adv.*

suffix /ˈsʌfɪks/ *noun* [C] (**GRAMMAR**) a letter or group of letters that you add at the end of a word and that changes the meaning of the word or the way it is used: *To form the noun from the adjective 'sad', add the suffix 'ness'.* ⊃ look at **affix**[2], **prefix**

suffocate /ˈsʌfəkeɪt/ *verb* [I, T] to die because there is no air to breathe; to kill sb by not letting them breathe air ▶ **suffocating** *adj.* ▶ **suffocation** /ˌsʌfəˈkeɪʃn/ *noun* [U]

suffrage /ˈsʌfrɪdʒ/ *noun* [U] (**POLITICS**) the right to vote in political elections: *universal suffrage* (= the right of all adults to vote) ◇ *women's suffrage*

suffragette /ˌsʌfrəˈdʒet/ *noun* [C] (**HISTORY, POLITICS**) a member of a group of women who, in the UK and the US in the early part of the twentieth century, worked to get the right for women to vote in political elections

sugar ⟨² A1⟩ /ˈʃʊɡə(r)/ *noun* **1** [U] a sweet substance that you get from certain plants: *Do you take sugar in tea?* **2** [C] (in a cup of tea, coffee, etc.) the amount of sugar that a small spoon can hold; a LUMP (= piece) of sugar **3** [C] any of various sweet substances that are found naturally in plants, fruit, etc: *Glucose and fructose are sugars.* ⊃ picture at **DNA, photosynthesis**

sugar beet (*BrE* *also* **beet**) *noun* [U] (**AGRICULTURE**) a plant with a large round root that sugar is made from

sugar cane *noun* [U] (**AGRICULTURE**) a tall tropical plant with thick STEMS (= the long central parts that leaves grow on) that sugar is made from

sugar lump *noun* [C] (*BrE*) (*also* **sugar cube** *BrE, AmE*) a small CUBE of sugar, used in cups of tea, coffee, etc.

sugary /ˈʃʊɡəri/ *adj.* very sweet

suggest ⟨² A2 O⟩ /səˈdʒest/ *verb* **1** ~ **sth** (**to sb**); ~ **doing sth**; ~ **that** … to mention a plan or an idea that you have for sb to discuss or consider: *Tony suggested a walk.* ◇ *Tony suggested going out for a walk.* ◇ *Tony suggested (that) we go out for a walk.* **2** to put an idea into sb's mind; to make sb think that sth is true: *What do these results suggest to you?* **3** ~ **sb/sth** (**for/as sth**) to say that a person, thing or place is suitable: *Who would you suggest for the job?* ⊃ look at **recommend**(1) **4** to say or show sth in an indirect way: *Are you suggesting the accident was my fault?*

suggestion ⟨² A2⟩ /səˈdʒestʃən/ *noun* **1** [C] a plan or an idea that sb mentions for sb else to discuss and consider: *May I make a suggestion?* ◇ *Has anyone got any suggestions for how to solve this problem?* ⊃ note at **opinion** **2** [U] putting an idea into a person's mind; giving advice about what to do **3** [C, usually sing.] (*formal*) a slight amount or sign of sth: *He spoke with a suggestion of a Scottish accent.* **SYN** **hint**[1]

suggestive /səˈdʒestɪv/ *adj.* **1** ~ (**of sth**) making you think of sth; being a sign of sth: *Your symptoms are more suggestive of an allergy than a virus.* **2** making you think about sex: *a suggestive dance/remark/posture* ▶ **suggestively** *adv.*

suicidal /ˌsuːɪˈsaɪdl/ *adj.* **1** people who are **suicidal** want to kill themselves: *to be/feel suicidal* **2** likely to have a very bad result; extremely dangerous: *a suicidal mission*

suicide ⟨²+ C1⟩ /ˈsuːɪsaɪd/ *noun* [U, C] the act of killing yourself deliberately: *Ben has tried to commit suicide several times.* ◇ *There have been three suicides by university students this year.*

suit[1] ⟨² A2⟩ /su:t/ *noun* [C] **1** a formal set of clothes that are made of the same cloth, consisting of a jacket and either trousers or a skirt: *He always wears a suit and tie to work.* **2** a piece of clothing or set of clothes that you wear for a particular activity: *a tracksuit/swimsuit* ⊃ look at **swimsuit, tracksuit** **3** one of the four sets of 13 PLAYING CARDS that form a PACK: *The four suits are hearts, clubs, diamonds and spades.* **IDM** **follow suit** → **FOLLOW**

suit[2] ⟨² B1⟩ /su:t/ *verb* [T] (not used in the progressive tenses) **1** to be convenient or useful for sb/sth: *Would Thursday at 9.30 suit you?* ◇ *He will help around the house, but only when it suits him.* **2** (used about clothes, colours, etc.) to make you look attractive: *That dress really suits you.*

suitable ⟨² B1 W⟩ /ˈsuːtəbl/ *adj.* ~ (**for sb/sth**); ~ (**to do sth**) right or appropriate for sb/sth: *The film isn't suitable for children.* ◇ *I've got nothing suitable to wear for a wedding.* **OPP** **unsuitable** ▶ **suitability** /ˌsuːtəˈbɪləti/ *noun* [U] ▶ **suitably** /ˈsuːtəbli/ *adv.*

suitcase /ˈsuːtkeɪs/ (*also* **case**) *noun* [C] a box with a handle that you use for carrying your clothes, etc. in when you are travelling ⊃ picture at **baggage**

suite ⚡+ **C1** /swiːt/ *noun* [C] **1** (**TOURISM**) a set of rooms, especially in a hotel: *the honeymoon/penthouse suite* ◇ *a suite of rooms/offices* ⊃ look at **en suite** **2** a set of two or more pieces of furniture of the same style or covered in the same material: *a three-piece suite* (= a SOFA and two ARMCHAIRS) **3** (**MUSIC**) a piece of music made up of three or more related parts, for example pieces from an OPERA: *Stravinsky's Firebird Suite* **4** (**COMPUTING**) a set of related computer programs: *a suite of software development tools*

suited /ˈsuːtɪd/ *adj.* [not before noun] **~ (for/to sb/sth)** appropriate or right for sb/sth: *She was ideally suited to the part of Eva Perón.*

sulk /sʌlk/ *verb* [I] to refuse to speak or smile because you want people to know that you are angry about sth ▶ **sulkily** /ˈsʌlkɪli/ *adv.* ▶ **sulky** *adj.* (**sulkier**; **sulkiest**)

sullen /ˈsʌlən/ *adj.* in a bad mood and not wanting to speak to people: *a sullen face/expression/glare* ▶ **sullenly** *adv.*

sulphide (*BrE*) (*AmE* **sulfide**) /ˈsʌlfaɪd/ *noun* [C, U] (**CHEMISTRY**) a COMPOUND of SULPHUR with another chemical element

sulphite (*BrE*) (*AmE* **sulfite**) /ˈsʌlfaɪt/ *noun* [C] (**CHEMISTRY**) a SALT that is found naturally in wine and that is added to some food products to make them last longer

sulphur (*BrE*) (*AmE* **sulfur**) /ˈsʌlfə(r)/ *noun* [U] (*symb.* **S**) (**CHEMISTRY**) a chemical element. Sulphur is a pale yellow substance with a strong unpleasant smell. ❶ For more information on the periodic table of elements, look at the **Reference Section** of this dictionary. ▶ **sulphurous** (*AmE* **sulfurous**) /-fərəs/ *adj.*: *sulphurous fumes*

sulphur dioxide (*BrE*) (*AmE* **sulfur dioxide**) *noun* [U] (*symb.* SO_2) (**CHEMISTRY**) a poisonous gas with a strong smell, that is used in industry and causes air pollution

sulphuric acid (*BrE*) (*AmE* **sulfuric acid**) /sʌlˌfjʊərɪk ˈæsɪd/ *noun* [U] (*symb.* H_2SO_4) (**CHEMISTRY**) a strong clear ACID

sultan /ˈsʌltən/ (*also* **Sultan**) *noun* [C] (**POLITICS**) the title of the RULER (= leader) in some Muslim countries

sultana /sʌlˈtɑːnə/ *noun* [C] a dried GRAPE with no seeds in it that is used in cooking ⊃ look at **raisin**

sultry /ˈsʌltri/ *adj.* (**sultrier**; **sultriest**) **1** (used about the weather) hot and uncomfortable **2** (used about a woman) behaving in a way that makes them sexually attractive

sum¹ ⚡ **B2** ❂ /sʌm/ *noun* [C] **1** an amount of money: *The industry has spent huge sums of money modernizing its equipment.* **2** [usually sing.] **the ~ (of sth)** (**MATHEMATICS**) the amount that you get when you add two or more numbers together: *The sum of two and five is seven.* **3** (**MATHEMATICS**) a simple problem that involves calculating numbers: *to do sums in your head*

sum² ⚡ **B2** ❺ /sʌm/ *verb* (-**mm**-)
PHRV **sum sth up** to describe in a few words the main ideas of what sb has said or written: *To sum up, there are three options here …* **sum sb/sth up** to form an opinion about sb/sth: *He summed the situation up immediately.*

summary¹ ⚡ **B1** ❂ /ˈsʌməri/ *noun* [C] (*pl.* -**ies**) a short description of the main ideas or points of sth but without any details: *A brief summary of the experiment is given at the beginning of the report.* **SYN** **precis** ▶ **summarize** ⚡ **B1** **W** (*BrE also* -**ise**) /-raɪz/ *verb* [T, I]: *Could you summarize the story so far?*

summary² /ˈsʌməri/ *adj.* [only before noun] (*formal*) **1** giving only the main points of sth, not the details: *a summary report* **2** done quickly and without taking time to consider whether it is the right thing to do or following the right process: *summary justice*

summation /sʌˈmeɪʃn/ *noun* [C] **1** [usually sing.] (*formal*) a summary of what has been done or said: *What he said was a fair summation of the discussion.* **2** (*formal*) a collection of different parts that forms a complete account or impression of sb/sth: *The exhibition presents a summation of the artist's career.* **3** (*AmE*) (**LAW**) a final speech that a lawyer makes near the end of a trial in court, after all the evidence has been given

summer ⚡ **A1** /ˈsʌmə(r)/ *noun* [C, U] the warmest season of the year, between spring and autumn: *Is it very hot here in summer?* ◇ *We're going away in the summer.* ◇ *this/next/last summer* ◇ *a summer's day* ⊃ picture at **season¹** ▶ **summery** /-məri/ *adj.*: *summery weather* ◇ *a summery dress*

summer school *noun* [C, U] (**EDUCATION**) courses that are held in the summer at a university or college

summertime /ˈsʌmətaɪm/ *noun* [U] the season of summer: *It's busy here in the summertime.*

summer time (*BrE*) *noun* [U] (**GEOGRAPHY**) the period during which in some countries the clocks are put forward one hour, so that it is light for an extra hour in the evening ⊃ look at **daylight saving time**

summing-up *noun* [C] (*pl.* **summings-up**) (**LAW**) a speech in which a judge gives a summary of what has been said in court before a VERDICT (= a decision) is reached

summit ⚡+ **C1** /ˈsʌmɪt/ *noun* [C] **1** (**GEOGRAPHY**) the top of a mountain **2** (**POLITICS**) an important meeting or series of meetings between the leaders of two or more countries

summon /ˈsʌmən/ *verb* [T] **1** (*formal*) to order a person to come to a place: *He was summoned to appear before magistrates.* ◇ *The boys were summoned to the head teacher's office.* **2** **~ sth (up)** to find strength, courage or some other quality that you need even though it is difficult to do so: *She couldn't summon up the courage to leave him.*

summons /ˈsʌmənz/ *noun* [C] (*pl.* **summonses**) (**LAW**) an order to appear in court

sumo /ˈsuːməʊ/ (*also* **sumo wrestling**) *noun* [U] (**SPORT**) a Japanese style of WRESTLING (= a sport in which two people fight and try to throw each other to the ground), in which the people taking part are extremely large: *a sumo wrestler*

sumptuous /ˈsʌmptʃuəs/ *adj.* (*formal*) very expensive and looking very impressive: *We dined in sumptuous surroundings.* ▶ **sumptuously** *adv.*

Sun. *abbr.* (in writing) = SUNDAY

sun¹ ⚡ **A1** /sʌn/ *noun* **1 the sun**, **the Sun** [sing.] the star that shines in the sky during the day and that gives the earth heat and light: *The sun rises in the east and sets in the west.* ◇ *the rays of the sun* ⊃ picture at **climate change**, **energy**, **food chain**, **moon**, **solar system** **2** [sing., U] light and heat from the sun: *Don't sit in the sun too long.* ◇ *Too much sun can be harmful.*
IDM **catch the sun** → CATCH¹

sun² /sʌn/ *verb* [T] (-**nn**-) **~ yourself** to sit or lie outside when the sun is shining in order to enjoy the heat

sunbathe /ˈsʌnbeɪð/ *verb* [I] to take off most of your clothes and sit or lie in the sun in order to get a TAN (= darker skin) ⊃ look at **bathe**

sunbeam /ˈsʌnbiːm/ *noun* [C] a line of light from the sun

sunbed /ˈsʌnbed/ *noun* [C] a bed for lying on under a special lamp that can turn the skin brown ⊃ look at **sunlounger**

sunblock /ˈsʌnblɒk/ *noun* [U, C] cream that you put on your skin to protect it completely from the harmful effects of the sun

sunburn /ˈsʌnbɜːn/ *noun* [U] (**HEALTH**) red painful skin caused by spending too long in the sun

sunburned /ˈsʌnbɜːnd/ (*also* **sunburnt** /ˈsʌnbɜːnt/) *adj.* suffering from SUNBURN

suncream /ˈsʌnkriːm/ *noun* [U, C] cream that you put on your skin to protect it from the harmful effects of the sun ⊃ look at **sunscreen**

Sunday ⓘ A1 /ˈsʌndeɪ, -di/ *noun* [C, U] (*abbr.* **Sun.**) the day of the week after Saturday

sundial /ˈsʌndaɪəl/ *noun* [C] a type of clock used in past times that uses the sun and the shadow from a pointed piece of metal to show what the time is

sundry /ˈsʌndri/ *adj.* [only before noun] (*formal*) of various kinds that are not important enough to be named separately
IDM **all and sundry** (*informal*) everyone

sunflower /ˈsʌnflaʊə(r)/ *noun* [C] a very tall plant with large yellow flowers, often grown for its seeds and their oil, which are used in cooking

sung /sʌŋ/ past participle of **sing**

sunglasses /ˈsʌnɡlɑːsɪz/ (*also* **dark glasses**, *informal* **shades** /ʃeɪdz/) *noun* [pl.] a pair of glasses with dark glass in them that you wear to protect your eyes from bright light

ˈsun hat *noun* [C] a hat that you wear to protect your head and neck from the sun

sunk /sʌŋk/ past participle of **sink**[1]

sunken /ˈsʌŋkən/ *adj.* **1** [only before noun] below the water: *a sunken ship* **2** (used about CHEEKS or eyes) very far into the face as a result of illness or age **3** [only before noun] at a lower level than the surrounding area: *a sunken bath/garden*

sunlamp /ˈsʌnlæmp/ *noun* [C] a lamp that produces ULTRAVIOLET light that has the same effect as the sun and can turn the skin brown

sunlight /ˈsʌnlaɪt/ *noun* [U] the light from the sun ⊃ picture at **energy, photosynthesis, shadow**[1]

sunlit /ˈsʌnlɪt/ *adj.* having bright light from the sun: *a sunlit terrace*

sunlounger /ˈsʌnlaʊndʒə(r)/ *noun* [C] a chair with a long seat that supports your legs, used for sitting or lying on in the sun ⊃ look at **sunbed**

Sunni /ˈsʊni, ˈsʌni/ *noun* (*pl.* **Sunni, Sunnis**) (**RELIGION**) **1** [U] one of the two main groups of the religion of ISLAM ⊃ look at **Shia** (1) **2** [C] a member of the Sunni religious group ⊃ look at **Shia** (2) ▶ **Sunnite** /-naɪt/ *adj.*

sunny /ˈsʌni/ *adj.* (**sunnier; sunniest**) having a lot of light from the sun: *a sunny garden* ◇ *a sunny day*

sunrise /ˈsʌnraɪz/ *noun* [U, C] the time when the sun comes up in the morning: *to get up at sunrise* ⊃ look at **dawn**[1] (1), **sunset**

sunroof /ˈsʌnruːf/ *noun* [C] (*pl.* **-roofs**) a part of the roof of a car that you can open to let air and light in

sunscreen /ˈsʌnskriːn/ *noun* [U, C] a cream or liquid that you put on your skin to protect it from the harmful effects of the sun ⊃ look at **suncream**

sunset /ˈsʌnset/ *noun* [U, C] the time when the sun goes down in the evening: *The park closes at sunset.* ◇ *a beautiful sunset*

sunshine /ˈsʌnʃaɪn/ *noun* [U] heat and light from the sun: *We sat down in the sunshine and had lunch.*

sunspot /ˈsʌnspɒt/ *noun* [C] (**ASTRONOMY**) a dark area that sometimes appears on the sun's surface

sunstroke /ˈsʌnstrəʊk/ *noun* [U] (**HEALTH**) an illness that is caused by spending too much time in very hot, strong sun: *Keep your head covered or you'll get sunstroke.*

suntan /ˈsʌntæn/ (*also* **tan**) *noun* [C] when you have a **suntan**, your skin is darker than usual because you have spent time in the sun: *to have/get a suntan* ◇ *suntan oil* ▶ **suntanned** (*also* **tanned**) *adj.*

super ⓘ+ B2 /ˈsuːpə(r)/ *adj.* (*informal, old-fashioned*) very good; wonderful: *We had a super time.* ▶ **super** *adv.*: *He's been super understanding.*

super- /ˈsuːpə(r)/ *prefix* **1** (in nouns, adjectives and adverbs) extremely; more or better than normal: *superglue* ◇ *super-rich* ◇ *superhuman* **2** (in verbs and nouns) above; over: *superimpose* ◇ *superstructure*

superannuation /ˌsuːpərˌænjuˈeɪʃn/ *noun* [U] (*especially BrE*) (**FINANCE**) money that you get, usually from your employer, when you stop working when you are old and that you pay for while you are working; the money that you pay for this ⊃ look at **pension**[1]

superb ⓘ+ C1 /suːˈpɜːb/ *adj.* extremely good, excellent ▶ **superbly** *adv.*

the ˈSuper Bowl™ *noun* [C] (**SPORT**) an AMERICAN FOOTBALL game played every year to decide the winner of the National Football League

superbug /ˈsuːpəbʌɡ/ *noun* [C] (**HEALTH**) a type of bacteria that cannot easily be killed by ANTIBIOTICS (= medicine that is used for destroying bacteria and curing infections) ⊃ look at **MRSA**

supercilious /ˌsuːpəˈsɪliəs/ *adj.* showing that you think that you are better than other people: *She gave a supercilious smile.* ▶ **superciliously** *adv.*

superconductor /ˈsuːpəkəndʌktə(r)/ *noun* [C] (**PHYSICS**) a substance that, at very low temperatures, allows electricity to flow completely freely through it

superficial /ˌsuːpəˈfɪʃl/ *adj.* **1** not studying or thinking about sth in a deep or complete way: *a superficial knowledge of the subject* **2** only on the surface, not deep: *a superficial wound/cut/burn* **3** (used about people) not caring about serious or important things: *He's a very superficial sort of person.* ▶ **superficiality** /ˌsuːpəˌfɪʃiˈæləti/ *noun* [U] ▶ **superficially** /ˌsuːpəˈfɪʃəli/ *adv.*

superfluous /suːˈpɜːfluəs/ *adj.* more than is wanted; not needed

superfood /ˈsuːpəfuːd/ *noun* [C] (**HEALTH**) a type of food that some people think is very good for you and helps to prevent disease

superhero /ˈsuːpəhɪərəʊ/ *noun* [C] (*pl.* **-oes**) (**ARTS AND MEDIA**) a character in a story, film, etc. who has unusual strength or power and uses it to help people; a real person who has done sth unusually brave to help sb

superhuman /ˌsuːpəˈhjuːmən/ *adj.* much greater than is normal: *superhuman strength*

superimpose /ˌsuːpərɪmˈpəʊz/ *verb* [T] ~ **sth (on sth)** to put sth on top of sth else so that what is below can still be seen: *The old street plan was superimposed on a map of the modern city.*

superintendent /ˌsuːpərɪnˈtendənt/ *noun* [C] **1** (*abbr.* **Supt**) (**LAW**) a police officer with a high position: *Detective Superintendent Waters* **2** a person who looks after a large building

superior[1] ⓘ+ C1 /suːˈpɪəriə(r)/ *adj.* **1** ~ **(to sb/sth)** better than usual or than sb/sth else: *He is clearly superior to all the other candidates.* **OPP** **inferior** **2** ~ **(to sb)**

having a more important position: *a superior officer*
3 thinking that you are better than other people
▶ superiority /suːˌpɪəriˈɒrəti/ *noun* [U]

superior² /suːˈpɪəriə(r)/ *noun* [C] a person of higher
position: *Report any accidents to your superior.*
OPP inferior

superlative /suːˈpɜːlətɪv/ *noun* [C] (**GRAMMAR**) the form
of an adjective or adverb that expresses its highest
degree: '*Most beautiful*', '*best*' and '*fastest*' are all
superlatives. ▶ superlative *adj.*

supermarket ⚆ A1 /ˈsuːpəmɑːkɪt/ *noun* [C] a very
large shop that sells food, drink, goods used in the
home, etc.

supermodel /ˈsuːpəmɒdl/ *noun* [C] a very famous and
highly paid fashion model

supernatural /ˌsuːpəˈnætʃrəl/ *adj.* **1** that cannot be
explained by the laws of science: *a creature with
supernatural powers* **2** the supernatural *noun* [sing.]
events, forces or powers that cannot be explained by
the laws of science: *I don't believe in the supernatural.*

supernova /ˈsuːpənəʊvə/ *noun* [C] (*pl.* supernovae /-viː/,
supernovas) (**ASTRONOMY**) a star that suddenly
becomes much brighter because it is exploding
⊃ look at **nova**

superpower /ˈsuːpəpaʊə(r)/ *noun* [C] (**POLITICS**) one of
the countries in the world that has very great military
or economic power and a lot of influence, for example
the US ⊃ look at **world power**

supersede /ˌsuːpəˈsiːd/ *verb* [T, often passive] to take the
place of sb/sth that existed or was used before and
has become old-fashioned: *Steam trains were
gradually superseded by electric trains.*

supersonic /ˌsuːpəˈsɒnɪk/ *adj.* (**PHYSICS**) faster than the
speed of sound

superstar /ˈsuːpəstɑː(r)/ *noun* [C] (**ARTS AND MEDIA**,
MUSIC) a singer, film star, etc. who is very famous and
popular

superstition /ˌsuːpəˈstɪʃn/ *noun* [U, C] a belief that
cannot be explained by reason or science: *According
to superstition, it's unlucky to walk under a ladder.*
▶ superstitious /-ʃəs/ *adj.*

superstore /ˈsuːpəstɔː(r)/ *noun* [C] a very large shop
that sells food or a wide variety of one particular type
of goods

superstructure /ˈsuːpəstrʌktʃə(r)/ *noun* [C]
(**ARCHITECTURE**) a structure that is built on top of sth,
for example the part of a building above the ground
⊃ look at **substructure**

supervise ⚆+ C1 /ˈsuːpəvaɪz/ *verb* [T, I] to watch sb/sth to
make sure that work is being done properly or that
people are behaving correctly: *Your job is to
supervise the building work.* ▶ supervision ⚆+ C1
/ˌsuːpəˈvɪʒn/ *noun* [U]: *Children should not play here
without supervision.* ▶ supervisor ⚆+ C1 *noun* [C]

supper /ˈsʌpə(r)/ *noun* [U, C] the last meal of the day,
either the main meal of the evening or a small meal
that you eat quite late, not long before you go to bed

supple /ˈsʌpl/ *adj.* that bends or moves easily; not stiff:
Children are generally far more supple than adults.
▶ suppleness *noun* [U]

supplement ⚆+ C1 /ˈsʌplɪmənt/ *noun* [C] something that
is added to sth else: *You have to pay a small
supplement if you travel on a Saturday.*
▶ supplement ⚆+ C1 /-ment/ *verb* [T] ~ sth (with sth): *to
supplement your diet with vitamins* ▶ supplementary
/ˌsʌplɪˈmentri/ *adj.*: *supplementary exercises at the
back of the book*

supple‚mentary ˈangle *noun* [C] (**GEOMETRY**) either of
two angles that together make 180° ⊃ look at
complementary angle ⊃ picture at **angle¹**

supplier /səˈplaɪə(r)/ *noun* [C] (**BUSINESS**) a person or
company that supplies goods

supply¹ ⚆ B1 🔊 /səˈplaɪ/ *verb* [T] (supplying; supplies;
pt, pp supplied) ~ sth (to sb); ~ sb (with sth) to give or
provide sth: *The farmer supplies eggs to the
surrounding villages.* ◊ *He supplies the surrounding
villages with eggs.*

supply² ⚆ B1 🔊 /səˈplaɪ/ *noun* [C] (*pl.* -ies) a store or an
amount of sth that is provided or available to be used:
The water supply was contaminated. ◊ *Food supplies
were dropped by helicopter.* ◊ *In many parts of the
country water is in short supply* (= there is not much
of it).

supˈply chain *noun* [C, usually sing.] (**BUSINESS**) the series
of processes involved in the production and supply of
goods, from when they are first made, grown, etc.
until they are bought or used

supˈply teacher (*BrE*) (*AmE* substitute teacher) *noun* [C]
(**EDUCATION**) a teacher employed to do the work of
another teacher who is away because of illness, etc.

support¹ ⚆ A2 🅦 /səˈpɔːt/ *verb* [T]
• HELP **1** to help sb/sth by saying that you agree with
them or it, and sometimes giving practical help such
as money: *Several large companies are supporting the
project.* ◊ *Which political party do you support?*
• GIVE MONEY **2** to give sb the money they need for food,
clothes, etc: *Jim has to support two children from his
previous marriage.*
• CARRY WEIGHT **3** to carry the weight of sb/sth: *Large
columns support the roof.*
• SHOW STH IS TRUE **4** to show that sth is true or correct:
What evidence do you have to support what you say?
• SPORTS TEAM **5** to have a particular sports team that
you like more than any other: *Which football team do
you support?*
• POP/ROCK CONCERT **6** (**MUSIC**) (used about a band or
singer) to perform in a pop or rock concert before the
main band or singer: *They were supported by a local
band.*
• IN COMPUTING **7** (**COMPUTING**) (used about a computer
or computer system) to allow a particular program,
language or device to be used with it: *The new
operating system isn't supported on this phone.*

support² ⚆ A2 🅦 /səˈpɔːt/ *noun* **1** [U] ~ (for sb/sth)
help and approval that you give, especially in order to
encourage a person or thing: *public support for the
campaign* ◊ *Steve spoke in support of the proposal.*
2 [C, U] something that carries the weight of sb/sth or
holds sth FIRMLY in place: *a roof support* ◊ *She held on
to his arm for support.* **3** [U] money to buy food,
clothes, etc: *She has no job, no home and no means of
support.* **4** [U] (**MUSIC**) a band or singer who performs
in a pop or rock concert before the main band or
singer: *They have announced the support for their UK
shows.*
IDM moral support → MORAL¹

supporter ⚆ B1 /səˈpɔːtə(r)/ *noun* [C] a person who
supports a political party, sports team, etc: *football
supporters*

supportive ⚆+ C1 /səˈpɔːtɪv/ *adj.* giving help or support
to sb in a difficult situation: *Everyone was very
supportive when I lost my job.*

suppose ⚆ A2 🆂 /səˈpəʊz/ *verb* **1** [T, I] to think or
believe that something is true or possible (based on
the knowledge that you have): *It isn't as simple as you
might suppose.* ◊ *What do you suppose could have
happened?* ◊ *I don't suppose that they're coming now.*
2 [I, T] used to make a suggestion, request or
statement less strong: *I don't suppose you'd lend me*

your car tonight, would you? ◊ 'Can we give Andy a lift?' 'Yes, **I suppose so**, if we must.' (= Yes, but I'm not happy about it.) **3** [T] to pretend that sth will happen or is true: *Suppose you won the lottery. What would you do?*

IDM **be supposed to do sth** **1** to be expected to do sth or to have to do sth: *The train was supposed to arrive ten minutes ago.* **2** to be considered or thought to be sth: *This is supposed to be the oldest building in the city.* **not supposed to do sth** to not be allowed to do sth: *This is secret and I'm not supposed to talk about it.*

supposedly ʔ+ **C1** /sə'pəʊzɪdli/ *adv.* according to what many people believe

supposing /sə'pəʊzɪŋ/ *conj.* if sth happens or is true; what if: *Supposing the plan goes wrong, what will we do then?*

supposition /ˌsʌpə'zɪʃn/ *noun* [C, U] an idea that a person thinks is true but which has not been shown to be true; an act of believing or claiming that sth is true

suppress ʔ+ **C1** /sə'pres/ *verb* [T] **1** to stop sth by using force **2** to stop sth from being seen or known: *to suppress the truth* **3** to stop yourself from expressing your feelings, etc: *to suppress laughter/a yawn*
▶ **suppression** /-'preʃn/ *noun* [U]

supremacist /su'preməsɪst/ *noun* [C] (**SOCIAL STUDIES**) a person who believes that the human group they belong to is better than others and should be in power: *a white supremacist*

supremacy /su'preməsi/ *noun* [U] ~ **(over sb/sth)** the state of being the most powerful: *The company has established total supremacy over its rivals.*

supreme ʔ+ **C1** /su'pri:m/ *adj.* the highest or greatest possible

Su͵preme 'Court = HIGH COURT (2)

supremely /su'pri:mli/ *adv.* extremely

Supt *abbr.* (in writing) = SUPERINTENDENT (1)

surcharge /'sɜ:tʃɑ:dʒ/ *noun* [C] an extra amount of money that you have to pay for sth

surd /sɜ:d/ = IRRATIONAL NUMBER

sure¹ ʔ **A1** /ʃʊə(r), ʃɔ:(r)/ *adj.* [not before noun]
1 having no doubt about sth; certain: *You must be sure of your facts before you make an accusation.* ◊ *I'm not sure what to do next.* ◊ *Craig was sure that he'd made the right decision.* ◊ *I think I had my bag when I got off the bus but I'm not sure.* **OPP** **unsure** **2** [not before noun] ~ **of sth**; ~ **to do sth** certain that you will receive sth or that sth will happen: *If you go and see them you can be sure of a warm welcome.* ◊ *If you work hard you are sure to pass the exam.* ⊃ note at **certain 3** that you can be certain of: *A noise like that is a sure sign of engine trouble.*
IDM **be sure to do sth** used to tell sb to do sth: *Be sure to text and tell me what happens.* **for sure** without doubt: *Nobody knows for sure what happened.* **make sure 1** to check that sth is in a particular state or has been done: *I must go back and make sure I closed the window.* **2** to take the action that is necessary: *Make sure you are back home by eleven o'clock.* **sure of yourself** confident about your opinions, or about what you can do **sure (thing)** (*AmE, informal*) yes: 'Can I borrow this book?' 'Sure thing.'

sure² ʔ **A2** /ʃʊə(r), ʃɔ:(r)/ *adv.* (*informal*) **1** used to say 'yes' to sb: 'Can I have a look at your newspaper?' 'Sure.' **2** (*especially AmE*) used to emphasize what you are saying: *I sure hope you're right.*

IDM **sure enough** as was expected: *I expected him to be early, and sure enough he arrived five minutes before the others.*

surely ʔ **B1** /'ʃʊəli, 'ʃɔ:li/ *adv.* **1** without doubt: *This will surely cause problems.* **2** used for expressing surprise at sb else's opinions, plans, actions, etc: *Surely you're not going to walk home in this rain?* ◊ 'Meena's looking for another job.' 'Surely not.' **3** (*AmE, informal*) yes; of course

surf¹ /sɜ:f/ *noun* [U] (**GEOGRAPHY**) the white part on the top of waves in the sea

surf² /sɜ:f/ *verb* [I, T] **1** (**SPORT**) to stand or lie on a SURFBOARD (= a special board) and ride on a wave towards the beach **2** ~ **the net/internet** (**COMPUTING**) to use the internet

surface¹ ʔ **B1** /'sɜ:fɪs/ *noun* **1** [C] the outside or top layer of sth: *Teeth have a hard surface called enamel.* ◊ *a broad leaf with a large **surface area*** ◊ *This tennis court has a very uneven surface.* ⊃ picture at **reflection 2** [C, usually sing.] the top layer of an area of water or land: *the earth's surface* ◊ *These plants float on the surface of the water.* **3** [C] the flat top part of a piece of furniture, used for working on: *a work surface* ◊ *kitchen surfaces* **4** [sing.] the qualities of sb/sth that you see or notice, that are not hidden: *Everybody seems very friendly but there are a lot of tensions **below/beneath the surface**.*

surface² /'sɜ:fɪs/ *verb* **1** [I] to come up to the surface of water **2** [I] to suddenly appear again or become obvious after having been hidden for a while: *All the old arguments surfaced again in the discussion.* **3** [I] (*informal*) to wake up or get up after being asleep **4** [T] to put a surface on a road, etc.

'**surface mail** *noun* [U] letters, packages, etc. that go by road, railway or sea, not by air ⊃ look at **airmail**

surfboard /'sɜ:fbɔ:d/ *noun* [C] (**SPORT**) a long narrow board used for SURFING

surfeit /'sɜ:fɪt/ *noun* [sing.] ~ **(of sth)** (*formal*) too much of sth

surfer /'sɜ:fə(r)/ *noun* [C] **1** (**SPORT**) a person who rides on waves standing on a SURFBOARD **2** (*informal*) (**COMPUTING**) a person who spends a lot of time using the internet

surfing /'sɜ:fɪŋ/ *noun* [U] **1** (**SPORT**) the sport of riding on waves while standing on a SURFBOARD: *to go surfing* **2** (**COMPUTING**) the activity of looking at different things on the internet in order to find sth interesting

surge ʔ+ **C1** /sɜ:dʒ/ *noun* [C] **1** ~ **(of sth)** a sudden strong feeling: *a surge of pity* **2** a sudden strong movement in a particular direction by a large number of people or things: *a surge forward* **3** ~ **(in/of sth)** a sudden increase in the amount or number of sth: *a surge in the demand for electricity* ◊ *a surge of interest*
▶ **surge** ʔ+ **C1** *verb* [I] (used with an adverb or a preposition): *The crowd surged forward.*

---

sure

confident ♦ convinced ♦ certain ♦ positive

These words all describe sb who knows without doubt that sth is true or will happen.

sure *Are you sure that's the answer?*

confident *He was confident that he would pass the exam.*

convinced *I'm convinced she's innocent.*

certain *Are you absolutely certain about this?*

positive (*informal*) *She was positive that he'd be there.*

surgeon ̃+ B2 /ˈsɜːdʒən/ *noun* [C] (**MEDICINE**) a doctor who performs surgery: *a brain surgeon* ➲ note at **hospital**

surgery ̃ B2 /ˈsɜːdʒəri/ *noun* (*pl.* -ies) (**MEDICINE**) **1** [U] medical treatment in which the body is cut open so that part of it can be removed, replaced or repaired: *to undergo surgery* ➲ look at **operation** (1), **plastic surgery** ➲ note at **hospital 2** [C, U] (*BrE*) the place or time when a doctor or dentist sees patients: *Surgery hours are from 9.00 to 11.30.* ➲ note at **doctor**[1]

surgical ̃+ C1 /ˈsɜːdʒɪkl/ *adj.* (**MEDICINE**) connected with medical operations: *surgical instruments* ▸ **surgically** /-kli/ *adv.*

surly /ˈsɜːli/ *adj.* (surlier; surliest) unfriendly and rude: *a surly expression*

surmount /səˈmaʊnt/ *verb* [T] to deal successfully with a problem or difficulty ➲ look at **insurmountable**

surname /ˈsɜːneɪm/ (*also* last name) *noun* [C] the name that you share with other people in your family: *'What's your surname?' 'Jones.'*

surpass /səˈpɑːs/ *verb* [T] (*formal*) to do sth better than sb/sth else or better than expected: *The success of the film surpassed all expectations.*

surplus ̃+ C1 /ˈsɜːpləs/ *noun* [C, U] an amount that is extra or more than you need: *the food surplus in Western Europe* ▸ **surplus** *adj.*: *They sell their surplus grain to other countries.*

surprise[1] ̃ A2 /səˈpraɪz/ *noun* **1** [C] something that you did not expect or know about: *What a pleasant surprise to see you again!* ◇ *The news came as a complete surprise.* ◇ *a surprise visit/attack/party* **2** [U] the feeling that you have when sth happens that you do not expect: *They looked up in surprise when she walked in.* ◇ *To my surprise they all agreed with me.* **IDM** take sb by surprise to happen or do sth when sb is not expecting it

surprise[2] ̃ A2 /səˈpraɪz/ *verb* [T] **1** to make sb feel surprised: *It wouldn't surprise me if you get the job.* **2** to attack or find sb suddenly and unexpectedly

surprised ̃ A2 /səˈpraɪzd/ *adj.* ~ to see, hear, find, etc. feeling or showing surprise: *I was very surprised to see Cara there. I thought she was still abroad.*

surprising ̃ A2 /səˈpraɪzɪŋ/ *adj.* that causes surprise: *It's surprising how many adults can't read or write.* ▸ **surprisingly** *adv.*: *Surprisingly few people got the correct answer.*

surreal /səˈriːəl/ *adj.* very strange; with images mixed together in a strange way like in a dream: *a surreal film/painting/situation*

surrealism /səˈriːəlɪzəm/ *noun* [U] (**ART, LITERATURE**) a twentieth-century style and movement in art and literature in which images and events that are not connected are put together in a strange or impossible way, like a dream, to try to express what is happening deep in the mind ▸ **surrealist** /-lɪst/ *adj., noun* [C]: *a surrealist painter/painting* ◇ *the surrealist Salvador Dali*

surrender ̃+ C1 /səˈrendə(r)/ *verb* **1** [I, T] ~ (**yourself**) (**to sb**) to stop fighting and admit that you have lost: *The hijackers eventually surrendered themselves to the police.* **2** [T] ~ **sb/sth (to sb)** (*formal*) to give sb/sth to sb else when you are forced to: *The police ordered them to surrender their weapons.* ▸ **surrender** *noun* [U, sing.]

surreptitious /ˌsʌrəpˈtɪʃəs/ *adj.* done secretly: *I had a surreptitious look at what she was writing.* ▸ **surreptitiously** *adv.*

surrogate /ˈsʌrəgət/ *adj.* used to describe a person or thing that takes the place of sb/sth else: *a surrogate mother* (= a woman who has a baby and gives it to

another woman who cannot have children) ▸ **surrogate** *noun* [C]

surround ̃ B2 /səˈraʊnd/ *verb* [T] ~ **sb/sth (by/with sth)** to be or go all around sb/sth: *The garden is surrounded by a high wall.* ◇ *Troops have surrounded the parliament building.*

surrounding ̃ B2 /səˈraʊndɪŋ/ *adj.* [only before noun] that is near or around sth

surroundings /səˈraʊndɪŋz/ *noun* [pl.] everything that is near or around you; the place where you live: *to live in pleasant surroundings* ◇ *animals living in their natural surroundings* (= not in zoos) ➲ look at **environment** (1)

surround sound *noun* [U] a system that uses several speakers placed around you so that you hear a more realistic sound

surveillance ̃+ C1 /sɜːˈveɪləns/ *noun* [U] the careful watching of sb who may have done sth wrong: *The building is protected by surveillance cameras.*

survey[1] ̃ A2 ⓦ /ˈsɜːveɪ/ *noun* [C] **1** a study of the opinions, behaviour, etc. of a group of people: *Surveys have shown that more and more people are getting into debt.* ◇ *to carry out/conduct/do a survey* **2** (**GEOGRAPHY**) the act of carefully measuring an area of land and making a map of it **3** (*BrE*) the act of examining a building carefully in order to find out if it is in good condition

survey[2] ̃ B2 /səˈveɪ/ *verb* [T] **1** to look carefully at the whole of sth: *We stood at the top of the hill and surveyed the countryside.* ➲ note at **examine 2** (**GEOGRAPHY**) to carefully measure and make a map of an area of land **3** (*BrE*) to examine a building carefully in order to find out if it is in good condition

surveyor /səˈveɪə(r)/ *noun* [C] **1** a person whose job is to examine and record the details of a piece of land **2** (*BrE*) (*AmE* inspector) a person whose job is to examine a building to make sure it is in good condition, usually done for sb who wants to buy it ➲ look at **quantity surveyor**

survive ̃ B1 /səˈvaɪv/ *verb* **1** [I, T] ~ (**on sth**) to continue to live or exist, especially in or after a difficult or dangerous situation: *More than 100 people were killed in the crash and only five passengers survived.* ◇ *How can she survive on such a small salary?* ◇ *to survive a plane crash* ◇ *Not many buildings survived the bombing.* **2** [T] to live longer than sb SYN **outlive** ▸ **survival** ̃+ B2 ⓞ /-ˈvaɪvl/ *noun* [U]: *A heart transplant was his only chance of survival.* ▸ **survivor** ̃+ B2 *noun* [C]: *There were five survivors of the crash.*

susceptibility /səˌseptəˈbɪləti/ *noun* [U, sing.] ~ (**to sth**) the state of being very likely to be influenced, harmed or affected by sth: *susceptibility to disease*

susceptible /səˈseptəbl/ *adj.* ~ **to sth** very likely to be influenced, harmed or affected by sth: *Some of these plants are more susceptible to frost damage than others.*

suspect[1] ̃ B2 /səˈspekt/ *verb* **1** [T, I] to believe that sth may happen or be true, especially sth bad: *The situation is worse than we first suspected.* ◇ *Nobody suspected that she was thinking of leaving.* ◇ *She strongly suspected that he was lying.* ➲ look at **unsuspecting 2** [T] ~ **sb (of sth/doing sth)** to believe that sb is guilty of sth, although you do not have definite proof: *I suspect Laura of taking the money.* ➲ noun **suspicion 3** [T] to not be sure that you can trust sb or believe sth: *I rather suspect his motives for offering to help.*

suspect[2] B2 /ˈsʌspekt/ *noun* [C] a person who is thought to be guilty of a crime: *The suspects are being questioned by police.* ⊃ note at **crime**

suspect[3] /ˈsʌspekt/ *adj.* possibly not true or not to be trusted: *to have suspect motives* ◇ *a suspect package* (= that may contain a bomb)

suspend + B2 /səˈspend/ *verb* [T] **1** ~ **sth (from sth) (by/ on sth)** to hang sth from sth else: *A bulb was suspended from the ceiling on a long wire.* **2** to stop or delay sth for a time: *Some rail services were suspended during the strike.* **3** ~ **sb (from sth)** (**EDUCATION**) to send sb away from their school, job, position, etc. for a period of time, usually as a punishment: *He was suspended from school for a week for stealing.* ⊃ noun **suspension**

su,spended ˈsentence *noun* [C] (**LAW**) a punishment given to a criminal in court that means that they will only go to prison if they commit another crime within a particular period of time: *He was given an 18-month suspended sentence for theft.*

suspender /səˈspendə(r)/ *noun* **1** [C, usually pl.] (*BrE*) a short piece of ELASTIC that women use to hold up their STOCKINGS **2** suspenders [pl.] (*AmE*) = BRACE[1] (2)

suspense /səˈspens/ *noun* [U] the feeling of excitement or worry that you have when you feel sth is going to happen, when you are waiting for news, etc: *Don't keep us in suspense. Tell us what happened.*

suspension + C1 /səˈspenʃn/ *noun* **1** [U, C] (**EDUCATION**) not being allowed to do your job or go to school for a period of time, usually as a punishment: *suspension on full pay* **2** [U, sing.] the act of delaying sth for a period of time ⊃ verb **suspend** **3** the suspension [U] the parts that are connected to the wheels of a car, etc. that make it more comfortable to ride in **4** [C, U] (**CHEMISTRY**) a liquid with very small pieces of solid matter floating in it; the state of such a liquid

su'spension bridge *noun* [C] (**ARCHITECTURE**) a bridge that hangs from thick steel wires that are supported by towers at each end

suspicion + C1 /səˈspɪʃn/ *noun* **1** [U, C] a feeling or belief that sth is wrong, that sb has done sth wrong or that you cannot trust sb/sth: *She was arrested on suspicion of murder.* ◇ *He is under suspicion of being involved in organized crime.* ◇ *I always treat smiling politicians with suspicion.* **2** [C] ~ **(that …)** a feeling that sth may happen or be true: *I have a suspicion that he's forgotten he invited us.* ⊃ verb **suspect**

suspicious + C1 /səˈspɪʃəs/ *adj.* **1** ~ **(of/about sb/sth)** feeling that sb has done sth wrong, dishonest or illegal: *We became suspicious of his behaviour and alerted the police.* **2** that makes you feel that sth is wrong, dishonest or illegal: *The old man died in suspicious circumstances.* ◇ *It's very suspicious that she was not at home on the evening of the murder.* ◇ *a suspicious-looking person* ▸ **suspiciously** *adv.*: *to behave suspiciously*

sustain + C1 ⓦ /səˈsteɪn/ *verb* [T] **1** to keep sb/sth alive or healthy: *Oxygen sustains life.* **2** to make sth continue for a long period of time without becoming less: *It's hard to sustain interest for such a long time.* **SYN** maintain **3** (*formal*) to experience sth bad: *to sustain damage/an injury/a defeat*

sustainable + B2 /səˈsteɪnəbl/ *adj.* **1** (**ENVIRONMENT**) involving the use of natural products and energy in a way that does not harm the environment: *sustainable forest management* **2** that can continue or be continued for a long time **OPP** unsustainable ▸ **sustainability** /səˌsteɪnəˈbɪləti/ *noun* [U]

sustenance /ˈsʌstənəns/ *noun* [U] (*formal*) **1** the food and drink that people, animals and plants need to live and stay healthy: *There's not much sustenance in a bowl of soup.* **2** the process of making sth continue to exist: *Elections are essential for the sustenance of parliamentary democracy.*

suture /ˈsuːtʃə(r)/ *noun* [C] (**MEDICINE**) a STITCH or STITCHES made when SEWING up a wound, especially after an operation ▸ **suture** *verb* [T]: *The wound needs to be cleaned and then sutured.*

SUV /ˌes juː ˈviː/ *noun* [C] (*especially AmE*) a type of large car, often with FOUR-WHEEL DRIVE, and made originally for travelling over rough ground (the abbreviation for 'sport utility vehicle')

SW *abbr.* (in writing) **1** = SHORT WAVE **2** (**GEOGRAPHY**) = SOUTH-WEST[1], SOUTH-WESTERN: *SW Australia*

swab /swɒb/ *noun* [C] (**MEDICINE**) **1** a piece of soft material used by a doctor, nurse, etc. for cleaning wounds or taking a small amount of a substance from sb's body for testing **2** an act of taking a small amount of a substance from sb's body with a swab: *to take a throat swab* ▸ **swab** *verb* [T] (-bb-)

swagger /ˈswæɡə(r)/ *verb* [I] to walk in a way that shows that you are too confident or proud ▸ **swagger** *noun* [sing.]

swallow[1] + B2 /ˈswɒləʊ/ *verb*
• FOOD/DRINK **1** [T, I] to make food, drink, etc. go down your throat to your stomach: *It's easier to swallow pills if you take them with water.*
• IN FEAR, ETC. **2** [I] to make a movement in your throat, often because you are afraid or surprised, etc: *She swallowed hard and tried to speak, but nothing came out.*
• USE ALL **3** [T] ~ **sth (up)** to use all of sth, especially money: *The rent swallows up most of our monthly income.*
• ACCEPT/BELIEVE **4** [T] to accept or believe sth too easily: *You shouldn't swallow everything they tell you!* **5** [T] to accept offensive remarks, criticisms, etc. without complaining: *I find her criticisms very hard to swallow.*
IDM hard to swallow → HARD[1]

swallow[2] /ˈswɒləʊ/ *noun* [C] **1** a small bird with long pointed wings and a tail with two points, that MIGRATES (= moves from one part of the world to another according to the season) **2** an act of SWALLOWING; an amount of food or drink that is SWALLOWED at one time

'swallow hole = SINKHOLE

swam /swæm/ past tense of **swim**

swamp[1] /swɒmp/ *noun* [C, U] (**GEOGRAPHY**) an area of soft wet land

swamp[2] /swɒmp/ *verb* [T] **1** to cover or fill sth with water: *The fishing boat was swamped by enormous waves.* **2** [usually passive] ~ **sb/sth (with sth)** to give sb so much of sth that they cannot deal with it: *We've been swamped with applications for the job.* **SYN** inundate

swan /swɒn/ *noun* [C] a large white bird with a very long neck, that lives on lakes and rivers

swap (*also* swop) /swɒp/ *verb* [I, T] (-pp-) ~ **(sth) (with sb)**; ~ **A for B** to give sth for sth else; to exchange: *When we finish these books, shall we swap* (= you have my book and I'll have yours)? ◇ *Would you swap seats with me?* ◇ *I'd swap my job for hers any day.* ▸ **swap** (*also* swop) *noun* [sing.]: *Let's do a swap.*
IDM change/swap places (with sb) → PLACE[1]

swarm[1] /swɔːm/ *noun* [C] **1** a large group of insects, especially bees, moving around together: *a swarm of bees/locusts/flies* **2** a large number of people together

swarm[2] /swɔːm/ *verb* [I] to fly or move in large numbers **PHR V** swarm with sb/sth to be full of people or things

swash /swɒʃ/ *noun* [sing.] (**GEOGRAPHY**) the flow of water up the beach after a wave has broken ⊃ look at **backwash** ⊃ picture at **longshore drift**

swat /swɒt/ *verb* [T] (-tt-) to hit sth, especially an insect, with sth flat

sway /sweɪ/ *verb* **1** [I] to move slowly from side to side: *The trees were swaying in the wind.* **2** [T, often passive] to influence sb: *Many people were swayed by his convincing arguments.*

swear ⚓ **B2** /sweə(r)/ *verb* (*pt* swore /swɔː(r)/; *pp* sworn /swɔːn/) **1** [I] ~ (**at sb/sth**) to use rude or bad language: *He hit his thumb with the hammer and swore loudly.* ◇ *There's no point in swearing at the car just because it won't start!* ⊃ look at **curse**[1] (1) **2** [I, T] ~ (**to do sth**); ~ (**that**) … to make a serious promise: *When you give evidence in court you have to swear to tell the truth.* ◇ *Will you swear not to tell anyone?* ◇ *I swear (that) I'll never leave you.*
PHR V **swear by sth** to believe completely in the value of sth **swear sb in** [usually passive] to make sb say officially that they will accept the responsibility of a new position: *The president will be sworn in next week.*

swearing /ˈsweərɪŋ/ *noun* [U] rude language that may offend people

ˈ**swear word** *noun* [C] (**LANGUAGE**) a word that is considered rude or bad and that may offend people

sweat /swet/ *verb* [I] **1** to produce liquid through your skin because you are hot, ill or afraid **2** ~ (**over sth**) to work hard: *I've been sweating over that problem all day.* ▶ **sweat** *noun* [U, C]: *He stopped digging and wiped the sweat from his forehead.* ◇ *He woke up in a sweat.* ⊃ look at **perspiration** at **perspire** ⊃ picture at **skin**[1]
IDM **sweat/work your guts out** → **GUT**[1]

sweater ⚓ **A1** /ˈswetə(r)/ *noun* [C] a KNITTED piece of clothing made of wool or cotton for the upper part of the body, with long SLEEVES and no buttons **SYN** **jersey, jumper, pullover**

sweatpants /ˈswetpænts/ *noun* [pl.] loose warm trousers/pants, usually made of thick cotton and worn for relaxing or playing sports in

sweatshirt /ˈswetʃɜːt/ *noun* [C] a piece of clothing with long SLEEVES for the top part of the body, usually made of cotton

sweatshop /ˈswetʃɒp/ *noun* [C] (**BUSINESS**) a place where people work for low wages in poor conditions

sweatsuit /ˈswetsuːt/ *noun* [C] a SWEATSHIRT and SWEATPANTS worn together, for relaxing or playing sports in

sweaty /ˈsweti/ *adj.* (**sweatier; sweatiest**) **1** wet with SWEAT: *I was hot and sweaty after the match and needed a shower.* **2** causing you to SWEAT: *a hot sweaty day*

swede /swiːd/ *noun* [C, U] (*BrE*) (*AmE* **rutabaga**) a large round yellow vegetable that grows under the ground

sweep[1] ⚓ **B2** /swiːp/ *verb* (*pt, pp* swept /swept/)
• **WITH A BRUSH** **1** [T, I] to clean the floor, etc. by moving dust, dirt, etc. away with a brush: *to sweep the floor* ◇ *I'm going to sweep the leaves off the path.* ◇ *Could you sweep under the table too?* ⊃ note at **clean**[1]
• **WITH YOUR HAND** **2** [T] (used with an adverb or a preposition) to remove sth from a surface using your hand, etc: *He swept the books angrily off the table.*
• **MOVE FAST** **3** [I, T] to move quickly and smoothly over the area or in the direction mentioned: *Fire swept through the building.* **4** [I] (used with an adverb or a preposition) to move in a way that impresses or is intended to impress people: *Five big black Mercedes swept past us.*
• **MOVE WITH FORCE** **5** [T] (used with an adverb or a preposition) to move or push sb/sth with a lot of force: *The huge waves swept her overboard.*
• **SEARCH** **6** [I, T] to move over an area, especially in order to look for sth: *His eyes swept quickly over the page.* ◇ *The army were sweeping the fields for mines.*
PHR V **sweep (sb/sth) aside** to not allow sb/sth to affect your progress or plans **sweep sth out** to remove dirt and dust from the floor of a room or building using a brush **sweep over sb** (used about a feeling) to suddenly affect sb very strongly **sweep (sth) up** to remove dirt, dust, leaves, etc. using a brush

sweep[2] /swiːp/ *noun* [C] **1** [usually sing.] the act of moving dirt and dust from a floor or surface using a brush: *I'd better give the floor a sweep.* **2** a long, curving shape or movement: *He showed us which way to go with a sweep of his arm.* **3** a movement over an area, especially in order to look for sth **4** = CHIMNEY SWEEP
IDM **a clean sweep** → **CLEAN**[1]

sweeper /ˈswiːpə(r)/ *noun* [C] **1** a person or thing that cleans surfaces with a brush: *He's a road sweeper.* ◇ *Do you sell carpet sweepers?* **2** (**SPORT**) (in football) the defending player who plays behind the other defending players

sweeping /ˈswiːpɪŋ/ *adj.* **1** (used about statements, etc.) too general and not accurate enough: *He made a sweeping statement about all politicians being dishonest.* **2** having a great and important effect: *sweeping reforms*

sweet[1] ⚓ **A2** /swiːt/ *adj.* **1** containing, or tasting as if it contains, a lot of sugar: *Children usually like sweet things.* ◇ *This cake's too sweet.* ⊃ look at **savoury, sour** (1) **2** (used about a smell or a sound) pleasant **3** (used especially about children and small things) attractive: *a sweet little kitten* ◇ *Isn't that little girl sweet?* **SYN** **cute 4** having or showing a kind character: *a sweet smile* ◇ *It's very sweet of you to remember my birthday!* ▶ **sweetness** *noun* [U]
IDM **have a sweet tooth** to like eating sweet things

sweet[2] ⚓ **A2** /swiːt/ *noun* (*BrE*) **1** [C, usually pl.] (*AmE* **candy** [U, C]) a small piece of chocolate, boiled sugar, etc., eaten between meals: *He was sucking a sweet.* ◇ *a sweet shop* **2** [C, U] (*BrE*) sweet food served at the end of a meal ⊃ look at **dessert, pudding** (1)

sweetcorn /ˈswiːtkɔːn/ (*AmE also* **corn**) *noun* [U] the yellow grains of a type of MAIZE (= a tall plant) that you cook and eat as a vegetable

sweeten /ˈswiːtn/ *verb* [T] to make sth sweet by adding sugar, etc.

sweetener /ˈswiːtnə(r)/ *noun* [U, C] a substance used instead of sugar for making food or drink sweet: *artificial sweeteners*

sweetheart /ˈswiːthɑːt/ *noun* **1** [sing.] (*informal*) used when speaking to sb, especially a child, in a very friendly way: *Do you want a drink, sweetheart?* **2** [C] (*old-fashioned*) a boyfriend or girlfriend

sweetly /ˈswiːtli/ *adv.* in an attractive, kind or pleasant way: *She smiled sweetly.* ◇ *sweetly-scented flowers*

ˌ**sweet poˈtato** *noun* [C, U] a vegetable that grows under the ground and looks like a red potato, but is orange inside and tastes sweet

swell[1] /swel/ *verb* (*pt* swelled; *pp* swelled, swollen /ˈswəʊlən/) **1** [I, T] ~ (**up**) to become or to make sth bigger, fuller or thicker: *After the fall her ankle began to swell up.* ◇ *Heavy rain had swollen the rivers.* **2** [I, T] to increase or make sth increase in number or size: *The crowd swelled to 600 by the end of the evening.* **3** [I] (used about feelings or sound) to suddenly become stronger or louder: *Hatred swelled inside him.*

swell² /swel/ *noun* [C, usually sing.] the slow movement up and down of the surface of the sea

swelling /'sweliŋ/ *noun* **1** [U] the process of becoming SWOLLEN (= bigger or fatter than usual): *The disease often causes swelling of the ankles and knees.* **2** [C] **(HEALTH)** a place on your body that is bigger or fatter than usual because of an injury or illness: *I've got a nasty swelling under my eye.*

sweltering /'sweltəriŋ/ *adj.* (*informal*) much too hot: *It was sweltering in the office today.*

swept /swept/ *past tense, past participle of* **sweep¹**

swerve /swɜːv/ *verb* [I] to change direction suddenly: *The car swerved to avoid the child.* ▸ **swerve** *noun* [C]

swift /swift/ *adj.* happening without delay; quick: *a swift reaction/decision/movement* ◊ *a swift runner* ▸ **swiftly** *adv.*

swig /swig/ *verb* [T] (-gg-) (*informal*) to take a quick drink of sth, especially alcohol ▸ **swig** *noun* [C]

swill /swil/ *verb* [T] ~ **sth** (**out/down**) to wash sth by pouring large amounts of water, etc. into, over or through it

swim 🔊 **A1** /swim/ *verb* (**swimming**; *pt* **swam** /swæm/; *pp* **swum** /swʌm/) **1** [I, T] **(SPORT)** to move your body through water: *Hundreds of tiny fish swam past.* ◊ *How long will it take her to swim the Channel?* **2** go **swimming** [I] to spend time swimming for pleasure: *I go swimming twice a week.* **3** [I] **be swimming (in/with sth)** to be covered with a lot of liquid: *The salad was swimming in oil.* **4** [I] to seem to be moving or turning: *The floor began to swim before my eyes and I fainted.* **5** [I] (used about your head) to feel confused: *My head was swimming with so much new information.*
▸ **swim** 🔊 **B1** *noun* [sing.]: *to go for/have a swim*
▸ **swimmer** *noun* [C]: *a strong/weak swimmer*

swimming 🔊 **A1** /'swimiŋ/ *noun* [U] **(SPORT)** the sport or activity of swimming

swimming bath *noun* [C] (*usually* **swimming baths** /'swimiŋ bɑːðz/ [pl.]) **(SPORT)** a public swimming pool, usually indoors

swimming pool (*also* **pool**) *noun* [C] **(SPORT)** a pool that is built especially for people to swim in; the building that contains this pool: *an indoor/outdoor/open-air swimming pool*

swimming trunks *noun* [pl.] **(SPORT)** a piece of clothing like short trousers that a man wears to go swimming: *a pair of swimming trunks*

swimsuit /'swimsuːt/ (*also* **swimming costume**) *noun* [C] **(SPORT)** a piece of clothing that a woman wears to go swimming ◗ look at **bikini**

swindle /'swindl/ *verb* [T] ~ **sb/sth** (**out of sth**) to trick sb in order to get money, etc. from them: *He swindled his sister out of her savings.* ▸ **swindle** *noun* [C]: *a tax swindle*

swine /swain/ *noun* **1** [C] (*informal*) a very unpleasant person **2** [pl.] (*old-fashioned*) **(AGRICULTURE)** pigs

swine flu *noun* [U] **(HEALTH)** a serious illness that affects pigs, or a similar illness that can be spread between humans

swing¹ 🔊+ **C1** /swiŋ/ *verb* (*pt, pp* **swung** /swʌŋ/) **1** [I, T] to move backwards and forwards or from side to side while hanging from sth; to make sb/sth move in this way: *The rope was swinging from a branch.* ◊ *She sat on the wall, swinging her legs.* **2** [I, T] (used with an adverb or a preposition) to move in a curve or make sb/sth move in a curve: *The door swung open and Rudi walked in.* ◊ *He swung the child up onto his shoulders.* **3** [I] to move or change from one position or situation

towards the opposite one: *She swung round when she heard the door open.* ◊ *His moods swing from one extreme to the other.* **4** [I, T] ~ **(at sb/sth)** to try to hit sb/sth: *He swung violently at the other man but missed.*

swing² 🔊+ **C1** /swiŋ/ *noun* **1** [sing.] a SWINGING movement or rhythm: *He took a swing at the ball.* **2** [C] a seat, a piece of rope, etc. that is hung from above so that you can SWING backwards and forwards on it: *Some children were playing on the swings.* **3** [C] a change from one position or situation towards the opposite one
IDM in full swing → **FULL¹**

swing voter (*AmE*) = **FLOATING VOTER**

swipe /swaip/ *verb* **1** [I, T] ~ **(at) sb/sth** to hit or try to hit sb/sth by moving your arm in a curve: *He swiped at the wasp with a newspaper but missed.* **2** [I, T] ~ **(sth) (on/across sth)** (on some mobile phones or small computer devices) to move content across a screen using your finger: *Swipe your finger across the screen to unlock the phone.* **3** [T] (*informal*) to steal sth **4** [T] to pass the part of a plastic card on which information is stored through a special machine for reading it: *The receptionist swiped my credit card.* ▸ **swipe** *noun* [C]: *She took a swipe at him with her handbag.*

swipe card *noun* [C] a small plastic card on which information is stored which can be read by an electronic machine

swirl /swɜːl/ *verb* [I, T] (often used with an adverb or a preposition) to move around quickly in a circle; to make sth do this: *Her long skirt swirled round her legs as she danced.* ◊ *He swirled some water round in his mouth and spat it out.* ▸ **swirl** *noun* [C]

Swiss roll /ˌswis 'rəʊl/ *noun* [C] a thin flat cake that is spread with jam, etc. and rolled up

switches

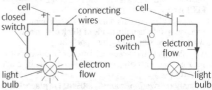

complete circuit:
• The charge flows.
• The light bulb is lit.

incomplete circuit:
• There is no flow of charge.
• The light bulb is not lit.

switch¹ 🔊 **B2** /swit∫/ *noun* [C] **1** a small device that you press or move up and down in order to turn a light or piece of electrical equipment on and off: *a light switch* **2** a sudden change: *a switch in policy*

switch² 🔊 **B1** /swit∫/ *verb* [I, T] **1** ~ **(sth) (over) (to/from sth)**; ~ **(between A and B)** to change or be changed from one thing to another: *I'm fed up with my glasses — I'm thinking of switching over to contact lenses.* ◊ *Press these two keys to switch between documents on screen.* ◊ *The match has been switched from Saturday to Sunday.* **2** ~ **(sth) (with sb/sth)**; ~ **(sth) (over/round)** to exchange positions, activities, etc: *We asked them if they would switch places with us.* ◊ *Somebody switched the signs round and everyone went the wrong way.*
PHR V switch off to stop thinking about sth or paying attention to sth **switch (sth) off/on** to press a switch in order to stop/start electric power: *Don't forget to switch off the cooker.* **switch (sth) over** to change to a different TV programme

switchboard /'swit∫bɔːd/ *noun* [C] the place in a large company, etc. where all the phone calls are connected

switched 'on adj. ~ (to sth) (informal) knowing about new things that are happening: We are trying to get people switched on to the benefits of healthy eating.

swivel /'swɪvl/ verb [I, T] (-ll-, AmE -l-) ~ (sth) (round) to turn around a central point; to make sth do this: She swivelled round to face me. ◇ He swivelled his chair towards the door.

swollen¹ /'swəʊlən/ past participle of swell¹

swollen² /'swəʊlən/ adj. thicker or wider than usual: Her leg was badly swollen after the accident. ➔ note at hospital

swoop /swuːp/ verb [I] 1 to fly or move down suddenly: The bird swooped down on its prey. 2 ~ (on sb/sth) (used especially about the police or the army) to visit or capture sb/sth without warning: Officers swooped on the vehicles as they left the ferry. ◇ Police swooped at dawn and arrested the man at his home. ▶ swoop noun [C]

swop /swɒp/ = SWAP

sword ℹ+ 🄲 /sɔːd/ noun [C] a long, very sharp metal weapon, like a large knife ➔ picture at weapon

swordfish /'sɔːdfɪʃ/ noun [C, U] (pl. swordfish) a large sea fish that you can eat, with a very long thin sharp upper JAW

swore /swɔː(r)/ past tense of swear

sworn /swɔːn/ past participle of swear

swot¹ /swɒt/ verb [I] (-tt-) ~ (for sth) (BrE, informal) (EDUCATION) to study sth very hard, especially to prepare for an exam: She's swotting for her final exams.
PHR V swot sth up | swot up on sth (BrE, informal) (EDUCATION) to study a particular subject very hard, especially to prepare for an exam

swot² /swɒt/ noun [C] (BrE, informal) (EDUCATION) a person who studies too hard

'SWOT analysis noun [C] (BUSINESS) a study done by an organization in order to find its strengths and weaknesses, and what problems or opportunities it should deal with HELP SWOT is formed from the first letters of 'strengths', 'weaknesses', 'opportunities' and 'threats'.

swum /swʌm/ past participle of swim

swung /swʌŋ/ past tense, past participle of swing¹

syllabic /sɪ'læbɪk/ adj. (LANGUAGE) 1 based on syllables: He invented syllabic scripts that are still used today. 2 (used about a consonant) forming a whole syllable, for example /l/ in middle

syllable /'sɪləbl/ noun [C] (LANGUAGE) a word or part of a word that contains one vowel sound: 'Mat' has one syllable and 'mattress' has two syllables. ◇ The stress in 'international' is on the third syllable.

syllabus /'sɪləbəs/ noun [C] (pl. syllabuses, syllabi /-baɪ/) (EDUCATION) a list of subjects, etc. that are included in a course of study ➔ look at curriculum

symbiosis /ˌsɪmbaɪ'əʊsɪs/ noun [U, C] (pl. symbioses /-'əʊsiːz/) 1 (BIOLOGY) the relationship between two different living creatures that live close together and depend on each other in particular ways, each getting particular benefits from the other: The birds live in symbiosis with the cattle, picking insects from their skin to eat. 2 a relationship between people, companies, etc. that is to the advantage of both ▶ symbiotic /-'ɒtɪk/ adj.: a symbiotic relationship ▶ symbiotically /-kli/ adv.

symbol ℹ 🄰🄲 🕓 /'sɪmbl/ noun [C] 1 ~ (of sth) a sign, an object, etc. that represents sth: The cross is the symbol of Christianity. ➔ note at sign¹ 2 ~ (for sth) a letter, number or sign that has a particular meaning: O is the symbol for oxygen.

symbolic ℹ+ 🄲 /sɪm'bɒlɪk/ (also symbolical /sɪm'bɒlɪkl/) adj. ~ (of sth) used or seen to represent sth: The white dove is symbolic of peace. ▶ symbolically /-kli/ adv.

symbolism /'sɪmbəlɪzəm/ noun [U] (ART, LITERATURE) 1 the use of symbols to represent things, especially in art and literature 2 (also Symbolism) a style in painting and poetry developed in France and Belgium in the late nineteenth century, which uses images and symbols to express ideas and emotions ▶ symbolist /-lɪst/ noun [C], adj.

symbolize (BrE also -ise) /'sɪmbəlaɪz/ verb [T] to represent sth: The deepest notes in music are often used to symbolize danger or despair.

symmetrical /sɪ'metrɪkl/ (also symmetric /sɪ'metrɪk/) adj. (GEOMETRY) having two halves that match each other exactly in size, shape, etc. OPP asymmetric ▶ symmetrically /-kli/ adv.

symmetry /'sɪmətri/ noun [U] (GEOMETRY) the state of having two halves that match each other exactly in size, shape, etc. ➔ picture at axis

sympathetic ℹ+ 🄱🄲 /ˌsɪmpə'θetɪk/ adj. 1 ~ (to/towards sb) showing that you understand other people's feelings, especially their problems: When Suki was ill, everyone was very sympathetic. ◇ I felt very sympathetic towards him. OPP unsympathetic 2 ~ (to sb/sth) being in agreement with or supporting sb/sth: I explained our ideas but she wasn't sympathetic to them. OPP unsympathetic ▶ sympathetically /-kli/ adv.

sympathize (BrE also -ise) /'sɪmpəθaɪz/ verb [I] ~ (with sb/sth) 1 to feel sorry for sb; to show that you understand sb's problems: I sympathize with her, but I don't know what I can do to help. 2 to support sb/sth: I find it difficult to sympathize with his opinions.

sympathizer (BrE also -iser) /'sɪmpəθaɪzə(r)/ noun [C] a person who agrees with and supports an idea or aim

sympathy ℹ 🄱🄲 /'sɪmpəθi/ noun (pl. -ies) 1 [U, C, usually pl.] ~ (for/towards sb) an understanding of other people's feelings, especially their problems: Everyone feels great sympathy for the victims of the attack. ◇ I don't expect any sympathy from you. ◇ I have no sympathy for Mark — it's his own fault. ◇ May we offer our deepest sympathies on the death of your wife. 2 sympathies [pl.] feelings of support or agreement: Some members of the party have nationalist sympathies.
IDM in sympathy (with sb/sth) in agreement, showing that you support or approve of sb/sth: Train drivers stopped work in sympathy with the striking bus drivers.

symphony /'sɪmfəni/ noun [C] (pl. -ies) (MUSIC) a long piece of music written for a large ORCHESTRA

symposium /sɪm'pəʊziəm/ noun [C] (pl. symposia /-ziə/, symposiums) a meeting at which experts have discussions about a particular subject; a small conference

symptom ℹ 🄱🄼 /'sɪmptəm/ noun [C] 1 (HEALTH) a change in your body that is a sign of illness: The symptoms of flu include a headache, a high temperature and aches in the body. ➔ note at doctor¹ 2 a sign (that sth bad is happening or exists): The riots are a symptom of a deeper problem. ➔ note at sign¹ ▶ symptomatic /ˌsɪmptə'mætɪk/ adj.

synaesthesia (also synesthesia) /ˌsɪnəs'θiːziə/ noun [U] (BIOLOGY) the fact of experiencing some things in a different way from most other people, for example experiencing colours as sounds or shapes as tastes

synagogue /'sɪnəgɒg/ *noun* [C] (**RELIGION**) a building where Jewish people go to pray or to study their religion

synapse /'saɪnæps, 'sɪ-/ *noun* [C] (**BIOLOGY**) a connection between two nerve cells ▶ synaptic /saɪ'næptɪk, sɪ-/ *adj.*: *the synaptic membranes*

sync (*also* **synch**) /sɪŋk/ *noun* (*informal*)
IDM **in sync** moving or working at exactly the same time and speed as sb/sth else: *The soundtrack is not in sync with the music.* **out of sync** not moving or working at exactly the same time and speed as sb/sth else

synchronize (*BrE also* **-ise**) /'sɪŋkrənaɪz/ (*also informal* **sync, synch** /sɪŋk/) *verb* [T] **1** ~ (**sth**) (**with sth**) to happen at the same time or to move at the same speed as sth; to make sth do this: *We synchronized our watches to make sure we agreed what the time was.* **2** ~ **sth** (**with sth**) to link data files between one computer or mobile device and another so that the information in the files on both machines is the same: *The phone lets you synchronize your calendar and contacts with your PC.*

synchronized swimming (*BrE also* **-ised-**) *noun* [U] (**SPORT**) a sport in which groups of people swimming move in patterns in the water to music

syncline /'sɪŋklaɪn/ *noun* [C] (**GEOLOGY**) an area of ground where layers of rock in the earth's surface have been folded into a curve that is lower in the middle than at the ends ⊃ look at **anticline**

syncopated /'sɪŋkəpeɪtɪd/ *adj.* (**MUSIC**) in **syncopated** rhythm the strong beats are made weak and the weak beats are made strong ▶ syncopation /ˌsɪŋkə'peɪʃn/ *noun* [U]

syndicate¹ /'sɪndɪkət/ *noun* [C] (**BUSINESS**) a group of people or companies that work together in order to achieve a particular aim

syndicate² /'sɪndɪkeɪt/ *verb* [T, usually passive] (**BUSINESS**) to sell an article, a photo, a TV programme, etc. to several different news companies, etc: *His column is syndicated throughout the world.*

syndrome ʔ+ **C1** /'sɪndrəʊm/ *noun* [C] **1** (**HEALTH**) a group of signs or changes in the body that are typical of an illness: *Down's syndrome ◇ Acquired Immune Deficiency Syndrome (Aids)* **2** a set of opinions or a way of behaving that is typical of a particular type of person, attitude or social problem

synergy /'sɪnədʒi/ *noun* [U, C] (*pl.* **-ies**) the extra energy, power, success, etc. that is achieved by two or more people or companies working together, instead of on their own

synonym /'sɪnənɪm/ *noun* [C] (**LANGUAGE**) a word or phrase that has the same meaning as another word or phrase in the same language: *'Big' and 'large' are synonyms.* ⊃ look at **antonym** ▶ synonymous /sɪ'nɒnɪməs/ *adj.* ~ (**with sth**): *Wealth is not always synonymous with happiness.*

synopsis /sɪ'nɒpsɪs/ *noun* [C] (*pl.* **synopses** /-'nɒpsiːz/) (**ARTS AND MEDIA, LITERATURE**) a short description of a piece of writing, a play, etc. **SYN** **summary¹** ▶ synoptic /-'nɒptɪk/ *adj.* (*formal*)

synovial /saɪ'nəʊviəl, sɪ-/ *adj.* (**ANATOMY**) connected with a type of JOINT (= a place where two bones meet) that has a MEMBRANE (= a thin layer of skin) containing liquid between the bones, which allows the JOINT to move freely: *a synovial joint/membrane*

syntax /'sɪntæks/ *noun* [U] (**GRAMMAR**) the system of rules for the structure of sentences in a language

synthesis ʔ+ **C1** /'sɪnθəsɪs/ *noun* (*pl.* **syntheses** /-θəsiːz/) **1** [U, C] ~ (**of sth**) the act of combining separate ideas, beliefs, styles, etc.; a mixture or combination of ideas, beliefs, styles, etc: *the synthesis of traditional and modern values ◇ a synthesis of art with everyday life* **2** [U] (**COMPUTING**) the production of sounds, music or speech using electronic equipment: *digital/sound/speech synthesis* **3** [U] (**BIOLOGY**) the natural chemical production of a substance in animals and plants: *protein synthesis* **4** [U] (**CHEMISTRY**) the artificial production of a substance that is present naturally in animals and plants: *the synthesis of penicillin*

synthesize (*BrE also* **-ise**) /'sɪnθəsaɪz/ *verb* [T] **1** (**CHEMISTRY**) to produce a substance by artificial means **2** (**MUSIC**) to produce sounds, music or speech using electronic equipment **3** to combine separate ideas, beliefs, styles, etc.

synthesizer (*BrE also* **-iser**) /'sɪnθəsaɪzə(r)/ *noun* [C] (**MUSIC**) an electronic musical instrument that can produce a wide variety of different sounds

synthetic /sɪn'θetɪk/ *adj.* **1** (**CHEMISTRY**) made by a chemical process; not natural: *synthetic materials/fibres* ⊃ note at **artificial** **2** (**LANGUAGE**) (used about a language) using changes to the ends of words rather than separate words to show the functions of words in a sentence ▶ synthetically /-kli/ *adv.*

syphilis /'sɪfɪlɪs/ *noun* [U] (**HEALTH**) a serious disease that passes from one person to another by sexual contact

syphon /'saɪfn/ = SIPHON

syringe /sɪ'rɪndʒ/ *noun* [C] **1** (**MEDICINE, SCIENCE**) a plastic or glass tube with a long hollow needle that is used for putting drugs, etc. into the body or for taking a small amount of blood out of the body ⊃ picture at **health** **2** (**SCIENCE**) a plastic or glass tube with a rubber part at the end, used for taking liquid in and then pushing it out ⊃ picture at **laboratory**

syrup /'sɪrəp/ *noun* [U] a thick sweet liquid, often made by boiling sugar with water or fruit juice: *peaches in syrup* ⊃ look at **treacle**

system ʔ **A2** ⊙ /'sɪstəm/ *noun* **1** [C] a set of ideas or rules for organizing sth; a particular way of doing sth: *We have a new computerized system in the library. ◇ The government is planning to reform the education system.* **2** [C] a group of things or parts that work together: *a central heating system ◇ a transport system* **3** [C] (**COMPUTING**) a set of computer equipment and programs that are used together: *an upgraded computer system* **4** [C] the body of a person or an animal; parts of the body that work together: *the central nervous system* **5** the system [sing.] (*informal*) the traditional methods and rules of a society: *You can't beat the system* (= you must accept these rules). **IDM** **get sth out of your system** (*informal*) to do sth to free yourself of a strong feeling or emotion

systematic ʔ+ **C1** ⊙ /ˌsɪstə'mætɪk/ *adj.* done using a fixed plan or method: *a systematic search* ▶ systematically ⊙ /-kli/ *adv.*

systemic /sɪ'stiːmɪk, -'stem-/ *adj.* **1** affecting or connected with the whole of sth, especially the human body **2** **systemic** chemicals or drugs that are used to treat diseases in plants or animals enter the body of the plant or animal and spread to all parts of it: *systemic weedkillers* ▶ systemically /-kli/ *adv.*

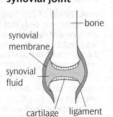
synovial joint

bone
synovial membrane
synovial fluid
cartilage   ligament

systems 'analyst *noun* [C] (**COMPUTING**) a person whose job is to look carefully at the needs of a company or an organization and then design the best way of working and completing tasks using computer programs

'system unit *noun* [C] (**COMPUTING**) the main part of a computer, separate from the keyboard, monitor and mouse, that contains all the other parts of the system

systole /'sɪstəli/ *noun* [C] (**HEALTH**) the part of the heart's rhythm when the heart PUMPS blood ⊃ look at **diastole**
▸ **systolic** /ˌsɪ'stɒlɪk/ *adj.*: *systolic blood pressure*

T t

T /tiː/ (*also* t) *noun* [C, U] (*pl.* T's, t's) the 20th letter of the English alphabet: *'Table' begins with (a) 'T'.*

ta /tɑː/ *exclamation* (*BrE, informal*) thank you

tab /tæb/ *noun* [C] **1** a small piece of cloth, metal or paper that is fixed to the edge of sth to help you open, hold or identify it: *You open the tin by pulling the metal tab.* **2** (*informal*) the money that you owe for food, drink, etc. that you receive in a bar, restaurant, etc. but pay for later **3** (**COMPUTING**) one of a number of small areas at the edge of a computer window that allows you to change the section of the website or piece of software that you are looking at **4** (**COMPUTING**) a fixed position in a line of a document that you are typing that shows where a piece of text or a column of figures, etc. will begin
IDM **keep tabs on sb/sth** (*informal*) to watch sb/sth carefully; to check sth

tabla /'tæblə/ *noun* [C] (**MUSIC**) a pair of small drums played with the hands and used in South Asian music, usually to accompany other instruments

table 🔑 **A1** /'teɪbl/ *noun* [C] **1** a piece of furniture with a flat top supported by legs: *a dining/bedside/coffee/kitchen table* ◇ *Could you lay/set the table for lunch?* (= put the knives, forks, plates, etc. on it) ◇ *Let me help you clear the table* (= remove the dirty plates, etc. at the end of a meal). **2** a list of facts or figures, usually arranged in rows and columns down a page: *Table 3 shows the results.* **3** = MULTIPLICATION TABLE

tablecloth /'teɪblklɒθ/ *noun* [C] a piece of cloth that you use for covering a table, especially when having a meal

'table manners *noun* [pl.] behaviour that is considered correct while you are having a meal at a table with other people

tablespoon /'teɪblspuːn/ *noun* [C] **1** a large spoon used for serving or measuring food (*also* **tablespoonful** /'teɪblspuːnfʊl/) (*abbr.* **tbsp**) the amount that a tablespoon holds: *Add two tablespoons of sugar.*

tablet 🔑 **A2** /'tæblət/ *noun* [C] **1** (**COMPUTING**) a small, flat computer that you can carry with you and that you work by touching the screen so that you do not have to use a mouse or a keyboard **2** (**MEDICINE**) a small round piece of medicine that you SWALLOW: *Take two tablets every four hours.* **SYN** **pill** ⊃ picture at **health** **3** a small amount of a substance in solid form

table tennis (*also BrE, informal* ping-pong) (*AmE* Ping-Pong™) *noun* [U] (**SPORT**) a game with rules like tennis in which you hit a light plastic ball across a table with a small round BAT ⊃ picture at **sport**

tabloid /'tæblɔɪd/ *noun* [C] (**ARTS AND MEDIA**) a newspaper with small pages, often with a lot of pictures and short articles, especially ones about famous people ⊃ note at **newspaper**

taboo /tə'buː/ *noun* [C] (*pl.* **-oos**) something that you must not say or do because it might shock, offend or make people embarrassed ▸ **taboo** *adj.*: *a taboo subject/word*

tabular /'tæbjələ(r)/ *adj.* presented or arranged in a table: *tabular data* ◇ *The results are presented in tabular form.*

tabulate /'tæbjuleɪt/ *verb* [T] to arrange facts or figures in columns or lists so that they can be read easily ▸ **tabulation** /ˌtæbju'leɪʃn/ *noun* [U, C]

tacit /'tæsɪt/ *adj.* understood but not actually said ▸ **tacitly** *adv.*

tack[1] /tæk/ *noun* **1** [U, sing.] a way of dealing with a particular situation: *If people won't listen we'll have to try a different tack.* **2** [C] a small nail with a sharp point and a flat head

tack[2] /tæk/ *verb* [T] **1** to fasten sth in place with TACKS (= small nails) **2** to fasten cloth together temporarily with long STITCHES that can be removed easily **PHR V** **tack sth on (to sth)** to add sth extra on the end of sth

tackle[1] 🔑 **B2** /'tækl/ *verb* **1** [T] to make an effort to deal with a difficult situation or problem: *The government must tackle the problem of rising unemployment.* ◇ *Firemen were brought in to tackle the blaze.* **2** [T] ~**sb (about sth)** to speak to sb about a difficult subject: *I'm going to tackle him about the money he owes me.* **3** [T, I] (**SPORT**) (in football, etc.) to try to take the ball from sb in the other team **4** [I, T] (**SPORT**) (in rugby and AMERICAN FOOTBALL) to stop sb running by pulling them to the ground

tackle[2] 🔑 **C1** /'tækl/ *noun* (**SPORT**) **1** [C] (in football, etc.) the act of trying to get the ball from another player **2** [C] (in rugby and AMERICAN FOOTBALL) the act of pulling sb to the ground to stop them running **3** [U] the equipment you use in some sports, especially fishing: *fishing tackle*

tacky /'tæki/ *adj.* (tackier; tackiest) **1** (*informal*) cheap and of poor quality and/or not in good taste: *a shop selling tacky souvenirs* **2** (used about paint, etc.) not quite dry; sticky

tact /tækt/ *noun* [U] the ability to deal with people without offending or upsetting them: *She handled the situation with great tact and diplomacy.*

tactful /'tæktfl/ *adj.* careful not to say or do things that could offend people **SYN** **diplomatic** **OPP** **tactless** ▸ **tactfully** /-fəli/ *adv.*

tactic 🔑 **C1** /'tæktɪk/ *noun* **1** [C, usually pl.] the particular method you use to achieve sth: *We must decide what our tactics are going to be at the next meeting.* ◇ *I don't think this tactic will work.* **2** tactics [pl.] the effective arrangement and use of military forces in order to win a battle

tactical 🔑 **C1** /'tæktɪkl/ *adj.* **1** connected with the particular method you use to achieve sth: *tactical discussions/planning* ◇ *I made a tactical error.* **2** designed to bring a future advantage: *a tactical decision* ▸ **tactically** /-kli/ *adv.*

ˌtactical 'voting *noun* [U] (*BrE*) (**POLITICS**) the act of voting for a particular person or political party, not because you support them, but in order to prevent sb else from being elected

tactless /'tæktləs/ *adj.* saying and doing things that are likely to offend and upset other people: *It was rather tactless of you to ask her how old she was.* **OPP** **tactful** ▸ **tactlessly** *adv.*

tadpole /'tædpəʊl/ *noun* [C] a young form of a frog when it has a large black head and a long tail ⊃ picture at **animal**

tae kwon do /ˌtaɪ ˌkwɒn 'dəʊ/ *noun* [U] (**SPORT**) a Korean system of fighting without weapons, similar to KARATE

tag¹ ʔ+ **B2** /tæg/ *noun* [C] **1** (often in compounds) a small piece of card, cloth, etc. fastened to sth to give information about it: *How much is this dress? There isn't a price tag on it.* **2** = QUESTION TAG **3** an electronic device that can be attached to a person, an animal or an object so that police, researchers, etc. know where the person, etc. is

tag² ʔ+ **B2** /tæg/ *verb* [T] (-gg-) **1** to fasten a TAG onto sth **2** to fasten an electronic TAG onto sb **3** to add a link to various users' profiles from a photo on a SOCIAL MEDIA website
PHRV **tag along** to follow or go somewhere with sb, especially when you have not been invited

'tag question = QUESTION TAG

t'ai chi /ˌtaɪ 'tʃiː/ *noun* [U] (**SPORT**) a Chinese system of exercises consisting of sets of very slow controlled movements

tail¹ ʔ **B1** /teɪl/ *noun*
- OF AN ANIMAL, ETC. **1** [C] the part at the end of the body of an animal, a bird, a fish, etc: *The dog barked and wagged its tail.* ⊃ picture at **animal**, **fertilization**
- OF A PLANE, ETC. **2** [C] the back part of an aircraft, etc. ⊃ picture at **airliner**
- JACKET **3** tails [pl.] a man's formal coat that is short at the front but with a long, divided piece at the back, worn especially at weddings
- SIDE OF A COIN **4** tails [pl.] the side of a coin that does not have the head of a person on it: *'We'll toss a coin to decide,' said my father. 'Heads or tails?'*
- PERSON **5** [C] (*informal*) a person who is sent to follow sb secretly to get information about them
IDM **can't make head nor/or tail of sth** → HEAD¹

tail² /teɪl/ *verb* [T] to follow sb closely, especially to watch where they go
PHRV **tail away/off** (*especially BrE*) to become smaller and weaker

tailback /'teɪlbæk/ *noun* [C] a long line of traffic that is moving slowly or not moving at all, because sth is blocking the road in front

tailbone /'teɪlbəʊn/ *noun* [C] (**ANATOMY**) the small bone at the bottom of the SPINE **SYN** coccyx ⊃ picture at **body**

tailgate¹ /'teɪlɡeɪt/ *noun* [C] **1** (*also* tailboard /'teɪlbɔːd/) a door at the back of a lorry that opens downwards and that you can open or remove when you are loading or UNLOADING the vehicle **2** the door that opens upwards at the back of a HATCHBACK (= a car that has three or five doors)

tailgate² /'teɪlɡeɪt/ *verb* [I, T] (*informal*) to drive too closely behind another vehicle

tailor¹ /'teɪlə(r)/ *noun* [C] a person whose job is to make clothes, especially for men

tailor² /'teɪlə(r)/ *verb* [T, usually passive] ~ sth (to/for sb/ sth) to make or design sth for a particular person or purpose: *programmes tailored to the needs of specific groups*

ˌtailor-'made *adj.* ~ (for sb/sth) made for a particular person or purpose and therefore very suitable **SYN** bespoke

tailpipe /'teɪlpaɪp/ *noun* (*AmE*) = EXHAUST¹ (2)

tailplane /'teɪlpleɪn/ *noun* [C] a small wing at the back of an aircraft ⊃ picture at **airliner**

tailwind /'teɪlwɪnd/ *noun* [C] a wind that blows from behind a moving vehicle, a runner, etc. ⊃ look at **headwind**

taint /teɪnt/ *noun* [C, usually sing.] (*formal*) the effect of sth bad or unpleasant that damages or harms the quality of sb/sth: *the taint of corruption* ▶ **taint** *verb* [T, often passive]: *Her reputation was tainted by the scandal.*

take ʔ **A1** /teɪk/ *verb* [T] (*pt* took /tʊk/; *pp* taken /'teɪkən/)
- CARRY/MOVE **1** to carry or move sb/sth; to go with sb from one place to another: *Take your coat with you — it's cold.* ◇ *Could you take this letter home to your parents?* ◇ *The ambulance took him to hospital.* ◇ *I'm taking the children swimming this afternoon.*
- NEED **2** to need sth/sb: *It took three people to move the piano.* ◇ *How long did the journey take?* ◇ *It took a lot of courage to say that.*
- PHOTOGRAPH **3** to photograph sth: *I took some nice photos of the wedding.*
- TRANSPORT **4** to use a form of transport; to use a particular route: *I always take the train to York.* ◇ *Which road do you take to Hove?* ◇ *Take the second turning on the right.* ⊃ note at **direction**
- IN YOUR HAND **5** to put your hand round sth and hold it (and move it towards you): *She held out the keys, and I took them.* ◇ *He took a sweater out of the drawer.* ◇ *She took my hand/me by the hand.*
- REMOVE **6** to remove sth from a place or a person, often without permission: *Who's taken my pen?* ◇ *My name had been taken off the list.* ◇ *The burglars took all my jewellery.*
- EAT/DRINK **7** to eat, drink, etc. sth: *Take two tablets four times a day.* ◇ *Do you take sugar in tea?*
- WRITE DOWN **8** to write or record sth: *She took notes during the lecture.* ◇ *The police officer took my name and address.* ⊃ note at **meeting**
- EXAM **9** (**EDUCATION**) to study a subject for an exam; to do an exam: *I'm taking the advanced exam this summer.* ⊃ note at **study²**
- ACTION **10** used with nouns to say that sb is performing an action: *Take a look at this article* (= look at it). ◇ *We have to take a decision* (= decide).
- MEASUREMENT **11** to measure sth: *The doctor took my temperature/pulse/blood pressure.*
- CONTROL **12** to capture a place by force; to get control of sb/sth: *The state will take control of the company.*
- ACCEPT **13** to accept or receive sth: *If you take my advice you'll forget all about him.* ◇ *Do you take credit cards?* ◇ *What coins does the machine take?* ◇ *I'm not going to take the blame for the accident.* ◇ *She's not going to take the job.*
- DEAL WITH STH BAD **14** to be able to deal with sth difficult or unpleasant: *I can't take much more of this heat.* **SYN** stand¹
- UNDERSTAND/REACT **15** to understand sth or react to sth in a particular way: *She took what he said as a compliment.* ◇ *I wish you would take things more seriously.*
- HAVE A FEELING **16** to get a particular feeling from sth: *He takes great pleasure in his grandchildren.* ◇ *When she failed the exam she took comfort from the fact that it was only by a few marks.*
- SIZE **17** (not used in the progressive tenses) to wear a certain size of shoes or clothes: *What size shoes do you take?*
- CONTAIN **18** (not used in the progressive tenses) to have enough space for sb/sth: *How many passengers can this bus take?*
- TEACH **19** ~ sb (for sth) (**EDUCATION**) to give lessons to sb: *Who takes you for English* (= who is your teacher)?
- IN GRAMMAR **20** (not used in the progressive tenses) to have or need a word to go with it in a sentence or other structure: *The verb 'depend' takes the preposition 'on'.*

• IN MATHEMATICS 21 (not used in the progressive tenses) **~ A (away) (from B); B~ (away) A** to reduce one number by the value of another: *Take 3 from 15 and you're left with 12.* ◊ *90 take away 5 is 85.*
IDM **be taken with sb/sth** to find sb/sth attractive or interesting **I take it (that …)** (used to show that you understand sth from a situation, even though you have not been told) *I imagine; I guess; I suppose: I take it that you're not coming?* **take it from me** believe me **take a lot out of sb** to make sb very tired **take a lot of/some doing** to need a lot of work or effort **❶** For other idioms containing **take**, look at the entries for the nouns, adjectives, etc. For example, **take place** is at **place**.
PHR V **take sb aback** → ABACK
take after sb (not used in the progressive tenses) to look or behave like an older member of your family, especially a parent
take sth apart to separate sth into the different parts it is made of
take sth away 1 to cause a feeling, etc. to disappear: *These pills will take the pain away.* **2** to buy cooked food at a restaurant, etc. and carry it out to eat somewhere else, for example at home ᴐ noun **takeaway** **take sb/sth away (from sb)** to remove sb/ sth: *She took the scissors away from the child.*
take sth back 1 to return sth to the place that you got it from **2** to admit that sth you said was wrong
take sth down 1 to remove a structure by separating it into the pieces it is made of: *They took the tent down and started the journey home.* **2** to write down sth that is said
take sb in 1 to make sb believe sth that is not true: *I was completely taken in by her story.* **2** to invite sb who has no home to live with you **take sth in** to understand what you see, hear or read: *There was too much in the museum to take in at one go.*
take off 1 (used about an aircraft) to leave the ground and start flying **OPP** **land²** **2** (used about an idea, a product, etc.) to become successful or popular very quickly or suddenly **take sb off** to copy the way sb speaks or behaves in a way that makes people laugh **take sth off 1** to remove sth, especially clothes: *Come in and take your coat off.* **OPP** **put sth on 2** to have the period of time mentioned as a holiday: *I'm going to take a week off.*
take sb on to start to employ sb: *The firm is taking on new staff.* ᴐ note at **job** **take sth on** to accept a responsibility or decide to do sth: *He's taken on a lot of extra work.*
take sb out to go out with sb (for a social occasion): *I'm taking Sarah out for a meal tonight.* **take sth out 1** to remove sth from inside a person's body: *He's having two teeth taken out.* ᴐ note at **tooth 2** to obtain a service ᴐ note at **insurance** **take sth out (of sth)** to remove sth from sth: *He took a notebook out of his pocket.* ◊ *I need to take some money out of the bank.* **take it out on sb** to behave badly towards sb because you are angry or upset about sth, even though it is not this person's fault
take (sth) over (BUSINESS) to get control of sth or responsibility for sth: *The firm is being taken over by a large company.* ◊ *Who's going to take over as assistant when Tim leaves?*
take to sb/sth to start liking sb/sth or doing sth well **take to sth/doing sth** to begin doing sth regularly as a habit
take sth up to start doing sth regularly (for example as a hobby): *I've taken up yoga recently.* **take up sth** to use or fill an amount of time or space: *All their time is taken up looking after the new baby.* **SYN** **occupy** **take sb up on sth 1** to say that you disagree with sth that sb has just said, and ask them to explain it: *I must take you up on that last point.* **2** (*informal*) to accept an offer that sb has made **take**

sth up with sb to ask or complain about sth: *I'll take the matter up with my MP.*

takeaway /ˈteɪkəweɪ/ (*BrE*) (*AmE* **takeout** /ˈteɪkaʊt/, **carry-out**) noun [C] **1** a restaurant that sells food that you can eat somewhere else **2** a meal that you buy at this type of restaurant: *Let's have a takeaway.*

'take-off noun [U, C] the moment when an aircraft leaves the ground and starts to fly: *The plane is ready for take-off.* **OPP** **landing**

takeover /ˈteɪkəʊvə(r)/ noun [C] (**BUSINESS**) the act of taking control of sth: *They made a takeover bid for the company.* ◊ *a military takeover of the government*

'take-up noun [U, sing.] the rate at which people accept sth that is offered or made available to them

takings /ˈteɪkɪŋz/ noun [pl.] (**FINANCE**) the amount of money that a shop, theatre, etc. gets from selling goods, tickets, etc.

talcum powder /ˈtælkəm paʊdə(r)/ (*also* **talc** /tælk/) noun [U] a soft powder that smells nice. People often put it on their skin after a bath.

tale ⚡**B2** /teɪl/ noun [C] **1** (**LITERATURE**) a story about events that are not real: *fairy tales* **2** a report or description of sb/sth that may not be true: *I've heard tales of people seeing ghosts in that house.*

talent ⚡**B1** /ˈtælənt/ noun [C, U] **~ (for sth)** a natural skill or ability: *She has a talent for painting.* ◊ *His work shows great talent.* ◊ *a talent contest/show* (= in which people perform to show how well they can sing, dance, etc.) ▶ **talented** ⚡**B1** adj.: *a talented musician*

talk¹ ⚡**A1** **S** /tɔːk/ verb [I] **~ (to/with sb) (about/of sb/sth)** to say things; to speak in order to give information or to express feelings, ideas, etc: *I could hear them talking downstairs.* ◊ *Can I talk with you for a minute?* ◊ *Nasreen is not an easy person to talk to.* ◊ *We need to talk about the plans for the weekend.* ◊ *He's been talking of going to Australia for some time now.* ◊ *Dr Hollis will be talking about Japanese art in her lecture.* **2** [I, T] to discuss sth serious or important: *We can't go on like this. We need to talk.* ◊ *Could we talk business after dinner?* **3** [T] to say things that are/ are not sensible: *He's the only politician who talks any sense.* ◊ *You're talking rubbish!* **4** [I] to discuss people's private lives: *His strange lifestyle started the local people talking.* **SYN** **gossip 5** [I] to give information to sb, especially when you do not want to: *The police questioned him for hours but he refused to talk.*
IDM **know what you are talking about** → KNOW¹ **talk/speak of the devil** → DEVIL **talk shop** to talk about your work with the people you work with, outside working hours
PHR V **talk down to sb** to talk to sb as if they are less intelligent or important than you **talk sb into/out of doing sth** to persuade sb to do/not to do sth: *She talked him into buying a new car.* **talk sth over (with sb)** to discuss sth with sb, especially in order to reach an agreement or make a decision

talk² ⚡**A2** **S** /tɔːk/ noun **1** [C] **~ (on/about sth)** a formal speech on a particular subject: *He's giving a talk on 'Our changing world'.* **SYN** **lecture 2** [C] **~ (with sb) (about sth)** a conversation or discussion: *I had a long talk with Tim about the problem.* **3** talks [pl.] (**POLITICS**) formal discussions between governments: *The Foreign Ministers of the two countries will meet for talks next week.* ◊ *arms/pay/peace talks* **4** [U] (*informal*) things that people say that are not based on facts or reality: *He says he's going to resign but it's just talk.* ᴐ look at **small talk**

talkative /ˈtɔːkətɪv/ adj. liking to talk a lot

tall 🔊 **A1** /tɔːl/ *adj.* **1** (used about people or things) of more than average height; not short: *a tall young man* ◇ *a tall tree/tower/chimney* **OPP short¹ 2** used to describe the height of sb/sth: *Claire is 5 feet tall.* ◇ *How tall are you?* ◇ *Nick is taller than his brother.* ➔ note at **measure²**

tally¹ /ˈtæli/ *noun* [C] (*pl.* -ies) a record of the number or amount of sth, especially one that you can keep adding to: *He hopes to improve on his tally of three goals in the past nine games.*

tally² /ˈtæli/ *verb* (tallying; tallies; *pt, pp* tallied) **1** [I] ~ (with sth) to be the same as or to match another person's account of sth, another set of figures, etc: *Her report of what happened tallied exactly with the story of another witness.* **2** [T] ~ sth (up) to calculate the total number, cost, etc. of sth

talon /ˈtælən/ *noun* [C] a long sharp curved nail on the feet of some birds, especially BIRDS OF PREY (= birds that kill other animals and birds for food) ➔ picture at **animal**

tambourine /ˌtæmbəˈriːn/ *noun* [C] (**MUSIC**) a musical instrument that has a round frame, sometimes covered with plastic or skin, with metal discs round the edge. To play it, you hit it or shake it with your hand. ➔ picture at **instrument**

tame¹ /teɪm/ *adj.* **1** (used about animals or birds) not wild or afraid of people: *The birds are so tame they will eat from your hand.* **2** boring; not interesting or exciting: *After the big city, you must find village life very tame.*

tame² /teɪm/ *verb* [T] to bring a wild animal under your control; to make sth easy to control

tamper /ˈtæmpə(r)/ *verb*
PHR V tamper with sth to make changes to sth without permission, especially in order to damage it

tampon /ˈtæmpɒn/ *noun* [C] a piece of cotton material with a special shape that a woman puts inside her body to ABSORB (= take in and hold) the blood that she loses once a month ➔ look at **sanitary towel**

tan¹ /tæn/ *noun* **1** [C] = SUNTAN **2** [U] a yellow-brown colour

tan² /tæn/ *verb* [I, T] (-nn-) (used about a person's skin) to become brown or make sth brown as a result of spending time in the sun: *Do you tan easily?* ▶ **tanned** *adj.*: *You're looking very tanned — have you been on holiday?*

tan³ /tæn/ *adj.* yellow-brown in colour

tandem /ˈtændəm/ *noun* [C] a bicycle with seats for two people, one behind the other
IDM in tandem (with sb/sth) working together with sth/sb else; happening at the same time as sth else

tangent /ˈtændʒənt/ *noun* [C] **1** (**GEOMETRY**) a straight line that touches a curve but does not cross it ➔ picture at **circle** **2** (**MATHEMATICS**) (*abbr.* tan) the RATIO of the length of the side opposite an angle in a RIGHT-ANGLED TRIANGLE (= a shape with three sides and one angle of 90°) to the length of the side next to it ➔ look at **cosine, sine**
IDM go off at a tangent (*AmE*) | **go off on a tangent** to suddenly start saying or doing sth that seems to have no connection with what has gone before

tangerine¹ /ˌtændʒəˈriːn/ *noun* **1** [C] a fruit like a small sweet orange with a skin that is easy to take off **2** [U] a deep orange-yellow colour

tangerine² /ˌtændʒəˈriːn/ *adj.* deep orange-yellow in colour

tangible /ˈtændʒəbl/ *adj.* that can be clearly seen to exist: *There are tangible benefits in the new system.* **OPP intangible**

tangle /ˈtæŋgl/ *noun* [C] a confused mass, especially of THREADS, hair, branches, etc. that cannot easily be separated from each other: *My hair's full of tangles.* ◇ *This string's in a tangle.* ▶ **tangled** *adj.*: *The wool was all tangled up.*

tango /ˈtæŋgəʊ/ *noun* [C] (*pl.* -os) a fast South American dance with a strong beat, in which two people hold each other closely; a piece of music for this dance ▶ **tango** *verb* [I] (tangoing; tangoes; *pt, pp* tangoed)

tank 🔊 **B2** /tæŋk/ *noun* [C] **1** a container for holding liquid or gas; the amount that a tank will hold: *a water/fuel/petrol/fish tank* ◇ *We drove there and back on one tank of petrol.* ➔ picture at **purification 2** a large, heavy military vehicle covered with strong metal and armed with guns, that moves on special wheels inside metal BELTS

tanker /ˈtæŋkə(r)/ *noun* [C] a ship or lorry that carries oil, petrol, etc. in large amounts: *an oil tanker* ➔ picture at **vehicle**

tanned /tænd/ *adj.* = SUNTANNED

Tannoy™ /ˈtænɔɪ/ *noun* [C] a system used for giving spoken information in a public place: *They announced over the Tannoy that our flight was delayed.*

tantalizing (*BrE also* -ising) /ˈtæntəlaɪzɪŋ/ *adj.* making you want sth that you cannot have or do: *A tantalizing aroma of cooking was coming from the kitchen.* ▶ **tantalizingly** (*also* -isingly) *adv.*

tantalum /ˈtæntələm/ *noun* [U] (*symb.* Ta) (**CHEMISTRY**) a chemical element. Tantalum is a hard silver-grey metal used in the production of electronic parts. ❶ For more information on the periodic table of elements, look at the **Reference Section** of this dictionary.

tantrum /ˈtæntrəm/ *noun* [C] a sudden explosion of anger, especially by a child

tap¹ 🔊 **B2** /tæp/ *verb* (-pp-) **1** [I, T] ~ sb/sth (on sth); ~ (away) (at sth) to touch or hit sb/sth quickly and lightly: *Their feet were tapping in time to the music.* ◇ *She tapped me on the shoulder.* ◇ *He was busy tapping away at his computer.* **2** [T, I] ~ (into) sth to make use of a source of energy, knowledge, etc. that already exists: *to tap into the skills of young people* **3** [T] to fit a device to sb's phone so that their calls can be listened to secretly

tap² 🔊 **B2** /tæp/ *noun* **1** (*especially BrE*) (*AmE usually* faucet) [C] a type of handle that you turn to let water, gas, etc. out of a pipe or container: *Turn the hot/cold tap on/off.* **2** [C] a light hit with your hand or fingers **3** [C] an act of fitting a device to sb's phone so that their calls can be listened to secretly **4** [U] = TAP-DANCING

'tap dance *noun* [U, C] a style of dancing in which you TAP the rhythm of the music with your feet, wearing special shoes with pieces of metal on them ▶ **tap-dancing** (*also* tap) *noun* [U]

tape¹ 🔊 **B1** /teɪp/ *noun*
• FOR STICKING **1** [U] a long narrow band of plastic, etc. with a sticky substance on one side that is used for sticking things together, covering electric wires, etc: *sticky/adhesive tape* ➔ look at **insulating tape, Sellotape™**
• FOR MUSIC **2** [U] (**ARTS AND MEDIA**) a long thin band of plastic material used for recording sound, pictures or information, especially before digital technology became available: *I had the whole concert on tape* (= recorded). **3** [C] (**ARTS AND MEDIA**) a small flat plastic case containing tape for playing or recording music

or sound: *a blank tape* (= a tape with nothing recorded on it) ◊ *to rewind a tape*
- FOR TYING TOGETHER **4** [C, U] a narrow piece of cloth that is used for tying things together or as a label
- IN A RACE **5** [C] a piece of material stretched across a race track to mark where the race finishes ◌ look at **red tape**

tape² /teɪp/ *verb* [T] **1** (ARTS AND MEDIA) to record sound, music, TV programmes, etc. using tape **2** ~ **sth (up)** to fasten sth by sticking or tying sth with tape

'tape measure (*also* **measuring tape**) *noun* [C] a long thin piece of plastic, cloth or metal with CENTIMETRES, etc. marked on it. It is used for measuring things.

'tape recorder *noun* [C] a machine that is used for recording and playing sounds on tape

tapescript /'teɪpskrɪpt/ *noun* [C] a written or printed copy of words that are spoken in a recording

tapestry /'tæpəstri/ *noun* [C, U] (*pl.* -ies) a picture or pattern that is made by WEAVING coloured wool onto heavy cloth; the art of doing this

tapeworm /'teɪpwɜːm/ *noun* [C] a flat WORM (= a long creature with a soft body and no legs) that lives in the INTESTINES (= the tube that carries food out of the stomach) of humans and animals

tapioca /ˌtæpi'əʊkə/ *noun* [U] hard white grains obtained from a CASSAVA plant often cooked with milk to make a sweet dish

tapir /'teɪpə(r)/ *noun* [C] an animal like a pig with a long nose, that lives in Central and South America and south-east Asia

'tap water *noun* [U] water that comes through pipes and out of TAPS, not water sold in bottles

tar /tɑː(r)/ *noun* [U] **1** a thick black sticky liquid that becomes hard when it is cold. Tar is obtained from coal and is used for making roads, etc. ◌ look at **Tarmac™** (1) **2** a similar substance formed by burning TOBACCO: *low-tar cigarettes*

tarantula /tə'ræntʃələ/ *noun* [C] a large poisonous spider covered with hair that lives in hot countries

▼ SYNONYMS

target

objective ◆ goal ◆ object ◆ end

These are all words for sth that you are trying to achieve.

target *attainment targets*

objective *the main objective of the project*

goal *He pursued his goal of becoming an actor.*

object *The object is to educate people about health.*

end (*formal*) *He joined the group for political ends.*

target¹ 🔲 **A2** **◉** /'tɑːɡɪt/ *noun* [C] **1** a result that you try to achieve: *Our target is to finish the job by Friday.* ◊ *So far we're right on target* (= making the progress we expected). ◊ *a target area/audience/group* (= the particular area, audience, etc. that a product, programme, etc. is aimed at) **2** a person, place or thing that people aim at when attacking, criticizing, etc: *Doors and windows are an easy target for burglars.* ◊ *The education system has been the target of heavy criticism.* **3** an object, often a round board with circles on it, that you try to hit in shooting practice: *to aim at/hit/miss a target*

target² 🔲 **B2** **◉** /'tɑːɡɪt/ *verb* [T, often passive] ~ **sth at/ on sb/sth** to try to attack sb/sth; to try to have an effect on a particular group of people: *The attacks targeted the centre of the city.* ◊ *The advertising campaign is targeted at teenagers.*

tariff /'tærɪf/ *noun* [C] **1** (ECONOMICS) a tax that has to be paid on goods coming into a country **2** a list of prices, especially in a hotel

Tarmac™ /'tɑːmæk/ *noun* [U] **1** a black material used for making the surfaces of roads ◌ look at **tar** (1) **2** the tarmac an area covered with a Tarmac surface, especially at an airport

tarn /tɑːn/ *noun* [C] (GEOGRAPHY) a small lake in the mountains

tarnish /'tɑːnɪʃ/ *verb* **1** [I, T] (used about metal, etc.) to become less bright and shiny; to make sth less bright and shiny **2** [T] to damage the good opinion people have of sb/sth

tarpaulin /tɑː'pɔːlɪn/ *noun* [C, U] a large sheet of strong material that water cannot pass through, used for covering things to protect them from the rain

tarragon /'tærəgən/ *noun* [U] a plant with leaves that have a strong taste and are used in cooking

tarsal /'tɑːsl/ *noun* [C] (ANATOMY) one of the small bones in the ankle and upper foot ◌ picture at **body**

tart¹ /tɑːt/ *noun* [C, U] an open PIE filled with sweet food such as fruit or jam

tart² /tɑːt/ *verb*
PHR V **tart sb/sth up** (*BrE*, *informal*) to decorate and improve the appearance of sb/sth

tartan /'tɑːtn/ *noun* **1** [U, C] a traditional Scottish pattern of coloured squares and lines that cross each other **2** [U] cloth made from wool with this pattern on it

task 🔲 **A2** **◉** /tɑːsk/ *noun* [C] a piece of work that has to be done, especially an unpleasant or difficult one: *Your first task will be to enter this data.* ◊ *to perform/ carry out/undertake a task* ▶ **task** *verb* [T, usually passive] ~ **sb (with sth)** (*formal*): *NATO troops were tasked with keeping the peace.*

'task force *noun* [C] **1** a military force that is brought together and sent to a particular place **2** a group of people who are brought together to deal with a particular problem: *The government has set up a task force to improve standards in schools.*

tassel /'tæsl/ *noun* [C] a bunch of THREADS that are tied together at one end and hang from curtains, clothes, etc. as a decoration

tassel on a cushion

tassel

taste¹ 🔲 **A2** /teɪst/ *noun*
- FLAVOUR **1** [C, U] the particular quality of different foods or drinks that allows you to recognize them when you put them in your mouth: *a sweet/bitter/sour/salty taste* ◊ *I don't like the taste of this coffee.*
- SENSE **2** [U] the sense you have that allows you to recognize different foods and drinks when you put them in your mouth: *I've got such a bad cold that I seem to have lost my sense of taste.*
- SMALL QUANTITY **3** [C, usually sing.] a small amount of sth to eat or drink that you have in order to see what it is like: *Have a taste of this cheese to see if you like it.*
- SHORT EXPERIENCE **4** [sing.] a short experience of sth: *That was my **first taste** of success.*
- RECOGNIZING QUALITY **5** [U] the ability to decide if things are suitable, of good quality, etc: *He has excellent **taste in** music.*

• WHAT YOU LIKE **6** [C, U] ~ **(for sth)** what a person likes or prefers: *She has developed a taste for modern art.* **IDM** **(be) in bad, poor, etc. taste** (used about sb's behaviour) (to be) unpleasant and not suitable: *Some of his comments were in very bad taste.*

taste² 🔊 **A2** /teɪst/ *verb* **1** *linking verb* ~ **(of sth)** to have a particular taste: *The pudding tasted of oranges.* ◇ *to taste sour/sweet/delicious* **2** [T] to be able to recognize tastes in food or drink: *Can you taste the garlic in this soup?* **3** [T] to test the taste of something by eating or drinking a small amount of it: *Can I taste a piece of that cheese to see what it's like?*

ˈtaste bud *noun* [C, usually pl.] (ANATOMY) one of the small structures on the tongue that allow you to recognize the different tastes of food and drink

tasteful /ˈteɪstfl/ *adj.* (used especially about clothes, furniture, decorations, etc.) attractive and well chosen: *tasteful furniture* **OPP** **tasteless** ▸ **tastefully** /-fəli/ *adv.*

tasteless /ˈteɪstləs/ *adj.* **1** having little or no taste: *This sauce is rather tasteless.* **OPP** **tasty** **2** likely to offend people: *His joke about the funeral was particularly tasteless.* **3** (used especially about clothes, furniture, decorations, etc.) not attractive; not well chosen **OPP** **tasteful**

tasty /ˈteɪsti/ *adj.* (tastier; tastiest) having a strong and pleasant taste: *spaghetti with a tasty mushroom sauce*

tattered /ˈtætəd/ *adj.* old and torn; in bad condition: *a tattered coat*

tatters /ˈtætəz/ *noun* [pl.] **IDM** **in tatters** badly torn or damaged: *Her dress was in tatters.*

tattoo /təˈtuː/ *noun* [C] (*pl.* -oos) a picture or pattern that is marked permanently on sb's skin ▸ **tattoo** *verb* [T] (tattooing; tattoos; *pt, pp* tattooed): *She had his name tattooed on her left hand.*

tatty /ˈtæti/ *adj.* (tattier; tattiest) (*informal*) in bad condition: *tatty old clothes*

taught /tɔːt/ past tense, past participle of **teach**

taunt /tɔːnt/ *verb* [T] to try to make sb angry or upset by saying unpleasant or cruel things ▸ **taunt** *noun* [C]

Taurus /ˈtɔːrəs/ *noun* [U] the second sign of THE ZODIAC (= twelve signs that represent the positions of the sun, moon and planets), the Bull; a person born under this sign

taut /tɔːt/ *adj.* (used about rope, wire, etc.) stretched very tight; not loose

tautology /tɔːˈtɒlədʒi/ *noun* [U, C] (LANGUAGE) a statement in which you say the same thing twice in different words, when this is unnecessary, for example 'They spoke in turn, one after the other.' ▸ **tautological** /ˌtɔːtəˈlɒdʒɪkl/ *adj.*

tavern /ˈtævən/ *noun* [C] (*old-fashioned*) a pub

tax 🔊 **B1** /tæks/ *noun* [C, U] ~ **(on sth)** (ECONOMICS) the money that you have to pay to the government so that it can provide public services: *income tax* ◇ *There used to be a tax on windows.* ⊃ note at **pay²** ▸ **tax** 🔊 **B1** *verb* [T, often passive]: *Alcohol, cigarettes and petrol are heavily taxed.*

taxable /ˈtæksəbl/ *adj.* on which you have to pay tax: *taxable income*

taxation /tækˈseɪʃn/ *noun* [U] **1** (ECONOMICS, POLITICS) the system by which a government takes money from people so that it can pay for public services: *direct/indirect taxation* **2** (ECONOMICS) the amount of money that people have to pay in tax: *to increase/reduce taxation* ◇ *high/low taxation*

ˈtax avoidance *noun* [U] (FINANCE, LAW) legal ways of paying only the smallest amount of tax that you have to ⊃ look at **tax evasion**

ˈtax evasion *noun* [U] (FINANCE, LAW) the crime of deliberately not paying all the tax that you should pay ⊃ look at **tax avoidance**

ˌtax-ˈfree *adj.* on which you do not have to pay tax

ˈtax haven *noun* [C] (ECONOMICS, FINANCE) a place where taxes are low and where people choose to live or officially register their companies because taxes are higher in their own countries

taxi¹ 🔊 **A1** /ˈtæksi/ (*also* taxicab /ˈtæksikæb/, cab) *noun* [C] a car with a driver whose job is to take you somewhere in exchange for money: *Shall we go by bus or get/take a taxi?*

taxi² /ˈtæksi/ *verb* [I] (used about an aircraft) to move slowly along the ground before or after flying

taxing /ˈtæksɪŋ/ *adj.* difficult; needing a lot of effort: *a taxing exam* ⊃ note at **difficult**

ˈtaxi rank *noun* [C] a place where taxis park while they are waiting for passengers

taxonomist /tækˈsɒnəmɪst/ *noun* [C] (SCIENCE) a scientist who arranges things into groups

taxonomy /tækˈsɒnəmi/ *noun* (*pl.* -ies) **1** [U] (SCIENCE) the scientific process of arranging things into groups ⊃ picture at **animal** **2** [C] one particular system of groups that things have been arranged in

taxpayer 🔊 **C1** /ˈtækspeɪə(r)/ *noun* [C] (ECONOMICS) a person who pays tax to the government, especially on the money that they earn

TB¹ 🔊 /ˌtiː ˈbiː/ *noun* [U] (HEALTH) a serious disease that affects the lungs (the abbreviation for 'tuberculosis')

TB² *abbr.* (in writing) (*pl.* TB) = TERABYTE

Tb *abbr.* (in writing) (*pl.* Tb) = TERABIT

TBA /ˌtiː biː ˈeɪ/ *abbr.* **to be announced** (used in notices about events): *party with live band (TBA)*

TBC /ˌtiː biː ˈsiː/ *abbr.* **to be confirmed** (used in notices about events): *The course will run from March 8–11 (TBC).*

tbsp *abbr.* (in writing) (*pl.* tbsp, tbsps) = TABLESPOON (2): *Add 3 tbsp sugar.*

TCP/IP /ˌtiː siː ˌpiː aɪ ˈpiː/ *abbr.* (COMPUTING) **transmission control protocol/internet protocol** (a system that controls the connection of computers to the internet)

tea 🔊 **A1** /tiː/ *noun* **1** [U, C] a hot drink made by pouring boiling water onto the dried leaves of the tea plant or of some other plants; a cup of this drink: *a cup/pot of tea* ◇ *weak/strong tea* ◇ *Two teas and one coffee, please.* ◇ *herbal/mint/camomile tea* **2** [U] the dried leaves of the tea plant: *a packet of tea* **3** [C, U] (*BrE*) a small afternoon meal of sandwiches, cakes, etc. and tea to drink, or a cooked meal eaten at five or six o'clock: *The kids have their tea as soon as they get home from school.* **IDM** **(not) sb's cup of tea** → CUP¹

ˈtea bag *noun* [C] a small paper bag with tea leaves in it, that you use for making tea

teach 🔊 **A1** 🔊 /tiːtʃ/ *verb* (*pt, pp* taught /tɔːt/) **1** [I, T] ~ **sb (sth/to do sth); ~ sth (to sb)** (EDUCATION) to give sb lessons or instructions so that they know how to do sth: *I teach in a primary school.* ◇ *My mother taught me to play the piano.* ◇ *Jeremy is teaching us how to use the software.* ◇ *He teaches English to foreign students.* **2** [T] to make sb believe sth or behave in a certain way: *The story teaches us that history often repeats itself.* ◇ *My parents taught me always to tell the truth.* ⊃ note at **religion** **3** [T] (*informal*) to make sb have a bad experience so that they are careful not to do the thing that caused it again: *All the seats are taken. That'll teach you to turn up half an hour late.* **IDM** **teach sb a lesson** to make sb have a bad experience so that they will not do the thing that caused it again

teacher 🔊 **A1** ❺ /ˈtiːtʃə(r)/ *noun* [C] (**EDUCATION**) a person whose job is to teach, especially in a school or college: *He's a teacher at a primary school.* ◇ *a maths/chemistry/music teacher* ➲ look at **head**¹ (7)

teacher ˈtraining *noun* [U] (**EDUCATION**) the process of teaching or learning the skills you need to be a teacher in a school

teaching 🔊 **A2** /ˈtiːtʃɪŋ/ *noun* **1** [U] (**EDUCATION**) the work of a teacher: *My son went into teaching.* ◇ *teaching methods* **2** [C, usually pl.] ideas and beliefs that are taught by sb/sth: *the teachings of Gandhi*

ˈtea cloth (*BrE*) = TEA TOWEL

teacup /ˈtiːkʌp/ *noun* [C] a cup that you drink tea from

teak /tiːk/ *noun* [U] the strong hard wood of a tall Asian tree, used especially for making furniture

team¹ 🔊 **A1** /tiːm/ *noun* [C + sing./pl. verb] **1** (**SPORT**) a group of people who play a sport or game together against another group: *a football team* ◇ *Are you in/on the team?* **2** a group of people who work together: *a team of doctors*

team² /tiːm/ *verb* **PHRV** **team up (with sb)** to join sb in order to do sth together: *I teamed up with Elena to plan the project.*

teammate /ˈtiːmmeɪt/ *noun* [C] a member of the same team or group as yourself

teamwork /ˈtiːmwɜːk/ *noun* [U] the ability of people to work together

teapot /ˈtiːpɒt/ *noun* [C] a container that you use for making tea in and for serving it

tear¹ 🔊 **B2** /teə(r)/ *verb* (*pt* tore /tɔː(r)/; *pp* torn /tɔːn/) **1** [T, I] to damage sth by pulling it apart or into pieces; to become damaged in this way: *I tore my shirt on that nail.* ◇ *She tore the letter in half.* ◇ *This material doesn't tear easily.* **SYN** **rip**¹ **2** [T] to make a hole in sth by force: *The explosion tore a hole in the wall.* **3** [T] (used with an adverb or a preposition) to remove sth by pulling violently and quickly: *Paul tore the poster down from the wall.* ◇ *He tore the bag out of her hands.* ◇ *I tore a page out of my notebook.* ◇ *She tore herself from his grasp.* **SYN** **rip**¹ **4** [I] (used with an adverb or a preposition) to move very quickly in a particular direction: *An ambulance went tearing past.* **PHRV** **tear sth apart** **1** to pull sth violently into pieces **2** to destroy sth completely: *The country has been torn apart by the war.* **tear yourself away (from sb/sth)** to make yourself leave sb/sth or stop doing sth **be torn between A and B** to find it difficult to choose between two things or people **tear sth down** to pull or knock down a building, wall, etc: *They tore down the houses and built a hotel.* **SYN** **demolish** **tear sth up** to pull sth into pieces, especially sth made of paper: *'I hate this photo,' she said, tearing it up.*

tear² 🔊 **B2** /teə(r)/ *noun* [C] a hole that has been made in sth by tearing it: *You've got a tear in the back of your trousers.* **IDM** **wear and tear** → WEAR²

tear³ 🔊 **B2** /tɪə(r)/ *noun* [C, usually pl.] a drop of liquid that comes from your eye when you are crying, etc: *I was in tears* (= crying) *at the end of the film.* ◇ *The little girl burst into tears* (= suddenly started to cry). **IDM** **shed tears** → SHED²

tearful /ˈtɪəfl/ *adj.* crying or nearly crying

tear gas /ˈtɪə ɡæs/ *noun* [U] a type of gas that hurts the eyes and throat and is used by the police, etc. to control large groups of people

tease /tiːz/ *verb* [I, T] to laugh at sb either in a friendly way or in order to upset them: *Don't pay any attention to those boys. They're only teasing.* ◇ *They teased her about her name.*

teaspoon /ˈtiːspuːn/ *noun* [C] **1** a small spoon used for putting sugar in tea, coffee, etc. **2** (*also* teaspoonful /ˈtiːspuːnfʊl/) the amount that a teaspoon holds

teat /tiːt/ *noun* [C] **1** (*BrE*) (*AmE* nipple) the rubber part at the end of a baby's bottle that the baby SUCKS in order to get milk, etc. from the bottle **2** one of the parts of a female animal's body that the young animals drink milk from

ˈtea towel (*also* tea cloth) *noun* [C] a small towel that is used for drying plates, knives, forks, etc.

tech /tek/ (*BrE, informal*) = TECHNICAL COLLEGE

techie (*also* techy) /ˈteki/ *noun* [C] (*informal*) (**COMPUTING**) a person who is expert in or enthusiastic about technology, especially computers

technetium /tekˈniːʃiəm/ *noun* [U] (*symb.* Tc) (**CHEMISTRY**) a chemical element. Technetium is a substance that is found naturally as a product of URANIUM or produced artificially from MOLYBDENUM. ❶ For more information on the periodic table of elements, look at the **Reference Section** of this dictionary.

technical 🔊 **B1** ❺ /ˈteknɪkl/ *adj.* **1** connected with the practical use of machines, methods, etc. in science and industry: *The train was delayed owing to a technical problem.* **2** connected with the skills involved in a particular activity or subject: *This computer magazine is too technical for me.*

ˈtechnical college (*also BrE, informal* tech) *noun* [C] (**EDUCATION**) a college where students can study mainly practical subjects

technicality /ˌteknɪˈkæləti/ *noun* [C] (*pl.* -ies) one of the details of a particular subject or activity

technically /ˈteknɪkli/ *adv.* **1** according to the exact meaning, facts, etc: *Technically, you should pay by 1 May, but it doesn't matter if it's a few days late.* **2** used about sb's practical ability in a particular activity: *He's a technically brilliant dancer.* **3** in a way that involves detailed knowledge of the machines, etc. that are used in industry or science: *The country is technically not very advanced.*

ˌtechnical supˈport (*also informal* tech support) *noun* [U] (**COMPUTING**) **1** technical help that a company gives to customers using their computers or other products **2** [+ sing./pl. verb] a department in a company that provides technical help to its workers or customers: *I called technical support and they fixed it.*

technician /tekˈnɪʃn/ *noun* [C] a person whose work involves practical skills, especially in industry or science: *a laboratory technician*

technique 🔊 **B1** ❺ /tekˈniːk/ *noun* **1** [C] a particular way of doing sth: *new techniques for teaching languages* ◇ *marketing/management techniques* **2** [U] the practical skill that sb has in a particular activity: *He's a naturally talented runner, but he needs to work on his technique.*

techno /ˈteknəʊ/ *noun* [U] (**MUSIC**) a style of popular music with a regular rhythm for dancing, that makes use of technology to produce the sound

techno- /ˈteknəʊ, teknə, tekˈnɒ/ *prefix* (in nouns, adjectives and adverbs) connected with technology: *a technophobe*

technocrat /'teknəkræt/ *noun* [C] (**POLITICS**) an expert in science, engineering, etc. who has a lot of power in politics and/or industry

technology 🔊 **A2** ⊙ /tek'nɒlədʒi/ *noun* [U, C] (*pl.* -ies) the scientific knowledge and/or equipment that is needed for a particular industry, etc: *developments in computer technology* ▸ **technological** 🔊+ **B2** ⓦ /ˌteknə'lɒdʒɪkl/ *adj.*: *technological developments* ▸ **technologist** /tek'nɒlədʒɪst/ *noun* [C]: *Technologists are developing a computer that can perform surgery.*

technophile /'teknəfaɪl/ *noun* [C] a person who is enthusiastic about new technology

technophobe /'teknəfəʊb/ *noun* [C] a person who is afraid of, dislikes or avoids new technology

ˌtech-'savvy *adj.* (*informal*) (**COMPUTING**) having a good knowledge and understanding of modern technology: *I don't have any tech-savvy friends who can help me link up my TV to the app.*

ˈtech support = TECHNICAL SUPPORT

techy *noun* [C] (*pl.* -ies) (*informal*) = TECHIE

tectonic /tek'tɒnɪk/ *adj.* (**GEOLOGY**) connected with the structure of the earth's surface ⊃ look at **plate tectonics**

ˈteddy bear (*also* teddy /'tedi/, *pl.* -ies) *noun* [C] a soft toy that looks like a bear

tedious /'tiːdiəs/ *adj.* boring and lasting for a long time: *a tedious train journey* **SYN boring**

tee /tiː/ *noun* [C] (**SPORT**) **1** a flat area on a GOLF COURSE from which players hit the ball **2** a small piece of plastic or wood that you stick in the ground to support a golf ball before you hit it

teem /tiːm/ *verb* **PHR V teem with sth** (*usually* be teeming with sth) (used about a place) to have a lot of people or things moving about in it: *The streets were teeming with people.*

teenage 🔊 **A2** /'tiːneɪdʒ/ *adj.* between 13 and 19 years old; connected with people of this age: *teenage children ◇ teenage magazines/fashion*

teenager 🔊 **A1** /'tiːneɪdʒə(r)/ *noun* [C] a person aged between 13 and 19 years old: *Her music is very popular with teenagers.* ⊃ look at **adolescent**

teens 🔊+ **B2** /tiːnz/ *noun* [pl.] the period of a person's life between the ages of 13 and 19: *to be in your early/late teens*

ˈtee shirt = T-SHIRT

teeth /tiːθ/ plural of **tooth**

teethe /tiːð/ *verb* [I] (used about a baby) when a baby **is teething**, its first teeth are starting to grow

ˈteething problems (*also* ˈteething troubles) *noun* [pl.] the problems that can develop when a person, system, etc. is new: *We're having a few teething problems with this new software.*

teetotal /ˌtiː'təʊtl/ *adj.* (used about a person) never drinking alcohol ▸ **teetotaller** (*BrE*) (*AmE* teetotaler) *noun* [C] ⊃ look at **alcoholic²**

TEFL /'tefl/ *abbr.* (**EDUCATION**) **Teaching English as a Foreign Language** (the teaching of English to people who do not speak it as a first language)

tel. *abbr.* (in writing) phone number: *tel. 01865 56767*

tele- /teli, telɪ, tə'le/ *prefix* (in verbs, nouns, adjectives and adverbs) **1** over a long distance; far: *telepathy ◇ telescopic* **2** connected with or using a phone or TV: *telesales*

telebanking /'telibæŋkɪŋ/ = TELEPHONE BANKING

telecommunications /ˌtelikəˌmjuːnɪ'keɪʃnz/ *noun* [pl.] the technology of sending signals, images and messages over long distances by radio, phone, TV, etc.

telecommute /ˌtelikə'mjuːt/ *verb* [I] (**BUSINESS**) to work from home, communicating with your office, customers and others by phone, email, etc. ▸ **telecommuter** *noun* [C] **SYN teleworker** ▸ **telecommuting** *noun* [U] **SYN teleworking**

teleconference /'telikɒnfrəns/ *noun* [C] (**BUSINESS**) a conference or discussion at which members are in different places and speak to each other using phone and video connections ▸ **teleconference** *verb* [I]

telegram /'telɪɡræm/ *noun* [C] a message that is sent by TELEGRAPH and that is then printed and given to sb

telegraph /'telɪɡrɑːf/ *noun* [U] a method of sending messages over long distances, using wires that carry electrical signals

ˈtelegraph pole *noun* [C] a tall wooden POLE that is used for supporting phone wires

telemarketing /'telimɑːkɪtɪŋ/ = TELESALES

telepathy /tə'lepəθi/ *noun* [U] the communication of thoughts between people's minds without using speech, writing or other normal methods

telephone¹ 🔊 **A1** /'telɪfəʊn/ (*formal*) (*also* phone) *noun* **1** [U] an electrical system for talking to sb in another place by speaking into a special piece of equipment: *Can I contact you by telephone? ◇ to make a telephone call ◇ What's your telephone number?* **2** [C] the piece of equipment that you use when you talk to sb by telephone: *I picked up the telephone and called my best friend.* ⊃ note at **phone¹** **IDM on the phone/telephone → PHONE¹**

telephone² /'telɪfəʊn/ *verb* [I, T] = PHONE²

ˌtelephone 'banking (*also* telebanking) *noun* [U] (**FINANCE**) activities relating to your bank account that you do using the phone

telephony /tə'lefəni/ *noun* [U] the process of sending messages and signals by phone

teleprompter /'telɪprɒmptə(r)/ (*especially AmE*) = AUTOCUE™

telesales /'telɪseɪlz/ (*also* telemarketing) *noun* [U] (**BUSINESS**) a method of selling things by phone: *He works in telesales.*

telescope /'telɪskəʊp/ *noun* [C] (**ASTRONOMY, PHYSICS**) an instrument in the shape of a tube with LENSES inside it. You look through it to make things that are far away appear bigger and nearer. ⊃ picture at **binoculars**

televise /'telɪvaɪz/ *verb* [T] (**ARTS AND MEDIA**) to show sth on TV: *a televised concert*

television 🔊 **A1** /'telɪvɪʒn/ (*also* TV) *noun* (**ARTS AND MEDIA**) **1** (*also* ˈtelevision set) (*also BrE, informal* telly) [C] a piece of electrical equipment with a screen on which you can watch programmes with moving pictures and sounds: *to turn the television on/off* **2** (*also BrE, informal* telly) [U] the programmes that are shown on television: *We watch television almost every night.* **3** [U] the system, process or business of sending out television programmes: *a television programme/series/show ◇ He works in television* (= for a television company). **IDM on (the) TV/television → TV**

teleworking /'teliwɜːkɪŋ/ *noun* [U] (*BrE*) (**BUSINESS**) the practice of working from home, communicating with your office, customers and others by phone, email, etc. **SYN telecommuting** ▸ **teleworker** /-kə(r)/ *noun* [C] **SYN telecommuter**

tell 🔊 **A1** /tel/ *verb* (*pt, pp* told /təʊld/)

• **GIVE INFORMATION** **1** [T] ~ sb (sth); ~ sb (that) … ; ~ sb (about sth); ~ sth (to sb) to give information to sb by speaking or writing: *She told me her address but I've forgotten it.* ◇ *He wrote to tell me (that) his mother had died.* ◇ *Tell us about your holiday.* ◇ to **tell the truth/a lie** ◇ to **tell a story** ◇ *Excuse me, could you tell me where the station is?* ◇ *He tells that story to everyone he sees.* **2** [T] ~ **sb (sth)**; ~ **sb (that)** … (used about a thing) to give information to sb: *This book will tell you all you need to know.* ◇ *The data tells us (that) many people in our region don't work full-time.*

• SECRET **3** [I] (*informal*) to not keep a secret: *Promise you won't tell!*

• ORDER **4** [T] ~ **sb to do sth** to order or advise sb to do sth: *The policewoman told us to get out of the car.*

• KNOW **5** [I, T] ~ **(that)** … to know, see or judge (sth) correctly: *'What do you think Jenny will do next?' 'It's hard to tell.'* ◇ *I could tell (that) he had enjoyed the evening.* ◇ **You can never tell** what he's going to say next. ◇ *I can't **tell the difference between** Dan's sisters.*

• DISTINGUISH **6** [T] ~ **A and B apart**; ~ **A from B** to see the difference between one thing or person and another: *It's very difficult to tell Tom and James apart.* ◇ *Can you tell Tom from his twin brother?*

• HAVE AN EFFECT **7** [I] ~ **(on sb/sth)** to have an effect on sb, especially a bad one: *I can't run as fast as I could — my age is beginning to tell on me!*

IDM **all told** with everyone or everything counted and included **I told you (so)** (*informal*) I warned you that this would happen **tell the time** to read the time from a clock or watch **(I'll) tell you what** (*informal*) used to introduce a suggestion: *I'll tell you what — let's ask Diane to take us.*

PHR V **tell sb off (for sth/doing sth)** to speak to sb angrily because they have done sth wrong: *The teacher told me off for not doing my homework.* **tell on sb** to tell a parent, teacher, etc. about sth bad that sb has done

telling /'telɪŋ/ *adj.* **1** having a great effect: *That's quite a telling argument.* **2** showing, without intending to, what sb/sth is really like: *The number of homeless people is a telling comment on today's society.*

telltale /'telteɪl/ *adj.* [only before noun] giving information about sth secret or private: *He said he was fine, but there were telltale signs of worry on his face.*

tellurium /te'ljʊəriəm/ *noun* [U] (*symb.* Te) (**CHEMISTRY**) a chemical element. Tellurium is a shiny silver-white substance that breaks easily. ❶ For more information on the periodic table of elements, look at the **Reference Section** of this dictionary.

telly /'teli/ *noun* [C] (*pl.* -ies) (*BrE, informal*) **1** = TV (1) **2** = TV (2)

temp¹ /temp/ *noun* [C] (*informal*) a temporary employee, especially in an office ▶ **temp** *verb* [I]

temp² /temp/ *abbr.* = TEMPERATURE: *temp 15°C*

temper /'tempə(r)/ *noun* **1** [C, usually sing., U] if you have a temper you get angry very easily: *Be careful of Paul. He's got quite a temper!* ◇ *You must learn to control your temper.* **2** [C] the way you are feeling at a particular time: *It's no use talking to him when he's **in a bad temper*. **SYN** **mood**
IDM **in a temper** feeling very angry and not controlling your behaviour **keep/lose your temper** to stay calm/to become angry ⊃ look at **bad-tempered**

temperament /'temprəmənt/ *noun* [C, U] a person's or an animal's character, especially as it affects the way they behave and feel: *to have an artistic/a fiery/a calm temperament* **SYN** **disposition**

temperamental /ˌtemprə'mentl/ *adj.* often and suddenly changing the way you behave or feel

temperate /'tempərət/ *adj.* (**GEOGRAPHY**) (used about a climate) not very hot and not very cold **SYN** **mesothermal** ⊃ picture at **ecosystem**

temperature ᴦ **A2** /'temprətʃə(r)/ *noun* [C, U] (*abbr.* temp) **1** the measurement of how hot or cold sth is: *Heat the oven to a temperature of 200°C.* ◇ *a high/low temperature* ◇ *an increase in temperature* **2** the measurement of how hot or cold a person's body is **IDM** **have a temperature** (*BrE*) (**HEALTH**) (used about a person) to be hotter than normal because you are ill **take sb's temperature** (**HEALTH**) to measure the temperature of sb's body with a special instrument (a THERMOMETER)

tempest /'tempɪst/ *noun* [C] (*formal*) a violent storm

tempestuous /tem'pestʃuəs/ *adj.* (*formal*) **1** involving a lot of angry argument and strong feeling: *a tempestuous relationship* **2** involving violent storms: *tempestuous seas*

template /'templeɪt/ *noun* [C] **1** a shape cut out of a hard material, used as a model for producing exactly the same shape many times in another material **2** a thing that is used as a model for producing other similar examples: *If you need to write a lot of similar letters, set up a template on your computer.*

temple ᴦ+ **B2** /'templ/ *noun* [C] **1** (**RELIGION**) a building where people pray to a god or gods: *a Buddhist/Hindu temple* **2** (**ANATOMY**) one of the flat parts on each side of the head, at the same level as the eyes and higher ⊃ picture at **body**

tempo /'tempəʊ/ *noun* [C, U] **1** (*pl.* tempi /-pi:/) (**MUSIC**) the speed of a piece of music: *a fast/slow tempo* **2** (*pl.* -os) the speed of an activity or event

temporal /'tempərəl/ *adj.* **1** (*formal*) connected with the real physical world, not spiritual or religious matters: *Although spiritual leader of millions of people, the Pope has no temporal power.* **2** (*formal*) connected with or limited by time: *spatial and temporal changes in rainfall patterns* **3** (**ANATOMY**) near the TEMPLE(S) (= the flat parts at the side of the head): *the right temporal lobe of the brain*

temporary ᴦ **B2** /'temprəri/ *adj.* lasting for a short time: *a temporary job* ◇ *This arrangement is only temporary.* **OPP** **permanent** ⊃ note at **job** ▶ **temporarily** ᴦ+ **B2** /-prərəli/ *adv.*

tempt ᴦ+ **C1** /tempt/ *verb* [T] ~ **sb (into sth/doing sth)**; ~ **sb (to do sth)** to try to persuade or attract sb to do sth, even if it is wrong: *His dream of riches had tempted him into a life of crime.* ◇ *She was tempted to stay in bed all morning.*

temptation /temp'teɪʃn/ *noun* **1** [U] a feeling that you want to do sth, even if you know that it is wrong: *I managed to **resist the temptation** to tell him what I really thought.* ◇ *He wanted a cream cake badly, but didn't **give in to temptation.** **2** [C] a thing that attracts you to do sth wrong or silly: *All that money is certainly a big temptation.*

tempting /'temptɪŋ/ *adj.* attractive in a way that makes you want to do or have sth: *a tempting offer*

ten ᴦ **A1** /ten/ *number* 10

tenacious /tə'neɪʃəs/ *adj.* not likely to give up or let sth go; determined ▶ **tenacity** /-'næsəti/ *noun* [U]

tenancy /'tenənsi/ *noun* [C, U] (*pl.* -ies) the use of a room, flat, building or piece of land, for which you pay rent to the owner: *a six-month tenancy* ◇ *It says in the tenancy agreement that you can't keep pets.*

tenant ᴦ+ **C1** /'tenənt/ *noun* [C] a person who pays rent to the owner of a room, flat, building or piece of land so that they can live in it or use it: *They had evicted* their *tenants for non-payment of rent.* ◇ *tenant farmers* (= ones who do not own their own farms) ⊃ look at **landlady** (1), **landlord** (1)

tend 🔊 **B1** ⊙ /tend/ *verb* **1** [I] ~ **to do sth** to be likely to do sth or to happen in a particular way because this is what often or usually happens: *Women tend to live longer than men.* ◇ *There tends to be a lot of heavy traffic on that road.* ◇ *My brother tends to talk a lot when he's nervous.* ◇ *I tend to think that we shouldn't interfere.* **2** [T, I] ~ **(to) sb/sth** to look after sb/sth: *Paramedics tended (to) the injured.*

tendency 🔊+ **B2** ⊙ /'tendənsi/ *noun* [C] (*pl.* -ies) ~ **(to do sth/towards sth)** something that a person or thing usually does; a way of behaving: *They both have a tendency to be late for appointments.* ◇ *The dog began to show vicious tendencies.* ◇ *She seems to have a tendency towards depression.*

tender¹ 🔊+ **C1** /'tendə(r)/ *adj.* **1** kind and loving: *tender words/looks/kisses* **2** (used about food) soft and easy to cut or bite: *The meat should be nice and tender.* **OPP** **tough** ⊃ note at **meat 3** (used about a part of the body) painful when you touch it ▸ **tenderly** *adv.* ▸ **tenderness** *noun* [U]

IDM **at a tender age** | **at the tender age of …** when still young and without much experience: *She went to live abroad at the tender age of 15.*

tender² /'tendə(r)/ *noun* [C] ~ **(for sth)** a formal offer to supply goods or do work at a stated price: *Several firms submitted a tender for the catering contract.* **SYN** **bid**²

tender³ /'tendə(r)/ *verb* **1** [I] ~ **(for sth)** to make a formal offer to supply goods or do work at a stated price: *Five different companies tendered for the building contract* (= stated a price for doing the work). **2** [T] ~ **sth (to sb)** (*formal*) to offer or give sth to sb: *He has tendered his resignation to the prime minister.*

tendon /'tendən/ *noun* [C] (ANATOMY) a strong, thin part inside the body that joins a muscle to a bone ⊃ look at **ligament** ⊃ picture at **arm**¹

tendril /'tendrəl/ *noun* [C] (BIOLOGY) a long thin part that grows from a climbing plant. A plant uses tendrils to fasten itself to a wall, etc.

tenement /'tenəmənt/ *noun* [C] a large building that is divided into small flats, especially in a poor area of a city

tenner /'tenə(r)/ *noun* [C] (*BrE, informal*) a ten pound note; £10

tennis 🔊 **A1** /'tenɪs/ *noun* [U] (SPORT) a game for two or four players who hit a ball over a net using a RACKET (= a piece of equipment that is held in the hand): *Let's play tennis.* ◇ *to have a game of tennis* ◇ *a tennis match* ❶ In tennis you can play **singles** (a game between two people) or **doubles** (a game between two teams of two people).

tenor¹ /'tenə(r)/ *noun* [C] (MUSIC) a fairly high singing voice for a man; a man with this voice: *Andrea Bocelli is a famous Italian tenor.* ❶ Tenor is between **alto** and **baritone**.

tenor² /'tenə(r)/ *adj.* [only before noun] (MUSIC) (used about a musical instrument) with a range of notes similar to that of a TENOR voice: *a tenor saxophone/ trombone*

tenpin bowling /ˌtenpɪn ˈbəʊlɪŋ/ *noun* [U] a game in which you roll a heavy ball towards ten objects that are like bottles in shape, and try to knock them down

tense¹ /tens/ *adj.* **1** (used about a person) not able to relax because you are worried or nervous: *She looked pale and tense.* **2** (used about an atmosphere or a

situation) in which people feel worried and not relaxed **3** (used about a muscle or a part of the body) tight; not relaxed

tense² /tens/ *verb* [T, I] ~ **(up)** to have muscles that have become hard and not relaxed: *She tensed up before the concert and didn't play well.*

tense³ /tens/ *noun* [C] (GRAMMAR) a form of a verb that shows if sth happens in the past, present or future

tension 🔊+ **B2** 🅦 /'tenʃn/ *noun* **1** [U] the condition of not being able to relax because you are worried or nervous: *I could hear the tension in her voice as she spoke.* **2** [C, U] bad feeling and lack of trust between people, countries, etc: *There are signs of growing tensions between the two countries.* **3** [U] (used about a rope, muscle, etc.) the state of being stretched tight; how tightly sth is stretched: *The massage relieved the tension in my neck.*

tent 🔊 **B1** /tent/ *noun* [C] a small structure made of cloth that is held up by POLES and ropes. You can use a tent to sleep in when you go camping: *to put up/take down a tent*

tentacle /'tentəkl/ *noun* [C] one of the long thin soft parts like legs that some sea animals have: *An octopus has eight tentacles.* ⊃ picture at **animal**, **jellyfish**

tentative /'tentətɪv/ *adj.* **1** (used about plans, etc.) uncertain; not definite **2** not behaving or done with confidence: *a tentative smile/suggestion* ▸ **tentatively** *adv.*

tenterhooks /'tentəhʊks/ *noun* [pl.]
IDM **(be) on tenterhooks** (to be) in a very nervous or excited state because you are waiting to find out what is going to happen

tenth¹ /tenθ/ *ordinal number* 10th

tenth² /tenθ/ *noun* [C] one of ten equal parts of sth

'tent peg = PEG¹ (2)

tenuous /'tenjuəs/ *adj.* very weak or uncertain: *The connection between Joe's story and what actually happened was tenuous.*

tenure 🔊+ **C1** /'tenjə(r)/ *noun* [U] a legal right to live in a place, hold a job, use land, etc. for a certain time

tepid /'tepɪd/ *adj.* (used about liquids) only slightly warm

terabit /'terəbɪt/ *noun* [C] (*abbr.* Tb) (COMPUTING) a unit of computer memory or data, equal to 10^{12} BITS (= the smallest units of information)

terabyte /'terəbaɪt/ *noun* [C] (*abbr.* TB) (COMPUTING) a unit of computer memory or data, equal to 10^{12} BYTES (= small units of information)

terbium /'tɜːbiəm/ *noun* [U] (*symb.* Tb) (CHEMISTRY) a chemical element. Terbium is a silver-white metal used in LASERS and X-RAYS. ❶ For more information on the periodic table of elements, look at the **Reference Section** of this dictionary.

term¹ 🔊 **A2** ⊙ /tɜːm/ *noun* [C] **1** (LANGUAGE) a word or group of words with a particular meaning: *What exactly do you mean by the term 'genius'?* ◇ *a technical term in computing* **2** (*AmE also* **trimester**) (EDUCATION) (especially in the UK) one of the three periods in the year during which classes are held in schools, universities, etc: *the autumn/spring/summer term* ◇ *an end-of-term test* ⊃ look at **semester 3** (MATHEMATICS) each of the various parts in a series, an EQUATION, etc.
IDM **in the long/short term** over a long/short period of time in the future

term² 🔊 **B2** 🅦 /tɜːm/ *verb* [T, often passive] (*formal*) to describe sb/sth by using a particular word or expression: *the period of history that is often termed the 'Dark Ages'*

terminal¹ ʔ+ **C1** /ˈtɜːmɪnl/ adj. (HEALTH) (used about an illness) slowly causing death: *terminal cancer*
▶ **terminally** /-nəli/ adv.: *a terminally ill patient*

terminal² ʔ+ **B2** /ˈtɜːmɪnl/ noun [C] **1** a large railway station, bus station or building at an airport where journeys begin and end: *the bus terminal* ◇ *Which terminal are you flying from?* **2** (COMPUTING) the computer that one person uses for getting information from a central computer or for putting information into it

terminal veˈlocity noun [U] (PHYSICS) the maximum speed that sth falling through air, water or a gas can reach before the effect of GRAVITY is balanced by the forces of FRICTION

terminate ʔ+ **C1** /ˈtɜːmɪneɪt/ verb [I, T] (formal) to end; to make sth end: *to terminate a contract/an agreement*
▶ **termination** /ˌtɜːmɪˈneɪʃn/ noun [U, C]

terminology ⓦ /ˌtɜːmɪˈnɒlədʒi/ noun [U, C] (pl. -ies) the special words and expressions that are used in a particular profession, subject or activity ⊃ note at **language**

terminus /ˈtɜːmɪnəs/ noun [C] (pl. termini /-naɪ/) the last stop or station at the end of a bus route or railway line

termite /ˈtɜːmaɪt/ noun [C] a small insect that lives in large groups, mainly in hot countries. Termites do a lot of damage by eating the wood of trees and buildings.

terms ʔ+ **B2** ⓞ /tɜːmz/ noun [pl.] **1** the conditions of an agreement: *Under the terms of the contract you must give a week's notice.* ◇ *Both sides agreed to the peace terms.* ◇ *My terms are £20 a lesson.* **2** a way of expressing yourself or of saying sth: *I'll try to explain in simple terms.* ⊃ note at **language**
IDM **be on equal terms (with sb)** → EQUAL¹ **be on good, friendly, etc. terms (with sb)** to have a friendly relationship with sb **come to terms with sth** to accept sth unpleasant or difficult **in terms of …** | **in … terms** used for showing which particular way you are thinking about sth or from which point of view: *The house would be ideal in terms of size, but it is very expensive.* ◇ *We must think about this in political terms.*

ternary form /ˈtɜːnəri fɔːm/ noun [U] (MUSIC) the structure of a piece of music in three sections, in which the third section is the same as the first

terrace /ˈterəs/ noun **1** [C] (BrE) (ARCHITECTURE) a line of similar houses that are all joined together in one block: *12 Albert Terrace* **2** [C] a flat area of stone next to a restaurant or house where people can have meals, sit in the sun, etc: *a sun terrace* ◇ *All rooms have a balcony or terrace.* ⊃ look at **patio** ⊃ look at **veranda 3** terraces [pl.] (BrE) (SPORT) the wide steps that people stand on to watch a football match **4** [C, usually pl.] (AGRICULTURE) one of a series of flat areas of ground that are cut into the side of a hill like steps so that crops can be grown there ⊃ picture at **floodplain**

terraced /ˈterəst/ adj. **1** (BrE) (used about a house) forming part of a line of similar houses that are all joined together **2** (AGRICULTURE) (used about a hill) having steps cut out of it so that crops can be grown there

terracotta /ˌterəˈkɒtə/ noun [U] red-brown CLAY (= a type of earth) that has been baked but not GLAZED (= covered in a clear shiny substance), and is used for making pots, etc.

terrain ʔ+ **C1** /təˈreɪn/ noun [U] (GEOGRAPHY) land of the type mentioned: *mountainous/steep/rocky terrain*

terˈrain park noun [C] (SPORT) an outdoor area with special features designed for winter sports, especially SNOWBOARDING (= moving over snow on a special board)

terrestrial /təˈrestriəl/ adj. **1** (BIOLOGY) (used about animals and plants) living on the land or on the ground, rather than in water, in trees or in the air **2** (ASTRONOMY) connected with the planet Earth: *terrestrial life* ⊃ look at **celestial**, **extraterrestrial 3** (ARTS AND MEDIA) (used about TV and BROADCASTING systems) operating on earth rather than from a SATELLITE

terrible ʔ **A1** /ˈterəbl/ adj. **1** very unpleasant; causing great shock or injury: *a terrible accident* ◇ *terrible news* ◇ *What a terrible thing to do!* **2** [not before noun] ill or very upset: *I feel terrible. I think I'm going to be sick.* ◇ *He felt terrible when he realized what he had done.* **3** (informal) very bad; of poor quality: *a terrible hotel/book/memory/driver* **4** [only before noun] used to emphasize how bad sth is: *in terrible pain/trouble* ◇ *The room was in a terrible mess.*

terribly ʔ+ **B2** /ˈterəbli/ adv. **1** very: *I'm terribly sorry.* **2** very much; very badly: *I played terribly.* ◇ *The experiment went terribly wrong.*

terrier /ˈteriə(r)/ noun [C] a type of small dog

terrific ʔ+ **C1** /təˈrɪfɪk/ adj. (informal) **1** extremely nice or good; excellent: *You're doing a terrific job!* **2** very great: *I've got a terrific amount of work to do.*
▶ **terrifically** /-kli/ adv.: *terrifically expensive*

terrified /ˈterɪfaɪd/ adj. ~ (of sb/sth) very afraid: *I'm absolutely terrified of snakes.* ◇ *What's the matter? You look terrified.*

terrify ʔ+ **B2** /ˈterɪfaɪ/ verb [T] (terrifying; terrifies; pt, pp terrified) to frighten sb very much

territorial /ˌterəˈtɔːriəl/ adj. [only before noun] connected with the land or area of sea that belongs to a country

terriˌtorial ˈwaters noun [pl.] the parts of a sea or an ocean that are near a country's coast and are legally under its control

territory ʔ+ **B2** ⓦ /ˈterətri/ noun (pl. -ies) **1** [C, U] (POLITICS) an area of land that belongs to one country: *to fly over enemy territory* **2** [C, U] an area that an animal has as its own **3** [U] an area of knowledge or responsibility: *Computer programming is Frank's territory.*

terror ʔ+ **B2** /ˈterə(r)/ noun **1** [U, sing.] very great fear: *He screamed in terror as the rats came towards him.* **2** [C] a person or thing that makes you feel afraid: *the terrors of the night* **3** [U] (POLITICS) violence and the killing of ordinary people for political purposes: *a campaign of terror* **4** [C] a person (usually a child) or an animal that is difficult to control: *Joey's a little terror.*

terrorism ʔ+ **B2** /ˈterərɪzəm/ noun [U] the use of violence for political purposes: *an act of terrorism*
▶ **terrorist** ʔ+ **B2** /ˈterərɪst/ noun [C], adj. ⊃ note at **criminal¹**

terrorize (BrE also -ise) /ˈterəraɪz/ verb [T] to make sb feel frightened by using or threatening to use violence against them: *The gang has terrorized the neighbourhood for months.*

terse /tɜːs/ adj. said in few words and in a not very friendly way: *a terse reply*

tertiary /ˈtɜːʃəri/ adj. **1** third in order, rank or importance: *the tertiary sector* (= the area of industry that deals with services rather than materials or goods) **2** (BrE) (used about education) at university or college level ⊃ look at **primary¹** (2), **secondary** (3)

ˈtertiary industry (also **service industry**) noun [U, C] (ECONOMICS) the part of a country's economy that provides services

TESL /ˌtesl/ *abbr.* (**EDUCATION**, **LANGUAGE**) **Teaching English as a Second Language** (the teaching of English as a foreign language to people who are living in a country in which English is either the first or the second language)

tessellation (*BrE*) (*AmE* **tesselation**) /ˌtesəˈleɪʃn/ *noun* [C, U] (**GEOMETRY**) an arrangement of shapes fitted closely together with no spaces in between, especially in a repeated pattern; the act of arranging sth in this way ▶ **tessellated** (*BrE*) (*AmE* **tesselated**) /ˈtesəleɪtɪd/ *adj.*

test¹ 🔒 **A1** 🔘 /test/ *noun* [C] **1** (**EDUCATION**) a short exam to measure sb's knowledge or skill in sth: *We have a spelling test every Friday.* ⊃ note at **study²** **2** (**MEDICINE**) a medical examination of a part of your body: *to have an eye test* **3** an experiment to find out if sth works or to find out more information about it: *Tests show that the new drug is safe and effective.* ◇ *to carry out/perform/do a test* **4** a situation or an event that shows how good, strong, etc. sb/sth is **IDM** **put sb/sth to the test** to do sth to find out how good, strong, etc. sb/sth is

test² 🔒 **A1** 🔘 /test/ *verb* **1** [T, I] ~ **sb (on sth)** to find out how much sb knows, or what they can do by asking them questions or giving them activities to perform: *We're being tested on irregular verbs this morning.* **2** [T, I] ~ **(sb/sth) (for sth)** (**MEDICINE**) to examine a part of the body to find out if it is healthy: *to have your eyes tested* ◇ *The doctor tested him for hepatitis.* **3** [T] ~ **sth (for sth)**; ~ **sth (on sb/sth)** to use or try a machine, substance, etc. to find out how well it works or to find out more information about it: *These cars have all been tested for safety.* ◇ *Do you think drugs should be tested on animals?*

testament /ˈtestəmənt/ *noun* [C, usually sing., U] ~ **(to sth)** (*formal*) something that shows that sth exists or is true: *The new model is a testament to the skill and dedication of the workforce.* ⊃ look at **New Testament**, **Old Testament**

ˈtest drive *noun* [C] an occasion when you drive a vehicle that you are thinking of buying so that you can see how well it works and if you like it ▶ **ˈtest-drive** *verb* [T]

testes /ˈtestiːz/ *plural of* **testis**

testicle /ˈtestɪkl/ (*also* **testis**) *noun* [C] (**ANATOMY**) one of the two male sex organs that produce **SPERM** (= the seed necessary for making babies)

testify 🔒+ **C1** /ˈtestɪfaɪ/ *verb* [I, T] (**testifying**; **testifies**; *pt, pp* **testified**) ~ **(that) …** ; ~ **for/against sb/sth** (**LAW**) to make a formal statement that sth is true, especially in a court of law: *The witness testified that the accused was with her on the morning of the crime.* ◇ *She refused to testify against her husband.*

testimony 🔒+ **C1** /ˈtestɪməni/ *noun* (*pl.* **-ies**) **1** [U, sing.] ~ **(to sth)** (*formal*) something that shows that sth else exists or is true: *The design was testimony to her architectural skill.* **2** [C, U] (**LAW**) a formal statement that sth is true, especially one that is made in court

testing 🔒+ **B2** /ˈtestɪŋ/ *noun* [U] the activity of testing sb/sth in order to find sth out, see if it works, etc.

testis /ˈtestɪs/ *noun* [C] (*pl.* **testes**) = **TESTICLE**

testosterone /teˈstɒstərəʊn/ *noun* [U] (**BIOLOGY**) a **HORMONE** produced in men's bodies that makes them develop male physical and sexual characteristics ⊃ look at **oestrogen**, **progesterone**

ˈtest tube *noun* [C] (**SCIENCE**) a thin glass tube that is used in chemical experiments ⊃ picture at **laboratory**

tetanus /ˈtetnəs/ *noun* [U] (**HEALTH**) a serious disease that makes the muscles, especially the muscles of the face, impossible to move. You can get tetanus by cutting yourself on sth dirty.

tether¹ /ˈteðə(r)/ *verb* [T] ~ **sth (to sth)** to tie an animal to sth with a rope, etc.

tether² /ˈteðə(r)/ *noun* **IDM** **at the end of your tether** → **END¹**

tetrahedron /ˌtetrəˈhiːdrən/ *noun* [C] (**GEOMETRY**) a solid shape with four flat sides that are **TRIANGLES** ⊃ picture at **solid²**

text¹ 🔒 **A1** 🔘 /tekst/ *noun* **1** [U] any form of written material: *a computer that can process text* **2** [C] a piece of writing that you have to answer questions about in an exam or a lesson: *a literary text* ◇ (*BrE*) *'Macbeth' is a set text* (= one that has to be studied for an examination) *this year.* **3** [C] = **TEXT MESSAGE**: *She sent me a text to say she would be late.* **4** [U] (**ARTS AND MEDIA**, **LITERATURE**) the main printed part of a book or magazine, not the notes, pictures, etc: *My job is to lay out the text and graphics on the page.* **5** [C] the written form of a speech, a play, an article, etc: *The newspaper printed the complete text of the interview.*

text² 🔒 **A2** /tekst/ *verb* [T, I] to send sb a written message using a mobile phone: *Text me when you're ready.* ◇ *She spends all her time texting.* ⊃ look at **SMS**

textbook 🔒+ **B2** 🔘 /ˈtekstbʊk/ *noun* [C] (**EDUCATION**) a book that teaches a particular subject and that is used especially in schools: *a history textbook*

textile /ˈtekstaɪl/ *noun* **1** [C] any type of cloth made by **WEAVING** or **KNITTING**: *cotton textiles* ◇ *the textile industry* **2** textiles [pl.] the industry that makes cloth: *He got a job in textiles.*

texting /ˈtekstɪŋ/ *noun* [U] the act of sending written messages using a mobile phone

ˈtext message (*also* **text**) *noun* [C] a written message that you send using a mobile phone

textspeak /ˈtekstspiːk/ *noun* [U] the kind of language that is typically used in **TEXT MESSAGES**, for example short forms of words

textual /ˈtekstʃuəl/ *adj.* connected with or contained in a text: *textual errors* ◇ *textual analysis*

texture 🔒+ **C1** /ˈtekstʃə(r)/ *noun* [C, U] the way that sth feels when you touch it: *a rough/smooth/coarse texture* ◇ *This cheese has a very creamy texture.*

thalamus /ˈθæləməs/ *noun* [C] (*pl.* **thalami** /-maɪ/) (**ANATOMY**) either of the two parts of the brain that control pain and feeling ⊃ picture at **brain**

thallium /ˈθæliəm/ *noun* [U] (*symb.* **Tl**) (**CHEMISTRY**) a chemical element. Thallium is a soft silver-white metal whose **COMPOUNDS** are very poisonous. ❶ For more information on the periodic table of elements, look at the **Reference Section** of this dictionary.

than¹ 🔒 **A1** /ðən/, *strong form* ðæn/ *conj.* **1** used when you are comparing two things: *You speak French much better than she does.* **2** used with expressions showing that one thing happens straight after another: *No sooner had we arrived than the problems started.*

than² 🔒 **A1** /ðən/, *strong form* ðæn/ *prep.* **1** used when you are comparing two things: *He's taller than his brother.* ◇ *London is more expensive than Madrid.* ◇ *I'd rather play tennis than football.* **2** used with *more* and *less* before numbers, expressions of time, distance, etc: *I've worked here for more than three years.*

thank 🔒 **A1** /θæŋk/ *verb* ~ **sb (for sth/for doing sth)** to tell sb that you are grateful: *I'm writing to thank you for the present you sent me.* ◇ *I'll go and thank him for offering to help.*

IDM thank God/goodness/heavens used for expressing happiness that sth unpleasant has stopped or will not happen: *Thank goodness it's stopped raining.*

thankful /'θæŋkfl/ *adj.* ~ (for sth); ~ (to do sth); ~ (that) ... pleased and grateful: *I was thankful for my thick coat when it started to snow.* ◊ *I was thankful to hear that you got home safely.* ◊ *I'm thankful that you and your family are safe.*

thankfully ⱡ+ **C1** /'θæŋkfəli/ *adv.* **1** used for expressing happiness that sth unpleasant did not or will not happen: *Thankfully, no one was injured in the accident.* **SYN** **fortunately** **2** in a pleased or grateful way: *I accepted her offer thankfully.* **SYN** **gratefully**

thankless /'θæŋkləs/ *adj.* involving hard work that other people do not notice or thank you for: *Being a housewife can sometimes be a thankless task.*

thanks¹ ⱡ **A1** /θæŋks/ *exclamation* **1** used to show that you are grateful: *Thanks!* '*How are you?*' '*Fine, thanks!*' **2** no thanks a polite way of refusing sth that sb has offered you

thanks² ⱡ **A1** /θæŋks/ *noun* [pl.] words that show that you are grateful
IDM thanks to sb/sth because of sb/sth: *We're late, thanks to you!* a vote of thanks → VOTE¹

Thanksgiving /ˌθæŋks'gɪvɪŋ/ (*also* ˌThanks'giving Day) *noun* [U, C] a public holiday in the US and in Canada: *Are you going home for Thanksgiving?*

▼ CULTURE

Thanksgiving Day is on the fourth Thursday in November in the US and on the second Monday in October in Canada. It was originally a day when people thanked God for the **harvest** (= the amount of crops gathered on a farm each year).

'**thank you¹** *noun* [C, usually sing.] ~ (to sb) an act, a gift, a comment, etc. intended to thank sb for sth they have done: *The actor sent a big thank you to all his fans.*

'**thank you²** *exclamation* ~ (for sth) an expression of thanks: *Thank you for your letter.*

that¹ ⱡ **A1** /ðæt/ *det., pron., conj.* **1** (*pl.* those /ðəʊz/) used to refer to a person or thing, especially when they are not near the person speaking: *I like that house over there.* ◊ *What's that in the road?* ◊ '*Could you pass me the book?*' '*This one?*' '*No, that one over there.*' **2** (*pl.* those) used for talking about a person or thing already known or mentioned: *That was the year we went to Spain, wasn't it?* ◊ *Can you give me back that money I lent you last week?* **3** /ðət, ðæt/ used as a relative pronoun to introduce a part of a sentence that refers to the person or thing already mentioned: *Where's the letter that came yesterday?* ◊ *The people that live next door are French.* **4** /ðət, ðæt/ used after certain verbs, nouns and adjectives to introduce a new part of the sentence: *She told me that she was leaving.* ◊ *I hope that you feel better soon.* ◊ *I'm certain that he will come.* ◊ *It's funny that you should say that.*
IDM that is (to say) used when you are giving more information about sb/sth: *I'm on holiday next week. That's to say, from Tuesday.* that's that there is nothing more to say or do: *I'm not going and that's that.*

that² ⱡ **B1** /ðæt/ *adv.* (used with adjectives, adverbs) as much as that: *30 miles? I can't walk that far.*

thatched /θætʃt/ *adj.* (used about a building) having a roof made of STRAW (= dried grass) or a similar material

thaw /θɔː/ *verb* ~ (sth) (out) **1** [I] (used about ice and snow) to turn back into water after being frozen: *Is the snow thawing?* **2** [I, T] to become, or to let frozen food become, soft or liquid ready for cooking: *The burgers are still thawing.* ◊ *Always thaw chicken out before you cook it.* ⊃ look at **melt** (1) ▸ thaw *noun* [C, usually sing.]

the ⱡ **A1** /ðə, before vowels ði, strong form ðiː/ *definite article* **1** used for talking about a person or thing that is already known or that has already been mentioned: *I took the children to the dentist.* ◊ *We met the man who bought your house.* ◊ *The milk is in the fridge.* **2** used when there is only one of sth: *The sun is very strong today.* ◊ *Who won the World Cup?* ◊ *the government* **3** used with numbers and dates: *I've seen this film.* ◊ *Friday the thirteenth* ◊ *I grew up in the 1990s.* **4** used with adjectives to name a group of people: *the French* ◊ *the poor* **5** (*formal*) used with a singular noun when you are talking generally about sth: *The dolphin is an intelligent animal.* **6** used with units of measurement, meaning 'every': *Our car does 40 miles to the gallon.* **7** used with musical instruments: *Do you play the piano?* **8** the well-known or important one: '*My best friend at school was Adele.*' '*You mean the Adele?*' **HELP** 'The' is pronounced /ðiː/ in this meaning. **9** the more, less, etc ... , the more, less, etc ... used for saying that the way in which two things change is connected: *The more you eat, the fatter you get.*

theatre ⱡ **A1** (*AmE* theater) /'θɪətə(r)/ *noun* **1** [C] (**ARTS AND MEDIA**) a building where you go to see plays, shows, etc: *How often do you go to the theatre?* **2** [U] (**ARTS AND MEDIA**) plays in general: *He's studying modern Russian theatre.* **SYN** **drama** **3** [sing., U] (**ARTS AND MEDIA**) the work of acting in or producing plays: *He's worked in (the) theatre for 30 years.* **4** [C, U] = OPERATING THEATRE

theatregoer (*BrE*) (*AmE* theatergoer) /'θɪətəgəʊə(r)/ *noun* [C] (**ARTS AND MEDIA**) a person who goes regularly to the theatre

theatrical ⱡ+ **C1** /θi'ætrɪkl/ *adj.* **1** [only before noun] connected with the theatre **2** (used about behaviour) dramatic or showing feelings, etc. in a very obvious way because you want people to notice you

theft ⱡ+ **B2** /θeft/ *noun* [U, C] (**LAW**) the crime of stealing sth: *There have been a lot of thefts in this area recently.* ◊ *The woman was arrested for theft.* ⊃ note at **criminal¹**

their ⱡ **A1** /ðeə(r)/ *det.* **1** of or belonging to them: *The children picked up their books and walked to the door.* **2** used instead of *his* or *her*: *Has everyone got their book?*

theirs ⱡ **B1** /ðeəz/ *pron.* of or belonging to them: *Our flat isn't as big as theirs.*

them ⱡ **A1** /ðəm, strong form ðem/ *pron.* (the object form of *they*) **1** used when referring to people or things as the object of a verb or preposition: *I'll phone them now.* ◊ '*I've got the keys here.*' '*Oh good. Give them to me.*' ◊ *We have students from several countries but most of them are Italian.* ◊ *They asked for your address so I gave it to them.* **2** used instead of *him* or *her*: *If anyone phones, tell them I'm busy.*

thematic /θɪ'mætɪk, θiː'm-/ *adj.* connected with the subject or subjects of sth: *the thematic structure of a text* ▸ thematically /-kli/ *adv.*: *The books have been grouped thematically.*

theme ⱡ **B1** ⊙ /θiːm/ *noun* [C] (**ART, LITERATURE**) the subject of a talk, a piece of writing or a work of art: *The theme of today's discussion will be 'Our changing cities'.*

'theme park *noun* [C] a park where people go to enjoy themselves, for example by riding on ROLLER COASTERS (= large machines that go very fast), and where much of the entertainment is connected with one subject or idea

themselves 🔊 **A2** /ðəm'selvz/ *pron.* **1** used when the people or things who do an action are also affected by it: *Helen and Sarah seem to be enjoying themselves.* ◇ *People often talk to themselves when they are worried.* **2** used to emphasize *they* or a plural subject: *They themselves say that the situation cannot continue.* ◇ *Did they paint the house themselves?* (= or did sb else do it for them?)
IDM (all) by themselves **1** alone: *The boys are too young to go out by themselves.* **2** without help: *The children cooked the dinner all by themselves.*

then 🔊 **A1** /ðen/ *adv.* **1** (at) that time: *In 1990? I was at university then.* ◇ *I spoke to him on Wednesday, but I haven't seen him since then.* ◇ *They met in 1941 and remained close friends from then on.* ◇ *I'm going tomorrow. Can you wait until then?* ◇ *Phone me tomorrow — I will have decided by then.* **2** next; after that: *I'll have a shower and get changed, then we'll go out.* ◇ *There was silence for a minute. Then he replied.* **3** used to show the logical result of a statement or situation: *'I don't feel at all well.' 'Why don't you go to the doctor then?'* ◇ *If you don't do any work then you'll fail the exam.* **4** used after words like *now, right, well,* etc. to show the beginning or end of a conversation or statement: *Now then, are we all ready to go?* ◇ *Right then, I'll see you tomorrow.*
IDM then/there again → AGAIN there and then | then and there → THERE

thence /ðens/ *adv.* (*old-fashioned or formal*) from there

theo- /θiːəʊ, θiːə, θiˈɒ/ *prefix* (in nouns, adjectives and adverbs) (**RELIGION**) connected with God or a god: *theology*

theodolite /θiˈɒdəlaɪt/ *noun* [C] (**GEOMETRY**) a piece of equipment that is used for measuring angles

theologian /ˌθiːəˈləʊdʒən/ *noun* [C] (**RELIGION**) a person who studies THEOLOGY

theology 🔊+ **C1** /θiˈɒlədʒi/ *noun* [U] (**EDUCATION**, **RELIGION**) the study of religion ▸ theological /ˌθiːəˈlɒdʒɪkl/ *adj.*

theorem /'θɪərəm/ *noun* [C] (**MATHEMATICS**) a rule or principle, especially in mathematics, that can be proved to be true: *Pythagoras' theorem*

theoretical 🔊+ **C1** 🔊 /ˌθɪəˈretɪkl/ *adj.* **1** based on ideas and principles, not on practical experience: *A lot of university courses are still too theoretical these days.* ⊃ look at **practical**[1] (1) **2** that may possibly exist or happen, although it is unlikely: *There is a theoretical possibility that the world will end tomorrow.* ▸ theoretically 🔊 /-kli/ *adv.*

theorist /'θɪərɪst/ (*also* theoretician /ˌθɪərəˈtɪʃn/) *noun* [C] a person who develops ideas and principles about a particular subject in order to explain why things happen or exist

theory 🔊 **B1** 🔊 /'θɪəri/ *noun* (*pl.* -ies) **1** [C, U] (**SCIENCE**) an idea or set of ideas that tries to explain sth: *the theory about how life on earth began* **2** [U] the general idea or principles of a particular subject: *political theory* ◇ *the theory and practice of language teaching* **3** [C] an opinion or a belief that has not been shown to be true
IDM in theory as a general idea that may not be true in reality: *Your plan sounds fine in theory, but I don't know if it'll work in practice.*

therapeutic /ˌθerəˈpjuːtɪk/ *adj.* **1** (**MEDICINE**) helping to cure an illness: *therapeutic drugs* **2** helping you to relax and feel better: *I find listening to music very therapeutic.*

therapeutics /ˌθerəˈpjuːtɪks/ *noun* [U] (**MEDICINE**) the area of medicine connected with the treatment of diseases

therapy 🔊 **B2** /'θerəpi/ *noun* **1** [U, C] (**MEDICINE**) treatment to help or cure a mental or physical illness, usually without drugs or medical operations: *to have/ undergo therapy* **2** [U] = PSYCHOTHERAPY: *She's in therapy.* ▸ therapist 🔊+ **B2** /-pɪst/ *noun* [C]: *a speech therapist*

there 🔊 **A1** /ðeə(r)/ *adv.* **1** used as the subject of *be, seem, appear,* etc. to say that sth exists: *Is there a god?* ◇ *There's a man at the door.* ◇ *There wasn't much to eat.* ◇ *There's somebody singing outside.* ◇ *There seems to be a mistake here.* **2** in, at or to that place: *Could you put the table there, please?* ◇ *I like Milan. My husband and I met there.* ◇ *Have you been to Bonn? We're going there next week.* ◇ *Have you looked under there?* **3** existing or available if needed: *Her parents are always there if she needs help.* **4** at that point (in a conversation, story, etc.): *Could I interrupt you there for a minute?* **5** used for calling attention to sth: *Oh look, there's Kate!* ◇ *Hello there! Can anyone hear me?*
IDM be there for sb to be available to help and support sb when they have a problem: *Whenever I'm in trouble, my sister is always there for me.* then/ there again → AGAIN there and then | then and there immediately; at that time and place there you are **1** used when you give sth to sb: *There you are. I've bought you a sandwich.* **2** used when you are explaining sth to sb: *Just press the switch and there you are!*

thereabouts /ˌðeərəˈbaʊts/ *adv.* (usually after *or*) somewhere near a number, time or place: *There are 100 students, or thereabouts.* ◇ *She lives in Sydney, or thereabouts.*

thereafter 🔊+ **C1** /ˌðeərˈɑːftə(r)/ *adv.* (*formal*) after that

thereby 🔊+ **C1** 🔊 /ˌðeəˈbaɪ/ *adv.* (*formal*) in that way

therefore 🔊 **B1** 🔊 /'ðeəfɔː(r)/ *adv.* for that reason: *The new trains have more powerful engines and are therefore faster.* **SYN** thus

therein /ˌðeərˈɪn/ *adv.* (*formal*) because of sth that has just been mentioned

thereupon /ˌðeərəˈpɒn/ *adv.* (*formal*) immediately after that and often as the result of sth

therm /θɜːm/ *noun* [C] a unit of heat, used in the UK for measuring a gas supply

thermal[1] /'θɜːml/ *adj.* **1** (**PHYSICS**) connected with heat: *thermal energy* **2** (used about clothes) made to keep you warm in cold weather: *thermal underwear*

thermal[2] /'θɜːml/ *noun* **1** thermals [pl.] clothes, especially underwear, made to keep you warm in cold weather **2** [C] (**GEOGRAPHY**) a flow of rising warm air

thermal 'imaging *noun* [U] (**PHYSICS**) the process of producing an image of sth or finding out where sth is, using the heat that comes from it: *The police were able to use thermal imaging to find the child.*

thermo- /θɜːməʊ, θɜːmə, θɜːˈmɒ/ *prefix* (in nouns, adjectives and adverbs) connected with heat: *thermostat*

thermometer /θəˈmɒmɪtə(r)/ *noun* [C] an instrument for measuring the temperature of the air or of sb's body

thermoplastic /ˌθɜːməʊˈplæstɪk/ *noun* [U] a plastic material that can be easily shaped and bent when it is heated, and that becomes hard when it is cooled ⊃ look at **thermoset**

Thermos™ /ˈθɜːməs/ (*also* ˈThermos flask) *noun* [C] a particular type of VACUUM FLASK (= a container with double walls with a VACUUM between them, used for keeping liquids hot or cold) ⊃ look at **vacuum**[1] (1)

thermoset /ˈθɜːməʊset/ *noun* [C] (**CHEMISTRY**) a substance that becomes permanently hard when it is heated ⊃ look at **thermoplastic** ▶ **thermosetting** *adj.*

the thermosphere /ðə ˈθɜːməsfɪə(r)/ *noun* [sing.] (**ASTRONOMY, GEOGRAPHY**) the region of the atmosphere above the MESOSPHERE, where the temperature increases with height ⊃ picture at **atmosphere**

thermostat /ˈθɜːməstæt/ *noun* [C] a device that controls the temperature in a house or machine by switching the heat on and off as necessary

thesaurus /θɪˈsɔːrəs/ *noun* [C] (*pl.* **thesauruses, thesauri** /-raɪ/) (**LANGUAGE**) a book that contains lists of words with similar meanings in groups

these /ðiːz/ plural of **this**

thesis ⸎+ B2 /ˈθiːsɪs/ *noun* [C] (*pl.* **theses** /ˈθiːsiːz/) **1** a long piece of writing on a particular subject that you do as part of a university degree: *He did his thesis on Japanese investment in Europe.* ⊃ look at **dissertation** **2** an idea that is discussed and presented with evidence in order to show that it is true

they ⸎ A1 /ðeɪ/ *pron.* (used as the subject of a verb) **1** the people or things that have been mentioned: *We've got two children. They're both boys.* ◇ *'Have you seen my keys?' 'Yes, they're on the table.'* **2** used instead of *he* or *she: Somebody phoned for you but they didn't leave their name.* **3** people in general or people whose identity is not known or stated: *They say it's going to be a mild winter.*

they'd /ðeɪd/ *short form* they had; they would

they'll /ðeɪl/ *short form* they will

they're /ðeə(r)/ *short form* they are

they've /ðeɪv/ *short form* they have

thick[1] ⸎ A2 /θɪk/ *adj.*
• DISTANCE BETWEEN SIDES **1** (used about sth solid) having a large distance between its opposite sides; not thin: *a thick black line* ◇ *a thick coat/book* ◇ *These walls are very thick.* OPP **thin**[1] **2** used for saying what the distance is between the two opposite sides of sth: *The ice was 6 centimetres thick.*
• TREES/HAIR **3** growing closely together in large numbers: *a thick forest* ◇ *thick hair* OPP **thin**[1]
• LIQUID **4** (used about a liquid) that does not flow easily: *thick cream* ◇ *This paint is too thick.* OPP **thin**[1]
• OF SMOKE, ETC. **5** (used about smoke, FOG, etc.) difficult to see through: *thick clouds of smoke* ◇ *There'll be a thick fog tonight.* OPP **thin**[1]
• WITH A LARGE AMOUNT **6** ~ **(with sth)** containing a lot of sth/sb close together: *The air was thick with dust.*
• STUPID **7** (*informal*) slow to learn or understand; stupid
• ACCENT **8** easily recognized as being from a particular country or area
▶ **thick** *adv.*: *Snow lay thick on the ground.*
IDM **have a thick skin** to be not easily upset or worried by what people say about you

thick[2] /θɪk/ *noun*
IDM **in the thick of sth** in the most active or crowded part of sth; very involved in sth **through thick and thin** all the time, even when there are difficult times and situations

thicken /ˈθɪkən/ *verb* [I, T] to become thicker; to make sth thicker

thickener /ˈθɪkənə(r)/ *noun* [C] a substance used to make a liquid thicker: *paint thickeners*

thickly /ˈθɪkli/ *adv.* **1** in a way that produces a wide piece or deep layer of sth: *Spread the butter thickly.* ◇ *thickly sliced bread* **2** ~ **wooded, populated, etc.** having a lot of trees, people, etc. close together: *a thickly wooded area* **3** in a deep voice that is not as clear as normal, especially because of illness or emotion

thickness /ˈθɪknəs/ *noun* [C, U] the quality of being thick or how thick sth is ⊃ look at **width** (1)

thick-ˈskinned *adj.* not easily worried or upset by what other people say about you OPP **thin-skinned**

thief ⸎ A2 /θiːf/ *noun* [C] (*pl.* **thieves** /θiːvz/) (**LAW**) a person who steals things from another person ⊃ note at **criminal**[1]

thigh /θaɪ/ *noun* [C] (**ANATOMY**) the top part of the leg, above the knee ⊃ picture at **body**

ˈthigh bone *noun* [C] (**ANATOMY**) the large thick bone in the top part of the leg above the knee SYN **femur** ⊃ picture at **body**

thimble /ˈθɪmbl/ *noun* [C] a small metal or plastic object that you wear on the end of your finger to protect it when you are SEWING

thin[1] ⸎ A2 /θɪn/ *adj.* (**thinner; thinnest**) **1** (used about sth solid) having a small distance between the opposite sides: *a thin book/shirt* ◇ *a thin slice of meat* OPP **thick**[1] **2** not growing closely together or in large amounts OPP **thick**[1] **3** having very little fat on the body: *How do you stay so thin?* OPP **fat**[1] **4** (used about a liquid) that flows easily; not thick: *a thin sauce* OPP **thick**[1] **5** (used about MIST, smoke, etc.) not difficult to see through OPP **thick**[1] ▶ **thin** *adv.*: *Don't slice the onion too thin.* ▶ **thinly** *adv.*: *thinly sliced bread* ◇ *thinly populated areas*
IDM **thin on the ground** → GROUND[1] **through thick and thin** → THICK[2] **vanish, etc. into thin air** to disappear completely **wear thin** → WEAR[1]

thin[2] /θɪn/ *verb* [I, T] (-nn-) ~ **(sth) (out)** to become thinner or fewer in number; to make sth thinner: *The trees thin out towards the edge of the forest.* ◇ *Thin the sauce by adding milk.*

thing ⸎ A1 ⑤ /θɪŋ/ *noun*
• OBJECT **1** [C] an object that is not named: *What's that red thing on the table?* ◇ *A pen is a thing you use for writing with.* ◇ *I need to get a few things at the shops.*
• EQUIPMENT **2 things** [pl.] clothes or tools that belong to sb or are used for a particular purpose: *I'll just go and pack my things.* ◇ *We keep all the cooking things in this cupboard.*
• ACTION/EVENT **3** [C] an action, an event or a statement: *When I get home the first thing I do is have a cup of tea.* ◇ *A strange thing happened to me yesterday.* ◇ *What a nice thing to say!*
• FACT **4** [C] a fact, subject, etc: *He told me a few things that I didn't know before.*
• YOUR LIFE **5 things** [pl.] the situation or conditions of your life: *How are things with you?*
• QUALITY/STATE **6** [C] a quality or state: *There's no such thing as a ghost* (= it doesn't exist). ◇ *The best thing about my job is the way it changes all the time.*
• WHAT IS NEEDED **7 the thing** [sing.] exactly what is wanted or needed: *That's just the thing I was looking for!*
• PERSON/ANIMAL **8** [C] used for expressing how you feel about a person or an animal: *You've broken your finger? You poor thing!*
IDM **be a good thing (that)** to be lucky that: *It's a good thing you remembered your umbrella.* **a close shave/thing** → CLOSE[3] **do your own thing** to do what you want to do, without thinking about other people

first/last thing as early/late as possible: *I'll phone her first thing tomorrow morning.* ◇ *I saw him last thing on Friday evening.* **for one thing** used for introducing a reason for sth: *I think we should go by train. For one thing it's cheaper.* **have a thing about sb/sth** (*informal*) to have strong feelings about sb/sth **take it/things easy** → EASY[2] **to make matters/things worse** → WORSE[1]

think[1] A1 /θɪŋk/ *verb* (*pt, pp* **thought** /θɔːt/)
• HAVE AN OPINION **1** [T, I] **~ (sth) (of/about sb/sth); ~ (that) ...** to have a particular idea or opinion about sth/sb; to believe: *'Do you think (that) we'll win?' 'No, I* ***don't think so.'*** ◇ *'Sue's coming tomorrow, isn't she?' 'Yes, I* ***think so.'*** ◇ *What did you think of the film?* ◇ *Gary's on holiday, I think.* ◇ *I think (that) they've moved to York but I'm not sure.*
• USE YOUR MIND **2** [I, T] **~ (about sth)** to use your mind to consider sth or to form connected ideas: *Think before you speak.* ◇ *What are you thinking about?* ◇ *He had to think hard* (= a lot) *about the question.*
• IMAGINE **3** [T, I] to form an idea of sth; to imagine sth: ***Just think*** *what we could do with all that money!*
• EXPECT **4** [T] to expect sth: *The job took longer than we thought.*
• IN A PARTICULAR WAY **5** [I] to think in a particular way: *If you want to be successful, you have to* ***think big.*** ◇ *We've got to* ***think positive.***
• INTEND **6** [I] **~ (that) ...** to intend or plan to do sth: *I think I'll go for a swim.*
• REMEMBER **7** [T] to remember sth; to have sth come into your mind: *Can you think where you left the keys?* ◇ *I didn't think to ask him his name.*
IDM **think better of sth/doing sth** to decide not to do sth; to change your mind **think highly, a lot, not much, etc. of sb/sth** to have a good, bad, etc. opinion of sb/sth: *I didn't think much of that film.* **think the world of sb** to love and admire sb very much
PHR V **think about/of sb/sth** to consider sb/sth when you are doing sth: *She never thinks about anyone but herself.* **think about/of doing sth** to consider doing sth: *We're thinking of moving house.* **think of sth** to create an idea in your imagination: *Who first thought of the plan?* **think sth out** to consider carefully all the details of a plan, an idea, etc: *a well-thought-out scheme* **think sth over** to consider sth carefully: *I'll think your offer over and let you know tomorrow.* **think sth through** to consider every detail of sth carefully: *He made a bad decision because he didn't think it through.* **think sth up** to create sth in your mind; to invent: *to think up a new advertising slogan*

▼ **SYNONYMS**

think

believe • feel • be under the impression • be of the opinion

These words all mean to have an idea that sth is true or possible, or to have a particular opinion about sb/sth.

think *Do you think he'll like it?*

believe *The police believe that the man may be armed.*

feel *We felt we were unlucky to lose.*

be under the impression *I was under the impression that she had finished the work.*

be of the opinion (*formal*) *We are of the opinion that this matter deserves your full attention.*

think[2] /θɪŋk/ *noun*
IDM **have a think (about sth)** (*informal*) to think carefully about something in order to make a decision about it: *I'm not sure. I'll have to have a think about it.*

thinker /ˈθɪŋkə(r)/ *noun* [C] **1** a person who thinks about serious and important subjects **2** a person who thinks in a particular way: *a quick/creative/clear thinker*

thinking[1] A2 /ˈθɪŋkɪŋ/ *noun* [U] **1** using your mind to think about sth: *We're going to have to do some quick thinking.* **2** ideas or opinions about sth: *This accident will make them change their thinking on safety matters.* ➲ look at **wishful thinking**

thinking[2] /ˈθɪŋkɪŋ/ *adj.* [only before noun] intelligent and using your mind to think about important subjects

ˈthink tank *noun* [C] (**POLITICS**) a group of experts who provide advice and ideas on political, social or economic issues

ˌthin-ˈskinned *adj.* easily upset by criticism or offensive remarks OPP **thick-skinned**

third[1] A1 /θɜːd/ *ordinal number* 3rd

third[2] A2 /θɜːd/ *noun* [C] **1** one of three equal parts of sth **2** (*BrE*) a result in final university exams, below first and second class degrees

ˌthird ˈclass *noun* **1** [U, sing.] (**TOURISM**) (especially in the past) the cheapest and least comfortable part of a train, ship, etc. **2** [U] (in the US) the class of mail used for sending advertisements, etc. **3** [U, sing.] (**EDUCATION**) the lowest standard of degree given by a British university

ˌthird-ˈclass *adj.* **1** (**TOURISM**) (especially in the past) connected with the cheapest and least comfortable way of travelling on a train, ship, etc. **2** (in the US) connected with the class of mail used to send advertisements, etc. **3** (**EDUCATION**) used to describe the lowest standard of degree given by a British university **4** less important than other people: *They are treated as* ***third-class citizens.*** ▶ **third class** *adv.*: *to travel third class*

ˌthird-deˈgree *adj.* [only before noun] **1** (**HEALTH**) used to describe the most serious of three kinds of burn, affecting the FLESH under the skin and leaving permanent marks ➲ look at **first-degree** (2), **second-degree** (2) **2** (*especially AmE*) (**LAW**) used to describe the least serious of three kinds of murder or some other crimes

thirdly /ˈθɜːdli/ *adv.* used to introduce the third point in a list: *We have made savings in three areas: firstly, defence, secondly, education and thirdly, health.*

ˌthird ˈparty *noun* [C] a person who is involved in a situation in addition to the two main people involved

the ˌthird ˈperson *noun* [sing.] **1** (**GRAMMAR**) the set of pronouns and verb forms used by a speaker to refer to other people and things: *'They are' is the third person plural of the verb 'to be'.* **2** (**LITERATURE**) the style of writing a novel, telling a story, etc. as the experience of sb else, using third person forms: *a book written* ***in the third person*** ➲ look at **first person, second person**

the ˌThird ˈWorld *noun* [sing.] (**GEOGRAPHY, SOCIAL STUDIES**) a way of referring to the poorer countries of Asia, Africa and South America, which is sometimes considered offensive: *the causes of poverty and injustice in the Third World* ◇ *Third-World debt* ➲ look at **First World** ❶ People now prefer to talk about **developing countries** or **the developing world**

thirst /θɜːst/ *noun* **1** [U, sing.] the feeling that you have when you want or need a drink: *to die of thirst* ◇ *Iced tea really quenches your thirst.* **2** [sing.] **~ (for sth)** a strong desire for sth: *a thirst for knowledge* ➲ look at **hunger**[1]

thirsty ʔ A1 /ˈθɜːsti/ adj. (thirstier; thirstiest) wanting or needing a drink: *I'm thirsty. Can I have a drink of water, please?* ⊃ look at **hungry** (1) ▸ **thirstily** /-stɪli/ adv.

thirteen ʔ A1 /ˌθɜːˈtiːn/ number 13 ▸ **thirteenth** /-ˈtiːnθ/ ordinal number, noun [C]

thirty ʔ A1 /ˈθɜːti/ **1** number 30 **2** the thirties noun [pl.] numbers, years or temperatures from 30 to 39 ▸ **thirtieth** /-əθ/ ordinal number, noun [C]
IDM in your thirties between the ages of 30 and 39

this ʔ A1 /ðɪs/ det., pron. (pl. these /ðiːz/) **1** used for talking about sb/sth that is close to you in time or space: *Have a look at this photo.* ◇ *These boots are really comfortable. My old ones weren't.* ◇ *Is this the book you asked for?* ◇ *These are the letters to be filed, not those over there.* ◇ *This chair's softer than that one, so I'll sit here.* **2** used for talking about sth that was mentioned or talked about earlier: *Where did you hear about this?* **3** used for introducing sb or showing sb sth: *This is my wife, Claudia, and these are our children, David and Vicky.* ◇ *It's easier if you do it like this.* **4** (used with days of the week or periods of time) of today or the present week, year, etc: *Are you busy this afternoon?* ◇ *this Friday* (= the Friday of this week) **5** (informal) (used when you are telling a story) a certain: *Then this woman said...* ▸ this ʔ B1 adv.: *The road is not usually this busy.*
IDM this and that | this, that and the other various things: *We chatted about this and that.*

thistle /ˈθɪsl/ noun [C] a wild plant with purple flowers and sharp points on its leaves, which is the national symbol of Scotland

thong /θɒŋ/ (AmE) = FLIP-FLOP

thorax /ˈθɔːræks/ noun [C] **1** (ANATOMY) the middle part of the body between the neck and the WAIST **2** the middle section of an insect's body, to which the legs and wings are connected ⊃ look at **abdomen** (2) ⊃ picture at **animal** ▸ **thoracic** /θɔːˈræsɪk/ adj.

thorium /ˈθɔːriəm/ noun [U] (symb. Th) (CHEMISTRY) a chemical element. Thorium is a white RADIOACTIVE metal used as a source of nuclear energy. ❶ For more information on the periodic table of elements, look at the **Reference Section** of this dictionary.

thorn /θɔːn/ noun [C] one of the hard sharp points on some plants and bushes, for example on ROSE bushes ⊃ picture at **flower**[1]

thorny /ˈθɔːni/ adj. (thornier; thorniest) **1** causing difficulty or argument: *a thorny problem/question* **2** having THORNS

thorough ʔ+ B2 /ˈθʌrə/ adj. **1** careful and complete: *The police made a thorough search of the house.* **2** doing things in a very careful way, making sure that you look at every detail: *Pam is slow but she is very thorough.* ▸ **thoroughness** noun [U]

thoroughbred /ˈθʌrəbred/ noun [C] an animal, especially a horse, of high quality, that has parents that are both of the same type ▸ **thoroughbred** adj.

thoroughly ʔ+ B2 /ˈθʌrəli/ adv. **1** in a careful and complete way: *to study a subject thoroughly* **2** completely; very much: *We thoroughly enjoyed our holiday.*

those /ðəʊz/ plural of **that**[1]

though ʔ B1 /ðəʊ/ conj., adv. **1** despite the fact that; although: *Though he had very little money, Alex always managed to dress smartly.* ◇ *She still loved him even though he had treated her so badly.*
SYN although **2** but: *I'll come as soon as I can, though I can't promise to be on time.* **3** (informal) however: *I quite like him. I don't like his wife, though.*
IDM as though → AS[2]

thought[1] /θɔːt/ past tense, past participle of **think**[1]

thought[2] ʔ A2 ❺ /θɔːt/ noun
• IDEA/OPINION **1** [C] an idea or opinion: *What are your thoughts on this subject?* ◇ *The thought of living alone filled her with fear.* ◇ *I've just had a thought* (= an idea).
• MIND **2** thoughts [pl.] a person's mind and all the ideas that are in it: *You are always in my thoughts.*
• ACT OF THINKING **3** [U] the power, process or act of thinking: *I need to give this problem some thought.*
• FEELING OF CARE **4** [C] a feeling of care or worry: *They sent me flowers. What a kind thought!*
• IN POLITICS, SCIENCE, ETC. **5** [U] particular ideas or a particular way of thinking: *a change in medical thought on the subject*
IDM deep in thought/conversation → DEEP[1] a school of thought → SCHOOL second thoughts → SECOND[1]

thoughtful ʔ+ C1 /ˈθɔːtfl/ adj. **1** thinking deeply: *a thoughtful expression* **2** ~ (of sb) (to do sth) thinking about what other people want or need: *It was very thoughtful of you to send her some flowers.* **SYN** kind[2] ▸ **thoughtfully** /-fəli/ adv. ▸ **thoughtfulness** noun [U]

'thought leader noun [C] (BUSINESS) a person whose views on a subject are important and have a strong influence ▸ **thought leadership** noun [U]

thoughtless /ˈθɔːtləs/ adj. not thinking about what other people want or need or what the result of your actions will be **SYN** inconsiderate ▸ **thoughtlessly** adv. ▸ **thoughtlessness** noun [U]

'thought-provoking ʔ+ C1 adj. making people think seriously about a particular subject: *a thought-provoking book*

thousand ʔ A1 /ˈθaʊznd/ number **1** 1 000 **HELP** Note that when you are counting you use **thousand** without 's': *There were over 70 thousand spectators at the match.* **2** a thousand, thousands (of) (informal) a large amount: *There were thousands of people there.* ❶ For more information about numbers, look at the **Reference Section** of this dictionary. ▸ **thousandth** /-znθ/ ordinal number, noun [C]

thrash /θræʃ/ verb **1** [T] to hit sb/sth many times with a stick, etc. as a punishment **2** [I, T] ~ (sth) (about/around) to move or make sth move in a wild way without any control: *We saw a man thrashing around in the water.* **3** [T] (informal) to defeat sb easily in a game, competition, etc.
PHR V thrash sth out to talk about sth with sb until you reach an agreement

thrashing /ˈθræʃɪŋ/ noun [C] **1** the act of hitting sb/sth many times with a stick, etc. as a punishment **2** (informal) a bad defeat in a game

thread[1] ʔ+ C1 /θred/ noun **1** [C, U] a long thin piece of cotton, wool, etc. that you use for SEWING or making cloth: *a needle and thread* **2** [C] the connection between ideas, the parts of a story, etc: *I've lost the thread of this argument.* **3** [C] (COMPUTING) a series of connected messages on a MESSAGE BOARD on the internet that have been sent by different people **4** [C] the raised line that runs around the length of a SCREW and that allows it to be fixed in place by turning it ⊃ picture at **bolt**[1]

thread[2] /θred/ verb [T] **1** to put sth long and thin, especially THREAD, through a narrow opening or hole: *to thread a needle* ◇ *He threaded the belt through the loops on the trousers.* **2** to join things together by putting them onto a string, etc.
IDM thread your way through sth to move through sth with difficulty, going around things or people that are in your way

threadbare /ˈθredbeə(r)/ *adj.* (used about material or clothes) old and very thin

threat ᵏ **B2** **W** /θret/ *noun* **1** [C, U] a warning that sb may hurt, kill or punish you if you do not do what they want: *to **make threats** against somebody* ◊ *He keeps saying he'll resign, but he won't **carry out** his threat.* **2** [U, usually sing.] the possibility of trouble or danger: *The forest is **under threat** from building developments.* **3** [C, usually sing.] a person or thing that may damage sth or hurt sb; sth that indicates future danger

threaten ᵏ **B2** /ˈθretn/ *verb* **1** [T] ~ **sb (with sth); ~ (to do sth)** to warn that you may hurt, kill or punish sb if they do not do what you want: *The boy threatened him with a knife.* ◊ *She was threatened with dismissal.* ◊ *The man threatened to kill her if she didn't tell him where the money was.* **2** [I, T] ~ **(sth) (with sth); ~ (to do sth)** to seem likely to do sth unpleasant: *Many species are now threatened with extinction.* ◊ *The wind was threatening to destroy the bridge.*

threatening /ˈθretnɪŋ/ *adj.* **1** expressing a threat of harm or violence: *threatening letters* ◊ *threatening behaviour* **2** (used about the sky, clouds, etc.) showing that bad weather is likely: *The sky was dark and threatening.* ▶ **threateningly** *adv.*: *He glared at her threateningly.*

three ᵏ **A1** /θriː/ *number* 3

three-ˈD (*also* 3-D) *noun* [U] the quality of having, or appearing to have, length, WIDTH and depth (= three DIMENSIONS): *These glasses allow you to see the film in three-D.* ◊ *a three-D image* ⊃ look at **two-dimensional** ▶ **three-D** (*also* 3-D, ˌthree-diˈmensional) *adj.*

ˈthree-star *adj.* (**TOURISM**) having three stars in a system that measures quality. The highest standard is usually represented by four or five stars: *a three-star hotel*

thresh /θreʃ/ *verb* [T] (**AGRICULTURE**) to separate grains of CORN, rice, etc. from the rest of the plant using a machine or, especially in the past, by hitting it with a special tool ▶ **threshing** *noun* [U]: *a threshing machine*

threshold ᵏ+ **C1** **W** /ˈθreʃhəʊld/ *noun* [C] **1** the ground at the entrance to a room or building **2** the level at which sth starts to happen: *Young children have a low boredom threshold.* **3** the time when you are just about to start sth or find sth: *We could be **on the threshold** of a scientific breakthrough.*

threw /θruː/ *past tense of* **throw**

thrift /θrɪft/ *noun* [U] the quality of being careful not to spend too much money ▶ **thrifty** *adj.* (**thriftier; thriftiest**)

ˈthrift shop (*AmE*) = CHARITY SHOP

ˈthrift store *noun* [C] (*AmE*) = CHARITY SHOP

thrill /θrɪl/ *noun* [C] a sudden strong feeling of pleasure or excitement ▶ **thrill** *verb* [T]: *His singing thrilled the audience.* ▶ **thrilled** ᵏ+ **C1** *adj.*: *He was absolutely thrilled with my present.* ▶ **thrilling** *adj.*

thriller /ˈθrɪlə(r)/ *noun* [C] **1** (**ARTS AND MEDIA, LITERATURE**) a play, film, book, etc. with a very exciting story, often about a crime **2** (**SPORT**) an exciting match or game: *a seven-goal thriller*

thrive ᵏ+ **C1** /θraɪv/ *verb* [I] to grow or develop well **SYN flourish** ▶ **thriving** *adj.*: *a thriving industry*

throat ᵏ **B1** /θrəʊt/ *noun* [C] **1** the front part of the neck: *The attacker grabbed the man by the throat.* ⊃ picture at **body 2** (**ANATOMY**) the back part of the mouth and the passage down the neck through which air and food pass: *She got a piece of bread stuck in her throat.* ◊ *I've got a sore throat.*

IDM **clear your throat** → CLEAR³ **have/feel a lump in your throat** → LUMP¹

throb /θrɒb/ *verb* [I] (-bb-) ~ **(with sth)** to make strong regular movements or noises; to beat strongly: *Her finger throbbed with pain.* ▶ **throb** *noun* [C]

thrombosis /θrɒmˈbəʊsɪs/ *noun* [C, U] (*pl.* **thromboses** /-ˈbəʊsiːz/) (**HEALTH**) a serious medical condition caused by a CLOT (= a thick mass of blood) forming in a BLOOD VESSEL (= tube) or in the heart ⊃ look at **deep vein thrombosis**

throne /θrəʊn/ *noun* **1** [C] the special chair where a king or queen sits **2 the throne** [sing.] the position of being king or queen

throng¹ /θrɒŋ/ *noun* [C] (*formal*) a large crowd of people

throng² /θrɒŋ/ *verb* [I, T] (*formal*) (used about a crowd of people) to move into or fill a particular place

throttle¹ /ˈθrɒtl/ *verb* [T] to hold sb tightly by the throat and stop them breathing **SYN strangle**

throttle² /ˈθrɒtl/ *noun* [C] the part in a vehicle that controls the speed by controlling how much fuel goes into the engine

through ᵏ **A1** /θruː/ *prep., adv.* **1** from one end or side of sth to the other: *We drove through the centre of London.* ◊ *to look through a telescope* ◊ *She cut through the rope.* ◊ *to push through a crowd of people* **2** from the beginning to the end of sth: *Food supplies will not last through the winter.* ◊ *We're halfway through the book.* ◊ *He read the letter through and handed it back.* **3** past a limit, stage or test: *He lifted the rope to let us through.* ◊ *She didn't get through the first interview.* **4** (*also* **thru**) (*AmE*) until, and including: *They are staying Monday through Friday.* **5** because of; with the help of: *Errors were made through bad organization.* ◊ *David got the job through his uncle.* **6** (*BrE*) connected by phone: *Can you put me through to extension 5678, please?*
PHR V **be through (with sb/sth)** to have finished with sb/sth

throughout ᵏ **B1** **S** /θruːˈaʊt/ *adv., prep.* **1** in every part of sth: *The house is beautifully decorated throughout.* ◊ *The match can be watched live on TV throughout the world.* **2** from the beginning to the end of sth: *We didn't enjoy the holiday because it rained throughout.*

throw ᵏ **A2** /θrəʊ/ *verb* (*pt* **threw** /θruː/; *pp* **thrown** /θrəʊn/)
• WITH YOUR HAND **1** [T, I] ~ **(sth) (to/at sb); ~ (sb sth)** to send sth from your hand through the air by moving your hand or arm quickly: *Throw the ball to me.* ◊ *Throw me the ball.* ◊ *Don't throw stones at people.* ◊ *How far can you throw?*
• PUT CARELESSLY **2** [T] (used with an adverb or a preposition) to put sth somewhere quickly or carelessly: *He threw his bag down in a corner.* ◊ *She threw on a sweater and ran out of the door.*
• MOVE WITH FORCE **3** [T] (used with an adverb or a preposition) to move your body or part of it quickly or suddenly: *Jenny threw herself onto the bed and sobbed.* ◊ *Lee threw back his head and roared with laughter.*
• MAKE SB FALL **4** [T] to cause sb to fall down quickly or violently: *The bus braked and we were thrown to the floor.*
• PUT IN A SITUATION **5** [T, usually passive] to put sb in a particular (usually unpleasant) situation: *We were thrown into confusion by the news.*
• UPSET/CONFUSE **6** [T] (*informal*) to make sb feel upset, confused or surprised: *The question threw me and I didn't know what to reply.*
• LIGHT/SHADE **7** [T] to send light or shade onto sth: *The tree threw a long shadow across the lawn.*

▶ **throw** *noun* [C]: *It's your throw* (= it's your turn to throw the DICE in a board game, etc.). ◇ *a throw of 97 metres*

PHRV **throw sth away** **1** (*also* **throw sth out**) to get rid of rubbish or sth that you do not want: *I threw his letters away.* **2** to waste or not use sth useful: *to throw away a good opportunity* **throw sth in** to include sth extra without increasing the price **throw sb out** to force sb to leave a place **throw sth out** **1** to decide not to accept sb's idea or suggestion **2** = THROW STH AWAY (1) **throw up** (*informal*) (**HEALTH**) to be sick **SYN** **vomit** **throw sth up** **1** (*informal*) (**HEALTH**) to be sick **SYN** **vomit** **2** to produce or show sth: *Our research has thrown up some interesting facts.* **3** to leave your job

throwaway /ˈθrəʊəweɪ/ *adj.* [only before noun] **1** used to describe sth that you say quickly without careful thought, sometimes in order to be funny: *a throwaway line/remark/comment* **2** (**BUSINESS**) (used about goods, etc.) produced at a low cost and intended to be thrown away as rubbish after being used: *We live in a throwaway society* (= a society in which things are not made to last a long time). ◇ *throwaway products* **SYN** **disposable**

ˈ**throw-in** *noun* [C] (**SPORT**) (in football and rugby) the act of throwing the ball back onto the playing field after it has gone outside the area

thru /θruː/ (*AmE*) = THROUGH (4)

thrush /θrʌʃ/ *noun* **1** [C] a bird with a brown back and brown spots on its chest: *a song thrush* **2** (*BrE*) (*AmE* yeast infection*) [U] (**HEALTH**) an infection that affects a person's VAGINA or mouth

thrust¹ /θrʌst/ *verb* [T, I] (*pt, pp* thrust) **1** to push sb/sth suddenly or violently; to move quickly and suddenly in a particular direction: *The man thrust his hands deeper into his pockets.* ◇ *She thrust past him and ran out of the room.* **2** to make a sudden forward movement with a knife, etc.

PHRV **thrust sb/sth upon sb** to force sb to accept or deal with sb/sth

thrust² /θrʌst/ *noun* **1** the thrust [sing.] the main part or point of an argument, a policy, etc. **2** [C] a sudden strong movement forward **3** [U] (**ENGINEERING, PHYSICS**) the force that is produced by an engine to push a plane, ROCKET, etc. forward

thud /θʌd/ *noun* [C] the low sound that is made when a heavy object hits sth else: *She fell to the ground and her head hit the floor with a dull thud.* ▶ **thud** *verb* [I] (-dd-)

thug /θʌɡ/ *noun* [C] a violent person who may harm other people

thulium /ˈθuːliəm, ˈθjuː-/ *noun* [U] (*symb.* Tm) (**CHEMISTRY**) a chemical element. Thulium is a soft silver-white metal. ❶ For more information on the periodic table of elements, look at the **Reference Section** of this dictionary.

thumb¹ ʔ+ **B2** /θʌm/ *noun* [C] **1** (**ANATOMY**) the short thick finger at the side of each hand ⊃ picture at **body** **2** the part of a glove, etc. that covers the thumb **IDM** **have a green thumb** → GREEN¹ **a rule of thumb** → RULE¹ **stand/stick out like a sore thumb** → SORE¹ **the thumbs up/down** a sign or an expression to show that something has been accepted/rejected or that it is/is not a success **under sb's thumb** (used about a person) completely controlled by sb: *She's got him under her thumb.*

thumb² /θʌm/ *verb* [I, T] ~ **(through) sth** to turn the pages of a book, etc. quickly **IDM** **thumb a lift** (*BrE*) to hold out your THUMB to cars going past, to ask sb to give you a free ride

ˈ**thumb drive** (*AmE*) = FLASH DRIVE

thumbtack /ˈθʌmtæk/ (*AmE*) = DRAWING PIN

thump /θʌmp/ *verb* **1** [T] to hit sb/sth hard with sth, usually your FIST (= closed hand): *He started coughing and Jo thumped him on the back.* **2** [I, T] to make a loud sound by hitting sth or by beating hard: *His heart was thumping with excitement.* ▶ **thump** *noun* [C]

thunder¹ /ˈθʌndə(r)/ *noun* [U] the loud noise in the sky that you can hear when there is a storm: *a clap/crash/ roll of thunder* ⊃ look at **lightning** ⊃ note at **storm¹**

thunder² /ˈθʌndə(r)/ *verb* [I] **1** when **it thunders**, there is a loud noise in the sky during a storm: *The rain poured down and it started to thunder.* **2** to make a loud deep noise like THUNDER: *Traffic thundered across the bridge.*

thunderbolt /ˈθʌndəbəʊlt/ *noun* [C] a flash of LIGHTNING that comes at the same time as the noise of THUNDER and that hits sth

thunderclap /ˈθʌndəklæp/ *noun* [C] a loud crash made by THUNDER

thunderstorm /ˈθʌndəstɔːm/ *noun* [C] a storm with THUNDER (= loud noises) and LIGHTNING (= flashes of light in the sky) ⊃ note at **storm¹**

Thursday ʔ **A1** /ˈθɜːzdeɪ, -di/ *noun* [C, U] (*abbr.* Thur., Thurs.) the day of the week after Wednesday

thus ʔ **B2** **W** /ðʌs/ *adv.* (*formal*) **1** like this; in this way: *Thus began the series of incidents which changed her life.* **2** because of or as a result of this: *He is the eldest son and thus heir to the throne.* **SYN** **therefore**

thwart /θwɔːt/ *verb* [T, often passive] ~ **sth; ~ sb (in sth)** (*formal*) to stop sb doing what they planned to do; to prevent sth happening: *to thwart somebody's plans/ ambitions/efforts* ◇ *She was thwarted in her attempt to gain control.*

thyme /taɪm/ *noun* [U] a HERB (= a type of plant) that is used in cooking and has small leaves and a sweet smell

thymine /ˈθaɪmiːn/ *noun* [U] (**BIOLOGY**) one of the four COMPOUNDS that make up DNA ⊃ picture at **DNA**

thyroid /ˈθaɪrɔɪd/ (*also* ˈ**thyroid gland**) *noun* [C] (**ANATOMY**) a small organ at the front of the neck that produces HORMONES that control the way in which the body grows and works

tibia /ˈtɪbiə/ *noun* [C] (**ANATOMY**) the inner and larger bone of the two bones in the lower part of the leg between the knee and foot **SYN** **shin bone** ⊃ look at **fibula** ⊃ picture at **body**

tic /tɪk/ *noun* [C] (**HEALTH**) a sudden quick movement of a muscle, especially in your face or head, that you cannot control: *He has a nervous tic.*

tick¹ /tɪk/ *verb* **1** [I] (used about a clock or watch) to make regular short sounds **2** (*BrE*) (*AmE* check*) [T] to put a mark (✓) next to a name, an item on a list, etc. to show that sth has been dealt with or chosen, or that it is correct: *Please tick the appropriate box.*
IDM **what makes sb/sth tick** the reasons why sb behaves or sth works in the way he/she/it does: *He has a strong interest in people and what makes them tick.*
PHRV **tick away/by** (used about time) to pass **tick sb/sth off** to put a mark (✓) next to a name, an item on a list, etc. to show that sth has been done or sb has been dealt with **tick over** (usually used in the progressive tenses) **1** (used about an engine) to run slowly while the vehicle is not moving **2** to keep working slowly without producing or achieving very much

tick² /tɪk/ *noun* **1** (*BrE*) (*AmE* check mark, check*) [C] a mark (✓) next to an item on a list that shows that sth has been done or next to an answer to show that it is correct: *Put a tick after each correct answer.* **2** [C] a small animal with eight legs, like an insect, that bites humans and animals and drinks their blood ⊃ picture at **animal 3** (*also* ticking) [U] the regular short sound that a watch or clock makes when it is working **4** [C] (*BrE, informal*) a moment

ticket ¹ **A1** /ˈtɪkɪt/ *noun* [C] **1** ~ **(for/to sth)** a piece of paper or card that shows you have paid for a journey, or that allows you to enter a theatre, cinema, etc: *two tickets for the Cup Final* ◇ *a one-way/return ticket to Glasgow* ◇ *a ticket office/machine/collector* ⊃ look at **season ticket 2** a piece of paper with a number or numbers on it, that you buy in order to have the chance of winning a prize if the number or numbers are later chosen: *a lottery/raffle ticket* **3** a piece of paper fastened to sth in a shop that shows its price, size, etc. **4** (LAW) an official piece of paper that you get when you have parked illegally or driven too fast telling you that you must pay money as a punishment: *a parking ticket*
IDM just the job/ticket → JOB

ticket tout (*BrE*) = TOUT

tickle /ˈtɪkl/ *verb* **1** [T, I] to touch sb lightly with your fingers or sth soft so that they laugh: *She tickled the baby's toes.* **2** [I, T] to produce or to have an uncomfortable feeling in a part of your body: *My nose tickles/is tickling.* ◇ *The woollen scarf tickled her neck.* **3** [T] to interest sb and make them laugh: *That joke really tickled me.* ▶ **tickle** *noun* [C]

ticklish /ˈtɪklɪʃ/ *adj.* if a person is **ticklish**, they laugh when sb touches them in a sensitive place: *Are you ticklish?*

tic-tac-toe /ˌtɪk tæk ˈtəʊ/ (*AmE*) = NOUGHTS AND CROSSES

tidal /ˈtaɪdl/ *adj.* (GEOGRAPHY) connected with the TIDES

tidal wave *noun* [C] (GEOGRAPHY) a very large wave in the sea that destroys things when it reaches the land, and is often caused by an earthquake **SYN tsunami** ⊃ note at **disaster**

tidbit /ˈtɪdbɪt/ (*AmE*) = TITBIT

tide ¹ **C+** /taɪd/ *noun* [C] **1** (GEOGRAPHY) the regular change in the level of the sea caused by the moon and the sun. At **high tide** the sea is closer to the land, at **low tide** it is further away and more of the beach can be seen: *The tide is coming in/going out.* ⊃ look at **ebb** ⊃ picture at **erosion 2** [usually sing.] the way that most people think or feel about sth at a particular time: *It appears that the tide has turned in the government's favour.*

tide ² /taɪd/ *verb*
PHR V tide sb over to give sb sth to help them through a difficult time

tidy ¹ **A2** /ˈtaɪdi/ *adj.* (tidier; tidiest) (*especially BrE*) **1** arranged with everything in good order: *If you keep your room tidy it is easier to find things.* **2** (used about a person) liking to keep things in good order: *Mark is a very tidy boy.* **SYN neat OPP untidy** ▶ **tidily** /-dɪli/ *adv.* ▶ **tidiness** *noun* [U]

tidy ² **A2** /ˈtaɪdi/ *verb* [I, T] (tidying; tidies; *pt, pp* tidied) ~ **(sth) (up)** to make something look neat by putting things in the place where they belong: *I spent all morning tidying.* ◇ *We must tidy up this room before the visitors arrive.*
PHR V tidy sth away to put sth into the cupboard, DRAWER etc. where it is kept so that it cannot be seen

tie ¹ **A2** /taɪ/ *noun* [C] **1** (*AmE also* necktie) a long thin piece of cloth worn round the neck, especially by men, with a KNOT at the front. A tie is usually worn with a shirt: *a striped silk tie* ⊃ look at **bow tie**

2 [usually pl.] ~ **(to/with sb/sth)** a strong connection between people or organizations: *personal/emotional ties* ◇ *family ties* **3** something that limits your freedom **4** a situation in a game or competition in which two or more teams or players get the same score: *There was a tie for first place.* **5** (MUSIC) a curved line written over notes of the same PITCH (= how high or low a note is) to show that they should be played or sung as one note ⊃ picture at **music**

tie ² **A2** /taɪ/ *verb* (tying; ties; *pt, pp* tied) **1** [T] to fasten sb/sth or fix sb/sth with rope, string, etc.; to make a KNOT in sth: *The prisoner was tied to a chair.* ◇ *Kay tied her hair back with a ribbon.* ◇ *to tie something in a knot* ◇ *to tie your shoelaces* **OPP untie 2** [T, usually passive] **be tied (to sth/doing sth)** to limit sb's freedom and make them unable to do everything they want to: *I don't want to be tied to staying in this country permanently.* **3** [I] ~ **(with sb) (for sth)** to have the same number of points as another player or team at the end of a game or competition: *Germany tied with Italy for third place.*
IDM have your hands tied → HAND¹
PHR V tie sb/yourself down to limit sb's/your freedom: *Having young children really ties you down.* **tie in (with sth)** to agree with other facts or information that you have; to match: *The new evidence seems to tie in with your theory.* **tie sb/sth up 1** to fix sb/sth in position with rope, string, etc: *The dog was tied up in the back garden.* **OPP untie 2** [usually passive] to keep sb busy: *Mr Jones is tied up in a meeting.*

tier /tɪə(r)/ *noun* [C] one of a number of levels

tiger /ˈtaɪɡə(r)/ *noun* [C] a large wild cat that has yellow fur with black STRIPES (= lines). Tigers live in parts of Asia. ⊃ picture at **lion ❶** A female **tiger** is called a **tigress** and a baby is called a **cub.**

tight ¹ **B1** /taɪt/ *adj.*
• FIRM **1** fixed FIRMLY in position and difficult to move or open: *a tight knot* ◇ *Keep a tight grip/hold on this rope.*
• CLOTHES **2** (used about clothes) fitting very closely in a way that is often uncomfortable: *These shoes hurt. They're too tight.* ◇ *a tight-fitting skirt* **OPP loose** ¹
• CONTROL **3** controlled very strictly and FIRMLY: *Security is very tight at the airport.*
• STRETCHED **4** stretched or pulled hard so that it cannot be stretched further: *The rope was stretched tight.*
• BUSY/FULL **5** not having much free time or space: *My schedule this week is very tight.*
• -TIGHT **6** -tight (in adjectives) not allowing sth to get in or out: *an airtight/a watertight container*
▶ **tightness** *noun* [U]

tight ² /taɪt/ *adv.* closely and strongly; tightly: *Hold tight so that you don't fall off.*

tighten ¹ **C1** /ˈtaɪtn/ *verb* [T, I] ~ **(sth) (up)** to become tight or tighter; to make sth tight or tighter: *His grip on her arm tightened.* ◇ *He tightened the screws as far as they would go.*
IDM tighten your belt to spend less money because you have less than usual available
PHR V tighten up (on) sth to cause sth to become stricter: *to tighten up security/a law*

tightly /ˈtaɪtli/ *adv.* closely and FIRMLY; in a tight manner: *Her eyes were tightly closed.* ◇ *He held on tightly to her arm.*

tightrope /ˈtaɪtrəʊp/ *noun* [C] a rope or wire that is stretched high above the ground on which people walk, especially as a form of entertainment

tights /taɪts/ (*BrE*) (*AmE* pantyhose) *noun* [pl.] a piece of thin clothing, usually worn by women, that fits tightly over the middle part of the body, legs and feet: *a pair of tights* ⊃ look at **stocking**

tilde /'tɪldə/ *noun* [C] (**LANGUAGE**) the mark placed over letters in some languages and some vowels in the International Phonetic Alphabet to show how they should be pronounced, as in *España, São Paulo* and /'kwæsɒ/ (*croissant*)

tile /taɪl/ *noun* [C] one of the flat, usually square, objects that are arranged in rows to cover roofs, floors, bathroom walls, etc. ⊃ picture at **building**, **overlap** ▶ tile *verb* [T]: *a tiled bathroom*

till¹ ʳ**B1** /tɪl/ *prep., conj.* (*informal*) = UNTIL

till² /tɪl/ (*also* **cash register**) *noun* [C] a machine used in shops, restaurants, etc. for keeping money in, and that shows and records the amount of money received for each thing that is sold: *Please pay at the till.*

till³ /tɪl/ *verb* [T] (*old-fashioned*) (**AGRICULTURE**) to prepare and use land for growing crops

tilt /tɪlt/ *verb* [I, T] to move, or make sth move, into a position with one end or side higher than the other: *The front seats of the car tilt forward.* ◇ *She tilted her head to one side.* ▶ tilt *noun* [sing.]

timber ʳ+ **C1** /'tɪmbə(r)/ *noun* **1** (*especially BrE*) (*also* **lumber** *especially in AmE*) [U] wood that is going to be used for building **2** [C] a large piece of wood: *roof timbers*

timbre /'tæmbə(r)/ *noun* [C] (*formal*) (**MUSIC**) the quality of sound that is produced by a particular voice or musical instrument

time¹ ʳ**A1** /taɪm/ *noun*

• HOURS, YEARS, ETC. **1** [U, sing.] a period of minutes, hours, days, etc: *As time passed and there was still no news, we got more worried.* ◇ *You're wasting time — get on with your work!* ◇ *I'll go by car to save time.* ◇ *free/spare time* ◇ *We haven't got time to stop now.* ◇ *I've been waiting a long time.* ◇ *Learning a language takes time.* **2** [U,C] ~ **(to do sth)**; ~ **(for sth)** the time in hours and minutes shown on a clock; the moment when sth happens or should happen: *What's the time?/ What time is it?* ◇ *Can you tell me the times of trains to Bristol, please?* ◇ *It's time to go home.* ◇ *It's time for lunch.* ◇ *By the time I get home, Alex will have cooked the dinner.* ◇ *This time tomorrow I'll be on the plane.* **3** [U, sing.] a system for measuring time in a particular part of the world: *eleven o'clock local time*

• OCCASION/EVENT **4** [C] an occasion when you do sth or when sth happens: *I phoned them three times.* ◇ *I'll do it better next time.* ◇ *Last time I saw him, he looked ill.* ◇ *How many times have I told you not to touch that?* **5** [C] an event or occasion that you experience in a certain way: *Have a good time tonight.* ◇ *We had a terrible time at the hospital.*

• PERIOD **6** [C] a period in the past; a part of history: *The nineteenth century was a time of great industrial change.* ◇ *In Shakespeare's times, few people could read.*

• IN A RACE **7** [C, U] the number of minutes, etc. taken to complete a race or an event: *What was his time in the 100 metres?*

IDM (**and**) **about time** (**too**) | (**and**) **not before time** used to say that sth should already have happened **ahead of your time** so modern that people do not understand you **all the time/the whole time** during the period that sb was doing sth or that sth was happening: *I searched everywhere for my keys and they were in the door all the time.* **at one time** in the past **SYN** previously **at the same time** → SAME¹ **at a time on each occasion:** *The lift can hold six people at a time.* ◇ *She ran down the stairs two at a time.* **at the time** at a particular moment or period in the past; then: *I agreed at the time but later changed my mind.* **at times** sometimes: *At times I wish we'd never moved house.* **before your time** before you were

born, or before you lived, worked, etc. somewhere **behind the times** not modern or fashionable **bide your time** → BIDE **buy time** → BUY¹ **for the time being** just for the present; not for long **from time to time** sometimes; not often **give sb a hard time** → HARD¹ **have a hard time doing sth** → HARD¹ **have no time for sb/sth** to not like sb/sth: *I have no time for lazy people.* **have the time of your life** to enjoy yourself very much **in the course of time** → COURSE **in good time** early; at the right time **in the nick of time** → NICK¹ **in time (for sth/to do sth)** not late; with enough time to be able to do sth: *Don't worry. We'll get to the station in time for your train.* **it's about/ high time** (*informal*) used to say that you think sb should do sth very soon: *It's about time you told him what's going on.* **kill time, an hour, etc.** → KILL¹ **on time** not too late or too early: *The train left the station on time.* **once upon a time** → ONCE¹ **take your time** to do sth without hurrying **tell the time** → TELL **time after time** | **time and (time) again** again and again **SYN** repeatedly

time² ʳ**B2** /taɪm/ *verb* [T] **1** to measure how long sb/ sth takes: *Try timing yourself when you write your essay.* **2** [often passive] to arrange to do sth or arrange for sth to happen at a particular time: *Their request was badly timed* (= it came at the wrong time). ◇ *She timed her arrival for shortly after three.*

'time-consuming *adj.* that takes or needs a lot of time

'time frame *noun* [C] the length of time that is used or available for sth: *We expect to complete the project within a fairly short time frame.*

timekeeper /'taɪmkiːpə(r)/ *noun* [C] a person who records the time that is spent doing sth, for example at work or at a sports event

'time lag = LAG²

timeless /'taɪmləs/ *adj.* (*formal*) that does not seem to be changed by time or affected by changes in fashion

'time limit *noun* [C] a time during which sth must be done: *We have to set a time limit for the work.*

timeline /'taɪmlaɪn/ *noun* [C] **1** a HORIZONTAL line that is used to represent time, with the past towards the left and the future towards the right **2** (**COMPUTING**) a list of all sb's activity on a particular SOCIAL MEDIA website, with the most recent activity shown first

timely ʳ+ **C1** /'taɪmli/ *adj.* happening at exactly the right time

,time 'off *noun* [U] time when you are not at work or at school: *I'm going to take some time off next month.*

timeout /'taɪmaʊt/ *noun* [C] (*AmE*) (**SPORT**) a short period of rest during a sports game

timer /'taɪmə(r)/ *noun* [C] a person or machine that measures time: *an oven timer*

times¹ /taɪmz/ *prep.* (**MATHEMATICS**) used when you are multiplying one figure by another: *Three times four is twelve.*

times² /taɪmz/ *noun* [pl.] used for comparing amounts: *Tea is three times as expensive in Spain as in England.*

'time signature *noun* [C] (**MUSIC**) a sign at the start of a piece of music, usually in the form of numbers, showing the number of beats in each BAR (= each of the equal units of time into which music is divided) ⊃ picture at **music**

timetable /'taɪmteɪbl/ *noun* (*especially BrE*) (*AmE usually* **schedule**) *noun* [C] **1** a list that shows the times at which sth happens: *a bus/train/school timetable* **2** a plan of when you hope or expect particular events to happen

'**time zone** *noun* [C] (**GEOGRAPHY**) one of the 24 areas that the world is divided into, each with its own time that is one hour earlier than that of the time zone immediately to the east

timid /'tɪmɪd/ *adj.* easily frightened; shy and nervous ▸ **timidity** /tɪ'mɪdəti/ *noun* [U] ▸ **timidly** *adv.*

timing ⓘ+ **B2** /'taɪmɪŋ/ *noun* [U] **1** the time when sth is planned to happen: *The manager was very careful about the timing of his announcement.* **2** the skill of doing sth at exactly the right time: *The timing of her shot at goal was perfect.*

timpani /'tɪmpəni/ *noun* [pl.] (**MUSIC**) a set of large metal drums (also called KETTLEDRUMS) ▸ **timpanist** /-nɪst/ *noun* [C]

tin ⓘ **B1** /tɪn/ *noun* **1** (*BrE*) (*also* ˌtin ˈcan, can *AmE, BrE*) [C] a closed metal container in which food is sold; the contents of one of these containers: *a tin of peas/beans/soup* **2** [C] (*BrE*) a metal container with a LID (= cover) in which paint, etc. is sold: *a tin of paint/varnish* **3** [C] a metal container with a LID for keeping food in: *a biscuit/cake tin* **4** [U] (*symb.* Sn) (**CHEMISTRY**) a chemical element. Tin is a soft silver-white metal that is often mixed with other metals. ❶ For more information on the periodic table of elements, look at the **Reference Section** of this dictionary. ▸ **tinned** *adj.*: *tinned peaches/peas/soup*

tinfoil /'tɪnfɔɪl/ = FOIL¹ (1)

tinge /tɪndʒ/ *noun* [C, usually sing.] a small amount of a colour or a feeling: *a tinge of sadness* ▸ **tinged** *adj.* ~ (**with sth**): *Her joy at leaving was tinged with regret.*

tingle /'tɪŋgl/ *verb* [I] (used about a part of the body) to feel as if a lot of small sharp points are pushing into it: *His cheeks tingled as he came in from the cold.* ▸ **tingle** *noun* [C, usually sing.]: *a tingle of excitement/anticipation/fear*

tinker /'tɪŋkə(r)/ *verb* [I] ~ (**with sth**) to try to repair or improve sth without having the proper skill or knowledge: *He's been tinkering with the car all day but it still won't start.*

tinkle /'tɪŋkl/ *verb* [I, T] to make a light high ringing sound, like that of a small bell; to make sth produce this sound ▸ **tinkle** *noun* [C, usually sing.]

tinnitus /'tɪnɪtəs/ *noun* [U] (**HEALTH**) an unpleasant condition in which sb hears ringing in their ears

'**tin opener** (*BrE*) (*also* ˈcan opener *especially in AmE*) *noun* [C] a tool that you use for opening a tin of food

tinsel /'tɪnsl/ *noun* [U] long strings of shiny material like metal, used as a decoration to hang on a Christmas tree

tint /tɪnt/ *noun* [C] a shade or a small amount of a colour: *white paint with a pinkish tint* ▸ **tint** *verb* [T, usually passive]: *tinted glasses* ◇ *She had her hair tinted.*

tiny ⓘ **B1** /'taɪni/ *adj.* (tinier; tiniest) very small: *the baby's tiny fingers*

tip¹ ⓘ **A2** /tɪp/ *noun* [C]
- ADVICE **1** ~ (**on/for sth/doing sth**) a small piece of useful advice about sth practical: *useful tips on how to save money*
- MONEY **2** a small amount of extra money that you give to sb who serves you, for example in a restaurant: *to leave a tip for the waiter* ◇ *I gave the porter a $5 tip.*
- END OF STH **3** the thin or pointed end of sth: *the tips of your toes/fingers* ◇ *the tip of your nose* ◇ *the southernmost tip of South America*
- FOR RUBBISH **4** (*BrE*) (*also* rubbish tip) a place where you can take rubbish and leave it **SYN** dump¹
- UNTIDY PLACE **5** (*BrE, informal*) a place that is very dirty or untidy

IDM (have sth) **on the tip of your tongue** to be sure you know sth but to be unable to remember it for the moment: *Their name is on the tip of my tongue. It'll come back to me in a moment.* **the tip of the iceberg** only a small part of a much larger problem

tip² ⓘ **B1** /tɪp/ *verb* (-pp-) **1** [I, T] to give sb a small amount of extra money (in addition to the normal charge) to thank them for a service: *She tipped the taxi driver generously.* **2** [I, T] (often used with an adverb or a preposition) to move so that one side is higher than the other; to make sth move in this way: *When I stood up, the bench tipped up and the person on the other end fell off.* **3** [T] (used with an adverb or a preposition) to make sth come out of a container by holding or lifting it at an angle: *Tip the dirty water down the drain.* ◇ *The child tipped all the toys onto the floor.* **4** [T, usually passive] ~ **sb/sth** (**as sth/to do sth**) (*especially BrE*) to think or say that sb/sth is likely to do sth: *He is widely tipped as the next prime minister.* **PHR V tip sb off** to give sb secret information **tip** (**sth**) **up/over** to fall or turn over; to make sth do this: *An enormous wave crashed into the little boat and it tipped over.*

'**tip-off** *noun* [C] (**LAW**) secret information that sb gives, for example to the police, about an illegal activity that is going to happen: *Acting on a tip-off, the police raided the house.*

Tipp-Ex™ /'tɪp eks/ *noun* [U] (*BrE*) a liquid, usually white, that you use to cover mistakes that you make when you are writing or typing, and that you can write on top of; a type of CORRECTION FLUID ▸ **tippex** *verb* [T] ~ **sth** (**out**): *I tippexed out the mistakes.*

'**tipping point** *noun* [C, usually sing.] the point at which a small change in a situation has a sudden and great effect or leads to an idea spreading quickly

tipsy /'tɪpsi/ *adj.* (*informal*) slightly drunk

tiptoe¹ /'tɪptəʊ/ *noun*
IDM on tiptoe standing or walking on the ends of your toes with your heels off the ground, in order not to make any noise or to reach sth high up

tiptoe² /'tɪptəʊ/ *verb* [I] to walk on your toes with your heels off the ground

tire¹ /'taɪə(r)/ *verb* [I, T] to feel that you need to rest or sleep; to make sb feel like this
PHR V tire of sth/sb to become bored or not interested in sth/sb any more **tire sb/yourself out** to make sb/yourself very tired: *The long walk tired us all out.* **SYN** exhaust¹

tire² /'taɪə(r)/ *noun* [C] (*AmE*) = TYRE

tired ⓘ **A1** /'taɪəd/ *adj.* feeling that you need to rest or sleep: *She was tired after a hard day's work.* ▸ **tiredness** *noun* [U]
IDM be tired of sb/sth/doing sth to be bored with or annoyed by sb/sth/doing sth: *I'm tired of this game. Let's play something else.* ◇ *I'm sick and tired of listening to the same thing again and again.*

tireless /'taɪələs/ *adj.* putting a lot of hard work and energy into sth over a long period of time without stopping or losing interest

tiresome /'taɪəsəm/ *adj.* that makes you angry or bored **SYN** annoying

tiring /'taɪərɪŋ/ *adj.* making you want to rest or sleep: *a tiring journey/job* **SYN** exhausting

tissue ⓘ+ **B2** /'tɪʃuː/ *noun* **1** [C] a thin piece of soft paper that you use to clean your nose and throw away after you have used it: *a box of tissues* **2** [U] (*also* tissues [pl.]) (**ANATOMY**, **BIOLOGY**) the mass of cells that form the bodies of humans, animals and plants: *muscle/brain/nerve/scar tissue* ◇ *Radiation can destroy the body's tissues.* ⊃ picture at **skin¹** 3 (*also* ˈtissue paper) [U] thin soft paper that you use for putting around things that may break

tit /tɪt/ *noun* [C] a small European bird. There are several types of tit.

IDM **tit for tat** something unpleasant that you do to sb because they have done sth to you

titanium /tɪ'teɪniəm, taɪ-/ *noun* [U] (*symb.* Ti) (**CHEMISTRY**) a chemical element. Titanium is a silver-white metal used in making various strong light materials. **❶** For more information on the periodic table of elements, look at the **Reference Section** of this dictionary.

titbit /'tɪtbɪt/ (*BrE*) (*AmE* **tidbit**) *noun* [C] **1** a small but very nice piece of food **2** an interesting piece of information

title¹ **☜ A1 ❺** /'taɪtl/ *noun* [C] **1** (**ARTS AND MEDIA**, **LITERATURE**) the name of a book, play, film, picture, etc: *I know the author's name but I can't remember the title of the book.* **2** a word that shows a person's position, profession, etc: *'Lord', 'Doctor', 'Reverend', 'Mrs' and 'General' are all titles.* ◇ *What is your name and job title?* **3** the position of being the winner of a competition, especially a sports competition: *Sue is playing this match to defend her title* (= to remain champion).

title² **☜ B2** /'taɪtl/ *verb* [T, usually passive] (**ARTS AND MEDIA**, **LITERATURE**) to give a book, piece of music, etc. a particular name: *Their first album was titled 'Please Please Me'.*

titled /'taɪtld/ *adj.* having a word, for example 'Duke', 'Lady', etc. before your name

title-holder *noun* [C] the person or team who won a sports competition the last time it took place

titration /taɪ'treɪʃn, tɪ-/ *noun* [U] (**CHEMISTRY**) the process of finding out how much of a particular substance is in a liquid by measuring how much of another substance is needed to react with it

titter /'tɪtə(r)/ *verb* [I] to laugh quietly, especially in an embarrassed or nervous way ▶ **titter** *noun* [C]

titular /'tɪtjələ(r)/ *adj.* [only before noun] (*formal*) having a particular title but no real power or authority: *the titular head of state* **SYN** **nominal**

T-junction *noun* [C] a place where two roads join to form the shape of a T

TLC /ˌtiː el 'siː/ *abbr.* (*informal*) **tender loving care** (care that you give sb to make them feel better): *What you need now is rest and a lot of TLC.*

TM /ˌtiː 'em/ *abbr.* = TRADEMARK

TNT /ˌtiː en 'tiː/ *noun* [U] a substance used to cause powerful explosions (the abbreviation for 'trinitrotoluene')

to¹ **☜ A1** /tə, before vowels tu, strong form tuː/ *prep.*, *infinitive marker* **1** in the direction of; as far as: *She's going to London.* ◇ *Turn to the left.* ◇ *Pisa is to the west of Florence.* ◇ *He has gone to school.* **2** used to show the person or thing that receives sth: *Give that to me.* ◇ *I am very grateful to my parents.* ◇ *What have you done to your hair?* ◇ *Sorry, I didn't realize you were talking to me.* **3** used to show the end or limit of a series of things or period of time: *from Monday to Friday* ◇ *from beginning to end* **4** (nearly) touching sth; directed towards sth: *He put his hands to his ears.* ◇ *They sat back to back.* ◇ *She made no reference to her personal problems.* **5** reaching a particular state: *The meat was cooked to perfection.* ◇ *His speech reduced her to tears* (= made her cry). **6** used to introduce the second part of a comparison: *I prefer theatre to opera.* **7** (used for expressing quantity) for each unit of money, measurement, etc: *How many dollars are there to the euro?* **8** (used to say what time it is) before: *It's ten to three* (= ten minutes before

three o'clock). **9** used to express sb's opinion or feeling about sth: *To me, it was the wrong decision.* ◇ *It sounded like a good idea to me.* ◇ *I don't think our friendship means anything to him.* **10** used for expressing a reaction or an attitude to sth: *To my surprise, I saw two strangers coming out of my house.* ◇ *His paintings aren't really to my taste.* **11** used with verbs to form the INFINITIVE: *I want to go home now.* ◇ *Don't forget to write.* ◇ *I didn't know what to do.*

to² /tuː/ *adv.* (used about a door) in or into a closed position: *Push the door to.*
IDM **to and fro** backwards and forwards

toad /təʊd/ *noun* [C] a small animal like a frog with rough skin and long back legs that it uses for jumping, that lives both on land and in water ⊃ picture at **animal**

toadstool /'təʊdstuːl/ *noun* [C] a plant without leaves, flowers or green colour, with a flat or curved top. Toadstools are usually poisonous. ⊃ look at **fungus (1)**, **mushroom**

toast /təʊst/ *noun* **1** [U] a thin piece of bread that is heated on both sides to make it brown: *a piece/slice of toast* ⊃ note at **cook¹** **2** [C] ~ (**to sb/sth**) an occasion at which a group of people wish sb happiness, success, etc., by drinking a glass of wine, etc. at the same time: *I'd like to propose a toast to the bride and groom.* ◇ *The committee drank a toast to the new project.* ⊃ look at **drink to sb/sth** at **drink¹** ▶ **toast** *verb* [T]

toaster /'təʊstə(r)/ *noun* [C] an electrical machine for making bread turn brown by heating it on both sides ⊃ note at **cook¹**

tobacco **☜+ C1** /tə'bækəʊ/ *noun* [U] the dried leaves of the tobacco plant that some people smoke in cigarettes and pipes

tobacconist's /tə'bækənɪsts/ *noun* [C] (*pl.* **tobacconists**) a shop where you can buy cigarettes, matches, etc.

toboggan /tə'bɒɡən/ *noun* [C] (**SPORT**) a type of flat board with flat pieces of metal under it, that people use for travelling down hills on snow for fun **SYN** **sledge** ⊃ look at **bobsleigh**

toccata /tə'kɑːtə/ *noun* [C] (**MUSIC**) a piece of music for a keyboard instrument that includes difficult passages designed to show the player's skill

today **☜ A1** /tə'deɪ/ *noun* [U], *adv.* **1** (on) this day: *Today is Monday.* ◇ *What shall we do today?* ◇ *School ends a week today* (= on this day next week). ◇ *Where is today's paper?* **2** (in) the present age; these days: *Young people today have far more freedom.* **SYN** **nowadays**

toddle /'tɒdl/ *verb* [I] **1** to walk with short steps like a very young child **2** (*informal*) (used with an adverb or a preposition) to walk or go somewhere

toddler /'tɒdlə(r)/ *noun* [C] a young child who has only just learnt to walk

toe¹ **☜ B1** /təʊ/ *noun* [C] **1** (**ANATOMY**) one of the small parts like fingers at the end of each foot: *the big/little toe* (= the largest/smallest toe) ⊃ picture at **body** **2** the part of a sock, shoe, etc. that covers the toes

toe² /təʊ/ *verb* (**toeing**; **toes**; *pt, pp* **toed**)
IDM **toe the (party) line** to do what sb in authority tells you to do, even if you do not agree with them

TOEFL™ /'təʊfl/ *abbr.* (**EDUCATION**, **LANGUAGE**) **Test of English as a Foreign Language** (a test of a person's level of English that is taken in order to go to a university in the US)

TOEIC™ /ˈtəʊɪk/ *abbr.* (**EDUCATION, LANGUAGE**) **Test of English for International Communication** (a test that measures your ability to read and understand English if it is not your first language)

toenail /ˈtəʊneɪl/ *noun* [C] (**ANATOMY**) one of the hard flat parts that cover the end of the toes ➴ picture at **body**

toffee /ˈtɒfi/ *noun* [U, C] a hard sticky sweet that is made by cooking sugar and butter together

toga /ˈtəʊɡə/ *noun* [C] (**HISTORY**) a loose outer piece of clothing worn by the citizens of ancient Rome

together¹ ⓘ Ⓐ1 Ⓢ /təˈɡeðə(r)/ *adv.* **1** with or near each other: *Can we have lunch together?* ◇ *They walked home together.* ◇ *I'll get all my things together tonight because I want to leave early.* ◇ *Stand with your feet together.* **2** so that two or more things are mixed or joined to each other: *Mix the butter and sugar together.* ◇ *Tie the two ends together.* ◇ *Add these numbers together to find the total.* **3** at the same time: *Don't all talk together.* **IDM** get your act together → ACT² together with in addition to; as well as: *I enclose my order together with a cheque for £15.*

together² /təˈɡeðə(r)/ *adj.* (*informal*) (used about a person) organized, capable: *I'm not very together this morning.*

togetherness /təˈɡeðənəs/ *noun* [U] a feeling of friendship

toggle¹ /ˈtɒɡl/ *noun* [C] **1** a short piece of wood, plastic, etc. that is put through a LOOP of THREAD to fasten sth, such as a coat or bag, instead of a button **2** (*also* ˈtoggle switch) (**COMPUTING**) a key on a computer that you press to change from one style or operation to another, and back again

toggle² /ˈtɒɡl/ *verb* [I, T] (**COMPUTING**) to press a key or set of keys on a computer keyboard in order to turn a feature on or off, or to move from one program, etc. to another: *He toggled between the two windows.*

toil /tɔɪl/ *verb* [I] (*formal*) to work very hard or for a long time at sth ▸ **toil** *noun* [U]

toilet ⓘ Ⓐ1 /ˈtɔɪlət/ *noun* [C] a large bowl with a seat, connected to a water pipe, that you use when you need to get rid of waste material from your body; the room containing this: *I need to go to the toilet* (= use the toilet).

ˈtoilet paper (*also* ˈtoilet tissue) *noun* [U] soft, thin paper that you use to clean yourself after going to the toilet

toiletries /ˈtɔɪlətriz/ *noun* [pl.] things such as soap or TOOTHPASTE that you use for washing, cleaning your teeth, etc.

ˈtoilet roll *noun* [C] a long piece of toilet paper rolled round a tube

ˈtoilet tissue = TOILET PAPER

token¹ /ˈtəʊkən/ *noun* [C] **1** a round piece of metal, plastic, etc. that you use instead of money to operate some machines or as a form of payment **2** (*BrE*) a piece of paper that you can use to buy sth of a certain value in a particular shop. Tokens are often given as presents: *a £10 book/gift token* ➴ look at **voucher** **3** something that represents or is a symbol of sth: *Please accept this gift as a token of our gratitude.*

token² /ˈtəʊkən/ *adj.* [only before noun] **1** done, chosen, etc. in a very small quantity, and only in order not to be criticized: *There is a token woman on the board of directors.* **2** (used about an amount of money) small, but given to show that you are serious about sth and will keep a promise or an agreement: *a token payment*

told /təʊld/ past tense, past participle of **tell**

tolerable /ˈtɒlərəbl/ *adj.* **1** quite good, but not of the best quality **2** of a level that you can accept or deal with, although unpleasant or painful: *Drugs can reduce the pain to a tolerable level.* **OPP** **intolerable**

tolerant /ˈtɒlərənt/ *adj.* ~ (of/towards sb/sth) able to allow or accept sth that you do not like or agree with: *As a society, we've become less tolerant of cruelty.* **OPP** **intolerant** ▸ **tolerance** ⓘ Ⓒ1 /-rəns/ *noun* [U] ~ (of/for sb/sth): *religious tolerance*

tolerate ⓘ+ Ⓒ1 /ˈtɒləreɪt/ *verb* [T] **1** to allow or accept sth that you do not like or agree with: *In a democracy we must tolerate opinions that are different from our own.* **2** to accept or be able to deal with sb/sth unpleasant without complaining: *The noise was more than she could tolerate.* ▸ **toleration** /ˌtɒləˈreɪʃn/ *noun* [U]

toll ⓘ+ Ⓒ1 /təʊl/ *noun* [C] **1** money that you pay to use a road or bridge: *motorway tolls* ◇ *a toll bridge* **2** [usually sing.] the amount of damage done or the number of people who were killed or injured by sth: *The official death toll has now reached 5 000.* **IDM** take a heavy toll/take its toll (on sth) to cause great loss, damage, suffering, etc.

tollbooth /ˈtəʊlbuːð/ *noun* [C] a small building by the side of a road where you pay to drive on a road or go over a bridge

tom /tɒm/ = TOMCAT

tomato ⓘ Ⓐ1 /təˈmɑːtəʊ/ *noun* [C] (*pl.* -oes) a soft red fruit that is often eaten without being cooked in salads, or cooked as a vegetable: *tomato juice/soup/sauce*

tomb /tuːm/ *noun* [C] a large GRAVE (= where a dead person is buried), especially one built of stone above or below the ground: *the tombs of the Pharaohs* ➴ look at **grave**¹

tomboy /ˈtɒmbɔɪ/ *noun* [C] a young girl who likes the games and activities that are traditionally considered to be for boys

tombstone /ˈtuːmstəʊn/ *noun* [C] a large flat stone that lies on or stands at one end of a GRAVE (= where a person is buried) and shows the name, dates, etc. of the dead person ➴ look at **gravestone**, **headstone**

tomcat /ˈtɒmkæt/ (*also* tom) *noun* [C] a male cat

tomography /təˈmɒɡrəfi/ *noun* [U] (**MEDICINE**) a way of producing an image of the inside of the human body or a solid object using X-RAYS or ULTRASOUND

tomorrow ⓘ Ⓐ1 /təˈmɒrəʊ/ *noun* [U], *adv.* **1** (on) the day after today: *Today is Friday so tomorrow is Saturday.* ◇ *See you tomorrow.* ◇ *I'm going to bed. I've got to get up early tomorrow morning.* ◇ *a week tomorrow* (= a week from tomorrow) **2** the future: *The schoolchildren of today are tomorrow's workers.*

ton ⓘ+ Ⓑ2 /tʌn/ *noun* **1** [C] a measure of weight; 2 240 pounds ❶ For more information about weights, look at the **Reference Section** of this dictionary. **2** tons [pl.] (*informal*) a lot: *I've got tons of homework to do.*

tone¹ ⓘ Ⓑ2 /təʊn/ *noun* **1** [C, U] the quality of a sound or of sb's voice, especially expressing a particular emotion: *'Do you know each other?' she asked in a casual tone of voice.* **2** [sing.] the general quality or style of sth: *The tone of the meeting was optimistic.* **3** [C] a shade of a colour: *warm tones of red and orange* **4** [C] a sound that you hear on the phone: *Please speak after the tone* (= an instruction on an answering machine). **5** [C] (**MUSIC**) one of the longer steps between the notes in a musical scale, for example between C and D, or between E and F♯ ➴ look at **semitone**

tone² /təʊn/ *verb* [T] ~ **sth (up)** to make your muscles, skin, etc. tighter and stronger, especially by doing exercise: *Massage can help tone up flabby skin.*
PHR V **tone sth down** to change sth that you have said, written, etc., to make it less likely to offend

ˌtone-'deaf *adj.* (**MUSIC**) not able to sing or hear the difference between notes in music

'tone poem *noun* [C] (**MUSIC**) a piece of music that is intended to describe a place or express an idea

tongs /tɒŋz/ *noun* [pl.] a tool with two long parts that are joined at one end, that you use for picking up and holding things ⇨ picture at **laboratory**

tongue 🔒 **B1** /tʌŋ/ *noun* **1** [C] (**ANATOMY**) the soft part inside the mouth that you can move. You use your tongue for speaking, tasting things, etc. ⇨ picture at **body**, **digestive system** **2** [U, C] the tongue of some animals, cooked and eaten **3** [C] (*formal*) (**LANGUAGE**) a language: *your mother tongue* (= the language you learned as a child)
IDM **on the tip of your tongue** → **TIP¹** **put/stick your tongue out** to put your tongue outside your mouth as a rude sign to sb **a slip of the tongue** → **SLIP²** (**with**) **tongue in cheek** done or said as a joke; not intended seriously

'tongue-tied *adj.* not saying anything because you are shy or nervous

'tongue-twister *noun* [C] (**LANGUAGE**) a phrase or sentence with many similar sounds that is difficult to say correctly when you are speaking quickly

tonic /'tɒnɪk/ *noun* **1** (*also* 'tonic water) [U, C] a type of water with bubbles in it and a rather bitter taste that is often added to alcoholic drinks: *a gin and tonic* **2** [C] a medicine or sth you do that makes you feel stronger, healthier, etc., especially when you are very tired: *A relaxing holiday is a wonderful tonic.*

tonight 🔒 **A1** /tə'naɪt/ *noun* [U], *adv.* (on) the evening or night of today: *Tonight is the last night of our holiday.* ◇ *What's on TV tonight?* ◇ *We are staying with friends tonight and travelling home tomorrow.*

tonne 🔒+ **B2** /tʌn/ (*pl.* tonnes, tonne) (*also* metric ton) *noun* [C] a measure of weight; 1 000 KILOGRAMS ⇨ look at **ton**

tonsil /'tɒnsl/ *noun* [C] (**ANATOMY**) one of the two small soft parts in the throat at the back of the mouth: *She had to have her tonsils out* (= removed in a medical operation). ⇨ picture at **body**

tonsillitis /ˌtɒnsə'laɪtɪs/ *noun* [U] (**HEALTH**) an illness in which the TONSILS hurt and become SWOLLEN (= bigger than usual)

too 🔒 **A1** /tuː/ *adv.* **1** (used before adjectives and adverbs) more than is good, allowed, possible, etc: *These boots are too small.* ◇ *It's far too cold to go out without a coat.* ◇ *It's too long a journey for you to make alone.* **2** (in positive sentences) in addition; also: *Red is my favourite colour but I hate green, too.* ◇ *Phil thinks you're right and I do too.* **3** used to add sth that makes a situation even worse: *Her purse was stolen. And on her birthday too.* **4** (usually in negative sentences) very: *The weather is not too bad today.*
IDM **be too much (for sb)** to need more ability than you have; to be more difficult than you can bear

took /tʊk/ past tense of **take**

tool 🔒 **A2** 🌐 /tuːl/ *noun* [C] a piece of equipment such as a HAMMER, that you hold in your hand(s) and use to do a particular job: *Hammers, screwdrivers and saws are all carpenter's tools.* ◇ *garden tools* ◇ *a tool kit* (= a set of tools in a box or a bag)

toolbar /'tuːlbɑː(r)/ *noun* [C] (**COMPUTING**) a row of symbols on a computer screen that show the different things that you can do

tools

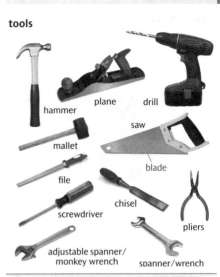

hammer
plane
drill
saw
mallet
blade
file
chisel
screwdriver
pliers
adjustable spanner/ monkey wrench
spanner/wrench

▼ VOCABULARY BUILDING

A **tool** is usually sth you can hold in your hand, for example a spanner or hammer. An **implement** is often used outside, for example for farming or gardening. A **machine** has moving parts and works by electricity, with an engine, etc. An **instrument** is often used for technical or delicate work: *a dentist's instruments.* A **device** is a more general word for a piece of equipment that you consider to be useful and that is designed to do one particular task: *The machine has a safety device that switches the power off if there is a fault.* A **device** is also a general word for a piece of computer equipment, especially a small one such as a smartphone.

toolbox /'tuːlbɒks/ *noun* [C] a box with a LID for keeping tools in

tooltip /'tuːltɪp/ *noun* [C] (**COMPUTING**) a message that appears when you move your mouse over an image, a link, etc. on a computer screen

toot /tuːt/ *noun* [C] the short high sound that a car HORN makes ▶ **toot** *verb* [I, T]: *Toot your horn to let them know we're here.*

tooth 🔒 **A1** /tuːθ/ *noun* [C] (*pl.* teeth /tiːθ/) **1** (**ANATOMY**) one of the hard white things in your mouth that you use for biting: *She's got beautiful teeth.* ⇨ look at **wisdom tooth** ⇨ picture on **page 766 2** one of the long narrow pointed parts of an object such as a COMB
IDM **by the skin of your teeth** → **SKIN¹** **gnash your teeth** → **GNASH** **grit your teeth** → **GRIT²** **have a sweet tooth** → **SWEET¹**

▼ VOCABULARY BUILDING

You **brush/clean** your teeth with a **toothbrush**. You clean between your teeth with special string called **dental floss**. If you have **toothache** (= pain in your teeth) or **tooth decay** (= a tooth that has gone bad), you should see a **dentist**. You might need a **filling**, or the tooth might have to be **taken out/extracted**. Some people have a **brace** (= a metal frame) to make their teeth straight, and people with no teeth can have **false teeth/dentures**.

toothache /'tuːθeɪk/ *noun* [U, C, usually sing.] (**HEALTH**) a pain in the tooth or teeth ⇨ note at **tooth**

structure of a tooth

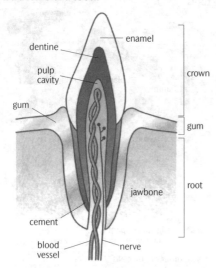

dentine
enamel
pulp cavity
crown
gum
gum
root
jawbone
cement
blood vessel
nerve

permanent teeth in an adult human

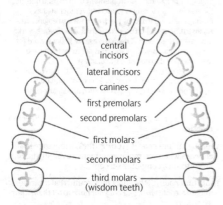

central incisors
lateral incisors
canines
first premolars
second premolars
first molars
second molars
third molars (wisdom teeth)

toothbrush /'tu:θbrʌʃ/ *noun* [C] a small brush with a handle that you use for cleaning your teeth ⊃ note at **tooth**

toothpaste /'tu:θpeɪst/ *noun* [U] a substance that you put on a brush and use for cleaning your teeth

toothpick /'tu:θpɪk/ *noun* [C] a short pointed piece of wood or plastic that you use for getting pieces of food out from between your teeth

top¹ ʔ **A2** /tɒp/ *noun*
• HIGHEST PART **1** [C] the highest part or point of sth: *The flat is at the top of the stairs.* ◇ *Snow was falling on the mountain tops.* ◇ *Start reading at the top of the page.* **OPP foot¹**
• FURTHEST POINT **2** [sing.] the end of a street, table, etc. that is furthest away from you or from where you usually come to it: *I'll meet you at the top of Broad Street.*
• FLAT SURFACE **3** [C] the flat upper surface of sth: *a desk/table/bench top*

• CLOTHING **4** [C] a piece of clothing that you wear on the upper part of the body: *a tracksuit/bikini/pyjama top* ◇ *I need a top to match my new skirt.*
• FOR A PEN, ETC. **5** [C] the cover that you put onto sth in order to close it: *Put the tops back on the pens or they will dry out.*
• HIGHEST POSITION **6** [sing.] **the ~ (of sth)** the highest or most important position: *to be at the top of your profession*
• TOY **7** [C] a child's toy that turns round very quickly on a point
IDM **at the top of your voice** as loudly as possible **get on top of sb** to be too much for sb to manage or deal with: *I've got so much work to do. It's really getting on top of me.* **off the top of your head** (*informal*) just guessing or using your memory without preparing or thinking about sth first **on top 1** on or onto the highest point: *a mountain with snow on top* **2** in control; in a leading position: *Josie always seems to come out on top.* **on top of sb/sth 1** on, over or covering sb/sth else: *Books were piled on top of one another.* ◇ *The remote control is on top of the TV.* **2** in addition to sb/sth else: *On top of everything else, the car's broken down.* **3** (*informal*) very close to sb/sth: *We were all living on top of each other in that tiny flat.* **over the top** (*abbr.* **OTT**) (*especially BrE, informal*) done with too much acting, emotion or effort

top² ʔ **A2** /tɒp/ *adj.* highest in position or degree: *the top floor of the building* ◇ *one of Britain's top businessmen* ◇ *at top speed* ◇ *She got top marks for her essay.*

top³ ʔ+ **C1** /tɒp/ *verb* [T] (-pp-) **1** to be higher or greater than a particular amount: *Inflation has topped the 10% mark.* **2** to be in the highest position in a list because you are the most important, successful, etc: *The band topped the charts for six weeks.* **3** [usually passive] **be topped (with sth)** if an item of food, a building, etc. **is topped** with sth, sth has been put on top of it: *cauliflower topped with cheese sauce* **IDM** **to top it all** (*informal*) used to introduce the final piece of information that is worse than the other bad things that you have just mentioned **PHR V** **top (sth) up** to fill sth that is partly empty: *Top the car up with oil before you set off.* ◇ *I need to top up my phone* (= pay more money so I can make more calls).

topaz /'təʊpæz/ *noun* [C, U] (**GEOLOGY**) a clear yellow SEMI-PRECIOUS stone

top-'class *adj.* of the highest quality or standard: *a top-class performance*

top 'hat *noun* [C] the tall black or grey hat that men sometimes wear on formal occasions

top-'heavy *adj.* heavier at the top than the bottom and likely to fall over

topic ʔ **A1** **⊙** /'tɒpɪk/ *noun* [C] a subject that you talk, write or learn about
IDM **on topic** connected with the subject that is being discussed: *Keep the text short and on topic.*

topical /'tɒpɪkl/ *adj.* **1** connected with sth that is happening now; that people are interested in at the present time **2** (**MEDICINE**) connected with, or put directly on, a part of the body

topless /'tɒpləs/ *adj., adv.* (used about a woman) not wearing any clothes on the upper part of the body so that her breasts are not covered

topmost /'tɒpməʊst/ *adj.* [only before noun] highest: *the topmost branches of the tree*

top-'notch *adj.* (*informal*) excellent; of the highest quality

topography /tə'pɒɡrəfi/ *noun* [U] (**GEOGRAPHY**) the physical characteristics of an area of land, especially the position of its rivers, mountains, etc.

topping /'tɒpɪŋ/ *noun* [C, U] something such as cream or a sauce that is put on the top of food to decorate it or make it taste nicer

topple /'tɒpl/ *verb* **1** [I] (often used with an adverb or a preposition) to become less steady and fall down: *Don't add another book to the pile or it will topple over.* **2** [T] to cause a leader of a country, etc. to lose their position of power or authority

top 'secret *adj.* (**POLITICS**) that must be kept very secret, especially from other governments

topsoil /'tɒpsɔɪl/ *noun* [U] (**AGRICULTURE**) the layer of soil nearest the surface of the ground ⊃ look at **subsoil**

top-up *noun* [C] (*BrE*) **1** a payment that you make to increase the amount of money, etc. to the level that is needed: *a phone top-up* (= to buy more time for calls) ◇ *Students will have to pay top-up fees* (= that are above the basic level). **2** (*informal*) an amount of a drink that you add to a cup or glass in order to fill it again: *Can I give anyone a top-up?*

Torah /'tɔːrə, tɔː'rɑː/ (*usually* the Torah) *noun* [usually sing., U] (**RELIGION**) (in the Jewish religion) the law of God as given to Moses and recorded in the first five books of the Bible

torch /tɔːtʃ/ *noun* [C] **1** (*AmE* flashlight) a small electric light that you carry in your hand **2** (*AmE*) = BLOWTORCH **3** a long piece of wood with burning material at the end that you carry to give light: *the Olympic torch*

tore /tɔː(r)/ past tense of **tear¹**

torment /'tɔːment/ *noun* [U, C] (*formal*) great pain and suffering in your mind or body; a person or thing that causes this: *to be in torment* ▸ **torment** /tɔː'ment/ *verb* [T]

torn /tɔːn/ past participle of **tear¹**

tornado /tɔː'neɪdəʊ/ *noun* [C] (*pl.* -oes) (**GEOGRAPHY**) a violent storm with very strong winds that move in a circle. Tornadoes form a tall column of air that is narrower at the bottom than at the top. ⊃ note at **storm¹**

torpedo /tɔː'piːdəʊ/ *noun* [C] (*pl.* -oes) a long narrow bomb that is fired under the water from a ship or SUBMARINE (= a ship that can travel UNDERWATER) and explodes when it hits another ship

torque /tɔːk/ *noun* [U] (**ENGINEERING, PHYSICS**) a force that causes machines, etc. to ROTATE (= turn around): *The more torque an engine has, the bigger the load it can pull in the same gear.*

torrent /'tɒrənt/ *noun* [C] a strong fast flow of sth, especially water: *The rain was coming down in torrents.*

torrential /tə'renʃl/ *adj.* (used about rain) very great in amount

torsion /'tɔːʃn/ *noun* [U] (**ENGINEERING, PHYSICS**) the action of TWISTING sth, especially one end of sth while the other end is held fixed

torso /'tɔːsəʊ/ *noun* [C] (*pl.* -os) (**ANATOMY**) the main part of the body, not the head, arms and legs

tort /tɔːt/ *noun* [C, U] (**LAW**) something wrong that sb does to sb else that is not criminal, but that can lead to action in a CIVIL court

tortilla /tɔː'tiːə/ *noun* [C] a type of very thin, round Mexican bread made with eggs and flour. It is usually eaten hot and filled with meat, cheese, etc.

tortoise /'tɔːtəs/ *noun* [C] a small animal with a hard shell that moves very slowly. A tortoise can pull its head and legs into its shell to protect them. ⊃ picture at **animal**

tortuous /'tɔːtʃuəs/ *adj.* **1** complicated, not clear and simple **2** (used about a road, etc.) with many bends

torture ᵻ+ **C1** /'tɔːtʃə(r)/ *noun* [U, C] **1** the act of causing sb great pain either as a punishment or to make them say or do sth: *His confession was extracted under torture.* **2** mental or physical suffering: *It's torture having to sit here and listen to him complaining.* ▸ **torture** ᵻ+ **C1** *verb* [T, often passive] ~ **sb (into doing sth)**: *Most of the prisoners were tortured into making a confession.* ◇ *She was tortured by the thought that the accident was her fault.* ▸ **torturer** *noun* [C]

Tory /'tɔːri/ *noun* [C] (*pl.* -ies) (**POLITICS**) a member of, or sb who supports, the British Conservative Party; connected with this party: *the Tory Party conference* ▸ **Tory** *adj.*

toss¹ ᵻ+ **C1** /tɒs/ *verb* **1** [T] to throw sth lightly and carelessly: *Bob opened the letter and tossed the envelope into the bin.* **2** [T] to move your head back quickly especially to show that you are annoyed or impatient: *I tried to apologize but she just tossed her head and walked away.* **3** [I, T] ~ **(up) (for sth)** to throw a coin into the air in order to decide sth, by guessing which side of the coin will land facing upwards: *to toss a coin* ◇ *There's only one ticket left. I'll toss you for it.* **4** [I, T] to move up and down or from side to side; to make sb/sth move in this way: *He lay tossing and turning in bed, unable to sleep.* ◇ *The ship was tossed about by huge waves.*

toss² /tɒs/ *noun* [usually sing.]
IDM **win/lose the toss** to guess correctly/wrongly which side of a coin will face upwards when it lands: *I won the toss and chose to serve first.*

tot¹ /tɒt/ *noun* [C] **1** (*informal*) a very small child **2** (*especially BrE*) a small glass of a strong alcoholic drink

tot² /tɒt/ *verb* (-tt-)
PHR V **tot (sth) up** (*informal*) to add numbers together to form a total

total¹ ᵻ **B1** ⊙ /'təʊtl/ *adj.* **1** being the amount after everyone or everything is counted or added together: *What was the total number of people there?* **2** used when you are emphasizing something, to mean 'to the greatest degree possible': *They ate in total silence.* ◇ *a total failure* **SYN** **complete¹**

total² ᵻ **B1** ⊙ /'təʊtl/ *noun* [C] the number that you get when you add two or more numbers or amounts together ▸ **total** ᵻ+ **C1** *verb* [T] (-ll-, *AmE* -l-): *His debts totalled more than £10 000.*
IDM **in total** when you add two or more numbers or amounts together: *The appeal raised £4 million in total.*

totalitarian /təʊˌtælə'teəriən/ *adj.* (**POLITICS**) in which there is only one political party that has complete power and control over the people ▸ **totalitarianism** *noun* [U]

totally ᵻ **B1** /'təʊtəli/ *adv.* completely: *I totally agree with you.*

totter /'tɒtə(r)/ *verb* [I] (often used with an adverb or a preposition) to stand or move in a way that is not steady, as if you are going to fall, especially because you are drunk, ill or weak

toucan /'tuːkæn/ *noun* [C] a tropical American bird with bright feathers and a very large BEAK (= the hard pointed part of a bird's mouth)

touch¹ ᵻ **A2** /tʌtʃ/ *verb* **1** [T] to put your hand or fingers onto sb/sth: *Don't touch that plate — it's hot!* ◇ *He touched her gently on the cheek.* ◇ *The police asked us not to touch anything.* **2** [I, T] (used about two or more things, surfaces, etc.) to be or move so close together that there is no space between them: *They were sitting so close that their shoulders touched.* ◇ *This bike is too big. My feet don't **touch the ground**.* **3** [T] to make sb feel sad, sorry for sb, grateful, etc: *Her story touched us all deeply.* ⊃ look at **touched 4** [T] (in negative sentences) to be as good as sb/sth in skill, quality, etc: *He's a much better player than all the others. No one else can touch him.*

IDM **touch wood** (*BrE*) (*AmE* **knock on wood**) an expression that people use (often while touching a piece of wood) to prevent bad luck: *I've been driving here for 20 years and I haven't had an accident yet — touch wood!*

PHR V **touch down** (used about an aircraft) to land
touch on/upon sth to mention or refer to a subject for only a short time

touch² 🔑 **B1** /tʌtʃ/ *noun*

- SENSE **1** [U] one of the five senses: the ability to feel things and know what they are like by putting your hands or fingers on them: *The sense of touch is very important to blind people.* ⊃ picture at **skin¹**
- WITH YOUR HAND **2** [C, usually sing.] the act of putting your hands or fingers onto sb/sth: *I felt the touch of her hand on my arm.*
- WAY STH FEELS **3** [U] the way sth feels when you touch it: *Marble is cold to the touch.*
- DETAIL **4** [C] a small detail that is added to improve sth: *The flowers in our room were a nice touch.* ◇ *She's just putting the finishing touches to the cake.*
- WAY OF DOING STH **5** [sing.] a way or style of doing sth: *She prefers to write her letters by hand for a more personal touch.*
- SMALL AMOUNT **6** [C, usually sing.] ~ **(of sth)** a small amount of sth

IDM **in/out of touch (with sb)** being/not being in contact with sb by speaking or writing to them: *During the year she was abroad, they kept in touch by email.* **in/out of touch with sth** having/not having recent information about sth: *We're out of touch with what's going on.* **lose touch** → LOSE **lose your touch** → LOSE

touchdown /'tʌtʃdaʊn/ *noun* **1** [C,U] the moment when a plane or SPACECRAFT lands **SYN** **landing 2** [C] (**SPORT**) (in the game of rugby) an act of scoring points by putting the ball down on the area of ground behind the other team's GOAL LINE **3** [C] (**SPORT**) (in the game of AMERICAN FOOTBALL) an act of scoring points by crossing the other team's GOAL LINE while carrying the ball, or receiving the ball when you are over the other team's GOAL LINE

touched /tʌtʃt/ *adj.* [not before noun] ~ **(by sth)**; ~ **(that)** ... made to feel sad, sorry for sb, grateful, etc: *We were very touched by the plight of the refugees.* ◇ *I was touched that he offered to help.*

touching /'tʌtʃɪŋ/ *adj.* that makes you feel sad, sorry for sb, grateful, etc. **SYN** **moving**

touchline /'tʌtʃlaɪn/ *noun* [C] (**SPORT**) a line that marks the side of the playing field in football, rugby, etc.

touchpad /'tʌtʃpæd/ (*also* **trackpad**) *noun* [C] a device that you touch in different places in order to operate a computer

touchscreen /'tʌtʃskriːn/ *noun* [C] (**COMPUTING**) a screen on a computer, phone, etc. that allows you to give instructions to the device by touching areas on it

'Touch-Tone™ *adj.* (used about a phone or phone system) producing different sounds when different numbers are pushed

touchy /'tʌtʃi/ *adj.* (**touchier; touchiest**) **1** ~ **(about sth)** easily upset or made angry: *He's a bit touchy about his weight.* **2** (used about a subject, situation, etc.) that may easily upset people or make them angry: *Don't mention the exam. It's a very touchy subject.*

tough 🔑 **B2** /tʌf/ *adj.*

- DIFFICULT **1** having or causing problems: *It will be a tough decision to make.* ◇ *He's had a tough time of it (= a lot of problems) recently.*
- STRICT **2** ~ **(on/with sb/sth)** not feeling sorry for anyone: *Don't be too tough on them — they were only trying to help.* ◇ *The government plans to get tough with people who drink and drive.*
- STRONG **3** strong enough to deal with difficult conditions or situations: *You need to be tough to go climbing in winter.* **4** not easily broken, torn or cut; very strong: *a tough pair of boots*
- MEAT **5** (used especially about meat) difficult to cut and eat ⊃ note at **meat**
- BAD LUCK **6** ~ **(on sb)** (*informal*) UNLUCKY for sb in a way that seems unfair: *It's tough on her that she lost her job.*

▶ **toughness** *noun* [U]

toughen /'tʌfn/ *verb* [T, I] ~ **(sb/sth) (up)** to become or to make sb/sth tough

toupee /'tuːpeɪ/ *noun* [C] a small section of artificial hair, worn by a man to cover an area of his head where hair no longer grows

tour 🔑 **A2** /tʊə(r), tɔː(r)/ *noun* **1** [C] ~ **(of/round/around sth)** (**TOURISM**) a journey that you make for pleasure during which you visit many places: *to go on a ten-day coach tour of around Scotland* ◇ *a sightseeing tour* ⊃ note at **travel²** **2** [C] (**TOURISM**) a short visit around a city, famous building, etc: *a guided tour round St Paul's Cathedral* **3** [C, U] (**MUSIC**, **SPORT**) an official series of visits that singers, musicians, sports players, etc. make to different places to perform, play, etc: *The band is currently on tour in America.* ◇ *a concert/cricket tour* ▶ **tour** 🔑 **B1** *verb* [T, I]: *We toured southern Spain for three weeks.*

tourism 🔑 **A2** /'tʊərɪzəm, 'tɔːr-/ *noun* [U] (**SOCIAL STUDIES**) the business of providing and arranging holidays and services for people who are visiting a place: *The country's economy relies heavily on tourism.*

tourist 🔑 **A1** /'tʊərɪst, 'tɔːr-/ *noun* [C] (**SOCIAL STUDIES**, **TOURISM**) a person who visits a place for pleasure ⊃ look at **sightseer**

'tourist class *noun* [U] (**TOURISM**) the cheapest type of ticket or accommodation that is available on a plane or ship or in a hotel

'tourist trap *noun* [C] (*informal*) (**TOURISM**) a place that attracts a lot of tourists and where food, drink, entertainment, etc. is more expensive than normal

touristy /'tʊəristi, 'tɔːr-/ *adj.* (*informal*) (**TOURISM**) attracting or designed to attract a lot of tourists: *The best beaches were far from the touristy spots.*

tournament 🔑+ **B2** /'tʊənəmənt, 'tɔːn-/ *noun* [C] (**SPORT**) a competition in which many players or teams play games against each other

tourniquet /'tʊənɪkeɪ/ *noun* [C] (**MEDICINE**) a piece of cloth, etc. that is tied tightly around an arm or a leg to stop the loss of blood from a cut or an injury

tousled /'taʊzld/ *adj.* (used about hair) untidy, often in an attractive way

tout /taʊt/ *verb* **1** [T, often passive] ~ **sb/sth (as sth)** to try to persuade people that sb/sth is important or valuable by praising them/it: *She's being touted as the next leader of the party.* **2** [I, T] ~ **(for sth)** (*especially BrE*) (**BUSINESS**) to try to persuade people to buy your goods or services, especially by going to them and asking them directly: *the problem of unlicensed taxi drivers touting for business at airports* **3** [I, T] (*BrE*) to sell tickets for a popular event illegally, at a price that is higher than the official price, especially outside a theatre, stadium, etc. ▶ **tout** (*also* **ticket tout**) *noun* [C] (*BrE*): *Touts are selling concert tickets at three times their original price.*

tow[1] /təʊ/ *verb* [T] to pull a car or boat behind another vehicle, using a rope or chain: *My car was towed away by the police.*

tow[2] /təʊ/ *noun*
IDM **in tow** (*informal*) following closely behind: *He arrived with his wife and five children in tow.*

towards 🔊 A2 /təˈwɔːdz/ (*also* **toward** /təˈwɔːd/) *prep.* **1** in the direction of sb/sth: *I saw Ken walking towards the station.* ◇ *She had her back towards me.* ◇ *a first step towards world peace* **2** near or nearer a time or date: *It gets cool towards evening.* ◇ *The shops get very busy towards Christmas.* **3** (used when you are talking about your feelings about sb/sth) in relation to: *Patti felt very protective towards her younger brother.* ◇ *What is your attitude towards this government?* **4** as part of the payment for sth: *The money will go towards the cost of a new minibus.*

towel 🔊 A2 /ˈtaʊəl/ *noun* [C] a piece of cloth or paper that you use for drying sb/sth/yourself: *a bath/hand/beach towel* ◇ *kitchen/paper towels* ⊃ look at **sanitary towel**, **tea towel**

towelling (*BrE*) (*AmE* **toweling**) /ˈtaʊəlɪŋ/ *noun* [U] a thick soft cotton cloth that is used especially for making bath towels

tower[1] 🔊 A2 /ˈtaʊə(r)/ *noun* [C] (**ARCHITECTURE**) a tall narrow building or part of a building such as a church or castle: *the Eiffel Tower* ◇ *a church tower*

tower[2] /ˈtaʊə(r)/ *verb*
PHR V **tower over/above sb/sth** **1** to be much higher or taller than the people or things that are near: *He towers over all his classmates.* **2** to be much better than others in ability or quality: *She towers over other dancers of her generation.*

tower block *noun* [C] (*BrE*) a very tall building consisting of flats or offices

towering /ˈtaʊərɪŋ/ *adj.* [only before noun] **1** extremely tall or high: *towering cliffs* **2** of extremely high quality: *a towering performance*

town 🔊 A1 /taʊn/ *noun* **1** [C] (**GEOGRAPHY**) a place with many streets and buildings. A town is larger than a village but smaller than a city: *Romsey is a small market town.* ◇ *The nearest town is 10 kilometres away.* **2 the town** [sing.] all the people who live in a town: *The whole town is talking about it.* **3** [U] the main part of a town, where the shops, etc. are: *I've got to go into town this afternoon.*
IDM **go to town (on sth)** (*informal*) to do sth with a lot of energy and enthusiasm; to spend a lot of money on sth **(out) on the town** (*informal*) going to restaurants, theatres, clubs, etc. for entertainment, especially at night

town ˈhall *noun* [C] a large building that contains the local government offices and often a large room for public meetings, concerts, etc. ⊃ look at **hall** (2)

town ˈplanner = PLANNER (1)

town ˈplanning (*also* **planning**) *noun* [U] the control of the development of towns and their buildings, roads, etc. so that they can be pleasant and convenient places for people to live in; the subject that studies this

townscape /ˈtaʊnskeɪp/ *noun* [C] (**ART**) a picture of a town ⊃ look at **cityscape**, **landscape**[1] (2)

townspeople /ˈtaʊnzpiːpl/ (*also* **townsfolk** /ˈtaʊnzfəʊk/) *noun* [pl.] people who live in towns, not in the countryside; the people who live in a particular town

tow truck (*AmE*) = BREAKDOWN TRUCK

toxic 🔊+ C1 /ˈtɒksɪk/ *adj.* **1** (**CHEMISTRY**) poisonous ⊃ picture at **safety** **2** (**FINANCE**) involving a high level of debt, where there is a high risk that the money will not be paid back: *toxic debt/loans* **3** (*informal*) unpleasant or harmful: *a toxic relationship*

toxicity /tɒkˈsɪsəti/ *noun* (*pl.* **-ies**) (**CHEMISTRY**) **1** [U] the quality of being poisonous; the degree to which sth is poisonous: *substances with high/low levels of toxicity* **2** [C] the effect that a poisonous substance has: *Minor toxicities of this drug include nausea and vomiting.*

toxicology /ˌtɒksɪˈkɒlədʒi/ *noun* [U] (**CHEMISTRY**) the scientific study of poisons ▶ **toxicological** /ˌtɒksɪkəˈlɒdʒɪkl/ *adj.* ▶ **toxicologist** /ˌtɒksɪˈkɒlədʒɪst/ *noun* [C]

toxin /ˈtɒksɪn/ *noun* [C] (**CHEMISTRY**) a poisonous substance, especially one that is produced by bacteria in plants and animals

toxoplasmosis /ˌtɒksəʊplæzˈməʊsɪs/ *noun* [U] (**HEALTH**) a disease that can be dangerous to a baby while it is still in its mother's body, caught from bacteria in meat, soil or animal waste

toy[1] 🔊 A2 /tɔɪ/ *noun* [C] an object for a child to play with: *The little boy continued playing with his toys.* ◇ *a toy shop* ▶ **toy** 🔊 A2 *adj.* [only before noun]: *a toy car/farm/soldier*

toy[2] /tɔɪ/ *verb*
PHR V **toy with sth** **1** to think about doing sth, perhaps not very seriously: *She's toying with the idea of going abroad for a year.* **2** to move sth about without thinking about what you are doing, often because you are nervous or upset: *He toyed with his food but hardly ate any of it.*

trace[1] 🔊+ C1 S /treɪs/ *noun* **1** [C, U] a mark, an object or a sign that shows that sb/sth existed or happened: *traces of an earlier civilization* ◇ *The man disappeared/vanished without trace.* **2** [C] ~ (of sth) a very small amount of sth: *Traces of blood were found under her fingernails.*

trace[2] 🔊+ B2 /treɪs/ *verb* [T] **1** ~ sb/sth (to sth) to find out where sb/sth is by following marks, signs or other information: *The wanted man was traced to an address in Amsterdam.* **2** ~ sth (back) (to sth) to find out where sth came from or what caused it; to describe the development of sth: *She traced her family tree back to the sixteenth century.* **3** to make a copy of a map, plan, etc. by placing a piece of TRACING PAPER (= paper that you can see through) over it and drawing over the lines

trace element *noun* [C] **1** (**CHEMISTRY**) a chemical substance that is found in very small amounts **2** (**BIOLOGY**) a chemical substance that living things, especially plants, need only in very small amounts to be able to grow well

tracery /ˈtreɪsəri/ *noun* [U] (**ARCHITECTURE**) a pattern of lines and curves in stone on the top part of some church windows

trachea /trəˈkiːə/ *noun* [C] (*pl.* **tracheae** /-ˈkiːiː/, **tracheas**) (**ANATOMY**) the tube in the throat that carries air from the throat to the lungs **SYN** **windpipe** ⊃ picture at **body**, **respiratory**

tracheotomy /ˌtræsiˈɒtəmi/ *noun* [C] (*pl.* **-ies**) (**MEDICINE**) a medical operation to cut a hole in sb's TRACHEA so that they can breathe

tracing /ˈtreɪsɪŋ/ *noun* [C] (**ART**) a copy of a map, drawing, etc. that you make by drawing on a piece of paper that you can see through placed on top of it

tracing paper *noun* [U] strong paper that you can see through that is placed on top of a drawing, etc. so that you can follow the lines with a pen or pencil in order to make a copy of it

track¹ 🔊 **A2** /træk/ *noun*
• FOR A TRAIN **1** [C, U] the two metal RAILS (= metal bars) on which a train runs: *The train stopped because there was a tree across the track.*
• FOR A RACE **2** [C] a piece of ground, often in a circle, for people, cars, etc. to have races on: *a running track*
• PATH **3** [C] a natural path or rough road: *Follow the dirt track through the forest.*
• MARKS ON THE GROUND **4** [C, usually pl.] marks that are left on the ground by a person, an animal or a moving vehicle: *The hunter followed the tracks of a deer.* ◇ *tyre tracks* ⊃ look at **footprint** (1)
• RECORDING **5** [C] (**MUSIC**) a recording of one song or piece of music: *the first track from her latest album* ⊃ look at **soundtrack**
IDM **keep/lose track of** sb/sth to have/not have information about what is happening or where sb/sth is **off the beaten track** → **BEAT¹** on the right/wrong track having the right/wrong idea about sth: *That's not the answer but you're on the right track.*

track² 🔊 **B2** /træk/ *verb* [T] to follow the movements of sb/sth: *to track enemy planes on a radar screen* **PHRV** **track** sb/sth **down** to find sb/sth after searching for them or it

track and 'field (*AmE*) = ATHLETICS

'track event *noun* [C] (**SPORT**) a sports event that consists of running round a track in a race, rather than throwing sth or jumping ⊃ look at **field event**

trackpad /ˈtrækpæd/ = TOUCHPAD

'track record *noun* [sing.] all the past successes or failures of a person or an organization: *He has a good track record in sales.*

tracksuit /ˈtræksuːt/ *noun* [C] a warm pair of soft trousers and a matching jacket that you wear for sports practice

tract /trækt/ *noun* [C] (**ANATOMY**) a system of organs or tubes in the body that are connected and that have a particular purpose: *the respiratory/digestive tract*

traction /ˈtrækʃn/ *noun* [U] **1** the action of pulling sth along a surface; the power that is used for doing this: *diesel/electric/steam traction* **2** (**MEDICINE**) a way of treating a broken bone in the body that involves using special equipment to pull the bone gradually back into its correct place: *He spent six weeks in traction after he broke his leg.* **3** the force that stops sth, for example the wheels of a vehicle, from sliding on the ground

tractor /ˈtræktə(r)/ *noun* [C] (**AGRICULTURE**) a powerful vehicle with two large and two smaller wheels, used especially for pulling farm machines

tractor

trade¹ 🔊 **B1** /treɪd/ *noun* **1** [U] (**ECONOMICS, SOCIAL STUDIES**) the buying or selling of goods or services between people or countries: *an international trade agreement* ◇ *Trade is not very good* (= not many goods are sold) *at this time of year.* **2** [C] a particular type of business:

the tourist/building/retail trade **3** [U, C] a job for which you need special skill, especially with your hands: *Jeff is a plumber by trade.* ◇ *to learn a trade* ⊃ note at **work²**

trade² 🔊 **B1** /treɪd/ *verb* **1** [I, T] ~ (**in sth**) (**with sb**) (**ECONOMICS, FINANCE, SOCIAL STUDIES**) to buy or sell goods or services: *to trade in luxury goods* ◇ *to trade in stocks and shares* ◇ *We no longer trade with that country.* ◇ *Our products are traded worldwide.* **2** [T] ~ **sth** (**for sth**) to exchange sth for sth else: *He traded a computer game for some concert tickets.*
PHRV **trade** sth **in** (**for sth**) to give sth old in part payment for sth new or newer: *We traded in our old car for a van.*

'trade balance = BALANCE OF TRADE

'trade deficit *noun* [C, usually sing.] (**ECONOMICS**) a situation in which the value of a country's imports is greater than the value of its exports

trademark 🔊 **C1** /ˈtreɪdmɑːk/ *noun* [C] (*abbr.* TM) a special symbol, design or name that a company puts on its products and that cannot be used by any other company

'trade name = BRAND NAME

trader /ˈtreɪdə(r)/ *noun* [C] (**ECONOMICS, SOCIAL STUDIES**) a person who buys and sells things, especially goods in a market or company shares

'trade route *noun* [C] (**HISTORY**) (in the past) the route that people buying and selling goods used to take across land or sea

trade 'secret *noun* [C] a piece of information, for example about how a particular product is made, that is known only to the company that makes it

tradesman /ˈtreɪdzmən/ *noun* [C] (*pl.* -men /-mən/) a person who brings goods to people's homes to sell them or who has a shop

trade 'union (*also* **trades union**) *noun* [C] (*both BrE*) (**BUSINESS**) an organization for people who all work in a particular industry. Trade unions try to get better pay and working conditions for their members.

trade 'unionist (*also* **trades unionist, unionist**) *noun* [C] (**BUSINESS**) a member of a TRADE UNION

trade winds /ˈtreɪd wɪndz/ *noun* [pl.] (**GEOGRAPHY**) strong winds that blow all the time towards the EQUATOR (= the imagined line around the middle of the earth) and then to the west

trading 🔊 **B2** /ˈtreɪdɪŋ/ *noun* [U] (**BUSINESS**) the activity of buying and selling things: *laws on Sunday trading* (= shops being open on Sundays) ◇ *Shares worth $8 million changed hands during a day of hectic trading.*

tradition 🔊 **A2** /trəˈdɪʃn/ *noun* [C, U] (**SOCIAL STUDIES**) a custom, belief or way of doing sth that has continued from the past to the present: *religious/cultural/literary traditions* ◇ *By tradition, the bride's family pays the costs of the wedding.*

traditional 🔊 **A2** 🔘 /trəˈdɪʃənl/ *adj.* **1** (**SOCIAL STUDIES**) being part of the beliefs, customs or way of life of a particular group of people, that have not changed for a long time: *It is traditional in Britain to eat turkey at Christmas.* **2** following older methods and ideas rather than modern or different ones: *traditional methods of teaching* ▸ **traditionally** 🔊 /-nəli/ *adv.*

traditionalist /trəˈdɪʃənəlɪst/ *noun* [C] a person who prefers tradition to modern ideas or ways of doing things ▸ **traditionalist** *adj.*

traffic¹ 🔊 **A1** /ˈtræfɪk/ *noun* [U] **1** all the vehicles that are on a road at a particular time: *heavy/light traffic* ◇ *We got stuck in traffic and were late for the meeting.* **2** the movement of ships, aircraft, etc: *air traffic* *control* **3** ~ **(in sth)** (LAW) the illegal buying and selling of sth: *the traffic in drugs/firearms*

traffic² /'træfɪk/ *verb* [T, I] (-ck-) ~ **(in)** sb/sth to move people in a way that is not legal, especially in order to make them work in bad conditions without proper payment; to buy and sell sth in a way that is not legal: *The women had been trafficked and forced into prostitution.* ◇ *human trafficking* ◇ *Smugglers were trafficking arms across the border to the rebels.*

traffic calming *noun* [U] (BrE) ways of making roads safer, especially for people who are walking or riding bicycles, by building raised areas, etc. to make cars go more slowly

traffic island (*also* **island**) *noun* [C] a higher area in the middle of the road, where you can stand and wait for the traffic to pass when you want to cross

traffic jam *noun* [C] a long line of cars, etc. that cannot move or that can only move very slowly: *to be stuck in a traffic jam*

trafficker /'træfɪkə(r)/ *noun* [C] a person who buys and sells sth in a way that is not legal: *a drugs trafficker*

trafficking /'træfɪkɪŋ/ *noun* [U] the activity of buying and selling sth in an illegal way: *drug trafficking* ▶ **trafficker** *noun* [C]: *a drugs trafficker*

traffic light *noun* [C, usually pl.] a sign with red, AMBER (= orange) and green lights that is used for controlling the traffic where two or more roads meet

traffic warden *noun* [C] (BrE) a person whose job is to check that cars are not parked in the wrong place or for longer than is allowed

tragedy ʔ+ B2 /'trædʒədi/ *noun* [C, U] (*pl.* -ies) **1** a very sad event or situation, especially one that involves death: *It's a tragedy that he died so young.* **2** (ARTS AND MEDIA, LITERATURE) a serious play that has a sad ending; plays of this type: *Shakespeare's 'King Lear' is a tragedy.* ◇ *I'm taking a course in Greek tragedy at Columbia.* ⊃ look at **comedy** (1)

tragic ʔ+ B2 /'trædʒɪk/ *adj.* **1** that makes you very sad, especially because it involves death: *It's tragic that she lost her only child.* ◇ *a tragic accident* **2** [only before noun] (LITERATURE) in the style of TRAGEDY: *a tragic actor/hero* ▶ **tragically** /-kli/ *adv.*

trail¹ ʔ+ C1 /treɪl/ *noun* [C] **1** a series of marks in a long line that is left by sb/sth: *a trail of blood/footprints* **2** a track, sign or smell that is left behind and that you follow when you are hunting sb/sth: *The dogs ran off on the trail of the fox.* **3** a path through the countryside

trail² ʔ+ C1 /treɪl/ *verb* **1** [I, T, I] to pull sth behind sb/sth; to be pulled along in this way: *The skirt was too long and trailed along the ground.* **2** [I] (used with an adverb or a preposition) to move or walk slowly behind sb/sth else, usually because you are tired or bored: *It was impossible to do any shopping with the kids trailing around after me.* **3** [I, T] ~ **(by/in sth)** (usually used in the progressive tenses) to be in the process of losing a game or a competition: *At half-time Liverpool were trailing by two goals to three.* **4** [I] (used about plants or sth long and thin) to grow over sth and hang downwards; to lie across a surface: *Computer wires trailed across the floor.*
PHR V **trail away/off** (used about sb's voice) to gradually become quieter and then stop

trailer ʔ+ C1 /'treɪlə(r)/ *noun* [C] **1** a truck, or a container with wheels, that is pulled by another vehicle: *a car towing a trailer with a boat on it* **2** (AmE) = MOBILE HOME (1): *a **trailer park** (= an area where trailers are parked and used as homes)* **3** (AmE) = MOBILE HOME (2) **4** (*especially* BrE) (ARTS AND MEDIA) a series of short pieces taken from a film and used to advertise it ⊃ look at **clip¹** (2) ⊃ note at **advertisement**

train¹ ʔ A1 /treɪn/ *noun* [C] **1** a type of transport that is pulled by an engine along a railway line. A train is divided into CARRIAGES (= sections for people) or WAGONS (= for goods): *a passenger/goods/freight train* ◇ *a fast/slow/express train* ◇ *to catch/take/get the train to Paris* ◇ *the twelve o'clock train to Bristol* ◇ *to get on/off a train* ◇ *Hurry up or we'll **miss the train**.* ◇ *You have to **change trains** at Hamburg.* **2** [usually sing.] a series of thoughts or events that are connected: *A knock at the door interrupted my **train of thought**.*

train² ʔ A2 /treɪn/ *verb* **1** [T, I] ~ **(sb/sth) (as/in/for sth)**; ~ **(sb/sth) (to do sth)** (EDUCATION) to teach a person or an animal the skills for a particular job or activity; to be taught in this way: *The organization trains guide dogs for the blind.* ◇ *There is a shortage of trained teachers.* ◇ *She trained as an engineer.* ◇ *He's not trained in anything.* ◇ *He's training to be a doctor.* ⊃ note at **job** **2** [I, T] ~ **(for sth)** to prepare yourself, especially for a sports event, by practising; to help a person or an animal to do this: *I'm training for the Boston Marathon.* ◇ *to train racehorses* **3** [T] ~ **sth (at/on sb/sth)** to point a gun, camera, etc. at sb/sth

trainee /ˌtreɪ'niː/ *noun* [C] a person who is being taught how to do a particular job ⊃ note at **job**

trainer ʔ A2 /'treɪnə(r)/ *noun* [C] **1** (BrE) (AmE **sneaker**) [usually pl.] a shoe that you wear for doing sport or as informal clothing ⊃ look at **plimsoll** ⊃ picture at **sport** **2** a person who teaches people or animals how to do a particular job or skill well, or to do a particular sport: *teacher trainers* ◇ *a racehorse trainer*

training ʔ A2 ⓦ /'treɪnɪŋ/ *noun* [U] **1** ~ **(in sth/doing sth)** the process of learning the skills that you need to do a job: *staff training in customer relations* ◇ *a training course* ⊃ note at **job** **2** the process of preparing to take part in a sports competition by doing physical exercises: *to be in training for the Olympics*

training college *noun* [C] (BrE) (EDUCATION) a college that trains people for a job or profession: *a police training college*

trainspotter /'treɪnspɒtə(r)/ *noun* [C] (BrE) **1** a person who collects the numbers of railway engines as a hobby **2** a person who has a boring hobby or who is interested in the details of a subject that other people find boring ▶ **trainspotting** *noun* [U]

trait ʔ+ B2 /treɪt/ *noun* [C] a quality that forms part of your character or personality

traitor /'treɪtə(r)/ *noun* [C] ~ **(to sb/sth)** a person who gives away secrets about their friends, their country, etc. ❶ A traitor **betrays** his/her friends, country, etc. and the crime against his/her country is called **treason**.

trajectory /trə'dʒektəri/ *noun* [C] (*pl.* -ies) the curved path of sth that has been fired, hit or thrown into the air: *a missile's trajectory*

tram /træm/ (BrE) (AmE **streetcar**, **trolley**) *noun* [C] a type of bus that works by electricity and that moves along special RAILS (= metal bars) in the road carrying passengers

tramp¹ /træmp/ *noun* **1** [C] a person who has no home or job and who moves from place to place **2** [sing.] the sound of people walking with heavy or noisy steps

tramp² /træmp/ *verb* [I, T] to walk with slow heavy steps, especially for a long time

trample /'træmpl/ *verb* [I, T] ~ **on/over sb/sth** to walk on sb/sth and damage or hurt them or it: *The boys trampled on the flowers.*

trampoline /ˈtræmpəˈliːn/ *noun* [C] (**SPORT**) a piece of equipment for jumping up and down on, made of a piece of strong material fixed to a metal frame by springs ▶ **trampoline** *verb* [I] ▶ **trampolining** *noun* [U]

trance /trɑːns/ *noun* [C] a mental state in which you do not notice what is going on around you: *to go/fall into a trance*

tranquil /ˈtræŋkwɪl/ *adj.* (*formal*) calm and quiet

tranquillize (*also* **-ise**) (*both BrE*) (*AmE* **tranquilize**) /ˈtræŋkwəlaɪz/ *verb* [T] (**MEDICINE**) to make a person or an animal calm or unconscious, especially by giving them or it a drug

tranquillizer (*also* **-iser**) (*both BrE*) (*AmE* **tranquilizer**) /ˈtræŋkwəlaɪzə(r)/ *noun* [C] (**MEDICINE**) a drug that is used for making people or animals calm or unconscious ➔ look at **sedative**

trans /trænz/ = TRANSGENDER, TRANSSEXUAL

trans- /trænz, træns/ *prefix* **1** (in adjectives) across; beyond: *transatlantic* ◇ *transparent* **2** (in verbs) into another place or state: *transplant* ◇ *transform*

transaction ̌+ **C1** /trænˈzækʃn/ *noun* [C] (**BUSINESS**) a piece of business that is done between people: *financial transactions*

transatlantic /ˌtrænzətˈlæntɪk/ *adj.* to or from the other side of the Atlantic Ocean; across the Atlantic: *a transatlantic flight/voyage*

transcend /trænˈsend/ *verb* [T] (*formal*) to go further than the usual limits of sth

transcribe /trænˈskraɪb/ *verb* [T] **1** ~ **sth (into sth)** to record thoughts, speech or data in a written form, or in a different written form from the original: *Clerks transcribe everything that is said in court.* ◇ *The interview was recorded and then transcribed.* **2** (**LANGUAGE**) to show the sounds of speech using a special PHONETIC alphabet **3** ~ **sth (for sth)** (**MUSIC**) to write a piece of music in a different form so that it can be played by another musical instrument or sung by another voice: *a piano piece transcribed for the guitar*

transcript ̌+ **C1** /ˈtrænskrɪpt/ (*also* **transcription**) *noun* [C] a written or printed copy of what sb has said: *a transcript of the interview/trial*

transcription /trænˈskrɪpʃn/ *noun* **1** [U] the act or process of representing sth in a written or printed form: *errors made in transcription* ◇ *phonetic transcription* **2** [C] = TRANSCRIPT: *The full transcription of the interview is attached.* **3** [C] something that is represented in writing: *This dictionary gives phonetic transcriptions of most headwords.* **4** [C] (**MUSIC**) a change in the written form of a piece of music so that it can be played on a different instrument or sung by a different voice

transducer /trænzˈdjuːsə(r)/ *noun* [C] (**PHYSICS**) a device for producing an electrical signal from another form of energy such as pressure

transept /ˈtrænsept/ *noun* [C] (**ARCHITECTURE**) either of the two wide parts of a church shaped like a cross, that are built at RIGHT ANGLES to the main central part ➔ look at **nave**

transexual /trænzˈsekʃuəl/ = TRANSSEXUAL

transfer¹ ̌ **B2** ◉ /trænsˈfɜː(r)/ *verb* (-rr-) **1** [I, T] ~ **(sb/sth) (from …) (to …)** to move, or to make sb/sth move, from one place to another: *He's transferring to our Tokyo branch next month.* ◇ *I'd like to transfer £1 000 from my deposit account* (= in a bank). ◇ *Transfer the data onto a memory stick.* **2** [T] ~ **sth (to sb)** to officially arrange for sth to belong to, or be controlled by, sb else: *She transferred the property to her son.*

▶ **transferable** *adj.*: *This ticket is not transferable* (= may only be used by the person who bought it).

transfer² ̌ **B2** ◉ /ˈtrænsfɜː(r)/ *noun* **1** [U, C] the act of moving or being moved from one place, job or state to another: *Paul is not happy here and has asked for a transfer.* **2** [U, C] the act of changing to a different vehicle or route during a journey: *The travel company will arrange airport transfers.* **3** [C] (*AmE*) a ticket that allows you to continue your journey on another bus or train **4** [C] (*especially BrE*) a piece of paper with a picture or writing on it that you can stick onto another surface by pressing or heating it

transference /ˈtrænsfərəns/ *noun* [U] the process of moving sth from one place, person or use to another: *the transference of heat from the liquid to the container*

transfigure /trænsˈfɪɡə(r)/ *verb* [T, often passive] (*formal*) to change the appearance of a person or thing so that they look more beautiful

transform ̌ **B2** ◍ /trænsˈfɔːm/ *verb* [T, I] ~ **(sb/sth) (from sth) (into sth)** to change sb/sth completely, especially in a way that improves sb/sth: *It has been transformed from a mining village to a skiing resort.* ◇ *Having a baby has transformed my life.* ◇ *The electric power industry is transforming.*
▶ **transformation** ̌+ **C1** ◍ /ˌtrænsfəˈmeɪʃn/ *noun* [C, U]

transformer /trænsˈfɔːmə(r)/ *noun* [C] (**PHYSICS**) a device for reducing or increasing the VOLTAGE (= strength) of a supply of electricity, usually to allow a particular piece of electrical equipment to be used ➔ picture at **generator**

transfusion /trænsˈfjuːʒn/ *noun* [C] (**MEDICINE**) the act of putting new blood into a person or an animal's body because they are ill: *a blood transfusion*

transgender /trænzˈdʒendə(r)/ (*also* **trans**) *adj.* (**SOCIAL STUDIES**) describing or connected with people who feel that their GENDER IDENTITY is different from their BIOLOGICAL sex: *the transgender community*

transgenic /ˌtrænzˈdʒenɪk/ *adj.* (**BIOLOGY**) (used about a plant or an animal) having GENETIC material introduced from another type of plant or animal: *transgenic crops* **SYN** **genetically modified**

transient /ˈtrænziənt/ *adj.* (*formal*) **1** continuing for only a short time: *the transient nature of speech* **SYN** **temporary 2** staying or working in a place for only a short time, before moving on: *a city with a large transient population* (= of students, temporary workers, etc.)

transistor /trænˈzɪstə(r)/ *noun* [C] (**ENGINEERING**) a small piece of electronic equipment that is used in computers, radios, televisions, etc.

transit ̌+ **C1** /ˈtrænzɪt/ *noun* **1** [U] the act of being moved or carried from one place to another: *The goods had been damaged in transit.* **2** [U, C, usually sing.] (**TOURISM**) the act of going through a place on the way to somewhere else: *the transit lounge at Singapore airport* ◇ *a transit visa* (= permission to pass through a country but not to stay there)

transition ̌ **B2** ◍ /trænˈzɪʃn/ *noun* [U, C] ~ **(from sth) (to sth)** a change from one state or form to another: *the transition from childhood to adolescence*
▶ **transitional** /-ʃənl/ *adj.*: *a transitional stage/period*

transition metal (*also* **transition element**) *noun* [C] (**CHEMISTRY**) one of the group of metals in the centre of THE PERIODIC TABLE (= a list of all the chemical elements). Transition metals are heavy, they melt only at high temperatures, they form coloured COMPOUNDS, they can combine with another element to form more than one COMPOUND and they often act as a CATALYST (= a substance that makes a chemical reaction happen faster).

transitive /ˈtrænzətɪv/ adj. (GRAMMAR) (used about a verb) used with a DIRECT OBJECT **OPP** **intransitive**
▸ **transitively** adv.

transitory /ˈtrænzətri/ adj. (formal) continuing for only a short time: *the transitory nature of his happiness* **SYN** **temporary**

translate ॄ **B1** /trænzˈleɪt/ verb [T, I] **1** ~ (sth) (from sth) (into sth) (LANGUAGE) to change sth written or spoken from one language to another: *This book has been translated from Czech into English.* ◌ look at **interpret** (2) ◌ note at **language** **2** ~(sth) (into sth) to change sth into a different form; to be changed into a different form: *I hope all the hard work will translate into profits.*

translation ॄ **B1** /trænzˈleɪʃn/ noun **1** [U] ~ (of sth) (into sth); ~ (from sth) (into sth) the process of changing sth that is written or spoken into another language: *an error in translation* ◊ *The systems are used for the online translation of text.* ◊ *He specializes in translation from Danish into English.* ◊ *The irony is lost in translation.* **2** [C, U] a text or word that has been changed from one language into another: *a rough translation* (= not translating everything exactly) ◊ *a literal translation* (= following the original words exactly) ◊ *I have only read Tolstoy in translation.* **3** [U] ~(of sth) into sth the process of changing sth into a different form: *the translation of theory into practice*

translator /trænzˈleɪtə(r)/ noun [C] a person who changes sth that has been written or spoken from one language to another ◌ look at **interpreter** ◌ note at **language**

translucent /trænzˈluːsnt/ adj. (formal) allowing light to pass through but not completely clear: *The sky was a pale translucent blue.* ◊ *His skin was translucent with age.* ◌ look at **opaque** (1), **transparent** ▸ **translucence** /-sns/ (also **translucency** /-snsi/) noun [U]

transmission **C1** **W** /trænzˈmɪʃn/ noun **1** [U] sending sth out or passing sth on from one person, place or thing to another: *the transmission of TV pictures by satellite* ◊ *the transmission of a disease/virus* **2** [C] (ARTS AND MEDIA) a TV or radio programme **3** [U, C] the system in a car, etc. by which power is passed from the engine to the wheels

transmit ॄ+ **B2** **W** /trænzˈmɪt/ verb [T, I] (-tt-) **1** (ARTS AND MEDIA) to send out TV or radio programmes, electronic signals, etc: *The match was transmitted live all over the world.* **2** (formal) to send or pass sth from one person or place to another: *a sexually transmitted disease*

transmitter /trænzˈmɪtə(r)/ noun [C] (ENGINEERING) a piece of equipment that sends out electronic signals, TV or radio programmes, etc.

transparency ॄ+ **C1** /trænsˈpærənsi/ noun [U] **1** the quality of sth, such as a situation or an argument, that makes it easy to understand: *They are demanding increased transparency about how public money is spent.* **2** the quality of something, such as glass, that allows you to see through it

transparent ॄ+ **C1** /trænsˈpærənt/ adj. that you can see through: *Glass is transparent.* **OPP** **opaque** ◌ look at **translucent**

transpiration /ˌtrænspɪˈreɪʃn/ noun [U] (BIOLOGY) the process of water passing out from the surface of a plant or leaf ◌ picture at **water cycle**

transpire /trænˈspaɪə(r)/ verb [I] **1** (not usually used in the progressive tenses) to become known; to be shown to be true: *It transpired that the gang had had a contact inside the bank.* ◊ *This story, it later transpired, was untrue.* **2** to happen: *You're meeting him tomorrow? Let me know what transpires.*

3 (BIOLOGY) when plants or leaves **transpire**, water passes out from their surface

transplant¹ /trænsˈplɑːnt/ verb [T] **1** (MEDICINE) to take out an organ or other part of sb's body and put it into another person's body **2** to move a growing plant and plant it somewhere else ◌ look at **graft** (1)

transplant² /ˈtrænsplɑːnt/ noun [C] (MEDICINE) a medical operation in which an organ, etc. is taken out of sb's body and put into another person's body: *to have a heart/liver/kidney transplant*

transport ॄ **A2** **W** /ˈtrænspɔːt/ noun [U] **1** (especially BrE) (AmE usually **transportation**) a system for carrying or taking people or goods from one place to another: *road/rail/sea transport* **2** (BrE) (AmE **transportation**) a vehicle or a method of travel: *Do you have your own transport* (= for example a car)? ◊ *I travel to school by public transport.* ◊ *His bike is his only means of transport.* **3** (especially BrE) (also **transportation** AmE, BrE) the activity or business of taking goods from one place to another using lorries, trains, etc.
▸ **transport** ॄ **B1** **W** /trænˈspɔːt/ verb [T]

transportation ॄ+ **B2** **W** /ˌtrænspɔːˈteɪʃn/ **1** (especially AmE) = TRANSPORT (1) **2** (AmE) = TRANSPORT (2) **3** = TRANSPORT (3)

transporter /trænˈspɔːtə(r)/ noun [C] a large vehicle used for carrying heavy objects, for example other vehicles: *a car transporter* ◌ picture at **vehicle**

transpose /trænˈspəʊz/ verb [T, often passive] **1** (formal) to change the order of two or more things **SYN** **reverse¹** **2** ~ sth (from sth) (to sth) (formal) to move or change sth to a different place or environment or into a different form: *The director transposes Shakespeare's play from sixteenth-century Italy to modern England.* **SYN** **transfer¹** **3** ~ sth (from sth) (to sth) (MUSIC) to write or play a piece of music or a series of notes in a different key ▸ **transposition** /ˌtrænspəˈzɪʃn/ noun [C, U]

transsexual (also **transexual**) /trænzˈsekʃuəl/ noun [C] a person whose sense of GENDER IDENTITY does not match their BIOLOGICAL sex, especially one who has a medical operation to change their sex organs
▸ **transsexual** (also **transexual**) (also **trans**) adj.

transverse /ˈtrænzvɜːs/ adj. located across sth: *A transverse bar joins the two posts.*

transverse ˈwave noun [C] (PHYSICS) a wave that VIBRATES (= makes very small, fast movements from side to side) at an angle of 90° to the direction that it is moving in ◌ look at **longitudinal wave**

transvestite /trænzˈvestaɪt/ noun [C] a person, especially a man, who wears clothes that are usually worn by a member of the opposite sex

trap¹ ॄ+ **B2** /træp/ noun [C] **1** a piece of equipment that you use for catching animals: *a mousetrap* ◊ *The rabbit's leg was caught in the trap.* **2** a clever plan that is designed to trick sb **3** an unpleasant situation from which it is hard to escape ◌ look at **death trap**

trap² ॄ+ **B2** /træp/ verb [T] (-pp-) **1** (usually passive) to keep sb in a dangerous place or a bad situation from which they cannot escape: *The door closed behind them and they were trapped.* ◊ *Many people are trapped in low-paid jobs.* **2** to force sb/sth into a place or situation from which they or it cannot escape: *Police believe this new evidence could help trap the killer.* **3** to catch an animal, etc. in a TRAP **4** to catch and keep or store sth: *Special glass panels trap heat from the sun.* **5** ~ sb (into sth/doing sth) to make sb do sth by tricking them: *She had been trapped into revealing her true identity.*

trapdoor /ˈtræpdɔː(r)/ noun [C] a small door in a floor or ceiling

trapeze /trəˈpiːz/ *noun* [C] a wooden or metal bar hanging from two ropes high above the ground, used by ACROBATS (= people who entertain an audience by performing difficult acts)

trapezium (*BrE*)
(*AmE* trapezoid)

trapezoid (*BrE*)
(*AmE* trapezium)

trapezium /trəˈpiːziəm/ *noun* [C] (**GEOMETRY**) **1** (*BrE*) (*AmE* **trapezoid**) a flat shape with four straight sides, one pair of opposite sides being PARALLEL and the other pair not PARALLEL **2** (*AmE*) = TRAPEZOID (1)

trapezoid /ˈtræpəzɔɪd/ *noun* [C] (**GEOMETRY**) **1** (*BrE*) (*AmE* **trapezium**) a flat shape with four straight sides, none of which are PARALLEL **2** (*AmE*) = TRAPEZIUM (1)
▸ **trapezoidal** /ˌtræpɪˈzɔɪdəl/ *adj.*: *a trapezoidal window*

trappings /ˈtræpɪŋz/ *noun* [pl.] clothes, possessions, etc. that are signs of a particular social position

trash /træʃ/ (*AmE*) = RUBBISH

ˈtrash can (*AmE*) = LITTER BIN

trashy /ˈtræʃi/ *adj.* (**trashier; trashiest**) of poor quality: *trashy novels*

trauma ʔ+ **C1** /ˈtrɔːmə/ *noun* [C, U] (an event that causes) a state of shock or the feeling of being very sad: *the trauma of losing your parents* ⊃ look at **stress¹** (1) ▸ **traumatic** /trɔːˈmætɪk/ *adj.*

traumatize (*BrE* also **-ise**) /ˈtrɔːmətaɪz/ *verb* [T, usually passive] to shock and upset sb very much, often making them unable to think or work normally

travel¹ ʔ **A1** /ˈtrævl/ *verb* (**-ll-,** *AmE* **-l-**) **1** [I] to go from one place to another, especially over a long distance: *Charles travels a lot on business.* ◇ *to travel abroad* ◇ *to travel by sea/air/car* ◇ *to travel to work* **2** [I] to go or move at/in a particular speed, direction or distance **3** [T] to make a journey of a particular distance: *They travelled 60 kilometres to come and see us.*
IDM **travel light** to take very few things with you when you travel

travel² ʔ **A1** /ˈtrævl/ *noun* **1** [U] the act of going from one place to another: *air/rail/space travel* ◇ *a travel bag/clock/iron* (= designed to be used when travelling) **2** **travels** [pl.] time spent travelling, especially to places that are far away

ˈtravel agency *noun* [C] (*pl.* **-ies**) (**TOURISM**) a company that makes travel arrangements for people (booking tickets, flights, hotels, etc.)

ˈtravel agent *noun* [C] (**TOURISM**) **1** a person whose job is to make travel arrangements for people **2** **travel agent's** (*pl.* **travel agents**) the shop where you can go to make travel arrangements, buy tickets, etc.

traveller ʔ **A2** (*BrE*) (*AmE* **traveler**) /ˈtrævələ(r)/ *noun* [C] **1** (**TOURISM**) a person who is travelling or who often travels **2** (*BrE*) a person who travels around the country in a large vehicle and does not have a permanent home anywhere ⊃ look at **Gypsy**

ˈtravel-sick *adj.* (**HEALTH**) feeling sick or VOMITING because of the movement of the vehicle you are travelling in ⊃ look at **airsick, carsick, seasick**

trawl¹ /trɔːl/ *verb* [I, T] **1** ~ **(through sth) (for sth/sb);** ~ **sth (for sth/sb)** to search through a large amount of information or a large number of people, places, etc. looking for a particular thing or person: *The police*

Travel is an uncountable word and you can only use it to talk about the general activity of moving from place to place: *Foreign travel is very popular these days.* When you talk about going from one particular place to another, you use **journey**. A journey can be long: *the journey across Canada,* or short, but repeated: *the journey to work.* A **tour** is a circular journey or walk during which you visit several places. You may **go on a tour** round a country, city, place of interest, etc: *a three-week tour around Italy* ◇ *a guided tour of the castle.* You often use **trip** when you are thinking about the whole visit (including your stay in a place and the journeys there and back): *They're just back from a trip to Japan. They had a wonderful time.* (**but**: *'How was the journey back?' 'Awful — the plane was delayed!'*) A trip may be short: *a day trip,* or longer: *a trip round the world,* and can be for business or pleasure: *How about a shopping trip to London this weekend?* ◇ *He's on a business trip to New York to meet a client.* An **excursion** is a short organized trip that you go on with a group of people: *The holiday includes a full-day excursion by coach to the capital.* You **go on** a journey/a tour/a trip/an excursion.

are trawling through their files for a similar case. ◇ *She trawled the shops for bargains.* **2** ~ **(for sth)** to fish for sth by pulling a large net with a wide opening through the water

trawl² /trɔːl/ *noun* [C] **1** a search through a large amount of information, documents, etc: *A trawl through the newspapers yielded two possible jobs.* **2** (*also* **ˈtrawl net**) a large net with a wide opening, that is pulled along the bottom of the sea by a boat in order to catch fish

trawler /ˈtrɔːlə(r)/ *noun* [C] a fishing boat that uses large nets that it pulls through the sea behind it

tray /treɪ/ *noun* [C] **1** a flat piece of wood, plastic, metal, etc. with slightly higher edges that you use for carrying food, drink, etc. on **2** a shallow plastic box, used for various purposes: *an ice tray* (= for making ice CUBES)

treacherous /ˈtretʃərəs/ *adj.* **1** (used about a person) that you cannot trust and who may do sth to harm you: *He was weak, cowardly and treacherous.* **2** dangerous, although seeming safe

treachery /ˈtretʃəri/ *noun* [U] the act of causing harm to sb who trusts you

treacle /ˈtriːkl/ (*BrE*) (*AmE* **molasses**) *noun* [U] a thick, dark, sticky liquid that is made from sugar ⊃ look at **syrup**

tread¹ /tred/ *verb* (*pt* **trod** /trɒd/; *pp* **trodden** /ˈtrɒdn/, **trod**) **1** [I] (*especially BrE*) (used with an adverb or a preposition) to put your foot down while you are walking: *Don't tread in the puddle!* ◇ *He trod on my foot and didn't even say sorry!* **2** [T] (used with an adverb or a preposition) to press down on sth with your foot: *Mud had been trodden into the carpet.*

tread² /tred/ *noun* **1** [sing.] the sound you make when you walk; the way you walk **2** [C, U] the pattern on the surface of a tyre on a vehicle, which is slightly higher than the rest of the surface

treason /ˈtriːzn/ *noun* [U] (**LAW**) the criminal act of causing harm to your country, for example by helping its enemies

treasure¹ ʔ+ **B2** /ˈtreʒə(r)/ *noun* **1** [U] a collection of very valuable objects, for example gold, silver, jewellery, etc: *to find buried treasure* **2** [C] something that is very valuable

treasure² /ˈtreʒə(r)/ *verb* [T] to consider sb/sth to be very special or valuable: *I will treasure those memories forever.*

'treasure hunt *noun* [C] a game in which people try to find a hidden prize by answering a series of questions that have been left in different places

treasurer /'treʒərə(r)/ *noun* [C] the person who looks after the money and accounts of a club or an organization

the Treasury /ðə 'treʒəri/ *noun* [sing.] (**ECONOMICS**, **POLITICS**) (in the UK, the US and some other countries) the government department that controls public money

treat¹ ⬧ **B1** ⊙ /triːt/ *verb* [T]
• BEHAVE TOWARDS SB/STH **1 ~ sb/sth (with/as/like sth)** to act or behave towards sb/sth in a particular way: *Teenagers hate being treated like children.* ◊ (*informal*) *They treat their workers like dirt* (= very badly). ◊ *You should treat older people with respect.* ◊ *to treat somebody badly/fairly/well*
• CONSIDER **2 ~ sth as sth** to consider sth in a particular way: *I decided to treat his comment as a joke.* **3** to deal with or discuss sth in a particular way: *The article treats this question in great detail.*
• GIVE MEDICAL CARE **4 ~ sb/sth (for sth)** (**MEDICINE**) to use medicine or medical care to try to make a sick or injured person well again: *The boy was treated for burns at the hospital.* ➲ note at **medical¹**
• USE A CHEMICAL **5 ~ sth (with sth)** to put a chemical substance onto sth in order to protect it from damage, clean it, etc: *Most vegetables are treated with insecticide.*
• PAY FOR STH SPECIAL **6 ~ sb/yourself (to sth)** to pay for sth or give sb/yourself sth that is very special or that they/you will enjoy: *Clare treated the children to ice creams* (= she paid for them).

treat² /triːt/ *noun* [C] something very pleasant that sb can enjoy, especially sth that you give sb or do for them: *I've brought some cream cakes as a treat.* ◊ *It's a real treat for me to stay in bed late.*
IDM **trick or treat** → TRICK¹

treatment ⬧ **B1** ⊙ /'triːtmənt/ *noun* **1** [U, C] **~ (for sth)** (**MEDICINE**) the use of medicine or medical care to cure an illness or injury; sth that is done to make sb feel and look good: *He is receiving treatment for shock.* ➲ note at **doctor¹**, **hospital**, **medical¹** **2** [U] the way that you behave towards sb or deal with sth: *The treatment of the prisoners of war was very harsh.* **3** [U, C] **~ (for sth)** a process by which sth is cleaned, protected from damage, etc.

treaty ⬧+ **C1** /'triːti/ *noun* [C] (*pl.* -ies) a written agreement between two or more countries: *to sign a peace treaty*

treble¹ /'trebl/ *verb* [I, T] (**MATHEMATICS**) to become or to make sth three times bigger: *Prices have trebled in the past ten years.* ▶ **treble** *det.*: *This figure is treble the number five years ago.*

treble² /'trebl/ *noun* (**MUSIC**) **1** [U] the high tones or part in music or a sound system: *to turn up the treble on the stereo* ➲ look at **bass** (1) **2** [C] a child's high voice; a boy who has a high singing voice ➲ look at **soprano 3** [sing.] a musical part written for a treble voice

tree ⬧ **A1** /triː/ *noun* [C] (**BIOLOGY**) a tall plant that can live for a long time. Trees have a thick wooden central part from which branches grow: *an oak/apple/elm tree*

'tree house *noun* [C] a structure built on the branches of a tree, usually for children to play on

treeline /'triːlaɪn/ *noun* [sing.] (**GEOGRAPHY**) the level of land, for example on a mountain, above which trees will not grow

trek /trek/ *noun* [C] **1** a long hard walk, lasting several days or weeks, usually in the mountains **2** (*informal*) a long walk: *It's quite a trek to the shops.* ▶ **trek** *verb* [I] (-kk-)

trellis /'trelɪs/ *noun* [C, U] a light frame made of long thin pieces of wood that cross each other, used to support climbing plants

tremble /'trembl/ *verb* [I] **~ (with sth)** to shake, for example because you are cold, frightened, etc: *She was pale and trembling with shock.* ◊ *His hand was trembling as he picked up his pen to sign.* ▶ **tremble** *noun* [C, usually sing.]

tremendous ⬧+ **C1** /trə'mendəs/ *adj.* **1** very large or great: *a tremendous amount of work* **SYN** **huge** **2** very good: *It was a tremendous experience.* **SYN** **great¹**

tremendously /trə'mendəsli/ *adv.* very; very much: *tremendously exciting* ◊ *Prices vary tremendously from one shop to another.*

tremolo /'tremələʊ/ *noun* [C] (*pl.* -os) (**MUSIC**) a special effect in singing or playing a musical instrument made by repeating the same note or two notes very quickly

tremor /'tremə(r)/ *noun* [C] (**GEOLOGY**) a slight shaking movement: *an earth tremor* (= a small earthquake) ◊ *There was a tremor in his voice.*

trench /trentʃ/ *noun* [C] **1** a long narrow hole dug in the ground for water to flow along **2** a long deep hole dug in the ground for soldiers to hide in during enemy attacks **3** (*also* **ocean trench**) (**GEOLOGY**) a long deep narrow hole in the ocean floor ➲ picture at **plate tectonics**

'trench coat *noun* [C] a long loose coat, worn especially to keep off rain, with a belt and pockets in the style of a military coat

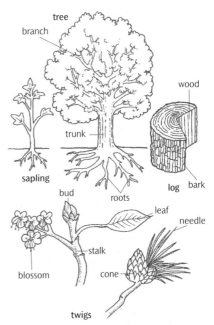

tree
branch
wood
trunk
sapling
bud
log bark
roots
leaf
needle
stalk
blossom
cone
twigs

trend¹ ⟨B1⟩ ⊙ /trend/ *noun* [C] ~ **(towards sth)** a general change or development: *The current trend is towards smaller families.* ◇ *He always followed the latest trends in fashion.*
IDM **set a/the trend** to start a new style or fashion

▼ COLLOCATIONS

trend

An amount can **be down/up (at)** or **be/remain unchanged (at)**: *The share price is down at 234p.* ◇ *The FT index was up 18.84 points.* ◇ *The 100 Share Index remained unchanged at 5297.* Something can **stand at** or **reach** a figure or an amount: *Second quarter sales stood at €18 billion.* ◇ *Customer confidence reached a 30-year high.* A share can **gain** or **lose** an amount: *The shares gained 19 cents to close at $4.38.* Markets, shares, profits, etc. **suffer** when there are economic problems: *Profit margins suffered when prices were lowered.* When amounts are **going up** they **climb**, **increase** or **rise**. When they go up suddenly, they **jump**, **rocket**, **shoot up** or **soar**: *Earnings per share climbed from 3.5p to 5.1p.* ◇ *The pound increased in value relative to the euro.* ◇ *Profits shot up by a staggering 25%.* ◇ *Oil prices have rocketed.* When amounts are **going down** they **decline**, **drop** or **fall**. When they go down suddenly, they **crash**, **plummet**, **plunge** or **slump**: *Banana exports crashed nearly 50%.* ◇ *The pound fell to a 14-year low against the dollar.* ◇ *Net income plummeted to USD 3.7 million.* ◇ *Sales have slumped by over 50%.*

---

trend² /trend/ **be trending** *verb* [I] (**COMPUTING**) to become a popular subject that is being discussed a lot on SOCIAL MEDIA: *What's trending on Twitter this morning?*

trending /ˈtrendɪŋ/ *adj.* being discussed a lot on SOCIAL MEDIA: *It's in the top ten trending topics on Twitter right now.*

trendy /ˈtrendi/ *adj.* (**trendier**; **trendiest**) (*informal*) fashionable

trespass /ˈtrespəs/ *verb* [I] to go onto sb's land or property without permission ▶ **trespasser** *noun* [C]

tri- /traɪ/ *prefix* (in nouns and adjectives) three; having three: *tricycle* ◇ *triangular*

trial ⟨B2⟩ /ˈtraɪəl/ *noun* [U, C] **1** (**LAW**) the process in court where a judge, and often a JURY (= members of the public), examine evidence and decide if sb is guilty of a crime or not: *He was on trial for murder.* ◇ *a fair trial* ⊃ note at **court¹**, **crime 2** an act of testing sb/sth: *New drugs must go through extensive trials.* ◇ *a trial period of three months*
IDM **trial and error** trying different ways of doing sth until you find the best one

trial 'run *noun* [C] an occasion when you practise doing sth in order to make sure you can do it correctly later

triangle /ˈtraɪæŋgl/ *noun* [C] **1** (**GEOMETRY**) a shape that has three straight sides: *a right-angled triangle* **2** (*AmE*) = SET SQUARE **3** (**MUSIC**) a metal musical instrument in the shape of a triangle that you play by hitting it with a metal stick ⊃ picture at **instrument**, **orchestra**

triangular /traɪˈæŋgjələ(r)/ *adj.* shaped like a TRIANGLE (= a shape with three straight sides)

triathlon /traɪˈæθlən/ *noun* [C] (**SPORT**) a sporting event in which people compete in three different sports, usually swimming, cycling and running ⊃ look at **biathlon**, **decathlon**, **pentathlon**

tribe ⟨B2⟩ /traɪb/ *noun* [C] (**SOCIAL STUDIES**) a group of people who have the same language and customs and who live in a particular area, often with one of the group as an official leader: *tribes living in the*

Amazonian rainforest ▶ **tribal** ⟨C1⟩ /ˈtraɪbl/ *adj.*: *tribal art*

tribulation /ˌtrɪbjuˈleɪʃn/ *noun* [C, U] (*formal*) great trouble or suffering: *the tribulations of modern life*

tribunal ⟨C1⟩ /traɪˈbjuːnl/ *noun* [C + sing./pl. verb] (**LAW**) a type of court with the authority to decide who is right in particular types of problem or situations where people disagree: *He is entitled to a review of his case by an impartial tribunal.*

tributary /ˈtrɪbjətri/ *noun* [C] (*pl.* -ies) (**GEOGRAPHY**) a small river that flows into a larger river

tribute ⟨C1⟩ /ˈtrɪbjuːt/ *noun* **1** [U, C] ~ **(to sb/sth)** something that you say or do to show that you respect or admire sb/sth, especially sb who has died: *At the funeral, her friends paid tribute to her life.* ◇ *A special concert was held as a tribute to the composer.* **2** [sing.] ~ **to sb/sth** a sign of how good sb/sth is: *The success of the festival is a tribute to the organizers.*

triceps /ˈtraɪseps/ *noun* [C] (*pl.* **triceps**) (**ANATOMY**) the large muscle at the back of the top part of the arm ⊃ look at **biceps** ⊃ picture at **arm¹**

trick¹ ⟨B1⟩ /trɪk/ *noun* [C] **1** something that you do to make sb believe sth that is not true or a joke that you play to annoy sb: *The thieves used a trick to get past the security guards.* **2** something that confuses you so that you see, remember, understand, etc. things in the wrong way: *It was a trick question* (= one in which the answer looks easy, but actually is not) **3** an action that uses special skills to make people believe sth which is not true or real as a form of entertainment: *to perform a magic trick* ◇ *a card trick* **4** [usually sing.] a clever or the best way of doing sth
IDM **do the job/trick** → JOB **play a joke/trick on sb** → JOKE¹ **trick or treat** a custom in which children dress up as witches, etc. and go to people's houses on Halloween (= the evening of October 31st) They say 'Trick or treat' and the people given them sweets: *to go trick or treating*

trick² ⟨B1⟩ /trɪk/ *verb* [T] to make sb believe sth that is not true: *I'd been tricked and I felt like a fool.*
SYN **deceive**
PHRV **trick sb into sth/doing sth** to persuade sb to do sth by making them believe sth that is not true: *He tricked me into lending him money.* **trick sb out of sth** to get sth from sb by making them believe sth that is not true: *Stella was tricked out of her share of the money.*

trickery /ˈtrɪkəri/ *noun* [U] the use of dishonest methods to trick sb in order to get what you want

triangles

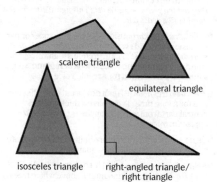

scalene triangle

equilateral triangle

isosceles triangle

right-angled triangle/
right triangle

trickle /ˈtrɪkl/ *verb* [I, T] **1** (used about a liquid) to flow in a thin line; to make sth flow in a thin line: *Raindrops trickled down the window.* **2** to go somewhere slowly and gradually; to make sth go somewhere slowly and gradually: *People began trickling into the hall.*
▸ **trickle** *noun* [C, usually sing.]: *a trickle of water*

tricky /ˈtrɪki/ *adj.* (**trickier**; **trickiest**) difficult to do or deal with: *a tricky situation*

tricycle /ˈtraɪsɪkl/ *noun* [C] a bicycle that has one wheel at the front and two at the back

trident /ˈtraɪdnt/ *noun* [C] a weapon used in the past that looks like a long fork with three points

trifle[1] /ˈtraɪfl/ *noun* **1** [C, U] (*BrE*) a type of cold DESSERT (= a sweet food) made from cake and fruit covered with CUSTARD (= a sweet yellow sauce) and cream **2** a trifle [sing.] (*formal*) (used as an adverb) slightly; rather **3** [C] (*formal*) something that is of little value or importance

trifle[2] /ˈtraɪfl/ *verb*
PHR V **trifle with sb/sth** (*formal*) to treat sb/sth without real respect: *He is not a person to be trifled with.*

trifling /ˈtraɪflɪŋ/ *adj.* very small or unimportant
SYN **trivial**

trigger[1] ʔ+ **C1** /ˈtrɪɡə(r)/ *noun* [C] **1** the part of a gun that you press to fire it: *to pull the trigger* **2** the cause of a particular reaction or event, especially a bad one **3** (**PSYCHOLOGY**) something that causes sb to feel anxious and upset, because it makes them remember a bad experience from the past

trigger[2] ʔ+ **B2** /ˈtrɪɡə(r)/ *verb* [T] **1** ~ **sth (off)** to make sth happen suddenly; to make a device start working: *The nuts in the salad triggered an allergic reaction.* ◇ *Smoke from the kitchen triggered off the fire alarm.* **2** (**PSYCHOLOGY**) to make sb upset or anxious, especially because they are made to remember a very bad experience they have had

trigonometry /ˌtrɪɡəˈnɒmətri/ *noun* [U] (**MATHEMATICS**) the type of mathematics that deals with the relationship between the sides and angles of TRIANGLES (= shapes with three straight sides)
▸ **trigonometric** /ˌtrɪɡənəˈmetrɪk/ *adj.* ▸ **trigonometrical** /-trɪkl/ *adj.*

trill /trɪl/ *noun* [C] (**MUSIC**) the sound made when two notes next to each other in the musical SCALE are played or sung quickly several times one after the other

trillion ʔ+ **B2** /ˈtrɪljən/ *number* one million million ❶ For more information about numbers look at the **Reference Section** of this dictionary.

trilogy /ˈtrɪlədʒi/ *noun* [C] (*pl.* -ies) (**ARTS AND MEDIA, LITERATURE**) a group of three novels, plays, films, etc. that form a set

trim[1] /trɪm/ *verb* [T] (-mm-) **1** to cut a small amount off sth so that it is tidy: *to trim your hair/fringe/beard* ◇ *The hedge needs trimming.* **2** ~ **sth (off sth)** to cut sth off because you do not need it: *Trim the fat off the meat.* **3** ~ **sth (with sth)** to decorate the edge of sth with sth ▸ **trim** *noun* [C, usually sing.]: *My hair needs a trim.*

trim[2] /trɪm/ *adj.* **1** (used about a person) looking thin, healthy and attractive **2** well cared for; tidy

trimester /traɪˈmestə(r)/ *noun* [C] **1** (**MEDICINE**) a period of three months during the time when a woman is pregnant: *the first trimester of pregnancy* **2** (*AmE*) = TERM[1] (2): *The school year is divided into three trimesters.*

trimming /ˈtrɪmɪŋ/ *noun* **1** trimmings [pl.] extra things that you add to sth to improve its appearance, taste, etc. **2** [U, C, usually pl.] material that you use for decorating the edge of sth

the Trinity /ðə ˈtrɪnəti/ *noun* [sing.] (**RELIGION**) (in Christianity) the union of Father, Son and Holy Spirit as one God

trinket /ˈtrɪŋkɪt/ *noun* [C] a piece of jewellery or an attractive small object that is not worth much money

trio ʔ+ **C1** /ˈtriːəʊ/ *noun* [C] (*pl.* -os) (**MUSIC**) **1** [+ sing./pl. verb] a group of three people **2** [+ sing./pl. verb] a group of three people who play music or sing together **3** a piece of music for three people to play or sing

trip[1] ʔ **A1** /trɪp/ *noun* [C] a journey to a place and back again, either for pleasure or for a particular purpose: *How was your trip to Turkey?* ◇ *We had to make several trips to move all the furniture.* ◇ *to go on a business/shopping trip* ➔ note at **travel**[2]

trip[2] ʔ **B2** /trɪp/ *verb* (-pp-) **1** [I] ~ **(over/up)**; ~ **(over/on sth)** to catch your foot on sth when you are walking, and fall or nearly fall: *Don't leave your bag on the floor. Somebody might trip over it.* ◇ *She tripped up on a loose paving stone.* **2** [T] ~ **sb (up)** to catch sb's foot and make them fall or nearly fall: *Linda stuck out her foot and tripped Barry up.*
PHR V **trip (sb) up** to make a mistake; to make sb say sth that they did not want to say: *The journalist asked a difficult question to try to trip the politician up.*

tripartite /traɪˈpɑːtaɪt/ *adj.* (*formal*) having three parts or involving three people, groups, etc: *tripartite discussions*

tripe /traɪp/ *noun* [U] **1** the LINING (= inside part) of a cow's or pig's stomach, which some people eat **2** (*informal*) something that sb says or writes that you think is NONSENSE or not of good quality

triple /ˈtrɪpl/ *adj.* [only before noun] having three parts, happening three times or containing three times as much as usual: *You'll receive triple pay if you work over the New Year.* ▸ **triple** *verb* [I, T]

the ˈtriple jump *noun* [sing.] (**SPORT**) a sporting event in which people try to jump as far forward as possible with three jumps. The first jump lands on one foot, the second on the other, and the third on both feet.

triplet /ˈtrɪplət/ *noun* [C] one of three children or animals that are born to one mother at the same time ➔ look at **twin**

triplicate /ˈtrɪplɪkət/ *noun*
IDM **in triplicate** **1** done three times: *Each sample was tested in triplicate.* **2** with three copies (for example of an official piece of paper) that are exactly the same: *Fill out the forms in triplicate.* ➔ look at **duplicate**[1]

tripod /ˈtraɪpɒd/ *noun* [C] a piece of equipment with three legs that you use for putting a camera, etc. on ➔ picture at **laboratory**

tripper /ˈtrɪpə(r)/ *noun* [C] (*BrE*) (**TOURISM**) a person who is visiting a place for a short time for pleasure: *a day tripper*

triptych /ˈtrɪptɪk/ *noun* [C] (**ART**) a picture that is painted or CARVED (= cut) on three pieces of wood placed side by side, especially one over an ALTAR (= the high table at the centre of a religious ceremony) in a church

triumph[1] ʔ+ **C1** /ˈtraɪʌmf/ *noun* [C, U] a great success or victory; the feeling of happiness that you have because of this: *The new programme was a triumph with the public.* ◇ *The team returned home in triumph.*

triumph[2] /ˈtraɪʌmf/ *verb* [I] ~ **(over sb/sth)** to achieve success; to defeat sb/sth: *France triumphed over Brazil in the final.*

triumphal /traɪˈʌmfl/ *adj.* done or made in order to celebrate a great success or victory

triumphant /traɪˈʌmfənt/ *adj.* feeling or showing great happiness because you have won or succeeded at sth ▶ **triumphantly** *adv.*

trivial /ˈtrɪviəl/ *adj.* of little importance; not worth considering: *a trivial detail/problem* ▶ **triviality** /ˌtrɪviˈæləti/ *noun* [C, U] (*pl.* -ies)

trivialize (*BrE also* -ise) /ˈtrɪviəlaɪz/ *verb* [T] to make sth seem less important, serious, etc. than it really is

trod /trɒd/ past tense of **tread**[1]

trodden /ˈtrɒdn/ past participle of **tread**[1]

troll /trɒl, trəʊl/ *noun* [C] (*informal*) a message to a discussion group on the internet that sb sends to make other people angry; a person who sends a message like this

trolley /ˈtrɒli/ *noun* [C] **1** (*AmE* **cart**) a piece of equipment on wheels that you use for carrying things: *a supermarket/shopping/luggage trolley* **2** (*AmE*) = **TRAM 3** (*BrE*) a small table with wheels that is used for carrying or serving food and drinks: *a tea/sweet/drinks trolley*

trombone /trɒmˈbəʊn/ *noun* [C] (**MUSIC**) a large musical instrument made of BRASS (= a yellow metal) that you play by blowing into it and moving a long tube backwards and forwards ⊃ picture at **instrument**, **orchestra**

troop 🔑+ B2 /truːp/ *noun* **1 troops** [pl.] soldiers **2** [C] a large group of people or animals ▶ **troop** *verb* [I] (used with an adverb or a preposition): *When the bell rang everyone trooped into the hall.*

trope /trəʊp/ *noun* [C] (**LITERATURE**) a word or phrase that is used in a way that is different from its usual meaning in order to create a particular mental image or effect. METAPHORS and SIMILES are tropes.

trophic level /ˌtrəʊfɪk ˈlevl, ˌtrɒf-/ *noun* [C] (**ENVIRONMENT**) each of several levels in an ECOSYSTEM (= all the plants and animals in a particular area and their relationship with their environment). Each level consists of living creatures that share the same function in the FOOD CHAIN and get their food from the same source. ⊃ picture at **food chain**

trophy 🔑+ C1 /ˈtrəʊfi/ *noun* [C] (*pl.* -ies) an object such as a large silver cup that you get for winning a competition or race

tropic /ˈtrɒpɪk/ *noun* (**GEOGRAPHY**) **1** [C, usually sing.] one of the two imaginary lines around the earth that are 23° 26′ north and south of the EQUATOR. The lines are called the Tropic of Cancer (= north) and the Tropic of Capricorn (= south). ⊃ picture at **earth**[1] **2 the tropics** [pl.] the part of the world that is between these two lines, where the climate is hot and wet

tropical 🔑 B2 /ˈtrɒpɪkl/ *adj.* (**GEOGRAPHY**) coming from, found in or typical of the parts of the world where the climate is hot and wet: *tropical fruit/fish* ◇ *a tropical island* ⊃ picture at **ecosystem**

tropism /ˈtrəʊpɪzəm, ˈtrɒp-/ *noun* [U] (**BIOLOGY**) the action of a living thing turning all or part of itself in a particular direction, towards or away from sth such as a source of light

the troposphere /ðə ˈtrɒpəsfɪə(r)/ *noun* [sing.] (**ASTRONOMY, GEOGRAPHY**) the lowest layer of the earth's atmosphere, between the surface of the earth and about 6 to 10 kilometres above the surface ⊃ picture at **atmosphere**

trot[1] /trɒt/ *verb* [I] (-tt-) **1** (used about a horse and its rider) to move forward at a speed that is faster than a walk ⊃ look at **canter**, **gallop 2** (used about a person or an animal) to walk fast, taking short quick steps

PHR V **trot sth out** (*informal*) to repeat an old idea rather than thinking of sth new to say: *to trot out the same old story*

trot[2] /trɒt/ *noun* [sing.] a speed that is faster than a walk **IDM** **on the trot** (*BrE*, *informal*) one after another; without stopping: *We worked for six hours on the trot.*

trotter /ˈtrɒtə(r)/ *noun* [C] a pig's foot

trouble[1] 🔑 A2 /ˈtrʌbl/ *noun* **1** [U, C] ~ **(with sb/sth)** a problem, difficulty or worry, or a situation causing this: *If I don't get home by eleven o'clock I'll be in trouble.* ◇ *I'm having trouble getting the car started.* ◇ *I'm having trouble with my car.* ◇ *financial troubles* ◇ *Marie is clever. The trouble is she's very lazy.* **2** [C, U] a situation where people are fighting or arguing with each other: *There's often trouble in town on Saturday night after the bars have closed.* **3** [U] illness or pain: *back/heart trouble* **4** [U] extra work or effort: *Let's eat out tonight. It will save you the trouble of cooking.* ◇ *Why don't you stay the night with us? It's no trouble.* ◇ *I'm sorry to put you to so much trouble.* **SYN** **bother**[2]

IDM **ask for trouble** → **ASK get into trouble** to get into a situation which is dangerous or in which you may be punished **go to a lot of trouble (to do sth)** to put a lot of work or effort into sth: *They went to a lot of trouble to make us feel welcome.* **take trouble over/with sth** | **take trouble to do sth/doing sth** to do sth with care **take the trouble to do sth** to do sth even though it means extra work or effort

trouble[2] B2 /ˈtrʌbl/ *verb* [T] **1** to make sb worried, upset, etc: *Is there something troubling you?* **2** ~ **sb (for sth)** (*formal*) (often used in polite requests) to interrupt sb because you want to ask them sth: *Sorry to trouble you, but would you mind answering a few questions?* **SYN** **bother**[1]

troubled 🔑+ C1 /ˈtrʌbld/ *adj.* **1** (used about a person) worried: *a troubled expression* **2** (used about a place, situation or time) having a lot of problems: *a troubled relationship*

troublemaker /ˈtrʌblmeɪkə(r)/ *noun* [C] a person who often deliberately causes trouble

troubleshoot /ˈtrʌblʃuːt/ *verb* [I, T] **1** (**BUSINESS**) to solve problems for an organization **2** to analyse and solve serious problems for a company or other organization **3** to identify and correct faults in a computer system **4** to find and correct faults in an electronic system or a machine

troubleshooter /ˈtrʌblʃuːtə(r)/ *noun* [C] (**BUSINESS**) a person who helps to solve problems in a company or an organization ▶ **troubleshooting** *noun* [U]

troublesome /ˈtrʌblsəm/ *adj.* causing trouble, pain, etc. over a long period of time **SYN** **annoying**

trough /trɒf/ *noun* [C] **1** (**AGRICULTURE**) a long narrow container from which farm animals eat or drink **2** (**GEOGRAPHY**) a low area or point between two higher areas ⊃ picture at **wave**[1]

troupe /truːp/ *noun* [C + sing./pl. verb] (**ARTS AND MEDIA**) a group of actors, singers, etc. who work together

trousers 🔑 A1 /ˈtraʊzəz/ (*especially BrE*) (*AmE usually* **pants**) *noun* [pl.] a piece of clothing that covers the lower body and is divided into two parts to cover each leg separately

trout /traʊt/ *noun* [C, U] (*pl.* trout) a common FRESHWATER fish that is used for food ⊃ picture at **animal**

trowel /ˈtraʊəl/ *noun* [C] **1** a small garden tool used for lifting plants, digging small holes, etc. ⊃ picture at **gardening 2** a small tool with a short handle and a flat metal part, used in building for spreading CEMENT, etc.

truant /'truːənt/ *noun* [C] (**LAW**) a child who stays away from school without permission ▶ truancy /-ənsi/ *noun* [U] ▶ truant *verb* [I]: *A number of pupils have been truanting regularly.*
IDM play truant (*BrE*) to stay away from school without permission

truce /truːs/ *noun* [C] an agreement to stop fighting for a period of time ⊃ look at ceasefire

truck ⚡**A2** /trʌk/ *noun* [C] **1** (*especially AmE*) = LORRY: *a truck driver* **2** (*BrE*) a section of a train that is used for carrying goods or animals: *a cattle truck*

'truck farming (*AmE*) = MARKET GARDENING

trudge /trʌdʒ/ *verb* [I] to walk with slow, heavy steps, for example because you are very tired

true ⚡**A1** ⓢ /truː/ *adj.*
1 right or correct: *Is it true that Adam is leaving? ◇ Read the statements and decide if they are true or false.* **OPP** false, untrue **2** real or exact, often when this is different from how sth seems: *The novel was based on a true story.* **OPP** false **3** having all the typical qualities of the thing mentioned: *How do you know when you have found true love?* **4** ~ (**to sb/sth**) behaving as expected or as promised: *He was true to his word* (= he did what he had promised). *◇ She has been a true friend to me.* ⊃ *noun* truth
IDM come true to happen in the way you hoped or dreamed: *My dream has come true!* too good to be true used to say that you cannot believe that sth is as good as it seems true to form typical; as usual true to life (used about a book, film, etc.) seeming real rather than invented: *I didn't think the film was at all true to life.*

WORD FAMILY
true *adj.* (≠untrue)
truth *noun* (≠untruth)
truthful *adj.* (≠untruthful)
truly *adv.*

▼ SYNONYMS

true

right ◆ correct ◆ exact ◆ precise ◆ accurate
These words all describe sth that cannot be doubted as fact and includes no mistakes.
true *All the rumours turned out to be true.*
right *That is the right answer.*
correct *Check that the details are correct.*
exact *The police need an exact description of the man.*
precise *Give precise details.*
accurate *Accurate records must be kept.*

true-'life *adj.* (**LITERATURE**) a **true-life** story is one that actually happened rather than one that has been invented

true 'north *noun* [U] (**GEOGRAPHY**) north according to the earth's AXIS (= an imagined line that goes through the earth's centre from north to south) ⊃ look at magnetic north

truly ⚡**B2** /'truːli/ *adv.* **1** (used to emphasize a feeling, statement, etc.) really; completely: *We are truly grateful to you for your help.* **2** used to emphasize that sth is correct or accurate: *I cannot truly say that I was surprised at the news.*
IDM well and truly → WELL[1]

trump /trʌmp/ *noun* [C] (in some card games) a card of the chosen SUIT (= one of the four sets) that has a higher value than cards of the other three SUITS during a particular game: *Spades are trumps.*

'trump card *noun* [C] a special advantage you have over other people that you keep secret until you can surprise them with it: *It was time for her to play her trump card.*

trumpet /'trʌmpɪt/ *noun* [C] (**MUSIC**) a musical instrument made of BRASS that you play by blowing into it. There are three buttons on it that you press to make different notes. ⊃ picture at **instrument**, **orchestra**

truncate /trʌŋ'keɪt/ *verb* [T, usually passive] (*formal*) to make sth shorter, especially by cutting off the top or end: *My article was published in truncated form. ◇ Further discussion was truncated by the arrival of tea.*

truncheon /'trʌntʃən/ (*BrE*) (*also* baton) *noun* [C] (**LAW**) a short thick stick that a police officer carries as a weapon

trundle /'trʌndl/ *verb* [I, T] (used with an adverb or a preposition) to move slowly and noisily; to make sth heavy move in this way: *A lorry trundled down the hill.*

trunk /trʌŋk/ *noun*
• TREE **1** [C] (**BIOLOGY**) the thick central part of a tree that the branches grow from ⊃ picture at **tree**
• ELEPHANT **2** [C] the long nose of an elephant ⊃ picture at **animal**
• CLOTHING **3** trunks [pl.] = SWIMMING TRUNKS
• PART OF A CAR **4** [C] (*AmE*) = BOOT[1] (2)
• LARGE BOX **5** [C] a large box that you use for storing or transporting things
• PART OF THE BODY **6** [C, usually sing.] (**ANATOMY**) the main part of the body (not including the head, arms and legs)

trust[1] ⚡**B2** ⓢ /trʌst/ *noun* **1** [U] ~ (**in sb/sth**) the belief that sb is good, honest, sincere, etc. and will not try to harm or trick you: *Our marriage is based on love and trust. ◇ I should never have put my trust in him.* ⊃ look at **distrust**, **mistrust** **2** [C, U] a legal arrangement by which a person or an organization looks after money and property for sb else, usually until that person is old enough to control it
IDM take sth on trust to believe what sb says without having proof that it is true: *I can't prove it. You must take it on trust.*

trust[2] ⚡**B2** ⓢ /trʌst/ *verb* [T] ~ **sb (to do sth)**; ~ **sb (with sth)** to believe that sb is good, sincere, etc. and that they will not trick you or try to harm you: *He said the car was safe but I just don't trust him. ◇ You can trust me not to tell anyone. ◇ You can't trust her with money.* ⊃ look at **distrust**, **mistrust**
IDM trust sb (to do sth) (*informal*) it is typical of sb to do sth: *Trust Alice to be late. She's never on time!*

▼ SYNONYMS

trust

depend on ◆ rely on ◆ count on ◆ believe in
These words all mean to believe that sb/sth will do what you hope or expect of them or that what they tell you is correct or true.
trust *Can I trust you to keep a secret?*
depend on *You can always depend on him for support.*
rely on *You can't rely on anything you read in the newspapers.*
count on *You can count on my help.*
believe in *He's a leader they can believe in.*

trustee ⚡**C1** /trʌ'stiː/ *noun* [C] (**BUSINESS**) a person who looks after money or property for sb else

trusting /'trʌstɪŋ/ *adj.* believing that other people are good, sincere, honest, etc.

trustworthy /ˈtrʌstwɜːði/ *adj.* that you can depend on to be good, sincere, honest, etc. ▸ **trustworthiness** *noun* [U]

truth ⓘ **B1** /truːθ/ *noun* (*pl.* truths /truːðz/) **1** the truth [sing.] what is true; the facts ~ **(about sth)**: *Please tell me the truth.* ◇ *Are you telling me the whole truth about what happened?* ◇ *The truth is, we can't afford to live here any more.* **2** [U] the state or quality of being true: *There's a lot of truth in what she says.* **3** [C] a fact or an idea that is believed by most people to be true: *scientific/universal truths* ◇ adjective **true**

truthful /ˈtruːθfl/ *adj.* **1** ~ **(about sth)** (used about a person) who tells the truth: *They were not truthful about their part in the crime.* ◇ *I don't think you're being truthful with me.* **SYN** **honest 2** (used about a statement) true or correct: *a truthful account* ▸ **truthfully** /-fəli/ *adv.*

try¹ ⓘ **A1** Ⓢ /traɪ/ *verb* (trying; tries; *pt, pp* tried) **1** [I, T] ~ **(to do sth)** to make an effort to do sth: *I tried to phone you but I couldn't get through.* ◇ *She was trying hard not to laugh.* ◇ *She'll try her best to help you.* ◇ *I'm sure you can do it if you try.* **2** [T] ~ **sth/doing sth** to do, use or test sth in order to see how good or successful it is: *'I've tried everything but I can't get the baby to sleep.'* *'Have you tried taking her out in the car?'* ◇ *Have you ever tried raw fish?* ◇ *We tried the door but it was locked.* **3** [T, often passive] ~ **sb (for sth)**; ~ **sth (LAW)** to examine evidence in a court of law in order to decide if sb is guilty of a crime or not: *He was tried for murder.* ◇ *The case was tried before a jury.* ◇ note at **court¹**
IDM **try your hand at sth** to do sth such as an activity or a sport for the first time
PHR V **try sth on** to put on a piece of clothing to see if it fits you properly: *Can I try these jeans on, please?* **try sb/sth out** to test sb/sth to find out if they or it are good enough

try² ⓘ **B2** /traɪ/ *noun* [C] (*pl.* tries) an occasion when you try to do sth: *I don't know if I can move it by myself, but I'll give it a try.* **SYN** **attempt²**

trying /ˈtraɪɪŋ/ *adj.* that makes you tired or angry: *a trying journey*

tsar (*also* czar) /zɑː(r)/ *noun* [C] **1** (**HISTORY, POLITICS**) the title of the **EMPEROR** (= the leader) of Russia in the past **2** (*informal*) (**POLITICS**) an official whose job is to advise the government on policy in a particular area: *the government's social media tsar*

tsarina (*also* czarina) /zɑːˈriːnə/ *noun* [C] (**HISTORY, POLITICS**) the title of the **EMPRESS** (= female leader) of Russia in the past

tsetse fly /ˈtsetsi flaɪ/ *noun* [C] an African fly that bites humans and animals and drinks their blood and can spread **SLEEPING SICKNESS**

T-shirt ⓘ **A1** (*also* **tee shirt**) *noun* [C] an informal shirt with short **SLEEVES** (= arms) and without buttons or a **COLLAR** (= a folded part around the neck)

tsp *abbr.* (in writing) (*pl.* tsp, tsps) = **TEASPOON** (2): *Add 1 tsp salt.*

T-square *noun* [C] a plastic or metal instrument in the shape of a T for drawing or measuring **RIGHT ANGLES** (= angles of 90°)

tsunami ⓘ **B2** /tsuːˈnɑːmi/ *noun* [C] (**GEOGRAPHY, GEOLOGY**) a very large wave in the sea caused, for example, by an earthquake ◇ look at **tidal wave** ◇ note at **disaster** ◇ picture at **plate tectonics**

tub /tʌb/ *noun* [C] **1** a large round container without a **LID**, used for washing clothes in, growing plants in, etc. **2** (*especially AmE, informal*) = **BATH¹ 3** a small plastic container with a **LID** that is used for holding food: *a tub of margarine/ice cream*

tuba /ˈtjuːbə/ *noun* [C] (**MUSIC**) a large musical instrument made of **BRASS** that makes a low sound ◇ picture at **instrument, orchestra**

tube ⓘ **B1** /tjuːb/ *noun* **1** [C] a long empty pipe: *Blood flowed along the tube into the bottle.* ◇ *the inner tube of a bicycle tyre* ◇ look at **test tube 2** [C] a long thin container made of soft plastic or metal with a **LID** at one end. Tubes are used for holding thick liquids that can be forced out of them by pressing: *a tube of toothpaste* ◇ picture at **aerosol 3** (*also* The Tube™) [sing.] (*BrE*) the underground railway system in London

tuber /ˈtjuːbə(r)/ *noun* [C] (**BIOLOGY**) the short thick round part of some plants, such as potatoes, which grows under the ground

tuberculosis /tjuːˌbɜːkjuˈləʊsɪs/ = **TB¹**

tubing /ˈtjuːbɪŋ/ *noun* [U] a long piece of metal, rubber, etc. in the shape of a tube ◇ picture at **laboratory**

TUC /ˌtiː juː ˈsiː/ *abbr.* **Trades Union Congress** (the association to which many British **TRADE UNIONS** belong)

tuck /tʌk/ *verb* [T] (used with an adverb or a preposition) **1** to put or fold the ends or edges of sth into or round sth else so that it looks tidy: *Tuck your shirt in — it looks untidy like that.* **2** to put sth into a small space, especially to hide it or to keep it safe: *The letter was tucked behind a pile of books.*
PHR V **tuck sth away 1** be tucked away to be located in a quiet place; to be hidden: *The house was tucked away among the trees.* **2** to hide sth somewhere; to keep sth in a safe place: *He tucked his wallet away in his inside pocket.* **tuck sb in/up** to make sb feel comfortable in bed by pulling the covers up around them **tuck in | tuck into sth** (*especially BrE, informal*) to eat with pleasure

Tudor /ˈtjuːdə(r)/ *adj.* (**HISTORY**) connected with the time when kings and queens from the Tudor family ruled England (1485-1603): *Tudor architecture*

Tuesday ⓘ **A1** /ˈtjuːzdeɪ, -di/ *noun* [C, U] (*abbr.* Tue., Tues.) the day of the week after Monday

tuft /tʌft/ *noun* [C] a small amount of hair, grass, etc. growing together

tug¹ /tʌɡ/ *verb* [I, T] (-gg-) ~ **(at/on sth)** to pull sth hard and quickly, often several times: *The little boy tugged at his father's trouser leg.*

tug² /tʌɡ/ *noun* [C] **1** (*also* **tugboat** /ˈtʌɡbəʊt/) a small powerful boat that is used for pulling ships into a port, etc. **2** a sudden hard pull: *She gave the rope a tug.*

tuition ⓘ+ **C1** /tjuˈɪʃn/ *noun* [U] ~ **(in sth)** (*formal*) (**EDUCATION**) teaching, especially to a small group of people: *private tuition in Italian* ◇ *tuition fees* (= the money that you pay to be taught, especially in a college or university)

tulip /ˈtjuːlɪp/ *noun* [C] a brightly coloured flower, shaped like a cup, that grows in the spring

tumble /ˈtʌmbl/ *verb* [I] (often used with an adverb or a preposition) **1** to fall down suddenly but without serious injury: *He tripped and tumbled all the way down the steps.* **2** to move in a particular direction in an untidy or relaxed way: *She opened her suitcase and all her things tumbled out of it.* **3** ~ **(down)** to fall suddenly and in a dramatic way: *The wall came tumbling down.* **4** to fall suddenly in value or amount: *House prices have tumbled.* ▸ **tumble** *noun* [C, usually sing.]

tumble dryer (*also* **tumble drier**) *noun* [C] (*BrE*) a machine that dries clothes by moving them about in hot air

tumbler /'tʌmblə(r)/ *noun* [C] a glass for drinking out of with straight sides and no handle

tummy /'tʌmi/ *noun* [C] (*pl.* -ies) (*informal*) = STOMACH¹ (2)

tumour (*BrE*) (*AmE* tumor) /'tjuːmə(r)/ *noun* [C] (**HEALTH**) a mass of cells growing in or on a part of the body where they should not, causing medical problems: *a brain tumour*

tumultuous /tjuː'mʌltʃuəs/ *adj.* very noisy, because people are excited: *tumultuous applause*

tuna /'tjuːnə/ (*pl.* tuna) (*also* 'tuna fish) *noun* [C, U] a large sea fish that is used for food: *a tin of tuna*

tundra /'tʌndrə/ *noun* [U] (**GEOGRAPHY**) the large flat Arctic regions of northern Europe, Asia and North America where no trees grow and where the soil below the surface of the ground is always frozen ⊃ picture at **ecosystem**

tune¹ ? **B2** /tjuːn/ *noun* [C] (**MUSIC**) a series of musical notes that are sung or played to form a piece of music: *The children played us a tune on their recorders.* **IDM** call the shots/tune → CALL¹ change your tune → CHANGE¹ in/out of tune **1** (**MUSIC**) (not) singing or playing the correct musical notes to sound pleasant: *You're singing out of tune.* **2** having/not having the same opinions, interests, feelings, etc. as sb/sth

tune² /tjuːn/ *verb* [T] **1** (**MUSIC**) to make small changes to the sound a musical instrument makes so that it is at the correct PITCH (= musical level): *to tune a piano/guitar* **2** to make small changes to an engine so that it runs well **3** [usually passive] ~ sth (in) (to sth) to move the controls on a radio or TV so that you can receive a particular station: *The radio was tuned (in) to the BBC World Service.* ◇ (*informal*) *Stay tuned for the latest news.* **PHR V** tune in (to sth) to listen to a radio programme or watch a TV programme tune (sth) up (**MUSIC**) to make small changes to a group of musical instruments so that they sound pleasant when played together

tuneful /'tjuːnfl/ *adj.* (used about music) pleasant to listen to

tungsten /'tʌŋstən/ *noun* [U] (*symb.* W) (**CHEMISTRY**) a chemical element. Tungsten is a very hard silver-grey metal used especially in making steel. ❶ For more information on the periodic table of elements, look at the **Reference Section** of this dictionary.

tunic /'tjuːnɪk/ *noun* [C] **1** a piece of clothing, usually without SLEEVES (= arms), that is long and not tight **2** (*BrE*) the jacket that is part of the uniform of police officers, soldiers, etc.

tunnel ? **B2** /'tʌnl/ *noun* [C] a passage built underground: *The train disappeared into a tunnel.* ▸ tunnel *verb* [I, T] (-ll-, *AmE* -l-): *The engineers tunnelled through solid rock.*

turban /'tɜːbən/ *noun* [C] (**RELIGION**) a covering for the head worn especially by Sikh and Muslim men. A turban is made by folding a long piece of cloth around the head.

turbine /'tɜːbaɪn/ *noun* [C] (**ENGINEERING**) a machine or an engine that receives its power from a wheel that is turned by the pressure of water, air or gas ⊃ look at **wind turbine** ⊃ picture at **energy**

turbocharger /'tɜːbəʊtʃɑːdʒə(r)/ (*also* turbo /'tɜːbəʊ/, *pl.* -os) *noun* [C] (**ENGINEERING**) a system in a car that sends a mixture of petrol and air into the engine at high pressure, making it more powerful

turbulent /'tɜːbjələnt/ *adj.* **1** in which there is a lot of sudden change, trouble, argument and sometimes violence **2** (used about water or air) moving in a violent way ▸ turbulence /-ləns/ *noun* [U]

turf¹ /tɜːf/ *noun* [U, C] (a piece of) short thick grass and the layer of soil below it: *newly laid turf*

turf² /tɜːf/ *verb* [T] to cover ground with TURF **PHR V** turf sb out (of sth) | turf sb off (sth) (*BrE*, *informal*) to force sb to leave a place

turkey /'tɜːki/ *noun* [C, U] a large bird that is often kept on farms for its meat; the meat of this bird. Turkeys are usually eaten at Christmas in the UK and at Thanksgiving in the US. ⊃ picture at **animal** **IDM** cold turkey → COLD¹

Turkish delight /ˌtɜːkɪʃ dɪ'laɪt/ *noun* [U, C] a sweet made from a substance like JELLY with a fruit taste and covered with fine white sugar

turmoil /'tɜːmɔɪl/ *noun* [U, sing.] a state of great noise or CONFUSION: *His mind was in (a) turmoil.*

turn¹ ? **A1** /tɜːn/ *verb*
• MOVE ROUND **1** [I, T] to move round a fixed central point; to make sth move in this way: *The wheels turned faster and faster.* ◇ *She turned the key in the lock.* ◇ *Turn the steering wheel to the right.*
• CHANGE POSITION/DIRECTION **2** [I, T] to move your body, or part of your body, so that you are facing in a different direction: *He turned round when he heard my voice.* ◇ *She turned her back on me* (= she deliberately moved her body to face away from me). **3** [I, T] to change the position of sth: *I turned the box upside down.* ◇ *He turned the page and started the next chapter.* ◇ *Turn to page 33 in your books.* **4** [I, T] to change direction when you are moving: *Go straight on and turn left at the church.* ◇ *The car turned the corner.* ⊃ note at **direction**
• BECOME **5** [I, T] (to cause) to become: *He turned very red when I asked him about the money.*
• AIM **6** *linking verb* to point or aim sth in a particular direction: *She turned her attention back to the TV.*
• AGE/TIME **7** *linking verb* (not used in the progressive tenses) to reach or pass a particular age or time: *It's turned midnight.*
IDM ❶ For idioms containing **turn**, look at the entries for the nouns, adjectives, etc. For example, **turn a blind eye** is at **blind**. **PHR V** turn (sth) around (*also* turn (sth) round *especially in BrE*) to change position or direction in order to face the opposite way, or to return the way you came: *This road is a dead end. We'll have to turn round and go back to the main road.* ◇ *He turned the car around and drove off.* turn away to stop looking at sb/sth: *She turned away in horror at the sight of the blood.* turn sb away to refuse to allow a person to go into a place turn back to return the same way that you came: *We've come so far already, we can't turn back now.* turn sb/sth down to refuse an offer, etc. or the person who makes it: *Why did you turn that job down?* ◇ *He asked her to marry him, but she turned him down.* turn sth down to reduce the sound or heat that sth produces: *Turn the TV down!* turn (from sth) into sth to become sth: *These caterpillars will turn into butterflies.* turn off (sth) to leave one road and go on another turn sth off to stop the flow of electricity, water, etc. by moving a switch, TAP, etc: *He turned the TV off.* turn sth on to start the flow of electricity, water, etc. by moving a switch, TAP, etc: *to turn the lights on* turn out (for sth) to be present at an event turn out (to be sth) to be in the end: *The weather turned out fine.* ◇ *The house that they had promised us turned out to be a tiny flat.* turn sth out to move the switch, etc. on a light or a source of heat to stop it: *Turn the lights out before you go to bed.* turn over **1** to change position so that the other side is facing out or upwards: *He turned over and went back to sleep.* **2** (used about an engine) to start or to

continue to run **3** (*BrE*) to change to another programme when you are watching TV **turn sth over 1** to make sth change position so that the other side is facing out or upwards: *You may now turn over your exam papers and begin.* **2** to keep thinking about sth carefully: *She kept turning over what he'd said in her mind.* **turn (sth) round** (*especially BrE*) = **TURN (STH) AROUND turn to sb/sth** to go to sb/sth to get help, advice, etc. ⊃ note at **religion turn up 1** to arrive; to appear: *What time did they finally turn up?* **2** to be found, especially by chance: *I lost my glasses a week ago and they haven't turned up yet.* **turn sth up** to increase the sound or heat that sth produces: *Turn the heating up — I'm cold.*

turn² 🔒 **A1** /tɜːn/ *noun* [C]

- TIME **1** [usually sing.] the time when sb in a group of people should or is allowed to do sth: *Please wait in the queue until it is your turn.* ◇ *Whose turn is it to do the cleaning?* **SYN** **go²**
- IN A VEHICLE **2** a change of direction in a vehicle: *to make a **left/right turn*** ◇ *a **U-turn** (= when you turn round in a vehicle and go back in the opposite direction)*
- IN A ROAD **3** (*especially AmE*) = **TURNING**
- MOVEMENT **4** the act of turning sb/sth round: *Give the screw another couple of turns to make sure it is really tight.*
- CHANGE **5** an unusual or unexpected change: *The patient's condition has **taken a turn for the worse** (= suddenly got worse).*

IDM **(do sb) a good turn** (to do) sth that helps sb **in turn** one after the other: *I spoke to each of the children in turn.* **take turns** (at sth) to do sth one after the other to make sure it is fair **the turn of the century/year** the time when a new century/year starts **wait your turn** → **WAIT¹**

turnaround /'tɜːnəraʊnd/ (*BrE also* **turnround**) *noun* [C, usually sing.] **1** (**TOURISM**) the amount of time it takes to UNLOAD a ship or plane at the end of one journey and load it again for the next one **2** the amount of time it takes to do a piece of work that you have been given and return it **3** a situation in which sth changes from bad to good: *a turnaround in the economy* **4** a complete change in sb's opinion, behaviour, etc: *They remain suspicious about the government's turnaround on education policy.*

turning /'tɜːnɪŋ/ (*BrE*) (*also* **turn** *especially in AmE*) *noun* [C] a place where one road leads off from another: *We must have taken a wrong turning.* ⊃ note at **direction**

'turning point *noun* [C] ~ **(in sth)** a time when an important change happens, usually a good one

turnip /'tɜːnɪp/ *noun* [C, U] a round white vegetable that grows under the ground

'turn-off *noun* [C] **1** the place where a road leads away from a larger or more important road: *This is the turn-off for York.* **2** [usually sing.] (*informal*) a person or thing that you do not find interesting or attractive: *I find beards a real turn-off.*

turnout 🔒+ **C1** /'tɜːnaʊt/ *noun* [C, usually sing.] the number of people who go to a meeting, sports event, etc.

turnover 🔒+ **C1** /'tɜːnəʊvə(r)/ *noun* [sing.] ~ **(of sth)** (**BUSINESS**) **1** the amount of business that a company does in a particular period of time: *The firm has an annual turnover of $50 million.* **2** the rate at which workers leave a company and are replaced by new ones: *a high turnover of staff*

turnpike /'tɜːnpaɪk/ *noun* [C] (*AmE*) a wide road, where traffic can travel fast for long distances and that drivers must pay a TOLL (= a sum of money) to use

turnround /'tɜːnraʊnd/ (*BrE*) = TURNAROUND

'turn signal (*AmE*) = INDICATOR (2)

turnstile /'tɜːnstaɪl/ *noun* [C] a metal gate that moves round in a circle when it is pushed, and allows one person at a time to enter a place ⊃ picture at **stile**

turntable /'tɜːnteɪbl/ *noun* [C] **1** the round surface on a RECORD PLAYER that you place the record on to be played **2** a large round surface that is able to move in a circle and onto which a railway engine is driven in order to turn it to go in the opposite direction

'turn-up *noun* [C] the bottom of the leg of a pair of trousers that has been folded over on the outside

turpentine /'tɜːpəntaɪn/ *noun* [U] a clear liquid with a strong smell that you use for removing paint or for making paint thinner

turquoise /'tɜːkwɔɪz/ *noun* **1** [C, U] a blue or blue-green SEMI-PRECIOUS stone **2** [U] a blue-green colour ▶ **turquoise** *adj.*

turret /'tʌrət/ *noun* [C] (**ARCHITECTURE**) a small tower on the top of a large building

turtle /'tɜːtl/ *noun* [C] **1** (*AmE also* **sea turtle**) an animal with a thick shell and skin covered in scales that lives in the sea ⊃ picture at **animal 2** (*AmE, informal*) any REPTILE with a large shell, for example a TORTOISE

turtleneck /'tɜːtlnek/ *noun* [C] **1** (*BrE*) a sweater with a high part fitting closely around the neck **2** (*AmE*) = POLO NECK

tusk /tʌsk/ *noun* [C] (**BIOLOGY**) one of the two very long pointed teeth of an elephant, etc. Tusks are made of IVORY (= a hard white substance like bone). ⊃ picture at **animal**

tussle /'tʌsl/ *noun* [C] ~ **(for/over sth)** a fight, for example between two or more people who want to have the same thing

tut /tʌt/ (*also* ˌtut-'tut) *exclamation* the way of writing the sound that people make when they think sth is bad ▶ **tut** *verb* [I] (-tt-)

tutor 🟢 /'tjuːtə(r)/ *noun* [C] (**EDUCATION**) **1** a private teacher who teaches one person or a very small group **2** (*BrE*) a teacher who is responsible for a small group of students at school, college or university. A tutor advises students on their work or helps them if they have problems in their private life. ⊃ note at **subject¹**

tutorial /tjuː'tɔːriəl/ *noun* [C] (**EDUCATION**) a lesson at a college or university for an individual student or a small group of students ⊃ note at **subject¹**

tuxedo /tʌk'siːdəʊ/ (*pl.* -os) (*also informal* **tux** /tʌks/) *noun* [C] (*AmE*) = DINNER JACKET

TV 🔒 **A1** /ˌtiː 'viː/ (*also* **television**) *noun* (**ARTS AND MEDIA**) **1** (*also* **television set**) (*also BrE, informal* **telly**) [C] a piece of electrical equipment with a screen on which you can watch programmes with moving pictures and sounds: *to switch/turn the TV on/off* **2** (*also BrE, informal* **telly**) [U] the programmes that are shown on TV: *Paul's watching TV.* **3** [U] the system, process or business of sending out TV programmes: *a TV presenter/series/documentary* ◇ *cable/satellite/terrestrial/digital TV*

IDM **on (the) TV/television** being shown by TV; appearing in a TV programme: *What's on TV tonight?* ⊃ look at **media** (1)

twang /twæŋ/ *noun* [C] the sound that is made when you pull a tight string or wire, etc. and then let it go suddenly ▶ **twang** *verb* [I, T]

tweed /twiːd/ *noun* [U] a type of thick rough cloth that is made from wool and used for making clothes

tweet¹ /twiːt/ *noun* [C] **1** (**COMPUTING**) a message sent using the Twitter SOCIAL MEDIA service **2** the short high sound made by a small bird

tweet² /twiːt/ *verb* [I] **1** (COMPUTING) to send a message using the Twitter SOCIAL MEDIA service **2** = TWITTER

tweezers /ˈtwiːzəz/ *noun* [pl.] a small tool consisting of two pieces of metal that are joined at one end. You use tweezers for picking up or pulling out very small things: *a pair of tweezers*

twelve ⚡A1 /twelv/ *number* 12 ᴐ look at **dozen**
▶ **twelfth** /twelfθ/ *ordinal number, noun* [C]

twenty ⚡A1 /ˈtwenti/ **1** *number* 20 **2** the twenties *noun* [pl.] numbers, years or temperatures from 20 to 29
▶ **twentieth** /-əθ/ *ordinal number, noun* [C]
IDM in your twenties between the ages of 20 and 29

twice ⚡A1 /twaɪs/ *adv.* two times: *I've been to Egypt twice — once last year and once in 1994.* ◇ *The film will be shown twice daily.* ◇ *Take the medicine twice a day.* ◇ *Prices have risen twice as fast in this country as in Japan.*

twiddle /ˈtwɪdl/ *verb* [I, T] ~ (with) sth to keep turning or moving sth with your fingers, often because you are nervous or bored

twig /twɪg/ *noun* [C] a small thin branch on a tree or bush

twilight /ˈtwaɪlaɪt/ *noun* [U] the time after the sun has set and before it gets completely dark; the small amount of light at this time ᴐ look at **dusk**

twin ⚡A2 /twɪn/ *noun* [C] **1** one of two children or animals that are born to one mother at the same time: *They're very alike. Are they twins?* ◇ *a twin brother/sister* ◇ *identical twins* ᴐ look at **triplet 2** one of a pair of things that are the same or very similar
▶ **twin** ⚡A2 *adj.* [only before noun]: *twin engines* ◇ *twin beds* ᴐ note at **hotel**

twinge /twɪndʒ/ *noun* [C] **1** (HEALTH) a sudden short pain: *He suddenly felt a twinge in his back.* **2** ~ (of sth) a sudden short feeling of an unpleasant emotion: *a twinge of fear/envy/regret*

twinkle /ˈtwɪŋkl/ *verb* [I] **1** to shine with a light that seems to go on and off: *Stars twinkled in the night sky.* **2** (used about your eyes) to look bright because you are happy ▶ **twinkle** *noun* [sing.]

twin town *noun* [C] one of two towns in different countries that have a special relationship: *Grenoble is Oxford's twin town.*

twirl /twɜːl/ *verb* [I, T] ~ (sb/sth) (around/round) to turn round and round quickly; to make sb/sth do this

twist¹ ⚡B1+ C1 /twɪst/ *verb*
• BEND **1** [T, I] to bend or turn sth into a particular shape, often one it does not go in naturally; to be bent in this way: *She twisted her long hair into a knot.* ◇ *Her face twisted in anger.* ◇ *He twisted his ankle while he was playing squash.* ᴐ note at **injure**
• TURN **2** [I, T] to turn a part of your body while the rest stays still: *She twisted round to see where the noise was coming from.* ◇ *He kept twisting his head from side to side.* **3** [T] to turn sth around in a circle with your hand: *She twisted the ring on her finger nervously.* ◇ *Most containers have twist-off caps.*
• OF A ROAD/RIVER **4** [I] (used about a road, etc.) to change direction often: *a narrow twisting lane* ◇ *The road twists and turns along the coast.*
• PUT/BE ROUND STH **5** [I, T] ~ (sth) (round/around sth) to put sth round another object; to be round another object: *The phone wire has got twisted round the table leg.*
• WORDS/FACTS **6** [T] to change the meaning of what sb has said: *Journalists often twist your words.*
IDM twist sb's arm (*informal*) to force or persuade sb to do sth

twist² ⚡B1+ C1 /twɪst/ *noun* [C] **1** the act of turning sth with your hand, or of turning part of your body: *She killed the chicken with one twist of its neck.* **2** an

unexpected change or development in a story or situation **3** a place where a road, river, etc. bends or changes direction: *the twists and turns of the river* **4** something that has become or been bent into a particular shape: *Straighten out the wire so that there are no twists in it.*

twisted /ˈtwɪstɪd/ *adj.* **1** bent or turned so that the original shape is lost: *After the crash the car was a mass of twisted metal.* ◇ *a twisted ankle* (= injured by being turned suddenly) **2** (used about a person's mind or behaviour) not normal; strange in an unpleasant way: *Her experiences had left her bitter and twisted.*

twit /twɪt/ *noun* [C] (*BrE, informal*) a stupid or annoying person

twitch /twɪtʃ/ *verb* [I, T] to make a quick sudden movement, often one that you cannot control; to cause sth to make a sudden movement: *The rabbit twitched and then lay still.* ◇ *He twitched his nose.*
▶ **twitch** *noun* [C]: *He has a nervous twitch.*

Twitter™ /ˈtwɪtə(r)/ *noun* [U] (COMPUTING) a SOCIAL MEDIA service that allows you to send out short messages about what you are doing or thinking, that people can access on the internet or on their mobile phones ᴐ look at **microblogging, tweet¹** (1)

twitter /ˈtwɪtə(r)/ (*also* tweet) *verb* [I] (used about birds) to make a series of short high sounds

two ⚡A1 /tuː/ *number* 2
IDM be in two minds (about sth/doing sth) → MIND¹ in two in two pieces: *The plate fell on the floor and broke in two.*

two-diˈmensional (*also* 2-ˈD) *adj.* (GEOMETRY) having or appearing to have length and WIDTH but no depth; flat ᴐ look at **three-D**

two-ˈfaced *adj.* (*informal*) not sincere; not acting in a way that supports what you say that you believe; saying different things to different people about a particular subject **SYN** hypocritical

two-ply *adj.* (used about wool, wood, etc.) with two THREADS or layers

two-star *adj.* (TOURISM) having two stars in a system that measures quality. The highest standard is usually represented by four or five stars: *a two-star hotel*

two-way *adj.* **1** moving in two different directions; allowing sth to move in two different directions: *two-way traffic* **2** (used about communication between people) needing equal effort from both people or groups involved: *Friendship is a two-way process.* **3** (used about radio equipment, etc.) used both for sending and receiving signals

tycoon /taɪˈkuːn/ *noun* [C] (BUSINESS) a person who is very successful in business or industry and who has become rich and powerful

tying /ˈtaɪɪŋ/ present participle of **tie²**

type¹ ⚡A1 ⊙ /taɪp/ *noun* **1** [C] ~ (of sth) a group of people or things that share certain qualities and that are part of a larger group; a kind or sort: *Which type of paint should you use on metal?* ◇ *Spaniels are a type of dog.* ◇ *You meet all types of people in this job.* ◇ *the first building of its type in the world* ◇ *I love this type/these types of movie.* **2** [sing.] (*informal*) a person of a particular kind: *He's the careful type.* ◇ *She's not the type to do anything silly.* ᴐ look at **typical** (1) **3** -type (in adjectives) having the qualities, etc. of the group, person or thing mentioned: *a ceramic-type material* **4** [U] letters that are printed or typed

type² ⚡ **B1** ~ **(sth in)** /taɪp/ *verb* [I, T] to write sth using a computer keyboard or TYPEWRITER: *Can you type?* ◇ *to type a letter* ◇ *Type in the filename, then press 'Enter'.* ▸ **typing** *noun* [U]: *typing skills*

typeface /'taɪpfeɪs/ *noun* [C] a set of letters, numbers, etc. of a particular design, used in printing: *I'd like the heading to be in a different typeface from the text.*

typewriter /'taɪpraɪtə(r)/ *noun* [C] a machine that you use for writing in print

typewritten /'taɪprɪtn/ *adj.* written using a TYPEWRITER or computer

typhoid /'taɪfɔɪd/ *noun* [U] (**HEALTH**) a serious disease that can cause death. People get typhoid from bad food or water.

typhoon /taɪ'fuːn/ *noun* [C] (**GEOGRAPHY**) a violent tropical storm with very strong winds ⊃ note at **storm¹**

typical ⚡ **A2** ⊘ /'tɪpɪkl/ *adj.* ~ **(of sb/sth) 1** having or showing the usual qualities of a particular person, thing or type: *a typical Italian village* ◇ *The stone used is typical of the area.* **OPP** **atypical, untypical** **2** happening in the usual way; showing what sth is usually like: *On a typical day, I receive about 50 emails.* **SYN** **normal¹** **3** behaving in the way you expect: *It was absolutely typical of him not to reply to my letter.*

typically ⚡ **B1** ⊘ /'tɪpɪkli/ *adv.* **1** in a typical case; that usually happens in this way: *Typically, the contracts were for five years.* **2** in a way that shows the usual qualities of a particular person, type or thing: *typically British humour*

typify /'tɪpɪfaɪ/ *verb* [T] (typifying; typifies; *pt, pp* typified) to be a typical mark or example of sb/sth: *This film typified the Hollywood westerns of that time.*

typist /'taɪpɪst/ *noun* [C] **1** a person who works in an office typing letters, etc. **2** a person who uses a computer keyboard or TYPEWRITER

typography /taɪ'pɒɡrəfi/ *noun* [U] the art or work of preparing books, etc. for printing, especially of designing how text will appear when it is printed ▸ **typographical** /ˌtaɪpə'ɡræfɪkl/ (*also* typographic /-fɪk/) *adj.*: *a typographical error* ◇ *typographic design* ▸ **typographically** /-kli/ *adv.*

tyranny /'tɪrəni/ *noun* [U] (**POLITICS**) the cruel and unfair use of power by a person or small group to control a country or state ▸ **tyrannical** /tɪ'rænɪkl/ *adj.*: *a tyrannical ruler* ▸ **tyrannize** (*BrE also* -ise) /'tɪrənaɪz/ *verb* [T, I]

tyrant /'taɪrənt/ *noun* [C] (**POLITICS**) a cruel leader who has complete power over the people in their country ⊃ look at **dictator**

tyre ⚡ **B1** (*BrE*) (*AmE* tire) /'taɪə(r)/ *noun* [C] the thick rubber ring that fits around the outside of a wheel: *a flat tyre* (= a tyre with no air in it)

U u

U¹ /juː/ (*also* u) *noun* [C, U] (*pl.* U's, u's) the 21st letter of the English alphabet: *'Understand' begins with (a) 'U'.*

U² /juː/ *abbr.* (*BrE*) **universal** (the label of a film that is suitable for anyone, including children) ⊃ look at **PG**

uber- (*also* über-) /'uːbə(r)/ *prefix* (in nouns and adjectives) of the best kind; to a very large degree: *an uber-cool restaurant*

ubiquitous /juː'bɪkwɪtəs/ *adj.* (formal) seeming to be everywhere or in several places at the same time; very common: *the ubiquitous bicycles of university towns* ◇ *the ubiquitous movie star, Tom Hanks* ▸ **ubiquitously** *adv.* ▸ **ubiquity** /-kwəti/ *noun* [U]

udder /'ʌdə(r)/ *noun* [C] (**AGRICULTURE**) the part of a female cow, etc. that hangs under its body and produces milk ⊃ picture at **goat**

UEFA /juː'eɪfə/ *abbr.* **the Union of European Football Associations** (the organization that controls the sport of football in Europe): *the UEFA cup*

UFO /ˌjuː ef 'əʊ, ˌjuː'fəʊ/ (*also* ufo) *noun* [C] (*pl.* UFOs) a strange object that some people claim to have seen in the sky and believe is a SPACECRAFT (= a vehicle from another planet) (the abbreviation for 'unidentified flying object') ⊃ look at **flying saucer**

ugh /ɜː, ʊx/ *exclamation* used in writing to express the sound that you make when you think sth is horrible

ugly ⚡ **B1** /'ʌɡli/ *adj.* (uglier; ugliest) **1** unpleasant to look at or listen to: *The burn left an ugly scar on her face.* ◇ *an ugly modern office block* **SYN** **unattractive** **2** (used about a situation) dangerous or threatening: *The situation turned ugly when people started throwing stones.* ▸ **ugliness** *noun* [U]

UHF /ˌjuː eɪtʃ 'ef/ *abbr.* **ultra-high frequency** (radio waves that move up and down at a particular speed and that are used to send out radio and TV programmes) ⊃ picture at **wavelength**

UHT /ˌjuː eɪtʃ 'tiː/ *abbr.* (*BrE*) **ultra heat treated** (used about foods such as milk that are treated to last longer): *UHT milk*

UI /ˌjuː 'aɪ/ *abbr.* = USER INTERFACE

UK /ˌjuː 'keɪ/ *abbr.* = UNITED KINGDOM: *She is Kenyan by birth but is now a UK citizen.*

ulcer /'ʌlsə(r)/ *noun* [C] (**HEALTH**) a painful area on the skin or inside the body that may lose blood or produce a poisonous substance: *a mouth/stomach ulcer*

ulna /'ʌlnə/ *noun* [C] (*pl.* ulnae /-niː/) (**ANATOMY**) the longer bone of the two bones in the lower part of the arm between the WRIST and the ELBOW ⊃ look at **radius** (3) ⊃ picture at **body**

ulterior /ʌl'tɪəriə(r)/ *adj.* [only before noun] that you keep hidden or secret: *Why is he suddenly being so nice to me? He must have an ulterior motive.*

ultimate¹ ⚡ + **B2** 🔊 /'ʌltɪmət/ *adj.* [only before noun] **1** being or happening at the end; last or final: *Our ultimate goal is complete independence.* **2** the greatest, best or worst: *This race will be the ultimate test of your skill.*

ultimate² /'ʌltɪmət/ *noun* [sing.] **the ~ in sth** (*informal*) the greatest or best: *This new car is the ultimate in comfort.*

ultimately ⚡ **B2** 🔊 /'ʌltɪmətli/ *adv.* **1** in the end: *Ultimately, the decision is yours.* **2** at the most basic level; most importantly

ultimatum /ˌʌltɪ'meɪtəm/ *noun* [C] (*pl.* ultimatums) a final warning to sb that, if they do not do what you ask, you will use force or take action against them: *I issued an ultimatum — either he paid his rent or he was out.*

ultra- /ˌʌltrə/ *prefix* (in nouns and adjectives) extremely: *ultra-modern*

ultrasonic /ˌʌltrə'sɒnɪk/ *adj.* (**PHYSICS**) (used about sounds) higher than humans can hear: *ultrasonic frequencies/waves/signals* ⊃ look at **infrasonic**

ultrasound /'ʌltrəsaʊnd/ *noun* **1** [U] (**PHYSICS**) sound that is higher than humans can hear **2** [U, C] (**MEDICINE**) a medical process that produces an image of what is inside your body: *Ultrasound showed she was expecting twins.*

ultraviolet /ˌʌltrəˈvaɪələt/ *adj.* (*abbr.* **UV**) (**PHYSICS**) connected with or using ELECTROMAGNETIC waves that are just shorter than those of VIOLET light in the SPECTRUM and that cannot be seen: *ultraviolet rays* (= that cause the skin to go darker) ⊃ look at **infrared** ⊃ picture at **wavelength**

ultra vires /ˌʌltrə ˈvaɪriːz/ *adv.* (**LAW**) beyond your legal power or authority

umami /uːˈmɑːmi/ *noun* [U] a taste found in some foods that is not sweet, SOUR, bitter, or like salt

umbilical cord /ʌmˈbɪlɪkl kɔːd/ *noun* [C] (**ANATOMY**) the tube that connects a baby to its mother before it is born ⊃ picture at **fertilization**

umbra /ˈʌmbrə/ *noun* [C] (*pl.* **umbras, umbrae** /-briː/) **1** the central part of a shadow where it is completely dark **2** (**ASTRONOMY**) a completely dark area on the earth caused by the moon, or a completely dark area on the moon caused by the earth, during an ECLIPSE (= a time when the moon is between the earth and the sun, or when the earth is between the moon and the sun) ⊃ look at **penumbra** (2) ⊃ picture at **shadow**¹

umbrella 🔒 **A1** /ʌmˈbrelə/ *noun* [C] an object that you open and hold over your head to keep yourself dry when it is raining: *to put an umbrella up/down*

umlaut /ˈʊmlaʊt/ *noun* [C] (**LANGUAGE**) the mark placed over a vowel in some languages to show how it should be pronounced, as over the *u* in the German word *für* ⊃ look at **acute accent, circumflex, grave**³, **tilde**

umpire /ˈʌmpaɪə(r)/ *noun* [C] (**SPORT**) a person who watches a game such as tennis or CRICKET to make sure that the players obey the rules ⊃ look at **referee** (1) ▶ **umpire** *verb* [I, T]

umpteen /ˌʌmpˈtiːn/ *pron.*, *det.* (*informal*) very many; a lot ▶ **umpteenth** /-ˈtiːnθ/ *det.*: *For the umpteenth time — phone if you're going to be late!*

UN /ˌjuː ˈen/ *abbr.* = UNITED NATIONS

un- /ʌn/ *prefix* **1** (in nouns, adjectives and adverbs) not; the opposite of: *unable* ◇ *unconsciously* ◇ *untruth* ◇ *un-American activities* (= against the interests of the US) **2** used in verbs that describe the opposite of a process: *unlock* ◇ *undo* ◇ *unfold*

unabated /ˌʌnəˈbeɪtɪd/ *adj.* (*formal*) without becoming any less strong: *The rain continued unabated.*

unable 🔒 **B1** /ʌnˈeɪbl/ *adj.* ~**to do sth** not having the time, knowledge, skill, etc. to do sth; not able to do sth: *She lay there, unable to move.* **OPP** **able** ⊃ noun **inability**

unacceptable 🔒+ **B2** /ˌʌnəkˈseptəbl/ *adj.* that you cannot accept or allow **OPP** **acceptable** ▶ **unacceptably** /-bli/ *adv.*

unaccompanied /ˌʌnəˈkʌmpənid/ *adj.* alone; without sb/sth else with you

unaccustomed /ˌʌnəˈkʌstəmd/ *adj.* ~**to sth/doing sth** (*formal*) not in the habit of doing sth; not used to sth: *He was unaccustomed to hard work.*

unadulterated /ˌʌnəˈdʌltəreɪtɪd/ *adj.* **1** used to emphasize that sth is complete or total: *For me, the holiday was sheer unadulterated pleasure.* **2** not mixed with other substances: *unadulterated foods* **SYN** **pure**

unadventurous /ˌʌnədˈventʃərəs/ *adj.* not willing to take risks or try new and exciting things

unaffected /ˌʌnəˈfektɪd/ *adj.* **1** not changed by sth **2** behaving in a natural way without trying to impress anyone **OPP** **affected**

unaffordable /ˌʌnəˈfɔːdəbl/ *adj.* costing so much that people do not have enough money to pay for it **OPP** **affordable**

unafraid /ˌʌnəˈfreɪd/ *adj.* [not before ~(to do sth) (*informal*) not afraid or worried about what might happen of conflict. ◇ *He's unafraid to speak* **OPP** **afraid**

unaided /ʌnˈeɪdɪd/ *adv.* without any

unalienable /ʌnˈeɪliənəbl/ *adj.* = INALIENABLE

unalterable /ʌnˈɔːltərəbl/ *adj.* (*formal*) that cannot be changed: *the unalterable laws of the universe*

unambiguous /ˌʌnæmˈbɪɡjuəs/ *adj.* clear in meaning; that can only be understood in one way

unanimous /juˈnænɪməs/ *adj.* **1** (used about a decision, etc.) agreed by everyone: *The jury reached a unanimous verdict of guilty.* **2** ~(in sth) (used about a group of people) all agreeing about sth: *The judges were unanimous in their decision.* ▶ **unanimously** *adv.*

unanticipated /ˌʌnænˈtɪsɪpeɪtɪd/ *adj.* (*formal*) that you have not expected or predicted

unapproachable /ˌʌnəˈprəʊtʃəbl/ *adj.* (used about a person) unfriendly and not easy to talk to **OPP** **approachable**

unarmed /ˌʌnˈɑːmd/ *adj.* having no guns, knives, etc. **OPP** **armed**

unashamed /ˌʌnəˈʃeɪmd/ *adj.* not feeling sorry or embarrassed about sth bad that you have done **OPP** **ashamed** ▶ **unashamedly** /-ˈʃeɪmɪdli/ *adv.*

unassuming /ˌʌnəˈsjuːmɪŋ/ *adj.* not wanting people to notice how good, important, etc. you are **SYN** **modest**

unattached /ˌʌnəˈtætʃt/ *adj.* **1** ~(to sb/sth) not connected to sb/sth else **2** not married; without a regular partner **SYN** **single**¹

unattainable /ˌʌnəˈteɪnəbl/ *adj.* impossible to achieve or reach: *an unattainable goal* **OPP** **attainable**

unattended /ˌʌnəˈtendɪd/ *adj.* not watched or looked after: *Do not leave bags unattended.*

unattractive /ˌʌnəˈtræktɪv/ *adj.* **1** not attractive or pleasant to look at **OPP** **attractive** **2** not good, interesting or pleasant

unauthorized (*BrE also* -ised) /ʌnˈɔːθəraɪzd/ *adj.* done without permission

unavailable /ˌʌnəˈveɪləbl/ *adj.* **1** ~(to sb/sth) that cannot be obtained: *Such luxury items were unavailable to ordinary people.* **2** not able or not willing to see, meet or talk to sb: *The minister was unavailable for comment.* **OPP** **available** ▶ **unavailability** /ˌʌnəveɪləˈbɪləti/ *noun* [U]

unavoidable /ˌʌnəˈvɔɪdəbl/ *adj.* that cannot be avoided or prevented **OPP** **avoidable** ▶ **unavoidably** /-bli/ *adv.*

unaware /ˌʌnəˈweə(r)/ *adj.* [not before noun] ~(of sb/sth) not knowing about or not noticing sb/sth: *She seemed unaware of all the trouble she had caused.* **OPP** **aware**

unawares /ˌʌnəˈweəz/ *adv.* by surprise; without expecting sth or being prepared for it: *I was taken completely unawares by his suggestion.*

unbalanced /ˌʌnˈbælənst/ *adj.* **1** (used about a person) slightly crazy **2** not fair to all ideas or sides of an argument **OPP** **balanced**

unbearable /ʌnˈbeərəbl/ *adj.* too unpleasant, painful, etc. for you to accept **SYN** **intolerable** **OPP** **bearable** ▶ **unbearably** /-bli/ *adv.*: *It was unbearably hot.*

unbeatable /ʌnˈbiːtəbl/ *adj.* that cannot be defeated or improved on: *unbeatable prices*

unbeaten /ʌnˈbiːtn/ *adj.* that has not been beaten or improved on: *Her world record remains unbeaten.*

⌐ievable /ˌʌnbɪˈliːvəbl/ *adj.* very surprising; ⌐fficult to believe **OPP believable** ⊃ look at **incredible** (1) ▶ **unbelievably** /-bli/ *adj.*: *His work was unbelievably bad.*

unbiased (*also* unbiassed) /ʌnˈbaɪəst/ *adj.* fair and not influenced by your own or sb else's opinions, desires, etc: *an unbiased judge* **SYN impartial OPP biased**

unblemished /ʌnˈblemɪʃt/ *adj.* not SPOILED, damaged or marked in any way: *The new party leader has an unblemished reputation.*

unblock /ˌʌnˈblɒk/ *verb* [T] to clean sth, for example a pipe, by removing sth that is blocking it

unborn /ˌʌnˈbɔːn/ *adj.* not yet born

unbroken /ʌnˈbrəʊkən/ *adj.* **1** continuous; not interrupted: *a period of unbroken silence* **2** that has not been beaten: *His record for the 1 500 metres remains unbroken.*

uncalled for /ʌnˈkɔːld fɔː(r)/ *adj.* (used about behaviour or comments) not fair and not appropriate: *That comment was quite uncalled for.* **SYN unnecessary**

uncanny /ʌnˈkæni/ *adj.* very strange; that you cannot easily explain: *an uncanny coincidence*

unceasing /ʌnˈsiːsɪŋ/ *adj.* (*formal*) continuing all the time: *unceasing efforts* ◇ *the country's history of unceasing conflict and division* ▶ **unceasingly** *adv.*: *The rain fell unceasingly.*

uncertain /ʌnˈsɜːtn/ *adj.* **1** ~ (about/of sth) not sure; not able to decide: *She was still uncertain of his true feelings for her.* **2** not known exactly or not decided: *He's lost his job and his future seems very uncertain.* **OPP certain** ▶ **uncertainly** *adv.* ▶ **uncertainty** ʔ+ **B2 W** /-tnti/ *noun* [U, C] (*pl.* -ies): *Today's decision will put an end to all the uncertainty.*

unchanged /ʌnˈtʃeɪndʒd/ *adj.* staying the same; not changed ⊃ note at **trend**[1]

uncharacteristic /ˌʌnˌkærəktəˈrɪstɪk/ *adj.* not typical or usual **OPP characteristic**[2] ▶ **uncharacteristically** /-kli/ *adv.*

uncharted /ˌʌnˈtʃɑːtɪd/ *adj.* **1** that has not been visited or investigated before; not familiar: *They set off into the country's uncharted interior.* ◇ (*figurative*) *The party is sailing in uncharted waters* (= a situation it has not been in before). **2** (**GEOGRAPHY**) not marked on a map: *The ship hit an uncharted rock.*

uncheck /ˌʌnˈtʃek/ *verb* [T] (**COMPUTING**) to click on a mark next to an answer or option on a computer in order to remove that mark

unchecked /ˌʌnˈtʃekt/ *adj.* if sth harmful is unchecked, it is not stopped from getting worse: *The fire was allowed to burn unchecked.* ◇ *The rise in violent crime must not go unchecked.* ◇ *The plant will soon choke ponds and waterways if left unchecked.*

uncle ʔ **A1** /ˈʌŋkl/ *noun* [C] your father's or mother's brother; your aunt's husband

unclear **W** /ˌʌnˈklɪə(r)/ *adj.* **1** not clear or definite; difficult to understand or be sure about: *His motives are unclear.* ◇ *Our plans are unclear at the moment.* ◇ *It is unclear whether there is any damage.* ◇ *Some of the diagrams are unclear.* **2** ~ (about sth); ~ (as to sth) not fully understanding sth; uncertain about sth: *I'm unclear about what you want me to do.* ◇ *The police are unclear as to the killer's motives.* **OPP clear**[1]

uncomfortable ʔ **B1** /ʌnˈkʌmftəbl, -ˈkʌmfət-/ *adj.* **1** not pleasant to wear, sit in, lie on, etc: *uncomfortable shoes* **2** not able to sit, lie, etc. in a position that is pleasant: *I was very uncomfortable for most of the journey.* **3** anxious, embarrassed or afraid and unable to relax; making you feel like this: *I felt very uncomfortable when they started arguing in front of me.* **OPP comfortable** ▶ **uncomfortably** /-bli/ *adv.*

uncommon /ʌnˈkɒmən/ *adj.* not existing in large numbers or in many places **OPP common**[1]

uncompetitive /ˌʌnkəmˈpetətɪv/ *adj.* (**BUSINESS**) not cheaper or better than others and therefore not able to compete equally: *an uncompetitive industry* **OPP competitive**

uncomplicated /ʌnˈkɒmplɪkeɪtɪd/ *adj.* simple and without difficulties or problems

uncompromising /ʌnˈkɒmprəmaɪzɪŋ/ *adj.* refusing to discuss or change a decision

unconcerned /ˌʌnkənˈsɜːnd/ *adj.* ~ (about/by sth); ~ (with sth) not worried about sth or not interested in it: *He seemed unconcerned about the noise the engine was making.* ◇ *Young people are often unconcerned with political issues.* **OPP concerned**

unconditional /ˌʌnkənˈdɪʃənl/ *adj.* without limits or conditions: *the unconditional surrender of military forces* **OPP conditional** ▶ **unconditionally** /-nəli/ *adv.*

unconnected /ˌʌnkəˈnektɪd/ *adj.* ~ (with/to sth) not related or connected in any way: *The two crimes are apparently unconnected.* **OPP connected**

unconscious ʔ **B2** /ʌnˈkɒnʃəs/ *adj.* **1** (**HEALTH**) in a state that is like sleep, for example because of injury or illness: *He was found lying unconscious on the kitchen floor.* **2** (used about feelings, thoughts, etc.) existing or happening without your realizing; not deliberate: *The article was full of unconscious humour.* **OPP conscious 3** ~ of sb/sth not knowing sth; not aware of sb/sth: *He was quite unconscious of the danger.* **SYN unaware** ▶ **unconsciously** *adv.* ▶ **unconsciousness** *noun* [U]

the un'conscious *noun* [sing.] (**PSYCHOLOGY**) the part of a person's mind with thoughts, feelings, etc. that they are not aware of and cannot control but that can sometimes be understood by studying their behaviour or dreams ⊃ look at **subconscious**

unconstitutional /ˌʌnˌkɒnstɪˈtjuːʃənl/ *adj.* (**LAW**) not allowed by the CONSTITUTION (= the basic laws or rules) of a country, a political system or an organization

uncontrollable /ˌʌnkənˈtrəʊləbl/ *adj.* that you cannot control: *I suddenly had an uncontrollable urge to laugh.* ▶ **uncontrollably** /-bli/ *adv.*

uncontrolled /ˌʌnkənˈtrəʊld/ *adj.* **1** (used about emotions, behaviour, etc.) that sb cannot control or stop **2** that is not limited or managed by law or rules ⊃ look at **controlled** (2)

unconventional /ˌʌnkənˈvenʃənl/ *adj.* not following what is done or considered normal or acceptable by most people; different and interesting: *an unconventional approach to the problem* **OPP conventional** ▶ **unconventionally** /-ʃənəli/ *adv.*

unconvinced /ˌʌnkənˈvɪnst/ *adj.* not believing or not certain about sth despite what you have been told: *I remain unconvinced of the need for change.*

uncountable /ʌnˈkaʊntəbl/ *adj.* (**GRAMMAR**) an **uncountable** noun cannot be made plural or used with *a* or *an*, for example *water, bread* and *information* **OPP countable**

uncouth /ʌnˈkuːθ/ *adj.* (used about a person or their behaviour) rude or socially unacceptable

uncover /ʌnˈkʌvə(r)/ *verb* [T] **1** to remove the cover from sth **OPP cover**[1] **2** to find out or discover sth: *Police have uncovered a plot to murder a top politician.*

uncultivated /ʌnˈkʌltɪveɪtɪd/ *adj.* (**AGRICULTURE**) (used about land) not used for growing crops

undecided /ˌʌndɪˈsaɪdɪd/ *adj.* **1** ~ **(about sb/sth)** not having made a decision: *I'm still undecided about whether to take the job or not.* **2** without any result or decision **OPP** **decided**

undemanding /ˌʌndɪˈmɑːndɪŋ/ *adj.* not needing a lot of effort or thought: *an undemanding job* **OPP** **demanding**

undemocratic /ˌʌndeməˈkrætɪk/ *adj.* against or not acting according to the principles of DEMOCRACY (= a system that supports equal rights for all people) **OPP** **democratic**

undeniable /ˌʌndɪˈnaɪəbl/ *adj.* clear, true or certain **SYN** **indisputable** ▶ undeniably /-bli/ *adv.*

under 🔵 **A1** /ˈʌndə(r)/ *prep., adv.* **1** in or to a position that is below sth: *We found him hiding under the table.* ◇ *The dog crawled under the gate and ran into the road.* **2** below the surface of sth; covered by sth: *Most of an iceberg is under the water.* ◇ *He was wearing a vest under his shirt.* **3** less than a certain number; younger than a certain age: *People working under 20 hours a week will pay no extra tax.* ◇ *Nobody under 18 is allowed in the club.* **4** experiencing a particular feeling, process or effect: *He was jailed for driving under the influence of alcohol.* ◇ *a building under construction* ◇ *The manager is **under pressure** to resign.* ◇ *I was **under the impression that** Bill was not very happy there.* **5** governed or controlled by sb/sth: *The country is now under martial law.* **6** according to a law, an agreement, a system, etc: *Under English law you are innocent until you are proved guilty.* **7** using a particular name: *to travel under a false name* **8** found in a particular part of a book, list, etc: *You'll find some information on rugby under 'team sports'.*

under- /ʌndə(r)/ *prefix* **1** (in nouns and adjectives) below: *undergrowth* ◇ *underground* **2** (in nouns) lower in age, level or position: *the under-fives* ◇ *the minister's undersecretary* **3** (used with verbs and adjectives) not enough: *undercooked food*

underarm¹ /ˈʌndərɑːm/ *adj.* **1** [only before noun] (ANATOMY) connected with a person's ARMPIT (= the part of the body under the arm where it joins the rest of the body): *underarm hair/deodorant* ◇ look at **armpit** **2** an **underarm** throw of a ball is done with the hand kept below the level of the shoulder

underarm² /ˈʌndərɑːm/ *adv.* if you throw, etc. **underarm**, you throw keeping your hand below the level of your shoulder

undercarriage /ˈʌndəkærɪdʒ/ (*also* **landing gear**) *noun* [C] the part of an aircraft, including the wheels, that supports it when it is landing and taking off ◇ picture at **airliner**

underclass /ˈʌndəklɑːs/ *noun* [sing.] (SOCIAL STUDIES) a social class that is very poor and has no power

underclothes /ˈʌndəkləʊðz/ = UNDERWEAR

undercook /ˌʌndəˈkʊk/ *verb* [T] to not cook food for long enough **OPP** **overcook**

undercover /ˌʌndəˈkʌvə(r)/ *adj.* (LAW) working or happening secretly: *an undercover reporter/detective*

undercurrent /ˈʌndəkʌrənt/ *noun* [C] ~ **(of sth)** a feeling, especially a negative one, that is hidden but whose effects are felt: *I detect an undercurrent of resentment towards the new proposals.*

undercut /ˌʌndəˈkʌt/ *verb* [T] (undercutting; *pt, pp* undercut) to sell sth at a lower price than other shops, etc.

underdeveloped /ˌʌndədɪˈveləpt/ *adj.* (ECONOMICS, GEOGRAPHY) used about a country, society, etc.) having few industries and a low standard of living ◇ look at **developed** (1), **developing** ◇ note at **HDI**

❶ 'A **developing country**' is now the usual expression. ▶ underdevelopment /-ləpmənt/ *noun* [U]

underdog /ˈʌndədɒg/ *noun* [C] (SPORT) a person, team, etc. who is weaker than others, and not expected to be successful: *San Marino were the underdogs, but managed to win the game 2–1.*

underestimate /ˌʌndərˈestɪmeɪt/ *verb* [T] **1** to guess that the amount, etc. of sth will be less than it really is **OPP** **overestimate** **2** to think that sb/sth is not as strong, good, etc. as they really are: *Don't underestimate your opponent. He's a really good player.* ▶ underestimate /-mət/ *noun* [C]

underfoot /ˌʌndəˈfʊt/ *adv.* under your feet; where you are walking: *It's very wet underfoot.*

underfunded /ˌʌndəˈfʌndɪd/ *adj.* (FINANCE) not having enough money to spend, with the result that it cannot function well

undergo 🔵+ **B2** 🔵 /ˌʌndəˈgəʊ/ *verb* [T] (*pt* underwent /-ˈwent/; *pp* undergone /-ˈgɒn/) to have a difficult or unpleasant experience: *She underwent a five-hour operation.*

undergraduate 🔵+ **C1** /ˌʌndəˈgrædʒuət/ *noun* [C] (EDUCATION) a student at college or university who is studying for their first degree ◇ look at **graduate¹** (1), **postgraduate** ◇ note at **subject¹**

underground¹ 🔵 **A2** /ˈʌndəgraʊnd/ *adj.* [only before noun] **1** under the surface of the ground: *an underground car park* ◇ note at **water¹** ◇ picture at **purification** **2** secret or illegal: *an underground radio station*

underground² 🔵 **A2** /ˌʌndəˈgraʊnd/ *adv.* **1** under the surface of the ground: *The cables all run underground.* **2** into a secret place: *She went underground to escape from the police.*

underground³ /ˈʌndəgraʊnd/ (*BrE*) (*AmE* **subway**) *noun* [sing.] a railway system under the ground

undergrowth /ˈʌndəgrəʊθ/ *noun* [U] bushes and plants that grow around and under trees

underhand /ˌʌndəˈhænd/ *adj.* secret or not honest

underlie /ˌʌndəˈlaɪ/ *verb* [T] (underlying; underlies; *pt* underlay /-ˈleɪ/; *pp* underlain /-ˈleɪn/) (*formal*) to be the basis or cause of sth: *It is a principle that underlies all the party's policies.*

underline /ˌʌndəˈlaɪn/ (*also* underscore /ˌʌndəˈskɔː(r)/ *especially in AmE*) *verb* [T] **1** to draw a line under a word, etc. **2** to show sth clearly or to emphasize sth: *This accident underlines the need for greater care.*

underlying 🔵+ **C1** 🔵 /ˌʌndəˈlaɪɪŋ/ *adj.* [only before noun] important but hidden: *the underlying causes of the disaster*

undermine 🔵+ **C1** /ˌʌndəˈmaɪn/ *verb* [T] to make sth, especially sb's confidence or authority, gradually weaker or less effective: *The public's confidence in the government has been undermined by the crisis.*

underneath /ˌʌndəˈniːθ/ *prep., adv.* under; below: *The coin rolled underneath the chair.*

the underneath *noun* [sing.] the bottom or lowest part of sth: *There is a lot of rust on the underneath of the car.*

undernourished /ˌʌndəˈnʌrɪʃt/ *adj.* (HEALTH) in bad health because of not having enough food or enough of the right type of food

underpants /ˈʌndəpænts/ (*BrE also* **pants**) *noun* [pl.] a piece of clothing that men or boys wear under their trousers

underpass /ˈʌndəpɑːs/ *noun* [C] a road or path that goes under another road, railway, etc.

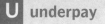

underpay /ˌʌndəˈpeɪ/ *verb* [T] (*pt, pp* **underpaid** /-ˈpeɪd/) to pay sb too little **OPP** **overpay**

underperform /ˌʌndəpəˈfɔːm/ *verb* [I] to not be as successful as was expected

underpriced /ˌʌndəˈpraɪst/ *adj.* something that is **underpriced** is sold at a price that is too low and less than its real value **OPP** **overpriced**

underprivileged /ˌʌndəˈprɪvəlɪdʒd/ *adj.* having less money, and fewer rights, opportunities, etc. than other people in society **OPP** **privileged**

underrate /ˌʌndəˈreɪt/ *verb* [T] to think that sb/sth is less clever, important, good, etc. than they or it really are **OPP** **overrate**

underscore¹ /ˌʌndəˈskɔː(r)/ *verb* [T] (*especially AmE*) = UNDERLINE

underscore² /ˈʌndəskɔː(r)/ *noun* [C] the symbol (_) that is used to draw a line under a letter or word and in computer commands and internet addresses

undershirt /ˈʌndəʃɜːt/ (*AmE*) = VEST (1)

underside /ˈʌndəsaɪd/ *noun* [C] the side or surface of sth that is below it **SYN** **bottom¹**

understaffed /ˌʌndəˈstɑːft/ *adj.* (**BUSINESS**) not having enough people working and therefore not able to function well: *We're very understaffed at the moment.*

understand 🔊 **A1** **S** /ˌʌndəˈstænd/ *verb* (not usually used in the progressive tenses) (*pt, pp* **understood** /-ˈstʊd/) **1** [T, I] to know or realize the meaning of sth: *I didn't understand the instructions. ◇ Please speak more slowly. I can't understand you. ◇ Do you understand what I'm asking you? ◇ I'm not sure that I really understand.* **2** [T] to know how or why sth happens or why it is important: *I can't understand why the engine won't start. ◇ As far as I understand it, the changes won't affect us.* **3** [T] to know sb's character and why they behave in a particular way: *It's easy to understand why she felt so angry.* **4** [T] (*formal*) to have heard or been told sth: *I understand (that) you have decided to leave.* **IDM** **give sb to believe/understand (that)** → BELIEVE **make yourself understood** to make your meaning clear: *I can just about make myself understood in Russian.*

understandable /ˌʌndəˈstændəbl/ *adj.* that you can understand ▸ **understandably** /-bli/ *adv.*: *She was understandably angry at the decision.*

understanding¹ 🔊 **A2** **O** /ˌʌndəˈstændɪŋ/ *noun* **1** [U, sing.] the knowledge that sb has of a particular subject or situation: *He has little understanding of how computers work. ◇ A basic understanding of physics is necessary for this course.* **2** [U] the ability to know why people behave in a particular way and to forgive them if they do sth wrong or bad: *She apologized for her actions and her boss showed great understanding.* **3** [C, usually sing.] an informal agreement: *I'm sure we can* **come to/reach an understanding** *about the money I owe him.* **4** [U] the way in which you think sth is meant: *My understanding of the arrangement is that he will only phone if there is a problem.* **IDM** **on the understanding that …** only if …; because it was agreed that …: *We let them stay in our house on the understanding that it was only for a short period.*

understanding² /ˌʌndəˈstændɪŋ/ *adj.* showing kind feelings towards sb **SYN** **sympathetic**

understate /ˌʌndəˈsteɪt/ *verb* [T] to say that sth is smaller or less important than it really is **OPP** **overstate**

understatement /ˈʌndəsteɪtmənt/ *noun* **1** [C] a statement that makes sth seem less important, impressive, serious, etc. than it really is: *'Is she pleased?' 'That's an understatement. She's delighted.'* **2** [U] the practice of making things seem less impressive, important, serious, etc. than they really are: *He always goes for subtlety and understatement in his movies.* **OPP** **overstatement**

understood /ˌʌndəˈstʊd/ past tense, past participle of **understand**

understorey (*AmE* **understory**) /ˈʌndəstɔːri/ *noun* [C] (*pl.* **-eys, -ies**) (**ENVIRONMENT**) a layer of branches and leaves below the main CANOPY (= top layer of leaves and branches) of a forest

understudy /ˈʌndəstʌdi/ *noun* [C] (*pl.* **-ies**) (**ARTS AND MEDIA**) an actor who learns the role of another actor and replaces them if they are ill

undertake 🔊+ **B2** **W** /ˌʌndəˈteɪk/ *verb* [T] (*pt* **undertook** /-ˈtʊk/; *pp* **undertaken** /-ˈteɪkən/) **1** to decide to do sth and start doing it: *The company is undertaking a major programme of modernization.* **2** to agree or promise to do sth

undertaker /ˈʌndəteɪkə(r)/ (*also* **funeral director**, *AmE also* **mortician**) *noun* [C] a person whose job is to prepare dead bodies to be buried and to arrange FUNERALS

undertaking **W** /ˌʌndəˈteɪkɪŋ/ *noun* [C, usually sing.] **1** a piece of work or business: *Buying the company would be a risky undertaking.* **2** ~ **(that … /to do sth)** a formal or legal promise to do sth: *He gave an undertaking that he would not leave the country.*

undertone /ˈʌndətəʊn/ *noun* [C] a feeling, quality or meaning that is not expressed in a direct way **IDM** **in an undertone** | **in undertones** in a quiet voice

undertook /ˌʌndəˈtʊk/ past tense of **undertake**

underused /ˌʌndəˈjuːzd/ *adj.* (*also formal* **underutilized**, *BrE also* **-ised** /ˌʌndəˈjuːtəlaɪzd/) not used as much as it could or should be

undervalue /ˌʌndəˈvæljuː/ *verb* [T] to place too low a value on sb/sth

underwater /ˌʌndəˈwɔːtə(r)/ *adj., adv.* existing, happening or used below the surface of water: *underwater exploration ◇ an underwater camera ◇ Can you swim underwater?*

underway (*also* **under way**) /ˌʌndəˈweɪ/ *adj.* [not before noun] already started

underwear 🔊 **B1** /ˈʌndəweə(r)/ *noun* [U] (*also formal* **underclothes** [pl.]) clothing that is worn next to the skin under other clothes

underweight /ˌʌndəˈweɪt/ *adj.* weighing less than is normal or correct **OPP** **overweight**

underwent /ˌʌndəˈwent/ past tense of **undergo**

underworld /ˈʌndəwɜːld/ *noun* [sing.] (**LAW**) the people and activities involved in crime in a particular place

underwrite /ˌʌndəˈraɪt/ *verb* [T] (*pt* **underwrote** /-ˈrəʊt/; *pp* **underwritten** /-ˈrɪtn/) to accept responsibility for an insurance policy by agreeing to pay if there is any damage or loss ▸ **underwriter** /ˈʌndəraɪtə(r)/ *noun* [C]

undesirable /ˌʌndɪˈzaɪərəbl/ *adj.* unpleasant or not wanted; likely to cause problems **OPP** **desirable**

undetectable /ˌʌndɪˈtektəbl/ *adj.* ~ **(to sb/sth)** impossible to see or find: *The sound is virtually undetectable to the human ear.*

undid /ʌnˈdɪd/ past tense of **undo**

undignified /ʌnˈdɪɡnɪfaɪd/ *adj.* causing you to look silly and to lose the respect of other people **OPP** **dignified**

undiminished /ˌʌndɪˈmɪnɪʃt/ *adj.* that has not become smaller or weaker: *They continued with undiminished enthusiasm.*

undiscovered /ˌʌndɪˈskʌvəd/ *adj.* that has not been found or noticed; that has not been discovered: *a previously undiscovered talent*

undisputed /ˌʌndɪˈspjuːtɪd/ *adj.* **1** that cannot be questioned or shown to be false; that cannot be argued against: *undisputed facts/evidence* **2** that everyone accepts or recognizes: *the undisputed champion of the world*

undisturbed /ˌʌndɪˈstɜːbd/ *adj.* **1** not moved or touched by anyone or anything **SYN untouched 2** not interrupted by anyone **3** ~ **(by sth)** not affected or upset by sth: *He seemed undisturbed by the news of her death.* **SYN unconcerned**

undivided /ˌʌndɪˈvaɪdɪd/ *adj.*
IDM get/have sb's undivided attention to receive all sb's attention give your undivided attention (to sb/sth) to give all your attention to sb/sth

undo /ʌnˈduː/ *verb* [T] (undoes /-ˈdʌz/; *pt* undid /-ˈdɪd/; *pp* undone /-ˈdʌn/) **1** to open sth that was tied or fastened: *to undo a knot/zip/button* **2** to destroy the effect of sth that has already happened: *His mistake has undone all our good work.*

undocumented /ˌʌnˈdɒkjumentɪd/ *adj.* **1** not supported by written evidence: *undocumented accusations* **2** not having the necessary documents, especially permission to live and work in a foreign country: *undocumented immigrants*

undone /ʌnˈdʌn/ *adj.* **1** open; not fastened or tied: *I realized that my zip was undone.* **2** not done: *I left the housework undone.*

undoubted /ʌnˈdaʊtɪd/ *adj.* definite; accepted as being true ▸ undoubtedly ?+ **C1** *adv.*

undress /ʌnˈdres/ *verb* **1** [I] to take off your clothes **2** [T] to take off sb's clothes **OPP dress¹** ▸ undressed *adj.*

undue /ˌʌnˈdjuː/ *adj.* [only before noun] (*formal*) more than is necessary or reasonable: *The police try not to use undue force when arresting a person.* ▸ unduly *adv.*: *She didn't seem unduly worried by their unexpected arrival.*

unearth /ʌnˈɜːθ/ *verb* [T] to dig sth up out of the ground; to discover sth that was hidden: *Archaeologists have unearthed a Roman tomb.*

unearthly /ʌnˈɜːθli/ *adj.* strange or frightening: *an unearthly scream*
IDM at an unearthly hour (*informal*) extremely early in the morning

unease /ʌnˈiːz/ (*also* uneasiness /ʌnˈiːzinəs/) *noun* [U] a worried or uncomfortable feeling **OPP ease¹**

uneasy /ʌnˈiːzi/ *adj.* **1** ~ **(about sth/doing sth)** worried; not feeling relaxed or comfortable **2** not settled; unlikely to last: *an uneasy compromise* ▸ uneasily /-zɪli/ *adv.*

uneconomic /ˌʌnˌiːkəˈnɒmɪk, -ˌek-/ *adj.* (**BUSINESS**) (used about a company, etc.) not making or likely to make a profit **OPP economic**

uneconomical /ˌʌnˌiːkəˈnɒmɪkl, -ˌek-/ *adj.* wasting money, time, materials, etc. **OPP economical** ▸ uneconomically /-kli/ *adv.*

unemployed ? **B1** /ˌʌnɪmˈplɔɪd/ *adj.* (**SOCIAL STUDIES**) **1** not able to find a job; out of work: *She has been unemployed for over a year.* **SYN jobless** ⊃ look at **work²** (1) **2** the unemployed *noun* [pl.] people who cannot find a job

unemployment ? **B1** /ˌʌnɪmˈplɔɪmənt/ *noun* [U] (**SOCIAL STUDIES**) **1** The number of people who are unemployed: *The economy is doing very badly and unemployment is rising.* **SYN joblessness** ⊃ look at

dole² **2** the situation of not being able to find a job: *The number of people claiming* **unemployment benefit** (= money given by the state) *has gone up.* **OPP employment**

unencumbered /ˌʌnɪmˈkʌmbəd/ *adj.* **1** not having or carrying anything heavy or anything that makes you go more slowly **2** (**FINANCE**) (used about property) not having any debts left to be paid

unending /ʌnˈendɪŋ/ *adj.* having or seeming to have no end

unequal /ʌnˈiːkwəl/ *adj.* **1** not fair or balanced: *an unequal distribution of power* **2** different in size, amount, level, etc. **OPP equal¹** ▸ unequally /-kwəli/ *adv.*

UNESCO /juːˈneskəʊ/ (*also* Unesco) *abbr.* (**SOCIAL STUDIES**) United Nations Educational, Scientific and Cultural Organization (an agency of the United Nations that was set up to encourage the exchange of information, ideas, and culture)

unethical /ʌnˈeθɪkl/ *adj.* not morally acceptable: *unethical behaviour/conduct* **OPP ethical** ▸ unethically /-kli/ *adv.*

uneven /ʌnˈiːvn/ *adj.* **1** not completely smooth, level or regular: *The sign was painted in rather uneven letters.* **OPP even²** **2** not always of the same level or quality ▸ unevenly *adv.*: *The country's wealth is unevenly distributed.*

un,even ˈbars = ASYMMETRIC BARS

unexceptional /ˌʌnɪkˈsepʃənl/ *adj.* not interesting or unusual ⊃ look at **exceptional**

unexpected ? **B2** /ˌʌnɪkˈspektɪd/ *adj.* not expected and therefore causing surprise ▸ unexpectedly *adv.*: *I got there late because I was unexpectedly delayed.*

unexploded /ˌʌnɪkˈspləʊdɪd/ *adj.* (used about a bomb, etc.) that has not yet exploded

unexplored /ˌʌnɪkˈsplɔːd/ *adj.* **1** (**GEOGRAPHY**) (used about a country or an area of land) that nobody has investigated or put on a map; that has not been explored **2** (used about an idea, a theory, etc.) that has not yet been examined or discussed THOROUGHLY

unfailing /ʌnˈfeɪlɪŋ/ *adj.* that you can depend on to always be there and always be the same: *unfailing devotion/support* ◇ *She fought the disease with unfailing good humour.* ▸ unfailingly *adv.*: *unfailingly loyal/polite*

unfair ? **B1** /ˌʌnˈfeə(r)/ *adj.* ~ **(on/to sb)** not right or fair according to a set of rules or principles; not treating people equally: *This law is unfair to women.* ◇ *The tax is unfair on people with low incomes.* ◇ *The referee warned him for unfair play.* **OPP fair¹** ▸ unfairly *adv.* ▸ unfairness *noun* [U]

unfaithful /ʌnˈfeɪθfl/ *adj.* ~ **(to sb/sth)** having a sexual relationship with sb who is not your husband, wife or partner **OPP faithful** ▸ unfaithfulness *noun* [U]

unfamiliar /ˌʌnfəˈmɪliə(r)/ *adj.* **1** ~ **(to sb)** that you do not know well: *This is an unfamiliar part of town to me.* **2** ~ **(with sth)** not having knowledge or experience of sth: *I'm unfamiliar with this author's work.* **OPP familiar**

unfashionable /ʌnˈfæʃnəbl/ *adj.* not popular at a particular time: *unfashionable ideas/clothes* **OPP fashionable** ⊃ look at **old-fashioned** (1)

unfasten /ʌnˈfɑːsn/ *verb* [T] to open sth that was fastened: *to unfasten a belt/button/chain/lock* **SYN undo OPP fasten**

unfavourable (*BrE*) (*AmE* unfavorable) /ʌnˈfeɪvərəbl/ *adj.* (*formal*) **1** not good and likely to cause problems or make sth difficult **OPP favourable** ⊃ look at **adverse**

2 showing that you do not like or approve of sb/sth ► **unfavourably** (*AmE* **unfavorably**) /-bli/ *adv.*: *In this respect, Britain compares unfavourably with other European countries.*

unfinished /ʌnˈfɪnɪʃt/ *adj.* not complete: *We have some unfinished business to settle.* ◊ *an unfinished drink/game/book* **OPP** **finished**

unfit /ʌnˈfɪt/ *adj.* **1** ~ **(for sth/to do sth)** not suitable or not good enough for sth: *His criminal past makes him unfit to be a politician.* **2** not in good physical health, especially because you do not get enough exercise **OPP** **fit²**

unfold 🔊+ **B2** /ʌnˈfəʊld/ *verb* [I, T] **1** ~ **(into sth)** to open out and become flat; to open out sth that was folded: *The sofa unfolds into a bed.* **OPP** **fold¹** **2** to become known, or to allow sth to become known, a little at a time

unforeseen /ˌʌnfɔːˈsiːn/ *adj.* not expected: *an unforeseen problem*

unforgettable /ˌʌnfəˈɡetəbl/ *adj.* making such a strong impression that you cannot forget it **SYN** **memorable**

unforgivable /ˌʌnfəˈɡɪvəbl/ *adj.* if sb's behaviour is **unforgivable**, it is so bad or unacceptable that you cannot forgive the person **SYN** **inexcusable** **OPP** **forgivable** ► **unforgivably** /-bli/ *adv.*

unfortunate 🔊+ **B2** /ʌnˈfɔːtʃənət/ *adj.* **1** not lucky: *It was an unfortunate accident.* **SYN** **unlucky** **OPP** **fortunate** **2** that you feel sorry about: *She described the decision as 'unfortunate'.*

unfortunately 🔊 **A2** /ʌnˈfɔːtʃənətli/ *adv.* used to say that a particular situation or fact makes you sad or disappointed, or gets you into a difficult position: *I'd like to help you but unfortunately there's nothing I can do.* ◊ *Unfortunately, I won't be able to attend the meeting.*

unfounded /ʌnˈfaʊndɪd/ *adj.* not based on or supported by facts: *unfounded allegations*

unfriend /ʌnˈfrend/ (*also* **defriend**) *verb* [T] to remove sb from your list of friends or contacts on SOCIAL MEDIA: *She broke up with her boyfriend, but she hasn't unfriended him.*

unfriendly /ʌnˈfrendli/ *adj.* ~ **(to/towards sb)** unpleasant or not polite to sb **OPP** **friendly¹**

unfurnished /ʌnˈfɜːnɪʃt/ *adj.* without furniture ➔ note at **flat¹**

ungainly /ʌnˈɡeɪnli/ *adj.* moving in a way that is not smooth or attractive

ungrateful /ʌnˈɡreɪtfl/ *adj.* not feeling or showing thanks to sb **OPP** **grateful** ► **ungratefully** /-fəli/ *adv.*

unguarded /ʌnˈɡɑːdɪd/ *adj.* **1** not protected or guarded **2** saying more than you wanted to: *an unguarded remark* **OPP** **guarded**

unhappily /ʌnˈhæpɪli/ *adv.* **1** in an unhappy way **SYN** **sadly** **2** unfortunately **OPP** **happily**

unhappy 🔊 **A2** /ʌnˈhæpi/ *adj.* (**unhappier; unhappiest**) **1** sad: *He had a very unhappy childhood.* **2** ~ **(about/at/with sth)** not satisfied or pleased; worried: *They're unhappy at having to accept a pay cut.* **OPP** **happy** ► **unhappiness** *noun* [U]

unharmed /ʌnˈhɑːmd/ *adj.* not injured or damaged; not harmed: *The hostages were released unharmed.*

UNHCR /ˌjuː en eɪtʃ siː ˈɑː(r)/ *abbr.* (SOCIAL STUDIES) **United Nations High Commission for Refugees** (an organization that helps and protects REFUGEES (= people who have been forced to leave their own country because of war, etc.))

unhealthy /ʌnˈhelθi/ *adj.* **1** (HEALTH) not having or showing good health: *He looks pale and unhealthy.* **OPP** **healthy** **2** likely to cause illness or poor health: *unhealthy conditions* **OPP** **healthy** **3** not natural: *an unhealthy interest in death* **OPP** **healthy**

unheard /ʌnˈhɜːd/ *adj.* [not before noun] not listened to or given any attention: *My suggestions went unheard.*

unˈheard-of *adj.* not known; never having happened before

unhelpful /ʌnˈhelpfl/ *adj.* not helpful or useful; not wanting to help sb: *an unhelpful response/reply* **OPP** **helpful** ► **unhelpfully** /-fəli/ *adv.*

unhurt /ʌnˈhɜːt/ *adj.* [not before noun] not injured or harmed: *He escaped from the crash unhurt.* **SYN** **unharmed** **OPP** **hurt²**

unhygienic /ˌʌnhaɪˈdʒiːnɪk/ *adj.* not clean and therefore likely to cause disease or infection **OPP** **hygienic**

uni- /juːni/ *prefix* (in nouns, adjectives and adverbs) one; having one: *uniform* ◊ *unilaterally*

UNICEF /ˈjuːnɪsef/ *abbr.* (SOCIAL STUDIES) **United Nations Children's Fund** (an organization that helps to look after the health and education of children all over the world)

unicellular /ˌjuːnɪˈseljələ(r)/ *adj.* (BIOLOGY) consisting of only one cell: *unicellular organisms*

unicorn /ˈjuːnɪkɔːn/ *noun* [C] (in stories) an animal that looks like a white horse with a long straight HORN on its head

unidentified /ˌʌnaɪˈdentɪfaɪd/ *adj.* whose identity is not known: *An unidentified body has been found in the river.*

uniform¹ 🔊 **A2** /ˈjuːnɪfɔːm/ *noun* [C, U] the set of clothes worn at work by the members of an organization or a group, or by some children at school: *I didn't know he was a policeman because he wasn't in uniform.* ► **uniformed** *adj.*

uniform² /ˈjuːnɪfɔːm/ *adj.* not varying; the same in all cases or at all times ► **uniformity** /ˌjuːnɪˈfɔːməti/ *noun* [U]

unify 🔊+ **C1** /ˈjuːnɪfaɪ/ *verb* [T] (**unifying; unifies;** *pt, pp* **unified**) to join separate parts together to make one unit, or to make them similar to each other ► **unification** /ˌjuːnɪfɪˈkeɪʃn/ *noun* [U]

unilateral /ˌjuːnɪˈlætrəl/ *adj.* (used about an action or a decision) done or made by one person, group or country that is involved in sth without the agreement of the other person, group, etc: *a unilateral declaration of independence* ➔ look at **multilateral** ► **unilaterally** /-trəli/ *adv.*

unimaginable /ˌʌnɪˈmædʒɪnəbl/ *adj.* (*formal*) impossible to think of or to believe exists; impossible to imagine: *unimaginable wealth* ► **unimaginably** /-bli/ *adv.*

unimportant /ˌʌnɪmˈpɔːtnt/ *adj.* not important: *unimportant details* ◊ *relatively/comparatively unimportant* ◊ *They dismissed the problem as unimportant.* **OPP** **important**

uninhabitable /ˌʌnɪnˈhæbɪtəbl/ *adj.* not possible to live in **OPP** **habitable**

uninhabited /ˌʌnɪnˈhæbɪtɪd/ *adj.* (used about a place or a building) with nobody living in it

uninhibited /ˌʌnɪnˈhɪbɪtɪd/ *adj.* behaving in a free and natural way, without worrying what other people think of you **OPP** **inhibited**

uninstall /ˌʌnɪnˈstɔːl/ *verb* [T] (COMPUTING) to remove a program from a computer: *Uninstall any program that you no longer need.* **OPP** **install**

unintelligible /ˌʌnɪnˈtelɪdʒəbl/ *adj.* impossible to understand **OPP** **intelligible**

unintended /ˌʌnɪnˈtendɪd/ *adj.* an **unintended** effect, result or meaning is one that you did not plan or intend to happen

unintentional /ˌʌnɪnˈtenʃənl/ *adj.* not done deliberately, but happening by accident: *Perhaps I misled you, but it was quite unintentional* (= I did not mean to). **OPP** **intentional** ▸ **unintentionally** /-ʃənəli/ *adv.*: *They had unintentionally provided wrong information.*

uninterested /ʌnˈɪntrəstɪd, -tres-/ *adj.* ~ **(in sb/sth)** having or showing no interest in sb/sth: *She seemed uninterested in anything I had to say.* **OPP** **interested** ⊃ look at **disinterested**

uninteresting /ʌnˈɪntrəstɪŋ, -tres-/ *adj.* not attracting your attention or interest; not interesting

union ⸦ **B1** /ˈjuːniən/ *noun* **1** [C] = TRADE UNION **2** [C] an organization for a particular group of people: *the Athletics Union* **3** [C] (**POLITICS**) a group of states or countries that have joined together to form one country or group: *the European Union* **4** [U, sing.] the act of joining or the situation of being joined

unionist /ˈjuːniənɪst/ *noun* [C] **1** = TRADE UNIONIST **2** Unionist (**POLITICS**) a person who believes that Northern Ireland should stay part of the United Kingdom **3** Unionist (**HISTORY**) a supporter of the Union during the Civil War in the US ▸ **unionism** /-ɪnɪzəm/ *noun* [U]

the Union Jack *noun* [sing.] the national flag of the United Kingdom, with red and white crosses on a dark blue background

unique ⸦ **B2** Ⓦ /juˈniːk/ *adj.* **1** not like anything else; being the only one of its type: *Shakespeare made a unique contribution to the world of literature.* **2** very unusual **3** ~ **to sb/sth** connected with only one place, person or thing: *This dance is unique to this region.*

unisex /ˈjuːniseks/ *adj.* designed for and used by both men and women: *unisex fashions*

unison /ˈjuːnɪsn/ *noun*
IDM **in unison** saying, singing or doing the same thing at the same time as sb else: *'No, thank you,' they said in unison.*

unit ⸦ **A2** Ⓞ /ˈjuːnɪt/ *noun* [C]
• SINGLE THING **1** a single thing that is complete in itself, although it can be part of sth larger: *The book is divided into ten units.* **2** (**BUSINESS**) a single item of the type of product that a company sells: *The game's selling price was $15 per unit.* ◇ *What's the **unit cost**?*
• GROUP OF PEOPLE **3** a group of people who perform a certain function within a larger organization
• IN A HOSPITAL **4** a department, especially in a hospital, that provides a particular type of care or treatment: *the intensive care unit*
• FURNITURE **5** a piece of furniture, especially a cupboard, that fits with other pieces of furniture and has a particular use: *matching kitchen units*
• MEASUREMENT **6** a fixed amount or number used as a standard of measurement: *a **unit of currency***
• SMALL MACHINE **7** a small machine that performs a particular task or that is part of a larger machine: *The heart of a computer is the central processing unit.*
• IN MATHEMATICS **8** any whole number from 0 to 9: *a column for the tens and a column for the units*

unitary /ˈjuːnətri/ *adj.* **1** (**POLITICS**) consisting of a number of areas or groups that are joined together and are controlled by one government or group: *a single unitary state* **2** (*formal*) single; forming one unit

unite ⸦+ **B2** /juˈnaɪt/ *verb* **1** [I] ~ **(in sth/doing sth)** to join together for a particular purpose: *We should all unite in seeking a solution to this terrible problem.* **2** [T, I] to join together and act in agreement; to make this happen: *Italy was united in 1861.* ◇ *Unless we unite, our enemies will defeat us.*

united ⸦ **A2** /juˈnaɪtɪd/ *adj.* joined together by a common feeling or aim

the United Kingdom *noun* [sing.] (*abbr.* UK) (**GEOGRAPHY**) England, Scotland, Wales and Northern Ireland

▼ CULTURE

The United Kingdom includes England, Scotland, Wales and Northern Ireland, but *not* the Republic of Ireland (Eire), which is a separate country. **Great Britain** is England, Scotland and Wales only. **The British Isles** include England, Scotland, Wales, Northern Ireland and the Republic of Ireland.

the United Nations *noun* [sing. + sing./pl. verb] (*abbr.* UN) (**POLITICS**) the organization formed to encourage peace in the world and to deal with problems between countries

the United States of America /ðə juˌnaɪtɪd ˌsteɪts əv əˈmerɪkə/ (*also* the United States) *noun* (usually used with a singular verb) (*abbr.* the US, the USA) a large country in North America made up of 50 states and the District of Columbia

unit trust (*BrE*) (*AmE* **mutual fund**) *noun* [C] (**BUSINESS**) a company that offers a service to people by investing their money in various different businesses

unity ⸦+ **B2** /ˈjuːnəti/ *noun* [U] the situation in which people are in agreement and working together

universal ⸦+ **B2** Ⓦ /ˌjuːnɪˈvɜːsl/ *adj.* connected with, done by or affecting everyone in the world or everyone in a particular group ▸ **universally** /-səli/ *adv.*

Universal Credit *noun* [U] (**SOCIAL STUDIES**) (in the UK) money given by the government to people who do not earn much, to help them pay for housing, the care of children, the cost of living while unemployed, etc.

universal indicator *noun* [C] (**CHEMISTRY**) a substance that changes to different colours according to whether another substance that touches it is an ACID or an ALKALI ⊃ picture at **pH**

the universe ⸦ **B2** /ðə ˈjuːnɪvɜːs/ *noun* [sing.] (**ASTRONOMY**) everything that exists, including the planets, stars, space, etc.

university ⸦ **A1** Ⓢ /ˌjuːnɪˈvɜːsəti/ *noun* [C] (*pl.* -ies) (**EDUCATION**) an institution that provides the highest level of education, in which students study for degrees and in which academic research is done: *Which university did you go to?* ◇ *I did history at university.* ◇ *a university lecturer*

Unix™ /ˈjuːnɪks/ *noun* [U] (**COMPUTING**) an OPERATING SYSTEM (= a set of programs that controls the way a computer works and runs other programs) that can be used by many people at the same time

unjust /ˌʌnˈdʒʌst/ *adj.* not fair or deserved: *an unjust accusation/law/punishment* ◇ *The system is corrupt and unjust.* **OPP** **just**[2] ▸ **unjustly** *adv.*

unjustified /ˌʌnˈdʒʌstɪfaɪd/ *adj.* not fair or necessary **SYN** **unwarranted** **OPP** **justified**

unkempt /ˌʌnˈkempt/ *adj.* (used especially about sb's hair or general appearance) not well cared for; not tidy: *greasy, unkempt hair* **SYN** **dishevelled**

unkind /ˌʌnˈkaɪnd/ *adj.* ~ **(to sb/sth)** unpleasant and not friendly: *That was an unkind thing to say.* ◇ *He was never actually unkind to them.* **OPP** **kind**[2] ▸ **unkindly** *adv.* ▸ **unkindness** *noun* [U]

unknown¹ 🔊 **B2** /ʌnˈnəʊn/ *adj.* **1** ~ **(to sb)** not known or identified: *The attacker's identity remains unknown.* ◇ *a species of insect previously unknown to science* **2** (used about people) not famous or familiar to other people: *an unknown actress* **OPP** **famous, well known**

IDM **an unknown quantity** a person or thing that you know very little about

unknown² /ʌnˈnəʊn/ *noun* **1 the unknown** [sing.] a place or thing that you know nothing about: *a fear of the unknown* **2** [C] a person who is not well known

unlawful /ʌnˈlɔːfl/ *adj.* (*formal*) (**LAW**) not allowed by the law **SYN** **illegal**

unleaded /ʌnˈledɪd/ *adj.* (used about petrol) not containing lead

unleash /ʌnˈliːʃ/ *verb* [T] ~ **sth (on/upon sb/sth)** to suddenly let a strong force, emotion, etc. be felt or have an effect: *The government's proposals unleashed a storm of protest in the press.*

unleavened /ʌnˈlevnd/ *adj.* (used about bread) made without any YEAST (= the substance that makes bread rise) and therefore flat and heavy

unless 🔊 **B1** /ənˈles/ *conj.* if … not; except if: *I was told that unless my work improved, I would lose the job.* ◇ *'Would you like a cup of coffee?' 'Not unless you've already made some.'* ◇ *Unless anyone has anything else to say, the meeting is closed.* ◇ *Don't switch that on unless I'm here.*

unlicensed /ʌnˈlaɪsnst/ *adj.* without a licence: *an unlicensed vehicle* **OPP** **licensed**

unlike¹ 🔊 **B1** /ʌnˈlaɪk/ *prep.* **1** different from; in contrast to: *He's extremely ambitious, unlike me.* ◇ *This is an exciting place to live, unlike my home town.* ◇ *She's unlike anyone else I've ever met.* **2** not typical of; unusual for: *It's unlike him to be so rude —* he's usually very polite.

unlike² /ʌnˈlaɪk/ *adj.* [not before noun] (used about two people or things) different from each other: *They are both teachers. Otherwise they are quite unlike.*

unlikely 🔊 **B1** 🅆 /ʌnˈlaɪkli/ *adj.* (unlikelier; unlikeliest) **1** ~ **(to do sth/that …)** not likely to happen; not expected; not PROBABLE: *I suppose she might win but I think it's very unlikely.* ◇ *It's highly unlikely that I'll have any free time next week.* **OPP** **likely¹** **2** difficult to believe: *an unlikely excuse* **SYN** **improbable**

unlimited /ʌnˈlɪmɪtɪd/ *adj.* without limit; as much or as great as you want **OPP** **limited**

unload /ʌnˈləʊd/ *verb* **1** [T, I] ~ **(sth) (from sth)** to remove things from a vehicle or ship after it has taken them somewhere: *We unloaded the boxes from the back of the van.* ◇ *Parking here is restricted to vehicles that are loading or unloading.* **OPP** **load²** **2** [T] ~ **sb/sth (on/onto sb)** (*informal*) to get rid of sth you do not want or to pass it to sb else: *He shouldn't try and unload the responsibility onto you.*

unlock /ʌnˈlɒk/ *verb* [T, I] to open the lock on sth using a key; to be opened with a key: *I can't unlock this door.* ◇ *This door won't unlock.* **OPP** **lock¹**

unlucky /ʌnˈlʌki/ *adj.* (unluckier; unluckiest) having or causing bad luck: *They were unlucky to lose because they played so well.* ◇ *Thirteen is often thought to be an unlucky number.* **OPP** **lucky** ► unluckily /-kɪli/ *adv.*

unmanageable /ʌnˈmænɪdʒəbl/ *adj.* difficult or impossible to control or deal with **OPP** **manageable**

unmanned /ʌnˈmænd/ *adj.* if a machine, a vehicle, a place or an activity is **unmanned**, it does not have or need a person to control or operate it

unmarried /ʌnˈmærɪd/ *adj.* not married **SYN** **single¹** **OPP** **married**

unmistakable /ˌʌnmɪˈsteɪkəbl/ *adj.* that cannot be confused with anything else; easy to recognize: *She had an unmistakable French accent.* ► unmistakable /-bli/ *adv.*

unmoved /ʌnˈmuːvd/ *adj.* not affected in an emotional way: *The judge was unmoved by the man's sad story, and sent him to jail.*

unnatural /ʌnˈnætʃrəl/ *adj.* different from what is normal or expected **OPP** **natural¹** ► unnaturally /-rəli/ *adv.*: *It's unnaturally quiet in here.*

unnecessary 🔊 **B1** /ʌnˈnesəsəri/ *adj.* more than is needed or acceptable: *We should try to avoid all unnecessary expense.* ◇ *All this fuss is totally unnecessary.* **OPP** **necessary** ► unnecessarily /-rəli/ *adv.*: *His explanation was unnecessarily complicated.*

unnerve /ʌnˈnɜːv/ *verb* [T] to make sb feel nervous or frightened or lose confidence: *His silence unnerved us.* ► unnerving *adj.*: *an unnerving experience* ► unnervingly *adv.*

unnoticed /ʌnˈnəʊtɪst/ *adj.* not noticed or seen: *He didn't want his hard work to go unnoticed.*

unobtainable /ˌʌnəbˈteɪnəbl/ *adj.* that cannot be bought or obtained

unobtrusive /ˌʌnəbˈtruːsɪv/ *adj.* avoiding being noticed; not attracting attention ► unobtrusively *adv.*: *He tried to leave as unobtrusively as possible.*

unofficial /ˌʌnəˈfɪʃl/ *adj.* not accepted or approved by a person in authority: *an unofficial strike* ◇ *Unofficial reports say that four people died in the explosion.* **OPP** **official¹** ► unofficially /-ʃəli/ *adv.*

unorthodox /ʌnˈɔːθədɒks/ *adj.* different from what is generally accepted, usual or traditional **OPP** **orthodox**

unpack /ʌnˈpæk/ *verb* [T, I] (**TOURISM**) to take out the things that were in a bag, case, etc: *to unpack clothes/ a suitcase* ◇ *When we arrived at the hotel we unpacked and went to the beach.* **OPP** **pack¹**

unpaid /ʌnˈpeɪd/ *adj.* **1** not yet paid: *an unpaid bill* **2** not receiving money for work done: *an unpaid assistant* **3** (used about work) done without payment: *unpaid overtime*

unparalleled /ʌnˈpærəleld/ *adj.* (*formal*) used to emphasize that sth is bigger, better or worse than anything else like it: *The book has enjoyed a success unparalleled in recent publishing history.*

unpleasant 🔊 **B1** /ʌnˈpleznt/ *adj.* **1** not pleasant or comfortable: *This news has come as an unpleasant surprise.* **2** not friendly or polite: *There's no need to be unpleasant; we can discuss this in a friendly way.* **OPP** **pleasant** ► unpleasantly *adv.*

unplug /ʌnˈplʌg/ *verb* [T] (-gg-) to remove a piece of electrical equipment from the electricity supply: *Could you unplug the printer, please?* **OPP** **plug sth in**

unpopular /ʌnˈpɒpjələ(r)/ *adj.* ~ **(with sb)** not liked by many people: *Her methods made her very unpopular with the staff.* **OPP** **popular** ► unpopularity /ˌʌnˌpɒpjuˈlærəti/ *noun* [U]

unprecedented 🔊+ **C1** /ʌnˈpresɪdentɪd/ *adj.* never having happened or existed before ⊃ look at **precedent**

unpredictable /ˌʌnprɪˈdɪktəbl/ *adj.* **1** that cannot be predicted because it changes a lot or depends on so many different things: *unpredictable weather* ◇ *The result is entirely unpredictable.* **OPP** **predictable** **2** if a person is **unpredictable**, you cannot predict how they will behave in a particular situation **OPP** **predictable** ► unpredictability /ˌʌnprɪˌdɪktəˈbɪləti/ *noun* [U]: *the*

▸ **unpredictably** /ˌʌnprɪˈdɪktəbli/ *adv.*

unprincipled /ʌnˈprɪnsəpld/ *adj.* without moral principles **SYN dishonest OPP principled**

unproductive /ˌʌnprəˈdʌktɪv/ *adj.* not producing very much; not producing good results: *I've had a very unproductive day.* **OPP productive** ▸ **unproductively** *adv.*

unprofessional /ˌʌnprəˈfeʃənl/ *adj.* not reaching the standard expected in a particular profession **OPP professional**¹

unpronounceable /ˌʌnprəˈnaʊnsəbl/ *adj.* (used about a word, especially a name) too difficult to pronounce

unproven /ˌʌnˈpruːvn/ *adj.* not proved or tested: *unproven theories* **OPP proven**

unprovoked /ˌʌnprəˈvəʊkt/ *adj.* (used especially about an attack) not caused by anything the person who is attacked has said or done

unpublished /ʌnˈpʌblɪʃt/ *adj.* not published: *an unpublished novel*

unqualified /ʌnˈkwɒlɪfaɪd/ *adj.* **1** not having the knowledge or not having passed the exams that you need for sth: *I'm unqualified to offer an opinion on this matter.* **OPP qualified 2** complete; total: *an unqualified success* **OPP qualified**

unquestionable /ʌnˈkwestʃənəbl/ *adj.* certain; that cannot be doubted **OPP questionable**
▸ **unquestionably** /-bli/ *adv.*: *She is unquestionably the most famous opera singer in the world.*

unravel /ʌnˈrævl/ *verb* [T, I] (-ll-, *AmE* -l-) **1** if you **unravel** THREADS, strings, wool, etc. that are TWISTED or they **unravel**, you separate them or they become separated: *I unravelled the tangled string and wound it into a ball.* **2** (used about a complicated story, etc.) to become clear; to make sth become clear

unreactive /ˌʌnriˈæktɪv/ *adj.* (**CHEMISTRY**) having chemical characteristics that do not change when mixed with another substance **OPP reactive**

unreal /ˌʌnˈrɪəl/ *adj.* **1** very strange and seeming more like a dream than reality: *Her voice had an unreal quality about it.* **2** not connected with reality: *Some people have unreal expectations of marriage.*

unrealistic /ˌʌnrɪəˈlɪstɪk/ *adj.* not showing or accepting things as they are: *unrealistic expectations* ◊ *It is unrealistic to expect them to be able to solve the problem immediately.* **OPP realistic** ▸ **unrealistically** /-kli/ *adv.*: *They're asking unrealistically high prices.*

unreasonable /ʌnˈriːznəbl/ *adj.* unfair; expecting too much: *I think she is being totally unreasonable.* ◊ *He makes unreasonable demands on his staff.* **OPP reasonable** ▸ **unreasonably** /-bli/ *adv.*

unregulated /ˌʌnˈregjuleɪtɪd/ *adj.* not controlled by means of rules

unrelated **W** /ˌʌnrɪˈleɪtɪd/ *adj.* **1** not connected; not related to sth else: *The two events were totally unrelated.* **2** not belonging to the same family: *They have the same name but are, in fact, unrelated.* **OPP related**

unrelenting /ˌʌnrɪˈlentɪŋ/ *adj.* continuously strong, not becoming weaker or stopping

unreliable /ˌʌnrɪˈlaɪəbl/ *adj.* that cannot be trusted or depended on: *He's totally unreliable as a source of information.* ◊ *Trains here are notoriously unreliable.* **OPP reliable** ▸ **unreliability** /ˌʌnrɪˌlaɪəˈbɪləti/ *noun* [U]: *the unreliability of some statistics*

unrepeatable /ˌʌnrɪˈpiːtəbl/ *adj.* **1** too offensive or shocking to be repeated: *He called me several unrepeatable names.* **2** that cannot be repeated or done again: *an unrepeatable experience* **OPP repeatable**

unrequited /ˌʌnrɪˈkwaɪtɪd/ *adj.* (*formal*) (used about love) not returned by the person that you love

unreserved /ˌʌnrɪˈzɜːvd/ *adj.* **1** (used about seats in a theatre, etc.) not kept for the use of a particular person **OPP reserved 2** without limit; complete: *The government's action received the unreserved support of all parties.* ▸ **unreservedly** /-ˈzɜːvɪdli/ *adv.*

unresolved /ˌʌnrɪˈzɒlvd/ *adj.* (*formal*) (used about a problem or question) not yet solved or answered; not having been resolved

unresponsive /ˌʌnrɪˈspɒnsɪv/ *adj.* ~ **(to sth)** (*formal*) not reacting to sb/sth; not giving the response that you would expect or hope for: *A number of patients were unresponsive to conventional treatments.*

unrest /ʌnˈrest/ *noun* [U] a situation in which people are angry or not happy and likely to protest or fight: *social unrest*

unrestrained /ˌʌnrɪˈstreɪnd/ *adj.* (*formal*) not controlled

unrestricted /ˌʌnrɪˈstrɪktɪd/ *adj.* not controlled or limited in any way: *We have unrestricted access to all the facilities.* **SYN unlimited OPP restricted**

unrivalled (*especially BrE*) (*AmE usually* **unrivaled**) /ʌnˈraɪvld/ *adj.* much better than any other of the same type: *His knowledge of Greek theology is unrivalled.*

unroll /ʌnˈrəʊl/ *verb* [T, I] to open (sth) from a rolled position **OPP roll**²

unruly /ʌnˈruːli/ *adj.* difficult to control; without discipline: *an unruly crowd* ▸ **unruliness** *noun* [U]

unsafe /ʌnˈseɪf/ *adj.* **1** (used about a thing, a place or an activity) not safe; dangerous: *The roof was declared unsafe.* ◊ *It was considered unsafe to release the prisoners.* ◊ *unsafe sex* (= sex without protection against disease) **2** (used about people) in danger of being harmed: *He felt unsafe and alone.* **3** (**LAW**) (used about a decision in court) based on evidence that may be false or is not good enough: *Their convictions were declared unsafe.* **OPP safe**¹

unsaid /ʌnˈsed/ *adj.* [not before noun] thought but not spoken: *Some things are better left unsaid.*

unsatisfactory /ˌʌnˌsætɪsˈfæktəri/ *adj.* not acceptable; not good enough **SYN unacceptable** ▸ **unsatisfactorily** /-rəli/ *adv.*

unsaturated fat /ʌnˌsætʃəreɪtɪd ˈfæt/ *noun* [C, U] (**HEALTH**) a type of fat found, for example, in nuts and seeds, that is considered to be healthier in the diet than other types of fat ⊃ look at **polyunsaturated fat**, **saturated fat**

unsavoury (*BrE*) (*AmE* **unsavory**) /ʌnˈseɪvəri/ *adj.* unpleasant; not morally acceptable: *His friends are all unsavoury characters.*

unscathed /ʌnˈskeɪðd/ *adj.* not hurt, without injury: *He came out of the fight unscathed.*

unscheduled /ʌnˈʃedjuːld/ *adj.* that was not planned in advance: *The plane made an unscheduled stop in Fiji.*

unscrew /ˌʌnˈskruː/ *verb* [T] **1** to open or remove sth by turning it: *Could you unscrew the top of this bottle for me?* **2** to remove the SCREWS (= pointed pieces of metal used for fixing things together) from sth

unscrupulous /ʌnˈskruːpjələs/ *adj.* being dishonest, cruel or unfair in order to get what you want **OPP scrupulous**

unseeing /ˌʌnˈsiːɪŋ/ *adj.* not noticing or really looking at anything although your eyes are open

unseemly /ʌnˈsiːmli/ *adj.* (*old-fashioned*) (*formal*) (used about behaviour, etc.) not polite; not right in a particular situation

unseen /ʌnˈsiːn/ *adj.* **1** that cannot be seen: *unseen forces/powers* ◊ *I managed to get out of the room unseen.* **2** not seen before: *unseen dangers/difficulties*

unselfish /ʌnˈselfɪʃ/ *adj.* giving more time or importance to other people's needs or wishes than to your own **OPP** **selfish** ➔ look at **selfless**

unsettle /ʌnˈsetl/ *verb* [T] to make sb feel upset or worried, especially because a situation has changed: *Changing schools might unsettle the kids.*

unsettled /ʌnˈsetld/ *adj.* **1** (used about a situation) that may change; making people uncertain about what might happen: *These were difficult and unsettled times.* ◊ *The weather has been very unsettled* (= it has changed a lot). **2** not calm or relaxed: *They all felt restless and unsettled.* **3** (used about an argument, etc.) that continues without any agreement being reached **4** (used about a bill, etc.) not yet paid

unsettling /ʌnˈsetlɪŋ/ *adj.* making you feel upset, nervous or worried

unshaven /ʌnˈʃeɪvn/ *adj.* not having SHAVED or been SHAVED recently: *He looked pale and unshaven.* ◊ *his unshaven face*

unsightly /ʌnˈsaɪtli/ *adj.* very unpleasant to look at: *an unsightly new building* **SYN** **ugly**

unskilled /ʌnˈskɪld/ *adj.* not having or needing special skill or training: *an unskilled job/worker* **OPP** **skilled**

unsolicited /ˌʌnsəˈlɪsɪtɪd/ *adj.* not asked for: *unsolicited praise/advice*

unsound /ʌnˈsaʊnd/ *adj.* **1** in poor condition; weak: *The building is structurally unsound.* **OPP** **sound³** **2** based on wrong ideas and therefore not correct or sensible

unspecified /ʌnˈspesɪfaɪd/ *adj.* not stated clearly or definitely: *The story takes place at an unspecified date.*

unspoiled /ʌnˈspɔɪld/ (*also* **unspoilt** /ʌnˈspɔɪlt/) *adj.* **1** (used about a place) beautiful because it has not been changed or built on **2** (used about a person) not made unpleasant, badly behaved, etc. by being praised too much: *Despite being one of the best-known singers in the world, she has remained unspoiled.* **OPP** **spoilt**

unspoken /ʌnˈspəʊkən/ *adj.* (*formal*) not stated; not said in words but understood or agreed between people: *an unspoken assumption*

unstable ❶ /ʌnˈsteɪbl/ *adj.* **1** likely to change or fail: *a period of unstable government* **OPP** **stable¹** **2** (used about a person's moods or behaviour) likely to change suddenly or often **OPP** **stable¹** **3** likely to fall down or move; not FIRMLY fixed **OPP** **stable¹** ➔ noun **instability**

unsteady /ʌnˈstedi/ *adj.* **1** not completely in control of your movements so that you might fall: *She is still a little unsteady on her feet after the operation.* **2** shaking or moving in a way that is not controlled: *an unsteady voice/step* **OPP** **steady¹** ▸ **unsteadily** /-dəli/ *adv.* ▸ **unsteadiness** *noun* [U]

unstressed /ʌnˈstrest/ *adj.* (used about a syllable) pronounced without emphasis **OPP** **stressed**

unstructured /ʌnˈstrʌktʃəd/ *adj.* without structure or organization

unstuck /ʌnˈstʌk/ *adj.* no longer stuck together or stuck down: *The label on the parcel had come unstuck.* **IDM** **come unstuck** to fail badly; to go wrong: *His plan came unstuck when he realized he didn't have enough money.*

unsubscribe /ˌʌnsəbˈskraɪb/ *verb* [I, T] ~ (**from sth**) (**COMPUTING**) to remove your email address from an internet MAILING LIST (= a list of the names and addresses of people to whom advertising material or information is regularly sent by a business or an organization)

unsuccessful /ˌʌnsəkˈsesfl/ *adj.* ~ (**in sth**) not achieving what you wanted to: *His efforts to get a job proved unsuccessful.* ◊ *They were unsuccessful in meeting their objectives for the year.* ◊ *She made several unsuccessful attempts to see him.* **OPP** **successful** ▸ **unsuccessfully** /-fəli/ *adv.*

unsuitable /ʌnˈsuːtəbl/ *adj.* ~ (**for sb/sth**) not right or appropriate for sb/sth: *This film is unsuitable for children under 12.* **OPP** **suitable**

unsure /ˌʌnˈʃʊə(r), -ˈʃɔː(r)/ *adj.* **1** ~ (**about/of sth**) not certain; having doubts: *I didn't argue because I was unsure of the facts.* **OPP** **certain, sure¹** **2** ~ **of yourself** not feeling confident about yourself: *He's young and still quite unsure of himself.*

unsurprising /ˌʌnsəˈpraɪzɪŋ/ *adj.* not causing surprise **OPP** **surprising** ▸ **unsurprisingly** *adv.*: *Unsurprisingly, the plan failed.*

unsuspecting /ˌʌnsəˈspektɪŋ/ *adj.* not realizing that there is danger ➔ look at **suspect¹** (1), **suspicious** (2)

unsustainable /ˌʌnsəˈsteɪnəbl/ *adj.* that cannot be continued at the same level, rate, etc. **OPP** **sustainable**

unsympathetic /ˌʌnsɪmpəˈθetɪk/ *adj.* **1** ~ (**towards sb**) not feeling or showing any sympathy **OPP** **sympathetic** **2** ~ (**to/towards sth**) not in agreement with sth; not supporting an idea, aim, etc: *How can you trust a government that is unsympathetic to public opinion?* **OPP** **sympathetic** **3** (used about a person) not easy to like; unpleasant: *I found all the characters in the film unsympathetic.*

untangle /ʌnˈtæŋgl/ *verb* [T] to separate THREADS that have become tied together in a confused way: *The wires got mixed up and it took me ages to untangle them.*

untapped /ʌnˈtæpt/ *adj.* available but not yet used: *untapped reserves of oil*

unthinkable /ʌnˈθɪŋkəbl/ *adj.* impossible to imagine or accept: *It was unthinkable that he would never see her again.* **SYN** **inconceivable**

unthinking /ʌnˈθɪŋkɪŋ/ *adj.* (*formal*) done, said, etc. without thinking carefully ▸ **unthinkingly** *adv.*

untidy /ʌnˈtaɪdi/ *adj.* (**untidier**; **untidiest**) **1** not tidy or well arranged: *an untidy bedroom* ◊ *untidy hair* **2** (used about a person) not keeping things tidy or in good order: *My flatmate is so untidy!* **OPP** **neat, tidy¹** ▸ **untidily** /-dɪli/ *adv.* ▸ **untidiness** *noun* [U]

untie /ʌnˈtaɪ/ *verb* [T] (**untying**; **unties**; *pt, pp* **untied**) to remove a KNOT; to free sb/sth that is tied by a rope, etc. **OPP** **fasten, tie²**

until ❓ **A1** /ənˈtɪl/ (*also* **till**) *prep., conj.* up to the time or the event mentioned: *The restaurant is open until midnight.* ◊ *Until that moment she had been happy.* ◊ *She waited until he had finished.* ◊ *We won't leave until the police get here* (= we won't leave before they come).

untold /ʌnˈtəʊld/ *adj.* [only before noun] very great; so big, etc. that you cannot count or measure it: *untold suffering*

untouched /ʌnˈtʌtʃt/ *adj.* **1** ~ (**by sth**) not affected by sth, especially sth bad or unpleasant; not damaged: *Some buildings had remained untouched by the explosion.* **2** (used about food or drink) not eaten or drunk: *She left her meal untouched.* **3** not changed in any way: *The final clause in the contract will be left untouched.*

untoward /ˌʌntəˈwɔːd/ *adj.* (used about an event, etc.) unexpected and unpleasant: *The security guard noticed **nothing untoward**.*

untrue /ʌnˈtruː/ *adj.* **1** not true; not based on facts: *These accusations are totally untrue.* ◇ *an untrue claim/statement* ◇ *It would be untrue to say that something like this could never happen again.* **OPP true 2** ~ **(to sb/sth)** (*formal*) not LOYAL to sb/sth; doing sth that hurts or damages sb/sth: *If he agreed to their demands, he would be untrue to his principles.*

untruth /ˌʌnˈtruːθ/ *noun* [C] (*pl.* untruths /ʌnˈtruːðz, -ˈtruːθs/) (*formal*) something that is not true; a lie ▶ **untruthful** /ʌnˈtruːθfl/ *adj.*

untying /ʌnˈtaɪɪŋ/ present participle of **untie**

untypical /ʌnˈtɪpɪkl/ *adj.* not typical or usual: *an untypical example* **OPP typical** ⊃ look at **atypical**

unused¹ /ʌnˈjuːzd/ *adj.* that has not been used

unused² /ʌnˈjuːst/ *adj.* ~ **to sth/doing sth** not having any experience of sth: *She was unused to getting such a lot of attention.*

unusual ↱ **A2** /ʌnˈjuːʒuəl, -ʒəl/ *adj.* **1** not expected or normal: *It's unusual for Joe to be late.* **OPP usual 2** interesting because it is different: *What an unusual hat!*

unusually /ʌnˈjuːʒuəli, -ʒə-/ *adv.* **1** more than is common; extremely: *an unusually hot summer* **2** in a way that is not normal or typical of sb/sth: *Unusually for her, she forgot his birthday.* **OPP usually**

unveil ↱ **C1** /ʌnˈveɪl/ *verb* [T] to show sth new to the public for the first time: *The president unveiled a memorial to those who died in the war.*

unvoiced /ʌnˈvɔɪst/ = VOICELESS

unwanted /ʌnˈwɒntɪd/ *adj.* not wanted: *an unwanted gift*

unwarranted /ʌnˈwɒrəntɪd/ *adj.* (*formal*) that is not deserved or for which there is no good reason: *unwarranted criticism*

unwelcome /ʌnˈwelkəm/ *adj.* not wanted: *To avoid attracting unwelcome attention he spoke quietly.* **OPP welcome¹**

unwell /ʌnˈwel/ *adj.* [not before noun] (**HEALTH**) ill; sick: *to feel unwell* **OPP well²**

unwieldy /ʌnˈwiːldi/ *adj.* difficult to move or carry because it is too big, heavy, etc.

unwilling /ʌnˈwɪlɪŋ/ *adj.* not wanting to do sth but often forced to do it by other people **OPP willing**

unwind /ʌnˈwaɪnd/ *verb* (*pt, pp* unwound /-ˈwaʊnd/) **1** [T, I] if sth that has been wrapped into a ball or around sth unwinds or you unwind it, it becomes, or you make it, straight, flat or loose again: *He unwound his scarf from his neck.* ⊃ look at **wind³ (2) 2** [I] (*informal*) to relax, especially after working hard: *After a busy day, it takes me a while to unwind.*

unwise /ʌnˈwaɪz/ *adj.* showing a lack of good judgement: *It would be unwise to tell anyone about our plan yet.* **SYN foolish OPP wise** ▶ **unwisely** *adv.*

unwitting /ʌnˈwɪtɪŋ/ *adj.* [only before noun] not realizing sth; not intending to do sth: *an unwitting accomplice to the crime* ▶ **unwittingly** *adv.*

unwrap /ʌnˈræp/ *verb* [T] (-pp-) to take off the paper, etc. that covers or protects sth

unzip /ʌnˈzɪp/ *verb* (-pp-) **1** [T, I] if you **unzip** a bag, piece of clothing, etc. , or if it **unzips**, you open it by pulling on the ZIP (= the device that fastens the opening). **OPP zip² 2** [T] (**COMPUTING**) to return a file to its original size after it has been COMPRESSED (= made smaller) **SYN decompress OPP zip²**

up¹ ↱ **A1** /ʌp/ *prep., adv.* **1** at or to a high or higher level or position: *The monkey **climbed up** the tree.* ◇ *I carried her suitcase up to the third floor.* ◇ *Put your **hand up** if you know the answer.* ◇ *I walked up the hill.* **2** in or into a VERTICAL position: *Stand up, please.* ◇ *Is he up* (= out of bed) *yet?* **3** used for showing an increase in sth: *Prices have gone up.* ◇ *Turn the volume up.* ⊃ note at **trend¹ 4** used with verbs of closing or covering: *Do up your coat. It's cold.* ◇ *She tied the parcel up with string.* ◇ *I found some wood to cover up the hole.* **5** to the place where sb/sth is: *She ran up to her mother and kissed her.* ◇ *A car drove up and two men got out.* **6** coming or being put together: *The teacher collected up our exam papers.* ◇ *Asif and Joe teamed up in the doubles competition.* **7** (used about a period of time) finished: *Stop writing. Your time's up.* **8** into pieces: *We chopped the old table up and used it for firewood.* ◇ *She tore up the letter and threw it away.* **9** used for showing that an action continues until it is completed: *Eat up, everybody, I want you to finish everything on the table.* ◇ *Can you help me clean up the kitchen?* **10** in a particular direction: *I live just up the road.* ◇ *Move up a little and let me sit down.* **11** in or to the north: *My parents have just moved up north.* ◇ *When are you going up to Scotland?* **12** (**COMPUTING**) working; in operation: *Are the computers back up yet?* **13** (*informal*) used for showing that sth has been made less good: *I really messed up when I told the interviewer I liked sleeping.* **IDM be up for sth 1** to be available to be bought or chosen: *That house is up for sale.* ◇ *How many candidates are up for election?* **2** (*informal*) to be willing to take part in an activity: *Is anyone up for a swim?* **be up to sb** to be sb's responsibility: *I can't take the decision. It's not up to me.* **not up to much** (*informal*) not very good: *The programme wasn't up to much.* **up against sth/sb** facing sth/sb that causes problems **up and down** backwards and forwards, or rising and falling: *He was nervously walking up and down outside the interview room.* **up and running** (used about sth new) working; being used **up there** (*informal*) among or almost the best, most important, etc: *I don't know if it's the best I've ever played, but it's up there.* **up to sth 1** as much/many as: *We're expecting up to 100 people at the meeting.* **2** as far as now: *Up to now, things have been easy.* **3** capable of sth: *I don't feel up to cooking this evening. I'm too tired.* **4** doing sth secret and perhaps bad: *What are the children up to? Go and see.* **what's up?** (*informal*) what's the matter?

up² /ʌp/ *noun*
IDM ups and downs the mixture of good and bad things in life or in a particular situation or relationship: *Every marriage has its ups and downs.*

up- /ʌp/ *prefix* (used in adjectives, verbs and nouns) higher; upwards; towards the top of sth: *upland* ◇ *upturned* ◇ *upgrade* ◇ *uphill*

up-and-coming *adj.* likely to be successful and popular in the future

upbeat /ˈʌpbiːt/ *adj.* (*informal*) positive and enthusiastic; making you feel that the future will be good: *The tone of the speech was upbeat.* **SYN optimistic**

upbringing /ˈʌpbrɪŋɪŋ/ *noun* [sing.] the way a child is treated and taught how to behave by their parents: *a strict upbringing*

upcoming ↱ **C1** /ˈʌpkʌmɪŋ/ *adj.* [only before noun] going to happen soon: *the upcoming presidential election*

update¹ 🔊 **B1** /ˌʌpˈdeɪt/ *verb* [T] **1** to make sth more modern **2** ~ sth; ~ sb (on sth) to put the most recent information into sth; to give sb the most recent information: *Our database of addresses is updated regularly.* ◇ *Shall I update you on what happened at the meeting?*

update² 🔊 **B1** /ˈʌpdeɪt/ *noun* [C] **1** ~ (on sth) a report or statement that gives the latest information: *an update on a news story* **2** (COMPUTING) the most recent improvements to a computer program that are sent to people using it

upfront /ˌʌpˈfrʌnt/ *adj.* **1** not trying to hide what you think or do: *He's been upfront about his intentions since the beginning.* **2** [only before noun] paid in advance, before other payments are made: *There will be an upfront fee of 4%.* ◯ look at **up front** at **front¹**

upgrade 🔊+ **C1** /ˌʌpˈgreɪd/ *verb* **1** ~ (from sth) (to sth) (COMPUTING) to make a machine, computer system, etc. more powerful and efficient: *Upgrading to new software can be expensive.* **2** [T] to improve the condition of a building, etc. in order to provide a better service: *to upgrade the town's leisure facilities* ◯ look at **downgrade 3** [T, often passive] ~ sb (to sth) (TOURISM) to give sb a better seat on a plane, room in a hotel, etc. than the one that they have paid for: *On the flight back, we were upgraded to business class.* **4** [T] ~ sb (to sth) to give sb a more important job ▶ **upgrade** 🔊+ **C1** /ˈʌpgreɪd/ *noun* [C]: *Frequent flyers qualify for a free upgrade.*

upheaval /ʌpˈhiːvl/ *noun* [C, U] a sudden big change, especially one that causes a lot of trouble

uphill /ˌʌpˈhɪl/ *adj., adv.* **1** going towards the top of a hill **OPP** **downhill 2** needing a lot of effort: *It was an uphill struggle to find a job.*

uphold 🔊+ **C1** /ʌpˈhəʊld/ *verb* [T] (*pt, pp* upheld /-ˈheld/) to support a decision, etc. especially when other people are against it

upholstered /ʌpˈhəʊlstəd/ *adj.* (used about a chair, etc.) covered with a soft thick material

upholstery /ʌpˈhəʊlstəri/ *noun* [U] the thick soft materials used to cover chairs, car seats, etc.

upkeep /ˈʌpkiːp/ *noun* [U] **1** the cost or process of keeping sth in a good condition: *The landlord pays for the upkeep of the building.* **2** the cost or process of providing children or animals with what they need to live

upland¹ /ˈʌplənd/ *noun* [C, usually pl.] (GEOGRAPHY) an area of high land that is located away from the coast: *the southern uplands of the country*

upland² /ˈʌplənd/ *adj.* [only before noun] (GEOGRAPHY) consisting of hills and mountains: *an upland area* ◇ *upland agriculture*

uplifting /ˌʌpˈlɪftɪŋ/ *adj.* producing a feeling of hope and happiness: *an uplifting speech*

upload¹ /ˌʌpˈləʊd/ *verb* [T] (COMPUTING) to send data to another computer, device or the internet **OPP** **download¹**

upload² /ˈʌpləʊd/ *noun* [C] (COMPUTING) data that has been moved to a larger computer system from a smaller one ◯ look at **download²** (1)

upmarket /ˌʌpˈmɑːkɪt/ *adj.* expensive and of high quality: *an upmarket restaurant* **OPP** **downmarket** ▶ **upmarket** *adv.*: *The company has been forced to move more upmarket.*

upon 🔊 **B1** /əˈpɒn/ *prep.* (*formal*) **1** = ON (1) **2** = ON (15) **3** = ON (17)

upper 🔊 **B2** ⊙ /ˈʌpə(r)/ *adj.* [only before noun] in a higher position than sth else; located above sth: *He had a cut on his upper lip.* **OPP** **lower¹** **IDM** **get, have, etc. the upper hand** to get into a stronger position than another person; to gain control over sb

ˌupper ˈcase *noun* [U] (LANGUAGE) letters that are written or printed in their large form: *'BBC' is written in upper case.* **SYN** **capital¹** **OPP** **lower case**

the ˌupper ˈclass *noun* [sing.] (*also* the upper classes [pl.]) (SOCIAL STUDIES) the groups of people that are considered to have the highest social position and that have more money and/or power than other people in society: *a member of the upper class/upper classes* ◯ look at **middle class**, **working class** ▶ **upper class** *adj.*: *They're upper class.* ◇ *an upper-class accent* ◯ look at **middle-class**, **working class**

uppercut /ˈʌpəkʌt/ *noun* [C] (SPORT) (in BOXING) a way of hitting sb on the CHIN (= the part of the face below the mouth), in which you bend your arm and move your hand upwards

ˌupper ˈhouse (*also* ˌupper ˈchamber, second chamber) *noun* [sing.] (POLITICS) one of the parts of a parliament in countries that have a parliament that is divided into two parts. In the UK it is the House of Lords and in the US it is the Senate. ◯ look at **lower house**

uppermost /ˈʌpəməʊst/ *adj.* in the highest or most important position: *Concern for her family was uppermost in her mind.*

upright /ˈʌpraɪt/ *adj., adv.* **1** in or into a VERTICAL position: *I was so tired I could hardly stay upright.* **SYN** **erect¹ 2** honest and responsible **IDM** **bolt upright** → BOLT³

uprising /ˈʌpraɪzɪŋ/ *noun* [C] (POLITICS, SOCIAL STUDIES) a situation in which a group of people start to fight against the people in power in their country **SYN** **insurrection**

uproar /ˈʌprɔː(r)/ *noun* [U, sing.] a lot of noise, CONFUSION, anger, etc.; an angry discussion about sth: *The meeting ended in uproar.*

uproot /ˌʌpˈruːt/ *verb* [T] **1** to pull up a plant by the roots: *Strong winds had uprooted the tree.* **2** to leave a place where you have lived for a long time; to make sb do this

uprush /ˈʌprʌʃ/ *noun* [sing.] (*formal*) a sudden upward movement

upset¹ 🔊 **B1** /ʌpˈset/ *verb* [T] (upsetting; *pt, pp* upset) **1** to make sb worry or feel unhappy: *The pictures of starving children upset her.* **2** to make sth go wrong: *to upset somebody's plans* **3** (HEALTH) to make sb ill in the stomach **4** to knock sth over: *I upset a cup of tea all over the tablecloth.*

upset² 🔊 **B1** /ʌpˈset/ *adj.* **1** [not before noun] worried and unhappy: *She was looking very upset about something.* **2** (HEALTH) slightly ill: *I've got an upset stomach.*

upset³ /ˈʌpset/ *noun* **1** [U, C] a situation in which there are unexpected problems or difficulties: *The company survived the recent upset in share prices.* **2** [C] a slight illness in your stomach: *a stomach upset* **3** [U, C] a situation that causes you to worry and feel sad: *It had been the cause of much emotional upset.* ◇ *She's had a few upsets recently.*

upshot /ˈʌpʃɒt/ *noun* [sing.] the ~ (of sth) the final result, especially of a conversation or an event

upside down /ˌʌpsaɪd ˈdaʊn/ *adv., adj.* with the top part turned to the bottom: *You're holding the picture upside down.* **IDM** **turn sth upside down 1** to make a place untidy when looking for sth: *I had to turn the house upside* down looking for my keys. **2** to cause large changes and CONFUSION in a person's life: *His sudden death turned her world upside down.*

upstairs ? A1 /ˌʌpˈsteəz/ *adv.* to or on a higher floor of a building: *to go upstairs* ◇ *She's sleeping upstairs.* OPP **downstairs** ▸ **upstairs** ? A2 *adj.* [only before noun]: *an upstairs window* ▸ **the upstairs** *noun* [sing.]: *We're going to paint the upstairs.*

upstream /ˌʌpˈstriːm/ *adv., adj.* (GEOGRAPHY) in the direction that a river flows from: *He found it hard work swimming upstream.* OPP **downstream**

upsurge /ˈʌpsɜːdʒ/ *noun* [C, usually sing.] ~ **(in/of sth)** a sudden increase of sth: *an upsurge in violent crime*

uptake /ˈʌpteɪk/ *noun*
IDM **quick/slow on the uptake** quick/slow to understand the meaning of sth: *I gave him a hint but he's slow on the uptake.*

upthrust /ˈʌpθrʌst/ *noun* [U] (PHYSICS) the force with which a liquid or gas pushes up against an object that is floating in it

uptight /ˌʌpˈtaɪt/ *adj.* (*informal*) nervous and not relaxed: *Relax! You're getting too uptight about it*

up to ˈdate *adj.* **1** modern: *up-to-date fashions* **2** having the most recent information

up-to-the-ˈminute *adj.* having the most recent information possible

upturn /ˈʌptɜːn/ *noun* [C] ~ **(in sth)** an improvement in sth: *an upturn in support for the government* OPP **downturn**

upturned /ˌʌpˈtɜːnd/ *adj.* **1** pointing upwards: *an upturned nose* **2** with the top part turned to the bottom: *an upturned boat*

upward /ˈʌpwəd/ *adj.* moving or directed towards a higher place: *an **upward trend** in exports* (= an increase) OPP **downward**

upwardly ˈmobile *adj.* (SOCIAL STUDIES) moving towards a higher social position, usually in which you become richer: *an upwardly mobile lifestyle*

upwards ? B2 /ˈʌpwədz/ (*also* **upward**) *adv.* **1** towards a higher place or position: *Place your hands on the table with the palms facing upwards.* **2** towards a higher amount or price: *Bad weather forced the price of fruit upwards.* **3** ~ **of sth** more than the amount or number mentioned: *You should expect to pay upwards of $150 for a hotel room.*

uranium /juˈreɪniəm/ *noun* [U] (*symb.* U) (CHEMISTRY) a chemical element. Uranium is a heavy silver-white RADIOACTIVE metal used mainly in producing nuclear energy: *Uranium is highly radioactive.* ❶ For more information on the periodic table of elements, look at the **Reference Section** of this dictionary.

Uranus /ˈjʊərənəs/ *noun* [sing.] (ASTRONOMY) the planet in the SOLAR SYSTEM that is seventh in order of distance from the sun

urban ? B2 ⓦ /ˈɜːbən/ *adj.* **1** (GEOGRAPHY) connected with a town or city: *urban development* ◯ look at **rural 2** [only before noun] (MUSIC) connected with types of music such as RHYTHM AND BLUES and HIP HOP that are played by black musicians: *the urban music scene*

urbane /ɜːˈbeɪn/ *adj.* (used especially about a man) good at knowing what to say and how to behave in social situations; appearing relaxed and confident ▸ **urbanely** *adv.* ▸ **urbanity** /-ˈbænəti/ *noun* [U]

urbanization (*BrE also* **-isation**) /ˌɜːbənaɪˈzeɪʃn/ *noun* [U] (GEOGRAPHY) **1** the process in which towns, factories, etc. are built in country areas **2** the process in which more and more people move to live in towns and cities from the country

urbanized (*BrE also* **-ised**) /ˈɜːbənaɪzd/ *adj.* (GEOGRAPHY) (used about an area, a country, etc.) having a lot of towns, streets, factories, etc. rather than countryside

Urdu /ˈʊəduː, ˈɜːduː/ *noun* [U] (LANGUAGE) the official language of Pakistan, which is also spoken in parts of India

urea /juˈriːə/ *noun* [U] (BIOLOGY) a clear substance that is found especially in URINE (= the liquid waste that is passed from the body when you go to the toilet)

ureter /juˈriːtə(r), ˈjʊərɪtə(r)/ *noun* [C] (ANATOMY) the tube that waste liquid from the body passes through to get from the KIDNEYS to the BLADDER

urethra /juˈriːθrə/ *noun* [C] (ANATOMY) the tube that carries liquid waste out of the body. In men and male animals SPERM (= the liquid produced by the male sex organs) also flows along this tube. ▸ **urethral** /-θrəl/ *adj.*

urge¹ ? B2 /ɜːdʒ/ *verb* [T] **1** ~ **sb (to do sth); ~ sth** to advise or try hard to persuade sb to do sth: *I urged him to fight the decision.* ◇ *Police urged caution on the icy roads.* ◯ note at **recommend 2** to force or encourage sb/sth to go in a certain direction: *He urged his horse over the fence.*
PHR V **urge sb on** to encourage sb: *The captain urged his team on.*

urge² /ɜːdʒ/ *noun* [C] a strong need or desire: *sexual/ creative urges*

urgent ? B2 /ˈɜːdʒənt/ *adj.* needing immediate attention: *an urgent message* ▸ **urgency** /-dʒənsi/ *noun* [U]: *a matter of the greatest urgency* ▸ **urgently** *adv.*: *I must see you urgently.*

urinal /juəˈraɪnl, ˈjʊərɪnl/ *noun* [C] a type of toilet for men that is attached to the wall; a room or building containing urinals

urinary /ˈjʊərɪnəri/ *adj.* (HEALTH) connected with URINE or the parts of the body through which it passes

urinate /ˈjʊərɪneɪt/ *verb* [I] (BIOLOGY) to pass URINE from the body

urine /ˈjʊərɪn, -raɪn/ *noun* [U] (BIOLOGY) the liquid waste that is passed from the body when you go to the toilet

URL /ˌjuː ɑːr ˈel/ *noun* [C] (COMPUTING) the address of a World Wide Web page (the abbreviation for 'uniform/ universal resource locator')

urn /ɜːn/ *noun* [C] **1** a special container, used especially to hold the ASHES (= the powder) that is left when a dead person has been CREMATED (= burnt) **2** a large metal container used for making a large quantity of tea or coffee and for keeping it hot

urology /juəˈrɒlədʒi/ *noun* [U] (MEDICINE) the scientific study of the URINARY system ▸ **urological** /ˌjuərəˈlɒdʒɪkl/ *adj.* ▸ **urologist** /juəˈrɒlədʒɪst/ *noun* [C]

US /ˌjuː ˈes/ (*often* **the US**) *abbr.* = UNITED STATES OF AMERICA

us ? A1 /əs, *strong form* ʌs/ *pron.* (used as the object of a verb, or after *be*) me and another person or other people; me and you: *Come with us.* ◇ *Leave us alone.* ◇ *Will you write to us?*

USA /ˌjuː es ˈeɪ/ (*often* **the USA**) *abbr.* = UNITED STATES OF AMERICA

usable /ˈjuːzəbl/ *adj.* that can be used

usage ? + B2 ⓦ /ˈjuːsɪdʒ, ˈjuːzɪdʒ/ *noun* **1** [U] the way that sth is used; the amount that sth is used **2** [C, U] (LANGUAGE) the way that words are normally used in a language: *a guide to English grammar and usage*

USB /ˌjuː esˈbiː/ *abbr.* (**COMPUTING**) the system for connecting other pieces of equipment to a computer (the abbreviation for 'universal serial bus'): *a USB port*

USB drive = FLASH DRIVE

use¹ 🔊 **A1** 🔊 /juːz/ *verb* [T] **1** ~ sth (as/for sth); ~ sth (to do sth) to do sth with a machine, an object, a method, etc. for a particular purpose: *Could I use your phone?* ◇ *The building was used as a shelter for homeless people.* ◇ *What's this used for?* ◇ *We used the money to buy a house.* ◇ *Use your imagination!* ◇ *That's a word I never use.* ◇ *A pen is used for writing with.* **2** to need or to take sth: *Don't use all the milk.* **3** to treat sb/sth in an unfair way in order to get sth that you want **PHR V** **use sth up** to use sth until no more is left

use² 🔊 **A2** 🔊 /juːs/ *noun* **1** [U, sing.] the act of using sth or of being used: *She kept the money for use in an emergency.* ◇ *The use of car share schemes is now widespread.* **2** [C, U] a purpose for which sth is used: *This machine has many uses.* **3** [U] the ability or permission to use sth: *He lost the use of his hand after the accident.* ◇ *She offered them the use of her car.* **IDM** **be of use (to sb)** be useful: *Will this jumper be of use to you or should I get rid of it?* **come into/go out of use** to start/stop being used regularly or by a lot of people: *Email came into widespread use in the 1990s.* **it's no use (doing sth) | what's the use of (doing sth)?** used to say that there is no point in doing something because it will not be successful or have a good result: *It's no use studying for an exam at the last minute.* ◇ *What's the use of trying?* **make use of sth/sb** to use sth/sb in a way that will give you an advantage

used 🔊 **B1** 🔊 *adj.* **1** /juːzd/ that has had another owner before: *a garage selling used cars* **SYN** **second-hand** **2** /juːst/ ~ to sth/doing sth familiar with sth because you do it or experience it often: *He's used to the heat.* ◇ *I'll never get used to getting up so early.*

used to 🔊 **A2** /ˈjuːst tə, before vowels and finally tu/ *modal verb* for talking about sth that happened often or continuously in the past or about a situation that existed in the past: *Did you use to believe in Father Christmas?* ◇ *He didn't use to speak to me.* ◇ *She used to live with her parents (= but she doesn't now).* ◇ *You used to live in Glasgow, didn't you?* ⊃ look at **would** (9)

useful 🔊 **A1** 🔊 /ˈjuːsfl/ *adj.* having some practical use; helpful: *a useful tool* ◇ *useful advice* ▸ **usefully** /-fəli/ *adv.* ▸ **usefulness** *noun* [U] **IDM** **come in useful** to be of practical help in a certain situation: *Don't throw that box away — it might come in useful for something.*

useless 🔊+ **B2** /ˈjuːsləs/ *adj.* **1** that does not work well; that does not achieve anything: *This new machine is useless.* ◇ *It's useless complaining/to complain — you won't get your money back.* **2** ~ (at sth/doing sth) (*informal*) (used about a person) weak or not successful at sth: *I'm useless at sport.* ▸ **uselessly** *adv.* ▸ **uselessness** *noun* [U]

user 🔊 **A2** /ˈjuːzə(r)/ *noun* [C] (often in compounds) (**COMPUTING**) a person who uses a service, machine, place, etc: *users of public transport* ◇ *computer software users*

user exˈperience *noun* [C] (*abbr.* UX) (**COMPUTING**) what it is like for sb to use a particular product such as a website, for example how easy or difficult it is to use: *The new features will improve the user experience.* ⊃ look at **user interface**

userˈfriendly *adj.* easy to understand and use: *You'll find this program very user-friendly.* ▸ **user-friendliness** *noun* [U]

ˈuser group *noun* [C] a group of people who use a particular thing and who share information about it, especially people who share information about computers on the internet

user ˈinterface *noun* [C] (*abbr.* UI) (**COMPUTING**) the way a computer gives information to a user or receives instructions from a user: *The new user interface has a simpler display.* ⊃ look at **user experience**

username /ˈjuːzəneɪm/ *noun* [C] (**COMPUTING**) the name you use in order to be able to use a computer program or system: *Please enter your username.*

usher¹ /ˈʌʃə(r)/ *noun* [C] a person who shows people to their seats in a theatre, church, etc.

usher² /ˈʌʃə(r)/ *verb* [T] (used with an adverb or a preposition) to take or show sb where to go: *I was ushered into an office.* **PHR V** **usher sth in** (*formal*) to be the beginning of sth new or to make sth new begin: *The agreement ushered in a new period of peace for the two countries.*

USP /ˌjuː es ˈpiː/ *noun* [C] (**BUSINESS**) a feature of a product or service that makes it different from others (the abbreviation for 'unique selling point/ proposition'): *You need to come up with a USP.*

usual 🔊 **A2** /ˈjuːʒuəl, -ʒəl/ *adj.* ~ (for sb/sth) (to do sth) happening or used most often: *It's usual for her to work at weekends.* ◇ *He got home later than usual.* ◇ *I sat in my usual seat.* **OPP** **unusual** **IDM** **as usual** in the way that has often happened before: *Here's Dylan, late as usual!*

usually 🔊 **A1** /ˈjuːʒuəli, -ʒə-/ *adv.* in the way that is usual; most often: *She's usually home by six.* ◇ *We usually go out on Saturdays.*

usurp /juːˈzɜːp/ *verb* [T] (*formal*) to take sb's position and/ or power without having the right to do this ▸ **usurper** *noun* [C]

UTC /ˌjuː tiː ˈsiː/ *abbr.* **Universal Time Coordinated** (the time based on ATOMIC CLOCKS (= very accurate and scientific clocks), used as the basis of legal time in most countries) ⊃ look at **GMT**

utensil /juːˈtensl/ *noun* [C] a type of tool that is used in the home: *kitchen/cooking utensils*

uterus /ˈjuːtərəs/ *noun* [C] (*pl.* uteruses, uteri /-raɪ/) (**ANATOMY**) the part of a woman or female animal where a baby develops before it is born **SYN** **womb** ⊃ picture at **fertilization** ▸ **uterine** /-raɪn/ *adj.*

utility 🔊+ **C1** 🔊 /juːˈtɪləti/ *noun* (*pl.* -ies) **1** [C] a service provided for the public, such as a water, gas or electricity supply: *the administration of public utilities* **2** [U] (*formal*) the quality of being useful **3** [C] (**COMPUTING**) a program or part of a program that does a particular task

uˈtility room *noun* [C] a small room in some houses, often next to the kitchen, where people keep large pieces of equipment, such as a washing machine

utilize 🔊+ **C1** 🔊 (*BrE also* -ise) /ˈjuːtəlaɪz/ *verb* [T] (*formal*) to make use of sth: *to utilize natural resources* ▸ **utilization** 🔊 (*BrE also* -isation) /ˌjuːtəlaɪˈzeɪʃn/ *noun* [U]

utmost¹ /ˈʌtməʊst/ *adj.* [only before noun] greatest: *a message of the utmost importance*

utmost² /ˈʌtməʊst/ *noun* [sing.] the greatest amount possible: *Resources have been exploited to the utmost.* ◇ *I will do my utmost (= try as hard as possible) to help.*

utopia /juːˈtəʊpiə/ (*also* Utopia) *noun* [C, U] a place or state that exists only in the imagination, where everything is perfect ▸ **utopian** /-piən/ (*also* Utopian) *adj.*

utter¹ /ˈʌtə(r)/ adj. [only before noun] complete; total: *He felt an utter fool.* ▶ **utterly** 🔊+ **C1** adv.: *It's utterly impossible.*

utter² /ˈʌtə(r)/ verb [T] (*formal*) to say sth or make a sound with your voice: *She did not utter a word* (= she did not say anything) *in the meeting.* ▶ **utterance** noun [C]

U-turn noun [C] **1** a type of movement where a car, etc. turns round so that it can go back in the direction it came from **2** (*informal*) a sudden change from one plan or policy to a completely different or opposite one ⊃ look at **about-turn**

UV /ˌjuː ˈviː/ abbr. = ULTRAVIOLET: *UV radiation*

uvula /ˈjuːvjələ/ noun [C] (*pl.* uvulae /-liː/) (**ANATOMY**) a small piece of FLESH that hangs from the top of the inside of the mouth just above the throat ⊃ picture at **body**

UX /ˌjuː ˈeks/ abbr. = USER EXPERIENCE

V v

V¹ /viː/ (*also* v) noun [C, U] (*pl.* V's, v's) the 22nd letter of the English alphabet: *'Velvet' begins with (a) 'V'.*

V² abbr. (in writing) (*pl.* V) = VOLT

v abbr. **1** /viː/ = VERSUS: *Liverpool v Everton* **2** (in writing) (*BrE, informal*) = VERY¹: *v good*

vacancy /ˈveɪkənsi/ noun [C] (*pl.* -ies) **1 ~ (for sb/sth)** a job that is available for sb to do: *We have a vacancy for a cleaner at our school.* **2** (**TOURISM**) a room in a hotel, etc. that is available: *The sign outside the hotel said 'No Vacancies'.*

vacant /ˈveɪkənt/ adj. **1** (used about a house, hotel room, seat, etc.) not being used; empty **2** (used about a job in a company, etc.) that is available for sb to take **3** showing no sign of intelligence or understanding: *a vacant expression* ▶ **vacantly** adv.: *She stared at him vacantly.*

vacate /vəˈkeɪt, veɪˈk-/ verb [T] (*formal*) to leave a building, a seat, a job, a hotel room, etc. so that it is available for sb else

vacation 🔊 **A1** /veɪˈkeɪʃn, vəˈk-/ noun **1** [U, C] (*AmE*) (**TOURISM**) = HOLIDAY (1): *The boss is on vacation.* **2** [C] (*BrE*) any of the periods of time when universities or courts of law are closed: *the Christmas/Easter vacation*

vaccinate /ˈvæksɪneɪt/ verb [T] [often passive] **~ sb (against sth)** (**MEDICINE**) to give a person or an animal a substance that protects the body from a disease, especially by INJECTING it (= putting it into the body through a needle): *Were you vaccinated against measles as a child?* ⊃ look at **immunize, inoculate** ▶ **vaccination** /ˌvæksɪˈneɪʃn/ noun [C, U]

vaccine /ˈvæksiːn/ noun [C] (**MEDICINE**) a substance that is put into the blood and that protects the body from a disease

vacuole /ˈvækjuəʊl/ noun [C] (**BIOLOGY**) an empty space inside a living cell ⊃ picture at **cell**

vacuum¹ 🔊+ **C1** /ˈvækjuːm/ noun [C] **1** (**PHYSICS**) a space that is completely empty of all substances, including air or other gases: *vacuum-packed foods* (= in a pack from which the air has been removed) ⊃ picture at **vacuum flask 2** [usually sing.] a situation from which sth is missing or lacking: *The writer criticized the moral vacuum in society.* **3** [usually sing.] the act of cleaning sth with a VACUUM CLEANER: *to give a room a quick vacuum*

vacuum² /ˈvækjuːm/ verb [T, I] to clean sth using a VACUUM CLEANER **SYN** **hoover**

vacuum cleaner (*BrE also* Hoover™) noun [C] an electric machine that cleans carpets, etc. by SUCKING up dirt ⊃ look at **cleaner** (2)

vacuum flask (*also* flask) (*both BrE*) (*AmE* ˈvacuum bottle) noun [C] a container with double walls with a VACUUM between them, used for keeping liquids hot or cold

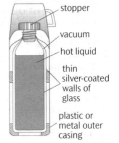

vacuum flask/ vacuum bottle

- stopper
- vacuum
- hot liquid
- thin silver-coated walls of glass
- plastic or metal outer casing

vagina /vəˈdʒaɪnə/ noun [C] (**ANATOMY**) the passage in the body of a woman or female animal that connects the outer sex organs to the WOMB (= the part where a baby grows)

vagrant /ˈveɪɡrənt/ noun [C] a person who has no home and no job, especially one who asks people for money

vague 🔊+ **C1** /veɪɡ/ adj. **1** not clear or definite: *He was very vague about how much money he'd spent.* ◇ *a vague shape in the distance* **2** (used about a person) not thinking or understanding clearly: *She looked vague when I tried to explain.* ▶ **vagueness** noun [U]

vaguely /ˈveɪɡli/ adv. **1** in a way that is not clear; slightly: *Her name is vaguely familiar.* **2** without thinking about what is happening: *He smiled vaguely and walked away.*

vain /veɪn/ adj. **1** failing to produce the result you want: *She turned away in a vain attempt to hide her tears.* **SYN** **useless 2** (used about a person) too proud of your own appearance, abilities, etc: *He's so vain — he looks in every mirror he passes.* ⊃ noun **vanity** ▶ **vainly** adv.

IDM in vain without success: *The firemen tried in vain to put out the fire.*

vale /veɪl/ noun [C] (**GEOGRAPHY**) a valley: *the Vale of York*

valency /ˈveɪlənsi/ noun [C, U] (*pl.* -ies) **1** (**CHEMISTRY**) a measurement of the power of an ATOM to combine with others, by the number of HYDROGEN ATOMS it can combine with or take the place of: *Carbon has a valency of 4.* **2** (**GRAMMAR**) the number of elements that a word, especially a verb, combines with in a sentence

valentine /ˈvæləntaɪn/ noun [C] **1** (*also* ˈvalentine card, ˈvalentine's card /ˈvæləntaɪnz kɑːd/) a card that you send, often without putting your name on it, to sb you love ❶ It is traditional to send these cards on **St Valentine's Day** (14 February). **2** the person you send this card to

valet¹ /ˈvæleɪ, -lɪt/ noun [C] **1** a man's personal servant who takes care of his clothes, serves his meals, etc. **2** (*BrE*) a hotel employee whose job is to clean the clothes of hotel guests **3** (*AmE*) a person who parks your car for you at a hotel or restaurant

valet² /ˈvælɪt/ verb **1** [T] (*BrE*) to clean a person's car carefully and completely, especially on the inside: *a car valeting service* **2** [I] to perform the duties of a VALET

valiant /ˈvæliənt/ adj. (*formal*) full of courage and not afraid ▶ **valiantly** adv.

valid ⚑+ **B2** Ⓦ /'vælɪd/ adj. **1** that is legally or officially acceptable: *This passport is valid for one year only.* **OPP invalid**[1] **2** based on what is logical or true; acceptable: *I could raise no valid objections to the plan.* ◇ *Jeff's making a perfectly valid point.* **OPP invalid**[1] ▸ **validity** ⚑+ **C1** Ⓦ /vəˈlɪdəti/ noun [U]

validate Ⓦ /'vælɪdeɪt/ verb [T] (formal) **1** to prove that sth is true: *to validate a claim/theory* **OPP invalidate** **2** to make sth legally recognized: *to validate a contract* **OPP invalidate** **3** to state officially that sth is useful and of an acceptable standard: *Check that their courses have been validated by a reputable organization.* ▸ **validation** Ⓦ /ˌvælɪˈdeɪʃn/ noun [U]

valley ⚑ **A2** /'væli/ noun [C] (GEOGRAPHY) the low land between two mountains or hills, which often has a river flowing through it ◯ look at **hanging valley**, **rift valley** ◯ picture at **glacial**

valour (BrE) (AmE **valor**) /'vælə(r)/ noun [U] (old-fashioned) great courage, especially in war: *the soldiers' valour in battle*

valuable ⚑ **B1** Ⓦ /'væljuəbl/ adj. **1** worth a lot of money: *Is this ring valuable?* **OPP valueless**, **worthless** **2** very useful: *a valuable piece of information*

valuables /'væljuəblz/ noun [pl.] the small things that you own that are worth a lot of money, such as jewellery, etc: *Please put your valuables in the safe.*

valuation /ˌvæljuˈeɪʃn/ noun [C] (FINANCE) a professional judgement about how much money sth is worth

value[1] ⚑ **B1** Ⓞ /'vælju:/ noun **1** [U, C] (FINANCE) the amount of money that sth is worth: *The thieves stole goods with a total value of $10 000.* ◇ *to go up/down in value* ◯ look at **face value 2** [U] (especially BrE) how much sth is worth compared with its price: *The hotel was good/excellent value* (= well worth the money it cost). ◇ *Package holidays give the best value for money.* **3** [U, sing.] the importance of sth: *to be of great/little/no value to somebody* ◇ *This bracelet is of great sentimental value to me.* **4 values** [pl.] beliefs about what is the right and wrong way for people to behave; moral principles: *a return to traditional values* ◇ *Young people have a different set of values.*

value[2] ⚑ **B2** Ⓢ /'vælju:/ verb [T] (valuing) **1** (not used in the progressive tenses) ~ sb/sth (as sth) to think sb/sth is very important: *Sandra has always valued her independence.* ◇ *I really value her as a friend.* **2** [usually passive] ~ sth (at sth) to decide the amount of money that sth is worth: *The house was valued at $150 000.*

value added tax = VAT

valueless /'vælju:ləs/ adj. without value or use **SYN worthless OPP valuable**

valve /vælv/ noun [C] **1** (ENGINEERING, PHYSICS) a device in a pipe or tube that controls the flow of air, liquid or gas, letting it move in one direction only: *a radiator valve* ◇ *the valve on a bicycle tyre* ◯ picture at **aerosol 2** (ANATOMY) a structure in the heart or in a VEIN (= a tube that carries blood to the heart) that lets blood flow in one direction only ◯ picture at **heart**

vampire /'væmpaɪə(r)/ noun [C] (in horror stories) a dead person who comes out at night and drinks the blood of living people

van ⚑ **A2** /væn/ noun [C] a road vehicle that is used for transporting things ◯ picture at **vehicle** **HELP** A van is smaller than a **lorry** and is always covered.

vanadium /vəˈneɪdiəm/ noun [U] (symb. V) (CHEMISTRY) a chemical element. Vanadium is a soft poisonous silver-grey metal used in making some types of steel.

❶ For more information on the periodic table of elements, look at the **Reference Section** of this dictionary.

vandal /'vændl/ noun [C] a person who damages sb else's property deliberately and for no purpose ◯ note at **criminal**[1] ▸ **vandalism** /-dəlɪzəm/ noun [U]: *acts of vandalism* ▸ **vandalize** (BrE also -ise) /-laɪz/ verb [T, usually passive]: *The children's play area had been vandalized.*

vanguard /'vænɡɑːd/ (usually **the vanguard**) noun [sing.] **1** the leaders of a movement in society, for example in politics, art, industry, etc: *The company is proud to be in the vanguard of scientific progress.* **2** the part of an army, etc. that is at the front when moving forward to attack the enemy

vanilla /vəˈnɪlə/ noun [U] a substance from a plant that is used to add taste to sweet food: *vanilla ice cream*

vanish ⚑+ **C1** /'vænɪʃ/ verb [I] **1** to disappear suddenly or in a way that you cannot explain: *When he turned round, the two men had vanished without trace.* **2** to stop existing: *This species of plant is vanishing from our countryside.*

vanishing point noun [C, usually sing.] (ART) the point in the distance at which PARALLEL lines appear to meet

vanity /'vænəti/ noun [U] the quality of being too proud of your appearance or abilities ◯ adjective **vain**

vantage point /'vɑːntɪdʒ pɔɪnt/ noun [C] a place from which you have a good view of sth: (figurative) *From our modern vantage point, we can see why the Roman Empire collapsed.*

vape[1] /veɪp/ verb [I, T] to smoke an E-CIGARETTE or similar device ▸ **vaping** noun [U]

vape[2] /veɪp/ noun [C] (informal) an electronic device, similar to an E-CIGARETTE, that produces VAPOUR usually containing NICOTINE, that you can take into your lungs through your mouth: *a ban on flavoured vapes*

vaporize (BrE also -ise) /'veɪpəraɪz/ verb [I, T] (CHEMISTRY, PHYSICS) to change into gas; to make sth change into gas ▸ **vaporization** (BrE also -isation) /ˌveɪpəraɪˈzeɪʃn/ noun [U]

vapour (BrE) (AmE **vapor**) /'veɪpə(r)/ noun [U, C] (CHEMISTRY) a mass of very small drops of liquid in the air, for example STEAM: *water vapour* ◯ note at **water**[1]

variable[1] ⚑+ **C1** Ⓞ /'veəriəbl/ adj. not staying the same; often changing ◯ picture at **resistor** ▸ **variability** /ˌveəriəˈbɪləti/ noun [U]

variable[2] ⚑+ **C1** Ⓞ /'veəriəbl/ noun [C] **1** a situation, number or quantity that can vary or be varied: *With so many variables to consider, it is difficult to calculate the cost.* ◇ *The temperature was kept constant throughout the experiment while pressure was a variable.* **2** (MATHEMATICS) a symbol that represents a quantity that can change in value during a CALCULATION **OPP constant**[1]

variance Ⓦ /'veəriəns/ noun [U, C] (formal) the amount by which sth changes or is different from sth else: *variance in temperature/pay* **IDM at variance (with sb/sth)** (formal) disagreeing with sb/sth

variant /'veəriənt/ noun [C] a slightly different form or type of sth

variation ⚑+ **B2** Ⓞ /ˌveəriˈeɪʃn/ noun **1** [C, U] ~ (in/of sth) a change or difference in the amount or level of sth: *There may be a slight variation in price from shop to shop.* ◇ *There was a lot of variation in the examination results.* **2** [C] ~ (on sth) a thing that is slightly different from another thing in the same general group: *All her films are just variations on a basic theme.* **3** [C] ~ (on sth) (MUSIC) any of a set of short pieces of music based on a simple tune repeated in a different and more complicated form: *a set of variations on a theme by Mozart*

varicose vein /ˌværɪkəʊs ˈveɪn/ *noun* [C] (**HEALTH**) a VEIN (= a tube that carries blood around the body), especially one in the leg, that has become SWOLLEN (= larger than normal) and painful ⊃ look at **deep vein thrombosis**

varied ʔ+ **C1** **W** /ˈveərid/ *adj.* having many different kinds of things or activities: *I try to make my classes as varied as possible.*

variety ʔ **A2** **O** /vəˈraɪəti/ *noun* (*pl.* -ies) **1** [sing. + sing./ pl. verb] ~ (**of sth**) a number of different types of the same thing: *There is a wide variety of dishes to choose from.* **2** [U] the quality of not being or doing the same all the time: *There's so much variety in my new job. I do something different every day!* **3** [C] ~ (**of sth**) a type of sth: *a new variety of apple called 'Perfection'* **4** [U] (**ARTS AND MEDIA**) a form of theatre or TV entertainment that consists of a series of short performances, such as singing, dancing and funny acts: *a variety show*

various ʔ **B1** **O** /ˈveəriəs/ *adj.* several different: *I decided to leave my job for various reasons.*

varnish /ˈvɑːnɪʃ/ *noun* [U] a clear liquid that you paint onto hard surfaces, especially wood, to protect them and make them shine ⊃ look at **nail polish** ▸ **varnish** *verb* [T]: *The doors are then stained and varnished.*

vary ʔ **B2** **O** /ˈveəri/ *verb* (varying; varies; *pt, pp* varied) **1** [I] ~ (**in sth**) (used about a group of similar things) to be different from each other: *The hotel bedrooms vary in size from medium to very large.* **2** [I] ~ (**from … to …**) to be different or to change according to the situation, etc: *The price of the holiday varies from £500 to £1 200, depending on the time of year.* **3** [T] to make sth different by changing it often in some way: *I try to vary my work as much as possible so I don't get bored.*

vascular /ˈvæskjələ(r)/ *adj.* (**BIOLOGY**) of or containing VEINS (= the tubes that carry liquids around the bodies of animals and plants)

vas deferens /ˌvæs ˈdefərenz/ *noun* [C] (*pl.* vasa deferentia /ˌveɪsə defəˈrenʃiə/) (**ANATOMY**) the tube through which SPERM (= cells produced by the sex organs of a male) pass from the TESTIS on their way out of the body

vase /vɑːz/ *noun* [C] a container that is used for holding cut flowers

vasectomy /vəˈsektəmi/ *noun* [C] (*pl.* -ies) (**MEDICINE**) a medical operation to stop a man being able to make a woman pregnant

vassal /ˈvæsl/ *noun* [C] **1** (**HISTORY**) a man in the Middle Ages who promised to fight and show support for a king or other powerful owner of land, in return for being given land to live on **2** (**POLITICS**) a country that depends on and is controlled by another country

vast ʔ **B2** /vɑːst/ *adj.* extremely big: *a vast sum of money* ◇ *a vast country* **SYN** **huge** ▸ **vastly** *adv.*: *a vastly improved traffic system*

VAT /ˌviː eɪ ˈtiː, væt/ *abbr.* (**FINANCE**) value added tax (a tax that is added to the price of goods and services): *Prices include VAT.*

the Vatican /ðə ˈvætɪkən/ *noun* [sing.] (**RELIGION**) the group of buildings in Rome where the POPE lives and works

vault¹ /vɔːlt/ *noun* [C] **1** a room with a strong door and thick walls in a bank, etc. that is used for keeping money and other valuable things safe **2** (**ARCHITECTURE**) a room under a church where dead people are buried: *a family vault* **3** (**ARCHITECTURE**) a high roof or ceiling in a church, etc., made from a

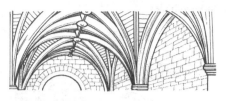

vault

number of ARCHES joined together at the top **4** (**SPORT**) a jump made by VAULTING ⊃ look at **pole vault**

vault² /vɔːlt/ *verb* [I, T] ~ (**over**) **sth** to jump over or onto sth in one movement, using your hands or a POLE to help you

vaulted /ˈvɔːltɪd/ *adj.* (**ARCHITECTURE**) made from a number of ARCHES joined together at the top; having a ceiling or roof of this shape: *The rooms are huge with high vaulted ceilings.*

VCR /ˌviː siː ˈɑː(r)/ *noun* [C] = VIDEO CASSETTE RECORDER

VDU /ˌviː diː ˈjuː/ *noun* [C] (**COMPUTING**) a screen on which you can see information from a computer (the abbreviation for 'visual display unit')

veal /viːl/ *noun* [U] the meat from a CALF (= a young cow) ⊃ note at **meat**

vector /ˈvektə(r)/ *noun* [C] **1** (**MATHEMATICS**) a measurement or a quantity that has both size and direction **2** (**HEALTH**) an insect, etc. that carries a particular disease from one living thing to another: *Mosquitoes are the vectors in malaria.* **3** the course taken by an aircraft

▾ **VOCABULARY BUILDING**

Scalars provide information about size (magnitude) such as distance, speed, mass, etc. **Vectors** provide two pieces of information (magnitude and direction) such as velocity, acceleration, force, etc.

veer /vɪə(r)/ *verb* [I] (used with an adverb or a preposition) (used about vehicles) to change direction suddenly: *The car veered across the road and hit a tree.*

veg /vedʒ/ *verb*
PHR V **veg out** (*informal*) to relax and do nothing that needs thought or effort: *I'm just going to go home and veg out in front of the telly.*

vegan /ˈviːgən/ *noun* [C] a person who does not eat meat or any other animal products at all ⊃ look at **vegetarian** ▸ **vegan** *adj.*

vegetable ʔ **A1** /ˈvedʒtəbl/ (*also informal* **veggie** *especially in AmE*) *noun* [C] a plant or part of a plant that can be eaten. Potatoes, beans and onions are vegetables: *vegetable soup*

vegetarian /ˌvedʒəˈteəriən/ (*also informal* **veggie**) *noun* [C] a person who does not eat meat or fish ⊃ look at **vegan** ⊃ note at **meat** ▸ **vegetarian** (*also* **veggie**) *adj.*: *a vegetarian cookery book*

vegetation /ˌvedʒəˈteɪʃn/ *noun* [U] plants in general; all the plants that are found in a particular place: *tropical vegetation*

veggie¹ /ˈvedʒi/ *adj.* (*informal*) = VEGETARIAN

veggie² /ˈvedʒi/ *noun* [C] (*informal*) **1** = VEGETARIAN **2** (*especially AmE*) = VEGETABLE

vehement /ˈviːəmənt/ *adj.* showing very strong (often negative) feelings, especially anger: *a vehement attack on the government*

large vehicles

lorry/truck

van

car transporter

tanker

vehicle 🔊 **A2** /'viːəkl/ *noun* [C] **1** something that transports people or things from place to place, especially on land, for example a car, lorry or bus: *Are you the owner of this vehicle?* **2** ~ **(for sth)** something that is used for communicating particular ideas or opinions: *This newspaper has become a vehicle for Conservative opinion.*

vehicular /və'hɪkjələ(r)/ *adj.* [only before noun] (*formal*) intended for vehicles or consisting of vehicles: *vehicular access* ◇ *The road is closed to vehicular traffic.*

veil /veɪl/ *noun* [C] a piece of thin material for covering the head and face of a woman: *a bridal veil*

veiled /veɪld/ *adj.* **1** not expressed directly or clearly because you do not want your meaning to be obvious: *a **thinly veiled** threat/warning/criticism* **2** wearing a VEIL: *a veiled woman*

vein 🔊+ **C1** /veɪn/ *noun* **1** [C] (**ANATOMY**) one of the tubes that carry blood from all parts of the body to the heart ⊃ look at **artery, jugular, varicose vein** ⊃ picture at **circulation** **2** [C] (**BIOLOGY**) any of the very thin tubes that form the frame of a leaf or an insect's wing **3** [C] a narrow area of a different colour in some types of stone, wood and cheese **4** [sing., U] a particular style or quality: *After a humorous beginning, the programme continued in a more serious vein.*

velar /'viːlə(r)/ *noun* [C] (**LANGUAGE**) a speech sound made by placing the back of the tongue against or near the back part of the mouth, for example /k/ or /g/ in *key* and *go* ▶ **velar** *adj.*

Velcro™ /'velkrəʊ/ *noun* [U] a material for fastening parts of clothes together. Velcro™ is made of NYLON (= a strong material) and is used in small pieces, one rough and one smooth, that can stick together and be pulled apart.

veld /velt/ *noun* [U] (**GEOGRAPHY**) flat open land in South Africa with grass and no trees

vellum /'veləm/ *noun* [U] **1** material made from the skin of a sheep, GOAT or CALF, used for making book covers and, in the past, for writing on **2** smooth cream-coloured paper used for writing on

velocity /və'lɒsəti/ *noun* [U] (**PHYSICS**) the speed at which sth moves in a particular direction: *a high-velocity rifle/bullet*

velodrome /'velədrəʊm/ *noun* [C] (**SPORT**) a track or building used for cycle racing

velour /və'lʊə(r)/ *noun* [U] a kind of cloth with a thick soft surface similar to VELVET

velvet /'velvɪt/ *noun* [U] a kind of cloth made of silk, cotton or other material, with a soft thick surface on one side only: *black velvet trousers*

vena cava /ˌviːnə 'keɪvə/ *noun* [C] (*pl.* **venae cavae** /ˌviːniː 'keɪviː/) (**ANATOMY**) a VEIN (= a tube that carries blood in the body) that takes blood without OXYGEN in it into the heart ⊃ picture at **heart**

vendetta /ven'detə/ *noun* [C] a serious argument between two people or groups, which lasts for a long time

'vending machine *noun* [C] a machine from which you can buy drinks, sweets, etc. by putting coins in it

vendor /'vendə(r)/ *noun* [C] a person who is selling sth ⊃ look at **purchaser**

veneer /və'nɪə(r)/ *noun* **1** [C, U] a thin layer of wood or plastic that is stuck onto the surface of cheaper wood, to give it a better appearance **2** [sing.] ~ **(of sth)** (*formal*) an outer appearance of a particular quality that hides what sb/sth is really like: *a thin veneer of politeness*

venetian blind /vəˌniːʃn 'blaɪnd/ *noun* [C] a covering for a window that has flat plastic or metal pieces going across it that you can turn to let in as much light as you want

vengeance /'vendʒəns/ *noun* [U] ~ **(on sb)** (*formal*) the act of punishing or harming sb in return for sth bad they have done to you, your friends or family: *He felt a terrible desire for vengeance on the people who had destroyed his career.* ⊃ look at **revenge**[1] **IDM with a vengeance** to a greater degree than is expected or usual: *After a week of good weather winter returned with a vengeance.*

venison /'venɪsn/ *noun* [U] the meat from a DEER (= a large wild animal) ⊃ note at **deer**

Venn diagram

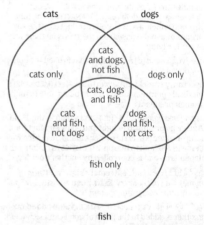

cats

dogs

cats only

cats and dogs, not fish

dogs only

cats, dogs and fish

cats and fish, not dogs

dogs and fish, not cats

fish only

fish

Venn diagram /'ven daɪəgræm/ *noun* [C] (**MATHEMATICS**) a picture showing SETS (= groups of things that have a shared quality) as circles that cross over each other, to show which qualities the different SETS have in common

venom /'venəm/ *noun* [U] **1** (**BIOLOGY**) the poisonous liquid that some snakes, spiders, etc. produce when they bite or STING you **2** (*formal*) extreme anger or hate and a desire to hurt sb: *She shot him a look of pure venom.* ▶ **venomous** /-nəməs/ *adj.*

vent /vent/ *noun* [C] an opening in the wall of a room or machine that allows air to come in, and smoke, STEAM or smells to go out: *an air vent* ◇ *a heating vent* ⊃ picture at **volcano**

ventilate /'ventɪleɪt/ *verb* [T, usually passive] to allow air to move freely in and out of a room or building: *The office is badly ventilated.* ▸ **ventilation** /ˌventɪ'leɪʃn/ *noun* [U]: *There was no ventilation in the room except for one tiny window.*

ventilator /'ventɪleɪtə(r)/ *noun* [C] **1** a device or an opening for letting fresh air come into a room **2** (MEDICINE) a piece of equipment that helps sb to breathe by sending air in and out of their lungs

ventral /'ventrəl/ *adj.* [only before noun] (BIOLOGY) on or connected with the under side of a fish or an animal ⊃ look at **dorsal**, **pectoral** ⊃ picture at **animal**

ventricle /'ventrɪkl/ *noun* [C] (ANATOMY) **1** either of the two lower spaces in the heart ⊃ picture at **heart 2** any space in the body that does not contain anything, especially one of the four main empty spaces in the brain

venture[1] ʔ+ C1 /'ventʃə(r)/ *noun* [C] a project that is new and possibly dangerous, because you cannot be sure that it will succeed: *a business venture*

venture[2] ʔ+ C1 /'ventʃə(r)/ *verb* [I] (used with an adverb or a preposition) to do sth or go somewhere new and dangerous, when you are not sure what will happen: *He ventured out into the storm to look for the lost child.* ◇ *The company has decided to venture into computer production.*

'venture capital *noun* [U] (FINANCE) money that is invested in a new company to help it develop, which may involve a lot of risk ⊃ look at **working capital**

venue ʔ B2 /'venjuː/ *noun* [C] the place where people meet for an organized event, for example a concert or a sports event

Venus /'viːnəs/ *noun* [sing.] (ASTRONOMY) the planet in the SOLAR SYSTEM that is second in order of distance from the sun ⊃ picture at **solar system**

veranda (*also* **verandah**) /və'rændə/ (*both especially BrE*) (*AmE usually* **porch**) *noun* [C] (ARCHITECTURE) a platform joined to the side of a house, with a roof and floor but no outside wall ⊃ look at **balcony** (1), **patio**, **terrace** (2)

verb /vɜːb/ *noun* [C] (GRAMMAR) a word or group of words that expresses an action (such as *eat*), an event (such as *happen*) or a state (such as *exist*) ⊃ look at **phrasal verb**

verbal ʔ+ C1 /'vɜːbl/ *adj.* **1** (LANGUAGE) connected with words, or the use of words: *verbal skills* **2** (LANGUAGE) spoken, not written: *a verbal agreement/warning* **3** (GRAMMAR) connected with verbs, or the use of verbs ▸ **verbally** /-bəli/ *adv.*

verbatim /vɜː'beɪtɪm/ *adj.*, *adv.* exactly as it was spoken or written: *a verbatim report* ◇ *He reported the speech verbatim.*

verdict ʔ+ C1 /'vɜːdɪkt/ *noun* [C] **1** (LAW) the decision that is made by the JURY (= a group of members of the public) in a court, which states if a person is guilty of a crime or not: *The jury **returned a verdict** of 'not guilty'.* ◇ *Has the jury **reached a verdict**?* ⊃ note at **court**[1] **2** ~ **(on sb/sth)** a decision that you make or an opinion that you give after testing sth or considering sth carefully: *The general verdict on the restaurant was that it was too expensive.*

verge[1] /vɜːdʒ/ *noun* [C] (BrE) the narrow piece of land at the side of a road, path, etc. that is usually covered in grass

IDM **on the verge of sth/doing sth** very near to doing sth, or to sth happening: *He was on the verge of a nervous breakdown.* ◇ *Scientists are on the verge of discovering a cure.*

verge[2] /vɜːdʒ/ *verb*
PHR V **verge on sth** to be very close to an extreme state or condition: *What they are doing verges on the illegal.*

verify ʔ+ C1 /'verɪfaɪ/ *verb* [T] (verifying; verifies; *pt, pp* verified) (*formal*) to check or state that sth is true: *to verify a statement* ▸ **verification** /ˌverɪfɪ'keɪʃn/ *noun* [U]

veritable /'verɪtəbl/ *adj.* [only before noun] (*formal*) a word used to emphasize that sb/sth can be compared to sb/sth else that is more exciting, more impressive, etc: *The meal was a veritable banquet.*

vermilion /və'mɪliən/ *adj.* bright red in colour ▸ **vermilion** *noun* [U]

vermin /'vɜːmɪn/ *noun* [pl.] small wild animals (for example RATS) that carry disease and destroy plants and food

vernacular /və'nækjələ(r)/ (*usually* the vernacular) *noun* [sing.] (LANGUAGE) the language spoken in a particular area or by a particular group of people, especially one that is not the official or written language

vernal /'vɜːnl/ *adj.* [only before noun] (*formal*) (GEOGRAPHY) connected with the season of spring: *the vernal equinox*

versatile /'vɜːsətaɪl/ *adj.* **1** (used about an object) having many different uses: *a versatile tool that drills, cuts or polishes* **2** (used about a person) able to do many different things: *She's so versatile! She can dance, sing, act and play the guitar!*

verse ʔ+ C1 /vɜːs/ *noun* (LITERATURE) **1** [U] writing arranged in lines that have a definite rhythm and often RHYME (= end with the same sound): *He wrote his valentine's message in verse.* SYN **poetry 2** [C] a group of lines that form one part of a song or poem: *This song has five verses.* SYN **stanza** ⊃ look at **chorus**[1] (1)

version ʔ B1 ◐ /'vɜːʃn/ *noun* [C] **1** a thing that has the same basic contents as sth else but that is presented in a different way: *Have you heard the live version of this song?* **2** a person's description of sth that has happened: *The two drivers gave very different versions of what had happened.*

versus ʔ+ W /'vɜːsəs/ *prep.* **1** (*abbr.* v, vs) used in sport for showing that two teams or people are playing against each other: *England versus Argentina* **2** used for showing that two ideas or things are opposite to each other, especially when you are trying to choose one of them: *It's a question of quality versus price.*

vertebra /'vɜːtɪbrə/ *noun* [C] (*pl.* vertebrae /-breɪ, -briː/) (ANATOMY) any of the small bones that are connected together to form the SPINE (= the column of bones down the middle of the back) ⊃ picture at **spine** (1) ⊃ picture at **body** ▸ **vertebral** /'vɜːtɪbrəl/ *adj.*

vertebrate /'vɜːtɪbrət/ *noun* [C] (BIOLOGY) an animal, a bird or a fish that has a BACKBONE OPP **invertebrate**

vertex /'vɜːteks/ *noun* [C] (*pl.* vertices /-tɪsiːz/, vertexes) **1** (GEOMETRY) a point where two lines meet to form an angle, especially the point of a TRIANGLE or CONE opposite the base **2** the highest point or top of sth

vertical ʔ+ B2 W /'vɜːtɪkl/ *adj.* (GEOMETRY) (used about a line, a pole, etc.) going straight up or down from a level surface or from top to bottom in a picture, etc: *a vertical line* ◇ *The cliff was almost vertical.* ⊃ look at

horizontal, perpendicular ⟳ picture at line[1]
▶ vertically /-kli/ adv.

,vertical inte'gration noun [U] (BUSINESS) the process of combining two or more companies so that a single company controls all of the stages of production

verve /vɜːv/ noun [U, sing.] energy, excitement or enthusiasm: It was a performance of verve and vitality.

very[1] 🔒 A1 ⑤ /'veri/ adv. (abbr. v) (used to emphasize an adjective or an adverb) extremely; in a high degree: very small ◇ very slowly ◇ I don't like milk very much. ◇ 'Are you hungry?' 'Not very.' ◇ They wanted the very best quality.

very[2] 🔒 🅱1 /'veri/ adj. [only before noun] 1 used to emphasize that you are talking about a particular thing or person and not about another: Those were his very words. ◇ You're the very person I wanted to talk to (= exactly the right person). 2 extreme: We climbed to the very top of the mountain. 3 used to emphasize a noun: The very thought of drink made her feel sick.
IDM before sb's very eyes → EYE[1]

vesicle /'vesɪkl/ noun [C] 1 (BIOLOGY) a small bag or hollow structure in the body of a plant or an animal 2 (HEALTH) a small place under the skin that is fatter because it is filled with liquid

vessel 🔒 🅲1 /'vesl/ noun [C] 1 (BIOLOGY) a tube that carries blood through the body of a person or an animal, or liquid through the parts of a plant: to burst/ rupture a blood vessel ⟳ look at blood vessel 2 (formal) a ship or large boat 3 a container for liquids, for example a bottle, cup or bowl: ancient drinking vessels ◇ The vessel contains liquid nitrogen.

vest /vest/ noun [C] 1 (AmE undershirt) a piece of clothing that you wear under your other clothes, on the top part of your body 2 (AmE) = WAISTCOAT

vested interest /ˌvestɪd 'ɪntrəst, -trest/ noun [C] a strong and often secret reason for doing sth that will bring you an advantage of some kind, for example more money or power

vestige /'vestɪdʒ/ noun [C] a small part of sth that is left after the rest of it has gone: the last vestige of the old system SYN trace[1]

vet[1] /vet/ (especially BrE) (AmE usually veterinarian /ˌvetərɪ'neəriən/) noun [C] a doctor for animals: We took the cat to the vet/to the vet's.

vet[2] /vet/ verb [T] (-tt-) to do careful checks before deciding if sb/sth can be accepted or not: All new employees at the Ministry of Defence are carefully vetted (= somebody examines the details of their past lives).

veteran 🔒 🅲1 /'vetərən/ noun [C] 1 a person who has very long experience of a particular job or activity 2 a person who has been a soldier, sailor, etc. in a war

veterinary /'vetnri, -trənəri/ adj. connected with the medical treatment of sick or injured animals: a veterinary practice ◇ veterinary medicine/science ⟳ look at vet[1]

veto /'viːtəʊ/ verb [T] (vetoing; vetoes) (pt, pp vetoed) to refuse to give official permission for an action or a plan, when other people have agreed to it: The prime minister vetoed the proposal to reduce taxation. ▶ veto noun [C, U] (pl. -oes): the right of veto

vexed /vekst/ adj. causing difficulty, worry and a lot of discussion: the vexed question of our growing prison population

VHF /ˌviː eɪtʃ 'ef/ abbr. (PHYSICS) very high frequency (a band of radio waves used for sending out a high quality signal): a VHF transmitter ⟳ picture at wavelength

via 🔒 🅱2 ⓦ /'vaɪə, 'viːə/ prep. 1 going through a place: We flew from Paris to Sydney via Bangkok. 2 by means of sth; using sth: These pictures come to you via our satellite link.

viable 🔒+ 🅲1 /'vaɪəbl/ adj. that can be done; that will be successful: I'm afraid your idea is not commercially viable. ▶ viability /ˌvaɪə'bɪləti/ noun [U]

viaduct /'vaɪədʌkt/ noun [C] a long, high bridge that carries a railway or road across a valley

vibes /vaɪbz/ noun [pl.] (also vibe /vaɪb/ [sing.]) (informal) a mood or an atmosphere produced by a particular person, thing or place: good/bad vibes ◇ The vibes weren't right.

vibrant 🔒+ 🅲1 /'vaɪbrənt/ adj. 1 full of life and energy; exciting: a vibrant city/atmosphere/personality 2 (used about colours) bright and strong

vibrate /vaɪ'breɪt/ verb [I, T] to move from side to side very quickly and with small movements; to make sth move in this way: When a guitar string vibrates it makes a sound. ◇ The male spider will vibrate one of the threads of the female spider's web. ▶ vibration /-'breɪʃn/ noun [C, U]

vibrato /vɪ'brɑːtəʊ/ noun [U, C] (pl. -os) (MUSIC) a shaking effect in singing or playing a musical instrument, made by making a note slightly higher and lower many times very quickly

vicar /'vɪkə(r)/ noun [C] (RELIGION) a priest of the Anglican church. A vicar looks after a church and its PARISH (= the area around the church and the people in it). ⟳ look at minister (2)

vicarage /'vɪkərɪdʒ/ noun [C] (RELIGION) the house where a VICAR lives

vicarious /vɪ'keəriəs/ adj. [only before noun] felt or experienced by watching or reading about sb else doing sth, rather than by doing it yourself: He got a vicarious thrill out of watching his son score the winning goal.

vice 🔒+ 🅲1 /vaɪs/ noun 1 [U] (LAW) criminal activities involving sex or drugs 2 [C] a moral weakness or bad habit: Greed and envy are terrible vices. ◇ My only vice is smoking. ⟳ look at virtue (2) 3 (especially BrE) (AmE usually vise) [C] a tool that you use to hold a piece of wood, metal, etc. FIRMLY while you are working on it: He held my arm in a vice-like (= very firm) grip. ⟳ picture at workbench

vice- /vaɪs/ prefix (in nouns) having a position second in importance to the position mentioned: the vice-captain

,vice 'chancellor noun [C] (EDUCATION) the head of a university in England, Wales and Northern Ireland who is in charge of the work of running the university ❶ Compare vice chancellor with chancellor, who is the official head of a university, but only has duties at various ceremonies.

,vice-'president noun [C] (abbr. VP) 1 (POLITICS) the person below the president of a country in rank, who takes control of the country if the president is not able to 2 (AmE) (BUSINESS) a person in charge of a particular part of a business company: the vice-president of sales

vice versa /ˌvaɪs 'vɜːsə, ˌvaɪsi/ adv. in the opposite way to what has just been said: Anna ordered fish and Maria chicken — or was it vice versa?

vicinity /və'sɪnəti/ noun
IDM in the vicinity (of sth) (formal) in the surrounding area: There's no bank in the immediate vicinity.

vicious ᵻ+ **C1** /ˈvɪʃəs/ *adj.* **1** cruel; done in order to hurt sb/sth: *a vicious attack* **2** (used about an animal) dangerous; likely to hurt sb ▸ **viciously** *adv.*
IDM **a vicious circle** a situation in which one problem leads to another and the new problem makes the first problem worse

victim ᵻ **B1** /ˈvɪktɪm/ *noun* [C] a person or an animal that is injured, killed or hurt by sb/sth: *a murder victim* ◊ *The children are often the innocent victims of a divorce.*

victimize (*BrE also* **-ise**) /ˈvɪktɪmaɪz/ *verb* [T] to punish or make sb suffer unfairly ▸ **victimization** (*BrE also* **-isation**) /ˌvɪktɪmaɪˈzeɪʃn/ *noun* [U]

ˌvictim supˈport *noun* [U] (**LAW**) a police service that helps people who are victims of crime

victor /ˈvɪktə(r)/ *noun* [C] (*old-fashioned*) the person who wins a game, competition, battle, etc.

Victorian /vɪkˈtɔːriən/ *adj.* (**HISTORY**) **1** connected with the time of the British queen Victoria (1837-1901): *Victorian houses* **2** having attitudes that were typical in the time of Queen Victoria ▸ **Victorian** *noun* [C]

victory ᵻ **B2** /ˈvɪktəri/ *noun* [C, U] (*pl.* **-ies**) success in winning a battle, a game, a competition, an election, etc: *Henderson led his team to victory in the final.*
▸ **victorious** /vɪkˈtɔːriəs/ *adj.: the victorious team*

video ᵻ **A1** /ˈvɪdiəʊ/ *noun* (*pl.* **-os**) **1** [U] a system of recording moving pictures and sound; a method of storing film: *Most of the film was shot on digital video.* **2** (*also* ˈvideo clip) [C] (**COMPUTING**) a short film or recording of an event, made using digital technology and viewed on a computer, especially over the internet **3** (*also* music video) [C] (**MUSIC**) a short film made by a pop or rock band to be shown with a song when it is played on TV or online: *She posted a series of videos on the internet.* **4** [C] a tape or CASSETTE used in the past for recording moving pictures and sound: *The movie was released on video in 1989.* **5** = VIDEO CASSETTE RECORDER ▸ **video** *verb* [T] (videoing; videos; *pt, pp* videoed): *We hired a camera to video the school play.*

ˌvideo casˈsette recorder (*also* video) *noun* [C] (*abbr.* **VCR**) (**ARTS AND MEDIA**) a machine used, especially in the past, to record and play films and TV programmes on video

videoconferencing /ˈvɪdiəʊkɒnfərənsɪŋ/ *noun* [U] a system that people in different parts of the world can use to have a meeting, by watching and listening to each other using video screens

ˈvideo game *noun* [C] a game in which you press buttons to control and move images on a screen

videophone /ˈvɪdiəʊfəʊn/ *noun* [C] (**ARTS AND MEDIA**) a type of phone with a screen that allows you to see the person you are talking to

view¹ ᵻ **A2** ◐ /vjuː/ *noun* **1** [C] what you can see from a particular place, especially beautiful countryside: *There are* **breathtaking views** *from the top of the mountain.* ◊ *a room with a sea view* **2** [U, sing.] the ability to see sth or to be seen from a particular place: *The garden was hidden from view behind a high wall.* ◊ *Just then, the sea* **came into view.** **3** [C] ~ **(about/on sth)** an opinion or a particular way of thinking about sth: *He expressed the view that standards were falling.* ◊ *In my view, she has done nothing wrong.* ◊ *She has* **strong views** *on the subject.* ᵓ *note at* **opinion, regard¹**
IDM **have, etc. sth in view** (*formal*) to have sth as a plan or an idea in your mind **in full view (of sb/sth)** → FULL¹ **in view of sth** (*formal*) because of sth; as a result of sth: *In view of her apology we decided to take no further action.* **a point of view** → POINT¹ **with a view to doing sth** (*formal*) with the aim or intention of doing sth

view² ᵻ **B1** ◐ /vjuː/ *verb* [T] **1** ~ **sb/sth (as sth)** to think about sth in a particular way: *She viewed holidays as a waste of time.* ᵓ *note at* **regard¹** **2** (*formal*) to watch or look at sth: *Viewed from this angle, the building looks much taller than it really is.*

viewer ᵻ **B1** **W** /ˈvjuːə(r)/ *noun* [C] a person who watches TV or a video on the internet

viewpoint ᵻ+ **B2** /ˈvjuːpɔɪnt/ *noun* [C] a way of looking at a situation; an opinion: *Let's look at this problem from the customer's viewpoint.* **SYN** **point of view**

vigil /ˈvɪdʒɪl/ *noun* [C, U] a period when you do not sleep all night for a special purpose: *All night she* **kept vigil** *over the sick child.*

vigilant /ˈvɪdʒɪlənt/ *adj.* (*formal*) careful and looking out for danger ▸ **vigilance** /-ləns/ *noun* [U]

vigilante /ˌvɪdʒɪˈlænti/ *noun* [C] (**LAW**) a member of a group of people who try to prevent crime or punish criminals in a community, especially because they believe the police are not doing this

vigour (*BrE*) (*AmE* **vigor**) /ˈvɪgə(r)/ *noun* [U] strength or energy: *After the break we started work again with renewed vigour.* ▸ **vigorous** /-gərəs/ *adj.: vigorous exercise* ▸ **vigorously** *adv.*

Viking /ˈvaɪkɪŋ/ *noun* [C] (**HISTORY**) a member of a human group of Scandinavian people who attacked and sometimes settled in parts of NW Europe, including Britain, in the eighth to the eleventh centuries

vile /vaɪl/ *adj.* very bad or unpleasant: *She's in a vile mood.* ◊ *a vile smell* **SYN** **terrible**

villa /ˈvɪlə/ *noun* [C] **1** (**TOURISM**) a house that people rent and stay in on holiday **2** a large house in the country, especially in Southern Europe

village ᵻ **A1** /ˈvɪlɪdʒ/ *noun* **1** [C] (**GEOGRAPHY**) a group of houses, sometimes with other buildings, for example a shop, school, etc., in a country area. A village is smaller than a town: *a small fishing village* ◊ *the village shop* **2** [sing. + sing./pl. verb] all the people who live in a village: *All the village is/are taking part in the carnival.*

villager ᵻ+ **C1** /ˈvɪlɪdʒə(r)/ *noun* [C] a person who lives in a village

villain /ˈvɪlən/ *noun* [C] **1** an evil person, especially in a book or play: *In most of his films he has played villains, but in this one he's a good guy.* ᵓ *look at* **hero** (2) **2** (*informal*) a criminal: *The police caught the villains who robbed the bank.*

villus /ˈvɪləs/ *noun* [C] (*pl.* **villi** /ˈvɪlaɪ, -liː/) (**BIOLOGY**) any one of the many small thin parts that stick out from some surfaces on the inside of the body (for example in the INTESTINE). Villi increase the area of these surfaces so that substances can be taken into the body more easily.

vindicate /ˈvɪndɪkeɪt/ *verb* [T] (*formal*) **1** to prove that sth is true or that you were right to do sth, especially when other people had a different opinion: *I have every confidence that this decision will be fully vindicated.* **2** to prove that sb is not guilty when they have been accused of doing sth wrong or illegal: *New evidence emerged, vindicating him completely.*

vindictive /vɪnˈdɪktɪv/ *adj.* wanting or trying to hurt sb without good reason: *a vindictive comment/person* ▸ **vindictiveness** *noun* [U]

vine /vaɪn/ *noun* [C] (**BIOLOGY**) the climbing plant that GRAPES (= small green or purple fruit that grow in bunches) grow on

vinegar /ˈvɪnɪɡə(r)/ noun [U] a liquid with a bitter taste that is made from wine. Vinegar is often mixed with oil and put onto salads.

vineyard /ˈvɪnjəd/ noun [C] (AGRICULTURE) a piece of land where GRAPES (= small green or purple fruit that grow in bunches) are grown in order to produce wine

vintage[1] /ˈvɪntɪdʒ/ noun [C] the wine that was made in a particular year or place; the year in which it was produced: *1999 was an excellent vintage.*

vintage[2] /ˈvɪntɪdʒ/ adj. [only before noun] **1 vintage** wine is of very good quality and has been stored for many years: *vintage champagne/port/wine* **2** (used about a vehicle) made between 1917 and 1930 and admired for its style and interest **3** typical of a period in the past and of high quality; the best work of the particular person: *a vintage performance by Robert De Niro*

vinyl /ˈvaɪnl/ noun [U] a strong plastic that can bend easily and is used to cover walls, floors, furniture, books, etc.

viola /viˈəʊlə/ noun [C] (MUSIC) a musical instrument with strings, that you hold under your CHIN and play with a BOW (= a long thin stick made of wood and hair): *A viola is like a large violin.* ⊃ picture at **instrument, orchestra**

violate ʔ+ C1 /ˈvaɪəleɪt/ verb [T] (formal) **1** (LAW) to break a rule, an agreement, etc: *to violate a peace treaty* **2** to not respect sth; to damage sth: *to violate somebody's privacy/rights* ▸ **violation** ʔ+ C1 /ˌvaɪəˈleɪʃn/ noun [U, C]: *(a) violation of human rights*

violence ʔ B2 ⓦ /ˈvaɪələns/ noun [U] **1** behaviour that harms or damages sb/sth physically: *They threatened to use violence if we didn't give them the money.* ◇ *an act of violence* **2** great force or energy: *the violence of the storm*

violent ʔ B1 /ˈvaɪələnt/ adj. **1** using physical strength to hurt or kill sb; caused by this behaviour: *The demonstration started peacefully but later turned violent.* ◇ *a violent death* ◇ **violent crime 2** very strong and impossible to control: *He has a violent temper.* ◇ *a violent storm/collision*

violently /ˈvaɪələntli/ adv. **1** with great energy or strong movement, especially caused by a strong emotion such as fear or hate: *She shook her head violently.* ◇ *to shiver violently* **2** very strongly or severely: *He was violently sick.* ◇ *They are violently opposed to the idea.* **3** in a way that involves physical violence: *The crowd reacted violently.*

violet[1] /ˈvaɪələt/ noun **1** [C] a small plant that grows wild or in gardens and has purple or white flowers and a pleasant smell **2** [U] a colour between blue and purple

violet[2] /ˈvaɪələt/ adj. between blue and purple in colour

violin /ˌvaɪəˈlɪn/ noun [C] (MUSIC) a musical instrument with strings, that you hold under your CHIN and play with a BOW (= a long thin stick made of wood and hair) ⊃ picture at **instrument, orchestra**

violinist /ˌvaɪəˈlɪnɪst/ noun [C] (MUSIC) a person who plays the VIOLIN

VIP /ˌviː aɪ ˈpiː/ noun [C] (informal) a famous or important person who is treated in a special way (the abbreviation for 'very important person'): *the VIP lounge at the airport* ◇ *give somebody the VIP treatment* (= treat sb especially well)

viper /ˈvaɪpə(r)/ noun [C] a small poisonous snake

viral /ˈvaɪrəl/ adj. **1** (HEALTH) like or caused by a virus: *a viral infection* **2** (COMPUTING) like a virus: *a viral video/email* (= that is sent on from one person to others, who then send it on again)

viral ˈmarketing noun [U] (BUSINESS) a way of advertising in which information about a company's products or services is sent by email to people who then send it on by email to other people they know

virgin[1] /ˈvɜːdʒɪn/ noun **1** [C] a person who has never had sex **2 the (Blessed) Virgin** /ðə ˌblesɪd ˈvɜːdʒɪn/ [sing.] (RELIGION) the Virgin Mary, mother of Jesus Christ

virgin[2] /ˈvɜːdʒɪn/ adj. in its original pure or natural condition, not changed, touched or made less good: *virgin forest/land/territory*

virginity /vəˈdʒɪnəti/ noun [U] the state of never having had sex: *to lose your virginity*

Virgo /ˈvɜːɡəʊ/ noun [U] the sixth sign of THE ZODIAC (= twelve signs that represent the positions of the sun, moon and planets), the Virgin; a person born under this sign

virile /ˈvɪraɪl/ adj. (used about a man) strong and having great sexual energy

virility /vəˈrɪləti/ noun [U] a man's sexual power and energy

virtual ʔ B2 /ˈvɜːtʃuəl/ adj. [only before noun] **1** (COMPUTING) made to appear to exist by the use of computer software, for example on the internet: *a virtual classroom/desktop/library* **2** being almost or nearly sth: *The country is in a state of virtual civil war.*

virtually /ˈvɜːtʃuəli/ adv. **1** almost, or very nearly, so that any slight difference is not important: *The building is virtually finished.* **2** (COMPUTING) by the use of computer programs, etc. that make sth appear to exist: *Check out our new hotel rooms virtually by visiting our website at …*

virtual ˈmemory (also **virtual ˈstorage**) noun [U] (COMPUTING) a feature of a computer's operating system that provides additional memory for applications using the computer's HARD DISK

virtual reˈality noun [U] (abbr. VR) (COMPUTING) images created by a computer that appear to surround the person looking at them and seem almost real

virtue ʔ+ C1 /ˈvɜːtʃuː/ noun **1** [U] (formal) behaviour that shows high moral standards: *to lead a life of virtue* **SYN** **goodness 2** [C] a good quality or habit: *Patience is a great virtue.* ⊃ look at **vice** (2) **3** [C, U] ~ **(of sth)**; ~ **(of being/doing sth)** an advantage or a useful quality of sth: *This new material **has the virtue** of being strong as well as very light.*
IDM **by virtue of sth** (formal) by means of sth or because of sth

virtuoso /ˌvɜːtʃuˈəʊsəʊ, -ˈəʊzəʊ/ noun [C] (pl. virtuosos, virtuosi /-ˈəʊsi, -ˈəʊzi/) (MUSIC) a person who shows very great skill at sth, especially playing a musical instrument

virtuous /ˈvɜːtʃuəs/ adj. behaving in a morally good way

virulent /ˈvɪrələnt/ adj. **1** (HEALTH) (used about a poison or a disease) very strong and dangerous: *a particularly virulent form of influenza* **2** (formal) very strong and full of anger: *a virulent attack on the leader*

virus ʔ A2 /ˈvaɪrəs/ noun [C] **1** (BIOLOGY, HEALTH) a living thing, too small to be seen without a MICROSCOPE (= a piece of equipment that makes small objects look bigger), that causes disease in people, animals and plants: *to catch a virus* ◇ *the flu virus* ◇ *HIV, the virus that can cause AIDS* ⊃ look at **bacteria, germ** (1) **2** a disease caused by a virus **3** (COMPUTING) instructions that are

virus

nucleic acid
protein
capsid
enzyme

put into a computer program in order to stop it working properly and to destroy information ➔ look at **viral** (2)

visa ₹+ **B2** /ˈviːzə/ noun [C] an official mark or piece of paper that shows you are allowed to enter, leave or travel through a country: *a tourist/work/student visa*

viscous /ˈvɪskəs/ adj. (**SCIENCE**) (used about liquids) thick and sticky; not flowing easily ▸ **viscosity** /vɪˈskɒsəti/ noun [U]

vise /vaɪs/ (*AmE*) = VICE (3)

visibility /ˌvɪzəˈbɪləti/ noun [U] the distance that you can see in particular light or weather conditions: *In the fog visibility was down to 50 metres.* ◇ *poor/good visibility*

visible ₹+ **B2** **W** /ˈvɪzəbl/ adj. that can be seen or noticed: *The church tower was visible from the other side of the valley.* ◇ *a visible improvement in his work* **OPP** **invisible** ➔ picture at **wavelength** ▸ **visibly** /-bli/ adv.: *Rosa was visibly upset.*

vision ₹ **B2** /ˈvɪʒn/ noun
- SIGHT **1** [U] (**HEALTH**) the ability to see; sight: *to have good/poor/normal/perfect vision*
- PICTURE IN YOUR MIND **2** [C] a picture in your imagination: *They have a vision of a world without weapons.* ◇ *I **had visions of** being left behind, but in fact the others had waited for me.*
- DREAM **3** [C] a dream or similar experience often connected with religion
- PLANS FOR THE FUTURE **4** [U] the ability to make great plans for the future: *a leader of great vision*
- TV/CINEMA **5** [U] the picture on a TV or cinema screen: *a temporary loss of vision*

visionary /ˈvɪʒənri/ adj. having great plans for the future: *a visionary leader* ▸ **visionary** noun [C] (*pl.* -ies)

visit[1] ₹ **A1** /ˈvɪzɪt/ verb [I, T] **1** to go to see a person or place for a period of time: *I don't live here. I'm just visiting.* ◇ *We often visit relatives at the weekend.* ◇ *She's going to visit her son in hospital.* ◇ *When you go to London you must visit the Science Museum.* **2** (**COMPUTING**) to go to a website on the internet

visit[2] ₹ **A1** /ˈvɪzɪt/ noun [C] **1** an occasion or a period of time when sb goes to see a place or person and spends time there: *the prime minister's **surprise visit** to the troops* ◇ *It's my first visit to New York.* ◇ *If you have time, **pay a visit to** the local museum.* ◇ *I decided it was time to **pay** him **a visit**.* ◇ *The family **made a visit to** England in the summer of 1923.* ◇ *We had a visit from the police last night.* ◇ *The prime minister is **on a visit** to Germany.* ➔ look at **flying visit 2** (**COMPUTING**) an occasion when sb looks at a website on the internet: *Visits to our website have doubled in a year.*

visiting /ˈvɪzɪtɪŋ/ adj. [only before noun] (**EDUCATION**) a **visiting** professor or LECTURER is one who is visiting for a fixed period at a particular university or college, but who normally teaches at another one

visitor ₹ **A1** /ˈvɪzɪtə(r)/ noun [C] **~ (to …)** **1** a person who visits a person or a place: *She's a frequent visitor to the US.* ◇ *How can we attract more visitors to our website?* **2** (**COMPUTING**) a person who looks at a website on the internet

visor /ˈvaɪzə(r)/ noun [C] **1** the part of a HELMET (= a hard hat) that you can pull down to protect your eyes or face **2** a piece of plastic, cloth, etc. on a hat or in a car that stops the sun shining into your eyes

vista /ˈvɪstə/ noun [C] (*formal*) **1** a beautiful view, for example of the countryside, a city, etc. **2** a variety of things that might happen or be possible in the future: *This job could open up whole new vistas for her.*

visual ₹ **B2** **W** /ˈvɪʒuəl/ adj. connected with seeing: *the visual arts* (= painting, sculpture, cinema, etc.) ▸ **visually** /-əli/ adv.: *The film is visually stunning.*

visual ˈaid noun [C] (**EDUCATION**) a picture, video, map, etc. that helps a student to learn sth

visualize (*BrE also* -ise) /ˈvɪʒuəlaɪz/ verb [T] to imagine or have a picture in your mind of sb/sth: *It's hard to visualize what this place looked like before the factory was built.*

vital ₹ **B2** /ˈvaɪtl/ adj. **1** very important or necessary: *Practice is vital if you want to speak a language well.* ◇ *vital information* ➔ note at **essential 2** full of energy **SYN** **lively** ▸ **vitally** /-təli/ adv.: *vitally important*

vitality /vaɪˈtæləti/ noun [U] the state of being full of energy

vitamin ₹ **B2** /ˈvɪtəmɪn/ noun [C] (**HEALTH**) one of several natural substances in certain types of food that are important to help humans and animals grow and stay healthy

vitamin ˈA = RETINOL

vitamin ˈB noun [U] (**HEALTH**) any one of a group of vitamins found in foods such as grains, meat and fish that are essential for the blood and the NERVOUS SYSTEM and for processing the food we eat

vitamin ˈC (*also* **ascorbic acid**) noun [U] (**HEALTH**) a vitamin found in fruits such as oranges and lemons, and in green vegetables: *Oranges are rich in vitamin C.*

vitamin ˈD noun [U] (**HEALTH**) any one of a group of vitamins found in meat such as LIVER, fish oils and eggs that are essential for healthy bones and teeth. **Vitamin D** is also produced by the action of the sun on the skin.

vitreous /ˈvɪtriəs/ adj. hard, shiny and clear like glass

vivacious /vɪˈveɪʃəs/ adj. (used about a person, usually a woman) full of energy; lively and happy

viva voce /ˌvaɪvə ˈvəʊtʃi/ (*BrE also* **viva** /ˈvaɪvə/) noun [C] (**EDUCATION**) a spoken exam, especially in a British university

vivid /ˈvɪvɪd/ adj. **1** having or producing a strong, clear picture in your mind: *vivid dreams/memories* **2** (used about light or a colour) strong and very bright: *the vivid reds and yellows of the flowers* ▸ **vividly** adv.

viviparous /vɪˈvɪpərəs/ adj. (**BIOLOGY**) (used about animals) that produce live babies from their bodies rather than eggs ➔ look at **oviparous**

vivisection /ˌvɪvɪˈsekʃn/ noun [U] (**BIOLOGY**) doing scientific experiments on live animals

vixen /ˈvɪksn/ noun [C] a female FOX (= a type of red-brown wild dog)

viz. /vɪz, ˈneɪmli/ adv. (*especially BrE, formal*) used to introduce a list of things that explain sth more clearly or are given as examples

VLE /ˌviː el ˈiː/ noun [C] (*BrE*) (**EDUCATION**) a software system for teaching and learning using the internet (the abbreviation for 'virtual learning environment')

ˈV-neck noun [C] an opening for the neck in a piece of clothing shaped like the letter V; a piece of clothing with a V-neck: *I went out and bought a navy V-neck.*

vocabulary /vəˈkæbjələri/ noun (*pl.* -ies) (**LANGUAGE**) **1** [C, U] all the words that sb knows or that are used in a particular book, subject, etc: *He has an amazing vocabulary for a 5-year-old.* ◇ *There are many ways to increase your English vocabulary.* ➔ note at **language 2** [C] all the words in a language: *New words are always coming into the vocabulary.*

vocal ᵏ+ **C1** /ˈvəʊkl/ *adj.* **1** [only before noun] connected with the voice **2** expressing your ideas or opinions loudly or freely: *a small but vocal group of protesters*

vocal cords *noun* [C] (**ANATOMY**) the thin bands of muscle in the back of the throat that move to produce the voice

vocalist /ˈvəʊkəlɪst/ *noun* [C] (**MUSIC**) a singer, especially in a band: *a lead/backing vocalist*

vocally /ˈvəʊkəli/ *adv.* **1** in a way that uses the voice: *to communicate vocally* **2** by speaking in a loud and confident way: *They protested vocally.*

vocation /vəʊˈkeɪʃn/ *noun* [C, U] a type of work or a way of life that you believe to be especially suitable for you: *Peter has finally found his vocation in life.*

vocational /vəʊˈkeɪʃənl/ *adj.* connected with the skills, knowledge, etc. that you need to do a particular job: *vocational training*

voˈcational school *noun* [C, U] (**EDUCATION**) (in the US) a school that teaches skills that are necessary for particular jobs

vocative /ˈvɒkətɪv/ *noun* [C] (**GRAMMAR**) (in some languages) the form of a noun, a pronoun or an adjective used when addressing a person or thing ▸ **vocative** *adj.*: *the vocative case* ɔ look at **accusative, dative, genitive, nominative**

vociferous /vəˈsɪfərəs/ *adj.* (*formal*) expressing your opinions or feelings in a loud and confident way ▸ **vociferously** *adv.*

vodka /ˈvɒdkə/ *noun* [U, C] a strong clear alcoholic drink originally from Russia

vogue /vəʊg/ *noun* [C, U] ~ (**for sth**) a fashion for sth: *a vogue for large cars* ◇ *That hairstyle is in vogue at the moment.*

voice¹ ᵏ **A2** /vɔɪs/ *noun*
- SOUND FROM THE MOUTH **1** [C, U] the sounds that you make when you speak or sing; the ability to make these sounds: *He had a bad cold and lost his voice* (= could not speak for a period of time). ◇ *to speak in a loud/soft/low/hoarse voice* ◇ *to lower/raise your voice* (= speak more quietly/loudly) ◇ *Shh! Keep your voice down!* ◇ *Jack is 13 and his voice is breaking* (= becoming deep and low like a man's). **2** *-voiced* (in adjectives) having a voice of the type mentioned: *husky-voiced*
- OPINION **3** [sing.] ~ (**in sth**) (the right to express) your ideas or opinions: *The workers want more of a voice in the running of the company.* **4** [C] a particular feeling, attitude or opinion that you have or express: *You should listen to the voice of reason and apologize.*
- IN GRAMMAR **5** the active/passive voice [sing.] the form of a verb that shows if a sentence is active or passive: *'Keats wrote this poem' is in the active voice.* ◇ *'This poem was written by Keats' is in the passive voice.*
IDM **at the top of your voice** → **TOP¹**

voice² /vɔɪs/ *verb* [T] to express your opinions or feelings: *to voice complaints/criticisms*

ˈvoice box *noun* [C] the area at the top of the throat that contains the VOCAL CORDS (= the muscles that move to produce the voice) **SYN** **larynx** ɔ picture at **body**

voiced /vɔɪst/ *adj.* (**LANGUAGE**) (used about consonants) produced by moving your VOCAL CORDS ɔ look at **voiceless**

voiceless /ˈvɔɪsləs/ *adj.* (*also* unvoiced) *adj.* (**LANGUAGE**) (used about consonants) produced without moving your VOCAL CORDS ɔ look at **voiced**

voicemail /ˈvɔɪsmeɪl/ *noun* [U] an electronic system that can store phone messages, so that sb can listen to them later ɔ look at **answering machine**

void¹ /vɔɪd/ *noun* [C, usually sing.] (*formal*) a large empty space: *Her death left a void in their lives.*

void² /vɔɪd/ *adj.* **1** ~ (**of sth**) (*formal*) completely lacking sth: *This book is totally void of interest for me.* **2** (used about a ticket, contract, decision, etc.) that can no longer be accepted or used: *The agreement was declared void.*

VoIP /vɔɪp/ *noun* [U] a phone system that allows users to make and receive calls using the internet (the abbreviation for 'voice over internet protocol')

vol. *abbr.* (in writing) = VOLUME (4): *The Complete Works of Byron, Vol. 2*

volatile /ˈvɒlətaɪl/ *adj.* **1** that can change suddenly and unexpectedly: *a highly volatile situation which could easily develop into rioting* ◇ *a volatile personality* **2** (**CHEMISTRY**) (used about a substance) that can easily change into a gas ▸ **volatility** /ˌvɒləˈtɪləti/ *noun* [U]

volcano

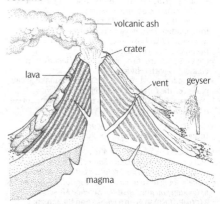
- volcanic ash
- crater
- lava
- vent
- geyser
- magma

volcano /vɒlˈkeɪnəʊ/ *noun* [C] (*pl.* -oes, -os) (**GEOLOGY**) a mountain with a CRATER (= a hole) at the top through which STEAM, LAVA (= hot melted rock), fire, etc. sometimes come out: *an active/a dormant/an extinct volcano* ◇ *When did the volcano last erupt?* ɔ note at **disaster** ▸ **volcanic** /-ˈkænɪk/ *adj.*: *volcanic rock/ash*

volcanology /ˌvɒlkəˈnɒlədʒi/ (*also* vulcanology) *noun* [U] (**GEOLOGY**) the scientific study of VOLCANOES

vole /vəʊl/ *noun* [C] a small animal like a mouse or RAT that lives in fields or near rivers ɔ picture at **food web**

volition /vəˈlɪʃn/ *noun* [U] (*formal*) the power to choose sth freely or to make your own decisions: *They left entirely of their own volition* (= because they wanted to).

volley /ˈvɒli/ *noun* [C] **1** (in tennis, football, etc.) a hit or kick of the ball before it touches the ground: *a forehand/backhand volley* **2** a number of stones, bullets, etc. that are thrown or shot at the same time: *The soldiers fired a volley over the heads of the crowd.* **3** a lot of questions, comments, offensive remarks, etc. that are directed at one person very quickly, one after the other: *a volley of abuse* ▸ **volley** *verb* [T, I]: *He volleyed the ball into the net.*

volleyball /ˈvɒlibɔːl/ *noun* [U] (**SPORT**) a game in which two teams of six players hit a ball over a high net with their hands while trying not to let the ball touch the ground on their own side

volt /vəult, vɒlt/ *noun* [C] (*abbr.* V) (PHYSICS) a unit for measuring electrical force

voltage /ˈvəultɪdʒ/ *noun* [U, C] (PHYSICS) an electrical force measured in VOLTS

volte-face /ˌvɒlt ˈfɑːs/ *noun* [sing.] (*formal*) a complete change of opinion or plan **SYN** about-turn

voltmeter /ˈvəultmiːtə(r)/ *noun* [C] (PHYSICS) an instrument for measuring VOLTAGE (= electrical force)

volume ᵻ B2 ⊙ /ˈvɒljuːm/ *noun* 1 [U, C] (PHYSICS) the amount of space that sth contains or fills: *What is the volume of this sphere?* ⊃ look at **area** (2) 2 [U, C] a large quantity or amount of sth: *the sheer volume* (= the large amount) *of traffic on the roads* 3 [U] (MUSIC) how loud a sound is: *to turn the volume on a radio up/down* ◇ *a low/high volume* 4 [C] (*abbr.* vol.) (LITERATURE) a book, especially one of a set or series: *The dictionary comes in three volumes.*

voluminous /vəˈluːmɪnəs/ *adj.* (*formal*) 1 (used about clothing) very large; having a lot of cloth: *a voluminous skirt* 2 (used about a piece of writing, a book, etc.) very long and detailed 3 (used about a container, piece of furniture, etc.) very large: *a voluminous armchair*

voluntary ᵻ+ B2 Ⓦ /ˈvɒləntri/ *adj.* 1 done or given because you want to do it, not because you have to do it: *He took voluntary redundancy and left the firm last year.* **OPP** **compulsory** 2 done or working without payment: *She does some voluntary work at the hospital.* 3 (used about movements of the body) that you can control **OPP** **involuntary** ▶ **voluntarily** /-trəli/ *adv.*: *She left the job voluntarily; she wasn't sacked.*

volunteer¹ ᵻ B1 /ˌvɒlənˈtɪə(r)/ *noun* [C] 1 a person who offers or agrees to do sth without being forced or paid to do it: *Are there any volunteers to do the washing-up?* 2 a person who joins the armed forces without being ordered to ⊃ look at **conscript**¹

volunteer² ᵻ B1 /ˌvɒlənˈtɪə(r)/ *verb* 1 [I, T] ~ (sth); ~ (to do sth) to offer sth or to do sth which you do not have to do or for which you will not be paid: *They volunteered their services.* ◇ *She frequently volunteers for extra work because she really likes her job.* ◇ *One of my friends volunteered to take us all in his car.* 2 [T] to give information, etc. or to make a comment or suggestion without being asked to: *I volunteered a few helpful suggestions.* 3 [I] ~ (for sth) to join the armed forces without being ordered to

vomit /ˈvɒmɪt/ *verb* [I, T] (HEALTH) to bring food, etc. up from the stomach and out of the mouth ▶ **vomit** *noun* [U]

voracious /vəˈreɪʃəs/ *adj.* (*formal*) 1 eating or wanting large amounts of food: *a voracious eater* ◇ *to have a voracious appetite* 2 wanting a lot of new information and knowledge: *a voracious reader* ▶ **voraciously** *adv.* ▶ **voracity** /-ˈræsəti/ *noun* [U]

vortex /ˈvɔːteks/ *noun* [C] (*pl.* vortexes, vortices /-tɪsiːz/) (PHYSICS) a mass of air, water, etc. that turns around very fast and pulls things into its centre

vote¹ ᵻ B1 /vəut/ *noun* 1 [C] ~ (for/against sb/sth) (POLITICS) a formal choice in an election or at a meeting in order to choose sb or decide sth: *The votes are still being counted.* ◇ *There were ten votes for, and 25 against the motion.* 2 [C] ~ (on sth) an occasion when a group of people vote on sth: *The democratic way to decide this would be to take a vote on it.* ◇ *Let's have a vote/put it to the vote.* 3 the vote [sing.] (POLITICS) the legal right to vote in political elections: *Women did not get the vote in this country until the 1920s.* 4 the vote [sing.] (POLITICS) the total number of votes in an election: *She obtained 30% of the vote.*

IDM **cast a/your vote** → CAST¹ **a vote of thanks** a short speech to thank sb, usually a guest, at a meeting, dinner, etc: *The club secretary proposed a vote of thanks to the guest speaker.*

vote² ᵻ B1 /vəut/ *verb* 1 [I, T] ~ (for/against sb/sth); ~ (on sth); ~ (to do sth) (POLITICS) to show formally a choice or an opinion, for example by marking a piece of paper or by holding up your hand: *Who did you vote for in the last general election?* ◇ *Very few MPs voted against the new law.* ◇ *After the debate we'll vote on the motion.* ◇ *They voted to change the rules of the club.* ◇ *I voted Liberal Democrat.* ◇ *46% voted in favour of* (= for) *the proposed change.* 2 [T, usually passive] to choose sb for a particular position or prize: *He was voted best actor at the Oscars.* ▶ **voter** *noun* [C] ▶ **voting** ᵻ+ B2 *noun* [U]: *Voting will take place on 1 May.*

ˈvoting booth = POLLING BOOTH

vouch /vautʃ/ *verb*
PHR V **vouch for sb/sth** to say that a person is honest or good or that sth is true or real: *I can vouch for her ability to work hard.*

voucher /ˈvautʃə(r)/ *noun* [C] (BrE) a piece of paper or an electronic document or code that you can use instead of money to pay for sth, or that allows you to pay less than the usual price for sth: *a gift voucher* ⊃ look at **token**¹ (2)

vow /vau/ *noun* [C] a formal and serious promise (especially in a religious ceremony): *to keep/break your marriage vows* ▶ **vow** ᵻ+ C1 *verb* [T] ~ (to do sth): *We vowed never to discuss the subject again.*

vowel /ˈvauəl/ *noun* [C] (LANGUAGE) any of the sounds represented in English by the letters a, e, i, o, or u ⊃ look at **consonant**

voyage /ˈvɔɪdʒ/ *noun* [C] a long journey by sea or in space: *a voyage to Jupiter* ▶ **voyager** *noun* [C]

VP /ˌviː ˈpiː/ *abbr.* = VICE-PRESIDENT

VPN /ˌviː piː ˈen/ *noun* [C] (COMPUTING) a system that allows you to connect to a private computer network over a public network such as the internet (the abbreviation for 'virtual private network')

VR /ˌviː ˈɑː(r)/ *abbr.* = VIRTUAL REALITY

vs *abbr.* (in writing) = VERSUS

VSO /ˌviː es ˈəu/ *abbr.* (BrE) **Voluntary Service Overseas** (a British organization that sends people to work in developing countries as volunteers)

VTOL /ˌviː tiː əu ˈel/ *abbr.* **vertical take-off and landing** (used to refer to an aircraft that can take off and land by going straight up or straight down)

vulcanized (BrE also -ised) /ˈvʌlkənaɪzd/ *adj.* treated with SULPHUR at great heat to make it stronger: *vulcanized rubber*

vulcanology /ˌvʌlkəˈnɒlədʒi/ *noun* [U] = VOLCANOLOGY

vulgar /ˈvʌlɡə(r)/ *adj.* 1 not having or showing good judgement about what is attractive or appropriate; not polite or well behaved: *vulgar furnishings* ◇ *a vulgar man/woman* 2 rude or likely to offend people: *a vulgar joke* ▶ **vulgarity** /vʌlˈɡærəti/ *noun* [U, C] (*pl.* -ies)

vulgar ˈfraction *noun* [C] (BrE) (AmE **common fraction**) (MATHEMATICS) a FRACTION (= a number less than one) that is shown as numbers above and below a line: ¾ and ⅝ are vulgar fractions. ⊃ look at **decimal**¹

vulnerable ᵻ+ C1 /ˈvʌlnərəbl/ *adj.* ~ (to sth) weak and easy to hurt in a physical or an emotional way: *Poor organization left the troops vulnerable to enemy attack.* **OPP** **invulnerable** ▶ **vulnerability** ᵻ+ C1 /ˌvʌlnərəˈbɪləti/ *noun* [U]

vulture /ˈvʌltʃə(r)/ *noun* [C] a large bird with no feathers on its head or neck, that eats dead animals ⊃ picture at **animal**

Vuvuzela™ /ˌvuːvuːˈzeɪlə/ *noun* [C] a long plastic instrument in the shape of a TRUMPET (= a musical instrument), that makes a very loud noise when you blow it and is popular with football fans in South Africa

W w

W¹ /ˈdʌblju:/ (*also* w) *noun* [C, U] (*pl.* W's, w's) the 23rd letter of the English alphabet: *'Water' begins with (a) 'W'.*

W² *abbr.* (in writing) **1** (*pl.* W) = WATT: *a 60W light bulb* **2** = WEST¹, WESTERN¹ (1): *W Cumbria*

wacky (*also* whacky) /ˈwæki/ *adj.* (wackier; wackiest) (*informal*) funny in a slightly crazy way

wad /wɒd/ *noun* [C] **1** a large number of papers, paper money, etc. folded or rolled together: *He pulled a wad of £20 notes out of his pocket.* **2** a mass of soft material that is used for blocking sth or keeping sth in place: *The nurse used a wad of cotton wool to stop the bleeding.*

waddle /ˈwɒdl/ *verb* [I] (often used with an adverb or a preposition) to walk with short steps, moving the weight of your body from one side to the other, like a DUCK (= a bird that lives on or near water)

wade /weɪd/ *verb* [I] (often used with an adverb or a preposition) to walk with difficulty through fairly deep water, mud, etc.
PHR V wade through sth to deal with or read sth that is boring and takes a long time

wadi /ˈwɒdi/ *noun* [C] (**GEOGRAPHY**) a valley or passage in the Middle East or North Africa that is dry except when it rains

wafer /ˈweɪfə(r)/ *noun* [C] a very thin, dry biscuit often eaten with ice cream

waffle¹ /ˈwɒfl/ *noun* **1** [C] a flat cake with a pattern of squares on it that is often eaten warm with SYRUP (= a sweet sauce) **2** [U] (*BrE, informal*) language that uses a lot of words but that does not say anything important or interesting: *The last two paragraphs of your essay are just waffle.*

waffle² /ˈwɒfl/ *verb* [I] ~ **(on) (about sth)** (*BrE, informal*) to talk or write for much longer than necessary without saying anything important or interesting

waft /wɒft/ *verb* [I, T] to move gently through the air; to make sth move in this way: *The smell of her perfume wafted across the room.*

wag /wæg/ *verb* [T, I] (-gg-) to make sth shake up and down or move from side to side; to move in this way: *The dog wagged its tail.*

wage¹ ⚡ **B2** /weɪdʒ/ *noun* [sing.] (*pl.* wages) (**FINANCE**) the regular amount of money that you earn for work: *a weekly wage of £200* ◇ *What's the national minimum wage* (= the lowest wage that an employer is allowed to pay by law)? ⊃ note at **pay²** ⊃ picture at **income**

wage² /weɪdʒ/ *verb* [T] ~ **sth (against/on sb/sth):** to begin and then continue a war, battle, etc: *to wage war on your enemy*

waggle /ˈwægl/ *verb* [T, I] (*informal*) to make sth move up and down or from side to side with quick, short movements; to move in this way

wagon /ˈwægən/ *noun* [C] **1** (*BrE*) (*AmE* freight car) an open section of a railway train that is used for carrying goods or animals ⊃ look at **truck** (2) **2** (*BrE also* waggon /ˈwægən/) a vehicle with four wheels pulled by animals and used for carrying heavy loads

waif /weɪf/ *noun* [C] a small thin person, usually a child, who looks as if they do not have enough to eat

wail /weɪl/ *verb* **1** [I, T] to cry or complain in a loud, high voice, especially because you are sad or in pain **2** [I] (used about things) to make a sound like this: *sirens wailing in the streets outside* ▶ **wail** *noun* [C]

waist /weɪst/ *noun* [C, usually sing.] **1** the narrowest part around the middle of the body: *She put her arms around his waist.* ⊃ picture at **body 2** the part of a piece of clothing that goes round the waist

waistband /ˈweɪstbænd/ *noun* [C] the narrow piece of cloth at the WAIST of a piece of clothing, especially trousers or a skirt

waistcoat /ˈweɪskəʊt/ (*BrE*) (*AmE* vest) *noun* [C] a piece of clothing with buttons down the front but no arms that is often worn over a shirt and under a jacket as part of a man's suit

waistline /ˈweɪstlaɪn/ *noun* [C, usually sing.] **1** (used to talk about how fat or thin a person is) the measurement or size of the body around the middle of the body **2** the place on a piece of clothing where your WAIST is

wait¹ ⚡ **A1** /weɪt/ *verb* [I] **1** ~ **(for sb/sth) (to do sth)** to stay in a particular place, and not do anything until sb/sth arrives or until sth happens: *Wait here. I'll be back in a few minutes.* ◇ *Have you been waiting long?* ◇ *If I'm a bit late, can you wait for me?* ◇ *I'm waiting to see the doctor.* **2** to be left or delayed until a later time: *Is this matter urgent or can it wait?*
IDM can't wait/can hardly wait used when you are emphasizing that sb is very excited and enthusiastic about doing sth: *The kids can't wait to see their father again.* **keep sb waiting** to make sb wait or be delayed, especially because you arrive late **wait and see** used to tell sb to be patient and to find out about sth later **wait your turn** to wait until the time when you are allowed to do sth
PHR V wait behind to stay in a place after others have left it: *She waited behind after class to speak to her teacher.* **wait in** to stay at home because you are expecting sb to come or sth to happen **wait on sb** to act as a servant to sb, especially by serving food to them **wait up (for sb)** to not go to bed because you are waiting for sb to come home

wait² ⚡ **A2** /weɪt/ *noun* [C, usually sing.] ~ **(for sth/sb)** a period of time when you wait
IDM lie in wait (for sb) → LIE¹

waiter ⚡ **A1** /ˈweɪtə(r)/ *noun* [C] a person whose job is to serve customers at their tables in a restaurant, etc.

'waiting list (*AmE also* 'wait list) *noun* [C] a list of people who are waiting for sth, for example a service or medical treatment, that will be available in the future: *to put your name on a waiting list*

'waiting room *noun* [C] a room where people can sit while they are waiting, for example for a train, or to see a doctor or dentist

waitress /ˈweɪtrəs/ *noun* [C] a woman whose job is to serve customers at their tables in a restaurant, etc.

waive /weɪv/ *verb* [T] (**LAW**) to say officially that a rule, etc. need not be obeyed; to say officially that you no longer have a right to sth

waiver /ˈweɪvə(r)/ *noun* [C] (**LAW**) a situation in which sb gives up a legal right or claim; an official document stating this

waltz **W**

wake¹ 🔊 **A1** /weɪk/ *verb* [I, T] (*pt* woke /wəʊk/; *pp* woken /ˈwəʊkən/) to stop sleeping; to make sb stop sleeping: *I woke early in the morning and got straight out of bed.* ◇ *Could you wake me at 7.30, please?* ➔ adjective **awake**

PHR V wake up to stop sleeping: *Wake up! It's nearly eight o'clock!* wake sb up **1** to make sb stop sleeping **2** to make sb become more active or full of energy: *She always has a coffee to wake her up when she gets to work.* wake up to sth to realize sth; to notice sth

wake² /weɪk/ *noun* [C] **1** an occasion before or after a FUNERAL when people meet to remember the dead person, traditionally held at night to watch over the body before it is buried **2** the track that a moving ship leaves behind on the surface of the water
IDM in the wake of sb/sth following or coming after sb/sth: *The earthquake left a trail of destruction in its wake.*

wakeboarding /ˈweɪkbɔːdɪŋ/ *noun* [U] (**SPORT**) the sport of riding on a short, wide board while being pulled along through the water by a fast boat ▸ **wakeboard** /-bɔːd/ *verb* [I]

waken /ˈweɪkən/ *verb* [I, T] (*formal, old-fashioned*) to stop sleeping or to make sb/sth stop sleeping: *She wakened from a deep sleep.*

ˈwake-up call *noun* [C] **1** (**TOURISM**) a phone call that you arrange to be made to you at a particular time, for example in a hotel, in order to wake you up: *I asked for a wake-up call at 6.30 a.m.* **2** ~ (**for sb/sth**) an event that makes people realize that there is a problem that they need to do sth about: *These riots should be a wake-up call for the government.*

walk¹ 🔊 **A1** /wɔːk/ *verb* **1** [I, T] to move or go somewhere by putting one foot in front of the other on the ground, but without running: *The door opened and Billy walked in.* ◇ *I walk to work every day.* ◇ *He walks with a limp.* ◇ *Are the shops within walking distance* (= near enough to walk to)? **2** [I] to move in this way for exercise or pleasure **3** [T] (used with an adverb or a preposition) to go somewhere with sb on foot, especially to make sure they get there safely: *I'll walk you home* if you don't want to go on your own. ◇ *He walked me to my car.* **4** [T] to take a dog out for exercise: *I'm just going to walk the dog.* ▸ **walker** *noun* [C]: *She's a fast walker.* ◇ *This area is very popular with walkers.*

PHR V walk off with sth **1** to win sth easily: *She walked off with all the prizes.* **2** to steal sth; to take sth that does not belong to you by mistake walk out (of sth) to leave suddenly and angrily: *She walked out of the meeting in disgust.* walk out on sb (*informal*) to leave sb for ever: *He walked out on his wife and children after 15 years of marriage.* walk (all) over sb (*informal*) **1** to treat sb badly, without considering their needs or feelings **2** to defeat sb completely: *He played brilliantly and walked all over his opponent.* walk up (to sb/sth) to walk towards sb/sth, especially in a confident way

walk² 🔊 **A1** /wɔːk/ *noun* **1** [C] an occasion when you go somewhere on foot for pleasure, exercise, etc: *We went for a walk in the country.* ◇ *I'm just going to take the dog for a walk.* ◇ *The beach is five minutes' walk/a five-minute walk from the hotel.* **2** [C] a path or route for walking for pleasure; an organized event when people walk for pleasure: *From here there's a lovely walk through the woods.* **3** [sing.] a way or style of walking; the speed of walking: *He has a funny walk.* ◇ *She slowed to a walk.*
IDM a walk of life a person's job or position in society

walkie-talkie /ˌwɔːki ˈtɔːki/ *noun* [C] (*informal*) a small radio that you can carry with you to send or receive messages

walking /ˈwɔːkɪŋ/ *noun* [U] the activity of going for walks in the countryside for exercise or pleasure

ˈwalking stick (*also* stick) *noun* [C] a stick that you carry and use as a support to help you walk ➔ look at **crutch** (1)

walkover /ˈwɔːkəʊvə(r)/ *noun* [C] an easy victory in a game or competition

wall 🔊 **A1** /wɔːl/ *noun* [C] **1** a solid, VERTICAL structure made of stone, BRICK, etc. that is built round an area of land to protect it or to divide it: *There is a high wall all around the prison.* **2** one of the sides of a room or building joining the ceiling and the floor: *He put the picture up on the wall.* **3** (**BIOLOGY**) the outer layer of sth such as an organ of the body or a cell of an animal or a plant: *the abdominal wall* ◇ *a cell wall* ➔ picture at **cell**, **fertilization** **4** a space on a SOCIAL MEDIA website where you can share messages, photos, etc. with other users
IDM up the wall (*informal*) crazy or angry: *That noise is driving me up the wall.*

wallaby /ˈwɒləbi/ *noun* [C] (*pl.* -ies) an Australian animal that moves by jumping on its strong back legs and keeps its young in a POUCH (= pocket of skin) on the front of the mother's body. A wallaby looks like a small KANGAROO.

walled /wɔːld/ *adj.* surrounded by a wall

wallet /ˈwɒlɪt/ (*AmE also* billfold) *noun* [C] a small, flat, folding case in which you keep paper money, plastic cards, etc. ➔ look at **purse¹** (1)

wallop /ˈwɒləp/ *verb* [T] (*informal*) to hit sb/sth very hard

wallow /ˈwɒləʊ/ *verb* [I] ~ (**in sth**) **1** (used about people and large animals) to lie and roll around in water, etc. in order to keep cool or for pleasure: *I spent an hour wallowing in the bath.* **2** to take great pleasure in sth (a feeling, situation, etc.): *to wallow in self-pity* (= to think about your unhappiness all the time and seem to be enjoying it)

wallpaper /ˈwɔːlpeɪpə(r)/ *noun* [U] **1** paper that you stick to the walls of a room to decorate or cover them **2** (**COMPUTING**) the background pattern or picture that you choose to have on the screen of your computer, mobile phone, etc. ▸ **wallpaper** *verb* [T, I]

ˌwall-to-ˈwall *adj.* **1** [only before noun] (used especially about a carpet) covering the floor of a room completely **2** (*informal*) continuous; happening all the time

wally /ˈwɒli/ *noun* [C] (*pl.* -ies) (*BrE, slang*) a silly or stupid person

walnut /ˈwɔːlnʌt/ *noun* **1** [C] a nut with a rough surface and a hard brown shell that is in two halves **2** (*also* ˈwalnut tree) [C] the tree on which these nuts grow **3** [U] the wood of the walnut tree, used in making furniture

walrus /ˈwɔːlrəs/ *noun* [C] a large animal with two TUSKS (= long teeth) that lives in or near the sea in Arctic regions

waltz¹ /wɔːls, wɔːlts/ *noun* [C] (**MUSIC**) a dance in which two people dance to music which has a rhythm of three beats; the music for this dance: *a Strauss waltz*

waltz² /wɔːls, wɔːlts/ *verb* **1** [I, T] to dance a WALTZ: *They waltzed around the floor.* ◇ *He waltzed her round the room.* **2** [I] (*informal*) (used with an adverb or a preposition) to go somewhere in a confident way: *You can't just waltz in and expect your meal to be ready for you.*

WAN /wæn/ *noun* [C] (**COMPUTING**) a system in which computers in different places are connected, usually over a large area (the abbreviation for 'wide area network') ⊃ look at **LAN**

wan /wɒn/ *adj.* looking pale and ill or tired

wand /wɒnd/ *noun* [C] a thin stick that people hold when they are doing magic tricks: *I wish I could wave a magic wand and make everything better.*

wander 🔊+ **B2** /'wɒndə(r)/ *verb* **1** [I, T] to walk somewhere slowly with no particular sense of direction or purpose: *We spent a pleasant day wandering around the town.* ◇ *He was found in a confused state, wandering the streets.* **2** [I] ~ **(away/off) (from sb/sth)** to walk away from a place where you ought to be or the people you were with: *We must stay together while visiting the town so I don't want anybody to wander off.* **3** [I] (used about sb's mind, thoughts, etc.) to stop paying attention to sth; to be unable to stay on one subject: *The lecture was so boring that my attention began to wander.*

wane¹ /weɪn/ *verb* [I] **1** to become gradually weaker or less important: *My enthusiasm was waning rapidly.* **2** (**ASTRONOMY**) (used about the moon) to appear slightly smaller each day after being full and round **OPP** **wax²**

wane² /weɪn/ *noun*
IDM **on the wane** becoming smaller, less important or less common

wangle /'wæŋgl/ *verb* [T] (*informal*) to get sth that you want by persuading sb or by having a clever plan: *Somehow he wangled a day off to meet me.*

wanna /'wɒnə/ a way of saying or writing 'want to' or 'want a' in informal speech: *I wanna go home now.*

wannabe /'wɒnəbi/ *noun* [C] (*informal*) a person who behaves, dresses, etc. like a famous person because they want to be like them

want¹ 🔊 **A1** /wɒnt/ *verb* [T] (not used in the progressive tenses)
• **WISH** **1** ~ **sth (for sth); ~ (sb) to do sth; ~ sth (to be) done** to have a desire or a wish for sth: *He wants a new bike.* ◇ *What do they want for breakfast?* ◇ *I don't want to discuss it now.* ◇ *I want you to stop worrying about it.* ◇ *I don't want Emma going out on her own at night.* ◇ *The boss wants this letter typed.* ◇ *They want Bhanot as captain.*
• **NEED** **2** (*informal*) used to say that sth needs to be done: *The button on my shirt wants sewing on.* ◇ *The house wants a new coat of paint.* **3** [usually passive] to need sb to be in a particular place or for a particular reason: *Mrs Lewis, you are wanted on the phone.* ◇ *She is wanted by the police* (= the police are looking for her because she is suspected of committing a crime).
• **SHOULD/OUGHT TO** **4** (*informal*) (used to give advice to sb) should or ought to: *He wants to be more careful about what he tells people.*
• **SEXUAL DESIRE** **5** to feel sexual desire for sb
IDM **what do you want?** used to ask sb in a rude or angry way why they are there or what they want you to do

want² /wɒnt/ *noun* (*formal*) **1** wants [pl.] something you need or want: *All our wants were satisfied.* **2** [U, sing.] a lack of sth: *He's suffering due to a want of care.*
IDM **for (the) want of sth** because of a lack of; because sth is not available: *I took the job for want of a better offer.*

wanting /'wɒntɪŋ/ *adj.* [not before noun] ~ **(in sth)** (*formal*) **1** not having enough of sth; lacking: *The children were certainly not wanting in enthusiasm.* **2** not good enough: *The new system was found wanting.*

wanton /'wɒntən/ *adj.* (*formal*) (used about an action) done in order to hurt sb or damage sth for no good reason: *wanton vandalism*

war 🔊 **A2** /wɔː(r)/ *noun* **1** [U, C] a state of fighting between different countries or groups within countries using armies and weapons: *The prime minister announced that the country was at war.* ◇ *to declare war on another country* (= announce that a war has started) ◇ *When war broke out* (= started), *thousands of men volunteered for the army.* ◇ *a civil war* (= fighting between different groups in one country) ◇ *to go to war against somebody* ◇ *to fight a war* **2** [C, U] very aggressive competition between groups of people, companies, countries, etc: *a price war among oil companies* **3** [U, sing.] ~ **(against/on sb/sth)** efforts to end or get rid of sth: *We seem to be winning the war against organized crime.* ⊃ note at **campaign¹**

war crime *noun* [C] (**LAW**) a cruel act that is committed during a war and that is against the international rules of war

ward¹ 🔊+ **C1** /wɔːd/ *noun* [C] **1** (**MEDICINE**) a separate room or area in a hospital for patients with the same kind of medical condition: *the maternity/psychiatric/surgical ward* ⊃ note at **hospital** **2** (*BrE*) (**POLITICS**) one of the sections into which a town is divided for elections **3** (**LAW**) a child who is under the protection of a court and who is cared for by a GUARDIAN (= somebody who is legally responsible for their care): *The child was made a ward of court.*

ward² /wɔːd/ *verb*
PHR V **ward sb/sth off** to protect or defend yourself against danger, illness, attack, etc.

warden /'wɔːdn/ *noun* [C] **1** a person whose job is to check that rules are obeyed or to look after the people in a particular place: *a traffic warden* (= a person who checks that cars are not parked in the wrong place) **2** (*especially AmE*) (**LAW**) the person in charge of a prison

warder /'wɔːdə(r)/ *noun* [C] (*BrE*) (**LAW**) a person whose job is to guard prisoners in a prison ⊃ look at **guard¹** (1)

wardrobe /'wɔːdrəʊb/ *noun* [C] **1** a large cupboard in which you can hang your clothes **2** [usually sing.] a person's collection of clothes: *I need a new summer wardrobe.*

ware /weə(r)/ *noun* **1** [U] (in compounds) things made from a particular type of material or suitable for a particular use: *glassware* ◇ *kitchenware* ⊃ look at **hardware** **2** wares [pl.] (*old-fashioned*) goods offered for sale

warehouse 🔊+ **C1** /'weəhaʊs/ *noun* [C] a building where large quantities of goods are stored before being sent to shops

warfare 🔊+ **C1** /'wɔːfeə(r)/ *noun* [U] the activity of fighting a war; types of war: *guerrilla warfare*

warhead /'wɔːhed/ *noun* [C] the part of a MISSILE (= a powerful exploding weapon) that explodes

warily, wariness → WARY

warlike /'wɔːlaɪk/ *adj.* liking to fight; good at fighting: *a warlike nation*

warm¹ 🔊 **A1** /wɔːm/ *adj.* **1** having a pleasant temperature that is fairly high, between cool and hot: *It's quite warm in the sunshine.* ◇ *I jumped up and down to keep my feet warm.* ⊃ note at **cold¹** **2** (used about clothes) preventing you from getting cold: *Take plenty of warm clothes.* **3** friendly, kind and pleasant: *I was given a very warm welcome.* **4** creating a pleasant, comfortable feeling: *warm colours* ▶ **the warm** *noun* [sing.]: *It's awfully cold out* here — I want to go back into the warm. ▶ **warmly** adv.: *warmly dressed* ◇ *She thanked him warmly for his help.*

warm² ʔ **B1** /wɔːm/ verb [T, I] ~ **(sb/sth) (up)** to make sb/sth warm or warmer; to become warm or warmer: *There's some meat left over from lunch, so we can warm it up (= heat it again) tonight.* ◇ *Come in and warm yourself by the fire.* ▶ **warming** ʔ+ **B2** noun [U]: *atmospheric warming*
PHR V **warm to/towards sb** to begin to like sb that you did not like at first **warm to sth** to become more interested in sth **warm up** to prepare to do an activity or a sport by practising gently: *The team warmed up before the match.*

ˌwarm-ˈblooded adj. (**BIOLOGY**) (used about animals) having a warm blood temperature that does not change if the temperature around them changes **OPP** **cold-blooded**

ˌwarm-ˈhearted adj. kind and friendly

warmonger /ˈwɔːmʌŋɡə(r)/ noun [C] a person, especially a politician or leader, who wants to start a war or encourages people to start a war ▶ **warmongering** noun [U]

warmth /wɔːmθ/ noun [U] **1** a fairly high temperature or the effect created by this, especially when it is pleasant: *She felt the warmth of the sun on her face.* **2** the quality of being kind and friendly: *I was touched by the warmth of their welcome.*

ˈwarm-up noun [C, usually sing.] **1** a short practice or a series of gentle exercises that you do to prepare yourself for doing a particular sport or activity **2** (**ARTS AND MEDIA**) a short performance of music, comedy, etc. that is intended to prepare the audience for the main show

warn ʔ **B1** /wɔːn/ verb **1** [T, I] ~ **(sb) (of sth)**; ~ **(sb) (about sb/sth)** to tell sb about sth unpleasant or dangerous that exists or might happen, so that they can avoid it: *When I saw the car coming I tried to warn him, but it was too late.* ◇ *The government is warning of possible terrorist attacks.* ◇ *He warned me about the danger of walking home alone at night.* **2** [I, T] ~ **(sb) against doing sth**; ~ **sb (not to do sth)** to advise sb not to do sth: *The radio warned against going out during the storm.* ◇ *I warned you not to trust him.*

warning ʔ **B1** /ˈwɔːnɪŋ/ noun [C, U] something that tells you to be careful or tells you about sth, usually sth bad, before it happens: *Many people continue to ignore warnings about the dangers of sunbathing.* ◇ *Your employers can't dismiss you without warning.*

warp /wɔːp/ verb **1** [I, T] to become bent into the wrong shape, for example as a result of getting hot or wet; to make sth become like this: *The window frame was badly warped and wouldn't shut.* **2** [T] to influence sb so that they start behaving in an unusual or shocking way: *His experiences in the war had warped him.* ▶ **warped** adj.

the ˈwarp noun [sing.] the THREADS on a LOOM (= a frame or machine for making cloth) that other THREADS are passed over and under in order to make cloth ᵓ look at **weft** ᵓ picture at **loom¹**

warpath /ˈwɔːpɑːθ/ noun
IDM **(be/go) on the warpath** (*informal*) to be very angry and want to fight or punish sb

warrant¹ ʔ+ **C1** /ˈwɒrənt/ noun [C] an official written statement that gives sb permission to do sth: *a search warrant* (= a document that allows the police to search a house)

warrant² ʔ+ **C1** /ˈwɒrənt/ verb [T] (*formal*) to make sth seem right or necessary; to deserve sth: *I don't think her behaviour warrants such criticism.*

warranty /ˈwɒrənti/ noun [C, U] (*pl.* -ies) a written statement that you get when you buy sth, which promises to repair or replace it if it is broken or does not work: *Fortunately my washing machine is still under warranty.* ᵓ look at **guarantee¹** (2)

warren /ˈwɒrən/ = RABBIT WARREN

warrior ʔ+ **C1** /ˈwɒriə(r)/ noun [C] (*formal*) a person who fights in a battle; a soldier

warship /ˈwɔːʃɪp/ noun [C] a ship for use in war

wart /wɔːt/ noun [C] (**HEALTH**) a small hard dry spot that sometimes grows on the face or body. It is caused by a virus. ▶ **warty** adj.

warthog /ˈwɔːthɒɡ/ noun [C] an African wild pig with two large outer teeth (TUSKS) and hard areas like WARTS on its face

wartime /ˈwɔːtaɪm/ noun [U] (**HISTORY**) a period of time during which there is a war

wary /ˈweəri/ adj. (warier; wariest) ~ **(of sb/sth)** careful because you are uncertain or afraid of sb/sth: *Since becoming famous, she has grown wary of journalists.* ▶ **warily** /-rəli/ adv. ▶ **wariness** noun [U, sing.] ᵓ note at **care¹**

was /wəz, *strong form* wɒz/ → BE¹

wash¹ ʔ **A1** /wɒʃ/ verb **1** [T, I] to clean sb/sth/yourself with water and often soap: *to wash your hands/face/hair* ◇ *That shirt needs washing.* ◇ *Wash and dress quickly or you'll be late!* ◇ *I'll wash (= wash the dishes), you dry.* ᵓ note at **clean¹** **2** [I] (often used with an adverb or a preposition) to be able to be washed without being damaged: *Does this material wash well, or does the colour come out?* **3** [I, T] (often used with an adverb or a preposition) (used about water) to flow or carry sth/sb in the direction mentioned: *I let the waves wash over my feet.* ◇ *The current washed the ball out to sea.*
IDM **wash your hands of sb/sth** to refuse to be responsible for sb/sth any longer: *They washed their hands of their son when he was sent to prison.*
PHR V **wash sb/sth away** (used about water) to carry sb/sth away: *The floods had washed away the path.* **wash (sth) off** to (make sth) disappear by washing: *The writing has washed off and now I can't read it.* ◇ *Go and wash that make-up off!* **wash out!** to be removed from a material by washing: *These grease marks won't wash out.* **wash sth out** to wash sth or the inside of sth in order to remove dirt: *I'll just wash out this bowl and then we can use it.* **wash (sth) up 1** (*BrE*) to wash the plates, knives, forks, etc. after a meal: *Whose turn is it to wash up?* **2** (*AmE*) to wash your face and hands: *Go and wash up quickly and put on some clean clothes.* **3** [often passive] (used about water) to carry sth to land and leave it there: *Police found the body washed up on the beach.*

wash² ʔ **A2** /wɒʃ/ noun **1** [C, usually sing.] an act of cleaning or being cleaned with water: *I'd better go and have a wash before we go out.* **2** [sing.] the waves caused by the movement of a ship through water
IDM **in the wash** (used about clothes) being washed: *'Where's my red T-shirt?' 'It's in the wash.'*

washable /ˈwɒʃəbl/ adj. that can be washed without being damaged

washbag /ˈwɒʃbæɡ/ (*also* **toilet bag**) (*both BrE*) (*AmE* **toiletry bag** /ˈtɔɪlətri bæɡ/) noun [C] a small bag for holding your soap, toothbrush, etc. when you are travelling

washbasin /ˈwɒʃbeɪsn/ (*also* **basin**) (*both especially BrE*) noun [C] a large bowl for water that has TAPS and is fixed to a wall, in a bathroom, etc. ᵓ look at **sink²**

,washed 'out *adj.* (used about a person) tired and pale: *They arrived looking washed out after their long journey.*

washer /'wɒʃə(r)/ *noun* [C] a small flat ring made of rubber, metal or plastic placed between two surfaces to make a connection tight ⊃ picture at **bolt**[1]

washing ₹ A2 /'wɒʃɪŋ/ *noun* 1 [U, sing.] the act of cleaning clothes, etc. with water: *I usually **do the washing** on Mondays.* 2 [U] clothes that need to be washed or are being washed: *Could you put the washing in the machine?* ◊ *a pile of dirty washing*

'washing machine *noun* [C] an electric machine for washing clothes

'washing powder *noun* [U] soap in the form of powder for washing clothes

,washing-'up *noun* [U] 1 the work of washing the plates, knives, forks, etc. after a meal: *I'll **do the washing-up.*** ◊ *washing-up liquid* 2 plates, etc. that need washing after a meal: *Put the washing-up next to the sink.*

washout /'wɒʃaʊt/ *noun* [C] (*informal*) an event that is a complete failure or doesn't happen, especially because of rain

washroom /'wɒʃruːm, -rʊm/ *noun* [C] (*AmE*) a toilet, especially in a public building

wasn't /'wɒznt/ *short form* was not

Wasp /wɒsp/ (*also* WASP) *noun* [C] (*especially AmE*) (**SOCIAL STUDIES**) a white American whose family originally came from northern Europe and is therefore thought to be from the most powerful section of society (the abbreviation for 'White Anglo-Saxon Protestant'): *a privileged Wasp background*

wasp /wɒsp/ *noun* [C] a small black and yellow flying insect that can STING ⊃ look at **hornet** ⊃ look at **bee** ⊃ picture at **animal**

wastage /'weɪstɪdʒ/ *noun* [U] using too much of sth in a careless way; the amount of sth that is wasted

waste[1] ₹ B1 /weɪst/ *verb* [T] 1 ~ sth (on sb/sth); ~ sth (in doing sth) to use or spend sth in a careless way or for sth that is not necessary: *She wastes a lot of money on magazines.* ◊ *He wasted his time at university because he didn't work hard.* ◊ *She wasted no time in decorating her new room* (= she did it immediately). 2 [usually passive] to give sth to sb who does not value it: *Expensive wine is wasted on me. I don't even like it.*

waste[2] ₹ B1 /weɪst/ *noun* 1 [U, sing.] ~ (of sth) using sth in a careless and unnecessary way: *It seems a waste to throw away all these old newspapers.* ◊ *If he gives up acting it will be a waste of great talent.* 2 [sing.] ~ (of sth) a situation in which it is not worth spending time, money, etc. on sth: *These meetings are a complete **waste of time.*** ◊ *They believe the statue is a **waste** of taxpayers' **money.*** 3 [U] material, food, etc. that is not needed and is therefore thrown away: *nuclear waste* ◊ *A lot of household waste can be recycled and reused.* ⊃ look at **rubbish** (1) 4 (*also* 'waste matter) [U] solid or liquid material that the body gets rid of: *The farmers use both animal and human waste as fertilizer.* ⊃ picture at **digestive system** 5 wastes [pl.] (*formal*) (**GEOGRAPHY**) large areas of land that are not lived in and not used: *the wastes of the Sahara desert*

IDM **go to waste** to not be used and so thrown away and wasted: *I can't bear to see good food going to waste!*

waste[3] ₹ B1 /weɪst/ *adj.* [only before noun] 1 no longer useful; that is thrown away: *waste paper* ◊ *waste material* 2 (used about land) not used or not suitable for use; not looked after: *There's an area of waste*

ground outside the town where people dump their rubbish.

wastebasket /'weɪstbɑːskɪt/ (*AmE*) = WASTEPAPER BASKET

wasted /'weɪstɪd/ *adj.* 1 not necessary or successful: *a wasted journey* 2 very thin, especially because of illness 3 (*slang*) suffering from the effects of drugs or alcohol

wasteful /'weɪstfl/ *adj.* using more of sth than necessary; causing waste

wasteland /'weɪstlænd/ *noun* [U, C] (**GEOGRAPHY**) an area of land that cannot be used or that is no longer used for building or growing things on

wastepaper basket /ˌweɪst'peɪpə bɑːskɪt/ (*BrE*) (*AmE also* wastebasket) *noun* [C] a container in which you put paper, etc. that is to be thrown away

watch[1] ₹ A1 /wɒtʃ/ *verb* 1 [T, I] to look at sb/sth for a time, paying attention to what happens: *I'm watching to see how you do it.* ◊ *We **watch** TV most evenings.* ◊ *Watch what she does next.* ◊ *I watched him open the door and walk away.* ◊ *I **watched in horror** as the car swerved and crashed.* 2 [T] to take care of sth for a short time: *Could you watch my bag for a second while I go and get a drink?* 3 [T, I] ~ (sb/sth) (for sth) to be careful about sth/sb; to pay careful attention to sb/sth: *Watch the cut for signs of infection.* ◊ *You'd better **watch what you say** to her. She gets upset very easily.* ◊ *Watch those two boys — they're acting suspiciously.*

IDM **watch your step** → STEP[1]

PHR V **watch out** to be careful because of possible danger or trouble: *Watch out! There's a car coming.* ◊ *If you don't watch out you'll lose your job.* **watch out for sb/sth** to look carefully and be ready for sb/sth: *Watch out for snakes if you walk through the fields.* **watch over sb/sth** to look after or protect sb/sth: *For two weeks she watched over the sick child.*

watch[2] ₹ A1 /wɒtʃ/ *noun* 1 [C] a type of small clock that you usually wear around your WRIST: *a digital watch* ◊ *a smart watch* ◊ *My watch is a bit fast/slow* (= shows a time that is later/earlier than the correct time). ⊃ look at **clock**[1] (1) 2 [sing., U] the act of watching sb/sth in case of possible danger or problems: *Tour companies have to **keep a close watch** on the political situation in the region.*

watchdog /'wɒtʃdɒg/ *noun* [C] a person or group whose job is to make sure that large companies respect people's rights: *a consumer watchdog*

watchful /'wɒtʃfl/ *adj.* careful to notice things

watchtower /'wɒtʃtaʊə(r)/ *noun* [C] a tall tower from which soldiers, etc. watch when they are guarding a place

water[1] ₹ A1 /'wɔːtə(r)/ *noun* 1 [U] the clear liquid that falls as rain and is in rivers, seas and lakes: *a glass of water* ◊ *All the rooms have hot and cold running water.* ◊ *drinking water* ◊ *tap water* ⊃ look at **freeze**[1] (1), **steam**[1] ⊃ picture at **distillation, energy, photosynthesis, purification, water cycle** 2 [U] a large amount of water, especially the water in a lake, river or sea: *Don't go too near the edge or you'll fall in the water!* ◊ *After the heavy rain several fields were **under water**.* 3 [U] the surface of an area of water: *Can you swim **under water**?* ◊ *I can see my reflection in the water.* 4 waters [pl.] (**GEOGRAPHY**) the water in a particular sea, lake, etc. or near a particular country: *The ship was still in British waters.*

IDM **keep your head above water** → HEAD[1] **pass water** → PASS[1]

water[2] ₹ B1 /'wɔːtə(r)/ *verb* 1 [T] to give water to plants 2 [I] (used about the eyes or mouth) to fill with liquid: *The smoke in the room was starting to **make** my*

▼ COLLOCATIONS

water

The water cycle is the constant circulation of water between the **atmosphere**, the **land** and the **sea**. **Evaporation** from oceans and lakes and **transpiration** from plants produces **water vapour** which forms **clouds** in the atmosphere. The water in the clouds then falls to the ground as **rain** or **snow**. Some drains off the surface into **rivers** and **lakes**, and some goes through the soil to **aquifers**. Eventually, all this water drains back into the sea and the cycle begins again.

▼ VOCABULARY BUILDING

When water is heated to 100° Celsius, it **boils** and becomes **steam**. When steam touches a cold surface, it **condenses** and becomes water again. When water is cooled below 0° Celsius, it **freezes** and becomes **ice**.

eyes water. ◇ *These menus will really **make** your **mouth water**.*

PHR V **water sth down** **1** to add water to a liquid in order to make it weaker **2** to change a statement, report, etc. so that the meaning is less strong or direct

waterbird /ˈwɔːtəbɜːd/ *noun* [C] a bird that lives near and walks or swims in water, especially rivers or lakes ➲ look at **seabird**

waterborne /ˈwɔːtəbɔːn/ *adj.* spread or carried by water: *cholera and other waterborne diseases* ➲ look at **airborne** (2)

ˈ**water buffalo** *noun* [C] (*pl.* **water buffalo**, **water buffaloes**) a large animal of the cow family, used for pulling vehicles and farm equipment in Asia

watercolour (*BrE*) (*AmE* **watercolor**) /ˈwɔːtəkʌlə(r)/ *noun* (**ART**) **1** **watercolours** [pl.] paints that are mixed with water, not oil **2** [C] a picture that has been painted with watercolours ➲ note at **art**

watercourse /ˈwɔːtəkɔːs/ *noun* [C] (**GEOGRAPHY**) a small river or an artificial channel for water

watercress /ˈwɔːtəkres/ *noun* [U] a water plant with small round green leaves that have a strong taste and are often eaten in salads

the ˈ**water cycle** *noun* [usually sing.] (**GEOGRAPHY**) the processes by which water passes between the earth's atmosphere, land and oceans

waterfall /ˈwɔːtəfɔːl/ *noun* [C] (**GEOGRAPHY**) a river that falls from a high place, for example over a rock, etc. ➲ picture at **glacial**

waterfront /ˈwɔːtəfrʌnt/ *noun* [C, usually sing.] (**GEOGRAPHY**) a part of a town or an area that is next to the sea, a river or a lake

waterhole /ˈwɔːtəhəʊl/ (*also* ˈ**watering hole**) *noun* [C] a place in a hot country where animals go to drink

ˈ**watering can** *noun* [C] a container with a long tube on one side that is used for pouring water on plants ➲ picture at **gardening**

ˈ**water lily** *noun* [C] a plant that floats on the surface of water, with large round flat leaves and white, yellow or pink flowers

waterlogged /ˈwɔːtəlɒgd/ *adj.* **1** (used about the ground) extremely wet: *Our boots sank into the waterlogged ground.* **2** (used about a boat) full of water and likely to sink

watermark /ˈwɔːtəmɑːk/ *noun* [C] a symbol or design in some types of paper, which can be seen when the paper is held against the light

watermelon /ˈwɔːtəmelən/ *noun* [C, U] a large, round fruit with a thick, green skin. It is pink or red inside with a lot of black seeds.

ˈ**water polo** *noun* [U] (**SPORT**) a game played by two teams of people swimming in a swimming pool. Players try to throw a ball into the other team's goal.

waterproof /ˈwɔːtəpruːf/ *adj.* that does not let water go through: *a waterproof jacket*

watershed /ˈwɔːtəʃed/ *noun* [C] **1** an event or a time that is important because it marks the beginning of sth new or different **2** (**GEOGRAPHY**) a line of high land where streams on one side flow into one river, and streams on the other side flow into a different river

waterside /ˈwɔːtəsaɪd/ *noun* [sing.] (**GEOGRAPHY**) the area at the edge of a river, lake, etc: *They strolled down to the waterside.* ◇ *a waterside cafe*

waterski /ˈwɔːtəskiː/ *verb* [I] (**SPORT**) to ski on water while being pulled by a boat

ˈ**water sports** *noun* [pl.] (**SPORT**) sports that are done on or in water, for example sailing and WATERSKIING

ˈ**water table** *noun* [usually sing.] (**GEOGRAPHY**) the level at and below which water is found in the ground

watertight /ˈwɔːtətaɪt/ *adj.* **1** made so that water cannot get in or out: *a watertight container* **2** (used about an excuse, opinion, etc.) impossible to prove wrong; without any faults: *His alibi was absolutely watertight.*

the water cycle

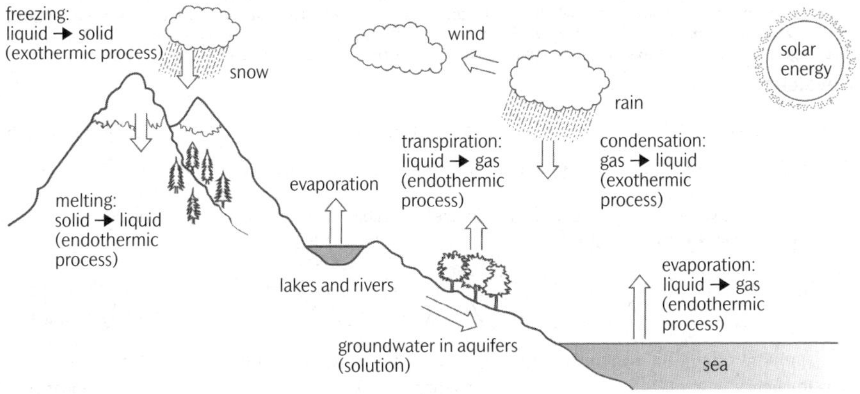
freezing:
liquid → solid
(exothermic process)
snow
wind
solar energy
rain
melting:
solid → liquid
(endothermic process)
evaporation
transpiration:
liquid → gas
(endothermic process)
condensation:
gas → liquid
(exothermic process)
lakes and rivers
evaporation:
liquid → gas
(endothermic process)
groundwater in aquifers
(solution)
sea

'water tower *noun* [C] a tall structure with a tank of water at the top from which water is supplied to buildings in the area around it ⊃ picture at **purification**

waterway /ˈwɔːtəweɪ/ *noun* [C] (**GEOGRAPHY**) a CANAL, river, etc. along which boats can travel

watery /ˈwɔːtəri/ *adj.* **1** containing mostly water: *watery soup* ◊ *A watery liquid came out of the wound.* **2** weak and pale: *watery sunshine* ◊ *a watery smile*

watt /wɒt/ *noun* [C] (*abbr.* **W**) a unit of electrical power: *a 60-watt light bulb*

waves

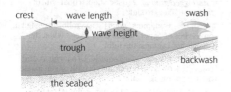

crest — wave length — swash
wave height
trough
backwash
the seabed

wave¹ 🔉 **A2** /weɪv/ *noun* [C]
• WATER **1** (**GEOGRAPHY**) a line of water moving across the surface of water, especially the sea, that is higher than the rest of the surface: *We watched the waves roll in and break on the shore.* ⊃ look at **tidal wave**
• SOUND/LIGHT/HEAT **2** (**PHYSICS**) the form that some types of energy such as sound, light, heat, etc. take when they move: *sound waves* ⊃ look at **long wave, medium wave, short wave** ⊃ picture at **diffraction, sound wave**
• MOVEMENT OF YOUR HAND **3** a movement of sth, especially your hand, from side to side in the air: *With a wave of his hand, he said goodbye and left.*
• FEELING/BEHAVIOUR **4** a sudden increase in a particular activity or feeling: *There has been a wave of sympathy for the refugees.* ◊ *a crime wave* ◊ *The pain came in waves.* ⊃ look at **heatwave**
• LARGE NUMBER **5** a large number of people or things suddenly moving or appearing somewhere: *There is normally a wave of tourists in August.*
• OF HAIR **6** a gentle curve in your hair ⊃ look at **perm**

wave² 🔉 **B1** /weɪv/ *verb* **1** [I, T] to move your hand from side to side in the air, usually to attract sb's attention or as you meet or leave sb: *She waved to me as the train left the station.* ◊ *I leant out of the window and waved goodbye to my friends.* **2** [T] (used with an adverb or a preposition) to move your hand in a particular direction to show sb/sth which way to go: *There was a policeman in the middle of the road, waving us on.* **3** [T] ~ **sth (about)** to hold sth in the air

and move it from side to side: *The crowd waved flags as the president came out.* ◊ *She was talking excitedly and waving her arms about.* **4** [I] to move gently up and down or from side to side: *The branches of the trees waved gently in the breeze.*
PHR V **wave sth aside/away** to decide not to pay attention to sth because you think it is not important
wave sb off to wave to sb who is leaving

waveband /ˈweɪvbænd/ = BAND (5)

wave-cut ˈplatform *noun* [C] (**GEOGRAPHY**) an area of land between the CLIFFS and the sea that is covered by water when the sea is at its highest level

waveform /ˈweɪvfɔːm/ *noun* [C] (**PHYSICS**) a curve showing the shape of a wave at a particular time

wavelength /ˈweɪvleŋθ/ *noun* [C] **1** (**PHYSICS**) the distance between two similar points on a wave of energy, such as light or sound **2** the size of a radio wave that is used by a particular radio station, etc. for sending out signals or programmes
IDM **on the same wavelength** → SAME¹

waver /ˈweɪvə(r)/ *verb* [I] **1** to move in a way that is not firm or steady: *His hand wavered as he reached for the money.* **2** to become weak or uncertain, especially when making a decision or choice: *He never wavered in his support for her.*

wavy /ˈweɪvi/ *adj.* (**wavier; waviest**) having curves; not straight: *wavy hair* ◊ *a wavy line* ⊃ picture at **line¹**

wax¹ /wæks/ *noun* [U] **1** a substance made from fat or oil that melts easily and is used for making CANDLES, POLISH, etc. ⊃ picture at **fractional distillation** **2** (**BIOLOGY**) a yellow substance that is found in your ears

wax² /wæks/ *verb* **1** [T] to POLISH sth with WAX **2** [T, often passive] to remove hair from a part of the body using WAX: *to wax your legs/have your legs waxed* **3** [I] (**ASTRONOMY**) (used about the moon) to seem to get gradually bigger until its full form can be seen **OPP** **wane¹**

ˈwax paper (*AmE*) = GREASEPROOF PAPER

waxwork /ˈwækswɜːk/ *noun* [C] **1** a model of sb/sth, especially of a famous person, made of WAX **2** **waxworks** (*pl.* **waxworks**) a place where WAX models of famous people are shown to the public

way¹ 🔉 **A1** 🔉 /weɪ/ *noun*
• METHOD/STYLE **1** [C] ~ **(to do sth); ~ (of doing sth)** a particular method, style or manner of doing sth: *What is the best way to learn a language?* ◊ *I've discovered a brilliant way of saving paper!* ◊ *They'll have to find the money one way or another.* ◊ *He always does things his own way.* ◊ *She smiled in a friendly way.*
• ROUTE **2** [C, usually sing.] the route you take to reach somewhere; the route you would take if nothing were stopping you: *Can you tell me the way to James Street?* ◊ *Which way should I go to get to the town*

wavelength

long wavelength

wavelength (metres)

short wavelength

| 10⁴ | 10³ | 10² | 10 | 1 | 10⁻¹ | 10⁻² | 10⁻³ | 10⁻⁴ | 10⁻⁵ | 10⁻⁶ | 10⁻⁷ | 10⁻⁸ | 10⁻⁹ | 10⁻¹⁰ | 10⁻¹¹ | 10⁻¹² | 10⁻¹³ |

radio waves | microwaves | infrared | visible light | ultra-violet | X-rays | gamma radiation

LW MW SW VHF UHF

red violet

| 10⁵ | 10⁶ | 10⁷ | 10⁸ | 10⁹ | 10¹⁰ | 10¹¹ | 10¹² | 10¹³ | 10¹⁴ | 10¹⁵ | 10¹⁶ | 10¹⁷ | 10¹⁸ | 10¹⁹ | 10²⁰ | 10²¹ |

low frequency

frequency (hertz)

high frequency

centre? ◇ *If you lose your way*, phone me. ◇ *We stopped on the way to Leeds for a meal.* ◇ *Can I drive you home? It's on my way.* ◇ *Get out of my way!* **3** [C] a path, road, route, etc. that you can travel along ⟳ look at **highway, motorway, railway** ⟳ note at **direction**
• DIRECTION **4** [C, usually sing.] a direction or position: *Look this way!* ◇ *That painting is the wrong way up* (= with the wrong edge at the top). ◇ *Shouldn't you be wearing that hat the other way round?* (= facing in the other direction) ◇ *He thought I was older than my sister but in fact it's the other way round* (= the opposite of what he thought). ⟳ look at **back to front** at **back**¹
• DISTANCE **5** [sing.] a distance in space or time: *It's a long way from London to Edinburgh.* ◇ *The exams are still a long way off.* ◇ *We came all this way to see him and he's not at home!*
IDM bluff your way through sth → BLUFF¹ by the way (*abbr.* BTW) (used for adding sth to the conversation) on a new subject: *Oh, by the way, I saw Mario in town yesterday.* change your ways → CHANGE¹ get/have your own way to get or do what you want, although others may want sth else give way to break or fall down: *The branch of the tree suddenly gave way and he fell.* give way (to sb/sth) **1** to stop or to allow sb/sth to go first: *Give way to traffic coming from the right.* **2** to allow sb to have what they want although you did not at first agree with it: *We shall not give way to the terrorists' demands.* go a long way → LONG¹ go out of your way (to do sth) to make a special effort to do sth the hard way → HARD¹ have a long way to go → LONG¹ in a big/small way used for expressing the size or importance of an activity: *'Have you done any acting before?' 'Yes, but in a very small way* (= not very much).' in a/one/any way | in some ways to a certain degree but not completely: *In some ways I prefer working in a small office.* in the way **1** blocking the road or path: *I can't get past. There's a big lorry in the way.* ◇ *Can you move that box — it's in my/the way.* **2** not needed or wanted: *I felt rather in the way at my daughter's party.* learn the hard way to understand or realize sth by having an unpleasant experience rather than by being told no way (*informal*) definitely not: *'Can I borrow your car?' 'No way!'* on your/the/its way coming or going: *He stopped for breakfast on the way.* out of the way no longer stopping sb from moving or doing sth pick your way across, over, etc. sth → PICK¹ under way having started and making progress: *Discussions between the two sides are now under way.* a/sb's way of life the behaviour and customs that are typical of a person or group of people

way² ⟨B2⟩ /weɪ/ *adv.* (*informal*) very far; very much: *I finally found his name way down at the bottom of the list.* ◇ *Matt's got way more experience than me.*

WC /ˌdʌblju: 'si:/ *noun* [C] (*old-fashioned*) toilet (the abbreviation for 'water closet')

we ⟨A1⟩ /wi, *strong form* wi:/ *pron.* the subject of a verb; used for talking about the speaker and one or more other people: *We're going to the cinema.* ◇ *We are both very pleased with the house.*

weak ⟨A2⟩ /wi:k/ *adj.*
• NOT STRONG **1** (used about the body) having little strength or energy; not strong: *The child was weak with hunger.* ◇ *Her legs felt weak.* **2** that cannot support a lot of weight; likely to break: *That bridge is too weak to take heavy traffic.*
• NOT POWERFUL **3** easy to influence; not firm or powerful: *He is too weak to be a good leader.* ◇ *a weak character*
• ECONOMY **4** not having economic success: *a weak currency/economy/market* **OPP** strong ⟳ note at **currency**

817 | **wear** | **W**

• LIQUID **5** (used about liquids) containing a lot of water, not strong in taste: *weak coffee* ◇ *I like my tea quite weak.*
• VOICE/SMILE **6** not easy to see or hear; not definite or strong: *a weak voice* ◇ *She gave a weak smile.*
• NOT GOOD AT STH **7** ~ (at/in/on sth) not very good at sth: *He's weak at maths.* ◇ *His maths is weak.* ◇ *a weak team* **OPP** strong
• ARGUMENT/EXCUSE **8** (used about an argument, excuse, etc.) not easy to believe: *She made some weak excuse about washing her hair tonight.*
► **weakly** *adv.*

weaken ⟨+ C1⟩ /'wi:kən/ *verb* **1** [T, I] to make sb/sth less strong; to become less strong: *The illness had left her weakened.* ◇ *The building had been weakened by the earthquake.* **OPP** strengthen ⟳ note at **currency** **2** [I, T] to become less certain or firm about sth; to make sb become less certain or firm about sth: *She eventually weakened and allowed him to stay.*

weak force *noun* [C] (**PHYSICS**) the natural force that can cause the parts of an ATOM to break apart ⟳ look at **electromagnetism, gravity** (1), **strong force**

weakness ⟨B2⟩ /'wi:knəs/ *noun* **1** [U] the state of being weak: *He thought that crying was a sign of weakness.* **OPP** strength **2** [C] a fault or lack of strength, especially in a person's character: *It's important to know your own strengths and weaknesses.* **OPP** strength **3** [C, usually sing.] ~ (for sth/sb) a liking for sb/sth that you find hard to resist: *I have a weakness for chocolate.*

wealth ⟨B2⟩ ⟨w⟩ /welθ/ *noun* **1** [U] (**FINANCE**) a lot of money, property, etc. that sb owns; the state of being rich: *They were a family of enormous wealth.* **SYN** riches [sing.] ~ of sth a large number or amount of sth: *a wealth of information/experience/talent*

wealthy ⟨B2⟩ /'welθi/ *adj.* (wealthier; wealthiest) having a lot of money, property, etc. **SYN** rich **OPP** poor

wean /wi:n/ *verb* [T] to gradually stop feeding a baby or young animal with its mother's milk and start giving it solid food

weapons

hilt

dagger   sword   spear

weapon ⟨B1⟩ /'wepən/ *noun* [C] an object that is used for fighting or for killing people, such as a gun, knife, bomb, etc.

weapon of mass de'struction *noun* [C] (*abbr.* WMD) a weapon such as a nuclear weapon, a CHEMICAL WEAPON or a BIOLOGICAL WEAPON that can cause a lot of DESTRUCTION and kill many people

wear¹ ⟨A1⟩ /weə(r)/ *verb* (*pt* wore /wɔː(r)/; *pp* worn /wɔːn/)
• CLOTHES **1** [T] to have clothes, jewellery, etc. on your body: *He was wearing a suit and tie.* ◇ *I wear glasses for reading.*
• EXPRESSION ON YOUR FACE **2** [T] to have a certain look on your face: *His face wore a puzzled look.*

- DAMAGE WITH USE **3** [I, T] to become thinner, smoother or weaker; to make sth become thinner, smoother or weaker because of being used or rubbed a lot: *These tyres are badly worn.* ◇ *The soles of his shoes had worn smooth.* **4** [T] to make a hole, path, etc. in sth by rubbing, walking, etc: *I'd worn a hole in my sock.*
- STAY IN GOOD CONDITION **5** [I] to last for a long time without becoming thinner or damaged: *This material wears well.*

IDM **wear thin** to have less effect because of being used too much: *We've heard that excuse so often that it's beginning to wear thin.*

PHR V **wear (sth) away** to damage sth or to make it disappear over a period of time, by using or touching it a lot; to disappear or become damaged in this way: *The wind had worn the soil away.* **wear (sth) down** to become or to make sth smaller or smoother: *The heels on these shoes have worn right down.* **wear sb/sth down** to make sb/sth weaker by attacking, persuading, etc: *They wore him down with constant arguments until he changed his mind.* **wear off** to become less strong or to disappear completely: *The effects of the drug wore off after a few hours.* **wear (sth) out** to become too thin or damaged to use any more; to cause sth to do this: *Children's shoes wear out very quickly.* **wear sb/yourself out** to make sb/yourself very tired: *She wore herself out walking home with the heavy bags.* ◇ look at **worn out**

wear² /weə(r)/ *noun* [U] **1** (usually in compounds) used especially in shops to describe clothes for a particular purpose or occasion: *casual/evening wear* ◇ *children's wear* **2** wearing or being worn; use as clothing: *You'll need jeans and jumpers for everyday wear.* **3** long use that damages the quality or appearance of sth: *The engine is checked regularly for signs of wear.*

IDM **wear and tear** the damage to objects, furniture, etc. that is the result of normal use the worse for wear → WORSE¹

weary /'wɪəri/ *adj.* (wearier; weariest) very tired, especially after you have been doing sth for a long time: *He gave a weary smile.* ▸ **wearily** /-rəli/ *adv.* ▸ **weariness** *noun* [U]

weasel /'wiːzl/ *noun* [C] a small wild animal with red-brown fur, a long thin body and short legs. Weasels eat smaller animals.

weather¹ 🔊 **A1** /'weðə(r)/ *noun* [U] the condition of the atmosphere at a particular place and time, including how much wind, rain, sun, etc. there is, and how hot or cold it is: **What's the weather like** *where you are?* ◇ *hot/warm/sunny/fine weather* ◇ *cold/wet/windy/wintry weather* ◇ *I'm not going for a run in this weather!*

IDM **make heavy weather of sth** → HEAVY under the weather (*informal*) not very well

▼ VOCABULARY BUILDING

Rain is drops of water that fall from the clouds. **Snow** is frozen rain. It is soft and white and often settles on the ground. **Sleet** is rain that is not completely frozen. **Hail** is rain frozen to ice. When it is only raining very slightly it is **drizzling**. When it is raining very hard it is **pouring**. **Fog** is like a cloud at ground level. It makes it difficult to see very far ahead. **Mist** is a thin type of fog. **Haze** is caused by heat. **Smog** is caused by pollution.

weather² /'weðə(r)/ *verb* **1** [I, I] (**GEOGRAPHY**, **GEOLOGY**) to change in appearance because of the effect of the sun, air or wind; to make sth change in this way: *This stone weathers to a warm pinkish-brown colour.* **2** [T]

to come safely through a difficult time or experience: *Their company managed to weather the recession and recover.*

'weather-beaten *adj.* (used especially about a person's face or skin) made rough and damaged by the sun and wind

'weather forecast (*also* forecast) *noun* [C] a description of the weather that is expected for the next day or next few days ◇ look at **weather¹**

weathering /'weðərɪŋ/ *noun* [U] (**GEOLOGY**) the action of sun, rain or wind on rocks, making them change shape or colour ◇ picture at **carbon cycle**, **erosion**, **rock¹**

weathervane /'weðəveɪn/ *noun* [C] a metal object on the roof of a building that turns easily in the wind and shows which direction the wind is blowing from

weave 🔊 **C1** /wiːv/ *verb* (*pt* wove /wəʊv/; *pp* woven /'wəʊvn/) ❶ In sense 2 **weaved** is used for the past tense and past participle. **1** [T, I] to make cloth, etc. by passing THREADS under and over another set of THREADS by hand or on a machine called a LOOM: *woven cloth* **2** [I, T] (used with an adverb or a preposition) to change direction often when you are moving so that you are not stopped by anything: *The cyclist weaved in and out of the traffic.*

web 🔊 **A2** /web/ *noun* **1** the Web, the web [sing.] = WORLD WIDE WEB: *a Web browser* **2** [C] a type of fine net that a spider makes in order to catch small insects: *A spider spins webs.* ◇ picture at **animal**

webbed /webd/ *adj.* (used about the feet of a bird or an animal) having pieces of skin between the toes ◇ picture at **animal**

webcam /'webkæm/ *noun* [C] (**COMPUTING**) a video camera that is connected to a computer so that what it records can be seen on a website or on another computer as it happens

webcast /'webkɑːst/ *noun* [C] (**COMPUTING**) a live broadcast that is sent out on the internet

webinar /'webɪnɑː(r)/ *noun* [C] (**BUSINESS**, **EDUCATION**) a talk or SEMINAR (= a meeting for discussion or training) that takes place on the internet

webmaster /'webmɑːstə(r)/ *noun* [C] (**COMPUTING**) a person who is responsible for the pages on a particular website

'web page *noun* [C] (**COMPUTING**) a document that is connected to the World Wide Web and that anyone with an internet connection can see, usually forming part of a website: *We learned how to create and register a new web page.*

website 🔊 **A1** 🌐 /'websaɪt/ *noun* [C] (**COMPUTING**) a place connected to the internet where a company, an organization or an individual person puts information

Wed. *abbr.* (in writing) = WEDNESDAY

we'd /wiːd, wɪd/ *short form* we had; we would

wedding 🔊 **A2** /'wedɪŋ/ *noun* [C] a marriage ceremony and often the party that follows it: *I've been invited to their wedding.* ◇ *a wedding dress/guest/present* ◇ *a wedding ring* (= one that is worn to show that a person is married)

wedge¹ /wedʒ/ *noun* [C] a piece of wood, etc. with one thick and one thin pointed end that you can push into a small space, for example to keep things apart: *The door was kept open with a wedge.*

wedge² /wedʒ/ *verb* [T] **1** to force sth/sb to fit into a small space: *The cupboard was wedged between the table and the door.* **2** (used with an adverb or a preposition) to force sth apart or to prevent sth from moving by using a WEDGE: *to wedge a door open*

Wednesday 🔊 **A1** /'wenzdeɪ, -di/ *noun* [C, U] (*abbr.* Wed.) the day of the week after Tuesday

wee /wiː/ *noun* [C, U] (*informal*) a child's word for the liquid waste that is passed from the body when you go to the toilet **SYN** **urine** ▶ **wee** *verb* [I]

weed¹ 🔊+ **C1** /wiːd/ *noun* **1** [C] a wild plant that is not wanted in a garden because it prevents other plants from growing properly **2** [U] a mass of very small green plants that floats on the surface of an area of water

weed² /wiːd/ *verb* [T, I] to remove WEEDS from a piece of ground, etc.
PHR V **weed sth/sb out** to remove the things or people that you do not think are good enough: *He weeded out all the letters with spelling mistakes in them.*

weedy /'wiːdi/ *adj.* (weedier; weediest) (*informal*) small and weak: *a small weedy man*

week 🔊 **A1** /wiːk/ *noun* [C] **1** (*abbr.* wk, wk.) a period of seven days, especially from Monday to Sunday or from Sunday to Saturday: *We arrived last week.* ◇ *He left two weeks ago.* ◇ *I haven't seen her for a week.* ◇ *I go there twice a week.* ◇ *They'll be back in a week/in a week's time.* **2** the part of the week when people go to work, etc., usually from Monday to Friday: *She works hard during the week so that she can enjoy herself at the weekend.* ◇ *I work a 40-hour week.*
IDM **today, tomorrow, Monday, etc. week** seven days after today, tomorrow, Monday, etc. **week in, week out** every week without a rest or change: *He's played for the same team week in, week out for 20 years.* **a week yesterday, last Monday, etc.** seven days before yesterday, last Monday, etc.

weekday /'wiːkdeɪ/ *noun* [C] any day except Saturday or Sunday: *I only work on weekdays.*

weekend 🔊 **A1** /ˌwiːk'end/ *noun* [C] Saturday and Sunday: (*BrE*) *The office is closed at the weekend.* ◇ (*especially AmE*) *The office is closed on the weekend.* ◇ *Have a good weekend!*

weekly¹ 🔊+ **B2** /'wiːkli/ *adj.* happening or appearing once a week or every week: *a weekly report* ▶ **weekly** *adv.*: *We are paid weekly.*

weekly² /'wiːkli/ *noun* [C] (*pl.* -ies) a newspaper or magazine that is published every week

weep /wiːp/ *verb* [I, T] (*pt, pp* wept /wept/) (*formal*) to let tears fall because of strong emotion; to cry: *She wept at the news of his death.*

the weft /ðə 'weft/ *noun* [sing.] the THREADS that are TWISTED under and over the THREADS that are held on a LOOM (= a frame or machine for making cloth) ⊃ look at **warp** ⊃ picture at **loom¹**

weigh 🔊 **B1** /weɪ/ *verb* **1** linking verb to have or show a certain weight: *I weigh 56 kilos.* ⊃ note at **measure²** **2** [T] to measure how heavy sth is, especially by using scales: *I weigh myself every week.* ◇ *Can you weigh this parcel for me, please?* **3** [T] ~ **sth (up)**; ~ **sth (against sth/sb)** to consider sth carefully: *You need to weigh up your chances of success.* ◇ *We shall weigh the advantages of the plan against the risks.* **4** [I] ~ **against sb/sth** to be considered as a disadvantage when sb/sth is being judged: *She didn't get the job because her lack of experience weighed against her.*
PHR V **weigh sb down** to make sb feel worried and sad: *He felt weighed down by all his responsibilities.* **weigh sb/sth down** to make it difficult for sb/sth to move (by being heavy): *I was weighed down by heavy shopping.* **weigh on sb/sth** to make sb worry: *The problem has been weighing on my mind* (= I have felt worried about it). **weigh sb/sth up** to consider sb/sth carefully and form an opinion: *I weighed up my chances and decided it was worth applying.*

weight¹ 🔊 **A2** **W** /weɪt/ *noun* **1** [U] how heavy sth/sb is; the fact of being heavy: *The doctor advised him to lose weight* (= become thinner and less heavy). ◇ *He's put on weight* (= got fatter). ◇ *The weight of the snow broke the branch.* **2** [C] a heavy object: *The doctor has told me not to lift heavy weights.* **3** [sing.] something that you are worried about: *Telling her the truth took a weight off his mind.* **4** [C] a piece of metal that weighs a known amount that can be used to measure an amount of sth, or that can be lifted as a form of exercise: *a 500-gram weight* ◇ *She lifts weights in the gym as part of her daily training.* ⊃ picture at **sport**
IDM **carry weight** → CARRY **pull your weight** → PULL¹

weight² /weɪt/ *verb* [T] **1** ~ **sth (down) (with sth)** to hold sth down with a heavy object or objects: *to weight down a fishing net* **2** [usually passive] to organize sth so that a particular person or group has an advantage or a disadvantage: *The system is weighted in favour of/ against people with children.*

weightless /'weɪtləs/ *adj.* having no weight, for example when travelling in space ▶ **weightlessness** *noun* [U]

weightlifting /'weɪtlɪftɪŋ/ *noun* [U] (**SPORT**) the sport or activity of lifting heavy metal objects ▶ **weightlifter** /-lɪftə(r)/ *noun* [C]

weight training *noun* [U] the activity of lifting WEIGHTS as a form of exercise: *I do weight training to keep fit.*

weighty /'weɪti/ *adj.* (weightier; weightiest) serious and important: *a weighty question*

weir /wɪə(r)/ *noun* [C] a type of wall that is built across a river to stop or change the direction of the flow of water

weird 🔊+ **B2** /wɪəd/ *adj.* strange and unusual: *a weird noise/experience* **SYN** **bizarre, strange** ▶ **weirdly** *adv.*

weirdo /'wɪədəʊ/ *noun* [C] (*pl.* -os) (*informal*) a person who looks strange or behaves in a strange way

welcome¹ 🔊 **A1** /'welkəm/ *verb* [T] **1** to be friendly to sb when they arrive somewhere: *Everyone came to the door to welcome us.* **2** to be pleased to receive or accept sth: *I've no idea what to do next, so I'd welcome any suggestions.* ▶ **welcome** 🔊 **A2** *noun* [C, U]: *Let's give a warm welcome to our next guest.*

welcome² 🔊 **A1** /'welkəm/ *adj.* **1** received with pleasure; giving pleasure: *You're always welcome here.* ◇ *welcome news* **OPP** **unwelcome** **2** ~ **to do sth** (*informal*) allowed to do sth: *You're welcome to use my bike.* **3** ~ **to sth** (*informal*) used to say that sb can have sth that you do not want yourself: *Take the car if you want. You're welcome to it. It's always breaking down.* ▶ **welcome** 🔊 **A1** *exclamation*: *Welcome to London!* ◇ *Welcome home!*
IDM **make sb welcome** to receive sb in a friendly way **you're welcome** used as a polite reply when sb thanks you for sth: *'Thank you for your help.' 'You're welcome.'*

welcoming /'welkəmɪŋ/ *adj.* **1** friendly towards sb who is visiting or arriving: *The locals were extremely welcoming.* ◇ *She gave me a welcoming smile.* **2** (used about a place) attractive and looking comfortable to be in: *His room was quiet, warm and welcoming.*

weld /weld/ *verb* [T, I] to join pieces of metal by heating them and pressing them together ⊃ look at **solder²**

welfare 🔊+ **B2** ⦿ /'welfeə(r)/ *noun* [U] **1** the general health, happiness and safety of a person, an animal or a group: *The doctor is concerned about the child's* welfare. **SYN** well-being 2 (SOCIAL STUDIES) the help and care that is given to people who have problems with health, money, etc: *education and welfare services* 3 (*AmE*) = SOCIAL SECURITY

welfare 'state *noun* [sing., C] (SOCIAL STUDIES) a system organized by a government to provide free services and money for people who have no job, who are ill, etc.; a country that has this system

well¹ ⚡ **A1** /wel/ *adv.* (better /'betə(r)/; best /best/) **1** in a good way: *You speak English very well.* ◇ *I hope your work is going well.* ◇ *You passed your exam! Well done!* ◇ *He took it well when I told him he wasn't on the team.* **OPP** badly **2** completely or fully: *Shake the bottle well before opening.* ◇ *How well do you know Henry?* **3** very much: *They arrived home well past midnight.* ◇ *She says she's 32 but I'm sure she's well over 40.* ◇ *This book is well worth reading.* **4** (used with *can, could, may* or *might*) probably or possibly: *He might well be right.* **5** (used with *can, could, may* or *might*) with good reason: *I can't very well refuse to help them after all they've done for me.* ◇ *'Where's Bill?' 'You may well ask (= I don't know either)!'* **IDM** as well (as sb/sth) in addition to sb/sth: *Can I come as well?* ◇ *He's worked in Japan as well as Italy.* augur well/ill for sb/sth → AUGUR bode well/ill (for sb/sth) → BODE do well **1** to be successful: *Their daughter has done well at university.* **2** to be getting better after an illness: *Mr Singh is doing well after his operation.* do well to do sth used to say that sth is the right and sensible thing to do: *He would do well to check the facts before accusing people.* may/might (just) as well used for saying that sth is the best thing you can do in the situation, even though you may not want to do it: *I may as well tell you the truth — you'll find out anyway.* mean well → MEAN¹ well and truly completely: *We were well and truly lost.*

well² ⚡ **A1** /wel/ *adj.* [not before noun] (better /'betə(r)/; best /best/) **1** (HEALTH) in good health: *'How are you?' 'I'm very well, thanks.'* ◇ *This medicine will make you feel better.* ◇ *Get well soon* (= written in a card that you send to sb who is ill). **2** in a good state: *I hope all is well with you.* **IDM** all very well (for sb) (*informal*) used for showing that you are not happy or do not agree with sth: *It's all very well for her to criticize* (= it's easy for her to criticize) *but it doesn't help the situation.* (just) as well (to do sth) sensible; a good idea: *It would be just as well to ask his permission.* it is just as well (that…) → JUST¹

well³ ⚡ **A1** /wel/ *exclamation* **1** used for showing surprise: *Well, thank goodness you've arrived.* **2** (*also* oh well) used for showing that you know there is nothing you can do to change a situation: *Oh well, there's nothing we can do about it.* **3** used when you begin the next part of a story or when you are thinking about what to say next: *Well, the next thing that happened was…* ◇ *Well now, let me see…* **4** used when you do not feel certain about sth: *'Do you like it?' 'Well, I'm not really sure.'* **5** used to show that you are waiting for sb to say sth: *Well? Are you going to tell us what happened?* **6** used to show that you want to finish a conversation: *Well, it's been nice talking to you.*

well⁴ ⚡+ **C1** /wel/ *noun* [C] **1** a deep hole in the ground from which water is obtained: *to draw water from a well* **2** = OIL WELL

well⁵ /wel/ *verb* [I] ~ (out/up) (used about a liquid) to come to the surface: *Tears welled up in her eyes.*

we'll /wiːl, wil/ *short form* we will; we shall

well ad'justed *adj.* (PSYCHOLOGY) (used about a person) able to deal with people, problems and life in general in a normal, sensible way ⊃ look at maladjusted

well 'balanced *adj.* **1** (used about a person) calm and sensible **2** (used about a meal, etc.) containing enough of the healthy types of food your body needs: *a well-balanced diet*

well be'haved *adj.* behaving in a way that most people think is correct

well-being ⚡+ **C1** *noun* [U] a state of being healthy and happy: *She was filled with a sense of well-being.*

well con'nected *adj.* (used about a person) having important or rich friends or relatives: *a well-connected family*

well 'done *adj.* (used about meat, etc.) cooked for a long time ⊃ look at medium¹ (2), rare (2)

well 'dressed *adj.* wearing attractive and fashionable clothes

well 'earned *adj.* that you deserve, especially because you have been working hard: *She's having a well-earned holiday.*

well 'educated *adj.* having had a high standard of education: *a well-educated person*

well 'fed *adj.* having good food regularly

well in'formed *adj.* knowing a lot about one or several subjects

wellington /'welɪŋtən/ (*also informal* welly) *noun* [C] (*BrE*) one of a pair of long rubber boots that you wear to keep your feet and the lower part of your legs dry: *a pair of wellingtons*

well 'kept *adj.* looked after very carefully so that it has a tidy appearance: *a well-kept garden*

well 'known *adj.* known by a lot of people **SYN** famous **OPP** unknown¹

well 'meaning *adj.* (used about a person) wanting to be kind or helpful, but often not having this effect

well 'meant *adj.* intended to be kind or helpful but not having this result

wellness /'welnəs/ *noun* [U] (*especially AmE*) (HEALTH) the state of being healthy

well 'off *adj.* having a lot of money: *They are much better off than us.* **OPP** badly off

well 'paid *adj.* earning or providing a lot of money: *The job is very well paid.* ◇ *well-paid managers*

well 'read *adj.* having read many books and therefore having a lot of knowledge

well-to-'do *adj.* having a lot of money, property, etc. **SYN** rich, wealthy

well-wisher *noun* [C] a person who hopes that sb/sth will be successful: *She received lots of letters from well-wishers before the competition.*

welly /'weli/ *noun* [C] (*pl.* -ies) (*BrE, informal*) = WELLINGTON

Welsh /welʃ/ *adj.* of or connected with Wales, its people or its language

went /went/ past tense of go¹

wept /wept/ past tense, past participle of weep

were /wə(r), strong form wɜː(r)/ → BE¹

we're /wɪə(r)/ short form we are

weren't /wɜːnt/ short form were not

west¹ ⚡ **A1** /west/ *noun* [U, sing.] (*abbr.* W) (GEOGRAPHY) **1** (*usually* the west) ~ (of…) the direction you look towards in order to see the sun go down; one of the points of the COMPASS (= the four main directions that we give names to): *Which way is west?* ◇ *Rain is spreading from the west.* ◇ *There's a road to the west of here.* ⊃ look at east¹ (1), north¹ (1), south¹ (1)

⊃ note at **compass** ⊃ picture at **compass** **2** the west, the West the western part of a country, region or city: *I live in the west of Scotland.* ◇ *The climate in the West is much wetter than the East.* **3** the West the countries of North America and Western Europe

west² 🔊 **A1** /west/ *adj., adv.* (**GEOGRAPHY**) **1** in or towards the west: *to travel west* ◇ *West London* **2 ~(of…)** nearer to the west than sth: *The island is 5 miles west of here.* **3** (used about a wind) coming from the west

westbound /'westbaʊnd/ *adj.* travelling or leading towards the west: *the westbound carriageway of the motorway*

the ˈWest Country *noun* [sing.] (**GEOGRAPHY**) the south-west part of Britain

the ˌWest ˈEnd *noun* [sing.] (**GEOGRAPHY**) the western part of central London where there are many shops, theatres, cinemas, etc.

westerly /'westəli/ *adj.* (**GEOGRAPHY**) **1** to, towards or in the west: *in a westerly direction* **2** (used about winds) coming from the west

western¹ 🔊 **B1** /'westən/ (*also* Western) *adj.* (**GEOGRAPHY**) **1** (*abbr.* W) in, of or from the west of a place: *western France* **2** from or connected with the western part of the world, especially Europe or North America

western² /'westən/ *noun* [C] (**ARTS AND MEDIA, LITERATURE**) a film or book about life in the past in the west of the United States

westerner /'westənə(r)/ *noun* [C] (**GEOGRAPHY**) a person who was born or who lives in the western part of the world, especially Europe or North America: *Westerners arriving in China usually experience culture shock.*

westernize (*BrE also* -ise) /'westənaɪz/ *verb* [T, usually passive] (**SOCIAL STUDIES**) to bring ideas or ways of life that are typical of western Europe and North America to other countries ▸ **westernized** (*BrE also* -ised) *adj.*: *a westernized society*

the West Indies /ðə ˌwest ˈmdɪz, -diːz/ *noun* [pl., + sing./ pl. verb] (**GEOGRAPHY**) a group of islands between the Caribbean and the Atlantic, that includes the Antilles and the Bahamas ▸ **West ˈIndian** *noun* [C], *adj.*: *The West Indians won their match against Australia.*

ˌwest-north-ˈwest *noun* [sing.] (**GEOGRAPHY**) (*abbr.* WNW) the direction that lies at an equal distance between west and north-west

ˌwest-south-ˈwest *noun* [sing.] (**GEOGRAPHY**) (*abbr.* WSW) the direction that lies at an equal distance between west and south-west

westwards /'westwədz/ (*also* westward /'westwəd/) *adv.* towards the west: *to fly westwards* ▸ **westward** *adj.*: *in a westward direction*

wet¹ 🔊 **A2** /wet/ *adj.* (wetter, wettest) **1** covered in a liquid, especially water: *wet clothes/hair/grass/roads* ◇ *Don't get your feet wet.* **OPP** **dry¹** **2** (used about the weather, etc.) with a lot of rain: *a wet day* **OPP** **dry¹** **3** (used about paint, etc.) not yet dry or hard: *The ink is still wet.* **4** (*BrE, informal*) (used about a person) without energy or enthusiasm ▸ **the wet** *noun* [sing.]: *Come in out of the wet* (= the RAINY weather).
IDM **a wet blanket** (*informal*) a person who is not enthusiastic about anything and who stops other people from enjoying themselves **wet through** extremely wet

wet² /wet/ *verb* [T] (wetting; *pt, pp* wet, wetted) **1** to make sth wet **2** (used especially of young children) to make yourself or your bed, clothes, etc. wet by letting URINE (= waste liquid) escape from your body

wetland /'wetlənd/ *noun* [C] (*also* wetlands [pl.]) (**GEOGRAPHY**) an area of land that is always wet

wetsuit /'wetsuːt/ *noun* [C] (**SPORT**) a piece of clothing made of rubber that fits the whole body closely, worn by people swimming UNDERWATER or sailing

we've /wiːv, *weak form* wiv/ *short form* we have

whack /wæk/ *verb* [T] (often used with an adverb or a preposition) (*informal*) to hit sb/sth hard

whacky /'wæki/ *adj.* (whackier; whackiest) = WACKY

whale /weɪl/ *noun* [C] a very large animal that lives in the sea and looks like a very large fish ⊃ picture at **animal**

whaling /'weɪlɪŋ/ *noun* [U] the hunting of WHALES

wharf /wɔːf/ *noun* [C] (*pl.* wharves /wɔːvz/) a platform made of stone or wood at the side of a river or the sea where ships and boats can be tied up

what 🔊 **A1** /wɒt/ *pron., det.* **1** used for asking for information about sb/sth: *What time is it?* ◇ *What kind of music do you like?* ◇ *She asked him what he was doing.* ◇ *What's their phone number?* **2** the thing or things that have been mentioned or said: *What he says is true.* ◇ *I haven't got much, but you can borrow what money I have.* **3** used for emphasizing sth: *What strange eyes she's got!* ◇ *What a kind thing to do!*
IDM **how/what about … ?** → ABOUT² **what?** used to express surprise or to tell sb to say or repeat sth: *'I've asked Alice to marry me.' 'What?'* ◇ *'Dad' 'What?' 'Can I have a dog?'* **what … for?** for what purpose or reason: *What's this little switch for?* ◇ *What did you say that for* (= why did you say that)? **what if … ?** what would happen if … ?: *What if the car breaks down?*

whatever¹ 🔊 **B1** 🄢 /wɒt'evə(r)/ *det., pron.* **1** any or every; anything or everything: *You can say whatever you like.* ◇ *He took whatever help he could get.* **2** used to say that it does not matter what happens or what sb does, because the result will be the same: *I still love you, whatever you may think.* ◇ *Whatever decision she makes I will support her.* **3** (used for expressing surprise or worry) what: *Whatever could have happened to them?*
IDM **or whatever** (*informal*) or any other or others of a similar kind: *You don't need to wear anything smart — jeans and a sweater or whatever.* **whatever you do** used to emphasize that sb must not do sth: *Don't touch the red switch, whatever you do.*

whatever² 🄢 **C1** /wɒt'evə(r)/ *adv.* **1** (*also* whatsoever) at all: *I've no reason whatever to doubt him.* ◇ *'Any questions?' 'None whatsoever.'* **2** (*informal*) used to say that it does not matter what happens or what sb does, because the result will be the same: *He promised to come back whatever.*

whatsoever 🄢+ **C1** /ˌwɒtsəʊ'evə(r)/ = WHATEVER² (1)

wheat 🄢+ **B2** /wiːt/ *noun* [U] **1** a type of grain that can be made into flour **2** (**AGRICULTURE**) the plant that produces this grain: *a field of wheat* ⊃ picture at **cereal**

wheel¹ 🔊 **A2** /wiːl/ *noun* [C] **1** one of the round objects under a car, bicycle, etc. that turns when it moves: *His favourite toy is a dog on wheels.* ◇ *By law, you have to carry a spare wheel in your car.* **2** a flat round part in a machine **3** = STEERING WHEEL: *Her husband was at the wheel* (= he was driving) *when the accident happened.*

wheel² /wiːl/ *verb* **1** [T] (often used with an adverb or a preposition) to push along an object that has wheels; to move sb about in/on a vehicle with wheels: *She wheeled her bike up the hill.* ◇ *He was wheeled back to* his bed on a trolley. **2** [I] to fly round in circles: *Birds wheeled above the ship.* **3** [I, T] to turn round suddenly: *Eleanor wheeled round, with a look of horror on her face.*

wheelbarrow /ˈwiːlbærəʊ/ (*also* **barrow**) *noun* [C] a type of small open container with one wheel and two handles that you use outside for carrying things ⊃ picture at **gardening**, **lever**

wheelchair /ˈwiːltʃeə(r)/ *noun* [C] a chair with large wheels that a person who cannot walk can move or be pushed about in

ˈ**wheel clamp** (*BrE*) = CLAMP¹ (2)

wheeze /wiːz/ *verb* [I] (**HEALTH**) to breathe noisily, for example if you have a chest illness

when¹ ⟨A1⟩ /wen/ *adv., conj.* **1** at what time: *When did she arrive? ◇ I don't know when she arrived.* **2** used for talking about the time at which sth happens or happened: *Sunday is the day when I can relax. ◇ I last saw her in May, when she was in London. ◇ He jumped up when the phone rang.* **3** since; as; considering that: *Why do you want more money when you've got enough already?*

when² ⟨A1⟩ /wen/ *pron.* what time: *Until when are you staying? ◇ 'I've got a new job.' 'Since when?'*

whence /wens/ *adv.* (*old-fashioned*) from where: *They returned whence they came.*

whenever¹ ⟨B1⟩ /wenˈevə(r)/ *conj.* **1** at any time that: *You can borrow my car whenever you want.* **2** every time that: *The roof leaks whenever it rains.* **3** used when the time when something happens is not important: *Don't worry. You can give it back the next time you see me, or whenever.*

whenever² /wenˈevə(r)/ *adv.* used in questions to mean 'when', expressing surprise: *Whenever did you find time to do all that cooking?*

where ⟨A1⟩ /weə(r)/ *adv., conj.* **1** in or to what place or position: *Where can I buy a newspaper? ◇ I asked him where he lived.* **2** in or to the place or situation mentioned: *the town where you were born ◇ She ran to where they were standing. ◇ Where possible, you should travel by bus, not taxi. ◇ We came to a village, where we stopped for lunch. ◇ Where maths is concerned, I'm hopeless.*

whereabouts¹ /ˌweərəˈbaʊts/ *adv.* where; in or near what place: *Whereabouts did you lose your purse?*

whereabouts² /ˈweərəbaʊts/ *noun* [pl.] the place where sb/sth is: *The whereabouts of the stolen painting are unknown.*

whereas ⟨B2⟩ ◎ /ˌweərˈæz/ *conj.* used for showing a fact that is different: *He eats meat, whereas she's a vegetarian.* **SYN** **while¹**

whereby ⟨+C1⟩ /weəˈbaɪ/ *adv.* (*formal*) by which; because of which: *These countries have an agreement whereby foreign visitors can have free medical care.*

whereupon /ˌweərəˈpɒn/ *conj.* (*formal*) after which: *He fell asleep, whereupon she walked quietly from the room.*

wherever¹ ⟨B2⟩ /weərˈevə(r)/ *conj.* **1** in any place: *You can sit wherever you like. ◇ She comes from Desio, wherever that is* (= I don't know where it is). **2** in all places: *Wherever I go, he goes.* **3** in all cases that **IDM** **or wherever** or any other place: *The students might be from Sweden, Denmark or wherever.*

wherever² /weərˈevə(r)/ *adv.* used in questions to mean 'where', expressing surprise: *Wherever did you learn to cook like that?*

whet /wet/ *verb* (-tt-)
IDM **whet sb's appetite** to make sb want more of sth: *Our short stay in Dublin whetted our appetite to spend more time there.*

whether ⟨B1⟩ ⓦ /ˈweðə(r)/ *conj.* **1** (used after verbs like *ask, doubt, know,* etc.) if: *He asked me whether we would be coming to the party.* **2** used for expressing a choice or doubt between two or more possibilities: *I can't make up my mind whether to go or not.*
IDM **whether or not** used to say that sth will be true in either of the situations that are mentioned: *We shall play on Saturday whether it rains or not. ◇ Whether or not it rains, we shall play on Saturday.*

whey /weɪ/ *noun* [U] the thin liquid that is left from milk after the solid part (called CURDS) has been removed

which ⟨A1⟩ /wɪtʃ/ *pron., det.* **1** used in questions to ask sb to be exact, when there are a number of people or things to choose from: *Which hand do you write with? ◇ Which is your bag? ◇ She asked me which book I preferred. ◇ I can't remember which of the boys is the older.* **2** used for saying exactly what thing or things you are talking about: *the houses which overlook the lake cost more. ◇ (formal) The situation in which he found himself was very difficult.* **3** used for giving more information about a thing, an animal or a situation: *We had to wait 16 hours for our plane, which was really annoying. ◇ My first car, which I bought as a student, was a Renault.*

whichever /wɪtʃˈevə(r)/ *det., pron.* **1** used to say what feature or quality is important in deciding sth: *You can choose whichever book you want.* **2** used to say that it does not matter which, as the result will be the same

whiff /wɪf/ *noun* [C, usually sing.] ~ **(of sth)** a smell, especially one that only lasts for a short time: *He caught a whiff of her perfume.*

while¹ ⟨A2⟩ /waɪl/ (*also formal* **whilst** /waɪlst/ *especially in BrE*) *conj.* **1** during the time that; when; at the same time as: *He always phones while we're having lunch. ◇ He always listens to the radio while he's driving to work.* **2** used when you are contrasting two ideas: *Some countries are rich, while others are extremely poor.* **SYN** **whereas**

while² ⟨B1⟩ /waɪl/ *noun* [sing.] a (usually short) period of time: *Let's sit down here for a while.*
IDM **once in a while** → ONCE¹ **worth sb's while** → WORTH¹

while³ /waɪl/ *verb*
PHRV **while sth away** to pass time in a lazy or relaxed way: *We whiled away the evening chatting and listening to music.*

whilst ⟨+C1⟩ /waɪlst/ (*especially BrE, informal*) = WHILE¹

whim /wɪm/ *noun* [C] a sudden idea or desire to do sth (often sth that is unusual or not necessary): *We bought the house on a whim.*

whimper /ˈwɪmpə(r)/ *verb* [I] to make weak crying sounds, especially with fear or pain ▶ **whimper** *noun* [C]

whine /waɪn/ *verb* **1** [I, T] to complain about sth in an annoying, crying voice **2** [I] to make a long high unpleasant sound because you are in pain or unhappy ▶ **whine** *noun* [C, usually sing.]

whip¹ /wɪp/ *noun* [C] **1** a long thin piece of leather, etc. with a handle, that is used for making animals go faster and for hitting people as a punishment: *He cracked the whip and the horse leapt forward.* **2** (**POLITICS**) (in the UK and the US) an official of a political party who makes sure that all members vote on important matters: *the chief whip*

whip² ʔ+ **C1** /wɪp/ *verb* (-pp-)
- HIT **1** [T] to hit a person or an animal hard with a WHIP, as a punishment or to make them or it go faster or work harder
- MOVE QUICKLY **2** [I] (used with an adverb or a preposition) to move quickly, suddenly or violently: *She whipped round to see what had made the noise behind her.* **3** [T] (used with an adverb or a preposition) to remove or pull sth quickly and suddenly: *He whipped out a pen and made a note of the number.*
- MIX **4** [T] ~ **sth (up)** to mix cream, etc. until it is light and thick: *whipped cream ◇ Whip up the egg whites with sugar.*

PHR V **whip through sth** (*informal*) to do or finish sth very quickly **whip sb/sth up** to deliberately try to make people excited or feel strongly about sth: *to whip up excitement* **whip sth up** to prepare food quickly: *to whip up a quick snack*

whir /wɜː(r)/ = WHIRR

whirl¹ /wɜːl/ *verb* [I, T] to move round and round very quickly in a circle; to make sb/sth move in this way: *The dancers whirled round the room. ◇* (*figurative*) *I couldn't sleep. My mind was whirling after all the excitement.*

whirl² /wɜːl/ *noun* [sing.] **1** the action or sound of sth moving round and round very quickly: *the whirl of the helicopter's blades* **2** a state of CONFUSION or excitement: *My head's in a whirl — I'm so excited.* **3** a number of events or activities happening one after the other: *The next few days passed in a whirl of activity.*

IDM **give sth a whirl** (*informal*) to try sth to see if you like it or can do it

whirlpool /'wɜːlpuːl/ *noun* [C] (**GEOGRAPHY**) a place in a river or the sea where currents in the water move very quickly round in a circle

whirlwind /'wɜːlwɪnd/ *noun* [C] (**GEOGRAPHY**) a very strong wind that moves very fast in a circle and causes a lot of damage **SYN** **tornado**

whirr (*also* whir) /wɜː(r)/ *verb* [I] to make a continuous low sound like the parts of a machine moving: *The noise of the fan whirring kept me awake.* ▶ whirr (*also* whir) *noun* [C, usually sing.]

whisk¹ /wɪsk/ *noun* [C] a tool that you use for beating eggs, cream, etc. very fast

whisk² /wɪsk/ *verb* [T] **1** to beat or mix eggs, cream, etc. very fast using a fork or a WHISK: *Whisk the egg whites until stiff.* **SYN** **beat¹** **2** (used with an adverb or a preposition) to take sb/sth somewhere very quickly: *The prince was whisked away in a black limousine.*

whisker /'wɪskə(r)/ *noun* [C] one of the long thick hairs that grow near the mouth of some animals such as a mouse, cat, etc. ᴐ picture at **animal, lion**

whisky (*BrE*) (*AmE* whiskey) /'wɪski/ *noun* (*pl.* -ies, -eys) **1** [U] a strong alcoholic drink that is made from grain and is sometimes drunk with water and/or ice: *Scotch whisky* **2** [C] a glass of whisky

whisper ʔ **B2** /'wɪspə(r)/ *verb* [I, T] to speak very quietly into sb's ear, so that other people cannot hear what you are saying ▶ whisper ʔ **B2** *noun* [C]: *to speak in a whisper*

whistle¹ /'wɪsl/ *noun* [C] **1** a small metal or plastic tube that you blow into to make a long high sound: *The referee blew his whistle to stop the game.* **2** the sound made by blowing a whistle or by blowing air out between your lips: *United scored just moments before the final whistle. ◇ He gave a low whistle of surprise.* **3** a sound made by air or STEAM being forced through a small opening, or by sth moving quickly through the air

whistle² /'wɪsl/ *verb* **1** [T, I] to make a musical or a high sound by forcing air out between your lips or by blowing a WHISTLE: *He whistled a tune to himself.* **2** [I] (used with an adverb or a preposition) to move somewhere quickly making a sound like a WHISTLE: *A bullet whistled past his head.*

white¹ **A1** /waɪt/ *adj.* **1** having the colour of fresh snow or milk: *a white shirt ◇ white coffee* (= with milk) **2** (**SOCIAL STUDIES**) (used about a person) belonging to or connected with a human group that has pale skin **3** ~ **(with sth)** (used about a person) very pale because you are ill, afraid, etc: *to be white with shock/anger/fear ◇ She went white as a sheet when they told her.*

IDM **black and white** → BLACK¹

white² **A1** /waɪt/ *noun* **1** [U] the colour of fresh snow or milk: *She was dressed in white.* **2** [C, usually pl.] (**SOCIAL STUDIES**) a member of a human group that has pale skin **3** [C, U] the part of an egg that surrounds the YOLK (= the yellow part) and that becomes white when it is cooked: *Beat the whites of four eggs.* **4** [C] the white part of the eye

IDM **black and white** → BLACK¹

whitebait /'waɪtbeɪt/ *noun* [pl.] very small young fish of several types that are fried and eaten whole

whiteboard /'waɪtbɔːd/ *noun* [C] a large board with a smooth white surface that teachers, etc. write on with special pens ᴐ look at **blackboard, interactive whiteboard**

white-'collar *adj.* (**SOCIAL STUDIES**) working in an office, rather than in a factory, etc.; connected with work in offices: *white-collar workers ◇ a white-collar job* ᴐ look at **blue-collar**

white 'elephant *noun* [C, usually sing.] something that you no longer need and that is not useful any more, although it cost a lot of money

'white goods *noun* [pl.] large pieces of electrical equipment in the house, such as WASHING MACHINES, etc.

white-'hot *adj.* (used about sth burning) so hot that it looks white

the 'White House *noun* [sing.] (**POLITICS**) **1** the large building in Washington D.C. where the US president lives and works **2** the US president and the other people in the government who work with him or her

white 'lie *noun* [C] a lie that is not very harmful or serious, especially one that you tell because the truth would hurt sb

white 'light *noun* [U] (**PHYSICS**) ordinary light that has no colour ᴐ picture at **prism**

whitewash¹ /'waɪtwɒʃ/ *noun* **1** [U] a white liquid that you use for painting walls **2** [U, sing.] an attempt to try to hide unpleasant facts about sb/sth: *The opposition say the report is a whitewash.*

whitewash² /'waɪtwɒʃ/ *verb* [T] **1** to paint WHITEWASH onto a wall **2** to try to hide sth bad or wrong that you have done

white 'water *noun* [U] (**GEOGRAPHY**) **1** a part of a river that looks white because the water is moving very fast over rocks: *a stretch of white water ◇ white-water rafting* **2** a part of the sea or ocean that looks white because it is very rough and the waves are high

whizz¹ (*also* whiz) /wɪz/ *verb* [I] (*informal*) (used with an adverb or a preposition) to move very quickly, making a high continuous sound; to do sth very quickly: *The racing cars went whizzing past/by.*

whizz² (*also* **whiz**) /wɪz/ *noun* [C, usually sing.] (*informal*) a person who is very good and successful at sth: *She's a whizz at crosswords.* ◇ *He's our new marketing* **whizz-kid** (= a young person who is very good at sth).

WHO / ˌdʌblju: eɪtʃ ˈəʊ/ *abbr.* (**MEDICINE**) **World Health Organization** (an international organization that tries to fight and control disease)

who 🔑 **A1** /hu:/ *pron.* **1** used in questions to ask sb's name, identity, position, etc: *Who was on the phone?* ◇ *Who's that woman in the grey suit?* ◇ *She wondered who he was.* **2** used for saying exactly which person or what kind of person you are talking about: *I like people who say what they think.* ◇ *That's the man (who) I met at Ann's party.* ◇ *The woman (who) I work for is very nice.* **3** used for giving extra information about sb: *My mother, who's over 80, still drives a car.* ❶ The extra information you give is separated from the main clause by commas.

who'd /hu:d/ *short form* who had; who would

whodunnit (*BrE*) (*also* **whodunit** *BrE, AmE*) / ˌhu:ˈdʌnɪt/ *noun* [C] (*informal*) (**ARTS AND MEDIA**, **LITERATURE**) a story, play, etc. about a murder in which you do not know who did the murder until the end

whoever 🔑+ **B2** /hu:ˈevə(r)/ *pron.* **1** the person or people who; any person who: *I want to speak to whoever is in charge.* **2** it does not matter who: *I don't want to see them — whoever they are.* **3** (used for expressing surprise) who: *Whoever could have done that?*

whole¹ 🔑 **A2** ❸ /həʊl/ *adj.* **1** complete; full: *I drank a whole bottle of water.* ◇ *Let's just forget* **the whole thing**. ◇ *She wasn't telling me* **the whole truth**. ➷ adverb **wholly** **2** [only before noun] used to emphasize how large or important sth is: *I'm going to be talking about* **a whole range** *of things today.* ◇ *I can't afford it — that's* **the whole point**. **3** not broken or cut: *Snakes swallow their prey whole* (= in one piece).

whole² 🔑 **B1** ❶ /həʊl/ *noun* **1** [sing.] **the ~ of sth** all that there is of sth: *I spent the whole of the morning cooking.* **2** [C] a thing that is complete or full in itself: *Two halves make a whole.* **IDM** **as a whole** as one complete thing or unit and not as separate parts: *This is true in Britain, but also in Europe as a whole.* **on the whole** generally, but not true in every case: *On the whole, I think it's a good idea.*

wholefood /ˈhəʊlfu:d/ *noun* [U] (*also* **wholefoods** [pl.]) food that is considered healthy because it does not contain artificial substances and is produced as naturally as possible

wholehearted / ˌhəʊlˈhɑ:tɪd/ *adj.* complete and enthusiastic: *to give somebody your wholehearted support* ▶ **wholeheartedly** *adv.*

wholemeal /ˈhəʊlmi:l/ (*also* **wholewheat**) *adj.* made from flour that contains all the grain including the outside layer: *wholemeal bread/flour*

whole note (*AmE*) = SEMIBREVE

wholesale /ˈhəʊlseɪl/ *adv., adj.* [only before noun] **1** (**BUSINESS**) connected with buying and selling goods in large quantities, especially in order to sell them again and make a profit: *They get all their building materials wholesale.* ◇ *wholesale goods/prices* ➷ look at **retail¹** **2** (usually about sth bad) very great; on a very large scale: *the wholesale slaughter of wildlife*

wholesaler /ˈhəʊlseɪlə(r)/ *noun* [C] (**BUSINESS**) a person or business that buys goods in large quantities and sells them to businesses, so they can be sold again to make a profit ➷ look at **retailer**

wholesome /ˈhəʊlsəm/ *adj.* **1** good for your health: *simple wholesome food* **2** having a moral effect that is good: *clean wholesome fun*

wholewheat /ˈhəʊlwi:t/ = WHOLEMEAL

who'll /hu:l/ *short form* who will

wholly 🔑+ **C1** /ˈhəʊlli/ *adv.* completely; fully: *George is not wholly to blame for the situation.*

whom 🔑 **B2** /hu:m/ *pron.* (*formal*) used instead of *who* as the object of a verb or preposition: *Whom did you meet there?* ◇ *He asked me whom I had met.* ◇ *To whom am I speaking?*

whooping cough /ˈhu:pɪŋ kɒf/ *noun* [U] (**HEALTH**) a serious disease, especially of children, that makes them COUGH (= send air out of their throats) loudly and not be able to breathe easily

whoops /wʊps/ *exclamation* (*informal*) used when you have, or nearly have, a small accident, or say or do sth embarrassing: *Whoops! I nearly dropped the cup.*

whoosh /wʊʃ, wu:ʃ/ *noun* [C, usually sing.] (*informal*) the sudden movement and sound of air or water going past very fast ▶ **whoosh** *verb* [I] (often used with an adverb or a preposition)

who're /ˈhu:ə(r)/ *short form* who are

who's /hu:z/ *short form* who is; who has

whose 🔑 **A2** /hu:z/ *pron., det.* **1** (used in questions to ask who sth belongs to) of whom?: *Whose car is that?* ◇ *Whose is that car?* ◇ *Those are nice shoes — I wonder whose they are.* **2** (used to say exactly which person or thing you mean, or to give extra information about a person or thing) of whom; of which: *That's the boy whose mother I met.* ◇ *My neighbours, whose house is up for sale, are splitting up.*

who've /hu:v/ *short form* who have

why 🔑 **A1** /waɪ/ *adv.* **1** for what reason: *Why was she so late?* ◇ *I wonder why they went.* ◇ *'I'm not staying any longer.' 'Why not?'* **2** used for giving or talking about a reason for sth: *The reason why I'm leaving you is obvious.* ◇ *I'm tired and that's why I'm in such a bad mood.* **IDM** **why ever** used to show that you are surprised or angry: *Why ever didn't you phone?* **why not?** used for making or agreeing to a suggestion: *Why not phone her tonight?* ◇ *'Shall we go out tonight?' 'Yes, why not?'*

wick /wɪk/ *noun* [C] the piece of string that burns in the middle of a CANDLE

wicked /ˈwɪkɪd/ *adj.* **1** morally bad; evil **2** (*informal*) slightly bad but in a way that is funny and/or attractive: *a wicked sense of humour* **3** (*slang*) very good: *This song's wicked.* ▶ **wickedly** *adv.* ▶ **wickedness** *noun* [U]

wicker /ˈwɪkə(r)/ *noun* [U] thin sticks of wood that bend easily and are crossed over and under each other to make furniture and other objects

wicket /ˈwɪkɪt/ *noun* [C] (**SPORT**) **1** (in CRICKET) either of the two sets of three VERTICAL sticks that the player throwing the ball tries to hit **2** the area of ground between the two wickets

wide¹ 🔑 **A2** ❿ /waɪd/ *adj.*
• MEASUREMENT **1** measuring a lot from one side to the other: *The road was not wide enough for two cars to pass.* ◇ *a wide river* **OPP** **narrow¹** ▶ noun **width 2** measuring a particular distance from one side to the other: *The box was only 20 centimetres wide.* ◇ *How wide is the river?* ➷ note at **measure²**
• LARGE NUMBER/AMOUNT **3** including a large number or variety of different people or things; covering a large area: *You're the nicest person in* **the whole wide world**! ◇ *a wide range/choice/variety of goods* ◇ *a manager with wide experience of industry*

• OPEN **4** fully open: *The children's eyes were wide with excitement.*

• NOT NEAR **5** not near what you wanted to touch or hit: *His first serve was wide* (= the ball did not land inside the tennis court).

wide² /waɪd/ *adv.* as far or as much as possible; completely: *Open your mouth wide.* ◇ *It was late but she was still wide awake.* ◇ *The front door was wide open.*

widely ῑ B2 Ⓦ /'waɪdli/ *adv.* **1** by a lot of people; in or to many places: *a widely held belief* ◇ *He has travelled widely in Asia.* ◇ *He's an educated, widely-read man* (= he has read a lot of books). **2** to a large degree; a lot: *Standards vary widely.*

widen ῑ+ C1 /'waɪdn/ *verb* [I, T] to become wider; to make sth wider: *The road widens just up ahead.*

wide-ranging *adj.* covering a large area or many subjects: *a wide-ranging discussion*

widespread ῑ+ B2 Ⓦ /'waɪdspred/ *adj.* found or happening over a large area; affecting a large number of people: *The storm has caused widespread damage.*

widget /'wɪdʒɪt/ *noun* [C] **1** (*informal*) used to refer to any small device that you do not know the name of **2** a small box on a web page that gives changing information, such as news items or weather reports, while the rest of the page remains the same

widow ῑ+ C1 /'wɪdəʊ/ *noun* [C] a woman whose husband or wife has died and who has not married again ▸ **widowed** *adj.*: *She's been widowed for ten years now.*

widower /'wɪdəʊə(r)/ *noun* [C] a man whose wife or husband has died and who has not married again

width ῑ+ C1 /wɪdθ, wɪtθ/ *noun* **1** [U, C] the amount that sth measures from one side or edge to the other: *The room is 8 metres in width.* ◇ *The carpet is available in two different widths.* ⊃ look at **breadth** (1), **length** (1) ⊃ note at **measure²** ⊃ picture at **dimension, wave¹** ⊃ adjective **wide** **2** [C] the distance from one side of a swimming pool to the other

wield /wiːld/ *verb* [T] **1** to have and use power, authority, etc.: *She wields enormous power in the company.* **2** to hold and be ready to use a weapon: *Some of the men were wielding knives.*

wiener /'wiːnə(r)/ (*AmE*) = FRANKFURTER

wife ῑ A1 /waɪf/ *noun* [C] (*pl.* wives /waɪvz/) the woman that sb is married to

Wi-Fi™ /'waɪ faɪ/ *noun* [U] (**COMPUTING**) a system for sending data over computer networks using radio waves instead of wires

wig /wɪg/ *noun* [C] a covering made of real or false hair that you wear on your head

wiggle /'wɪgl/ *verb* [I, T] (*informal*) to move from side to side with small quick movements; to make sth do this: *You have to wiggle your hips in time to the music.* ▸ **wiggle** *noun* [C]

wiggly /'wɪgli/ *adj.* (wigglier; wiggliest) (used about a line) having many curves in it

wigwam /'wɪgwæm/ *noun* [C] a type of tent that was used by some Native Americans in past times

wiki /'wɪki/ *noun* [C] (**COMPUTING**) a website that allows any user to change or add to the information it contains

wild¹ ῑ A2 /waɪld/ *adj.*

• ANIMAL/PLANT **1** (used about animals or plants) living or growing in natural conditions, not looked after by people: *wild animals/flowers/strawberries*

• LAND **2** (used about an area of land) in its natural state; not changed by people: *wild moorland*

• WITHOUT CONTROL **3** (used about a person or their behaviour or emotions) without control or discipline; slightly crazy: *The crowd went wild with excitement.* ◇ *They let their children run wild* (= behave in an UNCONTROLLED way).

• NOT SENSIBLE **4** not carefully planned; not sensible or accurate: *She made a wild guess.* ◇ *wild accusations/ rumours*

• LIKING STH/SB **5** ~ (about sb/sth) (*informal*) liking sb/sth very much: *I'm not wild about the band's new album.*

• WEATHER **6** with strong winds or storms: *It was a wild night last night.* SYN **stormy**
  ▸ **wildness** *noun* [U]

wild² /waɪld/ *noun* **1** the wild [sing.] (**ENVIRONMENT**) a natural environment that is not controlled by people: *the thrill of seeing elephants in the wild* **2** the wilds [pl.] places that are far away from towns, where few people live: *They live somewhere out in the wilds.*

wilderness /'wɪldənəs/ *noun* [C, usually sing.] **1** a large area of land that has never been used for building on or for growing things: *The Antarctic is the world's last great wilderness.* **2** a place that people do not take care of or control: *Their garden is a wilderness.*

wildfire /'waɪldfaɪə(r)/ *noun* [C] (**ENVIRONMENT**) a very big fire that spreads quickly and burns natural areas like woods, forests and open land

wildlife ῑ B2 /'waɪldlaɪf/ *noun* [U] animals, birds, insects, etc. that are wild and live in a natural environment

wildly /'waɪldli/ *adv.* **1** in a way that is not controlled: *She looked wildly around for an escape.* ◇ *His heart was beating wildly.* **2** extremely; very: *The story had been wildly exaggerated.*

wilful (*especially BrE*) (*AmE also* willful) /'wɪlfl/ *adj.* **1** done deliberately although the person doing it knows that it is wrong: *wilful damage/neglect* **2** doing exactly what you want, no matter what other people think or say: *a wilful child* ▸ **wilfully** (*AmE also* willfully) /-fəli/ *adv.*

will¹ ῑ A1 /wɪl/ *modal verb* (*short form* 'll /l/; *negative* will not /'wɪl nɒt/; *short form* won't /wəʊnt/) **1** used for talking about or predicting the future: *He'll be here soon.* ◇ *I'm sure you'll pass your exam.* ◇ *I'll be sitting on the beach this time next week.* ◇ *Next Sunday, they'll have been in England for a year.* **2** used for asking sb to do sth: *Will you post this letter for me, please?* **3** used for showing that sb is offering sth or wants to do sth, or that sth is able to do sth: *'We need some more milk.' 'OK, I'll get it.'* ◇ *Why won't you tell me where you were last night?* ◇ *My car won't start.* **4** used for ordering sb to do sth: *Will you all be quiet!* **5** used for saying that you think sth is probably true: *That'll be the postman at the door.* ◇ *He'll have left work by now, I suppose.* **6** (in positive sentences) used for talking about habits **HELP** If you put extra stress on **will** in this meaning, it shows that the habit annoys you: *He will keep interrupting me when I'm trying to work.*

will² ῑ B1 /wɪl/ *noun* **1** [C, U] the power of the mind to choose what to do; a strong and determined desire: *She has a will of iron.* ◇ *My father seems to have lost the will to live.* **2** [sing.] what sb wants to happen in a particular situation: *My mother doesn't want to sell the house and I don't want to go against her will.* **3** [C] (**FINANCE, LAW**) a legal document in which you write down who should have your money and property after your death: *You really ought to make a will.* ◇ *Gran left us some money in her will.* **4** -willed (in adjectives) having the type of will mentioned: *a strong-willed/weak-willed person*
IDM of your own free will → FREE¹

will³ /wɪl/ *verb* [T] to use the power of your mind to do sth or to make sth happen: *He willed himself to carry on to the end of the race.*

willing **B2** /'wɪlɪŋ/ *adj.* **1 ~ (to do sth)** happy to do sth; having no reason for not doing sth: *Are you willing to help us?* ◊ *She's **perfectly willing** to lend me her car.* ◊ *I'm not willing to take any risks.* **2** ready or pleased to help and not needing to be persuaded; enthusiastic: *a willing helper/volunteer* **OPP** **unwilling** ▸ **willingly** *adv.* ▸ **willingness** **C1** *noun* [U, sing.]

willow /'wɪləʊ/ (*also* 'willow tree) *noun* [C] a tree with long thin branches that hang down. Willows grow near water.

willpower /'wɪlpaʊə(r)/ *noun* [U] the ability to control your thoughts and actions in order to achieve what you want to do: *It takes a lot of willpower to lose weight.*

willy /'wɪli/ *noun* [C] (*pl.* -**ies** /'wɪliz/) (*informal*) a word used by children to refer to the PENIS (= the male sexual organ)

wilt /wɪlt/ *verb* [I] (**BIOLOGY**) **1** (used about a plant or flower) to bend and start to die, because of heat or a lack of water **2** (used about a person) to become weak or tired, often because of heat

wily /'waɪli/ *adj.* clever at getting what you want **SYN** **cunning**

wimp /wɪmp/ *noun* [C] (*informal*) a weak person who has no courage or confidence ▸ **wimpish** /'wɪmpɪʃ/ *adj.*

win **A1** /wɪn/ *verb* (**winning**; *pt, pp* **won** /wʌn/) **1** [I, T] to be the best, first or strongest in a race, game, competition, etc: *to win a game/match/championship* ◊ *I never win at table tennis.* ◊ *Which party do you think will win the next election?* **2** [T] to get money, a prize, etc. as a result of success in a competition, race, etc: *We won a trip to Australia.* ◊ *Who won the gold medal?* ◊ *He won the jackpot in the lottery.* **3** [T] to get sth by hard work, great effort, etc: *Her brilliant performance won her a great deal of praise.* ◊ *to win support for a plan* ▸ **win** **B1** *noun* [C]: *We have had two wins and a draw so far this season.*

IDM **win/lose the toss** → TOSS² **you can't win** (*informal*) there is no way of being completely successful or of pleasing everyone: *Whatever you do you will upset somebody. You can't win.*

PHR V **win sb around/over (to sth)** (*also* **win sb round (to sth)** *especially in BrE*) to persuade sb to support or agree with you: *They're against the proposal at the moment, but I'm sure we can win them over.*

wince /wɪns/ *verb* [I] to suddenly make an expression with your face that shows that you are embarrassed or feeling pain

winch /wɪntʃ/ *noun* [C] a machine that lifts or pulls heavy objects using a thick chain, rope, etc. ▸ **winch** *verb* [T] (used with an adverb or a preposition): *The injured climber was winched up into a helicopter.*

wind¹ **A2** /wɪnd/ *noun* **1** [C, U] (**GEOGRAPHY**) air that is moving across the surface of the earth: *There was a strong wind blowing.* ◊ *A gust of wind blew his hat off.* ◊ *gale-force/strong/high winds* ᗪ picture at **erosion**, **longshore drift 2** (*BrE*) (*AmE* gas) [U] (**HEALTH**) gas that is formed in the stomach: *The baby cries when he has wind.* **3** [U] the breath that you need for doing exercise or playing a musical instrument: *She stopped running to get her wind back.* **4** [U + sing./pl. verb] (**MUSIC**) the group of instruments that you play by blowing into them

IDM **get wind of sth** (*informal*) to hear about sth that is secret

wind² /wɪnd/ *verb* [T] **1** [usually passive] to cause sb to have difficulty in breathing: *She was winded by the punch in the stomach.* **2** to help a baby get rid of painful gas in the stomach by rubbing or gently hitting its back

wind³ **B2** /waɪnd/ *verb* (*pt, pp* **wound** /waʊnd/) **1** [I, T] (used with an adverb or a preposition) (used about a road, path, etc.) to have a lot of bends or curves in it: *The path winds its way down the cliff to the sea.* **2** [T] (used with an adverb or a preposition) to put sth long round sth else several times: *She wound the bandage around his arm.* **3** [T] to make sth work or move by turning a key, handle, etc: *He wound the car window down.* ◊ *He had forgotten to wind his watch.*

PHR V **wind down** (about a person) to rest and relax after a period of hard work, worry, etc. ᗪ look at **unwind** (2) **wind up** to find yourself in a place or situation that you did not intend to be in: *We got lost and wound up in a dangerous-looking part of town.* **wind sb up** to annoy sb until they become angry **wind sth up** to finish, stop or close sth

wind-blown /'wɪnd bləʊn/ *adj.* **1** carried from one place to another by the wind **2** made untidy by the wind: *wind-blown hair*

wind chill /'wɪnd tʃɪl/ *noun* [U] (**GEOGRAPHY**) the effect of low temperature combined with wind on sb/sth: *Take the **wind-chill factor** into account.*

windfall /'wɪndfɔːl/ *noun* [C] an amount of money that you win or receive unexpectedly

wind farm /'wɪnd fɑːm/ *noun* [C] (**ENVIRONMENT**) an area of land on which there are a lot of WIND TURBINES for producing electricity

winding /'waɪndɪŋ/ *adj.* with bends or curves in it: *a winding road through the hills*

'**wind instrument** *noun* [C] (**MUSIC**) a musical instrument that you play by blowing through it

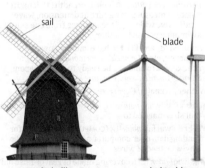

windmill   wind turbines

windmill /'wɪndmɪl/ *noun* [C] a tall building or structure with long parts called SAILS that turn in the wind. In past times windmills were used for making flour from grain. ᗪ look at **wind turbine**

window **A1** /'wɪndəʊ/ *noun* [C] **1** the opening in a building, car, etc. that you can see through and that lets light in. A window usually has glass in it: *Open the window. It's hot in here.* ◊ *a shop window* ◊ *These windows need cleaning.* **2** (**COMPUTING**) an area inside a frame on a computer screen, that has a particular program operating in it, or shows a particular type of information: *to create/open/close a window* **3** a time when you have not arranged to do anything and so are free to meet sb, etc.

'**window box** *noun* [C] a long narrow box outside a window, in which plants are grown

'**window ledge** = WINDOWSILL

windowpane /ˈwɪndəʊpeɪn/ *noun* [C] one piece of glass in a window

window seat *noun* [C] (**TOURISM**) a seat next to a window in a plane, train or other vehicle

window-shopping *noun* [U] looking at things in shop windows without intending to buy anything

windowsill /ˈwɪndəʊsɪl/ (*also* **sill, window ledge**) *noun* [C] the narrow shelf at the bottom of a window, either inside or outside

windpipe /ˈwɪndpaɪp/ *noun* [C] (**ANATOMY**) the tube in the throat that carries air from the throat to the lungs **SYN trachea** ➔ picture at **body**

windscreen /ˈwɪndskriːn/ (*BrE*) (*AmE* **windshield** /ˈwɪndʃiːld/) *noun* [C] the window in the front of a vehicle

windscreen wiper (*BrE*) (*also* **wiper**, *AmE* **windshield wiper**) *noun* [C] one of the two **BLADES** (= moving arms) with rubber edges that move across a **WINDSCREEN** to make it clear of water, snow, etc.

windsurf /ˈwɪndsɜːf/ *verb* [I] (**SPORT**) to move over water standing on a special board with a sail ▸ **windsurfing** *noun* [U]

windsurfer /ˈwɪndsɜːfə(r)/ *noun* [C] (**SPORT**) **1** (*also* **sailboard**) a board with a sail that you stand on as it moves over the surface of the water, pushed by the wind **2** a person who rides on a board like this

windswept /ˈwɪndswept/ *adj.* **1** (used about a place) that often has strong winds: *a windswept coastline* **2** looking untidy because you have been in a strong wind: *windswept hair*

wind turbine /ˈwɪnd tɜːbaɪn/ *noun* [C] (**ENGINEERING, ENVIRONMENT**) a tall structure that looks similar to a **WINDMILL** and is used for producing electricity ➔ picture at **energy, windmill**

windward /ˈwɪndwəd/ *adj.* on or towards the side of a hill, building, etc. towards which the wind is blowing **OPP leeward** ▸ **windward** *adv.*

windy /ˈwɪndi/ *adj.* (**windier; windiest**) with a lot of wind: *a windy day*

wine 🔊 **A1** /waɪn/ *noun* [U, C] an alcoholic drink that is made from **GRAPES**, or sometimes other fruit: *sweet/dry wine ◇ German wines* ➔ look at **beer**

winegrower /ˈwaɪnɡrəʊə(r)/ *noun* [C] (**AGRICULTURE**) a person who grows **GRAPES** (= green or purple fruit) for making wine

winemaker /ˈwaɪnmeɪkə(r)/ *noun* [C] a person who produces wine ▸ **winemaking** *noun* [U]

wine waiter *noun* [C] (**TOURISM**) a person who works in a restaurant serving wine and helping customers to decide which wine to choose **SYN sommelier**

wing 🔊 **B1** /wɪŋ/ *noun*
- OF A BIRD, ETC. **1** [C] one of the two parts that a bird, an insect, etc. uses for flying: *The chicken ran around flapping its wings.* ➔ picture at **animal**
- OF A PLANE **2** [C] one of the two long parts that stick out from the side of a plane and support it in the air ➔ picture at **airliner**
- OF A BUILDING **3** [C] a part of a building that sticks out from the main part: *the maternity wing of the hospital*
- OF A CAR **4** (*BrE*) (*AmE* **fender**) [C] the part of the outside of a car that covers the top of the wheels: *a wing mirror* (= fixed to the side of the car)
- OF A POLITICAL PARTY **5** [C, usually sing.] (**POLITICS**) a group of people in a political party that have particular beliefs or opinions: *He's on the right wing of the Conservative Party.* ➔ look at **left wing** (1), **right wing** (1)
- IN FOOTBALL, ETC. **6** (*also* **winger**) [C] (**SPORT**) (in football, etc.) a person who plays in an attacking position at one of the sides of the field **7** [C] (**SPORT**)

(in football, etc.) the part at each side of the area where the game is played: *to play on the wing*
- IN THEATRE **8** the wings [pl.] (**ARTS AND MEDIA**) (in a theatre) the area at the sides of the stage where the actors cannot be seen by the audience
IDM take sb under your wing to take care of and help sb who has less experience than you

wingspan /ˈwɪŋspæn/ *noun* [C] the distance between the end of one wing and the end of the other when the wings are fully stretched

wink /wɪŋk/ *verb* [I] **~ (at sb)** to close and open one eye very quickly, usually as a signal to sb ➔ look at **blink** (1) ▸ **wink** *noun* [C]: *He smiled and gave the little girl a wink. ◇ I didn't sleep a wink* (= not at all).
IDM forty winks → **FORTY**

winner 🔊 **A2** /ˈwɪnə(r)/ *noun* [C] **1** a person or an animal that wins a competition, game, race, etc: *The winner of the competition will be announced next week.* **2** [usually sing.] (*informal*) something that is likely to be successful: *I think your idea is a winner.* **3** (**SPORT**) a goal that wins a match, a hit that wins a point, etc: *Aguero scored the winner in the last minute.*

winning /ˈwɪnɪŋ/ *adj.* **1** [only before noun] that wins or has won sth, for example a race or competition: *The winning ticket is number 65. ◇ the winning horse* **2** attractive in a way that makes other people like you: *a winning smile*

winnings /ˈwɪnɪŋz/ *noun* [pl.] money that sb wins in a competition, game, etc.

winter 🔊 **A1** /ˈwɪntə(r)/ *noun* [U, C] the coldest season of the year, between autumn and spring: *It snows a lot here in (the) winter. ◇ this/next/last winter ◇ a cold winter's day* ➔ picture at **season**[1] ▸ **wintry** /-tri/ *adj.*: *wintry weather*

winter sports *noun* [pl.] (**SPORT**) sports that take place on snow or ice, for example skiing and **SKATING**

wintertime /ˈwɪntətaɪm/ *noun* [U] the period or season of winter

wipe[1] 🔊 **C1** /waɪp/ *verb* [T] **1** to clean or dry sth by rubbing it with a cloth, etc: *She stopped crying and wiped her eyes with a tissue. ◇ Could you wipe the table, please?* ➔ note at **clean**[1] **2 ~ sth from/off sth; ~ sth away/off/up** to remove sth by rubbing it: *He wiped the sweat from his forehead. ◇ Wipe up the milk you spilled.* **3 ~ sth (from/off) (sth)** to remove sound, information or images from sth: *I accidentally wiped the file. ◇ I tried to wipe the memory from my mind.* **PHR V wipe sth out** to destroy sth completely: *Whole villages were wiped out in the bombing raids.*

wipe[2] /waɪp/ *noun* [C] **1** the act of cleaning sth with a cloth: *He gave the table a quick wipe.* **2** a piece of paper or thin cloth that has been made wet with a special liquid and is used for cleaning sth: *a box of baby wipes*

wiper /ˈwaɪpə(r)/ = **WINDSCREEN WIPER**

wire[1] 🔊 **B2** /ˈwaɪə(r)/ *noun* [U, C] **1** metal in the form of thin **THREAD**; a piece of this: *a piece of wire ◇ Twist those two wires together. ◇ a wire fence* **2** (**ENGINEERING**) a piece of wire that is used to carry electricity: *phone wires* ➔ picture at **cable, light bulb, switch**[1]

wire[2] /ˈwaɪə(r)/ *verb* [T] **1 ~ sth (up) (to sth)** (**ENGINEERING**) to connect sth to a supply of electricity or to a piece of electrical equipment by using wires: *to wire a plug ◇ The microphone was wired up to a loudspeaker.* **2 ~ sth (to sb); ~ sb sth** (**FINANCE**) to send money to sb's bank account using an electronic system: *The bank's going to wire me the money.* **3** to join two things together using wire

wired /ˈwaɪəd/ *adj.* **1** (**COMPUTING**) connected to a device or computer network by wires: *wired headphones* **2** (*informal*) excited or nervous: *Too much coffee makes me feel wired.*

wireframe /ˈwaɪəfreɪm/ *noun* [C] (**COMPUTING**) a basic plan for a web page or website, showing the information on it and how it is arranged, but not showing details of what it will look like

wireless /ˈwaɪələs/ *adj.* (**COMPUTING**) not using wires: *wireless technology/communications*

ˌwire ˈwool = STEEL WOOL

wiring /ˈwaɪərɪŋ/ *noun* [U] (**ENGINEERING**) the system of wires that supplies electricity to rooms in a building or to parts of a machine

wiry /ˈwaɪəri/ *adj.* (**wirier; wiriest**) (used about a person) small and thin but strong

wisdom ⓘ+ **B2** /ˈwɪzdəm/ *noun* [U] the ability to make sensible decisions and judgements because of your knowledge or experience: *I don't see the wisdom of this plan* (= I do not think that it is a good idea).

ˈwisdom tooth *noun* [C] (**ANATOMY**) one of the four teeth at the back of the mouth that do not grow until you are an adult ⊃ picture at **tooth**

wise ⓘ **B2** /waɪz/ *adj.* **1** (used about actions) sensible; based on good judgement: *a wise choice* ◇ *It would be wiser to wait for a few days.* **2** (used about people) able to make sensible decisions and give good advice because of the experience and knowledge that you have ▶ **wisely** *adv.*
IDM none the wiser/worse → NONE²

wish¹ ⓘ **A2** /wɪʃ/ *verb* **1** [T] (not usually used in the present progressive tenses) ~ (**that**) to want sth that cannot now happen or that probably will not happen: *I wish I had listened more carefully.* ◇ *I wish that I knew what was going to happen.* ◇ *I wish I was taller.* ◇ *I wish I could help you.* **2** [I, T] ~ (**to do sth**) (*especially BrE, formal*) to want to do sth: *I wish to make a complaint about one of the doctors.* **3** [I] ~ **for sth** to think very hard that you want sth, especially sth that can only be achieved by good luck or magic: *She wished for her mother to get better.* ◇ *It's no use wishing for the impossible.* **4** [T] to say that you hope sb will have sth: *I rang him up to wish him a happy birthday.* ◇ *We wish you all the best for your future career.*

wish² ⓘ **A2** /wɪʃ/ *noun* **1** wishes [pl.] a hope that sb will be happy or have good luck: *Please give your parents my best wishes.* ◇ *Best wishes* (= at the end of a letter) **2** [C] a try at making sth happen by thinking hard about it, especially in stories when it often happens by magic: *Throw a coin into the fountain and make a wish.* ◇ *My wish came true* (= I got what I asked for). **3** [C] ~ (**to do sth**) a feeling that you want to have sth or that sth should happen: *I have no wish to see her ever again.* ◇ *Doctors should respect the patient's wishes.*

ˌwishful ˈthinking *noun* [U] ideas that are based on what you would like now, not on facts ⊃ look at **thinking¹**

wisp /wɪsp/ *noun* [C] **1** a small, thin piece of hair, grass, etc. **2** a small amount of smoke ▶ **wispy** *adj.*

wistful /ˈwɪstfl/ *adj.* thinking sadly about sth that you would like to have, especially sth in the past that you can no longer have: *a wistful sigh* ▶ **wistfully** /-fəli/ *adv.*

wit ⓘ+ **C1** /wɪt/ *noun* **1** [U, sing.] the ability to use words in a clever and funny way ⊃ adjective **witty** **2** -witted (in adjectives) having a particular type of intelligence: *quick-witted* ◇ *slow-witted* **3** [U] (*also* wits [pl.]) your ability to think quickly and clearly and to

make good decisions: *The game of chess is essentially **a battle of wits.***
IDM at your wits' end not knowing what to do or say because you are very worried **keep your wits about you** to be ready to act in a difficult situation

WORD FAMILY
wit *noun*
witty *adj.*
witticism *noun*
outwit *verb*

witch /wɪtʃ/ *noun* [C] (in past times and in stories) a woman who is thought to have magic powers ⊃ look at **wizard** (1)

witchcraft /ˈwɪtʃkrɑːft/ *noun* [U] the use of magic powers, especially evil ones

ˈwitch-hunt *noun* [C] the activity of trying to find and punish people who hold opinions that are thought to be unacceptable or dangerous to society

with ⓘ **A1** /wɪð, wɪθ/ *prep.* **1** in the company of sb/sth; in or to the same place as sb/sth: *I live with my parents.* ◇ *Are you coming with us?* ◇ *I talked about the problem with my tutor.* **2** having or carrying sth: *a girl with red hair* ◇ *a house with a garden* ◇ *the man with the suitcase* **3** using sth: *Cut it with a knife.* ◇ *I did it with his help.* **4** used for saying what fills, covers, etc. sth: *Fill the bowl with water.* ◇ *His hands were covered with oil.* **5** in competition with sb/sth; against sb/sth: *He's always arguing with his brother.* ◇ *I usually play tennis with my sister.* **6** towards, concerning or compared with sb/sth: *Is he angry with us?* ◇ *There's a problem with my visa.* ◇ *Compared with Canada, England has mild winters.* **7** used to say how sth happens or is done: *Open this parcel with care.* ◇ *to greet somebody with a smile* **8** including sth: *The price is for two people with all meals.* **9** in the care of sb: *We left the keys with the neighbours.* **10** because of sth; as a result of sth: *We were shivering with cold.* ◇ *With all the problems we've got, we're not going to finish on time.* **11** at the same time as sth: *I can't concentrate with you watching me all the time.*
IDM be with sb (on sth) to support sb and agree with what they say: *We're all with you on this one.* be with me/you to be able to follow what sb is saying: *I'm not quite with you. Say it again.*

withdraw ⓘ+ **B2** /wɪðˈdrɔː, wɪθˈd-/ *verb* (*pt* withdrew /-ˈdruː/; *pp* withdrawn /-ˈdrɔːn/) **1** [T] (**FINANCE**) to take money out of a bank account: *How much would you like to withdraw?* ⊃ look at **deposit¹** **2** [I, T] ~ (**sb/sth**) (**from sth**) to move back or away from a place; to make sb/sth do this: *The troops withdrew from the town.* **3** [I] ~ (**from sth**) to decide not to take part in sth: *Jackson withdrew from the race at the last minute.* **4** [T] ~ **sth** (**from sth**) to remove sth or take sth away: *to withdraw an offer/a statement*

withdrawal ⓘ+ **C1** /wɪðˈdrɔːəl, wɪθˈd-/ *noun* **1** [C] (**FINANCE**) the act of taking money out of your bank account; the amount of money that you take out: *to make a withdrawal* **2** [U, C] ~ (**of sb/sth**) (**from sth**) the act of moving or being moved back or away from a place: *the withdrawal of troops from the war zone* **3** [U] (**SOCIAL STUDIES**) the act of stopping doing sth, especially taking a drug; the period of time when sb is getting used to not taking a drug: *When he gave up alcohol he suffered severe withdrawal symptoms.*

withdrawn /wɪðˈdrɔːn/ *adj.* (used about a person) very quiet and not wanting to talk to other people

wither /ˈwɪðə(r)/ *verb* **1** [I, T] ~ (**sth**) (**away**) (used about plants) to become dry and die; to make a plant do this: *The plants withered in the hot sun.* **2** [I] ~ (**away**) to become weaker then disappear: *This type of industry will wither away in the years to come.*

withering /ˈwɪðərɪŋ/ *adj.* (used about a look, a remark, etc.) done to make sb feel silly or embarrassed: *a withering look*

withhold /wɪðˈhəʊld, wɪθˈh-/ *verb* [T] (*pt, pp* withheld /-ˈheld/) ~ **sth (from sb/sth)** (*formal*) to refuse to give sth to sb: *to withhold information from the police*

within[1] ʔ **B1** ⦿ /wɪˈðɪn/ *prep.* **1** in a period not longer than a particular length of time: *I'll be back within an hour.* ◇ *She got married, found a job and moved house, all within a week.* **2** not further than a particular distance from sth: *The house is within a kilometre of the station.* **3** not outside the limits of sb/sth: *Each department must keep within its budget.* **4** (*formal*) inside sb/sth: *The anger was still there deep within him.*

within[2] /wɪˈðɪn/ *adv.* (*formal*) inside: *Cleaner required. Apply within* (= come in and ask).

without[1] ʔ **A1** /wɪˈðaʊt/ *prep.* **1** not having or showing sth: *Don't go out without a coat on.* ◇ *He spoke without much enthusiasm.* **2** not using or being with sb/sth: *I drink my coffee without milk.* ◇ *Can you see without your glasses?* ◇ *Don't leave without me.* **3** used with a verb in the -ing form to mean 'not': *She left without saying goodbye.* ◇ *I used her phone without her knowing.*

without[2] /wɪˈðaʊt/ *adv.* not having or showing sth: *If there's no salt we'll have to manage without.*

withstand /wɪðˈstænd, wɪθˈs-/ *verb* [T] (*pt, pp* withstood /-ˈstʊd/) (*formal*) to be strong enough not to break, give up, be damaged, etc: *These animals can withstand very high temperatures.*

witness[1] ʔ **B2** /ˈwɪtnəs/ *noun* [C] **1** (*also* eyewitness) ~ **(to sth)** a person who sees sth happen and who can tell other people about it later: *There were two witnesses to the accident.* **2** (**LAW**) a person who appears in a court to say what they have seen or what they know about sb/sth: *a witness for the defence/ prosecution* ⊃ note at **court**[1] **3** (**LAW**) a person who sees sb sign an official document and who then signs it himself/herself
IDM **bear witness (to sth)** → BEAR[1]

witness[2] ʔ **B2** /ˈwɪtnəs/ *verb* [T] **1** to see sth happen and be able to tell other people about it later: *to witness a murder* **2** (**LAW**) to see sb sign an official document and then sign it yourself: *to witness a will*

ˈ**witness box** (*BrE*) (*AmE* ˈwitness stand) (*also* stand *BrE, AmE*) *noun* [C] (**LAW**) the place in court where people stand to give evidence

witticism /ˈwɪtɪsɪzəm/ *noun* [C] a clever and funny remark

witty /ˈwɪti/ *adj.* (wittier; wittiest) clever and funny; using words in a clever way: *a very witty speech* ⊃ noun **wit**

wives /waɪvz/ plural of **wife**

wizard /ˈwɪzəd/ *noun* [C] **1** (in stories) a man who is believed to have magic powers ⊃ look at **magician** (2), **witch 2** a person who is especially good at sth

wk (*BrE*) (*also* wk. *AmE, BrE*) *abbr.* (in writing) (*pl.* wks) = WEEK (1)

WMD /ˌdʌblju: em ˈdi:/ *abbr.* = WEAPON OF MASS DESTRUCTION

WNW *abbr.* (in writing) = WEST-NORTH-WEST

wobble /ˈwɒbl/ *verb* [I, T] to move from side to side in a way that is not steady; to make sb/sth do this: *Put something under the leg of the table. It's wobbling.* ◇ *Stop wobbling the desk. I can't write.* ▸ wobbly /-bli/ *adj.*

woe /wəʊ/ *noun* (*old-fashioned*) **1** woes [pl.] the problems that sb has **2** [U] great unhappiness
IDM **woe betide sb** used as a warning that there will be trouble if sb does/does not do a particular thing: *Woe betide anyone who yawns while the boss is talking.*

wok /wɒk/ *noun* [C] a large pan that is shaped like a bowl and used for cooking Chinese food

woke /wəʊk/ past tense of **wake**[1]

woken /ˈwəʊkən/ past participle of **wake**[1]

wolf /wʊlf/ *noun* [C] (*pl.* wolves /wʊlvz/) a wild animal that looks like a dog and that lives and hunts in a PACK (= group)

wolverine /ˈwʊlvəri:n/ *noun* [C] a wild animal that looks like a small bear, with short legs, long brown hair and a long tail

woman ʔ **A1** /ˈwʊmən/ *noun* [C] (*pl.* women /ˈwɪmɪn/) **1** an adult female person: *men, women and children* ◇ *Would you prefer to see a woman doctor?* **2** (in compounds) a woman who does a particular activity: *a businesswoman*

womanhood /ˈwʊmənhʊd/ *noun* [U] the state of being a woman

womanly /ˈwʊmənli/ *adj.* having qualities considered typical of a woman

womb /wu:m/ *noun* [C] (**ANATOMY**) the part of a woman or female animal where a baby grows before it is born **SYN** **uterus** ⊃ picture at **fertilization**

won /wʌn/ past tense, past participle of **win**

wonder[1] ʔ **B1** /ˈwʌndə(r)/ *verb* **1** [T, I] ~ **(about sth)** to want to know sth; to ask yourself questions about sth: *I wonder what the new teacher will be like.* ◇ *Vesna's been gone a long time — I wonder if she's all right.* ◇ *It was something that she had been wondering about for a long time.* ◇ *'Why did he say that?' she wondered.* **2** [T] used as a polite way of asking a question or of asking sb to do sth: *I wonder if you could help me.* ◇ *I was wondering if you'd like to come to dinner at our house.* **3** [I, T] ~ **(at sth)** to be very surprised by sth: *We wondered at the speed with which he worked.*

wonder[2] ʔ **B1** /ˈwʌndə(r)/ *noun* **1** [U] a feeling of surprise and pleasure that you have when you see or experience sth beautiful, unusual or unexpected: *The children just stared in wonder at the acrobats.* **2** [C] something that fills you with surprise and pleasure: *the wonders of modern technology*
IDM **do/work wonders (for sb/sth)** to have a very good effect on sb/sth: *Working in Mexico did wonders for my Spanish.* **it's a wonder (that)** … it's surprising that … : *It's a wonder we managed to get here on time, with all the traffic.* **no wonder** it is not surprising: *You've been out every evening this week. No wonder you're tired.*

wonderful ʔ **A1** /ˈwʌndəfl/ *adj.* extremely good: *What wonderful weather!* ◇ *It's wonderful to see you again.* **SYN** **fantastic** ▸ wonderfully /-fəli/ *adv.*

won't /wəʊnt/ *short form* will not

wood ʔ **A2** /wʊd/ *noun* **1** [U, C] the hard substance that trees are made of: *He chopped some wood for the fire.* ◇ *Pine is a softwood.* ⊃ picture at **building, tree** **2** [C] (*also* woods [pl.]) (**GEOGRAPHY**) an area of land that is covered with trees. A wood is smaller than a forest: *a walk in the woods*
IDM **touch wood** (*BrE*) (*AmE* **knock on wood**) → TOUCH[1]

woodcut /'wʊdkʌt/ *noun* [C] (**ART**) a print that is made from a pattern cut in a piece of wood

wooded /'wʊdɪd/ *adj.* (**GEOGRAPHY**) (used about an area of land) having a lot of trees growing on it

wooden ⚡ **A2** /'wʊdn/ *adj.* made of wood

woodland /'wʊdlənd/ *noun* [U, C] (**GEOGRAPHY**) land that has a lot of trees growing on it: *The village is surrounded by woodland.* ◇ *woodland birds* ⊃ picture at **ecosystem**

woodlouse /'wʊdlaʊs/ *noun* [C] (*pl.* woodlice /-laɪs/) a small grey creature like an insect, with a hard shell, that lives in wet soil or wood that is DECAYING (= being destroyed by natural processes) ⊃ picture at **animal**

wood pulp *noun* [U] wood that has been broken into small pieces and pressed until it is soft. It is used for making paper.

woodwind /'wʊdwɪnd/ *noun* [sing. + sing./pl. verb] (**MUSIC**) the group of musical instruments that are traditionally made of wood that you play by blowing into them ⊃ note at **instrument** ⊃ picture at **instrument, orchestra**

woodwork /'wʊdwɜːk/ *noun* [U] **1** the parts of a building that are made of wood such as the doors, stairs, etc. **2** the activity or skill of making things out of wood

woodworm /'wʊdwɜːm/ *noun* **1** [C] a small, soft, flat creature, the young form of a BEETLE, that eats wood, making a lot of small holes in it **2** [U] the damage to wood caused by these creatures

woof /wʊf/ *noun* [C] (*informal*) used for describing the sound that a dog makes ⊃ look at **bark**¹ (2)

wool ⚡ **B1** /wʊl/ *noun* [U] **1** the soft thick hair of sheep and some other animals **2** thick THREAD or cloth that is made from wool: *The sweater is 50% wool and 50% acrylic.* ⊃ look at **cotton wool**

woollen (*BrE*) (*AmE* woolen) /'wʊlən/ *adj.* made of wool: *a warm woollen jumper*

woolly (*BrE*) (*AmE* wooly) /'wʊli/ *adj.* (**woollier, woolier** /-ə(r)/; **woolliest, wooliest** /-liːst/) like wool or made of wool: *The dog had a thick woolly coat.* ◇ *long woolly socks*

word¹ ⚡ **A1** **⑤** /wɜːd/ *noun* **1** [C] (**LANGUAGE**) a single unit of language that expresses a particular meaning: *What's the Greek word for 'mouth'?* ◇ *What does this word mean?* **2** [C] a thing that you say; a short statement or comment: *Could I have a word with you in private?* ◇ *Don't say a word about this to anyone.* **3** [sing.] a promise: *I give you my word that I won't tell anyone.* ◇ *I kept my word to her and lent her the money.* ◇ *I trust him not to go back on his word.* **IDM a dirty word** → DIRTY¹ **have, etc. the last word** → LAST¹ **in other words** → OTHER **lost for words** → LOST² **not breathe a word (of/about sth) (to sb)** → BREATHE **not get a word in edgeways** (*BrE*) (*AmE* **not get a word in edgewise**) to not be able to interrupt when sb else is talking so that you can say sth yourself **put in a (good) word for sb** to say sth good about sb to sb else: *If you could put in a good word for me I might stand a better chance of getting the job.* **take sb's word for it** to believe what sb says without any proof **word for word 1** repeating sth exactly: *Sharon repeated word for word what he had told her.* **2** (**LANGUAGE**) translating each word separately, not looking at the general meaning: *a word-for-word translation*

word² /wɜːd/ *verb* [T, often passive] (**LANGUAGE**) to write or say sth using particular words: *The statement was carefully worded so that nobody would be offended by it.*

word class *noun* [C] (**GRAMMAR**) one of the classes into which words are divided according to their grammar, such as noun, verb, adjective, etc. **SYN part of speech**

wording /'wɜːdɪŋ/ *noun* [U, C, usually sing.] (**LANGUAGE**) the words that you use to express sth: *The wording of the contract was vague.* ⊃ note at **language**

word-'perfect *adj.* able to say sth that you have learnt from memory, without making a mistake

word processing *noun* [U] (**COMPUTING**) the use of a computer to write, store and print a piece of text: *I mainly use the computer for word processing.*

word processor *noun* [C] (**COMPUTING**) a type of small computer that you can use for writing letters, reports, etc. You can correct or change what you have written before you print it out.

wordsearch /'wɜːdsɜːtʃ/ *noun* [C] a game consisting of letters arranged in a square, containing several hidden words that you must find

wore /wɔː(r)/ past tense of **wear**¹

work¹ ⚡ **A1** /wɜːk/ *verb*
- DO A JOB/TASK **1** [I] ~ **(as sth) (for sb); ~ (at/on sth); ~ (to do sth)** to do sth that needs physical or mental effort, in order to earn money or to achieve sth; to have a job: *She's working for a large firm in Glasgow.* ◇ *I'd like to work as a newspaper reporter.* ◇ *Doctors often work extremely long hours.* ◇ *My teacher said that I wouldn't pass the exam unless I worked harder.* ◇ *I hear she's working on a new novel.* ◇ *I'm going to stay in tonight and work at my project.* ⊃ note at **job, office**
- MAKE AN EFFORT **2** [T] (used with an adverb or a preposition) to make yourself/sb work, especially very hard: *The coach works the players very hard in training.*
- MACHINE **3** [I, T] (used about a machine, etc.) to function; to make sth function; to operate: *Our phone hasn't been working for several days.* ◇ *We still don't really understand how the brain works.* ◇ *Can you show me how to work the photocopier?*
- HAVE A RESULT **4** [I] to have the result or effect that you want; to be successful: *Your idea sounds good but I don't think it will really work.* ◇ *The heat today could work in favour of the African runners.*
- USE MATERIALS **5** [T, I] to use materials to make a model, a picture, etc: *He worked the clay into the shape of a horse.* ◇ *She usually works in/with oils or acrylics.*
- MOVE GRADUALLY **6** [I, T] to move gradually to a new position or state: *Engineers check the plane daily, because nuts and screws can work loose.* ◇ *I watched the snail work its way up the wall.*
IDM ❶ For idioms containing **work**, look at the entries for the nouns, adjectives, etc. For example, **work from home** is at **home**.
PHR V work out 1 to develop or progress, especially in a good way: *I hope things work out for you.* **2** to do physical exercises in order to keep your body fit: *We work out to music at my exercise class.* **work out (at)** to come to a particular result or total after everything has been calculated: *If we divide the work between us it'll work out at about four hours each.* **work sb out** to understand sb: *I've never been able to work her out.* **work sth out 1** to find the answer to sth; to solve sth: *I can't work out how to do this.* **2** (**MATHEMATICS**) to calculate sth: *I worked out the total cost.* **3** to plan sth: *Have you worked out the route through France?* **work sb/yourself up (into sth)** to make sb/yourself become angry, excited, upset, etc: *He had worked himself up into a state of anxiety*

about his interview. **work sth up** to develop or improve sth with effort: *I'm trying to work up the energy to go out.* **work up to sth** to develop or progress to sth: *Start with 15 minutes' exercise and gradually work up to 30.*

work² ⚡ 🄰🄰 /wɜːk/ *noun*

- JOB **1** [U] the job that you do, especially in order to earn money; the place where you do your job: *It is very difficult to* **find work** *in this city.* ◇ *He's been* **out of work** *(= without a job) for six months.* ◇ *When do you* **start work***?* ◇ *I'll ask if I can* **leave work** *early today.* ◇ *I* **go to work** *at eight o'clock.* ◇ *The people* **at work** *gave me some flowers for my birthday.* ◇ *Police work is not as exciting as it looks on TV.* ⊃ look at **employment** (1) ⊃ note at **job**
- EFFORT **2** [U] something that requires physical or mental effort that you do in order to achieve sth: *Her success is due to sheer* **hard work***.* ◇ *I've got a lot of work to do today.* ◇ *We hope to* **start work** *on the project next week.*
- PRODUCT OF WORK **3** [U] something that you are working on or have produced: *a piece of written work* ◇ *The teacher marked their work.* ◇ *Is this all your own work?*
- BOOK/ART/MUSIC **4** [C] (**ARTS AND MEDIA**) a book, painting, piece of music, etc: *an early work by Picasso* ◇ *the complete works of Shakespeare*
- BUILDING/REPAIRING **5** works [pl.] (often in compounds) the act of building or repairing sth: *The roadworks are causing long traffic jams.*
- FACTORY **6** works [C + sing./pl. verb] (often in compounds) a factory: *The steelworks is/are closing down.* ⊃ note at **factory**
- IN PHYSICS **7** [U] the use of force to produce movement
- **IDM** **get/go/set to work (on sth)** to begin; to make a start (on sth)

▼ **VOCABULARY BUILDING**

Work is an uncountable noun. In some contexts we have to use **job**: *I've found work at the hospital.* ◇ *I've got a new job at the hospital.* **Employment** is the state of having a paid job and is more formal and official than **work** or **job**: *Many people are in part-time employment.* **Occupation** is the word used on forms to ask what you are or what job you do: *Occupation: student.* ◇ *Occupation: bus driver.* A **profession** is a job that needs special training and higher education: *the medical profession.* A **trade** is a job that you do with your hands and that needs special skill: *He's a carpenter by trade.*

---

workable /ˈwɜːkəbl/ *adj.* that can be used successfully: *a workable idea/plan/solution* **SYN** **practical¹**

workaholic /ˌwɜːkəˈhɒlɪk/ *noun* [C] a person who loves work and does too much of it

tools on a workbench

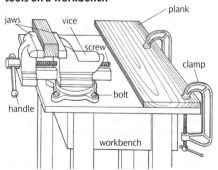

plank
jaws
vice
screw
clamp
bolt
handle
workbench

workbench /ˈwɜːkbentʃ/ *noun* [C] a long heavy table used for doing practical jobs, working with tools, etc.

workbook /ˈwɜːkbʊk/ *noun* [C] (**EDUCATION**) a book with questions and exercises in it that you use when you are studying sth

workday /ˈwɜːkdeɪ/ *noun* [C] **1** (*AmE*) = WORKING DAY (1): *an 8-hour workday* **2** = WORKING DAY (2): *workday traffic*

worker ⚡ 🄰🄰 /ˈwɜːkə(r)/ *noun* [C] **1** (often in compounds) a person who works, especially one who does a particular kind of work: *factory/office/farm workers* ◇ *skilled/manual workers* **2** a person who is employed to do physical work rather than organizing things or managing people: *Workers' representatives will meet management today to discuss the pay dispute.* **3** a person who works in a particular way: *a slow/fast worker*

work ethic *noun* [sing.] a person's attitude to work, especially the idea that hard work is a good habit: *They have a very strong work ethic.*

work experience *noun* [U] **1** (**BUSINESS**) the work or jobs that you have done in your life so far: *Please list your work experience and qualifications.* **2** (*BrE*) (**BUSINESS, EDUCATION**) a period of time that a young person, especially a student, spends working in a company as a form of training

workflow /ˈwɜːkfləʊ/ *noun* [C, U] (**BUSINESS**) the different stages that a particular piece or type of work passes through from the beginning until it is finished; the rate at which it passes through these stages

workforce ⚡⁺ 🄱🄱 /ˈwɜːkfɔːs/ *noun* [C + sing./pl. verb] **1** (**BUSINESS**) the total number of people who work in a company, factory, etc. **2** (**BUSINESS, SOCIAL STUDIES**) the total number of people in a country who are able to work: *10 per cent of the workforce is/are unemployed.*

workhouse /ˈwɜːkhaʊs/ *noun* [C] (**HISTORY, SOCIAL STUDIES**) (in England and Wales in the past) a building where very poor people were sent to live and given work to do

working¹ ⚡ 🄰🄰 🅦 /ˈwɜːkɪŋ/ *adj.* [only before noun] **1** employed; having a job: *the problems of childcare for working parents* **2** connected with your job: *He stayed with the same company for the whole of his* **working life***.* ◇ *The company offers excellent working conditions.* **3** good enough to be used, although it could be improved: *We are looking for somebody with a* **working knowledge** *of French.*
IDM **in working order** → ORDER¹

working² 🅦 /ˈwɜːkɪŋ/ *noun* **1** [U] the action of doing work: *Working with children requires patience.* ◇ *flexible working* **2** [C, usually pl.] **~ (of sth)** the way in which a machine, an organization, etc. works: *the workings of the human mind*

working capital *noun* [U] (**BUSINESS, FINANCE**) the money that is needed to run a business rather than the money that is used to buy buildings and equipment when starting the business ⊃ look at **venture capital**

the working class *noun* [sing. + sing./pl. verb] (*also the* working classes [pl.]) (**SOCIAL STUDIES**) the group of people in a society who do not have much money or power and who usually do physical work: *unemployment among the working class* ⊃ look at **middle class, upper class** ▶ working class *adj.*: *They're working class.* ◇ *a working-class family* ⊃ look at **middle-class, upper class**

working day *noun* [C] (*BrE*) **1** (*AmE* workday) the part of a day during which you work: *I spend most of my working day sitting at a desk.* **2** (*also* workday) a day on which you usually work or on which most people usually work: *Sunday is a normal working day for me.*

◇ *Allow two working days* (= not Saturday or Sunday) *for delivery.*

workings /'wɜːkɪŋz/ *noun* [pl.] the way in which a machine, an organization, etc. operates: *It's very difficult to understand the workings of the legal system.*

working 'week (*BrE*) (*AmE* **workweek**) *noun* [C] the total amount of time that you spend at work during the week: *a 40-hour working week*

work-life 'balance *noun* [sing.] the number of hours per week you spend working, compared with the number of hours you spend with your family, relaxing, etc: *We have a flexible working policy to ensure a healthy work-life balance.*

workload /'wɜːkləʊd/ *noun* [C] the amount of work that you have to do: *She often gets home late when she has a heavy workload.*

workman /'wɜːkmən/ *noun* [C] (*pl.* -men /-mən/) a man who does physical work

workmanlike /'wɜːkmənlaɪk/ *adj.* done, made, etc. very well, but not original or exciting: *The leading actor gave a workmanlike performance.*

workmanship /'wɜːkmənʃɪp/ *noun* [U] the skill with which sth is made

workmate /'wɜːkmeɪt/ *noun* [C] (*especially BrE*) a person that you work with, often doing the same job, in an office, a factory, etc. **SYN** **colleague**

work of 'art *noun* [C] (*pl.* **works of art**) (**ART, ARTS AND MEDIA, LITERATURE**) a painting, book, statue, etc. ⊃ note at **art**

workout 🔊+ **C1** /'wɜːkaʊt/ *noun* [C] a period of physical exercise, for example when you are training for a sport or keeping fit: *She does a 20-minute workout every morning.*

workplace 🔊+ **B2** /'wɜːkpleɪs/ *noun* [C] (*often the* **workplace** [sing.]) the office, factory, etc. where people work: *the introduction of new technology into the workplace*

work placement = PLACEMENT

worksheet /'wɜːkʃiːt/ *noun* [C] (**EDUCATION**) a piece of paper or an electronic document with questions or exercises on it that you use when you are studying sth

workshop 🔊+ **B2** /'wɜːkʃɒp/ *noun* [C] **1** a place where things are made or repaired ⊃ note at **factory** **2** a period of discussion and practical work on a particular subject, when people share their knowledge and experience: *a drama workshop*

workstation /'wɜːksteɪʃn/ *noun* [C] (**COMPUTING**) the desk and computer at which a person works; one computer that is part of a network of computers

worktop /'wɜːktɒp/ (*also* **'work surface**) *noun* [C] a flat surface in a kitchen, etc. that you use for preparing food, etc. on

work-to-'rule *noun* [C, usually sing.] a situation in which workers refuse to do any work that is not in their contracts, in order to protest about sth

workweek /'wɜːkwiːk/ (*AmE*) = WORKING WEEK

world 🔊 **A1** 🔵 /wɜːld/ *noun*
• THE EARTH/ITS PEOPLE **1** the world [sing.] (**GEOGRAPHY**) the earth with all its countries and people: *a map of the world* ◇ *the most beautiful place* **in the world** ◇ *I took a year off work to travel* **round the world.** ◇ *She is famous* **all over the world.** **2** [sing.] (in compounds) used before another noun to describe one of the most important people or things of their type in the world: *the* **world champion/championship/record/title** ◇ *the major world religions* **3** [C, usually sing.] (**GEOGRAPHY**) a

particular part of the earth or group of countries: *the western world* ◇ *the Arab world* ◇ *the Third World*
• AREA OF ACTIVITY **4** [C] (often in compounds) a particular area of activity or group of people or things: *the world of sport/fashion/politics* ◇ *the medical/business/animal/natural world*
• SOCIETY **5** [sing.] our society; the people in the world: *We live in a rapidly changing world.* ◇ *the modern world* ◇ *The whole world* *was waiting for news of the astronauts.*
• ANOTHER PLANET **6** [C] a planet with life on it: *Do you believe there are other worlds out there, like ours?* **IDM** **do sb a/the world of good** (*informal*) to have a very good effect on sb: *The holiday has done her the world of good.* **in the world** used to emphasize what you are saying: *Everyone else is stressed but he doesn't seem to have a care in the world.* ◇ *There's no need to rush — we've got all the time in the world.* ◇ *What* **in the world** *are you doing?* **the outside world** → OUTSIDE³ **think the world of sb/sth** → THINK¹

the ,World 'Bank *noun* [sing.] (**ECONOMICS**) an international organization that lends money to countries who are members at times when they are in danger or difficulty and need more money

world-'class *adj.* as good as the best in the world: *a world-class athlete*

world 'English *noun* [U] (**LANGUAGE**) the English language, used throughout the world for international communication, including all of its regional varieties, such as Australian, Indian and South African English

world-'famous *adj.* known all over the world

World 'Heritage Site *noun* [C] (**GEOGRAPHY**) a natural or MAN-MADE place that is recognized as having great international importance and is therefore protected

worldly /'wɜːldli/ *adj.* **1** [only before noun] connected with ordinary life, not with the spirit: *He left all his worldly possessions to his nephew.* **2** having a lot of experience and knowledge of life and people: *a sophisticated and worldly man*

'world music *noun* [U] (**MUSIC**) a type of pop music that includes influences from different parts of the world, especially Africa and Asia

world 'power *noun* [C] (**POLITICS**) a powerful country that has a lot of influence in international politics ⊃ look at **power¹** (7), **superpower**

world 'war *noun* [C] a war that involves a lot of different countries: *the Second World War* ◇ *the First World War/World War One*

worldwide 🔊 **B1** /,wɜːld'waɪd/ *adj., adv.* happening in all parts of the world: *The situation has caused worldwide concern.* ◇ *The product will be marketed worldwide.*

the ,World Wide 'Web (*also* the **Web** /ðə 'web/) *noun* [sing.] (*abbr.* WWW) (**COMPUTING**) the system for finding information on the internet, in which documents are connected to other documents using special links: *a Web browser/page* ⊃ look at **internet**

worm¹ 🔊+ **B2** /wɜːm/ *noun* **1** [C] a small creature with a long thin body and no eyes, bones or legs: *an earthworm* ⊃ picture at **food web** **2 worms** [pl.] (**HEALTH**) one or more worms that live inside a person or an animal and may cause disease: *He's got worms.* **3** [C] (**COMPUTING**) a computer program that is a type of virus and that spreads across a network by copying itself

worm² /wɜːm/ *verb* [T] **~ your way** (used with an adverb or a preposition) to move slowly or with difficulty in the direction mentioned: *I managed to worm my way through the crowd.*

PHR V worm your way/yourself into sth to make sb like you or trust you, in order to dishonestly gain an advantage for yourself

worn /wɔːn/ past participle of **wear**¹

worn out adj. **1** too old or damaged to use any more: *My shoes are completely worn out.* **2** extremely tired: *I'm absolutely worn out. I think I'll go to bed early.* ⊃ look at **wear**¹

worried ⚡A2 /'wʌrid/ adj. ~ (about sb/sth); ~ (that …) thinking that sth bad might happen or has happened: *Don't look so worried. Everything will be all right.* ◇ *I'm **worried sick** about the exam.* ◇ *We were **worried stiff** (= extremely worried) that you might have had an accident.*

worry¹ ⚡A2 /'wʌri/ verb (worrying; worries; pt, pp worried) **1** [I] ~ (about sb/sth) to think that sth bad might happen or has happened: *Don't worry — I'm sure everything will be all right.* ◇ *There's nothing to worry about.* ◇ *He worries if I don't phone every weekend.* **2** [T] ~ sb/yourself (about sb/sth) to make sb/yourself think that sth bad might happen or has happened: *What worries me is how are we going to get home?* ◇ *They worried themselves sick when he was away in the army.* ◇ *Don't worry yourself about it — I'll deal with it.* **3** [T] ~ sb (with sth) to annoy or upset sb: *I'm sorry to worry you with my problems but I really do need some advice.*
IDM not to worry it is not important; it does not matter

worry² ⚡B1 /'wʌri/ noun (pl. -ies) **1** [U] the state of worrying about sth: *His son has caused him a lot of worry recently.* **2** [C] something that makes you worry; a problem: *Crime is a real worry for old people.* ◇ *financial worries*
IDM no worries! (informal) it's not a problem; it's all right: *'Thanks for the lift.' 'No worries!'*

worrying /'wʌriɪŋ/ adj. that makes you worry: *a worrying development* ◇ *It is particularly worrying that nobody seems to be in charge.* ◇ *It's been a **worrying time** for us all.* ▶ worryingly adv.: *worryingly high levels of radiation*

worse ⚡A2 /wɜːs/ adj. (comparative of bad) **1** not as good as sth else; more unpleasant: *My exam results were far/much worse than I thought they would be.* **2** [not before noun] more ill; less well: *If you get any worse we'll call the doctor.* ▶ worse ⚡B2 noun [U]: *The situation was already bad but there was worse to come.*
IDM none the wiser/worse → NONE² to make matters/things worse to make a situation, problem, etc. even more difficult or dangerous than before the worse for wear (informal) damaged; not in good condition: *This suitcase looks a bit the worse for wear.* worse luck! (informal) unfortunately: *The dentist says I need three fillings, worse luck!*

worse² ⚡B1 /wɜːs/ adv. (comparative of badly) not as well as sth else: *She speaks German even worse than I do.*

worsen /'wɜːsn/ verb [I, T] to become worse; to make sth worse: *Relations between the two countries have worsened.*

worship¹ ⚡+ C1 /'wɜːʃɪp/ verb (-pp-, AmE -p-) **1** [T, I] (RELIGION) to show respect for God or a god, by saying prayers, singing with others, etc: *People travel from all over the world to worship at this shrine.* **2** [T] to love or admire sb/sth very much: *She worshipped her aunt.* ▶ worshipper noun [C]

worship² ⚡+ C1 /'wɜːʃɪp/ noun **1** [U] (RELIGION) the practice of showing respect for God or a god, by saying prayers, singing with others, etc.; a ceremony for this: *an act/a place of worship* **2** [U] a strong

feeling of love and respect for sb/sth **3** His, Your, etc. Worship [C] (formal) (LAW) a polite way of addressing or referring to a MAGISTRATE or MAYOR

worst¹ ⚡A2 /wɜːst/ adj. (superlative of bad) the least pleasant or suitable: *It's been the worst winter that I can remember.*

worst² ⚡B1 /wɜːst/ adv. (superlative of badly) the least well: *A lot of the children behaved badly but my son behaved worst of all!*

worst³ ⚡B2 /wɜːst/ noun [sing.] the most serious or unpleasant thing that could happen: *My parents always expect the worst if I'm late.*
IDM at (the) worst if the worst happens or if you consider sb/sth in the worst way: *The problem doesn't look too serious. At worst we'll have to make a few small changes.* if the worst comes to the worst if the worst possible situation happens

worth¹ ⚡B1 /wɜːθ/ adj. [not before noun] **1** having a particular value (in money): *How much do you think that house is worth?* **2** ~ doing, etc. used as a way of recommending or advising: *That museum's **well worth** visiting if you have time.* ◇ *The library closes in five minutes — it's not worth going in.* **3** pleasant or useful to do or have, even if it means extra cost, effort, etc: *It takes a long time to walk to the top of the hill but it's worth the effort.* ◇ *Don't bother cooking a big meal. It isn't **worth it** — we're not hungry.*
IDM get your money's worth → MONEY worth sb's while helpful, useful or interesting to sb

worth² ⚡B1 /wɜːθ/ noun [U] **1** the amount of sth that the money mentioned will buy: *20 pounds' worth of petrol* **2** the amount of sth that will last for the time mentioned: *two days' worth of food* **3** the value of sb/ sth; how useful sb/sth is: *She has proved her worth as a member of the team.*

worthless /'wɜːθləs/ adj. **1** having no value or use: *It's worthless — it's only a bit of plastic!* ⊃ look at invaluable, priceless, valuable (1) **2** (used about a person) having bad qualities

worthwhile ⚡+ C1 /ˌwɜːθ'waɪl/ adj. important, pleasant or interesting enough to be worth the cost or effort: *Working for so little money just isn't worthwhile.*

worthy ⚡+ C1 /'wɜːði/ adj. (worthier; worthiest) **1** ~ of sth/to do sth (formal) good enough for sth or to have sth: *He felt he was not worthy to accept such responsibility.* **2** that should receive respect, support or attention: *a worthy leader* ◇ *a worthy cause*

would ⚡A1 /strong form wʊd, weak form wəd, əd/ modal verb (short form 'd /d/; negative would not; short form wouldn't /'wʊdnt/) **1** used with like or love as a way of asking or saying what sb wants: *Would you like to come with us?* ◇ *I'd love a piece of cake.* **2** used as the past form of will when you report what sb says or thinks: *They said that they would help us.* ◇ *She didn't think that he would do a thing like that.* **3** used when talking about the result of an event that you imagine: *He would be delighted if you went to see him.* ◇ *She'd be stupid not to accept.* ◇ *I would have done more, if I'd had the time.* **4** used to describe a possible action or event that did not in fact happen, because sth else did not happen first: *If I had seen the advertisement in time, I would have applied for the job.* **5** used after wish: *I wish the sun would come out.* **6** ~ not do sth used to show that sb/sth was not willing or refused to do sth: *She just wouldn't do what I asked her.* **7** used for asking sb politely to do sth: *Would you come this way, please?* **8** used when you are giving your opinion but are not certain that you are right: *I'd say she's about 40.* **9** used for talking about things that often happened in the past: *When he was young he would often walk in these woods.* ➔ look at **used to 10** used for commenting on behaviour that is typical of sb: *You would say that. You always support him.*

'would-be *adj.* [only before noun] used to describe sb who is hoping to become the type of person mentioned: *advice for would-be parents*

wound¹ 🔒 **B2** /wuːnd/ *noun* [C] (**HEALTH**) an injury to part of the body, especially a cut, often one received in fighting: *a bullet wound*
IDM **rub salt into the wound/sb's wounds** → RUB

wound² 🔒 **B2** /wuːnd/ *verb* [T, often passive] **1** (**HEALTH**) to injure sb's body with a weapon: *He was wounded in the leg during the war.* ➔ note at **injure 2** to hurt sb's feelings deeply: *I was wounded by his criticism.*

wound³ /waʊnd/ past tense, past participle of **wind³**

wounded /'wuːndɪd/ *adj.* **1** (**HEALTH**) injured by a weapon, for example in a war: *wounded soldiers* ◇ *He was seriously wounded.* **2** feeling emotional pain because of sth unpleasant that sb has said or done: *wounded pride* **3** the wounded *noun* [pl.] (**HEALTH**) people who are wounded, for example in a war: *Paramedics tended to the wounded at the scene of the explosion.*

wove /wəʊv/ past tense of **weave**

woven /'wəʊvn/ past participle of **weave**

wow 🔒 **A2** /waʊ/ *exclamation* (*informal*) used for showing that you find sth impressive or surprising: *Wow! What a fantastic boat!*

'wow factor *noun* [sing.] (*informal*) a quality or feature that is extremely impressive: *The new stadium really has the wow factor.*

wrangle /'ræŋgl/ *noun* [C] **~ (with sb) (over sth)** a noisy or complicated argument: *The company is involved in a legal wrangle over copyrights.* ▸ **wrangle** *verb* [I]

wrap 🔒 **B2** /ræp/ *verb* [T] (**-pp-**) **1 ~ sth (up) (in sth)** to put paper or cloth around sth/sb as a cover: *to wrap up a present* ◇ *The baby was found wrapped in a blanket.* **2 ~ sth round/around sb/sth** to tie sth such as paper or cloth around an object or a part of the body: *The man had a bandage wrapped round his head.*
IDM **be wrapped up in sth** to be very involved and interested in sth/sb: *They were completely wrapped up in each other. They didn't notice I was there.*
PHR V **wrap (sb/yourself) up** to put warm clothes on sb/yourself

wrapper /'ræpə(r)/ *noun* [C] the piece of paper or plastic that covers sth when you buy it: *a sweet/ chocolate wrapper*

wrapping /'ræpɪŋ/ *noun* [U] paper, plastic, etc. that is used for covering sth in order to protect it: *Remove the wrapping before heating the pie.*

'wrapping paper *noun* [U] paper that is used for putting round presents

wrath /rɒθ/ *noun* [U] (*old-fashioned or formal*) very great anger

wreak /riːk/ *verb* [T] **~ sth (on sb/sth)** (*formal*) to cause great damage or harm to sb/sth: *Fierce storms wreak havoc at this time of year.*

wreath /riːθ/ *noun* [C] (*pl.* **wreaths** /riːðz/) a circle of flowers and leaves placed on a GRAVE (= place where sb is buried), etc. as a sign of respect for sb who has died

wreck /rek/ *noun* [C] **1** a ship that has sunk or been badly damaged at sea: *Divers searched the wreck.* **2** a car, plane, etc. that has been badly damaged, especially in an accident: *The car was a wreck but the*

lorry escaped almost without damage. **3** [usually sing.] (*informal*) a person or thing that is in a very bad condition: *He drove so badly I was a nervous wreck when we got there.* ▸ **wreck** *verb* [T]: *Vandals had wrecked the school hall.* ◇ *The strike wrecked all our holiday plans.*

wreckage /'rekɪdʒ/ *noun* [U] the broken pieces of sth that has been badly damaged or destroyed: *Investigators searched the wreckage of the plane for evidence.*

wrench¹ /rentʃ/ *verb* [T] **1** (used with an adverb or a preposition) to pull or turn sb/sth strongly and suddenly: *They had to wrench the door off the car to get the driver out.* ◇ (*figurative*) *The film was so exciting that I could hardly wrench myself away.* **2** to injure part of your body by turning it suddenly

wrench² /rentʃ/ *noun* **1** [C] (*especially AmE*) = SPANNER **2** [sing.] the pain or unhappiness that you feel because you have to leave sb/sth **3** [C] a sudden, violent pull or turn: *With a wrench I managed to open the door.*

wrestle /'resl/ *verb* [I, T] **~ (with) sb** (**SPORT**) to fight by trying to get hold of your opponent's body and throw them to the ground. People wrestle as a sport: *She tried to wrestle with her attacker.* ◇ *He managed to wrestle the man to the ground and take the knife from him.* **2** [I] **~ (with sth)** to try hard to deal with sth that is difficult

wrestling /'reslɪŋ/ *noun* [U] (**SPORT**) a sport in which two people fight and try to throw each other to the ground: *a wrestling match* ▸ **wrestler** /-slə(r)/ *noun* [C]

wretch /retʃ/ *noun* [C] a poor, unhappy person: *The poor wretch was clearly starving.*

wretched /'retʃɪd/ *adj.* **1** (used about a person) very unhappy or ill **SYN** **awful 2** [only before noun] (*informal*) used for expressing anger: *That wretched dog has chewed up my slippers again!*

wriggle /'rɪgl/ *verb* [I, T] **1 ~ (sth) (about/around)** to move about with short, quick movements, especially from side to side; to move a part of your body in this way: *The baby was wriggling around on my lap.* ◇ *She wriggled her fingers about in the hot sand.* **2** to move in the direction mentioned by making quick turning movements: *The worm wriggled back into the soil.*
PHR V **wriggle out of sth/doing sth** (*informal*) to avoid sth by making clever excuses: *It's your turn to wash up — you can't wriggle out of it this time!*

wring /rɪŋ/ *verb* [T] (*pt, pp* **wrung** /rʌŋ/) **~ sth (out)** to press and SQUEEZE sth in order to remove water from it

wrinkle¹ /'rɪŋkl/ *noun* [C] a small line in sth, especially one on the skin of your face that forms as you grow older: *She's got fine wrinkles around her eyes.* ◇ *Smooth out the wrinkles in the fabric.* ➔ look at **furrow (2)**

wrinkle² /'rɪŋkl/ *verb* [T, I] **~ (sth) (up)** to form small lines and folds in sth: *She wrinkled her nose at the nasty smell.* ◇ *My skirt had wrinkled up on the journey.* ▸ **wrinkled** *adj.*

wrist 🔒+ **B2** /rɪst/ *noun* [C] (**ANATOMY**) the narrow part at the end of the arm where it joins the hand ➔ picture at **body**

wristband /'rɪstbænd/ *noun* [C] a piece of material worn around the WRIST as a decoration, to take in SWEAT during exercise, or to show support for sth

wristwatch /'rɪstwɒtʃ/ *noun* [C] a watch that you wear on your WRIST

writ /rɪt/ *noun* [C] (**LAW**) a legal order to do or not to do sth, given by a court

write 🔊 **A1** **S** /raɪt/ *verb* (*pt* **wrote** /rəʊt/; *pp* **written** /'rɪtn/) **1** [I, T] to make words, letters, etc., especially on paper using a pen or pencil: *I can't write with this pen.* ◇ *Write your name and address on the form.* **2** [T, I] (**LITERATURE**) to create a book, story, song, etc. in written form for people to read or use: *Tolstoy wrote 'War and Peace'.* ◇ *He wrote his wife a poem.* ◇ *Who wrote the music for that film?* ◇ *I wanted to travel and then write about it.* **3** [I, T] ~ **(sth) (to sb)**; ~ **(sb) sth** to write and send a letter, an email, etc. to sb: *She phones every week and writes occasionally.* ◇ *She wrote that they were all well and would be home soon.* ◇ *I've written a letter to my son.*/*I've written my son a letter.* ◇ *I've written to him.* **4** [T] ~ **sth (out) (for sb)** to fill or complete a form, document, etc. with the necessary information: *The doctor wrote a prescription for me.* **PHR V** **write back (to sb)** to send a reply to sb **SYN** **reply** **write sth down** to write on paper, especially so that you can remember it **write in (to sb/sth) (for sth)** to write to an organization, etc. to ask for sth, give an opinion, etc. **write off/ away (to sb/sth) (for sth)** to write a letter to an organization, etc. to order sth or ask for sth **write sb/sth off** to accept or decide that sb/sth will not be successful or useful: *Don't write him off yet. He could still win.* **write sth off** to accept that you will not get back an amount of money you have lost or spent: *to write off a debt* **write sth out** to write the whole of sth on paper: *Can you write out that recipe for me?* **write sth up** to write sth in a complete and final form, often using notes that you have made

write-off *noun* [C] a thing, especially a vehicle, that is so badly damaged that it is not worth repairing

writer 🔊 **A1** /'raɪtə(r)/ *noun* [C] (**LITERATURE**) a person who writes, especially one whose job is to write books, articles, stories, etc.

write-up *noun* [C] an article in a newspaper or magazine in which sb writes what they think about a new book, play, product, etc.

writhe /raɪð/ *verb* [I] ~ **(about/around) (in sth)** to turn and roll your body about: *She was writhing around in pain.*

writing 🔊 **A1** /'raɪtɪŋ/ *noun* **1** [U] (**EDUCATION**) the skill or activity of writing words: *He had problems with his reading and writing at school.* **2** [U] (**LITERATURE**) the activity or job of writing books, etc: *It's difficult to earn much money from writing.* **3** [U] (**LITERATURE**) the books, etc. that sb has written or the style in which sb writes: *Love is a common theme in his early writing.* **4** [U] words that have been written or printed; the way a person writes: *This card's got no writing inside. You can put your own message.* ◇ *I can't read your writing, it's too small.* **5** **writings** [pl.] (**LITERATURE**) a group of pieces of writing, especially by a particular person on a particular subject: *the writings of Hegel* **IDM** **in writing** in written form: *I'll confirm the offer in writing next week.*

writing paper *noun* [U] paper for writing letters on

written[1] /'rɪtn/ past participle of **write**

written[2] 🔊 **B1** /'rɪtn/ *adj.* expressed in writing; not just spoken: *a written agreement* ◇ look at **spoken**[2] ◇ note at **language**

wrong[1] 🔊 **A1** /rɒŋ/ *adj.* **1** not right or correct: *the wrong answer* ◇ *You've got the wrong number* (= on the telephone). ◇ *I think you're wrong about Nicola — she's not lazy.* **OPP** **right**[1] **2** [not before noun] ~ **(with sb/ sth)** causing problems or difficulties; not as it should be: *You look upset. Is something wrong?* ◇ *What's wrong with the car this time?* ◇ *She's got something wrong with her leg.* **3** not the best; not suitable: *That's the wrong way to hold the bat.* ◇ *I think she married the wrong man.* ◇ *I like him — I just think he's wrong for*

the job. **OPP** **right**[1] **4** ~ **(to do sth)** not morally right or honest: *It's wrong to tell lies.* **OPP** **right**[1] **IDM** **get/start off on the right/wrong foot (with sb)** → FOOT[1] **get on the right/wrong side of sb** → SIDE[1] **on the right/wrong track** → TRACK[1]

wrong[2] 🔊 **B1** /rɒŋ/ *adv.* in a way that is not correct: *I always pronounce that word wrong.* ◇ *It isn't working. What am I doing wrong?* **OPP** **right**[2] **IDM** **get sb wrong** (*informal*) to not understand sb: *Don't get me wrong! I don't dislike him.* **go wrong** **1** to make a mistake: *I'm afraid we've gone wrong. We should have taken the other road.* **2** to stop working properly or to stop developing well: *My computer's gone wrong and I've lost all my work.*

wrong[3] 🔊 **B1** /rɒŋ/ *noun* **1** [U] behaviour that is morally bad or dishonest: *Children quickly learn the difference between right and wrong.* **2** [C] an action or situation that is not fair or legal: *A terrible wrong has been done. Those men should never have gone to prison.* **IDM** **in the wrong** (used about a person) having made a mistake; responsible for sth bad

wrong[4] /rɒŋ/ *verb* [T] (*formal*) to do sth to sb that is bad or unfair: *I wronged her when I said she was lying.*

wrongdoing /'rɒŋduːɪŋ/ *noun* [U, C] (*formal*) illegal or bad behaviour: *The company denies any wrongdoing.* ◇ look at **crime**

wrong-'foot *verb* [T] (*BrE*) to put sb in a difficult or embarrassing situation by doing sth that they do not expect

wrongful /'rɒŋfl/ *adj.* (*formal*) (**LAW**) not fair, not legal or not moral: *He sued the company for wrongful dismissal.*

wrongly /'rɒŋli/ *adv.* in a way that is wrong or not correct: *He was wrongly accused of stealing money.*

wrote /rəʊt/ past tense of **write**

wrought iron /ˌrɔːt 'aɪən/ *noun* [U] a form of iron used to make fences, gates, etc. ◇ look at **cast iron** ▸ **wrought-'iron** *adj.*: *wrought-iron gates*

wrung /rʌŋ/ past tense, past participle of **wring**

wry /raɪ/ *adj.* showing that you think sth is funny but also disappointing: *'Never mind,' she said with a wry grin. 'At least we got one vote.'* ▸ **wryly** *adv.*

WSW *abbr.* (in writing) = WEST-SOUTH-WEST

WTO /ˌdʌblju tiː 'əʊ/ *abbr.* (**ECONOMICS**) **the World Trade Organization** (an organization that encourages economic development and international trade)

WWW /ˌdʌblju: dʌblju: 'dʌblju:/ *abbr.* = WORLD WIDE WEB

X x

X /eks/ (*also* **x**) *noun* (*pl.* **X's**, **x's**) **1** [C, U] the 24th letter of the English alphabet: *'Xylophone' begins with (an) 'X'.* **2** [U] (**MATHEMATICS**) used to represent a number whose value is not mentioned: *The equation is impossible for any value of x greater than 2.* **3** [U] a person, a number, an influence, etc. that is not known or not named: *Let's suppose X knows what Y is doing.*

'X chromosome *noun* [C] (**BIOLOGY**) a CHROMOSOME that decides the sex of an animal or a plant. Two X chromosomes exist in the cells of human females. In human males each cell has one X chromosome and one Y CHROMOSOME.

xenon /ˈzenɒn, ˈziːn-/ *noun* [U] (*symb.* Xe) (**CHEMISTRY**) a chemical element. Xenon is a gas that is present in air and is used in some electric lamps. ❶ For more information on the periodic table of elements, look at the **Reference Section** of this dictionary.

xenophobia /ˌzenəˈfəʊbiə/ *noun* [U] (**SOCIAL STUDIES**) a fear or HATRED of foreign people and cultures ▶ **xenophobe** /ˈzenəfəʊb/ *noun* [C] ▶ **xenophobic** /ˌzenəˈfəʊbɪk/ *adj.*

Xerox™ /ˈzɪərɒks/ *noun* [C] **1** [U] a process for producing copies of letters, documents, etc. using a special machine **2** [C] a copy produced by Xerox™ or a similar process **SYN** **photocopy** ▶ **xerox** *verb* [T]

'X factor *noun* [sing.] a special quality, especially one that you need for success and that is difficult to describe: *She certainly has the X factor that all great singers have.*

XL /ˌeks ˈel/ *abbr.* **extra large** (used for sizes of things, especially clothes)

Xmas /ˈkrɪsməs, ˈeks-/ *noun* [C, U] (*informal*) (used as a short form in writing) Christmas

XML /ˌeks em ˈel/ *noun* [U] (**COMPUTING**) a system used for marking the structure of text on a computer, for example when creating website pages (the abbreviation for 'Extensible Markup Language')

'X-ray *noun* [C] **1** [usually pl.] (**MEDICINE, PHYSICS**) a kind of RADIATION that makes it possible to see inside solid objects, for example the human body, so that they can be examined and a photo of them can be made **2** (**MEDICINE**) a photo that is made with an X-ray machine: *The X-ray showed that the bone was not broken.* ⊃ look at **ray** ⊃ note at **hospital** ⊃ picture at **wavelength** ▶ **X-ray** *verb* [T]: *She had her chest X-rayed.*

xylem /ˈzaɪləm/ *noun* [U] (**BIOLOGY**) the material in plants that carries water and food upwards from the root ⊃ look at **phloem** ⊃ picture at **flower¹**

xylophone /ˈzaɪləfəʊn/ *noun* [C] (**MUSIC**) a musical instrument that consists of two rows of wooden bars of different lengths. You play it by hitting these bars with two small sticks. ⊃ look at **glockenspiel** ⊃ picture at **instrument**

Y y

Y /waɪ/ (*also* y) *noun* (*pl.* Y's, y's) **1** [C, U] the 25th letter of the English alphabet: *'Yawn' begins with (a) 'Y'.* **2** [U] (**MATHEMATICS**) used to represent a number whose value is not mentioned: *Can the value of y be predicted from the value of x?* **3** [U] a person, a number, an influence, etc. that is not known or not named: *Let's suppose X knows what Y is doing.*

yacht /jɒt/ *noun* [C] (**SPORT**) a boat with sails and often an engine, usually used for pleasure trips and racing: *a yacht race* ⊃ look at **dinghy** (1)

yachting /ˈjɒtɪŋ/ *noun* [U] (**SPORT**) the activity or sport of sailing or racing YACHTS

yachtsman /ˈjɒtsmən/ *noun* [C] (*pl.* -men /-mən/) a man who sails a YACHT in races or for pleasure

yachtswoman /ˈjɒtswʊmən/ *noun* [C] (*pl.* -women /-wɪmɪn/) a woman who sails a YACHT in races or for pleasure

yak /jæk/ *noun* [C] an animal of the cow family, with long HORNS (= hard pointed parts on its head) and long hair, that lives in central Asia

yam /jæm/ *noun* [C, U] the large root of a tropical plant that is cooked as a vegetable

yank /jæŋk/ *verb* [T, I] (often used with an adverb or a preposition) (*informal*) to pull sth suddenly, quickly and hard: *She yanked at the door handle.* ▶ **yank** *noun* [C]

yap /jæp/ *verb* [I] (-pp-) (used about dogs, especially small ones) to make short, loud noises in an excited way

yard 🔒 **B1** /jɑːd/ *noun* [C] **1** (*BrE*) an area outside a building, usually with a hard surface and a wall or fence around it: *a school/prison yard* ⊃ look at **churchyard, courtyard 2** (*AmE*) = GARDEN¹ **3** (usually in compounds) an area of land used for a particular type of work or purpose: *a shipyard/boatyard* ◇ *a builder's yard* ⊃ note at **factory 4** (*abbr.* yd) a measure of length; 0.914 of a metre or 36 inches. There are 3 feet in a yard: *Our house is 100 yards from the supermarket.* ❶ For more information about measurements, look at the **Reference Section** of this dictionary.

yardstick /ˈjɑːdstɪk/ *noun* [C] a standard with which things can be compared: *Exam results should not be the only yardstick by which pupils are judged.*

yarn /jɑːn/ *noun* **1** [C, U] THREAD (usually of wool or cotton) that has been SPUN (= prepared) and is used for KNITTING, etc. **2** [C] (*informal*) a long story that sb tells, especially one that is invented or is difficult to believe

yashmak /ˈjæʃmæk/ *noun* [C] a piece of material covering most of the face, worn by some Muslim women

yawn /jɔːn/ *verb* [I] to open your mouth wide and breathe in deeply, especially when you are tired or bored ▶ **yawn** *noun* [C]: *'How much longer will it take?' he said with a yawn.*

yaws /jɔːz/ *noun* [U] (**HEALTH**) a tropical skin disease that causes large red SWELLINGS (= places on the body that are bigger or fatter than usual)

yay /jeɪ/ *exclamation* (especially *AmE*, *informal*) used to show that you are very pleased about sth

'Y chromosome *noun* [C] (**BIOLOGY**) a CHROMOSOME that decides the sex of an animal or a plant. In human males each cell has one X CHROMOSOME and one Y chromosome. In human females there is never a Y chromosome.

yd *abbr.* (in writing) (*pl.* yds) = YARD (4)

yeah 🔒 **A1** /jeə/ *exclamation* (*informal*) yes

year 🔒 **A1** /jɪə(r), jɜː(r)/ *noun* (*abbr.* yr)
• TWELVE MONTHS **1** (*also* calendar year) [C] the period from 1 January to 31 December, 365 or 366 days divided into twelve months or 52 weeks: *last year/this year/next year* ◇ *The population of the country was over 66 million by the year 2018.* ◇ *Interest is paid on this account once a year.* ◇ *a leap year* (= one that has 366 days) ◇ *the New Year* (= the first days of January) **2** [C] any period of twelve months, measured from any date: *She worked here for 20 years.* ◇ *He left school just over a year ago.* ◇ *In a year's time, you'll be old enough to vote.* **3** [C] a period of twelve months in connection with schools, the business world, etc: *the school year* ◇ *the tax/financial year* ⊃ note at **form¹**
• AGE **4** [C, usually pl.] (used in connection with the age of sb/sth) a period of twelve months: *He's 10 years old today.* ◇ *a 6-year-old daughter* ◇ *This car is nearly 5 years old.* ◇ *The company is now in its fifth year.*

- IN SCHOOL/UNIVERSITY **5** [C] (*especially BrE*) (used in schools, universities, etc.) the level that a particular student is at: *My son is in year 10 now.* ◊ *The first years* (= students in their first year at school/university, etc.) *do French as a compulsory subject.* ◊ *He was a year below me at school.* ◔ note at **form**¹
- LONG TIME **6** years [pl.] (*informal*) a long time: *It happened years ago.* ◊ *I haven't seen him for years.* **IDM** all year round for the whole year donkey's years → DONKEY year after year | year in year out every year for many years

yearbook /'jɪəbʊk/ *noun* **1** a book published once a year, giving details of events, etc. of the previous year, especially those connected with a particular area of activity **2** (*especially AmE*) a book that is produced by students in their final year of school or college, containing photos of students and details of school activities

yearly /'jɪəli, 'jɜːli/ *adj., adv.* (happening) every year or once a year: *The conference is held yearly.*

yearn /jɜːn/ *verb* ~ **(for sb/sth)**; ~ **(to do sth)** (*formal*) to want sb/sth very much, especially sth that you cannot have **SYN** long³ ▸ yearning *noun* [C, U]

yeast /jiːst/ *noun* [U] a substance used for making bread rise and for making beer, wine, etc.

'yeast infection (*AmE*) = THRUSH (2)

yell ʔ+ **C1** /jel/ *verb* [I, T] ~ **(out) (sth)**; ~ **(sth) (at sb/sth)** to shout very loudly, often because you are angry, excited or in pain: *She yelled out his name.* ◊ *There's no need to yell at me; I can hear you perfectly well.* ▸ yell *noun* [C]

yellow ʔ **A1** /'jeləʊ/ *adj.* (yellower; yellowest) having the colour of lemons or butter: *a pale/light yellow dress* ▸ yellow ʔ **A1** *noun* [U, C]: *a bright shade of yellow* ◊ *the yellows and browns of the autumn leaves*

,yellow 'card *noun* [C] (**SPORT**) (used in football and rugby) a card that is shown to a player as a warning that they will be sent off the field if they behave badly again ◔ look at **red card**

,yellow 'fever *noun* [U] (**HEALTH**) a tropical disease that is passed from one person to another and that makes the skin turn yellow and often causes death

yellowish /'jeləʊɪʃ/ (*also* yellowy /'jeləʊi/) *adj.* slightly yellow in colour

,yellow 'journalism *noun* [U] (*AmE*) (**ARTS AND MEDIA**) newspaper reports that are EXAGGERATED (= made to seem larger, worse, etc. than they really are) and written to shock people

,yellow 'line *noun* [C] (*BrE*) a yellow line at the side of a road to show that you can only park there for a limited time: *double yellow lines* (= you must not park there at all)

yelp /jelp/ *verb* [I] to give a sudden short cry, especially of pain ▸ yelp *noun* [C]

yen /jen/ *noun* [C] (*pl.* yen) (**ECONOMICS**) the unit of money in Japan

yes ʔ **A1** /jes/ *exclamation* **1** used to give a positive answer to a question, for saying that sth is true or correct or for saying that you want sth: *'Are you having a good time?' 'Yes, thank you.'* ◊ *'You're married, aren't you?' 'Yes, I am.'* ◊ *'May I sit here?' 'Yes, of course.'* ◊ *'More coffee?' 'Yes, please.'* **OPP** no² **2** used for showing you have heard sb or will do what they ask: *'Waiter!' 'Yes, madam.'* **3** used when saying that a negative statement sb has made is not true: *'You don't care about anyone but yourself.' 'Yes I do.'* **OPP** no² ▸ yes *noun* [C] (*pl.* yeses): *Was that a yes or a no?*

yesterday ʔ **A1** /'jestədeɪ, -di/ *adv., noun* [U] (on) the day before today: *Did you watch the film on TV yesterday?* ◊ *yesterday morning/afternoon/evening* ◊ *I posted the form the day before yesterday* (= if I am speaking on Wednesday, I posted it on Monday). ◊ *Have you still got yesterday's paper?* ◊ *I spent the whole of yesterday walking round the shops.*

yet¹ ʔ **A2** /jet/ *adv.* **1** used with negative verbs or in questions for talking about sth that has not happened but that you expect to happen: *Has it stopped raining yet?* ◊ *I haven't seen that film yet.* ❶ In American English you can say: *I didn't see that film yet.* **2** (used with negative verbs) now; as early as this: *You don't have to leave yet — your train isn't for another hour.* **3** (used with SUPERLATIVES) until now/until then; so far: *This is her best film yet.* **4** from now until the period of time mentioned has passed: *She isn't that old; she'll live for years yet.* **5** (used especially with *may* or *might*) at some time in the future: *With a bit of luck, they may yet win.* **6** used with COMPARATIVES to emphasize an increase in the degree of sth: *a recent and yet more improbable theory*
IDM as yet until now: *As yet little is known about the disease.* yet again (used for expressing surprise or anger that sth happens again) once more; another time: *I found out that he had lied to me yet again.* yet another used for expressing surprise that there is one more of sth: *They're opening yet another fast food restaurant in the square.* yet to do, etc. that has not been done and is still to do in the future: *The final decision has yet to be made.*

yet² ʔ **A2** /jet/ *conj.* but; despite that: *He seems pleasant, yet there's something about him I don't like.*

yew /juː/ *noun* **1** [U, C] (*also* 'yew tree [C]) a small tree with dark green leaves and small red BERRIES **2** [U] the wood from the yew tree

'Y-fronts™ *noun* [pl.] (*BrE*) a type of men's underwear with an opening in the front in the shape of a Y the wrong way up

YHA /ˌwaɪ eɪtʃ 'eɪ/ *abbr.* **Youth Hostels Association** (an organization that exists in many countries and provides cheap and simple accommodation for people when they are travelling)

yield¹ ʔ+ **C1** ⓦ /jiːld/ *verb*
- PRODUCE **1** [T] (**AGRICULTURE, BUSINESS, FINANCE**) to produce or provide crops, profits or results: *How much wheat does each field yield?* ◊ *Did the experiment yield any new information?*
- STOP REFUSING **2** [I] ~ **(to sb/sth)** (*formal*) to stop refusing to do sth or to obey sb: *The government refused to yield to the hostage-takers' demands.* **SYN** give in (to sb/ sth)
- GIVE CONTROL **3** [T] ~ **sb/sth (up) (to sb/sth)** to allow sb to have control of sth that you were controlling: *The army has yielded power to the rebels.*
- MOVE UNDER PRESSURE **4** [I] (*formal*) to move, bend or break because of pressure: *The dam finally yielded under the weight of the water.* **SYN** give way
- IN A VEHICLE **5** [I] ~ **(to sb/sth)** (*AmE*) to allow other vehicles on a bigger road to go first: *You have to yield to traffic from the left here.* **SYN** give way (to sb/sth) **PHR V** yield to sth (*formal*) to be replaced by sth, especially sth newer: *Old-fashioned methods have yielded to new technology.*

yield² ʔ+ **C1** ⓦ /jiːld/ *noun* [C, U] (**AGRICULTURE, BUSINESS, FINANCE**) the total amount of crops, profits, etc. that are produced: *Wheat yields were down 5% this year.* ◊ *This will give a yield of 10% on your investment.*

yo /jəʊ/ *exclamation* (*slang*) used by some people when they see a friend; hello

yob /jɒb/ *noun* [C] (*BrE, informal*) a boy or young man who is rude, loud and sometimes violent or aggressive ⊃ look at **hooligan, lout** ▶ **yobbish** /ˈjɒbɪʃ/ *adj.*

yodel /ˈjəʊdl/ *verb* [I, T] (-ll-, *AmE* -l-) to sing or call in the traditional Swiss way, changing your voice frequently between its normal level and a very high level

yoga /ˈjəʊgə/ *noun* [U] a system of exercises for the body that helps you control and relax both your mind and your body

yogurt (*also* **yoghurt**) /ˈjɒgət/ *noun* [C, U] a white, thick liquid food made from milk: *plain/banana/strawberry yogurt*

yoke /jəʊk/ *noun* **1** [C] (**AGRICULTURE**) a long piece of wood fixed across the necks of two animals so that they can pull heavy loads together **2** [sing.] (*formal*) something that limits your freedom and makes your life difficult

yolk /jəʊk/ *noun* [C, U] the yellow part in the middle of an egg

you ⌥**A1** /weak form ju, strong form juː/ *pron.* **1** used as the subject or object of a verb, or after a preposition to refer to the person or people being spoken or written to: *You can play the guitar, can't you?* ◇ *I've told you about this before.* ▸ *Bring your photos with you.* **2** used with a noun, adjective or phrase when calling sb sth: *You idiot! What do you think you're doing?* **3** used for referring to people in general: *The more you earn, the more tax you pay.*

you'd /juːd/ *short form* you had; you would

you'll /juːl/ *short form* you will

young[1] ⌥**A1** /jʌŋ/ *adj.* (younger /ˈjʌŋgə(r)/; youngest /-gɪst/) not having lived or existed for very long; not old: *They have two young children.* ◇ *I'm a year younger than her.* ◇ *My father was the youngest of eight children.* ◇ *my younger brothers* **OPP** old
IDM **young at heart** behaving or thinking like a young person, although you are old

young[2] ⌥**B1** /jʌŋ/ *noun* [pl.] **1** the young (**SOCIAL STUDIES**) young people considered as a group: *The young of today are more ambitious than their parents.* **2** young animals: *Swans will attack to protect their young.*

youngish /ˈjʌŋɪʃ/ *adj.* quite young

youngster ⌥+ **C1** /ˈjʌŋstə(r)/ *noun* [C] a young person

your ⌥**A1** /strong form jɔː(r), weak form jə(r)/ *det.* **1** of or belonging to the person or people being spoken to: *What's your flat like?* ◇ *Thanks for all your help.* ◇ *How old are your children now?* **2** belonging to or connected with people in general: *When your life is as busy as mine, you have little time to relax.* **3** (*informal*) used for saying that sth is well known to people in general: *So this is your typical English summer, is it?* **4** (*also* **Your**) used in some titles: *your Highness*

you're /jʊə(r), jɔː(r)/ *short form* you are

yours ⌥**A2** /jɔːz/ *pron.* **1** of or belonging to you: *Is this bag yours or mine?* ◇ *I was talking to a friend of yours the other day.* **2** Yours used at the end of a letter: *Yours sincerely…/faithfully…* ◇ *Yours…*

yourself ⌥**A1** /jɔːˈself, weak form jə's-/ *pron.* (pl. **yourselves** /-ˈselvz/) **1** used when the person or people being spoken to both cause and are affected by an action: *Be careful or you'll hurt yourself.* ◇ *Here's some money. Buy yourselves a present.* ◇ *You're always talking about yourself!* **2** used to emphasize the

person or people who do the action: *You yourself told me there was a problem last week.* ◇ *Did you repair the car yourselves?* (= or did sb else do it for you?) **3** (*informal*) you: '*How are you?*' '*Fine, thanks. And yourself?*' **4** used when the person or people being spoken to both do an action and are also affected by the action: *You don't look yourself today.*
IDM **(all) by yourself/yourselves 1** alone: *Do you live by yourself?* **2** without help: *You can't cook dinner for ten people by yourself.*

youth ⌥**B1** /juːθ/ *noun* (pl. youths /juːðz/) **1** [U] the period of your life when you are young, especially the time before a child becomes an adult: *He was quite a good sportsman in his youth.* ⊃ look at **age**[1] (2), **old age 2** [U] the fact or state of being young: *I think that her youth will be a disadvantage in this job.* ⊃ look at **age**[1] (3) **3** (*also* the youth) [pl.] (**SOCIAL STUDIES**) young people considered as a group: *the youth of today* **4** [C] (**SOCIAL STUDIES**) a young person (usually a young man, and often one that you do not have a good opinion of): *a gang of youths*

youth club *noun* [C] (in the UK) a club where young people can meet each other and take part in various activities

youthful /ˈjuːθfl/ *adj.* **1** typical of young people: *youthful enthusiasm* **2** seeming younger than you are: *She's a youthful 50-year-old.*

youth hostel *noun* [C] (**TOURISM**) a cheap and simple place to stay, especially for young people, when they are travelling

you've /juːv/ *short form* you have

yo-yo[1] (*also* **Yo Yo™**) *noun* [C] (pl. yo-yos, Yo Yos) a toy that is a round piece of wood or plastic with a string round the middle. You put the string round your finger and can make the yo-yo go up and down.

yo-yo[2] *verb* [I] (often used with an adverb or a preposition) to keep changing in size, amount or quality from one extreme to another: *When I was young my weight yo-yoed up and down.*

yr (*also* yr. especially in AmE) *abbr.* (in writing) (pl. yrs) = YEAR

ytterbium /ɪˈtɜːbiəm/ *noun* [U] (*symb.* Yb) (**CHEMISTRY**) a chemical element. Ytterbium is a silver-white metal used to make steel stronger and in some X-RAY machines. ❶ For more information on the periodic table of elements, look at the **Reference Section** of this dictionary.

yttrium /ˈɪtriəm/ *noun* [U] (*symb.* Y) (**CHEMISTRY**) a chemical element. Yttrium is a grey-white metal used in MAGNETS. ❶ For more information on the periodic table of elements, look at the **Reference Section** of this dictionary.

yuan /juˈɑːn/ *noun* [C] (pl. yuan) (**ECONOMICS**) the unit of money in China

yuck /jʌk/ *exclamation* (*informal*) used for saying that you think sth is horrible: *It's filthy! Yuck!* ▶ **yucky** *adj.* (yuckier; yuckiest): *What a yucky colour!*

yummy /ˈjʌmi/ *adj.* (yummier; yummiest) (*informal*) tasting very good: *a yummy cake* **SYN** **delicious**

Z z

Z /zed/ (*also* z) *noun* [C, U] (pl. Z's, z's) the 26th letter of the English alphabet: '*Zero*' begins with (a) '*Z*'.

zany /ˈzeɪni/ *adj.* (zanier; zaniest) (*informal*) funny in an unusual and crazy way: *a zany comedian*

zap /zæp/ *verb* (-pp-) (*informal*) **1** [T] ~ **sb/sth (with sth)** to destroy, hit or kill sb, usually with a gun or other weapon: *It's a computer game where you have to zap aliens with a laser.* **2** [I, T] to change TV programmes very quickly using a REMOTE CONTROL (= an electronic device)

zeal /ziːl/ *noun* [U] (*formal*) great energy or enthusiasm: *religious zeal*

zealous /'zeləs/ *adj.* using great energy and enthusiasm ▸ **zealously** *adv.*

zebra /'zebrə, 'ziːb-/ *noun* [C] (*pl.* **zebra, zebras**) an African wild animal that looks like a horse, with black and white STRIPES (= lines) all over its body

zebra 'crossing *noun* [C] (*BrE*) a place where the road is marked with black and white lines and people can cross safely because cars must stop to let them do this ⟳ look at **pedestrian crossing**

zeitgeist /'zaɪtgaɪst/ *noun* [sing.] (*formal*) (**HISTORY**) the general mood, ideas, beliefs, etc. of a particular period of history: *Few novels capture the zeitgeist the way this one does.*

Zen /zen/ *noun* [U] (**RELIGION**) a Japanese form of Buddhism

zenith /'zenɪθ/ *noun* [C] **1** (**ASTRONOMY**) the highest point that the sun or moon reaches in the sky, directly above you **2** (*formal*) the time when sth is strongest and most successful **SYN** peak[1] **OPP** nadir

zero[1] 🔒 **A2** /'zɪərəʊ/ *number* (*pl.* -os) **1** (*BrE also* nought) [C] the figure 0 **2** freezing point in the Celsius system; 0°C: *The temperature is likely to fall to five degrees below zero* (= −5°C). **3** the lowest possible amount or level; nothing at all: *zero growth/inflation/profit*

zero[2] /'zɪərəʊ/ *verb* [T] (zeroing; zeroes; *pt, pp* zeroed) to turn an instrument, a control, etc. to zero **PHR V** zero in on sb/sth **1** to fix all your attention on the person or thing mentioned **2** to aim guns, etc. at the person or thing mentioned

zero-'carbon *adj.* (**ENVIRONMENT**) in which the amount of CARBON DIOXIDE produced has been reduced to nothing or is balanced by actions that protect the environment: *a zero-carbon house that uses no energy from external sources* **SYN** carbon-neutral

'zero-hours (*also* 'zero-hour) *adj.* [only before noun] (*BrE*) (**BUSINESS**) related to a contract of employment in which the employee only works when the employer needs them and the employee is only paid for the hours they actually work: *Workers on zero-hours contracts do not know how much they will earn from week to week.*

zero 'tolerance *noun* [U] (**LAW**) the policy of applying laws very strictly so that people are punished even for offences that are not very serious

zest /zest/ *noun* **1** [sing., U] ~ **(for sth)** a feeling of pleasure, excitement and enthusiasm: *She has a great zest for life.* **2** [U] the outer skin of an orange, a lemon, etc., when it is used in cooking

zigzag /'zɪgzæg/ *noun* [C] (**GEOMETRY**) a line with left and right turns, like a lot of letter W's, one after the other: *The skier came down the slope in a series of zigzags.* ◇ *a zigzag pattern/line* ⟳ picture at **line**[1] ▸ **zigzag** *adj.* [only before noun] ▸ **zigzag** *verb* [I] (-gg-)

Zika /'zɪːkə/ (*also* 'Zika virus) *noun* [U] (**HEALTH**) a disease, caused by the bite of a type of MOSQUITO, that may cause a serious condition in babies born to mothers who have the disease while they are pregnant

zilch /zɪltʃ/ *noun* [U] (*informal*) nothing

zillion /'zɪljən/ *noun* [C] (*especially AmE, informal*) a very large number

zinc /zɪŋk/ *noun* [U] (*symb.* Zn) (**CHEMISTRY**) a chemical element. Zinc is a blue-white metal that is mixed with COPPER to produce BRASS. ⟳ picture at **dry cell ❶** For more information on the periodic table of elements, look at the **Reference Section** of this dictionary.

zip[1] /zɪp/ (*BrE*) (*also* zipper *especially in AmE*) *noun* [C] a device consisting of two rows of metal or plastic teeth, that you use for fastening clothes, bags, etc: *to do up/undo a zip*

zip[2] /zɪp/ *verb* [T] (-pp-) **1** ~ **sth (up)** to fasten clothes, bags, etc. with a ZIP: *There was so much in the bag that it was difficult to zip it up.* **OPP** unzip **2** (**COMPUTING**) to COMPRESS a computer file (= make it smaller) **OPP** unzip

'zip code (*also* ZIP code) (*AmE*) = POSTCODE

zirconium /zɜːˈkəʊniəm/ *noun* [U] (*symb.* Zr) (**CHEMISTRY**) a chemical element. Zirconium is a hard silver-grey metal that does not CORRODE very easily. ❶ For more information on the periodic table of elements, look at the **Reference Section** of this dictionary.

zit /zɪt/ *noun* [C] (*informal*) a spot on the skin, especially on the face

zither /'zɪðə(r)/ *noun* [C] (**MUSIC**) a musical instrument with a lot of metal strings stretched over a flat wooden box, that you play with your fingers or a PLECTRUM (= a small piece of plastic, metal, etc.)

the zodiac /ðə 'zəʊdiæk/ *noun* [sing.] a diagram of the positions of the sun, moon and planets, that is divided into twelve equal parts, each with a special name and symbol called a 'sign of the zodiac'

zombie /'zɒmbi/ *noun* [C] (*informal*) **1** (in some African and Caribbean religions and in horror stories) a dead body that has been made alive again by magic **2** a person who seems only partly alive, without any feeling or interest in what is happening

zone[1] 🔒 **B2** /zəʊn/ *noun* [C] **1** an area or a region with a particular feature or use: *a war zone* ◇ *an earthquake/a danger zone* ◇ *a pedestrian zone* (= where vehicles may not go) **2** an area that is different from those around it, for example because sth special happens there **3** one of the areas that a larger area is divided into for the purpose of organization: *postal charges to countries in zone 2* **4** (**GEOGRAPHY**) one of the parts that the earth's surface is divided into by imaginary lines that are PARALLEL to the EQUATOR: *the northern/southern temperate zone* **IDM** in the zone (*informal*) in a state in which you feel confident and are performing at your best

zone[2] /zəʊn/ *verb* [T, usually passive] **1** ~ **sth (for sth)** to keep an area of land to be used for a particular purpose: *The town centre was zoned for office development.* **2** to divide an area of land into smaller areas ▸ **zoning** *noun* [U]

zoo /zuː/ *noun* [C] (*pl.* zoos) a park where many kinds of wild animals are kept so that people can look at them and where they are BRED (= kept in order to produce young), studied and protected

zookeeper /'zuːkiːpə(r)/ *noun* [C] a person who works in a ZOO, taking care of the animals

zoology /zuˈɒlədʒi, zəʊˈɒ-/ *noun* [U] (**BIOLOGY**) the scientific study of animals ⟳ look at **biology, botany** ▸ **zoological** /ˌzuːəˈlɒdʒɪkl, ˌzəʊə-/ *adj.* ▸ **zoologist** /zuˈɒlədʒɪst, zəʊˈɒ-/ *noun* [C]

zoom /zuːm/ *verb* [I] (used with an adverb or a preposition) to move or go somewhere very fast **PHR V** zoom in (on sb/sth) (used in photography) to show the object that is being photographed from closer, with the use of a ZOOM LENS: *The camera* *zoomed in on the actor's face.* **zoom out** (used in photography) to show the object that is being photographed from further away, with the use of a ZOOM LENS

'zoom lens *noun* [C] a device on a camera that can make an object being photographed appear bigger or smaller so that it seems to be closer or further away

zucchini /zu'ki:ni/ *noun* [C] (*pl.* zucchini, zucchinis) (*especially AmE*) = COURGETTE

zygote /'zaɪgəʊt/ *noun* [C] (**BIOLOGY**) a cell that starts the process of forming a baby person or animal, formed by the joining together of a male and a female GAMETE (= a cell that is provided by each parent)

Oxford Student's Dictionary
Writing Tutor

Using the Oxford Student's Dictionary to improve your writing

In the Writing Tutor you will find examples of essays, formal and informal emails, and various other types of writing commonly included in exams. You will also find advice about planning, organizing and writing your work, useful words and phrases, and tips to help you check your writing.

The Writing Tutor can help you prepare for the written component of tests such as IELTS, TOEFL™, TOEIC™ and B2 First. Further advice on academic writing and exam technique is given on Writing Tutor pages **2–5**.

Writing model

Each Writing Tutor section contains an example of a written text. Look carefully at:
- the content (what is being said)
- the structure and organization of the text
- the way the ideas and paragraphs are linked
- the language and style

Before you write

This section will help you to prepare for a writing task by suggesting ways that you can research topic areas, plan and organize your own writing, and develop good study habits.

While you are writing

This section gives you quick reminders and advice for each type of writing.

Language bank

Key words and phrases are highlighted in the writing models. Each Writing Tutor section also has a **Language bank**, which contains useful words and phrases that you can use for each type of writing. Check that you are familiar with these phrases and know how to use them correctly.

Checklist

Use this section to check and improve your work and correct mistakes.

Formal and informal writing

The language you use should be appropriate for the reader and the situation. Your writing should not be informal unless you are writing an informal letter or email. When you check your work, think carefully about these points:

Full/Short forms

We usually use short forms, for example *we've* rather than *we have*, in an informal context. In formal writing it is best to avoid short forms.

Choice of words and phrases

In formal writing you should use words and phrases that do not have the label *informal* or *slang* in the main part of the dictionary. Only use words and phrases marked *formal* if you are sure they are appropriate.

Sentence length

Using a lot of short sentences can appear very informal. In formal writing try to write longer sentences, using relative pronouns (e.g. *which*, *that*) and conjunctions (e.g. *but, or, although, because*). Avoid very long sentences, however, as these can be difficult to understand.

Abbreviations

You should avoid using abbreviations in formal writing, especially language typically used in text messages, on social media, etc., for example *IMO* (= in my opinion).

I, you and *we*

In essays and reports avoid using *you* and try to find alternatives to using *I* and *we*. For example:

✓ *The report shows…*
✗ *In this report I aim to show…*
✓ *A survey was carried out…*
✗ *I carried out a survey…*

Contents

The writing process

Stages of the writing process

When you write an essay, a letter or an email, whether it is for class, for an exam or for everyday life, you will produce the best piece of writing if you plan and write in an organized way.

1 PREPARATION STAGE

Think

Before you start, ask yourself some planning questions:

- What is the aim of this piece of writing?
  - To answer a specific essay or exam question
  - To convince others of your point of view
  - To show your understanding or knowledge of an idea or a topic to others, such as a teacher or lecturer
  - To communicate a request, complaint, etc. to somebody
- Who will read it?
  - A teacher or professor
  - Fellow students or colleagues
  - An employer
  - The general public

Your answers to these questions will help you to decide what information to include or leave out, how much research you need to do and how formal or informal your language should be.

For essay or exam questions read the question very carefully and identify the key task and topic words.

Explore

Think of as many ideas as possible related to the topic. You can make lists, create a table or draw a mind map.

Research

If you are not in an exam and have access to the internet or a library, do some research to find information and evidence to use in your writing. Make notes and keep a record of the sources.

Plan

Choose your best ideas and delete anything that is not relevant.

Write a plan, including an introduction, a development stage and a conclusion. Think about how to organize your ideas so that your piece of writing makes sense and is clear and consistent. Check that everything relates to your main aim and the essay or exam question.

Decide roughly how many words you will give to each part of your piece of writing.

2 WRITING STAGE

Draft

You are now ready to start writing your draft. Try to keep to your plan. At this stage think about the content rather than spelling and punctuation.

As you write check that you are using the appropriate level of formality. You can use informal or slang words and phrases if you are writing to a friend, but you do not usually use them in an essay.

If you are writing a letter or an email, make sure that you use an appropriate greeting and closing phrase. See Writing Tutor pages **18–20** for information about the type of language used in letters and emails.

Edit

If you are not in an exam, you will have the opportunity to write several drafts. Read your writing with a critical eye and edit your text. Ask yourself these questions:

- Does your text answer the question or achieve your aim?
- Does it make sense overall?
- Do you need to include more ideas, examples or quotes?
- Does it include anything that is not relevant?
- Have you met any word count requirements?

3 CHECKING STAGE

Proofread

Read your work again and check it very carefully for spelling, punctuation and grammatical errors. If you are not in an exam, you may find it helpful to ask somebody else to check your writing at this stage.

Effective writing

CHOOSE THE RIGHT WORD

Many learners find certain words confusing, for example *borrow* and *lend*. If you look up *borrow*, you will see the note 'look at **lend**' to help you work out which word to use. Many other entries in the dictionary include this type of note.

A lot of words in English have similar spellings and meanings but are used in different contexts and situations, for example the adjectives *alternate* and *alternative*. Many words are also different in British and American English, for example *holiday* (*BrE*) and *vacation* (*AmE*). Look up any words you are not certain about.

USE THE RIGHT WORDS TOGETHER

In order to write natural and correct English, you need to know which words are commonly used together (e.g. *make a mistake*). These combinations of words are called collocations. You can look up the main word (e.g. *mistake*) in the dictionary and look at the examples to find out which words it is used with. Collocations in examples are written in bold type. At some entries (e.g. *art*) you will find **Collocations** note boxes showing a range of collocations relating to particular subject areas.

USE THE CORRECT PREPOSITIONS, ADVERBS AND STRUCTURES

Some words are used with particular prepositions, adverbs and structures. For example, with the verb *like*, you can use the structure *like to do sth* (e.g. *I'd like to go on holiday*) or *like doing sth* (e.g. *I like going on holiday*). Patterns like this are shown in bold type at the start of an entry or a meaning.

USE LINKING WORDS

Use coordinating conjunctions like *and*, *but* and *or* to connect two pieces of information. To add information to the main part of a sentence, you can use subordinating conjunctions (e.g. *although*, *because*, *after*).

You can also use relative pronouns (e.g. *which*, *that*) to link short sentences and avoid repetition.

VARY YOUR LANGUAGE

Try to avoid using the same word or phrase too many times. Use the **Synonyms** note boxes in the main part of the dictionary, for example at *mention*, to find other words with the same meaning as a word you have already used. You will also find **SYN** (synonym) notes at a lot of entries, highlighting words with the same or nearly the same meaning as the word that you have looked up.

USE PHRASAL VERBS CORRECTLY

Phrasal verbs are verbs followed by an adverb, a preposition or both. In this dictionary phrasal verbs are listed at the end of the entry for the verb. The meaning of different phrasal verbs that include the same verb can be very different so make sure you look up any that you are not certain about.

CHECK YOUR WORK

Spelling

Check the spelling of plural forms, past tenses, *-ing* forms and comparative and superlative adjectives and adverbs. Remember that words that are similar to words in your own language may be spelled differently.

Punctuation

Take care with punctuation, particularly when using commas and apostrophes.

Grammar

Check whether the nouns you use are countable or uncountable, and take care with irregular verb endings. You can see a list of irregular verbs on the **Irregular verbs** pages in the reference section of the dictionary.

Answering exam questions

Your first priority at the beginning of an exam is to make sure that you really understand the exam question and address all the required parts. Questions can be considered in terms of three main components:

- Topic
- Focus
- Question types

Topic

The key words in a question help you identify the topic of the question. For example:

Describe the effects of climate change on wild animals in the Arctic over the last ten years.

In this case, the key words are *effects*, *climate change*, *wild animals*, *Arctic* and *ten years*.

When you write your answer, think about what the examiner wants you to demonstrate an understanding of.

Focus

Often, the wording of the question will include a word or phrase that either limits or expands the topic in a specific way. These phrases show you the focus of the question. Try to avoid common mistakes such as:

- covering too broad an area

  For example, if the question asks about the benefits of geothermal power in Iceland, think carefully about including information about geothermal power in Greenland or hydroelectric power in Iceland.

- writing with too narrow a focus

  For example, if you are asked to write about the effects of social media on young people, you should not write about its effects only on young teenagers.

- only answering half the question

  For example, if the question asks about the effects of taking up exercise in later life and whether or not the advantages outweigh the disadvantages, you need to discuss both parts of the question.

Question types

In an exam the type of information that you provide in your answer depends on the type of question being asked. Below are some of the main types of questions found in exams:

Comparing and contrasting

One type of comparison essay requires you to analyse the similarities and differences between two approaches, methods or things (e.g. exams and continuous assessment), and present their relative advantages and disadvantages. There is an example of this type of text on Writing Tutor pages **6–7**.

Some comparison essay questions ask you to read and compare two texts. The texts usually present two differing opinions on a topic (e.g. the advantages and disadvantages of globalization). You should be able to evaluate the two texts, identify the main points in both and say which puts forward its argument most successfully.

Discussing and giving opinions

Discussion essay questions either require you to analyse or discuss both sides of a question objectively, or to present an argument for one side or the other. In the latter case you should give reasons, evidence and examples to support your answer. There is an example of this type of text on Writing Tutor pages **8–9**.

Discussing problems and solutions

Problem and solution questions are a feature of many exams. You need to use your critical thinking skills and be able to analyse the problem. You also need to think creatively about how the problem could be solved and support your solutions with reasons, arguments and relevant examples from your own knowledge or experience. There is an example of this type of text on Writing Tutor pages **10–11**.

Writing a review

Some exam questions require you to write a review of a book or film. The review should contain details of the plot, setting, characters and themes. It should also include your opinion of the book or film, including its strong and weak points. Finally, the reviewer should say whether or not they think the reader should see the film or read the book. There is an example of this type of text on Writing Tutor pages **12–13**.

Describing charts, graphs and tables

You may be asked to summarize visual information in a particular graph, chart or table. It might show, for example, electricity supply trends over the last ten years. You should demonstrate your ability to select and report the main features of the graph, table or chart, and to describe and compare the data, identifying significant changes and trends. There is an example of this type of text on Writing Tutor pages **14–15**.

Describing a process

For some exams you will have to describe a natural or man-made process shown in a diagram. You need to show that you can describe the stages of the process logically and clearly, and explain the relationship between each stage. There is an example of this type of text on Writing Tutor pages **16–17**.

Writing letters and emails

Some exam questions may require you to write a formal letter or email. You should demonstrate your ability to clearly state why you are writing the letter or email and say directly but politely what you want the reader to do.

You may be asked to write an informal email that demonstrates the ability to understand a particular situation and respond appropriately.

There are examples of a formal and an informal email on Writing Tutor pages **18–20**.

Genres

It is important to be able to write different types of texts. Writing emails, letters, reports, reviews, articles, essays, summaries and stories requires you to know how to:

- choose the appropriate content for the context you are given
- lay out the text
- use the correct level of formality
- choose the appropriate vocabulary
- use grammar correctly

Key words

Here is a set of key task words that are used in exam questions:

analyse	separate a text into its parts in order to understand and explain it
compare	provide details of how two or more things are similar or different
contrast	highlight the differences between two or more things
describe	provide details of the appearance of a person, place or thing; provide details of a process or an event
discuss	describe/explain/analyse a topic or an argument
evaluate	judge the importance or validity of something
explain	give detailed reasons for an opinion or idea
give your opinion	say what you think about a situation or an argument, and support your opinion with relevant examples
outline	give only the main facts about an idea or a process
summarize	explain a text or information in a chart as concisely as possible, including only the most important facts and ideas

Writing a comparison essay

This type of comparison essay question requires you to describe the similarities and differences between two methods, approaches or things, and to analyse their relative advantages and disadvantages.

More and more people are choosing to read e-books rather than printed books. Do the advantages outweigh the disadvantages of this trend? (400–450 words)

INTRODUCTION

1 Give a short summary of the current situation.

DEVELOPMENT

2 Introduce the similarities (wide choice of books; pages are similar in tone and colour).

3 Introduce difference 1 (cost).

4 Introduce difference 2 (convenience).

5 Introduce difference 3 (space and storage).

6 Introduce difference 4 (reading experience).

7 Introduce difference 5 (technical aspects).

CONCLUSION

8 Give a conclusion based on the main points introduced in the development stage.

1 Nowadays many people are choosing to read e-books instead of printed books. While some people feel that this change is positive, others still prefer the print format. This essay will discuss the advantages and disadvantages of the trend towards e-books.

2 Buyers of both traditional books and e-books have access to a wide range of books. Reading an e-book is also similar to reading a printed book in some respects because e-reader screens look like the pages of a book in terms of tone and colour.

3 One key difference between e-books and printed books is that you need to buy a device — an e-reader — in order to read an e-book. You can then buy e-books online and download them onto the device. With printed books there is no such initial cost. Having said that, e-books tend to be cheaper to buy than printed books because printed books require paper, ink and binding. However, this advantage is balanced by the fact that an e-reader can be lost, stolen or damaged, which incurs a higher cost than simply losing a book.

4 Another advantage of e-books is that they can be bought and read almost immediately, as long as the user has internet access. On the other hand, buyers of printed books have to travel to a bookshop or order online and wait for the book to be delivered. Both take time and are less convenient than downloading an e-book.

5 E-books are stored on e-readers, which are small and light, so there is no issue with space or storage. In contrast, printed books can be heavy, and a collection of books can take up a large amount of space.

6 Another important factor is the reading experience. A lot of readers of printed books feel that the experience of holding a real book is preferable to holding an e-book. Printed books also have a cover, which adds an attractive visual element that an e-book does not have.

7 Finally, book lovers would argue that books cannot go wrong. The only 'working parts' are the paper pages, whereas e-readers are complex machines. They need regular recharging and an internet connection, which may not always be available. Over time they may become unreliable, which can negatively affect the reading experience.

8 In conclusion, the advantages of e-books outweigh the disadvantages, and it therefore seems likely that more and more people will turn to e-books. Nevertheless, it is ultimately up to the consumer to decide whether they prefer the high-tech convenience of e-books or the more traditional pleasure of printed books.

Before you write

- If you have a choice of essay questions, choose the question on the topic you are most familiar with.
- Read the question carefully several times. Underline the key task and topic words.
- Write as many ideas as you can on a blank piece of paper. For example:

E-books	Printed books	Both
+ cheaper + no need to go to bookshop + immediate access	+ only need to buy the book + people like having a physical object	• similar page tone and colour • wide range of titles
– have to buy an e-reader – device can be damaged or lost – battery can run out	– can take up a lot of space – heavy – have to travel to bookshop or order online	

- Cut any ideas that do not help you answer the question.
- Choose the structure of your essay (A or B) and organize your ideas into paragraphs:

   A: Introduction > Similarities > Differences > Summary and your opinion

   B: Introduction > Differences and similarities of aspect 1 > Differences and similarities of aspect 2, etc. > Summary and your opinion

While you are writing

- Include a fact or comment that captures the reader's interest in the introduction.
- Identify opportunities to develop your ideas and show your range of language.
- Use connecting words and phrases to make the structure of your essay clear to your readers.

Language bank

Identifying similarities	Identifying differences	
both X and Y…	*although/whereas/while X…, Y…*	*X is more/less… than Y*
like X, Y…	*in contrast (to Y), X…*	*X… Having said that, Y…*
one/another difference between X and Y is that…	*one/another difference between X and Y is that…*	*X… However/Nevertheless, Y…*
X and Y share…	*unlike Y, X…*	*X… On the other hand, Y…*
X is (not) as… as Y	*X is different from Y in that…*	*X…, but Y…*
X is similar to Y	*X is -er than Y*	*X…, whereas Y…*
X looks like Y		
X… Y also…		

Checklist

Have I…

- answered the question? . . . . ☐
- written about both the similarities and the differences? . . . . ☐
- organized my ideas into logical paragraphs? . . . . ☐
- used a range of phrases to compare and evaluate? . . . . ☐
- used linking words to help the reader follow what I have said? . . . . ☐
- given my opinion in the conclusion? . . . . ☐

Writing a discussion essay

A discussion essay question requires you to present an argument on a particular issue. For most discussion essay questions you should examine both sides of the issue and then give your opinion. Check the question carefully before you start writing to make sure you understand what is required. You should generally use formal language and use personal language only when it is appropriate. Your argument should be clearly organized and supported with information, evidence and reasons.

Tourism can have a negative impact on the people who live in tourist destinations. Discuss. (300–350 words)

INTRODUCTION

1 Introduce the topic and the two sides of the discussion.

DEVELOPMENT

2 Present reason 1 to support your case (damage to environment).

3 Present reason 2 to support your case (impact on local people).

4 Present evidence against your case (employment; infrastructure; culture).

CONCLUSION

5 Summarize the main points and give your opinion on the topic.

1 Tourism <u>can bring benefits to</u> the people who live in tourist areas in the form of increased investment, employment opportunities and income. However, <u>these benefits often come at a cost</u>. <u>A major question to be considered is</u> whether the benefits of tourism are worth the negative effects that the industry has on the people who live in tourist destinations.

2 <u>It is clear that</u> tourism <u>has its drawbacks</u>. The first of these is damage to the environment. Areas of natural beauty are destroyed by high-rise buildings, road systems and huge increases in population during the tourist season. <u>There is also often an increase in</u> air and noise pollution as the volume of traffic increases. Trees are cut down, coral reefs are damaged and lakes and rivers are polluted.

3 In addition, increased demand for land often <u>leads to</u> house prices rising beyond the level that many people who live in the area can afford. At the same time there may also be social problems such as crime and loss of local culture. <u>All of these factors can cause</u> the standard of living for many local residents to deteriorate.

4 Despite this, tourism also <u>brings some advantages</u>, especially in areas of low employment. Hotels, restaurants, shops and transport hubs provide jobs and income for many local people. <u>As a result</u>, these people may have a better quality of life. There is also often an improvement in the area's infrastructure in the form of airports and better road, rail and bus systems. Furthermore, <u>some may argue that</u> exposure to other cultures through interactions with tourists can help create a more open and enriched local culture.

5 In short, although tourism <u>can have a positive impact on</u> the people who live in tourist destinations, the negative effects of this industry need to be addressed. <u>In my opinion</u>, local communities and governments <u>should deal with these problems by</u> putting limits on development in tourist areas and restricting the number of tourists allowed to visit popular attractions.

Before you write

- Make notes on the topic, making sure that you include points for and against the argument. Do online research if possible. For example:

Disadvantages	Advantages
• damage to environment	• more jobs for local people
• increase in land and house prices	• improved standard of living
• crime	• better infrastructure
• loss of culture	• enriched culture

- Select the strongest ideas for both sides and add more detail to your notes, including supporting evidence and examples.
- Choose the structure of your essay (A or B) and organize your ideas into paragraphs:

  A: Introduction > Arguments for your case > Arguments against your case > Summary and your opinion
  (It is also possible to reverse the order of arguments for and against your case.)

  B: Introduction > Argument 1 for your case and counterargument > Argument 2 for your case and counterargument, etc. > Summary and your opinion

- Note down some useful vocabulary relating to the topic.

While you are writing

- Look carefully at the title or question and make sure you really answer it.
- Use general statements to convey the main ideas and then provide evidence, examples, details and reasons to support these statements.
- Use paragraph divisions and linking words and phrases to make the structure of your essay clear to your readers.

Language bank

Presenting an argument	Describing advantages and disadvantages	Describing consequences
a major question to be considered is...	*... brings some advantages (to...)*	*... leads to...*
in my opinion	*... can bring benefits (to...)*	*as a result (of this)*
it is clear/possible/likely/ important that...	*... can have a positive/negative impact on...*	*because of this*
... should deal with these problems by...	*... has its drawbacks*	*so*
some may argue that...	*there is often an increase/ a decrease/an improvement/ a deterioration in...*	*therefore*
	these benefits/advantages often come at a cost	*these factors can cause...*

Checklist

Have I...

- written about exactly what the task asked me to discuss?....................................... ☐
- presented both sides of the argument?... ☐
- organized my ideas into logically ordered paragraphs?................................... ☐
- used linking words and phrases to help the reader follow what I have said?................. ☐
- given my opinion in the conclusion?... ☐

Writing a problem and solution essay

A problem and solution essay contains an analysis of a problem followed by suggestions for solutions to address the problem. The solutions should be explained clearly and logically and be directly linked to the problem. Identifying key words in the question is essential.

INTRODUCTION

1 State the problem and its effects.

DEVELOPMENT

2 State cause 1 (growing population) and offer solutions (limit vehicles — congestion charges; road tolls; close off roads; encourage car sharing).

3 State cause 2 (road systems designed for less traffic) and offer solutions (build more roads; widen roads; introduce better traffic control systems).

4 State cause 3 (lack of alternatives for commuters) and offer solutions (offer better bus/train services; add more park-and-ride services; cycle paths).

5 State cause 4 (congestion during rush hour) and offer solutions (stagger commuting times; offer flexible working hours).

CONCLUSION

6 Summarize the causes of the problem and the solutions.

Traffic congestion is a serious problem in big cities. Why is this so and what could be done to resolve this issue? (300–350 words)

1 Traffic congestion is a serious problem in almost every major city in the world and leads to severe air pollution and extremely long commuting times. However, there are many measures that can be taken to address this issue.

2 The most obvious cause of traffic congestion is the growing population in many cities around the world. One solution is to try to limit the number of vehicles on the road. This could be done by introducing or increasing congestion charges and road tolls or closing off certain sections of the road system to traffic altogether. In cases where these options would be impractical, drivers should be encouraged to travel with one or more other drivers when commuting to work or school.

3 Another reason that cities are so congested is that many road systems were originally designed for much lower volumes of traffic. To resolve this issue, more roads could be built, roads could be widened and more effective traffic control systems such as traffic lights and road signs could be introduced. This would allow traffic to flow more smoothly on roads that often become congested.

4 In some cities the reason for traffic congestion is the lack of alternatives for commuters. One answer is to offer more attractive services such as more buses and upgraded train services. In addition, more park-and-ride services could be introduced. Adding more cycle paths would make cycling a safer and more practical option.

5 In many cities most commuters travel at the same time — during the rush hour. As a result, roads become very congested at certain times. This congestion could be reduced by staggering commuting times. This would require companies to encourage employees to work outside normal working hours.

6 In conclusion, traffic congestion is caused by too many cars using inadequate road systems, a lack of practical alternatives to driving and commuter behaviour. In my opinion, this issue could be resolved by improving road and cycle path systems, offering alternative forms of transport and encouraging people to change their commuting habits.

Before you write

- Read the question carefully several times. Underline the key task and topic words.
- Make sure you identify the main causes of the problem and solutions for each cause. Include only as many ideas as you can write about in the time given. Make notes on the key points:

Causes	Solutions
• road systems originally designed for much lower volumes of traffic	• reduce number of cars by making driving more expensive, e.g. introducing congestion charges • invest in better road systems
• not enough viable alternatives for commuters — inadequate public transport, lack of cycle lanes	• improve bus and train services • provide more cycle paths
• commuters all travelling at the same time, 'rush hour'	• stagger office hours and encourage flexible working

- Choose the structure of your essay (A or B) and organize your ideas into paragraphs:
  - **A: Introduction > Problem and solution 1 > Problem and solution 2, etc. > Conclusion**
  - **B: Introduction > Problems > Solutions > Conclusion**

While you are writing

- Try to convince the reader that the problem is important and needs to be solved.
- Explain your solutions clearly.
- Give your opinion in the conclusion.

Language bank

Describing problems and their causes	Giving solutions
as a result	*... could/should...*
consequently	*another way (forward) is to...*
one/another/the cause of X is (that)...	*one answer/solution is to...*
one/another/the reason for X is (that)...	*there are many measures that can be taken to address this issue*
one/another/the reason that...is (that)...	*this could be done by ...*
the most obvious cause of X is...	*this issue could be resolved by...*
X is a factor (in)...	*to resolve this issue,...*
X is caused by...	
X leads to...	

Checklist

Have I...
- stated the problem in the introduction?. . . . . ☐
- used a range of phrases to explain the causes of the problem? . . . . ☐
- suggested solutions that directly relate to the problem? . . . . ☐
- used linking words to help the reader follow what I have said? . . . . ☐
- summarized the solutions to the problem in the conclusion? . . . . ☐

Writing a book or film review

The main purpose of a book or film review is to give information to a potential reader or viewer so that they can decide whether or not they want to read the book or watch the film. A review typically contains facts about the setting, plot, characters and themes, and the reviewer's opinion of them. It should also include the positive and negative elements of the book or film. The review should end with a recommendation about whether or not to read the book or watch the film.

INTRODUCTION

1 Provide the main facts about the film and your overall impression/ opinion.

DEVELOPMENT

2 Describe the main interest of the story, but do not give away the ending (two main characters are very different; they don't like each other at first; will they fall in love?)

3 Mention any other interesting features and explain how these contribute to the overall success or failure of the book or film (various subplots; story concludes in positive way).

CONCLUSION

4 Give your opinion and say whether or not you think people should see the film or read the book.

Write a review of the best film you have seen recently. Give your opinion of the film and say whether or not you would recommend it. (250–300 words)

Pride and Prejudice (2005)

1 Deborah Moggach's highly entertaining film *Pride and Prejudice* is a film version of the classic novel by Jane Austen. The film is set in nineteenth-century England and depicts social life among the rural upper class. The plot deals with the relationship between a young woman and a rich, upper-class man.

2 The young woman, Lizzie, is intelligent, charming and independent, while the aristocrat, Mr Darcy, appears to be arrogant, awkward and cold. Their first meeting does not go well, and it seems that they will fall victim to the pride and prejudice of the title. However, the situation is complicated by their friends and family, and the question that keeps viewers gripped throughout the film is whether or not they will eventually overcome their first impressions and learn to like or possibly even love each other.

3 There are various subplots involving Lizzie's sisters and their relationships with various types of men. The clever interplay between these storylines keeps the viewer intrigued and amused. Some people may argue that the plot is overcomplicated and that the film loses direction occasionally, but I think that the story concludes in a positive and emotionally satisfying way.

4 The film is successful mainly because of the charming performances of the two main actors and a witty script that is contemporary despite the nineteenth-century setting. At the same time the film is a joy to watch, with wonderful camerawork capturing the beautiful English countryside. Some scenes reminded me of the highly successful film versions of Thomas Hardy's novels *Far From the Madding Crowd* and *Tess*. For anyone who loves classic, romantic stories, retold with style and wit, I would highly recommend this excellent film.

Before you write

- Watch the film or read the book and make notes about:
    - the type of film/book it is (e.g. romance, crime, comedy)
    - the setting (the time and place of the story)
    - the plot (what happens and why)
    - the characters and acting, if it is a film
    - your opinion, positive or negative, with reasons
- Choose the best points to include in your review.
- Organize your notes into logical paragraphs.

While you are writing

- Remember that the reader has not seen the film or read the book.
- Do not give details about the ending.
- Use your dictionary to find a range of suitable adjectives and synonyms to describe the type of book/film, the plot and the characters.
- Include both positive and negative aspects of the book/film.

Language bank

Giving general information about the book/film	Giving opinions
... is a film version of...	I believe/think (that)...
... is an account/a tale of...	I thoroughly enjoyed this book/film
the film/story focuses on...	I would advise against reading/seeing this book/film
the main characters are...	I would highly recommend this book/film
the novel/film depicts...	in my opinion
the plot deals with...	my favourite character is...
the story concludes in a/an... way	one possible flaw is that...
the story/film is set in...	some may argue that...
there are various subplots involving...	some scenes reminded me of...
written in..., this story begins with...	the book/film is a joy to read/watch
	the book/film is successful because...
	the writer/director excels at...

Checklist

Have I...

- given the name of the film or book in the first paragraph? .... ☐
- introduced facts about the author and setting?... ☐
- written about the story without giving away the ending? .... ☐
- given details about the characters?.. ☐
- recommended whether or not to read the book or watch the film in the conclusion? .... ☐

Describing graphs and charts

For some assignments and exams you are required to write a description and interpretation of a graph or chart. These are the most common types of graphs and charts:

- *Bar graphs* show different amounts in various categories using narrow rectangles of different heights.
- *Pie charts* are circles divided into sections that represent proportions of the whole.
- *Line graphs* show changes and trends over time.

Summarize the information shown in the graph, highlight the main trends and make comparisons where relevant. (250–300 words)

Huawei makes more phones than Apple
Smartphone makers' market share

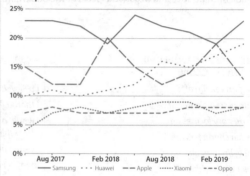

INTRODUCTION

1 Give a general description of what the graph represents.

DEVELOPMENT

2 Give a description of the main trends with supporting detail (Huawei — significant growth; Apple — seasonal peaks and troughs; Samsung — market leader but no significant increase).

3 Give details of the other trends (Oppo — share rose and fell gradually; Xiaomi — increase of 5%; both still had small share of market at end of period).

CONCLUSION

4 Highlight the main trends and explain their significance.

1 The graph shows the percentage of smartphones sold for the top five global manufacturers over the two-year period between May 2017 and May 2019.

2 In this period the sales of all five companies fluctuated, but only one, Huawei, showed significant growth. By the end of the period, Huawei's market share had almost doubled to nearly 20%. Apple was in a fairly strong position at the start and the end of the period with almost a 15% share of the market, and saw regular seasonal peaks and troughs between these two dates. By the end of the period Apple had moved from second to third place in terms of market share, but this may be a temporary effect. Samsung was the market leader at both the start and the end of this period, but the company's overall market share did not increase significantly over this time.

3 Oppo's market share rose and fell gradually, and Xiaomi's presence in the market increased by about 5%. However, at the end of the period both Xiaomi and Oppo still had a relatively small share of the overall market at around 8%, which was less than half that of Samsung.

4 In conclusion, the market share of all five companies changed by varying degrees over the two-year period. Huawei showed the most significant growth, Apple had the most dramatic seasonal fluctuations, and Samsung maintained its dominance of the smartphone market. Looking to the future, if these trends continue, Huawei may eventually overtake Samsung to become market leader.

Before you write

- Make sure that you understand the information presented in the graph.
- Make notes about:
  - what the information is about
  - what the numbers on each axis represent
  - what the lines on the graph represent
  - what changes the lines show
  - how the lines stand in relation to each other
  - which feature of the lines stands out most
  - what conclusions you can draw from the graph
- Organize your notes into logical paragraphs.

While you are writing

- Accuracy and clarity are key features of a good report. The language you use should be simple but academic in style.
- Organize the information so that you highlight the main trends or features in a logical way.
- Use specific words and phrases for describing graphs and charts.

Language bank

Summarizing data	Describing trends	Expressing quantities
between these two dates	*... doubled (to 70%)*	*25% of...*
by the end of the period	*... fluctuated*	*a greater/smaller proportion of... (than...)*
over a/the two-year period (between... and...)	*... had a series of rises/falls/recoveries*	*a quarter/third of...*
	... saw regular/occasional peaks/troughs	*fewer/more... than...*
the chart illustrates...	*... increased/decreased (by 60%)*	*half of...*
the figures show (that)...	*... increased/decreased significantly/gradually*	*more/less than half (that) of...*
the graph shows...	*... moved from second to third place (in terms of...)*	*over/under half (that) of...*
	... rose/fell (to 30%)	*the largest/smallest proportion of...*
	... showed (the most) dramatic/significant growth	*the percentage of...*
	... was in a strong position	*the vast majority of...*
	if these trends continue,... may...	*twice/three times as many... (as...)*

Checklist

Have I...

- shown that I understand the information presented in the graph? .... ☐
- included all the most important trends? .... ☐
- used a range of words and phrases to describe trends and quantities? .... ☐
- organized the description in a logical order? .... ☐
- summarized the main trends in my conclusion? .... ☐

Describing a process

You may be asked to write a description of a natural or man-made process shown in a diagram. The description should take the reader through each stage of the process step by step. It should mainly be written using the present simple passive form.

INTRODUCTION

1 Introduce and summarize the process. Include some useful background details.

DEVELOPMENT

2 Describe the initial stages in the process (chlorophyll helps tree/plant take in sunlight; water absorbed by roots; carbon dioxide enters plant).

3 Describe the remaining stages in the process (energy from sunlight used to process water and carbon dioxide, producing sugar and oxygen; sugar used by tree/plant to grow and deposited in leaves, etc.; oxygen enters atmosphere). Say how these stages are related to the initial stages.

CONCLUSION

4 Mention why the process is important (oxygen breathed by humans and other living organisms).

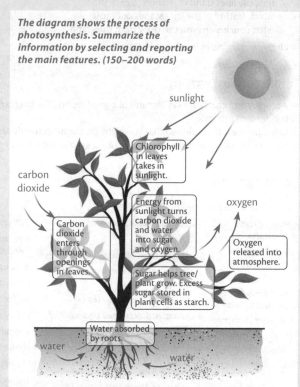

The diagram shows the process of photosynthesis. Summarize the information by selecting and reporting the main features. (150–200 words)

sunlight

carbon dioxide

Chlorophyll in leaves takes in sunlight.

Carbon dioxide enters through openings in leaves.

Energy from sunlight turns carbon dioxide and water into sugar and oxygen.

oxygen

Oxygen released into atmosphere.

Sugar helps tree/plant grow. Excess sugar stored in plant cells as starch.

Water absorbed by roots.

water

water

1 The diagram shows the main stages in the natural linear process of photosynthesis. Photosynthesis is the process by which plants and trees change light energy, carbon dioxide and water into sugar, oxygen and starch. There are six main stages in this process.

2 First of all, chlorophyll in the leaves of a tree or plant allows it to take in sunlight. Water in the soil is absorbed by the roots. At the same time carbon dioxide from the atmosphere enters the tree or plant through openings in the surface of the leaves.

3 Energy from the sunlight is used by the tree or plant to process the water and carbon dioxide, producing sugar and oxygen. The tree or plant uses the sugar to grow, and any extra sugar is stored in the plant cells as starch for later use. The oxygen enters the atmosphere.

4 The oxygen that is released into the atmosphere is breathed by humans and other living organisms. Photosynthesis is therefore one of the most essential processes for maintaining life on Earth.

Before you write

- Look at the diagram carefully and pick out the main features. Make sure that you understand the process.
- Note down the answers to the following questions:
  - Does the diagram show a natural or a man-made process?
  - Is the process cyclical (= it repeats itself and does not have a clear starting or end point) or linear (= it has a clear starting and end point)?
  - What is produced?
  - What is the sequence of events?
  - How does each stage relate to the next?

While you are writing

- Use formal and academic language.
- Make sure that your description of the process makes sense.
- You can use any essential vocabulary given in the diagram but do not copy whole sentences or phrases.
- Use a range of time expressions to describe the sequence of events.
- Use the present simple passive form where possible.

Language bank

Introducing the diagram	Describing the sequence of events	
... is the process by which...	*after that*	*secondly*
as you can see in the diagram	*at the same time*	*subsequently*
the diagram shows...	*finally*	*then*
there are... stages in this process	*first (of all)*	*next*
this is a diagram showing...	*firstly*	

Using the passive voice

When you talk about a process, use the present simple passive form of the verb to put the focus of the action on the object. The object goes at the beginning of the sentence:

__Water in the soil__ is absorbed by the roots.

Use *by* before the person or thing that performs the action at the end of the sentence:

Energy from the sunlight is used __by the tree or plant__...

Checklist

Have I...

- included all the stages in the process? .... ☐
- ordered the stages of the process in the correct sequence? .... ☐
- made the relationship between each stage clear? .... ☐
- written a description that matches the diagram? .... ☐

Writing emails

Emails can be used for formal correspondence such as job applications, neutral everyday correspondence and informal messages between friends and colleagues.

Writing an informal email

We generally use informal language when we write an email to somebody we know well, such as a family member, friend or work colleague. Some exams require candidates to write an informal email that demonstrates the ability to understand a particular situation and respond appropriately using one or more of the following functions:

- describing
- reporting
- suggesting
- persuading
- explaining
- giving information
- recommending

1 Write a 'Subject' line that clearly indicates what your email is about.

2 Use the appropriate form of address.

3 Start with a friendly greeting and refer to a previous text message or email.

4 Make a general comment about your friend's request and give your first recommendation.

5 Give your second and third recommendations.

6 Suggest when you might next contact your friend.

7 End with a closing phrase.

A friend is going to visit the town near where you live. She would like some advice about hotels. Write an email to her and recommend places to stay. (100–150 words)

1 Subject: Good hotels in Chester

2 Hi Greta,

3 How's it going? Thanks for your text message. Great to hear you're coming to Chester next month.

4 There are several hotels in this area, and I have a couple of suggestions for you. Firstly, I'd recommend a local hotel called The Townhouse. It's on Walton Street, and it's very quiet and reasonably priced. The rooms are quite small, but it's in an excellent location near the centre of town.

5 Another good option is the Royal Hotel. It's more expensive than The Townhouse, but it's VERY popular and there's an excellent restaurant next door. There's also a youth hostel near the station, which is clean and cheaper than the two hotels, but it can be a bit noisy at night.

6 Why don't you give me a call this evening and we can have a chat? Looking forward to meeting up.

7 All the best,
Daisy

Language bank

Starting your email

In an informal email use *Hi* or *Dear* followed by the reader's first name:

Hi Jenna,
Dear Sam,

great to hear (that)...
How are things?
How's it going?
I hope you're well
thanks for your text message/email

Making suggestions, giving information, etc.

I found the... really...
I have a couple of suggestions for you
I'd recommend...
it can bit very/quite/really...
it's more... than...
it's very/quite/really...
it's in a good location
let's...
Why don't we/you...?
you could...

Ending your email

looking forward to meeting up
have a good week
good luck with...

At the end of an informal email use one of the following closing phrases and a comma:

Best wishes,
All the best,
See you soon,

Use your first name on the next line after the closing phrase:

All the best,
Isla

Writing a formal email

We generally use formal language when we email somebody for the first time or when we are writing to a senior person of status, such as a professor or doctor. A good formal email is well planned, precise and clearly laid out.

1 The 'Subject' line should be short and clear.

2 Use the appropriate form of address.

3 Refer to any previous contact, for example a meeting or phone call. You should also explain why you are writing.

4 Give further details about the reason you are writing and the action you would like as a result.

5 Say what you want the reader to do or what you want to happen next.

6 End with a closing phrase.

You would like to carry out work experience in a hospital for two weeks in the summer holidays. Write an email to a doctor you met at a careers event. In your email:

- *explain your current situation*
- *ask about work experience*
- *give details about what you hope to achieve*

(150–200 words)

1 Subject: Work experience

2 Dear Dr Matthews,

3 Further to our conversation at the careers event in Oxford last week, I am writing to request a period of work experience at the Radley Infirmary. If possible, a period of two weeks starting at the end of July would be ideal.

4 As we discussed, I have just begun my final year of sixth form and I am hoping to attend medical school next year. Therefore, it would be very beneficial for me to gain some experience of working in a hospital environment. I am currently taking biology, chemistry, maths and history for my A levels. My aim is to become an expert in tropical diseases, which I understand is one of the Infirmary's specialist areas. I would be very grateful for the opportunity to gain some work experience in this field.

5 I look forward to your reply, and I would be happy to respond to any queries by email or phone. Please find my contact details below.

6 Yours sincerely,

Harry Grant

Mobile: +44 (0)3321 457690

Language bank

Starting your email

At the start of a formal email use one of the following opening phrases, with or without a comma:

Dear Sir/Madam, (reader is unknown)

To whom it may concern, (when writing to an institution rather than a person)

If the reader is known, use *Dear* and the person's title and family name, but not their first name:

Dear Professor Richardson,
Dear Ms Palmer,

Use *Dr* rather than *Doctor*:

Dear Dr Kingston,

Saying what you want

... would be ideal

I would be very grateful for...

I am writing to request...

if possible

it would be very beneficial for me to...

further to our conversation

as we discussed

Ending your email

I look forward to hearing from you

I look forward to your reply

please find my contact details below

At the end of a formal email use one of the following closing phrases and a comma:

Yours faithfully, (reader is unknown)

Yours sincerely, (formal, neutral)

Use your full name on the next line after the closing phrase. Do not use a title for yourself. You can include your contact details after your name:

Yours sincerely,
James Fielding
Mobile: 07731 450896

Before you write

- Make notes on the following:
  - Details of any previous correspondence
  - Your reason for writing
  - Any other relevant details
  - What future contact you will suggest
- Be clear about the purpose of the email and organize your ideas into paragraphs.

While you are writing

- Make the subject line short and relevant.
- Use a suitable greeting and closing phrase.
- Refer to a previous meeting, conversation or message.
- For formal emails:
  - state who you are and what your current situation is
  - state the purpose of the email clearly and politely
- For informal emails use suitable phrases for the relevant function (suggesting, explaining, etc.).
- Suggest how you or the reader will next get in touch.

Levels of formality

WHEN TO USE FORMAL, NEUTRAL AND INFORMAL LANGUAGE

When you write a letter or an email, you first need to consider how well you know the reader. Are they somebody you:

- are writing to for the first time or have never met? (formal or neutral)
- have written to or met before? (neutral)
- know very well, for example a friend or a close family member? (informal)

You also need to consider your relationship or status relative to the reader. Are they:

- a senior person of status, for example an academic, a manager or a doctor? (formal)
- somebody who provides a service or somebody in business outside your company? (neutral)
- somebody with the same or similar status as you, for example a classmate, a colleague at work or a friend? (informal)

The level of formality will determine the types of words and phrases you use in your correspondence.

REQUESTS AND INVITATIONS

In general, longer phrases indicate a higher level of formality while shorter, more direct phrases are used in less formal situations:

Formal	Informal
I would be very grateful if you could…	*Can you…?*
I would like to…/I wanted to…	*I want to…*
Would you care to join us for…?	*Do you want to come to…?*

EXCLAMATION MARKS, EMOTICONS AND INCOMPLETE SENTENCES (ELLIPSIS)

We only use these in informal emails:

Your presentation yesterday was amazing!   *Great lecture on Monday.*
I really enjoyed your talk on Monday ☺   *Loved your selfie.*

Checklist

Have I…

- used the appropriate level of formality in a consistent manner? .... ☐
- used an appropriate form of address, name format and closing phrase? .... ☐
- referred to any previous contact? .... ☐
- mentioned how you or the reader will next get in touch? .... ☐

Oxford Student's Dictionary
Speaking Tutor

Using the Oxford Student's Dictionary to improve your speaking

The dictionary can be just as helpful to you when you are preparing to speak as it is when you are writing. These pages show you how you can use it when you are getting ready for a speaking exam or when you are just interacting with other people in English.

At school as well as in conversation with friends, you have to put forward your own opinions, talk about yourself and everyday topics, and discuss other people's suggestions. In the Speaking Tutor you will find examples of these kinds of conversations.

Speaking model
In the Speaking Tutor you will find model texts that provide examples of how to speak and interact in various exam and speaking situations. Look carefully at these texts when you are preparing for a speaking test.

Before the exam
This section will help you to prepare for a speaking task by suggesting ways that you can practise your speaking and communication skills, research vocabulary areas, organize your ideas and develop good study habits.

During the exam
This section provides guidelines that you should try to remember when you are carrying out each type of speaking task.

Language bank
Key words and phrases are highlighted in the speaking models. Each Speaking Tutor section also has a **Language bank**, which contains useful words and phrases that you can use for each type of speaking task. Check that you are familiar with these phrases and know how to use them correctly.

Checklist
The checklist helps you check whether or not you have done everything you can to prepare for your speaking exam.

Preparing for speaking tests

Practise answering questions about yourself
Some exams require you to talk about yourself and answer the interviewer's questions. The section on Speaking Tutor pages **22–23** covers the types of questions the interviewer might ask and provides examples of the typical replies that will help you talk about yourself more clearly and accurately.

Practise using descriptive language
Some exams require you to talk continuously about a topic while the examiner checks your use of language and fluency. For this type of task you will need to learn phrases that help you to structure what you say and make your topic sound interesting. Examples of this type of language can be found on Speaking Tutor pages **24–25**.

Learn phrases for giving and justifying opinions
In some exams the test is carried out with a partner and you are required to take part in a discussion. You will be asked to put forward your opinions and to justify choices. The section on Speaking Tutor pages **26–27** highlights some of the functional language that you can use for this purpose.

Learn strategies for successful communication
You will not be able to produce perfect English sentences all the time, but there are strategies that you can use to keep a presentation or conversation going. For functional language that will help you communicate more successfully in all types of interactions, the section on Speaking Tutor page **28** provides a wide range of useful phrases.

Contents

Giving personal information

In some exams you will have a one-to-one interview with an examiner.
The aim of the test is to see how well you can communicate using spoken
English. The examiner is looking for fluency, accuracy, good pronunciation
and use of a range of grammatical structures and vocabulary.

Answer the examiner's questions about yourself, giving as much detail as possible.

What's your name, please?

> My name's Takeshi Nakamura.

Where are you from, Takeshi?

> I'm from Japan.

Whereabouts in Japan?

> Sapporo. It's the largest city on the island of Hokkaido.

Is that where you live?

> No, I live in Tokyo mostly — that's where I work. But I go back to Sapporo about twice a
> month to see my family. My mum and dad are a little elderly now and need somebody
> to check on them now and again.

What do you like most about where you live?

> The best thing about Tokyo is that you can eat in hundreds of different places. It's also
> pretty safe and easy to get around.

Can you tell me about what you do?

> I'm what some people call a 'salariman', so I work for a big corporation in Japan. I
> generally work long hours and take short holidays.

So what are you doing here?

> I'm currently doing an MBA at London Business School.

And what led you to take an MBA?

> Sorry, could you say that again?

Why did you decide to do an MBA?

> Well, there's a lot of competition for good jobs in Japan at the moment so I need to get
> ahead of the game. Fortunately, my company offered to sponsor me so it should work
> out financially in the long term.

It must be tough studying in a second language.

> Yes, to some extent that's true, but I'm already familiar with business concepts and
> business English, which means I don't have to worry too much about that side of it.
> Having said that, I have to admit that some of the written assignments are pretty tough.

And how important is English for your career?

> I hope English will help me to secure a position overseas or that it will at least improve
> my career prospects in my own country.

Speaking at CEFR level B2		
✓	Can interact with a degree of fluency and spontaneity that makes regular interaction with native speakers quite possible without strain for either party.	B2
✓	Has a good range of vocabulary and can vary formulation to avoid frequent repetition.	B2
✓	Does not make errors which cause misunderstanding.	B2
✓	Can correct slips and errors if he/she becomes conscious of them.	B2

Before the exam

- Prepare and learn the meaning of a list of questions that you might be asked.
- Do not write complete answers to possible questions and try to memorize them.
- Practise answering the questions with a friend.
- Record yourself practising your responses.
- Use and listen to as much English as possible.
- Practise saying your job title or the name of your course.

During the exam

- If you can, answer every question.
- Try to respond to questions as if you were in a normal conversation.
- Use grammatical structures and vocabulary you are confident with.
- Answer using the same tense as the question.
- Find ways to paraphrase words that you cannot remember.
- Make eye contact with the examiner.
- Ask the examiner to clarify any questions that you do not understand.
- Do not speak too quickly.
- Do not pause too long before responding.
- Do not give one-word answers or unnaturally long responses.

Language bank

Questions asking personal information	Giving personal information	Linking words and phrases
Can you tell me about…?	I hope English will help/improve…	also
How important is English for…?	I live in…	but
How long have you been studying English?	I work for…	fortunately
What do you like most about…?	I'm a/an…	having said that
What led you to…?	I'm currently…	well
What's your name?	my name's…	
Where are you from?		
Where do you live?		
Whereabouts in…?		
Why did you decide to…?		

Checklist

Have I…
- practised my answers with a friend?... ☐
- recorded myself giving my responses?.. ☐
- learned a range of linking words and phrases?.. ☐
- learned different ways of asking the examiner to clarify a question?......................... ☐

Talking about a topic

In some exams you are asked to talk about a topic for a short time. You are usually given a card containing details about the task at the beginning of the test and have a few minutes to prepare and make notes.

Describe a tourist attraction you once visited. You should say:

- **where you went**
- **when you went**
- **who you went with**
- **why you went**

1 Explain where you went, when you went and who you went with. Give some background information.

2 Give details about your journey to the place. Describe the appearance of the place and express your feelings or opinions.

3 Give a description of what happened next, including as much detail as possible.

1 One tourist attraction I visited a few years ago was the Eiffel Tower in Paris. I went there with my family — my mum, my sister and my grandparents. The main reason we went was that my grandparents had a dream of seeing it before they were too old. We went in late spring. The weather was wonderful, with blue skies and a warm breeze.

2 On the second day we took the underground, called the *Metro*, to Champ de Mars, the station nearest to the Eiffel Tower. When we came out of the station, we could only see the road and a few trees. My grandfather asked if I was sure this was the right stop and, to be honest, I wasn't certain, but we carried on and walked a little further down the road. We turned a corner and suddenly we saw the tower on our right. The five of us just stared upwards. The tower was absolutely huge but so elegant. Having seen it so many times in films and photos, it was quite extraordinary to see the real thing.

3 My mum and grandparents said they were happy just to sit nearby, take in the view and have an ice cream. My sister, on the other hand, had other ideas. 'Come on Stacey, let's go up the tower!' she said. She was ten and not afraid of anything. I, however, was a little older and had, how do you say, vertigo. I didn't want to disappoint her though, so I took a deep breath and said 'OK'. We bought our tickets and started climbing. The higher we climbed, the more scared I became. My legs started to shake. My sister bounded up the stairs as though she was at home. It seemed to take forever, but we finally got to the viewing platform — the view from the top was fantastic, and my sister was so excited. After we had taken a selfie, I was very glad to make our way back down to the ground, using the lift this time.

Speaking at CEFR level B2		
✓	Can give clear, detailed descriptions on subjects related to his/her field of interest.	B2
✓	Has a good range of vocabulary and can vary formulation to avoid frequent repetition.	B2
✓	Can use circumlocution and paraphrase to cover gaps in vocabulary and structure.	B2
✓	Can correct slips and errors if he/she becomes conscious of them.	B2

Before the exam

- Remind yourself of phrases for describing situations and giving opinions.
- Learn adverbs that will give more emphasis to your points (e.g. *definitely*, *really*).
- Look at past questions of this type for the exam that you are taking and practise responding as if you were in a real exam.

During the exam

- Try to base your talk on your personal experience rather than making up a story that did not happen.
- During the preparation time write down key words and actions rather than full sentences.
- Use the full time allowed when talking about your topic.
- Correct yourself briefly and continue if you make a mistake.
- Refer to your notes if you need to, but try to look at the examiner too.
- Do not start talking about a completely different topic.

Language bank

Describing situations, places, etc.	Using time expressions
he/she/it was very/absolutely/quite/so…	*a few years ago*
I went there with…	*after I/we had…*
… said (that)…	*finally*
the weather was…	*in late/early spring*
the… was/were very/absolutely/quite/so…	*on the second day*
they were very/absolutely/quite/so…	*suddenly*
we could see…	*when I/we…*

Making sentences sound more interesting

we went because… → the main reason we went was because/that…

I like the price → what I like about it is the price

it's special because it was a gift → the reason it's special is that it was a gift

I particularly liked the food → one thing I particularly liked was the food

Checklist

Have I…
- practised using sentence structures that make my points sound more interesting? . . . . ☐
- prepared and practised responding to past exam questions?. . . . . ☐
- learned a range of descriptive adjectives?. . . . . ☐
- learned different ways to correct myself if I make a mistake? . . . . ☐

Discussing opinions

You may be taking an exam where you and a partner have to discuss something, for example pictures that the examiner shows you. You may be asked to describe the pictures and interpret the ideas that they show. At the same time you may be required to express an opinion about them. You must make sure that you not only take part in the conversation, but that you also involve your partner.

Look at the pictures and discuss the following questions:
- *What are the good and bad points about a vegan diet?*
- *Which of the two pictures shows healthier food?*

Well, in my opinion, the best thing about a vegan diet is that it helps you to maintain a healthy weight. What do you think?

> I agree. And it's good for your overall health. I mean, on a vegan diet you have less chance of having heart problems, for example.

Yes, and vegan diets are generally better for the environment. I suppose a lot of people also avoid animal products because they're concerned about animal welfare.

> Uh huh, yeah, you're right. But on the other hand there are bad points too. I mean, you have to be careful that you get enough vitamins, don't you?

Yes, that's true. And other things like Omega-3. You have to make sure you get the right balance in your diet.

> Exactly. And it's really bad for you if you don't get enough calcium, which you get in dairy products like milk, right? What about you? What sort of diet do you have?

Not very healthy, I'm afraid. I feel a bit ashamed looking at the food in the first picture. And you?

> Me too. I don't eat much meat, but I eat too much fast food like pizza. So which diet do you think looks better in the pictures?

Well, let's see. I'd say that the diet in the first picture looks really healthy, but it makes me feel hungry.

> I know what you mean. But not in the second picture — there's a good balance of vegetables and fish.

Yes, and there's salad and potatoes.

> But there may be too many, what do you call it? The thing that gives you energy — 'car-' something.

Oh, carbohydrates. Yes, in the potatoes. But then again, individuals have to decide how much they eat, don't they? At least there's a choice.

> Yes, I suppose so. But some people don't have enough self-discipline. On the whole though, I think the diet in the second picture looks healthier.

I agree. And it looks tastier to me.

> That's true.

	Speaking at CEFR level B2/C1	
✓	Can take an active part in informal discussion in familiar contexts, commenting, putting point of view clearly, evaluating alternative proposals and making and responding to hypotheses.	B2
✓	Can initiate, maintain and end discourse appropriately with effective turn-taking.	B2
✓	Can relate own contribution skilfully to those of other speakers.	C1
✓	Has a good command of a broad lexical repertoire allowing gaps to be readily overcome with circumlocutions; little obvious searching for expressions or avoidance strategies. Good command of idiomatic expressions and colloquialisms.	C1

Before the exam

- Look at past questions of this type for the exam that you are taking and practise responding with a friend, as if you were in a real exam.
- Remind yourself of phrases you can use to express preferences, give reasons and justify choices.
- Learn different ways of inviting a response and responding to opinions.

During the exam

- Listen to what the other person says and respond to it.
- Use expressions like *Let's see* to give yourself some thinking time.
- Use questions or question tags like *isn't it?* to involve the other person in the conversation.
- Make sure you talk about each of the questions.
- Relate your comments to the photographs.
- Open out the discussion beyond the questions, but do not start talking about a completely different topic.
- Give personal opinions and relate the topic to your own life.
- Try not to give one-word answers.

Language bank

Giving opinions	Responding to opinions	Inviting a response
... is/are good/bad/better/worse for...	but (then again)	..., aren't they?
at least	exactly	..., doesn't he/she/it?
I suppose (that)...	I agree	..., don't you/they?
I think (that)...	I know what you mean	..., isn't he/she/it?
I'd say (that)...	I suppose so	..., right?
in my opinion	me too	And you?
it looks/seems... to me	that's true	Do you agree?
on the other hand	you're right	What about you?
on the whole		What do you think?
the best/worst thing about... is that...		

Checklist

Have I...

- learned key vocabulary relating to topic areas that might be covered in the exam? .... ☐
- practised responding to past exam questions with a partner? .... ☐
- learned different ways of inviting a response, including using question tags? .... ☐
- learned how to respond appropriately to comments and questions? .... ☐

Successful communication

Having a conversation in English does not mean that you have to produce perfectly formed sentences all the time. You should not worry that you might not know the exact word for something, or that you might not understand the meaning of everything that the other person says. Even in an exam situation you will be given credit for using strategies to keep the conversation running smoothly despite any gaps in your vocabulary or understanding. Here are some useful ideas to help you in everyday conversations or in more formal situations.

When you do not understand

When you are talking to somebody in English, you may not understand everything they say, but you can practise focusing on what is important. If you are asking for information, think about the key words that you will expect to hear. For example, if you are asking for directions, be prepared to hear words like *right*, *left*, *straight on*, etc. in the answer. Repeat key words back to the speaker to make sure you have understood correctly. Here are some useful phrases:

Saying that you do not understand
Sorry, I don't (quite) understand.
Sorry, I'm not sure I follow.

Checking that you understood correctly
Did you say five pounds fifty?
Do you mean 'pounds', as in money?
So are you saying...?

Asking what something means
Sorry, what does 'handy' mean?
What is 'cashback', exactly?

Asking for repetition
I beg your pardon? (formal)
Sorry?
Sorry, could you repeat that, please?
Sorry, what did you say your name was again?
Sorry, I missed what you said about... Could you tell me again?

Asking how you spell something
Could you spell that for me, please?
I haven't heard that name before. How do you spell it?

Asking somebody to speak more slowly
Could you speak more slowly, please?
Could you slow down a bit?
Sorry, that was a bit too fast for me.

When you do not know how to say something

Think about those words that are often used in dictionary definitions:

a type of...   *an organization that...*
a kind of...   *a person who...*
a device for...

They will help you explain what you mean even when you do not know the exact word.

Saying it another way
It's somewhere you go when you want to relax.
We saw a kind of animal with a long neck.

Saying that you don't know
I don't know how to say this in English — in German, we say...
I'm sorry, I can't think of the word in English.

Asking for a translation
How do you say 'bon appetit' in English?
What is the English equivalent of 'la bella figura'?

Explaining an idea from your language
I don't think there's an exact equivalent in English.
In my country, we normally say 'O-kaeri' when somebody arrives home.
Roughly speaking, 'hygge' means when you feel happy being with friends.

When you make a mistake

We all make mistakes when we speak, but it need not cause a problem if we can find a way to explain what we really meant. We also need time to think about what to say. There are expressions that we can use while we are thinking.

Words to use while you are thinking
Let me think for a moment.
Let's see,...
That's a good question.
Well,...

Correcting yourself
No, I meant...
..., or rather...
That's not exactly what I meant.
Sorry, I was trying to say 'price', not 'prize'.

Reference section

Contents

The language of literary criticism

Figurative language

Imagery is language that produces pictures in the mind. The term can be used to discuss the various stylistic devices listed below, especially **figures of speech** (= ways of using language to convey or suggest a meaning beyond the literal meaning of the words).

Metaphor is the imaginative use of a word or phrase to describe something else, to show that the two have the same qualities:
All the world's a stage
And all the men and women merely players.
(WILLIAM SHAKESPEARE, *As You Like It*)
In a **simile** the comparison between the two things is made explicit by the use of the words *as* or *like*:
I wandered lonely as a cloud
(WILLIAM WORDSWORTH, *Daffodils*)
Like as the waves make towards the pebbled shore,
So do our minutes hasten to their end.
(SHAKESPEARE, Sonnet 60)

Metonymy is the fact of referring to something by the name of something else closely connected with it, used especially as a form of shorthand for something familiar or obvious, as in 'I've been reading Shakespeare' instead of 'I've been reading the plays of Shakespeare'.

Allegory is a style of writing in which each character or event is a symbol representing a particular quality. In John Bunyan's *Pilgrim's Progress*, Christian escapes from the City of Destruction, travels through the Slough of Despond, visits Vanity Fair and finally arrives at the Celestial City. He meets characters such as the Giant Despair and Mr Worldly Wiseman, and is accompanied by Faithful and Hopeful.

Personification is the act of representing objects or qualities as human beings:
Love bade me welcome: yet my soul drew back,
Guilty of dust and sin.
(GEORGE HERBERT, *Love*)

Pathetic fallacy is the effect produced when animals and things are shown as having human feeling. For example, in John Milton's poem, *Lycidas*, the flowers are shown as weeping for the dead shepherd, Lycidas.

Patterns of sound

Alliteration is the use of the same letter or sound at the beginning of words that are close together. It was used systematically in Anglo-Saxon (= Old English) poetry but in modern English poetry is generally only used for a particular effect:
*On the **b**ald street **b**reaks the **b**lank day.*
(ALFRED, LORD TENNYSON, *In Memoriam*)

Assonance is the effect created when two syllables in words that are close together have the same vowel sound but different consonants, or the same consonants but different vowels:
*It seemed that out of battle I e**scaped***
Down some profound dull tunnel long since
* **scoop**ed...*
  (WILFRED OWEN, *Strange Meeting*)

Onomatopoeia is the effect produced when the words used contain similar sounds to the noises they describe:
murmuring of innumerable bees
(TENNYSON, *The Princess*)

Other stylistic effects

Irony is the use of words that say the opposite of what you really mean, often in order to make a critical comment.

Hyperbole is the use of exaggeration:
An hundred years should go to praise
Thine eyes and on thy forehead gaze
(ANDREW MARVELL, *To His Coy Mistress*)
An **oxymoron** is a phrase that combines two words that seem to be the opposite of each other:
Parting is such sweet sorrow
(SHAKESPEARE, *Romeo and Juliet*)
A **paradox** is a statement that contains two opposite ideas or seems to be impossible:
The Child is father of the Man.
(WORDSWORTH, *My heart leaps up...*)

Poetry

Lyric poetry is usually fairly short and expresses thoughts and feelings. Examples are Wordsworth's *Daffodils* and Dylan Thomas's *Fern Hill*.

Epic poetry can be much longer and deals with the actions of great men and women or the history of nations. Examples are Homer's *Iliad* and Virgil's *Aeneid*.

Narrative poetry tells a story, like Chaucer's *Canterbury Tales*, or Coleridge's *Rime of the Ancient Mariner*.

Dramatic poetry takes the form of a play, and includes the plays of Shakespeare (which also contain scenes in **prose**).

A **ballad** is a traditional type of narrative poem with short **verses** or **stanzas** and a simple **rhyme scheme** (= pattern of rhymes).

An **elegy** is a type of lyric poem that expresses sadness for someone who has died. Thomas Gray's *Elegy Written in a Country Churchyard* mourns all who lived and died quietly and never had the chance to be great.

An **ode** is a lyric poem that addresses a person or thing, or celebrates an event. John Keats wrote five great odes, including *Ode to a Nightingale*, *Ode to a Grecian Urn* and *To Autumn*.

Metre is the rhythm of poetry determined by the arrangement of stressed and unstressed, or long and short, syllables in each line of the poem.

Prosody is the theory and study of metre.

Iambic pentameter is the most common metre in English poetry. Each line consists of five **feet** (pentameter), each containing an unstressed syllable followed by a stressed syllable (iambic):

   /   /   /   /   /
The curfew tolls the knell of parting day
(GRAY, *Elegy*)

Most lines of iambic pentameter, however, are not absolutely regular in their pattern of stresses:

        /   /   /
Shall I compare thee to a summer's day?
(SHAKESPEARE, *Sonnet 18*)

A **couplet** is a pair of lines of poetry with the same metre, especially ones that rhyme:

For never was a story of more woe
Than this of Juliet and her Romeo.
(SHAKESPEARE, *Romeo and Juliet*)

A **sonnet** is a poem of 14 lines, written in iambic pentameter and with a fixed pattern of rhyme, often ending with a **rhyming couplet**.

Blank verse is poetry written in iambic pentameters that do not rhyme. A lot of Shakespeare's dramatic verse is in blank verse, as is Milton's epic *Paradise Lost*.

Free verse is poetry without a regular metre or rhyme scheme. Much twentieth-century poetry is written in free verse, for example T.S. Eliot's *The Waste Land*.

Drama

The different **genres** of drama include **comedy**, **tragedy** and **farce**.

Catharsis is the process of releasing and providing relief from strong emotions such as pity and fear by watching the same emotions being played out on stage.

A **deus ex machina** is an unexpected power or event that suddenly appears to resolve a situation that seems hopeless. It is often used to talk about a character in a play or story who only appears at the end.

Dramatic irony is when a character's words carry an extra meaning, especially because of what is going to happen that the character does not know about. For example, King Duncan in Shakespeare's *Macbeth* is pleased to accept Macbeth's hospitality, not knowing that Macbeth is going to murder him that night.

Hubris is too much pride or self-confidence, especially when shown by a tragic hero or heroine who tries to defy the gods or fate.

Nemesis is what happens when the hero or heroine's past mistakes or sins finally cause his or her downfall and death.

A **soliloquy** is a speech in a play for one character who is alone on the stage and speaks his or her thoughts aloud. The most famous soliloquy in English drama is Hamlet's beginning 'To be or not to be…'

Narrative

A **novel** is a **narrative** (= a story) long enough to fill a complete book. The story may be told by a **first-person narrator**, who is a character in the story and relates what happens to himself or herself, or there may be an **omniscient narrator** who relates what happens to all the characters in the third person.

A **short story** is a story that is short enough to be read from beginning to end without stopping.

The **denouement** is the end of a book or play, in which everything is explained or settled. It is often used to talk about mystery or detective stories.

Stream of consciousness is a style of writing used in novels that shows the continuous flow of a character's thoughts and feelings without using the usual methods of description or conversation. It was used particularly in the twentieth century by writers such as James Joyce and Virginia Woolf.

The periodic table of elements

The periodic table arranges all known elements according to their atomic numbers.

Periods →

- The horizontal rows of elements are called periods.
- A period contains elements with different properties.
- Each period (apart from the first) shows a trend from metallic to non-metallic properties.

Groups ↓

- The long vertical rows of elements are called groups.
- The groups are numbered 0 to 7.
- A group contains elements with similar chemical properties.
- Going down a group, the properties of the elements show trends.
- Hydrogen is unlike any other element — it is not part of a group.

Atomic mass

The **mass number** of an atom is the sum of the protons and neutrons in the nucleus of the atom.

223	223 = relative atomic mass
Fr	87 = atomic number
87	Fr = chemical symbol

Atomic number

The elements in the periodic table are arranged in order of increasing atomic number. This tells us the number of protons in the nucleus of the element. It also tells us the number of electrons in an atom.

Metals and non-metals

The black zigzag line divides the periodic table into metallic and non-metallic elements. The metals appear on the left and the non-metals appear on the right. There are many more metals than non-metals.

Transition elements

- These metals come between Group 2 and Group 3. They are generally hard metals with high boiling points.
- Many form coloured salts, for example copper(II) sulphate is blue, potassium manganate(VII) is purple and iron(II) sulphate is green.
- They form ions with different charges e.g. Cu^+ and Cu^{2+}, Fe^{2+} and Fe^{3+}. This means they can form different compounds with the same elements (e.g. copper(I) oxide Cu_2O, copper(II) oxide CuO).
- Some transition metals are useful catalysts for important reactions, for example vanadium(V) oxide in making sulphuric acid, iron for making ammonia and nickel for making margarine.

Groups: 1, 2, 3, 4, 5, 6, 7, 0

^{1}H, 1	

Transition elements

45 Sc 21	48 Ti 22	51 V 23	52 Cr 24	55 Mn 25	56 Fe 26	59 Co 27	59 Ni 28	64 Cu 29	65 Zn 30
89 Y 39	91 Zr 40	93 Nb 41	96 Mo 42	99 Tc 43	101 Ru 44	103 Rh 45	106 Pd 46	108 Ag 47	112 Cd 48
139 La 57	210 Hf 72	210 Ta 73	222 W 74	186 Re 75	190 Os 76	192 Ir 77	195 Pt 78	197 Au 79	201 Hg 80
227 Ac 89 *									

Elements not shown:
* 58–71 Lanthanoid series
* 90–103 Actinoid series
Elements that are produced artificially

Group 1 / 2:
7 Li 3, 9 Be 4
23 Na 11, 24 Mg 12
39 K 19, 40 Ca 20
85 Rb 37, 88 Sr 38
133 Cs 55, 137 Ba 56
223 Fr 87, 226 Ra 88

Groups 3–0:
11 B 5, 12 C 6, 14 N 7, 16 O 8, 19 F 9, 4 He 2
27 Al 13, 28 Si 14, 31 P 15, 32 S 16, 35 Cl 17, 20 Ne 10
70 Ga 31, 73 Ge 32, 75 As 33, 79 Se 34, 80 Br 35, 40 Ar 18
115 In 49, 119 Sn 50, 122 Sb 51, 128 Te 52, 127 I 53, 84 Kr 36
204 Tl 81, 207 Pb 82, 209 Bi 83, 210 Po 84, 210 At 85, 131 Xe 54
222 Rn 86

Names and symbols of the elements

NAME	SYMBOL	ATOMIC NUMBER	ATOMIC MASS	NAME	SYMBOL	ATOMIC NUMBER	ATOMIC MASS
actinium	Ac	89	227	mendelevium	Md	101	258
aluminium	Al	13	27	mercury	Hg	80	201
americium	Am	95	243	molybdenum	Mo	42	96
antimony	Sb	51	122	neodymium	Nd	60	144
argon	Ar	18	40	neon	Ne	10	20
arsenic	As	33	75	neptunium	Np	93	237
astatine	At	85	210	nickel	Ni	28	59
barium	Ba	56	137	niobium	Nb	41	93
berkelium	Bk	97	247	nitrogen	N	7	14
beryllium	Be	4	9	nobelium	No	102	259
bismuth	Bi	83	209	osmium	Os	76	190
boron	B	5	11	oxygen	O	8	16
bromine	Br	35	80	palladium	Pd	46	106
cadmium	Cd	48	112	phosphorus	P	15	31
caesium	Cs	55	133	platinum	Pt	78	195
calcium	Ca	20	40	plutonium	Pu	94	244
californium	Cf	98	251	polonium	Po	84	210
carbon	C	6	12	potassium	K	19	39
cerium	Ce	58	140	praseodymium	Pr	59	141
chlorine	Cl	17	35	promethium	Pm	61	145
chromium	Cr	24	52	protactinium	Pa	91	231
cobalt	Co	27	59	radium	Ra	88	226
copper	Cu	29	64	radon	Rn	86	222
curium	Cm	96	247	rhenium	Re	75	186
darmstadtium	Ds	110	281	rhodium	Rh	45	103
dysprosium	Dy	66	162	rubidium	Rb	37	85
einsteinium	Es	99	252	ruthenium	Ru	44	101
erbium	Er	68	167	samarium	Sm	62	150
europium	Eu	63	152	scandium	Sc	21	45
fermium	Fm	100	257	selenium	Se	34	79
fluorine	F	9	19	silicon	Si	14	28
francium	Fr	87	223	silver	Ag	47	108
gadolinium	Gd	64	157	sodium	Na	11	23
gallium	Ga	31	70	strontium	Sr	38	88
germanium	Ge	32	73	sulphur	S	16	32
gold	Au	79	197	tantalum	Ta	73	181
hafnium	Hf	72	178	technetium	Tc	43	99
helium	He	2	4	tellurium	Te	52	128
holmium	Ho	67	165	terbium	Tb	65	159
hydrogen	H	1	1	thallium	Tl	81	204
indium	In	49	115	thorium	Th	90	232
iodine	I	53	127	thulium	Tm	69	169
iridium	Ir	77	192	tin	Sn	50	119
iron	Fe	26	56	titanium	Ti	22	48
krypton	Kr	36	84	tungsten	W	74	184
lanthanum	La	57	139	uranium	U	92	238
lawrencium	Lr	103	260	vanadium	V	23	51
lead	Pb	82	207	xenon	Xe	54	131
lithium	Li	3	7	ytterbium	Yb	70	173
lutetium	Lu	71	175	yttrium	Y	39	89
magnesium	Mg	12	24	zinc	Zn	30	65
manganese	Mn	25	55	zirconium	Zr	40	91

Geographical names

These lists show the spelling and pronunciation of geographical names.

If there are different words for the country, adjective and person, all are given (e.g. **Denmark**; **Danish**; **a Dane**). To make the plural of a word for a person from a particular country, add -s except for *Swiss* and for words ending in -ese (e.g. *Japanese*), which stay the same, and for words that end in -man or -woman, which change to -men or -women.

(Inclusion in this list does not imply status as a sovereign state.)

COUNTRY OR CONTINENT	ADJECTIVE/PERSON
Afghanistan /æfˈgænɪstɑːn, -stæn/	Afghan /ˈæfgæn/
Africa /ˈæfrɪkə/	African /ˈæfrɪkən/
Albania /ælˈbeɪniə/	Albanian /ælˈbeɪniən/
Algeria /ælˈdʒɪəriə/	Algerian /ælˈdʒɪəriən/
America /əˈmerɪkə/	American /əˈmerɪkæn/
Andorra /ænˈdɔːrə/	Andorran /ænˈdɔːrən/
Angola /æŋˈɡəʊlə/	Angolan /æŋˈɡəʊlən/
Antarctica /ænˈtɑːktɪkə/	Antarctic /ænˈtɑːktɪk/
Antigua and Barbuda /ænˌtiːɡə ən bɑːˈbjuːdə/	Antiguan /ænˈtiːɡən/, Barbudan /bɑːˈbjuːdən/
Argentina /ˌɑːdʒənˈtiːnə/	Argentinian /ˌɑːdʒənˈtɪniən/, Argentine /ˈɑːdʒəntaɪn/
Armenia /ɑːˈmiːniə/	Armenian /ɑːˈmiːniən/
Asia /ˈeɪʒə, ˈeɪʃə/	Asian /ˈeɪʒn, ˈeɪʃn/
Australia /ɒˈstreɪliə/	Australian /ɒˈstreɪliən/
Austria /ˈɒstriə/	Austrian /ˈɒstriən/
Azerbaijan /ˌæzəbaɪˈdʒɑːn/	Azerbaijani /ˌæzəbaɪˈdʒɑːni/, Azeri /əˈzeəri/
(the) Bahamas /bəˈhɑːməz/	Bahamian /bəˈheɪmiən/
Bahrain /bɑːˈreɪn/	Bahraini /bɑːˈreɪni/
Bangladesh /ˌbæŋɡləˈdeʃ/	Bangladeshi /ˌbæŋɡləˈdeʃi/
Barbados /bɑːˈbeɪdɒs/	Barbadian /bɑːˈbeɪdiən/
Belarus /bel.əˈruːs/	Belarusian /ˌbeləˈruːsiən/, Belorussian /ˌbeləˈrʌʃn/
Belgium /ˈbeldʒəm/	Belgian /ˈbeldʒən/
Belize /bəˈliːz/	Belizean /bəˈliːziən/
Benin /beˈniːn/	Beninese /ˌbeniˈniːz/
Bhutan /buːˈtɑːn/	Bhutanese /ˌbuːtəˈniːz/
Bolivia /bəˈlɪviə/	Bolivian /bəˈlɪviən/
Bosnia and Herzegovina /ˌbɒzniə ən ˌhɜːtsəɡəˈviːnə/	Bosnian /ˈbɒzniən/, Herzegovinian /ˌhɜːtsəɡəˈvɪniən/
Botswana /bɒtˈswɑːnə/	Botswanan /bɒtˈswɑːnən/; person: a Motswana /mɒtˈswɑːnə/, people: Batswana /bætˈswɑːnə/
Brazil /brəˈzɪl/	Brazilian /brəˈzɪliən/
Brunei /bruːˈnaɪ/	Bruneian /bruːˈnaɪən/
Bulgaria /bʌlˈɡeəriə/	Bulgarian /bʌlˈɡeəriən/
Burkina Faso /bɜːˌkiːnə ˈfæsəʊ/	Burkinabe /bɜːˌkiːnəˈbeɪ/
Burma /ˈbɜːmə/ (officially Myanmar)	Burmese /bɜːˈmiːz/
Burundi /bʊˈrʊndi/	Burundian /bʊˈrʊndiən/
Cambodia /kæmˈbəʊdiə/	Cambodian /kæmˈbəʊdiən/
Cameroon /ˌkæməˈruːn/	Cameroonian /ˌkæməˈruːniən/
Canada /ˈkænədə/	Canadian /kəˈneɪdiən/
Cape Verde /ˌkeɪp ˈvɜːd/	Cape Verdean /ˌkeɪp ˈvɜːdiən/

COUNTRY OR CONTINENT	ADJECTIVE/PERSON
(the) Central African Republic /ˌsentrəl ˌæfrɪkən rɪˈpʌblɪk/	Central African /ˌsentrəl ˈæfrɪkən/
Chad /tʃæd/	Chadian /ˈtʃædiən/
Chile /ˈtʃɪli/	Chilean /ˈtʃɪliən/
China /ˈtʃaɪnə/	Chinese /tʃaɪˈniːz/
Colombia /kəˈlʌmbiə/	Colombian /kəˈlʌmbiən/
Comoros /ˈkɒmərəʊz/	Comoran /kəˈmɔːrən/
Congo /ˈkɒŋgəʊ/	Congolese /ˌkɒŋgəˈliːz/
(the) Democratic Republic of the Congo (DR Congo) /ˌdeməˌkrætɪk rɪˌpʌblɪk əv ðə ˈkɒŋgəʊ/	Congolese /ˌkɒŋgəˈliːz/
Costa Rica /ˌkɒstə ˈriːkə/	Costa Rican /ˌkɒstə ˈriːkən/
Côte d'Ivoire /ˌkəʊt diːˈvwɑː(r)/ ⊃ look at Ivory Coast	Ivorian /aɪˈvɔːriən/
Croatia /krəʊˈeɪʃə/	Croatian /krəʊˈeɪʃn/
Cuba /ˈkjuːbə/	Cuban /ˈkjuːbən/
Cyprus /ˈsaɪprəs/	Cypriot /ˈsɪpriət/
Czechia /ˈtʃekiə/, (the) Czech Republic /ˌtʃek rɪˈpʌblɪk/	Czech /tʃek/
Denmark /ˈdenmɑːk/	Danish /ˈdeɪnɪʃ/; a Dane /deɪn/
Djibouti /dʒɪˈbuːti/	Djiboutian /dʒɪˈbuːtiən/
Dominica /ˌdɒmɪˈniːkə/	Dominican /ˌdɒmɪˈniːkən/
(the) Dominican Republic /dəˌmɪnɪkən rɪˈpʌblɪk/	Dominican /dəˈmɪnɪkən/
East Timor /ˌiːst ˈtiːmɔː(r)/ ⊃ look at Timor-Leste	East Timorese /ˌiːst ˌtɪməˈriːz/
Ecuador /ˈekwədɔː(r)/	Ecuadorian, Ecuadorean /ˌekwəˈdɔːriən/
Egypt /ˈiːdʒɪpt/	Egyptian /iˈdʒɪpʃn/
El Salvador /ˌel ˈsælvədɔː(r)/	Salvadoran /ˌsælvəˈdɔːrən/, Salvadorean /ˌsælvəˈdɔːriən/
England /ˈɪŋglənd/	English /ˈɪŋglɪʃ/; an Englishman /ˈɪŋglɪʃmən/, an Englishwoman /ˈɪŋglɪʃwʊmən/
Equatorial Guinea /ˌekwətɔːriəl ˈgɪni/	Equatorial Guinean /ˌekwətɔːriəl ˈgɪniən/
Eritrea /ˌerɪˈtreɪə/	Eritrean /ˌerɪˈtreɪən/
Estonia /eˈstəʊniə/	Estonian /eˈstəʊniən/
Eswatini /ˌeswəˈtiːni/ ⊃ look at Swaziland	
Ethiopia /ˌiːθiˈəʊpiə/	Ethiopian /ˌiːθiˈəʊpiən/
Europe /ˈjʊərəp/	European /ˌjʊərəˈpiːən/
Fiji /ˈfiːdʒiː/	Fijian /fɪˈdʒiːən/
Finland /ˈfɪnlənd/	Finnish /ˈfɪnɪʃ/; a Finn /fɪn/
France /frɑːns/	French /frentʃ/; a Frenchman /ˈfrentʃmən/, a Frenchwoman /ˈfrentʃwʊmən/
Gabon /gæˈbɒn/	Gabonese /ˌgæbəˈniːz/
(the) Gambia /ˈgæmbiə/	Gambian /ˈgæmbiən/
Georgia /ˈdʒɔːdʒə/	Georgian /ˈdʒɔːdʒən/
Germany /ˈdʒɜːməni/	German /ˈdʒɜːmən/
Ghana /ˈgɑːnə/	Ghanaian /gɑːˈneɪən/
Great Britain /ˌgreɪt ˈbrɪtn/	British /ˈbrɪtɪʃ/; a Briton /ˈbrɪtn/
Greece /griːs/	Greek /griːk/
Grenada /grəˈneɪdə/	Grenadian /grəˈneɪdiən/
Guatemala /ˌgwɑːtəˈmɑːlə/	Guatemalan /ˌgwɑːtəˈmɑːlən/
Guinea /ˈgɪni/	Guinean /ˈgɪniən/
Guinea-Bissau /ˌgɪni bɪˈsaʊ/	Guinean /ˈgɪniən/
Guyana /gaɪˈænə, -ˈɑːnə/	Guyanese /ˌgaɪəˈniːz/

COUNTRY OR CONTINENT	ADJECTIVE/PERSON
Haiti /ˈheɪti/	Haitian /ˈheɪʃn/
Holland /ˈhɒlənd/ (officially the Netherlands)	
Honduras /hɒnˈdjʊərəs/	Honduran /hɒnˈdjʊərən/
Hungary /ˈhʌŋgəri/	Hungarian /hʌŋˈgeəriən/
Iceland /ˈaɪslənd/	Icelandic /aɪsˈlændɪk/; an Icelander /ˈaɪsləndə(r)/
India /ˈɪndiə/	Indian /ˈɪndiən/
Indonesia /ˌɪndəˈniːʒə/	Indonesian /ˌɪndəˈniːʒn/
Iran /ɪˈrɑːn, ɪˈræn/	Iranian /ɪˈreɪniən/
Iraq /ɪˈrɑːk, ɪˈræk/	Iraqi /ɪˈrɑːki, ɪˈræki/
Israel /ˈɪzreɪl/	Israeli /ɪzˈreɪli/
Italy /ˈɪtəli/	Italian /ɪˈtæliən/
(the) Ivory Coast /ˌaɪvəri ˈkəʊst/ ⊃ look at Côte d'Ivoire	Ivorian /aɪˈvɔːriən/
Jamaica /dʒəˈmeɪkə/	Jamaican /dʒəˈmeɪkən/
Japan /dʒəˈpæn/	Japanese /ˌdʒæpəˈniːz/
Jordan /ˈdʒɔːdn/	Jordanian /dʒɔːˈdeɪniən/
Kazakhstan /ˌkæzəkˈstɑːn, -ˈstæn/	Kazakh /ˈkæzæk/
Kenya /ˈkenjə/	Kenyan /ˈkenjən/
Kiribati /ˌkɪrɪˈbɑːti, ˈkɪrəbæs/	Kiribati /ˌkɪrɪˈbɑːti, ˈkɪrəbæs/, i-Kiribati /i ˌkɪrɪˈbɑːti, i ˈkɪrəbæs/
Korea /kəˈriːə/ ⊃ look at North Korea, South Korea	Korean /kəˈriːən/
Kuwait /kʊˈweɪt/	Kuwaiti /kʊˈweɪti/
Kyrgyzstan /ˌkɜːgɪˈstɑːn, -ˈstæn/	Kyrgyz /ˈkɜːgɪz/, Kyrgyzstani /ˌkɜːgɪˈstɑːni, -ˈstæni/
Laos /laʊs/	Lao /laʊ/, Laotian /ˈlaʊʃn/
Latvia /ˈlætviə/	Latvian /ˈlætviən/
Lebanon /ˈlebənən/	Lebanese /ˌlebəˈniːz/
Lesotho /ləˈsuːtuː, ləˈsəʊtəʊ/	person: a Mosotho /məˈsuːtuː, məˈsəʊtəʊ/, people: Basotho /bəˈsuːtuː, bəˈsəʊtəʊ/
Liberia /laɪˈbɪəriə/	Liberian /laɪˈbɪəriən/
Libya /ˈlɪbiə/	Libyan /ˈlɪbiən/
Liechtenstein /ˈlɪktənstaɪn, ˈlɪxt-/	Liechtenstein /ˈlɪktənstaɪn, ˈlɪxt-/, a Liechtensteiner /ˈlɪktenstaɪnə(r), ˈlɪxt-/
Lithuania /ˌlɪθjuˈeɪniə/	Lithuanian /ˌlɪθjuˈeɪniən/
Luxembourg /ˈlʌksəmbɜːg/	Luxembourg /ˈlʌksəmbɜːg/; a Luxembourger /ˈlʌksəmbɜːgə(r)/
Madagascar /ˌmædəˈgæskə(r)/	Madagascan /ˌmædəˈgæskən/, Malagasy /ˌmæləˈgæsi/
Malawi /məˈlɑːwi/	Malawian /məˈlɑːwiən/
Malaysia /məˈleɪʒə, -ˈleɪziə/	Malaysian /məˈleɪʒn, -ˈleɪziən/
(the) Maldives /ˈmɔːldiːvz/	Maldivian /mɔːlˈdɪviən/
Mali /ˈmɑːli/	Malian /ˈmɑːliən/
Malta /ˈmɔːltə/	Maltese /mɔːlˈtiːz/
(the) Marshall Islands /ˈmɑːʃl aɪləndz/	Marshallese /ˌmɑːʃəˈliːz/
Mauritania /ˌmɒrɪˈteɪniə/	Mauritanian /ˌmɒrɪˈteɪniən/
Mauritius /məˈrɪʃəs/	Mauritian /məˈrɪʃn/
Mexico /ˈmeksɪkəʊ/	Mexican /ˈmeksɪkən/
Micronesia /ˌmaɪkrəˈniːʒə, -ˈniːziə/	Micronesian /ˌmaɪkrəˈniːʒn, -ˈniːziən/
Moldova /mɒlˈdəʊvə/	Moldovan /mɒlˈdəʊvn/
Monaco /ˈmɒnəkəʊ/	Monégasque /ˌmɒnɪˈgæsk/
Mongolia /mɒŋˈgəʊliə/	Mongolian /mɒŋˈgəʊliən/, Mongol /ˈmɒŋgl/

COUNTRY OR CONTINENT	ADJECTIVE/PERSON
Montenegro /ˌmɒntɪˈniːgrəʊ/	Montenegrin /ˌmɒntɪˈniːgrɪn/
Morocco /məˈrɒkəʊ/	Moroccan /məˈrɒkən/
Mozambique /ˌməʊzæmˈbiːk/	Mozambican /ˌməʊzæmˈbiːkən/
Myanmar /ˈmjænmɑː(r)/ ɔ look at **Burma**	
Namibia /nəˈmɪbiə/	Namibian /nəˈmɪbiən/
Nauru /ˈnaʊruː/	Nauruan /naʊˈruːən/
Nepal /nəˈpɔːl/	Nepalese /ˌnepəˈliːz/
(the) Netherlands /ˈneðələndz/	Dutch /dʌtʃ/; a Dutchman /ˈdʌtʃmən/, a Dutchwoman /ˈdʌtʃwʊmən/
New Zealand (NZ) /ˌnjuː ˈziːlənd/	New Zealand /ˌnjuː ˈziːlənd/; a New Zealander /ˌnjuː ˈziːləndə(r)/
Nicaragua /ˌnɪkəˈrægjuə/	Nicaraguan /ˌnɪkəˈrægjuən/
Niger /niːˈʒeə(r)/	Nigerien /niːˈʒeəriən/
Nigeria /naɪˈdʒɪəriə/	Nigerian /naɪˈdʒɪəriən/
North Korea /ˌnɔːθ kəˈriːə/ ɔ look at **Korea, South Korea**	North Korean /ˌnɔːθ kəˈriːən/
North Macedonia /ˌnɔːθ mæsəˈdəʊniə/	North Macedonian /ˌnɔːθ mæsəˈdəʊniən/
Northern Ireland /ˌnɔːðən ˈaɪələnd/	Northern Irish /ˌnɔːðən ˈaɪrɪʃ/
Norway /ˈnɔːweɪ/	Norwegian /nɔːˈwiːdʒən/
Oman /əʊˈmɑːn/	Omani /əʊˈmɑːni/
Pakistan /ˌpɑːkɪˈstɑːn/	Pakistani /ˌpɑːkɪˈstɑːni/
Palau /pəˈlaʊ/	Palauan /pəˈlaʊən/
Panama /ˈpænəmɑː/	Panamanian /ˌpænəˈmeɪniən/
Papua New Guinea (PNG) /ˌpæpjuə ˌnjuː ˈgɪni/	Papua New Guinean /ˌpæpjuə ˌnjuː ˈgɪniən/
Paraguay /ˈpærəgwaɪ/	Paraguayan /ˌpærəˈgwaɪən/
Peru /pəˈruː/	Peruvian /pəˈruːviən/
(the) Philippines /ˈfɪlɪpiːnz/	Philippine /ˈfɪlɪpiːn/; a Filipino /ˌfɪlɪˈpiːnəʊ/, a Filipina /ˌfɪlɪˈpiːnə/
Poland /ˈpəʊlənd/	Polish /ˈpəʊlɪʃ/; a Pole /pəʊl/
Portugal /ˈpɔːtʃʊgl/	Portuguese /ˌpɔːtʃʊˈgiːz/
Qatar /kəˈtɑː(r), ˈkætɑː(r)/	Qatari /kəˈtɑːri/
the Republic of Ireland /ðə rɪˌpʌblɪk əv ˈaɪələnd/	Irish /ˈaɪrɪʃ/; an Irishman /ˈaɪrɪʃmən/, an Irishwoman /ˈaɪrɪʃwʊmən/
Romania /ruˈmeɪniə/	Romanian /ruˈmeɪniən/
Russia /ˈrʌʃə/	Russian /ˈrʌʃn/
Rwanda /ruˈændə/	Rwandan /ruˈændən/
Samoa /səˈməʊə/	Samoan /səˈməʊən/
San Marino /ˌsæn məˈriːnəʊ/	
São Tomé and Príncipe /ˌsaʊ təˌmeɪ ən ˈprɪnsɪpeɪ/	
Saudi Arabia /ˌsaʊdi əˈreɪbiə/	Saudi /ˈsaʊdi/, Saudi Arabian /ˌsaʊdi əˈreɪbiən/
Scotland /ˈskɒtlənd/	Scottish /ˈskɒtɪʃ/; a Scot /skɒt/
Senegal /ˌsenɪˈgɔːl/	Senegalese /ˌsenɪgəˈliːz/
Serbia /ˈsɜːbiə/	Serbian /ˈsɜːbiən/, Serb /sɜːb/
(the) Seychelles /seɪˈʃelz/	Seychellois /ˌseɪʃelˈwɑː/
Sierra Leone /siˌerə liˈəʊn/	Sierra Leonean /siˌerə liˈəʊniən/
Singapore /ˌsɪŋəˈpɔː(r)/	Singaporean /ˌsɪŋəˈpɔːriən/
Slovakia /sləˈvækiə/	Slovak /ˈsləʊvæk/, Slovakian /sləˈvækiən/
Slovenia /sləˈviːniə/	Slovene /ˈsləʊviːn/, Slovenian /sləˈviːniən/
(the) Solomon Islands /ˈsɒləmən aɪləndz/	a Solomon Islander /ˈsɒləmən aɪləndə(r)/
Somalia /səˈmɑːliə/	Somali /səˈmɑːli/

COUNTRY OR CONTINENT	ADJECTIVE/PERSON
South Africa /ˌsaʊθ ˈæfrɪkə/	South African /ˌsaʊθ ˈæfrɪkən/
South Korea /ˌsaʊθ kəˈriːə/ ⊃ look at Korea, North Korea	South Korean /ˌsaʊθ kəˈriːən/
South Sudan /ˌsaʊθ suˈdɑːn, -ˈdæn/	South Sudanese /ˌsaʊθ suːdəˈniːz/
Spain /speɪn/	Spanish /ˈspænɪʃ/; a Spaniard /ˈspænjəd/
Sri Lanka /ˌsriː ˈlæŋkə/	Sri Lankan /ˌsriː ˈlæŋkən/
St Kitts and Nevis /snt ˌkɪts ən ˈniːvɪs/	Kittitian /kɪˈtɪʃn/, Nevisian /niːˈvɪsiən/
St Lucia /snt ˈluːʃə/	St Lucian /snt ˈluːʃən/
St Vincent and the Grenadines /snt ˌvɪnsnt ən ðə ˈgrenədiːnz/	Vincentian /vɪnˈsenʃn/
Sudan /suˈdɑːn, -ˈdæn/	Sudanese /ˌsuːdəˈniːz/
Suriname /ˌsʊərɪˈnɑːm, -ˈnæm/	Surinamese /ˌsʊərɪnəˈmiːz/
Swaziland /ˈswɑːzilænd/ ⊃ look at Eswatini	Swazi /ˈswɑːzi/
Sweden /ˈswiːdn/	Swedish /ˈswiːdɪʃ/; a Swede /swiːd/
Switzerland /ˈswɪtsələnd/	Swiss /swɪs/
Syria /ˈsɪriə/	Syrian /ˈsɪriən/
Tajikistan /tæˌdʒiːkɪˈstɑːn, -ˈstæn/	Tajik /tæˈdʒiːk/
Tanzania /ˌtænzəˈniːə/	Tanzanian /ˌtænzəˈniːən/
Thailand /ˈtaɪlænd, -lənd/	Thai /taɪ/
Timor-Leste /ˌtiːmɔː ˈlesteɪ, ˈlest/ ⊃ look at East Timor	
Togo /ˈtəʊgəʊ/	Togolese /ˌtəʊgəˈliːz/
Tonga /ˈtɒŋə, ˈtɒŋgə/	Tongan /ˈtɒŋən, ˈtɒŋgən/
Trinidad and Tobago /ˌtrɪnɪdæd ən təˈbeɪgəʊ/	Trinidadian /ˌtrɪnɪˈdædiən/, Tobagan /təˈbeɪgən/, Tobagonian /ˌtəʊbəˈgəʊniən/
Tunisia /tjuˈnɪziə/	Tunisian /tjuˈnɪziən/
Turkey /ˈtɜːki/	Turkish /ˈtɜːkɪʃ/; a Turk /tɜːk/
Turkmenistan /tɜːkˌmenɪˈstɑːn, -ˈstæn/	Turkmen /ˈtɜːkmən/
Tuvalu /tuːˈvɑːluː/	Tuvaluan /ˌtuːvəˈluːən, ˌtuːˈvɑːluən/
Uganda /juˈgændə/	Ugandan /juˈgændən/
Ukraine /juːˈkreɪn/	Ukrainian /juːˈkreɪniən/
(the) United Arab Emirates (UAE) /juˌnaɪtɪd ˌærəb ˈemɪrəts/	Emirati /ˌemɪˈrɑːti/
(the) United Kingdom (UK) /juˌnaɪtɪd ˈkɪŋdəm/	British /ˈbrɪtɪʃ/; a Briton /ˈbrɪtn/
(the) United States of America (USA) /juˌnaɪtɪd ˌsteɪts əv əˈmerɪkə/	American /əˈmerɪkən/
Uruguay /ˈjʊərəgwaɪ/	Uruguayan /ˌjʊərəˈgwaɪən/
Uzbekistan /ʊzˌbekɪˈstɑːn, -ˈstæn/	Uzbek /ˈʊzbek/, Uzbekistani /ʊzˌbekɪˈstɑːni/
Vanuatu /ˌvænuˈɑːtuː/	Vanuatuan /ˌvænuˈɑːtuən/, ni-Vanuatu /ˌniː ˌvænuˈɑːtu/
(the) Vatican City /ˌvætɪkən ˈsɪti/	
Venezuela /ˌvenəˈzweɪlə/	Venezuelan /ˌvenəˈzweɪlən/
Vietnam /ˌviːetˈnɑːm, -ˈnæm/	Vietnamese /ˌviːetnəˈmiːz/
Wales /weɪlz/	Welsh /welʃ/; a Welshman /ˈwelʃmən/, a Welshwoman /ˈwelʃwʊmən/
Yemen /ˈjemən/	Yemeni /ˈjeməni/
Zambia /ˈzæmbiə/	Zambian /ˈzæmbiən/
Zimbabwe /zɪmˈbɑːbweɪ, -wi/	Zimbabwean /zɪmˈbɑːbwiən/

Irregular verbs

In this list you will find the infinitive form of the irregular verb followed by the past tense and the past participle. Where two forms are given, look up the verb in the main part of the dictionary to see whether there is a difference in the meaning.

INFINITIVE	PAST TENSE	PAST PARTICIPLE	INFINITIVE	PAST TENSE	PAST PARTICIPLE
arise	arose	arisen	draw	drew	drawn
awake	awoke	awoken	dream	dreamt, dreamed	dreamt, dreamed
babysit	babysat	babysat	drink	drank	drunk
bear	bore	borne	drive	drove	driven
beat	beat	beaten	dwell	dwelt, dwelled	dwelt, dwelled
become	became	become	eat	ate	eaten
befall	befell	befallen	fall	fell	fallen
begin	began	begun	feed	fed	fed
bend	bent	bent	feel	felt	felt
beseech	besought, beseeched	besought, beseeched	fight	fought	fought
beset	beset	beset	find	found	found
bet	bet	bet	fit	fitted (AmE usually fit)	fitted (AmE usually fit)
bid	bid	bid	flee	fled	fled
bind	bound	bound	fling	flung	flung
bite	bit	bitten	fly	flew	flown
bleed	bled	bled	forbear	forbore	forborne
blow	blew	blown	forbid	forbade	forbidden
break	broke	broken	forecast	forecast, forecasted	forecast, forecasted
breastfeed	breastfed	breastfed	foresee	foresaw	foreseen
breed	bred	bred	forget	forgot	forgotten
bring	brought	brought	forgive	forgave	forgiven
broadcast	broadcast	broadcast	forgo, forego	forwent, forewent	forgone, foregone
browbeat	browbeat	browbeaten	forsake	forsook	forsaken
build	built	built	freeze	froze	frozen
burn	burnt, burned	burnt, burned	get	got	got (AmE also, spoken gotten)
burst	burst	burst	give	gave	given
bust	bust, busted	bust, busted	go	went	gone, been
buy	bought	bought	grind	ground	ground
cast	cast	cast	grow	grew	grown
catch	caught	caught	hang	hung, hanged	hung, hanged
choose	chose	chosen	have	had	had
cling	clung	clung	hear	heard	heard
come	came	come	hide	hid	hidden
cost	cost, costed	cost, costed	hit	hit	hit
creep	crept	crept	hold	held	held
cut	cut	cut	hurt	hurt	hurt
deal	dealt	dealt			
dig	dug	dug			
dive	dived (AmE also dove)	dived			
do	did	done			

INFINITIVE	PAST TENSE	PAST PARTICIPLE	INFINITIVE	PAST TENSE	PAST PARTICIPLE
inlay	inlaid	inlaid	plead	pleaded (*AmE also* pled)	pleaded (*AmE also* pled)
input	input, inputted	input, inputted	proofread	proofread	proofread
keep	kept	kept	prove	proved	proved (*especially AmE* proven)
kneel	knelt (*especially AmE* kneeled)	knelt (*especially AmE* kneeled)	put	put	put
knit	knitted, knit	knitted, knit	quit	quit, quitted	quit, quitted
know	knew	known	read	read	read
lay	laid	laid	rebuild	rebuilt	rebuilt
lead	led	led	redo	redid	redone
lean	leaned (*BrE also* leant)	leaned (*BrE also* leant)	remake	remade	remade
			repay	repaid	repaid
leap	leapt, leaped	leapt, leaped	retell	retold	retold
learn	learnt, learned	learnt, learned	rethink	rethought	rethought
leave	left	left	rewind	rewound	rewound
lend	lent	lent	rewrite	rewrote	rewritten
let	let	let	rid	rid	rid
lie[1]	lay	lain	ride	rode	ridden
light	lit, lighted	lit, lighted	ring	rang, ringed	rung, ringed
lose	lost	lost	rise	rose	risen
make	made	made	run	ran	run
mean	meant	meant	saw	sawed	sawn (*AmE also* sawed)
meet	met	met			
mislay	mislaid	mislaid	say	said	said
mislead	misled	misled	see	saw	seen
misread	misread	misread	seek	sought	sought
misspell	misspelled, misspelt	misspelled, misspelt	sell	sold	sold
			send	sent	sent
mistake	mistook	mistaken	set	set	set
misunderstand	misunderstood	misunderstood	sew	sewed	sewn, sewed
mow	mowed	mown, mowed	shake	shook	shaken
offset	offset	offset	shear	sheared	shorn, sheared
outdo	outdid	outdone	shed	shed	shed
outgrow	outgrew	outgrown	shine	shone	shone
output	output	output	shoe	shod	shod
outrun	outran	outrun	shoot	shot	shot
overcome	overcame	overcome	show	showed	shown
overdo	overdid	overdone	shrink	shrank, shrunk	shrunk
overhang	overhung	overhung	shut	shut	shut
overhear	overheard	overheard	sing	sang	sung
overpay	overpaid	overpaid	sink	sank	sunk
override	overrode	overridden	sit	sat	sat
overrun	overran	overrun	slay	slew	slain
oversee	oversaw	overseen	sleep	slept	slept
oversleep	overslept	overslept	slide	slid	slid
overtake	overtook	overtaken	sling	slung	slung
overthrow	overthrew	overthrown	slink	slunk	slunk
pay	paid	paid	slit	slit	slit

INFINITIVE	PAST TENSE	PAST PARTICIPLE	INFINITIVE	PAST TENSE	PAST PARTICIPLE
smell	smelt (*BrE also* smelled)	smelt (*BrE also* smelled)	swim	swam	swum
sneak	sneaked (*especially AmE, spoken* snuck)	sneaked (*especially AmE, spoken* snuck)	swing	swung	swung
			take	took	taken
			teach	taught	taught
			tear	tore	torn
sow	sowed	sown, sowed	tell	told	told
speak	spoke	spoken	think	thought	thought
speed	speeded, sped	speeded, sped	throw	threw	thrown
spell	spelt, spelled	spelt, spelled	thrust	thrust	thrust
spend	spent	spent	tread	trod	trodden, trod
spill	spilled, spilt	spilled, spilt	undercut	undercut	undercut
spin	spun	spun	undergo	underwent	undergone
spit	spat, (*especially AmE* spit)	spat, (*especially AmE* spit)	underlie	underlay	underlain
			underpay	underpaid	underpaid
split	split	split	understand	understood	understood
spoil	spoiled (*BrE also* spoilt)	spoiled (*BrE also* spoilt)	undertake	undertook	undertaken
			underwrite	underwrote	underwritten
			undo	undid	undone
spread	spread	spread	unwind	unwound	unwound
spring	sprang	sprung	uphold	upheld	upheld
stand	stood	stood	upset	upset	upset
steal	stole	stolen	wake	woke	woken
stick	stuck	stuck	wear	wore	worn
sting	stung	stung	weave	wove, weaved	woven, weaved
stink	stank, stunk	stunk			
stride	strode	—	weep	wept	wept
strike	struck	struck	wet	wet, wetted	wet, wetted
string	strung	strung	win	won	won
strive	strove, strived	striven, strived	wind³	wound	wound
			withdraw	withdrew	withdrawn
sublet	sublet	sublet	withhold	withheld	withheld
swear	swore	sworn	withstand	withstood	withstood
sweep	swept	swept	wring	wrung	wrung
swell	swelled	swelled, swollen	write	wrote	written

be

Present tense			Past tense	
FULL FORMS	**SHORT FORMS**	**NEGATIVE SHORT FORMS**	**FULL FORMS**	**NEGATIVE SHORT FORMS**
I am	I'm	I'm not	I was	I wasn't
you are	you're	you aren't/you're not	you were	you weren't
he is	he's	he isn't/he's not	he was	he wasn't
she is	she's	she isn't/she's not	she was	she wasn't
it is	it's	it isn't/it's not	it was	it wasn't
we are	we're	we aren't/we're not	we were	we weren't
they are	they're	they aren't/they're not	they were	they weren't

Punctuation

Full stop (.)

A **full stop** is used at the end of a sentence, unless the sentence is a question or an exclamation:

We're leaving now.

It is often used in abbreviations (e.g., *a.m.*, *etc.*, *Jan.*).

Full stops are also used in internet and email addresses (said 'dot'):

http://www.oup.com

Comma (,)

A **comma** separates words in a list, although it is often omitted before *and*:

It's a play about children, fairies and pirates.

A comma also separates parts of a sentence:

Peter refuses to leave Neverland, but Wendy returns to her family.

In relative clauses, commas are used around a phrase that adds some new, but not essential, information:

The Pennine Hills, which are very popular with walkers, are situated between Lancashire and Yorkshire.

Do not use commas before or after a clause that defines the noun it follows:

The hills that separate Lancashire from Yorkshire are called the Pennines.

A comma is also used before a quotation and before or after direct speech:

Fiona said, 'I'll help you.'

'I'll help you', said Fiona, 'but you'll have to wait until Monday.'

Exclamation mark (!)

An **exclamation mark** is used at the end of a sentence to show surprise, joy, anger or shock:

'Don't speak to me like that!' she shouted.

What a glorious day for a wedding!

An exclamation mark is also used after an exclamation or a word describing a loud sound:

Bye!   Ow!   Crash!

Question mark (?)

A **question mark** is used at the end of a direct question:

'Can you drive?' asked Laura.

Do not use a question mark after an indirect question:

Jenny asked who the man was.

Brackets ( )

Brackets are used when the writer adds information, an explanation, a comment, etc. to something in the text. The text would still make sense if the information in brackets was removed:

Captain Hook (usually played by the same actor as Wendy's father) terrifies the children.

Numbers or letters used in sentences may also have a bracket after them or brackets around them:

The phone has three main advantages: 1) its compact size, 2) its low price and 3) the quality of its camera.

Dash (—)

Dashes are used when an additional comment or additional information is added to a sentence:

Peter is usually — but not always — played by a woman.

A dash can also be used near the end of a sentence before a phrase that sums up the rest of the sentence:

The burglars had taken the TV, the computer, the jewellery — everything of value.

Hyphen (-)

A **hyphen** is used in many cases where two words have been joined together to form one (e.g. *self-service*).

It is also sometimes used to link a prefix to a word (e.g. *non-violent*).

Hyphens are used in compound numbers (e.g. *thirty-four*).

They are also used to separate long words that will not fit on one line.

Colon (:)

A **colon** tells the reader that something is coming next, for example a list:
There is a choice of main course: spaghetti and meatballs, vegetable curry and fish and chips.

Semicolon (;)

A **semicolon** is used to divive two parts of a sentence:
She looked up and frowned; the boy ran away.

Apostrophe (')

An **apostrophe** replaces a missing letter or letters in contracted forms:
I'd (= I had)
isn't (= is not)
we'll (= we will)
won't (= will not)
We also use apostrophes with *s* to show that a person or thing belongs to somebody:
Daniel's mother
Eliza's scarf
my friend's car

With some clauses that end in *s*, another *s* is not always added:
James's/James' name
Notice the position of the apostrophe with singular and plural nouns:
the girl's keys (= the keys belonging to the girl)
the girls' keys (= the keys belonging to the girls)

Quotation marks (' ' or " ")

Quotation marks are used to show the words that somebody said:
'Come and see,' said Martin.
'Oh, no!' said Martin. 'Come and see what's happened.'
Angela shouted, 'Over here!'

They are also used to show what somebody thought, when the thoughts are presented like speech:
'Will they get here on time?' she wondered.

Quotation marks are also used around the titles of books, plays, films, etc.:
'Toy Story' was the first film I ever saw.
'Have you read "Emma"?' he asked.
This quotation is from 'The geology of Great Britain'.

Ellipsis (...)

An **ellipsis** is used to show that words have been left out, especially from a quotation or at the end of a conversation:
'Please help me, I can't...' He burst into tears.

Slash/Oblique (/)

A **slash** is used to separate alternative words or phrases:
a dessert and/or cheese
single/married/widowed/divorced

It is also used in internet and email addresses to separate the different elements (often said 'forward slash').

Expressions using numbers

Numbers

1	one	1st	first
2	two	2nd	second
3	three	3rd	third
4	four	4th	fourth
5	five	5th	fifth
6	six	6th	sixth
7	seven	7th	seventh
8	eight	8th	eighth
9	nine	9th	ninth
10	ten	10th	tenth
11	eleven	11th	eleventh
12	twelve	12th	twelfth
13	thirteen	13th	thirteenth
14	fourteen	14th	fourteenth
15	fifteen	15th	fifteenth
16	sixteen	16th	sixteenth
17	seventeen	17th	seventeenth
18	eighteen	18th	eighteenth
19	nineteen	19th	nineteenth
20	twenty	20th	twentieth
21	twenty-one	21st	twenty-first
22	twenty-two	22nd	twenty-second
30	thirty	30th	thirtieth
40	forty	40th	fortieth
50	fifty	50th	fiftieth
60	sixty	60th	sixtieth
70	seventy	70th	seventieth
80	eighty	80th	eightieth
90	ninety	90th	ninetieth
100	a/one hundred*	100th	hundredth
101	a/one hundred and one*	101st	hundred and first
200	two hundred	200th	two hundredth
1 000	a/one thousand*	1 000th	thousandth
10 000	ten thousand	10 000th	ten thousandth
100 000	a/one hundred thousand*	100 000th	hundred thousandth
1 000 000	a/one million*	1 000 000th	millionth

697	*six hundred and ninety-seven*
3 402	*three thousand, four hundred and two*
80 534	*eighty thousand, five hundred and thirty-four*

* You use *one hundred*, *one thousand*, etc. instead of *a hundred*, *a thousand*, etc. when it is important to stress that you mean *one* (not *two*, for example). In numbers over a thousand, you use a comma or a small space (e.g. *1,200*, *1 200*).

Roman numerals

I	one	V	five	IX	nine	L	fifty
II	two	VI	six	X	ten	C	a hundred
III	three	VII	seven	XV	fifteen	D	five hundred
IV	four	VIII	eight	XX	twenty	M	a thousand

Phone numbers

In phone numbers you say each number separately, often with a pause after two or three numbers:

509236 *five oh nine — two three six*

You can say *six six* or *double six* for 66:

02166 *oh two one **six six**/oh two one **double six***

If you are phoning a number in a different town, you have to use the **area code** before the number:

01865 *is the code for Oxford.*

If you are phoning somebody in a large firm, you can ask for their **extension number**:

(01865) 567672 x 4840 *(extension 4840)*

Fractions and decimals

½	a half	⅓	a/one third
¼	a quarter	⅖	two fifths
⅛	an/one eighth	⁷⁄₁₂	seven twelfths
¹⁄₁₀	a/one tenth	1½	one and a half
¹⁄₁₆	a/one sixteenth	2⅜	two and three eighths
0.1	(nought) point one	1.75	one point seven five
0.25	(nought) point two five	3.976	three point nine seven six
0.33	(nought) point three three		

Percentages and proportions

90% *of all households have a car.*
Nine out of ten *households have a car.*
Nine tenths *of all households have a car.*

The ratio of households that have a car to those that don't is **9:1/nine to one***.*

Mathematical expressions

+	plus	≠	is not equal to
−	minus	≈	is approximately equal to
×	times/multiplied by	>	is greater than
÷	divided by	≥	is greater than or equal to
=	equals	<	is less than
%	per cent	≤	is less than or equal to
3^2	three squared	√	square root
5^3	five cubed	$\sqrt[3]{\ }$	cube root
6^{10}	six to the power of ten		

$7 + 6 = 13$ *Seven plus six equals/is thirteen.*

$5 \times 8 = 40$ *Five times eight equals forty/Five eights are forty/Five multiplied by eight is forty.*

$\sqrt{9} = 3$ *The square root of nine is three.*

$\sqrt[3]{125} = 5$ *The cube root of one hundred and twenty-five is five.*

Temperature

In Britain, temperatures are now usually given in **degrees Celsius**, (although some people are still more familiar with **Fahrenheit**). In the United States, **Fahrenheit** is used, except in science.

To convert Fahrenheit to Celsius,	**68°F**
subtract 32 from the number,	− 32
then	= 36
multiply by five	× 5
and divide by nine.	÷ 9
	= **20°C**

Water freezes at 32°F and boils at 212°F.

The maximum temperature this afternoon will be 15°, and the minimum tonight may reach −5°/minus five.

She had a temperature of 102° last night, and it's still above normal.

Weight

Non-metric		Metric
	1 ounce (oz)	= 28.35 grams (g/gm/gms.)
16 ounces	= 1 pound (lb)	= 0.454 kilogram (kg)
14 pounds	= 1 stone (st/st.)	= 6.356 kilograms
8 stone	= 1 hundredweight (cwt)	= 50.8 kilograms
20 hundredweight	= 1 ton	= 1 016.04 kilograms

The baby weighed 8 lb 2 oz (eight pounds two ounces).
For this recipe you need 750 g (seven hundred and fifty grams) of flour.

Length and height

Non-metric		Metric
	1 inch (in.)	= 25.4 millimetres (mm)
12 inches	= 1 foot (ft)	= 30.48 centimetres (cm/cms)
3 feet	= 1 yard (yd)	= 0.914 metre (m)
1 760 yards	= 1 mile	= 1.609 kilometres (km)

flying at 7 000 feet
The speed limit is 30 mph (thirty miles per/an hour).
The room is 11' x 9'6" (eleven feet by nine feet six or eleven foot by nine foot six).
She's five feet four (inches).
He's one metre sixty (centimetres).

Area

Non-metric		Metric
	1 square inch (sq in.)	= 6.452 square centimetres (cm²)
144 square inches	= 1 square foot (sq ft)	= 929.03 square centimetres
9 square feet	= 1 square yard (sq yd)	= 0.836 square metre (m²)
4 840 square yards	= 1 acre	= 0.405 hectare
640 acres	= 1 square mile	= 2.59 square kilometres (km²)/ 259 hectares (ha)

an 80-acre country park
160 000 square miles of the jungle have been destroyed.

Cubic measurements

Non-metric		Metric
	1 cubic inch (cu. in.)	= 16.39 cubic centimetres (cc)
1 728 cubic inches	= 1 cubic foot (cu. ft)	= 0.028 cubic metre (cu. m)
27 cubic feet	= 1 cubic yard (cu. yd)	= 0.765 cubic metre

a car with a 1 500 cc engine

Capacity

	GB	US	Metric
20 fluid ounces (fl oz)	= 1 pint (pt)	= 1.201 pints	= 0.568 litre (l)
2 pints	= 1 quart (qt)	= 1.201 quarts	= 1.136 litres
4 quarts	= 1 gallon (gal.)	= 1.201 gallons	= 4.546 litres

I drink a litre of water a day.
a quart of orange juice

Dates

8 April 2005 (BrE)	Her birthday is on the thirteenth of July.
8th April 2005 (8/4/05) (BrE)	Her birthday is on July the thirteenth.
April 8, 2005 (4/8/05) (AmE)	Her birthday is July thirteenth. (AmE)

Years

1999	nineteen ninety-nine	2000	(the year) two thousand
1608	sixteen oh eight	2002	two thousand and two
1700	seventeen hundred	2020	twenty twenty

Age

When saying a person's age, use only numbers:

Sue is ten and Tom is six.
She left home at sixteen.

You can say 'a... -year-old/-month-old/-week-old, etc':

*Youth training is available to all **sixteen-year-olds**.*
*a **ten-week-old** baby*

To give the approximate age of a person:

13–19	in his/her teens	34–36	in his/her mid-thirties
21–29	in his/her twenties	37–39	in his/her late thirties
31–33	in his/her early thirties		

Times

There is often more than one way of telling the time:

Half hours

6.30	six thirty
	half past six
	half six (informal)

Other times

5.45	five forty-five	(a) quarter to six
2.15	two fifteen	(a) quarter past two
1.10	one ten	ten past one
3.05	three oh five	five past three
1.55	one fifty-five	five to two

In American English, *after* is sometimes used instead of *past*, and *of* instead of *to*.

With 5, 10, 20 and 25, the word *minutes* is not necessary, but it is used with other numbers:

10.25 twenty-five past ten
10.17 seventeen **minutes** past ten

Use o'clock only for whole hours:

*It's three **o'clock**.*

In slightly more formal language, *a.m.* (for times before midday) and *p.m.* (for times after midday) are used:

*School starts at 9 **a.m.***

Twenty-four hour clock

The twenty-four hour clock is used in official language:

13:52   thirteen fifty-two (1.52 p.m.)
22:30   twenty-two thirty (10.30 p.m.)

Pronunciation

The pronunciations given are those of younger speakers of Received Pronunciation, a widely recognized, non-regional accent of British English.

Consonants

p	**pen** /pen/	s	**see** /siː/
b	**bad** /bæd/	z	**zoo** /zuː/
t	**tea** /tiː/	ʃ	**shoe** /ʃuː/
d	**did** /dɪd/	ʒ	**vision** /ˈvɪʒn/
k	**cat** /kæt/	h	**hat** /hæt/
g	**get**/get/	m	**man** /mæn/
tʃ	**chain** /tʃeɪn/	n	**now** /naʊ/
dʒ	**jam**/jam/	ŋ	**sing** /sɪŋ/
f	**fall** /fɔːl/	l	**leg** /leg/
v	**van** /væn/	r	**red** /red/
θ	**thin** /θɪn/	j	**yes** /jes/
ð	**this** /ðɪs/	w	**wet** /wet/

(r) shows that the pronunciation will have /r/ only if a vowel sound follows immediately, as in **plaster of Paris**. Otherwise the /r/ sound is omitted.

/x/ represents a fricative sound, as in /lɒx/ for Scottish **loch**.

Vowels

iː	**see** /siː/	ʌ	**cup** /kʌp/
i	**happy** /ˈhæpi/	ɜː	**fur** /fɜː(r)/
ɪ	**sit** /sɪt/	ə	**about** /əˈbaʊt/
e	**bed** /bed/	eɪ	**say** /seɪ/
æ	**cat** /kæt/	əʊ	**go** /gəʊ/
ɑː	**father** /ˈfɑːðə(r)/	aɪ	**my** /maɪ/
ɒ	**got** /gɒt/	aʊ	**now** /naʊ/
ɔː	**saw** /sɔː/	ɔɪ	**boy** /bɔɪ/
ʊ	**put** /pʊt/	ɪə	**near** /nɪə(r)/
uː	**too** /tuː/	eə	**hair** /heə(r)/
u	**actual** /ˈæktʃuəl/	ʊə	**pure** /pjʊə(r)/

/i/ (without a length mark /ː/) represents a weak vowel that can be sounded as either /iː/ or /ɪ/, or a compromise between them. The sequence /iə/ can be pronounced /jə/, so **union** can be /ˈjuːniən/ or /ˈjuːnjən/.

/u/ (without a length mark /ː/) represents a weak vowel that varies between /uː/ or /ʊ/. If followed by a consonant sound, it can be pronounced as /ə/, and the sequence /ʊə/ can be pronounced /wə/, as in **actual** /ˈæktʃuəl/, /ˈæktʃwəl/.

Some words that come from French may retain a nasal vowel, indicated by the mark /˜/, as in **croissant** /ˈkwæsɒ̃/.

Stress

The mark /ˈ/ shows that the syllable that follows is said with more force (stress) than other syllables in the word. Weaker stresses may be marked with /ˌ/.

For many compounds the pronunciation of the individual words is not repeated. The stress is indicated on the written form, for example at ˌwell ˈknown.

A word or compound that has two stresses may show a shift of stress when used in a phrase. In the expression ˌwell ˈknown the main stress is on **known**, but in the phrase ˌwell-known ˈauthor the main stress is shifted to the noun that follows.

Strong and weak forms

Some pronunciations are labelled as strong or weak forms. The strong form should be used when the word is stressed, and usually when the word is at the end of a sentence.

Inflected forms

Many inflections are formed by adding a consistently pronounced suffix to a word. A pronunciation is only given where the pronunciation differs from the following, or for clarification:

-able	/əbl/	afford**able**
-ance	/əns/	avoid**ance**
-ant	/ənt/	repent**ant**
-ence	/əns/	insist**ence**
-er	/ə(r)/	few**er**
-est	/ɪst/	few**est**
-ing	/ɪŋ/	amplify**ing**
-ism	/ɪzəm/	liberal**ism**
-ist	/ɪst/	solo**ist**
-ity	/əti/	absurd**ity**
-ly	/li/	correct**ly**
-ment	/mənt/	adjust**ment**
-ness	/nəs/	eager**ness**
-y	/i/	crisp**y**

After vowels and voiced consonants:

-ed, -d	/d/	clubb**ed**
-es, -s	/z/	club**s**

After voiceless consonants:

-ed, -d	/t/	stopp**ed**
-es, -s	/s/	stop**s**

After /s z ʃ ʒ tʃ dʒ/:

-es, -s	/ɪz/	clutch**es**

After /t d/:

-ed, -d	/ɪd/	grad**ed**